CROSSWORD PUZZLE DICTIONARY

CROSSWORD PUZZLE DICTIONARY

4th Edition

ANDREW SWANFELDT

Harper & Row, Publishers
New York, Cambridge, Philadelphia, San Francisco
London, Mexico City, São Paulo, Singapore, Sydney

A hardcover edition of this book is published by Harper & Row, Publishers, Inc.

First PERENNIAL LIBRARY edition published 1985.

Library of Congress Cataloging in Publication Data

Swanfeldt, Andrew.
Crossword puzzle dictionary.
Reprint. Originally published: 4th ed. New York : Crowell, c 1977.
1. Crossword puzzles—Glossaries, vocabularies, etc. I. Title.
GV1507.C7S85 1985 793.73′2′0321 84-48628
ISBN 0-06-080762-8 (pbk.)

---

88 89 OPM 10 9 8

Publisher's Preface

Since its first appearance in 1940, the *Crossword Puzzle Dictionary*, compiled by Andrew Swanfeldt, has acquired such a widespread and loyal following among crossword fans that three successive improved and expanded editions have been needed to keep abreast of the demand.

The most notable improvement was the breakthrough device first incorporated in the 3rd edition: the Instant Finder System. On the surface it is a simple device—the answer words are listed according to the number of letters—but it was not, in fact, practical to produce a large book with this feature until the development of computer technology made it possible to count the letters by mechanical means.

Regrettably, Andrew Swanfeldt did not see the fruit of his years of research; he died soon after submitting the revised text for the 3rd edition. The publisher's staff, ably headed by Anne Vaughan, prepared his manuscript for processing by the computer.

This new edition is still very much a reflection of Mr. Swanfeldt's work: the publisher has kept practically all of his 3rd edition text (as well as the Instant Finder System). But the number of clues and answer words has been considerably increased. The result, we trust, is the most efficient and comprehensive puzzle dictionary of all.

The publisher is indebted, for all of the new material in the 4th edition, to lexicographer Sheila Brantley.

Abbreviations Used in This Book

abbr.	abbreviation	It.	Italian
Ar.	Arabic	L.	Latin
c.	capital	pert. to	pertaining to
comb. form	combining form	P.I.	Philippine Islands
D.	Dutch	pl.	plural
F.	French	Russ.	Russian
G.	German	Sc.	Scottish
Gr.	Greek	Sp.	Spanish
Ind.	Indian	W.	Welsh
Ir.	Irish	Yid.	Yiddish

A

A, a: an, ay; per **4** each
Greek: **5** alpha
Hebrew: **5** aleph
aa: 4 lava
aal, al: 8 mulberry
dye: **8** morindin
aalii: 4 tree, wood
aardvark: 8 anteater, edentate
Aaron: *associate:* Hur
brother: **5** Moses
burial place: Hor
father: **5** Amram
sister: **6** Miriam
son: **5** Abihu, Nadab **7** Eleazar, Ithamar
Aaronic: 9 Levitical
Aaron's rod: 7 mullein
ab-: off **4** away, from
aba: 4 robe **5** cloth **6** fabric **7** garment
abaca: 4 hemp **5** fiber, lupis **6** linaga
aback: 4 back **6** behind **8** backward, unawares
abaculus: 4 tile **7** tessera
abacus: 4 slab **5** stone **10** calculator
abaddon: 4 hell **5** hades
Abadite, Ibidite: 6 Muslim
abaft: aft **4** back, baft **5** abaff **6** astern, behind **8** rearward
abalienate: 8 alienate
abalone: ear **5** awabi, ormer, shell **6** asseir, sea-ear **7** mollusk
abandon: ego **4** cast, drop, flee, junk, quit **5** allay, ditch, expel, leave, remit, scrap, waive, yield **6** abjure, banish, desert, divest, disuse, maroon, recant, reject, relent, resign, vacate **7** discard, forsake **8** abdicate, forswear, rashness, renounce **9** surrender **10** enthusiasm, exuberance, relinquish
abandoned: bad **4** left, lost **7** corrupt, forlorn **8** derelict, flagrant, forsaken **9** desolated, destitute, dissolute, shameless, unbridled **10** dissipated, profligate **12** unrestrained
abandonment instrument: 6 waiver
abase: 5 lower, shame **6** bemean, debase, defame, deject, demean, depose, humble, lessen, reduce **7** degrade, depress, mortify **8** disgrace, dishonor **9** denigrate, humiliate **10** depreciate
abash: awe, cow **4** dash **5** shame **6** humble **7** mortify **8** bewilder, browbeat, confound **9** discomfit, embarrass, humiliate **10** disconcert, intimidate
abashed: 7 ashamed **8** sheepish
abate: ebb, end **4** fall, omit, slow, void, wane **5** allay, annul, let up, lower, quash, relax, remit, slake **6** deduct, lessen, reduce, relent **7** abolish, assuage, nullify, slacken, subside **8** decrease, diminish, mitigate, moderate **9** alleviate
abatement: 6 rebate **8** decrease **9** allowance, deduction, reduction **10** diminution, relaxation, subsidence
abatis: 8 obstacle **9** barricade **13** fortification
abba: 5 title **6** father
abbe: 4 monk **6** cleric, curate, priest **12** ecclesiastic
abbess: 4 amma **9** prelatess
abbey: 6 priory **7** convent, nunnery **8** cloister **9** monastery, sanctuary
pert. to: **8** abbatial
abbot: 5 coarb, abbas
assistant: **5** prior
abbreviate: cut **4** clip, dock **5** prune **6** digest **7** abridge, curtail, shorten **8** contract, condense, truncate **9** epitomize
abdicate: 4 cede, quit **5** demit, expel, leave, remit **6** depose, disown, forego, resign, retire, vacate **7** abandon **8** disclaim, renounce **9** surrender **10** disinherit, relinquish
abdomen: 5 belly, pleon, tharm **6** paunch
fluid in: **7** ascites
abduct: 4 lure, take **5** steal **6** kidnap **7** capture
abecedarian: 4 tyro **6** novice **7** learner **8** beginner, neophyte **9** fledgling **10** tenderfoot **12** alphabetical
abecederium: 4 book **6** primer
abed: 4 sick **7** resting, retired **8** sleeping

Abel: *brother:* 4 Cain, Seth
parent: Eve 4 Adam
Abelard's beloved: 7 Heloise
abele: 6 poplar
aberrant: 4 wild 7 deviant 8 abnormal, straying 9 wandering
aberration: 4 slip 5 error, fault, lapse, mania 8 delirium, delusion, insanity 9 deviation 12 eccentricity 13 hallucination
abet: aid, egg 4 back, help 5 boost, coach 6 assist, foment, incite, second, succor, uphold 7 connive, espouse, forward, further, support, sustain 8 advocate, befriend 9 encourage, instigate, subsidize 11 countenance
abettor: 6 fautor 8 advocate, promoter 9 accessory, auxiliary 10 accomplice 11 confederate, conspirator
abeyance: 9 cessation 10 expectancy, suspension 11 suppression
abhor: 4 hate, shun 6 detest, loathe 7 despise, dislike 8 execrate 9 abominate
abhorrence: 5 odium 6 hatred 7 disgust 8 aversion 9 antipathy 10 repugnance 11 detestation
Abi: *father:* 9 Zechariah
husband: 4 Ahaz
mother: 8 Hezekiah
abide: be 4 bear, bide, last, live, stay 5 await, delay, dwell, exist, pause, tarry 6 endure, linger, remain, reside, submit 7 sojourn, sustain 8 continue, tolerate 9 acquiesce, withstand
Abiel's son: Ner
abies: 4 firs 5 trees 10 evergreens
abigail: 4 maid
Abigail: *husband:* 5 David, Nabal
son: 5 Amasa
Abihail's husband: 8 Rehoboam
ability: can 5 force, power, skill 6 energy, talent 7 caliber, faculty, potency 8 aptitude, capacity, strength 9 dexterity, ingenuity 10 capability, competence, efficiency 11 proficiency
Abimelech's friend: 8 Ahuzzath
Abital: *husband:* 5 David
son: 10 Shephatiah
abject: low 4 base, mean, poor, sunk, vile 5 helot 6 paltry, sordid, supine 7 forlorn, ignoble, servile, slavish 8 beggarly, cringing, degraded, downcast, listless, wretched 9 groveling, miserable 10 despicable 12 contemptible
abjure: 4 deny 5 spurn 6 eschew, recall, recant, reject, resign, revoke 7 abandon, disavow, retract 8 abnegate, disclaim, forswear, renounce 9 repudiate
ablation: 7 aciurgy, surgery
ablaze: 4 alow 5 afire, alowe 7 burning, glowing, radiant 8 gleaming, inflamed
able: apt, can, fit 5 adept, smart 6 clever, facile, strong 7 capable 8 dextrous, skillful, suitable, talented, vigorous 9 competent, dexterous, effective, efficient, qualified, versatile 10 proficient
ablution: 4 bath 6 lotion 7 baptism, washing 9 cleansing
vessel: 5 basin 9 washbasin
abnegate: 4 deny 6 abjure, forego, refuse, reject 7 disavow 8 disclaim, forswear, renounce 10 relinquish
Abner: *cousin:* 4 Saul
father: Ner
abnormal: 5 queer, utter 7 erratic, unusual 8 aberrant 9 anomalous, eccentric, irregular, unnatural 10 exorbitant 11 exceptional 13 extraordinary
aboard: on 4 onto 6 across 7 athwart
abode: cot, dar, hut 4 bode, cell, flat, home 5 bower, house, manor, suite 6 estate 7 cottage, habitat, lodging, mansion 8 domicile, dwelling, tenement 9 apartment, residence 10 habitation
animal: zoo 9 menagerie
of Dead: Dar 4 Aaru, Hell 5 Aralu, Hades, Orcus, Sheol 6 Heaven 9 Purgatory
of gods: 4 Meru 6 Asgard 7 Asgarth, Olympus 8 Asgardhr
abolish: end 4 kill 5 abate, annul, erase, quash 6 cancel, recall, repeal, revoke, vacate 7 destroy, nullify, rescind 8 abrogate 9 eradicate 10 invalidate, neutralize 11 countermand, discontinue, exterminate
aboma: boa, bom 5 snake 7 serpent
abominable: 4 vile 6 odious 9 atrocious, execrable, loathsome 10 unpleasant 12 disagreeable
abominable snowman: 4 yeti 7 monster
habitat: 9 Himalayas
abominate: 4 hate 5 abhor 6 detest, loathe 8 execrate
abomination: 4 evil 5 crime, curse 6 horror, plague 7 disgust 8 aversion 9 antipathy 10 abhorrence, odiousness, repugnance 11 detestation
aboriginal: 5 first, natal 7 primary 8 original 9 beginning, primitive 10 indigenous
aborigine: 6 Indian, native, savage 10 autochthon
abortion: 7 failure 8 feticide, misbirth 9 foeticide 11 miscarriage, monstrosity 13 misconception
abortive: 4 idle, vain 6 futile 9 fruitless 12 unsuccessful
abound: 4 flow, teem 5 fleet, swarm 8 overflow 9 exuberate

abounding: 4 rife 5 flush 7 replete, teeming 8 abundant 9 luxuriant, plenteous, plentiful
prefix: 4 poly
about: in, re 4 in re, near, some 5 anent, astir, circa 6 active, almost, around 8 circiter 10 concerning, throughout 11 surrounding 13 approximately
prefix: amb
above: on, up; oer 4 atop, over, past, upon 6 beyond, higher 8 overhead, superior 9 exceeding, foregoing 12 transcendent
comb. form: 5 hyper, super, supra
abracadabra: 5 spell 11 incantation
abrade: rub 4 bark, file, fret, gall, rasp, sand, wear 5 chafe, erase, grate, grind 6 scrape 8 irritate 9 excoriate
abrader: 4 file, rasp 5 emery 6 grater, sander 7 grinder, scraper 9 sandpaper 10 grindstone
Abraham: *birthplace:* Ur
bosom: 6 heaven 8 paradise
brother: 5 Nahor
concubine: 5 Hagar
father: 5 Terah
grandfather: 5 Nahor
grandson: 4 Esau
nephew: Lot
shrine: 5 Caaba, Kaaba
son: 5 Isaac, Medan, Shuah 6 Midian, Zimran 7 Ishmael
wife: 4 Sara 5 Hagar, Sarah, Sarai 7 Keturah
abramis: 4 carp, fish 5 bream
abrasion: 4 gall, scar 9 attrition
abrasive: 4 sand 5 emery 6 pumice, quartz 7 erodent 8 corundum 9 sandpaper 11 rottenstone
abraxas: gem 5 charm, stone 6 amulet
abreast: 4 even 6 beside 8 parallel 9 alongside
of the times: 6 modern 7 popular
abret: 5 bread, wafer
abridge: cut 4 dock 5 brief, limit, rasee, razee 6 reduce, shrink 7 curtail, deprive, shorten 8 abstract, compress, condense, contract, diminish, retrench 10 abbreviate
abridgement: 6 digest, precis, sketch 7 epitome, summary 8 synopsis 9 lessening 10 compendium, diminution
abrii: 4 shed 5 cover 6 cavity, dugout 7 shelter
abrini: 8 licorice
abroad: off 4 asea, away 5 astir, forth 6 afield, astray, widely 7 distant
abrogate: 5 annul, quash, remit 6 cancel, repeal, revoke 7 abolish, nullify, rescind 8 overrule
abrogation: 9 abolition, cassation 11 dissolution
abrupt: 4 bold, curt, fast, rude 5 bluff, blunt, brief, hasty, quick, rough, sharp, sheer, short, steep, terse 6 craggy, rugged, sudden 7 angular, brusque, violent 8 headlong, vertical 9 impetuous 10 unexpected 11 precipitate, precipitous 12 disconnected 13 perpendicular, unceremonious
Abruzzi city: 4 Atri
Absalom: *captain:* 5 Amasa
father: 5 David
sister: 5 Tamar
slayer: 4 Joab
abscess: 4 boil, moro, sore 5 ulcer 6 fester, lesion 9 gathering
abscond: fly, run 4 bolt, flee, hide, quit 5 elope, scram 6 decamp, depart, desert, eloine, escape, levant 8 withdraw
absence: 4 lack, void, want 5 blank, leave 6 vacuum 7 vacancy 8 furlough 10 deficiency, withdrawal 13 nonappearance, nonattendance
absent: off, out 4 away, AWOL, gone 7 lacking, missing 8 absorbed 10 abstracted
absent-minded: 6 musing 8 distrait, dreaming 9 engrossed 10 abstracted 11 inattentive, preoccupied
absent without leave: 4 AWOL
absolute: 4 dead, fine, free, mear, meer, mere, plat, pure, rank, real, true 5 plumb, sheer, stark, total, utter, whole 6 entire, simple 7 certain, perfect, plenary 8 complete, explicit, implicit, positive 9 arbitrary, downright 10 autocratic, disengaged, peremptory 11 categorical, terminative, unalienable 13 authoritative, unconditional
monarch: 6 despot
absolutely: yea, yes 4 amen 6 wholly 8 evendown 10 thoroughly 13 unequivocally
absolution: 6 pardon 8 shriving 9 acquittal, cleansing, remission 11 exculpation, forgiveness
payment: 7 sin rent
absolve: 4 free 5 clear, remit 6 acquit, excuse, exempt, finish, pardon, shrive, unbind 7 cleanse, forgive, release 8 dispense, liberate, overlook 9 discharge, exculpate, exonerate, vindicate
absorb: eat, sop 4 soak, take 5 amuse, drink, merge, unite 6 devour, engage, engulf, imbibe, occupy 7 combine, consume, engross, immerse, occlude, swallow 10 assimilate 11 incorporate
absorbed: 4 deep, lost, rapt, sunk 6 absent buried, intent 7 plunged, riveted 8 immersed 9 engrossed 11 preoccupied
absorbent: 5 fomes

absquatulate: sit 5 elope, scram 6 decamp
abstain: 4 deny, fast 5 avoid, cease, spurn, waive 6 desist, eschew, forego, refuse, reject 7 forbear, refrain 8 restrain, teetotal, withhold
abstemious: 5 sober 7 ascetic 8 moderate 9 abstinent, temperate
absterge: 4 wipe 5 bathe, clean, purge, rinse
abstract: 4 cull, deed, draw, part, take 5 brief, ideal, steal 6 deduct, divert, precis, remove 7 abridge, excerpt, purloin, summary 8 abstruse, argument, separate, synopsis, withdraw 9 difficult, epitomize, recondite, summarize 10 compendium 11 abridgement, theoretical
being: ens 4 esse 5 entia (pl.)
abstruse: 4 dark, deep 6 hidden, mystic, remote, subtle, 7 obscure 8 abstract, acroatic, esoteric, profound 9 concealed, recondite 10 acroamatic, mysterious 16 incomprehensible
absurd: 4 wild 5 droll, false, inane, inept, silly 6 stupid 7 asinine, foolish 8 fabulous 9 fantastic, ludicrous, senseless 10 irrational, ridiculous 11 incongruous, nonsensical 12 inconsistent, inharmonious, preposterous, unreasonable
abundance: 4 flow, mort 5 depth, store 6 foison, plenty, riches, wealth 8 fullness, opulence 9 affluence, amplitude, plenitude 10 exuberance
suffix: ose
abundant: 4 free, lush, much, rife 5 ample, flush 6 galore, hearty 7 copious, fertile, fulsome, profuse, replete, teeming 8 fruitful, generous, numerous 9 abounding, bountiful, plenteous, plentiful 10 sufficient 11 overflowing
abuse: mar, tax 4 flay, harm, hurt, maul, rail, ruin, slam 5 crime, curse, fault, scold, spoil 6 berate, defile, ill-use, injure, insult, malign, misuse, punish, ravish, revile, vilify, yatter 7 affront, bedevil, deceive, falsify, misbede, miscall, obloquy, outrage, pervert, slander, traduce, upbraid, violate 8 dishonor, maltreat, misapply, mistreat, reproach 9 blaspheme, contumely, desecrate, disparage, invective, objurgate 10 adulterate, opprobrium, scurrility 12 vituperation
abusive: 4 foul 7 corrupt 8 cheating, insolent, libelous 9 offensive, perverted 10 calumnious, fraudulent, scurrilous 11 blasphemous 12 catachrestic, vituperative
abut: 4 join, rest 5 touch 6 adjoin, border 7 project
abutment: 4 pier 6 alette 8 buttress
abysmal: 4 deep 6 dreary 8 profound, unending, wretched 10 bottomless
abyss: pit 4 deep, gulf, hell, void 5 abysm, chaos, chasm, depth, gorge 6 bottom, vorago 7 gehenna 8 downfall, interval
Abyssinia: See **Ethiopia**
acacia: gum 4 tree 5 babul, boree, garad, myall, siris 6 arabic, coobah, locust 9 boobyalla 11 kameeldoorn
academic: 5 rigid 6 formal 7 classic, erudite, learned 9 scholarly 10 collegiate, scholastic 11 quodlibetic, theoretical 12 conventional
academy: 4 USMA, USNA 6 lyceum, manege, school 7 college, society 8 seminary 9 Annapolis, institute, West Point 10 university
Acadian: 5 Cajun
acaleph: 9 jellyfish
acantha: fin 5 spine, thorn 7 prickle
acanthopterygian: 4 bass, fish 5 perch
acarus: 4 mite, tick 6 insect
acaudal: 6 bobbed 7 anurous 8 ecaudate, tailless
accede: let 5 agree, allow, grant, yield 6 accord, assent, comply, concur 7 concede, conform, consent 9 acquiesce 11 acknowledge
accelerate: rev, run 4 race, urge 5 drive, hurry, speed 6 hasten 7 advance, forward, further, quicken 8 dispatch, expedite, increase 9 stimulate 11 precipitate
accelerator: 8 throttle
accent: 4 beat, burr, mark, tone 5 ictus, pitch, pulse, sound, throb 6 brogue, rhythm, stress 8 emphasis 9 emphasize, pronounce, underline 10 accentuate, inflection, intonation
accented: 7 marcato
syllable: 5 arsis
accentuate: 6 accent 9 emphasize, intensify
accept: 4 fang, take 5 admit, adopt, agree, allow, honor, marry 6 assent 7 approve, believe, embrace, espouse, receive 9 acquiesce 10 understand 11 acknowledge
acceptable: 7 welcome 8 pleasant 9 palatable 11 comfortable 12 satisfactory
accepted: 7 popular 8 admitted, approved, credited, orthodox, standard 9 canonical, prevalent 12 acknowledged, conventional, countenanced
access: way 4 adit, door, gate, path, road 5 entry, going, route 6 accost, avenue, entree, portal, street 7 advance 8 approach, entrance, paroxysm 9 admission 10 admittance, passageway 13 accessibility
accessible: 4 near, open 5 handy 6 at hand, patent 7 affable 8 familiar, pervious, sociable 9 available, reachable 10 attainable, convenient, obtainable, procurable 12 approachable

accession: 5 enter 8 addition, increase 9 agreement, inaugural, induction 11 acquisition, enlargement 13 reinforcement

accessorius: 5 nerve

accessory: 4 aide, ally, tool 5 extra, scarf 6 helper 7 abettor, adjunct 8 additive 9 adjective, appendage, assistant, auxiliary 10 accidental, accomplice, attachment, incidental, subsidiary 11 appurtenant, concomitant, confederate, contingency, subservient 12 accompanying, appurtenance, circumstance, contributary 13 accompaniment, supplementary

accident: hap 4 case, luck 5 event 6 chance, hazard, injury, mishap 7 fortune 8 calamity, casualty, disaster, fortuity, incident 9 mischance 10 misfortune 11 catastrophe, contingency, contretemps 12 misadventure

accidental: 6 casual, chance, random 9 dependent, extrinsic, haphazard, secondary 10 collateral, extraneous, incidental, undesigned, unexpected, unforeseen, unintended 11 conditional, subordinate 12 adscititious, adventitious, nonessential, unexpectedly 13 unintentional 14 unpremeditated

acclaim: cry 4 clap, hail, laud, root 5 cheer, claim, eclat, extol, shout 6 praise, salute 7 applaud, approve, commend, endorse, ovation, plaudit, welcome 8 applause 10 compliment 11 acclamation, approbation

acclimate: 5 inure 6 harden, season 8 accustom 9 habituate 10 naturalize 11 acclimatize

acclivity: 4 bank, brow, hill, rise 5 grade, pitch, slope, slant 6 ascent, height 7 incline 9 ascendant, ascendent 11 inclination

accolade: 4 Emmy, kiss, rite, sign 5 award, honor, medal, Oscar, token 6 salute, symbol 7 embrace 8 ceremony 9 laudation 10 salutation

accommodate: aid, bow, fit 4 give, help, hold, lend, suit 5 adapt, board, defer, favor, house, lodge, serve, yield 6 adjust, comply, favour, oblige, settle 7 conform 8 attemper, suitable 9 reconcile

accompaniment: 7 descant 9 accessory, obbligato

accompany: see 4 fare, join, lead 5 pilot 6 assist, attend, concur, convey, convoy, escort, follow, squire 7 coexist, conduct, consort 9 associate, companion

accomplice: pal 4 aide, ally, chum 5 buddy, crony 6 helper 7 abettor, partner 9 accessory, assistant, associate, colleague 10 cooperator 11 confederate 12 participator

accomplish: do; end, win 4 fill, work 5 enact, equip, forth 6 afford, attain, effect, finish, fulfil, manage 7 achieve, chevise, compass, execute, fulfill, furnish, operate, perfect, perform, realize, succeed 8 complete, contrive, dispatch, engineer 9 implement, negotiate 10 consummate, effectuate

accomplished: apt 4 able, done 5 adept, ended 6 expert 8 talented 10 proficient

accomplishment: art 4 deed, feat 5 craft, skill 8 learning 10 attainment 11 achievement, performance

accord: 4 give, jibe 5 agree, allow, atone, award, grant, tally, unity 6 accede, adjust, assent, bestow, beteem, comply, concur, settle, unison 7 comport, compose, concede, concert, concord, consent, consort, rapport, respond 9 harmonize, reconcile 10 compliance, conformity, correspond, permission 11 composition, concurrence

accordant: 4 even 7 attuned 8 agreeing, coherent, suitable 9 congruous, consonant 10 compatible, concentual, consistent, harmonious 11 concentuous, conformable 13 correspondent

accordingly: so 4 then, thus 5 hence 9 therefore, wherefore 12 consequently 15 correspondingly

accost: 4 hail, meet 5 board, greet, speak 6 halloo, salute, waylay 7 address, solicit 8 approach, confront, greeting 9 encounter

account: tab, 4 bill, deem, item, rate, sake, tale 5 chalk, count, judge, score, story, value, worth 6 credit, detail, esteem, profit, reckon, record, relate, report, repute 7 compute, explain, narrate, recital 8 consider, estimate, 9 advantage, biography, chronicle, discourse, inventory, narrative, reckoning, rehearsal, statement 10 commentary, importance, recitation 11 calculation, computation, description, enumeration, explanation

accountable: 6 liable 10 answerable, explicable 11 responsible 12 attributable

accountant: CPA 5 clerk 7 auditor 8 reckoner 10 bookkeeper, calculator

accoutre, accouter: arm, rig 4 gird 5 array, dress, equip 6 attire, clothe, outfit 7 furnish, provide

accoutrements, accouterments: 9 equipment, trappings

accredit: 5 allot, vouch 6 credit, depute 7 appoint, approve, ascribe, believe, certify, confirm, endorse, license 8 sanction 9 attribute, authorize 10 commission

accretion: 4 gain 6 growth 7 deposit, exudate 8 addition, abhesion, increase 9 coherence 11 enlargement

accrue: add 4 earn, gain, grow 5 arise, ensue, inure, issue 6 mature, result, spring 7 acquire, collect, redound 8 cumulate, increase

accumulate: 4 grow, heap, pile, save 5 amass, hoard, store, total 6 accrue, garner, gather, muster 7 collect 8 increase 9 aggregate

accumulation: 4 fund, heap, mass, pile 5 stack, store 6 budget 7 cumulus 8 dividend, interest 10 acervation, congestion, cumulation

accurate: 4 just, leal, nice, true 5 close, exact, right 6 strict 7 careful, correct, precise 8 faithful 9 veridical 10 particular

accursed: fey 6 cursed, damned, doomed 9 execrable, execrated 10 detestable 13 anathematized

accuse: tax 4 call, file, show, slur, wray 5 argue, blame 6 attack, charge, defame, indict 7 appeach, arraign, attaint, censure, impeach 8 chastise, denounce, reproach 9 challenge 10 calumniate 11 incriminate, recriminate

accuser: 7 charger, delator 8 libelant 9 plaintiff 10 prosecutor 11 complainant

accustom: use 4 haft, wont 5 adapt, enure, drill, inure, train 6 addict, season 7 consort, toughen 9 acclimate, habituate 10 naturalize 11 familiarize

ace: jot, one, pip 4 a-one, atom, card, hero, mark, tops, unit 5 adept, basto, flyer, point 6 expert 7 aviator 8 particle, quantity 10 topnotcher

acerb: 4 acid, sour, tart 5 acrid, harsh, sharp, surly 6 bitter, severe 10 astringent 11 acrimonious

acerbate: 8 embitter, irritate 10 exasperate

acetaldehyde: 5 ethyl 7 ethanal

acetic: 4 sour 5 sharp

acetic acid: 7 vinegar
salt: 7 acetate

acetylene: gas 5 tolan 6 ethine, tolane

ache: 4 hurt, long, pain, pang, pine 5 smart, throb, throe 6 desire, stitch, twinge 7 anguish 8 soreness

achieve: do; end, get, win 4 earn, gain 5 reach 6 afford, attain, effect, finish, obtain 7 compass, fulfill, produce, realize, succeed, triumph 8 complete, conclude, contrive 9 terminate 10 accomplish, consummate

achievement: act 4 deed, feat 6 action, career, result 7 exploit 9 execution, fosterage 11 performance 14 accomplishment

Achilles: *advisor:* 6 Nestor
charioteer: 9 Automedon
father: 6 Peleus
friend: 9 Patroclus
horse: 7 Xanthus
lover and captive: 7 Briseis
mother: 6 Thetis
slayer: 5 Paris
soldier: 8 Myrmidon
teacher: 6 Chiron 7 Centaur
victim: 6 Hector
vulnerable part: 4 heel

achiote: 4 tree 7 annatto, arnatta, arnatto

achira: 5 canna 8 acheiria, handless

acid: dry 4 keen, sour, tart 5 acrid, amino, eager, harsh, sharp, ulmic 6 biting, bitter, oleate 7 acetose, acetous, vinegar 9 corrosive 11 acrimonious
comb. form: oxy 4 acer
nitric: 10 aquafortis
pert. to: 7 oleatic
radical: 4 acyl 6 acetyl 7 malonyl, benzoyl

acidity: 4 acor 8 acerbity, verjuice
measure: 10 acidimeter

acknowledge: nod, own 4 aver, avow, sign 5 admit, allow, grant, thank, yield 6 accede, accept, answer, assent, avouch, reward 7 concede, confess, declare, observe, profess 8 disclose 9 recognize

acme: cap, top 4 apex, peak 5 crest 6 apogee, climax, crisis, height, heyday, summit, zenith 8 pinnacle 11 culmination

acolyte: boy 6 helper, novice 7 learner 9 satellite

acomia: 8 baldness

aconic acid: 4 salt 7 aconate

aconite: 4 bikh 6 remedy 9 monkshood

acorn: nut 4 mast 5 ovest
dried: 6 camata
edible: 7 ballote, bellote

acorn-shaped: 8 balanoid

acouchi: 5 elemi, resin 7 protium

acquaint: 4 know, tell 5 teach, verse 6 advise, inform, notify, school 7 apprise, apprize, possess 11 familiarize

acquaintance: 4 kith 6 friend 8 affinity, intimate 9 companion, knowledge 10 fellowship

acquainted: 7 versant 10 conversant

acquiesce: bow 5 abide, agree, chime, yield 6 accede, accept, assent, comply, concur, submit 7 concede, conform, consent

acquire: add, buy, get, win 4 earn, gain, grab, reap 5 adopt, amass, learn, reach, steal 6 attain, effect, obtain, secure, snatch 7 collect, conquer, procure, receive 8 contract 9 cultivate

acquit: 4 free 5 clear 6 behave, excuse, pardon, parole 7 absolve, amnesty, comport, conduct, release, requite 8 liberate, overlook 9 discharge, exculpate, exonerate, quitclaim, vindicate

acre: 4 land 5 field 6 arpent 7 measure 8 farmhold
one hundred: 7 hectare
quarter: rod 4 rood
acreage: 5 ranch 6 estate 8 farmland
acrid: 4 acid, keen 5 harsh, rough, sharp, surly 6 biting, bitter 7 caustic, pungent, reeking 8 unsavory, virulent 9 acidulous, corrosive 10 irritating
acrimonious: mad 4 acid, keen 5 acrid, angry, gruff, harsh, irate, sharp, surly 6 bitter 7 caustic 8 stinging 9 rancorous
acroamatic: 4 oral 6 arcane, secret 8 abstruse, esoteric, profound
acrobat: 4 zany 7 gymnast, tumbler 8 balancer 10 ropedancer 13 contortionist, schoenobatist
garment: 7 leotard
acrogen: 4 fern, moss
acropolis: 4 fort, hill 7 citadel
across: 4 over, span 6 aboard 7 athwart 8 opposite 9 crosswise 10 transverse
prefix: dia 5 trans
acrostic: 4 agla, game, poem 6 phrase, puzzle 9 crosswise 11 composition
act: do, go; ape, law 4 actu, bill, deed, feat, play, skit, turn, work 5 actus, drama, edict, emote, exert, feign, karma, model, scene, stunt 6 behave, bestir, decree 7 comport, execute, exploit, perform, portray, pretend, statute 8 function, pretense, simulate 9 ordinance, portrayal, represent 10 observance 11 impersonate, instruction, performance
by turns: 6 altern 9 alternate
suffix: ure
act for: 9 represent
act like: ape 7 imitate
act up: 5 emote 9 misbehave
action: 4 case, deed, fray, push, step, work 5 doing, edict, fight 6 affair, battle 7 conduct, process 8 behavior, conflict, function 9 animation, behaviour 10 deportment, enterprise 11 performance, transaction
field of: 4 bowl 5 arena, stage 7 stadium
legal: res 4 suit 5 actus 8 replevin 9 gravamina
pert. to: 9 practical
put out of: KO 7 disable
to recover property: 6 trover 8 replevin
word: 4 verb
active: 4 busy, pert, spry 5 about, agile, alert, astir, brisk, quick, ready, smart 6 hearty, lively, moving, nimble, prompt 7 kinetic 8 animated, athletic, diligent, spirited, vigorous 9 assiduous, effective, energetic, sprightly, unpassive 10 productive 11 industrious, progressive
activity: ado, gog, vir 4 life, stir 5 rally 6 action, bustle 8 business, exercise, function, movement
actor: ham 4 doer, hero, lead, mime, star 5 agent, extra, heavy, mimic 6 artist, mummer, player, stager 7 artiste, guisard, histrio, protean, stormer, trouper 8 aisteoir (Ir.), comedian, juvenile, stroller, thespian 9 performer, portrayer, tragedian 10 personator 11 barnstormer, entertainer, pantomimist, protagonist
cue: 4 hint, word 6 prompt
group of: 4 cast 6 troupe 7 company 8 troupers
lines: 4 role, side
part: 4 role
supporting: bit 5 super 6 walk-on 7 ripieno
actress: 4 diva, star 7 ingenue 8 thespian 9 soubrette 10 comedienne 11 entertainer
actual: 4 real, true 5 posit 6 bodily 7 factual, genuine 8 concrete, existing, material, positive, tangible 9 effective, veritable 11 substantial
actuality: 4 fact 5 being 6 verity 7 reality 9 existence, substance
actuate: egg, run 4 draw, move, urge 5 enact, impel, rouse, start 6 arouse, compel, incite, induce 7 agitate, animate, enliven, inspire, pointed, sharpen 8 motivate, persuade 9 instigate
acumen: wit 7 insight 8 keenness, sagacity 9 acuteness, mentality, sharpness 10 perception, shrewdness 11 discernment 12 perspicacity 14 discrimination
acute: 4 fine, high, keen 5 quick, sharp, smart, snell 6 astute, shrewd, shrill, subtle, urgent 7 intense, pointed 8 critical, incisive, poignant 9 ingenious, sensitive 10 discerning, perceiving 11 intelligent, penetrating 13 perspicacious 14 discriminating
ad-lib: 9 improvise
ad patres: 4 dead 8 deceased
adage: saw 4 dict 5 axiom, maxim, motto 6 homily, saying, truism 7 bromide, precept, proverb 8 aphorism, apothegm
Adah: *husband:* 4 Esau 6 Lamech
son: 5 Jabal, Jubal
Adam: *grandson:* 4 Enos 5 Enoch
rib: Eve
son: 4 Abel, Cain, Seth
teacher: 6 Raisel
wife, first: 6 Lilith
Adam-and-Eve: 9 puttyroot
Adam Bede author: 5 Eliot
adamant: 4 firm, hard 5 stony 8 obdurate 9 loadstone, lodestone 10 inflexible, unyielding

adamantine: 4 firm 5 stone 9 immovable 10 unyielding
pert. to: 5 boric
Adam's ale: 5 water
Adam's apple: 6 larynx
Adam's flannel: 7 mullien
Adam's needle: 5 yucca
adapt: apt, fit 4 suit 5 agree, apply, inure 6 adjust, change, comply, temper 7 arrange, conform, convert, prepare, qualify 8 attemper, equalize, regulate 9 acclimate, calculate, harmonize 10 assimilate 11 accommodate
adaptable: 7 pliable 8 flexuous 9 tractable 10 adjustable, changeable 11 conformable 12 reconcilable
add: say, sum, tot 4 gain, give, join, plus, tote 5 affix, annex, total, unite 6 accrue, append, attach, figure, reckon 7 accrete, augment, combine, compile, compute, enlarge, subjoin 8 increase 9 aggregate 10 supplement
adda: 5 scink, skink 6 lizard
added: and, eke 4 plus
adder: 5 krait, snake, viper 7 machine, serpent 13 mathematician
addict: fan 4 buff, user 5 fiend, hound, slave 6 devote 7 deliver, devotee, hophead, pothead 8 accustom, acidhead 9 habituate, mainliner 10 enthusiast
addiction: 5 habit 9 surrender 10 attachment 11 disposition, enslavement, habituation
addition: and, ell 4 also, else, plus 5 rider 6 prefix 7 addenda (pl.), adjunct, advance, codicil, joining 8 addendum, additory, increase 9 accession, accretion, amendment, appendage, extension 10 ascription 11 enlargement 12 augmentation
prefix: 5 super
additional: new 4 else, more 5 extra, fresh, other 7 besides, further 9 auxiliary
addle: 4 earn, home, idle, mire 5 amaze, filth, ripen, spoil 6 muddle, thrive 7 agitate, confuse 8 befuddle, bewilder, confound 9 fruitless
addled: 4 asea 5 empty, upset 6 putrid 7 spoiled, unsound 9 befuddled 10 bewildered
address: aim, sue, woo 4 call, hail, home, pray, tact, talk, turn 5 abode, apply, court, greet, poise, skill 6 accost, adjust, aplomb, appeal, devote, direct, eulogy, manner, salute, speech 7 consign, entrust, lecture, oration 8 approach, delivery, dispatch, facility, harangue, petition 9 dexterity, discourse, residence, statement 10 allocution, buttonhole, deportment, management, peroration 11 application
adduce: 4 cite, give, name 5 allay, argue, infer, offer, quote 6 allege, assign 7 advance, mention, present
ade: 8 beverage
adeps: fat 4 lard
adept: ace, apt 4 A-one, able 5 handy, sharp 6 adroit, artist, expert, versed 7 capable, dabster 8 skillful 9 alchemist, dexterous, masterful 10 consummate, conversant, proficient
adequate: due, fit 4 full, meet 5 ample, equal 6 enough, proper 7 condign 8 suitable 9 competent, effective 10 answerable, sufficient 12 commensurate, satisfactory 13 proportionate
Adhem: 4 Abou
adhere: 4 cleg, glue, hold 5 affix, cling, stick, unite 6 attach, cleave, cohere 7 accrete, persist 9 persevere
adherence: 8 devotion, fidelity 9 constancy 10 allegiance, attachment 11 concurrence 12 perseverance
adherent: ist, ite 4 aide, ally 6 factor, votary 8 believer, disciple, follower, partisan, servitor, upholder 9 supporter
suffix: ist, ite
adhesive: gum, wax 4 bond, glue, tape 5 epoxy, paste 6 cement, gluten, mastic, sticky, viscum 7 stickum 8 birdlime, mucilage 9 tenacious
adhibit: use 5 admit, affix, apply 6 attach 10 administer
adieu: 5 adios 6 good-by 7 good-bye 8 farewell 11 valediction
adipose: fat 4 hard, suet 5 fatty, obese, pursy, squat 6 tallow
adit: 5 entry, stulm 6 access 7 passage 8 approach, entrance 9 admission 10 passageway
adjacent: 4 near, next, nigh 5 close, handy 6 beside, hard by 7 against, meeting 8 abutting, touching 9 adjoining, bordering 10 contiguous, juxtaposed 11 neighboring 12 conterminous
adjective: 7 epithet 8 modifier 9 accessory, dependent
demonstrative: 4 that, this 5 these, those
limiting: the
suffix: ed, ic, il; ent, ial, ian, ile, ine, ish, ive, ous 4 ical, ular
verbal: 9 gerundive
adjoin: add 4 abut, butt, join 5 touch, verge 6 append, attach, border 7 contact 8 neighbor 9 juxtapose
adjourn: end 4 move, rise, stay 5 close, defer, delay 6 recess 7 suspend 8 dissolve, postpone, prorogue 11 discontinue 13 procrastinate
adjudge: try 4 deem, find, give, hold, rate 5 allot, award, grant, judge, order 6 assign,

decide, decree, ordain, regard 7 condemn 8 sentence 9 determine, forejudge 10 adjudicate

adjudicate: act, try 4 hear, pass, rule 5 judge 6 decide, esteem, reckon, regard, settle 8 consider, sentence 9 determine

adjunct: aid 4 help, word 5 annex 6 device, phrase 7 pertain, teacher 8 addition, appanage 9 accessory, appendage, associate, auxiliary, colleague 10 complement 11 contingency 12 appurtenance

adjure: ask, beg, bid 4 bind, pray 5 crave, plead, swear 6 appeal, charge 7 beseech, command, conjure, contest, entreat, request, unswear

adjust: fit, fix, set 4 form, free, gear, line, pare, rate, size, suit, trim, true 5 adapt, admit, align, frame 6 accord, attune, settle, temper, wangle 7 address, arrange, balance, conform, compose, dispose, justify, prepare, rectify 8 compound, regulate 9 harmonize 10 concinnate, coordinate, straighten 11 accommodate, systematize

adjutage: 4 pipe, tube 5 spout 6 nozzle 7 opening

adjutant: 4 aide, ally 6 helper 7 officer 9 assistant, auxiliary

bird: 5 crane, stork 6 argala 7 marabou

adjuvant: 4 aide 6 helper 7 helpful 9 assistant, auxiliary

admeasure: 4 mete 7 measure 9 ascertain, apportion, determine

Admetus' wife: 8 Alcestis

administer: run 4 deal, dose, give, rule 5 apply, treat 6 direct, govern, manage, settle, supply 7 adhibit, conduct, control, execute, furnish, husband 8 dispense 10 distribute 11 superintend

administration: 4 rule, sway 6 policy 7 regimen 10 regulation

administrator: 7 manager, trustee 8 director, executor 9 dispenser, executive, executrix

admirable: 4 high 7 amiable, capital, elegant, ripping 9 estimable, excellent, marvelous, wonderful

Admiralty island: 5 Manus

admire: 4 like, love 5 adore, extol, honor, prize, value 6 esteem, marvel, regard, revere, wonder 7 approve, delight, idolize, respect 8 venerate

admirer: fan 4 beau 5 beaux (pl.), lover, swain 7 devotee 10 dilettante

admission: fee 4 adit 6 access, charge, entree, ticket 7 consent, ingress 8 entrance 10 admittance, agregation, concession, confession, disclosure 15 acknowledgement

receipts: 4 gate

admit: ken, own 4 avow, take 5 agree, allow, enter, grant 6 accept, accede, adjust, assent, avouch, enroll, induct, permit, suffer 7 adhibit, concede, confess, include, profess, receive 8 initiate 9 recognize 11 acknowledge, matriculate

admixture: 5 alloy, blend, shade, tinge 6 flavor 7 mixture, soupcon 8 compound, infusion 11 composition

admonish: 4 warn 5 chide, scold 6 advise, enjoin, exhort, notify, rebuke, remind 7 caution, counsel, monitor, reprove 9 reprehend, sermonize

admonisher: 7 monitor

adnoun: 9 adjective

ado: 4 fuss, stir, to-do, work 6 bother, bustle, effort, flurry, hubbub, pother, ruckus 7 trouble, turmoil 9 commotion 10 excitement, hullabaloo

adobe: mud 4 clay 5 brick, house 6 mudcap

adolescence: 5 teens, youth 6 nonage 7 puberty 8 minority

adolescent: lad 4 girl, lass 5 young, youth 6 nubile, subdeb 7 hebetic 8 immature, teenager 9 pubescent

Adonis: *beloved:* 9 Aphrodite

slayer of: 4 boar

adopt: 4 take 6 accept, assume, borrow, choose, follow, foster 7 acquire, embrace, espouse, receive, welcome 8 advocate, maintain 9 affiliate 10 naturalize 11 appropriate

adorable: 6 lovely 7 angelic, lovable, winsome 8 charming, kissable 9 appealing 10 cuddlesome, delightful

adoration: 6 homage 8 devotion

adore: 4 dote, laud, love 5 honor 6 admire, esteem, praise, revere 7 glorify, idolize, worship 8 venerate

adorn: dub 4 deck, gaud, gild, pink, trim 5 array, begem, dight, drape, dress, grace, primp, prink 6 attire, bedeck, blazon, clothe, emboss, enrich, suborn, tassel 7 apparel, bedight, bedizen, commend, dignify, furnish, garnish, glorify, implume 8 beautify, decorate, emblazon, ornament 9 bespangle, caparison, embellish

Adriana's servant: 4 Luce

Adriatic: *city:* 6 Venice

island: Bua, Eso 7 Lagosta, Lastovo

peninsula: 6 Istria

port: 4 Pola 5 Fiume 6 Rimini 7 Trieste

resort: 4 Lido

river into: Po 4 Reno 5 Adige, Bosna, Drini, Kerka, Piave

wind: 4 bora 10 tramontana, tramontane (pl.)

adrift: 4 asea, lost 5 awaft, loose 6 afloat 8 derelict, floating, unmoored 10 unanchored

adroit: apt 4 deft, neat 5 adept, handy, ready, sharp, smart 6 artful, clever, expert, habile 7 cunning 8 dextrous, masterly, skillful 9 dexterous, ingenious, masterful 10 proficient 11 quick-witted, resourceful

adroitness: 4 ease, tact 5 knack 7 address 8 facility 9 dexterity, ingenuity

adulate: 4 fawn, laud 5 gloss, gloze 6 praise 7 flatter 10 compliment, overpraise

adulator: fan 5 toady 6 yes-man 9 flatterer, sycophant 10 bootlicker

adult: man 4 ripe 5 grown, imago, woman 6 mature, nubile 7 grown-up 8 seasoned 9 developed 12 marriageable

adulterate: cut, mix 5 alloy, alter, taint 6 debase, defile, dilute, doctor, weaken 7 corrupt, falsify 8 denature 11 contaminate

adulterated: cut 6 impure 8 spurious 11 counterfeit

adumbrate: 5 shade, vague 7 obscure 8 intimate 10 foreshadow, overshadow

aduncuous: 4 bent 6 hooked

adust: 5 burnt, fiery 6 gloomy, sallow 7 parched 8 scorched, sunburnt

advance: aid, pay 4 gain, help, laud, lend, lift, loan, move, near, nose, pass, push, rise 5 avant, boost, exalt, extol, favor, offer, raise, serve 6 adduce, allege, amount, assign, better, favour, hasten, stride, thrive 7 benefit, elevate, forward, further, improve, proceed, process, promote, propose, succeed 8 addition, heighten, progress 9 encourage, promotion 10 accelerate, aggrandize, appreciate

guard: van 8 vanguard

military: 8 anabasis, anabases (pl.)

slowly: 4 inch, worm 5 creep

advanced: far 5 ahead 11 enlightened, progressive

equally: 7 abreast

most: 8 foremost, headmost

advantage: use 4 boot, edge, gain, odds 5 avail, favor, start, stead 6 behalf, behoof, profit 7 account, benefit, exploit, further, utility 8 handicap, interest, leverage, overplus 9 emolument, privilege 11 opportunity, superiority

advantageous: 6 useful 9 expedient, favorable, strategic 10 auspicious, beneficial, commodious, favourable, profitable, propitious 11 encouraging

advent: 6 coming 7 arrival 8 approach 11 incarnation

adventitious: 6 casual 7 foreign 8 acquired, episodic 9 extrinsic 10 accidental, fortuitous, incidental 12 adscititious, nonessential

adventure: 4 gest, lark, risk 5 event, geste, peril, quest, 6 chance, danger, hazard, 7 fortune, venture 8 escapade, jeopardy 9 mischance 10 enterprise, experience 11 undertaking

story: 4 gest, yarn 5 geste

adventurer: 7 gambler 9 almogavar 10 filibuster 11 condottiere, condottieri (pl.), enterpriser 12 entrepreneur

adventuress: 7 demirep 12 demimondaine

adventurous: 4 rash 6 daring, errant 8 reckless 9 audacious, foolhardy, hazardous 10 courageous

adverb: *ending:* ly; ily

old: 4 erst

adversaria: 5 notes 10 miscellany 12 commentaries

adversary: foe 5 enemy, rival, Satan 6 foeman 8 opponent 10 antagonist, competitor

adverse: foe, ill 4 evil 5 loath 6 averse 7 awkward, counter, diverse, froward, opposed 8 contrary, opposing, opposite 9 diametric, reluctant, repugnant 10 afflictive, calamitous 11 conflicting, disinclined, unfavorable 12 antagonistic, inauspicious, unfavourable, unpropitious

adversity: woe 5 decay 6 misery, sorrow 7 illness, trouble 8 calamity, distress 9 suffering 10 affliction, misfortune 11 contrariety

advert: 4 heed 5 recur, refer 6 allude, attend, return, revert 7 observe 8 consider

advertise: 4 plug, warn 5 blurb, bruit, noise 6 blazon, inform, notify, parade 7 declare, exploit, observe, publish 8 announce, proclaim, skywrite 9 broadcast, publicize, spotlight 10 promulgate

advertisement: ad 4 bill, sign 5 blurb 6 dodger, notice, poster, teaser 7 affiche, placard 8 handbill 10 commercial

book jacket: 5 blurb

outdoor: 5 flyer 6 poster 7 marquee 9 billboard

advertiser: 6 barker 7 plugger, spieler 8 huckster

advice: 4 lore, news 6 notice 7 caution, counsel, opinion, tidings 8 monition 10 admonition, suggestion 11 instruction 12 consultation, deliberation 14 recommendation

seek: 6 huddle 7 consult

advisable: 6 proper 7 prudent 9 befitting, desirable, expedient

advise: 4 read, rede, warn 5 aread, areed, coach, guide 6 confer, exhort, inform, re-

veal **7** apprise, apprize, counsel **8** acquaint, admonish **9** encourage, recommend
adviser, advisor: **4** aide, tout **5** coach, tutor **6** doctor, lawyer, nestor **7** monitor, teacher **8** attorney, preacher **9** counselor, physician **10** admonisher, counsellor, instructor
advisory: **6** urging **7** prudent **9** expedient, hortative, hortatory
body: **5** board **7** cabinet, council
advocate: pro **4** abet **5** adopt, favor, plead **6** assert, backer, defend, lawyer **7** abettor, apostle, endorse, espouse, scholar, support **8** attorney, champion, partisan **9** apologist, barrister, counselor, paraclete, proponent, recommend **11** intercessor
of new laws: **9** neonomian
adytum: **6** shrine **7** sanctum **9** sanctuary
adz, adze: ax; axe **7** hatchet
Aeacus: *father:* **4** Zeus
son: **6** Peleus **7** Telamon
Aeetes' daughter: **5** Medea
Aegean Sea: *ancient peoples:* **5** Psara, Psyra **6** Samian **7** Leleges, Samiote
gulf: **5** Saros
island: Ios **4** Nios, Rodi, Scio **5** Chios, Melos, Naxia, Naxos, Paros, Patmo, Psara, Samos, Tenos, Thera **6** Ikaria, Ipsara, Kariot, Lemnos, Patmos, Rhodes, Skyros **7** Amorgos, Nikaria **8** Cyclades, Mytilene, Mytilini, Santorin, Sporades **10** Dodecanese, Samothrace, Samothrake **11** Castelrosso **12** Castellorizo
port: **4** Enos
river into: **6** Struma, Vardar **7** Marista
rock: Aex
Aegeon's wife: **7** Aemilia
aeger: ill **4** sick **6** excuse
Aegir's wife: Ran
aegis, egis: **6** shield **7** auspice, defence, defense **9** patronage **10** protection **11** sponsorship
Aegisthus' father: **8** Thyestes
Aegyptus: *brother:* **6** Danaus
father: **5** Belus
son: **7** Lynceus
Aello: **5** Harpy
Aeneas: *beloved:* **4** Dido
companion: **7** Achates
father: **8** Anchises
grandfather: **5** Capys
great-grandson: **4** Brut
mother: **9** Aphrodite
rival: **6** Turnus
son: Iulus **8** Ascanius
wife: **6** Creusa **7** Lavinia
Aeneid: *author:* **6** Vergil, Virgil
first word: **4** arma
hero: **6** Aeneas
second word: **8** virumque
third word: **4** cano
Aengus' mother: **5** Boann
Aeolian lyricist: **6** Sappho
Aeolus' daughter: **6** Canace **8** Halcyone
aeon, eon: age, era **5** cycle, Kalpa **6** period
aeonian, eonian: **7** eternal, lasting **8** infinite **11** everlasting
aerate: **6** aerify, charge **7** inflate **9** oxygenate, ventilate
aerial: **4** aery, airy **5** aeric, lofty **6** unreal **7** antenna **8** antennae (pl.), ethereal **9** imaginary **13** unsubstantial
aerialist: **10** trapeze man **11** entertainer
garment: **7** leotard
aerie: **4** nest **5** brood **9** penthouse
aeriform: **6** unreal **7** gaseous
aerify: **6** aerate, infuse **8** vaporize
aerobatics: **4** loop, roll **5** stunt
aerobe: **8** organism **9** bacterium
aerodrome: **7** airport **8** airfield
aerolite: **9** meteorite **10** brontolite
aeronaut: **5** pilot **8** operator, traveler
aeronautics: **7** science **8** aviation
pert. to: **4** aero
aerose: **6** brassy
aerostat: **7** airship, balloon **8** aircraft
aerugo: **4** rust **6** patina **9** verdigris
aery: **6** aerial **8** ethereal **9** visionary **11** incorporeal
aes: **4** coin **6** bronze
Aesculapian: **6** doctor **7** medical **9** medicinal, physician
Aesculapius' teacher: **6** Chiron
Aeson's son: **5** Jason
Aesop work: **6** Fables
character: ox; ant, ass, dog, fox **4** frog, hare, lion **5** eagle, mouse **8** tortoise **11** grasshopper
aesthetic, esthetic: **8** artistic, tasteful **9** beautiful
Aeta: Ita **8** Filipino **10** Philippino
Aether's father: **6** Erebus
Aetolian prince: **6** Tydeus
aevia: **8** alleluia
afar: off **4** away, saho **6** remote **7** distant
affable: **4** open **5** civil, frank, suave **6** benign, facile, urbane **7** amiable, likable **8** charming, familiar, friendly, gracious, pleasant, sociable **9** courteous **10** accessible **11** complaisant
affair: **4** case, duel **5** event, fight, levee, party, thing **6** action, battle, matter **7** concern **8** business, endeavor, intrigue, occasion **9** endeavour, rickmatic **10** engagement, proceeding **11** transaction **12** circumstance
affect: hit **4** melt, move, stir **5** allot, alter, fancy, feign, haunt, impel, mince, touch **6** aspire, assign, assume, change, desire,

soften, strike, thrill 7 attinge, concern, emotion, feeling, impress, operate, passion, pretend, profess 8 allocate, disposed, frequent, interest, simulate 9 cultivate, distemper, influence 11 counterfeit, disposition, hypothecate, inclination

each other: 8 interact

affectation: air 4 pose, sham 5 mince 7 display, foppery, grimace, pietism 8 fondness, pretense 9 arrogance, hypocrisy, mannerism

affected: 4 airy 5 ailed, apish, moved 6 formal, seized 7 minikin, smitten, stilted, touched 8 attacked, disposed, mannered 9 cherished, unnatural 10 artificial 11 pretentious

affection: 4 love 5 amour, heart 6 cherte, esteem, malady, regard 7 ailment, charity, emotion, feeling, symptom 8 fondness, tendency 10 attachment, friendship, propensity, tenderness 11 disposition, inclination

parental: 6 storge

affectionate: 4 fond, warm 6 ardent, doting, loving, tender 7 amorous, devoted, earnest, zealous 8 attached, parental, sisterly 9 brotherly

affeer: 6 affirm, assess

afferent: 4 bear 6 esodic 7 sensory 9 ascending 11 centripetal

affiance: 5 faith, trust 6 assure, engage, ensure, fiance, pledge, plight 7 betroth, promise 8 contract, reliance 9 assurance, betrothal 10 confidence

affiant: 8 deponent 9 affidavit

affidavit: 4 oath 7 affiant 9 statement 10 deposition 11 declaration

affiliate: 4 ally, unit 5 adopt, merge, unite 6 attach, branch, relate 7 ascribe, chapter, connect 9 associate 10 fraternize, subsidiary 11 incorporate

affinity: 6 family, liking 7 kinship, rapport 8 alliance, relation 10 attraction, conformity, connection 11 propinquity, resemblance 12 acquaintance, friendliness, relationship 13 companionship, consanguinity

affirm: 4 affy, aver, avow 5 posit, state, swear, vouch 6 allege, assert, attest, avouch, depose, ratify, verify 7 confirm, declare, profess, testify 8 maintain 9 predicate, pronounce 10 asseverate

affirmation: vow, yes 4 amen, oath, word 9 affidavit, assertion, statement 10 deposition 11 declaration, proposition 12 asseveration, ratification

by negative understatement: 7 litotes

affirmative: ay; aye, nod, yah, yea, yep, yes 4 amen, yeah 8 dogmatic, positive 10 cataphatic 11 affirmatory, declarative, predicative 12 conformative

affix: add, fix, pin 4 clip, join, nail, seal, 5 annex, stamp, unite 6 anchor, append, attach, fasten, settle, staple 7 adhibit, connect, entitle, impress, subjoin

afflatus: 4 fury 5 furor 6 frenzy, vision 7 impulse 9 breathing 11 inspiration

afflict: ail, rue, try, vex 4 hurt, pain, rack 5 array, beset, gripe, grill, harry, wound 6 burden, grieve, harass, humble, infect, pester, remord 7 chasten, oppress, torment, trouble 8 distress 9 overthrow, persecute

afflicted: sad 5 sorry 6 ailing, woeful 7 grieved, smitten 8 impaired, troubled 9 depressed, lacerated

affliction: woe 4 evil, loss, pain, sore 5 cross, grief 6 duress, misery, pathos, plague, sorrow 7 ailment, disease, illness, scourge, trouble 8 calamity, distress, hardship, severity, sickness 9 adversity, grievance, martyrdom 10 misfortune 12 wretchedness

afflue: 4 flow

affluence: 4 ease 6 afflux, influx, plenty, riches, wealth 7 fortune 8 opulence 9 abundance, concourse, plenitude, profusion, substance 10 prosperity 11 sufficiency

affluent: fat 4 rich 5 flush, river 6 stream 7 copious, flowing, opulent, wealthy 8 abundant 9 plenteous, tributary

afflux: 4 flow

afford: 4 bear, give, lend 5 grant, incur, spare, stand, yield 6 confer, manage, supply 7 achieve, forward, furnish, further, produce, provide 8 minister 10 accomplish

affray: 4 feud, fray, riot 5 alarm, brawl, broil, fight, melee, scare 6 attack, battle, fright, strife, terror, tumult 7 assault, contest, quarrel, scuffle, startle 8 frighten 9 encounter 11 disturbance

affright: cow 4 fear 5 alarm, daunt, dread, scare 6 agrise, appall, dismay 7 confuse, startle, terrify 8 frighten 10 intimidate

affront: cut 4 defy, slap 5 abuse, beard, peeve 6 harass, injure, insult, nettle, offend, slight 7 outrage, provoke 8 confront, disgrace, illtreat, irritate 9 encounter, indignity, sobriquet 10 soubriquet

affusion: 7 pouring 8 infusion

affy: 4 join, rely 5 trust 6 affirm 7 betroth, confide, espouse 8 affiance

afghan: rug 7 blanket 8 coverlet

Afghan: dog 5 hound Pashto 8 language

Afghan carpet: 5 Herat

Afghan fox: 6 corsac
Afghanistan: *carpet:* 7 Bukhara
city: 5 Cabul (c.), Herat, Kabul (c.) 6 Ghuzni 8 Kandahar
coin: pul 6 abbasi, anania 7 afghani
language: 6 Pashto, Pushto
mountain: 8 Sulaiman 9 Himalayas, Hindu Kush
native: 7 Sistani
pony: 4 yabu 5 yaboo
prince: 4 amir, emir 5 ameer, emeer
river: 5 Cabul, Indus 7 Hari Rud, Helmund 9 Archandab
tribe: 4 Safi, Ulus
aficionado: fan 7 amateur, devotee 8 follower
afield: 6 abroad, astray
afire: 4 alow 5 alowe, eager 6 ablaze, ardent 7 burning, flaming
afloat: 4 asea 5 awaft, awash 6 adrift, buoyed, natant 7 flooded, unfixed 8 floating
afoot: 5 about, astir 6 abroad 7 walking 9 unmounted
aforesaid: 5 ditto, named, prior 8 previous 9 foregoing 10 antecedent
aforethought: 8 prepense 10 deliberate 11 forethought 12 premeditated
aforetime: ere 8 formerly
afraid: rad (Sc.) 5 timid 6 aghast, craven, scared 7 afeared, alarmed, anxious, fearful, gastful 8 cowardly, ghastful, timorous 9 shrinking, terrified 10 affrighted, frightened 12 fainthearted 13 pusillanimous
afreet: 4 jinn 5 afrit, demon, giant, jinni 6 afrite
afresh: 4 anew, anon, over 5 again, newly 6 denovo, encore 8 repeated
Africa: *animal:* ayu 4 arui 5 civet, genet, okapi, potto, ratel, zebra, zoril 6 aoudad, aye-aye, quagga, serval 7 nandine 8 aardvark, pangolin, suricate
antelope: gnu, kob 4 bisa, guib, koba, kudu, oryx, tolo, topi, tora, zenu 5 addax, beisa, bongo, eland, nagor, oribi, peele 6 duiker, grimme, impala, koodoo, rhebok 7 blaubok, blesbok, boshbok, defassa, gemsbok, grysbok, reitbok, sassaby, stembok 8 blesbuck, bontebok, bosehbok, steenbok, steinbok 9 steenbock 10 duikerbuck, hartebeest
Arab tribe: 9 Battakhin
ash: 4 atar
ass: 6 quagga
aunt: 5 tanta
baboon: 5 drill 8 mandrill
bass: iyo
bat: 10 hammerhead
bean: 7 calabar
beer: 5 pombe
bird: 4 lory, taha 6 weaver 7 touraco, xurakoo 8 umbretti 9 hammerkop
blaubok: 5 etaac 8 antelope
boat: 4 dhow
boss: 4 baas
bread: 5 kisra
buffalo: 5 niare
burrowing animal: 6 gerbil 8 aardvark, suricate
bushman: 4 Qung
bustard: 4 kori 5 paauw
caffeine tree: 4 cola, kola
camp: 4 boma 5 lager 6 laager
canoe: 7 almadia, almadie
cape: ras 4 juby, vert, yubi
carnivore: 4 lion 5 hyena, ratel 7 cheetah, leopard
cataract: 8 Victoria
catfish: 4 shal 5 schal 6 docmac
cattle: 5 niata
cattle pen: 5 kraal 6 zareba 7 zareeba
charm: 4 juju 5 saffi, safie 6 grigri, saphie 8 greegree
chief: 4 kaid 8 caboceer
city: 4 Oran 5 Accra, Cairo, Dakar, Lagos, Rabat, Tunis 6 Bangui, Ibadan 7 Algiers, Tripoli, Yaoundi 8 Cape Town, Freetown, Khartoum, Monrovia, Pretoria 9 Timbuctoo 10 Addis Ababa, Alexandria, Casablanca 11 Brazzaville, Dar es Salaam 12 Johannesburg, Leopoldville 14 Elisabethville
civet: 7 nandine
cloak: 5 jelab 6 jellab
coin: 4 akey, pesa 5 rupie, toque
colonist: 4 Boer
colony: see *country* below
coney: das 6 dassie
conference: 6 indaba
corn: 6 mealie
corn lily: 4 ixia
country: 4 Chad, Mali, Togo 5 Egypt, Gabon, Ghana, Kenya, Libya, Natal, Niger, Sudan, Zaire 6 Angola, Gambia, Guinea, Malawi, Uganda 7 Algeria, Burundi, Dahomey, Lesotho, Liberia, Morocco, Nigeria, Senegal, Somalia, Tunisia 8 Cameroon, Ethiopia, Malagasy, Tanzania 9 Swaziland 10 Mozambique 11 Sierra Leone
dance: 4 juba
deity: 6 nyambe, nzambi
desert: 5 Igidi 6 Libyan, Sahara 8 Kalahari
desert region: erg
dialect: Twi 4 Akan, Geez, Saho, Taal 5 Bantu, Fanti 7 Swahili
dish: 8 couscous
district: 4 Rand, Tibu 5 Nubia 6 Ruanda

dog: 7 basenji
dried meat: 7 biltong
drink: 8 skokiaan
dunes: erg
eagle: 8 berghaan
enclosure: 5 bomar, kraal
farmyard: 4 werf
fetish: see *charm* above
finch: 7 senegal
fly: 5 kivus 6 tsetse
food: 6 paw-paw 7 cassava
fox: 4 asse 5 caama 6 fennec
fruit: 5 terfa 6 terfez
gangster: 7 tsotsis
garden: 6 shamba
garment: 4 haik, tobe 6 kaross
gazelle: 4 admi, cora, dama, kudu, mohr, nohr, oryx 5 ariel, mhorr 7 buffalo, dibatag 9 springbok
giraffelike animal: 5 okapi
gold region: 4 Rand
gorge: 5 kloof
grass: 4 alfa 5 fundi 7 esparto
grassland: 5 veldt
greenhorn: 5 ikona
groundnut: 5 gobbe
guard: 5 askar
gulf: 5 Gabes, Sidra 6 Guinea
gully: 5 donga 6 nullah
gun: 4 roer
harp: 5 nanga
headland: kop, ras
headman: 8 caboceer
helmet: 4 topi 5 topee
hemp: ife
hill: kop
hornbill: 4 tock
horse: 4 barb
horse disease: 5 surra
Hottentot: 4 Nama
house: 5 tembe
hunt: 6 safari
hut: 5 kraal, tembe
instrument: 5 nanga, rebab, zanze 6 balafo
iris: 4 ixia
Islamic sect: 9 Almohades
island: 6 Azores, Djerba 7 Bourbon, Comoros, Madeira, Reunion, Socotra 8 Canaries, St. Helena 9 Ascension, Cape Verde, Mauritius 10 Fernando Po, Madagascar, Seychelles 12 Prince Edward
jackal: 5 diebs
king: 5 negus 8 Selassie
lake: 4 Asal, Chad, Lifu, Tana 5 Abayo, chott, Moero, Mweru, Ngami, Nyasa, Rirwa, Shott, Tchad, Tsana, Tumba 6 Albert, Dembel, Dilolo, Nyanza, Nyassa, Rudolf, Shirwa 7 Leopold, Malumba 8 Victoria 9 Bangweulu, Stephanie 10 Tanganyika 12 Albert Edward
language: 5 Bantu, Hausa 6 Hamite 7 Swahili
legislature: 4 raad
lemur: 5 potto 6 maholi 8 kinkajou 10 angwantibo
lily: 4 aloe, ixia
livestock: fe
lynx: 7 caracal
mahogany: 9 cailcedra
measure: ton 4 doti, muid, rood, rope 5 curba, darah, mkono 6 morgen 7 schepel 8 Cape foot
monkey: 4 mona, mono, waag 5 patas 6 grivet, guenon 7 guereza 8 talapoin
mortar: 5 swish
mountain: 4 Pare 5 Atlas, Kenia, Natal 7 Cathkin, Kabylic 8 Cameroon 10 Drakenberg 11 Kilimanjaro
Muslim: 6 Berber
narcotic: 5 dagga
native(see also *people* below): Jur, Vai, Vei 4 Bari, Egbo 5 Bantu, Felup, Sotik 6 Fellup 7 Dahoman 8 Gabunese
nurse: aja 4 ayah
nut: 4 cola, kola
oak: 7 turtosa
old name: 5 Libya
ostrich: 4 rhea
palm: 4 doom, doum 6 raffia, raphia
palmyra: 6 ronier
pass: Nek
peasant: 4 kopi
people: Ga; Abo, Edo, Ewe, Ijo, Jur, Kru, Vai, Vei, Yao 4 Akim, Akka, Akra, Arab, Asha, Bari, Boni, Doma, Efik, Egbe, Ekoi, Golo, Habe, Hutu, Ibok, Kali, Leda, Lozi, Luri, Madi, Majo, Moor, Nama, Nuba, Riff, Sara, Suto, Tshi, Viti, Yako, Zulu 5 Afifi, Bantu, Batwa, Dinka, Hausa, Inkra, Kafir, Mandi, Masai, Mende, Pygmy, Sanye, Temne, Tutsi, Wa-yao 6 Berber, Damara, Djerma, Dorobo, Fulani, Hamite, Kikuyu, Somali, Sousou, Tuareg, Ubangi, Wabena 7 Ashanti, Bambute, Bapindi, Batonga, Dahoman, Kindiga, Malinke, Nilotic, Sandawe, Songhai, Voltaic
pigeon: 7 namaqua
pine: 6 ronier
plant: 4 ocra 5 argel, calla 6 arghel
plateau: 5 karoo
poison: 7 calabar
polecat: 5 zoril 6 musang
port: 5 Dakar 8 Freetown 10 Casablanca
Portuguese colony, former: 6 Angola
pygmy: 4 Akka 5 Afifi

reedbuck: 5 bohor, nagor 7 reitbok
region: 5 Nubia 6 Sahara
religious sect: 6 Coptic 7 Abelite
residence: 4 tato 5 kraal
rhinoceros: 6 umhofo
ridge: 4 rand
river: Job, Nun, Omo 4 Athi, Geba, Liba, Nile, Tana 5 Beira, Binue, Chobe, Congo, Kongo, Niger, Shari, Volta 6 Chinde, Gambia, Joliba, Rovuma, Sabaki, Ubangi 7 Atabara, Calabar, Limpopo, Semliki, Senegal, Zambesi 9 Crocodile
river bed: 5 donga
rosewood: 7 mulompi
scrub: 4 bito
seaport: Ibo 4 Oran 5 Dakar, Lagos, Tunis
secret society: Mau 6 Mau-Mau
servant: 4 volk
shallow lake: 5 chott, shott
sheep: 4 zenu
snake: boa 5 elaps, mamba 12 schaapsteker
soldier: 5 spahi 6 askari
sorcery: obe, obi 5 obeah
sorghum: 4 imfe 6 imphee
soup powder: 4 lalo
spear: 7 assagai, assegai
spiritual power: 4 ngai
squirrel: 5 xerus
stockade: 4 boma 6 zareba 7 zareeba
stork: 6 simbil 7 marabou
tableland: 5 karoo
tick: 6 tampan
title: 4 baas, sidi 5 bwana
tree: 4 akee, baku, bito, cola, etua, kola, moli, odum, olax, shea 5 abura, artar, bumbo, njave, odoom, sassy, siris, tenio 6 baobab, dukuma 7 assagai, assegai 8 gamdeboo 9 sassywood
tribe: See *people* above
valley: 4 daal, wadi, wady
village: 4 stad 5 kraal, stadt
wading bird: 4 ibis 8 ombrette
war dance: 7 calinda
wheat: 6 imphee
wild hog: 4 boar 7 warthog 9 boschvark
wild sheep: 4 arui 6 aoudad
wildcat: 6 serval
wind: 9 harmattan
witchcraft bean: 7 calabar
wolf: 4 aard
wood: 4 teak 5 ebony
worker: 4 volk
worm: loa

Afrikaans: 4 Boer, Taal
aft: 4 back, rear 5 abaft, after 6 astern, behind 9 posterior
opposite of: 4 fore
after: eft 4 anon, next, past 5 infra, later, since, apres (F.) 6 behind, beyond, follow, hinder 9 afterward, following, hereafter 10 subsequent, succeeding
awhile: 4 anon 5 later
prefix: 4 meta, post
after-dinner: 12 postprandial
afterbreast: 10 metathorax
aftermath: 4 loss 5 issue, rowen 6 eddish, effect, profit, result, sequel, upshot 7 stubble 11 consequence
aftermost: 4 last 8 hindmost
afternoon nap: 6 siesta
afternoon performance: 7 matinee
afterpiece: 5 epode, exode 8 postlude
aftersong: 5 epode
afterthought: 6 regret 7 remorse 15 reconsideration
in letter: PS10 postscript
afterward: 4 then 5 later 9 afterhend 10 thereafter 12 subsequently
afterwrist: 10 metacarpus
aga: 4 lord 5 chief 9 commander
wife: 5 begum
agacella: 8 antelope
Agag's slayer: 6 Samuel
again: bis, eft 4 anew, anon, back, more, over 6 afresh, denovo, encore, iterum (L.) 7 further 8 moreover
prefix: re
against: vs (abbr.); con, non 4 anti 5 anent 6 anenst, versus 7 opposed 8 adversus
prefix: ob 4 anti, para 6 contra
against the law: 7 illegal 8 unlawful
agal: 4 cord, rope
agalloch: 5 garoo 8 calambac 9 aloeswood, calambour, eaglewood
agallochum: 5 aloes
agama: 6 iguana, lizard
Agamemnon: *avenger:* 7 Orestes
brother: 8 Menelaus
daughter: 7 Electra 9 Iphigenia
father: 6 Atreus
rival: 9 Aegisthus
son: 7 Orestes
wife: 12 Clytemnestra
agape: 4 love, open 5 feast 6 gaping 7 yawning 10 bewildered
agar, agar-agar: 4 moss 6 gelose
agaric: 6 fungus
agasp: 5 eager 7 gasping 9 astounded
agate: taw 4 ruby 6 achate, marble, pebble, quartz 9 burnisher, drawplate 10 chalcedony
agave: 4 aloe 5 amole, datil 6 maguey, mescal, pulque 9 amaryllis
fiber: 4 pita 5 istle, sisal
Agaz: 6 Indian
age: eld, eon, era 4 aeon, olam, time 5 cycle, epoch, ripen, years 6 mature, mellow, pe-

riod, siecle, wither **7** century **8** duration, eternity, lifetime, majority, maturity **9** senectude **10** generation
geological: See **geology** *age*
modern: **6** atomic
pert. to: **4** eval **6** senile **9** geriatric
same: **6** coeval
aged: old **5** anile, hoary, olden, passe **6** feeble, infirm, mature, senile, ogyian **7** ancient, elderly **9** nestorian, senescent, venerable **10** antiquated
agee: **4** awry **5** agley, askew
ageless: **7** eternal **8** timeless
agency: **4** dint, hand **5** force, lever, means, moyen, proxy **6** bureau, medium, office **9** influence, operation **10** management **14** intermediation **15** instrumentality
news: AP; UPI **4** Tass **5** Domei **7** Reuter's
suffix: eer, fic, ier **4** ator, ific
agendum: **5** slate **6** record, ritual **7** liturgy, program **10** memorandum
Agenor: *daughter:* **6** Europa
father: **7** Antenor
son: **6** Cadmus
agent: spy **4** doer, gene, g-man, T-man **5** actor, buyer, cause, envoy, means, organ, proxy **6** broker, commis, dealer, deputy, factor, peskar, seller **7** bailiff, channel, coucher, facient, proctor **8** aumildar, emissary, executor, operator, promoter, salesman **9** canvasser, consignee, go-between, protector **10** commissary, instrument **11** facilitator **12** intermediary **14** representative
appoint: **6** depute **8** deputize
insurance: **11** underwriter
narcotics: **4** nark
native: **8** aumildar
servile: **6** minion
suffix: see **agency** *suffix*
symbol: Agt
agger: **4** road, tide **5** mound **7** rampart **9** earthwork **10** prominence
agglomerate: **4** heap, lump, mass, pile, wind **6** gather **7** cluster, collect **10** collection **12** conglomerate
agglutination: **8** adhesion
aggrandize: **4** lift **5** boost, exalt, raise **7** advance, augment, dignify, elevate, enlarge, magnify, promote **8** increase
aggravate: irk, nag, vex **4** load, twit **5** anger, annoy, taunt, tease **6** burden, pester, worsen **7** enhance, enlarge, magnify, provoke **8** aggrieve, heighten, increase, irritate **9** intensify **10** exacerbate, exaggerate, exasperate
aggregate: add, all, sum **4** bulk, mass **5** bunch, gross, total, unite, whole **6** amount, volume **7** collect **9** accretion, composite **10** accumulate, collection **11** combination, composition
aggregation: **4** herd **5** flock, group **7** cluster **9** congeries **10** assemblage, collection **11** association
aggression: war **4** raid **6** attack, injury **7** assault, offense **8** invasion **9** intrusion **11** provocation **12** encroachment
aggressive: **7** pushing **9** assertive **12** enterprising
aggressor: **9** assailant
aggrieve: try **4** harm, hurt, pain **5** harry, wrong **6** injure **7** afflict, oppress, trouble **8** distress **9** aggravate, persecute
aggrieved: **4** sore
aggroup: See **group**
aggry, aggri: **4** bead **5** charm
agha: See **aga**
aghast: **6** afraid **7** shocked **8** appalled **9** horrified, petrified, terrified
agile: **4** deft, fast, lish, spry, wiry **5** alert, brisk, lithe, quick, withy **6** active, lissom, lively, nimble, supple **7** lissome, salient, springy **8** dextrous **9** dexterous
agio: **5** batta **7** premium **8** discount, exchange **9** allowance, brokerage, deduction **10** percentage
agist: tax **4** feed, rate **5** graze **7** pasture
agitate: fan, irk, jar, vex, wey **4** fret, move, plot, rile, rock, seek, stir, teem **5** alarm, churn, drive, harry, rouse, shake **6** arouse, debate, devise, excite, foment, harass, incite, jumble, manage, rattle, ruffle, seethe **7** actuate, canvass, commove, concuss, discuss, disturb, perturb, revolve, trouble **8** activate, contrive, convulse, disquiet, distract, transact **10** administer, discompose
agitation: gog **4** fear, gust, heat **5** hurry, storm **6** bustle, energy, flight, flurry, jabble, quiver, tumult **7** emotion, ferment, flutter, rampage, tempest, turmoil **8** paroxysm, upheaval **9** carfuffle, commotion, confusion, estuation **10** combustion, ebullition, excitement, turbulence **11** trepidation **13** effervescence
prone to: **9** emotional
Aglaia: **5** Grace
aglet, aiglet: tab, tag **4** lace, stud **5** plate **7** pendant, spangle **8** hawthorn, staylace
agley: **4** awry **5** aside, askew, wrong
agnate: **4** akin **6** allied **7** cognate, kindred
agnomen: **4** name **5** alias **7** epithet, surname **8** cognomen, nickname
agnomination: **7** echoing **10** repetition **12** alliteration
agnostic: **7** doubter, skeptic **8** nescient **10** unbeliever **11** freethinker
agnus dei: **4** bell, lamb **6** prayer

ago: by 4 erst, past, syne, yore 5 agone, since
agog: 4 avid, keen 5 astir, eager 6 lively 7 excited 8 vigilant 9 expectant, impatient
agon: 6 debate 7 contest 8 argument, struggle
agonize: 4 bear, rack 6 strain, writhe 10 excruciate
agony: 4 pain, pang 5 dolor, grief, panic, throe, trial 6 aching 7 anguish, anxiety, emotion, torment, torture, travail 8 distress, paroxysm 9 suffering 11 tribulation
agora: 8 assembly
agouti, agouty: 4 paca 5 color 6 animal, rodent
agra: 4 pain 7 seizure
Agra tomb: 8 Taj Mahal
agrafe, agraffe: 4 hook 5 clamp, clasp 6 eyelet
agrarian: 5 rural 8 pastoral 10 campestral 12 agricultural
agree: fit, gee, pan, yes 4 gibe, jibe, side, suit 5 admit, allow, atone, grant, hitch, match, tally, yield, unite 6 accede, accord, assent, comply, concur, condog, cotton, engage, settle, square, submit 7 arrange, comport, concede, conform, consent, promise 8 coincide, contract, covenant, quadrate 9 acquiesce, congruous, co-operate, harmonize, reconcile, stipulate 10 astipulate, correspond, homologate
agreeable: 4 easy, good, joli, lief, nice 5 amene, jolie, ready, suave, sweet 6 comely, dulcet, savory 7 adapted, amabile, amiable, couthie, greable, welcome, willing 8 amenable, charming, grateful, pleasant, pleasing, sociable, suitable 9 accordant, appealing, compliant, consonant, desirable 10 acceptable, compatible, convenient, harmonious 11 acquiescent, conformable 13 companionable
render: 7 dulcify
agreeableness of letters: 6 eutony
agreeing: 11 consentient
agreement: nod 4 bond, deal, mise, pact 5 lease, terms 6 action, assent, cartel, treaty, unison 7 bargain, closure, compact, concert, consent, entente, harmony, oneness, paction, rapport 8 contract, sympathy 9 accedence, accession, character, collusion, communion, concordat, condition, congruity, consensus, convenant, indenture, statement, unanimity 10 accordance, compliance, compromise, conformity, consonance, conspiracy, convention, obligation 11 arrangement, concordance, concurrence, resemblance, stipulation 12 capitulation 13 understanding
in opinion: 9 consensus
written: 6 cartel 8 contract
agremens, agrements: 6 graces 9 amenities, ornaments 14 embellishments
agrestic: 5 rural 6 rustic 7 bucolic 10 unpolished
agricultural: 8 geoponic
agriculture: 7 farming, tillage 8 agronomy 9 husbandry 10 agrotechny
area: 11 breadbasket
building: 4 barn, silo
chemical: 10 fertilizer
college student: 5 aggie
comb. form: 4 agro
establishment: 4 farm 5 grove, ranch 7 orchard
god: 4 Nabu, Nebo, Thor 6 Faunus, Tammuz 8 Amaethon
goddess: Ops 5 Ceres 7 Demeter
machine: 4 disk, plow 5 baler, drill, mower 6 binder, harrow, header, reaper, seeder, tedder 7 combine, tractor 8 thrasher, thresher 9 separator 10 cultivator 11 caterpillar
overseer: 8 agronome 10 agronomist
pert. to: 7 georgic
science: 11 arviculture
worker: 4 okie, peon 5 Arkie 6 cocker, farmer 7 migrant, peasant 8 farmhand
agriculturist: 6 farmer, grower 7 planter, rancher 10 agricolist, husbandman, orchardist
agrimony: 4 hemp 6 bidens 7 borwort
Agrippina's son: 4 Nero
agrise: 5 abhor, dread 6 loathe 7 shudder, terrify, tremble 8 affright
aground: 6 ashore 7 beached 8 stranded
agrypnia: 8 insomnia 13 sleeplessness
agua: 4 toad 5 water
aguacate: 7 avocado
aguamas: 7 pinguin
ague: 5 chill, fever 7 malaria
ague tree: 9 sassafras
agueweed: 7 boneset, comfrey, gentian 10 eupatorium
aguja: gar 6 marlin 9 spearfish
Ahab: *daughter* 7 Athalia 8 Athaliah
father: 4 Omri
wife: 7 Jezebel
Ahasuerus: *minister:* 5 Haman
wife: 6 Vashti
Ahaz: *son:* 8 Hezekiah
wife: Abi
Ahaziah's sister: 9 Jehosheba 11 Jehosobeath
ahead: on 4 fore 5 afore 6 before, onward 7 forward, leading 8 adelante, advanced, anterior 9 preceding
prefix: pre
Ahinoam: *husband:* 4 Saul 5 David
son: 5 Amnon

Aholibamah's husband: 4 Esau
Ahriman's angel: div 4 deev, deva
ahu: 4 heap 5 mound 7 gazelle
ahuehuete: 5 cedar 6 sabino 7 cypress
ai: 5 sloth 8 edentate
aid: key 4 abet, back, beet, help, pony 5 allay, boost, coach, favor, grant, serve, treat 6 assist, favour, relief, remedy, rescue, second, succor, uphold 7 advance, forward, further, relieve, subsidy, support 8 befriend 9 alleviate, auxiliary 10 assistance, facilitate 11 collaborate, countenance
Aida: *composer:* 5 Verdi
father: 8 Amonasro
lover: 7 Radames
rival: 7 Amneris
aide: 6 deputy, second 7 officer, orderly 8 adjutant 9 assistant 11 subordinate 12 underofficer
aigrette: 5 egret, heron, plume, spray 8 feathers
ail: 4 fail, pain, pine 6 affect, bother, falter, suffer 7 afflict, decline, trouble 8 complain, distress 13 indisposition
Ailie: 5 Helen
ailment (see also **disease**): ail 6 malady 7 disease, illness 8 disorder, sickness, weakness 9 affection, complaint, infirmity 13 indisposition
aim: end, lay, try 4 bent, butt, goal, head, plan 5 essay, guess, level, point, sight, train 6 aspire, design, direct, esteem, intend, intent, object, scheme, strive 7 address, purpose 8 consider, endeavor, estimate 9 calculate, endeavour, intention, objective 10 aspiration, conjecture, estimation
aimless: 4 idle 5 blind 6 chance, random 8 drifting 9 desultory 10 undirected 11 purposeless
aimlessness: 8 flanerie
aine: 5 elder 6 senior
air: sky 4 aria, aura, lilt, mien, neon, pose, song, tell, tune, vent 5 beach (Sc.), ether, ozone, voice 6 aerate, aether, allure, aspect, broach, cachet, helium, manner, melody, ostent, regard, vanity, welkin 7 bearing, display, exhibit, krypton 8 attitude, behavior, carriage, sandbank (Sc.) 9 behaviour, semblance, ventilate 10 appearance, atmosphere, deportment 11 affectation, haughtiness 12 stratosphere
comb. form: aer, atm 4 aeri, aero, atmo
containing: 9 pneumatic
current: 4 wind 5 draft 6 breeze 7 draught
downward motion (pert. to): 9 katabatic
element: 5 argon, xenon 6 oxygen 8 nitrogen
in the: 5 aloft
measuring device: 9 aerometer, airometer
musical: see **melody**
overcast: 4 haze
upper: 5 ether 6 aether
air fleet arrangement: 7 echelon 8 squadron
air navigation officer: 8 avigator
air plant: 8 epiphyte
air pressure: 5 baric
air propeller: fan
air spirit: 5 Ariel, sylph
aircraft (see also **airplane**): 4 kite 5 blimp, plane 6 copter, glider 7 balloon, chopper 8 aerostat, airplane, autogyro, zeppelin 9 dirigible, orthopter 10 helicopter
carrier: 7 flattop
fleet formation: 7 echelon
manufacturer: 4 Vega 5 Astra 6 Bendix, Boeing, Curtis, Hughes, United, Vultee, Wright 7 Convair, Douglas, Grumman 8 Lockheed, American, Northrop, Republic
motorless: 6 glider
part: fin 4 keel, tail, wing 5 cabin 6 cabane 7 aileron, cockpit, nacelle 8 fusilage 9 empennage
pilotless: 5 drone
route: 6 skyway
route marker: 5 pylon
shelter: 6 hangar
unit: 5 squad 10 escadrille
vapor: 8 contrail
airing: 4 walk 6 pasear 8 exposure
airn: 4 iron
airplane (see also **aircraft**): jet, MIG, SST 4 gyro, zero 5 avion (F.), liner 6 bomber, copter, glider, 7 biplane, clipper, fighter 9 monoplane
inventor: 6 Wright
maneuver: 4 buzz, dive, loop, roll 8 nosedive 9 chandelle
operator: 5 flier, flyer, pilot 7 aviator 8 aeronaut
airport: 5 drome 8 airdrome, airfield 9 aerodrome
airs: 6 vanity 10 mannerisms, pretension 11 affectation, haughtiness, preciseness
airship: See **aircraft, airplane**
airt: See **direct**
airtight: 6 sealed 8 hermetic 12 impenetrable
airy: gay 4 cool, rare, thin 5 empty, huffy, light, merry 6 aerial, breezy, jaunty, jocund, lively 7 airlike, haughty 8 affected, animated, debonair, delicate, ethereal, flippant, graceful, trifling, volatile 9 sprightly, visionary, vivacious 11 atmospheric 13 insubstantial, unsubstantial
aiseweed: 8 goutweed

aisle: way 4 lane, walk 5 alley 7 passage 8 corridor 10 ambulatory, passageway

ait: oat eyot, holm, isle 5 islet

aitchbone: 9 natchbone

aith: 4 oath

aitu: god 5 demon 6 spirit

aizle: 5 ember, spark

ajaja: 4 bird 9 spoonbill

ajar: 4 open 10 discordant

Ajax's father: 7 Telamon

ajonjoli: 6 sesame

ajuga: 4 herb 7 bugloss 9 bugleweed

akia: 6 poison

akimbo: 6 angled

akin: sib 4 like, near, nigh 5 alike, close 6 agnate, allied 7 cognate, connate, germane, related, similar 10 correlated 11 appropriate 14 consanguineous

aku: 10 victorfish

akule: 4 fish 7 goggler

al, aal: 8 mulberry
dye: 8 morindin

ala: 4 axil, drum, wing 6 axilla, recess 8 winglike

Alabama: *city:* 5 Selma 6 Mobile 8 Anniston 10 Birmingham (c.)
county: Lee 4 Bibb, Clay, Dale, Hale, Pike 5 Coosa, Lamar 6 Etowah 7 Chilton
river: 5 Coosa
state flower: 9 goldenrod

alabarch: 10 magistrate

alabaster: 6 gypsum

alack: 4 alas 9 alackaday

alacrity: 5 haste, speed 8 celerity, rapidity 9 briskness, eagerness, readiness 11 promptitude, willingness 13 sprightliness

Aladdin's spirit: 4 jinn (pl.) 5 genie, genii (pl.)

a la diable: 7 deviled 8 seasoned

alameda: 4 mall, walk 9 promenade

Alamo: 4 fort, tree 6 battle, poplar, shrine 7 mission
hero: 5 Bowie 8 Crockett

a la mode: 4 mood 7 stylish 11 fashionable

alan: dog 9 wolfhound

alant: 10 sneezeweed

alantin: 6 inulin

alar: 6 pteric, winged 8 axillary, winglike 10 wing-shaped

alarm: din, SOS 4 bell, fear, gast 5 alert, broil, clock, larum, noise, panic, rouse, scare, siren, upset 6 affray, alarum, appall, arouse, attack, buzzer, dismay, excite, fright, outcry, signal, terror, tocsin 7 disturb, gloppen, startle, terrify, warning 8 frighten, surprise 9 commotion, diversion 11 disturbance, trepidation 13 consternation

alarmist: 9 pessimist, terrorist 11 scaremonger

alarum: See **alarm**

alas: ay; ach, heu, och, woe 5 alack, oimee 6 ochone 8 welladay, wellaway 12 interjection

Alaska: *animal:* 4 bear 6 Kadiak, Kodiak
auk: 5 arrie, murre
bear: 6 Kadiak, Kodiak
bird: auk 5 arrie, murre
blizzard: 5 purga
boat: 5 kayak, umiak 6 oomiac 7 angeyok, bidarka 8 bidarkee
city: 4 Nome 5 Sitka 6 Juneau (c.), Kodiak, Seward, Valdez 7 Cordova, Douglas, Klawock, Skagway 8 Latouche, Wrangell 9 Anchorage, Fairbanks, Ketchikan 10 Metlakatla, Petersburg
cotton grass: 10 eriophorum
fish: 4 atka 5 wacha 6 salmon 7 inconnu
garment: 5 parka
glacier: 4 Muir
highway: 5 Alcan
island: 4 Adak, Atka, Attu, Unga 5 Riska 6 Tanaka 8 Pribilof 9 Andreanof
island group: Fox, Rat 4 Near 8 Aleutian
liquor: 9 hoochinoo
mountain: Ada 4 Muir 5 Logan 8 McKinley 9 Blackburn 10 Saint Elias 11 Fairweather
native: auk 5 Aleut, Sitka 6 Ahtena, Eskimo 7 Tlingit 8 Aleutian
purchaser: 6 Seward
river: 4 Atna 5 Yukon 6 Copper, Innoko, Noatak, Tanana 7 Koyukuk, Susitna 9 Kuskokwim, Matanuska, Porcupine 10 Whitehorse
tree: 5 sitka 6 spruce

alate: ant 5 aphid 6 insect, winged

alb, albe: 7 camisia 8 vestment

albacore: 4 tuna 5 tunny 6 germon

Albania: *city:* 5 Berat 6 Avlona, Durres, Tirana (c), Tirane (c.), Valona 7 Chimara, Coritza, Durazzo, Elbasan, Koritza, Prevesa, Scutari 8 Tepeleni
coin: lek 5 franc 6 qintar
dialect: Geg 4 Cham, Gheg, Tosc, Tosk 7 Ghegish, Toskish
former king: Zog
lake: 7 Ochrida, Scutria
river: 4 Arta, Drin
soldier: 7 palikar

albatross: 4 bird 5 nelly 6 fabric 9 mallemuck

albeit: but, tho 5 altho 6 though 8 although 15 notwithstanding

albertin: 4 coin

Albion: 6 Anglia 7 England

albula: 4 fish 5 chiro

album: 4 book 6 record 8 register 9 scrapbook 10 collection
albumen seed: 9 endosperm
albuminoid: 7 elastin, keratin, protein 8 collagen
alburnum: 7 sapwood
alcalde, alcade: 5 judge 10 magistrate 11 burgomaster
alcazar: 6 castle, palace 8 fortress
Alcestis: *father:* 6 Pelias
husband: 7 Admetus
rescuer: 8 Heracles, Hercules
alchemist: 5 adept 8 hermetic
alchemy: art 5 magic 11 thaumaturgy
god: 6 Hermes
iron: 4 Mars
alchitran: oil 5 pitch 7 bitumen
Alcidice: *husband:* 9 Salmoneus
daughter: 4 Tyro
alcidine bird: auk 6 puffin 9 guillemot
Alcinous: *daughter:* 8 Nausicaa
wife: 5 Arete
Alcmaeon: *father:* 10 Amphiaraus
wife: 10 Callirrhoe
Alcmene's husband: 10 Amphitryon
alcohol (see also **alcoholic drink**): 5 ethyl, vinyl 6 liquor, methyl 7 ethanol 8 methanol
crystalline: 6 guaiol, talite 7 talitol
desire for: 10 dipsomania
liquid: 8 farnesol
radical: 4 amyl
solid: 6 sterin, sterol 11 cholesterol
standard: 5 proof
suffix: ol
alcoholic: 9 spiritous 11 dipsomaniac 12 intoxicating
alcoholic drink: ale, gin, rum 4 beer, grog, wine 5 julep, lager, negus, vodka 6 brandy, liquor, porter, whisky 7 liqueur, whiskey 8 cocktail, highball
Alcoran: 5 Koran
Alcott heroine: Jo; Amy, Meg 4 Beth
alcove: bay 4 nook 5 bower, niche, oriel 6 recess 7 cubicle, dinette, tablina (L. pl.) 8 alhacena (Sp.), tablinum 11 compartment
alder: arn (Sc.) 4 tree 5 shrub
genus: 5 almus
alderman: 6 bailie, senior 7 headman 10 magistrate
ale: mum 4 beer, bock, brew, flip 5 clink, lager, nappy, stout 6 alegar, liquor, porter, stingo, swanky 8 beverage, hugmatee
mixed with sweetener: 7 bragget
ale mug: 4 toby 5 stein
Alea: 5 light 6 Athena
alee: 5 ahead 7 leeward
opposite of: 5 stoss 8 aweather
alegar: ale
alehouse: pub 6 tavern 7 barroom 9 host-house
alembic: 5 still 6 retort, vessel 7 changer, furnace 9 distiller
Alençon product: 4 lace
alert: 4 gleg, warn, wary 5 agile, alarm, alive, awake, brisk, eager, ready, sharp, siren 6 active, alarum, bright, lively, nimble, prompt, tocsin 7 wakeful 8 vigilant, watchful 9 observant, wide-awake 11 circumspect
alette: 4 wing 8 abutment, door jamb
Aleut: 4 Atka 8 Unalaska
Aleutian Island: 4 Adak, Attu 5 Kiska, Umnak 6 Akutan, Amukta, Kodiak, Seguam 7 Kagamil 8 Amchitka, Unalaska
alewife: 4 fish 6 allice 7 herring, pompano, walleye 9 gaspereau (F.)
Alexander: *birthplace:* 5 Pella
horse: 10 Bucephalus
kingdom: 9 Macedonia
mistress: 8 Campaspe
victory: 5 Issus 6 Arbela
Alexandria: *bishop:* 10 Athanasius
magistrate: 8 alabarch
patriarch: 4 papa
theologian: 5 Arius
alfa: 7 esparto
alfalfa: hay 6 fodder, lucern 7 lucerne
alforja: bag 5 pouch 6 wallet 9 saddlebag
alga: 4 nori 6 desmid, diatom, nostoc 7 seaweed 8 rockweed
genus: 5 dasya 6 alaria, padina 10 gloeocapsa
study: 8 algology
algarroba: 4 tree 5 carob 6 calden
algate, algates: yet 6 always, wholly 10 completely, everywhere 15 notwithstanding
Algeria: 7 Algerie, Numidia
cavalryman: 5 spahi 6 spahee
city: 4 Bona, Oran 5 Blida, Media 7 Algiers (c.), Tlemcen 11 Constantine
department: 4 Oran 7 Algiers 11 Constantine
grass: 7 esparto
measure: pik 5 rebis, tarri 6 termin 9 pik halebi
monastery: 5 ribat
mountain: 5 Atlas
people: 5 Arabs 7 Berbers, Kabyles
river: 6 Shelif
ruler: bey, dey
seaport: 4 Bona, Bone, Oran, Orel
ship: 5 xebec
tirailleur: 5 Turco
weight: 4 rotl
algesia: 4 ache, pain 7 algesis
algid: 4 cold, cool 6 chilly, clammy

Algiers', native quarters: 6 Casbah, Kasbah

algodon: 6 cotton

algodoncillo: 7 majagua

Algonquin (see also **Indian**): Sac
spirit: 7 Manitou

Alhambra site: 7 Granada

Ali: *descendant:* 7 fatimid 8 fatimite
wife: 6 Fatima

Ali Baba: *brother:* 6 Cassim
word: 6 sesame

alias: 4 else, name 5 other, title 7 assumed, epithet, pen name 9 pseudonym, sobriquet

alibi: 4 plea 6 excuse 7 apology, pretext

Alice in Wonderland: *author:* 7 Carroll
character: cat 5 Queen 6 rabbit, Walrus 9 Mad Matter 11 Cheshire cat, White Rabbit

alien: ger 5 fremd, metic 6 exotic, remote 7 foreign, invader, strange 8 stranger, transfer 9 foreigner, immigrant, outlander, peregrine 10 irrelevant, tramontane 11 incongruous 12 inconsistent 13 unsympathetic

alienate: 4 part, wean 5 avert 6 convey, devest 8 amortize, disunite, estrange, separate, transfer, withdraw 10 abalienate

alienist: 12 psychiatrist

aliform: 8 winglike 10 wing-shaped

alight: 4 land, rest, stop 5 lodge, perch, roost 6 arrive, settle 7 descend, lighted 8 dismount 9 disembark

align, aline: 4 tram, true 5 array, range 6 adjust 7 arrange, marshal 10 straighten

alike: 4 akin, like, same 5 equal, twins 7 equally, similar, uniform 9 congruent, duplicate, identical
comb. form: iso

aliment: pap 4 food 5 broma, manna 6 viands 7 alimony, pabulum, rations 9 allowance, nutriment, substance 10 sustenance 11 nourishment

alimentation: 7 support 9 nutrition 10 sustenance 11 maintenance, nourishment

alimony: 7 aliment 9 allowance 11 maintenance

aline: See **align**

alive: 4 busy, keen, spry, vive (F.) 5 agile, alert, astir, brisk, quick, vital 6 extant, living 7 animate, vibrant 8 animated, existent, sensible, swarming 9 breathing, sensitive, sprightly, unexpired 14 unextinguished

alkali: lye, reh 4 kali, soda, usar
volatile: 7 ammonia

alkaline: *remedy:* 7 antacid
salt: 5 borax

alkaloid: 6 aricin, codein, conine, eserin 7 arabine, aricine, caffein, cocaine, codeine 8 atropine, caffeine, morphine 10 strychnine 13 physostigmine

all: sum 5 gross, quite, total, totum (L.), whole 6 entire, solely, wholly 7 plenary 8 entirely, everyone, totality 9 aggregate, everybody 10 altogether, completely, everything, thoroughly 11 exclusively
comb. form: pan 4 omni

all-fired: 7 extreme 9 excessive 10 inordinate

all in: 5 tired, weary

all-knowing: 10 omniscient

all right: OK; yes 4 okay 6 agreed 9 hunky-dory

all there: 4 sane

allanite: 6 cerite 7 mineral

allay: aid 4 calm, cite, cool, ease, help, hush 5 abate, allay, charm, check, quell, quiet, slake, still 6 adduce, pacify, quench, reduce, soften, soothe, stanch, subdue, temper 7 appease, assuage, comfort, compose, lighten, mollify, relieve, repress, staunch 8 mitigate, palliate 9 alleviate

allee: See **alley**

allege: 4 aver, avow, cite 5 offer, plead, quote, state, swear 6 adduce, affirm, assert, assign, charge, depose 7 advance, ascribe, declare, lighten, present, profess, propose 8 allegate, maintain 9 attribute 10 asseverate

alleged force: od 4 odyl

allegiance: tie 4 duty 5 honor 6 fealty, homage 7 loyalty, tribute 8 devotion, fidelity 9 constancy, obedience 10 obligation
violation of: 7 treason 9 treachery

allegory: 4 myth, tale 5 fable, story 7 parable 8 apologue, metaphor

alleviate: aid 4 ease, help 5 abate, allay 6 allege, lenify, lessen, pacify, soften, solace, soothe 7 assuage, compose, console, correct, lighten, relieve 8 diminish, mitigate, moderate, palliate 9 extenuate 11 tranquilize

alley: way 4 lane, mall, path, walk 5 allee, byway, chare, tewer 6 vennel 7 passage 10 passageway 12 thoroughfare
back: 4 slum

alliance: 4 pact 5 union 6 accord, fusion, league, treaty 7 compact, entente, society 8 affinity, agnation, covenant 9 coalition 10 federation, fellowship 11 association, combination confederacy, partnership 13 confederation

allice: 4 shad

allied: 4 akin 6 agnate, joined, linked, united 7 cognate, germane, kindred, related, similar 9 analogous

alligator: 5 niger 6 caiman, cayman, jacare, yacare 7 lagarto 9 crocodile
alligator pear: 7 avocado 8 aguacate
alliteration: 10 repetition 12 agnomination
allium: 4 leek 5 onion 6 garlic
allmouth: 6 angler
allocate: 4 deal, dole, mete, rate 5 allot, award, share 6 affect, assign 9 apportion 10 distribute
allonge: 4 pass 5 lunge, rider 6 thrust
allophanamide: 6 biuret 8 compound
allot: fix 4 cast, deal, dole, mete 5 award, grant, share 6 assign, bestow, depute, design, ordain, ration 7 appoint, destine, prorate, specify, tribute 8 allocate 9 apportion, attribute, authorize, prescribe 10 distribute
allow: let 4 bear, lend 5 admit, defer, grant, stand, thole, yield 6 accept, accord, assign, bestow, beteem, endure, permit, suffer 7 approve, concede, confess, suppose 8 consider, sanction, tolerate 9 authorize 11 acknowledge
allowance: fee 4 agio, edge, gift, hire, odds, size 5 leave, share 6 bounty, margin, salary 7 aliment, alimony, pension, portion, stipend 8 appenage, approval, discount, quantity, sanction, 9 admitting, allotment, conceding, deduction, reduction, tolerance 10 permission 11 appointment, approbation 13 authorization
short: 6 ration 9 scrimping
traveling: 7 mileage
weight: 4 tare, tret 7 scalage
allowing for that: if
alloy: mix 5 mokum 6 garble 7 mixture 9 admixture 10 adulterate, amalgamate
black copper: 6 niello
carbon and iron: 5 steel
Chinese: 7 paktong 8 packtong
copper and aluminum: 9 duralumin
copper, iron and zinc: 4 aich 7 paktong, rheotan 8 packtong
copper and tin: 6 bronze, oreide, oroide, pewter
copper and zinc: 5 brass 6 oreide, oroide 8 arsedine
costume jewelry: 6 oreide, oroide
fusible: 6 solder
gold and silver: 4 asem
gold-like: 6 oreide, oroide 8 doralium
heat resistant: 6 cermet 7 ceramal
lead and tin: 5 calin, terne 6 pewter
mercurial: 7 amalgam
nickel and silver: 8 alfenide
nickel and steel: 7 elinvar
nonferrous: 4 tula
pewter: 5 bidri
silver with copper or tin: 6 billon
sulphuric: 6 niello
tin: 5 terne 6 pewter
All's Well That Ends Well character: 5 Diana, Lafeu 7 Bertram
allspice tree: 7 pimento
allude: 4 hint 5 imply, point, refer 6 advert, relate 7 connote, mention, suggest 8 indicate, intimate 9 attribute, insinuate
allure (see also **lure**): air, woo 4 bait, draw, lead, lure, move, sway 5 angle, bribe, charm, court, decoy, snare, tempt 6 entice, entrap, induce, seduce 7 attract, beguile, ensnare 8 blandish, inveigle, persuade 9 captivate, fascinate, influence
allurement: 4 cord 6 glamor 7 gudgeon 9 incentive 10 enticement, temptation 11 fascination
allusion: 4 hint, twit 7 inkling, mention 8 innuendo, instance 9 quotation, reference 10 intimation
alluvial: *clay:* 5 adobe
deposit: mud 4 sand, silt, wash 5 delta, drift, geest 6 gravel, placer
fan: 5 delta
alluvion: 4 flow, wash 5 flood 10 inundation 11 overflowing
ally: pal 4 aide, join 5 union, unite 6 backer, friend, helper 7 connect, partner 8 adherent 9 affiliate, assistant, associate, auxiliary, colleague, supporter 10 accomplice 11 confederate
almanac: 4 ordo 8 calendar 9 ephemeris
almandine: 6 spinel, garnet 9 almandite
almighty: 5 great 7 extreme 8 powerful, puissant 10 omnipotent 12 irresistible
Almighty: God 7 Creator
almond: nut 5 badam 6 kanari
paste: 8 marzipan
pert. to: 10 amygdaline
syrup: 6 orgeat
almost: 4 nigh 5 anear, close 6 amaist, feckly (Sc.), nearly 13 approximately
prefix: pen 4 pene
alms: 4 dole, gift 6 aumous (Sc.), bounty, relief 7 charity, handout 8 donation, gratuity, offering, pittance 11 benefaction 12 philanthropy
box: 4 arca 7 poor box
dispenser: 7 almoner, almsman 11 eleemosynar
almshouse: 9 poorhouse, workhouse
almsman: 6 beggar, pauper
almuce: 4 hood 6 tippet 9 headdress
alodium, allodium: 6 estate 8 property
aloe: 4 pita 5 agave 6 maguey
compound: 5 aloin
extract: 5 orcin 7 orcinol
powder: 5 picra
aloes: 5 tonic 8 agalloch 10 agallochum

aloft: up 4 high 5 above 6 upward 7 skyward 8 overhead

aloha: 4 love 8 farewell, greeting, kindness 9 affection 10 salutation

alone: one 4 bare, lorn, only, sole, solo 5 aloof, apart, solus 6 single, unique 8 desolate, detached, isolated, separate, solitary 9 exclusive, matchless, unmatched 11 exclusively 12 incomparable, unparalleled 13 companionless, unaccompanied

comb. form: 4 soli

along: on; via 4 away, with 5 ahead 6 beside, onward 7 forward 8 parallel, together 10 lengthwise

alongside: at, by 5 close 6 aboard 7 abreast 8 parallel

prefix: 4 para

Alonso's son: 9 Ferdinand

aloof: shy 4 cold, cool 5 aback, alone, apart, proud 6 abeigh, frosty, remote, silent 7 distant, removed 8 detached, reserved, secluded, windward 11 indifferent

alopecia: 8 baldness 11 phalacrosis

alopecoid: 7 foxlike, vulpine

alouatte: 6 monkey

aloud: 4 oral 5 vocal 7 audible

alp: 4 peak 5 demon, mount, witch 8 mountain 9 bullfinch, nightmare

alpaca: 4 paco 5 llama

alpenstock: 5 staff 9 bergstock

alpha: 5 chief, debut, first

and omega: all 5 whole 6 entire

alphabet: 4 ABC's, order 6 primer, sarada 10 abcedarium

character: 4 ogam, ogum, rune 5 ogham 6 letter

pert. to: 11 abecedarian

Runic: 7 Futharc, Futhork

alphabetize: 7 arrange

Alpine: hat 5 stick 9 alpestral

dance: 5 gavot

dress: 6 dirndl

dwelling: 6 chalet

goat: 4 ibex 8 steinbok

herdsman: 4 senn

pass: col

plant: 9 edelweiss

primrose: 8 auricula

wind: 4 bora 5 foehn

Alps: *Austrian:* 5 Tirol, Tyrol

division of: 7 Bernese 8 Maritime 9 Lepontine

Italian: 9 Dolomites

mountain: 5 Blanc 7 Bernina 8 Jungfrau 10 Matterhorn

pass: 5 Cenis 7 Brenner, Simplon

tunnel: 5 Cenis 7 Arlberg, Gothard, Simplon 11 Loetschberg

Yugoslav: 6 Julian 7 Dinaric

already: een, now 6 before

Alsatian clover: 4 herb 6 alsike

also: and, eke, too, yet 4 erst, more, plus 5 ditto 7 besides, further 8 likewise, moreover 9 similarly

also-ran: 5 loser 9 candidate

altar: ara 5 table 6 autere, shrine 7 chancel, chantry 9 sanctuary

area: 4 apse

boy: 7 acolyte

carpet: 6 pedale

cloth: 6 coster 7 frontal

curtain: 6 coster, riddel

enclosure: 4 bema

hanging: 6 dorsal, dossal, dossel

ledge: 7 retable

platform: 8 predella

portable: 10 superaltar

screen: 7 reredos

top: 5 mensa

vessel: pyx 7 piscina

alter: 4 geld, move, turn, vary, veer 5 adapt, amend, break, emend, reset, shift 6 adjust, change, modify, mutate, revise, temper 7 convert 9 transform 11 interpolate

alter ego: 5 agent 6 friend 8 henchman

altercation: 4 spat, tiff 5 brawl, broil, fight 6 bicker, jangle, strife 7 contest, dispute, quarrel, wrangle 10 contention 11 controversy

alternate: 4 else, sway, vary 5 other, recur, shift 6 change, rotate, seesaw 8 intermit 9 oscillate 10 substitute 11 interchange, reciprocate

alternative: or 6 choice, either, option 8 election 10 preference

word introducing: 7 whether

althaea: 6 mallow

Althaea's husband: 6 Oeneus

althorn: sax 4 alto 7 saxhorn

although: een 4 even 5 while 6 albeit, though 7 despite 15 notwithstanding

altitude: 4 apex, peak 6 height 7 stature 9 elevation, loftiness

measuring device: 8 orometer 9 altimeter

altitude sickness: 7 soroche

alto: 4 part 6 singer 7 althorn, saxhorn 8 vocalist

altogether: all 5 quite 6 wholly 7 totally, utterly 10 completely, thoroughly 12 collectively

altruism: 10 generosity 11 benevolence 12 philanthropy 13 unselfishness

alture: 6 height

aludel: pot

alula: 4 lobe, wing

alum: 7 styptic 10 astringent

rock: 7 alunite

alumina: 5 argil

aluminum: *calcium silicate:* 7 epidote
discoverers: 4 Davy 6 Wohler
hydrousphosphate: 9 wavellite
oxide: 7 alumina
sulphate: 4 alum

alumnus: 4 grad 5 pupil 8 graduate

alure: 7 gallery, passage 10 ambulatory

alveary: 4 hive 7 beehive 9 alvearium

alveolar plasma: 11 trophoplasm

alveolate: 6 pitted 9 faveolate 11 honeycombed

always: ay; aye, een, e'er 4 ever 6 semper (L.), 7 algates, forever 8 evermore 9 eternally, uniformly 10 constantly, habitually, invariably 11 continually, perpetually, unceasingly 13 everlastingly

alyssum: 6 alison

am: See **be**

ama: cup 5 amula, cruet, diver 6 vessel 7 chalice 9 candlenut

amabile: 6 gentle, tender 9 agreeable

amability: 11 lovableness

Amadis' beloved: 6 Oriana

amadou: 4 punk 6 tinder 9 touchwood

amah: 5 nurse 7 servant

amain: 7 greatly 8 forcibly 9 violently 10 vigorously 11 exceedingly

Amalekite king: 4 Agag

amalgamate: mix 4 fuse, join 5 alloy, blend, merge, unite 6 mingle 7 combine 8 coalesce, compound 11 consolidate

Amalthea: 4 goat
horn: 10 cornucopia
nursling: 4 Zeus

amanita: 6 agaric

amanuensis: 6 penman, scribe, typist 8 recorder 9 scrivener, secretary 11 transcriber 12 stenographer

amara: 6 beetle

amaryllis: 4 girl, lily 5 agave 10 sweetheart 11 shepherdess

Amasa's father: 6 Jether

amass: 4 heap, mass, pile, save 5 gross, hoard, stack, store 6 gather 7 collect, compile 8 assemble 10 accumulate

amate: 4 tree 5 daunt, match 6 subdue 10 dishearten

amateur: ham 4 tiro, tyro 6 novice, votary 7 admirer, dabbler, devotee, fancier 8 beginner 10 dilettante, aficionado 15 nonprofessional

amative: 4 fond 6 ardent, loving 7 amatory, amorous 10 passionate

amaze: awe 4 stun 5 alarm 6 astony 7 astound, confuse, perplex, stagger, stupefy 8 astonish, bewilder, confound, dumfound, surprise 9 dumbfound, overwhelm

amazement: 5 ferly 6 frenzy, wonder 7 madness 13 consternation

Amazon: 5 river, woman 7 warrior
cetacean: 4 inia
discoverer: 8 Orellana
estuary: 4 Para
headstream: 7 Maranon
mat: 4 yapa
queen: 9 Hippolyta 12 Penthesileia
rain forest: 5 selva 6 silvas
tributary: Ica 4 Napo

ambage: 4 path 7 circuit, quibble 9 ambiguity 14 circumlocution

ambari: da 4 hemp 5 fiber 7 cordage

ambassador: 5 agent, envoy 6 deputy, legate, nuncio 8 diplomat, minister 9 messenger 10 ambassiate 12 intermediary 14 representative 15 plenipotentiary
pert. to: 8 legatine

amber: 4 gris 5 resin 6 yellow 8 amberoid, electrum 9 ambergris

amber-colored: 8 resinous

ambiance, ambience: 6 milieu 11 environment 12 surroundings

ambiguity: 6 ambage 7 paradox 9 duplexity, obscurity 10 hesitation 12 doubtfulness

ambiguous: 4 dark 5 vague 6 double 7 cryptic, dubious 8 doubtful 9 bifarious, equivocal, uncertain, unsettled 10 indefinite, indistinct, mistakable 11 problematic 12 inexplicable, questionable 13 indeterminate

ambit: 5 limit, scope, space 6 bounds, extent, sphere 7 circuit, compass 8 boundary, precinct 13 circumference

ambition: 4 goal, hope, wish 5 glory 6 desire 7 purpose 9 intention 10 aspiration

ambitious: 4 avid, bold, keen 5 eager, showy 7 emulous 8 aspiring

amble: 4 gait 7 meander, saunter

ambo: 4 desk 6 pulpit

Amboina button: 4 yaws

Amboina pine: 8 galagala

ambos: 5 incus

ambrosia: 5 honey 6 nectar

ambrosial: 6 divine 8 fragrant 9 delicious

ambry: 4 safe 5 chest, niche 6 closet, pantry, recess 7 almonry, armoire 8 armarium, cupboard 10 repository

ambulate: gad 4 hike, move, walk

ambush: 4 lurk, trap 5 await, blind, snare 6 waylay 7 forelay 9 ambuscade, ambuscado

ameer: See **emir**

ameliorate: 4 ease, help, mend 5 amend 6 better, reform 7 improve, promote 9 meliorate

amen: yea 5 truly 6 assent, verily, so-be-it 8 approval, sanction 9 assuredly, certainly 11 termination 12 ratification

Amen-Ra's wife: Mut

amenable: 4 open 6 liable, pliant 7 subject 9 tractable 10 answerable, responsive 11 accountable, responsible
amend: end 4 beet, mend 5 alter, emend 6 better, change, reform, remedy, repair, repeal, revise 7 convert, correct, improve, recover, rectify, redress, restore 8 chastise
amends: 6 reward 7 apology, redress 9 atonement, expiation 10 recompense, reparation 12 compensation, satisfaction
amenities: 8 agremens, niceties 9 agrements, etiquette 11 formalities
amenity: joy 6 comity 7 feature, suavity 8 civility, courtesy, mildness 9 geniality 10 gentleness 12 complaisance, pleasantness 13 agreeableness
ament: 4 cjat 5 idiot, moron 6 catkin 7 cachrys, cattail, gosling 8 imbecile, nucament
amerce: 4 fine 5 mulct 6 affeer, punish, sconce 7 condemn, forfeit 8 penalize
America (see also **North America, South America,** and specific countries, e.g., **Brazil, Canada, United States**): 8 New World 9 continent 10 hemisphere
animal: 4 puma 5 bison, tapir, vison 6 argali, marten, martin, ocelot, wapiti 7 musquaw, opossum 9 assapanic, chickaree
apple: 7 Roxbury
ash: 5 rowan, rowen
balsam: 4 tolu
boar: 7 musquaw
bird: 4 rhea, sora 5 colin, urubu 6 condor 7 shrupsh, tanager 8 squealer
butterfly: 7 viceroy
buzzard: 5 buteo 7 vulture
deer: 6 wapiti
discoverer of: 5 Cabot 7 Ericson 8 Columbus
elk: 6 wapiti
elm: 5 ulmus
finch: 5 junco
fir: 5 abies
lion: 4 puma 6 cougar
monkey: 4 titi
moth: io
plains: 6 pampas 7 prairie
rodent: 4 paca 6 gopher 8 capybara
shrub: 4 majo 5 guava, majoe, wahoo 10 frangipane, frangipani
tiger: 6 jaguar
toad: 4 agua, bufo, rana
tree: fir, lin, oak 4 pine 5 maple, savin 6 tupelo, walnut 7 hickory, redwood, sequoia 8 oneberry, zapetero
tropical tree: 5 acapu, balsa, dalli, guama, guara 6 babeen, grigri, grugru, mammee, pawpaw, sapota 7 wacapou 8 amarillo, sweetsop 10 manchineel
American: 4 Yank 6 Gringo, Yankee, Yanqui
American Indian: See **Indian** *American*
Amerind: 6 Eskimo, Indian, native 8 American
clan symbol: 5 totem
memorial post: xat
amethyst: gem 7 onegite
Amfortas' father: 7 Titurel
ami: 5 lover 6 friend
amiable: 4 kind, warm 5 sweet 6 loving, mellow, tender 7 affable, lovable, winsome 8 charming, engaging, friendly, pleasing 9 admirable, agreeable, courteous 11 kind-hearted
amicable: 8 friendly 9 peaceable 10 harmonious, neighborly
amice: 4 cape, cowl, hood 5 ephod 6 almuce, tippet, vakass 8 vestment
amid: in 5 among 6 amidst, during 7 amongst, between 10 surrounded
amino acid: 7 protein
amino compound: 7 diamide, diamine 8 triamine
amir: See **emir**
amiss: ill 4 awry, bias 5 agley, askew, wrong 6 astray, faulty 7 mistake 8 improper 9 erroneous, incorrect 10 inaccurate
amit: 4 lose
amity: 5 peace 6 accord 7 concord, harmony 10 friendship 12 friendliness
amm 6 abbess, mother
ammonia: 9 hartshorn 11 refrigerant
derivative: 4 amid, amin 5 amide, amine 6 anilid 7 anilide, diamine
ammoniac plant: 5 oshac
ammunition: 4 ammo, ammu, arms, shot 5 bombs 6 powder, shells 7 bullets 8 grenades, materiel, ordnance, shrapnel 9 munitions
case: 9 bandolier
depot: 7 arsenal
holder: gun 4 tray
wagon: 7 caisson
amnesia: 5 fugue, lapse 8 blackout 13 forgetfulness
amnesty: 6 pardon 11 overlooking
amnion: sac 6 serosa 8 membrane
amoeba, ameba: olm 7 proteus
amok, amuck: mad 5 crazy 6 crazed 7 violent 8 frenzied
amole: 4 salt, soap 5 agave, plant
Amon's son: 6 Josiah
among: in; mid 4 amid, with 5 amang, midst 6 amidst 7 between
prefix: epi
amor: 4 Eros, love 5 cupid 7 amoroso
amora: 5 rabbi
amoral: 7 neutral 8 nonmoral 9 objective
Amorc member: 11 Rosicrucian

amorous: 4 fond 6 ardent, erotic, loving, tender 7 amatory, fervent 10 passionate 12 affectionate
amorphous: 5 vague 8 formless, resinous 9 irregular, shapeless 14 uncrystallized
amort: 8 dejected, lifeless 9 inanimate 10 spiritless 11 discouraged
amortize: 7 destroy 8 alienate 9 liquidate 10 extinguish
amotion: 7 ousting, removal 11 deprivation
amount: gob, lot, sum 4 dose, feck, ream, rise, unit 5 chunk, price, reach, stack, store, total, whole 6 degree, dosage, extent, number 7 advance, scruple, signify, slather 8 increase, quantity 9 aggregate
fixed: 4 rate
indefinite: any 4 some
made: lot 5 batch
relative: 5 ratio 6 degree
small: bit, tot 4 dash, dite, flow, lick, wisp 5 pinch, shred, taste, trace 6 morsel, trifle 7 dribble, driblet, modicum 8 fragment, spoonful 10 pennyworth
smallest: jot 4 iota, whit 5 grain, least 7 minimum
amour propre: 5 pride 6 egoism, vanity 7 conceit 8 self-love
ampere unit: 4 volt, watt
ampersand: and 4 also, plus 9 character
amphibian: eft, olm 4 frog, hyla, newt, rana, toad 5 anura 7 caudate, proteus 8 tree toad 10 salamander
extinct: 5 eryop
family: 7 Ranidae
order of: 5 anura 7 aglossa
young: 7 tadpole 8 polliwog
amphibole: 7 edenite, oralite, uralite 9 tremolite 10 hornblende
Amphion: *father:* 4 Zeus 5 Iasus
mother: 7 Antiope
twin brother: 6 Zethus
wife: 5 Niobe
amphitheater: 4 bowl, oval 5 arena, cavea 6 circus 7 stadium 10 auditorium
Amphitrite: *father:* 6 Nereus
husband: 8 Poseidon
mother: 5 Doris
Amphitryon's wife: 7 Alcmena, Alcmene
amphora: jar, urn 4 cadi (pl.), vase 5 cadus 6 pelike
ample: 4 full, good, much, rich, wide 5 broad, great, large, roomy 6 enough, plenty 7 copious, liberal, opulent 8 abundant, adequate, generous, handsome, spacious 9 bounteous, bountiful, capacious, extensive, plenteous, plentiful, unstinted 10 munificent, sufficient
amplification factor: mu
amplify: mu; pad 5 farse, swell, widen 6 dilate, expand, extend, stress 7 augment, enlarge 8 ampliate, increase, lengthen, multiply 10 exaggerate
amputate: cut, lop 5 prune, sever 7 curtail 12 exarticulate
ampyx: 4 band 5 plate 6 diadem, fillet 9 headdress
amuck: See **amok**
amula: ama 6 vessel
amulet: gem 4 mojo 5 charm, saffi, safie, token 6 fetish, grigri, saphie, scroll 7 periapt 8 greegree, ornament, talisman 10 protection
Amulius' brother: 7 Numitor
amuse: 6 absorb, delude, divert, engage, please, tickle 7 beguile, disport, gratify 8 bewilder, distract 9 entertain 10 exhilarate
amusement: fad, fun 4 game, jest, play 5 mirth, sport 7 pastime 8 pleasure 9 avocation, diversion, merriment 10 recreation, relaxation 13 divertisement, entertainment
place (see also **entertainment:** ***place***): 4 park 5 movie 6 casino, cinema, circus, midway 7 theater
amusing: 5 droll, funny 7 comical, risible 8 humorous, pleasant 9 laughable, ludicrous, quizzical 10 ridiculous
Amy's sisters: Jo; Meg 4 Beth
Amycus: *enemy:* 5 Lycus 8 Dascylus
father: 8 Poseidon
friend: 8 Hercules
mother: 5 Melie
amygdala: 6 almond, tonsil
amyl: 6 pentyl, starch 7 alcohol
an: one 7 article
ana: 6 events 7 sayings 9 anecdotes, anthology 10 collection 11 memorabilia
anabasis: 7 advance 10 expedition
anabatic: 9 ascending
anaconda: boa 5 snake
Anacreon's birthplace: 4 Teos
anadem: 5 crown 6 diadem, fillet, wreath 7 chaplet, coronet, garland
anagogic: 6 occult 8 abstruse
anagram: 4 game 5 rebus 6 puzzle 9 logogriph 13 transposition
analabos: 5 cloak
analgesic: 5 opium 6 codein 7 anodyne, aspirin, codeine
analogous: 4 akin, like 5 alike 6 allied 7 cognate, related, similar 8 parallel 10 comparable, equivalent 11 correlative 13 correspondent
analogy: 10 congruence, proportion, similarity, similitude 11 resemblance
analysis: 4 test 5 study 8 solution, synopses 9 reduction, titration 10 exposition 13 investigation

analyze: 5 assay, parse, study, weigh 6 reduce 7 dissect, examine, resolve 8 diagnose, separate 9 decompose, determine
Anam: See **Annam**
Ananas: 5 anana 9 pineapple
Ananias: 4 liar
wife: 8 Sapphira
anarchist: 5 rebel 8 nihilist 10 antisocial
anarchy: 4 riot 5 chaos 6 revolt 7 license, misrule 8 disorder 9 confusion 11 lawlessness
anathema: ban 4 oath 5 curse 7 censure 9 blasphemy 11 imprecation, malediction 12 denunciation
Anatolia: 7 Armenia
goddess: Ma 6 Cybele
rug: 5 Tuzla
anatomize: 7 analyze, dissect
anatomy: 4 body 8 analysis, skeleton 9 structure
animal: 7 zootomy
microscopic: 9 histology
quick: 11 vivisection
Anaximander's principle: 7 apeiron
ancestor: 4 Adam, sire 5 elder 6 author, beldam, parent 7 beldame 8 forebear, relative 9 grandsire, precursor 10 forefather, forerunner, progenitor 11 predecessor
having common: 14 consanguineous
law: 6 stipes, stirps
remote: 6 atavus
worship: 10 ancientism
ancestral: 4 aval 6 avital, lineal 10 hereditary 11 patrimonial
ancestry: 4 race 6 family 7 descent, lineage 8 pedigree 9 paternity 11 antecedents
relating to: 6 atavic 9 atavistic
Anchises' son: 6 Aeneas
anchor: fix 4 bind, hook, moor, rest, stop 5 affix, berth, bower, kedge, rivet 6 attach, drogue, fasten, hermit, secure 7 chaplet, connect, grapnel, killick, support 9 anchorite
bill: pee 4 peak
hoist: 7 capstan
lift: cat
part: arm 4 palm 5 fluke, shank, stock
position: 5 atrip
ring: 4 tore 6 toroid
shaped: 8 ankyroid
tackle: cat
timber: 7 grouser
anchor bed: 9 billboard
anchorage: 4 dock, rade(Sc.) 6 harbor, refuge 7 moorage 8 berthage, location 9 roadstead
anchored: 4 stay
anchorite: 4 monk 6 hermit 7 ascetic, eremite, recluse, stylite 8 anchoret 9 pillarist
anchorman: key 5 emcee 6 editor 7 feature 8 mainstay 11 commentator
anchovy: 6 spratt 7 herring
sauce: 4 alec
ancient: eld, old 4 aged, auld(Sc.) 5 early, elder, hoary, olden 6 bygone, ensign 7 antique, archaic, archean, classic, oxygian 8 historic, obsolete, primeval, pristine 9 grandeval, primitive, venerable 10 antiquated 11 patriarchal
comb. form: 5 arche, paleo
Ancient of Days: God
ancilla: 6 helper 7 adjunct, servant 8 handmaid 9 accessory
ancillary: 9 auxiliary 10 subsidiary 11 subordinate
ancon: 5 elbow 6 corbel 7 console 9 olecranon
and: et(F., L.); ant, too 4 also, plus 7 besides, further 8 moreover 9 ampersand 10 connective 11 furthermore
and so forth: etc 4 more 6 others 8 etcetera
Andean: 5 grand, lofty 8 Peruvian
Andes: *animal:* 5 llama
bird: 6 condor
camel: 5 llama
deer: 4 pudu 6 vanada
grass: 4 ichu
tableland: 4 puna 6 paramo
tribe: 4 anti 5 campa
andiron: dog 7 cobiron, firedog, hessian
andradite: 6 aplome, garnet
android: 5 robot 9 automaton
Andromache's husband: 6 Hector
Andromeda: 5 heath, plant
father: 7 Cepheus
husband: 7 Perseus
mother: 10 Cassiopeia
ane: one 4 once
anecdote: 4 joke, tale, yarn 5 story 6 sketch 9 narrative
collection: ana
anele: 5 bless 6 anoint, shrive
anemia: 5 surra 6 surrah
anemic: low 4 pale, weak 6 watery 8 lifeless 9 bloodless 10 exsanguine
anemone: 9 buttercup 10 windflower
anent: on, re 5 about 6 anenst, beside, toward 7 against 8 opposite 9 regarding 10 concerning
aneroid: 9 barometer
anesthetic: gas 5 ether 6 acoine, obtuse, opiate 7 cocaine, dulling, menthol 8 sedative 9 novacaine 10 chloroform
anew: 4 over 5 again, newly 6 afresh, denovo, iterum(L.), 8 recently
anfractuous: 6 spiral 7 bending, sinuous, winding 8 tortuous
angel: 4 deva 5 daeva, seraf(Sp.), yaksa 6 backer, cherub, seraph, spirit, yaksha 7

sponsor 8 cherubim, guardian, seraphim 9 harbinger, messenger
apostate prince: 5 Eblis 7 Lucifer
biblical: 7 Gabriel, Raphael
bottomless pit: 7 Abaddon 8 Apollyon
of death: 6 Azrael 7 Sammael
Paradise Lost: 5 Uriel 6 Belial 7 Ariocha
worship: 5 dulia
angelfish: 9 chirivita, isabelita, isabelite
angelic: 7 saintly 8 cherubic, heavenly, seraphic 9 celestial 10 beneficent
angelica: 4 herb 7 jellica
angelico: 5 nondo
angelus: 4 bell 6 prayer 8 devotion
painter: 6 Millet
anger (see also **angry**): ire, irk 4 bile, fell, fury, gall, rage, rile, roil, teem 5 annoy, pique, wrath 6 choler, dander, enrage, excite, grieve, nettle, offend, rancor, spleen, temper 7 burning, dudgeon, emotion, incense, inflame, passion, provoke 8 acrimony, distress, irritate, vexation 9 displease 10 affliction, antagonism, antagonize, resentment 11 displeasure, indignation
express: 5 snort
Angevin: 11 Plantagenet
angle: ell, tee 4 cant, coin, fish, fork, knee, peak 5 arris, bevel, bight, coign, elbow, phase, point, slant 6 allure, aspect, canton, corner, scheme 7 bastion, perigon 8 decalage, fishhook, intrigue
acute: 6 akimbo
equal (pert. to): 8 isogonal, isogonic
external: 4 cant
forty-five degree: 6 octant
geological: 4 hade
having no: 6 agonic
mathematical: 6 octant, radian 9 incidence
measuring device: 10 semicircle
of branch and leaf: 4 axil
of keel and bowsprit: 6 steeve
of ore vein: 4 hade
without: 6 agonic
angler: 5 thief 7 rodster 8 allmouth, piscator 9 fisherman, sportsman
angleworm: ess
Anglian kingdom: 5 Deira
Anglo Saxon: *armor:* 7 hauberk
army: 4 fyrd
assembly: 4 moot, mote 6 mancus
coin: ora 5 sceat
council: 9 heptarchy
court: 4 leet 5 gemot 6 gemote
deity: Ing 4 Frey, Wyrd 5 Freyr
epic: 7 Beowulf
freeman: 5 thane, thegn
king: Ine 5 Edgar 6 Harold
king's council: 5 witan
letter: edh, eth, wyn 4 wynn 5 thorn
money: ora
nobleman: 4 earl 5 thane, thegn
poet: 4 scop
sheriff: 5 reeve 6 gerefa
slave: 4 esne
tax: 4 geld
village: ham
writer: 4 Bede
Angola: *coin:* 6 macuta, macute 7 angolar
river: 6 Coanza, Kunene, Kwanza
town: 6 Luanda(c.) 8 Benguela 10 Mossamedes
angora: cat 4 goat, hair, wool, yarn 6 rabbit
angry (see also **anger**): mad 4 grim, sore, wraw 5 cross, grame, huffy, irate, vexed, wroth 6 crouse, fuming, ireful 7 fretful, furious, iracund, painful 8 choleric, inflamed, rigorous, vehement 9 indignant, irascible, resentful 11 exasperated
anguilla: eel
anguish: woe 4 ache, pain, pang, rack 5 agony, dolor, grief, throe 6 misery, regret 7 remorse, torment, torture 8 distress
angular: 4 bone, bony, slim, thin 5 gaunt, sharp 6 abrupt 7 pointed, scrawny 8 angulose, angulous, cornered, rawboned
ani: 6 cuckoo 9 blackbird
anil: dye 6 indigo
anile: old 5 silly 6 doting, feeble, infirm, senile, simple 7 flighty, foolish 9 doddering 11 old-womanish
animadversion: 5 blame 6 remark 7 censure, comment, reproof, warning 8 monition, reproach 9 aspersion, criticism 10 perception, punishment 11 observation 12 chastisement, condemnation
animal (see also **amphibian, bird, carnivore, fish, insect, invertebrate, mammal, reptile, vertebrate**): 5 beast, biped, brute, fauna, gross, lusty 6 carnal, fleshy, mammal, rodent 7 sensual 8 creature, organism, physical 9 carnivore, marsupial, quadruped
arboreal: ai 4 unau 5 lemur, sloth 6 marten 7 dasyure, opossum, raccoon, tarsier
Biblical: 4 reem 8 behemoth
body: 4 soma
burrowing: 4 mole 6 badger, gopher, rabbit, wombat 8 squirrel 9 armadillo
class: 5 genus 6 genera(pl.)
coat: fur 4 hair, hide, pelt, skin, wool 6 pelage
collection: zoo 4 herd 5 drove 9 menagerie
crawling: 4 worm 5 snake
cross-bred: 4 mule 5 hinny 6 hybrid
doctor: vet 12 veterinarian
domestic: cat, cow, hog, pet, pig 4 mare, mule 5 horse, stock 6 cattle

draft: ox 4 mule, oxen(pl.) 5 horse 8 elephant
enclosure: pen, sty 4 cage, coop, cote, yard 5 hutch, kraal, stall 6 corral 7 pasture
equine: ass 5 horse, zebra
extinct: 8 dinosaur, mastodon
fat: 4 lard, suet 5 cetin 6 tallow 7 lanolin
feathered: 4 bird, fowl
feline: cat 4 pard 5 tiger 6 jaguar 7 cheetah
female: cow, dam, doe, ewe, gyp, hen, roe, sow 4 hind, mare, slut 5 bitch, filly, jenny, nanny, vixen 6 heifer 7 tigress
footless: 4 apod 5 apoda
group: gam, pod 4 herd, pack 5 drove, flock, pride 6 gaggle
hibernating: 4 bear
hunted: 4 game, prey
life: 4 bios 5 fauna
life (god of): 6 Faunus
lover: 8 zoophile 10 zoophilist
male: mas, tom 4 bull, jack, stag 5 steed, steer 8 stallion
many-footed: 6 insect 7 decapod, hexapod 8 multiped 9 centipede
marine: orc 4 brit, fish, inia, seal 5 coral, otter, polyp, salpa, whale 6 dugong, walrus 7 dolphin, manatee, rotifer 9 jellyfish 10 ctenophore, ctenophran
microscopic: 5 ameba, monad 6 acarid, amoeba 8 rhizopod 9 protozoan 10 animalcule
monkey-like: 5 lemur, loris
mythical: 4 faun 5 snark 6 acephal, bagwyn, bunyip, dragon, garuda 7 alborak, centaur, griffen, unicorn 8 dingmaul, minotaur 9 rosmarine
nocturnal: bat, owl 4 coon 5 lemur, ratel, tapir 6 possum, racoon 7 opossum
one-celled: 5 ameba, monad 6 amoeba 8 protozoa 9 protozoan
ovine: 5 sheep
pack: ass 4 mule 5 burro, camel, horse, llama 6 donkey
parasitic: 8 entozoon
pert. to: 7 leonine 8 zoologic
porcine: hog, pig 4 boar
pouched: 6 possum 7 opossum 8 kangaroo 9 marsupial
rabbit-like: 4 pika 6 marmot
ruminant: cow 4 deer, goat 5 camel, sheep 8 antelope
science: 7 zoology
scrawny: 5 scrag
symbol: 5 totem
ten-footed: 7 decapod
timid: 4 deer, hare 5 sheep
track: 5 spoor
undersized: 4 runt
ursine: 4 bear
vulpine: fox
water: 4 fish, seal 5 coral, otter, whale 6 beaver, walrus
winged: bat 4 bird
young: cub, kid, pup 4 babe, calf, colt, fawn, foal, lamb 5 bruin, chick, filly, puppy, whelp 6 kitten, lionet 8 chipling

animal and plant life: 5 biota

Animal Farm author: 6 Orwell

animalcule: fly 5 ameba 6 amoeba 7 rotifer 8 rotifera(pl.)

animate: pep 4 fire, move, perk, stir, urge 5 alive, brisk, cheer, drive, flush, imbue, impel liven, rouse 6 arouse, bright, ensoul, excite, incite, induce, living, prompt, vivify 7 actuate, comfort, enliven, inspire, quicken 8 activate, energize, inspirit, vitalize 9 encourage, stimulate 10 exhilarate, invigorate

animated: gay 4 glad 5 brisk, vivid, vital 6 active, ardent, blithe, lively 7 buoyant, jocular, sthenic 8 spirited, vigorous 9 sprightly, vivacious 12 enthusiastic

anime: 5 copal, elemi, resin, rosin 7 animato 9 oleoresin

animism: 8 naturism

animosity: 4 hate, 6 animus, enmity, hatred, malice, rancor 7 dislike 9 hostility 10 antagonism, opposition, resentment 11 acharnement, malevolence

animus: 4 mind, will 6 effort, spirit, temper 8 attitude 9 intention 10 antagonism 11 disposition, inclination

anion: ion 8 particle
opposed to: 6 cation

anise: 4 anet, dill 5 cumen 6 fennel

anisette: 7 cordial, liqueur

anisic acid salt: 7 anisate

anito: 6 spirit

Anius' daughter: 5 Elais

ankle: 4 coot, cuit, hock, tali(pl.), 5 talus, tarsi(pl.) 6 tarsus
comb. form: tar 5 tarso
ornament: 6 anklet
pert. to: 6 tarsal

anklebone: 5 talus 8 astragal 10 astragalus, hucklebone

anklet: 4 sock 6 fetter

anlage: 4 base 6 embryo, source 8 blastema, rudiment 10 primordium

ann: 7 stipend

anna: 4 coin 7 hoatzin 8 hoactzin

annal: 6 record 7 archive, history 8 register 9 chronicle 11 publication

annalist: 6 writer 8 recorder 9 historian 12 chronologist

Annam: *boat:* 6 gayyou 8 gaydiang
city: Hue(c.) 4 Haoi
division: 7 Tonquin 11 Cochin China

measure: ly; con, dam, gon, mao, ngu, quo, sao, tat, vai 4 chai, phan, that 5 shita, thouc 6 tac tao, troung
money: 4 quan
river: 6 Songka
tribe: Moi
weight: li; can, fan, hao, nen, yen 4 binh, dong
Annapolis student: 4 pleb 5 plebe 10 midshipman
annates: 6 bounty 8 benefice
annatto, annotto, arnatto: dye 4 tree 5 urucu 6 salmon 7 achiote
derivative: 7 orellin
anneal: 4 bake, fuse, heat 5 smelt 6 temper 7 inflame, toughen
annectent: 7 linking 10 connecting
annelid: 4 worm
fresh water: 4 naid
marine: 4 lurg 9 autolytus
annex: add, ell 4 join 5 affix, seize, unite 6 adject, append, attach, fasten 7 acquire, fixture, subjoin 8 addition 11 appropriate 12 appurtenance
Annie Oakley: 4 pass 6 ticket
annihilate: end 4 kill, raze, slay 5 annul, erase, wreck 6 devour, quench, reduce 7 abolish, destroy, expunge 8 decimate 9 eradicate, extirpate 10 extinguish, obliterate 11 exterminate
anniversary: 4 fete 5 feast 6 annual 7 jubilee 8 birthday, festival 11 celebration
hundreth: 10 centennial
one hundred fiftieth: 16 sesquicentennial
tenth: 9 decennial
third: 9 triennial
thousandth: 10 millennial 11 millenniary
twentieth: 12 vigentennial
wedding: see **wedding:** *anniversary*
annotate: 4 edit, note 5 gloss 6 remark 7 comment, explain 9 elucidate 10 illustrate
annotation: 7 scholia(pl.) 8 scholium
announce: bid, cry 4 bode, call, deem, tell 5 bruit 6 assert, blazon, herald, inform, report, reveal, steven 7 declare, divulge, publish 8 foretell, intimate, proclaim 9 advertise, broadcast, enunciate, pronounce 10 annunciate, promulgate
announcement: 4 hat 5 banns, blurb, edict 6 decree, dictum, notice 8 bulletin 9 manifesto 11 declaration 12 notification, proclamation
announcer: 4 page 5 crier, emcee 6 nuncio 7 gongman, spieler 8 nunciate 9 messenger
of coming events: 4 seer 6 herald 7 prophet 9 harbinger
annoy: dun, get, hox, ire, irk, nag, try, vex 4 bait, bore, fret, gall, grig, hale, harm, nark, pain, rile roil 5 chafe, chase, devil, harry, peeve, pique, spite, tease, upset, weary, worry 6 badger, bother, caddle, harass, heckle, hector, injure, molest, needle, nettle, offend, pester, rattle 7 disturb, trouble 8 distress, irritate 9 aggravate, displease, embarrass, incommode, persecute 10 exasperate 13 inconvenience
annoyance: 4 pest 5 thorn 6 insect 8 nuisance 11 disturbance 13 inconvenience
annual: 4 book 5 plant 6 flower, yearly 7 etesian 8 periodic, yearbook 11 anniversary, publication
annuity: 5 censo 6 income 7 pension, tontine
annul: 4 cass, undo, void 5 blank, elide, erase, quash, remit 6 cancel, negate, recall, repeal, revoke 7 abolish, cassate, nullify, rescind 8 abrogate, derogate, overrule 9 disaffirm 10 annihilate, extinguish, invalidate, neutralize, obliterate 11 countermand
annular: 6 banded, cyclic, ringed 8 cingular, circular
annulet: 4 ring 5 ridge 6 fillet 7 molding
annunciate: 8 announce
anoa: ox 8 sapiutan
anode: 9 electrode
deposit: 5 anion
anodic: 9 ascending
anodyne: 4 balm 6 opiate, remedy 7 soother 8 narcotic, sedative 10 painkiller, palliative
anoesia: 5 anoia 6 idiocy
anoint: oil, rub 4 balm, beat, cere, nard 5 anele, anoil, cream, crown, prune, slave, smear 6 chrism, grease, spread, thrash 7 moisten 8 chastise 10 consecrate
anole: 6 lizard
anomalous: odd 7 strange, unusual 8 aberrant, abnormal, atypical, peculiar 9 eccentric, irregular 10 dissimilar 11 exceptional
anomy: 7 miracle
anon: 4 once, soon 5 again, later 6 afresh, bedeen, bedene, thence 7 shortly 9 afterward, forthwith, presently 11 immediately, straightway
anonymous: 7 unknown 8 nameless, unavowed, unsigned 9 incognito
another: new 5 alias 6 second 7 further 9 different 10 additional
ansa: 4 loop 6 handle
anserine: 4 dull 6 stolid, stupid 9 gooselike
answer: do 4 echo, plea, suit 5 atone, avail, react, reply, serve 6 result, retort, return, result, ripost 7 defense, fulfill, respond, satisfy 8 pleading, rebuttal, repartee, response, solution 9 rejoinder 11 acknowledge 16 counterstatement
answerable: 5 equal 6 liable 7 fitting 8 adequate, amenable 10 equivalent 11 ac-

countable, responsible 12 commensurate 13 proportionate
ant: 4 anai, anay, mire 5 emmet 6 eciton, insect 7 pismire, termite 8 formicid, micraner 9 myramicid 10 formicidae(pl.), hymenopter, myrmicidae(pl.), 11 hymenoptera(pl.), 12 hymenopteron
comb. form: 6 myrmec 7 myrmeco
leaf-cutting: 4 atta
male: 9 ergataner 15 ergatandromorph
nest: 9 formicary
nonworker: 5 drone
queen: 4 gyne
stinging: 5 kelep
white: 4 anai, anay 7 termite
worker (comb. form): 6 ergate, ergato
ant bear: 8 aardvark 12 myrmecophaga
ant cow: 5 aphid
ant lion: 5 aphid 9 myrmeleon
ant shrike: 6 batara
anta: 4 pier 5 tapir 8 pedestal, pilaster
Antaeus: *enemy:* 8 Hercules
father: 8 Poseidon
mother: 4 Gaea
antagonism: 6 enmity 9 animosity, antipathy, hostility 10 opposition 11 contrariety
antagonist: foe 5 enemy, rival 7 battler, warrior 8 copemate, opponent, wrangler 9 adversary, combatant 10 competitor
antagonistic: 7 counter, hostile 8 contrary, inimical 9 dissonant
Antarctica: *bird:* 4 skua 7 penguin
explorer: 4 Byrd, Cook, Ross 5 Scott 7 Wilkins
mountain: 5 Siple 9 Admiralty
sea: 4 Ross
seal: 4 Ross 9 sterrinck
ante: pay 5 stake 6 before
anteater: 5 tapir 6 animal 7 echidna, tamandu 8 aardvark, aardwolf, edentate, tamandua
scaly: 5 manis 8 pangolin
antecedent: 4 fore 5 cause, prior 6 former, reason 7 premise 8 anterior, previous 9 foregoing, foretaste, precedent, preceding
antechamber: See **anteroom**
antedate: 7 precede, predate 10 anticipate
antediluvian: 10 antiquated
antelope (see also specific countries, e.g., **Africa:** *antelope*): gnu, sus 4 poku 5 eland, peron, takin, yakin 6 dik-dik, impala, mammal 7 bloubok, gazelle, gemsbok, leather, stembok 8 ruminant, steenbok 9 pronghorn 10 hartebeest
brown: 5 nagor
female: doe
forest: 5 bongo
four-horned: 6 chouka 7 chikara 10 chousingha
gazelle-like: 5 beira 7 gerenuk
genus: 4 oryx
goat-like: 5 goral, serow 7 chamois
golden: 6 impala
harnessed: 4 guib
large: gnu 4 aste, kudu, oryx 5 addax, beisa, bongo, eland 6 impala, koodoo, nilgai, nilgau 7 bubalis, defassa, gemsbok, sassaby 10 hartebeest
male: 4 buck
mountain: 7 chamois
mythical: 4 yale
pied: 8 bontebok
pronghorn: 6 cabree, cabrie, cabret, cabrit
reddish: 7 grysbok
royal: 5 ipete 9 kleeneboc
sheep-like: 5 saiga
short-maned: gnu 6 nilgau
small: 6 duiker, grimme 7 grysbok 9 duikerbok
tawny: 5 oribi
tiger-like: 8 agacella
young: kid
antelope-like: 5 bovid 6 bovine
Antelope State: 8 Nebraska
antenna: 4 horn, palp 6 aerial, feeler, lead-in
insect: 5 clava
radar: 7 scanner
Antenor: *father:* 8 Aesyetes
son: 6 Agenor 11 Archelochus
wife: 6 Theano
anterior: 5 front, prior 6 atloid, before 7 ventral 8 atlantal, previous 9 foregoing, preceding 10 antecedent
anteroom: 4 hall 5 foyer, lobby 8 entrance 9 vestibule 11 antechamber
anthelion: 4 halo 6 nimbus 7 antisun, aureole 10 countersun
anthem: 4 hymn, song 5 motet, psalm 9 antiphony, offertory 10 responsory
anther: tip 6 pollen, stamen
anthesis: 5 bloom 7 blossom 13 efflorescence
anthill: 4 bank 5 mound 9 formicary
anthology: ana 4 book 6 corpus 7 garland 9 potpourri 10 collection 11 compilation
Anthony Adverse author: 5 Allen
anthozoan: 5 coryl, polyp 7 anemone
anthropoid: ape, lar 5 orang 6 gibbon, simian 7 gorilla, primate, siamang 9 orangutan 10 chimpanzee, troglodyte
anthropophagite: 8 cannibal
anti: 6 contra 7 against, opposed
anti-aircraft: *fire:* 4 flak
gun: 5 archy 6 pom-pom

antic: 4 dido, fool, wild 5 caper, clown, comic, droll, prank, stunt 6 gambol 7 buffoon, caprice, gambado 9 grotesque, ludicrous 11 merry-andrew, monkeyshine
anticipate: 4 balk, hope 5 augur, await 6 divine, expect, thwart 7 devance, forerun, foresee, obviate, portend, prepare, prevene, prevent 8 antedate 9 apprehend, forestall, foretaste
anticipation: 5 odium 6 augury 9 intuition, prolepsis 11 forethought 12 presentiment 13 preoccupation
anticipator: 4 seer 6 omener 7 prophet, seeress 8 foreseer
antidote: 4 cure, soda 6 bezoar, emetic, remedy 10 preventive 11 restorative
Antigone: *mother:* 7 Jocasta
sister: 6 Ismene
Antilles: *god:* 4 Zeme
native: 5 Ineri
pearl: 4 Cuba
antimacassar: 4 tidy 5 doily
antimony: Sb 4 kohl 7 stibium
pert. to: 7 stibial
Antioch proselyte: 7 Nicolas
antipasto: 6 relish 9 appetizer, foretaste 12 hors d'oeuvres
antipathy: 6 enmity, nausea, rancor 7 disgust, dislike 8 aversion, distaste, loathing 9 disrelish, hostility 10 abhorrence, antagonism, reluctance, repugnance 11 contrariety, detestation 14 disinclination 15 incompatibility
antiquated: old 4 aged 5 passe 6 fossil, voided 7 ancient, archaic 8 obsolete, outdated, outmoded 9 primitive 12 antediluvian 13 superannuated
antique: 5 relic, virtu 9 venerable 12 old-fashioned
antiquity: eld 4 hpar, yore 5 relic 8 ancience, anciency, monument 9 anciently
antiseptic: 5 amido, amine, eupad, eusol, salol 6 iodine, phenol 7 alcohol, aseptic, loretin, sterile 8 creosote, metaphen 9 germicide 12 disinfectant
powder: 6 formin
antisocial: 7 hostile 11 anarchistic 12 misanthropic
antisociability: 14 anthropophobia
antispasmodic: 9 asadulcis
antithalian: 7 killjoy
antithesis: 8 contrast 9 antipodes 10 opposition
antitoxin: 4 sera(pl.) 5 serum
antler: 4 horn
bay: 9 bezantler
branch: bay, bey 4 beam, brow, snag, tine, tyne 5 crown, royal 7 speller 8 tresting
knob: 6 croche
main stem: 4 beam
unbranched: dag 4 horn 5 dague, spike 7 pricket 9 greenhorn
Antony and Cleopatra character: 4 Eros, Iras 5 Menas, Philo 6 Gallus, Taurus 7 Agrippa
antrum: 5 sinus 6 cavern, cavity
anuran: 4 toad 10 salientian
anurous: 8 tailless
Anu's consort: 4 Anat
anvil: 5 block 6 stithy 7 bickern 8 beakiron
bone: 4 amos 5 incus 7 incudes(pl.)
point: 4 horn, beak
tinsmith's: 5 teest
anxiety: 4 care, fear 5 alarm, anger, doubt, dread, panic, worry 7 caution, chagrin, concern, scruple, trouble 8 disquiet, suspense 9 misgiving 10 foreboding, perplexity, solicitude, uneasiness 12 apprehension
anxious: 4 agog 5 eager 6 uneasy 7 carking, unquiet 8 desirous, restless, watchful 9 disturbed, expectant, impatient
any: an; ary, oni 4 part, some 8 quantity 11 appreciable
anybody: one 7 someone
anything: 5 aught
anyway: 6 anyhow 12 nevertheless
Anzac: 7 soldier 10 Australian 12 New Zealander
aorist: 4 past 5 tense
aoristic: 10 indefinite 12 undetermined 13 indeterminate
aorta: 5 trunk 6 artery
aoudad: 4 arui 5 sheep
apa: 7 wallaba
apace: 4 fast 5 quick 7 quickly, rapidly 8 speedily
Apache: 4 Yuma 6 Indian 10 Chiricahua
beverage: 6 tiswin
chief: 7 Cochese 8 Geronimo
jacket: 6 bietle
Apache State: 7 Arizona
apar: 9 armadillo
apart: by 4 away, lone 5 alone, aloof, aside, riven, solus, split 6 atwain, lonely 7 asunder, enisled, removed, severed 8 divorced, secluded, separate 10 abstracted 11 dissociated
prefix: se; dia, dis
apartment: 4 digs, flat 5 abode, rooms, suite 7 chamber 8 building, dwelling, tenement 11 compartment
upper: 5 solar 6 sollar
apathetic: 4 calm, cold, cool, dead, dull 5 inert, stoic 6 torpid, supine 7 passive, unmoved 8 listless, sluggish 9 impassive, incurious, unfeeling 10 insensible, phleg-

matic 11 indifferent, unemotional 12 uninterested 13 dispassionate, sensationless
apathy: 6 acedia, phlegm, torpor 7 languor 8 doldrums 9 lassitude, unconcern 12 indifference
apatite: 7 ijolite
ape (see also **anthropoid**): 4 boor, copy, dupe, fool, maha, mime, mock 5 clown, magot, mimic 6 baboon, gelada, langur, monkey, parrot, simian 7 buffoon, copycat, emulate, imitate, portray, primate 8 imitator, simulate 10 anthropoid, quadrumane 11 impersonate
dog-headed: 4 aani 11 cynocephali(pl.) 12 cynocephalus
largest: 7 gorilla
like animal: 5 lemur
apeak: 8 vertical
apeman: 6 alalus 15 pithecanthropus
aper: 4 boar, mime, snob 5 clown 6 mocker 7 buffoon, copycat
apercu: 6 digest, glance, sketch 7 insight, outline 10 conspectus
aperitif: 5 drink 9 appetizer
apert: 4 bold, open 7 evident 9 outspoken 15 straightforward
aperture: gap, vue 4 hole, leak, pore, rima, slit, slot, vent 5 chasm, cleft, crack, mouth, stoma 6 window 7 fissure, opening, orifice, ostiole 8 loophole, spiracle 11 perforation
apex: tip, top 4 acme, cone, cusp, noon, peak 5 crest, point, spire 6 apogee, climax, crisis, summit, tittle, vertex, zenith 7 cacumen 8 fastigia(pl.), pinnacle 9 fastigium 11 culmination
covering: api
elbow: 5 ancon
ornament for: 6 finial
pert. to: 6 apical 9 cacuminal
rounded: 6 retuse
Aphareus: *brother:* 7 Lynceus
son: 4 Idas
aphid: 5 aphis, louse
aphorism: saw 5 adage, axiom, dicta(pl.), gnome, maxim, motto, sutra, sutta 6 dictum, saying 7 epigram, precept, proverb 8 apothegm 10 apophthegm
aphoristic: 6 gnomic 8 gnomical 10 proverbial
Aphrodite: 5 Venus 6 Urania 9 priestess
consort: 4 Ares
mother: 5 Dione
priestess: 4 Hero
son: 4 Eros 5 Eneas 6 Aeneas
temple site: 6 Paphos
apiary: 4 hive, skep 8 beehouse
apiece: per 4 each 8 seriatim 14 distributively
apina: 7 apoidea
apis: bee 8 honeybee
Apis' manifestation: 7 Serapis
apish: 5 silly 7 foppish 8 affected
apishamore: bed 7 blanket
aplomb: 4 tact 5 nerve, poise 6 surety 8 coolness 9 assurance, stability 10 confidence, resolution
apocopate: 5 elide 7 shorten
apocryphal: 4 sham 5 false 6 unreal 8 doubtful, fabulous, mythical, spurious 9 imitative 10 fictitious, unorthodox 11 counterfeit, uncanonical, unauthentic
Apocryphal book: 5 Tobit 6 Baruch, Esdras, Judith 9 Maccabees
apodal: 8 footless
apode: eel 5 moray
apogee: 4 acme, apex, peak 6 climax, zenith 11 culmination
apograph: 4 copy 6 ectype 7 replica 9 imitation 10 transcript
apoidea: bee 4 apis 5 apina 6 apidae
Apollo: 6 Delius 7 Phoebus
abode of: 7 Helicon
beloved of: 6 Cyrene, Daphne 8 Calliope
birthplace: 5 Delos
father: 4 Zeus 7 Jupiter
festival: 5 Delia 6 Carnea
instrument: 4 lute, lyre
mother: 4 Leto 6 Latona
oracle site: 6 Delphi
priest: 7 Calchas
sacred vale: 5 Tempe
sister: 5 Diana 7 Artemis
son: Ion
traveler: 6 Abaris
twin: 5 Diana
Apollyon: 5 Satan, devil 7 Abaddon 9 archfiend, Beelzebub, destroyer
apologetic: 5 sorry 9 defensive 10 remorseful
apologue: 4 myth 5 fable, story 7 parable 8 allegory
pert. to: 7 fabular
apology: 4 plea 5 alibi 6 amends, excuse, regret 11 explanation, vindication 13 justification 14 acknowledgment 15 acknowledgement
apoplexy: 4 esca 5 plant 6 stroke 12 black measles
apostate: rat 7 heretic, pervert, seceder 8 deserter, disloyal, recreant, renegade, turncoat 9 faithless 10 recidivist
apostle: 4 John, Jude, Paul 5 James, Judas, Peter, Silas, Simon 6 Andrew, Philip, Thomas 7 Matthew, teacher 8 Barnabas, disciple, follower, preacher 9 messenger 10 apprentice 11 Bartholomew
of Indies: 6 Xavier
pert. to: 7 petrine

to Franks: 4 Remi
to Gauls: 5 Denis
to Goths: 7 Ulfilas
apothecary: 8 druggist, gallipot 10 pharmacist, posologist
weight: 4 dram 5 grain, pound 7 scruple
apothegm, apophthegm: saw 4 dict 5 adage, axiom, dicta(pl.), gnome, maxim, sutra 6 dictum, saying, suttah 7 proverb 8 aphorism
apotheosize: 5 deify, exalt 7 elevate, glorify 10 consecrate
Appalachian range: 6 Ramapo
appall, appal: 4 stun 5 daunt, shock 6 dismay, reduce, revolt, weaken 7 astound, depress, disgust, dismiss, horrify, terrify 8 affright, astonish, enfeeble, frighten, overcome 10 discourage, dishearten
appalling: 5 awful 7 awesome 8 terrible, terrific 9 frightful, unearthly
appanage, apanage: 5 grant 7 adjunct 9 allowance, privilege, territory 10 dependency, perquisite 11 prerogative 12 appurtenance
apparatus (see also **device, instrument**): 4 gear, tool 6 dingus, gadget, graith, outfit 7 machine, utensil 8 equipage 9 appliance, equipment, machinery, mechanism, trappings 10 furnishing 11 contrivance 12 appurtenance
apparel (see also **dress, vestment**): 4 deck, fare, garb, gear, robe, wear 5 adorn, array, equip, tunic 6 attire, clothe, graith, outfit 7 costume, furnish, garment, prepare, raiment, vesture 8 clothing, wardrobe 9 embellish, equipment 11 habiliments
apparent: 4 open 5 clear, overt, plain 6 patent 7 certain, evident, glaring, obvious, seeming, visible 8 distinct, manifest, palpable, probable 9 appearant 10 ostensible 11 discernible, perceptible, unconcealed 12 unmistakable
apparition: 4 hant 5 dream, ghost, haunt, shade, spook 6 aspect, eidola(pl.), idolum, spirit, sprite, wraith 7 display, eidolon, fantasy, phantom, specter, spectre 8 phantasm, revenant 9 hobgoblin, semblance 10 appearance, phenomenon 13 demonstration
appay: 5 repay 6 please, reward 7 content, satisfy
appeach: 6 accuse 7 asperse, impeach
appeal: ask, beg 4 call, case, plea, seek, suit 5 apply, refer 6 accuse, adjure, avouch, invoke, prayer, summon 7 address, conjure, entreat, implore, request, solicit 8 approach, petition 9 challenge, importune 10 appelation, supplicate
appealing: 4 cute, nice 6 catchy, clever 8 pleasant 9 agreeable 10 attractive
appear: 4 come, dawn, look, loom, seem 5 arise, enter, issue, occur 6 arrive, beseem, emerge 7 compear(Sc.), develop
appearance: air, hue 4 form, idea, look, mien, show, view 5 blush, front, guise, sight 6 aspect, manner, ostent 7 arrival, display 8 illusion, presence, pretense 9 semblance 10 disclosure, likelihood, phenomenon 11 countenance, probability 13 manifestation
first: 4 dawn 5 debut 8 premiere
appease: lay 4 calm, ease, hush 5 allay, alone, mease(Sc.), quiet, slake 6 defray, pacify, please, soften, soothe 7 assuage, content, gratify, mollify, placate, satisfy 8 mitigate 10 conciliate, propitiate 11 tranquilize
appellation: nom (F.), 4 name, term 5 style, title 6 appeal 7 calling, epithet, surname 8 cognomen, nickname 9 sobriquet 11 description, designation 12 denomination, nomenclature
appellee: 9 defendant 10 respondent
appenage: See **appanage**
append: add, pin, tag 4 clip, hang, join 5 affix, annex 6 adjoin, attach, fasten 7 augment, subjoin 8 appendix
appendage: arm, awn, tab, tag 4 aril, barb, caud, flap, lobe, tail 5 ceras, rider 6 adnexa(pl.), bracht, palpus, suffix 7 adjunct, eodicil 8 addition, pendicle 9 accessory, belonging 10 dependency 12 appurtenance
appendix: 5 organ 6 append 7 addenda(pl.), 8 addendum 10 supplement
operation: 12 appendectomy
appertain: 5 refer 6 belong, relate 7 pertain
appetite: yen 4 lust, urge, zest 5 gusto, taste 6 desire, hunger, liking, orexis, relish 7 craving, longing, passion, wanting 8 cupidity, tendency 9 appetency 10 preference, propensity
abnormal: 4 pica 7 bulimia
excessive: 5 greed 8 gluttony, gulosity 10 polyphagia
pert. to: 7 oretic
voracious: 7 edacity 8 rapacity
appetizer: 5 sauce 6 canape, relish, savory 8 aperitif 9 antipasto 11 hors d'oeuvre
applaud: 4 clap, laud, root 5 cheer, extol 6 praise 7 acclaim, approve, commend, endorse 10 compliment
applauders: 6 claque
applause: 4 clap, hand 5 bravo, cheer, eclat, huzza, salvo 6 hurrah 7 acclaim, ovation 8 clapping, plaudits 11 approbation
device: 8 claptrap
applause-seeking: 9 captation

apple: 4 crab, pome 6 Esopus, pippin, russet 7 Baldwin, Fameuse, winesap, wealthy 8 Ben Davis, Cortland, Greening, Jonathan, McIntosh 9 Delicious, Oldenberg 10 Rome Beauty 11 Gravenstein, Northern Spy, Spitzenburg 12 Yellow Newton, York Imperial 17 Yellow Transparent
acid: 5 malic
blight: 5 aphid 8 eriosoma
cider-making: 8 coccagee
crushed: 6 pomace
dried: 6 beefin, biffin
family: 8 Malaceae
genus: 5 malus
immature: 6 codlin 7 codling
juice: 5 cider 9 applejack
juice (pert. to): 5 malic
old variety: 6 rennet
pastry: 7 strudel
pulp: 6 pomace
ribbed: 7 costard
seed: pip 7 putamen
seller: 6 coster 12 costermonger
shriveled: 9 crumpling
tree: 4 sorb 5 malus, papaw 6 pawpaw
wild: 4 crab 6 doucin

apple butter: 6 spread 9 condiment
apple grunt: pie 8 dumpling
apple of one's eye: 7 darling 8 favorite
apple-polish: 7 flatter
apple-shaped: 8 pomiform
applelike fruit: 4 pome
applesauce: 4 bunk, pulp 5 hokum 6 relish 7 baloney, dessert 8 nonsense
appliance (see also **tool**): 4 gear 6 device, gadget 7 utensil 9 implement 10 instrument 11 application, contrivance 12 appurtenance
applicable: apt, fit 4 meet 6 proper, useful 7 fitting, pliable 8 apposite, relative, relevant, suitable 9 compliant, pertinent 11 appropriate
applicant: 8 prospect 9 candidate, declarant
application: use 4 form 5 blank, topic 6 appeal, effort 7 address, request 8 petition, practice, sedulity 9 diligence 10 compliance 11 requisition
applique: 6 attach, design 8 ornament 10 decoration
apply: ask, put, rub, use 4 give, toil, work 5 adapt, grind, labor, liken, smear 6 appeal, appose, bestow, betake, comply, devote, direct, employ 7 adhibit, compare, conform, overlay, pertain, request, solicit, utilize 8 dedicate, petition 9 persevere 10 administer
appoggiatura: 8 ornament 9 grace note
appoint: arm, fix, set 4 call, deck, name 5 allot, array, award, crest, dight, elect, enact, equip, place 6 assign, assize, attach, decree, detail, devise, direct, ordain, outfit, settle, steven 7 arraign, confirm, destine, dispose, furnish, resolve 8 delegate, indicate, ordinate, nominate 9 designate, determine, establish, prescribe 10 constitute
as agent: 6 depute 8 delegate, deputize

appointment: 4 date 5 berth, order, tryst 6 billet, office, steven 7 command, station 8 position 9 allowance, equipment, interview, ordaining, ordinance 10 assignment, engagement, nomination, perquisite, rendezvous 11 assignation, designation 12 capitulation 13 establishment
apport: 4 port 5 rents 7 bearing, produce, tribute 13 contributions
apportion: lot 4 deal, dole, mete 5 allot, award, grant, paral, share 6 assess, assign, divide 7 arrange 8 allocate 10 distribute
apportionment: 4 deal 8 dividend, division 9 allowance 12 distribution
appose: add, put 5 apply, place
apposite: apt, pat 6 timely 7 germane 8 relative, relevant, suitable 9 pertinent 11 appropriate
appraise (see also **apprise**): 4 gage, rate 5 assay, judge, price, value 6 assess, esteem, evalue, ponder 7 adjudge, analyze, commend 8 estimate, evaluate 10 adjudicate, appreciate
appreciable: any 11 perceptible
appreciate: 4 feel, love 5 judge, prize, raise, value 6 admire, esteem 7 advance, apprize, approve, cherish, realize 8 increase, treasure
appreciation: 5 gusto 9 gratitude 11 recognition 12 gratefulness
apprehend: cop, nab, see 4 fear, know, note, take, view 5 catch, dread, grasp, gripe, intue, seize 6 arrest, detain, intuit 7 believe, capture, imagine, realize 8 conceive, discover, overtake, perceive 9 recognize 10 anticipate, appreciate, comprehend, understand
apprehensible: 6 noetic 7 sensate 12 intelligible
apprehension: 4 fear, fray 5 doubt, dread, worry 6 arrest, dismay 7 anxiety, concern 8 distrust, mistrust, suspense 9 awareness, misgiving, suspicion 10 cognizance, conception diffidence, foreboding, perception, solicitude, uneasiness 11 premonition 12 anticipation, intellection, presentiment 13 signification
apprehensive: apt 5 jumpy 6 morbid 7 nervous 9 cognizant, conscious 10 discerning
apprentice: 4 tyro 6 helper, jockey, novice 7 learner, trainee 8 beginner, servitor 9 draftsman

apres: 5 after 10 afterwards

apprise, apprize (see also **appraise**): 4 warn 5 learn, teach 6 advise, inform, notify, reveal 8 acquaint, disclose 9 ascertain 10 appreciate, certiorate

apprised: 5 aware 7 knowing

approach: try 4 adit, come, near, nere, road 5 board, coast, essay, stalk, verge 6 access, accost, advent, appeal, broach, impend 7 advance, seagate 9 introduce 11 approximate 13 appropinquate

approbation: 4 test 5 favor, proof, trial 6 assent, favour, praise, regard, repute 7 plaudit 8 applause, approval, sanction 9 allowance 10 admiration 11 attestation 12 commendation, confirmation

appropinquate: 8 approach

appropriate: add, apt, due, fit 4 akin, grab, meet, suit, take 5 annex, happy, right, steal, usurp 6 assign, assume, borrow, pilfer, pirate, proper, timely, worthy 7 apropos, cabbage, condign, convert, fitting, germane, grabble, impound, preempt, purloin, related 8 accroach, becoming, deserved, idoneous, relevant, suitable 9 attribute, pertinent 10 applicable, assimilate, confiscate, convenient, felicitous, plagiarize 11 conformable,

approval: 4 amen 5 eclat 6 assent 7 approof, support 8 sanction 10 imprimatur 11 approbation

approve: ok; try 4 like, okay, pass, test, vote 5 allow, favor, value 6 accept, admire, concur, ratify 7 applaud, certify, commend, confirm, consent, endorse, exhibit, indorse 8 accredit, manifest, sanction 9 authorize, establish 10 appreciate, experience 11 countenance 12 adscititious, authenticate

approximate: 4 near 5 about, circa, close 8 approach, estimate 10 resembling 11 approaching

approximately: 4 nigh 5 about 6 almost, around, nearly 7 roughly

appurtenance: 4 gear 5 annex 7 adjunct 8 appanage, appenage 9 accessory, apparatus, appliance, belonging

apricot: ume 4 ansu, tree 5 color, fruit 8 Blenheim
  confection: 5 mebos 6 meebos
  cordial: 7 perisco 8 periscot
  vine: 6 maypop

apron: bib 4 base, boot, brat, tier 5 cover 6 barvel, bishop, napron, runway, shield, tarmac, touser 7 gremial 8 lambskin, pinafore 9 barmcloth 10 coverslut, protection
  leather: 4 dick 6 barvel 7 barvell 8 barmskin

apropos: apt, fit, pat 4 meet 6 timely 8 relevant, suitable 9 opportune, pertinent 11 appropriate

apse: 5 niche 6 recess 10 projection

apt: fit, pat 4 able, deft, keen 5 adept, alert, happy, prone, quick, ready 6 clever, docile, liable, likely, suited 7 apropos, capable, fitting, willing 8 apposite, dextrous, disposed, idoneous, inclined, prepared, skillful, suitable 9 competent, consonant, dexterous, pertinent, qualified 10 proficient 11 appropriate

apteral: 8 apterous, wingless

apteryx: 4 bird, kiwi

aptitude: art 4 bent, gift, turn 5 craft, flair, knack 6 genius, talent 7 ability, faculty, fitness, leaning 8 capacity, instinct, tendency 10 propensity 11 disposition 12 suitableness

aqua: 5 water

aquamarine: gem 4 blue 5 beryl, color

aquarium: 4 bowl, pool, pond, tank 5 globe

aquatic plant: 4 lily 5 coral, lotus 6 enalid, sugamo 7 elatine, seaweed 10 hydrophyte

aqueduct: 4 duct 5 canal 7 channel, conduit, passage 9 conductor
  of Sylvius: 4 iter

aquifer: bed 6 bearer 7 stratum

aquila: 5 eagle

aquiline: 6 curved, hooked 7 curving 9 prominent

Aquinas work: 5 Summa

aquosity: 7 wetness 8 moisture 10 wateriness

ara: 5 macaw

Arab: 4 Oman, sleb, waif 5 gamin, horse, nomad, Saudi, tatar 6 Semite, urchin 7 Arabian, bedouin, Saracen 8 wanderer, Yemenite 9 Himyarite

araba: cab 5 coach, wagon 6 monkey 7 vehicle

Arabia: *abode:* dar 4 tent
  alphabet: See **Arabic:** *alphabet*
  ancient: 4 Saha 5 Sheba
  antelope: 5 addax
  author: 6 lokman
  banquet: 5 diffa
  bazaar: suq
  bird: 7 phoenix
  caliph: Ali 6 sharif, sherif 7 shareef, shereef
  caravan: 6 cafila
  chief: 4 amir, emir 5 ameer, emeer
  city: 4 Aden, Bida, Hail, Riad, Sana 5 Mecca, Mocha 6 Medina 7 Oneizah
  cloak: aba
  coffee: 5 mocha
  coin: 4 lari 5 carat, dinar, kabik, riyal
  cosmetic: 4 kohl

country: 4 Asir, Iran, Iraq, Oman 5 Egypt, Syria, Yemen 6 Arabia, Jordan 7 Lebanon
demon: 4 jinn 5 afrit, genie, jinni 6 afreet, jinnee
desert: Nyd 5 Ankaf, Dehna, Nefud 6 Syrian
dish: 8 couscous
division: 4 Oman, Suez 5 Mecca, Sinai 6 El Hasa, El Nejd, Mahara 7 El Yemen, Medinah 8 El Hedjaz, El Tehama 9 Hadramaut
drink: 4 bosa, boza 5 bozah 6 lebban
drum: 9 tara-booka
fabric: aba 4 haik
father: abu 4 abba, abou
flour source: 4 samh
garment: aba 4 haik 6 cabaan 7 burnous 8 burnoose
gazelle: 4 cora 5 ariel
goddess: 5 Allat
grammar: 7 ajrumya
gulf: 4 Aden, Oman
horse: 6 anezeh 8 kadischi, palomino
infantryman: 5 askar
jasmine: 4 bela 10 sampaquita
judge: 4 cadi
kingdom: 4 Nejd
land: 6 feddan
measure: den, saa 4 ferk, foot, kist 5 achir, barid, cabda, cafiz, covid, cuddy, makuk, mille, qasab, teman, woibe, zudda 6 artaba, assbaa, covido, feddan, gariba, ghalva 7 caphite, farsakh, farsang, kiladja, marhale, nusfiah
mountain: 4 Nebo 5 Horeb, Sinai
noble: 4 amir, emir 5 ameer, emeer
nomad: 7 Saracen
palm: 4 doom, doum
peasant: 6 fellah
peninsula: 5 Sinai
philosopher: 6 Farabi 8 Averroes
plant: kat 5 retem
prince (see also *ruler* below): 6 sherif 7 shereef
raiders: 8 fedayeen
river bed: 4 wadi, wady
romance: 5 antar 6 antara
ruler: 4 amir, emir 5 ameer, emeer
scripture: 5 Koran 7 Alkoran
shrine: 5 Kaaba
shrub: kat 5 alhaj, retem
tambourine: 4 taar 5 daira
tea shrub: kat
tent encampment: 5 douar
tribe: Aus 4 Asir, Irad, Tema 5 Kedar 7 Diendel, Shukria 9 Hagarenes
vessel: 4 dhow 6 boutre, sambuk
weight: 4 rotl 5 cheki, kella, nasch, nevat, ocque, oukia, ratel, toman, vakia 6 bokard, dirhem, miskal, tomand 8 farsalah
wind: 6 simoom, simoon

Arabian Nights: *bird:* roc 4 aqib
character: Ali 4 Sidi 5 Amina 7 Zobeide
dervish: 4 Agib
merchant: 7 Sindbad
poet: Kab 5 Antar
prince: 7 Alasnam
sailor: 6 Sinbad 7 Sindbad
sorceress: 5 Amine
youth: 7 Aladdin

Arabic: *alphabet:* ba, ta, ha, ra, za, fa, ya; tha, jim, kha, dal, zay, sin, sad, dad, ayn, qaf, kaf, lam, mim, nun, waw 4 alif, dhal, shin 5 ghayn
script: 5 neski

arabic acid salt: 7 arabate

arable: 7 fertile 8 plowable, tillable
land: 5 laine

araca: 4 tree 6 timber 10 terminalia

aracanga: 5 macaw

aracari: 6 toucan

araceous: 5 aroid
plant: 4 arum, lily, taro

arachnid: 4 crab, mite, tick 6 acarus, spider 8 scorpion 9 tarantula

arachnoid: 4 thin 5 hairy 8 araneous, delicate 10 cobweblike

Aram: 5 Syria
children: Uz; Hul 4 Mash 6 Gether
city: 5 arpad 6 arphad
deity: 6 Rimmon
nomads: 7 Akhlame

Aramaic: 6 Syriac 9 Samaritan

araneous: 4 thin 8 delicate 9 arachnoid 10 cobweblike

araphorostic: 7 unsewed 8 seamless

araponga: 8 bellbird

Arawakan: *Indian:* 4 Uran 5 Araua, Bares, Guana, Moxos, Piros 6 Campas 7 Atorais, Banivas, Jucunas, Lucayos, Tacanan, Ticunan 8 Lorenzan
language: 5 Taino

arbiter: 5 judge 6 critic, oddman, umpire 7 adviser, daysman, oddsman, overman, referee 10 arbitrator

arbitrary: 6 severe, thetic 7 willful 8 absolute, despotic, masterly 9 imperious 10 autocratic, capricious, highhanded, peremptory, tryannical 11 determinate 13 irresponsible

arbitrate: 6 decide 7 mediate 9 determine, intercede

arbitrator: ref 5 judge 6 umpire 7 arbiter, munsiff, referee 8 mediator 11 conciliator

arbor, arbour: bar 4 axle, beam 5 abode, bower, shaft 6 garden 7 mandrel, orchard, pergola, retreat, spindle, trellis 8 platform 11 latticework

arbustum: 5 copse 7 orchard 10 plantation

arc: bow 4 arch, bend, halo 5 curve, orbit, spark 6 radian 7 rainbow 9 spotlight
chord of: 4 sine
horizon: 7 azimuth
arc lamp rod: 6 carbon
arca: box 5 chest, paten 9 reliquary
arcade: 6 avenue, loggia, street 7 gallery, portico 8 arcature 9 collonade 10 passageway
Arcadia: 4 Eden 6 Arcady 8 paradise
huntress: 8 Atalanta
princess: 4 Auge
town: 4 Alea
woodland spirit: Pan
arcadian: 5 ideal, rural 6 rustic, simple 7 bucolic 8 pastoral, shepherd
arcane: 6 hidden, secret 10 mysterious
arcanum: 6 elixir, remedy, secret 7 mystery
Arcas: *father:* 4 Zeus
mother: 8 Callisto
son: 4 Azan 8 Apheidas
arch: arc, bow, coy, sly 4 bend, span 5 arcus, chief, curve, great, prime, saucy, vault 6 arcade, clever, fornix, impish 7 archway, cunning, eminent, roguish, support, waggish 9 principal 11 mischievous
inner curve of: 8 intrados
kind of: 4 flat 5 round, Tudor 6 lancet 7 rampant, trefoil 9 horseshoe, primitive, segmental 10 shouldered 11 equilateral 12 basket-handle, four-centered 13 three-cornered
memorial: 6 pailoo, pailou, pailow
molding: 9 accoclade
part: 8 keystone, springer, voussoir
pointed: 4 ogee 5 ogive
arch-enemy: 5 devil, Satan
archaic: old 7 ancient 8 historic, obsolete 9 venerable 10 antiquated 12 old-fashioned
archangel: 5 Satan, Uriel 7 Gabriel, Michael, Raphael
archbishop: 7 prelate, primate
archbishopric: see
archer: 4 Clim, Clym, Tell 5 cupid 6 bowman 9 Robin Hood 10 archerfish 11 Sagittarius
archery: *deity:* 6 Apollo 7 Artemis
locker: 6 ascham
lover: 11 toxophilite
target center: 5 clout
archetype: 4 idea 5 model 6 figure, sample 7 example, paragon, pattern 8 exemplar, original 9 prototype 10 manuscript
architect: 5 maker 6 artist, author 7 artisan, builder, creator, planner 8 designer 9 contriver, draftsman
architectural: 8 tectonic
architecture: *convexity:* 7 entasis
order: 5 Doric, Ionic 10 Corinthian
ornament: ove 5 gutta 6 dentil, rosace 7 rosette
style: 5 Doric, Greek, Ionic, Tudor 6 French, Gothic, Lancet, Modern, Norman 7 Baroque, Cape Cod, English, Italian, Moorish, Spanish 8 Academic, Colonial, Egyptian, Etruscan, Georgian 9 Byzantine, Palladian 10 Corinthian, Romanesque 11 Renaissance
archive: 5 annal 6 museum, record 7 library 8 document, register 9 chronicle
archon: 5 ruler 8 director, official 10 magistrate
arctic: icy 4 cold, cool, shoe 5 gelid, polar 6 boreal, chilly, frigid, galosh 8 northern, overshoe
Arctic: *base:* 4 Etah
bird: auk
canoe: 5 kayak, umiak 6 oomiak
current: 8 Labrador
dog: 7 samoyed 8 samoyede
explorer: Rae 4 Byrd, Eric, Kane, Ross 5 Davis, Peary 6 Baffin, Bering, Button, Greely, Hudson, Nansen 7 McClure, Wilkins, Wrangel 8 Amundsen 9 Frobisher, Stefanson 10 Willoughby
falcon: 9 gyrfalcon
gull (genus): 4 xema
headland: 5 Odden
inhabitant: 4 Lapp 5 Aleut 6 Eskimo 7 Alaskan 9 Laplander
jacket: 6 anorak
musk ox: 6 ovibos
native: 4 Lapp 5 Aleut 6 Eskimo 7 Alaskan 9 Laplander
plain: 6 tundra
plant: 5 ledum
sea: 7 Barents
sea animal: 6 narwal 8 narwhale
Arctic Sea gulf: Ob
Arcturus: 4 star
arcuate: 4 bent 5 bowed 6 arched, curved, hooked
ardent: hot 4 avid, fond, keen, warm 5 eager, fiery, rethe(Sc.) 6 ablaze, fervid, fierce 7 amorous, earnest, feeling, fervent, flaming, forward, intense, shining, zealous 8 desirous, vehement 9 impetuous, perfervid 11 inflammable 12 enthusiastic
ardor, ardour: 4 dash, elan, glow, heat, love, zest 5 gusto, verve 6 desire, fervor, mettle, spirit 7 ardency, passion 8 devotion, vivacity 9 animation, calenture, constancy 10 enthusiasm
arduous: 4 hard 5 lofty, steep 6 trying 7 onerous 8 exacting, tiresome, toilsome 9 difficult, laborious, strenuous 10 exhausting
are: 5 exist

area: 4 belt, size, zone 5 court, field, range, realm, scene, scope, space, tract 6 areola, extent, locale, region, sector, sphere, volume 7 areaway, circuit, compass, environ, expanse, purlieu, surface 8 district, province 9 bailiwick, extension, territory 12 neighborhood
measure: 6 parish
pert. to: 7 spatial

aread, areed: 4 read, tell, warn 5 guess 6 advise, decree, direct, divine 7 adjudge, counsel, declare, explain 9 interpret

areca: 4 palm 5 betel

arena: 4 area, oval, ring, rink 5 court, field, scene, scope, space, stage 6 circus, region, sphere, stadia(pl.), 7 cockpit, stadium, theater 8 province 10 hippodrome 12 amphitheater
sports: see **field** *athletic*

arenaceous: 5 sandy 6 gritty 8 sabulous

areola: pit 4 area, ring, spot 5 space 9 periphery 10 interstice

areometer: 10 hydrometer

Ares: 4 Mars
father: 4 Zeus
mother: 4 Enyo, Hera
sister: 4 Eris
son: 6 Cycnus

arete: 4 crag 5 crest, ridge, valor 6 virtue 8 fishbone 9 manliness 10 excellence

argala: 7 marabou 8 adjutant

argali: 5 sheep 6 aoudad

argent: 4 coin 5 money, white 6 silver 7 shining, silvery 9 whiteness

Argentina: *armadillo:* 6 peludo
barge: 7 chalana
city: 4 Acha, Azul, Goya, Puan 5 Bahia, Jujuy, Lanus, Salta 6 Blanca, Burras, Parana 7 Cordoba, La Plata, La Rioja, Mendoza, Rosario, Santa Fe, Tucuman 11 Buenos Aires (c.)
coin: 4 peso 7 centavo 9 argentino
cowboy: 6 gaucho
dance: 5 tango 6 cuando
estuary: 5 Plata
garment: 7 chiripa
Indian: 4 Lule
Indian village: 8 tolderia
measure: 4 sino, vara 5 legua 6 cuadra, fanega 7 manzana
mesquite: 6 calden 9 algarroba
mountain: 9 Aconcagua
plain: 5 pampa
port: 7 Rosario
province: 5 Chaco, Jujuy, Pampa, Rioja, Salta 6 Estero 7 Cordova, Formosa, Mendoza, San Juan, San Luis, Santa Fe, Tucuman 8 Santiago 9 Catamarca, Entre Rios, Patagonia 10 Corrientes
ranch: 8 estancia
river: 5 Negro, Plata 6 Parana, Salado 7 Vermejo 8 Colorado, Paraguay, Picomayo 9 Rio Grande
tree: 4 coco, tala 5 ambay, timbo
weight: 4 last 5 grano 7 quintal 8 tonelada

argil: 4 clay 7 alumina

argillaceous: 5 slaty 6 clayey, cledgy, doughy, spongy

argol, argal: 6 tartar

Argonaut: 5 Jason 8 wanderer 10 adventurer

Argos: *king:* 4 Abas 6 Danaus 7 Lynceus 8 Acrisius, Adrastus
princess: 5 Danae

argosy: 4 boat, ship 5 craft, fleet 6 vessel 7 galleon

argot: 4 cant 5 flash, lingo, slang 6 jargon, patois 7 dialect

argue: 4 moot, spar 5 cavil, orate, plead, prove, treat 6 accuse, adduce, caffle, debate, reason 7 arraign, contend, contest, discuss, wrangle 8 indicate, maintain, persuade 9 argy-bargy, discourse 11 expostulate, ratiocinate, remonstrate

argument: row 4 agon, case, fuss, plea, spar, text 5 clash, proof, set to, theme 6 combat, debate, hassle 7 dispute, polemic, rhubarb, summary 8 abstract, evidence 9 argy-bargy, discourse 10 indication 11 altercation, argey-bargey, controversy, disputation
conclusive: 6 corker 7 crusher 8 clincher 9 knockdown 11 sockdolager, sockdologer
fallacious: 7 sophism
negative side: con
positive side: pro
specious: rot 8 claptrap, nonsense 9 sophistry 10 paralogism
starting point: 7 premise

argumentative: 7 eristic 8 forensic 10 rhetorical 11 presumptive 12 disputatious 13 controversial

Argus-eyed: 8 vigilant

argute: 5 acute, sharp 6 shrewd, shrill, subtle 9 sagacious

argy-bargy, argey-bargey: 5 argue 6 haggle 7 dispute, wrangle

arhat: 4 monk 5 lohan, saint

aria: air 4 solo, song, tune 6 melody 7 arietta, ariette, sortita

arid: dry 4 bald, bare, dull, lean 6 barren, desert, jejune, meager 7 parched, sterile 8 withered 9 unfertile, waterless 10 desiccated, siccaneous 12 moistureless 13 uninteresting

ariel: 7 gazelle

Aries: ram
mother: 4 Enyo

aril: pod 7 arillus, coating 8 covering 9 appendage 10 integument
false: 8 arillode
ariose: 7 melodic 8 songlike 9 melodious
aris: See **arris**
arise: 4 flow, lift, rear, rise, soar, stem 5 awake, begin, exist, issue, mount, raise, stand, surge, tower, waken 6 accrue, amount, appear, ascend, attain, derive, emerge, happen, spring 7 develop, emanate, proceed 8 develope 9 originate
arista: awn 5 beard 9 appendage
aristocracy: 4 rule 5 class, elite 8 nobility 10 government, patriciate
aristocrat: 4 lord 5 noble 7 grandee, parvenu 9 patrician
aristocratic: 4 tony 7 high-hat
Aristophanes work: 5 Birds, Frogs
Aristotle: 5 Greek 11 philosopher
birthplace: 6 Thrace 7 Stagira
category: 4 time 5 place 6 action 7 quality 8 position, quantity, relation 9 passivity, substance 10 possession
disciple: 11 Peripatetic
father: 10 Nicomachus
school: 6 Lyceum
teacher: 5 Plato
arithmetic: 4 sums 8 textbook 11 mathematics
rule: 10 allegation
Arius' follower: 5 Arian
Arizona: *city:* 4 Yuma 5 Tempe 6 Tucson 7 Nogales, Phoenix
county: 4 Gila, Pima 5 Pinal 6 Apache, Mohave, Navajo 7 Cochise, Yavapai
desert: 7 Painted
flower: 7 saguaro
Indian: 4 Hopi, Pima, Yuma 6 Navaho, Navajo
river: 4 Gila
town: see *city* above
Arizona gourd: 11 calabazilla
ark: bin, box 4 boat, ship 5 barge, chest, hutch 6 basket, coffer, refuge, wangan 7 retreat, shelter, wanigan 8 flatboat
builder: Noe 4 Noah
resting place: 6 Ararat
Arkansas: *city:* 10 Booneville, Little Rock
county: Lee 4 Clay, Drew, Pike, Poke, Polk, Yell 5 Scott
mountains: 5 Ozark
arkose: 9 sandstone
arm: fin 4 limb, wing 5 bough, equip, fiord, firth, force, inlet, might, power, rifle 6 branch, energy, member, outfit, sleeve, tappet, weapon 7 flipper, forearm, fortify, furnish, prepare, protect, provide, support 8 soupbone, strength 9 appendage 10 instrument, projection 12 ramification
bone: 4 ulna 5 radii(pl.), ulnae(pl.) 6 humeri(pl.), radius 7 humerus
comb. form: 6 brachi 7 brachio
hollow at bend: 8 chelidon
joint: 4 ares 5 elbow, wrist
muscle: 6 biceps 7 triceps
part: 4 ares 5 elbow, wrist
pert. to: 8 brachial
armada: 4 army, navy 5 fleet 8 flotilla, squadron, warships
armadillo: 4 peva 5 poyou 6 mulita 7 tatouay 8 pangolin 10 pichiciago
giant: 4 tatu 5 tatou 6 peludo
small: 4 peba 11 quirquincho
three banded: 4 apar 5 apara 6 mataco
armamentarium: 5 store 6 armory 7 arsenal 8 armament, magazine 9 equipment 10 collection
armariolum: 5 ambry 8 armarium
armarium: 5 ambry 10 armariolum
armband: 7 maniple 8 brassard
Armenia: 5 Minni 8 Anatolia
angel or devil worshiper: 6 Yezidi
cap: 6 calpac
city: 6 Erivan(c.) 7 Erzurum, Yerevan
cumin: 7 caraway
lake: Van 8 Urumiyah
mountain: 6 Ararat, Taurus
people: 5 Gomer
river: Kur 4 Aras 5 Cyrus, Halys 6 Araxes, Tigris 9 Euphrates 10 Kizil-Trmak
town: see *city* above
armet: 6 helmet
armful: 6 yaffle
armhole: 4 mail, scye 7 armscye
armistice: 4 lull 5 peace, truce 9 cessation 10 suspension
armoire (see also **ambry**): 8 cupboard, wardrobe 12 clothespress
armor: 4 arms, egis, mail, tace 5 amure, plate, tasse 6 armour, brinie, brunie, byrnie, cuisse, graith, shield, tasset, tuille 7 cuirass, defense 8 materiel, ordnance 10 protection
arm: 8 brassard, brassart 9 gardebras
bearer: 6 squire 7 armiger, custrel
body: 4 tace 6 byrnie, corium, lorica 7 cuirass
cap: 10 cerveliere
elbow guard: 9 cubitiere
face: 6 beaver 7 ventail 8 aventail
foot: 7 chausse
horse: 5 barde 7 peitrel, peytrel, poitrel 8 poitrail, testiere
knee: 11 genouillere
leg: 4 boot, jamb 5 cuish, jambe 6 cuisse, greave, tuille 7 jambeau 11 braconniere
neck: 6 gorget 8 aventail, gorgelet
part: 6 lorica(L.)

shoulder: **7** ailette **9** epauliere
skirt: **4** tace **5** tasse **6** taslet, tasset
thigh: **5** cuish
throat: **6** gorget

armored: **6** mailed **8** equipped, ironclad, mailclad **9** panoplied **11** encuirassed

armpit: ala **5** oxter **6** axilla **7** axillae(pl.)
pert. to: **7** axillar

arms depository: **7** arsenal

army: **4** here, host **5** array, crowd, force, horde **6** cohort, legion, number, throng, troops **7** militia **8** soldiers, warriors **9** battalion, multitude
base: **5** depot
camp: **6** campoo(Ind.)
car: **4** jeep
chaplain: **5** padre
commission: **6** brevet
engineer: **6** sapper **7** pioneer
enlisted man in ranks: **7** mustang
follower: **6** sutler
mascot: **4** mule
meal: **4** chow
officer: tab **4** aide **5** major **7** captain, general **8** sergeant **9** centurion **10** lieutenant
pert. to: **7** martial **8** military
post: **4** base, camp, fort
postal abbreviation: APO
school: OCS, OTS **7** academy
storehouse: **6** armory **7** arsenal
unit: **5** corps, squad, troop **7** brigade, company, platoon **8** division, regiment **10** detachment
vehicle: **4** jeep, tank **9** half-track
wing: ala(L.)

army ant: **6** driver **9** legionary

arnotto: See **annatto**

aroba: See **araba**

aroid: **4** taro **5** apium, tania **6** tanier **8** araceous

aroint: **6** begone

aroma: **4** odor **5** nidor, savor, scent, smell, spice **6** flavor **7** bouquet, perfume **9** fragrance, redolence

aromatic: **5** balmy, spicy, sweet **7** odorous, piquant, pungent **8** fragrant, redolent
gum: **5** myrrh
herb: **4** mint, nard **5** anise, clary, nondo **8** lavender
seed: **5** anise, cumin **6** nutmeg **7** aniseed
spice: **4** mace **5** clove
tree: **6** balsam **8** huisache **9** sassafras
weed: **5** tansy

around: **4** near **5** about, circa **10** encircling, enveloping
prefix: **4** peri

arouse: **4** call, fire, move, spur, stir, wake, whet **5** alarm, awake, evoke, pique, raise, rally, rouse, roust, waken **6** awaken, excite, foment, incite, kindle, revive, summon, thrill **7** actuate, agitate, animate, enliven, incense, inflame **8** inspirit **9** stimulate

arpeggio: **5** sweep **7** roulade **8** division, flourish

arpent: **4** acre

arraign: try **4** cite **5** argue **6** accuse, charge, impute, indict, indite, summon **7** appoint, impeach **8** denounce **9** challenge, prosecute

arraignment: **6** charge **10** accusation

arrange: fix, set **4** edit, file, form, plan, size, sort, tier **5** adapt, aline, align, array, drape, ettle, frame, grade, range, score, space **6** adjust, design, devise, fettle, settle **7** bespeak, catalog, compone, compose, dispose, gradate, marshal, permute, prepare, seriate **8** classify, conclude, organize, regulate, tabulate **9** catalogue, collocate, construct, determine **10** distribute **11** alphabetize
mutually: **5** agree **7** concert

arranged alternately: **4** paly

arrangement: **4** deal **5** index, order, setup **6** scheme, system, treaty **8** contract **9** direction **10** allocation **11** composition, disposition, permutation **12** dispensation

arrant: bad **5** thief **6** outlaw, robber **7** vagrant **8** rascally **9** confirmed, downright, itinerant, notorious, shameless **11** unmitigated **13** thoroughgoing

arras: **7** drapery **8** tapestry

array: don, rig **4** army, busk, deck, doll, garb, host, pomp, robe **5** adorn, align, aline, dress, habit, order **6** attire, attrap, bedeck, clothe, finery, invest, plight, series **7** address, affaite, afflict, apparel, arrange, company, envelop, furnish, marshal **8** accouter, accoutre **10** assemblage **11** preparation

arrear: **4** debt **6** behind, unpaid **7** arriere **8** backward

arrect: **5** alert, erect **6** direct, raised **9** attentive

arrest: cop, fix, nab **4** balk, curb, grab, halt, hold, jail, keep, pull, sist, stay, stop **5** arret, catch, check, delay, pinch, seize, stunt **6** attach, collar, decree, detain, engage, hinder, pledge, retard, thwart **7** capture, custody, suspend **8** imprison, obstruct, restrain **9** apprehend, intercept, interrupt **11** concentrate

arresting: **8** pleasing, striking **10** impressive

arret: **5** edict **6** arrest, decree **8** decision, judgment

arride: **5** laugh, smile **6** please **7** delight, gratify

arrie: **5** murre

arris, aris: 4 pien 5 angle, piend
arrival: 5 comer 6 advent
arrive: 4 come, flow, gain, land 5 occur, reach 6 appear, attain, happen 7 compass
arrogance: 5 pride 6 hubris, hybris 7 conceit, disdain, egotism, hauteur 9 insolence 10 effrontery 11 affectation
arrogant: 4 bold 5 lofty, proud 6 lordly, uppish 7 forward, haughty 8 affected, assuming, cavalier, fastuous, impudent 9 audacious, conceited, insulting, presuming 10 hoity-toity 11 dictatorial, domineering, impertinent, overbearing, overweening 12 contemptuous, contumelious, presumptuous, supercilious
arrogate: 4 grab, take 5 claim, seize, usurp 6 assume
arrondissement: 4 ward 8 division
arrow: pin, rod 4 bolt, dart, reed 5 shaft 6 sprite, weapon 7 missile, pointer 9 indicator
case: 6 quiver
comb. form: 4 belo
feathered: 4 vire
maker: 6 bowyer 8 fletcher
part: 4 barb, butt, head, nock 5 shaft, stele 7 feather
pert. to: 8 sagittal
point: neb 4 barb
poison: 4 haya, inee, upas 5 urali 6 antiar, curare, sumpit, wagogo 7 woorali
rotating: 4 vire
arrow-shaped: 6 beloid 8 sagittal 9 sagittate
arrowroot: pia 4 musa 5 araru, canna, tacca, tikor 6 ararao
family: 11 marantaceae
Arrowsmith author: 5 Lewis
arrowstone: 9 belemnite
arrowweed: 7 pluchea
arrowwood: 8 viburnum 10 burrobrush
arroyo: 5 brook, creek, gulch, gully, hondo, zanja 6 ravine, stream 7 channel 11 watercourse
ars artium: 5 logic
arsenal: 6 armory, supply 8 dockyard, magazine 10 storehouse 13 armamentarium
arsenate: *copper:* 7 erinite
hydrous zinc: 7 adamite
red manganese: 9 sarkinite
arsenic: 6 poison 8 chemical
antimony: 10 allemonite
comb. form: 6 arseno
compound: 8 arsenide
sulfide: 7 realgar
trisulfide: 8 orpiment
arsenic acid salt: 8 arsenate
arsenillo: 9 atacamite
arsenopyrite: 7 danaite
arsis: 4 beat 5 ictus 6 accent, rhythm
opposed to: 6 thesis, theses (pl.)
arson: 4 fire 5 crime 7 burning 12 incendiarism
arsonist: 10 pyromaniac
art: ars(L.) 4 wile 5 craft, knack, magic, skill, trade 7 calling, cunning, faculty, finesse, science 8 artifice, business, learning, 9 dexterity, duplicity, ingenuity 10 profession 11 contrivance, cultivation
black: 5 magic 7 alchemy 8 wizardry 9 diablerie 10 demonology, necromancy 11 conjuration
fancier of: 6 votary 7 esthete, devotee 8 aesthete 10 dilettante 11 connoisseur
gallery: 5 salon 6 museum
manual: 5 craft, sloid, slojd, sloyd
school: 4 Dada 5 Dutch 6 ashcan, French, Paduan 7 Flemish, Italian, Lombard, Umbrian 8 American, eclectic, Milanese Scottish 9 Bolognese 10 Raphaelite
style: pop 4 Dada 5 genre 6 cubism 7 baroque, fauvism 10 surrealism 11 objectivism, primitivism 13 impressionism 14 abstractionism
Artemis: 4 Upis 5 Delia, Diana 6 Phoebe
brother: 6 Apollo
father: 4 Zeus
mother: 4 Leto
priestess: 9 Iphigenia
artel: 5 union 11 association, cooperative
artery: way 4 path, road 5 route 6 course, street, vessel 7 anonyma, conduit, highway 9 maxillary
main: 5 aorta 6 aortae(pl.)
neck: 8 caratoid
pulsation: 5 ictus
artful: apt, sly 4 foxy, wily 5 agile, suave 6 adroit, clever, facile, shrewd, smooth, tricky 7 crooked, cunning, politic, vulpine 8 stealthy 9 deceitful, deceptive, designing, dexterous, imitative, practical
artfulness: 8 subtlety 9 diplomacy, duplicity, stratagem 10 refinement
arthritis: 4 gout
arthron: 5 joint 12 articulation
arthropoda: 4 crab 6 phylum, spider
Arthur: See **King Arthur**
artichoke: bur 6 Canada, Cynara 7 Chorogi 9 Jerusalem
leafstalk: 5 chard
article: an, ye; one, the 4 item, term 5 essay, paper, piece, plank, point, story, theme, thing 6 clause, detail, object, report 7 feature 8 causerie, doctrine 9 condition, paragraph, statement 10 particular 11 composition, stipulation
French: la, le, un; les, une
German: das, der, die, ein

Spanish: el, un; las, los, una

articulate: 4 join 5 clear, speak, unite, utter, vocal 6 fluent, verbal 7 express, jointed 8 distinct 9 enunciate, pronounce 10 formulated 13 particularize

articulation: 5 joint, voice 6 arthra(pl.), suture 7 arthron 9 arthrosis, utterance 10 connection

artifice: art 4 gaud, hoax, plan, plot, ruse, wile 5 blind, cheat, dodge, feint, fraud, guile, skill, trick 6 cautel, deceit, device, 7 cunning, evasion, finesse, sleight 8 intrigue, maneuver, pretense, strategy, trickery 9 deception, expedient, imposture, ingenuity, invention, strategem 10 artfulness, subterfuge 11 contrivance, machination 13 ingeniousness

artificer: See **artisan**

artificial: 4 sham 5 faked, false 6 ersatz, forced, forged, unreal 7 assumed, bastard, feigned 8 affected, falsetto, spurious 9 insincere, synthetic, unnatural 10 factitious, fictitious, theatrical 11 adulterated, counterfeit 12 suppositious

artillery: 4 arms, guns 6 cannon 8 ordnance
emplacement: 7 battery
fire: 5 salvo 6 rafale 7 barrage
wagon: 6 camion 7 caisson

artilleryman: 6 gunner, lascar 8 topechee 9 cannoneer 10 bombardier

artiodactyl: ox; pig 4 deer, goat 5 camel, sheep 6 artiad 7 giraffe 8 antelope 12 hippopotamus

artisan: 5 smith 6 artist 7 artifex, workman 8 opificer, mechanic 9 artificer, craftsman, operative 14 handicraftsman

artist: dab 5 actor, adept 6 dancer, etcher, expert, fictor, master, singer, wizard 7 artisan, artiste, operant, painter, schemer 8 magician, musician, sculptor, sketcher 9 craftsman, performer 12 professional, practitioner
equipment: 5 brush, easel 7 palette
medium: oil 7 tempera 10 watercolor
primitive: 5 Moses
signature word: 5 fecit
workshop: 6 studio 7 atelier

artistic: 6 daedal, expert 8 esthetic 9 aesthetic

artless: 4 naif, open 5 frank, naive, plain 6 candid, rustic, simple 7 natural 8 innocent 9 guileless, ingenuous, untutored 10 unaffected 11 undesigning 15 unsophisticated

arts: *goddess:* 4 Muse 6 Athena
liberal: 5 logic 6 trivia(pl.) 7 grammar, trivium 8 rhetoric

arui: 5 sheep 6 aoudad

arum: 4 arad, taro 5 aroid, plant 10 cuckoopint
family: 7 araceae
water: 5 calla

arundinaceous: 5 reedy

Aryan: 4 Mede, Slav 9 Caucasian
deity: 6 Ormazd, Ormuzd
god of fire: 4 Agni
language: 8 Sanskrit
of India: 5 Hindu

as: for, qua 4 like, that, thus, when 5 equal, since, while 7 because, equally, similar 9 therefore
above: 5 ditto, ut sup 7 ut supra
far as: to
if: 5 quasi
she is: 4 dyce
stated: so 4 thus
usual: 6 solito
well as: and
written: sic, sta 4 stet

As You Like It character: 5 Celia 6 Jaques 8 Rosalind

Asa: 6 healer 9 physician
father: 4 Abia
son: 11 Jehoshaphat

asafetida: 4 hing 5 laser 6 ferula

ascend: up 4 rise, soar 5 climb, mount, scale, tower 7 clamber 8 escalate, progress

ascendancy: 4 sway 5 power 7 control, mastery, success 8 dominion, prestige 9 authority, influence, supremacy 10 domination 11 sovereignty 13 preponderance

ascent: sty 4 hill, ramp, rise, rist 5 glory, grade, mount, scend, slope, steps 6 stairs 7 incline, upswing 8 eminence, gradient 9 acclivity, ascension 11 advancement

ascertain: get 4 find 5 count, learn, prove 6 assure, attain 7 apprise, apprize, measure, unearth 8 discover 9 determine

ascetic: nun 4 monk, yogi 5 fakir, friar, stoic, Yogin 6 Essene, strict 7 austere, bhikshu, devotee, eremite, recluse, stylite 8 anchoret 9 anchorite 10 abstemious

ascot: tie 5 scarf 6 cravat 7 necktie 9 racetrack

ascribe: lay 4 aret 5 blame, count, guess, infer, refer 6 accuse, allege, arette, assign, attach, charge, credit, impute, reckon 8 accredit, dedicate, inscribe 9 affiliate, attribute

ascription: 8 addition 11 declaration
of praise: 6 gloria
popular: 6 repute

ascus: bag, sac

asea: 4 lost 6 addled, adrift 7 puzzled, sailing 8 confused 9 befuddled, uncertain 10 bewildered

aseptic: 5 clean 6 barren 7 sterile

Asgard: *bridge to:* 7 Bifrost
watchman: 8 Heimdall

ash: ase(Sc.), ron 4 coke, sorb, tree 5 artar, ember, rowan 6 cinder, corpse 7 clinker, residue 8 fraxinus
receptacle: bin, box, urn
reduce to: 7 cremate
tobacco: 6 dottel, dottle
ash holder: urn
ashamed: 7 abashed, hangdog 10 humiliated
Ashanti pepper: 5 cubeb
ashen: wan 4 gray, grey, pale 5 waxen 6 pallid 7 ghastly 8 blanched 9 cinereous 11 cineritious
Asher: *daughter:* 5 Serah 6 Beriah
father: 5 Jacob
son: 4 Usui 6 Jimnah
ashkoko: 4 cony 5 daman, hyrax
ashore: 7 aground, beached, 8 stranded
ashweed: 8 goutweed
Asia (see also **Asia Minor, Southeast Asia**): 4 East 6 Orient
ancient region: 4 Aria 5 Akkad, Sumer 6 Canaan 7 Babylon
animal: 5 bison 8 pangolin 10 chevrotain
antelope: 5 goral, serow 6 dzeren, dzerin, dzeron
ass: 6 onager, koulan
bean: soy 4 gram, soya 5 mungo
bird: 4 mina, myna 5 mynah, pitta 7 minivet 8 dotterel 9 brambling
blizzard: 5 buran
carnivore: 5 panda
cattle: 4 zobo
central: 6 Tatary
Christian: 5 Uniat
city: 4 Amoy, Sian 5 Dacca 6 Bagdad, Bombay, Singan 7 Comilla 9 Singapore
comb. form: 4 Indo
conjurer: 6 shaman
country: 4 Elam, Irak, Iran, Iraq, Laos, Siam 5 Accad, Akkad, Annam, Araby, Assam, Burma, China, India, Japan, Korea, Nepal, Syria, Tibet 6 Arabia, Malaya, Persia, Russia, Sikkim, Turkey 7 Armenia, Chaldea, Siberia, Vietnam 8 Cambodia, Pakistan, Thailand
crowfoot: 9 buttercup
deer: roe 4 axis
desert: 4 Gobi
disease: 4 yaws 7 cholera, malaria 9 trachoman
district: 7 Fartary
dog (wild): 5 dhole
drink: 5 airan
eskimo: 4 Yuit 6 Innuit
esplanade: 6 maidan
falcon: 6 laggar 8 lanneret
fiber: 4 hemp 5 ramie
fox: 6 corsac
gangster: 6 dacoit
gazelle: ahu 4 cora
goat: 4 tahr
goddess: 4 Anta
grass: 4 coix, munj
greeting: 6 salaam
herb: 4 hemp
holiday: Tet
horse: 6 tarpan
island: 4 Java 5 Japan, Luzon, Malay 6 Borneo, Ceylon 7 Celebes, Formosa, Sumatra, Wrangel 8 Mindanao, Sakhalin 11 Philippines
isthmus: Kra
jay: 7 sirgang
lake: Tai 4 Tami 6 Baikal 8 Balkhash
language: 5 Malay, Pamir, Tamil
lemur: 5 loris 6 macaco
lynx: 7 caracal
mammal: 5 panda 10 chevrotain
market: 6 bazaar
measure: mou 4 tael
medicine man: 6 shaman
millet: 4 dari
mink: 8 kolinsky
mongoose: 4 urva
monkey: 6 rhesus
mountain: 5 Altai, Sayan 6 Zagros 7 Everest 9 Himalayas, Hindu-Kush 14 Kanchininjinga
mystic: 5 fakir
nomad: 4 Arab 5 Tatar 6 Mongol 7 Kipchak
oasis: 4 merv
oil plant: 4 odal
owl: 4 utum
ox: yak
partridge: 6 seesee
peninsula: 5 Corea, Korea, Malay 6 Arabia 9 Kamchatka
people: Meo, Tai 4 Huns, Miao, Shan, Yuit 5 Kurds, Medes, Seres, Tatar, Todas 6 Tartar 10 Mongolians
pert to: 8 Chaldean
pheasant: 8 tragopan
plain: 4 chol
plant: tea 4 atis, odal, soya 5 akebi, betel
plant (fiber source): 5 ramie
region: 7 Siberia, Tartary
religion: 5 Islam 8 Buddhism, Hinduism
river: Ob; Ili, Obi 4 Amur, Lena, Onon, Yalu 5 Amoor, Eelee, Indus, Putra 6 Branma, Ganges, Mekong, Tigris 7 Hwang-Ho, Yang-Tse, Yeinsei 8 Chao Phya, Irawaddy 9 Euphrates
rodent: 4 pika 6 gerbil, marmot 7 gerbile
sandstorm: 6 simoon, tebbad
seaport: 5 Macao 6 Bombay 9 Singapore
shrub: tea
sea: 4 Aral, Azof 7 Caspian

sheep: sha **5** argal, urial **6** argali, bharal, nahoor, oorial
shrub: tea **4** tche, thea
snake: **6** bongar, daboia, jessur
squirrel: **8** jelerang **10** polatouche
storm: **5** buran **6** tebbad **7** monsoon, typhoon
tableland: **5** Tibet
tree: **4** asak, asok, dita, rata **5** asoka, siris **6** banyan, medlar, wampee
warehouse: **6** godown
weapon: **5** adaga
weight: **4** tael **5** catty
wolf: **6** chanco

Asia Minor (see also **Asia**): **8** Anatolia
animal: **5** daman
city: **4** Myra, Myus, Teos, Troy **5** Haran, Perga, Ushak **6** Aintab, Sardis, Tarsus **7** Ephesus, Miletus
coast: **5** Ionia
island: **5** Samos
mountain: Ida
mountain range: **4** Alai
region: **4** Aria **5** Caria, Eolis, Ionia, Troad, Troas **6** Pontus
river: **5** Halys **8** Monderez
sea: **6** Aegean
seaport: **5** Issus

aside: off **4** away, gone, near, past **5** agley, aloof, apart **6** aslant, astray, beside, beyond, byhand **7** lateral, private, whisper **8** reserved, secretly, separate, sidewise **9** alongside **10** indirectly

asinego: ass **4** fool

asinine: **4** dull **5** crass, dense, inept, silly **6** absurd, obtuse, simple, stupid **7** doltish, fatuous, foolish, idiotic **9** gooselike, senseless

ask: beg, sue **4** pray, quiz **5** claim, crave, exact, frayn, plead, query, speer(Sc.), **6** adjure, demand, expect, frayne, invite **7** beseech, bespeak, consult, entreat, implore, inquire, request, require, solicit **8** petition, question **9** obsecrate **11** interrogate

askance: **4** awry **5** askew **6** askant, askile **7** crooked **8** sideways **9** obliquely, suspicion **13** distrustfully

askew: cam **4** agee, alop, awry **5** agley, amiss, atilt **6** askant, aslant, atwist **7** asquint, crooked, oblique **9** distorted **10** catawampus

asleep: **4** dead, idle **6** latent, numbed **7** dormant, napping **10** motionless, slumbering **11** unconscious

asomatous: **10** immaterial **11** incorporeal

asp: **5** adder, aspen, snake, viper **7** serpent **8** ophidian
representative headdress: **6** uraeus

asparagus: **5** sprue

aspect: air **4** face, look, mien, side, view **5** angle, facet, guise, phase, sight, stage **6** glance, manner, visage **7** bearing, feature, outlook **8** carriage, prospect **9** semblance **10** appearance **11** countenance **13** consideration

aspen: aps, asp **4** tree **6** poplar **7** quaking **9** quivering, trembling, tremulous

asper: **4** coin **5** harsh, rough, stern **6** bitter

asperse: **4** spot, slur **5** abuse, decry, libel, spray **6** defame, defile, malign, revile, shower **7** appeach, blacken, detract, lampoon, slander, tarnish, traduce **8** besmirch, forspeak, sprinkle **9** bespatter, discredit, disparage **10** besprinkle, vituperate

aspersion: **7** baptism, calumny **8** innuendo

asperity: ire **5** rigor **8** acerbity, acrimony, hardship, severity, sourness, tartness **9** briskness, harshness, roughness **10** bitterness, difficulty, unevenness **11** crabbedness **16** disagreeableness

aspersorium: **4** font **5** basin, stoup **11** aspergillum

asphalt: **4** brea **7** bitumen **9** chapapote **10** wurtzilite **11** courtzilite

asphyxia: **5** apnea **6** apnoea **8** acrotism **11** suffocation

aspic: asp **5** jelly **7** gelatin **8** gelatine, lavender

aspirant: **9** candidate

aspiration: **4** goal **5** ideal **8** ambition

aspire: aim **4** hope, long, rise, seek, soar, wish **5** ettle, mount, tower, yearn **6** desire, ascend, attain

ass: **4** dolt, duff, fool, moke **5** burro, chump, cuddy, dunce, jenny, kiang, kulan, neddy **6** donkey, koulan, onager, quagga **7** asinego **8** imbecile **9** blockhead, simpleton **10** rattlepate
comb. form: ono
in lion's skin: **8** imposter
male: **4** jack

assai: **4** very **6** enough

assail: woo **4** pelt **5** assay, beset, stone, whack, whang **6** accuse, attack, bullet, hurtle, impugn, invade, malign, molest, rattle, scathe **7** assault, belabor, bombard **9** encounter **11** assassinate

assailant: **9** aggressor

Assam: *city:* **4** Ledo **10** Shillangle (c.)
dialect: Ao; Aka **5** Lhota
rubber: **7** rambong
silkworm: eri **4** eria
tribesman: Ao; Aka **4** Ahom, Garo, Naga

assart: **4** grub **8** clearing

assassin: **4** thag, thug **5** bravo **6** cuttle, killer, slayer **7** ruffian **8** murderer **9** cutthroat

Abel's: 4 Cain
Kennedy's: 6 Oswald, Sirhan
Lincoln's: 5 Booth

assation: 6 baking 8 roasting

assault: 4 beat, raid, slug 5 assay, brunt, onset, pound, smite, storm 6 affray, assail, attack, buffet, breach, charge, invade 7 attempt, bombard, violate 8 outburst 9 incursion, onslaught 10 aggression

assay: try 4 test 5 prove, trial 6 attack, effort 7 analyze, attempt, examine, tasting 8 analysis, appraise, endeavor, hardship 9 determine 10 affliction, experiment

assaying: 8 docimasy
cup: 5 cupel

assemblage: 4 army body, camp, crew, herd, host, mass, pack 5 bunch, crowd, drove, flock, levee, posse, salon, swarm 6 convoy, galaxy, hookup, throng 7 cluster 9 community 11 aggregation 13 constellation

assemble: fit 4 call, mass, meet 5 amass, piece, rally, unite 6 couple, gather, huddle, muster, summon 7 collect, convene, convoke, recruit 9 aggregate 10 congregate, foregather

assembly: hui 4 baud, bevy, diet, feis, moot, raad 5 forum, group, junta, party, press, setup, synod, troop 6 assize, gemote, powwow, senate 7 comitia, company, council, husting, meeting, session, society 8 audience, conclave, congress, tribunal 10 consistory, convention, parliament 11 convocation, legislature
ecclesiastical: 6 coetus 8 sederunt
full: 5 plena
people's: 7 folcmot, folkmot 8 folkmote, folkmout 9 folcgemot
place: 5 agora
room: 4 hall 10 auditorium

assembly line: 5 plant 7 factory, process

assent: aye, bow, nod, yea, yes 4 amen 5 admit, agree, yield 6 accede, accept, accord, chorus, comply, concur, submit 7 approve, concede, conform, consent 8 adhesion, sanction 9 acquiesce, subscribe 10 compliance, condescend 11 acknowledge

assert: say 4 aver, avow, cite 5 claim, plead, posit, state, swear, utter, vaunt, voice 6 affirm, allege, assure, avouch, defend, depone, depose, uphold 7 advance, betoken, contend, declare, protest, support 8 advocate, champion, maintain 9 attribute, predicate, vindicate 10 asseverate
positively: 5 swear

assertive: 8 dogmatic, positive 9 defensive, pragmatic 10 aggressive 11 affirmatory

assess: tax 4 cess, levy, mise, rate, scot, toll 5 cense, price, value 6 assize, charge, impose 7 measure 8 appraise, estimate 9 apportion

assessment: fee, tax 4 duty, levy, scot, toll 5 price, ratal, tithe, worth 6 extent, impost, surtax, tariff 7 scutage 9 valuation

assessor: 5 judge, rater 8 adsessor 11 adjudicator

assets: 5 goods, means, money 6 credit, wealth 7 capital, effects 8 accounts, property, resource 9 valuables

asseverate: say, vow 4 aver, avow 5 state 6 affirm, allege, assert, assure 7 assever, declare, protest

asseveration: 4 oath

assiduous: 4 busy 6 active 7 devoted 8 diligent, frequent, sedulous, studious 9 attentive, laborious, unwearied 10 persistent 11 industrious, painstaking, persevering, unremitting 13 indefatigable 14 unintermittent

assign: fix, set 4 cede, deal, dole, give, mete, rate, seal, show, sign 5 allot, allow, award, endow, refer 6 adduce, affect, allege, charge, convey, delate, depute, detail, reckon, select, settle 7 adjudge, advance, appoint, ascribe, consign, dispose, specify, tribute 8 allocate, delegate, transfer 9 apportion, attribute, designate, determine 10 commission, distribute 11 appropriate

assignation: 4 date 5 tryst 7 meeting 11 appointment

assignment: 4 duty, task 5 stent, stint 6 lesson 11 assignation

assimilate: mix 4 fuse 5 adapt, alter, blend, learn, merge 6 absorb, digest, imbibe 7 compare, concoct 8 resemble 9 transform 10 metabolize, understand 11 appropriate, incorporate

assist: aid 4 abet, back, help, join 5 avail, boost, coach, favor, nurse, serve, speed 6 attend, escort, prompt, second, squire, succor 7 benefit, relieve, support, sustain 8 befriend 9 accompany 10 facilitate

assistance: aid 4 alms, gift, help 5 heeze 6 relief, remedy 8 easement 9 patronage 11 furtherance

assistant: 4 aide, ally, hand, maid, mate, zany 5 clerk, groom, usher, valet 6 aidant, deputy, second 7 abettor, partner 8 adjutant, adjuvant, servitor 9 associate, auxiliary, secretary 10 accomplice 11 confederate, subordinate
to pastor: 6 curate

assistants: 4 crew 5 staff 7 retinue 9 entourage

assize: fix 4 oyer, rate 5 court, edict, trial 6 assess, decree 7 hearing, measure, session, sitting, statute 8 assembly, standard, tribunal 9 enactment, ordinance 10 regulation

associate: mix, pal 4 aide, ally, band, chum, join, link, mate, moop, moup, peer, yoke, wife 5 blend, buddy, crony 6 cohort, fellow, friend, helper, hobnob, mingle, relate, spouse 7 adjunct, comrade, connect, consort, husband, partner 8 copemate, federate, intimate 9 accompany, affiliate, assistant, attendant, coadjutor, colleague, companion, conrector, socialize 10 accomplice, fraternize 11 concomitant
in crime: 10 accomplice

association: 4 body, bond, club, gild 5 artel, guild, hansa, hanse, union 6 cartel, league, pledge 7 company, consort, society 8 alliance, converse, intimacy, sodality 9 syndicate 10 assemblage, fellowship, sisterhood 11 aggregation, brotherhood, combination, confederacy, conjunction, partnership 12 conversation 13 confederation
literary: 6 lyceum 9 athenaeum
merchants': 5 hanse
secret: 5 cabal, lodge
workers': 5 guild, union

association football: 6 soccer

assoil: rid 5 atone, clear, solve 6 acquit, pardon, refute 7 absolve, deliver, expiate, forgive, release, resolve 9 discharge

assonance: pun 5 rhyme 8 paragram 11 resemblance

assort: 4 file, rank, sort, type 5 group, order 8 classify

assortment: lot, set 4 olio 5 batch, group, suite 7 mixture 10 collection, miscellany

assuage: 4 calm, ease 5 abate, allay, delay, slake 6 lessen, modify, pacify, quench, reduce, soften, solace, soothe, temper 7 appease, comfort, mollify, relieve, satisfy 8 diminish, mitigate, moderate 9 alleviate 11 tranquilize

assuasive: 4 mild 7 lenient 8 lenitive, soothing 9 emollient

assume: don 4 dare, fang, mask, sham, take 5 adopt, cloak, elect, feign, indue, infer, raise, usurp 6 accept, affect, betake, clothe 7 believe, premise, pretend, receive, suppose, surmise 8 accroach, arrogate, simulate 9 undertake 11 appropriate, counterfeit

assumed: 5 alias 9 fictional, uncertain 10 artificial, fictitious, precarious 12 hypothetical, suppositious

assumed name: 5 alias 9 pseudonym

assuming: 5 lofty 8 arrogant, superior 10 assumptive 11 pretentious 12 presumptuous
different form: 7 protean

assurance: 4 seal 5 brass, faith, nerve, trust 6 aplomb, belief, credit, safety 7 courage, promise 8 audacity, boldness, coolness, firmance, security 9 certainty, certitude, impudence 10 confidence, effrontery 12 cocksureness

assure: 4 aver 5 hight 6 assert, avouch, ensure, insure, pledge, secure 7 betroth, confirm, declare, hearten, promise, protest 8 affiance, convince, embolden, reassure 9 ascertain, encourage, guarantee, vouchsafe 10 asseverate, certiorate, underwrite

assuredly: 4 amen 6 surely, verily 10 intrepidly, truthfully 11 indubitably, undoubtedly

Assyria: 5 Ashur, Assur 6 Asshur
capital: 5 Calah 7 Nineveh
city: 4 Hara, Opis 5 Al Sur, Calah 6 Arbela, Asshur, Kalakh 7 Antioch(c.), Nineveh(c.) 9 Dur Sargon
god: El, Zu; Ira, Sin 4 Adad, Anet, Asur, Nebo 5 Ashir, Ashur, Hadad, Ninip 6 Asshur, Nergal, Shamas
goddess: 4 Nana, Nine 5 Istar 6 Allatu, Ishtar 9 Sarpanitu
king: Pul 5 Belus 6 Sargon 8 Asnapper, Osnappar 9 Asenappar
measure: 4 cane, foot 5 makuk, gasab 6 artaba, gariba, ghalva 7 mansion
queen: 9 Semiramis
river: Zab 6 Adhiam

astart: 8 suddenly

asteism: 5 irony 8 derision, raillery, ridicule

aster: *family:* 10 carduaceae, compositae
herb: 5 alant 6 arnica 7 boneset 10 elecampane

asterisk: 4 mark, star

Asterius: 8 argonaut, minotaur
father: 10 Hyperasius
mother: 8 Pasiphae
wife: 6 Europa

astern: aft 4 baft, hind, rear 5 abaft, apoop 6 behind 7 occiput 8 backward

asteroid: 4 Eros, Hebe, Iris, Juno 5 Ceres, Flora, Irene, Metis, Vesta 6 Astrea, Egeria, Europa, Hygeia, Pallas, planet, Psyche, Thetis 7 Eunomia, Fortuna, Lutetia 8 Massalia, starfish, starlike, Victoria 9 Melpomene, planetoid 10 Parthenope, star-shaped
first: 5 Ceres
nearest earth: 4 Eros

asthmatic: 5 pursy 6 wheezy 7 panting, puffing

astipulate: 5 agree 6 assent 11 exstipulate

astir: up 4 agog 5 about, afoot, alert, going 6 active, moving, roused 7 abroach, excited 8 stirring, vigilant

Astolat's Lily Maid: 6 Elaine

astonish: awe 4 daze, stam 5 amaze 7 astound, impress, startle 8 bewilder, confound, surprise 11 flabbergast
astonished: 5 agape
astonishing: 8 fabulous
astonishment: 5 ferly 6 dismay, wonder 10 admiration 13 consternation
astound: 4 stun 5 amaze, appal, shock 6 appall 7 stagger, stupefy, terrify 8 astonish, confound 9 overwhelm
astragal: 5 talus 7 molding 9 anklebone
astrakhan: 5 apple, cloth 7 caracul, karakul
astral: 6 remote, starry 7 stellar 8 sidereal, starlike 9 visionary
astray: 4 awry, lost 5 agley, amiss, aside, wrong 6 abroad, afield, errant, erring, faulty 7 sinning 8 mistaken, straying 9 wandering
astride: 4 atop 7 acheval 8 spanning 9 astraddle 10 bestriding, straddling
astringent: 4 acid, alum, sour, tart 5 acerb, harsh, stern 6 severe, tannin 7 austere, binding, styptic 11 acrimonious, compressive, contracting 12 constrictive
extract: 7 catechu
gum: 4 kino
astrologer: 4 Josh 6 Merlin 9 stargazer 10 astronomer 11 Nostradamus
astronaut: 9 cosmonaut
American: 5 Glenn, Scott, White, Young 6 Aldrin, Anders, Borman, Cernan, Conrad, Lovell 7 Collins, Grissom, Schirra, Shepard 8 McDivitt, Mitchell, Stafford 9 Armstrong 10 Cunningham
Soviet: 7 Gagarin, Komarov
astronomer: 10 Hipparchus
astronomical: far 4 huge 5 great 6 uranic 7 distant, immense 8 colossal, infinite
instrument: aba 9 telescope 10 equatorial
measurement: 5 apsis 7 azimuth
Muse: 4 Clio 6 Urania
astute: sly 4 foxy, keen, wily 5 acute, canny, quick, sharp, smart 6 clever, crafty, shrewd 7 cunning, skilled 9 astucious, sagacious 10 discerning 14 discriminating
asunder: 5 apart, split 6 atwain, sunder 7 divided 8 divorced 9 separated
prefix: dis
asylum: ark 4 home, jail 5 altar, cover, grith, haven 6 bedlam, harbor, refuge 7 alsatia, hospice, retreat, shelter 9 sanctuary 11 institution
asymmetrical: 4 skew
asymmetry: 13 disproportion
at: al, au, by, to; als 5 atten, there 6 hereat
all: any, ava, eer 4 ever 5 aught 6 anyway, soever
hand: by 4 near, nigh 7 present
home: in; tea 4 here 5 levee, party 9 reception
last: 7 finally 10 ultimately
odds: out
once: now, PDQ 4 anon 5 amain 6 presto 9 instanter 11 immediately
that: 4 then 7 thereat, whereat 9 thereupon, whereupon
this: 6 hereon 8 hereupon
Ata, Aeta: Ita 7 Negrito
atabal, attabal: 4 drum 5 tabor 10 kettledrum
atacamite: 9 arsenillo
Atahaulpa: 4 Inca 6 Indian
ataman: 5 chief, judge 6 hetman 7 Cossack, headman
atap: 4 nipa, palm
atavism: 9 reversion
atavus: 8 ancestor 11 grandfather
atelier: 6 studio 7 bottega 8 botteghe(pl.), workshop
ates: 8 sweetsop
Athamas: *daughter:* 5 Helle
son: 7 Phrixos, Phrixus 8 Learchus
wife: Ino
athanor: 4 oven 7 furnace
Athapascan Indian: 4 Dene, Hupa 5 Hoopa
atheist: 7 doubter 8 agnostic 11 nonbeliever
Athena, Athene: 4 Alea, Auge, Nike 5 Alera, Areia 6 Ergane, Hippia, Hygeia, Itonia, Pallas, Polias 7 Minerva 8 Apaturia, Athenaia 9 Parthenos, Poliuchos, Promachos 10 Chalinitis 11 Chalcioecus, Tritogeneia
pert. to: 9 Palladian
temple: 9 Parthenon
Athens (see also **Attica, Greece**):
alien resident: 5 metic
assembly: 4 pnyx 5 boule
assembly platform: 4 bema
astronomer: 5 Meton
clan: obe
coin: 5 oboli 6 obolus 7 chalcus, chalkos
family: 11 Alcmaeonids 12 Alcmaeonidae
festival: 8 Apaturia, Athenaea 11 Scirophoria
founder: 7 Cecrops
general: 6 Nicias 7 Phocion 8 Zenophon
hill: 9 Acropolis 10 Lycabettus
historian: 8 Xenophon
king: 6 Codrus 7 Cecrops, Pandion
lawgiver: 5 Draco, Solon
magistrate: 5 draco 6 archon, dicast
marketplace: 5 agora
mountain: 6 Parnes
orator: 9 Isocrates
pert. to: 5 Attic
philosopher: 5 Plato 8 Socrates 9 Aristotle
platform: 4 bema 6 bemata(pl.)

rival: **6** Sparta
ruler: **6** archon
sculptor: **7** Phidias
seaport: **7** Piraeus
statesman: **8** Pericles **9** Aristides
temple: **4** Nike
Athens of: *America:* **6** Boston
Ireland: **7** Belfast
Switzerland: **6** Zurich
the North: **9** Edinburgh
the West: **7** Cordoba
athlete: pro **4** star **5** boxer **7** amateur, acrobat, gymnast, tumbler **8** wrestler **9** aerialist
athletic: **5** agile, burly, lusty, vital **6** brawny, robust, sinewy, strong **8** muscular, powerful, vigorous **9** acrobatic, energetic, strapping
contest: **4** agon, game, meet, race **8** Olympics
field: **4** oval, ring, rink **5** arena, court, green **6** course **7** diamond, stadium **8** gridiron
prize: cup **5** medal **6** ribbon
athletics: **5** games, sport **8** exercise
athwart: **6** aboard, across, aslant **7** oblique **8** sidewise, traverse **10** perversely
atlantal: **6** atloid **8** anterior, cephalic
Atlantic: *island:* **4** Cuba **6** Azores, Canary **7** Iceland **9** Greenland
seaport: **5** Colon **6** Boston **7** New York, Norfolk **8** Savannah **9** Baltimore **12** Philadelphia
Atlantides: **8** Pleiades **10** Hesperides
atlas: **4** bone, book, list, maps, tome **5** titan **8** mainstay
Atlas: *daughter:* **4** Maia **6** Merope **7** Alcyone, Calypso, Electra, Kelaine, Taygete **8** Asterope, Pleiades
mother: **7** Clymeme
atloid: **8** atlantal
atmosphere: air **4** aura, mood, tone **5** ether **6** frowst, miasma, nimbus, welkin **7** feeling, qualify **10** background **11** environment
disturbance: **5** storm **6** static
gas: **5** argon **6** oxygen **8** nitrogen
phenomenon: **6** aurora, meteor
prefix: **4** atmo **5** atmos
pressure: **10** barometric
atole: **4** meal **5** gruel **8** porridge
atoll: **4** reef **6** Bikini, island, Tarawa
atom: ace, bit, jot **4** haet, iota, mite, mote, whit **5** atomy, monad, shade, speck, tinge **7** atomize **8** molecule, particle, quantity **9** corpuscle, scintilla
adsorbed: **6** adatom
component: **6** proton **7** neutron
electrically charged: ion
nucleus: **6** proton
atomic: **4** tiny **6** minute **7** nuclear **9** molecular **13** infinitesimal
particle: **4** beta, pion **5** alpha, meson **6** photon **7** neutron
physicist: **4** Bohr, Rabi **5** Fermi, Pauli **7** Compton, Meitner
pile: **7** reactor
submarine: **5** Sargo, Skate **6** Triton **8** Nautilus
theory originator: **6** Dalton
atomize: **5** grate, spray **6** reduce **8** nebulize **9** devastate, pulverize
atomy: **4** atom, mite, mote **5** pygmy **8** skeleton
atone: **5** agree, amend **6** accord, redeem, repent **7** appease, expiate, restore **9** harmonize, reconcile **10** conciliate, propitiate
atonement: **7** penance **10** reparation **12** satisfaction
atonic: **7** unheard **9** voiceless **10** unaccented
atrabilious: **4** glum **6** gloomy, morose, sullen **10** melancholy
atramentous: **4** inky **5** black
Atreus: *brother:* **8** Thyestes
father: **6** Pelops
half brother: **10** Chrysippus
mother: **10** Hippodamia
slayer: **9** Aegisthus
son: **8** Menelaus **9** Agamemnon **11** Pleisthenes
wife: **6** Aerope
atrio: **6** atrium, valley **10** depression
atrip: **6** aweigh
atrium: **4** hall **5** atrio, court **6** cavity **7** auricle, chamber, passage **8** entrance
atrocha: **5** larva
atrociou bad **4** dark, rank, vile **5** awful, black, cruel, gross **6** brutal, odious, savage, wicked **7** heinous, ungodly, violent **8** grievous, horrible, terrible **9** execrable, frightful, nefarious **10** abominable, villainous
atrophy: **4** rust **5** stunt, tabes **6** shrink, starve, wither **8** stultify **10** emaciation
Atropos: **4** Fate
attach: add, fix, tag, tie **4** bind, glue, join, link, take, vest, weld **5** affix, annex, hitch, paste, seize, unite **6** accuse, addict, adhere, adjoin, append, arrest, cement, fasten, indict **7** adhibit, appoint, ascribe, connect, subjoin **9** affiliate, associate, garnishee
attache: **4** aide **8** diplomat
attached (see also **attach**): **4** fond **6** doting
at base: **7** sessile
to the land: **7** predial **8** praedial
attachment: **4** love **8** devotion, fondness **9** accessory, addiction, adherence, affection **10** engagement, friendship **11** inclination
attack: fit **4** bout, fray, pang, raid, rush, wade **5** alarm, assay, begin, beset, blitz, drive, fight, foray, ictus, onset, sally,

spasm, storm **6** accuse, action, affray, assail, battle, charge, invade, onrush, pounce, sortie, strike, stroke, thrust **7** assault, beseige, censure, descent, offense, potshot, seizure **8** paroxysm **9** diversion, encounter, onslaught **10** aggression

false: **5** feint

suicidal: **8** kamikaze

attacker: **9** aggressor **10** iconoclast

attain: get, hit, win **4** earn, gain, rise **5** reach, touch **6** accede, amount, arrive, aspire, effect, obtain, secure, strike **7** achieve, acquire, compass, procure, succeed **8** overtake **9** ascertain **10** accomplish, comprehend

attainment: **4** feat **5** skill **6** wisdom **14** accomplishment

attar: oil **4** atar **7** essence, perfume

attempt: try **4** dare, fist, mint, mird, osse, seek, shot, stab, wage **5** assay, begin, essay, frame, onset, start **6** attack, effort **7** venture **8** endeavor, exertion **9** undertake **10** enterprise, experiment

attend: go, ho; see **4** hear, heed, mind, tend, wait **5** await, guard, nurse, serve, treat, visit, watch **6** assist, convey, follow, harken, listen, shadow **7** consort **8** champion, minister **9** accompany

attendance: **4** gate **6** number, regard **8** presence **9** attention **11** application, expectation

attendant: **4** maid, page, zany **5** gilly, guide, usher, valet **6** escort, famuli(pl.), friend, minion, porter, squire, varlet, waiter **7** chobdar, courier, famulus, footboy, orderly, pageboy **8** chasseur, follower, henchboy, henchman **9** assistant, associate, attentive, companion **10** consequent, subsequent **11** chamberlain, concomitant **12** accompanying

attendants: **5** train, suite **7** cortege, retinue **9** entourage

attention: ear **4** care, heed, hist, note **5** study **6** notice, regard **7** achtung(G.), respect **9** diligence, obedience, vigilance **10** observance **11** observation **13** concentration, consideration

attentive: **4** wary **5** alert, awake, civil **6** intent, polite **7** careful, gallant, listful, mindful **8** studious, watchful **9** advertent, assiduous, courteous, listening **11** circumspect

attenuate: sap **4** thin **5** water **6** dilute, lessen, rarefy, reduce, weaken **7** slender **8** decrease, diminish, enfeeble, tapering **9** subtilize

attest: **4** seal **5** prove, swear, vouch **6** adjure, affirm, invoke **7** certify, confess, confirm, testify, witness **8** evidence, manifest **9** subscribe **12** authenticate

attic: **4** loft **6** garret **8** cockloft

Attic: **5** Greek **8** Athenian

Attic salt: wit

Attica (see also **Athens, Greece**): *alien:* **5** metic

festival: **5** Haloa **8** Diipolia **9** Diipoleia

legendary king: **6** Ogyges, Ogygos

township: **4** deme

valley: **6** Icaria

Attila: Hun **5** Etzel

attire: See **dress**

attitude: air, set **4** bias, mien, mood, pose **5** angle, phase, slant, stand **6** action, aspect, manner **7** bearing, feeling, posture **8** behavior, position **11** disposition

attorney: **4** doer **5** agent, proxy **6** deputy, factor, lawyer, legist, muktar **7** proctor **8** advocate **9** barrister, counselor, solicitor **10** counsellor

attract: **4** bait, draw, lure, pull **5** catch, charm, court, fetch, tempt **6** allure, engage, entice, invite, seduce **8** interest **9** captivate, fascinate, influence, magnetize

attracting: **9** allicient, attrahent

attraction: **4** card **6** magnet **7** gravity **8** affinity, penchant, witchery

attractive: **4** chic, cute, fair **5** bonny **6** lovely, pretty, taking **7** winning, winsome **8** alluring, charming, fetching, graceful **9** beautiful

attribute: fix, owe **4** mark, sign, type **5** asign, badge, blame, place, power, refer **6** allege, allude, assert, bestow, charge, impute, symbol **7** ascribe, pertain, quality **8** accredit, property **10** reputation **11** peculiarity **14** characteristic

attribution: **6** theory **8** etiology

attrition: **4** wear **5** grief **6** regret, sorrow **7** anguish **8** abrasion, friction **10** contrition

attune: key **4** tune **5** adapt, agree **6** accord, adjust, temper **7** prepare **9** harmonize

atua: **5** being, demon **6** spirit

atwain: **7** asunder

Au: **4** gold

au fait: **6** expert, proper **8** skillful **10** proficient

auberge: inn **7** albergo

auction: **4** cant, roup, sale, sell, vend **5** trade **6** barter, bridge **8** disposal

hammer: **5** gavel

platform: **5** block

price: bid **5** upset

audacious: **4** bold **5** brash, hardy, saucy **6** audace, brazen, cheeky, daring **7** forward **8** arrogant, fearless, impudent, insolent, intrepid, spirited **9** barefaced, bodacious, imprudent, shameless 10 courageous 11 adventurous, impertinent, venturesome 12 presumptuous

audacity: 5 nerve 7 courage 8 boldness, temerity 9 assurance, hardihood, impudence, insolence, sauciness 10 effrontery 12 impertinence

audible: 5 aloud, heard

audience: ear 4 fans 5 audit, court, house 6 public 7 gallery, hearing 8 assembly, auditory, tribunal 9 audiencia, interview, reception

audio-visual aid: 4 film, tape 5 slide

audit: 4 scan 5 check, probe 6 reckon, verify 7 account, examine, inquire, inspect 8 estimate

audition: 4 test 5 trial 6 tryout

auditor: CPA 6 censor, hearer 7 apposer, audient 8 disciple, listener 10 accountant, catechumen 11 comptroller

auditorium: 4 hall, room 5 cavea, odeum 7 theater 8 auditory

auditory: 4 oral, otic 5 aural 8 acoustic

auger: bit 4 bore, tool 5 grill 6 gimlet, wimble

aught: 5 owned 6 cipher, naught, worthy 7 nothing, valiant 8 anything, property 9 possessed

Augie March creator: 6 Bellow

augite: 8 pyroxene

augment: add, eke 4 grow 5 exalt, swell 6 append, dilate, expand, extend 7 amplify enhance, enlarge, improve, magnify 8 heighten, increase, multiply 9 increment 10 aggrandize

augur: 4 bode, omen, seer 6 auspex, divine 7 betoken, foresee, portend, predict, presage, prophet, promise, signify 8 forebode, foreshow, foretell, forewarn, indicate, prophesy 9 auspicate, 10 anticipate, conjecture, soothsayer 13 prognosticate

augury: 4 rite, sign 5 token 6 hansel, ritual 7 handsel 8 ceremony 10 foreboding, forerunner

august: 5 awful, grand, noble 6 solemn 7 exalted, stately 8 imposing, majestic 9 dignified, venerable 11 magisterial

Augustus' death place: 4 Nola

auk: 4 loom 5 arrie, lemot, noddy 6 puffin, rotche 7 dovekey, dovekie, 9 guillemot
family: 7 alcidae
genus: 4 alca, alle
razorbill: 4 falk 5 murre

aula: 4 hall, room 5 court 6 emblic

aumildar: 5 agent 6 factor 7 manager 9 collector

auncel: 7 balance

aunt: tia(Sp.) 4 bawd 5 tante(F.) 6 gossip 8 relative

aura: air 4 halo, odor 5 aroma, savor 6 breeze 7 buzzard, feeling 9 emanation 10 atmosphere, exhalation

aural: 4 otic 7 audible 9 auricular
appendage: ear

aureate: 6 golden, ornate, rococo, yellow 8 aurelian

aureole: 4 halo 5 crown, glory, light 6 corona, nimbus 8 gloriole

auricle: ear 5 pinna 6 atrium, earlet 7 trumpet
part: 7 earlobe

auricular: 4 otic 7 hearsay 12 confidential

aurochs: tur 4 urus 5 bison 6 wisent

Aurora: Eos 4 dawn 7 morning

auroral: 4 eoan, rosy 7 eastern, radiant

aurum: 4 gold

auscultate: 6 listen

auspex: 5 augur

auspicate: 5 augur 7 portend, predict 8 initiate 10 inaugurate

auspice: 4 care, egis, omen, sign 5 aegis 6 augury 7 portent 8 guidance 9 patronage 10 indication, protection 11 observation, sponsorship

auspicious: 4 fair, good 6 dexter 9 favorable, fortunate, opportune 10 favourable, propitious, prosperous 12 advantageous

Aussie: 9 Australia 10 Australian

austere: 4 cold, hard, sour 5 budge, grave, gruff, harsh, rigid, rough, sharp, stern, stiff 6 bitter, formal, severe, simple, somber, strict 7 ascetic, earnest, serious 8 rigorous 9 unadorned, unsmiling 10 astringent, forbidding, relentless 13 unembellished

Australia: *animal:* 4 tait 5 coala, koala, panda 6 bunyip, cuscus, wombat 7 dasqure, wallady 8 duckbill, kangaroo, platypus 9 bandicoot, phalanger
apple: 6 colane
badger: 6 wombat
bag: 5 dilli
bear: 5 coala, koala
beefwood: 5 belar
beverage: 4 kava
bird: emu 4 emeu, lory 5 arara, crake, grebe, stint 6 gannet, leipoa 7 bittern, boobook, bustard, figbird 8 berigora, dabchick, dotterel, lorikeet, lyrebird, morepork, whimbrel 9 bower-bird, cassowary, coachwhip, friarbird, stipiture, 10 paradalote, pratincole, sanderling
boomerang: 5 kiley, kilie
brushwood: 6 millee
bush: ake
bustard: 7 bebilya
cake: 6 damper 7 brownie
call: 5 cooee, cooey

cape: 4 Howe
cat: 7 dasyure
catfish: 6 tandan
cattle stealer: 6 duffer
cedar: 4 toon
channel: 5 cowal 9 anabranch, billabong
city: see *town* below
clover fern: 6 nardoo
cockatoo: 5 galah
coin: 4 dump
colonist: 8 sterling
countryman: 8 Billijim
crayfish: 5 yabby 6 yabbie
cycad: 5 banga
dog: 5 dingo 6 Kelpie
duckbill: 8 platypus
eucalyptus: 6 bimbil, mallee 7 carbeen
fern: 5 nardu 6 nardoo
fish: 4 dart, mado, mako 5 yabby 6 tandan, yabbie
flightless bird: emu 4 emeu
fruit: 5 nonda
gum tree: 4 kari 6 tewart, tooart, touart
herb: 8 piripiri
horse: 7 brumbee 8 yarraman
hut: 6 miamia
insect: 4 laap, lerp
island: 5 Timor 8 Tasmania
kangaroo: 4 joey 5 tungo 7 bettong
kiwi: roa
lake: 4 Eyre 5 Carey, Cowan, Frome, Moore, Woods 6 Austin, Barlee, Bulloo, Harris, Mackay 7 Amadeus, Blanche, Eyerard, Torrens 8 Carnegie, Gairdner 9 Macdonald 14 Disappointment
language: 6 yabber
lizard: 6 goanna
lorikeet: 6 parrot, warrin
mahogany: 6 jarrah 7 gunning
marsupial: 4 tait 5 koala 6 wombat 8 kangaroo
measure: 4 saum
mile: 4 naut
moth: 6 bogong
mountain: Ise 5 Bruce 6 Cradle, Garnet, Magnet, Morgan 7 Bongong 8 Cuthbert, Mulligan 9 Kosciusko, Murchison
mountain range: 7 Darling 8 Flinders
native: 4 Mara 5 binge 6 digger 7 Billjim 8 Warragal, Warrigal
no: 4 baal, bail, bale
ostrich: 4 emeu
owl: 7 boobook 8 morepoke, morepork
palm: 8 bangalow
parakeet: 6 budgie 7 corella 10 budgerigar
parrot: 4 lory 7 corella, lorilet 8 lorikeet 9 cockateel, cockatiel
pepper: 4 arva, kava, yava 6 ava-ava
petrel: 4 titi
phalanger: 5 ariel
plant: 5 lakea 6 correa 7 calomba, waratah 8 warratau
pine: 5 kauri, kaury
pond: 9 billabong
rat: 8 hapalote 9 hapalotis
ratite: 4 emeu
rifleman: 5 yager
river: Hay 4 Avon, Daly, Swan, Yule 5 Comet, Namoi, Paroo, Roper, Yarra 6 Barcoo, Barwon, Bulloo, Culgoa, Dawson, De Grey, Hunter, Isaacs, Murray, Nepean, Norman 7 Darling, Fitzroy, Georges, Gilbert, Lachlan, Staaten 8 Brisbane, Burdekin, Clarence, Drysdale, Flinders, Gascoyne, Georgina, Goulburn, Mitchell, Thompson, Victoria, Werribee, Wooramel 9 Ashburton, Fortescue, Macquarie, Murchison, Saltwater 10 Diamantina, Leichhardt 11 Murrumidgee
rustler: 6 duffer
shark: 4 mako
shield: 8 heelaman, heilaman, hielaman, yeelaman
snake: 6 elapid
soldier: 5 Anzac 6 digger, swaddy 7 Billjim
sorcerer: 5 boyla 6 boolya
spear: 7 womerah, wommala, woomera 8 wommerah, woomerah 9 woomerang
state: 8 Tasmania, Victoria 10 Queensland 13 New South Wales 14 South Australia 16 Western Australia 17 Northern Territory
territory: 5 Papua
thicket: 6 mallee
throwing stick: 5 kiley, kylie 7 womerah, wommala 8 hornerah, wommerah, woomerah 9 boomerang, woomerang
town: Ayr 4 Yass 5 Dubbo, Perth, Wagga 6 Albury, Casino, Darwin, Hobart, Mackay, Sydney 7 Geelong, Ipswich, Kogarah, Mildura, Warwick, Waverly 8 Adelaide, Brighton, Brisbane, Canberra (c.), Hamilton, Maylands, Richmond, Toowomba 9 Bankstown, Caulfield, Melbourne, Newcastle 10 Hurtsville, Townsville, Wollongong 11 Rockhampton
toy: 8 weet-weet
tree: 4 toon 5 belah, belar, boree, gidya, penda 6 gidgea, gidgee, gidyea, marara 7 alipata 8 beefwood, curajong, flindosa, flindosy, ironbark 9 koorajong 10 bunya-bunya
tulip: 7 waratah 8 warratau
valley: 5 Grose 8 Jamieson, Kangaroo, Megalong 11 Burragorang
war club: 5 waddy
weapon: 5 hulla, waddy 6 hullah 7 liangle 8 leeangle 10 hullanulla

wilderness: 7 outback
wombat: 5 koala
wood: emu
workman: 7 Billjim
Austria: *city:* 4 Graz, Linz, Wien(c.) 5 Gratz 6 Vienna(c.) 7 Noricum 8 Salzburg
coin: 5 ducat, krone 6 florin, heller, zehner 8 groschen 9 schilling
composer: 4 Berg 7 Strauss 8 Bruckner
crownland: 8 Dalmatia
dance: 6 dreher
former ruling family: 8 Habsburg, Hapsburg
legislature: 10 Herrenhaus
measure: 4 fass, fuss, joch, mass, muth, yoke 5 halbe, linie, meile, metze, pfiff, punkt 6 achtel, becher, seidel 7 klafter, viertel 8 dreiling 10 muthmassel 12 futtermassel
measure of weight: 4 marc, saum, unze 5 denat, karch, pfund, stein 7 centner, pfennig 8 vierling 9 quentchen
money: 5 ducat
native: 7 Styrian 8 Tyrolese
nobility: 6 Ritter
province: 4 Gorz 5 Tirol, Tyrol 6 Istria, Styria, Triest 7 Bohemia, Galicia, Moravia, Selesia 8 Bukowina, Carniola, Dalmatia, Gradisca, Salzburg 9 Carinthia 10 Vorarlberg
psychiatrist: 5 Adler, Freud
river: Inn, Mur 4 Elbe, Enns, Isar, Raab 6 Danube, Moldau
writer: 5 Kafka
austringer: 8 falconer
Austronesian language: 4 Niue 7 Tagalog
autarch: 6 despot 8 autocrat
authentic: 4 pure, real, sure, true 5 exact, right, valid 6 actual, proper 7 correct, genuine, sincere 8 bonafide, credible, official, original, reliable 9 veritable 10 authorized 11 trustworthy 13 authoritative
authenticate: 4 seal 5 prove 6 attest, verify 7 approve, confirm
author: 4 doer 5 maker, ruler 6 factor, parent, source, writer 7 creator, founder 8 ancestor, begetter, compiler, composer, inventor, producer 10 bookwright, instigator, originator
authoritative: 8 official, oracular, positive 9 canonical, effectual, imperious, masterful 10 conclusive, convincing, legitimate, peremptory 11 dictatorial, excathedral, magisterial
authority: 4 sway 5 adept, board, power, riche, right, title 6 artist, author, expert, regent, regime, weight 7 command, dynasty, scepter, sceptre, warrant 8 dominion, prestige, sanction 9 influence 10 ascendancy, ascendency, commission, competence 12 jurisdiction 13 authorization, justification
judicial: 4 banc
preponderant: 8 hegemony
symbol: 7 scepter
woman's: 7 distaff
authorize: let 4 vest 5 allow 6 clothe, permit, ratify 7 approve, empower, endorse, entitle, indorse, justify, license, warrant 8 accredit, delegate, legalize, sanction 10 commission, legitimize
authorless: 9 anonymous
auto: See **automobile**
auto court: inn 5 motel
auto race: 4 drag 5 derby
autobiography: 4 vita 6 memoir
autochthonous: 6 native 7 edaphic, endemic 10 aboriginal, indigenous
autocrat: 4 czar, tsar, tzar 5 mogul 6 Caesar, despot 7 autarch, monarch 8 dictator 9 sovereign
autocratic: 8 absolute 9 arbitrary 10 tyrannical
autograph: 4 name, sign 9 signature
automatic: 7 machine 10 automatous, mechanical, self-acting 11 instinctive, spontaneous
automaton: 5 golem, robot 7 android, machine
automobile: 4 heap, jeep 5 coupe, crate, racer, sedan 6 jalopy 7 flivver, machine, phaeton 8 roadster 11 convertible
army: 4 jeep
British: AC, MG 5 Alvis, Riley, Rover 6 Allard, Anglia, Austin, Consul, Humber, Jaguar, Jowett, Morgan, Morris, Rapier, Singer, Zephyr 7 Bentley, Daimler, Hillman, Sunbeam, Triumph 8 Berkeley, Vauxhall 10 Rolls-Royce 11 Austin-Healy, Hillman-Minx, Morris-Minor 12 Metropolitan 13 Sunbeam-Talbot
Czech: 5 Skoda
early: EMF, Reo 4 Alco, Benz, Cord, Knox, Moon, Olds, Sear, Star 5 Brush, Regal, Stutz 6 Auburn, Dupont, Duryea, Graham, Haynes, Kissel, Lozier, Marmon, Mercer, Saxson, Thomas, Winton 7 Autocar, Bugatti, La Salle, Maxwell, Oakland, Premier, Rambler, Simplex, Stevens, Tourist 8 Apperson, Chalmers, Chandler, Franklin, Mercedes, National, Overland, Peerless 9 Hupmobile 10 Cunningham, Duesenberg, Jackrabbit, Locomobile 11 Graham-Paige, Pierce-Arrow 12 Crane-Simplex, Owen-Magnetic, Pope-Hartford, White-Streamer 13 Baker-Electric, Ofeldt-Steamer, Stevens-Duryea, Wills-St.

Claire 14 Stanley-Steamer 16 Columbia-Electric 22 International Auto Buggy
Europe: BMW 4 Benz 5 Aston, Metro, Prinz, Skoda 6 Martin, Denzel, Isetta, Zodiac 7 Bugatti, Prefect 9 Facel-Vega
French: DB 5 Simca 7 Citroen, Panhard, Peugeot, Renault 8 Dauphine
German: DKW 4 Opel 6 Taunus 7 Goliath, Porsche, Weidner 8 Borgward, Rometsch, Wartburg 10 Golomobile, Lloyd-Wagon, Volkswagen 12 Mercedes-Benz
Italian: 4 Fiat 6 Lancia 7 Ferrari 8 Maserati 9 Alfa-Romeo
Japanese: 5 Honda 6 Datsun, Toyota 13 Pringe-Skylark
part: 4 hood 5 motor, trunk 6 engine 7 chassis, magneto, tonneau 8 ignition
Russian: Zim 6 Pobeda 9 Moskvitch
Swedish: 4 Saab 5 Volvo
supercharged: 6 hot rod
United States: 4 Ford, Jeep, Nash, Nova, Vega 5 Buick, Capri, Comet, Dodge, Edsel, Pinto 6 Cougar, De Soto, Duster, Hudson, Impala, LeMans, Torino, Willys 7 Caprice, Lincoln, Mercury, Montego, Mustang, Packard, Pontiac, Rambler, Ventura 8 Cadillac, Chrysler, Corvette, Imperial, Maverick, Plymouth 9 Chevrolet 10 Oldsmobile, Studebaker 11 Continental, Thunderbird

autonomous: 4 free 11 independent
autopsy: 8 necropsy 10 dissection 11 examination
autumn: 4 fall 6 season 8 maturity 11 harvest-time
auxiliary: aid, sub 4 aide, ally 6 branch, helper 7 abetter, abettor, adjunct, partner 8 adjutant 9 accessory, adminicle, ancillary, assistant, coadjutor, secondary, tributary 10 additional, foederatus, subsidiary, supporting 11 confederate, cooperating, subordinate, subservient
ava: 4 kava
avail: do; aid, dow, use 4 boot, help 5 serve, stead, value 6 moment, profit 7 benefit, bestead, succeed, suffice, utilize 9 advantage 10 assistance
available: fit 4 free, open 5 handy, ready 6 patent, usable 7 present 9 effectual, practical 10 accessible, attainable, convenient, obtainable 11 efficacious
aval: 8 acceptor, indorser 9 ancestral
avalanche: 5 slide 9 landslide
avale: 4 doff, flow, sink 5 abase, lower, yield 6 submit 7 descend 8 dismount
Avalon, Avilion: 4 isle 6 island
tomb: 6 Arthur
avania: tax 6 impost
avanious: 12 extortionate
avantgarde: 8 vanguard
avarice: 7 avidity 8 cupidity, rapacity
spirit of: 6 Mammon
avaricious: 5 close 6 greedy, hungry, stingy 7 gripple, miserly 8 covetous, grasping 9 niggardly, penurious 12 parsimonious
avast: 4 hold, stay, stop 5 cease
avatar: 8 epiphany 10 embodiment 11 incarnation
avaunt: 5 boast, vaunt 6 begone, depart 7 advance, forward 9 dismissal
ave: 4 bead, hail 6 prayer 8 farewell, greeting 10 salutation, veneration
avellane: nut 5 hazel 7 filbert
avelonge: 4 oval 6 oblong 8 slanting
avenaceous: 4 oaty 5 oaten
avenge: 5 repay, wrack 6 awreak, punish 7 requite, revenge 8 chastise 9 retaliate, vindicate
avenger: 7 nemesis 10 vindicator
avens: 4 geum, herb
avenue: rue(F.), way 4 gate, mall, pike, road 5 allee, alley, drive, entry 6 access, arcade, artery, street 7 opening 9 boulevard 10 passageway 12 thoroughfare
aveolate: 6 favose
aver: say 5 claim, prove, state, swear 6 affirm, allege, assert, assure, avouch, depose, verify 7 declare, justify, protest 9 predicate 10 asseverate 11 acknowledge
average: par, sum 4 duty, fair, mean, norm, rule, so-so 5 ratio, usual, value 6 charge, medial, median, medium, middle, normal, tariff 8 estimate, mediocre, moderate, ordinary, quantity, standard 10 proportion 13 approximation
averse: 4 loth 5 balky, loath 7 adverse, against, opposed 8 inimical, opposite 9 disliking, reluctant, unwilling 11 disinclined, unfavorable
aversion: 4 hate 5 odium 6 enmity, hatred, horror 7 disdain, disgust, dislike 8 distaste 9 antipathy 10 repugnance 11 abomination 12 estrangement 14 disinclination
avert: 4 bend, fend, move, shun, ward 5 avoid, deter, dodge, evade, parry, sheer, twist 6 defray, divert, retard, shield 7 deflect, expiate, prevent 8 alienate, estrange, forefend 9 forestall
aviary: 4 cage 5 house 6 volery 8 ornithon 9 birdhouse, enclosure
keeper: 8 aviarist
aviation: 6 flying 10 airplaning 11 aeronautics
maneuver: 8 Immelman
aviator: ace 5 flier, flyer, pilot 6 airman, flying, Icarus 8 operator
signal: out 4 over 5 roger

aviatrix: 13 Amelia Earhart

avid: 4 agog, keen, warm 5 eager 6 ardent, greedy, hungry, jejune 7 anxious, athirst, craving, longing 8 desirous, grasping 9 devouring

avidity: 7 avarice 8 cupidity 10 greediness

avifauna: 5 birds, ornis

avile: 5 abase 6 debase, vilify 10 depreciate

avital: 6 avitic 9 ancestral

avocado: 4 coyo, pear, tree 6 chinin 8 aguacate, alligato

avocation: 4 work 5 hobby, trade 7 calling 9 amusement, diversion 10 recreation

avocet: 4 bird 5 stilt 6 godwit, plover

avoid: 4 balk, quit, shun 5 annul, avert, dodge, elude, evade, feign, hedge, parry, shirk, slack, spair(Sc.), 6 blench, escape, eschew, refute, remove, vacate 7 abstain, evitate, forbear, forsake, refrain 8 sidestep

avoidance: 6 outlet 10 dismissing, withdrawal

avoirdupois weight: ton 4 dram 5 ounce, pound 7 long ton 13 hundredweight 17 long hundredweight

avolate: fly 6 escape 9 evaporate

avow: own 4 bind 5 admit, state 6 affirm, avouch, depone, depose, devote 7 confess, declare, justify, profess 8 maintain 11 acknowledge

avowal: 4 oath, word 14 representation

awa: 4 kava 8 milkfish

awabi: 8 abalone

await: 4 bide, heed, pend, wait 5 abide, tarry, watch 6 attend, expect, impend, waylay

awake: daw 4 stir, wake 5 alert, alive, aware, rouse 6 active, arouse, awaken, excite 7 careful, heedful 8 open-eyed, vigilant 9 attentive, conscious

awakening: 7 revival 14 expergefacient, expergefaction

award: 4 give, meed, mete 5 allot, grant, medal, prize 6 accord, addeem, assign, bestow, bounty, confer, decide 7 adjudge, appoint, consign, custody, keeping 8 accolade, sentence 9 apportion, determine, judgement 10 adjudicate

academic: 7 diploma 11 scholarship

cinema: 5 Oscar

television: 4 Emmy

aware: hep 4 reck, sure, wary 5 alert, alive 6 beware 7 knowing, mindful 8 apprised, apprized, informed, sensible, vigilant, watchful 9 cognizant, conscious 11 intelligent

away: awa(Sc.), fro, off, out, via 4 gone 5 along, apart, aside, forth, hence 6 abroad, absent, begone, onward, thence 7 distant, froward 8 fromward 9 fromwards, herehence

prefex: aph, apo

awe: cow 5 amaze, daunt, scare 6 fright, regard, terror, wonder 7 buffalo, respect 8 astonish, bewilder, overcome 9 fascinate, overpower 10 intimidate

aweband: 4 band, rope 5 check 9 restraint

aweigh: 5 atrip

awesome: 4 eery 5 awful, eerie, weird 6 solemn 7 dreaded, ghostly 9 appalling, unearthly

awful: 4 dire, ugly 6 august, horrid 7 awesome, fearful 8 dreadful, shocking, terrible 9 appalling, frightful 10 tremendous

awk: odd 6 clumsy 7 adverse 8 perverse

awkward: 4 gaum 5 gawky, inapt, inept 6 clumsy, gauche, rustic, uneasy 7 adverse, boorish, froward, loutish, stilted, uncouth, unhandy 8 bungling, clownish, lubberly, perverse, ungainly, untoward, unwieldy 9 graceless, inelegant, lumbering, maladroit, ponderous 10 backhanded, blundering, ungraceful, unskillful 11 heavy-handed 12 inconvenient

awl: 4 brog 5 brode, elsen, elson(Sc.) 6 elshin, gimlet

awn: ear 4 barb 5 beard 7 aristae, bristle 9 appendage

awning: 5 velum 6 canopy, tienda 8 velarium 9 shameeana, shamianah(Ind.)

fastening: 6 earing

awreak: 6 avenge 7 condemn

awry: 4 agee, bias 5 agley(Sc.), amiss, askew, gleed, gleyd, wrong 6 cammed 7 askance, asquint, crooked, oblique 8 perverse 9 distorted 10 crisscross

ax: adz 4 adze 5 hache 6 twibil 7 besague, boucher, cleaver, hatchet, twibill 8 tomahawk

blade: bit

butt: 4 poll

handle: 5 helve

axeman: 8 woodsman 9 lumberman 10 woodcutter 11 woodchopper

axial: 7 central

axilla: ala 6 armpit 8 shoulder

axiom: saw 5 adage, dicta(pl.), maxim, motto 6 byword, dictum, saying, truism 7 precept, proverb 8 aphorism, apothegm, sentence 9 principle 11 proposition

axis: 4 axle, deer 5 stalk 6 chitra 7 spindle

axle: bar, cod, pin 4 axis 5 arbor, shaft 6 axtree 7 mandrel, spindle

axletree pin: 8 linchpin

axolotl: 4 newt 10 salamander

axweed: 8 goutweed

ay: 9 champagne

ayah: 4 maid 5 nurse 9 nursemaid
aye, ay: pro, yea, yes 4 ever 6 always, assent 7 forever 11 affirmative, continually
aye-aye: 5 lemur
Azerbaijan city: 4 Baku(c.) 11 Elizavetpol 12 Yelisavetpol
Azores: *district:* 5 Horta
island: 4 Pico 5 Fayal 6 Flores
port: 5 Horta
volcano: 4 Pico

Aztec: *ball game:* 8 tlachtli
god: 4 Xipe 9 Xipetotic 11 Xiuhtecutli
language: 7 Nahuatl
myth: 4 Nana, Nata
stone: 9 temelactl 12 chalchihuitl
temple: 6 teopan 8 teocalli

azure: 4 biçe, blue 8 cerulean 9 cloudless, unclouded

azygous: odd 6 single

B

baa: 5 bleat
baahling: 4 lamb
Baal: god 4 idol 5 deity
consort: 6 Baltis
baba: 4 baby, cake, male 5 child
babacoote: 5 lemur
babassu: oil 4 palm, soap
babblative: 9 garrulous, talkative 10 loquacious
babble: 4 chat, gash 5 haver, prate 6 cackle, gabble, glaver, gossip, murmur, palter, tumult 7 blabber, blather, bluster, brabble, chatter, chipper, clatter, prattle, smatter, twaddle 8 glaister 11 stultiloquy
babel: din 5 clang, tower 6 jargon, medley, racket, tumult 7 discord 9 charivari, confusion
babiche: 5 thong 6 lacing, thongs
babillard: 4 bird 11 whitethroat
baboon: ape 4 papa 5 drill 6 chaema 7 babuina 8 mandrill
babul: gum, lac 4 tree, wood 6 acacia, mimosa
pod: 5 garad
babushka: 5 scarf 8 kerchief 11 grandmother
baby: 4 baba, babe, doll 5 bairn(Sc.), child, humor, spoil 6 coddle, fondle, infant, moppet, pamper, puppet, weanie(Sc.) 7 bambino(It.), papoose 9 youngster
carriage: 4 pram 6 gocart 8 stroller 12 perambulator
cry: mew 6 squall
food: pap 4 milk 6 pablum
outfit: 7 layette
shoe: 6 bootee
babyish: 6 simple 7 puerile 8 childish
Babylonia: *abode of the dead:* 5 Aralu
Adam: 5 Adapa
army officer: 11 samagarnebo
city: 5 Akkad 6 Calneh, Cunaxa, Cuthah
cycle of moon: sar 5 saros
division: 4 Elam 5 Sumer, Sumir
era: 5 sumer 10 Nabonassar
foe: 7 Elamite
god: Ea, Zu; Anu, Aya, Bel, Hea, Hes, Ira, Ler, Sin, Utu 4 Adad, Anat, Apsu, Baal, Gula, Irra, Nebo, Utug 5 Alala, Alalu, Dagan, Enlil, Etana, Ninib, Nusku, Siris, Urash 6 Ishtar, Nergal, Oannes, Tammuz 7 Ninurta, Shamash 8 Merodach 10 Adramelech 11 Adrammelech
goddess: Ai; Aya 4 Erua, Nana, Nina 5 Belit, Istar 6 Belili, Beltis, Ishtar 7 Mylitta
hero of myth: 5 Adapa, Etana 9 Gilgamesh
king: 14 Nebuchadnezzar, Nebuchadrezzar
language: 5 Accad, Akkad
mountain: 6 Ararat
people: 7 Elamite
priest: En
priestess: 5 Entum
region: 5 Aralu, Sumer, Sumir
river: 6 Tigris 9 Euphrates
ruler: 8 Exilarch
sea: 4 Nina
sun god's attendant: 6 Bunene
tower: 7 zikurat 8 ziggurat
waters: 4 Apsu
weight: 4 mina 5 maneh
Babylonian: 5 Accad 8 Sumerian
bacalao: 5 murre 7 codfish, grouper 9 guillemot
bacca: 5 berry
baccalaureate degree: B.A. 8 bachelor
baccarat: 4 game
player: 6 punter
term: 5 banco
variety of: 11 chemin-de-fer
baccate: 5 pulpy 7 berried
bacchanal: 7 devotee, reveler 8 carouser
Bacchanal's cry: 4 evoe 5 evohe
bacchante: 6 maenad 9 priestess
bachelor: 4 seal 6 garcon 8 benedict, celibate 11 holluschick 13 holluschickie(pl.)
bachelor button: 8 milkwort 10 bluebottle
bacillus: 4 germ 5 virus 7 microbe
back: aid, fro, tub, vat 4 abet, beck, hind, nape, nata, rear, tail 5 again, angel, chine, dorsa(pl.), notum, splat, spine, stern 6 assist, dorsum, second, trough, uphold, verify 7 cistern, endorse, finance, sponsor,

support, sustain 8 backward 9 encourage, posterior, reinforce 10 strengthen
at the: aft 5 abaff, abaft, arear 6 astern 7 postern
comb. form: 5 notus
lower part of: 4 loin
pain: 8 notalgia
pert. to: 6 dorsal, lumbar, tergal
prefix: re 5 retro
toward: aft 5 abaft 6 astern, dorsad 7 postern
back off: ebb 6 recede, retire 7 retreat, reverse 10 retrograde
back out: 4 funk 5 welsh 8 crawfish, withdraw
back scratcher: 7 strigil
Back Street author: 5 Hurst
back talk: lip 4 sass 9 insolence
backbite: 5 abuse 6 defame, vilify 7 asperse, slander
backbone: 4 grit, guts 5 chine, nerve, pluck, spina, spine 6 mettle, spinae, spirit 7 stamina 8 vertebra
backer: 5 angel
backgammon: 6 fayles 10 tricktrack
term: 4 blot 6 gammon
background: 4 rear 6 offing 7 setting 8 distance, training 9 education
backing: aid 6 lining, refuse 7 support 9 financing 10 embankment 11 endorsement
backlog: 7 reserve, surplus 12 accumulation
backslide: 4 fall 5 lapse 6 desert, revert 7 relapse 11 deteriorate
backward: fro, lax 4 back, dull, loth 5 arear, inapt, loath, unapt 6 astern, averse, bygone, stupid 7 bashful, laggard, lagging, reverse 8 dilatory, perverse, rearward 9 recessive, reluctant, unwilling 10 behindhand, hesitating, regressive, retrograde 11 unfavorable 13 retrogressive, retrospective, unprogressive
backwater: ebb 5 bayou 7 retract, retreat
backwoodsman: 4 hick 9 hillbilly
backwort: 7 comfrey
bacon: pig 4 pork 5 prize 6 rustic
fat: 5 speck
side: 6 gammon
slice: 6 rasher, collop
Bacon work: 12 Novum Organum
bacteria, bacterium: 4 germ 6 aerobe 7 aerobia, microbe 10 aerobacter
chain: 6 torula 7 torulae(pl.)
culture: 4 agar 8 agar-agar
dissolver: 5 lysin
free from harmful: 7 asepsis, aseptic
rod-shaped: 7 bacilli(pl.) 8 bacillus
vaccine: 8 bacterin
bacteriologist: *culture:* 4 agar
wire: 4 oese
bactrian: 5 camel
bad: big, ill, sad 4 evil, full, lewd, poor, qued, sick, vile 5 gammy, nasty, sorry, worst, wrong 6 arrant, faulty, nought, rotten, severe, sinful, wicked 7 baleful, baneful, corrupt, harmful, hurtful, immoral, inutile, naughty, noughty, spoiled, tainted, unlucky, unmoral, unsound, vicious 8 annoying, criminal, depraved, flagrant, inferior, unsuited 9 abandoned, atrocious, blemished, dangerous, defective, incorrect, injurious, offensive, perverted, worthless 10 aggravated, distressed, inadequate, iniquitous, pernicious, unsuitable 11 deleterious, displeasing, inopportune, unfavorable 12 disagreeable, inauspicious
comb. form: dys, mal 4 caco, kako
prefix: mal, mis
bad blood: 4 hate 5 anger 6 enmity 10 bitterness, resentment
bad debt: 7 default
bad habit: 4 vice
bad luck: 7 ambsace, ill wind 9 adversity 10 misfortune
badderlocks: 6 murlin 7 henware, seaweed 9 honeyware
badge: pin 4 mark, sign 5 token 6 emblem, ensign, symbol 8 insignia 10 cognizance
policeman: 4 star 6 busser, shield
badger: nag 4 bait, mele, pate 5 annoy, brock, brush, chevy, chivy, phani, rated, tease, worry 6 bauson, bother, chivvy, haggle, harass, hawker, heckle, pester, teledu, wombat 7 torment 8 carcajou, huckster, irritate 9 bandicoot, mistonusk 10 badgerweed 12 pasqueflower
cape: 4 cony 5 coney, daman, hyrax
Badger State: 9 Wisconsin
badgerweed: 12 pasqueflower
badigeon: 5 paste 6 cement 11 composition
badinage: 4 fool 5 joker 6 banter 8 raillery, trifling 9 badinerie
badly: ill 4 illy, sick 6 poorly, unwell 8 faultily, wickedly 9 viciously 11 imperfectly 12 disagreeable, unskillfully 13 unfortunately
baff: 4 bang, beat, blow, thud 6 strike, stroke 9 worthless
baffle: get 4 balk, foil, pose 5 cheat, check, elude, evade, fling, stump 6 blench, boggle, defeat, delude, infamy, outwit, resist, thwart 7 confuse, deceive, quibble 8 bewilder, confound, disgrace, juggling 9 confusion, discomfit, frustrate 10 circumvent, disappoint, disconcert
baft: 5 abaft 6 astern
bag: cod, net, pod, pot, sac 4 grip, poke, sack, trap, womb 5 belly, bouge, bulse, catch,

pouch, purse, scrip, seize, snare, steal **6** budget, cavity, entrap, pocket, sachet, valise, wallet **7** alforja, balloon, capture, gamebag, handbag, reticle, satchel **8** entrails, knapsack, reticule, suitcase **9** cartridge, container, gladstone, haversack **10** collection, pocketbook **11** portmanteau
botanic: sac **4** asci **5** ascus, spore
canvas: **7** musette
fishing net: **4** bunt, fyke
hop: **7** sarpler
muslin: **6** tillot
traveling: **9** telescope
bagatelle: **4** game **5** verse **6** trifle
baggage: **4** arms, gear, minx **5** huzzy, nasty, tents, trash, wench **6** harlot, refuse, trashy, trunks **7** clothes, effects, rubbish, valises **8** carriage, rubbishy, utensils **9** munitions, viaticals, worthless **10** prostitute **11** impedimenta
baggy: **5** loose **6** flabby, puffed
Baghdad: *capital:* **4** Irak
merchant: **6** Sinbad **7** Sindbad
bagman: **5** tramp **7** swagman **8** henchman **9** collector
bagnio: **4** bath **5** bagne **6** prison **7** brothel **8** hothouse
bagpipe: **5** drone **7** musette **8** zampogna **10** doodlesack, sordellina
mouthpiece: **4** muse
pipe: **6** drones **7** chanter
play: **5** skirl
player: **5** piper **7** doodler
sound: **5** skirl
tune: **4** port
bah: foh, pah, rot **5** faugh, pshaw **8** nonsense
Bahama Islands: **5** Abaco **6** Andros, Bimini **9** Eleuthera
capital: **6** Nassau
bahia: bay
baikie: **5** stake, stick
bail: dip **4** bond, hoop, lade, lave, ring, rynd, yoke **5** ladle, scoop, throw, vouch **6** bucket, handle, secure, surety **7** custody, deliver, release **8** bailsman, bulwarks, security **9** guarantee
bailiff: **4** hind **5** agent, reeve, staff **6** bailie, bailli, beadle, deputy, factor, grieve, office, porter, staves(pl.), varlet **7** sheriff, steward **8** huissier, overseer, tipstaff **9** constable **10** magistrate **12** understeward
farm: **4** hind
bailiwick: **4** area **6** domain, office **8** province **9** bailiffry, bailliage **12** jurisdiction
bain: **4** near **5** lithe, ready, short **6** direct, limber, supple **7** forward, willing
bairn: **5** child
bait: bad **4** bite, chum, feed, halt, lure **5** decoy, tempt, worry **6** allure, attack, badger, entice, harass, repast **7** fulcrum, gudgeon, provoke, torment **9** persecute **10** allurement, enticement, exasperate, inducement, temptation **11** refreshment
artificial: **6** hackle
bird enticing: **5** shrap **6** shrape
salmon fishing: **5** baker
baize: **6** fabric **7** drapery
bake: dry **4** cook, fire **5** batch, broil, grill, parch, roast **6** anneal, harden **7** biscuit **8** clambake
baker: **4** oven **6** baxter **7** furnace, roaster, utensil
sheet: pan
shovel: **4** pale, peel
tool: **4** pale, peel
baker's dozen: **8** thirteen
baker's itch: **4** rash **9** psoriasis
bakie: **6** trough, vessel
baking chamber: **4** kiln, oast, oven
baking dish: **7** cocotte, ramekin
baking ingredient: **4** soda **5** flour, yeast
baking soda: **9** saleratus
Bakongo goddess: **6** Nyambe, Nzambi
Balaam's beast: ass **6** donkey
balance: **4** even, rest **5** peise, poise, scale, weigh, weihe **6** adjust, equate, offset, sanity **7** residue **8** equality, equalize, serenity **9** composure, equipoise, remainder, stability **10** neutralize, steadiness **11** equilibrium **12** counterpoise
lose: **4** trip **7** stagger
weighing: **6** auncel
balancer: **7** acrobat, athlete, gymnast
balate: **7** trepang
balcony: **5** oriel, porch **6** piazza, sollar **7** balagan, gallery, mirador, pergola, terrace **8** brattice, verandah
church singer: **8** cantoria
projecting: **6** gazabo, gazebo
bald: **4** bare, base **5** crude, naked, plain **6** callow, paltry, pilled, simple **7** epilose, literal **8** glabrous, hairless **9** unadorned, uncovered **11** undisguised, unvarnished
Balder: *father:* **4** Odin
mother: **5** Frigg
murder weapon: **9** mistletoe
slayer: **4** Hoth, Loke **5** Hothr
son: **7** Forsete, Forseti
wife: **5** Nanna
balderdash: rot **5** trash **6** drivel, jargon **8** nonsense **9** balductum, rigmarole **10** flumdiddle
baldicoot: **4** coot, monk
baldmoney: **7** gentian **8** spicknel
baldness: **6** acomia **7** calvity **8** alopecia **10** calavities **11** phalacrosis
baldric, baldrick: **4** belt **6** girdle, zodiac **7** balteus, support **8** baltheus, necklace
bale: no; not, woe **4** evil, fire, harm, pyre **5** crate, death **6** ballot, bundle, sorrow **7**

package 8 compress, disaster 9 influence, suffering
of wool: 7 sarpler
Balearic Island: 5 Iviza 7 Cabrera, Majorca, Minorca 10 Formentera
language: 7 Catalan
measure: 5 palmo 6 misura, quarta, quarte 7 quartin 8 barcella, quartera
port: 5 Palma
weight: 5 artal, artel, cargo, corta, libra, mayor, ratel, rotel 8 quartano
baleen: 5 whale 9 whalebone
baleful: bad 4 evil 6 deadly, malign 7 noxious, ruinous 8 sinister, wretched 10 calamitous, pernicious 11 destructive
baleise: 4 flog
Bali (see also **Indonesia**):
dance: 5 ardja, baris, kriss 6 barong, ketjak, monkey 7 djanger 9 sanghyang 14 barong-landoeng
musical instrument: 7 gamelan 8 gamelang
religion: 8 Hinduism
rice field: 6 sawaii
balk: hue, jib, shy 4 beam, bilk, foil, heap, lick, loft, miss, omit, shun, skip, slip, stop 5 avoid, block, check, hunch, mound, rebel, reest(Sc.), ridge, waver 6 baffle, defeat, falter, hinder, impede, outwit, rafter, refuse, thwart 7 blunder, isthmus, mistake 8 omitting, overlook, skipping 9 discomfit, frustrate 10 disappoint 14 disappointment
Balkan: 4 Serb, Slav 7 Serbian 8 Albanian, Rumanian, Yugoslav
bandit: 6 haiduk, heydue 7 heyduck, heyduke
coin: 6 novcic
country: 6 Serbia, Servia 7 Albania, Rumania 10 Yugoslavia
instrument: 5 gusla, gusle
balky: 6 mulish 8 stubborn 9 obstinate
ball: bal(F.), bob, orb, toy 4 bead, pill 5 dance, globe, glome 6 bullet, muddle, pellet, pompon, rundle, sphere 7 confuse, mandrel, ridotto 8 spheroid 11 glomeration
lofted: fly, lob
low: 5 liner
minced meat: 5 pinda 7 rissole
wooden: 4 knur
ball and chain: 4 wife 6 burden
ball club: 4 nine, team 6 eleven
ball game: cat 5 rugby 6 pelota, soccer 7 cricket 8 baseball
ball of fire: 4 whiz 6 genius
ball up: 7 confuse, perplex
ballad: lai(F.) 4 lilt, poem, song 5 derry 6 ballet, sonnet 7 ballant, canzone
ballast: 4 load, trim 5 poise, stone 6 burden, gravel, weight 7 balance 9 saburrate
ballerina: 4 pony 6 dancer 8 danseuse
ballet: 5 dance, drama 6 ballad, masque 9 pantomime 12 choreography
leap: 4 jete
movement: 4 jete 5 brise 8 glissade
posture: 9 arabesque
skirt: 4 tutu
ballistic missile: 4 ICBM, IRBM
balloon: bag 5 blimp 6 expand, gasbag 7 airship, distend, inflate 8 aerostat 9 dirigible
basket: car 7 gondola, nacelle
ballot: 4 bale, poll, vote 5 elect, voice 6 billet, choice, ticket
cast: 4 vote
balm: oil 4 bito, daub, case 5 salve 6 balsam, embalm, lotion, relief, soothe, solace 7 anoint, anodyne, besmear, comfort, cure-all, heal-all, perfume, soother, unguent 8 mitigate, ointment 11 assuagement
horse: 10 citronella
of Gilead: 6 balsam
balmy: 4 mild, soft 5 bland, daffy, moony, spicy, sunny, sweet 6 gentle, insane 7 healing, lenient 8 aromatic, dressing, fragrant, soothing 9 assuaging 10 refreshing 11 odoriferous
balneary: 9 bathhouse
balneation: 4 bath
balneum: 4 bath 8 bathroom
baloney: 4 bunk 5 hooey 6 humbug 8 nonsense
balsa: 4 raft, tree, wood 5 float
balsam: 4 balm, riga, tree, tolu 6 storay 7 copaiba 8 bdellium, ointment
apple: 4 vine 7 creeper 8 amargosa, amargoso, ampalaya
Balt: Yod 4 Esth, Lett 8 Estonian 10 Lithuanian
balteus: 4 band, belt 7 baldric
Baltic: *barge:* 5 praam
city: 4 Riga 6 Danzig
gulf: 4 Riga
island: 4 Dago, Faro, Osel 5 Alsen, Oesel, Oland
language: 6 Lettic
seaport: 4 Kiel, Riga 5 Memel, Reval 6 Talinn
Baltic Sea: *canal:* 4 Kiel
river: 4 Oder, Odra 5 Dvina, Peene, Wilsa
Baluchistan: *native:* 4 Mari 5 Marri 6 Marree
province: Lus 5 Kalat 6 Khelat
balustrade: 6 barrer 7 parapet, railing 8 balconet, baluster, banister 10 balconette
Balzac character: 4 Nana 6 Goriot
bam: 4 hoax, sham 5 cheat, trick 7 wheedle

Bambi: 4 deer 7 animal
bambino: 4 baby 5 child 6 infant
bamboo: 4 cane, reed, tree
sacred: 6 nandin
sprouts: 5 achar
sugar: 9 tabasheer
woven: 6 sawali
bamboozle: 4 dupe 5 cheat, cozen, grill 6 cajole, humbug 7 buffalo, defraud, deceive, mystify, perplex 11 hornswoggle
ban: bar, woe 4 tabu, veto 5 banal, block, curse, edict, order, taboo 6 banish, enjoin, forbid, hinder, invoke, notice, outlaw 7 condemn, exclude 8 anathema, denounce, execrate, prohibit 9 interdict, proscribe 10 inhibition 11 forbiddance, imprecation, malediction 12 anathematize, denunciation, interdiction, proclamation 15 excommunication
Bana: *conqueror:* 7 Krishna
daughter: 4 Usha
banal: 4 flat 5 corny, inane, silly, stale, trite, vapid 6 jejune 7 trivial 9 hackneyed 11 commonplace 13 platitudinous
phrase: 6 cliche
banana: 4 musa 6 ensete 7 platano(Sp.) 8 plantain
bunch: 4 hand, stem
family: 4 musa 6 pesang 8 musaceae
leaf: 5 frond
wild: fei
banana fish: 6 albula 8 ladyfish
banana oil: 8 soft soap
Bananaland: 10 Queensland
band: bar, tie 4 belt, bond, came, cord, crew, fess, gang, girt, hoop, ring, zona, zone 5 ampyx, bandy, corse, label, strap, strip, tribe, unite, zonae(pl.) 6 armlet, binder, bundle, cohort, collar, collet, copula, fascia, fetter, fillet, girdle, hyphen, norsel, pledge, string, stripe, swathe, tether 7 aweband, bandeau, binding, circlet, company, fasciae(pl.), garland, orphrey, promise, shackle 8 banderol, biliment, bracelet, cincture, cingulum, faisceau, ligament, ligature, tressour, tressure 9 associate, banderole, bandoleer, guarantee, orchestra 10 obligation
armed: 5 posse
armor: 6 tonlet
brain: 6 ligula 7 ligulae
decorative: 7 cornice
garment fastening: 5 patte
narrow: 4 tape 5 stria 6 striae(pl.)
small: 8 bandelet 10 bandelette
bandage: 4 bind, tape 5 blind, clout, dress, sling, spica, truss 6 fettle, fillet, ligate, swathe 8 cincture, ligature 9 blindfold
fastener: 7 ligator
nose: 9 accipiter
surgical: 5 spica 6 fascia, spicae(pl.) 7 fasciae
bandeau: 4 band 5 strip 6 fillet
bandicoot: rat 6 badger
bandikai: 4 okra
bandit: 4 caco 5 bravo, thief 6 banish, outlaw, robber 7 bandido, brigand, ladrone 8 marauder, picaroon 10 highwayman
bandleader: 6 master 7 choragi, maestro 8 choragus 9 conductor
bandmaster: 5 Sousa
bandy: 4 band, cart, swap 5 trade 6 league, strive 7 chaffer, contend, discuss 8 carriage, exchange 11 reciprocate
bane: woe 4 evil, harm, kill, pest, ruin 5 curse, death, venom 6 injury, murder, poison, slayer 7 nemesis, scourge 8 mischief, murderer, nuisance
baneful: bad, ill 4 evil, vile 7 harmful, hurtful, noxious, ruinous 8 venomous 9 sinistral 10 pernicious
bang: rap 4 baff, beat, blow, dash, dock, drub, slam 5 blaff, clash, drive, excel, force, impel, pound, sound, thump, whack, whang 6 bounce, cudgel, energy, strike, thrash, thunge, thwack 7 sardine, surpass 8 forelock
into: hit 5 crash 7 collide
bang-up: 5 crack 6 tiptop 9 first-rate
bangle: 4 flap, roam 5 droop, waste 7 circlet, fritter, trinket 8 bracelet, ornament
Bani's son: Uel 4 Amzi 5 Amram
banish: ban 5 eject, exile, expel, fleme 6 bandit, deport, dispel, forsay, outlaw 7 abandon, condemn, dismiss, exclude 8 displace, relegate 9 ostracize, proscribe, transport 10 expatriate, repatriate
banished: 8 fugitive
banister: 7 railing 8 baluster 10 balustrade
bank: bar, bay, cop, rim, row 4 bink, brae, brew, caja, dike, dune, dyke, edge, hill, mass, pile, ramp, rive, sand, seat, tier, weir 5 banco, bench, bluff, brink, fence, levee, marge, mound, ridge, stack, share, shelf, shoal, shore, slope, stage, trust 6 causey, degree, depend, margin, reckon, rivage, strand 7 anthill, deposit, pottery, shallow 8 barranca, barranco, platform 9 acclivity, 10 depository, elevation, embankment
clerk: 6 teller
examiner: 10 accountant
requirement: 5 funds, money 6 assets 7 surplus 8 deposits
river: 4 ripa
bankroll: wad 5 bills 8 currency
bankrupt: sap 4 bung 5 broke, drain, smash, strip 6 busted, devour, ruined.

quisby 7 failure 8 beggarly, depleted 9 destitute, insolvent 12 impoverished

banner: 4 fane, flag, jack 5 color 6 ensign, fannon, pennon 7 leading, pennant, salient 8 banderol, foremost, gonfalon, standard, vexillum 9 banderole, exemplary, oriflamme 10 surpassing

banns: 4 bans 6 notice 12 proclamation

banquet: 4 fete, meal 5 feast 6 dinner, junket, regale, repast 8 carousal, festival
room: 8 cenacula(pl.) 9 cenaculum

banquette: way 4 seat 5 shelf 7 footway 8 platform, sidewalk 10 embankment

banshee: fay 5 fairy, sidhe 6 goblin

bant: 4 diet, fast 6 reduce

bantam: 4 cock 5 saucy 7 chicken 9 combative 10 diminutive
breed: 8 Sebright

banteng: ox 5 tsine

banter: kid, rag 4 fool, jest, joke, josh, mock, quiz, rail 5 borak, chaff, rally, roast, trick 6 delude, deride, haggle, satire 7 badiner, stashie 8 badinage, chaffing, raillery, ridicule 10 persiflage, pleasantry

bantering: 9 quizzical

bantling: 5 child 6 infant

Bantu: *dialect:* 6 Chwana 8 Sechuana
language: Ila 4 Suto 5 Ronga 6 Thonga 7 Nyanaja 8 Nyamwezi 10 Wanymawezi
people: 4 Baya, Bihe, Bule, Fang, Gogo, Gola, Guha, Hehe, Jaga, Luba, Maka, Nama, Vira, Yaka, Zulu 5 Duala, Kafir 6 Banyai, Damara, Kaffir, Waguha, Yakala 7 Swahili, Wachaga 8 Bechuana

banxring: 4 tana 6 tupaia

banyan: bur 4 burr 6 banian

banzai: cry 6 attack

baobab: 4 tree 7 tebeldi

baptism: 9 aspersion, cleansing, immersion 11 christening
robe: 7 Chrisom
vessel: 4 font 6 fontal, spring 7 piscina
water: 5 laver

baptize: dip 4 full, name 5 heave 6 purify 7 cleanse 8 christen, sprinkle

bar: ban, dam, fid, gad, law, rod 4 axle, band, bank, beam, bolt, cake, gate, hide, joke, lock, oust, pole, rail, reef, save, shut, stop 5 arbor, bench, bilco, block, close, court, deter, estop, fence, hedge, lever, perch, shade, shaft, strap, strip 6 billet, brooch, except, fasten, grille, hinder, meagre, saloon, stripe 7 barrage, barrier, confine, counter, exclude, prevent 8 conclude, handicap, obstacle, obstruct, preclude, prohibit, restrain, restrict, surround, tribunal 9 barricade, fastening, gatehouse, hindrance, interpose, ostracize 10 crosspiece, difficulty, impediment, inhibition, portcullis 11 obstruction
acrobat: 7 trapeze
bullion: 5 ingot
legally: 5 estop
millstone: 4 rynd
resisting pressure: 5 strut
supporting: fid, rod 9 stanchion
tamping: 7 stemmer
window: 5 jemmy, jimmy 7 forcing

barb: awn, bur, jag, mow 4 burr, clip, file, flue, hair, herl, hook, jagg 5 beard, horse, point, ridge 6 pigeon 7 bristle 8 kingfish 9 appendage 10 projection
anchor: 4 flue
feather: 4 harl, herl 5 ramus 7 pinnula, pinnule 8 pinnulae

Barbados: *capital:* 10 Bridgetown
liquor: rum
native: Bim

barbarian: Hun 4 boor, Goth, rude, wild 5 alien, brute 6 savage, vandal 7 ruffian 9 foreigner, untutored 10 Philistine, unlettered 11 uncivilized
North African: 6 Berber

barbarism: 4 cant 8 savagism, solecism 10 savageness

barbarity: 6 ferity 7 cruelty 8 ferocity, rudeness, savagery 9 brutality 10 inhumanity

barbarous: 4 fell, rude, wild 5 cruel 6 brutal 7 foreign, Hunnish, inhuman, slavish, uncivil 8 ignorant 9 ferocious, primitive 10 illiterate, outlandish, tramontane, unpolished 11 uncivilized 12 uncultivated

Barbary: ape 5 magot 6 simian
sheep: 6 aoudad
states: 5 Tunis 7 Algiers, Morocco, Tripoli

barbecue: 4 bake 5 broil, grill
rod: 4 spit 6 skewer

barbed: 4 bent 6 hooked 8 uncinate

barber: 6 Figaro, poller, shaver, tonsor 7 scraper, tonsure 11 chirotonsor

barber's itch: 8 ringworm

bard: 4 poet, scop 5 druid, runer, scald 6 singer 8 minstrel, musician
India: 4 bhat

Bard of Avon: 11 Shakespeare

bardy: 4 bold 7 defiant 9 audacious

bare: 4 bald, mere, nude 5 alone, crude, empty, naked, plain, stark, strip 6 barren, callow, denude, divert, divest, expose, histie, meager, meagre, paltry, pilled, reveal, simple 7 divulge, exposed, unarmed, uncover 8 desolate, disclose, stripped 9 unadorned, uncovered, worthless 10 threadbare 11 defenseless, unconcealed, unfurnished 13 unaccompanied

bare skin: 4 buff

barefaced: 7 glaring 8 impudent 9 audacious, shameless 11 undisguised
barefooted: 6 unshod 9 discalced
barely: 4 only 5 faint 6 hardly, merely, poorly 8 scantily, scarcely, slightly 13 unqualifiedly 14 insufficiently
barfly: 5 drunk, stiff 8 carouser
bargain: 4 deal, huck, mise, pact, pick, sale, sell 5 cheap, fight 6 barter, dicker, haggle, higglo, palter 7 chaffer, compact, contend, contest, traffic 8 contract, covenant, purchase, struggle 9 agreement, negotiate, situation, stipulate 10 engagement 11 transaction
bargain-basement: 5 cheap 6 tawdry
bargain for: 6 expect
barge: ark, box, boy, tow, tub 4 bark, boat, pram, raft, scow 5 foist, lunge, lurch, praam, scold, shrew, vixen 6 barque, berate, praham, rebuke, thrust, tender, vessel 7 gabbard, gabbart, gondola, lighter, omnibus 9 houseboat, interfere
charge: 10 lighterage
coal: 4 keel
bargeman: pug 6 bargee 7 huffler
barium sulphate: 6 barite
bark: bag, bay, rub, wap, yap, yip 4 boat, coat, howl, husk, peel, pelt, pill, rind, ross, ship, skin, yawp 5 balat, barca, barge, cough, shell, shout, strip 6 abrade, cortex, girdle, vessel 7 solicit, tanbark 8 cortices, covering
aromatic: 6 sintoc 7 canella 9 sassafras
at: 5 scold 6 rebuke
cloth: 4 tapa 5 tappa 8 mulberry
covered with: 9 corticate 10 corticated
medicinal: 4 coto 5 casca, madar, nudar, niepa 7 quinine 8 cinchona 9 sassafras
outer: 8 periderm
pert. to: 8 cortical
remove: 4 ross 5 scale
resembling: 8 cortical
rough: 4 ross
tanning: 5 alder
up the wrong tree: err 5 stray
barkeeper: 6 barman 7 tapster
barker: dog 6 jumper, pistol, tanner 7 spieler 9 solicitor
barking: 4 spud 7 latrant 9 latration
barking deer: 7 muntjac, muntjak
barley: 5 grain
ground: 6 tsamba
pert. to: 11 hordeaceous
steep: 4 malt
variety: big 4 bere, bigg
barman: 7 tapster 9 barkeeper, barrister 11 metalworker
barmy: 5 foamy, silly 6 frothy, yeasty 7 flighty, foolish, idiotic
barn: 4 byre 5 stall 6 stable 10 storehouse
storage area: bag, mow 4 loft 7 hayloft
barn dance official: 6 caller
barnacle: *genus:* 5 Lepas
plate: 5 terga(pl.), 6 tergum
barnstorm: 4 tour
barometric line: 6 isobar
baron: 4 peer 5 noble 7 freeman
baronet: sir 8 commoner
barony: han 4 rank 6 domain 7 dignity
baroque: 6 ornate, rococo 9 grotesque, irregular 11 extravagant
barrack: 4 camp 6 casern 7 cuartel(Sp.), 8 quarters
barraclade: 7 blanket
barracuda: 4 fish, spet 5 barry, pelon 6 becuna, picuda, sennet 10 guaguanche 12 guanchepelon
barrage: bar 6 attack, volley 7 barrier 9 cannonade 10 barricuade, obtruction
barranca, barranco: 4 bank 5 bluff 6 ravine
barras: 5 linen 7 galipot 8 gallipot
barrator: 5 bully, rowdy 7 fighter
barred: 6 ribbed 7 striped
barrel: fat, keg, tun, vat 4 butt, cade, cask, drum, knag 6 runlet, tierce, vessel 7 cistern, rundlet 8 cylinder, hogshead 9 container, kilderkin
herring: 4 cade
maker: 6 cooper
part: 4 side, hoop 5 stave
raising device: 9 parbuckle
stopper: 4 bung
support: 4 hoop 6 gantry 7 gauntry
barren: dry 4 arid, bare, dull, gast, geld 5 blunt, drape, empty, gaunt, stark, stern 6 desert, effete, fallow, histie, hungry, jejune, meager, stupid 7 sterile 8 impotent, treeless 9 exhausted, fruitless, infertile, penurious 10 unfruitful 12 unproductive, unprofitable
barren oak: 9 blackjack
barren privet: 7 alatern 9 houseleek
barrette: bar 8 ornament
barricade: bar 4 stop 5 block, close, fence 6 abatis, prison 7 barrage, defense, fortify 9 roadblock 11 obstruction 13 fortification
Barrie character: 5 Peter, Wendy
barrier: bar, dam 4 door, gate, line, wall, weir 5 bound, chain, fence, hedge, limit 6 hurdle, screen 7 barrage, parapet, railing 8 boundary, fortress, frontier, stockade 9 palisades, restraint 10 difficulty, partcullis, tournament 11 obstruction
movable: 4 bars, door 5 blind, shade 6 window 7 certain 8 shutters
barring: 4 save 6 except 7 without
barrio: 4 slum 6 ghetto 7 village

barrister: 6 barman, lawyer 7 counsel 8 advocate, attorney
barroom: pub 4 cafe 6 saloon 7 cantina(Sp.), doggery 8 dramshop, exchange
barrow: hod, hog 4 bank, dune, hill, mote 5 grave, gurry, mound 6 tumuli 7 hillock, trolley, tumulus 8 mountain
bartender: 7 tapster
barter: 4 chap, chop, cope, coup, hawk, sell, swap, vend 5 corse, trade, troke, truck 6 dicker 7 bargain, cambium, permute, traffic 8 commerce, exchange 9 excambion 11 reciprocate
Bartered Bride composer: 7 Smetana
bartizan: 6 turret 7 lookout
bas: low
bas-relief: 9 plaquette
basal: 5 basic 7 basilar 11 fundamental
basalt: 6 marble, navite 7 pottery
base: bed, low 4 clam, evil, foot, foul, lewd, mean, poor, root, stem, step, vile 5 basis, cheap, dirty, muddy, petty, snide 6 abject, bottom, common, ground, menial, paltry, podium, shabby, sordid, vulgar 7 bastard, caitiff, comical, debased, hangdog, hilding, housing, ignoble, servile, slavish, support 8 coistrel, coistril, degraded, infamous, inferior, pedestal, scullion, shameful, stepping, unworthy, wretched 9 absorbent, degrading, establish, worthless 10 despicable, foundation, villainous 11 ignominious 12 contemptible, dishonorable, disreputable 13 dishonourable
architectural: 5 socle 6 plinth
attached by: 7 sessile
military: HDQ 4 camp 5 depot 12 headquarters
structural: 6 plinth
base hit: 6 bingle, single
base on balls: 4 pass, walk
baseball: *field:* 7 diamond
founder: 9 Doubleday
hit: 4 bunt
official: ump 5 coach 6 umpire 7 manager
team: 4 nine
term: bag, bat, box, fan, fly, hit, lob, low, out, peg, RBI, run, tap, top 4 ball, bean, beat, bunt, burn, deck, foul, high, hill, hole, home, hook, miss, pill, pole, sack, save, turn, walk, wild 5 alley, apple, bench, booth, clout, coach, count, curve, drive, error, field, first, force, frame, glove, homer, lined, mound, pitch, plate, popup, punch, score, slide, swing, third 6 assist, batter, bungle, bottom, charge, clutch, double, dugout, groove, hitter, inside, lifted, lumber, middle, popout, putout, rubber, runner, screen, second, series, single, sinker, stance, strike, string, target, triple, wind-up 7 arbited, arbiter, battery, blooper, bullpen, circuit, cleanup, diamond, fielder, floater, infield, manager, nothing, outside, pitcher, side-arm, squeeze, stretch, thumbed 8 delivery, grounded, grounder, knuckler, outfield, pinch-hit, powdered, soupbone, spitball 9 full-count, hot corner, sacrifice, smothered, strike-out, two-bagger 10 scratch-hit 11 three-bagger
baseless: 4 idle 9 unfounded 10 gratuitous, groundless
basement: 4 base 6 cellar
bash: bat, lam 4 beat, blow, dent, mash, swat, wham, whop 5 abash, smash 6 bruise, strike
Bashan king: Og
Bashemath's husband: 4 Esau
bashful: coy, shy 4 helo 5 blate, heloe, timid 6 modest 7 daunted 8 backward, blushing, dismayed, retiring, sheepish, verecund 9 diffident, shrinking
Bashkir capital: Ufa
basic: 5 basal, vital 7 central 9 elemental 11 fundamental 13 indispensable
basil: 4 herb 5 plant, royal 6 fetter
basilica: 6 canopy, church, shrine, temple 7 Lateran
part of: 4 apse
basin: pan 4 bowl, dish, dock, ewer, font, tank 5 laver, stoup 6 chafer, marina, valley, vessel 7 cuvette, piscina 8 lavatory, receptor, washbowl 9 reservoir 10 aspersoria, depression 11 aspersorium
geological: 4 tala
basis: 4 base, fund, root, sill 5 axiom 6 bottom, ground 7 footing, premise, support 10 foundation, groundwork
bask: sun 4 beek, warm 5 acrid, bathe, enjoy, revel 6 bitter 7 rejoice 9 luxuriate
basket: ark, fan, ped 4 kipe, trug 5 cassy(Sc.), cesta, chest, crate, scull 6 cassie, coffin, dorsel, dorser, dosser, gabion, hamper, hoppet, panier 7 canasta, hanaper, pannier, scuttle 9 container 10 receptacle
coal mine: 4 corf
eel: 4 buck
fig: 4 caba 5 frail 6 tapnet
fire: 5 grate 7 cresset
fish: pot 4 caul, cawl, corf, hask, skip, weel 5 creel, crate, maund 6 courge, gabion, hamper 7 pannier
fruit: 6 pottle, funnet
material: 5 otate
twig: 6 wattle
water-tight: 7 wattape
wicker: cob 4 cobb, coop 5 willy 6 hamper 7 hanaper 8 bassinet
willow: 5 osier 7 prickle
work: 4 caba 5 cabas, slath 6 slarth

basket-ball team: 4 five 7 cagemen

Basque: 5 waist 6 scoter 7 Iberian
cap: 5 beret
dance: 7 auresca 8 aurrescu, zortzico
game: 6 pelota
language: 6 Uskara 7 Eskuara, Euskara, Euskera
people: 7 Euscara, Euscaro
petticoat: 8 basquine
province: 5 Alava 6 Biscay

bass: low 4 deep, fish 5 voice 6 singer 7 achigan, jewfish

bassinet: 6 basket, cradle

basswood: lin 4 bast 5 tilia 6 linden

bast: 4 bark, flax, hemp, jute 5 fiber, ramie 6 phloem 8 piassava

basta: 4 stop 6 enough

bastard: 4 base 5 false 6 cannon, galley, hybrid, impure 7 byspell, lowbred, mongrel 8 bantling, spurious 10 artificial 11 adulterated 12 illegitimate

baste: sew 4 beat, cane, cook, drub, lard, tack 6 cudgel, punish, stitch, thrash

bastion: *defensive:* 4 fort 13 fortification
shoulder: 6 epaule

bat: hit, wad 4 bate, beat, club, gait, lump, mass, swat, wink 5 brick, piece, spree, stick 6 aliped, backie(Sc.), baston, beetle, cudgel, racket, strike, stroke 7 flutter, noctule, vampire 8 bludgeon, serotine 9 reremouse 10 battledore, chiroptera, packsaddle 11 rattlemouse 12 chauvesouris, flittermouse
around: 4 roam 6 ponder 7 debate
European: 9 barbastel 11 barbastelle
species: 9 pipistrel 11 pipistrelle

Bataan: *bay:* 5 Subic
city: 7 Balanga

Batavia: 7 Jakarta 8 Djarkarta

batch: lot 4 mass, mess, sort 5 group 6 baking 7 mixture 8 quantity 10 collection

bateau: 4 boat

batfish: 6 diablo

bath: dip 4 bate, pert 5 therm 6 plunge, shower 7 balneum 8 ablution 10 natatorium
comb. form: 6 balneo
pert. to: 7 balneal
public: 7 piscine
sponge: 5 luffa 6 loofah
treatment by: 13 balneotherapy

Bath river: 4 Avon

bathe: bay, tub 4 bask, lave, stew, wash 5 embay 6 enwrap 7 immerse, pervade, suffuse 8 permeate

bathhouse: 6 cabana 8 balneary

bathing suit: 6 bikini, trunks 7 maillot

bathos: 8 comedown 10 anticlimax

bathroom: W.C.(abbr.) 6 hammam 8 sudatory 10 sudatorium 11 water closet

Bathsheba: *husband:* 5 Uriah
son: 7 Solomon

baton: rod 4 bend 5 staff, stick 6 baston, cudgel 7 bourdon, scepter, sceptre 9 truncheon

batrachian: 4 frog, toad

batsman: 6 batter, hitter 7 striker

batten: 6 enrich, fatten, thrive 9 fertilize

batter: ram 4 beat, dent, maim 5 clour, dinge, frush, paste, pound 6 bruise, hammer, hatter, hitter, pummel 7 batsman, bombard, cripple, destroy, shatter, striker 8 demolish

battery: *floating:* 4 cell 5 praam 7 parapet 9 artillery 11 bombardment
plate: 4 grid

battle: war 4 duel, fray, meet, tilt 5 brush, fight, joust 6 action, affray, combat 7 contend, contest, hosting, warfare 8 conflict, skirmish, struggle 9 encounter 10 engagement, tournament 11 competition
area: 5 arena, front 6 sector 7 terrain
cry: 6 slogan 9 catchword
formation: 5 herse 6 deploy
line: 5 front
order: 7 regalia 8 battalia
royal: 5 melee 9 scrimmage
site: 6 Shiloh 7 Bull Run 8 Manassas 10 Armageddon, Gettysburg
trophy: 5 medal, scalp 6 ribbon

Battle Hymn of the Republic author: 4 Howe

battleship: 7 carrier 11 dreadnaught 16 superdreadnaught

battologize: 6 repeat 7 iterate

batty: 5 crazy, silly 7 batlike, foolish

bauble: bow, toy 4 bead, gaud 6 button, gewgaw, trifle 7 trinket 8 gimcrack 9 plaything 10 knickknack

bauxite derivative: 8 aluminum

Bavaria: *beer:* 10 Wurzburger
city: Hof 6 Munich(c.), 8 Augsburg, Nurnberg, Ratisbon, Wurzburg 10 Regensburg
community: 6 Passau
division: 7 Neuburg 8 Schwaben 9 Franconia 10 Palatinate, Regensburg 13 Aschaffenburg
lake: 4 Wurm 5 Ammer, Chiem 8 Starbber
measure: 4 fass, fuss, rute 5 linie, metze, ruthe 6 massel, morgen 7 juchert, tagwerk 10 dreissiger
mountain: 6 Vosges 8 Watzmann 9 Zugspitze
river: Inn, Nab 4 Eger, Isar, Iser, Lech 5 Iller, Regen, Saale 7 Altmuhl, Wornitz
university site: 8 Erlangen
weight: 4 gran 9 quentchen

bawd: 4 aunt, hare 5 dirty 6 defile 7 commode 8 procurer 9 procuress 10 fruitwoman
bawdry: 5 mirth 6 filthy, finery, gaiety, gayety 9 obscenity
bawdy: 4 foul, lewd 5 dirty 7 obscene 8 unchaste
bawl: cry 4 howl 5 golly, shout 6 bellow, boohoo, outcry 8 glaister 10 vociferate
out: 5 scold 9 reprimand
bawling: 10 vociferous
bay: dam, ria, voe 4 bank, bark, cove, gulf, hole, hope, howl, loch(Sc.), roan, tree, yaup, yawp 5 bahia(Sp.), berry, bight, color, creek, fiord, fjord, fleet, haven, horse, oriel, sinus 6 laurel, recess, window 7 enclose, estuary, silanga, ululate 11 compartment, indentation
bird: 5 snipe 6 curlew, godwit, plover
camphor: 6 laurin
Bay State: 13 Massachusetts
bayard: 5 horse
bayardly: 5 blind 6 stupid
Baylor University site: 4 Waco
bayonet: 4 stab 5 knife 6 pierce, weapon
bayou: 5 brook, creek, inlet, river 6 outlet, stream 7 rivulet 9 backwater
Bayou State: 11 Mississippi
bazaar, bazar: 4 fair, fete, sale 5 agora, burse 6 market 7 canteen 8 emporium 9 bezesteen 10 exposition
bazoo: 4 talk 5 kazoo, mouth
be: are 4 live 5 abide, exist, occur 6 remain 7 breathe, subsist 8 continue
beach: 4 bank, moor, ripa, sand 5 coast, plage(F.), playa(Sp.), shore 6 ground, shilla, strand 7 hardway, seaside, shingle
beachcomber: 7 vagrant 8 vagabond
beachhead: van 7 landing 8 foothold
beacon: 4 mark, sign 5 baken, fanal, guide, phare 6 ensign, pharos, signal 7 cresset, seamark, warning 8 signpost 10 lighthouse, watchtower
light: 7 cresset, lantern
Beaconsfield: 8 Disraeli
bead: 4 drop, foam 5 sewan, sight 6 bauble, bubble, prayer, wampum 7 globule, molding, sparkle, trinket
string: 6 rosary 7 chaplet 8 necklace
beadel: 5 crier, macer, usher 6 bedell, bumble, herald 7 bailiff, officer 8 servitor, summoner 9 apparitor, messenger 10 mace-bearer
beadsman, bedesman: 6 beggar, hermit 10 petitioner
beady: 5 round, small 8 globular 10 glistening
beak: neb, nib 4 bill, nose, prow 5 lorum, snout 6 master, speron 7 molding, rostrum 8 mandible 10 magistrate 11 stipendiary
ship's: bow, ram 4 prow
without: 9 erostrate
beaker: cup 4 tass 5 bocal, bouse, glass 6 bareca, bareka, vessel
beam: bar, ray 4 balk, emit, glow, I-bar, sile(Sc), stud, T-bar 5 arbor, caber, flash, gleam, gleed, joist, light, shine, smile 6 binder, girder, rafter, timber, walker 7 bumpkin, chevron, radiate, support, trimmer 10 architrave
beaming: gay 4 rosy 6 bright, lucent 7 radiant, shining
beamy: 5 broad 6 joyous, lucent 7 massive, radiant 8 mirthful
bean: urd 4 chap, gram, head, Lima, pole 5 brain, skull 6 caster, collar, fellow, kidney, lentil, nipple, noggin, strike, thrash, trifle 7 calabar, frijole(Sp.) 11 castigation
Asian: 4 gram 5 mungo
climbing: 4 lima, pole
cluster: 4 guar
eye: 4 hila 5 hilum
kind: goa, soy, wax 4 lima, navy 6 castor, kidney, string 7 calabar
lima: 4 haba 5 sieva
locust: 5 carob
lubricant: ben
Mexican: 6 frejol, frijol 7 frijole
poisonous 4 loco 7 calabar
bean shooter: 8 catapult 9 slingshot
Bean Town: 6 Boston
bear: cub, lug 4 gest, tote, ursa 5 abide, allow, beget, breed, bring, brook, brown, bruin, carry, drive, geste, koala, Polar, press, stand, yield 6 afford, behave, endure, kadiak, kodiak, pierce, render, suffer, thrust, uphold 7 comport, conduct, forbear, grizzly, produce, support, sustain, undergo 8 forebear, tolerate 9 carnivore, transport 13 constellation
Alaskan: 6 kadiak, kodiak
genus 5 ursus
bear bane: 9 wolfsbane
bear bush: 8 inkberry
bear cat: 4 paud 9 binturong
bear down: 5 exert, press 6 stress 8 approach
bear-shaped: 8 ursiform
Bear State: 8 Arkansas
bear upon: 6 affect 7 concern
beard: ane, awn 4 avel, barb, defy 6 arista, goatee 7 affront, aristae, Vandyke 8 whiskers
grain: awn
bearded: 5 hairy 6 barbed 7 barbate, hirsute 9 whiskered 11 barbigerous

grain: rye **5** awned, wheat **8** aristate

bearer: **5** macer **6** beadle, porter **7** carrier **8** escudero, portator **9** supporter **10** pallbearer **11** gonfalonier

bearing: aim, air **4** gest, mien, orle, port **5** birth, front, geste, habit, poise, trend **6** allure, apport, aspect, course, gerent, manner, orient, thrust **7** address, conduct, meaning, posture, purport, support **8** amenance, attitude, behavior, carriage, demeanor, pressure, relation, tendency, yielding **9** behaviour, demeanour, direction, gestation, influence, personage, producing **10** cognizance, deportment **11** comportment, countenance **12** significance.

fine: **6** belair

heraldic: **4** ente, orle **5** pheon

plate: gib

beast: **4** bete(F.) **5** brute **6** animal **7** monster **8** blighter **9** quadriped

mythical: **4** ogre, Rahu **5** Apepi, giant, harpy, hydra, Rahab **6** dragon, ellops, Empusa, garuda, Geryon, gorgon, Kraken, scylla, sphinx, triton **7** centaur, chimera, echidna, figfaun, griffin, griffon **8** chimaera, minotaur **9** bucentaur **10** jabberwock **11** chichevache

pertaining to: **7** leonine

royal **4** lion

beast fly: **6** gadfly

beast of burden: ox; ass, yak **5** burro, camel, horse, llama **6** donkey, onager

beastly: **5** gross **6** brutal **7** bestial, brutish, inhuman, swinish **9** offensive **10** abominable, disgusting

beat: KO; bat, cob, dad, fan, fib, tap, taw, tew **4** baff, bang, bash, bate, belt, best, blow, bolt, bray, cane, chap, club, daud, ding, dint, drub, dump, dunt, fell, flap, flax, flog, frat, haze, lash, lump, maul, mill, pant, pelt, poss, prat, rout, scat, slam, tack, tick, tund, whip, whop **5** baste, berry, churn, clink, douse, feeze, fight, filch, flail, knock, pound, pulse, round, scatt, scoop, skelp, strap, threp, throb, thump, trump, whang, worst **6** accent, batter, beetle, bensel, buffet, cotton, cudgel, defeat, dowsel, feague, fettle, hammer, hamper, larrup, outrun, pummel, raddle, rhythm, squash, strike, stroke, swinge, switch, thrash, threap, threip, threpe, thresh **7** assault, battuta, belabor, blister, cadence, canvass, conquer, contuse, exhaust, fatigue, pulsate, reeshie, shellac, surpass, trounce, vibrate **8** belabour, fatigued, lambaste, overcome, shellack, slaister, vanquish **9** exhausted, pulsation, throbbing **10** assignment

back: **7** repulse

into plate: **8** malleate

beat it: **4** scat **5** scram **7** vamoose

beater: rab **4** maul, seal **5** caner, lacer **6** dasher, mallet **8** thresher **9** scrutcher

beatify: **6** hallow **7** enchant, glorify **8** sanctify

beatitude: joy **5** bliss **7** benison **9** happiness **11** blessedness

beau: **5** beaux(pl.), blade, dandy, flame, lover, spark, swell **6** garcon, escort, fellow, steady, suitor **7** admirer, bravery, courter, coxcomb, cupidon, gallant **8** follower

Beau Brummell: fop **5** dandy **7** coxcomb

beau geste: **5** favor

beau ideal: **5** model **8** paradigm

beau monde: **7** fashion, society

beaut: **4** lulu

beautician: **10** beautifier, cosmetiste(F.) **11** cosmetician

beautifier: **8** cosmetic

beautiful: **4** fair, fine, glad, mear, meer, mere **5** belle, bonny **6** blithe, bonnie, comely, decore, freely, lovely, poetic, pretty **7** elegant **8** charming, delicate, fairsome, gorgeous, graceful, handsome **9** exquisite

comb. form: bel **4** calo **5** calli

beautify: **4** gild **5** adorn, grace, hight, preen, primp, prune **6** bedeck **7** adonize, garnish **8** decorate, fairhead **9** embellish

beauty: **5** belle, charm, grace **6** looker, polish **10** comeliness, goodliness, loveliness **11** pulchritude

goddess: Sri **5** Freya, Venus **6** Freyja **7** Lakshmi **9** Aphrodite

lover: **7** esthete **9** aesthete

beaver: hat **4** coin **6** castor, rodent

cloth: **6** kersey

eater: **9** wolverine

skin: **4** plew

Beaver State: **6** Oregon

because: as, so; for **4** that **5** since **8** inasmuch

because of that: **7** thereby **9** therefore

bechance: **6** befall, chance

beche-de-mer: **4** grub, worm **6** pidgin **7** trepang **8** language

beck: vat **5** becon, brook

becken: **7** cymbals

beckon: bow, nod **4** wave **6** curtsy, summon **7** bidding, command, curtsey, gesture **10** salutation

becloud: **4** hide **5** bedim **6** darken **7** mystify, obscure **8** befuddle, overcast

become: get, wax **4** grow, pass, suit **5** adorn, befit, grace **6** accord, befall, beseem, betide, change **7** behoove, flatter

becoming: 4 good 5 right 6 comely, gainly 7 decorum, farrand, farrant 8 decorous, handsome, suitable 10 convenient 11 appropriate
becscie: 9 merganser
becuna: 9 barracuda
bed: cot, pad 4 base, bunk, doss, lair, plot 5 berth, couch, layer 6 bottom, couche(F.), litter, matrix, pallet, strata 7 channel, lodging, stratum 8 matrices, plancher 9 basegrave, stretcher 10 apishamore, foundation
feather: tye
small: cot 4 crib 6 cradle, pallet 7 hammock, truckle, trundle 8 bassinet
straw: 9 shakedown
bed stay: 4 slat
bedbug: 5 cimex 6 chinch 7 cimice(pl.) 8 conenose
bedding: 6 quilts, sheets 8 blankets 10 bedclothes
bedeck: gem 4 lard 5 adorn, array, dight, grace 8 ornament 9 embellish
bedevil: 5 abuse, annoy, worry 6 muddle, pester 7 bewitch, confuse, torment
bedim: fog 4 mist 5 cloud 6 darken 7 becloud, obscure
bedizen: 4 daub 5 adorn, array, dizen 6 bedaub 9 overdress
bedlam: 4 riot 5 noise, rudas(Sc.) 6 asylum, madman, tumult, uproar 7 lunatic, madness 8 madhouse 9 confusion
Bedouin: 4 Arab, Moor 5 nomad
head cord: 4 agal
official: 4 cadi 5 sheik
tribe: 4 Harb
bedridden: ill 6 ailing
bedrock: 5 nadir 6 bottom
bedroll: 6 bindle
bedroom: 4 flat 5 berth, cabin 11 compartment
bee: dor, fly 4 apis, ring 5 party 6 dingar, insect, notion, torque 7 stinger 9 gathering 11 hymenoptera 12 hymenopteron
colony of: 5 swarm, yeast
comb. form: api
family: 5 apina 6 apidae
female: 5 queen
genus: 4 apis
girl named for: 7 Melissa
house: gum 4 butt, hive, scap, skep 6 apiary 7 alveary, bee-butt 9 alvearium
house covering: 6 hackle
male: 5 drone
nose: 4 lora(pl.) 5 lorum
pert. to: 8 apiarian
pollen brush: 5 scopa 6 scopae(pl.), 9 sarothrum
beebread: 8 ambrosia
beech: 4 buck, tree 6 myrtle
genus: 5 fagus
beechnut: 4 mast
beef: 4 meat 5 gripe 8 complain
cut: 4 loin, rump, side 5 baron, chine, chuck, flank, roast, round, shank, steak 6 cutlet, saddle 7 brisket, knuckle, quarter, sirloin 8 short-rib, shoulder 9 aitchbone, rattleran 11 porterhouse
dried: 5 bucan, jerky, vifda, vivda 6 buccan 7 charqui
pickled: 5 bully
salted: 4 junk
spiced: 8 pastroma, pastromi
beefy: 5 hefty, heavy 6 brawny, fleshy, stolid
Beehive State: 4 Utah
beekeeper: 8 apiarist, skeppist 12 apiculturist
been: be; see
beep: 4 tone, toot 6 signal
beer: ale, mum 4 bock, brew, grog, scud(Sc.) 5 kvass, lager, stout 6 liquor, porter, stingo, swanky 8 beverage
barley: 5 chang
cask: 4 butt
ingredient: 4 hops, malt
king: 9 Gambrinus
maize: 5 chica 6 chicha
mug: see *vessel,* below
shop: pub 6 saloon
unfermented: 4 wort
vessel: mug 4 Toby 5 stein 6 flagon, seidel, tanker 8 schooner 9 blackjack
beer and skittles: fun 4 play
beery: 7 maudlin, muddled
beeswax substitute: 7 ceresin
beet: 5 chard, sugar 6 mangel 8 beetrave 9 vegetable
genus: 4 beta
Beethoven: *birthplace:* 4 Bonn
opera: 7 Fidelio
symphony: 5 fifth, first, ninth, sixth, third 6 eighth, Eroica, fourth, second 7 seventh 8 Pastoral
beetle: bat, bug, jut, ram 4 beat, goga, gogo, maul, stag 5 amara, drive, gogga, hispa, meloe 6 chafer, golach, goloch, jutout, mallet, pestle, scarab, weevil 7 prinoid, project 8 lowering, overhang 9 prioninae(pl.) 10 battledore, projecting
bark: 5 borer
bright: 7 ladybug
family: 10 elateridae 11 clavicornes, clavicornia
fire: 6 cucuyo
genus: 5 fidia
grain: 7 cadelle
grapevine: 6 thrips

ground: 5 amara
horny substance of: 6 chitin
mustard: 9 blackjack
rhinoceros: 4 uang
sacred: 6 scarab
wing cover: 5 shard
wood: 6 sawyer
beetle-browed: 6 morose 8 scowling
beetle-head: 6 plover 9 blockhead
befall: hap 4 come 5 occur 6 astart, become, betide, happen 7 pertain 8 bechance
befile: 4 soil 6 defile
befit: dow 4 suit 5 beset 6 become, behove, beseem, betide 7 behoove
beflum: 7 deceive
befog: 5 cloud 6 obsane 7 confuse, mystify
before: ere 4 said 5 ahead, afore, avant, coram(L.), first, forby, front, prior 6 forbye, former, rather, sooner 7 already, earlier, forward 8 anterior, hitherto 10 beforehand, heretofore, previously
prefix: pre, pro 4 ante, prae
before long: 4 anon, soon 9 presently
before now: ere 4 gone, over 6 erenow
befoul: 4 soil 5 dirty 6 bemire, defile 7 pollute 8 entangle 11 contaminate
befriend: aid 4 abet, help 5 favor 6 assist, favour, foster, succor 7 benefit, support, sustain 11 countenance
befuddle: 5 addle, besot 6 muddle 7 becloud, confuse, fluster, mystify, stupefy
beg: ask, bid, sue, woo 4 coax, pray, sorn(Sc.) 5 cadge, crave, mooch, plead 6 adjure 7 beseech, entreat, implore, request, solicit 8 petition 9 importune, panhandle 10 supplicate
beget: ean 4 bear, sire 5 breed, yield 6 author, create, father 7 acquire, engraff 8 engender, generate 9 germinate, procreate
begetter: 4 sire 6 author, father, mother, parent
beggar: 4 ruin 5 asker, randy, rogue 6 alsman, bacach, bidder, canter, devour, mumper, pariah, pauper, wretch 8 palliard, stroller 9 maunderer, mendicant, schnorrer, suppliant 10 impoverish, panhandler, petitioner, starveling 12 hallan-shaker
saint: 5 Giles
speech: 4 cant
beggarly: 4 mean, poor 5 cheap, petty, sorry 6 abject, paltry 8 bankrupt, indigent 10 despicable 12 contemptible
Beggar's Opera author: Gay 6 Brecht
begin: 4 fang, lead, open, rise 5 arise, enter, start 6 attack, spring 8 commence, inchoate, initiate 9 institute, introduce, originate 10 inaugurate
begin again: 4 anew, over 5 renew 6 resume 7 restart
beginner: 4 boot, tiro, tyro 5 rooky 6 novice, rookie 7 amateur, entrant, noviate, recruit, trainee, student 8 freshman, neophyte 9 candidate, debutante, postulate, 10 apprentice
beginning: egg 4 dawn, edge, germ, rise, root, seed 5 alpha, birth, debut, start 6 source 7 genesis, geneses(pl.), initial, nascent 8 entrance, exordium, inchoate, rudiment 9 embryonic, inception, incipient 10 conception, foundation, incunabula(pl.), initiation 11 incunabulum 12 commencement
begone: off, out 4 away, scat, shoo 5 scoot, scram 6 aroint, avaunt, depart 7 vamoose
begrudging: 6 loathe, grudge 7 envious, grumble 9 reluctant
beguile: fox 4 coax, foil, gull, lure 5 amuse, charm, cheat, cozen, elude, evade, trick 6 brique, delude, divert, entrap 7 deceive, ensnare, flatter, mislead 9 entertain
behalf: 4 part, sake, side 5 stead 6 affair, matter, profit 7 benefit, defence, support 8 interest 9 advantage
behave: act 4 bear, work 5 carry, react, treat 6 acquit, demean, deport, handle 7 comport, conduct, gesture, manager 8 function, regulate, restrain
behavior, behaviour: air 4 port, mien 5 guise 6 action, manner 7 bearing, comport, decorum 8 amenance, breeding, carriage 9 demeanour 10 deportment, governance
behead: 9 decollate 10 decapitate, guillotine
behemoth: 4 huge 5 beast, giant, hippo 7 monster
behest: bid, law 4 hest, rule 5 order 6 demand 7 command, mandate 10 injunction
behind: aft 4 past, rear, ward, rump 5 abaff, abaft, after, ahind(Sc.), arear, later, passe, tardy 6 arrear, astern 8 backward, dilatory 9 posterior 10 afterwards
behold: lo; eye, see, spy 4 ecce, espy, gaze, hold, keep, look, scan, stop, view, wait 5 sight, voila, watch 6 descry, regard, retain 7 discern, observe, witness 8 consider, maintain, perceive
beholden: 7 obliged 8 indebted
behoof: use 6 profit 7 benefit 8 interest 9 advantage
behoove: dow, fit 4 need, suit 5 befit, ought 6 belong, proper 7 require 8 suitable 9 incumbent
beige: tan 4 ecru 5 color, grege(F.) 10 unbleached
being: ens 4 self 5 entia, entre(F.), gnome, human, troll 6 animal, entity, extant, living, mortal, person 7 essence, present, re-

ality 8 creature, ontology, standing 9 actuality, existence 11 subsistence 12 constitution
abstract: ens 5 entia
actual: 4 esse
in front: 6 anteal
physiological: 4 bion
science of: 8 ontology
suffix: ure
beken: 7 commend, deliver, entrust, intrust
beknow: 7 confess 9 recognize 11 acknowledge
Bela's son: Ard, Iri 4 Uzzi 5 Ezbon
Bel's wife: 5 Belit 6 Beltis
belabor, belabour: ply 4 beat, drub, lash, work 6 assail, cudgel, hammer, hamper, thrash, thwack
belair: 7 bearing 10 deportment
Belait: 6 Europe
belamour: 5 lover 6 flower 8 ladylove
belated: 5 lated, tardy 7 delayed, overdue
belay: 5 beset 6 invest, waylay 7 besiege 8 encircle
belaying pin: 5 kevel 7 bollard
belch: 4 boke, bolk, galp, rasp 5 eruct 8 eructate 10 eructation
beldam, beldame: hag 4 fury 5 crone, jixen 6 alecto, erinys, virago 7 Jezebel 8 ancestor 9 Tisiphone 11 grandmother
beleaguer: 5 belay, beset 6 invest 7 assault, besiege 8 blockade, surround 9 encompass
belfry: 4 shed 5 tower 7 clocher 9 campanile
Belgian: 7 Fleming, Walloon
Belgian Congo: See **Zaire**
Belgium: *anthem:* 11 Brabanconne
city: Ans, Huy, Spa 4 Gand, Mons 5 Alost, Ciney, Eupen, Ghent, Jumet, Liege, Namur, Ypres 6 Bruges, Deurne, Lierre, Merxem, Ostend, Turnai 7 Antwerp, Berchem, Herstal, Hoboken, Ixelles, Louvain, Mechlin, Roulers, Seraing 8 Brussels(c.), Courtrai, Muscron, Turnhout, Verviers 9 Charleroi, Molenbeek 10 Anderlecht, Borgerhout, Schaerbeek
coin: 5 belga, franc 7 centime
commune: Ans, Ath, Ely, Hal, Mol, Spa 4 Aath, Boom, Geel, Genk, Lier, Niel, Roux, Zele 5 Aalst, Alost, Evere, Genck, Jette, Namur, Ronse, Uccle, Ukkel
endive: 7 witloof
Gaul tribe: 4 Remi 6 Nervii
horse: 9 Brabancon
marble: 5 rance
measure: vat 4 aune, last, pied 5 carat 6 perche 8 boisseau
province: Spa 5 Liege, Namur 7 Antwerp, Brabant, Hainaut, Limburg 8 Flanders 9 Luxemburg
river: Lys 4 Dyle, Leie, Maas, Yser 5 Meuse, Rupel, Senne 6 Dender, Ourthe, Sambre 7 Schelde, Scheldt
seaport: 6 Ostend
tribe: 9 Bellovaci
violinist: 5 Ysaye
weight: 4 last 5 carat, livre, pound 6 charge 7 chariot 8 esterlin
Belgrade native: 4 Serb
Belial: 5 devil, Satan
belie: 6 belong, defame 7 besiege, falsify, pertain, slander, traduce 8 disguise, strumpet, surround 9 encompass 10 calumniate, contradict 11 counterfeit 12 misrepresent
belief: fay, ism 4 mind, sect, view 5 credo, creed, dogma, faith, tenet, troth, trust 6 credit 7 opinion 8 credence, doctrine, reliance 9 assurance 10 confidence, conviction, persuasion
liable to: 7 credent 9 credulous
believe: wis 4 deem, trow, ween 5 judge, think, trust 6 accept, credit 7 suppose 8 accredit, consider, credence
believer: ist 8 adherent
in all religions: 7 omnist
in God: 5 deist 6 theist
in predestination: 13 particularist
Belili's brother: 6 Tammuz
belittle: 5 decry, dwarf, sneer 6 slight 7 detract 8 minimize 9 denigrate, discredit, disparage 10 depreciate
bell: 4 call, fair, gong, ring, roar 5 chime, cloak, codon, flare, knell, swell 6 bellow, bubble(Sc.), crotal, curfew, tocsin 7 blossom, campana, campane, corolla 9 beautiful 13 tintinnabulum
alarm: 6 tocsin
axle bearing: cod
clapper: 6 tongue
kind of: cow 4 door, gong, hand 5 ship's 6 church, jingle, school 8 electric
part: 7 baldric 8 baldrick
pert. to: 10 campanular 11 campanulate
ringer: 6 toller 12 carillonneur
room: 6 belfry
sound: 4 ding, dong, toll 5 knell 6 tinkle
tower: 6 belfry 9 campanile
bell, book, and candle: 15 excommunication
bell bottoms: 8 trousers
bell ear: 6 cannon
Bell for Adano author: 6 Hersey
bell-mouthed: 5 evase(F.)
bell-shaped: 11 campanulate
belladonna: 5 dwale, plant 6 remedy 7 manicon 8 narcotic 9 dwayberry 10 nightshade
extract: 7 atropin 8 atropine

bellbird: 6 shrike 8 arapunga
bellboy: 4 page 6 porter, redcap
Bellerophon: *father:* 7 Glaucus
spring: 7 Pelrene
belles-lettres: 10 literature
bellicose: mad 5 irate 7 hostile, warlike 8 militant 10 pugnacious 11 belligerent
belligerent: 7 hostile, warlike 8 choleric, fighting, jingoist 9 bellicose, combative, irascible, litigious, wrangling 10 pugnacious 11 contentious, quarrelsome 12 disputatious
Bellini: *opera:* 5 Norma
sleepwalker: 5 Amina
bellow: cry, low, moo, yap 4 bawl, beal, bell, roar, rout, yaup, yawp 5 belve, blart, croon, roust(Sc.), shout 6 buller, clamor 7 bluster, clamour, ululate 10 vociferate
bellware: 4 kelp
bellweed: 8 knapweed
bellwether: 5 sheep 6 leader
belly: bag, cod, gie(Sc.), gut, pod 4 bouk, kyte(Sc.) 5 bingy, bulge, pleon 6 hunger paunch 7 abdomen, stomach 8 appetite
bellying: 7 bunting
belong: 4 bear 5 apply, belie 6 inhere, relate 7 pertain 9 appertain
belongings: 4 gear 5 goods, traps 6 assets, estate 7 effects 8 chattels, property 9 household 10 appendages 11 possessions 13 appurtenances
beloved: 4 dear, idol 5 cheri(F.) 6 adored, cherie(F.) 7 darling 8 precious 9 inamorata, valentine
below: 4 alow, down 5 ablow, infra, sotto(It.), under 7 beneath 8 downward, inferior 10 downstairs, underneath
belt: 4 area, band, beat, blow, cest, gird, mark, ring, sash, zone 5 girth, strap, strip, tract, whack, zonar 6 bodice, cestus, cingle, fettle, girdle, invest, region, strait, stripe, zonnar, zonule 7 circuit, passage 8 cincture, encircle, surround 9 bandoleer, encompass 10 cummerbund, kummerbund
conveyor: 5 apron
ecclesiastical: 7 balteus 8 baltheus
non-Mohammedan: 5 zonar
sword: 7 baldric 8 boldrick
belted: 6 zonate 7 girdled 9 cinctured
bema: 4 pace, step 7 chancel
bemoan: 4 wail 6 grieve, lament, sorrow 7 deplore
bemuse: 5 addle 7 confuse 8 distract
bench: bar, pew 4 banc, seat 5 board, judge, ledge, stool 6 settee 7 discard
church: pew, pue 6 sedile(L.)
bench hook: 5 clamp
bend: bow, nid, ply, sag 4 arch, flex, kink, turn 5 angle, baton, bulge, crimp, crook, curve, stoop, twist 6 buckle, cotice, cotise, crouch, direct, divert, fasten, inflex, submit 7 bendlet, incline, refract 9 genuflect
backward: 6 retort
in timber: sny
bender: leg 5 drunk, spree 7 whopper 8 guzzling, sixpence
bending: 5 lithe 6 pliant, supple 7 anfract, flexion 8 flection
beneath: 5 aneth(Sc.), below, lower, under 6 aneath 10 underneath 11 underground
benedict: 4 mild 6 benign, kindly 7 blessed 8 bachelor, gracious, salutary 9 benignant, favorable, wholesome 10 propitious
Benedictine: 4 monk 7 Cluniac, liqueur
title: dom
benediction: 4 amen 6 prayer 7 benison 8 blessing 10 invocation
benefaction: 4 alms, boon, gift 7 benefit, present 8 benefice, donation, gratuity 11 beneficence
benefactor: 5 agent, angel, donor 6 friend, helper, patron, savior 8 promoter 14 philanthropist
benefice: feu 4 fief 5 favor 6 curacy, favour, living 7 benefit, rectory 8 kindness, vicarage 10 beneficium 11 benefaction
first fruit: 5 annat 6 annate
beneficence: 4 boon, gift 5 grace 6 bounty 7 charity 8 goodness, kindness 11 benefaction
beneficial: 4 good 6 useful 7 helpful 8 salutary 9 available, benignant, desirable, enjoyable, healthful, lucrative, wholesome 10 beneficent, profitable, salubrious 11 serviceable 12 advantageous, remunerative
beneficiary: 4 heir, user 5 donee 6 vassal 7 legatee 9 feudatory
benefit: aid, use 4 boon, boot, gain, gift, help, prow, sake 5 avail, boost 6 assist, behalf, behoof, better, profit, usance 7 advance, bespeak, concert, deserve, improve, service, utility 8 benefice, befriend, interest 9 advantage, emolument 11 benefaction, performance
benevolent: 4 good, kind 6 benign, loving 7 amiable, liberal 8 generous 9 benignant 10 altruistic, charitable, munificent 13 philanthropic
Bengal: *boat:* 5 batel 6 baulea 7 bauleah
capital: 5 Dacca
caste member: 6 baidya
city: see *town* below
cotton: 5 adati, adaty
district: 5 Dacca, Nadia
gentlemen: 5 baboo
grass: 6 millet
hemp: 4 sunn

measure: 5 cotta 6 cottah 8 chattack
native: Ebo, Kol 4 Eboe 6 Banian
quince: bel 4 bael, bhel
root: 10 cassumunar
singer: 4 baul
town: 5 Dacca(c.) 6 Madras 7 Barisal, Rangoon 8 Calcutta 9 Tittacarh
tree: 4 bola

benign: 4 boon, good, kind, mild 5 bland 6 genial, gentle 7 affable 8 benedict, gracious, salutary 9 benignant, favorable, wholesome 10 benevolent, favourable, propitious, salubrious

benison: 8 blessing 9 beatitude 10 invocation 11 benediction

Benjamin: *descendant:* 4 Aher
grandson: Iri
son: Ehi 4 Gera, Rosh

benne: 6 sesame

bent: aim, bow, set 4 bias, gift, turn 5 bound, bowed, crank, crump, flair, knack, prone, taste, trend 6 akimbo, biased, braced, courbe, course, curved, energy, genius, hooked, swayed, talent 7 crooked, curvant, flexion, flexure, impetus, leaning, leveled, pronate, purpose, stooped, tension 8 aptitude, declined, flection, penchant, tendency 9 curvature, direction, prejudice 10 determined, proclivity, propensity 11 disposition, inclination 13 prepossession 14 predisposition

benthonic plant: 6 enalid

benthos: 5 fauna, flora

benumb: nip 4 daze, dunt, numb, stun 5 daver 6 cumber, deaden 7 fretish, fretize, stupefy

benzine derivative: 6 phenol

Beowulf: 4 epic, poem

bequeath: 4 give, will 5 endow, leave, offer 6 bestow, commit, demise, devise, legate, quethe 7 bequest, commend 8 transmit 9 testament

bequest: 4 gift, will 6 legacy 8 bequeath, heritage, pittance 9 endowment

berate: jaw, nag 4 lash, rail 5 abuse, chide, scold, score 6 revile 7 censure, reprove, upbraid 8 chastise 10 vituperate

Berber: 4 Moor 6 Hamite, Kabyle 7 Haratin
chief: 4 caid, qaid
dialect: 6 Tuareg
tribe: 4 Daza, Riff, Tibu 6 Tuareg

Berea: 6 Aleppo

bereave: rob 5 strip 6 divest, sadden 7 deprive, despoil 10 dispossess

bereft: orb 4 lorn, lost, poor 7 forlorn 9 destitute 12 dispossessed

beret: cap, hat, tam 7 biretta, chapeau 8 berretta, chapeaux(pl.), headgear

berg: ice 4 floe 6 barrow 8 eminence, mountain

bergamot: 4 bose, mint, pear 5 snuff 6 orange 7 Bergama, essence, perfume

bergstock: 10 alpenstock

beriberi: 5 kakke

Berkshire: *race course:* 5 Ascot
village: 5 Ascot

Berlin park: 10 Tiergarten

berm, berme: 4 bank, edge, path 5 ledge, shelf 7 terrace

Bermuda: *arrowroot:* 5 aruru 6 ararao
barracuda: 4 spet
berry: 9 soapberry
capital: 8 Hamilton
catfish: 6 coelho
ceremony: 6 gombay
grass: 4 doob

berry: bay, dew, haw 4 beat, cran, rasp 5 acini, bacca, black, fruit, mound, salal, savin 6 acinus, baccae, burrow, sabine, thresh 7 currant, hillock
comb. form: 5 bacci
disease: 8 bluestem
medicinal: 5 cubeb
oil: 5 olive

berry-like: 7 baccate

berserk: mad 5 bravo 6 pirate 7 enraged, warrior 8 frenzied, maniacal

berth: bed, job 4 bunk, dock, slip 5 place 6 billet, office 7 lodging, mooring 8 position 9 anchorage, situation 11 appointment

bertha: 4 cape 6 cannon, collar

beryl: gem 5 jewel 7 emerald 10 aquamarine
green: 11 davidsonite
yellow: 8 heliodor

beryx: 8 alfonsin

beseech: ask, beg, sue 4 pray 5 crave, plead 6 adjure, appeal, obtest 7 entreat, implore, solicit 9 impetrate, obsecrate 10 supplicate

beseeching: 9 precative

beset: ply 4 sail, stud 5 allot, belay, harry, siege, spend 6 assail, attack, harass, infest 7 arrange, besiege, perplex 8 blockade, encumber, obstruct, surround 9 beleaguer

beshrew: 5 curse 8 execrate

beside: by 4 hear 5 along, aside 7 abreast 8 adjacent
comb. form: 4 para 5 juxta

besides: by; and, but, too, yet 4 also, else, over, then 6 beside, beyond, except 8 moreover 10 additional 11 furthermore

besiege: 4 gird, girt 5 belay, belie, beset, siege, storm 6 attack, pester, plague 7 solicit 8 surround 9 beleaguer

besmear: ray 4 balm, daub, soil 5 apply, cover, muddy, smear, sully, taint 6 bedaub 7 beslime, smother 8 besmirch
besmirch: 4 soil 5 smear, sully 6 smirch 7 asperse, blacken 8 discolor
besom: map 4 drab(Sc.), 5 broom, sweep 6 sloven(Sc.), 7 heather
besot: 4 dull 6 muddle, stupid 7 stupefy 8 befuddle 9 infatuate
bespangle: dot 4 stud, star 5 adorn 8 sprinkle
bespatter: 4 blot, dash, soil, spot 5 muddy, plash, stain, sully 6 sparge 7 asperse, scatter 8 reproach, sprinkle
bespeak: 4 cite, hint, show 5 argue, imply, order, speak 6 accost, attest, engage, steven 7 address, arrange, benefit, betoken, discuss, exclaim, reserve 8 foretell, indicate 9 stipulate
best: ace 4 a-one, beat, most, tops, wale 5 elite, excel, worst 6 choice, defeat, finest, flower, outwit, utmost 7 conquer, largest, optimum 8 greatest, outmatch, outstrip, vanquish 9 excellent, overmatch 11 superlative
comb. form: 5 arist 6 aristo
bestial: low 4 vile, wild 5 brute, feral 6 brutal, filthy 7 beastly, brutish, inhuman, sensual 8 depraved 10 irrational
bestir: 5 rouse
bestow: add, put, use 4 deal, dote, give 5 allot, allow, apply, award, besot, grant, lodge, place 6 accord, beteem, confer, demise, devote, divide, donate, employ, entail, extend, impart, render 7 collate, dispose, instate, present, quarter, tribute 8 bequeath 11 communicate
bestraddle: 8 bestride
bestride: 6 stride 8 straddle 10 bestraddle
bet: lay 4 ante, gage, play, plot, risk, wage 5 hedge, stake, wager 6 gamble, pledge
broker: 6 bookie 9 bookmaker
fail to pay: 5 welch, welsh
faro: 7 sleeper
roulette: bas 4 noir 5 carre 6 milieu 7 dernier, encarre, enplein
betake: go; hie 4 move 5 apply, catch, grant 6 assume, commit, repair, remove, resort 7 commend, journey
bete: 5 beast, silly 6 stupid 7 foolish
bete noir: 4 hate 5 dread 6 terror 7 bugaboo, bugbear
betel: 4 ikmo, itmo, siri
leaf: pan 4 buyo
betel palm: 5 areca
extract: 7 catechu
masticatory: pan 4 buyo
seed: 8 betel nut
Betelgeuse: 4 star
bethel: 6 chapel
Bethesda: 4 pool 6 chapel
bethink: 5 think 6 devise, recall 7 reflect 8 consider, remember 9 recollect 10 deliberate
Bethlehemite: 4 Boaz
Beth's sister: Jo; Amy, Meg
Bethuel's son: 5 Laban
betide: hap 5 befit, occur, trite 6 become, befall, chance, happen 7 betoken, presage
betimes: 4 anon, rath, soon 5 early, rathe 8 speedily 9 forthwith 10 seasonably 12 occasionally
betise: 5 folly 9 silliness, stupidity
betoken: 4 mark, note, show 5 augur 6 assert, betide, denote, evince, import 7 bespeak, express, forbode, oblique, portend, presage, signify 8 forebode, foreshow, indicate 9 symbolize 10 foreshadow 13 prognosticate
betray: 4 blab, blow, boil, gull, sell, sile, sing, tell, undo, wray 5 peach, spill 6 accuse, delude, descry, reveal, seduce, snitch, squeal 7 beguile, deceive, falsify, mislead 8 disclose, discover
betrayer: rat 5 Judas, skunk 7 seducer, traitor 8 derelict
betroth: 4 affy 6 assure, engage, ensure, pledge, plight 7 espouse, promise 8 affiance, contract, handfast
better: aid, top 4 mend 5 amend, emend, excel, safer, wiser 6 bigger, exceed, reform 7 advance, choicer, correct, greater, improve, promote, rectify, relieve, support, surpass 8 increase, superior 9 meliorate 10 ameliorate, preferable
better half: 4 wife
betting: *adviser:* 4 tout
figures: 4 odds
odds: 5 price
betty: 7 dessert
between: 4 amid 5 amell, among, entre(F.) 7 average, betwixt 12 intermediate
law: 5 mesne
prefix: dia 4 meta 5 inter
between the lines: 6 latent, secret
bevel: 4 blow(Sc.), cant, edge, push(Sc.) 5 angle, bezel, miter, mitre, slant, slope 6 aslant 7 chamfer, incline, oblique
corners: 5 splay
end of timber: 5 snape
out: 4 ream
beverage: ade, ale, nog, pop, tea 4 beer, grog, mead, milk, soda, wine 5 cider, cocoa, draft, drink, lager, leban, negus, morat, punch, treat, water 6 coffee, eggnog, liquid, liquor, nectar, posset 7 potable 8 cocktail, potation 9 metheglin 10 melicratum
alcoholic: see **alcoholic drink**

container: vat 6 kettle 7 charger 9 separator
extract: 4 kola
malted wheat: 6 zythem, zythum
mixed: 5 negus, punch, smash 6 bishop
mulberry and honey: 5 morat
Oriental: rak 4 sake 5 rakee 6 arrack
pepper: 4 kava
Polynesian: 4 kava
South American: 4 mate

bevy: 4 herd, pack 5 covey, drove, flock, group, swarm 6 flight, school 7 company 8 assembly 9 gathering, multitude 10 collection

bewail: cry, rue 4 keen, moan, sigh, wail, weep 5 mourn 6 bemoan, grieve, lament, plaint, sorrow 7 deplore 8 complain

beware: 4 cave, heed, shun 5 avoid, spend 6 eschew 7 warning

bewilder: fog 4 daze, foil, gaum 5 abash, addle, amaze, amuse, deave 6 baffle, bemist, bother, dazzle, muddle, puzzle 7 buffalo, confuse, mystify, perplex, stagger, stupefy 8 astonish, confound, distract, entangle, surprise 9 embarrass, obfuscate 10 spiflicate 11 spifflicate

bewildered: 4 asea, lost, mang 5 agape, dazed 8 confused, helpless 9 perplexed

bewilderment: awe, fog 4 daze 9 amazement, confusion 10 perplexity 11 distraction 13 embarrassment

bewitch: hex 5 charm, fasci, spell 6 enamor, entice, glamor, grigri, hoodoo, thrill 7 bedevil, delight, enchant, glamour 8 ensorcel, forspeak, greegree 9 captivate, ensorcell, fascinate

bewith: 9 makeshift 10 substitute

bewray: 4 show, tell 6 accuse, betray, expose, malign, reveal 7 divulge 8 disclose

bey: 6 beylic, beylik 8 governor

Beyle's penname: 8 Stendhal

beyond: by 4 free, over 5 above, aside, forby, ultra 6 forbye, yonder 7 besides, further 8 superior 9 hereafter
prefix: sur 4 meta 5 ultra
the sea: 11 ultramarine
the threshold: 12 ultraliminal

bezel, basil: rim 4 edge, ouch, seal 5 bevil, bezil, crown, facet 6 chaton, flange 8 template

bezezteen: 5 bazar 6 bazaar

bezzle: 5 drink, revel, waste 7 consume, plunder 10 gluttonize

bhagavat: 7 blessed

bhakta: 7 devotee 9 bhagavata, worshiper

bhalu: 4 bear

bhandar: 5 store 7 library 10 storehouse

bhandari: 7 steward 9 treasurer

bhang, bang: 7 hashish 8 narcotic 10 intoxicant
product of: 6 majoon

bhangi: 6 mehtar 7 sweeper

bharal: tur 5 sheep 6 nahoor

bhat: 4 bard 8 minstrel

bhikku: 4 monk 5 friar 6 priest 9 mendicant

bhikshu: 5 friar 7 ascetic 9 mendicant

bhoosa: 5 chaff, husks, straw

b'hoy: 5 rowdy 8 gangster

bhut: 5 ghost 6 goblin

Bhutan: *disease:* dha
pine: 4 kail
religion: 9 shamanism
robe: 6 bakkhu

bias: 4 awry, bent, sway 5 amiss, color, slant, slope 7 bigotry, incline, oblique 8 clinamen, diagonal, tendency 9 clinamina(pl.), prejudice, procedure 10 favoritism, partiality, prepossess, propensity 11 declination, disposition, favouritism, inclination 12 predetermine, predilection 13 prepossession

biased: 11 tendentious

bib: sip 4 brat, fish 5 apron, drink 6 tipple, tucker 7 bavette(F.), 9 neckpiece 10 protection

bibelot: 5 curio 7 trinket 8 ornament

Bible: *angel:* 5 Micah 7 Raphael
animal: 4 reem 5 daman 6 hydrax 8 behemoth
apocrypha: 5 Tobit 6 Baruch, Esdras, Jeremy, Judith, Syriac, Wisdom 7 Vulgate 8 Manasses 9 Maccabees 10 Septuagint 14 Ecclesiasticus
ascetic order: 6 Essene
battle scene: 10 Armageddon
book: Job 4 Acts, Amos, Ezra, Joel, John, Jude, Luke, Mark, Ruth 5 Hosea, James, Jonah, Kings, Micah, Peter, Titus 6 Daniel, Esther, Exodus, Haggai, Isaiah, Joshua, Psalms, Romans, Samuel 7 Ezekiel, Genesis, Hebrews, Matthew, Numbers, Obadiah, Timothy 8 Habakkuk, Jeremiah, Nehemiah, Philemon, Proverbs 9 Apocrypha, Ephesians, Galatians, Leviticus, Zechariah 10 Chronicles, Colossians, Revelation 11 Corinthians, Deuteronomy, Philippians 12 Ecclesiastes, Lamentations 13 Song of Solomon, Thessalonians
character: see *name* below
city: Ain, Dan 4 Arad, Aven, Cana, Elim, Elon, Gath, Gaza, Geba, Maon, Rome, Tyre, Zoar 5 Akkad, Arvad, Ashur, Assur, Joppa, Sidon, Sodom 6 Bethel, Biblos, Gadara, Jerico, Tarsus 7 Babylon, Nineveh 8 Gomorrah, Nazareth 9 Jerusalem
clan: 6 Shelah

country: Nod, Pul **4** Aram, Bela, Edam, Elam, Gath, Hali, Moab, Seba, Seir **5** Ammon **6** Canaan **7** Galilee, Samaria
garden: **4** Eden
giant: **4** Anak, Emim **7** Goliath
giant killer: **5** David
hunter: **6** Nimrod
judge: **4** Agog, Elon
king: Og; Asa, Gog, Iva **4** Agag, Ahab, Ahaz, Amon, Bera, Jehu, Omri, Reba, Saul **5** David, Herod, Hiram, Joram, Nadab, Rezin, Tidal, Zimri **6** Birsha, Hezion, Japhia, Jotham, Uzziah **7** Jehoram, Solomon
kingdom: **4** Elam, Moab **5** Judea, Judah **6** Israel **8** Chaldeae
land of plenty: **6** Goshen
liar: **7** Ananias
money: **4** beka **5** bekah **6** shekel
mountain: Hor **4** Ebal, Nebo, Peor, Sina, Sion, Zion **5** Heres, Horeb, Sinai, Tabor **6** Ararat, Gilead, Moriah, Olivet, Pisgah
name: Ai, Ar, Ir; Ahi, Asa, Eri, Eve, Evi, Hor, Iri, Koa, Lot, Ner, Ono, Reu, Toi, Uel, Uri **4** Abel, Acan, Acub, Adam, Ader, Adna, Ador, Agee, Aher, Aman, Anak, Anam, Aner, Aram, Arem, Arie, Asan, Asom, Ater, Aven, Azal, Cain, Cana, Dura, Edar, Edec, Edes, Eker, Enan, Enos, Eran, Esau, Etam, Gera, Irad, Iram, Isac, Mary, Neri, Obal, Omar, Oreb, Oren, Paul, Reba, Sami, Sara, Seth, Suba, Ucal, Vale **5** Ahlab, Allan, Amasa, Aroer, Bedan, Besai, Caleb, Elias, Ephai, Esrom, Hadad, Hanes Isaac, Mered, Nehum, Oseas, Peleg, Rahad, Tarah, Vania **6** Naaman, Pilate, Ramath **7** Abadias, Abigail, Antioch, Elmodam, Idithum, Sidrach, Tabitha
navigator: **4** Noah
ornament: **4** urim **7** thummin
patriarch: Reu **4** Seth, Shem **5** Jacob, Nahor, Peleg **6** Israel, Lamech
people: **4** Moab, Phut, Seba **5** Ammon **6** Hamite, Hivite, Kenite **7** Amorite, Dodanim, Moabite
plain: **5** Mamre **7** Jericho
plotter: **5** Haman
pool: **6** Siloam
priest: Eli **5** Aaron **6** Levite
pronoun: ye; thy **4** thee, thou **5** thine
prophet: **4** Amos, Ezra **5** Elias, Hosea, Jonah, Micah, Nahum **6** Elijah, Isaiah **7** Ezekial **8** Jeremiah
psalmist: **5** David
queen: Abi **5** Sheba **6** Esther, Vashti **7** Jezebel
region: **4** Enon **5** Ophir, Perea **6** Bashan
reproach: **4** raca
river: Zab **4** Nile **5** Abana, Arnon **6** Kishon, Jordan
ruler: see *king* above
scholar: **7** Biblist **9** Biblicist
sea: Red **4** Dead **7** Galilee **8** Tiberias **10** Gennesaret
shepherd: **4** Abel **5** David
spice: **5** myrrh **6** stacte **12** frankincense
spy: **5** Caleb
stone: **4** ezel **6** ligure
tower: **4** Edar **5** Babel
town: see *city* above
tribe: see *people* above
valley: **4** Baca, Elah **6** Shaveh, Siddim
version: Av, RV **4** Geez **5** Douay, Itala **6** Syriac **7** Vulgate **8** Bohairic **9** Apocrypha, King James **10** New English **15** Revised Standard
weed: **4** tare
witch's home: **5** Endor

Bible society: **7** Gideons
Biblical: **10** scriptural
bicker: war **4** bowl, spar, tiff **5** argue, brawl, cavil, fight **6** assail, attack, battle **7** contend, dispute, quarrel, wrangle **8** pettifog, skirmish, squabble **10** contention
bicycle: **4** bike **5** wheel
for two: **6** tandem
rider: **7** cyclist
bid: beg **4** call, hist, pray **5** clepe, offer, order **6** adjure, charge, direct, enjoin, invite, reveal, tender **7** command, declare, entreat, proffer **8** announce, proclaim, proposal
biddable: **6** docile **8** obedient
biddy: hen **7** chicken
bide: **4** face, stay, wait **5** abide, await, dwell, tarry **6** endure, remain, suffer **7** sojourn **8** continue, tolerate **9** encounter, withstand
bield: den **4** cozy **5** dwell **7** comfort, courage, hearten, protect, shelter **8** boldness, embolden **9** sheltered **10** confidence, habitation
bien, bein: **4** fine, good, snug **6** genial **8** pleasant, thriving **10** prosperous **11** comfortable
bier: **4** pyre **5** frame, grave **6** coffin, hearse, litter **7** support **10** catafalque, handbarrow
bifarious: **7** twofold **9** ambiguous
biff: **4** blow
bifid: **6** forked
bifocal: **4** lens
bifold: **6** double **7** twofold
bifurcation: wye **4** fork **5** split **6** branch **8** division
big: **4** bold, huge, vast **5** bulky, chief, grand, great, gross, large **6** mighty **7** bumping, eminent, leading, massive, pompous, violent **8** boastful, bouncing, enormous, gen-

erous, gigantic, imposing, pregnant **9** notorious **10** tremendous **11** magnanimous, outstanding, pretentious, threatening
Big Bend State: **9** Tennessee
big shot: VIP
big toe: **6** hallux
bigener: **4** mule **6** hybrid
bighorn: **5** sheep **6** argali, aoudad **8** cimarron
bight: bay **4** bend, coil, gulf, loop **5** angle, curve, inlet, noose **6** corner, hollow
bignou, biniou: **7** bagpipe
bigot: **6** cafard, zealot **7** fanatic **9** hypocrite
bigoted: **6** biased, narrow **9** hidebound, illiberal, sectarian **10** intolerant, prejudiced **12** narrow-minded
bijou: **5** jewel **7** trinket
bilbie: **6** refuge **7** shelter
bile: **4** boil, gall, hump **5** venom **6** choler, growth
bilge: **4** scum **5** bouge, bulge
bilingual: diglot
bilk: do; gyp **4** balk, hoax **5** cheat, cozen, trick **6** delude, fleece **7** deceive, defraud, swindle **9** frustrate **10** disappoint
bill: act, dun, law, neb, nib, tab **4** beak, note, peck **5** libel, score **6** caress, charge, indict, pickax, poster, strike **7** invoice, lampoon, mattock, placard, statute **8** billhook, document, headland, petition **9** memoranda(pl.), statement **10** broadsword, memorandum, promontory **13** advertisement
anchor: pee
five dollar: fin, vee
one dollar: **4** buck **8** frogskin
ten dollar: **7** sawbuck
bill of fare: **4** card, menu **5** carte
billabong: **8** waterway
billet: bar, gad, log **4** loop, note, pass, post **5** berth, enrol, house, lodge, order, stick, strap **6** ballot, enroll, harbor, letter, notice, ticket **7** bearing, epistle, harbour, missive, pollack **8** coalfish, document, firewood, ornament, position, quarters **11** appointment, requisition
billfish: gar **8** sailfish **9** spearfish
billiard: *cue:* **4** mace
shot: **5** carom, masse **7** bricole
rod: cue
billiards: **4** game, pool
billingsgate: **5** abuse **7** obloquy **8** ribaldry **12** vituperation
billionaire: **6** nabob
billow: sea **4** wave **5** bulge, float, surge, swell **6** ripple, roller **7** breaker **8** undulate
billowing: **5** tidal **7** surging
billy: caw **4** chap, club, goat, mate **6** cudgel, fellow **7** brother, comrade **8** billikin, bludgeon **9** blackjack
billycock: **5** derby **6** bowler
bin: ark, box, cub **4** bing, cart, crib, vina **5** frame, hutch, pungi, stall, storo, wagon **6** basket, bunker, hamper, manger, trough, within **9** container **10** receptacle
coal: **6** bunker
fish: **5** canch, kench
binate: **4** dual **6** double, paired **7** coupled, twofold
bind: jam, tie **4** gird, hold, tape **5** stick **7** confine
comb. form: **5** desmo
to secrecy: **4** tile, tyle
tightly: **4** frap
up in: **6** absorb
binder: **4** band, beam, bond, cord, rope **5** baler, cover, frame, lever **6** fillet, folder, girder, header **9** bondstone
binding: **4** band, cord, rope, tape **5** valid **6** edging, ribbon **7** galloon, mousing, webbing **9** stringent **10** astringent, obligatory **11** restraining, restrictive
limp: **4** yapp
bindle stiff: **4** hobo **5** tramp
binge: bow, hit **4** blow, soak **5** beano, party, spree **6** cringe **8** carousal **9** obeisance
bingo: **4** game, keno **5** lotto **6** brandy
biography: **4** life, vita(It.) **6** memoir **7** account, history, memoire(F.), recount
saint's: **11** hagiography
biological class: **5** genus **6** genera(pl.) **7** species
biological factor: id **4** gene **5** idant
biology: **7** ecology **8** genetics
biose: **11** disaccharid **12** disaccharide
biotic community: **5** biome
biotite: **4** mica **7** anomite
biplane: **4** spad **8** airplane
birch: **4** cane, flog, tree, whip **5** canoe **6** betula **7** hickory
bird: ani, daw, nun, pie, tit **4** avis(L.), crow, kite, lark, ruff, tern, wren **5** brant, egret, finch, hobby, pewee, pewit, raven, robin, snipe, terek, vireo **6** bulbul, dunlin, falcon, hoopoe, linnet, marten, mocker, oriole, phoebe, plover, shrike, thrush **7** bluejay, bustard, buzzard, catbird, flicker, halcyon, irrisor, jackdaw, kinglet, ortolan, peacock, redwing, skylark, sparrow, swallow, tanager, warbler, waxwing **8** airplane, bluebird, boatbill, bobolink, bobwhite, chicadee, grosbeak, kingbird, pheasant, redstart, starling, thrasher **9** blackbird, blackcock, brambling, bullfinch, goldfinch, partridge, phalarope, sandpiper **10** bufflehead, meadowlark, tropicbird, woodpecker **11** butcherbird, hummingbird **12** yellowhammer

adjutant: **5** stork **6** argala **7** hurgila, marabou
African: **4** taha **8** umbrette
American: **4** sora **5** robin, vireo **6** darter, fulmar, turkey **7** grackle, tanager **8** cardinal **10** bufflehead
Antarctic: **4** skua **7** penguin
aquatic: **4** duck, gull, loon, swan, tern **5** goose, grebe, small, terne **7** penguin **8** dabshick, flamingo
aquiline: **5** eagle
Arabian Nights: roc
Arctic: auk **6** fulmar
Asiatic: **4** mine, myna **5** pitta **7** hilltit **8** dotterel **9** brambling, feng-huang, fenghwang
Attic: **11** nightingale
Australian: emu, roa **4** emeu, lory **5** arara **6** leipoa **7** boobook, bustard **8** lorikeet, lyrebird, platypus **9** cassowary, coachwhip, friarbird, pardalote
black: ani, ano, daw, pie **4** crow **5** merle, raven **6** oriole **7** jackdaw **8** starling
brillant plumage: **4** tody **5** jalep **6** oriole, trogon **7** jacamar, tanager **8** pheasant
Central American: daw **4** crow, rave, rook **5** raven **6** magpie **7** corvine, jacamar **8** puffbird
crane-like: **5** wader **6** chunga
crow-family: daw, jay, pie **4** craw **5** raven **7** jackdaw
crying: **6** ramage **7** limphin
diving: auk
dressing of feathers: **5** preen
emu-like: **11** cassowaries
European: ani, daw, emu, mew, qua **4** oirl, darr, emeu, gled, kite, mall, moro, osel, rook, stag, whim, yite **5** amsel, boonk, glede, mavis, merle, ousel, ouzel, sacer, saker, serin, tarin, terek, terin, whaup **6** avocet, avoset, cushat, gaylag, godwit, linnet, loriot, marten, merlin, missel, redcap, whewer, windle, winnel, wranny **7** bittern, bustard, haybird, kestrel, motacil, ortolan, sakeret, starnel, whiskey, winnard, witwall **8** bargoose, chepster, dotterel, garganey, redstart, wheybird, whimbrel, wrannock, yoldring **9** brambling, gallinule, goldfinch, goosander, peregrine, swinepipe, wheybeard **10** chiffchaff, lammegeyer, turtledove, whitterick **11** capercailie, lammergeier **12** capercailzie
extinct: moa, roc **4** dodo, jibi, kiwi, mamo, rukh **7** offbird
finch-like: **7** chewink, tanager
fish-catching: **6** osprey **9** cormorant
flightless: emu, moa **4** emeu, kiwi **7** apteryx, ostrich, penguin, ratitae **9** solitaire
fly-catching: **8** redstart **9** solitaire
flying backwards: **7** swallow, humming
food: hen **5** capon **6** pullet, turkey **7** chicken, rooster
frigate: ioa, iwa **6** tropic
gallinaceous: **6** peahen **7** peacock, peafowl
game: **5** quail, snipe **6** grouse **8** pheasant
genus: **4** alca, crax, otis **7** certhia **9** apatornis
gull-like: **4** tern **6** jaeger
Hawaiian: io, oo; ava, ioa, iwa **4** iiwi, mamo, moho
heron family: **4** benu, ibis **7** bittern
honey eater: **4** moho
humming: ava **5** carib **7** colibri
insectiverous: owl **5** vireo
jay: gae **6** magpie
large: emu **4** emeu, guan **5** eagle **6** curlew, willet **7** bustard, megapod, ostrich, pelican, seriema **8** curassow, shoebill
lark-like: **5** pipit
long-billed: **5** snipe **7** pelican
long-legged: io **4** sora **5** heron, snipe, stilt, wader **6** avocet, avoset, curlew **7** seriema
long-necked: **4** swan **5** agami, crane, goose, geese(pl.), stork **7** ostrich
male: cob, tom **4** cock **5** drake **6** gander **7** peacock, rooster **11** chanticleer
marsh: **4** sora **5** snipe, stilt
meadow: **8** bobolink
Mexican: **6** jacana, towhee **7** jacamar
mythological: roc **5** hansa **6** simurg **7** phoenix, simurgh
New Zealand: kea, moa **4** kaka, kiwi, kulu, ruru, titi, weka **6** kakapo **7** apterix, apteryx **8** morepork, notornis **10** blightbird
nonpasserine: **4** tody **6** hoopoe, motmot **8** hornbill **10** kingfisher
Northern: auk **6** gannet, puffin
of Athena: owl
of Juno: **7** peacock
of paradise: **8** manucode
of prey: owl **4** hawk, kite **5** eagle, elant **6** eaglet, elanet, owelet **7** goshawk, vulture **9** accipeter
of Zeus: **5** eagle
oldest known: **13** archaeopteryx
oscine: **4** chat **6** dronge, oriole **7** tanager
ostrich-like: emu, moa **4** emeu, rhea **10** cassowarie
parrot-like: **11** budgereegah, budggerygah
parson: poe, tue, tui
parts of body: neb, nib **4** bill, cere, knee, lora, mala **5** lores **6** pecten, pileum, pinion, rostra, syrinx **7** ambiens **8** pectines(pl.)
passerine: **5** finch **7** sparrow, starnel **9** chatterer, coachwhip
pert. to: **5** avian, avine **8** ornithic **9** volucrine

pink: 8 flamingo
plover-like: 5 drome 7 lapwing
Poe's: 5 raven
predatory: owl 4 kite 5 yager 6 falcon, shrike 9 cormorant
protuberance at base of bill: 4 cere
rare: 8 rara avis
ratite: emu, moa 4 emeu 7 ostrich 9 cassowary
red-tailed: 4 koae
sacred: 4 ibis
sea: auk, ern 4 erne, gony, gull, smew, tern 5 eider, solan 6 gannet, petrel, puffin 7 pelican 9 albatross 10 shearwater
shore: ree 4 rail, sora 5 snipe, stilt, wader 6 avocet, avoset, curlew, plover, willet
Sindbad's: roc 4 rock, rukh
singing: 4 lark, wren 5 finch, mavis, robin, shama, veery, vireo 6 canary, linnet, mocker, oriole, oscine, thrush 7 mocking, robinet 8 bobolink, redstart 12 whippoorwill
small: tit 4 tody, wren 5 dicky, pipit, vireo 6 dickey, linnet, siskin, todies(pl.), tomtit 7 creeper, humming, sparrow, titlark, wheater 8 starling 9 didappers
South American: 4 guan, mina, myna 5 chaja, mynah 6 barbet, becard 7 cariama, oilbird 8 bellbird, boatbill, caracara, guacharo, hoactzin, puffbird
swallow-like: 4 cran 5 swift
swimming: 4 loon 5 grebe
talking: 4 crow, mina, mino, myna 5 mynah 6 parrot
tall: 6 avocet, avoset
tropical: ani 4 koae, tody 6 barbet, trogon
unfledged: gor 4 eyas 6 gorlin 8 bubbling, nestling
wading: 4 hern, ibis, rail, sora 5 crane, heron, snipe, stilt, stork 6 avocet, jacana 8 flamingo 9 sandpiper
web-footed: 4 duck, swan 5 drake, goose 6 avocet, avoset, gander
West Indies: 4 tody
white-tailed: ern 4 erne 5 egret
woodcock: 5 pewee
young: eya 4 gull 5 piper 7 flapper, nestler 8 birdikin, nestling 9 fledgling

bird cage: 6 aviary, pinjra, volary, volery 7 paddock
bird clapper: 9 scarecrow
bird crest: 4 tuft
bird eye: 12 cuckoo flower
bird nest: 4 aery, eyry 5 aerie, eyrie
bird of passage: 8 wanderer 9 transient
bird route: 6 flyway
birdman: 6 airman 7 aviator 13 ornithologist
birds: 4 aves
collective: 4 fowl
domesticated 7 poultry
bird's-eye view: 6 apercu
birdwoman: 8 aviatrix 9 aviatress, aviatrice
biretta, berretta: cap 5 beret 8 skullcap
biri: 9 cigarette
birl: 4 spin, toss, whir 5 whirr 6 rattle, rotate 7 revolve
birma: 6 calaba
birn: 5 brand 6 burden
birr: bur 4 blow, burr, push, rush, wind 5 force, storm, vigor 6 energy, thrust, onrush 7 impetus
birse: 6 temper 7 bristle 8 bristles 10 irritation
birsle: 5 broil, toast 6 scorch 9 scorching
birsy: 7 bristly 9 irritable
birth: 4 bear 6 burden, origin 7 descent, genesis, lineage 8 delivery, geniture, nascency, nativity 9 beginning, naissance, parentage 10 extraction
after: 9 postnatal
before: 8 prenatal
by: nee
goddess: 5 Parca
help with: 8 accouche
new: 10 renascence 11 Renaissance
nobleness: 6 eugeny
pert. to: 5 natal 13 primogenitive

birth flower: *April:* 5 daisy
August: 9 gladiolus
December: 9 poinsetta
February 8 primrose
January: 9 carnation
July: 8 sweet pea
June: 4 rose
March: 6 violet
May: 15 lily of the valley
November: 13 chrysanthemum
October: 6 dahlia
September: 5 aster

birth stone: *April:* 7 diamond 8 sapphire
August: 9 carnelian
December: 4 ruby
February: 8 amethyst
January: 6 garnet
July: 9 turquoise
June: 5 agate
March: 6 jasper 10 bloodstone
May: 7 emerald
November: 5 topaz
October: 5 beryl
September: 10 chrysolite

birthday: 11 anniversary, celebration
ode: 12 genethliacon
pert. to: 10 genethliac 12 genethliacal
birthmark: 4 mole 5 naeve, nevus 6 naveus 7 blemish, spiloma

pert. to: 7 naevoid
birthplace: 10 incunabula(pl.) 11 incunabulum
birthrate: 8 natality
birthright: 8 heritage
bis: 5 again, twice 6 encore, repeat 7 replica 9 duplicate
Biscay: *island:* Re; Yeu
language: 6 Basque
biscuit: bun 4 bake(Sc.), roll, rush, snap 5 scone, wafer 6 cookie 7 cracker, pentile, pretzel 8 hardtack 9 porcelain 11 earthenware
bisect: 4 fork 5 cross, halve, split 6 cleave, divide 8 separate
bishop: 4 pope 5 angel 6 archer, bustle, priest 7 pontiff, prelate, primate 8 director, overseer 9 clergyman, inspector 13 administrator 14 superintendent
apron: 7 gremial
assistant: 6 verger 9 coadjutor
buskin: 6 caliga 7 caligae(pl.)
cap: 4 hura 5 miter, mitre 7 biretta 8 berretta, mitrella
first year revenue: 5 annat 6 annate
jurisdiction: see 7 diocese
private room: 9 accubitus
robe: 6 chimar, chimer 7 chimere
staff: 7 crosier
stave: 6 baculi(pl.) 7 baculus
throne: 4 apse
title: 4 abba, anba 7 prelate, primate
vestment: alb 4 cope 6 chimer, rochet 7 gremial, tunicle 8 dalmatic 10 omophórion
bishopric: see 7 diocese 10 episcopacy, episcopate
bishop's weed: 4 ammi 6 ammeos 8 goutweed
bismar: 9 steelyard
bismer: 5 scorn, shame 8 reproach
bison: 6 bovine 7 aurochs, bonasus, buffalo
bisque: 4 soup 5 point 8 ceramics
bisson: 5 blind 8 blinding, purblind
bistro: bar 6 tavern 10 restaurant
bisulcate: 6 cloven
bit: ace, jot, ort, wee 4 atom, bite, curb, doit, food, iota, item, mite, mote, part, snap, tool, whit 5 blade, check, crumb, drill, pezzo, piece, scrap, shred, speck 6 bridle, cannon, eating, morsel, smidge, splice, tittle, trifle 7 morceau(F.), portion, scatche, smidgen, smidgin, smigeon, snaffle 8 fraction, fragment, quantity, smitchin, victuals 9 restraint
horse's curb: 6 pelham
Irish: 7 traneen
bit by bit: 9 gradually
bit part: 6 walk-on
bite: bit, cut, eat, nip 4 bait, cham, chew, food, gash, gnap, gnaw, hold, knap, meal, snap 5 chack, chamm, champ, cheat, pinch, seize, smart, snack, sting, trick 6 crunch, morsel, nibble, pierce 7 cheater, corrode, impress, partake, sharper, slander 8 lacerate, puncture, victuals 9 denticate
bite one's tongue: 6 regret
biting: 4 acid, hoar, keen 5 acrid, sharp, snell 6 bitter, rodent, severe 7 caustic, cutting, mordant, nipping, pungent 8 incisive, poignant, scathing, stinging 9 corrosive, sarcastic, trenchant, vitriolic
biting dragon: 8 tarragon
biting of nails: 12 phaneromania
bito: 4 balm, tree 7 hajilij
oil 6 zachun
bitt: 4 post 5 block
bitter: 4 acid, bask, gall, keen, sore, sour, tart 5 acerb, acrid, amara, bleak, harsh, irate, sharp 6 biting, picric, severe 7 austere, caustic, crabbed, cutting, galling, painful, pungent, satiric 8 poignant, stinging, virulent 9 malicious 11 acrimonious, distressful
bitter apple: 9 colocynth
bitter bush: 9 snakeroot
bitter gentian: 9 baldmoney
bitter grass: 9 colicroot
bitter oak: 6 cerris
bitter spar: 8 dolomite
bitter vetch: ers 5 vicia
bitter wintergreen: 10 pipsissewa
bittern: 4 bump 5 boonk, heron 6 kakkak
bitterness: rue 4 acor, bile, fell, gall 5 atter 6 enmity, malice, rancor 7 amarity 8 acerbity, acrimony, severity 9 amaritude, hostility, poignancy, virulence 11 malevolence
bitters: 4 amer(F.) 5 tonic 6 liquor
pert. to: 9 amaroidal
bittersweet: 10 confection, nightshade
bitterweed: 7 ragweed 9 horseweed 10 sneezeweed
bitterwort: 7 felwort 9 dandelion
bitumen: tar 5 pitch 7 asphalt 8 alkitran 9 alchitran, elaterite
bivalve: 4 clam, spat 6 cockle, diatom, mussel, oyster 7 mollusk, Pandora, scallop 10 brachiopod
genus: 5 pinna 6 anomia 7 toheroa 12 gastrochaena
bivocal: 9 diphthong
bivouac: 4 camp 5 etape, watch 6 encamp 10 encampment
biwa: 6 loquat

bizarre: odd 5 antic, dedal, outre, queer 6 quaint 7 curious 8 fanciful 9 eccentric, fantastic, grotesque 10 ridiculous 11 extravagant
Bizet opera: 6 Carmen
blab: 4 chat 5 blart, blate, clack 6 babble, betray, gossip, reveal, tattle 7 blabber, chatter 8 telltale
black: jet 4 calo, dark, ebon, foul, inky 5 dusky, murky, Negro, noire(F.), raven, sable, sooty 6 atrous, dismal, gloomy, pitchy, sullen 7 melanic, Negrito, swarthy, unclean 8 mournful 9 atrocious 10 blackamoor, calamitous, forbidding
and white: 11 chiaroscuro
comb. form: 4 atra, atro, mela 5 melan 6 melano
black and blue: 5 livid
spot: 6 bruise, shiner 10 ecchymosis
black art: 5 magic 7 alchemy 8 wizardy 10 necromancy 11 conjuration
black cod: 6 beshow
black death: 6 plague
black diamond: oil 4 coal 8 hematite
black earth: 4 mold 9 chernozem
black elder: 9 hackberry
black eye: 5 shame 6 bruise, shiner 7 scandal
black-eyed Susan: 6 ketmia 10 coneflower
black grunt: 10 tripletail
black hole: 4 cell 7 dungeon 8 solitary
black plague: 7 bubonic
Black Sea: *city:* 5 Batum 6 Odessa
old name: 6 Euxine
peninsula: 6 Crimea
pert. to: 6 Pontic
river to: Bug, Don 4 Prut 6 Danube 7 Dnieper 8 Dniester
black sheep: 7 deviate 9 reprobate
black widow: 6 spider 7 pokomoo
blackamoor: 5 bleck, Negro 7 negress
blackball: 4 pill 6 ballot 7 exclude, heeball 9 ostracize
blackberry: 6 agawam 8 dewberry
blackbird: ani, daw, pie 4 crow, merl 5 amsel, colly, merle, ousel, ouzel, raven 6 colley 7 jackdaw
blackboard: 5 slate
blackcap: 4 gull 7 warbler 8 chicadee, titmouse 9 raspberry
blackdamp: 9 chokedamp
blacken: ink, tar 4 char, soot 5 bleck, cloud, japan, sully 6 darken, defame, malign, vilify 7 asperse, slander, traduce 8 besmirch 10 calumniate
blackface: 5 actor, comic, sheep 8 boldface, minstrel
blackfin: 4 fish 5 cisco, sesis
blackfish: 5 whale 6 tautog 10 nigrescent
school: 5 grind
blackguard: 4 shag 5 gamin, guard, snuff 7 vagrant 8 criminal, hanger-on, vagabond 9 scoundrel
blackhead: 6 comedo
blackjack: oak 4 club, duck, flag, game, jack 5 billy 6 beetle, jerkin, vessel, weapon
blackleg: 4 scab, snob 7 disease, gambler 8 apostate, swindler 13 strikebreaker
blacklist: ban 4 veto
blackmail: 5 bribe 6 coerce, extort 7 payment, tribute
blackmailer: 5 ghoul 7 leecher
blackmailing: 8 chantage 9 extortion
Blackmore heroine: 10 Lorna Doone
blackout: 6 darken 8 darkness, scrounge 11 suppression
blacksmith: gow 5 shoer, smith 6 plover, smithy, stithy 7 farrier, striker 10 horseshoer
shop: 5 anvil, stith 6 smithy, stithy 8 smithery
blacksnake: 4 whip 5 racer, quirt
blackhorn: haw 4 sloe
Blackwater State: 8 Nebraska
blackwort: 8 comfrey
bladder: sac 7 blister, inflate, vesicle
comb. form: 4 asco
blade: bit, fop, oar 4 blow, bone, edge, leaf, shiv 5 blood, dandy, fluke, grain, knife, spark, spear, spire, sword 6 cutter, lamina, scythe, sickle 7 gallant, laminae(pl.), scapula 9 propeller
blae: blo 4 blue, gray 5 bleak, livid 7 sunless 10 unbleached
blague: lie 4 hoax 6 humbug 8 claptrap, raillery
blah: 4 bunk 8 nonsense
blain: 4 sore 5 bulla 7 blister, inflame, pustule 8 swelling
blake: wan 4 pale 6 yellow 9 colorless
Blake's symbol: 4 Zoas
blamable: 6 faulty 8 culpable 11 blameworthy 13 reprehensible
blame: 4 call, hurt, onus, twit 5 chide, fault, guilt, odium, shend 6 accuse, charge, dirdum, rebuke, revile, scance 7 ascribe, censure, condemn, obloquy, reproof, reprove, upbraid 8 reproach 9 challenge, criticism, inculpate 10 accusation 11 culpability, reprobation 12 reprehension 13 animadversion
deserving: 8 culpable
blameless: 7 perfect 8 innocent, spotless 9 faultless, righteous 14 irreproachable
blanch: 4 fade, pale 5 chalk, scald, white 6 argent, bleach, blench, whiten 8 etiolate 9 whitewash

bland: 4 kind, mild, oily, open, soft 5 suave 6 benign, genial, gentle, smooth, urbane 7 affable, amiable, lenient 8 gracious 9 benignant, courteous

blandish: 4 coax 5 charm 6 allure, blanch, cajole 7 flatter, wheedle 10 compliment

blank: 4 bare, flan, form, shot, void 5 annul, blind, break, clean, empty, range, space 6 vacant 7 nonplus, unmixed, vacuous 8 unfilled 9 colorless, downright, fruitless, frustrate

blanket: 4 brot, wrap 5 cotta, cover, layer, manta, quilt, sheet, throw 6 afghan, poncho, serape 8 coverlet 10 barraclade
cowboy: 5 sugan 6 soogan, sougan, sugann
goat's hair: 6 cumbly
horse: 5 manta
Indian: 6 stroud

blare: 4 peal 5 blast, noise 6 blazon 7 fanfare, tantara, trumpet 11 flamboyance

blarney: 5 stone 6 butter 7 flatter, wheedle 8 flattery

blase: 5 bored, sated, weary 8 satiated 9 surfeited 11 indifferent

blaspheme: 5 abuse, curse 6 revile 7 defame, profane 10 calumniate

blasphemy: 7 calumny, cursing, impiety 8 anathema, swearing 9 profanity, sacrilege 10 execration 11 imprecation, irreverence, malediction 12 vilification

blast: bub, nip, wap 4 bang, blow, gale, gust, ruin, wind 5 split, stunt 6 attack, blight, wither 7 bluster, explode, shatter, shrivel 8 dynamite, outburst, proclaim 9 discharge, explosion 10 detonation

blast furnace: *lower part:* 4 bosh
nozzle: 6 tuyere

blat: 5 bleat, blurt

blatant: 4 glib, loud 5 gross, noisy, silly, vocal 6 coarse, vulgar 8 brawling 9 bellowing, clamorous, inelegant, obtrusive 10 vociferous

blate: 4 blab, dull, pale, slow 5 blunt, prate, timid 7 bashful, ghastly 8 sheepish 9 diffident 10 spiritless

blather: 4 stir 5 bleat 6 babble 7 blither, prattle 8 nonsense 9 commotion

blaubok: 5 etaac 8 antelope

blaw: 4 blow, brag 5 boast

blaze: 4 burn, fire, glow, mark, shot 5 flame, flare, flash, glare, gleam, glory, shine, torch 6 bleeze 7 bonfire, pioneer 8 splendor 9 firebrand 10 effulgence 11 coruscation 13 conflagration

blazer: 6 jacket

blazon: 4 deck, show 5 adorn, blare, boast 6 depict, shield 7 declare, display, exhibit, publish 8 emblazon, inscribe 9 delineate, embellish 11 description, publication 14 representation

bleach: sun 5 chalk 6 blanch, blench, chlore, purify, whiten 7 decolor, lighten 8 etiolate

bleachers: 5 seats, stand 10 grandstand

bleaching vat: 4 keir, kier

bleak: dim, raw 4 blae, blay, cold, gray, pale 5 sprat 6 bitter, bleach, dismal, dreary, frigid, pallid 7 cutting 8 desolate 9 cheerless 10 depressing
fish: 4 blay, bley 5 sprat

blear: dim 4 blur, dull 6 darken 7 deceive, mislead 8 hoodwink, protrude

bleared: 4 inky 5 dusky 6 rheumy

bleat: baa 4 blat, blea 5 blart 7 blather, bluster, whicker

bleb: 4 blob 5 bulla 6 bubble 7 blister, pustule, vesicle 8 swelling

bleed: 4 flow, leak, shed 6 escape, extort 7 agonize

bleeding heart: 8 dicentra

blemish: mar 4 blot, blur, dent, flaw, gall, lack, mark, rift, scar, slur, spot, vice, want 5 blame, breck, crack, fault, mulct, speck, sully, tache, taint 6 blotch, breach, defame, defect, impair, injure, macula, macule, smirch, stigma 7 default, failing, fissure, maculae(pl.) 9 birthmark, deformity, discredit, disfigure 10 defacement, deficiency 12 imperfection 13 disfigurement
wood: 4 mote
wound: 4 scar 8 cicatrix 9 cicatrice

blench: 4 foil, shun, wile 5 avoid, elude, evade, quail, shake, shirk, trick 6 baffle, blanch, bleach, flinch, recoil, shrink 7 deceive 9 stratagem 10 disconcert

blend: mix 4 blot, fuse, join, meng 5 blind, cream, merge, shade, spoil, stain, tinge, unite 6 commix, dazzle, mingle 7 combine, confuse, corrupt, deceive, mixture, pollute 8 coalesce, tincture 9 admixture, associate, commingle, harmonize 10 amalgamate 11 incorporate

blended: 5 fondu, mixed 6 merged 7 mingled 9 confluent

blesbok: 5 nunni 8 antelope, blesbuck

bless: 4 keep, sain, wave 5 adore, anele, bensh(Yid.), extol, favor, guard, thank, wound 6 favour, hallow, praise, thrash 7 approve, beatify, glorify, protect 8 macarize, preserve, sanctify 10 consecrate, felicitate

blessed: 4 holy 5 happy 6 divine, joyful, sacred 8 benedict, bhagavat, blissful, hallowed 9 beatified, benedight 11 consecrated

blessing: 4 boon, gift 5 bliss, grace 6 praise 7 benison, worship 8 felicity 9 beatitude 10 benedicite, beneficent 11 benediction
blether: See **blather**
blight: nip 4 ruin, rust, smut 5 blast, frost 6 mildew, wither 7 destroy 9 frustrate
blimp: 7 airship, balloon, colonel
blind: bet, pot 4 ante, dark, dull, hood 5 blank, blend, dunch, shade, stake, wager 6 ambush, bisson, dazzle, screen, secret 7 aimless, bandage, benight, eclipse, execate, eyeless, obscure, pretext, shutter 8 abortive, artifice, bayardly, blinding, hoodwink, ignorant, involved, jalousie, outshine, purblind 9 benighted, concealed, deceitful, defective, insensate, intricate, senseless, sightless 10 incomplete, misleading, subterfuge
as a hawk: 4 seel
part of: 4 slat
printing for: 7 braille
blind alley: 7 dead end, impasse 8 cul-de-sac
blind god: 4 Hoth 5 Hoder, Hothr
blind me: 5 blimy
blind pig: 4 dive 6 saloon
blind spot: 6 hang-up 7 bigotry
blind staggers: gid 7 vertigo
blind worm: 5 orvet
blinder: 4 flap 5 bluff 7 blinker 8 hoodwink 9 blindfold 11 obstruction
blindfold: 4 dark 5 blink, bluff 7 bandage, blinder, obscure 8 heedless, hoodwink, reckless 9 concealed
blindness: 6 bisson, cecity 7 ablepsy, anopsia 8 ablepsia 9 ignorance
color: 13 achromatopsia 14 monochromatism
day: 11 hemeralopia
partial: 7 meropia 10 cecutiency
snow: 14 chiona-blepsia
blink: 4 shun, wink 5 blush, cheat, flash, gleam, shine, trick 6 glance, ignore, obtuse 7 blinter, condone, glimmer, glimpse, neglect, nictate, sparkle, twinkle 9 blindfold
blinker: eye 5 bluff, light 6 signal 7 blinder, goggles 8 coquette, hoodwink, mackerel
blinking: 5 utter 8 blooming, complete
blintze: 7 pancake
bliss: joy 4 Eden, kaif, seil(Sc.) 5 glory 7 delight, ecstacy, gladden, rapture 8 felicity, gladness, paradise, pleasure 9 happiness 11 contentment
place of: 4 Eden 6 Utopia 7 Elysium 8 Paradise
blissful: 4 holy 6 blithe 7 blessed, Elysian, Utopian 9 beatified, glorified
blister: 4 beat, bleb, blob, lash 5 blain, bulge 6 bubble, scorch 7 vesicle 8 vesicate 10 vesicatory
blithe: gay 4 glad 5 bonny, happy, jolly, merry 6 bonnie, jovial, joyous, lively 7 gaysome, jocular, winsome 8 cheerful, gladsome 9 sprightly
blitzkrieg: 4 raid 5 blitz 6 attack 11 bombardment
blizzard: 4 blow, gale, wind 5 purga 6 retort 9 snowstorm, squelcher
Blizzard State: 11 South Dakota
bloat: 5 puffy, swell 6 expand, tumefy 7 distend, ferment, inflate 8 drunkard
bloated: 5 bloat, cured 6 sodden, turgid 7 pompous
blob: lip, wen 4 bleb, blot, boil, daub, drop, lump, mark, mass 6 bubble, pimple, splash 7 blemish, blister, blossom, globule, postule, splotch 8 globular
bloc: 4 ring 5 cabal, party, union 6 clique 7 faction 11 combination
block: ame, bar, cob, dam, hob, nog, row, vol 4 bloc, cake, clog, cube, foil, head, mass, stop 5 check, chump, deter, nudge, parry, shape, spike, stump 6 hamper, hinder, impede, oppose, outwit, square, street, stymie, taplet, thwart 7 buckler, inhibit, outline, prevent 8 blockade, obstacle, obstruct, stoppage 9 barricade, blockhead, frustrate, hindrance 11 obstruction
architectural: 6 dentil, mutule
electrically insulated: 6 taplet
football: 4 clip
for shaping metal objects: ame
ice: 4 cube 5 serac
mechanical: 6 pulley
metal type: 4 quad, quod
nautical: 7 deadeye
perforated: nut
small: 7 tessera
blockade: dam 5 beset, block, siege 6 whisky 7 embargo 8 obstruct 9 beleaguer 11 obstruction, restriction
blockhead: ass, oaf 4 bust, coof, dolt, fool, mome 5 block, chump, cuddy, idiot, ninny 6 noodle 7 dizzard, half-wit, tomfool 8 beefhead, clodpate, gamphrel, hardhead 9 blockpate, grouthead, hoddy-peak, numbskull, screwball, simpleton 10 beetlehead, dunderhead, hoddy-doddy
blockhouse: 4 fort
bloke: man 4 chap, toff 6 fellow 9 personage
blonde: 4 fair 5 light 6 flaxen, golden, yellow
blood: kin, sap 4 gore, life, mood, race 5 blade, fluid, serum, stock 6 indred 7 gallant, kinship, kinsman, lineage, youstir(Sc.) 8 relation 9 lifeblood 14 consanguineous
comb. form: 4 hema, hemo 5 haemo
deficiency: 6 anemia 7 anaemia

disease: 8 leucemia, leukemia 9 leucaemia, leukaemia
fluid part: 5 serum 6 plasma 7 opsonin
mixed: See **hybrid**
of the gods: 4 icor 5 ichor
particle in: 7 embolus
poisoning: 6 pyemia 7 pyaemia, toxemia 10 septicemia
stagnation: 4 clot 5 cruor, grume 6 stasis, stases
strain: 4 race 5 stock 6 family
testing instrument: 13 hemabarometer 14 haemabarometer

blood and thunder: 6 uproar 8 violence 9 melodrama
blood brother: 6 friend 8 intimate
blood feud: 8 vendetta
blood fine: cro(Sc.) 4 eric 7 galanas, wergild 9 bloodwite
blood horse: 12 thoroughbred
blood money: cro 7 breaghe
blood pudding: 7 sausage
blood relationship: 7 kinsman 8 relative 13 consanguinity
blood vessel: 4 vein 5 hemad 6 artery 9 capillary
comb. form: vas
rupture: 6 rhexis

bloodbath: 8 massacre
bloodcurdling: 8 horrible 10 terrifying
blooded: 9 pedigreed 12 thoroughbred
bloodhound: 4 lyam, lyme
bloodless: 4 dead 6 anemic 7 anaemic, inhuman 8 lifeless 9 unfeeling 10 exsanguine
bloodroot: 7 puccoon 10 tetterwort
bloodshed: 5 death 7 carnage 8 violence 9 slaughter
bloodshot: red 8 inflamed
bloodstone: 10 chalcedony
bloodsucker: 5 leech 7 sponger 11 extortioner
bloodthirsty: 6 bloody, carnal 9 ferocious, murderous 10 sanguinary
bloody: 4 gory 5 cruel 6 cruent 8 bleeding, hematose, infamous 9 cruentous, ferocious, haematose, merciless, murderous 10 sanguinary 12 bloodstained, bloodthirsty, contemptible
bloodybones: 7 specter 9 hobgoblin
bloom (see also **flower**): dew 4 blow 7 blossom, blowing 8 floreate, flourish 13 efflorescence
bloomer: 5 error 6 blower 7 blunder, failure
bloomery: 5 forge 6 hearth 7 furnace
blooming: 4 rosy 5 green 6 abloom, florid
blooper: 5 error, radio 7 blunder, blowing, roseate 8 blinking 10 prospering.
blossom (see also **flower**): bud 4 blob 5 bloom 7 prosper 8 flourish 13 efflorescence
small: 8 floweret

blot: mar 4 blob, blue, daub, soil, spot 5 blend, erase, smear, speck, stain, sully 6 blotch, cancel, damage, efface, impair, macula, shadow, smirch, smudge, smutch, stigma 7 blemish, eclipse, expunge, maculae(pl.), obscure, tarnish 8 disgrace, reproach 9 bespatter 10 obliterate, stigmatize 12 obliteration 13 disfigurement
blotch: dab 4 blot, gout, spot 5 patch, smear, stain 6 macula, mottle, smirch, stigma 7 blemish, maculae(pl.), pustule, splotch 8 eruption, maculate
blouse: 5 shirt, smock, tunic 7 casaque 10 shirtwaist
bushman's: 5 bluey

blow: bob, cob, cop, dub, jab, pat, rap, tap, wap 4 ande, baff, bang, bash, beat, belt, biff, birr, blad, blaw, brag, buff, bump, chap, conk, crig, cuff, daud, dint, dird, drub, dunt, dush, fleg, gale, gowf, huff, jolt, knap, lash, mint, oner, pant, plug, puff, scud, slam, slap, slug, sock 5 binge, blade, blast, blizz, bloom, boast, brunt, burst, clink, clour, clout, clump, crump, curse, douse, dowse, filip, flack, flick, gowff, ictus, impel, knock, peise, shock, skite, slipe, sound, spend, storm, swipe, thump, whack, whang 6 bensel, bensil, betray, bounce, buffet, depart, dirdum, expand, fillip, flower, frolic, larrup, wallop 7 assault, attaint, bensail, bensall, bensell, blossom, blowout, bluster, boaster, destroy, inflate, publish, shatter, whample 8 boasting, calamity, confound, disaster, disclose 9 bastinado
in: 5 enter 6 arrive
mock: 5 feint
over: end 4 pass 7 subside
to: 5 treat
up: 5 scene 7 explode, inflate 8 dynamite, outburst

blower: fan 5 whale 6 puffer 7 bloomer 8 braggart 9 swellfish 11 sacheverell
blowfish: 6 puffer
blowfly: 10 bluebottle
blowgun: 10 peashooter
blowhard: 8 braggart
blowhole: 7 nostril 8 spiracle
blown: 5 stale, tired 6 opened 7 blossom, swollen, tainted 8 betrayed, flyblown, inflated 9 distended, exhausted, worthless
blowout: 4 blow, feed, meal 6 valley 10 depression
blowze: 5 trull, wench, woman 6 hoyden 8 slattern

blowzed: red 5 ruddy 7 flushed
blowzy: 5 dowdy 6 frowzy 10 disheveled, slatternly
blub: 4 bulb 5 swell 6 puffed 7 blubber, swollen
blubber: cry, fat 4 blub, foam, wail, weep 5 swell, thick, whine 6 bubble, flitch, medusa, nettle, seethe 7 blobber, bluster, swollen, whimper 9 disfigure
remove: 6 flense
whale: 5 fenks, speck 6 muktuk
blubbery: fat 5 obese 7 swollen 9 quivering 10 gelatinous 11 protuberant
bludgeon: bat, hit 4 club, mace 5 billy, stick 6 coerce, weapon
blue: low, sad, sky 4 aqua, bice, glum 5 azure, livid, perse, small 6 cobalt, gloomy, indigo, severe 7 celeste, gentian, learned, lobelia 8 cerulean, cynanine, dejected, literary 9 turquoise 10 despondent, melancholy
asbestos: 11 crocidolite
gray: 5 merle, pearl, slate 7 cesious 8 caesious
green: 4 bice, teal 5 beryl 8 calamine
red: 5 smalt 6 mallow 8 gridelin, mazarine 9 gris-de-lin
sheep: 6 bharal
blue blood: 5 noble 10 aristocrat 12 bluestocking
blue boneset: 10 mistflower
blue catalpa: 9 paulownia
blue-chip: 9 exemplary 11 prestigious
blue dandelion: 7 chicory
blue dye herb: 4 woad
Blue Eagle agency: NRA
blue earth: 10 kimberlite
Blue Grotto site: 5 Capri, Italy
blue gum: 4 tree 10 eucalyptus
Blue Hen State: 8 Delaware
blue huckleberry: 11 tangleberry
blue jaundice: 8 cyanosis
blue jeans: 5 levis 6 denims
blue Joe: 8 bluegill
blue John: 4 milk
Blue Law State: 11 Connecticut
blue-pencil: 4 edit 6 delete, redact
blue peter: 4 coot, flag 9 gallinule
blue-ribbon: top 4 best 7 supreme
Bluebeard's wife: 6 Fatima
bluebonnet: cap 4 Scot 7 bluecap 8 Scotsman 10 cornflower
bluebottle: 5 bluet 7 barbeau, blowfly 8 hyacinth
bluecap: 4 Scot 10 bluebonnet
bluefish: 4 bass, tuna 5 saury 8 weakfish
bluegill: 7 sunfish
bluegrass: poa 9 agropyron 10 andropogon
Bluegrass State: 8 Kentucky
bluejacket: gob, tar 6 sailor
bluejoint: 6 redtop
bluenose: 4 snob 8 moralist 11 Nova Scotian
bluepoint: 6 oyster
blueprint: map 4 plan, plot 5 draft, trace 6 sketch 7 diagram 9 cyanotype
bluer: 4 anil
bluerocket: 9 monkshood
blues: 4 song 5 dumps 6 cafard 7 megrims 10 melancholy, mulligrubs 11 despondency
bluestocking: 5 woman 12 intellectual
bluet: 5 plant 10 bluebottle 11 farkleberry
bluethroat: 7 warbler
bluey: 6 bundle 7 blanket
bluff: 4 bank, brag, curt, fool, rude 5 blunt, burly, cliff, frank, gruff, short, surly 6 abrupt, crusty 7 blinder, blinker, brusque, deceive, uncivil 8 barranca, barranco, churlish, hoodwink, impolite 9 blindfold, outspoken, precipice 13 unceremonious
Bluff King Hal: 5 Henry
blunder: err, mix 4 balk, bull, flub, gaff, roil, slip, stir 5 boner, botch, break, error, fault, lapse, misdo 6 boggle, bumble, bungle, gazabo, gazebo, mingle, muddle 7 bloomer, confuse, derange, failure, faux-pas, mistake, stumble 8 solecism 9 confusion, mismanage 11 disturbance
blunderbuss: gun 9 espingole
blunge: mix 5 blend 10 amalgamate
blunk: 6 bungle 9 mismanage
blunt: 4 bald, curt, damp, dull, flat 5 bluff, brusk, inert, plain, plump, stunt 6 clumsy, deaden, obtund, obtuse, stupid 7 brusque 8 hebetate 9 depressed, downright 10 point-blank 11 insensitive 13 unceremonious
mentally: 8 hebitate
blur: dim, hum 4 blob, blot, mist, soil, spot 5 blear, cloud, smear, stain, sully 6 mackle, macule, smudge, stigma 7 blemish, obscure 9 disfigure
blurb: ad 4 puff, rove 5 brief 6 notice 12 announcement, commendation 13 advertisement
blush: 4 glow, look 5 blink, color, flush, gleam, tinge 6 glance, mantle, redden 8 likeness 10 appearance, rubescence
blushing: red 4 rosy 5 ruddy 7 roseate 8 flushing 9 rosaceous 10 erubescent 11 embarrassed
bluster: 4 blow, huff, rage, rant 5 blast, bleat, boast, bully, noise, storm, swank 6 babble, bellow, bounce, hector, huffle, tumult 7 blubber, bravado, gauster, roister, swagger 8 boasting, bullying, threaten 9 confusion, gasconade 10 swaggering, turbulence 11 fanfaronade, rodomontade
bo, boh: 5 chief 6 leader 7 captain

boa: 5 aboma, scarf, snake 8 anaconda 9 neckpiece
boa contrictor: 5 snake 6 giboia
Boadicea's people: 5 Iceni
boar: hog, sus 4 aper 5 swine 6 barrow, hogget 8 sanglier 9 hoggaster
head: 4 hure
wound: 4 gore 5 ganch
board: 4 deal, diet, eats, fare, keep, lath, slat 5 enter, found, house, lodge, meals, panel, plank, stage 6 accost, planch, shield 7 cabinet, council, duoviri, enplane, entrain, planche 8 approach, tribunal 9 authority, shipboard 10 commission, management, provisions 11 switchboard 13 entertainment
boast: gab 4 blaw, blow, brag, crow, pomp, rave 5 brave, extol, exult, glory, prate, roose, scold, skite, vapor, vaunt 6 bounce, clamor, extoll, flaunt, menace(Sc.), outcry, splore 7 bluster, clamour, display, glorify, swagger 8 flourish, threaten 9 gasconade 11 rodomontade
boaster: 5 skite 6 crower, gascon, pedant 7 bouncer, bravado, cracker, ruffler 8 blowhard, braggart, cacofogo, fanfaron, glorioso, jingoist, rodomont 9 cacafuego 11 braggadocio
boastful: big 6 parado 8 fanfaron 9 gasconade, kompology 11 rodomontade, thrasonical
boat (see also **canoe, ship, vessel**): ark, cat, cot, gig, tub 4 bark, brig, carv, dory, junk, raft, scow, ship, skag, tack, trow, yawl 5 aviso, barca, barge, bully, canoe, coble, craft, dingy, ferry, ketch, liner, shell, skiff, skift, smack, xebec, zebec 6 baidak, bateau, carvel, chebec, cruise, cutter, dinghy, dugout, garvey, packet, vessel, zebeck 7 bateaus, chebeck, coracle, gondola, lighter, nacelle, pinnace, scooter, steamer 8 pessoner, schooner 9 submarine, transport 10 watercraft
coal cargo: 7 collier
comb form: 5 scapo
deck: 4 poop 5 orlop
engine-driven: 6 sampan
fishing: 8 bracozzo
flat-bottomed: bac 4 dory, punt, scow 5 barge 6 bateau
freight: 7 lighter
front: bow 4 prow
garbage: 6 hopper
harbor: tug 5 barge 7 bumboat
joint: 4 jerl
merchant: 6 argosy, holcad
ornamental: 9 navicella
part: bow 4 beam, deck, hold, keel, prow 5 bilge, cabin, stern 6 bridge, gunnel, kelson, saloon, thwart 7 capstan, gunwale, keelson, painter, scupper 12 companionway
pin: 5 thole
post: poy 4 biff 7 bollard, capstan 9 sternpost
power: tug
propellant: oar, row 4 pole 5 motor, scull
racing: gig 5 scull
ride: row 4 sail 6 cruise
round: 4 gufa 5 goofa 6 goofah
sailing: 4 pram, proa 5 praam, prahu
undersea: sub 9 submarine 11 submersible
boatman: 6 barger, Charon 7 hobbler, hoveler, huffler 8 hoveller 9 gondolier 10 barcajuolo
boatswain: 5 bosun 6 serang
whistle: 4 pipe
Boaz: *son:* 4 Obed
wife: 4 Ruth
bob: bow, cut, dab, job, rap, tap 4 ball, blow, buff, calf, clip, coin, cork, duck, grub, jeer, jerk, jest, knob, mock, worm 5 bunch, cheat, dance, filch, float, flout, shake, taunt, trick 6 bingle, buffet, curtsy, delude, pommel, strike, weight 7 bobsled, bobtail, cluster, curtesy, haircut, pendant, refrain 8 shilling 9 bobsleigh
bobac: 6 marmot
bobber: 4 cork, duck 5 float 6 bobfly 7 dropper 8 deadhead
bobbery: 6 hubbub, tumult 8 squabble 11 disturbance
bobbie, bobby: cop 4 bull 6 peeler 7 officer 9 policeman
bobbin: pin 4 cord, pirn, reel 5 braid, quill, spool 7 ratchet, spindle 8 cylinder 10 cuckoopint
frame: 5 ereel
pin: 7 spindle
bobble: dib 6 fumble
bobcat: 4 lynx
bobolink: 4 bird, reed 7 bunting, ortolan 10 butterbird
bobsled: bob 6 ripper
bobtail: bob, cur 4 dock 6 rabble, strunt(Sc.) 7 curtail 8 sheepdog 9 deficient 11 abbreviated
bobwhite: 4 bird 5 colin, quail
bocardo: 6 dokhma, prison 7 bokardo
Boccaccio work: 9 Decameron
bodacious: 8 reckless
bode: 4 omen, stop 5 augur, offer 6 herald 7 message, portend, presage 8 forebode, forecast, foreshow, foretell, indicate 9 messenger 10 inaugurate 13 foreshadowing, prognosticate
bodice: 4 jupe 5 choli, gilet, waist 6 basque, corset
bodiless: 9 trunkless 11 incorporeal

bodily: 5 solid 6 actual, carnal 7 fleshly, somatic 8 corporal, entirely, material, physical 9 corporeal 10 completely 11 corporeally, substantial

bodily motion: 5 shrug 7 gesture

boding: 7 ominous 10 foreboding, prediction, prognostic

bodkin: awl, pin 6 dagger, needle 7 hairpin, poniard 8 stiletto 9 eyeleteer

body: 4 bole, bouk, bulk, form, mass, nave, rupa, soma, stem 5 flesh, stiff, torso, trunk 6 corpse, corpus, extent, licham, person 7 cadaver, carcass, company 8 extensum, majority 9 curcurbit, substance 10 assemblage, foundation 11 association, corporation

anterior part of: 7 prosoma

armor: 4 tace 6 corium

away from center: 6 distal

cavity: 5 sinus 6 coelom 7 coelome

comb. form: 4 soma 6 somato

fluid: 5 blood, lymph, serum 6 plasma, saliva

heavenly: sun 4 luna, moon, star 5 comet 6 meteor, planet 8 asteroid, luminary

joint: hip 4 knee 5 elbow, wrist 8 shoulder

motion: 7 gesture

of men: 5 posse 10 authorized

of persons: 5 corps, posse

of water: bay, sea 4 gulf, lake, pond, pool 5 ocean 6 lagoon, sealet 9 reservoir

path: 5 orbit

pert. to: 5 somal 8 physical, systemic

wagon: box

wall: 6 paries, septum

body politic: 4 weal 9 community

bodyguard: 5 thane 6 escort 7 retinue, trabant 9 lifeguard

Boeotia: *capital:* 6 Thebes

region: 5 Ionia

Boer: *dialect:* 4 Taal

general: 5 Botha

bog: bug, car, fen, gog, hag 4 bold, carr, cess, mire, moor, moss, ooze, sink, slew, slue, syrt 5 marsh, saucy, swamp 6 morass, muskeg, slough 7 forward 8 quagmire 9 conceited

bog down: 4 mire 5 stall 6 bemire

bogey: bug, cow, hag 5 bogie, bogle, devil, gnome 6 boggle, booger, goblin 7 boggard, boggart, bugaboo, bugbear, gnomide, specter, spectre 9 hobgoblin, scarecrow 10 bullbeggar

boggle: jib, shy 4 balk, foil, stop 5 alarm, botch, demur, scare, start 6 baffle, bungle, goblin, shrink 7 bauchle, blunder, perplex, scruple 8 frighten, hesitate 9 dissemble, embarrass 10 difficulty

boggy: wet 4 miry, soft 5 gouty, fenny, haggy, mossy 6 quaggy, swampy 7 boggish, queachy

bogle: 5 alarm, scare 6 goblin

bogus: 4 fake, sham 5 false, phony 8 spurious 10 fictitious 11 counterfeit

bogy: See **bogey.**

Bohemian: 4 arty 5 gipsy, gypsy 6 Picard

dance: 6 redowa

boil: sty 4 bile, blob, buck, coct, cook, rage, sore, stew, stye, teem 5 botch, brede, steam 6 betray, bubble, buller, burble, decoct, seethe, simmer 7 anthrax, estuate, inflame 8 aestuate, ebullate 10 ebbulliate, effervesce

almost: 5 scald

down: 6 decoct

boiler: 4 reef 6 copper, kettle, retort 7 alembic, caldron, furnace 8 cauldron

plate: 4 sput

tube scaler: 6 sooter

boisterous: 4 gurl, loud, rude 5 burly, gurly, noisy, rough, windy 6 coarse, stormy, strong, unruly 7 furious, massive, roaring, violent 8 cumbrous, strident, vehement 9 clamorous, excessive, excitable 10 blustering, tumultuous, unyielding

bold: big, bog, yep 4 derf, pert, rash, rude, yepe 5 bardy, bield, brash, brave, brent, frack, freak, freck, gally, hardy, large, manly, nervy, peart, saucy, steep, stout 6 abrupt, audace, brassy, brazen, crouse, daring, fierce, heroic, strong 7 assured, dashing, defiant, forward, grivois, haughty, massive, valiant 8 arrogant, familiar, fearless, grivoise, immodest, impudent, intrepid, malapert, powerful, resolute 9 audacious, bodacious, confident, dauntless, imprudent, undaunted 10 courageous, forritsome 11 venturesome 12 enterprising, overassuming, presumptuous, stout-hearted 13 overconfident

boldness: 4 brow 5 bield, nerve, vigor 6 daring 7 bravery, courage 8 audacity, temerity 9 assurance, hardiesse, hardihood, hardiness 10 brazenness, confidence, effrontery 11 intrepidity, presumption 13 dauntlessness

bole: 4 clay, dose, stem 5 bolus, crypt, trunk 7 opening

bolero: 5 dance, waist 6 jacket

Bolero composer: 5 Ravel

bolide: 6 meteor 7 missile

Bolivia: *animal:* 6 vicuna

city: 5 La Paz(c.), Oruro, Sucre(c.) 6 Potosi 10 Chuquisaca, Cochabamba

coin: 5 tomin 7 bolivar, centavo 9 boliviano

district: 5 La Paz, Oruro 6 Elbeni, Potosi, Tarija 7 Colinas, El Chaco 9 Santa Cruz 10 Chuquisaca, Cochabamba
dried mutton: 7 chalone
Indian: Uro, Uru 4 Iten, Moxo, Uran 6 Arawak, Aymara, Charca, Chicha, Tacana 7 Aymaran, Puquina, Sirione 10 Chiriguano
lake: 8 Aullugas, Titacaca 11 Desaguadero
measure: 6 league 7 celemin
mountain: 5 Andes, Cusco, Cuzco 6 Sajama, Sorata 8 Illimani
plateau: 9 Altiplano
river: 4 Beni 5 Orton 6 Mamore 7 Guapore 8 Paraguay 9 Pilcomayo, San Miguel 10 Cordillera 11 Madre de Dios
weight: 5 libra, macro
boll: pod 4 bulb, grow, knob 5 onion 6 bubble 7 capsule, measure 8 pericarp 12 protuberance
boll weevil: 6 picudo
bollard: 4 bitt, post
bolo: 5 knife 7 machete, sundang 8 pacifist 9 defeatist
Bolshevist: 7 Russian 9 socialist
leader: 5 Lenin
bolster: aid, pad 6 pillow 7 cushion, support 8 compress, maintain
bolt: bar, pen, pin, rod, run 4 beat, dart, flee, gulp, lock, pawl, sift 5 arrow, bilbo, close, elope, flash, gorge, latch, rivet, shaft 6 assort, decamp, desert, fasten, flight, garble, pintle, purify, refine, secure, strong, toggle, winnow 7 missile, shackle, thunder 8 fastener, separate, stampede 9 lightning
bolus: cud 4 bole, clop, lump, mass, pill, rock
bomb: dud, egg 5 blare, shell 6 ashcan 7 bombard, grenade, marmite 9 pineapple 10 projectile 11 blockbuster
guide: fin
hole: 6 crater
bombard: 4 bomb 5 crump, shell 6 batter, bottle, strafe, vessel
bombardier: 6 gunner 12 artilleryman
bombardment: 5 blitz, siege 6 attack, rafale, strafe 9 cannonade
bombardon: 4 oboe, tuba 7 bassoon
bombast: gas, pad 4 rage, rant, rave 5 stuff 6 padded 7 bluster, stuffed, tympany 8 boasting 9 turgidity 11 rodomontade 12 altiloquence 14 grandiloquence
bombastic: 5 tumid, vocal 6 fluent, heroic, turgid 7 bombast, flowery, fustian, orotund, pompous, ranting, stilted 8 inflated 9 expansive, flatulent, grandiose, plethoric 10 lexiphanic 12 magniloquent
Bombay: *arrowroot:* 5 tikor
division: 4 Sind
fabric: 5 rumal
hemp: 4 sunn 6 ambary
mountain: Abu
native: 5 Parsi 6 Parsee
state: 4 Edar
town: 5 Miraj, Poona, Surat
vessel: 7 patamar
bombinate: hum 4 boom
bombproof chamber: 8 casemate
bombyx: eri 4 eria, moth 8 silkworm
bon ami: 5 lover 6 friend 10 sweetheart
bon mot: pun 4 jest, quip 9 witticism
bonafide: 7 genuine 9 authentic
bonanza: 4 mint 6 eureka 7 jackpot
Bonanza State: 7 Montana
bonasus: ox 5 bison 7 aurochs
bonbon: 5 candy, cream 6 dainty 7 caramel 8 confetto, confetti 9 sugarplum
bond: tie, vow 4 bail, band, duty, glue, knot, link, note, yoke 5 bound, chain, nexus 6 binder, cement, connex, engage, escrow, fetter, league, pledge 7 husband, manacle, shackle 8 adhesive, contract, covenant, guaranty, ligament, ligature, mortgage, security 9 agreement, composure, guarantee 10 constraint, husbandman, obligation 11 association, householder
chemical: 5 diene 7 valence
bondage: 4 yoke 7 helotry, serfdom, slavery 9 captivity, restraint, servitude, thralldom
bondsman: 4 carl, esne, peon, serf 5 churl, Helot, slave 6 stooge, surety, thrall, vassal 7 chattel, peasant, servant, villein
bondstone: 6 binder
bone: os; rib 4 ossa(pl.) 5 blade 6 fillet, radius 7 humerus
anvil: 5 incus 7 incudes(pl.)
arm: 4 ulna 6 radius 7 humerus
breast: 6 sterna(pl.) 7 sternum
cartilage: 6 ossein
cavity: 5 antra(pl.), sinus 6 antrum
cell: 10 osteoblast
change into: 6 ossify
comb. form: os 5 osteo
dorsal: 4 ilia(pl.) 5 ilium
elbow: 4 ulna
formation: 7 ostosis 10 parostosis
girdle: 12 sphenethmoid
manipulator: 9 osteopath
pert. to: 6 osteal 7 osseous
prefix: 4 oste
scraper: 6 xyster
bonefish: 8 ladyfish
bonelet: 7 ossicle
boner: 5 error 7 blunder, mistake
bones: 4 dice, ossa 8 skeletoa
boneset: 7 comfrey 8 hempweek 12 thoroughwort
boneyard: 5 store 6 supply 9 scrap heap

bonefire: 5 blaze
bongo: 4 drum 8 antelope
boniata: yam
boniface: 8 landlord 9 innkeeper
bonito: aku, atu 4 fish, nice 5 cobia 6 bonita, pretty, robalo 8 skipjack
Bonjour Tristesse author: 5 Sagan
bonne: 5 nurse 9 nursemaid 11 maidservant
bonnet: cap, hat 4 hood 5 cover, decoy, toque 6 capote, slouch 7 chapeau, coronet 8 headgear 9 headdress 10 accomplice, chinquapin
brim: 4 poke
string: 5 bride
bonnet monkey: 4 zati 5 munga
bonny, bonnie: gay 4 fine 5 merry, plump 6 blithe, pretty, strong 7 healthy 8 budgeree, handsome 9 beautiful 11 good-looking
bonnyclabber: 4 curd, milk, skyr
bonton: 5 elite
bonus: tip 4 gift, meed 5 award, bribe, bunce, pilon, prize, spiff 6 reward 7 cumshaw, premium, subsidy 8 dividend, lagnappe 9 allowance, lagniappe 12 compensation
bony: 4 hard, lank, leaw, thin 5 stiff, tough 6 osteal, skinny 7 osseous 8 skeletal
boo: 4 hoot, jeer 5 decry
boob: ass 4 fool 5 dunce, goony, neddy 6 nitwit
boobook: owl 6 cuckoo
booby: 5 dunce, idiot, loser, prize 6 sleigh, stupid 8 goosecap 9 simpleton
booby hatch: 4 jail 6 asylum
boodle: 4 swag 5 crowd, graft 6 noodle 7 plunder 8 caboodle
boohoo: sob 4 hoot, weep 5 shout 8 sailfish
boojum: 5 snark
book: mo; log, mss. 4 opus, text, tome 5 Bible, canto, diary, divan, enter, folio, liber, libri(pl.) 6 manual, record, volume 7 blotter, catalog, writing 8 brochure, document, libretto, register 9 catalogue, potboiler
accounts: day 5 bilan, liber 6 ledger 7 journal
alphabet: 9 abecedary
Apocrypha: 5 Tobit
back: 5 spine
best selling: 5 Bible
binding material: 5 cloth, paper 6 canvas 7 buckram, leather
blank: 5 album, diary 6 tablet
church music: 6 hymnal
collector: 12 bibliomaniac
cover ornamentation: 7 tooling
covering: 6 jacket 7 binding
design: 6 format, lay-out
destroyer: 11 biblioclast
devotional: 5 Bible 6 gospel, missal 7 diurnal, psalter
division: 7 chapter
elementary reading: 6 primer
fiction: 5 novel
group: 7 trilogy
Islam: 5 kitab, Koran
jacket notice: 5 blurb
large: 4 tome 5 folio
lover: 11 bibliophile
make-up: 6 format
manuscript: 5 codex, draft 7 codices(pl.)
map: 5 atlas
mass: 6 missal
navigator's: log 7 logbook 9 portolano
obscene: 11 pornography
of hours: 4 Hora 5 Horae(pl.)
of masses: 6 missal
of nobility: 7 peerage
of psalms: 7 psalter
page: 5 folio
palm: 4 tara 7 taliera
part: 4 leaf, page 5 cover 7 binding, chapter, section 9 signature
pert. to: 13 bibliographic
school: 6 primer, reader 7 grammar, speller 9 geography 10 arithmetic
size: 6 octavo, quarto 8 twelvemo 9 duodecimo
title page: 6 rubric
translation: 4 pony
words of opera: 8 libretto
yearbook: 7 almanac
Zoroastrian: 6 Avesta
book dealer: 10 bibliopole 11 bonguiniste
bookbinder: 12 bibliopegist
bookcase: 5 forel 6 forrel
bookkeeper: 7 auditor 10 accountant
bookkeeping term: 4 post 5 debit, entry 6 credit 9 statement
booklet: 8 brochure 10 literature
bookman: 6 bookie, dealer 7 scholar 9 publisher 11 litterateur
bookplate: 8 exlibris
bookworm: 6 reader 7 scholar 11 bibliophile
boom: jib 4 bump, crib, pole, roar, spar 5 croon 7 bumpkin, resound, support 8 bowsprit, flourish 9 bombilate, bombinate 10 prosperity
boomerang: 5 kiley, kalie 6 recoil 7 rebound 8 backfire, ricochet
boon: gay 4 bene, gift, good, kind 5 favor, grant, merry, order 6 benign, bounty, favour, goodly, jovial, prayer 7 benefit, command, present 8 blessing, intimate, petition 9 congenial, convivial, favorable 10 concession, prosperous 11 benefaction

boon companion: pal 4 chum 5 buddy
boondocks: 6 sticks 9 backwoods 10 wilderness
boondoggle: 6 trifle 9 goldbrick
boor: cad, oaf 4 Boer, carl, lout, pill 5 chuff, churl, clown, slave 6 carlot, clunch, hoblob, lubber, lummox, rustic 7 cauboge, grobian, peasant, villain 8 bosthoon 9 barbarian, roughneck 10 clodhopper, countryman, husbandman, tramontane
boorish: 4 rude 5 gawky, rough, surly 6 clumsy, rustic, sullen, vulgar 7 awkward, crabbed, hoblike, loutish, roister, uncouth 8 churlish, cloddish, clownish, lubberly, ungainly 9 bourgeois 10 uncultured, unmannerly
boost: aid 4 abet, back, help, lift, plug, push 5 coach, exalt, hoist, raise 6 assist, rear up 7 advance, commend, elevate, endorse, indorse, promote 8 increase 9 encourage 10 assistance 12 commendation
booster: 4 shot 9 injection 10 enthusiast
boot: pac, use 4 cure, gain, help, kick, shoe, sock 5 avail, booty, eject, jemmy, kamik, spoil 6 bootee, buskin, casing, crakow, enrich, fumble, galosh, sheath 7 benefit, galoshe 8 chassure(F.), covering 9 advantage, discharge, dismissal
  half: pac 4 pack 6 buskin, cocker 7 blucher, bottine 8 cothurni(pl.) 9 cothurnus
  heavy: pac 5 stogy 6 Brogan 8 Balmoral
  high-water: 5 wader
  loose-topped: 10 wellington
  riding: 5 jemmy 7 gambado
  small: 7 bottine 8 bottekin
Boot: 5 Italy
booted: 4 shod 7 ocreate
booth: 4 loge, shed, shop, sook 5 bothy, cabin, crame, house, stall, stand 6 tienda 7 balagan
bootleg: 7 illegal, illicit 11 clandestine 12 illegitimate 13 surreptitious
bootless: 7 useless 9 incurable 10 remediless, unavailing 12 unprofitable
bootlick: 4 fawn 5 toady 7 flatter
booty: 4 boot, gain, loot, pelf, prey, swag 5 cheat, graft, prize 6 spoils 7 despoil, pillage, plunder 10 chevisance
booze: 4 bout 5 budge, drink, spree 6 fuddle, liquor
boozer: pub 5 toper 6 bouser
boquet: See **bouquet**
bora: 4 wind
borax: 6 tincal
Bordeaux wine (see also **wine**): 5 Bourg, cosne, medoc 6 claret 7 Margauz
border: hem, rim 4 abut, brim, dado, eave, edge, line, nark, orle, rand, rund(Sc.), roon, side, trim 5 bound, braid, brink, coast, costa, flank, forel, frame, limit, march, marge, plait, skirt, strip, touch, verge 6 adjoin, costae, edging, forrel, fringe, impale, margin, purfle, stripe 7 bordure, confine, selvage 8 boundary, frontier, neighbor, tressour, tressure 9 extremity, periphery 10 sidepieces
  fluted: 5 frill
  ornamental: 4 dado
  wall: 4 dado, ogee 7 cornice
Border State (Civil War): 8 Arkansas, Delaware, Kentucky, Maryland, Missouri, Virginia 9 Tennessee 13 North Carolina
bordering: 6 edging 8 abutting, adjacent
bore: bit, irk, tap 4 drag, hole, pall, poke, push, ream, size, tide, tire, tool 5 annoy, augur, chink, drill, eagre, gauge, prick, punch, tewel, trick, weary 6 befool, gimlet, pierce, thrust, tunnel 7 caliber, calibre, carried, crevice, opening 8 aiguille, diameter 9 annoyance, penetrate, perforate, terebrate 11 perforation 12 buttonholder
Boreas: 4 wind 7 norther
  son: 5 Butes 6 Calais
borecole: 4 kail, kale
bored: 7 ennuyee(F.)
boredom: 5 ennui 6 tedium
borer: 6 insect 7 hagfish, termite 8 shipworm
boric acid salt: 6 borate
boring: dry 4 flat 6 broach, tiring 7 tedious 8 piercing, tiresome 9 wearisome 11 displeasing, penetrating 13 uninteresting
boring tool: bit 5 auger, drill 6 gimlet, wimble
born: nee(F.) 6 innate 7 nascsent, natural 9 delivered
  dead: 9 stillborn
  prematurely: 8 abortive
  well: 4 free 5 noble 7 eugenic
borne (see also **bear**): 4 rode 6 narrow 7 carried, endured
  by the wind: 6 eolian
Borneo (see also **Indonesia**): *ape:* 5 orang 9 orangutan
  city: 5 Bruni
  island near: 4 Java
  measure: 5 ganta 7 gantang
  mountain: 8 Kini-Balu
  native: 4 Dyak, Iban 5 Dayak
  pepper plant: ara
  pirates: 5 bajau
  river: 5 Bruni, Kajan
  sea: 4 Sulu
  seaport: 4 Miri 5 Balik, Papan
  snake: 5 boiga
  timbertree: 7 billian
  tribe: 4 Dyak, Iban 6 Dusuns
  weight: 4 para 6 chapah
boron: 5 borax, boric 7 ulexite

borough: 4 burg, town 5 brush, burgh 6 burgus, castle 7 citadel, village 8 fortress, township
borracho: 5 drunk 8 drunkard
borrow: 4 copy, loan, take 5 adopt, steal 6 pledge, surety 7 chevise, hostage, tithing 11 frankpledge
bosc: 4 pear
boscage: 4 wood 5 grove 7 thicket
bosh: end, rot 4 joke, show, talk, tosh 5 trash 6 bushwa, figure, flaunt, humbug, trivia 8 nonsense 9 poppycock
bosky: 5 bushy, tipsy, woody 7 fuddled 11 intoxicated
Bosnian native: 4 Slav 5 Croat
bosom: 4 barm(Sc.) 5 close, sinus 6 breast, cavity, desire, recess 7 beloved, embrace, inclose 8 intimate 9 cherished 11 inclination, indentation 12 confidential
boss: bur, pad 4 baas, buhr, burr, knob, stud 5 bully, chief, empty, knosp, order, owner 6 brooch, button, direct, emboss, hollow, manage, master, shield 7 capataz, cushion, foreman, hassock, headman, manager, phalera 8 director, domineer, overseer 9 supervise 10 politician, supervisor 12 protuberance 14 superintendent
logging camp: 5 bully
political: 7 cacique
shield: 4 umbo
bossy: cow 4 calf 11 dictatorial, domineering
Boston: 4 game 5 waltz 8 Beantown
district: Hub 7 Back Bay
leader: 7 Brahmin
bot: 5 larva
botanist: Ray 5 Brown 6 Mendel
botany: *angle:* 4 axil
cell: 5 spore
depression: 5 fovea 7 variole
botch: mar, mux 4 boil, mend, mess, sore 5 bitch, bodge, spoil 6 boggle, bumble, bungle, cobble, jumble, repair 8 swelling 10 hodge podge
botcher: 6 grilse, salmon 7 bungler, butcher, clouter, cobbler
botfly larva: bot
both: bo; two 7 equally
handed: 12 ambidextrous
prefix: bi 4 ambi
bother: ado, ail, nag, vex 4 fuss 5 annoy, deave, tease, worry 6 badger, bustle, dither, flurry, gravel, harass, meddle, moider, molest, pester, pother, puzzle, tamper 7 confuse, disturb, perplex, trouble 8 bewilder, irritate, nuisance
bothy: cot, hut 5 booth, lodge 6 bothie 8 barracks
bottle: jug 4 vial 5 cruet, cruse, flask, glass, gourd, house, phial 6 bundle, carafe, carboy, fiasco, flagon, magnum, vessel 7 canteen, costrel 8 building, decanter, demijohn, jeroboam, preserve 9 aryballos, aryballus, container
sealer: 6 capper
size: 4 pint, pipe 5 fifth, quart 6 magnum 8 jeroboam
small: 4 vial 5 ampul, cruet, phial 6 doruck, flacon 7 ampoule, costrel 8 decanter 11 vinaigrette
bottleneck: 7 barrier 8 blockade
bottom: bed 4 base, dale, fund, holm, lees, root 5 abyss, basis, dregs, floor, nadir 6 ground 7 bedrock, grounds, lowland, support, surface 8 buttocks, sediment 10 foundation, groundwork
boudoir: 4 room 5 cabin 7 bedroom, cabinet
bouffant, bouffante: 4 full 6 puffed 7 bulging
bough: arm, leg 4 limb, twig 5 shoot, spray, sprig 6 branch, ramage 7 gallows 8 offshoot, shoulder
bouillabaisse: 4 stew 7 chowder
bouillon: 4 soup 5 broth 8 consomme
boulder: 4 rock 5 stone
monument: 8 megalith
transported by ice: 7 erratic
boulevard: 6 avenue, street 7 highway 12 thoroughfare
boulevardier: 4 roue 5 dandy, idler
bounce: 4 bang, blow, brag, bump, fire, jump, leap, sack 5 boast, bound, bully, carom, chuck, eject, knock, scold, thump, verve 6 spirit, spring, strike 7 address, bluster, dismiss, rebound, swagger 8 proclaim, ricochet 9 discharge, explosion, expulsion 10 resilience
bouncing: big 5 buxom, lusty, stout 7 healthy 9 excessive
bound: dap, end, hop 4 bent, bind, bond, brow, butt, dart, girt, jump, leap, mere, ramp, scud, skip, stem 5 ambit, bourn, going, limit, ready, stend, sting, tiled, vault, verge 6 border, bounce, bourne, curvet, define, domain, finish, hurdle, oblige, prance, spring 7 barrier, certain, chained, closure, confine, costive, delimit, dressed, rebound, saltate, secured, trussed 8 boundary, confined, destined, enclosed, frontier, handfast, landmark, precinct, prepared, shackled 9 compelled, inhibited, obligated 10 borderland 11 constrained, termination 12 circumscribe 13 circumference
back: 5 carom 6 resile
by a vow: 6 votary
boundary: ahu, end, rim 4 dole, dool, edge, line, mear, meer, mere, meta, mete, term, wall 5 ambit, bourn, fence, hedge, limit, march, metae, mound, verge 6 border,

bourne, define 7 barrier, bounder, termini(pl.) 8 frontier, precinct, terminus 9 demarcate, perimeter 11 termination 13 circumference
comb. form: ori
bounder: cab, cad, cub 4 snob, rake, roue 7 dogcart
boundless: 4 vast 6 untold 7 endless, eternal 8 infinite 9 limitless, unlimited 10 immoderate, unconfined, unmeasured 11 illimitable, measureless 12 immeasurable, interminable
bountiful: 4 good, lush, rich 5 ample 6 freely, lavish 7 liberal, profuse 8 abundant, generous 9 bounteous, plenteous, plentiful 10 munificent
bounty: 4 boon, gift, meed 5 award, bonus, grant, valor, worth 6 reward, virtue 7 largess, premium, present, prowess, subsidy 8 goodness, gratuity, kindness 9 allowance 10 generosity, liberality, recompense 11 beneficence, munificence
Bounty captain: 5 Bligh
bouquet, boquet: 4 aura, odor 5 aroma, cigar, posey, spray 7 corsage, nosegay 9 fragrance 10 compliment 11 boutonniere
bourgeois: 6 common, stupid 7 boorish, burgher 8 mediocre 9 hidebound 12 capitalistic, conservative
bourn, bourne: 4 goal 5 bound, brook, limit, realm 6 bourne, domain, stream 7 rivulet 8 boundary 11 destination
bouse: cup 4 haul, lift, pull, tope 5 booze, drink 6 beaker 7 carouse
bout: go; job 4 turn 5 booze, essay, fight, match, round, set-to, trial 6 attack, fracas 7 attempt, carouse, circuit, contest, debauch, outside, without 8 conflict 10 knobkerrie
boutique: 4 shop
boutonniere: 6 boquet 7 bouquet 10 buttonhole
bovine: ox; bos, cow 4 bull, calf, dull, neat, slow, zebu 5 bison, steer 6 oxlike 7 patient, taurine 8 longhorn, sluggish
hybrid: 4 mule 6 catalo
genus: bos
bow: arc, nod, tie 4 arch, beck, bend, bent, duck, fold, knot, prow, stem, turn, wend 5 binge, conge, crush, curve, defer, kneel, noued, stoop, yield 6 archer, assent, bauble, buckle, curtsy, fiddle, ribbon, salaam, submit, swerve, weapon 7 depress, incline, inflict, rainbow 8 crescent, greeting 9 obeisance, prostrate
facing sea: 4 atry
of ship: 4 beak, prow, stem
oriental: 5 salam 6 salaam
toward: 5 afore
wood for: yew
bow-shaped: 6 arcate
bowdlerize: 6 censor 9 expurgate
bowed: 4 bent 5 kneed 6 arcate, curved 7 bulging
bowels: gut 5 belly, colon 8 entrails 10 compassion 11 disembowels, eviscerates
bower: 4 jack, nook 5 abode, arbor, joker, knave 6 anchor 7 berceau, chamber, cottage, embower, enclose, pergola, retreat, shelter
bowfin: 4 amia 6 lawyer 7 grindle, mudfish
bowie: tub 4 bowl, cask, pail 5 knife
Bowie State: 8 Arkansas
bowl: cap, cup, pan 4 coup 5 arena, basin, bowie, depas, phial, rogan 6 beaker, crater, syphus, tureen, vessel 7 stadium, whiskin
bowler: hat 5 derby 6 kegler 8 trundler
bowling: 7 tenpins
division: 5 frame
pin: 7 ninepin, skittle
place: 5 alley
score: 5 spare 6 strike
bowman: 5 cupid 6 archer
box: bin, lug, pix, pyx 4 arca, cage, caja, case, cist, crib, cuff, cyst, loge, pack, scob, seat, slap, slug, spar, stow, till, tray 5 barge, boist, buist, buxus, caddy, chest, clout, crate, fight, hutch, punch, shrub, stall, trunk 6 arcana(pl.), buffet, bunker, carton, casket, coffin, hopper, shrine, strike 7 arcanum, cabinet, caisson, casquet, cassone, confine, enclose, fostell, hanaper, package, trummel 9 container, fisticuff 10 receptacle
alms: 4 arca
ammunition: 7 caisson 9 bandoleer, bandolier
document: 7 hanaper
tea: 8 canister
box office: 4 gate 6 income 8 receipts
box sleigh: 4 pung
boxcar: 7 carrier
boxer: dog, hat, pug 5 champ 6 bantam 7 bruiser, fighter, sparrer 8 pugilist 11 heavyweight
hand covering: 5 cesti, glove 6 cestus
boxing contest: 4 bout 5 match
blow: jab 5 feint, punch
knockout: KO; TKO
pert. to: 6 fistic 10 pugilistic
boxwood: 4 tree 5 seron
boy: bub, lad, tad 4 chap, nino(Sp.), page, puer(L.) 5 buddy, chabo, child, gamin, knave, rogue, valet, youth 6 garcon, nipper, rascal, shaver, urchin 7 gossoon, servant 8 henchboy 9 stripling, youngster

boy friend: 4 beau 5 beaux(pl.) 6 steady 10 sweetheart

boycott: 4 shun 5 avoid, debar 9 blackball 10 ostracized

brabble: 5 argue 7 quarrel

brace: leg, tie, two 4 bind, case, frap, gird, mark, pair, prop, stay 5 nerve, strut 6 clench, couple, crutch, fasten, fathom, splint 7 embrace, refresh, stiffen, support 8 buttress, encircle 9 reinforce, stimulate, suspender 10 strengthen 11 mantelpiece

bracelet: 4 band, ring 5 chain 6 armlet, bangle, grivna 7 armilla, circlet, manacle, poignet 8 handcuff 10 calombigas

bracer: 5 drink, tonic 6 breeze 9 stimulant

brachyuran: 4 crab 10 crustacean

bracing: 5 crisp, quick, tonic 10 salubrious 11 stimulating 12 invigorating 13 strengthening

brack: 4 crag 5 brine, crack

bracken: 4 fern 5 plaid

bracket: 5 brace, class, level, shelf, strut 6 corbel, couple, sconce 7 console, fixture, spotted 8 category, speckled 9 merganser

brackish: 5 foist, salty 6 bracky, saline 7 saltish 8 nauseous 11 distasteful

bract: 5 glume, palea, palet 6 spadix, spathe

brad: pin 4 nail 5 rivet, sprig

brae: 4 bank, brow, hill 5 cleve, slope 6 cleeve, valley 8 hillside

brag: 4 blaw, blow, crow, defy, huff, yelp 5 bluff, boast, flird, preen, strut, vaunt 6 bounce, splore 7 display, gauster, roister, swagger 8 braggart, flourish, pretense, threaten 9 gasconade 11 rodomontade

braggadocio: 7 boaster 8 braggart, rodomont 9 swaggerer 10 pretension

braggart: 4 brag 5 boast 6 blower, crower, gascon, potgun 7 boaster, cracker, ruffler 8 bangster, blowhard, fanfaron, rodomont 9 renommist 10 burgullian 11 braggadocio, rodomontade

Bragi's wife: 4 Idun 6 Ithunn

Brahma: 5 Hindu 7 creator

first woman created by: 6 Ahalya

Brahman: 4 zebu 5 Aryan, Hindu 6 priest, pundit 9 Bostonian

land grant: 5 sasan

precept: 5 sutra, sutta

title: aya

braid: cue 4 band, jerk, lace, plat, trim 5 brede, fancy, freak, jiffy, lacet, onset, plait, pleat, queue, start, tress, trick, twine, vomit, weave 6 bobbin, border, moment, plight, ribbon, sennet, snatch, string 7 caprice, entwine, upbraid 8 brandish, ornament, reproach, soutache, trimming 9 deceitful, interlace 10 interweave

gold and silver: 5 orris

hemp: 5 tagal

knotted: 5 lacet

brain: mad 4 bean, harn(Sc.), mind, utac, wits 5 skull 6 psyche 7 furious 8 cerebrum(L.), conceive 9 intellect

box: pan 5 skull 7 cranium

comb. form: 7 cerebro

layer: 4 obex 6 cortex

membrane: 4 tela 8 meninges

operate on: 6 trepan

orifice: 4 lura

part: 4 aula 8 cerebrum 10 encephalon 11 pericranium

passage: 4 iter

pert. to: 8 cerebral 10 cerebellar, encephalic

tumor: 6 glioma

white matter: pia 4 alba, dura

brain trust: 5 panel 7 council 8 advisers

brainchild: 4 opus, work

brainless: 5 silly 6 stupid 7 foolish, witless 11 thoughtless

brainstorm: 9 confusion

brake: 4 cage, curb, drag, fern, rack, slow, trap 5 block, check, copse, delay, deter, snare, vomit 6 bridle, harrow, hinder, retard 7 dilemma, thicket 9 brushwood

brakeman: 6 brakie 8 trainman

bramble: 5 brier, thorn 6 bumble 10 cloudberry

brambly: 5 spiny 6 thorny 7 prickly

bran: 5 treat 6 cereal, chisel

branch: arm, bow 4 brog, bush, chat, fork, limb, part, rame, rami, snag, spur, stem 5 bough, creek, ramus, shoot, spray, sprig, vimen, withe 6 divide, member, outlet, raddle, ramage, ramify, stolon, stream 7 diverge, tendril 8 district, offshoot 10 department 11 bifurcation 12 ramification

angle of: 4 axil

of nerves: 4 rami(pl.) 5 ramus

pert. to: 5 ramal 6 remeal

branch herring: 7 alewife

branch-like: 5 ramal 6 ramose, ramous

branched: 5 forky 6 forked, ramate, ramose 7 cladine, cladose

branchia: 4 gill

brand: 4 birn, blot, burn, flaw, kind, mark, sear, smit, sort 5 buist, stain, stamp, sword, taint, torch 6 stigma 8 flambeau 9 cauterize, character, trademark 10 stigmatize

on stolen cattle: 4 duff

sheep: 4 smit

brandish: 4 dart, wave 5 bless, braid, shake, swing, wield 6 flaunt, hurtle 7 flutter, glitter, swagger, vibrate 8 flourish 9 coruscate, irradiate

brandling: 4 parr 9 earthworm

brandy: 4 marc 5 bingo 6 cognac 11 aguardiente(Sp.)
and soda: peg
cocktail: 7 sidecar, stinger 9 alexander
mastic: 4 raki 5 rakee
plum: 9 slivovitz

brank: 5 caper, mumps, strut 6 bridle, prance 7 pillory

brannigan: 5 brawl

brant: 4 rout 5 erect, goose, proud, quink, sheer, steep 7 steeply 8 straight

brash: 4 bold, rash 5 hasty, saucy, storm 6 attack 7 brittle, forward 8 impudent, tactless 9 irascible

brass: 4 cash 5 alloy, money, nerve 6 brazen 7 officer 9 impudence, insolence

brass hat (army slang)**:** 7 general, officer

brass tacks: 5 facts 10 essentials

brassard, brassart: 5 badge 6 bracer 7 armband

brassbound: set 5 rigid 10 inflexible

brassica: 4 cole, rape 6 turnip

brassy: 4 bold 6 aerose, brazen 8 impudent

brat: bib, imp 4 film, scum 5 apron, bairn, bilsh, child, cloak 6 infant, mantle, urchin 7 garment 8 clothing 9 offspring

bravado: 4 pomp 5 brave, pride, storm 6 bravor, hector 7 bluster, bombast, bravade, bravery, swagger 9 gasconade

brave: 4 bold, braw(Sc.), dare, defy, face, fine, game, good, prow 5 adorn, boast, bravo, bully, felon, hardy, manly, Roman, stout, vaunt 6 breast, daring, heroic, manful, plucky 7 bravado, gallant, soldier, swagger, valiant, venture, warrior 8 cavalier, defiance, embolden, fearless, intrepid, stalwart, superior, valorous, virtuous 9 challenge, dauntless, excellent, undaunted 10 courageous 11 venturesome 12 stouthearted

Brave New World author: 6 Huxley

bravery: 4 grit 5 valor 6 spirit, valour 7 bravado, bravura, courage, heroism 8 boldness 9 fortitude, gallantry, gentleman, hardihood

bravo: ole(Sp.), rah 4 thug 5 brave, bully 6 bandit, Indian 7 bravado, villain 8 applause, assassin 9 cutthroat, desperado

brawl: din, row 4 clem, fray, riot 5 broil, fight, melee, revel, scold 6 affray, bicker, fracas, habble, revile, rumpus, shindy, strife, tumult, uproar 7 brabble, discord, dispute, quarrel, scuffle, wrangle 8 complain, squabble 10 contention 11 altercation, disturbance

brawling: 5 noisy 7 blatant 9 clamorous 10 clamourous, vociferous 11 quarrelsome

brawn: 4 boar 5 flesh 6 fatten, muscle 8 strength 10 headcheese

brawny: 5 beefy 6 fleshy, robust, sinewy, strong, sturdy 7 callous 8 muscular, powerful, stalwart

bray: cry, mix, rub 4 beat, rout, tool 5 grind, noise, pound 6 bruise, heehaw, outcry, pestle, thrash, whinny

brazen: 4 bold, pert 5 brass, harsh, sassy 6 brassy 7 callous, forward 8 immodest, impudent, insolent, metallic 9 shameless

Brazil: *ant:* 9 tucandera
bird: ara, iva 4 soco 5 agami, macaw 6 arvara, darter, tiriba 7 maracan, seriema
city: Rio 4 Lapa, Para 5 Bahia, Belem, Ceara, Natal 6 Manaos, Santos 8 Brasilia(c.), Campinas, Sao Paulo 10 Pernambuco 11 Porto Alegre 12 Rio de Janeiro
coffee plantation: 7 fazenda
coin: 4 reis 5 conto, dobra 7 milreis 8 cruzeiro
dance: 5 samba 6 maxixe
discoverer: 6 Cabral
drink: 5 assai
duck: 7 muscovy
estuary: 4 Para
fiber: 4 imbe
fish: 8 arapaima
forest: 5 matta
Indian: 4 Anta 5 Acroa, Arara, Arana, Bravo, Carib, Guana, Hauri 6 Arawak, Caraja 7 Tariana 8 Amiranha, Araquaju, Botocudo
mammal: 5 tapir
measure: pe 4 moio, pipa, sack, vara 5 braca, fanga, legoa, milha, palmo, passo, tonel 6 canada, covado, cuarta, league, quarto, tarefa 7 alquier, garrafa 8 alqueire 9 pollegada, quartilho
monkey: *sai* 6 miriki 9 belzebuth
mountain: 5 Organ 8 Maririme 10 Serra do Mar 14 Serra dos Orgaos
palm: 4 jara 5 assai, inaja, tucum 6 babaca, jupati 7 babassu 9 barriguda
paste: 7 guarana
plant: 4 imbe, para, yage, yaje 5 caroa 7 ayapana, seringa 9 jaborandi
promontory: 4 frio
river: Apa 4 Para, Paru 5 Jurua, Negro, Purus, Xingu 6 Amazon, Parana 7 Madeira, Orinoco, Tapajos 8 Paraguay 9 Tocantins 12 San Francisco
rubber: ule 4 hule, Para 6 caucho
seaport: Rio 4 Para 5 Bahia, Belem, Natal 6 Santos 7 Pelotas
state: 4 Para 5 Bahia, Ceara, Goyas 6 Parana, Piauhy 7 Alagoas, Sergipe 8 Amazonas, Maranhao, Parahiba, Sao Paulo 10 Mato Grosso, Pernambuco 11 Minas

Geraes 13 Espirito Santo 14 Rio Grande do Sul, Santa Catharina 16 Rio Grande do Norte
tree: apa, ule 4 anda, assu, uhle 5 araca, tingi 6 biriba, brauna, satine 7 araroba, becuiba, gomavel, paraiba, seringa, wallaba 8 bakupari 10 barbatimao, dal guarabu
weight: bag 4 onca 5 libra 6 arroba, oitava 7 arratel, quilate, quintal 8 tonelada
wood: 6 embuia 8 kingwood
breach: gap 4 chap, flaw, gool, rent, rift 5 brack, breck, chasm, cleft, crack, pause, split, wound 6 bruise, harbor, hernia, hiatus, inroad, schism 7 assault, blemish, dispute, fissure, opening, quarrel, rupture 8 breaking, fraction, fracture, interval, trespass 9 violation 10 disruption, infraction 12 infringement, interruption 14 nonfulfillment 16 misunderstanding
of etiquette: 5 gaffe 8 solecism
breach pin: 4 tige
bread: bun 4 diet, fare, food, loaf, pone, roll, rush 5 batch 7 aliment, bannock(Sc.) 10 livelihood, sustenance
boiled: 4 cush 6 panada
browned: 5 toast 6 sippet 7 crouton
communion: 4 azym 5 azyme
crust: 4 rind
leavened: 5 kisra 6 cocket
Passover: 5 matzo 6 matzoh, matzos(pl.), matzot(pl.) 7 matzoth(pl.)
pert. to: 6 panary
unleavened: 4 azym 5 azyme 6 matzos 7 bannock, matzoth 8 afikomen
bread spread: 4 oleo 6 butter 9 margarine 13 oleomargarine
breadth: 4 span 5 brede, scope, width 6 extent 8 diameter, distance, latitude 9 amplitude, dimension
breadwinner: 6 earner, worker
break: gap 4 boon, bust, dash, hint, knap, pick, plow, rend, rent, rift, rive, ruin, rush, slip, snap, stop, tear 5 alter, blank, burst, cleft, crack, craze, frush, lapse, pluck, sever, smash, wound 6 bruise, change, cleave, defeat, hiatus, impair, lacuna, pierce 7 blunder, caesura, crackle, crevice, crumble, destroy, disable, dispart, disrupt, exhaust, fissure, lacunae(pl.), opening, respite, rupture, shatter 8 caesurae, fraction, fracture, interval, separate 9 interrupt, penetrate 10 invalidate 12 interruption 14 discontinuance
down: 7 debacle, failure 8 collapse 9 cataclasm 10 catabolism
in: 4 slip 5 stave 7 blunder 8 initiate 9 interrupt
of day: 4 dawn, morn 5 sunup 7 morning
out: 4 rash 5 erupt 6 escape
up: 5 split 7 disband, disrupt 8 disperse, dissolve, separate
breakable: 7 brittle, bruckle, friable 8 delicate
breakbone fever: 6 dengue
breaker: 4 surf, wave 6 billow, comber, roller
breakwater: cob, dam 4 cobb, dike, mole, pier, pile, quay 5 jetty 6 refuge 11 obstruction
bream: tai 4 fish, scup 5 broom 7 sunfish
sea: 4 shad 6 sargus
breast: 4 crop 5 bosom, brave, chest 6 thorax 9 encounter
ornament: 8 pectoral
breastbone: 6 sterna(pl.) 7 sternum, xiphoid 9 gladiolus
pert to: 7 sternal
breastplate: *armor:* 4 urim 6 gorget, lorica, shield 7 poitrel, thummin 8 poitrail
ecclesiastical: 4 urim
breastwork: 4 fort 5 redan 7 brattle, parapet, rampart 10 forecastle
breath: 4 ande, gasp, huff, life, pant, pech, puff, sigh, wind 5 pause, scent, smell, vapor, whiff 6 breeze, pneuma 7 halitus, instant, respite 10 exhalation
breathe: 4 ande, live, pant, pech, puff, sigh 5 exist, speak, utter 6 aspire, exhale, inhale, wheeze 7 afflate, emanate, respire, suspire
hard: 4 gasp, pant
breather: 4 rest 5 break, pause, truce 6 recess, repose 9 armistice
breathing: 5 alive 7 gasping 9 spiration 11 respiration
difficult: 7 dyspnea 8 dyspnoea
harsh: 4 rale
orfice: 4 nose, pore 5 mouth, nares 7 nostril 8 spiracle
smooth: 4 lene
sound: 4 rale 5 snore, snort 7 stridor
breathless: 4 dead 5 stale, tense 6 stuffy 10 motionless
bred well: 6 polite 7 genteel 9 pedigreed
breech: 4 bore, butt, doup 5 block 7 droddum 8 buttocks, derriere 9 posterior
breeches: 5 chaps, jeans, levis 8 jodhpurs, knickers, trousers 10 pantaloons
breeching: 4 rope 7 harness
breed: ilk 4 bear, kind, race, rear, sort 5 beget, brood, caste, cause, class, hatch, raise, stock, train 6 create, strain 7 educate, nourish, produce, progeny, species, variety 8 engender, instruct, multiply 9 offspring, orginate, propagate 10 generation
breeding: 6 origin 7 descent 8 behavior, training 9 education, gestation 10 deport-

ment, extraction 11 development, instruction

science: 8 eugenics

breeze: air 4 aura, blow, flaw, gale, gust, pirr, stir, wind 5 blast, rumor 6 breath, report, zephyr 7 freshen, quarrel, whisper 11 disturbance

land: 6 terral

breezy: 4 airy 5 brisk, fresh, windy 6 airish 9 vivacious

bressumer: 4 beam 6 girder, lintel 7 support

breve: 4 bird, mark, note, writ 5 brief, minium, order 6 letter 7 compose, precept 8 syllable

brevet: 6 confer 9 promotion 10 commission

breviary: 4 ordo 6 digest, portas 7 coucher, epitome, summary 8 abstract 10 compendium 11 abridgement

brevity: 9 briefness, shortness, terseness 11 conciseness 12 succinctness

brew: ale, mix 4 beer, boil, make, plot, pour 5 hatch 6 devise, dilute, foment, gather, liquor, seethe 7 concoct, incline, prepare 8 beverage, contrive

brewer: *grain:* rye 4 corn, malt 6 barley

vat: tun

yeast: 4 barm 6 leaven

briar: saw 4 pipe

bribe: fee, oil, rob, sop, tip 4 bait, gift, hire, meed 5 bonus, cuddy, graft, offer, steal, sugar, tempt 6 extort, grease, payola, suborn 7 corrupt 8 gratuity 10 allurement

bric-a-brac: 5 curio 7 bibelot 11 knickknacks

brick: 4 pave, tile 5 block, quarl, stone 6 fellow, quarle

handler: 6 hacker

oven: 4 kiln

sun-baked: bat 5 adobe

tray: hod

vitrified: 7 clinker

wood: nog 4 dook 6 scutch

bridal: 7 nuptial

bride: bar, tie 4 loop, rein, rose 6 bridle, kallah

bridesmaid: 9 attendant

bridewell: 4 gaol, jail 6 prison 9 workhouse

bridge: way 4 game, link, pons, pont, span 5 cross 6 ponton 7 auction, bascule, connect, pontoon, trestle, viaduct 8 contract, traverse 9 alcantara, gangplank

combination: 6 tenace

forerunner: 5 whist

lever: 7 bascule

of musical instrument: 5 magas 10 ponticello

part: 4 arch, deck, pier 5 cable, pylon 7 caisson 8 spandrel

player: 4 east, west 5 north, south

pontoon plank: 5 chess

score: leg

support: 4 pier 5 truss

term: bid, bye, leg, set 4 book, game, pass, ruff, slam, suit, void 5 raise, trick, trump 6 renege, revoke 7 finesse 9 part-score

bridle: bit 4 curb, rein, rule 5 brake, brank, bride, check, guard, guide, strut 6 direct, govern, halter, master, simper, subdue 7 blinder, control, repress, snaffle, swagger 8 restrain, suppress 9 restraint

noseband: 6 musrol 8 cavesson

brief: few 4 curt, list, rife, writ 5 blurb, breve, charm, pithy, quick, short, terse 6 abrupt, common, letter 7 abridge, compact, compose, concise, invoice, laconic, mandate, outline, precept, summary 8 breviate, condense, fleeting, succinct, syllabus 9 catalogue, condensed, ephemeral, memoranda(pl.), prevalent 10 compendium, memorandum, transitory 11 compendious

briefness: 7 brevity

brier, briar: 4 barb, pipe 5 thorn 6 similax

briery: 5 sharp, spiny

brig: 4 boat, jail 6 prison, vessel 10 guardhouse

brigand: 5 thief 6 bandit, pirate, robber 7 cateran, ladrone, soldier 8 picaroon 10 highwayman

bright: apt, gay 4 fine, glad, rosy 5 acute, aglow, alert, anime, beamy, clear, fresh, gemmy, light, lucid, nitid, quick, riant, sharp, smart, sunny, vivid, witty 6 cheery, clever, florid, garish, limpid, lively, lucent, orient 7 forward, fulgent, radiant, ringing, shining 8 animated, cheerful, flashing, gleaming, luminous, lustrous, splendid, splendor 9 brilliant, cloudless, effulgent, refulgent, sparkling 10 brightness, epiphanous, glistening, glittering 11 illustrious, intelligent, resplendent, transparent

brighten: 4 gild 5 cheer, clear, light, liven, shine 6 cantle, engild, polish 7 animate, burnish, enliven, furbish, lighten 8 illumine 9 irradiate

brightness: 5 eclat, flame, gleam, gloss, nitor, sheen 6 acumen, bright, fulgor, luster 7 clarity, fulgour, sparkle 8 splendor 9 clearness 10 brilliance, effulgence

brilliance: 4 fame 5 eclat, flame, glory 8 keenness, radiance, splendor 10 brightness, effulgence

brilliant: gay 4 good, keen, sage, wise 5 breme 6 bright, clever, signal 7 eminent, flaming, radiant, shining 8 dazzling, glorious, luminous 9 effective, prismatic, refulgent, sparkling 10 glittering 11 prismatical, resplendent 13 distinguished

brim: lip, rim, rut, sea 4 edge 5 bluff, brink, marge, ocean, verge, water 6 border, margin 8 copulate, strumpet 9 periphery

brimming: 4 full

brimstone: 6 virago 7 sulphur 8 spitfire

brindled: 5 tawny 7 flecked 8 streaked

brine: sea 4 main, salt 5 ocean, tears 6 pickle 8 marinade

preserve in: 4 corn, cure, salt

brine shrimp: 7 artemia

bring: 4 bear, take 5 carry, fetch 6 convey, deduce 7 conduce, procure, produce 9 transport

about: 5 cause 6 create 7 achieve 10 accomplish

back: 6 effect, recall, return, revive 7 produce, restore 8 occasion, retrieve, transact 9 instigate 10 consummate

forth: ean(Sc.) 4 bear 5 educe, hatch, incur 6 adduce, beteem 7 produce

forward: 7 present 9 introduce

in: 5 usher 6 import, report, return 9 introduce

near to: 6 appose

off: 7 achieve, succeed 8 complete

on: 6 induce

out: 7 display, publish

to: 11 resuscitate

to earth: 4 land

to light: 6 elicit, reveal 7 unearth 8 disclose, discover

to naught: 4 dash 6 negate 7 confute 9 frustrate

together: 4 join 5 unite 7 compile

up: 4 rear 5 nurse, raise, train 7 educate 11 regurgitate

up to date: 4 post 5 brief 6 inform

brink: end, eve, lip, rim, sea 4 bank, brim, edge, foss 5 marge, shore, verge 6 border, margin

briny: 5 brack, salty 6 saline

brioche: 4 roll 6 stitch 7 cushion, pudding, savarin

Briseis' lover: 8 Achilles

brisk: gay 4 busy, fast, keen, pert, racy, spry, yern 5 agile, alert, alive, budge, crisp, fresh, frisk, peart, perky, quick, sharp, smart, yerne 6 active, breezy, cocket, crouse, lively, nimble, snappy 7 allegro 8 animated, friskful, spirited 9 energetic, sprightly, vivacious 11 stimulating 12 effervescing

bristle: awn 4 barb, hair, seta, tela 5 birse, brush, parch, preen, setae, strut, toast 6 chaeta, palpus, ruffle, setula 7 chaetae, setulae, stubble

comb. form: 4 seti

surgical: 4 seta 5 seton

bristled: 7 horrent 8 echinate

bristlelike: 5 setal 8 setiform

bristling: 5 rough 6 hispid, horrid, setose, thorny 7 horrent, scrubby

brit, britt: 5 sprat 7 herring 10 crustacean

Britain: See **England**

British Columbia: *Indian:* 5 Haida 7 Shuswap

river: 6 Nicola

Britomartis: 7 Artemis 8 Dictynna

mother: 5 Carme

Briton: 4 Celt, Scot

Brittany: *ancient name:* 8 Armorica

canvas: 8 vandelas

king: Ban

native: 6 Breton

poetry: 6 soniou

saint: 4 Anne

brittle: 4 frow, weak 5 brash, candy, crisp, crump, eager, frail, frowy, frush, short 6 crispy, crumpy, feeble, fickle, frough, infirm, slight 7 brickle, bruckle, fragile, friable, froughy 8 delicate, snappish 9 breakable, crumbling, frangible, irritable 10 perishable

broach: air, awl, cut, pin, rod, tap 4 open, ouch, shed, spit, spur, stab, veer, vent 5 begin, dress, drift, prick, rimer, spool, voice 6 boring, brooch, launch, pierce, reamer 7 enlarge, publish, spindle, violate 8 approach, broacher, deflower, incision 9 introduce 11 perforation

broad: 4 deep, free, vast, wide 5 ample, beamy, large, plain, roomy, thick, woman 6 coarse 7 evident, general, grivois, liberal, obvious, platoid 8 grivoise, spacious, tolerant 9 capacious, expansive, extensive, outspoken 12 unrestrained 13 comprehensive

comb. form: 4 lati

broad-footed: 8 platypod

broad-minded: 7 lenient, liberal 8 Catholic, tolerant

broadbill: 4 bird, gaya, raya 5 scaup 8 shoveler 9 swordfish

broadcast: sow 4 seed, send 5 radio, strew 6 spread 7 publish, scatter 8 announce, televise, transmit 9 advertise

broadcloth: 6 cotton, fabric, woolen 7 suiting 8 material

broaden: 5 brede, widen 6 dilate, expand, extend, spread 7 ennoble 9 expatiate 10 generalize

broadside: 4 bill 5 salvo 8 circular

broadsword: 4 bill, kris 6 glaive, spatha 7 cutlass, Ferrara 8 claymore, scimitar

brobdingnagian: big 4 huge 5 giant 8 colossal, gigantic
brocade: 5 cloth 6 broche, kincab 8 baudekin 9 baldachin
brocard: 4 gibe, rule 5 maxim 6 speech 7 sarcasm 9 principle
brochure: 4 book 5 tract 8 pamphlet, treatise
brocket: 4 deer, pita, stag 5 brock 7 spitter
brogan: 4 shoe 5 stogy 6 brogue
brogue: 4 hose, shoe 5 fraud, trick 6 accent, brogan 7 dialect 8 trousers
broil: row 4 burn, char, feud, fray, heat 5 alarm, brawl, grill, melee, scrap 6 affray, birsle, braise, splore, tumult 7 brulyie(Sc.), contest, discord, dispute, embroil, garboil, quarrel 8 conflict, grillade 10 contention, dissension 11 altercation, disturbance
broiler: 4 bird 5 grill 7 chicken
broke: 8 bankrupt 9 insolvent, penniless
broken: 4 rent, torn 5 burst, gappy, rompu(F.), rough, tamed 6 hackly, ruined, shaken 7 crushed, fracted, reduced, subdued 8 outlawed, ruptured, weakened 9 cashiered, dispersed, fractured, shattered 10 incoherent, incomplete 11 fragmentary 12 disconnected, intermittent
broker: 5 agent 6 corser, dealer, factor, jobber 7 brogger, changer, courser, peddler, realtor, scalper 8 broacher, huckster, merchant 10 pawnbroker
brokerage: fee 4 agio 10 commission
brolly: 8 umbrella
bromide: 5 trite 8 compound, sedative 9 platitude
bronco: 5 horse 6 cayuse 7 broncho, mustang 9 estrapade(Sp.)
bronco buster: 6 cowboy, ginete
Bronte: 4 Anne 5 Emily 9 Charlotte
hero: 9 Rochester 10 Heathcliff
heroine: 8 Jane Eyre
pen name: 4 Bell
Bronx cheer: boo 9 raspberry
bronze: aes(L.), tan 4 bust 5 alloy, brown 6 statue
film: 6 patina
gilded: 6 ormolu
nickel: 11 cupronickel
pert. to: 7 aeneous
brooch: bar, pin 4 boss, ouch 5 cameo, clasp 6 fibula, plaque, shield 8 ornament 9 brochette
brood: fry, nye, set, sit 4 mope, nest, nide, race, weep 5 aerie, breed, covey, flock, group, hatch, issue, sedge, worry, young 6 cletch, clutch, family, litter, ponder 7 progeny, species 8 cogitate, incubate, meditate 9 multitude, offspring 11 contemplate
brook: run 4 bear, beck, burn, ghyl, gill, rill, rush, sike 5 abide, bayou, bourn, creek, stand 6 arroyo(Sp.), bourne, canada, endure, gutter, rindle, rivose, runlet, stream, suffer 7 comport 8 quebrada, tolerate 11 watercourse
brooklet: 4 beck, rill 6 rillet, runnel 7 rillock, rivulet 9 arroyuelo(Sp.)
broom: mop 4 fray, swab 5 besom, bream, brush, spart, sweep, whisk 8 splinter
broom plant: 5 hirse, spart 7 cyticus, genista, heather 8 deerweed
broomcorn millet: 5 hirse
broth: 4 bree, broo, soup 5 stock 6 brewis, jussal, jussel 7 pottage 8 consomme, jusshell
brothel: 4 crib, stew 6 bagnio, bordel 8 bordello
brother: bub, fra, kin, pal, sib 4 mate, monk, peer 5 billy, buddy, cadet, frere(F.), friar 6 fellow, fraile, frater(L.) 7 comrade, sibling
pert. to: 9 fraternal
brotherhood: 4 gild 5 guild, lodge 6 friary 8 bratstro, sodality 10 fellowship, fraternity 11 association 13 brotherliness, companionship, confraternity
brotherly: 4 kind 6 tender 9 fraternal 12 affectionate
brougham: 8 carriage
brought up: 4 cade
brow: top 4 brae, bree, edge, mien, snab(Sc.) 5 bound, brink, crest, front, ridge, slope 8 boldness, forehead 9 acclivity, gangplank 10 effrontery 11 countenance
browbeat: 5 abash, bully 6 hector 7 depress 10 disconcert, intimidate
brown: dun, tan 4 coin, cook, dark, sear 5 dusky, penny, sedge, sepia, tawny, tenne, toast, umber 6 gloomy, russet, sennet, tanned 9 half-penny
cocoa: 6 sahara
dark: 6 bister, bistre
light: tan 4 ecru, fawn 5 beige, khaki, tenne
purple: 4 puce
red: bay 4 cuba, roan 5 henna, sepia 6 auburn, russet, sorrel 8 chestnut
rich: 5 sepia
brown Bess: 6 musket
brown Betty: 7 pudding 10 coneflower
brown study: 10 absorption 11 abstraction
browned: 7 rissole
brownie: elk, nis 4 cake 5 cooky, nisse, urisk 6 goblin, uruisg(Sc.) 9 sandpiper
browse: 4 brut, crop, feed 5 graze 6 forage, nibble 7 pasture
bruin: 4 bear
bruise: 4 bash, bray, dent, dunt, hurt, maim, maul 5 break, crush, curry, delve, dinge,

pound 6 batter, breach, hatter, injury, mangle, shiner 7 contuse, dammish, disable 9 pulverize, triturate
bruised: 4 hurt 5 livid 6 humble 7 froisse
bruiser: 5 boxer 8 pugilist
bruit: din 4 fame, rale, tell 5 noise, rumor, sound 6 blazon, clamor, report 7 declare, hearsay
brume: fog 4 haze, mist, smog 5 vapor
brumous: 5 foggy, misty 6 hiemal, sleety 7 wintery
brunette: 4 dark 5 brown, brune, gipsy, gypsy 7 swarthy
brunt: jar 4 blow, jolt 5 clash, force, onset, shock 6 attack, effort, impact 7 assault 8 outburst
brush: 4 comb, fray, skim 5 broom, clean, copse, fight, graze, sweep 6 badger, battle, brosse(F.), stroke 7 thicket 8 skirmish 9 brushwood, encounter 11 undergrowth
brushwood: 4 rone 5 brake, brush, copse, frith, scrog, scrub 6 rammel 7 coppice, thicket
brushy: 5 hairy 6 shaggy 7 hirsute
brusque: 4 curt, rude 5 bluff, blunt, brusk, gruff, hasty, rough, short 6 abrupt 7 violent 8 cavalier, impolite 12 discourteous
brut: dry 6 browse
brutal: 5 cruel, feral, gross 6 carnal, coarse, savage 7 bestial, beastly, brutish, caddish, inhuman 8 ruthless 9 atrocious, barbarous, ferocious, insensate
brute: 5 beast, yahoo 6 animal, savage 7 ruffian 9 scoundrel
bryophyte: 4 moss 5 plant 9 liverwort
Brython: 5 Welsh 6 Celtic 7 Cornish
god: Dea, Ler 4 Bran 5 Dylan, Lludd 8 Amaethon
goddess: Don 8 Rhiannon 9 Arianrhod
bubal: 4 topi 8 antelope
bubble: air, bub 4 bead, bell(Sc.), bleb, blob, boil, boll, dupe, foam, glob, seed, suds 5 caper, cheat, empty 6 burble, delude, seethe, trifle 7 blister, blubber, deceive, globule 8 delusive 10 effervesce 11 speculation
bubbling: gay 8 effusive 9 sparkling
buccal: 4 oral
buccaneer: 6 pirate, rifler, robber, viking 7 corsair, mariner, spoiler 8 Picaroon 10 freebooter
standard: 5 roger
Bucephalus: 5 steed 7 charger
buck: fob, ram 4 boil, butt, deer, dude, male, prig, rear, soak, stag, toff, wash 5 dandy, steep 6 basket, dollar, oppose, resist 7 sawbuck 8 antelope, prickett, sawhorse 9 buckwheat
first year: 4 fawn
fourth year: 4 sore
buckaroo: 6 cowboy 8 horseman
buckboard: 8 carriage
bucket: tub 4 bail, bowk, cage, pail 5 cheat, scoop, skeel 6 bailer, drench, hoppet, situla(L.), vessel 7 swindle 8 cannikin
handle: 4 bail
molten glass: 7 cuvette
Buckeye State: 4 Ohio
buckle: bow 4 bend, curl, kink, tach, warp 5 clasp, marry, twist 6 fibula(L.) 7 contend, fermail, fibulae(L.pl.), grapple 8 fastener, struggle 10 distortion
part: 5 chape 6 tongue
buckler: 4 crab 5 block 6 shield 7 rotella, roundel, shutter
buckram: 6 fabric 7 precise 10 cuckoopint, stiffening
buckthorn: 5 rhamn 7 alatern, cascara 8 lotebush 9 alaternus, chaparral
buckwheat: 4 buck 8 sarrazin
buckwheat tree: 4 titi 6 teetee
bucolic: 4 idyl 5 local, naive, rural 6 farmer, rustic, simple 7 cowherd, eclogue 8 agrestic, herdsman, pastoral
bud: eye, gem, imp, pip 4 bulb, cion, germ, girl, grow, knop 5 child, graft, scion, shoot, youth 6 button, flower, germin, sprout 7 blossom, brother, gemmule 8 bourgeon 9 germinate
arrangement: 11 aestivation
social: deb 8 debutant 9 debutante
Buddha: Fo; Foh 7 Gautama 10 Shakyamuni
cause of infinite existence: 6 nidana
center: 5 Lassa, Lhasa
church: 4 Tera
column: lat
disciple: 6 Ananda
dryad: 6 Yaksha, Yakshi
enlightenment: 5 bodhi
evil spirit: 4 Mara
fate: 5 karma
fertility spirit: 6 Yaksha, Yakshi
festival: bon
final beatitude: 4 raga 7 nirvana
for justice: 6 dharna, dhurna
gateway: 5 toran, torii 6 torana
god: 4 deva
greater: 8 Mahayana
hatred: 4 dosa
hell: 6 Naraka
Japanese image: 8 Daibutsu
language: 4 Pali
lesser: 8 Hinayana
life cycle: 6 anicca
mendicant: 6 bhikku 7 bhikshu
monastery: 4 Tera 6 Vihara

monk: bo 4 lama 5 arhat, yahan 7 poongee 8 poonghee, poonghie, talapoin
monument: 5 stupa
mother: 4 Maya
novice: 5 goyim
paradise: 4 Jodo
passion: 4 raga
prayer: 4 mani
priest: 4 lama 7 mahatma
relic mound: 5 stupa
retribution: 5 karma
rock temple: 4 rath 5 ratha
sacred city: 5 Lassa, Lhasa
scripture: 5 sutra
sect: Zen 7 Jodo-shu
shrine: 4 tope 5 stupa 6 dagoba 7 chorten
son: 6 Rahula
stupa site: 9 Amaravati
throne: 5 asana
title: 7 Mahatma
tree: 5 pipal 6 botree
will to live: 5 Tanha

buddy: bo; boy, pal 4 mate 7 brother, comrade 8 tentmate 9 companion

budge: fur 4 move, stir 5 booze, brisk, stiff, thief 6 jocund, liquor, solemn 7 austere, pompous 8 movement 11 nervousness

budget: bag 4 boot, pack, plan, roll 5 batch, bunch, stock, store 6 bottle, bundle, parcel, socket, wallet 7 program 12 accumulation

buds: 8 burgeons, dehisces
pickled: 6 capers

buff: ox; bob, fan, tan 4 blow, coat, curt, firm 5 shine 6 buffet, polish, sturdy 7 leather, stammer, stutter 8 nonsense, seladang 10 enthusiast

buffalo: ox 5 anoa, buff, stag 5 bison, bugle 6 buffle, hamper 7 caribao, caribou, gazelle, overawe, timarau, zamouse 8 bewilder 9 bamboozle
large: 4 arna, arni 5 arnee
meat: 7 biltong
wild: 4 arna, arni 5 arnee 8 seladang

buffalo gourd: 11 calabazilla

buffalo tree: 10 rabbitwood

buffer: dog, pad 6 bumper, fender, pistol 7 cushion

buffet: bar, bob, box 4 beat, blow, buff, cuff, slap, toss 5 filip, smite, stool 6 abacus, batter, fillip, strike, strive, thrash 7 contend, counter, hassock 8 credence, credenza, cupboard 9 footstool, sideboard 10 affliction

bufflehead: 4 duck, fool 5 clown 6 buffle 9 merrywing

buffleheaded: 4 dull 6 stupid

buffoon: dor, wag, wit 4 aper, fool, jape, mime, mome 5 actor, antic, buffo, clown, comic, drole, droll, mimer 6 harlot, jester, mummer, stooge 7 playboy 8 balatron, gracioso, humorist, merryman, ridicule 9 harlequin 10 harlequina, hobby-horse 11 merry-andrew, Punchinello

bug: bog, dor 4 flaw, germ, idea, mite 5 bogey, bulge, roach 6 beetle, chinch, elater, insect, scheme 7 bellied, bugbear, forward, pompous 8 hemipter, hobbyist 9 conceited, hobgoblin, prominent 10 enthusiast, flashlight 11 hunchbacked
June: dor
lightning: 7 firefly
needle: 7 ranatra

bugaboo: 4 bogy, fear, goga, gogo, ogre 5 alarm, bogey, bogie, gogga 6 bodach, goblin 7 bugbear, specter, spectre 8 worricow(Sc.) 9 hobgoblin, scarecrow, worriecow(Sc.) 10 mumbo-jumbo

bugbane: 4 herb 9 hellebore 10 rattleroot

bugbear: See **bugaboo**

bugger: 4 chap 6 fellow, person, rascal 7 heretic 8 sodomite 11 Albigensian

buggy (see also **carriage**): 4 cart, shay, trap 5 nutty 7 caboose, foolish, vehicle 8 demented, infested, stanhope 9 gladstone

bughouse: 5 crazy, nutty 6 asylum, insane

bugle: ox 4 bead, horn 5 black 7 buffalo, bullock, clarion, trumpet
blare: 7 tantara
call: 4 taps 6 alerte(F.), sennet, tattoo 7 retreat 8 reveille
note: mot
yellow: iva

bugleweed: 4 mint 6 indigo

build: big 4 bigg, form, make, rear 5 edify, erect, found, frame, raise, set up, shape 6 create, gralth 7 fashion 8 assemble 9 construct, establish, fabricate
nest: 6 nidify
up: 7 enhance 8 increase 9 publicity 10 strengthen

builder: 5 maker 7 erector 8 tectonic 9 carpenter 11 constructor
labyrinth: 8 Daedalus
of wooden horse: 5 Epeus 6 Epeius

building: 4 casa(Sp.), pile 5 aedes, hotel, house 6 biggin, bottle, fabric 7 edifice, factory 8 dwelling 9 apartment, structure 10 storehouse 11 edification
addition to: ell 4 apse, wing 5 annex 6 lean-to
dilapidated: 7 rookery 8 firetrap, tenement
exhibition: 6 museum
farm: 4 barn, crib, shed, silo
gateway: 5 pylon
material: 4 iron, wood 5 brick, glass, steel 6 cement
medieval: 6 castle
part: ell 4 apse

projection: ell 4 apse, wing 5 annex 6 dormer, lean-to 7 cornice
public: 5 edile 6 aedile, casino, church, museum, temple 7 capitol, library, theater 10 auditorium
rib: 9 tierceron
round: 7 rotunda
sacred: 4 fane 6 church, mosque, temple 7 edicule 8 pantheon 9 cathedral
stately: 6 castle, palace 7 edifice, mansion
buirdly: 5 husky 6 strong 8 athletic
bulb: bud 4 blub, corm, knob, lamp, root 5 globe, swell, tuber 6 bulbus 9 expansion 12 protuberance
edible: yam 4 sego 5 onion 6 garlic, potato
bulbous: 5 round 7 swollen
bulbul: 4 bird, kala
Bulgar: 4 Slav 5 Tatar 6 Slavic 9 Bulgarian
Bulgaria: *assembly:* 8 Sobranje, Sobranye
capital: 5 Sofia
coin: lev, lew 8 stotinka
commune: 6 Sliven, Slivno 7 Sistova
liquor: 8 slivovic 9 slivovitz, slivowitz
measure: oka, oke 5 krine, lekha
river: 5 Mesta 6 Danube, Marica, Struma 7 Marista
ruler: 4 czar, tsar 5 Boris
town: 4 Ruse 5 Byclu, Sofia(c.), Stara, Varna 6 Bleven, Burgas, Plevna, Shumen, Shumla, Sliven, Slivno, Widdin, Zagora 7 Plovdiv, Sistova, Tirnova 8 Rustchuk 9 Silistria
weight: oka, oke 5 tovar
bulge: bag, bug, jut 4 bump, cask, hump, knob, lump 5 belly, bilge, bloat, bouge, flask, pouch, swell 6 billow, cockle, extend, pucker, wallet 7 blister 8 protrude 9 convexity, gibbosity 10 projection 11 indentation 12 protuberance
bulged: 5 bombe
bulging: 4 full 5 bombe, bowed, pudgy 6 convex 7 gibbous 8 bouffant
bulk: 4 body, heap, hold, hulk, hull, mass, pile, size 5 cargo, gross, might, power, stall, swell 6 expand, extent, figure, volume 7 bigness 8 majority, quantity 9 aggregate, dimension, largeness, magnitude 11 massiveness
bulkhead: 5 check 9 partition, structure
bulky: big 5 burly, gross, large, stout 6 clumsy, stody 7 hulking, massive, weighty 8 unwieldy 9 corpulent, policeman, ponderous
bull: cop 4 apis, jest, male, seal, slip, toro(Sp.), zebu 5 bobby, boner, drink, edict, error 6 bovine, letter, peeler, taurus(L.) 8 cajolery, document, flattery 9 detective, policeman, quadruped 10 zapaterito(Sp.)
angry: 5 gorer
castrated: 4 stot 5 steer 7 bullock
half man: 8 minotaur
hornless: 5 doddy 6 doddie
pert. to: 7 taurine
young: 4 stot(Sc.) 5 stirk 7 bullock
bull-like: 7 taurine
Bull Run: *battle:* 8 Manassas
hero: Lee
bull session: 4 talk 7 rapping 10 discussion
bulla: 4 bleb, case, seal 5 blain 7 vesicle
bullate: 8 puckered
bulldoze: cow, dig, ram 5 bully, force, scoop 6 coerce, pistol 8 browbeat, restrain
bulldozer: 5 bully 6 grader 7 machine
bullet: 4 ball, lead, shot, slug 6 pellet, sinker, tracer 7 missile
diameter: 7 caliber
fake: 6 pellet
bulletin: 4 memo 6 notice, poster, report 7 program 9 statement 11 publication 12 announcement
bullfight cheer: ole
bullfighter: 6 torero 7 matador, picador 8 capeador, matadore, toreador
foot: 6 torero
mounted: 8 toreador
bullfinch: alp, olp 4 monk, nope, olph, pope 5 hedge
bullheaded: 6 stupid 8 stubborn 9 obstinate 10 headstrong
bullion: bar 5 ingot, metal 6 billot
bullock: 4 stot 5 bugle, steer, stirk 6 bovine 9 quadruped
bull's eye: 6 target
bully: 4 boat, boss, fine, good, huff, mate 5 brave, bravo, great 6 bounce, harass, hector, jovial, tyrant 7 bluster, bouncer, bullock, darling, dashing, gallant, gauster, huffcap, roister, ruffian 8 bangster, barrater, barrator, browbeat, bulldoze, domineer, frampler 9 blusterer, bulldozer, companion, excellent, scrimmage 10 burgullian, intimidate, sweetheart
bulrush: 4 reed, rush, tule 5 sedge 6 bumble 7 cattail, papyrus, scirpus
bulwark: 4 bail, fort, wall 5 fence, mound 7 bastion, defence, defense, parapet, protect, rampart 10 breakwater 12 propugnacula(L.pl.) 13 propugnaculum(L.)
bum: beg, din 4 hobo 5 drink, drone, idler, mooch, tramp 6 frolic, guzzle, sponge 7 guzzler 8 vagabond
bumble: bee 4 veil 5 botch, drone, idler 6 beadle, bungle, jumble, muffle 7 bittern, blunder, bramble, bulrush, bungler
bumblebee: dor 6 bumbee, bumble, insect

bump: cry, hit 4 blow, boom, jolt, lump, whop 5 bulge, clout, knock, thump 6 bounce, nodule, strike 7 bittern, collide 8 swelling 10 projection 12 protuberance
bumper: 4 bowl, fine, good 5 facer, glass 6 buffer, fender, goblet 8 carangid
bumpkin: yap 4 beam, boom, clod, gawk, hick, lout, rube, swab 5 churl, clown, robin, yahoo, yokel 6 lummox 7 cauboge, hawbuck 9 chawbacon
bumptious: 8 insolent 9 obtrusive
bumpy: 5 rough 6 uneven
bun: jag, wig 4 boat, bunt, roll, stem, tail 5 stalk 6 rabbit 7 biscuit, chervil, stubble 8 squirrel 11 drunkenness
bunch: bob, set 4 bale, club, herd, hump, kick, pack, tuft, wisp 5 clump, fagot, flock, knoll, pahil(Ir.), thump 6 budget, bundle, finial, hobble, 8 quantity, swelling 9 aggregate 10 collection
of grapes: bob
pert. to: 5 comal
buncombe: rot 4 bunk 6 drivel 9 poppycock
bund: 4 band, quay 5 praya 6 league 7 society 10 embankment, federation 11 confederacy
bundle: lot, wad, wap 4 bale, band, bolt, garb, hank, pack, roll, swag 5 bunch, fadge, group, sheaf 6 bindle, fardel, fascis(L.), gather, number, packet, parcel 7 package 10 collection
maker: 5 baler
bundle of: *arrows:* 5 sheaf
firewood: 5 bavin
grain: 5 sheaf
sticks: 5 fagot 6 faggot
straw: 4 bolt
bung: 4 cork, dead, maul, plug, stop 5 plumb, purse, spile 6 parcel 7 smashed, squared, stopper, stopple, tampeon, tampion, tampoon 8 bankrupt, bunghole, 9 falsehood 10 pickpocket
bungalow: 5 house 7 cottage
bungle: err 4 goof, mess, muff 5 blunk, botch, spoil 6 boggle, bumble, foozle, fumble 7 bauchle, blunder 9 mismanage
bungling: 6 clumsy 7 awkward 9 maladroit, unskilled 10 blundering
bunk: bed, car 4 case 5 abide, berth, bunko, frame, hokum, hooey, leave, lodge, sleep, truck 6 bunkum, timber 7 baloney, boloney, chicory, hemlock, twaddle 8 buncombe, nonsense 9 crossbeam, skedaddle 10 humbuggery
bunker: bin, box 5 chest 6 hazard 8 obstacle, sandhole 11 compartment 12 entanglement
bunko: 5 bunco, cheat 6 scheme 7 swindle
bunt: bun 4 butt, push, sift, smut, tail 5 shove, 6 kernel, strike
bunting: 4 bird, flag, pape 5 dumpy, finch, plump 6 cotton, stocky, towhee, untidy 7 cowbird, etamine, garment, ortolan, rounded 8 bellying, bobolink, slovenly
bunyip: 4 sham 6 humbug, poster 8 impostor
buoy: dan 5 baken, elate, float, raise 6 marker 7 sustain 8 deadhead, levitate
mooring: 7 dolphin
trawling marker: dan
buoyant: gay 5 happy, light 6 blithe, floaty, lively 7 elastic, hopeful, lilting, springy 8 animated, cheerful, sanguine, spirited, volatile 9 resilient, vivacious 12 lighthearted
bur: See **burr.**
burble: 4 boil 6 bubble, gurgle, jabber, muddle, pimple 7 confuse, prattle, trouble 8 disorder
burbot: cod 4 fish, ling, lota 7 eelpout
burd: 4 lady 5 woman 6 maiden
burden: tax, vex 4 birn(Sc.), care, cark, clag, clog, duty, load, onus, seam 5 birth, cargo 6 charge, cumber, fardel, hamper, impose, lading, weight 7 ballast, fraught, freight, oppress, refrain, trouble 8 capacity, carriage, encumber, handicap, quantity 9 aggravate, grievance 10 imposition 11 encumbrance 14 responsibility
of complaint: 8 gravamen
with care: 4 cark
burden bearer: 4 Amos 5 Atlas
burdensome: 5 heavy 7 irksome, onerous, weighty 8 cumbrous, grievous, grinding 10 chargeable, cumbersome, oppressive 11 importunate, troublesome
burdock: 5 clite, lappa, plant 7 cadillo, clotbur, harebur, hurr-bur 9 cocklebur
bureau: 4 desk 5 chest 6 agency, office 7 dresser 10 chiffonier, department, escritoire
burg, burgh: 4 city, town 6 burgus 7 borough 9 community
burgeon: bud 4 grow 5 shoot 6 sprout
burgess: 7 citizen, freeman 8 commoner 10 magistrate
burglar: 4 yegg 5 thief 6 gopher, robber 7 yeggman 8 peterman 10 burglarize
burglary: 5 theft 7 larceny, robbery 8 stealage
burgomaster: 4 gull 5 mayor 7 alcalde 10 magistrate
burgoo, burgout: 4 soup, stew 5 gruel 7 pudding 8 porridge
burial: 9 interment 10 deposition
case: box 6 casket, coffin
ceremony: 7 funeral

litter: 4 bier
mound: low 5 grave 6 barrow 7 tumulus
pile: 4 pyre
place: 4 tomb 5 grave 7 pyramid 8 catacomb, cemetery, golgotha 9 graveyard, mausoleum 10 necropolis
preparation for: 4 cere 11 pollincture

buried (see also **bury**): 6 hidden 8 absorbed, imbedded

burin: 4 tool 6 graver

burke: 4 kill, slay 6 murder 7 smother

burl: 4 knot, lump 6 pimple 7 pustule 11 excrescence
in mahogany: roe

burlap: 5 gunny 6 fabric 7 bagging 8 wrapping
fiber: 4 hemp, jute

burler: 6 spiler 9 inspector

burlesque: ape, odd 4 copy, jest, mime 5 droll, farce, revue 6 comedy, overdo, parody 7 jocular, mockery, overact 8 ridicule, travesty 9 imitation, laughable, ludicrous 10 caricature
serenade: 9 charivari

burly: fat 5 bluff, bulky, heavy, husky, large, lusty, noble, obese, stout, thick, tramp 7 stately 8 imposing 9 corpulent, excellent, policeman 10 boisterous

Burma: *canopy:* 7 tazaung
chief: bo; boh, wun 4 woon
city: Ava 4 Pegu 5 Akyah, Prome 6 Lashio 7 Rangoon(c.) 8 Mandalay
dagger: dah 4 dout
deer: 6 thamin 7 thameng
demon: nat
district: 7 Toungoo
division: 4 Pegu 6 arakam
garment: 6 tamein
gate: 5 toran
gibbon: lar
girl: 4 mima
head hunter: 4 Naga
hill: 4 chin 6 kachin
hill dweller: Lai
knife: dah, dow
language: Wa; Lai 4 Chin, Pegu 6 Kachin
measure: dha, lan, tha 4 byee, dain, seit, taim, teng 6 palgat
musical instrument: 4 turr
native: Vu, Wa; Lai, Mon 4 Shaw 5 Karen 6 Kachin, Pequan
river: 6 Salwin, Sutang 7 Salween 8 Chindwin, Irrawadi 9 Irrawaddy
robber: 6 dacoit
sash: 7 tubbeck
skirts: 5 engis
spirit: nat
town: 4 Paan 5 Akyab, Manle 7 Bassein 8 Moulmein
traveler's shed: 5 zayat
tree: 4 acle 7 yamanai
tribe: Ao; Tai 4 Chin, Kuki, Shan, Thai, Tsin 6 Kachin, Karens 8 Kakhyens
tribesman: Lai
weight: mat, moo, vis 4 kait, ruay, viss 5 candy, tical, ticul

burn: 4 brew, char, fire, plot, raze, rill, sear, sere 5 adust, blaze, broil, brook, cense, flame, parch, scald, singe, waste, water 6 scorch, stream 7 combure, combust, consume, cremate, flicker, oxidize, rivulet, smolder 8 squander 9 cauterize 10 incinerate
midnight oil: 6 stay up 9 lucubrate
surface: 5 singe 6 scorch

burn up the road: 5 speed

burned: 5 baked 6 seared 7 charred 8 ustulate

burner: 6 Bunsen, censer 8 thurible

burning: hot 4 fire 5 afire, angry, blaze, calid, eager, fiery, flame, gledy 6 ablaze, ardent, fervid, torrid 7 caustic, cautery, fervent, flaming, glaring, glowing, mordant, shining 8 ardurous, exciting, inustion 9 consuming, cremating, inflaming 10 combustion, phlogistic 13 conflagration
bush: 5 wahoo
malicious: 5 arson
mountain: 7 volcano
taste: 5 acrid

burnish: rub 5 glaze, gloss 6 polish 7 furbish

burnisher: 4 tool 5 agate 6 buffer 7 frottom 8 polisher

burnoose, burnous: 5 cloak 7 garment 8 albornoz

burnsides: 5 beard 8 whiskers

burnt work: 10 pyrography

burr: nut, pad, rib 4 barb, birr, boss, buzz, halo, knob, ring, whir 5 briar, whirr 6 banyan, circle, corona, tunnel, washer 7 sticker 8 parasite 9 whetstone 10 sweetbread

burro: ass 6 donkey 9 quadruped

burrow: den, dig 4 heap, hole, mine, mole, root, tube 5 berry, couch, mound 6 furrow, tunnel 7 passage, shelter 8 excavate

bursa: sac 4 hall, sack 5 pouch 6 cavity 9 residence

bursar: 6 purser, terrar 7 boucher, cashier, student 9 treasurer

bursary: 8 treasury 11 scholarship

burse: 4 case, shop 5 bazar, purse 6 bazaar, bourse, pocket 8 exchange, treasury 11 scholarship

burst: pop 4 blow, bust, loss, rend, scat 5 blast, break, erupt, flash, reave, salvo,

scatt, split **6** broken, damage, injury, sprout **7** explode, rupture, shatter **8** outbreak, sundered **9** interrupt
forth: **5** erupt, sally **9** blasted
inward: **7** implode
burster: **4** gale **7** cracker **9** explosive
bursting: **8** erupting **10** dehiscence
comb. form: **6** rrhage **7** rrhagia
bury: **4** hide, mool, veil **5** cloak, cover, earth, grave, inter, inurn **6** entomb, hearse, inhume, shroud **7** bedelve, conceal, engross, immerse, repress, secrete **8** submerge **9** overwhelm
bus: **6** jitney **7** vehicle **9** charabanc
busby: cap, wig **8** bearskin **9** headdress
bush: tod **4** buss, butt **5** bosch, clump, grove, shrub **6** branch, tavern **7** boscage, cluster, thicket **11** advertising
bushed: **4** worn **5** spent **9** exhausted
bushel: foo(Sc.), gob, lot **4** full
quarter of: **4** peck
forty: wey
bushing: **5** drill **6** collet, lining **7** padding
machine: **6** sleeve
bushman: san(pl.) **4** gung, saan(pl.) **5** bushy **6** Abatoa, Abatua, Abatwa, rustic **8** woodsman
blanket: **5** bluey
bushmaster: **5** snake, viper
bushwa: **4** bosh, bull **5** hooey, trash **7** baloney **8** bodewash
bushwacker: **5** papaw **6** pawpaw, scythe **8** guerilla
bushy: **5** hooky **6** dumose, dumous **7** bushman, queachy
hair: **4** shag
heap: tod
business: ado, art, job **4** care, firm, fuss, game, line, task, work **5** cause, trade **6** affair, custom, matter, metier, office **7** calling, concern, trading, traffic **8** activity, commerce, industry, vocation **9** diligence, following, patronage, rickmatic **10** employment, enterprise, occupation, solicitude **11** disturbance, importunity, intercourse, transaction **13** attentiveness, establishment
custom: **9** patronage
memorandum: **4** note **7** agendum
place of: **4** mart, shop **5** store **6** market, office, shoppe **8** emporium
businessman: **9** executive
powerful: **6** tycoon
busk: hie **4** seek, stir, tack **5** array, dress **6** corset, hasten **7** prepare, stiffen
buskin: **4** boot, shoe **7** bottine, tragedy **8** cothurni(L. pl.), half-boot, stocking **9** brodequin, cothurnus(L.)
buss: **4** boat, bush, calf, deck, kiss **5** dress, smack **6** vessel **9** transport
bussock: **6** donkey
bussu: **4** palm **7** troolie
bust: **4** fail, ruin, tame **5** bosom, break, burst, chest, flunk, spree **6** bronze, demote, reduce, statue **7** degrade, dismiss, failure **8** bankrupt **9** blockhead
sculptured part: **5** gaine **6** pillar
bust-up: **5** party, spree **7** failure **8** collapse, outbreak **11** dissolution
bustard: **4** bird, kori **5** paauw **7** bebilya, houbara **8** gompaaum
genus: **4** otis **6** otidae
bustee: **4** slum **6** hamlet **7** village
buster: **4** crab, wind **5** blade, child, spree **6** fellow
bustle: ado **4** fray, fuss, stir, todo, whir **5** frisk, haste, whirr **6** bishop, energy, fissle, fistle, flurry, fustle, huddle, hustle, pother, racket, tumult, unrest, uproar **7** clatter, contend, scuffle **8** activity, struggle, tournure **9** agitation, commotion, stirabout
woman's: **6** bishop
busy: **4** fell **5** brisk **6** active, cident, intent, lively, occupy **7** engaged, humming, operose, trouble **8** diligent, employed, occupied, sedulous, tireless, untiring **9** assiduous, attentive, detective, laborious, officious, unwearied **11** industrious, painstaking, persevering, unremitting **13** indefatigable
busybody: **4** busy **5** snoop **7** marplot, meddler, snooper **8** factotum, quidnunc
but: lo, ma(It.); sed(L.), yet **4** mere, only, save **5** still **6** except, unless **7** besides, howbeit, however **12** nevertheless
butcher: **4** kill, slay **5** spoil **6** bungle, murder, vendor **7** botcher, britten **8** pigstick **9** slaughter **10** pigsticker **11** executioner, slaughterer
hook: **7** gambrel
rabbi: **8** shochtim
tool: saw **5** knife, steel **7** cleaver
butcher-bird: **6** shrike
butchery: **6** murder **7** carnage **8** massacre, shambles **9** martyrdom, slaughter **12** manslaughter **14** slaughterhouse
butler: **6** yeoman **7** servant, spencer, steward **10** manservant
butt: jut, mot, pit, ram, run, tup **4** buck, bunt, burt, bush, cart, cask, fool, goad, goal, goat, jolt, poll, push, stub, tope **5** bound, hinge, joint, mound, stump **6** breech, target, thrust **7** beehive, buttock, parapet, project **8** flatfish, flounder
cigar or cigarette: **5** snipe
one third: **5** terce **6** tierce

butte: 4 hill 7 picacho 8 mountain

butter: 4 shea 6 beurre(F.), cajole, spread 7 blarney, flatter
artificial: 4 oleo, suin 8 margarin 9 butterine, margarine 12 oleomargarin 13 oleomargarine
comb. form: 6 butyro
lump: pat
pert. to: 7 butyric
semifluid: ghi 4 ghee
shea: 5 galam 6 bambui, bambuk 7 bambara
tree: 4 shea 5 fulwa 8 phulwara
tub: 6 firkin

butter-and-eggs: 6 clover 7 ransted 8 ramstead, ranstead, toadflax

butterbur: 5 eldin, plant

buttercup: 6 flower 7 anemone 8 reindeer 10 butter-rose
fruit: 6 achene

butterfish: 6 blenny, gunnel

butterfly: io 4 kiho 5 satyr 6 idalia, morpho, ursula 7 admiral, buckeye, monarch, skipper, vanessa, viceroy 8 arthemis, cecropia, grayling 9 aphrodite, underwing 10 fritillary, lepidopter
expert: 13 lepidopterist
fish: 6 blenny
genus: 8 melitaea 10 heliconius
larva: 11 caterpillar
lily: 4 sego 8 mariposa
peacock: io

buttermilk: 8 sourdook(Sc.)

butterwort: 9 steepweed

buttery: 6 larder, pantry, spence 9 apartment, storeroom, wheedling 10 flattering

button: bud 4 boss, chin, hook, knob, knop 5 badge, catch, pearl 6 bauble, buckle 8 fastener
ornamental: 4 stud
part: 5 shank
three jewel: 6 troche

buttonhole: 4 loop, slit 6 detain, eyelet 11 boutonniere

buttress: 4 pier, pile, prop, stay 5 brace 7 support 8 abutment 11 counterfort

butty: 4 chum 6 worker 7 partner, workman 9 companion, middleman

buxom: 4 mild 5 jolly, plump, prone, sonsy 6 blithe, florid, humble, pliant, sonsie 8 bouncing, flexible, obedient, obliging, yielding 9 compliant, courteous, tractable 10 submissive 11 complaisant

buy: 4 chap, coff(Sc.), coup, gain, shop 5 bribe, trade 6 market, ransom, redeem, secure 7 acquire 8 purchase
cheaply: 4 snup
to sell at a profit: 7 regrate

buyer: 4 chap 5 agent 6 emptor, patron 7 chapman, shopper 8 customer, prospect 9 purchaser
stolen property: 5 fence

buying and selling: 11 nundination

buzz: hum 4 burr, call, hiss, huss, huzz, ring, whir 5 fancy, fling, phone, rumor 6 notion 7 whisper 9 bombilate, telephone

buzzard: 4 aura, fool, hawk, pern 5 buteo 6 beetle, curlew, stupid 7 vulture 9 senseless
bald: 6 osprey
honey: 4 pern

buzzer: bee 4 bell 5 alarm, badge 6 signal 7 whizzer 10 pickpocket, talebearer

by: at; ago, per 4 abut, anon, near, past 5 apart, aside, close 6 beside, toward 7 besides, through 9 alongside 10 concerning
means of: per 4 from, with 7 through
mouth: 4 oral

by-pass: 4 shun 5 evade, shunt 6 detour 7 circuit

bygone: 4 past, yore 5 olden 6 former 7 ancient, elapsed 8 backward, departed

byname: 6 byword 7 surname 8 cognomen, nickname 9 sobriquet

bypath: 4 lane 5 byway

byre: 4 barn 6 stable

Byron character: 4 Inez, Lara 6 Haidee 7 Don Juan

byssin: 4 flax 5 linen

byssoid: 7 cottony 9 fiberlike 10 byssaceous

bystander: 7 witness 9 spectator

byway: 4 lane, path 5 alley

byword: 5 axiom, motto 6 byname, phrase, saying 7 proverb 8 nickname 9 catchword

Byzantine: *capital:* 6 Nicaea 14 Constantinople
coin: 6 bezant
empress: 5 Irene
mosaic: 4 icon
scepter: 6 ferula

C

C: 7 hundred

Caaba: 6 shrine

caama: fox 4 asse 10 hartebeest

cab: 4 hack, taxi 6 hansom

cab driver: 5 cabby 6 cabbie, cocher(F.) 7 cochero(Sp.)

cabal: 4 plot, ring 5 junta, party 6 brigue, clique, scheme, secret 7 chatter, consult, council, dispute, faction, talking 8 intrigue 9 occultism, tradition 10 conspiracy 11 combination

pert. to: 9 factional

cabalistic: 6 mystic 10 mysterious

caballero: 6 knight 8 cavalier, horseman 9 gentleman

caballo: 5 horse

cabana: 9 bathhouse

cabaret: 4 cafe 5 table 6 tavern 9 nightclub 10 restaurant

cabbage: cab 4 chou, crib, kale, wort 5 filch, steal 6 pilfer, tailor 7 bowkail, purloin 8 borecole, colewort 11 appropriate, translation

daisy: 11 globeflower

family: 12 brassicaceae

salad: 4 slaw 8 coleslaw

seed: 5 colza

soup: 4 kale(Sc.)

tree: 7 angelin

variety: 4 cale, kale 5 colza, savoy 8 colewort, kohlrabi

cabbagehead: 5 dunce 9 screwball

cabbageworm: 6 looper 7 cutworm

cabby: 6 cabbie, cabman 9 cabdriver

caber: 4 beam, pole, spar 6 rafter

cabin: cot, den, hut 4 cave, cell, shed 5 booth, coach, hovel, lodge, shack 6 litter, saloon, shanty 7 bedroom, boudoir, cottage 9 stateroom

cabin boy: 7 grummet

cabin car: 7 caboose

cabinet: box 4 buhl, case 5 habut, board, chest 6 bureau, closet 7 almirah, boudoir, console, council, etagere, whatnot 8 cellaret, cupboard, ministry 10 chiffonier

cable: 4 boom, link, rope, wire 6 ganger 8 telegram

lifter: 7 wildcat

post: 4 bitt

cable car: 6 telfer 7 telpher

cabling: 7 molding 9 rudenture

cabochon: gem 5 stone 8 ornament

caboodle: kit, lot 10 collection

caboose: cab, car 5 buggy 6 galley

cabotin: 5 actor 9 charlatan

cabrilla: 4 bass 7 grouper

cacao: 4 bean 5 broma, cocoa 6 arriba 9 chocolate

shell extract: 6 martol

cache: 4 bury, hide 5 store 6 screen 7 conceal 8 treasure 10 storehouse

cachet: 4 seal 5 stamp, wafer

cachexia: 7 illness, wasting 9 morbidity 12 malnutrition

cacholong: 4 opal

cackle: 4 cank 5 clack, laugh 6 babble, gabble, giggle, gossip, keckle, titter 7 chackle, chatter, snicker, twaddle 8 laughter

cacoethes: 4 itch 6 desire

cacography: 11 misspelling

cacophonous: 5 harsh 7 raucous 8 jangling, strident 9 dissonant 10 discordant 11 unmelodious

cactus: 4 bleo 5 dildo, nopal, plant 6 cereus, chaute, chende, cholla 7 airampo, saguaro 8 chichope

drug: 6 peyote

fruit: 6 cochal

plantation: 7 nopalry

cad: cur 4 boor, chum, heel 5 churl 6 rascal, rotter 7 bounder, dastard 9 scoundrel

cadaver: 4 body 5 stiff 6 corpse 7 carcass 8 skeleton

cadaverous: 4 pale 5 gaunt 7 ghastly, haggard

caddis fly: 4 bait 5 cadew 6 cadbit 7 cadbait, cadbote

caddle: 4 fuss, mess 5 annoy, tease, worry 6 gossip 7 confuse, trouble 8 disarray 9 confusion 13 embarrassment

caddow: 5 quilt 7 jackdaw 8 coverlet
caddy: box, boy, can 5 chest
cade: keg, pet 4 cask, lamb 6 barrel, coddle 7 indulge, juniper
cadence: 4 beat, lilt, pace, tone 5 meter, metre, sound, swing, throb 6 rhythm, 8 clausula 10 modulation
cadent: 7 falling 10 descending, rhythmical
cadet: son 5 plebe, youth 6 embryo, junior 10 midshipman
cadew: 4 worm
cadge: beg, tie 4 bind, hawk 5 carry, mooch 6 peddle, sponge 8 scrounge
cadger: 6 dealer, hawker 7 carrier, packman, sponger 8 huckster
cadgy: 6 wanton 7 lustful 8 cheerful, mirthful
Cadmus: *daughter:* Ino 5 Agave 6 Semele 7 Autonoe
father: 6 Agenor
sister: 6 Europa
wife: 8 Harmonia
cadre: 4 core 5 frame, group 6 scheme 9 framework
caduceus: 4 wand 5 staff 6 symbol 7 insigne, scepter, sceptre
caducity: 5 lapse 8 senility 10 feebleness 14 perishableness
caecum: See **cecum**
Caen stone: 9 freestone, limestone
Caesar (see also **Augustus**): 6 tyrant 7 emperor
assassin: 6 Brutus 7 Cassius
capital: 4 Roma
colleague: 7 Bibulus
country conquered by: 4 Gaul
fatal day: 4 Ides
place of victory: 6 Actium
river crossed by: 7 Rubicon
sister: 4 Atia
site of famous message: 4 Zela
wife: 8 Cornelia 9 Calpurnia
caesura: 4 rest, stop 5 break, pause 8 interval 12 interruption
cafard: 5 bigot, blues 6 apathy, humbug 9 hypocrite 10 depression
cafe: 7 barroom, cabaret 8 teahouse 10 restaurant 11 coffeehouse
caffeine: 5 thein 6 theine 8 alkaloid 9 stimulant
cage: box, car, pen 4 coop 5 brake 6 aviary, basket, bucket, chapel, prison 7 chantry, confine 8 imprison, scaffold, strainer 9 enclosure, inclosure
cage hawk: mew 5 meute
caged: 4 pent
cagey, cagy: sly 4 wary
cahoots: 6 league 9 collusion 11 partnership
caiman: 6 cayman, jacare 9 alligator
Cain: 8 murderer 10 fratricide
brother: Pur 4 Abel, Seth
descendant: 6 Lamech
father: 4 Adam
land: Nod
mother: Eve
nephew: 4 Enos
son: 5 Enoch
cairn: 4 pike 5 mound 8 stoneman
cairngorm: 6 quartz
caisson: box 4 pont 5 chest, wagon 6 ponton 7 chamber, pontoon
disease: 5 bends
caitiff: 4 base, mean, vile 6 coward, wicked 7 captive 8 cowardly, prisoner, wretched 10 despicable
cajole: cog 4 coax, flam, palp 5 carny, cheat, curry, decoy, jolly, tease 6 carney, delude, entice, fraise, humbug, whilly 7 beguile, flatter, wheedle 8 blandish 9 bamboozle 10 honey-fogle
cajolery: 5 fraik 6 butter 8 flattery
cake: bar, bun, wig 4 bake, flae, fool, lump, mass, tart 5 batty, block, crust, scone, torte, wafer, wedge 6 barkle, cimbal, eclair, harden, nacket, pastry 7 bannock, oatcake, pancake 8 solidify 9 coagulate, simpleton 11 griddlecake
almond: 7 macaron 8 macaroon
boiled in honey: 8 teiglech
corn: 4 pone 7 fritter
custard: 6 eclair 9 creampuff
dough: 6 batter
filled: 4 flan
fried: 7 cruller 8 doughnut
griddle: 7 bannock(Sc.), crumpet, hotcake, pancake
plum: 4 baba
rich: 5 torte 8 madeline 9 madeleine
sacrificial: 6 hallah
seed: wig 4 wiff
small: bun 4 tart 5 batty 6 jumble 7 cupcake
tea: 5 scone
thin: 5 scone, wager 8 tortilla(Sp.)
unleavened: 5 matzo 6 damper 8 tortilla
cakewalk: 4 walk 5 dance, march, strut 6 prance
calaba: 4 tree 5 birma
calabash: 5 gourd 6 curuba
calaboose: jug 4 brig, gaol, jail 6 prison 8 bastille
caladium: 4 taro
calamanco: 5 manco 6 fabric 7 garment
calamitous: sad 4 dire, evil 5 black, fatal 6 bitter, dismal, tragic, woeful 7 adverse, baleful, direful, hapless, ruinous, unhappy, unlucky 8 grievous, tragical,

wretched 9 miserable 10 afflictive, deplorable, disastrous 11 distressful, unfortunate

calamity: 4 blow, evil, ruin 5 storm, wrack 6 misery, sorrow 8 accident, disaster, distress, fatality 9 adversity, mischance 10 affliction, misfortune 11 catastrophe, unhappiness 12 misadventure, wretchedness

calamus: pen 4 cane, reed 9 sweetflag

calangay: 8 cockatoo

calash: 6 calesa

calcar: 4 oven, spur 7 furnace

calcareous: See **calcite**

calced: 4 shod

calcite: *animal:* 8 skeleton
deposit: 4 spar, tufa 5 tatar 10 stalactite, stalagmite
soil with: 4 marl

calcium: *carbonate:* 4 tufa
oxide: 9 quicklime
sulphate: 5 hepar 6 gypsum

calculate: aim 4 plan, rate, tell 5 count, frame, think 6 design, expect, figure, number, reckon 7 average, compute, prepare 8 consider, estimate, forecast 9 determine, enumerate

calculation: 4 care 5 share 7 account, caution 8 forecast, prudence 9 logistics, reckoning 10 adjustment, discretion 11 computation

calculator: 5 table 6 abacus 7 soroban 10 accountant

Calcutta: *hemp* 4 jute
river: 5 Hugli 7 Hooghly
weight: 4 pank, raik 5 hubba, pally

calderite: 6 garnet

caldron, cauldron: pot, red, vat 4 afet 6 boiler, kettle, vessel 8 go-ashore

Caleb's son: Hur, Iru

Caledonia: 8 Scotland

Caledonian: 4 Pict, Scot 8 Scotsman

calefy: 4 heat, warm

calendar: 5 diary 7 almanac, calends, journal, kalends 8 register, schedule 9 repertory, ephemeris
church: 4 ordo
former: 6 Julian
French revolution: 6 Nivose 7 Floreal, Ventose 8 Brumaire, Fervidor, Gernubak, Messidor, Pluviose, Prairial 9 Fructidor, Thermidor 11 Vendemiaire

calenture: 4 fire, glow 5 ardor, fever 7 passion 9 sunstroke

calf: bob, boy, leg 4 buss, dolt 5 bobby, bossy, dogie, moggy, youth 6 bovine, muscle 7 bulchin, fatling 9 quadruped
flesh: 4 veal, veau(F.)
jelly: 7 fisnoga
motherless: 4 dogy 5 dogie 8 maverick
muscle: 9 plantaris
pert. to: 5 sural

Caliban: 5 beast, slave
adversary of: 8 Prospero
deity of: 7 Setebos
witch mother: 7 Sycorax

caliber: 4 bore, rank 6 degree, talent 7 ability, breadth, compass, quality 8 capacity, diameter

calibrate: 7 measure 11 standardize

calico: 4 girl 5 pinto, sallo, woman 6 salloo 7 spotted 8 goldfish 9 womankind 12 multicolored
horse: 5 pinto
mix colors for: 4 teer
pigment: 7 canarin 8 canarine
printing: 4 teer 5 fondu, lapis

calid: hot 4 warm 7 burning

Calif: 6 Caliph

California: *bay:* 8 Monterey
bulrush: 4 tule
capital: 10 Sacramento
condor: 8 gymnogyp
county: 4 Inyo, Kern, Lake, Napa, Yolo, Yuba 5 Butte, Costa, Glenn, Kings, Marin, Modoc 6 Alpine, Amador, Colusa, Contra, Fresno, Lassen, Madera, Merced, Nevada, Orange, Plumas, Obispo, Shasta, Sierra, Solano, Sonoma, Sutter, Tehama, Tulare 7 Alameda, San Luis, Trinity, Ventura 8 Del Norte, Eldorado, Humboldt, Imperial, Mariposa, Monterey, San Diego, Siskiyou, Toulumne 9 Calaveras, Mendocino, Riverside, San Benito, Santa Cruz, San Joquin 10 Los Angeles, Sacramento, Santa Clara, Stanislaus 12 San Francisco, Santa Barbara 13 San Bernardino
dam: 6 Shasta
desert: 6 Mohave, Mojave
fan palm: 7 erythea
fish: 5 reina, sprat
fort: Ord
Indian: 4 Hupa, Pomo, Seri, Yuma 5 Hoopa, Yurok 10 Weitspekan
island: 4 Goat, Mare 7 Anacapa 8 Alcatraz, Catalina, Coronado, Nicholas, Treasure 9 Farollone, San Miguel, Santa Cruz, Santa Rosa 11 San Clemente 12 Santa Barbara
lake: 5 Tahoe
laurel: 7 cajeput, cajuput
motto: 6 Eureka
oak: 5 roble 6 encina
observatory: 4 Lick 7 Palomar 8 Mt. Wilson
pass: 6 Donner, Sonora
peak: 6 Lassen, Shasta
plant: 7 tarweed

river: Eel, Mad, Pit 4 Kern 5 Kings, Smith 6 Merced, Salmon 7 Feather, Klamath, Russian, Salinas, Trinity 10 Sacramento, San Jacinto, Stanislaus
rockfish: 4 rena 5 reina, viuva 6 rasher 8 bocaccio
sea: 6 Salton
shrub: 5 salal 7 chamise, chamiso, tarbush 9 chaparral, manzanita
town: 4 Asti, Napa 5 Tracy 6 Arcata, Eureka, Fresno, Salina 7 Alameda, Arcadia
tree: 6 torrey 7 redwood, sequoia 12 Wellingtonia
valley: 4 Napa
wine area: 4 Napa
caliginous: dim 4 dark 5 misty 7 obscure
Caligula's horse: 9 Incitatus
caliph, calif: Abu, Ali 4 Bekr, Imam, Omar 6 Othman 9 caliphate
descendant: 5 Alide 7 Fatamid 8 Fatamite
fourth: Ali
calix: cup 7 chalice
calk: nap 4 copy, stop 5 close 7 occlude, silence
calking: 5 oakum
call: bid, cry, dub 4 cite, hail, name, page, stop, term, yell 5 claim, clepe, clock, elect, phone, rouse, shout, style, utter, visit, waken, yodel, yodle 6 accuse, appeal, arouse, demand, invite, invoke, muster, quethe, summon 7 address, appoint, collect, command, convene, convoke, entitle, impeach 8 announce, assemble, nominate, proclaim, vocation 9 challenge, reprimand, telephone, terminate 10 denominate
back: 6 revoke 8 retrieve
distress: S.O.S.
down: 5 scold 6 berate, invoke, rebuke 7 censure, reprove 8 denounce, execrate 9 reprimand
for: 4 page 5 exact 6 demand 7 request, require
forth: 5 evoke 6 arouse, elicit, invoke, signal, summon 7 evocate
off: end 6 cancel
out: 5 ascry, evoke 6 muster
to: 4 hail 5 ascry 6 accost, halloo 7 address
to attention: hop 6 remind
to mind: 4 cite 6 recall 8 remember
together: 6 muster, summon 7 convoke
call girl: 10 prostitute
Call of the Wild author: 6 London
callan, callant: boy, lad 4 chap 6 fellow 8 customer
calligrapher: 6 penman, writer 7 copyist 9 engrosser
calling: art, job 4 rank 5 trade 6 career, metier, naming, outcry 7 pursuit, station, summons 8 business, function, position, shouting, vocation 9 condition, summoning, utterance 10 employment, invitation, occupation, profession 11 appellation, convocation, undertaking 13 circumstances
Calliope's son: 7 Orpheus
Callisto's son: 5 Arcas
callous: 4 hard 5 horny, tough 6 brawny, obtuse, torpid 8 obdurate 9 indurated, unfeeling 11 hardhearted, indifferent 14 pachydermatous
callow: 4 bald, bare 5 crude, green 6 marshy 7 meadown 8 immature, unformed, youthful 9 unfledged 13 inexperienced 15 unsophisticated
calm: lee 4 cool, dill, easy, fair, hush, lull, mees(Sc.), mild, rest 5 abate, allay, charm, mease, peace, quell, quiet, sober, still, stoic 6 docile, gentle, irenic, pacify, placid, sedate, serene, smooth, soothe, steady 7 appease, assuage, halcyon, mollify, pacific, patient, placate, restful, unmoved 8 composed, decorous, peaceful, restrain, tranquil 9 collected, impassive, temperate, unexcited, unruffled 10 halcyonian, phlegmatic, unconfused 11 complacence, tranquilize, undisturbed 13 dispassionate, imperturbable 15 undemonstrative
calmness: 5 poise 6 repose 8 ataraxia, serenity 9 composure, placidity, quietness, sang-froid, stillness 10 equanimity 11 self-control, tranquility 12 peacefulness 13 impassiveness
calorie, calory: 5 therm 6 therme
calotte: 4 coif 6 summit
calumet: 4 pipe
calumniate: 4 slur 5 belie, libel 6 accuse, attack, defame, malign, revile, vilify 7 asperse, blacken, slander, traduce 9 blaspheme
calyx: 4 leaf 5 sepal
helmet-shaped: 5 galea
of flower: 8 perianth
cam: cog 4 awry, lobe 5 askew, catch, wiper 6 tappet 7 crooked, trippet 8 perverse
camail: 4 hood 5 guard 6 tippet
camalig: hut 5 cabin 10 storehouse
camara: 5 house 7 chamber
camarilla: 4 cell, ring 5 cabal, junta 6 clique 7 chamber, company 11 combination
camas, cammas: 5 plain 7 lobelia, prairie
Cambodia: *ancient capital:* 6 Angkor
capital: 8 Pnompenh
lake: 8 Tonle Sap
native: 5 Khmer
official name: 13 Khmer Republic
river: 6 Mekong
temple: 9 Angkor Wat
Camboria: 7 Camboja 8 Cambodge
Cambria: See Wales

cambric: 5 linen 7 batiste
Cambridge: *boat races:* 4 Lent
college official: 6 bedell
council: 5 caput
honor examination: 6 tripos
student: 5 sizar, spoon 6 optime
camel: 4 cont 6 mehari 7 tylopod 8 bactrian, ruminant 9 dromedary 10 camelopard
driver: 6 sarwan 8 cameleer
female: 4 naga
fermented milk: 5 kumys 6 koumis, kumiss 7 koumiss, koumyss
keeper: 4 obil
two-humped: 8 Bactrian
camellia: 8 japonica
Camelot: *lord:* 6 Arthur
magician: 6 Merlin
camel's hair: aba 5 cloth 6 camlet 8 cameline
garment: aba
cameo: gem 7 camaieu(F.), carving, relievo, rilievo, phalera 8 anaglyph 9 sculpture
cutting tool: 5 spade
stone: 4 onyx 8 sardonyx
camera: 7 chamber 10 department, instrument
part: 4 lens 6 finder 7 bellows, shutter
platform: 5 dolly
cameraman: 8 camerist, operator 12 photographer 13 projectionist
Cameroon: *inhabitant:* 4 Sara
river: 5 Shari
camion: bus 4 dray 5 truck, wagon 7 motorbus
camlet: 6 Angora, fabric, mohair 9 camelteen, camletine
Camorra: 5 Mafia
camouflage: 4 fake, hide 6 muffle, screen 7 conceal 8 disguise 9 deception
camp: 4 pest, tent 5 etape(F.), horde, siege, tabor 7 bivouac, shelter 8 quarters 10 settlement
follower: 5 bidar(Ind.) 6 gudget(Sc.)
pert. to: 7 castral
provision seller: 6 sutler
campaign: 5 drive, plain 7 canvass, crusade, solicit 9 champaign, operation
campanero: 8 arapunga, bellbird
campanile: 5 tower 6 belfry 7 clocher, steeple
camphol: 7 borneol
camphor: 7 menthol, asarone
campus: 4 quad 5 field 7 grounds
Camus work: 5 Rebel
can: cup, jug, may, tin 4 able, fire, jail 5 caddy, could, eshin, skill 6 vessel 7 ability, capable, dismiss 8 conserve, preserve 9 competent, container, discharge, knowledge 10 cleverness, receptacle
Canada: *airport:* 6 Gander
boat: 6 bateau 7 bateaux(pl.), batteau 8 batteaux(pl.)
city: 5 Banff, Levis, Sorel 6 Ottawa(c.), Regina 7 Calgary, Toronto 8 Edmonton, Montreal, Victoria, Winnipeg 9 Carstairs, Saskatoon, Vancouver
court decree: 5 arret
fur company employee: 8 voyageur
gannet: 6 margot
goose: 5 brant 6 honker
lake: 4 Cree, Gras, Seul 6 Louise, Teslin
land measure: 6 arpent, roture
lynx: 5 pishu
measure: ton 5 minot, perch, point 6 arpent 7 chainon
mountain: 4 Gold 5 Logan 7 Cascade, Rockies, St. Elias 9 Notre Dame 10 Laurentian, Shickshock
peninsula: 5 Gaspe
physician: 5 Osler
policeman: 6 mounty 7 mountie
poplar: 5 liard
porcupine: 5 urson 7 cawquaw
province: 6 Quebec 7 Alberta, Ontario 8 Manitoba 10 Nova Scotia 12 New Brunswick, Newfoundland, Saskatchewan 15 British Columbia 18 Prince Edward Island
river: 4 Back, Leaf 5 Peace, Trent 6 Albany, Fraser, Nelson, Ottawa, Skeena 8 Gatineau, Saguenay, Stickeen 9 Athabasca, Churchill, Great Bear, Great Fish, Mackenzie, Richelieu, St. Maurice 10 Coppermine, Great Slave, Peace Slave, St. Lawrence 12 Saskatchewan
territory: 5 Yukon 9 Northwest
Canadian: 6 Canuck
canadine: 8 alkaloid
canaille: mob 5 flour 6 rabble 7 rifraff
canal: cut 4 cano, duct, tube 5 ditch, drain, fossa(L.), graff, zanje 6 fossae(L.pl.), groove, strait, trench 7 acequia(Sp.), channel, conduit, raceway, towpath 8 aqueduct 10 waterspout 11 watercourse
dredging machine: 7 couloir
famous: Soo 4 Erie, Kiel, Suez 6 Morris, Panama 7 Welland
footpath: 7 towpath
Canal Zone: *city:* 6 Balboa
lake: 5 Gatun
canape: 6 relish 9 appetizer 11 hors d'oeuvre
canard: 4 hoax 9 grapewine 11 fabrication
canary: 4 bird 5 dance 6 singer 8 informer, squealer
forerunner of: 5 serin
canary broom: 7 genista
Canary Islands: 4 Roca 5 Ferro, Lobos, Palma, Clara 6 Gomero 7 Inferno 8 Graci-

osa, Rocca Sta., Tenerife 9 Lanzarote, Teneriffe 10 Allegranza 11 Grand Hierro 13 Fuerteventura
city: 6 Laguna 9 Santa Cruz(c.)
commune: 4 Icod
measure: 8 fanegada
mountain: 6 La Cruz 8 El Cumbre, Tenerife 9 Teneriffe 11 Gran Canaria
canary yellow: 6 meline
canasta: 4 game 5 cards, crate 6 basket, hamper
play: 4 meld
cancel: 4 blot, dele, omit 5 annul, erase, quash, remit 6 delete, efface, recall, remove, revoke 7 abolish, destroy, expunge, nullify, rescind, retract, scratch 8 abrogate 10 obliterate 11 countermand
cancion: 4 song 5 lyric
candent: hot 7 fervent, glowing
candescent: 7 glowing 8 dazzling 11 luminescent 15 autoluminescent
Candia: 5 Crete
candid: 4 fair, just, open, pure 5 blunt, clear, frank, naive 6 honest 7 artless, sincere 8 splendid 9 guileless, honorable, impartial, ingenuous, outspoken 10 immaculate 11 illustrious 15 straightforward
candidate: 7 nominee 8 aspirant, prospect 9 applicant
list: 4 leet 5 slate 6 roster
religious: 9 postulant
winning: 7 electee
Candiot, Candiote: 6 Cretan
candle: dip, wax 5 light, taper 6 cierge(F.) 9 chandelle
holder: 6 lampad, sconce, sconse 9 girandole 10 candelabra 11 candlestick
kind of: 8 bayberry
place of keeping: 9 chandlery
wax: 5 taper 6 bougie
candlelight: 4 dusk 8 twilight 9 nightfall
candlelighter: 5 spill 7 acolyte
candlenut tree: ama 5 kukui 6 bankul
candlestick: 6 lampad, sconce 8 flambeau, standard 9 flambeaux(pl.)
bracket: 6 sconce, sconse
branched: 5 jesse 8 dicerion, dikerion 9 girandole, tricerion, trikerion 10 chandelier 11 candelabrum
candlewood: 4 tree 5 shrub 9 coachwhip
candor, candour: 6 purity 8 fairness, kindness 9 frankness, innocence, unreserve, whiteness 10 brightness, brilliance, kindliness 12 impartiality 13 outspokenness
candy: 5 fudge, gundy, lolly, sweet, taffy 6 bonbon, comfit, nougate 7 brittle, caramel, congeal, fondate, flatter, sweeten 8 lollipop 9 granulate, sweetmeat 10 confection 11 crystallize
base: 7 fondant
mixture: 6 fourre
nut: 7 praline
pulled sugar: 5 taffy 6 penide
sugar: 7 fondant 8 alphenic
candytuft: 5 plant 6 flower, iberis
cane: rod 4 beat, dart, flog, pipe, reed, stem, tube, whip 5 birch, lance, staff, stick 6 bamboo, punish, rattan 7 calamus, hickory, malacca, scourge 9 crabstick
dense growth: 9 canebrake
knife: 7 machete
part: 7 ferrule
sugar: 7 sucrose
Canfield: 8 Klondike 9 solitaire
cangle: 7 dispute, quarrel, wrangle
canine (see also **dog**): cur, dog, fox, pup 4 fisc, wolf 5 canis(L.) 7 doglike
tooth: 7 laniary
caning: 6 rattan
canister: box 9 container
canker: 4 rust 6 infect 7 consume, corrode, corrupt, tarnish 9 verdigris
cannabis: 4 hemp
drug: 5 bhang 7 hashish 9 marijuana
Cannery Row author: 9 Steinbeck
cannibal: 6 savage 15 anthropophagite
cannikin: can, cup 4 pail 6 bucket
cannon: bit, gun 5 crack, thief 6 mortar 7 bastard 8 howitzer, ordnance 9 artillery 10 pickpocket
breech-end knob: 8 cascabel
early: 5 aspic, saker 7 robinet
fire: 7 barrage
firing stick: 8 linstock
fodder: 8 infantry
handle: 4 anse
muzzle plug: 7 tampion
part: 4 bore 5 chase 6 breech, muzzle 7 chamber, rimbase 8 cascabel, trunnion
shot: 5 grape
support: 8 trunnion
cannonade: 7 barrage
cannoneer: 12 artilleryman
cannot: 6 unable
cannular: 6 hollow 7 tubular
canny: sly 4 cozy, snug, wary, wily, wise 5 lucky, pawky, quiet 6 clever, frugal, gentle, shrewd 7 careful, cunning, knowing, prudent, quietly, thrifty 8 cautious, skillful, watchful 9 carefully, dexterous, fortunate, sagacious 10 cautiously 11 comfortable, sharpwitted
canoe: 4 boat, kiak, pahi, proa, waka 5 birch, kayak, prahu, skiff, umiak, waapa 6 ballam, dugout, oomiak, pitpan 7 almadia, bidarka, coracle, currane, pirogue
bark: 7 cascara

dugout: **5** banca **6** baroto, corial **7** pirogue, piroque **12** pambanmanche
large: pah **5** bungo
sailing: **4** proa **5** prahu
skin-covered: **4** kiak **5** bidar, kayak **7** baidara
war: **4** proa
canon: law **4** code, hymn, laud, list, rule, song **5** axiom, gorge, gulch, model, table, tenet **6** decree **7** precept, statute **8** decision, standard **9** catalogue, clergyman, criterion **10** regulation **12** constitution
enigmatical: **4** nodi(pl.) **5** nodus
resident: **8** stagiary
canonical: **8** accepted, orthodox **13** authoritative
hour: **4** laud, none, sext **5** matin, prime **6** tierce **7** vespers **8** compline
canonicals: alb **4** cope, cowl, robe **5** stole
canopy: sky **4** ceil, cope, dais, hood **5** shade, vault **6** awning, celure, finial, tester **7** marquee, shelter **8** covering **9** baldachin, baldaquin, pavillion **11** baldacchino
altar: **7** ciboria(pl.) **8** baldakin, ciborium **9** baldachin, baldaquin **10** baldachino **11** baldacchino
bed: **6** tester **7** sparver
canorous: **5** clear **7** musical **8** sonorous **9** melodious **10** euphonious
cant: tip **4** coax, heel, lean, list, nook, sing, tilt, turn **5** argot, bevel, chant, hield, lingo, lusty, merry, niche, pitch, share, slang, slant, slope, whine **6** careen, corner, herald, intone, jargon, lively, patois, snivel **7** auction, incline, portion, singing, wheedle **8** cheerful, pretense, vigorous **9** barbarism, hyprocrisy, vulgarism **10** intonation **13** colloquialism **17** sanctimoniousness
cantabank: **6** singer **7** chanter
cantaloupe, cantaloup: **9** muskmelon
cantankerous: **6** ornery **8** perverse **9** irritable, malicious **10** brabagious **11** contentious **12** crossgrained
cantata: **4** mote, poem **8** serenata **11** composition
cantatrice: **6** singer **9** chanteuse
canteen: K.T., P.X., bar **5** bazar, flask **6** bazaar **7** cantina
canter: jog, run **4** gait, lope, pace, rack **5** rogue **6** beggar, whiner **8** vagabond
Canterbury: *archbishop:* Odo **4** Lang **6** Anselm, Becket **7** Crammer
gallop: **5** aubin
canticle: ode **4** hymn, laud, song **5** canto **6** anthem, cantic, hirmos **7** bravura
church: **6** Te Deum, venite **10** magnificat
cantilena: **6** legato, melody **8** graceful
cantillate: hum **5** chant **6** intone, recite
cantina: bag **5** pouch, store **6** pocket, pommel, saloon **7** canteen
canting: **5** atrip, pious **12** hypocritical
cantle: **4** join, nook, part **5** cheer, piece, raise, slice **6** corner **7** portion, segment **8** brighten, fragment **11** cornerpiece
canto: air, fit **4** book, pace, song **5** verse **6** melody, passus
canton: **4** part **5** angle **6** corner **7** portion, quarter, section **8** district, division
cantor: **6** leader, singer **7** chanter, soloist **9** precentor
cantoria: **7** balcony, gallery
cantrip: **5** charm, spell, trick
cantus: **4** song **5** chant
canty: **6** lively **8** cheerful **9** sprightly
Canuck: **8** Canadian
canvas: **4** duck, sail, tarp, tent, tewk **5** scrim **6** burlap **7** picture, poldavy **8** painting
waterproof: **9** tarpaulin
canvasback: **4** duck **6** cheval
canvass: **4** beat, hawk, poll, sift **5** randy, study **6** debate, peddle, search **7** agitate, discuss, examine, solicit, trounce **8** campaign, consider **11** electioneer, investigate
canvasser: **5** agent **6** poller, rodman **7** counter **8** salesman
canyon: **5** cajon, chasm, gorge, gulch **6** arroyo, ravine
mouth: **4** abra
small: **6** canada
canzonet: air **4** song **5** canto **6** ballad **7** canzona, canzone **8** madrigal
caoba: **5** quira **8** mahogany, muskwood
caoutchouc: **6** rubber
source: ule **6** caucho
cap: fez, hat, lid, taj, tam, tip, top **4** acme, coif, cork, dome, eton, hood, hure, mate, topi **5** beret, chief, cover, crown, excel, match, outdo, seize, topee **6** arrest, beanie, bonnet, climax, cornet, helmet, puzzle, summit, turban **7** commode, ferrule, overlie, overtop, perplex, surpass **8** headgear, surprise, tarboosh **9** detonator, headpiece **11** mortarboard
child's: **5** mutch, toque **6** biggin, bonnet
close-fitting: **4** coif **5** toque **6** cloche **7** calotte
covering: **8** havelock
ecclesiastical: **5** beret **6** barret **7** biretta, galerum, galerus **8** barretta
hunter's: **7** montero
ignition: **4** fuse, fuze
military: **4** kepi **5** busby, shako
muslin: **5** mutch
part: **4** bill, peak **5** visor
Roman: **6** pileus
Scotch: tam **8** balmoral **9** glengarry **11** tamoshanter
sheepskin: **6** calpac **7** calpack

skull: 5 beame 6 callot, pileus 7 calotte, yamilke 8 yarmulka
steel: 10 cerveliere
cap-a-pie: 7 utterly 10 throughout
capa: 5 cloak 6 mantle
capability: 6 stroil 7 ability 8 capacity 9 potential 10 competence, efficiency
capable: apt, can, fit 4 able 5 adept 6 expert 7 skilled 9 competent, effective, efficient, qualified 10 proficient 12 accomplished
of being cut: 7 sectile 8 scissile
of being defended: 7 tenable
of being heard: 7 audible
of being molded: 7 plastic
of being touched: 8 tangible
of endurance: 4 wiry 5 tough
of extension: 7 tensile
of flying: 6 volant
of suffering: 8 passible 9 sensitive
render: 6 enable
capacious: 4 full, wide 5 ample, broad, large, roomy 6 goodly 8 captious, spacious 9 extensive 10 commodious 12 considerable
capacitate: 7 qualify
capacity: 4 bent, gift, size, turn 5 knack, power, skill, space 6 burden, extent, spread, talent, volume 7 ability, caliber, calibre, content, faculty, fitness 8 aptitude, strength 9 continent, endowment, intellect 10 capability, competence
Capaneus: *father:* 9 Hipponous
mother: 8 Astynome
son: 9 Sthenelus
wife: 6 Evadne
caparison: 4 deck, trap 8 covering 9 adornment 10 decoration
capatas: 4 boss 7 capataz(Sp.), foreman 8 overseer
capcase: bag 4 case 5 chest 10 receptacle
cape: ras 4 cope, gape, head, look, neck, ness, writ 5 amice, cappa, cloak, fanon, fichu, orale, point, sagum, stare, stole, talma 6 bertha, chapel, mantle, sontag, tabard, tippet 7 leather, manteel 8 headland, lambskin, mantilla 9 inverness, peninsula, sheepskin 10 projection, promontory
crocheted: 6 sontag
lace: 5 fichu 6 bertha 8 collaret
Cape anteater: 8 aardvark
Cape armadillo: 8 pangolin
Cape Colony plateau: 5 karoo 6 karroo
Cape Dutch: 9 Afrikaans
Cape elk: 5 eland
Cape gooseberry: 4 poha 12 ground cherry
Cape jasmine: 8 gardenia
Cape lancewood: 7 assagai
cape merchant: 10 supercargo
Cape polecat: 5 zoril 8 muishond
Cape Province: *people:* 4 Xosa 5 Pondo
Cape Ruby: 6 garnet, pyrope
Cape Verde: *capital:* 5 Praia
island: Sal 4 Fago
native: 5 Brava, Serer
Capek: *play:* RUR
creature: 5 robot
capel: 4 rock, wall 5 horse 6 quartz
caper: hop 4 dido, jump, leap, romp, skip, skit 5 antic, brank, dance, flisk, frisk, prank, sauce, shrub 6 cavort, frisco, frolic, gambol, gamond, prance, spring, tittup, vagary 7 corsair, courant, friscal, gambado 8 capricci(pl.), capriole, marigold 9 capriccio, condiment, privateer
family: 13 capparidaceae
capercaillie: 4 cock 6 grouse
courtship: lak
capernoited: 7 crabbed, peevish 9 irritable 11 intoxicated 12 muddleheaded
capernoitie: 4 head 6 noddle
capeskin: 7 leather 9 sheepskin
capful: 4 puff 8 quantity
capias: 4 writ 7 process
capillary: 6 minute 7 slender 8 filiform, hairlike
capillus: 4 hair
capilotade: 4 stew 5 sauce 6 ragout
capital: 4 cash, city, good, main, rare, seat 5 basic, chief, fatal, great, major, money, stock, vital 6 deadly, letter, mortal, primal, wealth 7 central, chattel, leading, radical, serious, weighty 9 copacetic, excellent, paramount, principal, prominent 10 pre-eminent 11 scrumptious
ancient: 4 Roma
impairment of: 7 deficit 9 depletion
provide: 4 back 5 angel 7 finance
capital punishment: 7 hanging 8 shooting 12 death penalty 13 electrocution
capitalist: 8 investor 9 plutocrat
capitano: 5 chief 7 captain, headman, soldier
capitate: 8 headlike
Capitol Hill group: 5 House 6 Senate
capitulate: 4 fall 5 agree, title, yield 8 headline 9 enumerate, surrender
caporal: 7 foreman, tobacco 8 overseer
capote: 4 hood 5 cloak 6 bonnet, mantle, topper 8 overcoat
capric acid salt: 6 rutate
caprice: fad 4 kink, mood, whim 5 antic, braid, fancy, freak, humor, quirk 6 maggot, notion, temper, vagary, whimsy 7 boutade, conceit, crochet, impulse, whimsey 9 capriccio 12 inconsistent
capricious: 5 dizzy, doddy, fluky, moody 6 fickle 7 comical, erratic, flighty, wayward 8 fanciful, freakish, humorous, unsteady,

volatile **9** arbitrary, crotchety, fantastic, humorsome, whimsical **10** changeable, inconstant
Capricorn: **4** Goat **6** beetle **13** Constellation
star within: **5** Deneb
capriole: **4** leap **5** caper **6** spring **9** headdress
capripede: **4** goat **5** satyr
caprylate: **4** acid, salt **5** ester **7** octoate
capsize: **4** coup, keel **5** upset **8** overturn
capstan: **4** drum **5** hoist, lever **8** cylinder, windlass
catch: **4** pawl
capsule: pod **4** boll, case, pill **5** shell, theco, wafer **6** ampule, sheath **7** ampoule **8** pericarp **9** cartridge, detonator **10** repository
captain: bo; boh **4** head **5** chief **6** leader, master **7** capitan, foreman, headman, manager, skipper **8** capitano, governor **9** centurion, commander, principal **14** superintendent
boat: gig
caption: **5** title **6** leader, legend **7** heading **8** headline, subtitle
captious: **5** testy **6** crafty, severe **7** carping, cynical, fretful, peevish **8** alluring, caviling, contrary, critical **9** capacious, insidious, irascible **10** capricious, censorious **12** faultfinding **13** hypercritical
captivate: win **4** take **5** catch, charm **6** allure, enamor, please, ravish, subdue **7** attract, bewitch, capture, enamour, enchant **8** enthrall, overtake **9** enrapture, fascinate, infatuate
captive: **5** slave **6** enamor **7** caitiff **8** prisoner
captivity: **4** bond **6** duress **7** bondage, serfdom, slavery **9** servitude, thralldom **10** subjection **11** confinement **12** imprisonment
captor: **5** taker **6** victor **7** catcher
capture: bag, cop, get, nab, net, win **4** fang, grab, hook, land, prey, take, trap, tree **5** catch, prize, raven, seize **6** arrest, collar, obtain **9** apprehend, captivate **10** circumvent **12** apprehension
capuche: **4** cowl, hood
Capuchin: **5** friar **6** monkey, pigeon
caput: top **4** head **7** chapter, council, section **8** division **9** paragraph
capybara: **6** rodent
car (see also **automobile**): box, bus **4** auto, jeep, rath **5** coach, hutch, ratha, sedan, train, wrong **6** basket **7** awkward, chariot, trailer, trolley, vehicle **8** roadster, sinister **10** automobile, left-handed **11** convertible
aerial cable: **6** telfer **7** telpher
armored: **4** tank
railroad: box, oil **4** club, flat, mail, tank **5** chair, coach, diner **6** buffet, hopper, parlor **7** baggage, caboose, express, freight, gondola, pullman, sleeper, tourist **9** furniture, passenger **12** refrigerator
car barn: **5** depot
carabao: **7** buffalo
caracara: **4** hawk
caract: See **character**
carafe: **6** bottle
caramel: **5** candy, sweet **6** bonbon **9** flavoring **10** confection
carapace: **5** crust, shell **6** lorica
carara: **9** coronopus
caravan: van **4** trek, trip **5** fleet **6** cafila, convoy, safari, travel **7** journey, vehicle
slave: **6** coffle
caravansary: inn **4** chan, khan **5** hotel, serai **6** hostel, imaret **8** choultry, hostelry **9** resthouse
carbine: gun **5** rifle **6** musket, weapon **7** escopet **9** escopette
carbohydrate: **5** sugar **6** starch **8** dextrose **9** cellulose
carbon: **4** coal, coke, copy, soot **6** crayon **7** replica **8** graphite
deposit: **4** soot
point: **6** crayon
carbonate: **4** burn, char, fizz **6** aerate **7** enliven **9** carbonize
carborundum: **5** emery **8** abrasive
carboy: jug **6** bottle
carbuncle: **4** boil **5** jewel **6** garnet **7** abscess
carcajou: **4** lynx **6** badger, cougar **9** wolverine
carcanet: **5** chain **6** collar **8** headband, necklace
carcass: **4** body **6** corpse **7** carrion
carcel: **4** jail **6** prison
carcoon: **5** clerk **7** manager
card: map, pam, wag **4** comb, menu, plan **5** chart, fiche, joker, tease **6** cartel, ticket **7** program **8** schedule **9** character, eccentric **10** attraction, pasteboard
spot: pip
wool: tum **4** comb, rove, toom
card game: lu; gin, hoc, loo, pam **4** bank, faro, hock, keno, ruff, skat, slam, snap, solo, spin, vint **5** beast, chico, cinch, comet, crimp, decoy, gilet, gleek, monte, omber, ombre, pedro, pique, pitch, poker, rummy, stuss, trump, two-up, waist, whist **6** basset, boston, bridge, casino, commit, ecarte, euchre, fantan, flinch, hearts, masset, piquet, rounce, sledge, smudge **7** baccara, bezique, cayenne, Chicago, canasta, cooncan, sevenup **8** baccarat, commerce, conquian, contract, cribbage, handicap, Napoleon, patience, pinochle, tresillo, vederuff **9** Newmarket, panguinui, solitaire **10** blackstone **11** everlasting, speculation

bid: 4 slam 6 misere
holding: 6 tenace
old: hoc, loo, pam 4 brag, ruff 5 comet, gilet, omber, ombre, trump 7 primero, reversi 8 penneech, penneeck
player who cuts: 4 pone
playing card: ace, pam, ten 4 jack, king, trey 5 basto(Sp.), deuce, joker, knave, queen, taroc, tarot
term: bid, bye, cat, pic 4 book, card, deal, hand, meld, pair, pass, suit 5 flush, raise, trump 6 renege, tenace, tricon 8 sequence, straight 9 doubleton, singleton 10 Yarborough
widow: 4 skat
wild: 5 joker

cardigan: 6 fabric, jacket, wampus 7 sweater

cardinal: 4 bird, main 5 basic, chief, cloak, color, vital 6 cleric 7 radical 9 principal 10 underlying
assembly at Rome: 7 college
notification of elevation: 9 biglietto
office: hat 6 datary 7 dataria
title: 8 eminence

cards (see also **card game**): 4 deck, pack, suit

care: 4 cark, cure, duty, fret, heed, mind, reck, soin(F.), tend, wish, yeme 5 grief, guard, nurse, pains, worry 6 burden, desire, grieve, lament, regard, sorrow 7 anxiety, auspice, caution, cherish, concern, keeping, scruple, thought, tuition 8 business 9 attention, diligence, direction, oversight 10 management, solicitude 11 calculation, heedfulness 12 watchfulness 14 responsibility
for: 4 like, mind, tend 5 guard, nurse, treat 6 foster, relish
requiring: 7 fragile 8 ticklish
under another's: 4 ward 6 charge 7 protege 10 apprentice

careen: dip 4 cant, heel, keel, list, tilt, veer 5 lurch, slope 7 incline

career: run, way 4 life, road 5 trade 6 charge, course, gallop 7 calling, pursuit, running 8 business, vocation 10 occupation, profession, racecourse 11 achievement

carefree: 4 easy 5 frank, happy 10 insouciant 12 lighthearted

careful: 4 wary 5 canny, chary, exact 6 eident, frugal 7 anxious, guarded, heedful, prudent, thrifty 8 accurate, cautious, diligent, discreet, dreadful, gingerly, mournful, troubled, vigilant, watchful 9 advertent, attentive, exquisite, observant, provident 10 economical, meticulous, respectful, respective, scrupulous, solicitous, thoughtful 11 circumspect, considerate, painstaking, punctilious

carefully: 7 charily 8 gingerly

careless: lax 4 cool, easy, lash, rash 5 slack 6 casual, overly, remiss, supine, untidy, unwary 7 languid 8 heedless, listless, reckless, slattern, slipshod, slovenly 9 forgetful, haphazard, negligent, unheeding, unmindful 10 neglectful, nonchalant, regardless 11 inadvertent, inattentive, indifferent, perfunctory, spontaneous, thoughtless, unconcerned

caress: coy, hug, pat, pet 4 bill, dant(Sc.), kiss, neck 6 coddle, cosset, fondle, pamper, stroke 7 cherish, embrace 10 endearment

caretaker: 6 keeper 7 janitor 9 custodian 11 housekeeper

Carew's love: 5 Celia

careworn: 5 lined

carfuffle: 6 flurry, ruffle 8 disorder 9 agitation 10 disarrange

cargador: 6 porter 7 carrier 9 stevedore

cargo: 4 bulk, load 6 burden, lading 7 freight 8 property, shipment 10 freightage
discarded: 6 jetsam
loader: 9 stevedore
space in ship: 4 hold
stabilizer: 7 ballast
take on: 4 lade, load
wrecked ship: 7 flotsam

Caribbean: *bird:* 4 tody
gulf: 6 Darien
island: 4 Cuba 6 Nassau

caribe: 4 fish 6 pirana, piraya 7 piranha

caribou: 4 deer 8 reindeer

carica: 4 tree 6 papaya, pawpaw

caricature: ape 4 copy, mock, skit 5 farce, libel, mimic, squib 6 overdo, parody, satire 7 cartoon 8 travesty 9 burlesque 12 exaggeration

caries: 5 decay 10 ulceration 11 saprodontia

carillon: 5 bells 6 chimes 12 glockenspiel

cark: vex 4 care, heed, load 5 cavil, pains, worry 6 burden, charge, harass 7 anxiety, perplex, trouble 8 distress

carl: lad 4 boor, hemp 5 churl, snarl 6 carlot, fellow, rustic 7 bondman, villein 10 husbandman, pinchpenny

carling: 6 rafter 7 support

Carmelite: 4 monk 5 friar
barefoot: 8 Teresian

carmen: 4 poem, song 11 incantation

Carmen composer: 5 Bizet

carmine: red 7 crimson, scarlet 8 coloring

carnage: 6 murder, pogrom 8 butchery, massacre 9 bloodshed, slaughter

carnal: 4 crow, lewd 6 animal, bodily, sexual, worldly 7 brutish, earthly, fleshly, secular, sensual 8 material, temporal 9 corporeal 11 unspiritual 12 bloodthirsty, unregenerate

carnation: 4 pink 5 flake 6 flower 7 picotee 9 grenadine(F.)

carnelian: 4 sard 10 chalcedony

carnival: 4 fete 7 revelry 8 festival 11 merrymaking

wild man: 4 geek

carnivore: cat, dog, fox 4 bear, coon, lion, lynx, mink, puma, seal, wolf 5 civet, coati, genet, hyena, otter, panda, pekah, ratel, sable, stoat, tiger 6 cougar, ermine, feline, ferret, jackal, jaguar, marten, ocelot, possum, serval, weasel 7 dasyure, genette, glutton, leopard, opposum, polecat, raccoon, tigress 8 mongoose 9 ichneumon

carnose: 6 fleshy

carob: 4 tree 6 locust 9 algarroba

carol: lay 4 noel, sing, song 5 ditty, yodel, yodle 6 alcove, warble 8 madrigal

Caroline island: Yap 4 Palu, Truk 5 Pelew 6 Ponape

carom: 4 shot 6 bounce, glance, strike 7 rebound 8 ricochet

carousal: 4 lark, orgy, riot, romp, toot 5 binge, feast, randy, revel, spree 6 frolic, shindy, splore 7 banquet, carouse, wassail 8 festival, jamboree 9 bacchanal

carouse: 4 bout 5 birle(Sc.), bouse, drink, revel, quaff, spree, toast 7 wassail 8 carousal

carp: nag 4 fish, sing, snag, talk, yerk 5 cavil, prate, scold, speak 6 censor, nibble, recite 7 censure, chatter, quibble 8 complain, goldfish 9 criticize, discourse

carpel: 9 carpophyl 10 carpophyll

carpenter: ant 6 framer, joiner, wright 8 tectonic 9 artificer 10 woodworker 12 cabinetmaker

machine: 5 lathe 6 planer, shaper

ship: 5 chips

tool: adz, awl, saw 4 adze 5 level, plane 6 gimlet, hammer, square 7 hatchet

carpet: mat, rug 4 kali 5 scold, tapet, tapis 6 fabric 8 covering 9 reprimand

design: 9 medallion

variety: 4 Agra 6 velvet, Wilton 7 ingrain 8 Brussels, moquette, Venetian 9 Axminster, broadloom

carping: 8 captious, caviling, critical 10 censorious 12 faultfinding 13 hypercritical

carplike fish: 4 dace, rudd

carpus: 5 wrist

carr, car: bog, fen 4 pool 5 grove

carrack, carack: 4 boat 7 galleon

carrageen: 4 alga, moss 7 seaweed

carriage: air, gig 4 gait, garb, hack, load, mien, shay 5 bandy, brake, break, buggy, coach, front, midge, poise, wagon 6 burden, convoy, landau, manner, surrey 7 baggage, bearing, conduct, gesture, hackney, phaeton, vecture, vehicle 8 behavior, demeanor, dormeuse, equipage, portance 9 behaviour, execution 10 conveyance, deportment, management 14 administration

baby: 4 pram 6 gocart 8 stroller 12 perambulator

closed: cab 4 hack, taxi 6 calash 7 caleche 8 brougham, clarence

covered: 6 Berlin, landau 7 ricksha 8 carryall, dearborn, stanhope

four-wheeled: 5 coupe 6 surrey, whisky 7 phaeton, whiskey 8 barouche, clarence, rockaway, victoria 9 chariotee, gladstone

French: 6 fiacre

one-horse: fly, gig 4 ekka (Ind.), shay, trap 5 sulky 6 dennet 7 cariole, dogcart 8 carriole

open: 7 dogcart, dos-a-dos 8 sociable

portable: 5 sedan

three-horse: 6 troika

two-seated: 6 tandem

two-wheeled: gig 4 shay, trap 5 essed, sulky, tonga 6 chaise, cisium, esseda, hansom 7 carreta, chariot, tilbury 8 carretta 9 caretella, carromata 11 jinrickshaw

carriage trade: 7 society

carried: 5 borne, giddy, toted 6 carted, lugged, wafted 8 drifting, ravished 10 abstracted 11 transported

carrier (see also **conveyance**): hod 4 ship 5 hamal, maoor, plane 6 bearer, cadger, hamaul, hammal, khamal, porter 7 drayman, flattop, hammaul, postman, remover 8 cargador, portator, railroad, teamster 9 messenger

carrion: 4 vile 6 corpse, refuse, rotten 7 carcass, corrupt 9 loathsome

Carroll character: 5 Alice 6 hatter, rabbit 7 duchess

carrot: 4 root 5 plant 6 daucus 10 enticement

deadly: 5 drias

family: 8 ammaicea

genus: 5 carum

top: 7 red-head

wild: 8 hilltrot 10 laceflower

carrottop: 7 redhead

carrousel: 4 ride 12 merry-go-round

carry: hug, jag, lug 4 bear, cart, gest, hold, lead, take, tote, tump 5 bring, cadge, geste, guide, poise 6 behave, convey, convoy, delate, derive, extend 7 conduct, contain, produce, support, sustain, undergo 8 continue, transfer, transmit 9 prosecute, transport 11 comportment

away: 4 kill, take 5 eloin, reave, steal 6 eloign, kidnap, remove 9 transport

on: 4 rant, rave, wage 6 manage 7 conduct, perform, proceed 8 continue, maintain, transact 9 misbehave, prosecute
out: 6 effect 7 execute, perform, sustain 8 complete
over: 4 tide 5 table 6 extend, shelve 8 contango, postpone, transfer
the day: win 7 prevail
carryall: bag, bus 4 case 8 carriage
carrying: 6 gerent 9 gestation
cart: 4 butt, char, dray, haul, tote, wain 5 araba, bandy, bogie, carry, sulky, tonga, wagon 6 charet, convey 7 chariot, hackery, trolley, trundle, tumbler, tumbrel, tumbril, vehicle 8 charette
farmer: 7 morfrey 8 morphrey
freight: 8 carreton
horse: 8 cartaver(Sc.)
license: 6 caroon 7 caroome, carroon
racing: 5 sulky
rope: 5 wanty(Sc.)
strong: 4 dray
two-wheeled: bin, gig 4 shay 5 dandy, sulky, tonga 6 reckla 7 tumbril 8 carretta(Sp.)
cartage: 7 drayage, haulage
carte: map 4 card, list, menu 5 chart 7 charter, diagram
cartel: 4 card, defy, pact, pool, ship 5 paper, trust 6 corner, letter, treaty 8 contract 9 agreement, challenge 10 convention
carter: 7 drayman, trucker 8 horseman, teamster
Carthage: *citadel:* 5 Bursa, Byrsa
emblem: 4 palm
foe: 4 Cato
founder: 4 Dido
general: 5 Hanno 8 Hannibal
god: 6 Moloch
goddess: 5 Tanit 6 Tanith
language: 5 Punic
magistrate: 7 suffete
pert. to: 5 Punic
queen: 4 Dido
subject: 6 Libyan
victor at Zama: 6 Scipio
Carthusian: 4 monk 7 eremite
monastery: 5 Pavia 7 Certosa
noted: 4 Hugh
superior: 5 prior
cartilage: 6 tissue 7 gristle
ossified: 4 bone
cartload: 6 fother
cartograph: map 4 plat 5 chart
carton: box 4 case 9 container 10 receptacle
cartoon: 10 caricature
cartoonist: 4 Arno, Capp, Ding, Nast 6 Disney
cartridge: bag 4 case 5 shell 7 capsule
holder: 4 clip
carucate: 4 hide, land 5 field
caruncle: 4 comb, gill 6 growth, wattle
carving: *in stone:* 5 cameo 8 intaglio 10 engrailing
pert. to: 7 glyphic, glyptic
relief: 5 cameo
carya: 5 pecan 6 pignut 9 bitternut
caryatid: 6 figure 9 priestess
male: cap 7 telamon
casa: 5 house 8 building, dwelling
casaba: 5 melon 9 muskmelon
Casanova: 4 rake, roue 5 lover
cascade: lin(Sc.) 4 fall, linn(Sc.) 5 force(Sc.) 8 cataract 9 waterfall
casco: 5 barge 7 lighter
case: bag, box, hap, pod 4 bunk, burr, deed, file, pack, pair, suit 5 brace, bulla, burse, casus, cover, crate, event, folio, state, theca, trial 6 action, affair, binder, carton, chance, coffin, couple, matter, quiver, sheath, survey 7 cabinet, capcase, capsule, enclose, envelop, example, holster, inclose, lawsuit, satchel 8 accident, argument, cupboard, envelope, instance, situated 9 cartridge, condition, container, happening 10 occurrence, receptacle, sabretache 11 contingency
book holder: 5 forel 6 forrel
cigar: 7 humidor
cosmetic: 7 compact
document: 7 hanaper
explosive: 5 shell 6 petard 11 firecracker
grammatical: 6 dative 8 ablative, genitive, vocative 9 objective 10 accusative, nominative
small: tye 4 etui 5 bulla, etwee 6 trouse
toiletries: 4 etui 5 etwee
case history: 5 story 6 record
casement: 6 window 8 covering
cash: 4 coin, cush, dump, dust, jack, jake 5 blunt, brass, clink, darby, dough, funds, money 6 specie 7 capital, hemlock 8 currency 10 spondulics
keeper: 6 bursar, teller 7 cashier 9 treasurer
cashbox: 4 till 6 coffer
cashew: nut 4 tree 7 maranon
casing: 4 boot, shoe, tire 5 gaine 6 coffin, collet, lining, sheath 8 covering 9 framework
cask: keg, tub, tun, vat 4 butt, cade, cowl, knag, pipe 5 bowie, bulge, foist 6 bareca, bareka, barrel, cardel, casque, firkin, tierce 7 barrico, fostell 8 cassette, hogshead, puncheon 9 kilderkin
bulge: 5 bilge
oil: 4 rier
orifice: 8 bunghole
rim: 5 chimb, chime

stave: lag
wine: fat, tun 4 butt, fust, pipe 6 tierce
casket: box, pix, tye 4 case, cask, cist, till, tomb 5 chest 6 Accera, chasse, coffer, coffin 7 casquet, fostell 8 cassette 9 reliquary
Caspian Sea: 5 Tates
ancient region: 7 Parthia
harbor: 4 Baku
river to: 4 Kura, Ural 5 Terek, Volga
casque: hat 4 cask 5 armor 6 helmet 9 headdress
Cassandra: 7 prophet, seeress
father: 5 Priam
cassation: 8 quashing 9 annulling, canceling 10 abrogation
cassava: 4 aipi, juca 5 aipim 6 casiri, manioc 7 tapioca
cassena: 6 yaupon
cassette: 6 casket, holder, sagger
cassia: 4 drug, herb, tree 5 senna, shrub
bark: 8 cinnamon
cassie: 6 basket 8 huisache
Cassiopeia: *daughter:* 9 Andromeda
husband: 7 Cepheus
cassock: 4 gown 5 gippo 6 priest 7 pelisse, soutane 9 clergyman
cassone: box 5 chest
cassowary: emu 4 bird 5 murup 6 moorup
cast: 4 hurl, mold, molt, shed, spew, tint, toss 5 eject, fling, found, heave, mould, pitch, shade, sling, throw, tinge 7 cashier, deposit, discard
aside: see *away* below
away: 4 jilt, junk, shed 5 scrap, wreck 6 maroon, reject 7 abandon, discard, dismiss 8 squander 9 shipwreck
down: 5 abase 6 abattu, deject, sadden 7 abattue, depress, destroy 8 demolish, dispirit 10 discourage
lots: 5 cavel
off: 4 free 5 untie 6 disown, unmoor 7 discard 9 eliminate
out: 5 eject, expel 6 banish
up: add 5 total, vomit 6 reckon 7 compute, measure 8 reproach
castaway: 4 waif 5 tramp 6 reject 7 outcast 8 derelict, stranded 9 shipwreck
caste: 4 rank 5 breed, class, grade, order 6 degree, status
group: 5 varna
merchant: 6 banian, banyan
priestly: 4 magi(pl.) 5 magus
caster: 4 vial 5 cruse, cruet, phial, wheel 6 castor, hurler, roller 7 pitcher, trundle
castigate: 5 emend, scare 6 berate, punish, revise, strafe, subdue 7 censure, chasten, correct, reprove 8 chastise, lambaste 9 criticize
castigatory: 5 penal 8 punitive 10 corrective
Castile: *hero:* Cid
province: 5 Avila, Soria
river: 4 Ebro, Esla 5 Douro, Duero
Castilian: 7 Spanish
casting: *mold:* die 6 matrix 7 matrice
rough: pig
castle: 4 fort, rock, rook 5 abode, morro 7 bastile, chateau, citadel 8 bastille, castillo, fastness, fortress 10 stronghold 13 fortification
in the air: 5 dream 6 vision 7 fantasy 8 daydream 9 imagining
part: 4 bawn, moat 6 donjon 10 drawbridge, portcullis
tower: 4 keep
wall: 6 bailey
warden: 6 disdar, dizdar 9 castellan
castor: hat 4 bean, star 6 beaver 7 leather
Castor: *and Pollux:* 5 twins 6 Gemini 8 Dioscuri
brother: 6 Pollux
father: 4 Zeus 9 Tyndareus
horse: 8 Cyllaros
mother: 4 Leda
slayer: 4 Idas
castor-bean poison: 5 ricin
castrate: gib 4 geld, spay, swig 5 alter, capon, prune 6 eunuch, neuter 7 evirate 8 caponize, mutilate 10 emasculate
casual: 5 stray 6 chance, random 7 cursory, natural, offhand 8 informal 9 haphazard, uncertain 10 accidental, contingent, fortuitous, incidental, nonchalant, occasional 11 indifferent 14 unconventional, unpremeditated
casualty: 4 loss 5 death 6 chance, hazard, injury, mishap 8 accident, disaster 9 mischance 10 misfortune 11 contingency 12 misadventure
casus: 4 case 5 event 8 occasion
cat: 4 flog, lion, lynx, pard, puma, puss 5 civet, felid, gatol(Sp.), moggy, ounce, pussy, tiger 6 cougar, feline, jaguar, malkin, mawkin, ocelot, tibert 7 cheetah, leopard, panther, tigress, wildcat 8 baudrons(Sc.) 9 carnivore, grimalkin 11 caterpillar 12 catamountain
breed: 4 Manx 5 alley, tabby 6 Angora 7 Maltese, Persian, Siamese
civetlike: 5 genet
comb. form: 5 aelur 6 aeluro
cry: mew 4 hiss, meow, miau, purr 5 miaou, miaow, miaul
disease: 9 distemper
Eugene Field's: 6 calico
female: 9 grimalkin
genus: 5 felis 7 felidae(pl.)

cat-o-nine-tails: 4 lash, whip 7 cattail
cataclysm: 5 flood 6 deluge 7 debacle 8 disaster, overflow, upheaval 11 catastrophe
catacomb: 4 tomb 5 crypt, vault 8 cemetery
catafalque: 4 bier 6 coffin
cataian: 5 thief 7 sharper 9 scoundrel
catalepsy: 6 trance 7 seizure
catalog, catalogue: 4 book, list, roll, rota 5 brief, canon, index 6 record, roster 7 arrange 8 classify, register, schedule 9 enumerate, inventory, repertory 11 systematize
Catalonia: *dance:* 7 sardana
marble: 8 brocatel 10 brocatelle
catamaran: 4 raft, trow 5 balsa, float 6 vessel 8 auntsary
catamount: 4 lynx, puma 6 cougar
cataplasm: 8 poultice
catapult: 5 throw 6 launch, onager 7 bricole 8 ballista, crossbow 9 slingshot
cataract: lin 4 linn 5 falls, flood 6 deluge 7 cascade, Niagara 8 Victoria 9 waterfall
cataria: 6 catnip
catarrh: 4 cold 5 rheum
catastrophe (see also **cataclysm**): 8 accident, calamity, disaster 10 denouement, misfortune
catbird: 7 mimidae
catcall: boo 4 hoot 6 deride
catch: bag, cop, get, nab, net 4 draw, hasp, haul, hawk, hold, hook, land, pawl, snap, stop, trap, tree 5 grasp, hitch, ketch, knack, seize, snare, trick 6 button, clutch, corner, detect, detent, engage, enmesh, entrap, snatch 7 attract, capture, ensnare, grapnel 8 entangle, overtake, surprise 9 intercept
sight of: 4 espy 6 descry
up with: 8 overtake
catchall: bag 6 basket 10 receptacle
catchfly: 5 plant 6 silene 7 campion
catching: 6 catchy 8 alluring 10 contagious, entrapping, infectious 11 captivating
catchwork: cue, tag 5 motto 6 byword, phrase, slogan
catchy: 9 appealing
cate: 4 food 6 viands 8 dainties 10 delicacies, provisions
catechism: 5 guide 6 manual 8 carritch 10 carritches(Sc.)
catechumen: 5 pupil 7 audient, auditor, convert 8 beginner, neophyte
categorical: 8 absolute, explicit 11 dictatorial, unequivocal, unqualified
category: 4 rank 5 class, genus, genre(pl.), order 6 family 7 species 8 division 12 denomination 14 classification
catena: 4 link 5 chain 6 series
catenate: 4 link 11 concatenate
cater: 4 feed 5 humor, serve, treat 6 pander, purvey, supply 7 provide
caterpillar: cat 4 muga 5 aweto, eruca, larva 6 canker, erucae(pl.), risper, woubit 7 tractor
caterwaul: cry 4 wail 5 miaul
catface: 4 scar
catfish: mud 4 cusk, elod, pout, raad, shal 5 bagre, raash 6 docmac, hassar, raasch, tandau 7 candiru 8 bullhead 9 sheatfish
genus: 13 saccobranchus
catgut: 4 cord, ropp 5 tharm 6 string, violin
cathartic: 8 lapactic, laxative 9 cleansing, purgative
cathedral: dom 6 church
passage: 5 slype
cathode: 9 electrode
catholic: 5 broad, papal 7 general, liberal 8 tolerant 9 universal 10 ecumenical
Catholic: See **Roman Catholic**
catkin: 5 ament, spike
catlike: 6 feline 8 stealthy 9 noiseless
catmint: nep, nip 4 herb
catnap: 4 doze
catnip: nep 6 catnep 7 cataria, catwort
Catoism: 9 austerity, harshness
Catreus: *daughter:* 6 Aerope 7 Clymene 9 Apemosyne
father: 5 Minos
mother: 8 Pasiphae
cat's-cradle: 7 ribwort
cat's-paw: 4 dupe, gull, tool 5 cully
cattail: 4 flag, musk, rush 5 ament, cloud, raupo, reree 6 catkin 7 bulrush, matreed
family: 9 typhaceae
cattle: 4 cows, dhan(Ind.), kine, neat, oxen 5 beefs, bulls, stock 6 beasts, beeves, steers 7 bovines
assemblage: 4 herd 5 drove
brand: 4 duff 5 buist
breed: 4 Nata, Zobo 5 Angus, Devon, Dutch, Niata(dwarf) 6 Durham, Belted, Jersey, Sussex 7 Brahman, Brangus, Kerries 8 Ayrshire, Bradford, Charbray, Guernsey, Hereford, Holstein, Longhorn 9 Red Polled, Shorthorn, Teeswater 10 Beefmaster, Brown Swiss 11 Charollaise, Dutch Belted 14 French Canadian, Santa Gertrudis
call: 4 sook
dealer: 6 drover, herder
dehorned: 5 muley 6 mulley
genus: bos
goddess: 6 Bubona
group: 4 herd 5 drove 7 creaght(Ir.)
plague: 10 rinderpest
shelter: 4 byre 5 barth
tick: 8 carapato
yard: 6 cancha

cattleman: 6 cowboy 7 byreman 8 stockman
catwalk: 7 footway, walkway
catwort: 6 catnip
Caucasia: *goat:* tur
ibex: zac
language: Laz, Udi 4 Andi, Avar, Laze, Lazi, Udic 5 Udish 7 Semitic 9 Itranican
race: 5 Aryan, Osset 6 Ossete
rug: 4 baku, kuba 5 chila 7 derbend
tribe: 4 Imer, Kurd, Laze, Lazi, Svan 5 Pshav 7 Kubachi
caucho: ule 4 tree 6 rubber
caucus: 7 council, meeting, primary 8 election
caudal: 4 rear 9 posterior
appendage: 4 tail
caudata: 4 newt 5 snake 10 salamander
cauk: 5 chalk 9 limestone
caul: web 4 cawl, trug, veil 7 network, omentum 8 membrane, tressour, tressure
cauldrife: 4 cold 6 chilly 8 chilling 9 cheerless
cauldron: See **caldron**
cauliflower: 7 cabbage 8 broccoli 9 disfigure
caulk, calk: 6 chinse 7 chintze
cauma: 4 heat 5 fever 6 warmth
cause: aim, gar(Sc.), key 4 case, chat, move, root, spur, suit 5 agent, basis, breed 6 create, effect, gossip, ground, induce, malady, motive, object, origin, reason, source, spring 7 concern, disease, lawsuit, produce, provoke 8 business, engender, movement, occasion 9 originate, wherefore 10 mainspring
causerie: 4 chat, plea, talk 6 debate 10 discussion 12 conversation
causes, science of: 8 etiology
causeuse: 4 sofa 9 tete-a-tete
causeway: way 4 dike, road 7 chausse(F.), highway
causey: dam, way 4 bank, pave, road 5 mound 6 street 7 highway 8 sidewalk
caustic: lye 4 tart 5 acrid, sharp 6 biting, bitter, severe 7 burning, cutting, erodent, mordant, pungent, satiric 8 alkaline, scathing, snappish, stinging 9 corrosive, sarcastic, satirical, vitriolic 10 malevolent 11 acrimonious
agent: 7 cautery, erodent
cauterize: 4 burn, char, fire, sear 5 brand, inust, singe 9 sterilize
caution: 4 care, heed, warn 6 advice, cautel, caveat, exhort 7 anxiety, counsel, precept, proviso 8 admonish, forecast, monition, prudence, wariness 9 diligence, vigilance 10 admonition, precaution, providence 11 calculation, forethought, reservation 12 watchfulness
cautious: 4 wary 5 alert, canny, chary, siker 6 fabian, sicker 7 careful, guarded, prudent 8 discreet, vigilant 10 scrupulous 11 circumspect
cavalcade: 4 raid, ride 5 march 6 parade, safari 7 journey, pageant 10 procession
cavalier: gay 4 curt, easy, fine 5 brave, frank, rider 6 escort, knight 7 brusque, gallant, haughty, offhand, soldier 8 Royalist 9 caballero, chevalier 10 disdainful 12 high-spirited, supercilious
Cavalleria Rusticana character: 4 Lola 5 Alfio 7 Turiddu
cavalry: 6 horses, troops 8 horsemen 10 knighthood
horse: 6 lancer
weapon: 5 lance, saber
cavalryman: 5 spahi 6 hussar, lancer, spahee 7 courier, dragoon, soldier, trooper 8 gendarme, horseman
cave: den, tip 4 cove, hole, lair, rear, sink, toss, weem 5 antre, cavea, crypt, speos, store, upset 6 beware, cavern, cavity, cellar, forgou, grotto, hollow, larder, luster, pantry, plunge 7 reserve, spelunk 8 collapse, overturn 9 storeroom
dweller: 10 troglodyte
researcher: 9 spelunker 12 speleologist
science of researching: 10 speleology
cave in: 5 stove, yield 6 submit 8 collapse
cavea: den 4 cage, cave 10 auditorium
caveat: 6 beware 7 caution, warning
cavern: 4 cave, grot, hole, lair, weem 5 antra(pl.), croft 6 antrum, cavity, grotto, hollow 7 spelunk
cavetto: 7 molding
caviar, caviare: ova, roe 4 eggs, ikra 5 ikary 6 relish 8 delicacy
source: 7 sterlet 8 sturgeon
cavie: 4 cage, coop 7 hencoop
cavil: 4 cark, carp, haft 6 haggle 7 quibble 9 criticise, criticize, exception, objection
caviling: 8 captious, picayune
cavity: bag, pit, sac 4 abri, cave, dalk, dent, hole, mine, vein, void 5 antra(pl.), atria(pl.), fossa, geode, lumen, mouth, sinus 6 antrum, atrium, camera, cavern, fossae(pl.), grotto, hollow, vacuum 7 cistern, vesicle 8 cul-de-sac 10 depression, excavation
anatomical: 5 antra(pl.), fossa 6 antrum, fossae(pl.)
brain: 6 coelia
gun: 4 bore
heart: 7 auricle 9 ventricle
lode: vug 4 voog, vugg, vugh
pert. to: 5 sinal 6 atrial, geodic
sac-like: 5 bursa 6 bursae(pl.)
skull: 4 aula 5 fossa, sinus
stone: 5 geode

cavort: 4 play 5 bound, caper 6 curvet, gambol, prance
cavy: 4 paca, pony 6 agouti, aperea, cayuse, rodent 8 capybara 9 guinea pig
caw: cry 4 call, cawl 5 croak, quark, quawk
cawl: 4 trug 6 basket
caxi: 4 fish 7 snapper
cay: See **key**
cayenne: 5 whist 6 canary, pepper 8 capsicum
cayuse: 4 cavy, pony 6 bronco 7 broncho
cease: end 4 halt, liss, quit, rest, stop 5 avast, douse, dowse, lisse, pause, peter 6 desist, devall, finish 7 abstain, refrain 8 intermit 9 terminate 11 discontinue
cease-fire: 5 truce 9 armistice
ceaseless: 4 ever 7 endless 8 unending 9 continual, incessant, unceasing
ceasing: 9 cessation
cecidium: 4 gall
cecity: 9 blindness
Cecrops' daughter: 5 Herse 8 Aglauros
cecum: pit 4 pore 6 cavity
cedar: 4 toon, tree 5 savin 6 deodar, sabina, sabine, savine 7 waxwing
camphor: 6 cedrol
green: 5 cedre(F.), color
moss: 8 hornwort
cede: 4 cess, give 5 award, grant, leave, waive, yield 6 assign, resign, submit 8 renounce, transfer 9 surrender 10 relinquish
cedrat: 6 citron
cedula: 8 document, schedule 11 certificate
ceil: 4 line 7 overlay 8 wainscot
ceilidh: 4 call 5 visit 12 conversation 13 entertainment
ceiling: 6 lining, screen, soffit 7 curtain, testudo 8 covering, paneling 10 testudines(pl.) 11 wainscoting
covering: 9 calcimine, kalsomine
division: 5 trave
mine: 5 astel
wooden: 8 plancher
Celebes: *bovine:* ox 4 anoa
island: 4 Muna
people: 6 toraja 7 toradja
celebrate: 4 keep, sing 5 extol, honor, revel 6 extoll, praise 7 glorify, observe 8 emblazon, eulogize, proclaim 9 solemnize 11 commemorate
celebrated: 4 kept 5 famed, noted 6 famous 7 eminent, feasted, renomme 8 glorious, observed, renowned 9 distingue, prominent 10 solemnized 11 conspicuous, illustrious 13 distinguished
celebration: 4 fete, rite 6 renown 9 celebrity, festivity
celebrious: 6 famous 7 festive 8 renowned, thronged 10 frequented
celebrity: VIP 4 fame, lion, name, star 5 eclat 6 renown, repute 11 celebration
celerity: 5 haste, hurry, speed 8 dispatch, rapidity, velocity 9 prestezza, quickness, swiftness
celery: *family:* 9 ammiaceae
wild: 8 smallage
celeste: 4 stop 5 pedal 7 sky-blue
celestial: 4 holy 6 divine, uranic 7 angelic, Chinese, ethered 8 empyreal, ethereal, heavenly
being: 5 angel 6 cherub, seraph 8 seraphim(pl.)
body: sun 4 star 5 comet 6 meteor, nebula, planet
elevation of mind: 7 anagoge
matter: 6 nebula
celibacy: 8 chastity
celibate: 6 chaste, single 8 bachelor, spinster 9 unmarried
cell: egg 4 cage, germ, jail 5 cabin, crypt, group, vault 6 cytode, prison 7 cellule, chamber, cubicle, dungeon 9 hermitage 10 ergastulum 11 compartment
bull: 5 toril 7 toriles(pl.)
coloring: 10 endochrome
colorless: 10 achroacyte, lymphocyte
connecting: 10 heterocyst
division: 7 spireme
generative: 6 gamete
group: 6 ceptor 7 cascade 8 blastema
layer: 8 blastula 10 blastoderm
lens-shaped: 8 lenticel
migratory: 9 leucocyte
pert. to: 6 cytoid
star-shaped: 10 astroblast
structural unit: 7 energid, nucleus 10 protoplast
study of: 8 cytology
substance: 5 linin
cell-like: 6 cytoid
cella: 4 naos
cellar: 4 cave 8 basement 9 storeroom
cellaret: 4 case 7 cabinet 8 tantalus 9 sideboard
cellular: 6 favose 7 areolar 8 faviform 9 alveolate
cellulose: *acetate:* 7 acetose
elastic: 5 rayon
celsitude: 6 height 8 altitude 10 exaltation
Celt: 4 Gael, Gaul, Manx 5 Irish, Welsh 6 Breton, Briton, Eolith 7 Cornish
Celtic: 4 Erse 7 Scotch
abbot: 5 coarb
chariot: 5 essed
chieftain: 6 tanist
divinity: 7 Taranis

foot soldier: 4 kern
giant: 5 Fomor
god: Ler 4 Leir, Llyr
harp: 5 telyn 11 clairschach
hero: 5 Fionn
language: 4 Erse, Manx 5 Irish, Welsh 6 Celtic, Cymric, Gaelic 9 Brythonic
peasant: 4 kern
priest: 5 Druid
sword: sax 4 seax

cembalo: 8 dulcimer 11 harpsichord

cement: fix 4 glue, join, knit, lime, lute 5 imbed, paste, putty, stick, unite 6 cohere, fasten, gulgul(Ind.), mortar, solder 7 asphalt 8 adhesive, hadigeon(F.), solidify 11 agglutinate
hydraulic: 4 paar
infusible substance: 4 lute
plastic: 8 albolite, albolith
quick-drying: 6 mastic
substance: 6 celite
window glass: 5 putty

cemetery: 6 litten 7 charnel 8 catacomb, Golgotha 9 graveyard 10 necropolis 11 polyandrium

cenchrus: 5 grass 6 millet

cenobite: nun 4 monk 5 friar 6 essene 7 recluse 8 monastic 9 anchorite

cenoby: 5 abbey 6 priory 7 convent

cense: 4 rank 6 assess, rating 7 perfume 8 estimate, position

censer: 8 thurible

censor: 6 critic 8 restrict, suppress 9 detractor

censorious: 6 severe 7 carping 8 blameful, captious, critical 9 satirical

censurable: 8 blamable, culpable 13 reprehensible

censure: 4 carp, flay 5 blame, chide, decry, judge, slate 6 accuse, berate, charge, rebuff, rebuke, remord, targue(Scot.), tirade 7 chasten, condemn, impeach, inveigh, reprove 8 disallow, reproach 9 challenge, criticize, reprimand 10 animadvert, exprobrate, vituperate 11 disapproval 12 reprehension 13 animadversion 15 discommendation

census: 4 list, poll 5 count 11 enumeration

cent: 4 coin 5 penny 6 copper

centaur: *bull's head:* 9 bucentaur
father: 5 Ixion
killed by Hercules: 6 Nessus

Centennial State: 8 Colorado

center, centre: cor, hub, mid 4 axis, core, foci(pl.), nave, seat 5 focus, heart, midst, pivot, spine 6 middle 7 lineman, nucleus 8 centrate 12 headquarters
away from: 6 distal
toward: 4 orad 5 entad 10 centerward

centerpiece: 7 epergne

centigrade: 5 scale 11 thermometer

centipede: 4 veri 6 earwig, golach, goloch 8 chilopod, myriapod 9 geophilus

central: mid 5 axial, basic, chief, focal, prime 6 median, middle 7 capital, centric, leading, pivotal, primary 8 dominant 11 equidistant

Central Africa: See **Africa**

Central America: *agave:* 5 sisal
ant: 5 kelep
bird: 7 jacamar 8 puffbird
canoe: 6 pitpan
country: 6 Panama 8 Honduras, Salvador 9 Costa Rica, Guatemala, Nicaragua
fishing boat: 6 cayuco
gopher: 7 quachil
Indian: 4 Maya 5 Carib
measure: 7 cantaro, manzana
monkey: 4 mono
mullet: 4 bobo
rodent: 4 paca
snake: 10 bushmaster
stockade: 4 boma
tragon: 4 bird 6 quezal 7 quetzal
tree: ebo, ule 4 eboe 5 amate 9 sapodilla
village: 4 boma
weight: 5 libra

Central Asia: See **Asia**

central cylinder: 5 stele

centric: 5 focal 6 middle, tarete 7 central 9 clustered 11 cylindrical 12 concentrated

centrifugal: 9 radiating

centripetal: 8 afferent

century: age 6 siecle(F.)
ten: 7 chiliad 10 millennium

century plant: 4 aloe 5 agave 6 maguey
fiber: 4 pita, pito

ceorl: 5 churl, thane 7 freeman, villein

cepa: 5 onion

cephalagia: 8 headache

cephalic: 8 atlantal, cerebral

cephalopod: 5 squid 6 cuttle 7 inkfish, octopus
secretion: ink

Cepheus: *daughter:* 9 Andromeda
wife: 10 Cassiopeia

ceral: 4 waxy 7 waxlike

ceramics: 5 tiles 7 pottery 9 stoneware
oven: 4 kiln
sieve: 4 laun

cerate: wax 4 lard 5 salve 8 ointment

ceratoid: 5 horny

ceratose: 5 horny

Cerberus: dog 7 monster 8 guardian 9 custodian

cere: wax 4 sere, wrap 6 anoint, embalm

cereal: rye 4 bean, bran, corn, mush, oats, rice 5 grain, maize, spelt, wheat 6 barley, farina, hominy 7 oatmeal, soybean 8 por-

ridge 9 buckwheat
coating: 4 bran
grass: oat, rye 4 ragi, rice 5 grain, wheat 6 barley, raggee
seed: 6 kernel
spike: ear
cereal grass genus: 6 secale
cerebral: 6 mental
cerebration: 7 thought
cerebrospinal axis: 4 cord 5 brain, spine
cerement: 6 shroud 9 cerecloth
ceremonial fuss: 10 panjandrum
ceremonious: 5 grand, lofty, stiff 6 formal, proper, solemn 7 precise, stately, studied 10 respectful 11 punctilious 12 conventional
ceremonious leave-taking: 5 conge
ceremony: 4 fete, pomp, rite, show, sign 5 state 6 augury, parade, powwow, review, ritual 7 display, pageant, portent, prodigy 8 accolade, function, marriage, occasion 9 formality, solemnity 10 ceremonial, observance 11 celebration
cerer: 10 undertaker
Ceres: 7 Demeter
mother: Ops
cerise: red 6 cherry
cerite: 7 mineral 8 allanite
cernuous: 7 nodding 8 drooping 9 pendulous
cero: 4 fish 6 sierra 7 cavallo, pintado
certain: 4 firm, real, sure, true 5 bound, clear, exact, fixed, plain, siker(Sc.) 6 actual, sicker, stated 7 assured, precise, settled 8 absolute, apparent, constant, official, positive, reliable, resolved, unerring 9 confident, steadfast, undoubted 10 dependable, inevitable, infallible, undeniable 11 determinate, indubitable, trustworthy 12 indisputable 13 incontestable 14 unquestionable 16 incontrovertible
certainly: 4 amen, ywis 5 iwiss, truly 6 certes, indeed, verily 7 hardily 8 forsooth
certie, certy: 5 faith, troth
certificate: 4 bond 5 check, libel, scrip 6 attest, ticket, verify 7 diploma, voucher 9 statement, testimony 10 credential 11 attestation, declaration, testimonial 13 certification
cargo: 8 navicert
debt: IOU 9 debenture
land: 6 amparo(Sp.)
medical, for ill student: 8 aegrotat
money owed: 9 debenture
certify: 4 avow, vise 5 swear 6 affirm, assure, depose, evince, verify 7 endorse, license, testify 9 determine, guarantee
under oath: 6 attest
certiorari: 4 writ 6 review
certiorate: 6 assure 7 apprise, certify
cerulean: 4 blue 5 azure 6 coelin 7 skyblue
cervine: elk 4 deer, stag 5 moose 6 cervid 8 cervidae(pl.), reindeer
cervix: 4 neck
cespitose: 6 matted, tufted 7 tangled
cess: bog, tax 4 cede, duty, levy, luck, rate, tyrf 5 slope, yield 6 impost 7 measure 9 surrender 10 assessment, estimation
cessation: end 4 halt, liss, lull, rest, stay, stop 5 letup, lisse, pause, truce 6 recess 7 ceasing, respite 8 interval, stoppage, surcease 9 armistice, remission 12 intermission, interruption 14 discontinuance
of being: 8 desition
cession: 8 yielding 9 surrender 10 compliance, concession
cesspool: 4 sump 7 cistern
cest: 4 belt 6 cestus, girdle
cesta: 6 basket
cetacean: orc 4 cete, orca 5 whale 6 beluga 7 dolphin, grampus 8 porpoise
blind: 4 susu
genus: 4 inia
cete: 5 whale 7 cetacea
Ceylon: *aborigine:* 4 Toda 5 Vedda 6 Veddah
bay: 4 Palk
boat: 4 done, doni 5 balsa, dhoni, doney 11 warkamoowee
city: 7 Colombo(c.)
coin: 4 cent
Dravidian: 5 Tamil
garment: 6 sarong
gooseberry: 10 ketembilla
governor: 6 disawa
hemp: 6 sina-wa
hill dweller: 4 Toda
language: 4 Pali 5 Tamil
measure: 4 para 5 parah
monkey: 4 maha 5 toque 6 langur, rilawa, rillow 10 wanderoock
moss: 4 agar, alga 5 jaffa 7 gulaman
native: 5 Vedda 6 Veddah
oak: 5 kusam
palm: 7 talipat, talipot
rat: 9 bandicoot
resthouse: 6 abalam
rice: 4 padi 5 paddy
rose: 8 cleander
seaport: 5 Galle
sedan: 6 tomjon, tonjon
skirt: 6 reddha
snake: 7 adjiger
soldier: 4 peon
tea: 5 pekoe
tree: 4 doon, tala 7 talipot
chabouk, chabuk: 4 whip
chabutra: 4 dais 7 terrace 8 platform

chack: 4 bite, snap 5 clack, snack 8 wheatear
chackle: 6 cackle, rattle 7 chatter
chacma: 6 baboon
chacra: 4 farm 5 milpa, ranch
chaeta: 4 seta 5 spine 7 bristle
chafe: irk, rub, vex 4 fret, frig, frot, fume, gall, heat, josh, rage, warm, wear 5 anger, annoy, grind, scold 6 abrade, banter, excite, fridge, harass, injury, nettle 7 incense, inflame 8 friction, irritate, raillery
chaff: guy, hay, pug 4 bran, caff(Sc.), guff, josh, quiz 5 borak, chyak, dross, glume, hulls, husks, straw, tease, trash 6 banter, bhoosa, chyack, refuse 7 tailing 8 raillery, ridicule
chaffer: 5 bandy, sieve, wares 6 buying, dicker, haggle, higgle, market 7 bargain, chatter, selling, traffic 8 exchange 9 negotiate 10 bargaining 11 merchandise
chaffinch: 7 robinet
chaffy: 5 scaly 7 acerose, acerous, paleate, trivial 9 bantering, worthless, 10 paleaceous
Chaillot resident: 8 madwoman
chain: guy, row, set, tew, tie, tye 4 bind, bond, file, gyve, join, link 5 cable, leash, suite, train 6 catena, chigon, collar, fasten, fetter, hobble, secure, series, string, tether 7 bobstay, catenae(pl.), connect, embrace, enslave, manacle, network, shackle 8 bracelet, restrain 9 constrain 10 chatelaine 13 concatenation
collar: 4 tore 6 torque
key: 10 chatelaine
mountain: 5 range, Rocky 7 Sierras
of quotations: 6 catena
of rocks: 4 reef
pert. to: 8 catenary
set with precious stones: 7 sautoir
chain cable: 4 boom
chain grab: 7 wildcat
chain-like: 8 catenate
chains: 7 bondage, serfdom
lady in: 9 Andromeda
chair: 4 seat 5 sedan, stool 6 office, pulpit, rocker
back: 5 splat
bath: 11 vinaigrette
bishop's official: 8 cathedra
cover: 4 tidy 12 antimacassar
decoration: 8 claw foot
easy: 6 morris, rocker
folding: 9 faldstool
litterlike: 4 kago
occupy: 7 preside
portable: 5 sedan
chairman: 4 head 5 emcee 8 director 9 moderator 10 supervisor
chaise: gig 4 shay 7 curicle 8 carriage
chaitya: 6 shrine 8 monument
chalcedony: 4 onyx, opal, sard 5 agate 6 jasper, quartz 7 opaline 9 carnelian 11 chrysoprase
orange: 4 sard
Chalcodon: *father:* 4 Abas
son: 9 Elephenor
Chaldea: *astronomical cycle:* 5 saros
city: Ur
measure: 4 cane, foot 5 makuk, qasab 6 artaba, gariba, ghalva 7 mansion
chalet: hut 5 cabin, house 7 cottage 8 lavatory
chalice: ama, cup 4 bowl 5 calix, grail 6 goblet 7 calices(pl.)
cover: 4 pall 8 animetta
chalk: 4 cauk, pale, scar, talc, tick 5 creta, score 6 blanch, bleach, crayon, credit, rubble, whiten 7 account 9 limestone, reckoning
chalky silicate: 4 talc
challenge: 4 call, dare, defy, gage 5 blame, brave, claim, query, stump 6 accuse, appeal, cartel, charge, dacker, daiker, demand, forbid, impugn, invite 7 arraign, censure, impeach, provoke, reprove, summons 8 question, reproach 9 exception, objection 10 controvert 11 impeachment
judge: 6 recuse
to a duel: 6 cartel
challenger: 7 duelist 8 pugilist
chamber: oda 4 cell, flat, hall, kiva, room 5 atria(pl.), bower, solar, soler 6 atrium, camara, camera, hollow, sollar 7 bedroom, caisson, cubicle, loculus 9 apartment, camarilla, vestibule 11 compartment
annealing: 4 leer
bombproof: 8 casemate
council: 10 consistory
drying: 4 kiln, oven
judge's: 6 camera
pert. to: 7 cameral
private: 5 adyta(pl.) 6 adytum 7 sanctum 8 conclave
underwater construction: 7 caisson
chamberlain: 6 factor 7 officer, servant, steward 9 attendant, chamberer, treasurer 10 camerlengo 14 superintendent
papal: 10 camerlengo, camerlingo
chambray: 5 cloth 6 fabric 7 gingham
chameleon: 5 anole, anoli 6 lizard
chameleonic: 6 fickle 10 changeable, inconstant
chamfer: 5 bevel, flute 6 furrow, groove 7 channel 11 countersink
chamois: 4 gems, skin 5 cloth, gemse 6 chammy, shammy, shamoy 7 leather 8 antelope

male: 7 gemsbok
champ: 4 bite, chaw, firm, hard, mash 5 field, gnash 7 trample 11 battlefield
champagne: ay 4 wine
center: 6 Troyes
champerty: 7 contest, rivalry 10 conspiracy
champion: ace, aid 4 abet, back, defy, hero 6 assert, attend, defend, squire, victor 7 espouse, fighter, protect 8 advocate, defender 9 challenge, combatant, firstrate 10 unexcelled
championship: 5 title 7 defense 8 advocacy 9 supremacy 10 leadership
champlevo: 6 enamel, inlaid
chance: die, hap, lot 4 case, dint, fate, luck, odds, risk, tide 5 ettle, stake 6 betide, casual, gamble, happen, hazard, mishap, random 7 aimless, fortune, stumble, venture 8 accident, casualty, fortuity 9 adventure, haphazard, happening, mischance 10 contingent 11 contingency, opportunity, probability
by: 5 haply
even: 6 tossup
favorable: 4 odds
chancel: *part:* 4 bema 5 altar
screen: 4 jube
seat: 6 sedile 7 sedilia(pl.)
chancery petitioner: 7 relator
chandelier: 6 pharos 7 fixture 11 candelabrum
chandelle: lob 4 turn, zoom 5 climb 6 candle 7 support
chandler: 6 dealer 10 chandelier 11 candlestick
chang: 4 beer 5 noise 6 uproar
change: mew 4 move, turn, vary, veer 5 adapt, alter, amend, break, coins, shift 6 modify, mutate, remove, revamp, revise, switch 7 commute, convert, deviate 8 revision, transfer 9 diversity, permutate, rearrange, transform, transmute, transpose, variation 10 alteration, correction, difference, transition 11 vicissitude 13 metamorphosis 15 diversification
appearance: 6 obvert
back: 6 return, revert
character of: 8 denature
color: dye 5 blush 6 redden
course: 4 tack, turn, veer 5 sheer
into: 6 become
music: 4 muta
subject to: 7 mutable 8 amenable, variable
changeable: 5 eemis, giddy, immis 6 fickle, fitful, mobile 7 bruckle, erratic, mutable, protean, variant 8 amenable, catching, unstable, volatile 9 alterable, irregular, mercurial, uncertain, unsettled 10 capricious, inconstant, irresolute 11 chameleonic
in form: 9 metabolic
changeling: oaf 4 dolt, fool 5 child, dunce, idiot 7 waverer 8 imbecile, renegade, turncoat 9 simpleton 10 substitute
changing: *color:* 11 allochroous
pattern and color: 13 kaleidoscopic
channel: gat, ree, rut 4 cano, cava, dike, duct, dyke, gool, gote, gout, pipe, vein, wadi, wady 5 canal, chase, ditch, drain, drill, flume, flute, glyph, media(pl.), regal, rigol, river, sinus, stria 6 arroyo, artery, furrow, groove, gutter, medium, rabbet, rivose, sluice, strait, stream, striae(pl.), trough 7 conduct, conduit, passage, rivulet, silanga, tideway 8 aqueduct, guideway
artificial: gat 4 leat 5 canal, drain, flume 6 sluice 7 drainer
brain: 4 iter
formed by cutting: 5 scarf
longitudinal: 6 rabbet
marker: 4 buoy
narrow: 6 furrow, strait
near port: 5 deeps
river: bed 6 alveni(pl.) 7 alvenus
ship: gat
vertical: 5 glyph
vital: 6 artery
water: gat 4 gote, gurt, leat, pipe, race 5 canal, drain, flume 6 sluice 7 conduit 8 aqueduct, millrace, tailrace
channel bone: 8 clavicle 10 collarbone
Channel Island: 4 Sark 8 Guernsey
measure: 4 cade 5 cabot
seaweed: 5 vraic
channelbill: 8 rainfowl
channeled: 7 voluted 8 furrowed 9 chamfered
channels: 5 media 6 striae
chanson: 4 song 5 lyric 6 ballad 7 refrain
chant: 4 cant, sing, song 5 carol, psalm 6 anthem, cantus, intone, warble 7 introit, worship 10 cantillate
chantage: 9 extortion 12 blackmailing
chanter: 6 cantor, singer 7 bagpipe 8 songster 9 chorister
chanteuse: 6 singer 10 cantatrice
chantey, chanty: 4 song
chanticleer: 4 cock 7 rooster
Chantilly: 4 lace
chantry: 5 altar 6 chapel, shrine
chanty, chantey: 4 song
chaos: pie 4 gulf, mess, void 5 abyss, babel, chasm 6 jumble 7 anarchy, mixture 8 disorder, shambles 9 confusion
primordial: 4 Apsu
utter: 6 tophet 7 topheth

Chaos: *Babylonian:* 4 Apsu
daughter: Nox, Nyx
Maori: 4 kore
primeval fluid of: Nu
son: 6 Erebus

chaotic: 5 snafu 7 muddled 8 confused, formless

chap: boy, buy, man, rap 4 bean, beat, blow, chip, chop, cove, duck, kibe, mash 5 billy, bloke, bully, buyer, chink, cleft, crack, knock, lover, split, trade, youth 6 barter, breach, bugger, callan, choose, fellow, shaver, strike, stroke 7 callant, chapman, chappie, fissure, husband, roughen 8 blighter, customer, division
odd: 6 galoot
old: 6 geezer
young: 6 gaffer

chaparral: 9 buckthorn

chapel: 4 cage, cape, cope, cowl, hood 5 cloak 6 bethel, church, shrine 7 chantry, service 8 bethesda 9 reliquary, sanctuary
private: 7 oratory
sailor's 6 bethel

chaperon: 4 hood 6 attend, duenna(Sp.), escort, matron 7 protect 8 guardian, trapping 10 escutcheon 11 gouvernante(F.)

chaplain: 5 padre 9 clergyman

chaplet: 4 bead, orle 5 crown 6 anadem, anchor, circle, fillet, rosary, trophy, wreath 7 coronal, coronet, garland 8 moulding, necklace, ornament

chapman: 4 chap 5 buyer 6 dealer, hawker, trader 7 peddler 8 customer, merchant

chaps: 4 boys, jaws, lads 5 flaws 8 breeches, overalls

chapter: 4 body, cell, post 5 caput, lodge 6 branch 7 correct, meeting, section 8 assembly 9 reprimand 10 contingent
member: 9 capitular

char: 4 burn, cart, sear 5 broil, chark, chore, singe, trout 6 scorch 7 blacken, chariot 8 sandbank 9 carbonize

charabanc: bus 5 coach 7 vehicle

charact: 6 emblem

character: 4 bent, card, kind, mark, mold, note, part, rune, sign, sort, tone 5 brand, fiber, stamp, tenor, token, trait, write 6 caract, emblem, figure, letter, mettle, nature, repute, stripe, symbol 7 edition, essence, engrave, impress, quality 8 inscribe 9 agreement, ampersand 10 reputation 11 disposition
assumed: 4 role
bad: 5 drole(F.)
chief: 4 hero, lead, star 7 heroine
group: 5 ethos
of a people: 5 ethos
vein: 6 streak
word-representing: 8 logogram 9 logograph

characteristic: 4 cast, mark, mien 5 trait 6 nature 7 feature, impress, quality, typical 8 property, symbolic 9 attribute, lineament 11 distinctive, pathognomic, peculiarity
individual: 9 idiopathy

characterize: 4 mark 6 define, depict 7 engrave, entitle, imprint, portray 8 describe, indicate, inscribe 9 delineate, designate, represent 11 distinguish

charade: 6 enigma, puzzle, riddle 7 picture, tableau

charco: 4 pool 6 puddle, spring

charcoal: 5 carbo, chark 6 carbon, fusain, pencil 7 blacken, drawing
animal: 9 boneblack
reduce to: 4 char

chard: 4 beet 7 thistle 9 artichoke

chare, char: job 4 lane, task, turn 5 alley, chore 6 finish, street 7 perform

charge: fee 4 bill, cark, cost, duty, fill, lien, load, onus, rate, rush, toll, ward 5 debit, onset, order, price, refer 6 accuse, adjure, allege, assess, attack, burden, career, credit, defame, demand, enjoin, impute, indict, tariff, weight 7 arraign, ascribe, assault, average, censure, command, concern, custody, expense, impeach, keeping, mandate, mission 8 chastise, overload 9 challenge, oversight 10 commission, impetition, impregnate, injunction, management 11 arraignment, encumbrance, incriminate, instruction 14 responsibility
customary: 4 dues
grazing: 5 agist
with gas: 6 aerate

chargeable: 6 costly, liable 7 weighty 9 expensive, important, momentous 10 burdensome 11 responsible, troublesome

charged: 5 tense 9 emotional 10 purposeful
with electricity: 4 live

chargeman: 7 blaster, foreman 10 batteryman

charger: 4 dish 5 horse, mount, plate, steed 6 vessel 7 accuser, courser, platter

charges: *boat carrying:* 7 boatage
legal: 4 dues, fees 5 costs 9 retainers
repairs to barrister's quarters: 9 detriment

charily: 8 frugally, gingerly 9 carefully 10 cautiously

chariness: 7 caution 9 frugality, integrity 11 heedfulness, sparingness

chariot: car 4 cart, char, wain 5 buggy, essed, wagon 6 charet, esseda, essede 7 vehicle 8 carriage, charette
for carrying image of god: 4 rath 5 ratha
Greek: 8 quadriga
Roman: 5 essed 6 esseda, essede

two-horse: 4 biga
chariotee: 8 carriage
charioteer: 5 pilot 6 auriga, driver 7 wagoner 9 charioter
charisma: 5 charm, power 6 impact
charitable: 4 kind 6 benign, humane 7 lenient, liberal 8 generous 9 favorable, forgiving, indulgent 10 beneficent, benevolent 12 eleemosynary 13 compassionate, philanthropic
charity: 4 alms, dole, gift, love, pity, ruth 5 mercy 6 bounty 7 handout, largess 8 lenience 9 affection 10 almsgiving, generosity, liberality, tenderness 12 philanthropy
dispenser: 7 almoner
charivari: 5 babel 8 serenade, shivaree 10 callithump 11 celebration
chark: cup 4 burn, char, coal, coke 5 glass 6 cinder, noggin 8 charcoal
charlatan: 5 cheat, faker, fraud, quack 7 cabotin, empiric 8 imposter, magician 9 pretender 10 medicaster, mountebank
Charlemagne: *brother:* 8 Carloman
conquest: 5 Avars
court hero: 6 Roland
father: 5 Pepin
knight: 4 Gano 7 Ganelon, Paladin
nephew: 7 Orlando
peer: 6 Oliver 7 Paladin
pert. to: 8 Caroline
sword: 7 Joyeuse
Charles' Wain: 4 Bear, Ursa 6 Dipper
Charlie Chan creator: 7 Biggers
charlock: 4 weed 5 kraut 7 mustard
charlotte: 7 custard, dessert
Charlotte Corday's victim: 5 Marat
charm: obi 4 calm, juju, jynx, mojo, play, song 5 allay, freet, freit, grace, obeah, magic, saffi, safie, spell, weird 6 allure, amulet, beauty, caract, enamor, entice, fetich, fetish, glamor, grigri, melody, please, scarab, saphie, soothe, subdue, summon 7 assuage, attract, beguile, bewitch, cantrip, conjure, control, delight, enamour, enchant, enthral, flatter, glamour, periapt, singing, sorcery 8 breloque, enthrall, entrance, greegree, practice, talisman 9 agreeable, captivate, fascinate, seduction 10 attraction, demonifuge 11 incantation
protective: 6 amulet
charmer: 5 siren 8 exorcist, magician, sorcerer 9 sorceress 11 spellbinder
charming: 7 amiable, eyesome, winning, winsome 8 adorable, delicate 9 agreeable, beautiful, glamorous 10 attractive, glamourous
charnel: 7 ghastly 8 cemetery 10 sepulchral
house: 7 ossuary 8 mortuary
Charon: 7 boatman 8 ferryman
payment to: 4 obol 6 obolus
river: 4 Styx
Charpentier opera: 6 Louise
charpoy: bed, cot
charqui: 4 beef, meat 5 jerky
chart: map 4 card, plat, plan, plot 5 carte, graph 6 record, scheme 7 diagram, explore, outline, project 8 document, platform 10 cartograph
chartaceous: 6 papery
charter: let 4 deed, hire, rent 5 carte, chart, grant, lease 6 charta, permit 9 privilege 10 commission, conveyance
chary: shy 4 dear, wary 5 chere, scant 6 frugal, prized, skimpy 7 careful, sparing 8 cautious, hesitant, precious, reserved, vigilant 9 diffident, reluctant, treasured 10 economical, fastidious, scrupulous 11 circumspect
Charybdis rock: 6 Scylla
chase: 4 hunt, shag, sick 5 annoy, catch, chevy, chivy, harry, score 6 chivvy, emboss, follow, frieze, furrow, gallop, groove, harass, hollow, indent, pursue, quarry, scorse, trench 7 channel, engrave, pursuit 8 ornament
away: 4 rout 5 drive
goddess: 4 Dian 5 Diana
chaser: ram 5 drink 8 airplane, engraver
chasm: gap, pit 4 gulf, rift 5 abyss, blank, canon, chaos, cleft, gorge 6 breach, canyon, hiatus 7 fissure 8 aperture, crevasse, interval
glacial: 7 crevass 8 crevasse
chasse: 4 step 5 glide 6 liquor, shrine 7 dismiss 9 reliquary
chasseur: 6 hunter 7 footman 8 huntsman 9 attendant
chassis: 5 frame
chaste: 4 pure 5 clean 6 decent, honest, modest, proper, severe, vestal 7 refined 8 celibate, innocent, virtuous 9 continent, undefiled 10 immaculate
chasten: 4 rate 5 abase, smite, smote, sober 6 humble, punish, refine, subdue, temper 7 afflict, censure, correct 8 chastise, moderate, restrain 9 castigate, reprimand 10 discipline
chastise: 4 beat, flog, lash, slap, trim, whip 5 amend, blame, scold, spank, strap, taunt 6 accuse, anoint, berate, charge, punish, purify, rebuke, refine, swinge, temper, thrash 7 chasten, correct, reprove, scourge, suspect 9 castigate
chastity: 6 purity, virtue 7 modesty 8 goodness
chasuble: 6 deacon 8 vestment
chat: mag 4 bird, chin, cone, coze, gist, talk, tove, twig 5 ament, cause, dally, point, prate, speak, spike 6 babble, branch, cat-

kin, confab, gabble, gibber, gossip, jabber, potato, samara 7 chatter, prattle 8 causerie, converse, spikelet, strobile 9 dalliance 11 confabulate 12 conversation

chateau: 5 house 6 castle 7 mansion 8 fortress

Chateaubriand work: 5 Atala

chatelaine: pin 4 etui, hook 5 chain, clasp, etwee, purse 6 brooch 8 mistress

chaton: 5 basil, bezel, bezil 7 setting

chatta: 8 umbrella

chattels: 4 gear 5 goods, money, wares 6 slaves 7 capital 8 bondsmen, property 9 livestock, principal
distraint: 4 naam
tenant's: 6 farleu, farley
to recover: 7 detinue

chatter: gab, jaw, mag, yap 4 blab, carp, chat, hack, rick, talk, tear, yirr 5 cabal, clack, garre, haver, prate, shake 6 babble, gabble, gibber, gossip, jabber, palter, rattle, shiver, tattle, yammer, yatter 7 blabber, brabble, chackle, chaffer, chipper, chitter, clitter, nashgob, prabble, prattle, shatter 8 verbiage 11 goosecackle
conjurer's: 10 hanky-panky

chatterbox: jay, mag 4 piet 5 clack 6 gossip, magpie 10 chatterbag, chattermag 13 chatterbasket

chattering: 8 babbling 9 prattling, talkative 10 loquacious

Chaucer: *inn:* 6 Tabard
Knight's Tale character: 7 Palamon
pilgrim: 5 reeve
title: Dan

chauffeur: 5 drive 6 driver 8 operator

chaussee: 4 road 6 street 7 highway 8 causeway

chaussure: 4 boot, shoe 7 slipper 8 footgear

chauve-souris: bat

chauvinism: 8 jingoism 10 patriotism

chavel: 4 gnaw 6 mumble, nibble

chaw: jaw, vex 4 chew, envy, mull 5 champ, grind 6 ponder 7 portion 8 ruminate 9 chawbacon, masticate

chawbacon: 4 chaw 5 yokel 6 rustic 7 bumpkin

chawn: gap 4 gape 5 cleft 6 cleave

cheap: low 4 base, poor, vile 5 close, gaudy, kitch, price, tight, tinny, value 6 abject, common, plenty, shoddy, sordid, stingy, tawdry, trashy 7 bargain, dealing 8 inferior, purchase 9 innkeeper 10 despicable 11 depreciated, inexpensive 12 contemptible

cheap jack: 6 hawker, pedlar, pedler 7 peddler 8 huckster 9 Cheap-John

cheat: do; bam, bob, cog, con, fob, gip, gum, gyp, nip 4 bilk, bite, clip, dupe, fake, flam, geck, gull, hoax, jilt, jouk, liar, mump, rook, sell, sham, sile, skin 5 blink, booty, bunco, bunko, cozen, cully, dodge, faker, fling, foist, fraud, gleek, gouge, guile, knave, mulct, rogue, scamp, spoil, trick, welsh 6 baffle, blanch, bubble, bucket, chiaus, chisel, chouse, daddle, delude, deride, doodle, duffer, fiddle, fleece, grease, humbug, illude, jockey, outwit, raddle, renege, shaver 7 abusion, beguile, deceive, defraud, escheat, faitour, finesse, foister, gudgeon, juggler, mislead, plunder, quibble, sharper, skelder, swindle 8 artifice, delusion, dry-shave, hoodwink, imposter 9 bamboozle, fainaigue, hypocrite, imposture, scoundrel, stratagem, victimize 10 mountebank 15 prestidigitator

cheater: 4 bite, gull 5 knave 6 bilker, topper 7 sharper 9 trickster

check: bit, dam, nab, nip, tab 4 balk, curb, damp, rein, snub, stay, stem, stop, stub, test, twit, were 5 abort, allay, block, brake, catch, chide, chink, choke, crack, daunt, delay, deter, draft, limit, quell, repel, stall, still, stunt, tally, taunt, token 6 arrest, attack, baffle, bridle, defeat, detain, detent, gravel, hinder, impede, oppose, outwit, quench, rabbet, rebate, rebuff, rebuke, scotch, stifle, ticket, verify 7 backset, command, control, inhibit, monitor, refrain, repress, reproof, reprove, repulse, setback 8 bulkhead, encumber, obstruct, restrain, withhold 9 constrain, frustrate, interrupt, overpower, reprimand, restraint, supervise 10 difficulty 11 certificate, counterfoil, examination

check growth of: 5 stunt 7 shorten

check in: 6 arrive 8 register

check out: die 5 leave 6 depart 7 confirm 11 investigate

check over: 7 examine, inspect

checker: 5 freak, freck 6 damper

checkerboard: 7 dambrod 8 damboard
marked like: 10 tessellate

checkered: 4 pied, vair 5 diced, plaid 6 motley 10 changeable, variegated 11 diversified

checkers: 4 game 6 damrod, drafts 8 draughts
move: 4 dyke, fife, huff 5 cross 7 bristol
opening: 6 souter
term: 4 king 5 block, crown

checkerwork: 7 tessera 8 tesserae(pl.)
inlay: 6 mosaic

checkmate: 4 gain, lick, stop, undo 6 baffle, corner, defeat, outwit, stymie, thwart 9 frustrate

checkrein: 4 curb 7 saccade

cheddar: 6 cheese

cheechako, chee-chaco: 10 tenderfoot

cheek: 4 chap, gall, gena, jole, jowl, leer, sass 5 bucca, chyak, genae(pl.), nerve, sauce 6 chyack, haffet, haffit 8 audacity, temerity 9 impudence
bone: 5 malar 6 zygoma
comb. form: 5 bucco
distended: 7 buccate
muscle: 10 buccinator
pert. to: 5 genal, malar 6 buccal
cheep: pip, yap, yip 4 hint(Sc.), peep, pule 5 chirp, creak(Sc.), tweet 6 squeak, tattle
cheer: ole(Sp.), rah 4 fare, food, root, viva, yell 5 bravo, elate, feast, heart, huzza, mirth, shout, whoop 6 cantle, gaiety, hurrah, huzzah, solace, viands 7 acclaim, animate, applaud, cherish, comfort, console, enliven, gladden, hearten, jollity, refresh, rejoice 8 applause, brighten, inspirit, pheasant, vivacity 9 animation, encourage, merriment 10 exhilarate, invigorate 11 acclamation, hospitality 13 entertainment, hospitability
burst: 5 salvo
cheerful: gay 4 cant, glad, gleg(Sc.), rosy 5 cadgy, canty, chirk, douce, happy, jolly, merry, peart, ready, sunny 6 blithe, bright, cheery, chirpy, crouse, genial, hearty, hilary, jocund, lively 7 buoyant, chipper 8 cheering, gladsome, homelike, sanguine 9 contented, lightsome, sprightly 10 enlivening 11 comfortable 12 lighthearted
cheerless: sad 4 cold, drab, glum, gray 5 bleak, drear 6 dismal, dreary, gloomy 7 forlorn, joyless 8 dejected 10 dispirited, melancholy 11 comfortless 12 disconsolate
cheese: 4 Brie, Edam, Jack 5 cream, Gouda, mysost, Swiss, Ziega 6 Barrie, Dunlop, Glarus, Zieger 7 Cheddar, cottage, Gruyere, Stilton 8 American, Parmesan 9 Camembert, Gammelost, Limburger, Roquefort 10 Gorgonzola, Neufchatel 11 Liederkranz
brown: 6 mysost
curdy: 4 trip
dish: 4 cake 6 fondue, omelet 7 rarebit, soufflé
green: 7 sapsago
large: 7 kebbock, kebbuck
milk whey: 5 ziega 6 zieger
Normandy: 7 angelot
pert. to: 6 caseic 7 caseous
poached: 10 gnocchetti
white: 11 Neufchatel
cheese maggot: 7 skipper
cheesecake: 7 dessert 10 photograph
cheeseparing: 6 penury 9 parsimony 10 stinginess
cheesy: 4 fine 5 cheap, smart 6 shabby, sleazy 7 caseous 9 excellent, worthless
cheetah: cat 5 youse, youze 7 guepard 8 gueparde
chef: 4 cook 9 cuisinier 10 cuisiniere
chela: 4 claw 5 slave 6 pincer 7 servant 8 disciple
chelicera: 8 mandible 9 appendage
chelonian: 6 turtle 8 tortoise
chemical: 4 acid, salt 7 alkalai 10 alchemical 13 iatrochemical
agent: 8 catalyst
compound: 4 imin 5 amide, azine, ceria, ester, imine, purin 6 boride 7 inosite, leucine, metamer
element: see **element:** *chemical*
measure: 4 dram, gram 5 liter, titer
salt: sal
suffix: ac, ol; ane, ein, ene, ile, ine, ion, ite, ole, ose 4 idin, olic 5 ylene
chemise: 5 shift, shirt, smock 6 camisa 8 lingerie
chemisette: 4 sham 6 guimpe
chemist: 7 analyst 8 druggist 9 alchemist 10 apothecary
vessel: 4 vial 5 ampul, cupel, phial 6 aludel, ampule, beaker, retort 7 ampoule
workroom: lab 10 laboratory
chequeen: 6 basket, sequin, zequin 8 zecchino
cheri, cherie: 4 dear 7 beloved, darling 9 cherished 10 sweetheart
cherish: aid, hug, pet 4 dote, hope, like, love, save 5 adore, cheer, cling, enjoy, nurse, prize, value 6 caress, esteem, faddle, fondle, foster, harbor, nestle, pamper, pettle, revere 7 comfort, embosom, embrace, indulge, nourish, nurture, protect, support, sustain 8 enshrine, inspirit, preserve, treasure 9 cultivate, encourage, entertain
cheroot: 5 cigar
cherry: 4 bing, duke, gean 5 morel 7 capulin, chapman, lambert, morello, oxheart 8 amarelle, napoleon 9 bigarreau
acid: 7 cerasin
color: red 6 cerise
extract: 8 cerasein
sour: 8 amarelle
sweet: 4 bing 7 lambert, oxheart
wild: 4 gean 7 marasca, mazzard
cherry finch: 8 hawfinch
cherry holly: 5 islay
cherry laurel: 7 cerasus
cherry orange: 7 kumquat
cherub: 5 angel 6 seraph, spirit 8 seraphim(pl.)
chervil: bun 4 herb
Cheshire district: 4 Hale 5 Hoole 6 Marple
chess: *draw game:* 9 stalemate

finish: 4 draw, mate 7 endgame 9 checkmate, stalemate
Japanese: 5 shogi
move: 5 debut 6 castle, fidate, gambit 10 fianchetto
opening: 5 debut 6 gambit 10 fianchetto
pert. to: 8 scacchic
piece: man 4 king, pawn, rook 5 horse, queen 6 bishop, castle, knight
chest: ark, box, kit 4 arca, bust, cist, cyst, fund, safe 5 ambry, bahut, front, hoard, hutch, trunk 6 basket, breast, bunker(Sc.), casket, coffer, coffin, hamper, locker, shrine, stripe, thorax 7 caisson, capcase, cassone(It.), commode, deposit, enclose 8 cupboard, treasury 9 container, strongbox 10 contention, receptacle, repository 11 controversy, gardeviance
alms: 6 almoin 7 almoign
animal: 7 brisket
bone: 5 costa
human: 6 breast, thorax
meal: 6 girnal, girnel
pert. to: 8 thoracic
sacred: ark 4 arca, cist
sound: 4 rale 7 rhonchi(pl.) 8 rhonchus
stone: 4 cist, kist
supply: 6 wangan, wangun 7 wanigan 8 wannigan
chesterfield: 4 coat, sofa 5 divan 8 overcoat 9 davenport
chestnut: 4 joke, ling, rata, tree 5 brown, horse 6 marron(F.), sativa 7 crenata, dentata
and gray: 4 roan
dwarf: 9 chincapin 10 chinquapin
genus of: 8 castanea
water: 4 ling 5 trapa
chevalier: 5 noble 6 knight 7 gallant 8 cavalier, horseman 10 greenshank
cheverel, cheveril: 6 pliant 7 elastic, kidskin 8 flexible
chevet: 4 apse 11 termination
chevin: 4 chub
chevisance: 5 booty, issue, spoil 6 remedy, supply 8 chivalry, resource 9 expedient, substance 10 enterprise, provisions 11 achievement, transaction
chevron: 4 beam, mark 5 glove 6 rafter, stripe 7 molding 10 gravystain
chevrotain: 4 napu 7 deerlet, kanchil, tragule
chevy: See **chivy**
chew: cud 4 bite, cham, chaw, gnaw, quid 5 chamm, grind, munch, rumen 6 mumble 8 meditate, ruminate 9 denticate, manducate, masticate
inability to: 8 amasesis
the rag: 6 gossip 7 chatter
chewing gum base: 6 chicle
chewink: 4 bird 5 finch, joree 6 towhee
chiastolite: 5 macle
chiaus: 5 cheat 8 sergeant, swindler 9 messenger
Chibcha: 4 zipa 5 zaque 6 Indian, zacqua
chic: 4 pert, posh, trig, trim 5 natty, nifty, smart 6 dapper, modish 7 elegant, stylish
chicadee: 8 titmouse
Chicago district: 4 Loop
chicanery: 4 ruse, wile 5 feint, trick 8 artifice, intrigue, trickery 9 deception, duplicity, sophistry, stratagem
chick: 4 girl, tick 5 child, natty 6 screen, sequin, sprout 7 chicken
chick-pea: 4 gram, herb 5 chich, cicer 8 garbanzo, garvance, garvanzo 9 garavance
chickadee: 8 titmouse
chickaree: 8 squirrel
chicken: hen 4 cock, fowl 5 biddy, capon, chick, child, chuck, fryer, layer, manoc, poult 6 chicky, pullet 7 broiler, rooster 8 cockerel 11 chickabiddy
breed: 7 Leghorn 9 Wyandotte 11 Rhode Island
raising device: 7 brooder
young: 5 chick, fryer, poult 6 pullet 7 broiler
chicken out: 4 quit 6 renege
chicken snake: 4 boba
chickenhearted: 5 timid 8 cowardly
chickweed genus: 6 alsine
chicle: gum 5 latex
chicory: 4 bunk, root 5 plant 6 endive 7 succory, witloof
family: 12 cichoriaceae
chide: 4 rail, rate 5 blame, check, flite, flyte, scold 6 berate, rebuff, rebuke, threap, threep, threpe 7 censure, reprove, upbraid, wrangle 8 admonish, reproach 9 objurgate, reprehend, reprimand
chief: bo; aga, big, boh, cap, cob, dux, mir 4 agha, arch, boss, duce, duke, head, high, khan, main, rais, raja, reis, tyee 5 alder, elder, first, great, major, prime, rajah, ruler, thane, titan, vital 6 adalid, cabeza, leader, master, rector, sachem, staple 7 capital, captain, central, eminent, foreman, overman, palmary, prelate, premier, supreme 8 dominant, especial, foremost, intimate, sagamore 9 chieftain, commander, paramount, principal, prominent 11 predominant
chiffonier: 6 bureau 7 cabinet, commode
chigger: 4 mite 6 chigoe, insect, jigger, red-bug
chignon: 4 knot 5 chain, twist 6 collar
chigoe: 4 flea 7 chigger
chilblain: 4 kibe, mule(F.) 5 blain 6 pernio

child (see also **children**): ben (Heb.), boy, bud, imp, kid, son, tad, tot 4 baba, babe, baby, bata, brat, chit, girl, page, tike, tyke 5 bairn(Sc.), chick, chiel(Sc.), gamin, issue 6 cherub, enfant, filius(L.), infant, moppet, urchin 7 bambino(It.), progeny 8 bantling, chiseler(Ir.), daughter 9 firstling, offspring, youngster 10 descendant 11 chickabiddy
advancement: 9 precocity
chubby: 8 rolypoly 10 butterball
comb. form: ped 4 paed, pedo 5 paedo
dainty: elf 5 fairy
homeless: 4 waif
illegitimate: 6 by-blow 7 bastard
killer: 11 infanticide
parentless: 6 orphan
patron saint: 8 Nicholas
pert. to: 6 filial
puckish: imp
roguish: 6 urchin
spoiled: 4 brat 5 mardy 7 cockney
street: 5 gamin
tiny: tot 4 babe, baby 6 infant, peewee
unmannerly: 7 smatche(Sc.)

childbirth: 5 labor 7 lying-in, travail 11 confinement, parturition
goddess: 4 Apet, Auge, Upis 5 Damia 6 Lucina 7 Auxesia

childish: 4 weak 5 naive, petty, silly 6 puling, simple, weanly(Sc.), young 7 asinine, babyish, foolish, kiddish, puerile, unmanly 8 bairnish, brattish, immature, juvenile 9 credulous, childlike, infantile, kittenish

childish talk: 7 prattle

childish walk: 6 toddle

childlike: 4 meek 6 docile, filial 7 babyish, dutiful 8 childish, innocent, trusting 9 confiding, frivolous 10 submissive

children: 7 progeny 9 offspring
dislike of: 9 misopedia 10 misopaedia
medical science: 10 pediatrics 11 paediatrics
room: 7 nursery
study: 8 pedology 9 paedology
tender of: 4 amah 6 sitter 9 nursemaid

Chile: *arborvitae:* 6 alerce, alerse
city: 6 Arauco, Cobija, Serena 7 Caldera, Copiapo 8 Coquimbo, Santiago(c.), Valdivia 10 Concepcion, Valparaiso
coastal wind: 5 sures
coin: 4 peso 5 libra 6 condor, escudo
desert: 7 Atacama
Indian: Ona
island: 5 Hoste
measure: 4 vara 5 legua, linea 6 cuadra, fanega
money: 6 condor
mountain: 5 Maipu, Pular
mountain range: 5 Andes
national police: 11 carabineros
province: 5 Arica, Aysen Maule, Nuble, Talca 6 Bio-Bio, Cautin, Chiloe, Curico 7 Atacama 8 Coquimbo, Santiago, Tarapaca, Valdivia 9 Aconcagua, Colchagua 10 Concepcion, Valparaiso 11 Antofagasta
river: Loa 5 Itata, Maipu, Maule 6 Bio-Bio, Chuapa, Lontue 7 Illapel 8 Valdivia
rodent: 10 chinchilla
seaport: 4 Lota, Tome 5 Arica 8 Coquimba
shrub: 5 lithi 6 pepino
tree: 4 brea, pelu, ulmo 5 coleu, rauli, roble 6 alerce, alerse, coigue, muermo
volcano: 6 Antuco, Lascar, Llaima 7 Calbuco
weight: 5 grano, libra 7 quintal
workman: 4 roto

chill: ice, raw 4 ague, cold, cool, dazy(Sc.) 5 algor, gelid, rigor, shake 6 frappe, freeze, frigid, frosty, shiver 7 depress, frisson, malaria 8 coldness 11 refrigerate

chilling: 4 eery 5 eerie

chills and fever: 4 ague 7 malaria

chilly: raw 4 cold, cool, lash 5 algid, bleak, hunch 6 arctic, frosty 9 cauldrife

chilver: 4 lamb

chimaera: 7 ratfish

chime: din, rim 4 bell, edge, peal, ring, suit, ting 5 agree, prate 6 accord, cymbal, jingle, melody 7 concord, harmony 8 singsong

chimera: 5 fancy 6 mirage 8 illusion

chimerical: 4 vain, wild 7 utopian 8 delusive, fanciful, romantic 9 fantastic, imaginary, unfounded, visionary

chimes: 5 bells 8 carillon

chimney: lum 4 flue, pipe, tube, vent 5 gully, stack, tewel 6 funnel 7 fissure, opening, orifice 10 smokestack
cover: 4 cowl 7 turncap
deposit: 4 soot
piece: 5 parel 6 mantel
post: 5 speer

chimney corner: 8 fireside 9 inglenook

chimpanzee: ape 5 pigmy 10 anthropoid, troglodyte

chin: jaw 4 chat 5 menta(pl.) 6 mentum
comb. form: 5 genio
double: 4 fold 7 buccula

china: 4 ware 6 dishes 7 ceramic, pottery 8 Cinchona, crockery 9 porcelain 11 earthenware
fine: 5 Spode 6 Sevres 7 Limoges 8 Wedgwood

China: *aborigine:* Yao 4 Mans, Miao 6 Mantzu, Yao-min 7 Miaotse, Miaotze

alloy: **7** paktong **8** packtong
ancient name: **4** Tsao **5** Seres **6** Cathay
antelope: **6** dzeren
arch: **6** pailoo, pailou, pailow
artichoke: **7** chorogi
bamboo: **7** whangee
banker: **6** shroff
bat: ia
bean: soy **6** cowpea
black tea: **6** oolong
boat: **4** bark, junk **6** sampan
brigand: **9** hunghutze, hunghutzu
Buddha: Fo; Foh
Buddhist paradise: **7** Chingtu
cabbage: **7** pakchoi
calculator: **7** suan pan, swan pan
canton: Fu **5** Hsein
city: Su; Nom, Ude **4** Amoy, Tsin, Wuhu **5** Jehol, Macao, Macau, Pekin **6** Canton, Fachan, Fuchau, Hankau, Hankow, Huchau, Kalgan, Nankin, Ningpo, Suchau, Swatow, Tsinan, Yunnan **7** Chengte, Chengtu, Chingtu, Fatshan, Foochow, Hanyang, Kaifeng, Lanchau, Nanking, Paoting, Taiyuen, Tunkuan, Wenchau, Wuchang, Yenping **8** Changsha, Chaochau, Fancheng, Hangchau, Hangchow, Kiaochau, Nanchang, Shanghai, Shaohing, Siangtan, Tengchau, Tientsin, Tungchau, Tunghwan, Yanphing **9** Changchau, Chinkiang, Chungking, Lienkiang **10** Chingkiang, Kingtechen
city (walled): **6** Peking
civet: **5** rasse
clay: **6** kaolin
cloth: sha **4** moxa, pulo, silk **6** nankin **7** nankeen
cloth-stiffening gelatin: **7** haitsai
coin: le, pu; fan, neu, sen **4** cash, cent, mace, tael, tiao, yuan **5** liang, tsien **6** dollar, ticket **9** candareen **10** Kupingtael **11** Haikwantael
comb. form: **4** Sino **5** Sinic
cooking style: **5** Honan **6** Fukien, Peking **8** Szechuan **9** Cantonese
cosmic order: tao
customs collector: **5** hoppo
decigram: li
deer: **8** elaphure
department: Fu **5** Hsien
dialect: Wu **4** Amoy **5** Hakka **6** Canton, Ningpo, Swaton **7** Foochow, Wenchow
dish: **4** rice **7** fooyung **8** fooyoung
division: **4** chow, Miao **5** Hsien **6** canton
dog: **4** chow, peke
dragon: **6** chilin
drink: **6** samshu
duck eggs: **5** pidan
dulcimer: **7** yang-kin
dynasty: Fo; Han, Sui, Wei, Yin **4** Chin, Chou, Hsia, Ming, Sung, Tang, Tsin, Yuan **5** Shang
exchange medium: **5** sycee
factory: **4** hong
festival: **9** Ching Ming
feudal state: Wei
figurine: **5** magot
fir: **5** nikko
fish: **7** trepang
flute: che **4** tche
fruit: **6** lichee, litchi
ginger: **9** galingale
god: **4** Ghos, Joss, Shen **5** Kuant
gong: **6** tamtam
gooseberry: **9** carambola
grass: bon **5** ramie
grass linen: **8** barandos
gruel: **6** congee, conjee
herb: tea **7** ginseng
herb genus: **7** nandina
houseboat: **5** tanka
idol: **4** joss **6** pagoda
indigo: **6** isatis
isinglass: **4** agar **8** agar-agar
island: **4** Amoy **5** Macao **6** Hainan **7** Formosa
jute: **7** chingma
laborer: **6** coolie
lake: **6** Po-yang **8** Tung-ting
language: Wu **4** Shan **8** Mandarin **9** Cantonese
lemon: **6** citron
magistrate: **8** mandarin
magnolia: **5** yulan
mandarin's residence: **6** oyamen
measure: ho, hu, ko, li, mu, pu, ta, to, tu, yu; cho, fen, tou, yan, yin **4** chih, fang, kish, quei, shih, teke, tsan, tsun **5** chang, ching, sheng, shing **6** kung ho, kung li, kung mu, tching, tchung **7** kung fen **8** kung chih, kung shih **9** kung ching, kung sheng
measure of distance: li
measure of weight: **4** chin **5** catty
mile: li
money (see also *coin* above): mo, pu **4** mace, tael, tiao **5** sycee, tsien
mongol: hu
mountain: Omi **4** Omei, Sung **5** Tsins **6** Inshan, Pu-ling **7** Alashan, Kuen-lun, Kuliang **8** Ta-yu-ling **9** Funiu-shan, Tsing-Ling
musical instrument: kin **5** cheng, sheng **7** samisen
Nationalist Party: **11** Kuomintang
noodles: **4** mein
nurse: ama **4** amah
official: **4** kuan, kwan **5** amban
oil: **4** tung

old name: 6 Cathay
orange: 7 kumquat 8 mandarin
ounce: 4 tael
ox. 4 zebu
pagoda: ta; taa 4 taag
parasol tree: 6 aogiri
peony: 6 moutan
pert. to: 4 Sino
philosopher: 4 Moti 5 Motzu 6 Laotse, Laotzu 9 Confucius
plant: tea, udo 4 rice, tche 5 ramie 7 ginseng
poet: 4 Li Po 7 Li Tai-Po
pony: 7 griffin
porcelain: 7 Celadon, Nankeen
porcelain glaze: 7 eelskin
porgy: tai
positive principle: 4 yang
pottery: 4 Kuan, Ming, Ting 5 Chien 7 boccaro, Tzuchou
pound: 5 catty
prefecture: fu
province: 4 Amur (Heilungkiang) 5 Chili, Honan, Hunan, Hupeh, Kansu 6 Fokien, Fukien, Shansi, Shensi, Yunnan 7 Kiangsi, Kiangsu, Kwangsi, Nganhui 8 Che-Kiang, Kweichau, Shantung, Szechuan, Szechwan 9 Kwangtung, Manchuria
provincial chief: 6 taoyin
puzzle: 7 tangram
race: 4 Lolo 5 Sinic, Soyot 6 Mongol
religion: 6 Taoism 12 Confucianism
river: Si; Han, Ili, Kan, Min, Pei, Wei 4 Hwai, Tung, Yuan, Yuen 5 Hwang, Peiho, Pieho, Tarim 7 Hoangho, Sikiang 12 Yangtsekiang
roller: 7 sirgang
salutation: bow 6 kowtow
sauce: soy
sea port: 4 Amoy, Wuhu 5 Aigun, Shasi 6 Antung, Canton, Chefoo, Dairen, Harbin, Ichang, Ningpo, Pakhoi, Swaton, Szemao, Wuchow, Yochow 7 Foochow, Hangkow, Hunchun, Lungkow, Mengtsz, Nanking, Nanning, Samshui, Santuao, Soochow, Wenchow 8 Changsha, Hangchow, Kiukiang, Kongmoon, Lungchow, Shanghai, Tengyueh, Tientsin, Tsingtao, Wanhsien 9 Chinkiang, Chungking, Kiungchow, Newchwang 10 Chiankiang 12 Chingwangtao 14 Lungchingstsun
secret society: hui 4 tong
sedge: 4 mati
shrub: tea 5 ramie
silk: sha 5 pekin, tasar 6 pongee, tussah 7 taysaam, tsatlee 8 shantung
silkworm: 4 sina 6 tussah, tusser 10 ailanthus
silver: 5 sycee
skiff: 6 sampan
sky: 4 tien
sleeping platform: 4 kang
society: 4 Hoey, Huey, Hung, Tong 5 Triad
squash: 6 cushaw
state(anc.): 4 Tsao 6 Cathay
stocks: 6 cangue
street: 6 hutung
student: 9 sinologue
sugar cane: 5 sorgo
taa: 6 pagoda
Tartar tribe: 4 Toda
tax: 5 likin
tea: cha 4 Tsia 5 bohea, congo, congu, Emesa, hyson
Temple: taa 6 pagoda
toy: 7 tangram
treaty port: 4 Amoy
tree: 5 nikko 6 kinkan, litchi 7 gingkgo, hagbush, kumquat 9 bandoline, soapberry
tribe: Hu 4 Shan, Toba
vegetable: udo
vine: 5 kudzu 7 yangtao
walking stick: 7 whangee
warehouse: 4 hong
wax: 4 cere, pela
weight: li; fen, hao, kin, ssu, tan, yin 4 chee, chin, mace, shih, tael 5 catty, chien, liang, picul, tsien 6 kung li 7 haikwan, kung fen, kung ssu, kung tun 8 king chin 9 candareen 10 kuping tael 11 haikwan tael
wind instrument: 5 cheng, sheng
wormwood: 4 moxa
China Sea: *gulf:* 4 Siam
island: 6 Hainan 7 Formosa
Chinaberry: 9 soapberry
chinch: 6 bedbug
chine: 4 back, grow 5 chink, crack, crest, ridge, spine 6 cleave, ravine, sprout 7 crevice, fissure 8 backbone
Chinese (see also **China**): 5 Cerai, Seres, Seric, Sinic 6 Mongol, Sinico 7 Asiatic, Cataian, Sangley 9 Celestial
pert. to: 5 Seric 6 Serian 7 Sinitic 8 Senesian
chink: gap 4 bore, cash, coin, kink, rent, rift, rime 5 boore, check, chine, cleft, crack, grike, money 6 cranny, sprain 7 chinkle, crevice, fissure 8 aperture 9 chaffinch 10 interstice
chinky: 5 rifty 6 rimose
Chinook: 4 wind 6 indian 8 Flathead
chief: 4 Tyee
god: 8 tamanoas
people: 7 tilikum 8 tillicum
powwow: 4 wawa
salmon: 7 quinnat
woman: 10 klootchman
Chinook State: 10 Washington

chinquapin: oak 6 bonnet 8 chestnut, wankapin 9 rattlenut
chinse: 4 calk, seam 5 close
chintz: 5 cloth 7 pintado
Chios: 4 Scio(It.) 5 Khios(Gr.) 6 island 10 Sakis-Adasi
chip: bit, cut, hew, nig 4 chap, clip, knap, nick, pare 5 crack, flake, piece, scrap, spale, spalt, waste 6 chisel 7 counter 8 fragment, splinter
of stone: 5 spall 6 gallet
chipmunk: 6 chippy, hackee, rodent 8 squirrel
chipper: gay 4 spry 5 chirp, perky 6 babble, cockey, lively 7 chatter, chirrup, twitter 8 cheerful
chirk: 5 chirp 6 lively 7 chirrup 8 cheerful
chirm: din, hum 5 chirp, croon, noise 6 clamor
chiro: 4 fish
chirognomy: 9 palmistry 10 chiromancy
chirography: 6 script 7 writing 10 engrossing 11 handwriting
chiromancy: 9 palmistry 10 chirognomy
chiroptera: bat
chirp: pip 4 peek, peep, pipe 5 cheep, chelp, chirk, chirl, chirm, chirt, tweet 7 chipper, chirrup, chitter, rejoice, twitter, wheetle
chirrup: 5 chirk, chirp, tweet 7 chipper
chirurgeon: 7 surgeon
chisel: cut, gad 4 chip, form, pare, tool 5 burin, carve, cheat, gouge, hardy 6 chesil, gravel, haggle 7 bargain, engrave, quarrel, shingle
ancient stone: 4 celt
engraving: 7 scooper, scorper
mine: gad 6 peeker
sculpture: 7 gradine 9 ebauchoir
stonemason's: 5 drove
toothed: 6 jagger
chiseled: 6 cisele(F.)
chiseler: 5 cheat, crook 6 gouger 9 bargainer
chiselled: 8 clearcut
chiselly: 6 gritty 8 gravelly 10 unpleasant 12 disagreeable
chit: dab, IOU 4 bill, girl, mind, note, rice 5 child, draft, shoot 6 infant, letter, sprout 7 voucher 9 offspring 10 memorandum
chitarra: 6 guitar
chitchat: 4 talk 6 banter, gossip 12 conversation
chiton: 4 gown, robe 5 tunic 7 mollusk
chitter: 5 chirp 6 shiver 7 chatter, twitter
chivalrous: 5 brave, civil, noble 6 gentle, polite 7 gallant, genteel, valiant, warlike 8 knightly 9 courteous, honorable
chive: cut 4 stab 5 clout, clove, knive, onion 6 bulbet
chivy, chivvy: run, vex 4 hunt, race 5 chase, tease 6 badger, flight, harass, pursue 7 pursuit, scamper, torment 8 maneuver 9 confusion
chlamys: 5 cloak 6 mantle 7 garment
chloral: 8 sedative
chloride: 4 salt 5 ester 7 calomel 8 compound
chlorine remover: 9 antichlor
chloroform: 4 kill 10 anesthetic
discoverer: 6 Liebig 7 Guthrie 9 Soubeiran
ingredient: 7 acetone
liquid used: 7 acetone
chobdar: 5 usher 9 attendant
chock: 5 block, chuck, cleat, wedge
chocolate: 5 candy, cocoa 8 beverage
family: 13 sterculiaceae
machine: 6 conche
powder: 5 cocoa 6 pinola
seed: 5 cacao
stick for mixing: 7 molinet
tree: 4 cola 5 cacao
choice: 4 a-one, best, fine, pick, rare, wale, weal, will 5 cream, elite, prime, voice 6 chosen, dainty, flower, option, picked, select 8 delicate, election, eximious, uncommon, volition 9 excellent, exquisite, recherche 10 preferable, preference 11 alternative
choicy: 6 choosy 10 fastidious
choir: 5 quire 6 chorus
leader: 6 cantor 9 precentor
member: 4 alto, bass 5 basso 7 songman, soprano 9 chorister
vestment: 4 gown 5 cotta 8 surplice
choke: dam, gag 4 clog, plug, quar 5 check, close, grane 6 hinder, impede, stifle 7 querken, repress, silence, smother 8 obstruct, stoppage, strangle, suppress, throttle 9 constrict, neckcloth, suffocate 10 extinguish
choke coil: 7 reactor
chokedamp: 9 blackdamp
choler: ire 4 bile, fury, rage 5 anger, wrath 6 spleen, temper 9 distemper 10 resentment 11 biliousness 12 irascibility
choleric: mad 5 angry, cross, fiery, huffy, testy 6 fumish, touchy 7 bilious, enraged, iracund, peevish, peppery, waspish 8 wrathful 9 impatient, irascible 10 passionate 11 belligerent, quarrelsome
render: 6 enrage
choose: opt 4 chap, cull, pick, vote, wale, weal 5 adopt, chuse, elect 6 prefer, select 7 embrace, espouse
choosy, choosey: 7 finical 9 selective 10 fastidious
chop: cut, hew, jaw, lop 4 chap, dice, gash, hack, hash, jowl, rive, slit 5 carve, cleft, crack, knock, mince, slash, stamp, trade,

truck, whang 6 barter, change, cleave, incise 8 exchange 9 cotolette
down: 4 fell, raze 5 level
eye of: 8 noisette
off: lop 4 drib 5 prune 8 amputate
chop-chop: 7 quickly 8 promptly
chophouse: 10 restaurant
Chopin's country: 6 France, Poland
chopping block: 7 hacklog
chopping tool: ax; axe 7 cleaver, hatchet
choppy: 5 rough
choragus: 6 leader 10 bandleader
chord: 4 cord, tone 5 nerve, triad 6 string, tendon 7 harmony 8 filament 9 harmonize
arc: 4 sine
harplike: 8 arpeggio
musical: 5 major, minor
ninth: 4 none
seventh: 6 tetrad
succession: 7 cadence
Chorda filum: 7 sealace
chore: job 4 char, duty, task 5 chare, stint 6 errand 9 housework
chorister: 6 singer 7 chanter 8 choirboy
chorten: 5 stupa 6 shrine 8 monument 9 reliquary
chortle: 5 laugh, snort 7 chuckle
chorus: 4 song 5 choir 6 accord, assent, unison 7 refrain, singers 8 response
girl: 6 dancer, singer 7 chorine
leader: 7 choragi(pl.) 8 choragus 9 conductor
chose: 5 thing
chosen: 5 elect, elite 7 elected 8 selected
Chosen: 5 Corea, Korea
chosen people: 10 Israelites
chough: 4 bird, crow
chouse: 4 dupe, gull, sham 5 chase, cheat, trick 6 harass 7 defraud 8 swindler 10 imposition
chow: dog 4 eats, food, grub, meal 6 fodder
chowchow: dog 4 bird, olio 7 mixture 8 mishmash 10 hodgepodge, miscellany
chowk: 5 bazar 6 bazaar, market
Christ: 4 Lord 7 Messiah, Saviour
christen: 4 name 7 baptize 10 denominate
Christian: 7 Gentile 8 Nazarene
early: 8 Galilean
Eastern: 6 Uniate
Egyptian: 4 Copt
persecuted: 6 martyr
unity: 7 irenics
Christian Science founder: 4 Eddy
Christiania: 4 Oslo
Christianity: *heretical sect:* 7 Docetae
love feast: 5 agape
martyr: 7 Stephen
symbol: 5 cross, orant 7 lehthus
theologian: 4 Kuhn 7 Aquinas, Niebuhr, Tillich 8 Bultmann 9 Augustine, deChardin 10 Bonhoeffor 11 Kierkegaard
writer: 6 Origen
Christ's thorn: 4 nabk, nubk 5 shrub 6 jujube
Christmas: 4 noel, yule 7 holiday 8 festival, nativity, yuletide
carol: 4 noel 5 nowel
crib: 6 creche
decoration: 5 holly 6 tinsel 9 mistletoe
midnight mass supper: 9 reveillon
Christmas Carol: *author:* 7 Dickens
character: Tim 7 Scrooge
Christmas rose: 9 hellebore
chromium: 7 element, mineral
group element: 7 uranium 8 tungsten 10 molybdenum
symbol: Cr
chromo: 7 picture 10 lithograph
chromolithograph: 7 picture
chronic: 5 fixed 6 severe 7 intense 8 constant 9 confirmed, continual, lingering, prolonged 10 continuous, inveterate 12 disagreeable
chronicle: 5 annal, diary 6 record 7 account, archive, history, recital 8 register 9 narrative
chronicler: 6 writer 8 compiler, recorder 9 historian 11 memorialist
chronology: 6 record 11 arrangement 14 classification
according to: 5 datal
error in: 9 prolepsis 11 anachronism
chronometer: 5 clock 9 metronome, timepiece 10 timekeeper
chronometry: era 4 date 5 epoch
chrysalis: 4 pupa 5 pupae(pl.)
chrysolite: 7 olivine, peridot
chrysoprase: 10 chalcedony
chthonian: 8 infernal
chub: 4 dace, dolt, fool, lout 5 chopa 6 chevin, shiner 8 fallfish, mackerel 9 hornyhead, squawfish
chubby: 5 chuff, fubsy, plump 6 choaty, rotund 8 rolypoly
chuck: hen, log, pig 4 beef, food, fowl, grub, hurl, jerk, lump, toss 5 chock, cluck, pitch, throw 6 bounce, collet 7 chicken, discard 9 dismissal
chuckle: 5 cluck, exult, laugh 6 giggle, titter 7 chortle
chuff: fat 4 boor 5 brick, churl, cross, miser, proud, sound, sulky, surly 6 chubby, elated, rustic 7 swollen 9 conceited 11 ill-tempered
chug: 4 puff

chum: cad, pal 4 bait, mate, pard 5 buddy, butty, crony 6 cobber, copain, friend 8 roommate 9 associate, companion
chump: ass 4 dolt, head 5 block 8 endpiece 9 blockhead, schlemiel, schlemihl
chunk: dab, gob, pat, wad 4 junk, slug 5 claut, piece, throw, whang
chunky: 4 game 5 lumpy, plump, squat, stout, thick
church: 4 tera(Jap.) 7 edifice 9 sanctuary, structure
altar end: 4 apse
altar offering: 8 altarage
attendant: 8 altarboy, choirboy
balcony: 8 cantoria
bench: pew, pue 4 seat
bishopric: see 7 diocese 10 episcopacy, episcopate
body of: 4 nave
calendar: 4 ordo
chapel: 7 oratory
congregation: 7 synaxis
council: 5 synod 6 Nicene
court: 4 Rota
deputy: 5 vicar 6 curate
dignitary: 4 dean, pope 5 abbot, canon 6 bishop 7 prelate, primate
dissenter: 7 sectary
district: 6 parish 7 diocese
dominion of: 11 sacerdotium
doorkeeper: 7 ostiary
early Christian: 8 basilica
endowed: 8 benefice
entrance chapel: 7 galilee
episcopacy: 7 prelacy
field: 5 glebe
government: 9 hierarchy
home: 5 manse 7 deanery 8 convento 9 parsonage
law: 5 canon
member: 11 communicant
morning service: 5 matin
officer: 5 elder, vicar 6 beadle, deacon, lector, sexton, warden 7 prelate, sacrist 8 reverend 9 clergyman, moderator, presbyter, sacristan 11 headborough
part of: 4 apse, bema, nave 5 altar, solea 7 chancel, narthex 8 cantoria, transept 10 clearstory, clerestory
prayer: 5 kyrie 12 kyrie eleison
property: 5 glebe
reader: 6 lector
recess: 4 apse
revenue: 5 tithe 8 benefice
Roman: 7 lateran 8 basilica
room: 6 vestry 7 galilee 8 sacristy
seat: pew, pue 5 bench 6 sedile 7 sedilia(pl.)
service: 4 mass, rite 5 matin 7 vespers, nocturn 8 evensong
stand: 4 ambo
stipend: 7 prebend
vault: 5 crypt
vessel: ama, pyx 4 font 5 amula 7 columba, piscina 9 colymbion 10 monstrance
vestry room: 8 sacristy
wall: 6 cashel
warden's aide: 7 hoggler
wing: 5 aisle
church council (previous to): 10 antenicene
churchgoer: 11 communicant
Churchill: *forte:* 5 prose
Order: 6 Garter
trademark: 5 cigar
churchly: 9 religious, spiritual
churchyard: 6 litten 8 cemetery 9 graveyard
churl: cad, man 4 boor, carl, gnof, hind, lout, serf 5 carle, ceorl, chuff, gnoff, knave, miser 6 bodach, carlot, lubber, rustic, vassal, yeoman 7 bondman, freeman, haskard, husband, niggard, peasant, villain, villein 10 countryman, curmudgeon
churlish: 4 mean 5 bluff, gruff, rough, surly 6 crabby, rustic, sordid, sulkly, sullen, vulgar 7 boorish, crabbed, uncivil, violent 9 illiberal 10 ungracious, unyielding 12 cross-grained
churn: 4 beat, kirn(Sc.), stir 5 drill, shake 7 agitate
part: 6 dasher
chute: 4 rush, tube 5 flume, hurry, rapid, shoot, slide 6 hopper, trough 7 decline, descent 8 downfall, stampede
cibarious: 6 edible
cibol: 5 onion 7 shallot
ciborium: pix, pyx 6 canopy, coffer, vessel
cicada: 6 cagale, cigala, locust
noise: 5 chirr
cicala: 6 locust 11 grasshopper
cicatrix: 4 mark, scab, scar, seam
cicatrization: 8 scarring
cicely: 5 myrrh
Cicero's target: 8 Catiline
cicerone: 5 guide, pilot 6 mentor, orator 7 courier 9 conductor
cichlid food dish: 5 bolti 7 sunfish
cid: Ruy 4 epic, hero, poem 5 Bivar, chief, title 9 commander
sword of: 6 colada, tizona
cider: 5 perry 6 perkin, swanky 8 beverage
pulp: 6 pomace
cienega: 5 marsh, swamp
cigar: 4 toby 5 claro, smoke 6 boquet, Corona, maduro, stogie 7 bouquet, cheroot, culebra 8 perfecto 9 Belvedere
crude: 7 cheroot, culebra

long thin: 8 panatela, panetela 9 panatella, panetella
cigarette: fag 4 biri, pill 5 cubeb, smoke 6 gasper, reefer 9 cigarillo
cigarfish: 4 scad 8 quiaquia
cilium: 4 hair, lash 7 eyelash 8 barbicel
cima: See **cyma**
cimarron: 5 slave 6 maroon 7 bighorn
cimbia: 4 band 6 fillet
cimex: 6 bedbug, insect
cimmerian: 4 inky 5 black 6 gloomy
cinch: 4 belt, gird, grip, pipe, snap 5 girth 6 fasten 8 sinecure 9 certainty
cinchona: 4 bark, tree
extract: 7 quinine
cinct: 4 girt 9 encircled
cincture: 4 band, belt, gird, halo, list, ring 5 girth 6 cestus, collar, fillet, girdle 7 baldric, compass 8 encircle 9 enclosure 11 environment, surrounding
cinder: ash 4 gray, slag 5 chark, dross, ember 6 scoria 7 clinker, lapilla, residue
cinders: 5 gleed, track
cinema (see also **motion picture**): 4 film, show 5 flick, movie 6 screen
cinerarium: urn 8 mortuary
cinerator: 6 ashery 9 crematory 11 incinerator
cinerous: 5 ashen
cingle: 4 belt 5 girth 6 girdle
cingular: 7 annular 8 circular
cingulum: 4 band 5 ridge 6 girdle
cinnabar: ore 7 mineral 9 vermilion
derivative: 11 quicksilver
cinnamic acid derivative: 7 sinapic
cinnamon: 4 tree 5 canel, spice 6 canela, canell, canelo, cassia 7 canella, canelle 8 barbasco
cinnamon apple: 8 sweetsop
cinnamon oak: 8 bluejack
cinnamon stone: 6 garnet 8 essonite
cinquefoil: 6 clover 7 frasier
cion: bud 5 graft, scion, shoot, uvula 10 descendant
Cipango: 5 Japan 6 Nippon
cipher: key, nil 4 code, null, zero 5 aught, ought 6 device, decode, figure, letter, naught, nought, number, symbol 9 nonentity 10 cryptogram
cipo: 4 vine 5 liana
cippus: 6 pillar 8 landmark 10 gravestone
circa: 5 about 6 around 13 approximation
Circassian: *dialect:* 6 Adighe 8 Cherkess 9 Abkhasian, Kabardian
king: 9 Sacripant
Circe: 5 siren 7 tempter 9 sorceress 11 enchantress
brother: 6 Aeetes
father: 6 Helios
island: 5 Aeaea
niece: 6 Medea
son: 5 Comus 9 Telegonus
circle: lap, set 4 disk, gyre, halo, hoop, loop, maru(Jap.), orbe, ring, rink, turn 5 class, crown, cycle, frame, group, monde, realm, rhomb, rigol, round, swirl, twirl 6 bezant, cirque, clique, collet, cordon, corona, diadem, girdle, rotate, rundle, spiral, system 7 chukkar, chukker, circlet, circuit, company, compass, coronet, coterie, enclose, revolve, ringlet 8 encircle, surround 9 circulate, encompass 13 circumference
around sun or moon: 6 corona
geographic: 6 tropic
great: 7 equator
heraldry: 7 annulet
longest chord: 8 diameter
luminous: 4 aura, halo 6 corona, nimbus
part of: arc 5 chord 6 degree, radius, secant, sector 7 segment
circlet: 4 band, hoop, ring 6 bangle, cirque 7 circuit 8 bracelet, headband
of light: 7 aureola, aureole
circuit: lap 4 area, bout, iter, loop, tour, zone 5 ambit, cycle, orbit, round, route 6 ambage, circle, detour 7 compass, itinera(pl.) 8 district 10 revolution 13 circumference
auxiliary: 5 relay
court: 4 eyre
circuitous: 4 mazy 6 curved 7 crooked, devious, oblique, sinuous, twisted, vagrant, winding 8 circular, flexuous, indirect, rambling, tortuous 9 ambagious, ambiguous, deceitful, underhand, wandering 10 roundabout, serpentine 12 disingenuous, labyrinthine
circular: 4 bill 5 libel, orbed, round 6 ringed 7 annular, cycloid, discoid, perfect 8 cingular, complete, encyclic, globular, pamphlet 9 orbicular 10 circuitous, roundabout 11 publication
indicator: 4 dial
motion: 4 eddy, gyre
plate: 4 disc, disk
circulate: air, mix 4 move, turn 6 rotate, spread 7 diffuse, publish 9 propagate 10 promulgate 11 disseminate
publicly: 6 report 9 broadcast
circumference: arc 5 ambet, girth 6 border, bounds, limits 7 circuit 8 boundary, surround 9 dimension, perimeter, periphery
circumlocution: 6 ambage 7 winding 8 verbiage 10 periphrase, redundancy, roundabout
circumscribe: 5 bound, fence, limit 6 define 7 confine, enclose, environ 8 encircle, restrain, restrict, surround 9 encompass

circumspect: 4 wary, wise 5 alert, chary 7 careful, guarded, prudent 8 cautious, discreet, watchful 9 attentive 10 deliberate
circumstance: fix 4 fact, item 5 event, phase, state 6 affair, detail, factor, pickle 7 element, episode 8 incident, position 9 condition, situation 10 occurrence, particular 11 environment, opportunity 12 surroundings
circumstantial: 5 exact 6 minute 7 precise 8 detailed 9 pertinent 10 incidental, particular 11 inferential 12 nonessential
circumstantiate: 7 support 8 evidence
circumvent: 4 balk, dupe, foil 5 cheat, check, cozen, evade, trick, 6 baffle, delude, entrap, outwit, thwart 7 capture, deceive, defraud, ensnare, prevent 8 surround 9 encompass, frustrate, overreach, underfong
circus: 4 ring 5 arena 6 circle, cirque 9 spectacle 10 hippodrome 12 amphitheater 13 entertainment
arena wall: 5 spina
column: 4 meta
employee: 5 clown, tamer
gear: 4 tent 5 rings 7 trapeze
rider: 8 desultor
cirque: 5 basin 6 circle, circus, corrie, recess 7 circlet, erosion
cirrus: 5 cloud 7 tendril 8 filament
cisco: 8 blackfin, whitefin
cist: box 4 tomb 5 chest 6 casket 7 chamber 9 cistavaen
cistern: sac, tub, vat 4 tank, well 6 cavity 7 cuvette 8 cisterna 9 reservoir, impluvium
cit: 8 townsman 9 tradesman 10 shopkeeper
citadel: arx 4 fort, hall 5 alamo, tower 6 castle 7 borough 8 fastness, fortress 10 stronghold 13 fortification
of Carthage: 5 Bursa, Byrsa
of Moscow: 7 Kremlin
citation: 6 notice 7 mention, summons 8 monition 9 quotation, reference 10 allegation 11 enumeration
cite: 4 call, tell 5 allay, quote, refer 6 accite, accuse, adduce, allege, arouse, avouch, excite, notify, repeat, summon 7 arraign, bespeak, excerpt, extract, mention 8 indicate
citizen: cit 5 voter 6 native 7 burgess, burgher, citoyen(F.), denizen, elector, freeman, oppidan 8 civilian, commoner, occupant, resident 9 citoyenne(F.) 10 inhabitant
suffix: ese, ian, ist, ite
citizenship: *admission to:* 14 naturalization 15 enfranchisement
pert. to: 5 civic
citrine: 5 color 7 rhubarb
citron: 4 lime 5 lemon 6 cedrat, yellow
citrullus: 7 pumpkin 10 watermelon
citrus: *belt:* 7 Florida 10 California
disease: 8 buckskin
drink: ade 5 juice
fruit: 4 lime 5 lemon 6 citron, orange 7 kumquat, tangelo 8 mandarin, shaddock 9 tangerine 10 grapefruit
city: 4 burg, dorp, town, urbs(L.) 5 ville 6 ciudad, staple 9 community 10 metropolis 12 municipality
celestial: 4 Zion
district: 4 slum 6 barrio, ghetto, uptown 8 business, downtown, red-light 11 residential
eternal: 4 Roma, Rome
hanging gardens: 7 Babylon
holy: 5 Mecca 6 Medina 9 Jerusalem
leaning tower: 4 Pisa
official: 5 mayor 7 manager, marshal 8 alderman 10 councilman
oldest inhabited: 8 Damascus
pert. to: 5 civic, urban 7 oppidan 9 municipal 12 metropolitan
problem: 4 riot, slum, smog 5 crime 6 ghetto 7 poverty, traffic
section: 4 ward 5 block, plaza 6 square
wicked: 5 Sodom 8 Gomorrah
City: *of Bells:* 9 Strasburg 10 Strasbourg
of Bridges: 6 Bruges
of Brotherly Love: 12 Philadelphia
of Churches: 8 Brooklyn
of David: 9 Jerusalem
of God: 6 church, heaven 8 Paradise
of God author: 9 Augustine
of Hundred Towers: 5 Pavia
of Kings: 4 Lima
of Lilies: 8 Florence
of Masts: 6 London
of Rams: 6 Canton
of Refuge: 6 Medina
of Saints: 8 Montreal
of Seven Hills: 4 Rome
of Violet Crown: 6 Athens
of Victory: 5 Cairo
Cius: 6 Gemlik
civet: cat, cit 5 rasse, zibet 6 bondar, musang, zibeth 7 fossane, nandine
civet-like animal: 5 genet
civic: lay 5 civil, suave, urban 6 polite, urbane 7 secular
civil: 4 hend 5 hende, suave 6 polite, urbane 7 affable, courtly, elegant, politic, refined 8 discreet, gracious, obliging, polished, wellbred 9 civilized, courteous 10 cultivated, respectful 11 complaisant 13 condescending
civil rights (extinction of): 9 attainder
Civil War: *admiral:* 8 Farragut

battle: 6 Shiloh 8 Antietam
commander: Lee 4 Pope 5 Ewell, Grant, Meade, Sykes 7 Forrest, Jackson
civil wrong: 4 tort
civilian: cit 5 civvy 7 citizen, teacher 12 noncombatant, practitioner
dress: 5 mufti
civility: 6 comity 7 amenity 8 courtesy 9 propriety 10 affability, compliance, politeness 11 complacence 12 complaisance
civilization: 6 kultur(G.) 7 culture 10 refinement 11 cultivation
civilize: 4 tame 5 teach, train 6 polish, refine 7 educate 8 humanize, urbanize 9 cultivate 11 domesticate
clabber: mud 4 mire 6 curdle, lopper 12 bonnyclabber
clack: 4 blab 5 chack, cluck, crack 6 cackle, gossip, rattle, tongue 7 chatter, clacket, clatter, prattle 10 chatterbox
clad: 5 drest, robed 6 beseen, decked 7 adorned, arrayed, attired, clothed, covered, dressed 8 sheathed
cladose: 6 ramose 8 branched
clag: mud 4 clog, clot, daub, mire 5 fault, stick 6 adhere, burden
claggum: 5 taffy 7 treacle 8 molasses 9 sweetmeat
claim: ask 4 aver, call, case, lien, mine, name 5 exact, right, shout, title 6 assert, demand, elicit 7 acclaim, derecho, pretend, profess, require 8 maintain, pretence, pretense, proclaim 9 challenge, homestead, postulate, vindicate 11 encumbrance
claimant: 7 usurper 9 pretender, arrogator
clairvoyance: 7 insight 8 sagacity 10 divination 11 discernment, penetration
clairvoyant: 4 seer 6 omener 7 prophet, seeress
clam: 4 base, clog, daub, glam, hush, mean 5 clamp, crash, glaum, grasp, grope, smear, stick 6 adhere, clutch, sticky 7 bivalve, clangor, mollusk, steamer 8 adhesive
genus of: mya
kinds of: 4 mega 5 blunt, chama, razor, solen 6 gweduc, quahog 7 geoduck, quahaug
clamant: 4 loud 6 crying, urgent 9 clamorous
clambake: 4 bake 5 movie, rally 6 defeat 7 failure 9 gathering 11 performance
clamber: 5 climb, scale 6 claver 7 rammack 8 scramble, struggle
clamjamfry: mob 5 crowd 6 rabble 7 rubbish
clammy: 4 damp, dank, soft, wack 5 moist, sammy 6 sticky, waughy
clamor: cry, din 4 bere, bunk, roar, rout, wail 5 blare, boast, bruit, noise, shout 6 bellow, hubbub, outcry, racket, tumult, uproar 7 stashie 10 hullabaloo, vociferate
clamorous: 4 loud 5 noisy 7 blatant, clamant, yelling 8 brawling, decrying 9 clamatory, turbulent 10 boisterous 11 openmouthed
clamp: lug, nip, pin 4 bolt, glam, grip, nail, vise 5 block, clasp, glaum 6 fasten 8 fastener, holdfast 10 clothespin
clan: set, sib 4 cult, race, sect, sept, unit 5 class, group, horde, party, tribe 6 clique, family 7 society 8 division 10 collection, fraternity
emblem: xat 5 totem
head of: 5 chief, elder, thane
pert. to: 6 tribal
clancular: 6 secret 11 clandestine
clandestine: bye, sly 4 foxy 5 privy 6 covert, hidden, secret 7 bootleg, furtive, illicit 8 phratria, stealthy 9 clancular, concealed 10 fraudulent 12 hugger-mugger 13 surreptitious
clang: din 4 ding, peal, ring 5 clank, clash, noise 6 jangle, timbre
clangor: din 4 clam, roar 5 clang 6 hubbub, uproar
clank: 4 ring 5 sound 6 rackle
clannish: 5 close 6 secret, tribal, united
clansman: 10 Highlander
clap: 4 bang, flap, peal, slap 5 cheer, clink, crack 6 poster, strike, stroke 7 applaud, chatter, plaudit 9 explosion 11 thunderpeal
clapper: 6 rattle, tongue 7 knacker, knocker
support: 7 baldric 8 baldrick
claptrap: 5 trash 6 blague, device 7 fustian 8 nonsense, trickery 10 pretension 11 insincerity
clarify: 5 clean, clear 6 purify, refine, render, settle 7 cleanse, explain, glorify 8 depurate, eliquate, simplify 10 illuminate 11 transfigure
clarinet: 4 reed, wind 10 instrument
mouthpiece: 4 birn
snake charmer's: 4 been
clarion: 5 clear 7 trumpet
clarity: 5 glory 8 splendor 9 clearness 10 brightness, brilliance 11 pellucidity
claro: 4 mild 5 cigar
clart: 4 clot, daub 5 smear, trash 6 sloven
clarty: 4 foul 5 dirty, gooey, muddy 6 sticky
clash: jar 4 bang, bolt, dash, news, slam 5 brawl, brunt, crash, fight, occur, prate, shock 6 affray, differ, gossip, hurtle, impact, strife, strike, tattle 7 collide, discord, scandal 8 argument, conflict 9 collision, interfere

clasp: hug, pin 4 fold, grab, grip, hasp, hold, hook, hoop, ouch, tach 5 cling, grasp, morse, preen, seize, tache 6 agrafe, brooch, buckle, clench, clutch, enfold, enwrap, fasten, fibula, gimmer, gimmor, infold 7 agraffe, amplect, embrace, entwine, fermail, tendril 8 barrette, fastener, surround 9 constrain, safety-pin 10 chatelaine

class: ilk 4 clan, kind, race, rank, sect, sort, type 5 breed, caste, genus, genre, grade, group, order, tribe 6 circle, family, gender, rating 7 seminar, species, variety 8 category, division 9 abteilung 11 description 12 denomination
animal: 5 genus 6 genera
biological: 5 genus 6 genera(pl.)
member: 4 coed 6 junior, senior 8 freshman 9 sophomore
pert. to: 7 generic

classic: 4 book 5 Attic, model 7 ancient 8 standard 9 venerable 11 composition, masterpiece

classical: 4 pure 5 Attic, Greek, Latin, Roman 6 chaste 8 academic, masterly 9 firstrate

classification: 4 file, rank, rate, sort 5 genre, genra(pl.), genus, grade, order, taxis 6 genera(pl.), rating, system 8 analysis, category, division, taxonomy 12 distribution

classify: 4 list, rank, rate, size, sort, type 5 grade, group, label, range 6 assort, codify, divide, ticket 7 arrange, catalog, dispose, marshal 8 register 9 catalogue, segregate 10 categorize, distribute

classy: 4 tony 5 nifty, slick, smart 7 stylish

clat: 4 clod, clot, mess 5 dirty, prate 6 bedaub, gossip 7 chatter

clatter: din, jar 5 clack, noise, rumor 6 babble, gabble, gossip, rackle, rattle, tattle 7 blatter, chatter, clutter, prattle, reeshie 9 commotion 11 disturbance

Claudia's husband: 6 Pilate

claudicant: 4 lame 7 limping

Claudius' wife: 9 Messalina

clause: 4 part 5 close, plank, rider 6 phrase 7 article, passage, proviso 8 sentence 9 condition, provision 10 conclusion 11 stipulation

claut: 4 hand, lump, rake, tear 5 chunk 6 clutch, scrape 7 handful, scratch

clavecin: 11 harpsichord

clavel: 6 lintel, mantel

claver: 5 prate 6 clover, gossip 7 chatter, clamber

clavichord: 6 spinet

clavicle: 4 bone 10 collarbone

clavis: key 8 glossary

clavus: 4 band, corn 5 strip 6 bunion 7 callous

claw: dig 4 clee, fawn, hand, hook, nail, pull, sere, tear, unce 5 chela, cloof, clufe, court, grasp, griff, seize, talon, uncus 6 clutch, nipper, scrape, ungula 7 crubeen, flatter, scratch, wheedle 8 lacerate

clawk: 4 claw 6 snatch 7 scratch

clay: cob, pug 4 bole, galt, loam, lute, marl, mire 5 argil, brick, cloam, earth, gault, loess, ochre, rabat, tasco 6 cledge, clunch, kaolin 8 lifeless 9 inanimate
bed: 5 gault
box: 6 saggar, sagger
building: 5 adobe, tapia
casting: 4 slip
comb. form: pel 7 argillo 10 argillaceo
constituent: 7 alumina
covered with: 6 lutose
deposit: 4 marl
fragment: bat
friable: 4 bole
layer: 4 lias 5 sloam
lump: 4 clag, clod
made of: 7 fictile
mineral: 7 nacrite
mold: dod
musical instrument: 7 ocarina
pert. to: 5 bolar
piece: 4 tile
pottery: 6 kaolin 7 kaoline
tropical: 8 laterite

claybrained: 4 dull 6 stupid

clayey: 5 bolar, heavy, malmy, marly 6 cledgy, lutose 9 argillous 12 argillaceous

clead: 6 attire, clothe

cleam: 4 daub 5 smear, stick 6 adhere 7 plaster

clean: fay, fey, hoe, mop 4 dust, fair, pure, smug, swab, trim, wash, wipe 5 bream, clear, curry, empty, feigh, grave, scour, scrub, smart 6 chaste, clever, kosher, purify 7 apinoid, cleanse, clearly, furbish, perfect 8 absterge, brightly, dextrous, entirely, renovate, spotless, unsoiled 9 destitute, dexterous, guiltless, speckless, undefiled 10 immaculate 11 butterworth, untarnished 13 unadulterated
Hebrew: 6 kosher

cleaner: 4 soap 5 borax, purer 6 ramrod 8 cleanser 9 detergent 10 dentifrice
fish: 6 scaler

cleaning agent: 4 soap 5 borax 9 detergent

cleaning implement: mop 4 swab 5 broom 6 ramrod 7 sweeper

cleanly: 4 pure 6 adroit, artful, chaste 7 correct, elegant 8 innocent, skillful 9 dexterous

cleanse: 4 farm, heal, soap, wash 5 brush, clean, dight, purge, rinse, scour, scrub 6

purify, refine 7 baptize, clarify, deterge, sweeten 8 renovate
cleanser: lye 10 clarifiant
cleansing: 4 bath 7 abluent, clysmic, washing 8 ablution, lavation 9 acquittal, cathartic, detergent 10 emundation 12 purification
cleansing agent: 4 soap 5 borax
cleansing process: 4 bath 7 washing
clear: net, rid 4 free, gain, open, over, pure, quit 5 atrip, breme, brent, clean, lucid, plain, prune, sharp, vivid 6 acquit, assoil, bright, candid, clever, exempt, fluted, limpid, lucent, patent, purify, settle, smooth 7 absolve, clarion, clarify, crystal, deliver, evident, glaring, graphic, lighten, obvious, release 8 apparent, brighten, definite, distinct, explicit, manifest, pellucid, revelant 9 cloudless, discharge, disengage, elucidate, enigmatic, exculpate, exonerate, extricate, vindicate 10 unconfused 11 disentangle, perspicuous, transparent 12 intelligible
as crystal: 7 evident, obvious
away: fay, fey 5 feigh 6 dispel 8 evacuate 9 eliminate, expurgate
out: 6 decamp, desert
up: 5 solve 6 settle
clear-cut: 5 lucid, sharp 7 concise 8 definite, distinct, incisive 9 chiselled 10 unconfused
clear-sighted: 10 discerning 13 perspicacious
clearing: *in woods:* 5 glade, tract 8 slashing
of land: 4 sart 6 assart
cleat: 4 bitt 5 block, chock, kevel, wedge 6 batten 7 bollard, coxcomb, support 9 butterbur
cleavage: 7 fission, fissure 8 division 9 partition 10 separation
cleave: cut, rip 4 chop, hold, join, link, part, rely, rend, rift, rive, slit, tear 5 break, carve, chawn, chine, clave, cleft, cling, clove, crack, sever, shear, split, stick 6 adhere, bisect, cohere, divide, pierce, sunder 7 dispart, fissure 8 separate
cleaver: ax; axe 4 froe, frow
cleche: 4 urde 5 urdee 11 cross-shaped
cleek: 4 club, hook, link 5 crook, pluck, seize 6 clutch, snatch 8 fishhook
clef: key 9 character
bass: eff
treble: gee
cleft: gap 4 chap, chop, fent, flaw, reft, rift, rima, rive 5 break, chasm, chawn, chink, clove, crack, crena, riven, split 6 breach, cleave, cloven, cranny, crotch, divide, recess 7 crevice, divided, fissure, opening 8 aperture, fracture
cleft-lip: 7 harelip
cleg: 4 gleg 6 gadfly 8 horsefly
Cleite: *father:* 6 Merops
husband: 7 Cyzicus
clem: 4 riot 5 brawl, fight 6 clútch, starve, thirst
clemency: 4 pity 5 mercy 6 lenity 7 quarter 8 kindness, leniency, mildness 10 compassion, indulgence
clement: 4 mild, soft, warm 6 gentle 7 lenient 8 merciful 9 forgiving 13 compassionate
clench: 4 fist, grip, grit, hold 5 brace, clasp, clint, close, grasp 6 clinch, clutch 9 interlock 10 strengthen
cleome: 5 caper
Cleopatra: *attendant:* 4 Iras 8 Charmian
killer: asp
lover: 6 Antony, Caesar 10 Mark Antony
river: 4 Nile
sister: 7 Arsinoe
Cleopatra's Needle: 7 obelisk
clepe: bid, cry 4 call, name 5 shout 6 appeal, invite, ínvoke, summon 7 address, mention
clepsydra: 5 clock
clergy: 4 cloth 9 clergyman
body of: 6 pulpit 7 college
clergyman: 4 abba, abbe, dean, Papa 5 canon, clerk, padre, pilot, prior, rabbi, vicar 6 bishop, cleric, curate, deacon, divine, domine, parson, pastor, priest, rector 7 cassock, prelate 8 cardinal, chaplain, minister, preacher, reverend 9 blackcoat, dignitary, presbyter 12 ecclesiastic
office: 4 cure 6 curacy 8 ministry 9 pastorate, priorship, rectorate
residence: 5 manse 6 priory 8 vicarage 9 parsonage
clergywoman: nun 8 rectress 9 priestess 10 religieuse
cleric: See **clergyman**
clerical clothing: alb 5 rabat, stole, amice, cloth, fanon, orale 6 collar 7 biretta
clerk: nun 4 monk 5 agent, write 6 cleric, commis, hermit, layman, priest, scribe, teller, yeoman 7 carcoon, compose, gomasta, scholar 8 employee, greffier(F.), recorder, salesman 9 assistant, clergyman, registrar 10 accountant 11 salesperson 12 ecclesiastic
court: 11 protonotary 12 prothonotary
passenger ship: 6 purser
clerkly: 7 learned, scribal 9 scholarly
cletch: 5 brood 6 clique, clutch, family 8 hatching
cleuch: 5 cleft 6 clough, ravine 7 descent
cleve, cleeve: 4 brae 5 cliff 8 hillside
clever: apt, sly 4 able, cute, deft, fine, gnib, hend, keen 5 agile, alert, clean, clear, handy, hende, lithe, quick, slick, smart,

witty 6 active, adroit, artful, astute, bright, expert, habile, heppen, neatly, nimble, pretty, shrewd 7 amiable, cunning, parlous 8 dextrous, handsome, obliging, skillful, talented 9 dexterous, ingenious 10 well-shaped 11 clean-limbed, dexterously, intelligent

cleverness: can 4 tact 5 skill 6 esprit 9 dexterity, ingenuity 10 adroitness, astuteness

clevis: 4 hake 5 copse 6 muzzle 7 fitting 10 connection

clew, clue: 4 ball, hint 5 globe, glome, skein 6 hurdle, thread

cliche: 6 truism 7 bromide 8 banality

click: 4 pawl, tick 5 agree, catch 6 detent 7 ratchet

click beetle: 6 elater

client: 5 ceile 6 patron 7 patient 8 customer, henchman, retainer 9 dependent

clientele: 9 following

cliff: hoe 4 crag, hill, rock, scar 5 bluff, cleve, heuch, heugh, scarp, shore, slope 6 cleeve, height 7 clogwyn 8 hillside, palisade 9 precipice

cliff-hanger: 8 suspense 9 melodrama

climate: 4 mood 6 region, temper 8 attitude 9 condition

climax: cap, top 4 acme, apex, near, peak, shut 5 mount, scale, tight 6 apogee, ascend, finish, opogee, summit, zenith 9 gradation 11 culmination

climb: gad 4 ramp, rise, shin 5 creep, grimp, mount, scale, speed(Sc.), twine 6 ascend, ascent, shinny 7 clamber

climb down: 7 descend 8 dismount

climb on: 5 mount, scale

climber: 6 rigger, scaler 11 mountaineer 12 alpenstocker

climbing device: 6 ladder

climbing plant: ivy 4 vine 5 liana, liane 7 creeper

clime: See **climate**

clinamen: 4 bias, turn 5 twist

clinch: fix, get, hug 4 bind, grip, nail, seal 5 clamp, cling, clink, clint, grasp, rivet, seize 6 clench, clutch, fasten, secure, snatch 7 confirm, embrace, grapple, scuffle 8 complete, conclude, holdfast 9 establish

cling: hug 4 bank, hang, hold, rely 5 clasp, stick, trust 6 adhere, cleave, clinch, cohere, depend, fasten, shrink, wither 7 cherish, embrace, shrivel 8 contract 9 persevere

clingfish: 6 testar

clink: ale, jug, put, rap 4 beat, blow, brig, cash, clap, coin, jail, move, ring, slap 5 latch, money, rhyme, seize 6 clinch, jingle, lockup, moment, prison, strike, tinkle 7 instant 9 assonance 10 guardhouse

clinker: 4 slag 5 waste

clinquant: 5 clink, showy 6 tinsel 8 tinseled 10 glittering

Clio's sister: 5 Erato

clip: bob, cut, dod, hug, lip, lop, mow, nip 4 barb, chip, coll, crop, dock, dodd, hold, pace, pare, poll, snip, trim 5 clasp, force, prune, shear 6 clutch, fasten, hinder, holder 7 curtain, curtail, embrace, scissor, shorten 8 diminish, encircle 9 encompass 10 abbreviate

clipper: 4 boat, ship 6 vessel 7 shearer, workman

clique: cot, mob, set 4 bloc, clan, club, gang, ring 5 cabal, group, junto, write 6 circle, cletch 7 coterie, faction 8 conclave, sodality 9 camarilla 11 combination

clit: 5 caked, close, heavy 6 doughy, sticky

clitter: 5 noise 6 rattle 7 chatter 10 stridulate

cloaca maxima: 5 drain, sewer

cloak: aba 4 brat, capa, cape, hide, mant, mask, pall, rail, robe, veil, wrap 5 capot, cover, guise, manta, manto, sagum 6 assume, bautta, capote, caster, chapel, dolman, mantle, mantua, pharos, screen, serape, shield, shroud, tabard, visite 7 bavaroy, chlamys, conceal, garment, manteau, manteel, pelisse, pretext, shelter, zimarra 8 albornoz, burnoose, disguise, intrigue, mantilla, palliate 9 dissemble 10 roquelaure 11 portmanteau

African: 5 jelab 6 jellab

Arabian: 7 feridgi, ferigee, ferijee 8 feridjee

baptismal: 7 chrisom

bishop's: 10 mantelleta

ecclesiastical: 4 cope

Greek: 6 abolla 7 chlamys

hooded: 6 camail

Indian: 5 choga

Jewish: 6 kittel 9 gaberdine

large-sleeved: 10 witzchoura

loose: 5 palla

monk's: 8 analabos

Punjabi: 5 choga

Roman: 5 sagum 7 alicula, paenula

Roman military: 10 paludament 11 paludamenta(pl.) 12 paludamentum

sleeveless: aba 6 dolman 7 paenula

Spanish: 4 capa 5 manta 6 mantle

worn over armor: 6 tabard

cloam: 4 daub 8 crockery 11 earthenware

clobber: 4 beat 5 patch, pound, smear 6 cobble, defeat, strike

cloche: hat, jar 4 bell 5 cover

clocher: 6 belfry 9 bell tower, campanile

clock: nef 4 bell, call, dial, gong, time 5 cluck, hatch, hurry, meter, watch 6 beetle, Big Ben, crouch 8 horologe, incubate, ornament, recorder 9 clepsydra, hourglass,

indicator, taximeter, timepiece 11 chronometer, speedometer
ancient water: 9 clepsydra
astronomical: 8 sidereal
maker: 9 horologer 10 horologist
part of: 4 dial 5 bundy 6 detent, foliot 8 pendulum, recorder
regulating body: 8 pendulum 10 escapement
ship-shaped: nef
weight: 5 peise
clocker: 5 timer 8 railbird 11 embroiderer
clockmaker: 9 horologer
clockwise: 6 deasil, dessil 7 deiseal 8 positive
clod: sod 4 clat, clot, dolt, dull, lout, lump, turf 5 clout, clown, divot, earth, glebe, gross, knoll, yokel 6 ground, stupid 7 bumpkin 9 coagulate 10 clodhopper
cloddish: 5 gross 6 stupid 7 boorish
clodhopper: 4 boor, clod, shoe 6 rustic 7 plowman
clodpate: 4 clot, dolt, fool 7 ramhead 8 clodpole, clodpoll, imbecile 9 blockhead
clog: gum, jam, log 4 clag, clam, cloy, curb, load, lump, shoe, skid, stop 5 block, check, choke, dance, sabot 6 adhere, burden, chopin, fetter, galosh, hamper, hobble, impede, pattern, remora, sandal, secque, weight 7 galoshe, perplex, shackle, trammel 8 coalesce, encumber, obstruct, overshoe, restrain 9 embarrass, hindrance, restraint 10 difficulty 11 encumbrance
with mud: 4 daub 6 daggle
cloggy: 5 heavy, lumpy 6 sticky
clogwyn: 5 cliff 9 precipice
cloister: 4 hall, stoa 5 abbey, aisle, stoae(pl.) 6 arcade, friary, immure, piazza, priory 7 closter, convent, nunnery 9 cloistral, enclosure, hermitage, monastery, sanctuary 11 ambulatoria(pl.) 12 ambulatorium
pert. to: 9 claustral, cloistral
Cloister and the Hearth author: 5 Reade
cloistered: 7 recluse 11 sequestered
cloistress: nun 10 religieuse(Fr.)
cloof, clufe: 4 claw, hoof 6 cleave
clop: 4 limp 5 sound 6 hobble
close: by; cap, end, hot 4 clit, firm, hard, hide, near, nigh, quit, seal, shut, slam, snug, stop 5 anear, block, cease, cheap, dense, finis, garth, gross, muggy, thick, tight 6 clause, clench, effect, expiry, finale, finish, narrow, nearby, period, stingy, strait 7 adjourn, compact, context, extreme, miserly, occlude, similar 8 accurate, adjacent, complete, conclude, familiar, imminent, intimate 9 barricade, extremity, niggardly, terminate 10 avaricious, conclusion 11 termination 12 parsimonious
a hawk's eyes: 4 seel
comb. form: 4 sten 5 steno
firmly: bar 4 lock, seal 5 tight 6 batten, cement
closefisted: 4 near 6 stingy 7 miserly 8 handfast 9 niggardly
closely: 4 just 6 almost, barely, narrow, nearly 9 compactly
closeness: 7 secrecy 8 fidelity, intimacy 9 parsimony, proximity 10 stinginess, strictness 11 conciseness, literalness 14 oppressiveness
closest: 4 next 7 nearest 9 proximate
closet: 4 ewry, room, safe 5 ambry, cuddy 6 armary, locker, pantry, secret 7 cabinet, conceal, private 8 conclave, cupboard, gardevin, wardrobe 9 gardevine 12 confidential
closing device: 4 lock 6 zipper
closure: end, gag 5 bound, limit 7 cloture 8 clausure 9 agreement, enclosure 10 conclusion 11 confinement, containment 12 entrenchment
clot: dot, gel 4 clag, clat, clod, gout, jell, lump, mass 5 clart, grume 6 balter, cotter 7 clodder, embolus, thicken 8 clodplate, coagulum, concrete, solidify 9 blockhead, coagulate 12 crassamentum
cloth (see also **fabric,** and names of individual fabrics: **cotton, linen, silk,** etc.): rag 5 bluet, toile(F.), tweed, twill 6 canvas, clergy, drapet, fabric, livery, napkin 7 acetate, drapery, garment, raiment, textile, worsted 8 dwelling, material, sheeting 10 cassinette
baptismal: 7 chrisom
bark: 4 tapa 9 tapa cloth
blemish: yaw 4 snag, tear 5 amper
camel's hair: aba 6 camlet
coarse: 4 duck 5 crash, gunny 6 burlap, linsey
crinkled: 5 crape, crepe 10 seersucker
dealer: 6 draper, mercer
decorative: see *ornamental* below
dryer: 6 tenter
dye method: tie 5 batik
figured: see *patterned* below
fine-textured: 4 mull, pima, silk 7 percale
finisher: 7 beetler
flaw in: 4 rase
flaxen: 5 linen
glazed: 5 tammy
goat's hair: 5 tibet 6 camlet, mohair
heavy: 9 petersham
hemp: 4 jute 5 gunny 6 baline, burlap, canamo

homespun: 4 kelt

instrument: 8 ringhead

knitted: 6 jersey, tricot

light: 6 tissue 7 challis, etamine

lining: 5 serge 8 sarcenet, sarsenet

measure: ell 4 nail

mesh: net 5 super, tulle 11 cheesecloth

metallic: 4 acca, tash

mourning: 5 crape, crepe

muslin: 5 adati

narrow: 4 tape 5 braid 6 edging, ribbon

old kind: 4 acca, tuke 5 tewke 6 samite

ornamental: 4 gimp, lace 6 lampas, riband 8 tapestry

poplin: 7 tabinet 8 tabbinet

print: 6 calico 7 percale

printer: 7 candroy

raised design: 7 brocade

remnant: 4 fent

ridge in: 4 wale

roll: 4 bolt

rug: mat 7 matting

satin: see **fabric**: *satin*

shop: 7 mercery

silk: see **fabric**: *silk*

soft: 5 panne, plush, surah 6 fleece 9 montagnac

stiff: 7 taffeta 9 crinoline

stretcher: 6 tenter

synthetic: 5 nylon, rayon 6 dacron 7 acetate

toweling: 5 terry

twilled: rep 4 jean 5 denim, serge

used as a dressing: 5 stupe

velvet: 5 panne

weatherproof: 4 tarp 6 canvas

woolen: 6 kersey

clothe: don, dub, rig, tog 4 deck, garb, gird, gown, robe, vest 5 adorn, array, clead, cleed, dress, endow, endue, frock 6 attire, enrobe, invest, swathe 7 address, apparel, vesture 8 accouter, accoutre 9 authorize, represent

clothes (see also **dress**): 4 duds, garb, gear, suit, tack, wear 5 habit 6 attire 7 apparel, baggage, costume, raiment, regalia, toggery, vesture 8 clothing, frippery, garments 9 vestments 10 bedclothes 11 habiliments

basket: 6 hamper

civilian: 5 mufti

dealer: 6 ragman 7 fripper 9 fripperer

informal: 5 smock 6 halter, shorts, slacks, trunks

pert. to: 8 vestiary 10 habilatory

presser: 7 sadiron

clothesmoth: 5 tinea

clothespress: 5 chest 7 armoire 8 wardrobe

clothing: (see also **garment**): 4 wear 6 attire 7 apparel

coarse: 4 brat 5 burel

protective: 5 armor

woman's: 6 fardel

cloud: fog, nue(F.) 4 blur, dust, haze, hide, mist 5 bedim, befog, gloom, nubia, stain, sully, swarm, taint, vapor 6 cirrus, damage, darken, deepen, defame, nebula, nimbus, screen, shadow, stigma 7 blacken, confuse, cumulus, eclipse, obscure, tarnish 8 overcast 9 obfuscate 10 overspread 11 thunderhead

comb. form: 5 nepho

kinds of: nue 4 rack, scud 6 cirrus, nebule, nimbus 7 cumulus, stratus, tornado 9 mare's tail

morning: 4 velo

pert. to: 7 nebular 12 nephological

study of: 9 nephology

wind-driven: 4 rack, scud

cloud-built: 4 airy 9 imaginary 13 unsubstantial

cloud-like: 7 nebular

cloudburst: 6 deluge 9 rainstorm

cloudless: 5 azure, clear 6 bright

cloudy: dim 4 dark, dull, hazy 5 filmy, foggy, misty, murky, shady 6 gloomy, lowery, opaque 7 blurred, clouded, nebular, obscure 8 confused, nubilous, overcast, vaporous 9 cloudlike 10 indistinct, lackluster

clough: 5 cleft 6 cleuch, cleugh, ravine, valley

clour: 4 blow, bump, dint 5 thump 6 batter

clout: bat, box, hit 4 beat, blow, bump, clod, club, cuff, join, mend, nail, slap, slug, swat 5 patch, smite 6 strike, target, thrash, washer 7 bandage 8 bosthoon 12 handkerchief

clouter: 7 botcher, cobbler

clove: gap 4 tree 5 cleft, spice 6 cleave, ravine

cloven: 5 cleft, split 9 bisulcate

cloven-footed: 8 fissiped

clover: red 5 lotus, medic, nardu 6 alsike, luxury, nardoo 7 alfalfa, comfort, lucerne, melilot, trefoil 10 prosperity

cloverleaf: fan 7 freeway 8 crossway

clown: hob, oaf 4 aper, boor, fool, goff, joey, lout, mime, mome, zany 5 churl, comic, mimer, punch, zanni(It.) 6 august, bodach, hobbil, jester, lubber, rustic, stooge 7 buffoon, bumpkin, peasant, playboy 8 merryman 9 harlequin, joculator 10 bufflehead, countryman, harlequina 11 merry-andrew, punchinello 13 pickle-herring

clown's allheal: 8 woudword 9 clownheal

clownish: raw 4 rude, zany 5 gawky, rough 6 clumsy, coarse, rustic 7 awkward, boorish, hoblike, ill-bred, loutish, uncivil 8 ungainly 9 untutored
cloy: 4 clog, glut, nail, pall, sate 5 gorge, prick 6 pierce 7 satiate, satisfy, surfeit
club: bat, hit, set 4 beat, cane, join, mace, maul, polt, team 5 billy, bunch, clout, kebby, lodge, order, staff, stick, unite, yokel 6 clique, cudgel, kebbie, menage, weapon 8 bludgeon, sorority, spontoon 9 blackjack, truncheon 10 fraternity, knobkerrie, shillelagh 11 association
famous: 5 Lambs 6 Friars 7 Garrick
kinds of: bat 4 arum, mere 5 billy, plant 6 nullah, tawkee, tawkin, taiaha 7 pantoon 8 spantoon, spontoon 9 blackjack, espantoon, truncheon 10 knobkerrie, pogamoggan 12 nullahnullah
social: 4 card 6 bridge, cercle 10 fraternity
woman's: 7 Sorosis 8 sorority
club moss: 8 buckhorn
club-shaped: 7 clavate
clubfoot: 7 talipes 9 deformity
clubfooted: 7 taliped
clubs: 4 suit 5 cards, basto
clubstart: 5 stoat
clubweed: 8 knapweed
cluck: hen 4 call, fuss 5 chuck, clack, click, clock, sound
clue: key, tip 4 ball, clew, hint, idea 5 guide, twine 6 thread 8 innuendo 10 indication, intimation, suggestion 11 fingerprint
clump: tod 4 blow, bush, heap, lump, mass, mott, tope, tuft 5 bunch, group, grove, patch, tread 6 clunch, dollop 7 cluster, thicket
clumsy: awk 4 numb, rude 5 blunt, bulky, gawky, hulky, inapt, inept, stiff 6 gauche 7 awkward, boorish, ill-made, unhandy 8 benumbed, bungling, clownish, footless, tactless, ungainly, unwieldy 9 lumbering, maladroit, misshapen 10 cumbersome 11 heavy-handed 13 inappropriate
clunch: 4 clay, lump 5 clump, lumpy 9 limestone
clung: 5 stiff 8 shrunken, starving 9 collapsed, shriveled, toughened
Cluny product: 4 lace
cluster: bog 4 bush, cyme, knot, lump, tuft 5 bunch, clump, group 7 bourock, cluther 8 fascicle 9 glomerule 10 collection 11 agglomerate, aggregation
fern spore: 4 sori(pl.) 5 sorus
fiber: nep
flower: 4 cime, cyme 5 ament, umbel 6 raceme 7 panicle 8 anthemia
flower-like: 7 rosette
growing in: 8 acervate
of seven stars: 8 Pleiades
clustered: 6 tufted 8 racemose 9 aciniform, aggregate, glomerate 10 coacervate
clutch: nab 4 clam, claw, clem, clip, fist, glam, grab, grip, nest 5 brood, catch, clasp, claut, cleek, glaum, grasp, gripe, hatch, lever, power, seize, talon 6 cleach, clench, cletch, clinch, retain, snatch 7 control 8 coupling
clutter: 4 mess 6 bustle 7 clatter 8 disorder 9 confusion 10 disarrange
Clymene's son: 5 Atlas
clyster: 5 enema 9 injection
Clytemnestra: *daughter:* 7 Electra
half-sister: 5 Helen
husband: 9 Agamemnon
mother: 4 Leda
paramour: 9 Aegisthus
son: 7 Orestes
cnemis: 4 shin 5 tibia 7 legging
coach: bus, car 4 hack, help 5 araba, cabin, prime, teach, train, tutor 6 advise, direct, fiacre(F.), saloon 7 adviser, prepare, tallyho 8 carriage, dormeuse 10 instructor, stagecoach
railway: 7 Pullman, sleeper
coach dog: 9 Dalmatian
coachman: fly 4 fish, jehu, whip 5 pilot 6 coachy, driver 7 coachee, coacher 8 yemschik
assistant: 10 postillion
Russian: 7 yamshik 8 yemschik 9 yamstchik
coadjuster: 6 bishop 7 partner 8 coworker 9 assistant, associate
coagulant: 6 rennet 7 styptic 8 gelatine
coagulate: gel, set 4 cake, clod, clot, curd, jell 5 quail 6 cotter, curdle, posset 7 clabber, congeal, thicken 8 solidify
coagulation: 4 gout 7 clotter
coal: 4 bass, fuel 5 chark, ember, gleed, stoke 6 carbon, cinder
agent: 6 fitter
bed: 4 seam
block: jud
carrying box: hod 7 scuttle
comb. form: 7 anthrac 8 anthraco
constituent: 4 goaf 6 carbon, ethene, phenol, pyrene 7 benzene 8 creosote 11 naphthalene
distillate: tar
dust: 4 coom, culm, smut, soot, swad 5 coomb
immature form of: 7 lignite
kind of: jud 4 dant, hard, soft 6 cannel 7 lignite 9 tasmanite 10 anthracite, bituminous
lump: cob
mine explosive: 9 Bobbinite

miner: 7 collier
miner's disease: 11 anthrocosis
mining implement: 7 breaker
oil: 8 kerosene
refuse: 4 coke, dust, slag 6 cinder 7 backing, clinker
size: cob, ett, nut, pea 4 lump 5 slack, stove 6 broken 8 chestnut 9 buckwheat
wagon: 4 corb, carf, tram
worker: 7 collier, geordie 8 chaffman
coal car part: 6 hopper
coalbin: 6 bunker
coalesce: mix 4 fuse, join 5 blend, merge, unite 6 embody 7 combine 10 amalgamate
coalescence: 5 union 6 fusion, league 11 combination
coalfish: sey 4 parr 5 cuddy 6 beshow, billet, cudden, podler, sarthe 7 baddock, glashan, pollack
coalition: 5 trust, union 6 fusion, league, merger 8 alliance 11 combination, confederacy, conjunction 13 confederation
coarse: low, raw 4 dank, hard, hash, lowd, loud, rank, rude, vile 5 bawdy, broad, crass, crude, dirty, gross, harsh, heavy, loose, randy, routh, thick 6 brutal, callow, common, earthy, impure, ribald, rustic, vulgar 7 blatant, fulsome, goatish, obscene, raucous, sensual 8 clownish, homespun, immodest, indecent, unchaste 9 inelegant, offensive, unrefined 10 boisterous, indelicate, unpolished
coast: 4 bank, land, ripa 5 beach, blide, shore, slide 6 adjoin, border, rivage, strand 7 seaside 8 approach, seaboard, seashore
area: 7 seaside 8 seacoast 9 coastline, shoreline
dweller: 7 orarian
pert. to: 7 coastal, orarian 8 littoral, riparian
projection: 4 cape, ness 8 headland 9 peninsula
Coast Guard: *boat:* 6 cutter
service-woman: 4 Spar
coaster: mat 4 sled 5 trout 8 toboggan 9 container
coat (see also **cloak**): 4 bark, daub, husk, rind, zinc 5 cloth, cover, crust, glaze, habit, layer, paint, plate, shell, terve 6 enamel, jacket, mantle, parget, pelage, veneer 7 garment, incrust, overlay, plaster, vesture 8 membrane, tegument 9 petticoat 10 integument
animal: fur 4 hair, hide, wool 6 pelage
fastener: 4 frog 6 button
Irish: 9 coatamore
kind of: pea 4 cape, jupe, mail, robe, sack, toga 5 armor, simar, tails 6 coatie, duster, jerkin, kirtle, mantle, reefer, rocket, topper 7 cassock, cutaway, haubeck, paletot, pelisse, surcoat, curcote, surtout 8 benjamin, mackinaw, overcoat 9 gaberdine, newmarket, redingote 12 chesterfield
neck: 6 george
part: 4 cuff 5 lapel, skirt 6 collar, george, pocket, sleeve
seaman's: 5 grego
soldier's: 5 tunic
coat of arms: 5 crest
pert. to: 8 heraldic
coati: 5 nasua 6 animal, narica
coating: 4 aril, film 6 patina, veneer 8 mucilage
coax: beg, coy, pet 4 cant, dupe, fawn, lure, urge 5 tease 6 cajole, cuitle, entice 7 beguile, cuittle, flatter, implore, wheedle 8 blandish, collogue, inveigle, persuade 9 influence 10 manipulate
coaxial: 12 conterminous
cob: ear, mew 4 beat, blow, gull, loaf, lump, mole, mule, pier, pony, swan, toss 5 block, break, chief, cnool, horse, outdo, piece, stump, throw, thump 6 basket, cobnut, leader, muffin, peapod, spider, strike 7 beating, seagull, surpass, threash 8 dumpling 10 breakwater
cobber: pal 4 chum, mate 6 friend 9 companion
tool: awl
cobble: 4 darn, make, mend, pave 5 botch, patch, stone 6 bungle, repair 7 clobber 11 cobblestone
cobbler: pie 4 snob 5 sheep, soler, sutor 6 souter 7 botcher, catfish, crispin, dessert, pompano, saddler 8 chuckler, scorpion 9 killifish, shoemaker
pitch: 4 code
cobbra: 4 head 5 skull
cobby: 5 stout 6 hearty, lively, stocky 10 headstrong
cobia: 4 fish 6 bonito
cobra: asp, nag 4 naga, naja 5 snake, viper 6 uraeus
genus: 4 naja
tree: 5 mamba
cobweb: net 4 trap 5 snare, wevet 8 gossamer 9 intricacy
cocaine: 4 snow 8 alkaloid, narcotic 10 anesthetic
source: 4 coca
Cochin-China: See **Vietnam**
cochleate: 6 spiral
cock: tap 4 bank, fowl, heap, kora, pile, rick 5 fugie, fight, gallo, shock, stack, strut, valve, yowle 6 faucet, leader 7 chicken, contend, gorcock, rooster, swagger 8 gamecock, malemass 10 cockalorum 11 chanticleer

gun: nab
cock-a-hoop: 4 awry 6 elated, lively 8 boastful, cockeyed
cock-and-bull story: lie 6 canard
cockade: 4 knot 5 badge 7 rosette
Cockade State: 8 Maryland
Cockaigne: 6 utopia 8 paradise
cockatoo: ara 5 arara, cocky, galah, macaw 6 abacay, cockie, parrot 8 calangay, gang-gang
genus: 7 cacatua, kakatoe
cockatrice: 7 serpent 8 basilisk
cockboat: cog 7 rowboat
cockchafer: 6 beetle
cocker: dog, pet 4 shoe 6 coddle, fondle, pamper, quiver, reaper 7 fighter, indulge, legging, nurture, spaniel
cockerel: 4 cock 6 bantam
cocket: 4 join, pert, seal 5 bread, brisk, merry, saucy 6 lively 7 mortise 8 document
cockeyed: 4 alop, awry 5 askew
cockfight: 4 game, spar 5 match 7 contest
cockfighting: 13 alectryomachy
cockhorse: 5 lofty, proud 7 astride, upstart 8 exultant
cockle: 4 boat, gall, gith, kiln, oast 5 bulge, shell, stove 6 darnel, pucker, ripple, wabble 7 mollusk, wrinkle 9 whimsical
cocklebur: 5 plant 7 burdock
cockpit: pit 4 ring, rink, well 5 arena, cabin, field 7 gallera
cocksure: 4 sure 5 cocky 8 confident
cocktail: 5 Bronx, drink 7 apertif, martini, sidecar 8 daiquiri 9 appetizer, Manhattan
cocky: 4 pert 6 crouse, farmer, jaunty 8 arrogant 9 conceited
cocoa, coco: 4 head, palm, tary 5 broma 6 yuntia 9 chocolate
cocoanut: 7 coquito
dried meat: 5 copra
fiber: 4 coir, kyar
cocoon: pod 4 clew, clue 5 shell 11 incunabulum
cod: bag, cor, pod 4 axle, bank, cusk, fish, fool, hoax, husk, rock 5 belly, pouch, scrod, torsk 6 burbot, codger, cultus, fellow, pillow 7 bacaloa, cushion
family: 7 gadidae
genus: 5 gadus
young: 5 scrod, sprag 7 codling
cod-like: bib 4 hake, ling 5 gadus
coda: 4 part 5 rondo 6 finale 10 conclusion
coddle: pet 4 baby, cade, cook 5 humor, nurse, spoil 6 caress, cocker, cotton, fondle, pamper 7 parboil
code: law 4 flag 5 canon, codex 6 cipher, digest, secret, signal 7 precept
inventor: 5 Morse
message: 6 cipher 10 cryptogram
coded message: 10 cryptogram
codex: 4 code 5 annal 9 formulary 10 manuscript
codfish: See cod
codger: cod 5 churl, crank, miser 6 fellow 7 niggard
codicil: 5 rider 6 sequel 8 appendix
codify: 5 index 6 digest 8 classify 11 systematize
coehorn: 6 mortar
Coelebs: 8 bachelor
coelenterate: 5 polyp 8 cnidaria
coerce: cow 4 curb, make 5 bully, check, drive, force 6 compel 7 concuss, enforce, repress 8 bludgeon, bulldoze, restrain, restrict 9 blackmail, constrain, terrorize 10 intimidate
coercion: 5 force 6 duress
Coeus' daughter: 4 Leto
coeval: 12 contemporary
coffee: *after dinner:* 9 demitasse
alkaloid: 7 caffein
bean: nib
beverage: Rio 4 Java, Kona 5 Milds, Mocha 6 Bogota, Brazil, Santos 7 Sumatra 8 Medellin 9 Maracaibo
maker: urn 5 silex
refuse: 6 triage
coffee house: inn 4 cafe
coffeeberry: 6 jojoba 7 cascara, soybean 8 peaberry 9 buckthorn, chaparral
coffeepot: 6 biggin 9 cafetiere
coffer: ark, box, dam 5 chest, hutch, trunk 6 casket, forcer, trench 7 caisson 8 ciborium, standard
coffin: 4 bier, case, cist, mold 6 basket, casing, casket 11 sarcophagus
cloth: 4 pall 5 cloak
support: 4 bier
cog: cam, lie 4 gear, jest 5 catch, cheat, cozen, tenon, tooth, trick, wedge, wheel 6 cajole 7 deceive, produce, quibble, wheedle 8 cockboat 9 fabricate, falsehood
cogent: 5 valid 6 potent, strong 7 telling 8 forcible, powerful 9 trenchant 10 conclusive, convincing, legitimate, persuasive
cogitate: 4 mull, muse, plan 5 think 6 ponder 7 connate, reflect 8 consider, meditate
cognate: kin 4 akin 5 alike 6 allied 7 kindred, related, similar 8 bandhava, relative
cognizance: ken 4 heed, mark 5 badge, crest 6 emblem, notice 7 bearing, cockade 9 knowledge 11 observation, recognition 12 apprehension
cognizant: 4 onto, ware 5 awake, aware 8 sensible 9 conscious 10 conversant 11 intelligent 12 apprehensive
cognize: 4 know 8 perceive 9 recognize

cognomen (see also **name**): 4 name 6 byname 7 agnomen, surname 8 nickname, patronym 11 appellation
cohabit: 4 live 5 dwell 6 occupy 8 accustom 9 accompany
coheir: 8 parcener 10 coparcener
cohere: fit 4 glue, suit 5 agree, cling, stick, unite 6 adhere, cement, cleave 7 connect 8 coincide 9 glutinate
coherence: 5 union 8 cohesion 9 congruity 10 accordance, connection, continuity 11 consistency
cohort: 4 band 7 company
coif, coiffe: cap 4 hood 6 beggin, burlet, hairdo 7 arrange 8 skullcap 9 headdress
coiffure: 6 hairdo 9 headdress
coign: 5 wedge 6 corner 8 position 10 projection
coil: ado, wip 4 ansa, clew, curl, fuss, hank, loop, roll, wind 5 helix, querl, tense, twine, twist 6 rundle, spiral, tumult, windup 7 haycock, ringlet, trouble 8 encircle 9 confusion, encounter 10 difficulty 11 convolution
electric: 6 teaser
coilet: 7 sinuous, tortile
coin: die, ori 4 cash, dime, make, mint 5 angle, brown, chink, clink, metal, money, quoin, shape, stamp, token, wedge 6 change, corner, create, invent, specie, strike 7 convert 8 currency 9 fabricate, neologize, originate 11 cornerstone
ancient: 4 obol 6 obolus
box: pyx 4 till 5 meter 8 register
collector: 11 numismatist
copper: 4 cent 5 penny, bodle, brown
counterfeit: 9 brummagem
difference: 5 value 11 seigniorage
edge corrugation: 7 reeding
front: 4 head 7 obverse
imperfectly minted: 8 brockage
kind of: lap, ora 4 dime, doit, mite, rial, rosa 5 cuyne, daric, disme, ducat, eagle, groat 6 bawbee, beaver, besant, bezant, cunzie 7 bezzant, carolus, crocard, louleau 8 bezantee, crockard 10 castellano
pert. to: 10 numismatic 12 numismatical
reverse side: 4 tail 5 verso
roll: 7 rouleau
science: 11 numismatics
silver: 4 batz, dime, dump, pina, tara 5 bezzo 6 tester, teston
stamper: 4 mill
weight: 6 shekel
coin new words: 9 neologize
coinage: 7 fiction, mintage
collector: 11 numismatist
coincide: gee 4 jibe 5 agree, tally 6 concur 9 harmonize 10 correspond
coincidence: 9 concourse 11 concurrence 12 concomitance, simultaneity
coincident: 4 even 8 together 9 consonant 10 concurrent 11 concomitant 12 contemporary 15 contemporaneous
coiner of new words: 9 neologian, neologist
coistrel: 4 base 6 menial, varlet 7 servile, soldier
coition: 7 meeting 10 attraction 11 conjunction
cojuror: 12 compurgator
coke: ask 4 coal, core, dope 5 chark 7 cocaine
cokes: 4 gull 9 simpleton
col: 4 pass 10 depression
colander: 5 sieve 7 utensil 8 strainer
colate: 6 filter, strain
Colchean: See **Colchis**
Colchis: *king:* 6 Aeetes
princess: 5 Medea
cold: flu 4 dead, dull 5 algid, bleak, frore, gelid, rheum, virus 6 arctic, chilly, frigid, frosty, wintry 7 catarrh, chilled, distant, glacial 8 reserved, rhigosis, unheated 9 apathetic, cheerless 10 insensible, spiritless 11 hyperborean, indifferent, unemotional 12 unresponsive 13 dispassionate, marblehearted 15 undemonstrative
comb. form: 4 cryo 5 frigo
pert. to: icy 5 gelid 6 frigid, frozen 10 frigorific
remedy: 13 antihistamine
cold and damp: raw 4 dank 5 bleak
cold-blooded: 7 callous 9 unfeeling 14 poikilothermal
cold feet: 4 fear 5 doubt 9 cowardice 12 apprehension
cold mist: 4 drow
cold-shoulder: 4 snub 6 ignore, rebuff
cold steel: 5 sword 6 dagger 7 bayonet
cold sweat: 4 fear 5 shock 11 trepidation
colder: 4 husk 6 refuse 7 rubbish
coleopthera insect: 6 beetle, insect, weevil
Coleridge's sacred river: 4 Alph
colewort: 4 cole, kale 7 cabbage
colic: 10 mulligrubs
coliseum: 4 hall 7 stadium, theater 8 building 12 amphitheater
coll: hug 4 clip, poll 5 prune 7 embrace
collaborate: aid 9 cooperate
collagen: 7 protein 10 albuminoid
collapse: 4 cave, fall, fold 5 crash, slump, wreck 6 bust-up 7 crumple, debacle, deflate, failure, flummox, smashup 8 contract, downfall 9 breakdown, telescope 11 prostration
collar: nab 4 band, eton, gill, grab, ring, ruff 5 chain, fichu, ruche, seize 6 bertha, gor-

get, tackle, torque 7 capture, chignon, circlet, shackle 8 cincture, neckband, necklace 9 neckpiece
horse: 6 hounce
jeweled: 8 carcanet
kind of: 4 ruff 5 fanon, orale, phano, ruche, rabat 6 cangue, carcan, rabato, rebato, 7 bargham, panuelo, 8 carcanet 10 chevesaile
collar cell: 10 choanocyte
collarbone: 8 clavicle
collared monad: 16 choanoflagellate
collate: 6 bestow, confer, verify 7 compare, emamine
collateral: 4 side 8 indirect, parallel, security 9 ancillary 10 subsidiary 11 accidential, concomitant, subordinate
collation: tea 4 meal 5 lunch 6 repast, sermon 7 address, reading 8 dejeuner, parallel, treatise 10 collection, comparison, conference 12 consultation, contribution
collator: 6 critic 7 machine
colleague: 4 aide, ally 5 unite 6 deputy 7 adjunct, consort, partner 8 confrere, conspire 9 assistant, associate
collect: tax 4 call, heap, levy, pile, pool, save 5 amass, glean, group, hoard, raise 6 accoil, accrue, confer, garner, gather, muster, prayer, sheave 7 compile, engross, impound 8 assemble, contract 9 aggregate 10 accumulate, congregate 11 agglomerate
collected: 4 calm, cool 5 sober 6 serene 8 composed 9 aggregate, clustered 10 coacervate 11 agglomerate 13 dispassionate
collection: ana 4 bevy, clan, olio 5 batch, group, store, suite 6 bundle, conger, sorite 8 assembly, caboodle 9 aggregate, anthology, collation, repertory 10 assemblage, assortment, cancionero
literary: ana 7 library 8 analects
miscellaneous: 4 olio 6 fardel
poems: 5 divan, sylva 9 anthology 10 cancionero
proper names: 11 onomasticon
wild animals: zoo 9 menagerie
collector: *bird egg:* 8 oologist
book: 11 bibliophile
coin: 11 numismatist
item: 5 curio 11 collectible
stamp: 11 philatelist
collectorship: 5 staff 6 office 9 residence 12 jurisdiction
colleen: 4 girl, lass, miss 5 belle 6 damsel, lassie, maiden
college (see also **university**): 5 lycee 6 school 7 academy 8 seminary 10 assemblage, university 11 institution 12 organization
accounts: 6 battel
building: gym, lab
campus: 4 quad 10 quadrangle
course: 5 major, minor 7 seminar
court: 4 quad
degree: A.B., B.A., B.S., C.E., D.D., M.A., M.D., M.S.; B.L.S., B.Sc., LL.B., LL.D., M.Sc., S.C.B., Ph.D. 5 Litt.D.
girl: 4 coed
graduate: 6 alumna, doctor, master 7 alumnus 8 bachelor
kind of: 9 electoral
living quarters: 4 dorm, hall
official: 4 dean 5 prexy 6 beadle, bursar, regent 7 proctor 9 president, registrar
pert. to: 8 academic 10 collegiate
professor: don 6 docent, doctor
session: lab 5 class 7 lecture, seminar 8 tutorial
student group: 4 frat 8 sorority 10 fraternity
term: 8 semester
treasurer: 6 bursar
tree: elm
U.S. oldest: 7 Harvard
U.S. woman's oldest: 9 Mt. Holyoke
collet: 4 band, ring 5 chuck 6 casing, circle, collar, flange, socket 7 bushing, ferrule 8 neckband
collide: hit, ram 4 bump, dash, hurt 5 clash, crash, wreck 6 hurtle, strike
collier: fly 4 boat 5 miner 6 plover, vessel 7 geordie
boy: 6 hodder
lung disease: 11 anthracosis
colliery: 4 mine
collieshangie: row 5 brawl 6 uproar 7 quarrel 8 squabble 11 disturbance
colliquate: 4 melt 7 liquefy
collision: 5 clash, crash, shock 7 smashup 8 clashing 9 encounter 10 opposition, percussion 12 interference
collocate: set 5 place 7 arrange
collogue: 4 coax, talk 5 gloze 6 confer 7 collude, flatter, wheedle 8 conspire, intrigue 12 conversation
colloquial: 8 familiar, informal 9 unstudied 14 conversational
colloquy: 4 chat, talk 6 parley 8 dialogue 9 discourse 10 conference 12 conversation
colluctation: 8 struggle 10 contention
collude: 4 plot 6 scheme 7 connive 8 collogue, conspire
collusion: 6 deceit 7 cahoots, secrecy 9 agreement 10 connivance
law: 5 covin
collusive: 8 covinous 10 fraudulent
colly: 4 dust, smut, soot 5 black, grime, sooty 9 blackbird
coloboma: 6 defect 7 fissure

Cologne: *German spelling:* 4 Koln
king: 6 Caspar, Jaspar
Colombia: *city:* 4 Cali 5 Neiva, Pasto, Tunja 6 Bogota(C.), Cucuta, Ibaque, Quibdo 7 Leticia, Popayan 8 Medellin 9 Cartagena, Manizales, San Andres 10 Santa Maria 11 Bucaramanga 12 Barranquilla 13 Villavicencio
coin: 4 peso, real 6 condor, peseta 7 centavo
gulf: 6 Darien
Indian: 5 Boros 6 Betoya, Chitas, Tahami, Yahuna 7 Tunebos 8 Guacicos, Morcotes, Pedrazas, Quimbaya, Sinsigas
mahogany: 7 albarco
measure: 4 vara 7 celemin
plant: 5 yocco
province: 5 Cauca, Choco, Huila, Valle 6 Boyaca, Caldas, Narina, Tolima, Vaupes 7 Bolivar 9 Antioquia, Atlantico, Magdalena, Santander 12 Cundinamarca
river: 4 Sinu, Tomo 6 Atrato, Atroto, Pattia, Yapura 7 Putumay 8 Guaviara 9 Magdalena
seaport: 6 Lorica 9 Cartagena 10 Santa Marta 12 Barranquilla
volcano: 5 Huila, Pasto 6 Purace
weight: bag 4 saco 5 carga, libra 7 quilate, quintal
colon: 4 coin 6 farmer 7 planter 8 colonist 10 husbandman
colonial teak: 8 flindosa
colonist: 5 colon 7 pioneer, settler 8 emigrant
colonize: 5 found 6 gather, settle 7 migrate 9 establish
colonizer: ant 6 oecist 7 settler
colonnade: row 4 stoa 7 pergola, portico, terrace 9 peristyle
colony: 5 swarm 9 community 10 dependency, settlement
colophon: 6 device, emblem
colophonite: 6 garnet 9 andradite
colophony: 5 resin, rosin
color (see also next entry): dye, hue 4 blee, cast, flag, tint, tone 5 badge, blush, paint, shade, stain, tenne, tinge 6 banner, ensign, redden 7 distort, pennant, pigment 8 standard, tincture 10 complexion
achromatic: 4 gray 5 black, white
change: 8 iridesce, opalesce
dull: dun 4 drab 5 terne
full of: 9 chromatic
graduation: 5 shade
healthy: tan
light: 4 tint
line of: 6 streak
malachite: 4 bice
mat white: 9 alabaster
mulberry: 7 morello
neutral: 4 ecru, gray 5 beige, black, white
painter: 6 Titian
pale: 6 pastel
primary: red 4 blue 5 black, green, white 6 yellow
quality: 4 tone
secondary: 5 green 6 orange, purple
shade of difference: 6 nuance
unhealthy: 6 sallow
uniform in: 4 flot
value: see *quality* above
varying: 10 iridescent, opalescent
color: For colors see their names: **red, green, purple,** etc.; for shades see main color. EXAMPLES: "reddish brown": see **brown;** "grayish green": see **green.**
color bar: 11 segregation 14 discrimination
color blindness: 9 Daltonism 13 achromatopsia 14 monochromatism
color organ: 8 clavilux
color photography inventor: 4 Ives
Colorado: *army camp:* 6 Carson
city: 5 Aspen, Delta, Lamar 6 Denver, Meeker, Pueblo 7 Alamosa, Boulder, Greeley, Manassa 8 Trinidad 10 Walsenburg
county: Ada 4 Baca, Bent, Mesa, Park, Weld, Yuma 5 Adams, Grand, Kiowa, Logan, Otero, Ouray 6 Custer, Denver, Elbert, Moffat 7 Conejos, Crowley, Dolores, Douglas, Jackson, Lincoln, Prowers 8 Arapahoe 9 Archuleta, Montezuma
fort: 5 Logan
Indian: Ute 8 Arapahoe
mountain: Oso 5 Eolus 7 Massive
mountain pass: 6 Alpine 7 Fremont 8 Marshall 9 Argentine, Tennessee 10 Cottonwood
mountain range: Elk 4 Book, Park, Roan 5 Raton 7 Sawatch
park: 5 Estes 9 Mesa Verde
peak: Oso 4 Yale 5 Baldy, Ethel, Evans, Grays, James, Pikes 6 Castle, Elbert, Long's, Maroon 7 Audubon, Harvard, Rosalie, Torreys 8 Arapahoe, Snowmass 9 Princeton
resort: 5 Aspen 7 Manitou
river: 4 Bear 5 Grand, Green, White, Yampa 7 Dolores, Laramie 8 Arkansas, Colorado, Gunnison
river tributary: 4 Gila
state flower: 9 Columbine
valley: 5 Estes
colorant: dye 4 anil 7 pigment
coloratura: 6 singer 7 soprano 8 vocalist
colored: 6 biased 9 distorted, prismatic 14 misrepresented
partly: 4 pied 6 motley 7 piebald 10 variegated
colorful: gay 5 vivid 9 brilliant

colorimeter: 10 tintometer
coloring: *cell:* 10 endochrome
matter: dye 5 morin 7 pigment 8 clorofil 10 endochrome 11 chlorophyll
colorless: wan 4 drab, dull, pale 5 ashen, blake, blank, plain 6 pallid 7 hueless, neutral 8 blanched 9 impartial 10 achromatic 11 transparent 13 uninteresting
colors, set of: 7 palette
colossal (see also **huge**): big 4 huge, vast 5 great, large 7 immense 8 enormous, gigantic 9 monstrous
colosseum: See **coliseum**
colossus: 5 giant, titan 6 statue 7 monster, prodigy
colporteur: 6 hawker 7 peddler 11 distributor
colt: gun 4 foal 5 filly 6 pistol 9 quadruped, youngster
coluber: 5 snake 7 serpent
colubrine: 6 crafty 7 cunning 9 snakelike
Columbia River rapids: 6 Dalles
Columbia University symbol: 4 lion
columbine: 4 bird, dodo 5 plant 6 flower 8 dovelike
Columbus: *birthplace:* 5 Genoa
burial place: 7 Seville
companion: 5 Ojeda
embarkation port: 5 Palos
patron: 8 Isabella 9 Ferdinand
ship: 4 Nina 5 Pinta 10 Santa Maria
son: 5 Diego
column: lat, row 4 file, line, post 5 shaft, stela, stele 6 pillar 7 support 8 cylinder, pilaster 9 formation
arrange in: 8 tabulate
base: 9 stylobate
part: 4 anta, fust 5 galbe, socle, scape, shank 6 plinth 7 entasis, capital 8 pilaster
pert. to: 8 columnar
shaped like human figure: 7 telamon 8 atlantes, caryatid
small: 5 stele
support: 5 socle
type of: 5 Doric, Ionic 10 Corinthian
columnar: 6 terete 7 stelene 8 vertical
columnist: 6 writer
columns: *series of:* 9 colonnade
set in: 7 tabular
without: 7 astylar
coma: 4 tuft 5 bunch, carus, sleep 6 stupor, torpor, trance 7 cluster 8 lethargy 13 insensibility
comate: 5 hairy 6 comose 9 companion
comatose: out 6 drowsy 9 lethargic 10 insensible
comb: 4 card, lash, rake 5 brush, clean, crest, curry, tease 6 smooth 11 disentangle
comb. form: 4 cten 5 cteno
flax: 6 hackle, heckle 7 hatchel
horse: 5 curry
comb jelly: 10 ctenophore
comb-like: 8 pectinal 9 pectinate
comb rat: 5 gundi
combat: war 4 bout, cope, duel, fray, meet, rush, tilt 5 clash, fight, joust, repel, set-to 6 action, battle, oppose, resist, strife 7 contend, contest, counter, scuffle 8 argument, conflict, struggle 9 encounter, withstand 10 antagonize, contention
challenge to single: 6 cartel
code: 6 duello
place: 5 arena
combatant: 6 dueler 7 battler, fighter 8 champion 10 contestant
combative: 6 bantam 8 militant 9 agonistic 10 pugnacious 11 agonistical, belligerent
comber: 4 wave 7 breaker 11 beachcomber
combinate: 6 joined 8 combined 9 betrothed
combination: key 4 bloc, gang, pact, pool, ring 5 cabal, junto, party, trust, union 6 cartel, clique, corner, merger 7 combine, consort, coterie, faction 8 alliance, ensemble 9 aggregate, camarilla, coalition, composite, composure, synthesis 10 concoction, conspiracy 11 association, coalescence, composition, confederacy, conjunction, corporation 12 undergarment 13 incorporation
combine: add, mix, wed 4 bloc, join, pool 5 blend, marry, merge, total, unite 6 absorb, concur, merger, mingle, splice 7 conjoin, conjure, machine 8 coalesce, compound, concrete, condense, contract, federate 9 construct, cooperate 10 amalgamate 11 combination, consolidate
combining form (see also **prefix, suffix**): For all definitions beginning with this phrase, look under main word or phrase. EXAMPLES: "combining form for cat": see **cat:** *comb. form;* "combining form for foot": see **foot:** *comb. form.*
comble: 4 acme, heap, load 6 summit
comboy: 6 sarong
combust: 4 burn 5 burnt 8 consumed 10 incinerate
combustible: 4 fuel, peat 5 fiery 9 irascible 10 accendible 11 inflammable
material: gas, oil 4 coal, coke, peat 6 tinder
combustion: 4 fire, heat 5 therm 6 tumult 7 burning 9 agitation, confusion, consuming, cremation, oxidation 12 inflammation 13 conflagration
residue: ash, gas 7 clinker
come: 4 grow 5 arise, issue, occur, reach 6 accrue, appear, arrive, befall, emerge, happen, spring 7 advance, develop, emanate 8 approach, practice 9 eventuate

a cropper: 4 fail, fall
across: 4 find, meet 9 encounter 10 contribute
after: 5 ensue 6 follow 7 succeed
again: 6 return
along: 4 fare 7 improve 8 progress
apart: 5 break
at: 6 attack
before: 7 precede, prevene 8 antecede
between: 8 alienate 9 interpose
by: get 4 gain 6 obtain 7 acquire, inherit
down with: 5 catch 8 contract
forth: 6 appear, emerge
from: 5 ensue 6 result
in: 5 crash, enter 6 arrive 7 intrude
into view: 4 loom 6 appear, emerge
of age: 6 mature
out: 6 appear, emerge, emerse, extend 8 protrude
to a head: 6 climax 9 suppurate
to nothing: end 4 stop 5 cease
to terms: 4 join 5 agree 6 assent, settle 7 approve, consent 8 coincide 9 acquiesce
together: 4 bump, join, meet 5 clash 7 collide, convene 8 assemble, converge
under: 7 subvene
up: 5 arise, occur 6 appear

comeback: 5 rally 6 answer, retort, return 7 rebound 8 recovery, repartee

comedian: wag, wit 4 card 5 actor, antic, clown, comic 6 jester 7 buffoon

comedown: 4 land 6 alight, bathos 7 descend

comedy: 5 drama, farce, revue 8 comoedia(L.), travesty 9 burlesque, slapstick
character: 9 Pantaloon
muse: 6 Thalia
pert. to: 7 thalian
symbol: 4 sock

Comedy of Errors servant: 4 Luce

comeling: 8 newcomer 9 immigrant, sojourner

comely: 4 fair, hend, pert 5 bonny, hende 6 decent, goodly, liking, lovely, pretty, proper 7 farrant 8 becoming, decorous, graceful, handsome, pleasing, suitable 9 agreeable, beautiful 10 gratifying, personable

comer: one 6 person 7 arrival

comestible: 4 food 5 manna, viand 6 edible 7 eatable, victual 8 esculent

comet: 6 meteor
discoverer: 5 Biela, Encke, Swift 6 Donati, Halley, Olbers 8 Kohoutek
part: 4 coma
tail: 8 streamer

comeuppance: 6 rebuke 7 deserts 12 chastisement

comfit: 5 candy 7 confect, praline 8 conserve, preserve 9 sweetmeat 10 confection

comfort: aid 4 ease, rest 5 bield(Sc.), cheer 6 endure, relief, repose, solace, soothe, succor 7 animate, assuage, cherish, confirm, console, enliven, gladden, refresh, relieve, support, sustain 8 inspirit, nepenthe, pleasure, reassure 9 encourage, well-being 10 strengthen 11 consolation

comfortable: 4 bein, bien, cosh, cozy, easy, like, snug, trig 5 comfy, scarf 7 relaxed 8 cheerful, euphoric, wristlet 9 contented 10 acceptable, commodious, complacent, gratifying 11 consolatory, encouraging

comforter: 4 puff 5 cover, quilt, scarf 6 tippet 7 cheerer 8 pacifier

comfortless: 7 forlorn 8 desolate 9 cheerless 12 inconsolable

comfrey: 5 daisy 9 blackwort

comic: 5 droll, funny 8 comedian, farcical 9 burlesque

comical: low 4 base 5 droll, funny, queer, witty 7 amusing, jocular, risible, strange, trivial 8 humorous, ticklish 9 diverting, laughable, ludicrous, quizzical, whimsical 10 capricious

coming: due 4 next 6 advent, future 7 arrival, forward 8 deserved 9 impending 11 approaching

coming out: 5 debut 8 issuance

command: bid 4 beck, bode, boon, call, fiat, hest, rule, sway 5 beken, check, edict, exact, force, hight, order, power, ukase 6 adjure, behest, charge, compel, degree, demand, direct, enjoin, govern, impose, master, ordain 7 appoint, behight, bidding, control, dictate, mandate, officer, precept, require 8 domineer, restrain 9 authority, direction, influence, ordinance, prescribe 10 commission 11 appointment
supreme: 9 hegemony
to a horse: gee, haw, hup 4 whoa

commander: cid, cio 4 head 5 chief 6 leader, master, rammer 7 captain, drungar, emperor, general, officer 10 commandant 11 commendador(Sp.) 13 generalissimo
of a thousand men: 9 chiliarch

commanding: 8 dominant, imposing 9 imperious, masterful 10 imperative 13 authoritative

commandment: law 4 rule 5 order 7 precept

commmando: 6 raider, ranger

comme il faut: 6 proper 7 fitting

commemoration: 5 award, medal 6 plaque 7 service 8 memorial 11 celebration 13 solemnization

commence: 4 fall, open 5 arise, begin, found, start 6 incept, spring 8 initiate 9 institute, originate
commencer: 4 tyro 8 beginner
commencing: 7 initial, nascent 9 incipient
commend: pat 4 give, laud 5 adorn, boost, extol, grace, offer 6 bestow, betake, commit, praise, resign 7 applaud, approve, bespeak, deliver, entrust, intrust 8 bequeath 9 predicate, recommend 10 compliment, ingratiate
highly: 5 extol 8 eulogize 10 panegyrize
to favor: 10 ingratiate
commendable: 4 good 6 worthy 8 laudable 9 exemplary, honorable
commensurate: 4 even 5 equal 6 enough 8 adequate 10 answerable, convenient 11 appropriate 12 proportional 13 corresponding, proportionate
comment: 4 note, talk, word 5 aside, gloss, gloze 6 notate, postil, remark 7 descant, discuss, explain, expound 9 criticise, criticism, criticize, discourse 10 animadvert, annotation, commentary 13 animadversion
commentaries: 10 adversaria
commentary: 5 gloss 6 memoir 7 account, comment 8 glossary, treatise
commentator: 6 critic, glozer 9 annotator, expositor, glossator, scholiast 10 glossarist 13 glossographer
commerce: 5 trade 6 barter 7 traffic 8 business, exchange 10 connection 11 interchange
vehicle: 5 truck
commercial: 9 mercature 10 mercantile 13 advertisement
commingle: mix 4 fuse, join 5 blend, merge, unite 6 mingle 7 combine, embroil 10 amalgamate
comminute: 4 mill 5 crush, grind 9 pulverize, triturate
commiseration: 4 pity 7 empathy 8 sympathy 10 compassion, condolence
commission: 4 send, task 5 board, trust 6 brevit, charge, demand, depute, errand, office, ordain, permit 7 command, consign, empower, mandate, mission, warrant 8 delegate, encharge 9 allowance, authority, authorize, brokerage, establish 10 constitute 11 instruction 12 compensation, dispensation, perpetration 13 authorization
commissioner: 5 envoy 7 officer 8 delegate
commissure: 4 seam 5 joint, miter, mitre 8 juncture 10 miter joint
commit: do 4 give 5 allot, refer 6 assign, betake, remand 7 command, confide, consign, deposit, entrust, intrust 8 bequeath, delegate, imprison, relegate 9 recommend 10 perpetrate
committee: 4 body 5 board, group, junta 7 council 9 executors, guardians
Commius' kingdom: 9 Atrebates
commixture: 7 mixture 8 compound
commode: cap 5 chest 8 cupboard 10 chiffonier
commodious: fit 5 ample, roomy 6 proper, useful 8 spacious, suitable 9 capacious 10 beneficial, convenient 11 comfortable, serviceable 12 advantageous
commodity: 4 ware 5 goods 6 staple 7 article
common: low 4 base 5 banal, brief, cheap, joint, stale, trite, usual 6 coarse, mutual, ornery, vulgar 7 average, current, general, generic, natural, plebian, popular, regular, trivial, unnoble 8 familiar, frequent, habitual, mediocre, ordinary, pandemic, trifling 9 bourgeois, customary, defective, hackneyed, prevalent, universal, unrefined 10 second-rate 11 commonplace
common effort: 8 teamwork
common fund: pot 4 pool 5 purse
common law: 6 custom 9 tradition
common man: 4 pleb 8 plebeian
common sense: 5 sense 8 judgment
common stock: 8 security
commoner: 5 ceorl, plebe 7 burgess, citizen, student 8 roturier 12 participator
commonly: *accepted:* 7 popular, vulgate
thought: 7 reputed 8 putative
commonplace: 4 dull, fade, worn 5 banal, daily, plain, prose, stale, trite, usual 6 common, garden, truism 7 humdrum, prosaic, tedious, trivial 8 ordinary 9 hackneyed 11 unimportant
remark: 5 style 6 cliche, truism 9 platitude
commonwealth: 5 state 6 public 9 community 10 commonweal, res publica
Commonwealth country: 6 Canada 8 Rhodesia 9 Australia 10 New Zealand
commotion: ado, din 4 bree, fray, fuss, heat, riot, stir, to-do, whir 5 alarm, flare, hurry 6 bustle, cathro(Sc.), fracas, flurry, garray, mutiny, pother, tumult, unrest, welter 7 clatter, tempest, turmoil 8 disorder, upheaval, uprising 9 agitation, confusion 10 concussion, convulsion, ebullition, excitement, turbulence 11 disturbance 12 perturbation
commune: 4 area, talk 5 argue, realm, share, treat 6 advise, confer, debate, import, parley, reveal 7 consult, discuss, divulge 8 converse, district, township 11 communicate, intercourse, participate 12 conversation

communicable: 4 open 5 frank 8 catching, sociable 9 knowledge, talkative 10 diffusible, infectious 13 communicative

communicant: 6 member 8 adherent 9 informant

communicate (see also **commune**): 4 tell 6 bestow, convey, impart, inform, reveal, signal 7 declare, dictate, divulge 8 converse

communication: 4 note 5 favor 6 favour, letter 7 message 8 telegram 9 communion 10 communique, connection

means: 4 drum, flag, note, post 5 phone, radio, smoke 6 letter, movies, speech, tomtom 9 telegraph, telephone 10 television

communion: 4 cult, host, mass, sect, talk 5 creed, faith, share, unity 6 church, homily 7 concord 8 antiphon, converse, viaticum 9 agreement, eucharist, sacrament 10 confession, fellowship 11 intercourse 12 conversation, denomination 13 communication, participation

case: 5 burse

cloth: 8 corporal 9 corporale

consecrated food: 5 hagia

cup: ama

plate: 5 paten

table: 5 altar

vessel: pyx

communique: 6 report 7 message 12 announcement 13 communication

communism: 8 Leninism 10 Bolshevism

communist: Red 6 Soviet

community: mir 4 body, burg, city 5 firca, state, thorp 6 cenoby, colony, hamlet, nation, polity, public 7 society, village 8 district, likeness, province, township 9 frequency 10 commonness 12 commonwealth, neighborhood

pert. to: 8 societal

commute: 5 alter 6 change, travel 7 convert 8 exchange 10 substitute 11 interchange

Comoro island: 6 Moheli

comose: 5 hairy 6 comous, tufted

compact: 4 bond, case, firm, hard, knit, pact, plot, snug, trim 5 brief, close, dense, gross, pithy, solid, terse, thick 6 vanity 7 bargain, concise, concord, serried 8 alliance, condense, contract, covenant, solidify, succinct 9 agreement, concordat 10 compaction, compressed, conspiracy, federation 11 compendious, concentrate, confederacy, consolidate, sententious 13 understanding

compadre: pal 5 buddy 6 friend 9 companion

companion: pal 4 chum, fere, mate, peer, twin, wife 5 buddy, bully, butty, crony, cully, matey 6 attend, comate, escort, fellow, friend, spouse 7 compeer, comrade, consort, husband, partner 8 compadre, helpmate 9 accompany, associate, attendant 11 concomitant 12 acquaintance

constant: 6 shadow

equal: 4 peer 7 compeer

faithful: dog 7 Achates

companionable: 6 social 7 cordial 8 gracious, sociable 9 agreeable

company: mob, set 4 band, bevy, body, core, crew, fare, fere, firm, gang, gest, ging, host, rout, team 5 coven, covey, crowd, flock, geste, group, guest, horde, party, squad, troop 6 actors, circle, clique, cohort, covine, curney(Sc.), throng, troupe 7 battery, college, consort, society, visitor 8 assembly 9 camarilla, cavalcade, concourse, gathering 10 fellowship 11 association, partnership 13 companionship

comparable: 4 like 7 similar 9 analogous

comparative: as 4 than 5 equal, rival 7 compeer 8 relative

suffix: er, or; ior

compare: vie 4 even 5 apply, liken, match, scale 6 confer, relate 7 collate, examine, senible 8 contrast, estimate 10 assimilate

comparison: 6 simile 7 analogy, parable 8 likeness, likening, metaphor 9 collation 10 conference, similitude 11 examination

compartment: bay, bin 4 cell, part 5 abode, stall 6 alcove, bunker, region 7 cellule, chamber, section 8 division 9 apartment 10 pigeonhole

granary: 8 grintern

compass: 4 area, gain, room, size 5 abmit, field, gamut, range, reach, scope 6 arrive, attain, bounds, circle, degree, device, effect, extent, sphere 7 achieve, caliber, circuit, confine, divider, enclose, environ, horizon, pelorus 8 boundary, cincture, circuity, surround 10 accomplish

beam: 7 trammel

card: 4 rose

housing: 8 binnacle

ink leg: pen

kind of: sun 4 gyro 5 solar

part: pen 4 airt, vane 5 rhumb 6 gimbal, needle 7 gimbals, trammel 8 trammels

pocket: 6 diacle

point: E., N., S., W.; N.E., N.W., S.E., S.W.; E.N.E., E.S.E., N.N.E., N.N.W., S.S.E., S.S.W., W.N.W., W.S.W. 4 airt 5 airth, rhumb 7 azimuth

sight: 4 vane

suspender: 6 gimbal

compassion: rue 4 pity, ruth 5 heart, grace, mercy, sorry 6 lenity 7 remorse 8 clemency, sympathy 10 condolence 12 misericordia 13 commiseration

compatible: 8 suitable 9 accordant, agreeable, congenial, congruous, consonant 10

consistent, harmonious 16 noncontradictory
compatriot: 10 countryman
compeer: 4 mate, peer, rank 5 equal, match 7 comrade 9 colleague, companion 11 comparative
compel: gar(Sc.) 4 make, move, urge 5 cause, drive, exact, force, impel, press 6 coerce, enjoin, extort, incite, oblige 7 actuate, command, dragoon, enforce, require 9 constrain, influence, instigate, overpower 11 necessitate, subjudicate
compelled: has 4 must 5 bound
compelling: 6 cogent 7 telling 8 forceful 9 demanding 10 conclusive, convincing, persuasive
compendious: 5 brief, short 6 direct 7 compact, concise 8 succinct 9 condensed 11 expeditious 13 comprehensive
compendium: 4 list 5 brief 6 apercu, digest, precis, sketch 7 catalog, compend, epitome, medulla, outline, summary 8 abstract, breviary, syllabus, synopsis 10 abridgment 11 compilation, composition, contraction 12 abbreviation
compensate: pay 4 jibe 5 agree, atone, repay, tally 6 recoup, reward, square 7 correct, redress, requite, restore, satisfy 8 compense 9 indemnify 10 recompense, remunerate 11 countervail 12 counterpoise 14 counterbalance
compensation: fee, pay, utu 4 hire 5 bonus, wages 6 amends, angild, gersum, offset, reward, salary 7 damages, payment, redress, stipend 8 pittance, requital 9 emolument, indemnity 10 recompense 11 restitution 12 counterpoise, remuneration, satisfaction 15 indemnification
compete: pit, vie 4 cope, tend 5 match, rival 6 strive 7 contend, contest, emulate
competent: apt, can, fit 4 able, good, meet, sane 5 adept, capax, smart 6 worthy 7 capable, endowed, skilled 8 adequate, suitable 9 effective, efficient, qualified 10 proficient, sufficient
competition: 4 game, heat 5 match, trial 7 contest, rivalry 8 conflict 9 emulation 10 contention, free-for-all, opposition
competitor: foe 5 enemy, rival 6 player 7 entrant 8 opponent 9 adversary, candidate, combatant 10 antagonist, contestant
Compiegne's river: 4 Oise 5 Aisne
compilation: ana 4 book, code 5 cento 6 digest 9 accretion 10 collection, compendium, confection
compile: add 4 edit 5 amass 6 gather, select 7 arrange, collect, compose, prepare 11 anthologize
compiler: 6 author, editor
complacent: 4 calm, smug 7 fatuous 9 satisfied 11 comfortable 13 self-satisfied
complain: ail, yip 4 beef, carp, fret, fuss, kick, moan, rule, wail, yelp, yirn 5 brawl, croak, croon, gripe, whine 6 bewail, charge, cotter, grieve, grizze, grouse, murmur, repine, yammer 7 deplore, grumble, protest 9 bellyache 11 expostulate
complainant: 5 asker 7 accuser, querent, relator 9 plaintiff
complaining: 9 plaintive, querulous
complaint: 6 lament, malady, plaint 7 ailment, disease, illness, protest 8 disorder, gravamen, jeremiad 9 exception, grievance 10 accusation 11 lamentation
complaisant: 4 able, easy, kind 5 buxom, civil, suave 6 polite, smooth, urbane 7 affable, amiable, lenient 8 gracious, obliging, pleasing 9 compliant, courteous, favorable 10 favourable 12 ingratiating
complect: 5 plait 7 embrace 9 interwine 10 interweave
complement: 4 crew, gang 5 force 6 amount 7 adjunct, obverse 10 completion, supplement 11 counterpart
complete: do; all, end 4 dead, deep, fill, full 5 close, every, plumb, quite, ripen, total, utter, whole 6 effect, entire, finish, intact, mature 7 achieve, execute, fulfill, germane, perfect, plenary, realize 8 absolute, blinking, circular, conclude, implicit, thorough 9 implement, surfeited, terminate 10 accomplish, consummate, effectuate 11 unqualified 12 wholehearted
completely: all 5 quite
completeness: 5 depth 9 entelechy
completion: end 6 finish 9 plenitude
complex: 4 hard, mazy 5 mixed 6 knotty 7 network, tangled, twisted 8 involved, manifold, syndrome 9 composite, difficult, entangled, intricate, perplexed 10 interlaced 11 complicated
of communities: 5 biome
complexion: hue 4 blee, look, rudd, tint 5 color, humor, state, tenor, tinge 6 aspect, temper 10 appearance
compliance: 7 harmony 8 civility 9 obedience 10 concession, submission 11 application 12 complaisance
compliant: 4 easy, oily 6 pliant, supple 7 ductile, dutiful, willing 9 indulgent 10 applicable, manageable, obsequious, sequacious 11 complaisant
complicate: 6 intort, puzzle, tangle 7 involve, perplex 8 bewilder
complicated: 4 hard 6 knotty, prolix 7 complex, gordian, snarled, tangled 8 involved 9 difficult, elaborate, embroiled, intricate, plexiform 10 disordered

complication: 4 node, plot 5 nodus, snarl 9 complexus, confusion, intricacy 10 difficulty, perplexity

compliment: 4 gift, laud 5 extol 6 boquet, eulogy, praise 7 adulate, applaud, bouquet, commend, flatter, tribute 8 encomium, flummery, gratuity 9 adulation, panegyric 12 blandishment, commendation, congratulate

compline: 4 hour 7 prayers, service

comply: 4 cede, obey 5 abide, adapt, agree, apply, yield 6 accede, accord, assent, enfold, submit 7 conform, embrace, observe 9 acquiesce 11 accommodate

component: 4 item, part, unit 6 factor, member 7 element 8 integral 10 compounder, ingredient 11 constituent

comport: act 4 bear, jibe, suit 5 agree, brook, carry, tally 6 accord, acquit, behave, demean, endure, square 7 conduct 9 behaviour, harmonize 10 correspond, deportment 11 comportance

comportable: 8 suitable 9 endurable, tolerable 10 consistent

comportment: 7 conduct, dealing 8 behavior, demeanor 9 behaviour, demeanour 10 deportment

compose: pen, set 4 calm, dite, form, lull, make 5 allay, brief, clerk, dight, order, write 6 accord, adjust, create, design, indite, settle, soothe 7 arrange, compone, concoct, conform, dispose, fashion, produce 8 compound, comprise, comprize, regulate 9 alleviate, construct, formulate 10 constitute 11 tranquilize

compose type: set

composed: 4 calm, cool 5 quiet, sober, wrote 6 demure, placid, sedate, serene 7 written 8 compound, decorous, tranquil 9 collected, composite, unruffled 13 dispassionate

composer: 4 poet 5 odist 6 author, writer 7 elegist 8 monodist, musician 10 compositor, typesetter

composition (see also **musical composition**): ana 4 mass, opus, work 5 cento, ditty, drama, piece, poesy, theme 6 accord, lesson, make-up, thesis 7 article, compost, mixture, picture, writing 8 acrostic, compound, fantasia 9 admixture, aggregate, composure, congruity, formation, invention, structure, synthesis 10 adjustment, compendium, composture, confection, manuscript 11 arrangement, combination, compositure, conjunction 12 constitution, construction

art of: 8 rhetoric

for two: 6 duetto 7 duetino

literary: ms(abbr.) 5 cento, drama, essay, novel, theme 6 satire, thesis 7 tragedy 8 treatise

metrical: 4 poem, rime 5 poesy, rhyme

mournful: 5 dirge

compositor: 4 type 6 setter 7 caseman, printer

compost: 6 mingle 7 compote, mixture 8 compound 10 composture, fertilizer 11 composition

composure: 4 bond, mien 5 quiet, union 6 repose 7 balance, posture 8 calmness, serenity 10 composture, equanimity, sedateness 11 combination, composition, tranquility

compote, compot: 4 bowl 5 fruit 7 dessert

compound: 4 fill, join 5 alloy, blend, ester, unite 6 adjust, jumble, medley, settle 7 amalgam, combine, complex, compone, compose, compost 8 ceromide 9 admixture, aggregate, composite, enclosure 10 amalgamate, commixture, compromise, concoction, confection, constitute, hodge-podge, settlement

alkaline: 4 soda

amorphous: 7 phenose

chemical: 4 amid, amin, azin, imid, imin 5 amide, amine, azine, azola, borid, ceria, ester, imide, imine, osone 6 borids 7 inosite, metamer, leucine 8 chloride

containing double bonds: 5 diene 6 triene

containing two hydroxyl groups: 4 diol

crystalline: 5 aloin, oscin 6 amarin, anisil, phenol 7 tropine

hypnotic: 7 trional

organic: 4 amin 5 amine, ester, ketol 6 ketole, ketone

compound interest: 9 anatocism

comprehend: get, see 4 know 5 grasp, imply, savvy, seize, sense 6 attain, digest, embody, fathom, follow, uptake 7 contain, discern, embrace, enclose, imagine, include, involve, realize 8 comprise, comprize, conceive, conclude, perceive 9 apprehend 10 understand

comprehensible: 8 exoteric, included 9 comprised 11 conceivable 12 intelligible

comprehension: 5 grasp 6 noesis 7 epitome, knowing, summary 9 inclusion, intension 10 conception 11 connotation

comprehensive: big 4 full, wide 5 broad, grand, large 7 concise, generic 8 encyclic, spacious 9 expansive, extensive, panoramic 11 compendious

compress: nip, tie 4 bale, bind, firm, wrap 5 cling, cramp, crowd, crush, press 6 gather, shrink 7 abridge, bolster, compact, curtail,

embrace, deflate, flatten, repress, squeeze 8 astringe, condense, contract, restrain 9 constrain, epitomize 11 consolidate
medical: 5 stupe 7 bandage, pledget
compressor: 4 pump 6 device 7 machine
comprise, comprize: 4 hold 5 cover, imply, seize 6 attach, confer, embody 7 compose, contain, embrace, enclose, include, involve 8 conceive, perceive 10 comprehend
comprised: 4 rapt 8 included 9 engrossed 14 comprehensible
compromise: 8 compound, endanger 9 surrender 10 concession
opposition to: 13 intransigence
compt: 4 neat 6 spruce 8 polished
comptroller: 7 auditor, officer 10 controller
compulsion: 4 need, urge 5 force 6 duress, stress 7 impulse 8 coaction, coercion 10 constraint
compulsory: coercive, forcible 10 imperative, obligatory
compulsory service: 6 angary 7 angaria, slavery
compunction: 5 qualm 6 regret, sorrow 7 remorse, scruple 9 misgiving 10 conscience, contrition, repentance
compute: add, sum 4 cast, rate 5 count, tally 6 assess, figure, number, reckon 7 account 8 estimate 9 calculate, enumerate
computer: 6 univac 7 machine
algebraic language: 5 algol
correct: 5 debug
information: 4 data 5 input 6 output
inventor: 7 Babbage
plan for action: 7 program
program symbol: 5 block
symbol system: 4 code
worker: 9 programer 10 programmer
comrade: pal 4 ally, chum, mate, peer 5 billy, buddy, crony 6 copain(F.), digger, fellow, frater, friend, hearty 7 brother 8 copemate 9 associate, companion
comte: 5 count
comtesse: 8 countess
con: rap 4 anti, know, lead, look, pore, read, scan 5 cheat, guide, knock, learn, steer, study 6 direct, peruse, regard, versus 7 against, deceive, examine, inspect, opposed, swindle 10 understand
conation: 4 will 7 conatus 8 tendency, volition 11 inclination
conative state: 5 nisus
concatenate: 4 join, link 5 chain, unite 7 connect 8 catenate
concave: 4 void 6 arched, dished, hollow 7 vaulted 8 incurved 9 depressed
concavity: dip, pit 4 bowl, dent, hole 6 crater, hollow
conceal: 4 bury, hide, mask, sile, veil 5 cache, cloak, couch, cover, feign 6 closet, emboss, pocket, screen, shroud 7 secrete 8 bescreen, disguise, ensconce, withhold 9 dissemble 10 camouflage
goods: 5 cache, eloin 6 eloign
concealed: 4 dern(Sc.) 5 blind 6 covert, hidden, latent, occult, perdue, secret, veiled 7 covered, larvate 8 abstruse 9 blindfold, disguised, insidious, recondite, withdrawn 11 clandestine
concealing: 10 obvelation
concede: own 4 cede 5 admit, agree, allow, grant, waive, yette, yield 6 accord, assent 7 confess 9 surrender 10 condescend 11 acknowledge
conceit: ego 4 idea 5 fancy, pride 6 notion, vagary, vanity 7 caprice, egotism, tympany 9 arrogance, conundrum 10 conception
conceited: bug 4 fess, vain 5 chuff, cocky, flory, huggy, proud 6 clever 8 arrogant, dogmatic, priggish, snobbish 9 pragmatic, whimsical 11 coxcombical, egotistical, opinionated
conceive: 4 form, make, plan, ween 5 begin, brain, dream, fancy, frame, think 6 devise, ideate, ponder 7 imagine, realize, suppose, suspect 8 comprise, comprize, contrive 9 apprehend, formulate 10 comprehend, understand
concent: 9 harmonize 10 accordance 11 consistency
concentrate: aim, fix 4 mass, pile 5 coact, exalt, focus, unify 6 arrest, attend, center, gather 7 compact, essence, thicken 8 approach, assemble, condense, contract 9 intensify 10 centralize 11 consolidate 12 conglomerate
concentration: 7 extract 10 absorption 11 application
concentration camp: 6 prison, stalag
concept: 4 idea 5 fancy, image 7 opinion, thought 11 disposition
conception: ens 4 idea 5 fancy, fetus, image 6 belief, design, embryo 7 conceit, purpose 8 notation 9 beginning 10 cogitation, impression 12 apprehension 13 comprehension
concern: 4 bear, care, firm, reck, sake 5 apply, cause, event, grief, touch, worry 6 affair, affect, behold, charge, employ, matter, regard 7 anxiety, article, company, disturb, involve, pertain, respect, trouble 8 business, interest 9 implicate, rickmatic 10 solicitude 11 corporation, distinguish 12 apprehension
concerned: 6 intent 7 anxious, worried 8 bothered
concerning: by, of, on, re; for 4 in-re 5 about, anent 6 anenst 9 regarding

concert: 4 plan 5 unite 6 accord, devise 7 arrange, benefit, concent, concord, consort, consult, harmony, recital 9 agreement 11 performance 13 entertainment
concert hall: 5 odeon, odeum
concertina: 9 bandonion
concession: 4 boon 5 favor, grant, lease 6 assent, favour, gambit 7 cession 9 admission, privilege 10 compliance, compromise 12 acquiescence 13 condescension 15 acknowledgement
conch: 5 shell 6 cockle, mussel
conchie, conchy: 8 objector
Conchobor's wife: 4 Medb
concierge: 6 porter, warden 7 janitor 9 attendant 10 doorkeeper
conciliate: get 4 calm, ease 5 atone 6 adjust, pacify 7 acquire, appease, concile, mollify, placate, satisfy 9 reconcile 10 propitiate
conciliatory: 4 mild 6 gentle, giving, irenic 7 lenient, pacific, winning 8 irenical, lenitive 9 forgiving 10 mollifying 12 propitiating
concilium: 7 council
concinnity: 7 harmony 8 elegance
concise: 4 curt, neat 5 brief, crisp, pithy, short, terse 7 compact, laconic, pointed, precise, serried 8 mutilate, pregnant, succinct 9 condensed 10 compedious, contracted 11 sententious 12 epigrammatic 13 comprehensive
concision: 6 schism 7 faction 8 division 10 mutilation
conclave: 6 closet 7 chamber, meeting 8 assembly
conclude: bar, end 4 rest 5 close, estop, infer, judge, limit 6 clinch, deduce, figure, finish, gather, reason, settle 7 achieve, arrange, confine, embrace, enclose, resolve, suppose 8 complete, dispatch, graduate, restrain 9 determine, speculate, terminate 10 comprehend
conclusion: end 4 amen, coda, last 5 finis 6 finale, finish, period, result, upshot 7 finding, outcome 8 epilogue, judgment 9 diagnosis, inference 10 conjecture, settlement 11 probability, termination
conclusive: 4 last 5 final, valid 6 cogent 7 certain, extreme, telling 8 decisive, definite, ultimate 10 convincing, peremptory 11 irrefutable 12 unanswerable 13 determinative
concoct: mix 4 brew, cook, plan, plot, vamp 5 frame, hatch 6 decoct, devise, digest, invent, refine, scheme 7 compose, perfect, prepare 8 compound, intrigue 9 fabricate 10 assimilate
concomitant: 9 accessory, associate, attendant, attending, companion, conjoined, cooperant 10 coincident, concurrent 11 synchronous 12 accompanying 13 accompaniment
concord: 4 part 5 agree, amity, peace, union, unity 6 treaty, unison 7 compact, concent, concert, harmony, oneness 8 covenant 9 agreement, communion, congruity 10 accordance, consonance
concordant: 8 unisonal 9 agreeable, congruous, consonant 10 harmonious 13 correspondent
concourse: 5 crowd, place, point 6 throng 7 company 8 assembly 9 affluence, frequency, gathering 10 assemblage, confluence 11 coincidence, concurrence, conjunction, cooperation
concredit: 6 commit 7 entrust, intrust
concrete: 4 clot, firm, hard, real 5 beton, solid, unite 6 actual 7 combine, congeal, special 8 coalesce, compound, tangible 9 concresce 10 particular
construction: 6 tremie 7 caisson
concretion: 4 clot, mess 5 pearl 6 nodule 8 calculus
concubine: 5 woman 7 adalisk 8 mistress 9 odalisque
concur: 4 jibe, join 5 agree, chime, unite 6 accede, accord, assent 7 approve, combine, consent 8 coincide, converge 9 acquiesce, cooperate 10 correspond
concurrence: 5 union 6 assent, bestow 7 consent, consort, meeting 8 adhesion 9 adherence, agreement, concourse 10 conspiracy 11 coincidence, conjunction
concurrent: 6 coeval, united 7 meeting 10 associated, coincident 11 concomitant, synchronous 12 accompanying
concuss: jar 4 jolt 5 clash, force, shake, shock 6 coerce 7 agitate
condalia: 9 chaparral
condemn: ban 4 damn, doom, file, fine 5 blame, decry, judge 6 amerce, attain, awreak, banish, detest 7 adjudge, censure, convict 8 denounce, reproach, sentence 10 confiscate, disapprove
condemnation: 4 doom 5 blame 7 censure, decrial 11 reprobation 13 animadversion 14 disapprobation
condense: cut 5 brief, unite 6 decoct, digest, harden, lessen, narrow, reduce, shrink 7 abridge, combine, compact, deflate, distill, shorten, thicken 8 compress, diminish, solidify 9 constrict, epitomize, evaporate, intensify 11 concentrate, consolidate
condensed: 4 curt 5 brief 7 compact, concise 8 absorbed 11 compendious
condenser: 4 cric 6 aludel
condescend: 5 deign, favor, grant, stoop 6 assent, oblige, submit 7 concede, descend 9 patronize, vouchsafe

condescension: 7 disdain 8 courtesy 10 affability, concession 12 complaisance
condign: due, fit 4 fair, just 6 severe, worthy 8 adequate, deserved, suitable 11 appropriate
condiment: rea 4 herb, kari, mace, sage, salt 5 caper, curry, sauce, spice, thyme 6 catsup, cloves, pepper, relish 7 chutney, cuminos, ketchup, mustard, paprika, vinegar 8 allspice, turmeric 9 appetizer, seasoning
container: 5 cruet
stand: 6 caster
condisciple: 7 student 12 schoolfellow
condite: 7 pickled 8 seasoned 9 preserved
condition: if 4 case, mode, rank, rote, term 5 angle, birth, cause, class, estre, facet, place, stage, state 6 estate, fettle, gentry, morale, plight, status 7 article, calling, premise, proviso, station 8 covenant, occasion, position 9 agreement, exception, provision, requisite, situation 10 limitation 11 predicament, stipulation 13 circumstances
comb. form: ate 4 ance, ancy, ence, ency 6 blasty
critical: 9 emergency
favorable: 4 odds
suffix: ile
conditional: 9 qualified 10 accidental
conditioned: 6 finite 7 limited
condolence: 4 pity, ruth 7 empathy 8 sympathy 10 compassion 13 commiseration
condone: 5 blink, remit 6 acquit, excuse, forget, ignore, pardon 7 absolve, forgive 8 overlook
condor: 4 coin 6 tiffin 7 vulture 8 gymnogyp
conduce: aid 4 help, hire, lead, tend 5 bring, guide 6 confer, effect, engage 7 advance, conduct, further, redound 10 contribute
conduct: act, run 4 bear, deed, gest, lead, mien, rule, wage 5 carry, geste, guard, guide, usher 6 action, attend, behave, convey, convoy, demean, deport, direct, escort, govern, manage, squire 7 bearing, channel, comport, conduce, conduit, control, execute, officer, operate 8 behavior, carriage, chaplain, demeanor, guidance, regulate, transact 9 accompany, behaviour, demeanour, supervise 10 administer, deportment, governance, government, proceeding 11 comportment, countenance, superintend
scandalous: 9 esclandre(F.)
conductor: cad 4 gude 5 guard 6 convoy, copper, escort, leader 7 cathode, maestro 8 aqueduct, cicerone, conveyor, director, employee 10 bandleader, propagator 11 impressario
stick: 5 baton
conduit: 4 duct, main, pipe, tube, wire 5 cable, canal, sewer 6 trough 7 channel, conduct, culvert, passage 8 aqueduct
cone: 4 chat 5 crack, solid, spire 6 bobbin, object 7 cluster, fissure, strobil 8 strobile 9 container
section: 8 parabola
cone-shaped: 5 conic 6 pineal 7 conical
conenose: 6 bedbug
conepate: 5 skunk
coney: See cony
confab: 4 chat, talk 6 powwow 7 prattle 10 conference 11 confabulate 12 conversation
confect: mix 4 form, make 6 pickle 7 prepare 8 preserve 9 construct
confection: 5 candy, dulce, sweet 6 bonbon, comfit, cimbal, dainty, nougat 7 caramel, confect, fondant, mixture, praline, sherbet, succade 8 compound, delicacy, preserve, sherbert 9 confiture, marmalade, sweetmeat 10 concoction 11 bittersweet, compilation, composition, preparation
Confederacy: *banknote:* 8 blueback
general: Lee 5 Bragg, Price 6 Morgan 7 Jackson 10 Beauregard
guerilla: 11 bushwhacker
president: 5 Davis
soldier: reb
vice-president: 8 Stephens
victory: 7 Bull Run 11 Chickamauga 16 Chancellorsville
confederate: aid, pal, reb 4 ally 5 rebel, stall, unite 6 league 7 abetter, abettor, conjure, fedarie, federal, partner 8 conspire, federate 9 accessory, assistant, associate, auxiliary 10 accomplice
confederation: 4 body 5 union 6 league 7 compact, society 8 alliance, covenant 9 coalition 10 conspiracy, federation 11 association, confederacy
confer: dub 4 give, meet, talk 5 award, endow, grant, treat 6 advise, bestow, donate, impart, invest, parley 7 commune, compare, conduce, consult, counsel, discuss, instate, present 8 comprise, converge 10 contribute, deliberate
conference: 4 talk 5 synod, trust 6 confab, huddle, parley, pow-wow 7 council, meeting, palaver 8 colloque, colloquy, congress 9 collation, comparing, discourse, interview 10 comparison, discussion 11 association 12 consultation, conversation
technique: 13 brainstorming
confess: own 4 avow, sing 5 admit, grant 6 attest, avouch, beknow, reveal, shrive 7 concede, divulge 8 disclose, discover, manifest 11 acknowledge

confession: 5 credo, creed 6 avowal, shrift, shrive 9 admission, communion, statement 10 profession

confetti: 4 tape 5 candy 7 bonbons 9 sweetmeat 10 confection
container: 8 cascaron

confidant: 8 intimate

confide: 4 affy, rely, tell 5 trust 6 commit, depend 7 believe, consign, entrust, intrust

confidence: 4 hope 5 bield, faith, trust 6 aplomb, belief, credit, mettle, morale, secret, spirit 7 courage 8 affiance, boldness, credence, reliance, sureness 9 assurance, certitude, hardihood, hardiness 10 effrontery 11 presumption 12 impertinence
game: 5 bunco, bunko 7 swindle
lack: 10 diffidence

confident: 4 bold, smug, sure 5 hardy, siker 6 crouse, secure, sicker 7 assured, certain, hopeful, reliant 8 constant, fearless, impudent, sanguine, trustful 9 dependent, undaunted 10 dogmatical 11 trustworthy 12 presumptuous

confidential: 5 bosom, privy 6 covert, secret 7 private, subrosa 8 esoteric, intimate 9 auricular 11 trustworthy
law: 9 fiduciary

configuration: 4 form 5 shape 6 figure 7 contour, outline 10 topography

confine: bar, box, dam, hem, new, pen, pin, sty, tie 4 bind, cage, coop, hasp, jail, keep, lock, seal 5 bound, cramp, delay, impen, limit, pinch, stint 6 border, compas, corral, fetter, forbar, hamper, hurdle, immure, impale, intern, pinion, pocket, tether 7 astrict, impound 8 boundary, conclude, imprison, restrain, straiten 9 carcerate, constrain, restraint 11 incarcerate 12 circumscribe

confined: ill 4 pent 5 bound, caged 6 sealed 7 cramped, cribbed, limited 8 impended, interned 9 impounded 10 cloistered 13 incommunicado
to select group: 8 estoeric

confinement: mew 8 clausure, firmance 9 captivity, restraint 10 childbirth, constraint, internment 11 contraction 12 accouchement, imprisonment
place of: mew, pen 4 brig, cage, coop, goal, jail, stir 5 limbo 6 asylum, corral, prison 7 dungeon 9 calaboose 12 penitentiary

confirm: fix, set 4 firm, seal 5 prove 6 affirm, assent, assure, attest, avouch, clinch, ratify, settle, verify 7 approve, comfort, endorse, fortify, sustain 8 accredit, convince, sanction, validate 9 approbate, establish 10 comprobate, strengthen 11 corroborate, countersign 12 adminiculate, authenticate, substantiate

confirmed: set 5 fixed 6 arrant, stable 7 chronic 8 habitual, ratified 9 fortified, initiated 10 encouraged, inveterate 11 established

confiscate: 4 grab 5 seize, usurp 7 condemn 9 sequester 11 appropriate

conflagration: 4 fire 5 blaze, fever 7 burning 10 combustion 12 inflammation

conflict: war 4 bout, duel, fray, rift 5 broil, brush, clash, fight, grips, mix-up 6 action, battle, combat, mutiny, oppose, strife 7 contend, contest, discord, warfare 8 disagree, militate, struggle 9 collision, encounter, rebellion 10 contention 11 competition
final: 10 Armageddon

conflicting: 7 adverse 10 contending 12 incompatible, inharmonious

confluence: 5 crowd 7 conflux, meeting 8 junction 9 concourse 12 assimilation

conform: go; fit 4 lean, obey, suit 5 adapt, agree, apply, yield 6 accede, adjust, assent, comply, settle, submit 7 compose 9 acquiesce, harmonize, reconcile 10 correspond 11 accommodate

conformist: 6 pedant 7 babbitt 9 precisian 10 philistine 11 reactionary

conformity: 7 harmony 8 affinity, likeness, symmetry 9 agreement, congruity, obedience 10 accordance, compliance, similarity, submission 11 affirmative 12 acquiescence, complaisance
to law: 6 dharma 8 legality

confound: mix 4 blow, dash, maze, rout, stam, stun 5 abash, addle, amaze, spend, spoil, waste 6 baffle, dismay, muddle, rattle 7 astound, confuse, confute, corrupt, destroy, flummox, perplex, stupefy 8 astonish, bewilder, distract, surprise 9 discomfit, dumbfound, embarrass, frustrate, overthrow 10 disconcert 11 intermingle

confraternity: 4 body 5 union 7 society 11 brotherhood

confrere: 6 fellow 7 comrade 9 colleague

confront: 4 defy, face, meet 5 beard, brave 6 oppose, resist 7 affront, compare 8 envisage, threaten 9 challenge, encounter

confuse: mix 4 dash, daze, maze, muss, rout 5 abash, addle, amaze, befog, blend, cloud, snarl 6 baffle, bemuse, bother, burble, caddle, flurry, fuddle, jumble, muddle, puzzle, rattle 7 bedevil, blunder, derange, fluster, mystify, nonplus, perplex, stupefy 8 befuddle, bewilder, confound, distract 9 barbulyie, discomfit, dumbfound, obfuscate 10 demoralize, disarrange, discompose, disconcert

confused: 4 asea, lost 5 foggy, muddy, vague 6 doiled, doited 7 chaotic, obscure 8 deranged 9 chagrined 10 bewildered, hur-

ly-burly, topsy-turvy, tumultuous 13 helter-skelter
confusion: din 4 coil, dust, fuss, harl, mess, moil, riot 5 babel, chaos, chevy, chivy, deray, mix-up, snafu, snarl, strow 6 babble, bedlam, caddle, chivvy, habble, hubbub, huddle, jabble, jumble, muddle, pother, rabble, rumpus, tophet, tumult, uproar, welter 7 farrage, blunder, bluster, clutter, farrage, flutter, garboil, topheth, turmoil, widdrim 8 disarray, disorder 9 agitation, commotion 10 hullabaloo, hurly-burly 11 disturbance, trepidation 12 hugger-mugger, perturbation 13 embarrassment
confute: 4 deny 5 rebut 6 expose, refute 7 silence 8 confound, convince, disprove, infringe, overcome 9 overwhelm
conge: bow 6 curtsy 7 license, molding 8 farewell, passport 9 clearance, dismissal 10 permission 11 leavetaking
congeal: gel, ice, set 4 geal, jell 5 candy 6 cotter, curdle, freeze, harden 7 stiffen, thicken 8 concrete, solidify 9 coagulate 11 crystallize
congealing agent: 6 pectin 8 gelatine
congee: 5 gruel 9 departure
congener: 4 kind, race 5 class, genus
congenial: 4 boon 5 natal 6 native 7 connate, kindred 10 compatible 11 sympathetic
conger: eel 8 cucumber
congeries: 4 mass 5 group 10 collection
congestion: jam 4 heap 8 crowding, stoppage 9 gathering 12 accumulation
conglaciate: 6 freeze 7 congeal
conglobation: 4 ball
conglomerate: 4 heap, mass, pile, rock 5 stack 9 clustered 10 assemblage 11 agglomerate 12 concentrated
Congo (see also **Zaire**): *tribe:* 4 Susa 6 Wabuma 7 Bangala
tributary: 4 Uele 6 Ubangi 7 Aruwima
congou: tea
congratulate: 4 laud 5 greet 6 salute 8 macarize 10 compliment, felicitate
congregate: 4 herd, mass, meet, teem 5 group, swarm, troop 6 gather, muster 7 collect, convene 8 assemble
congregation: 4 body, fold, host, mass 5 flock, swarm 6 church, parish 7 meeting, synaxes 8 assembly, brethren 9 gathering 10 collection 11 convocation
congress: 4 dail, diet 5 synod 7 council, meeting 8 assembly, conclave 10 conference, convention, parliament 11 convocation, legislature
Congress: *building:* 7 Capitol
member: 7 senator
upper house: 6 Senate
congressman: 14 representative
congruity: 6 accord 7 concord, fitness, harmony 8 symmetry 9 agreement, coherence 10 conformity, consonance 11 composition, consistency, correctness, suitability 13 compatability 14 correspondence
conical: 8 tapering
conifer: fir, yew 4 pine, tree 5 cedar, larch 6 spruce 7 pinacle, pinales
conium: 7 hemlock
conjecture: aim 4 plot, shot, view 5 augur, ettle, fancy, guess, opine 6 belief, divine, theory 7 imagine, opinion, presume, suppose, surmise, suspect 9 inference, speculate, suspicion 10 conclusion, estimation 11 contrivance, supposition
conjoined: 6 joined, linked 8 conjunct, touching 11 concomitant
conjoint: 8 combined 9 conjoined 10 associated 11 correlative 12 simultaneous
conjugal: 9 connubial 11 matrimonial
conjugate: 5 yoked 6 joined, united 7 coupled
conjunction: as, et, if, or; and, but, nor, tie 4 than 5 joint, since, union 7 coition, consort 9 coalition, concourse 10 connection 11 association, combination, composition, concurrence
conjuration: art 5 charm, magic, spell 6 voodoo 10 necromancy 11 incantation, legerdemain
conjure: 4 pray 5 charm, halse 6 adjure, invent, invoke 7 beseech, combine, entreat, imagine 8 conspire, contrive, exorcise, exorcize 10 supplicate 11 confederate
conjuror: 4 mage, sear 6 pellar, shaman, wizard 7 juggler, warlock 8 magician, sorcerer 9 coswearer, enchanter 15 prestidigatator
conk: 4 fail, head, nose 5 faint, knock, stall
Conlaech: *father:* 10 Cuchulainn
mother: 5 Aoife
connach: 5 spoil, waste
Connacht king: 6 Ailill
connate: 4 akin, born 5 fused 6 allied, inborn, innate 7 cognate 9 congenial 10 congenital
connect: tie 4 ally, bind, glue, join, knit, link 5 affix, chain, marry, unite 6 attach, bridge, cement, cohere, connex, couple, fasten, relate 7 combine 8 continue 9 affiliate, associate, correlate, interlock 11 communicate
Connecticut: *city:* 4 Avon 6 Bethel, Darien 7 Meriden 8 Hartford(c.)
river: 10 Housatonic
connection: tie 4 bond, link 5 nexus, union 6 family 7 contact, kinship 8 affinity, alliance, commerce, intimacy, junction, rela-

tive, syndetic **9** coherence, reference, relevance **10** continuity **11** association, conjunction, intercourse **12** articulation, relationship **13** communication

connective: **8** syndetic **11** conjunction

connective tissue: **6** fascia

conniption fit: **7** tantrum

connive: **4** abet, plot, wink **5** blink, cabal **6** assent, foment, incite **7** collude **8** intrigue, overlook

connoisseur: **5** judge **6** critic, expert **7** epicure, gourmet **8** gourmand **9** collector **11** cognoscente

connotation: **6** intent **7** meaning **10** denotation **13** comprehension, signification

connote: **5** imply **8** indicate

connubial: **7** marital **8** conjugal, domestic **11** matrimonial

conquer: get, win **4** beat, best, down, gain, lick, rout, tame **5** crush, daunt **6** defeat, evince, humble, master, reduce, subdue, victor **7** acquire, prevail, subject, triumph **8** overcome, surmount, vanquish **9** checkmate, discomfit, overpower, overthrow, overwhelm, subjugate

conqueror: **4** hero **6** victor, winner **12** conquistador

conquest: **7** mastery, triumph, victory **8** invasion

conquistador: **6** Cortez

consanguineous: **4** akin **7** kindred, related

consanguinity: **5** blood, nasab **7** kinship **8** affinity **12** relationship

conscience: **5** grace, inwit, qualm. sense **6** erinys, psyche, virtue **7** monitor, probity, scruple, thought **9** casuistry, punctilio **11** compunction

conscientious: **4** fair, just **5** exact, rigid **6** honest, strict **7** dutiful, upright **8** faithful **9** honorable **10** scrupulous **11** punctilious

conscious: **4** keen **5** alive, awake, aware **7** feeling, knowing **8** rational, sensible, sentient **9** attentive, cognizant, concerned **10** perceptive **12** apprehensive

consciousness: **9** awareness
loss of: **4** coma **5** faint **8** apoplexy

consciousness-altering: **11** psychedelic

conscript: **5** draft, enrol **6** enlist, muster **7** recruit

consecrate: vow **4** fain, seal **5** bless, deify, devot **6** anoint, hallow, ordain **8** sanctify, dedicate **10** inaugurate **11** apotheosize

consecrated: **5** blest **6** oblate, sacred, votive **8** hallowed
cloth: **11** antimension
oil: **6** chrism
thing: **6** sacrum

consent: **5** agree, allow, grant, yield **6** accede, accord, assent, beteem, comply, permit **7** approve **9** recognize **10** permission **11** concurrence **12** acquiescence

consequence: end **4** bore **5** event, fruit, issue, worth **6** effect, import, moment, repute, result, sequel, weight **7** concern, outcome **8** aftering, interest, occasion **9** aftermath, emanation, inference **10** importance **11** consecution **13** consideration

consequently: so **4** ergo, then, thus **5** hence, later **8** pursuant **9** therefore **11** accordingly **12** subsequently **13** consecutively

conservative: **4** safe, Tory **5** staid **6** stable **7** diehard **8** moderate **9** bourgeois **11** reactionary **12** preservative

conservatory: **6** school **7** academy **10** glasshouse, greenhouse

conserve: can, jam **4** save **5** guard, jelly **6** defend, secure, shield, uphold **7** husband, protect, sustain **8** maintain, preserve **9** sweetmeat

consider: see **4** deem, heed, mull, muse, rate **5** ettle, judge, study, think, weigh **6** behold, debate, expend, impute, ponder, reason, reckon, regard **7** account, believe, canvass, examine, inspect, reflect, suppose **8** cogitate, estimate, meditate, ruminate **9** calculate, entertain, speculate **10** adjudicate, deliberate **11** contemplate

considerable: **5** geyan(Sc.), large, smart, smert **7** notable, several **9** capacious, important **10** cognizable, noteworthy, remarkable **11** perceptible, significant

considerate: **4** kind, mild **6** gentle **7** careful, heedful, prudent, serious **8** delicate **9** observant, regardful **10** deliberate, reflective, respectful, thoughtful

consideration: **4** sake **5** price, topic **6** aspect, esteem, motive, notice, reason, regard **7** respect, thought **9** attention, deference, incentive, influence **10** importance, inducement, recompense, reputation **11** consequence

considering: if **5** since

consign: **4** doom, give, mail, send, ship **5** allot, award, dight, remit, shift, yield **6** assign, commit, devote, remand, resign **7** address, confide, deliver, deposit, entrust, intrust **8** delegate, relegate, transfer **9** recommend **10** commission

consignee: **5** agent **8** receiver

consist: lie **4** hold **5** exist, stand **6** inhere, reside **7** contain, embrace **8** comprise **9** harmonize

consistency: **4** body **5** union **6** degree **7** concord, harmony **8** firmness, solidity, symmetry **9** adherence, coherence, congruity

10 consonance, uniformity 11 composition, persistency 14 correspondence, substantiality

consistent: 4 firm 7 durable, logical, uniform 8 coherent, enduring, suitable 9 accordant, congruous, consonant 10 changeless, compatible, persisting

consociate: 9 associate 11 confederate

consolation: sop 4 fine 6 relief, solace 7 comfort 10 booby prize

console: 4 calm 5 allay, ancon, cheer, organ, table 6 solace, soothe 7 bracket, cabinet, comfort, relieve, support, sustain 9 alleviate, encourage

consolidate: mix 4 knit, mass, pool, weld 5 blend, merge, unify, unite 6 harden, mingle 7 combine, compact 8 coalesce, compress, condense, organize, solidify 10 amalgamate, strengthen 11 concentrate

consomme: 4 soup

consonance: 6 accord 7 harmony 9 resonance

consonant: 5 linis 6 dental, fortis, letter, sonant 7 palatal, spirant, unified 8 harmonic, suitable 9 accordant, agreeable, congruous 10 coincident, compatible, concordant, consistent, harmonious
hard: 6 fortis
hissing: 8 sibilant
pert. to: 7 palatal 9 fricative
smooth: 4 lene 5 lenis
voiceless: 4 lene, surd 6 atonic 7 spirate

consort: cot 4 aide, ally, join, mate, wife 5 group, unite 6 accord, attend, escort, mingle, spouse 7 company, concert, husband, partner 8 accustom, assembly 9 accompany, associate, colleague, companion, forgather 10 foregather 11 association, combination, concurrence, conjunction

consortium: 5 group 8 alliance

conspectus: 4 list 6 survey 7 outline 8 synopsis 11 abridgement

conspicuous: 5 clear, famed, plain 6 extant, famous, marked, patent, signal 7 eminent, glaring, notable, obvious, pointed, salient, visible 8 apparent, manifest, striking 9 egregious, prominent 10 celebrated, noticeable 11 discernable, distinctive, illustrious, outstanding, perspicuous 13 distinguished

conspiracy: 4 coup, plan, plot, ring 5 cabal, junto 6 scheme 7 compace 8 intrigue 9 agreement, champerty 11 combination, concurrence, confederacy, machination

conspire: 4 abet, plot 5 unite 6 league, scheme 7 collude, complot, conjure 8 contrive 9 cooperate 11 confederate

constable: cop 4 bull 6 beadle, harman, keeper, warden 7 bailiff, officer 8 tipstaff 9 policeman

constancy: 4 zeal 5 ardor 6 fealty 7 loyalty 8 devotion, fidelity 9 adherence, diligence, eagerness, integrity, stability 10 allegiance, attachment 11 earnestness 12 perseverance
symbol of: 6 garnet

constant: set 4 even, firm, leal, true 5 fixed, loyal, solid, still, tried 6 stable, steady 7 certain, chronic, durable, forever, lasting, regular, staunch, uniform 8 enduring, faithful, positive, resolute 9 confident, continual, immovable, incessant, permanent, perpetual, steadfast, unvarying 10 invariable, persistent, unwavering

Constantine: *birthplace:* 4 Nish
mother: 6 Helena
wife: 6 Fausta

Constantinople: See **Istanbul**

constate: 6 assert 9 establish

constellation (see also **star**): 5 group 6 dipper 7 cluster, pattern 10 assemblage 13 configuration
altar: Ara
archer: 11 Sagittarius
Argo division: 4 Vela
arrow: 7 Sagitta
balance: 5 Libra
bear: 4 Ursa
bird of paradise: 5 Apus
bull: 6 Taurus
Champion: 7 Perseus
charioteer: 6 Auriga
Charles' Wain: 6 Dipper
clock: 10 Horologium
compass: 5 Pyxis 8 Circinus
crab: 6 Cancer
crane: 4 Grus
cross: 4 Cruz
crow: 6 Corvus
crown: 6 Corona
dipper: 4 Ursa
dog: 5 Canis
dolphin: 9 Delphinus
dove: 7 Columba
dragon: 5 Draco
eagle: 6 Aquila
fish: 6 Pisces
goat: 9 Capricorn
herdsman: 6 Bootes
hunter: 5 Orion
lady, chained: 9 Andromeda
lady in the chair: 10 Cassiopeia
lion: Leo
lyre: 4 Lyra
maiden: 5 Virgo
northern: Leo 4 Coma, Lynx, Lyra, Ursa 5 Aries, Canes, Draco 6 Aquila, Auriga,

Bootes, Cancer, Cygnus, Gemini, Taurus 7 Cepheus, Lacerta, Pegasus, Sagitta 8 Hercules 9 Andromeda, Delphinus, Vulpecula 10 Cassiopeia
peacock: 4 Pavo
rabbit: 5 Lepus
ram: 5 Aries
sails: 4 Vela
southern: Ara 4 Apus, Argo, Crux, Grus, Pavo, Vela 5 Canis, Cetus, Hydra, Indus, Lepus, Libra, Mensa, Musca, Norma, Virgo 6 Antlia, Carina, Corvus, Crater, Dorado, Fornax, Pictor, Pisces, Puppis, Tucana, Volans 7 Columba, Phoenix, Sextans 8 Aquarius, Circinus, Sculptor, Scorpius 9 Centaurus, Chameleon, Monoceros, Reticulum 10 Horologium 11 Capricornus, Sagittarius 12 Microscopium
stern: 6 Puppis
swan: 6 Cygnus
twins: 6 Gemini
water bearer: 8 Aquarius
whale: 5 Cetus
winged horse: 7 Pegasus
wolf: 5 Lupus

consternation: 4 fear 5 alarm, panic 7 dismay, fright, horror, terror 9 amazement, trepidity 11 trepidation 12 befuddlement

constituent: 4 item, part 5 piece, voter 6 detail, factor, matter, member 7 elector, element 9 component 10 ingredient

constitute: fix, set 4 form, make 5 enact, forge, found, shape 6 depute, graith, ordain 7 appoint, compose, station 8 compound, comprise 9 determine, establish 10 commission

constitution: law 4 code 5 being, canon, humor, state 6 custom, health, nature, temper 7 charter 8 physique 9 enactment, ordinance, structure 11 composition, disposition 12 organization

Constitution: 9 Ironsides

Constitution State: 11 Connecticut

constitutional: 4 walk 6 innate 8 exercise 9 essential, organical 10 congenital

constrain: 4 bend, bind, curb, fain, urge 5 chain, check, clasp, cramp, deter, drive, force, impel, limit, press 6 coerce, compel, oblige, ravish, secure 7 astrict, confine, enforce, oppress, repress, violate 8 compress, distress, restrain 9 constrict 10 constringe 11 necessitate

constraint: 4 bond 5 force 6 duress, stress 7 reserve 8 coercion, distress, pressure 9 captivity, restraint, stiffness 10 compulsion, obligation 11 compression, confinement

constrict: tie 4 bind, curb, grip 5 choke, cramp, limit 6 hamper, shrink, strait 7 astrict, deflate, squeeze, tighten 8 astringe, compress, condense, contract, restrict 9 constrain 10 constipate, constringe
breath: 8 strangle

constrictor: boa 5 snake 6 python 8 anaconda 9 sphincter

constringe: See **constrict**

construct: 4 form, make, rear 5 build, dight, erect, frame, model 6 devise 7 arrange, combine, compose, confect, fashion 8 construe, engineer 9 fabricate, originate

construction: 7 synesis 8 building

constructive: 7 helpful 8 creative, implicit, inferred

construe: 5 infer, parse 6 render 7 analyze, dissect, explain, expound, resolve 9 construct, interpret, translate

consuetude: use 4 wont 5 habit, usage 6 custom 8 practice

consuetudinary: 6 manual, ritual

consul's recognition: 9 exequatur

consult: ask 5 cabal, refer 6 advise, confer, decree, devise 7 concert, counsel, discuss, meeting 8 consider, contrive, decision 9 agreement, determine 10 deliberate

consultant: 6 expert 7 adviser

consultation: 6 advice 7 council, counsel 9 collation, interview 10 conference, discussion 12 deliberation

consume: eat, use 4 burn, fret, rust, wear 5 drink, raven, spend, waste 6 absorb, absume, bezzle, canker, devour, engage, expend, perish 7 corrode, destroy, dwindle, engross, exhaust, swallow 8 squander 9 dissipate 10 incinerate, monopolize

consumer: 4 usee, user

consummate: end 4 fine, full, ripe 5 ideal, sheer 6 arrant, effect, finish 7 achieve, consume, crowned, perfect, perform 8 absolute, complete 9 culminate, exquisite 10 accomplish

consumption: use 5 decay, waste 7 expense 8 phthisis 11 destruction, expenditure 12 tuberculosis

contact: 4 abut, join, meet 5 touch, union 6 arrive, impact, syzyzy 7 meeting 8 junction, tangency, touching 10 connection, contiguity 11 contingency 13 juxtaposition

contagion: pox 5 taint, virus 6 miasma, poison 9 infection 13 contamination
preventative: 4 shot 8 antidote 10 alexiteric 11 prophylaxis

contagious: 7 noxious 8 catching 9 pestilent, spreading 10 infectuous

contain: 4 have, hold, keep 5 carry, check, cover, house 6 embody, retain 7 embrace, enclose, include, subsume, sustain 8 comprise, restrain 10 comprehend

container: bag, bin, box, can, cup, jug, keg, pan, pod, pot, tin, tub, urn, vat 4 cage, case, cask, crib, ewer, sack, silo, tank, vase 5 crate, cruet, gourd, pouch 6 barrel, basket, bottle, carboy, carton, hamper, hatbox, holder, shaker 7 bandbox, capsule, hanaper 8 canister, decanter, demijohn, hogshead, puncheon 10 receptacle

containing: For all phrases beginning with this word, see under the main word or phrase. EXAMPLES: "containing gold": see **gold** *containing;* "containing air": see **air** *containing.*

contaminate: 4 foul, harm, slur, soil 5 stain, sully, taint 6 befoul, debase, defile, infect, injure, poison 7 corrupt, debauch, pollute, tarnish, vitiate 8 dishonor 9 desecrate 10 adulterate

conte: 4 tale 9 narrative, novelette

contemn: 4 hate 5 flout, scorn, spurn 6 reject, slight 7 despise, disdain 8 contempt

contemplate: 4 muse, plan, scan, view 5 deign, study, think, weigh 6 ponder, regard, survey 7 propose, reflect 8 consider, meditate 9 speculate

contemplation: 5 study 6 musing, prayer, regard, theory 7 request 8 petition 9 intention 10 meditation 13 consideration

contemporaneous: 6 coeval, living, modern 7 current 8 existing, up-to-date 10 coincident 12 contemporary, simultaneous

contemporary: 6 coeval 7 current
comb. form: neo

contempt: 5 scorn, shame, sneer 6 slight 7 contemn, disdain, mockery 8 derision, disgrace 9 contumacy, contumely 10 disrespect 11 indignation
exclamation of: bah, foh 4 pooh

contemptible: low 4 base, mean, vile 5 cheap, petty, sorry 6 abject, paltry, scurvy, shabby, sordid, yellow 7 pitiful, scorned 8 beggarly, infamous, inferior, sneaking, unworthy, wretched 9 groveling, worthless 10 despicable 11 ignominious 12 dishonorable 13 insignificant

contemptuous: 7 haughty 8 arrogant, flouting, insolent, scornful 9 hubristic, insulting 10 despicable, disdainful 12 contemptible, supercilious

contend: vie, war 4 cope, race, wage 5 argue, bandy, brawl, claim, fight 6 assert, battle, bicker, buffet, bustle, combat, debate, oppose, reason, strive 7 bargain, compete, contest, dispute, quarrel 8 conflict, contrive, maintain, militate, squabble, struggle

contender: 7 entrant 10 contestant 11 protagonist

content: 4 calm, ease, gist, paid 5 happy 6 amount, please 7 appease, gratify, replete, satiate, satisfy, suffice, willing 8 capacity 9 satisfied 12 satisfaction

contented: 4 cozy 5 sated 8 cheerful 9 satisfied

contention: war 4 bait, bate, feud, riot, tiff 5 broil 6 combat, debate, strife 7 contest, discord, dispute, opinion, quarrel, rivalry, wrangle 8 argument, conflict, squabble, struggle, variance 9 rebellion 10 dissension, litigation 11 altercation, competition, controversy 12 disagreement

contentious: 7 peevish 8 perverse 9 litigious, wrangling 10 pugnacious 11 belligerent, quarrelsome 12 cantankerous, disputatious

contentment: 4 ease 5 bliss 8 pleasure 9 happiness 11 complacence 12 satisfaction 13 gratification

conterminous: 4 next 8 adjacent, proximal 9 adjoining

contest: bee, sue, try, vie 4 agon, bout, cope, duel, feud, fray, game, pitt, race, spar, tiff, tilt 5 broil, clash, fight, setto, trial 6 action, adjure, affray, battle, combat, debate, defend, oppose, resist, strife, strive 7 bargain, brabble, compete, contend, dispute, protest, tourney, warfare 8 argument, conflict, skirmish, struggle 9 champerty, encounter 10 controvert, tournament 11 altercation
kind of: 6 tryout 7 lawsuit 10 litigation

contestant: 4 vier 5 rival 6 player 7 agonist, entrant 8 finalist, prospect 9 combatant, candidate, contender, defendant, plaintiff 10 competitor 12 participator

contiguous: 4 next, nigh 6 nearby 8 abutting, adjacent, touching 9 adjoining, immediate, proximate 10 contacting 11 neighboring

continence: 6 virtue 8 chastity

continent: 4 Asia, land, mass 5 sober 6 Africa, chaste, Europe 7 content 8 capacity, mainland, moderate 9 Greenland, temperate 10 Antarctica, receptacle, restrained 12 South America
hypothetical: 8 Cascadia
lost: 8 Atlantis

contingency: 4 case 5 event 6 chance 7 adjunct, contact 8 fortuity, incident, prospect 9 accessory 11 possibility, uncertainty

contingent: 6 casual, chance 8 doubtful, touching 9 dependent 10 accidental, fortuitous 11 provisional
on discretion: 9 arbitrary

continual: 7 endless, lasting, regular, undying, uniform 8 constant, enduring, unbroken 9 ceaseless, connected, incessant, perennial, permanent, unceasing 10 continuous, invariable 11 everlasting, unremitting 12 imperishable 13 unintermitted, uninterrupted

continually: aye 4 ever 6 always, hourly, steady 7 endless, eternal, forever 9 perpetual 10 constantly 11 incessantly, unceasingly

continuance: 4 stay 5 delay 6 sequel 8 duration 9 endurance, procedure 10 continuity 11 adjournment 12 postponement, perseverance

continue: be 4 bide, dure, last, live, stay 5 abide, carry, exist, unite 6 beleve, endure, extend, remain, resume 7 beleave, connect, persist, proceed, prolong, sustain 8 protract 9 persevere

continued: 5 still 6 serial 7 chronic 8 constant 9 continual, extending 10 continuous, protracted

continuity: 6 script 8 cohesion, scenario 9 coherence 10 connection

contort: wry 4 bend, coil, turn, warp 5 gnarl, screw, twist, wrest 6 deform, writhe 7 distort, pervert 8 obvolute 9 convolute

contortionist: 7 acrobat

contour: 4 form, line 5 curve, graph, shape 6 figure 7 outline, profile 9 lineament 10 appearance, silhouette 13 configuration
outline: 13 configuration

contra: 6 offset 7 against, counter, opposed 11 contrasting 12 contrariwise

contraband: 5 goods 7 illegal, illicit 8 smuggled, unlawful

contract: get 4 bond, knit, pact 5 catch, cramp, incur, lease, limit 6 cartel, engage, lessen, narrow, pledge, pucker, reduce, shrink, treaty 7 abridge, bargain, compact, crumple, curtail, promise, shorten, shrivel, wrinkle 8 condense, covenant, restrict 9 agreement, betrothal, constrict, indenture 10 abbreviate, constringe, convention, obligation 11 arrangement, concentrate, stipulation
addition to: 5 rider 7 codicil
furnishing slaves: 8 assiento
part: 6 clause 7 proviso
unlawful: 10 chevisance

contraction: tic 5 cramp, spasm 6 intake, twitch 7 elision, epitome 9 gathering, reduction, shrinkage, stricture 10 abridgment, compendium, limitation 11 conciseness, confinement 12 abbreviation
common: een, eer, oer, oft, tis 5 arent, shant
heart: 8 systolic

contractor: 7 builder, remover 8 supplier

contradict: 4 deny 5 belie, rebut 6 forbid, impugn, negate, oppose, recant, refute 7 counter, gainsay 8 disprove 9 disaffirm 10 contravene, controvert

contradiction: 6 denial 7 paradox 8 antilogy

contradictory: 6 oppose 9 dissonant 12 incompatible, inconsistent

contraption: rig 4 tool 6 device, gadget 7 machine 11 contrivance

contrary: 5 snivy 6 averse, contra, ornery, snivey 7 adverse, counter, hostile, opposed, reverse, wayward 8 captious, contrair, inimical, opposite, perverse, petulant 9 refactory, repugnant, unpopular, vexatious 10 discordant, discrepant 11 prejudicial, unfavorable 12 antagonistic, cantankerous
to fact: 5 false
to law: 7 illegal 16 unconstitutional
to reason: 6 absurd

contrast: 6 strife 7 compare, contend 8 opposite 9 diversity 10 difference

contravene: 4 defy, deny 6 hinder, oppose, thwart 7 dispute, violate 8 infringe, obstruct 9 disregard 10 contradict

contravention: sin 4 vice 5 crime 6 breach 7 offense 9 violation 13 contradiction, transgression

contretemps: 4 slip 5 boner, hitch 6 mishap, scrape 8 accident 9 mischance 10 occurrence
music: 11 syncopation

contribute: aid 4 ante, give, help, tend 5 cause, grout 6 assist, bestow, concur, confer, donate, supply, tender 7 conduce, further 9 cooperate, subscribe

contribution: sum, tax 4 alms, boon, gift 5 essay, share 6 impost 7 article, largess, payment, present, renewal, writing 8 donation, offering 9 collation 10 imposition

contrite: 4 worn 5 sorry 6 humble, rueful 8 penitent 9 repentant, sorrowful

contrition: 7 penance, remorse

contrivance: art, gin 4 gear, plan, tool 5 shift 6 deceit, design, device, gadget, scheme 7 fiction, machine, project 8 adaption, artifice, resource 9 apparatus, appliance, doohickey, invention 10 conjecture, instrument 11 contraption

contrive: 4 brew, make, plan, plot 5 frame, fudge, hatch, weave 6 afford, design, devise, divine, invent, manage, scheme, wangle 7 achieve, agitate, concoct, consult, contend, fashion, procure, project 8 conspire, engineer, intrigue 9 fabricate, machinate 10 accomplish

contrived: pat 10 artificial

contriver: 8 Daedalus 9 architect 10 originator

control: law, run 4 curb, hold, rein, rule, sway 5 charm, check, grasp, gripe, guide, power, skill, steer 6 bridle, direct, empire, govern, handle, manage, regime, subdue 7 command, conduct, mastery, preside 8 attemper, dominate, dominion, hegemony, regulate, restrain 9 influence, ordinance, prescribe 10 ascendancy, manipulate, moderation, possession, regulation 11 predominate, superintend

controversial: 7 eristic 9 debatable, polemical 12 disputatious 13 argumentative

controversy: 4 spat, suit 5 chest 6 debate, strife 7 dispute, quarrel, wrangle 8 argument 10 contention, difference, difficulty, discussion, litigation 11 altercation 12 disagreement

controvert: 4 deny, face, moot 5 argue 6 debate, oppose, oppugn, refute 7 contest, dispute, gainsay 9 challenge 10 contradict

contumacious: 6 unruly 7 riotous 8 insolent, mutinous, perverse, stubborn 9 obstinate, seditious 10 disdainful, headstrong, rebellious, refractory, unyielding 11 disobedient, intractable 13 insubordinate

contumelious: 8 arrogant

contumely: 5 abuse, scorn 6 contek, insult 7 conteck, disdain 8 contempt, rudeness 9 arrogance 10 opprobrium 11 humiliation

contuse: 4 beat 5 pound 6 bruise, injure 7 squeeze

contusion: 4 blow, bump 6 bruise

conundrum: pun 4 whim 6 enigma, puzzle, riddle 7 conceit 8 crotchet

convalesce: 4 mend 7 recover 10 recuperate

convene: sit 4 call, meet 5 unite 6 gather, muster, summon 7 convoke 8 assemble, converge 10 congregate, foregather

convenience: 7 benefit, comfort 8 plumbing 9 appliance

convenient: fit 5 handy, ready 6 proper, useful 7 adapted, helpful 8 becoming, suitable 9 agreeable, available, congruous, favorable, opportune 10 accessible, commodious 11 appropriate 12 commensurate

convent: 5 abbey 6 priory 7 convent, meeting 8 cloister 9 community, monastery, sanctuary

head: 5 abbot 6 abbess 8 hegumene 10 hegumeness

member: nun 4 monk 8 cenobite

pert. to: 6 friary

reception room: 8 arlatory

room: 9 parlatory

superior: see *head* above

convention: 4 diet, feis, mise, rule 5 synod, usage 6 cartel, caucus, custom, treaty 7 decorum, meeting 8 assembly, congress, contract, covenant, practice 9 agreement, gathering, tradition 10 conference 11 convocation

conventional: 4 more 5 nomic, right, trite, usual 6 decent, formal, modish, proper 7 correct, regular 8 academic, accepted 9 customary, hidebound 10 ceremonial, stipulated 11 contractual

conventionalize: 7 conform, stylize

converge: 4 join, meet 5 focus 6 concur 8 approach

conversant: 5 adept 6 busied, expert, versed 7 skilled 8 familiar, occupied 9 concerned, practiced 10 acquainted, proficient

conversation: 4 chat, talk 6 confab, parley 7 conduct, palaver 8 behavior, chitchat, colloquy, dialogue, parlance 9 discourse 10 conference 11 association, interchange, intercourse 13 communication, interlocution

of three: 7 trialog 9 trialogue

private: 7 ceilidh(Sc.) 8 collogue 9 tete-a-tete

converse: 4 chat, chin, live, move, talk 5 dwell, speak 6 confer, homily, parley 7 commune, obverse, reverse 8 colloque, exchange, opposite 9 discourse 11 association, confabulate

convert: 4 turn 5 alter, amend, apply, renew 6 change, decode, direct, novice 7 restore, reverse 8 converse, neophyte, persuade 9 acetalize, proselyte, transform, translate, transmute, transpose 10 regenerate

convertible: 4 auto 7 soft-top 10 automobile, changeable, equivalent, reciprocal, synonymous 15 interchangeable

convex: 5 bowed 6 arched, camber, curved 7 bulging, gibbous, rounded 9 cymbiform 11 protuberant

molding: 5 ovolo, torus

convey: 4 bear, cart, cede, deed, lead, mean, pass, send, take, tote, will 5 bring, carry, grant, guide, hurry, steal 6 assign, convoy, delate, demise, devise, eloign, impart, import, remove 7 auction, conduct, deliver, dispone, dispose 8 alienate, bequeath, transfer, transmit 9 accompany, transport 11 communicate

conveyance: bus, car, sak 4 auto, cart, deed, sled, taxi, tram 5 grant, stage, theft, train, wagon 6 demise 7 charter, conduct, rattler, trailer, trolley, vecture, vehicle, waftage 8 carriage, carrying, stealing, transfer 9 transport 10 automobile 11 transmittal

public: el; bus, cab, car 4 taxi, tram 5 train 6 subway 7 omnibus, ricksha, steamer 8 airplane, elevated, railroad, rickshaw 10 jinricksha, jinrikisha

convict: 4 find 5 argue, felon, lifer, prove 6 attain, termer, trusty 7 attaint, captive, condemn, culprit 8 criminal, jailbird, prisoner, sentence 10 malefactor

collar: 6 carcan

conviction: 5 creed, dogma, faith, tenet 6 belief, credit 7 opinion 8 sentence

convinced: 4 sold, sure 6 assure, subdue 7 certain 8 overcome, positive 9 persuaded
convincing: 5 sound, valid 6 cogent, potent 7 telling 8 forcible 10 conclusive, persuasive
convivial: gay 4 boon 6 festal, genial, jovial, social 7 festive, jocular 8 reveling
convocation: 4 diet 5 synod 7 calling, council, meeting 8 assembly, congress 9 gathering 10 convention 12 congregation
convoke: bid 4 call, cite, meet 6 gather, muster, summon 7 convene 8 assemble
convolute: 4 coil, roll, wind 5 twist 6 tangle, writhe 7 contort 8 obvolute
convolution: 4 coil, curl, fold 5 gyrus, whorl 9 sinuosity
of brain: 5 gyrus
convolve: 5 twist 6 enwrap, enfold, infold, writhe
convolvulus: 4 vine
convoy: 4 lead 5 carry, guard, guide, pilot, watch 6 attend, convey, escort, manage 7 conduct 9 accompany, conductor, safeguard
convulse: 4 rock, stir 5 shake 6 excite 7 agitate, disturb
convulsion: fit 5 shrug, spasm, throe 6 attack, tumult, uproar 8 laughter, paroxysm 9 agitation, commotion 11 disturbance
cony: das 4 hare, pika 5 daman, dassy, ganam, hutia, hyrox, lapen 6 burbot, dassie, gazabo, gazebo, rabbit 7 ashkoko
catcher: 5 cheat 7 sharper 8 swindler
coo: 4 curr(Sc.), woot 6 murmer
coof: 4 dolt, lout 9 blockhead
cook: fix, fry 4 bake, boil, chef, make, sear, stew 5 broil, grill, poach, roast, shirr, steam 6 braise, decoct, sautee, seethe, simmer 7 prepare, process, servant 8 cusinero, magirist 9 cuisinier
in simmering liquid: 4 poach
one's goose: 5 spoil 6 defeat
partially: 7 parboil
cooked: 4 done
cookery: 7 cuisine, science 8 magirics
cookie, cooky: 4 cake, snap 6 hermit 7 brownie, oatcake 8 seedcake 10 confection, gingersnap
cooking: *art:* 7 cuisine 8 magirics
device: 4 etna 5 range, stove 7 brazier, griddle 10 rotisserie
odor: 5 nidor
pert. to: 8 culinary
room: 5 cuddy 6 galley 7 kitchen
vessel: pan, pot 4 etna, olla 6 caster, chafer, spider, tureen 7 broiler, griddle, roaster, skillet, steamer 8 colander, fleshpot 9 autoclave
cool: air, fan, ice 4 calm, cold 5 algid, allay, chill, fresh, gelid, nervy, sober, staid, whole 6 chilly, placid, quench, sedate, serene 7 unmoved 8 careless, cautious, composed, mitigate, moderate, tranquil 9 apathetic, collected, officious, temperate, unruffled 10 deliberate, nonchalant, unfriendly 11 indifferent, refrigerate, unconcerned 12 unresponsive 13 dispassionate, imperturbable 15 undemonstrative
one's heels: 4 wait
cooled: 6 frappe
cooler: 4 icer, jail, olla 5 drink 6 icebox, lockup, prison 11 refrigerant 12 refrigerator
coolie: 7 changar
cooling device: fan 7 freezer 12 refrigerator 14 air-conditioner
coolness: 5 nerve 6 aplomb 8 serenity 9 assurance
coom, coomb: 4 smut, soot 5 frame, grime 6 grease, refuse
coony: sly 4 cute, foxy 6 clever, crafty
coop: cot, cub, mew, pen, pot 4 cage, cote, jail 5 cramp, hutch 6 basket, corral 7 confine 9 enclosure 11 cooperative
cooperate: 4 tend 5 agree, coact, unite 6 concur 7 combine, conduce, connive 8 coadjute, conspire 10 contribute 11 collaborate
cooperation: 8 teamwork
cooperator: 9 auxiliary, colleague 10 accomplice
coordinate: 5 adapt, equal 6 adjust 7 arrange, syntony 8 classify 9 harmonize 10 concurrent
coordination: 4 bond 7 harmony, liaison 12 relationship
inability: 6 abasia
lack: 8 asynergy
coorie: 5 cower, stoop 6 crouch
cooser: 8 stallion
coot: 4 duck, fowl, rail 5 smyth 6 beltie, person, scoter 7 henbill 13 phalacrocorax
cooter: 4 idle 6 loiter, turtle 8 tortoise
cottie: nit 4 bowl, game 5 louse 6 vessel 8 grayback
cop: bag, nab, rob 4 bank, blow, bull, head, heap, lift, pile, trap, tube 5 catch, crest, filch, mount, quill, shock, snare, steal, stock, swipe 6 peeler, spider, strike 7 capture 9 patrolman, policeman
cop-out: 7 retreat 9 defection
copacetic: 4 fine 5 dandy, prime 6 snappy 7 capital 12 satisfactory
copaiba: 4 tree 6 balsam 9 oleoresin
copain: pal 4 chum 7 comrade
copal: 5 anime, resin
cope: vie, war 4 cape, duty, face 5 cappa, cloak, cover, dress, equal, fight, match, notch, rival, vault, wield 6 barter, canopy,

chapel, combat, mantel, muzzle, oppose, strike, strive 7 contend, contest 8 complete, exchange, struggle, vestment 9 encounter

copemate: 7 comrade, partner 9 associate 10 antagonist

Copenhagen: *park:* 6 Tivoli

shopping district: 7 Stroget

copestone: 5 crown 6 coping

copier: 4 stat 5 Xerox

copious: 4 full, good, lush, rich 5 ample, large 6 fluent, lavish 7 diffuse, flowing, fulsome, profuse, replete, teeming, uberous 8 abundant, affluent, numerous 9 exuberant, plenteous, plentiful, redundant 11 overflowing

copper: cu; cop 4 bull, cent 5 bobby, metal, penny 6 cuprum, peeler 9 butterfly, policeman

alloy: 5 brass 6 oroide 7 rheotan

arsenic sulfide: 8 enargite

coin: 4 cent 5 brown, penny

comb. form: 5 cupro 6 chalco

engraving: 9 mezzotint

sulphate: 7 vitriol

copper nickel: 9 niccolite

Copperfield's wife: 4 Dora 5 Agnes

copperhead: 5 snake, viper

coppice: 4 wood 5 copse, firth, grove 6 forest, growth 7 thicket 9 brushwood, underwood

Copreus: *father:* 6 Pelops

son: 10 Periphetes

victim: 7 Iphitus

copse: cut, hag 4 hasp, trim 6 clevis 7 coppice, shackle

Copt: 8 Egyptian 9 Christian 11 monophysite

dialect: 8 Bohairic

title: 4 anba

copula: 4 band, link 5 union 7 coupler

copy: ape 4 echo, edit, mime 5 dummy, image, mimic 6 ectype, effigy, follow, record 7 emulate, estreat, imitate, redraft, replica, reprint, tracing 8 apograph, likeness 9 abundance, antigraph, duplicate, imitation, reproduce 10 transcribe, transcript 11 counterpart 12 reproduction

kind of: 6 carbon, ectype 7 estreat, extract, pattern, replica 9 duplicate, facsimile

true: 7 estreat

copying: 7 mimicry 8 mimetism

copyist: 6 scribe 7 copycat 10 plagiarist

pert. to: 8 clerical

copyread: 4 edit

copyright: 6 patent

infringe: 6 pirate 10 plagiarize

coque: bow 4 loop 8 trimming

coquette: toy 5 dally, flirt 6 trifle 9 philander 11 hummingbird

coquettish: coy

coquila: 4 palm 6 cohune 7 attalea

cora: 7 gazelle

coral: red 4 pink 5 polyp 6 palule 8 skeleton, zoophyte 9 madrepore, millepore 10 stalactite

division: 7 aporosa

formation: 5 palus

island: key 4 reef 5 atoll

corbel: 5 ancon 6 timber 10 projection

corbie: 4 crow 5 raven

cord: rib 4 band, bind, bond, cord, welt 5 nerve, twine 6 bobbin, sennet, string, tendon 7 amentum, measure 10 aiquilette, cordeliere

drapery: 7 torsade

goat's hair: 4 agal

parachute: 7 ripcord

cordage: da 4 rope, coir, eruc, feru, hemp, imbe, jute 5 fiber 6 sennit 7 rigging

Corday's victim: 5 Marat

corded: 4 tied 6 repped, ribbed, welted 7 stacked, twilled

Cordelia: *father:* 4 Lear

sister: 5 Regan 7 Goneril

cordelle: tow 4 cord, rope 7 towline, towrope

cordial (see also **liqueur**): 4 real, warm 5 shrub 6 ardent, elixir, genial, hearty 7 liqueur, sincere, zealous 8 anisette, friendly, gracious, vigorous 9 courteous, unfeigned 10 hospitable

apricot: 8 periscot

flavoring: 7 aniseed

cordiality: 5 ardor 6 regard, warmth 10 friendship, heartiness

cordon: 4 cord 5 braid, group, guard 6 ribbon

bleu: 10 decoration

sanitary: 10 quarantine

core: cob, hub, nut 4 coke, gist, nave, pith 5 focus, heart, nowse, spool 6 center, centre, kernel, matrix, middle, nodule 7 company, corncob, essence, nucleus 9 substance

corf: tub 4 cage, corb, skip 5 creel 6 basket, dosser

corge: 5 score 6 twenty

corinne: 7 gazelle

Corinth's king: 7 Polybus

corium: 5 layer 6 dermis

cork: oak 4 plug 5 float, shive 6 bobber 7 soberin, stopper, stopple

pert. to: 7 suberic

tissue: 5 suber

wax: 5 cerin

corking: 4 fine 8 pleasing 9 excellent

corkscrew: 6 defect, spiral

corkwood: 5 balsa 6 blolly

cormorant: 4 bird, shag 5 norie, scart 6 gormaw, scarth 7 glutton 8 ravenous 13 phalacrocorax
young: 7 shaglet
corn: 4 salt, samp 5 grain, maize, mealy 6 clavis, heloma, kernel 7 callous 8 preserve 9 granulate
bread: 4 pone
dealer: 10 cornmonger
ear: cob 5 mealy 6 mealie, nubbin
food: 6 hominy
ground: 4 meal 5 grist
hulled: 4 samp 6 hominy
Indian: zea
knife: 7 machete
spike: cob, ear
corn bread: 4 pone 8 tortilla
Corncracker State: 8 Kentucky
corndodger: 4 pone 5 bread 8 dumpling
corned: 6 salted
cornel: 4 tree 6 cherry 7 dogwood
corner: in; get, wro 4 bend, cant, coin, nook, pool, trap, tree 5 angle, bight, catch, coign, elbow, herne, ingle, niche, quoin, trust 6 cantle, canton, coigne, cranny, recess 8 monopoly
cornerpiece: 6 cantle
cornerstone: 4 coin 5 basis, coign 6 coigne 7 support 9 curbstone 10 foundation
cornet: 4 horn 8 woodwind 10 instrument
cornflower: 7 barbeau 10 bluebottle
cornhouse: 7 granary 8 corncrib
Cornhusker State: 8 Nebraska
cornice: 4 band, drip, eave 5 crown 6 geison 7 molding 8 astragal
basket: 4 caul
diamond: 6 quartz
support: 5 ancon
wolframite: cal
cornmeal: 4 masa, samp 5 atole 7 hoecake 10 johnnycake
cornucopia: 4 horn
Cornwall: *castle:* 8 Tintagel
mine: bal 5 wheal
ore: 5 whits
Cornwallis' surrender site: 8 Yorktown
corny: 5 banal, stale, trite 11 sentimental
corolla: 4 bell 8 perianth
part: 5 galea, petal
corollary: 5 dogma 6 result, truism 7 adjunct, theorem 9 deduction, inference 11 consequence, proposition
geometric: 6 porism
corona: 5 cigar, crown, glory 6 fillet, rosary, wreath 7 aureole, circlet, garland, scyphus
coronation: 9 inaugural
stone: 5 Scone
coroner: 6 elisor 7 officer 8 examiner
coronet: 4 band, burr 5 crown, tiara 6 anadem, circle, diadem, timbre, wreath 7 chaplet
coronopus: 4 herb 6 carara
corporal: NCO 4 fano 5 fanon, fanum, phano 6 bodily
corporal punishment: 5 death 7 penalty 8 spanking, whipping
corporate: 6 united 8 combined 9 aggregate
corporation: 4 body, firm 5 trust 10 fellowship, foundation 11 association, combination
corporeal: 4 real 5 hylic, somal 6 actual, bodily, carnal 7 somatic 8 material, physical, tangible 11 substantial
corpse: DOA 4 body 5 mummy, relic, stiff 7 cadaver, carcass, carrion
fat of: 9 adipocere
pert. to: 7 deathly 10 cadaverous
corpulent: fat 5 bulky, burly, husky, obese, plump, stout 6 fleshy, portly, rotund 7 adipose, bellied, weighty 8 rolypoly
corpus: 4 body 8 writings 10 literature
corpuscle: 4 cell 9 leucocyte
lack of red: 6 anemia
redblood: 7 hematid 8 haematid 11 poikilocyte, schistocyte
corral: pen, sty 4 coop 5 atajo, pound 7 confine, enclose 8 stockage, surround 9 enclosure, inclosure
correct: O.K.; due, fit, fix 4 edit, lean, nice, okay, smug, true 5 amend, check, emend, exact, right 6 adjust, better, change, inform, proper, punish, rebuke, reform, remedy, repair, revamp, revise, strict 7 chasten, improve, perfect, precise, rectify, redress, reprove 8 accurate, chastise, definite, emendate, regulate, rigorous, truthful 9 castigate, faultless 10 immaculate, particular, scrupulous 11 punctilious 12 conventional
comb. form: 5 ortho
correctable: 10 corrigible
correlated: 4 akin 7 related
correlative: or; nor 4 then 5 equal, still 6 either, mutual 7 neither 8 analogue, conjoint 9 analogous 10 reciprocal 13 correspondent
correspond: fit, gee 4 jibe, suit 5 agree, match, tally, write 6 accord, concur, square 7 conport, respond 8 coincide, parallel, quadrate 9 analogous, harmonize 11 communicate
correspondence: 4 mail 7 analogy, letters, traffic 8 homology 9 assonance, congruity 10 similarity

correspondent: 8 quadrate, suitable 9 accordant, analogous, congruous 10 accomplice, concordant, equivalent 11 conformable, contributor, correlative
corresponding: *in sound:* 5 rimic 6 rhymic
part: 7 isomere
corrida: 9 bullfight
corridor: 4 hall 5 aisle, oriel 6 arcade 7 couloir, gallery 8 coulisse 10 passageway
corrie: 6 cirque, hollow
corrigible: 8 amenable 10 corrective, punishable 11 correctable
corroborant: 5 tonic 10 supporting 12 invigorating 13 strengthening
corroborate: 5 prove 7 confirm, support, sustain 9 establish 11 countersign 12 substantiate
corrode: eat 4 bite, burn, etch, gnaw, rust 5 decay, erode, waste 6 be-gnaw, canker, impair 7 consume
corrosive: 4 acid 6 ardent, biting 7 caustic, erosive, fretful, mordant 9 sarcastic 11 destructive 14 disintegrating
corrugate: 5 crimp 6 furrow, rumple 7 crinkle, crumple, wrinkle
corrugation: 4 fold 6 crease, pucker 7 wrinkle
corrupt: bad, low, rot 4 evil, vile 5 blend, bribe, spoil, stain, sully, taint, venal 6 augean, canker, debase, impure, poison, putrid, ravish, rotten 7 abusive, attaint, carrion, crooked, defiled, degrade, deprave, envenom, falsify, immoral, pervert, pollute, putrefy, violate, vitiate 8 confound, empoison 9 abandoned, dishonest 10 adulterate, demoralize, flagitious, profligate 11 contaminate, purchasable
corsage: 5 waist 6 bodice, boquet 7 bouquet, flowers
corsair: bug 6 pirate, robber 8 picaroon, rockfish 9 privateer 10 buccanneer
body: 5 armor, cover
corset: 4 belt, busk 6 girdle 7 support
covering: 8 camisole
strip: 4 bone, busk
Corsica: *seaport:* 6 Bastia
town: 7 Ajaccio
corslet: 6 bodice 8 corselet 11 breastplate
cortege: 5 suite, train 6 parade 7 retinue 10 procession
cortex: 4 bark, peel, rind 8 peridium
corundum: 4 ruby, sand 5 emeru, emery 7 alumina 8 abrasive, sapphire
coruscate: 5 blaze, flash, gleam, shine 7 glisten, glitter, radiate, sparkle 8 brandish 11 scintillate
corviform: 7 corvine 8 crowlike
corvine bird: daw 4 crow, rook 5 raven
coryza: 4 cold
symptom: 6 sneeze
cos: 7 lettuce, romaine
cosa nostra: 5 Mafia 9 syndicate
cosh: 4 neat, snug, tidy 5 happy, quiet, still 6 attack, lively, strike, weapon 7 assault 8 familiar, friendly 11 comfortable
cosher: pet 4 chat 5 feast, visit 6 pamper, sponge
cosmetic: 5 cream, henna, liner, paint, rouge 6 enamel, pomade, powder 7 mascara 8 lipstick
medicated: 6 lotion
paste: 4 pack
white lead: 6 ceruse
cosmic: 4 vast 7 orderly 8 catholic, infinite 9 universal 10 harmonious
opposed to: 7 chaotic
cosmonaut: See **astronaut**
cosmopolitan: 5 urban 8 ecumenic 10 ecumenical 13 sophisticated
cosmos: 5 earth, globe, order, realm, world 6 flower 7 harmony 8 universe
opposed to: 5 Chaos
Cossack: 4 Turk 5 tatar 6 ataman, hetman, tartar 7 Russian 10 cavalryman
captain: 6 Sotnik
chief: 6 ataman, hetman
district: 6 voisko
mount: 5 steed 7 charger
regiment: 4 polk, pulk
squadron: 6 sotnia, sotnya
village: 8 stanitza
whip: 5 knout
cosset: pet 4 lamb 6 caress, coddle, cuddle, fondle, pamper
cossette: 4 chip 5 slice, strip 9 schnitzel
cossid: 9 messenger
cost: 4 loss, pain 5 price, value 6 charge, outlay 7 expense 8 estimate 9 detriment, sacrifice, suffering 11 deprivation, expenditure 14 characteristic
costa: rib 4 side, vein 5 ridge 6 border, midrib
Costa Rica: *city:* 7 Heredia, San Jose(c.) 8 Alajuela
coin: 5 colon 7 centimo
measure: 6 fanega, tercia 7 cajuela, manzana 10 caballeria
mountain: 6 Blanco 8 Chirripo
people: 6 Guaymi 7 Guaymie
port: 10 Porto Limon 11 Punta Arenas
volcano: 5 Barba
weight: bag 4 caja
costate: 6 ribbed
costermonger: 6 coster, hawker, nipper 7 peddler

costly: 4 dear, fine, high, rich 6 lavish 8 gorgeous, precious, prodigal, splendid 9 dearthful, expensive, priceless, sumptuous 11 extravagant

costmary: 4 herb 5 plant, tansy 7 alecost

costrel: keg 4 head 5 flask 6 bottle

costume (see also **dress, vestment**): rig 4 garb, robe, sari, suit 5 dress, getup, habit 6 attire 7 apparel, clothes, raiment, uniform 8 clothing, ensemble 10 habiliment

costus root: 4 herb 6 pachak, pochok

cot: bed, hut, mat, pen 4 boat, coop, cote, fold 5 abode, cabin, couch, cover, house, stall 6 pallet, sheath, tangle 7 charpai, charpoy, cottage, shelter 8 bedstead, dwelling 9 sheepfold, stretcher 11 fingerstall

cote: cot, hut 4 coop, fold, shed, wine 5 house, quote 7 cottage, shelter 8 hillside, outstrip, vineyard 9 inclosure, sheepfold

Cote d'Azur: 7 Riviera

coterie: set 4 ring 5 junto, monde 6 circle, clique, galaxy 7 platoon, society 9 camarilla

cothamore: 8 overcoat 9 greatcoat

cothurnus: 4 boot 6 buskin

cotta: 6 mantle 7 blanket 8 surplice, vestment

cottage: cot, hut 4 bari, cosh 5 bower, cabin, house, lodge, shack 6 bohawn, cabana, chalet 7 shelter 9 hosthouse 10 guesthouse
 partition: 5 speer 6 hallan

cottage cheese: 9 smearcase

cotter, cottar: mat, pin, vex 4 clot 6 fasten, potter, pucker, shrink, toggle, wither 7 congeal, cottier, peasant, shrivel, villein 8 cottager, cotterel, entangle 9 coagulate

cotton: 4 beat, flog 5 agree, bayal, derry 6 coddle, dhurry, fabric, nankin 7 algodon, dhurrie, garment, succeed 8 perceive 9 harmonize 10 fraternize, understand
 and linen: 7 fustian
 cleaner: 5 willy 6 willow
 cloth: 4 baft, jean, lawn, leno, susi 5 bafta, bluet, denim, doria, khaki, lisle, manta, surat, terry, vichy, wigan 6 baline, calico, cangan, hum-hum 7 camboye, cotonia, galatea, jaconet, nankeen, percale, silesia
 cloth blemish: nit
 Egyptian: sak 4 Pima 5 sakel
 extraction: 5 bolly
 fabric: 4 leno
 fiber: 4 lint 6 stapel
 flowered: 6 chintz
 gauze: 4 leno
 handkerchief: 7 malabar
 knot in: nep 4 slub
 lawn: 7 batiste
 light: 7 etamine
 long-staple: 4 maco
 measure: lea 4 hank
 printed: 6 calico
 refuse: 8 grabbots
 seed pod: 4 boll 5 bolly
 seed remover: gin
 sheeting: 5 manta 6 muslin 7 percale 8 drilling
 striped: 5 bezan 7 express
 strong: 4 duck 5 scrim 6 canvas
 thread: 5 lisle
 twilled: 4 jean 7 silesia
 waste: 4 noil 6 linter

cotton gin inventor: 10 Eli Whitney

Cotton State: 7 Alabama

cottonseed kernel: 4 meat

cottontail: 4 hare 7 leveret

cottonwood: 4 tree 5 alamo 6 poplar

couch: bed, cot, lie 4 hide, lair, lurk, sofa 5 divan, inlay, lodge, press, skulk, slink, sneak, squat, stoop, utter 6 burrow, litter, pallet, settee 7 conceal, express, overlay, recline 8 disguise 9 accubitus(L.), davenport, embroider

couch grass: 5 quack, quick 6 quitch, scutch

couchant: 4 abed 5 prone 6 supine 7 lurking 9 crouching, squatting

cougar: cat 4 puma 7 panther 9 catamount

cough: 4 bark, hack 5 hoast 6 tussis 9 pertussis
 pert. to: 7 tussive

cough drop: 6 pastil, troche 7 lozenge 8 pastille

cough up: 4 ante 5 yield 10 contribute

coulee: 4 lava 5 gorge, gulch 6 ravine

council: 4 body, dael, diet, rede 5 board, boule, cabal, divan, junta, junto, synod 6 senate 7 cabinet, consult, meeting 8 assembly, conclave, congress, hustling, ministry 10 conference, consistory, federation 11 convocation 12 consultation
 church: 5 synod
 pert. to: 7 cameral
 political: 5 cabal, junta
 table cover: 5 tapis

councilman: 11 concionator

counsel: 4 lore, rede, rule, warn 5 chide 6 advice, advise, confer 7 caution 8 admonish, advocate, prudence 9 barrister, counselor, recommend 10 counsellor 11 exhortation, instruction 12 consultation, deliberation

counselor, counsellor: 4 sage 6 lawyer, mentor, nestor 7 adviser, advisor, counsel, proctor 8 attorney 9 barrister

counselor-at-law: 9 barrister

count: add, tot 4 bank, cast, earl, foot, graf, name, rely, tell, tote 5 comte(F.), judge, score, tally 6 census, depend, esteem, figure, impute, number, reckon 7 account, ascribe, compute 8 numerate, sanction 9 ascertain, calculate, enumerate

Count of Monte Cristo: 6 Dantes

count on: 4 lean, rely 6 expect

countenance: aid, mug 4 abet, brow, face, mien, puss, show, vult 5 favor, front 6 aspect, favour, visage 7 approve, bearing, conduct, endorse, feature, proffer, support 8 befriend, demeanor, sanction 9 demeanour, encourage, semblance 10 appearance 11 physiognomy

counter: bar 4 chip, dump, eddy, pawn 5 shelf, stand, table 6 combat, marker, oppose 7 adverse, contend, current 8 contrary, opposite 10 contradict

counter-irritant: 4 moxa 5 seton, stupe 6 arnica, iodine, pepper 7 mustard 8 liniment

counteract: 5 check 6 oppose, resist, thwart 7 balance, destroy, nullify 8 antidote 9 frustrate 10 compensate, neutralize 11 countermand 12 counterpoise

counterattack: 6 answer, charge

countercurrent: 4 eddy 5 swirl 9 whirlpool

counterfeit: tin 4 base, copy, coin, duff, fake, mock, sham 5 belie, bogus, dummy, false, feign, forge, fudge, phony, queer 6 affect, assume, forged, pseudo, tinsel 7 falsify, feigned, imitate 8 deformed, simulate, spurious 9 brummagem, disguised, dissemble 10 adulterate, artificial, fictitious, fraudulent

counterfoil 4 stub 5 check

countermand 4 stop 5 annul 6 cancel, forbid, recall, revoke 7 abolish, rescind, reverse 8 abrogate, prohibit 9 frustrate 10 counteract

counterpart: 4 copy, like, mate, twin 5 image, match 6 double 7 obverse 8 parallel 9 duplicate, facsimile 10 complement, equivalent, similitude

counterpoint: 4 foil 7 deecant 8 contrast 11 arrangement 13 juxtaposition

counterpoise: 6 offset 7 balance 8 equalize 10 compensate, counteract 13 counterweight 14 counterbalance

countersign: 4 mark, seal, sign 6 signal 7 confirm, endorse 8 consigne, password, sanction 9 signature, watchword 11 corroborate

countersink: 4 ream 5 bevel 7 chamfer

countertenor: 4 alto 8 falsetto

counting frame: 6 abacus

countless: 8 infinite 10 numberless 12 incalculable

country: 4 home, land, pais(Sp.) 5 addle, realm, state, tract, weald 6 ground, nation, people, region, sticks 8 district 9 champaign, territory 12 commonwealth
ancient: 4 Aram, Elam, Elis 5 Sheba
man: 4 jake, rube 5 swain, yokel 6 farmer, rustic 7 bumpkin, hayseed, plowman 10 compatriot, inhabitant
mythical: Oz
open: 4 moot, wold 5 heath, weald
pert. to: 5 rural 6 rustic 7 predial 8 agrestic, pastoral, praedial
place: 4 farm, peat 5 ranch, villa
reside in: 9 rusticate
road: 4 lane, path 5 byway

county: 4 seat 5 shire 6 domain, parish 7 borough 8 district

coup: buy 4 blow, plan, play 5 scoop, upset 6 attack, barter, strike, stroke 7 capsize, traffic 8 overturn 9 stratagem

coup-cart: 8 dumpcart

coup de grace: end 7 quietus 9 deathblow

coup d'etat: 9 stratagem 10 revolution

couple: duo, tie, two 4 bond, case, dyad, join, link, mate, pair, span, team, twin, yoke 5 brace, leash, marry, twain, unite 7 bracket, connect, coupler 8 assemble

coupled: 5 yoked 6 joined, wedded 7 gemalad 8 geminate 9 conjugate

coupler: 4 link, ring 7 drawbar, shackle, tirasse

couplet: 4 pair, poem 5 brace 7 distich

coupon: 4 form, slip, stub 5 check, stamp 7 portion

courage: 4 grit, guts, prow, sand, soul 5 heart, nerve, pluck, spunk, valor 6 daring, mettle, spirit 7 bravery, heroism, prowess 8 audacity, boldness, firmness, tenacity 9 assurance, fortitude, gallantry, hardihood 10 resolution
symbol of: 10 bloodstone

courageous: 4 bold, game 5 brave, hardy, manly, stout 6 daring, heroic, manful, plucky 7 gallant, spartan, staunch, valiant 8 fearless, intrepid, valorous 9 undaunted 11 adventurous 12 enterprising

courant, courante: 4 romp 5 caper, dance, music 6 letter 7 current, gazette, running 9 messenger, newspaper

courier: 4 post 5 guide, scout 7 estafet, orderly, postboy, soilage 8 cicerone, dragoman, estafeet, horseman 9 attendant, messenger 10 cavalryman

courlan: 4 bird 7 limpkin

course: lap, run, way 4 bent, flow, game, heat, line, mode, path, race, rill, rink, road, rote, went 5 cycle, drift, orbit, route, tenor, track, trail, trend 6 artery, career, cursus, gallop, manner, method, series, stream, street, system 7 beeline, conduct, highway, passage, pathway, process, routine, running, subject, traject 8 curricle, progress, sequence, tendency 9 direction 10 curriculum, proceeding, racecourse, succession 11 watercourse

alter: 4 veer 6 detour

easy: 4 pipe, snap 5 cinch 8 sinecure

habitual: rut, way 4 rote 7 regimen, routine

of action: 6 career 8 demarche 9 procedure

of study: 7 seminar 8 syllabus 10 curriculum

roundabout: 6 detour 11 indirection

courser: 5 horse, racer, steed 7 charger

court: bar, bid, see, sue, woo 4 area, body, quad, rota, seek, yard 5 arena, curea, curry, favor, forum, judge, patio, space, spark, tempt, train 6 allure, atrium, gemote, homage, invite, palace 7 address, attract, retinue, solicit 8 hustling, serenade, tribunal 9 attention, enclosure 10 quadrangle

action: 4 case, suit 5 trial

attendant: 5 staff 6 elisor, staves

bring into: sue 4 sist 6 arrest

call to: 4 oyes, oyez 7 summons 8 subpoena 11 arraignment

circuit: 4 eyre, iter

crier: 6 beadle

cry: 4 oyes, oyez

ecclesiastical: 10 consistory

exemption: 6 essoin

hearing: 4 oyer, suit 5 trial 6 action

inner: 5 patio

Mikado's: 5 dairi

minutes: 4 acta

of equity: 8 chancery

official: 5 clerk, crier, macer(Sc.) 7 bailiff

old: 4 leet 5 gemot 6 gemote 8 woodmote

order: 4 nisi, rule, writ 6 decree

panel: 4 jury

participant: 4 jury 5 crier, judge 6 elisor 7 pleader 8 advocate, talesman 9 defendant, plaintiff

pert. to: 5 aulic 10 fornaneous

session: set 4 oyer 6 assize 7 sitting 8 sederunt 11 downsitting

writ: 6 capias 7 summons 8 subpoena

court game: 6 tennis 9 badminton

court-martial: 8 drumhead

courteous: 4 fair 5 buxom, civil, suave 6 polite, urbane 7 affable, cordial, gallant, genteel, gentile, refined 8 debonair, gracious 9 attentive 10 complaisant, respectful 11 considerate, gentlemanly

courtesan: 10 prostitute

courtier: 4 bean 5 beaux(pl.), wooer 7 courter 8 courtman 9 attendant, courtling, flatterer

courtly: 4 hend 5 aulic, civil, hende 6 polite 7 elegant, refined, stately 8 polished 9 dignified

courtship: 4 suit 7 romance

courtyard: 4 area 5 patio 7 cortile 9 curtilage 10 quadrangle

cousin: coz, kin 4 akin 6 allied 8 relative

couthie: 4 smug 6 kindly, smooth 8 friendly, pleasant 9 agreeable 11 comfortable

couturier, couturiere: 8 designer 10 dressmaker

cove: bay, den 4 cave, chap, gill, hole, nook, pass 5 basin, bight, creek, inlet 6 fellow, hollow, recess, valley 7 molding

covenant: 4 bind, bond, mise, pact 5 agree 6 accord, cartel, engage, pledge, treaty 7 bargain, compact, concord, promise 8 alliance, contract, document 9 agreement, concordat, condition, stipulate, testament, undertake 10 convention 11 confederacy, stipulation

cover: cap, lid 4 coat, hide, mask, pave, roof, span, veil 5 drape, hatch 6 mantle, screen, shield 7 obscure, overlay, shelter

a bet: 4 fade

a fire: 4 bank

a hatch: 6 batten

ground: 5 speed 7 advance

the eyes: 9 blindfold

up: 4 hide 7 conceal

up for: 6 shield 7 protect

with mud: 6 belute

with straw: 6 thatch

with strips of bacon: 4 lard

covered: 4 clad, shod 5 mossy 6 covert, hidden 7 encased 8 screened 9 cleithral, concealed, panoplied, sheltered

covering: fur, hap 4 aril, bark, boot, case, hood, hull, husk, mask, pall, roof, tarp, tile 5 apron, armor, crust, quilt, shell, testa 6 awning, canopy, drapet, facing, heling, helmet, jacket, pelage, screen, sheath, shroud 7 capsule, ceiling, healing, overlay, pericap, wrapper 8 casement, clothing, coverlet, umbrella 9 coverture, operculum 10 integument 11 smokescreen

defensive: 5 armor 6 helmut 10 camouflage 11 smokescreen

seed: 4 aril

thin: 4 film 6 veneer

coverlet: 5 quilt, rezai, throw 6 afghan, caddow, spread 7 blanket 8 coverlid 9 comforter 11 counterpane

coverslut: 5 apron 7 garment

covert: den, lie, sly 4 lair 5 niche, privy 6 asylum, harbor, hidden, latent, masked, refuge, secret 7 covered, defense, harbour,

private, shelter, subrosa, thicket 9 concealed, disguised, insidious, shrubbery 10 underbrush 12 confidential
covet: 4 ache, envy, pant, want, wish 5 crave, yearn 6 desire, grudge, hanker
covetous: 4 avid, gair, gare 5 eager 6 frugal, greedy, stingy 7 miserly 8 desirous, grasping 9 mercenary 10 avaricious 12 parsimonious
covey: 4 bevy 5 brood, flock, hatch 7 company
covin, covine: 4 band, crew 5 fraud 7 company 8 assembly, trickery
cow: awe 4 beef, bogy, cowl, cush, faze, kine, vaca 5 abash, alarm, bossy, brock, bully, daunt, dompt, moggy, scare 6 bovine, goblin, heifer, subdue, vacha 7 bugbear, depress, overtop, squelch, terrify 8 browbeat, dispirit, frighten, threaten 9 quadruped 10 intimidate
barn: 4 byre 7 vaccary
barren: 5 drape
cud: 5 rumen
dung: 4 upla
group: 4 herd, kine 6 cattle
hornless: not 4 moil 5 doddy, muley 6 doddie, mulley 7 pollard
hybrid: 7 cattabu, cattalo
pasture: 7 vachery
sound: low, moo
young: 4 calf 5 stirk 6 heifer
cow-headed deity: 4 Isis
cow pilot: 4 fish 9 chirivita 10 damselfish
cowardly: shy 4 argh 5 timid 6 afraid, cowish, craven, yellow 7 caitiff, chicken 11 lily-livered 12 fainthearted 13 pusillanimous
cowbird: 7 bunting 9 blackbird
cowboy: 5 rider, roper, waddi 6 gaucho, herder 7 llanero, puncher, vaquero 8 buckaroo, buckayro, wrangler 10 cowpuncher 12 broncobuster
breeches: 5 chaps, levis 8 jodhpurs
contest: 5 rodeo
cowcatcher: 5 guard, pilot
cowed: 8 downcast 11 crestfallen
cower: 4 fawn 5 quail, stoop, toady, wince 6 coorie, cringe, crouch, hurkle, shrink
cowfish: 4 toro 7 manatee, sirenia
cowherd: 7 bucolic 8 herdsman, neatherd
cowl: cap, lid, tub 4 hood, monk 6 bonnet, vessel 7 capuche
cowle: 5 grant 7 amnesty 10 engagement 11 safe-conduct
cowled: 6 hooded 9 cucullate
cowpea: 5 sitao
cowpuncher: 6 cowboy 7 puncher
cowslip: 8 auricula, marigold, primrose
coxa: hip
coxcomb: fop, nob 4 buck, dude, fool, toff 5 cleat, dandy, hinge 7 princox 8 popinjay
coy: pal, shy 4 arch, coax, nice 5 aloof, chary, decoy, quiet, still 6 allure, caress, demure, modest, proper 7 bashful, distant 8 reserved 9 diffident 10 coquettish, disdainful, hesitating
Coyote State: 11 South Dakota
coypu: 6 nutria, rodent
coze: 4 chat, talk 6 gossip 8 converse
cozen, cosen: cog, con 4 bilk, gull 5 cheat, trick 6 chisel 7 beguile, deceive, defraud, swindle 8 hoodwink 9 bamboozle
cozy: 4 easy, safe, snug 5 bield 6 chatty, secure, toasty 8 covering, familiar, homelike, sociable 9 contented, gemutlich, talkative 11 comfortable
cozy retreat: den 4 lair, nest, nook 5 ingle
crab: gin 5 anger, maian, racer, winch 6 buster, cancer, grouse, heemit, peeler 7 buckler, fiddler, grumble 8 arachnid, irritate, windlass 9 horseshoe 10 crosspatch, crustacean, curmudgeon
abdomen: 5 apron
claw: 5 chela 6 nipper
fiddler: uca
genus: uca 6 birgus 7 squilla
suborder: 9 brachyura
crab apple: 5 malus, scrog
crabbed: 4 ugly 5 cabby, cross, testy 6 bitter, crusty, morose, rugged, sullen, trying 7 boorish, cramped, cornish, crooked, gnarled, knotted, obscure, peevish 8 churlish, contrary, petulant, vinegary 9 difficult, fractious, intricate, irregular 10 perplexing 11 intractable
crabgrass: 9 digitaria
crabstick: 4 cane 5 crank, stick 6 cudgel
crabwood: 8 andiroba
crack: gag, pop 4 a-one, bang, blow, chap, chip, chop, clap, cone, flaw, jest, jibe, joke, kibe, leak, quip, rend, rift, rime, snap, yerk 5 brack, break, check, chine, chink, clack, cleft, craze, split 6 cleave, cranny 7 blemish, crackle, crevice, crevise, fissure 8 fracture
crack down on: 6 attack 10 discipline
crack up: 5 amuse, crash, extol, smash 8 collapse 9 break down
crackbrain: 8 crackpot 9 screwball
crackbrained: 5 crazy, nutty 7 erratic 12 unreasonable
cracker: 4 bake, liar 5 wafer 7 biscuit, boaster, breaker, burster, redneck, snapper 8 braggart 11 firecracker
Cracker State: 7 Georgia
crackle: 4 snap 5 break, crack 7 brustle, crinkle, sparkle, sputter 9 crackling, crepitate

crackpot: 7 erratic, lunatic 9 screwball
cracksman: 4 yegg 7 burglar, peteman
cradle: bed, cot 4 rest, rock 5 cader, frame 6 creche 7 berceau, shelter 8 cunabula 9 framework 11 incunabulum
song: 7 lullaby 8 berceuse
wicker: 8 bassinet
craft (see also **boat**): art 4 boat 5 fraud, guile, skill, trade 6 deceit, metier, talent, vessel 7 ability 8 aptitude, artifice, vocation 9 dexterity 10 employment, occupation 12 skillfulness
craftsman: 4 hand 5 navvy 6 artist, writer 7 artisan, workman 8 mechanic 9 artificer
aid: cad
crafty: sly 4 arch, foxy, wily 5 adept 6 adroit, astute, callid, shrewd, subtle, tricky 7 cunning, vulpine 8 captious, fetching 9 cautelous, deceitful, ingenious 10 fallacious, fraudulent 13 Machiavellian 15 Mephistophelean
crag: tor 4 craw, neck, rock, scar, spur 5 arete, brack, cliff 6 throat 9 precipice
craggy: 5 rough 6 abrupt, knotty, rugged
crake: 4 bird, crow, rail, rook 5 raven 8 railbird
cram: wad 4 bone, fill, glut, pack, stow, urge 5 crowd, crush, drive, force, gorge, grind, learn, press, study, stuff, teach
crame: 4 tent 5 booth, stall
cramp: 4 coop, kink, pain 5 crick, crowd, pinch, stunt 6 hamper, hinder, knotty 7 confine 8 compress, contract, restrain, restrict 9 constrict, difficult 11 contraction
one's style: 5 queer 9 frustrate
cranberry: 7 pembina 8 bilberry, foxberry 9 mossberry, sourberry
habitat: bog
crane: job 4 bird, grus 5 davit, heron, jenny, raise, wader 6 sarsus 7 derrick 9 cormorant
arm: gib, jib
charges: 7 cranage
genus: 4 grus
Malayan: 5 sarus
neck: 4 gaze 5 stare
pert. to: 6 gruine
ship: 5 davit
small: 10 demoiselle
traveling: 5 jenny, titan
crane fly: 6 tipula
cranial nerve: 4 vagi(pl.) 5 vagus
root: 5 radix 7 radices(pl.)
craniometrical point: 5 inion 7 pterion, stenion
cranium: pan 4 head 5 skull 8 brainpan
nerve root: 5 radix
part: 7 calotte 8 calvaria
pert. to: 7 cranial
crank: wit 4 bent, sick, weak, whim, wind 5 brace, loose, rogue, shaky, winch 6 ailing, boldly, grouch, handle, infirm 7 awkward, bracket, fanatic, lustily 9 distorted, eccentric, sprightly 10 monomaniac, vigorously
crankle: 4 bend, turn 5 twist 6 zigzag
cranky: 4 ugly 5 crazy, cross, lusty, shaky, testy 6 ailing, infirm, sickly 7 crooked, grouchy 8 tortuous 9 crotchety, difficult, irritable
cranny: 4 hole, nook 5 chink, cleft, crack 6 corner 7 crevice, fissure
cranreuch: 4 rime 9 hoarfrost
crants: 6 wreath 7 garland
crap: 5 dregs, money 7 gallows, greaves, rubbish 8 nonsense, sediment
crape: 4 band, curl, friz 5 crepe, crimp, drape, gauze 6 shroud 8 mourning
crapehanger: 7 killjoy 10 spoilsport
crapulence: 7 surfeit 8 gluttony 11 overfeeding 12 intemperance, intoxication
crash: 4 fail, fall 5 blast, burst, cloth, crush, shock, smash, sound 6 fiasco 7 failure, shatter 8 collapse, splinter 9 collision
crass: raw 4 dull, rude 5 crude, dense, gross, rough, thick 6 coarse, obtuse, stupid 9 unrefined
cratch: 4 crib, rack 6 manger 7 grating
crate: box, car 4 case, crib 5 plane, seron 6 basket, cradle, encase, hamper, hurdle 7 canasta, vehicle 9 container 10 receptacle
bar 4 slat
crater: cup, pit 4 cone, hole 5 fovea 6 hollow 7 caldera
edge: lip
cravat: tie 4 teck 5 ascot, scarf, stock 7 bandage, necktie, overlay 8 crumpler 9 neckcloth 10 fourinhand 11 neckerchief
crave: ask, beg 4 long, need, pray, seek 5 covet, yearn 6 desire, hanker, hunger, thirst 7 beseech, entreat, implore, request, require, solicit 10 supplicate
craven: 6 afraid, coward, scared 7 dastard 8 cowardly, defeated, overcome, poltroon, recreant, sneaking 10 vanquished 12 fainthearted
craw: maw 4 crop 7 stomach 9 ingluvies
crawl: lag 4 drag, fawn, inch, ramp, swim 5 creep, kraal 6 cringe, grovel, scride 7 slither
crayfish: 5 yabby 6 yabbie 7 crawdad, lobster 8 cambarus, crawfish 9 ecrevisse 10 crustacean
crayon: 4 plan 5 chalk 6 pastel, pencil, sketch 7 drawing
craze: fad 4 flaw, mode, rage 5 break, crack, crush, furor, mania, vogue 6 defect, impair, madden, weaken, whimsy 7 derange,

destroy, fashion, shatter, whimsey 8 distract 9 bedlamize, infirmity 11 infatuation
crazed: mad, ree 4 amok, loco, wild, wood, zany 5 balmy, batty, daffy, dotty, manic, nutty, potty, wacky 6 coocoo, dottle, insane, looney 7 lunatic 8 deleerit, delieret, demented, deranged 10 crackbrain, distraught
creak: gig 4 rasp, yirr 5 cheep(Sc.), croak, grind, groan 6 squeak
cream: 4 beat, best 5 creme, elite, froth, sauce 6 bonbon 8 emulsion, ointment
cream of tartar: 5 argol
cream puff: 6 pastry 8 weakling
creamery: 5 dairy
creamy: 4 rich 5 reamy 6 smooth 8 luscious
crease: 4 fold, lirk, ruck, ruga, seam 5 crimp, pleat 7 crumple, wrinkle
create: 4 coin, form, make, plan 5 build, cause, forge, shape, write 6 design, invent 7 compose, fashion, imagine, produce 8 generate 9 establish, originate
creation: 5 world 6 cosmos, effect 7 fashion, product 8 creature, universe 10 production 11 masterpiece
creative: 9 demiurgic, inventive 10 productive 12 constructive
creativity: 6 genius
creator: 5 maker 6 author 8 designer 9 architect
creature (see also **animal**): man 4 tool 5 beast, being, slave, thing 6 animal, minion, person, wretch 8 hellicat(Sc.) 9 dependent 10 animalcule, individual
fabled: elf 5 gnome 6 dragon, merman 7 centaur, mermaid
ogre: 5 pixie 6 wyvern
creche: 4 crib 6 manger 7 nursery
credence: 5 faith, trust 6 belief, buffet, credit 8 credenza 10 acceptance, confidence 11 reliability 15 trustworthiness
credential: 7 voucher 8 credence 11 certificate, testimonial
credenza: 5 niche, shelf, table 6 buffet 8 credence, cupboard 9 sideboard
credible: 6 likely 7 credent 8 probable 9 authentic, plausible, reputable 11 trustworthy
credit: 4 loan 5 asset, chalk, faith, honor, merit, tenet, trust 6 belief, charge, esteem, impute, renown, repute, weight 7 ascribe, believe 8 accredit, credence 10 estimation
credulous: 4 fond 8 credible, gullible
creed: ism 4 cult, sect 5 credo, dogma, faith, tenet 6 belief 7 trowing 8 doctrine 10 confession
Christian: 6 Nicene 8 Apostle's
creek: bay, ria, rio 4 burn(Sc.), cove, kill, pill, rill, slue 5 bayou, bight, bogue, brook, crick, fleet, inlet, zanja 6 arroyo, estero, Indian, slough, stream 7 estuary, rivulet 11 watercourse
creel: 4 caul, cawl, rack, trap 6 basket
creem: hug 4 mash 5 crush 6 shiver 7 shudder, squeeze
creep: 4 fawn, inch, ramp 5 crawl, prowl, skulk, slink, steal 6 cringe, grovel, scride 7 cramble
creeper: ivy 4 shoe, vine, worm 5 snake 6 ipecac, romper, tecoma
creeping: 4 slow 7 reptant, servile 9 reptilian 11 reptatorial
creese: 4 kris, stab 5 sword 6 dagger, weapon
cremate: 4 burn 9 incremate 10 incinerate
Cremona: 5 Amati 6 violin
crena: 5 cleft, notch 7 scallop 11 indentation
crenic acid salt: 7 crenate
creole: 6 patois 7 mestizo
Creole State: 9 Louisiana
crepe: 6 fabric 7 frizzed, pancake 8 crinkled, wrinkled
crepitate: 4 snap 6 rattle 7 crackle
crepuscule: 8 twilight
crescent: 4 horn, lune, moon, rool 5 curve, lunar 6 lunule 7 lunette, menisci(pl.) 8 meniscus 10 semicircle
point: 4 cusp
crescent-shaped: 6 bicorn, lunate 7 lunular 9 semilunar
crescive: 7 growing 10 increasing
cresset: 5 torch 6 basket, beacon, signal 7 furnace 8 flambeau
crest: cop, tip, top 4 acme, apex, comb, edge, knap, peak, seal, tuft 5 chine, crown, plume, ridge 6 copple, crista, finial, height, helmet, summit 7 bearing 8 pinnacle, whitecap 10 cognizance
rugged 6 arete
crested: 6 muffed 7 crisate, crowned 8 pileated 9 coronated
crestfallen: 5 cowed 8 dejected 10 dispirited
creta: 5 chalk
cretaceous: 6 chalky
Crete: 6 Candia
cape: 4 krio 5 krios
city: Hag 5 Canea(c.), Khora 6 Kisamo, Malemi, Mallia, Meleme, Retimo 7 Kasteli 8 Nikolacs, Sphakion 9 Heraclion, Tympakion 11 Palaiokhora
earth spirit: 6 Curete
flier: 6 Icarus
goddess: 8 Dictynna
king: 5 Minos 9 Idomeneus
language: 6 Minoan
man of brass: 5 Talos
monster: 8 minotaur
mountain: *Ida* 9 Psiloriti
princess: 7 Ariadne

seaport: **5** Canea **6** Candia, Khania
Cretheus: *son:* **8** Amythaon
wife: **7** Biadice
cretin: **5** idiot
cretism: **5** lying **9** falsehood
cretose: **6** chalky
Creusa: *father:* **5** Priam
husband: **6** Aeneas
mother: **6** Hecuba
son: **8** Ascanius
crevasse: **5** chasm, split **8** cleavage
crevice: **4** bore, leak, nook, seam, vein **5** break, chine, chink, cleft, crack, grike **6** cranny **7** fissure, opening **8** crevasse, peep-hole **10** interstice
crew: men, mob, set **4** band, gang, herd, oars, team **5** hands, party, squad, staff **6** seamen, throng **7** company, faculty, members, retinue **8** equipage, mariners **10** assemblage, complement
crewel: **6** caddis **7** caddice **10** crewelwork, embroidery
crib: bed, bin, box, cab, cot, cub, hut, key **4** boom, dive, pony, rack, raft **5** boose, boosy, cheat, crate, frame, hovel, stall, steal **6** bunker, cratch, 'creche, manger, pilfer **7** purloin **8** cribbage **9** enclosure **10** plagiarize, storehouse
cribbage score: nob, peg
crick: **5** creek, hitch, spasm, twist
cricket: **4** game, grig **6** insect
genus: **7** gryllus
run: bye
side: ons
sound: **5** chirp **12** stridulation
team: **6** eleven
term: off, ons, rot **4** over **5** smick **6** yorker
crier: **6** beadle, herald, wailer **7** muezzin
crime: act, sin **4** evil **5** abuse, arson, blame, wrong **6** felony, murder, piacle **7** misdeed, offense **8** iniquity **9** violation **10** wickedness **11** abomination, malefaction **13** transgression
ecclesiastical: **6** simony
goddess of: Ate
organized: **10** underworld
scene of: **5** venue
Crimea: **4** Krym
city: **5** Kerch, Yalta **10** Sevastopol
people: **5** Tauri
river: **4** Alma
sea: **4** Azof, Azov
criminal: bad **4** yegg **5** crook, felon **6** guilty, inmate, nocent, slayer, wicked **7** convict, culprit, illegal **8** culpable, gangster **9** desperado, wrongdoer **10** blackguard, deplorable, flagitious, malefactor, malfeasant **11** blameworthy, disgraceful **13** reprehensible
habitual: **8** repeater **10** recidivist
refuge: **7** Alsatia **11** Whitefriars
crimonology branch: **8** penology
crimp: **4** bend, curl, fold, friz, pote, wave, weak **5** cramp, flute, frizz, pinch, plait **6** goffer, ruffle **7** crinkle, friable, gauffer, wrinkle **8** obstacle **9** corrugate **12** inconsistent
crimson: dye, lac, red **4** pink **6** bloody, maroon, modena **7** carmine, scarlet
crine: **4** hair, mane **6** shrink **7** shrivel
cringe: bow **4** bend, fawn, jouk **5** binge, cower, crawl, quail, sneak, stoop, wince, yield **6** crouch, grovel, shrink, submit **7** crinkle, distort, truckle
cringing: **6** abject **7** hangdog
cringle: orb **4** disk **6** eyelet, terret **7** grommet
crinite: **5** hairy **6** fossil
crinitory: **5** hairy **7** crinose
crinkle: **4** bend, curl, kink, turn, wind **6** pucker, ripple, rumple, rustle **7** crackle, wrinkle **9** corrugate **11** convolution
cripple: mar **4** halt, harm, hurt, lame, maim, wing **6** bacach, hobble, impair, injure, scotch, spavin, weaken **7** crapple, crumpet, disable, lamiter(Sc.) **8** handicap, mutilate, paralyze **9** hamstring **12** incapacitate
crisis: **4** acme, crux, pass, turn **5** panic, peril, pinch, trial **6** strait **8** decision, juncture **9** criterion, emergency **11** conjunction
having no: **9** acritical
crisp: new **4** cold **5** brisk, clear, curly, fresh, nippy, pithy, sharp, short, stiff, terse **6** biting, bright, lively **7** bracing, brittle, concise, cutting, friable **9** crackling
crispin: **4** coat **9** shoemaker
crisscross: **4** awry **7** network **8** confused **9** intersect
cristate: **6** ridged, tufted **7** crested
criterion: law **4** norm, rule, test, type **5** axiom, canon, gauge, nodel, proof **6** metric **7** measure **8** standard **9** yardstick **10** indication, touchstone
critic: **5** booer, judge, momus **6** carper, censor, expert, slater **8** collator, reviewer **9** detractor, literator **11** connoisseur, criticaster, faultfinder
critical: **4** edge **5** acute, exact **6** urgent **7** carping, exigent **8** captious, decisive, exacting **10** censorious, fastidious **12** faultfinding **14** discriminating
critical mark: **6** obelus **7** obelisk
criticism: **5** blame **6** review **7** comment **8** critique, diatribe, judgment **9** stricture **13** animadversion
criticize: hit, pan, rap, rip **4** carp, flay, slam, slur, yelp **5** blame, blast, cavil, judge, knock, roast **6** rebuke, review **7** censure,

comment, examine 8 critique 9 castigate 10 animadvert

Crius: *father:* 6 Uranus
mother: Ge 4 Gaea, Gaia
sister: 7 Eurybia

cro: 7 payment 12 satisfaction

croak: caw, die 4 gasp, kill 5 creak, quark, speak 7 forbode, grumble 8 complain

Croatia: *capital:* 5 Agram 6 Zagreb
city: 5 Fiume, Rieka
mountain: 6 Kapela
people: 4 Serb, Slav, Sorb, Wend 5 Sclav 6 Hrvati 7 Hervati, Slovene 8 Croatian, European

crochet: 4 hook, knit 5 braid, plait, weave 8 crotchet

crock: jar, pig, pot 4 smut, soil, soot 5 stool 6 critch, smudge 8 potsherd

crockery: 5 china, cloam 6 dishes, plates 11 earthenware

crocodile: goa 5 gator 6 cayman, gavial, jacare, mugger 7 reptile 9 alligator
genus: 11 goniopholis

crocus: 7 saffron

Croesus: 4 king 9 moneybags, plutocrat
country: 5 Lydia

croft: 4 farm 5 crypt, field, garth, vault 6 bleach, cavern

cromlech: 6 circle, dolmen 7 gorsedd 9 cyclolith

Cromwell: 4 Noll 6 Oliver
son-in-law: 6 Ireton
victory site: 6 Naseby

crone: hag 4 cive 5 witch 6 beldam 7 beldame 9 cailleach, cailliach

Cronus: *daughter:* 4 Hera 6 Hestia 7 Demeter
father: 6 Uranus
mother: 4 Gaea
wife: 4 Rhea

crony: pal 4 chum 9 associate, companion

crook: 4 bend, turn, warp 5 cheat, cleek, crump, curve, pedum, staff, thief, trick 7 crosier, crozier 8 artifice, swindler 10 camshachle(Sc.)

crooked: cam 4 agee, awry, bent 5 agley(Sc.), askew, false, gleed 6 akimbo, artful, aslant, crabby, crafty, curved, tricky, zigzag 7 askance, asquint, corrupt, crabbed, oblique, turning, twisted, winding 8 tortuous 9 dishonest, distorted, irregular 10 circuitous, fraudulent, misleading 12 dishonorable
comb. form: 5 ankyl 6 ankylo

croon: hum, low 4 boom, lull, sing, wail 5 chirm, whine 6 lament, murmur 8 complain

crop: cut, maw, top 4 clip, craw, knap, reap, trim, whip 5 fruit, quirt, shear 6 gather, gebbie, silage 7 curtail, harvest, tillage 8 gleaning, ingulies
goddess of: 6 Annona
second growth: 5 rowen
year's: 6 annona

cropper: 8 collapse, disaster

croquet: 5 roque

croquette: 5 cecil

crosier, crozier: 5 crook, cross, staff

cross: go; mix 4 ford, rood, span 5 angry, testy, trial 6 bisect, crabby, cranky, crouch, emblem, gibbet, grumpy, outwit, signum, sullen, symbol, thwart, touchy 7 athwart, crabbed, fretful, froward, oblique, peevish, pettish, potence 8 crotched, crucifix, petulant, snappish, suastica, swastika, traverse, vexillum 9 frustrate, intersect, irritable, plaintive 10 affliction, ill-humored, transverse 12 disagreeable
barred: 11 trabeculate
fiery: 8 crantara 9 crostarie
Greek: 6 fylfot
stroke: 5 serif 6 ceriph
swords: 4 duel 5 fight 6 combat
tau: 4 crux 5 ankih
type: 5 Greek, Latin, Papal 6 Celtic 7 Maltese 8 Egyptian
wires: 7 confuse

cross-examine: 5 grill 8 question

cross-grained: 7 gnarled 8 churlish, perverse 9 irascible 12 cantankerous

cross out: 4 dele 5 blank, erase 6 cancel, delete 9 eliminate

cross-rib: 4 arch 6 lierne

cross section: 4 part 14 representation

crossbar: 4 axle, rung 5 round 10 horizontal

crossbeam: bar 5 trave 6 girder

crossbow: 6 weapon 8 arbalest

crossbreed: 5 husky 6 hybrid 9 hybridize

crosshatch: 7 engrave

crossing: 7 passage 8 opposing

crosspatch: 4 bear, crab 6 grouch

crosspiece: bar 4 spar, yoke 5 grill 8 crossarm 10 doubletree

crossroads: 9 carrefour 12 intersection
goddess: 6 Hecate, Hekate, Trivia

crossruff: 6 seesaw 9 alternate

crosswise: 6 across 7 athwart 8 acrostic, diagonal

crotch: 4 fork, pole, post 5 cleft, notch, stake 9 stanchion

crotchet: fad 4 hook, whim 5 fancy 6 vagary 9 conundrum 11 peculiarity 12 eccentricity

crotchety: 6 cranky 10 capricious

crouch: 4 bend, fawn, ruck 5 cower, squat, stoop 6 cringe 7 scrooch

crouching: 8 couchant

crouse: 4 bold 5 brisk, cocky 6 lively 8 cheerful 9 confident

crouton: bit 5 toast 7 garnish

crow: aga, caw, cry, daw 4 bird, brag, rook 5 boast, exult, raven, vaunt 6 carnal, corvas 7 grapnel, jackdow, swagger 9 blackbird

cry: caw

pert. to: 7 corvine

crow-like: 7 corvine

crowbar: pry 5 jemmy, jimmy, lever 7 gablock 8 gavelock

crowd: jam, mob, set 4 bike, cram, herd, host, pack, push, rock, rout, stow, swad 5 bunch, cramp, crush, drove, flock, group, horde, posse, press, serry, shoal, swarm, three, wedge 6 boodle, clique, hubble, huddle, jostle, rabble, throng 7 bourock(Sc.), company, squeeze 9 multitude 10 assemblage, clamjamfry(Sc.), confluence

penetrate: 5 elbow 6 needle

crowded: 5 close, dense, thick 6 filled 7 bunched, compact, serried, stipate, stuffed, teeming 9 congested

crowder: 6 loader 7 fiddler 8 thatcher

crown: cap, top 4 coin, pate, peak, poll 5 adorn, basil, bezel, bezil, crest, miter, mitre, tiara 6 anadem, circle, climax, corona(L.), diadem, fillet, invest, laurel, potong, reward, summit, trophy, wreath 7 aureole, chaplet, coronet, garland, install 8 coronate, enthrone, pinnacle, surmount 9 headdress, sovereign

pert. to: 8 coronal

crown prince: 4 heir 8 atheling

cru: 8 vineyard

crucial: 5 acute 6 severe, trying 7 pivotal, telling 8 critical, decisive

cruciation: 7 torture

crucible: pot 4 dish, etna, test 6 cruset, retort 7 furnace

crucifix: pax 4 rood 5 cross

crucify: vex 4 hang, kill 5 harry 7 mortify, torment, torture 8 cruciate 9 persecute

crud: 4 curd 6 refuse 7 thicken

crude: raw 4 bald, bare, rude 5 crass, green, harsh, rough 6 callow, coarse, savage, unripe, vulgar 7 uncouth 8 immature, impolite 9 primitive, unglossed, unrefined, untrained 10 incomplete, unpolished 11 undeveloped 13 inexperienced

cruel: 4 fell, hard 5 harsh 6 bloody, brutal, fierce, savage, severe, unjust, unkind 7 bestial, brutish, inhuman, neronic 8 barbaric, diabolic, fiendish, inhumane, pitiless, ruthless, sadistic, tyrannic 9 atrocious, draconian, ferocious, heartless, merciless, rapacious, unfeeling 10 diabolical, sanguinary, vindictive 11 hardhearted

lover of: 6 sadist

cruet: ama, jar, jug 4 vial 5 cruse 6 bottle, caster, guttus, vessel 7 ampulla, burette 9 container

cruise: 4 boat, sail, trip 9 excursion

cruiser: 4 ship 6 vessel 7 warship

cruising: 4 asea

cruller: 7 olycook, olykock 8 doughnut 9 friedcake

crumb: bit, ort 5 piece 6 little, morsel 7 remnant 8 fragment

crumb covered: 7 breaded

crumble: rot 5 break, crush, decay, slake, spoil 6 molder, perish 7 moulder 9 decompose, pulverize 12 disintegrate

crumbly: 7 friable

crumpet: 4 cake 6 muffin 7 pikelet

crumple: 4 fold, muss 5 crush 6 crease, furrow, raffle, rumple 7 crunkle, wrinkle 8 collapse, contract 9 corrugate

crunch: 4 bite, chew 5 chomp, crump, crush, gnash, grind, munch, press 6 cranch 7 craunch, scrunch

cruor: 4 gore 5 blood

crural joint: 4 knee

crus: 5 shank

crusade: war 5 jehad, jihad 8 campaign 10 expedition

crusader: 7 pilgrim, Templar 8 reformer

enemy: 7 Saladin, Saracen

port: 4 Acre

crush: bow, jam 4 cram, dash, mash, mill, mull 5 brake, break, crash, craze, crowd, force, grind, press, quash, quell, smash, tread, unman 6 bruise, burden, crunch, squash, subdue, thwack 7 conquer, crumple, depress, destroy, oppress, overrun, repress, scrunch, scrunge, shatter, squeeze, squelch 8 compress, overcome, suppress 9 overpower, overwhelm, pulverize

crust: 4 cake, hull, rind 5 shell 6 eschar, harden 7 coating 8 pellicle

crustacean: 4 crab, flea, scud 5 louse, prawn 6 endite, isopod, shrimp 7 lobster, squilla 8 barnacle

appendage: 5 exite

claw: 5 chela

feeler: 7 antenna

genus: 5 eryon, hippa 6 tripos

group: 7 caridea

larva: 5 alima

limb: 6 podite

small: 6 isopod 7 copepod 8 barnacle

ten-footed: 4 crab

crusty: 4 curt 5 bluff, blunt, testy 6 morose 7 crabbed, peevish, pettish 8 snappish 11 ill-tempered
crux: nub 4 ankh, gist, pith 5 cross, point 6 puzzle, riddle 7 problem 10 difficulty
cry (see also **exclamation**): ho; boo, caw, cri(F.), fad, hue, ole, sob, yip 4 bawl, bump, call, evoe, hawk, hoot, howl, keen, mewl, pule, rage, scry, wail, weep, yell, yelp 5 clepe, crede, greet, groan, rumor, shout, sound, utter, vogue whewl, whine 6 bellow, boohoo, clamor, demand, lament, outcry, quethe, scream, shriek, slogan, snivel, squeal, squall, wimick, yammer 7 clamour, exclaim, fashion, screech 8 proclaim 11 acclamation, lamentation
court: 4 oyes, oyez
derisive: bah, boo 4 hiss, hoot 6 phooey 7 catcall
for: 4 need 6 demand, desire
gang's signal: 4 whyo
havoc: 8 mobilize
of approval: ole, rah 5 bravo
of pain: 4 ouch
of relief: 4 phew, whew
of sorrow: ay; woe 4 alas 5 alack
of triumph: aha 6 hurrah
out: 5 blame, crake, deery 7 censure, protest 8 complain, denounce
political: 6 slogan 10 shibboleth
Cry the Beloved Country author: 5 Paton
crying: 6 urgent 7 clamant, heinous 8 pressing, recreant 9 notorious 11 exclamatory
crying bird: 7 limpkin
crying hare: 4 pika
crying out: 10 childbirth 11 confinement
crypt: pit 5 croft, vault 6 cavern, grotto, recess 7 chamber 8 follicle 10 depression
cryptic: 4 dark 5 vague 6 hidden, occult, secret 7 obscure 9 enigmatic, recondite 10 mysterious 12 hieroglyphic
cryptogram: 4 code 6 cipher 11 cryptograph
crystal: ice 4 dial, hard 5 clear, glass, lucid 6 limpid, pebble 7 acicula, diamond 8 pellucid 11 crystalline, transparent
gazer: 4 seer 7 seeress
ice: 6 frazil
twin: 5 macle
crystalline: 4 pure 7 crystal 8 pellucid 11 transparent
acid: 7 alanine
compound: 5 alban 6 anisil, oscine 7 aconite, amarine 8 atropine
mineral: 4 mica, spar 6 quartz 7 apatite 8 boracite, elaterin
phenol: 5 orcin 6 orcine
pine tar: 6 retene
salt: 5 borax 8 analgene, racemate
structure: 6 sparry 8 siderite
substance: 4 urea 6 dulcin 9 scopoline
crystallize: 5 candy, sugar 7 congeal 8 solidify 9 granulate
ctenophora: 4 nuda 5 beroe 6 cestus
cub: fry, pen 4 bear, coop, shed 5 stall, whelp 6 lionet, novice 7 codling 8 reporter 9 youngster
Cuba: *asphalt:* 9 chapapote
beverage: 4 pina
bird: 6 trogon 8 tocororo
carriage: 7 volante
castle: 5 Morro
cigar: 6 Havana
city: 6 Guines, Havana(c.) 7 Palmira 8 Camaguay, Matanzas, Santiago 9 Cienfuego 10 Santa Clara 14 Puerto Principe
coin: 4 peso 7 centavo 8 cuarenta
dance: 5 conga, rumba 6 danzon, rhumba
dictator: 6 Castro 7 Batista
dollar: 6 gourde
fish: 6 diablo 7 viajaca
hutia: 6 pilori
measure: 4 vara 5 bocoy, tarea 6 cordel, fanega 10 caballeria
mountain: 6 Copper 11 Pinar del Rio 12 Guaniguanico 13 Pico Turquinos
province: 6 Havana 7 Oriente 8 Camaguey, Matanzas 10 Santa Clara 11 Pinar del Rio
rodent: 5 hutia 6 pilori
root: 7 malanga
rum: 7 Bacardi
secret police: 5 porra
snake: 4 juba
storm: 6 bayamo
tobacco: 4 capa 6 vuelta
tree: 4 cuya 5 culla
ward: 6 barrio
weapon: 7 machete
weight: 5 libra 6 tercio
cubage: 6 volume 7 content
cubbyhole: 4 nook
cube: cut, die 4 dice 5 block, solid 10 hexahedron
cube spar: 9 anhydrite
cubic: 5 solid 9 isometric
decimeter: 5 liter, litre
meter: 5 stere
shape: 6 cuboid
cubicle: bay 4 cell, noak, room 5 booth, niche 6 alcove
cubitus: 4 ulna 7 forearm
Cuchullin's wife: 4 Emer 5 Eimer
cuckoo: ani 4 bird, fool, gowk, koel 5 clock, crazy, silly 7 boobook 8 rainfowl
kind: 6 coucal, kobird 7 kowbird, wryneck 8 coccyzus
cuckoopint: 4 arum 5 aaron, plant 9 wake-robin

cucullate: 6 cowled, hooded 7 covered 10 hood-shaped
cucumber: 4 cuke, pepo 6 conger, pepino(Sp.) 7 gherkin 9 elaterium
cucurbit: 5 flask, gourd 6 vessel 7 alembic, matrass
cud: chew, quid 5 bolus, rumen 6 cudgel
cuddle: hug, pet 6 caress, cosset, fondle, nestle 7 embrace, snuggle
cuddy: ass 4 lout 5 bribe, cabin 6 donkey, galley, pantry 9 blockhead
cudgel: bat 4 beat, cane, club, drub, rack 5 baste, drive, kebby, kevel, staff, stave, stick 6 alpeen, ballow, baston, kebbie, thrash, weapon 7 belabor, bourdon 8 bludgeon, shillala 9 bastinado, crabstick, fustigate, truncheon 10 shillelagh
cue: nod, tip 4 hint, mast, tail, wink 5 braid, cluff, plait, queue, twist 6 prompt, signal 7 pigrail 9 catchword 10 intimation
cuff: box 4 bank, blow, gowf, slam, slap, slug, swat 5 clout, fight, gowff, miser, smite 6 buffet, codger, mitten, strike 7 scuffle 8 gauntlet, handcuff
cuirass: 4 mail 5 armor, loric, plate 6 lorica
cuisine: 4 food, menu 5 table 7 cookery
cuittle: 4 coax 6 tickle 7 wheedle
cul-de-sac: 6 pocket, strait 7 deadend, impasse 10 difficulty
culicid: 8 mosquito
cull: opt 4 dupe, gull, pick, sift, sort 5 elect, glean, pluck 6 assort, choose, gather, remove, select 8 separate
cully: 4 dupe, gull, mate 5 cheat, trick 7 deceive 9 companion
culm: 5 slack 6 refuse 7 deposit
culmen: top 4 acme 5 ridge
culmination: end 4 acme, apex, noon 5 crown 6 apogee, climax, summit, vertex, zenith 10 completion 12 consummation
culpa: 5 fault, guilt 10 negligence 12 carelessness
culpable: 6 faulty, guilty, laches 7 immoral 8 criminal 10 censurable 11 blameworthy 13 reprehensible
culprit: 5 felon 7 convict 8 criminal, offender 10 malefactor
cult: 4 clan, sect 5 creed 6 church, ritual, school 7 worship 12 denomination
cultivate: ear, hoe 4 disk, farm, grow, plow, rear, tend, till 5 nurse, raise, study, train 6 affect, foster, harrow, plough 7 acquire, cherish, educate, husband, improve, nourish, prepare 8 civilize 9 encourage
cultivated: 5 civil 6 polite 7 refined 8 cultured 12 domesticated
land: 4 farm 5 arada, tilth
cultivation: 7 culture, tillage 9 culturing, husbandry 10 refinement 12 civilization
art: 9 geoponics
cultivator: 6 farmer, harrow, tiller 7 grubber, husband 10 husbandman
culture: art 4 agar 5 taste 6 polish 7 tillage 9 knowledge 10 discipline, refinement 12 civilization
medium: 4 agar
culver: 4 dove 6 pigeon
culvert: 5 drain 6 bridge 7 conduit
cumbersome: 5 heavy 6 clumsy 7 onerous, weighty 8 cumbrous, unwieldy 10 burdensome
combrous: 8 clogging, unwieldy 9 difficult, vexatious 10 burdensome, cumbersome
cumin: 5 anise, cumic
cummer, kimmer: 4 girl, lass 5 witch, woman 6 friend 7 midwife 9 companion, godmother
cummerbund: 4 band, belt, sash
cumshaw: tip 5 bonus 6 thanks 7 present 8 gratuity
cumulate: 4 heap 6 gather 7 combine 10 accumulate
cunabula: 6 cradle
cuneal: 7 cuneate 11 wedge-shaped
cuneiform: 4 bone 6 wedged 7 writing 8 sphenoid
cunner: 5 canoe 6 nipper, wrasse
cunning: sly, wit 4 arch, cute, foxy. keen, wily 5 downy, guile, sharp, smart 6 adroit, artful, astute, callid, clever, crafty, deadal, deceit, shrewd, subtle, tricky, wisdom 7 curious, finesse, politic, vulpine 8 dextrous, skillful, stealthy 9 chicanery, colubrine, designing, dexterity, ingenious, knowledge, sagacious 10 fraudulent, witchcraft 13 Machiavellian
cup: ama, dop, mug, tyg 4 tass 5 bouse, calix, cruse, glass, grail, phial, stein, tazza 6 beaker, crater, goblet, noggin, potion, vessel 7 chalice, stirrup
assay: 4 test 5 cupel 6 beaker
diamond cutting: dop
eared: 6 quaich, quaigh
earthenware: mug
fungus: 6 aecium
handle: ear, lug
holder: 4 zarf
horn-shaped: 6 holmos
large: 5 grail, jorum
looped handles: 5 kylix 9 cantharus, kantharos
loving: tyg 5 award, prize
of tea: 5 forte, thing 6 metier
pastry: 7 dariole
resembling: 9 oalicular
small: 4 shot 5 chark, cruse 6 noggin 8 cannikin 9 demitasse
two-handled: tig, tyg 5 depas

cup-shaped: 10 cyathiform
cupbearer of the gods: 4 Hebe 8 Ganymede
cupboard: kas 4 case, safe 5 ambry, cuddy 6 buffet, closet, larder, pantry 7 armoire, cabinet, dresser 8 credenza 9 sideboard
cupel: 4 burn, test 6 refine
Cupid: Dan 4 Amor, Eros, love 7 Amorino
beloved of: 6 Psyche
mother: 5 Venus
cupidity: 4 lust 5 greed 6 desire 7 avarice, avidity, longing 8 appetite 12 covetousness
demon of: 6 Mammon
cupidon: 5 cupid
cupola: 4 dome, kiln 5 vault 6 turret 7 furnace, lantern, lookout
cur: dog, yap 4 fice, mutt, tike, tyke 5 feist 6 canine, messan, messin 7 bobtail, mongrel 9 goldeneye
curacao: 7 liqueur
Curacao island: 5 Aruba
curare: 5 urare, urari 6 oorali, poison
curassow: 4 bird, crax, mitu
curate: cur 4 abbe 5 agent 7 dominie 8 minister 9 assistant, clergyman
curative: 7 healing 8 remedial, salutary, sanative 9 medicinal 11 restorative
curator: 6 keeper 7 manager, steward 8 guardian, overseer 9 custodian 14 superintendent
curb: bit 4 foil, rein 5 brake, check, curve, guard, limit 6 arrest, bridle, govern, hamper, thwart 7 control, inhibit, repress, shackle 8 moderate, restrain, restrict, withhold 9 constrain, hindrance 10 hamshackle
curculio: 6 weevil
curd: 6 curdle 7 caseine, clabber, congeal 8 fleeting 9 coagulate
curdle: 4 earn(Sc.), leep, quar, sour, yern 5 quail, quarl, spoil 6 posset, quarle 7 clabber, congeal, thicken 8 condense 9 coagulate
agent causing: 6 rennet
cure: dry 4 boot, care, heal, heed, help, jerk, salt, save 5 reest, smoke 6 charge, curate, priest, remedy, season 7 restore, therapy 8 antidote, preserve
by salting: 4 corn
in sun: 6 rizzar
cure-all: 4 balm 5 avens 6 elixir, remedy 7 panacea 10 catholicon
curfew: 4 bell 6 signal
curio: 5 relic, virtu 7 bibelot 8 keepsake, souvenir 9 bric-a-brac, curiosity
curious: odd 4 nosy, rare 5 queer 6 prying, quaint 7 cunning, strange, unusual 8 freakish, meddling, peculiar, singular 9 intrusive, wondering 11 inquisitive
curl: 4 bend, coil, kink, lock, roll, wave, wind 5 acker, crisp, tress, twist 6 buckle, frowse, ripple, spiral, writhe 7 crimple, flexure, ringlet, tendril 11 convolution 12 heartbreaker
curled: 7 savoyed
curlew: 4 bird, fute 5 kioea, snipe, whaup 6 marlin 7 bustard
curlicue: ess 5 caper, curve 6 paraph 8 flourish
curling mark: tee
curly: 4 wavy 5 crisp 7 rippled 8 crinkled
curmudgeon: 4 crab 5 churl, miser 6 grouch 7 niggard
curn: 4 corn 5 grain
currant: 5 berry 6 raisin, rizzar
genus: 5 ribes
currency: 4 cash, coin 5 bills, money, scrip 6 specie 10 greenbacks
current: now, way 4 eddy, flow, flux, ford, rife, tide 5 drift, going, rapid, tenor, trend, usual 6 coeval, common, course, living, motion, moving, recent, stream 7 counter, flowing, general, present, running, thermal, torrent 8 frequent 9 prevalent 10 prevailing 11 electricity 15 contemporaneous
generator: 12 electromotor
measuring device: 7 ammeter
pert. to: 7 voltaic
currish: 4 base 7 cynical, ignoble 8 snarling 12 mean-spirited
curry: 4 comb, drub 5 clean, dress, groom 6 bruise, cajole, powder 7 prepare 9 condiment, seasoning
favor: 4 fawn 6 cajole, smooge
curse: ban 4 bane, blow, damn, oath 5 spell, swear 6 malign 7 beshrew, malison 8 anathema 9 blaspheme, imprecate, maranatha 10 execration, vituperate 11 deprecation, malediction 12 anathematize 13 excommunicate
cursed: bad 6 odious 8 blighted, virulent 9 execrable
cursory: 4 fast 5 brief, hasty, quick, short 6 fitful, speedy 7 passing, shallow 8 careless, rambling 9 desultory, irregular, transient 10 discursive, evanescent 11 superficial
curt: 4 buff, rude, tart 5 bluff, blunt, brief, brusk, short, terse 6 abrupt 7 brusque, concise 8 cavalier, succinct 9 condensed
curtail: cut, lop 4 clip, crop, dock, pare, stop 5 abate, short, slash, stunt 6 lessen, reduce, teaser 7 abridge, bobtail, shorten 8 diminish, minorate, retrench 9 decurtate, epitomize 10 abbreviate
curtain: end 4 boom, drop, mask, veil, wall 5 blind, drape, shade 6 purdah, screen, shroud 7 ceiling, conceal, drapery 8 portiere

half: 4 bise, cafe 5 brise
raiser: 9 forepiece
curtilage: 4 area, yard 5 court
curtsy, curtsey: bob, bow 4 beck 5 conge 9 obeisance
curvature (see also **curve**): arc 4 bool, curl 8 kyphosis, lordosis 9 arcuation, scoliosis
center locus: 7 evolute
convex: 6 camber
surface: 5 plane
curve: arc, bow, ess 4 arch, bend, curb, ogee, turn, veer 5 ambit, bight, crook, crump, swirl, twist 6 bought, spiral 7 circuit, concave, contour, curvity, ellipse, flexure, inflect, sinuate 8 parabola, sinusaid 9 convexity, curvature
cusp: 7 spinode
double point of: 6 acnode
kind: 9 parabolic 10 memniscate
mathematical plane: 5 polar
parallel to an ellipse: 6 toroid
curved: 5 round, wound 6 convex, hamate, turned 7 arcuate, arrondi, crooked, curvant 8 anchoral, aquiline, arciform
inward: 5 adunc 6 hooked 8 aduncous
curvet: hop 4 leap, lope, skip, turn 5 bound, caper, frisk, prank 6 cavort, frolic, gambol, prance 8 corvetta(F.) 9 courbette
cuscuta: 5 plant 6 dodder 8 parasite
Cush: *father:* Ham
son: 4 Seba 6 Nimrod
cushat: 4 bird, dove 6 pigeon
cushion: bag, cod, mat, pad 4 boss, seat 5 gaddi, squab 6 buffer, insole, jockey, pillow, sachet 7 bolster, hassock 9 upholster
stuffing: 4 baru, down 5 kapok 8 feathers
cusk: 4 fish, tusk 5 torsk 6 burbot
cusp: 4 apex, horn, peak 5 angle, point, tooth 6 corner 8 paracone 10 projection
custard: 4 flan 5 flawn 6 doucet, dowcet, dowset 8 flummery 9 charlotte
custard apple: 5 anona 6 annona, paw-paw 8 sweetsop
custodian: 5 guard 6 bailee, keeper, warden 7 curator, janitor 8 guardian 9 caretaker, protector
custody: 4 care 5 trust 6 charge 7 control, durance, keeping, tuition 11 safekeeping 12 guardianship
custom: fad, law, mos(L.), tax, use 4 duty, form, garb, mode, more, rite, rote, rule, toll, wont 5 habit, haunt, usage, vogue 6 dastur, impost 7 costume, fashion, tribute 8 business, practice 9 costumbre, patronage 10 consuetude, convention, observance 12 constitution
of peoples: 5 mores
with force of law: mos
customary: 5 nomic, usual 6 common 7 general 8 familiar, habitual, orthodox 10 accustomed 11 traditional 12 conventional 14 consuetudinary
customer: 4 chap 5 buyer 6 client, patron 7 callant, patient, shopper 8 prospect 9 purchaser
group: 9 clientele
customhouse: 6 aduana(Sp.), dogana(It.) 9 chophouse
customs: tax 4 cess, duty, levy, rate, toll 5 mores 6 tariff 7 trewage
officer: 8 douanier
cut: bob, hew, lop, mow, nip, rit 4 bite, chip, chop, clip, crop, dock, fell, gash, hack, knap, mode, nick, pare, raze, slit, snee, snip, snub, trim 5 carve, flick, knife, lance, mince, notch, prune, razee, scarp, sever, shear, shorn, slash, slice, slish, snick, split 6 ablate, bisect, broach, chisel, cleave, divide, excise, haggle, ignore, incise, lessen, mangle, reduce, scotch, slight, swinge 7 affront, curtail, whittle 8 lacerate, retrench 9 engraving, intersect
a melon: 5 allot 8 dispense
a rug: 5 dance
across: 5 slice 8 transect 9 intersect, transcend
along: go 5 speed
capable of being: 7 sectile
down: 4 pare 5 clear, slash 9 economize
in: mix 9 interpose, interrupt, introduce
in half: 5 halve 6 bisect, secant 8 dimidiate
in small pieces: 4 dice, hash 5 mince 6 sliver
off: lop, nig 4 clip, crop, drib, poll 5 elide, roach, shave 7 deprive, divorce, exscind 8 amputate, truncate 9 apocopate, intercept 10 disinherit
out: 6 exsect 7 exscind 9 eliminate
roughly: jag 4 hack, snag 7 butcher
short: bob 4 clip, crop, dock, poll 5 abort, check, clipt 6 arrest 7 curtail
slanting: 4 bias 5 bevel, miter, mitre
with die: 4 dink
with shears: 4 snip 5 shirl
wool: dod 4 dodd 5 shear
cut and dried: 5 trite
cutaneous: 6 dermal
cutaway: 4 coat
cute: coy 4 keen 5 coony, dinky, sharp 6 clever, pretty, shrewd 7 cunning 10 attractive
cuticle: 4 hide, skin 8 membrane, pellicle 9 epidermis 10 integument
blister: 4 bleb 5 bulla
ingredient: 5 cutin
cutis: 4 skin 5 derma 6 corium
cutlass: 5 sword 6 dusack, tesack 7 machete
cutout: 9 decoupage
cutpurse: 5 thief 10 pickpocket

cutter: 4 beef, boat, sled 5 bravo, sloop, smack 6 cotter, editor, sleigh, slicer 7 clipper, incisor, ruffian 9 cutthroat, foretooth
cutthroat: 5 bravo 7 ruffian
cutting: hag, raw 4 curt, keen, kerf, slip, tart, twig 5 acute, bleak, crisp, scion, scrap, scrow, sharp 6 biting, bitter, secant, severe 7 caustic, mordant, painful, satiric 8 chilling, incisive, piercing, poignant, wounding 9 sarcastic, trenchant 10 blustering 11 abridgement, curtailment 12 adulteration
edge: 5 blade
implement: ax; axe, bit, hob, saw 4 adze 5 knife, lathe, mower, plane, razor 6 chisel, reaper, scythe, shears 8 scissors
of last letter: 7 apocope
cuttle: 4 thug 5 bully, knife 7 ruffian 8 assassin 9 swaggerer
cuttlefish: 5 sepia, squid 7 octopus, scuttle
ink: 5 sepia
cuvette: pot, tub 4 tank 5 basin 6 bucket, trench 7 cistern
cyanogen compound: 7 cyanide
Cybele: 4 Rhea
sweetheart: 5 Attis
Cyclades Island: Ios, Zea 4 Keos, Milo, Nios, Sira, Syra 5 Delos, Melos, Naxia, Naxos, Paros, Syros, Tenos, Tinos 6 Andros 7 Amorgos
cycle: age, eon, era 4 aeon, bike 5 epoch, pedal, round, saros, wheel 6 circle, course, period 7 bicycle, circuit, vehicle 8 tricycle 10 revolution
cyclone: 4 gale, gust, wind 5 blast, storm 6 baguio 7 tornado, twister, typhoon 9 hurricane, windstorm
cyclopean: 4 huge, vast 6 strong 7 massive 8 colossal, gigantic 9 herculean
Cyclopes: 5 Arges 7 Brontes 8 Steropes
Cyclops: 5 giant 7 monster
feature: 6 one eye
cyclostome: 7 lamprey
Cycnus' father: 4 Ares
cygnet: pen 4 fowl, swan
cygnus: 4 swan
cylinder: 4 beam, drum, pipe, prim, tube 6 barrel, bobbin, gabian, piston, platen, roller 7 sleever
cylindrical: 5 round 6 terete 7 centric, tubular 8 teretial
cyma: 4 gola, gula, ogee 7 molding
cymar: 4 robe 5 shift, simar
cymbal: tal, zel 8 doughnut
cymbals: 6 becken, piatti
Cymbeline's daughter: 6 Imogen
Cymric: 5 Welsh
god of dead: 5 Pwyll
god of sky: 7 Gwydion
god of sun: 4 Lleu, Llew
god of underworld: 4 Gwyn
cynic: 5 Timon 7 doubter 9 pessimist 11 misanthrope
cynical: 6 sullen 7 currish, doglike 8 captious, snarling
cynosure: 8 lodestar, polestar
cypress: 9 belvedere
cyprinoid: See **fish**
Cyprus: *city:* 6 Paphos 7 Limasol, Nicosia(c.) 9 Famagusta
coin: 4 para 7 piaster
measure: oka, oke, pik 4 cass 5 donum, kouza 6 gomari, kartos 7 medimno
mountain: 7 Troodos
weight: oka, oke 5 moosa 6 kantar
cyrenaic: 7 hedonic
Cyrus: *daughter:* 6 Atossa
treasurer: 10 Mithredath
cyst: bag, sac, wen 5 pouch 6 ranula 7 vesicle
Cyzicus: *mother:* 6 Aenete
slayer: 5 Jason
wife: 6 Cleite
czar, csar: 4 Ivan, tsar, tzar 5 Peter 8 Nicholas
daughter: 8 czarevna, tsarevna
son: 10 czarevitch, tsarevitch
wife: 7 czarina, tsarina
Czechoslovakia: *capital:* 5 Praha 6 Prague
city: As 4 Asch, Brno, Eger, Hron 5 Opava, Praha, Tuzla 6 Aussig, Pilsen, Prague 7 Budweis, Teplitz 9 Pressburg 10 Bratislava 11 Reichenberg
coin: 5 ducat, haler 6 heller, koruna
county: Ung
dance: 5 polka 6 redowa 7 furiant
leader: 5 Benes
measure: lan, sah 4 mira 5 latro, liket, stopa 6 merice
mountain: 5 Tatra
munitions plant: 5 Skoda
province: 7 Bohemia, Moravia
reformer: 4 Huss
river: Vag, Vah 4 Eger, Elbe, Gran, Hron, Isar, Iser, Labe, Oder, Ohre, Waag 5 Nitra 6 Moldau
czigany: 5 gypsy

D

dab: dap, hit, pat **4** blow, chit, lump, peck, spot **5** clout, dight, smear **6** blotch, expert, strike **7** dabster, portion, splotch **8** flatfish, flounder
dabble: dib **4** mess **5** dally **6** dibble, meddle, paddle, potter, splash, tamper, trifle **7** moisten, spatter **8** sprinkle
dabbler: **7** amateur, dabster **10** dilettante
dabby: wet **4** damp **5** moist **8** adhesive
dabchick: **5** grebe
dabster: See **dab**
dace: **4** chub
dacoit: **6** robber **8** criminal **9** plunderer
dactyl: toe **6** finger **7** piddock
dactylogram: **11** fingerprint
dactylopodite: **6** pollex
dactyloscopy: **14** classification, identification
dad: **4** beat, blow, hunk, lump, papa **5** knock, thump **6** father, strike
daddle: **4** fist, hand **6** dawdle
daddy longlegs: **5** stilt **7** spinner, tipulid **8** arachnid
dado: **6** groove **7** solidum
daedal: **4** rich **6** varied **7** bizarre **8** artistic, skillful **9** ingenious, intricate **10** variegated
Daedalus: *son:* **6** Icarus
victim: **5** Talos
daemon (see also **demon**): **8** eudaemon
daffing: fun **7** fooling
daffodil: **5** dilly
daffy: See **daft**
daft: gay **4** luny, wild **5** balmy, crazy, giddy, potty, silly **6** insane **7** foolish, idiotic **8** imbecile
dag: jag **4** stab **5** slash **6** daggle, pierce **7** daglock
Dag's horse: **8** Hrimfaxi **9** Skinfaksi
Dagda's kin: **5** Boann **6** Aengus, Brigit
dagger: **4** dirk, itac(PI), kris, snee, spud, stab **5** crise, katar(Ind.), skean(Ir.) **6** anlace, bodkin, coutel, creese, diesis, kreese, panade, stylet, weapon **7** baslard, corteau, dudgeon, lalarao, poniard **8** puncheon, stiletto **10** misericord **11** misericorde
Burmese: dah, dow
handle: **4** hilt
Malay: **4** kris
Scotch: **4** dirk
stroke: **4** stab **8** stoccado
Dahomey people: Fon **4** Fong
daily: **4** aday **7** diurnal **9** hodiernal, newspaper, quotidian
daintily: **8** gingerly
dainty: **4** cate, nice, rare **5** acate, denty **6** bonbon, choice, costly, friand, mignon, minion, picked, scarce **7** elegant, finical, finicky, minikin **8** delicacy, delicate, mignard **9** exquisite, finicking, squeamish **10** confection, fastidious
dairy: **7** vaccary **8** creamery
food: **6** yogurt **7** yoghurt, yohourt **8** yoghourt
tool: **9** separator
dairymaid: dey **8** deywoman, milkmaid
dairyman: **7** milkman
dais: **4** seat **5** bench, podia(pl.), stage, table **6** canopy, podium, settle **7** estrade, terrace **8** chabutra, platform
daisy: **5** gowan, oxeye **6** shasta **10** moonflower
dak: **4** post
Dakota Indian: **5** Sioux **6** Mandan **7** Arikara **8** Arikaree
Daksha's father: **6** Brahma
Dalai Lama: **5** ruler **13** reincarnation
dale: **4** dell, dene, glen, vale **5** spout **6** bottom, dingle, trough, valley
dalles: **6** rapids
dalliance: toy **4** chat, play, talk **6** gossip, trifle, tousel, tousle
dally: toy **4** chat, fool, idle, jake, jauk, play, wait **5** delay, flirt, sport, tarry **6** dabble dawdle, linger, loiter, trifle
Dalmatia: *channel:* **7** Narenta
seaport: **7** Spalato
dam: bar, bay **4** stay, stem, stop, weir **5** block, check, choke, garth, mound **6** ani-

cut, causey, mother, parent 7 annicut, barrier 8 blockade, obstacle, obstruct, restrain
dama: 7 gazelle
damage: mar 4 blot, cost, harm, hurt, loss, ruin, teen 5 burst, cloud, spoil, wound 6 charge, deface, defect, impair, injure, injury, scathe 7 expense, scratch 8 accident, disserve, mischief, sabotage 9 detriment, disprofit, vandalism 10 impairment 11 deleterious, impeachment 12 disadvantage
pert. to: 5 noxal
damages: 5 award 7 payment
daman: 5 hyrax
Damascus: *people:* 6 Syrian
river: 5 Abana 6 Abanah, Barada 7 Pharpar
damask: 5 linen
dame: 4 lady 5 woman 6 matron
correlative: 4 sire
dammar: 5 resin, rosin
damn: 5 curse
damnable: 6 odious 8 infernal 9 execrable 10 detestable
damnation: 9 perdition
damned: 5 bally 6 bloody 8 accursed
damnum: 4 harm, loss 9 detriment
damourite: 4 mica 9 muscovite
damp: deg, fog, wet 4 dank, dewy, dull, mist, roky 5 dabby, humid, moist, muggy, musty, rafty, rainy, soggy 6 clammy, dampen, deaden, muffle, quench, stupor 7 bedewed, depress, moisten 8 dejected, dispirit, humidity, moisture 9 depressed, stupefied 10 discourage
damper: 5 bread 7 checker 8 register
damsel: 4 girl 6 maiden 8 donzella, princess 10 demoiselle
Dan: *prince:* 7 Ahiezer
town: 4 Elon
Danae's kin: 4 Zeus 7 Perseus 8 Acrisius
danaite: 12 arsenopyrite
dance: bal(F.), bob, hop 4 ball, frug, haka, hoof, prom, shag 5 caper, flisk, frike, frisk, rumba, tango, tread, stomp, twist, waltz 6 balter, Boston, hormos, masque, minuet, monkey 7 foxtrot, saltate 8 cotillon, fandango 9 allemande(G.), cotillion, farandole 10 roundabout, tripudiate
ancient: see *old* below
art of: 8 orchesis 12 choreography
ballroom: 5 polka, waltz 7 czardas, foxtrot, mazurka, twostep
basket-carrying: 11 calathiscus
ceremonial: 6 areito
chorus: 5 strut 6 cancan, cordax
college: hop 4 prom
country: hay, hey 7 argeers, auresca 8 aurrescu, haymaker 10 villanella
designer: 12 choregrapher 13 choreographer
drama: 6 ballet
English: 6 althea, morris
exhibition: tap 6 ballet
fast: see *lively* below
formal: 4 prom 5 pavan, paven, pavin 7 mazurka 9 farandole
gypsy: 7 farruca 10 zingaresca
Hawaiian: 4 hula
Hebrew: 4 hora
involuntary: 8 tricotee
Italian: 5 volta 8 courante 9 rigoletto 10 tarantella
Latin American: 5 conga, rumba, samba, tango 6 maxixe, rhumba 7 carioca, criolla
lively: jig 4 reel, trot 5 fling, galop, gavot, polka, rumba 6 bolero, branle, canary,, rhumba 7 coranto 8 galliard, rigadoon 9 allemande, schottish, shakedown, tambourin 10 corybantic 11 schottische
masked: 7 ridotto
modern: toe 4 dump, frug, pony, shag 5 twist 6 chacha, monkey 7 twostep 10 Charleston 12 mashed potato
movement: pas 4 jete, step 5 brise, coule, coupe 6 chasse, coupee 7 chassed, fouette, gambado 8 glissade 9 entrechat, pirouette
Muse: 11 Terpsichore
music: 10 gymnopedie
nineteenth-century: 7 tempete
old: 5 galop, gavot, loure, pavan, paven, pavin, rondo, volta 6 bource, branle, canary, carole, cebell, corant, minuet, morris, pavane 7 boutade, chaccon, chacona, coranto, courant, furlana, gavotte, lavolta 8 chaconne, faradole, gilliard 9 allemande, farandola, horedance, sarabande 10 tarantella, tarantelle
pert. to: 6 gestic 13 terpsichorean
Peruvian: 5 cueca
round: 5 carol, waltz 6 carole 10 Charleston
rustic: See *country* above
shoes: 4 taps 5 pumps 8 slippers, toeshoes
slow: 5 waltz 6 adagio, minuet, valeta
square: 7 argeers, lancers 8 lanciers 9 quadrille
step: See *movement* above
sword: 8 matachin 11 Flamborough
voluptuous: 5 belly 8 habanera
dance of death: 7 macaber, macabre
dancer: 6 artist, hoofer, happer 7 danseur 11 terpsichore 13 terpsichorean
Biblical: 6 Salome
female: 7 artiste, chorine 8 bayadere, coryphee, danseuse, devadasi 9 ballerina 15 terpsichorienne

garment: 7 leotard
instrument: 8 castanet
rope: nat
sword: 8 matachin
dancing: 7 saltant 11 choregraphy 12 choreography
dancing girl: See **dancer** *female*
dandelion: 7 chicory 10 bitterwort
stalk: 5 scape
dander: 5 anger, scurf 6 stroll, temper, wander 7 passion, saunter 8 dandruff
dandified 6 spruce 8 adonized
dandiprat: 5 dwarf, pygmy 6 urchin
dandle: 6 diddle, fondle, pamper
dandruff: 5 scurf
dandy: fop 4 beau, buck, dand, dude, fine, jake, prig, toff, yawl 5 dildo, swell 7 capstan, coxcomb, foppish, jessamy 8 sailboat 9 exquisite 11 scrumptious
female: 10 dandisette, dandizette
Dane: See **Denmark**
danger: 4 fear, risk 5 doubt, peril 6 hazard 7 pitfall, venture 8 distress, jeopardy 9 adventure
signal: 4 bell 5 alarm, siren 6 tocsin
dangerous: bad, rum 5 nasty 6 fickle 7 parlous 8 insecure 9 desperate 10 precarious
dangle: lop 4 hang, loll 5 droop, swing 7 shoggle, suspend
Danish: See **Denmark**
dank: wet 4 damp 5 humid, moist 6 clammy, coarse, dampen 7 drizzle, wetness 8 moisture
danseuse: 6 dancer 9 ballerina
danta: 5 tapir
Dante: *beloved:* 8 Beatrice
circle of hell: 5 Caina
illustrator: 4 Dore
patron: 5 Scala
verse form: 7 sestina
Danube: 5 Ister
fish: 4 huch 5 hucho
people: 6 Dacian
town: Ulm
tributary: 4 Drau, Raab, Raba 5 Drava, Drave, Siret
Danzig: *coin:* 6 gulden 7 pfennig
liqueur: 7 ratafia
dap: dab, dib, dip 4 skip 6 bounce, dibble 7 rebound
Daphne: 8 Mezereon
father: 5 Ladon
mother: 6 Creusa
Daphnis' lover: 5 Chloe
dapper: 4 neat, trim 5 natty 6 spruce 7 finical, foppish
dappled: 6 dotted 7 flecked, mottled, spotted 8 freckled 10 variegated
darbies: 8 manacles 9 handcuffs
Dardanelles: 10 Hellespont
dare: 4 dast, defy, face, osse, risk 5 brave 6 assume 7 attempt, venture 9 challenge, undertake
dare not: 5 dasn't 6 daurna
daredevil: 6 madcap 12 swashbuckler
daring: 4 bold, rash 5 brave, hardy, manly, nerve 6 heroic 7 courage 8 boldness, devilish, fearless 9 audacious 10 courageous, jeopardous 11 adventurous, venturesome
dariole: cup 5 shell
Darius: *father:* 9 Ahasuerus
prince: 6 Daniel
dark: dim, mum, sad, wan 4 dern, ebon, mirk, murk 6 black, blind, brown, cloud, dingy, dusky, faint, mirky, murky, shady, sooty, swart, unlit, vague 6 closed, cloudy, dimpsy, dismal, gloomy, opaque, swarth, wicked 7 melanic, obscure, rayless, stygian, swarthy 8 abstruse, darkling, gloomful, ignorant, lowering, sinister 9 ambiguous, atrocious, blindfold, Cimmerian, infuscate, recondite, secretive, tenebrous, uncertain, unlighted, unrefined 10 caliginous, indistinct, mysterious
dark-complexioned: 7 swarthy
dark horse: 9 candidate 10 contestant
darken: dim 4 dull 5 bedim, cloud, gloam, shade, sully, umber 6 deepen, shadow 7 becloud, benight, blacken, eclipse, obscure, opacate, perplex, tarnish 8 overcast 9 obfuscate, overcloud 10 overshadow
darkness: 4 dark, dern, dusk, murk 5 gloom, night, shade 6 shadow 7 dimness, privacy, secrecy 8 gloaming, iniquity, twilight 9 blackness 10 wickedness
realm: Po 6 Erebus
darling: jo; joe(Sc.), pet 4 dear, duck 5 aroon(Ir.), aruin, bully, cheri, deary, lieve, sweet 6 cherie, dautie(Sc.), dawtie(Sc.), minion, moppet 7 acushla(Ir.), pigsney, querida 8 favorite 9 favourite
darn: 4 mend 5 patch 6 repair
darnel: 4 tare, weed 5 grass 6 cockle
darner: 6 needle
dart: 4 bolt, flit, jouk, leap, plan 5 arrow, bound, fling, flirt, lance, skite, spear, speed, start 6 dartle, elance, method, scheme, spring 7 javelin, missile 9 flechette
throwing machine: 10 anisocycle
dart-like: 8 dartling, spicular
D'Artagnan: *companion:* 5 Athos 6 Aramis 7 Porthos
creator: 5 Dumas
Dartmouth College Location: 7 Hanover 12 New Hampshire
Darwin: *boat:* 6 Beagle
theory: 9 evolution

Darwinian: 12 evolutionist
das: 6 dassie
Das Kapital author: 4 Marx
dash: pep 6 bang, ding, elan, gift, hurl, line, pelt, race, ruin, rush, show, slam 5 abash, ardor, break, clash, crash, crush, fling, knock, smash, speed, spice, style, swash, throw 6 energy, hurtle, hyphen, shiver, spirit, splash, sprint, stroke, thrust 7 bravura, collide, depress, display, shatter, spatter, splotch 8 confound, gratuity, splinter 9 animation, bespatter, frustrate, overthrow
dasheen: 4 taro
dasher: 6 beater 7 plunger
dashing: 4 bold 5 bully, showy 6 swanky, veloce 7 stylish, swagger 8 spirited 11 fashionable
dastard: cad, sot 5 sneak 6 coward, craven 7 dullard 8 poltroon
dastardly: 4 foul
data: 5 facts 8 material 11 information
datary: 7 dataria
date: age, day, era 5 epoch, fruit 6 reckon 10 engagement, rendezvous 11 anniversary, appointment
erroneous: 11 anachronism
on coin: 7 exergue
dated: 5 passe 8 outmoded 12 old-fashioned 13 unfashionable
dateless: 8 timeless 10 immemorial
dating: 6 timing
datum: 4 fact, item 11 information
daub: 4 balm, blob, blot, clag, clam, clat, coat, gaum, soil 5 clart, cleam, cover, paint, slake, smear 6 bedaub, grease 7 besmear, plaster, splotch 8 slaister
daughter: 4 bint 5 fille, filly 6 alumna 7 cadette
pert. to: 6 filial
Daughter of Moon: 7 Nokomis
daunt: awe, cow, daw 4 daze, faze, stun, tame 5 abash, amate, break, check, deter, dompt 6 dismay, subdue 7 conquer, control, overawe, repress, stupefy, terrify 8 dispirit, overcome 10 disconcert, discourage, dishearten, intimidate
dauntless: 4 bold, good 5 brave 7 aweless 8 fearless, intrepid 9 undaunted 10 courageous
davenport: 4 desk, sofa 5 couch, divan 12 chesterfield
daver: 4 fade, stun 5 droop 6 benumb, wither 7 stupefy
David: *chief ruler:* Ira
companion: 6 Hushai
daughter: 5 Tamar
employer: 5 Nabal
favorite son: 7 Absalom
friend: 5 Ittai
kin: 5 Jesse, Tamar 6 Michal 7 Abigail, Absalom, Solomon
man of: Ira 4 Igal 7 Shammah
musician: 5 Asaph
prophet: 6 Nathan
scribe: 7 Shavsha
traitor to: 10 Ahithophel
valley of Goliath's death: 4 Elah
David Copperfield character: 4 Dora, Heep, Rosa 5 Agnes, James, Uriah 6 Dartle 8 Micawber 9 Wickfield 10 Steerforth
daviely: 10 listlessly 12 spiritlessly
Davy: 4 lamp
daw: 4 dawn, drab 5 color, daunt 6 magpie 7 jackdaw 8 slattern, sluggard 9 blackbird, simpleton
dawdle: lag 4 idle, poke 5 dally 6 daddle, daidle, diddle, linger, loiter, pickle, piddle, putter, trifle 7 finnick, quiddle
dawn: 4 morn 5 sunup 6 aurora 7 morning, sunrise 8 daybreak 9 beginning
comb. form: eo
goddess: Eos 5 Ushas 6 Aurora
pert. to: 4 eoan 7 auroral
symbol: dew
toward the: 8 eastward
dawny: 4 puny 5 small
day: yom(Heb.) 4 date, time 5 epoch 6 period 8 lifetime
before: eve 9 yesterday
early: see **daybreak**
father of: 6 Erebus
god of: 5 Horus
hot: 8 scorcher
joyful: 8 festival
judgment: 8 doomsday
pert. to: 6 ferial
day blindness: 11 hemeralopia
daybreak: 4 dawn, morn 5 sunup
daydream: 4 muse 6 vision 7 reverie
days: *fateful:* 4 Ides
fifty: 13 quinquagesima
fourteen: 9 fortnight
daysman: 6 umpire 7 arbiter 8 mediator
daze: fog 4 stun 5 daunt 6 astony, bemuse, benumb, dazzle, muddle, trance 7 confuse, stupefy 8 bewilder, dumfound
dazed: 4 asea 6 doiled, rotten 7 spoiled 8 astonied, withered 10 doitrified
dazzle: 4 daze 5 blind, glaik, shine 6 fulgor 7 eclipse 8 bewilder, outshine, surprise
dazzling: 5 flare, flash 6 garish 7 fulgent, glaring, radiant 8 gorgeous 9 brilliant 10 candescent, foudroyant 11 pyrotechnic
deacon: 5 adept 6 cleric, doctor, layman, master 10 adulterate
prayers: 6 ectene
stole: 7 orarion

dead: 4 bung, cold, dull, flat, gone, mort(F.), numb, tame 5 amort, inert, napoo, quiet, slain 6 asleep, lapsed, napooh, refuse 7 defunct, exactly, expired, extinct, insipid, sterile, tedious 8 absolute, complete, deceased, departed, inactive, lifeless, obsolete 9 apathetic, bloodless, inanimate, nerveless, unsalable 10 breathless, lusterless, monotonous, motionless, spiritless, unexciting 11 indifferent, ineffectual, inoperative 12 extinguished, unproductive, unprofitable
city of: 10 necropolis
house of: 4 tomb 5 grave 6 morgue 7 ossuary 8 mortuary 9 crematory, ossuarium
mass for: 5 black
region of: Po 5 Hades 6 Erebus
dead duck: 5 goner
Dead Sea: *city:* 5 Sodom
mountain: 6 Pisgah
pass: 8 Akrabbin
plateau: 4 Seir
river to: 5 Arnon 6 Jordan
territory: 4 Moab
Dead Souls author: 5 Gogol
deadbeat: bum 7 sponger 8 parasite
deaden: 4 damp, dull, kill, mute, numb, stun 5 blunt 6 benumb, dampen, muffle, obtund, opiate, retard, weaken 7 petrify, repress 8 amortize, enfeeble 10 devitalize
deadfall: 4 trap
deadhead: 6 bobber
deadhouse: 6 morgue 8 mortuary
deadline: 5 limit 8 boundary
deadlock: tie 4 draw 7 impasse 8 stoppage 9 stalemate 10 standstill
deadly: 4 dire, fell, mort 5 fatal 6 lethal, mortal 7 capital, deathly, fateful, ruinous 8 venomous, virulent 9 pestilent 10 implacable, pernicious 11 destructive, internecine
deadpan: 6 vacant 9 impassive
deaf: 5 dunch 9 unheeding
deaf and dumb person: 9 surdomute
deafness: 6 asonia 8 anacusia, anacusis, cophosis
cause: 4 stun 5 deave(Sc.)
deal: 4 dole, part, sale 5 allot, board, plank, sever, share, trade, wield 6 bestow, divide, handle, parcel 7 bargain, deliver, inflict, portion, scatter, wrestle 8 dispense, separate 9 apportion, negotiate 10 administer, distribute 11 transaction
in: 4 sell 5 trade 6 purvey
with: 4 cope 6 handle
dealbate: 5 white 8 whitened
dealer: 5 agent 6 badger, broker, cadger, jobber, monger, seller, trader 7 chapman 8 merchant, operator 9 middleman, tradesman 10 negotiator, trafficker 11 distributer, distributor
secondhand goods: 6 broker 10 pawnbroker
dealing: 7 trading, traffic 8 exchange 11 intercourse
shrewd: 6 deceit 9 chicanery
dean (see also **dene**): 5 doyen 6 senior, verger 8 official
dear: jo; gra, joe, pet 4 agra, cara(It.), cher(F.), fond, high, lief, near 5 chary, chere(F.), honey, loved 6 costly, dearly, scarce, severe, worthy 7 beloved, darling, lovable, pigsney, querida 8 esteemed, glorious, precious, valuable 9 cherished, expensive, heartfelt, honorable, important 10 sweetheart 12 affectionate
dearly: 6 deeply, keenly, richly 8 heartily 9 earnestly
dearness: 6 dearth
dearth: 4 lack, want 6 famine 7 paucity, poverty 8 dearness, scarcity 10 costliness, deficiency
death: end 4 bale, bane, doom, mors, mort(F.), obit 5 decay 6 demise, expiry, murder 7 decease, quietus 8 biolysis, rawbones 9 bloodshed, departure, forthfare 10 expiration, extinction, pestilence
after: 10 posthumous
angel of: 6 Azrael
aware of portending: fey
bringing: 6 funest
eternal: 9 perdition
goddess: Hel 4 Dana, Danu
march: 5 dirge 7 cortege, funeral
meditation: 11 thanatopsis
mercy: 10 euthanasia
notice: 4 obit 5 orbit 8 obituary
personification: 4 Mors 5 Ankou 6 Charos, Charus
put to: gas 4 hang, kill, slay 5 choke 6 murder, noyade, starve, stifle 7 garrote 8 strangle 9 suffocate 11 assassinate, electrocute
rate: 9 mortality
rattle: 4 rale
register: 9 necrology
song: 5 dirge, elegy 8 threnody
symbol of: 5 orant
type of: 5 lynch 6 halter, noyode 10 lapidation
death-defying: 4 bold, rash 6 heroic 9 audacious, imprudent
deathless: 7 eternal, undying 8 immortal 12 imperishable
deathlessness: 9 athanasia 11 immortality
deathlike: 7 deathly, ghastly, macaber, macabre 8 ghastful, moribund

deathly: 5 fatal 6 deadly, mortal 8 mortally 9 deathlike 11 destructive
deave: din 4 stun 6 bother, deafen 7 stupefy 8 bewilder
debacle: 4 rout 7 failure 8 collapse, stampede 9 breakdown, cataclysm
debar: 4 deny, tabu 5 estop, taboo 6 forbid, hinder, refuse 7 boycott, deprive, exclude, prevent, seclude, suspend 8 preclude, prohibit 9 foreclose, interdict 10 disqualify
debark: 4 land 9 disembark
debarrass: 7 relieve 12 disembarrass
debase: 5 abase, alloy, avile, lower, stoop 6 defile, demean, impair, reduce, revile, vilify 7 corrupt, degrade, deprave, traduce, vitiate 10 adulterate, degenerate, depreciate 11 deteriorate
debased: 4 base, vile 7 corrupt
debatable: 4 moot
debate: 4 agon, moot 5 argue, fight 6 reason, strife 7 agitate, canvass, contend, contest, discuss, dispute, examine, palaver, quarrel, wrangle 8 argument, consider, militate, question 9 dialectic, quodlibet 10 contention, controvert, deliberate 11 controversy 12 dissertation 13 argumentation
pert. to: 8 forensic
place of: 5 forum
stoppage of: 7 cloture
debater: 16 controversialist
debating: 11 contentious
association: 6 lyceum
debauch: 4 bout 5 spree, taint 6 defile, guzzle, seduce, splore, vilify 7 corrupt, deprave, mislead, pollute, violate 8 squander, strumpet 10 depreciate, hellbender 11 contaminate
debauched: 4 lewd 8 rakehell 9 dissolute
debauchee: rip 4 rake, roue 6 lecher 8 rakehell 9 libertine
debilitated: 4 weak 5 seedy 6 feeble, infirm, sapped 9 enervated
debility: 5 atony 7 languor 8 weakness 9 infirmity, lassitude 10 feebleness
debit: 4 loss 6 charge
deblaterate: gab 7 chatter
debonair: 4 airy 6 jaunty, polite 8 graceful, gracious
Deborah's husband: 8 Lapidoth
debouche: 4 exit 6 emerge, outlet 7 passage 9 emergence
debris: 5 trash, waste 6 refuse, rubble 7 rubbish 8 detritus
debt: sin 5 debit, fault 7 arrears 8 trespass 9 arrearage, liability 10 obligation
acknowledgement: IOU 4 bill, note
debtor: 6 dyvour
note: IOU
proceed against: 6 excuss
debut: 7 opening 8 entrance 9 beginning 12 introduction
debutant, debutante: bud, deb 5 dobby
decad: ten
decade: 9 decennium
decadent: 6 effete 7 decayed 9 declining 10 retrograde 12 deteriorated 13 retrogressive
decamp: 4 bolt 5 elope, scoot, vamos 6 depart, levant, mizzle, vamose 7 abscond, vamoose 8 clear out
decant: 4 emit, pour 6 unload 8 transfer
decanter: 6 carafe
decapitate: 6 behead 10 guillotine
decapod: 4 crab 5 prawn, squid 7 lobster 10 crustacean
decay: ebb, rot 4 conk, dote, doze, fade, fail, ruin 5 death, spoil, waste 6 caries, mildew, wither 7 decline, failure 8 decrease 9 adversity, decadence, decompose 11 destruction, deteriorate, dissolution 12 dilapidation, disintegrate, putrefaction 13 decomposition, deterioration 14 disintegration
comb. form: 5 sapro
dental: 6 caries
in fruit: 4 blet
decaying: 4 doty
decease: die 5 death 6 demise 9 departure 11 dissolution
deceased: 4 dead 7 defunct 8 departed
deceit: See **deception**
deceitful: 5 false, gaudy 6 fickle, hollow 7 sirenic 8 tortuous 9 faithless, insidious, insincere 10 circuitous, fallacious 11 disaffected 13 machiavellian
deceivable: 8 gullible
deceive: cog, con, lie 4 bilk, dupe, flam, fool, gaff, gull, hoax, jilt 5 abuse, blear, blend, blind, bluff, catch, cheat, cozen, cully, dodge, gleek, hocus, trick 6 baffle, beflum, befool, betray, bubble, delude, divert, humbug, illude 7 beguile, defraud, mislead 8 flimflam, hoodwink 9 bamboozle, frustrate 11 doublecross 12 misrepresent
deceiver: 6 trepan 7 juggler, sharper, warlock 8 magician
decelerate: 4 slow
decency: 7 decorum 9 propriety
decennium: 6 decade
decent: 4 fair 6 chaste, comely, honest, modest, proper, seemly 7 fitting, gradely, shapely 8 decorous 11 appropriate, respectable
deception: dor 4 dole, gaff, ruse, sham, wile 5 cheat, covin, craft, fraud, guile, magic, trick 6 cautel, deceit, humbug 7 blaflum, cunning, evasion, fallacy, fiction, knavery, pretext, slyness 8 artifice, falsedad(Sp.), intrigue, prestige, subtlety, trickery, trumpery, wiliness 9 chicanery, collusion, duplicity, falsehood, hypocrisy, imposture, mendacity, sophistry, treach-

ery **10** artfulness, camouflage, dishonesty, imposition, infidelity **11** contrivance, counterfeit, dissembling **13** deceitfulness, dissimulation

deceptive: **5** false **8** delusive, illusory **10** fallacious

decided: **4** firm, flat **6** formed **8** clear-cut, decisive **14** unquestionably

decima: **5** tenth, tithe

decimal base: ten

decimate: **7** destroy

decipher: **4** read **6** decode, detect, reveal **8** discover, indicate **9** translate

decision: end **4** doom, fiat, grit **5** arret, canon, pluck **6** crisis, decree, ruling **7** consult, verdict **8** finality, judgment, sentence **9** precedent **10** conclusion, resolution **12** adjudication **13** determination

maker: **5** judge **6** umpire **7** referee **9** executive

sudden: **4** whim **7** impulse

decisive: **5** final **6** crisic **7** crucial **8** critical **10** conclusive, peremptory

deck: tog **4** buss, dink, heap, pink, trig **5** adorn, array, cover, dizen, dress, equip, floor, prink, store **6** blazon, clothe, fettle **7** apparel, bedight, bedizen, feather **8** beautify, decorate, platform **9** embellish **10** overspread

kind: gun **4** boat, main, poop, spar **5** berth, orlop, upper **6** bridge **7** shelter **8** platform, splinter **9** hurricane, promenade **10** forecastle, protective

lowest: **5** orlop

part: **7** scupper

deck out: **5** adorn, array **6** attire

decked: **4** clad **6** beseen

deckle-edged: **5** erose

declaim: **4** gale, rant, rave **5** orate, speak, spout **6** recite **7** elocute, inveigh **8** denounce, harangue, perorate **9** discourse

declaration: **4** word **5** fuero, libel **6** oracle, placet **7** promise **9** affidavit, assertion, statement **10** allegation, deposition, exposition, intimation **11** affirmation, certificate, description, enunciation **12** announcement, asseveration, proclamation **13** advertisement, pronouncement **14** interpretation **15** acknowledgement

declare: bid, say, vow **4** aver, avow, deny, make, read, show, trow **5** aread, areed, posit, state **6** affirm, allege, assert, assure, avouch, blazon, depone, herald, indict, notify, relate **7** behight, express, profess, protest, signify, testify **8** announce, denounce, describe, indicate, maintain, manifest, proclaim **9** advertise, enunciate, nuncupate, pronounce **10** annunciate, asseverate, promulgate **11** acknowledge, communicate

in cards: **4** meld

declination: **4** bias **5** decay, slope **6** regret **7** decline, descent, refusal **8** swerving **10** declension **11** declinature, inclination **13** deterioration

decline: dip, ebb, set **4** bend, fade, fail, fall, flag, sink, turn, wane **5** chute, droop, heald, hield, lower, repel, slope, slump, stoop, stray **6** debase, refuse, reject, renege, weaken **7** descend, descent, deviate, disavow, dwindle, failure, forbear **8** decrease, forebear, languish, withdraw **9** decadence, declivity, recadence, repudiate **10** declension, retrograde **11** declination, degradation **13** deterioration

declining: **5** awane **8** decadent **13** deteriorating

declivity: **4** hang **5** cliff, scarp, slope **6** calade **7** decline, descent, hanging **9** acclivity, precipice

declivous: **5** prone **7** sloping

decoct: **4** boil, cook **5** smelt **6** excite, kindle, refine **7** extract **8** condense, diminish

decoction: **4** dish, sapa **5** drink **6** cremor **7** extract **8** infusion

decode: **8** decipher

decompose: rot **5** decay, spoil **7** putrefy

decorate: **4** bind, cite, deck, pink, trim **5** adorn, dress, inlay, panel **6** decore, emboss, parget **7** festoon, garnish, miniate **8** ornament, titivate **9** embellish

decorated: **6** ornate **7** damasse, wrought **9** sigillate

decoration: **4** bahl **5** medal **6** frieze, plaque, tinsel **7** epergne, garnish, regalis **8** flourish, ornament **9** furniture, sgraffito **10** chambranle, decorament, decorement, sgraffiato

metalware: **4** tole

military: DSC, DSM, DSO **5** medal **6** ribbon

pert. to: **8** medallic

decorative: **5** fancy **9** beautiful **10** ornamental

decore: **5** adorn **8** beautify, decorate

decorous: **4** calm, good, prim **5** grave, quiet, sober, staid **6** decent, demure, modest, polite, proper, sedate, seemly, serene, steady **7** fitting, orderly, regular, settled **8** becoming, composed, mannerly **9** befitting, dignified, unruffled **11** appropriate

decorticate: **4** flay, hull, husk, pare, peel, pill, skin **5** strip **6** denude **9** excoriate

decorum: **9** propriety **10** convention

decoy: **4** bait, lure, tole **5** drill, plant, shill, tempt **6** allure, entice, entrap, pigeon **8** inveigle **9** shillaber

decrease: ebb 4 drop, fall, loss, sink, wane 5 abate, decay, taper, waste 6 impair, lessen, shrink 7 decline, dwindle, slacken, subside 8 diminish, moderate, retrench 9 decession, decrement 10 diminution

decree: act, law 4 fiat, rede, rule, will 5 aread, areed, arret, canon, edict, enact, irade, order, tenet, ukase 6 arrest, assize, decern, dictum, firman, indict, ordain 7 adjudge, appoint, command, decreet, mandate, statute 8 decision, decretum, rescript, sentence 9 determine, enactment, ordinance, preordain 10 adjudicate, plebiscite 12 adjudication, announcement
authoritative: 5 arret, canon
imperial: 4 fiat
papal: 4 bull

decrement: 4 loss 5 waste 8 decrease 10 diminution

decrepit: 4 lame, weak, 6 feeble, infirm, senile 7 failing, invalid 9 bedridden

decrown: 6 depose 8 unthrone

decry: boo 4 slur 5 lower 6 lessen 7 asperse, censure, condemn, debauch, degrade, detract 8 belittle, derogate 9 discredit, disparage, underrate 10 depreciate, undervalue

decuman: 4 huge 5 large

decuple: 7 tenfold

decussate: 9 intersect

dedal: See **daedal**

dedicate: vow 6 devote, direct, hallow, oblate 7 ascribe 8 inscribe 9 nuncupate 10 consecrate

deduce: 4 draw, lead 5 bring, drive, infer, trace 6 derive, elicit, evolve, gather 7 extract 8 conclude

deduct: 4 bate, dock, take 5 abate, allow 6 defalk, remove 7 curtail 8 abstract, discount, separate, subtract

deduction: 4 agio 6 rebate 7 reprise 8 illation 9 corollary, induction

deed: act 4 case, fact, feat, fiat, gest 5 actum, actus, chart, doing, title 6 action, convey, escrow, pottah, remise 7 charter, exploit 8 transfer 10 instrument 11 achievement, performance 14 accomplishment
benevolent: 4 boon 5 favor 8 benefice
evil: sin 11 malefaction

deeds: 4 acta 9 res gestae

deem: say 4 hope, reck, tell 5 judge, opine, think 6 esteem, expect, ordain, reckon, regard 7 account, adjudge, believe, surmise 8 announce, consider, judgment, proclaim 10 adjudicate

deep: low, sea 4 howe, rapt 5 abyss, grave, great, gruff, heavy, ocean 6 hollow, intent 7 abysmal, intense, serious, unmixed 8 absorbed, abstruse, complete, powerful, profound, thorough 9 entangled, insidious, recondite 11 far-reaching

deepen: 5 cloud 6 darken 7 enhance, thicken 9 intensify 10 strengthen

deer: red, roe 6 animal, cervid, fallow, mammal 7 barking
antler: dag
Asian: 4 axis, maha, napu, shou, sika 5 maral 6 chitra, hangul, sambar 10 barasingha
barking: 7 muntjac, muntjak
cry: 4 bell
fallow: 4 dama
family: 8 cervidae
female: doe 4 hind
genus of: 8 cervilla
large: elk 5 moose 6 wapiti 7 caribou
male: 4 buck, hart, spay, stag 7 roebuck
meat: 5 jerky 7 charqui, venison
North American: elk 5 moose 6 wapiti
path: run 4 slot 5 trail
pert. to: 6 damine 7 cervine
small: roe 7 roebuck
South American: 4 pudu 6 guemal, guemul, vanada 7 brocket
young: 4 fawn, spay 7 spitter

deerlet: 4 napu 10 chevrotain

deface: mar 4 foul, ruin, scar 5 erase, shame, spoil 6 damage, defame, defoil, deform, defoul, efface, injure, injury 7 destroy, detract, distort, slander 8 disgrace, dishonor, mutilate, outshine 9 blemished, discredit, disfigure, disvisage, vandalize 10 disfeature

defame: 4 foul 5 abase, belie, cloud, libel, smear 6 accuse, charge, deface, infamy, injure, malign, vilify 7 asperse, blacken, blemish, debauch, detract, publish, scandal, slander, traduce 8 dishonor 9 blaspheme, denigrate 10 calumniate, defamation

default: 4 fail, flaw 5 error, fault 6 offend 7 blemish, failure, mistake, neglect, offense 8 omission 12 imperfection 13 nonappearance

defeasance: 6 defeat 7 undoing 9 overthrow

defeat: win 4 balk, beat, best, drub, foil, loss, rout, ruin, undo 5 break, check, facer, floor, skunk, worst, wrack 6 baffle, cumber, derout, master, thwack, weaken 7 conquer, deprive, destroy, preempt, reverse, shellac 8 overcome, vanquish, Waterloo 9 discomfit, disfigure, frustrate, overpower, overthrow, overwhelm 10 defeasance, defeatment, disappoint 12 discomfiture
at chess: 4 mate 9 checkmate

defeated: 4 lost 5 kaput 6 craven

defeatist: 4 Bolo 8 fatalist 9 handupper, pessimist 10 handsupper
defect: 4 flaw, lack, vice, want 5 craze, fault, minus 6 damage, desert, injury 7 blemish, debauch, detract, publish, scandal, slander, traduce 8 dishonor 12 imperfection
in cloth: 4 scob
in timber: 4 knot
without: 5 sound 7 perfect
defective: bad, ill 4 poor 6 faulty 7 halting 8 vitiated 9 deficient, imperfect 10 inaccurate, incomplete
defend (see also **defense**): 4 fend, hold, save, wear 5 guard, watch 6 assert, forbid, screen, secure, shield, uphold 7 contest, espouse, justify, prevent, protect, shelter 8 advocate, champion, conserve, maintain, preserve, prohibit 9 exculpate, patronage, vindicate
defendant: 8 appellee
answer: 4 plea 14 nolo contendere
defender: 11 propugnator
defense, defence (see also **fortification**): 4 egis, fort 5 aegis, alibi, fence, grith 6 answer, behalf, covert, sconce 7 contest, shelter 8 apologia, boundary, security 9 coverture, safeguard 10 protection 11 maintenance
in law: 6 answer
means of: 6 abatis
movement: 4 spar
outwork: 8 barbican
position: 7 rampart 10 bridgehead
unit: AAF 4 army, NATO, navy 5 SEATO 7 marines
defenseless: 4 bare 5 naked 7 unarmed 8 helpless 9 unguarded
defensible: 7 tenable 9 excusable
defensive: 9 shielding 10 apologetic
defer: boy 4 wait 5 delay, honor, yield 6 esteem, humble, retard, revere, submit 8 consider, postpone, prorogue, protract 13 procrastinate
deference: 6 homage, regard 9 obeisance
defiance: 6 defial
defiant: 4 bold 5 brave 6 daring 8 insolent 11 challenging
deficiency: 4 lack, want 5 fault, minus 6 dearth, defect 7 absence, blemish, deficit, failing, failure 8 scarcity, shortage 9 indigence 10 inadequacy 11 destitution, shortcoming 12 imperfection 13 insufficiency
deficient: 6 meager, meagre 7 bobtail
defile: gut 4 file, gate, gowl, hals, pass, soil 5 abuse, beray, dirty, gorge, smear, sully, taint 6 debase, infect, ravish 7 corrupt, deprave, distain, passage, pollute, tarnish, violate 8 dishonor, maculate 9 desecrate 10 adulterate 11 contaminate
defiled: 6 impure 7 unclean 8 maculate
definable: 6 finite
define: end, fix, set 4 mere, term 5 bound, limit 6 decide 7 clarify, delimit, explain, expound 8 describe, discover 9 demarcate, determine, interpret, prescribe 11 distinguish 12 characterize, circumscribe
definite: 4 sure 5 clear, final, fixed, sharp 7 certain, limited, precise 8 distinct, explicit, limiting 10 conclusive 11 determinate, determining, unequivocal 12 determinable, unmistakable
definitive: 5 final
deflect: 4 bend, warp 5 parry 6 divert, swerve 7 deviate, inflect, reflect, refract
deflower: 6 ravage, ravish 7 despoil, violate
Defoe character: 4 Moll, Xury 6 Crusoe, Friday
deform: mar 6 deface 7 blemish, contort, distort 8 disguise, dishonor, misshape 9 disfigure 10 disarrange
deformed: 7 crooked, hideous 8 formless 9 amorphous, loathsome, monstrous, shapeless, unshapely 11 counterfeit
deformity: 4 flaw 6 defect 7 blemish 13 disfigurement
of foot: 5 varus 7 talipes
defraud: rob 4 bilk, fake, gull, rook, trim 5 cheat, cozen, gouge, mulct, trick 6 chouse 7 deceive, swindle 8 dry-shave
defray: pay 5 avert 6 expend, prepay 7 appease, requite, satisfy 8 disburse 9 discharge, reimburse
deft: 4 neat, trim 5 agile, handy, quick 6 adroit, expert, heppen, nimble, spruce 7 deliver 8 dextrous, skillful 9 dexterous
defunct: 4 dead 7 extinct 8 deceased, departed, finished
defy: 4 dare, face 5 beard, brave, stump, tempt 6 forbid, reject 7 affront, despise, disdain, outface 8 champion, defiance, renounce 9 challenge, repudiate 10 contravene
deg: 6 dampen 8 sprinkle
degenerate: rot 6 debase 7 degrade, deprave 11 deteriorate
degradation: 7 descent 8 ignominy
degrade: 4 bust 5 abase, decry, lower, shame, strip 6 debase, demean, demote, depose, humble, reduce, vilify 7 corrupt, decline, depress 8 disgrace, dishonor 9 disparage, humiliate 10 degenerate, depreciate 11 deteriorate
degraded: 4 base 5 seamy 6 abject, fallen 7 debased, grieced 10 degenerate, diminished
degrading: 4 base 6 menial 8 shameful
degree: 4 bank, heat, rank, rate, rung, step, term, tier 5 class, grade, grece, honor, order, pitch, point, stage, stair 6 extent, me-

dium, soever 7 measure, station 8 quantity, standing 9 gradation 10 attainment
academic: A.B., B.A., B.S., C.E., D.D., M.A., M.D., M.S., B.L.S., B.Sc., L.L.B., L.L.D., M.Sc., Ph.D. 4 D.Lit. 5 Litt.D.
conferral: 10 laureation
equal: as
highest: sum 6 summit, utmost 7 extreme 8 cum laude
kind of: nth 5 third
seeker: 9 candidate
slight: ace, nth 4 hair, inch 5 shade 8 slightly 9 gradation

degust, degustate: 5 savor, taste 6 relish

dehisce: 4 gape

dehort: 4 urge 8 dissuade

dehydrate: dry 9 desiccate, evaporate

deific: 6 divine 7 godlike

deification: 10 apotheosis

deiform: 6 divine 7 godlike

deify: 10 consecrate 11 apotheosize

deign: 5 stoop 10 condescend

deigning: 11 patronizing

deity (see also **god** and next entry): god 4 deva, idol, muse 6 genius 7 creator, demigod, godling, godhead, godship 8 Almighty, divinity, governor
half-fish: Ea 6 Oannes
half-goat: 4 faun
hawk-eyed: Ra 5 Horus 6 Sokari 7 Sokaris
jackal-headed: 6 Anubis
tutelary: 5 genie, lares, numen 7 Hershef, penates

deity: For definitions using this word, see *god* and *goddess* under appropriate country or function. EXAMPLES: "Roman deity" see **Rome** *god;* "war deity" see **war** *god.*

deject: 5 abase, lower 6 humble, lessen 7 flatten 8 dispirit 9 overthrow 10 discomfort, discourage, dishearten

dejected: low, sad 4 damp, glum, sunk 5 amort 6 abased, gloomy, pining 7 alamort, humbled, unhappy 8 repining, wretched 9 cheerless, depressed, prostrate, woebegone 10 despondent, spiritless 11 crestfallen, downhearted 12 disconsolate, disheartened, fainthearted

dejection: 6 dismay 10 melancholy

dejeuner: 5 lunch 9 breakfast, collation

dekko: 4 look, peep

delapse: 5 lapse 7 descend

delate: 5 carry 6 accuse, assign, convey, inform, report, submit, tender 7 publish 8 denounce

Delaware: *county:* 4 Kent 6 Sussex
Indian: 6 Lenape
seaport: 5 Lewes
town: 5 Dover, Lewes 7 Chester 10 Wilmington

delay: lag 4 bode, mora, stay, stop, wait 5 abide, abode, allay, check, dally, defer, do mur, deter, dwell, frist, stall, tarry 6 arrest, belate, detain, dilate, dilute, dretch, hinder, impede, linger, loiter, quench, remora, retard, taigle, temper, weaken 7 adjourn, assuage, barrace, confine, prolong, respite 8 demurral, hesitate, macerate, mitigate, moration, obstruct, postpone, stoppage 9 detention, hindrance, lingering 10 cunctation, moratorium, suspension 13 procrastinate 15 procrastination

delayed: 4 late 5 tardy 7 belated, overdue

delaying: 8 dilatory

dele: 4 omit 5 erase 6 cancel, delete, efface, remove 7 expunge 9 eradicate, extirpate 10 obliterate

delectable: 5 tasty 8 pleasing 9 delicious, desirable, diverting, enjoyable 10 delightful 11 pleasurable

delegate: 4 name, send 6 assign, commit, depute, deputy, legate, nuncio 7 appoint, consign, empower, entrust 8 emissary, transfer 9 authorize, surrogate 10 commission 12 commissioner 14 representative

delegation: 7 mission 9 committee 10 deputation

delete: 4 dele, omit 5 erase, purge 6 cancel, remove 7 destroy, expunge 9 eliminate, eradicate 10 obliterate

deleterious: bad 7 harmful, hurtful, noxious 8 damaging 9 injurious, malignant 10 pernicious 11 destructive, detrimental, prejudicial

delf, delft: pit, sod 4 mine, pond 5 ditch, drain, grave 6 quarry

Delhi district: 5 Simla

Delian god: 6 Apollo

delibate: sip 5 taste 6 dabble

deliberate: 4 cool, pore 5 think 6 advise, confer, debate, ponder 7 bethink, consult, reflect, resolve, studies 8 consider, measured, meditate 9 determine, leisurely, speculate, voluntary 10 purposeful 11 circumspect, intentional 12 premeditated 13 dispassionate

deliberation: 7 counsel 10 reflection
without: 4 rash 8 headlong

Delibes ballet: 5 Naila

delible: 10 eradicable

delicacy: roe 4 cate, ease, nori, tact 5 acate, taste 6 caviar, dainty, delice, luxury, nicety 7 caviare, finesse 8 niceness, pleasure, subtlety 9 exactness, precision 10 daintiness, effeminity, femininity, refinement 13 gratification
lacking: 5 gross

delicate: 4 airy, fine, lacy, nice 5 frail, light, silky 6 dainty, minion, petite, puling, queasy, slight, tender 7 elegant, finical, fragile, minikin, refined, subtile, tenuous 8 araneose, araneous, charming, ethereal, graceful, luscious, migniard, pleasant 9 agreeable, beautiful, delicious, exquisite, palatable, sensitive 10 delightful, fastidious 11 comfortable, considerate

delicatessen: 11 charcuterie

delicious: 8 delicate 9 ambrosial, exquisite, luxurious, nectareal, nectarean 10 delectable, delightful, nectareous, voluptuous

delict: 7 offense 13 transgression

delight: joy 4 glee, love 5 bliss, charm, feast, mirth, revel 6 admire, divert, liking, please, ravish, regale 7 ecstasy, enchant, gladden, gratify, rapture, rejoice 8 entrance, gladness, pleasure, savoring 9 delectate, enjoyment, enrapture, happiness 11 delectation

in: 6 relish

delightful: 4 nice 6 savory 7 elysian 8 adorable, delicate, glorious 9 delicious 10 delectable 11 pleasureful

Delilah's paramour: 6 Samson 7 Sampson

delimit: See **define**

delineate: map 4 draw, limn, line 5 trace 6 blazon, depict, design, sketch, survey 7 outline, picture, portray 8 describe 9 represent 12 characterize

delineation: 10 expression

delinquency: 5 fault 7 failure, misdeed, offense 8 omission 9 violation 10 misconduct 11 malfeasance, misdemeanor, misfeasance

deliquesce: 4 give, melt 7 liquify 8 dissolve

delirious: mad 4 frey, gyte 5 manic 6 insane, raving 7 frantic, lunatic 8 brainish, deleerit, delieret, deranged, frenetic, frenzied 9 phrenetic 11 lightheaded

delirium: 4 fury, maze 8 idleness 10 aberration 13 hallucination

delirium tremens: 7 horrors 9 oenomania

delitescent: 6 latent

deliver: rid 4 bail, deal, free 5 serve, speak, utter 6 assoil, commit, convey, redeem, render, rescue, resign, succor, unbind 7 beteach, consign, declaim, dictate, present, release, relieve 8 dispatch, exorcise, exorcize, liberate 9 enunciate, pronounce, surrender 10 emancipate

deliverer: 7 drayman 9 preserver

deliverly: 6 deftly, nimbly 8 actively

delivery: 6 rescue 7 address 8 shipment 9 rendition 11 deliverance, parturition 12 accouchement

dell: den 4 dale, dean, dene, drab, glen, vale 5 trull, wench 6 dingle, ravine, valley

Delphi: 6 oracle, shrine

modern name: 6 Kastri

priestess: 5 Pythia

delphinium: 8 larkspur

delta: 8 alluvium, triangle

delude: bob 4 bilk, dupe, fool 5 cheat, elude, evade, trick 6 befool, bubble, illude 7 beguile, deceive, mislead 8 hoodwink 9 mislippen 10 circumvent

deluge: sea 4 flow 5 flood, swamp 8 inundate, overflow, submerge 9 cataclysm, overpower, overwhelm, rainstorm 10 overspread

delusion: 5 trick 6 mirage, vision 7 chimera, fallacy, fantasm 8 illusion, phantasm 9 deception 13 appersonation, hallucination

Buddhist: 4 moha

of grandeur: 11 megalomania

partner of: 5 snare

delusory: 8 delusive

delve: den, dig, dip, pit 4 cave, dint, mine 5 ditch, plumb 6 bruise, exhume, fathom, indent 7 impress 8 excavate, inscribe

demagogic: 8 factious

demagogue, demagog: 6 leader, orator, rouser 7 speaker

demand: ask, cry 4 call, need 5 claim, exact, order, query 6 charge, elicit, expect, summon 7 command, inquire, mandate, request, require 8 question 9 challenge 10 commission 11 requisition

demandable: due

demarcate: 6 demark 7 delimit 8 separate 12 discriminate

demean: 5 abase, lower 6 debase 7 degrade 8 demeanon, maltreat

demeanor: 4 mien, port 5 habit 6 action, havior 7 bearing, conduct 8 behavior, carriage, portance 9 treatment 10 deportment, management 11 comportment, countenance

demented: mad 4 luny 5 buggy, crazy, nutty 6 insane 7 fatuous

demerit: 4 mark 5 fault 6 desert

demesne: 5 manor, place, realm 6 domain, estate, region 8 district

Demeter: 5 Ceres

daughter: 4 Cora, Kore 8 Despoina 10 Persephone, Proserpina, Proserpine 11 Persephassa

headdress: 5 polos

mother: 4 Rhea

shrine: 9 anaktoron

demigod: 4 hero 7 godling

pert. to: 7 satyric

sylvan: 5 satyr

demirep: 11 adventuress

demise: 4 will 5 death 6 convey 7 decease 8 bequeath

demiss: 6 humble
demit: 5 lower 6 humble, resign 8 abdicate 10 relinquish 11 resignation
demiurgic: 8 creative
demoded: 5 passe
demoiselle: 5 crane 7 kaikara
demolish: 4 rase, raze, ruin 5 level, waste, wreck 6 batter 7 destroy, ruinate 9 devastate, overthrow
demon: hag, imp, nat 4 aitu, atua, ogre 5 devil, fiend, genie, lamia, Satan, witch 6 Abigor, afreet 7 villain, warlock 9 cacodemon 10 cacodaemon
assembly of: 6 sabbat
female: 6 empusa 8 succubus
Hebrew: 8 Asmodeus
Iroquois: 5 otkon
possessed by: 9 energumen
prince of: 9 Beelzebub
worship of: 11 demonolatry
Zoroastrian: 5 daeva
demoniac: 7 demonic, lunatic 8 devilish, diabolic, fiendish, infernal 10 diabolical
demonstrate: 4 show 5 prove 7 display, portray 8 manifest
demonstration: 4 show, sign 5 proof 9 manifesto, portrayal 10 apparition 12 illustration 13 manifestation
demonstrative: 4 that, this 5 these, those 8 effusive 9 ostensive 12 ostentatious
demoralize: 6 weaken 7 confuse, corrupt, deprave, pervert 9 undermine 10 discourage, dishearten 11 disorganize
demos: 4 deme 6 people 8 citizens, populace
Demosthenes: *follower:* 5 Bryan 6 orator
oration: 9 philippic
demote: 4 bust 6 reduce 7 degrade
demotic: 7 popular
demulcent: 8 soothing 9 softening 10 mollifying
demur: 4 stay 5 delay, doubt, pause 6 boggle, linger, object 7 scruple, suspend 8 hesitate, suspense 9 objection 12 irresolution
demure: coy, mim, shy 4 prim 5 grave, staid, suant 6 modest, sedate 8 composed, decorous
demurral: See **demur**
den: mew 4 cave, cove, dell, dive, glen, hole, lair, nest, room 5 bield, cabin, couch, haunt, study 6 burrow, cavern, covert, grotto, hollow, ravine 7 retreat 8 hideaway, snuggery, workroom
denary: 7 tenfold
dendroid 11 arborescent
dendrophilous: 8 arboreal
dene, dean: 4 dell, vale 5 mound 6 valley
denial (see also **deny**): no; nay
denizen: 6 native 7 citizen 8 resident 9 indweller 10 inhabitant

Denmark: *city:* 6 Odense 7 Aalborg, Aarhuus, Horsens, Randers 8 Elsinore 9 Helsingor 10 Copenhagen(c.) 13 Frederiksberg
anatomist: 5 Steno
animal: 7 aurochs
artist: 5 Bloch
astronomer: 5 Brahe
author: 5 Bajer 8 Andersen
borough: 4 borg
chief: 4 jarl, yarl
coin: ore 5 krone
comb. form: 4 Dano
composer: 4 Gade
county: Amt 4 Soro 7 Aalborg 8 Aabenraa
downs: 7 Klitten
embroidery: 6 hedebo
flag: 9 Dannebrog
inlet: Ise 5 fjord
island: Oe; Als 4 Aero 5 Faroe, Samso 7 Seeland
king: 4 Cnut, Knut 6 Canute 9 Christian
knighthood order: 9 Dannebrog
measure: ell, fod, mil, pot 4 alen, favn, rode 5 album, kande, linje, paegl, tomme 6 achtel, paegel, paegle, skeppe 7 landmil, oltonde, skieppe, viertel 8 fjerding 9 korntonde, ottingkar
musical instrument: 4 lure
parliament: 7 Rigsdag
peninsula: 7 Jutland
physicist: 4 Bohr
possession: 5 Faroe 6 St. John 7 Iceland 8 St. Thomas 9 Greenland, Santa Cruz
prince: 5 Ogier
river: Asa 4 Holm, Stor 5 Guden 7 Lonborg
seaport: 6 Aarhus
settlers: 6 Ostmen
tribunal: 7 Rigsret
weight: es; lod, ort, vog 4 eser(pl.), last, mark, pund, unze 5 carat, kvint, pound, quint, tonde 6 toende 7 centner, lispund, quintin 8 lispound, skippund 9 ship pound, skibslast 10 bismerpund
dennet: gig 8 carriage
denominate: 4 call, name 5 title 6 denote 8 christen, indicate, nominate 9 designate
denomination: 4 cult, sect 5 class, title 7 society 8 category 9 communion 11 appellation
religious: 7 Baptist 8 Lutheran 9 Methodist, Unitarian 12 Episcopalian, Presbyterian 14 Congregational
denotation: 4 sign 5 token
denote: 4 give, mark, mean, name, show 6 import 7 betoken, connote, express 8 indicate 9 designate, recommend, represent 10 denominate

denouement: end 5 issue 7 outcome 8 solution 11 catastrophe

denounce: ban 6 accuse, delate, descry, menace, scathe 7 arraign, condemn, declare, upbraid 8 proclaim, threaten 9 fulminate 10 stigmatize

de novo: 4 anew 5 again, newly 6 afresh

dense: 4 firm 5 close, foggy, gross, heavy, murky, silly, solid, thick 6 obtuse, stupid 7 compact, crowded, serried 11 thickheaded 12 impenetrable

density: 4 mass 11 compactness

dent: 4 bash, dint, nick 5 dinge, notch, tooth 6 batter, hallow, indent 7 blemish, depress 10 depression, impression 11 indentation

dental: See **dentistry, tooth**

dentate: 6 jagged 7 serrate, toothed

dentation: 5 serra 10 projection

denticulate: 7 serrate

denticulation: jag 5 tooth 8 denticle

dentil: 5 block

dentine, dentin: 5 ivory 6 enamel

dentistry: *appliance:* dam 4 burr
branch: 9 exodontia 11 orthodontia 12 orthodontics
plastic: 6 cement
tool: 6 scaler 7 forceps

denture: 5 teeth, plate

denude: 4 bare 5 scalp, strip 6 devest, divest 8 denudate 11 decorticate

denunciation (see also **denounce**): 6 threat 8 diatribe 9 philippic 11 malediction 12 proclamation

deny: nay 5 debar, repel 6 abjure, disown, forbid, impugn, negate, refuse, refute, reject, renege 7 confute, deprive, disavow, dispute, forsake, gainsay, protest 8 abnegate, disclaim, forswear, renounce, withhold 9 disaffirm 10 contradict, contravene, controvert

deodand: 7 forfeit

deodar: 5 cedar

depart: go; die, mog 4 blow, pass, quit, vary 5 found, leave, mosey, sever 6 begone, decamp, demise, desist, divide, perish, recede, retire, sunder 7 abscond, deviate, forsake, get away, retreat, vamoose 8 farewell, separate, withdraw

departed: 4 dead 6 bygone 7 defunct 8 deceased, decedent

department: 4 part 5 realm 6 branch, bureau, sphere 7 portion 8 division, province 11 subdivision

departure: 4 exit 5 death, exode 6 congee, egress 7 decease 9 decession 11 abandonment, forthfaring, leavetaking

depend: 4 bank, hang, lean, rely, rest, turn 5 count, hinge, trust 7 confide

dependable: 5 siker, solid 6 sicker 7 certain 8 reliable 11 trustworthy

dependency: 5 taluk 6 colony 7 apanage 8 appanage

dependent: 6 client, minion, sponge, vassal 7 sponger, subject 8 clinging, follower 9 adjective, corollary 10 accidental, contingent, sequacious 11 subordinate

depict: 4 draw, limn 5 paint 6 blazon 7 picture, portray 8 describe 9 delineate, represent 12 characterize

depilate: 4 husk 5 shave

depilatory: 5 rusma

depilous: 8 hairless

deplete: 5 drain, empty 6 reduce, unload 7 exhaust 8 diminish 10 impoverish

deplorable: sad 8 wretched 10 calamitous

deplore: rue 4 moan, sigh, wail 5 mourn 6 bemoan, bewail, grieve, lament, regret 8 complain

deploy: 6 unfold 7 display

deplume: 5 pluck, strip

depone: 5 swear 6 depose 7 testify

deponent: 7 affiant 10 incomplete

depopulate: 6 ravage 9 devastate, dispeople

deport: 5 exile 6 banish, behave, demean 7 bearing, conduct 9 transport 10 deportment

deportment: air 4 gest, mien 5 geste, havit 6 action, deport, manner 7 address, bearing, comfort, conduct 8 behavior, breeding, carriage, demeanor 9 behaviour, demeanour

depose: 4 aver 5 abase 6 affirm, assert, depone, divest, remove 7 degrade, deposit, testify 8 dethrone, displace 10 dispossess 11 disenthrone

deposit: lay, set 4 bank, cast, dump, fund, hock, pawn 5 chest, lodge, place, store 6 entomb, pledge, repose, settle 7 consign, deposit, entrust 10 deposition, depository
alluvial: 5 delta, geest
black: 4 soot
earthy: as; ore 4 asar(pl.), gobi, lode, marl, sand, silt 5 delta, eskar, esker, geest, loess, manto, trona 6 placer, sludge 7 alluvia, moraine 8 alluvium
geyser: 6 sinter
gold-containing: 6 placer
gravel: 5 apron
ore: vug
roric: dew
teeth: 6 tartar
wine cask: 6 tartar

deposition: 6 burial 7 deposit, opinion 8 sediment 9 affidavit, statement, testimony 10 allegation 11 declaration 12 displacement 13 precipitation

depository: 4 bank, safe 5 attic, vault 7 ossuary 10 repository
depot: 4 base, gare(F.) 6 aurang(Ind.), aurung 7 station 8 magazine, terminal, terminus 9 warehouse 10 storehouse
deprave: 5 taint 6 debase, defile, malign, revile 7 corrupt, pervert, vitiate 10 degenerate, depreciate
depraved: bad 4 evil, ugly, vile 6 rotten, wicked 7 bestial, immoral, vicious 9 abandoned, graceless 10 profligate 11 demoralized 12 incorrigible
depravity: 4 vice 8 villainy
deprecate: 4 pray 6 invoke 7 beseech 10 depreciate, disapprove, supplicate
deprecation: 8 petition 14 disapprobation
depreciate: 4 fall 5 abase, avile, decry, slump 6 debase, lessen, reduce, shrink 7 cheapen, debauch, degrade, deprave, depress, detract 8 belittle, derogate, disprize, disvalue, minimize 9 disparage, dispraise, extenuate 10 undervalue
depreciation: 4 agio 8 discount 9 misprison
depredate: rob 4 prey, raze 5 spoil 6 thieve 7 despoil, destroy, pillage, plunder
deprehend: 5 seize 6 detect 7 capture 8 discover 9 apprehend
depress: bow, cow 4 dash, dent, fall, sink 5 abase, appal, chill, crush, lower, slump 6 appall, dampen, dismay, humble, indent, lessen, sadden, weaken 7 degrade, flatten, oppress, repress 8 browbeat, diminish, dispirit, enfeeble 9 disparage, subjugate 10 depreciate, discourage, dishearten
depressed: 4 sick 6 gloomy, hipped, hollow, lonely, oblate, somber, triste 8 dejected, downcast 9 afflicted, debruised 10 spiritless 11 downhearted, melancholic
depressing: 5 bleak 6 dreary
depression: col, dip, gat, pit 4 delk, doke, fall, foss, howe 5 atrio, basin, cowal, crypt, dinge, fossa, fosse, nadir 6 cafard, cavity, crater, dismay, gulley, ravine, valley 7 alveola, blowout 8 doldrums 9 dejection 11 despondency 13 disparagement
between mountains: col
pert. to: 6 bathic
deprivation: 4 cost, loss, want 7 amotion 9 privation, restraint 10 diminution 11 destitution
deprive: bar, rob 4 bate, deny 5 debar, spoil, strip 6 amerce, defeat, depose, devest, dismay, divest, hinder, remove 7 abridge, bereave, cashier, despoil, exhaust 8 denature, desolate, evacuate 9 dismantle, forestall 10 dispossess
deprived: 4 reft
depth: 5 abyss, midst 8 deepness, strength 9 abundance, intensity 10 profundity 12 abstruseness, completeness, profoundness
depth charge: 4 mine 10 projectile
depths: 5 heart
depurant: 8 purifier 11 purificator
deputation: 7 mission 10 delegation
depute: 4 send 5 allot 6 assign, devote 7 appoint 8 delegate 10 commission, constitute
deputy: 4 aide 5 agent, envoy, proxy, vicar 6 commis, legate 7 bailiff 8 delegate 9 assistant, surrogate, vigilante 10 substitute
deracinate: 9 eradicate, extirpate
derange: 5 upset 7 disturb, perturb 8 displace, unsettle 9 interrupt 10 disarrange, discompose
deranged: 5 crazy 6 crazed 7 frantic 10 distraught, unbalanced
derangement: 5 mania 6 lunacy 7 madness, rummage 8 delirium, disorder, insanity 9 confusion 11 distraction, disturbance 12 irregularity 15 disorganization
deray: 8 disorder 9 confusion 11 disturbance
derby: hat 4 race, town 5 shire 6 bowler
derelict: 7 failure 8 betrayer, castaway 9 abandoned 10 delinquent, neglectful, unfaithful
derf: 4 bold 6 daring
deride: 4 geck, gibe, hoot, jape, jeer, mock, twit 5 fleer, rally, scoff, scorn, taunt 6 illude 8 ridicule
derision: 8 contempt
derive: get 4 draw, stem 5 carry, infer, trace 6 deduce, evolve, gather, obtain 7 extract, proceed, receive 9 originate
derm: 4 skin 7 cuticle
derma: 5 layer 6 corium, dermis
dermal filament: 4 hair
dern: 4 dark, darn, dire, evil, hide 5 drear 6 crafty, hidden, secret, somber, sombre 7 conceal 9 concealed, underhand
dernier: 4 last 5 final
dernier cri: 7 fashion, novelty
derogate: 5 annul, decry 6 lessen, repeal 7 detract, slander 8 restrict, withdraw 9 disparage 10 depreciate
derrick: jib, rig 4 lift, spar 5 crane, davit, hoist 6 tackle 7 gallows, hanging, hangman
part: jib, leg 4 boom
derring-do: 4 gest 8 audacity
derringer: 6 pistol, weapon
derry: 7 dislike 8 aversion
dervish: 5 fakir 6 fakeer
cap: taj
descant: 4 sing, song 6 melody, remark, warble 7 comment 9 discourse 11 observation 12 counterpoint, dissertation 13 accompaniment

descend: 4 fall, sink 5 avale, lower, stoop 6 alight, derive 7 decline, delapse 9 originate 10 condescend
descendant: son 4 cion, heir, seed 5 child, scion 9 offspring
descendants: 7 progeny 9 posterity 10 generation
descended from same mother: 5 enate 6 enatic
descent: 4 drop, fall 5 birth, chute, issue, scarp, slope, stock 6 escarp, strain 7 assault, decline, extract, lineage 8 ancestry, breeding, downfall, pedigree 9 avalanche, declivity, onslaught 10 declension, extraction, generation 11 declination, degradation, inclination
describe: 4 tell 6 define, depict, relate, report 7 declare, explain, express, narrate, outline, picture, portray, recount 8 inscribe 9 delineate, designate, discourse, enumerate, represent 10 transcribe 12 characterize
descry: see, spy 4 espy 5 sight 6 behold, betray, detect, reveal 7 discern, display 8 denounce, disclose, discover, perceive 9 determine 11 distinguish
Desdemona: *husband:* 7 Othello
traducer: 4 Iago
desecrate: 5 abuse 6 defile 7 pollute, profane, violate 8 unhallow 11 contaminate
desert: due, erg, rat 4 areg, arid, bolt, fail, flee, sand 5 waive, waste 6 barren, defect, lonely, renege, reward 7 abandon, abscond, demerit, forsake, hornada 8 desolate, renounce 9 backslide, wasteland 10 excellence, punishment, relinquish, wilderness
beast: 5 camel
driver: 8 cameleer 9 camelteer
dweller: 4 Arab 5 nomad
group: 7 caravan
hallucination: 6 mirage
pert. to: 6 eremic
rat: 10 prospector
region: erg
science: 9 eremology
ship: 5 camel
shrub: 5 retem 6 alhagi, raetam
train: 7 caravan
valley: 6 bolson
watering spot: 5 oasis
wind: 6 simoom, simoon 7 sirocco
desert candle: 5 plant 8 ocotillo
desert-like: dry 4 arid, sere
deserted: 6 lonely 7 forlorn 8 desolate, forsaken 9 abandoned 11 uninhabited
deserter: rat 6 bolter 8 apostate, fugitive, recreant, renegade
desertion: 14 tergiversation
deserve: 4 earn 5 merit, repay 7 benefit
deserved: 6 worthy 7 condign 11 appropriate
desiccate: dry 4 arid, sere 5 drain 9 dehydrate
desideratum: 4 need 6 desire
design: aim, end, map 4 draw, goal, idea, mean, plan, plot 5 allot, decor, drift, ettle, model, motif, shape 6 device, intend, intent, invent, layout, object, sketch 7 destine, diagram, fashion, outline, pattern, project, propose, purpose 8 contrive 9 calculate, delineate, intention 10 conception 11 contemplate, contrivance
of scattered objects: 4 seme
perforated: 7 stencil
skin: 6 tattoo
designate: set 4 mark, mean, name, show 5 label, style, title 6 assign, denote, intend, settle 7 appoint, entitle, specify 8 describe, identify, indicate 9 appellate, nuncupate 10 denominate 11 distinguish 12 characterize
designed: 8 prepense 11 intentional
designer: 7 planner, plotter, schemer 8 engineer 9 architect, intriguer
designing: 6 artful 7 cunning 8 planning, plotting, scheming 10 foreseeing, fraudulent, intriguing
desinential: 8 terminal
desipience: 5 folly 8 trifling
desipient: 5 silly 7 foolish
desirable: 7 amiable, welcome 8 desirous, eligible, pleasing, salutary 9 advisable, agreeable 10 beneficial
desire: yen 4 care, hope, itch, lust, need, urge, want, will, wish 5 ardor, bosom, covet, crave, mania, yearn 6 affect, aspire, hanker, hunger, prefer, thirst, yammer 7 craving, fantasy, inkling, longing, passion 8 appetite, cupidity 9 appetency, cacoethes 10 benedicite, desiderium
want of: 11 inappetence
desirous: 4 fain, fond 5 eager, frack, freck 6 ardent 7 willing, wishing 8 covetous, spirited 10 delectable, solicitous
desist: ho 4 ease, halt, quit, stop 5 cease 6 depart 7 forbear 11 discontinue
desk: pew 4 ambo 5 board, table 6 pulpit 7 lectern 8 prie-dieu 9 davenport, monocleid, secretary 10 escritoire, monocleide
desman: 4 mole 7 muskrat
Desmanthus: 5 Acuan
desmid: 4 alga 5 algae(pl.)
desolate: sad 4 bare, lorn, ruin, sack, sole 5 alone, bleak, drear, gaunt 6 desert, dreary, gloomy, gousty, lonely, ravage 7 destroy, forlorn, goustie, lacking 8 deprived, de-

serted, forsaken, solitary 9 abandoned, destitute, dissolute, woebegone 11 comfortless, uninhabited 12 disconsolate

desolation: woe 4 ruin 5 gloom, grief, havoc 6 ravage 7 sadness 10 gloominess, loneliness, melancholy 11 deprivation, destitution, destruction, devastation 12 solitariness
area of: 5 waste 6 desert

Desmodium: 7 trefoil

despair: 5 gloom 11 desperation, despondency 12 hopelessness

despect: 8 contempt

desperado: 6 bandit 7 ruffian 8 criminal 10 lawbreaker

desperate: mad 4 rash 7 extreme, frantic 8 headlong, hopeless, perilous, reckless 9 dangerous 10 despairing, despondent, infuriated, outrageous 11 precipitate 13 irretrievable

despicable: 4 base, vile 5 cheap, dirty 6 abject, paltry, shabby, sordid 7 caitiff, pitiful 8 unworthy, wretched 9 beggardly, miserable 11 ignominious 12 contemptible, contemptuous

despise: 4 defy, hate 5 scorn, scout, spurn 6 detest, loathe, slight 7 contemn, despite, disdain 8 disprize, misprize, vilipend 9 disregard

despite: vex 7 despise 15 notwithstanding

despiteful: 5 cruel 8 insolent 9 insulting, malicious 12 contemptuous, contumelious

despiteous: 5 cruel 8 pitiless 9 malicious, merciless 12 contemptuous

despoil: rob 4 poll, raid, ruin 5 booty, harry, reave, rifle, spoil, strip 6 divest, fleece, ravage, ravish, remove 7 bereave, deprive, disrobe, pillage, plunder 8 deflower, disarray, unclothe 9 depredate

Despoina: 4 Kore 10 Persephone

despondency: 6 misery 7 despair 10 depression, melancholy 11 desperation

despondent: sad 4 blue 8 dejected, downcast, hopeless 9 desperate, heartless 10 despairing 12 heavy-hearted

despot: 4 czar, tsar, tzar 6 satrap, tyrant 7 autarch, monarch 8 autocrat 10 autocratix

despotic: 6 lordly 8 absolute, dominant 9 arbitrary 10 tyrannical

despumate: 4 scum, skim 5 froth

dessert: ice, pie 4 cake 5 fruit, glace(Fr.) 6 eclair, mousse, pastry, sweets 7 banquet, pudding, sherbet, strudel 8 ice cream, Napoleon, sillabub 9 poundcake, sweetmeat 10 blanc-mange

destination: end 4 goal 5 bourn 6 bourne

destine: 4 doom, fate 5 allot 6 depute, design, devote, intend, ordain 7 appoint 9 designate, destinate 10 foreordain, predestine 12 predetermine

destiny: lot 4 dole, doom, fate 5 karma, stars 6 kismet 7 fortune 8 foredoom
goddess: 4 Fate, Norn 5 Moira 6 Ciotho, Laches 7 Atripos
oriental: 6 kismet

destitute: 4 poor 5 clean, needy 6 bereft, devoid, wasted 7 forlorn, lacking, wanting 8 bankrupt, beggared, defeated, deprived, desolate, forsaken, helpless, indigent 9 abandoned, defaulted, driftless 10 devastated, frustrated 12 disappointed, impoverished

destroy: eat, end, gut 4 blow, full, rase, raze, ruin, rush, slay, undo 5 break, craze, elide, erase, erode, fordo, havoc, quell, shend, smash, smite, spoil, stroy, wrack, wreck 6 blight, cancel, cumber, deface, defeat, delete, efface, famish, foredo, ravage 7 abolish, consume, expunge, forfare, nullify, overrun, perempt, ruinate, unbuild, whittle 8 amortize, confound, decimate, demolish, desolate, dissolve, infringe, mutilate, overturn, sabotage 9 depredate, devastate, discreate, dismantle, eradicate, extirpate, liquidate, overthrow 10 annihilate, counteract, disappoint, discomfort, extinguish, neutralize 11 assassinate, exterminate

destroyed: 5 kaput

destroyer: hun 6 vandal 7 warship 8 saboteur

Destroyer: 4 Siva

Destroying Angel: *fungus:* 7 amanita
Mormon: 6 Danite

destruction: end 4 bane, doom, loss, ruin 5 decay, havoc, waste 7 Abaddon(Heb.) 8 downfall, excision, shambles 9 holocaust, perdition 10 extinction, subversion
god: 4 Siva
goddess: Ara
of species: 8 genocide

destructive: 4 fell 5 fatal 6 deadly, mortal 7 baleful, deathly, fateful, harmful, hurtful, noisome, noxious, ruinous 8 wasteful 9 poisonous, truculent 10 catawampus, pernicious 11 catawampous, deleterious, internecine

desuetude: 6 disuse 12 obsolescence 14 discontinuance

desultory: 4 idle 5 hasty, loose 6 roving 7 aimless, cursory 8 rambling, unsteady, wavering 9 irregular, unsettled 10 discursive, inconstant 12 disconnected

detach: 5 sever 7 disjoin, isolate 8 disunite, separate, unfasten, withdraw 9 disengage

detached: 4 free 5 alone, aloof 8 unbiased 11 unconcerned, unconnected
detail: 4 item 6 assign, nicety, relate 7 account, appoint, article, itemize, minutia, narrate, specify 8 rehearse, salience 9 enumerate, narrative 10 particular 11 stipulation 12 circumstance 14 accountability 15 circumstantiate
detailed: 6 prolix 8 tiresome 9 wearisome 10 protracted
detain: 4 hold, keep, stay, stop 5 check, delay 6 arrest, hinder, retard 8 imprison, restrain, withhold
in time of war: 6 intern
detainment: 6 arrest 9 detention
detect: see, spy 4 espy, nose, spot 5 catch 6 descry, divine, expose, reveal 7 develop, discern, uncover 8 decipher, discover, overtake 9 deprehend
detection device: 5 radar
detective: tec 4 bull, dick 6 sleuth, tracer 7 gumshoe, scenter, spotter 8 flatfoot, operator, Sam Spade, The Saint 9 James Bond, Nero Wolfe 10 Martin Kane, Miss Marple, Nick Carter, Perry Mason, Peter Salem, Philo Vance 11 Charlie Chan, Ellery Queen, Green Hornet 12 investigator, Simon Templar 13 Hercule Poirot, Michael Shayne 14 Sherlock Holmes
story writer: 10 Ian Fleming 11 Ellery Queen 14 Agatha Christie 16 Arthur Conan Doyle 19 Earle Stanley Gardner
detector: 7 reagent
defect: 14 troubleshooter
storm: 7 sferics
detent: dog 4 pall, pawl 5 catch, click 7 ratchet
detention: 5 delay 7 capture 9 hindrance, restraint 10 arrestment, detainment
deter: bar 5 block, check, delay 6 hinder, retard 7 prevent 8 dissuade, restrain 9 constrain 10 discourage, dishearten, intimidate
deterge: 5 purge 7 cleanse
detergent: 4 soap 7 purging, smectic, solvent 8 cleanser 9 cleansing
deteriorate: 4 fail, wear 5 decay 6 debase, impair 7 decline, pervert 9 backslide 10 degenerate
determinable: 5 fixed 8 definite 9 judicable 10 mensurable, terminable
determinate: 7 certain 8 definite, resolute, resolved, specific 9 arbitrary 10 invariable 11 established
determinative: 5 final 7 shaping 8 limiting 9 directing 10 conclusive 13 authoritative
determine: end, fix, get 4 test 5 assay, award 6 assess, assign, decide, decree, define, descry, settle 7 adjudge, analyse, analyze, appoint, arrange, dispose, resolve 8 conclude 9 admeasure, arbitrate, ascertain, calculate, terminate 10 adjudicate, constitute, deliberate, predestine
determined: set 4 bent, firm 6 dogged, intent, mulish, sturdy 7 decided, settled 8 foregone, perverse, resolute, resolved, stubborn 9 obstinate, pigheaded 10 persistent, unyielding 12 determinable
deterrent: 9 hindrance 14 discouragement
detersion: 7 washing 8 ablution
detest: 4 damn, hate 5 abhor, curse 6 loathe 7 condemn, despise, dislike 8 denounce, execrate 9 abominate
detestable: 4 foul 6 horrid, odious 8 infamous 9 nefarious 12 antipathetic
dethrone: 6 depose, divest
detonate: 4 fire 5 blast 7 explode 9 fulminate
detonator: cap 7 torpedo 9 explosive
detour: 6 bypass 7 circuit 9 deviation
detract: 5 decry 6 defame, divert, villify 7 asperse, traduce 8 belittle, derogate, distract, minimize, protract, subtract, withdraw 9 disparage 10 depreciate
detraction: 7 calumny, scandal, slander
detriment: 4 cost, hurt, loss 5 damna(pl.), wound 6 damage, damnum, injury 8 mischief 9 disprofit 10 impediment 12 disadvantage
detrimental: 7 harmful, hurtful 9 injurious 10 pernicious 11 deleterious
detritus: 4 tuff 5 chaff, waste 6 debris 7 garbage, rubbish
deva: 5 angel, deity
Devaki's son: 7 Krishna
deval: 4 stop 5 cease, pause 9 cessation
devance: 8 outstrip 9 forestall 10 anticipate
devastate: 5 exile, havoc, waste 6 ravage 7 destroy, pillage, plunder, scourge 8 demolish 10 depopulate
devel: 4 blow 6 strike
develop, develope: 4 form, grow 5 arise, ripen 6 appear, detect, evolve, expand, flower, mature, reveal, unfold, unfurl 7 educate, enlarge, expound, uncover 8 disclose, discover, engender, generate, manifest 9 elaborate, germinate
development: 6 growth 7 stature 8 breeding, increase 9 evolution, expansion, formation, unfolding 11 elaboration
arrested: 7 aplasia
full: 8 maturity, ripeness
going back: 13 retrogression
devest: 5 strip 6 denude, divest 7 abandon, deprive, undress 8 alienate
Devi: *beneficent:* 5 Guari
consort: 4 Siva
fierce: 4 Kali
light: Uma

malignant: 5 Durga
riding a tiger: 6 Chandi
deviate: err, yaw 4 lean, miss, vary, veer 5 drift, lapse, sheer, stray 6 change, depart, detour, recede, squint, swerve, wander 7 decline, deflect, digress, diverge
from the norm: 6 mutate
from the vertical: 4 hade
deviation: 7 anomaly 11 declination
device: gin, mot 4 tool 5 drift, meter, motto, shift 6 design, emblem, gadget, scheme 7 compass, fiction, impresa, imprese, project, vehicle 8 artifice, fastener, gimcrack 9 apparatus, appliance, doohickey, expedient, invention, regulator, stratagem 10 concoction, instrument 11 contraption, contrivance
curve measuring: 9 rotameter
holding: 4 vise 5 clamp
devil: imp 4 bogy, Deil(Sc.), haze, mahu 5 annoy, bogey, bogie, demon, fiend, Satan, tease 6 Amamon, diablo(Sp.), diable(F.), pester 7 Amaimon, Apollyn, clootie, diaboli(pl.), dickens, gremlin, torment, warlock 8 diabolus, Mephisto 9 archfiend, Beelzebub, cacodemon, deevilick, diablotin 10 cacodaemon
Dante's: 8 Cagnazzo
pert. to: 7 satanic 10 diabolical
printer's: 10 apprentice
ruler: 10 diabolarch
tree: 4 dita
worship: 8 satanism
devil's bones: 4 dice
devil-may-care: 8 reckless
deviled: 9 a la diable
devilfish: ray 5 manta
devilish: 6 daring, rakish, wicked 7 demonic, extreme, hellish, inhuman, satanic 8 demoniac, diabolic, fiendish, infernal 9 excessive 10 diabolical 15 Mephistophelian
devilkin: imp
devious: 6 errant, roving, shifty, tricky 7 vagrant, winding 8 indirect, rambling, tortuous 9 eccentric, irregular 10 circuitous, farfetched, roundabout
devise: 4 plan, plot, will 5 array, frame, fudge, weave 6 convey, decoct, divide, divine, invent, scheme 7 appoint, arrange, bethink, concoct, consult, prepare 8 bequeath, contrive 9 construct, fabricate 10 distribute 11 distinguish
devitalize: 6 deaden 10 eviscerate
devoid: 4 free, void 5 empty 6 barren, vacant 7 wanting 9 destitute
devoir: 4 duty, task 6 effort
devolve: 4 pass 8 overturn, transfer, transmit
Devonshire: *boat:* 9 mumblebee
river: 4 Exe
devote: vow 4 ally, avow, doom, give 5 apply 6 addict, attach, bestow, depute, resign 7 address, consign, destine 8 dedicate, venerate 10 consecrate 11 appropriate
devoted: 4 true 5 liege, loyal, pious 6 devout, doomed, fervid 7 adoring, arduous, zealous 8 attached, constant, faithful 9 assiduous, religious 10 obsequious, venerating 11 whole-souled 12 affectionate, wholehearted
devotee: fan, nun 4 monk 6 votary, zealot 7 admirer, amateur, fanatic 8 follower, partisan 10 enthusiast
devotion: 4 aves(pl.) 6 bhakti, novena 7 loyalty, worship 8 fidelity
excessive: 13 ecclesiolatry
object of: 4 idol 5 totem 6 fetich, fetish
period of: 4 Lent 6 novena
devour: eat 4 fret 5 raven, waste 6 engulf 7 consume, engorge 10 annihilate
devout: 4 good, holy, warm 5 godly, pious 6 hearty, solemn 7 cordial, devoted, godlike, saintly, sincere 8 reverent 9 religious, righteous, spiritual 13 sanctimonious
devow: 7 disavow 8 disclaim, renounce
dew: 4 rime 5 bloom 7 moisten, refresh 8 moisture
dewlap: 4 jowl 7 wattles
dewy: 4 damp 5 moist, roral, roric 6 gentle, roscid 9 sparkling 10 refreshing
dexter: 5 right 6 honest 9 fortunate 10 auspicious 15 straightforward
dexterity: art 5 craft, knack, skill 6 stroil 7 ability, address, agility, aptness, cunning, finesse, sleight 8 aptitude, deftness, facility 9 adeptness, diplomacy, quickness, readiness 10 adroitness, cleverness, expertness, nimbleness
dextral: 10 auspicious 11 right-handed
dey: 5 pasha, ruler 7 servant 9 dairymaid
dhan: 6 cattle, wealth 8 property
diabetes remedy: 7 insulin, orinase
diablerie: 7 devilry, sorcery 8 demology, mischief
diabolical, diabolic: 5 cruel 6 wicked 7 demonic, hellish, inhuman, satanic, violent 8 demoniac, devilish, fiendish, infernal 9 demonical, fiendlike
diacope: cut 5 wound 8 incision
diacritic: 4 mark 5 tilde 6 umlaut 11 distinctive
diadem: 5 crown, tiara 6 anadem, circle, emblem, fillet 7 coronet 8 headband 11 sovereignty
diagnose: 7 analyze 8 identify
diagonal: 4 bias

diagram: map 4 plan, tree 5 carte, chart, epure(F.), graph 6 design, schema 9 blueprint
dial: 7 crystal 8 horologe 9 horoscope, indicator, telephone, timepiece
dialect: 5 argot, idiom, lingo 6 brogue, debate, patois, patter, speech 8 language 10 vernacular 11 phraseology
dialogue, dialog: 6 epilog, patter 8 epilogue 12 conversation
having nature of: 13 interlocutory 14 conversational
diameter: pi 4 bore 5 width
half: 5 radii(pl.) 6 radius
diamond: gem, ice 4 bort, rock 5 bortz, field, jager, jewel 7 lozenge 8 corundum 9 briolette
coarse: 4 bort
crystal: 7 glassie
cutter: 12 brilliandeer
famous: See **stone:** *famous*
fragments: 4 bort
glazier's: 6 emeril
holding device: dop 4 dopp
imitation: 5 paste 9 schlenter
necklace: 7 riviere(F.)
surface: 5 facet
diamond-hard: 7 adamant
Diamond State: 8 Delaware
Diana: 7 Artemis
father: 7 Jupiter
mother: 6 Latona
twin: 6 Apollo
diana monkey: 7 roloway
diaper: 6 hippen, hippin, napkin
diaphanous 5 sheer 11 transparent
diaphragm: 4 riff 7 midriff
pert. to: 7 phrenic
diary: log 6 record 7 journal 8 register 9 ephemeris
diaskeuast: 6 editor 7 reviser, revisor
diastase: 4 malt 6 enzyme
diatribe: 6 screed 8 harangue 9 criticism, invective, philippic 10 discussion 12 denunciation
Diaz de Bivar's title: Cid
dib: bob, dap, dip 5 rupee 6 dibble
dibble: dap, dib 6 dabble, trifle
dibs: 5 syrup
dice: 4 cube 5 bones 6 reject 7 checker
cheater: 6 topper
throw of six: 4 sice
trick: cog
dicer: 5 derby 7 gambler
dick: lad 4 dike, whip 5 agent, apron, ditch 6 fellow 8 flatfoot 9 detective
Dickens: *character:* Tim 4 Dora, Nell 5 Fagin 6 Cuttle 7 Dorritt, Podsnap 9 Bill Sikes, Uriah Heep
pen name: Boz
dicker: 4 swap 5 daker 6 barter, haggle 7 bargain, chaffer 8 exchange 9 agreement, negotiate
dickey, dicky: 4 weak 5 shaky 6 donkey, rumble 7 haddock 9 petticoat
dict: saw 5 adage, maxim 6 saying 8 apothegm 10 apophthegm
dictate: say 4 dite, tell 5 dicta(pl.), utter 6 dictum, enjoin, impose 7 command, deliver, require, suggest 9 prescribe 11 communicate
dictatorial: 6 lordly 7 pompous 8 arrogant, dogmatic, positive 9 imperious, masterful, pragmatic 10 autocratic, peremptory 11 categorical, domineering, magisterial, opinionated, overbearing 13 authoritative
diction: 5 style 6 phrase 8 language, parlance, verbiage 10 vocabulary 11 enunciation, phraseology
dictionary: 7 lexicon 8 wordbook 10 vocabulary 11 onomasticon
compiler: 13 lexicographer
geographical: gazetteer
poet's: 6 gradus
dictum: 5 adage, axiom, edict 6 decree, saying 7 dictate, opinion 8 apothegm 9 principle, statement
Dictynna: 11 Britomartis
did: See do
didactic: dry 7 preachy 10 moralistic
didacticism: 6 homily 8 pedantry
diddle: 4 hoax 6 befool, dandle, dawdle, jiggle, toddle 7 swindle
dido: 5 antic, caper, trick
Dido: *father:* 5 Belus
founder of: 8 Carthage
husband: 7 Acerbas
sister: 4 Anna
wooer: 6 Aeneas
die: dod 4 coin, fade, mold, seal, wane 5 croak, stamp 6 chance, depart, expire, finish, perish, vanish, wither 7 decease, succumb 8 languish, puncheon 9 plaything
loaded: 6 fulham, fullam
symbol: ace
die-hard: 4 Tory
diet: 4 fare, fast, food 5 board 6 reduce, viands 7 regimen 8 congress 10 convention 11 convocation, legislature
convalescent: 5 broth
rule of: 7 dietary
difference: 5 clash 6 change 7 discord, dispute 8 division 10 alteration, dissension, unlikeness 11 controversy, discrepancy 12 disagreement
different: 4 many 5 other 6 divers, sundry, unlike 7 diverse, several, unalike, un-

usual, variant, various 8 distinct, manifold, separate 9 disparate, divergent 10 dissimilar, variegated 11 diversified
differentiate: 8 contrast 11 distinguish 12 discriminate
difficult: 4 hard 5 cramp, crank, spiny 6 crabby, cranky, strait, uneasy, uneath 7 arduous, crabbed, diffuse, labored, obscure, painful, practic 8 abstract, puzzling, stubborn 9 difficile, intricate, laborious 11 complicated, troublesome
prefix: dys
difficulty: ado, bar, rub 4 clog, coil, node, nodi(pl.), snag 5 cheek, nodus 6 boggle, habble, hobble, plight, scrape, strait 7 barrier, pitfall, problem 8 asperity, obstacle, severity, struggle 9 hindrance 10 impediment 11 controversy, obstruction 12 complication, disagreement
lack of: 4 ease
pert. to: 5 spiny 7 crucial
diffidence: 5 doubt 7 modesty, reserve, shyness 8 distrust, humility, timidity 9 suspicion 10 hesitation 11 bashfulness 12 apprehension
diffuse: 4 full, shed 5 strew 6 derive, dilate, divide, expand, extend, prolix, spread 7 copious, perplex, pervade, publish, radiate, scatter, verbose 8 confused, disperse 9 circulate, difficult, dissipate, expatiate, garrulous, irradiate, propagate 10 widespread 11 disseminate
diffusion: 6 osmose 7 osmosis
diffusive: 7 osmotic
dig: hoe 4 claw, grub, howk, mine, moot, pion, poke, root 5 delve, dwell, graft, lodge, spade, start 6 burrow, exhume, plunge, thrust 7 unearth 8 excavate
dig out: 5 scoop, shove, spade 8 excavate
digest: 4 code 5 ripen 6 codify, mature 7 concoct, epitome, pandect, summary 8 condense 10 abridgment, assimilate, compendium, comprehend 11 abridgement
digestion: 7 eupepsy 8 eupepsia 9 dyspepsia
agent: 6 pepsin, rennin 7 maltase
ailment: 5 colic 6 gripes 7 pyrosis 9 dyspepsia 12 constipation
having good: 8 eupeptic
digger: pal 4 plow 5 miner 6 bildar, drudge 7 comrade, plodder 10 Australian 12 New Zealander
digging, fitted for: 7 fodient
dight: dab, rub 4 deck, wipe 5 adorn, dress, equip, order, raise, treat 6 manage, repair, winnow 7 appoint, consign, perform, prepare 9 construct
digit: toe 4 unit 5 thumb 6 figure, finger, number 7 dewclaw
podal: toe
shield for: cot 5 stall 7 thimble
diglot: 9 bilingual
dignified: 5 grand, lofty, manly, noble, staid 6 august, sedate, solemn 7 courtly, exalted, togated 8 ennobled, majestic 11 magisterial
dignify: 5 adorn, exalt, grace, honor 7 elevate, ennoble, promote
dignitary: don 4 raja 5 rajah 6 priest 7 prelate 9 clergyman
dignity: 4 rank 5 honor, pride, state 6 barony, repose 7 bearing, decorum, fitness, gravity, majesty, station 8 nobility 9 nobleness 10 excellence
digraph: 8 ligature
digress: 4 veer 6 swerve, wander 7 deviate, diverge 8 divagate 10 transgress
digression: 7 episode 8 excursus 9 excursion
dike, dyke: 4 bank, dick, pond, pool 5 digue, ditch, levee 7 channel 8 causeway 10 embankment 11 watercourse
dilapidation: 4 ruin 5 decay 9 disrepair 10 raggedness 14 disintegration
dilatation: 7 ectasia, ectasis 8 dilation
dilate: 5 delay, plump, swell, widen 6 expand, extend, spread 7 amplify, broaden, diffuse, distend, enlarge, inflate, prolong, stretch 8 disperse, increase, lengthen, protract 9 expatiate
dilatory: 4 slow 5 slack, tardy 6 fabian, remiss 8 backward, delaying, inactive, sluggish 10 behindhand 15 procrastinating, procrastinative
dilemma: fix 4 node 5 brake 8 quandary 11 predicament 12 complication
dilettante, dilettant: 5 lover 7 admirer, amateur, dabbler, dabster, esthete 8 aesthete
diligence: 4 heed 6 effort 7 caution 8 industry 9 constancy 11 application, earnestness, heedfulness
diligent: 4 busy, hard 6 active, eident, steady 7 careful, earnest, heedful, operose 8 cautious, constant, sedulous 9 assiduous, attentive, laborious 11 industrious, painstaking
dill: 4 calm 5 anise 6 pickle, soothe
seed: 4 anet
dillydally: lag, toy 4 loaf 5 stall 6 loiter, trifle 9 vacillate
dilute: dil(abbr.) 4 thin 5 delay, water 6 rarefy, reduce, weaken 8 diminish 9 attenuate, distemper
dim: wan 4 blur, dark, dull, fade, gray, hazy, mist, pale, veil 5 bleak, blear, dusky, faint, foggy, misty 6 bemist, cloudy, darken, dimpsy, gloomy, obtuse, shadow 7 darkish, eclipse, obscure, shadowy, tarnish 8 overcast 9 obfuscate 10 indistinct, mysterious 11 crepuscular

dime: 4 coin 5 disme
dimension: 4 bulk, size 5 scope 6 extent, height, length 7 breadth 9 magnitude, thickness 10 importance, proportion 11 measurement 13 circumference
diminish: ebb 4 bate, ease, fade, fret, melt, pare, sink, wane, wear 5 abate, lower, peter, taper 6 decoct, dilute, lessen, rebate, reduce, vanish, wither 7 abridge, assuage, curtail, deplete, depress, dwindle, qualify, relieve 8 adminish, condense, decrease, diminute, minorate, moderate, retrench 9 alleviate, epitomize, extenuate
diminution: 8 decrease 9 abasement, abatement, decrement 11 abridgement, attenuation, curtailment, degradation, deprivation, extenuation
diminutive: wee 4 tiny 5 banty, dwarf, petty, runty, small 6 bantam, little, petite 9 minuscule 11 disparaging
suffix: el, et, ie; cle, ole, ule 4 cula, ette 5 culus
dimmet: 4 dusk 8 twilight
dimness: 5 gloom 8 darkness 9 obscurity
dimple: 4 doke 6 ripple 8 fossette
din: bum 4 riot 5 alarm, bruit, clang, noise 6 clamor, hubbub, racket, rattle, steven, tumult, uproar 7 clamour, clangor, clatter, discord, turmoil 9 commotion, confusion 10 hullabaloo
dindle: 4 ring 6 quiver, thrill, tingle, tinkle, tremor 7 vibrate 9 vibration
dine: eat, sup 5 feast 6 regale
diner: 7 epicure
dinette: 6 alcove 10 kitchen set
ding: 4 beat, dash, push, ring 5 clang, drive, excel, fling, knock, pound, thump 6 stroke, thrash, thrust
dinge: 4 dent, dint 6 batter, bruise 10 depression
dinghy, dingy: 4 boat 5 skiff 7 rowboat, shallop
dingle: 4 dale, dell, glen, vale 6 valley
dingus: 6 gadget 9 doohickey, doohickus, doohinkey, doohinkus
dingy: dun 4 dark 5 dirty, dusky, grimy, ourie, smoky 6 dinghy 8 smirched
dining: *room:* 7 cenacle, dinette 9 refectory
science: 10 aristology
dink: 4 deck, neat, trim 7 elegant
dinkey: 10 locomotive
dinkum: 4 fair 5 truly 6 honest, square 7 genuine 8 honestly, reliable
dinky: 4 cute, neat, poor 13 insignificant
dinner: 4 meal 5 feast 6 repast 7 banquet 9 beanfeast
course: 4 nuts, soup 5 fruit, salad 6 entree 7 dessert
pert. to: 8 cenatory
dinornis: moa
dinosaur: 11 morosaurian, stegosauria, stegosaurus, triceratops, tyrannosaur 12 brontosaurus 13 tyrannosaurus
genus of: 10 diplodocus 11 apatosaurus
dint: 4 beat, blow, dent, nick 5 clour, delve, dinge, force, notch, onset, power, press, shock 6 attack, chance, effort, strike, stroke 7 imprint 8 efficacy, striking 10 impression 11 indentation
diocese: see 8 district 12 jurisdiction
division: 6 parish 8 parishen(Sc.)
Dione: *consort:* 4 Zeus
daughter: 9 Aphrodite
Dionysus: *attendant:* 6 Maenad
festival: 7 Agrania 8 Agrionia
mother: 6 Semele
pert. to: 7 Bromian
diopside: 7 alalite 8 pyroxene
diorite: 7 diabase
Dioscuri: 5 twins 6 Anaces, Castor, Gemini, Pollux
father: 4 Zeus 9 Tyndareus
mother: 4 Leda
sister: 5 Helen 12 Clytemnestra
diose: 14 glycolaldehyde
dip: sop 4 bail, drop, dunk, lade, sink, soak 5 delve, ladle, lower, slope 6 candle, hollow, plunge 7 decline, immerge, immerse, incline, moisten 8 submerge 10 depression, pickpocket
in water: 5 douse, rinse, souse
diploma: 6 degree 7 charter 11 certificate
diplomacy: 4 tact 9 dexterity 10 artfulness
diplomat: 4 dean 6 consul 7 attache 8 minister 10 ambassador
corps head: 4 dean 5 doyen
dipody: 6 syzygy
dipper: 5 ladle, scoop 10 pickpocket
dippy: mad 7 foolish 9 screwball
dipsomania: 9 potomania 10 alcoholism
dipteran: fly 4 gnat 8 mosquito
lobe of wing: 5 alula
dipthong, diphthong: ae, oe 7 bivocal
dird: 4 blow 5 thump 9 buffeting
dirdum: 4 blow 5 blame 6 rebuke, tumult, uproar 8 scolding 10 punishment
dire: 4 dern, evil 5 awful, fatal 6 deadly, dismal, funest, tragic, woeful 7 doleful, drastic, fearful 8 dreadful, horrible, terrible, ultimate 10 calamitous, oppressive, portentous 12 overpowering
direct: aim, bid, con 4 airt, bain, bend, boss, edit, even, flat, head, helm, lead, open, rein, sway, turn 5 apply, blank, coach, frank, guide, order, point, refer, steer, teach, train, utter, write 6 ensign, govern, handle, honest, impart, lineal, manage 7 address, appoint, command, conduct, control, convert, execute, express, officer, pre-

side 8 dedicate, instruct, marshall, regulate, straight 9 categoric, downright, immediate 10 administer, forthright, point-blank 11 categorical, compendious, superintend, superscribe 15 straightforward

direction: way 4 airt, bent, care, duct, east, road, rule, west 5 north, order, route, south, trend 6 course 7 address, bearing, command, control, mandate, precept 8 guidance, tendency 9 ordinance 10 injunction, management, regulation 11 appointment, arrangement, inclination, information, instruction 13 determination 14 superscription 15 superintendence
Biblical: 5 selah
court: 5 order
line of: 5 range
musical: see **musical direction**
pole to pole: 5 axial
printer's: 4 stet
without: 7 astatic

direction finder: 7 compass

directly: 4 soon 8 promptly 9 instantly, presently 11 immediately, straightway

director: 4 boss, head 5 coach, guide, pilot 6 archon, bishop, leader, rector 7 manager, prefect, trainer 8 governor, producer 9 conductor, intendant 13 administrator 14 superintendent

directors, board of: 10 management

directory: 9 phonebook 10 collection, directoire(F.)

dirge: 4 keen, song 5 elegy 6 hearse, lament 7 epicede 8 epicedia(pl.), threnody 9 epicedium

dirigible: 5 blimp 7 airship 8 Zeppelin 10 Hindenburg
part: fin 7 nacelle

dirk: 4 snee 5 skean, sword 6 dagger, weapon

dirl: 4 ring 6 pierce, thrill, tingle 7 vibrate

dirndle: 5 dress, skirt

dirt: fen, mud 4 dust, gore, muck, nast, soil 5 earth, filth, grime, trash 6 gravel, ground, refuse 7 mullock 8 muckment 9 excrement

dirty: low 4 base, clat, foul, soil 5 bawdy, cabby, dingy, foggy, grimy, gusty, horry, muddy, nasty, sully 6 bemire, clarty, defile, filthy, greasy, grubby, impure, mussed, smutty, soiled, sordid, stormy 7 begrime, brookie, bruckle, clouded, muddied, squalid, sullied, tarnish, unclean 10 despicable

dirty dig: 5 taunt

dirty look: 5 frown

Dis: 5 Pluto

disable: 4 lame, maim 5 break, gruel, wreck 6 bruise, dismay, weaken 7 cripple 9 hamstring 10 disqualify 12 incapacitate

disaccharide: 5 biose 7 lactose, maltose, sucrose 10 saccharose

disadvantage: 4 hurt, risk 6 damage, injury 7 penalty 8 handicap 9 detriment

disadvantageous: 7 hurtful 10 derogatory 11 detrimental, prejudicial, unfavorable

disaffected: 5 false 6 untrue 8 disloyal, forsworn, perjured, recreant 9 estranged, faithless, insidious 10 perfidious, traitorous 11 treacherous

disaffection: 6 deceit 7 disease, disgust, dislike 8 disorder 9 distemper, hostility 10 disloyalty, alienation, discontent 13 indisposition 14 disinclination

disaffirm: 4 deny 5 annul 7 reverse 9 repudiate 10 contradict

disagree: 4 vary 6 differ 7 dissent, quarrel 8 conflict

disagreeable: bad 4 sour, vile 5 cross, harsh, nasty 7 chronic, hateful 8 terrible 9 invidious, irritable, offensive, repugnant 10 abominable, forbidding, unpleasant 11 displeasing, distasteful 13 uncomfortable

disagreement: 5 clash, fight 7 discord, dispute, dissent, wrangle 8 variance 9 diversity 10 contention, difference, difficulty, dissension, dissidence, divergence, unlikeness 11 contrariety, controversy, discrepancy, displeasure, incongruity 16 misunderstanding

disallow: 6 forbid, reject 7 censure 8 disclaim, disprove, prohibit 10 disapprove

disappear: fly 4 fade, flee 6 vanish 7 evanish 8 evanesce

disappoint: 4 balk, bilk, fail, fall, mock, undo 6 baffle, defeat, delude, outwit, thwart 7 deceive, destroy, nullify 9 frustrate, mislippen

disappointment: rue 7 letdown 11 frustration

disapprobation: 5 odium 11 deprecation, disapproval 12 condemnation

disapproval: 4 booh, hiss, veto 7 catcall, censure 9 disliking 14 disapprobation

disapprove: 6 reject, resent 7 condemn, protest 8 disallow, disprove 9 deprecate

disarm: 6 subdue

disarrange: 4 muss 6 deform, ruffle 7 clutter, confuse, derange, disturb, rummage 8 dishevel, disorder, unsettle 9 dislocate 10 discompose, disconcert 11 disorganize

disarray: 4 mess 5 strip 6 caddle 7 despoil 8 dishevel, disorder 9 confusion 10 dishabille

disassociate: 8 separate 10 dissociate

disaster: woe 4 bale, blow, evil, ruin 6 mishap, stroke 7 reverse 8 accident, calamity, casualty, fatality 9 cataclysm, extremity, mischance 10 misfortune 11 catastrophe 12 misadventure

disavow: 4 deny 5 devow 6 abjure, disown, recant, refuse 7 decline, retract 8 abnegate, disclaim, renounce 9 repudiate

disband: 7 breakup, dismiss, release, scatter 8 dissolve 9 discharge 12 disintegrate

disbelieve: 5 doubt 6 reject 7 suspect 9 discredit

disbeliever: 7 atheist, heretic

disburden: rid 4 ease 7 relieve 9 exonerate 11 disencumber

disburse: 5 spend 6 defray, expend, outlay 10 distribute

disc: 4 dial 5 medal, paten, plate, quoit 6 record 7 platter

discalced: 6 unshod 10 barefooted

discard: 4 cast, jilt, junk, omit, oust, shed 5 chuck, ditch, scrap, shuck, sluff 6 disuse, divest, excuss, reject 7 abandon, cashier, dismiss, forsake 9 eliminate, repudiate

pile: 4 heap 5 trash 8 boneyard

discern: ken, see, spy 4 espy, read 5 sight 6 behold, descry, detect, notice 8 discover, perceive 10 understand 11 distinguish

discernible: 7 evident, visible 8 apparent, manifest 11 conspicuous, perceptible 15 distinguishable

discernment: eye 4 tact 5 flair, taste 6 acumen 7 insight 8 sagacity 9 sharpness 10 divination, perception, shrewdness 11 penetration 12 clairvoyance, perspicacity 14 discrimination

discharge: can 4 boot, cass, dump, emit, fire, free, pour, sack 5 eject, empty, expel, exude, shoot, speed 6 acquit, assoil, bounce, defray, effect, exempt, unlade, unload 7 absolve, cashier, disband, dismiss, exhaust, release, relieve 8 disgorge, displace, evacuate, mittimus 9 acquittal, dismissal, exculpate, exonerate, exudation, liquidate 10 discompose, liberation 11 acquittance, exoneration, performance, transaction

dishonorable: 7 bobtail, cashier

discharged from active service: 8 emeritus

disciple: ite 4 John, Mark 5 Judas, Peter, teach, train 6 hearer, punish 7 apostle, auditor, Matthew, scholar, student 8 adherent, follower 10 discipline

disciplinarian: 4 czar, tsar 6 tyrant 7 trainer 8 martinet

discipline: 4 whip 5 inure, teach, train 6 ferule, govern, punish 7 chasten, culture, educate, scourge 8 doctrine, instruct, learning, regulate, restrain, teaching, training, tutoring 9 education 10 punishment 11 instruction 12 chastisement

disclaim: 4 deny 5 devow 6 abjure, disown, refuse 7 disavow 8 abdicate, abnegate, disallow, renounce 9 repudiate

disclose: ope 4 bare, blow, open, tell 5 utter 6 betray, bewray, descry, expose, impart, reveal, shrive, unseal, unveil 7 confess, develop, display, divulge, exhibit, unclose, uncover 8 discover, indicate, manifest

disclosure: 6 expose 10 revelation

discolor: 4 fade, spot 5 stain, tinge 6 smirch, streak 7 distain, tarnish 8 besmirch

discoloration: 4 spot 5 stain

discolored: old 5 dirty, moldy 7 stained 8 ustulate 9 tarnished

discomfit: 4 rout 5 abash, upset 6 baffle, defeat 7 confuse, conquer, disturb, scatter 8 confound 9 embarrass, frustrate, overthrow 10 disconcert

discomfort: 4 pain 6 dismay, grieve, sorrow, unease 7 disturb 8 distress 9 annoyance, embarrass 10 discourage, uneasiness 11 displeasure 13 inconvenience 14 discouragement

discommendation: 5 blame 7 censure 8 reproach 9 dispraise

discommode: 7 trouble 9 incommode 13 inconvenience

discompose: 4 fret 5 upset 6 flurry, ruffle 7 agitate, confuse, derange, disturb, fluster, perturb 8 disorder, displace, disquiet, unsettle 9 discharge 10 disarrange, disconcert

disconcert: 4 faze 5 abash, daunt, feeze, upset, worry 6 baffle, blench, rattle 7 confuse, disturb, nonplus, perturb, squelch 8 browbeat, disorder 9 discomfit, embarrass, frustrate 10 disarrange, discompose 14 discountenance

disconnect: 4 undo 5 sever 6 divide 7 disjoin 8 dissolve, disunite, separate, uncouple

disconnected: 6 abrupt, broken 7 cursory 8 rambling 9 desultory, scattered 10 abstracted, disjointed, incoherent

disconsolate: sad 6 gloomy, woeful 7 forlorn 8 dejected, desolate, hopeless 9 cheerless, miserable, sorrowful 10 dispirited, melancholy 12 inconsolable

discontent: 8 disquiet 9 displease 10 dissatisfy, malcontent, uneasiness 11 displeasure 12 disaffection 15 dissatisfaction

discontinue: end 4 drop, quit, stop 5 break, cease, letup 6 desist, disuse, sunder 7 disrupt 8 intermit

discord: din, jar 5 broil 6 strife 7 faction 8 conflict, variance 9 cacophony, diversity 10 contention, difference, dissension, dissonance 12 disagreement
goddess of: Ate 4 Eris
discordant: 4 ajar 5 harsh 6 hoarse 7 jarring 8 contrary, jangling 10 discrepant 11 incongruous, quarrelsome 12 antagonistic, inconsistent, inharmonious 14 irreconcilable
musically: 8 scordato
serenade: 9 charivari
Discordia: 4 Eris
discotheque: 5 agogo 7 cabaret
discount: 4 agio 5 batta 6 rebate, reduce 9 allowance, deduction, disregard, reduction 12 depreciation
discourage: 4 carp 5 daunt, deter 6 dampen, deject, dismay 7 depress 8 dispirit, dissuade 10 discomfort, dishearten
discourse: 4 carp, talk, tell 5 orate, paper, speak, tract 6 eulogy, homily, parley, preach, sermon 7 account, address, comment, declaim, discuss, dissert, lecture, narrate, oration, prelect 8 argument, colloquy, converse, parlance, treatise 9 expatiate, narration, narrative, panegyric, sermonize, soliloquy 10 conference 11 description 12 conversation, dissertation
art of: 8 rhetoric
long: 6 screed, tirade 7 descant 9 philippic
discourteous: 4 rude 6 scurvy 7 uncivil 8 impolite, ungentle 10 unmannerly 11 ill-mannered, uncivilized 13 disrespectful
discover: see, spy 4 espy, find 5 learn 6 define, descry, detect, expose, invent, locate, reveal 7 confess, discern, display, divulge, exhibit, explore, uncover, unearth 8 decipher, disclose, manifest 9 apprehend, ascertain, deprehend 11 reconnoiter
discoverer: spy 5 scout 8 explorer, inventor 10 originator
discovery: 5 trove 6 espial 10 disclosure, revelation
gold: 6 strike
discreate: 7 destroy 10 annihilate
discredit: 5 decry, doubt, refel 6 deface 7 asperse, blemish, impeach, scandal, suspect 8 belittle, disgrace, dishonor, distrust 9 disparage, disrepute 10 disbelieve
discreet: 4 wary 5 civil 6 polite, silent 7 careful, guarded, politic, prudent 8 cautious, reserved, reticent 11 circumspect
discrepant: 8 contrary 9 different 10 discordant 11 disagreeing 12 inconsistent
discrepate: 6 differ 11 distinguish 12 discriminate
discrete: 8 distinct, separate
discretion: 4 tact 6 wisdom 8 courtesy 9 restraint 13 secretiveness
discriminate: 6 secern 8 perceive 9 demarcate 10 discrepate 11 distinguish 13 differentiate
discriminating: 4 nice 5 acute 6 astute 7 choosey 8 critical 10 discerning 11 distinctive
discrimination: 5 taste 6 acumen 11 discernment, distinction, penetration
discursive: 6 roving 7 cursory 8 rambling 9 desultory 10 digressive
discus: 4 disk 5 quoit
thrower: 10 Discobolus
discuss: air 4 moot 5 argue, bandy, treat 6 confer, debate, excuss, parley 7 agitate, bespeak, canvas, consult, dispute, dissert, examine, narrate 9 discourse, exagitate, ventilate 11 expostulate
discussion: 5 forum 6 hassel 8 causerie, diatribe, entreaty 12 dissertation
group: 5 class, panel 7 seminar
medium of: 5 forum
open to: 4 moot
disdain: tut 5 pride, scorn, spurn 7 contemn, despise 8 contempt 9 arrogance 11 haughtiness, indignation
disease: 4 harm 5 pinta 6 malady, morbus 7 ailment, illness, malaria, trouble, yellows 8 beriberi, distress, sickness 9 complaint, distemper, infirmity 10 discomfort, pestilence, uneasiness 12 disaffection
agent of: 4 germ 9 bacterium, contagium
animal: coe, pip, rye 4 rout 5 braxy, coath, colic, farcy, hoose, hooze, mange, nenta 6 amoeba, garget, hammer 7 dartars, spavins, takosis 8 asthenia, glanders, sacbrood 9 distemper, tularemia 11 myxomatosis, psittacosis
blood: 8 leucemia, leukemia 9 leucaemia
brain: 8 paranoia 13 schizophrenia
comb. form: nos 4 noso
contagious: pox 5 mumps 7 measles
crippling: 9 arthritis, sclerosis 10 rheumatism 13 poliomyelitis
declining stage: 9 catabasis
deficiency: 6 scurvy 8 pellagra
diver's: 5 bends 7 caisson
eye: 8 glaucoma, trachoma 9 pterygium 14 conjunctivitis
fatal: 5 lyssa 10 malignancy
favorable termination of: 5 lysis
fowl: pip 4 roup 7 perosis
fungus: 5 ergot, tinea
hair: 5 plica 7 xerasia 8 psilosis
heart: 8 aneurism, aneurysm
liver: 9 cirrhosis, hepatitis
local: 7 endemic

lung: 8 phthisis 9 emphysema, pneumonia 11 consumption 12 tuberculosis
nervous: see **mental disorder**
pert. to: 6 clinic, loimic 7 endemic
plant: fen 4 bunt, rust, scab, smut 5 ergot, speck 6 calico, coleur, mildew 7 erinose, viruela, walloon 8 brindled, melanose
prediction about: 9 prognosis
recognition of: 9 diagnosis
science of children's: 10 pediatrics 11 paediatrics
science of origin: 8 etiology
skin: 4 acne, pian, rash 5 favus, hives, psora, tinea 6 courap, dartre, eczema, herpes, lichen, tetter 7 scabies, serpigo 8 impetigo, ringworm 9 frambesia, psoriasis, xeroderma 10 framboesia 11 scleroderma
spreader: fly 6 vector 7 carrier
suffix: 4 itis
tropical: 5 sprue 7 malaria
wasting: 8 phthisic

disembark: 4 land 6 alight, debark

disembodiment: 4 soul 6 spirit

disembowel: gut 4 hulk 6 paunch 8 gralloch 10 eviscerate

disembroil: 8 untangle 9 extricate

disencumber: rid 4 free 9 disburden, disengage

disengage: 4 free 5 clear, untie 6 detach, evolve, loosen 7 release, unravel 8 liberate 9 extricate 11 disencumber, disentangle 12 disembarrass

disentangle: 4 comb, free 5 clear, loose, ravel 6 evolve, sleave 7 unravel 8 untangle 9 disengage, extricate 12 disembarrass

disenthrone: 6 depose

disfavor, disfavour: 5 odium 7 umbrage 9 disesteem 11 displeasure

disfigure: mar 4 blur, scar 6 deface, defeat, deform, injure, mangle 7 blemish 8 mutilate 10 disfashion

disgorge: 4 spew, vent 5 eject, empty, vomit 9 discharge 10 relinquish

disgrace: 4 blot, slur, soil, spot 5 abase, crime, odium, shame, stain 6 infamy 7 affront, attaint, degrade, scandal, slander 8 contempt, dishonor, ignominy, reproach 9 discredit, disesteem, disfigure, humiliate 10 attainture, defamation, opprobrium 11 displeasure, humiliation 13 disparagement

disgruntled: 4 sore 7 peevish

disguise: 4 hide, mask, mumm, veil 5 belie, cloak, couch, feign, gloze, guise 6 covert, deform, masque 7 conceal, obscure, pretend 8 palliate 9 coverture, dissemble, incognito 10 camouflage, intoxicate, masquerade 11 dissimulate

disgust: 5 repel, shock 6 degout(F.), horror, nausea, offend, revolt, sicken 8 aversion, distaste, loathing, nauseate 9 antipathy 10 abhorrence, repugnance 11 abomination 12 disaffection

disgusting: 4 foul, vile 5 nasty 6 filthy 7 beastly, fulsome, hateful, noisome, obscene 8 shocking

dish (see also **food**): cap 4 caup 5 basin, comal, nappy, paten, plate 6 bassie, critch, panada, patera, recipe, saucer, tureen 7 charger, cresset, epergne, patella, plateau, platter, ramekin, scuttle 9 casserole, clackdish
gravy: 4 boat
main: 6 entree

dishabille: 8 disarray, disorder, negligee

Dishan's son: Uz 4 Aran

dishearten: 5 amate, daunt 6 deject 7 depress, flatten, unnerve 8 dispirit 10 demoralize, discourage

disheartened: 6 gloomy 8 downcast

dishevel: 4 muss 6 ruffle, tousel, tousle, tumble 8 disarray, disorder 10 disarrange

dishonest: 4 foul, lewd 5 cronk, false 7 corrupt, crooked, knavish 8 indecent, shameful, unchaste 9 deceitful, repulsive 10 fraudulent, perfidious 12 dishonorable 13 untrustworthy

dishonor, dishonour: 5 abase, abuse, shame, stain 6 defame, defile, infamy 7 degrade, obloquy, violate 8 disgrace, ignominy, reproach 9 discredit, disparage, disrepute 10 defamation, disworship, opprobrium 11 contaminate, impeachment, irreverence 13 disparagement

dishonorable, dishonourable: 4 base, foul, mean 5 nasty 6 yellow 7 ignoble 11 disesteemed

dishwasher: 7 machine 8 domestic

disillusion: 10 disenchant

disinclination: 7 dislike 8 aversion, distaste 9 antipathy 10 reluctance, repugnance 12 disaffection

disinclined: 6 averse 9 reluctant, unwilling 10 indisposed

disinfect: 7 cleanse 9 sterilize

disinfectant: 5 iodin 6 iodine, phenòl 9 germicide 10 antiseptic

disingenuous: 5 false 10 circuitous

disinherit: 7 deprive 10 exheredate

disintegrate: 4 melt 5 decay, erode 7 crumble, disband 8 dissolve, separate 9 decompose

disinter: 6 exhume, unbury

disinterested: 4 fair 9 apathetic, impartial 11 unconcerned

disjasked, disjaskit: 5 jaded 7 decayed

disjoin: 4 part, undo 5 sever 6 detach, sunder 8 dissolve, disunite, separate 10 disconnect, dissociate

disjune: 9 breakfast
disk: 4 dial 5 cakra, medal, paten, plate, sabot, wheel 6 bezant, chakra, harrow, record, washer 7 medalet, phalera 9 cultivate, faceplate, medallion, millstone
hockey: 4 puck
metal: 4 flan, gong 6 ghurry, sequin 8 zecchino
pert. to: 6 discal 7 discoid
solar: 4 Aten
dislike: 4 loth, mind 5 loath 6 detest 8 aversion, distaste 9 antipathy, disesteem, disrelish 11 detestation, displacency, displeasure 12 disaffection 14 disinclination
comb. form: mis 4 miso
object of: 8 anathema
of children: 9 misopedia 10 misopaedia
dislocate: 5 splay 8 disjoint, displace 10 disarrange
dislodge: 5 expel 6 remove
disloyal: 5 false 6 untrue 9 faithless 10 inconstant, perfidious, unfaithful 11 disaffected, treacherous
dismal: sad, wan 4 dark, dire, dull, glum, gray 5 black, bleak, drear, sorry 6 dreary, gloomy, triste 7 doleful, ghastly, joyless, ominous, unhappy 8 dolorous, funereal, lonesome 9 cheerless, sorrowful 10 acherontic, calamitous, lugubrious, melancholy 11 unfortunate
dismantle: 4 rase, raze 5 strip 6 divest 7 deprive, destroy, uncloak 8 dismount
dismay: 4 fear, ruin 5 alarm, appal, daunt, dread 6 appall, fright, subdue, terror 7 depress, deprive, horrify, terrify 8 affright, confound 9 dejection 10 depression, discomfort, discourage 11 trepidation 12 apprehension 13 consternation 14 discouragement
dismember: 4 maim, part, rend 5 sever 6 mangle 7 dissect 8 disjoint, mutilate
dismiss: can 4 boot, bust, drop, oust 5 chuck, eject 6 banish, bounce, reject, remove 7 cashier, disband, discard 8 relegate 9 discharge, overthrow
dismissal: 5 conge 6 avaunt 8 mittimus
dismount: 5 avale 6 alight 9 dismantle
disobedient: 7 forward, froward, naughty, ungodly, wayward 8 mutinous 10 rebellious, refractory 11 intractable 12 contumacious 13 insubordinate
disoblige: 6 offend 7 affront
disorder: pie 4 mess, muss, riot 5 chaos, deray, snafu, touse 6 burble, jumble, litter, malady, mucker, muddle, ruffle, tousle, tumu't 7 ailment, clutter, confuse, derange, disturb, embroil, flutter, illness, misdeed, perturb, trouble 8 disarray, dishevel 9 commotion, complaint, confusion, distemper 10 disarrange, discompose, disconcert, misconduct 11 derangement, disorganize, disturbance, misdemeanor 12 disaffection, discomposure, irregularity 13 indisposition 14 disarrangement 15 disorganization
visual: 10 strabismus
disordered: 6 frouzy, frowsy, frowzy 10 topsy-turvy 11 lightheaded
disorderly: 5 randy 6 unruly 8 slipshod, slovenly 12 hugger-mugger, ungovernable, unmanageable
disorganize: 5 upset 7 confuse, derange, disband, disrupt 8 disorder, dissolve 10 disarrange
disour: 6 jester 11 storyteller
disown: 4 deny 6 reject 7 disavow, retract 8 abdicate, disclaim, renounce 9 reprobate, repudiate
disparage, desparage: 4 slur 5 abuse, decry, lower 6 slight 7 degrade, depress, detract, impeach 8 belittle, derogate, dishonor, disprize, minimize 9 discredit, dispraise, extenuate 10 depreciate
disparate: 7 unequal 8 separate 9 different 10 dissimilar 16 disproportionate
dispart: 4 open, rend, rive 5 break, sever, split 6 cleave, divide 8 separate
dispassionate: 4 calm, cool, fair 5 stoic 6 sedate, serene 8 composed, moderate 9 collected, impartial, temperate, unruffled 10 deliberate, unimpaired 12 unprejudiced
dispatch: rid 4 free, kill, mail, note, post, send 5 haste, hurry, speed 6 hasten 7 deliver, depeche(F.), dispose 8 celerity, conclude, expedite 9 quickness 10 accelerate, accomplish, promptness
dispatch boat: 5 aviso 6 packet
dispatcher: 8 trainman 9 motor boss
dispel: 6 banish 7 scatter 8 disperse 9 dissipate
dispend: 5 spend 6 expend 8 dispense, squander
dispendious: 6 costly 9 expensive 11 extravagant
dispensation: 4 plan 6 scheme 7 economy, license 9 allotment 12 distribution
dispense: 4 deal, dole 6 effuse, excuse, exempt, forego, manage 7 absolve, arrange, dispend 9 exemption 10 administer, distribute 12 dispensation
dispenser: 7 manager, steward 10 pharmacist 13 administrator
information: 4 tout 7 tipster 11 stoolpigeon
dispeople: 10 depopulate
disperse: sow 4 fray, part, rout 5 strew 6 dilate, dispel, sparse, spread, vanish 7 diffuse, scatter 8 separate, squander 9 dissipate 10 dispergate, distribute 11 disseminate

dispirit: cow 4 damp 5 daunt 6 deject 7 depress, flatten 10 discourage, dishearten, intimidate
dispirited: 6 abattu 7 abattue 8 downcast 9 cheerless, woebegone 11 crestfallen 12 disconsolate
dispiteous: 5 cruel 8 pitiless, spiteful
displace: 6 banish, depose, mislay, remove 7 derange 8 dislodge, misplace, supplant 9 discharge, dislocate, supersede 10 discompose
display: air 4 brag, pomp, show, wear 5 boast, emote, scene, sight, sport, stage 6 blazon, deploy, descry, expose, extend, flaunt, ostent, parade, reveal, uncase 7 approve, etalage, exhibit, flutter, pageant, uncover 8 ceremony, disclose, discover, emblazon, exercise, flourish, indicate, manifest, splendor 9 spectacle 10 exhibition 11 affectation, demonstrate 13 demonstration, manifestation
displease: vex 4 miff 5 anger, annoy, pique 6 offend 7 provoke 8 irritate 10 discontent, dissatisfy
displeasing: bad, dry 7 irksome 9 offensive 10 unpleasant 11 distasteful 12 disagreeable
displeasure: ire 5 anger, mumps, pique 6 injury 7 dislike, offense, trouble, umbrage 8 disfavor, disgrace, distaste 10 discomfort, discontent, resentment, uneasiness 11 indignation
show: cry 4 pout 5 frown
dispone: 8 transfer 10 distribute
disport: 4 play 5 amuse, frisk 6 divert, frolic, gambol
disposal: 8 bestowal 11 arrangement, disposition
dispose: set 4 bend, give, mind 5 array, order, place 6 adjust, attire, bestow, settle 7 appoint, arrange, prepare 8 dispatch, regulate 9 determine 10 distribute
disposed: apt 5 fixed, prone, ready 7 tending 8 arranged, inclined
disposition: 4 bent, bias, mood, turn 5 tache 6 affect, animus, health, nature, temper 7 concept 8 aptitude, attitude, disposal, posture 9 affection, character, diathesis 10 adjustment, management, proclivity, propension, propensity 11 arrangement, inclination, temperament 12 constitution, distribution, organization 14 relinquishment
dispossess: 4 oust 5 eject, evict, expel, strip 6 depose, divest 7 bereave, deprive 8 disseize
dispraise: 5 blame 7 censure 9 disparage 10 depreciate, detraction 13 disparagement 15 discommendation
disprize: 10 undervalue 13 underestimate
disproof: 10 refutation 11 confutation
disproportion: 9 disparity 10 inequality
disproportionate: 14 incommensurate
disprove: 5 rebut, refel 6 negate, refute 7 confute, explode 8 disallow, redargue 10 disapprove
disputable: 5 vague 6 unsure 7 dubious, fallible 8 doubtful, insecure 9 uncertain 10 indefinite, precarious
disputant: 6 arguer 7 debater
disputation: 7 polemic 8 argument 9 dialectic 10 discussion 11 controversy 12 conversation
disputatious: 7 eristic 13 argumentative
dispute: 4 deny, feud, fuss, moot, riot, spat 5 argue, brawl, broil, cabal, hurry 6 barney, bicker, cangle, dacker, daiker, debate, differ, fratch, haggle 7 brabble, contend, contest, discuss, dissert, faction, gainsay, quarrel, wrangle 8 argument, question, squabble 9 argy-bargy, encounter 10 contravene, controvert, litigation 11 altercation, controversy 12 disagreement
disqualify: 5 debar 6 outlaw 7 disable 9 indispose 12 incapacitate
disquiet: vex 4 fear, fret, pain 6 excite, unease, unrest 7 agitate, anxiety, disturb, inquiet, trouble, turmoil 9 incommode 10 discompose, discontent, uneasiness 12 inconvenience, restlessness
disquieted: 6 uneasy
disquisition: 5 essay 10 discussion
disregard: 4 omit 5 waive 6 forget, ignore, slight 7 despise, neglect 8 discount, disvalue, overlook 9 pretermit 10 contravene 11 inattention
disrelish: 7 dislike 8 distaste 9 antipathy
disreputable: low 4 base, hard 5 seamy, shady 7 raffish 8 shameful 13 discreditable
disrepute: 7 disfame 8 dishonor, reproach 9 discredit, disesteem
disrespect: 8 rudeness 9 disesteem, insolence 10 incivility 11 discourtesy
disrespectful: 7 uncivil 8 impolite, impudent 10 irreverent 11 impertinent
disrobe: 5 strip 6 divest 7 despoil, undress
disrupt: 4 rend, tear 5 break 7 disrump 11 discontinue, disorganize
dissatisfaction: 8 distaste 9 annoyance 10 discontent 11 displeasure
dissect: 7 analyze 9 anatomize, dismember
disseize: 10 dispossess
dissemble: 4 hide, mask 5 cloak, feign 6 boggle 7 conceal 8 disguise, simulate 11 counterfeit, dissimulate
dissembler: 9 hypocrite

disseminate: sow 5 strew 6 effuse, spread 7 diffuse, publish, scatter 8 disperse 9 circulate, propagate 10 distribute
dissent: 4 vary 6 differ 7 contend, protest 8 disagree 9 exception 10 dissidence 12 disagreement, nonagreement 13 nonconformity 14 nonconcurrence
signal of: nay
dissenter: 7 heretic 8 recusant 9 meetinger, protestor 10 Protestant 13 nonconformist
pert. to: 7 pantile
dissentious: 8 factious 11 contentious
dissepiment: 9 partition
dissert: 7 discuss, dispute 9 discourse
dissertation: 5 essay, theme, tract 6 debate, thesis, theses(pl.) 7 descant, lecture 8 treatise 9 discourse 10 discussion
Dissertation on a Roast Pig (author): 11 Charles Lamb
disservice: 4 harm 6 damage, injury 8 mischief
dissever: 4 part 6 sunder 8 disunite
dissidence: 7 dissent 12 disagreement 13 nonconformity
dissimilar: 6 unlike 7 difform, diverse 9 anomalous, different, disparate 13 heterogeneous
dissimulate: 5 feign 7 deceive, pretend 8 disguise 9 dissemble
dissipate: 4 fray 5 spend, waste 6 dispel, expend 7 diffuse, scatter, shatter 8 disperse, dissolve, embezzle, evanesce, squander 9 evaporate
dissocial: 7 selfish 8 unsocial 10 unfriendly
dissociate: 5 sever 7 disjoin 8 disunite, separate
dissolute: lax 4 lewd, wild 5 loose, slack 6 rakish, wanton 7 immoral, lawless 8 desolate, rakehell, reckless, uncurbed 9 abandoned, debauched, libertine, unbridled 10 licentious, negligence 12 unrestrained
dissolution: 4 ruin 5 decay 6 bust-up 7 breakup, decease, divorce 10 abrogation 14 disintegration
comb. form: lys
dissolve: end 4 fade, fuse, melt, thaw 5 fleet, solve 6 relent, unbind 7 adjourn, destroy, disband, disjoin, divorce, liquefy 8 discandy, disunite, separate 9 decompose, dissipate 10 deliquesce, disconnect 11 disorganize 12 disintegrate
dissolved: 6 solute
dissolving: 7 diluent
dissonant: 5 harsh 7 grating, jarring 8 jangling 10 discordant 11 cacophonous, incongruous, unmelodious 12 inconsistent, inharmonious, unharmonious 13 contradictory
dissuade: 5 deter 6 dehort, divert 10 discourage, disincline
distaff: 4 axis 5 woman 6 female
distain: 5 stain 6 defile 7 tarnish 8 discolor
distal: 6 remote 7 distant
angle: 4 axil
opposite of: 8 proximal
distance: 4 step 5 depth, range, space 7 farness, mileage, reserve, yardage 8 interval, outstrip 10 background, remoteness
measuring device: 6 stadia 8 odograph, odometer, viameter 9 pedometer, telemeter
on earth's surface: 8 latitude 9 longitude
distant: coy, far, off 4 afar, away, cold, yond 5 aloof 6 remote, yonder 7 faraway, foreign, removed 8 reserved 9 separated 10 discrepant
prefix: tel 4 tele
distaste: 6 degout 7 disgust, dislike 8 aversion 9 disrelish 11 displeasure 14 disinclination
distasteful: 7 hateful 8 brackish, nauseous, unsavory 9 loathsome, offensive, repugnant, repulsive 10 unpleasant 11 unpalatable 12 disagreeable
distemper: 4 soak 5 steep 6 choler, dilute, malady 7 ailment, disease, illness 8 disorder, sickness, unsettle 12 disaffection 13 indisposition
distend: 4 fill, grow 5 bloat, plump, swell, widen 6 dilate, expand, extend, spread 7 balloon, enlarge, inflate, stretch
distended: 4 wide 5 blown 8 patulous
distich: 7 couplet
distill, distil: 4 emit 6 infuse 7 trickle
distillation: 9 ascension
device: 6 retort 7 alembic
product: dew 6 liquor 7 spirits
tube: 7 matrass
distinct: 5 breme, clear, plain, vivid 7 diverse, legible, obvious, several, special 8 apparent, separate 9 different 10 articulate, individual 11 well-defined 13 distinguished
distinction: 4 note, rank 5 glory, honor 6 laurel, luster, lustre, renown 9 variation 10 prominence, reputation, separation 14 discrimination 15 differentiation
distinctive: 8 peculiar, talented 9 prominent 11 conspicuous 14 characteristic, discriminating
air: 6 cachet
distingue: 7 eminent 8 affected 10 celebrated
distinguish: 6 decern, define, descry, secern 8 perceive, separate 9 designate, punctuate 10 discrepate 12 characterize, discriminate 13 differentiate

distinguished: 5 noted 6 famous, marked 7 eminent, notable, special 8 distinct, laureate, renowned 9 brilliant, prominent 10 celebrated 11 conspicuous, illustrious 13 extraordinary

distort: 5 screw, twist 6 cringe, deface, deform 7 contort, pervert 10 camshachle, disfeature

distorted: wry 4 awry 5 askew, crank 7 crooked, gnarled 9 misshapen 10 anamorphic 11 anamorphous

distract: mad 5 amuse, craze 6 bemuse, divert, harass, insane, madden, moider, puzzle, twitch 7 agitate, confuse, disturb, embroil, perplex 8 bewilder, confound 9 tosticate 10 distraught

distraught: mad 6 crazed 7 frantic 8 deranged, distract 9 perplexed

distress: ail 4 hurt, need, pain, teen 5 agony, anger, annoy, dolor, grief, gripe, worry, wound 6 danger, dolour, grieve, harass, harrow, misery, sorrow 7 afflict, anguish, anxiety, disease, misease, oppress, perplex, torture, trouble 8 aggrieve, calamity, straiten 9 adversity, constrain, martyrdom, necessity 10 affliction, constraint, discomfort 11 tribulation

call: S.O.S. 6 mayday

distressing: sad 4 hard, sore 7 carking, fearful, painful 9 sorrowful 11 troublesome

distribute: 4 deal, dole, mete, sort 5 allot, issue, share 6 assign, assort, divide, expend, impart, parcel 7 arrange, dispose, prorate 8 allocate, classify, dispense, disperse, separate 9 apportion, partition 10 administer 11 disseminate

distributee: 4 heir

distributively: 4 each 6 apiece 9 severally 10 separately 12 individually, respectively

distributor: 6 dealer 10 colporteur

district: 4 area, slum, ward 5 harsh, tract, vicus(L.) 6 canton, member, parish, region 7 circuit, country, demesne, diocese, quarter 8 distrito, precinct, province, rigorous 9 community, territory 12 neighborhood 13 neighbourhood

theater: 6 rialto

District of Columbia: See **Washington, D.C.**

distrust: 4 fear 5 doubt 7 suspect 8 mistrust 9 suspicion 12 apprehension

distrustfully: 7 askance

disturb: vex 4 rile, roil 5 alarm, annoy, feeze, rouse, upset 6 harass, molest, ruffle, uncalm 7 agitate, commote, commove, derange, garboil, inquiet, perturb, trouble 8 convulse, disorder, disquiet, distract 9 discomfit, interfere, interrupt 10 disarrange, discomfort, discompose, disconcert

disturbance: 4 bree, dust, riot, rout 5 alarm, brawl, broil, deray, hurry, storm, strow, sturt, touse 6 affray, bother, breeze, cathro, fracas, hubbub, pother, rumpus, tumult, uproar 7 blunder, brulyie, brulzie, clatter, emotion, ferment, trouble, turmoil 8 business, disorder 9 agitation, annoyance, commotion, confusion, violation 10 convulsion, excitement 11 derangement, distraction, trepidation 12 discomposure, interruption, perturbation 13 collie-shangie(Sc.), inconvenience

emotional: 8 neurosis

ocean: 7 tsunami

disunite: rip 4 part 5 sever, untie 6 detach, divide, sunder 7 disband, disjoin, dissent, divorce, unravel 8 alienate, dissever, dissolve, estrange, separate 10 disconnect, dissociate

disuse: 6 misuse 7 abandon, discard 8 misapply 9 desuetude, disrepair 11 disaccustom, discontinue

disvalue: 9 disesteem, disregard 10 depreciate, undervalue

disyllabic foot: 7 trochee

disyoke: 6 unteam

dit, ditt: 4 poem, said, song 5 adage, ditty 6 saying 7 reputed 8 obstruct, surnamed 9 appointed 10 expression

ditch: rut, sap 4 delf, dick, dike, dyke, foss, gool, gout, ha-ha, holl, moat, rine, sike 5 canal, delft, delve, fence, fossa(L.), fosse, graff, graft, grave, rhine, zanja 6 fossae(pl.), gutter, trench, zanjon 7 abandon, channel, grindle, gripple, zanjona

side: 5 scarp

dite: 4 mite, song 5 ditty 6 indict, indite 7 compose, dictate, diction 11 composition

dither: 5 shake 6 bother, shiver 7 trouble 9 trembling

dithyrambic: 4 wild 10 boisterous

ditto: 4 same 6 repeat 8 likewise 9 duplicate

ditty: dit, lay 4 dite, poem, sing, song 5 theme, verse 6 saying 7 dictate 9 utterance 11 composition

diuretic: 8 evacuant

diurnal: 5 daily 9 ephemeral

divagate: 6 wander 7 digress

divan: 4 book, hall, room, sofa 5 couch, court 6 canape(F.), leewan, lounge, saloon, senate, settee 7 council 9 davenport 12 chesterfield

divaricate: 6 forked

dive: den 4 crib, duck, leap 5 haunt, swoop 6 header, plunge, resort 7 explore 8 submerge, tailspin 9 penetrate

kind of: 4 swan 6 gainer 8 jacknife

dive into: try 5 begin, start

diver: 4 loon 7 pearler, plunger 9 submarine 10 pickpocket
disease: 5 bends
gear: 4 tank 7 flipper
diverge: 6 branch, differ, divide, ramify, spread 7 deviate, digress 8 disagree
divers: 4 evil, many 5 cruel 6 sundry 7 several, various 8 perverse 9 different
diverse: 4 evil 6 motley, sundry, unlike, varied 7 adverse, several, various 8 distinct, perverse, separate, varietal 9 different, multiform 10 dissimilar 13 heterogeneous
comb. form: 4 vari
diversify: 4 vary 5 freck 7 variate 9 variegate 13 differentiate
with colors: 6 begary 7 begarie 9 bespatter
diversion: jeu 4 game, play 5 alarm, feint, hobby, sport 6 attack 7 pastime 9 amusement, avocation, merriment 10 deflection, recreation, relaxation 11 delectation, distraction 13 divertisement, entertainment
diversity: 6 change 7 discord, variety 10 difference, inequality 11 variegation 12 disagreement
divert: 5 amuse, relax 7 beguile, deflect, delight, detract, reflect 8 dissuade, distract, estrange, recreate 9 entertain
diverting: 5 droll 8 pleasant 9 laughable
divest: 4 bare, doff, reft 5 spoil, strip 6 delawn, denude, depose, devest 7 bereave, deprive, despoil, disrobe, uncover 8 denature, dethrone, unclothe 9 dismantle 10 disfurnish, dispossess
of sham: 6 debunk
divide: cut, lot 4 deal, fork, mere, part, rift, zone 5 cleft, divvy, sever, share, slice, space, split 6 bisect, branch, cleave, coteau, depart, devise, differ, parcel, ramify, sleave, sunder 7 aliquot, britten, diffuse, dispart, diverge, fissure, partake, prorate 8 classify, crossect, disunite, graduate, separate 9 apportion, dismember, intersect, multisect, partition, watershed 10 distribute
into feet: 4 scan
into parts: 4 paly 6 bisect, gobbet 7 quarter, trisect 9 bifurcate, septinate
divided: 4 ente, reft 7 fissate, partite 8 aerolate, areolate, camerate 10 incomplete
comb. form: 6 schist
dividend: 5 bonus
divider: 7 compass
dividing wall: 5 septa(pl.) 6 septum 9 partition
divination: 4 omen 6 augury 9 sortilege 11 discernment, rhabdomancy, sideromancy 12 clairvoyance 13 machairomancy
by dreams: 11 oneiromancy
by figures: 8 geomancy
by monstrosities: 11 teratoscopy
by rods: 7 dousing, dowsing
divine: 4 holy 5 aread, areed, guess, pious 6 detect, devise, halsen, priest, sacred 7 blessed, foresee, godlike, portend, predict, presage 8 ariolate, contrive, forebode, foreknow, foretell, heavenly, immortal, minister, perceive 9 ambrosial, celestial, clergyman, religious 10 anticipate, conjecture, superhuman, theologian 12 supernatural
artificer: 8 tvashtar, tvashtri
being: 4 deva
communication: 6 oracle
favor: 5 grace
gift: 5 grace
messenger: 7 apostle
render: 5 deify
spirit: 5 numen
word: 5 logos
work: 7 theurgy
Divine Comedy author: 5 Dante
divinely inspired: 7 entheal 8 entheate
diviner: 4 seer 5 augur, sibyl 7 augurer, prophet 8 haruspex 10 soothsayer 11 clairvoyant 14 prognosticator
diving: 8 plunging 10 acrobatics, submerging
bird: auk 4 loon 5 grebe
hazard: 5 bends
divinity: See **god; goddess**
divisible: 9 dividable, separable
division: 4 chap, clan, dole, neat, part, rift 5 group, realm, share 6 canton, schism, sector 7 roulade, section 8 arpeggio, category, cleavage 9 Abteilung, allotment, concision, departure, partition 10 department 11 bifurcation, compartment, disjunction 13 apportionment, disconnection, dismemberment
between torrid and temperate zones: 6 tropic
house: 5 estre
into hundred: 12 centuriation
plant: 15 archichlamydeae
play: act 5 scene
poem: 5 canto
political: 4 city, ward 5 state 6 county, parish 7 borough 8 district
property: 9 gavelkind
religious: 6 schism
shield: 4 ente, paly
social: 5 caste, class, tribe 6 clique
time: day, eon 4 aeon, week, year 5 month 6 decade, minute, moment, second 7 weekend 9 fortnight
word: 8 syllable
divisional: 10 fractional, separative

divorce: 5 sever 6 sunder 7 asunder 8 dissolve, disunion, disunite, separate 10 separation 11 dissolution
Jewish law: get 4 gett
mill: 4 Reno
divot: 4 clod
divulge: 4 bare, show, tell 5 voice 6 bewray, impart, reveal, spread, unfold 7 publish, uncover 8 disclose, discover, evulgate, proclaim 9 eliminate 11 communicate
divvy: 5 share 6 divide 7 portion
Dixie Land: 5 South
dizen: 7 bedizen 9 overdress
dizzard: 4 fool 6 jester 9 blockhead
dizziness: 6 megrim 7 vertigo 9 giddiness
pert. to: 5 dinic 7 dinical
with headache: 10 scotodinia
dizzy: 4 dunt 5 crazy, giddy 6 fickle, stupid 7 foolish 8 swimming, unsteady 10 capricious 11 lightheaded, vertiginous
djebel: 4 hill
Dnieper tributary: Bug 4 Psel, Sula 5 Desna, Psiol
do: act 4 bilk, dost, make, suit 5 avail, cheat, guise, serve, trick 6 answer, render 7 achieve, execute, perform, produce, satisfy, suffice 8 transact 10 accomplish, administer
musical: ut
poetic: 5 didst
do away with: rid 4 kill 7 abolish, destroy 9 liquidate 11 discontinue
do in: 4 kill 6 defeat 7 destroy
do out of: 5 cheat 7 deceive
do-re-mi: 4 song 5 money
do up: 4 wrap
do well: 7 prosper
dobbin: 4 mare
docent: 7 teacher 8 lecturer
docile: 4 calm, meek, tame 6 gentle 7 ductile, dutiful 8 biddable 9 tractable 10 manageable
dock: cut 4 bang, clip, moor, pier, quay 5 basin, wharf 6 marina, strunt 7 bobtail, curtail, shorten 8 canaigre 9 perforate
post: 4 pile 7 bollard
ship's: 4 slip 5 basin, berth
worker: 9 stevedore
yard: 7 arsenal
doctor: 4 dose 5 sugar, treat 6 deacon, healer, intern 7 teacher 9 internist, physician 11 aesculapian
aide: 5 nurse
animal: vet 10 veterinary 12 veterinarian
oath of: 11 hippocratic
specialist: 6 aurist, goofer, intern 7 interne, oculist, surgeon 9 hippiater, otologist 10 podiatrist 11 chiropodist, neurologist, optometrist, orthopedist 12 chiropractor, gynecologist, obstetrician, orthodontist, orthopaedist, psychiatrist, proctologist 13 cranioscopist, gynaecologist 15 ophthalmologist
doctrine: ism 4 doxy, lear, rule 5 credo, creed, dogma, maxim, tenet 6 belief, gospel, theory 7 article, opinion, precept 8 position 9 principle 10 discipline
pert. to: 10 dogmatical 12 teleological
secret: 7 esotery
single principle: 6 henism, monism
specific: 6 cabala, heresy, malism, Mishna 7 egotism, Mishnah 8 fatalism, hedonism 10 agathology, pragmatism 13 monarchianism
spreader: 12 propagandist
document: 4 bill, book, deed, writ 5 chart, lease, paper, teach 6 billet, patent, school 7 archive, missive, precept, writing 8 contract, covenant, instruct, mortgage 9 indenture 10 manuscript 11 instruction
addition: 5 rider 7 codicil 9 amendment
file: 7 dossier
original record: 8 protocol
provisional: 5 scrip
receptacle: 7 hanaper
signed by all parties: 8 syngraph
true copy: 7 estreat
dod, dodd: lop 4 clip, poll
Dodecanese Island: Coo, Cos 4 Caso, Lero, Simi, Syme 5 Leros, Lipso, Lisso, Patmo, Tilos 6 Calchi, Calino, Lipsos, Nisiro, Patmos 7 Nisyros, Piscopi 9 Karpathos, Scarpanto, Stampalia 10 Astropalia
dodder: 5 shake 6 totter 7 tremble
doddering: old 5 inane 6 infirm, senile 7 foolish
dodge: 4 duck, jink, jouk, ruse 5 avoid, cheat, elude, evade, shift, trick 6 escape 7 deceive, evasion 8 artifice, gilenyie 9 expedient 10 equivocate
dodger: 7 haggler 8 handbill 10 corndodger 13 advertisement
corn: 4 pone
doe: roe, teg 4 faun, hind 6 female
doer: 5 actor, agent, maker 6 author, factor, feasor 7 facient, manager 8 attorney, executor 9 performer
suffix: er, or; ast, eer, ier, ist 4 ator, euse, ster
does: 4 doth
doff: off 4 daff, vail 5 avale, douse, dowse, strip 6 divest, remove 7 undress
dog: cur, mut, pug, pup, yap 4 mutt, pawl, tike, tyke 5 canis(L.), pooch, puppy, whelp 6 bowwow, buffer, canine, detent, yapper 7 mongrel, yapster 9 carnivore
African: 7 basenji
Australian: 5 dingo
breed: pug 4 Dane 5 boxer, hound, Husky, pelon, sauki, spitz 6 Afghan, basset, bea-

gle, borzoi, Briard, collie, Eskimo, gun dog, poodle, setter, Sussex 7 Basenji, bulldog, griffon, harrier, Maltese, mastiff, Mexican, owtchar, pincher, pointer, Scottie, sleughi, spaniel, starter, terrier, whippet 8 Airedale, Alsatian, Aleutant, chow chow, coach dog, Doberman, elkhound, Flanders, foxhound, labrador, landseer, Malemute, Malinois, papillon, Pekinese, Pyrenees, Samoyede, Sealyham, shepherd, springer 9 boarhound, Brabancon, Chihuahua, dachshund, Dalmation, deerhound, Great Dane, greyhound, kerry blue, police dog, retriever, St. Bernard, schnauzer, shorthair, wolfhound, wolf spitz, Yorkshire 10 Bedlington, bloodhound, Boston bull, fox terrier, Manchester, otter hound, Pomeranian, Rottweiler, schipperke, toy terrier, weimaraner, wire-haired 11 bull terrier, Groenendael, ruby spaniel, Skye terrier 12 cairn terrier, field spaniel, gazelle hound, Gordon setter, gossett hound, Newfoundland, water spaniel, Welsh terrier 13 Boston terrier, Chesapeake Bay, cocker spaniel, Great Pyrenees, Prince Charles, yankee terrier 14 Chinese crested, clumber spaniel, highland collie, Tibetan spaniel 15 Brussels griffon, highland terrier, Riesenschnauzer 17 Bouvier de Flandres

close-haired: pug 5 boxer

Eskimo: 5 husky 7 samoyed 8 Malemute, samoyede

famous: 4 Asta, Fala, King, Tige, Toby 5 Devil 6 Feller, Lassie 8 Checkers 9 Rin-tin-tin 11 Strongheart

F.D.R.'s: 4 Fala

fox-like: 6 colpeo

genus: 5 canis

German origin: 5 boxer 8 Doberman 9 Drahthaar 10 Weimaraner

hauling: 5 husky 7 samoyed 8 Malemute, samoyede 9 Dalmatian

house: 6 kennel

howling of: 9 ululation

hunting: 4 alan, rach 5 aland, alant, hound, rache, ratch, toler 6 basset, borzoi, beagle, saluki, setter, talbot 7 courser, harrier, pointer 8 Elkhound 9 retriever, wolfhound 10 bloodhound

iron: 7 firedog

large: 4 alan, Dane 5 boxer, bawty 6 briard, bawtie, collie, police 7 mastiff 12 Newfoundland

long-haired: 4 alco, chow 7 spaniel

multi-headed: 8 cerberus

Orphan Annie's: 5 Sandy

pack: 8 canaglia, canaille

reward: 6 hallow

small: Pom, pug, pup 4 alco, fist, purp 5 ascob, foist 6 messan, messin 7 spaniel 8 Pekinese 9 chihuahua, Pekingese 10 Pomeranian

underworld: 8 Cerberus

upper lip: 5 flews

Welsh: 8 Sealyham

wild: 5 adjag, dhole, dingo 6 jackal 7 agouara 8 cimarron

dog days: 8 canicule

dog-like: 13 cynocephalous

dog rose: 5 bucky 6 canker 9 eglantine

fruit: hip

dog salmon: 4 keta

dog star: 4 sept, sopt 6 sirius

dogboat: pig

dogcart: 6 tumtum 7 bounder 8 gadabout

dogfish: hoe 4 huss, tope 9 roussette

dogged: 6 sullen 7 doggish, doglike 9 malicious, obstinate, tenacious 10 determined 12 pertinacious

doggerel: 6 trivia 9 burlesque

doggery: 7 barroom 8 grogshop

doggish: 5 sulky 7 currish, cynical, stylish 8 snapping

dogie: 5 stray

dogma: 5 creed, tenet 6 dictum 8 doctrine, document

pert. to: 9 levitical

dogmatic: 9 assertive, confident, pragmatic 10 intolerant, peremptory 11 affirmative, dictatorial, magisterial, opinionated, pragmatical

saying: 6 dictum 8 levitism

dogmatism: 10 positivism, pragmatism 11 intolerance 13 pontificality

Dogpatch depicter: 4 Capp

dogs: 4 feet

dogwood: 5 osier, sumac 6 cornel, cornus

flowering: 7 boxwood

genus: 6 cornus

doily: mat 6 napkin

doing: act 4 deed, stir 5 event 6 action 8 function

doings: ado 6 hustle 8 activity

doldrum: 5 dumps, ennui 6 tedium 7 dullard 8 confused, dullness 10 depression 12 listlessness

dole: lot 4 alms, deal, gift, goal, mete, part 5 allot, fraud, grief, guile, mourn, share 6 deceit, grieve, relief, sorrow 7 charity, dealing, destiny, handout, payment, portion 8 boundary, dispense, division, gratuity, landmark, pittance 9 allotment, apportion 10 distribute, misfortune 12 distribution

doleful: sad 5 drear, heavy 6 dismal, dreary, funest, rueful 7 flebile 8 dolesome, dolorous, mournful 9 sorrowful 10 lugubrious, melancholy

dolent: 9 sorrowful

dolente: 9 plaintive

dolesome: 6 dismal, gloomy 7 doleful 9 sorrowful

doll: toy 4 babe, baby 5 array, puppe(G.) 6 maumet, moppet, muneca(Sp.), poupee(F.), puppet 8 mistress 9 golliwogg 10 sweetheart

doll up: 5 adorn, dress

dollar: 4 bean, buck 5 berry, eagle 8 frogskin, simoleon

Doll's House heroine: 4 Nora

dolly: car 4 cart, doll, drab, tray 5 truck 7 carrier 8 mistress, slattern 10 sweetheart

dolor, dolour: 5 calor, grief 6 sorrow 7 anguish, sadness 8 distress, mourning 11 lamentation

dolorous: sad 6 dismal 7 doleful 8 grievous 9 sorrowful

dolphin, delphin: 4 fish, inia 6 dorado 8 porpoise 9 goosebeak 10 bottlenose

river: 5 bouto

dolt: ass, oaf 4 asse, calf, chub, clod, coof, dult, fool, moke 5 chump, dummy, dunce, idiot 6 befool, cudden, doodle 7 bluntie(Sc.), dawcock, dullard, half-wit 8 bosthoon, clodpate, imbecile, mooncalf, numskull 9 blockhead, ignoramus, simpleton 10 dunderhead

doltish: 4 dull 6 stupid 7 foolish, sottish 8 blockish, doltlike 11 thickheaded

domain: 5 bound, bourn, realm, scope, state, world 6 barony, bourne, empery, empire, estate 7 demesne 8 dominion, province 9 bailiwick 12 commonwealth

Dombey and Son: 6 Cuttle

dome: cap 4 cima 6 cupola 7 calotte, edifice

domed: 7 vaulted

domestic: 4 hind, maid 5 domal 6 hameil, hamelt, hamilt, homely, homish, housal, inland, inmate, native 7 servant 8 homebred, homemade, intimate 9 enchorial, home-grown

establishment: 6 menage

domesticate: 4 tame 6 entame 7 amenage, reclaim 8 civilize 10 naturalize 11 domiciliate

domicile: 4 home 5 abode, house 6 menage 8 dwelling 9 residence 10 habitation

identification: 9 doorplate

dominant: 5 bossy, chief 6 ruling 7 central, regnant, supreme 8 superior 9 ascendant, imperious, paramount, prevalent, principal 10 commanding, pre-eminent, prevailing 11 outweighing, predominant 12 preponderant 13 overbalancing

dominate: 4 rule 5 reign 6 govern 7 control 8 domineer 11 predominate

domination: 7 control 8 dominion 9 supremacy 10 ascendancy, ascendency 11 sovereignty 12 predominance 14 possessiveness

domine: 4 Lord, rule 6 master 9 clergyman 11 predominate

domineer: 4 boss, lord, rule 5 bully, feast, revel, tower 7 command, swagger 8 dominate, overlord 11 predominate

domineering: 6 lordly 7 haughty 8 arrogant, masterly 9 imperious, masterful 10 tyrannical 11 dictatorial, magisterial, overbearing

Dominican: 9 predicant

dominie: 6 pastor 9 pedagogue 12 schoolmaster

dominion: 4 rule, sway 5 realm, reign 6 domain, empire 7 control, dynasty, poustie, regency 9 authority, hierarchy, ownership, supremacy 10 ascendancy, ascendency, domination 11 sovereignty 12 jurisdiction

church: 11 sacerdotium

joint: 11 condominium

domino: die 4 mask

dominoes: 4 game 5 bones 7 ivories

dompt: cow 5 daunt 6 subdue

domus: 4 home 5 house

don: 4 wear 5 array, dress 6 assume, clothe, invest 8 nobleman 9 gentleman, professor 10 instructor

Don Juan's mother: 4 Inez

Don Quixote: *companion:* 11 Sancho Panza

steed: 9 Rosinante, Rozinante

Donar: 4 Thor

donate: gie(Sc.) 4 give 6 bestow 7 present 10 contribute

donatio: 4 gift 8 donation

donation: 4 gift 5 grant 7 donatio, present 10 foundation 11 benefaction 12 contribution

done: 4 over 5 baked, ended 6 cooked 7 through 8 finished 9 completed, exhausted 12 accomplished

donee: 7 heritor 8 receiver 9 recipient 11 beneficiary

donkey: ass 4 moke 5 burro, cuddy, dicky, neddy 6 dickey, onager 7 bussock, fussock 9 quadruped

comb. form: ono

cry: 4 bray 6 heehaw

donkey engine: 6 yarder

donna: 4 lady, wife 5 madam, woman 8 mistress

donor: 4 give 5 giver 10 benefactor 11 contributor 14 philanthropist
donsie: 6 ailing 7 sickish 9 squeamish
doodle: 4 dolt, draw 5 cheat 7 cartoon, trifler
doodlesack: 7 bagpipe
doodling: 9 scrolling
doohickey: 6 device, gadget 11 contrivance
doolee: 6 litter
doom: law, lot 4 damn, fate, ruin 5 death 6 decree, devote, steven 7 condemn, destine, destiny, fortune, statute 8 decision, sentence 9 destinate, enactment, judgement, ordinance 10 adjudicate, predestine 11 destruction, discernment 12 condemnation 13 righteousness
doomed: fey 5 fatal 8 accursed 9 sentenced
door: 4 gate 5 hatch 6 portal 7 barrier, doorway, opening, passage, postern 11 entranceway
back: 7 postern
cross piece: 6 lintel
fastener: bar 4 bolt, hasp, lock 5 catch 8 fastener
frame: 4 jamb
holder: 5 hinge
holy: 11 amphithyron
part: 4 jamb, knob, risp 5 panel 6 alette, lintel
storm: 6 dingle
trap: 4 drop
way: 4 exit 8 entrance
doorkeeper: 5 tiler, usher 6 durwan, porter, warden 7 durwaun, janitor, ostiary 8 huissier, janitrix 9 concierge(F.), janitress, ostiarius
doorknocker: 6 hammer, rapper
doorlatch: 8 haggaday
doormat: rug 8 weakling
doorpost: 4 durn, jamb 6 alette
doorway: 4 door, exit 6 portal 7 opening 11 entranceway
dope: hop 4 drug 5 opium, paste 6 heroin, opiate 7 predict, stupefy 8 narcotic 9 marijuana 13 nitroglycerin
doped: 10 narcotized, prophesied
dopester: 4 tout 6 touter 7 tipster
doppelganger: 6 double, spirit, wraith 10 apparition 11 counterpart
dor, dorr: bee 4 joke, mock 5 joker, scoff, trick 6 beetle 7 buffoon, deceive, mockery 9 deception 11 drumbledore
dorbel: 6 pedant
dorcas: 7 gazelle
dorian: 6 simple
Dorian festival: 6 Carnea 7 Carneia
doric: 6 rustic
Doric: *frieze bottom:* 6 taenia
frieze slab: 6 metope
Doris' king: 8 Aegimius
dormancy: 6 torpor 8 abeyance 10 quiescence
dormant: 5 fixed 6 asleep, latent, torpid 7 resting, sleeper 8 dormient, inactive, sleeping 9 quiescent, unaroused 10 stationary
dormer: 6 window 7 lucarne
dormeuse: 4 seat 5 coach 8 carriage, nightcap
dormient: 7 dormant 8 sleeping
dormitory: 4 dorm 5 house 8 quarters
monastery: 6 dorter 7 dortour
dormouse: 4 loir 5 lerot
pert. to: 7 myoxine
dornick: 5 linen
dorp: 4 city, town 5 thorp 6 hamlet, thorpe 7 village 8 township
dorsal: 5 notal 6 dorsel, dorser, dosser, tergal 7 hanging 9 posterior
opposed to: 7 ventral
pert. to: 5 notal 6 tergal
dorsum: 4 back
dorty: 5 saucy, sulky 7 haughty
dose: 4 bole 5 draft, treat 6 doctor, drench, potion 7 draught 8 quantity
doss: 4 tuft
dosseret: 6 abacus
dossil: 4 tent 6 spigot 7 pledget
dot: 4 clot, lump, mote, peck 5 dowry, point, speck 6 period 7 speckle, stipple 8 particle, sprinkle 9 bespangle 10 besprinkle, distribute
over the letter i: 6 tittle
dotage: 4 dote 5 folly 6 drivel 8 senility 10 feebleness, imbecility
dotard: 5 silly 6 senile 8 imbecile
dote: rot 4 dove, doze, love 5 adore, decay, endow 6 bestow, dotage, dotard, drivel, stupor 8 imbecile
doting: 4 fond
dotish,, doatish: 4 weak 7 foolish 8 imbecile
dotted: 7 spotted 8 speckled, stippled 9 scattered 11 distributed, diversified
dotterel: 4 dupe, gull, wind 6 plover 7 morinel
dottle: 4 fool, plug 5 silly 6 dotard
dotty: 5 crazy 6 feeble, spotty
doty: 10 discolored
Douay Bible: 4 Aree
double: ply 4 dual, fold, twin 5 duple, fetch 6 bifold, binary, binate, duplex 7 twofold 8 geminate 9 ambiguous, duplicate 11 counterpart
prefix: di
double dagger: 6 diesis
double dealing: 6 deceit
double-edged: 9 ancipital
double-hue: 7 bicolor

doublecross: 5 cheat 6 betray 7 deceive, swindle 9 treachery
doublecrosser: rat
doubled: 5 gemel
doublet: 9 pourpoint
doubling: 4 loop
doubloon: 4 coin, onza
doubly: 5 twice
doubt: 4 fear 5 demur, dread, query, waver 7 dubiate, scruple, suspect 8 distrust, dubitate, hesitate, mistrust, question 9 discredit, misgiving, suspicion 10 diffidence, disbelieve, indecision 11 uncertainty 12 apprehension
doubter: 5 cynic 7 skeptic 10 unbeliever
doubtful: 7 dubious, fearful, perhaps 8 dreadful, perilous, wavering 9 ambiguous, dangerous, diffident, equivocal, uncertain, undecided 10 apocryphal, hesitating, irresolute, suspicious 11 distrustful, vacillating 12 apprehensive, questionable, undetermined 13 problematical
doubtfulness: 9 ambiguity
douce: 4 neat, tidy 5 sober, sweet 6 genial, modest, sedate 7 prudent 8 cheerful, pleasant 10 hospitable
douceur: 5 bonus 9 pourboire
dough: 4 cash, duff 5 money, paste 6 noodle, sponge 7 brioche
doughnut: 6 cymbal, sinker 7 cruller, olycook, olykoek, simball 9 freidcake
doughty: 4 fell 7 valiant 8 intrepid
dour: 4 glum, grim, hard, sour 5 rough, stern 6 gloomy, morose, severe, strong, sullen 7 ominous 9 obstinate 10 inflexible
douse, dowse: 4 beat, blow, doff, duck, quit, stow 5 cease, rinse, souse 6 drench, plunge, strike, stroke 7 immerse 8 downpour 9 drenching 10 extinguish
douzepers: 4 Ivon, Oton 5 Ivory, Gerin, Ogier, peers 6 Anseis, Gerier, nobles, Oliver, Roland, Samson, Turpin 7 knights 8 Engelier, paladins 9 Berengier 17 Gerard de Rousillon
dove: 4 doze 5 color 6 culver, cushat, pigeon 7 namaqua, slumber
home: 4 cote
pert. to: 9 columbine
sound: 4 curr
young: 8 doveling
dovecot, dovecote: 9 columbary 11 columbarium
dovekey, dovekie: auk 4 alle 5 rotch, rotge 6 rotche 8 dovelike 9 guillemot
dovelike: 4 pure 6 dovish, gentle 7 lovable 9 columbine
dover: 4 doze, stun 6 drowse
dovetail: 5 tenon
dovish: 8 dovelike, harmless, innocent
dow: 4 dull, fade 5 avail, befit, endow 6 thrive 7 behoove, prosper
dowd: 5 frump
dowdy: 4 poky 5 frump, pokey 6 blowzy, shabby, untidy 8 slovenly 10 slatternly
dowel: peg, pin 4 coak 6 pintle
dower: dos 5 dowry, endow 7 portion 9 endowment
dowitcher: 5 snipe
down: 4 dowl, fell, flix, flue, fuzz, hill, lint 5 below, dowle, floor, fluff 6 bedown 7 hillock, plumage 9 overthrow
comb. form: bas(F.) 4 cata(Gr.)
poetic: 5 adown
prefix: de
down at the heel: 5 seamy, seedy
down in the mouth: 4 glum 7 unhappy 9 depressed 11 discouraged
down under: 8 Tasmania 9 antipodes, Australia 10 New Zealand
down wind: 7 leeward
down with: 4 a bas
downcast: sad 6 abject, gloomy 8 hopeless 9 depressed 10 despondent, dispirited, melancholy 11 discouraged 12 disheartened
downfall: pit 4 fate, ruin, trap 5 abyss 7 descent, undoing 8 collapse 9 precipice, ruination 11 destruction, ecroulement 12 degringolade
heavy: 7 torrent
downhearted: 8 dejected 9 depressed 10 melancholy
downpour: 4 pour, rain 5 douse, dowse, spill 7 torrent
downright: 4 flat, pure, rank 5 blank, blunt, plain, plumb, sheer, stark 6 arrant, direct 8 absolute, even-down, positive, thorough 10 completely, forthright, thoroughly 11 straightway 13 perpendicular, unceremonious 15 perpendicularly
downstairs: 5 below
downward: 5 below, lower 11 netherwards
poetic: 5 adown
slope: 9 declivity
downy: 4 soft 5 mossy, nappy, pilar, quiet 6 fluffy, placid 7 cunning, knowing 8 soothing
dowry: dos, dot 4 gift 5 dower 6 talent 7 portion 9 endowment
pert. to: 5 dotal
doxology: 13 glorification
doxy: ism 5 wench 6 harlot 7 opinion 8 doctrine
doyen: 4 dean
doze: nap, nod, rot 4 dote, dove 5 decay, dover, sleep, sloom 6 catnap, drowse, muddle, snooze 7 perplex, slumber, snoozle, stupefy
drab: box, daw 4 dell, drug, dull 5 besom, dolly, graze, wench, whore 6 malkin, poi-

son 7 prosaic 9 colorless 10 monotonous, prostitute 13 uninteresting
drachma: 4 coin, dram
one-sixth: 4 obol
draconian: 5 cruel 6 severe
Dracula: 5 demon, devil 7 vampire
home: 4 Bran 6 Risnov 9 Hunedoara
draff: 4 lees 5 dregs, drink 6 refuse 7 hogwash
draft: nip, sip 4 dose, dram, gust, levy, plan, swig, toot 5 drink, epure, swipe 6 drench, godown, minute, potion, redact, scroll, sketch, waucht, waught 7 drawing, outline, pattern, project 8 beverage, potation, protocol 9 conscript
draftsman, draughtsman: 6 drawer 7 tippler 9 architect
drag: lug, tow, tug 4 draw, hale, harl, haul, pull, snig, tear, tump 5 brake, drawl, rally, tease, trail, trawl 6 linger, school, taigle 7 grapnel
out: 6 elicit, extend 8 protract
through mud: 7 bemire
dragnet: 5 trawl 7 trainel
dragoman: 5 agent, guide 11 interpreter
dragon: 7 monster 8 basilisk
Biblical: 5 Rahab
biting: 8 tarragon
Chinese: 5 lung
Norse: 6 Fafner, Fafnir
Vedic: Ahi
dragonfly order: 8 odonata
dragoon: 10 cavalry-man, carabineer, carabinier
drain: dry, gaw, sap 4 delf, gout, grip, gurt, lade, milk, sike, sink 5 bunny, canal, delft, dreen, empty, fleet, gully, rhine(dial.), sewer, silver 6 filter, furrow, guzzle, siphon, syphon, trench, zanjon 7 acequia, alberca, channel, deplete, exhaust, grindle, gripple, zanjona 8 thurrock 9 undermine 11 watercourse
arched: 7 culvert
blood: 12 exsanguinate
forces: 5 spend
drainage: 4 adit
area: 5 basin
drainpipe: 6 leader
dram: nip 4 mite, slug 5 draft, drink 6 drachm 7 snifter 8 potation, quantity 11 indifferent
drama: 4 mime, play 5 opera 6 comedy 7 atellan, history, theater, tragedy 8 operetta, pastoral 9 pantomime 11 composition
court: 5 trial
division: act 5 scene
for single actor: 8 monodram
main act: 8 epitasis
part: 4 role
short: 4 skit 7 saynete
spectacular: 12 extravaganza
third most important actor: 11 tritagonist
dramatic: 4 wild 5 vivid 6 scenic 10 theatrical 12 melodramatic
expression system: 8 delsarte
representation: 13 impersonation
dramatist: 5 actor 10 playwright
drank: See **drink**
drape: 4 hang 5 adorn, cover, weave 7 curtain, hanging, valance
drapeau: 4 flag 8 standard
draper: 6 tailor
drapery: 5 baize, cloth 7 curtain, valance 8 mourning
drapet: 5 cloth 8 covering
drastic: 4 dire 5 harsh 7 extreme, radical 8 rigorous
drasty: 4 vile 9 worthless
draught: See **draft**
Dravidian (see also **India**): 4 Gond, Kota, Toda, Tulu 5 Arava, Gondi, Khond, Malto, Oraon, Tamil 6 Andhra, Brahui, Kodagu, Kurukh, Telegu, Telugu 8 Kanarese 9 Malayalam
demon: 4 bhut
tribe: 6 Badaga 7 Colleri, Collery 9 Colleries
draw: lug, tie, tow, tug 4 drag, duct, hale, haul, lade, limn, lure, pull 5 catch, educe, train 6 allure, deduce, depict, derive, design, elicit, entice, induce, inhale, select, sketch 7 attract, detract, extract, inspire, portray 8 inveigle 9 delineate, reproduce, statement
again: 5 remap 6 replat
away from: 6 shrink
back: 4 fawn 5 wince 6 cringe, rebate, recede, recoil, resile, retire, shrink 7 retract, retreat 9 deduction, hindrance
close: 4 near 5 steal 8 approach
finely: 4 etch
forth: tug 4 pull 5 educe 6 derive, elicit
near: hie 4 near 5 coast 8 approach
off: sap 5 drain 6 siphon, syphon 7 extract 8 abstract, withdraw
out: 4 lade, pump 5 educe 6 elicit, exhale 7 extract, tweezer 8 protract 9 exantlate 11 interrogate 12 cross examine
tight: 4 frap, furl, lace 5 brace, cinch 7 stretch
together: 4 coul, frap 8 assemble
draw game: 9 stalemate
drawer: 4 till
drawers: 5 pants 7 panties 9 shintiyan
chest of: 7 commode
drawing: 5 draft, envol, epure 7 hauling, pulling 8 traction 9 attrahent 10 attracting, extracting 11 delineation, centripetal

absent-minded: 8 doodling

exaggerated: 7 cartoon 10 caricature

instrument: 9 eidograph 10 pantograph

drawing room: 5 salon 6 parlor, saloon

drawl: 5 drant, drunt 6 draunt, loiter

drawlatch: lag 6 dawdle 11 latchstring 12 eavesdropper

drawn: 7 haggard

drawstring: 5 latch

dray: 4 cart 5 wagon 6 camion 7 go-devil

drayage: 7 cartage, haulage

drayman: 6 carter 7 carrier, remover, wagoner

dread: awe 4 fear, fray 5 awful, doubt 6 adread, agrise, dismay, eschew, horror, terror 7 anxiety, dismiss 8 affright, dreddour, terrible 9 reverence 12 apprehension

object of: 4 bogy 5 bogey, bogie 7 bugaboo, bugbear

dread of: See **fear**

dreaded: 7 awesome

dreadful: 4 dire 5 awful 6 grisly, horrid 7 careful, direful, fearful, ghastly, grimful, hideous 8 doubtful, ghastful, horrible, shocking, terrible, terrific 9 frightful 10 formidable

dreadnaught, dreadnought: 4 tank 7 warship 8 fearless 10 battleship

dream: 4 muse, reve(F.) 5 fancy 6 sweven, vision 7 fantasy, imagine, reverie, romance 8 phantasm 9 nightmare 10 apparition

god of: 8 Morpheus

interpretation: 13 oneirocritics 15 oneirocriticism

pert. to: 7 oneiric, somnial 9 oneirotic

dreamed: 7 fancied 8 visioned

dreamer: 4 poet 7 fantast 8 idealist 9 visionary 10 ideologist

dreaminess: 7 languor

dreamy: kef 4 soft 5 vague 6 poetic 7 faraway, languid, pensive 8 fanciful, soothing 9 visionary 11 imaginative

drear: 4 dern 5 gloom 6 dismal, gloomy 7 doleful, sadness 9 sorrowful 10 melancholy

dreary: sad 4 dire, dree, dull, flat 5 bleak, cruel, ourie 6 dismal, elenge, gloomy, gousty, lonely 7 doleful, goustie, howling, wilsome 8 grievous 9 cheerless, sorrowful 10 depressing, monotonous 11 distressful

dredge: mop 4 sift 5 scoop 6 deepen 8 excavate, springle 9 sweetmeat

dredger: 6 duster 9 sprinkler

dree: 4 dull, slow 5 grief 6 dismal, dreary, endure, suffer 7 tedious 9 suffering 10 persistent

dregs: 4 crap, faex, lees 5 draff, dross, feces, grout, magma 6 bottom, dunder, faeces, refuse 7 grounds, grummel, residue 8 grummels, remnants, sediment, settling 9 excrement, feculence 10 subsidence 12 crassamentum

drench: 4 dose, hose, sind, sink, soak 5 douse, dowse, draft, drink, drouk, drown, souse, steep 6 bucket, douche, imbrue, potion 7 immerse 8 permeate, saturate, submerge

drenched: wet 4 asop 6 soaked

dress (see also **garment, gown, robe, vestment**): don, dub, fig, ray, rig, tog 4 be-go, busk, buss, deck, garb, gear, gown, hone, knap, mill, rail, robe, suit, tire, trim, wear 5 adorn, array, curry, dight, equip, frock, guise, habit, magma, preen, primp, prink, prune 6 attire, broach, clothe, enrobe, fangle, fettle, graith, invest, outfit, revest, toilet 7 affaite, apparel, bandage, clothes, costume, garment, garnish, raiment, toggery, vesture 8 cleading, clothing, decorate, ornament, vestment 9 embellish, equipment, vestiture 10 garmenture, habiliment, habilitate, investment 12 accouterment, accoutrement

clerical: 5 cloth

cloth: 4 burl

court: 4 robe

feathers: 5 preen

flax: ted 5 dizen

gaudily: 5 primp, prink 6 dizene 7 bedizen

in full armor: 7 panoply

informal: 6 shorts, slacks 8 negligee 9 bluejeans

kind of: alb 4 huke 5 crape, crepe, ephod, get-up, mufti, tails, tenue, tunic, weeds 6 dirndl, finery, gaiter, kirtle, livery, tuxedo 7 regalia 8 lava-lava, negligee, peignoir 9 canonical, decollete, polonaise

leather: tan, taw, tew 5 curry

mean: 4 rags

odd: rig 5 getup

ornament: 4 frog, lace 5 jabot, ruche 6 sequin, zequin 7 ruching 8 chequeen, zecchino 10 embroidery

riding: 5 habit 8 breeches, jodhpurs

stone: nig 5 nidge, spall 7 scabble

surgically: 5 dight

trimming: 4 gimp, lace 5 braid

dress up: tog 5 preen, primp, prink

dressed: 4 clad 5 bound 7 habited

well: 4 braw 5 smart 7 dallack, stylish 9 spruced-up

dresser: 5 rober 6 bureau 7 modiste 8 cupboard 9 appreteur 10 escritoire

leather: 7 currier 8 levanter

scrupulous: 4 dude 7 preener 11 Beau Brummel

dressing: 7 beating 8 scolding 11 castigation

kind of: 4 lint 5 salve 7 pledget 8 ointment, remolade
dressing room: 7 camarin
dressing stone: 9 scotching
dressmaker: 5 sewer 6 seamer 7 modiste 8 stitcher 9 couturier 10 couturiere, seamstress
model: 7 manikin 8 mannikin 9 mannequin
dretch: 5 delay 6 dawdle 7 trouble
drew (see also **draw**): 8 eelgrass
dribble: 4 drip, drop
driblet: 5 piece
dried: See **dry**
dried out: 5 stale 6 effete
drift: sag 4 dene, dune, ford, herd, plot, tide, till 5 drove, fleet, float, flock, tenor, trend 6 broach, course, design, device, scheme, tunnel 7 impetus, impulse, pasture, purport 8 tendency 9 deviation 10 propulsion
along: 4 tide 5 float
sidewise: 4 crab 8 crescent
driftage: 7 flatsam 8 wreckage
drill: gad, sow, tap 4 bore, spud 5 auger, borer, churn, decoy, train, tutor, twirl, whirl 6 allure, entice, furrow, pierce, school, seeder, stoper 7 channel 8 exercise, instruct, practice 9 perforate
drilled: 9 practiced
drilling: 5 denim
drink (see also **beverage**): bib, bum, lap, peg, rum, sip, tea 4 dram, grog, horn, lush, mead, shot, slug, soak, swig, tiff, toot, tope 5 bever, booze, bouse, draft, julep, morat, punch, quaff, skink, sniff, snort, souse, toast, toddy, vodka 6 absorb, bezzle, bracer, chaser, coffee, drench, godown, guzzle, hooker, imbibe, potion, ptisan, swinge, tipple 7 diluent, draught, snifter, swallow 8 beverage, cocktail, highball, potation, refresco 9 decoction 10 intoxicant
alcoholic: ade, ale, gin, hum, rye 4 beer, beno, bosa, boza, chia, flip, mead, nipa, nogg, soma, swig 5 airah, bombo, bozah, bubud, bumbo, julep, lager, negus, posca, sling, vodka, zombi 6 brandy, casiri, caudle, fuddle, mescal, posset, rickey, zombie, 7 cobbler, guarapo, sidecar 8 aperitif, rumbarge, sangaree, tequilla 9 cointreau, ship belly 10 tangle-foot 13 whistle-belley
carbonated: fiz, pop 4 fizz, soda 9 gingerade, gingerale
Christmas: nog 7 wassail
farinaceous: 6 ptisan
frozen: 6 frappe
fruit: ade 5 assai, bland, julep, morat 6 rickey 7 ratafee, ratafia
honey: 4 mead 5 morat
hot: tod 5 cocoa, copus, negus, toddy 6 caudle
magic: 8 nepenthe
mixer of: 6 barman 9 barkeeper, bartender
molasses and vinegar: 6 swanky
money for: 8 bonamano 9 pourboire
much: 4 swig, tope 5 bouse, quaff, swill 6 waucht, waught 7 carouse
of gods: 6 nectar
Oriental: 4 sake
portion: 4 shot 5 ounce 6 dollop, jigger
Russian: 5 vodka
sassafras: 6 saloop
small: hum, nip, peg, tot 4 bull, dram, pony, shot 5 sniff, snort, tabor 6 chaser 7 diluent snifter
sweet: 6 nectar
Tatar: 6 kumiss
drinkable: 7 potable
drinker: sot 5 toper 6 bender 7 imbiber, intaker, quaffer 8 drunkard 9 inebriate
drinking: 5 bever 6 guzzle 8 carousal 10 poculation
bout: 4 orgy 5 binge, spree 6 fuddle, shindy, splore 7 gaedown, wassail 8 carousal, potation 11 downsitting
horn: 6 rhyton
salutation: 5 skoal 6 prosit
vessel: cup, mug 4 bowl, tass 5 glass, gourd, hanap, jorum, stein, stoop, stoup 6 beaker, cappie, dipper, goblet, noggin, patera, rumkin 7 bombard, canikin, hanaper, tankard 8 cannikin, schooner
drip: sie, sye 4 drop, leak, sile 5 eaves 7 dribble, dripple, trickle
frozen: 6 icicle
drive: cot 4 bang, bear, butt, cram, ding, goad, hunt, ride, send, spur, urge 5 chase, co-act, crowd, feeze, force, hurry, impel, infer, press, repel, roust, shove, sweep 6 attack, beetle, bensel, compel, cudgel, deduce, derive, hasten, plunge, propel 7 overtax 9 constrain
away: 5 chase, repel 6 banish, dispel 7 repulse
down: 4 tamp
frantic: 7 bedevil
out: 4 rout 5 exile, expel 9 eradicate
public: 9 esplanade
drive-in: 7 open-air 10 restaurant
drivel: 4 dote 5 drool 6 dotage, drudge, footle, menial, slaver 7 twaddle 8 nonsense
driveler: 4 fool 5 doter
driver: 4 jenu 5 drabi 6 cabman, caller, drover, jarvey, mallet 7 catcher, spanker, speeder 8 coachman, engineer, galloway, overseer, teamster 9 chauffeur, izvozchik, propeller 10 charioteer, taskmaster
of golden chariot: 6 Helios
drizzle: deg, mug 4 dank, haze, ling, rain, smur 5 misle, smurr 6 mizzle 8 sprinkle

drole: 7 buffoon
droll: odd 5 comic, drole, funny, merry, queer 6 jester, jocose 7 amusing, buffoon, comical, jocular, strange, waggish 8 farcical, humorous 9 burlesque, diverting, laughable, ludicrous, whimsical 10 ridiculous
drollery: wit 4 jest 5 farce, humor 10 buffoonery
drome: 6 ployer 7 airport
dromedary: 5 camel, delul 7 camelus, dromond
dromond: 7 warship
drone: bee, bum, hum 4 drum, slug 5 drant, idler, snail 6 bumble, draunt, lubber 7 bagpipe, humming, shirker, sleeper, speaker 8 loiterer, sluggard 9 bombilate
dronish: 4 slow 8 indolent, sluggish
drool: 6 drivel, slaver 7 slobber
droop: fag, lob, lop, sag 4 bend, drop, flag, hang, loll, pine, sink, wilt 5 daver, heald, hield 6 bangle, dangle, nutate, slouch 7 decline, flitter 8 languish
drooping: lop 4 limp 6 fluggy, nutant 7 nodding
of eyelid: 6 ptosis
on one side: 4 alop
drop: dap, sie, sye 4 bead, bede, blob, drib, drip, fall, gout, omit, shed, sile, sink, stop 5 droop, lower, minim, plump, plunk, slump 6 drappy, plunge 7 abandon, curtain, descent, dismiss, drappie, dribble, forsake, globule, guttula, guttule, plummet, release 8 decrease, quantity 10 relinquish 11 discontinue
lachrymal: 4 tear
syllable: 5 elide 7 elision
drop in: 5 enter 6 arrive 8 surprise
drop off: nap 4 doze 5 sleep 8 decrease
droplet: 7 globule
dropped: 6 fallen
dropper: 7 pipette
dropsical: 5 puffy 6 edemic 8 hydropic
dropsy: 5 edema
dross: 4 lees, scum, slag 5 chaff, dregs, sprue, waste 6 garble, refuse, scoria, scruff, sinter 7 cinders, leaving 9 recrement
iron: 6 sinter
drossel: 4 slut 5 hussy 6 drazel, drazil 9 dratchell
drought, drouth: 4 soka 6 thirst 7 aridity, dryness
drought plant: 9 xerophyte
drouk: 4 soak 6 drench 9 overwhelm
drove (see also **drive**): mob 4 sent 5 atajo, crowd, drift, flock 6 manada 7 disturb, trouble 8 driftway 10 assemblage
drover: 6 dealer, driver 8 herdsman
drovy, druvy: 5 muddy 6 filthy, turbid
drown: 6 drench 8 inundate
drowse: nod 4 doze 5 dover, sleep 6 snooze 7 slumber
drowsiness: 8 dullness 9 oscitance, oscitancy 10 sleepiness 12 sluggishness
drowsy: 4 dull, logy 5 noddy 6 sleepy, stupid, supine 7 lulling 8 comatose, oscitant, sluggish 9 somnolent, soporific 11 heavy-headed
drub: tap 4 bang, beat, blow, drum 5 array, curry, stamp, thump 6 cudgel, thrash 7 belabor, shellac 8 belabour, shellack
drubbing: 9 thrashing
drubly: 5 muddy 6 turbid 8 troubled
drudge: fag 4 grub, moil, plod, toil 5 grind, scrub, slave 6 digger, drivel, endure, slavey, suffer 7 hackney, plodder, slavery
literary: 4 hack 5 devil
drudgery: 4 moil, toil, work 5 labor, swink 7 faggery
piece of: fag
drug: 4 aloe, alum, dope, drab, dull, hemp, numb 5 hocus, japop, locus, opium, salol, senna, tonga, truck 6 heroin, ipecac, locust(pl.), opiate, peyote, peyotl 7 atebrin, stupefy, zedoary 8 medicine, nepenthe 9 asedulcis, marijuana 11 barbiturate, ipecacuanha 14 sulphapyridine
and ship: 8 shanghai
container: 7 capsule 8 gallipot
convulsion causing: 7 tetanic
crocus species: 7 saffron
for neuralgia: 5 tonga
Hippocratic: 5 mecon
of forgetfulness: 8 nepenthe
sleeping: 8 narcotic, sedative 12 somnifacient
drugged: 4 high 5 hyped 6 zonked 7 freaked 8 turned on 9 spaced out
drugget: mat, rug
druggist: 8 gallipot 10 apothecary, pharmacist 13 pharmaceutist
bible: USP
drugstore: 8 pharmacy
Druid: 6 priest
lodge: 4 cove
priestess of opera: 5 Norma
stone: 6 sarsen
symbol: 9 mistletoe
drum: 4 drub 5 drone, tabor 6 barrel, tambor, tympan 7 tambour, timbrel 8 cylinder, tympanum 9 reiterate
call to arms: 6 rappel
flourish: 7 roulade
kettle: 5 naker 6 atabal, nagara, timbal 7 attabal, timbale, timpano, timpani(pl.), tympani(pl.) 8 tympanum 9 tamburone
kind of: 4 base, gong, toph 5 gumbe, gumby, snare, tabor, tombe 6 kettle, tabour,

tam-tam, timbre, tom-tom 7 capstan, taboret, timbrel 8 bamboula, darbukka, derbukka, tabouret 9 darabukka, tambouret, tambourin
roll: 4 dian 5 diana
string: 5 snare
tighten cords: 4 frap
drumbeat: dub 8 berloque, breloque
at hour for sleep: 6 tattoo
drummer: 7 roadman 8 salesman
drumstick: 6 tampon
drunk: See **drunken**
drunkard: sot 4 soak 5 bloat, dipso, souce, souse, sowce, toper 7 fuddler, potshot, tippler, tosspot 8 borachio 9 alcoholic, inebriate 11 dipsomaniac
drunken: ree 4 gone 5 bousy, drown 6 blotto, fluffy 7 pickled, sottish 8 drenched, saturate, squiffed 9 drunkelew 10 inebriated 11 intoxicated
drunkenness: bun 7 potshot 9 inebriacy, inebriety 12 intoxication
bout of: 4 bust
drupelet: 5 acini(pl.) 6 acinus
dry: sec, ted 4 adry, arid, bake, brut, dull, geld, hask, sere, wipe 5 drain, hasky, parch, prosy, vapid, wizen 6 barren, boring, gizzen, jejune 7 brustle, insipid, sapless, sub-arid, sterile, thirsty, xerotic 8 tiresome 9 dehydrate, desiccate, drinkless, exsiccate, exsuccous, fruitless, pointless, sarcastic, waterless 10 desicated, evaporated, siccaneous, teetotaler 11 displeasing 12 moistureless, unprofitable 13 uninteresting
comb. form: ser, xer 4 xero
grass: hay
leather: sam
out: 5 steam, toast 6 rizzar 7 siccate
up: 4 sere 5 parch 6 shrink 9 dehydrate, desiccate, evaporate, exsiccate 10 dehumidify
dry goods: 4 wear 6 linens, napery
dry run: try 8 maneuver 9 rehearsal
dry shave: 5 cheat 7 defraud
dry spell: 7 drought
dryad: 5 nymph 6 yaksha, yakshi
dryness: 6 drouth 7 drought, siccity
abnormal: 7 xerosis 9 xerostoma 10 xerostomia
dryth: 6 thirst 7 drought, dryness
duad: 4 pair
dual: 4 twin 6 binary, double 7 twofold
dub: rub 4 blow, call, name, pool 5 adorn, array, dress, style, thump 6 clothe, puddle, smooth, strike 7 entitle 8 beginner, drumbeat, ornament 9 schlemiel, schlemihl
dubious: 8 doubtful, doubting 9 ambiguous, equivocal, uncertain, unsettled 10 disputable, precarious 12 questionable, undetermined
ducal: 5 noble
duck: bob, bow, mig, pet 4 chap, dive, jouk 5 dilly, dodge, douse, dowse, mommy, shirk, souse 6 fellow, person, plunge 7 darling, gadwall 9 sheldrake
black: 9 blackjack
bluebill: 5 scaup
brood: 4 team
dead: 5 goner
diving: 4 smew
eider: 4 colk, wamp
for cooking: 7 caneton
fresh-water: 4 teal
fresh-water genus: aix
genus: 4 anas 7 nettion
goldeneye: 7 gowdnie
group: 4 sord, team 5 skein
heraldic: 6 cannet 8 cannette
hooked-bill: 9 merganser
kind of: 4 smee, smew, teal 5 eider, scaup 6 scoter 7 mallard, pintail, scooter 9 merganser 10 bufflehead, butterball
longtailed: 6 hareld
male: 5 drake
Muscovy: 4 pato
old squaw: 6 quandy
Old World: 7 pochard 9 sheldrake
pert. to: 7 anatine
pintail: 4 smee, smew 8 piketail 11 querquedule
rare: 5 merse
ring-necked: 5 bunty
river: 4 smee, teal 7 pintail 8 piketail, shoveler 9 greenwing
ruddy: 6 bobber 9 blackjack
scaup: 9 blackjack
sea: 4 coot 5 eider, scaup 6 scoter 7 scooter 9 harlequin
tree: 7 yaguaza
wild: 4 teal 5 scaup 7 gadwall, mallard
wooden: 5 decoy
yellow-billed: 7 geelbec 8 geelbeck
young: 8 duckling
duck-on-the-rock player: 6 tenter
duck out: 4 flee 7 escape
duckbill: 8 platypus 10 mallangong
duckweed: 5 lemna
duct: vas 4 main, pipe, tube, vasa(pl.) 5 canal 7 conduit, ductule, leading, passage, trachea 8 aqueduct, guidance 9 direction
ductile: 4 soft 6 docile, facile, pliant 7 plastic, pliable, tensile 8 flexible, tractile 9 compliant, malleable, tractable 10 manageable, sequacious
ductless gland: 6 pineal, thymus

dud: 7 failure

dude: fop 5 dandy 6 dudine 7 coxcomb

stage door: 7 Johnnie

dudeen: 4 pipe

dudgeon: ire 5 anger, pique 6 dagger 10 resentment

duds: 7 clothes 8 clothing, garments

due: owe 4 just, meed, owed, toll 5 endow, endue, fated, owing 6 desert, extent, lawful, mature, proper, unpaid 7 exactly, fitting 8 adequate, directly, rightful, suitable 10 demandable, inevitable, sufficient 11 appropriate 12 attributable

duel: 4 tilt 5 fence, fight 6 affair, combat 7 contest 8 conflict

duelist: 7 fighter

aide: 6 second

duena: 8 landlady, mistress

duenna: 8 chaperon

dues: 5 tolls 6 droits 7 payment

duet: duo, two 7 twosome

upper part: 5 primo

duff: 5 alter, brand 7 pudding

duffer: 4 sham 5 cheat 6 hawker 7 peddler

dugong: 6 seacow

dugout: 4 abri, boat, cave 5 canoe, donga, dunga 6 cayuca, cayuco 7 pirogue, shelter 10 excavation

duke: duc(F.) 4 peer 5 chief 6 leader

dukedom: 4 duchy 7 ducatus

dulcet: 5 sweet 8 soothing 9 agreeable, melodious 10 harmonious

dulcimer: 6 citole, santir 7 cembalo, yang-kin 9 pantaleon

dull: dim, dow, dry, lax, mat, sad 4 clod, cold, dead, drab, dree, drug, dumb, flat, gray, grey, logy, mope, poky, slow, tame 5 besot, blate, blear, blind, blunt, crass, dingy, dunch, fishy, foggy, gross, heavy, inert, matte, moron, noose, plump, pokey, prose, prosy, shade, unapt, vapid 6 barren, bovine, cloudy, dampen, darken, deaden, dismal, dreary, drowsy, glassy, hebete, leaden, muffle, obtund, obtuse, sleepy, somber, stodgy, stolid, stupid, torpid, triste 7 blunted, doltish, humdrum, irksome, lumpish, mumpish, prosaic, sottish, stupefy, tedious, vacuous 8 backward, blockish, boeotian, hebetate, lifeless, listless, overcast, sluggish, stagnant, tiresome 9 apathetic, colorless, heavisome, inanimate, lethargic, pointless, saturnine, tarnished, tasteless, unfeeling 10 insensible, lusterless, melancholy, monotonous, slow-witted 11 claybrained, displeasing, heavy-headed, thickheaded 12 bufflehеaded 13 unimaginative

become: 4 pall 8 hebetate

finish: mat 5 matte

noise: 4 klop

dullard: 4 dolt 5 dunce, idiot, moron 6 stupid 7 dastard, doldrum, pothead

dullness: 7 dimness, doldrum, duncery, fatuity, languor 8 hebetude, slowness, vapidity 9 bluntness, oscitancy, platitude, stupidity 10 drowsiness

of hearing: 9 baryecoia

dulse: 7 seaweed

duly: 5 fitly 8 properly 9 regularly 13 appropriately

Dumas: *character:* 5 Athos 6 Aramis 7 Porthos

heroine: 7 Camille

dumb: 4 dull, mute 6 silent, stupid 9 senseless 10 speechless 11 meaningless 12 inarticulate, inexpressive

dumbbell: 9 screwball

dumfound, dumbfound: 4 daze, stun 5 amaze 7 confuse 8 confound, surprise 9 embarrass

dummy: 4 copy, dolt, mute, sham 6 silent 9 imitation 10 fictitious, figurehead 11 counterfeit

dump: sum 4 beat, cash, coin, fall, hole, jail, muse, nail 5 empty, house 6 grieve, plunge, unload 7 counter, deposit, reverie, sadness, storage 9 halfpenny 10 melancholy 11 despondency

dumping ground: 4 toom

dumpling: cob 7 gnoccho, gnocchi(pl.) 8 quenelle 10 appleberry

dumps: 8 doldrums

dumpy: 5 pudgy, squat

dun: tan 4 fort, urge 5 annoy, brown, crave, dingy, mound, sepia 6 pester, plague 7 swarthy 9 importune

dunce: ass 4 dolt, dult, gony 5 booby, idiot, ninny 6 hobbil, pedant 7 dullard, half-wit, sophist 8 numskull 9 ignoramus, simpleton 10 dunderhead

dunderhead: oaf 4 dolt 5 dunce 9 blockhead, numbskull

dune: bar 5 mound, towan 6 barkan 7 barchan, barkhan

dung: 4 gore, muck 5 filth, fumet 6 billet, manure, ordure 9 billeting, excrement, poppycock

dungeon: 4 cell, hell, hole 5 vault 6 donjon, prison 8 revolver 9 oubliette 10 ergastulum

dunghill: 5 mixen 7 mixhill 10 muckmidden

dunk: dip, sop 4 soak 5 steep 7 immerse, moisten

dunker: 7 tumbler

dunlin: 4 stib 9 sandpiper

dunt: 4 beat, blow 5 dizzy, knock, thump 6 benumb, bruise, strike, stupid 7 stupefy 10 heartthrob

duo: 4 duet, pair 6 couple
dupe: ape, fob, mug 4 coax, cull, fool, geck, gull, tool 5 cheat, cully, heald, mouth, trick 6 bubble, choose, delude, deride, plover, sucker, victim 7 catspaw, deceive, gudgeon, mislead, pidgeon, swindle 8 dotterel
dupery: 4 ramp
duple: 7 twofold
duplex: 6 double 7 twofold 8 dwelling
duplexity: 9 ambiguity
duplicate: bis 4 copy 5 alike, ditto, spare 6 double, repeat 7 estreat, mislead, replica, twofold 8 likeness 9 facsimile, reproduce 10 transcript 11 counterpart
duplicity: art 6 deceit 8 trickery 9 deception, falsehood 13 dissimulation
durable: 4 firm 6 stable, staple 7 lasting 8 constant, enduring 9 permanent 10 consistent, continuing, persistent 11 everlasting
durance: 6 duress 12 imprisonment
Durante byword: 8 Calabash
duration: age 4 span, term, time 5 space 6 period 7 durance 8 lifetime 9 extension 11 continuance
note: 4 time 5 clock
of ministerial charge: 9 pastorate
without beginning or end: 8 eternity
D'Urberville lass: 4 Tess
dure: 4 hard, last 5 rough 6 endure, severe, strong 7 sustain 8 continue
duress: 7 cruelty, durance 8 coercion, hardness, pressure 9 captivity, harshness 10 affliction, compulsion, constraint 12 imprisonment
durgah, dargah: 4 tomb 5 court 6 mosque, shrine
during: 4 time 5 while 6 whilst 7 pending 10 throughout
durra: 7 sorghum
durst: 8 ventured
dusk eve 5 gloom 6 dimmet, dimpsy 7 dimness 8 darkness, gloaming, twilight 11 crepusculum
dusky: dim, sad, wan 4 dark 5 adusk, brown, dingy, tawny 6 gloomy, somber, sombre, swarth 7 swarthy 8 blackish 10 melancholy
dust: row 4 dirt, pilm, smut 5 clean, flour, pouce, stive 6 pollen, powder 7 eburine, remains, turmoil 9 commotion, confusion 10 kryokonite 11 disturbance
measuring device: 9 koniscope
reduce to: 4 mull
speck: 4 mote
dust-like: 7 powdery
dusty: 5 adusk 6 poucey 9 pulverant
Dutch: See **Netherlands**
Dutch East Indies: See **East Indies, Indonesia**
Dutch Guiana: See **Surinam**
Dutch South Africa: See **South Africa**
Dutch uncle: oom
Dutchware blue: 5 delft
duteous: 7 dutiful 8 obedient 10 respectful 11 subservient
dutiful: 6 docile 7 duteous 8 obedient, reverent 9 childlike, compliant 10 submissive 11 reverential 13 conscientious
duty: job, tax 4 care, onus, role, task, toll 5 chore, stint 6 burden, charge, devoir, excise, exitus, heriot, impose, impost, rivage, tariff 7 average, bailage, service, station, tribute 8 function, malikana 10 allegiance, obligation
Hindu: 6 dharma
on commodities: 6 excise
shirking: 7 truancy
spell of: 5 shift, trick, watch
dux: 5 chief 6 leader
dwarf: elf 4 grig, grub, runt 5 crile, crowl, elves(pl.), Galar, gnome, midge, pigmy, pygmy, scrub, stunt, troll 6 ablach, droich, durgan, durgen, midget 7 blastie, manikin, overtop, Pacolet 8 belittle, Cercopes, homuncio, homuncle, huckmuck, nanander 9 dandiprat, homuncule 10 diminutive, homunculus, overshadow
king: 8 Alberich
race: 8 Nibelung 9 Nibelungs 10 Nibelungen
dwarfish: 5 pigmy, pygmy 6 grubby, nanoid 7 pigment, runtish, stunted
dwarfishness: 6 nanism
dwell: big, cot, dig 4 bide, bigg, haft, harp, live, stay 5 abide, bield, brood, delay, lodge, pause, tarry 6 linger, remain, reside 7 cohabit, inhabit 8 converse 9 expatiate 12 intermission, interruption
dweller: 6 tenant 8 habitant, occupant, resident 10 inhabitant
around city: 11 suburbanite
cave: 10 troglodyte
city: 8 urbanite
desert: 4 Arab 5 nomad 9 sourdough
earth: 9 tellurian
fellow: 6 inmate
formicary: ant
jungle: 5 beast 6 monkey
monastery: 8 cenobite
prairie: 9 plainsman
seacoast: 7 coaster 11 beachcomber
temporary: 6 lodger 7 boarder 9 transient
underground: 4 mold 5 gnome
dwelling: dar, hut 4 casa(It.), flat, haft, home, nest, slum, tent 5 abode, cabin, hotel, house, hovel, motel 6 duplex, shanty, teepee 7 cottage, lodging, mansion, trailer,

triplex 8 building, bungalow, domicile, tenement 9 apartment, habitance, residence 10 habitation
dwindle: 4 melt, pine, wane 5 peter, taper, waste 6 shrink 7 consume, decline 8 decrease, diminish, fordwine
Dyak: *blowgun:* 8 sumpitan
knife: 6 parang
Dyak Sea: 4 iban
dye: aal 4 anil, tint 5 color, eosin, fucus, imbue, stain, tinge 6 litmus, madder 7 aniline, toluene 8 colorant
blue: wad 4 anil, wade, woad
blue-red: 6 orchal, orchil
brown: 5 sumac 6 sumach
coal-tar: 6 magena
hair: 5 henna 6 rastik
indigo: al; aal 4 anil
morindin: al; aal
mulberry: al
purple: 8 murexide
quercitron bark: 6 flavin
red: 5 aurin, eosin 7 annatto, magenta 8 rhodamin 9 rhodamine 10 orseilline
red-brown: 5 henna
red-orange: 5 chica 7 fuchsin 8 morindin
source: 5 murex
violet: 6 archil
yellow: 4 weld, wold 5 arusa, woald, would
yellow-red: 6 anatta, anatto 7 annatto, annotto
dyeing apparatus: vat 4 ager
scrape: 6 harass
dyestuff: See **dye**
dying: 8 moribund
dynamic: 6 potent 8 forceful 9 energetic
dynamite: 5 blast 9 explosive
kind of: 6 dualin 7 dualine 9 fulgurite 10 kieselguhr
inventor: 5 Nobel
dynamo: 9 generator
in distributing system: 7 booster
inventor: 7 Faraday
part: 5 rotor 7 brushes 8 armature 10 commutator
dynast: 5 ruler 6 prince 8 governor
dynasty: 4 race 5 realm, ruler 6 prince 7 monarch 8 dominion, governor, lordship 10 succession 11 sovereignty
Chinese: Fo; Han, Yin 4 Isin, Ming
French: 5 Capet
dysentery: 7 toxemia 8 diarrhea, epidemic
remedy: 14 sulfaguanidine
dysphoria: 7 anxiety

E

ea: 5 river 6 stream
Ea's daughter: 4 Nina
each: ea; all, ilk, uch 4 ilka, uche 5 every 8 everyone
eager: hot 4 acid, avid, gair, keen, sour, warm, wave 5 afire, agasp, itchy, ready, sharp 6 ardent, greedy, hetter, intent 7 anxious, athirst, brittle, burning, excited, fervent, forward, provoke 8 desirous, irritate, spirited, vigorous, yearning 9 desireful, impatient, impetuous, strenuous 12 enthusiastic, forereaching
eagerness: gog 4 elan, zeal 5 ardor 6 fervor 7 ardency, avidity 8 alacrity, cupidity, fainness, fervency 9 alertness, constancy, readiness 10 enthusiasm, impatience 13 impetuousness
eagle: ern 4 erne, gier, tern 6 aquila, bergut, eaglet, formal, formel 8 allerion, bataleur, berghaan 9 ossifrage
Biblical: 4 gier
comb. form: 4 aeto
constellation: 6 Aquila
genus of: 10 haliaeetus
nest: 4 aery, eyry 5 aerie, eyrie
sea: ern 4 erne
eaglestone: 7 aétites
eagre: 4 bore, wave
ear: lug(Sc.) 4 hear, heed, obey, plow, till 5 auris(L.), spike 6 listen 7 auricle, hearing 8 audience 9 attention, cultivate
absence of: 6 anotia
bone: 5 ambos, incus 6 stapes 7 malleus, stirrup
canal: 5 scala
cavity: 6 meatus 7 cochlea
cleaning device: 8 aurilave
comb. form: oto 4 auri
covering: 4 muff 6 earcap, earlap 7 earmuff
doctor: 6 aurist 9 otologist
inflammation of: 6 otitis
middle: 4 drum 8 tympanum
near: 7 parotic
part of: 4 burr, lobe 5 helix, pinna 6 tragus
pert. to: 4 otic 5 aural 7 entotic 9 auricular
science of: 7 otology
ear shell: 7 abalone
ear stone: 7 otolite, otolith
earache: 6 otalgy 7 otalgia
earbob: 7 earring
eardrop: 7 earring, pendant
eardrum: 8 membrane, tympanum
eared seal: 5 otary
earl: 4 eorl, lord, peer 5 noble 8 nobleman
pert. to: 7 comital
earldom: 5 derby
earlet: 7 auricle
earlier: ere 4 erst, fore 5 elder 6 before, former, sooner 8 previous
early: air, ere, old 4 rath 5 forme, rathe 6 timely 7 ancient, betimes 9 matutinal, premature 10 forehanded
earmark: bit 14 identification
earn: get, win 4 fang, gain 5 addle, ettle, merit 6 obtain 7 achieve, acquire, chevise, deserve
earner: 6 winner, worker 11 breadwinner
earnest: 4 hard 5 grave, sober, staid 6 ardent, hearty, intent, sedate, solemn 7 engaged, forward, serious, sincere, zealous 8 diligent, emphatic 9 heartfelt 10 expressive, thoughtful 12 affectionate, wholehearted
earnest money: 5 arles 7 deposit, forfeit 8 security
earring: 4 grip 8 ornament 9 girandole
earshot: 7 hearing
earsplitting: 4 loud 5 shrill
earth: erd(Sc.), orb 4 bury, clay, dirt, grit, land, loam, marl, mool, muck, rock, soil, sory 5 glebe, globe, groot, inter, loess, regur, terra(L.), trass, umber, world 6 coarse, ground 7 tierras, topsoil 8 magnesia 10 terra firma
comb. form: geo
compound: 7 tierras
crust constituent: 6 silica
deposit: 4 marl, silt 5 loess 8 alluvium
dweller: 9 tellurian
god: Geg, Keb, Seb 5 Dagan

goddess: 4 Gaea 5 Ceres, Terra 6 Semele 7 Demeter
layer of: 5 sloam
lump of: 4 clod
metallic: ore
opposite side of: 9 Antipodes
pert. to: 4 geal 5 terra 8 telluric 9 planetary 11 terrigenous
pigment: 5 ochre, umber
prepare for seeding: 4 plow 5 spade 6 harrow 9 cultivate
ridge of: 4 kame 6 rideau
satellite of: 4 moon
science: 7 geodesy, geology 9 geography
surface gravel: 6 eratum 8 erratice
earth bob: 4 grub 6 maggot
earth hog: 8 aardvark
earth lodge: 5 hogan
earthborn: 11 terrigenous 13 autochthonous
earthbred: low 6 vulgar
earthdrake: 6 dragon
earthenware: 4 delf 5 china, cloam, crock, delft 7 biscuit, faience, pottery 8 crockery 9 porcelain, stoneware 10 terra-cotta
maker: 6 potter
peddler: 6 mugger
piece of: 5 shard
earthfall: 9 landslide
earthkin: 7 terella
earthling: 5 human 6 mortal
earthly: 6 carnal 7 mundane, secular, terrene, worldly 8 temporal 11 terrestrial
earthnut: 5 arnot, chufa 6 peanut 7 truffle
earthquake: 5 quake, seism 7 tomblor
measuring device: 10 seisometer
pert. to: 7 seismic
point directly above: 9 epicenter
science: 10 seismology
earthstar: 6 fungus 7 geaster
earthwork: 5 agger 7 rampart 10 breastwork 13 fortification
earthworm: ess 7 annelid, ipomoea
earthy: low 5 gross 6 carnal, coarse, fleshy 7 sensual 11 terrestrial
earwax: 7 cerumen
earwig: 6 golach, goloch
ease: 4 calm, rest 5 allay, knack, peace, quiet, relax 6 loosen, pacify, reduce, relief, repose, smooth, soften, soothe 7 appease, assuage, comfort, faculty, freedom, leisure, liberty, lighten, relieve, slacken 8 diminish, facility, mitigate, moderate, palliate, pleasure, security, unburden 9 alleviate, disburden, enjoyment 10 ameliorate, facilitate, relaxation, solicitude 11 contentment, naturalness, tranquillity 12 satisfaction
at: 6 degage, otiose 7 relaxed
ease off: 4 slow 5 slack
easel: 5 frame 7 support
easily: 6 gently, glibly 7 readily 8 smoothly
east: 4 Asia 6 Levant, Orient 9 direction
pert. to: 4 eoan 8 oriental
East Africa: See **Africa**
East Asia: *people:* 5 Seres
weight: 4 tras
East India: *agent:* 8 gomashta, gomastah
animal: 7 tarsier
aroid: 4 apii
arrowroot: 5 tikor
bark: 4 lodh 5 niepa
bead tree: nim 4 neem 6 neemba
bird: 4 baya
boatswain: 6 serang
broadbill: 4 raya
bush: 4 sola
cattle: 4 dhan, gaur
cavalry troop: 7 ressala
cheroot: 6 lunkah
civet: 6 musang
dancing girl: 4 dasi
disease: 5 lanas
drink: 4 nipa
dye: aal
dye tree: 4 dhak, toon
fish: 5 dorab 7 gourami
food: 4 sago
freight boat: 5 oolak
fruit: 6 durian, durion 8 belleric, cardamom 9 myrobalan
gateway: 5 toran 6 torana
granary: 4 gola
grass: 4 kasa, ragi, usar 5 glaga, ragee, raggi, raggy 6 glagah, raggie
gulf: 4 Boni
harbor master: 9 shabandar, shabunder
hawk: 5 bacha
hemp: 7 pangane
herb: pia, rea, til 4 chay, sola 6 sesame 7 roselle 8 eggplant
hog: 8 babirusa 9 babirussa 10 babiroussa
island: 4 Bali, Muna, Nias 5 Misal, Timor 6 Borneo 7 Celebes, Sumatra
juniper berry: 5 abhol
liquor: 6 arrack
maid: 4 ayah
mammal: 7 tarsier
mangrove: 7 ceriops
market: 5 pasar
measure: kit, kos 4 bouw, depa, rood, rope 5 depoh, kilan, parah, takar 6 bamboo, coyang 7 gantang, tjenkal, toenbak
millet: 4 dura 5 durra 6 dhurra
money: 4 bonk, duit
money changer: 6 shroff
monkey: 8 entellus
musical instrument: 4 bina, vina

muskmelon: 6 wungee
muslin: ban
nose flute: 6 upanga
nut: ben
palm: tal 4 nipa 7 jaggery, palmyra, tokopat
plant: da; rea 4 amil, jute, sola, sunn 5 benne 6 ambari, ambary, madder, sesame 7 ambaree
poison: 4 bikh
police chief: 7 darogah
post: dak 4 dawk
race: 4 swat
robber: 6 dacoit
rubber tree: saj
sailing vessel: 4 doni 5 dhoni
sardine: 4 lile
shrub: ak 4 odal, sola 5 mudar
snake: 7 bokadam
songbird: 5 shama
squirrel: 6 taguan
starch: 4 sago 5 tikor
sugar cane: 5 glaga 6 glagah 7 talthib
sword: 4 pata
tree: ach, bel, ber, bih, dar, eng, hur, mee, nim, saj, sal 4 alof, dhak, moli, neem, odal, poon, toon 5 dadap, fulwa, mahua, neeba, niepa, oodal, rohan, roman, salai, sapan, simal, siman, siris, sissu, tikur, uadal 6 banyan, chalta, chogak, deodar, illupi, sissoo, tikoor 7 champac, dhamnoo, gumihan, hollong, margosa 8 phulwbra 11 chaulmaugra, hursinghair
vehicle: 5 tonga
vessel: 7 patamar 8 gallivat
vine: 4 odal, soma
viper: 6 kupper
warrior: 5 singh
weight: 4 hoen, wang
wood: eng
wood apple: bel
xylophone: 5 saron

East Indies: See **East India**
Easter: 5 Pasch 6 Eostre, Pascha
first Sunday after: 9 Quasimodo
pert. to: 7 paschal
Sunday before: 4 Palm
eastern: 6 ortive 7 auroral
Eastern Church: *bishop:* 4 abba
choir platform: 5 solea
convent head: 8 hegumene
festival day: 8 apodosis
monk: 7 caloyer
prayer: 6 ectene, ektene
Eastland: 8 estriche
easy: 4 calm, cozy, eath, eith, glib, mild 5 cushy, light, suave 6 facile, gentle, secure, simple 7 lenient, natural 8 carefree, careless, cavalier, familiar, graceful, homelike, moderate, tranquil, unforced 9 compliant, indulgent, tractable, unhurried 10 manageable, unaffected 11 comfortable, complaisant, susceptible, unconcerned 13 unconstrained
easy job: 4 pipe, snap 5 cinch 8 sinecure
easy mark: 5 chump 6 sucker
easygoing: 6 placid 7 relaxed
eat: sup 4 bite, dine, fare, feed, fret, gnaw, grub, rust 5 erode, feast, munch, taste, waste 6 absorb, begnaw, devour, ingest, ravage 7 consume, corrode, destroy, swallow 9 manducate
between meals: 5 bever
by regimen: 4 diet
fastidiously: 7 epicure 8 gourmand
grass: 5 graze 6 forage
greedily: 4 cram, wolf 5 gorge, raven 6 gobble, goffle 8 gourmand 10 gormandize
pert. to: 7 dietary 8 dietetic, edacious
sparingly: 4 diet
sumptuously: 6 regale
eatable: 6 edible 8 esculent 10 comestible
eatage: 9 pasturage
eating: 6 dining 7 caustic, erosive 8 corrosive
eating-place: inn 4 cafe 5 diner, grill, hotel 6 tavern 7 automat, tearoom 8 grubbery 9 cafeteria, chophouse
eave: 7 cornice
eavesdrop: 6 harken 7 hearken
eavesdropper: 9 drawlatch
ebb: 4 fail, sink, wane 5 abate, decay 6 recede, reflux, retire 7 decline, subside 8 decrease, diminish 9 backwater
ebb and flow: 5 estus 6 aestus
ebbing: 5 awane 8 refluent 9 refluxing
Eber's son: 6 Joktan
ebon: 4 dark 5 black, sable
ebony: 5 black
eboulement: 9 landslide
ebriate: 9 inebriate 11 intoxicated
ebrious: 5 tipsy
ebullate, ebulliate: 4 boil
ebullience: 8 overflow
ebullient: 7 boiling 12 effervescent
ebullition: 7 ferment 8 outburst 9 agitation, commotion 10 excitement 12 fermentation 13 effervescence
ecaudate: 8 tailless
ecce: lo 6 behold
eccentric: odd 4 card 5 crank, queer 6 cranky 7 bizarre, devious, erratic, strange 8 abnormal, peculiar, singular 9 anomalous, erratical, irregular, quizzical, screwball, whimsical 15 idiosyncratical
eccentricity: 5 ferly 6 oddity 8 crotchet 9 queerness 10 aberration 11 peculiarity, strangeness 12 idiosyncrasy

ecclesiastic: 4 abbe 5 abbot, clerk 6 priest 7 prelate 9 clergyman
belt: 7 balteus 8 baltheus
council: 5 synod
court: 4 rota
garment: alb 4 cope 5 amice, fanon, orale, stole, cappa, rabat 6 callot 7 cassock, biretta, calotte 8 berretta
head: 6 rector
land: 5 glebe
living: 8 benefice
ruler: 8 hierarch
service: 5 matin
unit: 6 parish
ecclesiastics: 11 gens d'eglise
ecdysiast: 11 stripteaser
eche: 4 grow 7 enlarge 8 increase
echelon: 8 maneuver 11 arrangement
echidna: 8 anteater
food: 4 ants
three-toed: 6 nodiak
echinate: 5 spiny 7 bristly, prickly
echinoderm, armed: 8 starfish
echo: eco 4 ring 6 repeat, second 7 imitate, iterate, resound, respond, revoice 8 response 9 imitation 10 repetition 11 reverberate 13 reverberation
eciton: ant
eclat: 4 fame, pomp 5 glory 6 praise, renown, repute 7 acclaim, scandal 8 applause, facility, splendor 9 notoriety 10 brilliance, brilliancy 11 ostentation
eclectic: 7 liberal
eclipse: dim 4 bind, blot, hide 5 blind, cloud, shade, sully 6 darken, dazzle, exceed 7 obscure, travail 8 outrival 10 extinguish, overshadow 11 obscuration, occultation
demon of: 4 Rahu
shadow: 8 penumbra 9 penumbrae
eclogue: 4 idyl, poem 5 idyll 7 bucolic
ecology, oecology: 9 bionomics
economical: 5 chary 6 frugal, saving 7 careful, prudent, thrifty 9 provident
economics: *element:* 9 commodity
theoretical: 9 plutology
economize: 4 save 5 skimp, stint 6 scrimp 7 husband, utilize 8 retrench 9 housewife
economy: 6 saving, thrift 9 frugality, husbandry 10 compendium, providence
bad: 11 cacoeconomy
practice: 7 scraped 8 scrimped
ecostate: 7 ribless
ecru: 5 beige, linen 10 unbleached
ecstasy: joy 5 bliss, swoon 6 trance 7 delight, emotion, madness, rapture 9 enrapture, happiness, transport
ecstatic: 4 rapt 8 glorious 9 entranced, rapturous, rhapsodic 10 enraptured
ectad: 5 outer 7 outward 8 exterior
opposite of: 5 entad
ectal: 5 outer 8 exterior
ectype: 9 imitation
ecu: 4 coin 6 shield
Ecuador: *animal:* 6 vicuna
capital: 5 Quito
city: 4 Loja, Suyo 5 Banos, Guano, Luisa, Mocha, Piura, Quito, Zunga 6 Ambato, Cuenca, Ibarra, Patate, Pujili, Tulcan 7 Azogues, Cayambe, Guamote, Machala, Pelileo, Pillaro, Salcedo, Salinas, Squisil 8 Babahoyo, Cevallos, Cujibies, Guaranda, Pansaleo, Riobamba 9 Guayaquil, Latagunga 10 Esmeraldas 11 Puertoviejo
coin: 5 sucre 6 condor 7 centavo
Indian: 4 Cara 5 Palta 6 Canelo, Jibaro, Jivaro
island: 9 Galapagos
measure: 5 libra 6 cuadra, fanega
mountain: 7 Cayambe 8 Antisana, Cotopaxi 9 Cotacachi, Pichincha 10 Chimborazo
province: 4 Loja 5 Azuay, Canar, El Oro 6 Carchi, Guayas, Manabi 7 Bolivar, Los Rios 8 Cotapaxi, Imbabura 9 Pichincha 10 Chimborazo, Esmeraldas, Tungurahua
river: 4 Napo 5 Tigre 6 Ambato 7 Pastaza 9 Guayaquil 10 Esmeraldas
town: See **Ecuador:** *city*
tree: 5 balsa
volcano: 8 Antisana
ecumenic: 12 cosmopolitan
ecumenical: 7 liberal 8 catholic, tolerant 9 worldwide 12 cosmopolitan
ecumenical council: 4 Lyon 5 Lyons, Trent 7 Vatican
eczema: 6 herpes, tetter 9 malanders 10 dermatitis
edacity: 8 appetite, voracity 12 ravenousness
edaphic: 5 local 13 autochthonous
Edda: 4 saga
Eddaic god: 4 Odin
eddish: 6 arrish 7 eegrass 9 aftermath
eddo: 4 taro
eddy: 4 gulf, purl, weel 5 acker, gurge, shift, swirl, whirl 6 vortex 7 backset 9 whirlpool 14 countercurrent
eddying: 4 wale
edema: 5 tumor 6 dropsy 8 swelling 9 puffiness 12 intumescence
Eden: 6 heaven, utopia 7 arcadia, elysium 8 paradise
Edenic: 7 elysian, elysium 8 blissful 10 paradisaic
Edenite: 9 amphibole
edental: 9 toothless
edentate: ai 5 sloth 7 ant bear 8 aardvark, anteater, pangolin, tamandua 9 armadillo, toothless

Edessa's king: 5 Abgar
edge: hem, jag, lip, rim 4 bank, berm, brim, brow, rand, side, trim, whet 5 arris, berme, bevel, blade, brink, crest, frill, knife, marge, ruler, sidle, splay, verge 6 border, flange, impale, margin 7 margent, sharpen, selvage 8 boundary, keenness, selvedge 9 advantage, beginning, sharpness 10 escarpment
run along: 5 skirt
sharp: 5 beard
uneven: 4 wane, wany 5 waney
edged: 5 sharp, erose 7 crenate
edger: 7 whetter 9 sharpener
edging: hem 4 lace 5 frill, picot 6 border, fringe 7 binding 8 rickrack 10 embroidery
loop: 5 picot
edgrew, edgrow: 5 rowen 9 aftermath
edgy: 5 sharp 7 angular 8 critical, snappish 9 irritable
edible: 7 eatable 8 esculent 9 cibarious, vegetable 10 comestible
arum: 4 taro
fungus: 5 morel
gallingale: 5 chufa
mollusk: asi
parts of fruit: 4 pulp
rush: 5 chufa
seaweed: 4 agar 5 dulse, laver 6 delisk 8 agaragar
seed: pea 4 bean
tuber root: oca, uva, yam 4 beet, eddo, taro 6 turnip 7 parsnip 8 rutabaga
edict: act, ban, law 4 bull, fiat 5 arret, bando, bulla, irade, order, ukase 6 decree, dictum, notice 7 command, embargo, program, statute 9 ordinance, programma 12 announcement, proclamation
papal: 4 bull
edification: 7 edifice 8 building 11 instruction 13 enlightenment
edifice: 4 dome 6 church 8 building 9 structure 11 edification
kind: 6 palace, church, temple 7 capitol 10 tabernacle
edifier: 7 teacher
edify: 4 grow 5 build, teach 7 improve, prosper 8 instruct, organize 9 construct, establish
edile: 10 magistrate
Edina: 9 Edinburgh
Edinburgh: 5 Edina
part of: 5 Leith
edit: 5 emend 6 direct, redact, review, revise 7 arrange, compile, correct, prepare, publish, rewrite 8 copyread 9 supervise
edition: 4 kind 5 issue, print, stamp 6 source 7 version 9 character 10 extraction
kind of: 5 extra 7 revisal, reprint
editor: 8 redactor 9 emendator, publisher, redacteur 10 diaskeuast, journalist
room: 7 sanctum
Edom: 7 Idumaea
chieftain: 4 Iram
district: 5 Teman
king: 5 Hadad
mountain: Hor
Edomite's ancestor: 4 Esau
educate: 4 rear 5 breed, teach, train 6 expand, inform, school 7 develop, nurture 8 develope, instruct 9 cultivate, enlighten 10 discipline, strengthen 12 indoctrinate
educated: 4 bred 6 taught 7 trained 8 lettered, literate
education: 7 nurture 8 breeding, learning, training 9 erudition 10 background, discipline 11 scholarship
institution: 6 school 7 college 8 seminary 10 university
organization: PTA 6 lyceum
educator: 7 teacher
educe: 5 evoke 6 elicit, evolve 7 extract 9 eliminate
edulcorate: 7 sweeten
eegrass: 6 eddish 7 stubble
eel: ele 4 grig, ling, opah, snig 5 elver, moray, siren 6 conger, carapo, moreia, murene 7 eel pout, lamprey, muraena, sniggle, wriggle 8 Anguilla 9 snipefish
cut and cooked: 10 spitchcock
fish for: 7 sniggle
marine: 6 conger
migration: 7 eelfare
sand: 6 launce
trap: 6 eelpot
young: 5 elver
eel-shaped: 12 anguilliform
eelboat: 6 schuit
eeler: 9 fisherman
eelgrass: 9 grassweed
eellike: 10 anguilloid
eelpot: 4 trap
eelpout: 4 pout 6 burbot, guffer, yowler 10 muttonfish
eelworm: 4 nema
eely: 7 elusive, evasive, wriggly 8 slippery 9 wriggling
eemis, immis: 8 insecure 10 changeable
e'en: 4 even 7 evening
eerie, eery: 5 scary, timid, weird 6 dismal, gloomy, spooky 7 awesome, ghostly, macabre, strange, uncanny 8 eldritch, ghoulish 9 unearthly, unnatural, unworldly 10 frightened 11 phantomlike
efface: 4 blot, dele, rase, raze 5 erase 6 cancel, deface 7 destroy, dislimn, expunge 10 obliterate
effacement: 7 erasure

effect: 4 does, feck, prey 5 cause, close, eclat, enact, ettle 6 intent, result, sequel 7 achieve, acquire, compass, conduce, emotion, execute, fulfill, operate, outcome, perform, produce, purport, realize 8 complete 9 execution, influence 10 accomplish, consummate, expression, impression 11 consequence, fulfillment, performance 13 manifestation 14 accomplishment
of past experience: 5 mneme
of wind on a shot: 7 windage
effective: 4 able, real 5 siker 6 active, actual, causal, potent, sicker 7 capable, telling 8 adequate, forceful, powerful, striking, vigorous 9 brilliant, competent, effectual, efficient 10 perficient 11 efficacious, influential
effectiveness: 10 efficiency
effects: 5 goods 7 baggage 8 movables 10 belongings
effectual: 8 adequate, powerful 9 available, effective, efficient 10 perficient, sufficient 13 authoritative
effectuate: 6 fulfil 7 fulfill 8 complete 10 accomplish
effeminancy: 10 muliebrity
effeminate: 5 milky 6 female, tender, weakly 7 citizen, epicene, womanly 8 feminate, feminine, oversoft 9 emolliate 10 voluptuous 12 overdelicate 13 overemotional
effervesce: 4 huff 6 bubble
effervescence: 10 ebullition
effervescing: 5 brisk 9 ebullient
effete: 4 sere 5 spent 6 barren 8 decadent, moribund 9 exhausted
efficacious: 5 valid 6 mighty, potent 8 forcible, powerful, vigorous, virtuous 9 available, effective, officious, prevalent 10 legitimate 11 efficiently
efficaciousness: 10 efficiency
efficacy: 4 dint, feck 5 force, grace, might, power 6 virtue 7 potency 10 efficiency
efficiency: 5 power, skill 6 agency 7 ability 8 efficacy 10 capability, competence, competency 11 proficiency 13 effectiveness 15 efficaciousness
efficient: 4 able 6 potent 7 capable, feckful 8 powerful 9 competent, effective, effectual
efficiently: 13 efficaciously
effigy: 5 image 8 likeness 9 jackstraw
efflorescence: 5 bloom 7 blossom 8 anthesis
effluence: 5 issue 6 efflux 7 emanate 9 emanation
effluvium: 4 aura 9 emanation 10 exhalation
efflux: 7 outflow 8 effusion 9 effluence, emanation
effluxion: 7 outflow 9 effluence, emanation
effodient: 9 burrowing, fossorial
effort: try 4 dint, fist, toil 5 assay, brunt, drive, essay, labor, nisus, pains, power, trial 6 devoir, fizzle, fuffle, strain 7 attempt, trouble 8 endeavor, exertion, struggle 9 diligence 11 application
single: 4 solo 5 trice
violent: 4 adit 5 burst 8 struggle
effrontery: 4 brow, gall 5 front 8 audacity, boldness, temerity 9 hardihood, impudence, sauciness 10 confidence, incivility
effulgence: 5 blaze, glory 7 radiant 8 radiance, splendor 10 brightness, brilliance
effulgent: 6 bright 7 fulgent, radiant
effuse: 4 gush, shed 5 fling 7 emanate 8 dispense 11 disseminate
effussion: 6 efflux, foison
effusive: 5 gushy 7 gushing 8 bubbling 9 exuberant, rhapsodic 13 demonstrative
eft, evet: 4 newt 6 lizard, triton 10 salamander
eftsoon: 4 anon 5 again 9 afterward
egad: 4 ecod
egality: 8 equality 10 equanimity
egall: 5 equal
egeran: 11 vesuvianite
egeria: 7 adviser
egest: 4 void 7 excrete
egg: ova(pl.) 4 abet, goad, ovum, prod, seed, spur, urge 5 ovule, spore 6 incite 7 actuate, cokeney 9 instigate
case: 5 shell 6 ovisac 7 outheca
collector: 8 oologist
combining form: oo; ovi
fertilized: 4 zoon 7 oosperm
fish: roe 5 berry 6 caviar
insect: nit
measuring device: 7 oometer
nest: 6 clutch
part of: 4 yolk 5 shell, white 7 albumen, latebra
Philippine duck: 5 balut
prefix: oo
small: 5 ovule
tested: 7 candled
unfertilized: 8 oosphere
white of: 5 glair 7 albumen
egg case: 4 ovum 6 ovisac
egg on: 4 abet, goad, urge 6 incite
egg-shaped: 4 ooid, oval 5 ovate, ovoid 6 ooidal 7 obovoid, ovaloid, oviform
egg to anger: 7 provoke
egg yolk: 7 liaison 8 lecithin
egger: 4 moth
eggnog: nog 8 beverage
eggplant: 7 brinjal 8 brinjaul 9 berengena
eggs: roe 5 spawn 6 graine 7 ahuatle
feeding on: 9 ovivorous

poached in cream: 7 shirred
eggshell: 8 cascaron
Egil's brother: 6 Volund
egis: 5 aigis, armor 6 shield 7 defence, defense 10 protection
Eglah: *husband:* 5 David
son: 7 Ithream
eglantine: 8 eglatere, woodbine 10 sweetbrier 11 honeysuckle
Eglon's king: 5 Debir
ego: 4 self 7 conceit 11 personality, selfishness
egoism: 5 pride 6 oneism, vanity
egoist: 8 believer
egotism: 5 pride 6 vanity 7 conceit
egotistic: 7 selfish 9 conceited
egotistical: 7 selfish 9 conceited
egregious: 4 fine 5 gross 7 eminent 8 flagrant, shocking 9 excellent, prominent 10 remarkable 13 distinguished
egress: 4 exit 5 issue 6 outlet 7 outgate, passage, regress 9 departure
egret: 5 heron, plume 6 gaulin 8 gaulding
egrimony: 6 sorrow
Egypt: UAR 18 United Arab Republic
air god: Shu
animal: fox 4 adda, lynx 5 genet, hyena 6 jackal, jerboa 7 gazelle 9 ichneumon
antelope: 5 bubal
army chieftain: 6 sirdar
beer: 6 zythum
beetle: 6 scarab
bird: 6 sicsac
boat: 5 baris 8 dahabeah
body: Ka 4 Sahu
bottle: 6 doruck
bull: 4 apis
burial jar: 7 Canopus
calendar: 4 Ahet, Apap, Tybi 5 Choik, Payni, Shemu, Thoth 6 Hathor, Mechir, Mesore, Paophi 7 Pachons 9 Phamenoth, Pharmuthi
cap: fez
capital: 5 Cairo 10 Alexandria
cat-headed goddess: 4 Bast 5 Pakht
Christian: 4 Copt
city: No 4 Sais 5 Cairo, Gizeh, Luxor, Tanis 6 Abydos, Armant, Thebes 10 Alexandria
civilization: 6 Tasian
clover: 7 berseem
cobra: 4 haje
coin: 5 girsh, pound 7 piaster 8 millieme
concubine: 5 Hagar
cosmetic: 4 kohl
cotton: Sak 4 Pima
crocodile-headed god: 4 Sobk 5 Sebek
cross: 4 ankh
crown: 4 atef
dam: 4 sadd, sudd 5 Aswan
dancers: 7 ghawazi 8 ghawazee
deity: Hor, Mut, Nut 4 Anta, Apet, Bast, Isis, Maat, Sati 5 Anaka 6 Hathor, Seshat, Tefnut 7 Nepthys 8 Nechebit
descendant: 4 copt 6 fellah
desert: 5 Scete, Skete
dog: 6 saluki
drink: 4 bosa, boza 5 bozah
drug: 8 nepenthe
elysium: 4 Aalu
emblem: 4 aten 5 lotus
gateway: 5 Pylon
god: Set 4 Ptah, Seth 5 Thoth 6 Anubis 7 Serapis
goddess: Mut, Nut 4 Bast, Isis 5 Pakht 6 Sekhet 8 Nekhebet
governor: 5 Pasha
guard: 6 ghafir 7 ghaffir
gunde: 8 dragoman
hawk-headed god: 5 Horus
herb: 5 anise
instrument: 7 arghool, arghoul, sistrum
isthmus: 4 Suez
judge of the dead: 6 Osiris
king: So; Tut 4 Fuad, Mena 5 Menes 6 Ramses 7 Pharaoh, Ptolemy, Rameses 9 Amenhotep 11 Tutankhamen
laborer: 5 aperu
lake: 8 Menzaleh 13 Birket-el-Kurun
language: 6 Arabic, Coptic
lighthouse: 6 pharos
lily: 6 calla, lotos, lotus
lion-headed goddess: 4 Bast 5 Pakht 6 Sekhet
lizard: 4 adda 5 scink, skink
love goddess; 6 Hathor
lute: 5 nabla
maternity goddess: 4 Apet
measure: apt, dra, hen, rob 4 dira, draa, kada, khet, ocha, roub, theb 5 abdat, ardab, ardeb, cubit, farde, keleh, kilah, sahme 6 artaba, aurure, baladi, kantar, kedlah, robhah, schene 7 choryos, daribah, malouah, roubouh, toumnah 8 kassabah, kharouba 10 dira baladi, dira mimari, kerat kamel, nief keddah 11 feddan nasri
monarch: 7 Pharaoh
monument: 7 obelisk
mountain: 5 Sinai
native: 4 Copt 5 Nilot
negro: 6 Nubian
oasis: 4 Siwa 6 Dakhel 7 Farafra, Khargeh 8 Bahriyeh 12 Wah-el-Khargeh
official: 5 mudir
paper: 6 papyri 7 papyrus
peasant: 6 fellah
peninsula: 5 Sinai
Pharaoh's headdress: 7 pschent

plant: **5** cumin **6** cummin, lentil
province: **4** Giza
queen: **9** Cleopatra, Nofretete
relic: **5** mummy
river: **4** Bahr, Nile
rulers: **9** Ptolemeis
sacred bird: **4** ibis
sacred bull: **4** apis
sacred flower: **5** lotos, lotus
sanctuary: **5** secos, sekos
seal: **6** scarab
serpent: **5** apepi
shrub: kat
solar disk: **4** Aten
soul: Ba
stone: **7** rosetta
sun god: Ra; Tem, Tum **4** Atmu, Atum
symbol: uta **4** ankh **6** scarab
talisman: **5** angle
temple: **4** Idfu **5** Luxor **6** Abydos, Karnak, Osiris **7** Dendera
title: **4** atef **5** pasha **7** Pharaoh
tomb: **7** mastaba, pyramid
underworld: **4** Aaru, Duat **6** Amenti
vase: **7** canopic
viper: **8** cerastes
vulture-headed goddess: Mut **8** Nekhebet
waterway: **4** Nile
weight: ket, oka, oke **4** dera, heml, khar, okia, rotl **5** artal, artel, deben, kerat, okieh, ratel, uckia **6** hamlah, kantar **7** drachma, quintal
wind: **6** kamsin **7** chamsin, kamseen, khamsin **8** khamseen

Egyptian: **4** Arab, Copt **7** African, Ptolemy
Ehud's son: **6** Naaman
eident: **4** busy **7** careful **8** diligent
eider duck: **4** colk
eidetic: **5** vivid
eidolon: **4** icon **5** ghost, image **7** phantom **10** apparition
eight: eta(G.) **6** ogdoad
combining form: **4** octo
group of: **5** octad, octet **6** octave **7** octette
set of: **5** octad **6** ogdoad
eight-sided: **9** octagonal
eighth: *circle:* **6** octant
day after nones: **4** ides
order: **5** octic
eighty: pi(G.) **9** fourscore
Eire: **4** Erin
capital: **6** Tralee
legislature: **4** Dail
Eireannach: **8** Irishman
ejaculate: **5** blurt, eject **7** exclaim
ejaculation: **7** begorra **8** uttering **11** exclamation
eject: **4** boot, cast, emit, oust, spat, spew, spit, void **5** avoid, erupt, evict, expel, spout, spurt, vomit **6** banish, bounce **7** dismiss, exclude, extrude, obtrude **8** disgorge **9** discharge, ejaculate **10** disembogue, dispossess
ejection: **6** ouster **8** eviction **9** expulsion
eke: **4** also **7** augment, enlarge, husband, stretch **8** appendix, increase, lengthen, likewise **10** postscript, supplement
eking: **7** piecing **8** addition **12** augmentation
el: **4** bend
El Salvador: *coin:* **4** peso **5** colon **7** centavo
measure: **4** vara **6** fanega, tercia **7** botella, cajuela, manzana
weight: **4** caja
elaborate: **5** great **6** ornate, refine **7** develop, enlarge, labored, perfect **9** embellish, perfected **11** complicated, extravagant, painstaking
elaborated: **7** wrought **9** superfine
elaboration: **10** production **11** development
Elam: *capital:* **4** Susa
king: **12** Chedorlaomer
elan: **4** dash **5** ardor, gusto, verve **6** spirit, warmth **7** potency **9** eagerness **10** enthusiasm
elanet: **4** kite
elapse: go **4** pass, slip **6** expire
elasmobranch fish: ray
elastic: **6** garter, spongy **7** buoyant, springy **8** cheverel, cheveril, flexible, stretchy **9** expansive, resilient **10** propulsive
fluid: gas
material from whales: **6** baleen
elasticity science: **9** elaterics
elastin: **10** albuminoid
elate: **4** buoy **5** cheer, exalt, exult, flush, lofty, raise **6** excite, please, thrill **7** elevate, gladden, inflate, success **8** elevated, heighten, inspirit **9** stimulate **10** exhilarate
elated: **5** chuff, happy, vogie **6** jovial **7** excited, exulted, jocular **8** exultant, inflated, jubilant **9** cock-a-hoop
elater: **6** beetle **8** skipjack
elaterite: **7** bitumen
Elatha's son: **4** Bres
elation: joy **4** glee **10** exaltation
Elatus' daughter: **6** Caenis **7** Caeneus
Elbe tributary: **4** Eger, Iser
elbow: **4** bend **5** ancon, joint, nudge, shove **6** jostle
bend: **4** tope **5** drink
bone: **4** ulna **5** ulnae
pert. to: **5** ulnar **8** anconeal
elbowroom: **6** leeway
elcaja: **6** mafura
elchee, elchi: **5** envoy **10** ambassador
eld: **9** antiquity

elder: ain, iva 4 aine 5 prior 6 senior 7 ancient 8 ancestor, danewort 9 elderwort, presbyter 10 forefather
elderly: 4 aged, gray 6 senile
eldest: 5 eigne 6 oldest
eldritch: 4 eery 5 eerie, weird 7 uncanny 9 frightful
Eleanor's husband: 7 Henry II
eleatic: 11 xenophanean
elect: 4 call, pick 6 assume, choose, chosen, decide, prefer, select 9 legislate
election: 6 choice 9 balloting 10 plebiscite 11 alternative
majority of votes: 9 plurality
electioneer: 5 stump
elective: 8 optional 9 voluntary
elector: 5 voter 6 elisor 7 chooser 11 constituent
Electra: *brother:* 7 Orestes
father: 9 Agamemnon
husband: 7 Thaumas
mother: 12 Klytemnestra
son: 8 Dardanus
electric: 4 elod 6 static 8 magnetic
appliance: 4 iron, oven 5 dryer, mixer, stove 6 heater, washer 7 blender, broiler, toaster
carrier: 9 conductor
circuit regulator: 7 booster
coil: 5 tesla
conductor: 6 ohmage
current: AC., DC.
current meter: 7 ammeter 9 voltmeter
current moderator: 5 coder 9 rheometer 10 attenuator
device: 6 dynamo 8 divertor, rheostat 9 amplifier, capacitor, condenser
generator: 6 dynamo
instrument: 6 dynamo 8 rheostat, rheotome 9 condenser, generator
light: arc 4 neon 12 incandescent
measuring unit: es; amp, ohm, rel 4 volt, watt 5 barad, farad, henry, joule 6 ampere, proton 7 coulomb 8 kilowatt
motion: 14 electrodynamic
motor part: 10 commutator
od: 4 elod
particle: ion
pole: 5 anode 7 cathode
power: 7 wattage
resistance: 6 ohmage
safety device: 4 fuse
strength: 8 amperage
transmission: 5 radio
wave meter: 9 ondometer
electrify: 7 startle
electrocute: 7 execute
electrode: 5 anode 7 cathode, kathode
controlling electron tube: 4 grid
negative: 7 cathode, kathode
electronic tube: 6 triode, vacuum 8 klystron
electrum: 5 amber
Electryon: *brother:* 6 Mestor
daughter: 7 Alcmene
father: 7 Perseus
mother: 9 Andromeda
wife: 5 Anaxo
eleemosynary: 4 free 7 almoner 9 dependent 10 charitable, gratuitous
elegance: 4 chic 5 grace, taste 6 finery, luxury, polish 8 courtesy, grandeur, splendor 9 propriety, recherche 10 concinnity, refinement 12 gracefulness
elegant: 4 chic, dink, fine, posh 5 civil 6 dainty, dressy, facete, minion, superb, urbane 7 cleanly, courtly, featish, featous, genteel, minikin, refined 8 delicate, graceful, handsome, polished, tasteful 9 admirable, beautiful, excellent, exquisite 10 concinnous, fastidious
elegantly: 8 gingerly
elegiac: 8 mournful 9 plaintive
elegiacal: 8 mournful
elegist: 4 Gray, poet 6 Milton 10 Propertius
elegit: 4 writ
elegy: 4 poem, song 5 dirge 6 lament 7 epicede 9 epicedium 11 lamentation
element: 5 metal, stuff 7 essence 8 rudiment 9 component 10 ingredient 11 constituent, environment
chemical: tin(Sn) 4 gold(Au), Iron(Fe), lead(Pb), neon(Ne), zinc(Zn) 5 argon(A), boron(B), radon(Rn), xenon(Xe) 6 barium(Ba), carbon(C), cerium(Ce), cesium(Cs), cobalt(Co), copper(Cu), erbium (Er), helium(He), indium(In), iodine(I), nickel(Ni), osmium(Os), oxygen(O), radium(Ra), silver(Ag), sodium(Na) 7 arsenic (As), bismuth(Bi), bromine(Br), cadmium(Cd), calcium(Ca), gallium(Ga), hafnium(Hf), holmium(Ho), iridium(Ir), krypton(Kr), lithium(Li), mercury(Hg), niobium(Cb), rhenium(Re), rhodium(Rh), silicon(Si), sulphur(S.), terbium(Tb), thorium(Th), thulium(Tm), uranium(U), yttrium(Y) 8 actinium(Ac), aluminum(Al), antimony(Sb), astatine(At), chlorine(Cl), chromium(Cr), Europium(Eu), fluorine(F), hydrogen(H), illinium(Il), lutecium(Lu), masurium(Ma), nitrogen(N), platinum(Pt), polonium(Po), rubidium(Rb), samarium(Sm), scandium(Sc), selenium(Se), tantalum(Ta), thallium(Tl), titanium(Ti), tungsten(W), vanadium(V) 9 beryllium(Be), columbium(Cb), germanium(Ge), lanthanum(La), magnesium(Mg), manganese(Mn), neodymium(Nd), palladium(Pd), potassium(K), ruthenium(Ru),

strontium(Sr), tellurium(Te), virginium(Vi), ytterbium(Yb), zirconium(Zr) **10** dysprosium(Dy), gadolinium(Gd), molybdenum(Mo) **11** phosphorous(P), **12** praseodymium(Pr) **13** protoactinium(Pa)
combining power: **7** valence
decomposed: **5** anion
different weight: **7** isotope
even valence: **6** artiad
family: **7** halogen
minute: **5** monad
nonmetallic: **5** boron **6** bromin, iodine **7** bromine, silicon
nonvolatile: **6** barium
of air: **5** argon **6** oxygen **8** nitrogen
poisonous: **7** arsenic
rare earth: **6** erbium
elemental: **4** pure **5** basic **6** primal, simple **7** primary **10** elementary **11** fundamental, rudimentary
elemental spirit: **5** genie
elementary: **6** simple **7** initial **8** inchoate **9** elemental **10** rudimental, uncombined **11** fundamental, rudimentary
organism: **5** monad
reader: **6** primer
elemi: **5** anime, resin **9** oleoresin
pert. to: **7** elemine
elenge: **6** dreary, remote **7** tedious **9** miserable
elephant: cow **4** bull, calf **5** rogue, hathi **6** tusker, muckna **7** marmoth **8** oliphant, mastodon **9** pachyderm
call: **4** barr **7** trumpet
cry: **4** barr
dentin: **5** ivory
driver: **6** mahout
ear: **4** taro
enclosure: **5** kraal
extinct: **8** mastodon
goad: **5** ankus
group: **4** herd
keeper: **6** mahout
male: **4** bull
pert. to: **11** pachydermic
saddle: **6** howdah
seat: **6** howdah
trappings for: **5** jhool
trunk: **9** proboscis
tusk: **5** ivory **9** scrivello
young: **4** calf
elephant boy: **4** Sabu
elephantine: **4** huge **8** enormous, ungainly **9** ponderous
goddess: **4** Sati
elevate: **4** hain, lift, rear, rise **5** elate, erect, exalt, extol, heave, hoist, raise, setup, tower **6** uplift **7** advance, dignify, enhance, ennoble, glorify, promote **8** heighten, inspirit **10** exhilarate
elevated: el **4** high **5** great, lofty, noble, risen, steep **6** elated, raised, rising **7** exalted **8** majestic
elevation: **4** bank, hill, rise, toot **5** horst, mound, ridge **6** height, uplift **8** altitude, eminence, highness, swelling **10** exaltation
of mind: **7** anagoge
elevator: bin **4** cage, lift, silo **5** hoist **9** ascenseur
elf: fay, hob, imp, oaf, pug **4** fane, peri, pixy **5** dwarf, elfin, fairy, gnome, ouphe, pigmy, pixie **6** elfkin, goblin, sprite **7** brownie, incubus, succubi **8** succubus **10** changeling, leprechaun
elf dock: **10** elecampane
elfin: elf **5** child **6** urchin
elfish: **5** elfin **6** elvish, impish **7** elflike, tricksy **11** mischievous
elfland: **9** fairyland
elfwort: **10** elecampane
Elgin marbles: **10** sculptures
Eli: **4** Yale
son: **6** Hophni **8** Phinehas
Eliam's daughter: **9** Bathsheba
Elian: **8** Eretrian
elicit: **4** draw, milk, pump **5** claim, educe, evoke, exact, wrest, wring **6** deduce, demand, entice, extort, induce **7** extract **9** elicitate
elide: **4** omit, skip **5** annul **6** ignore **7** destroy, nullify **8** demolish, suppress **9** apocopate
eligible: fit **6** worthy **8** suitable **9** desirable, qualified
Elijah: **5** Elias **7** prophet **8** Tishbite
eliminate: **5** educe, expel **6** delete, except, ignore, remove **7** divulge, exclude, excrete, release, silence **8** separate
elimination: **9** excursion
Eliot: *hero:* **6** Marner
heroine: **6** Romola
eliquate: **4** melt **5** smelt **6** strain **7** clarify, liquate, liquefy
elision mark: **10** apostrophe
elisor: **7** elector
Elisha: *father:* **7** Shaphat
home: **11** Abelmeholah
servant: **6** Gehazi
Elissa: See Dido
elite: **4** best **6** choice, flower, select **9** oligarchy **10** uppercrust **11** aristocracy **12** quintessence
gathering: **6** galaxy
elixir: **6** spirit **7** arcanum, cordial, cureall, panacea **12** quintessence

of life: 6 amrita 7 amreeta
Elizabeth I: 4 Bess 6 Oriana
mother: 6 Boleyn
elk: 4 alce, deer 5 aland, eland, moose 6 sambar, wapiti 7 sambhur
genus of: 5 alces
ell: 6 alnage 8 addition
ellipse: 4 oval
ellipsoidal: 4 oval
elliptical: 4 oval 5 ovate
elm: *family of:* 8 ulmaceae
fruit of: 6 samara
rock: 5 wahoo
Elmo's fire: See **Saint Elmo's fire**
elocute: 7 declaim
elocution: 7 oratory 9 eloquence
elocutionist: 6 reader 7 reciter
elodian: 8 tortoise
eloge: 6 eulogy 7 oration 8 encomium 9 panegyric
elogium: 7 oration 11 inscription
eloign: 6 convey, remove 7 conceal
eloine: 7 abscond
elongate: 6 remove 7 stretch 8 lengthen, protract
elongated: 4 lank, long 6 linear, oblong 7 prolate, slender 9 stretched
elope: 6 decamp 7 abscond, getaway
eloquence: 6 facund 7 fluency, oratory 9 elocution, facundity, loftiness
teacher of: 6 rhetor
eloquent: 6 facund, fervid, fluent 7 renable 10 expressive, meaningful, oratorical, persuasive 11 impassioned, significant
else: or; ens 4 ense 5 other 7 besides, instead 9 otherwise 10 additional
elsewhere: 5 alibi
elt: 5 knead
elucidate: 5 clear, lucid 7 explain 8 simplify 9 interpret 10 illustrate
elude: 4 flee, foil, mock 5 avoid, dodge, evade 6 baffle, befool, delude, escape, illude 7 beguile, deceive 9 frustrate
elusive: 4 eely 6 subtle, tricky 7 elusory, evasive, subtile 8 baffling 9 lubricous 10 impalpable
elusory: 7 elusive, evasive
elver: eel
elves: See **elf**
elvish: 11 mischievous
Elysian: 8 beatific, blissful 10 delightful
Elysium: 4 Eden 8 Paradise
elytrin: 6 chitin
elytrum of beetle: 5 shard
emaciated: 4 lean 5 gaunt 6 peaked, skinny, wasted
emaciation: 5 niton, tabes 7 atrophy 8 marasmus 11 attenuation
emanant: 9 radiating
emanate: 4 flow 5 arise, issue 6 effuse 7 breathe, outcome, proceed, radiate 9 effluence, originate
emanation: 4 aura 5 aurae(pl.), niton 6 efflux 7 outcome 9 ectoplasm, effluence 10 exhalation 11 consequence
emanative: 7 issuant
emancipate: 4 free 7 manumit, release 8 liberate, unfetter 11 affranchise, enfranchise
emancipation: 7 freedom, release 10 liberation 11 deliverance, manumission 15 enfranchisement
emancipator: 5 freer, Moses 7 Lincoln 9 deliverer
emasculate: 4 geld 6 soften 8 castrate, enervate
embale: 4 pack
embalm: 4 balm, cere 5 mummy 6 balsam
embalmer: 5 cerer 10 undertaker
embankment: 4 bank, bund, dike, fill, quay 5 digue, levee, mound, revet 6 staith 7 backing 9 banquette
embar: 4 stop 6 hinder
embargo: 5 edict, order 8 blockade, stoppage 10 impediment, inhibition 11 prohibition, requisition
embark: 4 sail, ship 6 engage, enlist, invest
embarrass: 4 clog 5 abash, annoy, shame, upset 6 boggle, gravel, hamper, hinder, hobble, impede 7 confuse, flummox, nonplus 8 bewilder, confound, dumfound, encumber, entangle, handicap, obstruct, straiten 9 discomfit 10 complicate, disconcert
embarrassment: fix 5 shame 6 caddle, hobble 9 abashment, confusion 10 discomfort, impediment, perplexity 11 encumbrance, involvement 12 bewilderment, discomfiture, discomposure, entanglement 13 inconvenience
embassy: 7 ambassy 9 ambassade, embassage 10 ambassiate
embattle: 6 crenel 7 fortify
embattled: 7 crenele 8 crenelee, crenelle
embattlement: 7 parapet
embay: 5 bathe 7 shelter, suffuse 8 encircle, surround
embed: set 6 engage
embellish: 4 deck, gild, trim 5 adorn, dress, grace 6 bedeck, blazon, emboss, enrich, flower 7 apparel, bedrape, emblaze, garnish, varnish 8 beautify, decorate, flourish, ornament 9 elaborate, embroider
embellished: 6 florid, gested, ornate
embellishment: 7 agremen 8 agrement, mounting, ornament 9 fioritura, furniture, garniture 13 ornamentation
ember: ash 4 coal 5 aizle 6 cinder

embezzle: 5 steal 8 peculate, squander 9 dissipate
embezzlement: 5 theft
embitter: 4 sour 7 acidify, envenom 8 acerbate 9 acidulate 10 exacerbate, exasperate
emblaze: 5 adorn, honor 6 kindle 9 embellish
emblazon: 4 laud 5 adorn, extol 6 blazon 7 display, exhibit, glorify 9 celebrate
emblem: bar 4 aten, mace, orle, sign, star, type 5 badge, image, tiara, token 6 device, diadem, figure, sabcat, symbol 7 impresa, imprese, scepter, sceptre 8 allegory, colophon, insignia 9 character, laticlave, prototype 10 cognizance
of authority: 4 mace
of clan: 5 totem
of U.S.: 5 eagle
emblematic: 5 typal 7 typical 8 symbolic 10 figurative
emblic: 4 aula 5 aulae(pl.)
embodiment: map 6 avatar 11 incarnation 15 personification
of Ptah: 4 Apis
embody: 5 unite 7 contain 8 coalesce, organize 9 incarnate, personify 10 comprehend 11 incorporate
embolden: 5 bield, brave, nerve 6 assure 7 hearten 9 encourage, enhearten
embolism: 8 stoppage 9 occlusion 11 obstruction 13 intercalation
embolus: 4 clot
embosom, imbosom: 6 foster 7 cherish, enclose, shelter 8 surround
emboss: 4 boss, hide, knob 5 adorn, chase 6 indent 7 conceal, enclose, exhaust, inflate 8 ornament 9 embellish, embroider, insheathe
embossing: 8 celature
embowed: 5 bowed
embower: 5 bower
embrace: hug 4 clip, coll, fold, love, neck, side 5 adopt, bosom, brace, chain, clasp, cling, enarm, grasp, halch, halse, inarm 6 abrazo, accept, caress, clinch, comply, cuddle, enfold, huddle, inclip, infold, plight 7 amplect, cherish, contain, enclose, espouse, include, involve 8 accolade, complect, compress, comprise, comprize, conclude, encircle 9 encompass 10 comprehend 11 amplexation
embrangle: 7 confuse 8 entangle
embrocation: 6 arnica 8 liniment
embroider: tat 4 lace 5 couch, panel 6 emboss, frieze, stitch 8 ornament 9 embellish 10 exaggerate
embroidered: 5 brode 6 brodee 7 browden
embroidery: 4 lace 5 brede 6 bonnaz, edging, hedebo 7 orphrey 8 arrasene
figure: 6 etoile
frame: 7 taboret
hole: 6 eyelet
machine-made: 6 bonnaz
thread: 5 floss
embroil: 5 broil 6 jumble 7 perplex, trouble 8 disorder, distract, entangle 9 commingle, implicate 10 complicate
embrown: tan
embryo: 5 cadet, fetus, ovule 6 foetus 9 peritroch 10 conception
young: 8 blastema
embusque: 7 shirker, slacker
eme: 5 uncle 6 friend, gossip 8 relative
emeer, emir: 5 pasha, ruler
emend: 4 edit, mend 5 alter, amend 6 better, reform, repeal, revise 7 correct, improve, rectify, redress
emendate: 7 correct, rectify
emendator: 6 editor
emerald: 5 beryl, color, green 7 smaragd
Emerald Isle: 4 Erin 7 Ireland
emerge: dip 4 loom, rise 5 issue 6 appear, plunge 10 disembogue
emergence: 4 need 8 debouche, exigence 9 occurrence, outgrowth
emergency: 5 pinch 6 crisis, crises(pl.), strait 8 exigency, juncture 9 necessity
emergent: 6 rising
Emerson: *friend:* 7 Thoreau
philosophy: 17 transcendentalism
emery: 8 abrasive, corundum 11 carborundum
emetic: 8 evacuant
emetic holly: 6 yaupon
emeute: 6 tumult 8 outbreak
emigrant: 6 emigre 7 exodist, settler 8 colonist, stranger
emigrate: 4 move
emigre: 7 refugee
eminence: 4 berg, mote, note, rise, scar, toot 6 ascent, height, renown, rideau 9 elevation, loftiness 10 projection, prominence 12 protuberance 13 transcendency
eminent: big 4 arch, high 5 chief, great, lofty, noble, noted 6 famous, marked, signal 8 glorious, renowned, singular, towering 9 egregious 10 celebrated, noteworthy 11 conspicuous, illustrious, outstanding 13 distinguished
emir, emeer: 5 noble, ruler, title 6 leader, prince 8 governor 9 chieftain, commander
province: 7 emirate
emissary: spy 5 agent, scout 8 delegate
emission: 9 radiation
emissive: 8 exhalant
emit: 4 beam, cast, give, pour, send, shed, vent 5 avoid, eject, exert, exude, fling, is-

sue, utter 6 decant, evolve, exhale, expire 7 distill, exhaust, radiate 8 transmit 9 discharge, irradiate
heat: 4 glow
light: 4 glow 9 luminesce
offensive odors: 4 reek
emmer: 5 spelt, wheat
emmet: ant 7 pismire 8 formicid
emolliate: 6 soften 10 effeminate
emollient: 7 lenient 8 lenitive
emolument: 4 fees 5 wages 6 income, profit, salary 7 benefit, stipend 9 advantage 12 compensation
Emory University site: 7 Atlanta
emote: act 7 overact
emotion: ire 4 love 5 agony, anger, grief, heart 6 affect, effect, raptus, snivel 7 ecstasy, feeling, passion 8 gramercy, movement 9 affection, agitation, sentiment 11 disturbance 14 susceptibility
without: 9 apathetic
emotionable: 11 sensational
emotional: 7 emotive 9 rhapsodic 10 hysterical, passionate
emotionalism: 8 hysteria
emotionless: 5 staid 6 torpid 9 apathetic, unfeeling
empathy: 4 pity, ruth 8 affinity, sympathy 13 understanding
emperor: 4 czar, king, tsar 5 Akbar, ruler 6 sultan 7 Baginda, monarch 9 commander, imperator, sovereign
Holy Roman: 4 Otho, Otto
empery: 6 empire 8 dominion 11 sovereignty
emphasis: 6 accent, stress 8 salience
emphasize: 6 accent, betone, stress 9 punctuate 10 accentuate
emphatic: 7 earnest, marcato 8 enfatico, forcible, positive 9 energetic
empire: 4 rule, sway 5 power, realm, reign, state 6 domain, empery 7 control, kingdom 8 dominion 11 sovereignty
Empire State: 7 New York
empiric: 5 quack 8 impostor 9 charlatan 10 mountebank
emplacement: 7 battery 8 platform
employ: fee, use 4 busy, hire, wage 5 beset 6 bestow, engage, infold, occupy, supply 7 concern, enclose, involve, service, utilize 8 exercise
employed: 4 busy 6 unidle 7 engaged
employee: 5 clerk 11 salesperson
bank: 5 guard 6 teller 7 cashier 8 watchman 10 bookkeeper
minor: cog 6 helper 9 assistant
slaughterhouse: 5 sider
employees: men 4 help 5 hands
employer: 4 boss, user 6 gaffer 7 manager 12 entrepreneur
employment: use 4 task, toil, work 5 craft, trade, usage 7 calling, purpose 8 business, vocation 10 engagement, occupation, profession
empoison: 5 taint 6 poison 7 corrupt, deprave, envenom
emporium: 4 mart, shop 5 bazar, store 6 bazaar, market, staple
empower: 6 enable 7 entitle 8 delegate, deputize 9 authorize 10 commission
empresa: 5 motto 6 device 7 tsarina
empress: 5 queen, ruler
Byzantine: 5 Irene
Russian: 7 czarina, tsarina
empress tree: 9 paulownia
empresse: 6 ardent 9 impetuous
emprise, emprize: 9 undertake 10 enterprise
empt: 5 empty
emptiness: 4 void 7 inanity, vacancy, vacuity 9 inanition
emptio: 6 buying 8 purchase
empty: rid 4 bare, boss, dump, empt, farm, free, howe, idle, leer, pour, toom, void 5 addle, avoid, blank, drain, equal, expel, inane 6 barren, bubble, devoid, hollow, jejune, unload, vacant, vacate 7 deplete, exhaust, untaken, vacuate, vacuous 8 disgorge, evacuate, evanesce, negation, unfilled 9 discharge, moonshine 10 unburdened, unoccupied 11 rodomontade
comb. form: ken 4 keno
empty space: 4 void 5 blank 6 vacuum
emptying: 8 evacuant 9 avoidance
Empusa: 7 specter 9 hobgoblin
empyreal: 7 sublime 9 celestial
empyrean: 5 ether 7 heavens 9 firmament
emu: 4 rhea 6 ratite
emulate: ape, vie 4 copy 5 equal, excel, rival 7 compete, imitate
emulation: 6 strife 7 contest 10 contention 11 competition
emulator: 5 rival
emulsive: 9 softening
emyd: 6 turtle
enable: 7 empower, entitle, qualify
enact: 4 pass 6 decree, effect, ordain 7 actuate, appoint, perform, portray 9 legislate, personate, represent 10 constitute
enactment: law 4 doom 6 assize, decree 7 statute 12 constitution 14 representation
enactor: 6 player 10 legislator
enamel: 5 glaze, gloss, paint 6 aumail 7 dentine, schmelz 8 cosmetic, schmelze
enamelled: 10 variegated
enamelware: 7 Limoges

enamor, enamour: 4 love 5 charm 7 captive 9 captivate, fascinate
enamorata, inamorata: 5 lover 10 sweetheart
enamored, enamoured: 4 fond 5 epris 6 eprise 7 amorous, charmed, smitten 10 fascinated, infatuated
Enan's son: 5 Ahira
enarm: 4 lard 7 embrace, enhance
enarme: 5 strap
enate: 7 related
encamp: 4 tent 5 lodge, pitch 7 bivouac
encampment: 5 siege 7 bivouac, castrum(L.)
encase: 7 inclose
encave: 6 entomb
enchain: 6 fetter
enchant: 5 charm 6 delude, glamor 7 bewitch, delight, glamour 8 ensorcel 9 captivate, enrapture, ensorcell, fascinate, spellbind
enchanted: 4 rapt
enchanting: 10 bewitching
enchantment: hex 5 charm, magic, spell 7 chantry, gramary, sorcery 8 gramarye, witchery 9 chantment 10 necromancy, witchcraft 11 fascination, incantation
enchantress: 5 Circe, fairy, Medea 9 sorceress
encharge: 7 entrust 10 commission
enchase: 7 engrave
enchiridion: 6 manual 8 handbook
enchorial: 6 native 8 domestic
encina: oak
encipher: 4 code
encircle: orb 4 belt, clip, coil, gird, girt, hoop, pale, ring, rink, zone 5 belay, brace, embay, embow, girth, inorb 6 circle, emball, engirt, enlace, girdle, impale 7 betrend, embrace, enclose, environ, wreathe 8 cincture, ensphere, surround 9 encompass 12 circumscribe 13 circumference
encircled: 4 girt 6 ringed 10 surrounded
encircling: 6 around 8 encyclic
encircling band: 4 zone
encloak: 6 mantle
enclose: bay, box, hem, mew, orb, pin, rim 4 case, gird, pale, wall, yard 5 bound, bower, bught, chest, fence, hedge, house 6 bought, circle, corral, emboss, empark, employ, encase, encyst, enfold, enlock, impark, incase, picket, pocket 7 contain, embosom, embrace, envelop, harness, imbosom 8 comprise, comprize, conclude, encircle, imprison, palisade, surround 9 encompass 10 comprehend 12 circumscribe
enclosure: hag, haw, mew, pen, ree, sty 4 bawn, cage, coop, fold, sept, wall, yard 5 atajo, court, fence, kraal, pleck, pound, reeve 6 aviary, corral, cowpen, garden, hurdle, kennel, paling, prison 7 closure, paddock, puddock 8 cincture, clausure, cloister, sepiment
animal: pen, sty, par 4 yard, cage, cote, weir, yair, yare 5 booly, crawl, kench, gotra, kraal, atajo 6 booley, corral, runway, cancha, keddah 8 poundage 9 sheepcote
kind of: 4 bawn, boma, cage 5 bomar, carol, crawl 6 cruive 7 nacelle, paddock, stadium 8 delubrum, stockade 9 cofferdam
encomiast: 8 eulogist 10 panegyrist
encomium: 5 eloge 6 eulogy, praise 7 plaudit, tribute 9 panegyric 10 compliment
encompass: 4 be-go, belt, clip, gird, ring, wall 5 belie, beset 6 begird, circle, engird 7 embrace, enclose, environ, include 8 encircle, engirdle, surround 9 beleaguer, circulate 10 circumvent 12 circumscribe
encompassed: 5 bayed 6 begirt 10 surrounded
encompassing: 13 circumambient
encore: bis 5 again 6 recall, repeat 10 repitition
anti: boo 4 hiss 7 catcall
encore!: 5 again
encounter: 4 bide, coil, face, meet, rink 5 brush, fight, force, incur, onset 6 accost, affray, assail, attack, battle, breast, combat, oppose 7 address, affront, contest, counter, dispute, hosting 8 conflict, confront, skirmish 9 collision, interview 10 engagement, foregather, occurrence, tournament
courageously: 5 beard, brave 7 weather
encountered: 4 moot
encourage: 4 abet, back 5 boost, cheer, impel, nerve 6 advise, assure, exhort, foment, foster, incite, induce, second, uphold 7 advance, animate, cherish, comfort, confirm, console, enliven, forward, hearten, inspire, promote 8 embolden, inspirit, reassure 9 instigate, stimulate 10 strengthen 11 comfortable, countenance
encouragement: 5 flush 6 hurrah 7 fomento 9 incentive, patronage 11 fomentation
encouraging: 8 favoring 11 comfortable, inspiriting 12 advantageous
Encratite: 6 Tatian 9 Tatianist
encraty: 10 abstinence
encroach: 5 poach 6 invade, trench 7 impinge, intrude 8 entrench, infringe, intrench, trespass
encroachment: 6 inroad 10 aggression, infraction
encuirassed: 7 armored 8 loricate
encumber: 4 clog, load 5 beset, check 6 burden, hamper, hinder, impede, moider, re-

tard, saddle, weight 7 involve, oppress 8 entangle, handicap, obstruct, overcome, overload 9 embarrass 10 overburden
encumbered: 5 heavy
encumbrance: 4 clog, lien, load 5 claim 6 burden, charge 7 trouble 8 mortgage 9 cumbrance 10 impediment, perplexity 11 impedimenta(pl.) 13 embarrassment
encyclic: 8 circular 10 encircling 13 comprehensive
encyclopedia: 4 tome
encyclopedic learning: *person of:* 7 scholar 10 polyhistor
end: aim, tip 4 fate, goal, heel, stop, tail 5 amend, cease, close, death, ensue, finis, issue, limit, napoo, omega, raise, scrap, stash 6 define, design, expire, finale, finish, napooh, object, period, upshot, windup 7 abolish, achieve, closure, destroy, lineman, outgive, purpose, remnant 8 boundary, complete, conclude, dissolve, finality, surcease, terminal, terminus 9 cessation, determine, extremity, intention, objective, terminate 10 completion, conclusion, denouement, expiration 11 consequence, destruction, discontinue, termination 12 consummation 14 accomplishment
comb. form: 4 telo
loose: tag
musical: 4 coda, fine
remove: tip 4 clip
tending to: 5 telic
upper: tip 4 apex, head
End of World: 15 Gotterdammerung
end result: 7 product
endamage: 4 harm 6 injure
endanger: 6 hazard 7 imperil 10 compromise, jeopardize
endearing: 7 lovable 9 caressing
endearment: 6 caress
term of: hon 4 dear 5 aroon, honey 7 acushla, sweetie 10 mavourneen
endeavor, endeavour: aim, try 4 best, mint, seek 5 assay, essay, ettle, exert, study, tempt, trial 6 affair, effort, strife, strive 7 afforce, attempt 8 exertion, struggle 9 undertake
ended: 4 done, over, past 8 finished
endemic: 5 local
ending: 6 finale 11 termination
adjective: ic
adverbial: ly
having same: 11 coterminous 12 conterminous
participial: ed
superlative: est
endive: 7 chicory 8 escarole
endless: 7 eternal, forever, undying 8 immortal, infinite, unending 9 boundless, ceaseless, continual, incessant, perpetual, unceasing 10 continuous 11 everlasting, measureless 12 interminable 13 uninterrupted
endlessly: 7 forever
endlong: 5 along 10 lengthwise 14 longitudinally
endmost: 8 farthest, remotest
endoderm: 8 entomere
endorse, indorse: 4 back, sign 5 boost 6 second 7 approve, certify, support 8 advocate, sanction 9 authorize, guarantee 11 countenance
endorsement: 4 fiat, visa 5 rider 7 backing 8 approval, sanction 9 signature
endow: dow, due 4 dote, vest 5 dower, endue, equip, found, indue 6 clothe, dotate, enrich, invest 7 furnish, instate 8 bequeath
with bodily form: 11 materialize
with power: 8 energize
endowment: 4 gift 5 dower, dowry 6 talent 7 apanage, chantry 8 appanage, dotation 9 mentality 10 foundation
endpiece: 5 chump
endue: due 5 endow, teach 6 clothe, invest 8 instruct
endurable: 7 livable 8 bearable 9 tolerable 10 sufferable 11 supportable
endurance: 5 pluck 7 durance, stamina 8 gameness, hardship, patience, strength 9 fortitude, suffering 10 sufferance 11 continuance, persistance, resignation 12 perseverance
endure: vie, 4 bear, bide, dree, dure, last, tide, wear 5 abear, abide, allow, brook, stand, thole 6 abrook, drudge, harden, remain, suffer 7 comfort, forbear, persist, sustain, toughen, undergo 8 continue, forebear, tolerate 9 exantlate, withstand 10 strengthen
endured: 5 borne
enduring: 4 fast 6 biding 7 durable, eternal, lasting, patient 8 immortal, remanent 9 continual, perennial, permanent 11 everlasting 12 imperishable
endwise: 7 erectly
Endymion: *mother:* 6 Calyce
son: 7 Aetolus
loved by: 6 Selene
enemy: fae, foe 4 Axis, feid 5 devil, fiend, Satan 6 foeman 7 hostile 8 opponent 9 adversary, ill-wisher 10 antagonist, backfriend
energetic: 4 fast, hard, live 5 brisk, dashy 6 active, hearty, hustle 7 arduous 8 emphatic, forceful, forcible, vigorous 9 dynamical, strenuous 10 expressive 12 enterprising
energize: 7 animate

energumen: 7 fanatic 8 demoniac 10 enthusiast

energy: go; pep, vim, zip 4 bang, bent, birr, life 5 force, nerve, power, steam, vigor 6 intake, output, spirit 7 potency 8 activity, strength 9 animation
lack: 5 atony 6 anergy 7 aneuria
measuring device: 9 ergometer
pert. to: 7 actinic
potential: 4 edar 5 ergal
unit: erg 4 dyne 5 ergon, joule 7 atomerg, quantum 8 dinamode 9 megajoule 10 horsepower

enervate: sap 6 weaken 7 unnerve 8 enfeeble 9 enslumber 10 debilitate

enfeeble: 4 numb 5 shake 6 appall, deaden, impair, soften, weaken 7 depress 8 enervate 9 attenuate, undermine 10 debilitate

enfeebled: fey 4 numb 9 dissolute

enfilade: 4 rake

enfold: lap 4 wrap 5 clasp, cover, enrol 6 comply, enlace, enroll, enwrap, swathe 7 embrace, enclose, envelop

enforce: 5 exact 6 coerce, compel 7 execute, implant 9 constrain, prosecute

enfranchise: 4 free 7 deliver, manumit, release 8 liberate 10 emancipate

engage: 4 book, gage, hire, join, mesh, rent, sign 5 agree, catch, enter, lease, trade 6 absorb, arrest, embark, employ, enlist, induce, oblige, occupy, pledge 7 bespeak, betroth, conduce, consume, engross, involve, promise 8 contract, covenant, entangle, interest, persuade 9 interlock, undertake

engaged: 4 busy 5 hired 6 bonded, meshed 7 assured, earnest, entered, pledged, versant 8 embedded, employed, involved, occupied, promised 9 affianced, betrothed

engagement: 4 aval, date 5 cowle 6 affair, battle, escrow 7 bargain 9 betrothal, encounter 10 attachment, employment 11 appointment, involvement

engager: 6 surety

engaging: 5 sapid 6 taking 10 attractive 11 interesting

engastrimyth: 13 ventriloquist

engender: 5 beget, breed, cause 6 excite, gender 7 develop, produce 8 generate, occasion 9 procreate, propagate

engild: 8 brighten

engine: gas 5 motor, steam 7 turbine 8 gasoline 10 locomotive
covering: 4 cowl
kind of: gin, ram 4 goat 5 dinky, mogul 6 diesel, helper, mallet, pusher 7 turbine 8 dollbeer 10 locomotive
military: ram 4 tank 6 onager 7 robinet 8 ballista, helepole 9 espringal 11 ribaudequin
part: cam 4 gear 6 boiler, piston, stator 8 cylinder 9 crankcase 10 carburetor 12 differential, transmission
speed up: rev

engineer: 4 plan 6 driver, manage 7 planner, plotter 8 contrive, designer, inventor, maneuver 9 construct 10 accomplish 11 constructor, superintend
degree: C.E., E.E., M.E.

enginous: 6 crafty 9 ingenious

engirdle: 4 gird 9 encompass

engirt: 6 engird 7 envelop 8 encircle

England: 6 Albion 7 Britain 9 Britannia 12 Great Britain
aborigine: 4 Pict
actor: 4 Tree 5 Donat, Evans 6 Arliss 7 Burbage, Olivier 8 Guinness
actress: 4 Gwyn 5 Leigh, Terry
admiral: 6 Nelson, Rodney, Vernon
admirer of: 10 anglophile
air force: R.A.F.
Antarctic explorer: 5 Scott
apartment: 4 flat
apple: 6 beefin, biffin, coling, rennet 7 beaufin, costard 8 coccagee 9 guarenden, guarender
apron: 8 barmskin
archbishop: 4 Lang, Laud 6 Becket 7 Cranmer
architect: 4 Wren
art gallery: 4 Tate
bailiff: 5 reeve
bed: 4 doss
biologist: 6 Huxley
boat: 7 coracle
castle site: 7 Arundel, Windsor
cathedral city: Ely
cattle: 5 Devon
cattle tender: 7 byreman
Channel Island: 4 Sark
charity school scholar: 8 blue coat
cheese: 7 stilton, truckle
chinaware: 5 Spode 8 Wedgwood
church caretaker: 6 verger
church officer: 6 beadle
circuit court: 4 eyre
city: Ely 4 Bath, Hull, York 5 Derby, Erith, Leeds, Truro, Wigan 6 Bolton, Bootle, Exeter, Hanley, Jarrow, Leyton, London, Oldham, Rippon 7 Bristol, Burnley, Croydon, Grimsby, Halifax, Hornsey, Ipswich, Newport, Norwich, Preston, Reading, Salford, Seaford, Walsall, West Ham 8 Bradford, Brighton, Coventry, Dewsbury, Hastings, Plymouth, Rochdale, Wallasey, Wallsend 9 Birkehead, Blackburn, Devonport, Gateshead, Leicester, Liverpool, Rotherham, Sheffield, Smethwick, Stockport, Tottenham, Willesden 10 Aston Manor, Birmingham, Manchester, Nottingham,

Portsmouth, Sunderland, Warrington **11** Bournemouth, Northampton, Saint Helens, Southampton, Walthamstow **12** Huddersfield, Southshields, West Bromwich **13** Middlesbrough, South-end-on-sea, Wolverhampton **14** Stoke-upon-Trent, West Hartlepool **15** Barrow-in Furness **17** Newcastle-upon-Tyne
class: **4** form
clergyman: **4** Inge **5** Donne, Oates **6** Becket, Newman **7** Latimer
cloth: **5** tweed
coin: ora **4** rial, ryal **5** ackey, angel, crown, groat, pence, pound **6** bawbee, florin, guinea, seskin, teston **7** angelet, carolus **8** farthing, shilling, sixpence, twopence **9** dandiprat, fourpence, halfcrown, halfpenny, sovereign **10** threepence
composer: **4** Arne **5** Elgar, Neale **6** Delius, Handel **7** Britten, Stainer **8** Williams
conservative: **4** Tory
conspirator: **6** Fawkes
conveyance: **4** tram **6** waggon
county: **4** Kent **5** Derby, Devon, Essex, Hants, Shire **6** Dorset, Surrey, Sussex
court: **4** eyre, leet **5** gemot **6** gemote **8** hustling **9** Old Bailey
crown tax: **4** geld
dance: **6** morris
dandy: **4** toff
diarist: **5** Pepys **6** Evelyn
dramatist: **4** Shaw **5** Peele, Reade, Wilde **6** Coward, Dryden, Pinero **7** Marlowe **8** Beaumont, Fletcher **11** Shakespeare
early conqueror: **5** Horsa **7** Hengist
economist: **6** Keynes **7** Gresham, Ricardo
elevator: **4** lift
emblem: **4** Lion
entertainment: **4** busk **7** ridotto
essayist: **4** Elia, Lamb, Lang **5** Bacon **6** Steele **7** Addison
estate: **4** este
explorer: **4** Cook, Ross **5** Cabot, Drake, Scott **6** Hudson
field: **5** croft
fish: **5** sewen **8** dragonet
flood: **5** spate
flower: **4** rose
food dealer: **12** costermonger
forest: **5** Arden
freeman: **5** ceorl
game: **5** darts, rugby **6** soccer **7** cricket
gold: **4** rial, ryal
gun carrier: **4** bren
historian: **5** Acton, Grote **7** Toynbee **8** Macaulay
hog: **5** Essex
humorist: **4** Lear
inspector: **9** exciseman
invader: **4** Dane **5** Engle, Roman, Saxon **6** Norman
island: Man **4** Holy **5** Farne, Lundy **6** Scilly, Thanet, Walney **7** Ireland, Sheppey **8** Anglesey, Holyhead, Shetland **11** Isle of Wight
jacket: **4** Eton
king: Hal, Lud **4** Bran, Brut, Cnut, Cole, Knut, Lear **5** Brunt, Henry, James, Sweyn **6** Alfred, Arthur, Bladud, Cnaute, Edward, Egbert, George **7** Artegal, Elidure, Richard, Stephen, William **8** Gorboduc
laborer: **5** navvy
lake: **7** Derwent **8** Coniston **9** Ullswater **10** Windermere
land: **5** laine
law: **4** soke **6** esnecy **7** danelaw **9** common law
lawyer: **7** bencher **9** barrister, solicitor
liberal: **4** Whig
lunch: **6** tiffin
machine gun: **4** Bren, Sten
magistrate: **4** beak
man: **6** Briton **9** Britisher, Sassenach
measure: ell, pin, rod, ton, tun, vat **4** acre, bind, boll, comb, cran, foot, gill, goad, hand, hide, inch, last, line, mile, once, palm, peek, pint, pipe, pole, pool, rood, sack, span, trug, wist, yard, yoke **5** bodge, carat, chain, coomb, cubit, digit, float, floor, fluid, hutch, mimim, perch, point, prime, quart, skein, stack, truss **6** barrel, bovate, bushel, cranne, fathom, firkin, gallon, hobbet, jugrum, league, manent, oxgang, pottle, runlet, strike, sulung, thread, tieree **7** furlong, hobbitt, quarter, quarten, rundlet, spindle, tertian, virgate **8** carucate, chaldron, hogshead, landyard, puncheon, quadrant, standard **9** kilderskin, shaftment, shaftmont **10** barleycorn, barn gallon, winchester **13** tablespoonful
minister: **4** Peel, Pitt **7** Walpole **8** Disraeli
molasses: **7** treacle
monk: **4** Beda, Bede **5** Baeda
mountain: **7** Pennine **8** Cumbrian, Scawfell
news agency: **7** Reuters
noble family: **6** Talbot
nobleman (see also *title* below): **4** peer **6** milord
novelist: **5** Arlen, Hardy, Reade, Waugh, Wells **6** Austen, Bronte, Huxley, Sterne **7** Dickens **8** Fielding, Trollope
officer's civilian dress: **5** mufti
old kingdom: **6** Sussex
old letter: wen **5** thorn
order: **6** Garter
painter: **4** Opie **6** Turner **7** Hogarth, Millais, Poynter
pamphleteer: **5** Defoe, Swift

Parliament proceedings: **7** Hansard
party member: **4** Tory, Whig **7** Liberal **8** Laborite **9** Labourite **12** Conservative
patron saint: **6** George
peasant: **5** churl
pert. to: **8** Anglican **10** Anglo-Saxon
philosopher: **4** Hume **5** Bacon, Locke **6** Hobbes **7** Russell, Spencer **9** Whitehead
pirate: **4** Kidd **5** Drake **6** Morgan **7** Hawkins
poet: **4** Gray, Pope **5** Auden, Blake, Byron, Carew, Donne, Eliot, Keats **6** Brooke, Landor **7** Barrett, Caedmon, Shelley **8** Browning **9** Masefield **11** Shakespeare
policeman: **5** bobby **6** copper, peeler
pottery: **5** Spode
prairie: **4** moor **5** heath
printer: **6** Caxton
prison: **4** gaol
public school: **4** Eton **5** Rugby **6** Harrow **9** Sandhurst
queen: **4** Anne, Mary **8** Victoria **9** Elizabeth
racing town: **5** Ascot **10** Epsom Downs
rebel: **5** Essex, Tyler **8** Cromwell **10** Washington
resort: **4** Bath **8** Brighton
rifle: **7** Enfield
river: Dee, Esk, Exe, Nen, Ure, Wye **4** Aire, Avon, Eden, Nene, Ouse, Tees, Tyne, Wash, Wear **5** Alton, Dudin, Trent **6** Humber, Mersey, Ribble, Severn, Thames **7** Caulder **8** Walbrook
royal house: **4** York **5** Tudor **6** Stuart **7** Hanover, Windsor **9** Lancaster **11** Plantagenet
royal household officer: **7** equerry
royal residence: **7** Windsor
scientist: **6** Darwin, Huxley
seaman: **5** limey **6** rating
seaport: **4** Deal **5** Dover, Poole **8** Wallasey **9** Liverpool **11** Southampton
serf: **6** thrall
settler: **4** Jute, Pict **5** Angle, Saxon **6** Norman
sheep: **8** costwold **11** Wensleydale
shoemaker: **4** snob
sixpence: **5** sprat
slave: **4** esne
socialist: **6** Fabian
soldier: **5** tommy **7** redcoat **8** fusileer, fusilier **10** carabineer, carabinier
spy: **5** Andre
stable: **4** mews
statesman: **4** Eden, Grey, Peel, Pitt **5** Bevin, Simon **6** Attlee **7** Asquith, Baldwin **8** Disraeli **9** Churchill, Gladstone, MacDonald, Macmillan **10** Walsingham **11** Chamberlain, Lloyd George
stone monument: **8** cromlech
streetcar: **4** tram
tavern: pub
taxpayer: **9** ratepayer
tea muffin: **7** crumpet
thicket: **7** spinney
thrush: **5** mavis
title: **4** dame, duke, earl, king, lady, lord, peer **5** baron, noble, queen **6** knight, prince **7** baronet, duchess, marquis **8** baroness, countess, marquess, princess, viscount **11** marchioness, viscountess
tourist: **7** tripper
tribe: **5** Iceni
truck: **5** lorry
tutor: don
university: **6** London, Oxford **9** Cambridge
uplands: **5** downs
valley: **4** Eden, Tees, Tyne **5** coomb **6** coquet
weight: **5** stone

engorge: **4** glut **5** gorge **6** devour
engraft: **9** inoculate
engrave: cut **4** etch **5** carve, chase, grave, print, sculp **6** chisel, incise **7** enchase, impress, imprint, stipple **8** inscribe, ornament **9** character, sculpture
by dots: **7** stipple
engraver: **6** chaser, etcher, graver **7** artisan **13** siderographer
tool of: **5** burin
engraving: *wax:* **8** intaglio **9** cerograph, xylograph **11** glyptograph
instrument: **6** stylet
pert. to: **7** glyphic, glyptic
engross: **4** bury **5** amass **6** absorb, engage, enroll, enwrap, occupy **7** collect, consume, immerse **9** fascinate, overwhelm, preoccupy
engrossed: **4** rapt **6** intent
engrosser: **12** calligrapher
engrossing: **11** chirography
engulf: **5** swamp, whelm **6** absorb, devour **7** swallow **8** submerge **9** overwhelm
enhance: **4** lift **5** enarm, exalt, raise **6** deepen **7** augment, elevate, enlarge, greaten, improve, sharpen **8** heighten, increase **9** aggravate, intensify **10** exaggerate
enhearten: **8** embolden
enigma: **5** griph, rebus **6** riddle, sphinx **7** griphus, mystery, problem **9** conundrum
enigmatic: **6** mystic **7** cryptic, obscure **8** mystical, puzzling **9** equivocal **12** inexplicable
enisle: **7** isolate
enisled: **5** alone, apart **8** solitary
enjoin: bid **5** order **6** decree, forbid **7** command, dictate, require **8** admonish, prohibit

enjoyment: use 4 bask, ease, zest 5 gusto 6 liking, relish 7 delight 8 felicity, pleasure 9 happiness 11 delectation 12 satisfaction 13 gratification
enkerchief: 5 drape
enkindle: 7 incense, inflame 9 enlighten
enlace: tie 5 twine, twist, weave 6 enfold 7 entwine 8 encircle, entangle 10 interweave
enlarge: add, eke(Sc.) 4 grow, huff, ream 5 swell, widen 6 broach, dilate, expand, extend, fraise, spread 7 amplify, augment, distend, ·nhance, greaten, magnify, stretch 8 .ourish, increase 9 elaborate, expatiate, intumesce 10 aggrandize, exaggerate
enlarged: 8 varicose
enlargement: 9 accession, accretion 10 ampliation 13 magnification
enlarging gradually: 5 evase
enlighten: 5 edify, teach 6 inform 7 educate 8 enkindle, instruct 9 irradiate 10 illuminate
enlightened person: 10 illuminato
enlightenment: 5 bodhi 6 wisdom
enlist: 4 join 5 enter 6 embark, engage, enroll, induct 7 impress 8 register 9 volunteer
enlisted man: GI
enlistment: 5 hitch 7 listing
enliven: 4 warm 5 cheer, rouse 6 revive 7 animate, comfort, inspire, refresh 8 brighten, inspirit 9 encourage, stimulate 10 exhilarate, invigorate
enlivening: 6 genial 9 sprightly
enlock: 7 enclose
enmesh: 4 trap 5 catch 7 ensnare 8 entangle
enmity: war 4 feud 5 spite 6 hatred, malice, rancor 8 aversion 9 animosity, antipathy, hostility 10 antagonism, repugnance, resentment 11 malevolence
ennead: 4 nine 8 ninefold
ennoble: 5 exalt, honor, raise 6 uplift 7 dignify, elevate, glorify
ennui: 4 bore 6 tedium 7 boredom, doldrum
Enoch: *father:* 4 Cain 5 Jared
son: 4 Irad 10 Methuselah
enorm: 8 abnormal, enormous 9 monstrous 10 outrageous 13 extraordinary
enormous: big, gob 4 huge, ream, vast 5 enorm, great, large 6 heroic, mighty 7 immense 8 abnormal, colossal, gigantic 9 excessive, monstrous 10 gargantuan, prodigious, stupendous 11 elephantine
Enos: *father:* 4 Seth
grandfather: 4 Adam
grandmother: Eve
uncle: 4 Abel, Cain
enough: 4 enow 5 ample, basta 6 plenty 7 suffice 8 adequate 10 sufficient 12 satisfactory
enounce: 5 state, utter 8 proclaim 9 enunciate, pronounce
enow: 9 presently
enrage: 5 anger 6 grieve, madden 7 incense, inflame 9 infuriate 10 exasperate
enraged: 5 irate 7 berserk 8 choleric, maddened
enrapture: 6 ravish 7 ecstasy, enchant 8 enravish, entrance 9 captivate, fascinate
enraptured: 4 rapt 11 imparadised
enravished: 4 rapt 10 enraptured
enrich: 4 boot, lard 5 adorn, endow 6 batten, fatten 7 furnish 8 ornament 9 embellish, fertilize
enrobe: 6 attire, clothe
enroll, enrol: 4 join, list 5 enter, write 6 billet, enfold, enlist, induct, record 7 ascribe, impanel 8 initiate, inscribe, register 11 matriculate 13 immatriculate
enroot: 7 implant
ens: 5 being 6 entity 9 existence
ensaint: 8 canonize
ensconce: 4 hide 5 cover 6 settle 7 conceal, shelter 9 establish
ensemble: 5 decor, whole 7 costume 11 combination
ensiform: 6 ensate 7 xiphoid
ensign: 4 flag, sign 5 badge 6 banner, signal, symbol 7 officer 8 gonfalon, standard 9 oriflamme
of Othello: 4 Iago
of sovereignty: 7 regalia
papal: 8 gonfalon
ensilage: 4 feed 6 fodder, silage
enslave: 5 chain 7 slavish 8 enthrall
ensnare: net, web 4 mesh, trap 5 benet, catch, noose, snarl 6 allure, attrap, enmesh, entoil, entrap, tangle, trepan 7 beguile, springe 8 overtake 10 circumvent, intertwine
ensorcell, ensorcel: 5 charm 7 bewitch, enchant 9 fascinate
ensoul, insoul: 7 animate
ensuing: 4 next 9 following, resulting 10 subsequent, succeeding
ensure: 6 assure, insure, secure 7 betroth, espouse, warrant 8 affiance 9 guarantee
entablature: 10 trabeation
entad: 6 inward
opposite of: 5 ectad
entail: 6 impose 7 involve, require 11 necessitate
ental: 5 inner
opposite of: 5 ectal
entame: 11 domesticate
entangle: mat, web 4 foul, harl, knit, knot, mesh, mire 5 catch, ravel, snafu, snare,

snarl, twist **6** befoul, cotter, engage, enlace, enmesh, entrap, hankle, inmesh, puzzle **7** confuse, embroil, ensnarl, involve, perplex **8** bewilder, encumber **9** embarrass, embrangle, imbroglio **10** intertwine, interweave

entangled: **4** deep **5** cotty **7** complex **10** interwoven

entanglement: **4** knot **6** bunker **8** obstacle **13** embarrassment

entellus: **6** monkey

entente: **6** treaty **8** alliance **9** agreement **13** understanding

enter: **4** join, post **5** admit, begin, share **6** accede, appear, engage, enlist, enroll, entrer(F.), hamper, incept, pierce, record **7** intrude **8** initiate, inscribe, register **9** introduce, penetrate **11** matriculate

militarily: **6** invade

enter into: **10** participate

enter upon: **5** begin **6** embark

enteric: **10** intestinal

enterprise: **5** essay **6** action, spirit **7** attempt, emprise, project, venture **8** business, gumption **9** adventure **10** initiative, management **11** undertaking

enterpriser: **12** entrepreneur

enterprising: **4** bold **9** energetic **10** aggressive, courageous **11** progressive

entertain: **4** fete, hold **5** amuse, treat **6** divert, regale **7** beguile, cherish **8** consider, interest

entertainer: **4** host **5** actor **6** amuser, dancer, singer **7** actress, hostess, regaler, speaker **8** comedian, magician, minstrel **9** soubrette(F.) **10** comedienne

entertainment: **4** fare, fete, glee, play **5** board, cheer, feast, opera, revue, sport **6** kermis, shivvo **7** banquet, ceilidh(Ir.), concert, festine, festino, kermess, pastime, ridotto **8** function, musicale **9** amusement, diversion, festivity, reception, wayzgoose **10** recreation

of strangers: **9** xenodochy

place: **4** gaff, park **5** movie **6** casino, cinema, circus, midway **7** cabaret, theater, theatre

enthrall, enthral: **5** charm **7** enslave **9** captivate

enthrone: **5** crown, exalt **6** throne

enthusiasm: **4** elan, fire, zeal, zest **5** ardor, flame, furor, mania, verve **6** fervor, spirit **7** ardency **9** animation, eagerness **10** ebullience, fanaticism

enthusiast: bug, fan, nut **5** bigot **6** rooter, zealot **7** devotee, fanatic **8** follower **9** energumen

enthusiastic: **4** keen, warm **5** rabid **6** ardent **10** forthgoing

enthymeme: **8** argument **9** syllogism

entice: win **4** bait, coax, draw, lure, tole, wile **5** charm, decoy tempt **6** allure, cajole, incite, induce, invite, seduce **7** attract, bewitch **8** inveigle, persuade

entire: all **4** full, mear, mere **5** clean, every, quite, sound, stark, total, utter, whole **7** perfect, plenary **8** absolute, allwhole, complete, unbroken **9** exclusive, integrate, undivided **10** unimpaired **11** unqualified **12** undiminished

entitle: dub **4** call, name, term **5** affix **6** enable **7** empower, qualify **8** nominate **9** authorize, designate **10** denominate, habilitate **12** characterize

entity: ens **4** unit **5** being, thing **7** essence, integer **9** existence

entoil: **5** snare **7** ensnare

entomb: **4** bury **5** inter, inurn **6** encave, hearse, inhume

entourage: **5** train **7** retinue **9** associate, attendant

entracte: **8** interval **9** interlude **12** intermission

entrail: bag, gut **5** bowel **6** giblet, mugget **7** viscera **8** gigerium

entrain: **5** board

entrance: **4** adit, boca(Sp.), door, gate, hall **5** charm, debut, entry, foyer, mouth, stulm, toran **6** access, atrium(L.), entree, portal, ravish, torana, zaguam **7** delight, gateway, hallway, ingoing, ingress, initial, postern **9** admission, beginning, enrapture, fascinate, incursion, induction, overpower, threshold, vestibule **10** admittance **12** introduction

entranced: **4** rapt **8** ecstatic

entrant: **7** intrant, starter **8** beginner **11** participant

entrap: bag, net **5** catch, decoy, snare **6** allure, ambush, taigle(Sc.), tangle, trepan **7** beguile, ensnare **8** entangle, inveigle

entre(F.): **7** between

entreat: ask, beg, bid, sue **4** pray, seek **5** crave, plead **6** appeal, invoke **7** beseech, conjure, implore, prevail, request, solicit **8** persuade, petition **9** impetrate, importune **10** supplicate

entreaty: **4** plea, suit **8** petition **9** treatment **11** importunity, negotiation

entree: **5** entry **6** access **8** entrance **9** admission **10** permission

entrench, intrench: **6** invade **8** encroach, trespass

entrenchment: **7** closure

entrepot: **5** depot **9** warehouse **10** storehouse

entrepreneur: **7** manager **8** employer **10** impresario **11** enterpriser

entresol: **9** mezzanine

entrust, intrust: 4 give 6 commit 7 address, commend, confide, consign, deposit 8 delegate, encharge 9 concredit, recommend
entry: 4 adit, hall, item 5 debit 6 credit, entree, postea, record, ringer 7 ingress, passage 8 entrance, notandum, register 9 vestibule 10 adjustment, enlistment, enrollment
entwine: 4 lace 5 braid, twine, twist, weave 6 enlace 7 wreathe 9 interlace 10 intertwine
enucleate: 7 explain
enumerate: 4 tell 5 count 6 detail, number, recite, reckon, relate 7 compute, itemize, recount 8 estimate 9 calculate 13 particularize
enumeration: 4 list 6 census 7 account, catalog 9 catalogue
enunciate: 5 utter 7 declare, enounce 8 announce, proclaim 9 pronounce 10 articulate
enure: See **inure**
envelop, envelope: 4 case, coma, husk 5 cover, round 6 bemist, enfold, engirt, enwrap, infold, invest, muffle, sheath, shroud, swathe 7 enclose, environ, wrapper 8 enshpere, surround 9 chevelure 10 integument
of fruit: bur 4 burr
envenom: 7 corrupt, vitiate 8 embitter, empoison
envious: 7 jealous 8 enviable 9 invidious
environ: hem 4 gird 5 limit 6 girdle, suburb 7 envelop, inclose, involve, jealous, purlieu 8 district, encircle, surround 9 encompass, territory 12 circumscribe
environment: 6 medium, milieu 7 element, habitat, setting 8 ambiance, precinct
comb. form: eco
science of: 7 ecology
envisage: 4 face 8 confront 9 visualize
envision: 5 dream
envoy: 5 agent, envoi(F.) 6 deputy, legate 8 ablegate 9 messenger, missioner 10 ambassador 12 commissioner 14 representative 15 plenipotentiary
envy: 5 covet 6 grudge 8 begrudge, jealousy
enwrap: 4 roll 5 clasp 6 enfold, infold, kirtle 7 engross, envelop 8 convolve, envelope
enzyme: ase 6 cytase, lipase, olease, papain, pepsin, rennin, urease 7 adenase, amylase, casease, diatase, erepsin, ferment, guanase, inulase, maltase, pectase, pepsine, tannase 8 catalase, cytolist, eraptase, esterase, protease 9 biogenase, deamidase, deaminase, invertase, trehalase 10 amygdalase 11 gaultherase 14 acetaldehydase
leather-making: 7 tannase
opposite of: 5 azyme
eoan: 7 auroral
eolith: 4 celt
eon: age 8 eternity
eonic: 4 eral
epee: 5 blade, sword
epergne: 11 centerpiece
ephah: 7 measure
one-tenth: 4 omer
ten: 5 homer
ephelis: 7 freckle
ephemeral: 5 brief, vague 7 passant, passing 9 temporary, transient 10 evanescent, short-lived, transitory 11 impermanent
ephemeris: 5 diary 7 almanac, journal 8 calendar, magazine 10 periodical 11 publication
Ephialtes' slayer: 6 Apollo 8 Hercules
Ephraim's descendant: 7 Resheph
epi: 5 spire 6 finial 8 pinnacle
epic: 4 Edda, epos, saga 5 grand, Iliad, noble 6 epopee, heroic 7 Beowulf 8 epyllion, Ramayana 9 narrative 11 Mahabharata
epicarp: 4 husk, rind
epicede, epicedium: ode 4 song 5 dirge, elegy
epicene: 7 sexless 10 effeminate
epichoric: 5 local
Epictetus: 4 Stoic 10 philosopher
birthplace: 10 Hierapolis
expelled from: 4 Rome
home: 6 Epirus
epicure: 6 friand 7 glutton, gourmet 8 gourmand 10 gastronome 11 connoisseur
epicurean: 7 Apician 8 hedonist 9 luxurious
epidemic: flu 6 plague 8 pandemic 9 influenza 10 pestilence
epiderm appendage: 4 horn
epidermis: 7 cuticle
epigram: 4 poem 6 englyn 11 inscription
epigramatic: 7 concise, piquant, pointed
epigraph: 7 imprint 11 inscription 14 superscription
epilogue, epilog: 8 appendix 10 conclusion
Epimetheus: *daughter:* 7 Pyrrha
wife: 7 Pandora
epinard: 7 spinach
Epiphany: 9 uphellyaa(Sc.)
Epirus: *native:* 5 Greek 6 Epirot 7 Epirote
town: 6 Dodona
episcopacy: 9 bishopric
Episcopal parish head: 6 rector
Episcopalian: 9 prelatist
episcopate: 9 bishopric
episode: 5 event, scene, story 8 incident 9 happening
episperm: 5 testa
epistaxis: 9 nosebleed
epistle: 6 letter 7 missive, writing
epitaph: 8 hicjacet 11 inscription

epithet: 4 name, term 5 title 6 phrase 7 agnomen 9 sobriquet 10 soubriquet 11 appellation
epitome: 6 digest, precis 8 abstract, synopsis 9 comprisal, statement 10 compendium 11 abridgement, contraction 13 comprehension
epitomize: 6 resume 7 curtail 8 compress, condense, diminish 9 summarize 10 abbreviate
epityphlitis: 12 appendicitis
epoch: age, era 4 date, time 5 event 6 period
epochal: 4 eral
epode: 7 refrain 9 aftersong
epopee: 4 epic, epos
epoptic: 6 mystic
epure: 5 draft 7 diagram, drawing, pattern
equability: 10 equanimity
equable: 4 even, just 5 equal, suant 6 smooth, steady 7 uniform 8 tranquil 9 equitable
equal: par, tie 4 cope, egal(F.), even, fere, isos(Gr.), just, like, meet, peer, same 5 alike, level, match, rival 6 equate 7 abreast, compeer, emulate, equable, identic, uniform 8 adequate, equalize, tranquil 9 equitable, identical, unruffled 10 answerable, equivalent, tantamount 11 comparative, countervail 12 commensurate, counterpoise 13 unfluctuating
combining form: iso 4 equi, pari
equal-angled figure: 6 isogon
equalire: 4 even
equality: 6 equity, parity 7 balance, egality 8 evenness, fairness 12 impartiality
legal: 7 isonomy
equally: as 4 both 5 alike 6 evenly, justly
equanimity: 5 poise 7 egality 8 calmness, evenness, serenity 9 composure 10 equability 11 tranquility
equate: 7 balance 8 equalize
equatorial: 8 tropical
equestrian: 5 rider 7 vaquero(Sp.) 8 horseman
equidistant: 7 central, halfway
equilibrium: 5 poise 7 balance 9 equipoise
being in: 7 astatic
science: 8 astatics
equine: 4 colt, foal, mare 5 filly, horse, zebra
equine water sprite: 5 kelpy 6 kelpie
equip: arm, rig 4 deck, gear, gird, heel, reek 5 array, dress, enarm, endow 6 attire, fit out, outfit, suborn 7 apparel, appoint, bedight, furnish, prepare, qualify 8 accouter, accoutre 10 accomplish, habilitate
equipage: 4 crew 5 suite, train 6 supply 7 retinue, turnout 8 carriage 9 apparatus, furniture 10 habiliment
equipment: 4 gear 6 attire, tackle 7 fitment, harness, panoply 8 armament, material, mounting 11 appointment 13 paraphernalia
equipoise: 5 poise 7 balance 11 equilibrium
equiponderate: 14 counterbalance
equitable: 4 even, fair, just 5 equal, right 6 honest 7 equable, upright 9 impartial, righteous 10 reasonable
equitation: 12 horsemanship
equity: law 7 honesty, justice 8 equality, fairness 9 rectitude 11 uprightness 13 righteousness
equivalent: 9 identical 10 synonymous, tantamount
equivocal: 7 dubious, obscure 8 doubtful, puzzling 9 ambiguous, enigmatic, uncertain 10 indefinite, mysterious, perplexing, suspicious 12 questionable, undetermined 13 indeterminate, problematical
equivocate: lie 5 dodge, evade, shift 6 escape, palter, trifle, weasel 7 quibble, shuffle 11 prevaricate
equivogue: mot, pun 4 quip 9 witticism 10 paronomasia 12 adnomination
era: A.D., B.C.; age 4 aeon, date, time 5 epoch, stage 6 period
eradicate: 4 dele, weed 5 erase 6 delete, remove, uproot 7 abolish, destroy, outroot 9 extirpate 10 annihilate, deracinate 11 exterminate
eral: 7 epochal
erase: 4 blot, dele, rase, raze 5 annul 6 cancel, deface, delete, efface, excise, remove 7 destroy, expunge, scratch 9 eradicate 10 obliterate
erd: 4 land 5 earth 6 region
ere: 4 soon 5 early, prior 6 before 9 erewhile, formerly 9 aforetime 10 previously
Erebus: *parent:* 5 Chaos
sister: Nox
son: 6 Charon
erect: big 4 bigg, rear, step 5 build, exalt, setup, stand 6 arrect, uplift 7 address, elevate, upright 8 straight, vertical 9 construct, establish, institute 10 upstanding 13 perpendicular
erelong: 4 anon, soon
eremite: 6 hermit 7 ascetic, recluse 8 anchoret 9 anchorite
hut: 4 cell
erewhile: ere 10 heretofore
Erewhon: 6 utopia
ergastulum: 4 cell 7 dungeon
ergo: so 5 hence 9 therefore
erica: heath 7 heather
Erin: 4 Eire 7 Ireland 8 Hibernia 9 Innisfail
Erinys: 4 Fury 6 Alecto 7 Megaera 9 Tisiphone
Eriphyle: *brother:* 8 Adrastus
daughter: 8 Eurydice

father: 6 Talaus
son: 7 Alcmeon
Eris: *brother:* 4 Ares
daughter: Ate
missile: 5 apple
eristic: 12 disputatious 13 controversial
Eritrea: See **Ethiopia**
ermine: fur 5 stoat, white 6 weasel 7 ermelin, miniver
erode: eat 4 gnaw, wear 7 corrode, destroy 9 undermine 12 disintegrate
Eros: 4 Amor 5 Cupid
beloved: 6 Psyche
brother: 7 Anteros
father: 6 Hermes 7 Mercury
mother: 5 Venus 9 Aphrodite
erose: 6 uneven 9 irregular
erotic: 6 loving 7 amatory, amorous
err: sin 4 miss, slip 5 lapse, misgo, stray 6 bungle, wander 7 blunder, deviate, misplay, mistake 8 misjudge 10 transgress 12 miscalculate, misinterpret
errand: 5 chore 7 journey, mission
errand boy: 4 page 7 courier 9 messenger
errant: 5 stray 6 astray, erring 9 deviating, itinerant, wandering 10 journeying 11 adventurous
erratic: 5 queer, wacky 6 whacky 7 strange, vagrant 8 vagabond 9 eccentric, irregular, wandering 10 capricious, changeable
erratum: 5 error 7 mistake
errhine: 7 sneezer
erring: 6 astray, errant
erroneous: 5 amiss, false, wrong 6 untrue 7 erratic 8 mistaken, straying, wrongful 9 incorrect, wandering
error: sin 4 bull, flub, muff, slip 5 bevue, boner, fault, fluff, lapse 6 fumble, miscue 7 bloomer, blunder, default, erratum, fallacy, falsity, misplay, misstep, mistake, offense, rhubarb 8 solecism 9 violation 10 inaccuracy 12 irregularity, malformation
measuring device: 11 aberrometer
ers: 5 vetch
ersatz: 10 artificial, substitute 11 replacement
Erse: 5 Irish 6 Celtic, Gaelic 8 Scottish
erst: 8 formerly
erstwhile: 6 former 8 formerly 10 heretofore
eruca: 11 caterpillar
erudition: 4 lore 7 letters 8 learning 9 education, knowledge 11 instruction, scholarship
erupt: 5 burst, eject
eruption: 4 rush 5 rupia, storm 6 blotch 8 outbreak, outburst 9 commotion
Eryx: *father:* 5 Butes
mother: 5 Venus 9 Aphrodite
Esau: 4 Edom
brother: 5 Jacob
country: 4 Edom
descendant: 7 Edomite
father: 5 Isaac
father-in-law: 4 Elon
grandson: 6 Amalek
mother: 7 Rebekah
son: 5 Korha, Reuel 7 Eliphaz
wife: 4 Adah 10 Aholibamah
escapade: 5 prank, sally 7 runaway 9 adventure, excursion
escape: lam 4 flee, gate, jink(Sc.), miss, slip 5 avoid, dodge, elope, elude, evade, issue, spill 6 eschew, outlet 7 getaway, leakage, mistake, outflow 9 evaporate
means: 8 loophole
escargot: 5 snail
escarole: 6 endive
escarp: 5 scarp, slope
eschalot: 5 onion
eschar: 4 scab 5 crust
escheat: 4 fall 5 lapse 6 revert 7 forfeit
eschew: 4 shun 5 avoid 6 escape 7 abstain
escolar: 8 mackerel
escort: see 4 beau, lead, show 5 guard, usher 6 attend, convoy, squire 7 conduct, consort, gallant 8 cavalier, chaperon 9 accompany, attendant, bodyguard, safeguard
escritoire: 4 desk 6 bureau 9 secretary
escrow: 4 bond, deed
esculent: 6 edible 7 eatable 10 comestible
escutcheon: 6 shield
band: 4 fess 5 fesse
cord: 10 cordeliere
Esdras' angel: 5 Uriel
eserine: 13 physostigmine
eshin: tub 4 pail
esker, eskar: as 4 kame
Eskimo: *Aleutian Islands:* 4 Atka 5 Aleut, Husky
Asiatic: 4 Yuit 6 Innuit
bird: 4 fute
boot: 5 kamik
canoe: 5 cayak, kayak, umiak 6 oomiac, oomiak 7 oomiack
coat: 5 parka 6 parkee, temiak
Diomede Islands: 11 Yikirgaulit
dog: 5 husky 8 Malamute, Malemute
dwelling: 4 iglu 5 igloo, topek, tupek, tupik 9 barrabora
goddess: 5 Sedna
Greenland: Ita
knife: ulu
medicine man: 7 angakok, angakut, angekok, angekut 8 angekkok
mountain: 7 nunatak
settlement: 4 Etah
Siberian: 4 Yuit

sledge: 7 komatik
esne: 4 serf 7 bondman 8 hireling
esodic: 8 afferent
esophagus: 6 gullet
esoteric: 5 inner 6 mystic, secret 7 private 8 abstruse 9 recondite 10 acroamatic, mysterious 12 confidential
esoteric doctrine: 6 cabala
esoteric knowledge: 6 gnosis
ESP: 9 intuition 12 clairvoyance
espadon: 9 swordfish
espalier: 7 lattice, railing, trellis
Espanol: 7 Spanish
espantoon: 4 club 8 spontoon
esparto: 4 alfa
especial: 5 chief 8 peculiar, uncommon 10 particular
esperance: 4 hope 11 expectation
espial: spy 5 scout 6 notice 9 discovery 11 observation
espiegle: 7 roguish 10 frolicsome
espionage: 4 espy 6 spying
agent: spy
esplanade: 4 walk 5 drive 6 maidan, marina 9 promenade
esplee: 6 profit 7 product
espousal: 8 ceremony
espouse: wed 4 affy, mate 5 adopt, marry 6 defend, spouse 7 betroth, embrace, husband, support 8 advocate, maintain
esprit: wit 6 spirit 10 cleverness 12 intelligence
esprit de corps: 8 devotion
espy: see 4 spot 5 sight, watch 6 behold, descry, detect, locate, notice 7 discern, observe 8 discover 9 espionage
esquire: 7 armiger
ess: 4 worm 5 curve, sigma 7 sigmoid 8 curlicue, curlycue
essay: try 4 seek 5 chria(L.), paper, theme, tract, trail 6 effort, satire, thesis 7 article, attempt, venture, writing 8 endeavor, exertion, treatise 10 enterprise, experiment 12 disquisition, dissertation
essayist: 4 Elia, Lamb 5 Paine 6 Holmes, Steele 7 Addison, Emerson
esse: 5 being 9 existence
essence: ens 4 atar, core, crux, gist, odor, otto, pith, soul 5 attar, basic, being, heart, ottar, ousia(G.) 6 nature 7 element, extract, medulla, perfume 9 existence, principle, substance 10 extraction
Essene: 7 ascetic
essential: 5 per se, vital 7 needful 8 inherent, material 9 intrinsic, necessary 11 fundamental 13 indispensable 14 constitutional
essonite: 6 garnet
establish: fix, set 4 base, rear, rest, seat 5 build, edify, erect, found, plant, prove, setup, state 6 avouch, clinch, create, ground, locate, ordain, ratify, settle, verify 7 appoint, approve, confirm, enstate, install, instate, preempt 8 colonize, constate, ensconce, identify, radicate, regulate, validate 9 determine, institute, originate 10 accomplish, constitute 11 corroborate
established: 4 fast, firm, sure 7 certain
establishment: 4 mill 5 plant 6 ecesis, menage 7 dounset(Sc.), factory 8 business, hacienda
estafette: 7 courier 9 messenger
estancia(Sp.): 4 farm 5 ranch
estate: 4 alod, fief, home, pomp, rank 5 acres, allod, finca, habit, manor, state, taluk 6 domain, ground 7 alodium, demesne, dignity, dislay, fortune 8 allodium, freehold, hacienda, position, property, standing 9 condition, situation 11 latifundium
fourth: 5 press 9 newspaper
manager: 7 steward 8 executor, guardian 9 committee 13 administrator
owner: 9 hacendero
purchaser: 9 acquereur(F.)
rent deduction: 7 reprise
third: 9 tiers etat(F.)
to hold: 7 tenancy
esteem: 4 deem 5 adore, count, favor, honor, pride, prize, value, worth 6 credit, favour, regard, repute 7 account, opinion, respect 8 appraise, venerate 9 deference, reckoning, reverence 10 admiration, appreciate, estimation 13 consideration
ester: 6 oleate 7 acetate, tropate 8 compound, stearate
estero: 5 inlet 7 channel, estuary
Esther: 8 Hadassah
festival: 5 Purim
foster father: 8 Mordecai
husband: 6 Xerxes 9 Ahasuerus
esthesiometer: 10 tactometer
esthetic: See **aesthetic**
estimable: 4 good 5 solid 6 worthy 9 admirable, honorable 11 respectable
estimate: set 4 rank, rate 5 cense, guage, guess, judge, prize, value 6 assess, budget, esteem, reckon 7 average 8 appraise, consider 9 calculate 11 computation
low: 14 undervaluation
smallest: 7 minimum
too high: 8 overrate
estimation: air 4 fame 5 honor 6 regard, repute 7 opinion 9 judgement 10 conjecture
estivate: 6 summer
estoc: 5 sword
estocada: 6 thrust
Estonia: *city:* 5 Reval 7 Tallinn

coin: 4 sent 5 kroon 7 estmark
island: 4 Dago 5 Oesel, Saare
measure: tun 4 elle, liin, pang, sund, toll, toop 5 faden, verst 6 sagene, versta, verste 7 kulimet, verchoc, verchok, 8 tonnland 9 lofstelle
weight: 4 lood, nael, puud
estop: bar 4 fill, plug, stop 5 debar 6 hinder, impede 7 prevent 8 preclude, prohibit
estrade: 4 dais 8 platform
estrange: part, wean 6 divert 8 alienate, disunite
estray: 4 waif 5 dogie 6 wander
estreat: 4 copy, fine 5 exact 6 record 7 extract 9 duplicate
estrepe: 5 spoil
estuary: ria 5 firth, frith, inlet 6 estero
estuate: 4 boil 5 heave, surge 7 agitate
esurient: 6 greedy, hungry 9 voracious
et al: 6 others 9 elsewhere
etaac: 7 blaubok 8 antelope
etagere: 7 whatnot
etalon: 14 interferometer
etat: 5 state
etch: 7 engrave 8 inscribe
Eteocles: *father:* 7 Oedipus
kingdom: 6 Thebes
mother: 7 Jocasta
son: 8 Laodamas
eternal: 6 eterne 7 ageless, endless, lasting, unaging 8 enduring, immortal, timeless 9 boundless, continual, deathless, immutable, perpetual, unceasing 10 perdurable 11 everlasting 12 imperishable, unchangeable 13 uninterrupted
Eternal City: 4 Rome
eternal home: 6 heaven 8 paradise
eternal sleep: 5 death
eternal verity: 5 truth
eternally: ake, eer 4 ever 6 always 7 forever
eterne: 7 eternal
eternity: age, eon 4 aeon, olam
etesian: 6 annual 8 periodic
ethenol: 7 alcohol
etheostomoid: 4 fish 6 darter
ether: air, sky 5 ester 7 solvent 8 empyrean 10 anesthetic, atmosphere
ethereal, etherial: 4 aery, airy 6 aerial 7 airlike, etheric, fragile, slender 8 delicate, heavenly 9 celestial 10 spiritlike
ethical: 5 moral
ethics: *system of:* 8 hedonics
teacher of: 8 moralist
without: 6 amoral
Ethiopia: 4 Kafa 5 Kaffa 9 Abyssinia
ancient capital: 5 Meroe
animal: 4 kudu, lion, oryx 5 zebra 6 baboon, gelada, impala, jackal, monkey 7 gazelle, giraffe, redbuck 12 hippopotamus
area: 6 Amhara 7 Eritrea
battleground: 5 Adowa
bishop: 5 abuna
Catholic: 4 Cush, Geez 5 Uniat 6 Uniate
cattle: 5 sanga
cereal: 4 teff
city: 4 Axum, Gore 5 Adowa, Assab, Harar 6 Antalo, Asmara, Gondar, Harrar, Napata 7 Ankober, Gambela, Magdala 10 Addis Ababa(c.)
coin: 4 besa, harf 5 amole, girsh 6 kharaf, talari 7 ashrafi, piaster, tallero
district: 4 Shoa 5 Harer, Tigre 6 Amhara
dollar: 6 Levant, talari 12 Maria Theresa
emperor: 5 Negus 6 Memnon 7 Menelik 8 Selassie
fly: 4 zimb
garment: 6 chamma
governor: ras
Hamite: 4 Afar
lake: 4 Tana 5 Tanna, Tsana, Tzana 6 Dembel 8 Stefanie
language: Ago 4 Afar, Geez, Saho 5 Galla, Tigre 6 Harari 7 Amharic
lyre: 6 kissar
measure: tat 4 cubi, kuba 5 derah, messe 6 cabaho, sinjer, sinzer, tanica 7 entelam, farsakh, farsang, ghebeta
mountain: 9 Ras Dashan
people: 4 Kala 5 Bejas, Negro 6 Ethiop, Hamite, Harari 7 Somalis 10 Abyssinian
prince: ras
princess: 4 Aida 9 Andromeda
province: 4 Jima 5 Arusi, Gojam, Tigre, Wallo 6 Harage, Sidamo, Walaga 8 Bagemder, Gamagofa, Ilubabor
pygmy: 4 Doko
queen: 7 Candace
river: Omo 4 Baro, Gibe, Juba 5 Abbai, Albai, Giubo, Rahad, Webbe 7 Tacazze
tableland: 4 amba
title: ras 5 abuna, negus
torah: 5 tetel
tree: 4 koso 5 cusso
tribe: 4 Afar 5 Agows, Galas 6 Amhara, Tigres 7 Donakus, Somalis
violin: 7 masinko
weight: pek, 4 kasm, natr, oket, rotl 5 alada, artal, mocha, neter, ratel, wakea 6 wogiet 8 farasula 9 mutagalla
wolf: 7 kaberu
etiolate: 4 pale 6 bleach
etiquette: 4 form 6 manner 7 chanoyu, decorum 9 propriety
breach of: 8 solecism
etna: 4 lamp
Etruria: *city:* 4 Veii
god: 5 Tinia
goddess: Uni 6 Menfra

king: 4 Lars 7 Porsena
pert. to: 8 Etruscan
pottery: 8 bucchero
Etruscan (see also **Etruria**): 8 Etrurian, Tursenoi, Tyrrheni
ettle: aim 4 plan 6 aspire, design, intend, intent, nettle 8 endeavor
etui, etwee: 4 case 8 reticule 10 needlecase
etymology: 6 origin
etymon: 4 root 5 radix 7 radical
eucalyptus: *gum:* 4 kino
insect secretion: 4 laap, larp, lerp 5 laarp
Eucharist: *box:* pix, pyx
bread plate: 5 paten
cloth: 4 fano 5 fanon
cup: 5 calix 7 chalice
wafer vessel: 8 ciborium
wine vessel: ama 5 amula
Euchite: 8 satanist
Euclid: 11 philosopher
place of origin: 6 Megara
proposition: 11 asses' bridge 12 pons asinorum
eugenic: 8 wellborn
eulogistic: 9 laudatory 11 encomiastic, panegyrical 12 commendatory
eulogize: 4 laud 5 extol 7 glorify 9 celebrate
eulogy: 5 eloge 6 hesped(Heb.), praise 7 address, oration 8 encomium 9 panegyric 11 composition
eunuch: 7 gelding 8 castrate
pert. to: 8 spadonic
euphonium: 4 tuba
euphony: 5 meter 6 melody 7 harmony
euphorbia: 5 plant 6 spurge
euphoria: 4 ease 7 comfort 9 well-being
Euphrates tributary: 5 Habor 6 Tigris
euplexoptera: 6 earwig
Eurasia: *range:* 4 Ural 5 Urals
region: 6 Tatary
eureka red: 4 puce
Euripides: *hero:* Ion
heroine: 5 Helen, Medea
euripus: 4 flow 5 canal 6 strait 7 channel
Europa: *father:* 6 Agenor
husband: 8 Asterius
Europe: 9 continent
antelope: 7 chamois
ape: 6 baboon
ash: 4 sorb
badger: 5 brock
barracuda: 4 spet
bass: 6 brasse
bat: 8 serotine
bellflower: 7 rampion
bird: See **bird:** ***Europe***
bison: 7 aurochs
boar: sus(L.) 4 aper(L.)
boxing: 6 savate
broadcloth: 6 suclat
buckthorn: 7 alatern 9 alaternus
canal: 4 kiel
cavalryman: 4 Ulan 5 Uhlan 6 Hussar
cherry: 4 gean
city: Osb 4 Riga, Rome 5 Paris, Posen, Soest, Vichy 6 Berlin, Lisbon, Pilsen 9 Stockholm
clover: 6 alsike
coal basin: 4 Saar
coin: 5 ducat, taler 7 pistole
country: 5 Italy, Spain 6 France, Greece, Latvia, Norway, Poland 7 Austria, Belgium, Denmark, Finland, Germany, Holland, Hungary, Rumania 8 Bulgaria 9 Luxemburg 11 Switzerland
deer: roe 6 fallow
elder: 8 danewort
fish: id; gar, ide 4 blay, boce, dace, lote, rudd, tope 5 alose, barse, roach, ruffe, sprat, tench 6 barbel, besugo, braise, meagre, morgay, plaice, turbot 7 eperlan, homelyn, lavaret, osseter, picarel, topknot 8 John Dory, scirenga 9 John Doree
grape: 6 muscat
gulf: 4 Riga
herb: 4 dill, meum, woad 6 borage, lovage, yarrow 7 henbane 8 spicknel, tarragon
hundredweight: 7 zentner
industrial region: 4 Ruhr, Saar
invaders: 4 Huns 5 Alani, Alans, Arabs, Turks 7 Mongols
island: 4 Erin 5 Aland
juniper: 4 cade
kingdom: 5 Arles, Italy 6 Aragon, Norway, Sweden 7 Belgium, England, Holland, Navarre 11 Netherlands
lake: 5 Enare, Inari 6 Geneva
language: 5 Ugric
larkspur: 10 stavesacre
lavender: 5 aspic
lime: 4 teil
measure: aam 5 liter, metre
mint: iva 6 hyssop 9 horehound
mountain: Alp
mountain ash: 4 sorb 5 rowan, rowen
mountainous region: 4 Alps 5 Tyrol
mouse: 4 loir, vole 5 lerot
nationality: 4 Dane, Finn, Goth, Lapp, Lett, Pole, Serb, Slav 5 Croat, Swede, Welsh
oak: 4 holm 7 durmast
ox: 4 urus
peninsula: 7 Iberian
plain: 6 steppe
plant: 4 ulex 7 azarole, eelware 8 lavender 9 elderwort, escobilla 10 sneezewort
polecat: 7 fitchet, fitchew
rabbit: 4 cony 5 coney

republic: 4 Eire 5 Hesse 7 Andorra, Andorre
resort: Ems, Spa 5 Baden 7 Riviera
river: Po; Bug 4 Drau, Eder, Eger, Elbe, Oder, Oise, Ruhr, Saar, Ural 5 Meuse, Mosel, Rhine, Rhone 6 Danube 7 Narenta
rodent: erd 7 hamster
rustic: 7 peasant
sea: 4 Aral, Azov 5 North 6 Baltic
sedge: 5 chufa
squirrel: 5 sisel 10 polatouche
strait: 8 Bosporus
valley: 4 Ruhr
weasel: 5 stote 8 whitrack
wheat: 5 emmer 6 whizen 7 einkorn
worm: sao
Eurydice's husband: 7 Orpheus
Eurytus' daughter: 4 Iole
Euterpe: 4 Muse
lover: 7 Strymon
son: 6 Rhesus
evacuant: 6 emetic 8 diuretic, emptying 9 cathartic, purgative
evacuate: 4 void 5 empty, expel 6 vacate 7 deprive, excrete, exhaust, nullify, vacuate 9 discharge
evade: 4 bilk, foil, jouk, shun 5 avert, avoid, dodge, elude, shirk 6 baffle, blench, escape, illude 7 beguile
evaluate: 6 ponder 8 appraise
evanesce: 4 fade 5 empty 6 vanish 9 disappear, dissipate
evanescent: 7 cursory, evasive 8 fleeting, fugitive 9 ephemeral, fugacious, transient, vanishing 11 impermanent 13 infinitesimal
evangel: 6 gospel
Evangeline's home: 6 Acadia
evangelist: 4 John, Luke, Mark 6 Graham, Sunday, writer 7 apostle, Edwards, Matthew 8 disciple 9 McPherson, patriarch 10 revivalist
evaporate: dry 8 condense, vaporize 9 dehydrate
evasion: 4 jink 5 dodge, shift 6 escape 9 avoidance 10 subterfuge 12 equivocation
evasive: sly 4 eely 5 dodgy 6 shifty 7 elusive, elusory 9 deceitful 12 tergiversate
eve: 4 dusk 6 sunset 7 sundown 9 threshold
Eve: rib 6 female
even: een, tie 4 fair, just 5 aline, equal, exact, flush, grade, level, match, plain, rival, suant 6 direct, placid, smooth, square, steady 7 abreast, balance, equable, flatten, regular, uniform 8 moderate, parallel 9 equitable, impartial 10 coincident 15 straightforward
even if: tho 8 although
even-tempered: 4 calm, mild 5 plane, still 9 impartial
evener: 7 leveler 9 equalizer 10 doubletree
evening: eve 4 ereb(Heb.), sera(It.), soir(F.) 5 abend(G.) 6 sunset 8 eventide, twilight
party: 6 soiree
pert. to: 6 vesper 11 crepuscular
prayer: 6 vesper 7 vespers
song: 6 serena
star: 5 Venus 6 Hesper, Vesper 8 Hesperus
evenness: 8 equality 10 equanimity, uniformity
event: hap 4 case, fact, fate, feat, tilt 5 casus(L.), doing, epoch 6 factum(L.), result 7 episode, miracle, tragedy 8 incident, occasion 9 adventure, happening, milestone 10 occurrence, phenomenon 11 catastrophe, consequence, termination 12 circumstance
first: 6 opener 8 premiere
happy: hit 5 birth 7 godsend 8 marriage
eventful: 7 notable 9 important, momentous
eventide: 6 vesper 7 evening
eventual: 4 last 5 final 8 ultimate
eventuate: 6 result
ever: ay; aye, eer 6 always 7 forever 10 constantly 11 continually, perpetually
Everglade State: 7 Florida
Everglades: 5 marsh, swamp
evergreen: fir, ivy 4 ilex 5 heath, holly, savin 6 laurel, savine 7 jasmine 9 mistletoe 12 rhododendron
genus of: 4 olax 9 cupressus 11 pittosporum
tree: fir, yew 4 pine 5 carob, cedar 6 balsam, calaba, larche
everlasting: 6 eterne 7 aeonial, aeonian, durable, endless, eternal, forever, lasting, tedious 8 enduring, immortal, infinite, timeless 9 continual, incessant, perpetual, unceasing, wearisome 10 everduring, perdurable 12 imperishable 13 unintermitted, uninterrupted
everlasting flower: 6 orpine
everlastingly: 6 always 7 forever
evermore: 6 always
evert: 7 subvert 9 overthrow
every: all, ilk(Sc.) 4 each, ilka(Sc.) 6 entire 8 complete
everybody: all 8 everyone
everyday: 7 prosaic 8 ordinary
everything: all
evict: 4 oust 5 eject, expel 10 dispossess
evidence: 4 show 5 proof, scrip, token, trace 6 attest, reveal 7 exhibit, support 8 argument, manifest, muniment 9 testimony 10 indication 15 circumstantiate
piece of: 7 probate
evident: 5 apert, broad, clear, plain 6 patent 7 glaring, obvious, visible 8 apparent,

manifest, palpable **10** noticeable **11** discernible, indubitable, transparent **12** demonstrable

evil: bad, ill, sin **4** bale, base, harm, poor, vice, vile **5** crime, malum(L.), wrong **6** menace, wicked **7** adverse, corrupt, disease, hurtful, immoral, misdeed, noxious, satanic, unsound **8** calamity, depraved, disaster, improper, iniquity, mischief, sinister **9** injurious, malicious, malignant, malignity, offensive, worthless **10** malevolent, misfortune, pernicious **11** malefaction, unwholesome **12** unpropitious **14** unsatisfactory
combining form: mal
incarnation of: **5** Satan

evil spirit: imp **5** demon, devil **6** daemon
Hebrew: **8** Asmodeus
Iroquois: **5** otkon
Zoroastrian: **5** daeva

evildoer: **5** cheat, crook, felon **6** sinner **7** culprit, villain **8** criminal **9** miscreant **10** malefactor

evince: **4** show **5** prove **6** subdue **7** conquer, display, exhibit **8** indicate, manifest

evirate: **8** castrate **10** emasculate

eviscerate: gut **10** devitalize, disembowel, exenterate

evoke: **5** educe **6** arouse, elicit, summon **7** evocate

evolute: **6** evolve, unfold

evolution: **7** biogeny **8** maneuver **11** development

evolutionist: **9** Darwinian

evolve: **4** emit **5** educe **6** derive, unfold, unroll **7** develop, evolute **9** disengage **11** disentangle

evulgate: **7** divulge, publish

ewe: teg **5** crone, sheep **6** theave
old: **5** crone

ewer: jug **5** basin, udder **7** pitcher **9** container

ewest: **4** next **7** nearest

ex: **6** former

exacerbate: irk **5** tease **6** enrage, excite, worsen **7** provoke **8** embitter, increase, irritate **9** aggravate, infuriate **10** exasperate

exact: ask **4** even, fine, levy, true **5** wreak, wrest **6** compel, demand, elicit, extort, formal, minute, square, strict **7** careful, certain, command, correct, enforce, estreat, extract, literal, precise, regular, require **8** accurate, critical, explicit, rigorous, specific **9** religious **10** methodical, meticulous, scrupulous **11** punctilious **13** hypercritical **14** circumstantial
satisfaction: **6** avenge **7** revenge

exacting: **6** severe **7** arduous, exigent **8** pressing

exactly: due **4** dead **5** spang, truly **6** evenly, nicely **9** precisely

exactness: **8** delicacy, identity, severity

exaggerate: **6** extend, overdo **7** amplify, enhance, enlarge, magnify, romance, stretch **8** increase **9** aggravate, embroider, overstate

exaggerated: **5** outre **11** exceptional, extravagant

exaggeration: **9** hyperbole **10** caricature

exagitate: **6** harass **7** agitate, censure, discuss

exalt: **5** arear, elate, erect, extol, heeze, honor, raise, set up, tower **6** ascend, refine **7** advance, augment, dignify, elevate, enhance, ennoble, glorify, greaten, inspire, magnify, promote **8** enthrone, heighten **9** intensify **10** aggrandize

exaltation: **7** elation, rapture **9** celsitude, elevation **10** apotheosis

exalted: **4** high **5** grand, noble **7** haughty, sublime **11** illustrious, magnanimous

examen: **7** inquiry **11** examination **13** investigation

examination: **4** exam, oral, quiz, test **5** assay, audit, check, trial **6** examen, review, survey, tripos **7** autopsy, inquest, inquiry **8** necropsy, research, scrutiny **10** comparison, inspection **11** exploration, inquisition **13** consideration, investigation **14** reconnaissance
taker: **6** testee

examine: spy, try **4** feel, scan, sift, view **5** assay, probe, quest **6** candle, ponder **7** analyze, canvass, palpate, rummage **8** overhaul **10** introspect, scrutinize **11** expostulate, interrogate, reconnoiter, reconnoitre
critically: **4** sift **6** censor
judicially: try
secretly: spy **9** eavesdrop

examiner **6** censor, conner **7** analyst, auditor, coroner **9** inspector **10** inquisitor

example: **4** case, norm, tipe(Sp.), type **5** model **6** praxis, sample **7** pattern **8** exemplar, exemplum(L.), foregoer, instance, paradigm, specimen **9** precedent **11** description **12** illustration **15** exemplification

exanimate: **8** lifeless **9** inanimate **10** spiritless

exasperate: ire, irk **4** bait, gall, heat **5** annoy **6** enrage, excite, nettle **7** inflame, provoke, roughen **8** irritate **9** aggravate

exasperated: **5** wroth **9** indignant

excavate: dig **4** mine, mole, pion **5** delve, scoop **6** burrow, dredge

excavation: cut, pit **4** hole, mine **5** grave, stope **6** cavity, groove, trench
for ore: **4** mine **5** stope

into bank: 7 remblai
surface: 8 opencast
excavator: 6 bildar(Ind.), cleoid, digger 7 pioneer
exceed: top 4 best, pass 5 excel, outdo, outgo 6 better, outrun, outvie, overdo 7 eclipse, overtax, surpass 8 outrange, outstrip, overcome, overstep 9 overshoot, transcend 11 predominate
exceedingly: 4 tres(F.), very 5 amain 7 parlous 9 extremely
excel: cap, cob 4 best 5 outdo, outgo, shine 6 better, exceed 7 emulate, outpeer, surpass 8 outclass, outrival, outstrip 9 transcend
excellence: 5 arete(Gr.), merit 6 virtue 7 dignity 8 goodness 10 perfection
excellent: 4 best, braw(Sc.), fine, good 5 brave, bully, great, prime, super, wally(Sc.) 6 choice, famous, gentle, proper, select, spiffy, worthy 7 capital, corking, elegant, quality 8 eximious, generous, superior, valuable 9 admirable, first-rate 10 inimitable, preeminent 12 transcendent
excelse: 5 lofty 7 eminent
except: but 4 bate, omit, only 6 exempt, unless 7 besides, exclude 9 eliminate
exception: 5 demur 7 dissent, offense 9 complaint, condition, objection
exceptional: 4 rare 7 unusual 8 abnormal, uncommon 9 anomalous 10 remarkable 11 outstanding 13 extraordinary
excerpt: 4 cite 5 quote, scrap 7 extract
excess 4 over, plus, riot 5 flood 7 nimiety, overage, profuse, surplus 8 overmuch, overplus, plethora 10 exuberance, redundancy 11 excrescence, superfluity 12 intemperance 13 overabundance 14 superabundance
of solar year: 5 epact
excessive: too 4 over 5 enorm(Sc.), undue 6 de trop(F.) 7 extreme, nimious 8 allfired, enormous, horrible, overmuch 9 exuberant 10 boisterous, exorbitant, immoderate, inordinate 11 extravagant, intemperate 12 extortionate, unreasonable
excessively: 11 parlous
exchange: set 4 cash, chop, cope, mart, sell, swap, swop 5 bandy, bolsa, corse, store, trade, truck 6 barter, bourse, dicker, excamb(Sc.), market, resale, rialto, scorse, shoppe 7 barroom, chaffer, commute, dealing, traffic 9 excambion(Sc.), transpose 10 substitute 11 interchange, reciprocate 12 headquarters
business: 5 bolsa
medium: 7 coinage
rate: 4 agio 5 batta
exchequer: 4 fisc(Sc.) 5 purse 7 finance 8 treasury
excise: tax 4 duty, toll 6 impost, resect 7 exscind 8 alcabala(Sp.) 9 extirpate 10 overcharge
officer: 8 revenuer
excision: cut 7 erasure 9 expulsion 11 destruction, extirpation 15 excommunication
excitability: 12 irritability
excitable: 9 spasmodic
excite: 4 fire, spur, stir, urge 5 alarm, amove, anger, chafe, elate, impel, pique, rouse 6 arouse, awaken, decoct, foment, incite, kindle 7 agitate, animate, inflame, provoke 8 disquiet 9 electrify, galvanize, instigate, stimulate, titillate 10 exasperate, intoxicate
excited: hot 4 agog 5 eager, ranty 6 heated 7 fevered, wakened 8 flurried, startled
excitement: ado 4 stir 5 fever, furor, larry 6 warmth 7 widdrim(Sc.) 9 commotion 10 irritation 11 disturbance
exciting: 6 hectic 8 stirring, terrific
exclaim: 6 clamor, outcry 9 ejaculate
exclamation: ah, ai, ay, bo, ha, hi, ho, la, lo, oh, ow, so; aha, aie, bah, boo, fie, foh, hep, hey, hic, huh, och, oho, pah, poh, suz, tut, ugh, wow, yah 4 adad, ahem, alas, arra(Ir.), drat, egad, evoe, garn, hech, heck, hein(F.), hist, hoch(G.), hola, phew, pish, psha, pugh, rats, rivo, tush, wugg 5 alack, arrah(Ir.), bravo, faugh, feigh, heigh, holla, humph, ohone(Ir.), pshaw 6 clamor, hurrah, indeed, ochone(Ir.) 7 hosanna 9 alackaday, expletive 12 interjection
of contempt: foh, pah
of disgust: ugh 4 rats
of exhilaration: 4 evoe
of pain: ow 4 ouch
of sorrow: 4 alas 9 alackaday
of surprise: oh; aha, gee, oho, wow
of reproach: fie
exclude: bar 5 debar, eject, expel 6 banish, except, exempt, reject 7 foreign 9 blackball, eliminate, forestall, ostracize 13 excommunicate
exclusive: all 4 only, rare, sole 5 alone, whole 6 select 8 cliquish, entirely
excommunicate: 8 unchurch
excommunication: ban 8 excision
excoriate: 4 flay, gall 5 score, strip 6 abrade 11 decorticate
excrement: lee 4 dirt, dreg, dung, fece 5 faece 6 ordure, refuse
excrescence: 4 burl, lump, wart 6 excess, pimple 9 outgrowth, tubercule 11 superfluity
excrete: 5 egest 8 defecate 9 eliminate
excruciate: 4 rack 5 grind 7 agonize, torture
exculpate: 4 free 5 clear, remit 6 acquit, excuse, pardon 7 absolve, forgive, justify,

release 8 palliate 9 discharge, exonerate, vindicate

excursion: row 4 ride, sail, tour, trip 5 jaunt, sally, tramp 6 cruise, junket, outing, ramble, voyage 7 journey 8 campaign, escapade 10 digression, expedition

excusable: 6 venial 9 allowable 10 defensible, pardonable 11 justifiable

excuse: 4 plea 5 alibi, remit 6 acquit, essoin, pardon 7 absolve, apology, condone, essoign, essoine, forgive, pretext 8 dispense, occasion, overlook 9 exculpate, exonerate, extenuate, vindicate

for nonappearance: 6 essoin

for sickness: 5 aeger

excuss: 7 discard, discuss

execrable: bad 8 accursed, damnable, wretched 9 nefarious 10 abominable, detestable, horrifying

execrate: ban 5 abhor, curse 9 imprecate, objurgate 12 anathematize

execute: do; act 4 hang, kill, obey, play, slay 5 lynch 6 direct, effect, finish, manage 7 conduct, enforce, perform 8 complete 10 accomplish, administer 11 electrocute

execution: 7 garrote, technic 8 garrotte 9 technique 10 fulfilment 11 achievement, fulfillment

executioner: 7 butcher, hangman, headman, lockman 9 deathsman, Jack Ketch

executive: 4 dean 5 mayor 7 cashier, manager, premier 8 governor, official 9 president 13 administrator

executor: 4 doer 5 agent 8 enforcer 9 performer 13 administrator

exegesis: 10 exposition 11 explanation 14 interpretation

exegete: 6 critic 11 interpreter

exemplar: 5 model 7 example, pattern 9 archetype

exemplary: 8 laudable 11 commendable 12 praiseworthy

exemplification: 7 example 12 illustration

exemplify: 10 illustrate

exemplum: 7 example 12 illustration

exempt: 4 exon, free 6 fidate 7 exclude, release 8 excepted 9 discharge 11 exceptional

exemption: 7 freedom 8 immunity 12 dispensation

exenterate: 10 disembowel, eviscerate

exequy: 4 rite 7 obsequy 8 ceremony 10 procession

exercise: ply, ure, use 5 drill, etude, exert, longe 6 employ, lesson, parade, praxis, school 7 aufgabe, display, problem 8 activity, practice 9 athletics 10 exhibition, gymnastics, recitation 14 constitutional

system of: 8 aerobics

exercise book: 8 notebook

exerciser: 5 groom

exert: 4 emit 5 spend 6 reveal, strain 8 endeavor, exercise

exertion: 5 essay, labor, trial 6 action, effort, strife 7 attempt 8 endeavor

exfoliate: 5 scale 10 desquamate

exfoliation: 7 scaling

exhalation: 5 steam 9 effluvium, emanation 10 expiration 11 evaporation

exhale: 4 cast, emit 6 expire 7 breathe, respire 9 transpire

exhaust: sap 4 emit, fail, jade 5 break, drain, empty, peter, waste, weary 6 abrade, overdo 7 deplete, deprive, fatigue 8 evacuate 9 discharge 10 impoverish

exhausted: 4 done, worn 5 blown, spent, tired 6 barren, beaten, effete 7 emptied, fordone 8 consumed, foredone, forspent 10 forwearied

exhausting: 7 arduous

exhaustion: 7 fatigue 9 depletion, inanition, lassitude 11 exinanition, prostration

exheredate: 10 disinherit

exhibit: air 4 fair, show, show 5 stage 6 blazon, evince, expose, ostend, parade, reveal 7 approve, display, perform, produce 8 disclose, discover, emblazon, evidence, manifest 9 represent 11 demonstrate

exhibition: 4 fair, show 5 sight 6 salary 7 display, pageant, pension, present 8 exercise 9 allowance, cosmorama, spectacle 10 exposition, sustenance 11 maintenance 13 manifestation 14 representation

exhibitioner: 8 servitor

exhilarate: 5 cheer, elate 7 animate, enliven, gladden 10 invigorate

exhilarated: rad 9 ebullient

exhilaration: 6 gaiety 7 jollity 8 gladness, hilarity 9 merriment 10 joyousness

exhort: 4 urge, warn 6 advise, dehort, incite, preach 7 caution 8 admonish 9 encourage

exhortation: 6 advice 7 counsel 9 hortation

exhume: dig 5 delve 7 unearth 8 disinter, exhumate

exigency: 4 need, want 7 urgency 8 juncture

exigent: 5 vital 8 critical, exacting, pressing 13 indispensable

exiguity: 7 paucity

exiguous: 4 fine, tiny 5 scant, small, spare 6 meager, sparse 7 slender 10 diminutive

exile: 4 poor, ruin, thin 5 expel 6 deport, outlaw, scanty 7 outcast, refugee, slender 8 fugitive 9 devastate, foreigner, ostracize 10 banishment, expatriate 12 proscription

exility: 7 tenuity 8 fineness, subtlety, thinness 9 smallness 10 meagerness 11 slenderness

eximious: 6 choice, select 9 excellent
exinanition: 9 abasement 10 exhaustion 11 humiliation
exist: am, be, is; are 4 live
at same time: 15 contemporaneous
in name only: 7 nominal, titular
passively: 7 subsist 8 vegetate
existed: was 4 been, were, wert
existence: ens 4 esse, life, sein 5 being 6 entity, inesse 7 essence, reality 9 actuality
beginning of: 5 birth, origin 9 nascency
having no: 4 dead, null, void 7 defunct
pert. to: 5 ontal, ontic
existent: 4 real 5 alive, being 6 extant 8 existing
Existentialist leader: 6 Sartre
existing: 5 alive, being 6 extant
exit: 4 door, gate 5 going, leave 6 egress, exitus, outlet 7 outgate, passage 8 debouche 9 departure
exitus: 4 exit 5 issue 6 exodus, outlet 7 outcome
exlex: 6 outlaw
exode: 9 departure 10 afterpiece
exodus: 5 exody 6 exitus 9 migration
exonerate: 4 free 5 clear 6 acquit, excuse, exoner, unload 7 absolve, relieve 9 disburden, discharge, exculpate, vindicate
exorbitant: 5 undue 8 abnormal 9 deviating, excessive, wandering 10 immoderate, outrageous 11 extravagant 12 extortionate, unreasonable
exorcism: 5 charm, spell 9 expulsion 11 incantation
exordium: 7 preface 9 beginning 12 introduction
exoteric: 4 open 6 public 8 external, outsider
exotic: 5 alien 7 foreign, strange 9 glamorous, peregrine 10 extraneous, outlandish
expand: ope, wax 4 blow, bulk, flue, grow, open 5 splay, swell, widen 6 dilate, extend, spread, unfold, unfurl 7 amplify, balloon, broaden, develop, diffuse, display, distend, educate, enlarge, explain, inflate, stretch 8 dispread, increase, lengthen 9 disspread, expatiate, explicate, intumesce
expanded: 8 patulous
expanse: 4 area, room 5 reach, tract 6 extent, spread 7 stretch 8 separate
vast: 5 ocean 6 desert, empire
expansion: ala 6 growth 8 increase 9 extension 10 dilatation, distention 11 development, enlargement
expansive: 4 free 5 broad 6 genial 7 elastic, liberal 8 spacious 9 bombastic, diffusive, grandiose
expatiate: 5 dwell 6 dilate, expand, spread 7 broaden, descant, diffuse, enlarge
expatriation: 5 exile 10 banishment
expect: 4 deem, hope, stay, trow, wait, ween 5 await 6 attend, demand 7 require, suppose 9 calculate 10 anticipate
expectation: 9 esperance
expectorate: 4 spit
expedient: 4 wise 5 dodge, knack 6 device 7 politic, stopgap 9 advisable, makeshift 10 profitable 12 advantageous
expedite: hie 4 easy, free 5 hurry, speed 6 hasten 7 quicken 8 dispatch 9 expediate 10 accelerate, facilitate
expedition: 4 fare, trek 5 drave(Sc.), haste, hurry 6 safari, voyage 7 crusade, journey 8 progress 9 excursion
expeditious: 4 fast 5 hasty, quick, rapid, ready 6 prompt, speedy
expel: 4 oust 5 eject, evict, exile 6 banish, deport 7 exclude 8 dislodge, forjudge 9 discharge, eliminate, forejudge 10 dispossess, expatriate
expend: 5 spend, waste 6 occupy, ponder 7 dispend, overuse 9 dissipate 10 distribute
expenditure: 4 cost 5 outgo 6 outlay 10 lavishment 11 consumption 12 disbursement
expense: 4 cost, loss 5 batta, price 6 charge, gersum, outlay 8 overhead 11 consumption, expenditure 12 disbursement
expensive: 4 dear, high 6 costly, lavish 7 liberal 11 dispendious, extravagant
experience: see 4 feel, have, live, test 5 assay, skill, taste, trial 6 ordeal, suffer 7 calvary, feeling, undergo 9 adventure, knowledge
experienced: had, met 6 expert 7 veteran 9 practiced, underwent
experiment: try 4 test 5 assay, essay, trial 7 attempt
experimental: 9 empirical, tentative
expert: ace, dab 4 deft, good 5 adept 6 adroit, artist, au fait, clever, habile 7 artiste(F.), capable, skilled 9 authority 10 proficient 11 experienced 12 professional
expertness: 8 facility 9 dexterity, expertise
expiate: 5 atone, avert 6 assoil 10 propitiate
expiatory: 8 piacular
expiration: end 5 death 10 exhalation, extinction 11 termination
expire: die, end 4 emit 5 expel, lapse 6 elapse, exhale, perish
expiry: 5 close, death 10 extinction 11 termination
explain: 4 rede 5 aread, areed, gloze, solve 6 define, expand, unfold 7 expound 8 describe, exegesis, manifest 9 elucidate, enucleate, explicate, interpret 10 understand
explanation: key 7 account, apology 10 exposition 11 description 13 clarification

expletive: gee 4 bosh, egad, gosh, oath 5 begad

explicate: 6 expand, unfold 7 account, explain 9 interpret

explicit: 4 open 5 clear, exact, fixed, plain 7 express, precise 8 absolute, definite, implicit, positive, specific 9 categoric, outspoken 11 categorical, unambiguous, unequivocal 13 unconditional 14 discriminating

explode: 4 fire 5 blast, burst 8 backfire, detonate 9 fulminate

exploding meteor: 6 bolide

exploding star: 4 nova

exploit: act 4 deed, feat, gest, milk 5 geste, stunt 7 perform, success 9 advantage 11 achievement, performance

exploits: 9 res gestae(L.)

exploration: 5 probe 6 search 11 examinaion 13 investigation

explore: map 4 dive, feel 5 chart, range 8 discover

explorer: 4 Cook, Eric 5 Bruce, Cabot, Davis, diver, Drake 6 Baffin, Carter, Cortes, De Soto, Hearne, Hudson 7 pioneer, Pizarro, Raleigh 8 Amundsen, Columbus, Magellan, Vespucci 9 Frobisher 10 Chancellor, discoverer

explosion: pop 5 blast 6 blow-up, report 8 outburst 10 detonation

explosive: TNT 4 mine 6 amatol, powder, tonite 7 ammonal, lyddite, melnite 8 cheddite, dynamite, eruptive 9 fulminate, guncotton 10 detonative 13 nitroglycerin 15 trinitrotoluene

coal mine: 9 Bobbinite

device: cap 6 petard 9 initiator

high: TNT 7 cordite

igniter: 4 fuse

picric acid: 7 lyddite

place of manufacture: 4 Lydd

projectile: 5 shell 7 grenade 9 cartridge

sound: 4 bang, boom, chug 5 pluff, vroom

exponent: 9 explainer, expounder 11 interpreter 14 representative

expose: 4 bare, open, risk 5 strip 6 betray, detect, reveal, unmask 7 display, exhibit, expound, pillory, publish, uncover, unearth 8 disclose, discover, muckrake, ridicule, satirize, unclothe 10 exposition, jeopardize

exposed: 6 unsafe 11 unprotected

exposition: 4 fair 5 tract 6 expose 8 analysis, exegesis, exposure, treatise 10 exhibition, expounding 11 declaration, explanation 14 interpretation

expostulate: 5 argue 7 discuss, examine, protest 8 complain 11 remonstrate

expound: 5 gloze, treat 6 define, expose 7 develop, explain, exposit, express 8 construe 9 interpret

express: 4 vent 5 emote, opine, speak, state, utter, voice 6 denote, direct, phrase 7 declare, dictate, expound, testify 8 definite, describe, explicit, manifest 9 expatiate 10 articulate, particular, peremptory

appreciation: 5 thank

approval: 6 praise 7 applaud

pity: 6 bemoan

regret: 9 apologize

expression: 4 form, pose, show, sign, term, word 5 idiom, token, voice 6 byword, oracle, phrase, symbol 8 laconism 9 euphemism, statement, utterance 10 holophrase 11 delineation, holophrasis 13 manifestation 14 representation

facial: 4 grin, 5 laugh, scowl, smile 7 grimace

hackneyed: 6 cliche

mathematical: 8 equation

metaphorical: 6 figure

of approval: 4 clap 5 smile 7 ovation 8 applause

of assent: 6 placet

of contempt: bah, fie 4 geck, hiss 5 pshaw, sneer

of gratitude: 12 thanksgiving

of incredulity: 6 indeed

of opinion: 4 vote

of sorrow: ay 4 alas 11 lamentation

of weariness: 4 sigh

expressionless: 5 stony 6 vacant 8 toneless

expressive: 6 poetic 8 eloquent, emphatic 10 indicative 11 significant

expressly: 6 namely

expressway: 4 road 7 freeway, highway

exprobrate: 7 censure, upbraid 8 reproach

expugn: 5 storm 6 attack 8 vanquish

expulsion: 5 exile 6 bounce 8 ejection 10 banishment

expunge: 4 blot, dele 5 erase 6 cancel, delete, efface, excise 7 destroy, scratch 10 annihilate, obliterate

expurgate: 4 gelt 5 purge

exquisite: fop 4 dude, nice 5 dandy, exact 6 choice, dainty 7 careful, elegant, refined 8 affected, delicate 9 beautiful, delicious, excellent, matchless, perfected, recherche 10 consummate, farfetched, fastidious 12 accomplished 14 discriminating

exsanguine: 6 anemic 9 bloodless

exscind: 6 excise 9 extirpate

exsert: 8 protrude

exsiccate: dry

exsuccous: dry 7 sapless

extant: 5 alive, being 6 living 7 visible 8 existing, manifest 10 protruding 11 protuberant

extempore: 7 affloof(Sc.), offhand 9 forthwith 11 immediately 14 extemporaneous, unpremeditated

extend: eke, lie, run 4 grow, rise, span 5 bulge, cover, reach, renew, seize, widen 6 amount, deepen, deploy, dilate, expand, spread, strain 7 amplify, broaden, diffuse, display, distend, enlarge, overlap, overrun, proffer, prolong, radiate, stretch 8 continue, increase, lengthen, protract, protrude 10 exaggerate, generalize

extended: 4 long, open 12 outstretched

extending widely: far

extension: 4 area 5 scope 8 addendum, addition, duration, increase 9 expansion 11 enlargement 12 augmentation 13 amplification
building: ell 4 wing 6 lean-to
of time: 4 stay 7 respite 8 reprieve
trench: sap

extensive: 4 vast, wide 5 ample, broad, large 7 immense 8 expanded 9 capacious 10 widespread 11 far-reaching 13 comprehensive

extent: due, tax 4 area, body, bulk, levy, writ 5 ambit, limit, range, reach, scope, space 6 amount, attack, degree, spread 7 acreage, assault, breadth, compass, expanse, seizure 8 increase, latitude, quantity 9 dimension, extension, magnitude, territory, valuation 10 assessment

extenuate: 4 thin 5 gloze 6 excuse, lessen, weaken 8 diminish, palliate 9 alleviate, attenuate, disparage, underrate 10 depreciate 13 underestimate

extenuation: 10 dimunition

exterior: 5 ectad, ectal, outer, shell 6 extern 7 outside, outward, surface 8 external

exterminate: 5 expel 6 uproot 7 abolish, destroy 9 eradicate, extirpate 10 annihilate

extern: 7 outward 8 exterior, external 9 extrinsic

external: out 5 outer 6 extern 7 outside, outward 8 exterior 9 extrinsic 10 peripheral 11 superficial
comb. form: 4 ecto

extinct: 4 dead 7 defunct 8 quenched 12 extinguished

extinction: 5 death 6 expiry 9 abolition 10 expiration 11 destruction 12 annihilation, obliteration

extinguish: 4 dout 5 annul, choke, douse, dowse, quell 6 quench, stanch, stifle 7 destroy, eclipse, obscure, staunch 8 suppress 9 suffocate 10 annihilate

extinguished: 4 dead 7 extinct

extirpate: 4 dele 5 erase, expel 6 excise, uproot 7 destroy, exscind 8 supplant 9 eradicate 10 annihilate, deracinate 11 exterminate

extirpation: 8 excision 11 destruction, eradication 12 annihilation

extol, extoll: 4 laud 5 bless, exalt 6 praise 7 applaud, commend, elevate, enhance, glorify 8 emblazon, eulogize 9 celebrate

extort: 5 exact, force, wrest, wring 6 compel, elicit, wrench 7 extract 9 blackmail

extortion: 7 bribery 8 chantage, exaction, rapacity 10 oppression, overcharge

extortionate: 4 hard 9 excessive 10 exorbitant, oppressive

extortioner: 6 poller, shaver 11 blackmailer

extra: odd 4 more, orra(Sc.), over plus 5 added, spare 7 special, surplus 8 superior 9 accessory, lagniappe 10 additional

extract: dig, pry 4 cite, draw, pull 5 educe, exact, quote, steep, wring 6 decoct, deduce, derive, elicit, evulse, extort, remove, render 7 descent, essence, estreat, excerpt, exhaust, summary 8 withdraw 9 decoction, quotation 11 preparation
information: 4 pump

extraction: 5 birth, stock 6 origin 7 descent, essence, extract 8 breeding, tincture 9 parentage

extraneous: 5 outer 6 exotic 7 foreign 9 extrinsic 10 accidental

extraordinary: odd 4 rare, unco(Sc.) 5 byous(Sc.), enorm 6 signal 7 notable, special, strange, unusual 8 abnormal, singular, uncommon 9 irregular, monstrous, wonderful 10 additional, phenomenal, remarkable, surprising, tremendous 11 exceptional 13 distinguished

extravagance: ela

extravagant: 4 wild 5 outre 6 costly, heroic, lavish 7 baroque, bizarre, fanatic, nimious, profuse, vagrant 8 prodigal, reckless, romantic, wanderer, wasteful 9 excessive, expensive, fantastic, luxurious 10 exorbitant, thriftless 11 dispendious 12 unreasonable, unrestrained

extreme: 4 last, rank, sore 5 close, final, great, limit, ultra, undue, utter 6 heroic, severe, utmost 7 drastic, forward, howling, intense, outward, radical, violent 8 devilish, farthest, greatest, terrible, terrific 9 desperate, excessive, outermost, stringent, uttermost 10 conclusive, immoderate
comb. form: 4 acro, arch

extremely: so 4 very 6 mighty 10 mortacious 11 exceedingly

extremist: 7 radical

extremity: end, tip 4 need, tail 5 close, limit, verge 6 border 8 disaster, terminal 9 bitter end

extricate: 4 free 5 clear, loose 6 rescue 8 liberate, untangle 9 disengage 10 disembroil 11 disentangle

extrinsic: 5 every 7 foreign, outward 8 external 10 accidental, extraneous, incidental 11 unessential 12 adventitious, nonessential

extrude: 4 spew 5 eject, expel 7 project 8 protrude

exuberance: 6 plenty 8 overflow 9 abundance, profusion 11 excrescence 14 superabundance

exuberant: 6 lavish 7 copious, fertile, rampart 8 effusive 9 abounding, excessive, luxuriant, plentiful

exudation: gum, lac, sap, tar 5 pitch, resin, rosin 9 discharge, secretion

exude: 4 emit, ooze 5 sweat 7 secrete 8 perspire 9 discharge, percolate

exult: 4 crow, leap 5 boast, gloat, glory 6 spring 7 rejoice

exultant: 6 elated

exultation: joy 7 rapture 10 jubilation

exulted: 6 prided 7 vaunted

exuviate: 4 molt 5 moult

eyas: 4 bird 8 nestling

eye: ee(Sc.); orb 4 disc, gaze, glim, lamp, loop, mien, ogle, scan, view 5 glare, watch 6 behold, goggle, oculus(L.), peeper, regard, vision 7 blinker, observe, witness 10 scrutinize 11 discernment
black: 5 mouse 6 shiner
cavity: 5 orbit
colored portion: 4 iris
comb. form: 4 opia
cosmetic: 4 kohl, kuhl
covering: 6 eyelid 9 blindfold
defect: 4 cast 6 anopia, myopia 11 astigmatism
disease: 6 iritis 8 glaucoma, trachoma 14 conjunctivitis
doctor: 15 ophthalmologist
hollow: 5 orbit 6 socket
instrument for examining: 8 otoscope 14 ophthalmoscope
opening in: 5 pupil
part: 4 disc, iris, uvea 5 pupil 6 areola, cornea, retina
pert. to: 5 irian, optic 7 areolar, corneal, retinal 9 ocellated
protector: 5 patch, visor 7 blinker
pupil dilater: 8 atropine 10 belladonna
science: 13 ophthalmology
simple: 6 ocelli(pl.) 7 ocellus

eye-like: 9 ocellated

eyebrow: 4 bree(Sc.) 6 eebree(Sc.) 11 supercilium

eyedropper: 7 pipette

eyeglasses: 5 specs 6 lenses 7 lorgnon, nippers 8 monocles, pince-nez 9 lorgnette

eyelash: 4 lash 5 cilia(pl.) 6 cilium
dye: 7 mascara
loss: 9 madarosis

eyeless: 5 blind 9 sightless

eyelet: 6 agrafe, gromet, oillet 7 agraffe 8 peephole 10 buttonhole 11 perforation

eyeleteer: 6 bodkin 8 stiletto

eyelid: *drooping of:* 6 ptosis
pert. to: 9 blepharal

eyer: 8 beholder 9 spectator

eyeshot: 5 range, reach

eyesight: 4 view 5 sight 11 observation

eyesome: 11 good-looking

eyesore: 6 defect 7 blemish

eyetooth: 6 cuspid

eyewash: 6 excuse 8 flattery

eyot: ait 5 islet

eyra: 7 wildcat

eyrie: See **aerie**

Ezekiel: *father:* 4 Buzi
four beasts: 5 Aniel 6 Azriel, Haniel 7 Kafziel

F

fabes: 10 gooseberry
fabian: 8 cautious
fabiform: 10 bean-shaped
fable: 4 myth, tale 5 feign, story 6 legend 7 fiction, parable, untruth 8 allegory, apologue 9 falsehood, narrative 10 fabulosity
animal of: 6 dragon 7 centaur, unicorn
being of: 4 ogre 5 dwarf, giant, troll
bird of: roc 7 phoenix
collection: 8 bestiary
serpent of: 8 basilisk
fabric: rep, web 4 felt, repp 5 baize, beige, build, crepe, frame, lisle, rayon, serge, terry, tulle 6 creton, etoile 7 texture 8 cretonne, material 9 construct, cottonade
calico: 5 sallo 6 sallco
coarse: mat 5 crash 6 burlap
corded: rep 4 repp 5 pique
cotton: 4 susi 5 pique, wigan 6 burrah 7 buckram, galatea, hickory 8 bourette
cotton knit: 10 balbriggan
cotton of light quality: 4 leno 7 jaconet, organza 9 silka line
cotton mixture: 6 mashru 7 delaine, satinet, zanella 9 bombasine, grusaille
cotton print: 6 calico 7 percale 8 cretonne
cotton twilled: 5 denim, sallo 6 salico 7 fustian, silesia
cotton with silk embroidery: 8 agabanee
curtain material: 4 leno 5 scrim 6 moreen, velvet 7 silesia
dealer: 6 draper, mercer
finisher: 6 beetle
flag material: 7 buntine, bunting
heavy: 5 denim 6 canvas
linen: 4 crea(Sp.), ecru 5 carde, crash 6 barras 7 buckram, drabbet, sinelon
linen and cotton: 9 huckaback
linen of light quality: 4 lawn 5 scrim
lustrous: 6 poplin, sateen
medieval: 4 acca 6 samite
metallic: 4 lame
old: 9 ciclatoun
plaid: 6 tartan
printed: 5 batik 6 calico 7 challis
satin: 5 pekin 6 etoile
satin imitation: 6 sateen
sheer: 4 lawn 5 gauze, voile
silk: 4 alma, gimp, gros, ikat 5 caffa, carde, crepe, ninon, rumal, satin, surah 6 blatta, camaka, patola, samite 7 alamode, chiffon, taffeta, Xmantua, 8 barathea, bourette, sarcenet, sarsenet 9 charmeuse, levantine, matelasse 10 bombay-cine
silk (thin): 4 moff 5 tulle 6 pongee 7 hernani 8 eolienne
silk and cotton: 6 crepon, gloria 9 bombasine, bombazine
silk and linen: 8 brocatel 10 brocatelle
silk and wool: 6 crepon, gloria 7 challie, challis 8 eolienne
silk imitation: 5 rayon 7 satinet
silk mixture: kin 4 acca 5 balda 6 mashru 7 grogram 9 baldachin, baldaquin, farandine
silk-ribbed: rep 4 repp 6 faille 7 epingle 8 marocain
silk yarn: 7 schappe
straw: mat 7 matting
striped: aba
suiting: 6 dacron 7 acrilan
surface: nap
synthetic: 5 nylon, orlon, rayon 7 plastic
textile: rep 5 moire 7 etamine
texture: 4 woof
thin: 5 gauze 8 gossamer, tarlatan 9 grenadine
towel: 4 huck 5 terry
Turkish: 6 agaric 7 chekmak 8 cottonee 10 terry cloth
twilled: 4 alma 5 sallo, serge, surah 6 coburg, sallco 8 corduroy, shalloon, whipcord 9 bombasine, bombazine, gabardine, levantine, messaline, tricotine 10 kerseymere
unbleached: 5 beige
upholstery: rep 4 repp 6 frieze 7 tabaret
velvet-like: 5 panne 6 velure 8 duvetine 9 velveteen
waste material: 5 mungo

watered silk: **5** moire
waterproof: **8** burberry
white: **8** coteline
wide: **6** cotele
wool: **5** baize, beige, casha, serge, tweed **6** burnet, frisca, moreen **7** bolivia, debeige, delaine, droguet, frisado, frizado, hernani, worsted **8** cataloon, harateen, rattinet, zibeline **9** catalowne, gabardine, grenadine, harrateen, montagnac, zibelline
wool (coarse): **6** djersa, duffel, kersey, witney **7** bocking
wool dress: **5** beige **7** delaine **8** wildbore **9** grenadine
wool mixture: **7** delaine, zanella **9** grisaille
wool-ribbed: rep **4** repp **8** marocain
worsted: **7** etamine
woven: **4** lame **5** tweed, twill **6** tissue, tricot **7** blanket, damasse, textile

fabricate: **4** coin, form, make, mint **5** build, frame **6** devise, invent **7** concoct, fashion, produce **8** contrive **9** construct **11** manufacture
fabrication: lie **7** fiction, forgery, untruth **8** pretense **9** falsehood
fabricator: **4** liar **6** forger **12** manufacturer
fabricature: **9** structure **12** construction
fabula: **5** story
fabulist: **4** liar **5** Aesop, Grimm **6** fabler **8** Andersen **10** parabolist
fabulous: **7** feigned **8** mythical, romantic **9** legendary **10** apocryphal, fictitious **11** astonishing
facade: **4** face **5** front
face: map, mug, pan **4** dare, defy, dial, leer, line, meet, moue **5** cover, front, stand **6** facade, oppose, veneer, visage **7** feature, grimace, surface **8** confront, envisage **9** encounter, semblance **11** countenance, physiognomy
artery: **9** maxillary
bone: **5** malar **6** zygoma **7** maxilia **8** mandu-ble
covering: **4** mask, veil
defect: **7** harelip
false: **4** mask
guard: **6** beaver
ornament: **4** veil **5** jewel, patch **9** cosmetics
paint: **4** fard **6** parget
part: eye, jaw, lid, lip **4** brow, chin, nose **5** cheek
with masonry: **5** revet

face eastward: **9** orientate
face-to-face: **7** affront, vis-a-vis
face value: par
facer: **6** bumper **7** tankard
facet: **5** bezel, culet, phase
facete: **5** witty **9** facetious
facetious: **5** witty **6** facete, jocose **7** jocular **8** humorous, polished **9** laughable
facia: **5** plate **6** tablet
facient: **4** doer **5** agent
facile: **4** able, easy **5** quick, ready **6** expert, fluent, gentle **7** affable, lenient
facilitate: aid **4** ease, help **5** speed **6** assist **8** expedite
facility: art **4** ease **5** eclat, knack, skill **7** address, freedom **9** dexterity, readiness **10** adroitness, expertness, pliability
facing: **5** front, panel **6** veneer **7** surface **8** covering, opposite
inward: **8** introrse
outward: **8** extrorse

facsimile: **4** copy **5** model **7** replica **9** duplicate, imitation **10** similitude **11** counterpart
fact: **4** data(pl.), deed, fait(F.) **5** datum, event, truth **6** factum(L.) **7** keynote, lowdown, reality **9** actuality **12** circumstance
support: **15** circumstantiate

faction: **4** bloc, sect, side **5** cabal, junto, party **6** brigue, clique **7** dispute, quarrel **8** intrigue **9** concision **11** combination
factious: **9** seditious **11** dissentious
factitious: **4** sham **9** unnatural **10** artificial
factor: gen **4** doer, gene **5** agent, maker **6** author, detail **7** bailiff, factrix, steward **8** adherent, aumildar, gomashta, gomastah **11** chamberlain, constituent
factory: **4** mill, shop **5** plant **6** aurang, aurung **8** building, fabrique(F.), officina(Sp.), workshop **11** manufactory **13** establishment
book: **7** bindery

factotum: **5** agent **7** servant **8** handyman
factual: **4** real, true **6** actual **7** literal
factum: **4** fact **5** event **8** memorial
faculty: wit **4** ease, gift **6** talent **7** ability **8** aptitude, capacity
fad: **4** rage, whim **5** craze, fancy, hobby **7** crochet, fashion **9** amusement
faddle: **6** trifle **8** nonsense
fade: die, dim, dow, wan **4** flat, pale, vade, wilt **5** daver, decay, passe, peter **6** perish, vanish, wither **7** decline, insipid, lighten **8** diminish, discolor, dissolve, evanesce, languish **11** commonplace
camera device: **4** iris **9** diaphragm

faded: dim **4** dull **5** faint, passe
fadge: fit **4** suit **6** bundle **7** succeed
faerie: See **fairy**
Faerie Queen: *author:* **7** Spenser
character: Una **4** Alma **5** Guyon **6** Amoret **7** Artegal **8** Calidore, Gloriana **11** Britomartis

Faeroes: *district manager:* **4** foud
island: **6** Ostero

whirlwind: oe
Fafnir: *brother:* 5 Regin
slayer: 6 Sigurd 7 Sigurth 9 Siegfried
fag: 4 flag, tire, toil 5 droop, weary 6 drudge, menial 7 exhaust, fatigue, frazzle 9 cigarette
fagot, faggot: 5 fadge 6 bundle
faik: 6 lessen
fail: ebb 4 flag, fold, lose, sink, wane 5 flunk, peter 6 desert, falter 7 exhaust, flicker, founder 8 languish
failing: 5 fault 6 foible 7 blemish, frailty, weakness 9 infirmity 10 deficiency 11 delinquency, diminishing 12 imperfection
failure: dud 4 bust, flop, lack, loss, miss 5 bilge, decay, fault, lapse, lemon 6 fiasco, fizzle 7 bloomer, debacle, decline, default, neglect 8 abortion, collapse, omission 10 bankruptcy, deficiency 11 delinquency, miscarriage, shortcoming 13 deterioration 14 disappointment
fain: 4 fond, glad 5 eager 7 pleased, willing 8 desirous, inclined 11 constrained
fainaigue: 5 shirk 6 revoke, renege
faineant: 4 idle, lazy 5 idler 8 inactive, sluggard
fainness: 8 gladness 9 eagerness 11 willingness
faint: dim 4 dark, pale, pall, soft, weak 5 swoon, timid, waugh 6 evanid, feeble, sickly 7 feigned, languid, obscure, syncope 8 cowardly, delicate, languish, listless, sluggish, timorous 9 simulated 10 indistinct
fainthearted: 5 timid 6 afraid, craven 8 cowardly, timorous
faintness: 7 tenuity 8 weakness 9 dejection 10 feebleness 12 timorousness 16 faintheartedness
fair: 4 calm, even, just, mart 5 bazar, blond, clear, feria(L.), right 6 bazaar, blonde, decent, honest, kermis 7 exhibit, kermess 8 distinct, middling, unbiased 9 beautiful, equitable, impartial 10 auspicious, exhibition, reasonable 12 unprejudiced 13 disinterested, dispassionate
fair game: 4 butt, dupe 6 victim
fair-haired: 5 blond 6 blonde
fair-mindedness: 6 equity 7 justice
fairest: 6 flower
fairly: 4 well 7 plainly 8 properly, suitably 9 favorably, tolerably 10 handsomely 12 legitimately
fairness: 6 equity 7 honesty 8 equality 12 impartiality
fairy: elf, fay, hob, imp 4 peri, perl, pixy, puck, shee, vila 5 pixie, sidhe 6 faerie, spirit, yaksha, yakshi 7 banshee, sylphid 8 folletto 10 leprechaun 11 enchantress
abode: 4 shee 5 sidhe
air: 5 sylph
chief: 4 Puck
king: 6 Oberon
queen: Mab, Una 7 Titania
shoemaker: 10 leprechaun
spirit of death: 7 banshee
tricky: 4 Puck
fairy-like: 5 elfin
fairyland: 7 elfland
fait: 4 deed, fact
faith: 5 certy(Sc.), creed, troth, trust 6 belief, certie(Sc.), credit 8 affiance, reliance 9 bona fides 10 confidence
article: 5 tenet 8 credenda 9 credendum
faithful: 4 fast, feal, firm, leal, true 5 liege, loyal, pious, tried 6 honest, steady, trusty 7 devoted, sincere 8 accurate, constant 9 steadfast, veracious 13 conscientious
faithfulness: 8 fidelity
faithless: 5 false, punic 6 fickle, hollow, unjust, untrue 7 atheist 8 apostate, delusive, disloyal, shifting, unstable 9 deceptive, mercurial 10 inconstant, perfidious 11 disaffected, incredulous, treacherous 12 unsatisfying
faithlessness: 7 falsity, perfidy, untruth 8 betrayal 10 infidelity
faitour: 5 cheat 8 imposter
fake: 4 hoax, sham 5 bogus, cheat, false, feign, fudge, phony 7 falsify, furbish, pretend, swindle 8 simulate, spurious 9 imitation 10 fictitious, fraudulent 11 counterfeit, manufacture
comb. form: 5 pseud 6 pseudo
faker: 5 quack 6 humbug 7 peddler 9 charlatan, pretender
fakir: 4 monk, yogi 7 ascetic, dervish 9 mendicant
falbala: 7 flounce 8 furbelow, trimming
falcon: 4 hawk 5 hobby, saker 6 lanner, luggar, lugger, merlin, musket, tercel 7 kestrel 9 peregrine
bait: 4 lure
blind: 4 seel
genus: 5 falco
male: 6 tercel 7 tiercel
nestling: 4 eyas
strap for: 4 jess
falconer: 6 hawker 8 ostreger 10 austringer
summons: wo
fall: sag 4 drip, drop, flop, plop, ruin, ruse, sile, sink, slip 5 abate, cloit(Sc.), crash, hance, lapse, plump, rapid, shoot, slump 6 autumn, happen, perish, recede, season, topple, tumble 7 cascade, decline, degrade, depress, descend, devolve, dribble, escheat, plummet, retreat, stumble, subside 8 cataract, collapse, commence, decrease 9

backslide, prostrate, surrender 10 capitulate, depreciate, disappoint 11 precipitate
back: 6 recede 7 relapse, retreat
in: 4 cave 5 agree, lapse 6 concur 9 terminate
short: shy 4 fail, lack, miss
fall guy: 5 patsy 9 scapegoat
fallacious: sly 6 untrue 8 delusive, guileful, illusory 9 deceitful, deceptive, insidious 10 fraudulent, misleading 11 treacherous
fallacy: 5 error 6 idolum
fallal: 4 ruff 6 finery, gewgaw
fallfish: 4 chub
fallible: 7 errable
falling: 6 cadent 8 prolapse, windfall 10 subsidence
fallout: 9 radiation
fallow: 4 pale 6 barren 9 yellow-red, yellowish 12 uncultivated
fallow deer: 6 damine
false: 4 fake, sham 5 bogus, fause(Sc.), paste, phony, wrong 6 fickle, hollow, pseudo, untrue 7 bastard, crooked, feigned 8 disloyal, illusive, recreant, spurious 9 deceitful, deceptive, dishonest, erroneous, faithless, incorrect, insincere, irregular, pretended 10 apocryphal, artificial, calumnious, fictitious, groundless, mendacious, misleading, perfidious, traitorous, untruthful 11 counterfeit, disaffected, treacherous, unveracious 12 hypocritical
comb. form: 6 pseudo
falsehood: cog, fib, lie 4 flam, tale 5 fable 7 falsity, fiction, perfidy, romance, untruth 8 roorback 9 deception, duplicity, imposture, mendacity, treachery 10 pseudology 11 fabrication
falsify: lie 4 fake 5 belie, feint, forge 6 betray, doctor 7 violate 9 dissemble 10 adulterate 11 counterfeit
falsity: lie 5 error 7 untruth 9 falsehood, falseness, mendacity 13 deceitfulness, faithlessness 17 untrustworthiness
show: 5 belie 8 disprove
Falstaff: *follower:* Nym
ancient: 6 Pistol
prince: Hal
falter: 4 fail 5 pause, waver 6 boggle, flinch, totter 7 fribble, stumble, tremble 8 hesitate
faltering: 4 hink
Fama: 5 rumor
fame: 5 bruit, glory, honor, kudos, rumor 6 renown, report, repute 7 hearsay 9 celebrity 10 reputation
famed: 5 known, noted 7 eminent, renomee(F.) 11 illustrious, outstanding 13 distinguished
familiar: 4 bold, cozy, easy, free, tosh 5 usual 6 common, homely, versed 7 affable 8 frequent, habitual, intimate, sociable 9 customary, household, presuming, well-known 10 accustomed, conversant 12 acquaintance 13 unconstrained
familiarize: 4 haft 8 accustom 9 habituate 10 naturalize
family: lik, kin 4 clan 5 class, flesh, group, house 6 cletch 7 kindred, lineage, progeny 8 category 9 household 10 generation
head: 7 goodman, husband 9 patriarch 11 householder 13 pater familias(L.)
pert. to: 7 nepotic 12 genealogical
famine: 6 dearth, hunger 8 scarcity 10 starvation 11 destitution
famish: 4 kill 6 starve 7 destroy
famous: 5 grand, noted 6 namely 7 eminent, namable, notable 8 renowned 9 excellent, notorious 10 celebrated, celebrious 11 conspicuous, outstanding 13 distinguished
famulus: 7 servant 9 attendant
fan: 4 beat, cool 5 punka 6 basket, blower, colmar, punkah, rooter, shovel, spread, winnow 7 admirer, devotee 8 follower 9 flabellum, propeller 10 enthusiast
alluvial: 5 delta
form of: 7 plicate
fan-shaped: 10 flabellate
fanal: 5 light 6 beacon
fanatic: mad 5 bigot, crazy, rabid, ultra 6 zealot 7 devotee 8 frenetic 9 energumen, phrenetic 10 enthusiast, monomaniac 11 extravagant
fancied: 6 unreal 7 dreamed 9 imaginary 10 fictitious
fanciful: odd 5 ideal, queer 6 dreamy, quaint, unreal 7 bizarre, strange 8 romantic 9 conceited, fantasque, fantastic, grotesque, visionary, whimsical 10 capricious, chimerical, notionable 11 imaginative, unrealistic
fancy: fad 4 idea, love, maze, ween, whim 5 dream, freak, guess, humor 6 humour, ideate, liking, megrim, notion, ornate, vagary, vision, whimsy 7 caprice, chimera, conceit, crochet, fantasy, romance, suspect 8 chimaera, conceive, illusion, phantasm, phantasy 9 capriccio, fantaisie 10 conception, conjecture, decorative, impression, ornamental 11 imagination, inclination
fandango: 4 ball, tune 5 dance
fane: 4 flag 6 banner, church, temple 7 pennant 9 cathedral, sanctuary 11 weathercock
fanfare: 7 tantara 8 fanfaron, flourish 9 fanfarade 11 fanfaronade
fanfaron: 7 boaster, fanfare 8 braggart 9 swaggerer

fanfaronade: 7 bluster, fanfare 8 boasting 10 swaggering 11 ostentation
fanfoot: 5 gecko 6 lizard
fang: 4 earn, take, tusk, vang 5 begin, seize, snare, tooth 6 assume, obtain 7 capture, procure 9 undertake
fange: mud 4 dirt, mire
fangle: 4 mode 5 dress 6 geegaw 7 fashion
fanion: 4 flag 6 guidon
fanlight: 7 transom
fanon: 4 cape 5 orale 7 maniple
fantasque: 4 whim 5 fancy 7 fantasy 8 fanciful 9 fantastic
fantast: 7 dreamer 9 visionary
fantastic: odd 5 queer 6 absurd, unreal 7 bizarre 8 fanciful, freakish, romantic, singular 9 fantasque, grotesque, whimsical 10 capricious, chimerical 11 extravagant, imaginative 12 unbelievable
fantasy: 4 idea 5 dream, fancy 6 desire, vision 7 caprice, chimera, phantom, romance 8 chimaera, phantasm 9 fantasque 10 apparition 11 imagination, inclination 13 hallucination
fantoccini: 5 shows 7 puppets
fantod: pet 4 fuss 6 fidget
fantom: See **phantom**
far: 4 long 6 remote 7 distant
across: 4 wide
comb. form: tel 4 tele
down: 4 deep
far-reaching: 4 deep, vast 7 intense 8 profound
faraway: 6 dreamy, remote 7 distant 10 abstracted
farce: 4 mime 5 stuff 6 comedy 7 mockery 8 drollery 9 forcemeat
farceur: wag 5 joker
farcical: 5 comic, droll 7 Atellan 9 ludicrous 10 ridiculous
fardel: lot 4 furl, pack 6 bundle, burden 10 collection
fare: eat 4 diet, food, path, rate, wend 5 cheer, going, price, track, viand 6 happen, travel 7 journey, passage, proceed, prosper 8 progress 9 equipment, passenger, provision, sagaciate 10 expedition 11 nourishment 13 entertainment
farer: 8 traveler
farewell: ave(L.) 4 vale(L.) 5 adieu, adios, aloha, conge, final 7 goodbye, leaving, parting 9 bon voyage, departure 11 valedictory
farfetched: 6 forced 7 devious 8 strained 9 recherche 10 roundabout
farina: 4 meal 5 flour 6 starch
farinaceous food: oat, rye 4 meal 5 flour, grain, salep, spelt, wheat 6 barley, cereal 7 pudding 10 cornstarch
farm: 4 till 5 croft, empty, haras, ranch, range 6 barton, chacra, grange, rancho 7 cleanse, hennery, potrero 8 estancia, hatchery, hacienda 9 cultivate, farmstead
building: 4 barn, crib, shed, silo 7 farmery
grazing: 5 ranch
laborer: 4 hand, hind
machine: See **agriculture** *machine;* **machine** *farm*
steward: 7 granger
tenant: 6 cotter 7 cottier, cropper, metayer 12 sharecropper
farm out: let 4 hire
farmer: 4 tate 6 grower, tiller, yeoman 7 granger, hayseed, planter, plowman, rancher 8 producer 9 hacendero(Sp.), ploughman 10 cultivator, husbandman 13 agriculturist
Egyptian: 6 fellah 8 fellahin(pl.)
migratory: 4 Okie
South African: 4 Boer
farmhouse: 6 grange 7 caserio(Sp.), onstead(Sc.)
farming: 9 husbandry
farmland: 7 acreage
farmyard: 6 barton
farnesol: 7 alcohol
faro: 5 monte
bet: 7 sleeper
card: 4 soda
card combination: 5 split 6 cathop
player: 6 punter
Faroes: See **Faeroes**
farouche: shy 4 wild
farrago: 6 medley 7 mixture
farrier: 5 shoer, smith 10 blacksmith, horseshoer 12 veterinarian
farrow: pig, row 4 rake 6 litter
farseeing: 10 telescopic
farsighted: 6 shrewd 9 hyperopia, provident, sagacious 11 foresighted 13 hypermetropia
farther: 6 longer 7 remoter
farthest: 7 endmost, extreme, farmost, longest, outmost 8 remotest 11 farthermost
farthing: 4 coin 8 quadrans
fascia: 4 band, sash 6 fillet 7 molding
fascicle: 6 bundle 7 cluster
fascinate: 5 charm 6 allure, enamor 7 attract, bewitch, enchant, engross, philter, philtre 8 entrance, interest, intrigue 9 captivate, enrapture, spellbind
fascinating: 9 glamorous 10 attractive, glamourous
fascination: 5 charm, spell 11 enchantment
fashion: fad, ton(F.) 4 form, make, mode, mold, rage 5 craze, forge, frame, guise, model, mould, shape, style, vogue 6 create,

custom, design, fangle, invent, manner, method 7 compose, portray 8 contrive 9 construct, fabricate
fashionable: 5 dashy, smart 6 modish 7 a la mode, dashing, stylish
fashioned: 6 carved 7 wrought
fast: 4 firm, Lent 5 agile, apace, brisk, fixed, fleet, hasty, quick, rapid, stuck, swift 6 lively, secure, speedy, stable, starve 7 abiding, settled 8 enduring, faithful 9 immovable, indelible, steadfast, unfadable, velocious 10 abstinence, stationary, unyielding 11 expeditious
day of: 5 Ember
period of: 4 Lent
fasten: bar, fix, pen, pin, tag, tie 4 bend, bind, bolt, clip, gird, girt, glue, knit, lace, lash, link, lock, moor, nail, rope, seal, snib, soud, weld, wire 5 affix, annex, belay, brace, chain, clamp, clasp, cling, latch, paste, rivet, seize, strap, truss 6 anchor, attach, batten, cement, clinch, picket, secure, solder, staple, tether 7 connect, padlock 8 transfix
comb. form: 4 desm 5 desmo
fastener: bar, gib, nut, pin 4 agal, bolt, frog, hasp, lock, nail, snap 5 catch, clamp, clasp, latch, rivet, screw, strap, thong 6 buckle, button, hatpin, staple, zipper 7 latchet, padlock 8 staylace
fastidious: 4 fine, nice 5 chary, fussy, natty 6 choicy, choosy, dainty 7 choosey, elegant, finical, finicky, haughty, refined 8 critical, delicate, gingerly, overnice, scornful 9 exquisite, finicking, squeamish 10 meticulous, particular 14 overparticular
fastigate: 7 conical, pointed
fastness: 4 fort 6 castle 7 citadel 8 fortress 10 stronghold
fastuous: 7 haughty 8 arrogant 12 ostentatious
fat: oil, tub 4 lard, lipa, rich, suet 5 adeps, brosy, cetin, chuff, ester, fleck, gross, lipid, lipin, obese, plump, podgy, pudgy, pursy, squab, stout, thick 6 fleshy, grease, lipide, portly, pubble, stocky, tallow 7 adipose, blubber, fertile, fulsome, lanolin, opulent, pinguid, stearin 8 extended, fruitful, lanoline, stearine, unctuous 9 corpulent 10 profitable 11 flourishing
comb. form: pio 4 lipo, sebi 5 adipo, steat 6 steato
hard: 4 suet
liquid: 5 elain, olein 6 elaine, oleine
of geese: 6 axunge
pert. to: 6 adipic
render: try 4 lard
wool: 7 lanolin 8 lanoline
fat person: 4 lump 5 blimp, squab, tubby 8 roly-poly 12 humpty-dumpty
fata morgana: 6 mirage
fatal: fey 4 dire 6 deadly, doomed, funest, lethal, mortal 7 capital, fateful, ominous, ruinous 8 destined 9 condemned, prophetic 10 calamitous, disastrous, pernicious, portentous 11 destructive
fatality: 5 wreck 8 calamity, disaster
fatbird: 8 guacharo
fate: end, lot 4 doom, ruin 5 event, karma 6 chance, kismet 7 destiny, fortune, outcome 8 downfall 14 predestination
goddess: Ker 4 Nona, Norn 5 Morta, Tyche 8 Adrastea 9 Adrasteia
fated: 6 doomed 7 decreed 8 destined 10 inevitable
fateful: 5 fatal 6 deadly 7 ominous 9 momentous, prophetic 10 inevitable, portentous 11 destructive, predestined
Fates: *Greek:* 5 Moera, Moira 6 Clotho, Moerae 7 Atropos 8 Lachesis
Roman: 4 Nona 5 Decum, Morta, Parca 6 Parcae
father: bu(Ar.), pa; abu(Ar.), ama, dad, pop 4 abba, abou(Ar.), baba(Ar.), bapu, papa, pere(F.), sire 5 adopt, babbo, beget, daddy, friar, padre(Sp.), pater(L.), vader(Dan.) 6 old man, parent, priest 7 tatinek(Czech.) 8 beaupere(F.), generate 9 confessor, paternity, procreate 11 acknowledge
of English learning: 4 Bede
of geometry: 6 Euclid
of gods and men: 4 Zeus
of human race: 4 Adam
of plenty: 8 Abiathar
pert. to: 6 agnate 8 paternal
Father of Waters: 11 Mississippi
fatherhood: 9 paternity
fatherly: 8 parental, paternal
fathom: 5 brace, delve, solve 7 measure 9 penetrate
fathomless: 16 incomprehensible
fatidic: 9 prophetic
fatigue: fag 4 jade, tire 5 spend, weary 6 overdo, taigle(Sc.) 7 exhaust 8 fatigate
fatigued: 4 beat 8 tuckered 9 forjaskit, forjesket
fatiloquent: 9 fatidical, prophetic
Fatima: *husband:* Ali 9 Bluebeard
descendant: 7 Fatimid 8 Fatimite
sister: 4 Anne
stepbrother: Ali
fatness: 10 pinguitude
fatten: 4 lard 6 batten, enrich, thrive
fatty: 5 suety 6 greasy 7 adipose, pinguid 8 unctuous
fatty tumor: 6 lipoma

fatuous: 5 inane, silly 6 stupid, unreal 7 foolish, idiotic, witless 8 demented, illusory, imbecile 9 frivolous, insensate
faucal: 10 pharyngeal
faucet: tap 4 cock 5 valve 6 spigot 7 hydrant
faugh: bah
fault: sin 4 debt, flaw, flub, lack, slip, vice 5 abuse, blame, culpa(L.), error, guilt, lapse, tache(Sc.) 6 defect, foible, vitium(L.) 7 blemish, blunder, default, demerit, failure, frailty, mistake, neglect, offense 10 peccadillo 11 culpability, delinquency, misdemeanor 12 imperfection 13 transgression
in mining: 4 hade
faultfinder: 5 momus 6 carper, critic 7 caption, knocker, nagster
faultless: 4 pure 5 right 7 correct, perfect, precise 8 flawless 9 blameless 10 impeccable 13 unimpeachable 14 irreproachable
faulty: bad, ill 5 amiss, unfit, wrong 9 incorrect 10 inaccurate
faun: 5 satyr
of Praxiteles: 6 marble
fauna and flora: 5 biota
Faunus: *grandfather:* 6 Saturn
son: 4 Acis
Faust: *author:* 6 Goethe
composer: 6 Gounod
fautor: 6 patron 7 abetter, abettor, favorer 8 partisan 9 protector
faux pas: 4 bull, slip 5 boner, error, gaffe, lapse 6 booboo, bungle 7 blooper, misstep, mistake
faveolate: 6 favose 9 alveolate 11 honeycombed
favonian: 4 mild
favor, favour: aid, for, pro 4 boon, face, gree, help 5 bless, grace, leave, spare 6 esteem, letter, uphold 7 advance, feature, forward, support 8 advocacy, befriend, goodwill, kindness, resemble 9 patronage, privilege, subscribe 10 assistance, concession, indulgence, permission 11 accommodate, approbation, countenance 13 communication
pay: woo 5 court
favorable: 4 good, kind, rosy 5 clear 6 benign 7 benefic, optimal, popular 8 friendly, gracious, pleasing 9 approving, opportune 10 auspicious, charitable, convenient, propitious 12 advantageous
favored: 6 gifted 9 fortunate, preferred
favorer: 6 fautor 9 supporter
favorite: pet 6 minion 7 darling, popular
favoritism: 4 bias 8 nepotism 9 prejudice
favose: 8 aveolate 9 faveolate, honeycomb
fawn: 4 buck, deer, jouk 5 color, cower, crawl, kotow, toady, whelp 6 cringe, grovel, kowtow, shrink 7 adulate, flatter, hangdog, servile, toadeat, truckle 9 parasitic, sycophant 10 ingratiate
skin: 6 nebris
fay: elf, fit 4 join 5 fairy, unite 6 sprite
faze: 5 daunt, worry 10 disconcert
F.D.R.: See **Roosevelt, F.D.**
fe: 4 iron
feal: 5 loyal 7 conceal 8 faithful
fealty: 6 homage 7 loyalty 8 fidelity 9 constancy, obeisance 10 allegiance
fear: awe 5 alarm, doubt, dread, panic 6 danger, dismay, fright, horror, phobia, terror 7 anxiety, suspect 8 affright, disquiet, distrust, venerate 9 agitation, reverence, revulsion 10 solicitude 12 apprehension 13 consternation
of animals: 9 zoophobia
of being alone: 10 monophobia
of burial alive: 11 taphephobia
of cats: 12 aelurophobia, ailurophobia
of crowds: 11 ochlophobia
of darkness: 11 nyctophobia
of dirt: 10 mysophobia
of drafts: 10 aerophobia
of enclosed places: 14 claustrophobia
of fire: 10 pyrophobia
of great heights: 10 acrophobia
of open spaces: 11 agoraphobia
of pain: 10 algophobia
of poisons: 10 toxiphobia
of strangers: 10 xenophobia
of thunder: 12 brontophobia 13 tonitrophobia
of water: 11 hydrophobia
fearful: 4 dire 5 awful, pavid, timid 6 afraid 7 ghastly, nervous, panicky, worried 8 cautious, doubtful, dreadful, grewsome, gruesome, horrible, horrific, shocking, terrible, timorous 9 appalling, frightful, trembling 10 formidable, horrendous, meticulous 11 distressing 12 apprehensive
comb. form: 4 dino
fearless: 4 bold 5 brave 6 daring, heroic 7 impavid 8 intrepid 9 audacious, confident, dauntless, undaunted 10 courageous
fearsome: 5 timid 8 timorous 9 frightful
feasible: 6 likely 8 possible, probable, suitable 9 practical 10 reasonable
feast: eat, foy(Sc.), sup 4 dine, fete, luau, meal 5 festa, treat 6 regale, repast 7 banquet, delight, festino, gratify 8 festival, potlatch 10 burrakhana
comb. form: mas
Christian: 5 agape 9 eucharist
funeral: 5 arval, arvel, dirgy(Sc.), 6 arthel, averil, dirgie(Sc.)
January 6: 8 Epiphany
of lanterns: Bon

of lights: **7** Hanukka **8** Chanukah, Hanukkah
of lots: **5** Purim
of nativity: **9** Christmas
of tabernacles: **7** Succoth
of weeks: **8** Shabuoth
passover: **5** seder
feasting: **9** epulation
companion: **7** convive
feat: act **4** deed, gest **5** geste, stunt, trick **7** exploit, miracle **11** achievement, performance **14** accomplishment
feather: **4** deck, down, vane **5** adorn, penna, pinna(L.), pluma(L.), plume, quill, **6** clothe, fledge, fletch, hackle, pinion
barb: **4** harl, herl **7** pinnula
comb. form: **5** ptile
down: **4** dowl **5** dowle **7** plumule
mature: **10** teleoptile
quill: **5** remex **7** calamus
shaft: **5** scape
shank: **4** boot
shoulder: **4** cape
feather alum: **8** alunogen **12** halotrichite
feather-brained: **7** foolish **9** frivolous
feather-headed: **5** giddy **7** foolish
feather key: **6** spline
feather star: **8** comatula **9** comatulae(pl.), comatulid
feathered: **7** pennate, pinnate
feathers: *provide with:* **6** fletch
shed: **4** molt **5** moult
feathery: **6** fluffy
featly: **6** neatly, nimbly **8** graceful, properly
feature: **4** face **5** favor, motif, token, trait **6** aspect, favour **7** amenity, outline **8** salience **9** lineament **11** countenance **14** characteristic
natural: **9** geography
feaze: **4** fray **7** roughen, unravel, untwist
febris: **5** fever
feces, faeces: **4** dreg **5** drast, drest **6** ordure, refuse **8** sediment **9** excrement, feculence
feck: **5** value **6** amount **8** quantity
fecket: **9** waistcoat
feckful: **6** strong **8** powerful **9** efficient
feckless: **4** weak **9** shiftless, worthless
feckly: **6** almost, mostly
feculence: **5** dregs, feces **6** faeces **8** foulness **9** muddiness
fecund: **7** fertile **8** fruitful, prolific
fecundate: **9** fertilize, pollinate **10** impregnate
fed up: **5** bored **7** wearied **8** satiated **9** surfeited
fedarie: **10** accomplice **11** confederate
federacy: **8** alliance **11** confederacy
federation: **5** union **6** league, nation **8** alliance **11** association, confederacy
fedity: **8** impurity, vileness
fedora: hat
fee: **4** dues, feal, feul(Sc.), fier, hire, rate, wage **5** price **6** charge, dastur, employ, reward, salary **7** payment, stipend, storage, tribute **8** gratuity, malikana, retainer **9** allowance, bienvenne, emolument, pourboire **10** assessment, honorarium, perquisite, recompense **12** compensation
feeble: **4** flue, lame, mean, poor, puny, weak **5** faint **6** dotage, flabby, flimsy, foible, infirm, scanty, sickly, wankle, weanly **7** fragile, invalid, languid, queechy **8** decrepit, impotent, inferior, thewless(Sc.), yielding **9** miserable **10** inadequate, indistinct **11** debilitated
feeble-minded: **5** anile, dotty **7** moronic **10** irresolute **11** vacillating
feed: eat, hay **4** bait, bran, fill, glut, grub, meal, oats, sate **5** agist, gorge, grass, graze, nurse **6** fodder, foster, repast, suckle, supply **7** blowout, furnish, gratify, herbage, indulge, nourish, nurture, satiate, satisfy, surfeit, sustain **9** replenish
to excess: **4** glut **6** agrote, pamper **7** surfeit **8** overfill **9** crapulate
feeder: **9** tributary
fire: **6** stoker
feel: **5** grope, sense, touch **6** handle **7** examine, explore, sensate **8** perceive **10** appreciate, experience
feeler: **4** palp **6** palpus **7** antenna, smeller **8** proposal, tentacle
feeling: **4** pity, tact, view **5** humor, touch **6** morale **7** emotion, opinion, passion **8** attitude, sentient **9** affection, sensation, sentiment **10** atmosphere, experience, perception **11** sensibility **13** consciousness **14** susceptibility
capable of: **8** sentient
evocative of: **7** emotive
lack of: **8** numbness **9** apathetic, insensate **10** anesthesia **11** anaesthesia **13** insensibility
feet (see also **foot**): **4** dogs
feeze: **4** rush **5** drive **6** impact **7** disturb
fegary: **4** whim **5** prank **6** finery, gewgaw
feign: act **4** fake, seem, sham **5** avoid, fable, shape, shirk **6** affect, assume, invent **7** conceal, fashion, imagine, pretend, romance **8** disguise, simulate **9** dissemble, personate **11** counterfeit, dissimulate, make-believe
ignorance: **7** connive
sickness: **8** malinger
feigned: **5** false **6** pseudo **7** fictive **9** insincere **10** artificial, fictitious
feil: **4** neat **11** comfortable
feint: **4** ruse **5** shift, trick **7** falsify, feigned **8** pretense **9** diversion

in fencing: **5** appel
feirie: **6** active, nimble
feis: **8** assembly **10** convention
feist: dog, pup
feldspar: **6** albite, gneiss **7** odinite, syenite **9** anorthite **11** labradorite
yield: **6** kaolin
felicitate: **12** congratulate
felicitous: **5** happy
felicity: joy **9** happiness, well-being
felid: cat
felidae: cat
feline: cat, sly, tom **4** lion, lynx, pard, puma **5** civet, tiger **6** jaguar **7** cheetah, leonine, leopard, wildcat **8** stealthy **9** grimalkin **11** treacherous
breathing: **4** purr
felis: *domestica:* cat
leo: **4** lion
pardus: **7** leopard
fell: cut, fen, hew **4** down, hide, hill, moor, pelt, ruin, skin, very **5** cruel, eager, field, great, sharp **6** deadly, fierce, fleece, intent, mighty, savage, shrewd **7** brutish, crashed, doughty, hideous, inhuman, tumbled **8** mountain, spirited, vigorous **9** barbarous, ferocious, marshland, momentous, prostrate **11** destructive
fellah: **7** peasant
fellow (see also **man; person**): bo; cod, guy, lad, man **4** bean, beau, bozo, carl, chal, chap, cove, dick, duck, hind, mate, peer **5** billy, bloke, chiel, match **6** bugger, callan, chield, codger, hombre(Sp.), person, sirrah **7** callant, chappie, comrade, cullies, partner, scroyle **8** neighbor **9** associate, companion **10** sweetheart **12** contemporary
awkward: oaf **4** club, gawk, lout, slam **5** booby, clown **6** galoot **7** bumpkin **9** dromedary **11** hobble-de-hoy
beggardly: **8** bezonian
brutish: **5** yahoo
conceited: **7** dalteen
craven: **6** coward
dissolute: **4** rake, roue **9** debaucher
dull: **4** drip, fogy **5** fogey **8** codshead
fat: **7** glutton
fine: **5** brick, bully **7** bawcock **8** bonhomme(F.)
foolish: sop **4** goff
funny: wag, wit **4** card **5** clown
honest: **6** trusty **9** truepenny
idle: **6** footer, stocah
ignorant: **6** gobbin
lazy: bum **9** drawlatch
little: bub **5** caddy **6** birkie, caddie, shaver **9** dandiprat
mean: cad **4** boor, carl, pleb **5** bucko, bully, catso, cavil, churl, yahoo **6** fouter, foutre **7** cullion **8** blighter, coistrel, coistril, smatchet(Sc.)
old: **6** geezer, gleyde
old-fashioned: **4** fogy
queer old: **6** geezer **10** curmudgeon
ragged: **10** ragamuffin **14** tatterdemalion
reckless: **4** buck **5** blade **9** daredevil, hell-raker
rowdy: **6** roarer **8** larrikin
shrewd: **6** gazabo, gazebo
silly: **8** dotterel
stupid: ass **4** clod, daff, dolt, gump, hash, simp **5** booby, dunce, moron **6** bayard, foozle **8** codshead **9** blockhead, heavyhead **10** bufflehead **11** blunderbuss, blunderhead
tricky: **5** knave, scamp **6** rascal
vain: fop
worthless: bum, cur **5** rogue, scamp **6** budzat **7** bobtail, brothel, budzart, vaurien(F.) **9** schlemiel(Yid.), schlemihl(Yid.), scoundrel
fellowship: **5** guild, union **7** company **8** alliance **9** communion **10** membership **11** association, brotherhood, camaraderie, comradeship, corporation, familiarity, intercourse, partnership **12** acquaintance, friendliness **13** companionship
felly: rim **6** keenly **7** cruelly **8** bitterly, fiercely, savagely, terribly **11** barbarously **13** destructively
felo-de-se: **7** suicide
felon: **4** wild **5** cruel **6** fetlow, fierce, wicked **7** convict, culprit, villain, whitlow **8** criminal **9** murderous **10** malefactor
felony: **5** arson, crime **7** offense
felt: hat **6** fabric, sensed
felwort: **7** gentian
female: **4** girl, gyne **5** woman **6** weakly **7** feminal, womanly **8** feminine, ladylike, womanish **9** womanlike **10** effeminate
animal: cow, doe, ewe, hen **4** mare, slut **5** bitch, filly, jenny **6** sheder **7** lioness, tigress
assistant: **8** adjutrix **9** adjutrice
camel: **4** naga
comb. form: gyn **4** gyne, gyno
figure: **5** orant **8** caryatid
fish: **4** raun
fox: **5** vixen
monster: **6** gorgon
principle: **5** Sakti
red deer: **4** hind
saint: ste
sandpiper: **5** reeve
sheep: ewe
slave: **7** odalisk **9** odalisque
spirit: **7** banshee

warrior: 6 Amazon
feminine: 4 soft, weak 5 woman 6 female, tender 8 womanish 10 effeminate
femininity: 10 effeminacy, muliebrity 11 womanliness 12 womanishness
fere: 4 mate, peer 5 equal 9 companion
femme fatale: 5 siren 7 Lorelei
femoral: 6 crural
femur: 9 thighbone
fen: bog 4 carr, fowl, moor 5 marsh, snipe, swamp 6 morass 8 quagmire
fence: bar 4 bank, duel, ha-ha, pale, rail, wall 5 guard, hedge 6 paling, picket, raddle, rasper 7 barrier, bulwark, defense 8 palisade, palisado 9 enclosure 12 circumscribe
fish: net 4 weir
interwoven: 6 raddle
picket: 4 pale 6 paling
sunken: 4 ha-ha
fencer: 7 duelist, parrier 9 gladiator, swordsman
cry of: 6 touche 7 en garde
fencing: *attack:* 7 reprise
breastplate: 8 plastron
cry: 4 sasa
hit: 5 punto
maneuver: 5 appel
movement: 4 volt
position: 5 carte, prime, sixte, terce 6 octave, quarte, quinte, tierce 7 seconde, sep time
position of hands: 9 pronation 10 supination
redoubling of attack: 7 reprise
sword: 4 epee, foil 6 rapier
term: 4 bind 5 lunge 6 thrust, touche
thrust: 7 riposte
weapon: 4 epee, foil 5 saber, sabre, sword 6 rapier
fend: 4 ward 5 parry 6 defend, forbid, resist 7 support
fender: 5 guard 6 buffer, bumper, shield 11 splashboard
fenestra: 6 window 7 foramen, opening 8 aperture, fontanel
fennel: 4 hemp
fent: 4 slit 7 opening
fer-de-lance: 5 snake
feracious: 8 fruitful
feral: 4 wild 6 deadly, savage 7 bestial, untamed 8 funeral, unbroken 11 uncivilized 14 undomesticated
Ferdinand's wife: 8 Isabella
feretory: 6 chapel, shrine
feria: 4 fair 6 fiesta 7 holiday
ferine: 4 rude, wild 6 savage 7 untamed 9 barbarous, ferocious 11 uncivilized
ferly: 6 marvel, wonder 9 amazement 12 astonishment
fermail: 5 clasp 6 buckle
ferment: 4 barm, heat, turn, work, zyme 5 fever, yeast 6 enzyme, foment, tumult, uproar 7 agitate 8 disorder 10 ebullition, exacerbate, excitement, turbulence
fermenting mixture: bub
fern: 4 tara, weki 5 frond
climbing: 4 nito
edible: roi 4 tara
genus: 7 onoclea, osmunda 8 psilotum
kind of: 4 nito 5 brake 6 pteris 7 bracken 8 polypody 10 maidenhair
leaf: 5 frond
royal: 6 osmund
scale: 7 ramenta(pl.) 8 ramentum
fern-like: 7 pteroid 13 pteridophytic
ferocious: 4 fell, grim, wild 5 cruel, feral 6 bloody, brutal, fierce, raging, savage 7 inhuman, ominous, violent 8 pitiless, ravenous, ruthless 9 barbarous, malignant, merciless, murderous, rapacious, truculent 10 implacable, malevolent, relentless, sanguinary 11 remorseless 12 bloodthirsty
ferret: hob 4 tape 6 weasel 7 polecat
male: hob
ferric oxide: 5 rouge 6 powder
ferrotype: 7 tintype
ferrule: cap 4 ring, virl(Sc.) 6 collet, pulley, verrel 7 bushing, verrell
ferry: 4 pont, scow 7 traject
ferryman: 6 Charon
fertile: fat 4 rank, rich 5 gleby 6 fecund, hearty 7 teeming 8 abundant, fruitful, generous, prolific 9 exuberant, feracious, inventive, luxuriant, plenteous, plentiful 10 productive, profitable
render: 6 enrich
fertility god: 4 Frey 5 Freyr
fertilize: 6 batten, enrich 8 fructify 9 fecundate 10 impregnate, inseminate
fertilizer: 4 marl 5 guano, humus 6 alinit, manure, pollen, potash 7 compote, nitrate 8 nitrogen 11 phosphorous 14 superphosphate
ferule: rod 5 ruler 6 fennel, ferula 10 discipline, punishment
fervency: See **fervor**
fervent: hot 4 keen, warm 5 eager, fiery 6 ardent, bitter, fervid, fierce, raging, savage 7 boiling, burning, glowing, intense 8 vehement 9 religious 10 passionate 11 impassioned
fervid: hot 6 ardent, tropic 7 boiling, burning, fervent, zealous 8 vehement 9 impetuous 11 impassioned

fervor: 4 fire, heat, rage, zeal 5 ardor 7 passion 8 candency 9 eagerness, vehemence 10 enthusiasm 11 earnestness
fess: bar 4 band, pert 5 smart 6 lively 9 conceited
festa: 5 feast 7 holiday 8 festival
festal: gay 4 gala 5 gaudy 7 festive
fester: rot 4 scar 6 rankle 7 pustule, putrefy 9 cicatrice, cicatrize
festival: mas 4 fair, fete, gala, Holi 5 feast, feria, festa, gaudy, Haloa, Hooli, revel 6 fiesta, Hohlee 7 banquet, holiday 8 carnival, carousal 9 festivity
church: 4 Lent 6 Easter 9 Christmas
comb. form: mas
epiphany: 7 uphelya
festive: gay 4 gala 6 festal, genial, joyous 7 holiday, jocular 8 mirthful, sportive 9 convivial 10 celebrious 11 merry making
festivity: 4 gala 5 mirth, randy, revel 6 gaiety, splore 7 jollity 8 festival, function 9 festivity 10 joyfulness 11 celebration, merrymaking 12 conviviality 13 entertainment, glorification
god: 5 Comus 7 Bacchus 8 Dionysus
festoon: 6 wreath 7 garland 8 decorate
fetch: fet 4 gasp, tack, take 5 bring, sweep, trick 6 double, wraith 7 achieve, attract 8 artifice, interest 9 strategem
fetching: 6 crafty 8 alluring, pleasing, scheming 10 attractive 11 fascinating
fete: 4 fair, gala 5 bazar, feast 6 bazaar, fiesta, regale 7 banquet, holiday 8 ceremony, festival 9 entertain 11 celebration 13 entertainment
fetid: 4 foul, olid, rank 5 fusty, musty 6 putrid, rancid, rotten, virose 8 mephitic, stinking 9 offensive 10 malodorous
fetish, fetich: obi 4 idol, obia 5 charm, huaca, obeah, obiah, totem 6 grigri, voodoo 7 sorcery 8 greegree, talisman 10 mumbo-jumbo
fetter: 4 band, bond, find, gyve, iron 5 basil, chain 6 anklet, garter, hamper, hobble, hopple, impede 7 confine, enchain, manacle, shackle, trammel 8 restrain 9 restraint
fettle: 4 beat, deck, fuss, mull, tidy 5 dress, groom 6 repair, strike 7 arrange, bandage, harness 9 condition
fetus, foetus: 5 birth, child, young 6 embryo 10 conception
human: 10 homunculus
limbless: 5 ameli(pl.) 6 amelus
feud: 4 fray 5 broil 6 affray, enmity, strife 7 contest, dispute, quarrel 8 vendetta 9 hostility 10 contention
blood: 8 vendetta
feudal: *estate:* 4 feod, fief
jurisdiction: soc 4 soke
lord: 7 vavasor 8 suzerain, vavasour
penalty: 7 sursise
pert. to: 5 banal
tenant: 6 vassal 7 homager
tenure: 6 socage
feudatory: 4 fief 11 beneficiary
fever: 4 ague, fire 6 febris 7 ferment 9 calenture 10 excitement 11 temperature 13 conflagration
kind of: 4 ague 5 octan 6 dengue, sextan, sodoku 7 feveret, helodes, malaria, quartan 10 calentural 11 brucellosis
without: 8 apyretic
feverish: 5 fiery 6 hectic 7 excited, febrile, frantic 8 restless 9 overeager 11 impassioned
few: 4 less, some 5 scant 7 limited 8 exiguous
comb. form: 4 olig 5 oligo, pauci
fewness: 7 paucity
fey: 4 dead 5 fatal 7 unlucky 8 accursed 9 delirious, enfeebled, visionary
fez: cap 8 tarboosh
fiacre: 4 hack 5 coach
fiance: 5 trust 7 promise 8 affiance 10 confidence
fiasco: 5 crash, flask 6 bottle 7 failure
fiat: 5 edict, order 6 decree 7 command 8 decision, sanction 9 ordinance 12 announcement, proclamation
fib: lie, yed 4 beat, flaw, whid 6 pummel 9 falsehood 11 tarradiddle
fibber: 4 liar 12 prevaricator
fiber, fibre: 5 grain 6 strand, thread
band: 6 fillet
bark: 5 olona, terap
hat: 5 datil
kind of: nap, nep, tal, tow 4 adad, aloe, bast, buri, coir, eruc, feru, flax, hemp, ixle, jute, kyar, lint, marl, noil, pita, silk, sola 5 abaca, civil, erizo, floss, istle, istli, ixtle, kapok, linen, mudar, nylon, oakum, orlon, ramee, ramie, rayon, sisal 6 amiray, cotton, dacron, manila, raffia, staple 7 acetate, acrilan, castuli, haurizo, sabutan 8 filament, fibrilla, keratose 9 gamelotte 10 anodendron, escobadura
knot: nep
palm: 4 eruc 6 raffia 7 coquita, coquito
synthetic: 5 nylon, orlon, rayon 6 dacron 7 acetate, acrilan
yarn: 6 strand
fibril: 4 hair 8 filament
fibrin: 6 gluten
fibrose: 6 sinewy 7 stringy
fibula: 5 clasp 6 brooch, buckle 9 safety-pin
fickle: 4 gery 5 dizzy, false, giddy 6 mobile, puzzle, shifty, volage, wankle 7 casalty, caselty, cazelty, flatter, mutable 8 cassalty, casselty, gossamer, unstable, unsteady,

variable, volatile, wavering **9** changeful, dangerous, deceitful, faithless, unsettled **10** capricious, changeable, inconstant, irresolute, highheaded **11** treacherous, vacillating

fico: fig **4** snap **6** trifle

fictile: **6** molded **7** plastic

fiction: **4** tale **5** fable, false, novel **6** deceit, device, fabula, legend **7** coinage, fantasy, figment, forgery, romance **9** falsehood, invention **10** concoction, pretending **11** contrivance, dissembling, fabrication **14** counterfeiting

fictional: **7** assumed **11** make-believe

fictitious: **5** bogus, dummy, false, phony **7** assumed, feigned **8** fabulous, mythical, spurious **9** imaginary, imitative, pretended **10** apocryphal, artificial **11** counterfeit

fictive: **9** imaginary

fiddle: bow **4** viol **5** cheat, gique **6** potter, trifle, violin **7** swindle

fiddler: **4** crab **7** crowder, scraper **8** sixpence **9** violinist

fiddler crab: uca

fiddlesticks: **5** pshaw

fidelity: **5** troth, truth **6** fealty **7** honesty **8** adhesion, devotion, veracity **9** adherence, closeness, constancy **10** allegiance **12** faithfulness

symbol of: **5** topaz **7** diamond

fidget: **4** fike, fuss, roil **5** hotch, worry **6** brevit, fissle, fistle, fridge, fusser **7** nervous **8** restless **9** impatient **10** uneasiness **12** restlessness

fidgety: **5** fussy **6** uneasy **7** restive **8** restless **9** impatient

fiducial: **4** firm **7** trusted **8** trustful **9** confident **11** trustworthy

fiduciary: **7** trustee

fief: fee, han **4** feud **8** benefice **9** feudatory

field: lea, lot **4** acre, ager(L.), area, fell, list, mead, rand, wong **5** campo, champ, croft, glebe, paddy, range, rowen, sawah **6** arrish, campus, champe, furrow, ground, machar, meadow, sphere **7** compass, garston, paddock, terrain **8** clearing **9** grassland **11** battlefield

athletic: **4** oval, ring, rink **5** arena, court, green **6** course, stadia(pl.) **7** diamond, stadium **8** gridiron

common share: **4** dale

edge: **4** rand

extensive: **7** savanna **8** savannah

god: **4** Faun

goddess: **5** Fauna

pert. to: **8** agrarian, agrestic **10** campestral

Roman: **4** ager

stubble: **5** rowen

field mouse: **4** vole

field of blood: **4** ager **8** aceldama, akeldama **9** sanguinis

fieldwork: **5** lunet, redan **7** lunette **13** fortification

fiend: foe **5** demon, devil, enemy, Satan, trull **6** wizard

fiendish: **5** cruel **6** wicked **7** demonic **8** demoniac, devilish, diabolic **10** diabolical

fierce: **4** bold, fell, grim **5** breme, cruel, felon, rethe **6** ardent, gothic, hetter, raging, savage **7** brutish, fervent, furious, grimful, scaddle, violent **9** felonious, ferocious, impetuous, truculent **10** catawampus, forbidding, passionate **11** catawampous **13** catawamptious

fiercely: **4** fell **5** felly

fiery: hot, red **5** adust **6** ardent, flashy, ignite **7** burning, fervent, flaming, furious, glowing, parched, peppery, violent **8** choleric, feverish, frampoid, inflamed, spirited, vehement **9** hotheaded, impetuous, irascible, irritable **10** mettlesome, passionate, phlogistic **11** combustible, inflammable

fiesta: **4** fete **5** feria, party **7** holiday **8** festival **9** festivity

fife: **4** pipe **5** flute

fifty: nu(Gr.)

fig: rig **4** fico **5** array, breba, dress, eleme, elemi, pipal **6** trifle **7** furbish

basket: **5** cabas

crate: **5** seron

genus: **5** ficus

sacred: **5** pipal

Smyrna: **5** eleme, elemi

fig-shaped: **8** ficiform

Figaro: **6** barber

fight: box, war **4** beat, bout, clem, cock, cope, cuff, duel, flog, fray, mell, tilt, wage **5** brawl, clash, hurry, melee, scrap **6** affair, affray, barney, battle, bicker, combat, debate, impugn, oppose, resist, rippit, strife, strike, strive **7** bargain, contend, contest, ruction **8** conflict, militate, struggle **9** encounter, pugnacity **10** free-for-all **11** altercation **12** disagreement **13** combativeness

against the gods: **9** theomachy

fighter: pug **4** vamp **5** boxer **6** cocker **7** battler, duelist, soldier, warrior, **8** andabata, barrater, barrator, champion, pugilist, guerilla, scrapper **9** combatant, guerrilla

fighting: **7** warlike **8** militant **10** pugnacious **11** belligerent

street: **4** riot **5** brawl

fighting fish: **5** betta

figlike: **8** caricous

figment: **7** fiction **9** invention **11** fabrication

figuration: **4** form **5** shape **7** outline

figurative: 6 florid 7 flowery, typical 9 allegoric 10 rhetorical 12 emblematical
use of words: 5 trope
figure: hue, vol 4 bosh, form, idea, star 5 digit, image, magot, shape 6 emblem, number, symbol, tattoo 7 chiffer, chiffre, compute, contour, numeral, outline 8 likeness 9 archetype, calculate 13 configuration
geometrical: 4 cone, cube, lune 5 prism, rhomb, solid 6 circle, gnomon, oblong, sector, square 7 ellipse, lozenge, pelcoid, rhombus 8 crescent, pelecoid, pentacle, triangle 9 ellipsoid, rectangle 16 parallelepipedon
human form: 4 nude 5 dummy, glyph, orant 7 telamon 8 Atlantes, caryatid
many-sided: 4 cube 6 isogon 7 decagon, hexagon, nonagon, octagon, polygon 8 pentagon, tetragon 10 hexahedron, octahedron 11 icosahedron 12 dodecahedron 13 quadrilateral
of speech: 5 trope 6 aporia, simile 7 imagery 8 metaphor, metonymy
praying: 5 orant
symbolic: 6 emblem
figure out: 4 dope 5 solve
figured: 7 adorned, faconne(Fr.) 8 computed
figurine: 7 tanagra 9 statuette
motion picture: 5 Oscar
Fiji Island: *capital:* 4 Suva
chestnut: 4 rata
group: lau
drug: 5 tonga
filament: 4 dowl, hair, harl 5 fiber, fibre 6 mantle, strand, thread
lamp: 12 incandescent
filbert: nut 5 hazel
filch: bob, nim, rob 4 beat, fake, prig 5 fetch, steal 6 pilfer, strike 7 purloin
file: row 4 line, list, rank, rasp, rate, risp, roll, tool 5 grail, index, track 6 accuse, carlet, befoul, defile, rascal 7 arrange, condemn, graille, quannet 10 procession
combmaker's: 6 carlet
document: 7 dossier
flat: 7 quannet
filet: net 4 lace
filial: 9 childlike
filibeg: 4 kilt 5 skirt
filibuster: 5 orate 11 obstruction
filigree: 8 fanciful 13 unsubstantial
filing: 5 lemel 6 rasion 8 limation
Filipino: See **Philippines**
filippic: See **philippic**
fill: pad 4 cram, feed, glut, hold, pang, sate 5 estop, gorge 6 charge, fulfil, occupy 7 distend, enlarge, execute, fraught, fulfill, inflate, perfect, perform, pervade, plenish, satiate, satisfy, suffuse 8 complete, compound, permeate 9 replenish 10 accomplish, embankment 11 sufficiency
cracks: 4 calk, shim 5 caulk
with zeal: 7 enthuse
fille: 4 girl 8 daughter
filled: SRO 5 sated, solid 6 loaded 7 implete, replete 9 saturated 11 preoccupied
fillet: 4 band, bone, orle, orlo, sole, tape 5 ampyx, crown, label, miter, snood, stria, tiara, vitta 6 anadem, binder, cimbia, diadem, fascia, norsel, quadra, ribbon, striae(pl.), taenia, turban 7 bandage, bandeau, fasciae(pl.), molding, taeniae(pl.), tresson 8 bandelet, cincture, tressour, tressure 9 sphendone 10 bandelette
architectural: 6 cimbia, lintel, listel, regula, taenia
filling: *dental:* 5 inlay
fabric: 4 weft, woof
fillip, filip: 4 blow, flip, snap, urge 5 flash, flirt, flisk 6 buffet, moment 7 project 8 stimulus 9 stimulate
filly: 4 colt, foal, girl, mare 9 youngster
film (see also **motion picture**): 4 brat, haze, mist, scum, skin, veil 5 flake, layer 6 mother, patina 8 beeswing, negative, pellicle 10 photograph
filmy: 4 hazy 5 gauzy, misty, wispy 6 cloudy 7 clouded 8 gossamer 13 unsubstantial
filter: 4 sift, sile 5 drain, sieve 6 colate, purify, refine, strain 8 strainer 9 percolate
sugar: 4 clay
filth: fen 4 dirt, dung, gore, nast, slut 5 addle, gleet 6 defile, ordure, vermin 7 squalor 8 muckment 9 obscenity, scoundrel 10 acartharsy 11 acartharsia
filthiness: 5 mucor 7 squalor 8 cenosity
filthy: low 4 foul, miry, vile 5 dirty, drovy, gross, nasty 6 bawdry, impure, sordid 7 bestial, hoggish, obscene, squalid, unclean 8 sluttish 9 polluting 10 disgusting, licentious 11 disgraceful
fimbriate: hem 5 hairy 6 fringe
fin: arm 4 hand, keel 5 pinna 7 acantha, flipper, ventral
fin-footed: 8 pinniped
finagle, fenagle: 5 cheat, trick 6 revoke 7 deceive
final: 4 last 6 latter 7 dernier, extreme, outmost 8 decisive, definite, eventual, farewell, ultimate 9 uttermost 10 concluding, conclusive, definitive 11 terminating 13 determinating
final outcome: 5 issue 6 upshot
finale: end 4 coda 5 close, finis, fugue, shank 6 ending 7 closing 9 uttermost 10 conclusion 11 termination
finalist: 10 contestant

finality: end 11 termination 12 decisiveness 14 conclusiveness
finance: tax 4 back 5 goods 7 revenue 8 taxation, treasure 10 underwrite
finances: 5 funds, purse 6 assets 9 exchequer
financial: 6 fiscal 7 solvent 8 monetary 9 pecuniary
financing: 7 backing
finch: 4 fink, moro, pape 5 serin, terin 6 burion, citril, linnet, siskin 7 chewink, redpoll, senegal, tanager 8 amadavat 9 snowflake
find: get 5 catch 6 locate 8 discover
by keen search: 5 probe 6 ferret
find fault: nag 4 carp, crab, fret 5 cavil, scold 8 complain 9 belly-ache, criticise, criticize
find guilty: 7 convict
find out: 5 learn 6 detect 8 discover 9 ascertain
fine: cro, rum, tax 4 bein, bien, braw, eric, good, jake, levy, nice, pure 5 bonny, brave, bully, dandy, frail, mulct, noble, sharp, sheer, wally 6 amerce, bonnie, bright, clever, crafty, finish, gersum, ornate, proper, slight, spiffy, tender 7 cunning, elegant, estreat, forfeit, fragile, penalty, perfect, refined, tenuous 8 absolute, bloodwit, delicate, handsome, penalize, pleasant, skillful, splendid, superior 9 beautiful, bloodwite, excellent, ingenious, sensitive 10 consummate, fastidious, pulverized, punishment, surpassing
for killing: cro 7 wergild
for misdemeanor: 5 mulct
record of: 7 estreat
fineness: 5 trick 6 finery, purity 7 exility 8 delicacy 9 clearness
finery: 4 gaud, waly 5 wally 6 bauble, bawdry, beauty, fegary 7 gaudary 8 elegance, fineness, ornament 9 fallalery 10 hufty-tufty, lavishness
finespun: 4 hair, thin
finesse: art 5 cheat, skill 6 purity, serene 7 cunning 8 artifice, delicacy, subtlety, thinness 9 clearness, dexterity, stratagem 10 artfulness, refinement
Fingal's cave: *island:* 6 Staffa
kingdom: 6 Morven
fingent: 7 molding 10 fashioning
finger: toy 5 digit, index, pinky 6 handle, meddle, pilfer, pinkie 7 annular, minimus, purloin
comb. form: 6 digiti
guard for: cot 5 stall 7 thimble
inflammation of: 5 felon 7 whitlow
pert. to: 7 digital
resembling: 8 digitate
snap with: 5 filip 6 fillip
finger board: 4 fret
fingerlike: 6 dactyl
fingerling: 4 parr 8 troutlet
fingernail moon: 6 lunule
fingerprint: 11 dactylogram
mark: 4 arch, loop 5 whorl 9 composite
science: 12 dactyloscopy
finial: epi, tee, top 4 knot 5 bunch, crest, final 8 ornament, pinnacle
finical: 4 nice 5 fussy 6 choosy, dainty, dapper, jaunty, prissy, spruce 7 choosey, finicky, foppish, mincing 8 delicate 9 squeamish 10 fastidious, meticulous 11 overprecise 14 overscrupulous
finikin, finnikin: 6 pigeon
finis: end 4 goal 5 close 10 conclusion
finish: die, end 4 char, mill 5 bound, cease, chare, cheve, close enden(G.), glaze, limit 6 fulfil, windup 7 achieve, execute, fulfill, perfect, surface 8 complete, conclude, terminal 9 erudition, terminate 10 accomplish, completion, conclusion, consummate, perfection
dull: mat 5 matte
glossy: 6 enamel
finished: did, oer, pau 4 done, fine, gone, over, ripe 5 ended, kaput 6 closed, ornate 7 refined, stopped 8 climaxed, lustered, polished 9 completed, concluded, perfected, performed 10 terminated 11 consummated 12 professional
finisher: 4 eyer 5 ender 7 beetler 8 enameler
finishing line: 4 tape
finite: 7 limited 9 definable 10 restricted, terminable 11 conditioned
fink: 8 informer, squealer 13 strikebreaker
Finland: 5 Suomi
bathhouse: 5 sauna
city: Aba, Abo 11 Helsingfors
coin: 5 penni 6 markka
composer: 8 Sibelius
dialect: 5 Karel
division: 5 Ijore 9 Villipuri
forest god: 5 Tapio
fortress: 11 Suomenlinna
god: 6 Jumala
harp: 7 kantele
island: 5 Aland 6 Aaland
isthmus: 7 Karelia
lake: 5 Enare
language: 4 Avar, Lapp 5 Ugric 6 Magyar, Ostyak, Tarast 7 Samoyed 8 Estonian
measure: 5 kannu, tunna, verst 6 fathom, sjomil 7 tunland 8 ottinger, skalpund, tunnland
parliament: 9 Eduskunta
pert. to: 6 Suomic 7 Suomish
town: 5 Enare

tribe: 4 Veps, Wote 5 Vepse 6 Ugrian
Finlandia composer: 8 Sibelius
Finnegan's Wake author: 5 Joyce
fiord, fjord: ise 5 inlet
fippenny bit: fip
fir: 9 evergreen
genus: 5 abies
Firbolg queen: 6 Tailte 7 Talitiu
fire: can, feu(F.) 4 bale, burn, heat, zeal 5 ardor, arson, fever, gleed, light, shoot, stoke 6 arouse, excite, fervor, ignite, incite, kindle, spirit 7 animate, burning, dismiss, explode, fervour, glimmer, inflame, inspire 8 detonate, illumine, irritate, vivacity 9 calenture, cauterize, discharge, holocaust 10 combustion, enthusiasm, illuminate 12 inflammation 13 conflagration
artillery: 7 barrage
comb. form: 4 igni, pyro
containing: 7 igneous
fighter: 4 vamp
god: 4 Agni 6 Vulcan 10 Hephaestus
military: 4 flak 5 salvo 6 rafale 7 barrage
particle: arc 5 spark
pert. to: 7 igneous
sacrificial: 4 agni
set: 6 accend, ignite, kindle 7 inflame 8 enkindle, irritate
worshipper: 5 Parsi 6 Parsee 9 pyrolater 10 ignicolist
fire basket: 5 grate 7 cresset
fire extinguisher: 6 pyrene 9 pyroleter
fire feeder: 6 fueler, stoker
firearm: gun 5 piece, rifle 6 musket, pistol 7 demihag 8 revolver
fireback: 7 reredos 8 pheasant
fireboat: 8 palander
firebrand: 5 blaze 6 bleery
firebug: 10 incendiary, pyromaniac
firecracker: 5 squib 6 petard 7 cracker, snapper 9 skyrocket
firedamp: gas 7 methane
firedog: 7 andiron
fireman: 4 vamp 6 stoker, tizeur 9 fireeater
fireplace: 5 focus, fogon, forge, foyer, ingle 6 heath 8 cheminee
part: hob 6 mantel 9 ingleside 11 hearthstone
firer: 6 stoker 10 incendiary
fireside: 9 ingleside 11 hearthstone
firestone: 5 flint
firewood: 4 lena 5 fagot 6 billet, billot
fireworks: 4 gerb 5 gerbe 7 fizgigs, rockets 9 sparklers 10 girandoles 11 tourbillion 12 pyrotechnics
resembling: 11 pyrotechnic
firing: 4 fuel
firm: hui 4 buff, fast, hard, sure, trig 5 champ, dense, firma, fixed, hardy, house, loyal, rigid, solid, sound, stith, stout, tight 6 hearty, secure, settle, sinewy, stable, stanch, steady, stolid, strong 7 adamant, certain, compact, company, confirm, context, decided, durable, staunch, unmoved 8 constant, faithful, fiducial, obdurate, resolute, unshaken 9 backboned, establish, immovable, immutable, standfast, steadfast 10 consistent, determined, unslipping, unwavering, unyielding 11 established, partnership, substantial, substantive, well-founded
firmament: sky 7 heavens 8 empyrean
firmance: 9 assurance, stability 11 confinement
firmly fixed: 6 rooted, stable
firmness: 4 iron 7 courage 8 solidity, strength, tenacity 9 constancy, stability 10 immobility, steadiness 11 consistency 13 determination 15 indissolubility
firn: ice 4 neve, snow
first: 4 erst, head, high, main 5 alpha, chief, forme, nieve, prime 6 primal, primus 7 highest, initial, leading, primary 8 earliest, foremost, original 9 primitive, principal 10 aboriginal, primordial
comb. form: 5 proto
appearance: 5 debut 8 premiere
first-born: 5 eigne 11 protogenist
first class: 5 prime 9 excellent, topdrawer 10 first-cabin
first-rate: 4 A-one, good, jake 5 prime 6 tiptop 7 skookum 8 clipping, topnotch 9 admirable, excellent
firth: 4 kyle 5 frith, inlet 7 coppice, estuary
Firth of Clyde Island: 4 Bute
fisc: 9 exchequer
fiscal: 8 monetary 9 financial
fiscus: 8 treasury
fish: net 4 cast, quab 5 angle, drail, seine, troll 7 poisson(F.)
Alaska: 6 iconnu
ascending river from sea: 7 anadrom
Atlantic Coast: 4 opah, pogy 6 bunker, salema 7 alewife, bugfish, bughead, fatback, oldwife 8 bonyfish, menhaden 9 greentail 10 mossbunker
Australian: 4 mado 6 groper 7 grouper
bait: 5 killy 9 killifish
barbed tail: 8 stingray 9 stingaree
California: 4 rena 5 reina 6 rasher 9 garibaldi
carangold: 4 scad 5 jurel
carp: id; ide, orf
catfish: 6 hassar 9 sheatfish
caviar-yielding: 7 sterlet 8 sturgeon
cod: bib 4 cusk, hake, ling 5 torsk 6 gadoid 7 bacalao, beardie
colorful: 4 opah

cyprinoid: id; ide 4 dace
devil: ray 5 manta
eel-like: 4 link, opah 6 conger, cuchia 7 eelpout, lamprey
electric: 4 raad 7 torpedo
elongated: eel, gar 6 saurel
European: id; ide, rud 4 boce, dace, rudd, spet 5 alose, bleak, bream 6 angler, barbel, braice, meagre, plaice 7 gudgeon, lavaret, picarel
female: 4 raun 7 henfish
flat: dab, ray 4 butt, dace, sole 5 bream, fluke, skate 6 plaice, turbot 7 halibut, sanddab, sunfish, torpedo 8 flounder
Florida: 5 crunt 6 atinga, salema 7 burfish, tomtate 8 burrfish
food: cod, eel, gar, iki, sey 4 bass, boga, carp, haik, hake, scup, shad, sole, stew, tile, tuna 5 bolti, cisco, hilsa, jurel, siera, skate, smelt, trout 6 baleen, groupa, hilsah, mullet, pompon, salema, salmon, tautog, wahoon, weever, wrasse 7 alewife, escolar, garlopa, halibut, herring, pompano, pompoon, sardine, snapper 8 mackerel 9 barracuda 10 barracouta
fresh water: id; gar, ide, orf 4 bass, carp, chub, dace, orfe, pike, rudd 5 bream, loach, roach, tench 6 darter, redeye, sucker 7 crappie, mooneye
game: 4 bass, cero, tuna 5 trout 6 grilse, marlin, salmon, tarpon 8 grayling 9 swordfish
grunt: 5 ronco
Hawaiian: aku 4 ulua 5 akule, lania
herring: 4 shad, brit 5 sprat, sprot 7 alewife 8 pilchard
Japanese: tai, ay'u
kind of: id; cat, cod, dab, eel, gar, ide, orf 4 bass, carp, chub, dace, dorn, hake, hiku, jocu, lant, lija, ling, mado, masu, meat, mero, mola, opah, orfe, pega, peto, pike, pogy, pout, rena, roud, rudd, ruff, scad, scup, shad, sier, skil, sole, spot, spet, tope, ulua 5 bream, lance, midge, otter, perch, pogie, porgy, prane, roach, ruffe, scrod, seine, skate, smelt, trout, umbra, wahoo 6 barbel, caribe, launce, mullet, porgie, sauger, saurel, shiner, tomcod, turbot, wrasse 7 alewife, grunion, haddock, machete, pegador, pintado, piranha, poisson 8 gourhead, hardhead, pilchard, sturgeon 9 teleostei 10 candlefish
large: 4 cusk, opah 5 chiro, sargo, shark 6 bichir, tarpon 7 escolar, gourami, sennett 8 arapaima, sturgeon 10 blanquillo, maskalonge, maskinonge 11 muskellunge
little: see *small* below.
long: eel, gar 7 lamprey
mackerel-like: 4 cero 5 tunny 6 coelho 7 escolar, pintado
Mediterranean: 5 porgy, sargo 6 chivey 9 menominee
nest-building: 5 acara 11 stickleback
New England: 4 hake
New Zealand: ihi 5 hikus
newly-hatched: fry
Nile: 4 erse 5 saide
olive green: 7 lutfisk 8 ludefisk
one-horned: 9 monoceros
parasitic: 6 remora
pert. to: 7 piscine 8 ichthyic 9 piscatory
pike: gar 4 lude
pilot: 6 romero
ray-like: 5 skate
river: 8 arapaima 10 barramunda
rock: 4 rena 5 reina 8 buccacio
scaleless: 9 alepidote
serpentine: eel
shark-eating: som 4 pega 7 catfish
shell: 7 abalone
small: id; fry, ide, ihi 4 brit, dace, goby, spet 5 saury, sprat 6 blenny, cunner, limpet, minnow, riggle, sennet, shiner 7 sardine 8 halfbeak, seahorse, spearing
small bait: 5 killy 9 killifish
South American: 4 gogy, mapo 5 acara 6 acoupa, aimara, almara, caribe
sparoid: tai 5 porgy, sargo
spear-snouted: gar
star: 7 astoria
sucking: 6 remora
teleost: eel 6 iniomi
toad: 4 sapo 6 slimer
toothed: 7 piranha
total haul: 4 mess 5 catch
tree-climbing: 6 anabas
tropical: 8 coachman
tunny: 4 tuna
voracious: 4 pike 5 shark 6 caribe 9 barracuda
West Indies: 4 Boga, cero, sier 5 chopa 6 Blanco 7 guapena 12 walleyed pike
young: fry 4 parr 6 alevin
fish basket: pot 4 caul 5 creel, slath
fish gig: 5 spear
fish handler: 4 icer
fish hawk: 6 osprey
fish hide: 7 eelskin
fish limb: fin
fish net: 4 bunt 5 seine, trawl 6 sagene
fish net line: 5 meter
fish net mender: 8 beatster
fish peddler: 6 ripier, ripper 7 rippier
fish pole: pew
fish preserve: 6 warren
fish relish: 7 botargo
fish roe: 6 caviar 7 caviare

fish sauce: 4 alec 5 garum
fish spear: gig 7 trident
fish trap: 4 coop, fyke, weel, weir 5 willy 6 eelpot
fisher: 5 eeler, pecan 6 seiner, wejack 7 trawler, troller
fisherman: 5 eeler 6 angler, seiner 7 prawner, trawler 8 peterman, piscator 9 harpooner 11 Izaak Walton
fishery: 7 piscary 9 piscation
fishes: 5 raiae
fishhook: gig 5 angle, Kirby 6 Sproat 7 Kendall 8 Aberdeen, barbless, Carlisle, limerick
feathered: fly 5 sedge 6 hackle
fishing duck: 9 merganser
fishing gear: lam, rod, tew 4 cork, flew, flue, gaff, gimp, hook, line, reel, trot 5 cadar, cader, float, sedge, seine, snell, shood 8 trotline
fishing ground: 4 haaf
fishing vessel: 5 smack 6 seiner 7 trawler
fishlike: 8 ichthyic
fishline: 5 snell 7 boulter
fishmonger: 8 pessoner
fishpond: 7 piscina
fishwife: 9 buttwoman
fishy: 4 dull 6 vacant 10 improbable, lusterless, suspicious, unreliable 11 extravagant
fissate: 7 divided 8 fissured
fissile rock: 5 shale
fission: 8 breaking, cleavage, cleaving 9 splitting 12 reproduction
fissle: 4 fuss, hiss 6 bustle, fidget, rustle 7 whistle 9 fidgeting
fissure: gap 4 chap, cone, flaw, gool, leak, lode, rent, rift, rima, rime, seam, vein, vent 5 chasm, chine, chink, cleft, crack 6 cleave, cranny, divide, lesion 7 blemish, crevice, opening 8 aperture, cleavage, coloboma, crevasse, quebrada
fissured: 6 rimate 7 fissate, rimosed
fist: job 4 nave, neif 5 grasp, nieve 6 clench, clutch, daddle, effort, strike 7 attempt 8 puffball, tightwad 11 handwriting
fistic: 10 pugilistic
fisticuff: box
fistula: 4 pipe, reed, tube 5 sinus 6 cavity
fit: apt, fay, gee, pan, rig 4 able, ague, good, hard, meet, ripe, suit, well, whim 5 adapt, adept, besit, chink, fancy, ictus, ready, right, spasm 6 adjust, attack, become, behove, besort, habile, heppen, proper, seemly, stroke, strong, suited 7 adapted, behoove, capable, condign, conform, correct, healthy, prepare, qualify, tantrum 8 adequate, becoming, eligible, glooming, idoneous(L.), outbreak, paroxysm, passable, suitable, syncopes 9 befitting, competent, congruous, covenable, opportune, pertinent, qualified 10 applicable, commodious, correspond, convenient 11 accommodate, appropriate
out: 6 outfit 7 habille, prepare 9 equipment
together: fay 4 mesh, nest 5 panel 8 dovetail
fitful: 4 gery 7 cursory, flighty 8 restless, unstable, variable 9 impulsive, irregular, spasmodic, uncertain 10 capricious, convulsive 12 intermittent
fitly: pat 4 duly 6 gladly, meetly 7 happily 8 properly, suitably
fitness: 7 aptness, decency, decorum, dignity 8 aptitude, capacity, justness 9 rectitude 10 competence 11 suitability
fitout: 6 outfit 9 equipment
fitted: apt 4 able 6 suited 7 adapted 8 adjusted 9 qualified 10 convenient
for digging: 7 fodient, laniary
fitting: apt, due, pat 4 meet 5 happy 6 become, proper, seemly 8 decorous, graceful, suitable 9 befitting 10 adjustment, answerable, habiliment 11 appropriate
five: 4 cinq(F.), funf(G.) 6 cinque(It.) 7 epsilon(Gr), quinque(L.)
comb. form: 4 pent 5 penta
group of: 6 pentad
five-dollar bill: "V"; fin, vee
five-finger: 4 fish 5 oxlip, plant 10 cinquefoil
Five Nations: 7 Cayugas, Mohawks, Oneidas, Senecas 9 Onondagas
founder: 8 Hiawatha
five-year period: 6 pentad 7 lustrum
fivefold: 9 quintuple
fix: peg, pin, set 4 glue, mend, moor, nail, seal 5 affix, allot, found, imbed, limit, tryst 6 adjust, anchor, arrest, assign, assize, attach, cement, clinch, define, fasten, ficche, freeze, repair, revamp, settle, temper 7 appoint, arrange, confirm, delimit, dilemma, impress, imprint, prepare, station 8 renovate, transfix 9 determine, establish, stabilize 10 constitute 11 predicament 13 embarrassment
firmly: set 4 moor 5 brace, grave, imbed, stamp 6 anchor, cement, enroot 7 engraff
fixed: pat, set 4 fast, firm 5 siker, staid 6 frozen, intent, mended, sicker, stable 7 certain, dormant, settled, statary 8 arranged, attached, constant, definite, explicit, fastened, immobile, moveless, resolute, stubborn 9 immovable, indelible, inerratic, permanent 10 stationary 12 determinable, refrigerated
amount: 4 rate 6 ration 7 stipend 10 remittance
star: 4 Vega
fixer: 8 handyman

fixture: 5 annex 7 bracket, shelves 8 counters, shelving 10 furnishing
fizgig: 9 fireworks, whirligig
fizzle: 4 fuss 6 barney 7 failure, flivver, hissing 9 agitation
flabby: lax 4 fozy, lash, limp, weak 5 frush 6 feeble 7 flaccid
flabellate: 9 fan-shaped
flabent: 10 flickering
flaccid: 4 limp 6 flabby, flaggy 8 yielding
flack: 4 blow, flap 5 throb 6 stroke 7 flutter
flacker: 5 throb 7 flutter, tremble
flag: fag, sag, sod 4 fail, fane, pine, turf, waif, wilt 5 droop, woman 6 banner, colors, ensign, flower, pennon, signal 7 ancient, cattail, decline, drapeau, pennant 8 banderol, brattach, languish, standard, streamer, vexillum 9 banderole, flagstone, fourpence
kind of: 5 Roger 6 burgee, colors, danger, ensign, fanion, guidon, muleta 7 calamus, curtain, pennant 8 banderol, brattach, masthead, standard, streamer, vexillum 9 banderole, blackjack 10 Jolly Roger
flagellants: 4 albi
flagellate: 4 flog, whip 5 throw 6 thrash 7 flutter, scourge
flagellum: 4 whip 5 shoot 6 runner 7 scourge
flageolet: 4 pipe 6 zufolo 7 basaree, zuffolo
Hindu: 7 basaree
flagging: 4 weak 7 languid 10 spiritless
flaggy: 4 weak 7 flaccid, languid 8 drooping
flagitious: 6 wicked 7 corrupt, heinous 8 criminal, flagrant, grievous 10 scandalous, villainous
flagon: 5 stoup 6 bottle, vessel 7 flacket
flagrant: bad 4 rank 5 gross 6 odious, wanton, wicked 7 glaring, hateful, heinous, scarlet, violent 8 shameful 9 abandoned, atrocious, egregious, monstrous, nefarious, notorious 10 flagitious, outrageous, profligate, villainous
flagstone layer: 5 paver
flail: 4 beat, flog, whip 6 thrash, thresh
part: 7 swingle
flair: ray 4 bent, odor 5 skate, smell, taste 6 talent 7 leaning 8 aptitude 11 discernment
flake: 4 chip, film, flaw, rack, snow 5 fleck, flock, scale, strip 6 hurdle, lamina, paling 7 flaught 8 fragment
flaky: 5 scaly 7 laminar 8 laminose
flam: 4 whim 5 cheat, false, freak, trick 6 cajole, humbug, untrue 7 deceive, pretext, rubbish 8 drumbeat, illusory, nonsense, pretense 9 deception, deceptive, falsehood
flambeau: 5 torch 6 kettle 11 candlestick
flamboyant: 6 florid, ornate 7 flaming 9 flamelike 11 resplendent
flame: 4 fire, glow 5 ardor, blaze, flare, flash, glare, gleed, light 7 burning 9 affection 10 brightness, brilliance, sweetheart
fire without: 4 punk
movement: 4 dart, lick
flaming: 5 afire, fiery, vivid 6 ardent 7 blazing, burning, flaring 9 brilliant, consuming, flamelike 10 flamboyant, passionate 12 illuminating
Flanders capital: 5 Ghent
flanerie: 6 stroll 7 loafing 8 idleness 9 aimlessly, strolling 10 pillowcase
flaneur: 6 loafer 7 trifler
flank: 4 leer, side 5 thigh 6 border
flannel: 4 lana 6 stamin
flap: rob, tab, tag, wap 4 clap, flip, loma, slam, waff 5 alarm, flack, flaff, flipe, lapel, skirt 6 bangle, faffle, lappet, strike, tongue 7 aileron, blinder, flounce, flutter, swindle 9 appendage, operculum 10 epiglottis
furnished with: 5 lobed
flapper: 7 snicket 9 backfisch 10 backfische
flare: 4 bell, flue 5 blaze, flame, flash, fleck, fusee, light, torch 6 signal, spread 7 flicker 8 outburst 10 illuminate 11 ostentation
flaring: 4 bell, flue 5 evase(F.), gaudy 7 flaming, glaring 8 dazzling
flash: 4 pool 5 blash, blaze, burst, flare, flame, fluff, glaik, gleam, glent, glint, marsh, spark 6 bottle, fillip, glance 7 fouldre, glimmer, glimpse, glisten, glitter, instant, shimmer, sparkle 11 coruscation, fulguration, scintillate
flashing: 6 bright, flashy 7 forward 8 meteoric, snapping 9 fulgurant, fulgurous
flashy: gay 4 flat, gaud, loud 5 fiery, gaudy, showy 6 frothy, slangy, sporty 7 insipid, tinhorn 8 dazzling, flashing, vehement 9 impetuous 10 spiritless
flask: 4 olpe 5 betty, bulge, girba 6 bottle, fiasco, flacon, guttus 7 ampulla, canteen, matrass 8 cucurbit 9 aryballos
flask-shaped: 10 lageniform
flat: 4 dead, dull, fade, plat 5 abode, aflat, banal, blunt, level, molle, plane, prone, vapid 6 boring, dreary, flashy 7 decided, insipid, platoid, prosaic, uniform 8 directly, dwelling, lifeless, unbroken 9 apartment, downright, prostrate, tasteless 10 homaloidal, horizontal, monotonous, unanimated 12 unmistakable 13 uninteresting
comb. form: 5 plani
flat-nosed: 6 simous
flatboat: ark 4 scow 5 barge

flatfish: dab, ray 4 butt, dace, sole 5 bream, fluke 6 acedia, plaice, turbot 7 sanddab, sunfish, torpedo 8 floundor
flatiron: 7 sadiron
flatten: 4 even 5 level 6 deject, smooth 7 depress 8 compress, dispirit 9 prostrate 10 complanate, discourage, dishearten
flattened: 6 oblate 7 planate
flatter: 4 bull, claw, coax, fage, fume, palp 5 charm, float, gloze, honey, smalm 6 become, cajole, fickle, fleech, fraise, glaver, smooge, soothe 7 adulate, beguile, blarney, flether, flutter, wheedle 8 blandish, bootlick, collogue 10 compliment, ingratiate
flatterer: 6 cogger, glozer 7 soother 8 courtier 9 sycophant 10 assentator, greasehorn
flattering: 7 buttery, candied 11 assentatory
flattery: 4 bull, bunk 5 fraik, gloze, salve, taffy 6 butter, fleech 7 blarney, fawning, flether, palaver 8 cajolery 9 adulation 10 compliment 14 obsequiousness
flatulent: 5 gassy, windy 6 turgid 7 pompous, ventose 8 inflated 9 bombastic
flatworm: 9 trematode 13 plathelminth
flaunt: 4 bosh, wave 5 boast, vaunt 6 parade, trapes 7 display, flutter, traipse 8 brandish
flavicant: 6 yellow
flavor, flavour: 4 gamy, odor, rasa, salt, tang, zest 5 aroma, devil, sapid, sapor, sauce, savor, scent, taste, tinge 6 asarum, relish, season 7 perfume 8 hautgout, piquancy 9 fragrance
flavorable: 5 sapid, sipid 6 savory 9 palatable
flavoring material: 4 mint, sage 6 orgeat 7 cumarin 8 coumarin, cumarone 9 coumarone
flavorless, flavourless: 5 stale, rapid 9 tasteless
flaw: fib, gap, lie, mar 4 gall, hole, rase, rift, spot, wind 5 brack, cleft, crack, craze, fault, flake 6 breach, defect 7 blemish, default, fissure, nullify, violate, whitlow 8 fracture, fragment, gendarme 10 intoxicate 12 imperfection
flawless: 5 sound 7 perfect 9 faultless
flax: pob, tow 4 card, harl, lint 5 hards, hurds, linen, linin, pouce 6 bobbin
filament: 4 harl
holder: 7 distaff
prepare: ret
refuse: pob
remove seed: 6 ribble
tool: 7 hatchel, swingle
flaxen-haired: 4 bawn
flaxseed: 7 linseed
flay: 4 skin 5 strip 6 fleece 7 censure, pillage, reprove 9 excoriate 11 decorticate
flea: 6 chigoe 10 sandhopper
genus: 5 pulex
flebile: 7 doleful, tearful
fleck: fat 4 flea, flit, spot, tuft 5 flake, flare 6 dapple, streak, stripe 7 flutter, speckle 8 particle 9 variegate
fledgling, fledgeling: 5 squab
flee: fly, lam, run 4 bolt, fleg, loup, shun 5 elude, speed 6 escape, vanish 7 abandon, abscond, forsake 8 liberate 9 disappear, skedaddle
fleece: abb, jib, teg 4 bilk, fell, flay, gaff, wool 5 cheat, fleck, pluck, shear 6 toison 7 despoil
fleecy: 5 wooly 6 linten, woolly
fleeing: 7 fugient 8 fugitive
fleer: 4 gibe, grin, jeer, leer, mock 5 flout, laugh, scoff, sneer, taunt 7 grimace 8 derision
fleet: bay 4 fast, flit, navy, sail, skim, swim 5 creek, drain, drift, evand, float, flote, hasty, inlet, quick, rapid, swift 6 abound, argosy, armada, hasten, nimble, speedy 7 estuary 8 flotilla 10 evanescent, transitory
fleeting: 5 brief 6 caduke, volage 7 flighty, passing 8 caducous, fugitive 9 ephemeral, fugacious, transient 10 evanescent, transitory 11 impermanent
fleetings: 5 curds 9 skimmings
fleg: fly 4 flee, kick 5 fling, scare 6 fright
Flemish: *geographer:* 8 Mercator
painter: 5 Bouts 6 Mabuse, Massys, Rubens 7 Gossart, Memling, Patinir, van Eyck 8 Breughel, Brueghel, Gossaert, van Cleve 12 van der Weyden
flesh: kin 4 body, meat, race 5 stock 6 family, muscle 7 kindred, mankind 8 humanity 9 mortality 10 sensuality
appendage: 5 palpi(pl.) 6 palpus
formation: 8 sarcosis
kind of: 5 brawn 6 chevron, chiver 7 carrion
pert. to: 7 sarcoid
resembling: 7 sarcoid
fleshbrush: 7 strigil
flesh-eating: 11 carnivorous
fleshy: fat 5 beefy, human, obese, plump, pulpy, stout 6 animal, bodily, brawny, carnal 9 corpulent
fruit: 4 pear, pome 5 berry, drupe, melon 6 tomato
fleur-de-lis: lis, lys 4 iris, liss, luce, lucy
fleuret: 4 epee 5 sword 6 flower
flex: 4 bend
flexible: 4 limp, lush, soft 5 buxom, lithe, withy 6 limber, pliant, supple 7 ductile,

elastic, flexile, lissome, pliable, willowy 8 cheverel, cheveril, yielding 9 tractable 10 manageable
shoot: 4 bine
tube: 4 hose

flexile: 6 pliant 7 plastic, pliable 8 flexible 9 tractable, versatile

flexuous: 6 zigzag 7 relaxed 8 softened, wavering 9 adaptable 10 circuitous, flickering

flexure: 4 bend, bent, curl, fold 5 curve 6 bought

flichter: 6 quiver 7 flicker, flutter, vibrate

flick (see also **motion picture**): cut, hit 4 blow, flip, flit, snap, toss, whip 5 flisk, throw 6 flitch, propel 7 flutter

flicker: 4 fail, flit 5 flare, flunk, waver 6 fitter, shiver, yucker 7 blinter, flimmer, flitter, flutter, tremble 8 flichter 9 flaughter, palpitate 10 woodpecker

flickering: 7 flabent, lambent 8 flexuous, unsteady

flier: ace 5 pilot 6 airman 7 aviator 8 operator
female: 8 aviatrix 9 aviatress, aviatrice

flight: hop 4 bolt, rout 5 chevy, chivy, flock, scrap, volee 6 chivvy, exodus, hegira, hejira 7 flaught, migrate, mission, scamper 8 stampede, swarming 9 agitation, migration 12 perturbation
of fancy: 5 sally
of steps: 6 perron
of wild fowl: 5 skein
pert. to: 5 volar
put to: 4 rout

flightiness: 9 lightness

flightless bird: emu, moa 4 dodo, kiwi, weka 7 ostrich, penguin

flighty: 5 barmy, giddy, swift 6 fitful, nimshi, volage, whisky 7 foolish, giggish 8 fleeting, freakish 9 transient 10 capricious 11 harum-scarum 13 shuttlewitted

flim-flam: fob 5 freak, trick 6 humbug, tricky, trifle 7 swindle 8 nonsense, trifling 9 deception, deceptive 11 nonsensical

flimmer: 7 flicker, glimmer

flimsy: 4 limp, vain, weak 5 frail, gaudy 6 feeble, paltry, sleazy, slight 7 shallow, tenuous 10 gossamered 11 superficial 13 insubstantial, unsubstantial

flinch: 4 funk, game 5 feign, start, wince 6 blench, falter, flense, recoil, shrink

fling: 4 buzz, cast, dart, dash, ding, emit, fleg, gibe, hurl, kick, toss 5 cheat, dance, flirt, pitch, sling, sneer, throw, whang 6 baffle, effuse, hurtle, plunge, rebuff, spirit 7 flounce, repulse, sarcasm, scatter, swindle 9 overthrow

flint: 5 chert, miser, silex 6 quartz 9 firestone, skinflint

flintlock: 6 musket

flinty: 4 hard 5 cruel 8 obdurate

flip: tap 4 flap, snap, toss, trip 5 flick, flirt, slirt 6 fillip, limber, nimble, pliant, propel 7 journey 10 somersault

flipe: 4 flap, fold, peel

flippant: 4 airy, glib 6 fluent, limber, nimble 9 talkative

flipper: arm, fin, paw 4 hand

flirt: tap, toy 4 dart, fike, flip, gibe, jeer, jest, joke, mash, mock, play, toss 5 dally, flick, fling, throw 6 coquet, fillip, masher, spring, trifle 7 trifler 9 philander

flirtatious: coy 4 arch 10 coquettish

flit: 4 dart, flow, scud 5 fleck, fleet, flick, float, flurr, hover, quick, scoot, swift 6 nimble 7 flicker, flutter, migrate

flite, flyte: 4 gibe, jeer 5 chide, scold 6 strife 7 contend, dispute, quarrel, wrangle

flitter: rag 5 droop, hover, piece, waver 6 tatter 7 flicker, flutter, shuffle 8 fragment

flittermouse: bat

float: fly, sea 4 buoy, cork, flow, flux, hove, pont, raft, ride, sail, scow, soar, swim, waft, wave 5 balsa, drift, fleet, flood, hover, ladle 6 billow, bobber, bungey, ponton 7 flatter, flotter, pontoon 8 overflow 9 catamaran, podoscaph
aloft: 4 soar

floating: 4 free 5 awash, loose 6 adrift, afloat, flying, natant 7 movable 8 drifting, fluitant, shifting, variable 9 wandering

flocculent: 6 woolly

flock: mob 4 bevy, fold, herd, pack 5 brood, bunch, charm, covey, crowd, drift, drove, flake, fleck, group, sedge, shoal, swarm 6 flight, hirsel 7 company 9 multitude 10 assemblage 11 aggregation
kind of: nid, nye, pod 4 nide, sord 5 covey, sedge, tribe
pert. to: 6 gregal

flocks (god of): Pan

floe: 4 raft

flog: cat, tan 4 beat, cane, hide, lash, toco, toko, wale, whip 5 birch, excel, fight, flail, linge, quilt, skeeg 6 cotton, larrup, strike, switch, thrash 7 baleise, belabor, scourge, sjambok, surpass, trounce 8 slaister 10 flagellate

flood: sea 4 bore, flow, flux 5 eagre, float, spate 6 deluge, excess 7 debacle, freshet, torrent 8 alluvion, inundate, overflow 9 cataclysm 14 superabundance

flooded: 6 afloat 10 surrounded

floodgate: 5 hatch 6 sluice

floodlight: 5 klieg

floor covering: mat, rug 4 tile 5 tapis(Fr.) 6 carpet, planks 8 linoleum, oilcloth
floor plank: 5 chess
flop: 4 whop
flora: 6 plants 9 florilege 11 florilegium
flora and fauna: 5 biota
floreate: 5 bloom
Florence: *coin:* 6 florin 7 ruspone
devotees: 4 neri
family: 6 Medici
gallery: 6 Uffizi
iris: 5 ireos, orris
Florentine (see also **Florence**): 4 gold 6 finish
floret bract: 5 palea, palet
florid: 5 buxom, fresh, ruddy 6 ornate 7 flowery 8 blooming, rubicund, vigorous 10 figurative, flamboyant, rhetorical 11 embellished, full-blooded
Florida: *beach:* 4 Vero
city: 5 Miami, Ocala, Tampa 7 Orlando, Palatka, Pompano 8 Sarasota 9 Pensacola 11 Tallahassee(c.)
county: Bay, Lee 4 Clay, Dade, Gulf, Lake, Leon, Levy, Polk 5 Pasco
fish: 6 tarpon, tetard
fishing boat: 7 smackee
islands: 6 Bahama
palm: 5 royal
plain: 7 savanna 8 savannah
region: 10 Everglades
floss: 5 fluff, skein, waste 6 sleave, stream
flotage: 8 buoyancy
flotilla: 5 fleet
Flotow opera: 6 Martha
flotsam: 8 driftage
flounce: 4 flap, slam 5 fling, frill 6 ruffle 7 falbala, falbelo 8 flounder, furbelow, struggle
flounder: dab 4 butt, keel, roll, toss 5 bream, fluke, megin 6 grovel, muddle, plaice, turbot, wallow 7 flounce, plounce, stumble, sunfish, topknot, vaagmar, vaagmer 8 flatfish, struggle, vaagmaer
flour: *bleach:* 5 agene
diabetic: 9 aleuronat
maker: 6 miller
sifter: 6 bolter
sprinkle with: 6 dredge
testing device: 11 farinometer
wheat: 4 atta
flourish: 4 boom, brag, grow, riot, rise, show, wave 5 adorn, bloom, boast, cheve, gloss, quirk, vaunt 6 parade, paraph, thrive 7 blossom, display, enlarge, fanfare, prosper, roulade 8 arpeggio, brandish, curlicue, curlycue, increase, ornament 9 embellish 10 decoration 11 ostentation
flourishing fat 4 frim 5 green, palmy 7 florent 8 thriving 10 prosperous, successful
floury: 4 meal
flout: bob 4 gibe, jeer, mock 5 fleer, flite, flyte, frump, scoff, scorn, scout, sneer, taunt 6 deride, insult 7 jeering, mockery 8 betongue
flow: ebb, jet, run 4 bore, flit, flux, fuse, gush, hale, lava, lave, melt, pour, roll, shed, sile, teem, well 5 avale, drain, eagre, exude, fleam, float, flood, glide, issue, river, spill, spurt 6 abound, afflux, deluge, recede, stream 7 current, emanate, flutter, meander, spurtle 8 alluvion, inundate 9 streaming 10 menstruate, outpouring 12 menstruation
flower (see also **plant**): bud 4 best, blow, flag, iris, ixia, pink, posy, rose 5 aster, bloom, elite, lilac, pansy, tulip 6 azalia, crocus, dahlia, orchid, posies(pl.), unfold 7 blethia, blossom, develop, fairest, gentian 8 camellia, choicest, daffodil, freshest, gardenia, geranium, hyacinth, ornament 9 carnation, embellish, gladiolus 13 chrysanthemum
appendage: 5 bract
artificial: 7 rosette 8 gloxinia
band: 6 wreath
bell-shaped: 4 lily 5 tulip
blooming once a year: 6 annual
blue: 6 lupine 8 harebell
bud: 5 ament, caper 6 spadix
cluster: 4 cime, cyme 5 ament, bract, umbel 6 corymb, raceme 7 panicle 9 glomerule
of death: 8 asphodel
desert: 6 cactus
extract: 4 atar, otto 5 attar, ottar
fall: 5 aster 6 cosmos
of forgetfulness: 5 lotus
garden: 4 iris, ixia, lily, pink, rose 5 aster, canna, daisy, lilac, pansy, peony, phlox, tulip 6 asalia, olivia, orchid, violet 7 freesia, petunia, verbena 8 bletilla, camellia, daffodil, gloxinia, hyacinth, primrose 9 buttercup, carnation, gladiolus, narcissus 10 heliotrope, ranunculus 11 honeysuckle
goddess: 5 Flora
imaginary: 7 amarant 8 amaranth
large: 5 canna, peony
late-blooming: 5 aster
mass: 8 anthemia
meadow: 5 bluet
modest: 6 violet
obsolete: 5 pense
part: 5 calyx, sepal 6 anther, pistil, stamen 7 nectary, petiole 8 peduncle, perianth, pericarp
passion: 6 maypop
pink: 4 rose 7 rhodora

prickly: 4 burr
purple: 5 lilac, pense
receptacle: 4 vase 5 torus
spring: 4 iris 5 lilac, peony, tulip 7 arbutus 8 hepatica
stand: 7 epergne
stylized: lis
unfading: 7 amarant 8 amaranth
unknown kind: 8 belamour
white: 5 gowan
wild: 4 sage 5 bluet, daisy 6 lupine 7 anemone, arbutus 8 bluebell, hepatica 9 buttercup, innocence
wind: 7 anemone
yellow: 5 daisy, gowan, pense 7 jonquil 8 daffodil, marigold 9 buttercup

flower holder: pot 4 frog, vase 5 lapel
Flower State: 7 Florida
flowering: 7 flowery 8 anthesis, blooming 11 florescence
flowering plant: rue 4 arum 5 avens, calla, canna, comos, orpin, phlox, yucca, zamia 6 alalea, bareta, oxalis, spirea, teasel 7 barreta, gentian, lobelia, pavonia, petunia, rhodora, spiraea, tamarix, torenia, waratah 8 acanthus, ageratum, damewort, geranium, gerardia, valerian 9 candytuft, coreopsis, gloxinias, goldenrod, hollyhock, monkshood 10 pulsatilla, snapdragon
flowerless plant: 4 fern, moss 6 lichen 7 acrogen
flowerlike: 7 anthoid
flowerpot: 10 jardiniere
flowery: 6 florid 7 florent 9 flowering 10 figurative, flosculous
flowing: 4 flux 5 fluid, fluor, tidal 6 afflux, fluent 7 copious, current, cursive, emanent, fluxing 9 affluxion, emanation 10 transitive
together: 9 confluent
flu: 6 grippe
flub: 4 muff 5 error
fluctuate: 4 sway, vary, veer 5 waver 7 vibrate 8 undulate, unsteady 9 oscillate, vacillate 10 irresolute 12 undetermined
fluctuating: 8 unstable, unsteady
flue: net 4 barb, down, open, pipe, thin 5 flare, fluff, fluke 6 expand, feeble, funnel, sickly, tunnel 7 chimney, flaring, passage, shallow
fluency: 9 eloquence, profusion 10 smoothness
fluent: 4 glib 5 fluid, ready 6 facile, liquid, smooth, stream 7 copious, flowing, fluidic, renable, verbose, voluble 8 eloquent, flippant 9 talkative 13 talkativeness
fluff: nap 4 down, flue, lint, puff 5 flash, floss, whiff
fluffy: 4 soft 5 downy, drunk, fluey, fuzzy 6 linten 8 feathery, unsteady 12 undependable
fluid: ink 5 rasa 5 water 6 fluent, liquid, watery 7 flowing, fluible, fluxile, gaseous 8 floating, fluxible
kind of: gas, ink, oil, sap, tar 4 bile, icor, milk 5 blood, ether, grume, ichor, latex, nerol, plasm, serum 6 naptha 7 acetone, coaloil, tearlet 8 gasoline, kerosene
measure: rhe
pert. to: 7 humoral
without: 7 aneroid
fluidity unit: rhe
fluke: 4 fish, flue 5 blade 8 flounder
fluky: 8 unsteady 9 uncertain 10 capricious
flume: 4 leat 5 chute, gorge, water 6 ravine, sluice, stream 7 channel
flunk: 4 bust, fail 7 flicker
flunky, flunkey: 4 snob 5 toady 6 cookee 7 footman, servant, steward
flurry: ado 4 gust, stir 5 haste, skirl 6 bother, bustle, scurry, squall 7 confuse, flusker, fluster, flutter, fooster 9 agitation, carfuffle 10 discompose
flush: 4 even, glow, pool, rose 5 blush, elate, rouge, vigor 6 aflush, excite, lavish, mantle, morass, redden, thrill 7 animate 8 abundant, affluent, prodigal, rosiness 9 abounding, encourage 10 prosperous
flushed: red 4 ruby 5 aglow 6 florid 7 scarlet 8 vigorous 10 prosperous
flushing: 8 blushing 9 rubescent
fluster: 5 shake 6 flurry, fuddle, muddle, pother, rattle 7 confuse, flusker, fooster 8 befuddle, flustrum 10 discompose
flute: nay 4 fife 5 crimp 6 flauto, goffer, zufolo 7 chamfer, channel, gauffer, magadis, piccolo, zuffolo 8 flautino
ancient: 5 tibia
Hindu: bin 5 pungi
player: 5 piper 6 aulete 7 flutist, tootler 8 auletris, flautist
stop: 7 ventage
wood for: 5 kokra
fluting: 5 strix 7 gadroon, godroon, strigil 10 gadroonage, godroonage
flux: 4 flow, fuse, melt 5 float, flood, resin, rosin, smear, smelt 6 fusion, stream 7 euripus, flowing, outflow
fluxible: 5 fluid 7 pliable 8 changing 10 inconstant
fly: bee, hop 4 flee, fleg, flit, leap, melt, scud, soar, solo, whir, whiz, wing 5 agile, alert, float, midge, pilot, quick, sharp, whirr 6 aviate, insect, nimble, spring, vanish 7 avigate, avolate, knowing 8 coachman 9 disappear
African: 4 zimb 5 zebub 6 tsetse

enemy: 6 spider
fishing: bee 4 lure 5 nymph, sedge 6 Cahill 7 Babcock, grannom, huzzard 8 coachman, Ferguson, hare's ear 9 alexandra 10 Barrington
genus: 5 dacus
kind of: bee, bot, fag, mau, plu 4 gnat, kivu, zimb 5 alder, cadew, horse, midge, whame 6 breeze, gadfly, seroot, tsetse 7 butcher, collier, tachina 8 housefly 9 shoemaker 10 bluebottle 11 caterpillar, trichoptera
small: 4 gnat 5 midge
two winged: 8 dipteron
flyaway: 5 giddy 7 flighty 8 restless 12 unrestrained
flybane: 12 cinnamonroot
flyblow: 5 larva
flycatcher: 5 pewee 6 phoebe, yetapa 7 fielder, grignet, grinder
flyer: ace 5 pilot 7 Pegasus 8 aeronaut, operator
flying: 5 awing 6 flight, volant, waving 8 aviation, floating 9 fugacious
pert. to: 7 aviatic
flying adder: 9 dragonfly
flying boat: 8 seaplane 9 amphibian
flying body: 6 meteor
flying device: 4 kite 6 glider
Flying Dutchman heroine: 5 Senta
flying expert: ace
flying fish: 5 saury 7 gurnard
flying machine: 5 plane 8 aerostat 9 gyroplane 10 helicopter
flying mammal: bat
flying ship: 5 blimp 7 aeronat, biplane 8 airplane 9 amphibian, dirigible, monoplane 10 helicopter
Fo: 6 Buddha
foal: 4 colt 5 filly
foam: fob, sud 4 fume, head, scud, scum 5 frost, froth, spume, yeast 6 bubble, freath, lather 7 blubber
foaming: 6 yeasty 7 spumous
foamy: 5 barmy, spumy 6 frothy
fob: 4 buck, foam 5 cheat, froth, trick 6 impose, pocket 8 flimflam, imposter, ornament, swindler
focal: 7 central, centric, nuclear, nucleus 13 concentrative
focus: 4 foci(pl.) 5 point, train 6 center, hearth 8 converge 9 fireplace 11 concentrate
fodder: hay 4 feed, food, vert 5 mange 6 forage, silage 9 provender
kind of: ers, oat, rye 4 corn, rape 5 batad, maize, vetch, wheat 6 barley, clover, millet 7 alfalfa 8 deerweed 11 bitter vetch
storing place: 4 silo 5 bakie 6 haymow, silage 8 ensilage
trough for: 6 manger
fodgel: fat 5 plump, squat, stout
foe: 5 enemy, fiend, rival 7 adverse, hostile, opposer, saracen 8 opponent 9 adversary, ill-wisher 10 antagonist
foederatus: 4 ally
foeman: 5 enemy 9 adversary
fog: dag, rag 4 damp, daze, haar, haze, mist, moke, moss, murk, prig, roke, smog 5 bedim, brume, cloud, grass, vapor 6 nebula, salmon, stupor 7 obscure, pogonip 8 bewilder, moisture 10 aftergrass 12 bewilderment
foggy: dim 4 dull, hazy, moky, roky 5 dense, dirty, misky, misty, murky, rooky 6 cloudy, marshy 7 brumous, muddled, obscure 8 confused, nubilous 9 beclouded
foghorn: 5 siren
fogy: 6 foozle
foible: 4 weak 5 fault, ferly 6 feeble 7 frailty 8 weakness 9 infirmity 12 imperfection
foil: 4 balk, soil, tain 5 blade, blunt, elude, evade, stain, stump, sword, track, trail 6 baffle, blench, boggle, defeat, defile, outwit, stigma, stooge, thwart 7 beguile, failure, pollute, repulse, trample 8 disgrace 9 frustrate, overthrow 11 frustration
foist: 4 cask 5 barge, cheat, fudge, fusty 6 galley, suborn 7 swindle 8 brackish 9 rascality 11 interpolate
fold: bow, lap, pen, ply, wap 4 bend, cote, fail, flap, furl, loop, plie, ruga, tuck 5 clasp, crimp, drape, flipe, flock, layer, plait, pleat, plica, prank, sinus, yield 6 bought, crease, double, hurdle, infold, plight, pucker, rimple 7 crumple, enbrace, flexure, placate, plicate 8 surround 9 enclosure, overthrow, plicature
kind of: 4 loop 5 bight, lapel, plica, quire 6 bought, dewlap, octavo 7 plicate 9 replicate
of skin: 5 plica
folded: 4 shut 6 closed 7 plicate
folder: 5 cover, folio 6 binder 7 leaflet 8 pamphlet
folderol, falderal: 8 nonsense
foliage: 6 leaves 7 leafage
foliated: 5 lobed 7 spathic
folio: fo 4 case, leaf, page
folk: 6 daoine, people 7 friends 9 intimates, relatives
folklore: 4 myth 6 custom, history, legend 9 tradition 12 superstition
genie of: 7 sandman
folks: 6 people
folkway: mos 5 mores(pl.) 6 custom 7 pattern
folle: mad 8 reckless 11 extravagant
folletto: imp 5 fairy 6 goblin, spirit

follicle: 5 crypt
follow: 4 copy, hunt, next, seek, shag, tail 5 adopt, after, chase, ensue, snake, spoor, trace, track, trail 6 attend, pursue, result, shadow 7 imitate, observe, replace, succeed 8 practice, supplant 9 accompany, alternate, supervene 10 comprehend, understand
follow behind: dog, lag, tag 4 heel, hunt, nose, tail 5 hound, trace 6 shadow, trail 7 draggle 9 supervene
follower: fan, ist, ite, son 4 aper, beau, zany 5 gilly 6 bildar, ensuer, gillie, gudget, sequel, sulter, votary 7 devotee, grifter, pursuer, retinue, spaniel 8 adherent, disciple, henchman, partisan, retainer, servitor 9 attendant, caudatory, cuadrilla, dependent, satellite, successor 10 aficionado, sweetheart 11 cuadrillero
suffix: ite
following: 4 next, sect 5 after, suant, train 6 sequel 7 ensuing, sequent 8 business, trailing, vocation 9 clientele 10 posthumous, profession, sequential, subsequent, succeeding, successive
exact words: 7 literal
laws of arithmetical algebra: 6 scalor
folly: sin 6 betise, dotage, lunacy 7 daffery, daffing, foolery, foppery, madness, mistake 8 fondness, idleness, lewdness, morology, nonsense, rashness 9 silliness 10 imprudence, wantonness 11 foolishness 12 indiscretion
foment: 4 abet, brew, spur 5 rouse, stupe 6 arouse, excite, incite 7 agitate, ferment 9 encourage, instigate
fond: tid 4 dear, dote, fain, fool, fund, weak 5 silly, stock, store 6 ardent, befool, caress, dearly, doting, fondle, loving, simple, tender 7 amatory, amorous, beguile, browden, foolish, insipid 8 desirous, enamored, sanguine, trifling, uxorious 9 credulous, enamoured, indulgent, savorless 10 curcuddoch, infatuated, passionate 12 affectionate
of dainties: 6 friand 9 friandise
of drink: 8 bibulous
of hunting: 7 venatic
fonda: inn 5 hotel 6 fonduk 7 fondouk, funduck
fondle: pet 4 baby, coax, fond, neck, waly 5 daunt, wally 6 caress, cocker, coddle, cosset, dandle, pamper, stroke 7 cherish 8 blandish, canoodle
fondling: pet 4 fool 5 ninny 9 caressing, dalliance, simpleton
fondly: 4 fond 6 dearly 7 foolish 8 tenderly 9 foolishly 14 affectionately
fondness: gra 4 love 5 folly, taste 8 dearness, weakness 9 affection 10 attachment, tenderness 11 affectation, foolishness 12 predilection 15 Philotherianism
fondu: 6 cheese 7 blended
fons: 6 source 8 fountain
font: 4 pila 5 basin 6 source, spring 7 piscina 8 delubrum, fountain 10 aspersoria(pl.) 11 aspersorium
fontal: 8 original 9 baptismal
food: bit, pap 4 bite, cate, chow, diet, eats, fare, farm, gear, grub, meat, peck, prog 5 bread, broma, cheer, foray, scaff, tripe 6 fodder, foster, morsel, viands, wraith 7 aliment, edibles, handout, pabulum 8 flummery, grubbery, victuals 9 nutriment, provender 10 provisions, sustenance 11 nourishment
animal: 4 feed 5 grain, grass 6 fodder, forage 9 provender
choice: 4 cake 6 pastry
comb. form: 4 sito 5 troph 6 tropho
container: jar 4 bowl, dish, olla 5 crock, plate 6 saucer
craving for: 4 pica 7 bulimia
devotee: 7 epicure, gourmet
dislike of: 6 asitia 9 sitomania 10 cibophobia
dressing: 5 sauce
element: 6 gluten 7 protein, vitamin
farinaceous: 4 sago
garnish: 5 sauce
heavenly: 5 manna
invalid: pap 5 broth
kind of: pap, poi, sop 4 ants, chum, crum, mess, mush, sago 5 acate, balut, bread, broma, cates, gruel, jelly, manna, puree, salep, scaff, souse, tripe 6 cagmag, cereal, farina, forage, hominy, vivres 7 abalone, boscage, pemican, tapioca 8 ambrosia, aperient, beebread, pemmican 9 aperitive, rechauffe 10 rechauffee
list: 4 diet, menu 5 carte
of gods: 6 amrita 7 amreeta 8 ambrosia
pert. to: 8 cibarial 9 cibarious
protein: 4 fish, meat 6 cheese
provision of: 4 mess 6 ration 8 catering
seller: 6 grocer 7 viander
semidigested: 5 chyme
soft: pap
storage pit: 4 cist
southern: 4 okra, pone 5 gumbo 6 hominy 7 hoecake 11 chitterling
special dish: 4 hogo, olla, stew 5 bredi, pilaf, pilau, pilaw, pizza 6 haslet, hominy, majoon, omelet, panada, pilaff, ragout, salmis, scouse, sundae, zimmis 7 chowder, custard, rarebit, ravioli, souffle 8 cabeliau, hautgout, omelette, sillabub, sukiyaki 9 cabilliau, colcannon, galantine, succotash 10 salmagundi, shish-kebab

starchy: 8 macaroni 9 spaghetti 10 vermicelli
unclean: 4 tref
food and drink: 4 diet, fare 5 bouge, found 6 bouche 10 provisions
fool: ape, ass, cod, fop, fox, mug, nup, toy 4 butt, cake, chub, dolt, dupe, fond, gowk, gype, jape, jest, joke, mome, nizy, simp, toot, zany 5 bluff, clown, dally, goose, idiot, knave, moron, ninny, nizey, noddy, sammy, silly, snipe, spoof, trick 6 buffle, cudden, cuckoo, delude, dotard, dottle, jester, nidget, nimshi, nincom, nupson, tamper 7 asinego, buffoon, coxcomb, deceive, dizzard, foolish, fribble, gomeral, gomeril, haveral, haverel, mislead, omadawn, playboy, witling 8 badinage, driveler, fondling, hoodwink, omadhaun 9 blockhead, capocchia, driveller, fopdoodle, hoddy-peak, hoddy-poll, simpleton 10 bufflehead, hoddy-doddy, nincompoop
fool's gold: 6 pyrite
fool's paradise: 7 chimera 8 illusion
fool's stitch: 6 tricot
foolable: 8 gullible
foolhardy: 4 rash 11 adventurous 12 presumptuous
fooling: 6 banter 7 daffery, daffing 12 harlequinade
foolish: mad 4 bete, daft, fond, fool, rash, zany 5 barmy, batty, boggy, buggy, dizzy, gawky, goofy, goosy, inane, inept, noddy, silly 6 absurd, dotish, fondly, gotham, harish, mopish, simple, stupid, unwise 7 asinine, doatish, doltish, fangled, fatuous, flighty, foppish, gullish, idiotic, witless 8 fopperly, headless, heedless 9 brainless, childlike, desipient, doddering, imprudent, insensate, ludicrous, senseless 10 half-witted, hulver-head, indiscreet, irrational 12 preposterous 13 feather-headed 14 feather-brained
foolishness: 5 folly 6 barney, levity, rubble 8 fondness 9 absurdity 10 insipience
foot: paw, pes 4 base, hoof 6 gammon
animal: pad, paw 4 hoof 7 fetlock, pastern
armor: 7 chausse
comb. form: 4 pedi, pode
deformity: 5 varus
metric: 4 iamb 5 arsis, paeon 6 dactyl, iambic, iambus 7 anapest, spondee, triseme 8 bacchius, epitrite, molossus, trochee
pain: 8 talalgia
part: toe 4 arch 6 instep, tarsus, thenar 10 metatarsus
pert. to: 5 pedal, podal
poetic: See *metric* above
worked by: 5 pedal 7 treadle
foot bone: 6 cuboid, tarsus 8 scaphoid 10 astragulus, metatarsus
foot doctor: 10 podiatrist 11 chiropodist
foot lever: 5 pedal 7 treadle
foot-like part: pes
foot-loose: 4 free 10 ambulatory 11 untrammeled
foot soldier: 8 infantry
football: 5 rugby 6 rugger, soccer 7 pigskin
coach: 5 Jones, Morre, Stagg, Wilce 6 Bezdek, Dorais, Harlow, Rockne, Romney 7 Crisler, Heisman, Higgins 8 Morrison 9 Cavanaugh
kick: 4 punt 6 spiral
play: 4 buck, pass, punt 7 spinner
score: 4 down, goal 6 safety 9 touchback, touchdown
term: 6 onside 7 offside
footband: 6 canvas
footboy: 4 page 9 attendant
footed: 6 pedate
multiple: 7 bipedal, octopod 8 multiped
large: 7 megapod
footer: 4 fall, idle, jump 6 plunge, potter, trifle, walker
footfall: 5 tread
footgear: See **footwear**
foothold: 7 toehold
footing: par 5 basis, track 7 toehold 9 footprint
footle: 5 silly 6 drivel, potter, trifle 7 trivial, twaddle
footless: 4 apod 5 apoda, apode, inapt 6 apodal, clumsy, stupid 13 unsubstantial
footman: 6 flunky, lackey, varlet, walker 7 flunkey, footpad, servant 8 chasseur 10 pedestrian
footnote: 9 reference 11 explanation
footpad: pad 4 whyo 6 padder, robber 7 footman 10 highwayman
footpath: 4 lane 5 senda, trail 8 trottoir
footprint: 5 trace, track, tread
fossil: 9 ichnolite
rabbit: 5 prick
footrest: 4 rail 7 hassock 9 footstool
footrope: 5 horse 8 boltrope
footstalk: 7 pedicel, petiole 8 peduncle
footstep: 7 vestige
footstool: 4 mora 6 buffet 7 cricket, hassock, ottoman 8 footrest
footway: 4 path 9 banquette
footwear: pac 4 boot, clog, pack, shoe, sock 5 kamik, sabot 6 arctic, bootee, brogan, brogue, buskin, galosh, kamika(pl.), patten, rubber, sandal 7 galoshe, slipper 8 moccasin, overshoe, stocking
footy: 4 mean, poor 6 paltry
fooyoung, fooyung: 6 omelet 8 omelette

fop: 4 buck, dude, dupe, fool 5 dandy 7 coxcomb, jessamy 8 gimcrack, popinjay 9 exquisite

foppery: 9 absurdity

foppish: 5 apish, dandy, silly 6 dapper, spruce, stupid 7 fangled, finical, foolish 8 dandyish

foppishness: 13 dandification

for: 7 because 8 favoring 9 favouring 10 concerning

prefix: pro

for all voices: 5 tutti

for cash: 9 alcontado (Sp.)

for each: per

for example: e.g.

for fear that: 4 lest

for nothing: 6 gratis, lanyap 8 gratuity 9 lagniappe

for shame: fie

for temporary use: 4 jury

for that reason: 4 ergo(L.) 9 therefore

for which reason: 6 whence

forage: ers, oat, rye 4 corn, mast, raid, rape 5 grass, maize, raven, spoil, wheat 6 barley, browse, clover, fodder, millet, ravage, russud 7 alfalfa 8 deerweed 9 pasturage 10 provisions 11 bitter vetch

foramen: 4 pore

forane: 6 remote 7 foreign

foray: 4 rade, raid 5 melee 6 ravage, sortie 7 chappow, hership, pillage 9 incursion

forbear, forebear: 4 bear, help, shun, sire 5 avoid, forgo, spare 6 desist, endure, forego, parent 7 abstain, decline, refrain 8 ancestor 10 ancestress, forefather, foreparent

forbearance: 5 mercy 6 lenity 8 mildness, patience 9 tolerance 10 abstinence, self-denial 13 self-restraint

forbearing: 7 patient 8 tolerant 9 desisting

forbid: ban 4 defy, deny, fend, tabu, veto 5 debar, taboo 6 defend, enjoin, impede, refuse 7 forfend, forwarn, gainsay, inhibit 8 disallow, forefend, forspeak, preclude, prohibit 9 challenge, interdict, proscribe 10 contradict 11 countermand

forbiddance: ban 4 veto 12 interdiction, proscription

forbidden: 4 tabu 5 taboo 6 banned, denied 8 verboten 10 prohibited

Jewish law: 4 tref

Forbidden City: 5 Lhasa

forbidding: 4 grim 5 black, gaunt, stern 6 fierce, odious, strict 9 offensive, repellent 10 unpleasant 11 displeasing, prohibiting 12 disagreeable, interdicting

forbode: See **forebode**

force: gar, gut, vim, vis 4 bang, birr, clip, cram, dint, feck, make 5 co-act, drive, exert, farce, impel, might, peise, poach, power, press, repel, shear, stuff, wrest 6 coerce, compel, cudgel, energy, extort, oblige, ravish, stithy 7 ability, afforce, cascade, impetus, impulse, require, violate 8 coaction, coercion, efficacy, momentum, pressure, strength, validity, violence, virility 9 constrain, influence, puissance, restraint, waterfall 10 compulsion, constraint, constringe 11 necessitate

air upon: 4 blow

down: 4 tamp 5 stuff

into smaller space: 8 compress

kinds of: od 4 army, birr, dyne, elod, soul, task 5 agent, cadre, dynam, enemy, fohat, nerve, posse, steam, tonal 6 nature 7 voltage 8 bionergy, battalia, sanction 13 reinforcement

onward: 4 urge 6 propel

out: 5 evict 6 banish, unseat

producing rotation: 6 torque

to do without: 7 deprive

with full: 5 amain

forced: 7 labored 8 spurious 9 reluctant 10 artificial, compulsory, farfetched 11 constrained, involuntary, spontaneous 12 artificially

contribution: tax 4 duty, levy, toll 6 demand, excise, impost 7 tribute 8 exaction 10 assessment

feeding: 6 gavage

forceful: 6 mighty, strong, virile 7 dynamic, violent 8 eloquent, enfatico, forcible, vigorous 9 effective, energetic

forcemeat: 5 farce

forceps: 7 pincers 8 dentagra

forces: 4 army 6 troops

forcible: 5 stout, valid 6 cogent, mighty, potent 7 violent, weighty 8 emphatic, forceful, powerful, puissant, vigorous 9 energetic, impetuous, necessary 10 compulsory, convincing, impressive, obligatory 11 efficacious, influential

forcibly: 5 amain 6 hardly 9 violently 10 vigorously

ford: 4 wade, wath 5 drift 6 stream 7 current 8 crossing 9 wathstead

Fordham's team: 4 Rams

fore: van, way 5 afore, ahead, front, prior, track 6 former 7 earlier, further, journey 8 advanced, formerly 10 antecedent, previously

forearm: arm

bone: 4 ulna

pert. to: 7 cubital

forebear: See **forbear**

forebode, forbode: 4 bode, omen 5 augur, croak 6 divine 7 betoken, portend, predict, presage 8 foretell 13 prognosticate 15 prognostication

foreboding, forboding: 4 omen 5 black 6 augury, boding, gloomy 7 anxiety 8 bode-

ment, sinister 10 prediction 11 pessimistic, presagement 12 apprehension, presentiment
forecast: 4 bode 6 scheme 7 caution, foresee, fortune, predict 8 foredeem, foretell, prophesy 9 calculate, foregleam, forepoint, forescent, foretoken, prognosis 10 foreordain, prediction, prognostic 11 calculation, foredestiny 12 predetermine 15 prognostication
forecaster: 4 seer 6 oracle 8 dopester 11 nostradamus 13 meteorologist
foreclose: 5 debar 6 hinder 7 prevent 8 preclude
foredoom: 7 destiny 10 predestine
forefather: 4 sire 5 elder 6 parent 7 forbear 8 ancestor 9 grandsire 10 forerunner, progenitor
forefinger: 5 index
forefoot: paw, pud
forefront: van 5 front
foregather: 4 meet 7 consort, convene 8 assemble 9 encounter 10 fraternize
forego, forgo: 5 waive 7 abstain, neglect, precede, refrain 8 dispense, renounce
foregoer: 7 example 8 ancestor 10 forerunner 11 predecessor
foregoing: 4 past 5 above 8 anterior, previous 10 antecedent
foregone: 4 past 8 previous
conclusion: 9 certainty
forehanded: 5 early 6 timely 7 prudent, thrifty
forehead: 4 brow 5 frons, front 7 frontes 8 sinciput
pert. to: 7 metopic
prominence: 8 glabella
strap: 4 tump
foreign: 5 alien, fremd 6 exiled, exotic, forane, remote 7 distant, ecdemic, exclude, strange 8 barbaric, peregrin 9 barbarous, extrinsic, peregrine 10 extraneous, outlandish, tramontane 12 adventitious, exallotriote, exterraneous
comb. form: 4 xeno
geology: 7 epigene
foreign quarter: 6 barrio, ghetto 7 enclave
foreign service: *official:* 6 consul 7 attache 8 diplomat 10 ambassador
residence: 9 consulate
foreign to: 6 dehors
foreigner: 5 alien, haole 6 gringo, pakeha 7 greener, pardesi 8 outsider, stranger 9 barbarian, estranger, outlander 10 tramontane 12 ultramontane
forejudge: 7 adjudge
foreknow: 6 divine 7 foresee 9 prescient 11 preconceive
foreknowledge: 10 prescience
forel: 4 case 6 border, sheath 7 selvage 8 slipcase
foreland: 8 headland 10 promontory
forelay: 6 ambush, hinder, waylay 8 obstruct
forelock: 4 bang 6 cotter 8 linchpin
foreman: 4 boss 5 chief 6 gaffer, ganger, leader 7 capataz, captain, headman, manager, steward 8 overseer 9 chargeman 10 supervisor
foremost: 4 head, high, main 5 chief, first, forme, front, grand 6 banner 7 leading, supreme 9 principal
part: van 5 front
forensic: 8 forensal 10 rhetorical 13 argumentative
foreordain: 7 destine, foresay, predoom 8 forecast 9 preordain 10 predestine 12 predestinate, predetermine
forepart: 5 front 9 stomacher
of horse's hoof: toe
forerun: 6 herald, outrun 7 precede, prelude 8 announce 9 forestall, introduce, precourse, prefigure 10 anticipate, foreshadow
forerunner: 4 omen, sign 5 usher 6 augury, herald 8 ancestor, foregoer, fourrier 9 harbinger, messenger, precedent, precursor 10 forefather, foreganger, progenitor, prognostic 11 predecessor
foresaid: 9 aforesaid
foresee: 4 read 6 divine 8 forecast, foreknow 10 anticipate
foreseeing: 9 designing
foreshadow: 7 forerun 9 adumbrate, prefigure
foreshank: 4 shin
foreshow: 4 bode 5 abode, augur 7 betoken 8 foretell, prophesy 9 auspicate, foretoken 13 prognosticate
foresight: 6 vision 8 prudence 9 prevision 10 prescience, prevoyance, providence 11 forethought 12 anticipation 14 farsightedness
foresighted: 9 prescient, provident 10 farsighted
forest: 4 gapo, wood 5 Arden, glade, gubat, sylva(L.), taiga, waste 6 jungle, timber 7 boscage 8 caatinga, woodland 10 wilderness
deity: 4 faun 5 satyr 7 Aegipan
glade: 5 camas 6 camass, cammas 7 quamash
god: Pan 5 Tapio
love of: 9 hemophily
open place: 5 glade
pertaining to: 6 sylvan 7 nemoral 9 forestral
road: 4 ride 5 trail

subarctic: **5** taiga
treeless: **4** wold
warden: **6** ranger
Forest City: 8 Portland, Savannah **9** Cleveland
forest fire locator: 7 alidade
forester: 7 montero, treeman, woodman **8** woodsman
forestland for tillage: 7 thwaite
foretaste: 4 gust **6** teaser **8** prospect **12** anticipation
foretell: 4 bode, erst, read, spae **5** augur, insee, weird **6** divine **7** bespeak, foresay, portend, predict, presage **8** forebode, forecast, foreshow, prophesy, soothsay **9** predicate, prefigure, prophetic **10** vaticinate **13** prognosticate
foretelling: 9 fatidical, prophetic
forethought: 7 caution **8** prepense, prudence **9** foresight, provident **12** aforethought, anticipation **13** premeditation
foretoken: 4 omen **7** promise **8** forecast, foreshow, foresign **9** auspicate **10** presignify **13** prognosticate
foretold: 10 annunciate
foretooth: 5 biter **6** cutter **7** incisor
forever: ay; ake, aye **4** ever **5** etern **6** always, eterne **7** endless **8** eternity **9** endlessly, eternally, perpetual **10** constantly, invariably **11** ceaselessly, continually, everlasting, incessantly, perpetually, unceasingly **12** interminably, unchangeably **13** everlastingly
forewarn: 5 augur
forewarning: 7 portent **11** premonition
foreword: 5 proem **7** preface **8** preamble **12** introduction
forfeit: 4 fine, lose **5** crime, dedit, forgo **6** forego **7** escheat, misdeed, penalty **8** forfault
law **7** abandum
forfeiture: 4 fine **5** mulct **7** penalty **9** decheance **10** amercement
forfend, forefend: 5 avert **6** forbid, secure **7** prevent, protect **8** preserve, prohibit
forfex: 6 shears
forge: 4 mint **5** feign **6** smithy, swinge **7** falsify, fashion **8** bloomery **9** fabricate **11** counterfeit, fabrication, manufacture
nozzle: tew **5** tewel
on: **5** drive
tongs: tew
waste: **5** dross, sprue
wrought iron: **8** bloomery
forged: 10 artificial **11** counterfeit
forger: 5 smith **9** falsifier **10** coachsmith, fabricator
forgery: 4 sham **7** fiction **8** bloomery **11** counterfeit, fabrication **13** falsification
forget: 4 omit **7** neglect **8** overlook **9** disregard **11** disremember
one's lines: **5** fluff
forgetful: 8 careless, heedless **9** oblivious **10** neglectful **11** inattentive
forgetfulness: 7 amnesia, amnesty **8** oblivion
fruit of: **5** lotus
river of: **5** Lethe
forging: 11 fabrication
forgivable: 6 venial
forgive: 5 remit, spare **6** excuse, pardon **7** absolve, condone **8** overlook **9** exculpate
forgiven: 7 excused
forgiveness: 6 pardon **9** remission **10** absolution **11** condonation
forgiving: 6 humane **7** clement **8** merciful, placable **9** remissive **10** charitable
forgo, forego: 4 quit **5** leave **7** abstain, forbear, forfeit, forsake, neglect, refrain **8** agnegate, forebear, overlook, renounce **10** relinquish
forgoing: 5 above
forjudge, forejudge: 4 oust **5** expel **7** adjudge, condemn
fork: 4 tine **5** prong **6** bisect, branch, crotch, divide **7** fourche **10** divaricate, fourchette
kinds of: **4** croc, evil **5** graip, pikle, glack **7** biprong **9** tormentor
forked: 5 bifid **6** furcal **7** divided, furcate **8** branched **9** furciform **10** bifurcated **11** forficulate
forleave: 7 abandon
forlorn: 4 lorn, lost, reft **5** stray **6** abject, bereft, ruined **7** forfare **8** deserted, desolate, forsaken, helpless, hopeless, pitiable, wretched **9** abandoned, cheerless, desperate, destitute, miserable **10** friendless **11** comfortless **12** disconsolate
form: ame **4** blee, body, make, mode, mold, plan, rite, thew **5** bench, build, frame, guise, image, model, shape **6** adjust, create, figure, invent, manner, ritual, schema, sponge **7** arrange, compose, confect, contour, develop, fashion, outline, pattern, portray, produce, profile **8** ceremony, conceive, likeness, organize, schemata(pl.) **9** construct, etiquette, fabricate, formation, structure **10** appearance, constitute, expression, figuration, observance, similitude **12** conformation **13** configuration, questionnaire
carved: **8** statuary
display: **4** rack **7** manikin **9** mannequin
geometrical: see **figure:** *geometrical*
into arc: **5** embow
into ball: **8** conglobe
into chain: **8** catenate
into fabric: **4** knit

into network: 10 reticulate
literary: ode 5 novel, poesy 6 satire, sonnet 7 romance
liturgical: 6 litany 7 service
lyrical: 6 rondel 7 sestina, sestine(pl.)
of government: 6 polity
of greeting: bow 5 hello, salam 6 salaam, salute 7 curtsey
pert. to: 5 modal
formal: set 4 prim 5 exact, stiff 6 solemn 7 orderly, precise, regular, solward, starchy, stilted 8 academic, affected, formular, starched 9 essential, officious 10 ceremonial, methodical 11 ceremonious, punctilious, superficial 12 conventional
formality: 8 ceremony 15 conventionality
format: 4 size 5 shape, style 7 pattern
formation: 4 form, rank 9 structure 10 procession 11 composition, development 12 construction
bone: 7 ostosis 10 parostosis
cell: 6 tissue
flesh: 8 sarcosis
geological: lia 4 ione 5 atoll, ledge 6 schist 7 tapeats, terrain, terrane
military: 4 line 5 herse 7 echelon
sand: 4 dene, dune
formative: 7 plastic
forme: 5 bench, early, first 6 former 8 foremost
formed: 5 built 7 decided, matured, settled, wrought 10 constitute
at foot of mountain: 8 piedmont
by law: 9 corporate
crudely: 9 roughhewn
from above: 8 catogene
ingeniously: 5 dedal 6 daedal
of clustered grains (bot.): 7 grumose
on earth's surface: 7 epigene
former: ex; die, old 4 erst, fore, late, once, past 5 forme, gauge, guide, maker, prior 6 whilom 7 ancient, creator, earlier, further, pattern, quondam, templet 8 previous, sometime 9 aforetime, erstwhile 10 antecedent
prefix: ex
formerly: ere, nee 4 erst, fore, once, then 5 grave 7 onetime, quondam 8 sometime 9 aforetime, anciently, erstwhile 10 heretofore
formicary: ant 7 anthill, dweller
formicid: ant
formidable: 7 fearful 8 alarming, dreadful, menacing, terrible 11 redoubtable, threatening
formless: 5 arupa 7 anidian, chaotic 8 deformed 9 amorphous, shapeless 13 indeterminate
comb. form: 6 amorph 7 amorpho
Formosa city: 6 Taipei, Taiwan 7 Dai-Iloku
formula: law 4 rule 6 method, recipe, theory 7 receipt
formular: 5 model 6 formal, proper 7 regular 9 formulary
formulated: 6 stated 10 articulate
forsake: 4 deny, drop, flee, quit, shun 5 avoid, forgo, leave, waive 6 beleve, defect, depart, desert, forego, refuse, reject 7 abandon, beleave, discard 8 renounce, withdraw 9 surrender 10 relinquish
forsaken: 4 lorn 7 forlorn 8 deserted, desolate 9 abandoned, destitute
forset: bar 5 beset 6 invest, waylay 8 surround
forspeak: 4 help 5 avert, curse 6 forbid, hinder 7 asperse, bewitch, devance, exclude, forerun, obviate, prevent 8 renounce 9 intercept 10 anticipate
forswear: 4 deny 6 abjure, reject 7 abandon, perjure 8 abnegate, renounce
forsworn: 8 perjured 11 disaffected
fort: pa; dun, lis, pah 4 liss, shee 5 gotta, redan, sidhe 6 castle, strong 7 bastile, bastion, bulwark, citadel, fortify 8 bastille, castillo, fastness, fortress 10 blockhouse, protection, stronghold
sloping bank of: 6 glacis
forte: bag 5 skill, thing 6 metier 7 calling 8 strength 9 specialty
forth: out 4 away 6 abroad, manage, onward 7 forward 8 outdoors 10 accomplish
forthink: 6 regret, repent 10 reconsider
forthright: 7 frankly 9 downright 11 straightway 13 straightforth 15 straightforward
forthwith: now 6 bedene, believe, direct 7 betimes 8 directly 9 extempore, presently, therewith 11 immediately
fortification (see also **defense**): 4 boma, moat, wall 5 redan, tower 6 abatis, castle, glacis, shield 7 bastion, bulwark, citadel, parapet, rampart, ravelin, redoubt 8 fortress 9 barricade 10 stronghold 12 machiolation
kind of: 4 fort 5 redan 6 abatis, sconce 7 lunette, ravelin, redoubt, parados 8 ceinture, demilune, estacade 9 fortalice, bastionet
part: 5 redan 7 bastion, ravelin 8 barbette
fortify: arm, man 4 fort 5 spike 6 abatis, picket 7 bastile, confirm 8 bastille, embattle, fortress, palisade 9 barricade 10 invigorate, strengthen, stronghold
fortitude: 6 mettle 7 bravery, courage, heroism, stamina 8 strength 9 endurance 10 resolution 12 resoluteness 14 impregnability
fortress: 4 fort, keep 5 rocca 6 castle 7 alcazar, barrier, bastile, borough, castlet, cas-

trum, chateau, citadel, fortify **8** alcalzar, alcazava, bastille, chateaux(pl.), fastness **10** stronghold **13** fortification, propugnaculum
outwork of: **6** tenail **8** tenaille
fortuitous: **6** casual, chance, random **9** hazardous **10** accidental, contingent, incidental **12** adventitious
fortuity: **4** luck **6** chance **9** accidence
fortunate: edi, hap, sri **4** good, shri **5** faust, happy, lucky, shree **6** dexter **7** favored **8** gracious **10** auspicious, prosperous, successful
fortune: hap, lot **4** bahi, doom, fate, hail, luck **5** weird **6** chance, estate, mishap, riches, wealth **7** destiny, success **8** accident, hacienda **9** adventure **10** prosperity **13** circumstances
goddess: **5** Tyche
fortune teller: **4** seer **5** gypsy, sibyl, sybil **7** diviner, palmist
forty: **13** quadragesimal
forty days: **4** Lent
forty winks: nap **6** snooze
forty-five degree angle: **6** octant
forty-five inches: ell
forty-third asteroid: **4** Eros
43,560 square feet: **4** acre
forum: **5** court **8** tribunal
forward: on, to; aid, bog, bug **4** abet, bain, bold, free, help, pert, send, ship, step **5** ahead, along, brash, eager, favor, forth, frack, freck, front, hasty, ready, relay, remit, saucy, serve, spack, ultra **6** afford, ardent, avaunt, before, bright, coming, favour, forthy, hasten, onward, prompt **7** advance, earnest, extreme, further, promote, radical **8** adelante, arrogant, immodest, impudent, perverse, petulant, transmit **9** audacious, encourage, forthward, obtrusive, overready **10** accelerate, forritsome, precocious **11** disobedient, progressive
fosette: **5** ulcer **6** dimple, hollow
fossa: pit **4** foss, moat **5** canal, ditch, fosse, fovea, graff, grave **6** cavity, trench **10** depression
fosse (see also **fossa**): pit **4** hole, moat
fossil: **6** dolite **7** antique, lituite **8** calamite, conodont
egg: **7** ovulite
footprint: **7** ichnite
mollusk: **6** dolite
resin: **5** amber **8** retinite
science: **12** paleontology
shell: **6** dolite
toothlike: **8** conodont
worm track: **7** nereite
fossorial: **9** effodient
fostell: box **4** cask **6** casket
foster: **4** feed, food, help, rear **5** nurse **6** harbor **7** cherish, embosom, gratify, imbosom, indulge, nourish, nursing, nurture, promote, sustain **8** befriend, forester, nursling **9** cultivate, encourage, fosterage, offspring **11** nourishment
foster child: **5** nurry **7** stepson **12** stepdaughter
fosterage: **11** achievement
foudroyant: **8** dazzling, stunning **10** thundering
fougue: **5** ardor **11** impetuosity
foul: **4** base, hory, roil, vile **5** bawdy, black, dirty, grimy, horry, muddy, nasty, sully, weedy **6** clarty, defame, dirten, filthy, impure, malign, odious, putrid, rotten, soiled, unfair **7** abusive, defaced, fulsome, hateful, illegal, noisome, obscene, profane, smeared, squalid, unclean, vicious **8** entangle, indecent, stinking, wretched **9** dastardly, dishonest, loathsome, nastiness, obnoxious, offensive **10** detestable, disgusting, scurrilous **11** contaminate, unfavorable **12** dishonorable, inauspicious
foulard: tie **11** neckerchief **12** handkerchief
foulmouthed: **7** abusive, obscene, profane **10** scurrilous **11** opprobrious
foulness: **9** feculence
found: fix, try **4** base, cast, rest **5** board, build, endow, erect **6** attach, depart **8** equipped, practice, provided, supplied **9** establish, institute, originate, supported **10** foundation
foundation: bed **4** base, body, fund, gist, sill **5** basis, bases(pl.), found, stock **6** bottom, legacy, reseau, riprap **7** bedding, bedrock, chantry, roadbed **8** donation, pedestal **9** beginning, endowment **11** corporation **12** substructure
founder: **4** fail **6** author, caster, dismay, dynast **7** stumble **8** miscarry **9** supporter, undermine **10** maintainer **11** dumbfounder, establisher
metal: **5** yeter **6** yetter
founding: **8** settling
foundling: oaf **4** waif **6** infant, orphan **8** nursling
fount: **4** fons **6** source **8** fountain **9** reservoir
fountain: **4** fond, head, syke, well **5** fount **6** phiale, pirene, source, spring **7** bubbler **8** aganippe **9** reservoir **12** fountainhead
god of: **4** Fons
nymph: **5** naiad
Fountain of Youth site: **6** Bimini
fountainhead: **6** origin, source
four: IV
comb. form: **5** tetra

group of: 6 tetrad 7 guartet 8 quadriad 9 quartette
four-footed: 9 quadruped
Four Horsemen: war 5 death 6 famine 8 conquest
four hundred: 5 creme, elect, elite 6 select
four-in-hand: 7 necktie
four inches: 4 hand 7 measure
four-sided: 13 quadrilateral
fourchette: 4 fork 8 wishbone
fourflusher: 9 pretender
fourgon: car, van 5 wagon 7 tumbril
fourpence: 5 groat
fourrier: 9 harbinger 10 forerunner 13 quartermaster
fourscore: 6 eighty
foursome: 6 tetrad 7 quartet
fourth: 5 quart 6 fardel 7 quarter 8 quadrant
fourth estate: 5 press 10 newspapers
foveated: 6 pitted
fowl: hen 4 bird, cock 5 chick, chuck, manoc 7 chicken, rooster 8 volaille
kinds of: 4 keel, coot 5 malay, banty, snipe, poult, brant 6 Houdan, bantam, Sussex, rumkin 7 minorca, galeeny
fox: tod 4 fool 5 trick 6 canine, outwit 7 beguile, stupefy, vulpine 10 intoxicate, perplexity
foot: pad
hunter's cry: 4 soho 5 yoick
kinds of: cub 4 asse, stag 5 vixen, zorro 6 fennec, corsac 7 Reynard, karagan
scent of: 4 drag
fox trot: 5 dance
foxglove: 7 popdock
leaf: 9 digitalis
foxlike: 9 alopecoid
foxtail: 5 brush, grass
foxy: sly 4 wily 5 coony 6 shrewd 7 cunning, vulpine 10 fraudulent
foy: 4 gift 5 faith, feast
foyer: 5 lobby 6 hearth 8 anteroom, entrance 9 fireplace, greenroom
fra: 4 monk 5 friar 6 priest 7 brother
Fra Diavolo composer: 5 Auber
frab: nag 5 scold, worry 7 contend 8 struggle
fracas: 4 bout 5 brawl, melee, set-to 6 rumpus, uproar 7 quarrel 8 fraction 9 commotion 11 disturbance
fraction: bit 4 part 5 break, piece, scrap 6 breach, fracas, little 7 ruction, rupture 8 breaking, fracture, fragment
fractional: 7 partial
fractious: 4 ugly 5 cross 6 unruly 7 crabbed, peevish, waspish 8 perverse, snappish 9 irritable
fracture: 4 flaw, rend 5 break, cleft, crack 6 breach 7 rupture 8 fraction
fragile: 4 fine, frow, weak 5 frail, frowy, light 6 feeble, frough, infirm, slight 7 brickle, brittle, froughy, slender 8 delicate, ethereal 9 frangible
fragility: 8 delicacy 12 delicateness
fragment: bit, ort 4 blad, chip, flaw, grot, part, snip, wisp 5 broke, crumb, flake, groat, piece, relic, scrap, shard, sherd, shred, spall 6 gobbet, morsel, parcel, screed, sheard, sippet, sliver 7 cantlet, flinder, flitter, fritter, oddment, portion, remnant 8 fraction 10 smithereen
biographical: 8 anecdote
diamond: 4 bort
ice afloat: 5 brash
fragmentary: 5 hashy 6 broken
fragments: 5 frush 7 gubbins
literary: ana 7 analect
Fragonard painting: 7 Bathers
fragrance: 4 odor 5 aroma, scent, smell 6 flavor 7 flavour, incense, perfume 9 perfumery, redolence
fragrant: 5 balmy, olent, spicy 7 odorant, odorous, perfumy, scented 8 aromatic, redolent 9 ambrosial 11 odoriferous
fragrant ointment: 4 balm, nard
fragrant wood: 5 aloes, cedar
fraicheur: 5 chill 8 coolness 9 freshness
frail: 4 fine, puny, weak 5 crazy 6 basket, flimsy, infirm, sickly 7 brittle, bruckle, fragile 8 delicate 12 destructible 13 insubstantial
frailty: 5 fault 6 foible 7 failing 9 frailness, infirmity 10 peccadillo 12 imperfection
fraise: 4 fray, fuss, ream, ruff 6 cajole, defend, praise 7 defense, enlarge, flatter, pancake 8 cajolery 10 strawberry 11 disturbance
fraist: ask, try 4 seek 7 attempt 10 experience
fram: 5 spear
frambesia: 7 disease, sibbens, sivvens
frame (see also **framework**): go; bin 4 bunk, form, mold, plan, plot, sill 5 build, cadre, easel, panel, serve, shape, trave 6 abacus, adjust, binder, border, devise, fabric, invent, manage, profit, redact, resort, tenter 7 arrange, attempt, chassis, fashion, furnish, outline, portray, prepare, proceed, prosper 8 contrive, regulate 9 calculate, construct, fabricate, structure
kinds of: ame, mat 4 bier, calm, caum, gill, sash, sess, sime, sley 5 airer, cadar, cader, dekle, easel, grate, herse, knape, trave, scray 6 abacus, deckel, deckle, tenter 7 drosser, hayrack, taboret
frame of mind: 4 bent, mood 5 humor
frame-up: 4 plot 10 conspiracy

framework: 4 rack, sill 5 cadge, cadre, racke 6 replum, stroma 7 chassis, nacelle, trestle 8 skeleton

frampoid: 5 cross, fiery 7 peevish 8 spirited 9 vexatious 11 quarrelsome

franc: *piece of twenty:* 5 louis
twentieth part of: 7 centime

France: 4 Gaul 6 Gallia
airplane: 5 avion
among: 5 entre
ancient name: 4 Gaul 6 Gallia
and: et
annuity: 5 rente
appellation: nom
architect: 7 Lenotre 9 Corbusier
article: la, le, un; les, une
author: 4 Gide, Hugo, Loti, Sand, Zola 5 Benda, Camus, Dumas, Renan 6 Balzac, Proust, Racine, Sartre 8 Stendhal, Voltaire
axe: 5 hache
baby: 4 bebe 6 enfant
bachelor: 6 garcon
bacteriologist: 7 Pasteur
ball: bal
ballad: lai 7 virelai
bay: 6 Biscay
beach: 5 plage
beast: 4 bete
bed: lit 5 couche
beef: 5 boeuf
billiards: 7 bouchon
bitters: 4 amer
blessed: 4 beni 5 sacre
boat: 8 chaloupe
bond: 5 rente
boxing: 6 savate
boy: 6 garcon
brandy: 8 armagnac
brewery: 9 brasserie
brush: 6 brosse
butcher shop: 11 charcuterie
cafe: 9 estaminet
cape: 5 talma
capital: 5 Paris
card game: 6 ecarte 7 baccara 8 baccarat
cardinal: 7 Mazarin 9 Richelieu
care: 4 soin
cathedral city: 5 Reims, Rouen 6 Nantes, Rheims
champagne: Ay
chanteuse: 4 Piaf
chaperon: 11 gouvernante
cheese: 4 Brie 9 Roquefort
chemist: 5 Curie 7 Pasteur
chestnut: 6 marone, maroon
citizen: 7 citoyen
city: Ay; Aix, Pau 4 Caen, Metz, Nice, Riom, Sens, Vimy 5 Aries, Arles, Arras, Brest, Dijon, Harve, Lille, Lisle, Lyons, Nance, Nancy, Nerac, Nesle, Nimes, Paris, Reims, Rouen, Sedan Seine, Tours, Tulle, Vichy 6 Amiens, Angers, Calais, Lemans, Nantes, Pantin, Perret, Rennes, Rheims, Senlis, Sevres, Tarare, Toulon 7 Bareges, Ferrand, Limoges, Orleans, Roubaix, Valence 8 Bordeaux, Clermont, Mulhouse, Rochelle, Toulouse 9 Levallois, Marseille, Tourcoing 10 Saint-Denis, Strasbourg, Strassburg 11 Montpellier 12 Saint-Etienne
cleric: 4 abbe
cloth: ras 5 toile 8 blancard
cloud: nue
coffee house: 9 estaminet
coin: ecu, sol, sou 4 gros 5 agnel, blanc, blank, franc, obole, livre 6 denier, dizain, teston 7 centime, dizaine, testoon 8 cavalier, Louis d'or, Napoleon
commune: Pau 4 Auby, Bron, Dole, Laon, Loos, Orly, Reze, Vimy 5 Ancre, Rodez, Vichy 6 Pessac, Sanvic, Stains, Tarare
composer: 4 Lalo 5 Bizet, Ravel, Thome 6 Gounod, Halevy 7 Debussy
comrade: ami
concrete: 5 beton
conjunction: et
cordial: 8 anisette
cotton: 7 jasmine
couturier: 4 Dior
cowardly: 5 lache
cowboy: 6 baille 7 gardian
creamcake: 7 dariole
critic: 5 Taine
crown: ecu
curate: 4 abbe
custom: 9 Gallicism
daffodil: 10 polyanthus
daisy: 10 marguerite
dance: bal 5 gavot 6 branle, canary, cancan 7 bourree, boutade
dash: 4 élan
daughter: 5 fille
dead: 4 mort
dean: 5 doyen
dear: 4 cher
delicatessen: 11 charcuterie
department: Ain, Lot, Var 4 Aube, Aude, Cher, Eure, Gard, Gers, Jura, Nord, Oise, Orne, Tarn 5 Aisne, Corse, Doubs, Drome, Indre, Isere, Loire, Marne, Meuse, Rhone, Seine, Somme, Yonne 6 Allier, Ariege, Cantal, Creuse, Landes, Loiret, Lozere, Manche, Nievre, Sarthe, Savoie, Vendee, Vienne, Vosges 7 Ardeche, Aveyron, Correze, Dordgne, Gironde, Herault, Mayenne, Meurthe, Moselle 8 Ardennes, Calvados, Charente, Morbihan, Vaucluse 9 Finistere

designer: 4 Dior, Gres 5 Patou 6 Chanel 8 Givenchy 9 Courreges, St. Laurent 10 Balenciaga
devil: 6 diable
diplomat: 5 Segur, Senet 7 Ronsard
directory: 10 directoire
division: 6 canton 7 commune 10 department 14 arrondissement
division, ancient: 5 Arles 6 Arelas 7 Arelate 9 Aquitaine
doorkeeper: 9 concierge
dramatist: 5 Piron 6 Halevy, Racine, Sardou 7 Moliere
dressmaker: 9 couturier 10 couturiere
duke: duc
dungeon: 6 cachot
dynasty: 5 Capet 6 Valois
ecclesiastic: 4 abbe
egg: 4 oeuf
empress: 7 Eugenie
essayist: 4 Gide
evening: 4 soir
exclamation: 4 hein
F.B.I.: 15 Surete Nationale
farmhouse: mas
father: 4 pere
finally: 5 enfin
friar: 5 frere
friend: ami
gala: 4 fete
game: jeu 4 jeux(pl.)
god: 4 dieu
good: bon
goodbye: 5 adieu
green: 4 vert
hairdresser: 7 friseur
hat: 5 beret 7 chapeau 8 chapeaux
health: 5 sante
heaven: 4 ciel
here: ici
high: 5 haute
horse stable: 6 ecurie
husband: 4 mari
income: 5 rente
inn: 5 hotel 7 auberge
island: ile 4 Elba
judgment: 5 arret
king: roi 5 Louis, Capet
knife: 7 couteau
lace: 10 colberteen colbertine 12 Valenciennes
lake: 6 Annecy 7 Bourget
language: 7 Catalan 9 Provencal
laugh: ris 4 rire
laundry: 13 blanchisserie
leather: 4 cuir
lenten season: 6 Careme
liqueur: 5 creme 8 anisette 9 Cointreau
lord: 8 seigneur
lover: 5 amant
lyric: 6 rondel 7 descort, rondeau
magistrate: 7 echevin
maidservant: 5 bonne 7 lisette
marshal: Ney 4 Foch, Saxe 5 Murat 6 Petain
mask: 5 loups
mathematician: 5 Borel
me: moi
measure: pot 4 aune, line, mile, mine, muid, pied, sack, velt 5 arpen, carat, lieue, ligne, minot, perch, pinte, point, pouce, toise, velte 6 arpent, hemine, league, perche, quarte, setier 7 chopine, heminee, poisson, septier 8 boisseau, quartaut, roquille 9 decillion, quarteron 12 tonneau de mer
milk: 4 lait
money: See ***coin*** above
mountain: 4 Alps, Jura 6 Vosges 8 Auvergne, Cevennes, Cote d'Or, Pyrenees 9 Mont Blanc, Puy de Dome, Vignemale 10 Puy de Sancy
museum: 5 Musee
nail: 4 clou
name: nom
national anthem: 12 Marseillaise
national flower: 4 lily
no: non
noon: 4 midi
nose: nez
nothing: 4 rien
novelist: 4 Gide, Hugo, Loti, Zola 5 Camus, Dumas, Ohnet, Sagan, Verne 6 Halevy, Proust 7 Merimee 8 Flaubert
nursemaid: 5 bonne
of: de
officer: 7 prefect
old money: 6 besant
one: une
opera: 5 Faust, Manon 6 Carmen, Mignon
painter: 4 Dore 5 Corot, Degas, Manet, Monet 6 Cormon, Legros, Renoir, Vernet 7 Chardin, Deveria, Lorrain, Poussin, Watteau 8 Steinlen 9 Deschamps
palace: 6 elysee
pancake: 5 crepe
parish priest: 4 cure
Parliament chamber: 5 senat
party: bal
pastry shop: 10 patisserie
patron saint: 5 Denis, Denys 6 Martin
peer: duc 8 seigneur
philosopher: 4 Caro 5 Camus 6 Pascal, Sartre 8 Rousseau 9 Descartes
physicist: 5 Arago, Binet 6 Ampere
pocket: 5 poche
poem: dit, lai 7 rondeau
poet: 4 Labe 6 Racine 7 Rimbaud, Rostand 9 Deschamps, Desportes

police: 6 Surete 8 gendarme
porcelain: 7 Limoges
port: 4 Caen
preposition: de
president's residence: 6 elysee
pretty: 4 joli 5 jolie
priest: 4 abbe, cure, pere
pronoun: tu; moi 4 elle 6 tienne
psychologist: 5 Binet
pupil: 5 eleve
queen: 5 reine
rabbit: 5 lapin
race course: 7 Auteuil
railroad: 10 tortillard
railroad station: 4 gare
read: 4 lire
rear: 7 arrière
region: 6 Alsace
Republic calendar: 6 Nivose 7 Floreal, Ventose 8 Brumaire, Fervidor, Frimaire, Germinal, Messidor, Pluviose, Prairial 9 Fructidor, Thermidor 11 Vendemiaire
resort: Pau 4 Nice 5 Vichy 6 Cannes, Menton 7 Riviera
rest: 5 repos
restaurant: 6 bistro
Revolutionary hero: 6 Danton
Revolutionary leader: 5 Marat
Revolutionary radical: 7 Jacobin
river: Ain, Lot, Lys 4 Aire, Aude, Cher, Eure, Gard, Gers, Loir, Oise, Orne, Saar, Tarn, Yser 5 Adour, Aisne, Drome, Indre, Isere, Loire, Maine, Marne, Meuse, Rance, Rhone, Saone, Sarre, Seine, Seyre, Somme, Veste, Yonne 6 Allier, Ariege, Escaut, Loiret, Nievre, Sambre, Scarpe, Vienne 7 Ardeche, Durance, Garonne, Gironde, Moselle, Scheldt 8 Charente, Dordogne, Nantaise
roast: 4 roti 5 rotir
room: 5 salle
royal family: 5 Capet 6 Valois
saint: 5 Denis, Denys 6 Martin
savant: 7 Diderot
school: 5 ecole, lycee 8 Barbison, Barbizon
scientist: 5 Curie 7 Pasteur
sculptor: 5 Barye, Rodin 9 Bartholdi
sea: mer
seaport: 4 Caen 5 Brest, Havre 6 Calais, Toulon 8 Bordeaux 9 Dunkerque
shelter: 4 abri
shield: ecu 5 targe
shoe: 9 chaussure
shopgirl: 9 midinette
sister: 5 soeur
slang: 5 argot
soldier: 5 assis, poilu 6 Zouave 8 chasseur
son: 4 fils
song: 5 caira 6 aubade 7 Madelon, virelai, virelay
soul: ame
south: sud 4 Midi
spirit: ame 4 elan 6 esprit
stable: 6 ecurie
star: 6 etoile
state: 4 etat
stock exchange: 6 bourse
store: 8 boutique
story: 5 conte
street: rue
summer: ete
symbol: 4 lily 10 Fleur-de-lis
the: la, le; les(pl.)
theater: 5 odeon
then: 5 alors
ticket window: 7 guichet
title: duc 5 comte
tobacco: 5 tabac
town: 4 Agen, Aire, Caen, Sens, Sete 5 Douai, Ernee, Laval, Nerac, Ornes 6 Longwy, Sarlat, Tarbes, Troyes, Verdun 7 Castres 8 Le Perche, Rochelle
true: 4 vrai
Verdun battle: 4 Vaux
verse: 4 vers
verse form: lai 4 alba 6 rondel 7 ballade, virelay
very: 4 tres
vessel: 7 navette
vinegar: 8 vinaigre
vineyard: cru
waiter: 7 garcon
wall: mur
water: eau 4 eaux(pl.)
weight: 4 gros, marc, once 5 carat, livre, pound, tonne, uckia 7 tonneau 8 esterlin 9 esterling
who: qui
wicket: 7 guichet
wine: vin 4 Bois 8 sauterne 10 Roussillon
wine district: 5 Medoc 8 Burgundy 9 Champagne
wine shop: 6 bistro
woman: 5 femme
world: 5 monde
you: tu 4 vous
Franciscan: 8 Minorite, Capuchin 9 Cordelier
nun: 5 Clare
franchise: soc 5 grant 6 patent 7 license 8 freelage, suffrage 9 privilege
old English: soc 4 soke
francolin: 4 bird 5 titar 9 partridge
frangible: 7 brittle, fragile 9 breakable
frank: 4 free, open, rank 5 bluff, lusty, naive, plain 6 candid, direct, honest 7 artless, genuine, liberal, profuse, sincere 8 carefree, cavalier, generous, vigorous 9 ingen-

uous, luxuriant, outspoken 10 licentious, unreserved 15 straightforward, unsophisticated
frankincense: 8 olibanum
Frankish hero: 6 Roland
Franklin's nickname: 11 Poor Richard
frankly: 6 freely, openly 7 plainly 8 candidly 9 artlessly, liberally, sincerely, willingly 10 forthright 11 ingenuously 12 unreservedly 13 undisguisedly
frankness: 6 candor 7 freedom 8 openness 9 telltruth, unreserve
frankpledge: 6 borrow
Franks: 7 Salians
hero: 6 Roland
king: 5 Pepin 6 Clovis
law of: 5 Salic
peasant: 4 liti(pl.) 5 litus
vassal: 4 leud
frantic: mad 5 rabid 6 insane 7 furious, lunatic, violent 8 deranged, feverish, frenetic, frenzied 9 delirious, desperate, phrenetic 10 distracted, distraught
frap: 4 beat 5 brace 6 strike 7 tighten 10 strengthen
frappe: ice 4 iced 5 chill 6 cooled, freeze, frozen 9 milkshake
frat: 11 brotherhood
fratch: 7 dispute, quarrel, wrangle
frater: 7 brother, comrade
fraternal: 9 brotherly
fraternity: 4 club 8 sorority 10 sisterhood 11 brotherhood
fraternize: 6 cotton 9 affiliate, associate, forgather 10 foregather
fraud: 4 dole, fake, gaff, gaud, gull, jape, ruse, sham, wile 5 cheat, craft, faker, guile, hocus, quack, trick 6 brogue, deceit, humbug 7 defraud, knavery, roguery, swindle 8 artifice, impostor, subtlety, trickery, trumpery 9 collusion, deception, imposture, stratagem 10 imposition 11 fraudulency 13 circumvention
fraudulent: 4 fake, wily 5 snide 6 crafty, quacky 7 abusive, crooked, cunning 8 cheating, covinous, guileful, spurious 9 deceitful, deceiving, deceptive, designing, dishonest, horsefair, insidious, underhand 10 fallacious, misleading 11 clandestine, counterfeit, treacherous
fraught: 4 fill, lade, load 5 cargo, equip, laden 6 burden, supply 7 freight 9 freighted, transport
fraxinus: ash 4 tree
fray: 4 feud, fret, riot 5 alarm, broil, broom, dread, feaze, fight, melee, panic, ravel 6 affray, assail, attack, battle, bustle, combat, fraise, fridge, fright, inroad, terror, tumult 7 contest, frazzle, ruction, terrify 8 disperse, frighten 9 commotion, dissipate 12 apprehension
frayed: 4 worn 7 raveled 10 threadbare
freak: 4 bold, flam, lune, mood, whim 5 braid, fancy, fleck, humor, prank, sport 6 frolic, greedy, humour, megrim, streak, vagary, whimsy 7 caprice, checker, crochet, monster, whimsey 8 capricci(pl.), flimflam 9 capriccio, variegate 11 monstrosity 12 whimsicality
freakish: odd 6 screwy 7 curious, flighty 9 fantastic, whimsical 10 capricious
fream: 4 roar
freath: 4 foam 5 froth 6 lather
freck, frack: 4 bold, hale 5 eager, lusty, ready, stout 6 dapple, strong 7 checker, forward 8 desirous 9 diversify
freckle: 4 spot 7 ephelis, frecken, lentigo
remover: 6 adarce
Frederick I's nickname: 10 Barbarossa
Frederick the Great: 6 Alaric
free: lax, rid 4 liss, open, quit, void 5 broad, clear, enode, frank, lisse, loose, ready, siker, slake, spare, untie 6 acquit, adjust, beyond, degage, devoid, exempt, gratis, immune, lavish, loosen, remove, rescue, sicker, unbind 7 absolve, deliver, forward, grivois, inexact, leisure, liberal, manumit, outside, release, relieve, unbound, willing 8 abundant, detached, dispatch, distinct, expedite, familiar, floating, generous, grivoise, indigent, innocent, liberate, overfree, separate, unfasten, unhamper 9 discharge, disengage, exculpate, exonerate, expansive, extricate, foot-loose, guiltless, ingenuous, outspoken, separated, unbridled, unchecked, unimpeded, unleashed 10 autonomous, emancipate, gratuitous, immoderate, licentious, openhanded, unattached, uncombined, unconfined, unfettered, unimpaired, unreserved 11 disencumber, disentangle, independent, magnanimous, spontaneous, untrammeled 12 uncontrolled, unencumbered, unrestrained, unrestricted 13 communicative, unconstrained
from bacteria: 7 aseptic, sterile
from blame: 5 clear 6 acquit 7 absolve, relieve 9 exonerate
from bondage: 7 manumit 10 emancipate 11 affranchise
from dirt: 7 apinoid
from discount: net
from moisture: dry 9 dehydrate
from restraint: 5 untie
from suspicion: 5 clear, purge 6 acquit 7 absolve 9 exculpate, exonerate

free-for-all: 4 race 5 fight, melee 6 barney 11 competition

free of charge: 8 buckshee

free time: 4 rest 6 recess 7 leisure

freebooter: 5 rider 6 pirate 7 cateran, corsair 8 pillager 9 buccaneer, plunderer 10 filibuster

freed: 8 absolute 13 disencumbered

freedom: 4 ease 7 abandon, content, leisure, liberty, license, release 8 facility, freelage, immunity, latitude, openness 9 exemption, frankness, readiness 10 generosity, liberality, liberation 11 manumission, willingness 12 emancipation, independence 13 outspokenness 14 unreservedness
from activity: 4 rest 6 recess 7 respite
from fraud: 7 honesty 9 bonafides
from pain: 6 aponia
from strife: 5 peace
of access: 6 entree

freehold: 4 alod 5 allod 6 estate, tenure 7 alodium 8 allodium

freeholder: 6 yeoman

freeing: 8 acquital 11 manumission

freely: 4 lief 5 noble, nobly 6 gratis 7 frankly, largely, readily 8 heartily 9 beautiful, bounteous, bountiful, copiously, excellent, liberally, voluntary, willingly 10 abundantly, generously 11 beautifully, bounteously, bountifully, excellently, plenteously, plentifully, voluntarily 12 munificently 13 spontaneously 14 unobstructedly 15 unconditionally

freeman: 4 aire 5 ceorl, churl, thane, thegn 6 yeoman 7 burgess, burgher, citizen

Freestone State: 11 Connecticut

freethinker: 7 infidel, skeptic 8 agnostic 10 espritfort, unbeliever

freeze: ice 4 rime 5 chill 6 frappe, harden 7 chilled, congeal, impound 11 conglaciate, refrigerate

freezer: 4 icer

freezing: 4 cold 6 frigid, frosty

freight: 4 load 5 cargo, laden 6 lading 7 fraught 9 transport 10 freightage

freightage: 5 cargo 6 lading 7 freight

freighted: 5 laden 7 fraught

fremd: 5 alien 7 foreign, strange

French: See **France**

French-Belgian river: Lys 4 Yser

Frenchman: 4 Gaul 6 Picard 8 Parisian

frenetic, phrenetic: mad 4 wild 5 crazy, fresh 6 insane, madman 7 fanatic, frantic, madness, violent, zealous 9 delirious 10 distracted, ornamental, passionate 12 absent-minded

frenzied: 4 amok, mang 5 amoke, amuck, rabid 6 ramage 7 berserk, frantic, furious 8 frenetic, furibund, maddened 9 delirious

frenzy: mad 4 amok, fury, rage 5 amoke, amuck, furor, mania 7 frantic, madness, oestrus 8 delirium, insanity, maniacal 9 amazement 11 distraction

frequency: 5 crowd 6 throng 7 crebity 9 community, concourse 11 familiarity
unit: 7 fresnel

frequent: 5 haunt, howff, often, usual 6 affect, common, effect, hourly, sundry 7 current, enhaunt, prevail 8 familiar, habitual 9 assiduous, crebrouse, habituate 10 persistent

frequented places: 5 dives 6 haunts 7 resorts

frequenter: 7 habitue

frequently: oft 5 often 6 hourly 8 ofttimes 10 repeatedly

fresco: 5 mural, shade 8 coolness

frese: 4 bend, furl 5 slack 6 unbend 7 untwine

fresh: new 4 cool, good, pure, racy 5 brisk, green, ruddy, saucy, sound, sweet, vivid 6 breezy, bright, caller, florid, lively, recent, strong, unused 7 unfaded, untired, untried 9 obtrusive, unspoiled 10 additional, meddlesome, refreshing, unimpaired 12 invigorating, presumptuous
and lively: 4 racy

freshen: 5 renew 6 breeze, revive 7 refresh, sweeten

freshet: 5 spate 9 streamlet 10 inundation

freshly: 5 again

freshman: 5 bejan, frosh, plebe 6 bejant, novice

freshness: 4 verd 8 verdancy 9 fraicheur
lose: dry 4 fade, wilt 6 wither

fret: nag, rub, vex 4 care, fray, gall, gnaw, pout, rage, stew 5 chafe, grate, pique, tease, worry 6 abrade, devour, harass, murmur, nettle, plague, rankle, ripple, ruffle, strait 7 agitate, consume, disturb, grizzle, roughen 8 diminish, disquiet, irritate, vexation

fretful: 5 angry, cross 6 repine, sullen 7 carking, frecket, gnawing, peevish, pettish 8 captious, corroded, fretsome, petulant, restless 9 corrosive, impatient, irascible, irritable, plaintive, querulous 10 ill-humored, ill-natured

Freudian term: id; ego

Frey: *sister:* 5 Freya 6 Freyja
wife: 4 Gerd

Freya's husband: 4 Oder

friable: 5 crimp, crisp, crump, loamy, mealy
clay: 4 bole

friar: fra 4 fish, monk 5 frere 6 Bhikku, fraile, frater 7 Bhikshu, brother 8 monas-

tic 9 Carmelite 10 Franciscan 11 Augustinian
black: 9 Dominican
mendicant: 7 Servite
friary: 8 cloister 9 monastery 11 brotherhood
fribble: 4 fool 6 falter, totter, trifle 7 stammer 8 trifling 9 frivolity, frivolous
fricassee: 6 potpie 10 blanquette 11 blanc-manger
friction: rub 5 chafe 9 attrition 10 dissension
air: 7 windage
fridge: rub 4 fray 5 chafe 6 fidget 8 irritate
fried: 4 frit 7 sauteed
fried cake: 7 cruller 8 doughnut
friend: ami(F.), amy, eme, pal 4 ally, amie(F.), chum, kith 5 amigo(Sp.), amiga(Sp.), crony 6 bonami(F.), cummer, gimmer, kimmer 7 comrade, gremial, kinsman 8 cockmate, compadre, paramour, relative 9 associate, attendant, bonne amie(F.), broadbrim, companion, confidant 10 confidante 12 acquaintance
Friend: 6 Quaker
church founder: 9 George Fox
friendless: 7 forlorn
friendliness: 5 amity 8 affinity, amicable, goodwill 10 fellowship 13 companionship
friendly: sib 4 cosh, good, kind 5 chief, howdy 6 blithe, genial, homely, howdie 7 affable, amiable, amicous, cordial 8 amicable, homelike, intimate, sociable 9 favorable 10 favourable, hospitable 11 warmhearted
Friendly island: 5 Tonga
friendship: 5 amity 6 amitie 8 relation 9 affection 10 attachment
Friendship author: 6 Cicero
frier: 6 pullet
frieze: 4 kelt(Sc.) 5 adorn, chase 8 trimming 9 embroider 10 decoration
band: 6 taenia
frigate (see also **boat, ship**): 5 zabra(Sp.)
frigate bird: iwa
Frigg's son: 5 Baldr 6 Balder
fright: awe, cow 4 fear, fray, funk, gast 5 alarm, gliff, panic, scare, shock 6 affray, dismay, horror, schrik, terror 7 startle 13 consternation
frighten: awe, cow 4 fray, funk, hare, haze, shoo 5 afear, alarm, appal, gliff, hazen, scare 6 affray, appall, ascare, boggle 7 frecken, startle, terrify 8 affright 10 intimidate
frightened: 4 awed, eery, gast 5 eerie, timid 6 afraid 8 skittish
frightful: 4 grim 5 awful, ferly 6 horrid, ugsome 7 affreux, fearful, gashful, ghastly, hideous 8 alarming, dreadful, fearsome, horrible, horrific, shocking, terrible, terrific 10 horrendous, tremendous
frightfulness: 13 atrociousness 15 schrecklichkeit(Ger.)
frigid: icy 4 cold 5 acold, bleak 6 arctic, frosty 8 freezing
frill: 4 purl 5 jabot, ruche 6 ruffle 7 flounce 8 furbelow 9 balayeuse 11 chitterling
fringe: 4 loma 6 border, edging, margin 8 ciliella, trimming
fringed: 9 laciniate 10 frimbriate
frisk: 4 leap, skip, whid 5 brisk, caper, dance, flisk 6 curvet, frisco, frolic, gambol, lively, search 7 disport, friscal 8 caracole 10 frolicsome
frisky: gay 4 pert 6 lively 7 playful 8 frisking, sportive 10 frolicsome
frisson: 5 chill 6 quiver, shiver, thrill 7 shudder
frith: 4 help 5 firth, hedge 6 hurdle, wattle 7 coppice, estuary, freedom 8 liberate, security 9 brushwood, copsewood, underwood 10 protection
fritter: 5 shred, spend, waste 6 bangle 7 pancake, scatter 8 fragment
frivol: 6 trifle 9 frivolous
frivolity: 6 levity 7 fribble, inanity 8 nonsense 9 lightness
frivolous: gay 5 giddy, inane, petty 6 frivol, futile 7 fatuous, fribble, shallow, trivial 8 gossamer 9 childlike, worthless 11 lightheaded 14 featherbrained
frizzed: 5 crepe 6 crispy
fro: 4 away, back, from 5 hence, since 8 backward
frock (see also **dress**): jam 4 gown, slip, wrap 5 tunic 6 cleric, jersey, mantle 7 workman 9 gaberdine
frog: 5 frosh, frosk, jakie 6 peeper 7 paddock, quilkin 8 ferreiro 9 amphibian
order of: see *zoological order* below.
pert. to 6 ranine
rearing place: 7 ranaria(pl.) 8 ranarium
zoological order: 5 anura 6 anoura 9 salientia
frogman: 5 diver 7 swimmer
gear: 5 scuba
frohlich: gay 5 happy 6 joyous
froise: 7 pancake
frolic: bum, gay 4 blow, game, gell, jink, lark, orgy, play, ramp, romp 5 caper, freak, frisk, merry, prank, randy, sport, spree 6 curvet, gambol, plisky, prance, rollix, shindy, splore 7 disport, gammock, pliskie, scamper, stashie, wassail 8 carousal 9 gilravage 10 masquerade
frolicsome: gay 4 roid 5 gilpy 6 frisky, gilpey 7 jocular, waggish 8 espiegle, friskful, gamesome, sportive

from: fro
beginning to end: 4 over 7 through
head to foot: 7 capapie
here: 5 hence
that time: 6 thence
the egg: 5 ab ovo
the time that: 5 since
this time: 5 hence

front: bow, van 4 brow, face, fore, head, prow 5 afore 6 before, facade, facing, oppose, sector 7 forward, further, obverse 8 forehead, foremost, forepart 9 forefront 10 appearance, effrontery 11 countenance
toward the: 8 anterior

frontal: 6 sindon 7 metopic

frontier: 4 face 5 bound, march 6 border, oppose 7 barrier, defense 8 boundary

frontiersman: 4 Cody 5 Boone 6 Carson 7 settler

fronton: 7 jai-alai

frore: 4 cold 6 frosty, frozen

frost: ice, nip 4 foam, hoar, rime 7 failure

frosted: 4 iced 5 glace 6 frozen

frostfish: 5 smelt 6 tomcod 9 whitefish

frosting: ice, mat 5 icing

frosty: icy 4 cold, rimy 5 chill, frore, gelid, glary 6 frigid, froren 8 chilling, freezing

froth: fob 4 barm, foam, scum, suds 5 spume 6 freath, lather

frow: 4 frau, froe, wife 5 vrouw, woman

froward: 4 away 5 cross 7 adverse, awkward, peevish, wayward 8 contrary, perverse, petulant, untoward 9 obstinate 10 refractory, unyielding 11 disobedient, unfavorable 12 ungovernable

frown: 4 lour 5 gloom, glout, lower, scowl 6 glower, glunch 7 frounce

frowst, froust: 4 loll 5 stale 6 lounge, stuffy 10 atmosphere

frowsy, frowzy: 5 musty 6 blowzy 7 raffish, unkempt 8 slovenly 10 disordered

frozen: 4 hard 5 fixed, frore, gelid, glary 6 chilly, frappe, froren 7 chilled, frosted 8 hardened, immobile 9 congealed 10 unyielding 11 coldhearted 12 refrigerated 13 unsympathetic

fructify: 9 fertilize 10 impregnate

frugal: 4 mild 5 chary, roman, spare 6 saving 7 careful, sparing, thrifty 9 economize, provident 10 economical, unwasteful 12 parsimonious

frugality: 6 thrift 7 economy 9 chariness

fruit: fig 4 date, lime, pear, plum, pome 5 apple, berry, drupe, grape, lemon, melon, olive, peach 6 cherry, orange, result 7 apricot, azarole, product 8 dewberry 9 blueberry, nectarine, offspring, pineapple, tangerine 10 production
aggregate: 7 etaerio
apple-like: 4 pome 6 quince
astringent: 4 sloe
baccate: 5 berry
beverage: ade 4 wine
blackthorn: 4 sloe
buttercup: 5 akene 6 achene 7 achenia(pl.) 8 achenium
citrus: 4 lime 5 grape, lemon 6 orange 7 tangelo 9 tangerine
collective: 7 syncarp 10 syncarpium
cooked in syrup: 7 compote
decay: 4 blet
desert region: 5 terfa 6 terfez
dish: 7 compote
dried: 5 prune 6 orejon
dry: 5 regma 6 achene, samara
early maturing: 8 rareripe
elm tree: 6 samara
fleshy: 4 pear, plum, pome 5 berry, drupe, melon 6 tomato
fleshy part: 9 sarcocarp
goddess of: 6 Pomona
gourd family: 4 pepo
horseradish tree: ben
husk: 5 lemma
hybird: 7 tangelo
imperfect: 6 nubbin
juicy: 4 lime, pear, plum 5 grape, lemon, peach 6 orange 7 apricot 9 pineapple 10 grapefruit
layer: 7 epicarp
lime & lemon: 6 citron
many-seeded: 11 pomegranate
maple: 6 samara
mild acid: 5 guava
multiple: 4 cone
of rose: 11 cynorrhodon
of strawberry: 7 etaerio
oily: 5 olive
one-seeded: 5 akene 6 achene, samara 7 achenis(pl.) 8 achenium
palm tree: 4 date
peach-like: 7 apricot 9 nectarine
pear-shaped: fig 7 avocado
plum-like: 4 sloe
pome: 4 pear 5 apple 7 azarole
preserving: 6 medlar
pulp: pap
pulpy: uva 4 pome 5 drupe, grape, berry
red: 4 plum 5 apple 6 cherry 9 raspberry 10 strawberry
refuse: 4 marc
rind: 7 epicarp
rose-bush: hip
science of: 8 pomology
seed: pip, pit
spore: 6 aecium
stalk: 8 peduncle

stone: 4 paip, plum 5 drupe, peach, prune 6 cherry 7 apricot 9 nectarine
strawberry-family: 7 etaerio
tropical: fig 4 date 5 guava, gourd, mango 6 banana, papaya, pawpaw 9 sapodilla
vine: 5 grape
winged: 6 samara
withered: 6 nubbin
yellowish: 5 papaw 6 quince
fruit basket: 6 pottel, pottle
fruit bats: 8 pteropid 10 pteropidae
fruit dealer: 9 frontsman, fruiterer 11 greengrocer
fruit of Jove: 9 persimmon
fruit of paradise: 6 pomelo 10 grapefruit
fruit stone: pit 4 paip 6 pyrene 7 putamen
fruitful: fat 6 fecund 7 fertile 8 abundant, prolific 9 feracious, plenteous, plentiful, procreant 10 productive
fruitgrower: 8 fruitist 10 orchardist 11 palmologist 14 horticulturist
fruition: 8 pleasure 9 enjoyment 11 realization
fruitless: dry 4 geld, vain 5 addle, blank 6 barren 7 sterile, useless 8 abortive 10 profitless 11 ineffectual 12 unprofitable, unsuccessful
frump: vex 4 mock, snub, sulk 5 dowdy, flout 6 gossip 7 provoke 8 irritate
frush: din, rub 4 rush 5 break, carve, crush, onset 6 batter, debris, flabby, polish 7 brittle, scratch 9 fragments
frustrate: 4 balk, bilk, dash, foil, null, vain, void 5 baulk, blank, block, check, cross, crush, elude 6 baffle, blight, defeat, delude, outwit, scotch, thwart 7 deceive, nullify, prevent, useless 8 confound, infringe, nugatory 9 checkmate, discomfit 10 circumvent, counteract, disappoint, disconcert, neutralize 11 countermand, ineffectual 12 unprofitable
frustration: 4 foil 6 fiasco 12 discomfiture 15 disillusionment
fry: 4 sile 5 brook, roast, saute, young 9 offspring
frying pan: 6 spider 7 griddle, skillet
fubsy: 5 fubby, plump, short 6 chubby, stuffy
fuddle: 5 booze, tiple 6 muddle 7 fluster
fuddled: fap, ree 5 bosky, tipsy 7 muddled
fudge: 4 fake 5 candy, foist, hunch 6 devise, humbug 8 contrive, nonsense 9 interlope, makeshift 10 substitute 11 counterfeit
fuel: gas, oil 4 coal, coke, peat, wood 5 argal, argol, argul, stoke 6 acetol, elding, firing, petrol 7 pabulum 8 charcoal, gasoline, kerosene 9 petroleum 11 combustible
fuff: 4 puff 5 whiff 8 splutter
fuffy: 5 huffy, light, puffy
fugacious: 6 flying 8 fleeting, volatile 10 evanescent
fuggy: 6 smelly, stuffy
fugient: 7 fleeing 8 retiring
fugitive: 5 exile, fleme 6 emigré, exiled, outlaw 7 fleeing, refugee, roaming, runaway 8 banished, deserter, fleeting, runagate, unstable, vagabond, volatile 9 fugacious, strolling, transient, uncertain 10 evanescent
fugue: 4 fuga 9 ricercare
exponent: 4 Bach 6 Handel
Fukien river: Min
fulcrum: 4 bait, prop 5 thole 7 support
fulfill: 4 fill, full, meet 6 effect, finish, occupy 7 achieve, execute, perform, satisfy 8 complete 9 implement 10 accomplish, effectuate
fulfillment, fulfilment: 6 effect 9 execution 10 completion 11 performance, realization 14 accomplishment
fulgent: 6 bright 7 shining 8 dazzling 9 effulgent
full: bad 4 good 5 ample, round, sated, solid, total 6 entire, fulfil, honest 7 baptize, copious, destroy, diffuse, fulfill, fulsome, orotund, perform, plenary, replete, teeming, trample 8 adequate, bouffant, brimming, complete, resonant 9 bouffante, capacious, plentiful 10 consecrate, exhaustive 13 comprehensive
suffix: ose 5 itous, ulent
full-blooded: 6 florid 8 rubicund 12 thoroughbred
full force: 5 brunt
full-grown: 6 mature 9 developed
full of: *cracks:* 6 rimose
glands: 7 adenose
hollows: 8 lacunose
minute openings: 6 porous
sand: 7 arenose
sap or juice: 7 succous 9 succulent
thorns: 6 briary
twists: 5 kinky 7 winding
wrinkles: 6 rugose
fuller: 7 creaser
fuller's grass: 8 soapwort
fullness, fulness: 5 fulth 6 plenty 7 satiety 8 pleonasm 9 abundance, amplitude, plumpness, repletion 10 fleshiness, perfection 12 completeness
fully: 5 amply 6 wholly 7 clearly, largely, utterly 8 entirely, maturely 9 perfectly 10 abundantly, completely, distinctly 11 plenteously, plentifully
fulmar: 4 bird 5 nelly 7 malduck
fulminate: 7 explode, inveigh 8 detonate
fulsome: fat 4 foul, full 5 gross, plump, suave 6 coarse, wanton 7 copious, lustful, overfed 8 abundant, nauseous 9 offensive,

overgrown, repulsive, satiating, sickening 10 disgusting, indelicate, nauseating

fumble: paw 4 boot 5 abase, error 6 bobble, bungle, faffle, haffle, huddle, mumble

fume: 4 foam, odor, rage, rant, reek 5 ewder, fumet, smoke, storm, vapor 6 exhale 7 flatter, fumette 8 fumigate, outburst 10 exhalation

fumid: 5 smoky 8 vaporous

fun: gag, gig 4 game, gell, hoax, jest, joke, play 5 mirth, sport 6 gaiety, gayety 9 amusement, horseplay, merriment 10 pleasantry

function: act, run, use 4 duty, role, work 5 doing 6 action, office 7 calling, operate, service 8 activity, ceremony, occasion 9 festivity, gathering, operating, operation 10 occupation, profession, providence 11 performance 13 entertainment

social: tea 4 ball 5 party 6 soiree 9 reception

trigonometrical: 4 sine 6 cosine, secant 7 tangent

fund: 4 fond, pool 5 basis, stock, store 6 bottom, ground, supply 7 deposit, reserve 10 foundation, groundwork 12 accumulation

fundamental: 5 basal, basic, vital 7 basilar, organic, primary, radical 8 original, rudiment 9 elemental, essential, important, principle 10 elementary

funds: 4 caja, cash 5 money 9 resources

funebre: sad 7 funeral 8 funereal

funeral: 6 burial, dismal, exequy 7 cortege, funebre 8 exequial, funereal 9 forthfare, obsequies 10 sepulchral

bell: 5 knell

oration: 5 eloge 6 eulogy 8 encomium 9 panegyric

pile: 4 pyre

song: 5 dirge, elegy, elogy, nenia 6 elegie 7 elogium, epicede 8 threnody 9 epicedium

structure: 10 catafalque

funereal: 5 feral 6 dismal, solemn 7 funebre, funeral 8 mournful 9 funebrial, funebrous 10 funebrious

funest: sad 4 dire 5 fatal 7 doleful

fungus: 4 bunt, cepe, mold, rust, smut 5 ergot, fungo, morel, moril, uredo, yeast 6 agaric, fungal, mildew, oidium, telium 7 agarics, amanita, blewits, fungoid, fungous, geaster, truffle 8 amanitin, mushroom, puffball 9 stinkhorn, toadstool 10 fungaceous

edible: 4 cepe 5 morel 7 truffle 8 mushroom

parasitic: 5 ergot

fungus-like: 6 agaric

funk: 4 kick, odor, rage 5 shirk, spark 6 coward, flinch, fright, recoil, shrink 8 frighten 9 cowardice, touchwood

funnel: 6 hopper

funny: odd 5 comic, droll, queer 7 comical, jocular, risible, strange 8 humorous 9 laughable, ludicrous

funnyman: wit 8 comedian

fur: 4 flix, pell, pelt 5 budge, stole 6 furrow, pelage

coat: 6 pelage

collection of: 5 pelts 6 peltry

kind of: fox 4 mink, paen, scut, seal, vair, woom 5 budge, civit, coney, fitch, lapin, otter, sable 6 ermine, galyac, galyak, marten, martin, moutin, nutria 7 calabar, calaber, caracul, karakul, miniver, platina, sealine 8 karakule, ragondin 9 silver fox

piece: 5 stole

refuse: 4 kemp

fur-bearing animal: fox 4 mink, seal 5 genet, otter, sable 6 marten, martin

furbelow: 5 frill 6 ruffle 7 falbala, falbelo, flounce 8 trimming

furbish: fig, rub 4 fake, vamp 5 clean, scour 6 polish 7 burnish 8 renovate

Furies: 5 Dirae 7 Erinyes

individual: 6 Alecto, Erinys 7 Erinnys, Erinyes, Megaera 9 Tisiphone

furious: mad 5 angry, brain, irate, rabid 6 fierce, furied, insane, stormy 7 frantic, mankind, rushing, violent 8 frenzied, vehement, wrathful 9 impetuous, turbulent 10 boisterous, tumultuous, uproarious

furl: 4 fold, roll, wrap 5 frese 6 fardel, furdel, furdle

furlana: 5 dance, music

furlong: 5 stade 7 stadium 10 quarentene

furlough: 5 leave 6 permit 8 passport

furnace: 4 bosh, dome, kiln, oven 5 stove, tisar 6 calcar, cupola, heater 7 athanor, howells, rotator, smelter 8 bloomery, bruckner 9 scorifier 11 incinerator

part: 4 bosh, flue 5 grate

furner: 5 baker

furnish: arm 4 feed, give, lend 5 array, endow, equip, frame, indue 6 afford, graith, insure, render, supply 7 apparel, appoint, garnish, provide 8 minister, palisade 10 accomplish, administer

crew: man

with battlements: 9 crenelate

with meals: 5 board, cater

furnished: 5 boden, garni 8 equipped, provided, supplied 9 garnished

furnishing: 7 fitment 8 fixtures, muniment, ornament 9 adornment, apparatus, furniture 10 enrichment, habiliment

furniture: 6 graith, outfit 7 fitment, tallboy 8 equipage 9 equipment 10 decoration, encoignure, furnishing 13 embellishment

style: 6 Empire 8 Colonial, Sheraton 11 Chippendale, Hepplewhite, Renaissance
furor: 4 fury, rage 5 craze, mania 6 frenzy 7 madness
furrow: fur, rut 4 grip, plow, rout 5 chase, drain, drill, field, rigol, score, stria 6 groove, sulcus, trench 7 channel, crumple, windrow, wrinkle
furrowed: 6 rivose 7 sulcate, porcate 8 porcated 10 corrugated
furry: 5 hairy
furse: 4 whin 5 gorse
further: aid, and, yet 4 abet, also, fore, help, more 5 again, front, serve 6 afford, beyond, former 7 advance, earlier, forward, promote, remoter 8 moreover 9 advantage 10 accelerate, additional
furtherance: 6 assist 8 facility, progress 9 promotion 10 assistance 11 advancement
furthermore: and 7 besides 8 moreover
furthersome: 4 rash 7 helpful 11 venturesome 12 advantageous
furtive: sly 6 secret, sneaky 7 hangdog 8 mystical, sneaking, stealthy 10 creepmouse 11 clandestine
fury: ire 4 rage 5 anger, breth, furor, rigor, vixen, wrath 6 beldam, choler, frenzy 7 beldame, madness, oestrus 8 delirium, violence 9 furiosity, vehemence 10 fierceness, turbulence 11 indignation
fuse: 4 flux, frit, melt, weld 5 blend, smelt, unite 6 anneal, mingle, solder 7 liquefy 8 dissolve 10 amalgamate 11 incorporate
fusee: 5 flare, torch 6 signal
fusion: 4 flux 6 fusure, merger 8 alliance, blending 9 coalition 11 coalescence
fuss: ado, row, tew, vex 4 busk, fike, rout, spat, stir, todo 5 bearm, touse, whaup, worry 6 bother, bustle, caddle, fantad, fantod, fettle, fidget, fissle, fistle, fizzle, fraise, fuffle, fustle, pother, potter, tumult 7 dispute, friggle, fussock, quarrel, sputter, trouble 8 business 9 confusion 10 disconcert
fussy: 6 bustle, fidfad, spruce 7 fidgety, finical 8 overnice 10 fastidious, meticulous 14 overparticular
fustanella: 8 petticoat
fustian: 4 rant 5 tumid 7 bombast, pompous 8 claptrap, inflated 9 bombastic, worthless
fustigate: 4 beat, whip 6 strike
futile: 4 idle, vain 6 otiose 7 useless 8 hopeless, trifling 9 frivolous, worthless 11 ineffectual
futility: 11 uselessness 13 frivolousness
future: 5 later 6 coming 9 hereafter
fuzz: nap 4 down, lint 5 fluff 8 puffball
fyke: net
fylfot: 5 cross 6 emblem 8 swastika

G

Gaal's father: 4 Ebed
gab: lie, yap 4 talk 5 boast, mouth, prate, scoff 6 gossip 7 chatter, deceive, prattle
Gabael's son: 5 Aduel
gabardine: 5 cloth 6 fabric
gabbard, gabbart: 4 scow 5 barge 6 vessel 7 lighter
gabble: rai(Sc.), yap 4 cank, chat, talk 6 babble, cackle, gossip, habble, jabber, yabble 7 chatter, clatter, twaddle
gabbro: 4 rock 6 norite
gabelle: tax 4 duty 6 excise, impost
gaberdine: 4 coat, gown 5 frock, smock 6 mantle 7 garment 8 pinafore
gabi: 4 taro
gabirit: 4 mold 5 gauge, model
gable: 4 wall 6 dormer, pinion
gablock: See **gavelock**
Gabriel's instrument: 4 horn 7 trumpet
gaby: 4 fool 5 dunce 9 simpleton
gad: bar, rod 4 band, goad, roam, rope, rove, whip 5 climb, ingot, prowl, spear, spike, staff, stick, stray 6 billet, chisel, ramble, switch, wander 7 traipse 9 gallivant
Gad: *chieftain:* Ahi
descendant: Zia
father: 5 Jacob
mother: 6 Zilpah
son: Eri 5 Ezbon
tribe of: 6 Erites
gadfly: 4 pest 6 botfly 7 annoyer, oestrid, tabanid 8 busybody 9 breezefly
gadget: 4 tool 5 gibbe(Sc.) 6 device, doodad, jigger 9 doohickey 11 contrivance
Gadhelic: 4 Erse 6 Celtic, Gaelic
gadus: cod 4 fish
gadwall: 4 duck
gadzooks: 4 egad
Gaea: Ge 6 Tellus
consort: 6 Uranus
offspring: 5 Titan 6 Pontus, Titans, Uranus
parent: 5 Chaos
Gaelic (see also **Irish**): 4 Erse 8 Highland
clan: 4 Sept
hero: 6 Ossian
John: Ian
land distribution: 7 rundale
poem: 4 Duan
spirit: 5 kelpy 6 kelpie 7 banshee
warrior: 5 Dagda 6 Fenian
gaff: 4 hoax, hook, pick, spar, spur, talk 5 fraud, laugh, spear, trick 6 clamor, deceit, fleece, gamble, outcry 7 prating 8 raillery
gag: 4 gegg, hoax, joke 5 choke, heave, retch 6 muffle, muzzle 7 prevent, silence 8 obstruct, throttle 9 imposture 13 interpolation
gage (see also **gauge**): bet 4 pawn, risk 5 stake, wager 6 pledge 8 appraise, defiance, security 9 challenge
gain: buy, get, net, win 4 boot, earn, good, pelf, reap 5 clear, lucre, reach 6 attain, effect, income, obtain, profit, secure 7 achieve, acquire, advance, benefit, conquer, prevail, procure, realize 8 increase 9 accretion, advantage, increment 12 appreciation
ill-gotten: 4 pelf 5 graft, lucre 6 payola 9 extortion
gainly: 7 shapely 8 becoming, gainsome, graceful, suitable
gainsay: 4 deny 6 forbid, impugn, oppose, refute, resist 7 dispute 10 contradict, controvert
Gainsborough painting: 7 Blue Boy
gair: 4 keen 5 eager, piece 6 greedy, stingy 8 covetous 12 parsimonious
gait: bat, run, way 4 lope, pace, rack, step, trip, trot, volt, walk 5 amble, strut, tread 6 allure, canter, gallop 7 journey, shamble 8 distance
gaiter: 4 boot, spat 6 gaskin, puttee 7 cutikin(Sc.), legging 8 bootikin, gamashes 11 galligaskin
gala: gay 4 fete 5 merry 6 festal, fiesta 8 festival
galago: 5 lemur 6 monkey
Galahad: *father:* 8 Lancelot
mother: 6 Elaine
quest: 5 grail

Galapagos Islands resident: 8 tortoise
Galatea: *lover:* 4 Acis
suitor: 10 Polyphemus
galaxy: 6 nebula
gale: 4 blow, gust, wind 5 blast, storm 6 breeze, easter 7 declaim, tempest 8 outburst 9 hurricane, windstorm 11 northeaster, northwester, southeaster, southwester
galea: 6 helmet
Galen: 9 physician
Galician river: San 4 Styr
galilee: 5 porch 7 portico
Galilee: *ruler:* 5 Herod
town: 4 Cana, Nain 8 Nazareth, Tiberias 9 Capernaum
Galileo's birthplace: 4 Pisa
galimatias: 6 jargon 8 nonsense 9 gibberish
galipot, gallipot: sap 5 rosin 6 barras
gall: vex 4 bile, fell, flaw, fret 5 annoy, chafe, cheek, spite 6 abrade, harass, injure, poison, rancor 7 blemish 8 acerbity, cecidium, irritate, temerity 9 excoriate, impudence 10 bitterness, effrontery, exasperate
Gallagher's partner: 5 Shean
gallant: gay 4 beau, prow 5 blade, brave, bully, lover, noble, showy, swain 6 escort, heroic, polite, suitor 7 amatory, amorist, amorous, conduct, stately, younker 8 cavalier, cicisbeo(It.), galliard, handsome, polished, splendid 9 attentive, chamberer, chevalier, courteous 10 chivalrous, courageous 11 fashionable 12 high-spirited
gallantry: 7 bravery, courage 11 intrepidity
galled: mad, raw 4 sore 6 peeved 9 sensitive
galleon: 4 ship 6 carack, vessel 7 carrack
cargo: oro 4 gold
gallery: 5 alure, boyau(F.), porch, salon 6 arcade, dedans(F.), loggia, piazza 7 balcony, terrace, veranda 8 audience, brattice, cantoria, catacomb, corridor 9 promenade 10 ambulatory
galley: 4 aesc, tray 5 cuddy, foist 6 bireme, carvel, galiot, hearth 7 birling, birlinn, caravel, galliot, hexeris, kitchen, trireme, unireme 8 cookroom, crumster, galleass, hepteris, ramberge 9 caravelle 10 triaconter 13 tesseraconter
gallfly: 11 hymenoptera(pl.) 12 hymenopteron
galliard: 5 hardy 6 lively 7 gallant, valiant
Gallic: 6 French
gallimaufry: 4 hash 6 jumble, medley, ragout 7 mixture 10 hodgepodge
gallinae: 6 grouse, quails 7 rasores, turkeys 8 peafowls 9 curassows, pheasants
gallinule: hen 4 coot, fowl, rail
gallivant: gad 4 flit, roam 6 travel
galloon: 4 lace 8 trimming
gallop: run 4 gait, pelt 5 chase, speed 6 canter, career, course, hasten, pursue
galloping dominoes: 4 dice
gallows: 4 crap 5 bough 6 gibbet 7 potence
pert. to: 10 patibulary
galluses: 10 suspenders
gally: 5 worry 7 terrify 8 frighten
galoot: 6 fellow, marine, person 7 soldier 9 screwball
galore: 7 profuse 8 abundant 9 plentiful
galosh: 4 boot, clog, shoe 6 arctic, patten 8 overshoe
galvanize: 4 coat 6 excite 7 startle 9 stimulate
Galway islands: 4 Aran
galyak: fur, yak 6 cattle, hybrid
gam: leg 5 mouth, tooth, visit
gamb, gambe: leg 5 shank
gambado: 4 boot 5 antic, caper 6 spring 7 legging
gambit: 4 move 7 comment, opening 8 maneuver 9 launching
gamble: bet 4 dice, gaff, game, risk, spec 5 stake, wager 6 chance, hazard, plunge 9 speculate 11 uncertainty
gambler: 5 dicer, shill 6 carrow(Ir.), player 7 playman, plunger, sharper 8 blackleg, gamester 10 speculator
accomplice: 5 shill
gambling (see also **game:** *gambling*): *pert. to:* 8 aleatory
place: 4 Reno 6 casino
stake: pot 4 pool
gambol: hop 4 play 5 caper, frisk, prank 6 cavort, frolic
game: fun, jeu(F.) 4 lame, lark, plan, play, prey 5 brave, dodge, prank, sport, trick 6 course, frolic, gamble, gritty, plucky, quarry, racket, spunky 7 contest, foolery, pastime, project 8 enduring, resolute 9 amusement, diversion 10 courageous
ball: cat, tut 4 golf, polo, pool 5 fives, rugby 6 hockey, pelota, soccer, squash, tennis, tipcat 7 cricket, croquet 8 baseball, football, handball 9 billiards
board: 4 keno 5 bingo, chess, halma, lotto, salta 6 squail 7 pachisi 8 checkers, cribbage, parchesi, parchisi, scrabble 9 crokinole, parcheesi 10 backgammon
card: gin, hoc, loo, lus, nap, pam 4 bank, brag, faro, hock, jass, ruff, skat, slam, snap, solo, spin, vint 5 beast, chico, cinch, comet, crimp, decoy, gilet, gleek, monte, omber, ombre, pedro, pique, pitch, poker, rummy, stuss, trump, two-up, waist, whist 6 basset, birkie, boston, bridge, commit, ecarte, flinch, hearts, loadum, masset, piquet, rounce, sledge, smudge 7 bezique, canasta, cassino, cayenne, Chicago, cooncan, hundred, oldmaid, primero, reversi, sev-

en-up 8 baccarat(F.), commerce, conquian, contract, cribbage, handicap, napoleon, patience, penneeck, tresillo, videruff 9 cinq-cents, grabouche, montebank, new market, solitaire, tredrille 10 heartsette 11 everlasting, speculation
carnival: 5 darts 6 hoopla
confidence: 5 bunco, bunko
court: 5 roque 6 pelota, squash, tennis 7 jai alai 8 handball 9 badminton 10 volleyball
dice: 4 ludo 5 craps 7 pachisi 8 dominoes, trey-trip
gambling: 4 beno, faro, keno, pico 5 beano, bingo, boule, craps, keeno, lotto, monte(Sp.), pique, pitch, poker, rondo, stuss 6 brelan(F.), fan-tan(Ch.), piquet, policy 7 baccara, barbudi, primero, rondeau(F.) 8 baccarat, crackloo, roulette 9 black-jack, crackaloo, montebank, twenty-one, vingt-et-un(F.) 10 panguingui(Phil. Is.)
goal: run 4 home 5 first, score, spare, tally 6 basket, strike 9 touchdown
kind of: 4 mora(It.) 6 merels, morris, quoits 7 diabolo, loggats, loggets, marbles 9 philopena 10 jackstraws, spillikins
official: 5 judge, timer 6 umpire 7 referee, starter 8 linesman 10 timekeeper
outdoor: 4 polo 6 tennis 7 cricket, croquet 9 badminton
parlor: 4 dibs 5 jacks 7 matador 8 charades 13 tiddledywinks
pin: 7 bowling, kegling, tenpins 8 ninepins, skittles
racket: 5 bandy 6 squash, tennis 8 lacrosse 9 badminton
small: 4 bird, fowl
stewed in wine: 5 salmi 6 ragout
war: 10 kriegspiel
word: 6 crambo 7 anagram 8 acrostic, scrabble
gamekeeper: 8 warrener
gamester: 5 dicer 6 player 7 gambler, playman
gamete: 6 zygote 8 oosphere
gamin: tad 6 urchin 7 hoodlum
domain: 6 street
gaming cube: die
gammon: leg 4 bosh, dupe, foot, gull 5 bacon, cozen, feign, thigh 6 delude, humbug 7 beguile, deceive, mislead, pretend 10 backgammon
gammy: bad 4 lame, sore
gamp: 8 umbrella
gamut: 5 orbit, range, reach, scale 6 extent, series 7 compass
gamy: 5 spicy 7 lustful 8 spirited 10 malodorous 12 disreputable
ganch: 4 kill 6 impale 7 execute
gander: 5 goose 6 stroll, wander 9 simpleton
Gandhi: *name:* Bu; Aba, Abu 4 Abba, Abou, Bapu 7 Mahatma
publication: 7 Harijan
gandul: 6 loafer
ganef: 5 thief 6 rascal
gang: go; mob, set 4 band, crew, ging, pack, road, team, walk 5 group, horde, shift 6 clique, course, outfit, travel 7 company 9 pasturage 10 passageway 11 combination
member of: 4 b'hoy 5 rowdy, tough
Ganges River: *city:* 7 Benares
dolphin: 4 susu
goddess: 9 Gangadevi
vessel: 6 puteli 7 putelee
gangling: 5 lanky 7 awkward 9 spindling
ganglion: 5 tumor
gangplank: 4 brow 6 bridge 8 platform 9 gangboard
gangrene: rot 7 mortify 8 necrosis 9 sphacelus
gangster: 4 b'hoy, thug, whyo, yegg 5 rough, thief 6 bandit 7 mobster, ruffian 8 criminal, hireling
female companion: 4 moll
gangway: 7 couloir 8 corridor 10 passageway
gannet: 4 bird, fowl 5 goose, solan
family: 4 sula
ganoid fish: gar 6 bowfin 8 sturgeon
gaol: 4 brig, jail 6 prison
gaoler: 5 guard 6 warden
gap: col 4 flaw, pass, rent 5 break, breck, chasm, chawn, cleft, clove, meuse, notch, space 6 breach, hiatus, lacuna, ravine 7 fissure, lacunae(pl.), opening 8 aperture, interval, quebrada 10 interstice 12 interruption 13 discontinuity
gape: ope 4 cape, gasp, gaum, gaup, gawp, gaze, pant, rent, yaup, yawn, yawp 5 chawn, shout, stare 6 rictus, vacuum 7 dehisce 8 oscitate
gapeseed: 6 starer
gaping: 4 open 7 cracked, ringent
of plant capsule: 10 dehiscence
garage: 6 hangar, siding 8 building
garb (see also **dress**): 5 array, dress, habit, style 6 attire, bundle, clothe, custom, method 7 apparel, clothes, costume, fashion, raiment 8 carriage, clothing, vesiture, vestment 10 appearance, habiliment
kinds of: 4 toga 8 mourning 9 sackcloth
garbage: 5 offal, trash 6 bundle, faggot, refuse, scraps
garble: 4 bolt, cull, geld, sift, sort 5 alloy 6 jumble, mangle, refine, refuse, select 7 distort, pervert, rubbish 8 disguise, mutilate
garboil: 9 confusion 10 turbulence
garcon: boy, lad 6 waiter 8 bachelor

garden: 4 Eden, hall, park, yard 5 arbor, patch, tract 6 arbour 8 outfield 9 cultivate, enclosure 11 commonplace
implement: hoe 4 rake 5 mower 6 scythe, sickle, trowel, weeder
kind of: 4 herb 5 oasis, truck 6 cactus, flower, formal 7 kitchen 8 chinampa, kailyard(Sc.), kaleyard(Sc.) 9 botanical, terrarium, vegetable 10 zoological
protector: 7 Priapus
Garden City: 7 Chicago
garden plant: See **plant** *garden*
gardener: 9 topiarist 14 horticulturist
garfish: 8 hornbeak, hornfish
Gargantua's son: 10 Pantagruel
gargantuan: 4 huge, vast 5 giant 7 titanic 8 enormous, gigantic 9 monstrous
gargle: 9 mouthwash 11 collutorium
garish: 4 loud 5 cheap, gaudy, showy 6 bright, tawdry 8 dazzling 9 offensive
garland: bay, lei 4 band 5 crown, glory 6 anadem, corona, crants, diadem, laurel, rosary, wreath 7 chaplet, coronal, festoon 9 anthology
garlic: 4 moly, ramp 5 chive, clove 6 ramson
garment (see also **undergarment**): 4 brat, cape, coat, gear, gown, jupe, rail, robe, sari, vest 5 cloak, dress, habit 6 attire, kimono 7 apparel, leotard, raiment 8 vestment 10 investment
ancient: 4 toga 5 palla, stola 6 chiton 7 chlamys 8 himation
ecclesiastical: see **vestment**
infant's: 6 woolly 7 bunting
Malay: 6 cabaya, kabaya, sarong
medieval: 5 simar 6 kirtle, rochet, tabard 8 chausses
men's: cap, hat, tie 4 belt, coat 5 pants, shirt, short, socks 6 jacket, slacks 7 drawers 8 trousers 10 suspenders 11 windbreaker
mourning: 5 weeds
outer: 4 coat, wrap 5 cloak, dress, pants, parka, shawl, skirt, stole 6 jacket, slacks 7 sweater 9 coverslut, polonaise
protective: 4 brat 5 apron, armor, chaps, smock 7 cuculla 8 overalls, pinafore 9 coveralls, gaberdine
rain: 6 poncho 7 oilskin, slicker
sleeveless: aba 4 cape, vest 6 mantle 7 sweater 8 slip-over
upper: 4 coat, vest 5 jupon, shirt, tunic, waist 6 blouse, jersey, peplos, peplus 7 sweater 8 guernsey, slip-over
garn: 4 yarn 7 worsted 11 exclamation
garner: 4 reap 5 store 6 gather 7 collect, granary 10 accumulate
garnet: 5 jewel, stone 7 garnate 8 essonite
black: 8 melanite
deep-red: 9 almandine, almandite
green: 7 olivine
garnish: 4 trim 5 adorn, dress, equip 7 furnish 8 decorate, meringue, ornament 9 embellish
garret: 4 head 5 attic, solar, soler 6 gallet, soller, turret 7 mansard 8 cockloft 10 watchtower
garrot: 4 duck, fowl 9 goldeneye
garrote, garrotte: 4 kill 7 execute 8 strangle, throttle
garrulous: 5 talky, wordy 7 diffuse, voluble 8 fanfaron 9 talkative 10 long-winded, loquacious
garter: 4 garten 7 elastic 9 supporter
garth: dam 4 hoop, yard 5 close, girth 9 enclosure
garvey: 4 boat, scow
gas: 4 fuel, fume, reek, talk 5 radon, vapor 6 gossip, petrol 7 bombast 8 hydrogen 10 anesthetic, asphyxiate, illuminant
air: 4 neon 5 argon, ozone, xenon 6 oxygen 7 ammonia, krypton, sulfate 8 nitrogen
balloon: 6 helium
blue: 5 ozone
charcoal: 5 oxane
charge with: 6 aerate
colorless: 5 keten, ozone 6 arsine, ethane 7 ammonia
comb. form: aer 4 aero
inert: 5 argon, xenon 6 helium 8 nitrogen
inflammable: 6 butane, ethane 7 methane
marsh: 7 methane
mustard: 7 yperite
nitrogen and carbon: 8 cyanogen
oxygen: 5 ozone
poisonous: 6 arsine 7 mustard, stibine
gasbag: 7 balloon
gascon: 7 boaster 8 braggart 10 swaggering 12 swashbuckler
gasconade: 4 brag, crow 5 boast, vaunt 7 bluster, bravado 8 boasting
gaseous: 4 thin 5 fluid, light 7 tenuous 8 aeriform, gasiform, volatile 13 unsubstantial
gash: cut 4 bite, chop, slit, talk, trim, wise 5 sharp, slash, witty 6 babble, gossip, tattle 7 knowing 8 incision 9 talkative 11 well-dressed
gasket: 4 lute, ring, seal
gasoline: gas 6 petrol
gasp: 4 gape, pant 5 croak, fetch
gassy: 5 windy 8 inflated 9 flatulent
gast: 5 alarm, scare 8 frighten
gasthaus: inn 6 tavern
gastronome: 7 epicure 11 connoisseur
gastropod: 4 slug 5 harpa, oliva, snail 6 nerita, nerite, volute 7 mollusk 8 pteropod
ear-shaped: 7 abalone

marine: **5** cowry, murex **6** cowrie, limpet, tethys **7** aplysia
gat: gun **7** channel, passage **8** revolver
gata: **5** shark
gate: bar, dar, way **4** door, exit, hole, pass **5** hatch, valve **6** defile, escape, method, portal, wicket, zaguan **7** barrier, opening, postern **8** entrance **9** threshold, turnstile
flood: **6** sluice
gate money: fee **5** price **9** admission
Gates of Hercules: **9** Gibraltar
gatehouse: bar **5** lodge
gatekeeper: **6** porter, warden **8** guardian, watchman
gatepost: **4** durn
gateway: dar **5** pylon, toran, torii(Jap.) **6** portal, torana **8** entrance
gather: **4** bale, brew, cull, furl, herd, mass, meet, pick, rake, reap **5** amass, bunch, flock, glean, group, infer, pleat, pluck, raise, shirr **6** bundle, deduce, derive, garner, muster, scrape, summon **7** collect, compile, convene, convoke, harvest, recruit **8** assemble, colonize, compress, conclude, contract, increase **10** accumulate, congregate **11** agglomerate, concentrate **12** conglomerate
gatherer: **5** miser **7** gleaner **9** collector
gathering: bee, tea **4** bevy, fest, stag **5** crowd, party, troop **6** galaxy, plisse, shivoo, smoker **7** abscess, company, meeting, mooting **8** assembly, function, swelling **9** concourse **10** assemblage, collection, congestion, convention **11** contraction **12** accumulation, congregation
gauche: **4** skew **5** gawky **6** clumsy **7** awkward, twisted **8** tactless **10** left-handed
gaucho: **6** cowboy **8** herdsman
knife: **4** bolo
lariat: **5** bolas
weapon: **7** machete
gaud: **4** joke **5** adorn, fraud, paint, sport, trick **6** bauble, finery, flashy, gewgaw **7** trinket **8** artifice, ornament
gaudy: gay **4** loud **5** cheap, feast, showy **6** festal, flashy, flimsy, garish, tawdry, tinsel, tricky **7** brankie(Sc.), flaring, glaring, trinket **8** festival **9** brummagem, deceitful, flaunting, luxurious **11** pretentious **12** meretricious, ostentatious **13** entertainment
gaufre: **5** wafer **6** waffle
gauge, gage: **4** carp **5** judge **6** former **7** measure, scantle **8** estimate, udometer **9** indicator, manometer, manoscope **10** anemometer
Gaul: **6** France, Gallia(L.)
chariot: **5** esses **6** esseda, essede
city: **6** Alesia
god of thunder and rain: **7** Taranis
god of vegetation: **4** Esus
magistrate: **9** vergobret
people: **4** Remi
priest: **5** druid
river goddess: **8** Belisama
seer: **5** vates
gaulding: **4** bird **5** egret, heron
gaum: paw **4** daub, gape, heed, hold, mess **5** smear, stuff **8** perceive **9** attention **10** perception **13** understanding
gaunt: **4** bony, grim, lank, lean, slim, thin **5** spare **6** barren, hollow, meager, meagre **7** haggard, slender **8** desolate, rawboned **9** emaciated **10** attenuated, cadaverous, forbidding
gauntlet: **4** test **5** glove **6** ordeal
gauster: **4** brag **5** bully **6** gossip **7** bluster, swagger
Gautama: **6** Buddha **10** Siddhartha
wife: **6** Ahalya
gauze: **4** film, leno **5** crape, crepe, lisse **6** fabric, tissue **7** bandage
gavel: **4** mace, maul, rent **5** usury **6** hammer, mallet
gavelock: **4** gaff **5** lever, spear **7** crowbar, javelin
gavial: **9** crocodile
gaw: god **4** gape **5** drain **6** trench
Gawain: *brother:* **7** Gaheris
father: Lot
son: **5** Lovel **8** Florence, Gyngalyn
gawk: **4** gowk, left, lout **5** stare **6** gawney, lubber **7** bumpkin, rammack **9** simpleton **10** left-handed
gawky: **6** clumsy, gauche **7** awkward, foolish **8** clownish
gawn: tub **4** pail
gawney: **4** gawk **9** simpleton
gawp, gaup: **4** gape **5** stare **7** swallow **9** simpleton
gay: **4** airy, boon, daft, glad, gleg **5** bawdy, bonny, brisk, happy, jolly, loose, merry, riant, showy **6** blithe, bonnie, bright, flashy, frisky, garish, jocund, jovial, joyful, lively, wanton **7** festive, gleeful, jocular **8** cavalier, cheerful, colorful, mirthful, sportive **9** brillante, brilliant, convivial, sprightly, vivacious **10** frolicsome, licentious **12** lighthearted
gazabo: guy **6** fellow, person
gaze: eye, pry **4** gape, gouk, gowk, leer, look, moon, ogle, peer, porc, scan, toot **5** glare, gloat, sight, stare **6** behold, glower, regard
gazebo: **8** pavilion **11** summerhouse
gazelle: ahu, goa **4** admi, cora, dama, kudu, mohr, oryx **5** ariel, mhorr **7** buffalo, chikara, corinne **8** antelope **9** springbok
gazelle hound: **6** saluki

gazette: 7 courant, journal 9 newspaper
gazetteer: 5 atlas 6 writer 10 dictionary
Ge: See Gaea
geal: ice 5 jelly 7 congeal
gean: 6 cherry
gear: cam, cog, rig 4 food, tack 5 dress, equip, goods, stuff, tools 6 affair, aludel, doings, graith, liquor, matter, pinion, tackle, things, wealth 7 apparel, concern, harness, rigging, rubbish, trapeze 8 business, clothing, cogwheel, garments, material, ornament, property 9 equipment, mechanism, trappings, vestments 10 appliances, belongings, implements 12 appurtenance 13 accoutrements
geason: 4 rare 5 scant 6 scarce 12 unproductive
geaster: 9 earthstar
Geb: *daughter:* 4 Isis 8 Nephthys
father: Shu
son: Set 6 Osiris
wife: Nut
gecko: 6 lizard 7 tarente
gel: set 6 harden 7 congeal, thicken 8 solidify 9 coagulate
gelatin, gelatine: 6 collin 7 sericin 8 agar-agar
geld: dry 4 spay 5 alter, prune 6 barren, garble 8 castrate, mutilate 9 expurgate, fruitless 10 emasculate
gelid: icy 4 cold, iced 6 frozen
gell: fun 5 spree 6 frolic 8 carousal
gelt: 4 gold 5 money
gem: bud 4 keas, naif, onyx, opal, ruby, sard 5 agate, beryl, cameo, jewel, paste, pearl, stone, topaz 6 amulet, bedeck, garnet, muffin, scarab, spinel 7 diamond, emerald, paragon 8 intaglio, sapphire, tigereye 9 carnelian, germinate 10 aquamarine 11 masterpiece
blue: 8 sapphire 9 turquoise 10 aquamarine
face: 5 facet
green: 7 emerald, peridot 10 chrysolite
imperfect: 5 loupe
iridescent: 4 opal 5 pearl 7 cat's-eye 8 tigereye 9 moonstone
measure of weight: 5 carat
of fidelity: 5 topaz
of immortality: 7 emerald
of law: 4 ruby
of love: 8 amethyst
of peace: 7 diamond
of purity: 5 pearl
of truth: 8 sapphire
paste: 6 strass
purple: 8 amethyst
rectangular: 6 baguet 8 baguette
red: 4 ruby, sard 5 avena 6 garnet, pyrope 9 carnelian
relief-carved: 5 cameo
setting for: 4 ouch, pave 6 chaton
support: 7 setting
surface: 5 bezel, bezil, facet
Gem State: 5 Idaho
gemel: 4 twin 5 pairs, twins 6 hinged, paired 7 coupled, doubled
geminate: 6 binate, double 7 coupled
Gemini: 5 twins 6 Castor, Pollux
gemmule: bud 5 ovule
gemot, gemotte: 5 court 7 meeting 8 assembly
gemsbok: 4 oryx 8 antelope
gemutlich: 4 cozy 6 genial, kindly 8 cheerful 9 agreeable 11 comfortable, good-natured
gendarme: 7 soldier 9 policeman 10 cavalryman
gender: sex 4 kind, male, sort 5 class, genus 6 female, neuter 8 copulate, engender, generate
gene: 6 factor 10 determiner, uneasiness 13 embarrassment
genealogy: 4 tree 7 account, history, lineage, progeny 8 pedigree 9 offspring 10 generation
general: 5 broad, gross 6 common, leader 7 average, officer 8 catholic 9 commander, customary, prevalent, universal 10 prevailing, widespread
Civil War: Lee 5 Grant, Meade 7 Sherman
generalize: 5 widen 6 extend, spread 7 broaden
generate: 4 make 5 beget, breed, steam 6 create, gender 7 develop, produce 8 develope, engender 9 originate, procreate, propagate
generation: age, era 4 kind, race 5 breed, stock 6 family 7 descent, progeny 8 geniture 9 genealogy, offspring, posterity 11 abiogenesis, descendants, procreation
spontaneous: 11 abiogenesis
generative: 8 prolific 10 productive
generic: 12 encompassing 13 comprehensive
generosity: 7 largess 8 largesse
generous: big 4 free, good, kind, rich 5 ample, frank, noble 6 honest 7 fertile, liberal 8 abundant, gracious, handsome, highborn, spirited 9 bountiful, excellent, honorable, plenteous, unselfish, unstinted 10 benevolent, charitable, courageous, munificent, openhanded 11 magnanimous, stimulating, warmhearted
genesis: 5 birth 6 origin 9 beginning 11 origination
genet: 5 berbe, horse
genial: 4 bein, bien, warm 5 douce 6 benign, forthy, inborn, jovial, kindly, native 7

cordial, festive 8 cheerful, friendly, pleasant 9 benignant, expansive, gemutlich 10 enlivening, generative

genie: See **jinni**

genitor: 6 parent 7 creator 10 procreator

geniture: 5 birth 8 nativity 9 offspring 10 generation

genius: 5 genio 6 talent, wizard 8 aptitude 9 intellect 10 brilliance

Genoa: *coin:* 4 jane 8 genovino
family: 5 Doria
magistrate: 4 doge

genos: 4 clan, gens 6 family

genouillere: 7 kneelet 9 kneepiece

genre: 4 kind, sort, type 5 class, style 7 species 8 category 11 description 14 classification

gens: 4 clan 5 nomen 6 people

gent: 4 fine 5 noble 6 pretty 7 elegant 8 graceful

genteel: 4 nice 6 polite 7 stylish 8 graceful, lady-like, well-bred 11 fashionable

gentian: 6 flower 7 felwort 9 baldmoney

Gentile: 7 heathen 9 Christian

gentility: 8 breeding 10 refinement

gentle: moy 4 calm, deft, dewy, easy, fair, kind, meek, mild, soft, tame 5 bland, light, milky, quiet, sweet, tamed 6 benign, docile, facile, placid, polite, tender 7 amabile, bonaire, clement, gradual, lenient 8 amenable, dovelike, lenitive, maidenly, mansuete, moderate, peaceful, soothing, tranquil, well-born 9 courteous, excellent, honorable, tractable 10 chivalrous 11 considerate 13 compassionate
in music: 7 amabile

gentlemen: don, rye, sir 5 sahib, senor 6 bayard, mister 7 younker 8 cavalier 9 caballero

Gentlemen Prefer Blondes author: 4 Loos

gentlewoman: 4 lady

gentry: 4 rank 5 birth 6 people 8 gentrice 9 condition 10 gentlefolk

genty: 5 noble 7 genteel 8 graceful 9 courteous

genu: 4 bend 7 flexure

genuflect: 5 kneel

genuine: 4 leal, pure, real, true, vrai(F.) 5 frank, plain, pucka, pukka 6 actual, dinkum, honest 7 germane, gradely, sincere 8 bonafide 9 authentic, heartfelt, intrinsic, simon-pure, true-penny, unalloyed, unfeigned, veridical, veritable 10 legitimate 13 unadulterated 15 unsophisticated

genus: 4 kind, sort 5 class, order 6 gender 8 category 14 classification
pert. to: 7 generic

geode: 5 druse 6 nodule

geology: 12 earth science
age: 7 Permian 8 Cambrian, cenezoic, Devonian, Jurassic, mesozoic, Silurian, Triassic 9 paleozoic 10 Cretaceous, cryptozoic, Ordovician 13 Mississippian, Pennsylvanian
division: age, era 4 lias, lyas 5 epoch, trias
period: 6 eocene 7 miocene 8 pliocene, tertiary 9 oligocene 10 quaternary 11 pleistocene
remains: 7 fossils
science: 12 paleontology 13 palaeontology

geometry: *angle:* 9 incidence
curve: 6 spiral 7 ellipse, evolute 8 parabola, sinusoid
father: 6 Euclid
figure: 4 cone, lune 5 prism, rhomb 6 circle, gnomon, oblong 7 ellipse, rhombus 8 triangle
proposition: 7 theorem
ratio: pi
solid: 4 cube 5 prism 7 pyramid
surface: 5 nappe, torus

geoponic: 5 rural 11 agriculture 12 agricultural

Georgia (Caucasus): *city:* 6 Iberia, Kutais, Tiflis
island: 7 Sapelo
people: 4 Svan 5 Svane
queen: 6 Tamara 7 Thamara

Georgia (U.S.): *city:* 5 Macon 6 Dalton 7 Atlanta, Cordele
college: 5 Emory
county: Lee 4 Bibb, Clay, Cobb, Cook, Dade, Hall, Hart, Long, Pike, Polk, Tift, Ware 5 Bacon, Burke, Butts, Crisp, Early, Rabun, Troup

Geraint's wife: 4 Enid

germ: bud, bug 4 seed 5 spore, virus 6 embryo, germen, sprout 7 germule, microbe 8 rudiment 9 bacteriam, beginning 13 microorganism

germ cell: egg 4 ovum

German: 4 Goth 5 Boche, Saxon 6 Teuton

German measles: 7 rubello

germane: 4 akin, true 6 allied 7 genuine, related 8 relevant 9 pertinent 11 appropriate

Germany: *ancient:* 6 Almain 7 Almaine
ancient tribesman: 4 Jute 6 Teuton 9 Ostrogoth
angry: 4 bose
animal: 4 tier
article: das, der, des, die
artist: 5 Durer
association: 6 verein 12 gesellschaft
bacteriologist: 4 Koch
beautiful: 5 schon
blue: 4 blau
bread: 4 brot

bright: 4 hell
but: 4 aber
cake: 5 torte 9 lebkuchen 11 pfeffernuss
canal: 4 Kiel
capital: 6 Berlin
castle: 7 schloss
cheese: 4 kase
chicken: 4 huhn
child: 4 kind
Christmas: 11 Weihnachten
city: Aue, Ede, Ems, Ulm 4 Bonn, Gera, Jena, Kiel, Koln, Linz, Oder 5 Emden, Essen, Furth, Gotha, Hagen, Halle, Herne, Mainz, Pirna, Trier 6 Aachen, Altona, Barmen, Berlin, Bochum, Bremen, Cassel, Dessau, Erfurt, Kassel, Linden, Lubeck, Munich, Plauen 7 Breslau, Cologne, Crefeld, Dresden, Gorlitz, Hamburg, Hanover, Harburg, Krefeld, Leipzig, Mayence, Munchen, Munster, Potsdam, Rostock, Spandau, Stettin, Zwickau 8 Augsburg, Chemnitz, Dortmund, Duisburg, Freiburg, Liegnitz, Nurnberg, Steglitz, Wurselen, Wurzburg 9 Bielefeld, Brunswick, Darmstadt, Elberfeld, Flensburg, Karlsruhe, Magdeburg, Nuremberg, Offenbach, Osnabruck, Pforzheim, Remscheid, Stuttgart, Wiesbaden 10 Braunsberg, Dusseldorf, Heidelberg, Konigsberg, Oberhausen, Schoneberg, Tuttlingen 11 Lichtenberg, Saarbrucken 12 Ludwigshafen 13 Gelsenkirchen 14 Charlottenburg, Mannheim-on-Ruhr 15 Frankfort-on-Main, Frankfort-on-Oder
clever: 4 klug
clock: uhr
coal region: 4 Ruhr, Saar 5 Sarre
code: 5 Salic
coin: 4 mark 6 kronen, thaler 7 pfennig 8 groschen
cold: 4 kalt
day: tag
dead: tot
dear: 4 lieb
deep: 4 tief
dog: 4 hund
door: tur
early: 4 fruh
earth: 4 erde
evening: 5 abend
eye: 4 auge
field: 4 feld
forest: 4 wald
forest-keeper: 9 waldgrave
gnome: 6 kobold
good: gut
hair: 4 haar
hall: 4 aula, saal 5 diele
happy: 4 froh
head: 4 kopf
heart: 4 herz
highway: 8 autobahn
home: 4 heim
industrial area: 4 Ruhr
iron region: 4 Saar 5 Sarre
knight: 6 ritter
lake: 9 Constance
lancer: 4 ulan
language: 7 Deutsch
leaf: 5 blatt
letter: 5 brief
measure: aam, imi 4 last, sack, stab 5 carat, eimer, kanne, kette, maass 6 strich 7 klafter 8 scheffel, schoppen, stubchen 9 masskanne
mister: 4 herr
moon: 4 mond
mountain: 4 Alps, Berg, Harz
never: nie
nine: 4 neun
no: 4 nein
nobleman: 4 graf 5 adlig 6 junker, ritter 7 younker
overture: 8 vorspiel
parliament: 9 Bundestag, Reichstag
philosopher: 4 Kant 5 Hegel
port: 5 Emden 6 Bremen 7 Hamburg, Stettin
resort: Ems 5 Baden
river: Ems, Inn, Ulm 4 Alle, Eder, Eger, Elbe, Eser, Isar, Main, Oder, Ruhr, Saar 5 Aller, Hunte, Rhine, Saale, Spree, Werra, Weser 9 Constance
school: 10 realschule, volkschule 14 oberrealschule
shoe: 5 schuh
singing festival: 10 sangerfest 11 saengerfest
society: 4 bund 6 verein 10 turnverein 12 gesellschaft
son: 4 sohn
song: 4 lied
spa: see *resort* above
star: 5 stern
stone: 5 stein
teacher: 6 docent, dozent
tooth: 4 zahn
tower: 4 turm
two: 4 zwei
village: 4 dorf
vowel change: 6 umlaut
weight: lot
white: 5 weiss
wine: 4 hock, wein 5 Rhine 7 Moselle
woman: 4 frau, frow 8 fraulein
world: 4 welt
year: 4 jahr
young: 4 jung

germicide: 5 iodin 6 iodine 10 antiseptic 11 bactericide 12 disinfectant
germinate: bud, gem 5 geget, sprit 6 braird, evolve, sprout 7 develop 10 effloresce
geryon 7 monster
gesso: 5 paste 7 plaster
gest, geste: 4 deed, feat, jest, tale 5 route, stage 7 bearing, company, conduct, gesture, lampoon, romance 9 adventure 10 deportment
gestation: 7 bearing 8 breeding, carrying 9 pregnancy
gesticulate: 4 bend 6 motion 7 gesture
gesture: act, fig, nod 4 beck, bere, gest 5 geste, sneer 6 behave, motion, salute 7 posture 8 carriage 11 gesticulate 13 gesticulation
get: pen, win 4 earn, find, gain, take, trap 5 annoy, beget, catch, fetch, learn, reach, seize 6 appear, attain, baffle, become, corner, derive, induce, obtain, puzzle, secure, suffer 7 achieve, acquire, capture, conquer, possess, prepare, procure, realize, receive, recover 8 contract, irritate, overcome, persuade, retrieve, vanquish 9 ascertain, determine 10 comprehend, conciliate, understand
get along: 4 fare 5 hurry 7 advance, prosper, succeed 8 progress
get away: lam 4 flee, scat, shoo 6 escape
get back: 6 redeem 7 recover
get on: 4 fare 5 board 6 embark
get out: 5 scram 6 elicit, escape, reveal 8 evacuate
get-together: bee 4 stag 6 social 7 meeting
get up: 5 arise, array, dress, style 6 invent 7 arrange, costume, prepare 9 construct
get well: 4 heal 10 recuperate
getaway: lam 4 scat 5 elope, leave, start 6 depart, escape
gewgaw: toy 4 gaud 6 bauble, fangle, fegary, trifle 7 trinket 8 gimcrack 10 knickknack
gey: 4 very 5 quite 6 pretty, rather 9 tolerable 12 considerable
ghastful, gastful: 6 afraid 7 alarmed, ghostly 8 dreadful 9 frightful 10 frightened
ghastly: wan 4 grim, pale 5 ghast, lurid 6 dismal, gashly, gousty, grisly, pallid 7 charnel, deathly, fearful, gashful, goustie, hideous, macaber, macabre 8 dreadful, grewsome, gruesome, horrible, shocking, terrible 9 deathlike, frightful, horrified, terrified 10 cadaverous
ghat: 4 pass 5 range 7 landing 8 mountain
gherkin: 6 pickle 8 cucumber
ghost: hag 4 bhut, hant 5 bugan, duppy, shade, spook, umbra 6 daemon, spirit, sprite 7 eidolon, haunter, lemures(pl.), phantom, specter, spectre 8 guytrash, phantasm, revenant 10 apparition, glimmering 11 poltergeist
ghostly: 4 eery 5 eerie, scary, weird 6 spooky 7 gastful 8 ghastful, spectral 9 spiritual
ghoul: 4 ogre 5 fiend 7 vampire
ghoulish: 4 eery 5 eerie
giant: 4 Bara, eten, huge, ogre, rahu, Ymir 5 Argus, Cacus, jumbo, titan, troll 6 afreet, nozzle, ogress 7 Antaeus, Cyclops, monster, warlock 8 behemoth, Bellerus, colossus 9 monstrous 10 gargantuan, prodigious, tremendous
gibber: 5 stone 6 pebble 7 boulder, chatter
gibberish: 6 jabber, jargon 9 rigmarole 10 galimatias
gibbet: 4 stob, tree 6 cudgel 7 gallows, potence
gibbon: ape, lar 6 monkey, wou-wou 7 hoolock, siamang 10 anthropoid
gibbous: 6 convex, humped 7 hunched, rounded 11 hunchbacked, protuberant
gibe, jibe: 4 gird, jape, jeer, mock, quib, quip, twit 5 agree, fleer, fling, flirt, flout, gleek, scoff, sneer, taunt 6 deride, heckle 7 prepare, sarcasm 8 ridicule
giddy: 4 daff, daft 5 dizzy 6 fickle, giglot, volage 7 carried, flighty, glaiket, glaikit 8 halucket, heedless 9 frivolous, hellicate 11 hairbrained 13 featherheaded
gift: sop 4 bent, boon, dash, dole 5 bonus, bribe, dower, dowry, favor, grant, knack, pilon, power, token 6 bounty, donary, gersum, hansel, legacy, talent 7 aptness, benefit, faculty, handsel, largess, present, subsidy 8 aptitude, bestowal, blessing, donation, gratuity, largesse, offering, pittance, potlatch 9 endowment, gratitude, lagniappe, readiness 10 compliment 11 benefaction, beneficence, serendipity 12 contribution
gifted: 8 talented 9 ingenious
gig: fun, top 4 boat, fool, goad, joke, spur, whim 5 rouse, spear, sport 6 kibble 7 provoke 8 carriage, hilarity
gigantic: big 4 huge, vast 5 giant, large 7 immense, mammoth, titanic 8 colossal, enormous 9 cyclopean, gigantean, monstrous 10 gargantuan, prodigious
giggle: 5 tehee 6 teehee, titter 7 snicker, snigger
gila: 5 trout 6 lizard 10 woodpecker
Gilbert island: 5 Makin 6 Tarawa
gild: 5 adorn, tinge 7 overlay 8 brighten, inaurate 9 embellish
Gilda's father: 9 Rigoletto
gilded: 5 aural 6 aurate 7 aureate 8 inaurate 11 embellished

gilet: 4 vest 6 bodice 9 waistcoat
gill, ghyl: ivy 4 cove, girl, lass 5 brook 6 collar, ravine, stream, tipple, valley, wattle 10 sweetheart
four: 4 pint
gilt: hog, sow 4 gold 5 money 6 gilded, golden
gimcrack: fop, toy 6 bauble, flimsy, gewgaw, trifle 7 trinket, trivial 8 ornament, trumpery 9 frivolous 10 knickknack 13 unsubstantial
gimmer: ewe 5 clasp, hinge
gimp: jag, vim 4 trim 5 notch, orris 6 indent, spirit 7 cripple 8 trimming
gin: net 4 crab, grin, rack, sloe, trap 5 snare, trick 6 device, diddle, liquor, scheme 7 springe 8 artifice, beverage, schnapps 10 intoxicant 11 contrivance
ging: 4 crew, gang 5 troop 7 company, retinue
ginger: pep, vim 5 spice, vigor 6 mettle, revive, spirit 8 piquancy, spirited
genus: 8 zingiber
wild: 6 asarum
ginger cookie: 4 snap
ginger root: 4 race
gingerbread: 4 cake 5 money 6 wealth 8 trimming 13 pfefferkuchen(Ger.)
gingerbread tree: 4 doom
gingerly: 6 warily 7 charily 8 daintily 9 carefully, elegantly, finically, guardedly, mincingly 10 cautiously 12 fastidiously
gingham: 8 chambray
ginseng: 4 herb 5 panax 6 aralia
gipsy: See **gypsy**
giraffe: 5 piano 6 animal, spinet 10 camelopard
girasol, girasole: 4 opal 5 thorn 9 artichoke
gird: 4 belt, bind, gibe, girt, hasp, hoop, jerk, mock, yerk 5 brace, equip, scoff, sneer 6 clothe, fasten, girdle, secure 7 besiege, enclose, prepare, provide 8 engirdle, surround 9 encompass
girder: 4 beam 6 binder
girdle: obi 4 band, bark, belt, bind, cest, gird, ring, sash, zona, zone 5 girth, sarpe 6 bodice, cestus, circle, circum, corset, moocha, zonule 7 baldric, balteus, environ, equator, griddle 8 batheus, cincture, cingulum, encircle
girl: gal, sis 4 bint, chit, coed, gill, jill, lass, maid, minx 5 child, fille, filly, gilpy, quean, skirt, sylph, wench 6 amoret, calico, damsel, female, hoyden, kimmer, tomboy 7 camilla, colleen, flapper, ingenue 9 backfisch, debutante 10 jeune fille, sweetheart 11 maidservant
name: see **name** *female*
girlish: 5 sissy 7 artless 8 immature
girt: 4 gird 6 belted, fasten 7 besiege 8 prepared 9 encircled 13 circumference
girth: 4 band, belt, gird, hoop 5 cinch, cinct, garth, strap, width 6 girdle 7 girding, measure 8 cincture, encircle 13 circumference
gist: 4 core, crux, pith 5 heart, point 7 essence 10 foundation
gitano, gitana: 5 gipsy, gypsy
give: gie(Sc.) 4 cede, dole, emit, hand, mete 5 apply, endow, grant, serve, yield 6 accord, afford, bestow, commit, confer, denote, devote, donate, impart, render, supply 7 consign, dispose, furnish, intrust, present, proffer, propose 8 bequeath 9 surrender, vouchsafe 10 administer, contribute, deliquesce
give a hand: aid 4 abet, help
give away: 5 grant, yield 6 bestow, betray 7 present, succumb 8 disclose, telltale 9 sacrifice
give back: 4 echo 6 recede, remise, retire, return 7 replace, restore, retreat
give forth: 4 emit 8 eradiate
give in: 5 yield 6 relent 7 succumb 9 surrender
give off: 4 emit, quit 5 cease, exude, issue 7 publish
give out: 4 deal, emit, mete 5 exude, issue, peter, print 7 publish, release 9 circulate
give rise: 6 gender 7 produce 8 engender, occasion 9 originate
give up: 4 cede, emit, quit 5 demit, forgo, spare, waive, yield 6 betray, devote, forego, resign, reveal, vacate 7 abandon, deliver, despair, present 8 abdicate, renounce 9 sacrifice, surrender 10 relinquish
given: 5 fixed 6 stated 7 donated, granted 8 addicted, disposed, inclined 9 specified
givey: 4 soft
gizz: wig
gizzen: dry 5 leaky 7 parched 10 shrivelled
glabrous: 4 bald 6 smooth 8 levigate
glace: ice 6 glazed 8 polished
glacial: icy 4 cold 5 gelid 6 arctic, frigid, frosty, frozen 9 congealed
glacier: 6 icecap 7 iceberg
chasm: 6 crevas
deposit: as 4 asar(pl.) 5 eskar, esker 6 placer 7 moraine
direction: 5 stoss
fissure: 8 crevasse
fragment: 5 serac
hill: 4 paha 7 drumlin
ridge: as, os 4 kame, osar(pl.) 5 eskar, esker
snow: 4 neve
snow field: 4 firn, neve
glacis: 5 slope 6 buffer 7 incline
glack: 6 ravine, valley

glad: gay 4 fain 5 eager, happy, merry, sunny 6 blithe, bright, joyous 7 pleased, shining, willing 8 animated, cheerful, gladsome 9 beautiful, delighted, gratified, satisfied 11 exhilarated 12 lighthearted

gladden: 5 cheer, elate 6 please 7 gratify, rejoice

gladdy: 12 yellowhammer

glade: 4 vale 5 marsh 8 clearing
comb. form: 4 nemo

gladiator: 5 boxer 6 fencer 7 fighter
competition: 5 ludus
trainer: 7 lanista

gladness: joy 5 bliss, mirth 6 blithe 8 fainness, pleasure 9 happiness 12 cheerfulness, exhilaration

glaiket, glaikit: 5 giddy 6 stupid 7 foolish 11 lightheaded, thoughtless

glamor, glamour: 5 charm, magic, spell 7 bewitch, enchant, mystery, romance 9 fascinate

glamorous, glamourous: 6 exotic 8 alluring, charming, romantic 11 fascinating

glance: 4 gleg, leer, ogle, peek, peep, scan, scry, skew 5 blink, blush, flash, glent, gliff, glime, glint, glisk, prink 6 aspect, scance 7 glimpse

gland: 5 liver, lymph 6 carnel, thymus 7 adrenal, parotid, thyroid 8 exocrine 9 endocrine 11 paranephros
comb. form: 4 aden 5 adeno
edible: 5 liver 6 thymus
enlargement: 7 adenoma
secretion: 5 sebum 7 hormone
swelling: 4 bubo

glandular: 7 adenoid, adenose

glare: 4 gaze 5 blaze, flame, glaze, stare 7 glitter 8 radiance 9 showiness

glaring: 4 rank 5 clear, gaudy, glary, gross, plain, vivid 6 aglare 7 burning, evident, flaring, obvious, staring, visible 8 apparent, flagrant, manifest 9 barefaced 11 conspicuous

glary: 6 frosty, frozen 7 glaring, shining 8 slippery

glass: 4 frit, lens, pane 6 beaker, bottle, cloche, cullet, goblet, mirror 7 tumbler 9 barometer, telescope
alcohol: mug 4 pony 5 stein 6 rummer, seidel 8 schooner
colored: 5 smalt 7 opaline 10 aventurine
container: jar 6 bottle 7 matrass
design: 4 etch
molten: 5 metal 7 parison
partly fused: 4 frit
pert. to: 6 vitric
remove bubbles: 5 plane

glassmaking: *device:* 7 ironman
frame: 7 drosser
material: 4 frit 5 fritt
oven: 4 lehr

glassworker: 6 teaser

glasswort: 4 kali 5 plant 8 kelpwort

glassy: 4 hard 5 sharp 6 shrill 8 strident 9 apathetic 10 forbidding, lackluster, unwavering, unyielding

Glaucus: *father:* 8 Sisyphus
son: 11 Bellerophon

glaver: 7 flatter, wheedle

glaze: 4 coat, slip 5 cover, glare, sleet, stare 6 enamel, finish, polish, veneer, window 7 burnish, glidder, incrust, overlay, vitrify 8 couverte

glazier: 11 glassworker

gleam: ray 4 beam, glow 5 blink, blush, flash, glaik, glent, glint, glisk, sheen, shine 7 glimmer, glitter, shimmer, sparkle 8 radiance, splendor 9 coruscate 10 brightness 11 coruscation, scintillate

gleaming: 6 ablaze, bright

glean: 4 cull, reap 6 gather 7 collect

gleaning: 4 crop

glebe: sod 4 clod, land, soil 5 earth, field

glebe house: 5 manse 9 parsonage

glee: joy 4 song 5 mirth, sport 6 gaiety 7 delight, elation 8 hilarity 9 merriment 10 minstrelsy 12 cheerfulness 13 entertainment

gleeful: gay 5 merry 6 joyous 7 jocular 8 gleesome

gleek: 4 gibe, jest, joke

gleeman: 8 minstrel, musician

gleg: gay 4 keen 5 alert, quick, sharp 6 bright, lively, nimble 8 cheerful

glen: den 4 dale, dell, vale 5 griff, heuch, heugh, kloof 6 dingle, valley 10 depression

glent: 4 slip 5 flash, gleam, glint, shine 6 glance 7 sparkle

glib: pat 4 easy, oily 5 slick 6 casual, fluent, smooth 7 offhand, shallow, voluble 8 flippant, unforced 9 impromptu, talkative, unstudied 10 nonchalant, unthinking 11 superficial

glibbery: 6 smooth 8 slippery 10 changeable, unreliable

glide: 4 flow, sail, sile, skim, slip, soar 5 coast, creep, merge, slide, steal 6 glance 7 slither 8 glissade

gliding over: 6 labile 7 eliding

gliff: 4 look 5 scare, shock 6 fright, glance, moment 7 glimpse, instant 8 frighten

glim: bit, eye 5 light, watch 12 illumination

glimmer: 4 fire, glow 5 blink, flash, gleam 7 flimmer, glimpse, glitter, shimmer, sparkle

glimmering: 5 ghost

glimpse: 4 idea 5 blink, flash, glint, glisk, tinge, trace 6 glance, luster 7 glimmer, inkling

glint: 4 peep 5 flash, gleam, glent, shine 6 glance, luster 7 glimpse, sparkle 10 brightness

glisten: 5 flash, glisk, gliss, shine 7 glitter, sparkle 9 coruscate

glister: 5 shine 6 luster 7 sparkle

glitter: 5 flash, glare, gleam, glore, sheen, shine 6 scance 7 glimmer, glisten, glister, spangle, sparkle, twinkle 8 radiance 9 coruscate 10 brilliancy 11 coruscation, scintillate

glittering: 5 gaudy, gemmy 6 bright, fulgid 9 brilliant, clinquant, sparkling, twinkling

gloaming: eve 4 dusk 8 twilight

gloat: 4 gaze 5 exult

globe: orb 4 ball, clew 5 earth, monde, world 6 sphere 7 globule
half: 10 hemisphere
pert. to: 7 spheric

globular: 5 beady, round 6 beaded, globed 7 globose, spheric 9 globulous, orbicular, spherical 10 orbiculate

globule: 4 bead, blob, drop 6 bubble 7 droplet 8 particle, spherule

glockenspiel: 4 lyra 8 carillon 9 xylophone

glom, glaum: 4 take 5 steal, swipe, watch 10 understand

gloom: 4 dusk, murk 5 cloud, drear, frown 7 despair, dimness, sadness 8 darkness 9 dejection, heaviness, obscurity 10 cloudiness, depression, desolation, melancholy

gloomy: dim, sad, wan 4 blue, dark, dour, eery, glum 5 adusk, adust, black, brown, drear, dusky, heavy, moody, murky, stern 6 cloudy, dismal, dreary, morose, somber, sullen 7 clouded, obscure, stygian 8 darkling, darksome, detected, desolate, dolesome, downcast, overcast 9 cheerless, darkening, depressed, saturnine, tenebrous 10 depressing, despondent, foreboding, lusterless, melancholy, sepulchral, tenebrific 11 pessimistic 12 disconsolate, disheartened

glorify: 4 hery, laud 5 adore, adorn, bless, boast, exalt, extol, glory, honor, vaunt 6 praise 7 clarify, elevate, ennoble, magnify 8 emblazon, eulogize 9 celebrate 11 apotheosize

gloriole: 4 halo 7 aureole

glorious: 4 dear, mear, meer, mere 5 grand, noble 6 bright 7 eminent, haughty, radiant 8 boastful, ecstatic, gorgeous, renowned, splendid 9 hilarious, wonderful 10 celebrated, delightful 11 illustrious, intoxicated, magnificent, resplendent 12 praiseworthy, vainglorious

glory: 4 fame, halo 5 blaze, bliss, boast, eclat, exult, honor, kudos, pride 6 beauty, corona, heaven, praise, renown 7 aureole, clarity, garland, glorify 8 ambition, splendor 10 admiration, brilliancy, effulfgence, reputation 11 distinction 12 magnificence, resplendence

gloss: 4 glow 5 dodge, gloze, sheen, shine 6 blanch, enamel, excuse, luster polish, remark, veneer 7 burnish 8 annotate, flourish, palliate, pretense 9 semblance, sleekness 10 brightness, commentary 14 interpretation

glossal: 7 lingual

glossary: 6 clavis, claves(pl.)

glossy: 5 nitid, silky, sleek 6 bright, sheeny, smooth 7 shining 8 lustrous, polished, specious 9 plausible

glove: mit 4 cuff, mitt 6 mitten, sheath 7 chevron, dannock, gantlet 8 gauntlet
fabric: 4 silk, wool 5 nylon 6 cotton
leather: kid 4 napa 5 mocha, suede 7 pigskin
shape: 5 trank

glow: 4 beam, halo 5 ardor, blush, flame, flush, gleam, gloss, shine 6 warmth 7 glimmer 13 incandescence

glower: 4 gaze 5 frown, glore, scowl, stare

glowing: hot, red 5 aglow, fiery, vivid 6 ardent 7 burning, candent, fervent, radiant, shining 10 candescent

gloze: 4 fawn, glow, peer, pore 5 gleam, gloss, shine 6 speech 7 comment, deceive, explain, expound, flatter, wheedle 8 brighten, collogue, disguise, flattery, palliate, pretense 9 adulation, interpret

Gluck opera: 5 Orfeo 7 Alceste

glucose: 5 sugar 6 starch 7 sucrose 8 dextrose

glue: fix 5 mount, paste, stick 6 adhere, attach, cement, fasten, gluten, sizing 7 sericin 8 adhesive, mucilage

glum: 4 dour, grum 5 moody, surly 6 dismal, gloomy, glummy, glumpy, morose, sullen 8 dejected, frowning, overcast 10 melancholy 11 threatening

glume: 4 leaf 5 bract

glut: 4 cloy, fill, gulp, sate 5 draft, gorge 6 englut, excess, pamper 7 engorge, satiate, surfeit, swallow 8 overfeed, overload, plethora, saturate

gluten: gum 4 glue 7 fibrin 8 adhesive

glutinous: 4 ropy, sizy 5 gluey, gummy 6 sticky 7 viscous

glutton: hog, pig 4 gulo 5 gulch 6 lecher, rascal, wretch 7 epicure 8 gourmand 9 scoundrel 11 gormandizer
gluttonous: 6 greedy 7 hoggish 9 voracious
gnar, gnarr: 5 growl, snarl
gnarl: 4 gnaw, knor, knot, nurl 5 growl, knurl, snarl, twist 6 nibble, tangle 7 contort, distort
gnarled: 6 knarry, knotty, rugged 7 crabbed, knarred, twisted 12 crossgrained
gnash: 5 champ, grind
gnat: fly 4 pest 5 midge 6 insect
gnaw: eat 4 bite, chew, fret 5 erode, gnarl, waste 6 be-gnaw, chavel, nibble 7 corrode
gnede: 6 scanty 7 sparing
gnib: 5 ready, sharp 6 clever
gnome: elf, saw 5 adage, bogey, dwarf, elves(pl.), maxim, motto, pigmy, troll 6 goblin, kobold, sprite 8 aphorism, apothegm 10 apophthegm
gnomon: 4 nose 5 canon, style, tenet 9 indicator
gnostic: 4 wise 6 clever, shrewd 7 knowing 12 intellectual
gnu: 5 takin 6 mammal 8 antelope
go: be; act, bet, bid, die, gae, mog, run 4 fall, fare, gang, lead, mosy, move, pass, read, ride, turn, walk, wane, wend, work 5 break, elope, leave, occur, set-to, steal, visit 6 amount, attain, become, belong, betake, depart, elapse, follow, happen, intend, resort, result, retire, travel 7 conduce, operate, proceed, succeed 8 diminish, traverse, withdraw 9 circulate, harmonize, undertake
aboard: 6 embark 7 entrain
ahead: 7 proceed 8 continue, progress
around: 6 detour 10 circumvent
ashore: 4 land 6 debark 9 disembark
astray: err 8 aberrate, miscarry
away: 4 exit, scat, shoo 5 imshi, leave, scram 6 begone, depart, retire 7 amscray
back: ebb 6 recede, return, revert 7 regress, retreat 10 retrogress
back on: 6 betray, recede 7 abandon, retrace
before: 4 lead 7 precede 8 antecede
between: 7 mediate 9 interpose
down: sag 4 fall, sink 5 lower 7 decline, descend, founder 8 decrease 11 deteriorate
forward: 4 fare 7 advance 8 progress
into: 5 audit, delve, enter, probe 7 examine
mad: 4 rage, rave, roar 5 erupt
on: 5 enter 7 proceed 8 continue
over: 5 renew 7 retrace 9 backtrack
swiftly: run 5 scoot, speed
to and fro: 5 waver 6 totter, wig-wag 7 stagger 9 fluctuate, vacillate 11 shuttlecock
to glory: die 6 perish
to pot: die 4 fail 7 decline
up: 4 rise 5 arise, raise 6 ascend
go-between: 4 bhat 5 agent 7 arbiter 8 mediator 10 mouthpiece 11 internuncio 12 intermediary
go-cart: 4 pram 5 wagon 12 perambulator
goa: 6 mugger 7 gazelle
goad: egg, gad, rod 4 brod, dice, edge, move, prod, spur, urge, yerk 5 ankus, decoy, impel, pique, prick, sting, thorn 6 incite 7 inflame, stimuli(pl.) 8 irritate, stimulus 9 incentive, instigate, stimulate 10 incitement
goal: aim, end 4 base, butt, dole, hail, mark, mete 5 bourn, finis, score, tally 6 object 7 purpose 8 ambition 9 intention, objective 10 aspiration 11 destination 12 consummation
goat: kid, ram, tur 4 ibex, tahr 5 beden, billy, goral 6 alpaca, chamal, pasang, victim 7 markhor 8 aegagrus, ruminant 9 bouquetin, stambecco, steinbock
constellation: 9 Capricorn
disease: 7 takosis
flesh: 6 chevon
genus: 5 capra
god of: Pan
male: 4 buck 5 billy
pert. to: 6 capric 7 caprine, hircine
wild: 4 ibex
goatee: 5 beard
goatherd: 5 Damon
goatish: 4 lewd 6 coarse 7 caprine, hircine, lustful 9 salacious 10 lascivious
goatskin: 9 chevrette
gob: 4 hunk, lump, mass 5 chunk 6 sailor, seaman 7 mariner 8 quantity
gobbet: gob 4 lump, mass 5 piece 6 morsel 7 portion 8 fragment, mouthful
gobble: 4 gulp 6 gorble
Gobi Desert site: 4 Asia
goblet: cup 5 glass, hanap 6 vessel 7 chalice 8 standard
goblin: bog, cow, elf, hag, nis 4 bhut, pook 5 bogey, bogle, bucca, gnome, nisse, ouphe, pooka 6 boggle, booger, churel, kobold, sprite 7 brownie, bugaboo, bugbear 8 barguest, bogey-man, folletto, folletti(pl.)
god (see also **deity** and next entry): As, Ea, Ra, Ve; Ada, Ani, Asa, Bel, Bes, Geb, Keb, Ler, Min, Pan, Ran, Seb, Tiu, Tyr, Ull, Van 4 aitu, Amen, Amon, Aten, Aton, Baal, deus(L.), deva, dieu(F.), Frey, Hler, idol, Kama, Loke, Loki, Nora, Odin, Orra, Ptah, Rama, Surt, Thor, Vali, Yama, Zeus 5 Aeger, Aegir, Asura, Baldr, Brage, Brama, Donar, Freyr, Hades, image, Othin, Pluto, Shiva, Surtr, Woden 6 Apollo, Brahma, Cronus, Elohim, Ganesa, Hermes, Hoenir, Kronus, Marduk,

Njorth, Osiris, Saturn, Vulcan, Yahweh 7 Bacchus, creator, Forsete, godhead, Heimdal, Jehovah, Jupiter, Krishna, Mercury, Serapis, Vitharr 8 Almighty, Dionysus 9 Heindallr, Hlorrithi 10 Hephaestus 11 Ramachandra
false: 4 Baal 6 Mammon
love for: 5 piety 6 amadis, bhakti
god: For gods of specific localities, religions, or functions, see under the specific locality, religion, or function. EXAMPLES: "god of Thebes": see **Thebes** *god of;* "hindu god": see **Hinduism** *deity;* "god of war" : see **war** *god.*
God be with you: 5 adieu, adios 7 good bye
God blind me: 5 blimy
god-fearing: 5 pious 6 devout 9 religious
god-horse: 6 mantis
god-like: 5 pious 6 deific, devout, divine 8 immortal 9 religious
god of: For all definitions beginning with this phrase, see next important word. EXAMPLE: "god of flocks": see **flocks** *god of.*
goddess (see also **god**): Bau, Dis, Eir, Eos, Hel, Mut, Nut, Uma 4 Anta, Bast, Devi, Gaia, Hela, Hera, Isis, Juno, Kali, Nina, Norn, Saga, Urth, Wyrd 5 Belit, Ceres, Diana, Durga, Freya, Frigg, Gauri, Nanna, Venus 6 Athena, Aurora, Chandi, Freyja, Frigga, Hecate, Hestia, Shakti, Tiamat 7 Artemis, Asynjur, Demeter, Mylitta, Parvati 9 Aphrodite, Haimavati 10 Persephone, Proserpina
godfather: 7 sponsor
godforsaken: 8 desolate, wretched 9 neglected
godless: 6 wicked 7 impious, profane, ungodly 9 atheistic
godliness: 5 piety 13 righteousness
godling: 5 deity 6 godkin, godlet
woodland: 7 Selenus
godly: 5 pious 6 devout 8 gracious 9 religious, righteous
godmother: 6 cummer, kimmer 7 sponsor
gods' abode: 6 heaven 7 Olympus
God's body: 7 bodikin
Goethe drama: 5 Faust 6 Egmont
goety: 5 magic 10 necromancy
goffer, gauffer: 5 crimp, flute, plait
gog: bog 4 stir 8 activity, quagmire 9 agitation, eagerness
goggle: bug, eye 4 roll 5 stare 6 squint
goggler: 4 scad 5 akule
goggles: 8 blinkers
going: run, way 4 exit, fare, gait, gate, path, road 5 bound 6 access 8 behavior 9 departure 10 passageway
goiter: 6 struma 7 strumae(pl.)
gola: 4 cyma 7 granary 9 storeroom
Golan Heights town: 8 Kuneitra
gold: oro(Sp.) 4 gelt, gilt 5 aurum, metal 6 riches, wealth 7 bullion 9 clinquant
bar: 5 ingot
black: oil
comb. form: 4 auro
deposit: 6 placer
fool's: 6 pyrite
heraldry: or
imitation: 6 ormolu, oroide
measure of weight: 5 carat
pert. to: 4 dore 6 aurous
symbol: Au
thin sheet of: 4 foil 6 latten
uncoined: 7 bullion
gold braid: 5 orris
gold-brick: 7 swindle
Gold Bug author: Poe
gold-plate: 4 gild, gilt
golden: 4 gilt, rich 5 auric, blest, blond, goldy 6 aureal, blonde, goldie, mellow, yellow 7 aureate, aureous, halcyon, shining 8 aurelian, precious 9 aureoline, Pactolian, yellowish 10 auriferous
golden age: 9 siecle d'or(F.)
golden apple giver: 5 Paris
golden bough: 9 mistletoe
golden chain: 8 laburnum
Golden Fleece: *keeper of:* 6 Aeetes
land of: 7 Colchis
seeker: 5 Jason 8 Argonaut
ship used: 4 Argo
golden oriole: 5 pirol 6 loriot
goldeneye: cur 9 merrywing
goldenrod: 8 solidago
goldfinch: 8 graypate, greypate 12 yellowhammer
goldfish: 4 carp 6 calico 9 garibaldi, shubunkin
goldsmith: 7 artisan 9 artificer
crucible: 6 cruset
golem: 5 robot 9 automaton, blockhead
golf: *assistant:* 5 caddy 6 caddie
club: 4 iron, wood 5 baffy, cleek, mashy, spoon 6 brassy, driver, jigger, mashie, putter 7 brassie, midiron, niblick
course: cup 4 link 5 green, links
cry: 4 fore
cup: 5 Ryder 6 Walker
hazard: 4 trap 5 stymy 6 bunker, stymie
mound: tee
score: par 4 bogy 5 bogey, bogie, eagle 6 birdie, Nassau
stroke: 4 hook, loft, putt 5 drive, slice
target: cup 4 flag 5 green
term: lie, par, tee 4 baff, fore, hook 5 bogey, bogie, divot, dormy, eagle, green, slice, stimy 6 birdie, dormie, stymie, stroke 7 gallery

tournament: 4 open
goliath: 5 giant
Goliath: *home:* 4 Gath
place of death: 4 Elah
slayer: 5 David
gollar, goller: 4 roar 5 growl, shout 6 gurgle
golly: 4 oath, yell
Gomer: *father:* 7 Japheth
husband: 5 Hosea
gondola: car 4 boat 5 barge, coach
gone: 4 left, lost 6 ruined 8 absorbed, advanced, finished, involved
gone by: ago, o'er 4 over, past 5 agone 6 bygone, passed
Goneril: *father:* 4 Lear
sister: 5 Regan 8 Cordelia
gonfalon: 4 flag 6 banner, ensign
goober: 6 peanut
good: bon(F.), fit 4 able, bein, bien(F.), boon, braw, fine, full, gain, kind, nice, prow 5 ample, brave, bueno, bully, moral, nifty, pious, sound, valid 6 benign, devout, expert, profit, proper 7 copious, gradely, helpful, liberal, trained, upright 8 becoming, budgeree, decorous, friendly, gracious, interest, orthodox, pleasant, pleasing, salutary, skillful, suitable, virtuous 9 agreeable, bountiful, competent, dauntless, enjoyable, estimable, excellent, favorable, fortunate, indulgent, reputable, righteous, well-being 10 auspicious, beneficial, benevolent, courageous, gratifying, profitable, sufficient 11 pleasurable, respectable, responsible, well-behaved 12 considerable, satisfactory, stouthearted, well-disposed
good-bye, good-by: 4 tata 5 addio, adieu(F.), adios(Sp.), ciaou(It.) 6 so-long 7 cheerio 8 farewell
Good Earth author: 4 Buck
good-for-nothing: 4 orra 7 useless 8 spalpeen(Ir.) 9 worthless 10 ne'er-do-well, 11 rapscallion
good health: 5 skoal 6 prosit 7 slainte
good-looking: 4 fair 5 bonny 6 comely, pretty 7 eyesome, winsome 9 beautiful 10 personable
good luck: 7 fortune
image: 6 alraun
good-natured: 9 gemutlich
good spirit: 8 eudaemon
goodliness: 5 grace 6 beauty 8 goodness, kindness 10 comeliness, excellence
goodly: 4 kind 5 large 6 comely, portly 8 gracious, handsome 9 capacious, excellent 12 considerable
goodness: 6 bounty, purity, virtue 8 chastity, kindness 10 excellence, generosity, goodliness 11 beneficence, benevolence
goods: 4 fent, gear 5 stock, wares, wrack 7 chattel, finance 8 property 11 merchandise, possessions
cast overboard: 5 lagan, ligan 6 jetsam, lagend
in animal hides: 6 ceroon, seroon
in law: 4 bona
lost in shipwreck: 7 flotsam
smuggled: 10 contraband
stolen: 4 loot, pelf 5 booty, spoil 6 spoils
goodwill: 4 love 5 favor 9 readiness 10 heartiness 11 benevolence 12 friendliness
goody: 5 candy 9 sweetmeat
goof: 5 spoil 7 blunder
goofy: 5 silly 7 foolish 8 gullible
gool: 5 ditch 6 breach, sluice 7 channel, fissure
goon: sap 4 boob, dope, thug 6 bomber 7 slugger
goosander: 9 merganser
goose: 4 hiss 5 hansa, ninny, solan 6 cagmag, gander, goslet 7 gosling, widgeon 9 screwball, simpleton
cry: 4 honk, yang 5 cronk
flock: 4 raft 6 gaggle
genus: 4 chen 5 anser, brant
mackerel: 9 phalarope
male: 6 gander
pert. to: 8 anserine 9 grossular
resembling: 8 anserine
snow: 4 chen 5 brant, wavey 9 whitehead
tailor's: 8 flatiron
young: 7 gosling
gooseberry: 4 fabe 6 groser 7 currant 8 feaberry, goosegog 9 honey-blob
gooseflesh: 4 cold 7 pimples
goosefoot: 5 blite, plant, shrub
gooseherd: 7 gozzard
gopher: 4 tuza 6 rodent 8 squirrel
Gopher State: 9 Minnesota
Gorboduc's son: 6 Porrex
Gordian: 9 intricate 11 complicated
gore: mud 4 burt, dirt 5 blood, cruor, filth, slime 6 gusset, insert, pierce 9 penetrate
gorge: 4 fill, gaum, glut, pass, sate 5 cajon, canon, chasm, flume, gulch, gully, kloof, strid 6 canyon, coulee, defile, englut, nullah, ravine, valley 7 couloir, overeat, pitcher, satiate 8 quebrada 10 gluttonize
gorgeous: 4 vain 5 grand, showy 6 costly 8 dazzling, glorious, splendid 9 beautiful, luxurious 11 magnificent, resplendent
Gorgon: 6 Medusa, Stheno 7 Euryale
watcher for: 4 Enyo 5 Deino 6 Graeae(pl.) 8 Pephredo
gorilla: ape 10 anthropoid
gorse: 4 whin 5 furze 7 juniper
gory: 6 bloody 9 murderous 10 sanguinary 12 bloodstained

goshawk: gos 6 tercel
keeper: 8 ostreger 10 austringer
gospel: 7 evangel, tidings 8 doctrine, teaching 9 veritable
harmony of the four: 11 diatessaron
gossamer: web 5 filmy 6 cobweb 8 raincoat
gossip: cat, gab, gup 4 aunt, chat, clat, gash 5 cause, clack, clash, clepe, clype, crony, rumor 6 babble, caddle, callet, claver, gabble, glaver, norate, tattle 7 chatter, chin-wag, clatter, comment, gauster, nashgob, scandal, sponsor, tattler 8 informer, quidnunc 9 chatterer 10 newsmonger, talebearer, tattletale 11 scuttlebutt
gossoon: boy, lad 5 youth
got: see **get**
gotch: jug 7 pitcher
gote: 6 sluice, stream 7 channel
Goth: 8 Visigoth 9 barbarian, Ostrogoth
hero: 5 Wudga
last: 8 Roderick
Gothamite: 9 New Yorker
Gothic: 4 rude 5 rough 6 fierce 8 barbaric, Teutonic
gouge: 4 tool 5 cheat, fraud 6 cavity, chisel, groove 7 defraud 9 extortion 10 overcharge
Gounod opera: 5 Faust
gourd: 4 hole, pepo 5 melon, pepos 6 bottle, vessel 7 anguria 8 calabash, cucurbit 9 colocynth 11 chilacayote
rattle: 6 maraca
sponge: 5 loofa, luffa
gourmand: 7 epicure, glutton, gourmet 11 connoisseur
gourmandise, gormandize: 6 guttle
gourmet: 7 epicure 8 gourmand 11 connoisseur
gousty: 6 dreary 7 ghastly 8 desolate 13 preternatural
gout: 4 clot, drop 5 ditch, drain, taste 6 blotch, sluice, splash 7 channel, podagra 9 arthritis 11 coagulation, discernment
goutweed: 8 aiseweed
govern: run 4 curb, rein, rule, sway 5 guide, regle, steer 6 bridle, direct, manage, police 7 command, conduct, control, preside, refrain 8 dominate, regulate, restrain 9 influence, supervise 10 administer, discipline
governance: 7 control 10 government, management
governante, gouvernante: 8 chaperon 9 governess 11 housekeeper
governess: 6 abbess 8 mistress 11 gouvernante
governing: 6 regent 7 leading 11 gubernative
government: 4 rule 5 power 6 empire, habits 7 conduct, regency, regimen 8 demeanor, monarchy, republic 9 autocracy, democracy, hierarchy, oligarchy 10 governance, management 11 aristocracy, gubernation
agent: 5 envoy 6 consul 8 diplomat, minister 10 ambassador
art of: 8 politics 13 statesmanship
by a few: 9 oligarchy
by church: 9 hierarchy 10 hierocracy
by people: 9 democracy
by rich: 10 plutocracy
by three: 8 triarchy 11 triumvirate
by women: 8 gynarchy 11 gynecocracy
derived from: 9 political
head: 4 czar, king, tzar 5 queen 7 emperor, empress, premier 8 dictator 9 president 10 presidente
official: 6 syndic 10 bureaucrat
opposition to: 10 antarchism
representative: 6 consul 10 ambassador
science: 8 politics
system: 6 regime
without: 6 acracy 7 anarchy
governor: bey 4 lord 5 deity, nabob, pilot, ruler 6 author, dynast, grieve, rector, regent 7 captain, control, dynasty, manager, viceroy 8 director 9 president, regulator 10 gubernator, magistrate
castle: 6 alcaid 7 alcaide 9 castellan
gowk: 4 fool, gawk 6 cuckoo 9 simpleton
gowl: 4 howl, yell 5 whine 6 throat
gown (see also **dress, garment**): 4 robe, toga 5 frock, habit, manto, toosh 6 clothe, invest, mantua 7 garment
dressing: 4 robe 6 kimono 8 peignoir
loose: 6 banian, camise, chimer 7 cassock, chemise, chimere
Moslem: 4 jama 5 jamah
Goya painting: 4 Maja
goyle: 5 gully 6 hollow, ravine, valley
gozzard: 9 gooseherd
gra: 5 lover 6 liking 8 fondness 10 sweetheart
grab: nab, rap 4 boat 5 catch, clasp, grasp, seize 6 arrest, beclap, clutch, collar, snatch 7 capture, grapnel, grapple 11 appropriate
grabble: 4 grab 5 grope, seize 6 snatch, sprawl 7 grapple 11 appropriate
grace: 4 este 5 adorn, charm, favor, leave, mercy 6 beauty, become, bedeck, favour, polish, prayer, virtue 7 commend, dignify, gratify 8 beautify, easiness, efficacy, elegance, kindness 9 embellish, privilege 10 comeliness, goodliness, permission, refinement, seemliness 12 dispensation 14 attractiveness

Grace: 6 Aglaia, Charis, Thalia 10 Euphrosyne
mother of: 5 Aegle
graceful: 4 airy, easy, gent 5 genty 6 comely, gainly, mignon, seemly 7 elegant, fitting, genteel, tactful 8 charming, debonair, delicate 9 beautiful 11 appropriate
graceless: 4 ugly 5 cruel 7 awkward 8 depraved 9 abandoned, inelegant, merciless 10 ungracious 11 unfortunate
gracenote: 12 appoggiatura
graces: 8 agremens 9 agrements
gracile: 4 thin 6 slight 7 slender 8 graceful
gracious: 4 good, hend, kind, mild 5 civil, godly, happy, lucky, suave 6 benign, goodly, kindly 7 affable 8 benedict, debonair, generous, handsome, merciful, pleasing 9 benignant, courteous, favorable, fortunate 10 beneficent, forthgoing, regenerate 11 complaisant
grackle: 4 myna
gradation: 4 rank, step 5 scale, stage 6 climax, degree, series 8 position 10 exaltation, succession
grade: peg 4 mark, rank, rate, size, sort 5 class, level, order, stage 6 ascent, assort, degree, rating, select 7 incline, inspect 8 classify, gradient, graduate 14 classification
grader: 9 bulldozer
gradient: 4 ramp 5 grade, slope
gradino, gradin: 5 shelf 7 retable
gradual: 4 easy, slow 6 gentle 9 leisurely
graduate: 5 grade 6 alumna 7 alumnus
Graeae, Graiae: 4 Enyo 5 Deino 8 Pephredo
father: 7 Phorcus, Phorcys
sister: 6 Gorgon, Medusa 7 Gorgons
graff: 5 canal, ditch, fosse 6 trench
graft: dig 4 cion, toil, work 5 ditch, gravy, labor, scion, trade 6 boodle, inarch, trench 7 engraff 10 occupation
grafted: 6 united 8 attached
heraldry: 4 ente
grail: ama, cup 4 bowl 7 chalice, platter 8 sangraal, sangreal
knight of: 4 Bors 7 Galahad 8 Percival
grain: jot, rye 4 corn, curn, grit, meal, oats, rice, seed, wale 5 fiber, glebe, maize, scrap, spark, trace, wheat 6 barley, cereal, kernel, russud(Russ.) 7 granule, texture 8 particle 9 granulate
beard: awn
brewing: 4 malt
bundle: 5 sheaf
chaff: 4 bran, grit
coating: 4 bran
comb. form: 4 sito
disease: 4 smut 5 ergot
dried: 5 straw 6 groats, rissom, rizzom
ear of: 5 spike 6 ressum
foodstuff: 6 cereal
fungus: 5 ergot
funnel: 6 hopper
goddess of: 5 Ceres 7 Demeter
ground: 4 meal 5 flour, grist
line: 5 swath
measure: 6 thrave
mixture: 6 fodder 7 farrage 9 bullimong
outer membrane: 6 extine
parched: 7 graddan
price: 4 fiar(Sc.)
receptacle: bin 8 elevator
refuse: pug 5 chaff
scoop: 5 shaul
spike: ear
stack: 4 rick
tool: 5 flail
warehouse: 8 elevator
graip: 5 gripe
graith: 4 gear 5 adorn, build, dress, stuff 6 wealth 7 apparel, compose, furnish, prepare 8 material 9 apparatus, furniture 11 possessions 12 acoutrements 13 accouterments
gram: *one-tenth:* 8 decigram
molecule: mol 4 mole
gramary: 5 magic 7 grammar 8 learning 10 necromancy 11 enchantment
gramercy: 6 thanks 7 emotion
grammar: 6 syntax 9 accidence 11 linguistics
case: nom 6 dative 8 ablative, genitive, vocative 9 objective 10 accusative, nominative
describe: 5 parse
direct address: 8 vocative
example: 8 paradigm
term: 6 phrase, simile 8 metaphor
grampus: orc 4 orca 5 whale 7 cetacea, dolphin 8 cetacean, scorpion
granada: 11 pomegranate
granary: bin 4 gola 6 garnel, garner, girnal, girnel, grange 8 cornloft 9 cornhouse 10 repository, storehouse
grand: 4 epic, main 5 chief, great, lofty, noble, showy 6 august, epical, famous, superb, swanky 7 exalted, immense, stately, sublime 8 foremost, glorious, gorgeous, majestic, splendid 9 dignified, grandiose, principal, sumptuous 10 impressive, preeminent 11 ceremonious, illustrious, magnificent 13 comprehensive
Grand Canyon state: 7 Arizona
Grand Duke of Hell: 6 Abogor
grand slam: 4 vole 5 homer 7 home run
grandchild: oe, oy; oye
great: 5 ieroe

grandee: 6 bashaw 7 magnate 8 nobleman 10 clarissimo(It.)
grandeur: 4 pomp 5 state 6 parade 7 majesty 8 elegance, splendor, vastness 9 greatness, immensity, loftiness, nobleness, sublimity 10 augustness 12 magnificence
grandeval: 7 ancient
grandfather: 6 atavus 8 grandfer, gudesire(Sc.)
pert. to: 4 aval
grandiloquent: 6 heroic, turgid 7 pompous 9 bombastic 13 grandiloquous
grandiose: 4 epic 5 grand 6 turgid 7 pompous 8 imposing 9 bombastic, expansive, flaunting 10 impressive
grandmother: 6 beldam, granny, gudame(Sc.) 7 beldame, grandam, grannie 8 babushka(Russ.), grandame 9 eldmother
Devil's: 4 Baba
grange: 4 farm 7 granary 9 farmhouse
granger: 6 farmer
granite: 6 aplite 7 haplite, syenite 8 alaskite
granitic: 4 hard 7 austere 10 inflexible
grant: aid 4 boon, cede, gift, give, lend, loan, mise 5 admit, allot, allow, bonus, chart, cowle, spare, yette, yield 6 accede, accord, afford, assent, bestow, betake, beteem, bounty, confer, octroi, patent, permit, remise 7 adjudge, concede, consent, promise, subsidy, tribute 8 bestowal, donation, transfer 9 franchise, undertake 10 concession, permission, relinquish 11 acknowledge
granting: if 6 ceding, remise 7 lending 9 allowance, conceding
granular: 5 sandy 6 coarse, grainy 9 granulose
granulate: 5 grain 7 coarsen 11 crystallize
granule: 4 pill 5 grain 6 nodule, pellet 8 particle
grape: uva 5 Tokay 6 Agawam, Lalang, Malaga, Malage, Muscat 7 Catawba, Concord, Hamburg, Mission, Niagara 8 Delaware, Riesling, Thompson 8 muscadine 11 Scuppernong
acid: 7 racemic
cluster: 10 racemation
comb. form: 5 botry 6 botryo
conserve: 5 jelly, uvate
cultivation: 11 viniculture, viticulture
dried: 6 raisin
drink: 4 dibs, sapa, wine
fermentation: 6 cuvage(Fr.)
gatherer: 8 vintager
genus of: 5 vitis
juice: 4 dibs, must, sapa, stum
pert. to: 4 uval 10 botryoidal
refuse: 4 marc
residue: 4 marc, rape 6 pomace
seed: 6 acinus
spirit: 4 marc
sugar: 8 dextrose, fructose
grapefruit: 6 pomelo 8 shaddock
Grapes of Wrath: *author:* 9 Steinbeck
family: 4 Joad
grapevine: 4 caro 5 rumor 6 canard, report
pest: 10 phylloxera
graph: 5 chart 7 contour 8 quantity
graphic: 5 vivid 11 picturesque
graphite: 6 carbon
grapnel: 4 drag, grab 5 catch, seize 6 anchor 7 grapple
grapple: 4 grab, hold 5 grasp, gripe 6 buckle, clinch, tackle 7 contend, grabble, grapnel, gripple, seizing, seizure, wrestle 8 struggle
grasp: nap, see 4 clam, fist, glam, grab, grip, hand, hent, hold, holt, take 5 catch, clasp, glaum, gripe, seize, snare 6 clench, clinch, clutch, grappe, snatch 7 control, embrace, grapple, gripple, seizure 8 handfast 9 apprehend 10 comprehend, understand 13 comprehension
grasping: 4 avid, hard 6 greedy, grippy 7 miserly 8 covetous 10 avaricious 12 apprehension, parsimonious
adapted for: 10 prehensile, prehensive
grass (see also **cereal**): 4 lawn, reed, turf 6 darnel 7 hassock, herbage, pasture 9 colieroot, vetiveria 10 greensward
blade of: 7 traneen
dried: hay 6 fodder
fiber: 4 flax 5 istle, ramee, ramie 6 bhabar
fodder: 4 dura, gama 6 millet
forage: 7 setaria
genus of: 5 stipa 6 clover, lygeum 7 setaria
kinds of: eel, fog, hay, poa 4 alfa, bent, cane, diss, leaf, reed 5 avena, grama, sedge, spart, spike, stipa 6 enalid, marram, quitch, redtop, sesame, sorrel 7 esparto, traneen 8 calfkill 9 bouteloua
tuft: 7 tussock
grasschat: 8 whinchat
grasshopper: 4 grig 6 locust
grassland: lea 4 lawn, rakh(Ind.), vale 5 field, range, veldt 6 meadow 7 pasture, prairie
grassplot: 4 lawn 6 meadow
grassweed: 8 eelgrass
grate: jar 4 fret, grid, grit, rasp 5 grill, grind 6 abrade, basket, offend, prison, scrape 7 grating 8 imprison, irritate
grateful: 8 thankful 9 agreeable 12 appreciative
gratification: 4 gust 6 reward 8 delicacy, gratuity, pleasure 9 enjoyment 10 recompense 11 contentment 12 satisfaction
gratified: 4 glad 5 proud 7 pleased 9 delighted

gratify: 4 feed, sate 5 adorn, amuse, feast, grace, humor, wreak 6 arride, foster, pamper, please 7 appease, content, delight, flatter, gladden, indulge, requite, satisfy, welcome 9 gratulate 10 remunerate

grating: 4 grid, heck, rasp 5 grate, gride, grill, harsh, raspy, rough 6 cratch, grille, hoarse 8 gridiron, grinding, strident 9 dissonant 11 latticework

gratis: 4 free 10 gratuitous

gratitude: 4 gift 5 favor 6 thanks 7 tribute 8 gratuity 12 thankfulness

gratuitous: 4 free 6 gratis, wanton 8 baseless, needless 10 groundless 11 superfluous, unwarranted

gratuity: fee, tip 4 dash, dole, gift, vail 5 bonus, bribe, pilon, spiff 6 bounty 7 cumshaw, pension, present 8 bakshish, bonamano, buckshee, lagnappe 9 baksheesh, buona-mano, gratitude, lagniappe, pourboire 10 compliment 11 benefaction 13 gratification

grave: dig, pit 4 bier, bury, deep, foss, slow, tomb 5 carve, ditch, fossa, fosse, heavy, inter, sober, staid, suant 6 burial, grieve, hearse, sedate, solemn, somber, sombre, trench 7 austere, earnest, engrave, serious, steward 8 decorous, overseer, sermonic 9 important, momentous, ponderous, sepulcher 11 influential 13 authoritative

cloth: 8 cerement

comb. form: 5 serio

robber: 4 goul 5 ghoul

gravecloth: 6 sudary 8 cerement 9 cerecloth

gravedigger: 6 burier, fossor 7 fossore(pl.)

gravel: 4 dirt, grit, sand, stop 5 check 6 bother, chisel, eratum, sammel 7 perplex 8 alluvium, erratice 9 embarrass

graven: 6 etched 8 engraved 10 sculptured

graver: 5 burin 8 engraver, sculptor

gravestone: 5 blank, stela, stele 6 cippus, marker 8 monument 9 tombstone 11 sarcophagus

graveyard: 8 cemetery 10 churchyard

gravid: 8 pregnant

graviers: 4 dice

graving tool: 5 burin

gravity: 7 dignity 8 enormity, sobriety 9 heaviness, influence, solemnity 10 importance 11 earnestness, seriousness, weightiness 12 significance 13 momentousness 17 authoritativeness

law discoverer: 6 Newton

gravy: jus(F.) 4 lear 5 graft, juice, sauce

gravy boat: 9 sauceboat

gray: dim 4 ashy, dull, gris, hoar 5 ashen, bleak, hoary, lyard, lyart, slate 6 dismal, leaden, mature 7 elderly, grisard, grizzly, hueless, neutral 9 cheerless 10 achromatic

bluish: 7 cesious

comb. form: 5 polio

dark: 5 taupe 6 Oxford 8 charcoal

light: 4 ashy 5 pearl

Quaker: 5 acier

Gray's churchyard opus: 5 Elegy

gray matter: 4 obex 5 brain

gray whale: 7 ripsack

grayish: 7 grizzle 8 grizzled

graylag: 5 goose

grayling: 4 fish 9 butterfly

graze: 4 drab, feed, rase, skim 5 agist, brush, shave 6 browse, ripple, scrape 7 pasture

grazing ground: 4 colp 5 range 6 collop, meadow 7 pasture

grease: fat, oil 4 daub, lard, mort, seak, soil 5 bleck, bribe, cheat, cozen, smear 6 creesh(Sc.) 7 lanolin 9 lubricate, overreach

greaser: 6 stoker

greasewood: 5 chico, orach, yolky 6 orache

greasy: fat 4 oily, rich 5 dirty, fatty, gross, porky, thick 7 smeared 8 indecent, unctuous 10 indelicate 11 threatening

great: big 4 deep, fell, huge, much, rial, unco, vast 5 ample, chief, grand, large, yeder 6 grande(F.), heroic, mickle 7 capital, eminent, extreme, howling, immense, intense, titanic, violent 8 almighty, elevated, enormous, favorite, horrible 9 elaborate, excellent, important, prolonged 10 delightful, omnipotent 11 magnificent

comb. form: 4 mega 5 macro, megal

prefix: 4 arch

great albacore: 5 tunny 7 bluefin

great-aunt: 9 grandaunt

Great Barrier island: 4 Otea

great blue heron: 5 crane

Great Britain: See **England**

great deal: 4 gobs, lots

Great Divide: 7 Rockies

Great Expectations hero: Pip

Great Lake: 4 Erie 5 Huron 7 Ontario 8 Michigan, Superior

great many: lac 4 lakh

Great Sea: 5 Black 13 Mediterranean

Great White Brother: 7 Mahatma

greatcoat: 5 grego, jemmy, jimmy 8 overcoat 9 cothamore

greaten: 5 exalt 7 enhance, enlarge, magnify 8 increase

greater: 6 better 8 majority, mightier

greatest: 4 arch, best, most 6 utmost 7 extreme, noblest, supreme

greatly: 4 fell, much 5 amain, nobly

greatness: 8 grandeur 9 magnitude 11 magnanimity

greave: 5 armor, grove 7 thicket
greaves: 9 crackling
grebe: 4 fowl 8 dabchick
Grecia: 6 Greece
Grecian: 5 Greek 9 Hellenist
gree: 5 favor, prize 7 mastery 8 gladness, pleasure 11 superiority 12 satisfaction
Greece (see also **Athens, Sparta**): 6 Hellas
abode of gods: 7 Olympus
administrator: 10 amphodarch
alphabet: mu, nu, xi, pi; eta, rho, tau, phi, chi, psi 4 beta, zeta, iota 5 alpha, gamma, delta, theta, kappa, sigma, omega 6 lambda 7 epsilon, omicron, upsilon
altar: 7 eschara
ancient district: 4 Elis 5 Doris 6 Achaea, Achaia, Attica, Epirus, Hellas, Sparta 7 Epeiros, Macedon 12 Peloponnesus
Argolis valley: 5 Nemea
army corps: 6 evzone
assembly: 4 Pnyx 5 agora
avenging spirit: 6 Erinys
basin: 6 louter
beauty: 4 Lais
bondman: 6 penest
cape: 5 Malea 7 Matapan
castanet: 8 crotalum
Catholic: 5 Uniat 6 Uniate
chamber: 12 bouleuterion
chariot: 4 biga
church: 8 Orthodox
citadel: 9 Acropolis
city: 4 Elis 5 Barca, Chios, Drama, Eolis, Pella, Samos, Zante 6 Athens(c.), Edessa, Janina, Kozane, Larisa, Lesbos, Locris, Phocis, Phokis, Serrai, Serres, Sparta, Yanina 7 Corinth, Epeiros, Laconia, Larissa, Megaris, Rhodope 8 Ioannina, Komotine, Lassithi, Lessenia, Lessinia, Salonica, Salonika, Thessaly, Trikkala 9 Korinthos, Lasethion, Lasithion, Phthiotis, Rethymnon, Zakynthos 10 Negroponte 15 Alexandroupolis
clan: 4 obes 5 genos
cloak: 6 abolla 7 chlamys
coin: 4 mine, obol 5 hecte, nomas 6 lepton, phenix, stater 7 diobolo, drachma
colony: 4 Elea 5 Ionia
column: 5 Doric, Ionic 10 Corinthian
contest: 4 agon
counselor: 6 Nestor
courtesan: 5 Thais 7 Aspasia
cup: 5 depas
dialect: 5 Doric, Elean, Eolic, Ionic 6 Aeolic
dirge: 5 linos
district: 4 Arta, deme 5 Canea, Chios, Corfu, Drama, Evros, Khios, Pella, Samos, Zante 6 Achaea, Attica, Epirus, Euboea, Khania, Kozane, Lesbos, Phocis, Serrai, Yanina 7 Achaiam, Aetolia, Arcadia, Argolis, Boeotia, Corinth, Florina, Kavalla, Laconia, Larissa, Rhodope 8 Cyclades, Ioannina, Messenia, Rethymne, Salonica, Thessaly, Trıkkala 9 Acarnania, Korinthos, Lasithion, Macedonia, Phthiotis, Zakynthos 10 Cephalonia, Chalcidice, Khalkidike 11 Kephallenia
doom: ker
dramatist: 9 Aeschylus, Euripides, Sophocles 12 Aristophanes
enchantress: 5 Circe, Medea
epic: 5 Iliad 7 Odyssey
essence: 5 ousia
fabulist: 5 Aesop
Fate: 6 Clotho 7 Atropos 8 Lachesis
festival: 5 delia, haloa 8 Apaturia
flask: 4 olpe
fleet commander: 7 navarch
flute: 7 hemiope
folk dance: 7 romaika
foot-race course: 6 stadia(pl.) 7 diaulos, stadium
foot soldier: 7 hoplite
Fury: 6 Alecto, Erinys 7 Erinyes, Megaera 9 Tisiphone
galley: 6 bireme 7 trireme, unireme
garment: 5 tunic 6 abolla, chiton, peplos, peplus 7 chlamys
giant: 4 Otus 5 Mimas 7 Aloadae 9 Enceladus, Ephialtes
gift: 6 xenium
god: Dis, Pan 4 Ares, Eros, Zeus 5 Hades, Momus, Pluto, satyr 6 Apollo, Cronus, Hermes, Kronos, Nereus, Triton 7 Bacchus 8 Dionysus, Poseidon
god of love: 4 Eros
god of sea: 6 Triton 8 Poseidon
god of war: 4 Ares
god of wind: 6 Aeolus
goddess: Ge, Io; Ara, Ate, Eos, Not, Nyx, Ops 4 Alea, Dice, Dike, Enyo, Gaea, Gaia, Hebe, Hera, Leto, Nike 5 Horae, Irene, Metis, Moera, Niobe, Vesta 6 Athena, Eirene, Hecate, Hekate, Hestia, Selena, Selene, Semele 7 Ariadne, Artemis, Astarte, Demeter, Eunomia, Nemesis 9 Aphrodite
Gorgon: 4 Enyo 5 Deino 6 Graeae, Graiae, Medusa, Stheno 7 Euryale 8 Pephredo
governor: 6 eparch
gymnasium: 4 xyst 9 palaestra
hero: 4 Aias, Ajax, Idas 5 Jason 7 Cecrops, Theseus 8 Heracles
historian: 7 Ctesias 8 Polybius, Xenophon 10 Thucydides
hobgoblin: 6 Empusa
hunter: 5 Orion
huntress: 7 Artemis 8 Atalanta
instrument: 5 aulos 8 barbiton
invader: 6 Dorian

island: Ios, Kos, Nio 4 Keos, Milo, Paxi, Syra 5 Chios, Corfu, Crete, Delos, Khios, Krete, Melos, Milos, Naxos, Paros, Psara, Samos, Syros, Thera, Tinos, Zante 6 Andros, Candia, Cerigo, Ikaria, Ionian, Ithaka, Lemnos, Lesbos, Leukas, Patmus, Rhodes, Sifnos 7 Amorgos, Cythera, Kimolos, Kythera, Kythnos, Myconos, Mykonis, Serifus 8 Cyclades, Mytelene, Santorin 9 Antiparos, Santorini 10 Cephalonia, Samothrace 11 Anticythera
jar: 7 amphora
judge: 6 dikast 7 heliast
jug: 5 ascos
king: 5 Minos 6 Nestor
lake: 6 Copais
lawgiver: 5 Minos, Solon
legislative council: 5 boule
letter: see *alphabet* above
letter(primitive): san 5 koppa, sampi 7 digamma
lover: 7 Rhoecus
lyre player: 5 Arion
man of brass: 5 Talos
marker: 5 stela, stele
market place: 5 agora
marriage: 5 gamos
mathematician: 6 Euclid 10 Archimedes
measure: pik 4 bema, piki, pous 5 baril, cados, chous, cubit, diote, doron, pekhe, pygon, xylon 6 acaena, bachel, bacile, barile, cotula, dichas, hemina, koilon, lichas, milion, orgyia, palame, pechys, schene, xestes 7 amphora, choemix, cyathos, diaulos, hekteus, metreta, stadion, stadium, stremma 8 condylos, daktylos, dekapode, dolichos, medimnys, palaiste, plethron, spithame, stathmos 9 hemiekton, oxybaphon
monster: 5 Hydra
mountain: Ida 4 Oeta, Ossa 5 Athos, Parus, Visti 6 Othrys, Pelion, Pindus 7 Helicon, Olympus 8 Hymettus, Taygetus 9 Cambunian, Cithaeron, Parnassus, Psiloriti 10 Lycabettus, Pentelucus
musical interval: 6 ditone, meseme
musical note: 4 mese, nete
musical system: 5 neume
mustard: 6 sinapi
nome: see *district* above
numeral: mu, nu, xi, pi; eta, san 4 beta, zeta, iota 5 alpha, gamma, delta, theta, kappa, koppa, sampi 6 lambda 7 epsilon, digamma, omicron
nymph: 5 Oread 8 Arethusa
old testament: 10 Septuagint
overseer: 5 ephor
paradise: 7 Elysium
patriarch: 5 Arius
patriot: 6 klepht
peninsula: 4 Alte 5 Morea
people: 5 demos 6 Argive, Cretan, Ionian 7 Hellene, Spartan 8 Athenian
pert. to: 6 Ionian 8 Hellenic 9 classical 11 Panhellenic
philosopher: 4 Zeno 5 Galen, Plato 6 Thales 8 Diogenes 9 Aristotle 10 Pythagoras
physician: 5 Galen
pilaster: 4 anta
pillar: 5 stele
pitcher: 4 olla, olpe 8 oenochoe
platform: 4 bema 6 logeum
poem: 5 Iliad 7 Odyssey
poet: Ion 5 Arion, Homer 6 Pindar 9 Simonides, Sophocles
poetess: 5 Sapho 6 Sappho 7 Corinna
port: 4 Syra 5 Corfu 6 Patras 7 Piraeus
portico: 4 stoa, xyst
precinct: 7 temenos
priest: 4 papa
priestess: 4 Auge, Hero, Iole 8 Caryatid
promontory: 6 Actium
province: 4 nome 5 nomos 7 eparchy
resistance group: Eam 4 Elas
river: 4 Arta 5 Lerna 6 Peneus, Ruphia 7 Alpheus, Eurotas 8 Achelous, Arachtus 11 Aspropitamo 12 Basilipotamo
rose: 7 glaieul
sacred place: 6 abaton
sage: 5 Solon 6 Thales 8 Socrates
sanctuary: 5 hiera
sculptor: 5 Myron 7 Phidias
seaport: 4 Enos, Volo 5 Pylos 8 Salonica, Salonika 9 Gallipoli
senate: 5 boule
serpent: 4 seps
settler: 5 metic
shield: 5 pelta
ship: 4 saic 5 diota
shrine: 5 secos, sekos
skeptic: 5 Timon
slave: 5 helot 6 penest
slave woman: 5 Baubo, Iambe
soldier: 7 palikar
song: ode 5 melos, paeon
soothsayer: 7 Calchas
sorceress: 5 Circe, Medea, Siren
speech: 6 rhesis
statesman: 8 Pericles 9 Aristides 12 Themistocles
statue: 6 xoanon
storm wind: 6 lelaps 7 laelaps
subdivision: 5 phyle
temple: 4 naos 5 cella 7 Theseus
territory: see *district* above
theater: 5 odeon, odeum
time: 7 chronos

town: 4 Elea 5 Nemea 6 Actium 7 Eleusis 9 Pharsalus
township: 4 deme
tribal division: 7 phratry
underworld: Dis 5 Hades
valley: 5 Nemea
vase: 5 dinos
verse: 6 Alcaic
village: obe
weight: mna, oka, oke 4 mina 5 litra, maneh, minah, obole, pound 6 diobol, dramme, kantar, obolos, obolus, stater, talent 7 chalcon, chalque, drachma 8 diobolon, talanton 12 tetradrachma
wine pitcher: 4 olpc
word: 5 logos

greed: 7 avarice, avidity 8 cupidity, gulosity, voracity 11 miserliness
greedy: 4 avid 5 eager, gutty 6 stingy 7 miserly 8 covetous, esurient, grasping, ravenous 9 devouring, rapacious, voracious 10 avaricious, gluttonous, insatiable
Greek: See **Greece**
green: new, raw 4 bice, live, verd, vert(Fr.) 5 cedre, crude, fresh, mossy, virid, young 6 callow, recent, unripe 7 untried, verdant 8 blooming, gullible, ignorant, immature, inexpert 9 malachite, undecayed, unskilled, untrained 11 flourishing 13 inexperienced 15 unsophisticated
blue: 4 cyan, saxe 7 sistine
gray: 5 olive
pale: 7 celadon
shade: 4 nile 5 apple, kelly 6 bottle 7 emerald
woodbine: 7 peridot
yellow: 7 opaline
Green Mansions author: 6 Hudson
Green Mountain Boys' leader: 10 Ethan Allen
Green Mountain state: 7 Vermont
green peak: 10 woodpecker
greenback: 8 frogskin
greenery: 7 verdure
greengage: 4 plum
greenhorn: yap 4 jake, tyro 5 ikona 6 novice 9 cheechaco, cheechako 10 tenderfoot
Greenland: *base:* 4 Etah
discoverer: 4 Eric
Eskimo: Ita
geological division: 4 kome
town: 4 Etah 8 Godthaab 11 Julianehaab 12 Angmagssalik
greenlet: 5 vireo
greenroom: 5 foyer
greens: 5 salad
greenstone: 4 jade 7 pounamu 8 nephrite 9 malachite
greensward: 4 turf 5 grass
greet: cry 4 hail 5 halse 6 accost, salute 7 address, receive, welcome
greeting: ave, bow 4 hail 5 aloha, hello, salut(Fr.) 6 accost, salute 7 address, slainte, welcome 8 saluting 9 reception 10 salutation 12 commendation
gregarious: 6 gregal, social 8 sociable 11 amadelphous
grego: 5 cloak 6 jacket 9 greatcoat
gremlin: imp 5 devil
grenade: 4 bomb 5 shell 11 pomegranate
grenadier: 4 fish 7 rattail, soldier
grenier: 5 attic
gres: 8 ceramics 9 stoneware
Gretna Green visitor: 6 eloper
grey: See **gray**
Greya's husband: 4 Oder
greyhound: 4 grew 9 grewhound
grid: 5 grate 6 buccan 7 grating 8 gridiron
griddle: 5 grill 8 gridiron
griddle-cake: 7 crumpet, pancake 8 chapatty
gridiron: 5 field, grill 7 brander, grating, griddle
grief: woe 4 care, dole, dool, dree, harm, hurt, pain, ruth, teen 5 agony, dolor, tears, trial, wrong 6 dolour, mishap, regret, sorrow 7 anguish, chagrin, emotion, failure, offense, sadness, trouble 8 disaster, distress, hardship 9 grievance, suffering 10 affliction, desolation, heartgrief 11 lamentation
Grieg's dancer: 6 Anitra
grievance: 5 anger, grief 6 burden 8 gravamen, hardship 9 complaint, injustice 10 affliction, oppression 11 displeasure
grieve: rue 4 care, dole, pain, pine, sigh, 5 anger, grave, mourn, wound 6 bewail, enrage, lament, sadden, sorrow 7 afflict, bailiff, condole, manager, sheriff, steward, trouble 8 complain, distress, governor, overseer 10 discomfort
grieved: 4 sore 5 vexed 9 afflicted
grievous: sad 4 sore 5 heavy, sorry 6 bitter, dready, severe 7 heinous, intense 8 dolorous 9 atrocious 10 burdensome, calamitous, deplorable, flagitious, oppressive 11 gravaminous
griff: 4 glen 6 ravine
griffon: 4 lion 5 eagle 7 monster
grifter's henchman: 5 shill
grig: eel 5 annoy, dwarf 7 cricket, heather 8 irritate 9 tantalize 11 grasshopper
grigri: 5 charm 6 amulet, fetish 8 talisman
grike: 5 chink 6 ravine 7 crevice
grill, grille: vex 4 reja(Sp.) 5 broil, grate, harsh 6 offend 7 grating, griddle, torment 8 distress, gridiron, grillade, irritate 12 cross-examine

grilse: 5 trout 6 salmon 7 botcher

grim: 4 dour, sour 5 angry, cruel, gaunt, harsh, stern 6 fierce, grisly, horrid, raging, savage, sullen 7 furious, ghastly, hideous, ominous 8 horrible, pitiless, ruthless, sinister 9 ferocious, frightful, merciless, repellent 10 forbidding, inexorable, relentless, unyielding

grimace: mop, mow, mug 4 face, mock, moue, mowe, mump, sham 5 fleer, smirk, sneer 8 pretense 11 affectation

grimalkin: cat 6 feline, she-cat

grime: 4 dirt, smut, soil, soot 5 colly, sully 7 begrime

grimly: 4 grim 5 stern 7 hideous

grimp: 5 climb

grimy: 4 foul 5 dingy, dirty 6 grubby, soiled 7 swarthy 8 begrimed

grin: gin 4 girn 5 fleer, smile

grind: vex 4 bray, chaw, chew, grit, joke, mill, mull, whet 5 chafe, crush, gnash, grate, study 6 abrade, crunch, drudge, harass, pestle, polish, powder, satire 7 oppress, sharpen 8 satirize 9 blackfish, comminute, pulverize, triturate 12 steeplechase

grim: 4 dour, sour 5 angry, cruel, gaunt, harsh, stern 6 fierce, grisly, horrid, raging, savage, sullen 7 furious, ghastly, hideous, ominous 8 horrible, pitiless, ruthless, sinister 9 ferocious, frightful, merciless, repellent 10 forbidding, inexorable, relentless, unyielding

grinder: 5 molar, tooth, tutor 9 announcer 10 flycatcher, goatsucker

grinding: 7 grating 10 burdensome 12 excruciating

grindle: 5 ditch, drain 6 bowfin

gringo: 8 American 9 foreigner 10 Englishman

grip: bag 4 holt, vice 5 cinch, clamp, clasp, cleat, ditch, drain, grasp, gripe, seize, spasm 6 clench, clinch, clutch, furrow, gutter, handle, trench, valise 7 earring, grapple, handbag, handful 8 gripsack, handfast, handgrip 9 constrict 12 sceneshifter

gripe: 4 grip 5 grasp, pinch 6 clench, clutch, grouse, handle, harass, snatch, timber 7 afflict, control, grapple, handful, mastery, vulture 8 complain, distress 9 apprehend 10 affliction, oppression

griph, griphus: 6 enigma, puzzle, riddle

grippe, grip: flu 9 influenza

gripper: 6 nipper

gripping device: dog 4 hand, vise 5 tongs 6 pliers

gripple: 5 grasp 7 grapple 9 tenacious 10 avaricious

gripsack: 4 grip 7 handbag

griskin: 4 chop, loin 5 steak

grisly: 4 grim 7 ghastly, hideous 8 dreadful, grewsome, gruesome, horrible, terrible

grison: 5 huron 6 weasel

grist: lot 8 quantity 9 provision

gristle: 9 cartilage

grit: 4 sand, soil 5 earth, grain, grate, grind, nerve, pluck 6 clench, gravel 7 bravery, courage 8 decision 12 perseverance

grith: 5 mercy, peace 6 asylum, refuge 7 defense, quarter 8 security 9 sanctuary 11 self-conduct

gritty: 4 game 5 sandy 6 plucky 7 arenose, arenous 8 resolute, sabulous 10 persistent

grivet: 6 monkey

grivois: 4 bold, free 5 broad 8 indecent

grizzle: 4 fret 7 grayish, whimper 8 complain

grizzly: 4 bear

Grizzly Bear State: 10 California

groan: 4 moan 5 creak, grank, grunt

grocer: 7 epicier(F.) 11 storekeeper

grog: rum 5 drink, rumbo 6 liquor 8 beverage

groggery: 7 shebeen(Ir.)

groggy: 5 shaky, tipsy 8 unsteady, wavering 9 tottering

groom: 4 mafu, syce, tidy 5 curry, dress, mafoo, strap 6 fettle 7 hostler, marshal, prepare, servant, shopboy 8 coistrel 9 assistant 10 bridegroom, manservant, palfrenier 11 horsekeeper

grooming: 8 toilette

groove: rut 4 dado, rake, slot 5 canal, chase, flute, glyph, regal, rigol, scarf, shaft, stria, sulci(pl.) 6 furrow, gutter, hollow, rabbet, raglet, scrobe, striae(pl.), sulcus 7 channel, striate 10 excavation

groovy: 6 modern 9 excellent 10 marvellous

grope: 4 clam, feel, glam, test 5 glaum, probe, sound 6 handle 7 examine, grabble, gropple

grosbeak: 7 warbler 8 hawfinch

groser: 10 gooseberry

gross: big, fat, low, sum 4 bulk, clod, dull, mass, rank, rude 5 amass, broad, brute, bulky, burly, close, crass, dense, heavy, plain, rough, thick, total, whole 6 animal, brutal, coarse, earthy, entire, filthy, greasy, impure, vulgar 7 beastly, brutish, compact, fulsome, general, glaring, massive, obscene, obvious, sensual, swinish, witless 8 cloddish, flagrant, indecent 9 egregious, unlearned, unrefined 10 indefinite, indelicate, scurrilous

grot: 6 cavern, grotto

grotesque: 5 antic 7 baroque, bizarre 8 fanciful 9 fantastic, whimsical 11 incongruous 12 preposterous

grotto: den 4 cave, grot, hole 5 crypt, speos, vault 6 cavern, recess

grouch: 4 sulk 6 grouse 7 grumble

ground: 4 base, dirt, fund, land, root, soil 5 earth, field, train 6 bottom, estate, reason 7 country, premise, terrain 8 initiate 9 establish, territory 10 foundation, fundamenta(pl.) 11 fundamentum
kinds of: bog, lot 4 moor, acre, farm, plat, park 5 arada, glebe, tilth, range, marsh, swale, patch 6 meadow, calade, reseau, maidan 7 pasture, cripple, curragh
raised: 5 ridge 7 hillock, hummock

ground pine: iva

ground squirrel: 6 gopher 8 chipmunk

groundhog: 6 marmot 9 woodchuck

Groundhog Day: 9 Candlemas

groundless: 4 idle 5 false 8 baseless 9 unfounded 10 gratuitous 11 unwarranted

groundnut: 5 chufa, gobbe 6 goober, peanut

grounds: 4 lees 5 basis, dregs, grout 6 bottom 8 sediment
college: 6 campus
military: 4 camp, fort 8 presidio 11 reservation

groundwork: 4 base, fund 5 basis, bases(pl.) 6 bottom, fundus

group: fry, mob, set 4 bevy, gang, herd, mass, ring, sect, team 5 batch, brood, cabal, class, clump, drove, firca, flock, genus, horde, party, squad, suite, tribe 6 bundle, clique, family, galaxy, gather, nation 7 arrange, cluster, collect, company, consort 8 assemble, assembly, classify, division 10 assemblage, assortment, collection, congregate 11 aggregation
animal: 4 herd 5 drove
pert. to: 7 generic
suffix: ery

group together: 4 band, file, meet 7 cluster 8 assemble

grouper: 4 fish, hind, mero 5 guasa

grouse: 5 ganga, gripe 6 gorhen, grouch, repine 7 attagen, cheeper, gorcock, grumble 8 complain, squealer 9 gelinette, ptarmigan 10 whitebelly 12 capercaillie

grout: 4 less, root 5 dregs, larry 7 grounds 8 porridge

grouty: 5 cross, sulky 6 sullen

grove: 4 bush, hewt, tope, wood 5 copse, hurst, lucus(L.) 6 aboret, bosket, greave, pinery 7 alameda, boscage, boskage, bosquet, coppice, thicket
pert. to: 7 nemoral

grovel: 4 fawn, roll 5 crawl, creep 6 cringe, tumble, wallow 7 grabble 8 flounder

groveling: 6 abject 7 hangdog 12 contemptible

grow: age, bud, get, wax 4 come, eche, rise 5 edify, raise, swell 6 accrue, batten, become, expand, extend, thrive 7 augment, develop, distend, enlarge, improve, nourish 8 develope, flourish, increase 9 cultivate 10 accumulate

grow old: age 5 ripen 7 senesce

grower: 6 farmer, raiser 7 rancher 10 orchardist 13 agriculturist 15 arboriculturist

growing: 6 rising 8 crescive

growl: 4 gnar, gurl, gurr, wirr, yirr 5 gnarl, snarl 6 gollar, goller, mutter, rumble 7 grumble, maunder 9 complaint

grown: 5 adult, risen 6 mature 7 matured 8 expanded

grownup: man 5 adult 7 matured

growth: wen 4 rise 5 swell 7 stature 8 increase, swelling 9 accretion, expansion, heterosis 11 development, enlargement 12 augmentation
in clusters: 8 racemose
on another: 8 parasite
on surface: 9 epigenous
organic: 9 accretion
promoting: 8 nutrient 9 nutriment
retarding: 9 paratonic

grub: bob, dig, eat 4 chow, feed, food, moot, plod, root 5 dwarf, larva, stump 6 drudge, larvae(pl.), maggot, search 7 plodder 8 victuals

grubby: 5 dirty, grimy, small 8 dwarfish, slovenly

grudge: 4 envy 5 covet, pique, spite 6 grutch 8 begrudge 10 resentment

grue: ice 4 snow 6 shiver 7 shudder 8 particle

gruel: 5 atole 6 burgoo, crowdy 8 porridge, wangrace

gruesome, grewsome: 4 ugly 6 grisly, horrid, sordid 7 fearful, ghastly, hideous, macabre 8 horrible

gruff: 4 deep, sour 5 bluff, harsh, rough, surly 6 hoarse, morose, severe, sullen 7 austere, brusque, quarrel

grumble: 4 crab, hone, kick 5 croak, growl, munge, snarl 6 grouch, grouse, mumble, murmur, mutter, repine, rumble, yammer 7 channer, gnatter, gruntle, maunder 8 begrudge, complain

grumpy: 5 cross, moody, surly 7 grumphy

grunt: 4 fish 5 groan, snork, snort 6 grumph 7 gruntle

grutch: 6 grudge, murmur 8 complain

guacharo: 7 fatbird, oilbird

guaiol: 7 alcohol

Guam: *breadfruit tree:* 6 nangca, nangka

capital: **5** Agana
idol: **5** anito
native: **8** Chamorro
port: **4** Apra
guan: **4** bird, fowl **10** chachalaca
genus: **6** pipile **7** ortalis
guanaco: **5** llama
guar: **4** bean
guarantee: **4** bail, band, bond, seal **6** assure, avouch, ensure, insure, surety **7** certify, endorse, hostage, warrant **8** guaranty, security, warranty **9** assurance, vouchsafe
guarantor: **5** angel **6** backer, patron **7** sponsor **11** underwriter
guaranty: **4** bond, pawn, seal **6** pledge **7** warrant **8** security, warranty **9** guarantee
guarapucu: **4** fish, peto **5** wahoo
guard: **4** care, curb, herd, hold, keep, rail, tend, ward **5** bless, fence, hedge, watch **6** bantay, bridle, convey, custos, defend, dragon, escort, fender, gaoler, jailer, jailor, keeper, patrol, police, sentry, shield, warden **7** keeping, lineman, protect **8** conserve, preserve, restrain, security, sentinel, watchman **9** attention, custodian, protector, safeguard **10** cowcatcher, protection
foil: **6** button
line of: **6** cordon
on: **4** wary **5** alert, ready **8** vigilant, watchful **9** observant
guarded: **4** wary **6** manned **7** careful **8** cautious, defended, discreet, watchful **9** protected **11** circumspect
guardhouse: **4** brig **5** clink **6** prison **8** hoosegow
guardian: **4** herd **6** keeper, parent, pastor, patron, warden **7** curator, trustee, tutelar **8** defender, guardant **9** custodian, protector
church relics: **10** mystagogue
heavenly: **5** angel
legal: **7** trustee
pert. to: **7** tutelar **8** tutelary
subject of: **4** ward
watchful: **5** Argus **8** Cerberus
guardianship: **7** custody, keeping, tuition **8** custodia, tutelage **9** custodiae(pl.) **10** guardiancy
guasa: **7** grouper
Guatemala: *ant:* **5** kelep
city: **6** Salama **9** Guatemala **11** Ciudad Viega, Totonicapan **13** Quezaltenango
coin: **4** peso **7** centavo, quetzal
fruit: **4** anay
Indian: **4** Itxa, Ixil, Maya **5** Xinca
lake: **5** Dulce, Peten **7** Atitlan **10** Amatitland
measure: **4** vara **6** cuarta, fanega **7** cajuela, manzana **10** caballeria
port: **7** San Jose **10** Champerico, Livingston
river: **6** Chixoy, Pasion **8** San Pedro
volcano: **4** Agua **5** Fuego **7** Atitlan
Guaycuruan Indian: **4** Toba
gubbins: **6** refuse, scraps **9** fragments
gudame: **11** grandmother
gudesire: **11** grandfather
gudgeon: pin **4** bait, dupe, fish **5** cheat, pivot **7** journal **10** allurement
Gudrun: *brother:* **6** Gunnar
husband: **4** Atli
guenon: **4** mona **6** grivet, monkey
guerdon: **6** reward **8** requital **10** recompense
guess: aim **4** shot **5** areed, fancy, infer **6** divine **7** opinion, presume, surmise, suspect **8** estimate **9** speculate **10** conjecture
guest: **4** host **6** caller, inmate, lodger, patron, roomer **7** visitor **8** visitant
guesthouse: inn **5** hotel **11** caravansary
guff: **4** puff, talk **5** chaff, whiff **6** humbug
guffaw: **5** laugh **6** heehaw **8** laughter **10** horselaugh
Guiana: *cassava drink:* **7** paiwari
coin: bit
fowl: **4** keet
hut: **5** benab
river turtle: **8** matamata
tree: **4** dali, mora **5** dalli **6** camara
guidance: **4** duct, helm **7** auspice, conduct, guidage **8** steerage **9** direction **10** leadership, management **15** superintendence
guide: guy **4** airt, buoy, clue, lead, pole, rein, rule, show **5** airth, carry, longe, order, pilot, reign, steer, teach, treat, tutor, usher **6** bridle, convey, convoy, direct, former, govern, leader, manage **7** conduce, conduct, control, marshal, mercury **8** cicerone, director, instruct, polestar, regulate, textbook **9** catechism, conductor, guidebook, guidepost, itinerary, prescribe, regulator **11** superintend
guidebook: **8** baedeker, handbook **9** itinerary
guideway: **4** sley, slot **5** track **7** channel **8** slideway
guiding: **5** polar **7** leading
Guido: *fifth note:* sol
first note: ut
fourth note: fa
high note: la
highest note: E la
second note: re
third note: mi
guild, gild: hui **6** gremio **7** society **10** fellowship **11** association, brotherhood
merchant: **5** hansa, hanse **6** cartel

guile: 4 dole, wile 5 cheat, craft, fraud 6 deceit, humbug 7 cunning 9 duplicity, treachery
guileful: 9 deceitful, insidious 10 fallacious, fraudulent 13 Machiavellian
guileless: 5 naive 6 candid, honest 7 artless 8 innocent 9 ingenuous
guillemot: auk 4 loom, quet 5 murre 7 dovekey, dovekie
guillotine: 6 behead 10 decapitate
wagon for: 7 tumbrel, tumbril
guilt: sin 5 culpa, fault 6 piacle 7 offense 8 iniquity 10 wickedness 11 criminality, culpability
guiltless: 4 free 8 innocent 9 righteous
guilty: 6 nocent, wicked 7 correal 8 culpable
Guinea: *measure:* 7 jacktan
seaport: 4 Bata
tree: 4 akee, dali, mora 5 dalli
weight: 4 akey, piso, uzan 5 benda, seron 6 quinto 8 aguirage
guinea fowl: 4 keet 7 galeeny, pintado
guinea pig: 4 cavy
Guinevere's husband: 6 Arthur
guise: hue 4 form, garb, mask, mien 5 cloak, cover, dress, habit, shape 6 aspect, attire, deceit, manner 7 arrange, fashion 8 behavior, disguise, likeness, practice 9 semblance 10 appearance, masquerade
guitar: uke 5 sitar, tiple 6 sancho 7 samisen, ukulele 8 chitarra 10 calascione
guitarlike instrument: 4 lute, rota 7 bandore, pandora, samisen
half step in pitch: 5 dital
key: 5 dital
of India: 4 vina 5 sitar
play: 5 strum
small: uke 7 ukelele
guitguit: 6 pitpit
gula: 4 cyma, ogee 6 gullet, throat 7 molding
gulch: 4 gulp 5 canon, gorge, gully 6 arroyo, canyon, coulee, ravine 7 glutton
gulf: 4 eddy 5 abyss, chaos, chasm 6 vorago 9 barathrum, whirlpool 10 separation
Gulf of Mexico islet: cay
Gulf States: 5 Texas 7 Alabama, Florida 9 Louisiana 11 Mississippi
gull: mew 4 dupe, fool, geck, sell, tern 5 cheat, cokes, cully, fraud, larid, trick 6 chouse, nilgai, teaser, victim, whilly 7 cheater, deceive, defraud, gosling, mislead 8 dotterel, impostor 9 kittiwake 10 mountebank
kinds of: cob 4 skua 5 allan, annet, pewit 6 larine, teaser, waggel 11 burgomaster
pert. to: 6 larine, laroid
gullet: maw 6 throat, weason 7 weasand 9 esophagus
gullible: 5 goofy, green, naive 9 credulous
Gulliver: *author:* 5 Swift
flying island: 6 Laputa
human beast: 5 Yahoo
island kingdom: 8 Lilliput
gully: gut 4 sike 5 drain, gorge, goyal, goyle, gulch, knife, sword, zanja 6 arroyo, guttor, nullah, ravine, valley 7 couloir 11 watercourse
gulp: 4 glut, swig 5 gulch, quilt, swipe 6 glutch, gobble 7 swallow
gulp down: 4 bolt 6 englut
gum: 4 clog, hive, kino 5 cheat, nyssa, stick, trick 6 chicle, gluten, hashab, humbug, impede, tissue, tupelo 7 bilsted, gingiva 8 mucilage 10 eucalyptus 11 masticatory
derivative: 8 bassorin 10 tragacanth, traganthin 12 tragacanthin
kinds of: 5 tuart 6 acacia, acacin, balata, touart 7 acacine, dextrin
resin: 5 elemi, gugal, myrrh 6 salban 9 sagapenum 12 frankincense
gum tree: 5 xylan
gumbo: 4 ocra, okra, soup 7 melange
gumma: 5 tumor
gummy: 6 mastic 7 viscous 8 adhesive
gumption: 10 enterprise, initiative, shrewdness
gums: ula 7 alveoli
comb. form: ulo
pain in: 7 ulalgia
pert. to: 6 uletic 8 gingival
gun: gat, rod 5 rifle, tommy 6 cannon, heater, pistol, weapon 7 carbine, shotgun 8 revolver 9 matchlock 11 blunderbuss
barrel cleaner: 6 ramrod
kinds of: 4 bore, bren, roer 5 baril 6 ack-ack, archie, barker 7 aerogun, bazooka 8 amusette
mount: 6 turret
part: 4 lock 5 stock 6 barrel, hammer, muzzle, rammer, safety 7 trigger
platform: 11 emplacement
gunfire: 4 rake 5 salvo 6 strafe 7 barrage 8 enfilade
gunlock: *catch:* 4 sear
hammer: 7 doghead
pawl: 4 sear
gunner: 7 shooter 9 cannoneer 10 bombardier 12 artilleryman
gunny: tat 4 jute 6 burlap
gunpowder: 5 nitro
gunroom: 8 quarters
gunshot: pop
Gunther's uncle: 5 Hagen
gunwale: 8 portoise
gurge: 4 eddy 5 surge, swirl
gurgle: 6 gargle, gollar, goller, guggle
Gurkha's sword: 5 kukri
gurl: 4 howl 5 growl, snarl

gurnard: 6 elleck, rochet 8 dragonet
guru: 5 guide 7 teacher
gush: 4 flow, pour, teem 5 issue, smarm, spate, spout, spurt 6 effuse, stream 10 outpouring
gushing: 5 agush 7 teeming 8 effusive, unctuous
gusset: 4 gore 8 piecette
gussie: pig 5 swine
gust: bub 4 flan, gale, puff, scud, waft, wind 5 blast, draft, gusto, storm, taste, whiff 6 flurry, liking, relish, squall 8 outburst 9 enjoyment, foretaste 11 inclination 13 gratification
gusto: 4 elan, gust, zest 5 taste 6 liking, relish 12 appreciation
gusty: 5 windy 6 savory, stormy 7 gustful, squally 8 agitated 11 tempestuous
gut: 5 belly, force, gully 6 bowels, defile, strait 7 courage, destroy, passage, plunder, stamina, stomach 8 entrails, gluttony 9 intestine 10 disembowel, eviscerate
gutta: 8 ornament
gutta-percha: 5 latex 6 balata
gutter: 4 grip, sink 5 brook, ditch, gully, siver(Sc.) 6 groove, guzzle, trench, trough, vennel 7 channel, scupper 11 watercourse
guttural: 5 burry, harsh, velar 7 rasping, throaty
guy: kid, rod 4 josh, rope, stay, twit 5 chain, guide, spoof, tease 6 decamp, fellow, gazabo, gazebo, person 8 ridicule
guy rope: 4 stay, vang
guzzle: 4 tope 5 drain, drink 6 gutter, throat
guzzler: bum 6 bundur
gwyniad: 7 schelly
gymnast: 6 turner 7 acrobat, athlete, tumbler 8 balancer 10 gymnasiast
gymnastic: *stunt:* kip 9 handstand, headstand 10 handspring, headspring
swing: 7 trapeze
gyp: 5 cheat, steal 7 sharper, swindle 8 swindler 10 overcharge
gypsum: 6 parget 8 selenite 9 alabaster
resembling: 11 alabastrine
gypsy, gipsy: 4 calo 5 caird, nomad 6 Gitana, Gitano, roamer 7 czigany, tzigany, zincala, zincalo, zingana, zingano, zingara, zingaro 8 Bohemian, brunette, wanderer, zigeuner
boy: 4 chal
camp: tan
dance: 10 zingaresca
devil: 4 beng
dialect: 6 Romany 7 Rommany
fortune: 4 bahi
gentleman: rye
girl: chi 4 chai
horse: gri, gry
husband: rom
nongypsy: 4 gajo
paper: lil
Syrian: 5 Aptal
thief: 4 chor
village: gav
wife: 4 romi
gyrate: 4 gyre, spin, turn 5 twirl, whirl 6 rotate 7 revolve
gyrator: top
gyre: 4 ring 6 gyrate, vortex 7 circuit 10 revolution
gyrfalcon: 6 jerkin
gyve: 4 iron 5 chain 6 fetter 7 shackle

H

H: 5 aitch 8 aspirate
sound of: 8 aspirate
H-shaped: 5 zygal
haar: fog
habeas corpus: 4 writ
haberdashery: hat 5 shirt 6 gloves 7 necktie 8 menswear
habile: fit 4 able 6 adroit, clever, expert 8 skillful, suitable
habiliment (see also **dress, gown**): 4 garb 5 habit 6 attire 7 apparel, clothes, costume, raiment 8 billiment, clothing, equipage, fittings, ornament, vestment 9 equipment, faculties 11 furnishings
habilitate: 5 dress, equip 6 clothe 7 entitle, qualify
habit (see also **dress**): rut, use 4 coat, garb, gown, suit, vice, wont 5 array, guise, haunt, thews, usage 6 attire, clothe, custom, estate, groove 7 bearing, clothes, costume, garment 8 demeanor, habitude, practice, tendency 9 cacoethes 10 consuetude, deportment, habiliment
habitant: 7 dweller
habitat: 4 home 5 abode, range 6 patria 7 station 8 locality 11 environment
combining form: eco 4 oeco, oiko
habitation: 4 home, tent 5 abode, house, hovel, igloo 6 harbor, warren 7 harbour, lodging 8 domicile, dwelling, tenement 9 chaumiere(F.), residence
habited: 6 garbed, gowned 7 arrayed, clothed, dressed 9 inhabited 10 accustomed
habitual: 5 usual 6 common, hectic 7 regular 8 familiar, frequent, ordinary 9 customary 10 accustomed, inveterate
habituate: use 5 enure, inure 6 addict, season 8 accustom, frequent 9 acclimate, 11 acclimatize, familiarize
habitude: 5 habit 11 familiarity
habitue: 10 frequenter
hacendero: 6 farmer
Hachaliah's son: 8 Nemehiah
hachure: 4 line, mark 5 shade
hacienda: 4 farm 5 ranch 6 estate 7 finance 10 plantation 13 establishment
proprietor: 9 hacendado
hack: cab, cut, hag, hew 4 chop, taxi 5 coach, cough 6 drudge, fiacre, hacker, hackle, haggle, mangle 7 butcher, chatter, hackney, stammer, stutter 8 carriage, mutilate 9 mercenary
hack writer: 7 penster
hackberry: 8 oneberry 10 sugarberry
hackee: 8 chipmunk
hackle: 4 bait, comb, hack 6 heckle 11 stickleback
hackly: 5 rough 6 broken, jagged
hackney: nag 4 hack, pony 5 horse, noddy 6 drudge 8 carriage, hireling
hackneyed: old 4 worn 5 banal, stale, trite 6 common 7 forworn 8 foreworn 10 habituated, threadbare 11 commonplace, stereotyped
had: See **have**
Hades: dis, pit 4 hell 5 Orcus, Sheol 8 Tartarus 11 netherworld
god: 5 Pluto
inhabitant of: 7 hellion
lake to: 7 Avernus
mother: 4 Rhea
pert. to: 7 sheolic 8 infernal
river: 4 Styx 5 Lethe 7 Acheron
wife: 10 Persephone
hadj, hajj: 10 pilgrimage
haet: bit 4 atom, whit
haff: 6 lagoon
haffet, haffit: 5 cheek 6 temple
haft: 5 dwell 6 handle, settle 8 accustom, dwelling 11 familiarize
hag: bog, cut 4 bogy, hack, wood 5 copse, crone, demon, ghost, marsh, notch, rudas(Sc.), witch 6 beldam, goblin, harass, spirit 7 beldame, fatigue, haggard, pasture, terrify 8 harridan, quagmire 9 cailleach, cailliach, enclosure, hobgoblin
Hagar's son: 7 Ishmael
hagdon: 7 seabird 10 shearwater
hagfish: 5 borer

haggard: 4 bony, lank, lean, pale, thin, wild 5 drawn, gaunt, spare 6 hagged, wanton 7 anxious, haglike, untamed 8 harrowed, unchaste 9 suffering, untrained 10 cadaverous 11 intractable
Haggard novel: She
haggle: cut, hew 4 hack, prig 5 cavil 6 badger, banter, chisel, dicker, higgle, huckle, palter, scotch 7 bargain, chaffer, dispute, stickle, wrangle
haggler: 6 dodger 8 huckster
haggy: 5 boggy 6 uneven
hagioscope: 6 squint 7 opening
hagride: 4 ride 6 harass 7 torment
hail: ave 4 ahoy, call, goal 5 greet, sleet, sound, whole 6 accost, health, salute 7 address, fortune, graupel 8 greeting 10 salutation 13 precipitation
hain: 4 save 5 raise, spare 7 elevate
hair: fax, fur 4 barb, coma, mane, shag 5 crine, tress 6 crinet, nicety, trifle 7 bristle 8 capillus, filament, finespun 9 chevelure
accessory: 8 barrette
Angora goat: 6 mohair
braid: cue, pig 5 queue 7 pigtail
coarse: 4 kemp, seta, shag 7 bristle
comb. form: pil 4 pilo
curl: 7 ringlet
disease: 8 dandruff, psilosis
dye: 5 henna
excessive: 7 pilosis
false: rat, wig 6 peruke 7 periwig
fringe: 8 frisette, frizette
having: 6 pilose 7 barbate, hirsute, villous 8 crinated
horse: 4 mane 5 [illegible] 7 fetlock
intestinal: 6 villus
knot: bun 7 chignon
lock: 4 curl, feak, tate 5 flock, tress 6 berger 7 cowlick, elflock 8 lovelock 9 harigalds
loss: 8 alopecia, baldness
ornament: bow 4 comb 5 tiara 6 ribbon 7 coronet 8 barrette
pert. to: 6 crinal
plant: 6 villus
remover: 8 epilator 9 depilator, epilatory 10 depilatory
roll: 4 puff 5 twist 7 chignon 9 pompadour
short: 6 setula, setule
soft: 4 down 6 villus
unruly: mop 6 tousle 7 cowlick
white: 4 snow
hairbrained: 5 giddy 8 heedless, volatile
hairbreadth: ace 6 margin
haircloth: aba 6 cilice
haircut: 7 tonsure
hairdo: bob 4 glib(Ir.) 5 braid 6 bubble, marcel 7 beehive, pageboy, pigtail, shingle 8 bouffant, ponytail 9 horsetail
hairdresser: 7 friseur 8 coiffeur 9 coiffeuse
hairless: 4 bald 8 depilous
hairnet: 5 snood
hairpin: 4 bend 6 bodkin 8 bobbypin
hairy: 5 pilar 6 comate, comous, pilary, piline, pilose, shaggy 7 crinose, hirsute
Haiti: *bandit:* 4 caco
city: 12 Port-au-Prince
coin: 6 gourde
island: 4 Mona 6 Gonave
liberator: 9 Toussaint
magic: obi
ruler: 8 Duvalier
spirit: 4 baka, bako
sweet potato: 7 batatas
hake: 4 idle 5 tramp 6 loiter, trudge
Halakoth collection: 6 mishna 7 mishnah
halberd: 4 bill 6 glaive, weapon 8 battle-ax
halcyon: 4 bird, calm 5 happy, quiet 6 golden 8 peaceful, tranquil 9 unruffled 10 kingfisher
Halcyone: *father:* 6 Aeolus
husband: 4 Ceyx
hale: lug, tug, vex 4 draw, haul, heal, pull 5 annoy, frack, freck, sound 6 harass, hearty, robust, strong, summon, wholly 7 healthy 8 contract, vigorous
Halevy opera: 5 Juive
half: 4 demi, hemi, part, semi, term 6 moiety 7 partial, partner, portion 8 semester 11 imperfectly
half-ape: 5 lemur 7 tarsier
half breed: 5 metif, metis 6 mestee, metive, mustee 7 metisse, mestizo, mestiza, mulatto, mulatta 8 octoroon, quadroon
half brother: 7 half-sib 11 half-sibling
half circumference: 10 semicircle
half diameter: 6 radius
half-man: 4 faun 6 garuda 7 centaur 8 minotaur
half mask: 4 loup 6 domino
half-month: 9 fortnight
half-moon: 9 semilunar
figure: 4 lune
half-turn: 8 caracole
half-wit: 4 dolt 5 dunce 6 nimshi 9 blockhead
half-witted: 5 dotty, silly 7 foolish 9 senseless
halfbeak: ihi 5 balao
halfpenny: mag 4 dump 5 brown 6 bawbee
halfway: mid 7 midship, partial 9 equivocal, partially 11 equidistant
halibut steak: 6 flitch
Halicarnassian: 9 Dionysius, Herodotus
halicore: 6 dugong
halidom, halidome: 8 holiness, sanctity 9 sanctuary
Halifax citizen: 10 Haligonian

halite: sal 4 salt
halitus: fog 4 aura 5 vapor 6 breath 10 exhalation
hall: 4 aula, room, saal(G.) 5 entry, foyer, lobby, manor, odeon, odeum, salle 6 atrium, durbar, saloon 7 chamber, gallery, hallway, passage 8 anteroom, corridor 9 vestibule 10 auditorium, misericord, passageway 11 misericorde
music: 4 gaff 5 odeon, odeum
reception: 5 salon 6 parlor
student residence: 4 dorm 5 bursa 9 dormitory
hallanshaker: 5 scamp 6 beggar 8 vagabond
halloo: 5 shout 6 accost
hallow: 5 bless 8 dedicate 10 consecrate
hallowed: 4 holy
hallowed place: 4 fane 5 altar 6 bethel, chapel, church, shrine, temple 9 cathedral, synagogue
hallucination: d.t.'s 6 mirage 7 fantasy 8 delirium, delusion
halma: 4 game, jump
halo: arc 4 glow, nimb 5 glory 6 areola, areole, brough(Sc.), circle, corona, nimbus 7 aureola, aureole 8 cincture, gloriole
halogen: 6 iodine 7 bromine 8 chlorine 8 cyanogen, fluorine
halse, hals: col, hug 4 neck 5 greet 6 defile, salute, throat 7 conjure, embrace, entreat
halt: hop 4 bait, lame, limp, stem, stop 5 cease, hilch, hitch, pause, stand 6 arrest, desist, docked 7 limping 8 lameness, stoppage 9 cessation, mutilated, terminate
halter: 4 rope 5 leash, noose, strap, widdy 6 bridle, hamper 8 cavesson, restrain 9 hackamore
halting: 4 lame 7 limping 8 spavined 9 defective 10 hesitating 11 vacillating
halting place: 4 camp
halucket: 4 wild 5 crazy, giddy 10 halfwitted
ham: pig 4 port 7 amateur
Ham: *brother:* 4 Shem
father: 4 Noah
son: 4 Cush 6 Canaan
son's land: 8 Ethiopia
hamadryad: 5 nymph 6 baboon
hamate: 6 curved, hooked 7 hamular 8 hamiform
hameil: 5 homey 8 domestic
Hamilcar: 5 Barca
conquest: 5 Spain
home: 8 Carthage
son: 8 Hannibal
Hamite: *father:* 4 Abel
language: 4 Afar, Agao, Beja 5 Belin, Galla 6 Berber, Kabyle, Shilha, Somali, Zenaga 8 Cushitic, Numidian, Tamashek 9 Ethiopian, Gaetulian 11 Mauretanian
people: 4 Beja, Bogo 5 Fulah 6 Berber, Gallas, Somali
hamlet: 4 dorp 5 aldea(Sp.), casal, hamel, moray, vicus(L.) 6 bustee, casale(It.), thorpe 7 clachan(Sc.), village 10 settlement
Hamlet: *beloved:* 7 Ophelia
castle: 8 Elsinore
character: 7 Laertes, Ophelia 8 Gertrude, Polonius
country: 7 Denmark
friend: 7 Horatio
hammer: bit, tup 4 beat, claw, jack, maul, mell, reel, tack, tamp 5 gavel 6 batter, beetle, mallet, martel, pummel, sledge, strike, swinge 7 belabor 8 malleate 11 door-knocker
blacksmith's: 6 fuller, oliver
bricklayer's: 6 scutch
face: 4 trip
firearm: 4 cock 7 doghead
half-round: 6 fuller
head: 4 peen, poll
medical: 6 plexor 7 plessor
stone: 5 kevel, spall
hammerhead: 5 shark
hammock: 7 machila
hamper: bin, ped 4 beat, clog, curb, load, slow 5 block, cramp, crate, rusky(Sc.), seron(Sp.) 6 basket, burden, fetter, halter, hinder, hopple, impede, panier 7 buffalo, confine, hanaper, manacle, pannier, perplex, shackle, trammel 8 encumber, entangle, obstruct, restrain, restrict 9 container, embarrass
hamstring: hox 4 hock, lame 5 hough 7 cripple, disable
hamulus: 4 hook
Hananiah: *father:* 4 Azur
son: 8 Zedekiah
hanaper: 6 basket, hamper 10 receptacle
hance: 4 arch, fall 5 raise 6 lintel
hand: fin, paw, pud 4 claw, give, mano, mitt, neif, pass 5 claut (Sc.), grasp, nieve, power, share 6 clunch, daddle, famble, pledge, worker 7 ability, flipper, forepaw, laborer, proffer, workman 8 applause, bestowal, transmit 9 betrothal, craftsman, indicator, operative, signature 11 handwriting
back: 10 opisthenar
clenched: 4 fist
comb. form: 4 manu 5 chiro
covering: 4 mitt, muff 5 glove 6 cestus(L.) 7 gantlet 8 gauntlet
deformity: 11 talipomanus

hollow: **6** gowpen, gowpin
palm: **6** thenar
part: **4** palm **5** thumb **7** fingers
pert. to: **6** manual
without: **7** amanous
hand-me-down: 5 cheap **9** ready-made **10** secondhand
hand mill: 5 quern **7** grinder
hand out: 10 administer, distribute
hand over: 4 ante, cede **5** yield
hand-picked: 5 elite **8** selected
handbag: bag **4** etui, grip **5** cabas, etwee, purse **6** valise **7** satchel **8** gripsack, pochette, reticule
handball: *game:* **6** pelota **7** jai alai
point: ace
handbarrow: 4 bier
handbill: 5 libel **6** dodger **13** advertisement
handbook: 6 manual **9** guidebook **11** enchiridion
handbreath: 4 span **6** spread
handcar: 6 gocart **7** go-devil
handcloth: 5 towel **6** napkin **12** handkerchief
handcuff: 4 cuff, iron **5** darby **6** nipper **7** manacle **8** bracelet, handbolt, handlock
Handel: *composition:* **5** Largo
opera: **4** Nero **6** Xerxes
oratorio: **7** Messiah
handfast: 4 bind, grip **5** bound, grasp **7** betroth, manacle **11** closefisted
handful: 4 grip, wisp **5** claut, gripe **6** gowpen, gowpin, yaffle **7** maniple **8** quantity
handicap: bar, law **4** lame, lisp **6** burden, hinder, impede **7** stammer, stutter **8** encumber **9** advantage, embarrass **12** disadvantage
handicapper: 5 rater
handicraft goddess: 7 Minerva
handicraftsman: 7 artisan, workman **9** craftsman
handiwork: tat **7** sampler **10** embroidery
handjar: 5 knife **6** dagger **7** khanjar
handkerchief: 5 clout, fogle **6** madras **7** bandana, belcher, sneezer **9** barcelona, handcloth, muckender, neckcloth **11** neckerchief
handle: ear, fan, lug, nob, paw, ply, use **4** ansa, bail, bool, deal, feel, gaum, grip, haft, hank, hilt, knob **5** gripe, grope, helve, lever, shaft, swipe, touch, treat, wield **6** behave, direct, finger, manage **7** control **8** handgrip **10** manipulate
ancient: **4** ansa
bucket: **4** bail, bale
cup: ear
equipped with: **6** ansate
pail: **4** bail
printing press: **6** rounce
pump: **5** brake
scythe: **5** snath, snead, thole **6** snathe
sword: **4** haft, hilt
whip: **4** crop
handled: 5 dealt **6** ansate
handling: use **7** control **9** treatment **10** management
handlock: 8 handcuff
handout: aid **4** alms, dole, food, gift, meal, mete **5** snack **7** charity
handreading: 9 palmistry
hands: men **4** crew **8** pointers
hands off: 4 tabu **5** taboo
hand's spread: 4 span
handsel, hansel: 4 gift, luck, omen **5** money, token **6** augury
handsome: 4 braw(Sc.), fair, fine, pert **5** ample, belle, bonny, handy, ready **6** bonnie, clever, comely, goodly, heppen, limber **7** elegant, gallant, liberal **8** becoming, budgeree, generous, gracious, suitable **9** beautiful, dexterous **10** convenient, manageable **11** appropriate **12** considerable
handspring: 9 cartwheel
handstone: 4 mano
handwriting: 4 fist, hand **5** ronde **6** script **10** griffonage, manuscript **11** chirography
on the wall: **4** mene **5** tekel **8** upharsin
study of: **10** graphology
handy: 4 deft, near **5** adept, ready **6** adroit, clever, heppen **8** adjacent, dextrous, handsome, skillful **9** available, dexterous, versatile **10** accessible, convenient
Handy Andy's catch 5 Oonah
handyman: 5 fixer **8** repairer
hang: lop, sag **4** kilt, loll, pend, root **5** drape, droop, hinge, knack, slope, swing **6** append, dangle, depend, gibbet, talter **7** crucify, execute, stretch, suspend **9** declivity **11** inclination
around: **4** loaf **6** loiter
back: **6** falter **8** hesitate
down: **6** dangle **7** suspend
onto: **5** cling
hang fire: 4 pend **8** hesitate
hangar: 4 shed **6** garage, stable **7** shelter **9** penthouse
hangdog: 4 base **6** shifty **7** ashamed, fawning, furtive **8** cringing, sneaking **9** groveling
hanger-on: bur **5** toady **6** hangby, heeler **7** adjunct, dangler, slinger **8** bottomer, loiterer, onsetter, parasite **9** appendage, dependent, sycophant **10** blackguard
hanging: 5 arras, drape **6** celure, tippet **7** pendent, pensile, valance **8** inclined **9** declivity, execution, suspended **11** inclination
Hanging Gardens site: 7 Babylon

hangman: 6 hangie 9 Jack Ketch 11 executioner
hangnail: 6 agnail 10 backfriend
hangout: 5 joint 10 rendezvous
hangover: 8 residuum 11 aftereffect
hank: 4 coil, loop 5 skein 6 bundle, handle 7 control 9 influence
hanker: 4 long 5 crave, yearn 6 desire
hankle: 5 twist 6 fasten 8 entangle
Hannay: *creator:* 6 Buchan
special number: 10 thirty-nine
Hannibal: *father:* 8 Hamilcar
place of victory: 6 Cannae
Hanse merchant: 7 hansard
hansom: cab
hap: lot 4 case, luck, wrap 5 check, seize 6 befall, chance, clothe, snatch 7 fortune, venture 8 covering 9 happening 10 occurrence, prosperity
haphazard: 6 casual, chance, random 8 careless 10 accidental
hapless: 4 poor 7 unlucky 11 unfortunate
happen: 4 come, fall, fare 5 evene, occur 6 arrive, befall, betide, chance, mayhap 7 perhaps, stumble 9 eventuate, transpire
happen again: 5 recur
happening: hap 4 case, fact 5 event 6 chance, faring 7 episode 8 incident, occasion 10 occurrence
happily: 5 fitly, haply 6 gladly 7 luckily 10 gracefully 11 contentedly, fortunately, opportunely 12 felicitously, peradventure, prosperously, successfully 13 appropriately
happiness: joy 4 sele(Sc.), weal 5 bliss, mirth 6 felice 7 delight, ecstasy, felicia, rapture 8 felicity, gladness, hilarity 9 beatitude, enjoyment, eudaemony, transport, well-being 10 exaltation, prosperity 11 blessedness
god: 5 Ebisu
incapacity for: 9 anhedonia
happy: apt, gay 4 cosh, glad, gleg 5 blest, lucky, merry, ready, seely, sonsy, sunny 6 elated, sonsie 7 blessed, content, fitting, halcyon, radiant 8 carefree, frohlich, gracious, mirthful 9 contented, fortunate 10 felicitous, propitious, prosperous
happy-go-lucky: 9 easygoing
happy hunting ground: 6 heaven 8 paradise
Haran: *brother:* 7 Abraham
daughter: 6 Milcah
father: 5 Terah
son: Lot
harangue: nag 4 rave 5 orate, spiel 6 screed, sermon, speech, tirade 7 address, declaim, oration 8 diatribe, perorate 10 concionate
harass: fag, hag, nag, try, vex 4 bait, fret, gall, hake, hale, haze, jade, rack, raid, tire 5 annoy, beset, bully, chafe, chase, grind, gripe, harry, herry(Sc.), hurry, pique, tease, weary, worry 6 badger, bother, bucket, cumber, hatter, heckle, impede, molest, obsess, pester, plague, pother, scrape 7 afflict, affront, agitate, disturb, exhaust, fatigue, hagride, oppress, perplex, provoke, scourge, torment, trouble 8 distract, distress, irritate 9 exagitate, persecute, tantalize
harbinger: 4 camp, host 5 usher 6 herald 7 presage, shelter 8 fourrier, harbinge, harborer 9 messenger, precursor 10 forerunner
spring: 5 robin 6 crocus
harbor, harbour: inn 4 hold, port 5 haven 6 billet, breach, bunder, covert, foster, refuge 7 fairway, lodging, quarter, retreat, seaport, shelter 9 harborage
entrance: 4 boca
harbor master: 7 havener
harborage, harbourage: 6 harbor 7 shelter
hard: fit 4 acid, cold, dear, dere, dure, firm, iron, mean, oaky, sour 5 champ, close, cruel, hardy, harsh, horny, rigid, rocky, rough, solid, stern, stiff, stony 6 coarse, frozen, knotty, marble, robust, severe, steely, strict, strong 7 adamant, arduous, austere, callous, compact, earnest, intense, onerous, scleral 8 diligent, granitic, grasping, hardened, obdurate, renitent, rigorous, scleroid, toilsome 9 difficult, energetic, fatiguing, inclement, intricate, laborious, petrified, repelling, reprobate, resistant, strenuous, stringent, unfeeling, wearisome 10 inflexible, oppressive, perplexing, persistent, relentless, ungraceful, unyielding 11 complicated, distressing, impregnable, persevering, unremitting 12 disreputable, extortionate, impenetrable, incorrigible, unalleviated 13 unsympathetic
comb. form: dys
hard coal: 10 anthracite
hard corn: rye 5 wheat
hard drawn: 4 taut 5 tense
hard-shell: 9 confirmed, extremist
hard times: 9 recession 10 depression
harden: gel, set 4 bake, cake, salt, sear 5 beath, enure, inure, steel 6 endure, freeze, ossify, temper 7 congeal, petrify, stiffen, thicken, toughen 8 concrete, condense, indurate, solidify 11 acclimatize
hardened: 4 hard 5 caked 6 frozen, gelled, inured 7 callous, steeled 8 obdurate 9 abandoned, reprobate 10 impenitent, impervious inveterate, solidified 12 impenetrable

hardhead: 4 fish 5 whale 7 ribwort 8 knapweed, mackerel, menhaden 9 blockhead 10 niggerhead

hardheaded: 4 keen 6 shrewd 7 willful 8 stubborn 9 sagacious 10 longheaded 11 sharp-witted

hardhearted: 4 mean 5 cruel, stern 7 callous 8 obdurate, pitiless 9 unfeeling 13 marblehearted, unsympathetic

hardihood: 5 pluck, vigor 7 bravery, courage 8 audacity, boldness, temerity 9 hardiness, impudence, stoutness 10 confidence, effrontery, imprudence, resolution, robustness 11 intrepidity 13 audaciousness

hardly: 6 barely 7 faintly, hardily, harshly, roughly 8 forcibly, scarcely, severely, unfairly 11 unfavorably

hardness: 6 durity 8 severity, solidity 9 substance
measuring device: 9 durometer

hardpan: pan 7 bedrock 8 ortstein

hardship: 5 assay, rigor, trial 6 injury 7 penalty 8 asperity, hardness 9 endurance, grievance, injustice, privation 10 affliction

hardtack: 7 biscuit, galette(F.), pantile

hardwood: ash, oak 4 pelu, teak 5 maple 6 walnut 7 hickory 8 mahogany
genus: 7 quercus

hardy: 4 bold, firm, hard, rash, wiry 5 brave, lusty, manly, stout, tough 6 chisel, daring, robust, rugged, strong, sturdy 7 compact, spartan 8 galliard, intrepid, resolute, stubborn, vigorous 9 audacious, confident 10 courageous

Hardy heroine: 4 Tess

hare: dol 4 bawd(Sc.), pika 5 harry, lepus, tease, worry 6 malkin, rabbit 7 leporid, leveret 8 frighten, leporide
comb. form: lag 4 lago
female: doe
genus of: 5 lepus
male: 4 buck
pert. to: 8 leporine
tail: 4 scut
track: 4 file, slot
young: 7 leveret

harem: oda 4 odah 5 serai 6 serail, zenana 8 seraglio
male attendant: 6 eunuch
room: oda
slave: 9 odalisque

haricot: 4 stew 6 ragout

harish: 7 foolish

hark: 4 hear, heed hist 6 harken, listen 7 hearken, whisper

harl: 4 barb, drag, knot 5 leash, snarl 6 scrape, tangle 7 confuse, plaster, scraper 8 entangle 9 confusion

harlequin: 5 clown 7 buffoon 9 fantastic 11 masquerader

harlot: low, pug 4 base, doxy, lewd, slut 5 churl, knave, quean, rogue, whore 6 menial, rascal, wanton 7 buffoon, juggler 8 strumpet, vagabond 10 fricatrice, prostitute

harm: hob, ill 4 bale, bane, evil, hurt, pain, teen 5 abuse, annoy, grief, shend, wound, wrong 6 damage, damnum, injure, injury, scathe, sorrow 7 disease, impeach 8 disserve, endamage, nuisance 10 disservice, misfortune, wickedness 11 impeachment

harmful: bad 4 evil 5 nasty 6 nocent 7 baneful, hurtful, malefic, noisome, noxious 8 damaging, sinister 9 injurious 10 pernicious 11 contrarious, deleterious, detrimental, mischievous

harmless: 4 safe 6 dovish 9 innocuous 11 inoffensive

Harmonia: *father:* 4 Ares
husband: 6 Cadmus
mother: 9 Aphrodite

harmonious: 6 cosmic, dulcet 7 cordial, musical, spheral, tuneful 8 amicable, peaceful 9 accordant, agreeable, congruous, consonant, harmonial, melodious, peaceable 10 compatible, concentive, concordant 11 harmoniacal, symmetrical 12 proportional

harmonize: go; gee, key 4 jibe, tone, tune 5 adapt, agree, blend, chime, hitch, rhyme 6 accord, adjust, attune, cotton 7 concent, concord, consist, consort 9 reconcile 10 correspond, sympathize

harmony: 4 tune 5 amity, music, peace 6 cosmos, melody 7 concert, concord, rapport 9 agreement 10 accordance, atmosphere, conformity, congruence, consonance 11 cooperation
bring into: 6 attune
lack: 7 discord

harness: 4 gear 5 heald 6 fettle, tackle 7 enclose, hitch up 9 equipment, trappings
maker: 7 knacker, lorimer
part: bit, tug 4 hame, rein 5 blind, trace 6 billet, bridle, collar, saddle, terret 7 crouper 9 breeching, circingle, martingal, ridgeband, surcingle 10 breastband, crownpiece, martingale

harp: 4 arpa, koto, lyre 5 nanga 6 trigon 8 bedlamer 11 clairschach

harper: 4 coin 8 minstrel, musician

harpoon: 5 spear 7 javelin

harpsichord: 6 spinet 8 clavecin, virginal 12 clavicembalo

harpy: 5 Aello 7 Celaeno, Ocypete, Podarge 11 extortioner

harquebus: 6 hagbut 7 hackbut

harquebusier: 7 soldier 10 arcabucero
harridan: hag 5 crone, horse, vixen, woman 8 strumpet
harrier: dog 4 hawk
harrow: vex 4 disk, drag 5 brake, harry, wound 6 spader 7 oppress, torment 8 distress, lacerate 9 cultivate 10 cultivator
harrowed: 7 haggard
harry: rob, vex 4 sack 5 annoy, hound, hurry, spoil, steal, worry 6 harass, harrow, hector, plague, ravage 7 agitate, despoil, pillage, plunder, torment 9 persecute
harsh: raw 4 grim, hard, hask 5 acerb, acrid, asper, brute, crude, cruel, grill, gruff, raspy, rough, sharp, stern, stiff 6 bitter, brazen, coarse, severe, strict, sullen, unkind 7 austere, braying, drastic, grating, rasping, raucous 8 acerbate, catonian, clashing, croaking, district, guttural, jangling, rigorous, strident, ungentle 9 dissonant, inclement, insensate, repellent, squawking, truculent, unfeeling 10 astringent, discordant, oppressive, relentless 11 acrimonious, disagreeing 12 disagreeable
harshness: 5 rigor 6 duress 7 crudity, raucity 8 acerbity, acrimony, asperity, severity
hart: roe 4 deer, hert, stag 5 spade
hartebeest: 4 asse, tora 5 caama, kaama 6 lecama 8 antelope
hartshorn: 7 ammonia
harum-scarum: 4 rash, wild 7 flighty 8 reckless 11 thoughtless 13 irresponsible
Harun-Al-Rashid's wife: 7 Zobeide
haruspex: 7 diviner 10 soothsayer 14 prognosticator
Harvard book prize: 5 detur
harvest: 4 bind, crop, reap 6 foison, gather 8 ingather
festival: 6 Opalia
god: 5 Ceres 6 Cronus
goddess: Ops 5 Carpo
harvest home: 4 kern, kirn(Sc.)
harvester: 8 spalpeen
has: See **have**
hash: 4 chop 5 mince 6 jumble 7 mixture 11 gallimaufry, olla podrida
hashish: 4 hemp 5 bhang 8 cannabis
hashmark: 6 stripe
hask: dry 4 cold 5 harsh 6 coarse
hasp: 4 gird 5 catch, clasp 7 confine 8 fastener
hassle: 4 talk 6 hustle 7 quarrel, wrestle 8 argument, squabble 9 commotion 10 discussion
hassock: 4 boss, pess 5 grass, sedge 6 buffet 7 cushion, tussock 8 footrest 9 footstool
haste: hie 4 rush 5 hurry, speed 6 bustle, flurry 7 urgency 8 dispatch, rapidity 9 quickness, swiftness 10 expedition, nimbleness 11 festination, impetuosity 12 precipitance 13 precipitation
hasten: hie, run 4 pell, race, rush, trot 5 crowd, drive, fleet, hurry, speed 6 expede, gallop, scurry 7 advance, scamper 8 dispatch, expedite 9 festinate 10 accelerate 11 precipitate
hastily: 6 nimbly 8 speedily 11 impatiently 13 precipitately
hasty: 4 fast, rash 5 brash, fleet, quick, swift 6 abrupt, daring, nimshi, speedy, sudden 7 cursory, forward, hurried 8 headlong, pell-mell, succinct 9 hotheaded, hurrisome, impatient, impetuous 10 indiscreet 11 expeditious, precipitate, precipitous
hasty pudding: 4 mush 6 supawn 9 stirabout
hat: cap, dip, fez, lid, nab, tam 4 baku, felt, topi 5 beany, benjy, benny, beret, boxer, cordy, derby, dicer, kelly, terai, topee, toque 6 Alpine, beaver, boater, bonnet, bowler, castor, claque, cloche, fedora, panama, shovel, turban 7 biretta, caubeen, chapeau, Homburg, petasus, salacot, shallow 8 capeline, copatain, headgear, sombrero 9 Dunstable, stovepipe, wide-awake 10 belltopper 11 mortarboard
covering: 8 havelock
crown: 4 poll
ecclesiastic: 7 biretta
fiber: 4 felt, sola 5 straw
fur used in: 4 mink 5 coney 6 beaver, ermine 8 coonskin
ladies: 5 caddy, cooie 6 Breton, caddie, slouch 7 leghorn 8 duckbill 9 harlequin 12 Gainsborough
medieval: 6 abacot 7 bycoket
military: 5 shako
oilskin: 5 squam 9 sou'wester
opera: 5 crush, gibus 6 claque, topper
palm-leaf: 7 salacot
pert. to: 9 castorial
pith: 4 topi 5 topee
Quaker: 9 broadbrim
silk: lum(Sc.) 4 tile 5 opera 6 topper 7 catskin 8 gossamer
soft: 6 fedora
stovepipe: 8 caroline
straw: 6 boater
three-cornered: 7 tricorn
ventilated: 5 terai
hatch: 4 brew, door, gate, vent 5 breed, cleck, clock, cover 6 clutch, wicket 7 concoct 8 contrive, hatchway 9 floodgate
covering: 4 tarp
hatchel: 5 tease, worry 7 torment

hatchet: ax; adz, axe 4 adze, mogo 8 tomahawk
hatchet man: 4 tool 6 stooge 8 henchman
hatching: 6 cletch 8 breeding
hatchway: 7 scuttle
hate: 4 teen 5 abhor 6 detest, loathe, rancor, revile 7 contemn, despise 8 aversion 9 abominate, malignity 11 detestation
hateful: 4 foul 5 black 6 odious 7 heinous 8 flagrant 9 abhorrent, invidious, loathsome, malignant, obnoxious, offensive, revolting 10 abominable, detestable, disgusting, malevolent 11 distasteful 12 disagreeable
hatful: 4 lots, many, much 8 quantity
hatred: 5 odium 6 enmity, rancor 8 aversion 9 animosity, hostility, malignity 10 abhorrence, repugnance 11 abomination, detestation, malevolence
of argument: 8 misology
of children: 9 misopedia 10 misopaedia
of mankind: 11 misanthropy
of marriage: 8 misogamy
of strangers: 10 xenophobia
hatter: 5 worry 6 batter, bruise, harass 7 exhaust 8 milliner
haught: 4 high 5 noble 7 exalted, haughty
haughtiness: 4 airs 5 pride 6 morgue 7 hauteur 9 arrogance, insolence
haughty: 4 airy, bold, high 5 dorty, lofty, noble, proud 6 haught, snooty 7 exalted, fatuous, hontish, paughty, stately 8 arrogant, cavalier, glorious, scornful 9 imperious, masterful 10 disdainful, fastidious 11 domineering, magisterial, overbearing 12 contemptuous, presumptuous, supercilious
haul: lug, tow, tug 4 cart, drag, draw, hurl, pull, tote 5 bouse, catch, heave, trice 8 cordelle 9 transport
haulage: 6 towage 7 cartage, drayage
hauler: 7 tractor
haulm: 4 culm, stem 5 stems 6 stalks
haunch: hip 4 huck 5 hance 12 hindquarters
haunt: den 4 dive, hawf, lair, nest 5 ghost, habit, hawff, skill 6 custom, infest, obsess, resort, spirit 7 terrify 8 frequent, practice 9 companion 10 fellowship
haunted: 6 filled, spooky 8 infested
haunty: 6 unruly 8 restless
hautboy, hautbois: 4 oboe 10 strawberry
hauteur: 5 pride 9 arrogance 11 haughtiness
Havana suburb: 5 Regia
have: hae(Sc.), own 4 hold 5 enjoy 6 retain 7 contain, possess 10 experience
on: 4 wear
to do with: 4 deal
haven: bay, lee 4 hope, port 5 hotel, inlet 6 asylum, harbor, recess, refuge 7 shelter 9 sanctuary
haver: oat 6 babble, holder 7 chatter, maunder, twaddle 8 nonsense 9 possessor
haversack: bag
havior, haviour: 8 behavior, demeanor
havoc: hob 4 ruin 5 waste 7 destroy 9 devastate 10 desolation 11 destruction, devastation
haw: gee 4 sloe, yard 5 fence, hedge 8 hawthorn 9 enclosure
Hawaii: *ballad:* 4 mele
basket: ie
beverage: 4 kava 8 kava-kava
bird: io, oo; ioa, iwa 4 iiwi, koae, mamo, omao, ooaa 6 palila 8 drepanis
breechcloth: 4 malo
bush: See *shrub* below
canoe: 5 waapa
channel: 4 Auau
chant: 4 mele
city: 4 Hilo 7 Wailuku 8 Honolulu(c.)
cloak: 4 mamo 6 ahuula
cloth: 4 kapa, tapa 5 tappa
cookout: 4 luau
cord: aea
crater: 7 Kilauea
dance: 4 hula
discoverer: 4 Cook
district: 4 Puna, Kona
farewell, hello: 5 aloha
feast: 4 luau 7 ahaaina
fern: 4 heii 5 ekaha, uluhi 6 iwaiwa 7 amaumau
fiber: 4 pulu
fish: ahi 4 ulua 5 akule
fish poison: 4 hola 6 auhuhu
flower: 5 ilima
food: poi 4 kalo, taro
game: hei
garland: lei
garment: 6 holoku, muumuu 7 holomuu
god: 4 Kane 5 Wakea
goddess: 4 Pele
goose: 4 nene
grass: 6 emoloa
greeting: 5 aloha
harbor: 5 Pearl
hawk: io
herb: ape, pia 4 hola 5 awiwi 6 auhuhu
instrument: uke 7 ukalele, ukelele, ukulele
island: 4 Maui, Oahu 5 Kauai, Lanai 6 Hawaii, Niihau 7 Molokai 9 Kahoolawe
lava: aa 8 pahoehoe
loincloth: 4 malo, maro
lomilomi: rub 7 massage, shampoo
love: 5 aloha
massage: 8 lomilomi

morning glory: 5 koali
mountain: Kea 5 Mauna 7 Waianae 8 Mauna Loa
musical instrument: uke 7 ukulele
native: 6 Kanaka
octopus: hee
pantheon: 4 Kane
parrot fish: 5 lauia
partnership: hui
pepper: ava
pine: ie
pit for baking: imu
plant: pia 4 hala, taro 5 olona 8 pandanus
poem: 4 mele
porch: 5 lanai
precipice: 4 pali
priest: 6 Kahuna
raven: 5 alala
root: 4 taro
root paste: poi
seaweed: 4 limu
shaman: 6 Kahuna
shrub: 4 akia 5 akala, olona 6 aupaka
song: 4 mele
staple: poi 4 taro
starch plant: pia
starch root: pia 4 taro
swordfish: au
temple: 5 heiau
thrush: 4 amao 6 olomao
tree: koa 4 aulu, ohia 5 aalii, alani 7 amaumau, walahee 8 mokihana
valley: 5 Manoa
vine: 5 kaiwi 9 awikiwiki
volcano: 7 Kilauea 8 Mauna Kea, Mauna Loa
white man: 5 haole
wind: 4 kona
windstorm: 4 kona
woman: 5 haole
wreath: lei
yam: hoi

hawfinch: 8 grosbeak

hawk: io; cry, gos 4 eyas, kite, nyas, sell, vend 5 astur, cadge, catch, reach, retch 6 elanet, falcon, formal, formel, higgle, musket, osprey, peddle, rifler, tarcel, tarsel, tercel 7 buzzard, canvass, colport, harrier, kestrel, puttock, sparrow, vulture 8 brancher, caracara 9 accipiter 11 mortarboard
cage: mew
male: 6 tercel 7 tiercel
leash: 4 jess, lune
nest: 5 aerie
nestling: 4 eyas
pinion feather: 6 sarcel

hawk-headed deity: Ra

hawkbit: 9 dandelion

hawker: 6 badger, cadger, coster, duffer 7 chapman, mercury, packman, peddler 8 falconer, huckster 9 colporter 10 colporteur 12 costermonger

Hawkeye State: 4 Iowa

hawklike: 11 accipitrine

hawser: 4 line, rope
block: 4 bitt
post: 4 bitt 7 bollard

hawthorn: haw, may 5 aglet 6 aiglet 8 cockspur, maybloom, quickset

hay: bed, net 4 park 5 chaff, fence, grass, hedge 9 provender
bundle: mow 4 bale, rick, wisp 5 gavel, stack, truss 7 hayrick
kind of: 6 clover 7 alfalfa, timothy
line: 5 swath 7 windrow
second cutting: 5 rowen
spreader: 6 tedder
storage: mow 4 loft

haycock: 4 coil

hayfork: 4 evil 5 pikel

hayloft: mow 9 hay-tallat

hayseed: 5 yokel 6 farmer, rustic 10 countryman

hazard: die, lay, lot 4 risk 5 peril, stake 6 chance, danger, gamble 7 imperil, venture 8 accident, casualty, endanger, jeopardy 9 adventure 10 jeopardize

hazardous: 5 risky 6 chance, chancy, queasy, unsafe 8 insecure, perilous 9 dangerous, uncertain 10 fortuitous, jeopardous, precarious 11 adventurous

haze: fog 4 beat, film, mist 5 cloud, devil, scold, vapor 6 harass, vapour 7 drizzle 8 frighten

hazel: 8 noisette 11 avellaneous

hazelnut: nit 6 cobnut

Hazor king: 5 Jabin

hazy: dim 5 filmy, foggy, misty, smoky, thick, vague 7 nebular, obscure, unclear 8 nebulous 9 uncertain 10 indistinct

head: aim, cop, mir, nab, nob 4 bean, cape, coco, conk, crop, lead, pate, poll, tete(F.), turn 5 caput(L.), chief, chump, first, front, start, tibby 6 cabeza, cobbra, direct, garret, leader, manage, noggin, noodle, sconce, source, spring 7 captain, coconut, costrel, cranium, crumpet, leading, prelate 8 director, foremost, fountain, headland, initiate 9 intercept, president, principal 10 caper-nutie, headmaster, promontory 11 caper-noitie
army camp: 10 commandant
back part: 7 occiput
bald: 9 pilgarlic
boar: 4 hure
bone: 8 parietal

covering: cap, hat, tam **4** caul, hair, hood **5** beret, snood, toque
crown: **6** cantle
muscle: **11** occipitalis
ornament: hat, wig **4** hair, veil **5** tiara **7** coronet
part: **4** pate **5** scalp **6** earlap, temple **7** cranium
pert. to: **8** cephalic
shaven: **7** tonsure
shrunken: **7** tsantsa
side of: **4** lore **5** lorum **6** temple
top: **4** pate **5** scalp **7** coxcomb
head cook: **4** chef
head covering (see also **cap, hat**): cap, fez, hat, tam, wig **4** barb, coif, hair, hood **5** beret, scalp, snood **6** bonnet, coiffe, peruke, toupee **7** biretta, chapeau, periwig **8** berretta, maharmah, sombrero **9** rigolette **10** fascinator
head-shaped: **8** capitate
head to foot: **7** cap-a-pie
headache: **6** megrim **8** headwark, migraine **10** cephalagia
headband: **5** miter, mitre, vitta **6** diadem, fillet, infula **7** circlet, coronet **8** frontlet **9** sphendone
headdress: **4** caul, coif, pouf **5** ampyx, crown, cupee, miter, mitre, tiara, toque **6** almuce, bonnet, coiffe, faille, hennin, mobcap, pinner, turban **7** bandore, bycoket, coronet, topknot **8** biliment, binnogue, capriole, coiffure, stephane, tressure **9** rigolette
medieval: **6** abacot
military: **5** busby, shako **6** casque
sacerdotal: **5** miter **7** biretta
sacred: **6** uraeus
headgear: See **headdress**
headily: **6** rashly **9** violently
heading: **5** title, topic **7** caption **8** headline
topical: **5** trope
headland: ras **4** bill, cape, head, nase, naze, ness, peak **5** Morro, ridge, strip **8** foreland **10** promontory
headless: **4** rash **6** stupid **8** beheaded **10** acephalous
headline: **7** caption, feature, heading
headliner: **4** star **11** personality
headlong: **4** rash **5** hasty, steep **6** abrupt, sudden **8** reckless **9** desperate, headfirst, impetuous, impulsive **11** precipitate, precipitous
headman: **4** boss **5** chief **6** ataman, cabeza, hetman **7** capitan, captain, foreman **8** alderman, caboceer, capitano **11** executioner
headmaster: **4** head **9** principal **11** gymnasiarch
headpiece: See **headdress**
headquarters: **5** yamen **6** center **8** exchange, precinct
headstrong: **4** rash **5** cobby **6** unruly **7** hotspur, violent **8** stubborn **9** obstinate **10** bullheaded, forthright, hotspurred **11** intractable **12** contumacious, ungovernable
heady: **4** rash **7** huffcap, violent, willful **9** impetuous **11** precipitate **12** intoxicating
heal: **4** cure, hale, knit, mend, sain **5** amend **6** remedy, repair **7** restore **10** recuperate
heal-all: **4** balm **7** allheal, figwort, panacea
healer: asa **4** balm **6** doctor **9** naprapath **12** practitioner
healing: **5** balmy **8** covering, curative, sanative
agent: **6** balsam
goddess: Eir
pert. to: **7** medical **9** medicinal
science: **8** medicine **9** iatrology, latrology
health: **4** hale, hail **5** sante(F.), toast **7** slainte **8** eucrasia **11** disposition
goddess: **7** Minerva
poor: **4** sick **5** dawny
resort: spa
healthy: fit **4** hale, sane, well **5** bonny, hoddy **6** bonnie, hearty, robust **8** salutary, vigorous **9** wholesome **10** healthsome, salubrious
combining form: **4** sani
heap: ahu, cob, cop, mow **4** balk, bing, bulk, deck, dess(Sc.), hill, lump, mass, pile, pyre, raft, rick, ruck **5** amass, cairn, clump, crowd, spire, stack **6** burrow, hipple, jumble, plenty, throng **7** hourock, cumulus, hurrock **9** congeries, multitude **10** accumulate, collection, congestion, cumulation
hear: ear, see **4** feel, hark, heed, obey **6** attend, harken, listen **7** hearken **8** perceive **10** adjudicate
hear ye: **4** oyes, oyez
hearer: **7** audient, auditor **8** disciple, listener
hearing: ear **5** sound, trial **6** assize, report **7** earshot, lecture **8** audience, audition, scolding **9** attention, audiencia, interview, knowledge **10** attendance
court: **4** oyer
judicial: **5** trial **7** retrial
pert. to: **8** acoustic
hearken, harken: **4** hark, hear, heed, wait **6** attend, listen **7** inquire, whisper **9** eavesdrop
hearsay: **4** fame **5** rumor **6** report
hearse: **4** bier, bury, tomb **5** dirge, grave **6** coffin **8** monument, threnody

heart: ab; cor 4 core, gist, hati, love 5 cheer 6 center, centre, depths, middle, ticker 7 courage, emotion, essence, feeling 9 affection
cavity: 6 atrium
chamber: 7 auricle 9 ventricle
contraction: 7 systole
covering: 11 pericardium
expansion: 8 diastole
record: 17 electrocardiogram
stimulant: 8 thialdin 9 digitalis, thialdine 10 adrenaline, epinephrin 11 epinephrine
heart-shaped: 7 cordate
heartache: 4 pang 5 grief 6 sorrow
heartbeat: 5 pulse, throb 7 systole 9 pulsation
heartbreak: 5 grief 6 sorrow 7 tragedy
heartbroken: 12 inconsolable 13 brokenhearted, grief-stricken
heartburn: 4 envy 6 enmity 7 pyrosis 8 jealousy 10 cardialgia, discontent, heartscald, heartscaud
hearten: 5 cheer 6 spirit 7 refresh 8 embolden, inspirit, reassure 9 encourage
heartfelt: 4 dear, deep, real, true 7 earnest, genuine, sincere
hearth: 5 cupel, focus, fogon, foyer 8 bloomery, fireside
god: 6 Hestia
line: 6 fettle
heartily: 6 dearly, freely, warmly 8 actively, strongly 9 cordially, earnestly, profusely, sincerely, zealously, zestfully 10 abundantly, completely, vigorously 14 wholeheartedly
heartiness: 4 soul 8 goodwill, strength 9 soundness 10 cordiality
heartless: 5 cruel 8 hopeless, listless 9 merciless, unfeeling 10 despairing, despondent, spiritless 13 unsympathetic
heartsease, heartease: 5 pansy, peace 12 tranquillity
heartthrob: 4 dunt, love
heartwood: 4 dura 7 duramen
hearty: 4 firm, hale, real, rich, warm, well 5 cobby, heavy, sound 6 active, cheery, devout, robust, sailor, stanch 7 comrade, cordial, earnest, fertile, healthy, sincere, staunch 8 abundant, cheerful, heartful, vigorous 9 energetic, unfeigned, wholesome 10 nourishing 11 substantial, warmhearted
heat: ire 4 fire, mull, rage, warm 5 ardor, cauma, chafe, fever, roast, tepor 6 anneal, choler, degree, warmth 7 ferment, inflame, passion 8 fervency 9 agitation, animation, chauffage, commotion, vehemence 10 excitement 11 temperature 12 exasperation 14 passionateness
comb. form: 5 therm 6 calori, thermo
measure: 5 therm 6 calory, therme 7 calorie 10 centigrade, fahrenheit 11 calorimeter, pyronometer
pert. to: 7 thermic
quantity: 6 degree 11 temperature
unit of: 5 therm 7 calorie
white: 13 incandescence
heated: 7 excited 8 vehement 10 phlogistic
heater: 4 etna, oven 5 stove 6 boiler 7 choffer(Sc.), furnace 8 radiator
heath: 4 ling, moor 5 erica, plain
scrub: 9 chaparral
tree: 5 briar, brier
heathen: 5 pagan 6 ethnic, paynim 11 irreligious
deity: 4 idol
non-Jewish: 6 ethnic
non-Muslim: 7 infidel
heather: 4 grig, ling 5 erica
family: 9 ericaceae
heatless: 8 athermic
heautarit: 7 mercury 11 quicksilver
heave: gag 4 cast, haul, heft, hurl, lift, pant, pull, push, quap, toss 5 hoist, pitch, raise, scend, throw 7 elevate, estuate 8 struggle
heaven: sky 5 dyaus, ether, glory 6 Himmel(G.), welkin, zodiac 7 Elysium, Nirvana, Valhall, Vahalla 8 devaloka, empyrean, paradise 9 firmament
combining form: 5 urano
pert. to: 6 uranic 9 celestial
queen: 7 Astarte
heavenly: 6 divine 7 angelic, olympic, sublime, uranian 8 ethereal, supernal 9 angelical, celestial, celestine
heavenly being: 5 angel 6 seraph
heavenly belt: way 6 galaxy, nebula, zodiac
heavenly body: sun 4 luna, moon, star 5 comet 6 planet 8 luminary
heavenly city: 4 Sion, Zion
heavenly twins: 6 Castor, Gemini, Pollux
heaviness: 5 gloom 6 weight 7 gravity, sadness 9 thickness 10 oppression 12 sluggishness
heavy: 4 clit, deep, dull, logy, loud 5 actor, beefy, burly, dense, grave, gross, hefty, hoggy, massy, thick 6 clayey, cloggy, coarse, gloomy, hearty, leaden, stodgy, strong, stupid 7 doleful, intense, massive, onerous, serious, villain, violent, weighty 8 burdened, grievous, inactive, lifeless, lowering, overcast, pregnant, profound, sluggish 9 heavisome, laborious, lethargic, ponderous, saturnine 10 afflictive, burdensome, cumbersome, encumbered, oppressive 13 consequential
heavy-headed: 4 dull 6 drowsy, stupid

heavy-hearted: sad 10 despondent, melancholy
hebdomad: 4 week 5 seven
hebetate: 4 dull 5 blunt
Hebrew (see also **Israel, Judaism**): Jew 6 Semite 7 Semitic 8 Hebraean 9 Israelite
acrostic: 4 agla
alphabet: He, Pe; Mem, Nun, Sin, Taf, Tav, Tet, Vav, Yod, Yud 4 Alef, Ayin, Beth, Caph, Kaph, Koph, Ooph, Resh, Shin 5 Aleph, Cheth, Gimel, Lamed, Sadhe, Tsade, Zayin 6 Daleth, Samekh
ancestor: 4 Eber
clean: 6 kosher
dance: 4 hora
day: yom
gentile: goi, goy 5 goyim(pl.)
God: El 5 Eloah 6 Adonai, Elohim 7 Jehovah
greeting: 6 shalom
high priest: Eli 5 Aaron
infinity: 6 adalam
Jehovah: 5 Jahve, Yahve, Yahwe 6 Jahvah, Jahveh, Yahveh, Yahweh 7 Jahaveh
juniper: 4 ezel
lawbreaking: 6 averah
lesson: 9 Haphtarah
man: rab 5 bahur, hakam
measure: cab, hin, kab, kor 4 epha, ezba, omer, reed, seah 5 cubit, ephah, homer
month: Ab 4 Adar, Elul 5 Iyyar, Nisan, Tebet 6 Kislew, Shebat, Tammuz, Tishri, Veadar 7 Heshwan
name for God: 6 Adonai, Elohim, Yahweh 7 Jehovah
parchment: 6 mezuza 7 mezuzah
school: 5 heder, schul
scriptures: 4 Tora 5 Torah
son: ben
teacher: 5 rabbi
thief: 5 ganef, ganof, gonof 6 gonoph
title: rab 4 abba
weight: 4 beka, reba
Hebrides island: 4 Skye, Uist
hecatomb: 9 sacrifice, slaughter
heckle: nag 4 gibe 5 tease 6 badger, hackle, harass, hector, needle
hectic: 8 exciting, feverish, habitual, restless 11 consumptive 13 constitutional
hector: nag 5 bully, harry, worry 6 harass, heckle, plague 7 bluster, torment 8 braggart, browbeat, irritate 9 roisterer, swaggerer 10 intimidate
Hector: *companion:* 8 Diomedes
father: 5 Priam
mother: 6 Hecuba
rescuer: 6 Agenor
slayer: 8 Achilles
wife: 10 Andromache
Hecuba: *daughter:* 9 Cassandra
husband: 5 Priam
son: 5 Paris 6 Hector 7 Helenus 9 Deiphobus
hedenbergite: 8 pyroxene
hedge: bar, haw, hem 4 boma 5 beard, fence, frith, guard, skulk 6 hinder, hurdle, privet 7 barrier, enclose, protect 8 boundary, obstruct, quickset, separate, sepiment, straddle, surround 14 counterbalance
hedgehog: 6 urchin 7 echinus 8 herisson, hurcheon 9 porcupine
hedonic: 8 cyrenaic
heed: ear 4 care, cark, cure, gaum, hark, hear, mind, note, obey, reck 5 await, watch 6 attend, beware, harken, listen, notice, regard, remark 7 caution, hearken, observe, respect 8 consider 9 attention, diligence 10 cognizance, solicitude 11 observation
heedful: 4 wary 5 chary 6 attent 7 careful, mindful 8 diligent, watchful 9 advertent, attendant, attentive, observant 10 respectful 11 considerate
heedless: 4 rash 5 giddy 6 remiss, unwary 7 languid, witless 8 careless, reckless 9 blindfold, forgetful, negligent 10 incautious, indiscreet, insouciant, regardless, unthinking 11 hairbrained, inadvertent, inattentive, indifferent, lightheaded, thoughtless, unobservant
heehaw: 4 bray 6 guffaw 10 horselaugh
heel: cad, end, tip 4 calx, cant, knob, tilt 5 talon 6 careen 7 incline 12 protuberance
bone: 9 calcaneus
heeze: 4 help 5 exalt, hoist, raise 6 assist
heft: 5 heave, raise 6 strain, weight 8 exertion 9 influence 13 ponderousness
hefty: 5 heavy, rough 6 rugged 7 massive, weighty 8 vehement, vigorous
hegemonic: 6 ruling 7 leading 11 controlling, predominant
hegemony: 9 authority, influence 10 leadership
hegira, hejira: 6 exodus, flight 9 migration
heifer: 4 quey 5 stirk 10 colpindach(Sc.)
height: 4 acme, apex, mote 5 crest 6 summit 7 stature 8 altitude, eminence 9 celsitude, dimension, elevation, procerity, steepness 11 magnanimity
heighten: 4 lift 5 elate, exalt, raise 7 advance, augment, elevate, enhance 8 increase 9 aggravate, intensify
heinous: 6 crying, malign, odious, wicked 7 hateful 8 flagrant, grievous 9 atrocious, malicious, nefarious 10 flagitious, outrageous

heir: son 5 heres, scion 7 heritor, legatee 9 firstborn, inheritor, successor 11 beneficiary
heiress: 5 begum 8 heretrix, heritrix
Hejaz city: 5 Mecca
Hel: *dog:* 4 Garm
father: 4 Loki
mother: 9 Angurboda
realm: 7 Niflhel 8 Niflheim
held: See **hold**
Helen of Troy: *abductor:* 5 Paris
brother-in-law: 9 Agamemnon
daughter: 8 Hermione
half-sister: 12 Clytemnestra 13 Clytaemnestra
husband: 8 Menelaus
mother: 4 Leda
heliacal: 5 solar
helical: 6 spiral
helicon: 4 tuba
Helios: *daughter:* 5 Circe 8 Heliadae, Heliades
father: 8 Hyperion
son: 8 Phaethon
heliotrope: 6 Clytie
helix: 4 coil 6 spiral
hell: 5 limbo 6 prison 7 dungeon, inferno 9 barathrum
hell-bent: 8 reckless 10 determined
hellebore: 7 bugbane
Hellen: *father:* 9 Deucalion
son: 5 Dorus 6 Aeolus, Xuthus
Hellene: See **Greece**
Hellenistic school: 9 Pergamene
Hellespont: 11 Dardanelles
swimmer: 7 Leander
hellgrammite: 6 dobson 8 sialidae
hellier: 5 tiler 6 slater 8 thatcher
hellish: 6 wicked 7 stygian 8 devilish, diabolic, infernal 9 malignant 10 detestable, diabolical
hello: 8 greeting 10 salutation
helm: 5 helve, steer, wheel 6 direct, tiller 8 guidance
position: 4 alee 5 aport
helmet: cap 4 sola, topi 5 armet, galea, topee 6 casque, heaume, morion, salade, sallet 7 basinet 8 schapska 9 casquetel, headpiece
part: 4 bell 5 crest 7 ventail 8 aventail
helmet-shaped: 7 galeate
helmsman: 5 pilot 9 steersman
Heloise's lover: 7 Abelard
helot: 4 serf 5 slave 6 vassal 7 bondman
help: aid, bot, S.O.S. 4 abet, boot, bote, cure, lift, mend, rede, tide 5 avail, boost, favor, frith, heeze, serve, speed, stead 6 assist, favour, relief, remedy, repair, succor 7 advance, benefit, forbear, forward, further, improve, promote, relieve, support, sustain 8 befriend, facility 9 adminicle, alleviate, forestall 10 assistance, contribute, facilitate, strengthen
helper: aid 4 ally 5 aider 7 abetter, abettor, striker 8 adjutant, adjutrix, helpmate 9 adjutrice, assistant, samaritan 10 apprentice, benefactor
helpful: 4 good 6 aidant, useful 8 adjuvant, helpsome, salutary 9 auxiliary 10 beneficial, profitable 11 furthersome
helpless: 4 numb, weak 6 unable 7 forlorn 8 unaiding 9 destitute, powerless 10 bewildered, unsupplied 11 defenseless, incompetent, unprotected 12 irremediable
helpmate: 4 wife 6 helper 8 helpmeet 9 companion
helpmeet: See **helpmate**
helve: 4 haft 5 lever 6 handle
Helvetian: 5 Swiss 6 Suisse
hem: 4 edge, seam 5 hedge 6 border, edging, margin, stitch 7 confine, enclose, environ, inclose 8 surround 9 fimbriate
hem in: 5 beset, limit 6 impale 7 enclose, inclose 8 surround
hematite: 7 iron ore
hemeralopia: 6 defect 9 blindness
hemi: 4 half
hemlock: 4 bunk, herb, tree 5 tsuga 6 conium
poison: 6 conium
hemmel: 4 shed 5 hovel 7 shelter 11 outbuilding
hemp: ife, pua, tow 4 bang, carl, flax, harl, jute, rine, sunn 5 abaca, bhang, istle, ramie, sisal, sizal 6 ambary, banana, cabuja, cabuya, fennel, manila 7 hashish
hen: pea 4 fowl, rail, wife 5 biddy, chuck, woman 6 gorhen, nester, pullet, towdie 7 chicken 9 gallinule
hen coop: 4 cavy(Sc.) 5 cavie
feature: 4 nest
henbane: 10 nightshade
hence: so; fro 4 away, ergo(L.), thus 5 since 7 hereout, thither 9 therefore 11 accordingly
henceforth: 6 thence 12 henceforward
henchboy: boy 4 page 9 attendant
henchman: 4 page 6 gillie, squire 7 mobster 8 follower 9 attendant, supporter
Hengist: *brother:* 5 Horsa
daughter: 6 Rowena
Henley's poem: 8 Invictus
henna: dye 6 alcana 7 alcanna
Henry II: *adversary:* 6 Becket
drama about: 15 The Lion in Winter
surname: 5 Anjou 11 Plantagenet
wife: 7 Eleanor
Henry VII's surname: 5 Tudor
Henry VIII: Hal
first wife: 9 Catherine

second wife: **4** Anne
third wife: **4** Jane
fourth wife: **4** Anne
fifth wife: **9** Catherine
sixth wife: **9** Catherine
hent: get **5** catch, grasp, reach, seize **6** intent, obtain **11** opportunity
hepar: **5** liver
Hephaestus' wife: **6** Charis **8** Charites
heppen: fit **4** deft, neat **5** handy **6** clever **8** handsome **11** comfortable
heptad: seven **11** septivalent
Hera: **4** Juno
husband: **4** Zeus
mother: **4** Rhea
rival: Io
son: **4** Ares
herald: **4** bode **5** crier, usher **6** beadle, Hermes **7** declare, forerun **8** announce, blazoner, foretell, proclaim **9** harbinger, introduce, messenger, precursor **10** forerunner
heraldry: *band:* **4** fess **5** fesse
bastardy mark: **4** bend **5** baton **7** bendlet **8** sinister
bearing: **4** orle
bell: **7** compane **10** campanella
blood-red: **6** murrey
chaplet: **4** Orle
charge: vol **7** boterol, saltier, saltire **8** boteroll, tressour, tressure
circle: **6** bezant
cross: **4** paty **5** patee, patte **6** ermine, moline, pattee **7** erminee, patonce, saltier, saltire
device: **4** ente, orle **5** crest **6** altier
fleur-de-lis: lis, lys
gold: or
grafted: **4** ente
green: **4** vert
keylike: **4** urde
knot: **4** Lacy, Wake **5** Bowen, Dacre **7** Heneage **8** Stafford **9** Bourchier **10** Harrington
leg: **4** gamb, jamb **5** gambe, jambe
line: **4** unde
scattered: **4** seme
shield: **10** escutcheon
tincture: or **5** tenne **6** argent
triangle: **5** giron
winged: **4** aile
wreath: **4** orle **5** torse
herb: iva **4** anet, balm, dill, leek, mint, moly, sage, wort **5** anise, basil, chive, plant, sedge, thyme **6** annual, borage, catnip, clover, lovage, sesame, yarrow **7** caraway, oregano, parsley **8** marjoram, tarragon
aromatic: **4** anet, dill, hemp, mint, nard, sage **5** anise, basil, clary, nondo, tansy, thyme **6** catnip, fennel, hyssop **7** chervil, mustard **8** wormseed **9** basilmint, spearmint
bitter: rue **4** aloe, woad **7** aletris, boneset **8** centaury **10** turtlehead
bog: **5** calla **9** steepweed, steepwort
climbing: **4** faba **5** vicia
coarse: **5** tansy **6** eringo, eryngo **7** leafcup **8** pokeweed
flowering: **7** anemone, dittane **8** stapelia **9** celandine
genus: iva **4** ruta **5** canna, cicer, cruca, galax, gavra, inula, lemna, loasa, rheum **6** aralia, asarum, cassia, dondia, isatis, mentha, nerine **7** anemone, cirsium, hedeoma, torenia **8** psoralea **9** grindelia
medicinal: rue **4** aloe **5** senna, sumac, tansy **6** arnica, lovage, tutsan **7** aconite, boneset
mythical: **4** moly
narcotic: **4** hemp
perennial: pia **4** balm, irid **5** sedum **6** fennel, madder, yarrow **7** bugbane, lopweed **8** sainfoin, soapwort **9** digitalis
poisonous: **4** loco **6** conium **7** hemlock, henbane **9** hellebore
salad: **6** endive **7** chicory **10** watercress
shoot: udo
sweet-scented: **8** woodruff
trinity: **8** hepatica
woody: rue
herbage: **5** grass **7** foliage, pasture
herbbane: **9** broomrape
herculean: **4** huge **10** superhuman
Hercules: *capitve:* **4** Iole
companion: **5** Hylas
friend: **6** Iolaus
lion's home: **5** Nemea
mother: **7** Alcmene
stone: **9** loadstone
sweetheart: **4** Iole
victim: **5** Hydra
wife: **4** Hebe **8** Deianira
herd: mob **4** crew, ruck **5** bunch, crowd, drift, drove, flock, group, guard **6** hirsel, pastor, rabble **7** creaght, shelter **8** guardian **9** associate **10** assemblage, congregate **11** aggregation
herdsman: **5** booly **6** booley, cowboy, drover, gaucho, herder **7** bucolic, vaquero **8** garthman, ranchero(Sp.), wrangler
god: **5** Pales
here: ici(F.), **4** army, host **5** ready **6** hither **7** present
hereafter: **5** after, later **6** beyond, future
hereditary: **6** innate, lineal **8** heirship **9** ancestral, descended **11** inheritable, patrimonial
heredity: **4** line **10** inheritance
factor: **4** gene

heresy: 7 dissent 10 radicalism 11 unorthodoxy 13 nonconformism
heretic: 7 Patarin 8 Patarine 9 dissenter, miscreant, sectarian 10 schismatic, unbeliever 13 nonconformist
heretofore: 4 erst 6 before 8 erewhile, formerly, hitherto, previous 9 erstwhile
heritage: 9 heritance, patrimony 10 birthright 11 inheritance
heritor: 4 heir 5 donee 9 inheritor
heritrix, heretrix: 7 heiress
herl: fly 4 barb
hermaphrodite: 9 androgyne 10 androgynus
Hermes: 7 Mercury
birthplace: 7 Cyllene
cap: 7 petasos, petasus
father: 4 Zeus
mother: 4 Maia
son: 7 Evander 9 Autolycus
winged cap: 7 petasos, petasus
winged shoes: 7 talaria
hermetic: 8 airtight 9 alchemist
Hermione: *father:* 8 Menelaus
husband: 7 Orestes 11 Neoptolemus
mother: 5 Helen
hermit: 4 monk 5 clerk 6 anchor 7 ascetic, eremite, incluse, inclusa, recluse, stylite 8 anchoret, beadsman, bedesman, inclusus, marabout 9 anchorite
hut: 4 cell
hermit crab: 8 pagurian
hermitage: 7 ashrama 8 cloister 9 monastery, reclusery
hermitical: 8 eremitic
hernia: 6 breach 7 rupture
hero: ace 4 idol 5 darer 7 demigod 8 champion 9 conqueror 10 topnotcher 11 protagonist
deified: 7 demigod
legendary: 6 Amadis, Roland 7 Paladin
Hero's lover: 7 Leander
Herodias: *daughter:* 6 Salome
husband: 5 Herod
heroic: 4 bold, epic, huge 5 brave, great, large, noble 6 daring, epical 7 extreme, gallant, spartan, valiant 8 enormous, fearless, intrepid, powerful 9 bombastic 10 courageous 11 extravagant, illustrious, magnanimous, outstanding, venturesome 13 grandiloquent
heroin: 4 drug 8 narcotic
heroine: 11 demigoddess
heroism: 5 valor 6 valour 7 bravery, courage 9 fortitude 13 unselfishness
heron: 4 hern, rail, soco 5 crane, egret, herne, quawk, wader 7 bittern, hernser, quabird 8 aigrette, gaulding, heronsew 9 cormorant, herneshaw, heronsewe, heronshaw
genus: 5 ardea
herpes 6 eczema 8 shingles
herring: 4 raun 7 alewife, anchovy 8 scud-dawn
barrel: 4 cade, cran
catch: 4 tack
family: 8 pilchard
female: 4 raun
fry: 4 sile
genus: 6 clupea
head: cob
lake: 5 cisco
young: 4 brit 5 sprat, sprot
Hersey setting: 5 Adano
hership: 4 loot, raid 5 foray
Hertha: 4 Erda 7 Nerthus
hery: 6 praise 7 glorify, worship
hesitancy: 10 hesitation, indecision, reluctance
hesitant: 4 loth 5 chary, loath 8 timorous 9 reluctant
hesitate: 4 wait 5 delay, demur, doubt, pause, stall, waver 6 boggle, falter, loiter, scotch 7 stammer
hesitating: coy 4 hink 7 halting 8 backward, doubtful 9 ambiguous 10 indecisive 11 vacillating
hesped: 6 eulogy 7 oration
Hesperides: 5 Aegle 6 Hestia 7 Hespera 8 Arethusa, Erytheia, Erytheis
Hesperus: *father:* 8 Astraeus
mother: Eos
hessonite: 6 garnet
hest: bid 6 behest, pledge 7 command, precept, promise 10 injunction
Hestia: *father:* 6 Cronus
mother: 4 Rhea
hetaera, hetaira: 8 mistress, paramour 9 companion
heterogeneous: 5 mixed 6 motley, unlike 7 diverse 10 dissimilar 13 miscellaneous 14 indiscriminate
Heteroousian: 5 Arian
hetman: 6 ataman 7 headman
heu: 4 alas
heugh, heuch: 4 bank, crag, glen 5 cliff, shaft 6 hollow
hew: cut 4 chip, chop, fell, hack 5 carve, wound 6 haggle, strike, stroke
hex: 4 jinx 7 bewitch
hexad: 6 sextet
hexadecene: 6 cetene
hexastich: 6 sestet, stanza 7 strophe
hexoctahedron: 10 adamantoid
heyday: joy, May 4 acme 8 wildness 14 frolicsomeness

Hezekiah: *kingdom:* 5 Judah
mother: Abi

Hg: 7 mercury

hi: 8 greeting 10 salutation

hiatus: gap 5 break, chasm 6 breach, lacuna 7 opening 8 interval 12 interruption

Hiawatha: *grandmother:* 7 Nokomis
mother: 7 Wenonah

Hibernia: 4 Erin 7 Ireland

hiccup, hiccough: 4 burp 5 spasm 9 singultus

hick: 4 jake, rube 6 hiccup, rustic 7 bumpkin

hickory: 5 pecan 9 bitternut, shellbark

hidage: tax

hidalgo: 8 nobleman

hidden: 4 lost 5 inner, overt, perdu 6 arcane, buried, cached, closed, innate, latent, masked, occult, secret, veiled 7 arcanum, covered, cryptic, obscure, recluse 8 screened, secluded, secreted 9 concealed, invisible, recondite 10 mysterious 11 clandestine, delitescent 12 subterranean

hide: bar, kip, lie 4 bury, coat, dern, fell, hill, hood, lurk, pelt, skin, stow, veil 5 cache, cloak, cloud, couch, cover, derne(Sc.), skulk 6 huddle, screen, shroud 7 abscond, conceal, eclipse, leather, secrete, shelter 8 carucate, disguise, ensconce, hoodwink, palliate, suppress, withhold 9 dissemble 10 camouflage
cleaning instrument: 6 slater
measured in: 8 hidation
remove hair from: 4 moon
undressed: kip 4 pelt
worker: 6 tanner

hideaway: den 4 cave, lair 7 retreat

hidebound: 6 narrow 7 bigoted, miserly 9 barkbound, bourgeois, illiberal, niggardly 10 restrained 12 conventional

hideous: 4 fell, grim, ugly 5 awful 6 grisly, horrid, odious, ogrish 7 ghastly, ogreish 8 deformed, dreadful, grewsome, gruesome, horrible, shocking, terrible 9 dismaying, frightful, revolting 10 detestable, discordant, terrifying

hideout: mew 4 lair 5 cache

hides: 4 furs 5 skins 6 peltry

hiding: 7 secrecy 8 flogging 9 coverture

hie: 5 haste, hurry, speed 6 betake, hasten, scurry, strive 8 expedite

hield: 4 heel, lean, tilt 5 droop, slope, yield 7 decline, incline

hiemal: 6 wintry

hierarchical: 9 episcopal

hieroglyphic: 7 cryptic 9 illegible

hieroglyphics key: 7 Rosetta

higgle: 6 haggle 7 bargain, chaffer

high: alt 4 dear, haut(F.), main, much, tall 5 acute, chief, first, lofty, sharp, steep 6 costly, shrill 7 eminent, exalted, haughty, violent 8 elevated, foremost, piercing, towering 9 admirable, expensive, important, principal, turbulent 10 tumultuous 11 mountainous
combining form: 4 alti

high-and-mighty: 8 arrogant 9 imperious 11 overbearing

high-brow: 7 egghead 14 intelligentsia

high-class: 6 classy 10 first-class

high-flying: 7 icarian 11 pretentious

high-handed: 6 lordly 8 arrogant, despotic 9 arbitrary 11 dictatorial, domineering, overbearing

high-hat: 4 snub 8 snobbish 12 aristocratic

high-pitched: 6 shrill 8 inclined

high-pressure: 8 forceful, pressing 9 insistent 10 aggressive

high-priced: 4 dear 6 costly 9 expensive

high priest: Eli

high sea: 4 main

high-sounding: 7 fustian, pompous 8 imposing 9 bombastic 10 altisonant

high-spirited: 5 fiery 6 lively 7 gallant 8 cavalier 10 mettlesome

high-strung: 5 tense 7 nervous 9 excitable

high-toned: 7 stylish 8 elevated 9 dignified 11 fashionable

highborn: 5 noble 8 generous 12 aristocratic

highbred: 7 genteel, refined

higher: 8 superior

highest: 6 upmost 8 bunemost, overmost

highest point: 4 acme 6 zenith

Highland war cry: 6 slogan

Highlander (see also **Scotland**): 4 Celt, Gael, Kelt, Scot 6 Tartan 8 clansman 9 Gluneamie
dance: 4 reel 5 fling
language: 4 Erse
pouch: 6 sporan 7 sporran
weapon: 8 claymore, skeandhu

highroad: 7 highway

highway: way 4 bahn(G.), iter(L.), path, pike, road 5 Alcan 6 Appian, artery, causey, course, rumpad, street 7 Lincoln 8 autobahn, causeway, chaussee(F.), highroad, turnpike 9 boulevard 12 thoroughfare

highwayman: pad 5 rider, thief 6 bandit, padder, robber 7 brigand, footpad, ladrone 8 hightoby 9 bandolero

Highwayman: *author:* 5 Noyes

hike: 4 jerk, toss, walk 5 march, raise, throw, tramp

hilarious: mad 5 funny, merry, noisy 6 jovial 7 jocular 8 mirthful 9 ludicrous

hilarity: gig, joy 4 glee 5 mirth 6 gaiety 7 jollity 9 happiness, joviality, merriment 10 joyousness 12 cheerfulness, exhilaration
hilch: 4 halt, limp
hill: ben, hoe, kop, pap, tor 4 bank, brae, bult, dagh, dune, fell, heap, hide, knap, knob, loma, mesa 5 bargh, butte, cerro(Sp.), cliff, cover, hurst, morro, mound, mount 6 ascent, barrow, copple, djebel 7 colline, picacho 9 acclivity, elevation, monadnock
glacial: 4 kame, paha 7 drumlin
Jerusalem: 6 Olivet
range: 5 ridge
sand: 4 dene, dune
top of: tor 4 peak 6 summit
hillock: 4 tump 5 croft, hurst, knoll, kopje, mound, toman(Sc.)
over grave: 7 tumulus
hillside: 4 brae, cote 5 cleve, cliff, falda(Sp.), slade, slope 6 cleeve
hilly: 5 steep
hilt: 6 handle 8 handgrip
hilum: 5 porta 7 nucleus
Himalaya: *animal, bear-like:* 5 panda
antelope: 5 goral, serow
bear: 5 bhalu
bearcat: 5 panda
cedar: 6 deodar
cypress: 6 bhutan
dweller: 8 Nepalese
goat: 4 kras, tahr, tair, thar
oxen: yak
peak: Api 7 Everest
pheasant: 5 monal
sheep: 6 bharal, nahoor
swamp: 5 Terai
tableland: 5 Tibet
Himavat's daughter: 4 Devi
himene, himine: 4 hymn, song
himself: 4 ipse(L.)
Himyarite: 4 Arab 7 Axumite, Sabaean
Hinayana Buddhism: 5 shojo 6 lesser
hind: doe, lad, roe 4 back, chap, stag 6 fellow, rustic, worker 7 bailiff, peasant, servant, steward 8 cabrilla, domestic 9 posterior 11 hindquarter
hinddeck: 4 poop
hinder: bar, let 4 slow 5 after, block, cheat, check, choke, cramp, debar, delay, deter, embar, estop, hedge 6 arrest, detain, hamper, harass, impede, impend, injure, retard, scotch 7 deprive, forelay, impeach, inhibit, prevent 8 encumber, handicap, obstruct, preclude, prohibit 9 embarrass, foreclose, forestall, interrupt, posterior
hindmost: 4 last, rear 9 aftermost
hindrance: bar, rub 4 clog, curb, snag, stop 5 block, check, delay, hitch 6 arrest 7 barrier 8 obstacle 9 detention, deterrent, restraint 10 difficulty, impediment 11 impeachment, obstruction 12 interruption
Hindu (see also **India**): 4 Babu, Koli, Sikh 5 Tamil 6 Gentoo, Hindoo 8 Kolarian
abode of gods: 4 Meru
adherent: Sik 4 Jain, Seik, Sikh 5 Jaina, Seikh
age of world: 4 yuga
alphabet: 6 Sarada
ancestral race: 5 Aryan
apartment: 5 mahal
Aryan race: 4 Swat
ascetic: 4 jogi, sadh, yati, yogi 5 sadhu
atheist: 7 nastika
book: 4 Veda 6 Tantra 11 Yajna-valkya
calendar: Pus 4 Jeth, Asin, Kaur, Magh 5 Asarh, Sawan, Katik, Aghan, Chait 6 Bhadon, Kartik, Phagun 7 Baisakh, Sarawan, Phalgun
call to prayer: 4 azan
caste: Dom, Mal, Meo 4 Dasi, Gola, Koli, Kori, Mali, Pasi, Teli 5 Goala, Palli, Sudra 6 Babhan, Soodra 7 Brahman
caste member: Jat 4 Jain 6 Banian, Banyan, Rajput, Vaisya 7 Rajpoot 9 Kshatriya, Vakkaliga
charm: 6 mantra
chief: mir 6 sirdar
coin: ana, pai, pie 4 anna, pice 5 paisa, rupee
congregation: 5 samaj, somaj
convert to Islam: 6 shaikh
cremation: 4 sati 6 suttee
dancer: 8 devadasi
deity: Dev 4 Deva, Dewa, Maya, Rama, Yama 6 Ganesa, Varuna, Vishnu 7 Ganesha, Krishna 9 Jagannath 10 Jagannatha, Juggernaut 11 Ramachandra
demon: 4 Bali, Bhut, Ketu, Rahu 5 Asura 6 Daitya
devotee: 4 yati
disciple: 4 sikh
divine being: dev 4 deva
doctrine: 5 Karma 6 dharma
drink: 4 soma
duty: 6 dharma
ejaculation: om, um
essence: 4 rasa, rata 5 atman 6 amrita
family: 5 gotra
female energy: 5 Sakti 6 Shakti
festival: 4 Holi, mela 6 Dewali, Hoolee 7 Dashara
flute: bin 5 pungi
garment: 4 sari 5 saree
gentleman: 4 babu 5 baboo, sahib

god (see also *deity* above): 4 Agni, Deva, Kama, Siva, Vayu, Yama 5 Asura, Shiva, Simia 6 Brahma, Ganesa, Skanda, Varuna 7 Ganesha
goddess: Sri, Uma, Vac 4 Devi, Kali, Shri, Vach 5 Durga, Gauri, Sakti, Shree, Ushas 6 Chandi, Shakti 7 Parvati 9 Haimavati
guitar: 5 sitar
headdress: 5 rumal
heaven: 5 dyaus
hermitage: 7 ashrama
hero: 4 Nala, Rama
holy book: 4 Veda 6 Sastra
holy sage: 5 rishi
hymn: 6 mantra
idol worship: 5 arati
incarnation: 6 avatar
Indra: 5 Sakka, Sakra
king: 4 Nala 5 Sesha 6 Shesha
lady: 4 devi, rani 5 ranee
language: 4 Pali, Urdu 5 Hindi, Tamil 8 Sanskrit 10 Hindustani
lawgiver: 4 Manu
leader: 5 Nehru 6 Gandhi, sirdar
life principle: 4 jiva 5 atman, prana
literature: 4 Veda 5 sruti 6 shruti
loincloth: 5 dhoti
magic: 4 jadu, maya 5 jadoo
magician: 5 fakir 6 fakeer
mantra: om, um
master: 5 sahib
mendicant: 4 naga 7 bairagi, vairagi 8 sannyasi
mental discipline: 4 yoga
monastery: 4 muth
monkey god: 7 Hanuman
month: see *calendar* above
mother goddess: 6 matris
mystic: 4 yogi
noble: 5 rajah 8 maharaja
non-violence: 6 ahimsa
offering: 4 bali, lepa 5 pinda
paradise: 7 Nirvana
patriarch: 5 pitri
philosophy: 4 yoga 5 tamas
poem: 8 Ramayana 11 Mahabharata 12 Bhagavad-Gita
poet: 6 Tagore
policeman: 5 sepoy
prayer rug: 4 asan 5 asana
priest: 5 hotar
prince: 4 raja, rana 5 rajah 8 maharaja 9 maharajah
princess: 4 rani 5 ranee
pundit: 5 swami
queen: 4 rani 5 ranee 8 maharani 9 maharanee
religion: 5 Prana 7 Jainism, Sivaism 8 Shivaism
rice: 4 boro
rite: 5 achar
ruler: 5 rajah
scripture: Li; rig 4 Veda 5 Sruti 6 Purana, Sastra, Smriti, Tantra 7 Shastra
sect: 4 Sikh, siva 6 Aghori
social division: 5 caste
soldier: 4 Sikh 5 sepoy
soul: 4 atma 5 atman
spirit: 4 Jiva, Mara 5 Asura, Atman, Prana 7 Muktama
supreme being: 6 Vishnu
teacher: pir 4 guru
temple: 4 deul 6 vimana
title: aya, sri 4 mian, raja, shri, sidi 5 rajah, sahib, shree, swami 7 bahadur
tower: 5 stupa
triad god: 4 Siva
tunic: 4 jama 5 jamah
unknown god: Ka
unorthodox: 4 Jain 5 Jaina
Upanishad: 4 Isha, Veda 7 Vedanta
worship: 4 puja 5 pooja

Hindustan: Ind
language: 4 Urdu 5 Hindi
tribesman: 4 toda

hinge: har 4 butt, hang, turn 5 gemel, joint, pivot, stand 6 depend, gimmer, gimmor, hingle, lamina, pintle

Hinnom Valley: 7 Gehenna

hint: cue, tip 4 clew, clue, time, turn 5 cheep(Sc.), imply, trace 6 allude, moment 7 inkling, mention, suggest 8 allusion, innuendo, intimate, occasion 9 catchword, insinuate 10 indication, intimation, suggestion 11 insinuation

hip: hop 4 coxa, huck, limp, miss, skip 6 haunch, huckle
pert. to: 7 sciatic

hip boots: 6 waders

hipbone: 5 ileum, ilium

hippie: mod 5 rebel 6 copout

Hippocrates: *birthplace:* kos
drug: 5 mecon, opium

hippodrome: 5 arena 6 circus 7 contest

hippopotamus: 6 seacow 9 pachyderm

hire: buy, fee, let, use 4 rent, sign, wage 5 bribe, lease, price, wages 6 employ, engage, retain, reward, salary 7 charter, conduce, stipend 9 allowance 12 compensation

hireling: 4 esne, serf 5 slave 8 gangster 9 mercenary

hirple: 4 limp 6 hobble

hirsel: 4 herd, land 5 flock

hirsute: 5 hairy, rough 6 coarse, shaggy

hispid: 7 bristly 8 strigose, strigous

hiss: 4 hish, sizz, whiz 5 whizz 6 fissle, fistle 8 goose cry 10 assibilate

hissing: 6 fizzle 8 sibilant 9 sibilance
hist: 4 hark, hush
historian: 8 annalist 10 chronicler
history: 4 tale 5 drama, story 6 annals, memoir, record 7 account 8 relation 9 biography, chronicle, genealogy, narrative
muse: 4 Clio
histrion: 5 actor
histrionics: 6 acting 11 theatricals
hit: bat, lam, lob, ram, rap, tap 4 bump, bunt, cast, club, slog, slug, sock, swat, wham 5 clout, flick, knock, smack, smite, smote, throw, touch 6 attain, batted, bingle, strike 7 collide, success 8 bludgeon 10 production, succession
hit-or-miss: 6 casual, chance, habnab 8 careless 9 haphazard
hitch: hop, tie, tug 4 halt, hook, join, knot, limp, pull 5 agree, catch, crick, hotch, marry, unite 6 attach, enlist, hobble 8 obstacle, stoppage 9 harmonize, hindrance 10 enlistment, impediment 11 contretemps, obstruction
hitchhiker: 8 stowaway
hither: 4 here
hitherto: ago, yet 6 before
Hitler: *aerie:* 13 Berchtesgaden
chosen race: 5 Aryan
follower: 4 Nazi
hitter: 6 batter 7 batsman, slugger
Hittite: *ancestor:* 4 Heth
capital: 6 Pteria
storm god: 6 Teshub, Teshup
hive: 5 store, swarm 6 apiary 9 multitude
hives: 5 uredo 7 allergy 9 urticaria
ho: 4 long, stop 5 yearn 6 attend, desist
hoar: 4 cold, gray, rime 5 hoary, musty, stale 6 biting 7 ancient 9 antiquity, venerable 13 venerableness
hoard: 4 save 5 amass, chest, hutch, stock, store 6 supply 7 husband 8 quantity, treasure, treasury 10 accumulate, collection
hoarder: 5 miser 6 storer 9 treasurer
hoarfrost: rag 4 rime 9 cranreuch(Sc.)
hoarse: 5 gruff, harsh, rocky, rough 7 grating, raucous 10 discordant
hoarseness: 4 frog 5 croup
hoary: old 4 aged, gray, hoar 5 moldy, mossy, musty 7 ancient, hoarish, whitish 9 canescent, venerable
hoax: bam, cod, fun, hex, kid 4 bilk, fake, gaff, gegg, gunk, joke, ruse, sell, sham 5 bluff, cheat, spoof, trick 6 canard, diddle, humbug, string 7 deceive 8 artifice 9 bamboozle, deception 11 hornswoggle
hob: elf, peg, pin, tap 4 game, mark, nail, nave 5 clown, fairy, ledge 6 ferret, rustic, sprite 7 mandrel 8 mischief 10 countryman, projection
hobbil: 4 dolt 5 clown, dunce, idiot
hobble: 4 clog, clop 5 bunch, cramp, hitch 6 fetter, hopple 7 cramble, perplex, shackle, spancel 9 embarrass 10 difficulty, perplexity 13 embarrassment
hobbledehoy: lad 5 youth
hobbler: 5 pilot 7 boatman, hoveler, laborer 8 retainer 12 longshoreman
hobbly: 5 rough 6 uneven
hobby: fad 5 horse 6 falcon 7 pastime 9 avocation, diversion
hobgoblin: bug, elf, hag, imp 4 bogy, Puck 5 bogey, bogie, bugan, poker, spook 6 boodie(Sc.), sprite 7 bugaboo 8 boggle-bo, worricow(Sc.) 9 coltpixie 10 apparition
hobo: bo; boe, bum 5 tramp 7 vagrant 8 vagabond
hock: ham, hox 4 pawn 5 ankle, hough, thigh 6 mallow, pledge 9 hamstring 10 houghsinew
hocket: 6 hiccup 8 obstacle 12 interruption
hockey: 5 bandy 6 shinny
disk: 4 puck
goal: 4 cage
hocus: 4 drug 5 cheat, fraud 7 deceive 8 cheating, deceiver, trickery 10 adulterate
hocus-pocus: 5 cheat, trick 6 humbug 7 juggler 8 flimflam, quackery 9 trickster 12 charlatanism
hod: 4 soil 6 barrow 7 scuttle
hoddy-doddy: 4 fool 5 snail 7 cuckold 9 blockhead
hodgepodge: ana 4 mess, olio, stew 5 cento 6 medley 7 mixture 10 hotchpotch, miscellany 11 gallimaufry, ollapodrida 12 mingle-mangle
hoe: dig 4 brod, hill, till 5 clean, cliff, padle, worry 6 sarcle, scrape 7 dogfish, trouble 8 griffaun 9 cultivate 10 promontory
hog (see also **pig**): sow 4 bene, boar, dime, galt, gilt 5 shoat, shote, swine 6 barrow 7 hogling 8 shilling 9 boschvark 10 backfatter
breed: 5 Essex 9 Hampshire
food: 4 mash 5 slops, swill 6 acorns
genus: sus
young: pig 5 shoat
hog peanut: 8 earthpea
hog plum: 4 amra
hog side: 6 flitch
hog thigh: ham
hogfish: 8 scorpene
hoggish: 5 hoggy 7 selfish, swinish 10 gluttonous
hognut: 5 ouabe 6 pignut 8 earthnut
hogo: 5 taint 6 flavor, stench
hogshead: 4 cask 6 barrel, hogget, vessel
hogtie: 4 clog 6 fetter, hamper
hogwash: 5 draff 7 pigwash

hoi polloi: mob 6 masses, rabble 8 populace
hoick: 4 lift, yank
hoist: cat, gin 4 jack, lift 5 boost, crane, davit, heave, heeze, horse, lewis, raise, setup, winch 7 derrick, elevate 8 elevator
hoist sail: 4 swig
hoistman: 8 bandsman 9 engineman
hoity-toity: 5 giddy, proud 6 snooty 7 flighty, haughty 8 arrogant 11 harum-scarum, patronizing, thoughtless 13 irresponsible
hokum: 4 bunk 11 foolishness
hold: own 4 bind, bite, bulk, clip, fill, have, hook, keep, rely, seat, stow, tend 5 avast, carry, catch, grasp, guard, rivet 6 adhere, arrest, behold, cleave, clench, defend, detain, harbor, occupy, retain 7 adjudge, contain, control 8 interest, maintain, thurrock 9 entertain 10 possession, stronghold
hold a brief for: 6 defend 8 advocate
hold back: dam 4 stem, stop 5 deter 6 detain, retard 7 inhibit, repress 8 restrain
hold fast: hug 5 cling, stick 6 cohere
hold forth: 5 offer 7 exhibit 8 continue, maintain, propound
hold in custody: 4 jail 6 detain, intern
hold off: 5 avert 7 refrain
hold on: 4 stop, wait 7 forbear 8 continue
hold out: 4 last 6 endure 7 exclude, protend 8 continue
hold up: rob 4 halt, lift, rein 5 boost, check, raise 7 display, exhibit, robbery, support, sustain
hold water: 5 sound 10 consistent
holder: 5 haver 6 tenant 9 container 10 receptacle
holdfast: 5 clamp, miser 6 clinch 7 support 9 tenacious 10 persistent
holding: 5 asset 6 estate, tenure 8 property
adapted for: 10 prehensile
hole: bay, den, pit 4 bore, cave, cove, deep, dump, flaw, gate, gulf, leak, mine, nook, peck, rent, vent 5 abyss, chasm, shaft 6 burrow, cavern, cavity, cranny, crater, eyelet, grotto, hollow, pierce, prison, recess 7 dungeon, mortise, opening, orifice, ostiole 8 aperture, bunghole, peephole 10 excavation 11 perforation, predicament
instrument for making: awl 4 bore 5 drill 8 stiletto
wall: 4 muse 5 meuse, niche
Holi, Hoolee: 8 festival
holia: 4 fish 6 salmon
holiday: 4 fete 5 feria, festa, merry 6 fiesta, jovial, outing 7 festive, playday 8 festival, vacation 9 convivial, Mardi Gras
holiness: 5 piety 7 halidom 8 halidome, sanctity 9 sanctuary 11 saintliness 13 righteousness
Holland: See **Netherlands**
holler: 4 yell 6 shriek 7 protest
hollow: den, dip 4 boss, cave, cove, deep, dent, doke, glen, hole, holl, howe, huck, lean, thin, vain, void 5 bight, chase, cuppy, empty, false, gaunt, goyal, goyle, heugh, scoop, sinus, stria 6 cavern, cavity, cirque, groove, hungry, socket, sunken, vacant 7 concave, muffled, unsound 8 alveolus, fossette, specious 9 cavernous, deceitful, depressed, faithless, worthless 10 depression, sepulchral 11 treacherous 12 unsatisfying
comb. form: 5 coelo
hollow-eyed: 7 haggard
hollowed: 7 glenoid
hollowed out: 6 cavate
hollowness: 6 vanity 7 vacuity
holly: 4 assi, holm, ilex 5 yapon, yupon 6 hulver, yaupon, youpon
pert. to: 6 ilicic
holm: ait 5 holly, islet 7 bottoms, lowland
holm oak: 4 ilex 5 holly
Holmes' word: 10 elementary
holobaptist: 12 immersionist
holocaust: 9 sacrifice 11 destruction
holster: 4 case 7 housing 8 scabbard
holt: den 4 grip, hill, hold, lair, wood 5 copse, grasp 7 retreat
holy: 5 pious, sacre(F.), saint, santo 6 devout, divine, hallow, sacred 7 blessed, perfect, sainted, saintly 8 blissful, hallowed 9 inviolate, sanctuary, spiritual 10 sacrosanct 13 sanctimonious
combining form: 5 hagio
Holy City: 4 Kiev, Rome, Zion 5 Mecca, Lhasa, Medina, Moscow 7 Benares 9 Allahabad, Jerusalem
Holy Grail: 8 Sangraal, Sangreal
castle: 9 Monsalvat
knight: 7 Galahad
Holy Joe: 9 clergyman
Holy Land: 9 Palestine
pilgrim: 6 palmer
holy oil: 6 chrism
Holy One: God 6 Christ 7 Jehovah 12 Supreme Being
Holy Roman emperor: 4 Otho, Otto
Holy Rood: 5 cross 8 crucifix
holy statue: 4 icon, ikon 5 ikono
holy water: *font:* 5 paten
receptacle: 5 stoup
sprinkler: 11 aspergillum

homage: 5 honor 6 eulogy, fealty, regard 7 loyalty, manrent, ovation, respect 9 adoration, deference, obeisance, reverence 10 allegiance
homager: 6 vassal
homaloidal: 4 even, flat
homard: 7 lobster
hombre: guy, man 6 fellow
Homburg: hat 4 felt
home: den 4 nest 5 abode, being, domus, house 6 asylum, estate, maison(F.), 7 habitat, hospice, village 8 domicile, dwelling 9 homestead, residence 10 habitation 11 hearthstone
at: 4 chez(F.)
wheeled: 7 trailer
home base: den 5 plate
homeborn: 6 native 10 indigenous
homefelt: 6 inward 7 private
homelike: 4 cozy 5 homey 6 homely, homish 8 cheerful, friendly, homesome 11 comfortable
homeliness: 9 plainness 10 simplicity 11 domesticity 17 unpretentiousness
homely: 4 rude, ugly 5 plain 6 hameil, hamelt, hamilt, kindly, simple 7 plainly 8 domestic, familiar, friendly, homelike, intimate 9 unsightly 10 intimately 12 unpretending 13 unpretentious
homemade: 5 plain 6 simple 8 domestic
Homer: *birthplace:* 5 Chios
character: 4 Ajax 6 Nestor 8 Achilles, Odysseus
poem: 5 Iliad 7 Odyssey
Homeric: 4 epic 6 epical
homesickness: 9 nostalgia
homespun: 4 kelt(Sc.), rude 5 plain 6 coarse
homestead: 4 toft, tref(W.) 7 onstead
homicide: 6 murder
homilist: 8 preacher
homily: 5 adage 6 sermon 8 assembly 9 communion, discourse 11 exhortation
hominy: 4 bran, corn, samp 5 grits
homo: man
Homo Americanus: 6 Indian
Homo sapiens: man
homogeneity: 8 equality, identity, sameness
homogeneous: 4 like 5 equal, solid 7 similar 10 comparable
homologous: 9 identical
homonym: 7 synonym 8 namesake
homunculus: 5 dwarf 7 manikin
Honduras: *city:* 4 Yoro 6 Cedros, Iriona 7 Gracias 9 Juticalpa 11 Tegucigalpa(c.)
coin: 4 peso 7 centavo, lempira
Indian: 4 Ulua, Ulva 5 Lenca
measure: 4 vara 5 milla 6 mecate, tercia 7 cajuela, manzana 10 caballeria
mountain: 5 Ceiba, Colon
port: 8 Truxillo 10 San Lorenzo
river: 4 Ulua 5 Aguan, Negro 6 Patuca, Sulaco 9 Choluteca 10 Chemelicon
weight: 4 caja
hone: 4 long, pine 5 delay, dress, strop 6 lament 7 grumble, sharpen 8 oilstone 9 whetstone
honest: 4 fair, full, just, open 5 frank, roman 6 candid, chaste, decent, dexter, dinkum, proper, rustic, square 7 genuine, sincere, upright 8 bonafide, faithful, rightful, reliable, straight, suitable, truthful, virtuous 9 equitable, guileless, honorable, ingenuous, veracious 10 creditable 11 trustworthy 13 conscientious, incorruptible, unadulterated 15 straightforward
honestly: 5 truly 6 dinkum, justly 8 directly 9 telltruth
honesty: 5 honor 6 equity 7 decency, justice, probity 8 fairness, fidelity, veracity 9 constancy, integrity 10 generosity, liberality 11 uprightness 12 suitableness, truthfulness 13 honorableness 15 trustworthiness 19 straightforwardness
honesty plant: 8 moonwort
honey: mel 4 dear, niel(F.) 5 sweet 6 nectar 7 flatter 8 precious
combining form: 5 melli
fermented drink: 4 mead
source: bee 6 nectar
honey badger: 5 ratel
honey bear: 8 kinkajou
honey buzzard: 4 hawk, pern
honey eater: iao 6 manuao
honeybee: 7 deseret 8 angelito
disease: 8 sacbrood
honeyberry: 4 tree 5 genep, genip
honeycomb cell: 7 alveola 8 alveolus
honeycombed: 6 favose, pitted 8 alveolar
honeydew: 5 melon 6 mildew, orange
honeyed: 5 sweet 6 sugary 7 candied 11 mellifluous
honeysuckle: 6 azalea, widbin
Hong Kong: *bay:* 4 Mirs
city: 8 Victoria
coin: 4 cent 6 dollar 13 British dollar 14 Hong Kong dollar
honor: 4 fame, fete, prow 5 adore, exalt, glory, grace, izzat 6 credit, decore, esteem, homage, laurel, praise, regard, repute, revere 7 dignify, dignity, emblaze, ennoble, glorify, honesty, respect, worship 9 celebrate, deference, reverence 10 estimation, reputation
pledge: 6 parole
honorable: 4 dear 5 moral, noble, white 6 gentle, honest 7 upright 8 generous, hon-

orary 9 dearworth, estimable, reputable 10 creditable 11 commendable, illustrious, magnanimous, meritorious, respectable
honorarium: fee, tip 6 reward, salary 7 douceur, payment 8 gratuity
Honshu: *bay:* Ise
port: 4 Kobe
hood: cap 4 coif, cowl, hide 5 amice, blind 6 biggin, bonnet, burlet, camail, canopy, chapel, tippet 7 calotte, capuche, surtout 8 capsheaf, caputium, chaperon, covering
academic: 8 liripipe, liripoop
monk's: 4 atis, cowl 5 atees
saddle: 8 tapadera, tapadero
vehicle: 6 bonnet, capote
hooded: 9 cucullate 10 capistrate
hoodlum: yap 5 rowdy 6 goonda 8 hooligan
hoodoo: 4 jinx 5 Jonah 6 voodoo 7 bewitch, unlucky
hoodwink: 4 fool, hide, wile 5 blear, blind, bluff, cheat, cosen, cover, cozen 6 befool, delude 7 blinder, blinker, deceive, mislead 9 blindfold
hooey: 4 bunk 6 bunkum 7 baloney, boloney 8 buncombe, nonsense
hoof: 4 clee, foot, walk 5 cloof, cloot, cluif, dance, tramp 6 ungula
hoofer: 6 dancer, walker
hook: 4 barb, gaff, hake, hock, hold, huck 5 catch, cleek, hamus, hitch, larin, seize, steal 6 agrafe, anchor, larree, pilfer, tenter 7 agraffe, capture, grunter, hamulus, hitcher 8 crotchet 10 chatelaine
hook money: 5 larin 6 larree
hooka, hookah: 4 pipe 7 nargile 8 narghile 9 narghileh
hooked: 6 hamate 7 hamular, uncinal 8 ankyroid, aquiline, uncinate
hookey player: 6 truant
hooligan: 6 loafer 7 ruffian
hooly: 4 slow, soft, wary
hoop: 4 bail, band, ring, tire 5 clasp, garth, girth, shout 6 circle, frette 7 circlet, trundle 8 encircle, surround
hoopskirt: 9 crinoline
hoosegow: jug 4 jail 6 lockup, prison 10 guardhouse
hoosh: 4 lift, urge 5 boost, hoist
Hoosier State: 7 Indiana
hoot: boo 4 jeer, whoo 5 shout, whoop 6 boohoo 7 ululate
Hoover Dam lake: 4 Mead
hop: fly, hip 4 dope, halt, jump, leap, limp, skip 5 bound, dance, hitch 6 flight, gambol, spring
hop back: vat
hop kiln: 4 oast
hop-o'-my-thumb: 5 dwarf 6 midget
hop stem: 4 bine
hopbush: 6 akeake
hope: 4 deem, spes(L.), want, wish 5 haven, trust 6 aspire, desire, expect, morale 7 cherish, confide 8 prospect, reliance 9 esperance 10 aspiration 11 expectation 12 anticipation
goddess of: 4 Spes
lack of: 7 despair
symbol of: 4 opal
hopeful: 8 sanguine 9 confident, expectant 10 optimistic
hopeless: 4 gone, vain 6 futile 7 forlorn, useless 8 downcast 9 desperate, heartless, incurable 10 despairing, despondent, desponding, remediless 11 ineffectual 12 disconsolate, irremediable 13 irrecoverable, irretrievable
hophead: 6 addict
Hophni: *brother:* 8 Phinehas
father: Eli
Hopi Indian: 4 Moki 5 Moqui
god: 7 Kachina, Katcina 8 Katchina
hoplite: 7 soldier
hopper: box 5 chute 6 dancer, leaper 10 receptacle
hoppet: 4 yard 6 basket, bucket
hopple: 6 fetter, hamper, hobble 8 entangle
hopscotch: 7 pallall
stone: 5 potsy 6 peever
hopvine: 4 bine
Horae: 4 Dike 6 Eirene 7 Euromia
horde: 4 army, camp, clan, pack 5 crowd, group, swarm 6 legion, throng 9 multitude
horehound: 6 henbit
Horite chief: 4 Seir
horizon: rim 4 edge, goal 8 prospect
horizontal: 4 flat 5 level
hormigo: 5 quira 7 ant tree
horn: 4 scur, tuba 5 brass, bugle, cornu, drone, siren 6 antler, cornet, rhyton 7 antenna, trumpet 8 oliphant 9 alpenhorn 10 cornucopia
blast: 4 mort, toot 7 fanfare, tantara 9 tantarara
combining form: 4 kera
crescent moon: 4 cusp
deer: 4 tine 5 prong 6 antler
drinking: 6 rhyton
Hebrew: 6 shofar 7 shophar
player: 6 bugler 9 cornetist, trumpeter
without: 5 doddy 6 doddie, polled 7 acerous
hornbill: 4 bird, tock 6 homrai
genus of: 7 buceros
hornet: 4 wasp
hornpipe: 4 tune 5 dance 8 matelote
hornswoggle: 4 hoax 9 bamboozle
horny: 4 hard 8 ceratoid 9 calloused 10 semiopaque
hornyhead: 4 chub

horologe: 4 dial 5 clock, watch 9 timepiece
horoscope: 4 dial 7 diagram
horrendous: 7 fearful 8 horrible 9 frightful
horrible: 4 dire, grim 5 great 6 grisly, horrid 7 fearful, ghastly, hideous, horrent 8 dreadful, gruesome, horrific, shocking, terrible 9 atrocius, excessive, frightful, horrified, nefarious 10 horrendous, tremendous
horrid: 4 grim, ugly 5 awful, rough 6 rugged 7 hideous 8 dreadful, grewsome, gruesome, horrible, shocking 9 bristling, frightful, obnoxious, offensive, revolting 10 detestable, terrifying 13 objectionable
horrific: 7 fearful 8 horrible 9 frightful 10 horrifying
horrified: 6 aghast 7 ghastly
horrify: 5 shock 6 appall, dismay
horrifying: 8 horrific 9 execrable
horror: 4 fear 5 dread 6 terror 8 aversion 10 abhorrence 11 abomination, detestation 13 consternation
hors d'ouevre: 6 canape, relish 7 zakusha 8 apertif 9 antipasto, appetizer
Horsa's brother: 7 Hengist
horse: gee, nag, pad 4 barb, mare, plug, prad 5 brock, caple, capul, draft, filly, hobby, hoist, mount, pacer, raise, shier, steed, waler 6 cheval, equine, geegee, ladino, pelter, rouncy 7 caballo(Sp.), cavallo(Sp.), cavalry, charger, clipper, courser, hackney, mustang, saddler, sheltie, sleeper, stepper, trestle 8 bathorse, cartaver(Sc.), footrope, jackstay 10 breastband
Achilles': 7 Xanthus
ankle: 4 hock
breastplate: 7 peytrel, poitrel
breed: 4 Arab, Barb 5 Shire 6 hunter, Morgan 7 Belgian, harness, Suffolk, trotter 8 Galloway, Normandy, Shetland 9 Percheron 10 Clydesdale
brown: bay 6 sorrel 8 chestnut
buyer: 5 coper 6 trader 7 knacker
calico: 5 pinto
color: bay 4 pied, roan 5 pinto 6 calico, sorrel 8 chestnut, palomino, schimmel
combining form: 5 hippo
command: gee, haw, hup 4 whoa 6 giddap
covering: 9 caparison
cry: nie 5 neigh 6 whinny
dappled: 4 roan 5 pinto 7 piebald
dark: 4 zain
dealer: 7 chanter, scorser
disease: 5 surra 6 heaves, lampas 7 lampers, quittor, spavins 9 distemper
docked-tail: 6 curtal 8 cocktail
draft: 4 aver 5 aiver, hairy
driver: 6 jockey 7 sumpter 8 coachman
farm: 6 dobbin
feeding box: 6 manger
female: 4 mare, yaud 5 filly
foot: 4 frog, hoof 7 coronet, fetlock, pastern
forehead: 8 chanfrin
gait: run 4 lope, pace, rack, trot, vott, walk 6 canter, gallop
genus: 5 equus
goddess of: 5 Epona
golden: 8 palomino
gray: 8 schimmel
guide: 4 rein 5 longe
harness: 5 pacer 7 trotter
hired: 4 hack 7 hackney
horned: 7 unicorn 9 monoceros
leg: 6 instep 7 fetlock
lover: 10 hippophile
male: 4 stud 6 entire 7 gelding 8 stallion
measure: 4 hand
menage: 6 school 7 academy
pace: 4 lope, trot 5 amble 6 canter
pack: 5 bidet 7 sumpter
pair: 4 span, team
pert. to: 6 hippic
piebald: 5 pinto
prehistoric: 8 Eohippus
racing: 4 turf
rearing: 6 pesade
relay: 6 remuda
round-up: 5 rodeo
saddle: cob 5 mount 7 palfrey
small: cob, nag, tit 4 pony 5 bidet, genet 6 cayuse, jennet(Sp.) 8 galloway, Shetland
sorrel: 4 roan 8 chestnut
spirited: 4 Arab 5 steed 6 rearer 7 courser
stable of: 6 string
talking: 5 Arion
track slope: 6 calade
trainer: 5 valet
trapping: 6 tackle 7 harness 9 caparison
trotting: 6 Morgan
turn: 7 passade
war: 5 steed 7 charger, courser 8 destrier
white-streaked face: 4 shim 5 blaze, reach
wild: 6 bronco, brumby, tarpan 7 mustang 8 warragal, warrigal
winged: 7 Pegasus
working: 4 aver 5 aiver 6 dobbin
worn-out: nag 4 hack, jade, moke, plug 5 crock, skate 6 garran, garron, gleyde 7 knacker 8 harridan 9 rosinante
horse-and-buggy: rig 12 old-fashioned
horse collar: 7 bargham(Sc.)
horse mackerel: 4 fish, scad 5 atule, tunny 6 bonita, saurel
horse opera: 7 western
horse tackle: 7 harness
horseback: *on:* 7 a cheval(F.)
horsefly: 4 cleg 5 clegg 6 botfly, gadfly
horsehair: 4 mane 9 haircloth

horsehide: 8 cordovan
horsekeeper: 5 groom 7 hostler
horselaugh: 5 snort 6 guffaw, heehaw
horseman: 5 rider 6 carter, cowboy centaur, courier, vaquero 8 buckaroo, chevalier 10 cavalryman, equestrian 12 broncobuster, equestrienne
horseman goad: 4 spur
horsemanship: 6 manege 10 equitation
rearing: 6 pesade
sidewalk: 4 volt
turn: 8 caracole
horsemen: 7 cavalry 11 equestrians
horseradish tree: ben 5 behen
horseshoe: *point:* 6 sponge
spur: 4 calk
rim: web
horseshoer: 7 farrier 10 blacksmith
horsewhip: 4 flog 5 quirt 7 chabouk
horticulturist: 8 gardener
Horus: Ra, Re
brother: 6 Anubis
father: 6 Osiris
mother: 4 Isis
hory, horry: 4 foul 5 dirty 6 impure
hose: 4 sock, tube, vamp 5 water 6 drench 8 stocking
Hosea's wife: 5 Gomer
hospice: inn 5 house 6 asylum, imaret 9 hospitium
hospitable: 5 douce 6 cheery 7 cordial 8 friendly 9 receptive 10 hospitious
hospital: 6 creche, refuge, spital 9 infirmary 10 sanatorium 11 xenodochium 12 ambulatorium
attendant: 5 nurse 7 orderly
mobile: 9 ambulance
user: 7 patient
hospitality: 7 welcome 10 cordiality
to strangers: 9 xenodochy
host: inn 4 army, here 5 crowd, guest, swarm 6 housel, legion, myriad, throng 7 company, lodging 8 landlord 9 harbinger, multitude, sacrifice 10 assemblage 11 entertainer
receptacle for: pyx 5 paten 8 ciborium
hostage: inn 5 hotel 6 pledge 8 security 9 guarantee
hostel: inn 5 hotel, lodge 7 lodging 12 lodginghouse 13 entertainment
hostelry: inn 5 hotel 6 hostel, hostry, tavern 11 caravansary 12 lodginghouse
hostile: foe 5 black, enemy, fremd 7 adverse, opposed, warlike 8 contrary, inimical 9 resisting 10 malevolent, unfriendly 11 belligerent 12 antagonistic 13 unsympathetic
hostility: 4 feid, feud 6 animus, enmity, hatred, rancor 7 ill-will, warfare 9 animosity, antipathy 10 antagonism, bitterness, opposition, resistance 12 disaffection 14 unfriendliness, vindictiveness
hosting: 6 battle 9 encounter, gathering, incursion
hostler: 5 groom 6 ostler 9 innkeeper, stableman
hot: 5 acrid, calid, eager, fiery, spicy 6 ardent, biting, fervid, recent, strong, sultry, torrid, urgent 7 burning, excited, fervent, flaming, glowing, intense, lustful, peppery, pungent, thermal 8 sizzling, vehement 9 impatient, impetuous 10 passionate
hot cakes: 7 kneepad, pancake 11 griddle cake
hot-tempered: 7 iracund 8 choleric 9 irascible
hot-water bottle: pad, pig
hotbed: 4 nest
hotchpotch: 4 stew 6 jumble 8 hotchpot 9 tripotage(F.) 10 hodgepodge
hotel: inn 5 fonda, haven, house 6 hostel, imaret, tavern 7 gasthof, hostage 8 building, dwelling, gasthaus 11 caravansary 12 caravanserai, lodginghouse
auto: 5 motel
keeper: 4 host 7 padrone 8 boniface, hotelier
hothead: 5 raver 7 inciter 11 reactionary
hotheaded: 5 fiery, hasty 8 reckless 9 impetuous
hothouse: 6 bagnio 10 greenhouse
hotspur: 4 rash 6 madcap 7 violent 8 reckless 9 impetuous 10 headstrong
Hottentot: *dialect:* 4 Gona, Kora, Nama
garment: 6 kaross
instrument: 4 gora 5 gorah, goura
tribe: 4 Gona, Kora, Nama 6 Damara, Griqua 7 Sandawe, Sandawi
war club: 10 knobkerrie
hound: dog 4 hunt 5 harry 6 addict, talbot 7 harrier 9 persecute
tail: 5 stern
hounds: 4 pack 8 avantlay
hour: *canonical:* 4 none, sext
class: 6 period
lights out: 4 taps 6 curfew
hourly: 5 brief, horal 6 horary, recent 7 quickly 8 frequent 9 continual 10 frequently 11 continually
hourglass: 5 clock 7 shapely
house: cot, hut 4 casa(It.), cote, dorm, dump, firm, flat, flet, haus(G.), home, nest 5 abode, bahay, booth, cabin, cover, dacha, domus(L.), hovel, lodge, manor, shack, villa 6 biggin, billet, bottle, camara, casino, duplex, family, grange, maison(F.), palace, shanty 7 cabildo, chateau, cottage, enclose, mansion, quarter, shelter, thea-

ter 8 ancestry, audience, building, domicile, dwelling, tenement 9 dormitory, playhouse, residence 10 habitation
cluster: 4 dorp 6 hamlet 7 village
combining form: eco
commercial: 4 firm 5 store 8 emporium
eating: inn 4 cafe 6 tavern 9 chophouse 10 restaurant
English royal: 5 Tudor 6 Stuart 7 Windsor
guest: inn 5 hotel 11 caravansary
Newfoundland: 4 tilt
Oriental: 5 serai
pert. to: 5 domal
public: inn 5 hotel 6 hostel, tavern 7 hospice 8 hostelry
religious: 4 kirk 6 chapel, church, priory, temple 9 cathedral, synagogue 10 tabernacle
Russian: 4 isba 5 dacha
summer: 6 gazebo 9 belvedere
Upper: 6 Senate
house organ: 8 magazine 10 periodical
house servant: 4 maid 8 domestic
houseboat: 5 barge 6 wangan, wangun 7 wanigan 8 dahabeah, wannigan
housefly: 4 pest 5 musca 6 insect
household: 5 meiny 6 common, family, housal, menage 8 familiar 9 belonging
gods: 5 Lares 7 Penates
regulation: 6 thrift 7 economy 9 husbandry
housekeeper: 6 matron 7 janitor 8 janitrix 9 caretaker, janitress
housel: 9 Eucharist
houseleek: 8 sengreen
housemaid: 6 duster 7 servant
houseplant: ivy 5 aphis, calla 6 coleus 7 begonia, violets 11 asphidistra
housewarming: 6 infare
housewife: 8 hausfrau(G.) 9 economize
housework: 5 chore 8 drudgery
housing: box, pad 4 cowl 5 cover, niche 6 garage 7 shelter 8 covering 10 protection
Houston college: 4 Rice
hove: See **heave**
hovel: hut, sty 4 crib, hulk, hull, shed 5 cabin, hutch, lodge 6 cruive, hemmel, shanty 7 shelter 10 tabernacle
hoveler: 7 boatman, hobbler
hover: 4 flit 5 float, pause 7 flitter, flutter
howdy, howdie: 7 midwife 10 salutation
howe: 4 deep 5 empty, lowly 6 hollow, humble, hungry 10 depression
however: but, tho, yet 5 still 6 though 8 although 10 howsomever 12 nevertheless 15 notwithstanding
howf, howff: 4 loaf 5 haunt, lodge 6 resort, tavern 7 shelter, sojourn 8 frequent
howitzer: 6 cannon
howl: bay, cry, wow(Sc.) 4 bawl, gowl, gurl, hurl, wail, wawl, yawl, yell, yowl, yowt 5 whewl 6 lament, steven 7 ululate
howling: 4 wild 5 great 6 baying, dreary, savage 7 extreme, ululant 10 pronounced
howling monkey: 5 araba
howsoever: 8 although
howsomever: 8 although 12 nevertheless
hox: 4 hock 5 annoy, worry 6 pester 7 trample 9 hamstring
hoyden, hoiden: 4 romp, rude 6 blowze, tomboy 7 ill-bred 10 roistering
Hreidmar's son: 5 Otter, Regin 6 Fafnir, Reginn
huaca: 4 holy, idol, tomb 6 fetish, sacred, shrine, temple
hub: 4 core, nave 6 center, centre
Hub: 6 Boston
hubble: 5 crowd 6 hubbub, uproar
hubble-show: 6 rabble 9 commotion, confusion
hubbub: ado, din 4 stir 5 noise 6 clamor, hubble, racket, rumpus, tumult, uproar 7 bobbery 8 hubbuboo 9 commotion, confusion 11 disturbance
hubby: 7 husband
hubristic: 4 vain 7 insolent 8 arrogant 12 contemptuous
huck: hip 4 husk 6 haunch, higgle 7 bargain
huckle: hip 6 haunch
huckleberry: 9 blueberry
family: 9 ericaceae
Huckleberry Finn: *author:* 9 Mark Twain 13 Samuel Clemens
character: Jim
huckster: 5 adman, cheap 6 badger, broker, cadger, cagier(Fr.), hawker 7 haggler, peddler 8 regrater, retailer 9 middleman
hud: 4 hull, husk 5 shell
huddle: hug 4 hide, raff 5 crowd, hurry 6 bustle, fumble, jumble, mingle 7 conceal, embrace, scrunch 8 assemble, disorder 9 confusion 10 conference 14 conglomeration
Hudibras author: 6 Butler
hue: 4 balk, blee, form, tint 5 color, guise, shade, shout, tinge 6 aspect, clamor, depict, figure, outcry 7 clamour 8 shouting 10 appearance, complexion
hueless: 4 gray 9 colorless
huff: dod, pet 4 blow, brag, puff 5 bully, peeve, swell 6 hector 7 bluster, enlarge 8 boasting, offended
huffcap: 5 bully, heady 6 strong 9 blusterer 10 blustering, swaggering
huffy: 4 airy 5 fuffy, puffy, windy 7 pettish 8 arrogant 9 conceited 10 swaggering

hug: lug 4 clip, coll 5 carry, clasp, cling, creem, halse, press 6 cuddle, huddle, huggle 7 cherish, embrace, squeeze

huge: big 4 stor(Sc.), vast 5 enorm, giant, great, jumbo, large 6 heroic 7 banging, bumping, immense, massive, monster 8 colossal, enormous, gigantic, titanic 9 monstrous, pyramidal 10 gargantuan, prodigious, tremendous, unmeasured 11 elephantine

hugger-mugger: sly 6 jumble, muddle, secret 7 secrecy 8 confused, secretly 9 confusion 10 disorderly 11 clandestine 13 clandestinely

hui: 4 firm 5 guild 7 society 8 assembly 11 partnership

huisache: 4 wabe, wabi 5 aromo, shrub 6 cassie 7 popinac

huitain: 6 octave, stanza

huke: 4 cape 5 cloak, dress

hulk: 4 bulk, hull, loom, ship 5 hovel 10 disembowel

hulking: 5 bulky, hulky, husky 7 loutish, massive 8 unwieldy

hull: hud, hut, pod 4 bulk, hulk, husk, shed 5 hovel, shell, strip 8 covering 11 decorticate

grain: 4 bran

hullabaloo: ado, din 5 noise 6 clamor, hubbub, racket, tumult, uproar 7 clamour 9 confusion

hulver: 5 holly

hum: 4 blur, buzz, huss, huzz, sing, whiz 5 croon, drink, drone, feign, whizz 6 murmur 9 bombinate 11 bombilation, bombination

human: 6 humane, mortal 7 hominid 9 enigmatic

comb. form: 7 anthrop 8 anthropo

human being: man 6 mortal, person 7 Adamite 8 creature

humane: 4 kind 6 kindly, tender 8 merciful 9 forgiving 11 sympathetic 13 compassionate, tenderhearted

humanitarian: 14 philanthropist

humanity: 5 flesh 6 lenity 8 kindness 9 mortality

humanize: 6 refine 8 civilize

humble: low 4 mean, meek, mild, poor 5 abase, abash, lower, lowly, plain, stoop 6 debase, deject, demean, demiss, modest, reduce, simple 7 afflict, conquer, degrade, depress, mortify 8 contrite, deferent, disgrace, reverent 9 humiliate 10 submissive

humbug: gum, kid, pah 4 bosh, flam, guff, hoax, sham 5 cheat, faker, fraud, fudge, guile, trick 6 barney, blague, bunkum, cafard, cajole, gammon 7 deceive, flummer, mislead 8 flimflam, flummery, huckmuck, pretense 9 bamboozle, deception, imposture, stratagem 10 flumdiddle 11 flumadiddle

humdinger: 4 oner 6 corker

humdrum: 4 dull 7 irksome, prosaic 10 monotonous 11 commonplace, indifferent 13 uninteresting

humect: wet 7 moisten

humerus: 4 bone

humid: wet 4 damp, dank 5 moist 6 sultry 8 humorous, vaporous

humidity: 8 dampness

humiliate: 5 abase, abash, shame 6 debase, humble 7 degrade, mortify 8 belittle, disgrace

humility: 7 modesty 8 meekness, mildness 9 lowliness 10 diffidence

humming: big 5 brool 6 strong 7 buzzing, droning 8 frothing, seething 13 extraordinary

humming bird: ava 5 carib 6 hummer 8 froufrou 9 sheartail

genus of: 6 sappho

hummock: 4 hump 5 knoll

humor, humour: pet, tid, wit 4 baby, mood, whim 5 fancy, freak, vapor 6 levity, megrim, please, temper 7 caprice, gratify, indulge 8 drollery, moisture 11 inclination, temperament

humorist: wag 5 joker

humorous, humourous: 5 comic, droll, funny, humid, moist 6 watery 7 amusive, comical, jocular, playful 8 pleasant 9 facetious, laughable, whimsical 10 capricious

hump: 4 bile, hunk, lump 5 bouge, bulge, bunch, crump, hunch, mound, ridge 6 gibber, gibbus, hummie 7 hummock 12 protuberance

humpback: 9 hunchback 10 huckleback

Humperdinck girl: 6 Gretel

Hun: 6 vandal 9 barbarian

leader: 5 Etzel 6 Attila

Hunan river: 4 Yuan, Yuen

hunch: 4 balk, bend, hump, hunk, lump, push 5 fudge, shove 6 chilly, frosty, thrust 9 intuition 12 protuberance

Hunchback of Notre Dame: 9 Quasimodo

hundred: 7 cantred, cantref

combining form: 5 centi, hecto

division into: 12 centuriation

hundred-eyed being: 5 Argus

hundred percent: 6 entire 7 genuine, perfect 9 unalloyed 13 thoroughgoing 14 unquestionable

hundred years: 7 century 9 centenary

Hundred Years' War battle: 6 Cressy

hundredfold: 8 centuple 12 centuplicate

hundredweight: cwt 6 cental 7 quintal

hung: See **hang**

Hung Wu: 4 Ming

Hungary: *army:* 6 Honved 9 Honvedseg
cavalryman: 6 Hussar
city: 5 Erlau 8 Budapest(cap.), Debrecen, Szegedin 9 Budapesth, Debreczin, Kecskemet 16 Hodmezo-Vasarhely
coin: 4 gara 5 balas, pengo 6 filler, korona
commune: Mor
composer: 5 Lehar 6 Bartok
dance: 7 czardas
dog: 4 puli 6 kuvasz
gypsy: 7 tzigane
hero: 5 Arpad
lake: 7 Balaton 9 Blaten See 13 Neusiedler See
measure: ako 4 hold, joch, yoke 5 antal, itcze, marok, metze 7 huvelyk, merfold
mountain range: 10 Carpathian
people: 6 Magyar
poet: 5 Arany
river: 4 Raab 5 Drave, Maros 6 Danube, Poprad, Theiss 7 Vistula
Slav: 5 Croat 8 Croatian
weight: 7 vamfont 8 vammazsa
wine: 5 tokay
hunger: 4 long, want 5 belly 6 desire, famine, starve 7 craving 8 appetite, voracity 9 esurience
abnormal: 7 bulimia 10 polyphagia
hungry: 4 avid, howe, poor 6 barren, hollow, jejune 7 uneaten 8 esurient, hungered 10 avaricious
hunk: dad 4 daud, hump, lump 5 hunch, piece
hunks: 5 miser
hunt: dig 4 drag, seek 5 chase, chevy, chivy, delve, drive, hound, probe, quest, stalk, track, trail 6 chivvy, ferret, follow, forage, hunter, pursue, search, shikar 11 inquisition
god of: 5 Ninip 6 Apollo
hunted: 4 game, prey
hunter: 4 hunt 5 jager, yager 6 chaser, nimrod 7 stalker 8 chasseur, huntsman 9 sportsman
assistant: 5 gilly, jager
attendant: 5 gilly(Scot.) 6 gillie
mythological: 5 Orion
Golden Fleece: 5 Jason
patron saint: 6 Hubert
hunting: *cry:* yoi 4 toho 5 chevy, chivy, hoick 6 chivvy, hoicks, yoicks
expedition: 6 safari
game: 6 shikar, venery
horn note: 4 mort
pert. to: 7 venatic
hunting dog: 5 hound 6 basset, beagle, setter 7 pointer
huntress: 5 Diana 7 Artemis 8 Atalanta
huntsman: 5 jager 6 hunter 7 catcher, venerer 8 chasseur
changed into stag: 7 Actaeon
Hur's son: Uri
hurdies: 4 hips, rump 8 buttocks
hurdle: pen 4 clew, fold, leap 5 bound, cover, crate, frith, hedge 6 raddle 7 barrier, confine 8 obstacle, surmount 9 enclosure
hurdy-gurdy: 4 lira, rota
hurkle: 5 squat 6 crouch
hurl: 4 cast, dash, haul, howl, hurl, pelt, roar, send, toss, turn 5 fling, heave, pitch, sling, smite, throw, twist, whang 6 elance 9 overthrow
hurlement: 6 tumult 9 confusion
hurly: 6 uproar 7 turmoil 9 confusion
hurly-burly: 4 hurl 5 storm 6 tumult, uproar 8 confused 9 confusion 10 tumultuous
huron: 6 grison
hurrah: joy 5 cheer, huzza, shout 7 triumph 8 applause 13 encouragement
hurricane: 4 wind 5 storm 7 cyclone, prester, tempest 8 chubasco 9 hurricano, windstorm
center of: eye
hurried: See **hurry**
hurry: ado, hie, run 4 pass, pell, race, rese, rush, scud, stir, trot, urge, whir 5 drive, fight, haste, impel, slide, speed, worry 6 convey, harass, hasten, hustle, scurry, tumult 7 agitato(It.), dispute, quarrel, quicken 8 dispatch, expedite 9 agitation, commotion 10 expedition 11 disturbance, festination, precipitate
hurst: 4 hill, wood 5 copse, grove 7 hillock 8 sandbank
hurt: 4 harm, maim, pain 5 abuse, blame, grief, sorry, wound 6 damage, grieve, impair, injure, injury, mittle, scathe, strike 7 afflict, collide, hurting 8 distress, mischief, nuisance 9 detriment 12 disadvantage
hurtful: bad 4 evil 6 nocent 7 baneful, malefic, noisome, noxious 10 pernicious 11 deleterious, destructive, detrimental, prejudicial
hurtle: 4 dash 5 clash, fling, whirl 6 assail, jostle 7 collide 8 brandish
husband: eke, man, rom 4 bond, buck, chap, keep, mate, save 5 churl, hoard, marry, store 6 manage, spouse, tiller 7 consort, espouse, partner, plowman, steward 8 conserve 9 cultivate, economize 10 cultivator, husbandman
more than one: 9 polyandry
property right: 7 curtesy
husbandman: 4 bond, boor, carl 5 colon 6 farmer, tiller 7 acre-man, husband 8 agricole 10 cultivator

husbandry: 6 thrift 7 economy 8 managery 11 cultivation
god: 6 Faunus
hush: tut 4 calm, clam, hist, lull 5 allay, quiet, still 6 soothe 7 appease, repress, silence
husk: cod, hud 4 bark, bran, coat, hulk, hull, leam, rind 5 lemma, scale, shack, shell, shuck, straw, strip 6 colder 7 envelop, epicarp 8 covering, envelope 11 decorticate
husks: 5 chaff 6 bhoosa
Husky: dog 6 Eskimo
huss: 7 dogfish
hussar: 7 soldier 10 cavalryman
headdress: 5 busby
uniform jacket: 6 dolman
hussy: 4 jade 5 besom(Sc.), gipsy, gypsy, madam, quean 7 drossel 9 housewife 11 housekeeper
hustle: 4 push 5 crowd, hurry, shove 6 bustle, jostle, thrust 7 pushing 8 activity
hustler: 6 peeler 8 go-getter
hut: cot 4 bari, cote, crib, hulk, shed 5 benab, bohio, bothy, cabin, choza, house, hovel, humpy, hutch, kraal, lodge, scale, shack, toldo, wurly 6 bohawn, canaba, chalet, gunyah, gunyeh, rancho, shanty 7 balagan, bourock, camalig, cottage, huddock, wickiup 8 barabara, chantier
fisherman's: 4 skeo
hermit's: 4 cell
military: 6 Nissen
mining: coe
shepherd's: 5 bothy
hutch: ark, bin, box, car, hut, pen 4 coop 5 chest, hoard, hotch, hovel 6 coffer, humped, shanty 7 hunched, shelter 9 inclosure
huzza: 5 cheer, shout 6 hurrah, huzzah 9 roisterer
huzzar: 6 hussar
huzzy: See **hussy**
hyacinth: 7 greggle 8 bluebell, harebell
hyalite: 4 opal
hybrid: 5 blend 7 mongrel 9 composite
bovine: 7 cattalo
dog: 4 mutt 7 mongrel
horse and ass: 4 mule 5 hinny
horse and zebra: 7 zebrula, zebrule 8 zebrinny
zebra and donkey: 7 zebrass
hydra: 5 polyp 7 serpent
hydrant: 4 plug 6 faucet
hydraulic engine: ram
hydrazoate: 4 azid 5 azide
hydrocarbon: 6 butane, carane, nonane, retene 7 benzene, olefine, pentane
gaseous: 6 ethane, ethene
liver oil: 8 pristane
tree: 7 terpene
hydrocyanic acid: 7 prussic
hydrogen: gas 5 arsin 6 arsine
hydromel: 4 mead 5 aloja 10 melicratum
hydrometer: 9 aerometer
hydromica: 4 mica 9 muscovite
hydrophobia: 5 lyssa 6 rabies
hydrophyte: See **aquatic plant**
hygienic: 8 sanitary
hymenopteron: ant, bee 4 wasp 6 sawfly 7 gallfly 9 ichneumon
hymn: ode 4 sing, song 5 psalm 6 himene, himine, hirmos, hirmus 7 introit 8 canticle 11 recessional 12 processional
following psalm: 9 sticheron
funeral: 5 dirge
praising: 4 pean 5 paean
ritual: 8 encomium
sung in unison: 6 choral 7 chorale 9 plainsong
tune: 6 choral 7 chorale
victory: 9 epinicion, epinikion
hyoscyamus: 8 narcotic
hyperbole: 12 exaggeration 13 overstatement
Hyperborean sage: 6 Abaris
hypercritical: 7 carping 8 captious 12 overcritical, supercilious
Hyperion: *daughter:* Eos 6 Selene
son: 6 Helios
hyphen: 4 band, dash
hypnotic: 6 opiate 8 narcotic 9 soporific 12 somnifacient
hypnotic condition: 4 coma 6 trance 8 lethargy
hypnotism: 5 sleep 8 hypnosis 9 mesmerism
hypnotist: 6 Mesmer 9 mesmerist
hypnotize: 5 charm 9 mesmerize
hypnum: 4 moss
hypochondria: hyp 6 megrim
hypocrisy: 4 cant 10 simulation
hypocrite: 6 Levite 7 Tartufe
hypocritical: 4 nice 5 exact, false 7 bigoted, canting, carping 8 captious, specious 9 deceptive, insincere 11 dissembling, pharisaical 13 sanctimonious
hypostatic: 5 basic 9 elemental
hypotenuse: 5 slant
hypothesis: ism 6 system, theory 9 postulate 10 assumption 11 supposition
hypothetical being: ens 6 entity
hypocrisy: 6 deceit
hyrax: 8 procavia
Hyrtacus' son: 5 Nisus
hyssop: 4 mint 11 aspergillum
hysteria: 6 nerves
hysterical: 9 emotional 12 uncontrolled

I

I, Claudius author: 6 Graves
I do not wish to contend: 14 nolo contendere(L.)
I have found it: 6 eureka
I understand: 5 roger
Iago's wife: 6 Emelia
Iasion's father: 4 Zeus
Iberian: 4 Pict
ibex: tur, zac
ibis: 5 guara, stork 9 gourdhead
Ibsen: *character:* Ase 4 Gynt, Nora
native country: 6 Norway
play: 11 Rosmersholm
Icarian: 4 rash 6 daring 9 foolhardy
Icarius' daughter: 7 Erigone 8 Penelope
Icarus' father: 8 Daedalus
ICBM: 5 Atlas 6 weapon 7 missile
ice: 4 cool, geal, grue(Sc.), rime 5 chill, frost, glace(F.) 6 freeze 7 congeal, diamond, hauteur 10 confection 11 refrigerant, refrigerate
crystals: 4 snow 5 frost
floating: 4 berg, floe
fragment: 5 brash
glacier: 4 neve 5 serac
mass: 4 berg, floe
patch: 4 rone(Sc.)
pendant: 6 icicle
sea: 6 sludge
sheet: 4 floe
slushy: 4 sish
ice cream dish: 4 soda 6 frappe, sundae 7 parfait
ice river: 7 glacier
icebox: 6 cooler 12 refrigerator
icecap: 7 calotte
Iceland: *assembly:* 7 Althing
bishopric: 5 Holar 8 Skalholt
capital: 9 Reikjavik, Reykjavik
coin: 5 aurar, eyrir, krona
epic: 4 Edda
giant: 4 Atli
hero: 4 Bele
language: 5 Norse
legislature: 7 Althing
measure: fet 4 alin, lina 5 almud, turma 6 almenn, almude, ferfet, pottur 7 fathmur, feralin, fermila, oltunna, sjomila 9 korntunna 10 ferfathmur, kornskeppa, thumlungur 11 angjateigur 12 tundagslatta 13 ferthumlungur
mountain: 5 Jokul 10 Orafajokul
musician or poet: 5 scald, skald
volcano: 4 Laki 5 Hekla
weight: 4 pund 5 pound 11 tunna smjors
ichneumon: 8 mongoose 11 hymenoptera(pl.) 12 hymenopteron
ichnography: map
ichnolite: 6 fossil 9 footprint
ichthyosis: 9 sauriosis
icicle: 7 shoggle
limestone: 10 stalactite, stalagmite
icing: 7 topping 8 frosting
icon, ikon: 5 image 6 eidola(pl.), idolon, symbol 7 eidolon, picture 8 portrait 12 illustration
iconolater: 9 worshiper
iconoscope: 6 finder
icterine: 9 yellowish
icterus: 8 jaundice
ictus: fit 4 blow 6 attack, stress, stroke
icy: 4 cold 5 gelid 6 arctic, frigid, frosty 8 chilling
Idaho: *capital:* 5 Boise
county: Ada 5 Butte, Katah, Lewis
motto: 12 esto perpetua
nickname: 8 Gem State
river: 7 Kutenai, Kutenay 8 Kootenai, Kootenay
town: 5 Boise, Nampa 7 Preston 9 Pocatello
Idas' consort: 8 Marpessa
ide: orf
idea: 4 idee(F.) 5 fancy, ideal, image 6 design, figure, notion 7 conceit, concept, fantasy, inkling, opinion, project, thought 8 gimcrack 9 archetype 10 appearance, cogitation, conception, impression, reflection
comb. form: 4 ideo
impracticable: 7 chimera 8 chimaera
prompting action: 6 motive

ideal: 5 dream, model 6 mental 7 paragon, perfect, Utopian 8 abstract, fanciful, standard 9 imaginary, visionary 10 aspiration, conceptual, consummate 12 intellectual

ideal state: 4 Eden 6 Oceana, Utopia

ideate: 5 fancy 7 imagine 8 conceive 9 prefigure 11 preconceive

identic: 4 same 5 equal

identical: one 4 same, self, very 5 alike, equal, samen(Sc.) 8 selfsame 10 equivalent, tantamount

identify: 4 mark, name 5 brand, prove 7 earmark 9 designate, establish

identity: 4 name 5 unity 7 oneness 8 sameness 9 exactness 11 homogeneity
false: 5 alias

ideologist: 7 dreamer 8 theorist 9 visionary

idiasm: 11 peculiarity 12 idiosyncrasy

idiocy: 7 anoesia, fatuity

idiograph: 9 signature, trademark

idiom: 6 phrase 11 peculiarity

idiosyncrasy: way 6 idiasm, manner 11 peculiarity 12 eccentricity

idiot: oaf 4 dolt, fool 5 booby, dunce 6 cretin, hobbil, nidget 7 dullard, omadawn 8 imbecile, omadhuan 9 blockhead, simpleton 10 changeling

idiotic: 4 daft, zany 5 barmy, inane 7 asinine, fatuous, foolish 9 senseless

idle: 4 lazy, loaf, sorn(Sc.), vain 5 dally, empty, shool 6 asleep, cooter, dawdle, futile, loiter, otiant, otiose, unused, vacant 7 aimless, loafing, sluther, useless 8 baseless, faineant, inactive, indolent, slothful, trifling 9 desultory, unfounded, worthless 10 groundless, unemployed, unoccupied 11 ineffectual

idle talk: 5 rumor 6 gossip

idleness: 5 folly 6 vanity 7 inertia 8 flanerie, inaction, laziness 9 silliness 10 inactivity 15 lightheadedness

idler: bum 4 hake 5 drone 6 bodaud, bumble, loafer, stocah 7 faitour 8 faineant, loiterer

Idmon: *father:* 6 Apollo
killer: 4 boar
mother: 6 Cyrene
ship: 4 Argo

idol: god 4 Baal, hero 5 afgod, image, satyr 6 fetish 7 phantom 8 impostor 9 pretender
matinee: 4 star

idolater: 5 pagan 6 adorer 7 Baalite 9 worshiper

idolatrous: 5 pagan

idolize: 5 adore 6 admire, revere 7 worship 8 venerate

idolon: 5 image 6 eidola(pl.) 7 eidolon, phantom 10 apparition

idolum: 7 fallacy 8 phantasm

idoneous: apt, fit 8 suitable 11 appropriate

idyl, idyll: 4 poem 7 eclogue

idyllic: 7 bucolic 8 pastoral

if: si(F., It., L.) 8 granting, provided 9 supposing

i'faith: 5 truly 6 indeed

iffy: 8 doubtful

igloo: hut 4 home

igneous rock: 4 trap 6 basalt, gabbro 7 granite, periodot

ignite: hot 4 fire 5 fiery, light 6 ardent, kindle

ignition cap: 4 fuse, fuze

ignoble: low 4 base, mean, vile 6 adject, sordid 8 shameful 11 disgraceful 12 dishonorable

ignominious: 4 base 6 odious 8 infamous, shameful 9 degrading 10 despicable, mortifying 11 disgraceful, humiliating 12 contemptible, dishonorable

ignoramus: 4 dolt 5 dunce 6 nitwit

ignorance: 6 agnosy

ignorant: 4 dark 5 green, young 6 stupid 7 artless, unaware, uncouth 8 nescient, untaught 9 unlearned, unskilled, untutored 10 illiterate, unlettered 11 unconscious

ignore: cut 4 omit, snub 5 blink, elide 6 slight 7 neglect 8 overlook 9 disregard, eliminate

Igorot, Igorrote: 6 Bontok 7 Nabaloi 8 Kankanai
chief: Apo

iguana: 6 lizard 7 tuatara

Iguvine: 7 Umbrian 8 Eugubine

ihi: 4 fish 7 skipper 8 halfbeak 9 stichbird

Ihlat: 8 Sunnites

ijolite: 7 apatite, calcite 8 titanite

ikary: 6 caviar

ikbal: 7 arrival 8 prestige 10 prosperity

ikey: 5 proud

ikon: 5 image 6 symbol 7 picture 8 portrait 12 illustration

ikona: 9 greenhorn, simpleton

ikra: 6 caviar

ilex: 5 holly

Iliad: 4 epic, poem
character: 4 Ajax 5 Priam 6 Hector 8 Achilles 9 Agamemnon, Cassandra

ilium: 4 bone

Ilium, Ilion: 4 Troy

ilk: 4 each, kind, same, sort 5 breed, class, every 6 family

ill: bad 4 evil, harm, poor, sick 5 amiss, badly, wrong 6 ailing, faulty, wicked 7 adverse, ailment, baneful, noxious, trouble, unlucky 8 improper 9 adversity, defective 10 indisposed, iniquitous, misfortune 11 unfortunate
prefix: mal

ill at ease: 7 awkward

ill-boding: 4 dire 12 inauspicious
ill-bred: 6 hoiden, hoyden 7 plebian, uncivil 8 clownish, impolite, malapert 9 bourgeois 11 impertinent
ill-favored: 4 ugly 9 offensive 10 unpleasant 12 disagreeable
ill-humor: tid 5 anger 7 dudgeon
ill-humored: 5 cross 6 cranky, morose 7 fretful, peevish
ill-natured: 4 dour 5 nasty, surly 6 crabby 7 fretful
ill-smelling: 5 fetid 10 malodorous
ill-tempered: 5 cross, moody 6 crusty 7 bilious
ill-treat: 5 abuse 8 maltreat
ill will: 5 spite 6 animus, malice, mauger 9 hostility
showing: 7 hostile 8 choleric 9 bellicose, irascible, litigious, wrangling 10 pugnacious 11 belligerent, contentious, quarrelsome 12 disputatious
ill-wisher: foe 5 enemy
illation: 9 deduction 11 inferential
illegal: 4 foul 7 bootleg, illicit 8 unlawful 10 contraband
illegitimate: 7 bastard, bootleg, unusual 8 abnormal, improper, spurious, unlawful, wrongful 9 illogical
illiberal: 6 stingy 7 bigoted 8 churlish 9 hidebound 13 ungentlemanly
illicit: 7 bootleg, illegal 8 improper, unlawful 10 contraband
illimitable: 4 vast 8 infinite 9 boundless 11 measureless 12 immeasurable
Illinois: *county:* Lee 4 Cook, Ogle, Polk 6 Hardin
river: 5 Spoon
town: 4 Pana 5 Alton, Elgin 6 Aurora, Breese, Joliet, Moline 7 Decatur, Wheaten 8 Streator 10 Springfield(c.)
illiterate: 6 unread 8 ignorant, untaught 9 barbarous, unlearned, untutored 10 unlettered
illness: 5 colic 6 malady, morbus 7 ailment, cachexy, disease 8 cachexia, disorder, sickness 9 complaint, distemper 10 affliction, wickedness 13 indisposition
feign: 8 malinger
mental: See **mental disorder**
illogical: 7 invalid 12 inconsequent
illude: 4 bilk, mock 5 cheat, elude, evade 6 delude, deride 7 deceive
illume: See **illuminate**
illuminant: gas 9 petroleum
illuminate: 4 fire 5 adorn, flare, light 6 illume, kindle 7 clarify, emblaze, lighten 8 brighten, illumine 9 enlighten, irradiate 10 illustrate
illumination: *device:* 4 lamp 5 torch 7 lantern 10 flashlight
in eclipse: 8 penumbra
measure: 4 phot
illumine: See **illuminate**
illusion: 5 fancy 6 mirage 7 chimera, fallacy, mockery, phantom 8 delusion 9 deception 10 appearance
illusive: 4 flam 5 false 6 unreal 7 fatuous 8 illusory 9 deceitful, deceptive, fantasmal 10 fallacious, phantasmal 16 phantasmagorical
illusory: See **illusive**
illustrate: 5 adorn 7 picture 9 elucidate, exemplify, represent 10 illuminate
illustration: 4 icon, ikon 7 example, exempla(pl.) 8 exemplum, vignette 13 demonstration 15 exemplification
illustrator: 6 artist
illustrious: 5 famed, grand, noble, noted 6 bright, candid, heroic 7 eminent, exalted 8 glorious, renowned 9 honorable 10 celebrated 11 conspicuous 13 distinguished
ilvaite: 6 yenite
image: god 4 copy, form, icon, idol, ikon 5 eikon, image 6 effigy, eidola(pl.), emblem, figure, idolon, statue, symbol 7 eidolon, phantom, picture, portray 8 likeness 9 semblance, simulacre 10 conception, reflection, similitude, simulacrum
good luck: 6 alraun
maker: 10 iconoplast
mental: 4 idea 6 recept 7 concept 8 phantasm 10 conception
pert. to: 6 iconic 10 simulacral
rainbowlike: 7 spectra(pl.) 8 spectrum
religious: 4 icon
stone: 5 herma 6 hermae(pl.)
televised: 5 video
wooden: 4 tiki 6 xoanon
worship: 5 arati 8 idolatry
image-breaker: 10 iconoclast
image-like: 10 simulacral
image-worshiper: 8 idolator 9 conolater
imaginary: 5 ideal 6 unreal 7 fancied, feigned 8 mythical, notional 9 fantastic, visionary 10 artificial, chimerical, fictitious
imagination: 5 fancy 7 fantasy
imaginative: 6 dreamy, poetic 8 fanciful 9 fantastic
imagine: 4 ween 5 dream, fancy, feign, think 6 vision 7 picture, suppose, surmise 8 conceive, envision 9 apprehend 10 comprehend, conjecture
imago: bee
imam: 5 calif 6 caliph
last: 5 Mahdi

imaret: 7 hospice 11 caravansary, caravaserai
imbar: 5 guard 7 fortify
imbecile: 4 dolt, dote 5 anile, daffy, idiot, moron 6 cranky, dotard, dotish 7 fatuous 9 driveling 10 changeling, half-witted
imbed: fix 5 embed, inset 6 cement
imbibe: sip 4 soak 5 drink, imbue, steep 6 absorb 7 swallow 8 saturate 10 assimilate
imbosom: 7 cherish, embrace, shelter
imbricate: 5 tiled 6 scaled
imbroglio: 12 disagreement 16 misunderstanding
imbrue: wet 4 soak 5 stain, steep 6 defile, drench 7 moisten 8 saturate
imbue: dye 4 soak 5 steep, tinge 6 imbibe, infuse, leaven 7 animate, ingrain, inspire, instill, pervade 8 permeate, saturate, tincture 9 inoculate 10 impregnate
imburse: pay 10 recompense
imidogen compound: 4 imid, imin 5 imide, imine
imitant: 9 imitation 11 counterfeit
imitate: ape 4 copy, echo, mime, mock 5 mimic 6 follow, repeat 7 copycat, emulate 8 resemble, simulate 9 dissemble 11 counterfeit
imitation: 4 copy, echo, fake, sham 5 dummy, paste 6 parody 7 imitant 9 emulation, facsimile, imitative, schlenter
derisive: 7 mimicry, mockery
fantastic: 8 travesty
imitation gem: 5 glass, paste
imitation pearl: 6 olivet
imitator: 4 mima 5 mimae(pl.)
immaculate: 4 pure 5 clean 6 candid, chaste 7 correct, perfect 8 innocent, spotless, unsoiled 9 faultless, undefiled, unspotted, unstained, unsullied
immalleable: 10 unyielding
immane: 4 huge, vast 5 great 6 fierce 7 immense, inhuman 9 atrocious, monstrous
immanent: 8 inherent 9 intrinsic 10 indwelling
immaterial: 6 slight 8 trifling 9 asomatous, spiritual 10 impalpable, intangible 13 insignificant, unsubstantial
immatriculate: 6 enroll 11 matriculate
immature: 5 crude, green, young 6 callow, unripe 7 girlish, puerile, untried 8 youthful 9 premature 10 incomplete, unfinished 11 undeveloped
immaturity: 5 youth 6 nonage 7 infancy 10 callowness, unripeness
immeasurable: 7 immense 8 infinite 9 boundless, unlimited 10 indefinite 11 illimitable, measureless 12 immensurable
immediate: 4 next 6 direct 7 instant 8 imminent 9 proximate 10 contiguous, succeeding
immediately: now 4 anon 6 presto 8 directly 9 extempore, forthwith, presently
immemorial: 7 ageless, ancient 8 dateless 11 prehistoric, traditional
immense: 4 huge 5 grand, great, large 7 titanic 8 enormous, gigantic, infinite 9 extensive, monstrous 10 prodigious, unmeasured 12 immeasurable
immensurable: See **immeasurable**
immerge: See **immerse**
immerse: dip 4 bury, duck 5 bathe, douse, dowse, souse 6 absorb, drench, plunge 7 engross, ensteep, immerge
immigrant: 8 comeling
Israel: 6 halutz 7 chalutz
imminent: 9 impending
immitigable: 10 implacable
immobile: set 4 firm 5 fixed, inert 6 frozen, stable 8 moveless 9 immovable 10 motionless, stationary
immoderate: 4 free 5 undue 7 extreme 9 boundless, excessive, voracious 10 exorbitant, inordinate 11 intemperate 12 unreasonable
immodest: 4 bold 6 brazen, coarse 7 forward, obscene 8 indecent, unchaste 9 shameless 10 indecorous
immolation: 9 sacrifice
immoral: bad 4 evil 5 loose, wrong 7 corrupt, vicious 8 culpable, depraved, indecent 9 dissolute 10 licentious 11 unwholesome
immortal: 6 divine 7 endless, eternal, godlike 8 enduring 9 ceaseless, deathless 11 amaranthine, everlasting 12 imperishable 13 incorruptible
immortality: 8 athanasy 9 athanasia 13 deathlessness 15 everlastingness
Hindu: 6 amrita
immovable: pat, set 4 fast, firm 5 fixed, rigid 7 adamant 8 constant, immobile, obdurate 9 steadfast 10 adamantine, stationary
immunity: 7 freedom 9 exemption 11 unrestraint
immunize: 7 vastate 9 inoculate 10 haffkinize
immunizer: 5 serum 7 vaccine
immure: 4 wall 7 confine 8 cloister, imprison 11 incarcerate
immutable: 4 firm 7 eternal 10 invariable, unchanging 11 unalterable 13 unadulterated
Imogen's mother: 9 Cymbeline
imp: bud, elf 4 brat, cion, slip 5 child, demon, devil, graft, rogue, scamp, scion 6 sprite, urchin 7 gremlin, implant, progeny 8 dev-

ilkin, folletto, folletti(pl.) 9 hobgoblin, offspring 13 mischiefmaker 15 flibbertigibbet
impact: 4 pack, slam 5 brunt, feeze, shock, wedge, whang 6 stroke 7 impulse
impair: mar 4 blot, harm, hurt, wear 5 break, spoil, waste 6 damage, debase, injure, lessen, reduce, sicken, weaken 7 blemish, impeach, vitiate 8 decrease, enfeeble
impaired: 9 afflicted
impala: 7 rooibok 8 rooyebok
impale: 4 edge, spit 5 spear, spike 6 border, pierce 7 confine 8 encircle, surround
impalpable: 7 elusive 10 immaterial, intangible
impar: odd 7 unequal
impark: 7 enclose
impart: 4 give, lend, tell 5 share, yield 6 bestow, confer, convey, direct, impute, reveal 7 divulge, inspire, instill 8 disclose, discover 10 distribute 11 communicate
impartial: 4 even, fair, just 6 candid 8 unbiased 9 colorless, equitable 12 irrespective 13 disinterested, dispassionate
imparting motion: 7 kinetic
impassable: 5 solid 10 impervious
impasse: 8 cul-de-sac(F.) 9 stalemate
impassible: 9 impassive, unfeeling 11 unendurable
impassioned: 6 fervid 7 fervent 8 eloquent, feverish
impassive: 4 calm 5 stoic 6 serene, stolid 7 passive 9 apathetic 10 impassible 13 imperturbable
impatient: hot 5 eager, hasty, testy 7 fidgety, fretful, peevish 8 choleric, petulant, restless 9 irascible, irritable
impavid: 8 fearless
impeach: 4 call, harm 6 accuse, charge, hinder, impair, impede, indict 7 appeach, arraign, censure, prevent 9 challenge, discredit, disparage
impeachment: 4 harm 6 damage, injury 8 dishonor, reproach 9 challenge, hindrance 10 accusation, impediment 11 obstruction
impeccable: 9 faultless
impecunious: 4 poor 9 penniless
impede: gum, let 4 clog 5 block, check, choke, delay, estop 6 fetter, forbid, hamper, harass, hinder, retard, stymie 7 impeach, prevent 8 encumber, handicap, obstruct, preclude 9 embarrass
legally: bar 5 debar, estop
impediment: bar, bur, rub 4 clog, snag 5 hitch 6 defect, malady, remora 7 embargo 8 obstacle 9 detriment, hindrance 10 difficulty 11 encumbrance, impeachment, obstruction 13 embarrassment
impedimenta: 7 baggage
impel: pat 6 blow, goad, move, send, spur, urge 5 drive, feeze, force, hurry 6 compel, excite, incite, induce 7 actuate 8 motivate 9 constrain, encourage, influence, instigate, stimulate
impelling force: 7 impetus 8 momentum
impend: 4 hang, loom 6 menace 8 approach
impending: 8 imminent, menacing 9 hindering 11 threatening
impenetrable: 4 hard 5 dense 8 airtight, hardened 10 impervious 11 inscrutable 12 unfathomable
impenitent: 8 hardened, obdurate 11 unrepentant
imperative: 8 pressing, verb form 9 imperious, mandatory 10 commanding, compulsory, peremptory
imperator: 6 leader 7 emporer, general
imperceptible: 10 insensible, intangible 13 inappreciable, indiscernible 17 indistinguishable
imperfect: 4 cull, poor 5 rough 6 faulty, second 9 defective 10 inadequate, incomplete, unfinished
prefix: mal 5 atelo
imperfection: 4 flaw, vice 5 fault 6 defect, foible 7 blemish, default, failing, frailty 8 weakness 10 deficiency 11 shortcoming
imperfectly: 4 half 5 badly
imperial: 5 regal, royal 6 kingly 8 majestic
cap: 5 crown
domain: 6 empery, empire 8 emperies(pl.)
officer: 8 palatine
imperial woodpecker: 9 ivorybill
imperil: 4 risk 6 expone, hazard 8 endanger 10 jeopardize
imperious: 6 lordly 7 haughty 8 arrogant, despotic, dominant, pressing 10 commanding, imperative, tyrannical 11 dictatorial, domineering, magisterial, overbearing 13 authoritative
imperish: 6 impair, injure
imperishable: 7 eternal, undying 8 enduring, immortal 9 continual, deathless 11 everlasting 14 indestructible
impermanent: 8 fleeting 9 ephemeral, temporary, tentative, transient 10 evanescent
impersonal: 4 cold 7 general
impersonate: act, ape 4 pose 6 typify 9 exemplify, personify
impersonator: 5 actor 7 actress
impertinence: 4 sass 8 audacity 9 insolence 10 confidence, incivility 11 impropriety, irrelevance
impertinent: 4 rude 5 sassy, saucy 7 ill-bred 8 arrogant, impudent 9 audacious, officious 10 inapposite 12 inconsequent 13 disrespectful

imperturbability: 8 ataraxia

imperturbable: 4 cool 6 placid, serene 8 tranquil 9 impassive 10 phlegmatic

impervious: 5 tight 8 hardened 10 impassable 12 impenetrable

impetition: 6 charge 10 accusation

impetrate: 7 beseech, entreat, procure

impetuosity: 5 haste 6 fougue

impetuous: hot 4 ramp, rash 5 eager, fiery, hasty, heady, sharp 6 abrupt, ardent, fervid, fierce, flashy, sudden 7 furious, hotspur, violent 8 forcible, headlong, vehement 9 impulsive 10 hotspurred 11 precipitate

impetus: 4 bent, birr, fard 5 drift, faird, force 6 swinge 7 impulse 8 momentum, stimulus 9 incentive

imphee: 5 plant 7 sorghum

impi: 8 soldiers, warriors

impiety: 9 blasphemy 11 irreverence, ungodliness

impignorate: 6 pawned 7 pledged

impinge: 6 strike 8 encroach

impious: 6 unholy 7 godless, profane, ungodly 9 atheistic, nefandous, undutiful 10 irreverent 11 irreligious

impish: 6 elfish 7 warlock 11 mischievous

implacable: 6 deadly 9 ferocious 11 immitigable 12 unappeasable 14 irreconcilable

implant: sow 4 root 5 infix, inset 6 enrace, enroot, infuse 7 enforce, engraft, impress, inspire, instill 9 inculcate, inoculate, insinuate, introduce

implement (see also **tool**): 4 gear 7 enforce, fulfill, utensil 8 complete, material 9 apparatus, appliance 10 accomplish, instrument

ancient: 4 celt 6 amgarn, eolith 9 paleolith

baker's: 4 peel

barbed: 7 harpoon

cleaning: mop 4 swab 5 broom, brush 6 vacuum 7 sweeper

cutting: 5 knife, mower, razor 6 reaper, scythe, shears 8 scissors 9 jackknife 11 pocketknife

enlarging: 6 reamer 7 dilator

farm: 4 disc, disk, plow, rake 6 seeder, tiller 7 tractor

furcate: 4 fork

garden: hoe 4 rake 5 mower 6 sickle, weeder

grasping: 5 tongs 6 pliers 8 tweezers

hand printing: 6 brayer, roller

hide cleaning: 6 slater

kind of: 5 dolly 6 fraise, mortar, pestle, rabble 7 mattock, sadiron, scraper

kitchen: pot, pan 5 corer 6 kettle 7 skillet, spatula

lifting: pry 5 lever, tongs

logging: 4 tode 5 peavy, peevy 6 peavey, peevey

nap-raising: 5 tease 6 teasel, teasle, teazel, teazle

pounding: 4 maul 6 hammer, pestle

printer's: 5 biron, press

reaping: 5 mower 6 reaper, scythe, shears, sickle

shovel-like: 5 scoop, spoon 6 trowel

surgical: 7 scalpel 9 tenaculum

threshing: 5 flail

war: 6 armory, onager, petard

implete: 6 filled 7 replete

implicate: 7 concern, embroil, entwine, involve 10 interweave

implicit: 5 tacit 8 absolute, complete, explicit 12 constructive

implied: 5 tacit 6 hinted 11 inferential

implore: ask, beg 4 coax, pray 5 crave, plead 6 appeal 7 beseech, entreat, solicit 8 petition 10 supplicate

imply: 4 hint 5 infer 6 infold 7 connote, involve, premise, signify 8 comprise, intimate 9 insinuate, predicate 10 comprehend

impolite: 4 rude 5 bluff, crude, rough 7 ill-bred, uncivil 10 indecorous, ungracious, unmannerly, unpolished 12 discourteous 13 disrespectful

impolitic: 6 unwise 10 indiscreet 11 inexpedient, injudicious 12 undiplomatic

imporous: 5 close, dense, solid

import: 5 sense, value 6 convey, denote 7 betoken, meaning, signify 8 indicate 9 substance

tax: 4 duty 6 tariff

importance: 4 bore 6 moment, weight 7 account, gravity 8 prestige 9 dimension 11 consequence 13 consideration

to be of: 6 matter

important: 4 dear, high 5 grave, great 6 urgent 7 pompous, serious 8 eventful, material 9 momentous, ponderous 10 chargeable 11 considerate, fundamental, influential, significant 12 considerable 13 consequential

important person: VIP 6 bigwig 7 magnate

importunate: 6 urgent 7 teasing 8 exigeant, pressing 9 exigeante 10 burdensome 11 inopportune, troublesome

importune: beg, dun, nag, ply, woo 4 urge 5 plead 6 appeal 7 entreat, solicit 10 supplicate

importunity: 8 business, entreaty

impose: fob 4 dupe, fool, levy, sorn 6 burden, charge, delude, entail 7 blaflum, command, dictate, inflict, obtrude

impose upon: fob 4 dupe, palm

imposing: big 5 burly, proud 6 august 7 stately 9 grandiose, pyramidal 10 com-

manding, impressive, obligatory 11 outstanding
imposition: tax 4 duty, levy 5 fraud, gouge, trick 6 burden, chouse 7 penalty 8 artifice 9 deception, imposture
impossible: 13 impracticable
impost: tax 4 duty, levy, task, toll 6 annale, avania, custom, excise, surtax, tariff, weight 7 tribute 8 chaptrel
India: 5 abwab
salt: 7 gabelle
impostor: fob 4 gull, idol, sham 5 cheat, fraud, gouge, quack 6 bunyip 7 empiric, faitour 8 deceiver 9 charlatan, pretender 10 mountebank
imposture: gag 4 sham 5 cheat, fraud, trick 6 deceit, humbug 8 artifice, delusion 9 deception, falsehood 10 imposition
impotence: 7 acratia 8 weakness 10 feebleness
impotent: 6 barren, unable 7 sterile 9 powerless
impound: 5 seize, store 6 freeze 7 collect 11 appropriate
impouring: 6 influx
impoverish: 4 ruin 6 beggar, weaken 7 deplete, exhaust
impoverished: 4 poor 8 bankrupt
impracticable: 10 impossible
impractical: 9 visionary
imprecate: 4 pray 5 curse 6 invoke 8 execrate 10 supplicate
imprecation: ban 4 oath 5 curse 8 anathema 9 blasphemy 10 execration 11 deprecation, malediction
impregnability: 9 fortitude
impregnable: 4 hard 12 inexpugnable
impregnate: 4 soak 6 charge, infuse, leaven 8 fructify, permeate, saturate 9 fecundate, fertilize
impresa: 5 maxim, motto 6 device, emblem 7 proverb
impresario: 7 manager 9 conductor, projector 12 entrepreneur
impress: fix 4 bite, levy, mark, seal, tool 5 affix, brand, delve, infix, press, print, stamp 6 enlist 7 engrave, implant, impress, imprint 9 character, inculcate, influence 14 characteristic
impressed: 4 awed 8 affected
impression: 4 dent, dint, idea, mark 5 fancy, print, stamp 6 effect, signet 7 opinion 8 reaction 10 conception
printing: 6 macule
impressionable: 7 plastic 9 sensitive 10 responsive 11 susceptible
impressionist painter: 5 Manet, Monet 6 Renoir 8 Pissarro
impressive: 5 grand 6 solemn 8 forcible, imposing 9 arresting, grandiose
imprevu: 10 unforeseen
imprimatur: 7 license 8 approval, sanction
imprint: fix 4 dint, mark 5 press, stamp 7 engrave, impress 12 characterize
imprison: 4 cage, jail, seal 5 grate, limit 6 arrest, commit, detain, immure 7 confine, enclose 8 restrain 9 carcerate 11 incarcerate
imprisonment: 6 arrest, duress 7 durance 8 coercion 9 captivity, restraint 11 confinement 13 incarceration
improbable: 5 fishy 8 unlikely
impromptu: 7 offhand 9 extempore 14 extemporaneous
improper: ill 4 evil 5 amiss, undue, unfit, wrong 6 unjust 7 illegal, illicit 8 indecent, shameful, unseemly 9 incorrect 10 inaccurate, indecorous, indelicate, unbecoming 12 illegitimate
improperly: 5 amiss
impropriety: 5 shame 8 solecism 12 impertinence
improve: 4 grow, help, mend 5 amend, edify, emend, moise 6 better, enrich 7 advance, augment, benefit, correct, enhance, perfect, promote, rectify, retouch 9 cultivate, intensify, meliorate 10 ameliorate
improvident: 8 prodigal, wasteful 9 negligent 10 thriftless 11 thoughtless
improvise: 5 ad-lib 6 devise, invent 7 compose 8 contrive 11 extemporize
music: 4 vamp
imprudent: 4 rash 6 unwary, unwise 7 foolish 8 reckless 10 incautious, indiscreet 11 injudicious 12 shortsighted
impudence: lip 4 gall 5 brass, cheek, folly 8 audacity 9 arrogance, assurance, hardihood, insolence 10 confidence, effrontery 11 presumption 13 shamelessness
impudent: 4 bold, pert, rude 5 brash, sassy, saucy 6 brazen 7 forward 8 insolent 9 barefaced, officious 11 impertinent 13 disrespectful
impugn: 4 deny 5 fight 6 assail, resist 7 gainsay 9 insinuate 10 contradict
impulse: 4 urge 5 drift, force 6 impact, motive 7 impetus 8 instinct 9 incentive 11 instigation
blind: ate
characterized by: 7 sensory
divine: 8 afflatus
traveling: 10 wanderlust
impulsive: 5 quick 6 fitful 8 headlong 9 impellent, impetuous
impure: 4 foul, hory, lewd, vile 5 dirty, gross, mixed 6 coarse, filthy, unholy 7 bastard, defiled, obscene, unclean, vicious 8 indecent, inferior, unchaste 10 unhal-

lowed 11 adulterated, incongruous, unwholesome
impurity: 6 defect, fedity 8 solution 9 pollution 10 corruption
impute: 4 give 5 count 6 charge, credit, impart, reckon 7 arraign, ascribe 8 consider 9 attribute
impy: 11 mischievous
in: at 4 amid, into, nook 5 among 6 corner 7 arrived 9 incumbent
a bad way: 4 sick 5 upset
a chamber: 8 incamera
a flutter: 7 pitapat
a frenzied manner: 5 amuck
a row: 4 arow 6 alined, serial 7 aligned
a standing position: 7 statant
a vertical line: 5 apeak
abeyance: 7 pending
abundance: 6 galore, plenty
accordance with: 8 pursuant
addition: too, yet 4 also, more, plus 5 aside 7 besides
advance: 5 ahead 6 before
another direction: 4 away
any case: 4 ever
any event: 15 notwithstanding
as much: 5 since 7 because
capacity of: qua
case: 4 lest
common: 5 alike
company of: 4 with
concert: 8 together
contact: 9 attingent
due course: 4 soon 11 opportunely
Dutch: 9 disgraced
equal degree: as
every way: 5 fully 6 wholly 7 totally 8 entirely 10 completely, thoroughly
excess: too 4 over
existence: 6 extant
fact: 5 truly 6 indeed 7 de facto(L.)
favor of: pro
few cases: 6 seldom
good season: 5 early 6 betime
great need: 7 straits
manner of: ala
name only: 7 nominal 10 supposedly
place of: for 5 stead 7 instead
prefix: en, il
regard to: 5 anent
same place: 4 ibid
shape: fit 4 neat, trim 5 ready
so far as it is: qua
spite of: 4 over 6 mauger, maugre 7 despite
stitches: 6 amused 8 laughing
store: 8 awaiting
that case: so 4 then
the case of: 4 in re(L.)
the center of: 4 amid
the interim: 9 meanwhile
the know: hep, hip
the main: 9 generally
the manner of: a la
the mood: 5 eager 7 willing
the raw: 4 nude 10 dishabille
the red: 5 broke 8 bankrupt, strapped
the same period: 15 contemporaneous
the time of: 6 during
this: 6 herein
this way: 4 thus
toto: all 5 whole 8 complete 10 completely
truth: 6 certes, indeed, verily 8 forsooth
what way: how 7 quomodo
year of: 4 anno
inability: 9 impotence 10 incapacity 12 incompetence
to articulate: 7 anaudia
to chew: 8 amasesis
to comprehend: 11 acatalepsia
to name correctly: 9 paranomia
to read: 6 alexia
to speak: 6 anepia
to stand erect: 7 astasia
to swallow: 7 aphagia
to understand speech: 7 aphasia
inaccessible: 12 unattainable 14 inapproachable, unapproachable
inaccuracy: 5 error 7 mistake
inaccurate: 5 loose 6 faulty, unjust 7 inexact 8 improper 9 defective, imperfect 10 unfaithful
Inachus's daughter: Io
inaction: 8 idleness 9 inertness
temporary: 5 pause 6 recess 7 abeyant, respite
inactive: lax 4 dead, idle, slow 5 heavy, inert, prone, slack, still 6 latent, otiose, supine 7 dormant, passive 8 dilatory, faineant, indolent, sleeping, slothful, sluggish 9 quiescent, recumbent, sedentary 10 unemployed
inadequate: bad 4 lean 6 feeble 9 deficient, imperfect 12 insufficient
perilously: 7 Icarian
inadvertence: 10 negligence 12 carelessness, heedlessness 15 thoughtlessness
inadvisable: 4 rash 10 indiscreet
inalterable: 9 steadfast
inamorato: 7 amorado 8 amoretto
inane: 5 empty, silly, vapid 6 vacant 7 fatuous, foolish, idiotic, vacuous 8 trifling 9 doddering, frivolous, pointless, senseless, worthless 11 nonsensical 13 characterless
inanimate: 4 dead, dull, flat 5 brute, inert 6 stolid 8 lifeless 10 insensible 11 insensitive, unconscious
inanition: 7 fasting 9 emptiness

inanity: 7 vacuity 9 emptiness, frivolity, silliness 10 flimsiness, triviality 13 senselessness
inapposite: 10 irrelevant 11 impertinent 13 inappropriate
inappreciable: 10 invaluable 13 imperceptible
inappropriate: 5 inept, undue 6 clumsy 10 unsuitable
inapt: 5 inept 6 clumsy 7 awkward 8 backward 10 amateurish, unsuitable
inarch: 5 graft
inarm: 7 embrace
inarticulate: 4 dumb, mute
inartistic: 9 tasteless
inasmuch: as; for 5 since 7 because
inattention: 7 neglect 9 disregard 10 negligence
inattentive: lax 6 absent, remiss 8 careless, heedless 9 forgetful, negligent, unheeding, unmindful 10 abstracted, neglectful 11 inadvertent, thoughtless 13 inconsiderate
inaugurate: 4 open 5 augur, begin, start 6 induct 7 install 8 initiate 9 auspicate, introduce 10 consecrate
inauspicious: bad 4 foul 7 adverse, ominous 8 sinister 12 unpropitious
inauthentic: 5 false 6 mythic, unreal 8 doubtful, spurious 9 ambiguous, uncertain 10 apocryphal, fictitious
inborn: 6 inbred, innate, native 7 connate, natural 8 inherent 10 congenital
inborn desire: 7 conatus
inbreak: 6 inroad 8 invasion 9 incursion
inbred: 6 inborn, innate 10 congenital
Inca: 9 Atahualpa
clan: 5 ayllu
empire: 4 Peru
god: 4 Inti 5 Choun, Iraya 6 Chasca 9 Uiracocha, Viracocha 10 Pachacamac
king: 9 Atabalipa, Atahualpa
priests: 6 Amauta
ruler's sister-wife: 5 Ccoya
incalculable: 6 untold 9 boundless, countless, uncertain 11 illimitable 12 immeasurable
incandescence: 4 glow, heat
incantation: 5 chant, charm, dawut, magic, spell 6 carmen(L.) 7 sorcery 9 cantation 11 conjuration, enchantment
incapable: 6 unable 11 inefficient, unqualified 12 disqualified
incapacitate: 4 lame 7 cripple, disable 10 disqualify
incarcerate: 4 jail 6 immure 7 confine 8 imprison 9 carcerate
incarnate: 6 embody 8 embodied
incarnation: 6 advent, avatar, Christ 10 embodiment
of Vishnu: 4 Rama
incase: 5 cover 7 enclose 8 surround
incasement: 11 emboitement
incautious: 4 rash 6 unwary 8 careless, heedless, reckless 9 impolitic, imprudent, unguarded 10 indiscreet
incendiarism: 5 arson
incendiary: 4 goon 5 firer 9 seditious 12 inflammatory
incense: 5 anger 6 arouse, enrage, incite 7 provoke 8 enkindle, irritate 9 instigate
burner: 6 censer 8 thurible
spice: 6 balsam, stacte
vessel: 6 censer 7 navette(F.)
incentive: 4 goad, spur 5 spark 6 motive 7 impetus, impulse 8 stimulus 9 influence 10 incitement, inducement 11 provocation 13 consideration, encouragement
incept: 8 commence 9 undertake
inception: 6 origin 9 beginning, reception 10 initiation 12 commencement
incessant: 6 steady 7 endless, eternal 8 constant 9 ceaseless, continual 11 everlasting, unremitting
incessantly: 7 forever 11 continually, unceasingly
inch: 5 uncia
one-thousandth: mil
three-quarters of: 5 digit
inch along: 4 worm
inch forward: 4 edge 7 crowhop
inches: *forty-five:* ell
four: 4 hand
nine: 4 span
39.37: 5 meter
two and one-quarter: 4 nail
inchmeal: 9 gradually
inchoate: 5 begin 8 commence, initiate 9 incipient 10 incomplete
inchpin: 10 sweetbread
incident: 5 event 7 episode 8 accident, casualty, occasion 9 happening 11 contingency
incidental: 6 casual 8 episodic 9 accessory, extrinsic 10 accidental, contingent, fortuitous, occasional 12 adventitious 14 circumstantial
incidentally: 6 byhand, obiter 7 apropos
incinerate: 4 burn 7 combust, consume, cremate
incinerator: 7 furnace 9 crematory
incipient: 6 induct 7 initial 8 inchoate 10 commencing, inaugurate
incise: cut 4 chop, etch, rase 5 carve 7 engrave
narrowly: 9 laciniate
incision: cut 4 gash, slit 5 lance 6 broach, scotch 10 laceration
incisive: 5 acute, sharp 6 biting 7 cutting 9 sarcastic 11 penetrating

incisor: 6 cutter 9 foretooth
incite: egg, hie 4 abet, fire, goad, move, prod, sick, spur, urge 5 impel, sting 6 arouse, compel, entice, excite, exhort, foment, induce 7 actuate, agitate, animate, commove, provoke 8 motivate 9 encourage, instigate, stimulate
incitement: 6 motive 8 stimulus 9 incentive
incivility: 8 rudeness 9 surliness 10 disrespect, effrontery 11 discourtesy 12 churlishness, impertinence 14 unmannerliness
inclemency: 8 asperity
inclement: raw 4 hard, rude 5 harsh, rough 6 severe, stormy 8 rigorous 10 unmerciful
inclination: 4 bent, bias, broo, hang, love, urge, will 5 bevel, fancy, heald, hield, slant, taste, tenor, trend 6 affect, animus, ascent, device 7 conatus, descent, fantasy, hanging, inkling, leaning 8 penchant, tendency 9 acclivity, affection, direction, proneness 10 attachment, proclivity 11 declination, disposition 12 predilection 13 prepossession
incline: apt, bow, dip, tip 4 bend, brew, cant, heel, lean, list, ramp, tend, tilt 5 bevel, grade, heald, hield, humor, shape, slant, slide, slope, trend 6 careen, humour 7 upgrade
inclined: apt, dip 4 fain, wont 5 alist, atilt, prone 6 biased, leaned 7 hanging 8 addicted, affected 11 predisposed
inclip: 7 embrace, enclasp, inclasp
inclose: hem, pen 4 case 5 embar 6 encase, incase 7 environ
inclosed: 8 interior
inclosure: ree(Sc.) 8 sepiment 10 impalement
animal: pen, sty 4 cage, cote, fold 5 hutch, kraal 6 corral
include: 7 contain, embrace, involve 8 comprise, comprize 9 encompass 10 comprehend
incognito: 7 unknown 8 disquise
incoherent: 6 broken 9 illogical 11 incongruous 12 disconnected, inconsequent, inconsistent
income: 4 gain 5 rente(F.) 6 profit, return 7 produce, revenue 8 interest, proceeds, receipts 9 emolument
pert. to: 7 tontine
receiver: 7 rentier
incommensurate: 7 unequal 12 insufficient 16 disproportionate
incommode: vex 5 annoy 6 molest, plague 7 trouble 8 disquiet 9 disoblige 10 discommode 13 inconvenience
incomparable: 8 peerless 9 matchless, unequaled, unrivaled 10 surpassing 11 superlative 15 incommeasurable
incompatible: 9 repugnant 11 conflicting, incongruous 12 inharmonious 13 contradictory, unsympathetic 14 irreconcilable
incompetence: 9 inability, unfitness 10 disability
incompetent: 5 inept, unfit 6 unable 8 helpless 9 incapable, unskilled 10 untalented 11 inefficient, unqualified 12 insufficient
incomplete: 5 blind, crude, rough 6 broken, undone 7 divided, lacking 8 immature, inchoate 9 defective, imperfect, partially 10 unfinished
incomprehensible: 8 abstruse 9 graspless 10 fathomless, mysterious, unreadable 11 unthinkable 12 unimaginable 13 unconceivable 14 unintelligible
inconclusive: 10 indefinite 11 ineffective
incondite: 5 crude 9 unrefined 10 unpolished
incongruity: 9 inharmony 10 dissonance 11 incoherence 12 disagreement 13 inconsistency 14 unsuitableness
incongruous: 5 alien 6 absurd, impure 9 grotesque 10 discordant, unsuitable 12 disagreeable, inconsistent, inharmonious 13 inappropriate
inconsequent: 7 invalid 9 illogical 10 irrelevant 11 unimportant 12 inconsistent 13 inconsecutive
inconsiderable: 5 petty 7 trivial 8 careless, unworthy 10 negligible 13 inconsiderate
inconsiderate: 4 rash 6 unkind 8 careless 9 imprudent, negligent 10 incautious, indiscreet, neglectful 11 improvident, injudicious, thoughtless 14 inconsiderable
inconsistent: 5 crimp 6 absurd 9 dissonant 10 capricious, discordant, discrepant, incoherent, inconstant 13 contradictory 14 irreconcilable
inconsolable: 11 comfortless, heartbroken 12 disconsolate
inconstant: 6 fickle 7 bruckle 8 disloyal, fluxible, variable 9 desultory, faithless 10 capricious, changeable 12 inconsistent
incontestable: 4 sure 7 certain 10 undeniable 11 indubitable
incontrovertible: 7 certain 10 undeniable
inconvenience: 5 annoy 8 disquiet 9 annoyance, incommode 10 discomfort, discommode, uneasiness 11 awkwardness, disturbance 12 discomfiture 13 embarrassment
inconvenient: 7 awkward, unhandy 8 annoying 10 unsuitable 11 troublesome 12 unreasonable
incorporate: mix 4 fuse, join 5 blend, merge, unite 6 absorb, embody 10 assimilate
incorporation: 10 absorption 11 combination

incorporeal: 4 aery 8 bodiless 9 asomatous, spiritual, sprightly 13 unsubstantial
incorrect: bad 5 false, wrong 6 faulty 9 erroneous
incorrect naming of objects: 9 paranomia
incorrigible: 4 hard 9 abandoned
incorruptible: 4 just 6 honest 7 upright
incrassate: 7 stupefy, swollen, thicken 10 inspissate
increase: add, eke, wax 4 eche, gain, grow, rise, rist 5 boost, raise, swell 6 accrue, amount, better, dilate, expand, extend, gather, growth 7 amplify, augment, enhance, enlarge, greaten, inflate, magnify 8 addition, ampliate, flourish, heighten, multiply 9 accession, advantage, aggravate, expansion, extension, increment, intensify 10 accelerate, accumulate, aggrandize, appreciate 11 aggravation, development, enlargement 12 augmentation 13 amplification 15 intensification
comb. form: 4 auxo
in sound: 9 crescendo
possessions: 5 amass 6 enrich
salary: 5 raise
incredulous: 8 doubting 9 faithless, skeptical
incremate: 7 cremate
increment: 4 gain 6 growth, income 8 increase 12 augmentation
increscent: 6 waxing 7 growing 9 enlarging 10 increasing
incriminate: 6 accuse 7 impeach
incrust: 4 coat 5 glaze 6 barkle
incubate: 5 brood
incubator: 8 couveuse 11 eccaleobion
incubus: 4 load 5 demon 6 burden, spirit 9 hindrance, nightmare 10 impediment 11 encumbrance
inculcate: 5 infix 6 infuse, instil 7 implant, impress, instill
inculpate: 5 blame 11 incriminate
incumbent: 9 impending 11 threatening
incunabulum: 6 cocoon, cradle, origin 7 infancy 9 beginning 10 birthplace
incur: 8 contract 9 encounter
incurable: 8 hopeless 10 remediless 11 irreparable 12 irremediable 13 irretrievable
incurious: 9 apathetic 11 unconcerned, uninquiring 12 uninterested
incursion: 4 rade(Sc.), raid 5 foray 6 inroad 7 assault, descent, hosting 8 invasion 10 dragonnade
incurved: 7 concave
incus: 5 ambos, anvil
indebted: 8 beholden 9 obligated
indecency: 8 impurity 9 immodesty, indecorum, obscenity 10 indelicacy
indecent: 4 foul 5 gross, nasty 6 coarse, greasy, impure 7 grivois, immoral, obscene 8 grivoise, immodest, improper, unseemly 9 dishonest 10 scurrilous
indecipherable: 9 illegible
indecision: 5 doubt 9 hesitancy 10 hesitation 11 uncertainty, vacillation 12 irresolution
indecorous: 4 rude 6 coarse 7 uncivil 8 immodest, impolite, improper, unseemly 10 unbecoming
indeed: aru, yea 4 awat(Sc.), iwis, ywis 5 truly 6 i'faith 8 forsooth
indefatigable: 4 busy 8 tireless, untiring 9 assiduous 10 persistent, unwearying 11 persevering
indefensible: 11 inexcusable 12 unpardonable 13 insupportable
indefinite: 5 loose, vague 7 inexact, neutral 8 aoristic 9 ambiguous, equivocal, uncertain, unlimited 10 inexplicit 12 inconclusive
pronoun: any, one 4 some
indehiscent fruit: uva
indelible: 4 fast 5 fixed 9 permanent 10 inerasable 12 ineffaceable, ineradicable, inexpungible
indelicate: raw 5 broad, gross 6 coarse, greasy 7 fulsome 8 impolite, improper, unseemly 9 offensive, unrefined 10 indecorous, unbecoming
indemnification: 10 reparation 11 restitution
indemnify: pay 6 recoup 9 reimburse 10 compensate, recompense
indemnity: 7 amnesty 9 exemption 10 protection 12 compensation
indent: jag 4 dent, gimp 5 chase, delve, inlay, notch, press, stamp, tooth 6 bruise, emboss 7 depress
indentation: bay 4 dent, dint, doke, nick 5 bulge, choil, crena, notch 6 crenae(pl.), dimple, recess 8 crenelet 10 impression
indented: 6 dented, jagged, milled 7 notched, sinuous 9 crenelate, impressed 10 undulating
indenture: 5 notch 8 contract 9 agreement
independence: 7 freedom 10 competency
independent: 4 free 5 proud 9 sovereign, uncoerced 11 self-centred 12 self-centered, uncontrolled, unrestricted
independently: 5 apart 10 absolutely
indestructible: 10 inviolable 12 imperishable
indeterminate: 5 vague 8 formless 9 uncertain, unlimited
indetermined: 9 ambiguous, equivocal
index: 4 file, list 5 table 7 catalog 9 catalogue, repertory

India (see also **Hindu**): *abuse:* **4** gali **5** galee
acrobat: nat
agent: **4** amin **5** ameen **6** muktar **8** gomashta, gomastah
air conditioner: **5** tatty
alphabet: **6** Sarada **10** Devanagari
ambassador: **5** vakil **6** vakeel
ancestor: **4** Manu **5** Pitri
animal, ox-like: **4** zebu
antelope: **5** sasin **6** nilgai, nilgau **7** chikara, nilghai
apartment: **6** zenana
army officer: **4** naig, naik **6** naigue, naique **7** jemadar, jemidar
astrologer: **5** joshi
attorney: **6** muktar
awning: **9** shamianah
baby: **4** baba
bandit: **6** dacoit
bard: **4** bhat
bathing place: **4** ghat **5** ghaut
bazaar: **5** chawk, chowk
bean: urd
bear: **4** balu **5** baloo
bearer: **6** sirdar
bed: **7** charpai, charpoy
bed cover: **9** palampore
bedstead: **7** charpao, charpoy
bill of exchange: **5** hundi
bird: **5** shama **8** amadavat, amaduvad **9** amaduvade
blight: **4** soka
boat: **7** almadia, almadie, masoola
bodice: **5** choli
body servant: **6** sirdar
boy: **6** chokra, Mowgli
bracelet: **6** sankha
bread: **8** chapatty, chupatty
breakfast: **5** hazri
brick: **6** soorki, soorky **7** soorkee
British founder: **5** Clive
buck: **5** sasin
buffalo: **4** arna **5** arnee
bulbul: **4** kala
butter: ghi **4** ghee
buzzard: **4** tesa
cabinet: **6** almura, almyra **7** almirah, almyrah
calico: **5** saloo **6** salloo
cannabis: **5** ganja
canoe: **5** tanee
cape: **4** divi
capital: **5** Delhi
carpet: **4** agra
carriage: **4** ekka **5** bandy, tonga **6** gharri, gharry
cashmere: **5** ulwan
caste: Jat, Mal, Meo **4** Ahir, Gola, Mali **5** Dhoby, Sansi **6** Dacoit, Dhanuk, Dhobie, Lohana, Vaisya **7** Agarwal, Brahmin, Dhangar, Vaishya
cavalryman: **5** sowar **6** risala **7** ressala
cedar: **6** deodar
chamber: **4** Kiva **8** Tahkhana
charm: **6** mantra
chief: mir **4** raja, rana **5** rajah **6** sirdar
church: **5** samaj
cigarette: **4** biri
city: See *town* below.
civet: **5** rasse, zibet **6** zibeth
clarinet: **4** been
class: **5** caste
clerk: **4** babu **5** baboo
cloak: **5** choga
cloth: **7** dhurrie
coast: **7** Malabar
coin: lac, pie **4** anna, dawm, fels, hoon, lakh, pice, tara **5** abidi, crore, paisa, rupee
college: Tol
colonialist: **5** Clive
combining form: **4** Indo
cook: **8** bawarchi
corn: zea
coronation: **8** abhiseka
court official: **5** nazir
cowrie: **5** zimbi
crane: **5** sarus
crocodile: **6** gavial, muggar, mugger, muggur
crop: **4** rabi
cymbal: tal
dagger: **5** katar
dais: **8** chabutra
dance: **6** nautch **7** cantico
dancer: nat **8** bayadere
deer: **4** axis **5** kakar **6** chital, chitra, sambar, sambur **7** cheetal, cheetul
demon: **4** bhut **5** asura **6** daitya
deputy: **5** nabob, nawab
desert: **4** Thar
devil tree: **4** dita
dialect: **4** Urdu **5** Hindi, Tamil **7** Prakrit
dignitary: **5** rajah
dill: **4** soya
disease: **5** agrom
district: **4** Sibi **5** Nasik, Patna, Simla **6** Zillah **7** Malabar, Nellore **8** Mofussil
dog: **5** dhole **6** pariah
drama: **6** nataka
Dravidian: **5** Arava, Tamil
drink: **4** soma **6** arrack
drinking pot: **5** lotah
drought: **4** soka
drug: **5** bhang
dust storm: **7** shaitan, sheitan
earth: **5** regur

educated man: 4 babu 6 pundit
educated woman: 7 pundita
elephant: 5 hathi
elephant driver: 6 mahout
epic: 8 Ramayana 11 Mahabharata
fabric: 6 tanjib, zenana
falcon: 6 shahin 7 shaheen
fan: 5 punka 6 punkah
father: 4 babu
festival: 4 Holi, mela
fiber: 6 ambary
fig tree: 5 pipal 6 peepul
fish: 5 dorab
flower: 5 lotus
founder of Mogul dynasty: 5 Baber
fruit: bel
garment: 4 sari 5 burqa, saree
god: 4 Deva, Yama 5 Shiva
goddess: 4 Amma 5 Amman
gossip: gup
government: 6 sircar
governor: 5 nazim
grass: 4 kusa 5 kusha, roosa 6 bhabar, darbha, doorba
griddlecake: 8 chapatty
grinding stone: 4 mano 6 metate
grove: 5 Sarna
guard: 7 daloyet
guide: 7 shikari 8 shikaree
hall: 6 durbar
handkerchief: 7 malabar
harem: 6 zenana
harvest: 4 rabi
heiress: 5 Begum
hemp: kef 4 bang, carl, kaif, keef 5 bhang, ramie 7 chirata
herb: pie 6 sesame 7 curcuma, tumeric, zeodary
hero: 4 Rama
holy: sri 4 shri 5 shree
holy man: 5 fakir, sadhu 6 saddhu
house: 5 mahal 8 bungalow
impost: 5 abwab
instrument: 5 ruana, sarod 7 sarinda
intoxicant: 4 soma
jungle: 5 shola
justice: 7 adawlut
king: 4 Nala, raja 5 rajah
knife: dah
laborer: 4 toty 7 totyman
lady: 7 sahibah
lake: 4 jhil 5 jheel 6 Chilka, Kolair
language: 4 Urdu 5 Hindi, Tamil 6 Siouan, Telugu 8 Sanskrit
law opinion: 5 futwa
leader: 5 Nehru 6 Gandhi
legal claim: hak 4 hakh
leopard, hunting: 7 cheetah
literature: 7 akhyana
loincloth: 5 dhoti
lord: 4 mian
mahogany: 4 toon 5 toona
mail: dak 4 dawk
mangrove: 5 goran
master: 5 saheb, sahib
matting: 5 tatta
meal: ata 4 atta
measure: ady, dha, gaz, gez, guz, jow, kos, lan, ser 4 byee, coss, dain, dhan, hath, jaob, koss, kunk, moot, para, rati, raik, seit, taun, teng, tola 5 bigha, cahar, covid, crosa, danda, denda, drona, garce, gireh, hasta, krosa, pally, parah, ratti, salay, yojan 6 adhaka, amunam, angula, covido, cudava, cumbha, geerah, lamany, moolum, mushti, palgat, parrah, ropani, tipree, unglee, yojana 7 adoulie, dhanush, gavyuti, khahoon, niranga, prastha, vitasti 8 okthabah
merchant: 5 banya 6 banian 8 soudagur 9 brinjaree
millet: 4 joar
money: See *coin* above
mountain: 4 Meru 5 Ghats 7 Siwalik, Vindhya 8 Suleiman 9 Himalayas, Hindukush, Nilghiris 12 Neilgherries
mulberry: al; aal, ach 6 alroot
musical instrument: 4 vina 5 ruana
muslin: 5 adati, dorea, doria 6 gurrah 9 charkhana
narcotic: 4 bang 5 bhang 7 hashish
native: 5 Hindu, Sepoy, Tamil 8 Assamese 10 Hindustani
nonviolence: 6 ahimsa
nurse: 4 amah, ayah, dhai
old money: 5 mohur
ox: 4 zebu
peasant: 4 ryot
people: 4 Bhil 5 Kotar 6 Hubshi, Badaga
pheasant: 5 monal 6 monaul, moonal
pipe: 6 hookah
poetic name: Ind
policeman: 4 peon 5 sepoy
priest: 5 mobed, mulla 6 mullah
prince: 4 bana, rana 5 rajah
princess: 4 rani 5 begum, ranee
property: 4 dhan
province: 4 Dhar, Jath, Jind 5 Assam, Berar, Bihar 6 Bengal, Gujara, Kerala, Madras, Mysore, Orissa, Punjab 7 Kashmir, Manipur 9 Rajasthan 11 Utar Pradesh 13 Andhra Pradesh, Madhya Pradesh 14 Himachi Pradesh
Punjabi caste: 5 Sansi
Punjabi people: 4 Sikh
queen: 4 rani 5 begum, ranee 8 maharani
race: 5 Hindu 9 Dravidian
rainy season: 6 varsha 7 monsoon

region: 7 Malabar
religion: 5 Islam 8 Buddhism, Hinduism
rice: 4 boro
river: Ai; Dor 4 Kosi, Kusi, Sind 5 Bhimi, Indus, Kabul, Rapti, Tapti 6 Chenab, Ganges, Kistna, Sutlej 7 Cauvery, Irawadi, Krishna 8 Godavari, Hydaspes, Nerbudda, Vindhyas 9 Irrawaddy 10 Bhagirathi 11 Brahmaputra
rubber: 10 caoutchouc
rule: raj
ruler: 4 rana 5 nawab, rajah
sacred grove: 5 Sarna
saffron: 7 tumeric, zedoary
sage: 6 pandit, pundit
seaport: 6 Bombay, Madras 8 Calcutta
servant: 4 maty 6 bearer 10 mussalchee
sheep: 5 urial 6 oorial
shirt: 6 banian
shrine: 6 dagaba, dagoba
silk: 4 muga 6 cabeca
silkworm: eri
snake: 5 krait
soldier: 4 peon 5 sepoy 6 gurkha
song: 4 raga
spinning wheel: 6 charka 7 charkha
state: see *province* above
storm: 5 tufan 7 peesash
sun worshiper: 5 parsi 6 parsee
supreme court: 6 Sudder
tapir: 8 saladang
tariff: 6 zabeta
tax: 10 chaukidari
teacher: 4 guru 5 akhun, mulla 6 akhund, mullah, pandit, pundit 7 akhoond
tenant: 4 ryot
title: sri 4 mian, raja 5 sahib, singh 6 sirdar 7 gaekwad, gaekwar, gaikwar, sahibah 8 guicowar 9 ahluwalia
tower: 5 minar
town: 4 Agra, Gaya, Puna, Rewa 5 Adoni, Akola, Arcot, Bhera, Dacca, Daman, Delhi, Girot, Kalpi, Naida, Patan, Patna, Poona, Salem, Simla, Surat 6 Ajmere, Ambala, Bareli, Baroda, Bhopal, Bombay, Dum-Dum, Howrah, Indore, Jaipur, Lahore, Madira, Madras, Madura, Meerut, Multan, Muttra, Musore, Nagpur, Rampur 7 Aligarh, Benares, Calicut, Cawnpur, Dinapir, Gwalior, Jodhpur, Karachi, Laswari, Lucknow, Rangoon, Rangpur 8 Amritsar, Bhatinda, Bhatpara, Calcutta, Cawnpore, Dinapore, Jabalpur, Kolhapur, Mandalay, Mirzapur, Peshawar, Sholapur, Srinagar 9 Ahmadabad, Allahabad, Berhampur, Berhampir, Bhagalpur, Bungalore, Cuddalore, Darjiling, Gorakhpir, Hyderabad, Kurrachee, Moradabad, Nagapatam, Srirangam 10 Darbhangah, Darjeeling, Haidarabad, Jubbulpore, Rawalpindi, Saharanpur 11 Barrackpore 12 Shahjahanpur, Trichioopoli
tree: bel, dar, lin, sal 4 dita, myxa, shoq, teak 5 anjan, pipal, salai 6 banyan, deodar 7 majagua
tribe: Ao; Gor 4 Bhil 6 Badaga 7 Sherani, Shirani
turban: 8 seerband
vessel: 4 doni 6 shibar
viceroy: 5 nabob, nawab
village: 5 abadi 6 mouzah
weight: moo, pai, ser, vis 4 bhar, dhan, drum, kona, myat, pala, pank, pice, raik, rati, ruay, seer, tank, tola, yava 5 adpao, bahar, candy, catty, hubba, masha, maund, pally, pouah, ratti, retti, tical, ticul, tikal 6 abucco, dhurra, karsha, ruttee 7 chittak, peiktha 8 chittack
wheat: 4 suji 5 sujee
wife's cremation: 6 suttee
wild ox: 4 gaur
wine: 5 shrab
wood: eng, sal 4 toon 5 kokra

Indian (see also **India**): red 5 indic 7 redskin 9 aborigine
acricultural: 6 Pawnee
Alaska: 5 Aleut
Aleutian: 4 Attu
Algonquin: Sac 4 Cree, Sauk 5 Miami 6 Abnaki, Micmac, Ottawa, Sokoki 7 Arapaho, Mohican, Ojibway, Shawnee 8 Cheyenne, Delaware, Illinois 9 Blackfoot 10 Montagnais 11 Massachuset
American: Aht, Kaw, Oto, Red, Sac, Ute 4 Cree, Dene, Erie, Hopi, Ioni, Iowa, Otoe, Pima, Tana, Taos, Yuma, Zuni 5 Banak, Caddo, Coree, Creek, Huron, Kania, Kansa, Keres, Kiowa, Miami, Omaha, Osage, Piute, Sioux, Tinne 6 Abnaki, Apache, Dakota, Kansas, Lenape, Mohave, Mojave, Navaho, Navajo, Nootka, Oneida, Ottawa, Paiute, Pawnee, Redman, Sambos, Seneca, Siwash 7 Abenaki, Amerind, Arapaho, Choctaw, Keresan, Redskin 8 Apalachi, Cherokee, Chippewa, Comanche, Hitchiti, Iroquois, Kickapoo, Onondaga, Pokonchi, Sagamore, Seminole, Shoshone 9 Algonquin, Apalachee, Chickasaw, Winnebago 10 Muskhogean 12 Narragansett
Arawakan: 5 Guana
Arikara: Ree
Arizona: 4 Pima, Yuma 6 Navaho, Navajo
Athapascan: 4 Dene, Hupa 5 Hoopa, Tinne 6 Apache, Navaho, Navajo, Tinneh
blanket: 6 stroud 9 strouding
Bolivia: Uro 4 Iten, Moxo 6 Aymara 10 Chiriguano
Brazil: 5 Bravo 7 Tariana

British Columbia: 7 Gitksan
Caddoan: Ree 4 Adai, Ioni, Waco 6 Eyeish, Hainai 7 Andarko, Arikara 8 Arikaree 9 Nachitoch
Calgary: 5 Sarsi
California: 4 Pomo
Canadian: 4 Cree, Dene 5 Tinne 6 Tinneh 7 Sanetch 9 Athabasca 10 Athabascan
Cariban: 4 Yaos 5 Arara, Trios 6 Caribs, Oyanas 7 Akawais, Aparais, Chaymas, Macusis 8 Arecunas, Bakairis, Woyaways, Yauapery 9 Tamanacos 11 Cumanagotos 12 Maquiritares
ceremonial chamber: 4 kiva
chief: 6 sachem 8 sagamore
child: 7 papoose
Copehan: 6 Wintun
corn: zea 4 samp 5 maize
council: 6 powwow
craft: 5 canoe, kayak 6 dugout
Dakota: Ree
daughter of moon: 7 Nakomis, Nokomis
Delaware: 6 Lenape
female: 5 squaw 6 mahala, mahaly
festival: 8 potlatch
fighter: 5 Boone, Miles 6 Custer
flathead: 7 Chinook
Fuegian: Ona 6 Yahgan 8 Alikuluf
game: 6 canute
Great Lake: 4 Erie 5 Huron
Great Spirit: 6 manito
guardian spirit: 5 totem
hatchet: 8 tomahawk
headdress: 7 topknot
Hopi: 4 Moki 5 Moqui
hut: 5 hogan, toldo 6 wikiup 7 wickiup
Iroquois: 4 Erie 6 Oneida, Seneca 7 Wyandot 9 Hochelaga
Keresan: Sia
liquor: 9 firewater
lodge: 5 tepee
man: 4 buck 5 brave, chief 6 sannup
Manitoba: 4 Cree
meal bread: 8 corncake
memorial post: xat 5 totem
Missouri: 5 Osage
moccasin: pac
money: 6 seawan, wampum 7 seawant
Muskhogean: 5 Creek 8 Hitchiti
Nebraska: 4 Otoe 5 Omaha
Nevada: 6 Digger, Paiute
New Mexico: Sia 4 Tano, Taos 5 Keres
New York: 4 Erie 6 Oneida, Seneca 9 Tuscarora
North Carolina: 5 Coree 7 Buffalo
Northwest: 4 Cree
Oklahoma: 5 Creek, Kansa, Osage 6 Pawnee, Quapaw 7 Choctaw 8 Cherokee
Oregon: 5 Modoc
Orinoco Valley: 9 Guahiribo
Panama: 4 Cuna 6 Guaymi 7 Guaymic
Paraguay: 8 Guayaqui
Paru River: 8 Araquaju
Payaguas: 4 Agaz
peace pipe: 7 calumet
Peban: 5 Yagua
Peru: 4 Ande, Cana, Inca, Inka, Peba, Yutu 5 Boros, Campa, Carib, Panos 6 Aymara, Jibaro, Jiyaro, Kechua, Lamano 7 Quechau
pillar: lat, xat
Piman: 5 Opata
Platte River: 6 Pawnee
pony: 6 cayuse
porridge: 4 samp
potato: 4 yamp 9 breadroot
prayer stick: 4 paho
Pueblo: 4 Hopi, Moki, Piro, Tana, Taos
Quapaw: 5 Ozark
Quechuan: 4 Inca
Rio Grande: Tao
Salishan: 7 Tulalip
Seminole chief: 7 Osceola
Shoshone: Ute 4 Hopi, Otoe, Utah 5 Piute 6 Paiute 8 Comanche
Sioux: Kaw, Oto 4 Otoe 5 Omaha, Osage 6 Biloxi, Hidata, Saponi, Tutelo
snake dancer: 4 Hopi
sorcery: ob; obe, obi
South American: Ges, Ona 4 Inca 5 Aztec, Carib
spirit: 5 totem 7 Manitou
tent: 5 tepee 6 wigwam
Tierra del Fuego: Ona 4 Agni
token of victory: 5 scalp
Uchean: 5 Uchee, Yuchi
Utah: Ute 5 Piute 6 Paiute
Vancouver Island: Aht 5 Sooke 9 Ehatisaht
Venezuela: 5 Carib 6 Timote 7 Timotex 8 Guarauno
village: 6 pueblo
Virginia: 8 Powhatan 10 Algonquian
Wakashan: 6 Nootka
wampum: 4 peag 5 peage
warrior: 5 brave
Washington: Aht, Hoh 5 Lummi, Makah 6 Callam
weapon: 8 tomahawk
Western: Kaw 4 Seri
wigwam: 5 tepee
Wisconsin: Sac
woman: 5 squaw
Wyoming: 4 Crow 5 Kiowa
Xingu River: 5 Aneto
Yucatan: 4 Maya
Yukian: 4 Yuki 5 Wappo 7 Huchnom
Zuni Land: 6 Cibola

Indiana: *and Ohio River:* 6 Maumee

bird: **8** cardinal
city: **4** Peru **5** Floyd **6** Brazil, Fowler, Marion, Muncie **7** Bedford, Hammond, Laporte **8** Danville **10** Huntington **11** Bloomington **12** Indianapolis(c.), Kendallville **14** Jeffersonville
county: **8** Lagrange
flower: **6** zinnia
native: **7** Hoosier
tree: **5** tulip

indicate: say **4** bode, cite, mark, read, show **5** argue, augur, point **6** allude, denote, evince, import, reveal **7** bespeak, betoken, connote, declare, display, signify, specify **8** decipher, disclose, evidence, manifest, register **9** designate **10** denominate **12** characterize

indicated: **6** marked, signed **9** betokened

indicating: *chemical group:* azo
literal transcript: sic
succession: **7** ordinal

indication: **4** clew, clue, hint, mark, note, omen, sign **5** proof, token, trace **6** augury, signal **7** auspice, symptom **8** argument, evidence **10** denotation **11** designation **13** manifestation

indicative: **10** expressive **13** argumentative

indicator: **4** dial, hand, sign, vane **5** arrow, clock, gauge, index **6** gnomon, marker **7** indices(pl.), pointer **11** annunciator **15** telethermometer

indices: **5** files **6** tables **8** pointers

indicium: **4** mark, sign **5** token **10** appearance, indication

indict: **4** bill, dite **6** accuse, attach, charge, decree **7** arraign, impeach **8** proclaim

indictive: **8** declared **9** appointed **10** proclaimed

indictment: **10** accusation

indifference: **6** apathy **8** coldness, froideur **9** aloofness **10** negligence **11** insouciance **12** carelessness, heedlessness, lukewarmness **13** insensibility, pococurantism

indifferent: ill **4** cold, cool, dead, dram, sick, soso **5** aloof, blase, blaze, shrug, stoic **6** casual, poorly, supine **7** neutral, uneager **8** careless, listless, mediocre **9** apathetic, Laodicean **10** nonchalant, regardless **11** adiaphorous, pococurante **12** nonessential

indigence: **4** lack, need, want **6** penury **7** beggary, poverty **10** deficiency

indigene: **6** native

indigenous: **5** natal **6** inborn, innate, native **7** endemic, natural **8** homeborn, inherent **10** aboriginal **13** autochthonous

indigent: **4** free, poor, void **5** needy **7** lacking, wanting **8** beggarly **9** destitute, penniless **11** impecunious, necessitous

indigestion: **6** apepsy **7** apepsia

indign: **8** unworthy **10** undeserved **11** disgraceful, undeserving

indignant: **5** angry, irate, wroth **7** annoyed **8** incensed, wrathful **11** exasperated

indignation: ire **4** fury **5** anger, wrath **7** disdain **8** contempt **11** displeasure

indignity: cut **6** insult, slight **7** affront **13** disparagement

indigo: **4** anil, blue
artificial source: **6** isatin
bale of: **6** seroon
derivative: **5** indol **6** indole
natural source: **4** anil **7** indican
shrub: **4** anil
wild genus: **8** baptisia

indigo bunting: **4** bird **5** finch

indirect: **4** side **7** devious, oblique **8** circular **9** dishonest **10** circuitous, collateral, misleading, roundabout
expense: **8** overhead

indirectly: **5** aside

indiscernible: **13** imperceptible **17** indistinguishable

indiscreet: **4** rash **5** hasty, silly **6** unwise **7** foolish, witless **8** careless, heedless **9** impolitic, imprudent, unadvised **10** incautious **11** injudicious **12** undiscerning **13** inconsiderate

indiscretion: **5** folly **8** fredaine **10** imprudence

indiscriminate: **5** mixed **7** mingled **9** wholesale **13** heterogeneous

indispensable: **5** basic, vital **7** exigent **9** essential, requisite **10** imperative

indisposed: ill **4** sick **6** ailing **8** unsuited **11** disinclined **12** disqualified

indisposition: ail **6** malady **7** ailment, illness, malaise **8** disorder, sickness **9** distemper **10** discomfort, reluctance **12** disaffection **13** unwillingness

indisputable: **4** sure **7** certain, evident **8** positive **10** undeniable **11** indubitable **12** irrefragable **13** incontestable **14** unquestionable **16** incontrovertible

indissolubility: **8** firmness

indistinct: dim **4** dark, hazy **5** faint, misty, vague **6** cloudy **7** blurred, obscure, shadowy **9** ambiguous, unrefined **10** indefinite **17** indistinguishable

indistinctly: **6** feeble

indite: pen **4** dite **5** write **7** compose **8** inscribe

individual (see also **person**): one **4** oner, self, sole, unit **6** person, single **7** special **8** distinct, selfsame, solitary **9** identical **11** inseparable
combining form: **4** idio
of compound animal: **4** zoon
physiological: **4** bion

selfish: 6 egoist
smug: 4 prig
individuality: 5 selty 7 oneness 14 indivisibility, inseparability
rare: 5 seity
individually: 9 severally 10 personally 14 distributively
individuate: 9 undivided 11 inseparable
Indo-Aryan: Jat 6 khatri, Rajput
diety: 5 Indra
Indo-China: *dialect:* ao
former kingdom: 4 Anam 5 Annam
language: Ao, Hu, Wa; Aka, Lai, Lao, Sai, Tai, Yao 4 Bama, Mrus, Shan, Thai 7 Burmese
linguist stock: Tai
native: see *people* below
people: Mru, Tai 4 Naga
race: see *people* above
region: 4 Laos 5 Annam
river: Te
state: 4 Laos 5 Burma 7 Vietnam 8 Cambodia, Thailand
tree: eng, mee
Indo-European: 4 Lett, Serb, Slav 5 Aryan, Croat, Czech
language: 5 Indic 6 Baltic, Celtic, Italic, Slavic 7 Iranian 8 Albanian, Germanic, Hellenic
Indo-Iranian: 5 Aryan
Indo-Portuguese: *Christian half-caste:* 5 Topas, Topaz 6 Topass
measure: 5 covid 6 covido
indoctrinate: 5 imbue, teach, tutor 7 educate 8 instruct
indolence: 5 scorn, sloth 7 inertia, languor
indolent: 4 idle, lazy 5 inert 6 otiose, supine 7 dronish 8 inactive, slothful, sluggish
indomitable: 10 invincible 11 intractable 13 unconquerable
Indonesia: *base:* Lae
capital: 7 Jakarta
coin: 6 rupiah
Indian: Ata
island: 4 Bali, Java 5 Timor 6 Flores, Lombok 7 Madoera, Sumatra 8 Soembowa 9 New Guinea
lake: 4 Toba
law: 4 adat
Luzon: 6 Igorot
market: 5 pasar
measure: 4 depa 5 depoh
news agency: 5 Aneta
people: 6 Tapiro
priest caste: 8 brahmana
pyramid: 5 stupa
race: 4 Dyak 6 Battak, Bontok, Ifugao, Igorot, Manobo 7 Lampong
sea gypsy: 6 selung
shop: 4 toko
tribe: Ata 4 Atta
volcano: 4 Awoe 5 Agung, Raung
weight: 6 soekoe
wind: 5 brubu 7 broeboe
indorse: See **endorse**
Indra: 5 Sakka, Sakra
dragon: 6 Vritra
elephant: 8 Airavata
father: 8 Tvashtri
food: 4 soma
heaven capital: 9 Amaravati
indubious: 7 certain
indubitable: 4 sure 7 assured, certain, evident 8 apparent 10 infallible, undeniable 12 irrefragable 13 incontestable 16 incontrovertible
induce: get 4 draw, lure, urge 5 infer, tempt 6 elicit, suborn 7 actuate 8 persuade 9 encourage, influence
induced: led 5 moved, urged 6 caused 7 allured, engaged, enticed, incited 8 impelled 9 motivated, persuaded 10 instigated
inducement: 4 bait 5 prize 6 motive, reason 9 incentive, influence 10 enticement 13 consideration
induct: 5 enrol 6 enlist, enroll 7 install 8 initiate 9 introduce 10 inaugurate
inductance unit: 5 henry
inductile: 10 inflexible, unyielding
induction: 8 entrance 9 accession, deduction 10 initiation 12 commencement, introduction
indue: 5 endow 6 assume, clothe, invest 7 furnish
indulge: pet 4 cade, feed, waly 5 favor, humor, wally 6 cocker, favour, foster, humour, pamper, please 7 cherish, gratify
in antics: 7 skylark
in fault finding: 5 cavil
in recreation: 4 play
in revelry: 5 roist
to excess: 6 pamper
indulgence: 5 favor, spree 6 favour 8 clemency, humoring 9 tolerance 13 gratification 17 self-gratification
indulgent: 4 easy, fond, good, kind, mild 7 lenient 8 tolerant 9 compliant 10 charitable
indurate: 5 inure 6 harden 9 calloused
indurated: 4 hard 5 inure 7 callous, scleral 8 hardened, obdurate, scleroid, stubborn 9 sclerotic
Indus tribesman: Gor
industrial magnate: 6 tycoon
industrious: 4 busy 6 active 7 zealous 8 diligent, sedulous 9 assiduous 11 painstaking 13 indefatigable

industry: 5 labor, skill 8 business 9 assiduity, diligence, ingenuity 10 occupation

indweller: 7 denizen 9 sojourner 10 inhabitant

indwelling: 8 immanent, inherent 9 immanence

inearth: 4 bury 5 inter

inebriacy: 11 drunkenness 12 intemperance

inebriate: sot 5 drunk 6 excite 7 ebriate 8 drunkard 9 stupefied 10 exhilarate, intoxicate 11 intoxicated

inebriated: 5 drunk

ineffable: 11 unspeakable, unutterable 13 indescribable, inexpressible 15 unpronounceable

ineffaceable: 9 indelible 12 ineradicable

ineffectively: 6 feebly

ineffectual: 4 dead, idle, vain, weak 6 futile 7 useless 8 hopeless, nugatory 9 fruitless, frustrate 10 unavailing 11 inefficient 13 inefficacious

inefficient: 4 poor 6 unable 7 useless 11 incompetent

inelastic: 4 limp 10 inflexible, unyielding

inelegant: 6 vulgar 7 awkward, blatant 9 graceless

ineluctable: 4 sure 5 fated 6 doomed 7 certain 10 inevitable 11 inescapable

inept: 4 dull, slow 5 unfit 6 absurd, clumsy 7 awkward, foolish 8 backward, unsuited 10 unbecoming, unsuitable 11 incompetent 13 inappropriate

inequal: 5 rough 6 uneven 7 unequal

inequality: 4 odds 9 disparity, diversity 10 unevenness 13 disproportion

inequity: 9 injustice 10 unfairness

ineradicable: 7 lasting 9 indelible, permanent 12 ineffaceable

inerrable: 8 unerring 10 infallible

inerrant: 8 unerring 10 infallible

inerratic: 5 fixed 7 settled 11 established

inert: 4 dead, dull, lazy, slow 5 still 6 stupid, supine, torpid 7 passive 8 immobile, inactive, indolent, lifeless, slothful, sluggish 9 apathetic, lethargic 10 motionless, phlegmatic

inertia: 5 sloth 8 idleness 9 indolence

inesculant: 8 inedible

inessential: 9 extrinsic 11 unimportant

inestimable: 9 priceless 10 invaluable 12 incalculable

inevitable: due 5 fated 7 certain, fateful 11 ineluctable, unavoidable

inexact: 4 free 5 rough 10 inaccurate

inexorable: 4 grim 5 stony 6 strict 7 ominous 8 rigorous 9 unbending 10 inflexible, relentless, unyielding 11 unrelenting

inexorability: 5 rigor

inexpedience: 6 unwise 9 imprudent 10 indiscreet 11 inadvisable 12 unprofitable 15 disadvantageous

inexpedient: 6 unwise 9 impolitic, imprudent 10 indiscreet 11 inadvisable, injudicious 12 unprofitable 15 disadvantageous

inexpensive: 5 cheap 6 frugal

inexperienced: raw 5 crude, green, naive, young 6 callow 7 untried 8 inexpert 10 amateurish

inexpert: 5 green 9 unskilled

inexplicable: 9 ambiguous, enigmatic 12 supernatural 13 preternatural

inexpressible: 8 nameless 9 ineffable 11 unutterable

inexpressive: 4 dull, dumb 13 unintelligent

infallible: 4 sure 7 certain 8 inerrant, unerring 9 inerrable, unfailing 11 indubitable

infamous: 4 base 6 bloody, odious 8 shameful 9 nefarious 10 detestable 11 ignominious 12 contemptible

infamy: 5 stain 6 baffle, defame 8 disgrace, dishonor, reproach 10 opprobrium

infancy: 10 incunabula(pl.) 11 incunabulum

infant: 4 babe, baby 5 child, minor 7 bambino, chrisom 8 bantling 9 foundling

in law: 5 minor

Indian: 7 papoose

murder: 11 infanticide

infantile paralysis: 13 poliomyelitis

infantryman: 6 doggie 7 dogface 8 fusilier 9 musketeer

infare: 12 housewarming

infatuate: 5 besot 6 befool 9 captivate

infatuated: mad 4 fond 6 engoue 7 engouee 8 enamored 9 enamoured

infatuatedness: 7 fatuity

infatuation: ate 4 rave 5 craze, folly 6 beguin 9 engoument 10 engouement

infeasible: 13 impracticable

infect: 5 taint 6 canker, defile, poison 7 pollute 11 contaminate

infection: 6 malady, plague 7 disease, illness

freedom from: 7 asepsis

infectious: 8 catching 9 vitiating 12 demoralizing, pestilential

infelicitous: 7 unhappy 11 unfortunate

infelicity: 6 misery 10 misfortune 11 unhappiness 12 wretchedness

infer: 4 hint 5 drive, educe, guess, imply 6 adduce, deduce, derive, gather 7 surmise 8 conclude, construe

inferal: 7 stygian

inference: 9 corollary, deduction 10 assumption, conclusion, derivation 11 consequence

inferential: 7 implied 8 illative 9 deductive

inferior: bad 4 base, cull, less, poor 5 baser, below, lower, minor, petit, petty, snide, worst 6 cagmag, common, feeble, impure, lesser, nether 7 cheaper, humbler, unequal 8 mediocre 9 underling 10 inadequate 11 subordinate 12 contemptible 13 insignificant

infernal: 7 avernal, hellish, satanic, stygian 8 all-fired, damnable, devilish, diabolic 9 tartarean 10 acherontic, demoniacal, diabolical

infernal machine: 4 bomb

inferno: 4 fire, hell

infertile: 4 poor 6 barren 7 sterile

infest: vex 5 beset, haunt 6 plague 7 overrun, torment

infester: 8 nuisance

infidel: 5 deist, pagan 6 giaour, Kaffir, paynim 7 atheist, skeptic 8 agnostic 10 unbeliever 11 freethinker

infiltrate: 4 leak, seep

infinite: 6 Ananta 7 endless, immense 9 boundless, countless, limitless, unlimited 11 everlasting, illimitable, measureless 12 immeasurable, interminable

absorption into: 7 nirvana

infinitesimal: 4 tiny 5 small 6 atomic, minute 10 evanescent

infinity: 4 olam 8 eternity

infirm: old 4 lame, weak 5 anile, crank, crazy, frail 6 cranky, feeble, senile, sickly 7 brittle, casalty, caselty, cazelty, craichy, dowless, dwaible, dwaibly, fragile 8 cassalty, casselty, decrepit 9 doddering 10 irresolute 11 debilitated, vacillating

infirmary: 8 hospital

infirmity: 4 vice 7 ailment, disease, failing, frailty 8 debility, sickness, weakness 10 feebleness

infirmness: 8 weakness

infix: 5 inset 6 insert 7 engrave, implant, impress, ingrain, instill 9 inculcate

inflame: 4 boil, fire, goad, heat, stir 5 anger, blain, chafe 6 anneal, arouse, enrage, excite, kindle, madden, rankle, redden 7 inflame 8 enkindle, irritate 10 exasperate

with love: 6 enamor

with rage: 6 madden

inflamed: red 5 angry, fiery 6 ablaze

inflaming: 7 burning

inflammable: 5 fiery 6 ardent, tinder 7 bitumen, piceous 9 excitable, irascible, irritable 10 accendible 11 combustible

inflammation: 4 fire 10 combustion, phlegmasia 13 conflagration

kind of: 4 gout 5 felon 6 iritis, omitis, otitis 7 coxitis, gonitis, rickets 8 adenitis, cystitis, myositis, rachitis, sarcitis 9 arthritis, gastritis, phlebitis, rhachitis 12 encephalitis 13 poliomyelitis

suffix: 4 itis

inflate: 4 blow, fill 5 bloat, elate, swell 6 aerify, dilate, emboss, expand, tumefy 7 bombast, distend 8 increase

inflated: 4 blew 5 blown 6 elated, turgid 7 aerated, bellied, bloated, bombast, dilated, fustian, pompous, swollen 8 expanded 9 bombastic, distended, flatulent, plethoric

inflect: bow 4 bend 5 curve 7 deflect 8 modulate

inflection: 4 tone

of words: 8 paradigm

inflex: 4 bend 7 inflect

inflexibility: 8 acampsia

inflexible: 4 dour, hard 5 eager, rigid, stiff, stony 6 strict 7 adamant 8 granitic, obdurate, rigorous 9 immovable, inelastic, unbending 10 implacable, inexorable, relentless 14 uncompromising

inflict: 4 deal 5 wreak 6 impose

great pain: 7 torture

vengeance: 5 wreak

infliction: 7 scourge

inflorescence: 6 raceme

axial circle of: 5 whorl

inflow: 6 influx, infuse

influence: win 4 bale, coax, egis, hank, heft, lead, move, pull, rule, sway 5 bribe, force, impel, lobby 6 affect, aspect, compel, effect, govern, induce, infuse, leaven, miasma, motive, sphere 7 attinge, attract, bearing, command, control, gravity, impress, inspire, mastery 8 hegemony, persuade, prestige, reaction 9 authority 10 ascendancy, ascendency, attraction, inducement 13 consideration

by fixed idea: 6 obsess

by reward: 5 bribe

region of: 5 orbit 6 sphere

influence peddling: 8 intrigue, lobbying

influenced: 6 biased 8 affected

easily: 7 pliable

influential: 5 grave 6 potent 8 forcible 9 effective, important, momentous

influenza: flu 5 virus 10 coqueluche

influx: 4 tide 6 inflow 7 illapse 9 affluence, influence, inpouring

infold: lap 4 fold, wrap 5 clasp, twine 6 employ, enwrap 7 embrace, envelop 8 envelope

inform: 4 post, tell 5 train 6 advise, notify, preach 7 apprise, apprize, educate, lighten 8 acquaint, instruct 9 advertise 11 communicate

informal: 8 sociable 10 colloquial 13 unceremonious 14 unconventional

conversation: 4 chat
information: 4 data(pl.), dope, news, word 5 aviso, datum 6 notice 7 tidings 9 direction, knowledge 11 instruction
condensed: 6 digest
detailed: 7 dossier
giver: spy 4 fink 5 stool 7 stoolie 8 informer, squealer, telltale 10 tattletale 11 stoolpigeon
personal: 7 dossier
informative: 11 instructive 12 enlightening
informed: up; hep, hip 4 wise 5 aware 6 posted 7 knowing 8 apprised 11 enlightened
informer: spy 4 fink, tout 5 stool 6 canary, gossip, pigeon, teller 7 delater, delator 8 observer, squealer, telltale 9 informant 10 discoverer, talebearer
military: spy 5 agent
infortune: 4 Mars 6 Saturn 7 Mercury 10 misfortune
infra: 5 after, below, under
infraction: 6 breach 8 trespass 10 intrustion 12 encroachment, infringement 13 transgression
infrequency: 6 rarity 8 rareness, solitude 9 isolation 12 uncommonness
infrequent: 4 rare 6 scarce, seldom, sparse 8 sporadic, uncommon, unwonted 10 occasional
infrequently: 6 rarely, seldom 12 occasionally
infringe: 6 defeat, refute 7 confute, destroy, intrude 8 encroach, trespass 9 frustrate
upon: 7 violate
infringement: 6 breach 8 trespass 9 violation 10 infraction 13 transgression 14 nonfulfillment
infuriate: vex 6 enrage, madden 7 enfelon
infuscate: 6 darken 7 obscure
infuse: 5 spoil, steep 6 aerify 7 engrain, implant, instill 9 inculcate, influence, insinuate, introduce
infusion: tea 7 extract 8 affusion, tincture 9 admixture, decoction
malt: 4 wort
infusoria: 10 vorticella
ingang: 5 porch 8 entrance 10 intestines
Inge play: 6 Picnic
ingeminate: 6 repeat 8 redouble 9 reiterate
ingenious: 4 cute, fine 5 acute, dedal, sharp, smart, witty 6 adroit, clever, crafty, daedal, gifted, subtle 7 cunning 8 dedalian, enginous, skillful, talented 9 daedalian, deviceful, inventive 11 intelligent, resourceful
ingeniousness: 5 skill 8 artifice
ingenuity: art 7 address, cunning 8 artifice 10 adroitness, cleverness 11 originality 13 inventiveness
ingenuous: 4 free, naif 5 frank, naive, noble, plain 6 candid, honest, innate, simple 7 artless, sincere 8 freeborn, innocent 9 guileless 10 unaffected, unreserved 15 unsophisticated
ingenuousness: 7 naivete 9 innocence
ingest: eat 7 swallow
ingle: 4 fire 5 blaze, flame 9 fireplace
inglenook: 11 cornerstone
ingleside: 8 fireside
ingluvies: 4 craw, crop
ingoing: 8 entrance
ingot: *metal:* gad, pig
worker: 6 barman
ingrained: 6 imbued, innate, native 7 inhered 9 saturated 10 inveterate
ingratiate: 4 fawn 7 commend, flatter 9 insinuate, introduce
ingredient: 7 element 9 component 11 constituent
baking: 4 alum, soda 5 yeast
cough-syrup: 8 glycerin
facial: 5 cream, rouge 6 powder 7 lanolin 8 lanoline
incense: 6 stacte
ink: 6 tannin
varnish: lac 5 drier, resin, rosin
ingress: 4 adit 5 entry 8 entrance
ingrowing nail: 7 acronyx
inhabit: 5 dwell 6 occupy, people, settle 7 possess 9 establish
inhabitant: cit 6 inmate, native, people, tenant 7 citizen, denizen, dweller 8 habitant, resident
desert: 4 Arab 5 nomad
earliest known: 9 aborigine
foreign: 5 alien 10 alienicola
local: 6 native
moon: 8 selenite
northern: 11 septentrion
suffix: ese, ite
inhabited: 5 lived 7 dwelled, habited, peopled 9 populated
inhabiting: *caves:* 7 spelean 8 spelaean
ground: 11 terricolous
grove: 7 nemoral
island: 7 nesiote
lake: 9 lacustral
marsh: 10 limnophile
sea: 7 pelagic
inhale: 4 draw 7 attract, breathe, respire 9 embreathe
inharmonious: 6 absurd, atonal 7 jarring 9 dissonant, unmusical 10 discordant 11 conflicting 12 antagonistic
inhere: 6 belong, innate 7 ingrain

inherent: 6 inborn, innate 7 infixed 8 immanent 9 essential, immanence, intrinsic 10 indwelling, subsistent 13 indispensable
inheritable: 10 hereditary
inheritance: 6 legacy 8 heirship, heredity, heritage 9 cleronomy, heritance
by first-born: 13 primogeniture
portion: 8 legitime
restricted: 10 entailment
Scotch law: 5 annat
seizer: 6 abator
inherited: 6 native
inheritor: 4 heir 7 heiress, heritor, legatee
inheritrix 7 heiress
inhibit: 4 curb 5 check 6 forbid, hinder 8 prohibit, restrain 9 interdict
inhibition: ban, bar 7 embargo 9 restraint 11 prohibition 12 interdiction
inhuman: 4 fell 5 cruel 6 brutal, savage 7 beastly, bestial, brutish 8 devilish 9 barbarous, bloodless, ferocious 10 diabolical
inhumane: 5 cruel 6 brutal
inhumanity: 7 cruelty 9 barbarity
inhume: 4 bury 5 inter 6 entomb 7 deposit
inimical: 6 averse, frosty 7 hostile 8 contrary 9 repugnant 10 unfriendly 11 unfavorable
iniquitous: bad, ill 5 wrong 6 sinful, unjust, wicked 9 nefarious
iniquity: sin 4 evil, vice 5 crime, guilt 8 darkness 9 injustice 10 wickedness
initial: 5 first 6 letter, paraph 7 opening 8 entrance, monogram 9 beginning, incipient 10 commencing, elementary
design of: 8 monogram
initial payment: 4 ante, down 7 deposit
initiate: 4 head, open 5 admit, begin, enrol, start 6 enroll, ground, induct 7 install, instate 8 commence, inchoate 9 introduce, originate 10 inaugurate
initiation: 9 admission, beginning, induction 10 admittance, introduced 12 commencement
initiative: 5 getup 6 energy 8 aptitude, gumption, petition
injection: 4 hypo 5 enema
injudicious: 6 unwise 9 impolitic, imprudent 10 indiscreet 11 inexpedient
injunction: 4 hest, writ 5 order 6 behest, charge 7 mandate, precept, process 9 direction
injure: mar 4 harm, hurt, maim 5 abuse, spoil, sully, wound, wrong 6 impair, insult 7 affront, cripple 8 maltreat 9 disfigure
by bruising: 7 contuse
by scorching: 4 burn, char 5 singe
injured: 9 aggrieved
injury: ill, mar 4 bane, evil, harm, hurt, loss, risk, scar, tort 5 burst, chafe, wound, wrack, wrong 6 damage, deface, lesion, mayhem, scathe, trauma 7 hurting, scratch 8 crepance, hardship, nuisance, traumata(pl.) 9 contusion, detriment, injustice 10 aggression, disservice, impairment 11 displeasure, impeachment 12 disadvantage
causing: 7 malefic 9 traumatic
pert. to: 5 noxal
sense of: 7 umbrage
injustice: 5 wrong 6 injury 8 hardship, inequity, iniquity 9 grievance 10 imposition, unfairness
ink: 7 blacken 8 millrynd
pert. to: 10 atramental
ink fish: 5 squid 6 cuttle
inkling: 4 hint, idea 5 rumor, scent 6 desire, report 7 glimpse 10 glimmering, intimation 11 inclination
inky: 5 black 9 cimmerian 11 atramentous
inlaid: 6 mosaic 9 champleve, decorated
inland: 8 domestic, interior
sea: 4 Aral 5 Black
inlay: 5 adorn, couch 6 insert 7 enchase 8 ornament 9 marquetry
work: 6 mosaic 9 certosina, certosino, champleve
inlet: oe; arm, bay, cay, geo, gio, ria 4 cove, hope, rias(pl.), slew, sloo, slue 5 admit, bayou, bight, creek, fiord, firth, fjord, fleet, haven, inlay, sound 6 estero, slough, strait 7 estuary, orifice 8 entrance
coastline: 5 bight 6 strait
inmate: 5 guest, lifer 6 termer 8 domestic, occupant, prisoner 10 inhabitant
harem: oda
inmost: 8 intimate 9 innermost
inn: pub 4 host, khan 5 fonda, hotel, house, serai, tambo, venta 6 fonduk, harbor, hostel, hostry, imaret, public, tavern 7 albergo, auberge, boliche, fondaca, fondouk, fonduck, gasthof, harbour, hospice, hostage 8 choultry, gasthaus, hostelry, wayhouse 9 hosthouse 10 harbergage, herbergage 11 caravansary 12 caravanserai
innards: 4 guts 7 numbles 8 entrails
innate: 4 born 6 inborn, inbred, inhere, native 7 connate, natural 8 inherent 9 ingrained, intrinsic 10 congenital, hereditary 11 instinctive 14 constitutional
inner: ben 5 ental 6 inside, inward 8 esoteric, interior, internal
comb. form: ent 4 ento 5 ental
innermost: 6 inmost
innet: 7 ensnare
Innisfail: 4 Eire, Erin 7 Ireland
innkeeper: 4 host 5 cheap 7 hostler 8 boniface, caupones, traiteur 10 aubergiste
innocence: 6 purity 7 naivete 11 sinlessness 13 guiltlessness

symbol of: **7** diamond
innocent: 4 free, naif **5** bluet, naive **6** chaste, dovish, simple **7** artless, chrisom, cleanly, upright **9** blameless, childlike, guileless, guiltless, ingenuous, stainless **10** immaculate, unblamable **12** simpleminded **15** unsophisticated
Hebrew: **8** zaccheus **9** zacchaeus
innocent one: 4 babe, lamb **5** child **6** infant
innocuous: 8 harmless, innocent **9** innoxious **11** inoffensive, unoffending
innovation: 6 novity **7** novelty
innuendo: 4 clue, hint, slur **8** allusion **10** intimation **11** implication, insinuation
innumerable: 4 many **6** legion, myriad
Ino's grandfather: 6 Agenor
inoculate: 6 immune **7** engraft, implant
inodorous: 8 odorless **9** scentless
inoffensive: 8 harmless **9** innocuous
inoperative: 4 dead
inopinate: 10 unexpected
inopportune: bad **8** ill-timed, untimely **10** malapropos **11** importunate **12** unseasonable
inorb: 8 encircle
inordinate: 5 undue **8** all'fired **9** excessive **10** disorderly, immoderate **11** unregulated **12** unrestrained
inorganic: 7 mineral
inquest: 5 quest **6** search **7** inquiry **11** examination **13** investigation
official: **7** coroner
inquiet: 6 uneasy **7** disturb **8** disquiet, restless **9** disturbed
inquire: ask, esk(Sc.) **4** seek **5** frayn, price, query, spere **6** demand, frayne, harken **7** examine, hearken **8** question **11** interrogate, investigate
inquirer: 5 asker **6** seeker **7** zetetic **8** searcher
inquiring: 7 curious
inquiry: 5 query **6** examen **7** examine **8** question, research **11** examination **13** investigation
for lost goods: **6** tracer
inquisition: 4 hunt **6** search **11** examination **13** investigation
inquisitive: 4 nosy **5** nosey **6** prying **7** curious **8** meddling **10** meddlesome
inquisitiveness: 9 curiosity
inquisitor: 5 prier **6** tracer **8** examiner
inroad: 4 raid **5** foray **6** breach **8** invasion **9** incursion, irruption **12** encroachment
insane: mad **4** daft, luny **5** balmy, crazy, daffy, loony, manic **6** cranky, crazed **7** frantic, furious **8** bughouse, demented, deranged, distract, frenetic **9** delirious, phrenetic, psychotic
house for: **6** asylum, bedlam
to make: **6** dement **7** derange
insanity: 5 folie, mania **6** frenzy, lunacy **7** madness, vesania **8** delirium, dementia **9** psychosis **10** aberration, alienation **11** derangement
temporary: **7** amentia
insatiable: 6 greedy **9** voracious
insatiate: 10 insatiable **11** unsatisfied
inscribe, enscribe: 4 etch **5** delve, enter, stamp, write **6** blazon, enroll, indite, scroll **7** ascribe, engrave **8** dedicate, describe **9** character **12** characterize
inscribed: 8 lettered **9** dedicated
on stone: **10** lapidarian
with Teutonic characters: **5** runed
inscription: 6 legend **7** epigram, writing **8** epigraph **11** description **14** superscription
appropriate: **5** motto
end of book: **8** colophon
explanatory: **6** tituli(pl.) **7** titulus
on coins: **5** sigla
tomb: **7** epitaph
inscrutable: 6 secret **10** mysterious **12** impenetrable, inexplorable, unfathomable **16** incomprehensible
insculpture: 7 carving **11** inscription
insect: ant, bee, bug, fly **4** flea, gnat, goga, gogo, lice, mite, moth, tick, wasp **5** emmet, gogga, roach **6** beetle, earwig, mantis, spider, weevil **7** cricket, katydid, termite **9** bumblebee, centipede
adult: **6** imago
antenna: **4** palp **6** feeler
back surface: **5** notum
chirping: **7** cricket
destructive: **5** scale **7** termite **8** predator
dipterous: **8** mosquito
eye: **6** ocelli(pl.), stemma **7** ocellus
female: **4** gyne
genus of: **4** nepa **5** emesa **6** acarus, cicada, cicala, mantis, termes
hard covering: **6** chitin
hymenopterous: ant, bee **4** wasp **6** sawfly **7** gallfly **10** ichneumons
immature: **4** pupa **5** larva **6** larvae(pl.) **9** chrysalis
insectivorous bird: **5** pewee, vireo **8** redstart **10** flycatcher
kind of: dun, loa **5** aphid, aphis, bicho, borer **6** cicada, earwig, tremex, tsetse, vermin **7** attacus, Diptera, stinger **9** centipede, ephemeral
long-legged: **5** emesa
molting of: **7** ecdysis
order: **7** diptera **17** palaeodictyoptera
organ: **8** plantula **9** plantulae(pl.)
parasitic: **4** lice **5** louse
part of: **4** nota **5** chirr, media, palps **7** antenna **8** pronotum, tentacle

pert. to: 11 entomologic
plate: 6 scutum
resin: lac
science: 10 entomology
secretion: lac
small: 4 flea, gnat, mite 5 aphid, aphis, micro, midge 6 garfly 8 bullhead
social: ant, bee 5 emmet
stage: 4 pupa 5 imago, larva 6 instar 9 chrysalis
stinging: ant, bee 4 wasp 6 hornet 7 sciniph 12 yellowjacket
trap: web
winged: bee 4 wasp 6 hornet 12 yellowjacket
wingless: 4 flea 6 aptera(pl.)
insecticide: DDT 9 hellebore
insecure: 5 eemis, immis, loose, risky, shaky 6 infirm, unsafe, unsure 7 casalty, caselty, cazelty 8 cassalty, casselty, perilous, unstable 9 dangerous, hazardous 10 precarious
insecurity: 5 peril
insee: 8 foretell
inseminate: sow 7 implant, instill 9 fertilize 10 impregnate
insensate: 4 surd 5 blind, harsh 6 brutal, stupid 7 brutish, fatuous, foolish 9 senseless, unfeeling, untouched 10 insensible
insensibility: 4 coma, damp 6 apathy, torpor, trance 8 lethargy 9 analgesia 10 anesthesia 11 insentience 12 indifference
insensible: 4 dull 7 brutish 8 obdurate 9 inanimate, insensate, unfeeling 10 insentient 11 insensitive, meaningless, unconscious 13 imperceptible
insensitive: 5 blunt 9 inanimate, unfeeling 10 insensible, insentient 16 unimpressionable
insentient: 10 insensible 11 insensitive
insert: 5 foist, infix, inlay, inset 9 interpose 11 intercalate, interpolate
for growth: 5 graft 7 engraft
triangular: 4 gore 5 wedge
insertion: 5 inset
kind of: 5 shinn 11 parenthesis 13 interpolation 13 intercalation
of sound in word: 10 epenthesis
inset: 4 gore 5 imbed, infix, panel 6 gusset, insert 7 appoint, engraft, implant 9 insertion
insheathe: 6 emboss
inside: 5 inner 6 lining, within 8 interior 9 partition
toward: 5 entad 6 inward
inside out: 7 everted
insidious: 4 deep 6 covert 7 cunning 8 guileful 9 concealed, deceitful 10 fallacious, fraudulent 11 disaffected, treacherous
insight: ken 11 discernment 12 clairvoyance
insignia: 4 mark 5 badge 6 emblem
kind of: tie 7 caducei(pl.), regalia 8 caduceus
insignificance: 10 effacement
insignificant: 4 puny 5 dinky, petit, petty 6 paltry 7 trivial 8 inferior, trifling 9 minuscule, senseless 10 immaterial 12 contemptible
part: bit 4 iota 5 tithe 8 molehill
insincere: 5 false 7 feigned 9 deceitful, deceptive 12 hypocritical
insinuate: 4 hint 5 imply 6 allude, infuse 7 implant, instill 9 introduce, penetrate 10 ingratiate, serpentine
insinuation: 4 hint 8 innuendo
insipid: dry 4 dead, fade, flat, fond, pale, pall, tame 5 bauch, prosy, stale, tepid, vapid, waugh 6 flashy, jejune 7 prosaic 8 lifeless 9 pointless, tasteless 10 monotonous, spiritless, unanimated 13 uninteresting
insipience: 9 stupidity 11 foolishness
insist: 6 demand 9 persevere
insistence: 7 urgency 11 persistence
insnare: web 4 trap 5 benet, noose 6 enmesh, trapan, trepan
insolence: 5 nerve 6 insult 8 audacity 9 arrogance, contumacy, contumely, impudence 11 haughtiness, presumption 12 impertinence
insolent: 4 pert, rude 5 bardy 6 brazen 7 abusive, defiant 8 arrogant, impudent 9 audacious, hubristic 11 overbearing 12 contemptuous, contumelious
insolvency: 7 failure 10 bankruptcy
insolvent: 5 broke 6 busted, ruined 8 bankrupt 9 destitute 12 impoverished
insomnia: 7 ahypnia 8 agrypnia
insouciant: 4 calm 8 carefree, heedless 10 unbothered 11 indifferent, unconcerned
inspect: pry, see 5 aview, grade, visit 6 peruse 7 examine 8 consider 9 supervise 10 scrutinize
inspection: 4 oyer 6 parade, review 8 scrutiny 11 examination
inspector: 6 bishop, conner, sealer 8 examiner, overseer
inspiration: 4 muse 6 breath 8 afflatus 9 afflation 10 aspiration
poetic: 7 pierian
pretender to: 6 eolist
inspire (see also **inspirit**): 4 draw, fire, move, stir 5 exalt, imbue 6 aspire, inhale 7 actuate, animate, enliven, implant 8 motivate 9 encourage, influence, stimulate
inspired: 5 vatic

inspirit (see also **inspire**): 4 stir 5 cheer, elate, rouse 7 cherish, comfort, hearten, quicken 10 invigorate

inspissate: 7 thicken 8 condense 10 incrassate

instability: 8 fluidity 11 flexibility 12 unsteadiness 13 changeability 14 disequilibrium

install: 4 seat, vest 6 induct, invest 7 instate 8 initiate 9 establish 10 inaugurate

installation: 9 vestiture

instance: 4 case, sign, urge 5 token 7 example, present, request, symptom 8 presence 9 importune 10 succession 11 demonstrate, instigation

instancy: 7 urgency 8 pressure 9 imminence 10 insistence 17 instantaneousness

instant: 4 urge 5 clink, flash, gliff, glisk, trice 6 breath, minute, moment, second, urgent 7 solicit 8 pressing 9 handwhile, immediate 11 importunate

instantly: now 4 just 8 directly

instate: set 5 endow 6 bestow, confer, invest 7 install 8 initiate 9 establish

instead: 4 else 6 in lieu 10 equivalent, substitute

of: for

instigate: egg 4 abet, goad, move, prod, sick, spur, urge 5 impel 6 compel, excite, foment, incite, prompt, suborn 7 provoke 8 motivate 9 encourage, stimulate

instigator: 6 author 10 ringleader

instill: 5 imbue, infix 6 impart, infuse 7 implant, pervade 9 inculcate, insinuate

instinct: 5 knack 7 impulse 8 aptitude 11 instigation

instinctive: 6 innate 7 natural 8 inherent, original 9 automatic, intuitive 11 involuntary, spontaneous

institute: 5 begin, erect, found 6 asylum, ordain 7 academy 8 academie, initiate, organize 9 establish, originate 10 inaugurate

institution: 6 clinic, school 7 academy, college 8 hospital, seminary 10 university 12 constitution

instruct: 4 lead, show 5 breed, coach, drill, edify, guide, teach, train, tutor 6 direct, inform, preach 7 counsel, educate 8 document 9 enlighten 10 discipline 12 indoctrinate

instruction: act 4 lore, news, tora 5 torah 6 advice, assize, charge, lesson 7 precept, tuition 8 practice 9 erudition, knowledge 10 commission 12 propaedeutic

art of: 8 pedagogy

period: 4 term, year 7 quarter, session 8 semester 9 trimester

place of: 13 conservatoire

instructive: 8 didactic, sermonic

instructor: don 5 coach, tutor 6 docent, mentor 7 acharya, teacher, trainer 9 preceptor, professor

instrument (see also **apparatus; device; tool**): 4 deed, writ 5 agent, means 6 medium 7 utensil, writing 9 appliance, implement 11 contrivance

altitude: aba 9 altimeter 10 altazimuth

board: 5 panel

calculating: 6 abacus 9 sliderule

copying: 10 hectograph

cutting: 5 knife, razor 6 scythe, shears, sickle 8 scissors

for studying motion: 11 stroboscope

musical: See **musical instrument**

percussion: 12 Glockenspiel

sacred: 4 urim

sealed: 4 deed 5 crypt, vault 6 escrow

sharp-edged: 5 knife, razor 6 scythe, shears, sickle 7 cutlery 8 scissors

surveying: 7 transit 10 theodolite

instrumental: 5 organ 6 needed, useful 7 helpful, organic 11 ministerial

instrumentalist: 5 luter 6 harper 7 flutist, harpist, pianist 8 minstrel 9 cornetist 10 trombonist

instrumentality: 5 means 6 agency, medium

insubordinate: 5 rebel 6 unruly 7 riotous 8 mutinous, perverse 9 seditious 10 headstrong, refractory, unyielding 11 disobedient, intractable 12 contumacious

insubstantial: 4 airy, thin 5 frail 6 flimsy 10 intangible 12 apparitional

insufficient: 4 bare, poor 5 short 6 feeble, scanty, scarce 7 unequal, wanting 9 deficient 10 inadequate 14 incommensurate

insular: 8 islander, isolated 9 separated

insulate: 7 isolate 8 isolated 9 segregate 10 quarantine

material to: 4 cork 6 Kerite, rubber

insulated: 5 isled, taped

insulator: 4 tape 5 cleat

insult: cag 4 slap, slur 5 abuse, flout, frump 6 offend, revile 7 abusion, affront, offense, outrage 9 contumely, indignity, insolence

insulting: 4 rude 8 arrogant 9 offensive 10 despiteful, scurrilous 11 opprobrious 12 contumelious

insurance: 8 guaranty, warranty 9 assurance 10 protection

computer: 7 actuary 8 adjuster

payee: 11 beneficiary

system: 7 tontine

insure (see also **ensure**): 6 assure 7 furnish 10 underwrite

jointly: 8 coinsure

insurgent (see also **insubordinate**): 5 rebel 10 rebellious

insurmountable: 10 impassable, invincible 11 insuperable 13 unconquerable
insurrection: 6 mutiny, revolt, rising 9 rebellion
insusceptible: 6 immune 9 unfeeling
intact: 5 sound, whole 8 complete, unbroken 9 undefiled, undivided, uninjured, untouched 10 unimpaired
intaglio: cut, gem 9 represent
intake: net 4 gain, gate 6 profit 8 receipts 11 contraction
intangible: 5 vague 10 immaterial, impalpable 13 imperceptible, insubstantial
integer: one 5 whole 8 integral
integral: 5 whole 8 totality
integrate: mix 4 join 5 unite 6 entire
integrity: 7 honesty, probity 9 chariness, constancy
integument: 4 aril, coat 5 testa 7 cuticle, envelop 8 covering, envelope 10 investment
intellect: wit 4 mind, nous 5 brain 6 genius, reason 9 mentality 12 intelligence
limited in: 7 moronic
intellection: 6 notion 9 cognition, knowledge 12 apprehension 13 comprehension, understanding
intellectual: 5 ideal 6 brainy, mental, noetic, sophic 7 egghead 8 highbrow 9 epistemic
intelligence: 4 chit, mind, news, word 5 sense 6 esprit, notice, wisdom 8 learning 13 understanding
used alone: 6 noesis
without: 4 dull 5 inane 6 stupid
intelligence test deviser: 5 Binet, Simon
intelligencer: spy 9 informant, messenger 10 newsmonger
intelligent: 5 acute, aware, smart 6 bright, mental 7 knowing 8 rational, sensible 9 cognizant 13 understanding
intelligentsia: 13 intellectuals
intelligible: 5 clear, plain 10 conceptual 11 perspicuous 12 apprehensive 13 apprehensible, intellectible, suprasensuous 14 comprehensible
intemperate: 4 pure 6 severe 7 extreme 9 excessive, inclement, inviolate, undefiled 10 immoderate, inordinate 12 ungovernable
intend: aim 4 mean, mint, plan 5 allot, ettle 6 design 7 destine, purpose
intended: 6 fiance 7 fiancee
intense: hot 4 deep, hard, keen 5 acute, great, heavy, vivid 6 ardent, severe, strong 7 chronic, earnest, extreme, fervent, violent, zealous 8 grievous, powerful, strained, vehement 9 assiduous, excessive, strenuous 11 far-reaching
intensify: 5 exalt 6 deepen 7 enhance 8 condense, heighten, increase 9 aggravate 10 accentuate 11 concentrate
intensity: 5 depth 6 chroma, timbre
intensive: 7 intense 8 vehement 9 ascensive
intent: aim 4 deep, dole(Sc.), fell, rapt 5 eager, ettle, fixed, tense 6 design, effect 7 earnest, meaning, purpose 8 absorbed, diligent, sedulous 9 attentive, engrossed, intention, steadfast 10 determined
intention: aim, end 4 goal, hent, will 6 animus, attent, design, intent, object 7 meaning, purpose 11 designation 13 contemplation
intentional: 8 designed 9 voluntary 10 deliberate
inter: 4 bury 5 earth, grave 6 entomb, inhume
interagent: 6 medium 12 intermediary
intercalary: 8 inserted 12 intercalated, interpolated
intercalary month: 6 Veadar
intercalate: 7 insert 9 insinuate, interpose 11 interpolate
intercede: 7 mediate 9 arbitrate, interpose, intervene
intercept: 4 bury, head 5 catch 8 gaincope, retrench 9 forestall, interrupt
intercessor: 8 advocate, mediator
interchange: 4 vary 7 commute, permute 8 converse, exchange 9 alternate 10 transposal 11 reciprocate 12 conversation
interchangeable: 10 reversible 11 convertible
intercolumniation: 7 eustyle, systyle 8 diastyle 10 araeostyle
interconnection: 5 nexus
intercourse: 7 dealing 8 business, commerce, converse 9 communion 10 connection, fellowship 12 conversation 13 communication
interdict: ban 4 veto 5 debar, fence 6 forbid 7 inhibit 8 prohibit 9 proscribe
interdiction: 4 tabu 5 taboo
interest: 4 good 5 fetch 6 behalf, behoof, engage, profit 7 attract, concern 8 sympathy 9 advantage, anatocism, entertain, fascinate
exorbitant: 5 usury
in law: 5 right, title
lose: 4 tire
rate: 5 yield
without: 6 jejune 9 apathetic
interested: 4 rapt 6 caring
interfacing: 7 dineric
interfere: 5 barge, clash 6 meddle, tamper 7 collide, disturb, intrude 8 obstruct, sabotage 9 interpose, intervene
interference: 6 static

interferometer: 6 etalon

interim: 8 interval, meantime

interior: ben 5 ental, inner 6 inland, inside 8 midlands

interjection: aw, lo; boo, hic, rah 4 ahem, alas, amen, egad, ouch, well 6 aroint 7 criminy 11 exclamation

interlace: mat 5 braid, twine, weave 6 pleach, raddle 7 entwine 9 interfret, interlink 10 intertwine, interweave 11 interpolate

interlaced: 7 complex

interlock: 4 knit 5 unite 6 clench, engage 9 interlace 11 interrelate

interlocution: 12 conversation 13 communication

interlocutory: 12 intermediate

interlope: 6 insert 7 intrude, obtrude 8 trespass 11 intermeddle, interpolate

interlude: 5 truce 6 verset 8 entracte, ritornel 10 ritornelle

short: 6 verset

intermediary: 5 agent 6 medium 8 mediator 9 go-between 10 ambassador, interagent

intermediate: 5 mesne 6 median, middle 7 between 10 interposed 11 intervening

interminable: 7 endless, eternal 8 infinite, timeless, unending 9 boundless, limitless, unlimited

interminably: 7 forever

intermingle: 8 intermix 10 infiltrate

intermission: 4 rest, stop 5 dwell, pause 6 devall, recess 7 respite 8 entracte, vacation 9 cessation 10 suspension 13 interposition 14 discontinuance

intermittent: 6 broken, fitful 8 periodic 9 recurrent, spasmodic 11 alternating, interrupted 12 pretermitted

intermix: 6 mingle 10 interweave

intern: 6 doctor, inhume 7 confine, trainee

internal: 5 inner 6 inward, mental 8 enclosed 9 spiritual

combustion engine part: 5 timer

international: 9 world-wide

International: 4 song 9 Comintern

international business: 6 cartel

international organization: UN; WHO 4 NATO 5 SEATO 6 UNESCO

internecine: 6 deadly

interpellation: 7 summons 10 prevention 12 interception, intercession, interruption

interpolate: 5 alter 6 insert 9 introduce 11 intercalate

interpose: 6 thrust 7 intrude, mediate 9 intercede, interfere, intervene

interpret: 4 read, rede 5 aread, areed, gloze 6 decode, define, expose, render 7 explain, expound 8 construe 9 elucidate, explicate, translate 10 literalize, understand

interpretation: 5 gloss, sense 6 oracle 7 anagoge 8 exegesis 11 declaration

of science: 8 exegesis 12 hermeneutics

interpreter: 5 ulema 7 exegete 8 exponent 9 exegesist, hermeneut 11 oneirocritic

interpretive: 11 explanatory, hermeneutic 12 constructive

interrogate: ask 5 query 7 examine, inquire 8 question

interrogation: 4 quiz 5 probe, query 7 inquest 8 question 11 examination

interrogation mark: 7 eroteme

interrogative: how, who, why 4 what, when 5 where 8 question

interrupt: 4 stop 5 break, burst, cease, check 6 arrest, hinder, thwart 7 derange, disturb, suspend 8 obstruct 9 intercept, pretermit 11 discontinue

interruption: gap 5 dwell, pause 6 breach, hiatus 7 caesura 9 cessation 12 intermission

intersect: cut 4 meet 5 cross 6 divide, pierce 9 decussate

intersection: 6 secant 7 chiasma

interstice: 4 mesh, pore, seam 5 chink, crack, space 6 areola, areole, cranny 7 crevice 8 interval

pert. to: 7 areolar

intervolve: 4 coil, roll, wind 5 twist

intertwine: 4 knit, lace 5 twist 6 tangle 7 ensnare, ensnarl, entwine 8 entangle 9 interlace 10 intertwist

intertwist: 10 intertwine

interval: gap 4 rest, span 5 break, space 6 breach, hiatus, recess 7 caesura, respite 8 entracte 9 cessation 12 intermission

at irregular: 12 sporadically

musical: 5 fifth, ninth, sixth, tenth, third 6 fourth, octave, second 7 seventh

intervene: 7 mediate 9 intercede, interpose

intervening: 5 mesne(law) 12 intermediate

interview: see 7 consult, hearing 8 audience, question 9 encounter 10 conference 12 consultation

interweave: mat 4 plat 5 braid, plait 6 enlace, raddle, splice, wattle 8 entangle, intermix 9 interlace

intestinal: 7 enteric

intestine: gut 5 inner 6 inward 7 viscera 8 domestic, internal

comb. form: 6 entero

part: ile 5 ileum, ilium

pert. to: 7 enteric

intice: See **entice**

intimacy: 8 affinity 10 connection

intimate: sib 4 boon, hint, homy, near 5 bosom, chief, close, homey, imply 6 allude, chummy, homely, inmost, secret 7 signify, suggest 8 announce, domestic, familiar, friendly, informal, personal 9 associate, confidant 11 contubernal 12 acquaintance, confidential

intimately: 4 inly

intimation: 4 clue, hint, wind 5 scent 6 notice 7 inkling 10 suggestion 11 declaration

intimidate: awe, cow 5 abash, bully, daunt, deter, scare 6 hector 7 overawe, terrify 8 browbeat, dispirit, frighten 9 blackmail, terrorize

into: 4 unto 5 among, until 6 inside

prefix: en

that: 9 thereinto

intolerance: 9 misoneism

intolerant: 6 narrow 7 bigoted 8 dogmatic 9 illiberal, impatient 10 prejudiced

intonation: 4 sing 5 chant, sound 7 sonance

intonational: 7 tonetic

intone: 4 cant, sing 5 chant 8 modulate 10 cantillate

intort: 4 curl 5 twist

intoxicant (see also **alcoholic drink, liquor**): fox, gin, rum 4 wine 5 drink 6 excite, liquor 7 whiskey 9 inebriate, stimulate

intoxicated: 4 high, shot, tosy 5 bosky, drunk 6 boiled, soused, stewed 7 excited, screwed 8 besotted, glorious 9 crapulous 10 crapulated, inebriated, tosticated 11 capernoited

intoxicating: 5 heady

intracellular: 8 histonal

intractable: 6 unruly, wilful 7 haggard, restive 8 indocile, mutinous, obdurate, perverse, stubborn 9 obstinate 10 headstrong, refractory 11 disobedient, unteachable 12 contumacious, ungovernable 14 uncontrollable

intrada: 7 prelude 12 introduction

intranquillity: ado 12 restlessness

intransigent: 7 radical 14 irreconcilable, uncompromising

intrepid: 4 bold 5 brave, hardy, nervy 6 daring, heroic 7 assured, doughty, gallant, valiant 8 fearless, resolute, valorous 9 dauntless, dreadless, nerveless 10 courageous

intrepidity: 4 guts 5 nerve, valor 6 daring 7 bravery, courage 8 boldness

intricate: 4 hard 5 dedal 6 daedal, knotty 7 complex, Gordian, sinuous 8 involved 9 Daedalian, difficult, involuted 10 perplexing 11 complicated 12 labyrinthine

intrigue: 4 plot 5 cabal, charm 6 brigue, deceit, design, scheme 7 faction 8 artifice, collogue 9 fascinate 10 concoction, conspiracy 11 machination

intrinsic: 4 real, true 6 inborn, inbred, innate, native 7 genuine, natural 8 immanent, inherent, intimate 9 essential, necessary 11 inseparable 13 indispensable

intrinsically: 5 per se

introduce: 5 begin, enter, start, usher 6 broach, herald, infuse, insert 7 forerun, implant, precede, preface, present, sponsor 8 approach, initiate 9 insinuate 10 ingratiate

introduction: cue 5 debut, proem 7 intrada, introit, isagoge, preface, prelude 8 entrance, exordium, foreword, preamble, prologue, protasis 11 preparation

of new word: 7 neology

to treatise: 7 isagoge

introductory: 8 exordial 9 prefatory, prelusive

introductory cry: 4 hear, oyes, oyez

introit: 8 entrance 12 introduction

intromit: 5 admit 6 insert

intrude: 6 invade, meddle 7 obtrude 8 infringe, trespass 9 interfere, interlope, interpose

intruder: 8 outsider

intrusion: 10 aggression, infraction

intrusive: 7 curious

intrust: See **entrust**

intuit: 4 feel 5 sense 8 perceive 9 apprehend

intuition: 5 hunch 8 instinct

inulase: 6 enzyme

inunction: 8 ointment 9 anointing

pert. to: 7 aliptic

inundate: 4 flow 5 drown, flood 6 deluge 8 overflow, submerge 9 overwhelm 10 overspread

inundation: 8 alluvion

inure, enure: 5 steel 6 harden, season 7 toughen 8 accustom 9 habituate 10 discipline 11 acclimatize

inurn: 4 bury 6 entomb

inustion: 7 burning 13 cauterization

inutile: bad 7 useless 8 unusable 9 worthless 12 unprofitable

inutterable: See **unutterable**

invade: 4 raid 6 irrupt, offend 7 assault, intrude, overrun 8 encroach, entrench, intrench, trespass

invader: Hun 4 Pict 6 raider 8 intruder

invalid: 4 null 6 feeble, infirm, sickly 8 nugatory 11 ineffective 14 valetudinarian

invalidate: 4 undo 5 annul, break 7 abolish

invaluable: 8 precious 9 priceless 11 inestimable 13 inappreciable

invariable: 4 same 6 steady 7 uniform 8 constant 9 continual, immutable 10 unchanging 11 determinate 12 unchangeable

invariably: 6 always 7 forever

invasion (see also **invade**): 6 inroad 9 incursion 10 aggression

invective: 5 abuse, taunt 6 tirade 7 railing 8 diatribe, reproach 12 vituperation

inveigh: 9 fulminate

inveigle: 4 coax, lure 5 snare 6 allure, entice, entrap 8 persuade

invent: 4 coin, form, make, vamp 5 feign, forge, frame 6 create, design, devise, patent 7 concoct, fashion 8 contrive, discover, engineer 9 fabricate, improvise, originate 11 manufacture

invention: 7 fiction, figment

inventive: 6 adroit 7 fertile 9 ingenious

inventor: 6 author, coiner 7 creator 8 engineer 10 discoverer, originator

airplane: 6 Fokker, Wright

baseball: 9 Doubleday

condensing steam engine: 4 Watt

cotton gin: 7 Whitney

dynamite: 5 Nobel

electric light: 6 Edison

electric motor: 9 Davenport

elevator: 4 Otis

gun: 4 Colt 9 Remington

internal combustion engine: 6 Lenoir 7 Daimler

logarithm: 6 Napier

phonograph: 6 Edison

photography: 6 Niepce, Talbot

power loom: 10 Cartwright

printing: 9 Gutenberg

printing press: Hoe

radio: 7 Marconi 8 de Forest

safety lamp: 4 Davy

sewing machine: 4 Howe 6 Lester

steam locomotive: 10 Stephenson

steamboat: 5 Fitch 6 Fulton, Rumsey

telegraph: 5 Morse

telephone: 4 Bell

television: 6 Nipkow

wireless: 7 Marconi

inventor's right: 6 patent

inventory: 4 list 7 account, catalog, listing 8 register, schedule 9 catalogue

inveracity: fib, lie 9 falseness

inverse: 8 opposite

invert: 4 turn 7 reverse

invertebrate: 4 worm 5 polyp 6 insect, sponge 7 mollusk 8 arachnid 12 coelenterate

group: 7 radiata

invest: don 4 belt, gird, gown, robe, vest, wrap 5 array, crown, dress, endow, endue, imbue 6 clothe, confer, embark, ordain 7 envelop, install, instate 8 accredit, enthrone, surround

investigate: pry 4 nose 5 probe, study, trace 6 search 7 examine, explore, inquire 8 research 10 scrutinize

investigator: 6 prober, tracer 9 detective

body of: 4 jury 5 panel 9 committee

investiture: 7 clothes, vesture 8 clothing

investment: 7 garment 8 vestment

list: 9 portfolio

investor: 10 capitalist, shareowner 11 stockholder

inveterate: 6 rooted 7 chronic 8 habitual, hardened 9 confirmed, ingrained

invidious: 6 odious 7 envious, hateful 9 malignant 12 disagreeable

invigorate: pep 5 brace, cheer, nerve, renew 6 vivify 7 animate, enliven, fortify, refresh 9 stimulate 10 exhilarate, strengthen

invigorating: 5 tonic 11 corroborant

invincible: 10 unbeatable 11 indomitable

inviolate: 4 holy 6 sacred 9 undefiled, unstained 10 inviolable, sacrosanct 13 incorruptible 14 indestructible

invisible: hid 6 unseen 10 indistinct, unapparent 13 undiscernible

Invisible Empire: 4 Klan

invitation: bid 4 call 7 bidding 8 biddance, entreaty 9 challenge

initials: 4 RSVP

invite: ask, bid 4 call 5 court 6 allure, entice 7 attract, provoke, request, solicit

invocation: 4 plea 6 prayer, sermon 7 benison 8 entreaty 11 benediction

invoice: 4 bill 5 brief 7 account 8 manifest 9 statement

invoke: 4 call, pray 6 appeal, attest 7 conjure, entreat, provoke, solicit 9 imprecate 10 supplicate

involucre: 5 whorl 7 rosette 8 envelope

involuntary: 6 forced 9 reluctant, unwilling 11 instinctive, spontaneous

involute: 6 curled, rolled 8 involved

involve: 4 wrap 5 imply, snare 6 bemist, employ, engage, entail, tangle 7 concern, embrace, ensnare 8 comprise, comprize, encumber, entangle 9 implicate 10 complicate, comprehend

involved: 7 complex 12 labyrinthine

inward: 5 entad, inner 6 inside 8 homefelt, interior 10 internally

Io: *father:* 7 Inachus

guard: 5 Argus

son: 7 Epaphus

iodine: *combining form:* iod 4 iodo

compound: 6 iodide

salt: 6 iodate

source: 4 kelp

substitute: 7 aristal
treat with: 6 iodate
Iolcus king: 6 Pelias
ion: *negative:* 5 anion
positive: 6 cation, kation
Ion: *father:* 6 Apollo
mother: 6 Creusa
Ionia: *coin:* 4 obol 5 obolo
gulf: 4 Arta
island: 5 Corfu, Zante 6 Cerigo, Ithaca 7 Kythera 10 Cephalonia
monk: 5 Aidan
iota: bit, jot 4 atom, whit 6 tittle 8 particle
Iowa: *college:* Coe
county: 5 Adair, Onawa 7 Wapello
religious sect: 5 Amana
town: 4 Ames 5 Anita 7 Ottumwa 9 Davenport, Oskaloosa
tree: oak
ipecac: 4 evea
substance: 7 emetine
Iphicles: *brother:* 8 Heracles, Hercules
mother: 7 Alcmene
son: 6 Iolaus
Iphis' daughter: 6 Evadne
iracund: 8 choleric 9 irascible
irade: 5 edict 6 decree
Irak: See **Iraq**
Iran: 6 Persia
almond: 5 badam
angel: Mah
assembly: 6 Majlis, Mejlis
bed: 4 sofa 5 divan
bird: 6 bulbul
books: 5 Koran, Yasna 6 Avesta, Gathas, Yashts 8 Vendidad, Vispered
capital: 7 Teheran
carpet: 4 Kali 7 Hamadan
caste: 4 magi
chief: Mir
city: 4 Amol 7 Teheran(c.)
coin: pul 4 asar, cran, kran, lari, rial 5 bisti, daric, dinar, larin, shahi, toman 6 shahee, stater 7 ashrafi, kasbeke, pahlavi
comedy: 7 temacha
country: 4 Elam 5 Media
demigod: 4 Yima
demon: 7 Apaosha, Ahriman
diadem: taj
dynasty: 6 Safavi, Seljuk 7 Safavid, Safawid 10 Sassanidae
fire-worshipper: 5 Parsi 6 Parsee
founder: 5 Cyrus
garment: 6 chedar
god: 6 Ormazd 7 Mithras
governor: 4 khan 6 satrap
grass: 6 millet
hat: fez 6 turban
hero: 4 Yima
javelin: 5 jerid 6 jeerid
king: 4 shah 6 Darius, Xerxes 7 Jamshid, Jamshyd 9 Giamschid 10 Artaxerxes
Koran student: 5 hafiz
lake: 5 Niriz, Urmia 6 Sahweh 8 Urumiyeh
language: 4 Zend 7 Pahlavi, Pehlevi
measure: guz, mou, zar, zer 4 cane, foot 5 gareh, jerib, kafiz, makuk, qasab 6 artaba, charac, chebel, gariba, ghalva, ouroub 7 capicha, chenica, farsakh, farsang, mansion, mishara 8 parasang, piamaneh, sabbitha, stathmos 9 collothun, colluthun
moon: 4 Mahi
mountain: 4 Kush 5 Hindu 6 Ararat, Elburz 8 Demavend 11 Parapanisus
New Year's Day: 7 Nowroze
nomad: 4 Luri
oil center: 6 Abadan
Parliament: 6 Majlis, Mejlis
peasant: tai
people: Lur, tai 4 Kurd, Mede, sart 5 Kajar, Mukri, nomad, Perse, Tajik 6 Iranic, Tadjik 7 Hadjemi, Persian
poet: 4 Omar 5 Saadi
port: 7 Bushire 11 Bandar Abbas
province: 4 Yezd
religion founder: 9 Zoroaster 11 Zarathustra
religious doctrine: 6 babism 7 babiism
revenue officer: 9 tahsildar 10 tahseeldar
river: 4 Mand, Mund 5 Karun 6 Tigris 8 Safid Rud 9 Euphrates, Kizil Uzen
ruler: 4 shah 6 atabeg, atabek, satrap, sultan
saint: 6 Safavi 7 Safavid, Safawid
screen: 6 purdah
sect: 5 Shiah, Sunni 6 Shiite, Sunnee 7 Sunnite
supreme deity: 6 Ormazd
tapestry: 7 susanee
tax collector: 9 tahsildar 10 tahseeldar
tent-maker: 4 Omar
throne room: 5 aiwan
tiara: 7 cidaris
title: mir 4 azam, shah 5 mirza
tobacco: 6 tumbak, tumbek 7 tumbaki, tumbeki
town: Fao, Kom 5 Niriz, Resht 6 Kasvin, Kerman, Meshed, Shiraz, Tabriz, Tauris 7 Hamadan, Ispahan, Tabreez 9 Balfroosh
traders: 4 sart
trumpet: 6 kerana 7 kerrana
vessel: 6 aftaba
water-pipe: 5 hooka 6 calean, hookah 8 narghile 12 hubble-bubble
water wheel: 5 noria
weight: ser 4 dram, dung, rotl, sang, seer 5 abbas, artal, artel, maund, pinar, ratel 6

batman, dirhem, gandum, karwar, miscal, miskal, nakhod 7 abbassi 8 tcheirek 9 saddirham

Iraq: *capital:* 6 Bagdad 7 Baghdad
coin: 5 dinar
district: 5 Basra
town: 5 Amara, Basra

irascible: 5 brash, fiery, hasty, irate, techy, testy 6 snappy, touchy 7 fretful, peevish 8 captious, choleric, petulant, snappish 9 impatient, splenetic 10 passionate 11 bad-tempered, belligerent, combustible, hot-tempered 13 quick-tempered

irate: mad 5 angry, het up, wroth 6 bitter, wrathy 7 angered, enraged, furious 8 incensed, provoked, wrathful 9 indignant, irascible

ire: vex 4 fury, heat, rage 5 anger, annoy, wrath 6 choler, temper 8 asperity, vexation 9 vehemence 10 exasperate, resentment 11 displeasure 12 exasperation

Ireland: 4 Eire, Erin 5 Ierne, Irena 7 Ivernia 9 Innisfail
ancestor: Ir; Mil 6 Miledh 8 Milesius
assembly: 6 aenach, aonach
basket: 7 skeough
battle cry: abu
bay: 6 Galway
boat: 7 pookaun 8 pookhaun
cabstand: 6 hazard
cap: 6 barrad
capital: 4 Tara 6 Dublin
cattle: 5 Kerry
chamber of deputies: 4 Dail
chemist: 5 Boyle
chieftain: 6 Tanist
church: kil
church steward: 7 erenach
clan: 4 sept 5 Cinel
club: 8 shillala 9 shillalah, shillelah 10 shillelagh
coin: rap 4 real
cordial: 10 usquebaugh
county: 4 Cork, Down, Mayo 5 Cavan, Clare, Kerry, Louth, Meath 6 Antrim, Armagh, Galway, Offaly, Tyrone, Ulster 7 Donegal, Kildare, Leitrim, Wexford, Wicklow 8 Fermangh, Kilkenny, Limerick, Longford, Monaghan 9 Tipperary, Westmeath 11 Londonderry
dagger: 5 skean
dance: 10 rinkafadda, rinncefada
dirge: 4 keen
dish: 4 stew
dramatist: see *playwright* below
epic tales: 4 tain, tana(pl.)
exclamation: och 4 arra 5 arrah, ohone
fair: 6 aenach, aonach
fairy: 4 shee 5 sidhe 7 banshee, banshie 10 leprechaun
festival: 4 feis
fort: Lis 4 rath
freebooter: 8 rapparee
freeman: 4 aire
fuel: 4 peat
garment: 4 inar
goblin: 5 pooka
god's mother: Ana, Anu
god of love: 5 Dagda 6 Aengus, Oengus
god of sea: Ler
goddess: 4 Badb, Bodb, Dana
good-for-nothing: 8 spalpeen
groggery: 7 shebeen
harvester: 8 spalpeen
herring: 8 scud-dawn
holiday: 10 Whitmonday
infantryman: 4 kern
islands: 4 Aran
king: Ri; Rig 5 Ardri
king's home: 4 Tara
lamentation: 6 ochone
landholding system: 7 rundale
lawyer: 6 brehon
legislature: 4 Dail 10 Oireachtas
liquor: 6 poteen 7 potheen
lord: 6 tanist
luck: 4 cess
measure: 4 mile 6 bandle
melody: 7 planxty
moccasin: 9 pampootee, pampootie
monk: 6 culdee
monk's cell: kil 4 kill
mountain: 7 Wicklow 10 Carrantual 11 Lugnaquilla 13 Macgillicuddy
musical festival: 4 feis
musical instrument: 4 harp, lyre
name: 4 Sean 5 Moira
national emblem: 8 shamrock
negative: 5 sorra
novelist: 4 Shaw
oath: 5 bedad
old capital: 4 Tara
parliament: 4 Dail
patriot: 5 Emmet 6 Oakboy
patron saint: 7 Patrick
peasant: 4 kern 5 kerne
peat: gor
people: 4 Celt, Erse, Gael 6 Celtic 9 Hibernian
person: 4 aire, kern 5 kerne, paddy 7 shoneen 8 spalpeen 10 Eireannach
pert. to: 6 Celtic, Gaelic
pig: 5 bonav
playwright: 4 Shaw 5 Synge, Wilde, Yeats 6 O'Casey
poem: 6 amhran
poet: 5 Moore, Wilde, Yeats

priest: 5 druid
princess: 6 Iseult
proprietor: 6 tanist
Protestant: 9 Sassenach
province (see also *county* above): 6 Ulster 7 Munster 8 Leinster 9 Connaught
republicanism: 9 Fenianism
revolutionist: 6 Fenian
river: Lee 4 Bann, Deel, Erne, Suir 5 Boyne, Clare, Feale, Flesk, Foyle, Laune 6 Bandon, Barrow, Liffey, Martin 7 Munster, Shannon 10 Blackwater
robber: 8 woodkern
saint: 5 Aidan 7 Patrick
salutation: 6 a chara
seaport: 4 Cobh 6 Tralee
servant: 5 biddy
society: 4 aire
soldier: 6 bonagh 8 rapparee
soldiers' quartering: 7 bonaght 8 bonaught
song: 4 rann
spirit: see *fairy* above
steward: 7 erenach 8 herenach
stock: 4 daer
straw load: 5 barth
surgeon: 6 Colles
sweetheart: gra
symbol: 4 harp 8 shamrock
tax: 7 bonaght 8 bonaught
tenant: 4 saer
tenure: 6 sorren 7 sorehon
term of endearment: 5 aroon, aruin 7 acushla, alannah, asthore 9 avourneen 10 mavourneen
town: 4 Cork 5 Adare 6 Dublin, Lurgan 8 Limerick 9 Killarney, Tipperary 10 Abbey Feale 12 Castle Island
tribesman: see *person* above
trout: 7 gilaroo
verse: 4 rann
whiskey: 6 poteen 10 usquebaugh
white: 4 bawn
womanhood: 4 emer
writing system: 4 ogam 5 ogham

irenic: 4 calm 5 irene 7 henotic, pacific 8 irenical, peaceful 12 conciliatory
iridescence: 9 irisation
iridescent: 6 irised 7 opaline 9 prismatic 10 opalescent
iridium: *pert. to:* 6 iridic
symbol: ir
iris: lis 4 ixia 5 orris, sedge 6 orrice 7 rainbow 10 Florentine 11 ambassadeur
comb. form: 4 irid
family: 4 irid 8 tileroot
layer: 4 uvea
part: 4 uvea 6 argola 7 argolae(pl.)
pert. to: 5 irian
problem of: 6 iritis 8 aniridia

Irish (see also **Ireland** *people*): 6 Celtic, Gaelic 9 Hibernian
Irish bit: 7 traneen
Irish confetti: 6 bricks
Irish dividend: 10 assessment
Irish Free State: See **Ireland**
Irish pennant: 6 thread 8 raveling
Irish Sweepstakes: 7 lottery
irk (see also **ire**): vex 4 bore 5 anger, annoy, chafe, peeve, tease, upset, weary 6 nettle 7 trouble 8 irritate 10 exasperate
irksome: 4 dull 6 tedium 7 humdrum, painful, tedious 8 tiresome 9 fatiguing, wearisome 10 burdensome, monotonous, unpleasant 11 displeasing
irne: 4 iron
iron: fer(F.) 4 gyve, hard, irne 5 goose, metal, power, press 6 fetter, trivet, robust, strong, yetlin 7 manacle, shackle, yetling 8 firmness, gridiron, handcuff, hematite, siderite 10 unyielding
comb. form: 6 sidero
compound: 5 steel
containing: 6 ferric
dross: 6 sinter
magnet: 8 armature
lump: pig
marking: 7 brander
meteoric: 8 siderite
pert. to: 6 ferric
sulphate: 7 ilesite
symbol: Fe
Iron City: 10 Pittsburgh
iron sand: 6 iserin
ironclad: 7 armored, monitor
ironer: 6 mangle 7 presser
ironic: 7 satiric 9 sarcastic
irons: 6 chains 7 garters 8 creepers, shackles
ironwork: 8 ferament
ironworker's tool: 6 lifter
irony: 6 satire 7 asteism, sarcasm 8 ridicule 13 dissimulation
Iroquois Indian: 4 Erie 5 Huron, Litre 6 Cayuga, Mohawk, Neuter, Oneida, Seneca 7 Wyandot 8 Cherokee, Nottoway, Onondaga 9 Conestoga, Tuscarora 10 Tionontati
irradiance: 11 irradiation
irradiate: ray 4 beam, emit 6 bright 7 diffuse, radiate 8 brighten 9 enlighten 10 illuminate 11 illuminated
irrational: 4 surd 5 brute 6 absurd, stupid 7 bestial, brutish, foolish 9 senseless 10 ridiculous 12 preposterous, unreasonable 13 unintelligent
irrational number: 4 surd
irreclaimable: 4 lost 8 hopeless 9 abandoned 11 irrevocable

irreconcilable: 9 repugnant 10 discordant, implacable 12 incompatible, inconsistent, intransigent
irrecoverable: See **irreclaimable**
irredeemable: See **irreclaimable**
irrefutable: 10 conclusive
irregular: 4 wild 5 erose, false 6 ataxic, fitful, rugged, spotty, uneven, unlike 7 atactic, crabbed, crooked, cursory, devious, erratic, snatchy, unequal, wayward 8 abnormal, atypical, sporadic, unlawful, unstable, unsteady, variable 9 anomalous, desultory, eccentric, unsettled 10 changeable, disorderly, immoderate 11 intemperate 12 uncontrolled, unsystematic 13 extraordinary
irregularity: 5 error 7 anomaly 8 disorder 11 derangement 12 perturbation
irrelevant: 9 unrelated 10 inapposite 11 inessential, unessential 12 inconsequent
irreligious: 5 pagan 6 wicked 7 godless, heathen, impious, profane
irremediable: 8 helpless, hopeless 9 desperate, incurable 11 irreparable 13 irretrievable
irreproachable: 8 spotless 9 blameless, faultless
irresistible: 8 almighty 10 resistless 11 ineluctable 12 spellbinding
irresolute: 6 fickle, infirm, unsure 8 doubtful, unstable, wavering 9 uncertain, undecided 10 changeable, inconstant 11 fluctuating 12 undetermined
irresponsible: 8 carefree 10 fly-by-night 11 harum-scarum 12 undependable 13 unaccountable
irretrievable: See **irremediable**
irreverence: 7 impiety 8 dishonor 9 blasphemy, impudence, profanity
irrevocable: 4 firm 5 final 6 stable 9 immutable 11 unalterable
irrigate: wet 5 water 6 sluice 7 moisten
irritable: 4 edgy 5 birsy, cross, fiery, techy, testy 6 cranky, ornery, tetchy, touchy 7 fretful, iracund, peevish, pettish 8 snappish 9 excitable, fractious, impatient, querulent 11 capernoited 12 disagreeable
irritate: get, irk, nag, rub, vex 4 crab, fret, gall, goad, grig, rasp, rile, roil 5 anger, annoy, chafe, cross, frump, grate, peeve, pique, spite, sting, tease 6 abrade, badger, bother, enrage, excite, fridge, harass, hector, madden, needle, nettle, ruffle 7 affront, incense, provoke 8 acerbate 9 aggravate, displease, stimulate 10 exacerbate, exasperate
irritating: 5 acrid 8 rankling
irritation: 4 itch, sore 5 birse 6 temper
is: 6 exists 10 represents 11 personifies
is not: nis, nys
Isaac's kin: 4 Esau 5 Jacob 7 Abraham
isagoge: 12 introduction
Iseult: *beloved:* 7 Tristan
husband: 4 Mark
Ishmael: 5 rover 6 pariah 7 outcast
kin: 5 Hagar 7 Abraham 8 Nebaioth
Ishtar's lover: 6 Tammuz
isinglass: 4 mica
Isis: *kin:* 5 Horus 6 Osiris
mother: Nut
shrine: 5 Iseum 6 Iseium
son: 4 Sept
Islam: *adherent:* 6 Moslem, Muslim
festival: Eed
founder: 7 Mahomet
holy city: 5 Mecca 6 Medina
judge: 4 cadi
law: 5 sheri 6 sharia, sheria 8 sheriyat
paradise: 5 jenna
place of pilgrimage: 5 Caaba, Kaaba 6 Kaabeh
priest: 4 imam
scriptures: 5 Koran
tambourine: 5 daira
island: ait, cay, ile(F.), key 4 calf, eyot, holm, ilot, inch(Sc.), isle, Qais 5 atoll, holme, islet, islot 8 insulate
group: 5 Faroe, Samoa 8 Antilles, Caroline, Marshall 11 archipelago
mythical: 4 Meru 6 Avalon, Bimini 8 Atlantis
pert. to: 7 insular
snake-free: 4 Erin
Island of Saints: 7 Ireland
isle: See **island**
Isle of Man: *city:* 4 Peel 6 Ramsey 7 Douglas 10 Castletown
division of: 5 Treen
judge: 8 deemster, dempster
legislature: 7 tynwald
measure: 6 kishen, kishon
mountain: 8 Snaefell
part: 4 Ayre
pert. to: 4 Manx
watering place: 4 Ryde
islet: See **island**
ism: 5 ology, tenet 6 belief 8 doctrine 10 hypothesis
follower of: ist, ite
isolate: 4 isle 6 detach, enisle, island 7 seclude 8 insulate, separate 9 segregate, sequester 10 quarantine
isolated: 4 sole 5 alone 6 lonely 7 insular 8 singular, solitary
Isolde's lover: 7 Tristan
Israel (see also **Hebrew, Judaism**):
anthem: 7 Hatikva 9 Hattikvah
child: 5 sabra

city: 5 Jaffa, Joppa 9 Jerusalem(c.)
dance: 4 hora
desert: 5 Negeb
dust storm: 8 khamseen
government body: 7 Knesset 9 Sanhedrin
judge: 4 Elon 6 Samson 7 Sampson, Shamgar 8 Jephthah
king: 4 Ahab, Jehu, Omri, Saul 5 David, Pekah 7 Jehoram, Solomon 8 Jehoahaz, Jeroboam, Pekahiah
labor federation: 9 Histadrut
labor party: 5 Mapai
land of plenty: 6 Goshen
lawgiver: 5 Moses
measure: cab, cor, hin, kab, kor, log 4 bath, epha, ezba, omer, reed, seah 5 cubit, ephah, homer, kaneh, qaneh 11 handbreadth
plain: 6 Sharon
priest: Eli
seaport: 4 Acre 5 Aqaba, Elath, Haifa 7 Tel Aviv
settlement: 6 moshav 7 kibbutz
tribe: Dan 4 Aser, Levi 5 Asher 6 Reuben

issuance: 5 issue 6 sortie 7 issuing 9 emanation 12 distribution

issue: end, son 4 come, emit, fate, flow, gush, pour, send 5 arise, child, sally, spout, topic, utter 6 accrue, egress, emerge, escape, exitus, expede(Sc.), source, upshot 7 descent, edition, emanate, fortune, outcome, problem, proceed, progeny 9 effluence, offspring 10 denouement, distribute

issuing: 9 affluence, affluxion

ist: 7 devotee 8 adherent, believer, disciple, follower

Istanbul: 9 Byzantium 14 Constantinople
part: 4 Pera 5 Fanar
patriarch: 9 Nestorius

isthmus: 4 neck 6 strait 9 peninsula

istle fiber: 4 pita, pito

it may be: 5 haply

Ita: Ata 4 Aeta 7 Negrito

italicize: 9 emphasize, underline 10 underscore

Italy: *actress:* 4 Duse
article: et, il
artist: 7 Cellini
astronomer: 6 Secchi 7 Galileo
author: 5 Dante
card game: 5 tarot
carriage: 7 vettura
cathedral: 5 duomo
cereal: 5 arzun
cheese: 6 Romano 8 Parmesan
chest: 7 cassone
city: Bra, Ora 4 Alba, Asti, Bari, Este, Lodi, Nola, Pisa, Pola, Roma, Rome 5 Aosta, Fiume, Genoa, Lucca, Massa, Milan, Ostia, Padua, Parma, Pavia, Siena, Trent, Turin, Udine 6 Ancona, Foggia, Mantua, Modena, Naples, Spezia, Venice, Verona 7 Bologna, Catania, Ferrara, Leghorn, Livorno, Marsala, Messina, Palermo, Perugia, Pompeii, Ravenna, Taranto, Trieste 8 Brindisi, Cagliari, Florence, Sorrento 11 Alessandria
coin: 4 lira, sudo, tari 5 grano, paoli, soldo 6 ducato, sequin, teston, zequin 8 chequeen, zecchino 9 centisimo
commune: Bra 4 Atri, Como, Dego, Este, Nola 5 Asola, Eboli 6 Rivoli
composer: 5 Verdi 7 Puccini 8 Mascagni 9 Scarlatti
condiment: 6 tamara
country: 7 Etruria
dance: 5 volta 8 courante 9 rigoletto 10 tarantella
deity: 4 faun
department: 4 Roma 5 Marca 6 Apulia, Emilia, Umbria 7 Liguria, Sicilia, Tuscana, Venetia 8 Calabria, Compania, Piemonte, Sardinia 9 Lombardia 10 Basilicata 13 Aruzzi e Molise
dictator: 9 Mussolini
engraver: 8 Raimondi
entertainment: 6 ridoto
estate: 11 latifundium
family: 4 Asti, Este 5 Amati, Cenci 6 Medici
festival: 5 festa
food: 5 pizza 7 ravioli 10 zabaglione
gentleman: ser 6 signor
god: 5 Liber, Picus 6 Consus
goddess: Ops 4 Juno 5 Diana, Salus, Venus 6 Pomona 7 Feronia, Minerva
grape: 6 verdea
guessing game: 4 mora
gulf: 7 Salerno
hamlet: 5 casal 6 casale
hero: 7 Orlando
holiday: 5 festa
house: 4 casa 6 casino
immigrant: 6 guinea
infant cupids: 7 amorini
inlay work: 6 tarsia
inn: 7 locanda
innkeeper: 7 padrone
instrument: 10 colascione
island: Cos 4 Elba 5 Capri, Leros 6 Ischia, Lipari, Sicily 8 Sardinia
king: 4 Rene 5 Murat 6 Alonso
lady: 5 donna 7 signora
lake: 4 Como 5 Garda 6 Albano, Lugano 7 Bolsena 8 Maggiore 9 Trasimene
land: 7 maremma
landlord: 7 padrone
leader: 4 duce
limestone: 7 scaglia
lover: 7 amoroso

macaroni: 5 pasta
magistrate: 7 podesta
marble: 7 carrara
master: 7 padrone
mayor: 6 syndic
measure: pie 4 orna 5 canna, carat, palma, piede, punto, salma, staio, stero 6 barile, miglio, moggio, rubbio, tavola, tomolo 7 boccale, braccio, secchio 8 giornata, polonick, quadrato
medieval faction: 4 Neri
millet: 4 buda, moha 5 mohar, tenai
monk 5 padre 6 abbate
mountain: 4 Alps 5 Amaro, Somma 8 Vesuvius 9 Apennines, Appennino
musician: 5 Guido
native: 5 Italo 6 Tirano 7 Sienese 9 Calabrian
naval base: 7 Taranto
needlework: 8 trapunto
noblewoman: 8 marchesa
omelet: 8 frittata
opera: 4 Aida 5 Norma, Tosca 9 Pagliacci
opera house: 5 Scala
organization: 7 Balilla
painter: 4 Reni, Tisi 5 Colle, Lippi, Lotto 6 Crespi, Guardi, Sacchi, Titian 7 Amigoni, di Credi, di Paolo, Raphael, Robusti, Strozzi, Tiepolo 8 Bronzino, Cagliari, Mainardi, Sassetta 9 Correggio, del Piombo, Giorgione, Veneziano 10 Botticelli, Caracciolo, Tintoretto
painting: 9 tenebrosi
part: toe
patriot: 9 Garibaldi
peasant: 9 contadini, contadino
people: 5 Latin, Oscan, Roman 6 Sabine, Tuscan 8 Venetian
philosopher: 7 Rosmini
physicist: see *scientist* below
pie: 5 pizza
plays: 7 Vangeli
poet: 4 Redi 5 Dante, Tasso
poetic name: 7 Ausonia
police officer: 6 sbirri, sbirro
policeman: 11 carabiniere, carabinieri
porridge: 7 polenta
port: 6 Rimini
possession: 6 Dhalak 7 Eritrea, Tripoli 10 Somaliland
pottery: 8 majolica
prelate: 4 Rici
priest: fra
prince: 4 Asti, Este
printer: 6 Bodoni
procession: 5 corso 7 trionfi, trionfo
province: 4 Bari, Este, Pola, Roma, Zara 5 Aosta, Cuneo, Parma, Udine 6 Istria, Verona 7 Salerno
region: 5 Carso
resort: 4 Lido
river: Po 4 Adda, Arno, Liri 5 Adige, Melfa, Oglio, Piave, Tiber 6 Panora, Rapido, Tevere, Ticino 7 Rubicon, Secchia, Trebbia 8 Volturno 10 Garigliano
rock: 7 scaglia
saint: 4 Neri
sausage: 6 salami
scientist: 5 Fermi, Volta 7 Galileo, Galvani
sculptor: 5 Leoni 6 Canova 7 Bernini 8 Canonica 9 Egenesean
sea: 8 Adriatic
seaport: Aci 4 Bari, Mola, Pola, Zara 5 Genoa, Ostia, Trani 7 Otranto, Trieste
secret society: 5 Mafia 7 Camorra 9 Carbonari
section: 7 maremma
shore: 4 riva
soldier: 10 carabineer, carabinier 11 bersagliere, carabinieri
song: 10 villanella, villanelle
soprano: 5 Patti
soup: 8 minestra 10 minestrone
spice: 6 tamara
straits: 7 Messina, Otranto
stream: 4 rivo
summer house: 6 casino
theme: 4 tema
theologian: 7 Peronne
town: Bra 4 Alba, Elea, Este, Meda, Pisa 5 Acqui, Aosta, Capua, Genoa, Milan, Parma, Teano 6 Naples, Napoli, Torino 7 Bologna, Caserta 9 Caporetto
university: 5 Padua
vessel: 9 trabacolo 10 trabascolo
violin maker: 5 Amati
violinist: 7 Corelli, Tartini
volcano: 4 Etna 5 Somma 8 Vesuvius 9 Stromboli
weight: 5 carat, libra, oncia, pound 6 denaro, libbra, ottava 11 chilogrammo
wind: 7 sirocco
wine: 4 Asti 6 Barolo, Massic 9 Vernaccia

itch: 4 reef, yeuk(Sc.) 6 desire 9 cacoethes, hankering 10 irritation
ite: 8 adherent, disciple, follower
item (see also **object**): ad, bit 5 entry, scrap, thing, topic 6 detail 7 account, article, product 8 personal 9 paragraph 10 particular 12 circumstance
curious: ana
itemize: 9 enumerate
iterate: See **reiterate**
Ithaca king: 8 Odysseus
Ithunn's husband: 5 Brage, Bragi

itinerant: 6 errant, roving 7 migrant, nomadic 8 traveler, wanderer 9 migratory, transient, traveling, unsettled, wandering 11 peripatetic
itinerary: 4 plan, tour 5 guide, route 6 record 8 roadbook 9 guidebook
itinerate: 6 travel 9 traveling
itineration: 4 eyre, tour 7 circuit, travels
Ivan the Terrible: 4 Tsar
wife: 9 Anastasia
Ivanhoe: *author:* 5 Scott
character: 4 Tuck 5 Isaac 6 Cedric, Rowena
ivory: 6 creamy, dentin 7 dentine, ivoride, ribzuba 8 ribazuba
carving: 9 toreutics
rasping: 5 scobs
ivy: tod 4 gill, hove 6 hedera, hibbin
crowned with: 9 hederated
pert. to: 7 hederic
poison: 5 sumac 6 sumach
Ixion's descendants: 8 Centaurs
ixtle: 4 pita 5 fiber, istle
izzat: 5 honor 6 credit 8 prestige 10 reputation

J

jaal: 4 goat, ibex 5 beden
jab: hit, jag 4 poke, prod, stab 5 lunge, punch 6 thrust
Jabal's father: 6 Lamech
jabber: 4 chat 6 burble, gabble 7 chatter 9 gibberish
jabberwocky: 4 tove 6 slithy 7 brillig 8 nonsense 9 rigmarole
jabiru: 4 ibis 5 stork
jabot: 5 frill
jacare: 6 caiman
jacent: 5 prone 9 recumbent
jack: nob 4 card, lift 5 knave, money 6 wenzel 8 zapetero
group of 4: 8 quatorze
jack-in-the-pulpit: 4 herb 5 plant 7 figwort
jack-of-all-trades: 6 tinker
jack tree: 4 jaca
jackal: 5 diebs
jackanapes: ape, fop 4 beau 5 dandy 6 monkey 7 coxcomb
jackass: 4 dolt, fool 5 dunce 6 donkey, nitwit 9 blockhead
comb. form: ono
jackdaw: coe, daw 6 caddow 7 dawcock 9 blackbird
jacket: 4 bajo, coat, Eton 5 acton, grego, wamus 6 anorak, banian(Ind.), bietle, blazer, bolero, dolman, reefer, sliver, wammus, wampus 7 cassock, doublet, ristori, spencer 8 camisole, chaqueta, hanselin 9 habergeon, peajacket 10 carmagnole(F.), roundabout 11 nightingale
knitted: 5 gansy 6 gansey, sontag 7 sweater 8 cardigan, penelope
sleeveless: 4 vest 6 bolero
jackknife: 6 barlow
jackpot: all 5 award 8 windfall
jackrabbit: 4 hare
jackstay: 4 rope 5 horse, staff
jackstones: 4 dibs
Jacob: *brother:* 4 Edom, Esau
daughter: 5 Dinah
descendant: 6 Levite 9 Israelite
father-in-law: 5 Laban
new name: 6 Israel
parent: 5 Isaac 7 Rebekah
retreat: 5 Haran
son: Dan, Gad 4 Aser, Levi 5 Asher, Judah 6 Bononi, Joseph, Reuben, Simeon 7 Gershon, Zebulun 8 Benjamin, Issachar, Naphtali
vision(scene): 6 Bethel
wife: 4 Leah 6 Rachel
jade: fag, nag 4 hack minx, plug, tire 5 hussy, weary 6 harass 7 exhaust, fatigue, hilding, pounamu 8 nephrite 10 greenstone
jaded: 4 worn 5 blase, tired, weary 6 dulled 7 wearied 9 exhausted, forjaskit, forjesket
jaeger: 4 bird, gull, skua 6 hunter 7 diamond 8 huntsman
jag: dag, jab, rag 4 barb, hair, load, mess, stab 5 carry, notch, prick, scrap, shred, slash, souse, spree, tooth 6 indent, tatter 7 bristle, pendant, portion 8 quantity 13 denticulation
jagged: 5 erose, rough, sharp 6 hackly, ragged 7 cutting
jaguar: 5 ounce
jai alai: 4 game 6 pelota
court: 7 fronton
racket: 5 cesta
jail: can, jug 4 brig, dump, gaol, keep, stir 5 clink, pokey 6 asylum, carcel, cooler, lockup, prison 7 hoosgow 8 bastille, hoosegaw, hoosegow, imprison 9 calaboose 11 incarcerate
jailer, jailor: 4 caid 5 guard 6 gaoler, keeper, warden 7 alcaide, turnkey
Jairite: Ira
jake: 4 fine, hick, rube 5 dandy 6 rustic 9 first-rate, greenhorn
jako: 6 parrot
jalousie: 5 blind 7 shutter
jam: 4 bind 5 crowd, crush 6 spread 7 squeeze 9 marmalade 10 congestion
Jamaica dogwood: 8 barbasco
ginger alcohol: 4 jake
James' father: 7 Zebedee

jangle: 4 ring 6 bicker 7 prattle, quarrel, wrangle 11 altercation
jangling: 5 harsh 9 dissonant 10 discordant 11 cacophonous
janitor: 6 porter 9 caretaker 10 doorkeeper 11 housekeeper
japan: 7 lacquer, varnish
Japan: 5 Nipon 6 Niphon, Nippon
abacus: 7 soroban
abalone: 5 awabi
aborigine: 4 Aino, Ainu
alcoholic beverage: 4 sake, saki
alloy: 5 mokum
allspice: 12 chimonanthus
apricot: ume 4 ansu
art design: 5 notan
baron: 6 daimio, daimyo
battle cry: 6 banzai
bay: ise
biwa: 6 loquat
boxes: 4 inro
brake: 6 warabi
brazier: 7 hibachi
brocade: 7 nishiki
Buddha: 5 Amida, Amita
Buddhist festival: Bon
Buddhist sect: Zen 7 Jodo-shu, Shin-shu
bush clover: 4 hagi
button: 7 netsuke
calculator: 6 abacus 7 soroban
calisthenics: 4 judo
cape: 4 mino
capital: 5 Tokyo
cherry: 4 fuji
chess: 5 shogi
chevrotain: 4 napu
church: 4 tera
circle: 4 maru
city: Ome 4 Kobe, Kura, Nara, Ueda 5 Atami, Kioto, Kyoto, Nikko, Osaka, Otaru, Tokio(c.), Tokyo(c.), Ujina 6 Nagoya, Sasebo, Sendai 7 Fukuoka, Niigata, Okayama, Okazaki, Sapporo 8 Hako Date, Kamakura, Kanazawa, Kumamoto, Nagasaki, Wakatama, Yokahama, Yokosuka 9 Hiroshima, Kagoshima, Tokushima 11 Akamagaseki
clan: 7 Satsuma
class: eta, roi 6 heimin 7 kwazoku, samurai, shizoku
clogs: 4 geta
clover: 4 hagi
coin: bu; rin, sen, yen 4 oban 5 koban, obang, tempo 6 cobang, ichebu, ichibu, itzebu, itzibu, kobang 7 itzeboo, itziboo
combine: 8 zaibatsu
composition: 6 haikai
costume: 7 netsuke
court: 5 dairi
crepe: 8 chirimen
crest: mon 7 kikumon
dancing girl: 6 geisha
deer: 4 sika
deity: 9 Amaterasu
dextrose: ame
dish: 7 tempura 8 sukiyaki
dog: 6 tanate
door: 6 fusuma
drama: no
drink: 4 mate, sake, saki
drum: 5 tarko
dye process: 5 yuzen
earthenware: 5 banko 8 rakuware
emperor: 6 Makado 8 Hirohito
emperor's title: 5 Tenno 6 Mikado
ethics: 7 Bushido
explosive: 7 shimose
fabric: 6 birodi 7 habutai, nishiki 8 chirimen, habutaye
family concern: 8 zaibatsu
fan: ogi
felicitation: 6 banzai
festival: Bon 7 Matsuri
fish: ayu, tai, tho 4 fugu, funa
flag: 7 sunflag
flower: 9 nelumbium
flute: 4 fuye
game: go 5 goban 6 gobang
garment: 5 haori 6 kimono, mompei
gateway: 5 torii
girdle: obi
girdle receptacle: 4 inro
girl: 6 geisha, mousme 7 mousmee
god: 5 Ebisu, Hotei 6 Benten 7 Daikoku, Jurojin 8 Bishamon 10 Fukurokuju
goddess: 9 Amaterasu
governor's title: 6 shogun, taikun, tycoon
harp: 4 koto
herb: udo
island: Iki 4 Oita 5 Bonin, Hondo, Kuril, Sikok 6 Honshu, Kiushu, Kiusiu, Kurile, Kyushu, Niphon, Riu-kiu 7 Cipango, Loo-Choo, Shikoku 8 Hokkaido
kelp: 4 kome
lacquer: 6 urushi
lake: 4 Biwa
legislature: 4 Diet
litter: see *palanquin* below
loquat: 4 biwa
lyric: 5 haiku, hokku
magnolia: 5 yulan
measure: bu, jo; boo, cho 4 hiro 5 tsubo 11 kujira-shaku
measure of distance: ri
measure of land: se; tan

measure of weight: mo; fun, kin, kon, rin, shi 4 kati, kwan, niyo 5 carat, catty, momme, picul 6 kwamme 8 hiyak-kin 11 komma-ichida
medicine case: 4 etui, inro
metalwork: 5 zogan
Mikado: 5 dairi
monastery: 4 tera
money: mo, ro
money of account: mo; rin, yen
mountain: Usu 4 Fuji 5 Asama, Hondo, Yesso 6 Asosan, Kiusiu 7 Fujisan 8 Fujiyama
music and dancing: 7 san-gaku 8 sarugaku
musical instrument: 4 fuye, koto 5 tarko 8 samisen, truyume
nautical mile: 5 kairi
news service: 5 Domei
nobility: 7 kwazoku
opened by: 5 Perry
ornament: 4 inro
outcast: eta 5 ronin
overcoat: 4 mino
pagoda: taa
painting style: 4 kano 7 ukiyoye
palanquin: 4 kago 5 cango 7 norimon
paper mulberry: 4 kozo
paper screen: 5 shoji
peninsula: Izu
people: 4 Aino, Ainu 6 Nippon 9 Nipponese
persimmon: 4 kaki 7 Hyakume
pine: 5 matsu
plant: udo 5 kudzu 6 sugamo
plum: 6 kelsey
porcelain: 5 Hizen, Imari 6 Hirado 9 Nabeshima
port: 4 Kobe 5 Hiogo, Osaka, Otaru 7 Niigata 8 Hakodate, Nagasaki, Wakatama, Yokohama
porter: 5 akabo
potato: imo
prefecture: 5 ehime 9 Yamaguchi
province: Ise 5 Iwaki 6 Yamato 7 Satsuma
quince: 8 japonica
radish: 6 daikon
receptacle: 4 inro
religion: 6 Shinto 8 Buddhism 9 Shintoism
rice cake: ame
rice flour: ame
rice paste: ame
rice wine: 4 sake
river: 4 Yalu 8 Tonegawa
robe: 6 kimono
ruler: 6 shogun
salad plant: udo
salmon: 4 masu
samurai: 5 ronin
sash: obi
screen: 5 shoji
seaweed: 4 nori
self-defense: 4 judo 7 jujitsu, jujutsu
Shinto temple: Sha 5 Jinja 6 Jinsha 7 Yashiro
ship: 4 maro, maru
shoe: 4 geta, zori
shrub: 4 fuji 5 goumi 8 japonica
silk: 7 habutai 8 chirimen, habutaye
silkworm: 7 yamamai
silkworm disease: uji
sock: 4 tabi
song: uta
sovereign: 5 tenno
storm: 7 tsunami
street: 5 Ginza
suicide: 7 seppuku 8 hara-kari, hara-kiri, hari-kari, kamikaze
suntree: 7 hinokis
sword: 5 catan 6 cattan 8 wacadash
sword guard: 5 tsuba
syllabic writing: 4 kana
tea ceremony: 7 chanoyu
tea girl: 6 mousme 7 mousmee
temple: 4 tera
throne: 6 shinza
title: 4 kami 6 shogun
tortoise shell: 5 bekko
tree: 4 kozo, sugi 5 akeki, kiaki, yeddo 6 urushi 7 camphor 8 akamatsu 10 shirakashi
untouchable: eta
vehicle: 7 ricksha 8 rickshaw 10 jinricksha, jinrikisha
velvet: 6 birodi
verse: 5 tanka
vine: 5 kudzu
volcano: Aso 4 Fuji 5 Asama, Asame 6 Asosan 8 Fujiyama 9 Asamayama
wall: 5 shoji
windstorm: 5 taifu
winged being: 5 tengu
wrestling: 4 judo, Sumo 7 jujitsu, jujutsu 8 jiujitsu, jiujutsu
writing: 4 kana
zitherharp: 4 koto
Japanese-American: 5 Issei, Kibei, Nesei, Nisei 6 Kibbei, Sansei
japaneer: 9 varnisher
jape: 4 fool, gibe, jeer, jest, jibe, jipe, joke, mock 5 fraud, trick 6 deride
japery: 10 buffoonery
Japeth: *father:* 4 Noah
son: 5 Magog, Tubal 7 Meshech
japonica: 4 bush 5 shrub 8 camellia
jar: jug, ola, urn 4 jolt, olla, vase 5 banga, clash, cruse, shake, shock 6 croppa, hydria, krater, tinaja 7 agitate, amphora, clatter, concuss, discord 10 jardiniere
fruit: 5 mason

rubber: 4 lute
top: lid
two-handled: 7 amphora
wide-mouthed: 4 ewer
jardiniere: jar, jug, urn 4 vase 5 stand 7 garnish 9 flowerpot
jargon: 4 cant 5 argot, idiom, lingo, slang 6 pidgin 9 baragouin, gibberish 10 balderdash 11 grimgribber
jarl: 4 earl 7 headman 9 chieftain
jarring: 5 rough 9 dissonant 10 discordant
jasmine: 4 bela 5 papaw 6 flower 7 jessamy
Jason: *father:* 5 Aeson
love: 6 Creusa
men: 9 Argonauts
ship: 4 Argo
teacher: 7 Cheiron
uncle: 6 Pelias
wife: 5 Medea
jasper: 6 morlop, quartz 10 bloodstone
jauk: 5 dally 6 trifle
jaundice: 4 bias, envy 7 gulsach, icterus 8 jealousy 9 prejudice
jaunt: 4 ride, trip 5 sally, tramp 6 ramble 7 journey 9 excursion
jaunty: 4 airy 5 cocky, perky, showy, smart 7 finical, stylish 8 debonair 9 debonaire, sprightly
Java: *arrow poison:* 4 upas
badger: 5 ratel 6 teledu
berry: 5 cubeb
carriage: 4 sado 5 sadoo
city: 7 Batavia, Jakarta 8 Samarang, Surabaya 9 Surakarta 10 Jokjokarta
civet: 5 rasse
community: 5 Dessa
cotton: 5 kapok
dancers: 6 bedoyo
drama: 6 topeng
Dutchman: 6 blanda
fabric: 4 ikat
fig tree: 7 gondang
grackle: beo
island: 4 Bali
lomboy: 4 plum
measure: 4 paal 5 palen
mountain: 4 Gede 5 Lawoe 6 Raoeng 7 Semeroe, Slameta 8 Soembing
musical instrument: 5 saron 6 bonang, gender 7 gambang, gamelan 8 gamelang
orchestra: 7 gamelan 8 gamelang
ox: 7 bantens
pepper: 5 cubeb
plum: 5 duhal 6 jambul, lomboy 7 jambool
port: 7 Batavia 8 Surabaya
puppet show: 6 wajang, wayang
rice field: 5 sawah
speech: 5 krama, ngoko
straw: 6 peanit
sumac: 6 fuyang
temple: 5 candi 6 chandi, tjandi
tree: 4 upas 6 antiar 7 gondang
village: 5 Dessa
weight: 4 amat, pond, tali, 5 pound
wild dog: 5 adjag
Java almond: 7 talisay
Java cotton: 5 kapok
Javan squirrel: 8 jelerang
Javanese skunk: 6 teledu
javelin: 4 dart 5 lance, spear 7 assagai, assegai, harpoon
cord: 7 amentum
jaw: maw 4 chaw, chop, talk 5 scold 6 jabber 7 chatter 8 scolding
lumpy: 13 actinomycosis
muscle: 8 masseter
part: 4 chin
pert. to: 5 malar 7 gnathic
jawab: 5 reply 6 answer 7 balance 8 building
jawbone: 7 maxilla
Jayhawker: 6 Kansan
Jayhawker State: 6 Kansas
jazz: hot 4 cool 5 funky, swing 6 modern 7 ragtime 11 barrelhouse, progressive
jealous: 6 yellow 7 envious 10 suspicious 11 mistrustful
jeer: bob, boo 4 gibe, hoot, jape, jibe, mock 5 fleer, flite, flout, scoff, scout, sneer, taunt 6 deride 8 ridicule
jeering: 6 glaiks 7 sarcasm
Jehiada's wife: 9 Jehosheba 12 Jehoshabeath
Jehoahaz's mother: 7 Hamutal
Jehoiachin's successor: 9 Salathiel
Jehoshaphat: *father:* Asa
son: 4 Jehu
Jehovah: 4 Jave 5 Jahve, Yahve, Yahwe 6 Jahvah, Jahveh, Yahveh, Yahweh 7 Jahaveh
jehu: 6 driver
Jehu's father: 11 Jehoshaphat
jejune: dry 4 arid, avid, dull, flat 5 empty, inane, prosy, trite, vapid 6 barren, hungry, meager 7 insipid, sterile 8 foodless, lifeless
jell: 9 coagulate 11 crystallize
jellify: gel 5 jelly
jelly: gel 4 geal, sapa 5 aspic, kisel 6 cullis, pectin, spread 7 fisnoga, gelatin 8 gelatine
animal: 7 gelatin 8 gelatine
meat: 5 aspic
vegetable: 6 pectin
jellyfish: 6 medusa 7 acaleph
group: 10 discophora
part: 10 exumbrella
jellylike: 10 gelatinous
jennet: ass 5 horse 6 donkey

jeofail: **7** mistake **9** oversight
jeopardize: **6** expose **7** imperil **8** endanger
jeopardous: **6** daring **11** venturesome
jeopardy: **4** risk **5** peril **6** danger, hazard, menace **9** adventure
jequirity: **8** licorice
Jerahmeel's son: **4** Oren **5** Achia
jeremiad: **6** lament, tirade **9** complaint
jerez: **6** sherry
Jericho: *publican:* **8** Zaccheus **9** Zacchaeus
woman: **5** Rahab
jerk: bob, tic, tit **4** hike, lipe, shog, yank, yerk **5** chuck, hitch, pluck, tweak
jerkin: **4** coat **6** jacket, salmon **9** blackjack, waistcoat
jerky: **5** wagon **7** charqui **8** saccadic, staccato
jeroboam: **4** bowl **6** bottle, goblet
jersey: **6** gansey **7** sweater
Jersey tea: **11** wintergreen **12** checkerberry
Jerusalem: **4** Sion, Zion **5** Salem
captor: **4** Omar
garden: **10** Gethsemane
mosque: **4** Omar
mountain: **4** Sion, Zion **6** Moriah, Olivet
oak: **7** ambrose
pert to: **14** Hierosolymitan
pool: **6** Siloam **8** Bethesda
priest: **5** Zadoc, Zadok
prophetess: **4** Anna, Anne
region: **5** Perea
spring: **5** Gihon **6** Siloam
temple treasury: **6** Corban
thorn: **6** retama
town: **14** Hierosolymitan
Jerusalem artichoke: **5** tuber **7** girasol **8** girasole **10** topinambou
Jerusalem corn: **5** durra
Jerusalem haddock: **4** opah
jess: **5** strap, thong **7** binding
jessamy: fop **5** dandy
Jesse: *father:* **4** Obed
son: **5** David
jest: bob, cog, fun **4** bull, fool, gaud, jape, joke, mime, quip, skit **5** bourd, droll, flirt, gleek, sport **6** banter, japery, trifle **8** drollery **9** burlesque **10** jocularity
jester: **4** fool, mime **5** clown, droll **6** disour **7** buffoon, dizzard **8** merryman **9** joculator **11** merry-andrew
Jesuit: *founder:* **6** Loyola
motto: **4** A.M.D.G.
saint: **5** Regis
Jesuits' bark: **8** cinchona
jet: **4** ebon, gush **5** black, ladle, raven, spout, spurt **6** nozzle **8** fountain, spouting
jet-assisted takeoff: **4** JATO
Jethro's daughter: **8** Zipporah
jetty: **4** mole, pier **5** groin, wharf **6** groyne
jeu: **4** game, play **9** diversion
jeune fille: **4** girl, miss
Jew (see also **Hebrew, Judaism**): **6** Essene, Semite
ascetic: **6** essene
harp: **8** guimbard
horn: **6** shofar
jewel: gem **4** opal, ruby, sard **5** beryl, bijou(F.), regal **6** garnet **7** diamond **8** amethyst, ornament
box: **6** casket **7** casquet
case: tye
connoisseur: **10** lapidarist
set: **6** parure
weight: **4** tola
jeweler: **7** gemmary
glass: **5** loupe
jewelry: **10** bijouterie
alloy: **6** oreide, oroide
artificial: **5** paste **6** strass **7** costume
cutting device: dop
false: **5** paste **6** strass **7** costume
piece: **4** ring **6** brooch **8** bracelet, necklace
set: **6** parure **8** lavalier, necklace **9** lavaliere **10** lavalliere
setting: **4** pave
Jezebel: **4** fury **6** virago
husband: **4** Ahab
victim: **6** Naboth
jib: gib **4** balk, boom, sail
jibe: See **gibe**
jiffy: **5** braid, flisk, hurry, trice **6** gliffy, moment, second **7** instant
jig: top **4** boat **5** dance, prank **6** fiddle **8** carriage, fishhook
jigger: cup **4** club **5** glass **6** bridge, gadget **7** support
jiggle: jar **5** dance, shake **6** diddle, teeter
jihad, jehad: war **6** strife **7** contest, crusade **8** campaign
jill: **4** girl **5** woman **10** sweetheart
jilt: mau **4** girl, gunk **5** cheat, woman **6** begunk, mitten, reject **7** abandon, deceive, discard
jimmy: bar, pry **4** neat, spot **5** dandy, jemmy **6** spruce **7** crowbar **9** greatcoat
Jimsonweed: **6** datura
jingle: **4** ring **5** clank, clink, rhyme, verse **6** tinkle **7** chinkle
jingoist: **10** chauvinist
jinni: **5** genie **6** afreet, Alukah, jinnee, Yaksha, Yakshi(fem.)
jinx: hex **5** jonah **6** hoodoo
jitters: **5** panic **6** dither **11** nervousness
jittery: **5** jumpy **7** fidgety, nervous
jivatma: ego **5** atman
Joan of Arc: **7** Pucelle
counselors: **6** voices
victory: **7** Orleans

Joan's spouse: 5 Darby
job: 4 char, duty, snap, task 5 chare, chore 8 sinecure
Job: *daughter:* 5 Kezia 6 Jemima
friend: 6 Bildad, Zophar 7 Eliphaz
home: Uz
Job's tears: 4 coix 5 adlai, adlay, grass, plant
jobber: 6 dealer 10 wholesaler
Jocasta: *daughter:* 6 Ismene 8 Antigone
husband: 7 Oedipus
son: 7 Oedipus 8 Eteocles 9 Polynices 10 Polyneices
jockey: 4 gull 5 rider, trick 6 fellow, laddie, outwit 8 maneuver 10 manipulate
kind of: 4 disk
jocose: dry 5 droll, merry
jocular: gay 4 airy 5 droll, funny, jolly, merry, silly, witty 6 blithe, elated, jocose, jocund, jovial, joyous, lively, ribald 7 comical, festive, gleeful, jesting, playful, waggish 8 animated, cheerful, gladsome, humorous, mirthful, sportive 9 burlesque, convivial, facetious, hilarious, vivacious 10 frolicsome
joculator: fod 4 mime 6 jester 7 juggler 8 conjurer, jongleur, minstrel 11 entertainer
jog: bob, mog 4 lope, poke, prod, shog, trot 5 dunch, nudge 6 canter 7 refresh 9 stimulate
joggle: 5 hotch 7 shoggle
John: Ian 4 Ivan, Juan, Sean
John Brown's Body author: 5 Benet
John of Gaunt: 9 Lancaster
John the Baptist: *father:* 7 Zachary 9 Zachariah, Zacharias
mother: 9 Elizabeth
johnnycake: 4 pone 7 hoecake
Johnson grass: 7 sorghum
join: add, fay, mix, tie, wed 4 abut, affy, ally, club, fuse, knit, knot, link, mate, meet, seam, team, weld, yoke 5 annex, atone, blend, chain, clout, enrol, enter, graft, hitch, marry, merge, miter, nally, piece, unite 6 adject, adjoin, assist, attach, cantle, cement, cocket, concur, couple, engage, enlist, enroll, mingle, solder, splice, suture 7 combine, conjoin, connect, consort, mortise 8 accouple, coalesce, compound, copulate 9 associate 10 amalgamate, articulate, consociate 11 incorporate
joined: 8 conjugal
joiner: 7 splicer 9 carpenter 10 woodworker
joining: 6 syzygy 8 abutting, addition
joint: ell, hip, tee 4 ares, butt, coxa, knee, node, seam 5 alula, ancle, ankle, cross, elbow, hinge, scarf, tenon, wrist 6 arthra(pl.), mutual, rabbet, resort 7 arthron, calepin, hangout, knuckle, pastern 8 coupling 12 articulation
pert. to: 5 nodal 9 articular
plant stem: 6 phyton 8 phytomer
put out of: 9 dislocate
right angle: ell, tee
turned outward: 6 valgus
without: 10 acondylose, acondylous
wooden: 5 tenon
joist: 4 beam 7 sleeper 8 studding
joke: dor, egg, fun, gag, gig, pun 4 fool, gaud, gibe, hoax, jape, jest, jibe 5 flirt, prank, rally, sport, tease 6 banter, humbug 7 bromide 8 chestnut
joker: out, wag, wit 4 card 5 catch 6 gagger, jester 7 farceur 9 mistigris
Joktan: *father:* 4 Eber
son: 5 Ophir
joll: 5 lurch
jollity: fun 5 cheer, mirth, revel 6 gaiety, gayety 7 revelry 8 hilarity 9 amusement, festivity, joviality, merriment 11 merrymaking 12 cheerfulness, exhilaration 13 jollification
jolly: 5 buxom, rally 6 cajole, jovial, mellow 7 jocular 11 merrymaking
jolly boat: 4 yawl
jolt: jar 4 blow, bump, butt, shog 5 knock, shake, shock 6 jostle, jounce
Jonah: 4 jinx 7 prophet
deliverer: 5 whale
jongleur: See **joculator**
Jonson comedy: Fox 7 Epicene, Volpone 9 Alchemist
Jordan: *region:* 5 Perea 6 Basham
joree: 7 chewink
Joseph: *brother:* Dan, Gad 4 Levi 5 Asher, Judah 6 Reuben, Simeon 7 Zebulun 8 Benjamin, Issachar, Naphtali
buyer: 8 Potiphar
father: 5 Jacob
mother: 6 Rachel
son: 4 Igal 7 Ephraim
josh: guy, kid, rib 4 joke 5 chaff, spoof, tease 6 banter, string
Joshua: *associate:* 5 Caleb
burial place: 5 Gaash
father: Nun
place of importance: 7 Aijalon
Joshua tree: 5 yucca
Josiah: *father:* 4 Amon
mother: 7 Jedidah
son: 8 Jehoahaz 9 Jehoiakim
joss: 4 idol 5 image 8 divinity
jostle: jar, jog 4 jolt, push, shog 5 crowd, elbow, shove 6 hurtle, hustle
jot: ace, bit 4 atom, iota, whit 5 grain, minim, point 6 tittle 8 particle

jouk: 4 dart, duck, fawn, hide 5 cheat, dodge, evade, skulk 6 cringe
jounce: 4 jolt 5 shake 6 bounce
journal: log 5 diary, paper 6 record 7 daybook, gazette, gudgeon, logbook 8 magazine 10 periodical
keeper: 7 diarist
journalist: 6 editor 8 reporter 9 columnist
journey: go; run 4 eyre, fare, iter(L.), ride, sail, tour, trek, trip 5 jaunt, route 6 errand, travel, voyage 7 circuit, odyssey, passage, travail 8 navigate 9 excursion 10 expedition, pilgrimage 13 peregrination
course of: 9 itinerary
division of: lap, leg
pert. to: 6 viatic 11 peripatetic
journeying: 6 errant
joust: 4 tilt 6 combat 7 tourney 10 tournament
field: 4 list
ready to: 5 atilt
jovial: gay 4 boon 5 bully, jolly, merry 6 elated, genial, jocose, jocund, joyous 7 jocular 9 convivial, hilarious
jowl: jaw 4 chop 5 cheek 6 dewlap, wattle 7 jawbone
joy: 4 gaud, glee 5 bliss, mirth, revel 6 gaiety, gayety 7 delight, ecstasy, elation, rapture, revelry 8 felicity, gladness, hilarity, pleasure 9 beatitude, festivity, happiness, rejoicing, transport 10 exultation, joyfulness, joyousness 12 cheerfulness, exhilaration
Muse: 4 Tara
joya: 5 jewel
joyless: 6 dismal 9 cheerless
joyous: gay 4 glad 5 merry 6 blithe, festal, festus 7 blessed, gaudful, festive, gleeful, jocular 8 cheerful, gleesome, mirthful 9 blitheful, delighted
Jubal's father: 6 Lamech
jubilant: 6 elated 8 exulting 9 rejoicing 10 triumphant
Judah (see also **Judea**):
brother: 4 Levi 6 Joseph, Reuben, Simeon
daughter-in-law: 5 Tamar
descendant: 4 Anub, Boaz 5 David, Jesse 9 Jerahmeel
father: 5 Jacob
king: 4 Ahaz 6 Uzziah
mother: 4 Leah
queen: 8 Athaliah
son: Er 4 Onan
Judaism (see also **Hebrew, Israel**):
abode of the dead: 5 Sheol
ascetic: 6 essene
Bible: 4 Tora 5 Torah
Bible text: 5 miqra
Book of Psalms: 8 Tehillim
bread: 5 echem, matzo 6 hallah, matzos 7 matzoth 8 afikomen
butcher: 6 shohet 8 shochtim
cabalistic book: 5 Zohar
calendar: see *month* below
ceremony: 8 habdalah
community: 6 aljama 8 kehillah
confession of sins: 5 Alhet 7 Ashamnu
convert: ger
Day of Atonement: 9 Yom Kippur
devil: 6 Belial
dispersion: 5 golah 8 diaspora
doctor of law: 6 scribe
doctrine: 6 Mishna 7 Mishnah 8 Kodashim
drum: 4 toph
festival: see *holiday* below
garment: 5 shawl, talis 7 tallith
harp: 5 nebel
healer: Asa
heretical doctrine: 7 Karaism
holiday: 5 Pesah, Purim 6 Pesach, Succos, Sukkos 7 Sukkoth 8 Hanukhah, Lagbomer, Shabouth 9 Tishahbab 11 Rosh Hashana 12 Simhath Torah
horn: 6 shofar 7 shophar
immigrant: 4 oleh 6 halutz 7 chalutz
instrument: 4 asor 5 nebel
instrument player: 9 psalterer, psaltress
judge: 7 shophet
land: 4 Zion
law: 4 Chok, Tora 5 Torah 6 Chukah, Talmud 7 Halacha, Halakah 8 Kashruth
lawgiver: 5 Moses
liturgy: 6 Maarib, Minhah 9 Shaharith
lyre: 4 asor
marriage broker: 8 shadchen
marriage custom: 8 levirate
meat inspection: 7 bedikah
miter: 7 petalon
month: Ab 4 Adar, Iyar, Elul 5 Tebet, Nisan, Sivan 6 Tishri, Kislev, Shebat, Beadar, Tammuz 7 Heshvan
mourning period: 6 Shivah
New Year: 11 Rosh Hashana
Old Testament division 11 Hagiographa
patriarch: 5 Isaac
patriot family: 8 Maccabee
pioneer: 6 halutz 7 chalutz
poems: 6 yigdal 8 Azharoth
prayer: 5 Alenu, Shema 7 Geullah
prayer book: 6 mahzor, siddur
priest: 4 Ezra 5 Aaron, Cohen 6 Levite
priestly caste: 7 Cohanim, Levites
prophet: 4 Amos, Ezra 5 Elias, Hosea, Jonah, Micah, Nahum 6 Daniel, Elijah, Elisha, Haggai 8 Habakkuk, Jeremiah 9 Zechariah
prophetess: 6 Huldah
proselyte: ger

psalm of praise: 6 hallel
redeemer: 4 goel
revelation: 5 Torah
ritual: see *ceremony* above
sabbath: 8 Saturday
sacred objects: 4 urim
sage: 4 Agur
scarf: 5 abnet 7 tallith
scroll: 11 Sepher Torah
sect member: 6 Essene, Hassid
skullcap: 6 kippah 7 yamilke 8 yarmulka
song: 8 hatikvah 9 hattikvah
spirit: 8 Asmodeus
synagogue: 5 schul
tassel: 6 zizith
teacher: 5 rabbi
temple precentor: 6 cantor
trumpet: 6 shofar 7 shophar
vestment: 5 ephod
women's organization: 8 Hadassah

Judas: 7 traitor 8 betrayer
place of suicide: 8 Aceldama, Akeldama

Judea (see also **Judah**):
ancient name: 5 Judah
governor: 6 Pilate
king: Asa 4 Ahaz, Amon 5 Herod 7 Jehoram 8 Manesseh 10 Jehoiachin 11 Jehosphaphat
place: 5 Berea

judge: try 4 deem, gage 5 count, court, gauge, opine, trier 6 critic, decide, dicast, puisne, umpire 7 account, adjudge, arbiter, believe, referee, shamgar, suppose 8 consider, deemster, dempster, estimate, sentence 9 criticise, criticize, determine 10 adjudicate, appreciate, arbitrator, chancellor
bench: 4 banc 6 bancus
chamber: 6 camera
circuit: 4 iter
entry of, after verdict: 6 postea
gavel: 4 mace
group: 5 bench
junior or subordinate: 6 puisne
kind: 6 deputy 9 assistant
of Hades: 5 Minos
of the dead: 6 Osiris
robe: 4 toga

judgment 4 deem, doom 5 arret, award, sense, taste 6 steven 7 censure, opinion, verdict 9 criticism 10 astuteness, visitation 11 sensibility
lack of: 6 acrisy
left to one's: 13 discretionary

judicable: 12 determinable

judicial assembly: 5 court

judiciary: 5 bench
document: 4 writ 8 decision

judicious: 4 wise 9 sagacious 10 discerning

Judith: *husband:* Manasses
victim: 10 Holofernes

juego: 4 game, play

jug jar 4 ewer, jail, olla, toby 5 ascos, askos, ascus, buire, cruse, gotch 6 gomlah, lockup, prison, tinaja, urceus 7 pitcher 8 cruisken 9 container, cruiskeen 10 bellarmine, jardiniere 13 schnabelkanne
shaped like a man: 4 Toby

Juggernaut 6 Vishnu

juggle: 7 conjure, shuffle 10 manipulate

juggler: 5 cheat 6 harlot 8 conjurer, conjuror, deceiver, jongleur 14 legerdemainist

jugglery: 8 trickery 9 deception 10 escamotage(F.), hanky-panky 13 sleight-of-hand

Jugoslavia: See **Yugoslavia**

juice: jus(F.), oil, sap 4 broo 6 cremor 8 gasoline 10 succulence 11 electricity
apple: 5 cider
fruit: rob 4 must, stum, wine 5 cider 6 casiri 7 vinegar
plant: sap 4 milk 5 latex 6 achete

juicy: 4 frim, racy 5 spicy 6 lively 7 piquant 9 succulent

juju: 5 charm 6 amulet, fetish

jujube: ber, elb

julep: 5 drink 8 beverage

Juliet: *betrothed:* 5 Paris
father: 7 Capulet
lover: 5 Romeo

jumble: 4 hash, heap, mess, raff, stir 5 botch, shake 6 bumble, huddle, medley, muddle 7 agitate, confuse, embroil 8 disorder, riffraff 9 confusion 10 hodgepodge 12 hugger-mugger

jump: hop, lep 4 leap, loup, lowp 5 bound, caper, halma, scold, vault 6 prance, spring 7 saltate
stick for: 4 pogo, pole

jumper: 5 dress 6 blouse, jacket

jumpy: 7 jittery, nervous 12 apprehensive

junco: 5 finch 8 snowbird

junction: 4 axil, seam 5 joint, union 6 suture 7 contact, meeting 8 crossing, juncture 10 confluence, connection

juncture: 4 pass 5 union 6 choice, crisis, strait 7 quandry 8 exigency, junction 9 emergency 11 conjuncture, predicament

June bug: dor 4 dorr

June grass: poa

Jungfrau: 4 peak 8 mountain
site of: 4 Alps

jungle: 5 shola
dweller: 5 beast, snake 6 savage

junior: son 6 puisne 7 younger 8 namesake

juniper: 4 cade, ezel 5 gorse, retem, savin 6 sabine, savine

junk: 4 boat, bunk, dope, drug, lump, rush 5 chunk, scrap, waste 6 heroin, refuse 7 discard, rubbish 8 nonsense 9 narcotics
junker: 5 noble 6 German 12 conservative
junket: 4 trip 5 feast 6 picnic 9 excursion 13 entertainment
Juno: 4 Hera
consort: 7 Jupiter
special messenger: 4 Iris
junta: 7 council 8 tribunal 9 committee 10 government
junto: 5 cabal 6 clique 7 coterie, faction 11 combination
jupe: 4 coat 5 shirt, skirt, stays, tunic 6 bodice, jacket
Jupiter: 4 Jove, Zeus
angel: 7 Zadkiel
consort: 4 Juno
daughter: 4 Bura 7 Minerva
epithet: 6 Stator
lover: Io
Roman temple: 7 Capitol
satellite: Io 6 Europa 8 Ganymede, Callisto
son: 6 Castor, Pollux
Jupiter Pluvius: 4 rain
jural: 5 legal 8 juristic
Jurassic division: 4 Lias
juridical: 5 legal 7 juridic
jurisdiction: law, see, soc 4 soke 5 venue 6 county, parish 7 diocese 8 dominion 9 authority, bailiwick, patronate 10 patriarchy 13 collectorship
ecclesiastical: see 6 parish 7 deanery, diocese
jurisprudence: law
juror: 7 assizer, juryman 8 talesman
group: 4 jury 5 panel
jury: 5 panel
additions: 5 tales 8 talesmen
attempt to influence: 9 embracery
form: 7 impanel
person: 8 talesman
summons: 6 venire
just (see also **joust**): due, fit 4 even, fair, only, true 5 equal, exact, legal, valid 6 candid, honest, merely, normal, purely, simply 7 correct, equable, upright 8 accurate, unbiased 9 equitable, impartial 10 legitimate
justice: law 6 equity 7 honesty, nemesis
god: 7 Forsete, Forseti, Forsite
goddess: 4 Maat
pert. to: 9 juridical
seat: 4 banc 5 court 6 bancus 8 tribunal
justification: 6 excuse 7 apology 9 authority, rationale
justify: 4 avow 6 adjust, defend, excuse 7 support, warrant 8 maintain, sanction 9 authorize, exculpate, vindicate
jut: 4 butt 5 bulge 6 beetle 7 project 8 overhang, protrude 10 projection
jute: 4 desi 5 gunny 6 burlap 7 sacking
Jutlander: 4 Dane
jutting: 7 salient
juvenile: 5 actor, young 8 immature, youthful 11 undeveloped
Juventas: 4 Hebe
juxtaposition: 7 contact 8 nearness 9 adjacence, adjacency, proximity 10 contiguity

K

kaama: 10 hartebeest
kaddish: 6 prayer 8 doxology
kae: 7 jackdaw
kaffeeklatsch: 6 social 9 gathering 11 get-together
Kaffir, Kafir: 4 Xosa 5 Bantu, fondo, Tembu 8 Matabele
corn: 7 sorghum
language: 4 Xosa
servant: 6 umfaan
warriors: 4 Impi
weapon: 4 keri, kiri 10 knobkerrie
Kafka character: 4 Olga
kaiser: 5 ruler 7 emperor
kaka: 6 parrot
genus: 6 nestor
kakapo: 6 parrot
kaki: 4 bird 5 stilt 9 persimmon
kakkak: 7 bittern
kale: 4 cole 5 green 7 cabbage, collard 8 colewort
kalends: 7 calends
kali: 5 plant 6 carpet 8 saltwort
Kali's husband: 4 Siva 5 Shiva
kalinite: 4 alum
Kalmuck, Kalmuk: 5 Eleut 6 Mongol
Kamchatka: *codfish:* 6 wachna 9 wachnacod
salmon: 6 mykiss
kamias: 7 bilimbi
Kanaka: 8 Hawaiian 10 Melanesian, Polynesian 11 Micronesian
kanari: 6 almond
Kandh language: Kui
kangaroo: 'roo 5 bilbi, bilby 6 turatt 7 bettong, wallaby 8 bettonga, boongary, forester 11 macropodian
female: doe, gin, roo
male: 6 boomer
young: 4 joey
kangaroo rat: 7 potoroo
Kansas: *county:* 4 Reno
fort: 5 Riley
river: 5 Osage
town: 4 Iola 5 Dodge, Lyons, Paola, Sedan 6 Salina, Topeka(c.) 7 Abilene 8 Lawrence 11 Leavenworth
tree: 10 cottonwood
Kant's category: 7 quality 8 modality, quantity, relation
kaput: 6 broken, ruined 8 defeated 9 destroyed
karakul: 5 sheep
Karelian lake: Seg
karma: 4 fate 7 destiny
Kartvelian: 4 Svan 5 Svane
karyotin: 9 chromatin
kasha: 4 mush 5 grain 6 cereal
Kashmir: *alphabet:* 6 sarada
capital: 8 Srinagar
deer: 6 hangul
official: 6 pundit
river: 6 Jhelum
katchung: 6 peanut
kava: ava, awa
bowl: 5 tanoa
kayak: 5 canoe
kazoo: 5 gazoo
kea: 6 parrot
Keats poem: 5 Lamia
kebbie: 4 club 5 stick 6 cudgel
ked: 4 tick
kedge: 6 anchor
keek: spy 4 look, peep
keel: vat 4 ship 5 upset 6 careen, carina 7 capsize, carinae(pl.) 8 flounder, navigate
part: 4 skag, skeg
right angle to: 5 abeam
without: 9 ecarinate
keel over: 4 seel 7 capsize
keel-shaped: 8 carinate
keelbill: ani
keeling: 7 codfish
keen: yap(Sc.) 4 avid, fell(Sc.), gleg(Sc.), nice, wide 5 acute, awake, eager, sharp 6 ardent, astute, bewail, biting, clever, hearty, lament, severe, shrewd 7 cunning, fer-

vent, intense, parlous, pungent 9 trenchant 10 hardheaded 12 enthusiastic 13 perspicacious

keenly: 6 dearly

keenness: 4 edge 6 acumen, genius, talent

keep: 4 fend, hold 5 board, guard, lodge, place 6 arrest, behold, detain, stable 7 confine, contain, husband 8 fortress, maintain, preserve, restrain, withhold 9 celebrate 10 livelihood
going: 7 sustain

keep back: bar, dam, hap 6 detain 7 reserve

keep in: 6 retain

keep on: 8 continue

keep out: 4 save 5 debar 7 exclude, reserve 8 withhold

keeper: 5 guard 6 alcade, alcaid, custos, pastor, warden 7 alcaide, alcayde, curator 8 custodes(pl.), guardian 9 constable, custodian 10 maintainer
of golden apple: 5 Ithun
of marches: 8 margrave
of park: 6 ranger

keeping: 4 care 5 award, guard, trust 6 charge 7 custody 10 caretaking, possession 11 maintenance 12 guardianship

keepsake: 5 token 7 memento 8 giftbook, souvenir

keest: sap 6 marrow 9 substance

keeve: tub, vat 5 basin

kef: 7 languor, tobacco 8 euphoria 10 dreaminess 12 tranquillity

keg: cag 4 cade, cask 6 barrel 7 barrico
open: 6 unhead

kegler: 6 bowler

kelly: hat 5 color, derby, green

kelp: 5 varec 6 varech 7 seaweed 8 bellware(Sc.)

ken: 4 know(Sc.), view 5 admit, sight 7 discern, insight 9 knowledge, recognize 10 cognizance, understand 13 understanding

kench: bin

Kenilworth author: 5 Scott

kennel: 5 drain, sewer 6 cannel, gutter, stable 9 enclosure

Kent: *freedman:* 4 laet
sheep: 6 romney
tribal law: 4 laes

kentledge: 5 metal 7 ballast

Kentucky: *college:* 5 Berea
county: 4 Owen 6 Harlan
town: 5 Benge, Berea 7 Paducah 10 Louisville

Kentucky bluegrass: Poa

Kentucky coffee tree: 6 bonduc, chicot

Kenya: *lake:* 6 Rudolf
native: 5 Masai
reserve: 5 Masai

kerchief: 5 curch(Sc.) 7 panuelo 8 headrail 12 handkerchief

kerchoo: 6 sneeze
answer to: 10 gesundheit 11 God Bless you

Keresan Indian: Sia

kerf: cut 4 slit 5 notch 6 groove 7 cutting

kermis, kermess: 4 fair 8 carnival 11 celebration

kernel: nut 4 bunt, core, meat, pith, seed 5 acini(pl.), grain 6 acinus, nuclei(pl.) 7 nucleus

kestrel: 6 falcon, fanner 7 stannel 9 windhover

ketch: 4 boat, saic 8 sailboat

ketone: 7 acetone, camphor, shogaol 8 acridone, civetone, deguelin 9 heptanone 14 cyclopentanone
oily: 5 irone 6 carone

kettle: pot, vat 4 cazo(Sp.) 5 lebes 6 hollow 7 caldron 8 cauldron, flambeau 9 teakettle 10 kettledrum
nose: 5 spout

kettledrum: 5 naker, tabor 6 atabal, nagara(Ind.), timbal 7 attabal, timbale, timpano, timpani(pl.), tympani(pl.)

kevel: bar, bit, peg 4 bolt 5 cleat, staff 6 cudgel 7 bollard

key: cay, fin 4 clef, isle, quay, reef 5 dital, islet, pitch 6 claves(pl.), clavis, island, opener, spline, tapper 7 digital 8 clavecin, solution, tonality 11 explanation
notch: 4 ward
part: bit
pert. to: 5 tonal, tonic
skeleton: 4 gilt 5 screw 7 twirler

key chain: 10 chatelaine

keyboard: 6 manual 7 clavier 8 pedalier 10 claviature

keyed up: 4 agog 5 eager 7 excited 10 stimulated

keynote: do 5 theme, tonic, topic 7 feature

keynoter: 4 boss 6 orator

keystone: 8 voussoir

Keystone State: 12 Pennsylvania

khedive's estate: 5 daira

Khmer Republic: See **Cambodia**

Khnemu's consort: 6 Anukit

Khyber Pass tribe: 6 Afridi

kiang: ass

kibble: 5 grind 6 bucket

kibblings: 4 bait

kibe: 4 chap, sore 5 crack

kibitzer: 7 adviser, meddler 9 spectator

kick: toe 4 boot, fleg, funk(Sc.), punt, yerk 5 bunch, fling 6 fitter(Sc.), object, recoil 7 grumble 8 complain 10 calcitrate, enthusiasm

kickshaw: toy 6 bauble

kid: guy 4 hoax, joke 5 child, suede, tease 6 banter 7 fatling, leather 8 cheverel, cheveril 9 youngster
kidcote: 6 prison
kidnap: 6 abduct
kidney: 4 neer
comb. form: 4 reni
pert. to: 5 renal
kidney-shaped: 8 reniform
kidney stone: 4 jade 8 calculus, nephrite 10 nephrolith
Kilauea goddess: 4 Pele
kilderkin: 4 cask 6 barrel 7 measure
Kilimanjaro peak: 4 Kibo
kill: 4 fake, hang, slay 5 croak, fordo, stone 6 deaden, diddle, famish, foredo, murder 7 achieve, execute, poniard 8 deathify, dispatch, lapidate 9 slaughter 11 assassinate
by stoning: 8 lapidate
by strangling: 7 garotte, garrote
killed: 4 slew 5 slain 9 immolated
killer: 6 gunman 7 soldier, torpedo 8 genocide, homicide, murderer 10 triggerman 11 infanticide
of relative: 8 filicide 9 matricide, parricide, patricide 10 fratricide, sororicide
killer whale: orc 4 orca 7 grampus
killing: 6 murder 7 slaying 8 homicide 9 euthanasy, martyrdom, slaughter 10 euthanasia
of brother or sister: 10 fratricide
of father: 9 patricide
of king: 8 regicide
of mother: 9 matricide
of self: 7 suicide
of small child: 11 infanticide
Kilmer poem: 5 Trees
kiln: 4 oast, oven 5 clamp, stove, tiler 6 cockle 7 furnace
kiloliter: 5 stere
kilt: 4 hang 5 pleat 6 fasten 7 filibag
pouch for: 7 sporran
kilter: 5 order 9 condition
kimmer: 4 girl 5 witch 6 cummer, friend
kimono sash: obi
kin: (see also **kinship**): 4 clan, race, sept 5 flesh, tribe 6 family 7 kindred, kinfolk, related 8 affinity, cousinry, kinsfolk, relation, relative 12 relationship
kind: ilk, kin 4 boon, gest, good, kith, mild, soft, sort, type 5 breed, class, genre, genus, geste, order 6 benigh, blithe, gender, genera(pl.), genial, gentle, goodly, humane, kindly, tender 7 amiable, clement, couthie, species, variety 8 amicable, benedict, friendly, generous, gracious, merciful 9 benignant, brotherly, favorable, indulgent, squeamish 10 benevolent, charitable, favourable, generation 11 considerate, description, kindhearted, sympathetic 13 compassionate
comb. form: 4 geno
same: 10 homogeneal
kindle: 4 beet, fire, move 5 beete, brood, light, young 6 alight, arouse, decoct, excite, ignite, illume, incite, litter 7 animate, emblaze, inflame, inspire, provoke
kindling: 5 fagot 6 faggot, sticks, tinder 7 akindle
kindness: 5 aloha 6 bounty 8 benefice 9 benignity 11 beneficence
kindred: kin, sib 5 blood, flesh 6 allied, family 7 cognate, kinsmen 8 affinity, kinsfolk 9 congenial 12 relationship
kine: 4 cows 6 cattle
kinetic: 6 active
king: dam, rex(L.), rey(Sp.), roi(F.) 4 czar, tzar 5 ruler 7 cacique, regulus 9 sovereign
chamber: 9 camarilla
child: 6 prince 8 princess
domestic officer: 8 palatine
family: 7 dynasty
legendary: Lud 4 Bran 5 Hogni, Lludd, Midas, Sesha 6 Oberon, Shesha 11 Prester John
murderer: 8 regicide
personnel: 5 thane 6 avener 7 avenuer, dapifer, viceroy
pert. to: 5 regal 6 regnal
symbol: 7 scepter, sceptre
title: Sir 4 Sire 7 Majesty 8 Highness
King Arthur: *abode:* 6 Avalon
birthplace: 8 Tintagel
character: 6 Elaine, Merlin
court site: 7 Camelot 8 Caerleon
crowner: 6 Dubric
death place: 6 Camlan
father: 5 Uther
fool: 7 Dagonet
forest: 7 Calydon
foster brother: Kay
hound: 6 Cavall
jester: 7 Dagonet
knight: Kay 6 Gareth, Gawain, Modred 7 Galahad 8 Lancelot, Tristram 9 Percivale
lady: 4 Enid
lance: Ron
magician: 6 Merlin
mother: 7 Igraine
nephew: 6 Gareth 7 Mordred
parent: 5 Uther 7 Igraine
queen: 8 Guinever 9 Guinevere
shield: 7 Pridwin
sister: 7 Morgain 11 Morgan le Fay
sword: 9 Excalibur
King Canute's consort: 4 Emma
king clover: 7 melilot

king crab: 7 limulus
King Henry IV character: Hal 5 Blunt, Henry, Percy, Poins 6 Scroop
King Lear: See **Lear**
king of beasts: 4 lion
king's evil: 8 scrofula
king's yellow: 8 orpiment
kingdom: 5 realm, world 6 empire, region
kingfish: 4 barb, haku, opah 6 bagara
kingfisher: 7 halcyon
kingly: 5 regal, royal 6 regnal 7 basilic, leonine 8 imperial, majestic
kink: 4 bend, curl, loop 5 bunch, chink, cramp, quirk, snarl, twist 6 buckle, tangle 7 caprice 11 peculiarity
kinkajou: 5 potto 6 mammal
kinship (see also **kin**): 5 blood, nasab 8 agnation, nearness 10 connection 11 propinquity 13 consanguinity
father's side: 5 agnat 6 agnate 8 agnation
mother's side: 5 enate 7 enation
kinsman (see also **kin, kindred**): 4 ally 6 friend 8 bandhava 9 rishtadar
kiosk: 8 pavilion 9 newsstand
kipe: 6 basket
Kipling: *poem:* 6 L'Envoi
tale: Kim
kirtle: 4 coat, gown 5 cover, dress, skirt, tunic 6 enwrap 7 garment 9 petticoat
Kish: *father:* Ner
son: 4 Saul
kismet: 4 fate 7 destiny
kiss: 4 bass, buss 5 smack 6 caress 8 osculate
kiss-me-quick: 6 bonnet
kiss of peace: pax
Kiss sculptor: 5 Rodin
kist: box 4 cist 5 chest 6 locker
kit: bag, box, cat, lot, set 6 kitten, outfit 7 catling 8 caboodle 10 collection
kitchen: ben(Sc.) 4 chil(Ind.) 5 calan(P.I.) 6 chilla(Ind.) 7 cuisine 8 scullery
pert. to: 8 culinary
ship's: galley
tool or utensil: 5 corer, ricer 6 beater, grater, opener, sifter 7 spatula 8 colander, strainer
kitchen garden: 7 olitory
kith: 6 friend 10 associates 12 acquaintance
kittenish: coy 6 frisky 7 playful 8 childish
kittiwake: 4 gull 5 annet
kitty; 4 bowl, pool 6 stakes
kiwi: roa 7 Apteryx
kleptomaniac: 5 thief 7 filcher 8 pilferer
Klondike: See **Alaska**
kloof: 4 glen 5 gorge 6 ravine, valley
knabe: boy
knack: art 4 ease, gift, hang 5 catch, skill, trick 8 facility 9 dexterity 10 adroitness
knap: cut, rap, top 4 bite, blow, chip, crop, hill, snap 5 break, crest, knoll 6 nibble, strike, summit 7 hilltop
knapsack: bag 6 wallet
knapweed: 5 bluet 7 harweed 8 bellweed, clubweed, hardhead, harshwee 10 harebottle
knarred: 6 knarry, knotty 7 gnarled
knave: boy, nob, pam 4 fool, jack 5 cheat, churl, losel, rogue, scamp 6 harlot, rascal, varlet 7 villain 9 miscreant, scoundrel, trickster
knavery: 5 fraud 8 mischief 10 dishonesty 12 sportiveness
knead: elt(Sc.), mix 5 malax 7 massage 8 malaxate 9 masticate 10 manipulate 11 incorporate
knee: bow 5 joint 10 supplicate
armor: 11 genouillere
bend: 5 kneel
bone: 7 patella
knee breeches: 8 knickers 12 smallclothes
kneecap: 7 patella
kneel: 4 genu 9 genuflect
kneeling desk: 8 prie-dieu
kneepan: 6 rotula 7 patella
knell: 4 bell, omen, ring, toll 6 stroke, summon 7 warning 8 proclaim
knickknack: toy 6 bauble, bawble, gadget, gewgaw, trifle 7 novelty, trinket 8 gimcrack, kickshaw
knife: cut 4 bolo, cane, corn, shiv, snee, stab 5 bowie, bread, chive, corer, gully, kurki, sword 6 barong, campit, colter, coutel, cuttle, dagger, trevet, worker 7 carving, machete, spattle, spatula, whittle, yatagan 8 belduque, serpette
case: 6 sheath
maker: 6 cutler
one-bladed: 6 barlow
plaster and paint: 7 spatula
sharpener: 4 hone 5 steel, stone
surgical: 6 catlin 7 catling, scalpel
knight: sir 5 eques 6 equite, Ritter 8 banneret, cavalier 9 caballero, caveliere, chevalier
attendant: 6 squire
banner: 8 gonfanon
cloak: 6 tabard
famous: 7 Caradoc, Cradock, Galahad 9 Lohengrin
fight: 5 joust
horse: 7 charger, palfrey
rank above: 7 baronet
servant: 4 page 6 varlet
title: sir
wife: 4 lady
wreath: 4 orle
knight-errant: 7 paladin

knight of the road: 4 hobo 5 tramp
knighthood: 8 chivalry
confer: dub
knightly: 5 brave 9 courteous 10 chivalrous
knit: 4 bind, heal, join, mend, purl 5 plait, unite, woven 6 cement, fasten 7 conjoin, connect, crochet, wrinkle 8 contract, entangle 10 intertwine 11 compaginate, consolidate
knitted blanket: 6 afghan
knitter: 6 legger
knitting: 5 craft 9 handiwork
rod: 6 needle
term: 4 purl 7 castoff
knob: bob, bur, nub 4 boss, buhr, burr, club, heel, knot, lump, node, tore, umbo 5 bulge 6 button, croche, emboss, handle, pommel 12 protuberance
pointed: 6 finial
knobby: 5 gouty, hilly 6 knotty
knobkerrie: 4 club 5 stick
knobstick: 4 cane, club 5 stick 8 blackleg
knock: con, dad, hit, rap, tap, wap 4 beat, blow, bolt, bump, chap, chop, dash, daud, ding, dunt, hill(Sc.), jolt, knap, polt, poss, rout, slay 5 pound, thump 6 bounce 7 hillock(Sc.) 9 criticize 12 faultfinding
knock down: 4 fell 5 floor 9 prostrate
knock-kneed: 6 valgus
knock off: rob 4 kill, stop 6 deduct 8 overcome 11 discontinue
knock out: 4 daze, stun 6 defeat 7 exhaust 8 paralyze
knockabout: 5 actor, sloop, yacht
knockout: K.O. 4 kayo 5 facer
knoll: 4 knap, knob, lump 5 mound 7 hillock
knop: 5 knosp 6 button 8 ornament
knot: bow, nep, tie 4 bond, burl, burr, harl, knag, knar, knob, knur, loop, lump, node, snag 5 gnarl, hitch, knurl, nodus, snarl 6 finial, granny, nodule, puzzle, tangle 7 chignon, cockade, laniard, lanyard, rosette 8 entangle 12 entanglement, protuberance
running: 4 slip 5 noose
pert. to: 5 nodal
knotted: 5 noded 6 knotty 7 crabbed, nodated 9 intricate
knotted lace: 7 tatting
knotty: 4 hard 5 gouty 6 craggy 7 complex 9 difficult, intricate 10 perplexing
know: can, con, ken(Sc.), wis, wot 4 wist 7 realize 8 perceive 9 recognize 10 comprehend, experience, understand
know-it-all: 6 smarty 8 wiseacre
know-nothing: 8 agnostic 9 ignoramus 11 scissorbill
knowing: 4 able, gash, wise 5 cagey, downy, leery, smart, witty 6 scient, shrewd 7 gnostic, sapient, stylish 8 informed 9 cognitive, conscious, gnostical, wide-awake 10 experience, perceptive 11 intelligent 13 comprehension
knowledge: ken 4 lore 6 wisdom 7 cunning, hearing, science 8 learning, sapience 9 cognition, erudition 10 cognizance, experience 11 information, instruction 12 acquaintance 13 enlightenment, understanding
instrument: 7 organon
lack of: 9 ignorance, nescience
object of: 7 cognita(pl.), scibile 8 cognitum
pert. to: 7 gnostic
seeker: 10 philonoist
slight: 7 inkling, smatter 8 sciolism 10 smattering
summary: 13 encyclopaedia
systematized: 7 science
universal: 9 pantology
known: 5 couth, famed 6 famous 7 notable 8 familiar, renowned 9 notorious
knucklebone: 4 tali(pl.) 5 dolos, talus 7 dolosse(pl.)
kobird: 6 cuckoo
kobold: nis 5 gnome 6 goblin 7 Hodeken(G.) 10 nissespire
koel: 4 bird 6 cuckoo
kohl: 8 antimony
kohlrabi: 6 turnip
kokoon: gnu
kokopu: 4 fish, para
kola: nut 6 jackal
kopecks (100): 5 ruble
kopje: 4 hill 5 mound 7 hillock
Koran: 7 Alcoran
compiler's son: Ali
division: 4 Sura
interpreter: 5 ulema 7 alfaqui 8 alfaquin
pert. to: 9 alcoranic
register: 5 sijil 6 sijill
Korea: 6 Chosen
money: won 4 hwan
peninsula: 6 Ongjin
river: Kum 4 Hans, Look, Yalu 5 Imjin 7 Naktong
soldier: ROK
town: 5 Fusan, Heijo(c.), Kanko, Keijo(c.), Kimpo, Moppo, Rigen, Seoul(c.) 6 Andong, Antung, Gunzan, Inchon, Jushin, Kaeson, Keishu, Pochon, Rashin, Reigui, Wonzan 7 Capyong, Kenjiho, Moonsan, Samchok, Seishin 8 Chunchon, Pingyang 9 Chinnampo, Chuminjun, Shingishu
weight: kon
kosher: fit 4 pure 5 clean 6 proper 8 Kashruth 9 undefiled
meat maker: 6 porger
opposite of: 4 tref
kra: ape 7 macaque
kraal: 5 crawl 9 enclosure

krimmer: fur 4 skin 8 lambskin
Krishna: 6 Vishnu 10 Juggernaut
grandson: 9 Aniruddha
mother: 6 Devaki
paradise: 6 Goloka
kudo: 4 fame 5 glory 6 praise, renown 8 prestige 9 extolling
kudu: 8 antelope
kulak: 6 farmer 7 peasant
kumiss: 5 drink
Kurd: 7 Persian
ancestors: 9 Gordyaean
Kurile island: 6 Iturup
Kurland Peninsula inhabitant: 4 Lett
kurrajong: 4 tree 5 shrub 6 calool
kurtosis: arc 9 curvature
Kwantung seaport: 6 Dairen
kyphosis: 8 humpback 9 curvature, hunchback
Kyushu: See Japan

L

L: 5 fifty
La Boheme: *composer:* 7 Puccini
heroine: 4 Mimi
laagte: 6 bottom, valley
Laban's daughter: 4 Leah 6 Rachel
label: tab, tag 4 band 5 brand 6 docket, lappet, tassel 8 classify 9 designate 10 definition
labellum: lip 5 petal
labile: 8 unstable
labium: lip
labor: 4 moil, task, toil, work 5 sweat, yakka 6 effort, labour, stress, strive 7 travail 8 business, drudgery, exertion, industry, struggle 11 lucubration
labor organization: AFL, CIO, UMW 5 union, ILGWU
laboratory equipment: 5 pipet 6 beaker, retort
labored: 5 heavy 6 forced 8 strained 9 difficult, elaborate
laborer: man 4 hand, hind, peon, prol 5 cooly, plebe 6 coolie, toiler, worker 7 bracero, dvornik, hobbler, wetback, workman 10 bluecollar
laborious: 4 hard 5 heavy 7 arduous, operose, tedious 8 diligent 9 assiduous, difficult 11 displeasing, painstaking
Labrador retriever: 12 Newfoundland
Labrador tea: 5 ledum 8 gowiddie 9 evergreen
labyrinth: 4 maze 7 circuit
labyrinthine: 8 involved, puzzling, tortuous 9 intricate 11 complicated
lac: 4 milk 5 resin 6 veneer
lace: gin, net, tat 4 band, beat, cord, lash, line 5 braid, noose, plait, snare, twine, unite 6 fasten, ribbon, string 7 ensnare, entwine, laniard, lanyard 8 biliment, openwork 9 embroider, interlace 10 embroidery, intertwine, shoestring
barred: 6 grille
edge: 5 picot
frilled: 5 jabot, ruche
front: 5 jabot
gold and silver: 5 orris
kind: 5 lisle, orris, tulle 7 alencon, allover, guipure, macrame, potlace 9 Alostlace 10 colberteen, colbertine 12 Valenciennes
knotted: 7 tatting
loop in: 5 picot
make: tat
opening: 6 eyelet
lacerate: cut, rip 4 bite, rend, rive, tear 6 harrow, mangle
laceration: rip 4 tear 5 wound
lacework: See **lace**
lachrymose: sad 5 teary, weepy
laciniate: 7 fringed
lacis: 4 lace 7 network
lack: 4 need, void, want 5 fault, minus 6 dearth 7 absence, failure, paucity, poverty 8 scarcity 9 indigence 10 deficiency 11 destitution
lackadaisical: 4 blah 7 languid 8 listless 10 spiritless 11 sentimental
lackaday: 4 alas
lackey: 5 toady, valet 7 footman, servant
lacking: shy 5 short 6 absent, barren 7 wanting 8 desolate 9 deficient, destitute
lackluster: 4 dull 6 cloudy 8 dullness
Laconia: *capital:* 6 Sparta
people: Obe
laconic: 5 brief, pithy, short, terse 7 concise, pointed, summary 8 succinct
lacquer: 7 shellac, varnish
lactate: 4 salt 5 actol, ester
lacteal: 5 milky
lacuna: gap 5 break
lacy: 7 weblike 8 delicate
lad: boy, tad 4 carl, dick, hind 5 caddy, youth 6 caddie, shaver 9 stripling 10 adolescent
on call: 4 page 7 bellboy 9 messenger
serving: 7 gossoon 8 coistrel, coistril
ladder: run, sty 4 stee 7 scalade
on fortification: 8 escalade
step: 7 ratline
ladderlike: 6 scalar

lade: dip 4 bail, draw, lave, load, ship 5 drain, scoop 6 burden, charge, weight 7 fraught, freight
laden: 4 lade 7 fraught 9 freighted, oppressed
ladies' man: 4 beau
lading: 4 load 5 cargo 6 burden 7 freight 10 freightage
ladle: dip 4 bail 5 scoop, serve, spoon 6 dipper
ladrone: 5 rouge, thief 6 bandit, robber 7 brigand 10 highwayman
Ladrone island: 4 Guam 6 Saipan 8 Marianas
lady (see also **woman**): 4 burd, dame, dona(Sp.), rani(Ind.) 5 begum(Ind.), donna(It.), madam, ranee(Ind.) 6 domina(L.), female, senora(Sp.) 7 signora(It.) 11 gentlewoman
noble: 5 queen 7 duchess 8 countess, princess
young: 7 damozel 10 demoiselle, jeune fille(F.)
lady-killer: 4 wolf 5 sheik 7 Don Juan 8 Casanova
Lady of the Lake: 5 Ellen
lady's maid: 5 woman 9 tirewoman
lady's thumb: 9 peachwort, persicary
ladybird: bug 6 beetle
genus: 9 epilachna
ladyfish: oio 6 wrasse
ladylike: 6 female, polite 7 genteel 8 feminine
ladylove: 5 amour, lover 8 mistress 10 sweetheart
Laertes: *father:* 8 Acrisius
son: 7 Ulysses
wife: 8 Anticlea
laet: 8 freedman
lag: 4 flag, rift, tire 5 delay, stave, tarry, trail, weary 6 dawdle, linger, loiter 9 drawlatch 10 dillydally 11 retardation
lager: ale 4 beer 5 drink 8 beverage
laggard: 4 slow 6 remiss 8 backward, loiterer, sluggish 9 straggler
lagging: 5 tardy 8 backward
lagniappe: tip 4 gift 5 bonus, pilon 7 present 8 gratuity
lagomorph: 4 hare, pika 5 coney 6 rabbit
lagoon: 4 cove, haff, pond, pool 5 liman 6 laguna(Sp.)
Lagoon Islands: 6 Ellice
laic: 6 layman 7 secular 15 nonprofessional
laid-down: 5 posed 6 thetic 8 academic 10 prescribed 11 traditional
lair: den, lie 4 holt, rest 5 haunt 6 cavern 7 hideout, retreat 8 quagmire
Lais: 7 Burmese
laissez-faire: 8 inactive, tolerant 9 donothing, unconcern 11 philosophic 12 indifference, mercantilism 15 individualistic, noninterference
laity: 6 laymen
Laius' son: 7 Oedipus
lake: red, sea 4 loch, mear, mere, pond, pool, shat, shot, tarn 5 chott, color, lough, shott 7 pigment
deposit: 5 trona
highest: 8 Titicaca
Indian: 4 Erie
marshy: 5 liman
Lake Chad: *people:* 4 Maba
river: 5 Shari
Lake State: 8 Michigan
lakelet: 4 pond
lakhs (100): 5 crore
lam: hit 4 bash, beat 6 thrash
Lamaism: *dignitary:* 8 hutukhtu
priest: 6 Getsul
stupa: 7 Chorten
lamasery: 9 monastery
lamb: ean 4 yean 5 agnus(L.) 6 agneau(F.), cosset 7 chilver, fatling, hogling
hand-raised: hob
leg of: 5 gigot
pet: 4 cade 6 cosset
Lamb of God: 8 Agnus Dei
Lamb's penname: 4 Elia
lambskin: 4 case 5 suede 6 bagdad 7 baghdad
lambent: 7 glowing, radiant 8 wavering 9 brilliant 10 flickering
lame: 4 game, halt 5 gammy 6 feeble 7 cripple, halting 8 crippled, decrepit, disabled, handicap 9 defective, hamstring 12 incapacitate
Lamech: *son:* 5 Jabal, Jubal 9 Tubalcain
wife: 4 Adah 6 Zillah
lament: cry, rue 4 care, howl, keen, moan, pine, sigh, wail, weep 5 croon, dolor, dirge, elegy, greet, grief, mourn 6 bemoan, bewail, beweep dolour, grieve, lament, ochone, outcry, plaint, regret, repent, repine, yammer 7 condole, deplore, elegize 8 jeremiad 9 complaint
lamentable: sad 8 wretched 11 distressing
lamia: 5 witch 7 vampire 9 sorceress
lamina: 5 blade, flake, hinge, layer
laminated: 5 flaky 6 scaled 7 fissile, spathic, tabular 8 foliated, lamellar
lamp: 4 davy, etna 5 light, torch 7 lantern 8 lanthorn 9 veilleuse
safety: 4 davy
lampblack: 4 soot
lamplighter: 5 match, spill, torch
lampoon: 5 squib 6 satire 8 ridicule, satirize 10 pasquinade
lamprey: eel 6 ramper
migration: 7 eelfare

lanai: 5 porch 7 veranda
lanate: 5 wooly 6 woolly
Lancashire section: 6 Eccles
lance: cut 4 dart, hurl 5 joust, spear 6 faucre, lancet, launch, pierce, weapon 7 javelin
head: 5 morne
Lancelot's lover: 6 Elaine
lancer: 4 ulan 5 uhlan 7 soldier, spearer 10 cavalryman
lancet: 5 fleam
lancinate: 4 stab 5 gouge 6 pierce 8 lacerate
land: erd 4 ager(L.), soil 5 catch, earth, glebe, realm, shore, terra(L.) 6 alight, arrive, debark, ground 7 acreage, capture, country, terrene 9 disembark, territory
alluvial: 5 delta
ancestral: 5 ethel
arid: see **desert**
barren: see **wasteland**
body: 9 continent
church: 5 glebe 8 abadengo
cultivated: 4 farm 5 arada, arado, ranch, tilth 7 orchard, tillage
dealer: 7 realtor
depressed: 6 graben
elevated: alp 4 hill, mesa 5 mound, ridge 7 plateau 8 mountain
grazing: 5 field, plain, range 6 meadow 7 pasture
heritable: 4 alod, fief, odal 5 allod 7 alodium 8 allodium
hilly: 4 down
householder's: 6 barton, casate 7 demesne
in foreign territory: 7 enclave
living on: 11 terrestrial
low: 4 vale 5 carse(Sc.) 6 polder, valley 9 intervale
measure: ar; are, rod 4 acre, mile, rood 5 meter, perch 6 decare
mythical: 4 Eden 6 Utopia 7 Erewhon, Lemuria 9 Shangri-La
narrow: 4 neck 6 strake 7 isthmus 9 peninsula
open: 4 moor, vega, wold 5 heath, slash, weald
owned: see *heritable* above
pasture: ham 5 grass 6 meadow
pert. to: 11 continental
piece: lot 4 acre, farm 5 laine, ranch, range, solum (law) spong 6 estate
plowed: 5 arada, arado, field 6 arable, fallow, furrow 7 thwaite
point of: 4 cape, ness, spit
profit: 4 crop, rent 7 esplees
public: 4 parc, park
reclaimed: 6 polder 7 novalia(Sc.)
river drained: 5 basin
sandy: 4 dene
tilled: see *plowed* above
treeless: 5 llano 6 steppe 7 prairie, savanna 8 savannah
triangular: 4 gore
uncultivated: 5 heath, waste 6 desert, forest
uplifted: 5 horst
waste: see **wasteland**
waterlocked: ile(F.) 4 isle 6 island
watery: bog 4 flow, moor 5 marsh, swamp 6 morass 7 maremma(It.)
Land of Cakes: 8 Scotland
Land of the Midnight Sun: 6 Norway
Land of Nod: 5 sleep
Land of Plenty: 6 Goshen
Land of Promise: 7 Canaan 9 Palestine
Land of Rising Sun: 5 Japan
land's end guardian: 8 Bellerus
landed: See **estate; land**
landholder: 5 laird 6 coscet, yeoman
landholding: 6 tenure
landing: 8 arrivage
kind: 5 crash 10 three-point
place: 4 dock, pier 5 wharf 7 airport 8 airplace, arrivage
landlady: 5 duena 7 hostess 8 mistress 9 concierge
landlord: 4 host 5 laird(Sc.) 6 lessor
landmark: 4 copa, dole, dool, mere 5 bound, cairn, senal(Sp.) 9 milestone
landscape: 4 plan 5 plant, scene 7 scenery, paysage, picture 8 decorate
landslide: 9 avalanche 10 eboulement
landsman: 6 lubber, sailor
lane: way 4 char, path, race 5 aisle, alley, byway, chare, tewer 6 boreen, bypath, gullet, street, throat, vennel 7 pathway 8 footpath 10 passageway
Langobard king: 6 Alboin
language: 4 chib 5 argot, idiom, lingo, slang 6 jargon, speech, tongue 7 dialect, diction
ancient: 4 Pali 5 Aryan, Greek, Latin 6 Hebrew 7 Chinese 8 Sanskrit
artificial: 9 Esperanto
change: 8 misquote 9 interpret, translate 10 paraphrase
classical: 5 Greek, Latin
common: 6 French, German 7 Chinese, English, Italian, Russian, Spanish
Cretan: 6 Minoan
dead: 5 Latin
figurative: 7 imagery
international: od, ro; ido 7 volapuk 9 esperanto
nonmetrical: 5 prose
pert. to: 8 semantic
pompous: 4 bull, wind 7 bombast, oratory 8 rhetoric
principles: 7 grammar

Romance: **5** Latin **6** French **7** Catalan, Italian, Spanish **8** Rumanian **10** Portuguese
sacred: **4** Pali
secret: **5** argot
Semitic: **6** Arabic, Hebrew
spoken: **7** diction **13** pronunciation
unintelligible: **9** gibberish
languid: **4** dull, slow, weak **6** dreamy, tender **8** indolent, listless, lovesick, sluggish **9** lethargic **11** indifferent
languish: die **4** fade, fail, flag, long, pine, wilt **5** droop, dwine, faint, swoon **6** linger, repine **7** decline
languor: kef **4** kaif, keef, kief **5** ennui **7** boredom **8** debility **9** lassitude **10** stagnation
langur: **6** monkey **8** wanderoo
lanky: **4** lean, slim, tall, thin **5** gaunt, rangy, spare **6** gangly, meager, meagre, skinny **7** haggard, slender **8** gangling, ungainly **9** elongated **12** loose-jointed
lanose: **5** wooly **6** woolly
lantern: **4** lamp **5** bowet **8** absconce
lanyard, laniard: **4** cord, knot, rope
Laodamia's father: **7** Acastus
Laodicean: **8** lukewarm **9** apathetic **10** uninvolved **11** indifferent
Laomedon's son: **8** Tithonus
lap: sip **4** fold, lick, wash **5** drink, slurp **6** circle, cuddle, enfold, infold **7** circuit
lap robe: rug **5** throw **6** afghan **7** blanket
lapactic: **8** laxative **9** cathartic
lapel: **5** rever **6** revers
lapidary: **7** jeweler **8** engraver **9** gem cutter
instrument: dop **4** dial
lapidate: **4** pelt **5** stone
lapin: **6** rabbit
Lapland: *animal:* **8** reindeer
city or town: **4** Kola **6** Kiruna
sled: **4** pulk **5** pulka
lappet: **4** lobe **5** label **6** fabric
lapse: err **5** break, error, fault **6** expire **7** delapse, escheat, failure, relapse **8** caducity, slipping **9** backslide
lapsed: **4** dead, null, void
laputan: **6** absurd, dreamy **7** utopian **9** visionary **10** unfeasible **11** impractical
lapwing: **5** pewit **6** plover
lar: **6** gibbon
larboard: **4** left, port
larceny: **5** theft **7** looting, robbery **8** burglary, stealage
lard: fat, oil **4** mort **5** adeps(L.), baste, enarm, inarm **6** enrich, fatten, grease
larder: **4** cave **6** pantry, spence, spense **8** cupboard
large: big **4** bold, free, huge, main, vast, waly **5** ample, broad, bulky, burly, enorm, giant, great, hulky, massy, wally **6** goodly, heroic **7** copious, immense, liberal, massive, titanic, weighty **8** colossal, enormous, gigantic **9** capacious, extensive, plentiful **12** considerable **13** comprehensive
comb. form: **5** macro
largess, largesse: **4** gift **6** bounty **7** charity, present **10** generosity, liberality **11** beneficence
lariat: **4** rope **5** lasso, noose, reata(Sp.), riata(Sp.)
loop: **5** honda, hondo **6** hondoo, hondou
larix: **5** larch **7** larches
lark: **6** frolic **7** carouse **8** carousal
larkspur: **10** delphinium
larrigan: **8** moccasin
larrup: **4** beat, blow, flog, whip
larry: hoe **5** grout, noise **6** mortar **9** confusion **10** excitement
larva: bot, fly, loa **4** bott, grub **5** eruca **6** botfly, woubit **7** atrocha, oestrid **8** cercaria, horsefly **11** caterpillar
aquatic: **12** hellgrammite
beetle: **4** grub
larvate: **6** masked **7** covered **9** concealed
lascar: **6** sailor **12** artilleryman
lascivious: **6** wanton **7** blissom **9** lecherous, salacious, seductive **10** libidinous, licentious
lash: **4** beat, bind, blow, flog, lace, whip, yerk **5** slash **6** berate, fasten, strike, stroke, swinge **7** belabor, eyelash, scourge
lasket: **8** latching
lass: gal **4** gill, girl, maid, miss **5** trull, woman **6** cummer, kimmer, lassie, maiden **7** colleen **10** sweetheart **11** maidservant
lassitude: **5** ennui **7** languor **8** debility, lethargy **10** exhaustion
lasso: **4** rope **5** noose, reata(Sp.), riata(Sp.) **6** lariat
last: **4** dure, tail **5** abide, final, omega **6** endure, latest, utmost **7** dernier, extreme, tail-end **8** continue, eventual, hindmost, rearmost, ultimate **9** aftermost **10** concluding
but one: **6** penult
long: **7** outwear **9** perendure
Last of the Mohicans: **5** Uncas
Last Supper: *representation:* **4** cena
room: **7** cenacle
lasting (see also **last**): **6** stable **7** chronic, lasting, eternal **8** constant **9** perennial, permanent, steadfast **11** everlasting
briefly: **9** ephemeral, temporary
latch: **5** catch, sneck **6** fasten **8** fastener
latchet: tab **5** thong
late: new **4** sere **5** tardy **6** former, recent **7** belated, overdue **8** neoteric, serotine **10** behindhand
comb. form: neo

latent: 6 hidden 7 dormant 9 concealed, potential, quiescent, suspended 11 undeveloped
later: 4 anon, soon 5 after, newer 6 behind, future, puisne 7 elderly, neozoic 9 hereafter, posterior, presently 10 subsequent 12 subsequently
lateral: 4 side 8 indirect, sideward
latest: 4 last 6 newest
latex: 5 juice 6 rubber 9 secretion
lath: 4 slat 5 spale, stave
attachment: 7 setover
operator: 6 turner
part: 7 mandrel
lather: 4 foam, soap, suds 5 froth 6 freath
Latin (see also **Rome**): 5 Roman 7 Italian, Romanic
barracks: 6 canaba
bath: 7 balneum
booth: 7 taberna
bowl: 6 patina
boxing glove: 6 cestus, ceston
boy: 4 puer
bronze: aes
building: 5 aedes
cape: 5 sagum 6 byrrus
cistern: 9 impluvium
connective: et
contract: 5 nexum
couch: 9 accubitum
deity: 4 deus
dish: 4 lanx 6 lances, pateral, patina
food: 5 cibus
foot: pes
for example: 4 vide
force: vis
friend: 6 amicus
garland: 6 corona
ghosts: 7 lemures
grammar: 5 donat, donet
grammatical case: 6 dative 8 ablative, genitive, vocative 10 accusative, nominative
hope: 4 spes
hour: 4 hora
javelin: 4 pile 5 aclys, pilum
life: 4 vita
ornament: 5 bulla
post: 4 meta
pronoun: tu; ego, hic 4 ille, ipse, iste
ram: 5 aries
rite: 4 orgy 5 sacra
roof opening: 10 compluvium
seat: 5 sella
shelter: 7 taberna
towel: 5 mappa
trumpet: 4 tuba 6 buccin 7 buccina
Latinus' daughter: 7 Lavinia
latite: 4 lava
latitude: 5 scope, width 6 extent 7 breadth, freedom 8 distance
complement: 10 colatitude
measure: 6 degree 8 parallel
zero degrees: 7 equator
latrant: 7 barking 8 snarling 11 complaining
latrine: 5 privy 6 toilet
latter: 4 last 5 final 6 latest
Latter Day Saints: 7 Mormons
latterly: 4 anew 6 lately 8 recently
lattice: 6 pinjra(Ind.) 7 trellis 8 espalier
latticework: 5 arbor, grate 6 arbour 7 grating
Latvia: *city:* 4 Riga(c.) 5 Libau 6 Dvinsk, Libava 8 Dunaburg 10 Daugavpils
coin: lat 6 rublis 7 kapeika 8 santimas
measure: 4 stof 5 kanne, stoff, verst 6 kulmet, sagene, versta, verste 7 verchoc, verchok 8 krouchka, kroushka, pourvete 9 deciatine, lofstelle 10 tonnstelle
parliament: 6 Saeima
people: 5 Letts
river: Aa
university site: 4 Riga
weight: 9 liespfund
laud: 4 lute 5 extol 6 extoll, praise 7 adulate, applaud, cittern, commend, glorify, magnify 8 emblazon, eulogize 9 panegyric 10 compliment
laudable: 9 allowable, exemplary 12 praiseworthy
laugh: 4 gaff, haha 5 fleer, snort 6 cackle, giggle, guffaw, hawhaw, nicker, titter 7 chortle, grizzle, snicker 9 cachinate
disposed to: 7 risible
incipient: 4 grin 5 smile
pert. to: 8 gelastic
laughable: odd 5 comic, droll, funny, merry, queer, witty 7 amusing, comical, risible, strange, waggish 8 gelastic, humorous, sportive 9 burlesque, diverting, facetious, grotesque, ludicrous 10 ridiculous
laughing: 5 riant
laughing bird: 4 gull, loon 5 pewit 10 woodpecker
laughing owl: 5 wekau
laughter: 5 mirth, risus(L.)
pert. to: 7 risible
launder: tye 4 wash
laundry: 4 wash 10 laundromat 13 blanchisserie(F.)
laureate: 13 distinguished
laurel: bay 4 fame 5 honor 6 daphne, myrtle, tarata, trophy 7 garland, taratah 9 spoonwood 11 distinction
lava: aa, oo 4 slag 5 ashes 6 coulee, latite, scoria, verite 7 clinker 8 pahoehoe
fragment of: 8 lapillus

sheet of: 6 coulee
lavabo: 5 basin 8 washbowl 9 cleansing
lavaliere, lavalier: 7 pendant
lavation: 4 bath 6 lavage 7 washing 9 cleansing
lavatory: 5 basin 8 washbowl, washroom
lave: 4 bail, lade, pour, wash 5 bathe, rinse
lavender: 6 pastel, purple, violet
laver: 5 basin 6 trough, vessel 7 cistern
Lavinia: *father:* 7 Latinus
husband: 6 Aeneas
mother: 5 Amata
lavish: 4 free, lash, rank, wild 5 flush, spend, waste 7 opulent, profuse 8 prodigal, reckless, splendid, squander 9 bountiful, expensive, exuberant, impetuous, luxuriant, sumptuous, unstinted 10 immoderate 11 extravagant, magnificent 12 unrestrained 13 superabundant
law: act, bar, ius(L.), jus(L.), lex(L.) 4 code, doom, rule, Tora 5 canon, edict, mesne, sutra, Torah 6 custom, decree, equity, noetic, sutrah, suttah 7 derecho, justice, precept, statute 8 handicap 9 enactment, ordinance, principle 11 commandment, legislation 12 constitution, jurisdiction 13 jurisprudence
action: res 4 suit 5 actus 8 replevin 9 gravamina
body of: 4 code
breaker of: 5 felon 6 sinner 8 criminal
claim: 4 lien
contrary to: 7 illegal, illicit 8 unlawful 16 unconstitutional
decree: 4 nisi 5 edict
degree: LLD
delay: 4 mora
document: 4 deed, writ 6 capias, elegit
expounder of: 6 jurist
goddess: 4 Maat
male succession: 5 Salic
man of: 5 judge 6 jurist, lawyer 7 counsel, justice 8 attorney 9 barrister
Manu: 5 sutra, sutta
offender: 8 criminal 9 desperado, wrongdoer
offense: 4 tort 5 crime, malum 6 delict
oral: 5 parol 11 nuncupative
order: 4 writ
permitted by: see **lawful**
pert. to: 5 legal 7 canonic 9 canonical, judiciary 11 legislative
philosophy of: 13 jurisprudence
prevent by: 5 estop
warning: 6 caveat

lawful: due 5 legal, licit, valid 7 canonic, ennomic 10 legitimate
lawgiver: 5 Moses
lawless: 4 lewd 6 unruly 7 illegal 8 anarchic 9 dissolute 10 anarchical, disorderly, tumultuous
lawlessness: 4 riot 6 mutiny 7 anarchy, license 10 illegality
lawmaker: 5 solon 7 senator 10 legislator
lawn: 5 arbor, grass, sward 6 arbour 7 batiste 9 grassland, grassplot, grasswork
lawsuit: 4 case
one engaged in: 8 litigant
subject: res
lawyer: 6 avocat(F.) 8 attorney, commoner 9 barrister, counselor 10 counsellor
bad: 7 shyster 11 pettifogger
lax: 4 dull, free, limp, open, pave, slow 5 loose, slack, tardy 6 remiss 7 lenient 8 backward, careless, inactive 9 dissolute, negligent 10 unconfined 11 inattentive 12 unrestrained
lay: bet, put, set 4 bury, poem, rest, song 5 carol, ditty, place, quiet, stake, still, wager 6 ballad, entomb, hazard, impose, impute, melody 7 appease, ascribe, deposit 14 unprofessional 15 nonprofessional
lay aside: 5 table 6 shelve 7 abandon, discard, neglect
lay away: See **lay by**
lay bare: 4 show 5 strip 6 denude, expose, reveal 7 uncover
lay by: 4 hive, save 5 amass, cache, hoard, store 7 deposit, husband, reposit 8 treasure 10 accumulate
lay down: set 5 posit 9 establish, surrender
lay hold of: 4 grab, grip 5 grasp, gripe, seize 9 apprehend
lay out: 4 plan 5 set up, spend 6 expend, extend, invest
lay up: See **lay by**
lay waste: 6 harass, ravage 7 destroy 8 desolate 9 depredate, devastate
layer: bed, hen, ply 4 coat, film, fold, seam, tier, zona 5 paver 6 folium, lamina, veneer 7 bedding, provine, stratum 8 laminate 10 substratum
of coal: 4 seam
of stones: 4 dess
of wood: 6 veneer
pert. to: 7 stratal
layered: 7 laminal, laminar 8 tunicate
layman: 4 laic
laymen: 4 laic 5 laity
layout: 4 plan 6 design, make-up 7 pattern
lazar: 5 leper
lazy: 4 idle, laze 5 inert 8 indolent, slothful, sluggard
lea: 6 meadow 7 pasture 9 grassland
leach: wet 7 moisten 9 lixiviate, percolate
lead: con, van, wad 4 head, lode, star, wadd 5 carry, first, guide, krems, metal, pilot, steer, usher 6 bullet, ceruse, convey, de-

duce, direct, escort, induce, manage **7** command, conduct, pioneer, precede **8** graphite, instruct, outstrip **9** influence
astray: **4** lure **6** allure, delude, entice, seduce **7** deceive, mislead, pervert **8** inveigle
color: **4** dull, gray **5** livid, olive
ore: **6** galena
paste: **6** strass
pig: **6** fother
sounding: **7** plummet
sulphide: **6** galena
leaden: **4** dull, gray **5** heavy **8** plumbean, sluggish **9** plumbeous
leader: bo; boh, cob, dux **4** cock, duce, duke, head, line, wire **5** chief, coach, pilot, sinew, snell **6** cantor, Fuhrer(G.), tendon **7** captain, demagog, foreman, Fuehrer(G.) **8** caudillo, choragus, headsman, preceder **9** chieftain, demagogue, drainpipe, principal **10** bellwether **11** condottiere, gymnasiarch
ecclesiastical: fra **4** pope **5** rabbi **6** bishop, father, priest **8** cardinal, minister, preacher **10** evangelist
leadership: **8** guidance, hegemony **9** authority
leading: big **4** duct, head, main **5** ahead, chief, first **6** banner **7** capital, central, guiding, premier, stellar **8** foremost **9** conducive, directing, governing, hegemonic, inductive, principal **11** controlling
leaf: ola, ole, pan **4** foil, olay, olla, page **5** blade, bract, folio, frond, palet, scale, sepal **6** areola, insert, spathe **7** tendril
angle with branch: **4** axil
aperture: **5** stoma
appendage: **6** ligula, stipel **7** stipule
aromatic: see **herb**
circle: **7** corolla
division: **4** lobe
edge: **9** crenation
fern: **5** frond
floating: pad
kind: **5** calxy, petal, sepal **7** corolla
part: pen **4** axil **5** costa, stoma **6** pagina **7** petiole, stomate
secretion on: **4** lerp
set: **5** calyx **7** corolla
vein: rib **5** costa
leafage: **7** foliage
leaflet: **5** pinna, tract **6** folder **7** booklet **8** pamphlet
leafstalk: **6** celery
leafy: **5** green, shady **6** foliar **7** sepaled
league: **4** bond **5** union **7** compact **8** alliance, covenant **9** coalition **10** federation **11** association, combination, confederacy **13** confederation
League of Nations city: **6** Geneva
Leah: *father:* **5** Laban
sister: **6** Rachel
son: **6** Simeon
leak: **4** drip, hole, loss, ooze, seep **5** crack **6** escape **7** channel, crevice, fissure
leaky: **6** gizzen
leal: **4** just, real, true **5** legal, loyal **6** lawful **7** correct, genuine **8** accurate, faithful
leam: **4** husk
lean: **4** bend, cant, lank, mean, poor, rely, slim, tend, thin, tilt **5** gaunt, lanky, scant, spare **6** depend, hollow, meager, meagre, skinny **7** conform, deviate, haggard, incline, recline, scrawny, slender **8** rawboned, scragged **9** deficient, emaciated **10** inadequate **12** unproductive
lean-to: hut **4** shed **5** shack
Leander's sweetheart: **4** Hera, Hero
leaning: **7** pronate **8** penchant **9** accumbent
leap: fly, hop **4** dart, dive, jump, loup, skip **5** bound, caper, exult, frisk, lunge, salto, vault **6** bounce, breach, cavort, curvet, gallop, gambol, hurdle, hurtle, spring **7** saltate **8** capriole **9** ballotade, entrechat
leap year: **10** bissextile
leaping: **7** salient, saltant **9** caprizant, saltation
lear: **4** lore **6** lesson **8** learning
Lear: *daughter:* **5** Regan **7** Goneril **8** Cordelia
dog: **4** Tray
follower: **4** Kent
learn: con, get **4** find, here, lere **6** master **7** acquire, apprise, apprize, realize **8** memorize **9** ascertain
learned: wot **4** blue, read, sage, wise **6** astute, doctus **7** clerkly, cunning, erudite **8** lettered, literary, literose **9** scholarly **10** omniscient
learner: **5** pupil **7** scholar, trainee **8** disciple, opsimath **10** apprentice
learning: art **4** lear, lore **6** wisdom **7** cunning **8** pedantry **9** education, erudition, knowledge **10** discipline, experience **11** scholarship
display of: **8** pedantry
love of: **9** philology
man of: **6** pundit, savant **7** scholar, teacher **9** philomath, professor **12** intellectual
lease: let **4** hire, rent **6** demise, engage, rental, tenure **7** charter **8** contract **10** concession
leash: **4** bind, cord, harl, jess, lune **5** strap **6** couple, tether
least: **6** fewest, little, lowest **7** minimal, minimum **8** shortest, smallest **9** slightest
leather: tan **4** napa, whip, yuft(Russ.) **5** balat, leder, strap **6** thrash
artificial: **7** keratol

drying: sam 4 samm 5 sammy
fine: kid 6 vellum
finish: 4 buff
inspector: 6 sealer
kind: elk, kid, kip 4 bock, buff, calf, doze, napa, roan, seal, vici 5 aluta, basil, mocha, suede, trank 6 castor, levant, oxhide, skiver 7 buffalo, canepin, chamois, morocco, saffian 8 cheverel, cheveril, Cordovan
napped: 5 suede
pare: 5 skive
piece of: 4 rand, welt 5 clout, strap, thong 6 latigo
prepare: tan, taw
sheepskin: 4 roan 6 skiver
tool: 6 skiver
waste: 6 tanite
worker: 6 chamar, tanner 8 chuckler
leatherback: 6 turtle
leatherneck: 6 marine
leave: go; let 4 bunk, exit, quit 5 favor, forgo, grace, scram 6 beleve, decamp, depart, desert, entail, favour, forego, forlet, permit, retire, vacate 7 abandon, beleave, forsake, getaway, liberty, license 8 bequeath, emigrate, furlough, vacation 9 allowance 10 permission, relinquish
behind: 11 outdistance
in the lurch: 6 desert, maroon, strand
leave of absence: 5 exeat 8 furlough
leave off: 4 quit, stop 5 cease, elide 6 desist 10 abbreviate
leave out: 4 omit, skip 5 elide
leave-taking: 5 adieu, conge 6 congee 7 parting 8 farewell 9 departure
leaven: 5 imbue, yeast 7 lighten 10 impregnate
leaves (see also **leaf; leave**): 7 foliage
having: see **leafy**
medicinal: 5 senna
leavings: See **lees; rubbish**
Lebanon: *castle:* 5 Saida, Sidon, Toron 8 Beaufort
city: 4 Arca, Tyre 5 Ehden, Saida 6 Beirut(c.) 7 Tripoli 8 Beyrouth 9 Broummana
dance: 6 dabkeh
fort: 6 Byblos
money: 5 livre 7 piastre
mountain: 4 Mzar 7 Sannine 8 Kadischa, Kenisseh
people: 4 Arab
river: 5 Lycos 6 Damour, Litani 8 Kasemieh
seaport: 4 Tyre 6 Beirut 8 Beyrouth
tree: 5 cedar
lech: 4 slab 8 capstone, monument
lecher: 7 glutton 8 gourmand, parasite 9 debauchee, libertine
lecherous: 4 lewd 7 boarish, goatish, lustful 9 salacious
lectern: 4 ambo, desk 10 escritoire
lecture: 5 scold 6 lesson, preach, sermon 7 address, hearing, lection, oration, prelect 9 discourse, sermonize 12 dissertation
lecturer: 6 docent, reader 9 prelector, professor
led: See **lead**
Leda: *lover:* 4 swan, Zeus
son: 6 Castor, Pollux
ledge: 4 berm, sill 5 bench, berme, shelf 7 retable
ledger: 4 tome 6 record
lee: 5 haven 7 shelter 10 protection
opposite of: 5 stoss 8 windward
leech: 8 parasite 9 blackmail 11 bloodsucker
leer: 4 face, lear, lehr, loin, look, lust, ogle, void 5 empty, flank, fleer, smirk 6 entice, unlade 7 grimace
leery, leary: 4 wary 7 knowing 10 suspicious 11 distrustful
lees: 5 draff, dregs, dross, grout 6 bottom, dunder, refuse, ullage 7 grounds 8 emptings, sediment, settling 9 excrement
leeward: 4 alee
drift: 4 crab
Leeward group island: 5 Nevis 7 Antigua, Barbuda, St. Kitts 8 Anguilla, Dominica, Windward 10 Montserrat
leeway: 4 room 5 space 9 elbowroom
left: 4 port 8 larboard
toward: haw 5 aport 9 sinistrad
left-handed: car 6 gauche 8 southpaw 9 portsided
left-over: See **lees; rubbish**
leftist: red 7 radical 13 revolutionary
leftward: 5 aport
leg: gam 4 gamb, hoof, limb, prop, walk 5 bough, brace, gambe, shank 6 bender, gammon 8 cabriole
armor: 4 jamb 6 greave
bone: 4 shin 5 femur, ilium, tibia 6 fibula
in heraldry: 4 gamb
muscle: 8 peroneus 9 peronaeus
ornament: 6 anklet
part: 4 calf, crus, knee, shin 5 ankle, thigh 11 anticnemion
pert. to: 6 crural
legacy: 4 gift 6 legate 7 bequest 8 windfall 10 foundation
inheritor: 4 heir 7 legatee
legal (see also **law**): 5 licit, valid 6 lawful 7 juridic 9 juridical 10 authorized, legitimate
legal matter: res
legal right, by: 6 ex jure
legal tender: 4 cash, coin 5 money 6 dollar, specie

legalize: 9 authorize
legate: 5 envoy 6 deputy, legacy, nuncio 8 bequeath, delegate 9 messenger 10 ambassador 14 representative
legatee: 4 heir
joint: 6 coheir
legend: 4 edda, lore, myth, saga, tale 5 fable, story 6 record 7 fiction, proverb 9 tradition
legerdemain: 5 magic 6 deceit 8 trickery 9 conjuring
legging: 4 spat 5 chaps 6 cnemis, cocker, puttie 7 bottine, gambado 8 bootikin, chivarra, chivarro, gamashes 11 galligaskin, spatterdash 12 antigropelos
legible: 8 distinct, readable 14 understandable
legion: 4 army, host 9 multitude
legislate: act 5 elect, enact
legislation: act, law 7 statute
legislative: 12 nomothetical
legislative body: 4 diet, rada 5 house, junta 6 senate 7 althing 8 congress 9 Reichstag 10 parliament
legislator: 5 solon 7 enactor, senator 8 lawmaker 9 statesman
legislature: 4 Dail, diet 6 senate 8 assembly, congress
legitimate: 4 fair, just, real, true 5 legal, licit, valid 6 cogent, lawful 7 genuine 11 efficacious
legume: pea, pod, uva 4 bean, soya 5 pulse 6 lentil, loment 9 vegetable
lei: 6 wreath 7 flowers, garland
leisure: 4 case, free, idle, time 5 otium(L.), spare 6 otiose 7 freedom 10 relaxation, unemployed, unoccupied 11 convenience, opportunity 12 unproductive
leisurely: 4 slow 7 gradual 12 deliberately
leman: 5 lover 8 mistress, paramour 10 sweetheart
lemma: 5 bract 8 membrane
lemonade: 5 drink 6 cooler 8 beverage
lemur: 4 maki, vari 5 avahi, indri, loris, potto 6 aye-aye, colugo, galago, macaco, maholi 7 half-ape, semiape, tarsier 8 kinkajou 9 babacoote 10 angwantibo
lend: 4 loan 5 grant, prest 6 afford, impart, settle 7 advance, furnish 11 accommodate
lene: 6 smooth 9 consonant 11 unaspirated
length: 4 pace, term 7 yardage 9 dimension
measure: mil 4 foot, inch, yard
lengthen: eke 6 dilate, expand, extend 7 amplify, produce, prolong, stretch 8 elongate, increase, protract
lengthwise: 5 along 7 endlong, endways 14 longitudinally
lengthy: 4 long 8 extended 10 protracted
lenient: lax 4 easy, kind, mild 6 facile, gentle, humane 7 clement 8 lenitive, merciful, mitigant, relaxing, soothing, tolerant 9 assuasive, emollient, softening 10 charitable, forbearing, palliative
Leningrad: 9 Petrograd
lens: 4 unar 5 toric 7 bifocal 8 meniscus 10 anastigmat
Lent: 6 Careme(F.)
Lenten: 5 plain 6 meager, meagre, somber, sombre 8 meatless 14 unostentatious
lentigo: 7 freckle
lentil: 6 legume
Leo star: 7 Regulus
leonine: 8 lionlike, powerful
leopard: cat 4 pard 5 ounce 7 cheetah, panther
lepidopter: 4 moth 9 butterfly
leprechaun: elf 5 fairy
leprosy: 5 lepra
lerot: 8 dormouse
Les Miserables author: 4 Hugo
lesion: cut 4 sore 5 ulcer, wound 6 injury 7 fissure
less: 5 fewer, minus, under 7 smaller 8 inferior
lessee: 6 leaser, renter, tenant 7 huurder(D.)
lessen: 4 bate, ease, wane 5 abase, abate, decry, lower, peter 6 impair, reduce, soften, shrink, weaken 7 amenuse, assuage, curtail, depress, relieve 8 belittle, condense, contract, decrease, derogate, diminish, minimize, mitigate, palliate, retrench, truncate 9 alleviate, attenuate, disparage, extenuate 10 depreciate 11 deteriorate
lesser: 5 minor
lesson: 4 lear, task 5 moral, study 6 rebuke 7 example, lecture, precept, reading, reproof, warning 8 exercise 10 assignment 11 composition, instruction
lessor: 8 landlord
lest: 8 anaunter
let: 4 hire, rent 5 allow, lease, leave 6 hinder, impede, permit, suffer 7 prevent 8 obstacle 9 hindrance
fall: 4 drop, slip 5 lower, spill 7 mention
forth: 4 emit
in: 5 admit, enter 6 insert
let it stand: sta 4 stet
letdown: 5 slump 8 comedown, drawback 10 anticlimax, relaxation, slackening
lethal: 5 fatal 6 deadly, mortal, poison 9 poisonous 12 death-dealing
lethargic: 4 dull 5 heavy, inert 6 drowsy, sleepy, torpid 8 comatose, sluggish 9 apathetic
lethargy: 5 sopor 6 stupor, torpor
Lethe: 8 oblivion 13 forgetfulness
Leto: 6 Latona
daughter: 7 Artemis
father: 5 Coeus

mother: 6 Phoebe
son: 6 Apollo
Lett: 4 Balt 7 Latvian
letter: 4 bull, chit, line, note 5 breve, brief, chain, favor, vowel 6 billet, cartel, charta, favour, screed, symbol 7 collins, courant, epistle, message, missile, missive 9 consonant, semivowel 13 communication, semiconsonant
Anglo-Saxon: edh, eth, wen, wyn 4 wynn
decorated: fac
sloping: 6 italic
letter carrier: 6 correo(Sp.) 7 mailman, postman 9 messenger
letter for letter: 9 literally, literatim
lettered: 7 learned, stamped 8 educated, literate 9 inscribed
lettuce: *kind of:* cos 4 head, leaf 6 butter 7 romaine, simpson
sea: 4 alga 5 laver
letup: 7 respite 9 abatement, cessation
leucite: 5 lenad 9 amphigene
levant: 5 wager 6 decamp 7 abscond
Levant: 4 East 6 Orient 13 Mediterranean
garment: 6 caftan
river: 4 wadi, wady
ship: 4 jerm, saic
valley: 4 wady
levee: 4 bank, dike, dyke, pier, quay 6 durbar 9 reception 10 embankment
level: aim, par 4 even, flat, rase, raze, true 5 equal, grade, peavy, plane, point, scalp 6 evenly, peavey, peavie, smooth 7 flatten, uniform 8 demolish 10 horizontal 12 standardized
comb. form: 5 plani
social: 5 caste, class
tool: 5 plane 6 gimbal
level-headed: 8 sensible
lever: bar, lam, pry 5 helve, jemmy, jimmy, peavy, pedal, prise, swipe 6 binder, garrot, peavey, peavie, tappet, tiller 7 crowbar, treadle 9 rockshaft
part: 7 fulcrum
leveret: 4 hare 8 mistress
Levi: *descendant:* 6 Levite 7 Gershon
father: 5 Jacob
son: 6 Kohath
leviathan: 4 ship 5 titan, whale 6 dragon
levigate: 6 polish, smooth
levin: 9 lightning
levitate: 4 rise 5 float
levity: 5 humor 6 gaiety, humour 8 buoyancy 9 frivolity, lightness, silliness 11 foolishness
levy: tax 4 cess, fine, wage 5 exact, stent 6 assess, extent, impose, impost 7 collect 10 assessment, imposition
lewd: 4 base, rude 5 bawdy 6 carnal, coarse 7 lustful, obscene, rammish, sensual 8 unchaste 9 debauched, dissolute, lecherous, salacious 10 lascivious, libidinous, licentious 12 pornographic
lexicographer: 6 author 8 compiler 9 onomastic
lexicon: 7 calepin 10 dictionary 11 onomasticon
Leyte capital: 8 Tacloban
liability: 4 debt, loan 5 debit 6 burden 10 obligation
liable: apt 8 amenable 10 answerable 11 accountable, responsible
liaison: 4 bond 8 intimacy, intrigue
liana: 4 cipo 5 plant
liang: 4 tael
liar: 5 cheat 6 fibber 7 Ananias, cracker 8 deceiver, fabulist 10 fabricator 11 pseudologue 12 prevaricator, pseudologist 14 misrepresenter
lias: 4 rock 9 limestone
libation: 5 drink 8 potation
libel: 4 bill 4 defame, malign, vilify 7 calumny, lampoon, request, scandal, slander 8 circular, handbill, roorback 10 calumniate, defamation 11 certificate, declaration 12 supplication
libelant: 7 accuser
liberal: 4 free, good, open 5 ample, broad, frank, noble 6 honest 7 electic, profuse 8 eclectic, generous, handsome 9 benignant, bounteous, bountiful, expansive, expensive, plenteous, plentiful 10 benevolent, charitable, ecumenical, munificent
Liberal: 4 Whig
liberate: rid 4 flee, free 5 clear, loose, remit 6 acquit, redeem, rescue 7 deliver, manumit, release 8 unfetter 9 discharge, disengage, extricate 10 emancipate
Liberia: *boatman:* Kru
city: 8 Buchanan, Marshall, Monrovia(c.) 10 Greenville
measure: 4 kuba
people: Gi; Kru, Kwa, Vai, Vei 4 Kroo, Toma 5 Bassa, Gibbi, Greba 6 Krooby, Kruman 7 Krooboy, Krooman
river: 5 Manna 8 San Pedro
libertine: 4 rake, roue 7 sceptic 9 debauchee, dissolute 11 freethinker
liberty: may 4 ease, play 5 leave, right 7 freedom, license 9 privilege 11 presumption
library: 7 bhandar 8 atheneum 9 athenaeum 11 bibliotheca
libretto: 4 book 5 words
Libya: *city:* 7 Tripoli
measure: 4 drah 5 bozze, donum, jabia, teman 6 barile 7 mattaro
measure of weight: 4 kele 5 uckia 6 gorraf 7 termino 8 kharouba

oasis: 5 sebka
seaport: 5 Derna, Derrn 6 Tobruk 7 Bengazi 8 Benghazi
wind: 7 sirocco
Libya's child: 5 Belus 6 Agenor
lice: See **louse**
license: tax 5 exeat, leave 6 patent, permit 7 dismiss, freedom, liberty 8 escambio, passport, sanction 9 approbate, authority, authorize, franchise 10 permission 11 imprimateur, unrestraint
licentious: gay, lax 4 free, lewd 5 frank, loose 6 unruly 7 immoral, obscene 9 dissolute 10 lascivious, profligate 12 pornographic, uncontrolled, unrestrained
lichen: 4 moss
derivative: 6 archil, litmus
genus: 5 usnea 7 evernia 10 pertusaria
lich-house: 8 mortuary
licit: 5 legal 6 lawful 9 permitted
lick: lap, win 4 flog 5 slake 6 thrash 7 conquer 8 overcome, vanquish
licorice: 5 abrin, anise 8 absinthe 9 jequirity
pill: 6 cachou
seed: 9 jequirity
lid: cap, hat, top 5 cover 7 shutter 9 operculum
lie: cog, fib, gab 4 bask, cram, flaw, hide, loll, rest 5 exist 6 covert, extend, grovel, remain, repose 7 cracker, crammer, deceive, falsify, falsity, pronate, untruth 8 position, roorback 9 deception, fabricate, falsehood, mendacity, prostrate 10 equivocate, inveracity, taradiddle 11 fabrication, prevaricate, tarradiddle 13 prevarication
in ambush: 4 lurk 6 hugger 9 insidiate
Liebestraum composer: 5 Liszt
Liechtenstein: *capital:* 5 Vaduz
monetary unit: 5 rappe
lief: 4 dear, fain 5 leave 6 freely, gladly 7 beloved, happily 8 pleasing, precious 9 willingly 10 permission
liege: 5 loyal 6 vassal 7 devoted, subject 8 faithful, overlord 9 sovereign
lien: 5 claim 6 charge 8 mortgage 9 trust deed 11 encumbrance, garnishment
lieu: 5 place, stead 7 instead
lieutenant: 4 zany
lieve: See **lief**
life: vie 6 blood, hours 6 biosis, energy, spirit 8 vitality, vivacity 9 animation, biography, existence 11 anilopyrine
animal: 4 bios 5 biota, fauna
comb. form: bio
god of: 6 Faunus
pert. to: 5 vital 6 biotic, mortal 8 biotical
plant: 4 bios 5 biota, flora
principle: 5 atman, prana, tenet
professional: 6 career
science: 7 anatomy, biology, zoology 12 paleontology
sea: 5 coral 8 halibios, plankton
simple form: 5 ameba 6 amebic, ameoba 7 amoebic, amoebae(pl.)
staff of: 5 bread
without: 4 dead 5 azoic 9 inanimate
life insurance: 7 tontine
life jacket: 7 Mae West
life-like: 9 realistic
lifeless: 4 arid, dead, dull, flat 5 amort, heavy, inert, vapid 6 anemic, jejune, torpid 7 anaemic 8 inactive 9 bloodless, exanimate, inanimate, powerless, tasteless 10 spiritless, unanimated
comb. form: 4 abio
lifer: 7 convict
lifetime: age, day, eon 4 aeon 5 being 8 duration
lift: pry 4 help, jack, perk, rear 5 boost, exalt, heave, hoick, hoist, hoosh, raise, scend 6 cleach, cleech 7 derrick, elevate, enhance 8 elevator, heighten
ligament: 4 band, bind, bond 6 artery 7 bandage
comb. form: 5 desmo
ligan, lagan: 6 debris
ligate: 4 bind 7 bandage
ligature: tie 4 band, bond 6 taenia 7 bandage
light: dey, gay 4 airy, deft, easy, fire, glim, lamp, mild, moon, neon, soft 5 agile, blond, fanal, filmy, flaky, flame, flare, merry, torch 6 alight, beacon, bright, candle, floaty, gentle, ignite, kindle, lively, lumine, nimble, pastel, volant 7 buoyant, cresset, flyaway, fragile, trivial 8 brighten, cheerful, delicate, ethereal, gossamer, graceful, illumine, luminary, luminous, trifling 10 illuminate
circle: 4 halo 7 aureola, aureole
cloud: 6 nimbus
faint: 7 glimmer, shimmer 9 starlight 10 glimmering, shimmering
globe: 4 bulb
god: 5 Baldr 6 Balder
kind of: arc 4 lamp 5 klieg, torch 7 lantern 9 headlight 10 flashlight 12 incandescent
measure: lux, pyr, rad 5 lumen 6 Hefner
overpower with: 6 dazzle
portable: 4 lamp 5 flare, taper, torch 6 candle 7 lantern 10 flashlight
reflector: 4 lens 6 mirror
refractor: 5 prism
science: 6 optics
source: sun
unit: lux, pyr 4 phot 5 lumen
without: 4 dark 5 blind 7 aphotic

lighten: 4 ease, fade 5 allay, clear 6 alight, allege, bleach, illume, leaven 7 gladden, relieve 8 brighten 9 alleviate 10 illuminate

lightening: 10 levitation

lighter (see also **light**): 4 scow 5 barge, spill 7 fidibus, gabbard, gabbart, pontoon 8 chopboat

lightheaded: 5 dizzy, giddy 6 fickle 7 flighty, glaiket, glaikit 8 flippant, heedless, unstable, unsteady 9 delirious, frivolous 10 disordered, inconstant 11 thoughtless

lighthearted: gay 4 glad 5 merry 7 buoyant 8 carefree, cheerful, gleesome, volatile 9 vivacious

lighthouse: 5 phare 6 beacon, pharos 7 seamark, warning

lightness: 6 levity

lightning: 4 bolt 5 levin
defier of: 4 Ajax
pert. to: 8 fulgural
protective device: 8 arrester

lightning bug: 7 firefly

lightning rod: 8 arrester

lightning stone: 9 fulgurite

lights: 5 lungs

lights out: 4 taps

ligneous: 5 woody

lignite: 4 coal

ligula: 4 band

ligulate: 11 strap-shaped

likable: 6 genial 7 winning 8 charming, pleasant 10 attractive

like: as 4 love, same 5 alike, enjoy, equal 6 admire, prefer, relish 7 similar 9 analogous, semblance 10 preference, synonymous 11 counterpart, homogeneous
suffix: ar, ic; ose

like a: For definitions beginning with these words, see following important words. EXAMPLES: "like a cat" : see **catlike;** "like a house": see **house:** *pert. to.*

likelihood: 10 appearance 11 probability 14 verisimilitude

likely: apt 5 prone 6 liable 7 tending 8 credible, feasible, probable, suitable 9 promising 11 verisimilar

liken: 5 apply 7 compare 10 assimilate

likeness: 4 copy, form, twin 5 guise, image 6 effigy, figure, statue 7 analogy, parable, picture, replica 8 parallel, portrait 9 duplicate, facsimile, imitation, semblance, simulacre 10 comparison, photograph, similarity, similitude, simulacrum 11 counterfeit 12 reproduction 14 representation

likewise: and, nor, not, too 4 also 5 ditto 7 besides 8 moreover

liking: goo 4 gust, lust 5 fancy, gusto, taste 6 comely 7 delight 8 affinity, appetite, fondness, penchant, pleasing, pleasure 9 affection 10 sensuality 12 predilection

lilac: 5 mauve 7 syringa

Lilith's successor: Eve

lilliputian: 4 tiny 5 petty, small 6 midget 7 dwarfed

lilt: air 4 sing, song, tune 7 cadence

lily (see also **water lily**): ki, ti 4 aloe, ixia, sego 5 calla, niobe, tiger, water, yucca 6 titree 8 mariposa
family: 9 liliaceae
genus: 7 bessera

lily iron: 7 harpoon

Lily Maid of Astolat: 6 Elaine

lily of France: 10 fleur-de-lis

lily of the valley: 6 mugget, mugwet 10 convallily
family: 15 convallariaceae

lily-of-the-valley tree: 8 sourwood 10 fetterbush, pepperbush

lily-shaped: 7 crinoid

lima: 4 bean

liman: bay 5 marsh 6 lagoon 7 estuary

limation: 6 filing 9 polishing

limb: arm, fin, leg 4 wing 5 bough 6 branch, member 7 flipper, pleopod, support
adapted for swimming: 8 nectopod
flexion: 9 anaclasis

limber: 4 bain, flip, limp 5 lithe 6 pliant, supple, swanky 8 flexible, flippant, handsome, yielding

limbo: 4 hell 9 purgatory

lime: 5 color, green 6 cement, citrus
pendent: 10 stalactite
phosphate: 7 apatite

lime tree: 4 teil 6 linden, tupelo

limen: 9 threshold

limestone: 4 calp, cauk, malm 5 chalk, ganil, poros(Gr.) 6 clunch, marble, oolite 7 hurlock 8 peastone, pisolite

limey: 6 sailor 7 soldier 10 Englishman

limit: end, fix 4 curb, mete 5 ambit, bound, bourn, check, fence, hedge, scant, stint, verge 6 border, bourne, curfew, define, extent, finish 7 astrict, barrier, closure, confine, environ, extreme 8 boundary, conclude, contract, deadline, restrain, restrict, terminal, terminus 9 condition, constrain, extremity 10 limitation 11 restriction, termination 12 circumscribe 13 determination, qualification
combining form: ori

limited: few, ltd 5 local, scant 6 finite, narrow, scanty, strait 8 reserved 9 parochial 10 restricted 11 topopolitan

limiting: 10 relational

limitless: 4 vast 8 infinite 9 boundless, unbounded, unlimited 11 measureless

limn: 4 draw 6 depict, sketch 7 portray 8 describe 9 delineate
limp: hop, lax 4 himp, soft, thin 5 hilch, hitch, loose 6 flabby, flimsy, hirple, hobble, limber, wilted 7 flaccid 8 drooping, flexible 9 inelastic 13 unsubstantial
limpid: 4 pure 5 clear, lucid 6 bright 7 crystal 8 pellucid 11 translucent, transparent
limping: 4 halt 10 claudicant
limy: 6 sticky 7 viscous
Lincoln: *friend:* 5 Speed
portrayer of: 6 Massey
secretary of state: 6 Seward
secretary of war: 7 Stanton
son: Tad
wife: 4 Mary
linden: lin 4 lime, teil 8 basswood
genus of: 5 tilia
line: pad, ray, row, wad 4 axis, ceil, cord, dash, etch, face, file, mark, mere, race, rein, rope, rule, seam, wire 5 curve, front, leger, queue, route, serif, snell, steen, stich, stria, swath 6 border, ceriph, cordon, fettle, hawser, isobar, metier, nettle, streak, string, stripe, suture 7 barrier, carrier, contour, radiant, scratch 8 boundary, crossbar, isotherm, wainscot 9 delineate
comb. form: 4 lino
conceptual: 6 agonic, tropic 7 equator, isother 8 latitude, meridian 9 longitude
diagonal: 4 bias
geometrical: arc, ess 4 cant, sine 6 secant 7 tangent 8 parallel 9 asymptote
mathematical: 6 vector
nautical: 6 earing, hawser, ratlin 7 marline, painter, ratline
of soldiers: 4 file, rank 6 column
pertaining to: 5 filar 6 linear
raised: 4 weal, welt 5 ridge
with boards: 8 wainscot
lineage: 4 race 5 birth, blood, caste, tribe 6 family, havage, stirps 7 descent, stirpes(pl.) 8 ancestry, heredity, pedigree 9 genealogy 10 progenitor
lineal: 6 direct, racial 9 ancestral 10 hereditary
lineament: 7 feature 14 characteristic
linear: 9 elongated
lineate: 7 striped 8 streaked
lined: 5 ruled 6 notate 7 striate 8 careworn 9 lineolate
lineman: end 5 guard 6 center, tackle 7 wireman
linen: 4 brin, crea(Sp.), lawn 5 toile 6 barras, damask, dowlas, forfar 7 brabant, cambric, dornick 13 linsey-woolsey
fabric: 7 taffeta
household: 6 napery, sheets
source: 4 flax
yarn: lea
liner: 4 boat, ship 6 vessel 7 steamer 9 steamship
wrecked: 7 Titanic
lines: net 7 network, reticle
ling: 4 fish, hake 5 heath 6 burbot 7 heather 8 chestnut
linger: lag 4 drag, stay, wait 5 dally, delay, dwell, hover, tarry 6 dawdle, loiter, remain
lingerie: 9 underwear 11 underthings
lingering: 4 slow 7 chronic
lingo: 4 cant 5 argot 6 jargon, patter, tongue 7 dialect 8 language 10 vernacular
lingot: 4 mold 5 ingot
lingua: 6 glossa
lingual: 7 glossal 10 linguistic, tonguelike
linguist: 8 polyglot 9 pantoglot 10 vocabulist 11 interpreter, philologist
linguistics: 7 grammar 9 philology
lingy: 5 agile 6 active, healthy, limber, nimble 8 heathery
linhay: 4 shed 8 outhouse
liniment: 11 embrocation
lining: 5 stean, steen 7 backing, ceiling 8 wainscot 12 wainscotting
link: tie 4 join, yoke 5 cleek, nexus, torch, unite 6 braced, catena, copula, couple, course, fasten 7 conjoin, connect 8 catenate 10 connection, golf course 11 concatenate
series: 5 chain 13 concatenation
linking: 9 annectant, annectent
linn, lin: 4 pool 6 linden, ravine 8 cataract 9 precipice, waterfall
linnet: 5 finch, twite 9 gorsebird
linseed: 8 flaxseed
lint: 5 fluff 7 charpie 8 raveling
lintel: 5 hance 6 clavel 7 transom
lion: 4 puma, star 5 simba 6 cougar, roarer 9 carnivore, celebrity
group: 5 pride
hair: 4 mane
winged, with woman's head: 6 sphinx
young: cub 6 lionet
Lion of God: Ali
lionlike: 7 leonine
lip: rim 4 brim, edge, kiss 5 brink, labia(pl.) 6 labium, margin 7 labella 8 labellum
comb. form: 5 labio
ornament: 6 labret
part: 8 philtrum
pert. to: 6 labial 11 labiodental
lipa: fat
liparoid: 5 fatty
liparous: 5 obese
lipless: 8 achilary
lipoma: 5 tumor
lipped: 7 labiate

liquefy: 4 fuse, melt 6 fusile 7 liquate 8 dissolve, eliquate 10 colliquate, deliquesce

liqueur: 5 creme, noyau 6 genepi 7 cordial, ratafee 8 anisette, beverage 9 cointreau 11 benedictine

liquid: 5 fluid 6 fluent, watery 8 beverage
colorless: 5 water 7 alcohol
container: cup, jar, jug, mug, pan, pot 4 etna, ewer, vase, vial 5 cruse, glass, phial 6 boiler, bottle, bucket, goblet, kettle 7 creamer, pitcher 8 decanter, demijohn
gasified: 5 steam, vapor
inflammable: see *volatile* below
measure: 4 pint 5 ounce 6 gallon, tierce
oily: 6 cresol, octane 7 aniline, picamar
particle form: 4 mist 5 spray
sweet: 5 sirup, syrup 7 treacle 8 molasses
volatile: gas 5 ether 6 butane 7 alcohol, ligroin 8 gasolene, gasoline, ligroine

liquidate: 6 settle 8 amortize 9 discharge

liquor (see also **liqueur**): ale, bub, dew, gin, rum, rye 4 arak, bang, beer, beno, brew, grog, nipa, raki, sake, saki, soma 5 bhang, booze, budge, lager, pisco, stout 6 arrack, brandy, porter, pottle, scotch, stingo, strunt, tipple 7 bitters, whiskey 8 beverage 9 moonshine
bad: 5 smoke 6 rotgut 10 balderdash
cabinet: 8 cellaret
crude: 5 hooch 6 rotgut 9 hoochinoo, moonshine
drugged: 5 hocus 6 mickey 10 mickey-finn
manufacturer: 6 abkari 9 distiller
measure: 4 dram 5 rouse 7 snifter
mix with: 4 lace
mixture: 5 bogus 7 bragget
residue: 4 must 5 dregs 8 heeltaps
server: 6 barman 7 barmaid, skinker, tapster 9 barkeeper, bartender
shop: bar 6 saloon, tavern 7 shebeen
vessel: ama, keg 4 bowl 5 amula, flask 6 barrel, bottle, flagon 7 bombard, psykter, stamnos 8 cruisken, decanter 9 cruiskeen

lira (one-twentieth): 5 soldo

liripipe, liripoop: 4 hood, task 5 scarf 6 lesson, tippet

lirk: 6 crease 7 wrinkle

lish: 5 agile, quick 6 active, nimble

lisk: 4 loin 5 flank, groin

lisp: 7 prattle

lissome, lissom: 5 agile, lithe 6 limber, nimble, supple 8 flexible

list: tip 4 bill, cant, cast, file, item, keel, leet, memo, ordo, roll, rota, rote, tilt 5 brief, canon, index, panel, scrip, slate 6 careen, docket, roster 7 catalog, incline 8 manifest, register, schedule, tabulate 9 catalogue, inventory, portfolio, repertory 10 repertoire 11 enumeration

listen: ear 4 hark, hear, heed, note 5 audit 6 attend, harken 7 hearken 8 overhear 9 eavesdrop 10 auscultate

listener: 6 hearer 7 audient

lister: 8 assessor 9 appraiser 10 cataloguer

listful: 9 attentive

listing: 5 atilt 7 tilting, tipping 8 register 10 enlistment, enrollment
individual: 4 item 5 entry

listless: 4 dull 5 faint, inert 6 abject, drowsy, supine 7 languid 8 careless, heedless, sluggish 9 apathetic, heartless 10 spiritless 11 indifferent 13 uninteresting

listlessness: 8 doldrums

litany: 6 ectene, ektene, prayer 8 rogation 11 orapronobis

liter: kan(D.) 7 measure

literal: 4 bald, dull 5 exact 7 factual, precise, prosaic 8 verbatim 13 unimaginative

literary: 6 versed 7 bookish, erudite, learned 8 lettered 9 scholarly

literate: 6 reader, writer 8 educated, lettered

literati: 14 intelligentsia

literator: 6 critic

literature: 7 letters
extracts: 9 anthology
form: 5 novel 6 poetry 7 fiction 9 technical 10 nonfiction, scientific 11 pornography

lithe: 4 bain, slim 6 clever, limber, lissom, pliant, supple, svelte 7 lissome, slender 8 flexible

lithograph: 6 chromo

Lithuania: *city:* 5 Kovno(c.), Memel, Vilna
coin: lit 5 litas, marka 6 centas, fennig 7 ostmark 8 auksinas, skatikas
dialect: 5 Zmudz
lowlander: 5 Zhmud 10 Samogitian
railroad junction: 5 Vilna

Lithuanian: 4 Balt, Lett 5 Zhmud 6 Litvak 7 Yatvyag

litigant: 4 suer 6 suitor 7 accuser

litigation: 4 moot, suit 7 contest, dispute, lawsuit 10 contention, discussion
one involved in: 8 barrater, barrator, litigant

litigious: 10 disputable 11 belligerent, contentious 14 controvertible

litten: 7 lighted 8 cemetery 10 churchyard

litter: bed, hay 4 bier, mess, raff 5 cabin, couch, dooly, mulch, straw, trash, young 6 doolie, refuse 7 cacolet, mullock, rubbish, rummage 8 brancard(F.), disorder 9 offspring, stretcher 10 untidiness

litterateur: 7 bookman

little: sma(Sc.), wee 4 poco(It.), puny, tiny 5 crumb, petit, small 6 petite 8 fraction 10 diminutive
comb. form: 5 steno

little finger: 7 minimus
little toe: 7 minimus
Little Women: Jo; Amy, Meg 4 Beth
author: 6 Alcott
surname: 5 March
littoral: 7 coastal
lituite: 6 fossil
liturate: 7 spotted
liturgy: 4 rite 6 ritual 7 service
livable: 8 bearable 9 endurable, tolerable
live: 4 fare, room 5 abide, alive, dwell, exist, green, vital, vivid 6 reside 7 animate, blazing, breathe, subsist 8 animated, continue, converse 9 energetic 10 experience
in: 7 inhabit
in the country: 9 rusticate
passively: 8 vegetate
permit to: 5 spare 8 reprieve
livelihood: 4 keep 5 being 6 living
liveliness: 6 spirit 8 vitality
lively: gay, vif(F.) 4 airy, cant, fast, pert, racy, vive, yare 5 agile, alert, alive, brisk, canty, chirk, cobby, desto(It.), fresh, peart, peppy 6 active, blithe, bright, cheery, chirpy, cocket, crouse, dapper, frisky, nimble, snappy 7 allegro(It.), animate, animato(It.), buoyant, chipper 8 animated, galliard, spirited 9 energetic, sprightly, vivacious
liven: 5 cheer 7 animate 8 brighten
liver: 4 foie 5 hepar 8 tomalley
disease: 9 cirrhosis, hepatitis
fluid: 4 bile
pert. to: 7 hepatic
liverwort: 4 moss 8 agrimony, hepatica 9 bryophyte
genus: 6 riccia
livery: 7 uniform 8 clothing
livestock: 6 cattle 7 chattel
livid: 4 blae, blue 5 bleak 10 discolored
living: 4 keep 5 alive, being, vivid 6 extant 7 animate 8 animated, benefice 10 livelihood, sustenance 11 subsistence
again: 6 reborn 9 redivivus
correct: 7 regimen 11 orthobiosis
off others: 8 entozoic 9 parasitic, raptorial
together: 11 contubernal
Livonian river: Aa
lixiviate: 5 leach
lixivium: lye
lizard: dab, eft 4 adda, dabb, dhab, evet, gila, ibid, newt, seps, uran 5 agama, anoli, dhabb, gecko, gekko, goana, scink, skink, varan, waran 6 ameiva, anolis, dragon, goanna, iguana, lacert, moloch, worral, worrel 7 cheecha, geitjie, monitor, saurian, tuatera 8 basilisk 9 chameleon, galliwasp 10 chuckwalla 12 scheltopusik
comb. form: 5 sauro
family: 12 xenosauridae
genus: uta 5 agama 0 ameiva
mammal similar to: 10 salamander
lizard-like: 8 iguanoid
llama: 6 alpaca
habitat: 5 Andes
llanero: 6 cowboy 8 herdsman
llano: 5 plain 7 lowland, prairie
Llyr's son: 4 Bran 7 Branwen
lo: but 4 ecce(L.), look 6 behold 7 observe
load: jag 4 clog, jagg, lade, onus, pack, tote, stow 5 cargo, weigh 6 burden, charge, hamper, lading, steeve, weight 7 fraught, freight, oppress 8 carriage, encumber 9 aggravate, exonerate 10 adulterate 11 encumbrance
small: jag 4 jagg 5 hurry
loader: 9 stevedore
loadstone: See **lodestone**
loaf: 4 idle, laze 6 dawdle, loiter, lounge 10 dilly-dally
loafer: bum 4 hood 5 idler 7 flaneur, hoodlum, lounger 8 hooligan, larrikin 11 chairwarmer
loam: rab 4 silt 5 loess, regur(Ind.) 6 cledge
constituent: 4 clay, lime 5 chalk
deposit: 4 silt 5 loess
loan: 4 dhan(Ind.), lend 5 prest 6 borrow 7 advance 10 obligation, provisions 13 accommodation
loan shark: 6 usurer
loath, loth: 6 averse, odious 7 hateful 8 backward 9 reluctant, repulsive, unwilling
loathe: 4 hate 5 abhor 6 detest 7 adverse, condemn, despise, dislike 9 abominate
loathsome: 4 foul, ugly, vile 7 carrion, cloying, hateful 8 abhorent, deformed 9 offensive, repellent, repugnant 10 abominable, detestable, disgusting 11 distasteful
lob: hit 4 bowl, lots, lout, lump, step, till, toss, vein 5 droop, stair, throw 6 propel 7 pollack 9 chandelle
lobate: 8 lobelike
lobby: 4 hall, room 5 foyer 8 anteroom, coulisse 9 enclosure, vestibule
lobbyist: 8 promoter 12 propagandist
lobe: 5 alula 6 alular, earlap, lappet, lobule
lobelike: 6 lobate
loblolly: 4 mush, pine, tree 5 gruel 6 puddle 7 mudhole
lobo: 4 wolf
lobster: *claw:* 5 chela 6 nipper
female: hen
part: 4 claw 6 pincer, telson, thorax
roe: 5 coral
trap: pot 5 creel 6 bownet
lobster pot: pot 4 corf 5 creel, trunk

local: 7 bucolic, endemic, limited, topical 8 regional, specific 10 restricted
locale: 4 loci(pl.), site 5 locus(L.), place, scene 6 region 9 situation
locality: 4 loci(pl.), seat, site, spot 5 locus, place, situs 6 region 7 habitat 8 district, position 12 neighborhood
localize: 7 situate 8 pinpoint
locate (see also **place**): sat 4 espy, find, seat, show, site, spot 5 stand, trace 6 settle 7 situate, station 8 discover 9 establish
located: 7 bestead
locatio: 7 leasing, letting
location: 4 area, seat, site, spot 5 place, scene, situs 6 ubiety 7 habitat 9 situation
loch: bay 4 lake, pond, pool 5 lough
loci: See **locus**
lock: 4 bolt, curl, frib, hank, hasp 5 latch, sasse, tress 6 fasten 7 confine, cowlick 8 fastener
part: 4 bolt 5 stump 8 cylinder
locker: 6 ascham
lockjaw: 7 tetanus, trismus 11 ankylostoma
remedy: 11 antitetanic, antitetanus
lockman: 11 executioner
lockup: jug 4 jail 5 clink 6 cooler 7 hoosgow 8 hoosegaw, hoosegow 9 calaboose
loco: mad 5 crazy 6 insane
locomotive: 5 dolly, mogul 6 diesel, dinkey, engine, mallet 8 electric
part: cab 5 pilot
service car: 6 tender 7 coalcar
Locrine: *daughter:* 7 Sabrina
father: 4 Brut
locus: 4 area, site 5 place 8 locality
locust: 5 bruke, cicad 6 cicada, cicala, cigala 11 grasshopper
wingless: 4 weta
locust bird: 7 grackle 8 starling
locust plant: 5 senna
locust tree: 5 carob 6 acacia
locustberry: 5 drupe, nance 9 glamberry
lode: 4 path, road, vein 5 canal, drain, ledge 6 course 7 deposit, fissure 8 waterway
cavity: vug 4 vugg, vugh
lodestone, loadstone: 6 magnet 7 adamant 8 terrella 9 magnetite
lodge: dig, lie 4 club 5 board, couch, dwell, hogan 6 alight, bestow, encamp, hostel 7 deposit 8 harbinge 11 brotherhood
lodger: 5 guest 6 roomer, tenant
lodging: bed, hut, inn 4 camp, gite(F.), host, howf, nest, room, tent 5 abode, cabin, hotel, house, hovel, howff 6 billet, tavern, teepee, wigwam 7 mansion 8 barracks, dwelling, hostelry, quarters 9 dormitory, harborage, residence 10 habitation, harbourage
cost: 4 rent
loess: 4 loam, silt
loft: bin 4 balk 5 attic
lofty: 4 aery, epic, high, tall 5 aerie, elate, grand, noble, proud, steep 6 aerial, Andean, andine 7 Andesic, arduous, eminent, haughty, sublime 8 arrogant, assuming, elevated, eloquent, majestic 9 cockhorse, dignified, overproud 11 magisterial, mountainous
log: 4 clog, wood 5 diary 6 billet, loggat, logget, record, timber 7 journal
kind: 4 slab 5 splat 8 puncheon
mass: 5 drive
revolve: 4 birl 7 logroll
log gin: 6 jammer
logarithm: *unit:* bel
inventor: 6 Napier
loge: box 4 room 5 booth, stall
logger: 6 sniper 9 lumberman 10 lumberjack, woodcutter 11 woodchopper
boot: pac 4 pack
loggerhead: 4 head 6 turtle 9 blockhead
loggerheads: 4 odds, outs
loggets, loggats: 4 game
loggia: 7 gallery
logging: *sled:* 4 tode 7 travois 8 travoise
tool: 4 pevy 5 peavy, peevy 6 nigger, peavey
logic: 9 reasoning
inductive: 7 epagoge
specious: 7 sophism
term: 5 ferio, lemma 7 ferison
logical: 4 sane 5 sound, valid 8 coherent, rational 10 consistent, reasonable
logion: 5 maxim, motto 6 saying 11 observation
logogriph: 5 rebus 6 puzzle, riddle 7 anagram
logroll: 4 birl
logy: 4 dull 5 heavy 6 drowsy 8 sluggish
lohan: 4 monk 5 Arhat
Lohengrin: *character:* 4 Elsa 8 Parsifal
composer: 6 Wagner
loincloth: 5 pagne
loir: 8 dormouse
Loire: *river:* 5 Liger
town: 6 Nantes
loiter: lag 4 idle, loaf 5 dally, delay, drawl, shool, tarry 6 cooter, dawdle, linger 7 saunter 8 hesitate
loiterer: 4 slug 5 drone, idler 7 laggard 8 sluggard
Loki: *child:* Hel 4 Hela, Nare, Nari
mother: 9 Angrbodha
wife: 5 Sigyn
loll: 4 hang 5 droop, tarry 6 dangle, froust, frowst, lounge, sprawl 7 recline
loma: 4 hill
lombard: 6 cannon
Lombardy: *king:* 6 Alboin

lake: 4 Como
lomilomi: rub 7 massage, shampoo
lomita: 4 hill
London: *bus conductor:* 6 clippy
coffee shop: 5 Wills
district: 4 Soho 5 Acton 7 Adelphi, Alsatia, Mayfair
fish market: 12 Billingsgate
gallery: 4 Tate
monument: Gog 5 Magog 8 Cenotaph
porter: 6 George 8 Georgina
promenade: 4 Mall
roisterer: mun
society: 7 Mayfair
square: 9 Leicester
stables: 4 mews
street: 4 Bond 6 Savile 7 Wardour 9 Cheapside, Haymarket
suburb: Kew
theater: 7 Adelphi
timepiece: 6 Big Ben
Londoner: 7 Cockney
lone: 4 sole 5 alone, apart 6 single 7 retired 8 solitary 9 unmarried 12 unfrequented
Lone Ranger's companion: 5 Tonto
Lone Star State: 5 Texas
loneliness: 8 solitude 9 dejection, isolation 10 depression, desolation 12 lonesomeness
lonely: 4 lorn, sole 5 alone, apart 6 dismal, dreary 7 deavely, forlorn 8 deserted, desolate, lonesome, secluded, solitary 11 sequestered 12 unfrequented
long: far 4 hone, hope, pine 5 yearn 6 aspire, hanker, hunger, prolix, thirst 7 lengthy, tedious 8 extended, tiresome 9 elongated, prolonged, wearisome 10 protracted
and slender: 5 lathy, reedy 6 linear 9 elongated
for: 4 miss, want, wish 5 covet, crave 6 desire
long ago: 4 yore
long dozen: 8 thirteen
long-suffering: 7 patient 8 patience 9 endurance 10 forbearing
long-winded: 6 prolix 9 garrulous
longe: 4 rein, rope 5 guide, strap, trout 8 exercise
Longfellow hero: 8 Hiawatha
longheaded: 4 wise 6 shrewd 10 hardheaded 11 foresighted
longing: yen 6 desire 7 athirst, craving, wistful 8 appetite, cupidity, yearning 9 nostalgia 10 desiderium
longitudinally: 7 endlong 10 lengthwise
longshoreman: 9 stevedore
loo: pam 8 napoleon
look: lo; con, pry, see 4 gaze, leer, ogle, peek, peep, peer, pore, scan, seem, skew 5 blush, dekko, fleer, glare, gliff, glime, gloat, gloom, glout, lower, sight, smile, snoop, stare 6 aspect, behold, gander, glance, glower, glunch, regard, search, squint, visage 7 observe 8 demeanor 10 appearance
look after: 4 tend 6 attend
look at: eye, see 4 glom, view 6 behold, regard 7 examine, observe
look back: 6 recall, relive, review 7 rethink 8 remember 10 retrospect
look down on: 7 despise
look for: 4 seek 5 await 6 expect 10 anticipate
look forward to: 5 await 6 expect 10 anticipate
look into: 5 study 7 examine, inspect 11 investigate
look like: 8 resemble
look over: 6 ignore, survey 8 overlook 9 disregard 11 reconnoiter, reconnoitre
look toward: 4 face
looker-on: 8 audience, beholder 9 bystander, spectator
lookout: 6 conner 7 atalaya(P.I.) 8 bantayan(P.I.), cockatoo 10 watchtower
looks (see also **look**): 4 face 8 features 10 attraction
loom: auk 4 hulk, loon, tool 5 dobby, weave 6 appear, emerge, gentle, puffin, vessel 7 machine 9 guillemot, implement 10 receptacle
part: bar, lam 4 caam, leaf, reed, sley 5 easer, lathe 6 hanger, heddle 7 harness
loon: nut, sap 4 dolt, lout 5 diver, rogue, scamp, wabby 6 cobble, rascal
loop: eye, tab 4 ansa, coil, fold, hank, kink, knot, oese 5 bight, bride, coque, honda, hondo, noose, picot, terry 6 becket, billet, circle 7 circuit, curette, folding 8 doubling 11 aiguillette
loop-shaped: 9 fundiform
loophole: out 4 muse 5 meuse, oilet 6 escape, eyelet 7 opening 8 aperture, weakness
loose: gay, lax 4 floa, free, open 5 baggy, bulgy, crank, loose, relax, slack, vague 6 coarse, dangly, random, unlash, wobbly 7 immoral, movable, relaxed, unbound, unleash 8 insecure, unstable, withdraw 9 desultory, dissolute, unbridled, unchecked 10 indefinite, licentious, unattached, unconfined, unfastened 11 untrammeled 12 uncontrolled, unrestrained 14 unconventional
loose ends: 4 dags 5 bored 7 tagrags 8 restless
loose-jointed: 5 lanky, rangy 6 clumsy, wobbly 7 rickety 10 ramshackle
loosen: pry 4 ease, free, undo 5 relax, untie 7 slacken 8 liberate, unfasten 9 disengage, extricate 11 disentangle

loot: rob, sum 4 sack, swag 5 booty, strip 6 pilfer, ravage, spoils 7 pillage, plunder
receipt of: 9 theftbote

lop: bob, cut, dod 4 clip, flop, hang, sned(Sc.), snip, trim 5 droop, prune, slice 6 dangle 7 pendant, pendent 8 truncate

lope: jog 4 gait 6 canter 7 dogtrot

lopper: 4 clot 6 curdle 7 clabber 9 coagulate

lopsided: 4 alop 7 crooked 10 unbalanced

loquacious: 5 gabby 6 verbal 7 prating 8 cackling 9 garrulous, talkative 10 babblative, chattering

loquacity: 9 garrulity

loquat: 4 biwa

lord: aga 4 agha, earl, peer, rule, tsar 5 liege, ruler 6 domine, master, prince 7 marquis, vavasor 8 domineer, governor, nobleman, seigneur, suzerain, vavasour, viscount 9 dominator
attendant: 5 thane

Lord have mercy upon us: 5 Kyrie 12 Kyrie eleison

Lord High Executioner: 4 Koko

Lord Jim author: 6 Conrad

Lord's Prayer: 11 Paternoster

lordly: 5 proud 6 uppish 8 arrogant, despotic 9 imperious, masterful 10 tyrannical 11 dictatorial, domineering, magisterial, overbearing

lordship: 7 dynasty 10 allegiance

lore: 4 lear 6 advice, wisdom 7 counsel 8 learning 9 erudition, knowledge, tradition 11 instruction

Lorelei: 5 siren

lorgnette: 8 eyeglass 10 opera glass

lorica: 5 shell 7 cuirass 8 corselet

lorikeet: 6 parrot

loriot: 6 oriole

loris: 5 lemur

lorn: 6 bereft 7 forlorn 8 desolate, forsaken, lonesome 9 abandoned

Lorraine: *capital:* 4 Metz
river: 4 Saar

lose: 4 amit, fail, miss 5 waste 6 defeat, mislay 7 forfeit 9 dissipate

losel: bum 6 loafer 10 ne'er-do-well

loss: 4 cost, leak, ruin, toll 5 price, waste 6 damage, damnum, defeat, injury, ullage 7 expense, failure 8 amission, decrease 9 decrement, detriment, privation 10 affliction, bankruptcy 11 bereavement, deperdition, deprivation, destruction

lost: 4 gone, lorn 5 perdu(F.) 6 absent, hidden, ruined 7 forlorn, mislaid, strayed 8 absorbed, confused, defeated, estrayed, obscured, prodigal 9 abandoned, forfeited, perplexed, reprobate, subverted 10 abstracted, bewildered, dissipated, overthrown 11 preoccupied 13 irreclaimable

Lost Horizon author: 6 Hilton

lot: hap 4 dole, doom, fate, land, luck, much, plat, plot 5 batch, field, grist, group, share, weird 6 amount, bundle, chance, divide, hazard, parcel 7 destiny, fortune, portion 8 caboodle, quantity 9 allotment, apportion 13 apportionment
appointment by: 9 sortition
miscellaneous: 6 fardel, joblot

Lot: *father:* 5 Haran
grandson: 7 Moabite
nephew: 7 Abraham
place of flight: 5 Sodom
sister: 6 Milcah
son: 4 Moab

lotion: 4 balm, wash 6 loture 8 ablution, linament

lots: 4 gobs 5 scads 6 plenty

lottery: 6 raffle 10 sweepstake

lotto: 4 keno 5 bingo, keeno

lotus, lotos: 7 nelumbo 10 chinquapin

lotus bird: 6 jacana

lotus tree: 4 sadr 9 persimmon

loud: 5 gaudy, heavy, noisy, showy, vivid 6 coarse, flashy, vulgar 7 blatant, clamant, obvious, raucous 8 emphatic, strepent, vehement 9 clamorous, insistent, turbulent, unrefined 10 blustering, boisterous, stentorian, tumultuous, vociferous 11 thersitical 12 obstreperous

louder: 9 crescendo

lough: sea 4 lake, loch, pool 5 water

Louisiana: *county:* 6 parish
decree: 5 arret
dialect: 6 creole
native: 5 Cajun 6 creole
parish: 4 Winn 5 Allen, Caddo, Union 6 Acadia, De Soto, Iberia, Sabine, Tensas, Vernon 9 Iberville, Vermilion 10 Evangeline 11 Plaquemines
town: 4 Begg 6 Gretna 10 Shreveport
university: LSU 6 Tulane

lounge: 4 idle, loaf, loll, sofa 5 bange, couch, divan, relax 6 froust, frowst, loiter

loup: 4 flee, jump, leap

louse: nit 5 aphid, aphis 6 cootie, slater

lousy: 9 pedicular 10 pediculous

lout: bow, oaf 4 bend, boor, clod, coof, dolt, fool, gaum, gawk, hulk 5 clown, cuddy, stoop, yahoo, yokel 6 curtsy, lubber 7 bumpkin, grobian

loutish: 4 rude 5 crude 6 clumsy, gauche(F.), stupid 7 awkward

lovable, loveable: 4 dear 7 amative, amiable 8 adorable, dovelike 9 endearing

love: gra(Ir.), loe(Sc.), loo(Sc.) 4 dear, dote, like 5 adore, aloha, amore(It.), amour(F.), Cupid, fancy, liebe(G.), lover 6 enamor 7

charity, embrace, idolize 8 fondness, goodwill, idolatry 9 adoration, affection 10 attachment, sweetheart 11 inclination
comb. form: 4 phil 5 philo
god of: 4 Amor, Ares, Eros, Kama 5 Bhaga, Cupid
goddess of: 5 Athor, Freya, Venus 6 Freyja, Hathor, Ishtar 9 Aphrodite
science of: 9 erotology
token of: 6 amoret
love apple: 6 tomato
love feast: 5 agape 7 banquet 9 gathering
love knot: 6 amoret
love-potion: 5 charm 7 philter, philtre 11 aphrodisiac
love story: 7 romance
lovebird: 6 parrot
loveliness: 6 beauty 11 pulchritude
lovelock: 4 curl 5 tress 12 heartbreaker
lovely: 5 sweet 6 loving, tender 7 amiable, amorous, angelic 8 adorable, angelina, charming, graceful 9 beautiful 10 attractive
lover: ami(F.), gra(Ir.) 4 beau, chap 5 amant(F.), leman, Romeo 6 adorer, amadis, amante(F., fem.), bonami 7 admirer, amateur, amorist, amoroso, Don Juan, gallant 8 belamour, Lothario 9 bonne amie(fem.), enamorata, inamorata 10 dilettante, sweetheart 11 philanderer
meeting place: 5 tryst
patron saint: 9 Valentine
rustic: 7 Celadon
lovesick: 6 pining 7 longing 11 languishing
loving: 4 fond 6 erotic, lovely 7 adorant, amative, amatory, amorous 9 affecting 12 affectionate
comb. form: 4 phil 5 phile
loving cup: tig, tyg 5 prize
low: bas(F.), moo 4 base, bass, blue, deep, hill, mean, neap 5 dirty, gross, snide 6 bellow, coarse, common, earthy, feeble, filthy, humble, humbly, slight, sordid, vulgar 7 bestial, ignoble, plebian, shallow, slavish 8 dejected 9 depressed, earthbred 10 melancholy 11 undignified, unfavorable 12 contemptible, disreputable
lowan: 4 bird 6 leipoa, mallee
Low Country: 7 Belgium, Holland 9 Luxemburg 11 Netherlands
low-lived: 4 mean 10 despicable 12 contemptible
low-necked: 9 decollete
low tide: ebb 4 neap
lowbred: 5 crude 6 coarse, vulgar 11 ill-mannered
lower: dip 4 alow, bate, drop, sink, vail 5 abase, abate, baser, below, decry, demit, frown, glare, scowl, under 6 bemean, debase, deepen, demean, derate, glower, humble, lessen, meaner, nether, reduce 7 beneath, degrade, depress, descend, subside 8 diminish, downward 9 disparage 10 depreciate, nethermore
lowering: 4 dark 5 heavy 6 beetle, cloudy, gloomy, lowery, sullen 8 overcast 11 threatening
lowest: 5 least, nadir 6 bottom 7 bedrock 10 nethermost
lowing (see also **low**): 7 mugient 9 bellowing
lowland: 4 flat, holm, spit 5 terai(Ind.) 6 valley 7 bottoms
Lowlander (see also **Scotland**): 4 Scot 9 Sassenach
language: 6 Lallan 7 Lalland
lowly: 4 base, mean, meek 6 humble, modest 7 ignoble 12 unpretending 13 unpretentious
lox: 6 salmon
loy: 4 tool 5 spade
loyal: 4 feal, firm, leal, true 5 liege, pious 6 stanch 7 devoted, staunch 8 constant, faithful
loyalty: 6 homage 10 allegiance
Loyalty island: Uea 4 Lifu, Uvea
Loyolite: 6 Jesuit
lozenge: 4 pill 5 candy 6 jujube, pastil, tablet, troche 7 diamond 8 pastille
lubber: 4 boor, gawk, lout 5 churl, drone 8 landsman
lubricate: oil 4 dope 6 grease 7 moisten
lubricous: 4 lewd 6 shifty, tricky, wanton 7 elusive 8 slippery, unstable 10 lascivious
luce: 4 pike
lucent: 5 clear, lucid 6 bright 7 shining 11 translucent, transparent
lucerne, lucern: 7 alfalfa
lucid: 4 sane 5 clear 6 bright, lucent 7 crystal, shining 8 luminous, pellucid 11 resplendent, translucent
lucidity: 6 sanity 7 clarity
Lucifer: 5 devil, Satan
luck: hap, lot, ure 4 cess, eure, fate 5 deuce 6 chance, hansel 7 ambsace, fortune, handsel, success 8 fortuity 9 mischance
bringer: 5 Jonah 6 clover, mascot 9 horseshoe 10 rabbit-foot
stroke of: 5 fluke
token for: 5 charm 6 amulet, mascot 7 periapt
lucky: 5 canny, happy, sonsy 6 sonsie 8 gracious 9 fortunate 10 propitious, prosperous, successful 12 providential
lucrative: 6 paying 7 gainful 10 beneficial, productive, profitable 12 remunerative
lucre: 4 gain, loot, pelf 5 booty, money 6 profit, riches, wealth

ludicrous: 5 antic, awful, comic, droll, funny 6 absurd 7 comical, foolish, risible 8 farcical 9 burlesque, laughable 10 ridiculous
luff: 4 sail
lug: box, ear 4 drag, draw, pull, tote, worm, haul 5 carry 10 projection
lugubrious: sad 6 dismal 7 doleful 8 mournful
lukewarm: 5 tepid
lull: 4 calm, hush, rock 5 allay, quiet, still 6 pacify, soothe 7 compose 8 calmness, mitigate 9 cessation 11 tranquilize
lullaby: 5 baloo, balow
lumber: 4 raff, wood 6 refuse, timber
lumbering: 7 awkward
lumberman: 6 logger, sawyer, scorer 10 lumberjack
boot: pac
hook: 5 peavy 6 peavey
sled: 4 tode 7 travois 8 travoise
luminary: sun 4 star 5 light 12 illumination, intellectual
lumine: 5 light 8 illumine
luminous: 5 clear, lucid 6 bright 7 shining 9 brilliant 11 illuminated, transparent 14 phosphorescent
lummox: 4 boor, lout 5 yahoo 7 bumpkin, bungler
lump: bat, cob, dab, dad, dot, gob, nub, wad 4 beat, blob, burl, cake, clog, clot, daud, heap, hump, hunk, knob, knot, mass 5 bulge, claut, clump, clunk, hunch, wedge 6 dollop, gobbet, nodule, nugget 12 protuberance
lumpfish: 6 paddle
lumpish: 4 dull 5 heavy, inert 6 stodgy, stupid 8 sluggish 9 shapeless
lumpy: 5 rough 6 choppy
lunacy: 5 folly, mania 7 madness 8 delirium, insanity 9 craziness 11 derangement
lunar (see also **moon**): 6 lunate 8 crescent 9 satellite
lunatic: mad 6 insane, madman 7 frantic 8 demoniac 9 bedlamite 10 moonstruck
lune: 5 leash 8 crescent
lung: *comb. form:* 5 pulmo
disease: 11 anthracosis
having: 9 pulmonate
sound: 4 rale
lunge: jab 4 foin, leap, stab 5 barge, longe, lurch, pitch 6 plunge, thrust
luny: 5 crazy 8 demented
lupine: 6 fierce 7 wolfish 8 ravenous, wolflike
lurch: rob 4 jolt, reel 5 barge, cheat, fraud, lunge, pitch, steal, trick 6 careen, career, swerve 7 stumble
lure: 4 bait, draw, trap 5 decoy, snare, tempt 6 allure, entice, seduce 7 attract, beguile, pitfall 8 inveigle 10 allurement, attraction, enticement
lurer: 4 bait 5 siren 7 trapper
lurid: wan 4 pale 5 gaudy, livid 6 dismal, gloomy 7 ghastly, hideous 8 gruesome, shocking, terrible
lurk: 4 hide 5 skulk, slink, sneak 6 ambush
luscious: 4 rich, ripe 5 sweet 6 creamy 7 cloying 8 delicate 9 delicious 10 voluptuous
lush: 4 soft 5 drunk 6 limber, mellow 9 alcoholic, luxuriant, succulent 11 intoxicated
lusory: 7 playful 8 sportive
lust: 6 desire, liking 7 passion 8 appetite, cupidity 11 inclination
luster, lustre: 4 cave, naif 5 sheen, shine, water 6 polish 7 glister 8 schiller, splendor 11 distinction, iridescence
lusterless: mat, wan 4 dead, dull 5 faded, fishy 6 gloomy 9 tarnished
lustful: hot 4 gamy, lewd 5 cadgy 7 fulsome, rammish 9 lecherous, salacious
lustrous: 5 nitid 6 glossy, orient 7 radiant 8 nitidous 9 brilliant 11 illustrious, transparent
lusty: 4 cant 5 crank, frack, frank, freck, hardy 6 cranky, gawsie, robust, strong, sturdy 8 bouncing, vigorous
lute: tar 4 clay, ring 6 cement 7 dyphone 10 instrument
luxe: 8 elegance, richness
Luxemburg: *measure:* 5 fuder
river: 7 Moselle
luxuriant: 4 lush, rank, rich 5 frank 6 lavish 7 fertile, opulent, profuse, teeming 8 prolific 9 exuberant 10 voluptuous
luxuriate: 4 bask, riot 5 revel
luxurious: 4 posh, rich 5 gaudy 6 costly 7 elegant, opulent 8 gorgeous, sensuous 9 sumptuous 11 comfortable, extravagant
luxury: 8 delicacy
lover of: 8 Sybarite
Luzon: *city:* 5 Gapan 6 Ilagan 10 Cabanatuan
dialect: 6 Itaves
mountain: Iba
people: Ata, Ita 4 Aeta, Atta 5 Tagal 6 Aripas, Arupas, Igorot, Isinay, Itaneg 7 Igorote, Italone, Tagalog
seaport: 6 Aparri, Manila
volcano: 5 Mayon
lyam: 5 leash 10 bloodhound
lycanthrope: 8 werewolf
lycee: 6 lyceum, school
Lycian city: 4 Myra 6 Sardis
Lydia: *king:* 5 Gyges 7 Croesus
river: 8 Pactolus
lye: 6 potash 7 caustic 8 lixivium
pert. to: 8 lixivial

lying: 4 flat 5 awald, awalt, prone 6 supine 8 couchant 9 dishonest, mendacity 10 pseudology
lying-in: 11 confinement 12 accouchement
lymph: sap 5 water 6 plasma, spring
lynch: 4 hang 6 murder 7 execute
Lynette's knight: 6 Gareth
lynx: cat 5 pishu 6 bobcat, lucern 7 caracal 8 carcajou
Lyra star: 4 Vega
lyrate: 9 spatulate
lyre: 4 asor, harp 6 kissar, trigon 7 cithara, kithara, testudo
lyre turtle: 11 leatherback
lyric: lai, lay, ode 4 alba, odic, poem 5 epode, gazel, melic 6 ghazel, poetic, rondel 7 cancion, canzone(It.), descort, rondeau 9 dithyramb
Muse: 5 Erato 8 Polymnia 10 Polyhymnia
lyrical: 6 epodic 7 sestina
lyrichord: 11 harpsichord
lyssa: 6 rabies 11 hydrophobia

M

Maacah: *father:* Talmai
husband: 5 David 8 Rehoboam
son: Asa 6 Abijah 7 Absalom
mabolo: 4 plum 7 camagon
macabre: 4 eery, grim 5 eerie 7 ghastly 8 grewsome, gruesome 9 deathlike
macaca: 5 lemur 6 monkey
macadam: tar 8 pavement
macaque: 4 bruh 6 monkey, rhesus
macaw: ara 4 arra, bird 5 arara 6 parrot 7 maracan 8 aracanga, ararauna
Macbeth: *character:* 5 Angus 6 Banquo
title: 5 Thane
victim: 6 Duncan
maccaboy: 5 snuff
mace: dod, rod 4 club, maul, rush 5 spice, staff 6 mallet 7 swindle
bearer: 6 beadle
royal: 7 scepter, sceptre
Macedonia: *king:* 5 Abgar
mountain: 5 Athos 7 Olympus 8 Olympiad
people: 6 Greeks 8 Serbians 9 Albanians 10 Bulgarians
statesman: 9 Antipater
macer: 6 beadle, bearer 8 swindler
macerate: ret 4 soak 5 steep
machete: 4 bolo, fish 5 blade, knife 6 guitar
Machiavellian: 4 wily 6 crafty 7 cunning 8 guileful 9 deceitful 11 treacherous
Machiavelli's book: 6 Prince
machila: 7 hammock
machin: 7 macaque
machinate: 4 plan, plot 5 cabal 6 scheme
machination: 4 plan, plot 5 cabal 6 scheme 8 artifice, intrigue 10 conspiracy 11 contrivance
machine: car 4 auto 5 robot 6 device, engine 9 apparatus, appliance, automatic, automaton, mechanism 10 automobile 11 contrivance, machination 12 organization
hydraulic: 9 telemotor
part: cam 5 rotor, wheel 6 piston, stator, tappet
machine gun: 4 Sten 5 Maxim 7 Gatling 9 Hotchkiss 10 chatterbox
place: 4 nest
macilent: 4 lean, thin 9 emaciated
mackeral: 4 scad 5 akule, atule, tunny 7 escolar, tassard 8 hardhead
genus: 7 scomber
net: 7 spiller
young: 5 spike 6 tinker 7 blinker
mackerel bird: 7 wryneck 9 kittiwake
mackle: See **macula**
macle: 8 chrystal 11 chiastolite
macula: 4 blot, blur, spot 5 stain 6 blotch, mackle, macule 7 blemish
maculate: 6 defile, impure 7 speckle 8 besmirch
mad: 4 gite, gyte, hyte(Sc.) 5 angry, crazy, folle, irate, rabid, vexed 6 frenzy, insane 7 enraged, foolish, frantic, furious 8 demented, frenetic, incensed, maniacal 9 desperate, fanatical, hilarious, phrenetic, psychotic 10 distracted, distraught, infatuated, infuriated 11 fantastical 12 arreptitious, unreasonable
Madagascar: *animal:* 6 aye-aye, tanrec, tenrec 7 tendrac
city: 7 Mojanga 8 Tamatave 10 Tananarive, Tananarivo 12 Antananarivo(c.)
civet: 7 fossane
island group: 7 Aldabra
lemur: 5 avahi, indri 6 aye-aye 9 babacoote
measure: 7 gantang
native: 4 Hova 8 Sakalava
palm: 6 raffia
people: 4 Hova
tree: 11 antankarana
tribe: 4 Bara 5 Hovas 8 Betsileo, Malagasy, Sakalava 13 Betsimasaraka
madam, madame: Mme., Mrs. 4 bawd, lady 5 donna, hussy, title, wench 6 senora 8 mistress 9 courtesan
madcap: 4 wild 7 hotspur 8 reckless
madder: al; aal 7 munjeet 8 dyestuff
family: 9 rubiaceae
made: 10 artificial
Madeira: *capital:* 7 Funchal

wine: 4 bual 5 tinta, tinto 7 malmsey, sercial 8 verdelho
mademoiselle: 4 miss
madhouse: 5 chaos 6 asylum, bedlam 8 bughouse
madid: wet 5 moist
madman: 6 maniac 7 furioso, lunatic 8 frenetic 9 phrenetic, psychotic
madness: ire 4 fury 5 folly, furor, mania 6 bedlam, frenzy, lunacy, rabies 7 dewanee, ecstasy, widdrim 8 delirium, dementia, insanity 9 amazement, furiosity, nosomania, phrenetic 11 derangement
Madras: *district:* 7 Malabar, Nellore
hemp: 4 sunn
measure: 4 para 5 cawny, manei, parah 6 cawney, mercal, ollock, olluck, parrah, puddee
town: 5 Adoni, Arcot 7 Calicut
weight: ser 4 cash, powe, seer 5 fanam 6 pagoda, pollam 7 chinnam, varahan 8 mangelin
madrepore: 5 coral 6 fossil
Madrid promenade: 5 Prado
madrigal: ode 4 glee, poem 5 lyric 6 verses
Maecenas: 6 patron
maelstrom: 4 eddy 5 swirl 7 current, turmoil 9 whirlpool
maenad: 9 bacchante
maestro: 6 master 7 teacher 8 composer 9 conductor 10 bandleader 11 choirmaster 13 kapellmeister
di-cappella: 11 choirmaster 13 kapellmeister
maffle: 6 muddle, mumble 7 confuse, stammer 8 bewilder, squander
mag: 4 chat 6 magpie 7 chatter, magneto 8 titmouse 9 halfpenny 10 chatterbox
Magadha king: 9 Bimbisara 10 Ajatasatru
magadis: 5 flute 9 monochord
magazine: 4 pulp 5 depot 7 almacen, arsenal, chamber, journal 9 ephemeris, reservoir, warehouse 10 periodical, repository, storehouse 11 armamentary
mage: See **magician**
magenta: dye 7 fuchsia
maggot: 4 grub, mawk, whim 5 larva, mathe 6 gentle, notion 7 caprice
magi: 5 Sages 6 Gaspar 8 Melchior 9 Balthasar
gift of: 4 gold 5 myrrh 12 frankincense
magic: art 4 rune 5 fairy, obeah, spell, turgy 6 glamor, voodoo 7 glamour, gramary, sorcery 8 brujeria(Sp.), gramarye 9 deception, diablerie 10 necromancy, witchcraft 11 conjuration, enchantment, legerdemain, thaumaturgy 12 invultuation
act of: 11 conjuration
lantern: 11 epidiascope 12 stereopticon
perform: hex 6 sorcer 7 conjure
pert. to: 6 goetic
staff: 4 wand 7 rhabdos 8 caduceus
symbol: 5 charm 6 caract 8 pentacle
tree: 13 polemoniaceae
word: om, um 5 selah 6 presto, sesame, shelah 11 abracadabra
Magic Mountain: *author:* 4 Mann
character: 7 Castorp
magical: 5 goety 6 goetic, occult 8 charming 10 bewitching 11 necromantic
magician: 4 mage, magi 5 magus 6 goetic, Merlin, wabeno, wizard 7 juggler 8 conjurer, conjuror, mandrake, sorcerer 9 archimage, charlatan, enchanter 11 entertainer, necromancer, thaumaturge 13 thaumaturgist 15 prestidigitator
assistant: 6 famuli(pl.) 7 famulus
manual: 8 grimoire
motion: 4 pass
magirist: 4 cook
magisterial: 5 lofty, proud 6 august, lordly 7 haughty, stately 8 arrogant, dogmatic 9 dignified, imperious 11 dictatorial, domineering, overbearing 13 authoritative
magistrate: 4 beak, doge 5 edile, judge 6 alcade, alcaid, archon, bailie, bailli, syndic 7 alcaide, alcalde, bailiff, burgess, podesta(It.) 8 alderman, governor, mittimus, official 11 burgomaster
orders: 4 acta(pl.) 5 actum
magma: 4 rock 5 dregs 8 sediment
basalt: 10 limburgite
magnanimous: big 4 free 5 lofty, noble 6 heroic 7 exalted, liberal 8 generous 9 honorable, unselfish, unstinted 10 high-minded, high-souled 13 disinterested
magnate: 4 lord 5 mogul, noble 6 bashaw, tycoon 7 grandee, richman 10 clarissimo 11 millionaire
magnesian limestone: 8 dolomite
magnesium: *silicate:* 4 talc
sulphate: 7 loweite
symbol: Mg
magnet: 7 terella 8 solenoid, terrella 9 loadstone, lodestone
end: 4 pole
pole: red
type of: bar 9 horseshoe
magnetic: 5 polar 10 electrical
unit: 5 weber
magnetize: 4 lure 7 attract 9 captivate
magnific: 4 vast 5 grand 7 pompous, sublime
magnificent: 4 rial, rich 5 grand, great, noble, regal 6 august, lavish 7 exalted, stately, sublime 8 glorious, gorgeous, palatial, splendid, striking 9 beautiful, sumptuous 10 munificent

magnificence: 4 pomp
magnify: 4 laud 5 exalt, extol 6 praise 7 enhance, enlarge, glorify, greaten 8 increase 9 aggravate, overstate 10 exaggerate
magniloquent: 6 turgid 9 bombastic 13 grandiloquent
magnitude: 4 bulk, mass, size 6 extent 7 bigness 9 dimension, greatness
magnolia: 5 yulan
magnum: 6 bottle
magnum opus: 4 work 11 achievement
magot: ape 6 figure
magpie: daw, mag, pie 4 pica, piet, piot, pyat, pyet 5 madge, ninut, scold 9 chatterer, haggister
diver: 4 smew
shrike: 7 tanager
magsman: 8 swindler
maguari: 5 stork
maguey: 4 aloe 5 agave, plant 7 cantala
magus: 4 magi 8 magician
Magyar: 6 Ugrian 9 Hungarian
maha: 4 deer
mahajan: 11 moneylender
mahala: 5 squaw
mahogany: 4 toon 6 acajou, totara 7 albarco, gunnung 8 bangalay 9 cailcedra
maholi: 5 lemur
Mahomet: See **Mohammed**
Mahometan: See **Muslim**
Mahound: 5 devil 8 Mohammed
mahout: 6 driver, keeper
mahu: 5 devil
mahua butter: 6 phulwa
Maia's son: 6 Hermes
maid: may 4 ayah, girl, help, lass 5 bonne, woman 6 damsel, maiden, slavey, virgin 7 Abigail, ancilla, colleen, servant 8 domestic, suivante 9 attendant, cameriera, tirewoman
changed to heifer: Io
changed to spider: 7 Arachne
mythical: 5 nymph
Maid of Astolat: 6 Elaine
Maid of Orleans: 4 Joan 7 Pucelle
maiden: deb 4 girl, jill, lass 5 nymph, sylph 6 damsel 7 damosel, damozel 8 damozell 9 damosella, damoysell, debutante
maiden duck: 8 shoveler
maiden name: nee
maidenhair: 4 fern 8 adiantum
tree: 6 ginkgo
maidenly: 6 gentle, modest, virgin
mail: bag 4 post, send, ship 6 wallet 8 dispatch
boat: 6 packet
coat: see **armor**
maim: 4 hurt 6 mangle 7 cripple, disable 8 mutilate 9 dismember
main: sea 4 duct, high, pipe 5 chief, first, grand, ocean, prime 7 capital, conduct, conduit, leading, purpose 8 foremost 9 principal
main gauche: 6 dagger
Main Street author: 5 Lewis
Maine: *bay:* 5 Casco 13 Passamaquoddy
bird: 9 chickadee
city: 4 Bath, Milo, Saco 5 Hiram, Orono 6 Bangor 7 Augusta(c.) 9 Skowhegan
county: 5 Waldo
lake: 5 Moose 6 Sebago
motto: 6 dirigo
mountain: 5 Kineo 8 Katahdin
port: 6 Bangor 8 Portland
river: 4 Saco 8 Kennebec
symbol: 4 pine
university town: 5 Orono
mainferre: 5 armor 8 gauntlet
mainland: 8 fastland 9 continent
mainsheet: 4 rope
mainstay: key 7 support
maintain: 4 avow, bear, fend, hold, keep 5 argue, claim 6 affirm, allege, assert, avouch, defend, retain, uphold 7 bolster, contend, declare, espouse, justify, support, sustain 8 conserve, preserve 9 vindicate
again: 8 reassert
maintainable: 7 tenable
maintenance: 5 batta 6 upkeep 7 alimony, probend 10 livelihood
maison: 5 house
de sante: 6 asylum 8 hospital 10 sanatorium
maize: 4 corn, samp 5 grain 7 mealies
genus: Zea
majagua: hau 4 baru, bola 5 guana 8 balibago 12 algodoncillo
majestic: 5 grand, lofty, noble, regal, royal 6 august, kingly 7 leonine, stately, sublime 8 elevated, imperial, splendid 9 dignified, sovereign 11 magnificent
major: wig 5 chief 7 capital, greater, officer 8 superior 9 principal
music: dur
major-domo: 7 bailiff, steward 9 seneschal
Majorca city: 5 Palma
majority: age 4 body, more, most 6 quorum 7 greater
make: do; cut, gar(Sc.) 4 coin, form 5 build, force, frame, shape 6 compel, create, invent, render 7 compose, confect, fashion, prepare, produce 8 contrive, generate 9 construct, fabricate 11 manufacture
suffix: fy; ify

make-believe: 4 sham 5 feign, magic 7 feigned, fiction, pretend 8 pretense
make do: eke 9 improvise
make fun of: rib 5 scoff 8 ridicule
make known: 6 impart, reveal 7 divulge, publish, uncover 8 disclose, discover, proclaim 9 advertise, publicize
make over: 4 redo 6 revamp 9 refashion
make up: 8 complete, cosmetic
make up for: 5 atone 10 compensate
maker: 4 doer 6 author, factor 7 creator 8 declarer, inventor 9 architect 10 originator 12 manufacturer
makeshift: 4 rude 9 temporary
maki: 5 lemur
makluk: 4 seal
mal: bad 4 evil
de mer: 11 seasickness
du pays: 12 homesickness
Malabar: *bark:* 5 ochna
canoe: 5 tonee
monkey: 8 wanderoo
palm: 7 talipot
people: 4 Nair
malacca: 4 cane 5 stick
Malacca: *measure:* 4 asta
weight: kip
malachite: 4 bice 7 azurite, mineral
maladive: ill 4 sick 6 sickly, unwell 9 unhealthy
maladroit: 6 clumsy 7 awkward, unhandy 8 bungling, inexpert
maladventure: 6 mishap 8 escapade
malady (see also **disease**): 7 ailment, illness 8 disorder, sickness 9 affection, complaint, distemper 10 affliction 13 indisposition
malagma: 7 plaster 8 poultice
malanders: 6 eczema
malapert: 4 bold 5 saucy 7 ill-bred 8 impudent 9 unskilled
malapropism: 7 mistake
malapropos: 11 inopportune
malar: 6 zygoma 8 zygomata(pl.) 9 cheekbone
malaria: 4 agie, ague 5 chill, fever, miasm 6 miasma
antidote: 7 quinine
carrier: 8 mosquito 9 anopheles
malarkey: 6 drivel 8 nonsense
malaxate: 5 knead
Malaya: *almond:* 6 kanari
ape: lar
archipelago: See *island* below
boat: 4 proa 5 praam, prahu 6 praham 7 cougnar
buffalo: 7 carabao 8 seladang
Christian: 7 Ilokano
coin: tra 4 trah 7 tampang
condiment: 6 sambal, sambei 7 semball
crane: 5 sarus
disease: 4 amok, lata 5 amuck, latah
form of address: 4 tuan
fruit: 8 rambutan
garment: 6 sarong
island: Aru, Goa, Kei, Oma 4 Bali, Buru, Gaga, Java, Sulu 5 Ambon, Arroe, Arrou, Banca, Banda, Buton, Ceram, Misol, Sangi, Sumba, Timor 6 Boefon, Boeroe, Borneo, Flores, Jilolo, Lombik, Madura, Musool, Sangir, Soemba, Talaur, Waigeu 7 Amboina, Amboyna, Celebes, Morotai, Salwati, Sumatra, Sumbawa 8 Belitong, Billiton, Djailolo, Moluccas, Soembawa, Tanimbar, Tenimber 9 Belitoeng, Halmahera, New Guinea, Singapore, Timorlaut 10 Sandalwood
isthmus: Kra
jacket: 4 baju
knife: 4 cris, kris 5 crise 6 crease, creese, kreese, parang
language: 7 Tagalog
mammal: 10 chevrotain
measure: 4 tael, wang
mountain: 6 Gunong, Gunung
musical instrument: 7 anklong
ox: 5 tsine 7 banteng
palm: 4 ejoo, sago 5 areng 6 arenga, gebang, gomuti, nibong, nibung 7 talipot
parrot: 4 lory 6 lories
people: Ata 5 Bajau, Tagal 6 Aripas, Semang 7 Bisayan, Tagalog, Visayan
pepper: 4 siri 5 sirih
pewter: 4 trah
rice field: 5 sawah
state: 5 Kedah, Perak 6 Johore
title: 4 tuan
town: 7 Malacca
tree (see also *palm* above): 4 upas 5 kapur, niepa, terap 6 durian, durion
ungulate: 5 tapir
malconformation: 9 imperfect 16 disproportionate
malcontent: reb 5 rebel 6 uneasy 8 agitator, Frondeur 10 discontent, rebellious 12 discontented
Maldives' capital: 4 Male
male: man, mas 4 gent 5 manly 7 mankind, manlike, mannish 9 masculine
animal: tom 4 buck, bull, hart, jack, stag, stud 8 stallion
figure: 7 telamon
gelded: 4 galt 5 steer 6 eunuch 7 gelding
malediction: ban 5 curse 7 malison, slander 8 anathema 9 blasphemy 11 imprecation 12 denunciation
malefactor: 5 felon 7 convict, culprit 8 criminal, evildoer, offender 9 wrongdoer
malefic: 7 harmful, hurtful 11 mischievous

malevolence: 4 evil, hate 5 pique, spite 6 enmity, hatred, malice, rancor 8 ferocity 9 animosity, hostility, malignity 10 bitterness

malevolent: 4 evil 7 hateful, hostile 9 rancorous 11 ill-disposed

malfeasance: 5 crime, wrong 8 trespass 11 delinquency

malheur: 10 misfortune

malice: 5 pique 6 enmity 9 animosity 13 maliciousness

malicious: 4 evil 5 catty, depit 6 bitter 7 heinous 8 sinister, spiteful 9 felonious, malignant, rancorous, resentful 10 calumnious, despiteful, despiteous, malevolent 11 ill-disposed 12 cantankerous, unpropitious
action: 5 arson 8 sabotage 9 vandalism
intention: 6 animus

malign: 4 evil, foul 5 abuse, curse, libel 6 bewray, defame, revile, vilify 7 asperse, baleful, blacken, deprave, hurtful, slander 8 virulent 10 calumniate, pernicious

malignant: 4 evil 6 wicked 7 hateful, heinous, hellish, noxious, vicious 8 spiteful, venomous, virulent 9 cancerous, felonious, ferocious, invidious, malicious, poisonous, rancorous 10 rebellious 11 deleterious

malignity: 10 malignancy

malikana: fee 4 duty 7 payment

malison: 5 curse 11 malediction

malkin: cat, mop 4 drab, hare 6 sponge 8 slattern 9 scarecrow

mall: 4 walk 5 allee, alley 6 mallet 7 meeting 9 promenade

mallard: 4 duck
genus: 4 anas

malleable: 4 soft 7 ductile, pliable

mallemuck: 6 fulmar, petrel 9 albatross

mallet: tup 4 club, mace, mall, maul, mell(Sc.) 5 gavel, madge 6 beater, beetle, driver, hammer
hatter's: 6 beater
presiding officer's: 5 gavel
wooden: 4 maul 6 beetle

maline: net

mallow: maw 4 hock, weed 5 altea 6 escoba 7 althaea, gemauve

malm: 4 marl 9 limestone

malmsey: 4 wine 5 grape 7 madeira

malnutrition: 7 cachexy, wasting 8 cachexia

malodorous: 4 rank 5 fetid 6 putrid, smelly 7 noisome 9 odiferous

malt: 8 diastase
beverage: ale 4 beer, brew 5 lager, stout 6 zythem
froth: 4 barm
ground: 5 grist
infusion: 4 wort
vinegar: 6 alegar
worm: 5 toper 7 tippler

Malta: *capital:* 7 Valetta
coin: 5 grain, grano
hamlet: 5 casal 6 casale
island: 4 Gozo 6 Comino
measure: 4 salm 5 canna, salma 7 caffiso
suburb: 7 Florian
weight: 4 rotl, salm 5 artal, artel, parto, ratel, salma 6 kantar
wind: 7 gregale 8 levanter

Malta fever: 11 brucellosis

maltose: 6 amylon

maltreat: 5 abuse, dight 6 defile, defoul, demean, huspel, huspil, misuse, mohock

malty: 5 drunk

malum: 4 evil 5 wrong 7 offense

malvaceous plant: 4 okra 6 cotton, escoba, mallow 7 althaea

malvasia: 5 grape

mameluke: 5 slave 7 servant

Mamers: 4 Ares, Mars

mammal (see also **animal**): cat 5 beast, ovine, swine 6 bovine, equine, feline, monkey, rodent 7 primate 8 edentate, ruminant, ungulant 9 carnivore, marsupial
amphibious: 5 otter
antlered: elk 4 deer 5 moose 7 caribou 8 reindeer
aquatic: 4 seal 5 otter, shark, whale 6 desman, dugong, manati, rytina, walrus 7 dolphin, manatee, sealion 8 sirenian 12 hippopotamus
aquatic order: 4 cete 7 cetacea
arboreal: ai 5 lemur, sloth 6 fisher, monkey 7 glutton, opposum, raccoon 8 banxring, kinkajou 9 orangutan
armored: 9 armadillo
badgerlike: 5 ratel 8 balisaur
bearlike: 5 panda
bovine: ox; bos, cow 4 bull, calf, zebu 5 bison, steer 7 taurine 8 longhorn
burrowing: 4 mole 6 badger, gopher, wombat 8 squirrel 9 armadillo
camel-like: 7 guanaco
caprine: 4 goat
carnivorous: 9 carnivore
cetacean: see *aquatic* above
civetlike: 5 genet
coat: fur 4 hide, skin 6 pelage
cud-chewing: 8 ruminant
deerlike: 10 chevrotain
desert: 5 camel
dolphinlike: 4 inia
domestic: cat, cow, dog 5 horse, sheep 6 cattle

edentate: 7 ant bear 8 anteater, pangolin, tamandua
equine: 4 colt, foal, mare 5 filly, horse, zebra 8 stallion
extinct: 6 rytina 8 mastodon
feline: cat 4 lion, lynx, puma 5 ounce, tiger 6 bobcat, cougar, jaguar, ocelot, serval 7 leopard, panther
fish-eating: 5 otter
fleet: 4 deer, hare 8 antelope
flying: bat
fur-bearing: 4 coon, mink 5 coypu, otter, sheep, skunk 6 badger, ermine, marten, martin, nutria, rabbit 7 genette, raccoon 8 squirrel
giraffe-like: 5 okapi
gnawing: 6 rodent
hands different from feet: 6 bimana
hedgehog-like: 6 tenrec
herbivorous: 5 daman, tapir 6 bovine, dugong, equine 7 manatee 8 ruminant 9 orangutan 10 rhinoceros 12 hippopotamus
highest order: 7 primate
horned: ox; cow 4 gaur, goat, reem 5 bison 7 buffalo, unicorn 8 antelope, reindeer, seladang 10 rhinoceros
insectivorous: bat 6 tenrec 7 tendrac
large: 5 whale 7 mammoth 8 behemoth, elephant, mastodon 10 rhinoceros 12 hippopotamus
largest: 5 whale
lemurine: 5 potto
leopard-like: 4 lion, lynx, pard, puma 5 tiger 6 cougar, jaguar, ocelot 7 polecat, wildcat
llama-like: 6 vicuna
lowest order: 9 marsupial 11 marsupialia
marine: see *aquatic* above
marsupial: 4 tait 5 koala 7 opossum 8 kangaroo
meat-eating: 9 carnivore
mole-like: 6 desman
monkey-like: 5 lemur, loris
mouselike: 5 shrew
musteline: 5 otter, ratel
nocturnal: bat 5 hyena, lemur, ratel, tapir 6 macaco, racoon 7 raccoon, tarsier 8 kinkajou, platypus
omnivorous: hog, pig 5 swine
ovine: 5 sheep
plantigrade: 6 racoon 7 raccoon
porcine: hog, pig 4 boar 5 swine 7 peccary
pouched: 9 marsupial
raccoon-like: 5 coati
retentive: 8 elephant
rhinoceros-like: 5 tapir 14 baluchitherium
ring-tailed: 4 coon 5 lemur
ruminant: ox; yak 4 deer, goat 5 bison, camel, llama, moose, okapi, sheep, steer 6 alpaca, cattle, chewer, vicuna 7 buffalo, giraffe 8 antelope
scaled: 8 pangolin
shelled: 7 armadillo
short-tailed: 7 bobtail
skunk-like: 5 zoril
slow-moving: 5 loris, sloth
smallest: 5 shrew
snake-eating: 8 mongoose
spiny: 6 tenrec 9 porcupine
thick-skinned: 8 elephant 9 pachyderm 10 rhinoceros
toothless: 8 edentate
tropical: 5 coati, rhino 7 peccary 9 coati-modi 10 coati-mundi, rhinoceros
tusked: 6 walrus 7 mammoth 8 elephant, mastodon
ursine: 4 bear 5 panda
viverrine: 8 falanaka
vulpine: fox 4 wolf
web-footed: 5 otter
wing-footed: 6 aliped
winged: bat
zebra-like: 6 quagga

mammock: 4 tear 5 break, scrap 6 mangle
mammon: 6 riches, wealth
mammoth: 5 large 8 gigantic
man (see also **fellow, person**): bo; guy, vir(L.) 4 aner(Gr.), chal, chap, homo(L.), male, mann(G.), uomo(It.), work 5 bloke, chiel, guard, homme(F.), human, valet 6 andros(Gr.), chield, hombre(Sp.), mensch(-Yid.) 7 counter, fortify, homines(L.pl.), husband, laborer, mankind, operate 8 creature 9 anthropos(Gr.)
aged: vet 4 cuff, sire 5 senex(L.), uncle 6 gaffer, stager 7 grandpa, starets(Russ.) 8 grandpop 9 grandsire, patriarch 10 Methuselah 11 grandfather 12 octogenarian
bad-tempered: 6 bodach 10 curmudgeon
bald: 9 pilgarlic 10 pillgarlic
big: cob
brass: 5 Talos
brave: 4 hero, lion
coarse: 5 churl, knave 7 ruffian
comb. form: 4 homo 5 andro 8 anthropo
conceited: 7 coxcomb
cruel: 4 ogre 7 monster, ruffian, villain
cunning: 5 rogue 7 shyster 9 trickster 10 mountebank
dissolute: 4 roue
eccentric: 6 codger
effeminate: 9 androgyne
elderly: see *aged* above
enlisted: GI 6 rating, sailor 7 private, soldier 8 sargeant

fashionable: fop 4 dude 5 dandy 10 Corinthian 11 Beau Brummel 12 boulevardier
handsome: 6 Adonis
hard-pressed: Job
hardheaded: 5 boche
henpecked: 10 hoddy-doddy 11 milquetoast
impetuous: 7 hotspur
important: VIP 4 hero, name 5 nabob 7 grandee
ladies': 4 beau 5 beaux(pl.)
learned: PhD 4 bhat 6 doctor, pundit savant 7 erudite, scholar, teacher 8 literati 9 literatus, professor 11 philologist
little: 6 mankin, shrimp, squirt 8 homuncio 10 homunculus
mechanical: 5 robot 9 automaton
medicine: 6 priest, shaman
money: 9 paymaster
mother of: Eve 6 Cybele
newspaper: 6 editor 8 reporter 9 columnist 10 journalist
objectionable: oaf 4 boor 5 bully 8 wiseacre
of all work: 4 joey, mozo 8 factotum, handyman
of letters: 6 savant 11 litterateur
of straw: 6 figure 9 nonentity
of the world: 6 layman 10 secularist 11 cosmopolite 12 sophisticate
old: see *elderly* above
old-clothes: 4 poco
outdoor: 6 camper, hunter 7 athlete 9 fisherman
personifying: 15 anthropomorphic
pert. to: 5 human 6 humane, mortal
political: 7 senator 8 diplomat 9 statesman 10 ambassador 11 assemblyman 14 representative
poor: 6 pauper 7 peasant 8 beadsman, bedesman
primitive: 6 savage 8 urmensch(Yid.)
resembling: 7 android 10 anthropoid
rich: 5 Midas, nabob 6 tycoon 7 Croesus, magnate 9 plutocrat 10 capitalist 11 billionaire, millionaire
science: 9 ethnology 12 anthropology
self-important: 10 cockalorum
shadowless: 6 ascian
single: 4 stag 7 widower 8 bachelor, celibate
unattractive: 4 clod, goon, jerk, lout, rube, slob 5 yokel 6 lummox 7 fathead 10 clodhopper
undercover: spy 5 agent 9 detective 12 investigator
unemployed: 6 batlan, batlon(Yid.)
unmarried: see *single* above
white: 6 buckra 7 cachila(P.I.) 8 paleface
wicked: 7 villain
wise: 4 sage, seer 5 solon 6 nestor 7 Solomon
worthless: bum 4 hobo 5 idler, tramp
young: boy 5 youth 6 varlet
man fungus: 9 earthstar
Man of Destiny: 17 Napoleon Bonaparte
Man of Galilee: 11 Jesus Christ
man of God: 5 rabbi, saint 6 pastor, priest 7 ascetic, prelate 8 minister 12 ecclesiastic
man-of-war: 7 frigate, soldier, warrior
deck: 5 orlop
Man O'War: 5 horse 6 winner
Man Without a Country: *author:* 4 Hale
character: 5 Nolan
manacle: 4 bond, cuff, iron 5 chain, darby 6 fetter, hamper 7 confine, shackle 8 handcuff 9 restraint
manada: 4 herd 5 drove, flock
manage: man, run 4 boss, head, lead, rule 5 dight, frame, guide, order, steer, wield 6 convoy, demean, direct, govern, handle 7 conduct, control, dispose, execute, husband, operate, oversee 8 contrive, dispense, engineer, maneuver 9 supervise 10 accomplish, administer, manipulate
frugally: 6 eke out 7 husband 9 economize
hard to: 6 ornery
manageable: 4 easy, tame, yare 6 docile, wieldy 7 ductile, pliable 8 flexible, maniable, workable 9 compliant, tractable 10 governable
management: 4 care 6 agency, charge, menage 7 address, economy, gestion 8 carriage, demeanor 9 demeanour, governail, ordinance 10 enterprise, governance 11 generalship
good: 6 eutaxy 7 eutaxie
poor: 11 cacoeconomy
manager: 4 doer 6 gerent, grieve 7 captain, curator, foreman, steward 8 aumildar 12 entrepreneur
managery: 7 cunning 8 artifice 9 frugality, husbandry 10 management 11 managership
Manasseh: *city:* 4 Aner
son: 4 Amon, Jair
manatee: 6 seacow 8 sirenian
Manchuria: *city:* 5 Hulan, Kirin 6 Harbin, Mukden 9 Niuchwang
province: 5 Jehol
river: 4 Amur, Liao, Yalu
manciple: 5 slave 7 servant, steward 8 purveyor
mandarin: 6 orange 7 Chinese 9 tangerine
residence: 5 yamen
mandate: 4 writ 5 brief, order 6 behest, charge, decree, demand, firman 7 bidding, command, precept 9 direction 10 commission, injunction, referendum
mandatory: 10 imperative, obligatory
mandible: jaw 4 beak 9 chelicera
part: 5 molar

mandrel: hob 4 axle, ball, pick 5 arbor 7 spindle
mandrill: 6 baboon
manducate: eat 4 chew 9 masticate
mane: 4 hair, juba 5 brush 6 grivna 8 encolure
manege gait: 4 lope, trot, volt
maneuver: 4 ploy 6 deploy, jockey, tactic 7 echelon 8 artifice, contrive, engineer 9 evolution, stratagem 10 manipulate
aviation: 4 loop, spin 7 echelon, flathat 9 chandelle, Immelmann
military: 6 tactic
manful: See **manly**
mang: 8 frenzied 10 bewildered
manga: 6 poncho
manganese symbol: Mn
mange: eat 4 itch, meal, scab 6 fodder, scurvy
cause of: 4 mite 6 acarid
manger: bin, box 4 crib, meal 5 stall 6 trough 7 banquet
mangle: cut, mar 4 hack, maim 6 bruise, garble, ironer, smooth 8 calender, lacerate, mutilate 9 dismember
mango: 4 tree 5 bauno, fruit
bird: 6 oriole 11 hummingbird
fish: 9 threadfin
tree: 4 tope
mangrove: 4 tree 5 goran, shrub
mangy: 4 mean 5 seedy 6 ronion, ronyon, scurvy, shabby 7 squalid 12 contemptible
manhandle: 4 maul
mani: 6 peanut
mania: 5 craze, furor 6 frenzy, furore 7 madness, passion 8 delirium 9 cacoethes 11 derangement
buying: 9 oniomania
stealing: 11 kleptomania
maniable: See **manageable**
maniac: 6 madman 7 lunatic
maniacal: mad 6 crazed, insane 8 demented, deranged 9 psychotic 10 hysterical
manic: 9 afflicted
manicure: cut 4 clip, pare, trim 6 polish
manifest: 4 open, show 5 argue, clear, index, overt 6 attest, evince, extant, graith, patent, reveal 7 approve, confess, declare, develop, display, evident, exhibit, explain, express, glaring, invoice, obvious, signify, visible 8 apparent, develope, disclose, discover, evidence, indicate, palpable 11 conspicuous, demonstrate, discernible, indubitable, perspicuous 12 indisputable, unmistakable
manifestation: 4 sign 5 phase 6 effect, ostent
manifesto: 5 edict 7 placard 8 evidence 9 statement 11 declaration 13 demonstration
manifold: 4 many 7 various 8 multiple, numerous 9 different, multifold, multiplex, replicate 12 multifarious
manikin: 4 puny 5 dwarf, model, pygmy 7 phantom 8 homuncio, homuncle 9 homuncule, homunculi(pl.), mannequin 10 diminutive, homunculus
Manila: *airfield:* 5 Clark
creek: 6 estero
hemp: 5 abaca, abaka 6 banana
hero: 5 Dewey
nut: 6 peanut
river: 5 Pasig
Manila Bay boat: 6 bilalo
manioc: 7 cassava, tapioca
manipulate: rig, use 4 work 5 treat, wield 6 handle, manage 7 control, operate
manis: 8 anteater, pangolin
mankind: man 4 Adam, male 5 flesh, world 6 humans, people 8 humanity
division: 4 race 5 tribe 6 people
hater: 11 misanthrope
manlike: 4 male 5 manly 7 android, mannish 9 masculine 10 anthropoid
manly: 4 bold, male 5 brave, hardy, noble 6 daring 7 manlike, mannish 8 resolute 9 dignified, masculine, undaunted 10 courageous
Mann character: 7 Castorp
manna: 7 Godsend 10 gazangabin
mannequin: See **manikin**
manner: air, way 4 cost, form, mien, mode, more, thew 5 guise, trick 6 aspect, course, method 7 address, bearing, fashion, quomodo 8 attitude, behavior 9 behaviour, technique 10 appearance, deportment
law: 4 modi(pl.) 5 modus
mannerism: 4 mode, pose 5 trait 7 bearing 11 affectation, peculiarity
mannerly: 4 nice 5 civil, moral 6 decent, polite, seemly 8 decorous
manners: 5 lates 8 courtesy 9 amenities, etiquette
Mannus' father: 6 Tuisto
mano: 4 hand 9 handstone
manoc: 4 fowl 7 chicken, rooster
manor: 4 hall 5 abode, house 6 estate 7 mansion
land: 6 barton 7 demesne
manred: 6 homage 9 vassalage
manse: 7 rectory
manservant: 4 help, mozo, syce 5 gilly(Sc.), groom, valet 6 Andrew, butler, garcon, gillie 8 factotum
manship: 5 honor 6 homage 7 courage, manhood 8 courtesy, humanity 9 manliness

mansion: 4 hall, home, stay 5 abode, house, manor, siege 7 chateau, lodging, sojourn 8 chateaux(pl.), dwelling 9 residence
papal: 7 Lateran
manslaughter: 6 murder 7 killing, slaying 8 butchery
mansuete: 4 kind, tame 6 gentle
manta: 4 wrap 5 cloak, cloth 7 blanket, bulwark, shelter 8 mantelet 9 devilfish
mantegar: ape
manteel: See **mantle**
mantel: 4 arch, beam 5 brace(Sc.), ledge, shelf, stone 6 clavel, lintel 10 manteltree
mantelet: 4 cape 5 cloak 6 mantle, screen, shield 7 shelter 8 galapago
mantilla: 4 cape 5 cloak
mantis crab: 7 squilla
mantle (see also **cloak**): 4 brat, capa, cape, coat, cope, hood, mant, robe 5 blush, cover, manto 6 capote, kittel 7 encloak, manteau, manteel, whittle 8 envelope, mantelet, mantilla 10 witzchoura
manto: 4 gown 5 cloak 6 mantle, mantua
mantoid: 6 mantis
mantra: om 4 hymn 5 charm, spell
mantua: 4 gown 5 cloak, manto 9 overdress
manual: 4 book 7 clavier, didache 8 grimoire, handbook 9 catechism 11 enchiridion
art: 5 craft
manuduction: 5 guide 7 leading 8 guidance 9 direction 12 introduction
manufactory: 7 factory
manufacture: 4 fake, make 5 forge 6 invent 7 confect, produce 9 fabricate
manufactured: 4 made 10 artificial
manufacturer: 8 employer 9 fabricant, operative 10 fabricator 12 entrepreneur 13 industrialist
manumission: 7 freedom, freeing, release 10 liberation 11 deliverance 12 emancipation
manure: 4 dung 5 addle 7 compost 10 composture
manuscript: MS 4 copy 5 codex 7 papyrus, writing 8 document 9 archetype, minuscule 11 composition, handwriting
back: 5 dorso
space: 6 lacuna
copier: 6 scribe
mark: 5 obeli(pl.) 6 obelus
many: 4 fele, raff 6 divers 7 diverse, several, various 8 manifold, numerous 9 different, multifold, multitude 10 multiplied
prefix: 4 poly, vari 5 multi
many-footed: 8 multiped
many-sided: 9 versatile 12 multilateral
mao: 7 peacock
Maori: *bird:* poe, tue, tui
canoe: 4 waka
charm: 7 heitiki
chief: 5 ariki
clan: ati 4 hapu
club: 4 mere, patu, rata
compensation: utu
dance: 4 haka
food: kai
fort: pa; pah
hen: 4 weka
hero: 4 Maui
house: 5 whare 8 wharekai 9 wherekura 12 wharewananga
over: umu
priest: 7 tuhunga
raft: 4 moki 6 moguey
sect: 7 Ringatu
store: 6 pataka
tatooing: 4 moko
tree: 5 mapau 6 manuka 9 tanehakas
tribe: Ati 4 Hapu
village: pa; pah 4 kaik 5 kaika 6 kainga
wages: utu
weapon: 4 mere, patu, rata
map: 4 card, plan 5 carte, chard, chart, image 6 design, sketch, survey 7 diagram, epitome, explore, outline, picture 8 roadbook 9 delineate 10 cartograph, embodiment 14 representation
book: 5 atlas
copier: 10 pantograph
maker: 7 charter 8 Mercator 12 cartographer
townsite: 4 plat
weather line: 6 isobar
maple: 4 acer
cup: 5 mazer
derived from: 6 aceric
family: 9 aceraceae
sap: 5 humbo
scale: 10 pulvinaria
seed: 6 samara
spout: 5 spile
mar: 4 amar, blot, scar 5 botch, spoil 6 damage, deface, deform impair, injure, mangle 7 blemish 8 obstruct 9 disfigure
marabou: 5 stork 6 argala 7 faleric 8 adjutant, marabout
maral: 4 deer
maranatha: 5 curse
maranon: 6 cashew
marasca: 6 cherry 10 maraschino
marasmus: 5 waste 10 emaciation 13 contabescence
maraud: 4 loot, raid, rove 7 pillage, plunder
marauder: 6 bandit, pirate 7 cateran(Sc.)
marble: 4 cold, hard 5 agate, rance, stone 6 basalt 7 cipolin 8 brocatel, dolomite 9 unfeeling 10 brocatelle

game: taw
mosaic: 7 tessera
playing: mib, pea, taw 4 doby 5 alley, dobie 6 glassy 7 shooter
slab: 5 dalle(F.)
Marble Faun: *author:* 9 Hawthorne
character: 5 Hilda
marble flower: 5 poppy
marblehead: 6 fulmar
marbler: 6 carver 8 sculptor
marc: 6 refuse 7 residue
marcato: 6 marked 7 pointed 8 accented, emphatic
march: 4 hike, trek 5 route, troop 6 border, defile, parade 8 boundary, frontier, smallage 9 cavalcade 10 procession
day's: 5 etape
horsemen: 9 cavalcade
spirited: 9 quickstep
March 15: 4 ides
March King: 5 Sousa
March sisters: Jo; Amy, Meg 4 Beth
marchland: 8 frontier 10 borderland
marcid: 4 weak 7 decayed, tabetic 8 withered 9 exhausted 10 emaciating
marcor: 5 decay 7 maramus
Mardi Gras: 8 carnival
king: Rex
mare: yad 4 jade, yade, yaud(Sc.) 5 gilot, horse, meare 6 dobbin, equine, grasni
young: 5 filly
mare's nest: 4 hoax 5 trick 8 disorder 9 confusion
mare's tail: 5 cloud 6 cirrus
margarine: 4 oleo
marge: See **margin**
margin: hem, lip, ori, rim 4 bank, brim, edge, orae(L.), rand, side 5 brink, shore, verge 6 border, fringe, leeway 7 margent
narrow: 4 hair
note: 7 apostil 8 scholium 10 annotation
set in: 6 indent
Marianas: 4 Guam 6 Saipan
marigold: 5 boots, caper, gools 6 buddle 7 cowslip, elkslip, golland
genus: 7 tagetes
marijuana: boo, hay, pot, tea 5 grass
cigarette: mu 6 greefa, griffo, moocah, mooter, muggle, reefer 7 mohasky 8 joy-smoke, loco weed, Mary Jane 9 Indian hay 10 bambalacha, Mary Warner, Mary Weaver 11 giggle-smoke
cigarette holder: 6 crutch
user: 7 pothead
marina: 4 dock 5 basin 9 esplanade, promenade
marinade: 5 brine 6 pickle 8 marinate
marinal: 6 marine, sailor, saline 7 mariner 8 nautical
marine: tar 5 jolly, naval, water 7 aquatic, marinal, mariner, oceanic, pelagic 8 halimous, maritime, nautical 9 aequoreal 11 leatherneck
crustacean: 8 barnacle
instrument: aba 5 radar 7 pelorus, sextant
plant: 4 alga 5 algae 6 enalid 7 seaweed
science: 10 oceanology 12 oceanography
skeleton: 5 coral
slogan: 6 gungho
marine animal: orc 4 salp 5 coral, polyp 9 jellyfish
marine fish: 8 menhaden
mariner: gob, tar 5 Jacky 6 galoot, sailor, seaman 7 buscarl 8 buscarle, seafarer, waterman 9 aequoreal
card: 5 chart
compass card: 4 rose
compass points: 6 rhumbs
marinheiro: 6 acajou
marionette: 6 puppet 10 bufflehead
marital: 9 connubial 11 matrimonial
maritime: See **marine**
marjoram: 4 herb, mint 6 origan
mark: dot, hob, tee 4 belt, goal, line, note, rist, scar, wale 5 badge, brand, grade, label, score, stamp, track, watch 6 accent, beacon, caract, denote, notice, target 7 betoken, blemish, earmark, impress, imprint, insigne, observe 8 identify, insignia(pl.), standard 9 character, designate 10 indication 11 distinguish 14 characteristic
bad: 7 demerit
diacritical: 5 breve, tilde 6 macron, umlaut 7 cedilla(F.)
down: 5 lower
out: 6 cancel, define 7 measure 10 obliterate
possessive: 10 apostrophe
printer's: 4 dele, fist, stet 5 caret, obeli 6 dagger, diesis, obelus 7 obelisk
pronunciation: see *diacritical* above
punctuation: 4 dash 5 colon, comma 6 period 8 dieresis 9 diaeresis, semicolon 11 parenthesis, parentheses(pl.)
question: 7 erotema, eroteme
reference: 4 star 6 dagger 8 asterisk
tiny: dot
white: 5 rache, ratch
with critical notes: 8 annotate
Mark Antony's wife: 7 Octavia
Mark Twain's name: 22 Samuel Langhorne Clemens
markaz: 8 district 11 subdivision
marked: 5 fated 7 eminent 10 emphasized 11 conspicuous, outstanding
with lines: 5 ruled 6 gyrose, linear, notate
marker: peg 5 arrow 6 scorer, signal 7 brander, counter, monitor 8 bookmark,

marksman, recorder 9 milestone 10 gravestone
air course: 5 pylon
floating: 4 buoy
market: 4 gunj(Ind.), mart, sale, sell, shop, sook 5 agora(Gr.), bazar, gunge, halle, pasar, plaza, store, tryst 6 bazaar, rialto, shoppe 7 chaffer 8 cheaping, debouche(F.), emporium
marketable: 8 vendible
markhor: 4 goat
marksman: 4 shot 6 sniper
marl: 4 clay, malm 6 manure 7 marlite 9 greensand 10 fertilizer, overspread
marli: 4 lace 5 gauze, tulle
marlin: 6 curlew, godwit 9 spearfish
marlinespike: fid 4 skua 6 Jaeger
marlock: 4 ogle 5 prank, sport, trick 6 frolic
marmalade: jam 6 sapote 8 preserve
quince: 8 co-diniac, quiddany
tree: 5 mamie
marmit: pot 6 kettle
marmoset: 4 mico 6 monkey, sagoin, wistit 7 tamarin, wistiti
marmot: 5 bobac 6 rodent 8 burrower, whistler 9 woodchuck
marmota: 8 arctomys 9 woodchuck
maroon: 6 enisle, strand 7 isolate, reddish 8 cimarron, purplish
marooner: 6 pirate 9 buccaneer
Marpessa's abductor: 4 Idas
marplot: 7 meddler, snooper 8 busybody 9 addle-plot
Marquand character: 4 Moto 5 Apley, Wayde 6 Pulham 7 Goodwin
marquee: 4 tent 6 canopy
marquetry: 5 inlay
marquis: 4 peer
marriage: 5 match 6 splice 7 wedding, wedlock 9 matrimony
absence of: 5 agamy
broker: 9 schatchen(Yid.)
comb. form: 4 gamy
forswearer: 8 celibate
fourth: 9 tetragamy
god: 5 Hymen
goddess: 4 Hera
hater of: 10 misogamist
more than one husband: 9 polyandry
more than one wife: 6 bigamy 8 polygamy
notice: 5 banns
of aged: 8 opsigamy
of gods: 8 theogamy
open to slaves: 12 contubernium
outside tribe: 7 exogamy
pert. to: 7 marital, spousal 8 hymeneal 9 connubial, endogamic
portion: dot 5 dowry
second: 6 digamy
secret: 9 elopement
to promise: 7 betroth 8 affiance
to two people: 6 bigamy
marriageable: 6 nubile
married: 5 wived 6 wedded 8 espoused 9 connubial
married person: 4 wife 6 spouse 7 husband 8 benedict
marrow: 4 best, pith 5 reest(Sc.) 6 inmost, medula 7 essence, medulla
bones: 5 knees
marry: 4 join, mate, wive, yoke 5 cleek, hitch, unite 6 buckle, couple 7 espouse, husband
Mars: 4 Ares 6 planet, war god
discoverer of satellites: 4 Hall
inner moon: 6 Phobos
pert. to: 5 Arean 7 Martian
planet belt: 5 Libya
planet spot: 5 oasis, oases(pl.)
priests of: 5 Salii 6 Deimos
region (dark): 4 mare
twin sons: 5 Remus 7 Romulus
Marseillaise author: 13 Rouget de Lisle
marsh: bog, fen, hag 4 jeel, mire, moor, slew, sloo, slue 5 flash, liman, slash, swale, swamp 6 morass, palude, slough 7 cienaga, maremma(It.) 8 quagmire 9 everglade
bird: 4 sora 5 snipe, stilt
crocodile: goa
elder: iva
fever: 7 helodes
gas: 7 methane 8 firedamp
grass: 4 tule 5 sedge, spart
hawk: 7 harrier
marigold: 5 boots
pert. to: 8 paludine
salt: 6 salina 7 corcass
shrub: 8 moorwort
marsh plant genus: 6 caltha 7 elatine
marshal: 4 lead 5 align, aline, array, groom, guide, usher 6 direct, parade 7 arrange, farrier, officer 8 official
marshland: fen 4 fell
marshmallow: 5 altea
marshwort: 9 cranberry
genus: 4 sium
marshy: wet 5 fenny 6 callow 7 helodes, paludal, paludic 8 paludine 9 paludinal
lake: 5 liman
marsupial: 4 tait 5 coala, koala 6 possum, wombat 7 dasyure, opossum 9 bandicoot
Australian: 4 tait 6 cuscus 7 dasyure 8 kangaroo 9 phalanger
bearlike: 5 coala, koala 6 wombat
genus: 10 diprotodom
mart: 4 fair 5 bazar 6 bazaar, market, rialto 8 emporium
martel: 6 hammer

marten: fur 5 sable 6 animal, fisher, martin
beech: 4 foin
genus: 7 mustela
stone: 4 foin
martial: 7 warlike 8 military
Martial's writing: 7 epigram
Martian: 5 Arean
comb. form: 4 areo
martin: 7 swallow
martinet: 6 tyrant 14 disciplinarian
Martinique: *garment:* 4 jupe
volcano: 5 Pelee
martyr: 5 saint 8 sufferer 10 sacrificer
first Christian: 7 Stephen
royal: 7 Charles
martyrdom: 7 killing, passion, torment, torture 8 butchery, distress 10 affliction
place of: 8 Golgotha
marvel: 5 ferly 6 admire, wonder 7 miracle, portent 8 astonish 9 horehound 12 astonishment
marvelous: 7 strange 8 wondrous 9 excellent 10 improbable, incredible
Maryland: *city:* 9 Baltimore
county: 4 Kent 5 Cecil 6 Howard, Talbot
founder: 7 Calvert
race track: 5 Bowie
mas: 9 masculine
masa: 8 cornmeal
Masada: *builder:* 5 Herod
defender: 6 zealot
enemy: 4 Rome
historian: 8 Josephus
masculine: mas 4 male 5 manly 6 strong, virile 7 manlike, mannish
mash: 4 chap, mess, ogle 5 champ, cream, crush, flirt, smash 6 muddle 7 farrago, mixture, trouble
mashal: 7 parable, proverb
masher: 4 chap 5 flirt, ricer
masjid: 6 mosque
mask: 4 hide, veil 5 cloak, cover, guise, visor 6 screen 7 conceal, curtain 8 defilade, disguise 9 dissemble
half: 4 loup(Fr.) 6 domino(Fr.)
top knot on: 5 onkos
masked: 6 covert 7 larvate, obscure 8 larvated
masker: 6 domino, mummer
maskery: 10 masquerade
maslin: 5 brass 7 mixture 9 potpourri
mason: 7 builder 11 stoneworker
mixing rod: rab
Masons: *doorkeeper:* 5 tiler
order: 8 Templars
masonry: 6 ashlar 7 blocage 9 stonework
masquerade: 5 guise 8 disguise
mass: bat, gob 4 blob, body, bulk, clot, heap, lump, size, swad 5 amass, batch, gross, group, store 6 gather, gobbet, prayer 7 phalanx, service 8 assemble 9 aggregate, magnitude 10 accumulate, assemblage, congregate 11 agglomerate, composition, compositure, concentrate, consolidate 12 congregation
book: 6 missal
cloudlike: 6 nebula 7 nebulae(pl.)
comb. form: mas
confused: cot 5 chaos 6 welter 9 imbroglio 10 hotchpotch
directory: 4 ordo
for dead: 7 requiem
musical number: 5 Credo, Kyrie 6 Gloria 7 Sanctus
of particulars: 9 aggregate
pert. to: 5 molar
small: dab, pat, wad 4 floc
tangled: mop 4 shag
mass meeting: 5 rally
Massachusetts: *cape:* Ann
city: 4 Lynn 5 Acton, Salem 6 Boston(c.), Hadley, Lowell, Malden, Quincy, Wianno, Woburn 7 Chelsea, Metheun, Waltham 8 Brockton, Plymouth 9 Braintree, Cambridge, Worcester 10 Framingham 11 Charlestown, Springfield, Summerville
flower: 7 arbutus
island: 9 Nantucket 15 Martha's Vineyard
mountain: Tom
mountain ridge: 7 Taconic
oyster: 6 Cotuit
port: 5 Salem 6 Boston
school: 7 Andover
state flower: 7 arbutus
massacre: 6 pogrom 7 carnage 8 butchery 9 slaughter
massage: rub 5 knead
massager: 7 masseur 8 masseuse
massed: 7 serried
Massenet's opera: 5 Manon, Thais
massive: big 4 bold, huge 5 beamy, bulky, gross, heavy, large, massy 7 hulking, weighty 9 cyclopean, ponderous 10 boisterous
mast: cue 4 spar 5 stick 6 forage 8 beechnut
against: 5 aback
crosspiece: fid
inclination from perpendicular: 4 rake
middle: 8 mainmast
wood for: ash 4 poon
mastaba: 4 tomb 8 platform
master: get, man, rab 4 baas, boss, lord, mian, rule, sire 5 chief, rabbi, sahib(Ind.), tutor 6 bridle, buckra, defeat, doctor, domine, govern, humble, subdue 7 captain, conquer, maestro, padrone(It.) 8 amaister, overcome, regulate, surmount, vanquish 9 commander, overpower, preceptor, subjugate 10 proprietor

comb. form: 4 arch 5 archi
Eton: 4 beak
fencing: 7 lanista
harbor: 7 havener, havenor
hard: 6 despot, Legree
of house: 13 paterfamilias
pert. to: 6 herile
ship's: 7 captain, skipper
Master of Arts: A.M., M.A.
master of ceremonies: M.C. 5 emcee
master stroke: 4 coup
masterful: 6 lordly 7 haughty 8 arrogant, masterly 9 arbitrary, imperious 10 commanding 11 dictatorial, domineering, magisterial, overbearing 13 authoritative
mastermind: 4 plan 6 expert 8 wiseacre
masterpeice: 4 coup 7 triumph 10 masterwork 11 chef d'oeuvre
mastery: 4 gree 5 gripe 7 control, victory 8 conquest, facility 9 influence
mastic: 5 gummy 8 adhesive
masticate: 4 chaw, chew 5 crush, gnash, grind 6 crunch 9 manducate
masticatory: gum 7 chewing
mastiff: dog 5 burly 7 massive
mastodon: 5 giant 7 mammoth
mat: cot, rug 4 felt 5 doily, platt, snarl 6 carpet, cotter, petate(Sp.), tangle 7 cushion, drugget, gardnap 8 entangle 10 interweave, lusterless
mat grass: 4 nard
Mata Hari: spy 5 agent
Mataco: 4 apar 6 Indian 9 armadillo
matador: 11 bullfighter
adversary: 4 bull, toro
garment: 4 cape
staff: 6 muleta
sword: 7 estoque
matagasse: 11 butcherbird
match: go; cap, pit, tir(F.) 4 bout, cope, even, mate, pair, peer, side, spar, suit, team, wife 5 amate, equal, fusee(F.), marry, rival, tally, torch, vesta 6 fellow, spouse 7 compare, compeer, contest, husband, lucifer(Eng.) 8 equalize, lampwick, marriage 9 allumette(F.) 10 candlewick, correspond 11 counterpart, countervail, parallelize
matched: 6 paired, teamed
matchless: 5 alone 6 unlike 8 peerless 9 exquisite, unequaled 10 inimitable 12 incomparable
matchlock: gun
mate: cap, pal, wed 4 fear, fere, join, pair, peer, wife 5 billy, buddy, bully, cully, feere, marry, match 6 bunkle, cobber, couple, fellow, spouse 7 brother, compeer, comrade, consort, espouse, husband, partner 9 associate, companion 10 yokefellow
matelot: 6 sailor
mater: ma; mom 4 mama 6 mother
materia medica: 7 acology
material (see also **cloth, fabric, substance**): 4 data, gear 5 goods, stuff 6 bodily, carnal, graith, matter 7 weighty 8 physical, tangible 9 corporeal, essential 12 nonspiritual
discard: 4 junk, slag 5 scrap, trash, waste 6 refuse 7 rubbish
glass-like: 5 plass
raw: ore 6 staple
materialism: 8 hylonism
materialize: 5 reify
materiel: 8 supplies 9 apparatus, equipment
maternal: 8 motherly
relation: 7 enation
matey: 9 companion 13 companionable
matezite: 7 pinitol 10 caoutchouc
matgrass: 4 nard 8 fogfruit
math: 6 mowing 9 monastery 10 arithmetic 11 mathematics
mathe: 4 grub 6 maggot
mathematician: 5 adder 7 figurer
mathematics: *abbreviation:* Q.E.D.
branch: 7 algebra, geodesy 8 calculus, geometry 9 logarithm 10 arithmetic 12 trigonometry
constant (arbitrary): 9 parameter
deduction: 8 analysis
diagram: 5 graph
equation: 4 surd
exercise: 7 problem
factor: 10 quaternion
function: 4 sine 6 cosine
instrument: 6 sector 7 compass 8 arbalest
irrational number: 4 surd
line: 6 vector
number: 5 digit 12 multiplicand
operation: 7 operand
operator: 5 nabla 10 quaternion
proposition: 7 theorem
quantity: 6 scalar
ratio: pi 4 sine 8 derivate
symbol: 7 faciend, operand 12 multiplicand
term: 4 root, sine 6 cosine
mathemeg: 7 catfish
mathes: 7 mayweed
matie: 7 herring
matin: 4 call, song 6 prayer 9 matutinal
song: 6 aubade
matinee: 5 party 6 soiree 8 negligee 9 reception 13 entertainment
matinee idol: 4 lion, star 5 actor
matka: 4 seal
matranee: 7 servant, sweeper
matrass: 4 tube 5 flask 6 bottle 8 bolthead
matriculate: 5 adopt, enter 6 enroll 8 register 10 naturalize 13 immatriculate

matrimonial: 7 nuptial, spousal 8 conjugal, hymeneal 9 connubial
matrimony: 7 wedlock 8 marriage
matrix: bed, die, mat 4 form, mold, womb 5 plasm 6 gangue 7 pattern
plate: 6 stereo
matron: 4 dame, wife 5 widow 11 housekeeper
matte: 7 regulus
matter: pus 4 gear, malm, mass 5 solid, topic 6 affair, behalf 7 article, concern, problem, signify, trouble 8 business, material 11 constituent
law: res
particle: 4 atom
pert. to: 5 hylic
property: 4 mass 7 inertia
rarefied: fog, gas 4 mist 5 vapor 6 miasma
matter of fact: 7 literal, prosaic 9 pragmatic 11 utilitarian
matthiola: 5 stock
mattock: ax; axe 4 bill 5 tubal 6 twibil 7 twibill
mattress: 6 pallet
cover: 4 tick 7 ticking
mature: age, old 4 aged, form, gray, grow, ripe 5 adult, grown, ripen 6 accrue, autumn, decoct, digest, mellow, season 7 develop 8 complete, develope
maturing: 8 rathripe 9 ratheripe
matutinal: 5 early, matin
Mau Mau land: 5 Kenya
maud: rug 5 plaid, shawl
maudlin: 5 beery, corny, tipsy 7 tearful, weeping 10 lachrymose 11 sentimental
mauger: 5 spite 7 ill-will 9 unwilling 15 notwithstanding
Maugham: *heroine:* 5 Sadie
play: 4 Rain
maul: paw 4 beat, bung, club, mace, mall, mell, moth 5 abuse, gavel, staff 6 beater, beetle, bruise, hammer, mallet 9 manhandle
maumet: god, guy 4 doll, idol 5 image 6 puppet
maund: beg 6 basket, hamper
maunder: 5 growl, haver 6 beggar 7 grumble
Maupassant character: 4 Fifi
Maurois subject: 4 Hugo, Sand 5 Byron, Dumas 6 Proust 8 Disraeli
Mauser: arm, gun 5 rifle 6 weapon 7 firearm
mausoleum: 4 tomb 8 baradari(Ind.)
mauve: 5 lilac 6 purple, violet
mauvetaupe: 5 copra
maux: 8 slattern, slipshod 10 prostitute
mavis: 6 thrush
maw: 4 craw, crop 6 gullet, mallow 7 stomach
mawk: 6 maggot
mawkish: 5 vapid 6 sickly 8 nauseous 9 squeamish 10 disgusting 11 sentimental
maxilla: jaw 4 bone
maxim: saw 4 dict, rule, word 5 adage, axiom, gnome, logia(pl.), moral, motto 6 logion, saying 7 brocard, precept, proverb 8 aphorism, apothegm, doctrine, moralism 9 erudition, principle 10 apophthegm
maximum: 4 most, peak 5 limit 7 highest, largest 8 greatest
may: can 4 mote 5 might, shall 6 maiden 8 possible
May: *festival:* 7 Beltane
goddess: 4 Maia
May curlew: 8 whimbrel
May gowan: 5 daisy
Maya: *day:* 5 uayeb
month: 5 uinal
people: Mam 8 Pokonchi
year: 4 haab
mayapple: 8 mandrake
maybe: 7 perhaps 11 possibility, uncertainty
maybird: 6 thrush
maycock: 5 melon 6 maypop, plover
mayfish: 9 killifish
mayflower: 7 arbutus 8 hawthorn, marigold 10 stitchwort 12 cuckooflower
Mayflower's sister ship: 9 Speedwell
mayfly: dun
mayfowl: 8 whimbrel
mayhap: 6 happen 7 perhaps 12 peradventure
mayor: 5 maire(F.) 7 alcalde(Sp.) 8 official 10 magistrate 12 burgomeister(G.)
maze: 4 daze 5 amaze, fancy 7 confuse, stupefy 8 bewilder, confound, delirium, delusion 9 amazement, deception, labyrinth 12 bewilderment
mazed: 4 lost 5 dazed 10 bewildered
mazer: 4 bowl
mazy: 7 complex 9 intricate 10 circuitous, perplexing
mead: 5 drink 6 meadow 8 hydromel 9 metheglin
meadow: ing, lea 4 mead, vega, wish, wong 5 field, haugh 6 saeter 7 pasture 9 grassland, grassplot
piece of: 5 swale
meadow bell: 8 harebell
meadowlark: 6 medlar
meadowmouse: 4 vole 8 arvicole
meadowsweet: 7 spiraea
meager: bar 4 arid, bare, lank, lean, poor, slim, thin 5 gaunt, scant, spare 6 barren, jejune, lenten, meagre, narrow, pilled,

scanty, scarce, sparse 7 scranny, starved, sterile, tenuous 9 emaciated 10 inadequate
meagerness: 7 exility
meal: tub 4 bite, dune, feed, menu 5 feast, flour, lunch, padar, salep, snack 6 bucket, dinner, morsel, nocake, repast, supper 7 banquet, blowout, potluck 8 sandbank 9 breakfast, collation, pulverize
army: 4 chow, mess
coarse: 5 grout 7 cribble 8 gurgeons
last course: 7 dessert
light: tea 5 lunch, snack 6 tiffin
main dish: 6 entree
wheat: 4 atta(Ind.)
meals: 5 board
mealy: 4 pale 6 floury, spotty 7 friable, starchy 8 farinose 9 personate 11 farinaceous
mealy back: 6 cicada
mean: low 4 base, clam, hard, lean, norm, poor 5 argue, footy, nasty, petty, ratty, snide, snivy, sorry 6 abject, chetif, coarse, common, denote, design, dirten, feeble, humble, intend, medial, medium, middle, narrow, paltry, pilled, snivey, sordid 7 average, caitiff, ignoble, pitiful, purport, purpose, signify 8 baseborn, beggarly, churlish, recreant, shameful 9 niggardly, penurious, truculent 11 disgraceful, hardhearted 12 contemptible, dishonorable, intermediate, parsimonious
mean line: 9 bisectrix
meander: 4 roam, turn, wind 5 amble 6 wander 8 straggle 9 labyrinth
meaning: 5 sense 6 import, intent, spirit 7 anagoge, bearing, purport, purpose 9 intending, intention, knowledge 10 definition 11 designation 12 apprehension, significance 13 signification, understanding
without: 4 null
meanly: 6 humbly, poorly 8 beggarly, shabbily
means: 4 cost 5 agent 6 agency, method 7 quomodo 8 averages 10 instrument 11 wherewithal 12 intermediary
financial: 5 funds 7 capital 9 resources
of livelihood: 4 work 5 labor, trade 8 vocation 10 profession
support: 4 hold 6 income 7 aliment 11 maintenance
meantime: 7 interim 8 interval
meanwhile: 9 adinterim
mear: 8 boundary
measles: 7 rubeola
measly: 4 mean 6 skimpy, slight 9 worthless 12 contemptible
measure (see also **measuring instrument**): pe 4 bole, boll, cess, gage, mete, rule, span, tape, time 5 clock, gauge, girth, meter, ruler, scale 6 assize, degree, stadia 7 battuta, caliper 8 odometer, tapeline 9 admeasure, calculate, criterion, rotameter
area: ar; are, rod 4 acre 6 decare
astronomical: 7 azimuth
Biblical: cab, hin, kor, log 4 epha 5 cubit, aphah, homer
cable: 4 naut
capacity: 4 cask, gill, orna, peck, pint 5 liter, quart 6 barrel, bushel, gallon
cloth: ell 4 yard
cubic: 4 cord 5 stere 10 hectostere
cut wood: 4 cord
degree of angle: arc
distance: see *length* below
dry: 4 bale, peck 6 bushel
energy: erg 5 ergon, joule
established: 8 standard
fish: vog 4 cran(Sc.) 5 crane, crans
flexible: 4 tape 8 tapeline
heat: 5 therm 6 calory, therme 7 calorie 10 centigrade, fahrenheit
horse: 4 hand
land: ar; are, rod 4 acre, area, mile, rood 6 decare 7 hectare, kiliare
length: dra, ell, pik, rod 4 foot, inch, knot, mile, nail, pace, pole, yard 5 cubit, digit, meter, metre, perch, toise(F.) 6 league, micron, mikron 9 decimeter, kilometer 10 centimeter, hectometer, millimeter
liquid: aam, keg 4 gill, pint 5 lagen, liter, quart 6 barrel, gallon, magnum, minims, runlet, tierce 7 rundlet 8 hogshead 9 hectolite, kiloliter
loudness: 4 phon
medicinal: 4 dram 5 minim, ounce 7 scruple
nautical: 4 knot 6 fathom
paper: 4 page, ream 5 quire, sheet
printer's: em, en 4 pica 5 agate, empen
short: 6 ullage
sound: bel
space: 6 parsec
time: day 4 hour, week, year 5 month 6 decade, minute, moment, second
water depth: 5 sound
weight: ton 4 bale 5 carat, liter, ounce, pound 9 kiloliter 10 hectoliter
wheat: 4 trug
wine: tun 4 butt, pipe
wire: mil 5 stone
work: erg 5 ergon
yarn: lea 4 heer, typp 6 denier 7 spindle
Measure for Measure character: 5 Elbow, Froth, Lucio 6 Angelo, Juliet
measured: 7 careful, guarded 10 deliberate
measureless: 4 vast 7 endless, immense 8 infinite 9 boundless, limitless, unbounded, unlimited 11 illimitable 12 immeasurable
measurement: 9 dimension 11 mensuration

pert. to: 6 metric 11 dimensional
measuring instrument: 4 gage, tape 5 chain, gauge, meter, ruler 7 alidade 8 measurer, tapeline 9 container, yardstick 13 saccharimeter
acidity: 10 acidimeter
heat: 11 calorimeter
lumber: 6 scaler
surveying: 11 stratameter
thickness: 7 caliper
measuring wheel: 8 odometer 12 perambulator
meat: 4 beef, food, gist, lamb, pork, veal 5 flesh 6 chevon, mutton 7 chilver, venison 9 nutriment
ball: 7 rissole 9 croquette, fricandel 11 fricandelle
bony: 5 scrag 9 spareribs
cured: ham 5 bacon 6 flitch, salame, salami 7 biltong, bultong, sausage 8 pastrami, pastroma 9 biltongue
cut: ham, rib 4 chop, loin 5 flank, roast, steak 6 cutlet, rasher 7 icebone, sirloin 9 aitchbone
dish: 5 pasty 6 potpie, ragout 7 goulash, haricot, ravioli 8 fricando 10 fricandeau
dish with vegetables: 4 olla, stew 8 mulligan 9 lobscouse 10 lobscourse
dried: 5 jerky 7 biltong, bultong, pemican 8 pemmican 9 biltongue
frozen: 5 frigo
ground: 7 rissole, sausage 9 hamburger
jelly: 5 aspic
pie: 5 pasty 7 rissole
pin: 6 skewer
potted: 7 rillett 8 rillette
roasted: 5 brede, cabob, kabob
sauce: 4 A-one 5 caper, gravy 14 Worcestershire
slice: 6 collop
smoking place: 5 bucan
unwholesome: 6 cagmag
meated: fed 8 fattened
meatless: 6 lenten, maigre
meatman: 7 butcher
meatus: 4 burr, duct 5 canal 7 foramen, passage
meatworks: 8 abattoir 14 slaughterhouse
meaty: 5 pithy, solid 11 substantial
Mecca (see also **Muslim**): *deity:* 5 Hobal, Hubal
mosque: 5 Caaba, Kaaba 6 Kaabeh
pilgrim's dress: 5 ihram
pilgrimage: 4 hadj
mechanic: erk(F.) 7 artisan, workman 8 operator 9 artificer, craftsman, operative
mechanical: 9 automatic 10 uninspired 11 automatical, involuntary, perfunctory, stereotyped
mechanical man: 5 robot 9 automaton
mechanical part: 5 rotor 6 stator, tappet
mechanics branch: 7 statics 8 dynamics
mechanism: 4 gear, tool 9 apparatus, machinery
driving: 9 propeller
eccentric: cam
self-moving: 8 automata(pl.) 9 automaton
meconin: 7 opianyl
medal: 4 disk 5 badge 6 plaque 7 medalet 10 decoration
medallion: 4 coin 8 ornament 11 contorniate, contorniato
Medb's consort: 6 Ailill
meddle: 4 nose 5 snoop 6 dabble, finger, monkey, potter, tamper 7 intrude 9 interfere
meddler: 7 marplot 8 busybody
meddlesome: 4 busy 5 fresh 7 curious 8 meddling 9 officious 10 handersome
Mede: 5 Aryan, Mesne 6 Median
caste: 4 magi
king: Evi
Medea: *father:* 6 Aeetes
husband: 5 Jason
rival: 6 Creusa
media: See **medium**
medial: 6 middle 8 ordinary
median: 4 mean 6 medial, middle 7 average, central 12 intermediate
Median: See **Mede**
mediate: 7 referee 8 ruminate 9 arbitrate, intercede, interpose
mediator: 7 daysman 9 go-between 10 ambocepter, interagent 12 intermediary
medic: 6 clover, doctor, intern, medico 7 luterne, student, surgeon 8 resident 9 physician
false: 10 medicaster
medical: 6 iatric 11 aesculapian
medical officer: 7 coroner
medical student: 6 extern, intern 7 externe, interne 8 resident
medicinal: 6 curing 7 healing 8 salutary 9 relieving 11 aesculapian
bark: 6 cartex
berry: 5 cubeb
capsule: 6 cachet
compound: 4 pill, sera 5 hepar, iodin, serum 6 iodine 7 turpeth
nut: 4 cola
plant (see also *root* below): rue 4 aloe 5 ergot, senna, tansy 6 arnica, cohosh, ipecac 7 chirata 8 valerian
remedy: 8 antidote
root (see also *plant* above): 5 artar, jalap, orris 6 seneca, senega 8 licorice
solution: 8 tincture
tablet: 4 pill 6 troche 7 lozenge

medicine: 4 drug 5 tonic 6 physic, remedy 7 placebo 10 abirritant, alterative
amount: 4 dose 6 dosage
comb. form: 5 iatro, iatry
institution: 6 clinic 8 hospital
instrument: see **surgery instrument**
mild: 6 tisane
noncuring: 6 ptisan
patent: 7 nostrum
vessel: 4 vial 5 ampul, phial 6 ampule 7 ampoule 8 gallipot
medicine dropper: 7 pipette
medicine man: 4 piay 6 doctor, shaman 8 magician, sorcerer 9 physician
mediety: 6 moiety
medieval: *battle:* 4 Acre
coin: 9 bracteate
dagger: 6 anlace
fiddle: 4 giga
fort: 11 Carcassonne
gown: 6 cyclas
helmet: 5 armet 6 heaume
lyric: 4 alba
prayer book: 7 portass
shield: ecu
weapon: 5 lance, oncin 7 gisarme 8 crossbow
Medina (see also **Muslim**): Aus
citizen: 5 Ansar
mediocre: 4 mean, soso 6 common, medium 7 average 8 middling, ordinary, passable 11 commonplace, indifferent
meditate: 4 chew, mull, muse, pore 5 brook, study, think, watch, weigh 6 ponder, reason 7 reflect, revolve 8 cogitate, consider, ruminate 10 deliberate 11 contemplate
meditation: 4 yoga 8 higgaion 14 omphaloskepsis
meditative: 7 pensive
mediterranean: 6 inland 7 midland 10 landlocked
Mediterranean: sea
boat: nef 4 saic 5 setee, xebec, zebec 6 galiot, mistic, settee, tartan, zebeck 7 felucca, mistico, polacre
coast: 7 Riviera
country: 5 Italy 6 France, Greece 7 Algeria
Eastern: 6 Levant
falcon: 6 lanner
fish: aco 6 remora
fruit: 5 olive 7 azarole
galley: 6 galiot
grass: 4 diss
gulf: 5 Tunis
island: 4 Elba 5 Capri, Crete, Ibiza, Iviza, Malta 6 Candia, Cyprus, Ebusus, Lesbos, Lipari, Rhodes, Sicily 7 Majorca, Panaria 8 Sardinia 9 Stromboli
pert. to: 9 Levantine
port: 5 Tunis 7 Tunisia
resort: 4 Nice 6 Menton 7 Mentone
shrub: 7 azarole
storm: 7 borasca, borasco
tree: 5 carob 6 mastic 7 azarole
wind: 6 otesan, solano 7 gregale, mistral, sirocco 8 levanter 10 euroclyden
medium: 4 mean 5 media(pl.), midst, organ 6 degree, medial 7 average, channel, psychic 8 mediator 10 instrument, interagent 11 environment 12 intermediary, intermediate
communication: 4 note 5 cable, phone, radio 6 letter 9 telegraph, telephone 10 television
culture: 4 agar
news: TV 5 radio 7 journal 8 magazine 9 newspaper 10 periodical, television
medlar: 4 lark, tree 5 fruit 6 mespil
medley: 4 olio 6 jumble 7 farrago, melange, mixture 8 mingling 9 bariolage(F.), potpourri 10 hodgepodge 11 gallimaufry 12 mingle-mangle
musical: 8 fantasia
medrick: 4 gull, tern
medulla: 4 pith 6 marrow 7 essence, summary 10 compendium
Medusa: 6 Gorgon 7 blubber 9 jellyfish
offspring: 7 Pegasus 8 Chrysaor
representation: 9 Gorgoneum
sister: 6 Stheno 7 Euryale
slayer: 7 Perseus
meed: due 4 gift 5 award, bribe, merit, repay, worth 6 desert, reward 7 bribery 10 excellence, recompense
meek: 4 deft, kind, mild 5 lowly 6 docile, gentle, humble 7 pacific, patient 8 moderate, sheepish, yielding 9 childlike, spineless 10 spiritless, submissive
meerkat: 6 monkey 8 suricate
meerschaum: 7 seafoam 9 sepiolite
meet: fit, kep(Sc.), sit 4 duel, face, join, tidy 5 equal, occur, touch, tryst 6 battle, combat, confer, gather, proper 7 contact, convene, fitting, fulfill 8 assemble, assembly, confront, moderate, suitable 9 encounter, forgather, gathering, intersect 10 congregate, experience, foregather 11 appropriate
athletic: 8 gymkhana 10 tournament
meeting: 4 mall, moot 5 gemot, rally, union 6 caucus, gemote, huddle, parley 7 coition, consult, session 8 adjacent, assembly, conclave, congress, junction 10 concurrent, conference, confluence, rendezvous 11 convocation
meeting place: 4 fora(pl.) 5 forum
meetinger: 9 dissenter
meg: 6 guinea 9 halfpenny

Meg's sisters: Jo; Amy 4 Beth
megagamete: 11 macrogamete
megalithic chamber: 6 dolmen
megaphone: 8 vamphorn
megapod: 4 bird 5 maleo 6 leipoa
Megara king: 5 Nisus
megrim: 4 whim 5 blues, fancy, freak, humor, whiff 7 vertigo 8 flounder, headache 9 dizziness 12 hypochondria
Mehitabel: cat
companion: 6 Archie 9 cockroach
creator: 7 Marquis
Mekong River: *site:* 4 Asia 7 Vietnam
tribe: Moi
mel: 5 honey
melancholia: 6 athymy 7 athymia
melancholy: sad 4 blue, dram, dull, dump, glum 5 dolar(L.), drear, dusky, gloom 6 dismal, somber, sombre, sorrow, yellow 7 chagrin, doleful, pensive, sadness, unhappy 8 atrabile, downcast, tristful 9 cheerless, dejection, plaintive 10 allicholly, depression, desolation 11 despondency, downhearted 12 disconsolate, heavy-hearted, hypochondria, mournfulness
Melanesia: *language:* 5 Santo
people: 4 Fiji
melange: 4 olio 6 medley 7 mixture
melanic: 5 black
melanous: 4 dark 6 brunet 8 brunette
meld: 4 play 5 unite
mele: 4 poem, song 5 chant, lyric 6 ballad
melee: row 4 fray, riot 5 brawl, fight, foray, mix-up 6 affray, fracas, ruckus 7 ruction, scuffle 8 dogfight, skirmish
melicocca: 5 genip
melicratum: 4 mead 8 beverage, hydromel
melilotus: 6 clover
meliorate: 6 better, soften 7 improve 10 ameliorate
melisma: 7 cadenza
melissa plant: 4 mint
Melita: 5 Malta
Melkarth: 4 Baal 6 Moloch
mell: mix 4 maul 5 fight, honey 6 beetle, hammer, mallet, meddle, mingle
mellifluous: 7 honeyed, sugared
mellow: age 4 aged, rich, ripe, soft 5 ripen 6 mature, tender 7 matured 8 patinate
melodeon: 9 seraphine
melodious: 6 ariose, arioso, dulcet 7 lyrical, melodic, musical, tunable, tuneful 8 canorous 10 harmonious
melodist: 6 singer 8 composer 9 harmonist
melodramatic: 8 dramatic 9 emotional 10 theatrical 11 sensational
melody: air, lay 4 aria, lilt, note, raga(Ind.), solo, song, tune 5 charm, dirge, music, theme 6 strain 7 arietta, harmony, rosalia, sortita 9 cantilena 11 tunefulness
characterization: 6 ariose, arioso
counter: 7 descant
outline: 5 melos
pert. to: 6 plagal
unaccompanied: 4 solo 6 monody
meloid: 6 beetle
melon: 4 musk, pepo 5 gourd, water 6 casaba, papaya 7 Persian 8 honeydew 10 cantaloupe, paddymelon
melon pear: 6 pepino
melongena: 8 eggplant
melos: 4 song 6 melody
melt: rin(Sc.), run 4 flow, flux, fuse, thaw 5 smelt, sweal 6 render, soften 7 dwindle, liquefy 8 discandy, dissolve, eliquate 10 colliquate, deliquesce 12 disintegrate
down: 6 render 7 liquefy
partly: 4 frit
Melville: *character:* 4 Ahab 5 whale
novel: 4 Omoo 5 Typee
member: 4 limb, part 5 organ 6 branch, fellow 7 section 8 district 11 communicant
new: 6 novice 7 entrant 8 neophyte 10 apprentice
oldest: 4 dean
membership: 4 seat 10 fellowship
membrane: web 4 caul, coat, skin, tela 5 amnia(pl.), lemma, telae(pl.) 6 amnion, amnios, retina 7 cuticle, eardrum, velamen 8 striffen
diffusion through: 7 osmosis
fold of: 5 plica
fringe: 4 loma
of bird: 4 cere
spore: 6 intine
weblike: 4 tela
memento: 5 relic, token 6 trophy 8 keepsake, reminder, souvenir
memo: 4 chit 8 reminder
memoir: 4 note 5 eloge 6 record, report 7 history 8 memorial 9 biography, narrative 10 commentary
memorabilia: ana
memorable: 7 namable, notable, special 9 reminding 10 remarkable 11 reminiscent 13 distinguished, extraordinary
memorandum: 4 bill, note, stub 5 brief 6 agenda(pl.) 7 agendum, memento, minutes, notanda(pl.), proctol 8 notandum, notation, reminder
book: 5 diary 6 agenda 7 tickler 8 calendar
legal: 5 jurat
memoria: 6 chapel, church, shrine, temple 9 reliquary
memorial: ahu 5 facta(pl.), relic 6 factum, memoir, record, trophy 8 mnemonic, mon-

ument 11 remembrance 12 recollection 13 commemorative
carved: 5 totem
stone: 5 cairn 6 statue 9 mausoleum
memorist: 8 prompter
memory: 4 mind, rote 8 memorial 9 retention 11 remembrance 12 recollection, reminiscence 13 retrospection
aid: 8 mnemonic, reminder 10 anamnestic
goddess: 9 Mnemosyne
loss: 5 blank, lethe 7 amnesia, aphasia 13 forgetfulness
pattern: 6 engram
pert. to: 6 mnesic 7 mnestic 8 mnemonic
vivid: 7 eidetic
memory book: 5 diary 9 scrapbook
Memphis (see also **Egypt**):
chief: Evi
god: Ra 4 Ptah
men: 4 crew 6 people
armed body: 4 army 5 posse
party: 4 stag 6 smoker
section of Greek church: 6 andron
wise: 4 Magi 6 Gaspar 8 Melchior 9 Balthasar, Balthazar
menace: 5 boast, peril 6 impend, threat 8 denounce, jeopardy, threaten 9 fulminate
menacing: 10 formidable
menage: 4 club 7 society 8 domicile 9 household 10 management 12 housekeeping
menagerie: zoo 10 collection
menald: 8 speckled 10 variegated
menaspis: 5 shark
mend: fix, sew 4 beet, darn, heal, help, knit 5 amend, beete, botch, clout, emend, moise, patch 6 better, cobble, repair, solder 7 improve, restore 10 ameliorate, convalesce
mendacity: lie 5 lying 6 deceit 7 falsity, untruth 9 falsehood
mendelevium symbol: Md
mender: 6 tinker 7 cobbler 9 repairman
mendicant: 4 monk 5 fakir 6 beggar, begger, bhikku, fakeer, frater, gosain, gusain 7 ajivika, bhikshu
Menelaus: *brother:* 9 Agamemnon
daughter: 8 Hermione
father: 6 Atreus
steersman: 7 Canopus
wife: 5 Helen
meng: mix 5 blend 6 mingle
menhaden: 4 fish, pogy 5 pogie, porgy 8 bonyfish 10 mossbunker
young: 7 sardine
menial: fag 4 base 6 drivel, harlot, sordid, stocah, varlet 7 servant, servile, slavish 8 coistrel, coistril, servitor 9 degrading, underling
meniscus: 4 lens
mennom: 6 mennon, minnow
Mennonite: 5 Amish
meno: 4 less
Menominee whitefish: 6 chivey
Menotti character: 5 Amahl
mensk: 5 adorn, favor, grace, honor 6 credit 8 ornament 9 reverence 12 graciousness
mensuration: 11 measurement 13 determination
mental: 5 ideal 7 phrenic 11 intelligent 12 intellectual
mental aberration: fog 4 daze, haze 5 lapse 6 stupor 7 doldrum, madness 8 insanity
mental defective: 5 idiot, moron 8 imbecile 9 retardate
mental disorder: 6 ataxia 7 aphasia 8 neuritis, neurosis, paranoia 9 melomania, paranomia, psychosis 11 megalomania 12 hypochondria 13 schizophrenia
specialist: 12 psychiatrist
mental faculties: 4 mind, wits
mental image: 4 idea 5 dream, idola(pl.) 6 idolum 7 fantasy 8 phantasm 10 conception
mental state: 5 blues 6 morale 7 doldrum 8 euphoria
mentality: 4 mind 5 sense 6 acumen, reason 9 endowment, intellect 11 rationality 12 intelligence
mentiferous: 10 telepathic
mention: 4 cite, hint, mind, name 5 clepe, refer, speak, trace 6 allude, denote, notice, record 7 specify, vestige 8 allusion, citation 9 statement 10 indication
implied: 11 connotation
mentioned: 8 foresaid 9 aforesaid
mentor: 4 guru 7 monitor, teacher 9 counselor 10 counsellor, instructor
menu: 4 card, meal 5 carte 10 bill of fare
part of: 4 soup 5 salad 6 entree 7 dessert, special 9 appetizer
Mephistophelean: sly 4 evil 6 crafty
Mephistopheles: 5 devil, Satan
mephitic: 4 foul 6 deadly 7 noxious
mephitis: 4 odor 5 smell 6 stench
mercantile: 7 trading 10 commercial
mercenary: 4 hack 5 venal 6 sordid 7 Hessian 8 covetous, hireling, vendible 10 galloglass(Sc.) 11 gallowglass 13 stipendiarian
merchandise: 4 ware 5 goods, wares 7 chaffer
cheap: 5 borax 7 camelot, schlock
pert. to: 10 emporeutic
merchant: 4 Seth(Ind.) 6 dealer, seller, sutler, trader, vender, vendor 7 chapman, goladar, howadji, vintner 8 purveyor 9 tradesman 10 shopkeeper 11 storekeeper
group: 5 guild, hansa 6 cartel

wholesale: 6 packer
Merchant of Venice: 7 Antonio
character: 5 Tubal 6 Portia 7 Jessica, Lorenzo, Nerissa, Shylock
merchant vessel: 6 argosy, holcad 8 bilander, indiaman
merciful: 6 benign 7 sparing 9 benignant, forgiving 10 charitable
merciless: 4 grim 5 cruel 6 savage 8 pitiless 9 ferocious, graceless, heartless 10 despiteous, relentless
mercurial: 6 clever, lively, shrewd 8 changing, thievish 9 faithless 10 inconstant
mercury: 5 azoth, guide, thief 6 hawker 9 messenger 11 quicksilver
derivative: 11 quicksilver
symbol: Hg
Mercury: 6 Hermes, planet 9 newspaper
son: 5 Cupid
staff: 8 caduceus
winged cap: 7 petasos, petasus
winged shoes: 7 talaria
mercury subchloride: 7 calomel
mercy: law 4 pity, ruth 5 grace, grith 6 lenity 7 charity 8 clemency, humanity, kindness, lenience, leniency, mildness 9 tolerance 10 compassion, indulgence, tenderness 11 forbearance, forgiveness
show: 5 spare 6 pardon 7 forgive 8 reprieve
mercy killing: 10 euthanasia
mere: but, sea 4 bare, club, lake, mear, pool, pond, pure, sole 5 bound, limit, plain, sheer, utter 6 divide, entire, famous, scarce, simple 7 unmixed 8 absolute, boundary, glorious, landmark, trifling 9 beautiful, undiluted 11 unqualified
merely: 4 also, just, only 5 quite 6 anerly
merganser: 4 smee, smew 5 harle, robin 7 becscie, bracket, garbill 9 goosander
merge: 4 fuse, join, meld 5 blend, unify, unite 6 absorb, mingle 7 combine, conjoin 8 coalesce 9 commingle 10 amalgamate 11 consolidate, incorporate
mericarp: 8 hemicarp
meridian: 4 noon 6 midday 11 culmination
meringue 5 icing
merino: 4 wool 5 sheep 6 fabric 7 Delaine
merit: 4 earn, meed 5 worth 6 desert, reward 7 deserve 10 condignity, excellence
merited: fit 7 fitting 8 adequate, suitable
meritorious: 8 valorous 9 honorable
merkin: mop
merlin: 6 falcon
Merlin: 4 poem 8 magician 9 alchemist
Merlin's grass: 9 quillwort
mermaid: 5 nymph, siren 6 merrow
mero: 5 guasa 7 grouper
Merob's alphabet: 8 Armenian
meropia: 9 blindness
meropodite: 5 meros
meros: 5 thigh
merriment: fun 5 deray 9 amusement, diversion 11 galliardise
merrow: 7 mermaid
merry: gai(F.), gay 4 agog, airy, boon, cant, glad 5 bonny, droll, happy, jolly, sunny 6 blithe, bonnie, cocket, hilary, jocose, jocund, jovial, joyous, lively 7 gleeful, jocular 8 cheerful, chirping, gamesome, gleesome, mirthful, pleasant, sportive 9 hilarious, sprightly 10 blithesome, frolicsome 11 exhilarated 12 lighthearted
merry andrew: 4 zany 5 antic, clown, joker 6 jester 7 buffoon 8 merryman
merry-go-round: 8 carousel 9 carrousel
Merry Widow composer: 5 Lehar
Merry Wives of Windsor character: Nym 4 Ford 5 Robin 6 Fenton, Pistol
merrymaking: 5 jolly, revel 6 splore 7 festive, revelry, wassail 8 carnival 9 festivity, merriment 12 conviviality
merrythought: 8 wishbone
merrytrotter: 5 swing 6 seesaw
merrywing: 9 goldeneye 10 bufflehead
merse: dip 5 marsh 6 plunge 7 immerse
merycism: 10 rumination
mesa: 7 plateau 8 plateaux(pl.) 9 tableland
mescal: 5 cacti(pl.), drink 6 cactus, peyote, peyotl
mesel: 5 leper 7 leprosy
mesh: net 4 moke 5 snare 6 areola, engage, macula, tangle 7 areolae, ensnare, maculae(pl.), netting, network 8 entangle 10 reticulate
mesial: 6 median, middle
mesmerize: 9 hypnotize
mesne: 6 middle 11 intervening 12 intermediate
Mesopotamia: 4 Irak, Iraq
ancient city or town: Ur 6 Nippur 7 Babylon
captives' place: 5 Halah
city: 5 Mosul 6 Bagdad(c.) 7 Edessan, Kerbela
people: 5 Iraki, Iraqi 7 Aramean
river: 6 Tigris 9 Euphrates
wind: 6 shamal
mesosperm: 9 secundine
mesotais: 4 base 10 groundmass
mespil: 6 medlar
mesquin: 4 mean 6 shabby, sordid
mesquite: 9 algarroba
genus: 8 prosopis
mess: jag, row 4 clat, jagg, meal, mull, muss, soil 5 batch, botch, cauch, dirty, lelee 6 bungle, dabble, jumble, litter, muddle, rumple, tousle 7 crumple, mixture, wrin-

kle 6 disarray, dishevel, disorder, scramble, slaister, squabble 9 commotion, confusion 10 hodgepodge, picklement
message: 4 bode, line, memo, news, note, wire, word 5 cable 6 brevet, letter 7 bodword, depeche, mission, missive, tidings 9 memoranda 10 communique, memorandum 13 communication
good news: 7 evangel
Messalina: 6 wanton 10 prostitute
husband: 8 Claudius
messenger: 4 bode, page, sand, toty 5 angel, envoy, miler 6 beadle, chiaus, herald, legate, nuncio 7 apostle, carrier, courant, courier, hi-carra, mercury, prophet, totyman 8 hi-carrah, minister, nunciate, portator 9 harbinger 10 ambassador, evangelist, forerunner 11 internuncio
mounted: 6 cossid(Ind.) 7 courier, estafet 9 estafette
of the gods: 6 Hermes 7 Mercury
Messiah: 6 Christ, Savior 7 prophet, Saviour
Messina Strait rock: 6 Scilla, Scylla
messy: 5 dirty 6 untidy
mestive: 8 mournful
mestizo: 5 cross, metis 7 mixture
met (see also **meet**): 7 measure, opposed 11 measurement
metad: rat
metagnomy: 10 divination
metagnostic: 10 unknowable
metal: ore, tin 4 gold, iron, lead, zinc 6 cobalt, copper, oroide, pewter, radium, silver, sodium, spirit 7 bullion, gallium, mercury 9 potassium, substance
alloy: 5 brass, steel
bar: gad 5 ingot
base: 5 dross, sprue
box: 8 canister
cake: 4 slag
clippings: 7 scissel
containing: 13 metalliferous
crude: 5 matte
decorate: 4 etch 6 emboss 9 damascene, damaskeen
decorative: 6 chrome, niello
deposit: 4 lode
disc: 5 paten 6 patten
fastener: pin 4 bolt, brad, nail 5 rivet, screw 6 cotter, solder
filings: 5 lemel
heavy: 6 osmium 7 uranium
impure mass: 7 regulus
layer: 4 seam 5 stope
leaf: 4 foil
lightest known: 7 lithium
lump: pig 4 slug 6 nugget
magnetized: 13 electromagnet
mixture: 5 alloy
nonexpanding: 5 invar
oblong piece: sow
patch: 6 solder
plate: gib
rare: 4 zinc 6 cerium, erbium 7 iridium, terbium, uranium, yttrium 8 lutecium, platinum
refuse: 4 slag 5 dross 6 scoria
scrap: 6 filing
shaper: 5 swage
sheet: 4 foil 5 lames, plate 6 lamina, latten, tagger
spike: gad
stannic: tin
strip: 6 spline
suit: 4 mail 5 armor
test: 5 assay
tin-like: 7 cadmium
unrefined: ore
vein: 4 lode
waste: 4 slag 5 dross 6 scoria 9 recrement
worker: 5 smith 6 barman 7 riveter 8 tinsmith 9 goldsmith 11 coppersmith, silversmith
metallic: 6 brazen 13 metalliferous
content: ory
metamere: 6 somite 8 somatome
metamerism: 12 segmentation
metamorphose: 6 change 9 transform, transmute 16 transubstantiate
metamorphosis: 4 pupa 6 change 8 mutation
metaphor: 5 trope 6 simile 8 allegory 10 comparison 11 tralatition
faulty or mixed use of: 11 catachresis
metaphorical: 10 figurative
metaphysical being: ens 5 entia(pl.)
metastrophe: 11 interchange
metayer: 6 farmer
mete: 4 dole, give, goal, post 5 allot, award, bound, limit, stake 7 measure 8 allocate 9 apportion 10 distribute
meteor: 5 bolis, Cetid, comet, Lyrid 6 Antlid, bolide, Lyraid 8 aerolite, fireball 9 Andromede 10 Andromedid
August: 8 Perseids
November: 6 Leonid
meteorite: 8 aerolite, aerolith, siderite 9 asiderite 10 siderolite
meteorological instrument: 6 bolide 9 barometer 11 thermometer
meteorologist: 10 forecaster
meter: 4 beat, time 5 metre, verse 6 rhythm 7 cadence, measure 8 measurer
cubic: 5 liter, litre, stere
one-hundredth: 10 centimeter
one-millionth: 6 micron
one-tenth: 9 decimeter

one-thousandth: 10 millimeter
square: 7 centare
unit: 4 mora 5 morae(pl.)
meterist: 10 verse-maker
meters: *10:* 9 decameter
100: 10 hectometer
100 square: ar; are
1,000: 9 kilometer
10,000: 10 myriameter
methane hydrocarbon: 8 paraffin 9 paraffine
metheglin: 4 mead 8 beverage
mether: cup
method: way 4 dart, form, garb, mode, rule 5 means, order, style, usage 6 course, manner, system 7 fashion, formula, process 9 procedure, technique 11 orderliness
customary: *rut* 5 habit 7 routine
methodical: 5 exact 6 severe 7 precise
methodize: 8 regulate
Methuselah: *father:* 5 Enoch
grandson: 4 Noah
son: 6 Lamech
methyl: *cyanide:* 7 nitrile
ethyl ketone: 8 butanone
ketol: 6 acetol
meticulous: 4 neat, nice, prim 5 fussy, timid 7 careful, fearful, finical 10 fastidious, scrupulous
metier: 4 line 5 trade 7 calling 8 business 10 occupation, profession
metis: 8 octoroon 9 halfbreed
metric: 8 criteria(pl.) 9 criterion
measure: ar; are 5 carat, liter, litre, meter, stere, tonne 6 decare, hectar, micron, miglio 7 centare, deciare, dekiare, hectare, kiliare, manzana, myriare 8 centiare, dekagram, milliare 9 decaliter, decameter, decastere, deciliter, decimeter, decistere, dekaliter, dekameter, dekistere, kiloliter, kilometer, kilostere, megameter 10 centiliter, centimeter, centistere, dekadrachm, hectoliter, hectometer, hectostere, microliter, milliliter, millimeter, millistere, myrialiter, myriameter 15 micromillimeter
metrical beat: 5 ictus
metrical foot: 4 iamb 6 iambic, iambus 7 anapest
accented syllable: 5 arsis
four syllables: 6 syzygy
three short syllables: 8 tribrach
two syllables: 7 spondee, trochee
two together: 6 dipody
metrist: 4 poet 9 metrician
metronome: 5 timer
metropolis: see 4 city, seat 6 center
metropolitan: cit 5 chief, urban 7 bishops, leading 9 principal
mettle: 4 fire 5 ardor, nerve, pluck, spunk 6 ginger, spirit 7 bravery, courage 9 fortitude
Metz's river: 7 Moselle
meuse: gap 4 hole, lurk 7 conceal, opening 8 loophole
mew: den 4 cage, cast, coop, gull, maas(Sc.), molt, shed 5 miaow, miaul 6 change 7 conceal, confine, enclose, garages, stables 8 spicknel 9 enclosure 11 concealment, confinement
mewl: cry, mew 6 squall 7 whimper
Mexico: *agave:* 5 datil 6 zapupe
alcoholic beverage: 6 mescal, pulque 7 tepache, tequila
American: 6 gringo
annuity: 5 censo
antelope: 9 pronghorn
bean: 6 frejol, frijol 7 frijole
bedbug: 8 conenose
beverage: 4 chia
bird: 6 jacana, towhee 7 jacamar, tinamou 8 zopilote
blanket: 6 serape
bread: 6 tamale
brigand: 7 ladrone
bull: 4 toro
cactus: 6 bavoso, chaute, chende, mescal 8 alicoche, chichipe 11 alfilerillo
candlewood: 8 ocotillo
cat: 6 margay
chaps(leather): 10 chaparajos, chaparejos
city: 4 Leon, Tula 5 Tepic 6 Colima, Jalapa, Juarez, Merida, Mexico(c.), Oaxaca, Puebla, Potosi 7 Durango, Orizaba, San Luis, Tampico 8 Culiacan, Mazatlan, Monterey, Saltillo, Vera Cruz, Victoria 9 Chihuahua, Luis Potos 10 Hermosillo 11 Guadalajara
cloak: 5 manta 6 serape
cockroach: 9 cucaracha
coin: 4 peso 5 adobe 6 azteca 7 centavo, piaster
conqueror: 6 Cortes, Cortez
cottonwood: 5 alamo
dish: 5 atole, tamal 6 tamale 9 enchilada
dollar: 4 peso
drug: 7 damiana
early dweller: 4 Maya 5 Aztec
fiber: 4 pita 5 istle, sisal 6 catena
fish: 6 salema 7 totuava
garment: 5 manga 6 serape 7 chiripa
gopher: 4 tuza 7 quachil
grapefruit: 7 toronja
grass: 5 otate 7 sacaton, zacaton 8 hanequen, hanequin
guardian spirit: 6 nagual
hero: 4 Diaz 6 Juarez
hog: 7 peccary

house: 5 jacal
Indian: see *people* below
ivy: 6 cobaea
laborer: 4 peon 7 bracero, wetback
lake: 7 Chapala
land owner: 8 ranchero
laurel: 7 madrona
masonry: 5 adobe
mat: 6 petate
measure: pie 4 alma, vara 5 almud, baril, jarra, labor, legua, linea, sitio 6 almude, fanega 7 pulgada 9 cuarteron, cuartillo 10 caballeria
measure of weight: bag 4 onza 5 carga, libra, marco 6 adarme, arroba, ochava, tercio 7 quintal
mixed blood: 7 mestizo
mountain: 7 Orizaba 12 Citlaltepetl, Ixtaccihuatl, Popocatepetl
musical instrument: 6 clarin, guiros 7 cabacas, maracas 11 chiapanecas
onyx: 6 tecali
orange: 7 choisya
painter: 6 Orozco, Rivera
pancake: 5 arepa
peasant: 4 peon
peninsula: 7 Yucatan
people: Mam 4 Cora, Maya, Seri, Xova 5 Aztec, Hauve, Lipan, Nahau, Opata, Otomi, Yaqui, Zoque 6 Indian, Mixtec, Otonia, Toltec 7 Haustec, Tepanec, Zacatec, Zapotec 8 Totonaco, Zacateco 9 Campesino 10 Cuitlateca, Cuitlateco
plant: 4 chia 5 agave, amole, datil, jalap, sotol 6 chaute, maguey, slavia 7 tequila 8 acapulco 9 sabadilla
plantation: 8 hacienda
porridge: 5 atole
porter: 5 tamen
ranch: 8 hacienda
resort: 8 Acapulco
river: 6 Panuco 7 Tabasco
rubber tree: ule
sandal: 8 gauracha, guarache, guaracho, huarache, huaracho
sandwich: 4 taco
sauce: 7 tabasco
scarf: 6 rebozo, tapalo
shawl: 6 serape
shrub: 6 anagua, anaqua, colima 7 choisya
state: 6 Colima, Sonora 7 Durango, Hidalgo, Sinaloa, Tabasco, Yucatan 9 Michoacan
sugar: 7 panocha
tea: 6 basote 7 apasote 9 alpasotes
thong: 5 romal
tree: ule 4 sero 5 abeto, amapa, ebano, ocote 6 chacte, colima, mezcal, sabino 7 capulin, colorin 8 chaparro, ulmaceae 9 ahuehuete, canadulce 10 anacahuita
village: 6 ejidos, tecali
volcano: 6 Colima 7 Jorullo 9 Paricutin 12 Popocatepetl
weight: 4 onza
yucca: 5 isote

mezereon: 5 shrub 6 daphne 8 camillia
mezzanine: 5 story 7 balcony 8 entresol
mias: 9 orangutan
miasma: 7 malaria
miaul: mew 4 meow, wraw 5 miaou, miaow, miaul 9 caterwaul
mib: 6 marble
mica: 4 talc 5 glist 7 biotite 8 silicate 9 damourite, hydromica, isinglass, muscovite 10 lepidolite
micaceous: 7 talcose
Micah: 7 prophet
son: 5 Abdon
miche: 4 lurk 5 skulk, sneak 6 pilfer 7 conceal
Michelangelo work: 5 Pieta
micher: 5 cheat, thief 6 truant 8 panderer
Michigan: *city:* 4 Alma, Caro 5 Flint, Ionia 7 Detroit, Lansing(c.) 8 Muskegon 9 Marquette
county: 4 Kent
motto: 6 Tuebor
river: 4 Cass 5 Huron
state flower: 5 apple
mickle: 4 much 5 great
mico: 6 marmoset
micraner: ant
micro: 4 moth
microbe: 4 germ 8 bacillus, organism
microcosm: 5 world 7 village 8 universe 9 community
Micronesia island: 4 Guam, Wake 5 Palau 6 Bikini, Ellice, Saipan
microorganism: 4 germ 5 virus 6 aerobe 7 aerobia 8 aerobium 9 autoblast, spirillum 10 spirochete 11 spirochaete
microscopic: 5 small 6 minute 9 engyscope
microspore: 6 pollen
microsporophyll: 6 stamen
mid: See **midst**
mid-European: 4 Slav 7 Slovene
mid-wifery: 10 obstetrics
midday: 4 noon 8 noontide
intermission: 5 lunch 7 nooning 8 noon hour
nap: 6 siesta
middle: 4 mean 5 mesne, midst, waist 6 center, centre, centry, median, mesial 7 average, central, centric 11 intervening 12 intermediate 13 intermediator

combining form: mes 4 medi, meso
way: 6 midway 7 halfway 10 moderation
Middle Ages: See **medieval**
Middle East: 6 Levant
middleman: 5 agent, butty 6 dealer, trader 8 huckster, retailer 9 go-between 12 interlocutor, intermediary
middling: 4 fair, soso 6 fairly, medium 8 mediocre, moderate, ordinary, somewhat 10 moderately
middlings: 4 feed
midge: fly 5 fish, gnat 5 dwarf, stout 6 insect, midget, punkie 8 carriage
midget: 5 dwarf, small 9 miniature
Midianite: *king:* Hur 4 Reba
prince: Evi, Zur
midnoon: 4 noon 6 midday
midrib: 5 costa 6 costae(pl.)
midshipman: 5 cadet 6 reefer
midst: 4 amid, mean 5 among, depth 6 amidst, center, centre, medium, middle, mongst 7 between, halfway, setting 11 surrounding
midwife: 4 baba, dhai(Ind.), gamp 5 howdy 6 cummer, howdie, kimmer 7 hebamme 9 gracewife 11 accoucheuse, finger-smith
mien: air, eye 4 brow, vult 5 guise 6 aspect, manner, ostent 7 bearing, conduct 8 attitude, behavior, carriage, demeanor 9 behaviour, demeanour 10 appearance, deportment 11 countenance
miffed: 5 sulky, vexed 8 offended 10 displeased
mig: 4 duck 6 marble
migale: 5 mouse, shrew
migeloid fish: 4 bobo
might: arm 4 mote 7 ability
mighty: big 4 bulk, fell, vast, very 5 felon, great 6 potent, strong 7 violent 8 enormous, forceful, forcible, powerful, puissant, vigorous 9 extensive, extremely, gigantean 10 omnipotent 11 efficacious
migniard: 6 dainty, minion 7 mincing 8 delicate, mistress
mignon: 5 small 6 dainty, petite 8 delicate, graceful
mignonette: 6 reseda
vine: 7 Madeira, tarweed
migraine: 4 whim 8 headache 10 hemicrania
migrant: See **migratory**
migrate: 4 flee, flit, move, pass, trek 8 colonize, transfer
migration: 5 exode 6 exodus, flight
migratory: 6 roving 7 nomadic 9 peregrine, wandering
bird: 4 duck 5 goose, robin
farm worker: 4 Okie
mihrab: 4 slab 5 niche 7 chamber
Mikado: 9 sovereign
court: 5 dairi
office: 9 mikadoate
mike: 10 microphone
milady: 4 dame 5 madam 10 noblewoman 11 gentlewoman
Milan opera house: 5 Scala
milarite: 8 silicate
mild: moy 4 calm, easy, kind, meek, soft, tame 5 balmy, bland, claro 6 benign, gentle, humble 7 clement, lenient 8 benedict, favonian, gracious, lenitive, merciful, moderate, soothing, tranquil 9 assuasive, forgiving, indulgent, temperate 10 forbearing, mollifying 11 considerate
milder: 6 molder
mildew: 4 mold, rust 5 mould 6 blight, fungus 8 honeydew
genus of: 7 erysibe 8 erysiphe
mildness: 6 comity
mile: *nautical:* 4 knot, naut
one-eighth: 7 furlong
mileage: 8 distance
milepost: 5 stela, stele 6 marker, stelae
miler: 6 runner
milestone: 8 milepost
milfoil: 6 yarrow 9 ahartalav
milieu: 11 environment 12 surroundings
militant: 7 martial, soldier, warlike 8 fighting 9 combating, combative 10 aggressive
military (see also **army, troop**): 7 martial
advance: 5 drive 8 anabasis 11 penetration 12 breakthrough
adventurer: 10 filibuster
area: 6 sector
assistant: 4 aide 8 adjutant
base: 4 camp 5 depot, field 7 billets 8 barracks, quarters 10 encampment
call: 6 tattoo
chest: 5 funds
cloak: 5 sagum
command: 4 halt 6 at ease 9 attention
commander: 7 marshal
commission: 6 brevet
engine: ram 6 cannon, onager 7 robinet 8 catapult, mangonel
force: 5 guard 6 legion, troops 7 reserve
formation: 4 file, line 7 echelon
front: 5 lines 6 sector
guard: 6 patrol
hat: 4 kepi 5 shako 6 helmet
hat covering: 8 havelock
horsemen: 7 cavalry, Hussars
informer: spy
inspection: 5 drill 6 parade, review
landing point: 9 beachhead
machine: 4 jeep, tank
maneuver: 6 tactic
messenger: 7 estafet

obstruction: 6 abatis 7 abattis
officer: 5 major 7 captain, colonel, general 8 corporal, sergeant 9 brigadier, subaltern 10 lieutenant
operations: 8 campaign, strategy
order: 7 command
organization: 5 cadre
pit: 10 trou-de-loup
police: M.P. 9 gendarmes 12 constabulary
punishment: 9 strappado
quarters: 4 camp 7 billets 8 barracks
rank: 6 brevet 8 banneret
salute: 5 salvo
signal: 7 chamade
staff officer: 4 aide
storage place: 7 arsenal
supplies: 8 materiel, ordnance
survey: 11 reconnoiter
unit: van 4 rear 5 cadre, corps, squad, troop 7 company, platoon, 8 division, regiment
vehicle: 4 jeep, tank 6 camion 7 caisson
weapon: 4 croc 6 onager 7 robinet 8 ballista 9 catapault
work: 4 fort
militate: 5 fight 6 debate 7 contend 8 conflict
milk: lac 4 lait(F.) 5 drain, nurse 6 elicit, suckle
coagulator: 6 rennet
comb. form: 4 lact 5 lacti, lacto
curdled: 6 yogurt 7 clabber, yoghurt, yogourt 8 yoghourt
curdler: 4 ruen 6 rennet
deodorizer: 7 aerator
derived from: 6 lactic
fermented: 5 kefir, kumys 6 koumis, koumys, kumiss 7 koumiss, matzoon
first after delivery: 9 beestings, biestings, colostrum
food: 10 lacticinia
mouse: 6 spurge
pail: soa, soe 5 bowie
pert. to: 6 lactic 7 lactary, lacteal
preparation: 9 lactarene, lactarine
protein: 6 casein
sap: 5 latex
selling place: 5 dairy 9 lactarium
separator: 7 creamer
sour: 4 whig 6 blinky
sugar: 7 lactose
thickened part: 4 curd
watery: 8 blue John
watery part: 4 whey
with: 6 aulait(F.)
milk and honey: 10 prosperity
milk-and-water: 4 weak 7 insipid
milk glass: 7 opaline
milk leg: 9 phlebitis
milkfish: awa 6 sabolo
milkman: 7 chalker 8 dairyman
milksop: 5 sissy 7 cockney 11 mollycoddle
milkweed; *down:* 4 silk
family: 14 asclepiadaceae
fluid: 5 latex
milkwood: 9 paperbark
milkwort family: 12 polygalaceae
milky: 4 meek, mild, tame 5 timid, white 6 chalky, gentle 7 lacteal, opaline 8 timorous 10 effeminate
Milky Way: 6 galaxy
black spaces in: 9 coalsacks
mill: box 4 beat, nurl 5 crush, dress, fight, grind, knurl, shape, thief 6 finish, powder, thrash 7 factory, machine 8 snuffbox, vanquish 9 comminute, transform 12 housebreaker
beetle: 9 cockroach
bill: adz
end: 7 remnant
kind of: 5 quern 7 central 8 arrastra, arrastre, trapiche
race: 4 lade
run: 7 average 8 millrace, ordinary
sail: 4 vane
mill-wheel: *current:* 8 millrace
float: 5 ladle
millclapper: 10 chatterbox
millcourse: 8 millrace
millefleurs: 7 perfume
millenarian: 8 chiliast
millennium: 6 utopia 8 paradise
millepede: 8 myriapod
millepore: 5 coral
miller: ray 4 moth 5 boxer 7 harrier 8 pugilist 10 flycatcher
miller's thumb: 4 bird 7 warbler 8 cottidae, titmouse 9 goldcrest
millerite: 8 sulphide
millesimal: 10 thousandth
millet: 4 buda, moha 5 bajra, bajri, chena, cumbu, hirse, milly, mohar, proso, tenai 6 bajree, hureek 7 zaburro 8 cenchrus
millimeter: *one millionth:* 15 micromillimeter
one thousandth: 6 micron
milliner: 6 hatter
millions of millions: 9 trillions
millpond: dam
millrace: 4 lade(Sc.) 10 millcourse
below wheel: 8 tailrace
millrind: 6 moline
millstone: 6 burden 7 grinder 9 albatross 10 affliction
support: 4 rind, rynd
millstream: 5 fleam
Mills bomb: 7 grenade
milo: 5 grain
milpa: 6 chacra

milt: 6 spleen
mim: shy 4 prim 5 quiet 6 demure, modest
mime: ape 4 aper, copy, jest 5 actor, clown, drama, farce, mimer, mimic 6 jester 7 buffoon, imitate 9 represent
chief: 9 archi-mime
mimeograph: 7 stencil
mimer: 4 mime
mimesis: 7 mimicry
mimic (see also **mime**): 4 mima, mimo(G.), mock 6 parrot 7 copy-cat, copying, mimetic 9 burlesque 11 counterfeit
mimic thrush: 11 mockingbird
mimicry: 4 echo 5 apery, apism 7 mimesis 8 parrotry 9 imitation 10 camouflage
mimidae: 7 catbird 8 thrasher 11 mockingbird
mimmock: 6 dainty 10 fastidious
mimosa: 4 tree 6 acacia
mimsey: 4 prim 7 prudish
min: 5 ruler 6 memory, prince, remind 8 remember 11 remembrance
mina: 5 money
minar: 4 myna 5 tower
minaret: 4 lamp 5 tower 10 lighthouse
minatory: 8 menacing 11 threatening
minaway: 6 minuet
mince: cut 4 chop, hash 6 affect 7 finnick 9 subdivide 11 affectation
minced oath: gad, gee, lud 4 drat, heck
mincemeat: 5 gigot
minchery: 7 nunnery
minchiate: 5 tarot
mincing: 5 fussy 7 finical, minikin
mincingly: 8 gingerly
mind: min(Sc.) 4 care, chit, heed, obey, reck, tend, will 5 besee, brain, manas(Ind.), watch 6 animus, burrow, memory, notice, psyche, regard 7 dislike, dispose 9 intellect, mentality 11 inclination, remembrance 12 intelligence, recollection
keep in: 9 entertain
origin and development: 13 psychogenesis
pert. to: 6 mental, noetic 7 phrenic 13 psychological
split: 13 schizophrenic
state of: 4 mood, tune
Mindanao: *gulf:* 5 Davao
island: 5 Samal
language: Ata
people: Ata 5 Lutao 6 Bagobo, Illano, Lutayo
town: 4 Dapa
volcano: Apo
mindful: 5 aware 7 heedful 9 attentive, observant, regardful
mine (see also **mining**): my; bal, dig, mio(Sp.), pit, sap 4 delf, hole, meum(It.) 5 bargh, delft, delve 6 cavity, gopher, threat 7 gallery, passage 8 colliery 10 excavation
basket: 4 corf
ceiling: 5 astel
coal: rob
deposit: 4 lode, vein
entrance: 4 adit 5 stulm
excavation: 5 stope
floor: 4 sill
gold: 9 Homestead(S.D.)
guardian: 5 gnome
passage: 4 sill 5 stope
platform: 6 sollar, soller
product: ore 4 coal, iron
prop: 5 sprag
refuse: 4 dead 5 attle
reservoir: 4 sump 8 standage
rich: 4 lode 7 bonanza 8 golconda
roof support: nog
shaft: 4 sump
surface: 6 placer
sweeping device: 8 paravane
tunnel: 4 adit 5 stulm
vein: 4 lode
wagon: 4 tram
waste: gob 4 goaf 7 rubbish
worker: 5 cager, miner 6 canary 7 cageman, trapper 8 onsetter
mine run: 6 common 7 average 10 unassorted
mine-thrower: 6 minnie 11 minenwerfer
miner (see also **mining**): 6 dammer(Sc.), digger, sapper 7 collier
miner's anemia: 15 ancylostomiasis
miner's consumption: 8 phthisis
miner's worm: 8 hookworm
mineral (see also **ore, metal**): cal, tin 5 irite 6 barite, iolite 7 alumite, ataxite, uralite 9 celestite, galactite, inorganic, uraninite 10 gadolinite, retinalite
amorphous: 6 pinite
black: jet 4 coal 5 irite 6 cerine, yenite 7 knopite, niobite 8 graphite 10 minguetite
blue-green: 5 beryl
brittle: 7 euclase
brown: 6 cerine, egeran, rutile 8 lederite 9 elaterite
calcium and magnesium: 8 diopside
calcium carbonate: 7 calcite 8 calcspar
combining form: 4 lite
crystalline: 4 spar 6 yenite 7 apatite, felsite, felspar, knopite 8 boracite, elaterin, felspath
deposit: 4 lode, nest, vein 6 placer
deposit cavity: vug 4 voog, vugg, vugh
earth like: 5 glebe
fibrous: 8 asbestos, oakenite
flaky: 4 mica
gray-green: 7 edenite

gray-white: 5 trona 14 chromiumptrona
green: 7 alalite, apatite, epidote, erinite, prasine, uralian 9 demantoid
gunpowder: 5 niter
hard: 6 spinel 7 adamant 8 corundum, spinelle
lustrous: 4 spar 7 blendes 8 smaltine, smaltite
magnetic: 9 lodestone
mixture: 5 magma
native: ore
non-combustible: 8 asbestos
non-metallic: 4 spar 5 boron 6 gangue, iodine
plaster of paris: 6 gypsum
potash: 4 alum
potassium sulphate: 8 misenite
quartz-like: 4 opal
rare: 7 euclase, thorite
red: 5 balas 6 garnet, rutile
salt: 4 alum
seam: 4 vein
silicate: 4 mica
smelting: ore
soft: 4 talc 6 gypsum
spot: 5 macle
tallow: 11 hatchettine
tar: 4 brea 6 maltha
transparent: 4 mica 5 fluor
vitreous: 4 spar 7 apatite
wax-like: 9 ozocerite
white: 6 barite 8 smaltine, smaltite
yellow: 4 iron 5 topaz 6 pyrite
yellowish green: 7 epidote

mineral jelly: 8 vaseline
mineral oil: 5 colza
mineral spring: spa 4 well
mineral water: 6 selter 7 seltzer
Minerva: 6 Athena, Athene
shield: 5 aegis
ming: 6 remind 7 mention, recount 8 remember
minge: 5 midge
mingle: mix 4 amix, fuse, join, meng, mool 5 admix, blend, merge, unite 6 huddle 7 blender, combine, compost 8 coalesce, compound, intermix 9 associate, commingle 10 amalgamate 11 consolidate
mingle-mangle: 6 medley 7 mixture 10 hodgepodge
mingwort: 8 wormwood
mingy: 4 mean 6 stingy
minhag: 6 custom, manner 7 conduct
miniate: 5 paint 8 decorate, luminate 9 rubricate
miniature: 4 copy, tiny 5 small, teeny 6 little, minute 8 painting, portrait 9 lineament, miniating 10 diminutive 11 rubrication 12 illumination 14 representation
minikin: 6 dainty 7 elegant, mincing 8 affected, delicate 10 diminutive
minim: jot 4 drop, fish 6 minnow, minute 7 tiniest 8 smallest 9 miniature 10 diminutive
minimize: 6 reduce 7 detract 8 belittle 9 disparage 10 depreciate
minimum: 5 least 6 lowest
minimuscular: wee 4 tiny 5 small
mining: 4 gwag
chisel: gad
deposit: 4 lode, nest, vein 6 placer
extraction: ore, tin 4 gold, lead 6 silver 8 diamonds 11 quicksilver
instrument: 4 dial
lamp: 4 davy
nozzle: 5 giant
partition: 8 brattice
place: 6 minery, mining
shack: coe
terms: hat 4 hade 6 clinic
tool: van
waste: 5 attle
minion: 4 idol, neat 5 lover 6 dainty, pretty 7 darling, elegant 8 creature, delicate, favorite, ladylove, mistress, paramour 9 underling
minister: 4 tend 5 angel, serve 6 afford, attend, cleric, curate, divine, pander, parson, pastor, supply 7 furnish, provide, servant 8 executor, preacher, reverend 9 attendant, clergyman, upstander 10 administer, ambassador
home: 5 manse 9 parsonage
minestrone: 4 soup
minitant: 11 threatening
Minnesota: *city:* Ely 6 Duluth, Winona 7 Bemidji, Mankato 8 Owatonna 9 Rochester 11 Minneapolis
county: 4 Cass, Clay, Cook, Lake, Lyon, Pine, Polk, Pope, Rice, Rock, Todd 5 Dodge, Swift 6 Aitkin, Benton, Carver, Dakota, Isanti, Nobles, Ramsey, Roseau, Sibley, Steele, Wadena, Waseca, Wilkin 7 Kanabec, Kittson, Stearns, Stevens 8 Hennepin 10 Pennington
iron range: 6 Cuyuna, Mesabi 9 Vermilion
lake: Red 7 Bemidji 10 Minnewaska 12 Winniboshish
minnow: 5 guppy 6 baggie
minor: 4 less 5 petit, petty, youth 6 infant, lesser, slight 7 smaller 8 inferior 11 subordinate 15 inconsequential
minorate: 7 curtail 8 diminish
minority: 6 nonage 10 immaturity
Minos: *child:* 7 Ariadne, Phaedra
country: 5 Crete
father: 4 Zeus
lover: 6 Scylla

mother: 6 Europa
slayer: 7 Cocalus
wife: 8 Pasiphae
Minotaur: *father:* 4 bull
home: 9 labyrinth
mother: 8 Pasiphae
owner: 5 Minos
slayer: 7 Theseus
minster: 6 church 9 cathedral, monastery
minstrel: 4 bard, bhat(Ind.), moke, poet 6 harper, jockey, singer 7 gleeman, goliard, Pierrot 8 jongleur, musician 9 blackface, troubador 10 gleemaiden, mountebank, troubadour 11 entertainer
accompanist: 7 harpist
minstrel show: *endman:* 5 bones
middleman: 12 interlocutor
part: 4 olio
minstrelsy: 4 glee
mint: aim, iva 4 blow, coin, sage 5 basil, feint, money, thyme 6 catnip, hyssop, intend, mentha, ramona 7 attempt, dittany, potherb, purpose, venture 8 bergamot, calamint, endeavor, lavender, marjoram 9 fabricate, horehound
charge: see *levy* below
family: 9 lamiaceae
genus of: 7 melissa 10 moluccella
geranium: 8 costmary
herb family: 4 balm 5 basil 6 hyssop
levy: 8 brassage 11 seigniorage
mintage: 5 stamp 7 coinage
minuend: 6 lessen 8 diminish
minuet: 5 dance
movement: 7 scherzo
minus: 4 lack, less 6 defect, devoid 7 lacking, without 8 negative, subtract 10 deficiency
minuscule: 4 tiny 5 petty, small 6 minute 10 diminutive, manuscript 13 insignificant
minute: jot, wee 4 mite, nice, note, time, tiny 5 draft, exact, petty, small 6 atomic, little, moment, record, slight, tittle 7 instant, minutia, precise 8 detailed, trifling 9 memoranda(pl.) 10 memorandum 13 imperceptible 14 circumstantial
glass: 9 hourglass
minutely: 7 exactly 9 continual, unceasing
minutes: 4 acta 5 actum 6 record
minutiae: 7 details, trifles 11 particulars
minx: dog 4 girl, jade 5 woman
Minyae king: 7 Athamas
minyan: 6 quorum
mir: 4 head 5 chief 9 community
Mira: 4 star
constellation: 5 Cetus
mirabilia: 7 marvels, wonders 8 miracles
mirac: 6 mirach 7 abdomen
miracle: 4 feat 5 anomy 6 marvel, wonder 10 occurrence, phenomenon
scene of: 4 Cana
wheat: 7 Poulard
worker of: 8 magician 11 thaumaturge
miraculous: 9 unnatural 12 supernatural
mirador: 5 oriel 6 loggia, turret 7 balcony 10 watchtower
mirage: 5 serab 7 chimera 8 delusion, illusion 10 phenomenon, refraction
Miranda's father: 8 Prospero
mirandous: 8 wondrous
mirate: 6 wonder
mird: toy 6 meddle 7 attempt
mire: bog, mud, wet 4 glar, moil, ooze, slew, slob, sloo, slud, sluo 5 addle, embog, glaur(Sc.), marsh, sluig, slush, stall, swamp 6 defile, slough, sludge 7 clabber, sludder 8 entangle
mire duck: 7 mallard
Miriam: *brother:* 5 Aaron, Moses
father: 5 Amram
mother: 8 Jochebed
mirific: 9 wonderful
mirky: See **murky**
mirror: 5 glass 7 reflect 8 speculum 9 girandole
pert. to: 9 catoptric 11 catoptrical
mirth: fun, joy 4 glee 5 cheer 6 bawdry, gaiety, levity, spleen 7 delight, jollity 8 gladness, hilarity, laughter 9 festivity, happiness, merriment 10 jocularity, joyousness 12 cheerfulness
god: 5 Comus
mirthful: 5 cadgy
miry: 5 boggy, muddy 6 claggy, clashy, filthy, lutose 7 guttery
mis: 5 amiss, wrong
misadventure: See **misfortune**
misanthrope: 5 cynic, hater, Timon
misanthropic: 7 cynical 10 antisocial
misapplication: 5 abuse 6 disuse 10 perversion
misappropriate: 5 steal
misbear: 9 misbehave
misbede: 5 abuse, wrong 6 injure
misbegotten: 7 bastard 12 illegitimate
misbehave: 7 disobey, misbear, mislead
misbeliever: 7 heretic, infidel 9 miscreant
misbirth: 8 abortion
miscalculate: err 9 overshoot
miscall: 5 abuse 6 revile 7 slander
miscarriage: 5 lapse 6 mishap 7 failure, misdeed, mistake 8 abortion 9 mischance 11 misdemeanor 13 mismanagement
miscarry: err 5 misgo 7 founder
miscellaneous: 5 mixed 6 sundry, varied 8 assorted 13 heterogeneous 14 indiscriminate
miscellany: 4 olio 10 adversaria, hodgepodge

mischance: See **misfortune**
mischief: ate, hob, ill **4** bane, evil, harm, hurt **5** prank, wrack **6** damage **7** cantrip **9** devilment, diablerie **10** disservice
god: **4** Loki
goddess: Ate **4** Eris
mischiefmaker: elf, imp, wag **5** knave, rogue
mischievous: sly **4** arch, impy **5** elfin, hempy **6** elfish, elvish, impish **7** harmful, knavish, malefic, mocking, naughty, parlous, roguish, teasing, waggish **8** prankish, sportive, venomous **9** injurious
mischievous child: imp **4** brat, limb **5** devil, scamp **6** monkey **7** hellion
miscible: **7** mixable
misconception: **8** abortion **16** misunderstanding
misconduct: **7** offense **8** disorder **9** mismanage **11** delinquency, malfeasance, misbehavior, misdemeanor
mark of: **7** demerit
miscreant: **5** knave **6** rascal, wretch **7** heretic, infidel, villain **8** criminal **9** heretical, scoundrel **10** unbeliever **11** misbeliever, unbelieving **12** unscrupulous
miscue: **4** miss, slip **5** error **7** mistake
misdeed: sin **5** crime, wrong **7** forfeit, offense **8** disorder **11** delinquency **13** transgression
misdemeanor sin **5** crime, fault **6** delict **7** misdeed **8** disorder **11** delinquency **12** misdemeanant
misdirect: **7** pervert
mise: **4** levy, pact **5** grant **6** layout, treaty **8** immunity **9** agreement, privilege
misease: **7** poverty **8** distress **10** discomfort, uneasiness
misenunciation: **9** lallation
miser: **4** cuff **5** churl, flint, hayne, hunks, Nabal **6** codger, huddle, nipper, snudge, wretch **7** hoarder, niggard **8** holdfast **9** skinflint **10** curmudgeon
miserable: bad **4** dawy **6** abject, chetif, elenge, feeble **7** forlorn, pitiful **8** pitiable **10** despicable, discomfort, inadequate **12** disconsolate **13** commiserative
miserere: **4** boss **7** bracket
misericord: **4** hall, pity **5** mercy **6** dagger **9** refectory **10** compassion
miserly: **4** mean **5** close, gnede **6** greedy, grippy, stingy **8** covetous, grasping **9** penurious, scrimping **10** avaricious **12** parsimonious
misery: woe **4** ache, pain **5** agony **6** sorrow **7** anguish, avarice, poverty, sadness, squalor **8** calamity, distress **9** adversity, privation, suffering **10** affliction, depression, misfortune **11** despondency, unhappiness **12** covetousness, wretchedness **13** niggardliness **14** unpleasantness
misfare: **6** mishap **8** miscarry **9** misbehave **10** misfortune
misfeasance: See **malfeasance**
misfortune: woe **4** dole, evil, harm, slip **5** grief **6** misery, mishap, scathe **7** ill-luck, misfare, reverse, trouble **8** accident, calamity, casualty, disaster **9** adversity, holocaust, infortune, mischance **10** affliction, ill-fortune **11** catastrophe, contretemps, miscarriage **12** misadventure
misgiving: **5** doubt, qualm **7** anxiety **12** apprehension
misgo: err **8** miscarry
misguess: err
misguide: **5** abuse **6** injure **7** mislead **8** maltreat **9** misbehave, misdirect, misgovern, mismanage
mishap: See **misfortune**
mishmash: **4** olio **6** jumble **10** hodgepodge
Mishnah: **6** Talmud **9** scripture
pert. to: **7** tannaic **8** Mishnaic
section: **4** Moed **5** Aboth
supplement: **8** Toseftas
misinterpret: err **4** warp
misjudge: err
misky: **5** foggy, misty
mislay: **4** lose
misle: **4** mist, rain **6** mizzle **7** drizzle
mislead: **4** dupe, fool **5** blear, cheat **6** betray, delude, humbug **7** beguile, debauch, deceive **8** hoodwink, misguide **9** duplicate, mismanage
misleading: **5** false **7** crooked **10** fallacious, fraudulent
mismanage: **5** blunk **6** bungle
misplace: **4** lose **6** mislay
misplay: err **5** error **6** renege
misprision: **5** scorn **6** slight **7** despite, mistake **8** contempt, misprise, misprize **10** misconduct **11** misdemeanor **12** depreciation **14** undervaluation **16** misunderstanding
mispronunciation: **8** cacology
misrepresent: lie **5** belie **6** garble **7** deceive
miss: err, fau, hip **4** balk, chit, fail, lack, lass, lose, muff, omit, skip, slip, snab, want **5** lapse, title **6** escape, lassie, miscue **7** deviate, failure **8** fraulein(G.), mistress, overlook, senorita(Sp.), spinster **9** signorina(It.) **10** desiderate, jeune fille, prostitute **12** mademoiselle(F.)
missay: **5** abuse **6** vilify **7** slander
missel: **9** mistletoe
misshapen: **4** ugly **6** clumsy **8** deformed **9** distorted, misformed, monstrous **11** counterfeit

missile (see also **guided missile**): 4 bola, bolt, dart, shot 5 arrow, shaft, spear 6 bullet, weapon 7 missive, outcast 8 brickbat 9 boomerang 10 projectile
pert. to: 9 ballistic
missing: out 4 lost 6 absent
mission: 6 charge, errand 7 message 10 commission, delegation, deputation
missionary: 6 Marist 7 apostle
Mississippi: *county:* 5 Amite 8 Pontotoc
flower: 8 magnolia
mussel: 8 deerhorn
nickname: 5 Bayou
town: 5 Yazoo 6 Biloxi 7 Jackson, Memphis, Natchez 8 Gulfport, Tutwiler
Mississippi River: *mouth:* 4 pass
source: 6 Itasca
Mississippian: 15 Eocarboniferous
missive: 4 note 6 billet, letter 7 epistle, message, missile 8 document
love: 9 valentine
Missouri: *bird:* 8 bluebird
county: 4 Cass, Cole 5 Adair, Bates, Boone, Lewis, Scott, Taney 6 Benton, Dallas, Maries, Mercer, Pettis, Putnam, Shelby 7 Clinton, Johnson, Webster 8 Reynolds, Stoddard, Sullivan 9 Bollinger 10 Montgomery, Saint Clair
gourd: 11 calabazilla
monogram: HST
river: 5 Osage
skylark: 5 pipit
town: 5 Edina 7 Clayton, Sedalia
misspelling: 10 cacography
misspend: 4 lose 8 squander
misstep: 4 slip, trip 5 error 7 faux pas
mist: dag, dim, fog, hag, rag, ure(Sc.) 4 blur, damp, drow(Scot.), film, haze, moke, scud, smog, smur, soup 5 bedim, brume, cloud, dabby, drisk, misle, smurr, vapor 6 mizzle, serein, shadow 7 mystery 9 obscurity 13 precipitation
mistake: err 4 balk, bull, slip 5 amiss, boner, error, fault, folly 6 astray, erring, escape, miscue, renege 7 blunder, default, erratum, rhubarb 10 inaccuracy 12 inadvertence 13 misconception 15 misapprehension
mistaken: 5 wrong
mister: don, sir 4 herr(G.) 5 senor(Sp.), title 6 signor(It.) 8 monsieur(F.)
mistletoe: 7 allheal, gadbush
family: 12 loranthaceae
mistonusk: 6 badger
mistreat: 5 abuse 7 violate
mistress: 4 amie, doll, dozy 5 amiga, dolly, donna, duena, leman 7 hataera, hetaira, hostess 8 gudewife(Sc.), guidwife, ladylove 9 chamberer, concubine, courtesan, courtezan, governess 10 chatelaine, sweetheart
mistrust: 5 doubt 8 distrust 12 apprehension
misty: 4 roky 5 rouky, vague 10 indistinct 13 unilluminated 14 unintelligible
misunderstanding: 6 breach 7 quarrel 9 imbroglio 12 disagreement
misuse: 5 abuse 6 disuse 7 abusion, pervert 8 maltreat, mistreat 9 misemploy
mite: bit 4 atom, dite, dram, tick 5 acari(pl.), atomy, speck 6 acarid, acarus, minute, smidge 7 acarina, chigger, smidgen, smidgin 8 acaridan, arachnid, particle, smidgeon, smitchin
miter: 4 belt 5 frank, mitre, tiara 6 fillet, girdle, gusset, tavern 8 headband 9 headdress
flower: 8 cyclamen
Jewish part: 7 Petalon
mithridate: 8 antidote 9 electuary 12 alexipharmic
mitigate: 4 balm, bate, cool, ease, tone 5 abate, allay, delay, mease(Sc.), relax, remit, slake 6 lessen, pacify, soften, temper 7 appease, assuage, mollify, qualify, relieve, sweeten 8 diminish, lenitive, moderate, palliate 9 alleviate, meliorate
mitt: mit 5 glove 6 mitten
mitten: 4 cuff, jilt, mitt 5 glove, hands
mittimus: 4 writ 6 notice 7 quietus, warrant 9 discharge, dismissal 10 magistrate
mittle: 4 hurt 8 mutilate
mix: pug 4 amix, fuse, join, meng, stir 5 admix, alloy, blend, cross, knead, merge, unite 6 jumble, mingle, muddle, wuzzle 7 blunder, confect, confuse, shuffle 8 coalesce, compound, confound 9 associate, commingle 10 amalgamate 11 incorporate, intermingle
with water: 5 slake 6 dilute, weaken
mix-up: 5 fight, melee 6 tangle 8 conflict 9 confusion
mixable: 8 miscible
mixed: 6 impure, motley 7 piebald 11 farraginous 13 heterogeneous 14 indiscriminate
mixed blood: See **hybrid**
person of: 5 metis 6 Baluga, Ladino, mestee, mustee 7 mestizo, metisse, mulatta, mulatto
mixed metaphor: 11 catachresis
mixen: 7 mixhill 8 dunghill
mixer: 5 party, paver 9 bartender
mixhill: 5 mixen 8 dunghill
mixture: 4 hash, mash, olio 6 batch, blend 6 medley 7 amalgam, compost, farrage, far-

rago, melange 8 blendure 9 admixture, potpourri 10 concoction, hodgepodge 11 composition 12 mingle-mangle

mizar star: 5 alcor

mizmaze: 9 confusion 12 bewilderment

mizzle: 4 mist, rain 5 misle 6 decamp 7 confuse, drizzle, speckle 9 disappear, misinform

mizzy: bog 8 quagmire

mnemonic: 8 memorial

Mnemosyne: 6 Memory

consort: 4 Zeus

daughters: 5 Muses

father: 6 Uranus

mo: 4 book 6 moment, volume

moa: 4 bird 6 ratite 8 dinornis 13 dinornithidae

moab: hat

Moab: *city:* Kir

descendant: 7 Moabite

famous woman: 4 Ruth

god: 7 Chemosh

king: 5 Eglon, Mesha

mountain: 4 Nebo

people: 5 Emims

moan: cry 4 sigh, wail 5 groan 6 bemoan, bewail, grieve, lament 7 deplore, whimper 8 complain 9 complaint 11 lamentation

as the wind: 4 sugh 5 sough

moat: 4 foss, lake, pond 5 ditch, fossa, fosse 6 trench

mob: set 4 crew, gang, herd, rout 5 cohue, crowd, drove, flock, group, volge 6 clique, masses, rabble 7 undress 9 multitude 10 dishabille, prostitute

member: 6 rioter

rule: 7 anarchy 8 violence

worship: 9 mobolatry

mobbish: 7 lawless 10 disorderly

mobile: mob 6 fickle, vision 7 movable 8 populace 9 wandering 10 changeable

moble: 4 wrap 6 muffle 8 movables 9 furniture

mobsman: 10 pickpocket

mobster: 8 gangster

Moby Dick: 5 whale

author: 8 Melville

character: Pip 6 Daggoo, Parsee 7 Ishmael

pursuer: 4 Ahab

moccasin: pac 4 pack, shoe 5 snake, tegua 6 loafer 7 slipper 8 larrigan 11 cottonmouth

moch: 4 moth

mocha: 6 coffee 7 leather

stone: 5 agate

mochy: 4 damp 5 misty, moist, muggy

mock: ape, bob, dor, gab 4 gibe, gird, jape, jeer, leer, sham 5 bourd, elude, false, fleer, flirt, flout, frump, hoker, mimic, scoff, sneer, taunt 6 banter, deride 7 deceive, grimace, imitate 8 ridicule 9 imitation 10 disappoint 11 counterfeit

brawn: 10 headcheese

cucumber: 5 apple

nightingale: 7 warbler 8 blackcap

orange: 7 seringa, syringa, syringe

ore: 10 sphalerite

plane: 8 sycamore

mocker: 4 bird 7 flauter 11 mockingbird

nut: 7 hickory

mockery: 5 bourd, farce, glaik, irony 6 satire 7 hething, sarcasm 8 futility, illusion, travesty 9 burlesque

mocking: 8 fleering

mockingbird: 8 imitator, songster

genus: 5 mimus

mod: 4 bold, free 6 modern 7 offbeat

mode: cut, fad 4 form, thew 5 modus, order, state, style, vogue 6 course, custom, fangle, manner, method, regime, system 7 fashion 10 convention

model: act, sit 4 form, mold, norm, plan, plot, pose, type 5 canon, ideal, shape 6 design, sitter 7 example, fashion, manikin, paragon, pattern, templet 8 ensample, exemplar, formular, fugleman, mannikin, paradigm, specimen, standard, template 9 archetype, construct, exemplary, facsimile, flugelman, mannequin, miniature, precedent, prototype

moderate: 4 bate, calm, ease, easy, even, meek, mild 5 abate, lower, slake, sober 6 ease-up, frugal, gentle, lessen, soften, temper 7 average, control 8 attemper, decrease, diminish 9 abstinent, alleviate, temperate 10 abstemious, reasonable 12 conservative 13 dispassionate

moderating: 9 remissive

moderation: 7 control 9 restraint 10 abstinence, diminution, governance, limitation, mitigation 11 restriction 13 temperateness

moderator: 6 umpire 7 arbiter 8 mediator

modern: new 4 late 6 latter, recent 8 neoteric

comb. form: ne; neo

modernize: 8 renovate

modest: coy, mim(Sc.), shy 4 deft, prim 5 douce, lowly 6 chaste, decent, demure, humble 7 bashful 8 decorous, maidenly, reserved, retiring, verecund, virtuous 9 diffident 10 unassuming 13 unpretentious

modicum: bit 6 amount 7 portion, soupcon

modify: 4 edit, tone, vary 5 alter, limit 6 change, master, temper 7 assuage, qualify 8 attemper, mitigate, moderate 9 influence

modish: 4 chic

modiste: 7 stylist 8 milliner 9 couturier 10 dressmaker
modulated: 5 toned 7 changed, intoned 8 softened, tempered 9 inflected, regulated
modulation: 9 inflexion 10 inflection
modus: way 5 means 6 manner, method
mog: jog 4 move, plod, walk 6 depart
moggan: leg 6 sleeve 8 stocking
moggy: cat, cow 4 calf 8 slattern 9 scarecrow
mogo: 7 hatchet
moguey: 4 moki, raft 5 mokhi
mogul: 4 lord 5 nabob, ruler, Tatar 6 Tartar 7 magnate 8 autocrat 9 Mongolian, personage 10 locomotive
capital: 4 Agra
emperor: 5 Akbar
moha: 6 millet
Mohammed: 7 Mahomet, Mahound 8 Muhammed
birthplace: 5 Mecca
daughter: 6 Fatima
descendant: Ali 5 Hasan 6 Hosein, Husain, She-rif 7 Ibrahim, She-reef
father: 8 Abdallah
flight from Mecca: 6 hegira, hejira
follower: 6 Wahabi 7 Wahabee, Wahabit, Wahhabi 8 Wahabite
horse: 7 Alborak
nephew: Ali
son-in-law: Ali
successor: 5 Calif 6 Caliph
title: 4 Iman
tomb: 6 Medina
uncle: 8 Abu-Talib
wife: 5 Aisha 6 Avesha, Ayesha 7 Khadija
Mohammedan: See **Muslim**
Mohammedanism: 5 Islam
moho: 4 bird, rail 9 gallinule
mohock: 6 attack 8 maltreat
mohr: 7 gazelle
moider: 4 toil 5 worry 6 bother, wander 7 perplex, smother 8 distract, encumber
moieter: 6 roller
moiety: 4 half, part 5 share 7 portion
moil: bar 4 mire, soil, spot, tire, toil 5 labor, taint, weary 6 defile, drudge 7 torment, trouble, turmoil 8 drudgery, vexation 9 confusion 10 defilement
moire: 7 watered
moise: 4 mend 6 thrive 7 improve
moist: 4 dank 5 humid, rainy 6 clammy 8 humorous
moisten: dew, dip, ret, wet 4 moil 5 bedew, leach 6 anoint, dabble, dampen, humect, humify, imbrue, sparge 8 irrigate, sprinkle 9 humectate
moisture: fog 4 bree(Sc.), drip, drop 5 humor, vapor, water 6 humour, liquid 8 aquosity, humidity
excess: 5 edema
remove: dry 4 wipe 5 wring 9 dehydrate
moisture-laden: 6 sodden
moistureless: dry 4 arid 6 burned 7 parched 8 scorched 10 desiccated
mojo: 4 Moxo 5 charm 6 amulet 7 majagua
mokaddam: 5 chief 7 headman
moke: fog, net 4 dolt, mesh, mist 5 horse 6 donkey 7 network 8 minstrel 9 performer
moki: 4 raft 9 trumpeter
moko: 9 tattooing
moko-moko: 6 lizard
mokum: 5 alloy
molar: 5 tooth 7 grinder 8 grinding
molarimeter: 11 thermometer
molasses: 5 syrup 7 claggum, treacle 8 theriaca 10 blackstrap
molave: 5 vitex
mold: die, fen 4 calm, cast, caum, core, form, mool, mull, must, soil 5 frame, humus, knead, model, mould, plasm, shape 6 coffin, matrix, mildew 7 fashion, matrice, moulage, pattern 9 ceroplast, character
opening: 6 ingate
part: 5 nowel, sprue
pert. to: 5 humic
pouring hole: 5 sprue
moldable: 7 fictile
Moldavia: *Rumania capital:* 4 Iasi
department: 4 Iasi 5 Jassy
measure: 7 faltche
molder: rot 5 decay 7 crumble
molding: ess 4 bead, beak, cima, cove, cyma, gula, ogee, reed, tore 5 angle, arris, conge, ogive, ovolo, splay, talon, thumb, torus 6 baguet, baston, fascia, fillet, listel, nebule, reglet, scotia 7 annulet, beading, cavetto, cornice, fingent, reeding, shaping 8 astragal, bageette, bezantee 9 trochilus
case: 5 chape
combination: 9 ledgement
concave: 4 gula 5 oxeye 7 cavetto
convex: 5 torus
curved: 4 ogee 6 nebule
flat: 6 fillet
ogee: 5 talon
pedestal: 7 surbase
rounded: 5 ovolo, torus 6 billet
rule for: 6 screed
moldy: 5 fusty, hoary, mucid, musty, stale 7 foughty 8 mildewed
mole: cob 4 cobb, pier, pile, quay 5 fault, jetty 6 anicut, burrow, rodent 7 annicut, barrier 8 excavate, starnose, tunneler 10 breakwater 12 imperfection
cricket: 9 churrworm
genus: 5 talpa
mole-like animal: 4 tape 6 desman
molecast: 8 molehill

molecule: *component:* 4 atom
gram: mol 4 mole
molehead: 8 pierhead
moleskin color: 5 taupe
molest: vex 5 annoy, tease 6 assail, bother, harass, pester 7 disturb, trouble 9 incommode, interfere 10 discommode
molge: 8 triturus
moliminous: 7 massive 9 laborious, momentous
moline: 8 millrind
molition: 6 device, effort 11 contrivance
molka: 10 cloudberry
moll: gal 5 wench 8 mistress 9 companion 10 prostitute
mollescent: 9 softening
mollhern: 5 heron
mollichop: 8 delicate
mollicrush: 4 beat, chop 9 pulverize
mollify: 4 bate, calm, ease 5 allay, relax, sleek 6 pacify, relent, soften, soothe, temper 7 amolish, appease, placate, sweeten 8 mitigate 9 attempter 10 conciliate
mollifying: 4 mild 9 demulcent
mollitious: 8 sensuous 9 softening, luxurious
molluscous: 6 flabby 9 spineless
mollusk: 5 snail, whelk 6 chiton, limpet 7 abalone 10 cuttlefish
bivalve: 4 leda, spat 5 chama 6 cockle, mussel, oyster 7 scallop
cephalopod: 8 argonaut
conical-shaped: 6 limpet
eight-armed: 7 octopus
fresh water: 7 etheria
gastropod: 4 slug 5 snail, whelk 7 abalone 12 taenioglossa
genus: 4 arca, leda(pl.) 5 eolis, ledum
group: 8 pteropod
large: 5 chama
larval: 7 veliger
marine: asi 4 welk 5 murex 7 abalone, scallop 8 nautilus
one shell: 5 snail 8 univalve
shell: 4 test 5 cowry, testa 6 cowrie, testae
shell concretion: 5 pearl
shell-less: 4 slug
teeth: 6 radula
ten-armed: 5 squid
used for bait: 5 squid 6 limpet
wrinkled shell: 6 cockle
young: 4 spat
molly: 4 moll 6 basket 7 milksop 9 mallemuck 11 mollycoddle
mollycoddle: 6 coddle, pamper
moloch: 6 lizard
molt: mew 4 cast, mute, shed 5 moult 8 exuviate
molten rock: 4 lava 5 magma
molting: 7 ecdysis
Molucca island: 5 Banda, Ceram 6 Maluku 7 Amboina 9 Halmahera
moly: 4 herb 6 garlic
molybdenum symbol: Mo
momble: 6 jumble, tangle
mome: 4 fool 5 clown 6 critic 7 buffoon 9 blockhead
moment: mo; sec 4 gird, hint, tick, tide, time 5 avail, braid, clink, filip, gliff, point, trice, value 6 fillip, minute, second, weight 7 instant 9 handwhile, twinkling 10 importance 11 consequence 13 signification
critical: 4 inch, nick 6 crisis, crises
particular: 4 then, when
momentary: 9 ephemeral, transient 10 transitory 13 instantaneous
momentous: 4 fell 5 grave 7 fateful, serious, weighty 8 eventful 9 important, ponderous 10 chargeable 11 influential
momentum: 5 force, power 7 impetus
momist: 5 momus
mommy: 4 duck 5 mammy 6 mother
momus: 6 critic, momist 8 ridicule 11 faultfinder
mon: 5 badge
monachist: 7 monkish
monad: 4 atom, unit 5 deity, henad 8 particle, zoospore
monarch: 4 csar, czar, tsar, tzar 5 ruler 6 despot, prince 7 dynasty, emperor 8 autocrat 9 butterfly, potentate, sovereign
monarchal: 5 regal, royal 8 imperial
monarda: tea 4 mint 5 plant 8 bergamot
monastery: 5 abbey, badia 6 friary, mandra, priory 7 convent, hospice, minster, nunnery 8 cloister, lamasery 9 sanctuary
Carthusian: 7 certosa
haircut: 7 tonsure
head: 5 abbot 7 hegumen
officer: 5 prior
room: 4 cell
superior: 5 prior
title: dom
monastic: 4 monk 5 friar 6 oblate 7 ascetic, monkish, recluse 8 abbatial, cenobite 9 cenobitic 10 conventual
monde: 5 globe, mound, world 6 circle 7 coterie, society
monetary: 9 financial, pecuniary
money (see also **bill, coin**): oof, tin, wad 4 bill, cash, coin, cush, dubs, dump, gelt, gilt, grig, jack, jake, kale, loot, lour, mina, moss, pelf 5 blunt, brass, bread, bunce, chink, clink, dough, funds, livre, lucre, maneh, rhino 6 argent, boodle, change, flimsy, hansel, mazuma, siller(Sc.),

spense, steven, wampum, wealth 7 chattel, handsel, lettuce, ooftish 8 currency 9 spondulix 10 spondulics
ancient: aes
blood: cro 7 breaghe
bag: 4 fels 6 follis, wealth 8 follicle
box: 4 arca, safe, till 5 chest 6 drawer 8 register
bribe: 6 boodle
broker: 7 changer
certificate: 5 scrip
changer: 5 saraf, seraf 6 shroff
chest for: 7 brazier
coinage: 4 mint
coined: 6 specie
counterfeit: 5 queer 6 boodle
cowrie: 6 shells
dealer: 6 broker
depreciation: 4 agio 9 inflation
earnest: 5 arles(Sc.), arrha 6 hansel 7 deposit, handsel 8 handgeld
gambler's: 6 barato
gate: 9 admission
gift: 4 alms 7 bequest, charity 9 endowment
given to lord: 6 farleu, farley
found: 5 trove 8 treasure
hearth: 6 fumage
held: 6 escrow
hole for: 4 slot
hook: 4 lari 5 larin 6 larree
lender: 6 banker, usurer 7 shylock 9 loanshark 10 pawnbroker
lots of: pot 4 heap, mint, pile
maker: 4 mint 7 moneyer
manual of exchange values: 7 cambist
metal: 4 coin 6 change, specie 7 coinage
overdue: 7 arrears
oversupply: 9 inflation
paid down: 4 cash 7 deposit 11 downpayment
paper: 4 bill, kale 6 flimsy 7 lettuce
premium: 4 agio
ready: 4 cash 5 asset, darby 9 alcontado(Sp.)
roll of coin: 7 rouleau
sent: 10 remittance
shell: 4 peag 5 cowry, peage, sewan, uhllo 6 cowrie, seawan
small amount: 4 mite 7 peanuts 11 chickenfeed
sorter: 6 teller 7 cashier
standard bank: 5 banco
transactions: 7 banking, finance
unit: ora, yen 4 lira, mark, mina, peso, real, tael 5 franc, krona, krone, maneh, pound, ruble, rupee 6 dollar, piatre, talent 7 drachma, guilder, milreis, piaster 8 cruzeiro
without: 4 poor 5 broke 11 impecunious
money of account: ora
money plant: 9 moneywort
moneyed: 4 rich 6 heeled 7 wealthy 8 affluent
moneyer: 6 banker, coiner, minter 13 counterfeiter
weight: 4 mite 5 blank, droit, perit
moneylender: 6 usurer 10 pawnbroker
mong: mix 5 crowd 6 barter, mingle 7 mixture, traffic 8 mingling 11 intercourse
monger: 6 dealer, trader
mongler: 9 sandpiper
Mongolia: *ass:* 8 chigetai
caravan leader: 5 bashi
city: 4 Urga 5 Kobdo 14 Ulan Bator Khoto
coin: 5 mungo 6 tugrik
conjurer: 6 shaman
conqueror: 9 Tamerland 11 Genghis Khan
desert: 4 Gobi
dynasty: 4 Yuan
fuel: 5 argal, argol, argul
measure: lan
monk: 4 lama
people: Hu; Lai, Rai 4 Garo, Lapp, Shan 5 Asian, Eleut, Tatar 6 Buriat, Tartar 7 Asiatic, Kalmuck, Khalkha 8 Annamese, Oriental 9 Mongoloid
priest: 6 shaman
province: 6 Chahar
religion: 9 Shamanism, Shintoism 12 Confucianism
river: Pei 4 Onon 5 Peiho
tent: 4 yurt
weight: lan
Mongoloid: See **Mongolia** *people*
mongoose: 4 urva 5 lemur 9 ichneumon
Kipling's jungle book: 14 Rikki-Tikki-Tavi
mongrel: cur, dog, mut 4 mutt 6 hybrid 7 bastard, piebald 9 sandpiper
whitefish: 8 tullibee
monial: nun
moniker: 4 name 5 alias 8 nickname
monish: 8 admonish
monition: 5 order 6 advice, notice 7 caution, summons, warning 8 citation 10 admonition, indication, intimation 11 instruction 13 animadversion
monitor: 4 ibid 6 lizard, mentor, nozzle 7 inciter 8 ironclad, reminder 9 catamaran 10 instigator
bug: 8 conenose
lizard: 4 uran 5 varan
monk: dom, fra 4 saki 5 clerk, friar, padre(Sp.) 7 devotee 8 anchoret, cenobite, monastic 9 anchorite, baldicoot, bullfinch, hieronach
Buddhist: bo 4 lama 5 arhat, goyim, yahan 6 bhikku 7 bhikshu, poongee 8 poonghee, poonghie, talapoin
cap: 5 kulah 6 kullah

Eastern Church: **7** caloyer, starets
haircut: **7** tonsure
hood: **4** cowl
Muslim: **7** dervish
Roman Catholic: **6** Culdee **8** Capuchin, Trappist
time in monastary: **9** monachate
monk's-head: **9** dandelion
monkey (see also **ape**): lar **4** fool, sime **5** burro **6** meddle, nisnas, simian, tamper, trifle **7** colobin **9** catarhina, catarhine **10** catarrhina, catarrhine
African: **4** waag **5** potto **6** grivet, vervet
American: **4** saki **5** acari **6** grison, miriki **7** ouakari **8** marmoset, orabassu **9** beelzebub
Asiatic: **4** douc **5** toque **6** langur **7** macaque
bearded: **8** entellus
beautiful: **7** guereza
bonnet: **4** zati
Callicebus: **5** yapok **6** yapock
capuchin: sai **7** sapajou
cebine: sai
Diana: **7** roloway
entellus: **7** hanuman **10** hoonoo-maun
genus of: **5** cebus **8** alouatta
god: **7** Hanuman
grivet: **4** tota
handsome: **4** mona
howling: **4** mono **5** araba **7** gauriba, stentor **8** alouatta
large: **5** sajou
long-tailed: sai **4** maha **5** patas **6** guenon, langur **7** hanuman **8** entellus, telapoin, wanderoo
macaque: **6** rhesus
proboscis: **4** kaha **7** noseape
purple-faced: **8** wanderoo
rhesus: **6** bandar
saki: **6** couxia, couxio
small: **4** titi **6** apelet, teetee **7** apeling **8** marmoset
spider: **6** ateles, coaita **9** belzebuth
squirrel: **6** samiri
tailless: ape
monkey bear: **5** koala
monkey bread: **6** baobab
monkey flower: **7** mimulus **8** toadflax
monkey-nut: **6** peanut
monkey pot: **5** fruit
monkey with: **6** meddle **9** interfere
monkey wrench: **7** spanner
monkeyboard: **9** footboard
monkeyshines: **6** antics, pranks, tricks **7** aperies
monkish: **7** ascetic **8** monastic
monkshood: **4** atis **5** atees **7** aconite **8** napellus
monoceros: **7** sawfish, unicorn **9** swordfish
monochord: **7** harmony, magadis **9** agreement, sonometer
monocle: **8** eyeglass
monocleid: **4** desk **7** cabinet
monocracy: **9** autocracy
monodist: **6** singer, writer **8** composer
monody: ode **4** poem, song **5** dirge **7** oration
monogram: **6** cipher, sketch **7** outline **8** initials **9** character
monolith: **6** menhir, pillar, statue **8** monument
monologue: **9** soliloquy
monomachy: **4** duel **6** combat
monomaniac: **5** crank **12** single-minded
monophone: **9** homophone
Monophysite: **4** Copt **8** Jacobite
monoplane: **5** Taube
monopole: **8** emporium, monopoly **11** combination
monopolize: **7** engross
monopoly: **5** grant, right, trust **6** cartel, corner **7** appalto, charter, control **9** privilege, syndicate
monosaccharide: ose **5** sugar
monostele: **8** prostele
monotonous: **4** dead, drab, dull, flat, same **6** dreary **7** humdrum, tedious, uniform **8** unvaried **9** wearisome **10** repetitive
monotony: **9** treadmill
monoxylon: **4** boat **5** canoe
monster (see also **beast**): **4** gowl, huge, ogre **5** bilsh, freak, giant, teras **6** geryon, sphinx **7** centaur, chimera, warlock
combining form: **5** terat **6** terato
fabled: **5** Argus, harpy **6** gorgon, sphinx **8** basilisk, Minotaur **9** bucentaur
female: **5** harpy **6** gorgon
fire-breathing: **6** dragon **7** chimera
handless: **8** acheirus
headless: **9** acephalus
human: **5** teras **6** terata
medical: **5** teras
nine-headed: **5** hydra
short-limbed: **9** nanomelus
study of: **10** teratology
two-bodied: **7** disomus
two-headed: **10** dicephalus
winged: **5** harpy
without hind limbs: api **4** apus
monster-like: **8** teratoid
monstrous: **4** huge, vast **5** enorm, large **7** hideous, immense, strange, titanic **8** colossal, deformed, enormous, flagrant, gigantic, horrible, shocking, **9** atrocious, unnatural **10** outrageous, prodigious, stupendous, tremendous **12** overpowering, overwhelming **13** extraordinary

Montana: *river:* Sun 4 Milk 5 Teton 6 Willow 7 Madison, Shields 8 Missouri 11 Yellowstone
town: 4 Kipp 5 Butte, Havre, Libby 6 Circle, Helena, Laurel 8 Anaconda, Billings, Browning, Glendive, Lewiston, Missoula 9 Kalispell
montant: 6 rising 8 mounting
montanto 5 sword 10 broadsword
Monte Cristo: *author:* 5 Dumas
hero: 6 Dantes
monteith: 4 bowl 12 handkerchief
Montenegro coin: 4 para 6 florin 7 perpera
montero: cap 6 ranger 8 forester, huntsman, mountain
Montezuma cypress: 9 ahuehuete
month: *comb. form:* 4 meno
excess of calendar over lunar: 5 epact
following: 7 proximo
half: 9 fortnight
preceding: 6 ultimo
present: 7 instant
monticule: 4 hill 5 mount 7 hillock 8 monticle, mountain
montilla: 6 sherry
Montmorency: 6 sherry
Montrachet: 8 Burgundy
monture: 5 horse, mount
monument: 4 tomb 5 cairn, relic, vault 6 bilith, effigy, hearse, menhir, record, statue 7 chaitya, chhatri, funeral 8 bilithon, cenotaph, cromlech, memorial, monolity 9 antiquity, sepulcher 10 gravestone
pillar-like: 5 stela, stele 6 stelae
moo: low 6 bellow
mooch: beg, bum 4 loaf 5 cadge, skulk, sneak, steal 6 loiter, pilfer, sponge 7 vagrant
moocha: 6 girdle
mood: tid(Sc.) 4 tune, vein, whim 5 freak, humor 6 humour, temper 7 caprice, feeling 10 atmosphere 11 disposition
assumed: 4 pose
recollection of past: 13 retrospection
moody: sad 4 glum 6 gloomy, grumpy, sullen 7 pensive 8 brooding 9 depressed 10 capricious 11 ill-tempered
mool: 4 bury, mold, soil 5 earth, grave 6 mingle 7 crumble
mools: 10 chilblains
moon: orb 4 Dian, Luna, lune(F.) 5 Diana, lunar 6 Phoebe 7 Cynthia, selenic 8 satelles, selenian 9 satellite
above: 10 superlunar
age at beginning of calendar year: 5 epact
apogee: 5 apsis
area on: 4 mare
aspect: 5 phase
astronaut: 6 Aldrin 9 Armstrong
combining form: 5 selen
crescent: 7 menisci 8 meniscus
crescent point: 4 cusp, horn 6 apogee 7 perigee
distance between apogee and perigee: 5 apsis
festival: 8 neomenia
first quarter: 8 crescent
geographer: 13 selenographer
god: Sin 6 Nannar
goddess: 4 Luna 5 Diana, Tanit 6 Hecate, Hekate, Salena, Selene, Tanith 7 Artemis, Astarte
inhabitant: 8 Selenite
instrument: 11 selenoscope
Jupiter's: Io
mock: 10 paraselene
new: 6 phasis
perigee: 5 apsis
pert. to: 5 lunar 7 selenic
phase: 7 horning
picture: 11 selenograph
position: 6 octant
spacecraft: 6 Apollo
Uranus': 5 Ariel
valley: 4 rill 5 cleft, rille
vehicle: LEM
moon fern: 8 moonwort
moon lily: 10 moonflower
moon-mad: 7 lunatic
moon-shaped: 6 lunate
half: 10 semilunate
moon valley: 5 rille
moonack: 9 woodchuck
moonbeam: ray
moonbill: 4 duck
mooncalf: 4 dolt, mole 7 monster 11 monstrosity
mooncreeper: 8 moonseed 10 moonflower
moondown: 7 moonset
mooned: 8 crescent
moonery: 7 madness
moonet: 9 satellite
moonfall: 7 moonset
moonfish: 4 opah 7 sunfish 9 spadefish
moonflower: 5 daisy, oxeye 6 achete
moonglow: 9 moonlight
moonish: 7 flighty 10 capricious
moonlighting: 4 raid 9 adventure 10 expedition 11 moonshining
moonman: 5 gipsy 6 robber
moonraking: 13 woolgathering
moonshine: 4 idle 5 empty, month, sauce 6 liquor 7 trivial, whiskey 8 nonsense 10 balsamweed
moonsick: 7 lunatic
moonstone: 10 hecatolite
Moonstone author: 7 Collins

moony: 5 round, silly 6 dreamy 8 listless
moor: bog, fen, fix 4 fell 5 heath, lande, marsh, swale, swamp 6 anchor, fasten, secure
Moor: 6 Berber, Moslem, Muslim 7 Bedouin, Othello, Saracen 8 Moroccan
moor blackbird: 5 ouzel
moor buzzard: 7 harrier
moor evil: 9 dysentery
moor game: 6 grouse 8 moorfowl
moor hawk: 7 harrier
moorage: 8 berthage 9 anchorage
moorbird: 6 grouse
moorburn: 7 quarrel 9 illtemper
moorcock: 6 grouse 9 blackcock
Moore character: 5 Lalla, Rookh
moorfowl: 6 grouse
moorhen: 4 coot 9 gallinule
Moorish: 8 Moresque
alcazar: 8 Alhambra
garment: 5 jupon 7 burnous 8 albornoz, burnoose
horse: 4 barb
judge: 4 cadi
kettledrum: 5 tabor 6 atabal
opiate: 4 kief
palace: 8 Alhambra
moorland: fen 5 moose
moose: elk 4 alce 5 eland
genus: 5 alces
mooseberry: 10 hobblebush
moot: dig 4 grub, plea, root, tell 5 argue, plead, speak 6 debate 7 discuss, meeting 8 argument, assembly, complain, disputed 9 debatable, encounter, gathering, undecided 10 discussion, litigation
mooth: wet 4 damp 5 misty
mop: 4 pout, swab, wash, wipe 5 bunch, clean 6 merkin, moppet, scovel 7 cleanse, grimace
mope: 4 pout, sulk 5 brood
mopish: 6 gloomy 7 foolish 8 confused
moppet: tot 4 baby, doll, tike 5 child 7 darling, toddler 9 youngster
mopsy: son 6 moppet 8 slattern
moquette: 6 carpet 10 upholstery
mora: 5 delay, stool 7 default 9 footstool 12 postponement
mora tree: 6 fustic
moral: 4 good, pure 5 ethic 7 dutiful, epimyth, ethical, upright 8 priggish, virtuous 9 honorable, righteous
fable: 8 apologue
failure: sin
law: 9 Decalogue
teaching: 5 maxim 7 precept 8 apologue 9 preaching 10 preachment 11 edification
morale: 4 hope, mood, zeal 6 spirit 8 morality 9 condition 10 confidence
morals: 6 ethics
description: 10 ethography
morass: bog, fen 4 flow, quag 5 flush, marsh, swamp 8 quagmire
morass weed: 8 hornwort
moration: 5 delay
Moravian city: 4 Brno, Zlin 5 Brunn
moray: eel 6 conger, hamlet 7 muraena
morbid: 4 sick 6 grisly 8 diseased, gruesome, horrible 9 debatable unhealthy 11 unwholesome 12 apprehensive, pathological
morbilli: 7 measles
morbus: 7 disease, illness
mordant: 4 keen 5 sharp 6 biting 7 burning, caustic, pungent 8 scathing 9 corrosive, sarcastic
more: piu 4 also, mair, plus 5 again, extra 6 custom, manner 7 folkway, further, greater 10 additional, convention
or less: 4 some
than: 4 over 5 above
than enough: too 9 excessive
than one: few 4 many 6 couple, plural 7 several
than this: yea
More opus: 6 Utopia
morel: 8 mushroom 10 nightshade
morena: 8 brunette
moreover: and 4 also, then 5 again 7 besides, further 8 likewise 11 furthermore
morepork: 4 peho, ruru 7 boobook
morgay: 7 dogfish
morglay: 5 sword
morgue: 8 mortuary 9 deadhouse, stolidity 11 haughtiness, impassivity
moribund: 5 dying 6 effete 8 decadent, decaying 10 acherontic, terminated
morindin dye: al
morinel: 8 dotterel
moringa oil: ben
morion: 6 helmet, quartz 8 cabasset
mormo: 7 bugbear 10 shemonster
Mormon: 6 Danite 8 mandrill
brothers: 7 Danites
emblem: bee
founder: 5 Smith
officer: 5 elder
priesthood: 7 Aaronic 11 Melchizedek
prophet: 6 Moroni
Mormon State: 4 Utah
Mormonweed: 6 flower, mallow
morning: 4 dawn, morn 5 matin 6 aurora 7 sunrise
concert: 6 aubade
coat: 7 cutaway
performance: 7 matinee
pert. to: 5 matin, wight 7 matinal 9 matutinal
prayer: 5 matin 6 matins

reception: 5 levee
morning glory: nil 7 gaybine, ipomoea
family: 14 convolvulaceae
morning star: 4 Mars 5 Venus 6 Saturn 7 Daystar, Jupiter, Lucifer, Mercury
moro: 5 finch
Moro: *chief:* 4 Dato 5 Datto
dialect: 4 Sulu
island: 8 Mindanao
knife: 6 barong
people: 4 Sulu 5 Lanao, Yakan
priest: 4 atli 5 sarip
sailboat: 5 vapit
morocco: 7 leather
imitation: 4 roan
Morocco: *cape:* Nun
city (see also *port* below): Fez 4 Assa 5 Rabat 6 Rabbat 7 Morocco 9 Marrakech
coin: 4 okia, rial 5 okieh 8 mouzouna
district: Sus 4 Riff
emperor: 9 Miramolin 11 Miramomolin
government: 7 Maghzen, Makhzan, Machzen
hat: fez
island: 7 Madeira
Jews' quarter: 8 El Millah
measure: 4 sahh 6 fanega, tomini
military expedition: 5 harka
mountain: Rif
people: 4 Moor 6 Berber, Kabyle, Moslem, Muslim 7 Maghzen, Makhzan, Makhzen
port: 5 Ceuta, Rabat 6 Agadir, Rabbat, Tetuan 7 Mogador, Tangier 8 El Araish, Laraiche 10 Casablanca
ruler: 6 she-rif, sultan 7 she-reef
soldier: 5 askar
tree: 4 arar 5 argan 6 alerse 8 sandarac
weight: 4 rotl 5 artal, artel, gerbe, ratel 6 dirhem, kintar 7 quintal
morology: 5 folly 8 nonsense
moron: 4 dull, fool 5 ament 6 stupid 7 dullard 8 imbecile, sluggish
moronic: 4 dull 6 stupid 7 idiotic 8 sluggish
morose: 4 dour, glum, grum, sour 5 gruff, moody, sulky, surly 6 crusty, gloomy, sullen 7 crabbed, clumpse, clumpst, crooked, unhappy 8 strounge 9 splenetic 10 embittered, ill-humored
moroseness: 8 asperity
morphia: 8 morphine
morphine derivative: 6 heroin
morro: 4 hill 5 bluff, point 6 castle 8 headland
Mors: 5 death
morse: 5 clasp 6 brooch, walrus
Morse code signal: dit, dah
morsel: bit, ort 4 bite, snap 5 crumb, piece, scrap, snack 6 tidbit, titbit 7 morceau, rarebit 8 fragment
morsing: 7 priming
morsure: 4 bite 6 biting
mort: 4 dead, lard 5 death, fatal 6 deadly, grease, salmon 9 abundance
mortacious: 4 very 9 extremely
mortal: 4 dire 5 being, fatal, human 6 deadly, lethal 7 capital, deathly, fleshly 8 grievous 9 extremely 10 implacable 11 destructive
mortar: 5 compo, putty 6 cannon, cement, holmos, petard 7 perrier
carrier: hod
mixer: rab
tray: hod
mortarboard: cap 4 hawk
Morte d'Arthur author: 6 Malory
mortgage: 4 bond, deed, lien 5 trust 6 pledge, wadset(Sc.) 11 encumbrance
giver: 6 lienee
receiver: 6 lienor
mortician: 10 undertaker
mortification: 5 shame 7 chagrin 8 gangrene, necrosis, vexation 11 humiliation 13 embarrassment
mortified: 10 sphacelate
mortify: 5 abase, abash, spite 6 ashame, humble, offend 7 crucify
mortifying: 11 ignominious
mortise: 6 cocket
complement of: 5 tenon
law: 8 amortize
machine: 7 slotter
mortuary: 4 gift 6 morgue 7 funeral 9 deadhouse, lich-house, sepulcher
car: 6 hearse
morvin: 7 mallein
mosaic: 5 tiled, tiles
formed like a: 10 tesselated
mosaic gold: 6 ormolu
piece: 7 tessera
moschate: 5 musky
Moscow citadel: 7 Kremlin
Moses: 6 leader 8 lawgiver
brother: 5 Aaron
emissary: 5 Caleb
father: 5 Amram
father-in-law: 6 Jethro
law: 4 Tora 5 Torah 10 Pentateuch
mother: 8 Jochebed
mountain: 4 Nebo
sister: 6 Miriam
son: 7 Eliezer, Gershom
successor: 6 Joshua
wife: 8 Zipporah
mosey: 4 mosy 5 amble 6 depart, ramble, stroll, wander 7 shuffle
mosker: 5 decay 6 molder

Moslem (see also **Muslim**): 7 Islamic, Saracen 9 Moslemite, Mussulman 10 Mohammedan
mosque: 4 jami, mosk 5 Caaba, Kaaba 6 church, dargah, durgah, Kaabeh, Kiblah, masjid, shrine, temple
official: 4 imam 5 imaum
student: 5 softa
tower: 7 manarat, minaret 8 minarete
warden: 5 nazir
mosquito: 5 aedes 7 culicid 11 gallinipper
genus of: 5 aedes, Culex 9 Anopheles
killer: 8 culicide
larvae: 8 wigglers
mosquito bee: 5 karbi 8 angelito
mosquito boat: P.T.
mosquito fish: 8 gambusia
mosquito hawk: 9 dragonfly, nighthawk
mosquito plant: 4 mint 10 pennyroyal
Mosquito State: 6 Jersey
moss: bog, fog, rag 5 swamp, usnea 6 lichen, morass 9 bryophyte, treebeard
animalcule: 8 bryozoan
club: 7 lycoped
edible: 4 agar 8 agaragar
like: 7 hepatic
moss cheeper: 5 pipit 7 bunting
moss coral: 8 bryozoan
moss corn: 10 silverweed
moss duck: 7 mallard
moss fruit: 11 sporogonium
moss-grown: 10 antiquated 12 old-fashioned
moss hammer: 7 bittern
moss polyp: 8 bryozoan
moss-trouper: 6 raider 8 marauder
mossback: 4 fogy 5 fogey
mossberry: 9 cranberry
mossbunker: 8 menhaden
mosshead: 9 merganser
mosswort: 9 bryophyte
mossy: 4 dull 5 baggy, downy, green, hoary 6 marshy, stupid 7 covered 9 abounding, overgrown
most: 4 best 5 chief 6 utmost 7 maximum 8 majority 9 principal
mostly: 6 feckly
mot: 4 butt, mark, moat, word 5 motto, piece 6 device 7 epigram, opinion
mote: dot, may 4 atom, hill, iota 5 atomy, match, might, speck, squib, stalk, straw 6 barrow, fescue, height, trifle 7 tumulus 8 eminence, particle
motel: inn 5 hotel
motet: 4 song 6 anthem 11 composition 12 contrapuntal
moth: io 5 tinea 6 bogong, lappet, mallet, miller, tineah, tinean, tineid 7 tineina 8 chloasma, forester 11 yellowshell
family: 7 arctiid, tineina 9 arctiidae
genus of: 5 sesia
larva: 11 caterpillar
spot: 8 chloasma, fenestra
suborder: 10 heterocera
moth-eaten: 4 worn 7 decayed 8 decrepit, out-dated
moth hawk: 10 goatsucker
moth hunter: 10 goatsucker
mother: dam 4 dame, womb 5 adopt, dregs, mamma, mater(L.), nurse 6 foster, matron, native, origin, parent, patron 7 nurture 8 genetrix 10 ancestress
comb. form: 5 matri
of believers: 5 Aisha 6 Ayesha
of gods: 4 Rhea 9 Brigantia
of Gracchi: 8 Cornelia
of Graces: 5 Aegle
of man: 6 Cybele
of months: 4 moon
of presidents: 8 Virginia
of sorrows: 4 Mary 6 Virgin
of states: 8 Virginia
one delivery: 7 unipara
related on side of: 6 enatic
spiritual: 4 amma
three deliveries: 7 tripara
two deliveries: 6 bipara
Mother Carey's chicken: 6 petrel
Mother Carey's goose: 6 fulmar
Mother Carey's hen: 6 petrel
mother gate: 4 bord 7 tramway
Mother Hubbard: 4 gown 5 dress
mother-in-law: 9 eldmother
mother of coal: 8 charcoal
mother of pearl: 5 nacre
mother superior: 6 abbess
mother's mark: 9 birthmark
mothered: 5 thick 6 viscid
motherland: 4 home 10 fatherland
motherly: 8 maternal
motion (see also **bodily motion**): 4 fard, idea, move 5 faird 6 unrest 7 gesture, impulse, propose, request, suggest 8 movement, petition, proposal 10 suggestion 11 application, inclination 13 gesticulation
circular: 4 gyre 10 revolution
convulsive: 11 vellication
due to: 7 kinetic
expressive: 7 gesture
impetuous: 6 bensel, bensil 7 bensail, bensall, bensell
pert. to: 7 kinetic 9 kinematic 11 kinematical
producing: 6 motile
quality: 8 momentum
rate: R.P.M. 4 time 5 speed, tempo 11 steerageway
science: 10 ballistics, kinematics

transmitter: cog 4 belt, gear
upward: 5 scend 8 upthrust
motion picture: 4 film, show 5 flick, movie, talky 6 cinema 7 flicker 9 photoplay
arc lamp: 5 kleig, klieg
award: 5 Oscar
cowboy & Indian: 7 Western
machine: 9 projector 11 kinetoscope 12 animatograph, theatrograph 13 cinematograph 14 cinematographe
outline: 6 script 8 scenario
pert. to: 9 cinematic
play: 5 movie 6 cinema 9 photoplay
prize: 5 Oscar
term: pan 4 shot, take 6 retake 7 reverse
motionless: 4 dead 5 inert, rigid, still 6 asleep 8 becalmed, immobile, stagnant, stagnate, stirless 9 quiescent, sedentary 10 breathless
motivate: 4 move 5 impel 6 incite, induce 7 inspire 9 influence, instigate, stimulate
motive: 4 sake, spur 5 cause 6 object, reason 7 impulse, purpose 8 pressure, stimulus 9 incentive, objective 13 consideration
ostensible: 7 pretext
motley: 4 fool 5 mixed 6 jester 7 diverse, mottled, piebald 9 checkered 10 variegated 13 heterogeneous
man of: 4 fool 6 jester 7 Pierrot
motmot: 4 bird
motor: car 4 auto, ride 6 engine 7 kinetic, machine 8 motorcar 10 automobile
electric: 6 dynamo
hand-powered: 9 baromotor
part: cam 4 coil 5 rotor 6 piston, stator 9 capacitor 10 carburetor
rotary: 7 turbine
motor-bike: 10 motorcycle
motor-boat: 8 palander
motor court: inn 5 motel
motor speed control: 8 rheocrat
motorman: 8 engineer, operator
motte: 5 grove
mottled: 4 pied, roed 5 pinto 6 motley 7 brocked, clouded, dappled, piebald, spotted 8 blotched 10 variegated 11 varicolored
motto: mot 4 word 5 adage, axiom, gnome, maxim 6 device, saying 7 empresa, precept 8 aphorism 10 shibboleth
mouche: 5 patch
mouchoir: 12 handkerchief
moue: 4 face, pout 7 grimace
mouflon, moufflon: 5 sheep
mould: See **mold**
moulding: See **molding**
moulrush: 7 pollack
moult: See **molt**
moulting: See **molting**
mound: ahu, cop, dam, dun, tee 4 balk, bank, butt, denc, dher, doon, dune, heap, hill, hump, pile, terp 5 agger, berry, cairn, dheri, globe, huaca, knoll, stack, toman(-Scot.) 6 barrow, bounds, burrow, causey 7 bourock, bulwark, hornito, rampart, tumulus 8 boundary 9 elevation 10 embankment
pert. to: 7 tumular
prehistoric: 4 terp
mound bird: 8 megapode
Mound City: 7 St. Louis
mound of light: 8 kohinoor
mount: 4 glue, hill, pony, rise 5 arise, climb, horse, paste, steed 6 ascend, aspire 8 escalate, increase, mountain 10 promontory 13 fortification
by ladder: 8 escalade
horizontal bar: kip
two-legged: 5 bipod
Mount Etna city: 7 Catania
Mount Everest peak: 6 Lhotse
Mount Helicon fountain: 8 Aganippe
Mount Ida nymph: 6 Oenone
Mount of Olives: 6 Olivet
Mount Parnassus fountain: 8 Castalia
Mount Rainier: 6 Tacoma
mountain (see also **peak**): ben(Scot.), kop 4 berg, dagh, fell, mont(F.) 5 onlay 6 barrow, bundoc 8 bundocks
base of: 8 piedmont
beyond: 10 tramontane 11 transalpine
Biblical: See **Bible:** *mountain*
burning: 7 volcano
combining form: oro 4 oreo
depression: col
devil: 6 moloch
formation: 7 orogeny 9 orogenesy 10 orogenesis
gap: see *pass* below
highest: 7 Everest
lake: 4 tarn
low: 5 butte
mythical: Kaf, Qaf 4 Meru 5 candy, glass 7 Helicon 9 Parnassus
nymph: 5 dryad, oread
pass: col, gap 4 cove, duar, gate, ghat 5 ghaut, gorge, kotal 6 defile
pasture: alp 6 saeter
pert. to: 10 orological
range: 4 Alps, Ghat, Ural 5 Andes, chain, Coast, ridge, Rocky, Teton, White 6 Alatau 7 Rockies, Sierras 8 Cascades, Catskill, Pyrenees 9 Allegheny, Blue Ridge, Himalayas 10 San Jacinto 11 Appalachian, San Gorgonio
ridge: 4 aret, peak, spur 5 arete, crest 6 sierra, summit 7 sawbuck
rocky: 7 nunatak

science: 7 orology
sickness: 4 veta 7 soroche
snow: 5 jokul
study: 7 orology 9 orography
sunset reflection: 9 alpenglow
trail marker: 5 cairn
mountain andromeda: 10 fetterbush
mountain ash: 4 sorb 5 rowan, rowen
mountain badger: 6 marmot
mountain balsam: fir
mountain banana: fei
mountain barometer: 8 orometer
mountain beaver: 8 sewellel
mountain bluet: 8 centaury
mountain cat: 4 lynx 6 bobcat, cougar 10 cacomistle
mountain climber: 10 alpestrian
equipment: 4 rope 5 piton
mountain climbing: 8 alpinism
peg: 5 piton
mountain cock: 12 capercaillie
mountain curassow: 10 oreophasis
mountain dew: 7 bootleg, whiskey 9 moonshine
mountain duck: 9 harlequin, sheldrake
mountain finch: 9 brambling
mountain flax: 8 centaury
mountain fringe: 8 fumitory, wormwood
mountain goat: 4 ibex
mountain ivy: 6 laurel
mountain leather: 12 palygorskite
mountain lion: 6 cougar
mountain magpie: 10 woodpecker 11 butcher-bird
mountain mint: 5 basil 8 calamint
mountain oak: 8 chestnut
mountain panther: 5 ounce 6 cougar 7 leopard
mountain parrot: kea
mountain partridge: 4 dove 5 quail
mountain pheasant: 6 grouse
mountain quail: 9 partridge
mountain raspberry: 10 cloudberry
mountain rose: 6 laurel
mountain snow: 4 neve
mountain spinach: 5 orach 6 orache
Mountain State: 7 Montana
Mountain States: 4 Utah 5 Idaho 6 Nevada 7 Arizona, Montana, Wyoming 8 Colorado 9 New Mexico
mountain tea: 11 wintergreen
mountaineer: 5 Aaron 7 climber, hillman 9 hillbilly
song: 5 yodel
mountainlike: 7 etiolin
mountainous: 4 high 5 alpen 6 alpine, rugged 8 elevated 10 alpestrine
mountaintop: 4 cone, peak 6 summit
mountebank: 4 gull 5 cheat, quack 7 empiric 8 impostor, minstrel 9 charlatan, pretender
aid: 4 zany
mounting: 7 setting 9 equipment 13 embellishment
mounting horizontal bar method: kip
moup: 6 nibble 9 associate
mourn: rue 4 dole, erme, long, sigh, wail, weep 6 bemoan, bewail, grieve, lament, murmur, sorrow 7 deplore 8 mourning
mournful: sad 5 black 6 woeful 7 doleful, elegiac, pitiful 8 funereal 9 elegiacal, plaintive, sorrowful, threnodic, woebegone 10 lamentable, lugubrious, melancholy 11 distressing
mourning: 4 garb 5 dolor 6 dolour 7 drapery
bride: 5 plant 8 scabious
dress: 5 black, crape, weeds 6 sables
group: 7 cortege
song: 5 dirge
mouse: erd, pry 4 girl, hunt, knot 6 bruise, rodent 8 black-eye
comb. form: mys
field: 4 vole 7 harvest
leaping: 6 jerboa
male: 4 buck
meadow: 5 voles
milk: 6 spurge
pert. to: 6 murine
mouse deer: 10 chevrotain
mouse-ear: 8 hawkweed 9 chickweed
mouse hare: 4 pika
mousebird: 4 coly 6 shrike
mouselike: shy 4 drab 5 mousy, quiet, timid 6 murine 8 retiring
mouser: cat 8 detective
mouseweb: 6 cobweb 8 gossamer
mousing: 6 prying 7 binding 8 prowling 9 rapacious 11 inquisitive
mousle: 6 rumple
mousse: 7 dessert, mossboy
mousy: 4 drab 5 quiet, timid
moutan: 5 peony, plant 6 flower
mouth: os; gab, gan, gob, mow, mug, mun, ora 4 boca(Sp.), dupe 5 front, stoma 6 cavity, gebbie(Sc.), mumble, rictus 7 flummer, opening, stomata 8 entrance 9 impudence
away from: 6 aborad, aboral
combining form: ori 5 stome
deformity: 7 harelip
disease: 4 noma 6 canker 10 stomatitis
muscle: 7 caninus
of furnace: 5 bocca
of river: 5 delta, firth
part: lip 5 uvula 6 palate 7 pharynx
pert. to: 4 oral 6 rictal 7 oscular, palatal 8 stomatic
projecting: 5 spout

roof: 6 palate
tissue: gum
toward: 4 orad
with open: 5 agape
mouth organ: 9 harmonica
mouth-watering: 8 alluring 9 delicious
mouthful: lot, sup 4 bite, gulp 6 gobbet
mouthpiece: 5 bocal 6 lawyer 8 attorney
mouthwash: 9 collutory 11 collutorium
mouthy: 9 bombastic, talkative
mouton: fur, spy 4 wool 9 sheepskin
movable: 5 loose 6 fickle, mobile, motile 8 exorable, floating 10 changeable, inconstant 11 ephelcystic 12 figuratively
move (see also **go**): go; act, gee, mog 4 goad, pass, play, spur, stir 5 budge, cause, clink, impel, rouse, shift, start, sweep 6 affect, arouse, bestir, betake, excite, incite, induce, kindle, motion, prompt, quetch, remble, remove 7 actuate, advance, agitate, animate, inspire, migrate, propose, provoke, suggest 8 converse, emigrate, maneuver, motivate, transfer 9 influence, instigate, stimulate
along: mog 5 mosey, scram 7 maunder
away: shy 8 emigrate
back: ebb 6 recede 7 retreat
back and forth: wag 4 flap, rock, tack 5 dodge, weave 6 falter, teeter, wabble, wiggle, wigwag, zigzag 7 shuttle 9 oscillate
false: 4 balk 5 feint 7 misstep
first: 10 initiative
forward: 4 edge 5 drive, forge, surge 7 advance 8 progress
furtively: 5 skulk, slink, sneak
heaven and earth: try 6 strive
heavily: lug 6 lumber, trudge
in: 6 occupy 7 inhabit
in water: 4 swim, wade
inwardly: 6 enmove
noiselessly: 4 slip 5 creep, glide, skulk, slink, sneak, steal 6 tiptoe 9 pussyfoot
noisily: 6 bustle 7 clatter, rollick
obliquely: 4 edge, joll, skew, slue 5 sidle
on wheels: 4 roll 7 trundle
quickly: fly 4 dart, dash, flit, jump, leap, race, scud, scur, whir 5 bound, hurry, scoot, skirr, spank, sweep, start 6 career, gallop, hurtle, scurry, spring
restlessly: 6 kelter, twitch
rhythmically: bob, jig, jog 5 dance, march
round and round: 4 eddy 5 swirl, twirl
sinuously: 5 snake 6 writhe
slowly: lag, mog 4 edge, inch, worm 5 crawl 6 trudge 7 crowhop
smoothly: 4 slip 5 glide, skate, slide
together: 5 unite 8 converge
moveless: See **immovable**
movement: 5 tempo, trend 6 rhythm
biological: 5 taxis
capable of: 6 mobile, motile
music: 4 moto
surface 6 seiche
movie: See **motion picture**
moving: 7 current 8 ambulant, pathetic, poignant, touching 9 transient 10 ambulatory
moving about: 8 ambulant 10 ambulatory
moving part: cam, cog 5 rotor, wheel
moving picture: See **motion picture**
moving staircase: 9 escalator
mow: bin, cut, lay, mew 4 barb, clip, goaf, heap, mass, math, pile, rick 5 mouth, stack 6 scythe, sickle 7 grimace 8 haystack 9 cornfield
mowana: 6 baobab
mowed strip: 5 swath 6 swathe
Mowgli: *elephant:* 5 Hathi
friend: 5 Akela, Baloo
mowie: 9 stackyard
mowing: 7 mockery 8 derision 10 meadowland
mowland: 6 mowlot 10 meadowland
mowth: 6 mowing
moxie berry: 9 snowberry
moy: 4 mild 6 demure, gentle 8 affected
moyen: way 5 means 6 agency, course 8 property 9 influence, substance
Mozambique native: Yao
Mozart opera: 6 Figaro
mubarat: 7 divorce
mucago: 5 mucus 7 coating 8 mucilage
much: 4 fele, high, lots, many 5 great, heaps, scads 6 mickle 7 gaylies, geylies, greatly 8 abundant, uncommon 9 multitude
comb. form: 4 poly 5 multi
music: 5 molto
Much Ado About Nothing character: 4 Hero 6 Ursula 7 Antonio, Claudio, Leonato
mucid: 5 moldy, musty, slimy 6 mucous
mucilage: gum 5 paste 6 arabin, mucago 8 adhesive
mucilaginous: 5 gluey, slimy 6 sticky, viscid 8 adhesive
muck: 4 dirt, dung, mess 5 filth, money, slime, waste 6 manure, refuse, wealth
muckle: 4 fret 6 bother
mucoid: See **mucous**
mucor: 9 hoariness, moldiness 10 filthiness
mucous: 5 moist, slimy 6 mucoid 7 viscous 8 blennoid, muculent
mud fen 4 dirt, glar, gore, mire, ooze, slob, slud 5 glaur, gumbo, slime, slush, waise 6 sludge 7 clabber, sludder, sluther 12 offscourings
deposit: 4 silt
hole: pan 6 puddle, wallow 8 quagmire

living in: 10 limicolous
pert. to: 7 luteous
mud bath: 10 illutation
mud dab: 8 flounder
mud dabbler: 9 killfish
mud dauber: 4 wasp
mud devil: 10 hellbender
mud eel: 5 siren
mud lark: 5 gamin 6 magpie, urchin 8 shoveler 10 meadowlark
mud mark: 7 mudflow
mud peep: 9 sandpiper
mud puppy: 10 hellbender, salamander
mud snipe: 8 woodcock
mud sunfish: 4 bass 8 warmouth
mud volcano: 5 salse
mudar: 6 yercum
Mudcat State: 11 Mississippi
muddle: mix 4 ball, daze, doze, mess 5 addle, besot, snafu 6 bemuse, burble, fuddle, jumble, pother 7 bedevil, blunder, confuse, fluster, mystify, perplex, stupefy 8 befuddle, bemuddle, bewilder, confound, disorder, flounder 9 confusion 10 intoxicate 12 hugger-mugger
muddled: ree 4 asea 5 beery, crazy, drunk, foggy, tipsy
muddy: 4 miry, roil 5 dirty, drovy, druvy, slaky, vague 6 claggy, clarty, clashy, cloudy, drubly, lutose, sludgy, slushy, turbid 7 clouded, guttery, obscure, sensual 8 confused, feculent 9 besmeared, spattered 11 bespattered
mudfish: 6 bowfin
mudhold: 4 slew, sloo, slue 6 slough
mudworm: ipo 9 earthworm
mudwort: 7 mudweed
muezzin's call to prayer: 4 adan, azan
muff: fur, vex 4 flub 5 crest, error 6 bungle, warmer 8 irritate
muffet: 5 mufty, muggy 11 whitethroat
muffetee: 7 muffler, wrister 8 wristlet
muffin: cob, gem 5 bread, scone 7 crumpet, popover
muffle: gag 4 damp, dull, mute, wrap 6 bumble, dampen, deaden, shroud 7 silence 8 envelope 10 camouflage
muffled: 6 hollow
muffler: 4 mute 5 scarf 6 tippet 8 silencer
mufflin: 8 titmouse
mufti: 4 alim 8 assessor, civilian, clothing, official 9 expounder
mufty: See **muffet**
mug: cup 4 cram, dupe, face, fool, toby 5 mouth, mungo, pulse, sheep, stein, study 6 noggin, seidel 7 assault, canette, drizzle, goddard, grimace, tankard 8 schooner 10 photograph
muga: 11 caterpillar
mugger: goa 4 thug 6 tinker 7 peddler, puncher 9 crocodile
mugget: 6 mugwet 8 woodruff
muggins: 4 dupe, fool, game 9 simpleton
muggy (see also **muffet**): 4 damp, fozy 5 humid, moist, moldy
mughouse: 8 alehouse, pothouse
mugweed: 7 mugwort
mugwet: 8 woodruff
muir: 4 moor
mulatto: 5 metis
mulberry bird: 8 starling
mulberry family: 8 Moraceae
mulberry fig: 8 sycamore
mulberry tree: 4 more
mulch: 5 cover, straw 6 litter 7 compost, sawdust
mulct: 4 balk, fine, scot 5 cheat 6 amerce, defect, fleece, punish 7 blemish, deceive, defraud, forfeit, penalty 8 penalize 10 amercement, forfeiture
mule: 4 mewl, mool, mute 5 coble, hinny 6 hybrid 7 bat-mule, slipper, tractor 9 chilblain 10 locomotive
cry: 4 bray 6 heehaw
driver: See **muleteer**
group: 5 atajo, drove
leader in pack train: 8 cencerro
male: 4 jack
spinning: 7 ironman
untrained: 9 shavetail
mule killer: 6 mantis
muleteer: 4 peon 6 driver 7 arriero(Sp.), skinner 9 almocrebe
mulga: 6 shield, wattle
mulish: 5 balky 6 hybrid, sullen 7 sterile 8 perverse, stubborn 9 obstinate, pigheaded 10 determined
mull: cow 4 crag, dust, heat, mess, mold, muse 5 cloth, crush, grind, snout, spice, think 6 fettle, muslin, muzzle, ponder, powder 7 crumble, failure, rubbish, squeeze, sweeten 8 cogitate, consider, ointment, snuffbox 9 pulverize 10 promontory
mullein: 5 torch 6 agleaf 8 hagtaper 9 torchwort 10 hare's-beard
mullet: 4 bobo, liza 6 harder, puffin
mullet hawk: 6 osprey
mulligan: 4 stew
mulligatawny: 4 soup
mulligrubs: 5 blues, colic, sulks
mullock: 4 dirt 6 litter, refuse 7 rubbish
mulloway: 7 jewfish
mulmul: 6 muslin
multicolored: 4 pied 6 calico 7 dappled, spotted
multifarious: 7 diverse 8 manifold
multifold: 4 many 8 manifold, numerous
multiform: 7 diverse

multiple: 4 many 6 plural 8 numerous
multiplier: 7 facient
multiply: 5 breed 6 spread 7 amplify, augment, magnify 8 increase 9 reproduce
by eight: 11 octuplicate
by ten: 7 decuple
multitude: mob 4 army, heap, hive, host, many, mass, much, ruck 5 crowd, drove, flock, horde, shoal, swarm 6 legion, myriad, nation, throng
multitudinous: 8 manifold, numerous
mum ale 4 beer, dark 5 still 6 mother, silent 7 silence 9 voiceless 10 speechless 13 chrysanthemum
mumble 4 chew, mump 5 mouth 6 chavel, chavle, faffle, fumble, haffle, murmur, mutter, palter, patter 7 flummer, grumble
mumbo-jumbo: 4 idol 6 fetich, fetish 7 bugaboo
mummer: 4 mime 5 actor 6 guiser, player 7 buffoon 9 performer, puppeteer
mummery: 6 acting 8 puppetry 9 hypocrisy
mummy: 5 relic 6 corpse 7 cadaver, carcass
mummy apple: 6 papaya
mump: 5 cheat, sulks 6 mumble, mutter 7 grimace 10 sullenness 11 displeasure
mumper: 6 beggar 8 impostor
mumps: 5 brank
mumruffin: 8 titmouse
mun: it; him, may 4 face, must, them 5 mouth, shall
munch: eat 4 chew 5 champ 6 growse, growze
mundane: 6 cosmic 7 earthly, prosaic, secular, terrene, worldly 8 temporal 11 terrestrial
mungo: mug 8 mongoose
municipality: 4 city, town 7 cabildo
pert. to: 5 civic
munificent: 4 free 5 ample 6 lavish 7 liberal 8 generous 9 bounteous, bountiful 10 benevolent
muniment: 6 record 7 defense 8 document, evidence, writings 9 valuables 11 furnishings 13 fortification
munitions: 7 baggage, weapons 10 ammunition
munity: 9 privilege
Munro's penname: 4 Saki
muntjac, muntjak: 4 deer 6 kidang
muraena: 5 moray
mural: 4 wall 8 painting
muralist: 6 Benton, Giotto, Orozco, Rivera 7 Cimabue, da Vinci
murchy: 8 mischief
murder: 4 bane, kill, slay 5 death 7 butcher, carnage, killing, murther 8 homicide 9 slaughter 11 assassinate 12 manslaughter
brother: 10 fratricide
father: 9 patricide
fine: cro 7 wergild 9 bloodfine
infant: 11 infanticide
king: 8 regicide
mother: 9 matricide
own child: 9 prolicide
parent: 9 parricide
prophet: 8 vaticide
sister: 10 sororicide
son or daughter: 8 filicide
spouse: 10 mariticide
wife: 9 uxoricide
woman: 8 femicide
murderous: 4 gory 5 felon 6 bloody, brutal 9 ferocious 10 sanguinary 12 bloodthirsty
mure: 4 meek, soft, wall 6 gentle, demure, immure, modest
murgeon: 7 grimace, grumble
muriatic: 12 hydrochloric
murid: rat 8 disciple
murky: dim 4 dark 5 black, dense, foggy, mirky, misty, thick 6 gloomy 7 obscure 12 impenetrable
murmur: coo, hum, pur 4 curr, fret, huzz, purl, purr, sugh 5 brool, grank, sough 6 babble, grutch, hummer, mumble, mutter, repine 7 grumble, whisper 8 complain 9 grumbling
nasal: hum
murphy: 6 potato
murrain: 6 plague 10 pestilence
murther: 6 murder
Musa: 6 banana
muscadine: 5 grape 11 scuppernong
muscle: 4 thew 5 brawn, flesh, sinew, teres 6 lacert 8 strength
affection: 5 crick 6 abasia, ataxia
column: 10 sarcostyle
contracting: 7 agonist
curve: 7 myogram
expansion: 7 dilator
lifting: 7 levator
limb-straightening: 8 extensor
round: 5 teres
segment: 8 myocomma
spasm: 5 tonus
straight: 6 rectus
stretching: 6 tensor
sugar: 7 inosite 8 inositol
trapezius: 10 cucullaris
triangular: 7 deltoid
turning: 7 evertor, rotator
two-headed: 6 biceps
muscovado: 5 sugar
Muscovite: Red 4 mica, Russ 7 Russian
mica: 4 talc
prince: 4 Ivan

muscular: 5 thewy 6 brawny, robust, sinewy, strong, torose, torous 8 athletic, vigorous

muse: 4 dump, mull 5 dream, think 6 loiter, ponder, trifle 7 reflect 8 cogitate, consider, meditate, ruminate 9 amusement 10 meditation 11 contemplate

Muse: 4 Clio 5 Erato 6 Thalia, Urania 7 Euterpe 8 Calliope, Pierides, Polymnia 9 Melpomene 10 Polyhymnia 11 Terpsichore

birthplace: 6 Pieria

epithet: 7 Pierian

father: 4 Zeus

Fountain: 8 Aganippe

home: 5 Aonia 7 Helicon

mother: 9 Mnemosyne

mountain: 9 Parnassus

of astronomy: 6 Urania

of comedy: 6 Thalia

of dancing: 11 Terpsichore

of eloquence: 8 Calliope

of epic poetry: 8 Calliope

of history: 4 Clio

of love poetry: 5 Erato

of lyric poetry: 5 Erato

of music: 7 Euterpe

of pastoral poetry: 6 Thalia

of sacred poetry: 8 Polymnia 10 Polyhymnia

of tragedy: 9 Melpomene

seat of worship: 6 Pieria

museful: 6 silent 10 meditative, thoughtful

musery: 4 play 9 amusement

musette: air 4 oboe 7 bagpipe, gavotte

museum: 10 repository

custodian: 7 curator

director: 7 curator

mush: cut 5 atole, crush, gruel, march, notch, sepon 6 indent, sepawn, supawn, travel 7 confuse, journey, pudding, suppawn 8 flattery, porridge, sagamite, umbrella 14 sentimentality

mushroom: 4 grow 6 agaric, spread 7 parvenu, upstart

cap: 6 pileus

disease: 5 flock

edible: 5 morel 11 chanterelle

fairy-ring: 10 champignon

like: 7 fungous

part of: 4 gill 5 stipe, trama 6 pileus 7 annulus 8 basidium, hymenium, sterigma 12 basidiospore

poisoning: 8 mycetism

poisonous: 7 amanita 9 toadstool

stem: 5 stipe

mushy: 4 soft, weak 5 gushy, thick 8 effusive, yielding

music (see also **melody, song,** and entries under **musical**): air, art 4 tune 7 harmony

aftersong: 5 epode

beat: 5 ictus, pulse, tempo 6 rhythm

change to another key: 10 modulation 13 transposition

chord: 5 triad

flourish: 7 roulade

for eight: 5 octet

for five: 7 quintet

for four: 7 quartet

for nine: 5 nonet

for one: 4 soli, solo

for seven: 6 septet

for six: 6 sextet 7 sestole 8 sestolet

for three: 4 trio

for two: duo 4 duet

god: 6 Apollo

half tone: 8 semitone

machine for: 5 radio 7 juke-box, pianola 8 musicbox 10 gramophone, phonograph

major scale: 5 gamut

major third: 6 ditone

mania for: 9 melomania

melodic phrase: 9 leitmotif, leitmotiv

morning song: 6 aubade

Muse: 7 Euterpe

notation system: 5 neume

outdoor: 6 aubade 8 serenade

patron saint: 7 Cecilia

simple song: air, lay 4 tune

symbol: bar, key, tie 4 clef, flat, note, rest, slur 5 brace, sharp, staff

syncopated: 4 jazz

theme: 4 tema

timing device: 9 metronome

music hall: 4 gaff, odea(pl.) 5 odeum, odeon

musical: 4 show 5 lyric, revue 7 lyrical, melodic 8 harmonic, rhythmic 9 melodious 10 harmonious

musical comedy: hit 4 flop, show 5 revue 6 review 7 musical

musical composition: 4 glee, opus 5 cento, fugue, opera, rondo 6 ballad, sonata 7 ballade, boutade, cantata, chanson, prelude, scherzo, virelai 8 berceuse, concerto, nocturne, operetta, oratorio, serenata, serenade, sonatina, symphony 9 cabaletta, interlude 10 intermezzo

aria-like: 6 arioso

choral: 5 motet 7 chorale 9 plainsong

dancer's: 10 gymnopedie

dawn: 6 aubade

declamatory: 10 recitative

ending: 4 coda, fine 6 finale

exercise: 5 etude, study

feature: 5 motif, theme

interlude: 6 verset

jazz: rag 4 jive 5 bebop, blues, swing 7 ragtime 12 boogie-woogie
opera: 5 scena
poetic: ode
prelude: 6 verset
religious: 4 mass 5 motet, psalm 6 anthem 7 cantata 8 oratorio
round: 5 canon, fugue, troll
suite: 7 partita

musical direction: *above:* 5 sopra
accented: 8 sforzato 9 sforzando
again: DC, DS; bis 6 da capo 8 dal segno
all: 5 tutti
always: 6 sempre
animated: 7 animato 9 spiritoso
ardent: 7 ardente 12 appassionato
as written: sta
begin now: 7 attacca
below: 5 sotto
bold: 6 audace
bowed: 4 arco
bright: 5 anime
cold: 6 freddo
continue: va
devout: 6 divoto
dignified: 8 maestoso
disconnected: 8 staccato
dying away: 7 calando
emotional: 12 appassionato
emphatic: 7 marcato
evenly: 10 eugalmente
everyone: 5 tutti
excited: 7 agitato 9 spiritoso
fast: 4 vivo 5 tosto 6 presto, veloce, vivace 10 tostamente
faster: 7 stretto
freely: 9 ad libitum
furious: 7 furioso
gay: 7 giocoso
gentle: 5 dolce
half: 5 mezzo
heavy: 7 pesante
held: 6 tenuto
hurried: 7 agitato
in the style of: 4 alla
joyous: 7 giocoso
leap: 5 salto
less: 4 meno
little: 4 poco
little by little: 9 poco a poco
lively: 6 vivace 7 allegro, animato, giocoso
loud: 5 forte 10 fortissimo
louder: 9 crescendo
lovingly: 7 amabile, amoroso
lyric: 5 erato
majestic: 8 maestoso
marked: 7 marcato
moderate: 7 andante 8 moderato
more: piu
more rapid: 7 stretta, stretto
much: 5 molto
muted: 5 sorda
passionless: 6 freddo
plaintive: 7 dolente
playful: 7 giocoso 10 scherzando
plucked: 9 pizzicato
proceed: va
quick: 4 vite 5 tosto 6 presto 7 schnell
quick time: 9 alla breve
quickening: 11 affrettando
repeat: bis 6 ancoro 7 ripresa
sadly: 7 dolente 8 doloroso
sharp: 8 staccato 9 sforzando
silent: 5 tacet
singing: 9 cantabile
sliding: 9 glissando
slow: 5 grave, largo, lento, tardo 6 adagio 7 andante 9 larghetto
slower: rit 6 ritard 10 ritardando
slowing: 11 rallentando
smooth: 6 legato
so much: 5 tanto
soft: 5 dolce, piano 10 pianissimo
softer: 10 diminuendo 11 decrescendo
solemn: 5 grave
somewhat: 4 poco
spirited: 7 animato 9 spiritoso
stately: 7 pomposo
strong: 5 forte 10 fortissimo
sustained: 6 tenuto 9 sostenuto, sustenuto
sweet: 5 dolce
tempo irregular: 6 rubato
thrice: ter
throughout: 6 sempre
together: 8 ensemble
too much: 6 troppo
tranquil: 7 calmato
turn: 9 gruppetto
twice: bis
very: tre 4 tres 5 assai, molto 7 dimolto
with: con

musical disc: 6 cymbal, record 9 recording

musical drama: 5 opera 8 operetta, oratorio

musical event: 5 opera 6 ballet 7 concert, recital 8 musicale, oratorio

musical instrument: 4 drum, fife, gong, harp, horn, lute, lyre, oboe, reed, tuba 5 banjo, flute, organ, piano, viola 6 cornet, guitar, spinet, violin 7 bassoon, ocarina, piccolo, saxhorn, trumpet, ukelele 8 castanet, clarinet, dulcimer, mandolin, trombone 9 euphonium, flageolet, saxophone 11 violoncello
aid: 4 pick 8 diapason, plectrum 9 metronome, pitch pipe
ancient: 4 asor 5 rocta 6 rappel, sabeca 7 cithera, serpent 9 pantaleon
bass: 5 cello 11 violoncello

brass: 4 horn, tuba 5 bugle 6 tromba 7 althorn, helicon, saxhorn, trumpet 8 altohorn, trombone 10 French horn
China: kin
East Indies: 4 bina
Egypt: 7 sistrum
helicon: 4 tuba
Java: 7 gamelon 8 gamelang
keyboard: 5 organ, piano 6 spinet 7 celesta, clavier 8 melodeon 9 accordion 10 clavichord, concertina, pianoforte 11 harpsichord
lute-like: 7 angelot, bandore, cithern, cittern 9 bandurria 10 colascione
lyre-like: 4 asor 6 cither, zither 7 cithara, kithara
medieval: 5 rebab, rocta 7 chrotta
Mexico: 5 guiro 6 clarin 7 cabacas, maracas 11 chiapanecas
mouthpiece: 4 reed 6 fipple
oboe-like: 5 shawm 7 musette
old: 5 rebec 7 cittern, gittern
percussion: 4 drum, gong 5 bells, traps 6 maraca 7 cymbals, marimba, timpani, tympani 8 triangle 9 castanets, xylophone 10 tambourine 12 glockenspiel
piano-like: see *keyboard* above
reed: 4 oboe 7 bassoon 8 clarinet 9 saxophone 11 English horn
six-stringed: 6 guitar
stringed: oud, uke 4 asor, bass, harp, lute, lyre, viol, vina 5 banjo, cello, rebec, ruana, viola 6 citole, fiddle, guitar, rebeck, violin, zither 7 bandore, cythara, gittern, pandura, samisen, theorbo, ukelele 8 autoharp, dulcimer, mandolin 11 harpsichord, violoncello
supplementary: 7 ripieno
two-necked: 7 theorbo
viol-like: 5 rebec, ruana 6 rebeck 7 claviol 8 claviole
wind: jug, sax 4 fife, horn, oboe, reed, tuba 5 brass, bugle, flute, organ 6 cornet 7 althorn, bagpipe, bassoon, clarion, ocarina, panpipe, piccolo, saxhorn, serpent, trumpet 8 altohorn, clarinet, recorder, trombone, zampogna 9 flageolet, harmonica, saxophone 10 French horn 11 sarrusphone
xylophone-like: 7 marimba

musical interval: 5 fifth, major, minor, sixth, third 6 ditone, fourth, octave, second, unison 7 perfect, seventh, tritone 9 augmented 10 diminished

musical medley: 4 olio 5 cento

musical note (see also **musical syllable**): 5 breve, minim, neume 6 quaver 9 semibreve

musical piece: See **musical composition; song**

musical program: 5 opera 7 concert, recital 8 musicale

musical rhythm: 4 beat, time 5 ictus, meter, pulse, swing, tempo
measuring device: 9 metronome

musical scale (see also **musical syllable**): 5 gamut

musical sign: 5 segno
entrance: 5 presa
hold: 7 fermata, formata
key: 4 flat 5 sharp 7 natural
pitch level: 4 clef
silence: 4 rest
slur: 8 ligature
smooth: 4 slur
staff: bar

musical syllable: do, fa, la, mi, re, si, ti, ut; sol
ancient: ce, ut; alt, are, ela 5 elami, neume 7 alamire

musical term: *arrangement:* 7 ridotto
ballad style: 8 a ballata
between acts: 8 entracte
cadence: 4 half 6 plagal 7 perfect 9 deceptive, imperfect
chapel-style: 9 a cappella
dance-style: 7 da ballo
embellishment: 8 ornament 9 fioritura 12 appoggiatura
ending: 4 coda
florid: 7 bravura
flourish: 7 cadenza
half note: 5 minim
half tone: 8 semitone
major key: dur
melodic phrase: 5 motif 9 leitmotif, leitmotiv
melos: 4 song 6 melody
minor key: 4 moll
movement: 4 moto
note: 5 breve, neume
refrain: 5 epode 8 repetend
repeat: 5 rondo 7 reprise
run: 6 volata 9 glissando
shake: 5 trill 7 tremolo
soft pedal: VC 7 celeste
third: 6 tierce
thirty-second note: 14 demisemiquaver
three-note chord: 5 triad
time: see **musical rhythm**
tones: 5 chord
tremble: 5 trill 7 tremolo, vibrato
triplet: 6 tercet, triole
two notes: 5 duole
unaccompanied: 9 a cappella
upbeat: 5 arsis
vocal part: 5 canto

musical theme: 4 tema 5 motif 9 leitmotif, leitmotiv
musician: 4 bard 5 piper 6 singer 7 drummer, flutist, gleeman, pianist 8 bandsman, composer, flautist, minstrel, organist 9 cornetist, performer, serenader, violinist 10 trombonist 11 clarinetist, saxophonist
group: 4 band, duet, trio 5 choir, nonet 6 chorus, septet, sextet 7 nonetto, quartet 8 ensemble, septette, sextette 9 orchestra, quartette
patron saint: 7 Cecelia
musing: 7 reverie 10 meditation, meditative 13 contemplation
musk: 4 deer 7 perfume
musk beaver: 7 muskrat
musk cat: 5 civet
musk cavy: 5 hutia
musk cucumber: 11 cassabanana
musk deer: 10 chevrotain
musk hog: 7 peccary
musk lorikeet: 8 parakeet
musk mallow: 8 abelmosk
musk shrew: 6 desman
muskeg: bog 5 marsh
muskellunge: 4 pike
musket: 4 hawk 5 fusil 6 falcon 7 bundock, bundook, dragoon, firearm 8 biscayen 9 flintlock
Musketeers: *Three:* see **Three Musketeers**
muskmelon: 6 atimon, casaba 10 cantaloupe
muskrat: 5 shrew 6 desman
Muslim, Moslem (see also **Islam, Mohammed**): 4 Moro 6 Paynim 7 abadite, Islamic, Saracen 9 Mahometan, Mussulman 10 Mohammedan
ablution: 4 widu, wudu, wuzu
Alexandria sect: 6 Senusi
angel: 6 Azrael 7 isrefel, israfil 8 israfeel
annual fast: 7 Ramadan
antenuptial settlement: 4 mahr
ascetic: 4 sufi 5 fakir 6 fakeer
bazaar: 4 sook
belt: 5 zonar 6 zonnar
Berber dynasty: 6 Hafsid 7 Hafsite
Bible: 5 Coran, Koran 7 Alcoran
bier: 5 tabut
blood relationship: 5 nasab
calendar: 5 Rabia, Rajab, Safar 6 Jumada, Shaban 7 Ramadan, Shawwal 8 Zu'lhijah, Zu'lkadah 9 Mulharram
call to prayer: 4 adan, azan
cap: taj 5 kulah 6 kullah
caravansary: 6 imaret
caste: 5 mopla 6 moplah
chief: 4 rais, sidi 5 datto, sayid, sheik
city (sacred): 5 Mecca 6 Medina
coin: 5 dinar
convert: 5 ansar
council: 5 Ulema
creed: 5 Sunna
crusade: 5 jehad, jihad
decree: 5 irade
deity: 5 Allah, Eblis
demon: 5 afrit, eblis, jinni 6 jinnee
dervish: 6 Sadite, Santon
divorce: 5 ahsan, talak 7 mubarat
fast days: 7 Ramadan
festival: Eed 6 Bairam
freethinker: 7 Saracen 9 Aladinist
garment: 4 izar 6 jubbah
god: 5 Allah
guide (spiritual): pir
headdress: fez, taj 5 kulah 6 kullah, turban
hermit: 8 marabout
holy book: 5 Koran
holy city: 5 Mecca 6 Medina
holy war: 5 jehad, jihad
infidel: 5 kafir 6 kaffir
judge: 4 cadi, cazi, imam, kazi 5 hakim, imaum
lady: 5 begum
law: 5 halal 7 sheriat
lawyer: 5 mufti
leader: 4 amir, emir 5 ameer, emeer
men's quarters: 8 selamlik
messiah: 5 Mahdi
minaret crier: 7 muezzin
minister of state: 6 vizier
monastery: 5 tekke
month: see *calendar* above
mosque: 6 masjid
mystic: 4 Sufi
mysticism: 6 Sufism
name: Ali
nymph: 5 houri
officer: aga
official: 5 hajib, mufti
orthodox: 5 hanif 7 Sunnite
people: Laz 4 Lazi, Moro, Sufi, Swat 5 Hanif, Isawa, Salar, Samal, Sunni, Swati 6 Dehgan, Senusi 7 Bazigar, Senousi, Senussi 8 Senusite 9 Senussian
physician: 5 hakim 6 hakeem
pilgrim: 4 haji 5 hadji, hajji
pilgrimage: 4 hadj
pilgrim's dress: 5 ihram
prayer: 5 namaz, salat
prayer call: 4 adan, azan
priest: 4 imam 5 imaum 6 wahabi
priests (body): 5 ulema
prince: 4 amir, emir, seid 5 ameer, emeer, nawab, sayid
princess: 4 tola 5 begum
religion: 5 Islam
ruler: aga 4 amir, emir 5 ameer, emeer, hakim, nawah 6 hakeem, sultan

saber: 7 yatagan 8 scimitar, scimiter, yataghan
sacred book: See *Bible* above
saint: Pir 5 Abdal 6 Santon 8 Marabout
salutation: 5 salam 6 salaam
sect: 5 Isawa 6 Wahabi 7 Abadite, dervish, Sunnite 8 Ahmadiya, Sifatite
shrine: 5 Kaaba 6 Kaabeh
spirit: 4 jinn(pl.) 5 genie, jinni 7 jinnyeh
spiritual adviser: pir
student: 5 softa
supreme being: 5 Allah
teacher: 4 alim, imam 8 mujtahid
title: sid 4 said, sidi 5 nawab, sayid 6 sayyid
warrior: 7 Saracen
washing: 4 widu, wudu, wuzu
women's quarters: 5 harem
muslin: ban 4 mull 5 adati, dorea, doria, shela 6 cossas, gurrah, shelah 7 beteela, organdy 8 nainsook, seerhand, sheeting 9 charkhana, womanhood 10 femininity
muss: See **mess**
mussel: 4 naid, unio 5 naiad 6 mucket, nerita 8 deerhorn
genus of: 8 modiolus
part: 6 byssus
mussitate: 6 mutter
Mussolini's son-in-law: 5 Ciano
Mussulman: See **Muslim**
must: 4 bood, mold, musk, sapa, stum 5 juice, ought, shall 6 refuse 10 obligation
mustang: 5 pinto 6 bronco 7 broncho
mustard: 5 nigra, senvy 6 senapi 7 cadlock 8 charlock
chemical: 5 allyl
family: 12 brassicaceae
genus of: 7 sinapis
pod: 7 silicle
mustard plaster: 8 sinapism
musteline animal: 6 weasel
muster: 4 call 5 erect 6 gather, roster, sample, summon 7 collect, marshal, pattern 8 assemble 10 accumulate, congregate
out: 7 disband, release 9 discharge
mustiness: 4 fust, mold
musty: 4 dull, sour 5 fusty, hoary, moldy, rafty, stale, trite 6 rancid 7 foughty, spoiled 10 antiquated
Mut: *child of:* 5 Chons
husband: 4 Amen, Amon
mutable: 6 fickle 8 variable 9 alterable 10 changeable, inconstant 11 vacillating
mutate: 4 vary 5 alter 6 change, modify
mutation: 6 change, revolt 9 posthouse 10 revolution, succession 11 vicissitude
mute: mum 4 dumb, lene, surd 6 deaden, muffle, silent 7 mourner, muffler 8 deadener, silencer 9 voiceless 10 speechless 12 inarticulate
mutilate: mar 4 hack, maim 6 deface, garble, injure, mangle, mittle(Sc.) 7 cripple, destroy 9 disfigure, dismember
mutinous: 6 unruly 9 seditious, turbulent 10 rebellious, refractory, tumultuous 11 disobedient, intractable 12 contumacious 13 insubordinate
mutiny: 6 revolt, strife 9 commotion 12 insurrection
mutt: cur, dog 7 mongrel 9 blockhead
mutter: 5 growl 6 mumble, murmur, patter 7 channer, grumble, maunder 9 mussitate
mutton: 4 meat 5 sheep 6 candle 10 prostitute
dried: 5 vifda, vivda
leg: 5 cabob, gigot 7 wabbler, wobbler
muttonbird: oii 6 petrel 10 shearwater
muttonchop: 7 whisker 8 burnside
muttonfish: 4 sama 5 pargo, porgy 7 eelpout, mojarra
muttonhead: 5 dunce 9 blockhead, screwball
mutual: 6 common 10 reciprocal, responsive
mutuality: 13 interrelation
mux: 4 mess 5 botch
muzhik: 7 peasant
muzz: 6 muddle
muzzle: gag 4 grub, nose, root 5 snout 6 clevis, muffle 7 sheathe 8 restrain 10 respirator
muzzy: 4 dull 5 fuzzy 7 blurred, muddled 8 confused 10 depressive
My Last Duchess author: 9 Browning
mycold: 7 fungold
mykiss: 6 salmon
myna: 7 grackle
myomorph: rat 5 mouse 6 rodent
myopic: 8 purblind 11 nearsighted 12 shortsighted
myotic: 6 eserin 7 eserine
myriad: 9 countless 11 innumerable 13 multitudinous
myriapod: 9 centipede
myrmicid: ant
myrmidon: 8 adherent, follower, henchman
myrrh: gum 4 tree 5 resin
myrtle: 8 ramarama 10 periwinkle 11 candleberry
myself: 5 masel(Sc.)
mysterious: dim 4 dark 5 runic 6 arcane, mystic, occult, secret 7 cryptic, uncanny 8 abstruse 9 equivocal, recondite, sphinxine 12 inexplicable, unfathomable
mystery: 4 rune 5 craft, trade 6 cabala, enigma, puzzle, riddle, secret 7 arcanum, esotery 8 thriller, whodunit
mystery novel award: 5 Edgar

mystic: 4 seer 5 epopt, runic 6 occult, orphic, secret 7 cryptic, epoptic, obscure 8 anagogic, esoteric, symbolic 9 enigmatic, recondite 10 cabalistic, mysterious
art: 6 cabala
initiate: 5 epopt
Moslem: 4 Sufi
secret sect: 5 cabal
word: om, um 4 evoe 7 abraxas 11 abracadabra

mystical: 4 dark 6 occult, secret 8 symbolic 9 spiritual
significance: 7 anagoge

mysticism: 6 cabala 8 cabalism

mystify: 5 befog 6 muddle, puzzle 7 becloud, confuse, perplex 8 befuddle, bewilder 9 bamboozle, obfuscate

myth: 4 saga, tale 5 fable, fancy, story 6 legend 7 parable 9 apocrypha

mythical: 9 imaginary 10 fictitious

N

nab: hat 4 grab, head 5 catch, seize 6 arrest, clutch, nibble, snatch 7 capture 9 apprehend
Nabal: *home:* 4 Maon
wife: 7 Abigail
nabob: 5 nawab 6 deputy 7 viceroy 8 governor 9 plutocrat 10 viceregent 11 billionaire
Nabokov novel: Ada 4 Pnin 6 Lolita
nacelle: 7 shelter 11 compartment
nacket: boy 4 cake 5 lunch
nacre: 9 shellfish 10 conchiolin 13 mother-of-pearl
nadir's opposite: 6 zenith
nag: tit 4 frab, fret, gnaw, jade, pony, twit 5 annoy, cobra, hobby, horse, scold, snake, tease 6 badger, berate, bother, harass, heckle, hector, padnag, pester, wanton 7 hackney 8 harangue, irritate 9 aggravate
naga, nag: 5 cobra, snake
nagor: 8 antelope, reedbuck
nahoor: sha, sna 5 sheep, urial 6 bharal, oorial
Nahor: *father:* 5 Serug
grandson: 7 Abraham
son: 5 Terah
wife: 6 Milcah
Nahuatlan: 5 Aztec
naiad: 5 nymph 6 mussel
naif: See **naive**
nail: cut, fix, hob 4 brad, brag, brod, claw, cloy, dump, spad, stub, stud, tack, trap 5 affix, catch, clout, grope, spike, sprig 6 clinch, detain, fasten, hammer, secure, unguis, ungula 7 capture 8 fastener, sparable, spikelet 9 finishing, intercept
drive at a slant: toe
headless: 5 sprig
ingrowing: 7 acronyx
marking on: 6 lunule
perforated: 4 spad
shoemaker's: 4 brad 8 sparable
nais: 5 naiad, nymph
naissance: 5 birth
naive: 5 frank 6 simple 7 artless 8 childish, untaught 9 childlike, guileless, ingenuous, untutored, unworldly 10 unaffected 13 inexperienced, unphilosophic 15 unsophisticated
naked: 4 bare, nude, open 6 cuerpo 7 exposed 8 manifest 9 unadorned, unclothed, uncovered 11 defenseless, unprotected
namaycush: 5 lunge, togue, trout
namby-pamby: 7 insipid 10 wishy-washy 11 sentimental
name: dub, nom(F.) 4 call, term 5 claim, clepe, count, nemme, nemne, neven, nomen, style, title 6 adduce, appeal, monica, select 7 appoint, behight, enstyle, entitle, epithet, intitle, mention, moniker 8 christen, delegate, identify, identity, monicker, monniker, nominate 9 designate 10 denominate, denotation, reputation 11 appellation, designation 12 denomination, nomenclature
added: 6 agname 7 agnomen
assumed: 5 alias 6 anonym 9 incognito, pseudonym, sobriquet 10 nom de plume, soubriquet
backwards: 6 ananym
based on location: 7 toponym
Biblical: See **Bible:** *name*
derivation: 7 eponymy
family: 7 eponymy, sirname, surname 8 cognomen
female: Ada, Amy, Ann, Ava, Dot, Ena, Eva, Eve, Fay, Ida, Ina, Jen, Lil, Lou, Mae, May, Meg, Nan, Pam, Pat, Rae, Una, Zoe 4 Alma, Alta, Anna, Anta, Avis, Caro, Cora, Dian, Dona, Dora, Edla, Edna, Ella, Elsa, Enid, Erma, Etta, Eula, Fifi, Gail, Inez, Irma, Kate, Katy, Lena, Lida, Lila, Lois, Lola, Lona, Lora, Lula, Meta, Mina, Nena, Nina, Nita, Nora, Olga, Prue, Rena, Reta, Rita, Sara, Suke, Suky, Susy, Tess, Vera 5 Adele, Agnes, Aimee, Alice, Alida, Aline, Alsie, Anita, Annie, Aphra, Bella, Betsy, Betty, Celia, Clare, Delia, Della, Doris, Dulce, Edith, Eilen, Elain, Elena, Elise, Ellen, Elsie, Essie, Ester, Ethel, Ettie, Flora, Freda, Genie, Greta, Helen, Hilda, Irene, Janet, Karen, Laura, Lelia, Leona,

Lucia, Lydia, Maida, Maria, Moira, Molly, Norah, Norma, Paula, Rhoda, Sally, Sarah, Sukey, Sukie, Susan, Susie, Tecla, Wilma **6** Adelai, Alicia, Annice, Arline, Connie, Dagmar, Daphne, Dorcas, Elaine, Esther, Fedora, Flavia, Frieda, Gertie, Gloria, Gratia, Hedwig, Hermia, Honora, Isabel, Janice, Jennie, Lenora, Lenore, Louisa, Louise, Muriel, Pamela, Persis, Sallie, Sandra, Sheila, Zebina **7** Abigale, Belinda, Cecilia, Celeste, Dolores, Eleanor, Emaline, Estelle, Eveline, Felicia, Heloise, Imogene, Juanita, Madelon, Mildred, Rosalia, Rosalie, Susanna, Waunita, Zulinde **8** Arabella, Drusilla, Hermiona, Hyacinth, Patricia **9** Anastasia
first: **9** praenomen
list: **11** onomasticon
masculine: Al, Ed, Si; Abe, Alf, Asa, Ben, Cal, Dan, Eli, Gil, Gus, Guy, Hal, Ian, Ike, Ira, Lem, Len, Lon, Moe, Nat, Ned, Ole, Pat, Ray, Rex, Roy, Sam, Sid, Ted, Tex, Tim, Ugo, Vic **4** Abel, Adam, Alan, Alex, Alva, Amos, Axel, Bart, Bert, Carl, Dian, Dick, Earl, Emil, Enos, Eric, Esme, Evan, Ezra, Gene, Hugh, Igor, Ivan, Joab, Joel, Knut, Leon, Levi, Luke, Lynn, Marc, Mark, Neal, Neil, Noah, Noel, Olaf, Otto, Owen, Paul, Phil, Pius, Rene, Saul, Stan, Tony, Zeke **5** Aaron, Abiel, Abner, Abram, Agard, Allan, Alvan, Angus, Anton, Basil, Biron, Bryan, Bryon, Byron, Caleb, Cecil, Cliff, Clive, Denis, Edgar, Elias, Elihu, Elmer, Emery, Eneas, Enoch, Ernie, Erwin, Ethan, Felix, Floyd, Giles, Hiram, Isaac, Jabez, Judah, Leigh, Leroy, Lloyd, Louis, Lysle, Moses, Nahum, Nigel, Orson, Peleg, Percy, Peter, Reuel, Roger, Rollo, Roman, Rufus, Silas, Titus, Urban, Uriah, Uriel, Zebee **6** Adolph, Adrian, Alaric, Albert, Alexis, Alfred, August, Austin, Caesar, Calvin, Caspar, Cedric, Daniel, Decius, Dexter, Donald, Dudley, Duncan, Dwight, Edmund, Egbert, Harvey, Hubert, Isaiah, Israel, Jairus, Jarvis, Joshua, Josiah, Jotham, Junius, Kasper, Lemuel, Lester, Lucius, Luther, Manuel, Marcus, Marion, Murray, Naaman, Nathan, Pierre, Reuben, Roland, Roscoe, Rupert, Samuel, Steven, Teague, Theron, Tobiah, Vergil, Victor, Vivian, Walter, Wilbur **7** Abraham, Anatole, Bertram, Chester, Clement, Dominic, Douglas, Eleazar, Elliott, Erasmus, Erastus, Eustace, Everard, Everett, Ezekiel, Flavius, Gabriel, Gifford, Gilbert, Godfrey, Isidore, Japheth, Lazarus, Leonard, Leopold, Lorenzo, Malachi, Maurice, Obadiah, Patrick, Phineas, Raphael, Raymond, Raymund, Rowland, Russell, Seymour, Stanley, Stephen, Ulysses, Zachary, Zebedee, Zebedei, Zebedia **8** Adelbert, Algernon, Alphonso, Benjamin, Claudius, Clifford, Ebenezer, Emmanuel, Fernando, Frederic, Gamaliel, Geoffrey, Gustavus, Hezekiah, Ignatius, Jeremiah, Laurence, Lawrence, Napoleon, Nehemiah, Octavius, Percival, Schuyler, Silvanus, Terrence, Thaddeus, Zebadiah **9** Anatasius, Archibald, Celestine, Cornelius, Demetrius, Ferdinand, Frederick, Lafayette, Launcelot, Llewellyn, Marcellus, Nathaniel, Rodolphus, Rudolphus, Siegfried, Sigismund, Silvester, Zachariah, Zacharias **10** Maximilian, Theophilus
objectionable: **7** caconym
pet: **8** nickname **9** sobriquet
tablet: **5** facia
nameable: 6 famous **7** notable **9** memorable
named: 6 yclept **7** ycleped
nameless: 7 bastard, obscure **9** anonymous, unnamable **12** illegitimate **13** indescribable, unmentionable
namely: viz **5** noted, to wit **6** famous **8** scilicet **9** expressly, videlicit **10** especially **12** specifically
namesake: 6 junior
nandu: 4 rhea
nanism: 12 dwarfishness
nanny: 4 goat **5** nurse
nanny plum: 10 sheepberry
nanpie: 6 magpie
Naomi: 4 Mara
daughter-in-law: **4** Ruth **5** Orpah
husband: **9** Elimelech
son: **6** Mahlon **7** Chilion
naos: 5 ceila **6** shrine, temple
nap: nod **4** calk, doze, fuzz, lint, pile, shag, wink **5** fluff, grasp, seize, sleep, steal **6** siesta, snooze
nape: nod **5** nucha, nuque **6** scruff **7** niddick
napery: 5 linen
Naphtali: *census taker:* **4** Enan
mother: **6** Bilhah
son: **4** Guni **5** Jezer **7** Jahziel, Shallum
naphtha: 9 petroleum
napkin: 5 cloth, doily, towel **6** diaper **8** kerchief **9** handcloth, serviette **11** neckerchief **12** handkerchief
Naples: *biscuit:* **10** ladyfinger
coin: **6** carlin **7** carline
king: **5** Murat
secret society: **7** Camorra
napless 10 threadbare
Napoleon: *battle:* Ulm **4** Acre, Jena **7** Dresden **8** Borodino, Waterloo **10** Austerlitz
birthplace: **7** Corsica
brother: **5** Louis **6** Jerome, Joseph, Lucien
brother-in-law: **5** Murat
island of exile: **4** Elba

marshal: Ney
nickname: 5 Boney
place of victory: 5 Ligny 10 Austerlitz
sister: 5 Elisa, Maria 8 Carlotta, Carolina
wife: 9 Josephine

nappy: ale 4 dish 5 downy, heady, wooly 6 liquor, strong 7 foaming
napu: 7 deerlet 10 chevrotain
narcotic (see also **marijuana**): kat 4 bang, dope, junk 5 bhang, dagga, ether, opium 6 heroin, opiate 7 anodyne, cocaine, hashish 8 hasheesh, hypnotic, morphine, takrouri 9 soporific 10 bella-donna, hyoscyamus, stramonium
dose: 5 locus
package: 4 deck 6 bindle
plant: kat 4 coca, cuca, hemp, kaat, khat 5 dutra, poppy
seller: 6 pusher 7 peddler

nard: 5 spice 6 anoint 7 rhizome 9 spikenard
nardoo: 6 clover
nargileh: 4 pipe 5 hooka 6 hookah 7 coconut
narial: 6 rhinal
nark: spy, vex 5 annoy 8 informer, irritate 10 spoilsport 11 stool pigeon
narrate: 4 tell 5 state 6 detail, recite, relate, report 7 discuss, recount 8 describe, rehearse 9 chronicle, discourse
narrative: 4 epic, myth, saga, tale 5 conte, drama, fable, story 6 legend 7 account, episode, history, parable 8 allegory, anecdote 9 narration
narrator: 9 reconteur
narrow: 4 mean 5 close, scant, sound, taper 6 biased, linear, meager, meagre, strait, strict 7 bigoted, limited 8 condense, contract 9 constrict, hidebound, illiberal, niggardly 10 prejudiced, restricted, straighten, ungenerous 11 reactionary 12 parsimonious 13 circumscribed
combining form: 4 sten 5 steno

narrowminded: 6 biased 7 bigoted
narsinga: 7 trumpet
narthex: 5 porch 7 portico 9 vestibule 10 antetemple
nasab: 7 kinship 13 consanguinity
nasal: 6 narine, rhinal, twangy
nascency: 5 birth 6 origin 7 genesis 9 beginning
naseberry: 9 sapodilla
nashgab: 6 gossip
nasi: 9 patriarch
nasicorn: 10 rhinoceros
nastika: 7 atheist
nasty: bad 4 foul, mean, ugly 5 dirty 6 filthy 7 harmful, obscene, squalid 8 indecent 9 dangerous, malicious, offensive 10 disgusting, ill-natured, nauseating, unpleasant 12 disagreeable, dishonorable 13 objectionable
nasutiform: 8 noselike
nat: 5 demon 6 spirit
natal: 6 native 7 gluteal 10 congenital
natant: 6 afloat 8 floating, swimming
natator: 7 swimmer
natatorium: 4 bath, pool
natchbone: 9 aitchbone
nation: 4 host, race 5 caste, class, state 6 people 7 country 9 community, multitude
symbol: 4 flag 5 crest

national: 7 citizen, federal 11 gentilitian
National Guard member: 10 militiaman
native: 5 natal 6 genial, inborn, innate, normal 7 citizen, endemic, natural 8 domestic, inherent, original, resident 9 aborigine, congenial, ingrained, unbranded 10 congenital, indigenous, inhabitant
nativity: 5 birth 8 geniture 9 horoscope
natrium: NA 6 sodium
nattle: 4 gnaw 6 nibble
natty: 4 chic, neat, tidy, trig, trim 5 smart 6 spruce 10 fastidious
natural: 4 born, easy 5 usual 6 common, cretin, inborn, inbred, innate, native, normal 7 regular 8 inherent, ordinary, physical 9 primitive, unassumed unfeigned 10 congenital 13 unenlightened
naturalize: 5 adopt 8 accustom 9 acclimate 11 acclimatize, domesticate, familiarize
nature: 4 kind, sort, type 7 essence 9 character 11 disposition, temperament
divinity: 5 nymph
god: Pan
goddess: 6 Cybele 7 Artemis
same: 10 homogeneal

naught: 4 evil, zero 5 aught, ought 6 cipher, nought, wicked 7 nothing, useless 9 worthless
naughty: bad 4 evil 5 wrong 6 wicked 7 obscene, wayward 8 improper 10 indelicate 11 disobedient, mischievous
nauntle: 4 fuss 5 raise, strut 6 potter
naupathia: 11 seasickness
nausea: 4 pall 7 disgust 8 loathing, sickness 10 queasiness
nauseating: 5 nasty, waugh 7 fulsome 8 brackish 9 loathsome, sickening 10 disgusting 11 distasteful
nautical (see also **navigation**): 5 naval 6 marine 7 oceanic 8 maritime
cry: 4 ahoy
flag: 6 cornet, pennon
instrument: 7 compass, sextant
mile: 4 knot
term: 4 atry 5 abaft, abeam, alist, avast

nautilus: 7 mollusk 9 argonauta

Navaho hut: 5 hogan
naval stores: tar 5 pitch 8 supplies 10 turpentine
nave: hob, hub, nef 4 apse, body, fist 5 aisle, nieve
navel: 9 umbilicus
navigate: 4 keel, sail 5 steer 6 direct, manage 7 journey, operate
navigation: 7 nautics 8 cabotage 10 seamanship
call: 4 ahoy 5 avast, belay
hazard: fog, sub 4 mine 9 submarine
instrument: aba 7 compass, pelorus, sextant
measure: ton 4 knot, seam 6 fathom 7 renning, sea mile 12 cable's length
signal: 4 bell, flag
term: 4 atry 5 abeam, atrip
navigator: 5 flyer, navvy, pilot 6 airman 7 aviator, copilot, laborer 8 aeronaut, seafarer, spaceman
navite: 6 basalt
navvy: 7 laborer 9 navigator
navy: 5 fleet
board: 9 admiralty
depot: 4 base
force: 5 fleet 6 armada 8 squadron
jail: 4 brig
officer: 4 aide, mate 5 bosun 6 ensign 7 admiral, armorer, captain 8 armourer 9 commander, commodore 10 lieutenant
vessel: PT; sub 7 carrier, cruiser, flattop, gun boat 9 destroyer, submarine, transport 10 battleship
wireless operator: 6 sparks
nawab: 5 nabob, ruler 7 viceroy
nay: no; nai, not 4 deny, nyet(Russ.) 5 flute, never 6 denial, refuse 7 refusal 8 negative 11 prohibition
naysay: 6 denial 7 refusal
nayword: 6 byword 7 proverb 9 watchword
naze: 8 headland 10 promontory
Nazi: 9 Hitlerite
police: SS 7 Gestapo
symbol: 6 fylfot 8 swastika
nazim: 7 viceroy 8 governor
neal: 6 anneal, temper
neanic: 8 immature, youthful
neap: 4 tide
near: by; gin, kin, nar(Sc.) 4 bain, dear, hend, nigh 5 anear, anent, aside, close, handy, hende 6 almost, around, beside, climax, narrow, stingy 7 advance, similar, thrifty, vicinal 8 adjacent, approach, intimate 9 niggardly, thriftily 10 contiguous, juxtaposed 11 approximate, closefisted 12 parsimonious 13 propinquitous
Near East: 6 Levant
ketch: 4 saic
nearest: 4 next 5 ewest(Sc.) 7 closest 9 proximate
nearsighted: 6 myopic 12 shortsighted
neat: gim 4 cosh(Sc.), deft, dink, feil(Sc.), nice, prim, pure, snod(Sc.), snug, tidy, tosh, trig, trim 5 clean, compt, dinky, douce, natty 6 adroit, cattle, clever, dapper 7 concise, orderly, precise, refined, unmixed 8 skillful, tasteful 9 dexterous, shipshape, undiluted 10 concinnous, meticulous
neath: 5 below 7 beneath
neatherd: 7 cowherd 8 herdsman
neb: nib, tip 4 beak, bill, nose 5 snout
Nebraska: *bird:* 10 meadowlark
city: 5 Omaha
river: 6 Platte
nebris: 8 fawnskin
nebula: sky 5 vapor 6 galaxy 10 atmosphere
nebulize: 7 atomize
nebulous: 4 hazy 5 foggy, misty, vague 6 cloudy 7 clouded, unclear 8 nebulose 10 indefinite, indistinct
necessarily: 8 perforce
necessary: 5 privy, vital 6 toilet 7 needful 8 forcible, integral 9 essential, mandatory, requisite 10 inevitable, undeniable 11 unavoidable, water-closet 13 indispensable
necessitate: 5 force, impel 6 compel, entail, oblige 7 require 9 constrain
necessity: 4 food, must, need, want 5 drink 7 ailment, poverty, urgency 8 distress 9 emergency 11 destitution
neck: pet 4 cape, crag, crop, hals, kiss 5 halse 6 caress, cervix, collum, fondle, strait 7 channel, embrace, isthmus
armor: 6 gorget
artery: 7 carotid
back of: 4 nape 5 nucha, nuque 6 scruff
comb. form: 6 cervic 7 cervico
muscle: 8 scalenus
part: 4 gula 7 withers
pert. to: 7 jugular 8 cervical
piece: bib, boa 5 amice, rabat, scarf, stole 6 collar 8 kerchief
neck and neck: tie 4 even 5 close
neckatee: 11 neckerchief
neckband: 6 collar, collet 10 collar-band
neckcloth: bib, boa 4 ruff 5 amice, choke, jabot, rabat, ruche, scarf, stole 6 choker, collar, cravat, dickey 7 bur-dash, pannelo 8 kerchief 9 barcelona 11 neckerchief
neckerchief: 4 gimp 7 belcher 8 kerchief, nectatee 12 handkerchief
necklace: 4 rope, torc 5 beads, chain, noose 6 collar, grivna, locket, torque 7 baldric, chaplet, haltern, necktie, riviere 8 baldrick, carcanet, lavalier 9 esclavage, lavaliere 10 lavalliere

necktie: bow, tie 4 band 5 ascot, scarf 6 cravat 10 four-in-hand
necktie party: 7 hanging 8 lynching
necrologue: 8 obituary
necromancy: art 5 goety, magic 7 grammary, sorcery 8 gramarye, wizardry 11 conjuration, enchantment
necropolis: 8 cemetery
necropsy: 7 autopsy
nectar: 5 honey 8 ambrosia
nectar bird: 7 sunbird
nedder: 5 adder
neddy: 6 donkey
nee: 4 born 8 formerly
need: 4 lack, want 5 crave 6 behove, demand, desire 7 behoove, poverty, require, urgency 8 distress, exigency 9 emergency, extremity, indigence, necessity, requisite 10 compulsion, dependence, obligation, retirement 11 destitution
needful: 5 vital 8 integral 9 essential 13 indispensable
needle: sew 4 acus(L.), darn 5 annoy 7 acicula, provoke, spicule 10 strengthen
combining form: acu
hole: eye
type: 4 sail 5 blunt, style 6 bodkin, stylus 7 darning, obelisk 8 knitting 10 hypodermic, phonograph, upholstery
needle bug: 7 ranatra
needle gun: 5 rifle 6 Dreyse
needlefish: gar 8 pipefish
needlelike: 6 acuate 7 acerate, acerose, acerous, aciform 8 acicular, belonoid
needleman: 6 tailor
needless: 10 gratuitous 11 superfluous, unnecessary
needlewoman: 10 seamstress
needlwood: 10 needlebush
needlework: 6 sewing 7 sampler, seaming, tatting 8 knitting 9 hemstitch 10 embroidery, crocheting
needy: 4 poor 9 penniless
neep: 6 turnip
ne'er-do-well: bum 5 losel, loser 9 schlemiel, worthless 11 incompetent
nef: 4 nave 5 clock
nefandous: 9 execrable
nefarious: 6 wicked 7 heinous, impious 8 flagrant, horrible, infamous 9 atrocious 10 detestable, iniquitous, villainous
nefast: 6 wicked
negate: 4 deny 5 annul 6 refute 7 nullify
negation: not 5 empty 6 denial 7 refusal 9 annulment, blankness, nonentity 10 refutation 13 contradiction, nullification
negative: no, ne; nae(Sc.), nay, non(F.), nor, not 4 film, veto 5 minus, never 7 neutral
prefix: il, im, in, ir, un; dis, non
neglect: 4 fail, omit, slip 5 fault, forgo, shirk 6 forego, forget, ignore, slight 7 default, failure 8 omission 9 disregard, oversight, pretermit 10 negligence 11 inattention 12 inadvertence, indifference
neglectful: lax 6 remiss 8 careless, derelict, heedless 9 dissolute
negligee: 4 robe 7 undress 8 peignoir 9 nightgown 10 dishabille
negligence: 7 laxness 9 disregard
negotiable: 12 transferable
negotiate: 4 deal 5 treat 6 dicker 7 bargain, chaffer, discuss 8 transact 10 accomplish
negotiation: 6 treaty 8 entreaty
negus: 8 beverage
neigh: 6 whinny
neighbor: 6 adjoin, border fellow
neighborhood: 4 area 5 venue 6 locale, region 7 section 8 district, vicinage, vicinity 9 community, proximity, territory 11 propinquity
neighboring: 4 nigh 6 near-by 7 vicinal 8 adjacent 10 contiguous
neither: not
nema: 7 eelworm 9 roundworm
nemesis: 4 bane 7 avenger
nemoral: 6 sylvan
neophyte: 4 tyro 5 epopt 6 novice 7 amateur, convert 8 beginner 9 proselyte 10 catechumen
neoteric: new 4 late 6 modern, recent
nep: 6 catnep, catnip 7 catmint
Nepal: *city:* 5 Palan 8 Bhatgaon, Katmandu 9 Khatmandu
cloth: 5 khadi 6 changa
coin: 5 mohar
mountain: 7 Everest 11 Dhawalagiri 12 Kinchinjinga
people: Rai 4 Aoul 5 Bokra, Hindu, Limbu, Murmi, Newar, Tharu 6 Bhotia, Gurkha, Lepcha 7 Kiranti 8 Gorkhali
river: 4 Kusi 6 Gandak 7 Karnali
ruler: 4 Rana
sheep: 6 bharal, nahoor, nayaur
tree: sal 4 toon 5 sisoo
nepenthe: 7 anodyne
nephew: 6 nepote(Sc.)
nephrite: 4 jade 6 pounam 10 greenstone
nepote: 6 nephew
nepotism: 9 patronage 10 favoritism
Neptune: sea 5 ocean 6 seagod
consort: 7 Salacia
emblem: 7 trident
Ner's son: 5 Abner
Nereides: *father:* 6 Nereus
mother: 5 Doris
steed: 8 seahorse
Nero: 6 tyrant 7 emperor, fiddler
mother: 9 Agrippina

successor: 5 Galba
victim: 5 Lucan 6 Seneca
wife: 7 Octavia, Poppaea
Nero Wolfe creator: 5 Stout
nerve: 4 grit 5 cheek, pluck, sinew, spunk, vigor 6 aplomb, daring, energy 7 courage 8 audacity, boldness, coolness, embolden, strength, temerity 9 encourage 10 brazenness, invigorate, resolution
apparatus: 6 sensor
cell: 5 cyton 6 cytone
center: 8 ganglion
combining form: 4 neur 5 neuro
cranial: 5 optic, vagus
inflammation: 8 neuritis
malady: tic 8 neuritis
operation: 10 neurolysis
pathway: 4 rete 5 hilum 8 ganglion
pert. to: 5 neuro 6 neural
root: 5 radix
sensory: 8 afferent
tissue: 8 cinerea
tumor: 7 neuroma 9 neurinoma 11 neurocytoma 12 neuromatosis
nerve cell: 4 axon 6 neuron
extension: 4 axon 6 neurite
framework: 6 stroma
process: 4 axon 5 axone 7 neurite
nerveless: 4 dead, weak 5 brave, inert 8 unnerved 9 foolhardy, powerless 10 courageous
nervous: 5 jumpy, timid 6 fidget, sinewy, touchy 7 fearful, fretful, jittery 8 neurotic, timorous 9 excitable, sensitive 10 highstrung 12 apprehensive
nervous disorder: See **mental disorder**
nervous system: *center:* 5 brain
description of: 11 neurography
nomenclature: 9 neuronymy
science: 9 neurology
nervy: 4 bold 6 brazen, sinewy, strong 7 jittery, nervous 8 impudent, vigorous 9 excitable
nescient: 7 infidel 8 agnostic, ignorant
ness: 4 cape 6 suffix 8 headland 10 promontory
nest: den, web 4 aery, bike, dray, drey, eyry, home 5 abode, aerie, eyrie, haunt, nidus, swarm 6 cuddle, hotbed 7 lodging, retreat 9 residence 10 nidificate
builder of: ant, bee 4 bird, wasp
eagle's: 4 aery 5 aerie
insect's: 5 nidus
squirrel's: 4 dray, drey
nester: 7 settler 8 squatter 11 homesteader
nestle: pet 4 nest 6 cuddle, pettle(Sc.) 7 cherish, shelter, snuggle
nestling: 4 baby, bird, eyas, nest 7 retreat 9 fledgling
nestor: 4 sage 7 adviser, advisor 9 counselor 10 counsellor
net: bag, gin, web 4 caul, flan, gain, lace, lawn, mesh, moke, neat, pure, rete, toil, trap, trim, weir 5 clean, clear, gauze, lacis, seize, snare, tulle, yield 6 bright, cobweb, entrap, maline, profit 7 dragnet, ensnare, network, protect, rinsing, shelter 8 meshwork 9 reticulum 10 reticulate 13 unadulterated
fishing: lam 4 flew, flue, fyke 5 seine, trawl 6 sagene 7 trammel
hair: 5 snood
interstice: 4 hole, mesh
net-winged: 12 neuropteroid
nether: 5 lower, under 8 downward
Netherlands: 7 Holland
bailiff: 6 schout
cheese: 4 Edam 5 Gouda 7 cottage
city: Ede 5 Asten, Breda, Hague 6 Aalten, Arnhem, Leiden 7 Commune, Haarlem, Utrecht 8 Aalsmeer 9 Amsterdam, Groningen, Rotterdam 10 Gravenhage
coin: 4 cent, doit, raps 5 ryder 6 florin, gulden, stiver 7 ducaton, escalan, escalin, guilder, stooter 8 ducatoon 9 dubbeltje 12 rijksdaalder
commune: Ede, Epe 4 Echt 5 Breda, Doorn, Hague 6 Dongen, Leyden 9 Amsterdam, Rotterdam 11 Doniawestal
council: 7 heemrad 8 heemraad, heemraat
fishing boat: 4 tode 6 hooker
former colony: 4 Java 6 Borneo 7 Celebes, Sumatra 9 New Guinea
gin: 8 schnapps
inlet: 9 Zuider Zee
island: 5 Texel 7 Ameland 8 Vlieland 9 Schelling
island group: Aru 5 Arroe, Arrou
lake: 7 Haarlem
legislative assembly: 4 Raad
measure: el; aam, ahm, aum, ell, kan, kop(pl.), mud, vat, zak 4 duim, lood, mijl, rood, rope, voet 5 anker, carat, roede, stoop, wisse 6 bunder, koppen, legger, maatje, muddle, mutsje, streep 7 leaguer, schepel 8 mimgelen, okshoofd, steekkan 10 vingerhoed
native: 5 Dutch 8 Dutchman
painter: Lis 4 Hals, Kalf, Neer 5 Helst, Steen 6 Leyden 7 De Houch, Hobbema, Seghers, Vermeer 8 Kroninck, Mostaert, Ter Borch 9 Rembrandt 10 Van de Velde 11 Van Ruisdael 19 Geertgen Tot Sint Jans
people: 5 Dutch 7 Flemish, Frisian
possessions: 4 Saba 7 Curacao, Surinam
pottery: 4 delf 5 delft 11 Dutch Guiana, St. Eustacius

province: Epe 7 Brabant, Drenthe, Holland, Limburg, Utrecht, Zeeland 9 Friesland, Groningen 10 Gelderland, Overijssel
reclaimed land: 6 polder
river: Eem 4 Leck, Maas, Rijn, Waal, Ysel 5 Meuse, Rhine, Yssel 6 Ijssel, Kromme 7 Scheldt
scholar: 7 Erasmus
sheriff: 6 schout
town hall: 9 stadhouse
uncle: eme, oom
vessel: 4 koff 5 yanky 6 schuit, schuyt
weight: ons 4 last, lood, pond 5 bahar, grein, pound 6 korrel 7 wichtje 8 esterlin, 9 esterling
woman: 4 frau, frow
netlike: 9 reticular
netop: 5 crony 6 friend 9 companion
netting: 4 lint, mesh 7 network
nettle: vex 4 fret, line 5 annoy, cnida, ettle, peeve, pique, sting 6 henbit, ruffle, splice 7 affront, blubber, knittle, provoke 8 irritant, irritate 9 urticacea 10 exasperate
nettle cell: 10 nematocyst
family: 10 Urticaceae
genus of: 10 parietaria
network (see also **net**): 6 plexus, reseau
neume: 6 pneuma
neural: 6 dorsal
neuralgia: 9 costalgia
neuter: 6 gender 7 neither, neutral, sexless 9 impartial
neutral: 4 gray 8 middling, negative 9 colorless 10 achromatic, indefinite 11 adiaphorous, indifferent 12 noncombatant
comb. form: 6 neutro
neutralize: 5 annul 7 abolish, balance, destroy, nullify, vitiate 9 frustrate 10 counteract 11 countervail 14 counterbalance
neutralizer: 6 alkali
Nevada: *lake:* 5 Tahoe
town: Ely 4 Elko, Reno 6 Carson, Fallon, Minden, Sparks 7 Sulphur 8 Lovelock, Mesquite 9 Henderson 10 Winnemucca
neve: 4 firn, snow 7 glacier
never: nay, nie(G.), not 4 nary, ne'er
nevertheless: but, yet 5 still 7 how-be-it, however 9 howsoever,, natheless 10 howsomever
nevus: 4 mole 5 tumor 7 spiloma 9 birthmark
new: neu(G.) 4 late, noval(L.) 5 fresh, green, novel 6 modern, recent, unused 7 foreign, strange, untried 8 neoteric, original, untested 10 additional, promethean, unfamiliar 11 fashionable, modernistic 12 unaccustomed 13 inexperienced
combining form: neo
New Caledonia: *bird:* 4 kagu
seaport: 5 Numea
New Deal agency: CCC, NRA, TVA
New England: *aristocrat:* 7 Brahmin
chair: 6 Carver
inhabitant: 6 Yankee
of the West: 9 Minnesota
settler: 7 Pilgrim, Puritan
New Guinea: *bay:* Oro
city: Lae 4 Daru 5 Soron 6 Rabaul
export: 5 copra
gulf: 4 Huon 5 Papua
hog: 4 bene
island: Aru 5 Ceram, Papua
island group: 7 Solomon
mountain: 6 Albert 8 Victoria 9 Carstensz 10 Wilhelmina
parrot: 4 lory
people: 5 Karon 6 Papuan
port: Lae 4 Daru
river: Fly 5 Sepik 7 Amberno 10 Strickland 15 Kaiserin Augusta
section: 8 Bunagona
New Hampshire: *academy:* 6 Exeter
city: 5 Dover, Keene 6 Antrim, Exeter, Nashua 7 Hanover, Laconia
county: 4 Coos
lake: 7 Sunapee
river: 4 Saco
state flower: 5 lilac
New Hebrides Island: Epi 4 Tana 5 Efate
port: 4 Vila
New Jersey: *city:* 6 Verona 7 Bayonne, Raritan, Trenton
river: 6 Ramapo 7 Raritan
New Mexico: *county:* 4 Mora, Taos
resort: 4 Taos
river: 4 Gila 5 Pecos
state flower: 5 yucca
New Testament (see also **Bible**): *book:* 4 Acts, John, Jude, Luke, Mark 5 James, Peter, Titus 6 Romans 7 Hebrews, Matthew, Timothy 8 Philemon 9 Ephesians, Galatians 10 Colossians, Revelation 11 Corinthians, Philippians 13 Thessalonians
gospel: 4 John, Luke, Mark 7 Matthew
letter: 7 epistle
New York: *canal:* 4 Erie
city: Rye 4 Avon, Erie, Rome, Troy 5 Ilion, Nyack, Olean, Owego, Tioga, Utica 6 Albany, Cohoes, Elmira, Esopus, Geneva, Goshen, Gotham, Ithaca, Malone, Oneida, Oswego 7 Buffalo, Endwell 8 Saratoga 10 Binghamton 11 Skaneateles 12 Niagara Falls
county: 4 Erie 5 Tioga, Wayne, Yates 6 Cayuga, Monroe, Oneida, Oswego, Seneca 7 Chemung, Genesee, Niagara, Ontario, Orleans, Steuben, Tompkin, Wyoming 8 Al-

legany, Onondaga, Schuyler 9 Chatauqua, Courtland 10 Livingston 11 Cattaraugus
early land owner: 7 patroon
harbor entrance: 14 Ambrose channel
Indian tribe: 6 Seneca
lake: 6 Cayuga, Croton, Oneida, Seneca 7 Saranac 8 Onondaga 11 Skaneateles
law: 6 Baumes
resort: 7 Saranac
river: 5 Tioga 6 Harlem, Hudson 7 Genesee, Niagara 8 Canisteo, Cohocton
state flower: 4 rose
university: 7 Colgate, Cornell 8 Columbia

New York City: 6 Gotham
island: 5 Ellis 6 Staten 7 Bedloes, Liberty, Welfare 9 Governors, Manhattan 10 Blackwells
prison: 5 Tombs
street: 4 Wall 6 Bowery
subway: BMT, IND, IRT

New Zealand: *anteater:* 7 echidna
bird: kea, moa, oii, poe, roa 4 kaka, kiwi, koko, kulu, ruru, titi, weka 6 kakapo 7 apteryx, wrybill 8 morepork, notornis
city: see *town* below
clay: 4 papa
dance: 4 haka
fern: 4 weki 5 pitau, wheki
fish: ihi 5 hikus
flax: 8 harakeke
flightless bird: 4 weka 7 apteryx
fort: pa; pah, pau
grass: 6 toetoe
gun: 6 tupara
heron: 6 kotuku
hut: 5 whare
island: 4 Otea 7 Stewart
kiwi: moa, roa 7 apteryx
lake: Ada 4 Gunn, Ohau, Rere 5 Hawea, Okaro, Taupo 6 Fergus, Pukaki, Rotoma, Sylvan, Teanau, Tekapo, Wanaka 7 Brunner, Diamond, Kanieri, Okareka, Rotoiti, Rotoroa, Rotorua 8 Okataina, Paradise, Rotoaira, Tarawera, Wakatipu 9 Manapouri, Rotokawau 10 Rotomahana 12 Rerewhakaitu, Waikaremoana
mahogany: 6 totara
mountain: 4 Cook 5 Ohope 6 Egmont 7 Aorangi, Pihanga, Raupehu, Ruapehu, Tauhara, Tauhera 8 Aspiring, Tarawera, Tauranga 9 Blackburn, Messenger, Ngauruhoe, Tongariro 10 Ngongotaha, Tapuaenuka
national bird: 4 kiwi
ostrich: moa
owl: 4 ruru
palm: 5 nikau
parrot: kea 4 kaka 6 kakapo
people: Ati 5 Arawa, Maori 7 Ringatu
pine: 4 rima 6 totara 9 kahikatea
port: Lae 7 Aukland, Dunedin 10 Wellington
reptile: 7 tuatara, tuatera
river: 7 Waikato 8 Wanganui 9 Taramakau, Tongariro, Whakapapa 10 Rangitikei 11 Waimakariri
settlement: pa; pah, pau
shark: 4 mako
shrub: 4 tutu
song: 6 waiata
spa: 5 Aroha 7 Rotorua, Tearoha
storehouse: 5 whata
town: 5 Levin, Otaki, Taupo 6 Foxton, Napier, Nelson, Oamaru, Picton, Timaru 7 Dunedin, Raetihi, Rotorua 8 Auckland, Gisborne, Hamilton, Hastings, Tauranga, Wanganui 9 Ashburton, Greymouth, Masterton, Whangarei 10 Dannenirke, Palmerston, Queenstown, Wellington 12 Christchurch, Invercargill
tree: ake 4 hino, kopi, mako, miro, pelu, puka, rata, rimu, tawa, toro, toru, whau 5 hinau, hinou, karui, mahoe, maire, mapau, ngaio 6 ake-ake, karaka, kowhai, manuka, puriri, tarata, titoki 7 akepiro, taratah, wahahen 8 hiropito, makomako 9 kaiwhiria 10 pohutukawa
vine: aka
volcano: 6 Egmont 7 Ruapehu 9 Ngauruhoe
wages: utu
welcome: 8 haeremai

newcomer: 7 settler 8 comeling 9 immigrant

newel: 4 post

newfangled: 5 novel 6 modern

Newfoundland: *cape:* 4 Race
log house: 4 tilt

newly: 4 anew 5 again 6 afresh, lately 8 recently

news: 4 word 6 notice 7 tidings 11 information, instruction 12 intelligence
agency: AP, UP; DNB, INS, UPI 4 Tass(-Russ.) 5 Domei 7 Reuters 13 International
gatherer: 8 reporter
media: TV 5 radio 7 journal 8 magazine 9 newspaper 10 periodical, television
statement: 8 bulletin

newsboy: 7 camelot

newsmonger: 6 gossip 7 tattler 8 reporter

newspaper: 4 News 5 daily, paper, sheet, Times 6 Herald 7 courant, Gazette, Mercury, tabloid, Tribune 9 newsprint 11 publication
article: 4 item
collectively: 5 press

employee: **6** editor **7** printer **8** pressman, reporter **9** columnist, linotyper **10** cartoonist, compositor, journalist **12** photographer **13** correspondent
file: **6** morgue
hoax: **6** canard
part of: ear **6** banner, sports **8** obituary **9** editorial
newsstand: **5** booth, kiosk, stall
newt: ask, eft **4** evet **6** lizard, triton **7** axolotl **10** salamander
next: **4** then **5** after, ewest(Sc.), neist(Sc.) **7** closest, ensuing, nearest **9** adjoining, following, immediate, proximate **10** contiguous, succeeding **12** conterminous
next to: **6** almost, beside, nearly **8** adjacent
nexus: tie **4** link **10** connection **15** interconnection
nib: pen **4** beak, bill **5** point, prong
nibble: eat, nab **4** bite, gnaw, knap **6** browse **7** chimble, gnabble, gnatter
Nicaragua: *city:* **4** Leon **6** Masaya **7** Granada, Managua **9** Choluteca **10** Chinandega
coin: **4** peso **7** centavo, cordoba
lake: **7** Managua
measure: **4** vara **5** cahiz, milla **6** suerte, tercia **7** cajuela, estadal, manzana **10** caballeria
river: **4** Coco, Tuma **5** Wanks **7** San Juan
weight: bag **4** caja **8** tonelada
nice: **4** fine, good **5** exact **6** bonita, dainty, minute, peachy, queasy, subtle **7** elegant, finical, genteel, precise, prudish, refined **8** delicate, exacting, pleasant, pleasing **9** agreeable, appealing, exquisite, squeamish **10** appetizing, delightful, discerning, fastidious, particular, scrupulous **11** considerate, punctilious, scrumptious **13** hypercritical **14** discriminating
niche: **4** apse, nook **6** alcove, covert, recess **7** edicule, retreat **9** habitacle
nick: cut, nob **4** chip, slit **5** cheat, notch, tally, trick **6** arrest, record **7** defraud **9** indention
nickel alloy: **5** invar
nickel compound: **8** argenton
nickelodeon: **7** jukebox
nickname (see also **penname, pseudonym**): **6** agname, byword **7** misname, moniker **8** cognomen, monicker **9** sobriquet **10** soubriquet
James Boswell: **5** Bozzy
Winston Churchill: **6** Winnie
Georges Clemenceau: **5** Tiger
Benjamin Disraeli: **5** Dizzy
Thomas Edison: **17** Wizard of Menlo Park
Dwight Eisenhower: Ike
Elizabeth I: **11** Virgin Queen
Frederick I: **10** Barbarossa
Ernest Hemingway: **4** Papa
Andrew Jackson: **10** Old Hickory
Abraham Lincoln: **9** Honest Abe
Louis XIV: **7** Sun King
Joe Louis: **11** Brown Bomber
Mary I: **10** Bloody Mary
Napoleon I: **14** Little Corporal
Napoleon II: **7** L'Aiglon
Richard Nixon: **10** Tricky Dick
Henry Percy: **7** Hotspur
William Pitt: **13** Great Commoner
Richard I: **11** Lion-Hearted
Richard III: **10** Crouchback
Babe Ruth: **7** Bambino **12** Sultan of Swat
Joseph Stilwell: **10** Vinegar Joe
Charles Stratton: **8** Tom Thumb
nicknaming: **12** prosonomasia
nictate: **4** wink **5** blink, twink **7** twinkle **9** nictitate
niddick: **4** nape
nide: **5** brood
nidge: **5** shake **6** quiver
nidget: **4** fool **5** idiot
nidification: **7** nesting
nidor: **5** aroma, savor, scent
nidus: **4** nest
nieve: **4** fist, hand, neif
niff-naff: **6** trifle
nifty: **4** good **5** smart **7** stylish
Nigeria: *people:* Aro, Ebo, Edo, Ibo, Ijo, Vai **4** Beni, Eboe, Efik, Ejam, Ekoi, Nupe **5** Benin
port: **5** Lagos **7** Calabar
province: Isa **4** Nupe, Ondo **5** Warri
river: Oli
town: Aba, Ede, Isa **4** Bidi, Offa **5** Lagos **6** Ibadan, Yakoba **9** Ogbomosho
tree: **5** afara
walled city: **4** Kano
niggard: **8** scrimper **9** skinflint **10** curmudgeon
niggardly: **4** mean **5** close **6** narrow, scanty, stingy **7** miserly **8** churlish, wretched **10** avaricious **11** closefisted **12** parsimonious
niggle: **6** potter, putter, trifle
nigh: at **4** near **5** close **6** almost, nearly **8** adjacent **10** contiguous **11** neighboring
night: **4** nuit(F.) **8** darkness
comb. form: **4** nyct **5** nycti, nycto
goddess: Nox, Nyx
goddess of: Nyx **6** Hecate
pert. to: **9** nocturnal
night bird: **10** shearwater **11** nightingale
night blindness: **10** nyctalopia
night-wandering: **11** noctivagant
nightcap: **6** biggin
nightchurr: **10** goatsucker
nightclub: **7** cabaret

nightfall: een, eve 4 dusk, even 8 twilight
nightingale: 8 philomel 9 philomela
nightjar: 5 potoo 9 nighthawk 10 goatsucker
nightmare: 5 dream, fiend 7 incubus 9 cauchemar(F.), ephialtes
nightshade: 5 morel 7 henbane, morelle 10 belladonna 11 bittersweet
nigrescent: 9 blackfish
nihil: 7 nothing
nihilist: 9 anarchist
nil: 4 zero 7 nothing
Nile: *bird:* 4 ibis 7 wryneck
boat: 5 baris 6 nuggar 8 dahabeah
captain: 4 rais, reis
dam: 5 Aswan
falls: 5 Ripon
fish: 5 saide 8 mormyrid 9 mormyroid
houseboat: 8 dahabeah
island: 4 Roda
people: 4 Madi 5 Nilot
plant: 4 sudd 5 lotus
reptile: 9 crocodile
river gauge: 9 nilometer
town: 5 Cairo, Rejaf 7 Rosetta
tributary: 6 Atbara, Kagera
nilgai: 8 antelope
nim tree: 4 neem 7 margosa
nimb: 4 halo
nimble: 4 deft, lish, spry 5 agile, alert, fleet, quick 6 active, adroit, clever, feirie, lissom, lively, prompt, volant 9 dexterous 11 quick-witted
nimbly: 6 featly 9 deliverly
nimbose: 6 cloudy, stormy
nimbus: 4 halo 5 cloud, vapor 6 gloria 7 aureole 10 atmosphere
nimiety: 6 excess 10 redundancy
nimmer 5 thief
nimrod: 5 ruler 6 hunter, tyrant
nimshi: 4 fool 7 halfwit
nincompoop: 4 dolt, fool 5 moron, ninny 9 simpleton
nine: 6 ennead 8 ninefold
based on: 8 novenary
comb. form: 5 ennea
days' devotion: 6 novena
group of: 5 nonet 6 ennead
inches: 4 span
nine-eyes: 7 lamprey
nine-headed monster: 5 Hydra
nine-killer: 6 shrike
ninepin: 6 kayles 7 skittle 8 skittles
ninny: See **nincompoop**
ninth: 5 nonus(L.)
ninut: 6 magpie
Niobe: *brother:* 6 Pelops
father: 8 Tantalus
husband: 7 Amphion
sister-in-law: 5 Aedon
nip: cut, sip 4 bite, clip, dram, tang 5 check, clamp, draft, drink, frost, pinch, seize, sever, steal, sting 6 blight, catnip, snatch, tipple, twitch 7 squeeze 8 compress 10 pickpocket
nipa: 4 atap, palm 5 attap, drink 6 liquor
nipcheese: 5 miser 6 purser
nipper: boy, lad 4 claw, grab 5 biter 6 cunner, pliers, urchin 7 forceps, incisor, pincers 8 pincenez 9 handcuffs 10 eyeglasses
Nippon: See **Japan**
nippy: 5 brisk, quick, sharp 6 active, biting, nimble 7 nipping 8 vigorous
nisse: 6 goblin, kobold, sprite 7 brownie
nisus: 6 effort 7 impulse 8 endeavor, striving
Nisus' daughter: 6 Scylla
nit: egg, nut 5 speck 6 insect 8 hazelnut
niter, nitre: 5 peter, petre 6 potash 9 saltpeter
combining form: 5 nitro
nither: 5 blast 6 debase, shiver 7 tremble 9 humiliate
nithing: 6 coward 7 dastard
nitid: 6 bright, glossy 7 glowing, radiant 8 lustrous, nitidous
nitrate: 4 salt 5 ester
sodium: 5 niter, nitre
nitrocotton: 9 guncotton
nitroform: 15 trinitromethane
nitrogen: 9 quinoline
combining form: az; azo
compound: 7 ammonia
niveau 5 level
nivenite: 9 uraninite
niveous: 5 snowy 8 snowlike
nix: no 6 goblin, nobody, sprite 7 nothing
Njorth: *daughter:* 5 Freya 6 Freyja
son: 4 Frey 5 Freyr
wife: 6 Skathi
no: na(Sc.), ne; nae(Sc.), naw, nay, nea(Sc.), nit, nix, non(F.) 4 nein(G.), nyet(Russ.), play 5 drama 6 denial 7 refusal
no one: nix 6 nobody
Noah: *dove:* 7 Columba
father: 6 Lamech
grandson: 4 Aram
great-grandson: Uz; Hul
place of debarkation: 6 Ararat
raven: 6 Corvus
son: Ham, Sem 4 Shem 7 Japheth
wine cup: 6 Crater
nob: 4 head, jack
nobble: 5 bribe, cheat, steal 7 swindle 12 incapacitate
nobby: 4 chic 5 swell 7 stylish 9 excellent, first-rate 11 fashionable
noble: 4 epic, fine, free, gent, good, pure, rial 5 burly, ducal, grand, ideal, lofty, manly,

proud 6 august, epical, famous, heroic 7 eminent, exalted, gallant, liberal, soulful, stately, sublime 8 elevated, generous, glorious, nobleman, precious, renowned, splendid 9 chevalier, dignified, excellent, honorable 10 idealistic, noblewoman 11 illustrious, magnanimous, magnificent

noble pine: 10 pipsissewa

nobleman: don 4 duke, earl, lord, peer 5 barin(Russ.), baron, count 6 knight, varlet 7 grandee(Sp.), hidalgo, marquis 8 marquess 10 aristocrat

pert. to: 5 ducal 6 lordly

nobleness of birth: 6 eugeny

noblewoman: 4 lady 7 duchess, peeress 8 baroness, countess, marquise 10 marquisess 11 marchioness

nobody: 4 none 9 nonentity

nocent: 6 guilty 7 harmful, hurtful, noxious 8 criminal

noctambulism: 12 somnambulism

noctuid: 4 moth, worm

noctule: bat

nocturnal: 5 night 7 nightly 11 nightwalker

nocturnal mammal: bat 5 lemur

nocturne: 7 lullaby 8 serenade

nocuous: See **noxious, poisonous**

nod: bow 4 beck, bend, doze, wink 5 droop 6 assent, beckon, drowse, nutate, salute 7 signify 8 nutation

nodding: 6 nutant 7 annuent 8 cernuous

noddy: auk 4 fool 5 ninny 6 fulmar, noodle 7 hackney 9 simpleton

node: bow 4 bump, knob, knot, lump 5 joint, nodus 6 nodule 7 dilemma, granule 8 swelling, tubercle 10 difficulty 12 complication, protuberance

nodule: 4 auge, node 5 geode 7 noblock 9 septarium

noel: 5 carol 9 Christmas

noetic: 12 intellectual

nog: ale, peg, pin 5 block 6 eggnog, noggin 8 beverage, treenail

noggin (see also **noodle**): cup, mug, nog 4 pate

noir: 5 black

noise (see also **sound**): air, din 5 bruit, rumor 6 gossip, norate, report

noiseless: 5 quiet, still, tacit 6 silent 7 catlike

noisemaker: 4 bell, horn 6 rattle

noisette: 5 hazel

noisome (see also **noxious**): 4 foul 5 fetid 7 harmful, hurtful 8 stinking 9 offensive 10 disgusting, malodorous, pernicious 11 destructive, unwholesome

noisy: 4 loud 6 clashy 7 blatant 8 brawling, clattery, strepent 9 clamorous, hilarious, turbulent 10 boisterous, tumultuous, vociferous 12 obstreperous

noll: See **noodle**

nom: 4 name 10 nominative

nom de plume: 7 pen name 9 pseudonym

noma: 5 ulcer

nomad: 4 Arab, Luri, Moor 5 Alani, gypsy, rover 6 roamer, roving 7 Bedouin, Saracen, scenite 8 wanderer

nomadic: 9 itinerant

nomadism: 10 wanderlust

nome: 4 Elis 5 nomos 8 nomarchy, province 10 department

nomen: 4 gens, name

nomenclature: 4 list, name 8 glossary, register 9 catalogue, recounter 10 dictionary, vocabulary 11 appellation, designation

nomic: 8 ordinary 9 customary 12 conventional

nominal: 6 slight, unreal 7 titular, trivial 8 platonic 11 theoretical 13 unsubstantial

nominalist: 8 Occamist 9 terminist

nominate: 4 call, leet(Sc.), name 5 slate 7 appoint, entitle, propose, specify 10 denominate

nominee: 9 candidate

nomothetical: 11 legislative

non-kosher: 4 tref

non-Mahometan: 5 Kafir

nonage: 10 immaturity 12 youthfulness

nonaspirate: 4 lene

nonbeliever: 5 pagan 7 atheist 8 agnostic

nonce: 7 present 8 occasion

noncentric: 8 acentric

nonchalant: 4 cool 6 casual 8 careless 10 insouciant 11 indifferent 13 imperturbable

nonclerics: lay 4 laic

noncombatant: 8 chaplain, civilian, observer

noncompliance: 7 refusal 10 obstinance 13 recalcitrance

nonconcurrence: 7 dissent

nonconductor: 5 resin

nonconforming: 9 anomalous

nonconformist: 5 rebel 6 hippie 7 beatnik, heretic 8 bohemian 9 dissenter

nonconformity: 6 heresy 7 dissent 9 recusance, recusancy 10 dissidence 13 individualism

nondependent: 11 independent

nondescript: 13 indescribable 14 indeterminable

none: no; nae 4 nane(Sc.), neen

nonentity: 4 zero 6 cipher 7 nothing

nonessential: 9 extrinsic 10 adiaphoron 11 unnecessary 12 adventitious 14 circumstantial
nonesuch: 5 apple, model 7 paragon 8 paradigm 9 matchless, nonpareil, unequaled, unrivaled
nonexistent: 4 null 8 nonbeing
nonfestal: 6 ferial
nonfulfillment: 6 breach 12 infringement
nongrata: 9 unwelcome
nongypsy: 4 gajo
nonobjective: 8 abstract
nonobservance: 9 violation
nonpareil; 4 best 7 paragon, perfect, unequal 8 nonesuch, peerless 9 unrivaled
nonpasserine bird: 4 tody 6 hoopoe, motmot 8 hornbill 10 kingfisher
nonphysical: 7 psychic 9 psychical
nonplus: 5 blank, stump, trump 6 puzzle 7 perplex 9 embarrass
nonpositive: 8 negative 9 privative
nonproductive: 6 barren 7 sterile 10 unfruitful
nonprofessional: lay 4 laic 7 amateur
nonsense: bah, pah, rot 4 blah, bosh, buff, bunk, flam, tosh 5 blash, folly, fudge, haver, hooey, stite(Sc.) 6 bunkum, drivel, faddle, folder 7 blarney, blather, buncome, inanity, twaddle 8 blahblah, blathery, falderal, folderol, flimflam, trumpery 9 absurdity, fandangle, frivolity, moonshine, poppycock, silliness 10 balderdash, flapdoodle, flumdiddle, galimatias, triviality 11 flumadiddle, foolishness, monkeyshine 12 fiddle-dee-dee, flummadiddle, flummydiddle 16 preposterousness
nonsolid: 5 fluid 6 liquid
noodle: 4 bean, fool, head, nizy, noll, pate 5 ninny, nizey, noddy 6 boodle, noddle, noggin 9 blockhead, simpleton 10 caper-nutie 11 caper-noitie
nook: in; out, wro 4 cant, cove, glen, hole 5 angle, herne, niche 6 cantle, corner, cranny, recess 7 crevice, retreat
noon: 6 midday 8 meridian 11 culmination
noose: tie 4 bond, dull, grin, loop, trap 5 bight, grane, honda, snare, widdy 6 entrap, halter, lariat 7 ensnare, execute, laniard, lanyard, springe 8 slip-knot
armed with: 10 laquearian
nope: 9 bullfinch
nor: ner 7 neither 8 negative 10 connective
norate: 5 noise, rumor 6 gossip
nori: 4 alga 7 seaweed
noria: 5 wheel
norie: 9 cormorant
norite: 6 gabbro
norm: 4 rule, type 5 gauge, model, norma 7 average, pattern 8 standard, template
norma: 4 mold 5 gauge 6 square 7 pattern
normal: 5 usual 7 natural, regular, typical
Normandy: *beach:* 5 Omaha
capital: 4 Caen 5 Rouen
conqueror: 5 Rollo 10 Eisenhower
department: 4 Eure, Orne 6 Manche 8 Calvados
duke: 5 Rollo
town: 7 Saint-Lo
Norn: 4 fate, Urth, Wyrd 5 Skuld 9 Verthandi
Norse (see also **Scandinavia**): 4 mink 8 Teutonic 9 Icelandic, Norwegian 12 Scandinavian
abode of gods: 6 Asgard
alphabet: 5 runic
bard: 5 scald, skald 7 sagaman
chieftain: 4 jarl
demigoddess of destiny: Urd
demon: 4 Mara, Surt 5 Surtr
epic: 4 Edda
explorer: 4 Eric
fate: 4 Norn
first man: 4 Askr
first woman: 5 Embla
giant: 4 Atli, Loke, Loki, Natt, Norn, Nott, Wate, Ymer, Ymir 5 Jotun, Mimer, Mimir, Thrym 6 Fafnir, Jotunn
god (see also *giant* above): As, Ve; Asa, Ase, Ran, Tiu, Tyr, Ull, Zio 4 Frey, Hler, Hoth, Loke, Loki, Odin, Surt, Thor, Vali 5 Aeger, Aegir, Aesir(pl.), Baldr, Brage, Bragi, Donar, Freyr, Gymir, Othin, Surtr, Vanir(pl.), Wodan, Woden, Wotan 6 Balder, Hoenir, Njorth 7 Forsete, Forseti, Heimdal, Vitharr 9 Heimdallr, Hlorrithi
goddess: Dis, Eir, Hel 4 Frea, Hela, Nora, Saga, Urth, Wyrd 5 Freya, Frigg, Nanna 6 Freyja, Frigga 7 Asynjur
goddess of earth: 4 Erda
king: 4 Atli
mythological wolf: 6 Fenrir
night: 4 Natt, Nott
nobleman: 4 yarl
poem: 4 rune
poet: 5 scald, skald
saint: 4 Olaf 5 Olaus
sea serpent: 6 Kraken 7 Midgard
tale: 4 saga
toast: 5 skoal
viking: 5 Rollo
watchdog: 4 Garm 5 Garmr
world tree: 8 Ygdrasil
norsel: 4 band, line 6 fillet
North Africa: *antelope:* 5 addax 7 gazelle
country: 7 Algeria, Tunisia
fruit: fig 4 date
lyre: 6 kissar
measure: 4 rotl

oasis: **4** wadi, wady
people: **4** Moor **5** Nilot **6** Hamite
port: **4** Sfax
sheep: **6** aoudad
valley: **4** wadi, wady
North America: *bird:* **6** fulmar **7** grackle **8** cardinal, killdeer, kingrail **10** bufflehead
discoverer: **5** Cabot
herb: **4** sego
Indian: see **Indian**
marmoset: **7** tamarin
mountain: **5** Logan **8** McKinley
orchids: **9** arethusas
owl: **7** wapacut
people: **7** Mexican **8** American, Canadian
reindeer: **7** caribou
thrush: **5** robin
tree: lin **4** mabi, sorb, titi **5** balsa, papaw **6** balsam, pawpaw, redbud, tupelo **7** catalpa, hickory **8** basswood, oneberry, sweetsop **9** sassafras
North Atlantic: *island:* **7** Britain, Iceland, Ireland **9** Manhattan
seagull: **4** skua
North Britain: **8** Scotland **9** Caledonia
North Carolina: *cape:* **4** Fear **8** Hatteras
college: **4** Elon
county: **4** Ashe **5** Anson, Avery **6** Lenoir
people: **7** Buffalo, Tarheel
river: Tar **5** Neuse **6** Pee Dee
town: **5** Boone **6** Durham, Lenoir, Oxford, Whynot **7** Edenton, Raleigh, Roxboro
North Dakota: *city:* **5** Fargo, Minot
county: **6** Traill
North Pole discoverer: **5** Peary
North Sea: *arm:* **9** Skagerrak, Skager-Rak
canal: **4** Kiel
river: **5** Weser
North Star: **7** polaris **8** loadstar, lodestar, polestar **10** tramontane
North Vietnam: *capital:* **5** Hanoi
city: **8** Haiphong
gulf: **6** Tonkin
monetary unit: **4** dong
north wind: **6** boreas
northeaster: **4** blow, gale, wind **5** storm
northern: **6** boreal **13** septentrional
Northern Bear: **6** Russia
Northmen: See **Norse**
Northumberland river: **4** Tyne
Norway: *bird:* **4** rype
boat: **4** pram **5** praam **6** praham
capital: **4** Oslo
cart: **11** stolkjaerre
chieftain: **4** jarl
city: see *town* below
coin: ore **5** krone
counties: **5** amter
county: amt **5** fylke **6** fylker(pl.), Tromso **7** Finmark
dance: **7** halling
embroidery: **9** hardanger
goblin: **5** nisse **6** kobold
governor: **6** amtman
haddock: **8** rosefish
inlet: **5** fiord, fjord
language: **5** Norse
measure: fot, mal, pot **4** alen, maal **5** kande **6** fathom **7** skieppe **9** korntonde
mountain: **5** Sogne **6** Kjolen **7** Numedal **8** Telemark, Ustetind **9** Blodfjell, Harteigen, Ramnanosi **10** Galdhoepig, Glitretind, Hallingdal, Vibmesnosi **11** Myrdalfjell **14** Hallingskarvet, Hardangerjokul, Skagastolstind
parliament: **8** Storting **9** Storthing
plateau: **5** Dovre, fjeld **9** Hardanger
river: Oi; Ena **4** Tana **6** Lougen, Glomma
ruler: **6** hersir
saint: **4** Olaf **5** Olaus
town: Nes **4** Oslo(c.), Voss **5** Bjort, Hamar, Skein, Skjak **6** Bergen, Horten, Larvik, Narvik **7** Alesund, Drammen **9** Stavanger, Trondhjem **10** Kristiania(c.) **11** Christiania(c.)
weight: lod **4** mark, pund **9** skaalpund **10** bismerpund
nose: neb, nez(F.), pry, spy **4** beak, conk, lora(pl.) **5** lorum, scent, smell, sniff, snoop, snout **6** detect, muffle, muzzle, nozzle, search, socket **7** advance, perfume **8** discover, informer, perceive **9** proboscis **11** investigate
cartilage: **6** septum
inflammation: **6** coryza **8** rhinitis
large: **6** nasute
medicine: **7** errhine
muscle: **7** nasalio
openings: **5** nares
partition: **5** vomer
pert. to: **5** nasal **6** narial, rhinal
snub: **6** simous
nosebleed: **9** epistaxis
nosegay: **4** odor, posy **5** scent **6** boquet **7** bouquet, perfume
nosegay tree: **10** frangipani
nosepiece: **5** nasal **6** nozzle **8** noseband
nosey: See **nosy**
nosh: **4** chew **5** munch, snack
nosocomium: **8** hospital
nostalgia: **7** longing **10** melancholy **12** homesickness
nostic: **12** paragerontic
Nostradamus: **4** seer **7** prophet **10** forecaster
nostril: **4** nare **5** nares(pl.), naris(pl.) **6** thrill
pert. to: **5** naric **6** narial, narine

nostril-shaped: 8 nariform
nosy: 6 prying 7 curious 8 fragrant 10 malodorous 11 inquisitive
not (see also **non**): na(Sc.); nae(Sc.), nay, nor 4 baal, bail, bale, nott 5 shorn 6 nought, polled, shaven 7 neither 8 hornless, negation, negative 11 nothingness
any: no; nul 4 nane(Sc.), nary, none
at all: 5 never 6 noways, nowise
either: 7 neither
final: 13 interlocutory
otherwise than: 6 merely
prefix: il, im, ir, un, non
the same: 5 other 7 another 9 different
notable: V.I.P. 6 fabled, famous 7 eminent, storied 8 eventful, historic 9 memorable, notorious 10 noteworthy, remarkable 12 considerable 13 distinguished, extraordinary
notal: 6 dorsal
notandum: 4 note 5 entry 9 memoranda(pl.) 10 memorandum
notar: 6 notary
notarize: 6 attest 7 certify
notary: 5 notar(Sc.), noter 7 graffer, notable 8 notebook, observer, official 9 notorious, scrivener
chief: 11 protonotary 12 prothonotary
notation: 4 memo, note 7 marking 10 annotation 14 representation
phonetic: 5 Romic
notator: 5 noter 8 recorder 9 annotator
notch: cut, dag, gap, hag, jag 4 cope, dent, dint, gimp, hila(pl.), kerf, nick, step 5 crena, grade, hilum, score, tally 6 crenae(pl.), crotch, defile, degree, indent, record, scotch 7 crenate, serrate 8 undercut 9 indenture 11 indentation
notched: 5 erose 7 crenate, serrate 8 crenated, serrated
irregularly: 5 erose
note: I.O.U., jot, see 4 bill, chit, fame, heed, line, mark, memo, name, sign, sole, song, tone, tune 5 label, sound, token 6 billet, letter, minute, notice, record, regard, remark, renown, report 7 betoken, comment, message, missive, notanda(pl.), observe 8 annotate, breviate, dispatch, eminence, notandum, perceive 9 character 10 indication, memorandum, prominence, reputation 11 distinction, observation
accompanying: 8 overtone
bank: 6 finnip, flimsy 8 frogskin
bugle: mot
explanatory: 8 scholium 10 annotation
highest: ela
marginal: 6 postil 7 apostil 9 apostille
middle: 4 mese
musical: 4 half 5 breve, whole 6 eighth 7 punctus, quarter 9 semibreve
prisoner's: 4 kite
promissory: bon
writer: 9 annotator
note well: N.B.(L.) 8 nota bene(L.)
notebook: log 5 diary 6 street 7 journal 10 adversaria
notecase: 10 pocketbook
noted: 9 distingue, well-known 10 celebrated 11 illustrious
notes: *literary:* ana
miscellaneous: 10 adversaria
noteworthy: 7 eminent, notable 10 remarkable 11 outstanding 12 considerable
nothing: nil 4 free, luke, nill, zero 5 aught, nihil 6 naught, nought, trifle 7 useless 10 triviality 12 nonexistence, unimportance 14 insignificance
nothing but: 4 mere, only
nothous: 8 spurious 12 illegitimate
notice: ad; ban, see 4 espy, heed, idea, mark, mind, news, note, sign 5 await, quote 6 advice, billet, espial, notion, regard, remark 7 affiche, article, discern, mention, observe, warning 8 apprisal, citation, civility 9 attention 10 cognizance, intimation 11 garnishment 12 announcement, intelligence, notification 13 consideration
book: 5 blurb
death: 4 obit 8 obituary
favorable: 4 rave
honorable: 8 citation
leave of: 8 mittimus
marriage: ban 4 bans 5 banns
official: 5 edict 8 bulletin 12 proclamation
paid: ad 13 advertisement
Patent Office: 6 caveat
refuse: 6 ignore
noticeable: 7 evident, notable, salient 8 striking 9 prominent 10 noteworthy, remarkable 11 conspicuous, outstanding, significant
notification: 6 notice
notify: bid 4 cite, page, tell, warn 6 inform 7 apprise, declare, frutify, publish 8 acquaint
notion: bee 4 buzz, idea, idee, view, whim 5 fancy, image 6 belief, desire, maggot, notice, theory, vagary 7 conceit, inkling, opinion, thought 9 intention 10 conception 11 inclination
notoriety: 5 eclat 9 publicity
notorious: big 5 known 6 arrant, crying, famous, notour 7 evident 8 apparent, flagrant, infamous, manifest 11 conspicuous
notum: 4 back
notus: 9 southwind

notwithstanding: yet 4 even 6 algate, mauger, maugre 7 algates, despite, however 8 although 12 nevertheless
nougat: 5 candy 8 nut shell 10 confection
nought: bad, nil 4 zero 5 wrong 7 nothing, useless 9 worthless 10 wickedness
noun: 4 name, word 11 substantive
form: 4 case 6 gender
indeclinable: 6 aptote
kind of: 6 common, proper
suffix: ac, et, ia, ic; ent, ery, ial, ier, ing, ion, ior, ist 4 ence 5 orium
verbal: 6 gerund
nourish: 4 feed, grow 5 breed, nurse 6 foison, foster, suckle, supply 7 cherish, support, sustain, develop 9 cultivate, stimulate
nourishing: 4 alma 6 alible, hearty 8 nutrient 9 alimental, nutritive 10 alimentary
nourishment: 4 food, meat 5 manna 6 foison 7 aliment, pabulum 9 nutriment 10 sustenance 13 nutritiveness 14 nutritiousness
nous: 4 mind 6 reason 9 intellect
nova: new
Nova Scotia: 6 Acadia, Acadie
bay: 5 Fundy
cape: 5 Canso, Sable 6 Breton, George
mountain ash: 8 dogberry
people: 8 Acadians 9 bluenoses
port: 5 Truro
novel: new 4 book 5 fresh, story 6 recent 7 fiction, romance, strange, unusual 8 original, uncommon 10 newfangled
cut: 11 abridgement 12 condensation
novelette: 5 conte
novelty: fad 6 change 10 innovation
novice: dub 4 puny, tiro, tyro 5 rooky 6 rookie, tyrone 7 amateur, convert, learner 8 beginner, freshman, neophyte 9 greenhorn 10 apprentice 11 abecedarian
novitiate: 9 probation 14 apprenticeship
now: noo(Sc.) 4 here 5 today 7 present 9 forthwith 11 immediately
nowise: 5 navis
nowt: ox 4 lout, oxen 6 cattle 7 bullock 9 blockhead
noxious: ill 4 evil 6 nocent 7 baneful, harmful, hurtful, nocuous, noisome, vicious 8 virulent 9 injurious, miasmatic, poisonous 10 pernicious 11 deleterious, destructive, unwholesome 12 insalubrious
noy: 4 harm 5 annoy
nozzle: 4 nose, vent 5 snout
nuance: 5 shade
nub: 4 core, crux, gist, hang, knob, knot, knub, lump, neck, snag 12 protuberance
nubia: 4 wrap 5 cloud
nubile: 12 marriageable
nubilous: 5 foggy, misty, vague 6 cloudy 7 obscure 10 indefinite
nucament: 5 ament
nucha: 4 nape
nucleus: 4 core 5 focus, umbra 6 kernel
pert. to: 8 nucleate
starch: 4 hila(pl.) 5 hilum
nude: 4 bare 5 model, naked 6 statue 7 denuded, picture 8 painting, stripped 9 unclothed, uncovered, undressed
nudge: jog, nog 4 knub, lump, poke, push 5 block, elbow
nudibranch: 7 mollusk
nudist: 7 Adamite 12 gymnosophist
nugatory: 4 vain 7 invalid, trivial 8 trifling 9 frustrate, worthless 11 ineffectual
nugget: 4 hunk, lump, mass, slug
nuisance: 4 harm, hurt, pest 6 injury 9 annoyance 13 inconvenience
null: nil 7 nullify 11 nonexistent 13 insignificant
nullah: 5 gorge, gully 6 ravine
nullifidian: 7 skeptic
nullify: 4 flaw, null, undo, void 5 abate, annul, elide 6 cancel, negate, repeal 7 abolish, destroy 8 abrogate, evacuate 9 frustrate 10 counteract, disappoint, invalidate, neutralize
nullo: 4 game, task
numb: 6 asleep, benumb, deaden, stupid, torpid 7 stupefy 8 enfeeble, helpless 9 incapable 10 insensible
number: sum 4 curn(Sc.), data(pl.), many, mort, slew, herd, host 5 count, datum, digit, scads, score, total 6 bundle, encore, figure, myriad, reckon, hirsel 7 chiffer, chiffre, compute, decimal, several 8 numerate, quantity, fraction 9 aggregate, calculate, enumerate, multitude 10 collection, complement, percentage
cardinal: one, two 4 four 5 three
dice: 4 sise
indeterminate: 7 umpteen, zillion
irrational: 4 surd
ordinal: 5 first, third 6 second
prime: one, two 4 five 5 seven, three 6 eleven 8 thirteen
pure: 6 scalar
suffix: st, th; eth
third power: 4 cube
under ten: 5 digit
whole: 7 integer
numbles: 7 innards nombles 8 entrails
numen: 5 deity 6 spirit 8 divinity
numerable: 11 enumerative
numeral: 4 word 6 figure, letter
style: 5 Roman 6 Arabic
numerate: 6 number

numerical group: duo 4 trio 5 octet 6 sextet 7 octette, quartet, twosome 8 foursome, sextette 9 threesome
numerous: 4 lots, many 7 copious, crowded 8 abundant, multiple, thronged 9 multifold, plentiful
Numidia: *bird:* 10 demoiselle
city: 5 Hippo
nun: 4 bird, snew 5 clerk 6 pigeon, sister, vestal 7 confine, devotee 8 titmouse, votaress 9 priestess 10 cloistress
chief: 6 abbess
Franciscan: 5 Clare
headdress: 6 wimple
Latin: 5 Vesta
order: 6 Marist 8 Trappist 9 Dominican, Lorettine
Nun's son: 6 Joshua
nun moth: 7 tussock
nunbird: 6 monase
nunciate: 9 announcer, messenger
nuncio: 6 legate 8 delegate 9 messenger 14 representative
nuncupate: 7 declare 8 dedicate, inscribe, proclaim 9 designate
nuncupative: 4 oral 9 unwritten
nunnery: 5 abbey 7 convent 8 cloister
head: 6 abbess
nunni: 7 blesbok 8 antelope
nuphar: 12 nymphaeaceae
nupson: 4 fool
nuptial: 6 bridal, genial 7 marital, wedding 11 matrimonial
nur: 5 gnarl
nurse: 4 amah, ayah, baba, care, feed, rear, tend 5 bonne(F.), mammy, nanny 6 attend, cradle, foster, norice, suckle 7 cherish, nourice, nourish, nurture, promote
nurse shark: 4 gata
nursery: 6 creche
nursling: 4 baby 9 foundling
nurture: 4 diet, feed, food, rear 5 nurse, train 6 cocker, foster 7 cherish, educate 8 breeding, training 9 education, nutriment
nut: bur, guy, nit 4 burr, cola, core, head, kola, nute, pili, task 5 acorn, betel, crank, hazel, pecan 6 almond, Brazil, cashew, fellow, peanut, pyrene 7 filbert, hickory, problem 8 beechnut, chestnut 9 eccentric 11 undertaking
collective: 4 mast 5 shack
edible part: 6 kernel
ivory: 4 anta
kola: 5 bichy 9 gourou-nut
medicinal: 4 cola, kola
palm: 5 betel, lichi 8 cocoanut
pert. to: 5 nucal
tropical: ben 4 cola, kola
Nut: *daughter:* 4 Isis 8 Nephythys
son: Ra
nut-bearing: 10 nuciferous
nut-brown: 5 hazel 6 walnut 8 chestnut
nut coal: 10 anthracite
nut grass: 5 sedge
nutate: nod 5 droop
nutbreaker: 10 nutcracker
nutcake: 8 doughnut
nutcracker: 6 xenops 7 pillory 8 nuthatch 9 nutpecker 10 nutbreaker
nuthook: 6 beadle 9 constable
nutmeg: *covering:* 4 mace
family: 13 myristicaceae
Nutmeg State: 11 Connecticut
nutpecker: 8 nuthatch
nutramin: 7 vitamin
nutria: fur 5 coypu
nutrice: 5 nurse
nutrient: 10 nourishing
nutrify: 7 nourish
nutriment: 11 nourishment
nutrition: 11 nourishment 12 alimentation
nutritious: 10 nourishing
nutritive: 10 nourishing
nutty: 4 gaga 5 buggy, queer, spicy 7 amorous, piquant 8 demented, pleasant 10 unbalanced 12 crackbrained, enthusiastic
nuzzle: 5 nurse 6 foster, nestle 7 snuggle
nye: 4 eyas, nest, nide 5 brood
nylon: 5 crepe, ninon, tulle
nymph: 5 Aegle, naiad, siren, oread, sylph 6 nereid 7 Corycia 9 hamadryad
Arcadian: 6 Syrinx
beloved of Narcissus: 4 Echo
Cretan: 8 Cynosura
hills: 5 Oread
laurel tree: 6 Daphne
Messina Strait: 6 Scylla
Mount Ida: 6 Oenone
mountain: 5 Oread
Muslim: 5 houri
ocean: 5 siren 6 Nereid 7 Galatea, Oceanid 10 Callirrhoe
pursued by Apollo: 6 Daphne, Syrinx 8 Arethusa
queen: Mab
sea bird: 6 Scylla
water: 4 Nais 5 Naiad 6 Egeria, Lurlei, Undine 7 Apsaras, Hydriad, Lorelei 8 Arethusa
wood: 5 Dryad 6 Nereid 9 Hamadryad
nymphaea: 7 Castaly 8 Castalia, Castalie
nyssa: 6 tupelo
nystagmus: tic
Nyx, Nox: *brother:* 6 Erebus
daughter: Day 4 Eris 5 Light 10 Hesperides
father: 5 Chaos
husband: 5 Chaos 6 Erebus
son: 6 Charon

O

O. Henry: 6 Porter
oaf (see also **fool**): 4 boor, dolt, lout 5 clown, idiot, yokel 9 blockhead, foundling, schlemiel, schlemihl, simpleton 10 changeling
oafish: 6 stupid
oak: 5 roble 6 barren, cerris, encina 7 ambrose, durmast, turtosa 8 chaparro 9 blackjack
bark: 4 crut
bitter: 6 cerris
black: 10 quercitron
blight: 5 louse
comb. form: 6 querci
evergreen: 4 holm
family: 8 fagaceae
fruit: 5 acorn 6 camata
fungus: 10 armillaria
gall: 8 oakapple
holm: 4 ilex 5 holly
immature fruit: 6 camata
seed: 5 acorn
tannin: 6 queric 9 quercinic
white: 5 roble
young: 8 flittern
oak beauty: 4 moth
oak fern: 8 polypody
oak web: 10 cockchafer
oaky: 4 hard
oam: 5 steam
oar: row 5 aloof, rower 6 paddle, propel 7 oarsman 9 propeller
blade: 4 palm, peel
collective: 6 oarage
fulcrum: 7 oarlock
part: 4 loom
short: 5 scull
steering: 5 swape, swipe
oarlock: 5 thole 7 rowlock
oarsman: 5 rower 6 stroke 7 sculler
oasis: ojo, spa 4 merv, wadi, wady
oast: 4 kiln, oven
oat: ait(Sc.) 5 grain 6 angora 7 egilops 8 aegilops
genus: 5 avena
head: 7 panicle
oaten: 10 avenaceous 11 farinaceous
oath: vow 4 aith 5 aithe, curse, haith 6 appeal, pledge 7 serment 8 anathema 9 affidavit, expletive, profanity, swearword 10 adjuration, obligation 11 affirmation, imprecation
mild: 4 darn, drat, ecod, egad, gosh 5 golly 7 gee-wizz
take: 5 swear
oatmeal: 8 porridge
oats: *paid as rent:* 7 avenage
unthreshed: 6 oathay
obclude: 4 hide
obduction: 7 autopsy
obdurate: 4 firm, hard 5 rough, stony 6 inured, rugged 7 adamant 8 hardened, stubborn 9 calloused, immovable, obstinate, unbending, unfeeling 10 impenitent, inflexible, insensible, persistent, unyielding 11 hardhearted, intractable, unrepenting 13 unsusceptible
obeah: 5 charm 6 fetish, voodoo
Obed: *father:* 4 Boaz
mother: 4 Ruth
son: 4 Jehu 5 Jesse 7 Azariah
obedience: 5 order 7 control 8 docility 10 compliance, conformity, submission 12 jurisdiction
obedient: 7 duteous, dutiful, heedful, mindful, obeying 8 biddable, yielding 9 attentive, observing, tractable
obedient plant: 10 dragonhead
obeisance: bow 5 binge, conge, salam 6 congee, curtsy, fealty, homage, saalam 7 curtsey 9 abaisance, deference, reference 10 submission 14 respectfulness
obelisk: 4 mark 5 pylon, shaft 6 dagger, guglia, guglio, needle, obelus, pillar 8 monument
Oberon: 4 king, poem 5 fairy, opera
wife: 7 Titania
obese: fat 5 plump, pudgy, pursy, stout 6 fleshy, pyknic, rotund 8 blubbery, liparous 9 corpulent
obey: ear 4 hear 7 execute

obfuscate: dim 6 darken 7 confuse, mystify, obscure, perplex, stupefy 8 bewilder 9 obfuscous
obi: 4 sash 5 charm, obeah 6 fetich, fetish, girdle
obit: 5 death 6 notice 8 obituary 9 obsequies 10 necrologue
obiter: 12 incidentally
object: aim, end 4 goal, item 5 argue, cavil, demur, thing 6 design, entity, motive, oppose, target 7 dislike, protest, purpose, quarrel 9 challenge, intention, interpose 10 disapprove 11 expostulate, remonstrate
rare: 5 curio 7 antique
sacred: 4 urim
object lesson: 7 example
object to: 4 mind
objection: but 6 cheson 7 chesoun 9 exception
legal: 5 demur
objectionable: 4 vile 6 horrid 9 obnoxious, offensive 11 exceptional 12 disagreeable
objective: aim, end 4 goal 6 motive, realty, target 7 purpose 8 detached 9 intention 10 impersonal
objet d'art: 4 vase 5 curio, virtu 7 bibelot 8 figurine
objurgate: 5 abuse, chide 6 berate, rebuke 7 reprove, upbraid 8 execrate
oblate: 4 monk 8 dedicate, monastic
opposite of: 7 prolate
oblation: 6 corban 7 charity 8 devotion, offering 9 sacrifice
obligate: 6 fasten, oblige
obligation: vow 4 band, bond, debt, duty, loan, must, oath, onus 6 pledge 7 promise 8 contract 9 agreement, liability 10 allegiance, compulsion 11 obstruction 12 indebtedness 14 responsibility
obligato: 13 accompaniment
obligatory: 7 binding, bounden 8 forcible, imposing 9 mandatory
oblige: 4 pawn 6 engage, please 7 gratify, require 8 mortgage, obligate 9 constrain 11 necessitate
obliged: 8 beholden
obliging: 4 kind 5 buxom, civil 6 clever 7 amiable 9 agreeable, courteous 11 complaisant 13 accommodating
oblique: 4 awry, bias, skew 5 askew, bevel, cross, slant 6 aslant, aswash 7 askance, crooked, evasive, scalene 8 inclined, indirect, sidelong, sideways, sidewise, slanting 9 slantways, slantwise, underhand 10 circuitous 12 disingenuous
render: 5 splay
obliterate: 4 blot, dele, rase, raze 5 annul, erase 6 cancel, delete, efface, sponge 7 expunge 10 annihilate, extinguish
obliteration: 7 erasure, removal 10 extinction
oblivion: 5 Lethe 6 pardon 7 amnesty 13 forgetfulness
producer of: 8 nepenthe
oblong: 8 avelonge 9 elongated 11 rectangular
rounded: 7 ellipse
obloquy: 5 abuse, odium 6 infamy 7 calumny, censure 8 disgrace, dishonor 12 reprehension, vituperation
obnoxious: 4 foul, vile 6 horrid, odious, rancid 7 hateful 9 offensive, verminous 13 objectionable
oboe: 4 reed 5 shawn 6 surnai, surnay 7 hautboy, musette 8 szopelka
obrok: tax
obscene: 4 foul, lewd, nast 5 bawdy, gross, nasty 6 coarse, filthy, impure, vulgar 7 profane 8 immodest, indecent 9 loathsome, offensive, repulsive 10 disgusting, licentious 12 pornographic
obscuration: 7 eclipse
obscure: dim 4 blot, blur, dark, hazy, hide 5 bedim, befog, blind, faint, foggy, inner, murky, vague 6 bemist, cloudy, darken, darkle, gloomy, mystic, remote 7 becloud, conceal, confuse, cryptic, eclipse, shadowy, unknown, unnoted 8 abstruse, darkling, disguise, mystical, nameless, obstruse, oversile 9 ambiguous, blindfold, difficult, enigmatic, equivocal, recondite, undefined 10 caliginous, extinguish, indistinct, overshadow 14 uncomprehended
obsecrate: 4 pray 7 beseech, entreat 8 petition 10 supplicate
obsequious: 5 slick 7 devoted, dutiful, fawning, servile, slavish 8 obedient, toadying, toadyish 9 attentive, compliant 10 submissive 11 subservient
obsequy: 4 rite 6 exequy, ritual 7 funeral 8 ceremony
observance: act 4 form, rite, rule 6 custom, regard 8 ceremony, practice 9 attention, deference 11 observation 12 constitution
religious: 6 Novena 9 sacrament
observant: 5 alert 7 careful, mindful 8 watchful 10 perceptive 11 considerate
observation: 4 heed, note 6 remark 7 auspice, autopsy, descant
preliminary: 5 proem
observatory: 4 Lick 5 tower 7 lookout, Palomar 11 Mount Wilson
observe: lo; eye, see, spy 4 espy, heed, keep, look, nark, note, obey, tout, wait, yeme 5 study, watch 6 athold, behold, follow, notice, regard, remark 7 comment, discern,

respect, witness 8 perceive, preserve 9 advertise, celebrate, solemnize 10 animadvert, scrutinize
observer: 8 audience, informer, onlooker 9 bystander, spectator 11 stool-pigeon
obsess: 5 beset, haunt 6 harass 9 preoccupy
obsession: 5 craze, mania 6 hang-up 7 passion 8 idee fixe(F.) 13 preoccupation
obsidian: 5 lapis
obsignate: 4 seal 5 stamp 6 ratify
obsolescence: 9 desuetude
obsolete: old 4 dead 5 passe 7 ancient, archaic, outworn 8 out-dated, outmoded 9 discarded 10 antiquated 12 old-fashioned
obstacle: bar, dam, let 4 snag 5 block, hitch 6 bunker, hocket, hurdle 7 barrier 9 hindrance 10 difficulty, impediment 11 obstruction 12 entanglement
insurmountable: 7 impasse
obstetrician: 10 accoucheur
obstetrics: 9 maieutics
obstetrix: 7 midwife
obstinate: set 4 dour 5 balky, sulky, tough 6 assish, dogged, mulish, sullen, unruly 7 froward, willful 8 crotched, obdurate, perverse, stubborn 9 foreright, pigheaded 10 bullheaded, determined, headstrong, inflexible, persistent, refractory, selfwilled 11 intractable, opinionated 12 contumacious, pertinacious, recalcitrant
obstreperous: 5 noisy 6 unruly 9 clamorous 10 boisterous, vociferous
obstriction: 10 obligation
obstruct: bar, dam, dit, gag, mar 4 clog, ditt, stop 5 beset, block, check, choke, delay, hedge 6 arrest, cumber, forbar, hamper, hinder, impede, oppose, retard 7 barrier, forelay, occlude 8 blockade, encumber, incumber 9 barricade, embarrass, interfere, interrupt 10 filibuster 11 fillibuster
obstruction: 4 snag 5 gorce, hitch 7 barrace, barrage, barrier, blinder 8 embolism, obstacle 10 difficulty, impediment 11 impeachment
obtain: beg, bum, eke, get, win 4 earn, fang, gain, hent, reap 5 cadge, ettle, reach 6 attain, derive, secure, sponge 7 achieve, acquire, capture, chevise, prevail, procure, receive, succeed
by threat: 6 extort
obtainable: 9 available
obtent: 6 design 7 purpose
obtest: 7 beseech 10 supplicate
obtrude: 5 eject, expel 6 impose
obtruncate: lop
obtrusive: 5 fresh, pushy 7 blatant, forward, pushing 9 intrusive 10 aggressive 12 presumptuous
obtund: 4 dull 5 blunt, quell 6 deaden
obtuse: dim 4 dull 5 blink, blunt, crass, dense 6 stupid 8 boeotian, hebetate, purblind 11 insensitive
obvelation: 7 veiling 10 concealing
obverse: 4 face 5 front 8 converse 10 complement 11 counterpart
obviate: 7 prevent 8 preclude 9 forestall
obvious: 4 open 5 broad, clear, gross, overt, plain 6 patent 7 evident, glaring, visible 8 apparent, distinct, manifest, palpable 11 conspicuous
obvolute: 9 contorted, convolute 11 overlapping
oca: 5 tuber 6 oxalis, sorrel
occasion: 4 hint, sele, time 5 casus, cause, event, nonce, slant 6 excuse 7 pretext 8 ceremony, engender, exigency, function, incident 9 condition, happening
festive: 7 holiday
occasional: odd 4 orra 5 stray 6 daimen 8 sporadic 10 infrequent
occasionally: 7 betimes 9 sometimes
occasive: 7 setting 8 westward
Occidental: 4 West 6 ponent 7 Western 9 Hesperian, Westerner
occlude: 5 close 6 absorb 8 obstruct
occult: 5 magic 6 hidden, mystic, secret, voodoo 7 alchemy, cryptic 8 esoteric, mystical 9 concealed, recondite 10 mysterious, necromancy 11 supernormal 12 supernatural 13 imperceptible
science: 9 esoterics
occultation: 7 eclipse 13 disappearance
occultism: 6 cabala
occupant: 6 inmate, tenant 7 citizen, dweller 10 inhabitant
occupation: job 4 note, toil, work 5 graft, trade 6 career, metier, tenure 7 calling, pursuit 8 business, function, industry, vocation 10 employment, profession
transient: 5 hobby 9 avocation
occupied: 4 rapt
occupy: sit, use 4 busy, fill, hold, take 6 absorb, employ, engage, expend, fulfil, tenant 7 cohabit, engross, fulfill, oversit, pervade, possess 8 interest
occur: be 4 come, meet, pass 5 clash 6 appear, arrive, befall, betide, happen
again: 5 recur 6 repeat
occurrence: hap 4 case 5 event 7 episode 8 incident 9 encounter, happening 12 circumstance
supernatural: 7 miracle
unusual: 6 oddity
ocean (see also **sea**): 4 brim, deep, main 5 brine 6 Arctic, Indian 7 Pacific 8 Atlantic 9 Antarctic
approach: 7 seagate
floating matter: 5 algae 7 flotsam

mammal: 5 whale
periodic motion: 4 tide
phenomenon: 4 tide
swell: sea
Oceania: 6 Malaya 9 Australia, Melanesia, Polynesia 10 Micronesia, New Zealand 11 archipelago
Oceanid: 5 nymph
Oceanus: *daughter:* 5 Doris 7 Oceanid 8 Eurynome
father: 6 Uranus
mother: 4 Gaea
sister: 6 Tethys
wife: 6 Tethys
ocellus: eye 6 stemma
ocelot: cat 7 leopard
ocher: rud, sil 5 tiver 6 abraum 7 almagra
black: 4 wadd
ocrea: 6 sheath
octahedrite: 7 anatase
octapody: 9 octameter
octave: 4 utas 5 eight 6 eighth
Octavia: *brother:* 8 Augustus
husband: 6 Antony
octet: 7 huitain
octopean: 7 octopus
octopus: 5 polyp, poulp 6 poulpe 7 polypus 8 octopean 10 cephalopod
arm: 8 tentacle
secretion: ink
ten arms: 7 decapod
octoroon: 5 metis 6 mestee, mustee 7 metisse
octose: 5 sugar
octroi: tax 5 grant 9 privilege 10 concession
octuple: 9 eightfold
ocuby: rum
ocular: 5 optic 6 visual
odd: awk 4 fell, left, lone, orra(Sc.), rare 5 droll, extra, funny, impar, outre(F.), queer, weird 6 quaint, uneven 7 azygous, bizarre, curious, strange, unusual 8 fanciful, freakish, peculiar, singular, unpaired 9 burlesque, eccentric, fantastic, grotesque, unmatched, whimsical 10 occasional 13 extraordinary
oddity: 5 quirk 8 crotchet, quiddity 12 eccentricity, idiosyncrasy
oddly: 6 featly
oddman: 6 umpire 7 arbiter, referee
oddment: ort 5 scrap 7 remnant 8 fragment
odds: 7 dispute, quarrel 8 variance 9 advantage 10 dissension 13 probabilities
odds and ends: 4 orts 6 refuse, scraps 7 mixture, seconds 8 remnants 9 leftovers
ode: 4 hymn, poem 5 lyric, paean, psalm 7 epicede 8 canticle 9 epicedium
birthday: 12 genethliacon
kind of: 8 pindaric
part: 5 epode
victory: 9 epinicion, epinikion
odeon: 4 hall 5 odeum 7 gallery, theater
Oder tributary: 6 Neisse
odeum: 5 odeon
odic: 5 lyric
odiferous: 11 odoriferous
Odin: 5 Wodan, Woden, Wotan
brother: Ve 4 Vili
descendant: 5 Scyld
father: Bor
hall: 7 Valhall 8 Valhalla
horse: 8 Sleipner
maiden: 8 Valkyrie
mother: 6 Bestla
ring: 8 Draupnir
son: Tyr 4 Thor, Vali 5 Baldr 6 Balder
spear: 7 Gungnir
sword: 4 Gram
wife: 4 Fria, Rind 5 Frigg, Rindr 6 Frigga
wolf: 4 Gere, Geri 5 Freki
odious: 4 foul, loth, vile 5 loath 7 hatable, hateful, heinous, hideous 8 damnable, flagrant, infamous 9 abhorrent, invidious, obnoxious, offensive, repugnant 10 abominable, detestable, disgusting, forbidding 11 ignominious, opprobrious
odium: 6 stigma 8 aversion, disfavor 9 antipathy 14 disapprobation
odograph: 9 pedometer
odontalgia: 9 toothache
odor: 4 fume, funk, nose, olid, tang 5 aroma, ewder, fetor, flair, fumet, nidor, odour, scent, smell, stink 6 breath, flavor, foetor, repute, stench 7 bouquet, essence, flavour, fumette, perfume 9 fragrance, redolence 10 estimation, reputation
odoriferous: 5 balmy, olent 7 odorous 9 odiferous
Odysseus: See **Ulysses**
Odyssey: *author:* 5 Homer
sorceress: 5 Circe
oecist: 9 colonizer
oecodomic: 13 architectural
oeconomus: 7 manager, steward
Oedipus: *brother-in-law:* 5 Creon
daughter: 6 Ismene 8 Antigone
father: 5 Laius
mother: 7 Jocasta
refuge: 7 Colonus
son: 8 Eteocles 9 Polynices 10 Polyneices
victim: 5 Laius 6 Sphinx
wife: 7 Jocasta
oeillade: 4 ogle 6 glance
Oeneus: *father:* 8 Porthaon
kingdom: 7 Calydon
mother: 6 Euryte
wife: 7 Althaea
Oenomaus daughter: 10 Hippodamia

oestrid fly larva: bot
oestrus: 4 fury 5 sting 6 desire, frenzy 7 impulse 8 stimulus
oeuvre: 4 opus, work
of (see also next entry): de(F.); van(D.) 4 from 5 about 10 concerning
of: For all definitions beginning with this word, see under following main word or phrase. EXAMPLES: "of the country": see **country** *pert. to;* "of necessity": see **necessity** *of*
off: 4 away, doff, gone 5 aside, wrong 6 absent, cuckoo, remote 7 distant, further, removed
off-scouring: 5 filth 6 refuse 7 garbage, rubbish
offal: 5 gurry, waste 6 refuse 7 carrion, garbage, leaving, rubbish 8 gralloch
offend: cag, sin, vex 4 hurt, miff 5 abuse, anger, annoy, grate, grill, pique, shock, wrong 6 aguilt, attack, grieve, insult, revolt 7 affront, default, mortify, outrage, violate 9 disoblige, displease 10 transgress
offended: 4 huff, sore 7 froisse
offender: 7 culprit
offense: 4 mala(pl.) 5 crime, error, fault, guilt, malum 6 felony, pritch 7 misdeed, umbrage 8 peccancy, trespass 9 indignity 10 aggression, peccadillo, resentment 11 delinquency, misdemeanor
civil: 11 stellionate
law: 5 delit 6 delict 8 delictum
moral: 4 evil
offensive: bad 4 foul 5 fetid 6 coarse, horrid 7 beastly, fulsome, hateful, noisome 8 invading 9 loathsome, obnoxious, repugnant 10 aggressive, disgusting, forbidding, ill-favored, scurrilous, ungracious, unpleasant 11 distasteful 12 disagreeable 13 objectionable
offer: bid 4 bode, tend 6 adduce, allege, tender 7 advance, commend, present, proffer, propine, propose, suggest 8 avertment, bequeath, overture 9 volunteer
last: 9 ultimatum
solemn: 6 pledge
offering: 4 gift 6 corban 7 present 9 sacrifice
religious: 7 deodate 8 anathema, oblation
sacrificial: 5 hiera 7 sphagia(pl.) 8 sphagion
offering block: 4 aloe
offhand: 4 curt 6 casual 7 brusque 8 cavalier, informal 9 impromptu 10 improvised 11 extemporary 14 extemporaneous, unpremeditated 15 autoschediastic 16 extemporaneously
office: 4 post, wike 5 place, wiken 6 bureau 7 camarin, station 8 function, position 9 bailiwick, situation 10 commission 11 appointment 13 collectorship
chief: 7 manager
divine: 9 akoluthia
help: 5 clerk 6 typist 9 secretary 12 stenographer
machine: 5 Xerox 9 stenotype 10 calculator, mimeograph, typewriter 11 comptometer
of third hour: 5 terce
paid without work: 8 sinecure
purchase or sale: 8 barratry
put in again: 7 re-elect 9 re-instate
seeker of: 7 nominee 9 candidate
officeholder: in 6 winner 8 official, placeman
officer: 4 aide 5 usher 6 direct, ensign, manage, tindal 7 command, conduct, general 8 adjutant
assistant: 4 aide
college: 4 dean 6 bursar 10 chancellor
future: 5 cadet
law: cop 7 bailiff, marshal, sheriff 9 constable, detective, patrolman, policeman
naval: 4 mate 5 bosun 6 ensign, yeoman 7 admiral, captain, striper 9 boatswain, commander, commodore 10 lieutenant
noncommissioned: 4 mate 5 chief 8 corporal, sergeant
presiding: 6 archon 7 speaker 8 chairman 9 moderator, president
warrant: 5 bosun 9 boatswain
officers: 5 staff
official: 6 formal 9 escribano(Sp.), executive, officious 10 authorized, bureaucrat, magistrate 11 ceremonious 13 authoritative
administrative: 5 reeve 6 gerefa 9 executive
assistant: 4 aide
city or town: 5 mayor 7 manager, marshal 8 alderman 10 councilman
civil: 5 judge, mayor 7 bailiff, marshal, sheriff 8 governor 9 constable, patrolman, policeman, president 10 magistrate
corrupt: 7 grafter
despotic: 6 satrap
excise: 8 reveneur 9 revenooer
former: aga
government: 6 syndic
judicial: 8 assessor, recorder 9 treasurer 11 comptroller
local: 6 bailie(Sc.), grieve 7 burgess
public: 6 notary
state: 8 minister 9 secretary
officiate: act 6 supply 7 perform 9 celebrate
officious: 4 busy, cool, pert 6 formal 8 arrogant, impudent, informal, official 10 impersonal, meddlesome 11 efficacious, impertinent, pragmatical 12 contemptuous 14 supererogatory 16 superserviceable
offing: 7 picture 10 background

offset: 6 contra 7 balance 10 compensate, complement 12 counterpoise
offshoot: rod 5 bough, scion 6 branch, sprout
offspring: fry, imp, kid, son 4 brat, chit, seed 5 brood, child, fruit, issue, scion 6 foster, result 7 outcome, produce, product, progeny 8 children, daughter, geniture 9 genealogy, youngster 10 descendant, generation
oficina: 5 works 6 office 7 factory 10 laboratory
oflete: 5 wafer 8 oblation, offering
often: 6 common 8 frequent, repeated 10 frequently 11 continually
ogdoad: 5 eight
ogee: See **molding**
Ogier: 4 Dane, hero 6 prince 8 Norseman
ogle: eye 4 gaze, leer 5 stare 7 examine
ogre: 5 demon, giant 6 tyrant, yaksha, yakshi 7 bugaboo, monster
ogtiern: son 4 lord 6 master
ogygian: 7 ancient 8 primeval
oh: ach(G.) 4 ouch
Ohio: *college:* 5 Hiram, State 7 Antioch 10 Wittenberg
county: 4 Erie, Ross
town: Ada 5 Akron, Berea, Cadiz, Niles, Xenia 6 Canton, Dayton, Girard, Lorain, Toledo 7 Bucyrus 8 Columbus, Sandusky 9 Cleveland 11 Chillicothe 13 Yellow Springs
oii: 10 muttonbird
oil: ben, fat, ile 4 balm, fuel 5 bribe, oleum 6 aceite, anoint, chrism, grease 7 lanolin 9 lubricate, petroleum
blasting: 14 nitroglycerine
bone: 6 olanin
butter: 4 ghee
cedar and juniper: 8 alkitran 9 alchitran
coal: 8 photogen
comb. form: 4 oleo
derived from: 5 elaic, oleic
in skin: 5 sebum
linseed: 6 carron
liquid compound: 5 olein
mineral: 7 naphtha
orange-blossom: 6 neroli
pert. to: 5 oleic
prefix: ol
salt: 7 bittern
torch: 7 lucigen
vegetable: 8 macassar
vessel: 4 drum, olpe 5 cruet, cruse 6 tanker 7 cresset
whale: 5 sperm
oil beetle: 5 meloe
oil bottle: 5 cruet
oil cask: 4 rier
oil fish: 7 escolar
oil lamp: 7 coal-oil 8 kerosene
oil plant: 6 sesame
oil rock: 5 shale 9 limestone
oil tree: 4 eboe, tung 5 mahwa
oil well: 6 gusher
oilbird: 8 guacharo
oilcan: 5 oiler
oilcloth: 8 linoleum
oiler: 6 oilcan, tanker
oillet: 6 eyelet
oilseed: til 4 teel 6 sesame 7 linseed 8 rapeseed 10 castorbean, cottonseed
oilstone: 4 hone 5 shale 9 whetstone
oily: fat 4 glib 5 bland, soapy, suave 6 greasy, oleose, supple 7 pinguid 8 slippery, unctuous 9 compliant, plausible 10 oleaginous 11 subservient
ointment: 4 balm, mull, nard 5 salve 6 balsam, cerate 7 unguent 9 spikenard
application: 11 embrocation
Biblical: 9 spikenard
dry: 9 xeromyron, xeromyrum
hair: 6 pomade 7 pomatum
oil: 6 carron, cerate 7 oleamen
veterinary: 8 remolade 9 remoulade
wax: 6 cerate
Oise tributary: 5 Aisne
Oisin's father: 4 Finn
oisivity: 8 laziness
ojo: 5 oasis
okay: ok 4 okeh 7 approve, correct
oket: 5 ounce
Okie: 7 migrant
Okinawa capital: 4 Naha
Oklahoma: *county:* 6 Garvin
mountain: 5 Ozark
people: 5 Okies 7 Sooners
river: Red
state flower: 9 mistletoe
town: Ada 4 Alva, Enid, Hugo 5 Miami, Sayre, Tulsa 6 Beaver, Edmond, El Reno, Guymon, Idabel, Kansas, Lawton, Pawnee 7 Buffalo, Cordell, Cushing, Newkirk, Shawnee 8 Anadarko, Cheyenne, Coalgate, Eldorado 9 Drumright, Stillwell, Wilburton 10 Kingfisher 11 Pauls Valley
tribe: 4 Otoe
university: 6 Norman 10 Stillwater
okra: 5 bendy, gumbo 6 bendee 8 bandikai
olam: 8 eternity, infinity, universe
old: agy, ald, eld 4 aged, auld 5 anile, hoary, stale 6 former, infirm, mature, senile, shabby 7 ancient, antique, archaic 8 medieval, obsolete 9 doddering, hackneyed, senescent, venerable 10 antiquated 11 experienced 12 antediluvian
old age: 10 senescence 11 senectitude
Old Bailey: 4 gaol, jail 6 prison

Old Bay State: 13 Massachusetts
old boy: man 6 alumni(pl.) 7 alumnus
Old Dominion State: 8 Virginia
Old Faithful: 6 geyser
old-fashioned: 5 passe 6 fogram, fogrum, quaint 7 ancient, antique, archaic 8 obsolete 9 primitive 10 antiquated
Old Franklin State: 9 Tennessee
Old Gooseberry: 5 devil, satan
Old Hickory: 13 Andrew Jackson
Old Line State: 8 Maryland
old maid: 8 cardgame, spinster
Old Noll: 14 Oliver Cromwell
Old Rough and Ready: 6 Taylor
Old Sod: 4 Erin 7 Ireland
Old Testament: See **Bible**
old-womanish: 5 anile
Old World: *ape:* 6 baboon 10 catarrhina, catarrhine
carnivore: 5 genet
dish: 5 tansy
falcon: 5 saker
goat: 4 ibex
lizard: 5 agama 9 chameleon
mouse: 6 jerboa
olden: 6 bygone
older: 5 elder 6 senior 8 ancestor 11 forefathers 12 predecessors
oldest: 4 dean 6 eldest
olea: 5 olive
oleaginous: 4 oily
oleander: 11 rhododaphne 12 rhododendron
olecranon: 5 ancon
olefin: 6 alkene
olena: 8 turmeric
olent: 11 odoriferous
oleo: 9 margarine
oleomargarine: 9 butterine, margarine
oleoresin: 5 anime, elemi, tolus 7 copaiba 10 turpentine
oleum: oil
olfact: 5 smell
olfaction: 7 osmesis 8 smelling
olid: 5 fetid
olinda bug: 6 weevil
olio: 4 stew 6 medley 7 melange, mixture 8 mishmash 9 potpourri 10 collection, hodgepodge, miscellany
oliphant: 4 horn 8 elephant
oliprance: 4 romp, show 7 jollity 11 merry-making, ostentation
olitory: 6 garden 7 potherb
olive: 4 olea 9 appetizer
enzyme: 6 olease
overripe: 5 drupe
pert. to: 9 oleaceous
stuffed: 6 pimola
wild: 8 oleaster
oliver: 6 hammer
olivet: 5 pearl
olivine: 10 chrysolite
olla: jar, jug, pot
ollapodrida: 4 hash, olio, olla 6 medley 10 assortment, hodgepodge, miscellany
olm: 10 salamander
ology: ism 7 science
oloroso: 6 sherry
olp: 4 olph 9 bullfinch
olpe: 5 flask 6 vessel 7 pitcher
olycook: 7 cruller, olykoek 8 doughnut
Olympic cupbearer: 4 Hebe 8 Ganymede
Olympus: *deity:* see **Greece:** *god*
pert. to: 7 exalted, godlike, Olympic 8 heavenly, majestic 9 celestial
Oman money: 5 ghazi
Omar Khayyam's country: 4 Iran 6 Persia
omber card: 5 basto
omega: end 4 last
omelet: 5 amlet 8 fooyung
omen: 4 bode, omen, sign 5 augur, boder, freet, freit, token 6 augury, handel, hansel 7 auspice, portent, presage, warning 8 bodement, forebode, foresign 9 foretoken 10 foreboding, forerunner, indication, prediction 11 premonition
omentum: 4 caul
omer: 4 unit 7 measure
ten: 4 epha 5 ephah
ominous: 4 dour, grim 5 fatal 6 dismal 7 fateful 8 menacing, sinister 9 prophetic 10 inexorable, portentous 11 threatening
mark: 4 dele 5 caret 7 ellipse 10 apostrophe
pretended: 10 paralepsis, paralipsis
tacit: 7 silence
omission: cut 5 error 7 default, failure 9 exclusion, oversight
mark of: 5 caret
of vowel: 7 elision
omit: cut 4 balk, dele, drop, miss, skip, slip 5 abate, elide, spare 6 beleve, cancel, delete, except, forget, ignore 7 beleave, discard, neglect 8 overlook 9 disregard, pretermit
omneity: 7 allness
omnibus: bus 5 barge 10 shillibeer
omnipotent: God 4 able 5 deity, great 6 arrant, mighty 8 almighty, powerful 9 unequaled, unlimited 11 all-powerful
omnipresent: 10 ubiquitous 12 ubiquitarian
omniscient: 4 wise 7 learned 8 powerful 10 all-knowing, allwitting 11 everpresent
omnitude: 7 allness 8 totality 12 universality
omoplate: 7 scapula
omphalos: hub 4 boss, knob 5 navel 6 center
Omri: *daughter:* 8 Athaliah
successor: 4 Ahab

on: 4 atop, upon 5 about, above, ahead, along, anent 6 anenst, within 7 forward 10 concerning
account of: for
all sides: 5 about 6 around
and on: 4 ever 7 forever, tedious
behalf: for
other side: 4 over 6 across
on the contrary: 6 rather
on the other hand: but 7 however 8 although 11 nonetheless 12 contrariwise, nevertheless
on time: 6 prompt
on what account: why
Ona: 7 Fuegian
onager: ass 8 catapult
Onam's son: 4 Jada 7 Shammai
once: ane(Sc.) 4 anes(Sc.), anis(Sc.), erst 5 aince(Sc.) 6 former 7 quondam 8 formerly, whenever
in a while: 9 sometimes 12 occasionally
more: 4 anew, echo 5 again 6 encore, repeat
upon a time: 8 formerly
once-over: 6 survey 8 scrutiny
oncorhynchus: 6 salmon
ondoyant: 4 wavy
one: ae(Sc.), an; ain(Sc.), ane(Sc.), ein(G.), tae(Sc.), una, une(F.), yae(Sc.) 4 same, sole, some, unal, unit 5 alone, unity 6 person, single, unique, united 7 numeral, pronoun 8 unbroken 9 singleton, undivided, unmarried 10 individual
after another: 8 serially, seriatim 11 consecutive 12 successively
by one: 6 apiece, singly 10 separately
comb. form: uni 4 mono
one-chambered: 10 unicameral
one-colored: 13 monochromatic
one-footed: 6 uniped
one-sided: 6 biased, uneven, unfair, unjust 7 bigoted, partial 10 prejudiced, unilateral
one-spot: 4 buck 6 dollar
one tenth: 5 tithe
one thousand: mil
one twenty-fourth: 5 carat
oneberry: 9 hackberry
onefold: 6 simple, single 7 sincere 9 guileless
onegite: 8 amethyst
O'Neill heroine: 4 Anna
oneism: 6 egoism, monism
oneness: 7 concord 8 identity, sameness 9 agreement 11 singularity
oner: 6 corker 9 humdinger
onerous: 4 hard 5 heavy 7 arduous, onerose 8 exacting 9 laborious 10 burdensome, cumbersome, oppressive
onetime: 8 formerly
onfall: 5 onset 6 attack
onion: 4 boll, cepa, leek 5 cibol, pearl 7 Bermuda, onionet, shallot 8 eschalot, rareripe, scallion
genus: 6 allium
onkos: 7 topnot
onlepy: 4 only, sole 8 solitary 9 unmarried
onlooker: 5 gazer 7 witness 8 audience, beholder 9 bystander, spectator 10 rubberneck
only: 4 just, lone, mere, sole 5 afald 6 anerly, barely, merely, simple, single, singly, solely 9 allenarly, excepting 11 exclusively
onomasticon: 7 lexicon 10 dictionary
onomatopoeic: 6 echoic
onrush: 4 birr 6 attack
onset: 4 dash, dint, fard, rese, rush 5 braid, brunt, faird, frush, start 6 attack, charge 7 assault, attempt, brattle 9 beginning, encounter, onslaught 12 commencement
onslaught: 5 onset 6 attack 7 assault, descent
onstead: 9 farmhouse, homestead
Ontario: *capital:* 7 Toronto
town: 4 Galt 9 Kitchener
onto: 4 atop 6 aboard
onus: 4 duty, load 6 burden, charge 10 obligation
onward: 4 away 5 ahead, along, forth 7 forward
onyx: 10 chalcedony
oodles: 4 heap 5 scads 8 lashings 9 abundance
oolong: tea
oomiack, oomiak: 4 boat
oomph: 5 vigor 6 energy
oont: 5 camel
oopak: tea
oorali: 6 currare
oorial: sha 5 urial
ooze: bog, mud 4 drip, leak, mire, seep, slob 5 exude, gleet, marsh, slime, weeze 6 sludge 8 transude 9 percolate
opah: 4 fish 5 cravo
opal: gem 5 noble, resin 7 girasol, hyalite 8 girasole 10 chalcedony
variety: 8 menilite 9 cacholong
opalescent: 7 opaline 8 irisated 10 iridescent
opaque: 4 dark, dull 6 obtuse, stupid 7 obscure 8 eyeshade 13 unilluminated 14 unintelligible
open: dup, ope 4 ajar, flue, free, undo 5 agape, apert, begin, clear, frank, lance, overt, naked, plain, start, untie 6 candid, direct, expand, expose, honest, patent, unbolt, unfold, unfurl, unlock, unseal, unstop 7 artless, dispart, obvious, sincere, unclose 8 apparent, commence, disclose,

dispread, explicit, extended, initiate, manifest, patulous, unfasten **9** disspread, originate, uncovered **10** accessible, forthright, inaugurate, unreserved **11** unconcealed **13** undissembling **15** straightforward
bursting: **10** dehiscence
fully: **4** wide **5** agape **7** yawning **9** dehiscent, full-blown
partly: mid **4** ajar
open-eyed: **5** awake **8** vigilant, watchful **9** receptive **10** discerning
opener: key **4** knob **5** latch **6** seseame **8** aperient
openhanded: **4** free **7** liberal **8** generous **9** receptive **10** munificent
opening: os; gap, ora(pl.) **4** bore, door, fent, gate, hole, pass, rift, rima, slit, slot, span, vent **5** brack, cleft, debut, mouth, start, width **6** avenue, breach, hiatus, lacuna, outlet, portal, spread **7** crevice, fissure, orifice **8** aperture, overture **11** opportunity
enlarge: **4** ream
escape: **4** muse **5** meuse
having: **10** fenestrate
in chess: **6** gambit
mouth-like: **5** stoma **7** stomata(pl.)
slitlike: **4** rima
small: **4** pore **5** chink **6** cranny, eyelet **7** foramen, pinhole **8** foramina(pl.)
openmouthed: **6** gaping, greedy **8** ravenous **9** clamorous **10** vociferous
openwork: **7** tracery
opera: **4** Aida **5** Faust **6** Boheme, Carmen, Otello **7** Fidelio **8** Falstaff, Parsifal, Traviata, Walkyrie **9** Lohengrin, Pagliacci, Rheingold, Rigoletto, Trovatore **10** Magic Flute, Tannhauser **11** Don Giovanni **16** Marriage of Figaro
comic: **5** buffa
division: **5** scena
horse: **7** Western
kind: **4** soap **5** horse **8** burletta
part: **4** aria
soap: **6** serial **9** melodrama
solo: **4** aria
song: **4** aria **7** sortita **8** cavatina **9** cabaletta
soprano: **4** Bori **5** Eames, Patti **6** Callas, Farrar
star: **4** diva
tenor: **6** Caruso
opera glass: **9** lorgnette **10** binoculars
opera house: **7** theater
operant: **9** operative
operate: go; act, man, run **4** work **6** affect, effect, manage **7** conduct **10** accomplish
by hand: **10** manipulate
operation: **4** deed **6** agency **7** process **8** creation, function **9** actuation, influence, procedure **10** production **11** maintenance, transaction
operative: **4** hand **6** artist **7** artisan **8** mechanic **9** detective
beyond itself: **9** transeunt
for past: **11** retroactive
operator: **5** agent, quack **6** dealer **7** manager, operant, surgeon **9** conductor, operative **10** mountebank
operculum: lid **4** flap **8** covering
operose: **4** busy **8** diligent **9** laborious **11** industrious
ophidian: asp, eel **5** snake **6** conger **7** reptile, serpent
ophthalmic: **6** ocular
opiate: **4** dope, drug, hemp **5** dwale, opium **6** deaden **7** anodine, anodyne **8** hypnotic, narcotic **9** paregoric
opificer: **7** workman **9** artificer
opine: **4** deem **5** judge **6** ponder **7** suppose
opinion: **4** idea, view, ween **5** dicta(pl.), guess, tenet **6** advice, belief, dictum, esteem, notion, repute **7** concept, feeling, thought **8** decision, doctrine, estimate, judgment **9** sentiment **10** conjecture, conviction, deposition, estimation, expression, evaluation, impression, persuasion **10** apprehension
erroneous: **13** misconception
expression: **4** vote
preconceived: **9** prejudice
united: **9** unanimous
unorthodox: **6** heresy
opinionated: **8** dogmatic **9** conceited, obstinate **11** dictatorial
opinions: *collected:* **9** anthology, symposium
professed: **5** credo
opium: **4** drug **10** intoxicant
alkaloid: **6** codein **7** codeine **8** morphine, narcotin **9** narcotine, papaverin **10** papaverine
camphorate tincture: **9** paregoric
concentrated form: **6** heroin
derivative: **7** meconic
Egyptian: **8** thebaine
poppy seed: maw
prepared: **6** chandu **7** chandoo
opossum: **9** marsupial
mouse: **7** marmosa, marmose **8** marmouse
water: **5** yapok **6** yapock
oppidan: **5** civic, urban **8** townsman
oppilate: **4** clog **5** block **8** obstruct
opponent: foe **5** enemy **7** opposer **9** adversary, assailant **10** antagonist

opportune: fit, pat 5 ready 6 timely 8 suitable 9 favorable, well-timed 10 auspicious, convenient, favourable, seasonable
opportunely: 7 apropos, happily
opportunity: 4 hent, sele 5 slant 6 chance 7 opening 8 occasion 9 advantage 12 circumstance
oppose: pit, vie 4 buck, cope, face, meet, stem, wear 5 argue, block, check, cross, fight, front, rebel, rebut, repel 6 breast, combat, object, oppugn, resist 7 contest, counter, gainsay 8 conflict, confront, contrast, frontier, obstruct 9 encounter, withstand 10 calcitrate, contradict, contravene, controvert
opposed: 4 anti 6 averse 7 adverse, against, hostile 8 contrary 11 contrariant
opposer: 8 opponent
opposite: 5 anent, polar 6 across, anenst, averse, facing 7 adverse, counter, inverse, reverse 8 contrary, contrast, converse 9 antipodal, repugnant 10 antipodean 12 antagonistic 13 contradictory
opposite to: 7 abreast, subtend
opposition: 5 atilt 9 animosity, collision, hostility, renitency 10 resistance 11 contrariety
oppress: 4 load, rape, thew 5 crush, grind, weigh, wrong 6 burden, defoil, defoul, extort, harass, harrow, ravish, subdue 7 afflict, depress, overlay, repress, trample 8 distress, encumber, pressure, suppress 9 constrain, overpower, overthrow, overwhelm 10 extinguish
oppressed: 5 laden 9 debruised 10 heavy-laden
oppression: 8 dullness 9 grievance, lassitude 11 obscuration
oppressive: 4 dire, hard 5 close, harsh, heavy 6 severe 7 onerous 8 rigorous 10 hardhanded 11 gravaminous, heavy-handed, overbearing 12 extortionate
oppressor: 4 csar, czar, Nero, tsar, tzar 6 tyrant
opprobrium: 5 abuse, odium, scorn 6 infamy, insult 7 calumny, offense, scandal 8 disgrace, dishonor, reproach 9 contumely 10 disrespect
oppugn: 6 oppose
oppugnacy: 9 hostility 10 antagonism
oppugnation: 6 attack 10 opposition
Ops: *associate:* 6 Consus
consort: 6 Saturn
daughter: 5 Ceres
festival: 6 opalia
son: 4 Zeus 8 Poseidon
opt: 4 cull, pick 5 elect 6 choose, decide, select
optic: eye 6 ocular, visual
optical: 6 ocular
instrument: 4 lens 6 alidad 7 alidade 9 eriometer, optometer, periscope, telescope 10 microscope, teinoscope 11 stereoscope 15 ultramicroscope
organ: eye
optimistic: 4 rosy 6 joyous 7 hopeful, roseate 8 sanguine
option: 6 choice 7 refusal 9 privilege 11 alternative
optional: 8 elective 9 voluntary 10 permissive
opulent: fat 4 rich 5 ample 6 lavish 7 profuse, wealthy 8 abundant, affluent 9 luxuriant, plentiful
opus: 4 work 11 composition
overlabored: 11 lucubration
oquassa: 5 trout
or: aut(L.), ere 6 either 11 alternative
heraldry: 4 gold 6 yellow
oracle: 4 seer 5 sibyl
pert. to: 8 pythonic
oracular: 4 otic 5 vatic 7 vatical 9 prophetic 10 mysterious 11 dictatorial 13 authoritative
orage: 5 storm 7 tempest
oral: 5 aloud, parol, vocal 6 sonant, spoken, verbal 7 uttered 9 unwritten 10 acroamatic
orange: 4 mock 5 chino, color, hedge, Navel, Osage 6 bodock 7 Seville 8 bergamot, chinotti, mandarin, Valencia 9 tangerine
genus: 6 citrus
heraldry: 5 tenne
membrane: 4 zest
mock: 7 seringa, syringa, syringe
piece: 4 lith(Sc.) 7 segment
red: 7 saffron
seed: pip
seedless: 5 navel
variety: 5 blood, navel, osage 7 seville
Orange Bowl site: 5 Miami
orange-flower oil: 6 neroli
orange-shaped: 6 oblate
orangeat: 9 orangeade
orangeberry: 9 cranberry
orangebird: 7 tanager
orangeleaf: 6 karamu
orangelike fruit: bel 9 tangerine
orangewood: 5 Osage
orangutan: ape 4 mias 5 orang, pongo, satyr 7 primate 11 orangoutang
orate: 5 plead, speak, spiel, spout 7 address, declaim, lecture 8 harangue 9 discourse, speechify 10 filibuster 11 expostulate
oration: 6 sermon 7 concion 9 panegyric
funeral: 5 eloge 6 eulogy 7 elogium, encomia(pl.) 8 encomium

orator: 6 rhetor 7 demagog, speaker 8 cicerone, ciceroni(pl.) 9 demagogue, plaintiff 10 petitioner 11 rhetorician, spellbinder
oratorian: 6 priest
oratorical: 8 eloquent 10 rhetorical
oratorio: 7 Messiah, Seasons
coda in: 7 stretta
oratory: 6 chapel 9 elocution, eloquence
orb: eye, sun 4 ball, moon, star 5 earth, globe 6 circle, planet, sphere 7 circuit, enclose 8 encircle, surround
orbed: 5 lunar, round
orbit: 4 path 5 track 6 socket 7 circuit, ellipse
point: 5 apsis, syzgy 6 apogee, epigee 7 apsides(pl.), perigee
orc: 4 orca 5 whale 7 grampus
orchard: 5 arbor 6 arbour, garden 8 arbustum 9 enclosure 10 plantation
orchestra: 4 band 5 group 8 ensemble
section: 4 wind, wood 5 brass 6 string 7 timpany
orchestra bells: 12 glockenspiel
orchestra circle: 7 parquet 8 parterre
orchestrate: 5 score 7 arrange, compose
orchid: 5 faham, petal, vanda 6 purple 7 aerides, calypso, lycaste, pogonia, vanilla 8 arethusa, labellum
appendage: 8 caudicle
dried tubers: 5 salep
genus of: 5 vanda 6 laelia 10 gymnadenia 14 gymnadeniopsis
leaves: 4 faam 5 faham
meal: 5 salep
petal: 8 labellum
tuber: 5 salep 7 cullion
Orcus: 5 Hades
ordain: 4 deem 5 allot, enact, order 6 decree 7 adjudge, appoint, arrange, behight, command, destine, install, prepare 9 establish, prescribe 10 adjudicate, commission, constitute
ordeal: 4 gaff 5 trial 10 experience
order: ban, bid 4 boon, fiat, form, ordo, rank, rule, sect, will 5 align, array, class, dight, edict, genus, grade, guide 6 billet, charge, cosmos, decree, degree, demand, direct, enjoin, genera(pl.), graith, kilter, manage, method, ordain, police, series, system 7 adjudge, arrange, bespeak, bidding, command, compose, dispose, embargo, mandate, ordines(pl.), precept, process, society 8 decision, neatness, organize, regulate 9 direction, directive, procedure 10 injunction, succession 11 appointment, instruction
back: 6 remand 8 recommit
connected: 8 seriatim
cosmic: tao 4 rita
good: 6 eutaxy 7 eutaxie
grammar: 5 taxis
lacking: 5 amiss, messy, mussy 7 chaotic, unkempt 8 confused 10 disarrayed
law: 4 writ 7 summons 8 subpoena
Parliamentary: 9 procedure
writ: 7 precipe
orderly: 4 aide, tidy, trim 6 batman 7 regular 8 decorous, obedient 9 peaceable, regularly, shipshape 10 law-abiding 11 well-behaved
ordinal: 4 book 6 number 7 orderly, regular
ordinance: law 4 doom, fiat, rite 5 bylaw, edict 6 assize, decree 7 control, decreta(pl.), statute 8 decretum 9 direction, sacrament 10 management, regulation 11 appointment
ordinary: 4 lala, ruck, soso 5 nomic, plain, prose, usual 6 common, normal 7 average, natural, prosaic, trivial, vulgate 8 everyday, habitual, mediocre 9 customary 11 commonplace
ordinate: 7 appoint, orderly, regular 8 moderate 9 temperate 10 methodical
ordnance: 4 guns 5 armor, orgue 6 petard 7 weapons 8 basilisk 9 artillery, torpedoes 10 ammunition, serpentine
ordo: 5 order 7 almanac
ore (see also **mineral**): tin 4 gold, iron, lead 5 favor, glory, grace, honor, mercy, metal 6 copper 7 respect, seaweed 8 clemency 9 reverence
crusher: 5 dolly
deposit: 4 lode 5 scrin 7 bonanza
fusing: 8 smelting
horizontal layer: 5 stope
impure: 6 speiss
iron: 5 ocher, ochre 8 hematite 9 magnetite
layer: 4 seam 5 stope
lead: 6 galena
loading platform: 4 plat
mercury: 8 cinnabar
refuse: 6 scoria 8 tailings
separator: 6 vanner
silver: 10 stephanite
sluice: 5 trunk
tin: 5 scove
tungsten: 4 cals
washing trough: 6 strake
worthless: 5 matte
oread: 5 nymph
Oregon: *capital:* 5 Salem
coin: 6 beaver
county: 4 Coos 5 Curry 7 Gilliam, Klamath, Malheur, Wallowa, Yamhill 8 Umatilla 9 Deschutes, Multnomah, Tillamook
crab apple: 7 powitch
fabled monster: 7 Big Foot 9 Sasquatch
Indian tribe: 4 Coos

mountain: 4 Hood 5 Coast 7 Cascade
river: 5 Rogue 7 Klamath 8 Columbia 9 Deschutes 10 Willamette
town: 4 Bend 7 Medford 8 Portland
university site: 6 Eugene
wind: 7 chinook
oreortyx: 5 quail
Orestes: *father:* 9 Agamemnon
friend: 7 Pylades
mother: 12 Clytemnestra
sister: 7 Electra
wife: 8 Hermione
orf, orfe: ide 4 fish
orfevrerie: 7 jewelry
organ: 6 medium 9 equipment 10 instrument
auricular: ear
barrel: 8 autophon
bristle-like: 4 seta
cactus: 7 saguaro
desk: 7 console
elongated: 8 tentacle
essential: 5 brain, heart, liver, lungs 6 viscus 7 viscera(pl.)
fish: 8 drumfish
flutter device: 7 tremolo
footlike: pes
gallery: 4 loft
interlude: 6 verset
lymphoid: 6 tonsil
note: 9 tremolant
of insect: 7 stinger
of living bodies: 8 organism
of motion: 6 muscle
of volition: 5 manas
olfactory: 4 nare, nose
opening: os; ora(pl.)
optical: eye
part: 4 reed, stop
piano: 9 melopiano
pipe: 4 reed 5 flute 7 mixture
portable: 5 regal
prelude: 6 verset
reed: 9 harmonium
respiratory: 4 lung
sawlike: 5 serra
secreting: 5 gland
sensory: ear, eye 4 nose
speech: lip 6 throat, tongue
tactile: 6 feeler
organ stop: 5 quint, viola 7 celesta, tertian 8 diapason, dulciana, gemshorn, register 9 rohrflute 10 quindecima
adjust: 10 registrate
bell-like: 8 carillon
labial: 7 melodia
reed: 4 oboe 7 bassoon 8 possaune
storm-imitating: 5 orage
string: 5 gamba
two banks of pipes: 7 tertian
organic: 6 inborn 7 natural 8 inherent 9 organlike 11 fundamental 12 instrumental 14 constitutional
body: 5 zooid
compound: 5 amine, ketol
radical: 5 ethyl
organism: 5 plant 6 aerobe, animal
bacterial: 4 germ 7 microbe
body: 4 soma 6 somata(pl.)
elementary: 5 monad
minute: 5 ameba, monad, spore
pelagic: 6 nekton
process: 6 miosis 7 meiosis
vegetable: 4 tree 5 plant
organization: 5 setup 11 association, disposition 12 constitution
business: 4 firm 5 guild 11 cooperative, corporation, partnership 13 establishment
college: 4 frat 6 alumna, alumni(pl.) 7 alumnus 8 sorority 10 fraternity
political: 4 bloc 5 party
secret: K.C.; K.O.P., P.E.O., W.O.W. 4 B.P.O.E., Elks, frat 5 lodge, mafia, Moose 6 apache, maffia, Masons 8 sorority 9 Foresters, Maccabees 10 fraternity, Freemasons 11 underground
skeleton: 5 cadre
social: 4 club 5 forum
veterans: A.V.C., D.A.V., G.A.R., S.A.R., V.F.W. 5 Fidac 6 AMVETS 14 American Legion 21 Veterans of Foreign Wars
women's: D.A.R., W.A.F., W.R.C. 8 sorority
organize: 4 form 5 edify 6 embody 7 arrange 8 regiment
organized: 7 organic 10 systematic
organized body: 4 army, navy 5 corps, posse
organology: 10 phrenology 12 splanchnology
organophone: 9 harmonium
organoscopy: 10 phrenology
orgueil: 5 pride 11 haughtiness
orgy: 4 lark, romp 5 revel, spree 6 frolic, shindy 7 revelry, wassail 8 carousal, ceremony 10 observance 11 celebration, merrymaking
Oriana: *father:* 8 Lisuarte
lover: 6 Amadis
oribi: 8 antelope, bleekbok
oriel: bay 6 recess, window 7 balcony, gallery, portico 8 corridor
orient: 4 dawn 5 adapt, place 6 adjust, locate 7 sunrise 11 accommodate
Orient: 4 Asia, East 6 Levant
animal: 4 zebu
archangel: 5 Uriel
bearer: 5 hamal
beverage: 6 arrack

bow: **6** salaam
cap: **7** calpack
caravansary: **4** khan **5** serai **6** imaret
carriage: **10** jinricksha **11** jinrickshaw
cart: **5** araba
chief: **4** khan
Christian: **4** Uniat
coin: sen, yen **5** dinar
commander: ras **4** amir, emir, rais, reis **5** ameer, emeer
corn: **4** para
cosmetic: **4** kohl
council: **5** Divan
cymbal: zel
deity: Bel
destiny: **6** Kismet
disease: **8** beri-beri
dish: **5** pilau, pilaw
drug: **6** heroin **7** hashish
drum: **7** anacara
dulcimer: **6** santir
dwelling: dar
emperor: **6** sultan
fan: ogi
fish: tai
food: **4** rice **5** salep
garment: aba
gate: dar
guitar: **5** sitar
inn: **5** serai
liquor: **4** sake, saki
litter: **5** dooli, dooly **6** dooley, doolie
lute: tar
manservant: **5** hamal
mansion: **5** yamen
market: **5** bazar **6** bazaar
measure: dra, mao
measure of weight: **4** kati, rotl, tael **5** abbas, bhaar, catty, picul **6** cantar, kantar, miskal
money of account: rin
monkey: **7** macaque
musical instrument: tar **5** sitar, surna, suray **6** santir **7** samisen
name: Ali
nomad: **5** Tatar **6** Tartar
nurse: **4** amah, ayah
oboe: **5** surna, suray
pagoda: tea
people: Tai, Tho **4** Sere **5** Asian, Tatar **6** Indian, Korean, Muslim, Tartar **7** Chinese, Eastern **8** Japanese **9** Easterner, Levantine **10** Mohammedan
pine: **5** matsu
pipe: **7** nargile **8** harghile, nargileh
plane-tree: **7** cheenar
porter: **5** hamal
rest house: **4** khan **5** serai
rice dish: **5** pilaf, pilau, pilaw
rice paste: ame
ruler: **4** amir, emir, khan, shah **5** ameer, calif, emeer **6** caliph, sultan
saber: **6** tulwar **7** tulwaur **8** scimitar
sailing ship: **4** dhow
sailor: **6** lascar
salutation: **5** saheb, salam **6** kowtow, salaam
sash: obi
sauce: soy
sea captain: ras **4** rais, reis
shoe: **6** sandal
silkworm: **6** tussah, tusseh, tusser **7** tussore
slipper: **7** baboosh **8** babouche
smoking apparatus: **7** nargile **8** narghile, nargileh
tamarisk: **4** atle **5** atlee
tambourine: **5** daira
taxi: **7** ricksha **8** rickshaw
tea: cha
title: aga **4** amir, baba **5** pasha **6** huzoor
tower: **6** pagoda
tree: **4** atle **5** atlee
vessel: **4** dhow, saic
wagon: **5** araba
weight: **4** mann, tael **5** artal(pl.)
whip: **6** chabuk **7** chabouk
wind: **7** monsoon
worker: **5** cooly

oriental: **5** pearl **6** bright, ortive, rising **7** eastern, shining **8** lustrous, pellucid, precious **9** ascending, brilliant **11** resplendent

Oriental rug: **4** Baku, Kali **5** Herez, Mahal, Saruk, Senna, Sumak **6** Kashan, Kerman, Kirman, Meshed, Pamiri, Sarouk, Shiraz, Soumak, Tabriz **7** Bokhara, Bukhara, Chinese, Hamadan, Isfahan, Ispahan, Karajas, Meshhed **8** Lerestan, Sedjadeh **9** Kurdistan **10** Kermanshah
pattern: **7** ainaleh

orifice: **4** hole, vent **5** inlet, mouth **6** cavity, outlet **7** chimney, opening, ostiole **8** aperture
in brain: **4** lura

origin: nee **4** rise, root, seed **5** birth, cause, start **6** nature, parent, source **7** genesis, lineage **8** nascence, nascency **9** beginning, inception, naissance, parentage **10** extraction, incunabula(pl.) **11** incunabulum, provenience **12** commencement, fountainhead
foreign: **7** ecdemic
on earth: **7** epigene

original: new **5** first, novel **6** fontal, native, primal, primer **7** primary **8** pristine **9** authentic, inventive, primitive **10** aboriginal **11** fundamental, primigenial

originally: **5** first **9** initially, primarily **10** inherently

originate: 4 coin, make, open, rise 5 arise, begin, breed, cause, found, start 6 create, derive, devise, invent 7 causate, emanate, produce 8 commence, contrive, discover, generate, initiate 9 construct, establish, institute
origination: 7 genesis 9 etymology
originator: 6 author
oriole: *family:* 9 icteridae
golden: 5 pirol 6 loriot
Orion: 5 Rigel 13 constellation
hound: 6 Aratus
slayer: 7 Artemis
orison: 6 prayer, speech 7 praying
oristic: 10 definitive 11 determinate
Orkney Island: *capital:* 8 Kirkwall
fishing ground: 4 haaf
hut: 4 skio
inlet: voe
island: Hoy 6 Pomona, Sanday
land: 4 odal, udal 6 udaler 7 udalman 8 udalborn
largest: 6 Pomona
tower: 5 broch
orle: 6 border, fillet, wreath 7 bearing, chaplet
orlean: 7 annatto
orlop: 4 deck
ormer: 7 abalone
ormolu: 4 gilt, gold 5 alloy 7 varnish
ornament (see also **decoration**): dub, fob, pin 4 etch, gaud, gear, tool, trim, waly 5 adorn, braid, chase, decor, gutta, inlay, wally 6 amulet, attire, bedaub, bedeck, billet, brooch, edging, emboss, enrich, finery, flower 7 agremen, engrave, garnish, spangle, trinket 8 agrement, applique, decorate, flourish, lavalier 9 arabesque, billiment, embellish, embroider, lavaliere 10 decorament, furnishing, habiliment, lavalliere 11 garnishment 13 embellishment
apex: 6 finial
bell-shaped: 9 clochette
Biblical: 4 Urim
boat-shaped: nef
claw-like: 6 griffe
crescent-shaped: 6 lunula 7 lunette, lunulae(pl.)
delicate: 7 tracery
diamond-shaped: 10 epigonatia(pl.) 11 epigonation
dress: 4 frog, lace 5 jabot 6 sequin, zequin 7 spangle 8 chequeen, zecchino 10 embroidery
flowerlike: 7 rosette
hanging: 6 bangle, fringe, tassel 7 pendant
magical: 6 amulet
mantel: 7 bibelot
neck: 5 chain 6 choker, gorget 8 necklace
pagoda: tee
pendant: 6 anadem, bangle, tassel 7 earring 8 lavalier 9 lavaliere 10 lavalliere
protuberant: 4 boss
scroll-like: 6 volute
silver: 6 tinsel
spiral: 5 helix 7 helices(pl.)
terminal: 6 finial
tufted: 6 pompon, tassel 7 pompoon, rosette
ornamental: 7 elegant 8 fanciful 10 decorative
ornamented: 6 ornate, tawdry 9 elaborate
ornate: gay 4 fine 5 fancy, showy 6 florid 7 aureate, flowery 9 elaborate, unnatural 10 flamboyant 11 overadorned
ornery: 4 mean 7 crabbed 8 stubborn 9 irritable 12 cantankerous
ornithologist: 7 Audubon, birdman
ornithon: 6 aviary
orogeny: 8 upheaval
orotund: 4 full 5 clear, showy 6 mellow, strong 7 pompous 8 resonant 9 bombastic
Orozco specialty: 5 mural
orp: 4 fret, weep
orphan: 5 Annie 9 foundling
orpheum: 7 theater
Orpheus: *birthplace:* 6 Pieria
father: 6 Apollo
instrument: 4 lyre
mother: 8 Calliope
wife: 8 Eurydice
orphrey: 4 band 10 embroidery
orpiment: 7 arsenic
orpit: 7 fretful
orra: odd 10 occasional, unemployed 13 miscellaneous
orris: 4 gimp, lace 5 braid 7 galloon
ort: bit 5 crumb, scrap 6 morsel, refuse 7 leaving, remnant 8 fragment
orthodox: 4 good 6 proper 7 canonic, correct 8 accepted, standard 9 canonical, customary 12 conventional
orthographer: 7 speller
ortive: 7 Eastern
ortolan: 4 bird, rail 7 bunting 8 bobolink, wheatear
ortstein: 7 hardpan
oryx: 7 gazelle, gemsbok 8 antelope
os: 4 bone 5 eskar, esker, mouth 7 opening
Osaka Bay port: 4 Kobe
oscillate: wag 4 rock, sway, vary 5 swing, waver, weave 7 vibrate 9 fluctuate, vacillate
oscillation: 11 trepidation
oscine: 9 scopoline
oscitant: 4 dull 6 drowsy, gaping, sleepy, stupid 7 yawning 8 careless, sluggish 9 apathetic

osculate: 4 buss, kiss
ose: 6 glucid 7 glucide 13 monosaccharid 14 monosaccharide
osier: rod 5 wand 6 basket, sallow, willow 7 dogwood, wilgers
Osiris: *brother:* Set 4 Seth
crown: 4 atef
enemy: Set 4 Seth 7 brother
father: Geb, Keb, Seb
mother: Nut
recorder: 5 Thoth
sister: 4 Isis
son: 5 Horus 6 Anubis
wife: 4 Isis
Osmanli: 4 Turk
osmesis: 8 smelling 9 olfaction
osprey: 4 bird, hawk, ossi
ossature: 8 skeleton
osse: 4 dare 7 attempt, presage, promise 8 prophesy 9 recommend, utterance
osseous: 4 bone, bony 6 osteal 10 ossiferous
ossianic: 7 flowery, pompous 9 bombastic
ossicle: 4 bone 5 incus 6 stapes 7 bonelet, malleus
ossifrage: 5 eagle 6 osprey 11 lammergeier
ossify: 6 harden
ossuary: urn 4 tomb 5 vault 10 depository, receptacle
ostend: 4 show 6 reveal 7 exhibit 8 manifest 11 demonstrate
ostensible: 7 seeming 8 apparent, specious 9 pretended, professed
ostensorium: pix, pyx 10 monstrance
ostent: air 4 mien 5 token 7 display, portent 10 appearance 13 manifestation
ostentation: 4 show 5 eclat, flare 6 parade 7 display, flutter, pageant, portent, presage 8 flourish, pretense 9 showiness, spectacle 10 exhibition 11 fanfaronade
ostentatious: 4 arty, loud 5 gaudy, showy 6 sporty 7 obvious, pompous 8 fastuous 9 elaborate, flaunting 11 pretentious
osteoma: 5 tumor
osteria: inn 6 tavern
ostiole: 4 pore 5 stoma 7 orifice, stomata(pl.) 8 aperture
ostler: 7 hostler 9 stableman
ostracize: bar 4 snub 5 exile 6 banish, reject 7 exclude 9 blackball, proscribe 10 expatriate
ostracon: 8 potsherd
ostreger: 8 falconer
ostrich: 4 rhea 5 nandu
extinct: moa
feather: boa, boo 5 plume
ostrichlike bird: emu 4 emeu
Otaheite: 6 Tahiti
otalgia: 7 earache
otary: 4 seal
Othello: 4 Moor
character in play: 6 Bianca, Cassio, Emilia
friend: 4 Iago
wife: 9 Desdemona
other: 4 else, more 5 ither(Sc.) 6 former 7 further 9 distinct 9 different 10 additional
combining form: 5 heter 6 hetero
other-worldly: fey 9 imaginary, spiritual
otherness: 8 alterity 9 diversity
others: 4 rest
and: 4 et al 6 et alii
otherwise: or 4 else 5 alias 6 aliter 11 differently
otic: 5 aural 8 auditory, oracular 9 auricular
otiose: 4 idle, lazy, vain 6 futile, otiant 7 sterile, useless 8 inactive, indolent, reposing 10 unemployed 11 ineffective, superfluous
otium: 7 leisure
otologist: 6 aurist
ottavino: 7 piccolo
otter: fur 4 fish 6 tackle 7 annatto 8 paravane
genus: 5 lutra
sea: 5 kalan
ottoman: 4 pouf, seat 5 couch, divan, stool 6 fabric 9 footstool
Ottoman (see also **Turkey**): 4 Turk 5 Osman 6 Othman
court: 5 porte
governor: 5 pasha
imperial standard: 4 alem
leader of: 5 Osman
poetry couplet: 4 beyt
province: 7 Vilayet
subject: 4 Raia 5 Rayah
ouachitite: 4 dike
ouakari: 6 monkey
oubliette: 7 dungeon
ouch: oh 5 adorn, bezel, clasp 6 brooch, fibula 7 fibulae(pl.) 8 ornament 11 exclamation
ought: 4 bood, must, zero 6 cipher, naught, nought, should 7 behoove
ouija board part: 10 planchette
ounce: ure 6 weight 7 measure
sixteenth of: 4 dram
oundy: 4 wavy 5 curly 6 waving
ouphe: elf 6 goblin
our: wir(Sc.) 5 notre(F.) 7 pronoun 10 possessive
ourie: 4 cold 5 dingy 6 dreary
ousia: 6 nature 7 essence 9 substance
oust: bar 5 eject, evict, expel 6 banish, remove 7 dismiss 8 forjudge 9 forejudge 10 dispossess
out: 4 away 5 forth 6 absent, begone, issued 8 external 9 published 12 disadvantage
at elbows: 5 seedy

of: 4 from 6 dehors
of date: old 5 passe 10 antiquated
of kilter: 4 alop, awry 6 broken
of line: 4 awry 5 askew
of order: 5 amiss, kaput 6 faulty 9 deficient
of place: 5 inept 13 inappropriate
of play: 4 dead, foul
of, prefix for: ec, ex; ect, exo 4 ecto
of sight: 5 great 6 hidden 7 extreme
of sorts: 5 cross 7 peevish
of the ordinary: odd 5 novel 6 unique 7 strange, unusual 8 peculiar, uncommon 9 different
of the way: 5 aside 6 afield, remote 10 far-fetched
of this world: 4 fine 6 superb

out-and-out: 5 sheer, utter 6 arrant, wholly 8 absolute, complete
outage: 4 vent 6 outlet 10 suspension 12 interruption
outas: 6 clamor, outcry
outback: 7 country 10 wilderness
outbear: 4 bear, lead 7 sustain 8 outcarry
outbearing: 8 arrogant, demeanor 10 projection
outbraid: 4 draw 5 eject 7 upbraid
outbreak: fit 4 riot 5 burst 6 bust-up, emeute(F.), ruckus, tumult 7 boutade, outcrop, ruction 8 eruption 12 insurrection
new: 13 recrudescence
sudden: 5 spurt
outbreeding: 7 exogamy
outbuilding: 4 barn, shed 5 privy 6 barton, garage, hemmel 8 outhouse 9 backhouse
outburst: 4 fume, gale, gust, rage, tiff 5 blast, brunt, flare 6 blower, blow-up, tirade 7 outcrop, tantrum, torrent 8 eruption, outbreak 9 explosion 10 ebullition, outpouring
outcast: 5 exile, leper, ronin 6 outlet, pariah 7 missile 8 castaway, chandala, rejected, vagabond 10 expatriate
outclass: 5 excel 6 outwit 7 surpass 8 outcraft
outcome: 4 fate 5 issue 6 effect, exitus, outlet, result, sequel, upshot 7 emanate 9 aftermath, emanation 10 conclusion, denouement 11 consequence
outcraft: 8 outclass
outcrop: 5 ledge
outcry: ga; cry, hue, yip 4 bawl, bray, yell 5 alarm, boast, noise, shout 6 clamor, racket, shriek, steven 7 calling, clamour, exclaim, protest, screech, shil-loo 8 proclaim 9 objection 11 lamentation 12 vociferation
outdate: 7 outmode 9 antiquate
outdistance: 7 surpass 8 outstrip
outdo: cap, cow 5 excel 6 defeat, exceed 7 nonplus, surpass 8 overcome
outdoors: 5 forth 7 outside
outer: 5 alien, ectad, ectal, utter 7 foreign, outside 8 exterior, external 10 extraneous
Outer Mongolia capital: 4 Urga 9 Ulan Bator
outermost: 5 final, utter 6 utmost 7 extreme, outward 8 farthest, remotest 9 extremest, outermost, uttermost
outface: 4 defy 6 resist, subdue 8 overcome
outfield: 6 garden 7 pasture 8 moorland
outfit: kit, rig 4 gang, gear, suit, team, unit 5 equip 6 attire, fitout 7 furnish 8 equipage 9 equipment, furniture, grubstake 12 organization 13 paraphernalia
outflow: 4 flux 5 drain 6 efflux, escape
outgo: 4 exit 5 excel, issue, outdo 6 efflux, egress, exceed, outlay, outlet, outrun 7 outcome, outflow, product, surpass 11 expenditure, outdistance
outgrowth: 8 offshoot 9 emergence 11 excrescence
outhouse: 4 shed 5 privy 6 biggin 7 latrine
outing: 4 stay, trip 6 picnic 7 holiday 8 vacation 9 excursion
outknee: 6 bowleg
outlandish: 5 alien 6 exotic, remote 7 bizarre, foreign, strange, uncouth 8 peculiar 9 barbarous, fantastic, grotesque 10 tramontane
outlaw: ban 4 caco 5 exile, exlex, fleme, ronin 6 arrant, bandit, banish 8 fugitate, fugitive, prohibit 9 proscribe 10 disqualify, expatriate
outlawed: 7 illegal, illicit
outlay: 4 cost 7 expense 11 expenditure 12 disbursement
outlet: 4 exit, vent 5 issue 6 egress, escape, exitus 7 opening, outcast, outcome 9 avoidance
outline: map 4 form, plan 5 brief, chart, draft, frame, shape, trace 6 design, figure, sketch 7 contour, profile, summary 8 describe, skeleton, synopsis 9 delineate, perimeter 10 compendium, figuration, silhouette 11 delineation 13 configuration
outlive: 7 outlast, survive
outlook: 4 view 5 vista 6 aspect 7 purview 8 frontage, prospect 10 perception 11 expectation
medical: 9 prognosis
outlying district: 7 purlieu
outmoded: 5 dated, passe 7 antique 8 obsolete, outdated
outpeer: 8 outclass
outpost: 7 station 8 forepost 10 settlement
outpour: 4 flow 7 outflow 8 outburst

output: cut 5 expel, power, yield 6 energy 10 production
outrage: 4 rape 5 abuse 6 insult, offend, ravish 7 abusion, affront, offense, violate
outrageous: 5 enorm 7 heinous, obscene, ungodly 8 flagrant, shocking 9 atrocious, desperate, execrable, monstrous 10 exorbitant
outre: 7 bizarre, strange 9 eccentric 11 exaggerated, extravagant
outreach: 5 cheat 6 exceed, extend, outwit, search 7 deceive, project, surpass 8 protrude 9 overreach
outright: 5 total, whole 6 direct, openly, wholly 8 complete, entirely 9 downright 15 straightforward
outrival: 5 excel 6 outvie 7 eclipse
outroot: 9 eradicate, extirpate
outrun: 4 beat, cote 6 exceed 7 forerun 9 forespeed
outset: 5 start 9 beginning
outshine: 5 blind, excel 6 dazzle, deface 7 distain, surpass
outside: 4 bout, free 8 exterior, external
comb. form: ect 4 ecto
outsider: 5 alien 8 stranger 9 extranean(Sc.), foreigner
outspoken: 4 bold, free 5 bluff, blunt, broad, frank 6 candid, direct 7 artless 8 explicit 10 unreserved 12 unrestrained
outstanding: big 4 arch, rare 5 famed, noted 6 famous, heroic, marked, unpaid 7 eminent 9 principal, prominent, unsettled 10 noticeable, pre-eminent, projecting 11 conspicuous, exceptional, uncollected, unfulfilled 13 distinguished
outstretched: 5 stent(Sc.) 8 extended
outstrip: cap, top, win 4 best, cote, lead, pass 5 excel, out do 6 exceed 7 devance, surpass 8 distance 9 transcend
outvie: 8 outstrip
outward: 5 ectad, outer, overt 6 exodic, extern, formal 7 extreme, visible 8 apparent, exterior, external, obsolete 9 extrinsic 11 superficial
outweighing: 8 dominant 12 preponderant
outwit: fox 4 balk, best, foil 5 block, check, cross 6 baffle, jockey, thwart 9 checkmate, frustrate 10 circumvent, disappoint
outwork: 6 tenail 7 defense, lunette, ravelin 8 tenaille
ouzel: 4 piet 5 colly, ousel 6 thrush 8 whistler 9 blackbird
oval: 7 ellipse, stadium 8 avelonge 10 elliptical 11 ellipsoidal
ovary: 6 germen
ovate: 9 egg-shaped
inversely: 7 obovate
ovation: 8 applause 10 exultation
oven: 4 kiln, oast 5 baker 6 calcar 7 furnace
annealing glass: 4 leer, lehr
goddess of: 6 Fornax
oven mop: 6 scovel
over: oer, sur(F.), too 4 also, anew, done, uber(G.), upon 5 above, again, clear, ended, extra, vault 6 across, beyond, excess 7 surplus, through 8 finished 9 completed, excessive 10 terminated 11 consummated, superfluous
and above: 7 besides 11 therewithal
combining form: sur 5 hyper, super, supra
prefix: sur 5 super, supra
overabundance: 6 excess 7 surplus 8 plethora
overact: 5 emote 9 burlesque 10 exaggerate
overage: 6 excess 7 surplus
overalls: 5 chaps 10 chaparajos, chaparreras, chaparejos 11 chaparreras
overassuming: 4 bold
overbalance: 8 dominate
overbearing: 5 proud 6 lordly 7 haughty 8 arrogant, bullying, insolent, snobbish, subduing 9 imperious 10 disdainful, high-handed 11 dictatorial, domineering, magisterial 12 overpowering, supercilious
overburden: 8 encumber 9 surcharge
overbusy: 5 fussy
overcast: dim, sew 4 bind, dark, dull 5 cloud, heavy 6 cloudy, darken, gloomy, lowery 7 accloud, becloud, clouded
overcharge: gyp 6 excise 9 extortion
overcloud: dim 6 darken 7 obscure
overcoat: 5 benny 6 capote, raglan, slipon(Sc.), ulster 7 paletot(F.), surtout, topcoat 9 balmacaan, greatcoat, inverness 12 chesterfield
close fitting: 7 surtout
loose: 6 raglan 7 paletot
sleeveless: 9 inverness
overcome: awe, get, win 4 beat, best 5 charm, crush, daunt, fordo 6 appall, beaten, craven, defeat, exceed, foredo, master 7 confute, conquer 8 convince, encumber, outstrip, overbear, overturn, suppress, surmount, vanquish 9 overpower, overthrow, overwhelm, prostrate
overcrowded: 9 congested
overdo: 6 exceed 7 exhaust, fatigue 8 overcook, overwork 9 burlesque 10 caricature, exaggerate
overdue: 4 late 5 tardy 7 arrears, belated, delayed
overeager: 8 feverish
overeat: 5 gorge 7 satiate 8 gourmand 10 gluttonize
overfed: 7 fulsome
overflow: 4 slop, swim, teem, vent 5 float, flood, spate, spill 6 abound, debord, deluge, outlet 7 overrun 8 alluvion, inundate

9 abundance, cataclysm 10 ebullience, exuberance
overflowing: 5 awash 7 copious
overgrown: 7 fulsome
overhang: jut 6 beetle 7 project, suspend
overhasty: 4 rash 6 daring 8 headlong
overhaul: 7 examine 8 renovate 9 forereach
overhead: 5 above, aloft 7 expense
overissue: 9 inflation
overjoyed: 6 elated 8 jubilant 9 delighted
overlapping: 8 obvolute 9 imbricate
overlay: cap, lap 4 ceil, coat 5 couch, cover, glaze, plate 6 cravat, spread, veneer 7 encrust, oppress, overlie 8 covering 10 overburden 11 superimpose
overload: 4 glut 6 charge 8 encumber
overloaded: 9 plethoric
overlook: 4 balk, miss, omit, skip 5 forgo 6 acquit, excuse, forego, forget, ignore, manage 7 absolve, condone, inspect, neglect 9 disregard
overlord: 5 liege 6 despot, satrap, tyrant 8 suzerain
overlying: 8 brochant
overman (see also **overseer**): 5 chief 6 leader 7 arbiter, foreman, referee 8 overseer 9 overpower
overmatch: 4 best 6 exceed 7 surpass 8 vanquish
overmodest: 4 prim 7 prudish
overmuch: too 6 excess 7 surplus 9 excessive
overnice: 5 fussy 7 precise 8 dentical 10 fastidious
overplus: 6 excess 7 surplus 9 advantage
overpower: awe 4 rout 5 crush, whelm 6 compel, defeat, deluge, master, subdue 7 conquer 8 convince, entrance, overbear, overcome, vanquish 9 enrapture, overthrow, overwhelm
overpowering: 4 dire 6 fierce 8 dazzling, stunning
overreach: do 5 cheat 6 grease, nobble, outwit 10 circumvent
overready: 7 forward
override: 4 veto 6 defeat 7 nullify
overrule: 4 veto 8 abrogate
overrun: 5 crush 6 infest, ravage, spread 7 destroy 9 overwhelm
overs: 5 boots
overseas address: APO
oversee: 5 watch 6 survey 7 examine, inspect 9 supervise 11 superintend
overseer (see also **overman**): 4 boss 5 ephor(Gk.), grave, reeve 6 bishop, censor, driver, gaffer, grieve 7 baliff, caporal, curator, foreman, manager 8 banksman, martinet 9 inspector 10 acequiador, supervisor 14 superintendent
agricultural: 8 agronome
spiritual: 6 pastor, priest
overshadow: dim 5 cover, dwarf 6 darken 7 eclipse, obscure 8 dominate 9 adumbrate
overshoe: gum 4 boot 6 arctic, galosh, golosh, patten, rubber 7 flapper
overshoot: 6 exceed
oversight: 4 care 5 error, lapse, watch 6 charge 7 blunder, control, mistake 8 omission 9 direction 10 inspection, negligence 11 supervision 12 surveillance 15 superintendence
overskirt: 6 peplum 7 pannier
oversleeve: 6 armlet
overspread: 4 deck, pall 5 brede, cloud, cover 6 deluge
overstate: 7 magnify 10 exaggerate
overstep: 6 exceed 10 transgress
overt: 4 open 6 patent, public 7 obvious 8 apparent, manifest
overtake: 5 catch 6 attain, detect 7 ensnare 9 apprehend, captivate
overtask: 5 drive
overtax: 6 exceed
overthrow: tip 4 dash, down, fell, foil, fold, hurl, raze, rout, ruin, rush 5 allay, evert, fling, upset, worst, wrack 6 defeat, unseat 7 afflict, conquer, destroy, dismiss, ruinate, unhorse 8 confound, demolish, overcome, overturn, reversal, supplant, vanquish 9 discomfit, overpower, overwhelm, prostrate 10 defeasance 11 destruction 12 discomfiture
overtime: 8 extended
overtire: tax
overture: 5 offer, proem 7 opening, prelude 8 aperture, proposal 11 proposition
opera: 8 sinfonia
overturn: tip 4 cave, coup, tilt 5 throw, upset 6 topple 7 capsize, destroy, pervert, reverse, subvert 8 overcome 9 overthrow, overwhelm
overweening: 8 arrogant
overwhelm: 4 bury 5 amaze, cover, crush, drouk, swamp 6 defeat, deluge, engulf, quench 7 confute, conquer, engross, oppress 8 astonish, inundate, overturn, submerge 9 overpower, overthrow
overword: 7 refrain
Ovid: *birthplace:* 5 Sulmo
burial place: 4 Tomi 5 Tomis
work: 5 Fasti 7 Tristia 13 Metamorphoses
ovine: 5 sheep 9 sheeplike
female: ewe
ovoid: 5 ovate 7 egg-like, obovoid, oviform
ovule: egg 4 seed 6 embryo 7 gemmule, seedlet
integument: 7 primine
ovum: *egg:* 4 seed 5 spore

combining form: ova
owala tree: 4 bobo
owe: due, own 7 possess 9 attribute
ower: 6 debtor
owl: 4 lulu, momo 5 wekau 7 boobook, harfang, woolert 8 billy-wix, moreport 10 gillhooter, hob-houchin
barn: 5 madge
call: 4 hoot
genus of: 5 ninox
pert. to: 8 strigine
plumed eye area of: 4 disk
short-eared: 4 momo
small: 4 utum 6 howlet
young: 4 utum 5 owlet
Owl and Pussycat author: 4 Lear
own: ain(Sc.), owe 4 avow, have, hold, nain(Sc.) 5 admit 7 concede, confess, possess 9 recognize 11 acknowledge
ownership: 5 title 7 tenancy 8 dominium 11 condominium 14 proprietorship
owse: 8 quagmire
ox: yak 4 anoa, aver, beef, buff, gaur, musk, reem, zebu 5 bison, bugle, gayal, steer, tsine 6 bovine 7 banteng, buffalo 8 seladang 9 quadruped
extinct: 4 urus
harness: 4 yoke
pert. to: 5 bovid 6 bovine 7 taurine
small: 4 runt
stall: 5 boose
wild: 4 gaur 8 seladang
oxalis: oca 5 plant 6 sorrel
oxen: 6 cattle
yoke: 4 span
oxeye: 4 boce 5 aster 6 dunlin
oxford: 4 shoe 5 cloth 7 college 10 saddleshoe, university
Oxford: *Earl of:* 6 Harley 7 Asquith
examination: 6 greats
library: 8 Bodleian
officer: 5 bedel 6 beadle
scholar: 4 demy
scholarship: 6 Rhodes
oxhead: 4 dolt 9 blockhead
oxidation: 4 rust
oxide: *aluminum:* 7 alumina
barium: 6 baryta
calcium: 4 lime
hydrocarbon radical: 5 ether
iron: 4 rust
sodium: 4 soda
strontium: 8 strontia
oxidize: 4 rust 7 calcine
oxlike: 6 bovine 7 taurine
oxlip: 8 primrose
oxter: arm 6 armpit
oxtongue: 7 alkanet, bugloss
oxyacantha: 8 hawthorn
oxygen: gas
acid: 7 chloric 9 sulphuric
allotropic: 5 ozone
binary: 5 oxide
oxygenate: 6 aerate
oyez: 4 hear 6 attend 9 attention
oyster: 6 huitre 7 bivalve, mollusk
bed: 4 park, stew 5 layer 6 clair 9 oysterage
eggs: 5 spawn
fossil: 9 ostracite
gatherer: 7 tongman
genus: 6 ostrea
kind of: 6 native 9 bluepoint
phylum: 8 mollusca
rake: 5 tongs
shell: 4 husk, test 5 shuck
spawn: 5 culch 6 cultch
tree: 8 mangrove
young: 4 spat
oyster catcher: 4 bird 5 tirma
oyster grass: 4 kelp
oyster plant: 7 salsify
oysterfish: 6 tautog 8 toadfish
Oz books author: 4 Baum
Ozark State: 8 Missouri
ozone: air

P

pa, pah: dad, paw **4** fort, papa **5** daddy **6** father **7** village **8** stockade **10** settlement
pabulum: **4** food, fuel, prog **6** cereal **7** aliment, support **9** nutriment **10** sustenance
pac, pack **4** boot **8** moccasin
paca: **4** cavy, lava **5** agout, labba **6** rodent
pace: way **4** clip, gait, lope, pass, rack, rate, step, trot, walk **5** amble, canto, speed, tempo, tread **6** canter, gallop, strait **7** channel, chapter, dogtrot, measure, passage **8** platform **10** passageway
pacer: **5** horse **9** pacemaker
pachisi: **4** game, ludo
pachyderm: **8** elephant **10** rhinoceros **12** hippopotamus
pacific: **4** calm, meek, mild **5** irene **6** irenic, placid, serene **8** irenical, peaceful, tranquil **9** appeasing, peaceable **12** conciliatory
Pacific coast state: **6** Oregon **10** California, Washington
Pacific Islands: *archipelago:* Aru **4** Sulu **5** Malay, Samoa **6** Tulagi
bird: **4** kagu
cloth: **4** tapa
collective name: **7** Oceania
grass: **4** neti
military base: **4** Guam
region: **9** Polynesia
tree: kou **4** ipil, taro **7** dasheen, madrona, madrono **8** eddyroot
Pacific Ocean: *archipelago:* **4** Sulu **5** Malay, Samoa
discoverer: **6** Balboa
island: Ie; Lae, Yap **4** Guam, Truk, Wake **5** Leyte, Samoa **6** Tahiti **8** Tasmania **9** Carolines, Marquesas
shark: **4** mako
"stepping stones": **9** Aleutians
pacifier: sop **4** ring **6** nipple
pacifist: **8** appeaser, peacenik
pacify: **4** calm, ease, lull **5** abate, allay, quiet, still **6** serene, soften, soothe **7** appease, assuage, mollify, placate **8** mitigate **9** alleviate, reconcile **10** conciliate, propitiate **11** tranquilize
pack: wad **4** bale, cram, gang, load, stow, tamp **5** crowd, flock, horde, steve, store, truss **6** barrel, bundle, duffle, embale, encase, fardel, impact, wallet **8** knapsack
of cards: **4** deck
pack animal: ass **4** mule **5** burro, camel, horse, llama **6** donkey
package: pad **4** bale **6** bundle, packet, parcel
packer: **5** baler, roper **6** canner
packet: **4** boat **6** bundle, parcel
packing: **4** rags **5** gauze, paper, straw, waste **7** stowage
box: **5** crate
clay: **4** lute
material: **6** gasket, baline **9** excelsior
water-tight: **6** gasket
packing plant: **7** cannery
Pacolet: **5** dwarf, horse
pact: **6** cartel, treaty **7** bargain, compact **8** alliance, contract, covenant **9** agreement
Pactolian: **6** golden
pad: mat, wad, way **4** boss, path, road, walk **5** quilt, stuff, tramp **6** basket, buffer, jockey, pillow, tablet, trudge **7** bolster, bombast, cushion, footpad **8** footfall **10** highwayman
padcloth: **7** housing **11** saddlecloth
padding: **7** packing, robbery, wadding **8** stuffing
paddle: oar, row **4** spud, wade **5** aloof **6** dabble, toddle **8** lumpfish
paddlefish: **9** spadefish **10** shovel-fish
paddock: lot **4** frog, park **5** field **6** sledge **9** enclosure
paddockstone: **10** greenstone
paddockstool: **9** toadstool
Paddy: **8** Irishman
paddywhack: **4** beat, blow **9** thrashing
Paderewski opera: **5** Manru
padlock: **4** lock **6** fasten **7** closing **8** fastener
padre: **4** monk **6** cleric, father, priest **8** chaplain

padrona: 8 landlady, mistress
padrone: 6 master, patron 8 landlord 9 innkeeper
paean, pean: ode 4 hymn, song 6 praise
pagan: 6 ethnic, paynim 7 heathen, infidel 8 idolator 10 idolatrous, unbeliever 11 nonbeliever
god: 4 Baal, idol
page: boy 4 call, leaf 5 child, folio, sheet 6 donzel, summon, varlet 7 footboy, servant 8 henchboy, henchman 9 attendant, messenger
beginning: 4 leaf 7 flyleaf
book: 5 folio 6 cahier
lady: 8 escudero
left-hand: vo 5 verso
number: 5 folio 10 pagination
paper: 5 sheet
reverse: 5 verso
right-hand: 5 recto
title: 5 unwan 6 rubric
pageant: 4 pomp, show 6 parade 7 tableau 8 aquacade 9 spectacle 10 exhibition, procession
pageantry: 8 splendor 11 ostentation
Pagliacci: *character:* 5 Nedda, Tonio
composer: 11 Leoncavallo
pagoda: taa 6 temple 10 kryailteyo 11 summerhouse
finial or ornament: tee
pagurian: 4 crab
pah: pa 5 nasty 6 humbug 8 improper
paha: 4 hill 5 ridge
Pahlavi's realm: 4 Iran
paideutics: 8 pedagogy
pail: can, cog(Sc.), pan, soa, soe 4 beat, bowk, gawn, meal, trug, 5 bowie, cogue(Sc.), eshin, skeel 6 bucket, coggie(Sc.), harass, piggin, situla(L.), thrash, vessel 7 collock, situlae(pl.) 8 cannikin
paillette: 7 spangle
pain: 4 ache, agra, care, cark, harm, hurt, pang 5 agony, cramp, grief, sting, thraw(Sc.), throe, wound 6 grieve, twinge 7 afflict, algesis, anguish, penalty, torture, travail, trouble 8 disquiet, distress 9 suffering 10 affliction, algophilia, discomfort, punishment
comb. form: 5 algia
darting: 6 twinge
dull: 4 ache
pert. to: 6 asonal 7 algetic
relayer: 5 nerve
sensitiveness to: 7 algesia
painful: 4 sare, sore 5 angry 6 bitter 7 irksome 8 exacting 9 difficult, laborious 11 painstaking
painkiller: 6 opiate 7 anodyne, aspirin 8 reliever 9 analgesic, paregoric
pains: 4 care, work 5 labor 6 effort 7 trouble 8 exertion
painstaking: 4 busy 7 careful 8 diligent, exacting 9 assiduous, elaborate, laborious
paint: 4 coat, daub, gaud, limn 5 color, feign, fucus, rouge, stain 6 bedaub, depict, enamel 7 besmear, portray, pretend 8 decorate, disguise
combining form: 5 picto
glossy: 6 enamel
painted: 5 pinto 6 fucate 10 artificial, variegated
painter: 6 artist 7 artiste, panther, workman 9 decorator
painting: oil 5 mural 6 canvas 10 watercolor
equipment: 5 brush, easel, paint 6 canvas, pallet 7 palette
medium: oil 7 gouache, tempera 10 watercolor
one-color: 8 monotint 10 monochrome
plaster: 5 secco 6 fresco
sacred: 5 pieta
scenic: 5 scape 8 seascape 9 cityscape, landscape
small: 9 miniature
style: 5 genre
three panels: 8 triptych
wall: 5 mural, panel 6 fresco
pair: duo, two 4 case, diad, duad, dyad, mate, span, team, yoke 5 brace, match, unite 6 couple
paisano: 7 peasant 10 countryman
Paisley: 5 shawl 6 design, fabric 7 pattern
Pakistan: *city or town:* Dir 6 Lahore, Multan, Quetta
province: 4 Sind, Swat 5 Kalat, Sindh 6 Khelat 11 Baluchistan
pass: 5 Bolan
pal: 4 ally, chum, pard 5 buddy, crony 6 cobber, digger, friend 7 comrade, partner 9 associate, companion 10 accomplice 11 confederate
palace: 5 court, serai 6 castle, palais(F.) 7 alcazar, edifice, mansion 8 Alcalzar 9 pretorium 10 praetorium
officer: 7 paladin 8 palatine
papal: 7 Lateran
paladin: 4 hero, peer 6 knight 8 champion, douzeper
palaestra: 6 school 9 gymnasium
palamate: 9 web-footed
Palamedes: *enemy:* 7 Ulysses
father: 8 Nauplius
mother: 7 Clymene
war: 6 Trojan
Palamon: *rival:* 6 Arcite
wife: 6 Emelye

palanquin: 4 kago 5 dooli, dooly, palki, sedan 6 doolee, dooley, doolie, litter, palkee 10 conveyance
palatable: 5 sapid, tasty 6 savory 8 delicate, pleasing 9 agreeable, delicious 10 acceptable
render: 4 salt 5 spice 6 season
palatal: 5 front, velar 8 gutteral 9 consonant
palate: 5 taste 6 relish 7 gourmet
pert. to: 6 uranic
soft: 4 cion, vela(pl.) 5 uvula, velum
palatial: 5 large 6 ornate 7 stately 11 magnificent
palantine: 4 cape 7 officer, paladin 8 palatial
palaver: 4 talk 6 debate, glaver, parley 7 chatter, flatter, wheedle 8 cajolery, flattery 10 conference 12 conversation
pale: dim, wan 4 ashy, fade, grey, gull, lily, pall, sick 5 ashen, blake, blate, bleak, faint, fence, livid, lurid, stake, stick, white 6 anemic, blanch, chalky, feeble, pallid, pastel, picket, region, sickly, whiten 7 anaemic, enclose, ghastly, haggard, insipid, obscure, whitish 8 encircle, etiolate 9 colorless
paleness: 6 pallor
Palestine: *animal:* 5 daman
ancient city: 8 Ashkelon
coin: mil 5 pound
conquerors: 5 Turks
country: 4 Edom 9 Philistia
god: 4 Baal
Jewish: 5 Erets, Eretz 7 Yisrael, Yisroel
lake: 5 Merom 7 Galilee 8 Tiberias
landmark: Dan
language: 7 Aramaic
mammal: 5 daman
measure: 5 cubit, donum 6 sacred
mountain: 4 Ebal, Nebo, Zion 6 Carmel, Gilead, Hermon, Moriah, Olives, Pisgah 7 Gerizim 8 Jebel Tur
part: 4 Gaza 5 Haifa 6 Canaan, Ghazze
people: 7 Amorite
plain: 6 Sharon
port: 4 Acre 5 Haifa, Jaffa
province: 7 Galilee
region: 5 Perea 6 Bashan
river: 6 Jordan
town: Tob 4 Bire, Cana, Gaza 5 Endor 6 Ghazze 7 Samaria 9 Jerusalem
weight: 4 rotl, zuza
palestra, palaestra: 6 school 9 gymnasium
palet: 5 quoit
paletot: 8 overcoat 9 greatcoat
palfrey: 5 horse
palimpsest: 6 tablet 9 parchment
palindrome: 7 sotadic
paling: 4 pale 5 fence, flake, limit, stake 6 picket 7 fencing 9 enclosure
palinode: 10 retraction 11 recantation
Palinurus: 9 steersman
palisade: 5 cliff, fence, stake 7 barrier, enclose, fortify, furnish 8 espalier, surround 9 implement
pall: 4 bore, cloy, pale, sate 5 cloak, cloth, faint, qualm, stale, weary 6 mantle, nausea 7 disgust, satiate 8 animetta, covering
Pall Mall site: 7 West End
palladium symbol: Pd
pallbearer: 6 bearer
pallet: bed, cot, pad 5 couch, quilt 7 blanket 8 mattress, plancher 9 headpiece
palliard: 6 beggar, lecher, rascal 8 vagabond
palliasse: 6 pallet 8 mattress
palliate: 4 ease, hide 5 cloak, cover, gloss, gloze 6 lessen, soften 7 conceal, shelter 8 disguise, mitigate 9 alleviate, exculpate, extenuate
pallid: wan 4 ashy, pale, paly 5 bleak, white 7 ghastly 9 colorless
pallion: bit 5 piece 6 pellet
pallium: 4 band, pall 5 cloak 6 mantle 8 himation
palm: 4 hide 6 palmus(Lat.), thenar, trophy 7 conceal
betel nut: 5 areca, bonga
beverage: 5 assai
cabbage: 8 palmetto
climbing: 6 rattan
coconut: 4 coco
fan-leafed: 7 talipat, talipot, taliput 8 palmetto
feather: 5 howea 6 gomuti 7 urucuri, urucury
fiber: tal 4 buri 6 raffia
food: nut 4 sago 5 fruit
juice: 4 nipa, sura 5 taree, toddy
kind: ti 4 jara 5 assai, royal, tucum 6 bacaba, tucuma 7 babassu, jaggery, tokopat 8 bangalow
leaf: ola, ole 4 olay, olla 5 frond
low: 5 bussu 6 trooly, trouie, ubussu
palmyra: ola, ole, tal 4 brab, olla 6 ronier
pert. to: 6 palmar 8 frondous 10 palmaceous
pith: 4 sago
reader: 7 palmist
sap: 5 toddy
seeds: 4 nipa
spiny: 6 grigri, grugru
starch: 4 sago
stem: 4 cane 5 ratan 6 rattan
stemless: 5 curua
thatch: 4 nipa 9 barriguda
wing-leaved: 6 cohune
palm-leaf mat: 4 yapa

palm off: 5 foist
palma: 5 yucca
palmary: 5 chief, palmy 6 palmar 8 superior 9 principal 10 pre-eminent, victorious
palmate: 4 flat 5 broad, lobed 6 palmed, webbed
palmed: 7 palmate
palmer: 5 louse 6 stroll, travel, votary, wander 7 pilgrim 15 prestidigitator
Palmetto State: 13 South Carolina
palmistry: 10 chirognomy, chiromancy
practicer: 11 chiromancer
palmodic: 5 jerky
palms down: 7 pronate
palmy: 7 palmary 10 prosperous, triumphant 11 flourishing
Palmyra's queen: 7 Zenobia
palmyra tree: 4 brab 7 talipot
palp: 6 feeler, palpus 7 flatter 8 tentacle
palpable: 4 rank 5 plain 6 patent 7 audible, evident, obvious, tactile 8 apparent, distinct, manifest, tangible 10 noticeable, perceptive 12 recognizable
palpebra: 6 eyelid
palpebrate: 4 wink
palpitation: 4 beat, pant 7 flicker, flutter 9 pulsation, quivering, throbbing, trembling
palsied: 5 shaky 7 shaking 9 paralyzed, tottering, trembling
palter: fib, lie 6 babble, haggle, mumble, trifle 7 chatter, quibble 10 equivocate 11 prevaricate
paltock: 6 jacket 7 doublet
paltry: 4 bald, bare, base, mean, puny, vile 5 footy, petty, trash 6 chetif, flimsy, trashy 7 pitiful, rubbish, trivial 8 picayune, trifling 9 worthless 10 despicable 12 contemptible 13 insignificant
paludal: 6 marshy 8 paludine
pampas: 6 plains
cat: 6 pajero
pamper: pet 4 baby, cram, delt(Sc.), glut 5 spoil 6 caress, cocker, coddle, cosher, cosset, cuddle, dandle, fondle, posset 7 cherish, cockney, gratify, indulge, satiate, forwean
pamphagous: 10 omnivorous
pamphlet: 5 tract 6 folder 7 booklet, catalog, leaflet 8 brochure 9 catalogue
pan: fit, tab 4 part, wash 5 agree, basin, unite 6 frache(F.), lappet, vessel 7 cranium, hardpan, portion, subsoil 8 brainpan, ridicule 9 criticize 10 acetabulum
coal burner: 5 grill 7 brazier
frying: 6 spider 7 skillet
gold-washing: 4 tina 5 batea
Pan: 6 Faunus
father: 6 Hermes
instrument: 4 pipe, reed
place of worship: 7 Arcadia
son: 7 Silenus 8 Seilenos
panacea: 4 cure 6 elixir, remedy 7 allheal, cure-all, heal-all 8 nepenthe 10 catholicon 11 panchreston
panache: 5 plume
panachure: 8 mottling
panal: 7 biscuit
Panama: hat 6 Darien
city: 5 Colon 6 Panama 9 Aspinwall, Cristobal
coin: 6 balboa
gulf: 6 Darien
measure: 7 celemin
river: 5 Sambu, Tuira 7 Chagres
rubber: 8 Castilla
tree: 4 yaya 6 alfaje, cativo
Panama Canal: *dam and locks:* 5 Gatun 10 Miraflores
engineer: 9 de Lesseps
lake: 5 Gatun
port: 5 Colon 9 Cristobal
panatela: 5 cigar
panax: 4 herb
pancake: 5 arepa(Sp.), flawn 6 blintz, fraise, froise 7 blintze, fritter, hotcake 8 flapjack 11 griddlecake
delicate: 5 crepe
panda: wah 6 animal 7 bearcat
pandemonium: 5 noise 6 tumult, uproar 8 disorder 9 confusion
pander: 4 bawd, pimp 5 cater 7 whiskin 8 procurer 9 go-between, procuress
Pandora: *brother:* 10 Prometheus
daughter: 6 Pyrrha
husband: 10 Epimetheus
pane: 5 glass 7 section
panegyric: 5 eloge, elogy 6 eulogy, praise 7 encomia(pl.), oration, tribute, writing 8 encomium 9 discourse, laudation
panel: 4 jury 5 group 6 tympan 8 decorate
paneling: 4 wall 7 ceiling
panfish: 4 crab, king 9 horseshoe
pang: 4 ache, cram, fill, gird, pain, tang 5 agony, spasm, stuff, throe 6 twinge 7 anguish, travail 8 paroxysm 9 heartache
Pangim native: 4 Goan
pangolin: 5 manis 8 anteater, edentate
order: 9 pholidota
panhandle: beg 5 cadge
Panhandle State: 12 West Virginia
panic: 4 fear, fray, funk 5 alarm, chaos, scare 6 fright, terror 8 stampede 13 consternation
panjandrum: 7 magnate 9 personage
pannier, panier: bag, ped 5 seron 6 basket, dorsel, dorser, dosser, pantry 9 overskirt

horse: 6 curagh 7 currach, currack, curragh, currock
panoply: 5 armor 6 armour
panorama: 4 view 5 scene, sweep, vista 7 picture, scenery 9 cyclorama
panpipe: 6 syrinx 8 zampogna
pansy: 9 heartease 10 heartsease
pant: 4 ache, beat, blow, gasp, puff 5 heave, throb, yearn 7 pulsate 9 palpitate 11 palpitation
Pantagruel: *companion:* 7 Panurge
father: 9 Gargantua
mother: 7 Badebec
pantalan: 5 wharf 8 platform
Panthea's husband: 9 Abradatus
pantheon: 6 temple
panther: cat 4 pard, puma 6 cougar, jaguar 7 leopard, painter
pantile: 4 tile 7 biscuit 8 hardtack
panting: 8 anhelose, anhelous 10 anhelation
pantomimist: 4 mime 5 actor 7 Marceau
pantry: 4 cave 5 ambry 6 closet, larder 7 buttery, pannier, pantler 8 cupboard
pants: 5 jeans 7 drawers 8 trousers 10 pantaloons
leather: 5 chaps 10 chaparajos, chapareras, chaperejos, lederhosen(G.) 11 chaparreras
panuelo: 6 collar, ruffle 8 kerchief 9 neckcloth
pap: 4 teat 6 nipple 8 emulsion, mammilla
papa pa; dad, paw, pop 6 baboon, father, potato, priest 7 vulture
papal (see also **Pope**): 9 apostolic 10 pontifical
papal court: see 5 curia
papaya: 5 papaw 6 pawpaw
paper: 5 essay, theme 6 cartel, report 7 journal, writing 8 document 9 monograph, newspaper, wallpaper 10 periodical 11 credentials, examination 12 dissertation 13 unsubstantial
absorbent: 7 blotter 9 towelling
case: 4 file 5 folio 6 binder
collection: 7 dossier
currency: 5 scrip
damaged: 5 broke, casse, salle 6 cassie
design: 9 watermark
detachable: tab 4 stub 6 coupon
fine: 5 linen 6 vellum
folded once: 5 folio
gummed: 5 label, stamp 6 paster 7 sticker
hard: 6 pelure
large-size: 5 atlas
legal: 4 writ
medicinal: 6 charta
official: 5 targe 8 document
pad: 6 tablet
piece: 5 scrip, sheet
postage-stamp: 6 pelure
pulp: 4 ulla
quantity: 4 page, ream 5 quire, sheet 6 bundle
scroll: 9 parchment
size: cap 4 copy, demi, demy, pott 5 atlas, crown, folio, legal 7 bastard, emperor 8 foolscap, imperial 9 colombier
thin: 6 pelure, tissue 9 onionskin
untrimmed edge: 6 deckle
writing-size: cap 8 foolscap
paper money: 4 bill, cash 7 lettuce 8 frogskin 9 greenback
papilla: bud 6 pimple
papist: 8 Catholic
papoose: 4 baby
pappy: pa; dad, paw 4 papa, soft 5 mushy 6 father
papule: 6 pimple
papyrus: 4 reed 6 biblos, biblus, scroll 7 bulrush
repository: 5 capsa
par: by 5 equal 6 normal 7 average 8 equality 9 enclosure 11 equivalence
par value: 4 face 7 nominal
parable: 4 myth, tale 5 fable, story 6 apolog, byword 7 byspell 8 allegory, apologue, forbysen 10 comparison, similitude
parabola: arc 5 curve
parachute: *material:* 4 silk 5 nylon
part: 4 pack 6 canopy 7 harness, ripcord
paraclete: 6 helper 7 pleader 8 advocate, consoler 9 comforter 11 intercessor
parade: 4 pomp, show, walk 5 march, strut 6 flaunt, review, stroll 7 cortege, display, exhibit, marshal 8 ceremony, flourish, grandeur, splendor 9 advertise, pageantry, promenade, strollers 10 callithump, pretension, procession 12 magnificence
paradigm: 5 model 7 example, pattern
Paradise: 4 Eden 5 bliss 6 Aidenn, heaven 7 Elysium
Buddhist: 4 Jodo
fool's: 5 limbo
Muslim: 5 Jenna
river: 5 Gihon
Paradise Lost angel: 5 Ariel, Uriel
paraffin: 6 alkane
paragon: gem 4 type 5 ideal, model 7 pattern 9 nonpariel
paragram: pun
paragraph: 4 item, sign 5 caput 7 initial 8 material
Paraguay: *city:* Ita 8 Asuncion(c.) 9 Paraguari, Villa Rica
coin: 4 peso
Indian: 7 Guarani

measure: pie 4 line, lino, vara 5 legua, linea 6 cordel, cuadra, cuarta, fanega, league
money: 7 guarani
river: Apa 6 Parana 8 Paraguay 9 Tibiquare
tea: 4 mate 5 yerba
weight: 7 quintal
parakeet: 6 parrot, wellat 8 paraquet 10 budgerygah 11 budgereegah
parallel: 4 even 5 along, equal, match 8 analogue 10 collateral 11 counterpart
render: 9 collimate
parallelism: 6 simile 10 similarity 11 resemblance 14 correspondence
parallelogram: 5 rhomb 6 oblong, square 9 rectangle
paralogist: 7 sophist
paralysis: 5 cramp, palsy 7 paresis 10 holoplexia 11 monoparesis
with: 7 paretic 9 paralytic
paralyzed: 4 numb 7 palsied 8 benumbed, crippled
paramount: 5 above, chief, ruler 7 capital, supreme 8 dominant, superior, suzerain 10 pre-eminent, proprietor
lord: 5 liege
paramour: 5 leman, lover, wooer 6 amoret, friend 10 sweetheart
female: 7 hetaera, hetaira 8 mistress
paranomasia: pun
paranymph: 10 bridesmaid
parapet: 4 butt, wall 5 redan 7 bulwark, railing, rampart 10 breastwork 12 embattlement 13 fortification
part of: 5 crete
V-shaped: 5 redan
paraphernalia: 4 gear 9 apparatus, equipment, trappings 10 belongings 11 furnishings
paraphrase: 6 reword 7 version 9 translate 11 translation
parasite: bug, bur 4 burr, moss 5 leech, toady, virus 6 fungus, sponge 7 sponger 8 hanger-on 9 mistletoe, sycophant
animal: 8 entozoan
blood: 4 tryp
marine: 6 remora, sponge
plant: 9 entophyte
trout: sug
parasol: 8 sunshade, umbrella 11 bumbershoot
paratrooper cry: 8 Geronimo
paravane: 5 otter
Parcae: See **Fates**
parcel: lot 4 deal, mete, pack, part 5 bulse, bunch, group, piece 6 bundle, divide, packet 7 package, portion 8 fragment 10 collection, distribute
parch: dry 4 burn, sear 5 roast, toast 6 scorch 7 bristle, brustle, graddan, shrivel
parched: 4 arid, sere 5 fiery 6 gizzen, torrid
parchment (see also **paper, scroll**): 6 charta
book cover: 5 forel 6 forrel
fine: vel 6 vellum
manuscript: 10 palimpsest
piece: 8 membrane
roll: 4 pell 6 scroll
pard: pal 4 chum 5 tiger 7 leopard, panther, partner 9 companion 10 camelopard
pardesi: 9 foreigner, outlander
pardie, pardi: 6 indeed, surely, verily 9 certainly
pardo: 7 mulatto
pardon: 5 mercy, remit, spare 6 assoil, excuse 7 absolve, amnesty, condone, forgive 8 reprieve, tolerate 9 exculpate, remission 10 absolution, indulgence 11 forgiveness
general: 7 amnesty
stall: 12 confessional
pardonable: 6 venial 9 excusable
pare: cut 4 chip, peel, skin 5 shave 6 reduce, remove, resect 7 curtail, whittle 8 diminish 11 decorticate
paregoric: 7 anodyne
pareil: 4 mate 5 equal 8 equality
parel: 7 apparel 11 mantelpiece
parella, parelle: 6 lichen
parent: dad, dam 4 mama, papa, sire 5 daddy, mater(L.), pater 6 author, father, mother, origin 7 forbear, genitor 8 ancestor, begetter, forebear, guardian, producer 10 forefather, progenitor
parentage: 5 birth 6 family, origin 10 extraction, parenthood
parget: 4 coat 6 gypsum 7 plaster 8 decorate 9 whitewash
pariah: 7 Ishmael, outcast
parian: 6 marble, market 9 porcelain
Paris: *airport:* 4 Orly
district: 7 Auteuil
father: 5 Priam
first bishop: 5 Denis, Denys
mother: 6 Hecuba
palace: 6 Elysee, Louvre 9 Tuileries
police: 5 flics 6 Surete
river: 5 Seine
Roman name: 7 Lutetia
stock exchange: 6 bourse
suburb: 5 Passy
subway: 5 metro
thug: 6 apache
wife: 6 Oenone
parish: 12 congregation
head: 6 pastor, priest 8 minister
officer: 10 borsholder
official: 9 vestryman

paristhmion: 6 tonsil
parity: 7 analogy 8 equality 10 similarity 11 resemblance
park: hay 4 stop 7 commons, paddock 10 playground
parlance: 4 talk 7 diction 9 discourse 11 phraseology 12 conversation
parlay: 5 wager 6 paroli
parley: 5 speak, treat, utter 6 confer, paroli 7 discuss, palaver 9 discourse 10 conference, discussion 12 conversation
parliament: 4 diet 5 senat(F.) 7 council 8 congress, converse 9 parleying 10 conference
member: 4 lord
parlous: 4 keen 5 risky 6 clever, shrewd 7 cunning 8 perilous 9 dangerous 11 exceedingly, excessively, mischievous 13 disconcerting
parnassian: 4 poet
paroch: 9 clergyman
parody: 4 skit 6 satire 8 travesty 9 burlesque, imitation 10 caricature
paroemia: 7 proverb
parole: 6 pledge 7 promise
paronomasia: pun 12 agnomination
paroxysm: fit 4 pang 5 agony, spasm, throe 6 access, attack, orgasm 8 epitasis, outburst 9 agitation 10 convulsion 12 exacerbation
parrot: ara 4 copy, echo, jako, lory 5 arara, mimic, polly 6 repeat, tiriba 7 corella 8 cockatoo, lorikeet, lovebird, parakeet 9 cockateel, cockatiel
disease: 11 psittacosis
genus: 9 psittacus
gray: 4 jako
green: 5 cagit
hawk: hia
like: 5 arine 11 psittaceous
long-tailed: 5 macaw
monk: 4 loro
owl: 4 kaka 6 kakapo
part of bill: 4 cere
sheep-killing: kea
small: 8 lovebird, parakeet
parrot fish: 4 scar 5 lania 6 scarus 9 labroidea
parry: 4 fend, ward 5 avoid, block, evade 6 thwart 7 deflect, evasion
parse: 7 analyse, analyze, diagram 8 construe
Parsee: See **Parsi**
Parsi: 11 Zoroastrian
holy book: 6 Avesta
priest: 5 mobed 6 dastur 7 destour, dustoor
parsimonious: 4 mean, near 5 close, scant, spare 6 frugal, narrow, skimpy, sordid, stingy 7 miserly, sparing 8 covetous, grasping, wretched 9 illiberal, mercenary, niggardly, penurious 10 avaricious, economical, ungenerous 17 narrowheartedness
parsley: 5 cumin 6 eltrot
derivative: 5 apiol 6 apiole
genus: 12 petroselinum
relative: 6 celery
parsley camphor: 6 apiole
parson: 6 rector 8 minister, preacher 9 clergyman, guidepost
parson bird: poe, tui 4 rook
parson-in-the-pulpit: 10 cuckoopint
parsonage: 5 manse 7 rectory 9 pastorium
part (see also **parts**): 4 deal, dole, half, role, rove, side, some, twin 5 piece, quota, sever, share 6 behalf, canton, cleave, depart, detail, divide, member, sunder 7 disjoin, element, portion, section, segment 8 alienate, disperse, dissever, disunite, division, estrange, fraction, fragment, separate 9 abteilung(G.), apportion, dismember 10 department 11 constituent
baglike: sac
basic: 4 core, pith 7 essence
central: 4 core 5 focus, solar 6 nuclei(pl.) 7 nucleus
choice: 5 cream, elite 6 marrow 7 essence
coarse: 5 dregs
comb. form: 4 demi, hemi, meri, semi
distinct: 4 unit 7 article
essential: 4 core, gist, pith 6 factor
final: 5 shank
hardest: 5 brunt
highest: top 4 apex 5 crest 6 summit
inmost: 4 core 5 heart 6 center
main: 4 body 5 trunk
minor: bit, cog
moving: 5 rotor
narrow: 4 neck
revolving: 5 rotor 7 rotator
root-like: 7 radicle
small: bit, jot 4 atom, iota, mite 5 tithe 6 detail, moiety 7 snippet
suddenly: 4 rend, snap
uppermost: top 4 peak 6 upside 7 topside
part with: 4 give, lose, sell 5 leave 6 donate 7 abandon
partage: 4 part 5 share 7 portion 8 division
partake: 4 bite 5 share 6 divide 11 participate
of: use
partan: 4 crab
parted: 7 partite
parten: 6 impart 7 partake
Parthian ruler: 7 Arsaces
parti-colored: 4 pied 7 piebald 10 variegated

partial: 4 half, part 6 biased, unfair 7 colored, halfway 8 coloured, inclined, one-sided, partisan 10 fractional, incomplete, prejudiced 11 predilected, predisposed
prefix: 4 demi, semi
participant: 5 party 8 partisan 10 accomplice 12 participator 13 participating
participate: 4 join, side 5 enter, share 7 compete, partake 9 cooperate
particle: ace, bit, dot, gru, jot 4 atom, grue, iota, mite, mote, whit 5 fleck, grain, shred, speck 6 smidge, tittle 7 smidgen, smidgin 8 smidgeon, smitchin
affirmative: yes
burnt: 6 cinder
co-ordinating: or
cosmic: 5 meson
electrified: ion 5 anion 6 proton
incandescent: 5 spark
minute: jot, ort, ray 4 atom, iota, mite, mote 5 grain, speck 7 granule, ramenta(pl.) 8 molecule, ramentum 9 scintilla
negative: nor, not
pluvial: 4 drop
small: see *minute* above
particular: 4 item, nice 5 fussy, thing 6 detail, minute 7 article, careful, correct, precise, special, unusual 8 accurate, concrete, detailed, especial, exacting, itemized, specific 10 fastidious, noteworthy 11 scrumptious 12 circumstance 13 extraordinary 14 circumstantial
particularly: 9 expressly
parting: 5 death 8 farewell 11 leavetaking
parting shot: 5 taunt
partisan: 4 pike 5 staff 6 biased, fautor 7 devotee 8 adherent, follower, partizan 9 truncheon 10 factionary, factioneer, interested
unwavering: 6 zealot 8 stalwart
partite: 6 parted 7 divided 9 separated
partition: 4 wall 5 septa(pl.) 6 divide, screen, septum 7 enclose, portion, scantle 8 cleavage, division 9 severance 10 distribute, enterclose, separation 11 compartment 13 apportionment
partitioned: 7 septate
partlet: hen 5 woman
partner: pal 4 ally, half, mate, wife 5 butty 6 fellow, sharer 7 comrade, consort, husband 8 camarada 9 associate, coadjutor, colleague, companion 10 accomplice 11 confederate, participant
comedian's: 6 stooge
paid: 6 gigolo
partnership: hui 4 firm 7 cahoots, company 14 compagnieschap(D.)
partridge: 4 yutu 5 titar 6 chukar, chukor, seesee 7 tinamou 9 francolin
flock: 5 covey
young: 7 cheeper 8 squealer
partridgeberry: 9 snowberry
parts (see also **part**): *innermost:* 10 penetralia
together: 9 adhesions
totality: 5 unity
two: 6 binary
parturition: 7 travail 8 delivery 10 childbirth
party (see also **political party**): bal(F.) 4 clan, drum, sect, side 5 cabal, group 6 comite, fiesta, person 7 company, faction 9 gathering 10 detachment 11 association, combination 12 participator
afternoon: tea 9 reception
evening: 4 ball 6 soiree
guilty: 7 culprit
men's: 4 stag 6 smoker
reconnaissance: 6 patrol
seashore: 6 picnic 8 clambake
party man: 8 partisan
parure: 5 adorn 6 paring 7 apparel, peeling 8 ornament
parvenu: 4 snob 6 arrive 7 upstart 9 arriviste 12 nouveauriche, nouvellerich
Pascal work: 7 Pensees
Pasch, Pascha: 6 Easter 8 Passover 10 Good Friday
paschal: 4 lamb 6 supper 8 Passover 11 celebration
pasear: 4 walk 6 airing 9 promenade
pasha: dey 4 emir
territory: 8 pachalic, pashalic, pashalik
Pashur's father: 9 Malchijah
Pasiphae: *children:* 7 Ariadne, Phaedra
husband: 5 Minos
pasqueflower: 6 badger 10 badgerweed
pasquinade: 5 squib 6 satire 7 lampoon, pasquil
pass: go; col, end, gap 4 abra, beal(Sc.), comp, cove, fare, ghat, hand, lane, pace, step, wend 5 canto, enact, ghaut, gorge, hurry, kotal, lapse, lunge, occur, relay, smite, spend, utter, yodel 6 billet, convey, defile, elapse, exceed, happen, passus, permit, ticket, twofer 7 allonge, approve, devolve, passage, undergo 8 beallach, surmount 10 abjudicate, permission 11 Annie Oakley 13 complimentary
slowly: 4 drag
without touching: 5 clear
pass around: 5 skirt 6 detour
pass away: die 6 expire, perish, vanish 8 transfer 9 disappear, surrender
pass by: 4 cote, omit, skip 6 forego, ignore 8 overlook 9 disregard
pass off: con 5 foist

pass over: die 4 omit, skip 5 cross 6 elapse, expire, excuse, ignore 8 overlook, transfer, traverse 9 disregard
lightly: 4 skim
quickly: 4 scan, scud
smoothly: 5 elide
pass through: 5 cross 6 pierce 7 pervade 8 permeate, traverse 9 penetrate
pass up: 6 reject 7 decline 9 disregard
passable: fit 4 fair, soso 7 genuine 8 adequate, mediocre, moderate, traveled 9 navigable, navigated, tolerable, traversed 10 admissable
passage: gat, gut, wro 4 adit, belt, door, duct, exit, fare, flue, ford, gang, gate, hall, iter, lane, pass, pawn, race, ramp, slip 5 aisle, allee, alley, alure, atria(pl.), entry, going, gorge, meuse 6 access, arcade, atrium, avenue, burrow, course, defile, egress, strait, travel, tunnel, voyage 7 channel, couloir, estuary, gangway, itinera(pl.), journey, transit 8 aqueduct, corridor, crossing 9 ventiduct 10 bottleneck 12 thoroughfare
air: 4 flue 9 ventiduct
between two walls: 5 slype
covered: 6 arcade
literary: 4 text 7 excerpt 9 quotation
mine: 5 stope
one outlet: 7 impasse 8 cul-de-sac
scripture: 4 text
subterranean: 4 mine 6 tunnel 8 cuniculi(pl.) 9 cuniculus
passageway: 5 aisle
passant: 4 past 7 current, cursory, passing, walking 9 ephemeral, excelling 10 proceeding, surpassing, transitory
passe: 4 aged, past, worn 5 faded 7 demoded 8 obsolete, outmoded 10 antiquated 12 old-fashioned 13 superannuated
passementerie: 8 trimming
passenger: 4 fare 8 ferryman, traveler, wayfarer
passerby: 9 saunterer
passerine bird: 7 sparrow 8 starling
passing: 7 cursory 8 elapsing, fleeting 9 departing, ephemeral, exceeding 10 pre-eminent, transitory, surpassing
passion (see also **mania**): ire 4 fire, fury, heat, love, lust, raga, rage, zeal 5 anger, ardor 6 affect, choler, desire, fervor 7 emotion, feeling, fervour 8 appetite 9 calenture, martyrdom 10 affliction, enthusiasm
passion flower: 6 maypop
family: 14 passifloraceae
passionate: 4 fond 6 fervid, fierce 7 amorous, flaming, peppery 8 frenetic 9 irascible, phrenetic 11 impassioned 12 affectionate
passionless: 4 cold 6 freddo(It.)
passive: 5 inert, stoic 6 stolid 7 patient 8 inactive, yielding 9 apathetic, impassive 10 submissive
passover: 5 phase
Passover: 5 Pesah 6 Pesach
bread: 5 matzo 6 matzos 7 matzoth 8 afikomen
festival: 5 Seder
pert. to: 7 paschal
songs of praise: 6 hallel
story: 7 haggada 8 haggadah
passport: 5 conge 6 dustuk 7 dustuck 8 furlough
endorsement: 4 visa, vise
passus: 4 pace, part, step 5 canto 8 division
password: 11 countersign
past: by; ago 4 gone, yore 5 after, agone, aside, ended, since 6 behind, bygone 8 foregone 9 completed, foregoing 11 antecedents
immediate: 9 yesterday
pert. to: 8 historic
tense: 11 perteritive
pasta: 7 ravioli 8 macaroni 9 spaghetti
paste: hit, pap 4 beat, blow, duff, glue, pate 5 cream, dough, false, punch, stick 6 attach, batter, fasten, strass 7 filling 8 adhesive, mucilage 9 imitation
aromatic: 6 pastil 7 pastile 8 pastille
dried: 7 guarana
pasteboard: 4 card, sham 6 flimsy
pastel: 6 crayon 7 picture
pastern: 6 hobble, hopple, tether 7 shackle
Pasternak novel: 7 Zhivago
pasticcio: 4 olio 6 jumble, medley 9 patchwork, potpourri 10 hodgepodge
pastime: 4 game 5 hobby, sport 9 amusement, diversion 10 yesteryear 13 entertainment
pastor: 4 herd 5 angel, rabbi 6 curate, keeper, priest, rector 7 dominie 8 guardian, minister, shepherd 9 clergyman
pastoral: 4 poem 5 drama, rural 7 bucolic, idyllic, romance
god: Pan
pert. to: 8 agrestic, geoponic
pipe: 4 reed
place: 7 Arcadia
poem: 4 idyl 5 idyll 7 eclogue, georgic
pastry (see also **cake, pie**): pie 4 flan, huff, tart 6 eclair 7 carcake(Sc.), strudel 8 napoleon, turnover
garnish: 5 cream, fruit 8 meringue
shell: 7 dariole, timbale
pasturage: 4 gang 6 eatage, forage 7 herbage

pasture: hag, ham, ing, lea 4 heaf, hoga 5 agist, drift, grass, graze, veldt 6 meadow, saeter 7 grazing, vaccary 8 herdwick 9 grassland 10 agostadero
god: Pan
pasturer: 7 grazier 8 herdsman
pasty: pie 6 doughy
pasty cement: 6 mastic
pat: apt, dab, tap 4 blow 5 fitly, fixed, impel, throw 6 caress, soothe, strike, stroke, timely 7 apropos, fitting, readily 8 suitable 9 immovable, opportune, pertinent 10 seasonable 12 commendation
Patagonia: *cavy:* 4 mara
deity: 7 Setebos
rodent: 4 cavy, mara
tree: 6 alerce, alerse
patamar: 7 courier 9 messenger
patand: 4 base 6 plinth
patch: bit 4 mend, vamp 5 bodge, clout, clump, cover, piece, scrap 6 blotch, cobble, dollop, parcel, revamp, solder 7 clobber, remnant
of woods: 5 motte
patchwork: 5 cento 6 jumble, scraps 9 fragments 10 hodgepodge
pate: pie, top 4 head 5 crown, paste, pasty, patty 6 badger, noggin
patella: pan 4 dish, vase 7 kneecap, kneepan
paten: 4 arca, disc, dish, disk 5 plate 6 vessel
patent: 4 arca, open 5 berat(Orient), overt, plain 7 evident, license, obvious 8 apparent, archives, enduring, manifest 9 available, franchise 10 accessible, university 12 unobstructed
notice: 6 caveat
pater: 6 father, priest
paterissa: 7 crosier
paternal: 8 fatherly
kinsman: 6 agnate
paternity: 6 father, origin 10 authorship, fatherhood 12 fatherliness
path: pad, rut, way 4 fare, lane, line, road, walk 5 alley, byway, going, piste, route, track, trail 6 camino, casaun, comino, course, groove 7 footway, highway, towpath
hill: 4 berm 5 berme 6 roddin 7 borstal, rodding 8 borstall
math: 5 locus
pathetic: sad 5 teary 7 pitiful 8 stirring 9 affecting
pathic: 7 passive 8 catamite 9 suffering
pathological: 4 sick 6 morbid
pathway: run 4 lane, path 6 course, roddin 7 rodding
patience: 4 calm 8 stoicism 9 composure, endurance, fortitude 10 submission 11 forbearance, resignation 12 acquiescence
patient: 4 case, meek 6 bovine
patinize: 6 patine
patio: 5 court 9 courtyard
patisserie: 4 shop 6 pastry
patois: 6 Creole 7 dialect
patriarch: 4 Enos, Levi, Nasi, Noah 5 elder 7 ancient 9 venerable
patrician: 5 noble 10 aristocrat 12 aristocratic
patrimony: 8 ancestry, heritage
patriot: 10 chauvinist, countryman 11 compatriate
song: 6 anthem 7 America
patrocinium: 9 patronage 10 protection
patrol: 5 guard, scout, watch 7 protect 10 detachment
patrolman: cop 5 guard 9 inspector, policeman
patron: 5 buyer, guest 6 client, fautor 7 sponsor 8 advocate, champion, customer, defender, guardian 9 protector, supporter 10 benefactor
stock exchange: 5 buyer 6 seller, trader
patron saint: *of beggars:* 5 Giles
of children: 8 Nicholas
of cripples: 5 Giles
of England: 6 George
of Ireland: 7 Patrick
of lawyers: 4 Ives, Yves
of musicians: 7 Cecilia
of sailors: 4 Elmo
of Scotland: 6 Andrew
patronage: 5 aegis, favor 6 custom, favour 7 auspice, fomento 8 business 10 assistance 13 encouragement
patronize: 5 deign 10 condescend
patroon: 5 tract 6 patron 9 supporter 10 proprietor
land: 5 manor
patten: 4 base, clog, foot, shoe 5 skate, stand, stilt 6 sandal 7 support 8 overshoe, snowshoe
patter: 4 cant, talk 5 lingo 6 jargon 7 blatter, chatter
pattern: 4 form, norm, plan 5 bysen, draft, epure, guide, ideal, model, plaid 6 checks, design, format, former, sample, stripe 7 example,, project, stencil, templet 8 exemplar, forbysen, paradigm, specimen, template 9 archetype, ensampler, precedent
patulous: 4 open 8 expanded 9 distended, spreading
paucity: 4 lack 6 dearth 7 fewness 8 exiguity, scarcity 13 insufficiency
paughty: 4 pert 5 saucy 7 haughty
Paul: *associate:* 5 Demas, Titus
birthplace: 6 Tarsus
companion: 5 Silas 7 Artemas 8 Barnabas
original name: 4 Saul

place of conversion: 8 Damascus
pauldron: 5 armor 6 splint
paunch: 5 belly, rumen 7 abdomen, stomach 8 potbelly 10 disembowel, eviscerate
pauper: 6 beggar 8 indigent
pause: 4 halt, lull, rest, stop, wait 5 abide, break, cease, delay, demur, dwell, hover, selah, tarry 6 breach, breath, falter, stance 7 caesura, respite 8 breather, caesurae(pl.), hesitate, intermit 9 cessation 10 hesitation 12 intermission, interruption
paut: paw 4 poke 5 stamp 6 finger
pavane: 5 dance
pave: lay 4 path, stud, tile 5 cover, floor 6 causey, cobble, smooth 7 overlay, prepare 10 facilitate, macadamize
pavid: 5 timid 6 afraid 7 fearful
pavilion: 4 flag, tent 5 kiosk 6 canopy, ensign, litter 8 covering 9 gloriette
paving: 4 flag, sett 5 block, brick, dalle, paver, stone 6 cobble, Tarmac 7 asphalt 9 flagstone
pavis: 5 cover 6 shield 7 protect
pavo: 7 peacock 13 constellation
paw: pud, toe 4 foot, gaum, hand, maul, paty 5 patte 6 fumble, handle, pattee 7 crubeen, flipper 8 forefoot
pawky: sly 4 arch, bold 5 canny, saucy 6 crafty, lively, shrewd 7 cunning, forward
pawl: cog, dog 4 bolt, sear, tent, trip 5 catch, click 6 detent, pallet, tongue 7 ratchet
pawn: 4 gage, hock, soak 6 lumber, pledge 7 counter, hostage, peacock 8 chessman, guaranty 11 impignorate
pawnbroker: 6 broker
Pawnee: 6 Indian
rite: 4 hako
pawnie: 7 peacock
pawpaw: 5 papaw 6 papaya 7 immoral, naughty 8 indecent 11 bushwhacker 15 euphemistically
pax: 5 board, peace 6 friend, tablet 10 friendship, osculatory
pay: fee, tip 4 ante, foot, meet, rent, wage 5 repay 6 defray, reward, salary 7 imburse, requite, satisfy, stipend, tribute 9 indemnify, reimburse 10 compensate, recompense, remunerate 11 retribution 12 compensation
attention: 4 heed 6 listen
back: 6 rebate, refund 9 reimburse, retaliate
extra: 5 batta, bonus 8 kickback
for: buy 4 rent 8 purchase
homage: 5 adore, honor
out: 5 spend 6 expend 8 disburse 10 distribute
up: 4 ante 6 settle 9 liquidate
payable: due 5 owing 11 outstanding
paying: 10 profitable
paymaster: 6 bakshi, bukshi, purser 7 bukshee(Ind.) 8 buckshee 9 treasurer
payment: cro, fee, tax 4 bill, dolc, dues, duty, feal, fine, gale, levy, toll 5 gavel, price 6 pledge, rebate, return, reward, tariff 7 alimony, annuity, customs, pension, stipend, trewage, tuition 8 defrayal, requital 9 acquittal, allowance, discharge, honoraria(pl.) 10 honorarium, recompense, remittance 12 compensation, contribution
demand: dun 4 bill
evade: 4 bilk 7 default
failure: 13 nonredemption
immediate: 4 cash 9 alcontado(Sp.)
on delivery: COD
press for: dun
without: 4 free 6 gratis
paynim: 5 pagan 7 heathen, infidel 10 Mohammedan
payoff: fix 5 bribe 6 climax 9 reckoning 10 settlement
payola: 5 bribe
payong: 8 umbrella
paysage: 7 picture 9 landscape
Pb: 4 lead
pea: dal 4 gram, seed 5 arhar, chick, cicer, pease 6 gandul, legume, pigeon 7 carmele, catjang 8 garvanro 12 peavetchling
dove: 7 zenaida
family: 8 fabaceae
finch: 9 chaffinch
flour: 9 Erbswurst
pod: 5 quash
sausage: 9 Erbswurst
seeds: 5 pulse
shaped: 8 pisiform
vine: 8 earthpea
peaberry: 11 coffeeberry
peabird: 6 oriole 7 wryneck
peace: pax(L.), paz(Sp.) 4 calm, ease, liss, rest 5 amity, grith, lisse, quiet 6 repose 7 concord, harmony 8 ataraxia, security, serenity 9 armistice, heartease 10 heartsease 11 tranquility
goddess: 5 Irene
pledge: 11 Frankpledge
symbol: 4 dove, toga 5 olive
peace pipe: 7 calumet
peaceable: 6 gentle 7 pacific, solomon 11 undisturbed
peaceful: 4 calm 5 still 6 irenic, placid 7 halcyon 8 irenical 11 undisturbed
peach: 4 blab 6 accuse, betray, indict, inform 7 impeach, whittle
family: 12 amygdalaceae
grafted on quince: 9 melocoton

kind: **6** Carman, Crosby, Salwey **7** Elberta **8** Crawford, quandang, quandong, quantong **9** freestone, nectarine **10** clingstone
origin: **5** China
stone: **7** putamen
peachwort: **9** persicary
peachy: **4** fine, nice **9** beautiful, excellent
peacock: mao **4** pavo, pawn
fan: **9** flabellum
feather fiber: **4** marl
female: **6** peahen
pert. to: **8** pavonine
tail spot: eye
peacock bittern: sun
peacock blue: **4** paon **7** pigment
peacock butterfly: io **4** kiho
peacock fish: **6** wrasse
peacock flower: **9** poinciana
peacock heron: **7** bittern
peacock ore: **7** bornite **12** chalcopyrite
peafowl: **6** peahen **7** peacock
peag, peage: tax **4** toll **5** beads **6** pedage, wampum
peak: Alp, ben, pic(F.), top, tor **4** acme, apex, cima, cusp, dent, dolt, pico(Sp.) **5** crest, crown, point, slink, sneak, steal **6** shrink, summit **7** epitome, maximum **8** aiguille, headland, pinnacle **9** ascendant, ascendent, simpleton **10** promontory
ice: **5** serac
ornament: epi **6** finial
rocky: alp **4** crag
snow-capped: **7** calotte
peaked: wan **4** pale, thin **5** drawn **6** picked, sickly **9** emaciated
peal: **4** clap, ring, toll **5** chime **6** appeal, shovel **7** resound, summons, thunder **8** carillon
Peale Island: **4** Habe
pean, paean: ode **4** hymn, song
peanut: **4** mani **5** pinda **6** goober, pindal **7** beennut **8** earthnut, earthpea, grassnut, katchung
pear: **4** bosc **5** melon **6** beurre, burrel, warden, winter **7** kieffer, prickly **8** ambrette, Bartlett, bergamot **9** alligator **10** chaumontel
squash: **5** perry **7** chayote
pear-shaped: **8** pyriform
pearl: gem **5** nacre, onion **6** bouton, orient **9** margarite
artificial: **6** olivet
of great luster: **6** orient
seed: **7** aliofar
pearl blush: **7** rosetan
pearl moss: **9** carrageen
Pearl of Antilles: **4** Cuba
pearl opal: **9** cacholong
pearlbird: **6** barbet
pearlweed: **6** sagina **8** sealwort
pearlwort: **6** sagina
pearly: **8** nacreous
peart: **4** pert
peasant: **4** bond, boor, hind, kern(Ir.), kopi, peon, ryot, serf **5** churl, kerne(Ir.), knave, kulak, swain **6** cotman, cottar, cotter, farmer, fellah, rascal, rustic **7** bondman, laborer, paisano(Sp.) **9** chopstick, contadino(It.) **10** countryman
crop sharing: **7** metayer
pease: pea **5** quiet **6** pacify **7** appease **9** reconcile
pease brose: **7** pottage **8** porridge
peaseweep: See **peesweep**
pease crow: **4** tern
peashooter: **6** blower **7** blowgun **11** beanshooter
peat: gor(Ir.), pet **4** fuel, turf **6** lawyer, minion **7** darling **8** favorite **11** combustible
bog: **4** cess, moss
cutter: **5** piner(Sc.)
spade: **5** slane
peatwood: **11** loosestrife
peau d'ange: **6** fabric, finish **9** angelskin
peavey, peavy: **4** hook **5** lever
peba: **9** armadillo
pebble: **5** scree, stone **6** gravel, quartz, sycite **7** chuckie, crystal **10** chuckstone
pebble-shaped: **9** calciform
peccadillo: **5** fault **7** offense **8** mischief
peccant: **6** morbid, sinner **7** corrupt, sinning **9** incorrect, unhealthy
peccary: **6** warree **7** tagassu, tayassu **8** javelina
pech: **4** pant, sigh **6** breath **7** breathe
pecht: **4** pict **5** fairy, gnome, pygmy
peck: dab, dot, nip **4** bill, carp, food, hole, jerk, kiss **5** pitch, prick, throw **6** nibble, stroke **7** chimble, measure
at: nag **4** twit **5** tease **6** attack, harass
four: bu. **6** bushel
pecker: **4** nose **5** eater **6** feeder **7** courage, spirits **10** resolution, woodpecker
pectase: **6** enzyme
peculate: **5** steal **6** misuse **8** embezzle **11** appropriate
peculiar: odd **5** queer **6** unique **7** curious, special, strange, unusual **8** especial, singular **9** eccentric, exclusive **10** particular **11** distinctive **14** characteristic
combining form: **4** idio
peculiarity: **4** kink **5** quirk, trait, twist **6** idiasm **9** attribute **12** idiosyncracy
of expression: **5** idiom **6** idioma, idiome
pecuniary: **9** financial
ped: **6** basket, hamper, panier **7** pannier
pedagogue: **5** tutor **6** pedant **7** dominie, teacher **12** schoolmaster

pedal: 5 lever 7 treadle
coupler: 7 tirasse
piano: 7 celeste
pedant: 4 prig 5 dunce, tutor 6 dorbel, purist, tassel 9 pedagogue 12 bluestocking, schoolmaster
pedantic: 7 bookish 8 teaching 10 didascalic, moralistic
peddle: 4 hawk, sell 5 cadge, trant 6 higgle, meddle, piddle, retail 7 colport
peddler: 5 faker 6 broker, coster, duffer, hawker, seller 7 camelot, chapman 8 huckster, pitchman 12 carpetbagger, costermonger
pedestal: 4 anta, base 6 pillar, podium 7 support 10 foundation
part: die 4 dado 5 socle 6 plinth, quadra
put on: 7 idolize 8 enshrine
pedestrian: ped 4 dull, slow 6 hoofer, walker 7 footman, prosaic 11 commonplace 13 unimaginative
pedicel: ray 4 stem 5 scape, stalk 8 peduncle 9 footstalk
umbel: ray
pedigree: 6 stemma 7 descent, lineage 8 ancestry, stemmata 9 genealogy
pedometer: 8 odograph 12 perambulator
pedum: 5 crook, staff
peduncle: 7 pedicel
peek: 4 peep
peekaboo: 4 game 6 bopeep, peep-bo 7 peepeye
peel: 4 bark, harl, hull, pare, rind, skin 5 flipe, slipe, stake, strip 6 shovel 7 undress 8 palisade, stockade 11 decorticate
peeler: 4 crab 5 bobby, corer 7 hustler 8 pillager 9 policeman
peeling: 4 rind, skin 6 paring
peep: pry, spy 4 peek, peer, pule, skeg 5 cheep, chirp, dekko, glint, snoop, tweet 6 glance, squeak
hawk: 7 kestrel
show: 5 raree
peeper: eye, Tom 4 frog
peepeye: 8 peekaboo
peephole: 4 hole 6 eyelet 7 crevice, eyehole
peeping: 4 nosy 5 nosey 11 inquisitive
peer: pry, vis. 4 duke, earl, fear, fere, gaze, look, lord, mate, peep 5 baron, equal, feere, gloze, match, noble, rival, stare, stime(Sc.), styme(Sc.), thane(Sc.) 6 appear, fellow 7 compeer, comrade, marquis 8 nobleman, superior, viscount 9 associate, companion 12 contemporary
residence: 6 barony
Peer Gynt: *author:* 5 Ibsen
character: 4 King 6 Anitra
composer: 5 Grieg
mother: Ase
peerage: 4 rank 7 dignity
peerdom: 8 equality
peerless: 9 matchless, nonpareil, unrivaled 11 superlative
peesoreh: 7 meminna
peesweep: 5 pewit 7 lapwing 10 greenfinch
peetweet: 9 sandpiper
peeve: irk 6 grudge, nettle 8 irritate 9 annoyance
peevish: 5 cross, techy, testy, wemod 6 crusty, hipped, snarly, sullen, touchy 7 crabbed, frecket, fretful, froward, pettish, spleeny, waspish 8 captious, choleric, crotched, frampoid, petulant, sawshach, snappish 9 fractious, impatient, irascible, irritable, plaintive, splenetic 10 ill-humored 11 caper-noited, contentious, disgruntled
peewee: 4 bird, lark 7 lapwing
peg: fix, hob, nob, nog, pin 4 plug, scob, step 5 cleat, dowel, drink, perch, piton, prong, spill, stake, throw, tooth 6 degree, dowell, marker, reason 7 pretext, support 8 fastener
pega, pagador: 6 remora
pegall: 6 basket
Pegasus: *rider:* 11 Bellerophon
source: 6 Medusa
Peggotty's niece: 5 Emily
Pego: See **Burma**
peho: 8 morepork
peignoir: 4 gown 5 dress 6 kimono 7 wrapper 8 negligee 9 housecoat 12 dressing-gown
peise: 4 blow 5 force, poise 6 impact, weight 7 balance, measure, oppress
pelage: fur 4 hair, pelt
pelagic: 6 marine 7 aquatic, oceanic 9 thalassic
Peleg: *father:* 4 Eber
son: Reu
Peleus: *brother:* 7 Telamon
father: 6 Aeacus
son: 7 Pelides 8 Achilles
wife: 6 Thetis
pelf: rob 4 gain 5 booty, lucre, money, spoil, trash 6 pilfer, refuse, riches, wealth 7 despoil, rubbish
pelham: bit
Pelican State 9 Louisiana
pelike: jar 4 vase 7 amphora 8 amphorae
pell: 4 pelt
pellar: 6 wizard 8 conjurer
pellet: wad 4 ball, pill, shot 5 bolus, stone 6 bullet, pilule 7 granule
pellicle: 4 film, scum, skin 5 crust 7 cuticle
pellock: 8 porpoise
pellucid: 5 clear 6 bright, limpid 7 crystal 11 crystalline, translucent, transparent

pelmet: 7 valance
Peloponnesus: *city:* 6 Sparta
people: 7 Moreote
river god: 7 Alpheus
Pelops: *father:* 8 Tantalus
son: 6 Atreus 8 Thyestes
wife: 10 Hippodamia
pelota: 7 jai-alai
pelt: fur 4 beat, blow, cast, dash, fell, hide, hurl, pell, push, skin 5 fitch, flung, hurry, stone 6 gallop, hasten, pelage, refuse, strike, thrust 7 rawhide, rubbish 8 woolfell
dealer: 7 furrier
peltast: 7 soldier
peltmonger: 7 furrier
peltry: 4 furs 5 pelts
peludo: 9 armadillo
pelvis: *bone:* 4 ilia 5 ilium, pubes 7 ischium
pert. to: 5 iliac
pen: cot, cub, get, mew, pin, sty 4 bolt, cage, coop, fold, jail, yard 5 bught, crawl, hutch, kraal, quill, write 6 bought, corral, cruive, fasten, hurdle, indite, record, stylus, zareba 7 calamus, compose, confine, zareeba 9 enclosure 12 penitentiary
kind: ink 8 fountain 9 ball-point 12 stylographic
point: neb, nib 4 stub
seller: 9 stationer
pen-like: 7 styloid
pen name (see also **nickname, pseudonym**): 6 anonym 9 pseudonym 10 nom de plume
Francois Arouet: 8 Voltaire
Henri Beyle: 8 Stendhal
Charlotte Bronte: 10 Currer Bell
Emily Bronte: 9 Ellis Bell
Samuel Clemens: 9 Mark Twain
Charles Dickens: Boz
Charles Dodgson: 12 Lewis Carroll
Amandine Dupin: 10 George Sand
Mary Ann Evans: 11 George Eliot
Benjamin Franklin: 11 Poor Richard
Charles Lamb: 4 Elia
Alexei Peshkov: 10 Maxim Gorky
Jean Baptiste Poquelin: 7 Moliere
William S. Porter: 6 O. Henry
Jacques Thibault: 13 Anatole France
Louis Viaud: 10 Pierre Loti
pen text: 5 ronde
penal: 8 punitive, punitory
penalize: 4 fine 5 mulct 6 punish
penalty: 4 fine, loss, pain 5 mulct 6 amende, amerce 7 forfeit 8 hardship 10 forfeiture, punishment 12 disadvantage
pay: **aby 4 abye**
penance: 6 sorrow 7 remorse 9 atonement, penitence, suffering 10 contrition, repentance
pencel: 4 flag 6 pennon 8 streamer 9 pennoncel
penchant: 4 bent 5 taste 6 liking 7 leaning 8 fondness 10 attraction 11 inclination
pencil: red, wad 4 blue, lead, wadd 8 charcoal 9 eversharp 10 mechanical
pert. to: 6 desmic
worn-down: 4 stub
pendant, pendent: bob, jag 4 jagg, pend, tail 5 aglet 6 aiglet, tassel 7 pensile, support 8 gamaliel, lavalier 9 lavaliere, pendulous, suspended, undecided
pending: 6 during
pendulous: lop 7 hanging 8 swinging
Penelope: *father:* 7 Icarius
father-in-law 7 Laertes
husband: 7 Ulysses 8 Odysseus
suitor: 7 Agelaus
penetralia: 6 secret 7 privacy
penetrate: 4 bore, dive, gore, stab 5 break, enter, imbue 6 fathom, ficche, pierce 7 discern, pervade 8 permeate 9 insinuate, perforate 10 understand
penetrating: 5 acute, sharp 6 astute, shrewd, shrill, subtle 7 knowing 8 incisive 9 sagacious 10 insightful 11 clairvoyant 14 discriminating
penetration: 6 acumen 13 understanding
penguin: auk 6 Johnny
genus: 9 eudyptula
home: 4 pole 7 rookery 10 penguinery
large: 7 emperor
small: 6 Adelie
peninsula: 4 neck 6 penile 10 chersonese
penitence: rue 6 regret 7 remorse 10 contrition, repentance 11 compunction
season of: 4 Lent
penitent: 4 ruer 5 sorry 6 humble
penitentiary: jug, pen 4 jail, stir 5 tench 6 prison 8 big-house
penman: 6 author, scribe, writer 10 amanuenses, amanuensis 12 calligrapher
penmanship: 4 hand 6 script 7 writing
pennant: 4 fane, flag, whip 5 roger 6 cornet, banner, pennon, pinion 8 streamer 9 banderole
yacht: 6 burgee
pennate: 9 penniform
penniless: 4 poor 5 broke, needy 8 bankrupt 9 insolvent 11 impecunious
pennon: 4 flag, wing 6 banner, pinion 7 feather, pennant
Pennsylvania: *borough:* 5 Avoca, Sayre 9 Homestead
coal-mining town: 6 Jermyn
county: 7 Venango

founder of: 4 Penn
people: 5 Amish
port: 4 Erie
sect: 5 Amish
river: 6 Beaver, Lehigh 9 Allegheny, Conemaugh 10 Schuylkill 11 Monongahela, Susquehanna
town: Ono 4 Erie, York 5 Avoca 6 Easton, Sharon 7 Lebanon, Reading 8 Steelton
penny: 5 brown, pence 6 copper, saltee, stiver
penny-pinching: 6 stingy 7 miserly
penology: 11 criminology
Pensees author: 6 Pascal
pensile: 7 pendent
pension: 7 payment, stipend, subsidy, tribute 8 gratuity 9 allowance 10 exhibition
pensive: 5 sober 6 dreamy, musing 7 wistful 10 meditative, melancholy, reflective, thoughtful 13 contemplative
pent: 5 caged 8 confined, enclosed
pentacle: 4 star
pentastitch: 4 poem 6 stanza 7 strophe
Pentateuch: law 4 tora 5 Bible, torah
first book: 7 Genesis
pentene: 7 amylene
Pentheus: *grandfather:* 6 Cadmus
mother: 5 Agave
penthouse: 4 roof, shed 5 aerie 6 hangar 7 pentice 8 dwelling 9 apartment, treehouse
pentyl: 4 amyl
penurious: 4 mean, poor 6 barren, scanty, stingy 7 miserly, wanting 8 indigent 9 destitute 10 avaricious 12 parsimonious
penury: 7 beggary, poverty 9 privation
peon: 4 hand, pawn, serf 5 slave 6 thrall 7 footman, laborer, peasant, soldier 9 attendant, constable, messenger, policeman
state of: 7 peonage
peony: 4 piny 5 plant 6 flower, mouton
people (see also **person**): kin, men 4 folk, gens, herd, pais(law) 5 demos, gentée(Sp.), laity, stock 6 daoine, gentry 7 tilikum-(Ind.) 8 canaglia(It.), canaille(F.), populate, tillicum(Ind.) 11 inhabitants
aggregation: 5 tribe
ancient: 4 Seba 5 Itali, Medes 6 Greeks, Romans 7 Sabines 8 Grecians 9 Assyrians, Egyptians, Etruscans
ape-shaped skull: 9 proghathi
body: 4 race 6 nation 7 society 8 assembly, populace 9 citizenry, community 10 public Rais
group: mob 4 army, band, team 5 corps, crowd, posse 6 chorus, troupe, throng 7 company, coterie 8 assembly 9 orchestra 11 association
headless: 8 Acephali
mythical: 8 Acephali
pert. to: 6 ethnic 7 demotic
present: 5 class, crowd 10 assemblage, attendance 12 congregation
well-bred: 9 gentility
pep: go; vim 4 dash 5 verve, vigor 6 energy, ginger 7 animate, quicken 9 animation, briskness, encourage, stimulate 10 initiative, invigorate, liveliness
peplos: 5 scarf, shawl
peplum: 5 shawl 8 kerchief 9 overskirt
pepo: 5 gourd, melon 6 squash 7 pumpkin 8 cucumber
pepper ava, hot, red 4 kava, siri 5 betel, green, sirih, sweet 7 paprica, paprika 8 capsicum, kavakava, pimiento
beverage: 4 kava 8 kavakava
grass: 5 cress
package: 6 robbin
shrub: 4 cava, kava
species: 5 betel 7 cayenne
pepper-and-salt: 4 gray 7 mottled
pepper picker: 5 Peter, Piper
pepper plant: ava 5 chile, chili 6 chilli
peppermint camphor: 7 menthol
peppery: hot 5 fiery 7 piquant, pungent 8 choleric, spirited, stinging 9 irritable 10 passionate
Pequod's captain: 4 Ahab
per: by 4 each 7 through
per se: 6 itself 8 directly 11 essentially 13 intrinsically
peract: 7 perform
peradventure: hap 5 doubt, maybe 6 chance, mayhap 7 happily, perhaps 8 possibly 11 uncertainty
perambulate: 4 walk 6 ramble, stroll 8 traverse 9 promenade
perambulator: 5 buggy 12 baby-carriage, pushwainling
perceive: see 4 feel, hear, know, note 5 scent, sense, smell, taste, touch 6 behold, descry, divine, notice 7 discern, observe, realize, sensate 8 comprise, comprize 9 apprehend, recognize 10 articulate, comprehend, understand 11 distinguish 12 discriminate
perceivable: 11 perceptible
perceiving: 5 acute
percentage: 4 agio, part 5 share 6 profit 7 portion, rake-off 9 advantage
perceptible: 7 tactile, visible 8 palpable, sensible, tangible 10 cognizable 11 appreciable, discernible, perceivable 12 intelligible
perception: 6 acumen 9 sensation 13 animadversion, consciousness
capable of: 8 sentient
perceptor: 5 tutor
perch: bar, peg, rod, sit 4 fish, jook, mado, okow, pike, pole, pope 5 barse, light, roost,

ruffe, staff **6** alight, sauger, settle, weapon, zingel **9** trumpeter
perchance: **5** haply, maybe **7** perhaps **8** possibly
Percheron: **5** horse
perchers: **7** rooster **10** Incessores
percolate: **4** ooze, seep, sift, silt **5** exude, leach **6** filter, strain
percolator: **6** biggin
percussion instrument: **4** drum, gong, trap **6** cymbal **7** marimba **8** triangle **9** xylophone **10** tambourine **12** glockenspiel
percylite: **7** boleite
perdition: **4** hell, loss, ruin **9** damnation **11** destruction
perdrigon: **4** plum
perdue, perdu: **6** hidden **9** concealed
perdurable: **7** durable, eternal, lasting **8** enduring **9** permanent **11** everlasting
Pere Goriot author: **6** Balzac
peregrinate: **6** travel, wander **7** journey, sojourn **8** traverse
peregrine: **4** hawk **5** alien **6** exotic, falcon **7** foreign, pilgrim, strange
perempt: **5** quash **6** defeat **7** destroy
peremptory: **5** final, utter **7** express **8** absolute, decisive, dogmatic, positive **9** arbitrary, imperious **10** conclusive, imperative **11** dictatorial **13** authoritative
perennial: rue **4** tree **5** carex, liana, liane, peony, plant, sedum **6** banana **8** enduring, geophyte, toadflax **9** continual, permanent, perpetual, unceasing **12** neverfailing
perfect: all **4** fill, fine, holy, pure **5** exact, ideal, right, ripen, sheer, sound, utter, whole **6** entire, finish **7** concoct, correct, improve, plenary, precise, sinless, spheral **8** absolute, accurate, circular, complete, finished, flawless, thorough **9** blameless, elaborate, exquisite, faultless, righteous **10** accomplish, consummate, immaculate, satisfying
combining form: **5** teleo
perfection: **4** acme, pink **5** ideal **7** fulness, paragon **8** fullness, maturity **10** excellence
realm of: **6** Utopia
perfectly: **5** quite **10** altogether
perfecto: **5** cigar
perfervid: **6** ardent
perficient: **6** actual **10** proficient
perfidious: **5** false, snaky **8** disloyal, spiteful **9** dishonest, faithless, felonious **10** traitorous **11** disaffected, treacherous
perfidy: **7** treason **8** apostasy **9** defection, treachery **10** disloyalty, infidelity **13** faithlessness
perforate: eat **4** dock **5** drill, punch **6** pierce, pounce, riddle **9** penetrate, torebrate **10** foraminate
perforation: **4** bore, hole **6** broach, eyelet, tresis **7** stencil **8** aperture
perform: do; act **4** char, fill, full, play **5** chare, dight, enact, exert **6** effect, fulfil, render **7** achieve, execute, exhibit, exploit, fulfill, furnish, gesture **8** transact **10** accomplish, perpetrate
again: **7** re-enact
inadequately: **6** bungle
while moving about: **11** peripatetic
with ceremony: **9** solemnise, solemnize
performance: act **4** deed, feat, show, test, work **5** stunt **6** acting, action, effect **7** benefit, concert, exploit, matinee **8** feasance, function **9** discharge, execution, rendition **10** completion, fulfilment **11** fulfillment **12** consummation **14** accomplishment
daytime: **7** matinee
first: **8** premiere
individual: **4** soli, solo
standard: **5** bogey
performer: **4** doer, moke **5** actor, shine **6** artist, worker **7** artiste **8** executor, thespian
company: **6** troupe
diligent: **5** plier **6** drudge **7** plugger
low-grade: **9** hamfatter
supplementary: **7** ripieno
top-notch: ace **4** star
perfume: **4** atar, nose, otto **5** aroma, attar, cense, irone, myrrh, ottar, scent, smell **6** chypre, flavor **7** essence, flavour, incense, odorize, sweeten **8** bergamot, fumigate **9** fragrance
base: **4** musk **5** civet **6** neroli **9** ambergris
container: **4** vial **5** phial **6** censer
medicated: **6** pastil **7** pastile **8** pastille
oriental: **5** myrrh
pad: **6** sachet
shrub source: **8** abelmosk
with burning spice: **5** cense
perfumed cherry: **7** mahaleb
perfumer: **6** censer, sachet **8** atomizer, pomander, thurible
perfunctory: **8** careless **10** mechanical **11** indifferent, superficial
pergola: **5** arbor, bower **6** arbour **7** balcony, trellis **9** colonnade
perhaps: **4** haps **5** maybe **6** ablins, belike, happen, mayhap **7** ablings **8** doubtful, possibly, probably **9** perchance
peri: elf **5** fairy, houri **6** sprite
periapt: **5** charm **6** amulet
pericarp: pod **4** boll **5** berry
Pericles: *consort:* **7** Aspasia
ward: **10** Alcibiades

pericranium: 4 head 5 brain
periculum: 4 risk 5 peril 6 danger
peril: 4 risk 6 crises, crisis, danger, hazard, menace 7 apperil, imperil 8 jeopardy 9 adventure 10 insecurity
perilous: 8 doubtful 9 desperate
perimeter: rim 7 outline 8 boundary 9 periphery 13 circumference
period: age, dot, end, eon, era 4 aeon, span, stop, term, time 5 avail, close, cycle, epact, epoch, spell, stage 6 season 8 duration, semester 10 conclusion 11 termination
critical: 6 crises, crisis
festive: 7 holiday 8 vacation
holding: 6 tenure
infinite: 8 eternity
penitential: 4 Lent
playing: 4 half, hand 5 frame, round 6 inning 7 chukkar, chukker, quarter
sleep: 6 godown 11 hibernation
tertiary: 6 eocene 7 neocene
time: day 4 hour, week, year 5 month 6 decade, minute, second 7 century 9 fortnight
periodic: 4 eral 6 annual 7 etesian, regular 8 seasonal 12 intermittent
periodical: 5 daily, paper 6 annual, review, Tatler 7 etesian, journal, tabloid 8 bulletin, magazine 9 ephemeris, newspaper, Spectator
peripatetic: 8 rambling 9 itinerant, wandering
peripheral: 5 outer 6 distal 7 distant 8 confined, external
periphery: lip, rim 4 brim, edge 5 ambit, limit 6 areola, areole, border 7 areolae, outside 8 environs 9 perimeter 13 circumference
periphrastic: 14 circumlocutory
perique: 7 tobacco
perish: die 4 fade, fall, ruin 6 depart, expire 7 consume, crumble, forfare, succumb
perishable: 6 caduke 7 brittle
peristyle: 9 colonnade 10 peripteral
perite: 7 skilled
peritomy: 12 circumcision
peritoneum: 8 covering, membrane
fold of: 7 omentum
peritroch: 5 larva 6 embryo
periwig: wig 6 peruke, toupee 10 periwinkle
periwinkle: 5 color, snail 6 mussel, myrtle
perjink: 4 neat, nice 7 precise
perjure: 8 forswear 9 aperjurer
perk: 5 preen, prink 7 smarten 8 animated 9 percolate 10 perquisite
perkin: 5 cider
permanent: 5 fixed 6 stable 7 abiding, durable, lasting 8 constant, enduring 9 continual, headdress, perennial 10 continuing
permeable: 6 porous
permeate: 4 fill 5 bathe, imbue 6 drench 7 pervade 8 saturate 9 penetrate
permirific: 8 wondrous
permission: 5 leave 7 consent, license
to use: 4 loan
permit: let 4 leve, pass 5 admit, allow, conge, favor, grace, grant, leave 6 accord, beteem, dustuk, entree, favour, suffer 7 consent, dustuck, license, pompano, warrant 8 furlough, tolerate 9 authorize 10 permission
travel: 8 passport
permutation: 6 change 10 alteration 11 interchange 13 rearrangement
pern: 7 buzzard
pernicious: bad 4 evil 5 fatal 6 deadly, malign, wicked 7 baleful, baneful, harmful, hurtful, noisome, noxious, ruinous 10 villainous 11 deleterious, destructive, detrimental
pernio: 9 chilblain
peronate: 5 mealy, wooly
perorate: 7 address, declaim 8 harangue
perpendicular: 4 sine 5 erect, plumb, sheer 6 abrupt 7 apothem, upright 8 binormal, vertical 9 downright
perpetrate: do 6 commit, effect 7 perform
perpetual: 5 etern 7 endless, eternal 8 constant, unending 9 continual, incessant, perennial, permanent, unceasing 10 continuous 11 everlasting 14 unintermittent
perpetually: 4 ever 6 always 7 forever
perpetuate: 8 continue, eternize, maintain, preserve
perplex: cap 4 clog, doze 5 amaze, beset 6 baffle, boggle, bother, cumber, darken, gravel, hamper, harass, hobble, muddle, pother, puzzle, twitch 7 bedevil, confuse, diffuse, embroil, mystify, nonplus 8 babulyie, bewilder, confound, distract, distress, entangle 9 bamboozle, obfuscate 10 complicate
perplexed: 4 asea 5 upset 7 anxious 8 troubled 10 distraught
perplexing: 4 hard 6 crabby 7 carking, complex, crabbed 9 equivocal 11 complicated
perplexity: fog 4 knot 6 tangle 7 anxiety, trouble 9 intricacy 11 encumbrance 13 embarrassment
perquisite: fee, tip 6 income 7 adjunct, apanage 8 appanage, appenage, gratuity 9 accessory 11 appointment, prerogative 12 appurtenance 13 accompaniment
presidential: 4 veto
perquod: 7 whereby
Perry Mason creator: 7 Gardner
perse: 4 blue
Perse: *daughter:* 5 Circe 8 Pasiphae

father: **7** Oceanus
husband: **6** Helios
son: **6** Aeetes, Perses
persecute: 4 bait **5** annoy, harry, hound, wrack, wrong **6** harass **7** afflict, oppress, torment, torture
persecuted: 7 refugee
Persephone: 4 Kore **8** Despoina
daughter: **4** Cora, Kore
father: **4** Zeus
husband: **5** Hades, Pluto
mother: **7** Demeter
Perseus: *father:* **4** Zeus
grandfather: **8** Acrisius
mother: **5** Danae
star of: **4** Atik **5** Algol
victim: **8** Acrisius
wife: **9** Andromeda
perseverance: 4 grit **8** patience, tenacity **9** assiduity, constancy, diligence, endurance **10** insistence, steadiness **11** continuance, persistence, pertinacity **12** continuation **13** indefatigable, steadfastness
persevere: 4 tore
persevering: 4 busy **11** unremitting
Persia (see also **Iran**): *ancient inhabitant:* **4** Mede
apple: **6** citron
assembly: **6** majlis, meklis
bug: **5** miana
carpet: see *rug* below
cat: **6** Angora
chief officer: **5** dewan, diwan
deer: **5** maral **6** fallow
elf or fairy: **4** peri
gate: bab
gazelle: **4** cora
goddess: **7** Anahita
measure: gaz, guz, zer
lynx: **7** caracal
mightingale: bulbul
old coin: **5** daric
poet: **4** Omar, Sadi **5** Hafiz
rug: **4** Kali **5** Saruk, Senna **6** Sarouk **7** Isfahan, Ispahan, Teheran **8** Serabend
ruler: **4** shah
scriptures: **5** Koran
tick: **8** miana bug
wheel: **5** noria **7** tympana **8** tympanum
Persian Gulf: *kingdom:* **7** Chaldea
port: **7** Bushire
province: **4** Fars
wind: **6** shamal, sharki **7** shurgee
persiennes: 6 blinds
persiflage: 6 banter **8** raillery
persimmon: 7 chapote
family: **5** ebony **9** ebenaceae
persist: 4 last **6** endure, insist, remain **8** continue **9** persevere
persistent: 4 dree, hard **6** gritty **7** durable **8** constant, enduring, frequent, holdfast, obdurate, resolute, stubborn **9** assiduous, continued, tenacious **10** consistent, continuing, determined, relentless **11** persevering **13** indefatigable
person (see also **people**): guy, man, one, urf **4** body, chap, self, soul **5** being, child, human, wight, woman **6** entity, fellow **10** individual
amusing: **8** comedian, comedien **10** comedienne
bad-luck carrier: **4** jinx **5** jonah
baptized: **10** illuminato **11** illuminatus
base: **7** caitiff, hangdog
bearing the blame: **4** goat
beatified: **6** beatus
betrothed: **6** fiance **7** fiancee
blamed for others: **4** butt, goat **9** scapegoat
brilliant: **6** genius **10** mastermind
callow: **6** gorlin, smarty **7** gosling
canonized: **5** saint
careless: **6** tassel **11** pococurante
charitable: **9** samaritan
cheery: **8** optimist
contemptible: cad, yap **4** heel, toad **7** bauchle
cunning: **8** slyboots
deranged: nut **7** lunatic **10** monomaniac, psychopath
despicable: **5** hound **6** rotter **10** blackguard
detested: **8** anathema
disgruntled: **8** sorehead
dull: **5** dunce, moron **8** imbecile **9** blockhead, defective
eighty-year old: **12** octogenarian
enterprising: **8** go-getter
fearless: **10** fearnaught, fearnought **11** dreadnaught, dreadnought
fifty-year old: **15** quinquagenarian
foolish: sop **4** zany **5** clown **6** dotard **7** halfwit **9** simpleton
forty-year-old: **14** quadragenarian
good-luck carrier: **6** mascot
gray-headed: **7** grisard
guilty: **7** culprit
half-grown: **6** haflin **8** halfling **9** stripling
held as pledge: **7** hostage
holy: ste.(F.) **5** saint
horned: **7** cornute
ill: **7** invalid, patient
indefinite: one **6** anyone **7** anybody, so and so, someone **8** somebody
indifferent to pleasure or pain: **5** stoic
injured: **6** victim **8** casualty
learned: **6** pundit, savant **7** scholar **9** professor **12** intellectual
left-handed: **9** portsider
loud-voiced: **7** stentor

married: 4 wife 6 spouse 7 husband
middle-class: 9 bourgeois 11 bourgeoisie
mischievous: imp 4 pest
named after another: 8 namesake
ninety-year-old: 12 nonagenarian
non-Jewish: 7 gentile
of distinction: VIP 4 star 7 notable
of mixed blood: 7 mestizo, mulatto 8 octoroon 9 half-breed
one-hundred-year-old: 11 centenarian
overnice: 4 prig
perfidious: 5 snake 7 serpent, traitor
proposed for office: 7 nominee
rapacious: 4 wolf 5 harpy, shark
representing another: 5 mimic, proxy 9 alternate
rude: 4 boor 7 caveman
scolding: 9 catamaran
second: you 4 thou
seventy-year-old: 14 septuagenarian
shiftless: bum 7 drifter
sick: 5 ailer 7 invalid, patient 9 aegrotant
sixty-year-old: 12 sexagenarian
skilled: 5 adept 6 artist, master, talent 7 artisan 8 mechanic
small: 5 dwarf 6 midget, poppet
sponsored by another: 7 protege
studious: 5 grind, porer
stupid: ass 4 boob, clod, coot, dolt, fool, gump, moke 5 bucca, clout, moron, stirk, stock, stupe, sumph 6 boodle, duffer, gander 7 dullard 8 bonehead, dumbbell, gamphrel 9 boeoetian, simpleton
timid: 11 milquetoast
trustworthy: 7 standby
unmarried: 6 maiden 8 bachelor, celibate, spinster
unusual: 4 oner
wealthy: 5 nabob 9 plutocrat 10 capitalist 11 millionaire 12 millionnaire
white: fay 4 ofay 5 haole 6 albino 7 abiculi, redneck
young: 8 chipling 9 stripling 14 whippersnapper

personable: 6 comely 7 shapely 8 handsome 10 attractive 11 good-looking, well-favored
personage: 6 shogun, tycoon 7 magnate
personal: own 7 private 8 intimate
comb. form: 4 idio
personality: ego 4 self 8 selfhood 11 disposition 13 individuality
split: 13 schizophrenia
personate: See **impersonate**
personification: 10 embodiment 11 incarnation 14 representation
of rumor: 4 Fama
of truth: Una
personified: 9 incarnate
personify: 6 embody 9 represent 11 impersonate
personnel: 5 staff 9 employees
perspicacious: 4 keen 5 acute 6 shrewd 10 discerning, perceptive 11 penetrating
perspicacity: 6 acumen
perspicuous: 5 clear, lucid, plain 8 manifest 11 conspicuous, translucent, transparent 12 intelligible
perspiration: 5 sudor, sweat 8 hidrosis, sweating 9 exudation 10 ephidrosis
pert. to: 7 sudoric
sheep: 5 suint
persuade: get, win 4 coax, gain, sway, urge 5 argue, suade 6 allure, assure, engage, entice, induce 7 entreat 8 convince, inveigle 9 influence
persuaded: 7 pliable 8 gullible 9 credulous
persuasion: 6 belief
persuasive: 6 cogent 8 eloquent 9 impelling
pert: 4 bold 5 alert, alive, bardy, brisk, cocky, quick, sassy, saucy, smart 6 active, clever, cocket, comely, dapper, frisky, lively 7 forward, paughty 8 handsome, impudent, insolent, petulant 9 exquisite, officious, sprightly 11 flourishing
pert girl: 4 minx
pertain: 5 belie 6 befall, belong, relate 7 concern 9 accessory, appertain
pertaining to: For all definitions beginning with this phrase, see under following main word or phrase, EXAMPLES: "pertaining to gold": see **gold** *pert. to; "pertaining to the sun": see* **sun** *pert. to.*
suffix: ac, ar, ic; ese, ile
pertinacious: 4 firm 6 dogged 8 adhering, stubborn 9 obstinate, tenacious 10 determined, inflexible, persistent, unyielding
pertinent: apt, fit, pat 6 proper, timely 7 adapted, apropos, germane, telling 8 apposite, relative, relevant 10 applicable, felicitous 11 appropriate 12 appurtenance
pertinentia: 6 things 8 fixtures
perturb: 5 upset, worry 7 agitate, confuse, derange, disturb, trouble 8 disorder 10 discompose, disconcert
perturbation: 6 flight, pother 7 turmoil 9 commotion 10 uneasiness 12 irregularity
pertuse: 7 pierced, punched 10 perforated
pertussis: 5 cough 13 whooping cough
Peru: *animal:* 5 llama 6 alpaca
bark: 8 cinchona
city: Ica 4 Lima(c.) 5 Cuzco, Paita 6 Callao 7 Iquitos 8 Arequipa
coin: sol 5 libra 6 dinero 7 centavo
cormorant: 6 Guanay
dance: 5 cueca
department: Ica, Yca 4 Lima 5 Cusco, Cuzco, Piura, Tacna, Tagna

emblem of nobility: 6 llautu
empire: 4 Inca, Ynca
fog: 5 garua
goddess: 4 Mama
hillock: 4 loma
inn: 5 tambo
king: 7 cacique
lake: 8 Titicaca
liquor: 5 pisco
llama: 4 paco 6 alpaca
mark of nobility: 6 llautu
measure: 4 topo, vara 5 galon 7 celemin 8 fanegada
partridge: 4 yutu
people: 4 Ande, Cana, Inca, Inka, Peba, Yutu 5 Boros, Campa, Carib, Panos 6 Aymara, Jibaro, Jiyaro, Kechua, Lamano 7 Quechau
plant: oca 6 ulluco 7 rhatany
relic: 5 huaco
river: Ica 5 Rimac, Santa 7 Maranon, Ucayale 8 Apurimac, Huallaga, Urubamba 11 Paucartambo
rodent: 10 chinchilla
ruler: 4 Inca, Inka
shrub: 6 shansa
skin disease: uta
tableland: 4 puna
tavern: 5 tambo
tinamou: 4 yutu
tree: 6 bucare 8 cinchona
tuber: oca
volcano: 5 Misti
weight: 5 libra 7 quintal
wind: 4 puna 5 sures

peruke: wig 6 toupee 7 periwig
perukier: 8 wigmaker
perula: 6 mentum
peruse: con 4 read, scan 5 study 6 handle, survey 7 examine, inspect 9 supervise
pervade: 4 fill 5 bathe, imbue 6 occupy 8 permeate, traverse 9 penetrate
pervading: 9 prevalant, universal 10 widespread
perverse: awk 4 awry, wogh, wraw 6 divers, wicked, wilful 7 awkward, distort, diverse, forward, froward, wayward 8 backward, camshach, contrary, crotched, petulant 9 camsteary, camsteery, difficult, fractious 10 determined 11 contentious, contrarious, disobedient, intractable 12 cantankerous, contumacious
perversely: 7 athwart
pervert: 4 ruin, skew 5 abuse, twist, upset 6 debase, divert, garble, invert, misuse, poison 7 contort, corrupt, deprave, distort, vitiate 8 apostate, misapply, overturn, renegade 9 misdirect 10 demoralize 12 misinterpret
perverted: bad 6 wicked 7 vicious
pervious: 9 permeable 10 accessible
pervulgate: 7 publish
Pescadores: *island:* 4 Hoko
town: 4 Mako
peshkar: 5 agent 7 steward 8 minister 10 accountant
peshkash: tax 7 present, tribute 8 offering
pesky: 6 plaguy 8 annoying 9 pestering, vexatious 11 troublesome 12 disagreeable
peso: 4 coin
silver: 4 duro
pess: 7 hassock
pessimism: 5 gloom 7 despair 8 cynicism
pessimistic: 6 gloomy 7 alarmed, cynical
pessoner: 4 boat, ship 10 fishmonger
pest: 4 bane, weed 5 mouse 6 insect, plague, vermin 8 epidemic, nuisance 10 pestilence
pester: dun, nag, rib 5 annoy, devil, tease, worry 6 badger, bother, harass, molest 7 torment, trouble 9 aggravate
pestiferous: 4 evil 11 mischievous
pestilence: 4 pest 5 death 6 plague 7 disease 8 epidemic
pestilent: 6 deadly 7 noxious 9 poisonous 10 contagious, infectious
pestle: 4 bray 5 grind 6 beetle, bettle, muller
vessel: 6 mortar
pet: cat, dog 4 coax, daut(Sc.), dawt(Sc.), dear, duck, huff, neck, sulk, tiff 5 drunt, humor, quiet, spoil 6 caress, coddle, cosher, cuddle, dautie(Sc.), dawtie(Sc.), faddle, fantad, fantod, fondle, pamper, stroke 7 cherish, darling, indulge, tantrum 8 favorite, fondling 9 cherished, favourite
petal: ala 4 alae
petal-bearing: 8 petalous
petals: 7 corolla
without: 9 apetalous
petard: 11 firecracker
petasus, petasos: cap, hat
peteman: 9 cracksman 10 safeblower
peter: 4 fade, fail, wane 5 cease 7 dwindle, exhaust 8 diminish
Peter: 4 czar, rock 5 saint, Simon
father: 5 Jonas
Peter Pan: *author:* 6 Barrie
dog: 4 Nana
pirate: 4 Smee
peterman: 5 thief 7 burglar 9 fisherman
petiole: 4 stem 5 stalk 8 peduncle 9 leafstalk 10 mesopodium
petit: 4 mean 5 minor, small 6 little 13 insignificant
petite: 4 trim 6 demure 10 diminutive
petition: ask, beg, sue 4 bill, boon, plea, pray, suit, wish 5 apply, orate, plead 6 appeal, prayer, steven 7 address, entreat, implore, oration, request, solicit 8 entreaty

10 supplicate 11 application, deprecation 12 supplication 13 contemplation
petitioner: 5 asker 6 beggar, seeker 8 appealer, beadsman, bedesman 9 applicant
chancery: 7 relator
petitor: 10 petitioner
peto: 5 wahoo
Petrarch's love: 5 Laura
petrean: 5 rocky
petrel: 4 titi 5 mitty 7 assilag 8 allamoth 9 allamonti, allamotti, mallemuck
petrifying: 7 numbing 9 deadening, hardening 10 petrescent, terrifying 11 fossilizing
Petrograd: 9 Leningrad
petrol: gas 8 gasoline
petroleum: oil 10 illuminant
by-product: 6 butane, deisel 7 propane 9 propylene
product: wax 4 coke 5 ethyl 6 petrol 7 alcohol, asphalt, canadol, naphtha 8 gasoline, kerosene, paraffin 9 righolene
petrosal: 4 hard 5 stony 7 petrous
petticoat: 4 kilt, slip 5 jupon, pagne 6 kirtle 7 whittle 8 basquine, halfslip, vasquine 9 undercoat, waistcoat 10 fustanella, underskirt 11 farthingale
tails: 7 teacake 9 shortcake
pettifogger: 6 lawyer 7 shyster 8 attorney
pettish: 8 petulant
pettle: 6 cuddle, nestle, potter 7 cherish, indulge
petty: 4 base, mean, orra, puny 5 minor, small 6 paltry, puisne 7 trivial 8 childish, inferior, nugatory, trifling 9 frivolous, minuscule 10 diminutive 11 subordinate, unimportant 12 contemptible 13 insignificant 14 inconsiderable
fault: 10 peccadillo
matter: 6 fidfad
morel: 9 spikenard 10 nightshade
whin: restharrow
petulant: 4 pert 5 cross, huffy, saucy, short, testy 6 petted, sullen, wanton, wilful 7 forward, fretful, peevish, wayward 8 contrary, immodest, insolent, perverse 9 impatient, irascible, irritable, plaintive, querulous 10 ill-humored
pew: 4 desk, seat, slip 5 bench, bught, stall 6 bought
pewee: 10 flycatcher
pewter: tra 5 bidri, bidry 6 bidery, bidree 7 biddery
peyote: 5 plant 6 cactus, mescal, peyotl
Phaedo's school: 5 Elian
Phaedra: *father:* 5 Minos
husband: 7 Theseus
stepson: 10 Hippolytus
phaeton: 8 carriage
phalacrocorax: 4 coot 9 cormorant
phalacrosis: 8 alopecia, baldness
phalanger: 5 tapoa
phalera: 4 boss, disk 5 cameo
phantasm: 5 dream, fancy, vapor 7 phantom 8 delusion
phantasmal: 6 unreal 10 transitory
phantasy: 5 fancy
phantom: 4 idol 5 bogle, ghost, idola, image, shade, umbra 6 eidola(pl.), idolon, idolum, spirit 7 eidolon, fantasy, specter, spectre 8 illusion, phantasm 10 apparition
Phaon's consort: 6 Sappho
Pharaoh: 7 Rameses
ancestor: Ra
Pharaoh's chicken: 7 vulture
Pharaoh's fig: 8 sycamore
Pharaoh's mouse: 9 ichneumon
phare: 6 pharos
pharisaical: 12 hypocritical
pharmaceutical: dia 7 mellite
pharmacist: 8 druggist 9 dispenser 13 pharmaceutist
pharmacy weight: 5 obole 6 obolus
pharos: 5 cloak 6 beacon 7 lantern 10 chandelier, lighthouse
phase: 4 side 5 angle, facet, stage 6 aspect 8 passover 13 manifestation
phasm: 6 meteor 7 phantom 10 appearance
pheasant: 5 cheer, monal 6 monaul, moonal, pukras 7 kallege 8 fireback, tragopan
breeding-place: 4 stew
brood: nid, nye 4 nide
nest: 4 nide
pheasant cuckoo: 6 coucal
pheasant duck: 7 pintail 9 merganser
pheasant finch: 7 waxbill
phenate: 9 phenolate
Phenicia: See **Phoenicia**
phenol: 6 orcine, thymol 9 germicide
derivative: 4 anol
phenolate: 7 phenate
phenomenal: 7 unusual 13 extraordinary
phenyl salicylate: 5 salol
pheon: 7 bearing
phial: cup 4 bowl, vial 6 bottle, vessel
Phidias' statue: 6 Athena
philabeg: 4 kilt
philander: 5 flirt 10 flirtation
philanthropic: 6 humane 10 altruistic, benevolent, charitable 12 humanitarian
philanthropist: 5 donor 10 benefactor
philanthropy: 4 alms 10 almsgiving
universal: 15 omnibenevolence
philippic: 6 screed, tirade 8 diatribe
Philippines: *animal:* 5 civet, lemur
ant: 4 anai, anay
archipelago: 4 Sulu
attendant: 5 alila

banana: 7 saguing
barracks: 7 cuartel
beer: 7 pangasi
bird: 6 abacay
boat: 5 balsa, banca 8 balangay, barangay
breadfruit: 4 rima 8 casmansi
brigand: 7 ladrone
buffalo: 7 carabao, timarau, timerau
canoe: 5 banca, vinta 6 baroto
capital: 8 cabecera
carriage: 9 carretela, carromata
chief: 4 dato 5 datto, Iloco 7 Ilocano, Ilokano
Christianized tribe: 5 Bicol, Bikol, Tagal, Vicol 7 Bisayan, Tagalog, Visayan
city: Iba 4 Agoa, Cebu, Naga 5 Albay, Davao 6 Aparri, Baguio, Cavite, Ilagan, Manila(c.) 7 Dagupan
coconut meat: 5 copra
coin: 4 peso 7 centavo
cyclone: 6 baguio
dagger: 4 itac 7 balarao
deity: 5 Dagon
discoverer: 8 Magellan
drink: 4 beno, vino 5 bubud 7 pangasi
farmer: lao, tao
fern: 4 nito
fetish: 5 anito
fiber: 4 eruc 6 buntal 9 pineapple
fish: 8 langaray
food: 4 baha, taro
forest: 5 gubat
fort: 4 Gota 10 Corregidor
garment: 4 saya
grass: 5 cogon
guerrilla: Huk
gulf: 5 Davao, Ragay
hardwood: 4 ipil 5 narra
hat: 7 salacot
hemp: 5 abaca 6 manila
house: 5 bahay
idol: 5 anito
island: 4 Cebu 5 Batan, Bohol, Leyte, Luzon, Panay, Samal, Samar 6 Negros 7 Masbate, Mindora, Palawan, Paragua 8 Mindanao
kitchen: 5 calan
knife: 4 bolo, itac 7 balarao, machete
lake: 4 Taal 5 Lanao
language: 4 Moro 5 Bicol, Tagal 6 Ibanag 7 Ilocano, Tagalog, Visayan
lighthouse: 4 faro
liquor: 4 beno 7 pangasi
litter: 7 talabon
lizard: 4 ibid
mammal: 7 tarsier
mango: 5 bauno 7 pahutan
market-day: 7 tiangue
measure: 4 loan 5 braza, caban, cavan, chupa, ganta 6 apatan, balita, quinon
measure of weight: 5 catty, fardo, picul, punto 6 lachsa 7 quilate 8 chinanta
mother: ina
mountain: Apo, Iba 5 Mayon
mountaineer: 8 mentesco
mudfish: 5 dalag
muskmelon: 6 atimon
Muslim: 4 Moro
native: see *people* below
nut: 4 pili
oil: 5 cebur
pagan: 6 Italon
palm: 4 nipa 6 anahao, anahau
parrot: 5 cagit
peasant: tao
people: Ata, Ati, Ita, Tao 4 Aeta, Atta, Etas, Moro, Sulu 5 Bicol, Bikol, Tagal, Vicol 6 Igorot, Timaua, Timawa 7 Bisayan, Tagalog, Visayan 8 Filipino, Igorrote 10 Philippino
plant: aga 4 alem 5 abaca, baroi, batad 6 agamid
plum: 6 sapote
port: 4 Cebu 6 Cavite, Iloilo
priest: 7 pandita
province: 4 Abra 5 Albay 6 Iloilo
raft: 5 balsa
reptile: 6 python
rice: 4 paga 5 barit, bigas, macan
river: 4 Abra, Agno 5 Pasig 7 Cagayan 8 Mindanao, Pampanga
road: 4 daan
rope tree: 4 nabo 5 anabo
sapodilla: 5 chico
sarong: 8 padadion
sea: 4 Sulu
sentinel: 6 bantay
servant: 4 bata 5 alila
shirt: 4 baro
shrub: 4 alem, nabo 6 anilao
silk: 10 alcaiceria
skirt: 4 saya
slave: 6 alipin
slipper: 7 chinela
soap vine: 4 gogo
spirit: 5 anito
stream: 4 ilog
sword: 6 barong 8 campilan
termite: 4 anai, anay
textile: 4 pina, saba 7 sina-may
thatch: 4 nipa
timber: 5 cahuy
tree: dao, iba, tua, tui 4 acle, anam, ates bogo, dita ifil, ipil, supa 5 almon, amaga anabo, balao, balau, bayok, betis, bulak guijo, ligas, tabog, yacal 6 alagao, alagau alupag, amuyon, anagap, aranga, bancal banuyo, bataan, batino, botong, dungon lanete, marang, molave 7 amuguis amuyong, anabong, apitong, banilad

binukau, hapiton, mambong, tindalo **8** almaciga, bitanhol, macaasim, malapaho, tanguile **9** alintatad, batikulin, batitinan **10** batikuling **11** alibangbang, balinghasay
tree bark: aga **6** agamid
vine: iyo
volcano: Apo **4** Mayo
watchtower: **7** atalaya **8** bantayan
water buffalo: **7** carabao
water-jar: **5** bango
weapon: **4** bolo
white man: **7** cachila
wine: **4** beno
wood: **4** teak **5** ebony, narra **6** sandal
yam: ubi, uve
Philistine: **9** barbarian, hypocrite
city: **4** Gath
giant: **7** Goliath
god: **4** Baal **5** Dagan, Dagon
foe: **6** Samson
philomel: **11** nightingale
Philomela: **11** nightingale
father: **7** Pandion
sister: **6** Procne
philosopher: **4** Kant, sage **5** Plato, Renan, Solon **6** Nestor, Seneca **7** Emerson **8** Socrates, Voltaire **9** Epictetus
disciples: **4** sect **6** school
of Syracuse: **4** Dion
philosophical: **4** wise **8** rational **9** temperate, unruffled
philosophy: **4** yoga **7** dualism **8** stoicism **9** esoterics **10** empiricism, esthetics, pragmatism **17** transcendentalism
philter, philtre: **5** charm **6** potion **7** amatory **9** fascinate
phlebotomize: **5** bleed **8** venesect
phlegm: **5** gleet **10** equanimity
phlegmasia: **12** inflammation
phlegmatic: **4** calm, cool, dull, slow **5** inert **6** watery **7** viscous **8** composed, sluggish **9** apathetic, impassive **13** imperturbable
phloem: **4** bast
phlogistic: **5** fiery **6** heated **7** burning, flaming **11** impassioned **12** inflammatory
phoca: **4** seal
Phoebad: **7** seeress **9** priestess **10** prophetess
phoebe: **4** bird **5** pewee, pewit **6** peewee **10** flycatcher
Phoebe: **5** Diane **6** Selene **7** Artemis
Phoebus: Sol, sun **6** Apollo
Phoenicia: *city:* **4** Tyre **5** Sidon
colony: **8** Carthage
dialect: **5** Punic
god: **4** Baal
goddess: **5** Tanit **6** Baltis, Tanith **7** Astarte
***goddess of love:* 7 Astarte**
king: **6** Agenor
seaport: **5** Sidon
phonetic: **4** oral **5** vocal
notation system: **5** romic
sound: **7** palatal
phonograph record: **4** disk **7** platter
phony: **4** fake, sham **5** bogus, false **8** impostor, spurious **9** charlatan **10** fictitious **11** counterfeit
Phorcys: *child:* **5** Ladon **6** Gorgon, Graeae(pl.)
father: **6** Pontus
mother: **4** Gaea
phosphate: **6** ehlite **7** apatite **9** wavellite
photocopy: **4** stat **5** print
photoengraving: **15** heliotypography
photograph: mug **4** film, snap, X-ray **7** picture, tintype **8** likeness, portrait, snapshot **9** ferrotype, pictorial **10** cheesecake, heliograph **13** daguerreotype
bath: **5** fixer, toner **7** reducer **9** developer
chemical: **5** metal, toner
color tool: **5** blimp
developer: **5** ortol **6** amidol **9** revelator
fixing agent: **4** hypo
instrument: **8** enlarger
inventor: **6** Niepce, Talbot **8** Daguerre
kind: **5** panel, still **6** motion **7** boudoir, cabinet, diamond **8** imperial, passport, portrait **9** pictorial **10** commercial, scientific **12** composograph **13** carte de visite
negative: **4** film
printing: **7** ozotype
photographer: **9** cameraman
photology: **6** optics **7** photics
photometric unit: pyr, rad
phrase: mot **4** term, word **5** idiom, state **6** clause, cliche, saying, slogan **7** adjunct, diction, epigram, epithet, thought **8** acrostic **9** catchword, leitmotif **10** expression
phraseology: **7** dialect, diction, wording **8** parlance
phratry: **4** clan
phrenetic: **8** frenetic
phrenic: **6** mental
Phrixos: *father:* **7** Athamus
mother: **7** Nephele
sister: **5** Helle
Phrygia: *enthusiast:* **9** Montanist
god: **4** Atys **5** Attis **8** Sabazios
king: **5** Midas
river: **7** Meander
town: **5** Ipsus
phylactery: **5** charm **6** amulet **8** talisman
phyletic: **6** racial **12** phylogenetic
phyma: **5** tumor **6** nodule
physic: **5** purge **9** cathartic
physical: **6** bodily **7** natural, somatic **8** material **9** corporeal, somatical

physician: asa, doc 5 curer, medic, quack 6 doctor, intern, healer, medico 7 interne 8 restorer 10 consultant, medicaster 11 aesculapian, philosopher 12 practitioner

association: AMA

combining form: 5 iatro

group: AMA 5 panel, staff

symbol: 8 caduceus

physicist: 10 naturalist

physiognomy: mug 4 face 8 portrait 11 countenance

physique: 4 body 6 figure 8 strength 10 appearance 12 constitution

physostigmine: 5 esere 6 eserin 7 eserine

piacle: sin 5 crime, guilt 7 offense 8 piaculum

pian: 4 yaws 9 frambesia 10 framboesia

piano: 5 grand 6 softly, spinet 7 clavial, quietly, upright 8 pianette 10 anemochord, pianoforte

dumb keyboard: 9 digitoria 10 digitorium 11 finger board

early: 6 spinet

key: 7 digital

keyboard: 7 clavier

notes: 6 octave

pedal: 7 celeste

pedal keyboard: 8 pedalier

piatti: 7 cymbals

piazza: 5 porch 7 gallery, portico, veranda

pic: 4 peak 8 picayune

picacho: 4 hill 5 butte

picador: wit 6 jester 7 debater 11 bullfighter

picadura: 7 tobacco

picaro: 5 knave, rogue, tramp 7 sharper 8 vagabond

picaroon: 5 rogue, thief 6 bandit, pirate, rascal 7 brigand, corsair 9 hooka-roon 10 adventurer

Picasso painting: 8 Guernica

picayune: 4 mean 5 small 6 little

pichiciago: 9 armadillo

pick: 4 gaff, pike, wale 5 adorn, beele, cavil, elect, elite, pluck 6 choice, gather, pickax, twitch 7 bargain, diamond 8 plectrum

on: 5 abuse, annoy, tease 9 criticize

out: 4 cull, sort 5 glean 6 assort, choose, select

pickax: 4 bill, pick 6 tubber, twibil 7 mattock, twibill

picked: 4 trim 5 spiny 6 dainty, peaked, spruce 7 pointed 8 stripped 10 fastidious

picket: peg 4 pale, post 5 fence, stake 6 fasten, paling, tether 7 enclose, fortify

pickle: 4 alec, dill, mess, peck 5 achar, brine 6 capers, dawdle(Sc.), muddle, nibble, piddle, pilfer(Sc.), trifle(Sc.) 7 chutney, condite, confect, gherkin, vitriol 8 marinate 11 predicament

mixed: 6 higdon

pickled: 5 drunk, soust 6 soused 11 intoxicated

pickling herb: 4 dill

pickpocket: dip 4 bung, hook, wire 5 diver, filer, thief 6 buzzer, cannon, dipper, figboy, hooker, ratero(Sp.), robber 7 foister, mobsman, stealer 8 clyfaker 11 fingersmith

helper: 4 duke 5 shill, stall 6 bulker

pickup: 5 truck 6 bracer, chippy 8 recovery 9 stimulant 10 hitchhiker 11 improvement, stimulation 12 acquaintance

again: 6 resume

Pickwick Papers author: 7 Dickens

picnic: 5 gipsy, gypsy 6 junket, outing

picot: 4 loop

picotee: 9 carnation

pictograph: 5 glyph

picture (see also **motion picture**): oil 4 copy, icon, idea, ikon 5 ikono, image, photo, print, scene, vinet 6 chromo, crayon, depict, marine, pastel 7 diorama, etching, explain, imagine, paysage(F.), portray, porture, reflect, tableau 8 describe, likeness, makimono, painting, panorama, portrait, seascape, triptych, vignette 9 delineate, landscape, miniature 10 illustrate, impression, photograph, watercolor 16 chromolithograph

border: mat 5 frame

composite: 7 montage

drawn with heated instrument: 11 pyrogravure

painted on wall: 5 mural

section: 7 gravure

small: 5 cameo 9 miniature 15 microphotograph

stand: 5 easel

viewer: 9 projector 11 alethoscope, stereoscope

Picture of Dorian Gray author: 5 Wilde

picture puzzle: 5 rebus 6 jigsaw

pictured: 11 counterfeit

picturesque: 5 vivid 6 quaint, scenic 7 graphic 8 informal, scenical, striking

picuda: 9 barracuda

piddle: toy 4 pick, play 6 dawdle, putter, trifle

piddling: 6 paltry 7 trivial, useless 13 insignificant

pie: 4 mess, tart 5 chaos, flawn, graft, patty, pasty 6 jumble, magpie, pastry, tourte 7 cobbler, dessert, mixture 8 crustade, turnover 9 blackbird, confusion

meat: 5 pasty 7 rissole

with ice cream: 7 a la mode
piebald: 4 pied, piet, pyot 5 mixed, motly, pinto 6 bauson 7 mongrel, mottled 10 variegated 12 multicolored 13 heterogeneous
piece: bat, bit, cob, eke 4 chip, gare, hunk, join, mend, part, slab, slat, snip, stub, tate(Sc.) 5 crumb, flake, patch, pezzo(It.), scrap, sheet, shred, slice, strip 6 cantle, gobbet, morsel, parcel, sliver 7 cantlet, driblet, flinder, flitter, morceau(F.), oddment, portion, section, segment, snippet 8 assemble, dribblet, fraction
tapering: 4 gore, shim 6 gusset
piece of eight: 4 peso(Sp.) 6 escudo(Sp.)
piece out: eke 10 supplement
piece together: 4 form, make 5 unite
pied: 7 piebald
pied antelope: 8 bontebok
pieplant: 7 rhubarb
pier: cob 4 cobb, dock, mole, pile, quai, quay 5 groin, stilt, wharf 6 bunder 7 landing, support 8 buttress, pilaster 10 breakwater
architectural: 4 anta
base: 5 socle
pierce: dag, rit 4 bear, bite, bore, brod, cloy, dirl, gore, hole, stab, tang 5 break, drill, enter, gride, lance, probe, smite, spear, spike, stick, sting 6 broach, cleave, empale, ficche, impale, riddle 7 discern, poniard 8 puncture 9 intersect, lancinate, penetrate, perforate 10 comprehend
with horn: 4 gore
with stake: fix 6 impale
pierced: 5 ajour
piercer: awl
piercing: 4 fell, high, keen, tart 5 clear, sharp 6 shrill 7 cutting, pungent 8 poignant 9 searching 10 foraminate
Pierus: *consort:* 4 Clio
son: 10 Hyacinthus
piet: 5 ouzel 6 magpie 10 chatterbox, chattering
piety: 4 pity 7 loyalty 8 devotion, holiness, religion 9 godliness, reverence 10 compassion, devoutness
pig (see also **hog**): far, ham, hog, sow 4 boar, pork 5 bacon, chuck, crock(Sc.), ingot, shoat, shote, swine 6 farrow, gussie, porker 7 casting, dogboat, glutton, grumphy(Sc.) 8 grumphie(Sc.), pressman, sixpence
female: sow 4 gilt
lead: 6 fother
litter: far 6 farrow
male: 4 boar 6 barrow
metal: bar 5 ingot
pert. to: 7 porcine
pickled feet of: 5 souse
red variety: 5 Duroc
tender: 9 swineherd
young: elt 4 gilt, runt 5 grice(Sc.), piggy, shoat, shote, snork 6 bonham, farrow, piggie, piglet 7 teatman 9 gruntling
pig bed: sty 4 sand
pig deer: 8 babirusa 9 babirussa 10 babiroussa
pig hickory: 6 pignut
pig iron ballast: 9 kentledge
pig latin: 5 argot
pig potato: 7 cowbane
pig rat: 9 bandicoot
pigboat: sub 9 submarine
piggy bank: 6 pishke 7 knippel, pushkeh
pigs and whistles: 4 ruin 8 fragment, wreckage
pigeon: 4 barb, bird, dodo, dove, dupe, gull 5 decoy, pluck, squab, wonga 6 coward, culver, cushat, dodlet, fleece, isabel, pouter, turbit 7 cropper, fantail, jacobin, namaqua, pintado, swallow, tumbler 8 squealer 9 frillback, harlequin 10 sweetheart, turbitteen, turtledove, wonga-wonga
call: coo
carrier: 5 homer 6 homing 8 horseman 10 scandaroon
clay: 5 skeet 6 target
domestic: nun 4 barb, ruff, runt, spot 9 satinette, trumpeter
extinct: 4 dodo 9 passenger
feed: 7 saltcat
genus of: 7 columba
hawk: 6 falcon, merlin
pert. to: 9 columboid 12 peristeronic
short-beaked: 4 barb
tooth-billed: 6 dodlet
young: 5 piper 8 squealer
pigeon blood: red 6 garnet
pigeon grass: 7 foxtail 9 crabgrass 12 bristlegrass
pigeon hawk: 6 merlin
pigeon house: 7 dovecot 9 columbary
pigeon-livered: 4 meek, mild 6 gentle
pigeon pea: dal, tur 4 herb, seed 5 arhar 6 gandul 7 cajanus, catjang
pigeon woodpecker: 7 flicker
pigeonberry: 8 pokeweed 9 Juneberry 11 coffeeberry
pigeonhearted: 5 timid 8 cowardly 14 chickenhearted
pigeonhole: 6 shelve 7 arrange, cubicle 8 classify
pigeonry: 7 dovecot 8 dovecote
piggery: 4 pigs 6 pigsty 8 crockery(Sc.)
piggish: 4 mean 6 filthy, greedy 7 selfish 8 stubborn 10 gluttonous
pigheaded: 7 willful 8 perverse, stubborn 9 obstinate 10 determined

piglike animal: 7 peccary
pigment: 4 lake 5 color, paint 8 colorant
absence of: 8 alphosis
applied to canvas: 7 impasto
black: tar 5 sepia 7 melanin
blood: 10 hemoglobin
blue: 4 bice 5 smalt 7 veriter
blue-gray: 4 bice
blue-white: 4 zinc
brown: 5 sepia, umber 6 bister, bistre, sienna 7 melanin
green: 4 bice 7 veriter
kind: 7 aniline, rubiate 8 alizarin, massicot 9 alizarine
red: 7 amatito, realgar, turacin
yellow: 5 ocher, ochre 7 etiolin 8 orpiment
pigmy: See **pgymy**
pignus: 4 pawn 6 pledge
pigpen: sty
pigsconce: 7 pighead
pigskin: 5 glove 6 saddle 8 football
pigsney: 4 dear 7 darling 10 sweetheart
pigsticker: 4 sled 5 sword 7 butcher 11 pocketknife
pigtail: 5 braid, queue
pigwash: 5 swill 7 hogwash
pika: 6 rodent
pike: ged(Sc.) 4 dore, fish, gedd(Sc.), luce, pick, road 5 cairn, point, spike, tower 6 beacon, pickax, summit 7 highway 8 poulaine 9 spearhead 11 muskallonge, muskallunge, muskellunge
pike perch: 4 dory 6 sauger
pikel, pikle: 7 hayfork 9 pitchfork
pikelet: 7 crumpet
piker: 5 thief, tramp 6 coward 7 gambler, quitter, shirker, vagrant 8 pilferer, tightwad 10 speculator
pilar: 5 downy, hairy
pilaster: 4 anta 5 antae 6 column
Pilate: 10 procurator
prisoner: 8 Barabbas
tribunal: 9 Gabbatha
wife: 7 Claudia
pilchard: 7 sardine
smoked: 6 fumado
pile: cop, mow, nap 4 bank, bing, cock, dass(Sc.), dess(Sc.), heap, mass, mole, pier, rick, sess, shag 5 amass, crowd, spile, stack, stake 6 pillar 7 fortune 8 buttress 10 accumulate, breakwater, coacervate
funeral: 4 pyre 5 mound
hay: 4 cock, rick 5 stack
rubbish: 4 dump
stone: 5 cairn, scree
pile driver: 6 beetle
weight: tup
pile up: 5 amass, stack
pileup: 4 heap, mass 8 accident 9 collision
pilewort: 6 ficary
pilfer: rob 4 hook, loot, pelf, take 5 filch, sneak, steal, swipe 6 finger, snitch 7 purloin 8 scrounge
pilgrim: 5 ihram 6 palmer 8 crusader, traveler, wanderer, wayfarer 9 sojourner 12 peregrinator
bottle: 7 ampulla, costrel
garb at Mecca: 5 ihram
ship: 9 Mayflower, Speedwell
to Holy Land: 6 palmer
Pilgrim's Progress: *author:* 6 Bunyan
character: 5 Demas
pilgrimage: 4 hadj, trip 7 journey
pill: 4 ball, goli, pare, peel, pool 5 bolus, creek, strip 6 pellet, pilule 7 capsule, granule, pitcher, placebo 11 decorticate
pill bug: 5 louse 6 slater
pillage: 4 flay, loot, prey, sack 5 booty, foray, harry, rifle, spoil, strip 6 maraud, rapine, ravage 7 despoil, plunder 8 expilate, spoliate 9 depredate, devastate
pillager: 6 peeler 10 freebooter
of Rome: 6 Alaric
pillaging: 9 predatory
pillar: lat 4 pile, post 5 cippi(pl.), pylon, shaft, stela, stele 6 cippus, column, stelae(pl.), steles 7 obelisk, osiride, support 8 pilaster, pillaret 9 totem pole
capital: 7 chapiter
pert. to: 6 stelar
resembling: 6 stelar
series of: 9 colonnade
without: 7 astylar
pillar-like: 6 stelar
pillar saint: 7 stylite
pillar-stone: 8 monument 11 cornerstone
pillarist: 7 stylite
Pillars of Hercules: 5 Abila, Calpe 9 Gibraltar
pillbox: cap, hat 7 shelter 8 brougham 11 emplacement 13 fortification
pilled: 4 bald, bare 6 barked, peeled, shaven 8 tonsured 12 decorticated
pillion: 6 saddle 7 cushion
pillory: 4 joug(Sc.), thew 5 stock, trone
pillow: cod, pad 5 block 7 bolster, cushion, support
stuffing: 5 eider, kapok 6 dacron
pillowcase: 4 sham, slip 5 cover, linen 8 flanerie
pilm: 4 dust
pilon: 4 gift 5 bonus 7 present 8 gratuity, lagnappe 9 lagniappe
pilose: 5 hairy
pilot: ace, fly 4 lead 5 flyer, guide, steer 6 leader 7 aviator, conduct, hobbler 8 chap-

lain, coxswain, director, governor, helmsman, preacher 9 clergyman, cockswain, steersman 10 cowcatcher
test for: 4 solo
pilot bird: 6 plover
pilot fish: 6 remora, romero 9 whitefish
pilot snake: 4 bull 10 copperhead
pilot whale: 9 blackfish
pilotweed: 7 compass 9 rosinweed
pilous: 5 hairy 6 pilose
pilum: 6 pestle 7 javelin
Piman Indian: 5 Opata
pimento: 7 paprika 8 allspice
pimple: 4 blob, burl, flaw 6 burble, papule 7 bubukle
pin: fed, fix, hob, nog, peg, pen, tit 4 axle, bolt, coak, dart, join, lill, scob 5 affix, arrow, badge, dowel, preen, rivet, spile, stake, style 6 bobbin, broach, brooch, cotter, fasten, pintle, secure, skewer 7 confine, enclose, eyebolt, gudgeon, jewelry, skittle, spindle, trenail 8 fastener, kingbolt, linchpin, ornament, spilikin, transfix 9 spillikin 10 chatelaine
for fastening meat: 6 skewer
machine: 6 cotter
oar: 5 thole
rifle: 4 tige
wooden: fid, peg 5 dowel
pin grass: 9 alfilaria
pin plant: 5 tacca
pin-wing: 6 pinion
pinafore: 4 slip 5 apron, dress, smock 6 daidly(Sc.) 8 sundress 9 gaberdine
Pinafore: *author:* 7 Gilbert 8 Sullivan
Pinales: 5 trees 6 shrubs 11 Coniferales
pinbone: 7 hipbone
pince-nez: 5 specs 7 glasses, lorgnon 10 eyeglasses, spectacles
pincers: tew 5 chela 6 pliers, tenail 7 forceps 8 tenaille
pinch: nip, rob, wry 4 bite, raid 5 cramp, gripe, hinch, steal, stint, tweak 6 arrest, crisis, extort, snatch, snitch, twince 7 confine, squeeze 8 contract, straiten 9 emergency, vellicate
pinch bar: pry 5 lever
pinchbeck: 4 sham 5 alloy, cheap 8 spurious 11 counterfeit
pinchpenny: 4 carl 5 miser, stint 9 niggardly
Pindaric: ode
pine: ara, fir, iva, lim 4 ache, flag, hone, tree 5 cedar, droop, dwine, kauri, kaury, larch, pinon, vacoa, waste, white, yearn 6 balsam, grieve, lament, pandan, repine, spruce, totara, vacona, vacoua, wither 7 dwindle 8 galagala, languish, Northern 9 evergreen, Norwegian
acid: 5 pinic
exudation: 5 resin, rosin
fruit: 4 cone
grove: 7 pinetum
leaf: 6 needle
mahogany: 6 totara
product: tar 5 resin 10 turpentine
pine bark aphid: 10 phylloxera
pine family: 8 pinaceae
pine gum: 8 sandarac
pine knot: 7 dovekie
pine siskin: 5 finch
pine tar: 6 retene
Pine Tree State: 5 Maine
pine tulip: 10 pipsissewa
pineapple: 4 bomb, pina(Sp.) 5 anana(It.) 7 grenade 8 ornament 10 decoration
family: 12 bromeliaceae
genus of: 6 ananas
segment: pip
pineapple weed: 8 marigold
pinecone: 4 clog 8 strobile
pinfold: 4 jail 5 pound
ping: 4 push, urge 5 prick
pinguid: fat 5 fatty
pinguin: 7 aguamas
pinguitude: 7 fatness, obesity 8 oiliness 10 greasiness
pinhead: 4 fool 5 clown
pinion: pin, tie 4 bind, gear, wing 5 quill 7 confine, disable, feather, pennant, shackle, trundle 8 cogwheel, restrain
pink: cut 4 deck, rose, rosy, stab, tint 5 adorn, color, coral, prick 6 flower, minnow, pastel, pierce, salmon 7 blossom, radical 8 decorate, grayling 9 carnation, embellish
family: 15 caryophyllaceae
genus of: 6 silene
pink needle: 9 alfilaria
pink pill: 7 cure-all
pinkeen: 6 minnow
pinkeye: 14 conjunctivitis
pinnace: 4 boat, ship 5 woman 6 tender 9 procuress 10 prostitute
pinnacle: epi, tee, top, tor 4 acme, apex, peak 5 crest, crown, serac 6 finial, needle, summit 8 gendarme
glacial: 5 serac
rocky: tor
pinnate: 9 feathered 11 featherlike
pinniped: 4 seal 6 walrus
pinnula: 4 barb
Pinocchio author: 7 Collodi 9 Lorenzini
pinochle score: 4 meld
pinpoint: aim, dot, fix 5 exact, point 6 trifle 7 precise
pintado: 4 cero, fish, sier 6 chintz, pigeon, sierra 7 siering

pintail: 4 duck, smee

pintle: 4 bolt 5 hinge, dowel

pinto: 4 pied, pony 5 horse 6 calico 7 mottled, painted, piebald

pinxter flower: 6 azalea 11 honeysuckle

pion: dig 8 excavate

pioneer: 5 miner 6 digger 7 settler 8 colonist, explorer 9 excavator

pious: 4 good, holy 5 froom, godly, loyal 6 devout, devine, pietic 7 canting, goddard, godlike, piteous 8 faithful 9 religious 11 reverential 13 sanctimonious

pip: 4 paip, peep, seed, spot 5 cheep, chirp, speck

pipe: oat 4 cask, duct, flue, lead, main, reed, tube 5 briar, canal, drain, spout, stack 6 dudeen, leader, outlet, tubule 7 calumet, conduit, fistula, larigot 8 mirliton(F.)

ashes: 6 dottle

bend: el 5 elbow

clay: TD 4 tile 5 straw 12 churchwarden

connection: ell, tee 5 cross, elbow

end: 4 taft 6 nozzle

joint: "T", "Y"; ell, tee, wye 5 cross, elbow 7 calepin 8 coupling

Oriental: 5 hooka 6 hookah 7 nargile 8 narghile, nargileh 12 hubble-bubble

part: 4 bowl, stem

pastoral: oat 4 reed

pert. to: 6 tubate

player: 5 fifer 8 shepherd

smoke: 5 tewel

steam: 5 riser

stove: 4 flue 5 tewel 7 chimney

pipe dream: 4 hope 7 chimera 8 illusion

pipe wrench: 8 Stillson

pipeline: 7 channel, conduit

Piper's son: Tom

piperly: 7 trivial 9 worthless

pipette: 6 taster 7 dropper

measuring: 11 stactometer

piping: 6 edging, tubing

pipistrel, pipistrelle: bat

pipit: 6 wekeen 7 titlark

pippin: 5 apple

piquancy: 4 salt 6 flavor, ginger 7 flavour

piquant: 4 racy, tart 5 salty, sharp, spicy, tasty, zesty 6 biting, bitter 7 peppery, pungent 8 poignant, stinging 11 provocative, stimulating

pique: 4 fret, goad 5 annoy, pride, spite, sting 6 excite, grudge, harass, malice, nettle, offend, pritch, strunt 7 dudgeon, offense, provoke, umbrage 8 irritate, vexation 9 annoyance, displease 10 irritation, resentment 11 displeasure

piqued: 5 pouty

piquet: *score:* pic

tricks: 5 capot

pirate: 4 Kidd 5 rover 6 robber 7 brigand, corsair, omnibus 8 algerine, marauder, picaroon, predator 9 buccaneer, privateer 10 freebooter, plagiarize

flag: 5 Roger

gallows: 7 yardarm

piripiri: 4 weed 5 birch, mapau

pirl: 4 spin 5 twine, twist

pirn: 4 reel 5 spool 6 bobbin

pirogue: 5 canoe

pirol: 6 oriole

piscation: 7 fishery, fishing

piscator: 6 angler 9 fisherman 11 piscatorian

piscina: 4 tank 5 basin 8 fishpond 9 reservoir

piscine appendage: fin

Pisgah summit: 4 Nebo

pishogue, pishoge: 5 spell 7 sorcery 10 witchcraft

pismire: ant 5 emmet

pismo: 4 clam

piste: 4 path 5 spoor, track, trail

pistil: 6 carpel

pistle: 4 tale 5 story 7 epistle

pistol: dag, gat, gun, rod 6 barker, buffer 7 dungeon 8 bulldoze 9 automatic, derringer

case: 7 holster

lock: 5 rowet

piston: 7 plunger

pit: 4 butt, delf, foss, hell, hole, mine, pool, seed, sump, trap, weem, well 5 abyss, chasm, delft, delve, fossa, fosse, fovea, grave, shaft, snare, stone 6 cavern, cavity, fossae, hollow, oppose 7 abaddon, cockpit 8 downfall 9 barathron, barathrum, waterhole 10 depression, excavation 11 indentation

bottomless: 7 Abaddon

of peach: 4 seed 7 putamen

of theater: 7 parquet

small: 7 alveola, foveola 8 alveolus, foveolae

pit viper: 4 habu 8 lachesis 10 bushmaster, copperhead

pitch: dip, key, tar 4 cant, cast, hurl, line, roll, send, tone, toss 5 fling, heave, lunge, lurch, resin, rosin, throw 6 accent, encamp, patter, plunge, totter 7 asphalt, bitumen 8 alkitran 9 alchitran

above: 5 sharp

apple: 5 copei, cupay

below: 4 flat

high in: alt

pipe: 9 epitonion

pitch-color: 7 piceous

pitchblende: 6 radium 7 uranium

pitcher: jar 4 ewer, olla, olpe, toby 5 buire, gorge, gotch, ollae, olpae 6 carafe, heaver, hurler, tosser, urceus 7 canette, creamer 8

cruisken, oenochoe 9 container, cruiskeen 10 ballplayer
false move: 4 balk
left-handed: 8 southpaw
motions: 6 windup
place: 5 mound
pitcher plant: 8 nepenthe 10 cephalotus, sarracenia 12 chrysamphora, darlingtonia
pitcher-shaped: 9 urceolate 10 ascidiform
pitchfork: 4 evil 5 pikel, pikle 8 sheppeck, sheppick
pitchhole: 5 cahot
piteous: 5 pious 6 devout, moving, tender 7 pitiful, pitying 8 pitiable, touching 13 compassionate
pitfall: 4 lure, trap 5 snare 6 danger 10 difficulty
pith: jet, nub 4 core, crux, gist, meat, pulp 5 force, vigor 6 kernel, marrow 7 essence, medulla, nucleus 8 strength
full of: 5 heady, meaty, terse 7 concise
pith helmet: 5 topee
pith tree: 7 ambatch
pithy: 5 crisp, meaty, terse 7 compact, concise, laconic 11 sententious 12 apothegmatic
plant: 4 sola
saying: mot 5 maxim 9 witticism
pitiful: sad 4 mean 6 rueful, woeful 7 forlorn, piteous 8 pathetic, pitiable 9 miserable, sorrowful 10 despicable, lamentable 12 contemptible
pitiless: 4 grim 5 cruel, stony 6 savage 8 ruthless 9 ferocious, merciless 10 despiteous, dispiteous, relentless 11 hardhearted
pitpit: 8 guitguit
pittance: bit 4 alms, dole, gift, mite, song 6 trifle 7 bequest
pitted: 7 foveate, opposed, scarred 9 alveolate 10 pockmarked 11 honeycombed
pity: 4 ruth 5 mercy, piety 6 pathos 8 clemency, sympathy 10 compassion, condolence, tenderness 11 commiserate 13 commiseration
Pius: 4 Pope
Pius II: 6 Aeneas 7 Silvius
pivot: toe 4 slew, slue, turn 5 hinge, swing 6 evener, swivel 7 gudgeon
pivot pin: 6 pintle 8 kingbolt
pivotal: 5 polar 7 central, crucial 8 cardinal
pixie, pixy: elf 5 fairy 6 sprite
pixilated: 5 dotty
placable: 4 calm 8 peaceful 9 agreeable, forgiving, peaceable
placard: 4 bill, post, sign 6 poster 7 affiche 9 manifesto 12 proclamation 13 advertisement
placate: 4 calm 5 quiet, sooth 6 pacify, please, soothe 7 appease 10 conciliate
place: lay, put, set 4 area, calm, city, lieu, loci, post, room, seat, site, spot, town 5 being, court, estre, locus, plant, posit, siege, situs, space, stead 6 bestow, locale, locate, region, repose, square 7 allodge, bestead, demesne, deposit, dispose, situate, village 8 dwelling, location, locality, position 9 collocate, residence, situation
again: 6 reseat 7 replace
apart: 6 enisle 8 separate
before: 6 appose, prefix
beneath: 9 infrapose
between: 6 insert 9 interpose
business: 5 plant, store 6 office
by itself: 7 isolate
camping: 5 etape
combining form: gea 4 gaea
end for end: 7 reverse
hiding: mew 4 cave
holy: 6 shrine
in a row: 5 align, aline
in the sun: 5 glory 11 recognition
intermediate: 5 limbo
little hiding: 5 niche
market 4 mart 5 agora
meeting: 5 tryst 10 rendezvous
one inside another: 4 nest
side by side: 9 collocate, juxtapose
trial: 5 venue
placebo: 8 medicine 11 preparation
placed: 7 bestead
placid: 4 calm, even, mild 5 downy, quiet, suant 6 gentle, serene 8 peaceful, tranquil 9 unruffled 11 undisturbed 13 imperturbable
placket: 4 slit 6 pocket 7 opening
pladaroma: 5 tumor
plage: 4 zone 5 beach 6 region 7 country 8 transept
plagiarism: 4 crib 5 theft 6 piracy
plagiarize: rob 4 crib 5 steal 6 borrow, pirate, thieve 7 purloin
plague: dun, pox, vex 4 fret, pest, twit 5 annoy, harry, tease, worry 6 harass, hector, pester, wanion 7 scourge, torment, trouble 8 calamity, epidemic, irritate, nuisance 9 annoyance 10 affliction, pestilence 11 infestation
carrier: rat
pert. to: 6 loimic
plaguy: 6 vexing 9 vexatious 12 disagreeable
plaice: 8 flounder
plaid: 4 maud 5 cloth 6 design, tartan 7 bracken, garment, pattern 9 checkered 11 crossbarred
plain: lea 4 bald, bare, chol, down, even, fair, mead, mere, mesa, moor, open, vega, wold

5 blair, blunt, broad, camas, campo, clear, corah, frank, gross, heath, homey, llano, veldt 6 camass, cammas, coarse, cuesta, graith, homely, humble, lenten, meadow, pampas, simple, steppe, tundra, undyed 7 artless, certain, evident, genuine, glaring, legible, obvious, prairie, quamash, savanna 8 apparent, campagna(It.), campaign, distinct, explicit, flatland, homemade, homespun, ordinary, savannah, tailored 9 champaign, downright, outspoken, primitive, unadorned, unfigured, untwilled 10 unaffected 11 perspicuous, transparent, undisguised 12 altiplanicie 13 unembellished 15 straightforward
depression 5 swale
elevated: 4 mesa 7 plateau
Olympic games: 4 Elis
salt-covered: 5 flats 6 salada
treeless: 5 llano, pampa, veldt 6 tundra 7 prairie, savanna 8 savannah
upland: 4 wold 5 weald

plainstone: 6 paving 9 flagstone

plaint: 6 lament 9 complaint 11 lamentation

plaintiff: 4 suer 7 accuser 9 recoverer 11 complainant

plaintive: sad 5 cross 7 elegiac, fretful, peevish, pettish 8 dolorous, mournful, petulant, repining 9 lamenting, sorrowful 10 melancholy 11 complaining 12 discontented

plait: cue 4 fold, knit 5 braid, brede, crimp, pleat, weave 6 border, gather, goffer, pleach, plight, wimple 7 gauffer 8 complect 9 gathering 10 interweave

plaited: 7 browden

plan: aim, map 4 card, dart, form, game, idea, plat, plot 5 draft, epure, ettle, frame 6 budget, decoct, design, devise, intend, layout, method, policy, scheme, sketch, system 7 arrange, concert, diagram, draught, drawing, outline, program, project, purpose 8 conspire, contrive, engineer, platform, prepense, schedule 9 calculate, machinate, stratagem 10 concoction 11 arrangement, contemplate, contrivance, preconceive, precontrive, premeditate

planate: 5 plane 9 flattened

plancher: bed 4 slab 5 board, floor, plank 6 pallet 7 ceiling 8 planking, platform

plancier: 6 soffit

plane (see also **airplane**): 4 even, flat, soar 5 glide, level 6 aequor, chinar, smooth 7 surface 8 sycamore
block: 5 stock
handle: 4 toat, tote
inclined: 5 chute, shute
kind of: 4 iron, jack 5 block 6 router 8 grooving, tounging
on same: 8 coplanar

plane figure: *boundary:* 9 perimeter
four angles: 8 tetragon
nine-sided: 7 nonagon

plane iron: bit 5 blade

plane-tree: 8 sycamore

planer: 6 shaper 8 surfacer

planet: orb 4 Mars, moon, star 5 Earth, Pluto, Venus 6 Saturn, sphere, Uranus 7 Jupiter, Mercury, Neptune 8 asteroid, terrella, wanderer 9 satellite
brightest: 5 Venus
cone: 8 strobile
course: 5 orbit
nearest sun: 7 Mercury
newest: 5 Pluto
orbit: 7 ellipse
orbit point: 5 apsis, nadir 6 apogee, zenith 8 parigree
path: 5 orbit
period: 9 alfridary
red: 4 Mars
relation to another: 5 trine 7 sextile 10 opposition 11 conjunction
ruling: 9 dominator
satellite: 4 moon
shadow: 5 umbra

planeta: 5 cloak

planetarian: 10 astrologer

planetarium: 6 orrery

planetary: 7 erratic 9 wandering, world-wide 10 astrologer 11 terrestrial

planeticose: 9 wandering

planetoid: 8 asteroid

plangor: 4 wail 11 lamentation

planisphere: 9 astrolabe

plank: 4 deal, slab 5 board, slate, stone 6 lumber, timbor 8 plancher 10 gravestone
breadth: 6 strake
increasing bearing surface: 5 shole
lengthwise: 8 stringer

plank down: pay 7 advance, deposit

planking: 8 flooring

planner: 9 architect

plant: fix, set, sow, spy 4 arum, bush, fern, herb, hide, rape, root, seed, slip, trap, tree, weed, wort 5 berry, clote, decoy, found, fruit, grain, place, shoot, shrub, sotol, spice, trick, works 6 annual, clover, flower, legume, scheme, settle, teasel 7 alyssum, aquatic, creeper, cutting, factory, furnish, pungent, sapling 8 aromatic, building, business, geophyte, narcotic, radicate 9 detective, establish, perennial, seasoning, succulent, swindling, vegetable 13 establishment

acid-juice: 5 ribes 6 nettle 8 knotweed 9 smartweed
aconite: 4 bikh
amaryllis family: 5 agave
ambrosia genus: 7 ragweed
ammoniac: 5 oshac
apiaceous: 4 ache
apoplexy: 4 esca
appendage: 7 stipule
aquatic: see **aquatic plant**
arboreal: 4 tree
aromatic: see **aromatic**
arrowroot-yielding: 7 curcuma
arum family: 4 arad, taro 5 aroid, calla
aster family: 5 oxeye, tansy 8 fleabane
asteraceous: 5 daisy
bayonet: 5 datil
bean family: 6 lupine 8 licorice 9 liquorice
benthonic: 6 enalid
bitter: ers, rue 9 colicroot
blue-blossomed: 6 lupine 8 ageratum
body: 6 cormus
bog genus: 5 abama 10 narthecium
bramble: 5 briar, furze, gorse, thorn
branched: 4 bush, tree 5 shrub
breathing organ: 5 stoma 7 stomata(pl.)
bulbous: 5 camas 6 camass, cammas, nerine 7 quamash
cabbage family: 4 rape
cactus family: 5 dildo 6 cereus, mescal
cactus-like: 8 stapelia 9 xerophyte
capsule: pod
carrot-like: 7 parsnip
cassia genus: 5 senna
catnip family: nep 6 nepeta
celery family: 5 anise
celery-like: udo
cell: 6 gamete
chlorophyll-rich: 4 alga 5 algae(pl.)
chromatophore-lacking: 6 albino
class: 4 alga 5 algae(pl.)
climbing: ive, ivy 4 bine, vine 5 liana, liane, vetch 6 byrony, smilax 7 creeper
clover-like: 5 medic 7 calomba
coloring matter: 8 clorofil 10 endochrome 11 chlorophyll
corn lily: 4 ixia
crocus family: 4 irid
crossbred: 6 hybrid
crowfoot family: 5 peony 8 clematis
cruciferous: 5 cress 7 alyssum
cryptogamous: 4 moss
cuticle: 5 cutin
cyperaceous: 5 sedge
decorative: ivy 4 bush, fern 6 flower
desert: 5 agave 6 alhagi, cactus
dipsacus genus: 6 teasel
disease: 4 scab, smut 5 ergot 7 blister
division: 15 archichlamydeae
dock-like: 6 sorrel
dry-climate: 5 xerad 9 xerophyte 10 ombrophobe
dwarf: 5 cumin
dye: 4 anil, weld, woad, wold 5 henna, woald, would 6 kamala, madder, wurras, wurrus 7 alhenna, orselle
dye-yielding: 4 anil, woad 5 henna, sumac 6 madder 7 alkanet
ebony family: 6 ebenad
embryo: 8 plantule
environmentally modified: 4 ecad
erica genus: 5 heath 7 heather
Euphorbia genus: 6 spurge
exudation: gum, sap 4 milk 5 latex, resin, rosin
fabaceous: pea
family: 7 araceae
fernlike: 8 filicoid
fiber: see **fiber**
flag-family: 4 irid
floating: 7 frogbit
flowering: see **flowering plant**
forgetfulness-causing: 5 lotus
fragrant: 5 orris 8 angelica
garden: 4 geum, iris, ixia, rose 5 aster, calla, canna, daisy, pansy, phlox, poppy, stock, viola 6 bellis, bletia, celery, clivia, cosmos, crocus, lupine, oxalis, zinnia 7 agathea, alyssum, anchusa, anemone, begonia, celosia, clarkia, gazania, gerbera, godetia, lettuce, lobelia, muscari, petunia, primula, statice, verbena 8 ageratum, arctotis, cyclamen, daffodil, dianthus, herebell, hyacinth, larkspur, marigold, myosotis, scabiosa, sparaxis, sweet pea, tithonia, watsonia 9 amaryllis, calendula, campanula, candytuft, carnation, centaurea, cinararia, coreopsis, digitalis, gladiolus, hollyhock, linararia, narcissus, nicotiana, penstemon, portulaca 10 delphinium, gaillardia, gypsophila, marguerite, ranunculus, snapdragon, sweet basil, wallflower 11 dusty miller, forget-me-not, helichrysum, hunnemannia, Madonna Lily, shasta daisy 12 nierembergia, rhododendron, salpiglossis, sweet William 13 chrysanthemum, dimorphotheca, glory of the sun 14 canterbury bell 15 Star of Bethlehem 16 spring snowflakes
genus: 4 dion
geography: 14 phytogeography
gourd family: 5 melon
grain: oat, rye 4 corn 5 wheat 6 barley
grass: 5 avena
grass cloth: 5 ramee, ramie
grass-like: 5 sedge
grassland: 6 baccar 7 bacchar

growing from inside: **7** endogen **9** endogenae(pl.)
growing from outside: **6** exogen
growth layer: **7** cambium
growth on: **4** gall
habitat: **4** ecad
hawthorn: **7** azarole **9** mayflower
head: bud, bur **4** burr **5** fruit **6** flower
healing: **7** sanicle
heather family: **4** ling **5** erica
herbaceous: see **herb**
honey-secreting organ: **7** nectary
house: see **houseplant**
interior chaff: **5** palea, palet
iridaceae: **4** irid
iris family: **4** irid, ixia **7** freesia
joined to another: **5** graft
joint: **4** node
juice: see *exudation* above
leguminous: see **legume**
liliaceous: **4** aloe, leek **5** onion **9** birthroot
lily family: **4** aloe, sego **5** lotos, lotus, yucca **6** camass
linen-producing: **4** flax
main axis: **4** stem **5** stalk, trunk
male: mas **16** androgametophore
mallow family: **5** altea **6** escoba
manufacturing: **4** mill
marine: see **aquatic plant**
marsh: **4** fern, reed **7** bulrush, cattail
masculine: see *male* above
medicinal: hop, oak **4** aloe, dill, flax, herb, lime, sage **5** buchu, elder, erica, guaco, jalap, peony, poppy, senna, tansy **6** arnica, carrot, catnep, catnip, fennel, garlic, ipecac, kousso, laurel, nettle **7** aconite, boneset, calamus, camphor, caraway, catechu, copaiba, ephedra, gentian, hemlock, henbane, juniper, lobelia, mullein, mustard, parsley, rhubarb, saffron **8** barberry, camomile, crowfoot, foxglove, licorice, plantain, rosemary, valerian, wormwood **9** asparagus, bearberry, buckthorn, chamomile, colchicum, coltsfoot, dandelion, liquorice, monkshead **10** assafetida, pennyroyal, peppermint, stavesacre **11** assafoetida, bittersweet
microscopic: **5** spore
millet: **5** hirse
mock orange: **7** syringa
modified by environment: **4** ecad
moss-like: **6** orpine **7** hepatic
mottled leaf: **8** ratsbane
multicellular: **9** metaphyte
mushroom-type: **6** fungus
mustard family: **4** woad **5** cress **6** radish **7** alyssum
native: **8** indigene
nettle family: **4** hemp
nightshade family: **6** tomato
oil-yielding: **4** odal **6** sesame
old-world: **5** lotus
one-seeded fruit: **9** olacaceae
onion family: **4** leek
onion-like: **5** chive **7** shallot
opening: **5** stoma **7** stomata(pl.)
packing: **7** cannery
painful to touch: **5** briar, thorn **6** nettle **8** knotweed **9** smartweed
parsley family: **4** dill **5** anise
part: **6** stamen, stipel **7** tendril
pert. to: **6** agamic **7** botanic, vegetal **9** botanical **10** vegetative
pigment-lacking: **6** albino
poaceae: **5** grass
pod: **4** boll
poisonous: **4** atis **6** datura **7** amanita **8** oleander
poisonous to cattle: **4** loco **8** calfkill, locoweed
poisonous to fowls: **7** henbane
poppy family: **9** celandine
pore: **8** lenticel
potato-like: oca
preserving: **4** dill **7** cannery
prickly: **5** briar, brier, cacti(pl.), thorn **6** cactus, nettle, teasel **7** thistle **9** tearthumb
rat poison: **8** oleander
reproductive organ: **5** spore
root: **5** radix
rope: **4** hemp
rose family: **5** avens
round-leaved: **9** pennywort
salad: **5** cress **6** celery, endive, greens **7** lettuce, romaine **8** purslane **10** watercress
scented: **4** mint **6** catnip **7** catmint
science: **6** botany
seasoning: **8** tarragon
sedge family: **5** carex
seed: nut, pip **4** bulb **5** grain **6** button **7** putamen
seedless: **4** fern
seller: **7** florist
shoot: rod **4** cion **5** scion, sprig **6** stolon
silk: **5** floss
soap: **5** amole
solanaceous: **7** tobacco
sour-juice: **6** sorrel
starch: pia **4** arum, taro **7** cassava
stem: **4** bine **5** shaft **6** caulis
stem joint: **4** node
stem tissue: **4** pith **6** phloem
tanning: **5** sumac
tapioca-yielding: **6** casava, casave, casavi **7** cassava
tequila-yielding: **5** agave
thistle family: **5** aster
thorny: see *prickly* above

three-leaved: 9 trifolium
trailing: 7 arbutus
tropical: 4 arum, palm, taro 5 agave, altea, canna, liana, liane, yucca, zamia 6 pepino 7 dasheen, hamelia 8 mangrove, redwithe
tufted: 4 moss
twining: see *climbing* above
type: 6 exogen
urticaceous: 6 nettle
valerian genus: 4 nard
verbenaceous: 7 lantana
vetch family: ers
vine: ivy 5 liana
wall: ivy
water-side: 5 sedge
wild-growing: 9 agrestial
woody: 4 bush, tree, vine 5 shrub
woody-vine genus: 5 vitis
xyloid: 4 tree
young: 4 cion 5 scion, shoot 6 sprout 7 vinelet 8 seedling
yucca-like: 5 sotol
plant life: 5 flora 10 vegetation
plant louse: 5 aphid
secretion: 4 laap, lerp 5 laarp
plant raising: *pert. to:* 13 floricultural
Plantagenets: 7 Angevin
plantain: 4 weed 6 banana, wabron 8 balisier
family: 14 plantaginaceae
plantain eater: 7 touraco
plantation: 4 farm 6 estate 8 hacienda
cacti: 7 nopalry
coffee: 5 finca 7 cafetal, fazenda
coniferous tree: 7 pinetum
oak tree: 9 quercetum
sugar: 8 trapiche
trees: 6 forest 7 orchard
willow: 4 holt 6 osiery
planter: 5 sower 6 farmer, grower, seeder 7 pioneer, settler 8 colonist 13 agriculturist
government by: 11 plantocracy
planting stick: 6 dibble
plantling: 8 plantlet
plaque: pin 5 medal 6 broach, brooch
plash: 4 pool 5 blash, hedge 6 pleach, puddle, splash 9 bespatter
plashy: wet 6 marshy
plasm: 4 mold 6 matrix
plasma: 5 lymph 11 trophoplasm
plaster: 4 daub, harl, teer, tere 5 cleam, cover, gatch, gesso, grout, salve, smalm, smear 6 mortar, parget
artist's: 5 gesso
coarse: 5 grout 6 parget, stucco
of Paris: 6 gypsum
stone: 6 gypsum
support: 4 lath
tool: 7 spatula
wax: 6 cerate
plastered: 5 drunk 11 intoxicated
plasterer: 5 mason
plastic: 4 soft 5 gesso 7 ductile, fictile, flexile, pliable 8 flexible 9 formative 14 impressionable
cotton-sizing: 7 viscose
dentist's: 6 cement
plastosome: 12 chondriosome
plastron: 7 calipee 8 trimming 11 breastplate
plat: lot, map 4 boat, flat, plan, slap 5 braid, chart, level, plain, plait 6 buffet 7 flatten, plateau 8 straight 9 tableland 10 interweave 15 straightforward
platanist: 4 susu
platano: 6 banana
plate: cut, gib 4 coat, disc, dish, disk, lame, tile 5 aglet, armor, facia, scute, stove 6 aiglet, discus, lamina, platen, tagger, veneer 7 lamella, laminae, overlay 8 assiette, lamellae, laminate 9 silverize
communion: 5 paten 6 patina
cooking: 4 grid
for throwing: 6 discus
from matrix: 6 stereo 10 stereotype
glass: 4 pane
horny: 5 scute
perforated: dog 4 grid 7 stencil
pitcher's: 4 slab
ship-shaped: nef
stereotype: 6 cliche
thin: 6 lamina 7 lamella
plate bone: 7 scapula
plate mark: 8 hallmark
plateau: 4 dish, mesa, seir 5 fjeld 6 hamada, plaque, salver 7 hammada, uplands 9 altiplano, tableland 12 altiplanicie
plateholder: 8 cassette
platen: 6 roller
platform: map 4 bank, bema, dais, deck, plan 5 bench, chart, floor, stage 6 bemata(pl.), podium, pulpit 7 estrade, program, rostrum, tribune 8 chabutra, plancher 9 banquette, gangplank, vestibule
church: 5 solea
fort: 8 barbette
mining: 6 sollar, soller
nautical: 7 maintop
reloading: 6 staith
salt-manufacturing: 6 hurdle
ship: 7 foretop, maintop 9 gangplank
sleeping: 4 kang
temple: 5 dukan
theater: 7 logeion
wheeled: 5 float
platic: 9 imperfect
platinum: *combining form:* 6 platin 7 platino

crude: **7** platina
symbol: Pt
wire: **4** oese
platitude: 6 cliche, truism **7** bromide **8** dullness, flatness **9** staleness, triteness **10** triviality **11** commonplace **15** commonplaceness
Plato: *idea:* **5** eidos
knowledge: **6** noesis
school: **7** Academe
work: **4** Meno **5** Crito **6** Phaedo **7** Apology, Gorgias, Sophist, Timaeus **8** Republic
platoid: 4 flat **5** broad
platonic: 9 spiritual, visionary **10** idealistic **11** impractical, theoretical
body: **4** cube **10** hexahedron, octahedron **11** icosahedron, tetrahedron **12** dodecahedron
philosophy follower: **9** academist
platoon: set **4** team, unit **5** squad **6** volley **7** coterie **8** division **9** formation
Platoon School: 4 Gary
platter: 4 dish, lanx(L.) **5** ashet(Sc.), grail, plate **7** charger
platter-shaped: 10 scutellate
platyfish: 8 moonfish
platypus: 8 duckbill
plaudit: 4 clap **6** praise **8** applause, approval, encomium **11** acclamation, approbation
plausible: 4 oily **6** glossy **7** colored **8** coloured, credible, specious **10** applausive, ostensible, plauditory
Plautus: *character:* **5** miles(L.) **7** soldier
forte: **6** comedy
language: **5** Latin
play: act, fun, jeu(F.), hit, toy **4** game, jeux(F.), move, romp **5** charm, dally, drama, enact, flirt, sport **6** cavort, frolic, gambol, rollix **7** disport, execute, perform **9** amusement, dalliance, diversion, pantomime **10** recreation **13** entertainment
badly: err **4** miff **6** bobble
ball: **5** begin **6** resume **9** cooperate
complication: **4** node
festival: **9** festspiel
kind: **4** auto **5** farce **6** comedy, one-act **7** musical, tragedy **8** burletta **9** melodrama, pantomime **13** curtain-raiser
musical: **5** opera **8** burletta, operetta
on words: pun
outline: **8** scenario
part: act, bit **4** acte(F.), role **5** exode, scene **7** prelude **8** epilogue, epitasis, prologue
possum: **4** sham **5** feign **7** pretend
put on: **5** stage **7** produce
silent: **9** pantomime
playa: 4 lake **5** basin, beach
playboy: 4 fool **5** clown, idler **6** madcap **7** buffoon
playday: 7 holiday
play out: 6 finish, unreel
played out: 5 tired **8** finished **9** exhausted
player: man **4** cast, star **5** actor **6** leader **7** enactor, gambler **8** gamester, thespian **10** competitor, contestant
card: **4** pone **6** dealer, eldest
leading: **4** star
poor: dub, dud, sub **12** second-string
strolling: **9** serenader, troubador **10** troubadour **11** barnstormer
player piano: 7 pianola
playful: 5 merry **6** frisky, joking, lusory, wanton **7** jocular **8** gamesome, humorous, playsome, sportive **10** frolicsome
playground: 4 park, yard
playhouse: 5 house, movie **6** cinema **7** theater
playing cards: 4 deck **6** tarots
hand: cat **4** deal
playlet: 4 skit
playman: 7 gambler **8** gamester
playmate: pal **6** friend
playock: 9 plaything
playroom: den, gym **7** nursery
playsome: 7 playful
plaything: die, toy **4** hoop **6** bauble, trifle
playtime: 6 recess
playwright: 6 author **9** dramatist
plea: sue **4** suit **6** abater, answer, appeal, excuse, prayer **7** apology, pretext, request, solicit **8** argument, entreaty, petition, pretense **12** supplication **14** nolo contendere
to end: **6** abater
pleach: 5 plait, plash **9** interlace
plead: beg, sue **5** orate **6** allege, assert **7** beseech, entreat, implore, solicit **8** advocate, appealed, petition **9** importune, intercede **10** supplicate
pleading: 4 oyer **6** answer **8** demurrer **9** suppliant **10** litigation **12** supplication
pleasant: gay **4** bien(F.), fine, good, hend, joli, nice, waly **5** bigly, cushy, douce(F.), hende, hoddy, jolie, lepid, merry, sweet, wally **6** genial **7** amiable, amusing, farrand, farrant, jesting, jocular, leesome(Sc.), playful, winsome **8** delicate, gracious, humorous, pleasing, sportive **9** agreeable, appealing, diverting, enjoyable, laughable, sprightly **10** acceptable, delightful, gratifying
pleasantness: 7 amenity
pleasantry: fun **4** jest, joke **6** banter **7** jesting **10** jocularity **11** gauloiserie **13** facetiousness

please: 4 suit 5 agree, amuse, elate, humor 6 arride, humour 7 aggrate, appease, content, delight, gladden, gratify, indulge, placate, satisfy
pleased: 4 fain 5 apaid, happy 8 gladsome
pleaseship: 10 litigation
pleasing: 4 glad, lief 5 amene, sooth 6 comely, eesome(Sc.), liking 7 roseate 8 fetching, pleasant 9 desirable, favorable, palatable 10 attractive, delectable, favourable 11 pleasureful
pleasurable: 7 hedonic 8 pleasant
pleasure: fun, joy 4 ease, este, gree, will 5 bliss, mirth, sport, treat 6 gaiety 7 delight, jollity 8 delicacy, fruition, gladness, hilarity 9 amusement, diversion, enjoyment, happiness, merriment 10 beneplacit 11 beneplacity, contentment, delectation 12 cheerfulness 13 gratification
god: Bes
ground: 4 park 9 pleasance
insensitiveness to: 9 anhedonia
pert. to: 7 hedonic
philosophy of: 8 hedonism
seeker: 5 sport 7 epicure, playboy 8 hedonist
pleat: 4 fold, kilt, shir 5 braid, prank 7 plicate
pleater: 8 plicator
plebe: 5 toast 8 commoner, freshman
plebeian: 4 snob 6 coarse, common, vulgar 7 illbred, lowborn 8 baseborn, ordinary
plebiscite: 4 vote 6 decree 7 mandate 10 referendum
pleck: 4 spot 5 speck, stain 9 enclosure
plectrum: 4 pick 5 uvula 6 fescue, tongue 7 malleus
pledge: bet, vas(L.), vow 4 adhi, band, bond, gage, hand, hest, hock, oath, pawn, seal, wage, word 5 siker, skoal, toast, troth 6 arrest, assure, borrow, commit, engage, lumber, parole, plight, sicker 7 betroth, earnest, espouse, hostage, promise 8 affiance, contract, guaranty, mortgage 9 assurance, certainty, sacrament 11 association, impignorate
security for: 5 gager
pledger, pledgor: 6 pawner
pledget: 4 swab 8 compress
Pleiad of Alexandria: 5 Homer 6 Aratus 8 Nicander 9 Lycophron 10 Apollonius, Theocritus 11 Callimachus
Pleiades: 4 Maia 6 Merope 7 Alcyone, Celaeno, Electra, Sterope, Taygeta 8 Asterope
constellation: 6 Taurus
father: 5 Atlas
mother: 7 Pleione
Pleione's offspring: 8 Pleiades
plenary: 4 full 6 entire 7 perfect 8 absolute, complete 11 unqualified
plenipotentiary: 5 envoy 8 minister 10 ambassador
plenitude: 6 plenty
plenteous: 9 plentiful
plenteously: 6 freely
plentiful: 4 full, rich, rife 5 ample, sonsy 6 galore, plenty, sonsie 7 copious, fertile, liberal, opulent, profuse 8 abundant, affluent, fruitful, generous, prolific 9 abounding, bounteous, bountiful, exuberant, plenteous 10 productive
plenty: 4 enow, heap, raff 5 ample, cheap, fouth 6 enough, foison, scouth 7 copious(L.) 8 fullness, opulence 9 abundance, affluence, plenitude, plenteous 10 exuberance, luxuriance, perfection, sufficient 11 copiousness, sufficiency 12 completeness
goddess: Ops
horn of: 10 cornucopia
plenum: 5 space 8 assembly, fullness, plethora
pleon: 6 telson 7 abdomen
pleonasm: 8 fullness 10 redundancy
plethora: 4 glut 6 excess 8 fullness 9 repletion 13 overabundance 14 superabundance
plethoric: 6 turgid 8 inflated, overfull 9 bombastic 10 overloaded
pleurapophysis: rib
pleurocarpous: 11 cladanthous, cladogenous
plexiform: 4 rete 5 retia 7 complex 9 intricate 11 complicated
plexus: 4 rete 5 retia 6 tangle 7 network
pliable: 4 easy, limp, soft, waxy 5 lithe 6 limber, pliant, supple 7 bending, ductile, flaccid, flexile, plastic, tensile 8 flexible, fluxible, informal, tractile, workable, yielding 9 adaptable, compliant, malleable, tractable 10 applicable 13 unconstrained
pliant: 4 flip 7 willowy 8 cheverel, cheveril 10 sequacious
plicate: 4 fold 5 pleat
plight: 4 fold, risk 5 array, braid, plait, state 6 engage, pledge, status 7 betroth, embrace, promise 8 position 9 betrothal, condition 10 difficulty 11 predicament
plinth: 4 base, orlo 5 block, couch, stone, table 6 course 8 skirting 9 baseboard
flat: 4 orlo
Pliny's birthplace: 4 Como 5 Comum
plod: dig, mog, peg 4 grub, slog, toil, tore, vamp, work 6 drudge, trudge
plop: 5 plump
plot: map 4 land, plan, plat 5 cabal, chart, draft, story 6 design, devise, scheme, secret 7 compact, connive, diagram, outline

8 conspire, contrive, engineer, intrigue, scenario 9 insidiate, machinate 10 conspiracy 11 machination
garden: bed 8 parterre
ground: lot 5 grave 7 terrain
inventor: 8 schemist
play: 4 node
plouk, plook: 4 knob 6 pimple
plounce: 6 plunge 8 flounder
plout: 4 dash 5 plash 6 splash
plover: 4 bied, crab, dupe 5 drome, sandy 6 kildee, piping 7 collier, killdee, lapwing 8 dotterel, killdeer, Wilson's 9 courtesan, turnstone 10 beetle-head, blacksmith
plow, plough: dig, ear 4 farm, mole, rove, till 5 break 6 digger, furrow 9 cultivate
handle: 5 stilt
kind of: 4 snow 5 sulky 6 gopher, lister, rotary, shovel 7 breaker 8 stirring, turnplow 9 moldboard 14 prairiebreaker
knife: 6 colter 7 coulter
part: 4 hale 5 sheth, slade, stilt 6 sheath 9 plowshare, sharebeam
plow spade: 9 plowstaff
plowgang: 4 area, land 6 bovate(Sc.), oxgang
plowhead: 4 beam 5 frame 6 clevis
plowing: 7 aration
plowland: 4 area 7 measure 8 carucate
plowman: 6 farmer, rustic, tiller 7 acreman, husband 10 clodhopper, countryman
command: gee, haw
plowman's-spikenard: 4 herb 8 aromatic 12 cinnamonroot
plowshare, ploughshare: 6 colter 7 coulter
bone: 5 vomer
ploy: 4 bend, joke 5 sport, trick 6 frolic, tactic 7 pastime 8 escapade 11 merrymaking
pluck: rob, tug 4 grit, jerk, pick, pull, sand, tear 5 cheek, nerve, spunk, strip, twang 6 daring, finger, fleece, gather, snatch, spirit, twitch 7 bravery, courage, deplume, plunder 8 decision, gameness 9 endurance, fortitude, hardihood 10 resolution
plug: peg, tap, tit 4 blow, bung, calk, cork, slog 5 boost, caulk, estop, knock, punch, shoot, spile, spill 6 dottle, tampon 7 bouchon, pledget, stopper, stopple, tampeon, tampion, tampoon 9 advertise
cannon muzzle: 7 tampion
clay: bod 4 bott
medical: 4 clot 7 embolus
wall: 6 outlet
water: 7 hydrant
plug bib: 6 spigot
plug cock: 6 spigot
plug hat: 4 tile 5 gibus 6 topper
plug-ugly: 4 thug 5 rowdy, tough 7 ruffian 8 gangster
plugboard: 11 switchboard
plum: hog 4 amra, coco, gage, sloe 5 drupe, duhat, icaco, prune 6 damson, jambul, sapote 7 bullace, jambool 9 greengage 10 amatungula
date: 6 sapote
dried: 5 prune
family: 12 amygdalaceae
sapodilla: 5 chico
seed: pit 7 putamen
wild: 4 sloe
plum-colored: 4 puce
plum curculio: 6 weevil
plum duff: 7 pudding
plum weevil: 8 curculio
plumage: 4 down 5 dress 6 hackle 7 floccus 8 feathers 9 adornment
plumb: 4 bung 5 delve, probe, solve 6 chunky, fathom, plunge 7 explore, plummet 8 absolute, complete, entirely, vertical 9 downright 10 absolutely, straighten, understand 13 perpendicular
plumbago: ore 4 lead 5 plant 8 graphite, leadwort
plumbeous: 4 dull 6 leaden
plumber: 5 piper
plume: 4 tuft 5 crest, egret, preen, pride, prize, prune 6 aigret, plumet 7 feather, panache 8 aigrette, plumelet 9 plumicorn
plummet: 4 drop, fall, lead 5 plumb 6 weight
plump: fat 4 back, drop, fall, plop, sink, tidy 5 bonny, buxom, obese, plunk, stout 6 bonnie, chubby, dilate, flatly, fleshy, portly, rotund 7 bluntly, distend, fulsome, support 9 downright
plunder: gut, rob 4 boot, loot, pelf, prey, raid, sack, swag 5 booty, cheat, harry, pluck, poach, raven, reave, rifle, spoil, steal, strip 6 bezzle, boodle, creach(Sc.), creagh(Sc.), dacoit, maraud, pilfer, pirate, rapine, ravage, ravish, spoils 7 despoil, pillage, ransack 8 predator, spoliate 9 depredate, devastate
plunderer: 5 thief 6 bandit, vandal 8 marauder, predator 10 freebooter
plunge: bet, dig, dip 4 cave, dive, duck, dump, pool, sink 5 douse, dowse, drive, fling, lunge, merse, plumb, souse 6 absorb, emerge, footer, gamble, thrust 7 immerge, immerse 8 submerge
plunger: ram 6 risker 10 speculator
plunk: 4 drop, flop, pull, push, sink, toss 5 drive, pluck, plump, sound, throw 6 dollar, strike
plunther: 4 plod 8 flounder
plurality: 8 majority 9 multitude
plus: add 4 more, over 5 extra 6 excess 8 addition, positive
Plutarch work: 5 Lives

Pluto: Dis 5 Hades
kingdom: 5 Hades
wife: 10 Persephone, Proserpina
plutocrat: 5 nabob
plutonium symbol: Pu
Plutus: *father:* 6 Iasion
mother: 7 Demeter
ply: web 4 bend, fold, mold, sail, urge, work 5 beset, layer, plait, wield 6 double, handle, travel 7 belabor, shuttle 8 belabour, exercise 9 importune, thickness
with drink: 5 birle
pneuma: 4 soul 5 neume 6 breath, spirit 9 breathing
pneumonia: 5 lobar, viral 9 bronchial
Po tributary: 4 Adda 9 Cispadane
poach: ram 4 boil, cook, poke, push, stab, stir 5 drive, force, shirr, spear, steal, steam 6 pierce, thrust 7 trample 8 encroach, trespass
poacher: 7 lurcher, stalker, widgeon
Pocahontas: *father:* 8 Powhatan
husband: 5 Rolfe
pochard: 4 duck, fowl, smee 6 dunker
pochette: 6 violin 7 handbag 8 envelope
pock: pit 4 scar 6 pimple 7 pustule
pocket: bin, cly, fob 4 poke, prat, sack 7 cantina, conceal, confine, enclose
ore: 4 lode 7 bonanza
water: 6 tinaja 7 alberca
pocketbook: bag, fob, lil 4 poke 5 burse, pouch, purse 6 wallet 8 billfold 12 portemonnaie
poco: 6 little 8 slightly, somewhat
pococurante: 9 apathetic 10 nonchalant 11 indifferent
pocosin, pocoson, pocosen: 5 marsh, swamp
pod: bag, bur, cod, kid, sac 4 aril, boll, hull, swad 5 belly, carob, pouch, shell, shuck 6 legume, loment 7 silicle
podesta: 5 judge, mayor 8 executor, governor, official 10 magistrate
podgy: fat 5 pudgy, squat
podium: 4 base, dais, wall 8 pedestal, platform 12 substructure
Poe: *bird* 5 raven
house: 5 Usher
poem: 5 Raven 6 Lenore 7 Ulalume
poem: ode 4 duan, epic, raff, rann(Ir.), rime, song, vers(F.) 5 canto, ditty, elegy, ionic, lyric, poesy, raffe, stave, verse 6 ballad, carmen, epopee, eulogy, iambic, jingle, poetry, screed, sonnet, tercet 7 ballade, dimeter, sestina, triolet, virelay 8 acrostic, doggerel, hexapody, senarius, trimeter 9 hexameter, hexastich, monometer, octameter, soliloquy 10 tetrameter 11 acatalectic
break in rhythm: 6 cesura 7 caesura
bucolic: 8 pastoral
division of: see *part* below
eight-line: 7 triolet
foot: 4 iamb 6 iambus 7 anapest, spondee
four-line: 8 quatrain
fourteen-line: 6 sonnet
heroic: 4 epic
line: 8 trimeter 9 hexameter 12 decasyllabic
love: 6 erotic
lyric: 4 alba
medieval: lai 4 alba
melodic: 5 lyric
moral: dit
mournful: 5 elegy
narrative: 4 epos
node: 4 plot
nonsensical: 8 doggerel, limerick
part: fit 4 feet, foot, line 5 canto, epode, stich, verse 6 epilog, prolog, stanza 7 refrain 8 epilogue, prologue
pastoral: 4 idyl
pert. to: 4 odic
religious: 4 hymn 5 psalm
rural: 7 eclogue, georgic
satirical: dit(F.) 6 iambic, parody
seven-line: 10 heptastich
short: dit(F.) 5 ditty 6 sonnet 7 epigram 8 rondelet
six-line: 9 hexastich
six-stanza: 7 sestina
ten-line: 6 dizain 7 dizaine 9 decastich
poems: 5 poesy, verse 6 poetry
collection: 5 sylva
poesy: 4 poem 5 motto, verse 7 nosegay
poet: 4 bard, fili, scop 5 odist, rishi 6 lyrist 7 dreamer, imagist, metrist 8 idyllist, minstrel 9 bucoliast, 13 cinque-centist
humorous: 4 Lear, Nash
inferior: 5 rimer 6 rhymer 8 rimester 9 poetaster, poeticule, rhymester, versifier
inspiration: 4 Muse
poetic: 4 odic 5 lyric 6 dreamy 8 romantic 9 beautiful 11 imaginative
poetical: 8 sonnetic
poetry: *accented foot:* 5 arsis
god: 5 Bragi
inspiring to: 7 helicon
muse: 5 Erato 6 Thalia 8 Calliope
pogonip: fog
pogrom: 6 attack 8 massacre 9 slaughter
pogy: 8 menhaden
poi: 4 food 5 paste
source: 4 taro
poietic: 8 creative
poignant: 4 keen, tart 5 acute, sharp 6 biting, bitter, moving 7 cutting, piquant, pointed, pungent 8 piercing, pricking

poind: 4 sell 5 seize 7 impound

point: aim, dot, jag, jet, jot, neb, nib, res, tip, wit 4 apex, barb, cape, crux, cusp, foci, gist, horn, peak, pith, pole, show, spit, spot 5 angle, focus, issue, level, prong, refer, sense, taper 6 allude, apices, cruces(pl.), degree, direct, tittle 7 apicula(L.), apiculi(L.), article, feature, meaning 8 apiculae(L.), apiculus(L.), emphasis, indicate, salience 10 promontory

cardinal: 4 east, west 5 north, south

compass: E., N., S., W.; N.E., N.W., S.E., S.W.; E.N.E., E.S.E., N.N.E., N.N.W., S.S.E., S.S.W., W.N.W., W.S.W. 4 airt 5 airth

final: dot, end 6 period

finishing: 4 tape

highest: sum 4 acme, apex, noon, peak 6 apices, apogee, maxima, summit, zenith 7 maximum 8 meridian, pinnacle

land: 4 hook, spit

law: res

lowest: 4 zero 5 nadir 6 bottom, pergee

pert. to: 6 apical

scoring: ace, run 5 punto 6 sponge

spear: gad

strong: 5 forte

supporting: 5 pivot 7 fulcrum

to the: 8 relevant 9 pertinent

turning: 4 tide 6 crisis, crises

utmost: 7 extreme

vibration: 4 node

weak: 4 flaw 5 fault 6 foible

point-blank: 7 blankly, bluntly, exactly 8 directly 9 perfectly, precisely 10 completely 13 unqualifiedly

point of view: eye 5 angle, sight, slant

pointed: 5 acute, tangy, terse 6 acuate, marked, picked 7 actuate, capapie, concise 8 aculeate, piercing, poignant, spicated, stinging 9 acuminate, apiculate, fastigate 11 conspicuous

pointer: arm, dog, tip 4 clue, hand, hint 5 index 6 fescue, gnomon 7 indices 9 indicator

pointless: 4 dull 5 blunt, inane, silly, vapid 6 stupid 7 insipid

points: *three:* 11 tricuspidal

twelve: 4 pica

pointsman: 7 flanker 9 switchman

poise: tee 5 carry, weigh 6 aplomb 7 balance, ballast, bearing, support, suspend 8 calmness, carriage, liberate, maintain 9 equipoise, stability 10 equanimity 11 equilibrium 12 counterpoise 14 counterbalance

poison: fig 4 bane, drab, gall 5 atter, taint, venin, venom, virus 6 amarin, infect, miasma 7 amarine, arsenic, corrupt, pervert, vitiate 8 empoison, ptomaine 11 contaminate

ant: 10 formmicide 11 formicicide

arrow: 4 haya, inee, upas 5 urali, urare, urari 6 curare, curari

comb. form: 5 toxic 6 toxico

hexapod: 11 insecticide

kind: 4 bikh 5 abrin, nabee, ricin 6 antiar 7 arsenic, tanghin

pert. to: 9 arsenious

tree: 4 upas

poison ash: 5 sumac 6 sumach 9 torchwood

poison dogwood: 5 sumac 6 sumach

poison fish: 4 fugu 6 weever 8 scorpion, toadfish

poison flag: 4 iris

poison flower: 11 bittersweet

poison ivy: 5 sumac 6 laurel

poison tobacco: 7 henbane

poisoned: 6 sepsis

poisonous: 5 toxic 6 virose 7 noxious 8 virulent 9 malignant 11 destructive

fish: 4 fugu

fungus: 7 amanita

gas: 6 arsine 8 phosgene

herb: 8 aconitum

lizard: 4 gila

plant: 8 mandrake 10 nightshade

weed: 4 loco

poisonwood: 5 sumac 10 manchineel

poisson bleu: 7 blue cat, catfish 8 grayling

poitrel: 5 armor, plate 6 armour 9 stomacher 11 breastplate

poke: bag, dig, hat, jab, jog 4 blow, bore, brod, prod, root, sack 5 nudge, probe, punch, purse 6 bonnet, dawdle, loiter, meddle, pocket, potter, putter, sleeve, thrust, wallet 7 dawdler, intrude, tobacco 8 slowpoke 10 pocketbook

poker: rod 4 dart, game

drawing by: 10 pyrography

forerunner: 7 primero

form: 4 draw, stud

stake: pot 4 ante 5 chips

pokewood: 5 pocan 6 garget 8 inkberry

family: 14 phytolaccaceae

pokey, poky: 4 dull, mean, slow 5 dowdy 6 narrow, shabby, stuffy 7 tedious 8 trifling

Poland: 7 Polonia 8 Sarmatia

cake: 4 baba

carriage: 7 britska

city: 4 Lodz 5 Brest, Posen, Vilna 6 Cracow, Gdynia, Grodno, Krakow, Lublin, Tarnow, Warsaw 7 Beuthen, Lemberg, Litovsk 8 Gleiwitz, Tarnopol 9 Bialystok, Bielostok, Byelostok

coin: 5 ducat, grosz, marka, zloty 6 fennig, halerz, korona

commune: 4 Ruda 5 Plock, Radom
composer: 6 Chopin
dance: 7 mazurka 9 krakowiak, polonaise 11 cracovienne
dollar: 5 dalar
dynasty: 5 Piast
island: 5 Wolin
measure: cal 4 mila, morg, pret 5 linja, morga, sazen, stopa, vloka, wloka 6 cwierc, korzec, kwarta, lokiec 7 garniec 9 kwarterka
nobleman: 7 starost
parliament: 4 Seim, Sejm, Seym 5 Senat
people: 4 Slav 5 Marur 8 Silesian
river: San 4 Styr 5 Dwina, Seret 6 Niemen, Pripet, Strypa 7 Vistula 8 Dniester, South Bug
scientist: 5 Curie
szlachta: 6 gentry 8 nobility 9 landowner
title of address: 4 Pani
weight: lut 4 funt 5 uncya 6 kamian 7 centner, skrupul

polar: 6 Arctic 7 pivotal 8 opposite
polar explorer: 4 Byrd
polar plant: 9 rosinweed
pole: bar, pew, poy, rod, xat 4 axis, boom, brog, mast, palo(Sp.), pike, prop, spar, wand 5 caber, guide, nader, perch, sprit, staff, stake, stick, stool, sweep, totem 6 crotch 7 barling
circle: 11 circumpolar
electric: 5 anode 7 cathode, kathode 9 electrode
fishing: rod
pert. to: 5 polar
tribal: xat 5 totem
vehicle: 4 cope, neap 5 thill
pole fluke: 8 flounder
pole horse: 7 wheeler
pole strip: 8 template
polecat: 5 skunk, zoril 6 ferret, musang 7 fitchet, fitchew, foumart
polehead: 7 tadpole
polemic: 8 argument 9 disputant 10 discussion 11 disputation 12 disputatious 13 argumentative, controversial
polenta: 4 mush 8 porridge
polestar: 5 guide 8 lodestar 10 tramontane
police: 5 guard, watch 6 govern, patrol 7 protect, rurales 8 officers 11 carabinieri(It.) 12 constabulary
headquarters: 4 tana 7 station 8 bargello, barracks 9 marshalcy
line: 6 cordon
officer: 6 kotwal 8 bargello
organization: PAL
vehicle: car, van 7 cruiser 8 prowl car, squad car
policeman: cop 4 bull 5 bobby, bulky, burly, rural, sepoy 6 bobbie, copper, peeler 7 crusher, gumshoe, officer, trooper 8 flatfoot, gendarme(F.) 9 burkundaz, constable, patrolman 11 burkundauze, carabiniere(It.)
badge: 6 buzzer, shield
club: 5 billy 9 espantoon, truncheon 10 nightstick
policy: wit 4 plan 6 wisdom 8 contract, prudence, sagacity 9 diplomacy, principle 10 artfulness, management, shrewdness 14 administration
polish: rub 4 buff 5 frush, glaze, gloss, grind, rabat, scour, sheen, shine, slick 6 finish, luster, lustre, rabbat, refine, smooth 7 burnish, culture, furbish 8 brighten, civilize, elegance, lapidate, levigate, urbanity 10 refinement
polish off: end 4 kill 6 finish
polished: 4 fine 5 compt, suave 6 polite 7 gallant
polisher: 5 rabat(F.) 8 abrasive
polishing: 8 frottage, limation
polishing material: 4 sand 5 emery, rabat 6 pumice
polite: 5 civil, suave 6 gentle, smooth, urbane 7 correct, courtly, cunning, gallant, genteel, refined 8 cultured, debonair, decorous, discreet, polished 9 courteous, debonaire 10 cultivated, debonnaire 11 complaisant
politesse: 10 politeness 11 cleanliness, courtliness 12 decorousness
politic: 4 wary, wise 5 suave 6 artful, crafty, shrewd 7 prudent 8 discreet 9 expedient, politique, provident, sagacious 10 diplomatic 12 unscrupulous
political: *division:* 4 city, town, ward 5 shire, state 6 county 8 province 9 community
gathering: 5 rally 6 caucus
group: 4 bloc, ring 5 cadre, party 6 caucus 7 faction, machine
hanger-on: 6 heeler
incumbents: ins
influence: 5 lobby
list: 5 slate
political party: G.O.P. 4 Tory, Whig 5 labor 9 Communist, Socialist 10 Democratic, Republican 12 Conservative
principles: 8 platform
program article: 5 plank
unit: 4 city, East, ward, West 5 state 6 county, parish 7 borough, hundred, kingdom 8 district 9 sultanate
politician: 7 schemer, senator, statist 9 intriguer, president, statesman 16 congressionalist
politico: 9 statesman 10 politician
polka dot: 4 spot 6 circle

poll: cow 4 clip, coll, head, list, trim 5 count, shave, shear 6 fleece, survey 7 canvass, despoil, listing 8 counting, register 9 enumerate
pollack: 4 fish, pool 6 billet 7 baddock(Sc.) 8 coalfish
pollan: 9 whitefish
pollard: cow 4 bran, deer, goat, stag, tree 5 sheep
polled: 8 hornless
pollen: 4 dust, meal 5 flour
pollen brush: 5 scopa 6 scopae
pollen grain: *mass:* 8 pollinia 9 pollinium
pollenization: 5 xenia
poller: 6 barber 9 plunderer 11 extortioner, taxgatherer
pollex: 4 inch 5 digit, thumb 7 phlange
pollicitation: 7 promise 8 proposal
pollinate: 9 fecundate
pollinosis: 8 hay fever
polliwog: 7 tadpole
pollute: 4 foul, soil 5 dirty, smear, stain, sully, taint 6 befoul, defile, ravish 7 corrupt, debauch, profane, violate, vitiate 9 desecrate 11 contaminate
pollution: 5 filth 8 impurity 11 uncleanness
Pollux: *brother:* 6 Castor
father: 4 Zeus
mother: 4 Leda
polo: *division:* 7 chucker, chukker
mount: 4 pony 5 horse
stick: 6 mallet
team: 4 four
Polonius: *daughter:* 7 Ophelia
son: 7 Laertes
Polony: 6 Polish 7 sausage 9 polonaise
polt: 4 blow, club 5 knock, thump
poltergeist: 5 ghost 6 spirit
poltfoot: 8 clubfoot
poltroon: cad 4 idle, lazy 6 coward, craven 7 dastard 8 cowardly, sluggard 9 dastardly
polverine: 6 potash 8 pearlash
polyandrium: 8 cemetery
polychromatic: 10 variegated 12 multicolored
polygamy: 6 bigamy
polygon: 4 ngon 6 square 7 decagon, hexagon, nonagon, octagon 8 pentagon, triangle
equal sides: 6 isagon
nine sides: 7 nonagon
twelve sides: 9 dodecagon
Polynesia: *apple:* 4 hevi
baking pit: umu
banana: fei
beverage: 4 kava, kawa
breech cloth: 4 malo
burial place: ahu
butterfly: io
chestnut: 4 rata
cloth: 4 tapa
dance: 4 siva
dragon: ati
fern: 4 tara
garment: 5 pareu
god: Oro 4 Tane, Tiki
goddess: 4 Pele
herb: pia
homeland: 7 Havaiki
island: 4 Fiji 5 Samoa 7 Phoenix, Tokelau
language: 7 Tagalog
magical power: 4 mana
memorial: ahu
oven: umu
people: Ati 5 Malay, Maori 6 Kanaka, Samoan, Tongan 8 Hawaiian, Tahitian 9 Marquesan
pepper plant: 4 avas
pigeon: 4 lupe
pine: ara 4 hala
plant: 4 taro
ruler: 7 faipule
sky: 5 langi
sling: ma
spirit: 4 Atua
statue: 4 Tiki
tree: ti 4 ahia, rata
wages: utu
yam: ube, ubi, uve, uvi
polyp: 5 hydra, tumor 6 seapen 7 anemone, hydroid
skeleton: 5 coral
polytrophic: 9 versatile
Polyxena: *father:* 5 Priam
lover: 8 Achilles
mother: 6 Hecuba
pomade: 5 salve 7 pomatum, unguent 8 cosmetic, ointment
pome: 4 ball, pear 5 apple, fruit, globe 6 quince, sphere
pomegranate: 6 granet 7 granate, grenade
sirup: 9 grenadine
pomelo: 8 shaddock 10 grapefruit
Pomerania: *capital:* 7 Stettin
city: 6 Anklam
island: 5 Rugen 6 Usedom
river: 4 Oder
Pomeranian: dog
pomme de terre: 6 potato
pommel: bat 4 beat, knob 6 handle 12 protuberance
bag: 7 cantina
pomp: 4 fare 5 boast, pride, state 6 estate, parade 7 cortege, display, pageant 8 ceremony, grandeur, splendor 9 pageantry, spectacle 10 ceremonial 11 ostentation 12 magnificence

Pomp and Circumstance composer: 5 Elgar
pompano: 4 fish 7 alewife 9 poppy fish
Pompeii: *archeologist:* Mau
heroine: 4 Ione
pom-pom: gun 6 cannon
pompon: 4 ball, tuft 8 ornament 13 chrysanthemum
pompous: big 7 bloated, fustian, orotund, stately, stilted 9 bombastic, flatulent, grandiose 10 altisonant, pontifical 11 altiloquent, dictatorial, magnificent, pretentious, stateliness 12 ostentatious 13 grandiloquent, self-important
Ponchielli opera: 8 Giaconda
pond: dam, lum 4 delf, dike, dyke, lake, mere, pool, tarn 5 delft 6 lagoon 7 lakelet
fish: 7 aquaria, pisoina 8 aquarium
frog: 7 ranaria 8 ranarium
oyster: 6 claire
pond dogwood: 10 buttonbush
pond duck: 7 mallard
pond hen: 4 coot
ponder: 4 chaw, mull, muse, pore 5 brood, opine, weigh 6 reason 7 reflect, revolve 8 appraise, cogitate, consider, evaluate, meditate, ruminate 10 deliberate 11 contemplate
ponderous: 5 bulky, grave, heavy, hefty, massy 7 awkward, massive, weighty 8 unwieldy 9 important, momentous 11 elephantine
pondfish: 7 sunfish
pondokkie: hut 5 hovel
pone: 4 lump, turf 8 swelling 10 johnnycake
pongee: 4 silk 5 cloth 6 fabric 8 shantung
pongy: 4 monk 6 priest 8 Buddhist
poniard: 4 kill, stab 6 bodkin, dagger, pierce, stylet 8 stiletto
pont: 5 ferry, float 6 bridge 7 caisson, pontoon 9 ferryboat
pontiff: 4 pope 6 bishop
pert. to: 5 papal 7 sistine
pontifical: 5 papal 7 pompous 8 dogmatic
pontoon: 4 boat 5 barge, float 6 bridge, vessel 7 caisson
plank: 5 chess
pony: cab, cob, nag 4 crib 5 glass, horse 6 garran, liquor 7 hackney, measure
kind: 5 pinto, tatoo 6 cayuse, Exmoor 8 Shetland
student's: 4 crib, trot
pooch: dog 6 barbet 7 mongrel
pooh-pooh: 8 ridicule 9 denigrate
pook: 4 heap, pile, pull 5 pluck, stack
pooka: 6 goblin 7 specter
pool: car, dib(Sc.), dub(Sc.), lin, pit, pot 4 carr, dike, dyke, game, jeel, linn, loch, mear, meer, mere, pond, tank, tarn 5 flash, flush, funds, kitty, lough, plash, stake, trunk, trust 6 cartel, charco, flodge, lagoon, plunge, puddle, salina 7 alberca, carline, combine, jackpot, plashet 8 monopoly 9 billabong, billiards, reservoir, resources 10 natatorium 11 combination
ball: cue 4 spot 6 ringer
poon tree: 4 dilo 5 domba, keena 8 mastwood
poonghie: See **pongy**
poop: 4 deck, fool, gulp, seat 5 cheat, cozen, stern 8 hinddeck 10 nincompoop 11 information
poor: bad, ill 4 bare, base, lean, mean 5 cheap, dinky, naked, needy, seedy 6 abject, barren, feeble, humble, hungry, paltry, pilled, scanty, shabby 7 hapless, sterile, unlucky 8 indigent, inferior 9 defective, destitute, emaciated, imperfect, infertile, penurious 10 inadequate, ungenerous 11 impecunious, inefficient, unfortunate 12 contemptible, insufficient 13 improverished, insignificant 14 unsatisfactory
Poor Clare: nun 6 sister
poor joe: 5 heron
poor John: cod 4 food, hake
poor man's pepper: 9 stonecrop 11 peppergrass
poor man's soap: 8 hardhack
poor man's weatherglass: 9 pimpernel
poor soldier: 9 friarbird
poor-spirited: 4 base 8 cowardly
poorer: 5 worse 8 inferior
poorhouse: 9 almshouse, workhouse
poorly: 13 disparagingly
pop: 4 dart 8 beverage 9 explosion
popadam: 4 cake 5 wafer 6 cookie
popdock: 8 foxglove
pope: 4 ruff 6 bishop, priest, puffin, shrike 7 pontiff 9 bullfinch, patriarch
answer: 8 rescript
cape: 5 fanon 7 mozetta 8 mozzetta
collar: 5 orale
court: 5 Curia
court office: 6 datary 7 dataria
court officer: 6 datary
crown: 5 tiara 9 triregnum
envoy: 6 legate 7 nuntius 8 ablegate
epistle: 8 decretal
headdress: 5 miter, mitre
letter: 4 bull
line: 6 papacy
name: Leo 4 John, Pius 5 Peter, Ratti, Urban 6 Adrian 7 Gregory, Zachary 8 Benedict
palace: 7 Lateran, Vatican
pert. to: 5 papal
seal: 5 bulla
veil: 5 orale 6 fannel

Popeye's sweetheart: Oyl 5 Olive
popinac: 8 huisache
popinjay: 6 parrot 8 parakeet 10 woodpecker
poplar: 4 liar 5 abele, alamo, aspen, bahan, bolle, garab 7 populus 9 tacamahac 10 cottonwood
white: 4 abele, aspen
Poppaea's husband: 4 Nero
poppy: 5 plant 6 blaver, canker, flower 7 coprose, papaver, ponceau 8 foxglove 10 coquelicot
herb family: 9 celandine
seed: maw
poppycock: rot 4 bosh, dung 8 nonsense
populace: mob 4 mass 5 demos, plebs 6 people
popular: lay, pop 6 common, simple 7 demotic, favored 8 accepted, favorite 9 prevalent, well-liked 11 proletarian 12 nontechnical
popularity: 5 vogue
populate: 6 occupy, people 7 inhabit
population: 9 habitancy 11 inhabitants
count: 6 census
study: 10 larithmics
porbeagle: 5 shark
porcelain: 4 frit 5 china 7 biscuit
ancient: 5 murra
clay: 6 kaolin 7 kaoline
furnace: 5 hovel
kind of: 6 Sevres 7 Celadon, Dresden, Limoges 8 Haviland 9 Wedgewood
porch: 4 door, stoa 5 lanai, plaza, stoae(pl.), stoop 6 harbor, loggia, piazza 7 balcony, galilee, gallery, portico, terrace, veranda 8 entrance 9 colonnade
church: 7 galilee
sun: 7 solaria(pl.) 8 solarium
swing: 6 glider
porcine: 7 piglike
porcupine: 5 urson 7 cawquaw 8 hedgehog
disease: 10 ichthyosis
genus of: 7 hystrix
spine: 5 quill
porcupine anteater: 7 echidna
porcupine fish: 6 diodon
porcupine grass: 5 stipa
quill: pen
pore: con 4 gaze 5 gloze, stare, stoma, study 6 ponder 7 foramen, opening, orifice, ostiole, stomata(pl.) 8 lenticel, meditate
plant: 8 lenticel
porgy: tai(Jap.) 4 fish, scup 6 besugo, pagrus 7 margate, pinfish 8 menhaden 9 spadefish
pork: ham, pig 5 bacon, money, swine 6 hamhog 7 griskin, sausage 8 position
porker: hog, pig 5 swine
porkfish: 4 sisi
porky: fat, pig 6 greasy 9 porcupine
pornographic: 4 lewd 7 obscene 10 licentious
porphyry: 4 rock
porpoise: 4 inia 6 seahog 7 dolphin, pellock(Sc.) 8 gairfish
porrect: 6 extend, tender 7 present
porret: 4 leek 5 onion 6 garlic 8 scallion
porridge: 4 samp 5 atole, brose(Sc.), grout, gruel 6 burgoo 7 brochan, burgout, oatmeal, polenta, pottage 9 stirabout 11 skilligalee
container: 6 bicker
port: 4 gate, toal, left, wine 5 carry, haven 6 apport, harbor, market, portal, refuge 7 bearing, harbour, meaning, purport, shelter 8 carriage, demeanor, larboard 9 demeanour, transport 10 deportment 11 destination
portable: 6 mobile 7 movable 8 bearable
bathtub: 4 tosh
bed: cot 8 rollaway
chair: 5 sedan
lamp: 7 lantern
stove: 4 etna
portal: 4 arch, door, gate 7 gateway 8 entrance
portance: 7 bearing, conduct 8 carriage, demeanor
portcullis: bar 4 door, gate, shut 5 grate, herse 7 grating, lattice
porte-monnaie: 5 purse 10 pocketbook
portefeuille: 9 portfolio
portend: 4 bode 5 augur 6 divine 7 betoken, forbode, predict, presage 8 forebode, foretell, prophesy 10 foreshadow
portent: 4 omen, sign 5 event 6 marvel, ostent, wonder 7 meaning, prodigy 8 ceremony 10 prognostic 11 forewarning
portentous: 4 dire 5 fatal, grave 6 solemn 7 fateful, ominous 10 impressive 11 significant
porter: ale 5 carry, hamal, stout 6 bearer, durwan, hamaul, hammal, khamal, redcap, suisse 7 bailiff, carrier, durwaun, dvornik(Russ.), gateman, hummaul, janitor 8 beverage, cargador, janitrix 9 attendant, concierge, janitress, transport 10 doorkeeper
porteress: See **portress**
Portia: *alias:* 9 Balthazar
lover: 8 Bassanio
maid: 7 Nerissa
portia tree: 5 bendy
portico: 4 stoa(Gr.), xyst 5 porch, stoae(Gr., pl.) 6 atrium, piazza, xystus 7 narthex, pteroma, terrace, veranda 9 colonnade, pteromata(pl.) 10 ambulatory, antetemple

long: 6 xystus 7 veranda
potiere: 5 drape 7 curtain
portion: bit, cut, dab, dot, jag, lot, nip 4 chaw, deal, dole, dunt, fate, jagg, part, some 5 allot, allow, divvy, dower, dowry, endow, piece, quota, ratio, share 6 canton, divide, dowery, gobbet, moiety, parcel, rasher, ration 7 destiny, helping, scruple, section, segment, serving 8 legitime, quantity 9 allotment, allowance, apportion 10 distribute 13 apportionment
portly: fat 5 obese, stout 6 goodly 7 stately 8 imposing, majestic 9 corpulent, dignified
portmanteau: bag 4 case 6 valise 8 suitcase 9 carpetbag, gladstone
Porto Rico: See **Puerto Rico**
portoise: 7 gunwale 8 portlast
portrait: 4 copy, icon, ikon 5 image 7 picture 8 likeness 10 similitude
pert. to: 6 iconic
sitting: 6 seance
portray: act 4 draw, form, limn, mime, show 5 enact, frame, graph, image, paint 6 depict 7 fashion, picture 8 describe 9 delineate, pantomime, represent 11 demonstrate
portrayal: 8 portrait
portreeve: 5 mayor 7 bailiff, officer
portress, porteress: 6 porter 9 charwoman 10 doorkeeper
Portugal: *brandy:* 11 aguardiente
city: 4 Ovar 5 Braga, Evora 6 Guarda, Lisbon, Oporto 7 Coimbra 8 Braganca
coin: rei 4 peca, real 5 conto, coroa, dobra, indio 6 dobrao, escudo, macuta, macute, pataca, pataco, testao, tostao, vintem 7 centavo, crusado, moidore, patacao 8 equipaga
colony: Diu, Goa 5 Damao, Macao, Timor 6 Angola, Guinea 8 Principe, Sao Thome 10 Mozambique 11 Cape de Verde
commune: 5 Braga
district: 4 Tete 5 Evora
explorer: Cao 4 Diaz
festival: 9 chamarita
former money: 5 dobra
guitar: 7 machete
harbor: 4 Faro, Ovar 5 Macao 6 Aveiro, Lisbon, Oporto, Vianna 7 Setubal 8 Figueira
island: 6 Angola, Azores 7 Madeira 8 Principe, Sao Thome
Jew: 8 Sephardi 9 Sephardim(pl.)
legislature: 6 cortes
liquid measure: 6 canada
measure: pe 4 alma, bota, meio, moio, pipa, vara 5 almud, braca, fanga, geira, legoa, linha, milha, palmo 6 almude, covado, quarto 7 alquier, estadio, ferrado, selamin 8 alqueire, tonclada 9 pollegada, quartilho
money: rei 4 peca 5 dobra 8 johannes
mountain: 15 Serra d'Estrella
navigator: 4 Gama 8 Magellan
noble: see *title* below
people: 7 Iberian
poet: 7 Camoens
province: 4 Ovar 5 Beira, Minho 6 Azores 7 Algarve, Madeira 8 Alemtejo 11 Estremadura 12 Traz-os-Montes
river: 4 Sado 5 Douro, Duero, Minho, Tagus 7 Mondego 8 Guadiana
saint: Sao
song: 4 fado
title: dom 4 dona 6 senhor 7 fidalgo, senhora 9 senhorita
vessel: 7 caravel
weight: 4 grao, onca, once 5 libra, marco 6 arroba, oitava 7 arratel, quintal 9 escropulo
porwigle: 7 tadpole
posada: inn 5 hotel
posaune: 8 trombone
pose: set, sit 4 airs 5 model, place 6 baffle, puzzle, stance 7 nonplus, posture 8 attitude, position, propound 9 mannerism 10 disconcert, expression 11 affectation, impersonate 12 attitudinize
Poseidon: 7 Neptune(L.)
father: 6 Cronus
mother: 4 Rhea
scepter: 7 trident
servant: 7 Proteus
son: 6 Albion, Triton 7 Alebion, Antaeus, Antaios
wife: 10 Amphitrite
poser: 5 facer 6 puzzle 7 problem 8 question
posh: 5 smart 6 spruce, swanky 7 elegant 9 luxurious
posit: 6 affirm, assert, assume 9 postulate
position (see also **place**): job, lie, set 4 loci(pl.), pose, post, rank, site 5 cense, coign, locus, place, situs, stand 6 billet, coigne, estate, locale, office, plight, stance, status 7 calling, posture 8 attitude, doctrine, location, sinecure, statuses(pl.) 9 condition, gradation, situation 11 affirmation, appointment, disposition 12 circumstance
change: 4 move
correct: 8 oriented
defensive: 4 fort 10 bridgehead
relative: 5 grade 8 standing
with little work: 8 sinecure
positional: 6 situal
positive: set 4 plus, sure 6 actual, thetic 7 assured, certain 8 absolute, complete, constant, dogmatic, emphatic, explicit 9 assertive, confident, downright, empirical, practical 10 peremptory 11 affirmative,

dictatorial, opinionated, unqualified **13** authoritative, overconfident
positively: **5** truly **6** really **8** actually **9** certainly, obviously **11** indubitably
positivism: **7** Comtism **11** materialism
founder: **5** Comte
positure: **7** posture **11** arrangement, disposition **13** configuration
poss: **4** beat, dash, push **5** drive, knock, pound, stamp **6** thrust
posse: **4** band
possess: get, owe, own **4** have **5** reach **6** occupy **7** inhabit **8** dominate, maintain
possessed: mad **8** demoniac
possession: **4** aver, hold **5** aught **6** havior, seisin, wealth **7** control, dewanee, haviour, mastery **8** property **9** ownership
family: **8** heirloom
legal: **5** title **6** estate
of goods by finding: **6** trover
take: **5** seise
time: **5** lease
possessions: **5** goods **6** graith
possessor: **10** proprietor
posset: **4** turn **6** curdle, pamper **8** beverage **9** balductum, coagulate
possibility: **11** eventuality
possible: may **6** likely **8** feasible, probable **9** potential **10** contingent **11** practicable
possibly: may **5** maybe **7** perhaps
possum: **7** opossum **9** marsupial, phalanger
comic strip: **4** Pogo
play: **4** sham **5** feign **7** pretend
post: set **4** dole, dool, fort, mail, polo, ride, send **5** cippi(pl.), newel, place, stake, stock **6** assign, cippus, column, inform, office, pillar, travel **7** courier, placard, station **8** announce, dispatch, garrison, position **9** advertise, situation, sternpost **11** publication
airplane race: **5** pylon
boat rope: **7** bollard, capstan
easy: **4** pipe, snap **8** sinecure
middle: **8** kingpost
post chaise: **4** jack **5** coach **8** carriage
post office: **6** correo(Sp.)
letter box: **8** apartado(Sp.)
postage: **5** stamp
stamp design: **6** burele **8** burelage, spandred
postbox: **7** mailbox
postboy: **7** courier, yamshik(Russ.) **8** yemschik **9** postilion, yamstchik(Russ.)
postdate: **9** afterdate
postea: **5** entry **6** record
poster: **4** bill, clap, sign **7** affiche, courier, placard, sticker **10** billposter **13** advertisement

posterior: **4** back, hind, rear **6** behind, caudal, dorsal, hinder **10** subsequent
posterity: **6** sequel **10** generation **11** descendants
postern: **4** door, exit, gate **7** private **8** entrance **10** undercover
postfix: **6** append **7** suffix
postiche: wig **6** switch, toupee **8** pretense **9** imitation **14** counterfeiting
postil: **6** homily **7** comment **10** commentary
postilion: **7** postboy
postpone: **4** stay, wait **5** defer, delay, remit, table **6** remand, retard, shelve **7** adjourn, prolong **10** pigeonhole **11** subordinate **13** procrastinate
postponement: **4** mora **5** morae(pl.) **7** respite **8** reprieve **10** ampliation
postprandial: **11** after-dinner
postulant: **9** applicant, candidate **10** petitioner
postulate: **5** claim, posit **6** assume, demand **7** premise, require **10** hypotheses(pl.), hypothesis **11** proposition **12** prerequisite
posture: **4** pose **6** stance **7** bearing, gesture **8** attitude, carriage, position **9** composure
erect: **11** orthostatic
posy: **5** motto, verse **6** flower, legend **7** bouquet, nosegay **9** sentiment **11** composition
pot: bag, pan, win **4** dixy, pool **5** abyss, crewe, dixie, drink, kitty, shoot **6** aludel, basket, cruset, posnet, secure, vessel **7** caldron, capture, cuvette **8** cauldron, crucible, potation **11** deteriorate
arch: **4** kiln
earthen: **4** olla **5** crock, cruse **6** chytra
handle: **4** bool
hat: **5** derby **6** bowler
lead: **8** graphite
wheel: **5** noria
pot-au-feu: **4** soup, stew
pot liquid: **6** brewis
pot-rustler: **4** cook
potable: **5** drink **8** beverage **9** drinkable
potage: **4** soup **5** broth
potash: **4** kali **5** niter, nitre, salin **6** alkali, saline **8** pearlash
potassium: *compound:* **4** alum **6** chrome, potash
sulphate: **4** alum
potation: **4** bout, dram **5** draft, drink **6** liquid, liquor **7** spirits **8** beverage, drinking
potato: ima, oca, yam **4** chat, papa, spud **5** rural, tuber **6** murphy **7** manroot
beetle: **8** hardback
bud: eye
disease: pox **4** curl
dish: **8** au gratin **9** lyonnaise, scalloped
family: **10** solanaceae
planting ridge: **4** ruck

seed part: eye
starch: 6 farina
sweet: 6 batata, comote, patata 7 batatas, ocarina
Potato State: 5 Idaho, Maine
potbank: 7 pottery
potboiler: 4 book 8 painting 9 potwaller
potboy: 8 Ganymede 9 cupbearer
pote: 4 kick, poke, push 6 thrust
poteen, potheen: 6 whisky
potence: 5 cross 6 gibbet 7 gallows
potency: vis 5 force, might, power, vigor 6 energy 8 efficacy, strength, vitality 9 fertility
potent: 4 able 6 cogent, mighty 7 dynamic 8 powerful, puissant, virulent 9 effective, efficient 10 convincing 11 influential
potentate: 4 amir, emir 5 ameer, emeer, mogul, ruler 6 moghul, prince 7 monarch 9 sovereign
potential: 6 latent, mighty 8 possible 10 unrealized 11 influential, possibility, undeveloped
potentiality: 5 power
potgun: 6 pistol, popgun 8 braggart
pothead: 9 blackfish
pother: ado, row, vex 4 fuss, stir 5 worry 6 bother, bustle, harass, muddle, uproar 7 fluster, perplex, trouble 9 commotion, confusion 11 disturbance 12 perturbation
potherb: 4 kale, mint, wort 5 chard 6 greens 7 mustard, spinach
pert. to: 7 olitory
pothole: 6 tinaja
pothook: rod 4 hake, nine 5 crook 6 collar, scrawl
pothouse: 6 tavern 8 alehouse
potiche: jar 4 vase
potion: 4 brew, dose, drug 5 draft, drink 6 drench 7 draught, philter, philtre 8 nepenthe
sleeping: 5 dwale 6 opiate 8 narcotic 9 soporific 10 belladonna
potlatch: 4 gift 5 feast
potomania: 10 dipsomania
potpie: 4 stew 9 fricassee
potpourri: jar 4 olio, stew 6 medley 7 mixture 9 anthology 10 miscellany 11 salamagundi
potrero: 6 meadow 7 pasture
potsherd: bit 4 chip 5 shard 8 fragment
potshot: 5 shoot 6 assail, attack
potstone: 8 steatite
pottage: 4 soup 6 brewis 8 porridge
pottah: 4 deed 5 lease 11 certificate
potted: 5 drunk 11 intoxicated
potter: fad, pry 4 fuss, mess, poke, push 6 cotter, dabble, dacker, daiker, dawdle, dodder, fiddle, footer, footle, loiter, meddle, putter, tamper, tinker, trifle 7 cloamer, fossick, saunter 8 ceramist 10 ceramicist
potter's clay: 5 argil
potter's field: 8 Aceldama, cemetery
potter's wheel: 4 disk 5 lathe, palet, throw 6 jigger, pallet
pottery: 4 bank, ware 5 china, delft 7 Keramos(F.) 8 ceramics 9 delftware, Kerami-kos(Gr.), stoneware 11 earthenware
decorating paste: 9 barbotine
dish: 7 ramekin
enameled: 8 majolica
firing box: 6 saggar, sagger 7 saggard
fragment: 5 shard, sherd
kind: uda(Ind.) 4 delf 5 delft 6 basalt 7 aretine, bocraro 8 bucchero, Majolica, vitreous 9 delftware, sigillate 12 buccheronero
maker: 6 potter 8 ceramist
mineral: 8 feldspar
pert. to: 7 ceramic
pottle: pot 6 basket, liquor 7 tankard
potty: pot 5 crazy, dotty, petty 7 foolish, haughty, trivial 9 eccentric 12 supercilious
pouch: bag, cod, pod, sac 4 cyst, sack 5 bulge, bursa, purse 6 budget, gipser, pocket, sporan 7 alforja, gipsire, mailbag, saccule, silicle, sporran 9 spleuchan 10 pocketbook
Highlander's: 7 sporran
pouch bone: 9 marsupial
pouched: 9 sacculate
dog: 4 wolf
marmot: 8 squirrel 11 spermophile
pouf: 4 bang, puff 7 ottoman 9 hairdress
poule: 6 wanton 10 prostitute
poulp, poulpe: 7 octopus
poultry: 4 fowl 5 ducks, geese 7 pigeons, turkeys 8 chickens 9 pheasants 10 guinea fowl
breed: 6 Ancona 7 Dorking, Leghorn 12 Plymouth Rock 14 Rhode-Island Red
dealer: 6 eggler
disease: pip 4 roup
dish: 9 galantine
farm: 7 hennery
yard: 6 barton
pounamu: 4 jade 8 nephrite 10 greenstone
pounce: nab 4 leap, pink, poke, stab 5 pound, prick, punch, stamp, swoop, talon 6 emboss, spring, thrust 8 ornament 9 comminute, perforate
pound: lb. 4 beat, bray, ding, maul, pond, tamp, unit 5 knock, thump 6 bruise, hammer, powder, weight 7 contuse 9 enclosure, pulverize
poundage: 6 charge, weight 8 distrain 9 constrain, enclosure 11 confinement
pounder: 6 pestle
pour: 4 emit, flow, gush, hale, lave, pass, rain, teem, tide, toom(Sc.), vent, well 5

birle, drain, empty, heald, hield, issue, spout, utter **6** affuse, decant, effuse, libate, stream **8** downpour **9** discharge
pourboire: fee, tip **7** douceur **8** gratuity **9** buona-mani(pl.), buona-mano
pout: bib, mop **4** moue, sulk **5** boody, pique **7** catfish, eelpout **8** bullhead **9** sulkiness
poverty: **4** lack, need, want **6** dearth, penury **7** paucity, tenuity **9** indigence **10** inadequacy, scantiness **11** destitution, inferiority
powder: **4** abir(Ind.), dust, kish, mull, talc **5** boral, boron, flour, grind **6** empasm, pollen, pounce, yttria **7** araroba, aristol, malarin, saponin, tripoli **8** cosmetic, sprinkle, tannigen **9** pulverize **10** epiplastic
case: **9** bandolier
container: **4** horn **7** arsenal **8** magazine
make: **4** bray **5** grind **7** calcine **9** pulverize
smokeless: **6** filite, poudre **7** cordite **8** amberite
powdered: **4** seme **5** semee **6** floury
power: arm, art, vis **4** bulk, dint, gift, hand, iron, rial, sway, thew **5** force, might, state, steam, vigor, vires(pl.), wield **6** agency, effort, empire, energy, foison, throne **7** ability, command, control, potence, potency, stamina **8** capacity, efficacy, momentum, strength, virility **9** authority, dominator, influence, intensity, puissance **10** domination, efficiency **12** jurisdiction, potentiality
comb. form: **4** dyna
deprive of: **4** maim **7** impeach **8** dethrone **12** deparliament
intellectual: wit **5** brain **6** genius
lack: **5** atony
natural: od **4** odyl **5** odyle
partnership: **9** champerty
provide with: **5** endue, endow
superior: **10** prepotency **12** predominance
symbol: **5** sword **7** scepter, sceptre
third: **4** cube
unit of: HP; RPM **4** watt
unlimited: **11** omnipotence
power of attorney: **5** agent **10** procurator
powerboat: **5** yacht **9** motorboat
powerful: **4** able, bold, deep **5** stout **6** brawny, cogent, heroic **7** feckful, leonine **9** effective, effectual **10** dominating **11** efficacious
powerless: **4** weak **6** feeble, unable **8** helpless, impotent, lifeless
Powhatan: *daughter:* **10** Pocahontas
pownie: **4** pony
powwow: **6** confer, priest **7** meeting **8** assembly, ceremony, congress, conjurer **10** conference
poyou: **6** peludo **9** armadillo
praam: **4** pram
prabble: **7** quarrel **8** squabble
prabhu: **4** lord **5** chief **6** writer
practic: **6** artful, shrewd **7** cunning **8** decision(Sc.) **9** practical, practiced
practical: **5** utile **6** actual, beaten, usable, useful **7** practic, working **8** feasible, possible, workable **9** available, practiced, pragmatic **11** pragmatical, utilitarian
example: **6** praxis
joke: **4** hoax **5** prank, trick
practically: **6** almost, nearly **9** virtually **13** substantially
practice: do; ply, rut, try, use **4** plot, rote **5** apply, canon, cause, drill, habit, trade, train, usage **6** custom, follow, praxic **7** perform **8** exercise, intrigue, rehearse **9** construct, negotiate **10** experience
pert. to: **9** pragmatic
sharp: **4** game **5** dodge, fraud, usury **6** deceit **9** chicanery
practiced: **7** practic, skilled, veteran **10** conversant
practico: **5** guide **7** skilled **11** experienced
practitioner: **5** agent **6** artist, healer, novice **7** learner, plotter, schemer **8** civilian **9** assistant
prad: **5** horse
praenomen: **4** name **5** Caius, Gaius, Titus **9** first-name
pragmatic: **7** skilled **8** dogmatic, meddling **9** conceited, empirical, officious, practical **10** meddlesome, systematic **11** dictatorial, opinionated, pragmatical
Prague: **4** Prag **5** Praha
river: **6** Moldau, Vltava
prairie: bay **5** camas, llano, plain **6** camass, cammas, steppe **7** quamash **9** grassland **10** prairillon
clump of trees in: **5** motte
mud: **5** gumbo
plant: **5** camas **6** camass
prairie anemone: **12** pasqueflower
prairie antelope: **9** pronghorn
prairie apple: **9** breadroot
prairie berry: **9** trompillo
prairie breaker: **4** plow
prairie chicken: **6** grouse
prairie crocus: **12** pasqueflower
prairie dog: **6** marmot **11** wishton-wish
prairie dog weed: **8** marigold
prairie pigeon: **6** plover **9** sandpiper
prairie potato: **9** breadroot
prairie schooner: ark **5** wagon
Prairie State: **8** Illinois
prairie wolf: **6** coyote
prairieweed: **10** cinquefoil
praise: **4** hery, laud, tout **5** adore, allow, alose, bless, extol, glory, honor, kudos, roosa, roose **6** eulogy, extoll, kudize **7** ac-

claim, adulate, applaud, commend, encomia(pl.), glorify, hosanna, magnify, plaudit, tribute 8 applause, appraise, blessing, encomium, eulogize, macarism 9 adulation, celebrate, panegyric 10 compliment, panegyrize 11 approbation 12 commendation 13 glorification
ascription of: 6 Gloria
praiseworthy: 9 exemplary 13 complimentary
praising: 9 laudative
Prakrit: 7 Bahlika 8 language 11 Dakshinatya
praline: 5 candy 10 confection
pram, praam: 4 boat, cart 5 barge 8 carriage, stroller 12 perambulator
prana: 9 principle
prance: 5 brank, caper, dance, strut 6 cavort, frolic 7 swagger
prancer: 5 horse, rider
prandium: 4 meal 6 dinner, repast
prank: jig 4 dido, fold, lark, prat 5 adorn, antic, caper, freak, pleat, shine, trick 6 curvet, fegary, frolic, gambol 8 capricci(pl.), escapade, mischief 9 capriccio 11 monkeyshine
prase: 6 quartz 10 chalcedony
prat: 4 push 5 nudge, prank, trick
prate: gab 4 blab, buck, bukh, carp, chat, talk 5 blate, boast, clack, clash 6 babble, claver, tattle, tongue 7 blatter, chatter, deblate, prattle, twaddle 8 harangue 11 deblaterate
prattle: 4 gaff, lisp 5 prate 6 cackle 7 blather, blether, clatter 9 bavardage 11 confabulate
prawn: 10 crustacean
praxis: 6 action, custom 8 practice
pray: ask, beg, bid, sue 5 daven(Heb.) 6 appeal, invite, invoke 7 beseech, conjure, entreat, implore, request 8 petition 10 supplicate
praya: 4 road 5 beach 6 strand 9 esplanade 10 waterfront
prayer: ave 4 bead, bede, bene, boon, plea, suit 5 grace, matin 6 appeal, ectene, ektene, errand, orison 7 Angelus, bidding, collect, complin, gayatri, oration, request, savitri 8 compline, entreaty, petition 9 competory, precation 10 paratheses(pl.), parathesis, requiescat 11 benediction, paternoster 12 intercession, supplication
call: 4 adan, azan, bell 5 chime 6 oremus
chancery: 7 relator
day's last: 7 complin 8 compline
form of: 5 chant 6 litany
group: 12 comprecation
nine-day: 6 novena
set: 9 akoluthia
short: 5 grace 11 benediction
prayer bead: 6 rosary
prayer book: 6 missal, portas, ritual 7 brevary, portass 9 porthouse
prayer desk: 8 prie-dieu
prayer rug: 5 asana
prayer shawl: 5 orale 7 tallith
prayer tower: 7 minaret
praying figure: 5 orant
preach: 4 sugh 5 sough, teach 6 exhort, inform 8 advocate, homilize, instruct, moralize, proclaim 9 discourse, predicate, sermonize 10 concionate
preacher: 6 parson, rector 8 minister 9 clergyman, predicant, pulpiteer
preachment: 6 sermon 7 lecture 9 discourse 11 exhortation
preachy: 8 didactic 10 moralistic
preamble: 7 preface
preannounced: 10 annunciate
prebend: 4 land 7 stipend 9 allowance
prebendary: 5 canon
precarious: 5 risky 7 assumed, dubious 8 insecure, perilous, unstable 9 dangerous, hazardous, uncertain, unsettled 11 unwarranted
precative: 10 beseeching 12 supplicating
precaution: 4 care 6 cautel 7 caution
precede: 4 lead 5 usher 6 forego 7 forerun, predate, preface 8 antecede, antedate 9 introduce
precedence: pas 8 priority
right: pas
precedent: 5 model, usage 7 example 8 decision, standard
preceding: 5 first 8 anterior
precentor: 6 cantor
precept: law 4 hest, rule, tora, writ 5 adage, axiom, breve, brief, maxim, order, sutra, torah 6 lesson 7 caution, command, mandate 8 doctrine, document, teaching 9 direction, principle 10 injunction 11 commandment, instruction
preceptive: 8 didactic 9 mandatory 11 instructive
preceptor: 5 tutor
precinct: 5 ambit, bound 6 hieron 7 temenos 8 boundary, district, environs 9 enclosure
precious: 4 dear, rare, very 5 chere(F.), loved 6 costly, valued 7 beloved 8 affected, esteemed, valuable 9 extremely 10 fastidious 11 overrefined
precious stone: See **gem**
precipice: lin 4 crag, drop, linn, pali, scar 5 bluff, brink, cliff, steep 7 clogwyn 8 downfall 9 declivity
precipitate: 4 fall, floc, hurl, rash 5 hasty, heady, hurry, speed, throw 6 abrupt, has-

ten, sudden, tumble, unwary 8 headlong, settling, slapdash 9 desperate, impetuous, impulsive 11 precipitous

precipitation: dew 4 hail, mist, rain, snow 5 haste, sleet 8 downpour 9 hastening 10 deposition 11 impetuosity 12 acceleration

precipitous: 5 sheer, steep 6 steepy 7 prerupt 11 precipitate

rock: 4 crag, scar 5 steep

precis: 7 epitome, summary 8 abstract 11 abridgement

precise: 4 even, nice, prim 5 exact, stiff 6 formal, minute, strict 7 buckram, certain, correct, finicky, literal, starchy 8 accurate, definite, delicate, explicit, overnice, priggish 9 faultless, veracious 10 ceremonial, fastidious, particular, scrupulous 11 ceremonious, painstaking, punctilious 14 circumstantial

preclude: bar 4 stop 5 avert, close, debar, estop 6 forbid, hinder, impede 7 obviate, prevent 9 foreclose

precocious: 6 unripe 7 forward 9 premature

preconceive: 5 dream 6 ideate, scheme 8 foreknow

precursor: 6 herald 8 ancestor, foregoer 9 harbinger, messenger 10 forefather, forerunner 11 predecessor

precursory: 11 preliminary, premonitory 12 introductory

predatory: 7 robbing 9 pillaging, piratical, rapacious, raptorial 10 plundering, predacious

bird: owl 4 hawk 5 eagle

insect: 6 mantis

predestine: 4 doom, fate 6 decree, ordain 7 destine, predoom 8 foredoom 9 determine, forepoint, preordain 10 foreordain 11 foredestine 12 predetermine

predetermine: 4 bias 6 decree 7 destine, predict 8 forecast 9 prejudice 10 prepossess

predicament: fix 4 hole, stew 5 state 6 pickle, plight, scrape 7 dilemma 8 quandary 9 condition, situation

predicant: 5 friar 8 preacher 9 dominican

predicate: cry 4 aver 5 imply 6 affirm, assert, preach 7 commend, declare, foresee, involve, predict 8 foretell, proclaim

predict: 4 bode, dope, omen 5 augur, weird 6 divine, halsen 7 forbode, presage 8 forebode, forecast, prophesy, soothsay 9 auspicate, predicate 13 prognosticate

prediction: 5 weird 7 bodword 12 forespeaking, vaticination

predictor: 4 seer

predilection: 4 bent, bias 8 fondness, tendency 9 prejudice 10 partiality, preference, propensity 11 inclination 14 predisposition, susceptibility

predisposed: 5 prone 6 biased 7 partial

predisposition: 12 predilection

predominant: 6 ruling 8 dominant, reigning, superior 9 ascendant, ascendent, hegemonic, prevalent 10 dominating, noticeable, prevailing 11 controlling, outstanding 12 preponderant

predominate: 6 domine, exceed 8 domineer

pree: try 5 taste 6 sample

preeminent: big 4 star 5 grand 7 capital, palmary, ranking, supreme 8 dominant, superior 9 excellent, prominent 10 surpassing 11 outstanding

preempt: 5 usurp 9 establish 10 monopolize 11 appropriate

preen: pin, sew 4 perk, trim 5 adorn, clasp, dress, plume, press, primp, prink, prune 6 bodkin, brooch, smooth, spruce, stitch

preface: 5 front, proem 6 herald 7 forerun, precede, prelude 8 exordium, foreword, preamble, prologue 9 introduce 11 preliminary 12 forespeaking, introduction, introductory

prefect, praefect: 4 dean 7 monitor, officer 8 director, minister, official 9 president 10 magistrate

prefecture: 7 eparchy(Gr.) 8 district

prefer: opt 4 like 5 elect, favor 6 desire, favour, rather, select

preferable: 6 better

preference: 6 choice 8 appetite, priority 11 alternative 12 predilection

prefigure: 4 type 6 ideate, typify 7 forerun 8 foretell 10 foreshadow

prefix (see also **combining form, suffix**): For all definitions beginning with this word, look under main word or phrase. EXAMPLES: "prefix for two": see **two:** *prefix;* "prefix for within": see **within:** *prefix.*

pregnable: 10 assailable, expugnable, vulnerable 11 conquerable

pregnancy: 6 cyesis

pregnant: big 5 heavy 6 gravid 7 fertile, teeming, weighty 8 enceinte, fruitful, prolific 9 abounding, gestating, potential 10 germinable

prehend: 5 seize

prehistoric: 10 immemorial

preindicate: 7 presage 8 prophesy

prejudice: 4 bent, bias, harm, hurt 6 damage, hatred, impair 7 bigotry 9 suspicion 10 partiality, prepossess 11 inclination, intolerance 12 disadvantage, predetermine, predilection, prejudgement 13 prejudication

prejudicial: 8 contrary 9 injurious 11 contrarious, detrimental

prelate: 4 head 5 chief 6 abbess, bishop, priest 7 primate 8 superior 9 dignitary 10 archbishop 12 ecclesiastic

prelector: 6 reader 8 lecturer 9 professor 10 discourser, praelector

preliminary: 5 prior 7 preface 8 entrance, previous, proemial 9 prefatory, threshold 10 antecedent 11 preparatory

prelude: 6 verset 7 descant, intrada, opening, preface 8 overture, ritornel 10 ritornelle 12 introduction

premature: 6 unripe 8 immature, untimely 10 precocious 12 unseasonable

premeditate: See **meditate**

premeditation: 11 forethought 12 aforethought

premier: 5 chief 7 leading 8 earliest, foremost 9 principal

premise: 6 ground 9 postulate 10 assumption 11 proposition

premium: 4 agio 5 bonus, prize, spiff 6 bounty, deport, reward 8 lagnappe 9 lagniappe 10 recompense

premonition: 4 omen 5 hunch 6 notice 7 bodword, warning 9 forescent 10 foreboding 11 forewarning, information 12 apprehension, presentiment

preoccupied: 4 lost, rapt 6 absent, filled 8 absorbed 9 engrossed

preordain: 10 predestine

preparation: 5 array 7 extract, product 8 cosmetic 9 condiment, decoction 10 confection 11 arrangement 12 introduction

place of: 10 laboratory, paratorium

without: 5 ad lib 8 careless 9 impromptu

prepare: arm, fit, fix, get, set 4 bush, busk, gibe, gird, make, pave, suit, tibe 5 adapt, alert, coach, curry, dight, equip, ettle, frame, groom, prime, ready, train 6 adjust, devise, graith 7 address, affaite(F.), apparel, arrange, concoct, confect, dispose, furnish, provide, qualify 8 accustom, compound, instruct, rehearse 9 calculate, condition, construct 10 concinnate

for the press: 4 edit 6 redact, revise

prepared: apt 4 yare

prepaschal period: 4 Lent

prepense: 8 designed 11 forethought 12 aforethought, premeditated

preponderance: 6 weight 9 dominance 10 ascendancy, ascendency, prevalence 12 predominance

preponderate: 4 sink 7 incline, surpass

prepose: 6 prefix 7 preface

preposition: at, by, in, on, to, up; but, for, off, out, tae(Sc.) 4 from, into, onto, over, unto, upon, with 5 about

prepossess: 12 predetermine

prepossessing: 10 attractive

prepossession: 4 bent, bias 9 prejudice 10 absorption 11 inclination 12 predilection 14 predisposition

preposterous: 6 absurd, screwy 7 foolish 9 grotesque, senseless 10 irrational, ridiculous 11 nonsensical

prerequisite: 9 postulate

prerogative: 5 right 7 apanage 8 appanage, appenage, priority 9 privilege 10 precedence

eldest son's: 6 esnecy

prerupt: 11 precipitous

presage: 4 bode, omen, osse, sign 5 augur, token 6 augury, betide, divine, import 7 betoken, forbode, meaning, portend, portent, predict, warning 8 forebode, foretell, prophecy, prophesy 9 foretoken, harbinger 10 foreboding, prediction, prognostic 11 foreknowing, preindicate 12 apprehension, presentiment 13 prognosticate

presbyter: 5 elder 6 priest 7 prester 8 minister 9 clergyman

presbytery: 5 court 7 council, rectory 9 residence

prescience: 9 foresight 11 omniscience 13 foreknowledge

prescind: 6 detach 7 isolate 8 abstract, separate

prescribe: set 5 allot, guide, limit, order 6 define, direct, ordain, outlaw 7 appoint, command, control, dictate 9 prescript 10 invalidate

prescribed: 6 thetic

prescript: 9 prescribe

prescription: rx 6 recipe

presence: 4 mien 5 being 6 spirit 7 bearing, company, dignity, spectre 8 assembly 9 influence 10 apparition, attendance, deportment

prefix: oxy

present: now 4 boon, gift, give, here 5 adsum(L.), being, bonus, cuddy, grant, nonce, offer, ready, today 6 adduce, allege, bestow, bounty, confer, donate, render, tender 7 cumshaw, display, exhibit, largess, perform 8 donation, gratuity, lagnappe 9 collected, introduce, lagniappe, personate 10 exhibition 11 benefaction, efficacious

again: 5 rerun

pert. to: 6 modern 7 current 12 contemporary

to guest or stranger: 6 xenium

with another: 8 collocal

present-day: 7 current 12 contemporary

presentiment: 10 foreboding 11 premonition 12 apprehension

presently: 4 anon, enow, soon 7 shortly 8 directly 9 forthwith 11 immediately
preservation: 11 safekeeping
preservative: 4 salt 5 spice 7 alcohol, vinegar 8 creosote 12 conservative
preserve: can, dry, jam, tin 4 corn, cure, keep, salt, save 5 bless, guard, jelly, spare, store, uvate 6 athold, comfit, defend, govern, retain, secure, shield, uphold 7 compote, condite, confect, forfend, protect, succade, sustain 8 conserve, forefend, maintain 9 confiture, safeguard
preside: 6 direct 7 control 8 moderate, regulate
president: mir 4 head 5 ruler 8 governor 9 sovereign
successor: 9 designado(Mex.)
President (U.S.): (1, 1789-97) George Washington; (2, 1797-1801) John Adams; (3, 1801-09) Thomas Jefferson; (4, 1809-17) James Madison; (5, 1817-25) James Monroe; (6, 1825-29) John Quincy Adams; (7, 1829-37) Andrew Jackson; (8, 1837-41) Martin Van Buren; (9, 1841) William Henry Harrison; (10, 1841-45) John Tyler; (11, 1845-49) James K. Polk; (12, 1849-50) Zachary Taylor; (13, 1850-53) Millard Fillmore; (14, 1853-57) Franklin Pierce; (15, 1857-61) James Buchanan; (16, 1861-65) Abraham Lincoln; (17, 1865-69) Andrew Johnson; (18, 1869-77) Ulysses S. Grant; (19, 1877-81) Rutherford B. Hayes; (20, 1881) James A. Garfield; (21, 1881-85) Chester A. Arthur; (22, 1885-89) Grover Cleveland; (23, 1889-93) Benjamin Harrison; (24, 1893-97) Grover Cleveland; (25, 1897-1901) William McKinley; (26, 1901-09) Theodore Roosevelt; (27, 1909-13) William H. Taft; (28, 1913-21) Woodrow Wilson; (29, 1921-23) Warren G. Harding; (30, 1923-29) Calvin Coolidge; (31, 1929-33) Herbert Hoover; (32, 1933-1945) Franklin D. Roosevelt; (33, 1945-1953) Harry S. Truman; (34, 1953-1961) Dwight D. Eisenhower; (35, 1961-1963) John F. Kennedy; (36, 1963-1969) Lyndon B. Johnson; (37, 1969-1974) Richard M. Nixon; (38, 1974-1977) Gerald R. Ford; (39, 1977-) Jimmy Carter
last name: 4 Ford, Polk, Taft 5 Adams, Grant, Hayes, Nixon, Tyler 6 Arthur, Carter, Hoover, Monroe, Pierce, Taylor, Truman, Wilson 7 Harding, Jackson, Johnson, Kennedy, Lincoln, Madison 8 Buchanan, Coolidge, Fillmore, Garfield, Harrison, McKinley, Van Buren 9 Cleveland, Jefferson, Roosevelt 10 Eisenhower, Washington
nickname: Abe, Cal, Ike 5 Teddy
presignify: 7 presage 8 intimate 9 foretoken
press: hug 4 bale, bear, bind, cram, dint, iron, mash, spur, thew, urge 5 brize, brizz, chest, chirt, crowd, crush, drive, force, knead, preen, serry, wring 6 compel, crunch, impact, roller, smooth, throng 7 armoire, embrace, entreat, flatten, impress, imprint, scrunge, smasher, squeeze 8 calender, compress, straiten, wardrobe 9 constrain, embarrass, emphasize, importune 10 constipate, newspapers
corrector: 11 proofreader
critic: 6 censor
press down: 4 tamp
pressed: 5 dense 7 compact, serried
presser: 5 baler 6 ironer, mangle
of skins: 7 sammier
pressing: 6 urgent 7 exigent 8 exacting 9 imperious 10 imperative 11 importunate
pressman: 7 printer
pressure: 4 heat, push 5 force 6 duress, stress 7 bearing, squeeze 8 exigency, instancy 10 affliction, constraint, impression, oppression 11 compression
equal: 8 isobaric
gauge: 9 manometer, manoscope
unit: 4 atmo, dyne 5 barad 7 mesobar
pressure group: 5 lobby
pressure measuring instrument: 10 piezometer
prest: 4 duty, loan 7 advance, pressed
prester: 4 vein 5 snake 6 priest 7 serpent 9 hurricane, presbyter, whirlwind
prestidigitator: 6 palmer 7 juggler 8 conjurer, magician
prestige: 6 renown 7 sorcery 8 illusion 9 deception, influence 10 importance, prominence
presto: 7 passing, quickly 8 suddenly 11 immediately 13 instantaneous
presumably: 8 probably 10 ostensibly, supposedly
presume: 5 guess 6 impose 7 daresay, suppose, venture 8 arrogate 9 postulate 10 conjecture, presuppose
presumptuous: 4 bold 5 fresh 7 forward, haughty, icarian 8 arrogant, assuming, familiar, impudent, insolent 9 audacious, confident, foolhardy 11 adventurous, venturesome
presuppose: 6 assume
pretend: act 4 pose, seem, sham 5 claim, feign 6 affect, allege, assume, gammon 7 profess 8 disguise, simulate 11 dissimulate, make-believe
pretended: 4 fake 5 false 7 colored, reputed 8 coloured, intended, proposed 10 fictitious, ostensible
pretender: fop 4 fake, idol, snob 5 cowan(Sc.), faker, quack 6 poseur, seemer 8

aspirant, claimant, deceiver, impostor 9 charlatan 10 mountebank 11 fourflusher 12 dissimulator

pretense, pretence: act, peg 4 brag, cant, flam, plea, ruse, sham, show 5 claim, cloak, cover, feint, gloze, study, trick 6 excuse, humbug, tinsel 7 fiction, grimace, potiche, pretext 8 artifice, occasion 9 deception, moonshine, semblance 10 appearance, assumption, subterfuge 11 affectation, fabrication, make-believe, ostentation 13 stalking-horse

pretentious: big 4 arty 5 gaudy, showy 7 pompous 8 affected, assuming 11 highfaluten, highfalutin 12 highfaluting, ostentatious

pretermit: 4 omit 6 ignore 7 neglect, suspend 8 intermit 9 disregard, interrupt

preternatural: 6 gousty 7 goustie 8 abnormal, uncommon 9 irregular 12 supernatural

pretext: 8 pretense

pretty: gay, toy 4 cute, deft, fair, gent, joli 5 bonny, jolie, lindo(Sp.) 6 bonita, bonito, bonnie, clever, comely 7 dollish 8 betcheri, budgeree 9 beautiful, ingenious 10 attractive, knickknack, moderately

prevail: win 5 reign 6 induce, obtain 7 persist, succeed, triumph 8 dominate 11 predominate

prevail: *upon:* 4 urge 6 allure, induce 7 entreat 8 persuade

prevalent: 4 rife 6 common, potent 7 current, general 8 dominant, powerful 9 extensive 10 prevailing, successful, victorious, widespread 11 efficacious, influential

prevaricate: fib, lie 5 evade 7 quibble, shuffle 10 equivocate

prevarication: 10 subterfuge

prevene: 7 prevent

prevent: bar, gag, let 4 balk, bind, save, stop, warn 5 avert, debar, deter, estop 6 defend, forlet, hinder, impede, resist, thwart 7 forfend, impeach, obviate, prevent 8 antevert, forefend, preclude, prohibit, restrain 9 foreclose, forestall, frustrate 10 anticipate, circumvent
by law: 5 estop

preventive: 12 prophylactic 13 precautionary

previous: ere 4 erst, fore, past 5 prior, supra 6 before, bygone, former 7 earlier 8 anterior, foregone, untimely 9 foregoing, preceding, premature 10 antecedent, beforehand, heretofore 11 unwarranted

prevision: 8 forecast 9 foresight 10 prescience, prevoyance 13 foreknowledge 15 prognostication

prewar: 10 antebellum

prey: 4 feed 5 booty, raven, ravin, seize, spoil 6 quarry, ravage, ravine, victim 7 capture, plunder 9 victimize
living on: 9 predatory

prey upon: 4 feed 5 seize 9 victimize

Priam: *daughter:* 6 Creusa 8 Polyxena 9 Cassandra
grandfather: 4 Ilus
servant: 7 Agelaus
son: 5 Paris 6 Hector 7 Helenus, Troilus 9 Deiphobus, Polydorus
wife: 6 Hecuba

price: fee 4 cost, fare, fiar(Sc.), fier(Sc.), hire, rate 5 cheap, value, worth 6 charge, ransom, reward 7 expense 8 appraise, evaluate 10 estimation, excellence 12 preciousness 13 consideration
maintain: peg
reduced: 4 sale 7 bargain
rising: 4 boom 9 inflation

priceless: 4 rare 6 absurd, costly, unique 7 amusing 8 valuable 10 invaluable 11 inestimable

prick: dot, jag 4 brod, brog, cloy, drob, goad, jagg, ping, pink, prod, stab, tang 5 briar, point, smart, spine, sting, thorn 6 broach, cactus, incite, nettle, pierce, skewer, tingle 7 bramble, pricker, prickle 8 puncture

prick song: 7 descant

pricket: 4 buck 5 spike 11 candlestick

pricking: 8 poignant

prickle: 4 seta 5 setae(pl.), sieve 6 basket 7 acantha, aculeus, spicula(pl.) 8 spiculum

prickly: 5 burry 8 echinate
animal: 8 hedgehog 9 porcupine
plant: 6 cactus, nettle
seed coat: bur 4 burr
shrub: 4 rose 5 briar

prickly heat: 4 rash 8 eruption

prickly pear: 4 tuna 5 nopal 7 opuntia

pride: 5 glory, pique, plume, valor 6 egoism, esteem, spirit, vanity 7 conceit, disdain, egotism, elation, hauteur, respect 8 nobility, splendor, valiancy 9 arrogance, insolence, loftiness 10 lordliness, self-esteem 11 haughtiness, self-conceit, self-respect 12 independence 15 self-approbation 16 superciliousness

Pride and Prejudice: *author:* 6 Austen
character: 5 Darcy 9 Elizabeth

prier, pryer: 10 inquisitor

priest: en; fra 4 abbe, club, cura, cure(F.), imam, lama, papa(It.), pere(F.) 5 clerk, druid, hotar(Ind.), imaum, mulla, padre(Sp.), rabbi, sarip, vicar 6 bhikku, bishop, cleric, dastur, divine, father, gallah(Heb.), mullah, oblate, rector, vestal, wahabi 7 cassock, destour, dustoor, prester, tuhunga, wahabee, wahhabi 8 minister 9 clergyman, dignitary, orato-

rian, priesteen 10 hierophant, priestling 12 ecclesiastic
army: 5 padre 8 chaplain
assistant: 7 acolyte
cap: 7 biretta
garment: alb 4 cope, robe 5 ephod, habit 8 scapular 9 vestments
habit ornament: 4 urim
headdress: 9 saghavart
high: Eli 5 Aaron 7 pontiff
neckpiece: 5 amice, stole
pert. to: 10 sacerdotal
scarf: 5 rabat 7 maniple
server: 7 acolyte
surplice: 5 ephod
voodoo: 5 mambu 6 hungan 7 gangang
priesthood: 9 sacerdocy 11 sacerdotage
priestly: 10 sacerdotal
prig: beg, fop, pan 4 buck 5 dandy, filch, plead, prink, prude, steal, thief 6 haggle, pilfer, purist, tinker 7 bargain, entreat, pitcher 8 pilferer 9 precision 10 pick-pocket
prigger: 5 thief
priggish: 4 prim, smug 8 thievish 11 over-precise
prill: 4 rill 6 button, nugget, pellet, stream
prim: mim, set 4 neat, nice 5 stiff 6 demure, formal, proper 7 correct, precise, prudish 8 accurate, decorous 10 ceremonial
prima donna: 4 diva, lead, star 6 singer 7 actress
famous: 4 Lind 5 Patti 7 Russell 13 Schumann Heink
primary: 4 main 5 chief, first, prime 6 primal 7 capital, central, initial 8 earliest, original, primeval, pristine 9 elemental, primitive, principal 10 elementary, pre-eminent, primordial 11 fundamental
primate: ape, man 5 lemur, orang 6 bishop, monkey 8 marmoset 9 orangutan 10 anthropoid, archbishop 11 orangoutang
prime: 4 size 5 coach 7 prepare, primary 9 copacetic, excellent, undercoat
of life: 5 bloom 6 heyday
prime minister: 7 premier
primer: 8 hornbook, textbook 11 abecedarium
primeval: 6 primal 7 ancient, ogygian 8 original, pristine 9 primitive
primitive: 5 basic, crude, first, rough 6 simple 7 ancient, archaic, primary, priscan, radical 8 barbaric, original, pristine 9 underived 10 aboriginal, antiquated 11 uncivilized 12 old-fashioned
primogenial: 6 primal 7 primary 8 original 9 primitive
primordial: 5 first 7 primary 9 elemental 11 fundamental
primordium: 6 embryo, origin 8 rudiment
primp: 5 adorn, dress, preen, prink
primrose: 5 oxlip, spink(Sc.) 7 cowslip, primula 8 auricula
family: 11 primulaceae
primus: 5 first, stove
prince: bey, ras 4 amir, emir, raja, rial 5 alder, ameer, emeer, ruler 6 despot, dynast, satrap 7 dynasty, monarch 8 archduke 9 potentate, princekin, princelet, sovereign 10 princeling
allowance: 8 appenage
pine: 10 pipsissewa
title: 6 serene
Prince of: *Apostles:* 8 St. Peter
Darkness: 5 devil, Satan 7 Ahriman 9 Beelzebub
Destruction: 6 Timour 9 Tamerlane
Evil Spirits: 7 Sammael
Liars: 5 Pinto
Peace: 7 Messiah
the Ode: 7 Ronsard
the Sonnet: 15 Joachim du Bellay
princedom: 4 rank 11 sovereignty 12 jurisdiction
princely: 5 noble, regal, royal 6 kingly 10 munificent 11 magnificent
princeps: 4 head 5 first, pagus 7 headman
princess: 5 begum(Muslim), ranee (Muslim)
loved by Cupid: 6 Psyche
loved by Zeus: 6 Europa
mythological: 8 Atalanta
Princeton symbol: 5 tiger
principal: top 4 arch, head, high, main, star 5 chief, first, grand, major, prime 6 leader, staple 7 capital, captain, chattel, leading, palmary, primary, stellar 8 cardinal, dominant, foremost 9 important, preceptor 10 headmaster 11 outstanding
comb. form: 4 arch 5 archi
principle: law 4 rule 5 axiom, canon, dicta(pl.), maxim, prana, tenet 6 dictum 7 brocard, essence, precept, theorum 8 doctrine 9 integrity 11 fundamental, uprightness
accepted: 5 axiom
embodiment: 6 avatar
first: 4 base, seed 5 basis 8 rudiment 10 fundamenta(pl.) 11 fundamentum
general: 9 generalia 12 generalities
statement: 5 credo, creed, motto
vital: 4 soul 5 anima
principles: 5 creed
princox: fop 7 coxcomb
prink: 4 deck, perk, wink 5 adorn, dress, preen, primp, prune 6 bedeck, glance

print: 4 copy, film 5 issue, stamp 6 fabric 7 edition, engrave, impress, publish 8 negative 9 engraving, newspaper 10 impression

printer: 4 typo 8 letterer, pressman 11 typographer 12 lithographer
aid: 5 devil
cross stroke: 5 serif 6 ceriph
direction: tr.; cut 6 delete

printing: *block:* 4 wood 7 edition 8 linoleum
blurred appearance: 5 macul
color: 17 chromolithography
error: pi; pie 6 errata(pl.) 7 erratum
form: cut, die, mat 5 frame 6 matrix 7 matrice
implement: 5 biron 6 brayer, dabber, dauber
ink spreader: 6 brayer
mark: 4 dash, dele, list, stet 5 caret, obeli, tilde 6 dagger, diesis, obelus 7 obelisk 8 ellipses
measure: em, en 4 pica 5 agate, empen
metal block: 4 quad
plate: 6 stereo 10 stereotype
press part: 6 platen, roller, rounce 7 frisket
process: 6 offset 7 braille, typeset 8 cerotype 10 photolitho 11 lithography 14 photoengraving
second: 7 reissue
space block: 4 quad
system for the blind: 7 braille
type for spacing: 4 quad, slug

prion: 6 petrel

prionid: 6 beetle

prior: ex; ere 4 fore, past 5 elder 6 before, former 7 earlier 8 anterior, previous 10 antecedent 11 retroactive

priority: 8 position 9 privilege 10 precedence, preference 11 superiority

priory: 5 abbey 7 nunnery 8 cloister 9 monastery, sanctuary

priscan: 7 ancient 9 primitive

prism device: 8 iriscope

prismatic: 9 brilliant 10 iridescent 12 orthorhombic

prison: gib, jug 4 brig, cell, gaol, hell, hole, jail, keep, quod, rock, stir 5 bagne, clink, grate 6 bagnio, carcel, carcer, cooler, lockup 7 Atlanta, Bocardo, college, dungeon, Gehenna, hoosgow, kidcote, Newgate 8 Alcatraz, Bastille, hoosegaw, hoosegow, Sing Sing 9 Bridewell, calaboose, enclosure 10 guardhouse, panopticon 11 Leavenworth 12 penitentiary
guard: 5 screw
keeper: 5 guard 6 gaoler, jailer, jailor, keeper, warden 7 turnkey
naval or ship: 4 brig
room: 4 cell, hole, tank 7 dungeon 8 solitary
sentence: rap
spy: 6 mouton

prisoner: con 5 lifer 6 detenu(F.), inmate 7 caitiff, captive, convict, detenue(F.), parolee 9 collegian 10 emancipist 11 probationer
exchange agreement: 6 cartel

Prisoner of the Vatican: 4 Pope

prisoner of war: PW; P.O.W. 7 kriegie

prissy: 4 prim 5 fussy 7 finicky, precise, prudish 9 sissified 11 over-refined

pristav, pristaw: 8 official, overseer 12 commissioner

pristine: new 4 pure 5 early, fresh 7 ancient, primary 8 original 9 primitive, unspoiled, untouched 11 uncorrupted

pritch: 5 prick, spike, staff 6 pierce

privacy: 7 privity, retreat, secrecy 8 darkness, solitude 9 seclusion 10 penetralia 12 hugger-mugger

privado: 6 friend 8 intimate 9 confidant

private: 6 closet, covert, secret 7 soldier 8 esoteric, homefelt, personal, secluded, solitary 10 unofficial 12 confidential, unpublicized
comb. form: 4 idio

private eye: 6 tailer 9 detective, operative 12 investigator

privateer: 4 Kidd 5 caper 6 pirate 7 corsair, drumler 8 drumbler

privately: 5 aside

privation: 4 loss, want 6 misery 8 hardship 11 deprivation, destitution

privet: 5 hedge, ibota, shrub 7 alatern, ibolium 9 houseleek

privilege: law, soc, use 4 soke 5 favor, grace, grant, right 6 favour, patent 7 charter, liberty 8 easement, immunity 9 advantage, exemption, franchise 10 concession 11 prerogative

privy: wc 4 gong 6 cloaca, hidden, secret, toilet 7 cloacae(pl.), furtive, private 8 familiar, intimate, out-house 9 backhouse, confidant, necessary 11 clandestine, water-closet 12 confidential 13 surreptitious

prix: 5 prize

prize: cup, pry 4 gree(Sc.), prix(F.), tern 5 award, bacon, booty, lever, medal, plate, purse, stake, value 6 esteem, glaive, reward, trophy 7 capture, premium, seizure 8 estimate, leverage, purchase, treasure 10 appreciate

prizefight: go 4 bout 5 match 7 contest
customer demand: K.O.
ring: 5 arena

prized: 4 dear 5 chary

pro: for 8 advocate, favoring 9 favouring 12 professional

probability: 4 odds 6 chance 10 appearance, likelihood, likeliness 11 credibility

probable: 6 likely 8 credible, feasible

probably: 6 belike, likely

probation: 4 test 5 trial 6 parole 9 novitiate 11 examination

probe: 4 acus, tent, test 5 grope, sound 6 pierce, search, seeker, stylet, tracer 7 examine, explore 9 penetrate 10 ankylomele, instrument, scrutinize 11 exploration, investigate 13 investigation

probity: 7 honesty 9 integrity, rectitude 11 uprightness

problem: nut, sum 4 crux, knot 5 hydra, poser 6 enigma, riddle 8 question 9 situation

problematical: 8 doubtful 9 ambiguous, equivocal, uncertain, unsettled 12 questionable

proboscis: 4 nose 5 snout, trunk

proboscis monkey: 4 kaha

procacious: 4 pert 8 impudent, insolent, petulant

Procas' son: 7 Amulius, Numitor

procavia: 5 hyrax 10 hyracoidea

procedure: 6 tactic 7 process, program, routine

proceed: go 4 fand, fare, move, pass, wend 5 arise, frame, issue 6 derive 7 advance, emanate, forthgo 8 continue, progress 9 originate

laboriously: mog 4 plod, plow, slog, wade 6 trudge

rapidly: run 5 speed 6 gallop

proceeding: 4 acta(pl.), step 5 actum, doing 6 affair, afflux, course 7 conduct, measure 9 affluxion, procedure 11 transaction

proceeds: 4 loot 5 booty 6 income, profit, return 8 stealage

procerity: 6 height 8 tallness

process: 4 cook, writ 5 lapse, order 6 capias, course, manner, method, notice, system 7 advance, mandate, summons 8 progress 9 operation, procedure, sterilize 10 injunction

procession: 4 file 5 march 6 course, exequy, litany, parade 7 cortege, pageant 9 cavalcade, formation, recession

prochein: 4 next 7 nearest

proclaim: bid, cry 4 call, deem, toot, tout 5 blare, blast, blaze, claim, grede, knell, voice 6 blazon, bounce, defame, herald, indict, outcry, preach 7 declare, divulge, enounce, publish 8 announce, denounce, forspeak 9 advertise, celebrate, enunciate, forespeak 10 promulgate

proclamation: ban 4 bans, fiat 5 bando(Sp.), banns, blaze, edict, ukase 6 notice 7 bidding, placard 9 manifesto 11 publication 12 announcement, annunciation, denunciation, notification, promulgation

proclivity: 4 bent 6 talent 7 leaning 10 propensity 11 disposition, inclination

Procne: *husband:* 6 Tereus

sister: 9 Philomela

procrastination: 5 delay, stall 9 deferment 10 cunctation, inactivity 12 dilatoriness, postponement

procreant: 8 fruitful 9 producing 10 generating

procreate: 4 sire 5 beget 7 produce 8 engender, generate

procreation: 8 virility 9 offspring 10 generation, production

Procris: *father:* 10 Erechtheus

husband: 8 Cephalus

proctor: 5 agent, proxy 6 patron 7 steward 8 advocate, attorney

procumbent: 5 prone

procurable: 10 accessible

procure: get 4 fang, find, gain 5 bring 6 effect, obtain, secure, suborn 7 acquire, chevise, receive 8 contrive 9 impetrate

procurer: 4 bawd, pimp

procuress: 4 bawd, hack 7 commode

prod: egg, jab 4 brog, goad, poke, urge 6 incite, thrust

prodigal: 5 flush 6 lavish 7 liberal, profuse, spender, wastrel 8 abundant, generous, wasteful 10 profligate, squanderer 11 extravagant, spendthrift, squandering

prodigious: 4 huge 5 giant 7 amazing, immense 8 enormous, gigantic 9 marvelous, monstrous, wonderful 10 portentous, tremendous 11 astonishing 13 extraordinary

prodigy: 4 omen, sign 6 marvel, ostent, wonder 7 miracle, portent 8 ceremony

prodition: 7 treason 8 betrayal 15 treacherousness

prodrome: 7 symptom

produce: do 4 bear, form, make, show 5 breed, carry, cause, shape, stage, yield 6 create, effect, fruits 7 exhibit 8 engender, generate 9 fabricate, offspring 10 production, vegetables 11 manufacture

new: 6 create, invent 9 originate

producer: 6 author, farmer, grower, parent 7 creator 8 director 12 manufacturer

product: 4 item 5 fruit 6 number, result 9 offspring, outgrowth

production: 4 work 5 fruit 6 output 11 performance

productive: 4 rich 6 active, parous 7 fertile 8 creative, fruitful, sonorous 10 generative 11 originative

proem: 7 preface, prelude 8 foreword, overture, preamble 12 introduction

profanation: 9 sacrilege
profane: hoa 4 foul 5 abuse 6 debase, defile, defoil, defoul, unholy, vulgar, wicked 7 godless, impious, obscene, secular, ungodly, violate, worldly 8 temporal 9 desecrate, vulgarize 10 irreverent, unhallowed 11 blasphemous 12 unsanctified
profanity: 4 oath 5 curse 9 blasphemy
profess: own 4 avow 5 admit, claim 6 affect, affirm, allege 7 confess, declare, protest 8 proclaim 11 acknowledge
professed: 9 pretended 10 ostensible
profession: art 5 craft, faith, forte, trade 6 avowal, career, metier(F.) 7 calling 8 function, vocation 9 following 10 employment, occupation
professional: pro 4 paid 5 hired 6 expert 7 artiste, skilled, trained 8 finished
professor: don, fly 7 teacher
proffer: bid 4 give, hand 5 offer 6 extend, tender 11 countenance
proficiency: 5 skill 7 ability, aptness 9 adeptness 10 capability, competence, efficiency, expertness 14 accomplishment
proficient: 6 actual, versed 9 effective, effectual 10 conversant
profile: 4 form 6 figure 7 contour, drawing, outline 10 silhouette 14 representation
profit: net, pay, use 4 boot, gain, good, help, mend, nett 5 avail, frame, lucre, melon 6 behoof, return 7 account, benefit, bestead, revenue, utility 8 increase, interest 9 advantage, emolument 12 remuneration
receiver of: 6 pernor
profitable: fat 8 repaying 9 expedient
profitless: 9 fruitless 12 unprofitable
profligate: 6 rioter 7 corrupt, riotous, spender, vicious, wastrel 8 depraved, flagrant, prodigal, rakehell, wasteful 9 abandoned, dissolute, reprobate 10 licentious 11 extravagant
profound: low 4 deep, sage, wise 5 heavy 7 abysmal, intense 8 abstruse, unbroken 9 recondite, sagacious 10 acroamatic, exhaustive 11 far-reaching 12 unfathomable
profuse: 4 lush 5 frank 6 galore, hearty, lavish 7 copious, liberal 8 abundant, generous, prodigal, wasteful 9 bountiful, exuberant, luxuriant, plentiful 10 munificent 11 extravagant, overflowing
profusion: 6 galore 8 opulence 9 affluence 11 prodigality
prog: 4 food 5 prick, prowl, tramp 6 forage 7 vagrant 8 supplies 9 provender
progenitor: 4 sire 6 parent 8 ancestor 10 forefather, foreparent, forerunner
progeny: imp, son 4 race, seed 5 breed, brood, brook, child, issue, scion, shoot 6 family, strain 8 children, daughter 9 genealogy, offspring 10 generation 11 descendants
prognostic: 4 omen, sign 5 token
prognosticate: 4 bode 5 augur 6 divine 7 betoken, forbode, forerun, portend, predict, presage 8 forebode, forecast, foreshow, foretell, prophesy 9 foretoken, hariolate
prognosticator: 4 seer 5 augur 6 divine 7 augurer, diviner, prophet 9 predictor 10 soothsayer
program: 4 card, list, show 5 draft, edict 6 agenda, notice 7 agendum, catalog, outline 8 bulletin, playbill, schedule, syllabus 9 broadcast 10 prospectus 12 proclamation
programma: 5 edict 6 decree 7 preface 12 prolegomenon
progress: 4 fare, flow, grow, tour, wend 5 march 6 course, growth, motion 7 advance, circuit, develop, headway, improve, journey, proceed 10 betterment, expedition 11 development, furtherance, improvement
planned: 7 telesia, telesis
progression: 5 stage 8 sequence 10 succession
progressive: 6 active, onward 7 forward, liberal 9 advancing, ascensive 12 enterprising
prohibit: ban, bar, bid 4 stop, veto 5 debar, estop, fence 6 defend, enjoin, forbid, hinder, outlaw 7 forfend, forwarn, prevent 8 disallow, forefend 9 interdict, proscribe 11 countermand
prohibited: 4 tabu 5 taboo 7 illegal, illicit 8 unlawful, verboten(G.)
prohibiting: 8 vetitive
prohibition: ban, nay 4 veto 7 embargo 8 estoppel 12 interdiction
prohibitionist: dry
project: jet, jut, lap 4 abut, apse, barb, butt, game, idea, plan, send, task 5 filip, shoot 6 beetle, design, device, fillip, scheme 7 extrude, imagine, pattern, problem 8 contrive, proposal, protrude 9 intention 10 enterprise 11 contrivance, proposition, undertaking
projectile: 4 bomb, dart, rock, shot 5 arrow, shell 6 bullet, rocket 7 missile, torpedo 8 shrapnel 9 cartridge
curve: 8 parabola
pert. to: 9 ballistic
projecting: 6 beetle 7 salient
projection: arm, cam, ell, hob, hub, jag, lee, lug, toe 4 apse, barb, croc, fang, lobe 5 bulge, crena, redan, socle, tenon, tooth 6 corbel, crenae(pl.), dormer, lobule, tappet 7 cornice, empathy 8 abutment, ejection,

eminence 9 crenation 10 protrusion 12 protuberance
projector: 8 bioscope 13 cinematograph, kinematograph
projet: 4 plan 5 draft
prolapse: 7 falling
prolate: 9 elongated
opposite of: 6 oblate
proletarian: 4 mean, rude 6 coarse, vulgar 7 laborer, working
prolific: 6 birthy, fecund 7 fertile, teeming 8 fruitful 9 abounding, plentiful 10 generative 11 propagative 12 reproductive
prolix: 5 wordy 7 diffuse, prosaic, tedious, verbose 8 tiresome 9 prolonged, wearisome 10 longwinded, protracted 11 displeasing 13 uninteresting
prolocutor: 6 orator 7 speaker 8 advocate, chairman 9 spokesman 10 mouthpiece
prolong: 5 defer 6 extend 8 continue, lengthen
prolonged: 5 great 6 prolix 7 chronic, delayed, dilated 8 extended 9 continued, postponed, sostenuto, sustained 10 lengthened, protracted
prom: 4 ball 5 dance
promenade: 4 deck, hall, mall, walk 5 prado(Sp.) 6 avenue, marina, parade, pasear(Sp.) 7 alameda, gallery 9 boardwalk, esplanade
Prometheus: *father:* 7 Iapetus
gift to man: 4 fire
mother: 7 Clymene
promethium symbol: Pm
prominence: 4 cusp 5 agger 8 eminence, prestige, salience 10 colliculus, promontory 11 distinction
prominent: 5 chief 6 marked, signal 7 capital, eminent, notable, obvious, salient 8 aquiline, manifest 9 egregious 10 celebrated, noticeable, projecting 11 conspicuous, distinctive 13 distinguished
promise: vow 4 band, hest, hote, oath, osse, sure, word 5 agree, grant, hight 6 assure, behest, engage, parole, pledge, plight 7 behight, betroth, fianced 8 affiance, contract, covenant 9 assurance, betrothal, foretoken 10 convenable, engagement, obligation 11 declaration
oral stipulation: 6 cautio 9 cautiones(pl.)
Promised Land: 6 Canaan
promissory note: I.O.U. 5 check 6 pledge
promontory: hoe 4 bill, cape, head, mull, nase, naze, ness, peak, scaw, skaw, spit 5 mount, point 8 headland 10 projection, prominence
promote: aid 4 help 5 boost, exalt, nurse, raise, speed 6 better, foster, prefer 7 advance, dignify, elevate, forward, further 9 advantage, encourage, patronize 10 aggrandize
promoter: 5 agent 7 abetter, abettor, booster, hustler 8 broacher, lobbyist
promotion: 6 brevet 7 advance 10 graduation, preferment 11 advancement, furtherance
prompt: apt, cue 4 move, yare(Sc.) 5 alert, quick, ready, yeder 6 active, assist, excite, nimble, remind 7 animate, forward 8 punctual 11 expeditious
prompter: aid 4 cuer 7 readier
promptly: 4 soon, tite(Sc.) 8 directly
promptness: 8 alacrity, dispatch
promulgate: 7 declare, publish 8 announce, proclaim 9 advertise
prone: apt 4 bent, flat 5 buxom 6 agroof, agrufe, agruif, supine 7 passive 8 addicted, disposed, inclined, pronated 9 declivous, groveling, prostrate, recumbent 10 decubitous
prong: nib, peg 4 fang, fork, horn, tine 5 point, tooth 6 branch
prongbuck: 9 pronghorn, springbok
prong key: 7 spanner
pronghorn: 4 deer 6 cabree, cabret, cabrie, cabrit 8 berrendo
pronoun: he, it, me, my, we, ye; any, her, him, his, its, one, our, she, thy, you 4 mine, ours, that, thee, them, they, this, thou, your 5 their, these, thine, those 6 itself, myself 7 herself, himself, oneself, ourself 8 yourself 9 ourselves 10 themselves, yourselves
demonstrative: 4 that, this 5 these, those
interrogative: who 4 whom 5 whose
substantive: who 7 whoever 9 whosoever
pronounce: 4 pass 5 speak, utter 6 affirm 7 behight, declare, deliver, enounce 8 announce 9 enunciate 10 articulate
indistinctly: 4 slur
pronounced: 6 marked 7 decided, howling 12 unmistakable
pronouncement: 5 dicta(pl.) 6 dictum 9 manifesto, statement 11 declaration 12 announcement
pronto: 5 quick 7 quickly 8 promptly 11 immediately
pronunciation: 4 burr, lisp, slur 5 drawl, twang
correct: 8 orthoepy 9 phonology
incorrect: 7 cacoepy 8 psellism 9 psellisum
pronunciation mark: 5 tilde 8 dieresis 9 diacritic
proof: 4 test 5 trial 6 result 7 approof, probate, exhibit, outcome 8 argument, evidence 9 testimony 10 indication 11 appro-

bation 12 confirmation, impenetrable, verification 13 certification, demonstration

proofreader mark: lc, tr; cap 4 dele, stet 5 caret, space

prop: leg, nog 4 stay 5 appui, brace, shore, sprag, staff, stell(Sc.), stilt 6 scotch, shorer 7 fulcrum, support, sustain 8 buttress 10 strengthen

propaganda: 4 plan 5 ideas 6 scheme, system 8 doctrine 12 brainwashing

propagation: 12 continuation

propagate: 5 breed 7 diffuse 8 engender, generate, increase, multiply 9 circulate 11 disseminate

propel: gun, row 4 flip, move, pole, push, send, urge 5 drive, flick, force, impel, shove 7 project

propeller: fan, fin, oar 4 vane 5 screw 6 driver, paddle
arm: 4 vane

propensity: yen 4 bent, bias 6 liking 7 aptness, avidity 8 appetite, tendency 9 affection, proneness 10 proclivity, propension 11 disposition, inclination 12 predilection

proper: due, fit 4 fair, fine, good, meet, prim 5 right, stiff 6 behove, chaste, comely, decent, honest, modest, sedate, seemly, strict 7 behoove, correct, fitting, seeming 8 accurate, decorous, formular, suitable 9 advisable, allowable, befitting, beseeming, excellent 10 commodious, convenient, scrupulous 11 appropriate, respectable

properly: 6 featly, gladly 7 gradely

property: lot, res 4 acre, alod, aver, bona, dhan(Ind.), gear 5 addle, allod, asset, aught, glebe, goods, manor 6 domain, estate, havier, realty, wealth 7 acquest, alodium, chattel, haviour, holding 8 allodium 9 acensuada, attribute, homestead 11 appropriate, possessions 14 characteristic
act to regain: 8 replevin
bride's gift to husband: dos 5 dowry
charge against: 4 lien
conveyor of: 7 alienor, grantor
deceased wife's gift to husband: 8 courtesy
destruction of: 8 sabotage
found on the thief: 6 mainor
personal: 7 chattel
real: 4 land 7 acreage
receiver: 7 alienee
settle: 6 entail
settlement: dos
stolen: 4 loot, pelf 5 booty, lucre, spoil
suit for: 6 trover
transferring party: 7 alienor
wanton destruction of: 5 arson 8 sabotage 9 vandalism

property right: 4 lien 8 easement

prophecy: 5 weird 6 oracle 8 bodement 9 utterance 10 prediction 11 declaration, foretelling 12 vaticination
pert. to: 9 vaticinal

prophesy: 4 dope, osse, spae 5 aread, areed, augur 6 divine 7 predict, presage 8 ariolate, forecast, foreshow, foretell 10 vaticinate 11 preindicate 13 prognosticate

prophet: 4 Amos, John, seer 5 augur, Elias, fatal, Hosea, Syrus 6 divine, Elijah, Elisha, leader, mantis, oracle 7 augurer, diviner, Malachi, teacher 8 Mohammed, Muhammed, presager 9 John Smith 10 soothsayer 11 vaticinator

prophetess: 5 Sibyl 7 Pythian, seeress 9 Cassandra

prophetic: 5 vatic 6 mantic 7 fateful, fatidic, vatical 8 foretell, oracular 9 prescient 10 divinatory, predictive, presageful, signifying 11 fatiloquent, foretelling, nostradamic 12 vaticinatory 14 interpretative

propine: 5 offer 6 pledge 7 present, propose

propinquity: 7 kinship 8 affinity, nearness, vicinity 9 proximity 12 neighborhood, relationship 13 appropinquity, neighbourhood

propitiate: 5 atone 6 pacify 7 appease, expiate, satisfy 9 reconcile 10 conciliate

propitious: 4 rosy 5 happy, lucky 6 benign 8 benedict 9 benignant, favorable, opportune, promising 10 auspicious, benevolent, favourable, prosperous 12 advantageous

proponent: 6 backer 8 advocate

proportion: 4 part, rate 5 quota, ratio, share 7 analogy, portion, prorate 8 relation 9 dimension

proportionate: 5 equal 7 ratable 8 adequate 10 answerable, equivalent 11 symmetrical 12 commensurate, proportional

proportionately: 6 fairly 7 prorata 10 adequately

proposal: bid 4 plan 5 offer 6 design, feeler, motion, scheme 7 project 8 overture 10 nomination, suggestion 11 proposition

propose: 4 give, moot, move 5 state 6 allege, design 8 propound 11 contemplate

proposition: 5 axiom, offer, point 6 affair, porism 7 premise, project, theorem 8 offering, overture, proposal, question 9 corollary, postulate, situation, statement 11 affirmation, undertaking
antecedent: 6 premise 7 premiss
preliminary: 5 lemma 7 lemmata(pl.)

propound: 4 pose 5 posit, state 7 propose

proprietor: 5 owner 6 master, tanist 7 lairdie

propriety: See also **proper** 4 code, rule 7 customs, manners, quality 8 behavior, ele-

gance, standard 9 attribute, etiquette 13 possessorship
propugnator: 8 defender 10 vindicator
propulsion: jet 5 drift 8 ejection 9 expulsion
prorate: 5 allot 6 assess, divide 9 apportion 10 distribute, proportion
prorogue: 5 defer 6 extend 7 adjourn, prolong 8 postpone, protract
prosaic: 4 drab, dull, flat 5 prosy 6 prolix, stolid, stupid 7 humdrum, insipid, tedious 8 tiresome, unpoetic 10 unexciting 11 commonplace 12 matter-of-fact 13 unimaginative, uninteresting
proscenium: 5 stage
front area: 5 apron
proscribe: ban 4 tabu 5 exile, taboo 6 banish, forbid, outlaw 8 prohibit 9 interdict, ostracize
prose form: 5 novel, story, tract 7 fiction, romance 8 treatise 10 nonfiction
prosecute: sue 4 urge 5 carry, chase, hound 6 accuse, charge, follow, indict, pursue 7 enforce 8 continue
prosecutor: D.A. 7 accuser, relator
proselyte: 5 alien 7 convert 8 neophyte, newcomer
to Judaism: ger
Proserpine: See **Persephone**
proseuche: 7 oratory 9 synagogue
prosit: 5 toast 10 salutation
prosody: 5 meter
prospect: 4 hope, mine, view 5 buyer, scene, vista 6 aspect 7 outlook 8 customer, exposure 9 applicant, candidate, foretaste 10 contestant
prospective: 5 lofty 6 future, likely 7 eminent 8 expected, prospect 9 provident 11 anticipated, perspective
prospector: 9 sourdough
prosper: dow, hie, wax 4 fare 5 cheve, edify, frame, speed 6 thrive 7 blossom 8 flourish
prosperity: up; hap, ups 4 boom, weal 5 ikbal 6 thrift, wealth 7 fortune, success, welfare 9 happiness, well-being
god: 4 Frey
goddess: 5 Salus
symbol: 9 turquoise
Prospero: *daughter:* 7 Miranda
servant: 5 Ariel
slave: 7 Caliban
prosperous: up 4 bein, bien, boon 5 flush, happy, lucky, palmy, sonsy 6 sonsie 7 well-off 8 thriving 9 favorable, fortunate 10 auspicious, propitious, successful 11 flourishing
prostitute: bat, cat 4 aunt, drab, hack, trug 5 broad, venal, whore 6 callet, debase, harlot 7 baggage, brothel, corrupt, Cyprian, hackney 8 berdache, commoner, customer, infamous, occupant 9 courtesan, courtezan 10 crosha-bell, hobby-horse, licentious 12 streetwalker 13 commercialize
customer: 4 john
reformed: 8 Magdalen
prostitution house of: 6 bordel 7 brothel 8 bordello
prostrate: bow 4 fell, flat 5 prone 6 fallen, supine 7 exhaust 8 dejected, helpless, overcome 9 collapsed, flattened, overthrow, recumbent 10 subjugated, submissive
prosy: dry 4 dull 6 jejune 7 humdrum, prosaic, tedious 11 commonplace, displeasing 13 unimaginative
protagonist: foe 4 hero 5 actor, agent, enemy 6 leader 7 heroine 8 advocate, champion, defender 9 contender, principal, spokesman
protasis: 11 conditional, proposition 12 introduction
protean: 10 changeable
protect: arm 4 bind, hill, save, wear 5 bield, bless, guard, hedge, shade 6 assert, defend, insure, patent, police, screen, shield 7 bulwark, cherish, forfend, shelter, tuition 8 champion, conserve, forefend, preserve 9 copyright
protecting: 7 tutelar 8 tutelary
protection: bib, lee 4 egis, fort, moat, pass 5 aegis, apron, armor, frith, guard, shell, smock 6 amulet, armour, patent, safety 7 auspice, defence, defense, parapet, shelter, tuition, umbrage 8 passport, security 12 preservation
protector: 5 guard 6 fautor, patron, shield 8 defender, guardian 9 custodian
protectorate: 11 condominium
protege: 4 ward
proteid: 6 alexin 7 albumin 9 legumelin
Proteida family: olm 7 proteus 8 necturus 11 salamanders, typhlomolge
protein: 6 avidin, casein, fibrin 7 albumin, edestin, mucedin 8 aleurone, creatine, prolamin
group: 8 globulin
poison: 5 abrin, ricin 6 ricine
source of: egg 4 bean, meat, milk 6 cheese, lentil
protest: 4 aver, beef, deny, kick 5 demur 6 affirm, assert, assure, holler, object, plaint 7 contest, declare, dissent, testify 8 complain 9 complaint, objection, stipulate 10 asseverate 11 expostulate, remonstrate 12 remonstrance
Protestant: 9 dissenter
sect: 9 orangeist
proteus: olm 6 amoeba

Proteus: *friend:* 9 Valentine
love: 6 Silvia
wife: 5 Julia
protograph: 7 writing 9 holograph 12 illustration
protoplasm: 5 ameba, spore 6 amoeba 7 sarcade
outer layer: 9 ectoplasm
substance: gel
protoplasmic: 10 archetypal, primordial
prototype: 5 model 6 emblem 7 pattern 8 antetype, original 9 archetype
protozoan: 5 ameba 6 amoeba 8 rhizopod
genus of: 7 arcella
order: 6 lobosa
parasitic: 5 ameba 6 amoeba 8 amoebida
protract: 4 spin 5 defer, delay 6 dilate, extend 7 detract, prolong 8 continue, elongate, lengthen, protrude
protrude: jut 5 blear, bulge 7 extrude, project 9 interfere
protruded: 6 extant
protuberance: nub, wen 4 boll, boss, bulb, bump, heel, hump, knob, knot, lobe, lump, node, snag, umbo 5 bulge, bunch, caput, hunch, torus 8 eminence, swelling 9 gibbosity 10 projection, prominence, protrusion
rounded: 4 hump, umbo
protuberant: 6 convex, extant 7 bottled, gibbous 8 blubbery
proud See also **pride**): 4 ikey 5 brant, chuff 7 haughty, stately, valiant 8 imposing 9 cockhorse 10 impressive 11 magisterial, overbearing 12 presumptuous, supercilious
prove: try 4 aver, fand, pree, test 5 argue, essay, nurse, prive(Sc.) 6 argify, argufy, evince, verify 7 confirm, justify, probate 8 identify, manifest 9 ascertain, establish 11 corroborate, demonstrate
provenance: 6 origin, source 10 derivation 11 provenience
provender: hay 4 corn, feed, food, oats, prog 5 grain, straw 6 fodder 7 prebend 10 provisions
provenience: 10 provenance
proverb: saw 4 word 5 adage, axiom, maxim, motto 6 ballad, byword, enigma, saying 7 byspell, parable 8 allegory, aphorism, forbysen
proverbial: 11 sententious
provide: 5 cater, equip, stock, store, yield 6 afford, foison, purvey, ration, render, supply 7 chevise, furnish 8 accouter, accoutre 9 stipulate 10 contribute
provided: if; but 5 boden, found 6 sobeit 8 afforded, supplied 9 furnished 13 conditionally
provided that: if, so
providence: 8 function, guidance
provident: 4 wise 6 frugal, saving 7 careful, prudent, thrifty 8 cautious, discreet 9 farseeing 10 economical, farsighted 11 foresighted
providential: 5 lucky 9 fortunate
province: 4 area, nome 5 arena, range, realm, shire, tract 6 colony, domain, eparch, region, sphere 7 country, emirate 8 district, division 9 bailiwick, territory 10 department, palatinate 12 jurisdiction
pert. to: 5 nomic
provincial: 4 rude 5 crude, local 6 narrow, rustic 7 insular, limited 9 parochial 10 uncultured 11 countrified 15 unsophisticated
provision: 4 fare, food 5 board, cater, grist, stock, store 6 clause, supply, wraith 7 proviso 9 condition
seller: 6 sutler
provisional: 4 iffy 7 aeolian 9 provisory, temporary, tentative 10 contingent 11 conditional
provisions: 4 cate, chow, fare, food 5 board, bouge, terms 6 forage, stocks, stores, viands 7 rations 9 provender 10 chevisance
search for: 6 forage
stock of: 6 larder 8 magazine
proviso: 5 salvo 6 clause 7 article, caution 9 condition 11 stipulation
provisory: 11 provisional
provocative: 7 agacant 8 agacante 9 provoking 10 aggressive 11 stimulating
provoke: ire, vex 4 bait, move, spur, stir 5 anger, annoy, cause, eager, evoke, frump, pique, start, tease 6 arouse, excite, harass, incite, invite, invoke, nettle, summon 7 affront, incense, quicken 8 irritate 9 aggravate, challenge, displease, forthcall, stimulate 10 exasperate
provost: 4 head 5 chief 6 jailer, keeper 7 prefect 8 director, official 10 magistrate 13 administrator 14 superintendent
prow: bow 4 beak, nose, stem 5 brave, prore 6 steven 7 gallant, rostrum, valiant 9 honorable 10 courageous
prowess: 5 skill, valor 6 valour 7 bravery, courage 9 ingenuity 10 excellence
prowl: 4 lurk, roam 6 brevit, ramble, wander
proximal: 4 next 7 nearest 9 proximate 12 conterminous
proximate: 4 next 6 direct 8 proximal 9 immediate
proximity: 8 nearness, nighness, vicinage, vicinity 9 adjacence, closeness 10 contiguity 11 propinquity 13 approximation, juxtaposition

proxy: 5 agent, power, vicar 6 agency, deputy 7 proctor 8 function 9 authority 10 procurator, substitute
prudence: 10 management 11 calculation
prudent: 4 sage, wary, wise 5 canny, chary, douce, siker 6 frugal, sicker 7 careful 8 cautious, discreet, sensible 9 advisable, cautelous, provident, sagacious 10 economical, forehanded 11 circumspect, considerate, foresighted 14 forethoughtful
prudish: 4 nice, prim 8 priggish 10 overmodest
prune: cow, cut, lop 4 clip, coll, frog, geld, plum, sned(Sc.), trim 5 dress, fruit, plume, preen, purge, rasee, razee, shave 6 anoint 7 tonsure 8 castrate 9 simpleton
pruning knive: 8 serpette
prurient: 4 lewd 7 itching, longing, lustful 10 lascivious
pruritis: 4 itch
Prussia: *bay:* 4 Kiel 6 Danzig 10 Pomeranian
city: 4 Kiel 5 Essen 6 Aachen, Altena, Berlin, Tilsit 7 Breslau, Hanover, Munster, Stettin 9 Frankfort, Magdeburg 10 Dusseldorf, Konigsberg 14 Charlottenburg
district: 7 Stettin
island: 5 Rugen 6 Usedom, Wollin 7 Frisian
lagoon: 4 haff 7 Frische 8 Kurische 11 Pommerische
lancer: 4 Ulan 5 Uhlan
land-holding aristocracy: 6 Junker
legislature upper house: 10 Herrenhaus
measure: 4 fuss, rute, zoll 5 fuder, meile 6 morgen, oxhoft 8 scheffel
mountain: 4 Harz 7 Sudeten 11 Schneekoppe 13 Riesengebirge
province: 5 Posen 6 Berlin, Saxony 7 Hanover, Prussia, Silesia 9 Pomerania, Rhineland 10 Westphalia 11 Brandenburg, East-Prussia, Hesse-Nassau, West-Prussia 12 Hohenzollern 17 Schleswig-Holstein
river: Ems 4 Alle, Eder, Elbe, Oder, Saar 5 Memel 6 Niemen, Pregel 7 Vistula 8 Passarge, Weichsel
seaport: 4 Kiel 5 Emden
spa: Ems
university town: 5 Halle
weight: 4 mark 9 quentchen
prussiate: 4 salt 7 cyanide 12 ferricyanide, ferrocyanide
pry: spy 4 gaze, lift, move, nose, peek, peep, peer 5 jemmy, jimmy, lever, mouse, prize, raise, snoop 6 potter 7 crowbar 8 leverage, scrounge 10 scrutinize
prying: 4 nosy 5 nosey 7 curious 11 inquisitive
psalm: ode 4 hymn, poem, song 11 composition
collection: 6 hallel 7 psalter
kind: 4 laud 6 hallel, Venite 7 Cantate, introit 8 Miserere
opening communion: 7 introit
sign: 5 selah
word of punctuation: 5 selah
psalmist: 5 David 6 cantor, writer 8 composer 9 precentor
psalterium: 4 lyra 6 omasum 7 stomach 9 manyplies
psammite: 9 sandstone
pseudo: 4 fake, mock, sham 5 bogus, false 7 feigned 8 spurious 9 pretended, simulated 11 counterfeit
pseudologist: 4 liar
pseudonym (see also **nickname, pen name**): 5 alias 6 anonym 7 anonyme
Lev Bronstein: 11 Leon Trotsky
Josip Broz: 4 Tito
Iosif Dzhugashvili: 12 Joseph Stalin
Adolf Schicklgruber: 11 Adolf Hitler
Vladimir Ulyanov: 13 Vladimir Lenin
psittaceous: 10 parrotlike
psyche: 4 mind, soul 6 spirit
psychiatrist: 4 Jung 5 Adler, Freud 6 shrink 7 analyst 8 alienist
psychic: 9 animastic
psychic power: ESP
psychotic: mad 5 crazy 6 insane 10 disordered 12 unreasonable
Ptah's wife: 6 Sekhet
ptarmica: 10 sneezewort
ptarmigan: 4 bird, ripa, rype 6 grouse
pteric: 4 alar 8 winglike
pteroid: 8 fernlike, winglike
ptisan: tea 5 drink 6 tisane 9 decoction
Ptolemy: *astronomy work:* 8 almagest
wife: 12 Philadelphia
ptomaine: 6 poison
pub: bar, inn 5 hotel 6 boozer, tavern
pubble: fat 5 plump
public: inn 4 open 5 overt, state 9 community
discussion: 5 forum
record office: 7 archion 8 archives
service: 7 railway, utility 9 telegraph, telephone 10 waterworks
way: 4 road 5 alley 6 bridge, tunnel 7 highway 8 turnpike 9 boulevard
publican: 6 farmer, keeper 9 catchpole, catchpoll, collector
publication: 4 book 5 paper 6 annals, blazon, digest 7 booklet 8 pamphlet 9 ephemeris 10 periodical 12 notification, proclamation, promulgation
examiner: 6 censor
make-up: 6 format
permit: 7 release
preliminary: 9 prodromus

prepare for: 4 edit
regular: 10 periodical
publicist: 5 agent, solon 6 writer 10 journalist
publicity: air 7 buildup 9 promotion 11 advertising, information
publish: air 4 blow, edit, vent 5 issue, print 6 blazon, defame, delate, expose 7 diffuse, divulge, release 8 announce, evulgate, forspeak, proclaim, promulge 9 advertise, forespeak 10 promulgate 11 disseminate
without authority: 6 pirate 10 plagiarize
publisher: 6 editor, issuer 7 printer 8 broacher 10 journalist
copy: 5 blurb 8 colophon 12 announcement
Puccini: *heroine:* 4 Mimi
opera: 7 La Tosca
puck: elf 4 disk 5 fairy 6 roller, sprite, strike 9 hobgoblin 10 goatsucker
pucker: 4 fold 5 bulge, purse, reeve, smock 6 cockle, cotter, lucken 7 wrinkle 8 contract
puckered: 7 bullate
puckfist: 8 braggart, puffball
puckish: 8 annoying, pucklike 10 mysterious 11 mischievous
pud: paw 4 hand 7 pudding 8 forefoot
pudding: 4 duff, mush, sago 6 burgoo, hackin, haggis(Sc.), panada 7 burgout, custard, dessert, hacking, sausage, tapioca 8 roly-poly 9 stir-about
puddle: dub 4 plud, pond, pool 5 plash, swamp 6 charco, flodge 7 plashet 8 quagmire
puddock: 7 paddock
pudency: 7 modesty 11 bashfulness, prudishness 13 embarrassment 14 shamefacedness
pudgy: fat 5 dumpy, plump, squat 7 bulging 8 roly-poly
peublo: 4 town 7 village
Pueblo: 4 Hopi
assembly hall: 6 estufa
ceremonial chamber: 4 kiva
village: 4 taos
puerile: 4 weak 5 silly, young 7 babyish, foolish, trivial 8 childish, immature, juvenile, unworthy, youthful 10 unthinking
Puerto Principe: 8 Camaguey
Puerto Rico: *bark:* 4 mabi
beverage: 4 mabi
bird: 4 rola 7 yeguita
breadfruit: 7 castana
city: 5 Ponce 6 Dorado 7 Arecibo, San Juan(c.) 8 Mayaguez
conqueror of: 5 Miles
fish: 4 sama, sisi
island: 4 Mona
measure: 6 cuerda 10 caballeria
person of mixed blood: 6 gibaro
tree: 4 mora 5 yagua, yaray 8 guayroto 9 guaraguao
puff: 4 blow, chug, flam(Sc.), flan, fuff, gust, pant, pegh(Sc.), pouf, waff, waft 5 fluff, whiff
puff up: 5 bloat, swell 6 tumefy 7 distend, inflate
puffball: 4 fist, fuzz 8 fuzzball
puffbird: 6 barbet 8 barbacou
genus: 6 monasa
puffed up: 5 large 6 astrut 7 souffle 8 bouffant, imposing, inflated 9 bombastic, bouffante 11 pretentious
puffer: 6 blower 8 blowfish
puffin: auk 4 bird
puffy: 4 soft 5 pursy 6 flabby
pug: dog, elf 4 clay, plug, poke, puck 5 boxer, chaff, churn, dwarf, knead, track 6 harlot, refuse, sprite, thrust 7 trample 8 mistress, pugilist 9 footprint, hobgoblin
pug-nosed: 5 camus
puggy 6 monkey(Sc.) 10 sweetheart
pugilist: lug 5 boxer 7 battler, bruiser, fighter
assistant: 6 second 7 handler
pugilistic: 6 fistic
pugnacious: 7 warlike 8 fighting 9 bellicose, combative 10 aggressive 11 belligerent, contentious, quarrelsome
puisne: 4 puny 5 judge, later, petty 6 feeble, junior 10 subsequent 11 subordinate 13 insignificant
puissance: 4 army, host 5 force, might, power, vigor 8 potency 8 strength 12 forcefulness
puissant: 6 mighty, strong 8 powerful
puke: 4 wool 5 vomit
pukka, pucka: 4 good, real 7 genuine 8 complete 9 authentic 11 substantial 13 thoroughgoing
pulchritude: 5 grace 6 beauty 10 comeliness, excellence, loveliness
pule: cry 4 peep 5 cheep, whine 6 repine, snivel 7 whimper 8 complain
puling: 4 puly 6 sickly 7 babyish 8 childish, delicate
pull: lug, tew, tit, tow, tug, wap 4 claw, drag, draw, duct, hale, haul, jerk, yank, yerk 5 bouse(naut.), heave(naut.), hitch, pluck, tweak 6 arrest, twitch 7 attract, revulse, stretch 9 influence
apart: rip 4 rend, tear 8 separate
away: 5 wrest 6 remove 8 withdraw
down: 4 raze 7 destroy 8 demolish
off: pug 6 avulse, manage 7 succeed
one's freight: 5 leave 6 depart
one's leg: 4 hoax 7 deceive 8 hoodwink
out: 7 extract 9 extirpate 10 deracinate

through: **7** recover, succeed
up: **5** elate, trice
pullet: hen **4** fowl **5** frier **6** earock(Sc.) **7** pollard **8** poullard
pulley: **4** ring **5** fusee, fuzee, wheel **6** sheave
part: **4** arse, drum **6** rigger
Pullman: car **5** coach **7** sleeper
pullulate: bud **4** teem **5** swarm **9** germinate
pulp: pap **4** marc, mash, mass, pith **5** chyme, magma **6** pomace **7** bagasse
machine: **9** macerater
pulpit: **4** ambo, bema, desk **5** chair, stage **7** lectern, rostrum **8** platform, scaffold
pulpy: **6** fleshy
pulque: **5** drink **6** liquor, mescal
pulsate: **4** beat, move, pant **5** throb **6** quiver, strike, thrill **7** vibrate
pulsation: **5** ictus
pulsatory: **8** rhythmic **9** pulsatile, pulsative, systaltic, throbbing
pulse: mug **7** battuta **8** sphygmus
pulverize: **4** bray, meal, mull **5** crush, grind **6** bruise **7** atomize **8** demolish, levigate **9** comminute, triturate **12** contriturate
pulverized: **4** fine
pulverizer: **13** disintegrator
pulverulent: **5** dusty **7** crumbly, powdery **8** powdered
puly: **6** puling
puma: cat **6** cougar **7** panther **9** carnivore
pumice: **8** abrasive
pummel: fib **4** beat, maul **5** thump **6** batter, hammer
pump: gin, rum **4** jack **6** racker **7** stirrup, syringe **10** pulsometer
handle: **5** sweep, swipe
pumpernickel: **5** bread
pumpkin: **4** pepo **6** citrul, squash
head: **4** dolt **7** Puritan **9** blockhead
pumpkinseed: **7** sunfish **8** bluegill **10** butterfish
pun: mot **4** beat, joke **5** knock, pound **7** quibble **8** paragram **9** calembour, conundrum **11** paronomasia
punch: ade, jab **4** glog, poke, prod **5** douse, dowse, drink, negus, paste **6** pierce, strike **7** mattoir **8** beverage, puncture **9** perforate
Punch: **5** clown **7** buffoon, journal **8** magazine **10** periodical
first editor of: **5** Lemon
puncheon: die **4** cask, post, stud, tool **5** punch, stamp **6** timber
puncher: **6** cowboy **7** cowpoke **10** cowpuncher, perforator
Punchinello: **5** clown **7** buffoon
punctilious: **4** nice **5** exact **6** formal, proper **7** careful, correct, precise **8** exacting **10** ceremonial, scrupulous **11** ceremonious **13** conscientious
punctual: **6** prompt
punctuate: **4** mark **9** emphasize **11** distinguish
punctuation mark: dot **4** dash **5** colon, comma, quote **6** hyphen, period **8** ellipsis **9** semicolon **10** apostrophe **11** parenthesis
puncture: **4** bite, hole, stab, vent **5** prick, wound **6** pierce **9** perforate **11** perforation
pundit: **4** sage **5** swami **6** nestor **7** Brahman, scholar, teacher
pung: **4** sled **6** sleigh
pungent: hot **4** fell, keen, racy, tart **5** acrid, acute, cress, minty, salty, sharp, smart, spicy, tangy **6** biting, bitter, pepper **7** caustic, peppery, piquant **8** aromatic, piercing, poignant, stinging **10** expressive, irritating **11** acrimonious, stimulating
pungi: bin **4** pipe **5** flute
pungled: **8** shrunken **9** shriveled
Punic: **7** dialect **9** faithless **11** treacherous **12** Carthaginian
Punic faith: **8** betrayal **9** treachery
punish: **4** beat, fine, whip **5** abuse, mulct, scold, slate, smite, spank, strap, wreak **6** amerce, strike **7** chasten, correct, corrige, revenge, scourge **8** chastise, penalize **9** castigate **10** discipline **13** excommunicate
punishing: **8** grueling **9** gruelling
punishment: **4** loss, pain **5** peine(law), wrack **6** desert, dirdum, ferule **9** suffering **13** animadversion
device: rod **6** stocks
freedom from: **8** impunity
spare: **6** acquit **7** absolve **9** exculpate, exonerate
punitive: **5** penal **8** punitory **9** punishing **10** vindictive
Punjab: See **India**
punk: bad **4** fuel, poor **5** conch, tramp **6** amadou, tinder **8** beginner, elephant, inferior, strumpet **9** beginning, miserable, touchwood, worthless **10** prostitute
punkah: fan
punt: **4** boat, kick **6** gamble
punter: **5** poler **6** bettor **7** scalper
puny: **4** weak **5** dawny, frail, petty, small **6** feeble, puisne, sickly, slight **8** droghlin, inferior **9** unskilled **13** inexperienced, insignificant
pupa: **9** chrysalis
case: **5** theca
pupil: **4** tyro **5** cadet, eleve(F.), minor, plebe, youth **6** junior, senior **7** ecolier(F.), learner, scholar, student **8** disciple, neophyte, freshman **9** sophomore
pupilage: **6** nonage **10** immaturity
puppet: **4** baby, doll, tool **5** image **8** drollery **9** neuropast **10** marionette
show: **6** wajang, wayang

puppy: fop 5 whelp
pur: 4 purr
purblind: 5 blind 6 bisson, obtuse
purchasable: 5 venal 7 corrupt, salable 9 available 10 marketable
purchase: buy 5 acate, cheap, yield 6 emptio, income, obtain, return 7 acquire, bargain, emption 11 acquisition
back: 6 redeem, regain
purchaser: 5 buyer 6 emptor, patron, vendee 8 co-emptor, customer 9 acquereur 13 adjudicataire
purdah: 6 screen 7 curtain 9 seclusion
pure: 4 fine, good, mear, meer, mere, neat, nice, pute, true 5 clean, clear, fresh, moral, sheer, utter 6 candid, chaste, simple, vestal, virgin 7 cleanly, genuine, perfect, refined, sincere, sinless, unmixed 8 absolute, complete, dovelike, filtered, innocent, virtuous, zaccheus(Heb.) 9 authentic, blameless, downright, elemental, faultless, guiltless, stainless, unalloyed, undefiled, unsullied 10 immaculate 11 crystalline, unblemished, uncorrupted, unqualified 13 unadulterated 15 unsophisticated
puree: 4 mush, soup 8 porridge
purely: 6 solely, wholly
purfle: hem 6 border 7 outline 8 decorate, ornament, trimming
purgative: 5 jalap 6 physic 8 evacuant 9 cathartic 10 alviducous
purgatory: 5 limbo
purge: rid 5 clear 6 physic, purify, remove, seethe 7 cleanse, deterge 8 absterge 9 exculpate, expurgate
purification: 9 catharsis
purify: 5 clean, clear, purge 6 bleach, filter, refine 7 baptize, clarify, cleanse, distill, epurate 8 depurate, lustrate, renovate 9 elutriate
Puritan: 9 Roundhead
puritanic: 6 strict 7 denying 8 rigorous
purl: rib 4 eddy, knit 5 frill, swirl 6 murmur, purfle, stitch
purlieu: 5 haunt 7 environ 12 neighborhood
purloin: 4 crib 5 filch, steal, swipe 6 finger, pilfer, pirate 7 cabbage 8 abstract 10 plagiarize
purple: 4 plum 5 grape, lilac, mauve, royal 6 blatta, emblem, maroon, ornate, tyrian, violet 7 cassius 8 amaranth, imperial, lavender 9 cathedral, elaborate
dye: 7 cassius
land of: 4 Tyre
seller of: 5 Lydia
purple coneflower: 9 echinacea
purple copper ore: 7 bornite
Purple Heart: 5 award, medal, order
purple ragwort: 4 herb 6 jacoby
purport: 4 feck, gist, mean 5 drift, sense, tenor 6 effect, import, intent, object 7 bearing, meaning 9 intention, substance
purpose: aim, end, use 4 bent, goal, main, mean, plan, sake 5 avail 6 design, intend, intent, motive 7 mission 9 intention, objective, predesign 10 cogitation, conception, employment, resolution 13 determination
alleged: 7 pretext
lackin: 9 driftless
purposive: 5 telic 12 teleological
purpure: 6 purple
purr: hum 5 noise, sound 6 murmur
purse: bag, cly 4 bung, poke 5 bulse, burse, money, pouch 6 pucker, wallet 7 almoner, handbag 8 coco-wort, finances, treasury 9 exchequer 10 pocketbook 12 portemonnaie
purse crab: 5 ayuyu
purser: 6 bursar 7 boucher, cashier 9 paymaster, treasurer
pursue: run 4 hunt, seek 5 chase, chevy, chivy, hound, stalk 6 chivey, chivvy, follow, gallop 7 proceed 8 continue 9 prosecute
pursuer: 6 hunter 8 huntress
pursuit: 5 scent 7 calling 10 occupation
means: 7 dragnet
pursy: fat 5 obese, puffy 7 swollen, wealthy 9 asthmatic
purulent: 4 foul 5 pussy
purvey: tax 5 cater 6 supply 7 furnish, procure, provide 10 assessment
purveyor: 6 seller, sutler 7 caterer 9 victualer
push: go; pop, por 4 birr, bore, bunt, butt, ding, dush, pelt, ping, pole, porr, poss, prod, urge 5 bevel(Sc.), boost, crowd, drive, elbow, force, heave, hunch, impel, nudge, press, shove 6 clique, effort, energy, expand, extend, hustle, jostle, potter, propel, thrust 7 advance, promote 10 enterprise 14 aggressiveness
along: 4 prod 5 nudge
down: 7 detrude
in: 5 stove
pushy: 5 bossy 7 forward 9 officious
pusillanimous: 4 tame 5 timid 6 afraid 8 cowardly 10 irresolute 12 fainthearted
puss: cat 4 face, girl, hare 5 mouth, woman 8 baudrons(Sc.)
pustule: 4 blob, burl 5 achor, blain 6 blotch, pimple 7 blister 8 eruption, swelling
put (see also **place**): lay, set 4 cast, push, urge 5 clink, drive, fixed, force, impel

place, state, throw **6** appose, attach, bestow, incite, thrust **7** deposit, express **9** attribute, constrain
away: **4** kill **5** store **6** murder **7** consume
back: **6** demote **7** replace, restore
before: **7** apposed, present
by: **4** save **5** store **6** reject
down: **6** humble, record **7** degrade, depress **8** suppress **9** deposited
forth: **4** show **5** exert, offer **7** extrude, propose, publish **9** circulate
forward: **7** prepose, propone
in: **4** ante **5** defer, delay, elude **6** baffle, divert, insert **7** discard, enclose **8** postpone **9** frustrate
off: fob **4** doff, haft **5** defer, delay, evade, table **6** divert, shelve **7** discard **8** deferred, postpone
on: act, don **5** apply, endue, indue **7** assumed, feigned, pretend **10** exaggerate
out: irk, vex **4** oust **5** anger, annoy, eject, evict, exile, expel **6** banish, deport, retire **7** publish **8** displace, distress **9** ostracize **10** discompose, disconcert, expatriate, extinguish **14** discountenance
over: **4** bilk, hoax **5** cheat, trick **7** deceive
together: add **5** piece, unite **6** gather, muster **7** collect **8** assemble **9** construct **10** congregate
up: can **4** post **5** build, erect
up with: **4** bear, take **5** brook, stand **6** endure **7** stomach **8** tolerate
putrefy: rot **5** decay **6** fester **7** corrupt **9** decompose **12** disintegrate
putrid: **4** foul **7** friable, noisome, vicious **8** depraved **10** putrescent **11** displeasing **12** disagreeable
puttee: **4** spat **6** gaiter **7** legging
putting area: **5** green
putty: **6** cement
puxy: **6** swampy **8** quagmire
puzzle: cap, get **5** glaik, griph, pinon, poser, rebus, stick **6** baffle, enigma, fickle, riddle **7** anagram, charade, confuse, foitter, griphus, mystery, mystify, nonplus, paradox, perplex **8** acrostic, bewilder, distract, entangle, intrigue **9** conundrum **10** difficulty, disconcert, palindrome
puzzled: **4** asea
puzzling: **9** equivocal
pygarg: **5** addax **6** osprey
Pygmalion: *sister:* **4** Dido
offspring: **6** Paphos, Paphus
sister's husband: **8** Sichaeus
statue: **7** Galatea
victim of: **8** Sichaeus
pygmy, pigmy: elf **4** pixy, runt **5** atomy, dwarf, gnome, minim, short **8** dwarfish **9** dandiprat **10** chimpanzee
pygmy musk deer: **10** chevrotain
pygostyle: **4** bone **5** vomer
pyknic: **5** solid, squat **6** stocky, sturdy **8** muscular **9** endomorph, squatness **11** endomorphic
pylon: **4** post **5** tower **6** marker **7** gateway **8** monument
Pylos' king: **6** Nestor
pyramid: **4** heap **6** accrue **8** increase
builder of largest: **6** Cheops
inhabitant: **5** Khufu **6** Cheops
site: **4** Giza **7** Cholula
pyramidal: **4** huge **8** enormous, imposing
pyre: **4** bale, bier **6** suttee
pyrene: pip **4** seed **5** stone
Pyrenees: *bandit:* **8** miquelet
chamois: **5** izard
mountain peak: **5** Aneto
people: **6** Basque
republic: **7** Andorra
resort: Pau
pyriform: **10** pear-shaped
pyromaniac: **7** firebug **8** arsonist
pyrotechnics: **9** fireworks
pyrotechnical device: **8** pinwheel
pyroxene: **6** augite **8** diopside **11** schefferite **12** hedenbergite
Pythagoras' birthplace: **5** Samos
Pythias' friend: **5** Damon
python: **5** snake **7** serpent
slayer: **6** Apollo
pythonic: **4** huge **8** inspired, oracular **9** monstrous
pyx, pix: box **4** case, test, vase **5** assay, capsa, carry, chest **6** casket, coffer, vessel **8** binnacle, ciborium, preserve **10** tabernacle

Q

Q: cue 5 queue
Qatar's capital: 4 Doha
q.e.d.: 21 quod erat demonstrandum
qua: as 4 bird 5 heron 7 quabird
quabird: 5 heron
quack: cry 5 couch, faker, fraud 6 crocus 8 impostor 9 charlatan, pretender 10 mountebank
quad: 4 quod 5 block 6 campus, person 7 sibling, quadrat 10 quandrangle
quadra: 6 fillet, listel, plinth
quadragenarian: 8 fortyish
quadragesimal: 5 forty 6 Lenten
quadrangle: 5 court 8 tetragon
quadrant: 4 gill 6 fourth 8 farthing 9 antimeter 10 instrument
quadrate: 4 suit 5 agree, ideal 6 square 7 perfect, squared 8 balanced 9 rectangle 10 correspond 13 correspondent
quadriga: 4 cart 6 horses 7 chariot
quadrille: 5 cards, dance
quadroon: 6 hybrid 7 mulatto
quadrumane: ape 6 monkey 7 gorilla 10 chimpanzee
quadruped: 6 mammal 10 fourlegged
quaere: 5 query 7 inquiry 8 question
quaff: sip 5 draft, drink 6 waught
quag: 5 quake 6 quiver 8 quagmire
quaggy: 4 miry, soft 5 boggy 6 flabby, spongy 7 queachy 8 yielding
quagmire: bog, gog, hag 5 marsh, swamp 6 morass
quahog: 4 clam
quail: cow 4 bird 5 colin, cower, quake, shake 6 blench, cringe, curdle, flinch, recoil, shrink, tremor, turnix 7 massena, tremble 8 bobwhite 9 coagulate, courtesan, partridge
flock of: 4 bevy 5 covey
young: 7 cheeper 8 squealer
quail snipe: 9 dowitcher
quaint: odd 4 nice 6 crafty 7 antique, curious, strange, unusual 8 fanciful, graceful, peculiar, singular 9 whimsical
quake: 4 quag, rese 5 shake, waver 6 quiver, shiver, tremor 7 shudder, tremble, vibrate 10 earthquake
Quaker: Fox 4 Penn 6 Friend 9 broadbrim
Quaker City: 12 Philadelphia
Quaker gray: 5 acier
Quaker-ladies: 5 bluet 11 meadowsweet
Quaker State: 12 Pennsylvania
Quaker's founder: 9 George Fox
quaking: 5 aspen, quaky 6 trepid 9 trepidity
qualification: 7 ability 8 aptitude 9 condition, endowment, knowledge, requisite 10 adaptation, capability, competence, experience 11 acquirement, designation, restriction 12 capacitation, modification
qualified: 8 eligible
qualify: fit 5 abate, adapt, equip, limit 6 enable, modify, soften, temper 7 assuage, entitle, prepare 8 diminish, mitigate, moderate, restrain, restrict 10 habilitate
quality: 4 cost, kind, rank, rate, sort, thew, tone 5 class, grade, power, quale, taste, trait 6 nature, status, strain, virtue 7 caliber, calibre, element 8 capacity, nobility, property 9 attribute, character 10 excellence 11 superiority 14 accomplishment, characteristic
of tone: 6 timbre 9 resonance
qualm: 4 drow, pall 5 spasm 6 attack, nausea, regret, twinge 7 scruple 8 sickness 9 faintness, misgiving 11 compunction 16 faintheartedness
quamash: 5 camas 6 camass, cammas 7 prairie
quandary: fix 4 pass 6 pickle 7 dilemma, nonplus 11 predicament 12 bewilderment
quannet: 4 file
quant: 4 pole
quantity (See also **amount**): ace, any, bit, jag, jot, lot, sea, sum 4 atom, bulk, dash, dose, dram, drop, feck, iota, lick, lots, mass, mort, much, raff, raft, slew, unit 5 batch, bunch, grist, hoard, scads, stack, store 6 amount, capful, degree, extent, hir-

sel, morsel, number, weight 7 average, handful, modicum, portion, slather 8 dribblet 9 allowance 10 pennyworth
fixed: 8 constant
full: 10 complement
irrational: 4 surd
per unit: 4 rate
prescribed: 4 dose 6 dosage
without direction: 6 scalar
Quantrill's men: 7 raiders
quantum: 4 unit 6 amount 7 portion 8 quantity
quarantine: ban 7 exclude, isolate 8 restrain 9 interdict
quaranty: 5 court
quarentene: 4 rood 7 furlong
quark: caw 5 croak, quawk
quarl, quarle: 4 tile 5 brick
quarrel: row 4 feud, fuss, spat, tiff 5 brawl, broil, cavil, flite, flyte, scene, scrap 6 affray, barney, bicker, breach, breeze, cangle, chisel, debate, fracas, fratch, hassle, jangle, quarry, strife 7 contend, dispute, faction, rhubarb, wrangle 8 argument, disagree, squabble 9 upscuddle 10 contention 11 altercation, controversy 13 collie-shangie 16 misunderstanding
quarrelsome: 7 fratchy, hostile 8 brawling, choleric, frampoid, petulant 9 bellicose, irascible, irritable, litigious 10 discordant, pugnacious 11 belligerent, contentious 12 disputatious 13 argumentative
quarry: 4 delf, game, prey 5 chase, delft 6 latomy, object, ravine 7 latomia, quarrel
quart: 6 fourth 7 measure
four: 6 gallon
metric: 5 liter, litre
one-eighth: 4 gill
two: 6 flagon
quartan: 5 fever 7 malaria
quarter: 4 coin, span 5 allot, grith, house, lodge, tract 6 assign, bestow, canton, charge, fourth, harbor, supply 7 bearing, furnish, harbour, shelter 8 clemency, contrada, contrade(pl.), district, division 9 apportion, dismember 11 forbearance
quarters: 4 camp, room 7 billets, lodging, shelter 8 barracks 9 dormitory
nautical: 6 fo'c'sle 7 gunroom 8 steerage, wardroom 10 forecastle
winter: 10 hibernacle
women's: 5 harem
quarter note: 8 crotchet
quartz: 4 onyx, sand, sard 5 agate, flint, prase, silex, topaz 6 jasper, silica 7 citrine, crystal, rubasse, sinople 8 amethyst 9 carnelian 10 calchedony
quartzite: 9 itabarite, sandstone
quash: 4 cass, drop, void 5 abate, annul, crush, quell, shake 6 cancel 7 abolish, cassare, destroy, pumpkin, shatter 8 abrogate, suppress 9 overthrow
quat: 4 boil, glut, quit(Sc.) 5 squat 6 pimple, squash 7 blister, pustule, satiate
quaternion: 6 tetrad 8 quatrain
turning factor: 6 versor
quaver: 5 shake, trill 6 quiver 7 tremble, tremolo, vibrate 9 vibration
quaw: 8 quagmire
quawk: caw 5 heron 7 screech
quay: key 4 bund, dock, mole, pier, wall 5 levee, quell, wharf 6 bunder, subdue 7 landing 10 embankment
quean: 4 jade 5 hussy, wench 6 harlot
queach: fen 7 thicket
queachy: 5 boggy, bushy 6 marshy, quaggy, swampy
queasy: 5 timid 8 delicate, qualmish, ticklish, troubled 9 hazardous, nauseated, squeamish, uncertain, unsettled 10 fastidious 11 embarrassed 13 uncomfortable
Quebec: *acre:* 6 arpent
cape: 5 Gaspe
county: 5 Laval
patron saint: 4 Anne
peninsula: 5 Gaspe
town: 5 Sorel
vehicle: 7 caleche
quebrada: gap 5 brook, creek, gorge 6 ravine, stream 7 fissure 8 brooklet
Quechua: 4 Inca 6 Indian
queechy: 4 puny, weak 5 small 6 feeble, sickly
queen: 4 fers, rani(Ind.) 5 ranee(Ind.), reine(F.) 6 regina 7 monarch 9 sovereign
widowed: 7 dowager
queen it: 8 domineer 9 tyrannize
queen of fairies: Mab, Pam, Una 7 Titania 8 Gloriand
Queen Anne's lace: 6 carrot
Queen City: 10 Cincinnati
Queen of the Adriatic: 6 Venice
Queen of the Antilles: 4 Cuba
Queen of the East: 7 Zenobia
queen of gods: 4 Hera, Juno, Sati
Queen of Hearts: 9 Elizabeth
Queen of Heaven: 4 Hera, Mary, moon 7 Astarte
Queen of Isles: 6 Albion
Queen of Palmyra: 7 Zenobia
Queen of Sheba: 6 Balkis
queen of spades: 5 basta
Queen of Thebes: 5 Dirce
queen of underworld: Hel 4 Hela
queen's arm: 6 musket
queen's-delight: oil 4 herb 9 perennial, queenroot
queen's-flower: 6 myrtle 9 bloodwood
queenly: 5 noble, regal, royal 7 reginal

Queensland: *river:* 8 Brisbane
seaport: 8 Brisbane
queer: odd, rum 4 sham 5 comic, droll, drunk, faint, funny, giddy, rally, spoil 6 banter, insane 7 comical, erratic, strange, unusual 8 abnormal, doubtful, fanciful, humorous, peculiar, qualmish, ridicule, singular, spurious 9 dishonest, eccentric, fantastic 10 homosexual, suspicious 11 counterfeit, intoxicated 12 questionable
queest: 8 ringdove
queet: 4 coot
quell: 4 calm, cool, damp, dash, kill, quay 5 allay, check, crush, quash, quiet, still 6 obtund, pacify, reduce, soothe, spring, stanch, stifle, subdue 7 assuage, destroy, repress, satisfy 8 fountain, suppress 9 overpower, overwhelm 10 extinguish
quelque-chose: 6 trifle
queme: fit 4 neat, snug, tidy 5 handy, quiet 6 comely 7 fitting, satisfy 8 pleasant, suitable 9 agreeable
quench: 5 delay, slake
quenelle: 8 meatball 9 forcemeat
quercus: oak 4 tree 9 evergreen
querent: 8 inquirer 9 plaintiff 11 complainant
querida: 5 lover 10 sweetheart
querist: 8 inquirer 10 questioner
querken: 5 choke 6 stifle
querl: 4 coil 5 twirl, twist
quern: 4 mill 7 grinder
quernstone: 9 millstone
querulous: 7 fretful, peevish, whining 9 complaint, plaintive, quizzical 11 complaining 12 querimonious
query: ask 5 doubt 6 demand, quaere 7 inquire, inquiry 8 question 9 challenge 11 interrogate
quest: ask 4 hunt, seek 6 search 7 examine, inquest, journey, pursuit, seeking 9 adventure 10 enterprise, expedition
question: ask 4 crux, quiz 5 doubt, grill, poser, query, scout, targe(Sc.) 6 appose, cruces(pl.), debate, demand, quaere, riddle, shrive 7 dispute, inquire, inquiry, problem, scruple, stumper 9 catechise, catechize, challenge, interview 10 discussion 11 examination, interrogate, proposition 12 interpellate 13 interrogation, interrogative, investigation
denoting: 15 interrogational
rhetorical: 10 eperotesis
question mark: 7 erotema, eroteme
questionable: 4 moot 7 dubious, suspect 9 ambiguous, equivocal, uncertain
questionnaire: 4 form, poll
quetch: 4 stir 6 twitch
quetzal: 6 trogon
queue: cue 4 line 5 braid 7 pigtail
quey: 6 heifer
quiaquia: 4 scad 9 cigarfish
quibble: cog, pun 4 carp, quib 5 cavil, cheat, evade 6 ambage, baffle, haffle 7 brabble, evasion, shuffle 9 previcate 10 equivocate 12 equivocation
quica: 7 opossum, sarigue
quick: apt, yap 4 deft, fast, flit, lish, live, spry, vite(F.), yare 5 acute, agile, alert, alive, apace, brisk, fiery, fleet, hasty, rapid, ready, sharp, swift, tosto(It.), yeder 6 abrupt, active, lively, moving, nimble, prompt, speedy, sudden, volant 7 intense 8 animated, dextrous, shifting, vigorous 9 dexterous, impatient, sensitive, sprightly 10 celeritous, perceptive 11 expeditious 12 invigorating
quick bread: 7 muffins 8 biscuits 9 cornbread
quicken: 4 whet 5 hurry, speed 6 arouse, excite, hasten, incite, revive, vivify 7 animate, enliven, provoke, refresh, sharpen 8 expedite, inspirit 9 reanimate, stimulate 10 accelerate 11 resuscitate 12 reinvigorate
quicker than: ere
quicklime: 5 rusma
quickly: 4 fast, rath, soon, vite(F.) 5 alive, apace 6 belive, hourly, presto, pronto 7 rapidly 8 promptly, speedily, vigorous
quickness: 6 acumen 7 acidity 8 dispatch, progress, pungency, sagacity 9 acuteness 10 expedition
quicksand: 4 flow, syrt, trap 6 danger, syrtis
quickset: 5 hedge 7 thicket 8 hawthorn
quicksilver: 7 mercury 9 heautarit
quid: cud, fid 4 chaw, chew 5 pound, trade 6 barter, return 8 exchange, quiddity 9 sovereign
quiddany: 5 jelly, sirup
quiddit: 7 quibble 8 subtlety
quiddle: 6 dawdle, trifle
quidnunc: 5 frump 6 gossip, tatler 8 busybody
quiescent: 5 quiet, still 6 latent, static 7 dormant, resting 8 inactive, sleeping 10 motionless
quiet: sh; coy, pet 4 calm, cosh, dead, ease, fair, hush, lull, mild, rest, tame 5 allay, downy, inert, peace, privy, sober, still 6 gentle, hushed, merely, modest, placid, repose, secret, sedate, serene, settle, silent, smooth, soothe, static, stilly 7 appease, compose, halcyon, restful, retired, silence 8 composed, decorous, peaceful, secluded, tranquil 9 alleviate, contented, noiseless, peaceable, placidity, quiescent, reposeful, unruffled 10 motionless, silentness, unmo-

lested 11 clandestine, tranquilize, undisturbed

quietus: 5 death 6 repose 8 mittimus 11 acquittance

quiff: 4 girl, puff 5 whiff 8 forelock

quill: cop, pen 5 remex, spina 6 bobbin, pinion 7 remiges(pl.), spindle

porcupine: pen 5 spine

quillet: 4 tube 5 tract 7 quibble

quilt: pad, sew 4 gulp 5 eider 6 caddow, pallet, stitch 7 blanket, comfort, swallow 8 coverlet 9 comforter 11 counterpane

quink: 5 brant

quinoa: 5 seeds 7 pigweed

quinoline derivative: 7 analgen

quintuplets: 6 Dionne 7 Fischer

quip: mot, pun 4 gibe, jest, joke 5 sally, taunt 6 saying 7 quibble

quire: 4 fold 5 choir, paper

quirk: 4 kink, quip, turn 5 clock, knack, sally, trait, twist 6 groove, strike 7 caprice, evasion 8 flourish 9 deviation 10 subterfuge 11 peculiarity 12 equivocation

quirquincho: 5 pichi 6 peludo 9 armadillo

quirt: 4 whip 5 romal

quis: 8 woodcock

quisling: rat 7 traitor

quit: rid 4 free, stop 5 avoid, cease, clear, forgo, leave, repay 6 acquit, depart, desist, forego, resign, vacate 7 abandon, forsake, release, relieve 8 abdicate, absolved, liberate, renounce 9 surrender 10 relinquish 11 discontinue

quitclaim: 6 acquit 7 release 14 relinquishment

quite: all 4 very 5 stark, truly 6 really, wholly 7 totally, utterly 8 entirely 10 altogether, completely, positively 12 considerably

quite so: 7 exactly 9 precisely

quittance: 5 repay 6 return 7 requite 8 reprisal, requital 9 departure, discharge, repayment 10 recompense 11 acquittance

quitter: 4 seal, slag 5 piker 6 coward 7 shirker

quiver: 4 case, quag, tirl(Sc.) 5 bever, quake, quick, shake, thirl(Sc.), trill 6 active, arrows, bicker, cocker, dindle, lively, nimble, quaver, sheath, shiver, tremor 7 frisson, tremble, vibrate 8 flichter 9 palpitate, vibration

quivering: 5 aspen 6 ashake, didder 7 aquiver 8 blubbery

quiverleaf: 5 aspen

quixotic: 7 utopian 9 visionary 10 chivalrous, idealistic 11 impractical 13 impracticable

quiz: ask 4 exam, hiss, hoax, jest, joke, mock, test, whiz 5 chaff, probe 7 examine 8 instruct, question, ridicule 11 examination, questioning

quizzical: odd 7 amusing, comical, teasing 9 bantering, eccentric, perplexed

quizzing glass: 7 monocle 8 eyeglass

quod: jug 4 jail 5 court 6 prison

quodlibet: 6 debate, medley 8 fantasia, subtlety

quoin: 4 coin 5 angle, wedge 6 corner 8 keystone, voussoir

quoit: 4 disc, ring 5 throw 6 discus 8 cromlech

mark aimed at: tee

pin: hob

quomodo: 5 means 6 manner

quondam: 6 former 7 onetime 8 sometime

quonset hut: 6 prefab

British type: 6 Nissen

quop: 5 throb

quorum: 5 group 7 council 8 majority

quota: 4 part 5 share 6 divide, rating 8 dividend 10 contingent, proportion

quotation: 5 price, quote

quotation mark: 9 guillemet(F.)

quote: 4 cite, cote, name, note 5 motto, refer 6 adduce, allege, allude, notice, repeat, select 7 excerpt, extract, passage 9 quotation, reference, selection 10 memorandum

quoth: 4 said 5 spoke

quotha: 6 indeed 8 forsooth

quotidian: 5 daily 7 trivial 8 everyday, ordinary 9 recurring 11 commonplace

quotient: 6 result

quotity: 5 group 10 collection

R

R: ar; rho **6** letter
Ra: Re; Shu, Tem, Tum **4** Aten **5** Horus **7** Chepera, Khepera, Sokaris **9** Harmachis
bull form: **5** Bacis
child: Mu; Mat, Shu **4** Maat **5** Athor
parent: Geb, Keb, Nut, Seb **5** Neith
wife: **4** Mout
raad: **7** catfish
rab: **6** beater
rabat: **5** rabbi **8** polisher
rabato, rebato: **4** ruff **6** collar
rabban: **6** master **7** teacher
rabbet: **5** check **6** groove, recess **7** channel
rabbi: **4** lord **5** amora **6** master, rabbin **7** amoraim, tannaim, teacher **8** sabaraim, saboraim **9** clergyman
assistant: **6** cantor
school: **7** yeshiva **8** yeshibah, yeshivah **9** yeshiboth(pl.)
wife: **9** rebbetzin
rabbit: bun, doe **4** buck, cony, hare, tyro **5** bunny, capon, coney, lapin(F.) **6** coward, novice, rodent, tapeti
fur: **4** cony, rack, scut **5** coney, lapin
genus: **5** lepus
shelter: **5** hutch **6** burrow, warren **7** clapper
tail: fud(Sc.) **4** scut
young: **4** rack **6** gazabo, gazebo **7** starter
rabbit-ear: **6** cactus **8** toadflax
rabbit fever: **9** tularemia
rabbit flower: **8** foxglove, toadflax
rabbit-foot: **5** charm **8** talisman
rabbit-meat: **9** archangel
rabbit tobacco: **10** balsamweed
rabbit vine: **9** groundnut
rabbitfish: **8** chimaera
rabbitmouth: **10** harelipped
rabbitry: **5** hutch **6** warren
rabbit's-mouth: **10** snapdragon
rabbit's-root: **12** sarsaparilla
rabble: mob **4** herd, raff, rout **5** crowd **6** ragtag **7** bobtail **8** canaglia, canaille, riffraff **9** confusion **10** clamjamfry, hubble-shoo, hubble-show **11** commonality
rabble-rouser: **6** ragtag **8** agitator **9** demagogue
Rabelaisian: **5** bawdy **6** earthy
rabid: mad **6** raging **7** frantic, furious, violent, zealous **8** frenzied, virulent **9** fanatical **12** enthusiastic
rabies: **5** lyssa, lytta **7** madness **11** hydrophobia
raccoon: **4** coon **6** mapach **7** mapache
related animal: **5** coati, panda
race: cut, ilk, run **4** dash, gest, herd, kind, lane, line, root, rush, slit, sort, stem, stud **5** blood, breed, brood, caste, chevy, chivy, class, corso, flesh, geste, hurry, relay, speed, stock, track, tribe **6** arroyo, bicker, broose, chivvy, course, family, groove, hasten, hurdle, nation, people, slalom, sprint, stirps, strain **7** bombast, channel, contend, contest, dynasty, lineage, regatta, running, scamper, scratch **8** marathon **9** holethnos, **10** freeforall, generation, passageway **11** competition, descendants, watercourse
combined form: **4** gend, geno
division: **7** Negroid **9** Caucasian, Mongolian
human: man **7** mankind **9** mortality
mixed: see **person:** *of mixed blood*
murder: **8** genocide
pert. to: **6** ethnic
series: **7** regatta
science: **9** athletics, ethnology
starting line: **7** scratch
race board: **9** gangplank
race ginger: **10** gingerroot
raceabout: **5** sloop **8** roadster
racecourse: **4** heat, oval **6** career, circus, course **7** raceway
marker: **4** meta **5** pylon
racehorse: **6** maiden, mantis, plater
racer: **4** crab **5** miler, snake **6** runner **7** courser, serpent **8** sprinter **9** turntable **10** blacksnake
racetrack: **4** oval, turf **10** hippodrome
tipster: **4** tout

raceway: 5 canal 7 channel, fishway 8 millrace

Rachel: *children:* 6 Joseph 8 Benjamin
father: 5 Laban
husband: 5 Jacob
sister: 4 Leah

rachis: 4 stem 5 spine 8 backbone

rachitis: 7 rickets

rack: bar, fly, gin, jib 4 bink, crib, gait, pace, path, scud, skin, tree 5 airer, brake, creel, flake, horse, stand, touse, trace, track, vapor 6 course, cratch, gantry, harass, strain, wrench 7 agonize, grating, oppress, pathway, stretch, torment, torture, vestige 9 framework 10 excruciate, foresaddle

racket: bat, din 4 shoe 5 bandy, dodge, noise, trick 6 bustle, clamor, crosse, hubbub, outcry, scheme, strike 7 clangor, clatter, pattern, revelry 8 snowshoe 10 battledore, turbulence 11 merrymaking
jai alai: 5 cesta

rackle: 5 clank 6 rattle 7 clatter 8 reckless 9 impetuous 10 headstrong

raconteur: 8 narrator 11 storyteller

racy: 5 brisk, fresh, smart, spicy, swift 6 lively, risque 7 piquant, pungent, zestful 8 indecent, spirited, stirring, vigorous 10 suggestive 12 exhilarating

rad: 5 eager, quick, ready 6 afraid, elated 11 exhilarated

Radames' love: 4 Aida

raddle: rod 4 beat 5 color, ocher, twist 6 branch, cudgel, thrash 10 interweave

radial: ray 8 quadrant

radian: arc 7 auroral

radiance: 4 beam, glow 5 glare, gleam, glory, nitor, sheen, shine 6 luster 7 glitter, glowing, shining 8 lambency, splendor 9 brilliant 10 brightness, brilliancy, effulgence, refulgence

radiant: 7 auroral 11 resplendent

radiate: 4 beam, emit 5 shine 6 spread 7 diffuse, emanate 9 coruscate, irradiate 10 illuminate

radiating: 6 radial 8 stellate 11 centrifugal

radiation detector: 6 geiger

radiator: 6 heater

radical: red 4 root, surd 5 basal, basic, rebel, ultra 7 capital, drastic, extreme, forward, leftist, organic, support 8 cardinal, complete 9 extremist 10 foundation, iconoclast 11 fundamental 12 intransigent 13 revolutionary
chemical: ion 4 amyl, aryl 6 acetyl, adenyl, adipyl 7 tartryl 8 aluminyl

radicate: 9 establish

radicle: 7 rootlet

radio: set 8 portable, wireless 9 broadcast, radiogram 10 transistor 12 walkie-talkie
detector: 5 radar
frequency: 5 audio
interference: 6 static
operator: ham 6 sparks 11 broadcaster
part: 5 diode 8 detector, selector
rating: 6 Hooper
signal check: 7 monitor
wave: 5 micro, short

radish: 5 radis(F.) 7 cadlock

radium: *discoverer:* 5 Curie
emanation: 5 niton, radon
source: 7 uranite

radius: ken 5 orbit, range, spoke, sweep 6 extent, length
pert. to: 6 radial

radix: 4 root 6 etymon 7 radical

raff: 4 heap, raft, rake 5 trash 6 huddle, jumble, litter, lumber, rabble, timber 7 rubbish 8 leavings, riffraff

raffish: low 5 cheap 6 flashy, frowsy, tawdry 7 unkempt 9 worthless 11 disgraceful 12 disreputable

raffle: 4 raff 6 jumble, rabble, refuse, tangle 7 drawing, lottery, rubbish, serrate 8 entangle, riffraff

raft: cow 4 crib, floe, heap, moki, raff, spar 5 balsa, barge, float 6 rafter 9 catamaran, transport 10 collection
part: 5 brail

raft-breasted: 6 ratite

raft duck: 5 scaup 7 redhead 8 bluebill

rafter: 4 balk, beam, firm, raft, viga 7 carline, chevron

rafty: 4 damp 5 musty, stale 6 rancid

rag: jag 4 mock, rail, rate, tune 5 annoy, dance, scold, scrap, shred, tease 6 banter, harass, rumpus, tatter, uproar 7 quarrel, ragtime, remnant, wrangle

ragamuffin: 14 tatterdemalion

rage: fad, ire 4 beef, fret, fume, funk, fury, heat, rant, rave, tear 5 anger, chafe, craze, furor, mania, storm, wrath 6 choler, fervor, frenzy, furore, temper 7 amentia, bluster, bombast, emotion, fashion, fervour, passion, thunder 8 insanity, violence 9 vehemence 10 enthusiasm

ragged: 5 harsh, rough 6 jagged, shaggy, uneven 7 shreddy, unkempt 8 strident, tattered 9 defective, dissonant, imperfect, irregular 10 straggling, unfinished 11 dilapidated

ragged jacket: 4 seal

ragged lady: 5 guara 11 love-in-a-mist

ragged sailor: 10 bluebottle, cornflower

raggedy doll: Ann 4 Andy, Anne

raggle: cut 6 groove

raggy: 6 ragged

raging: 4 grim 5 rabid 6 fierce 7 fervent, rageous 8 furibund 9 ferocious
raglan: 6 sleeve 8 overcoat
ragout: 4 hash, stew 5 salmi 6 salmis 7 goulash, haricot 8 salpicon 10 capilotade 11 gallimaufry
ragpicker: 6 bunter 10 chiffonier(F.) 11 chiffonnier(F.)
ragshag: 11 masquerader
ragwort: 5 plant 8 ambrosia
rah: 5 cheer 6 hurrah
raid: 4 tala 5 foray 6 attack, creach(Sc.), creagh(Sc.), forage, harass, inroad, invade, maraud, piracy 7 chappow, despoil, hership 8 invasion 9 chevachie, incursion, roadstead, cavalcade
rail: bar, jaw 4 coot, flow, gush, jest, rant, rate, slat, sora 5 abuse, array, chide, cloak, crake, dress, guard, heron, plank, scoff, scold, soree, track 6 banter, berate, callet, revile, septum 7 arrange, bidcock, bilcock, clocker, footrest, garment, inveigh 8 decorate, Rallidae(pl.), reproach 9 spectator
genus of: 4 sora 6 rallus
railing: bar 5 fence 7 barrier, parapet 8 balconet, banister, espalier, rabulous 9 guardrail 10 balconette, balustrade 12 vituperation
raillery: 4 gaff 5 chaff, sport 6 banter, blague 8 badinage, ridicule 10 persiflage
railly: 4 jest, mock 5 rally 8 ridicule
railroad: 4 herd, line, push, rush 5 hurry, track 8 ceinture, monorail 9 transport
branch: 4 stub 6 feeder
bridge: 7 trestle, viaduct
car: 5 diner 6 parlor 7 caboose, coal-car, parlour, Pullman, sleeper
center: 7 station 8 terminal, terminus 10 roundhouse
cross rail: 4 frog
flare: 5 fusee
signal: 5 fusee 9 semaphore
station: 4 gare(F.) 5 depot
switch: 4 frog
tie: 6 timber 7 sleeper
worker: 6 boomer, porter 7 fireman 8 engineer, strapper 9 conductor
railway: 5 train 6 subway 8 elevated, jackstay, monorail 9 funicular
raiment: See **dress**
rain: dag, fog 4 mist, pour 5 blizz, blout, misle, plash, spate, storm 6 deluge, mizzle, serein, shower 7 drizzle 8 downpour, sprinkle 10 cloudburst 13 precipitation
check: 4 stub 12 postponement
fine: 4 mist 7 drizzle
god: 8 Parjanya
icy: 4 hail, snow 5 sleet
pert. to: 7 pluvial
unit of measure: 4 inch
rain bird: 6 plover
rain cloud: 5 nimbi(pl.) 6 nimbus
rain forest: 5 selva
rain gage: 8 udometer 10 hyetometer 11 pluviograph, pluviometer 15 hyetometrograph
rain glass: 9 barometer
rain leader: 9 downspout
rain-loving: 12 ombrophilous
rain tree: 5 saman, zaman 6 zamang 8 genisaro
rainbow: arc, bow 4 iris
goddess: 4 Iris
measuring device: 12 spectrometer
pert. to: 6 iridal
rainbow chaser: 9 visionary 11 doctrinaire
rainbow-like: 6 iridal 10 iridescent
raincoat: 4 mino 6 poncho, ulster 7 slicker 10 mackintosh, trenchcoat
rainfall: *pert. to:* 6 hyetal
rainfowl: 6 cuckoo 10 woodpecker 11 channelbill
rainspout: 4 rone(Sc.) 10 waterspout
rainworm: 8 nematode 9 earthworm
rainy: wet 4 damp 5 moist 7 flooded 8 cluttery
season: 7 monsoon
rais, reis: 4 head 5 chief, ruler 7 captain
raise: up; end 4 buoy, grow, hain, heft, hike, levy, lift, rear, rise, stir 5 arear, boost, breed, crane, dight, elate, exalt, hance, heave, heeze, hoist, horse, rouse, set-up, start, trice 6 arouse, ascend, assume, awaken, cantle, create, emboss, excite, gather, incite, leaven, muster, obtain, remove, uplift 7 address, advance, chevise, collect, elevate, enhance, ennoble, lighten, present, procure, produce, promote 8 heighten, increase 9 cultivate, establish, institute, intensify, originate, propagate 10 aggrandize, appreciate, invigorate
raised: 4 hove 6 arrect, enleve(F.)
raisin: 5 lexia, zibeb 7 currant
raj: 4 rule 5 reign 11 sovereignty
rajah: 4 king 5 chief 6 prince 9 dignitary
wife: 4 rani 5 ranee
Rajmahal creeper: 4 jiti, vine
rake: gad, rue, rut 4 path, raff, roue, rove, trip 5 claut, glean, track 6 gather, groove 7 collect, gleaner, scratch 8 enfilade, rakehell 9 debauchee 11 inclination
with gunfire: 8 enfilade
rakehell: 4 rake 7 immoral 9 debauched, debauchee, dissolute 10 profligate
rake-off: 4 take 6 profit, rebate 10 commission, percentage
rakish: 4 lewd, pert 7 roguish 9 dissolute
rale: 6 rattle

rallidae: 5 coots, rails, wekas 6 crakes 10 gallinules
rally: 4 drag, mock 5 chaff, noise, rouse 6 arouse, attack, banter, deride, revive 7 recover, reunite 8 assemble, raillery, ridicule 10 recuperate, strengthen 11 concentrate
rallying cry: 6 slogan
ram: hit, pun, tup, wad 4 buck, butt, tamp, teap 5 Aries, crash, sheep, stuff 6 batter, beetle, chaser, rancid, strike, wether 7 collide, plunger 8 bulldoze
ram cat: tom 4 male
Rama's bride: 4 Sita
ramage: 4 wild 5 bough, rough 6 unruly 7 untamed 8 branches, frenzied, wildness
ramage hawk: 8 brancher
ramass: 6 gather 7 collect
ramate: 8 branched
ramble: gad 4 roam, rove, walk 5 jaunt, prowl, range 6 stroll, travel, wander 7 saunter 8 straggle 9 excursion
rambling: 7 cursory, devious 9 desultory, wandering 10 circuitous, discursive 11 peripatetic 12 disconnected
rambunctious: 4 wild 6 unruly 10 boisterous, disorderly, rampageous 12 obstreperous 14 uncontrollable
ramekin: pan 4 dish 9 casserole
ramentum: 5 palea, palet 6 paleae(pl.), scales 7 shaving 8 particle
ramhead: arm 4 hook 5 lever 8 clodpate
ramie, ramee: 4 hemp, rhea 5 fiber
ramification: arm 4 rami(pl.) 5 ramus 6 branch, spread 8 division, offshoot 9 branching 10 divergence 12 embranchment
rammack: 4 rush
rammel: 5 trash 9 brushwood 11 undergrowth
rammish: 4 rank 5 rammy
Ramona author: 7 Jackson
ramose: 7 cladose 8 branched 9 branching
ramp: rob 4 bank, rage, walk 5 crawl, creep, slope, storm 6 dupery, unruly 7 incline, rampage, swindle 8 gradient, platform 9 helicline 10 cuckoopint
rampageous: 4 wild 6 unruly 9 rampaging 10 boisterous
rampant: 4 rife 6 fierce 7 violent 9 unchecked 10 rampageous, widespread 11 extravagant, flourishing, threatening 12 unrestrained 14 uncontrollable
rampart: 4 wall 5 agger, mound, redan 6 vallum 7 barrier, bulwark, parapet, ravelin 10 embankment 13 fortification
part: 4 spur
ramper: 7 lamprey
rampire: dam 7 fortify, rampart 10 embankment, strengthen
Ramses' goddess: 4 Anta
ramshackle: 5 loose, shaky 7 rickety 10 disorderly, dissipated, tumble-down
ramstam: 8 headlong, reckless 10 headstrong 11 thoughtless
ramus: 6 branch 10 branchlike
rance: 5 stone 6 marble
rancel: 6 search 7 ransack
ranch: 4 casa, farm, tear 5 finca, pluck 7 acreage, scratch 8 estancia, hacienda 9 estantion
worker: 4 hand 5 owner 6 cowboy, farmer 7 cowpoke, rancher 8 herdsman, ranchero(Sp.), ranchman
rancho: 5 ranch
rancid: 4 rank, sour 5 musty, stale 6 frowsy 7 spoiled 8 stinking 9 obnoxious, offensive 10 unpleasant
rancor, rancour: ire 4 gall, hate 5 spite 6 enmity, hatred, malice 8 rankling 9 animosity, antipathy, hostility 10 bitterness
rand: 4 edge 5 ridge, strip 6 border, margin
randan: row 4 boat 5 spree 7 rampage
random: 5 loose, stray 6 casual, chance 7 aimless 9 desultory, haphazard 10 accidental, fortuitous 11 purposeless
randy: 5 crude, revel, shrew 6 beggar, coarse, frolic, virago, vulgar 7 canvass 8 carousal 9 festivity 10 disorderly 12 unmanageable
range: ken, row 4 ally, area, farm, line, rank, roam, rove 5 align, aline, blank, class, field, gamut, order, reach, ridge, scope, space, stove, stray 6 extent, ramble, series, sphere, stroll, tether, wander 7 arrange, compass, explore, habitat, saunter 8 classify, distance 9 cookstove, grassland 11 systematize
range-finder: 6 stadia 9 mekometer, telemeter 10 trekometer
ranger: 4 seal 5 rover, sieve 6 keeper, warden 8 commando, rangeman, wanderer
Rangoon's state: 4 Pegu
rangy: 8 spacious
rank: row 4 army, file, foul, line, rate, sort, tier 5 array, caste, cense, class, frank, genus, grade, gross, order, proud, range, space 6 barony, coarse, degree, estate, fertid, gentry, mighty, rancid, rating, series, status, strong 7 caliber, calibre, calling, compeer, copious, corrupt, dignity, extreme, fertile, froward, glaring, haughty, noisome, overfed, peerage, quality, rammish, station, stratum, swollen, violent 8 absolute, abundant, classify, division, eminence, estimate, flagrant, gentrice, headlong, indecent, palpable, position, powerful, vigorous 9 condition, downright, ex-

cessive, exuberant, formation, graduation, hierarchy, luxuriant, offensive, overgrown, plentiful 10 coordinate 11 arrangement, distinction 14 classification
deprive of: 4 bust 5 break 6 depose 7 cashier
mark of: 6 stripe
military: PFC 5 major 7 captain, colonel, general, private 8 banneret, corporal, sergeant 10 lieutenant
rankle: 4 fret, gall 6 fester, rancor 7 inflame 8 irritate, ulcerate
rann: 5 verse 6 stanza, strain
ransack: 4 loot, rake, sack 5 rifle, steal 6 search 7 pillage, rummage
ransom: buy, fee 5 atone, price 6 redeem, rescue 7 deliver, expiate, release 9 redeeming 13 consideration
money: 10 redemptory
rant: 4 fume, rage, rail, rand, rave, riot, song, tune 5 dance, revel, scold, spout 6 frolic, speech, steven 7 bluster, bombast, carouse, declaim, fustian 9 discourse 11 merrymaking, rodomontade 13 jollification
rantipole: 4 wild 6 rakish, unruly 9 termagant
ranty: 4 wild 7 excited
ranula: 4 cyst 8 swelling
rap: bob, box, con, hit, tap 4 blow, chap, grab, knap, tirl 5 blame, clink, clout, knock, seize, smite, steal, utter 6 snatch, strike, thwack 7 deliver 8 sentence 9 criticize, criticism, enrapture, transport 10 punishment
rapacious: 6 greedy 8 covetous, grasping, revening, ravenous 9 ferocious, voracious 10 avaricious, predacious
rapacity: 5 ravin 7 edacity 8 appetite 9 extortion
rape: 4 file, rasp 5 abuse, haste, hasty, hurry, quick, seize 6 defile, pomace, ravish, turnip 7 dispoil, hastily, pillage, plunder, robbery, scratch, violate 9 violation 10 plundering, spoliation
rapeseed: 5 colza
Raphael: 5 angel 9 archangel
conqueror of: 8 Asmodeus
raphe: 4 line, seam 5 joint 6 suture
rapid: 4 fast 5 chute, fleet, quick, steep, swift 6 abrupt, moving, speedy 10 fastmoving 11 expeditions
rapidity: 5 haste 8 celerity, velocity
rapidly: 5 apace
rapier: 5 bilbo, sword 6 verdun 7 ricasso
blade heel: 7 ricasso
part of: 5 forte 6 foible
rapine: 4 rape
rapparee: 6 robber 8 vagabond 9 plunderer 10 freebooter
rappee: 5 snuff
rapport: 6 accord 7 harmony 8 affinity, relation 9 agreement 12 relationship
rapscallion: 5 rogue 6 rascal, wretch 8 rascally 11 ne'er-do-well 14 good-for-nothing
rapt: 4 deep 5 tense 6 intent 8 absorbed, ecstatic 9 comprised, enchanted, engrossed, entranced, transport 10 enraptured 11 preoccupied, transported
raptorial: 11 accipitrine
raptorial bird: owl 4 hawk 5 eagle 7 vulture
rapture: 5 bliss 6 trance 7 delight, ecstasy 8 rhapsody 9 enrapture, happiness, transport 10 exultation
rare: odd, raw 4 fine, good, nice, thin 6 choice, dainty, geason, scarce, seldom, unique 7 antique, capital, curious, extreme, special, tenuous, unusual 8 precious, uncommon, unwonted 9 beautiful, excellent, exclusive, exquisite, scattered, underdone 10 infrequent 11 distinctive, exceptional 13 distinguished, extraordinary
rarefied: 4 thin 7 diluted, ethered, gaseous, refined 8 aethered 10 attenuated
rarity: 5 curio, relic 6 geason 7 antique 8 rareness
ras: 4 cape 6 prince 8 headland 9 commander
rascal: boy, cad, imp 4 file, loon 5 foist, gipsy, gypsy, knave, rogue, scamp 6 ablach, budzat, coquin, harlot 7 budzart, glutton 8 hosebird, scalawag, sealpeen, widdifow 9 miscreant, reprobate, scallawag, scoundrel, trickster 11 rapscallion
rascally: 4 base, mean 6 arrant 9 dishonest, worthless 11 furciferous, mischievous
rase: 4 raze
rash: cut, mad 4 bold 5 brash, erase, hardy, hasty, heady, hives, scamp, shave, slash, uredo 6 daring, eczema, scrape, unwary 7 foolish, hotspur, icarian, scratch 8 careless, eruption, headlong, heedless, reckless, temerous 9 desperate, exanthema, foolhardy, foreright, impetuous, imprudent, overhasty, urticaria, venturous 10 headstrong, hotspurred, incautious, indiscreet, unthinking 11 adventurous, furthersome, harum-scarum, precipitate, precipitous, temerarious, thoughtless, venturesome 13 adventuresome, efflorescence
rasher: 5 slice 7 portion 8 rockfish
rashness: 4 rese 5 folly 6 acrisy 8 temerity
Rasores: 8 Columbae, Gallinae
rasorial: 10 scratching
rasp: rub 4 file 5 belch, eruct, grate 6 scrape 8 bogberry, irritate 9 raspberry

rasping: 5 harsh, raspy, rough 6 hoarse, rasion 7 raspish, raucous 8 guttural 9 offensive

rasse: 5 civet

rasure: cut 6 filing 7 erasing, erasure, rasping, scratch, shaving 8 scraping 12 obliteration

rat: pad 4 scab 6 rodent, vermin 8 betrayer, deserter, informer, renegade, squealer 9 councilor, counselor 11 stool-pigeon 13 doublecrosser
genus: 6 spalax
kind: 5 metad, zemmi, zemni 6 tosher
poison: 8 ratsbane

rat hare: 4 pika

ratafia: 4 noyau 7 biscuit, cordial, liqueur

rataplan: 8 drumbeat

ratch: bar 4 rend 7 ratchet, stretch 8 distance

ratchet: 4 pawl 5 click 6 bobbin, detent

rate: fee, tax 4 fare, file, pace, rank 5 abuse, blame, chide, grade, price, scold, score, tempo, value 6 assess, assize, charge, reckon, regard, tariff 7 account, censure, chasten, despise, quality, reprove 8 appraise, classify, consider, estimate, evaluate 10 proportion 14 classification

rate of exchange: 4 agio 5 batta

ratel: 6 badger

ratfish: 8 chimaera

rathe, rath: 4 soon 5 eager, early, quick 6 prompt, speedy 7 betimes 8 promptly, speedily

rather: ere 4 erer 5 prior 6 before, choice, liever, sooner 7 earlier, quickly 8 somewhat 10 preferably, preference 11 immediately

rather than: ere

ratify: 4 amen, pass, seal 6 affirm, enseal, verify 7 approve, confirm 8 roborate, sanction 9 authorize, establish

ratihabition: 8 sanction 12 ratification

rating: 4 rank 5 cense, class, grade 6 rebuke 8 estimate, scolding, standing 9 reprimand 10 evaluation 14 classification

ratio: pi; cos 4 rate, sine 5 quota, share 6 cosine, degree, ration 7 average, portion 8 relation 10 percentage, proportion 11 capacitance

ratiocination: 5 logic 7 thought 8 argument 9 reasoning

ration: 4 dole, food, mete 5 allot, ratio, share 6 divide 7 portion 8 relation 9 allotment, allowance 10 distribute 11 calculation

rational: 4 sane 5 sober 7 logical 8 sensible 10 reasonable 11 intelligent 13 philosophical

rational integer: 4 norm

rational principle: 5 logos

rations: 8 buckshee 10 provisions

ratite: emu, moa 4 bird, emeu 7 ostrich 9 cassowary
genus: 7 apteryx 8 dinornis

ratoon: 5 shoot, stalk 6 spring, sprout

rattail: 5 braid 7 pigtail

rattan: 4 cane, lash, palm, sega, whip 5 noose, thong 6 punish, switch, wicker

ratter: cat, dog 8 betrayer

rattle: din 4 birl, rale, rick, stun, tirl 5 addle, annoy, clack, rouse, scold, upset 6 assail, racket, uproar 7 agitate, chatter, clapper, clatter, clitter, confuse, fluster, gnatter, maracas 9 crepitate, embarrass 10 disconcert

rattlebrained: 5 giddy 9 frivolous 11 empty-headed, harebrained

rattlemouse: bat

rattlepate: ass 4 dolt 9 chatterer 11 rattlebrain

rattleroot: 7 bugbane

rattlesnake: 8 cascavel, crotalus 9 sistrurus 10 crotalidae(pl.) 11 massasaugas

rattlesnake-bite: rue

rattlesnake fern: 9 sporangia

rattlesnake herb: 9 baneberry

rattlesnake pilot: 10 copperhead

rattle-top: 7 bugbane

rattletrap: 5 ratty 7 gewgaws, rickety 10 ramshackle 11 knickknacks

ratton: rat

ratty: 4 mean 6 shabby 10 rattletrap 11 dilapitated

ratwa: 7 muntjac

raucous: dry 4 loud 5 harsh, noisy, rough 6 coarse, hoarse 7 braying, rasping 8 strident 11 cacophonous

raun: roe 5 spawn

raupo: 7 cattail

ravage: eat 4 loot, prey, ruin, sack 5 foray, harry, havoc, spoil, waste 6 forage 7 despoil, destroy, overrun, pillage, plunder, violate 8 deflower, desolate 9 devastate 10 depopulate, desolation 11 despoilment, devastation

rave: 4 rage, rant 5 blurb, crush, storm 7 bluster, bombast, declaim 8 harangue 11 infatuation 12 commendation

ravel: run 4 comb, fray, rail 5 snarl 6 runner, sleave, tangle, unwind 7 crumble, involve, railing, unravel, untwist, unweave 8 entangle, separate 11 disentangle

ravelin: 8 demilune 13 fortification

raveling: 4 lint 6 thread

raven: 4 crow 5 black 9 blackbird
genus: 5 corvus
of Odin: 5 Hugin

Raven: *author:* Poe
character: 6 Lenore

ravenous: 6 greedy, hungry, lupine, toothy 8 edacious 9 cormorant, ferocious, rapacious, voracious 10 catawampus, gluttonous 12 catawampious 13 catawamptious
ravine: den, gap, lin 4 dell, ghyl, gill, linn, sike, wadi, wady 5 canon, chine, clove, ditch, flume, glack, gorge, goyal, goyle, griff, grike, gulch, gully, kloof, strid 6 arroyo, canyon, cleuch, clough, coulee, gulley, hollow, nullah 8 barranca, barranco, quebrado 10 depression
raving: 6 raging 8 frenzied 9 delirious 10 incoherent, irrational 12 arreptitious
ravish: rob 4 rape 5 abuse, charm, force, harry, seize 6 defile, snatch 7 afforce, corrupt, delight, despoil, enchant, plunder, violate 8 deflower, entrance 9 captivate, constrain, enrapture
ravishment: 7 ecstasy, rapture
raw: 4 cold, damp, dazy(Sc.), lash, nude, rare 5 bawdy, bleak, chill, crude, green, harsh, naked 6 abrade, chilly, unfair 7 cutting, natural, obscene 8 immature, indecent, uncooked 9 inclement, unexposed, unrefined, unskilled, untrained 10 indelicate, unfinished, unprepared, unseasoned 11 uncivilized, unpracticed, unprocessed 12 uncultivated 13 inexperienced
rawboned: 4 lean 5 gaunt 7 angular, scrawny
rawhide: 4 pelt, whip 5 knout, quirt, thong
ray: 4 beam, beta, dorn, soil 5 array, dress, flair, gleam, gleed, light, manta, order, shine, sight, skate 6 defile, glance, obispo, radial, streak, stripe, vision 7 besmear, homelyn, radiate, raiment 9 irradiate, selachian 10 perception, vertebrate 11 arrangement, irradiation
fish: 4 dorn 5 skate
penetrating: 5 gamma
rayon: 5 moire, ninon, tulle 6 faille, pongee 7 taffeta
yarn size: 6 denier
raze, rase: cut, rub 4 rage, ruin, tear 5 erase, graze, growl, level, shave 6 efface, incise, scrape 7 destroy, scratch, subvert 8 demolish, dismantle 9 depredate, overthrow, prostrate 10 obliterate
razee: cut 5 prune 6 reduce 7 abridge
razor: 4 clam 6 shaver
kind: 7 rattler 8 electric
sharpen: 4 hone 5 strop
razorback: hog 5 ridge 10 roustabout
razorbill: auk 7 skimmer
razor stone: 10 novaculite
razz: 5 chaff, tease 6 banter, deride, heckle 8 ridicule
razzia: 4 raid 5 foray 9 incursion
razzle-dazzle: 5 spree 6 dazzle 7 confuse 8 hilarity 9 confusion
re: 5 anent 9 regarding 10 concerning
Re: See **Ra**
reach: toe 4 come, gain, hawk, hent, ryke(Sc.), seek, span, spit 5 grasp, retch, scope, vomit 6 advene, affect, amount, arrive, attain, extend, extent, strive 7 achieve, expanse, possess, stretch 9 culminate, penetrate 10 accomplish
under: 7 subtend
reachable: 10 accessible
reaching: 6 effort 8 profound
reaction: 4 kick 5 start 6 answer 7 tropism 8 response 9 influence 10 impression, opposition
read: con 4 lire(F.), pore, scan, skim, tell 5 aread, areed, drone, guess, solve, study 6 advise, browse, peruse, relate 7 counsel, declare, discern, foresee, learned 8 decipher, describe, foretell, indicate 9 interpret, supervise
ability to: 8 literacy
inability to: 6 alexia
metrically: 4 scan
superficially: 4 skim
readable: 7 legible
reader: 6 lector, lister, primer 7 reciter 8 lectrice, lecturer 9 assistant 10 instructor 11 proofreader 12 elocutionist
readiness: art 4 ease, gift 6 graith 7 address, freedom 8 alacrity, facility, goodwill, volition 9 dexterity, eagerness, quickness 10 promptness 12 preparedness
reading: 6 lesson 7 lection, lecture, perusal, recital, version 9 collation 10 prelection
ready: apt, fit 4 free, glib, here, pret(F.), ripe 5 alert, apert, bound, eager, handy, happy, point, quick 6 active, adroit, facile, fluent, prompt 7 forward, willing 8 cheerful, dextrous, handsome, prepared, skillful 9 agreeable, available, dexterous 10 convenient 11 expeditious 12 unhesitating
real: 4 very, true, vrai(F.) 5 being, loyal 6 actual, hearty 7 certain, cordial, factual, genuine, gradely, literal, sincere 8 existent, faithful, tangible 9 authentic, effective, heartfelt, intrinsic, unfeigned, veritable 10 unaffected
real estate: 4 alod 5 allod, lands 6 realty 8 freehold, premises, property, tenement 13 hereditaments
claim: tax 8 mortgage 9 trust deed 11 encumbrance
pert. to: 7 predial
realistic: 5 vivid 8 lifelike
realization: 8 fruition

realize: get 4 gain, know 5 sense 6 effect, obtain 7 achieve, acquire, convert, fulfill 8 complete, conceive 9 apprehend 10 accomplish, appreciate, understand
really: ara 5 quite, sooth 6 indeed 8 actually
realm: 4 land 5 bourn, clime 6 bourne, circle, domain, empire, region, sphere 7 country, demesne, dynasty, kingdom, terrene 8 division, dominion, province 9 territory 10 department 11 sovereignty 12 jurisdiction
realty: 7 honesty, loyalty, royalty 8 fidelity, property 10 possession
ream: 4 bore, draw, foam, scum 5 bevel, cream, froth, widen 7 enlarge, stretch 11 countersink
reamer: 5 drift 6 broach
reanimate: 5 rally, renew 6 revive 11 resuscitate 12 reinvigorate
reap: cut 4 crop, rake 5 glean 6 garner, gather 7 acquire, collect, harvest
rear: aft, end, fix 4 back, buck, cave, grow, last, lift, rere, tail 5 abaft, breed, build, erect, nurse, raise, stern, train 6 astern, behind, foster, nursle 7 arriere(F.), educate, elevate, nurture 9 construct, establish, posterior 10 background, forthbring
toward: aft 5 abaft 6 astern
rearing by horse: 5 stend 6 pesade
rearhorse: 6 insect, mantis
rearward: 8 backward 10 retrograde
reason: peg 4 mind, nous 5 argue, brain, cause, logic, sense, think 6 debate, ground, motive, ponder, sanity 7 meaning 8 argument, converse 9 discourse, intellect, rationale, wherefore 10 moderation, understand 11 expostulate, ratiocinate, rationality, rationalize 12 plausibility 13 consideration, understanding
alleged: 7 pretext
deprived of: 8 demented
pert. to: 6 noetic
want of: 5 folie 7 amentia, madness 8 insanity
reasonable: 4 fair, just 8 feasible 9 equitable 11 inexpensive
reasoning: 5 logic 8 argument 10 conclusion 13 argumentation
basis of: 7 premise
reassure: 6 assure 7 comfort, hearten 8 reinsure 9 encourage
reata, riata: 4 rope 5 lasso 6 lariat
reave: rob 4 tear 5 burst, seize, split 7 bereave, pillage, plunder
reb: 5 rebel
rebate: 5 check 6 lessen, reduce, refund, weaken 8 diminish, discount 9 abatement, deduction, reduction, remission
rebec: 4 lyre 5 sarod, rebab 6 fiddle, violin
Rebekah: *brother:* 5 Laban
father: 7 Bethuel
husband: 5 Isaac
mother: 6 Milcah
sister: 5 Laban
son: 4 Esau 5 Jacob
rebel: 4 rise 6 oppose, revolt 8 renegade 9 insurgent
rebellion: 6 mutiny, putsch, revolt 8 defiance, sedition, uprising 10 resistance, revolution 12 disobedience, insurrection, renunciation 15 insubordination
rebellious: 10 refractory 12 contumacious, recalcitrant
rebirth: 7 revival 10 conversion, renascence 11 renaissance 13 reincarnation
reboant: 7 echoing 13 reverberating
rebound: dap 4 echo, stot 5 bound, carom 6 bounce, carrom, recoil, re-echo, resile, return, spring 7 reflect, resound 8 ricochet 9 boomerang 11 reverberate
rebuff: cow 4 scat, slap, snub 5 check, chide, fling, repel, scold, spurn 6 lesson 7 censure, refusal, reprove, repulse 9 rejection, reprimand
rebuke: nip, tsk, tut 4 beat, snub, tush 5 barge, blame, check, chide, scold 6 berate, dirdum, lesson, rating 7 downset, lecture, repress, reproof, reprove 8 admonish, chastise, reproach, restrain 9 criticism, criticize, reprehend, reprimand 10 correction 11 comeuppance, reprobation
rebus: 6 enigma, puzzle, riddle
rebut: 5 reply 6 oppose, rebuff, refute, revile 7 repulse 8 disprove 10 contradict
recalcitrant: 5 rebel 6 unruly 7 defiant 9 obstinate 10 calcitrant, rebellious, refractory
recall: 5 annul 6 cancel, encore, remind, repeal, revoke 7 abolish, bethink, rescind, retrace, retract, summons 8 remember, withdraw 9 recollect, reminisce 11 countermand
recant: 6 abjure, revoke 7 abandon, disavow, retract 8 renounce, withdraw 9 repudiate 10 contradict
recapitulate: sum 5 essay 6 repeat, review 7 restate 8 argument 9 enumerate, reiterate, summarize
recapture: 6 recall, regain, retake 7 recover 9 reacquire
recede: ebb 6 depart, retire 7 deviate, regress, retreat 8 withdraw 10 retrograde
receipt: 4 stub, take 6 acquit, apocha, binder, recipe 7 formula 11 acquittance 15 acknowledgement
receive: get 4 take 5 admit, adopt, greet, reset 6 accept, assume, derive, obtain 7 acquire, procure 9 affiliate

receiver: 4 host 5 donee, fence 6 pernor, porter 7 breaker, catcher, hostess, renticr 8 cymaphen, receptor 9 collector, condenser, treasurer 12 receptionist
of property in trust: 6 bailee 7 trustee
of stolen goods: 5 fence
recense: 6 review, revise
recension: 6 review 8 revising 9 reviewing 11 enumeration, examination
recent: new 4 late 5 fresh 6 modern 7 current 8 neoteric
comb. form: neo
recently: 4 anew 8 latterly
receptacle: bin, box, can, cup, fat, pan, pot, tub, urn, vat 4 case, cell, cist, crib, etus, font, inro, pail, tray, vase, well, tank 5 basin, chest, etwee, torus 6 basket, bottle, bucket, carton, holder, hopper, trough 7 capcase, cistern, hanaper, humidor, pitcher 8 canister, receiver 9 cannister, container, continent, reservoir 11 chalkotheke
reception: tea 5 levee, party 6 accoil, durbar, soiree 7 accueil, ovation, receipt, welcome 8 greeting 9 admission, collation 10 admittance 13 entertainment
morning: 5 levee
place: 4 hall 5 atria(pl.), foyer, salon 6 atrium, parlor 7 parlour 9 vestibule
receptive: 9 acceptant, recipient 10 hospitable
receptor: 5 basin 8 receiver 10 dispositor
recess: ala, bay 4 apse, cave, cove, grot, hole, nook 5 ambry, cleft, crypt, niche, sinus 6 alcove, closet, grotto, rabbet, retire 7 adjourn, conceal, retreat, seclude 8 interval, vacation 9 cessation, embrasure, recession, remission, seclusion 10 retirement, suspension 11 withdrawing 12 intermission
recessive: 8 backward, receding
Rechab's son: 7 Jonadab
recherche: 4 rare 6 choice 8 uncommon 9 exquisite 10 farfetched
recidivation: 7 relapse 8 apostasy 11 backsliding
recipe: 7 formula, pattern, receipt 12 prescription
recipient: 4 heir 5 donee 7 alienee, devisee, legatee 8 receiver 9 receiving, receptive
reciprocal: 6 mutual 9 alternate 11 convertible, correlative
comb. form: 6 allelo
reciprocate: 5 bandy, repay 6 return 8 exchange 9 alternate 10 recompense 11 countervail, interchange
recital: 4 saga, tale 5 story 6 report 7 account, concert, program 8 relation 9 narration, narrative, rehearsal, statement 10 recitation, repetition 11 declamation, description, enumeration
recitation: 7 reading, recital
recitative: 5 scena 9 narrative
recite: say 4 carp, scan, tell 5 chant, spout 6 intone 7 recount 9 enumerate 10 cantillate 12 recapitulate
reciter: 6 anteri, diseur(F.) 7 diseuse(F.) 8 narrator 12 elocutionist
reck: 4 care, deem, heed, mind 7 concern 8 estimate
reckless: 4 bold, rash 5 blind, folle, perdu 6 madcap, perdue 7 hotspur 8 careless, headlong, heedless 9 blindfold, bodacious, daredevil, desperate, dissolute, hotheaded, imprudent 10 neglectful, regardless 11 adventurous, extravagant, harum-scarum, indifferent, thoughtless 13 inconsiderate, irresponsible
reckon: 4 aret, date, deem, rate, rely, tell 5 audit, count, think 6 arette, impute, number, regard, repute 7 account, ascribe, compute, include, suppose 8 consider, estimate, numerate 9 calculate, enumerate 10 adjudicate 11 connumerate
reckoner: 5 abaci, brain 6 abacus 9 tabulator 10 calculator 11 comptometer
reckoning: 4 rate, scot, shot 5 chalk, score 6 compot, esteem
machine: I.B.M. 5 adder, brain 6 abacus 9 tabulator 10 calculator
reclaim: 4 save, tame 5 train 6 ransom, recall, redeem, reform, repair, rescue, revoke 7 recover, restore, salvage 8 civilize, empolder 10 regenerate 11 domesticate
reclaimed land: 6 polder
recline: lay, lie, sit 4 lean, loll, rest 6 repose 7 incline
reclining: 5 lying 6 supine 7 leaning, lolling, passive, resting 8 reposing 9 accumbent, recumbent
recluse: nun 4 monk 6 hermit, hidden, secret 7 eremite 8 anchoret, secluded, solitary 9 anchoress, anchorite, cloistral 10 cloistered 11 sequestered
recognizance: 4 rank 5 badge, token 6 avowal, pledge, symbol 10 cognizance, obligation, profession 11 recognition
recognize: ken, own, see 4 avow, know, note, spot 5 admit, greet 6 accept, acknow, agnize, beknow, recall, review, revise, salute 7 consent, correct, recover 8 identify, perceive 9 apprehend 10 appreciate 11 acknowledge, distinguish
recoil: shy 4 kick 5 quail, wince 6 flinch, shrink 7 rebound, retreat, reverse 8 withdraw 12 repercussion
recollect: 6 recall 7 bethink 8 remember

recollection: 4 mind 6 memory 8 memorial 9 anamnesis 11 remembrance 12 reminiscence

recommence: 6 resume

recommend: 4 tout 5 refer 6 advise, commit, denote 7 commend, consign, counsel, entrust 8 advocate

recommit: 6 remand

recompense: fee, pay 5 repay 6 amends, bounty, reward, salary 7 premium, requite 8 requital 9 gratulate, indemnify, reimburse, repayment 10 compensate, remunerate 11 reciprocate, restitution, retribution 12 compensation, remuneration 13 consideration, gratification

without: 4 free 6 gratis

reconcile: 4 wean 5 agree, atone 6 accord, adjust, pacify, regain, settle, shrive, square 7 absolve, conform, expiate, explain, restore, reunite, satisfy 9 harmonize 10 conciliate, propitiate

recondite: 4 dark, deep 6 hidden, mystic, occult 7 cryptic, obscure 8 abstract, abstruse, esoteric, profound 9 concealed

reconnaissance: 6 survey

reconnoiter: spy 5 scout 6 survey 7 examine, explore, inquire 8 discover

record: log, tab 4 acta(pl.), book, dope, file, memo, note, past, roll 5 actum, annal, chart, diary, enrol, enter, entry, graph, score 6 agenda, enroll, legend, memoir, postea, report 7 account, archive, blotter, calends, catalog, dossier, estreat, history, journal, kalends, rotulet 8 calendar, memorial, register 9 catalogue, chronicle, itinerary, narration 10 background, chronology, memorandum, transcribe, transcript

historical: 6 annals

holder: 4 file 6 binder 7 cabinet

keeper: 8 recorder 9 registrar

of arrest: 7 blotter

of ship: log

of travel: 9 itinerary

official: 4 acta(pl.) 5 actum

personal: 5 diary 7 journal

recorded proceeding: 4 acta(pl.) 5 actum

recorder: 5 flute, judge 8 greffier, register 9 cartulary, registrar 10 chartulary

recording device: 4 tape 5 meter

recount: 4 deem, tell 5 count 6 recite, reckon, relate, repeat, retail 7 account, include, narrate 8 describe, rehearse 9 enumerate

recoup: 7 recover 9 indemnify, reimburse 10 compensate, recuperate

recover: get 5 amend, rally, upset 6 obtain, recoup, reform, regain, rescue, resume, retake 7 reclaim, recruit, restore, salvage 8 overcome, retrieve 9 repossess 10 convalesce, recuperate

recovery: 13 convalescence

law: 6 trover

recreant: 5 false 6 coward, craven, crying, wretch, yellow 7 traitor 8 apostate, betrayer, cowardly, deserter, disloyal, yielding 10 traitorous, unfaithful 11 disaffected 12 mean-spirited

recreation: 4 meal, play 5 dance, hobby, sport 6 picnic 7 renewal 9 amusement, avocation, diversion 10 relaxation 11 delassement, refreshment 12 regeneration 13 divertisement, entertainment

time: 6 recess 7 holiday 8 vacation

recrement: 4 scum 5 dregs, dross, spume 6 refuse, scoria

recruit: 4 bleu(F.), boot 5 raise, rooky 6 gather, muster, revive, rookie, supply 7 draftee, private, recover, refresh, restore, soldier 8 assemble, bezonian, inductee 9 reinforce, replenish 10 recuperate, strengthen

rectangle: 6 oblong, square

rectifier: 5 diode

rectify: 5 amend, emend, right 6 adjust, better, purify, refine, reform, remedy 7 correct, distill 8 emendate, regulate 10 straighten

rectitude: 6 equity, virtue 7 fitness, honesty 10 straitness 11 uprightness 12 straightness

rector: 4 head 5 chief, ruler 6 leader, priest 7 proctor 8 director, governor, minister 9 clergyman, conrector 10 headmaster, proproctor

rectory: 5 manse 8 benefice 9 parsonage

recumbent: 4 idle 5 lying 7 leaning, resting 8 inactive, reposing 9 reclining

recuperate: 4 heal, rest 5 rally 6 recoup, regain 7 recover 9 reimburse 10 convalesce

recur: 6 advert, repeat, return 7 rearise, reoccur 8 reappear

recurrent: 9 recurring, returning 11 reappearing 12 intermittent

recusant: 9 dissenter 11 dissentient 12 nonconformer

red: 4 lake, puce, rosy, ruby 5 canna, color, coral, fiery, gules, peony, roset, ruddy 6 cerise, cherry, claret, garnet, maroon, rubric, sienna, titian 7 carmine, crimson, glowing, leftist, magenta, nacarat, radical, roseate, Russian, scarlet 8 amaranth, blushing, inflamed, rubicund 9 anarchist, bloodshot, Bolshevik, communist, Muscovite, vermilion 10 erubescent 12 bloodstained

antique: 5 canna
brown: 5 sepia 6 russet, sorrel
dye: aal, lac 4 chay, choy 5 aurin, eosin 6 aurine 8 morindin
marked with: 6 rubric
purplish: 4 lake 6 claret
yellow: 4 lama 5 aloma, brass, ochre, tenne 6 alesan, orange 7 saffron 9 alabaster, peachblow
red ape: 9 orangutan
red arsenic: 7 realgar
red-backed sandpiper: 6 dunlin
red bell: 9 columbine
red-bellied snipe: 9 dowitcher
red benjamin: 9 birthroot
red blotch: 10 adustiosis
red box: 8 official 12 bureaucratic
red bug: 7 chigger
red cedar: 5 savin 6 sabine, savine 7 juniper 8 flindosa
red cell: 11 erythrocyte
red chalk: 6 ruddle
red cobalt: 9 erythrite
red copper ore: 7 cuprite
red corpuscle deficiency: 6 anemia
Red Cross founder: 6 Barton
Red Cross Knight: 6 George
wife: Una
red deer: roe 4 hart, hind, spay, stag
red-faced: 7 blowzed, flushed 8 blushing
red fever: 10 erysipelas
red fir: 4 pine 6 spruce 7 Douglas
red gum: 10 eucalyptus, strophulus
red honeysuckle: 5 sulla
red lead ore: 8 corcoite
red man: 6 Indian
red pepper: 5 chile, chili 6 chilli
red perch: 8 rosefish
Red Planet: 4 Mars
Red Sea: 9 Erythrean
gulf: 4 Suez 5 Aqaba
island: 5 Perim
peninsula: 5 Sinai
port: 9 Leningrad
red viper: 10 copperhead
red willow: 5 osier 6 cornel
redact: 4 edit 5 draft, frame 6 reduce, revise
redan: 7 rampart 8 fortress 10 breastwork 13 fortification
redargue: 6 accuse, refute 7 confute, convict, reprove 8 disprove, reproach
redbelly: 4 char 7 grouper 8 terrapin
redbird: 7 tanager 8 cardinal 9 bullfinch
redbird cactus: 7 jewbush
redbreast: 5 robin
redbud tree: 5 judas
redcap: 6 porter 7 carrier, specter, spectre 8 tarboosh 9 goldfinch, policeman
redden: 5 blush, flush, rouge
rede: saw 4 plan, tale, tell 5 story 6 advice, advise, relate, scheme 7 counsel, explain, narrate, predict, proverb 9 interpret, narration 10 prediction 11 explanation 14 interpretation
redeem: buy 4 save 6 ransom, regain, rescue 7 deliver, fulfill, reclaim, recover, release, restore 8 liberate 10 repurchase
redeye: 4 rudd 5 vireo 6 whisky 7 sunfish 10 copperhead
redhead: 5 finch 7 pochard 10 woodpecker
redmouth: 4 fish 5 grunt
redolence: 4 balm, odor 5 aroma, odour, scent, smell 7 perfume 9 fragrance, sweetness
redouble: 6 reecho, repeat 7 reprise, retrace 10 ingeminate
redoubt: 6 schanz 10 breastwork 13 fortification
redoubtable: 5 dread 8 fearsome 10 formidable
redound: 5 react 6 accrue, recoil, return 7 conduce, resound 11 reverberate
redress: 5 amend, emend 6 adjust, relief, remedy 7 correct, relieve 10 compensate, reparation 12 compensation, satisfaction
redshank: 4 bird, clee
redshirt: 9 anarchist 11 Garibaldian 13 revolutionist
reduce: cut 4 bant, bate, bust, diet, ease, pare, raze, thin 5 abase, abate, annul, break, level, lower, scale, slash, smelt 6 appall, change, debase, demote, depose, derate, dilute, equate, humble, impair, lessen, rebate, refine, subdue, weaken 7 abridge, assuage, commute, conquer, curtail, degrade, deplete, whittle 8 attemper, condense, contract, decrease, diminish, discount, emaciate, minimize, retrench 9 subjugate 10 annihilate, bantingize, depreciate
to half: 9 dimidiate
sail: 4 reef
reduced: 6 broken 7 dwarfed 9 vestigial
reduction: cut 5 slice 6 rebate 7 cutting, meiosis 8 analysis, discount 11 contraction, degradation 12 annihilation
redundancy: 7 nimiety 8 pleonasm, verbiage 8 plethora 9 verbosity 11 periphrasis
redundant: 5 wordy 6 lavish, prolix 7 copious, diffuse, verbose 9 excessive, exuberant 10 pleonastic 11 overflowing, superfluous 12 overabundant, tautological 13 superabundant 17 circumlocutionary
redwing: 6 thrush 9 blackbird, francolin
redwood: 7 Sequoia
ree: 4 bird, ruff 9 sandpiper, sheepfold
Ree: 7 Arikara

re-echo: 7 redoubt, resound 8 resonate 11 reverberate

reed: sag 4 dart, junk, pipe, sley, stem 5 arrow, grass, spear, stalk 7 bulrush, calamus, fistula
loom: 4 sley

reed organ: 9 harmonium

reedbird: 7 warbler 8 bobolink

reedbuck: kob 4 koba 5 bohor, nagor 7 reitbok 8 antelope 9 waterbuck

reeder: 8 thatcher

reedy: 4 thin 11 arundineous

reef: bar, cay, key 4 cayo, itch, lode, vein 5 atoll, mange, shoal 6 boiler 7 shorten 8 eruption
mining: 4 lode, vein
sail: 4 furl 7 shorten

reefer: 4 coat, eton 5 miner 6 jacket, oyster 9 cigarette 10 midshipman

reek: rig 4 emit, fume, heap, pile, vent 5 equip, exude, smell, smoke, steam, vapor 6 exhale, stench 7 seaweed 8 mountain 10 exhalation

reel: 4 drum, pirn(Sc.), roll, spin, sway, swim, wind 5 dance, lurch, spool, swift, swing, waver, whirl, wince 6 bobbin, hammer, tooter, totter, wintle 7 stagger 8 titubate, windlass
fishing: 4 pirn

reelrall: 9 confusion 10 topsy-turvy 11 disturbance

reem: 4 uris 7 unicorn

reese: 6 scorch

reeve: pen 4 pass, wind 5 twist 6 pucker, thread 7 bailiff, wrinkle 9 enclosure, sheepfold

refection: 4 food 5 drink, lunch 6 repast 11 refreshment

refectory: 4 mess 10 dining hall
monastery: 6 frater

refel: 6 refute, reject 7 deceive, repulse 8 disprove 9 discredit

refer: 4 cite, harp, send 5 recur 6 advert, allude, appeal, assign, charge, commit, direct, impute, regard, relate, return 7 ascribe, consult, mention, specify 8 identify 9 affiliate, appertain, attribute

referee: 5 judge 6 decide, umpire 7 arbiter 8 mediator 10 arbitrator
decision: nod

reference: 5 quote 6 aspect 7 respect 9 relevance 10 connection, pertinence 12 relationship 13 recommendance 14 recommendation

reference book: 5 atlas 7 almanac 8 handbook, syllabus 10 dictionary 12 encyclopedia

referendum: 4 vote 7 mandate 10 plebiscite

refine: 5 exalt, smelt 6 decoct, filter, finish, polish, purify 7 clarify, cleanse, concoct, elevate, improve, perfect 8 chastise, separate 9 cultivate, elaborate, subtilize 12 spiritualize

refined: 4 nice 5 civil 6 artful, chaste, polite, urbane 7 courtly, elegant, genteel 8 delicate, graceful, highbred 9 courteous, exquisite 10 fastidious

refinement: 7 finesse

refining cup: 5 cupel

reflect: 4 echo, muse, pore 5 think 6 divert, mirror, ponder 7 bethink, deflect 8 cogitate, consider, meditate, ruminate 9 reproduce 10 deliberate 11 contemplate, reverberate

reflected: 8 specular

reflection: 4 idea 5 image 6 musing 7 thought 8 likeness 10 cogitation, meditation, rumination 12 deliberation 13 consideration, contemplation
measuring device: 11 albedograph

reflective: 7 pensive

reflex: 4 bend, fold, turn 7 reflect 11 involuntary

reflux: ebb 6 ebbing, euripi(pl.), reflow 7 euripus 9 refluence, returning

refont: 6 recast

reform: 4 mend, trim 5 amend, emend, prune, renew 6 better, direct, punish, remass, repair, revise 7 censure, correct, improve, rebuild, reclaim, rectify, redress, reprove, reshape, restore 8 instruct 10 regenerate 11 reformation

refract: 6 dimish, impair 7 deflect, reflect

refraction: *device:* 4 lens 5 prism 9 telescope
pert. to: 10 anaclastic

refractory: 6 immune, unruly 7 froward, restive 8 contrary, perverse, stubborn 9 camsteary, camsteery, obstinate 10 rebellious, unyielding 11 contrarious, disobedient, intractable 12 contumacious, ungovernable, unmanageable, unresponsive 13 insusceptible

refrain: bob 4 curb, shun 5 avoid, cease, check, epode, forgo 6 chorus, forego, govern 7 abstain, forbear 8 forebear, response, restrain, withhold
music: fa, la 4 aria, song 5 derry

refresco: 5 drink 11 refreshment

refresh: 4 rest 5 bathe, cheer, renew, slake 6 caudle, revise, revive 7 comfort, enliven, freshen, hearten, quicken, restore 8 recreate, renovate 9 reanimate, replenish 10 invigorate, strengthen 12 reinvigorate

refreshing: 4 dewy 5 balmy, tonic 11 refectorial, refrigerant

refreshment: 8 refresco

refrigerant: ice 6 cooler 7 ammonia, coolant, cooling

refrigerate: ice 4 cool 5 chill 6 freeze
reft: 5 cleft 7 divided, forlorn 8 bereaved, divested
refuge: ark 4 home, port, rock 5 haven 6 asylum, bilbie, covert, harbor, resort 7 crannog(Sc.), harbour, retreat, shelter 8 crannoge(Sc.), hospital 9 sanctuary 10 protection, rendezvous, subterfuge
refugee: d.p. 5 exile 6 emigre 8 fugitive
refulgent: 6 bright 7 glowing, radiant, shining 8 splendid 9 brilliant 11 resplendent
refund: 5 repay 6 rebate 9 reimburse, repayment
refurbish: 5 renew 6 polish, revamp 7 freshen 8 brighten, renovate
refusal: no; nay, vee
refuse: nay, ort 4 balk, coom, culm, deny, dirt, dreg, junk, marc, nite, pelf, pelt, veto 5 chaff, coomb, crawm, debar, drast, drest, dross, grith, offal, renig, repel, scrap, trash, waste, wrack 6 debris, forbid, garble, litter, lumber, reject, renege 7 backing, baggage, decline, disavow, forsake, garbage, gubbins, leaving, mullock, rubbish, repulse 8 disclaim, renounce, withhold 9 excrement, repudiate
coffee beans: 6 triage
grape: 4 marc
metal: 4 slag 5 dross 6 scoria
table: ort 5 scrap
wine: 4 lees
refute: 4 deny, meet 5 avoid, rebut, refel 6 assoil 7 confute 8 disprove, infringe, redargue 9 overthrow 10 contradict
serving to: 8 elenctic 10 elenctical
regain: 6 recoup 7 recover 8 retrieve
regal: 5 jewel, royal 6 groove, kingly 7 channel, stately 8 imperial, majestic, splendid
regale: 4 dine, fete 5 feast, treat 7 delight, gratify 9 entertain
regalia: 5 crown, dress 6 finery 7 emblems, ensigns, scepter, symbols 8 costumes, insignia 11 decorations 13 paraphernalia
regality: 5 right 7 country, kingdom, royalty 8 kingship 9 privilege, territory 11 sovereignty 12 jurisdiction
regalo: 4 gift 6 dainty 7 banquet, present 8 delicacy
Regan: *father:* 4 Lear
sister: 7 Goneril 8 Cordelia
regard: air, awe, con, eye 4 care, deem, gaze, heed, hold, look, mind, note, rate, sake, view, yeme 5 honor, think, treat, watch 6 admire, aspect, attend, behold, esteem, glance, homage, notice, remark, repute, revere 7 adjudge, concern, observe, respect 8 consider, estimate, interest, relation 9 adoration, affection, attention, deference, reference 10 admiration, appearance, attendance, estimation, veneration 11 contemplate 13 consideration, contemplation
regarding: 5 about, anent 6 anenst
regardless: 9 negligent 10 neglectful
regatta: 4 race
regency: 4 rule 8 dominion 10 government
regenerate: 5 renew 6 reborn, redeem, reform, revive 7 convert, newborn, reclaim, restore 8 gracious, recreate, renovate
regent: 5 ruler 6 ruling 7 regnant, teacher 8 governor 9 governing
of sun: 5 Uriel
regimen: 4 diet, rule 6 system 7 control, hygiene 10 government, regulation 14 administration
regiment: 4 alai 5 cadre, order 11 systematize
flag: 6 pennon
member: 9 grenadier
nucleus: 5 cadre
officer: 5 boots 7 colonel
regina: 5 queen
region: des, erd, gay 4 area, belt, zone 5 clime, place, realm, space, tract 6 locale, sphere 7 climate, country, demesne, kingdom 8 district, division, latitude, province, vicinity 9 territory 12 neighborhood 13 neighbourhood
comb. form: 5 nesia
infernal: 5 Hades 7 Avernus 8 Tartarus 10 underworld
pert. to: 5 areal
surrounded by alien power: 7 enclave
upper: 5 ether
warm: 7 tropics
woodless: 4 wold 5 llano, plain, weald 6 desert, meadow, steppe 7 pasture, savanna 8 savannah
regional: 5 local 9 sectional 10 provincial
register: lid 4 book, list, roll, rota 5 album, annal, diary, enrol, enter, entry, slate 6 agenda, docket, enlist, enroll, record, roster 7 ascribe, calends, catalog, certify, coucher, kalends, license, stopper 8 archives, bookmark, calendar, recorder, registry, schedule 9 catalogue, chronical, inventory, registrar 10 enrollment 11 certificate, matriculate 12 authenticate, registration
cash: 6 damper
legal: 6 docket
of deaths: 9 necrology
registrar: 8 greffier, recorder, register
regius: 4 king 5 royal 13 professorship
regle: 4 rule 6 govern 10 regulation
reglet: 5 strip 7 molding
regnal: 5 royal 6 kingly

regnant: 6 regent, ruling 8 dominant, reigning 9 prevalent 10 widespread 11 predominant
regorge: 5 vomit 8 disgorge
regress: 6 egress, return 10 retrograde, withdrawal 13 retrogression 14 retrogradation
regressive: 8 backward
regret: rew, rue 4 miss, ruth 5 grief, mourn, sorry, spurn 6 lament, repent, repine, sorrow 7 bethink, deplore, dislike, remorse 8 aversion, distress, forthink 9 penitence 10 misgivings, repentance 11 compunction, lamentation 14 disappointment
regular: 4 even 5 exact, sober, usual 6 formal, normal, proper, serial, stated, steady 7 amiable, correct, ordered, orderly, typical, uniform 8 complete, constant, decorous, formular, habitual, ordinary, ordinate, periodic, pleasant, rhythmic, rotative, standard, thorough 9 continual, customary, isometric 10 consistent, dependable, methodical, systematic 11 symmetrical
regulate: set 4 pace, rule, time 5 frame, guide, order 6 adjust, behave, direct, govern, settle 7 arrange, compose, conduct, control, correct, dispose, rectify 8 attemper, modulate 9 establish 10 discipline 11 standardize
regulating box: 8 rheostat
regulation: law 5 bylaw, canon, regle 6 assize, normal 7 precept, regimen, repulse, statute 8 ordinary 9 ordinance 14 administration
regulator: 5 valve
electricity: 9 rheometer
regulus: 4 king, star 5 matte, ruler
rehash: 7 restate 9 rechauffe
rehearse: say 4 cite, tell 5 drill, quote, speak, train 6 detail, recite, relate, repeat 7 mention, narrate, recount 8 describe, instruct 9 enumerate 12 recapitulate
rehoboam: hat 4 bowl 6 flagon 8 jeroboam
Rehoboam: *father:* 7 Solomon
son: 6 Abijah
reif: 7 plunder, robbery
reign: raj 4 rule, sway 5 guide, power, realm 6 empire, govern 7 kingdom, prevail 8 dominate, dominion 9 authority, dominance 10 prevalence 11 predominate, sovereignty
pert. to: 6 regnal
reimburse: pay 5 repay 6 defray, recoup, refund 7 replace 9 indemnify 10 compensate, recompense, remunerate
reimkennar: 8 sorcerer 9 sorceress
Reims: 4 Loin, Remi
rein: 4 curb, slow, stop, turn 5 check, guide, leash, strap 6 bridle, direct, govern, haunch, kidney 7 control, repress 8 restrain 9 hindrance
reindeer: 6 tarand 7 caribou
genus: 8 rangifer
Santa's: See **Santa Claus** *reindeer*
reinforce: 4 back 5 brace, reman 6 second 7 afforce, support 10 strengthen
reinforcement: 4 sput 9 accession
reinstate: 6 revest
reinvigorate: 7 quicken, refresh
reit: 5 sedge 7 seaweed
reiterate: 4 drum, harp 6 repeat, resume 8 rehearse 10 ingeminate 12 recapitulate
reject: 4 defy, snub 5 eject, repel, scorn, scout, spurn, vomit 6 abjure, disown, rebuff, recuse, refuse 7 cashier, decline, discard, dismiss, disobey, forsake 8 abnegate, castaway, disallow, forswear, relegate, renounce 9 blackball, ostracize, reprobate, repudiate 10 disapprove, disbelieve 13 excommunicate
rejoice: 5 cheer, elate, exult 6 please 7 delight, gladden 8 jubilate 10 exhilarate, tripudiate
rejoin: 5 reply 6 answer 7 respond, reunite
rekindle: 6 revive 7 relight
relache: 10 relaxation 12 intermission
relapse: 4 fall, sink, slip 5 lapse 7 setback, subside 9 backslide 10 recurrence 11 backsliding 12 recidivation
relate: 4 ally, tell 5 apply, refer, state 6 allude, detail, recite, report 7 connect, declare, narrate, pertain, recount, restore 8 describe, rehearse 9 appertain, associate, correlate, enumerate
related: kin 4 akin 7 cognate, germane, kindred 9 affiliate, connected 10 becousined 11 appropriate
on father's side: 6 agnate
on mother's side: 5 enate 6 enatic 7 cognate
relation: sib 5 blood, ratio 6 degree, family, status 7 account, bearing, history, kinship 8 affinity, relative, standing 10 connection, friendship 12 relationship 13 consanguinity
local: 6 ubiety
mutual: 11 correlation
second term of: 7 relatum
relative: pa, eme, kin 4 aunt, mama, papa 5 aunty, niece, uncle 6 auntie, cousin, father, friend, mother, nephew, sister 7 brother, kindred, kinsman, sibling 8 ancestor, apposite, relation, relevant 9 connected, kinswoman, pertinent 10 pertaining 11 comparative 13 corresponding, proportionate
female line: 6 bandju
maternal: 5 enate
relative amount: 5 ratio 6 ration

relatives: 7 kinfolk 8 cousinry, kinsfolk
favoritism to: 8 nepotism
relax: 4 ease, open, rest 5 abate, loose, remit 6 divert, lessen, loosen, reduce, soften, unbend 7 mollify, release, relieve, slacken 8 mitigate
relaxation: 6 repose 7 detente(F.), relache 9 amusement 10 recreation 11 delassement
relaxed: 4 lash 7 lenient 8 flexuous
relay: 4 post, race 5 spell 6 remuda(Sp.), supply 7 forward, relieve, station 8 avantlay, transmit
release: 4 bail, drop, free, liss, trip, undo, vent 5 lisse, relay, remit, slake, untie 6 acquit, assoil, demise, exempt, loosen, parole, remise, rescue, spring 7 absolve, deliver, disband, freedom, manumit, publish, relieve, unleash, unloose 8 liberate, mitigate, unfasten 9 acquittal, discharge, disengage, eliminate, exculpate, extricate 10 emancipate, liberation, relinquish 11 acquittance, deliverance 12 emancipation
relegate: 5 exile 6 banish, commit, deport, remove 7 consign, dismiss
relent: 4 melt 5 abate, yield 6 soften 7 abandon, liquefy, mollify, slacken 8 dissolve 10 deliquesce
relentless: 4 grim, hard 5 harsh, stern, stony 6 strict 8 pitiless, rigorous 9 ferocious, immovable, merciless 10 inexorable, inflexible, persistent 11 unremitting
relevant: apt 6 timely 7 apropos, germain, germane 8 apposite 9 connected, pertinent 10 applicable 11 appropriate, referential
relevate: 5 raise 7 relieve, restore
reliable: 4 true 5 tried 6 dinkum, honest, steady, trusty 7 certain 9 authentic 10 dependable 11 trustworthy
reliance: 4 hope 5 trust 6 belief 8 affiance 10 confidence, dependence
relic: 5 curio, mummy 6 corpse, hallow, remain 7 antique, leaving, memento, remnant, residue 8 memorial, souvenir
pert. to: 9 reliquary
relic cabinet: 6 etager 7 etagere, whatnot
relict: 5 widow 7 widower 8 survivor
relief: bot 4 alms, boot, bote, dole 15 indemnification
ornamental: 4 fret 7 relievo
relieve: aid 4 beet, ease, free, help, liss 5 abate, allay, beete, erase, lisse, raise, relay, slake, spare, spell 6 assist, lessen, remedy, remove, succor 7 assuage, comfort, console, deliver, lighten, redress, release, support, sustain, unloose 8 diminish, mitigate 9 alleviate, debarrass, disburden, discharge, exonerate
religieuse: nun 6 sister
religieux: 4 monk 5 pious 9 religious
religion (see also next entry): 4 cult, sect 5 piety 6 voodoo 7 service, worship 8 devotion, fidelity 9 adoration, voodooism 10 conformity, observance, profession 17 conscientiousness
sect: 5 alogi
study of: 8 theology
system of: 5 faith
religion: See also under specific religions. EXAMPLES: "Jewish god", see **Judaism:** *god of:* "Islamic priest," see **Islam:** *priest*
religious: 4 holy 5 exact, godly, pious 6 devout, divine 7 fervent, godlike, zealous 8 devouted, faithful, monastic 9 pietistic, spiritual 10 devotional, scrupulous 13 conscientious
belief: 5 credo, creed
brotherhood: 8 sodality
denomination: 4 sect
devotion: 6 novena
directory: 4 ordo 7 ordines(pl.)
festival: 6 Easter 8 Passover
formally: 5 rigid 6 strict 8 orthodox 9 pharasaic
image: 4 icon
military order member: 7 Templar
observance: 4 fast, Lent 5 Purim
offering: 5 tithe 7 deodand 8 oblation
reformer: 4 Huss, Knox 6 Luther
sayings: 5 logia
relinquish: 4 cede, drop, quit 5 demit, forgo, grant, leave, waive, yield 6 desert, forego, remise, resign 7 abandon, dispose, forsake 8 abdicate, abnegate, disgorge, renounce 9 surrender
reliquary: box 4 apse, arca 5 apsis, arcae(pl.), chest 6 casket, chasse, shrine 7 chorten
reliquiae: 6 relics 7 remains
relish: 4 dash, gust, like, tang, zest 5 achar, enjoy, gusto, sauce, savor, taste 6 canape, degust, flavor, palate, savour 7 delight, flavour 8 appetite, hautgout 9 appetizer, degustate, enjoyment, seasoning 11 inclination
kind: 5 achar, curry 6 catsup, caviar 7 botargo, chutney, mustard
relucent: 6 bright 7 radiant, shining 9 refulgent
reluct: 5 fight 6 revolt 8 struggle
reluctance: 6 revolt 8 aversion 9 adversion, hesitancy 10 opposition, repugnance, resistance 13 indisposition, unwillingness 14 disinclination
reluctant: 4 loth 5 loath 6 averse, forced 7 adverse 8 backward, grudging, hesitant, opposing 9 resisting, unwilling 11 disinclined
reluctate: 5 repel 6 oppose 9 repudiate

rely: 4 bank, base, hold, hope, lean, rest 5 count, rally, trust 6 belong, cleave, depend, expect, lippen, reckon, repose 7 believe, confide

Remagen's river: 5 Rhine

remain: be; lie 4 bide, last, rest, stay, wait 5 abide, dwell, hover, stand, tarry, thole 6 endure, linger, reside 7 persist 8 continue

remainder: 4 rest, stub 5 stump 7 balance, remanet, remnant, residue, surplus 8 leavings, residual, residuum 9 leftovers

remains: 4 dust 5 ashes, relic, ruins, trace 6 corpse, fossil 7 vestige 9 remainder

remand: 6 commit 7 consign 8 recommit

remanent: 7 further, lasting, remains 8 enduring 9 permanent, remainder 10 additional 13 supplementary

remark: say 4 barb, heed, note, word 5 aside, gloss, state, write 6 notice, regard 7 comment, descant, express, observe 8 indicate, perceive 9 aspersion, platitude 10 animadvert, annotation, commentary, expression 11 distinguish, observation

embarrassing: 5 boner, break 7 blooper, faux pas

witty: gag, mot 4 quip 5 sally 7 sarcasm 9 witticism

remarkable: 7 notable, strange, unusual 8 uncommon 9 egregious, wonderful 11 exceptional 12 considerable 13 extraordinary

remble: 4 move, stir 6 remove

remedy: aid, bot 4 balm, boot, bote, cure, drug, gain, hale, heal, help 5 amend, salve, topic 6 arcana(pl.), relief, repair 7 arcanum, correct, cure-all, nostrum, panacea, placebo, rectify, redress, relieve 8 antidote, curative, medicine 9 treatment 10 assistance, catholicon, chevisance, corrective, reparation 13 counteractive

imaginary: 6 elixir 7 panacea

quack: 7 nostrum, placebo

soothing: 4 balm 6 balsam

remember: 6 ideate, recall, record, remind, reward 7 bethink, mention 9 recollect, reminisce 11 commemorate

remembrance: 4 gift, mind 5 token 6 memory, minnie, notice, trophy 7 memento, mention 8 allusion, keepsake, memorial, souvenir 9 discourse, reference 10 impression 11 inscription 12 recollecting

remex: 5 quill 7 feather

remind: 6 recall

reminder: cue 4 hint, memo, note, prod, twit 7 memento, monitor 10 admonition

reminiscence: act 4 fact 5 power 6 memory 9 recalling 10 experience 11 memorabilia, remembering, remembrance 12 recollection

remise: 4 deed 5 remit 6 giving, return 7 release, replace, respite 8 granting 9 remission, surrender 10 remittance

remiss: lax 4 lazy, mild, pale 5 slack, tardy 6 gentle 7 diluted, languid, lenient, relaxed 8 careless, derelict, dilatory, heedless, moderate 9 dissolved, liquefied, negligent 10 neglectful 11 inattentive, thoughtless 13 irresponsible

remission: 4 liss 5 lisse 6 rebate 9 abolition, cessation, lessening 10 diminution

remit: pay 4 bate, send 5 abate, defer, enter, refer, relax 6 cancel, excuse, insert, pardon, resign, return, submit 7 abandon, absolve, forgive, forward, readmit, release, restore, slacken, suspend 8 abrogate, liberate, mitigate, moderate, postpone, recommit, transmit 9 exculpate, surrender

remittance: 9 allowance

remnant: bit, end, ort, rag 4 dreg, fent, left, part, rest, stub 5 crumb, piece, relic, scrap, trace, wrack 7 leaving, portion, remains, residue 8 fragment 9 remainder 10 suggestion

remodel: 6 change, recast 7 rebuild 11 reconstruct

remolade: 5 sauce 8 dressing, ointment

remonstrance: 10 benedicite 13 expostulation

remonstrate: 5 argue 6 object 7 declare, profess, protest 8 complain 11 demonstrate, expostulate

remora: 4 clog, drag, fish, pega 5 delay 7 pegador 9 hindrance 10 impediment

remord: 5 taint 6 excite, ponder, rebuke 7 afflict, censure, remorse 8 remember

remorse: rue 4 pity, ruth 5 grief, qualm 6 regret, sorrow 7 penance 8 distress 9 penitence, repentent 10 compassion, contrition 11 compunction

remote: far, off 4 afar, cool 5 alien, aloof, faint, vague 6 forane, slight 7 distant, faraway, foreign, removed 8 secluded, separate 10 abstracted, impersonal, unfriendly 12 inaccessible

goal or end: 5 Thule

more: 7 endmost, further 8 ulterior

most: 6 ultima 9 diametric

remove: rid 4 bate, dele, doff, fire, free, kill, move, oust, pare, raze, rend, sack, void, weed 5 amove, apart, avoid, elide, eloin, erase, evict, expel, strip 6 betake, cancel, change, convey, deduct, delete, depose, disbar, distal, eloign, recall, remble, retire, uproot 7 deprive, despoil, dismiss, extract, uncover, whittle 8 abstract, disclose, discover, dislodge, displace, relegate, sepa-

rate, supplant, transfer **9** eliminate, eradicate, translate **10** disconnect **11** assassinate
clothing: **5** strip **7** disrobe, undress
from office: **4** oust **6** depose
ice: **7** defrost
impurities: **5** smelt **6** filter, refine
legally: **4** oust **6** disbar
to another place: **8** transfer
removed: off **4** away, move **5** aloof, apart **6** remote **7** distant **10** abstracted
remover: **6** porter **7** carrier, drayman, solvent **9** scavenger **10** contractor
remuneration: pay **5** wages **6** reward **7** payment, stipend **8** requital **9** emolument, repayment **10** recompense **12** compensation, satisfaction **13** consideration, gratification, reimbursement
remunerative: **10** beneficial, profitable
Remus: *brother:* **7** Romulus
father: **4** Mars
foster mother: **4** wolf
mother: **4** Rhea
slayer: **7** Romulus
renable: **4** glib **5** ready **6** fluent **8** eloquent
renaissance: **7** rebirth, revival **10** renascence
renal: **7** nephric **9** nephritic
Renard: See **Reynard**
rencounter: **4** duel, meet **5** clash, fight **6** action, battle, combat, debate **7** collide, contest, meeting **8** conflict **9** collision, encounter
rend: cut, rip **4** pull, rent, rive, slit, tear **5** break, burst, sever, split, wrest **6** breach, cleave, divide, enrive, pierce, remove, screed, sunder **7** abscind, dispart, disrupt, rupture **8** fracture, lacerate, separate **9** dismember **12** disintegrate
render: do; pay, put, try **4** emit, give, make, melt **5** treat, yield **6** depict, recite, repeat, return, submit **7** clarify, deliver, exhibit, extract, furnish, inflict, payment, perform, present, requite, restore **8** transmit **9** interpret, represent, surrender, translate **10** contribute
rendezvous: **4** date, meet **5** place, tryst **6** refuge **7** hangout, meeting, retreat **8** assemble, mobilize **9** agreement, gathering **11** appointment
rendition: **8** delivery **9** surrender **11** deliverance, performance, translation **14** interpretation
renegade: rat **5** rebel **6** bolter **7** traitor **8** apostate, deserter, fugitive, renegado, turncoat **10** changeling
renege, renig: **4** deny **5** welsh **6** desert, refuse, revoke **7** decline **8** renounce
renew: **4** beet **5** beete **6** extend, refill, repair, repeat, resume, revamp, revive **7** freshen, rebuild, refresh, replace, restore **8** reassume, re-create, renovate **9** replenish **10** invigorate, recommence, regenerate, rejuvenate **11** re-establish, resuscitate **12** redintegrate
renitent: **7** opposed **8** opposing **9** obstinate, resistant **12** recalcitrant
rennet: lab **5** apple **6** curdle, keslop **7** earning(Sc.) **8** cheeslep, cheeslip, earnings(Sc.), membrane **9** coagulate
ferment: **6** enzyme, rennin
renomme: **8** renowned **10** celebrated
renounce: **4** cede, defy, deny **5** cease, forgo, renay, renig, waive **6** abjure, desert, disown, forego, forlet, forsay, recant, reject, renege, repeal, resign **7** abandon, disavow, forsake, retract **8** abdicate, abnegate, disclaim, forspeak, forswear, renounce **9** repudiate, surrender **10** abrenounce, relinquish **12** abrenunciate
renovate: **4** redo **5** alter, clean, renew **6** purify, repair, resume, revive **7** cleanse, furbish, refresh, replace, restore **10** invigorate, regenerate
renown: rap **4** fame, note **5** eclat, glory, kudos, rumor **6** report **7** acclaim **8** eminence **9** celebrity **10** reputation **11** celebration, distinction
renowned: **5** known **11** illustrious
rent (see also **rend**): let, pay **4** gape, hire, hole, rime, toll **5** censo, chink, cleft, crack, cuddy, gavel, gorge, lease, share, split, yield **6** breach, engage, income, profit, return, reward, schism **7** fissure, opening, revenue, rupture, tribute
high: **8** rackrent
paid: tac
transfer: **6** attorn
rental: **4** cost, list **5** house **8** schedule **9** apartment
rente: **6** income **7** annuity, revenue
renter: **6** lessee, tenant **8** occupant
renverse: **7** reverse **8** overturn **9** overthrow
reopen: **6** resume **10** recommence
rep: **5** cloth **6** fabric
repair: fix **4** darn, heal, help, mend **5** amend, patch, piece, refit, renew **6** remedy, return, revamp, revive **7** correct, rebuild **8** renovate
repairman: **6** tinker **7** cobbler **8** mechanic
repand: **4** bent, wavy **6** uneven
reparation: **4** bote **6** amende, amends, reward **7** damages, redress **8** requital **9** amendment, atonement, indemnity, repairing **10** recompense **11** restitution **12** compensation, distribution, partitioning **14** redistribution
repartee: wit **5** reply **6** retort **7** riposte
repast: tea **4** bait, feed, food, meal **5** bever, feast, snack, treat **6** dinner **7** banquet **8**

mealtime 9 collation, refection 11 refreshment
pert. to: 8 prandial
repatriation: 6 return 11 restoration
repay: pay 4 meed 5 appay 6 avenge, profit, punish, refund, return, reward 7 deserve, requite, restore 9 gratulate, reimburse, retaliate 10 compensate, recompense, remunerate 11 reciprocate
repeal: 5 amend, annul, emend 6 appeal, cancel, recall, revoke 7 abolish, rescind, retract, reverse 8 abrogate, derogate, renounce, withdraw
repeat: bis(It.), din 4 cite, echo, rame 5 ditto, quote, recap, recur 6 encore, parrot, resume, retell 7 iterate, recount, reprise, restate 8 redouble 9 duplicate, reiterate 10 ingeminate, repetition 11 battologize 12 recapitulate
music: bis
performance: 6 encore
sign in music: 5 segno
repeatedly: oft 5 often 10 frequently 11 continually 12 continuously
repeater: gun 5 rifle, watch 6 pistol 7 firearm 10 recidivist
repel: 4 beat, stop 5 check, debar, force 6 combat, defend, oppose, rebuff, refuse, reject, remove, resist 7 decline, disgust, repulse 9 vanquish 10 extinguish
repellent: 4 grim 5 harsh 9 repugnant 10 forbidding
repent: rue 5 atone 6 grieve, lament, regret 7 reptant 8 crawling, creeping, forthink, penitent
repentance: 4 pity, ruth 5 shame 7 penance, remorse 9 attrition, penitence 10 contrition 11 compunction
repentant: 11 penitential
repercussion: 4 blow 6 impact, recoil 7 rebound 8 reaction 10 reflection 11 reiteration 12 ballottement 13 reverberation
repertory: 4 list 5 index 7 theater, theatre 8 calendar, magazine, treasury 9 catalogue 10 collection, storehouse
repetition: bis 4 copy, echo, rote 5 rondo 6 dilogy, encore 7 replica, tremolo 9 iteration, rehearsal 10 redundancy 12 reproduction
mechanical: 4 rote 8 anaphora
of homologous parts: 6 merism
of idea: 8 pleonasm 9 tautology
of others: 7 echolia, mimicry 9 echolalia
of sound: 4 echo
repine: 4 fail, fret, pine, wane 5 mourn 6 grouse, lament, regret 7 grumble, whimper 8 complain, languish
replace: 4 stet 5 reset, stead 6 follow 7 relieve, restore, succeed 8 supplant 9 reimburse, supersede 10 substitute
replacement: 6 ersatz 9 successor 10 substitute
replenish: 4 feed, fill 5 renew, store
replete: fat 4 full, rife 5 sated, stout 6 filled, gorged 7 bloated, implete, stocked, stuffed 8 complete 9 abounding, surfeited
replevy: 5 seize 6 attach, redeem 7 recover
replica: 5 image 6 carbon, ectype 8 likeness 9 facsimile 10 repetition 12 reproduction
replicate: 4 bend, fold 5 reply 6 repeat 8 manifold, repeated 9 duplicate, multifold
reply: 4 echo, fold, sass 5 rebut 6 answer, oracle, re-echo, rejoin, repeat, retort, return 7 respond, retract, riposte 8 repartee, response 9 rejoinder 11 replication
report: pop 4 fame, tell, word 5 bruit, noise, rumor, state, story 6 breeze, cahier(F.), delate, digest, recite, relate, repeat, return, rumour 7 account, crackle, hansard, hearing, hearsay, inkling, narrate, recital, summary 8 announce, describe 9 circulate, grapevine, narration, narrative
false: fib, lie 6 canard 7 slander 8 tall-tale 12 misstatement
reporter: cub 6 legman, writer 7 newsman 9 columnist 10 journalist
symbol: 6 thirty
repose: lay, lie, set, sit 4 calm, ease, rely, rest, seat 5 peace, place, quiet, sleep 6 relief 7 compose, confide, deposit, dignity, recline, replace, restore, support 8 calmness, serenity 9 composure, quietness 10 relaxation, repository 11 downsitting 12 requiescence, tranquillity
reposit: 7 deposit, replace
repository: ark, box 4 bank, file, safe, shop 5 ambry, capsa, chest, vault 6 closet, museum 7 arsenal, capsule, granary, storage 8 magazine, treasury 9 confidant, reliquary, sepulcher, warehouse 10 depository, storehouse
reposoir: 5 altar
repossess: 6 regain 7 recover
reprehend: 4 warn 5 blame, chide 6 rebuke 7 censure, reprove 8 admonish, disprove 9 reprimand
reprehensible: 8 criminal, culpable
represent: act 4 show 5 enact 6 clothe, denote, depict, typify 7 exhibit, express, picture, portray, produce, profess 8 describe, simulate 9 delineate, designate, exemplify, reproduce, symbolize 10 substitute 11 impersonate 12 characterize
representation: map 4 icon, idol, ikon 5 chart, graph, image, model 6 avowal, blazon, sample 7 account, diagram 8 likeness, notation 9 portrayal, statement 10 simili-

tude 11 histrionics, performance, portraiture
favorable: 14 recommendation
representative: 4 heir 5 agent, envoy 6 consul, deputy, legate 7 tribune 8 delegate, executor, exponent, salesman 10 ambassador 12 illustrating, illustrative 13 administrator
repress: 4 bury, curb, hush, rein, stop 5 check, choke, crush, daunt, press, quell 6 bridle, deaden, reduce, stifle, subdue 7 depress 8 compress, restrain, suppress, withhold 9 constrain, overpower
reprieve: 5 defer, delay 6 escape 7 respite, suspend 8 postpone 12 postponement
reprimand: 4 call 5 check, chide, slate 6 rebuff, rebuke 7 censure, chapter, chasten, repress, reproof, reprove 9 reprehend 12 reprehension
reprint: 4 copy
reprisal: 7 revenue 8 requital
reprise: 8 reassume 10 compensate, recommence, repetition 12 reprehension
reproach: 4 blot, slur, twit 5 abuse, blame, braid, chide, shame, shend, sully, taunt 6 accuse, infamy, rebuke, revile, stigma, vilify 7 censure, condemn, reprove, traduce, upbraid 8 besmirch, disgrace, dishonor 9 bespatter, challenge, contumely, descredit, disrepute, invective 10 correction, exprobrate, opprobrium, scurrility 11 impeachment 12 vilification 13 animadversion 15 discommendation
old word of: 4 raca
reprobate: 4 hard 5 Satan, scamp 6 disown, rascal, reject 7 abandon, condemn, corrupt, vicious 8 castaway, denounce, hardened 9 blameable, reprehend, scoundrel 10 censurable, condemned, disallowed 11 blameworthy, disapproved 12 unprincipled 13 reprehensible
reproduce: 4 copy, draw 6 repeat 7 imitate 8 multiply 9 duplicate, propagate, represent 11 reconstruct
asexually: 5 clone
reproduction: 6 ectype 7 fission, replica 8 likeness 9 photostat 11 counterpart 13 proliferation
reproductive: 8 prolific
reproductive cell: 6 gamete
reprove: 4 flay, rate, slam 5 blame, check, chide, roast, scold, shame 6 berate, rebuff, rebuke, refute, reject 7 censure, confute, correct, lecture, upbraid 8 admonish, carritch, chastise, disgrace, disprove, redargue, reproach 9 castigate, challenge, objurgate, reprehend, reprimand, reprobate 10 administer, animadvert, carritches 11 epostulate
reptant: 8 crawling, creeping
reptile: 4 croc, worm 5 snake 6 turtle 8 dinosaur, tortoise 9 alligator, crocodile, pterosaur 10 dinosauria(pl.), predentate 11 pterodactyl, pterosauria(pl.)
age: 8 Mesozoic
edible: 6 iguana, turtle
legless: 4 apod 5 snake
pert. to: 7 saurian 8 ophidian
scale: 5 scute
study of: 11 herpetology
reptiles: *age of:* 8 Mesozoic
group: 6 sauria
reptilian: low 4 mean 5 snaky 6 lizard, sneaky 7 reptant, saurian, serpent 8 crawling, creeping, ophidian 9 groveling, malignant 10 despicable
republic: 5 state 9 democracy 10 commonweal, government 12 commonwealth
imaginary: 7 Oceania
world's smallest: 5 Nauru
Republic author: 5 Plato
repudiate: 4 defy, deny 6 abjure, disown, recant, refuse, reject 7 decline, disavow, discard, divorce, retract 8 abrogate, disclaim, renounce 9 disaffirm
repugn: 6 oppose, resist
repugnance: 5 odium 6 enmity, hatred 7 disgust, dislike 8 aversion, distaste, loathing 9 antipathy, hostility, repulsion 10 abhorrence, antagonism, opposition, reluctance 11 abomination, contrariety, incongruity 13 inconsistency 14 disinclination 15 incompatibility 16 disagreeableness 17 contradictoriness
repugnant: 8 inimical 9 offensive, repellent 10 refractory 12 disagreeable 14 irreconcilable
repulse: 4 deny, foil, rout 5 check, fling, rebut, refel, repel 6 defeat, denial, rebuff, refuse, reject 7 exclude, refusal 9 rejection
repulsion: ug(Sc.) 7 dislike 8 aversion, distaste 10 repugnance
repulsive: 4 dain, evil, loth, ugly, vile 5 loath, toady 6 odious 7 fulsome, hateful, loathly 9 offensive, repellent, repugnant 10 disgusting, forbidding 11 distasteful, gorgonesque
repurchase: 6 redeem
reputable: 4 good 8 credible 10 creditable 11 responsible
reputation: 4 fame, lose, name, note, odor 5 glory, honor, izzat, odour, stamp 6 credit, honour, renown, repute 7 respect 9 attribute, character 11 distinction 13 consideration
loss of: 7 scandal
repute: 4 fame 5 honor, worth 6 credit, esteem, regard, revere 7 account, respect,

suppose 9 character 10 ascription, estimation
reputed: dit 8 putative
request: ask, beg, sue 4 plea, pray, suit, wish 5 apply, crave, order 6 appeal, behest, demand, invite 7 entreat, prithee, solicit 8 entreaty, petition, rogation 11 application 12 solicitation, supplication
formal: 8 rogation
requiem: 4 hymn, mass, rest, song 5 chant, dirge, peace, quiet 7 service
requiescat: 4 wish 6 prayer
requiescence: 6 repose
requin: 5 shark 8 man-eater
require: ask 4 lack, need 5 claim, crave, exact, force 6 behove, compel, demand, enjoin, entail, expect, oblige 7 behoove 9 postulate 11 necessitate
requirement: 4 duty 9 formality, requisite
requisite: 4 need 7 needful 9 condition, essential 11 requirement 13 indispensable
requisition: 5 order 6 billet, demand 9 embargo, request 11 application, requirement
requital: 7 guerdon 8 reprisal 9 vengeance 11 antapodosis, retribution
requite: pay 5 atone, repay 6 acquit, avenge, defray, return, reward 7 deserve, gratify, revenge 9 retaliate 10 compensate, recompense
reredos: 4 wall 6 screen 7 drapery 9 backplate, partition
reree: 7 cattail
reremouse: bat
rerun: 6 replay, reshow
res: 5 point, thing 6 matter
resale: 8 exchange
resay: 6 repeat 7 iterate
rescind: 4 void 5 annul 6 cancel, repeal, revoke 7 abolish, retract 8 abrogate 11 countermand
rescissible: 9 revokable 11 rescindable
rescript: 5 order 6 answer, decree 9 rewriting 11 counterpart
rescue: 4 free, save 6 ransom, redeem, succor 7 deliver, reclaim, recover, release, salvage 8 delivery, liberate 9 extricate 11 deliverance
rese: 4 rage, rush 5 hurry, onset, quake, shake 7 impulse, tremble 8 rashness
research: 7 inquiry 11 examination 13 investigation 15 experimentation
reseau: net 6 ground 7 network 10 foundation
resect: 6 excise
reseda: 10 mignonette
resemblance: 5 image 6 simile, symbol 7 analogy 8 affinity, likeness, vicinity 9 agreement, imitation, semblance 10 comparison, similarity, similitude 12 assimilation 14 representation
one bearing: 6 ringer
resembling: 4 like 5 alike 11 approximate
resentment: ire 4 gall 5 anger, depit, pique, spite 6 animus, choler, enmity, grudge, hatred, malice, rancor, spleen 7 dudgeon, umbrage 8 acrimony 9 animosity, annoyance, hostility, malignity 10 irritation 11 displeasure, indignation
reserve: 4 cash, cave, fund, keep, save 5 spare, stock, store 6 assets, retain, supply 7 backlog, bespeak, caution, modesty, shyness, silence, surplus 8 coldness, distance, forprise, preserve, withhold 9 exception, reservoir, restraint, retention, reticence 10 constraint, diffidence, discretion, limitation, substitute 11 reservation, taciturnity
reserved: coy 4 cold 5 aloof, staid, taken 6 sedate 8 backward, cautious 15 incommunicative, uncommunicative
reservoir: vat 4 font, pond, pool, sump, tank 5 basin, fount, stope, store 6 cenote, supply 7 cistern, favissa, forebay, piscina, reserve 8 favissae(pl.), fountain
re-set: 4 help 5 abode, alter 6 harbor, refuge, resort, succor 7 receipt, receive, replace, secrete, shelter 9 receiving 10 receptacle
reseiance: 5 abode 9 residence
reside: big, lie 4 bigg, live, room, stay 5 abide, dwell, habit, lodge 6 remain, settle 7 inhabit, sojourn, subside 8 habitate
residence: 4 home, seat, shed 5 abode, house, villa 6 biding, castle, palace 7 habitat, mansion 8 domicile, residuum, sediment 9 apartment 10 habitation, villanette 13 collectorship
resident: cit 6 lessee, tenant 7 burgess, citizen 8 inherent, occupant
residue: ash 4 dreg, lees, marc, orts, rest, silt, slag 5 ashes, dregs 6 cinder, excess, relics, sludge, sordes 7 balance, remains, remnant 8 leavings, remanent, residuum, sediment 9 remainder
residuum: 8 hangover 9 remainder
resign: 4 cede, quit 5 demit, remit, yield 6 devote, submit 7 abandon, consign, deliver 8 abdicate, renounce 9 surrender 10 relinquish
resignation: 8 patience 9 endurance 12 acquiescence
resile: 6 recede, return 7 rebound, retract, retreat 8 withdraw
resiliency: 4 tone 8 buoyancy 10 elasticity
resilient: 5 toned 7 buoyant, elastic, springy 8 bouncing, stretchy 9 recoiling, returning 10 rebounding

resin, rosin: alk, gum, lac, tar 4 aloe, balm, tolu 5 amber, anime, animi, copal, damar, elemi, gugal, gugul, loban, myrrh, pitch 6 balsam, charas, dammar, derrid, elemin, googul, salban, storax 7 acouchi, ambrite, aroiera, copalba, copaiva, derride, exudate, fluavil, galipot, hartite, ladanum, retinol 8 alkitran, bdellium, fluavile, gedanite, glessite, guaiacum, labdanum, retinite, sandarac 9 alchitran, colophony, elaterite 11 colophonium 12 frankincense
fossil: 5 amber 8 glessite
gum: 5 gugal 6 mastic
incense: 8 sandarac
purified: 7 shellac
varnish: 5 anime, copal

resinous tree: fir 4 pine 6 balsam

resist: 4 buck, fend 5 rebel, repel 6 baffle, combat, defeat, defend, impugn, oppose, wither 7 contest, prevent 9 frustrate, gainstand, withstand

resistance: 6 rebuff 7 defence, defense 9 hostility, renitence 10 antagonism, oppugnance 13 recalcitrance

resistance box: 8 rheostat

resistant: 4 hard 8 obdurate, renitent

resolute: 4 bold 5 fixed 7 animose, animous 8 positive, resolved, stalwart, unshaken 9 unbending 10 unwavering

resolution: vow 4 grit, thew 5 heart, nerve 7 purpose, resolve, verdict 8 analysis, backbone, decision, firmness, proposal, strength 9 assurance, certainty, constancy, fortitude, hardihood, statement, sternness, stoutness 10 conviction, separation, steadiness 11 intrepidity, persevering 12 deliberation, faithfulness, perseverance, resoluteness 13 determination, inflexibility, steadfastness 14 simplification 15 disentanglement

resolve: 4 free, melt 5 relax, untie 6 answer, assoil, dispel, inform, loosen, reduce, remove, settle 7 appoint, dispose, explain, liquefy, scatter, unravel 8 conclude, dissolve, enfeeble, persuade, separate

resonant: 7 ringing, vibrant 8 sonorous, sounding 10 resounding 11 reverberant

resort: go; spa 4 howf 5 crowd, haunt, howff, joint, place, visit 6 betake, casino, refuge, return, revert, throng 7 company 8 frequent, habitual, recourse 10 assemblage, honkeytonk
health: spa 9 sanatoria(pl.) 10 sanatorium, sanitarium
place of: 5 haunt 7 purlieu

resound: 4 echo, peal, ring 5 clang 6 reecho 11 reverberate

resounding: 8 plangent

resourceful: apt 5 sharp 7 fertile

resources: 5 funds, means, money 6 assets, stocks, stores 7 resorts 8 reserves, supplies, supports 10 expedients 12 contrivances
guardian: 15 conservationist

respect: awe 4 heed 5 defer, honor, value 6 admire, esteem, homage, regard, revere 7 concern, neglect, observe, respite, tribute, worship 8 postpone, venerate 9 attention, deference, reference, reverence 10 admiration
act of: 6 devoir
pay: 5 greet 6 salute

respectable: 4 good 6 decent, honest, proper 7 fausant 9 estimable, honorable, reputable 10 creditable 11 presentable

respectful: 5 civil 7 careful, duteous 11 ceremonious

respective: 4 each 6 sundry 7 partial 9 regardful 10 individual, particular

respiration: 6 breath 7 eupnoea 9 breathing
difficulty: 4 rale 5 cough 7 dyspnea 8 dyspnoea
normal: 7 eupnoea

respire: 4 live, sigh 6 exhale, inhale 7 breathe

respite: 4 lull, rest 5 delay, pause 6 recess 7 leisure 8 interval, reprieve, surcease 9 cessation 10 suspension 12 intermission, postponement

resplendent: 6 bright 7 aureate, blazing, radiant, shining 8 dazzling, glorious, gorgeous, lustrous, splendid 9 brilliant, refulgent 10 epiphanous, flamboyant

respond: 4 echo, feel 5 react, reply, write 6 accord, answer, pillar, rejoin, retort, return 8 response 10 correspond

response: 4 word 5 verse 6 anthem, chorus, phrase 7 refrain 8 sentence

responsible: 8 amenable 9 accordant, reputable 10 answerable, dependable, sufficient 13 correspondent

responsibility: 4 care, onus 6 burden, charge 9 liability 10 obligation 11 reliability 14 accountability 15 trustworthiness

responsive: 6 mutual 8 amenable 9 sensitive 11 sympathetic

res publica: 5 state 8 republic 10 commonweal 12 commonwealth

rest: lay, lie, set, sit 4 calm, ease, hang, lair, lean, liss, prop, rely, seat, slip, stay, stop 5 abide, ceast, found, lisse, pause, peace, quiet, relax, renew, repos(F.), sleep, stand 6 alight, cesura, depend, desist, remain, repose, settle 7 balance, caesura, comfort, leisure, refresh, remains, remnant, reposal, residue, respite, shelter, support, surplus 8 breather, interval, lodgment, vacation 9 cessation, establish, quietness, remainder, stillness 10 immobility, inactivity, relaxation 11 refreshment 12 intermission, peacefulness, tranquillity

in reading: 7 caesura

noonday: nap 6 siesta

rest house: inn 4 chan, khan 5 hotel, serai 6 abalam, hostel, tavern 7 chhatri

restate: 6 reword 8 reassert

restaurant: inn 4 cafe 5 diner, hotel 6 bistro, tavern 7 automat, beanery, cabaret, tearoom 9 cafeteria, chophouse, hashhouse 10 rotisserie, steakhouse 11 rathskeller(G.)

restful: 5 quiet 8 peaceful

resting: 4 abed 6 asleep, latent 7 dormant

restitution: 6 amends, return 8 recovery 10 recompense, reparation 11 restoration 12 compensation 13 reimbursement

restive: 5 balky 6 uneasy, unruly 7 fidgety, nervous 8 restless, stubborn 9 impatient 10 refractory 12 unmanageable

restless: 6 fidget, fitful, haunty, hectic, roving, uneasy 7 agitato(It.), fidgety, fretful, inquiet, restive, unquiet 8 agitated, feverish, stirring 9 disturbed, impatient, sleepless, unsettled, wandering 10 disquieted, reposeless 12 discontented

restoration: 10 reparation 11 restitution

restorative: 7 anodyne 8 salutary

restore: 4 cure, heal, mend 5 amend, atone, renew, repay, right 6 redeem, refund, repair, return, revive 7 convert, rebuild, recover, replace 8 renovate 9 reinstate, resurrect 10 regenerate 11 reconstruct, re-establish, resuscitate 12 redintegrate, rehabilitate

printer's mark: 4 stet

restrain: bar, dam 4 bate, bind, calm, clog, curb, hold, rein, rule, stay, stop 5 chain, check, cramp, deter, guard, limit, still, stint 6 arrest, behave, bridle, coerce, detain, fetter, forbid, govern, halter, hamper, hinder, pinion, tether 7 abridge, abstain, chasten, command, confine, contain, control, deprive, forbear, inhibit, prevent, repress, shackle, trammel 8 attemper, compesce, compress, conclude, imprison, prohibit, restrict, suppress, withhold 9 constrain, detention 12 circumscribe

restrained: 6 severe 8 reserved 9 hidebound 11 disciplined

restraint: bit 5 force 7 barrier, durance, reserve 9 avoidance, reticence 10 internment

restrict: bar 4 curb 5 bound, cramp, limit, scant, stint 6 censor, coerce, hamper, modify, ration 7 astrict, confine, repress, tighten 8 contract, derogate, prohibit, restrain, straiten 9 constrict 12 circumscribe

restricted: 5 local 6 finite, narrow, strait 9 parochial 10 provincial

restriction: 10 regulation 11 reservation 13 qualification

restrictive: 7 binding 8 limiting 9 stringent

resty: 5 quiet 6 rancid 7 restive 8 sluggish

result: go; end, sum 4 leap, rise 5 ensue, event, fruit, issue, score, total 6 accrue, effect, follow, sequel, spring, upshot 7 outcome, proceed, redound 8 aftering, decision 9 aftermath, eventuate, terminate 10 conclusion 11 achievement, consequence, termination

result in: 5 cause

resume: 5 renew 6 reopen, repeat, review 7 epitome, summary 8 continue, reoccupy, synopsis 9 epitomize, reiterate, summarize 10 abridgment, recommence 12 recapitulate 14 recapitulation

resurrection: 7 rebirth, revival 11 restoration

resuscitate: 6 revive 7 quicken, restore 8 revivify

ret: rot, sop 4 soak 5 steep 6 dampen

retable: 5 ledge, shelf 6 gradin 9 framework

retail: 4 hawk, sell vent 5 trade 6 barter, peddle, relate, repeat

retailer: 6 dealer 8 huckster, merchant

retain: 4 hire, hold, keep, save 6 adhere, athold, behold, employ 7 contain, prevent, reserve 8 maintain, preserve, remember, restrain 9 entertain, recollect

retainer: fee 4 cage, hewe 5 frame 6 menial, minion, vassal 7 hobbler 8 follower 9 burkundaz 11 burkundauze

retaining: 9 retentive

retaliate: 5 repay 6 avenge, punish, retort 7 requite, revenge

retaliation: 6 talion 8 reprisal, requital 11 retribution

retard: 4 slow 5 brake, catch, defer, delay, deter, trash 6 belate, deaden, detain, hinder, impede 8 encumber, obstruct, postpone, restrain 10 decelerate

retardant: 8 obstacle

retardation: lag

retch: gag 4 hawk, spit 5 reach, vomit 6 expand, extend, strain 7 stretch

rete: 6 plexus 7 network

retem: 7 juniper

retention: 6 memory 7 holding, keeping 8 learning 10 retainment 11 maintenance, remembering

retepore: 8 bryozoan

rethe: 5 cruel 6 ardent, fierce, severe

retiarius: 9 gladiator

retiary: 6 meshed, telary 7 netlike
reticent: 4 dark 6 silent 7 sparing 8 discreet, reserved, retiring, taciturn 9 secretive 10 mysterious 15 uncommunicative
reticule: bag 4 etui 5 cabas, etwee 6 pocket, sachet 7 handbag, reticle, workbag
reticulum: net 7 network, stomach 8 meshwork
retinaculum: 6 frenum
retinue: 4 band, crew, ging, rout, suit, tail 5 harem, meiny, suite, train 6 attend, escort 7 cortege, service 8 equipage 9 entourage, retainers 10 attendance, attendants
retire: go; ebb 5 leave 6 depart, recede, recess, remove, vanish 7 pension, retreat 8 withdraw 9 disappear, sequester
retired: 4 abed, lone 5 quiet 6 secret 7 private, recluse 8 abstruse, emeritus, reserved, secluded, solitary 9 recondite
retiring: shy 5 timid 6 modest 7 bashful, fugient 8 reserved 9 diffident 11 unobtrusive
retort: mot 4 quip, turn 5 facer, repay, reply, sally 6 answer, recoil, return, ripost 7 alembic, cornute, respond, riposte 8 blizzard, repartee 9 retaliate
retortion, retorsion: 7 bending 8 reprisal, twisting 10 reflection
retract: 4 bend 6 abjure, cancel, disown, recall, recant, remove, repeal, retire, revoke 7 disavow, prevent, rescind, retreat 8 restrain, withdraw 9 repudiate
retraction: 8 palinode
retral: 8 backward 9 posterior 10 retrograde
retreat: den 4 abri, cave, holt, lair, nest, nook, rout 5 arbor, bower 6 arbour, asylum, harbor, recede, recess, refuge, retire 7 harbour, privacy, retiral, shelter 8 solitude, withdraw 9 departure, hibernate, sanctuary, seclusion 10 rendezvous, retirement, sanitarium, withdrawal
underground: 4 abri, cave
retrench: cut 4 bate, omit, pare 6 delete, excise, lessen, reduce, remove 7 abridge, curtail, repress 8 decrease, diminish 9 economize, intercept
retrenchment: 5 ditch 7 parapet, rampart 8 traverse 10 breastwork 12 entrenchment
retribution: pay 6 return, reward 7 nemesis, revenge, tribute 8 requital 9 vengeance 10 punishment, recompense
goddess of: Ate
retrieve: 6 recall, regain, revive 7 recover, restore 8 discover 10 recuperate
retrograde: 4 slow 6 recede, retral 7 decline, inverse, opposed, regress 8 backward, contrary, decadent, inverted, rearward, withdraw 9 catabolic, reversely 10 degenerate, retrogress 11 deteriorate
retrogression: 7 regress 8 fallback 9 decadence 12 degeneration 14 retrogradation
retrogressive: 8 backward
retrospective: 6 review 8 backward 11 retroactive 13 contemplative
retund: 4 dull 5 blunt 6 refute, subdue 9 attenuate
return: lob 4 bend, turn 5 recur, remit, repay, yield 6 advert, answer, profit, render, report, retort, revert 7 regress, replace, reprise, requite, respond, restore, revenue, reverse 8 requital, response 9 repayment, retaliate, reversion 10 recompense, recurrence 11 reciprocate, replacement, restoration 12 reappearance 13 reciprocation
Return of the Native author: 5 Hardy
Reuben: *brother:* 6 Joseph
father: 5 Jacob
mother: 4 Leah
Reuel's father: 4 Esau
reunite: 6 rejoin 9 reconcile
reus: 9 defendant
revamp: 5 renew
reveal: bid 4 bare, blab, jamb, open, show, tell, wray 5 exert 6 betray, bewray, descry, detect, expose, impart, unveil 7 confide, develop, display, divulge, exhibit, uncover 8 announce, decipher, develope, disclose, discover, evidence, manifest, revelate 11 communicate
reveille: 4 call, dian 5 diana, levet 6 signal
revel: joy 4 orgy, riot, wake 5 feast, randy, spree, watch 6 bezzle, gavall, high-go 7 carouse, delight, revelry, roister 8 carnival, carousal, domineer, festival 9 celebrate, festivity 11 celebration, merrymaking 12 conviviality
revelant: 9 pertinent
revelation: 4 tora 5 torah 9 discovery 10 disclosure 13 manifestation
reveler, reveller: 8 bacchant 9 bacchanal, roisterer 10 merrymaker
cry: 4 evoe
revenant: 5 ghost 7 specter 9 recurring 10 apparition
revendicate: 7 reclaim, recover
revenge: 6 avenge 7 requite 8 requital 9 retaliate 11 retribution
revenue: 4 rent 5 yield 6 income, profit, rental, return 7 finance 8 interest
reverberate: 4 echo, ring 6 re-echo, return 7 reflect, resound
reverberating: 7 reboant 8 resonant 12 repercussive 13 reverberatory
revere: 4 love 5 adore, honor 6 admire, esteem, regard, repute 7 respect, worship 8 venerate

reverence: awe 4 fear 5 dread, piety 6 homage 8 devotion 9 deference, obeisance, solemnity
gesture of: 8 kneeling 11 genuflexion 12 genuflection
reverend: sri 4 holy 5 abbot 6 clergy, sacred 9 clergyman, monsignor
reverent: 6 humble 7 dutiful
reverie: 5 dream 6 musing, vision 7 fantasy 8 daydream
revers: 5 lapel
reverse: 5 annul, upset 6 defeat, invert, regard, repeal, revoke 7 abolish, backset, convert, subvert 8 backward, contrary, converse, disaster, opposite, overturn 9 disaffirm, overthrow, transpose 10 misfortune 11 countermand
reversion: 6 return
to state: 7 escheat
to type: 7 atavism
reversional: 9 atavistic
revert: 5 react 6 advert, return, revive 7 escheat, recover, reverse 9 backslide 11 antistrophe
revest: 4 robe 5 dress 6 attire, clothe 8 reinvest 9 reinstate
review: 4 edit 5 recap 6 parade, resume, survey 7 account 8 ceremony, critique 9 criticise, criticism, criticize, re-examine 10 certiorari, inspection, periodical, reconsider, retrospect 11 examination
revile: 4 hate, rail 5 abuse, blame, brawl, scold 6 debase, malign, vilify 7 deprave 8 reproach 9 blaspheme 10 calumniate
revince: 6 refute
revise: 4 edit 5 alter, amend, emend 6 change, redact 7 correct, improve, recense 8 readjust 9 castigate, reexamine, supervise
reviser, revisor: 10 diaskeuast
revival: 6 recall 7 rebirth 11 renaissance 12 reproduction 13 recrudescence
revive: daw 4 wake 5 rally, renew, rouse 6 return 7 enliven, freshen, quicken, recover, refresh, restore 8 reawaken, recreate, rekindle, revivify 9 reanimate, refreshen, resurrect 10 regenerate, rejuvenate 11 resuscitate 12 reinvigorate
revoice: 4 echo 5 refit 7 restore
revoke: 5 adeem, annul, check, renig 6 cancel, recall, recant, renege, repeal 7 abolish, fenagle, finagle, prevent, repress, rescind, retract, reverse 8 abrogate, restrain, withdraw 9 fainaigue 11 countermand
revolt: 5 rebel, repel 6 mutiny, offend 7 retreat 8 renounce, sedition, uprising 9 rebellion 12 insurrection, renunciation
revolting: 4 ugly 6 horrid 7 hateful, hideous 8 shocking 9 loathsome, offensive, repellent, repulsive 10 disgusting, nauseating
revolution: 4 gyre, turn 5 cycle 7 circuit 8 disorder, rotation, uprising 9 overthrow, rebellion 12 renunciation
revolutions per minute: RPM 4 revs
revolve: con 4 birl, roll, spin, turn, whir 5 recur, swing, trend, twirl, wheel, whirl, whirr 6 circle, gyrate, ponder, rotate 7 agitate, reflect, trundle 8 consider, meditate 10 deliberate
revolver: gat 6 pistol 7 firearm
revolving: 4 orby 6 rotary
part: 5 rotor 7 rotator
revue: 4 show 9 burlesque 13 entertainment
revulsion: 4 fear 6 change 8 reaction 9 reversion 10 withdrawal
reward: fee, pay, utu 4 heed, hire, meed, rent 5 ameed, award, bonus, check, crown, merit, medal, prize, repay, wages, yield 6 bounty, gersum, notice, profit, regard, return, salary, trophy 7 guerdon, premium, success 8 requital 9 honoraria(pl.) 10 compensate, honorarium, recompense, remunerate 11 retribution 12 compensation, remuneration 13 gratification
rewarding: 7 helpful 10 beneficial
rewrite: 4 edit 6 revise
rex: 4 king
Reynard: fox
rezai: 8 coverlet
rhamn: 9 buckthorn
rhapontic: 7 rhubarb 8 pieplant 9 knapweeds
rhapsodic: 8 ecstatic, effusive 9 emotional
rhea: emu 4 emeu 5 nandu 8 avestruz(Sp.)
Rhea: Ops
child: 4 Hera, Zeus 5 Hades 6 Hestia 7 Demeter 8 Poseidon
father: 6 Uranus
husband: 6 Cronus
rhema: 4 term, verb, word
rheoscope: 12 galvanoscope
rheotome: 11 interrupter
rhesus: 6 monkey 7 macaque
rhetor: 6 master, orator 7 teacher
rhetorical: 6 florid 8 forensic 10 figurative, oratorical
rhetorician: 6 master, orator, writer 7 speaker, teacher
rhetorics: *digression:* 6 ecbole
diminution: 7 litotes
figure of speech: 6 aporia, simile 7 epandos 8 metaphor 10 apostrophe 12 alliteration, onomatopoeia 15 personification
rheum: 4 cold 7 catarrh 8 rhinitis
rheumatism remedy: 5 salol 9 salacetol
rheumatism weed: 10 pipsissewa

rhexis: 7 rupture
rhinal: 5 nasal 6 narial
rhine: 5 ditch, drain 6 runnel
Rhine: *city:* 8 Mannheim
magic hoard: 9 Rheingold, Rhinegold
nymph: 7 Lorelei
pert. to: 7 Rhenish
tributary: Aar, Ill 4 Aare, Lahn, Main, Ruhr, Waal
wine: 7 Moselle
rhino: 4 cash 5 money 10 rhinoceros
rhinoceros: 5 abada, topan 6 borele, umhofo 7 keitloa, upeygan
black: 6 borele
cousin of: 5 tapir
feature: 4 horn
rhinoceros beetle: 4 uang
rhinoceros bird: 9 beefeater
rhipidion: 8 flabella(pl.) 9 flabellum
rhizoid: 8 rootcell
rhoda: 4 rose
Rhode Island founder: 13 Roger Williams
Rhodes: *ancient wonder:* 8 Colossus
festival: 10 Chelidonia
Rhodesia: *language:* Ila
people: 10 Balokwakwa
rhododaphne: 8 oleander
rhoeadales: 5 poppy
rhomboid: 13 parallelogram
rhonchus: 4 rale 7 snoring 8 croaking 9 whistling
Rhone: *town:* 5 Arles
tributary: 5 Isere, Saone
rhubarb: 5 error 6 hassle 7 mistake, yawweed 8 argument, pieplant 9 butterbur, rhapontic 10 discussion
derived from: 5 rheic
genus: 5 rheum
rhus tree: 5 sumac 6 sumach
rhyme: 5 verse 9 harmonize
rhymester: 4 poet 6 rhymer 8 rimester 9 poetaster
rhyptic: 9 detergent
rhythm: 4 beat, lilt, time 5 clink, meter, pulse, swing, tempo 7 cadence, measure
break in: 7 caesura 8 caesurae(pl.)
instrument: 4 drum 7 cymbals 8 triangle 9 tamborine
monotonous: 8 singsong
rhythmic: 6 poetic 8 metrical 9 recurrent
ria: bay 5 creek, inlet
rial: 4 king 5 great, noble, power, royal 6 prince 8 splendid 9 excellent 11 magnificent
rialto: 4 mart 6 bridge, market 8 exchange
rialty: 4 pomp 5 power, state 6 estate 8 grandeur 10 ceremonial
riant: gay 6 bright 8 cheerful, laughing, smiling
riata: 4 rope 5 lasso, reata 6 lariat
rib: 4 bone, hair, purl, stay, wale 5 costa, ridge, tease 6 costae(pl.), lierne 7 bristle, support 9 cotelette, tierceron
pert. to: 6 costal 7 costate
ribald: low 6 coarse, rascal, vulgar 7 obscene 9 offensive 10 irreverent, scurrilous 11 blasphemous
riband: 6 ribbon
ribband: bar 4 spar 5 plank, strip 6 bridge, timber 9 scantling
ribbed: 6 barred, corded 7 costate
fabric: rep 5 twill 6 faille
ribbet: 5 rybat 6 rabbet, rebate
ribble row: 6 string 9 rigmarole
ribbon: bow 4 tape 5 braid, corse, padou, reins, shred, snood, strip, taste 6 cordon, fillet, riband, silver, taenia, tatter 7 binding, taeniae(pl.) 8 banderol, decorate, tressour, tressure 9 banderole
badge: 6 cordon
binding: 6 lisere
ribbon-fish: 4 fish 7 cutlass, oarfish 8 bandfish, dealfish
ribbon gum: 8 eucalypt
ribbon-like: 8 taeniate, taenioid
ribbon worm: 9 nemertine
ribless: 8 ecostate 9 decostate
ribwort: 8 hardhead, plantain
rice: 4 boro, chit, paga, twig 5 arroz(Sp.), bigas, canin, macan, pilaf, pilau, stick 6 branch 7 risotto 9 brushwood
boiled with meat: 5 pilaf, pilau
drink: 4 sake 5 bubud 7 pangasi
field: 4 padi 5 paddy
husk: 4 shud 5 shood
inferior: 4 chit
milk: 5 gruel 7 pudding 8 porridge
paste: ame
polishings: 5 darac
rice rail: 4 sora
ricebird: 7 bunting, sparrow 8 bobolink 9 gallinule
riceroot grass: 9 broomroot
rich: fat 4 dear, oofy 5 ample, opime 6 absurd, costly, creamy, daedal, fruity, greasy, hearty, mellow, mighty, oofier, potent 7 copious, fertile, moneyed, opulent, orotund, pinguid, wealthy 8 abundant, affluent, generous, luscious, powerful, valuable, well-to-do 9 abounding, bountiful, elaborate, laughable, luxuriant, plentiful, sumptuous 10 productive 12 concentrated, preposterous
man: 5 Midas, nabob 7 Croesus 9 plutocrat
richard: 9 plutocrat
richdom: 6 wealth 8 richness
riche: 4 rule 5 realm, reign 9 authority
Richelieu's successor: 7 Mazarin

riches: 4 gold, pelf, weal 5 lucre, worth 7 fortune 8 treasure
demon of: 6 Mammon
region of: 8 Eldorado
worship of: 10 plutomania
rick: 4 goaf, heap, pile 5 noise, scold, stack, twist 6 jingle, rattle, sprain, wrench 7 chatter
rickety: 4 weak 5 crazy, shaky 6 feeble, senile 7 unsound 8 unstable 9 tottering 10 ramshackle
rickmatic: 6 affair 7 concern 8 business
rickshaw: 6 samlor
ricochet: 4 skip 5 carom 6 bounce, glance 7 rebound
rictus: 4 gape, mask
rid: 4 free 5 clear, empty 6 assoil, remove, rescue 7 deliver, relieve 8 dispatch, liberate 9 eradicate 11 disencumber
ridder: 4 sift 5 sieve
riddle: ree 4 crux, sift 5 aread, areed, griph, rebus, sieve 6 enigma, pierce, puzzle 7 griphus, mystery, perplex 8 disprove, separate 9 conundrum, criticize, perforate
riddler: 8 screener
ride: 4 dosa 5 drive, float, motor, tease 6 harass 7 hagride, journey, torment 8 ridicule 9 carrousel, cavalcade, excursion 12 merry-go round
to hounds: 4 hunt
without power: 5 coast, glide
rideau: 5 mound, ridge
rident: 5 riant 7 smiling 8 grinning, laughing
rider: 6 clause, cowboy, jockey, knight 7 allonge 8 addition, bucaayro, buckaroo, cavalier, desultor, horseman 9 amendment, performer, straddler 10 equestrian, freebooter, highwayman, horsewoman 11 endorsement, mosstrooper 12 bronco-buster, equestrienne(fem.)
ridge: as, os; aas, rib, top 4 aret, asar, back, balk, bank, barb, bult, dene, dune, gold, kame, lira, loma, osar(pl.), rand, reef, ring, ruck, ruga, seam, spur, wale, wave, weal, welt 5 arete, arris, bargh, chine, costa, crest, eskar, esker, hause, oesar(pl.), rugae(pl.), serac, spine, stria, varix, wheal, whelk 6 costae(pl.), crista, rideau, striae(pl.) 7 annulet, costula, cristae(pl.), hogback, porcate, varices(pl.), wrinkle, yardang 8 costulae(pl.), headland, sastrugi, zastrugi 9 elevation, razorback
anatomical: 5 spine, stria
cloth: 4 wale
glacial: 5 esker
pert. to: 7 cardinal
shell: 5 varix 7 varices(pl.)
skin: 4 wale, welt
ridge oak: 9 blackjack
ridged and furrowed: 7 porcate
ridicule: guy, pan 4 gibe, jeer, mock, quiz, razz, twit 5 borak, chaff, irony, roast, scout, sneer, taunt 6 banter, deride, expose, satire 7 asteism, buffoon, lampoon, mockery, pillory, sarcasm 8 derision, raillery, satirize 9 burlesque
deity: 5 Momus
object of: 13 laughingstock
ridiculous: 5 droll 6 absurd 7 amusing 8 farcical 9 laughable, ludicrous 10 irrational, outrageous 12 preposterous
riding: 9 chevachie 10 equitation
costume: 5 habit
pants: 8 jodhpurs
shoe: 8 solleret
riding school: 6 manege
riding whip: 4 crop 5 quirt
ridotto: 6 resort 7 redoubt, retreat 8 festival 9 gathering 10 masquerade 11 abridgement, arrangement 13 entertainment
riem: 5 strap, strip, thong
Rienzi composer: 6 Wagner
rier: 4 cask
rife: 5 brief 7 current, replete 8 abundant, numerous 9 abounding, plentiful, prevalent 10 prevailing, widespread
riff: 6 riffle, ripple 7 midriff 9 diaphragm
Riff: 6 Berber
riffle: 4 plow, reef 5 rapid, shoal 6 rattle 7 shallow, shuffle 11 obstruction
riffraff: mob 4 raff, scum 5 trash 6 rabble, refuse 7 rubbish 9 sweepings
rifle: arm, gun, rob 4 tige 5 reeve, steal 6 furrow, groove, weapon 7 bundock, carbine, despoil, escopet, firearm, pillage, plunder, ransack 8 bandhook 9 chassepot, escopette
accessory: 6 ramrod
ball: 5 minie
instrument: 7 bayonet
kind of: 6 Garand, Mauser 7 Enfield 9 Remington 10 Winchester 11 Springfield
magazine: 6 Mauser
pin: 4 tige
rifleman: 5 jager, yager
rift: lag 4 flaw, rive 5 belch, break, chasm, cleft, crack, rapid, split 6 breach, cleave, divide 7 blemish, fissure, opening, shallow 8 division
rig: fig, fit, fix 4 fool, gear, hoax, wind 5 dress, equip, rifle, storm, trick 6 lateen, outfit, square, tackle 7 arrange, costume, derrick, ransack, swindle, turnout 8 accouter, accoutre, carriage, equipage 9 apparatus, equipment 10 manipulate 11 contraption
part of: 4 spar

riga: 6 balsam
Riga Gulf island: 5 Oesel
Riga native: 4 Lett 7 Latvian
rigadoon: 5 dance
rigescence: 8 numbness 9 stiffness
rigging part: 4 gear, spar 5 ropes
right: fit, gee, hak 4 fair, good, hakh, real, sane, soke, true 5 droit, sound 6 angary, dexter, equity, lawful, normal, patent, proper 7 correct, derecho, fitting, genuine, liberty, rectify, redress, upright 8 becoming, courtesy, easement, interest, straight, suitable, usufruct, virtuous 9 authority, equitable, faultless, franchise, privilege 11 appropriate, certificate, prerogative
comb. form: 6 dextro
exclusive: ex 7 patents 10 concession
law: 5 droit
of way: 8 easement
proprietary: 8 interest
royal: 7 regalia
right-angled: 10 orthogonal, rectangled 11 rectangular
right down: 4 very 8 complete, thorough 10 positively, thoroughly
right hand: 6 dextra 7 dextera
right-hand page: 5 recto
right-handed: 7 dextral 8 dextrous 9 dexterous
righteous: 4 good, holy, just 5 godly, moral, pious, zadoc, zadok 6 devout, worthy 7 perfect, sinless, upright 8 virtuous 9 blameless, equitable, guiltless
righteousness: 9 rectitude
rightful: due 4 fair, just, true 5 legal 6 honest, lawful, proper 7 fitting, upright 9 righteous 11 appropriate
rightist: 4 Tory 11 reactionary 12 conservative
rigid: set 4 firm, hard, taut 5 fixed, stark, stern, stiff, stony, tense 6 marbly, severe, strait, strict 7 austere 8 rigorous 9 immovable, stringent, unbending 10 inflexible, motionless, unyielding
rigmaree: 4 coin 6 trifle
rigmarole: 8 nonsense 10 balderdash
rignum: 9 horsemint
rigol: 4 ring 6 circle, furrow, groove 7 channel
Rigoletto: *composer:* 5 Verdi
role: 5 Gilda
rigor, rigour: 4 fury 7 cruelty 8 asperity, hardship, rigidity, severity, violence 9 austerity, harshness, rigidness, sharpness, stiffness 10 difficulty, exactitude, puritanism, strictness 13 inflexibility
rigorous: 5 angry, rigid, stern 6 severe, strait, strict 7 correct, drastic, precise 8 accurate 9 inclement 10 inexorable, oppressive, relentless
rikk: 10 tambourine
rile: vex 4 roil 5 anger, annoy, upset 7 agitate, disturb 8 irritate 9 turbidity
rill: 5 brook, creek, crick, ditch 6 course, furrow, groove, runnel, trench 7 rillock, rivulet 8 brooklet 9 arroyuelo(Sp.), streamlet
rim: lip 4 bank, brim, edge, orle, ring, tire 5 basil, bezel, bezil, brink, somma, verge 6 border, flange, margin, shield 7 enclose, horizon 8 boundary 9 perimeter
horseshoe: web
pipe: 6 flange
rail: 6 flange
wheel: 4 tire 5 felly, 6 felloe
rima: 5 cleft 7 fissure 8 aperture 10 breadfruit
rimash: 9 hackberry
rimate: 8 fissured
rime: ice 4 hoar, poem, rent, rung, step 5 chink, crack, frost, rhyme, verse 6 freeze 7 fissure, versify 8 aperture 9 cranreuch(Sc.), hoarfrost
rimple: 4 fold 6 crease, ripple, rumple 7 wrinkle
rimption: lot 9 abundance
Rinaldo's steed: 6 Bayard 7 Bajardo
rind: 4 bark, husk, melt, peel, skin 5 crust, waste 6 cortex 7 clarify, epicarp, peeling 8 cortices(pl.)
rindle: 5 brook 6 runnel 7 rivulet
ring: bee, cut, rim, set 4 bail, band, cric, ding, dirl, echo, gyre, halo, hank, hoop, link, lute, peal, toll, tore 5 anlet, arena, bague, bezel, chime, clang, group, knell, longe, ridge, rigol 6 arenae, border, brough(Sc.), chaton, circle, circus, clique, collar, collet, corona, dindle, dingle, famble, gasket, girdle, terret, tingle, tinkle, toroid 7 annulet, annulus, circlet, coterie, curette, ferrule, grommet, resound, ringlet, tanbark, vibrate 8 bracelet, cincture, encircle, surround 9 archivolt, enclosure, encompass 10 racecourse 11 reverberate 14 tintinnabulate
carrier: 9 go-between
comb. form: 4 gyro
gem setting: 5 bezel 6 chaton
of chain: 4 link
of rope: 7 grommet
pert. to: 7 annular
stone: gem
to hold reins: 6 terret
to tighten joint: 6 washer
wedding: 4 band
ring finger: 5 third

ring ouzel: 6 thrush
ring plover: 5 sandy
ring-shaped: 7 annular 8 annulate 9 annulated
ring-tailed cat: 8 cacomixl 9 cacomixle 10 cacomistle
ring-worm: 5 tinea 7 serpigo 8 milleped 9 millepede
ringdove: 4 dove 6 cushat, pigeon 10 turtledove
ringed: 6 wedded 7 engaged, married 8 annulate, circular 9 annulated, decorated, encircled 10 surrounded
ringed worm: 7 annelid
ringent: 6 gaping
ringing: 4 clam 6 bright 7 orotund 8 resonant
ringle-eye: 7 walleye
ringleader: 10 instigator
ringlet: 4 curl, lock, ring 5 tress
rings: *interlocking:* 6 gimmal
series: 4 coil
rink: man 4 hero, race, ring 9 encounter
rinner: 6 runner
rinse: 4 lave, sind(Sc.), wash 5 douse 6 douche, gargle, sluice 7 cleanse
rinthereout: 5 tramp 7 vagrant 8 vagabond
rio: 5 river 6 coffee, stream
riot: din 4 clem 5 brawl, feast, melee, revel 6 affray, bedlam, clamor, excess, pogrom(Russ.), tumult, uproar 7 dispute, quarrel, revelry 8 carousal, debauche, disorder, outburst, sedition, uprising 9 commotion, confusion, luxuriate 10 donnybrook 11 dissolution, disturbance
riotous: 4 loud, wild 5 loose 6 wanton 10 boisterous, profligate 11 saturnalian 12 contumacious, unrestrained
rip: hag, rit 4 rend, rent, rive, tear 6 sunder 8 disunite, harridan, lacerate 9 debauchee 10 laceration
rip-roaring: 5 noisy 6 lively 8 exciting 9 hilarious 10 boisterous, uproarious
ripa: 4 bank 5 beach, shore 6 strand
ripe: fit, rob 4 aged, bank 5 adult, ready, rifle 6 addled, august, mature, mellow 7 plunder 8 complete, finished, seashore 9 developed, full-grown, perfected, riverbank 10 consummate, seasonable 11 intoxicated
early: 8 rareripe
ripen: age 4 grow 6 mature, mellow 7 develop, improve, perfect, prepare
riposte, ripost: 5 reply 6 retort, return, thrust 8 repartee
ripper: 7 bobsled 9 bobsleigh
rippet: 4 romp 6 uproar 7 quarrel
ripping: 4 fine 8 splendid 9 admirable, excellent 10 remarkable
ripping iron: 8 ravehook
rippit: 5 fight
ripple: cut, lap 4 curl, fret, purl, riff, tear, wave 5 acker, graze 6 cockle, dimple, rimple 7 crinkle, scratch, wavelet, wrinkle 8 undulate
ripple grass: 7 ribwort
rise: 4 flow, grow, hulk, loom, rare, rear, soar, stem, well 5 arise, begin, climb, issue, mount, reach, rebel, stand, start, surge, swell, tower 6 amount, appear, ascend, ascent, aspire, assume, attain, derive, emerge, growth, mature, revolt, spring, thrive 7 adjourn, advance, elevate, emanate, prosper, succeed 8 eminence, flourish, increase, levitate 9 ascension, beginning, elevation, originate
again: 7 resurge 9 resurrect
and fall: 4 tide 5 heave 6 welter
riser: 4 pipe, step
risible: 5 funny 7 amusing 9 laughable, ludicrous
rising: 5 arist 6 orient, ortive 7 montant, nearing 8 gradient, uprising 9 ascendant, ascendent, ascension 11 approaching 12 extumescence, insurrection
risk: 4 dare, gage, wage 5 peril, stake 6 chance, danger, expose, gamble, hazard, injury, plight, plunge 7 imperil, venture 8 exposure, jeopardy 9 adventure 12 disadvantage
risky: 7 parlous
risley: 7 acrobat
risp: bar, rub 4 file, rasp, stem, tirl, wisp 5 grass, stalk 7 bulrush, scratch
risper: 11 caterpillar
risque: 4 racy 5 risky 6 daring 9 audacious, hazardous 10 suggestive
rissle: 4 pole 5 staff, stick
rist: 4 mark 5 wound 6 ascent 7 engrave, scratch 8 increase 12 insurrection, resurrection
risus: 5 laugh 8 laughter
rit: cut, rip 4 slit, tear 5 split 6 pierce 7 scratch
ritardando: 9 retarding 11 rallentando
rite: 4 cult, form, orgy 5 sacra 6 augury, exequy, novena, prayer, ritual 7 liturgy, obsequy 8 accolade, accolate, ceremony 9 ordinance, procedure, sacrament, solemnity 10 ceremonial, initiation, observance
Ritter: 6 knight
ritual: 4 cult, form, rite 7 liturgy, obsequy 8 ceremony 9 obsequies(pl.) 10 ceremonial
ritus: 5 usage 6 custom
ritzy: 6 modish 7 elegant 9 expensive, luxurious 11 fashionable
rivage: 4 bank, duty 5 coast, shore
rival: vie 4 even, peer 5 equal, match 7 compete, emulate, feuding 8 corrival, emula-

tor, opponent 9 adversary, competing 10 antagonist, competitor, contending 11 comparative
rivalry: 11 competition
rive: rip, rob 4 bank, plow, pull, rend, rent, rift, tear 5 break, cleft, shore, split, steal 6 arrive, cleave, pierce, sunder, thieve, thrust 7 dispart 8 lacerate 9 disembark
rivel: 6 shrink 7 shrivel, wrinkle
river: ea; ree, ria(Sp.), rio(Sp.), run 4 wadi, wady 5 bayou, waddy 6 stream 7 channel 8 effluent 9 abundance 11 watercourse
arm: 7 estuary 9 tributary
bank: 4 rand, ripa 5 levee
channel: bed 6 alveus
comb. form: 6 potamo
current: 4 eddy 6 rapids
dam: 4 weir
gauge: 9 nilometer
god: 7 Alpheus, Inachus 8 Achelous
horse: 5 hippo
ice: 7 glacier
inlet: 5 bayou 6 slough
island: ait 4 holm
Kubla Khan's: 4 Alph
land: 5 carse(Sc.), flats
living in: 9 amphibian, rheophile
log run: 9 sluiceway
mouth: 4 beal(Sc.), lade 5 delta 7 estuary
mythical: 4 Styx
nymph: 4 nais 5 naiad
obstruction: 4 snag 5 gorce
of oblivion: 5 Lethe
passage: 4 ford 7 estuary
pert. to: 5 amnic 6 rivery 7 fluvial, potamic 8 riverine 9 fluminose, fluminous
sacred: 5 Ganga 6 Ganges
siren: 7 Lorelei
small: 5 brook, creek, tchai 6 stream 7 rivulet 8 riverlet 9 streamlet
thief: 6 ackman
underworld: 4 Styx 5 Lethe 7 Acheron
winding part: ess
river dog: 10 hellbender
river duck: 4 teal
river horse: 5 hippo 12 hippopotamus
river mussel: 4 unio
River of Forgetfulness: 5 Lethe
River of Hate: 4 Styx
River of Sorrows: 7 Acheron
riverbank: 4 ripa, ripe 5 levee
riverbed: 4 wadi, wady 5 waddy
riverboat: ark 5 barge 7 rowboat, towboat 8 flatboat
riverside: 4 bank 5 shore
riverweed family: 13 podostemaceae
rivet: fix 4 bolt, brad 6 clinch, fasten 8 fastener
riviere: 8 necklace
rivose: 5 brook 6 gutter 7 channel
rivulet: 4 burn, rill 5 bache, bayou, bourn, brook, creek 6 bourne, rindle(Sc.), runlet, runnel, stream 7 channel 9 streamlet
rix: 4 reed, rush
rixatrix: 5 scold 6 virago
rixy: 4 tern
rizzar: dry 4 cure 6 drying 7 currant
rizzom: ear 5 stalk, straw 8 particle
roach: bug, cut 4 fish, hill, rock, roll, soil, spot 6 braise 7 sunfish 9 cockroach
road: way 4 fare, gang, iter, path, raid, ride 5 agger, bargh, going, itero(pl.), route 6 avenue, camino, career, causey, chemin, course, street 7 calzada(Sp.), estrada, gangway, highway, itinera(pl.), journey, passage, railway 8 beallach, causeway, chaussee(F.), cul-de-sac, pavement, railroad 9 direction, incursion, roadstead 10 expedition
bend: 7 hairpin
character: 4 hobo 5 tramp 10 hitchhiker
country: 4 lane
edge: 4 berm 8 shoulder
machine: 4 harl 5 paver 6 grader 9 bulldozer
menace: 7 speeder
military: 5 agger
surface: tar 6 bricks, gravel, stones 7 macadam 8 concrete, pavement
road book: map 9 gazetteer, itinerary
road goose: 5 brant
road runner: 6 cuckoo 7 paisano(Sp.)
roadhouse: inn 6 tavern
roadman: 7 drummer, peddler 8 salesman 9 canvasser
roadster: 5 horse 7 bicycle 8 runabout
roadtrack: 9 roadstead
roadweed: 8 plantain
roam: err, gad 4 roil, rove 5 prowl, range, stray 6 bangle, ramble, stroll, travel, wander 7 meander 8 straggle 9 gallivant
roamer: 5 gipsy, gypsy, nomad 8 fugitive 12 peregrinator
roan: bay 5 horse 9 sheepskin
Roanoke bell: 7 cowslip
roar: cry, din 4 beal, bell, bere, boom, bray, clap, hurl, rote, rout, yell 5 blart, brool, fream, laugh 6 bellow, buller, outcry, steven 7 thunder 8 shouting
roaring: 4 loud 5 aroar, brisk, noisy 7 riotous 10 boisterous, disorderly, stentorian
roaring game: 7 curling
roaring Meg: 6 cannon
roast: fry 4 bake, cook, razz, roti(F.) 5 asado(Sp.), brede, grill, parch 6 assate, banter 7 torrefy, torrify 8 ridicule 9 criticize
meat on stick: 5 cabob, kabob
prepare: 5 truss

roasting stick: 4 spit 6 skewer
rob: cop 4 fake, flap, loot, pelf, take 5 bribe, filch, harry, pilch, pinch, pluck, raven, reave, rifle, spoil, steal, strip, touch 6 burgle, pilfer, pirate, ravish, shrive, snatch, snitch, thieve 7 bereave, defraud, deprive, despoil, pillage, plunder 10 plagiarize
Rob Roy: 5 canoe
robber: 4 goul, yegg 5 ghoul 6 arrant, bandit, dacoit, pirate 7 brigand, corsair, footpad, ladrone, yeggman 8 marauder 9 bandolero, buccaneer, privateer 10 depredator, highwayman
robe (see also **dress, gown**): aba 4 skin, vest, wrap 5 array, camis, camus, cloak, cover, cymar, simar, talar, tunic 6 caftan, chimer, clothe, dolman, invest, kimono, mantle, revest 7 chimere, costume, garment, vesture 8 clothing, covering, vestment 10 sticharion
robin: 4 lout, tody 6 oriole, thrush 7 bumpkin, chewink 8 trimming 10 cuckoopint, toxalbumin
Robin Goodfellow: 4 Puck 5 fairy 6 sprite 9 hobgoblin
Robin Hood: *chaplain:* 9 Friar Tuck
follower: 4 John 9 Friar Tuck
sweetheart: 6 Marian
robin sandpiper: 9 dowitcher
robinet: 6 cannon 9 chaffinch
Robinson Crusoe: *author:* 5 Defoe
companion: 6 Friday
roborant: 5 tonic 13 strengthening
roborate: 6 ratify 10 strengthen 11 corroborate
roborean: 5 oaken, stout 6 strong
robot: 5 golem 7 android 9 androides, automaton
drama about: RUR
robust: 4 hale, hard, iron, rude 5 hardy, lusty, rough, sound, stout, wally 6 brawny, coarse, hearty, rugged, sinewy, strong, sturdy 7 healthy 8 athletic, muscular, vigorous 10 boisterous
roc: 4 bird 6 simurg 7 simurgh, soldier
rocca: 4 hold, keep 6 donjon 8 fortress
rochet: 5 cloak, frock 7 camisia, garment, gurnard 8 vestment
rock: dag, ore, tor 4 clay, crag, lull, peak, reef, reel, roll, scar, shog, spar, sway, trap, tufa, tuff, wash 5 agate, brack, candy, chert, cliff, earth, flint, geest, lytta, prase, scree, shake, shale, shaul, slate, stane(Sc.), stone, wacke 6 aplite, basalt, dacite, egeran, gneiss, gravel, issite, oolite, pebble, refuge, rognon, schist, silica, sinter, teeter, totter 7 adinole, akerite, alunite, defense, diamond, gondite, granite, griesen, support, tremble, vibrate 8 andesite, banakite, dolomite, laterite, obsidian, porphyry, psephite, rhyolite 9 epidosite, flagstone, oscillate, phanerite 10 greenstone, promontory 11 petrography
boring tool: 6 trepan
cavity: vug 4 vugg 5 druse, geode
clay: 8 ganister
comb. form: 5 petro
debris: 5 talus 8 detritus
decomposed: 6 gossan
discarded: 5 attle
finely broken: 4 sand
fissile: 5 shale
flintlike: 5 chert 6 quartz
fold: 8 syncline 9 anticline
fragments: see *debris* above
glacier deposit: 7 moraine
glacier-transported: 7 erratic
igneous: 4 boss, sial, sima, trap, tufa 5 trass 6 basalt, domite, latite 7 diabase, diorite, felsite, ijolite, peridot 8 extaxite, ijussite, porphyry 11 agglomerate
laminated: 4 mica 5 shale, slate
liquid: aa 4 lava
mythical: 6 Scylla
nodule: 5 geode
pert. to: 6 petric 7 petrean
point: 4 crag, peak
science: 9 petrology
strata: see *fold* above
suffix: ite, yte
volcanic: 4 lava, tufa, tuff
rock badger: 4 cony
rock bass: 6 red-eye
rock bottom: 6 lowest 8 cheapest
rock dove: 9 guillemot 10 rockpigeon
rock eel: 6 gunnel
rock falcon: 6 merlin
rock geranium: 8 alumroot
rock goat: 4 ibex
rock grouse: 9 ptarmigan
rock hind: 7 grouper
rock hopper: 7 penquin
rock kangaroo: 7 wallaby
rock oak: 8 chestnut 10 California, chinquapin
rock oil: 9 petroleum
rock plant: 4 moss 6 lichen
rock rabbit: 5 hyrax
rock snake: 5 krait 6 phthon
rock starling: 5 ouzel
rock tar: 9 petroleum
rock tripe: 6 lichen
rock wren: 4 bird
rockaway: 8 carriage
rockbell: 9 columbine
rockbird: 5 murre 9 sandpiper
rocker: 5 chair, skate 6 cradle
rocket: 4 weld, wold 5 slate, woald, would 9 satellite 11 firecracker

end of combustion: 7 burnout
landing: 7 reentry 10 splashdown
launcher: 7 bazooka
launching: 4 shot 8 blastoff
rockfish: 4 bass, rena 5 perch 7 grouper 9 killifish 10 priestfish
rockling: 4 fish, gade
rockrose: 6 cistus
rocky: 4 hard, weak 5 dizzy, shaky, stony 6 cliffy 7 petrean 8 obdurate, unsteady 9 unfeeling
Rocky Mountain: *goat:* 8 antelope
park: 5 Estes
peak: 5 Logan, Pikes
range: 5 Teton 7 Wasatch
sheep: 7 bighorn
wind: 7 chinook
rococo: 4 arty 9 fantastic
rod: bar, gad, guy, rab, rib 4 axle, bolt, came, cane, crop, goad, I-bar, lath, pole, prod, race, scob, spit, wand, wire 5 arrow, baton, board, lytta, osier, perch, power, scion, spoke, staff, stick, stock, strip, tribe 6 baculi(pl.), batten, broach, carbon, etalon, eyebar, ferule, needle, pistol, piston, pontil, raddle, skewer, switch, toggle 7 baculus, caliper, crowbar, distaff, measure, scepter, sceptre, spindle, stemmer, support, tringle, tyranny 8 arrester, offshoot, revolver 9 authority 10 oppression 12 chastisement
bundle: 6 fasces
divination by: 7 dowsing 11 rhabdomancy
movable: 6 piston
square: 5 perch
rod-like: 6 rhabdo 7 virgate
rodd: 8 crossbow
rode goose: 5 brant
rodent: jap, rat 4 cavy, cony, cypu, degu, hare, mole, paca, pica, pika, utia, vole 5 aguti, hutia, jutia, lerot, mouse, ratel, zokor 6 agouti, agouty, beaver, biting, cururo, gerbil, gopher, gundie, jerboa, marmot, murine, rabbit, weasel 7 chincha, hamster, leveret, muskrat 8 capibara, capybara, dormouse, gerbille, leporide, sewellel, squirrel, viscacha, vizcacha 9 porcupine 10 chinchilla
aquatic: 6 beaver 7 muskrat
genus: mus
jumping: 6 jerboa
pert. to: 8 rosorial
rodeo: 7 roundup 9 enclosure 10 exhibition
rodge: 7 gadwall
rodman: 4 thug 10 highwayman
rodney: 5 idler 7 shirker 8 vagabond
rodomontade: 4 brag, rant 5 boast, empty 7 bluster, bombast 8 boastful, boasting, braggart
rodster: 6 angler 9 fisherman
roe: ra; ova, pea 4 deer, eggs, hart, hind 5 coral, spawn 6 caviar 7 caviare
roebuck: 4 girl 9 chevreuil
Roentgen's discovery: 4 X-ray
roestone: 6 oolite
rog: 4 pull, stir 5 shake 6 jumble
rogan: 4 bowl 10 receptacle
rogation: law 6 decree, litany, prayer 7 inquiry, request 8 petition 12 supplication
rogue: boy, gue, imp, wag 4 hemp, kite 5 catso, cheat, crank, decry, gipsy, gypsy, hempy, knave, scamp, shark, tramp 6 beggar, canter, coquin, harlot, pirate, rascal, wander 7 corsair, erratic, hellion, sharper, vagrant, villain, waggish 8 picaroon, swindler, vagabond 9 scoundrel, trickster 10 frolicsome, stigmatize 11 rapscallion
pert. to: 10 picaresque
roguery: 5 fraud 8 mischief, trickery 15 mischievousness
roguish: sly 4 arch 5 pawky 6 wanton 7 playful, puckish 8 espiegle, sportive 9 dishonest, fun-loving 12 unscrupulous
roid: 5 rough 6 severe 7 riotous, roguish 10 frolicsome 12 unmanageable
roil vex 4 foul, roam, romp, rust, stir 5 anger, annoy, muddy, rouse 6 cloudy, fidget, ruffle, wander 7 blunder, disturb 8 irritate 9 displease, unsettled
roily: 6 turbid
roister: 4 brag, rude 5 bully, revel, spree 7 bluster, boorish, reveler, swagger, violent 9 gilravage
roistering: 6 hoiden, hoyden
rojo: 6 Indian 7 redskin
roke: fog 4 mist, stir 5 smoke, steam, vapor 8 moisture
roker: ray 8 rockling 9 thornback
roky: 4 damp 5 foggy, misty, smoky 6 hoarse
Roland: *beloved:* 4 Aude
emperor: 11 Charlemagne
enemy: 4 Gano 7 Ganelon
friend: 6 Oliver
horn: 7 Olivant
horse: 10 Veillantif
sword: 8 Durendal
role: bit 4 cast, duty, part 6 office 8 business, function 9 character 13 impersonation 16 characterization
leading: 4 star
roll: bun, gad, rob 4 bolt, coil, file, flow, furl, list, pell, roam, rota, seel, sway, turn, wind, wrap 5 cadre, frisk, lurch, shift, surge, swing, trill, troll, wheel 6 bundle, enroll, enwrap, goggle, grovel, roster, rotate, scroll, spiral, tumble, wallow, wander, welter, whelve, wintle 7 biscuit bri-

oche, revolve, rissole, stagger, swagger, trundle **8** cylinder, flounder, register, undulate
of hair: bun **7** chignon
roll back: 5 lower **6** reduce **7** repulse
roll in: 4 flow **6** arrive, wallow, welter
roll up: 4 furl **5** amass **6** arrive, gather **10** accumulate
roller: 4 band, wave **5** finer, inker, swath **6** canary, caster, fascia, fillet, pigeon, platen, rowlet, sponge **7** bandage, breaker, presser, sirgang, tumbler **8** cylinder **9** surcingle
rolleyway: 4 road **5** track **7** gangway, tramway
rollick: 4 romp **5** sport **6** frolic
rollicking: gay **6** jovial, lively **8** careless **9** hilarious
rolling stock: 4 cars **7** coaches, engines **8** cabooses, Pullmans, sleepers **11** locomotives
rolling weed: 10 tumbleweed
rollix: 7 rollick
rolltop: 4 desk
roly-poly: 5 dumpy, pudgy, round **6** portly, rotund **7** pudding
rom: 4 buzz **5** gipsy, gypsy
romaine: cos **5** plant **7** lettuce
romal: 5 thong
Roman: 5 brave, Latin **6** frugal, honest, simple **7** Italian
Roman Catholic: *cassock:* **7** soutane, zimarra
church: **7** lateran
ecclesiastic: **7** Rosmini
priest: **4** abbe(F.) **6** father **8** sacerdos **9** monsignor
skullcap: **9** zucchetto
society: **7** Jesuits
romance: woo **4** gest, tale **5** court, dream, fable, fancy, feign, geste, novel, story **6** affair **7** chimera, fantasy, fiction, romanza **9** falsehood, sentiment **10** exaggerate **12** exaggeration
Romance language: 6 French **7** Catalan, Italian, Spanish **8** Rumanian **9** Provencal **10** Portuguese
Romanese: 7 gypsies **9** Walachian
romantic: 6 poetic, unreal **8** quixotic **9** imaginary, visionary **10** idealistic **11** extravagant
Romany, Rommany: 5 gipsy, gypsy
tongue: **7** Romanes
romanza: 7 fiction, romance
Rome (see also **Latin**): **4** Roma
abode of gods: **7** Olympus
adviser to king: **6** Egeria
amphitheater: **9** colosseum
apostle: **4** Neri, Paul
army unit: **6** cohort
army wing: ala
assembly: **5** forum **6** senate **7** comitia
attendant: **7** aliptes **8** aleiptes
augur: **6** auspex
author (see also *biographer, historian, poet,* below): **5** Pliny, Varro
authority symbol: **6** fasces
basilica: **7** lateran
barracks: **6** canaba
battle array: **5** acies
biographer: **5** Nepos **9** Suetonius
boy: **4** puer **8** camillus
brothers: **5** Remus **7** Romulus
building: **5** aedes
Caesar's title: **9** imperator
captain: **9** centurion
carriage: **5** essed
chief god: **4** Jove **7** Jupiter
citadel: arx
clans: **4** gens
cloak: **4** toga
coin: as; aes **5** asses(pl.), aurei(pl.), semis **6** aureus, dinder, solidu, triens **7** denarii(pl.), siliqua **8** decussis, denarius, sesterce, sesteria(pl.) **9** sesterium **10** sestertius, victoriate **11** victoriatus
comedy: **5** exode
comedy writer: **6** Cicero **7** Plautus, Terence
concert hall: **5** odeum
conqueror: **6** Alaric
conspirator: **8** Catiline
contract: **5** nexum
couch: **9** accubitum
court: **5** atria(pl.) **6** atrium
custodian: **10** neocorates
date: **4** Ides
district: **5** Pagus **7** Pontine **8** Pomptine
diviner: **5** augur **6** auspex
division: **5** curia
earthwork: **5** agger
emperor: **4** Nero, Otho, Otto **5** Galba, Nerva, Titus **6** Caesar, Julian, Trajan **7** Hadrian **8** Augustus, Claudius, Domitian, Tiberius **9** Vespasian **10** Elagabalus **11** Constantine
empress: **7** Eudocia
encampment: **7** castrum
entrance hall: **5** atria(pl.) **6** atrium
family: **7** familia
farmer: **7** colonus **8** agricola
Fate: **4** Nona **5** Morta, Parca **6** Decuma, Parcae(pl.)
fighter: **9** gladiator
fortress: **7** castrum
founder: **5** Remus **7** Romulus
galley: **6** bireme **7** trireme
garment: **4** toga **5** palla, sagum, stola, stole, togae(pl.), tunic

general: 5 Sulla, Titus 6 Antony, Marius, Scipio 8 Agricola
god: Dis, Lar, Sol 4 Amor, Jove, Mars 5 Comus, Cupid, Fauns, Janus, Lares, manes, Orcus, Pluto 6 Faunus, Vulcan 7 Jupiter, lemures, Neptune, penates, Phoebus, Vatican 8 Dispater, Morpheus, Quirinus 11 Aesculapius
god of dead: 5 Orcus
god of death: 4 Mors
god of fire: 6 Vulcan
god of love: 4 Amor
god of mirth: 5 Comus
god of sea: 7 Neptune
god of sleep: 8 Morpheus
god of sun: Sol
god of underworld: Dis 5 Pluto
god of war: 4 Mars
god of wind: 5 Eurus 6 Boreas
god of wine: 7 Bacchus
goddess: dea(L.), Lua, Nox, Ops, Pax 4 Caca, Juno, Luna, Maia, Paca 5 Ceres, Diana, Epona, Terra, Venus, Vesta 6 Aestas, Annona, Aurora, Lucina, Rumina, Tellus, Vacuna 7 Bellona, Fortuna, Minerva 8 Libitina 9 Abudantia, Discordia, Felicitas
goddess of agriculture: Ops 5 Ceres
goddess of beauty: 5 Venus
goddess of flowers: 5 Flora
goddess of hearth: 5 Vesta
goddess of hope: 4 Spes
goddess of hunting: 5 Diana
goddess of love: 5 Venus
goddess of marriage: 4 Juno
goddess of moon: 4 Luna
goddess of night: Nox
goddess of peace: Pax
goddess of plenty: Ops
goddess of underworld: 10 Proserpina
goddess of vegetation: 5 Ceres
goddess of war: 7 Bellona, Minerva
goddess of wisdom: 7 Minerva
greeting: ave
guard: 6 lictor
hall: 5 atria(pl.) 6 atrium
hat: 7 petasos, petasus
helmet: 5 galea 6 galeae(pl.)
highway: via 4 iter 5 itero(pl.) 6 Appian, 7 itinera(pl.)
holiday: 4 ides 5 feria 6 feriae(pl.)
hill: 7 Caelian, Viminal 8 Aventine, Palatine, Quirinal 9 Esquiline 10 Capitoline
historian: 4 Livy 5 Nepos
javelin: 4 pile 5 aclys, pilum
judge: 5 edile 6 aedile
jurist: 5 Gaius
king: 7 Romulus, Servius, Tullius 12 Ancus Martius 13 Numa Pompilius 15 Tullus Hostilius 18 Tarquinius Superbus
lake: 4 Nemi
language: 5 Latin
law: fas, lex 4 cern
leader: dux
magistrate: 5 edile 6 aedile, censor, pretor 7 praetor, tribune
marble: 7 cipolin
measure: pes, urn 4 mile, pace, urna 5 actus, clima, cubit, juger 6 culeus, dolium, gradus, hemina, modius, palmus, passus, saltus, versus 7 amphora, congius, cyathus, digitus, stadion, stadium 8 centuria, hereduim, quadrant 9 decempeda, millarium, sextarius 10 acetabulum, quartarius
measure of weight: as; bes 4 pood 5 asses(pl.), libra, uncia 6 duella 7 dodrans, sextula, solidus 8 sicilium 9 scrupulus, scrupulum
military formation: ala 6 alares(pl.) 7 phalanx
military machine: 7 terebra
military unit: 6 cohort, legion 7 maniple
military vessel: 6 bireme 7 trireme
naturalist: 5 Pliny
nymph: 6 Egeria
official: 5 augur, edile 6 aedile, lictor 7 prefect, tribune 8 irenarch 9 nestorian
ox: 4 urus
palace: 5 chigi 7 lateran
palace troops: 9 palatines
peace: 5 Irene
people: 5 Laeti 7 Sabines 8 plebians 10 patricians
pert. to: 9 classical
philosopher: 4 Cato 6 Seneca
physician: 9 archiater 11 Aesculapius
pillager: 6 Alaric
pin: 4 acus
poet: 4 Ovid 5 Cinna, Lucan 6 Horace, Vergil, Virgil 7 Juvenal, Terence 8 Catullus, Tibullus 10 Propertius
port: 5 Ostia
praenomen: 5 Aulus, Caius, Gaius, Titus 6 Appius 7 Quintus, Spurius 8 Tiberius
priest: 5 epulo 6 flamen 7 luperci
priestess: 6 vestal
procurator: 5 Felix 6 Pilate
province: 5 Dacia 7 Cilicia
queen of goddesses: 4 Juno
regulator: 6 censor
religious law: fas
river: Po 5 Tiber
road: 4 iter
room: ala 5 atria(pl.) 6 atrium 7 tablina(pl.) 8 fumarium, tablinum
rural deity: 6 Faunus
saint: 4 Neri
section: 5 Ostia

senate division: **5** curia
senate emblem: **9** laticlave
senate house: **5** curia
shield: scuta(pl.) **6** ancile, scutum **7** ancilia(pl.), clypeus
spirits of dead: **5** manes
standard: **7** labarum, vexilla(pl.) **8** vexillum
standard-bearer: **9** vexillary
statesman: **4** Cato **5** Pliny **6** Caesar, Cicero, Seneca **7** Agrippa **8** Maecenas
tax gatherer: **8** publican
temple: **4** naos **5** cella **8** pantheon
treasurer: **8** quaestor
veteran: **7** emeriti(pl.) **8** emeritus
weight: see *measure of weight* above
writing tablet: **7** diptych

Romeo: *beloved:* **6** Juliet
enemy: **6** Tybalt
father: **8** Montague
friend: **8** Mercutio
rival: **5** Paris

rommack: **4** play, romp **7** rummage

romp: **4** hoit, play, roil **6** frolic, hoiden, hoyden **7** carouse, courant, gammock **8** carousal, courante

Romulus: *brother:* **5** Remus
father: **4** Mars

rond: **4** rand **5** shred **6** border

rondure: **5** round **6** circle, sphere **9** plumpness, roundness

rone: **5** brake **7** thicket **9** brushwood

rood: **5** cross **7** measure **8** crucifix

roodebok: **6** impala

roof: **5** cover **7** palate, shelter **8** covering
border: **4** eave
comb. form: **5** stego
style: hip **4** dome, flat, nave, sark **5** gable, spire **6** cupola **7** cricket, gambrel, mansard **9** penthouse, pyramidal **10** jerkinhead
timber: **6** after
window: **6** dormer

roofing material: tar, tin **4** tile **5** paper, slate, straw, terne **6** copper, gravel, shakes, thatch **7** pantile **8** shingles

rook: **4** bird, crow **5** cheat, raven, steal **6** castle **7** defraud, sharper, swindle **8** swindler

rookery: **8** building

rookie, rooky: **4** tyro **6** novice **7** recruit, trainee **8** beginner

rooky: **4** roky **5** foggy **6** rookie, untidy **8** rascally **9** swindling **10** disheveled

room: ala, ben, den **4** aula, cell, hall, loge, sala(Sp.), seat **5** atria(pl.), aulae(pl.), cubby, divan, kiosk, lodge, place, salle(F.), salon, scope, space **6** atrium, casino, leeway, reside, saloon, scouth **7** boudoir, cabinet, chamber, cubicle, expanse, gallery, lodging, rotunda, theater **9** apartment, garderobe **10** auditorium
conversation: **6** exedra **7** exedrae(pl.) **11** drawing room
eating: **4** nook **7** cenacle, kitchen **8** cenacula(pl.) **9** cenaculum, refectory
private: **7** boudoir
provision: **4** ewry **5** ewery **6** larder **7** pantry **8** cupboard
reading: den **5** study **7** library
sleeping: **5** lodge **6** dormer **7** barrack, bedroom **8** roomette **9** dormitory
storage: **4** loft, shed **5** attic **6** cellar **9** storeroom

roomer: **5** guest **6** lodger, tenant **7** boarder

rooms: **4** flat **5** suite **9** apartment

roomy: **5** ample, broad, spacy **8** spacious **9** capacious **10** commodious

roorback, roorbach: lie **4** hoax **6** canard **7** fiction **9** falsehood

roose: **5** boast, extol, vaunt **6** praise

Roosevelt, F. D.: *dog:* **4** Fala
mother: **4** Sara

roost: sit **4** nest, pole, rest **5** abode, perch, sleep **6** alight, garret **7** lodging, support

rooster: **4** cock **5** gallo(Sp.) **11** chanticleer

root: dig **4** base, bulb, core, grub, moot, rout, stem **5** basis, cheer, grout, plant, radix, shout, tuber **6** bottom, etymon, ground, origin, settle **7** radical, radices(pl.), rootlet, support **9** beginning, establish **10** foundation
dyeing: **6** madder
edible: oca, roi, rue, uva, yam **4** beet, eddo, taro **5** orris, tania **6** carrot, ginger, orrice, radish, turnip **7** parsnip **8** rutabaga **9** sassafras
fragrant: **5** orris
outer layer: **7** exoderm
pert. to: **7** radical
principal: **7** taproot
pungent: **11** crinkleroot
starch: **4** arum

root out: **4** stub **6** evulse **9** eradicate, extirpate **10** deracinate

rooted: **10** inveterate

rooter: fan **10** enthusiast

rootlet: **7** radicle, rhizoid

rootstock: **6** stolon

rope: gad, guy, tie, tow **4** bind, cord, hemp, line, stay **5** cable, longe, riata, sheet, widdy **6** binder, fasten, halter, hawser **7** aweband, binding, bobstay, bollard, cordage, halyard, marline, painter **8** inveigle, prolonge
animal's: **5** leash **6** halter, tether
fiber: **4** coir, flax, jute **5** istle, sisal **6** cotton, Manila

holder: 6 becket
loop: 5 bight, noose 6 becket, parral, parrel
restraining: 6 tether
ship's: tye 4 colt, rode, stay, vang 5 sheet 6 hawser, inhaul, parral, parrel, ratlin, shroud 7 halyard, lanyard, painter, ratline
throwing: 5 lasso, reata, riata 6 lariat
ropedancer: 7 acrobat 9 funambulo 11 funambulist
roper: 6 cowboy, packer
ropery: 6 banter 7 roguery
roque: 7 croquet
roric: 4 dewy, rory 5 roral 6 roscid
rosaceous: 4 rosy 5 rosal 8 blushing
rosary: 4 bede 5 beads 7 chaplet, garland 8 beadroll
rose (see also **rise**): ris 5 delta, flush 6 flower, nozzle 7 rambler, rosette 9 hellebore
family: 8 rosaceae
kind of: dog 4 moss, musk
oil: 4 atar, otto 5 attar, ottar
part: 5 petal
Rose City: 8 Pasadena, Portland
rose of Sharon: 6 althea
rose parakeet: 7 rosella
rose pogonia: 10 snakemouth
rosebay: 8 oleander
rosemary: 9 rosmarine
rosette: 7 cockade 8 ornament
rosilla: 10 sneezeweed
rosin: See **resin**
Rosinante: nag 4 jade, plug 5 horse, steed
rosiness: 5 blush, flush
ross: 4 bark, peel 5 waste 8 exterior
roster: 4 list, roll, rota 5 slate
rostrum: 4 beak, dais 5 snout, stage 6 pulpit 7 lectern, tribune 8 platform 9 proboscis
rosy: red 4 pink 5 ruddy 6 bright, florid 7 auroral, flushed, roseate 8 blooming, blushing, cheerful, rubicund 9 favorable, promising, rosaceous 10 favourable, optimistic
rot: ret 4 bosh, dote, doze, joke 5 chaff, decay, spoil, tease, trash 6 banter, fester, perish 7 corrupt, putrefy, rubbish, twaddle 8 nonsense 9 decompose, poppycock 10 degenerate 13 decomposition
rot grass: 9 flukewort 10 butterwort
rota: 4 list, roll 5 court, round 6 course, roster 8 register
rotate: 4 pass, roll, spin, turn 5 twirl, wheel, whirl 6 gyrate 7 perform, revolve, trundle 8 rotiform 9 alternate
rotation: 4 eddy 6 torque, vortex 9 pirouette
part: cam 4 axle 5 rotor, wheel
rote: 4 list 5 learn 6 course, custom, memory, repeat, system 7 routine 8 practice 9 automatic, condition 10 memorizing, repetition
rotiform: 6 rotate
rotor: 7 spinner 8 impeller
rotten: bad 4 evil, foul 5 fetid, nasty 6 putrid 7 carrion, corrupt, decayed, spoiled, tainted, unsound 8 depraved, unstable 9 offensive, putrefied 10 abominable, decomposed, putrescent, undermined 12 disagreeable 13 disintegrated 14 unsatisfactory
comb. form: 4 sapr 5 sapro
rotter: cad 7 shirker, slacker 10 blackguard
rotula: 6 troche 7 kneepan, lozenge, patella
rotund: 5 obese, plump, round, stout 6 chubby, portly 7 rounded 8 rolypoly, sonorous 9 spherical
roturier: 7 freeman 8 commoner
roue: rip 4 rake 9 debauchee, libertine
rouge: red 5 blush, color, flush, paint, score 6 redden, ruddle 8 cosmetic
rough: 4 hard, rude 5 acrid, brute, crude, hairy, harsh, husky, lumpy, raggy, rowdy, seamy, stern, surly, uncut 6 abrupt, broken, choppy, coarse, crabby, craggy, hoarse, jagged, rugged, severe, shaggy, uneven 7 austere, boorish, bristly, brusque, grating, hirsute, inexact, jarring, raucous, ruffian, ruffled, uncivil 8 churlish, clownish, gangster, impolite, obdurate, unplaned 9 imperfect, inclement, turbulent, unrefined 10 boisterous, discordant, incomplete, tumultuous, unpleasant, unpolished 11 approximate, tempestuous
roughen: 4 chap, fret, shag 5 feaze 7 engrail 10 exasperate
roughneck: 4 boor 5 rowdy, tough 7 sweater
roughness: 7 crudity 8 acrimony, asperity
rouky: 4 roky 5 foggy, misty
roulade: run 8 arpeggio, division, flourish
roulette: 10 epicycloid 11 epitrochoid 12 hypotrochoid
bet: bas 4 noir 5 carre, rouge 6 milieu 7 dernier, encarre, enplein
rounceval: 5 giant, large 6 virago 9 termagant
round: 4 beat, bout, full, rung 5 group, large, orbed, plump 6 circle, curved, period, rotund 7 bulbous, circuit, liberal 8 circular, complete, globular, rolypoly 9 spherical 11 cylindrical
round clam: 6 quahog
round dance: hay, ray 5 polka, waltz 7 roundel 9 roundelay, schottish 11 schottische

round robin: 6 letter 7 contest 8 document, petition 9 cigarfish 10 tournament
Round Table knight: Kay 6 Gawain 7 Caradoc, Cradock, Gaheris, Galahad 8 Lancelot, Tristram 9 Percivale
roundabout: 5 about, dance 6 detour 7 devious 8 circular, indirect, tortuous 10 circuitous, farfetched 13 approximately 14 circumlocution, circumlocutory
rounded: 4 oval 5 bombe, ovate 6 convex, rotund 7 arrondi, bunting, gibbous 8 circular 10 labialized
roundel: 4 guze
rounder: 4 roue 5 sport 8 criminal, drunkard, preacher 11 spendthrift
roundhead: 5 Swede 7 Puritan
roundup: 5 rodeo 9 gathering
roundworm: 4 nema 7 ascaris
roup: 4 sale 6 clamor 7 auction 8 shouting
rouse: daw, hie 4 call, move, stir, wake, whet 5 alarm, amove, awake, raise, rally, start, toast, upset, waken 6 arouse, awaken, bestir, bumper, excite, foment, frolic revive 7 actuate, agitate, animate, disturb, enliven, startle 8 carousal, festival, inspirit 9 stimulate
Rousseau hero: 5 Emile
roussette: 5 shark 7 dogfish
roust: 4 roar, stir, tide 5 rouse 6 bellow, tumult 7 current, roaring 9 bellowing
rout: ado, low, mob 4 band, beat, bray, dart, fuss, roar, root 5 crowd, knock, noise, scoop, shout, snore, snort, troop 6 bellow, clamor, defeat, furrow, rabble, search, strike, throng, tumult, uproar 7 company, confuse, debacle, repulse, retinue, retreat, rummage, slumber, trouble 8 assemble, assembly, confound, disperse, shouting, stampede, vanquish 9 bellowing, discomfit, hurricane, overpower, overthrow, overwhelm 11 disturbance 12 dicomfiture
route: way 4 gest, lane, line, path, road 5 geste, march, trail 6 course, skyway 7 circuit, journey 9 direction, itinerary
circuitous: 6 detour
straight: 7 beeline
routh: 6 plenty 8 abundant 9 abundance, plentiful
routine: rut 4 rote 5 grind, habit, round, troll 6 course, groove, system 8 habitual 9 treadmill
rove: go; gad 4 move, part, pass, plow, roam, turn 5 prowl, range, stray 6 maraud, pierce, ramble, stroll, wander 8 straggle
rover: 5 nomad 6 pirate 7 corsair, Ishmael, migrant, vagrant 8 gadabout 9 itinerant
roving: 6 errant 7 cursory, devious 9 desultory 10 discursive
row: air, oar 4 bank, dust, file, fuss, line, list, rank, spat, tier 5 align, aline, brawl, broil, garry, noise, scull, swath 6 barney, clamor, paddle, pother, propel, rumpus, swathe 7 dispute, quarrel, ruction 8 argument, squabble 9 catalogue, commotion, excursion 11 disturbance 13 collieshangie
form in: 4 line 5 align, aline
rowan tree: ash 4 sorb
rowboat: cog, gig 4 dory, skif 5 canoe, cobil, coble, scull, skiff, skift 6 caique, galley, randan, wherry
stern: 7 transom
rowdy: 4 b'hoy, rude 5 rough, tough 6 roarer, tricky 7 hoodlum, vicious 8 larrikin 9 obstinate 10 boisterous
rowel: 4 spur 5 wheel 6 circle
rowen: 5 field 9 aftermath
rower: oar 6 punter 7 oarsman
rowing: 6 randan 8 sculling
royal: 4 real, rial, stag, true 5 basil, regal 6 august, kingly 7 stately 8 imperial, majestic, princely, splendid 9 excellent, sovereign 11 magnificent, monarchial
royal agaric: 8 mushroom
Royal Canadian Mounted Police: 7 Mountie
royal rock snake: 6 python
royal standard: 4 flag 6 banner, emblem
royalist: 4 Tory 8 Cavalier
royalty: 5 share 6 emblem 7 kingdom 8 kingship, nobility 10 kingliness, percentage 11 sovereignty
denoting: 5 crown 6 ermine, purple 7 scepter
symbol: 6 ermine
royet: 4 wild 6 unruly 7 romping 11 mischievous
rub: 4 bark, bray, buff, fret, rasp, wear, wipe 5 chafe, dight, feeze, grind, scour, smear 6 abrade, anoint, fridge, polish, scrape, smooth, stroke 7 burnish, massage 8 friction, irritate, obstacle 9 hindrance, triturate 10 difficulty, impediment
rub down: 4 comb 5 curry 7 massage
rub elbows: 9 associate 10 fraternize
rub out: 4 kill 5 elide, erase 6 cancel, efface, murder 7 expunge 10 obliterate
rubber: 4 band 5 brick 6 caucho, cutter, eraser 7 ebonite, masseur 8 masseuse, overshoe, polisher 9 vulcanite 10 caoutchouc
juice: 6 achete
source: 5 latex
substitute: 7 factice
synthetic: 4 buna
tree: 7 seringa
Rubber City: 5 Akron
rubber tree: ule 4 para 6 caucho 7 seringa 10 caoutchouc
rubbish: ket(Sc.), 4 flam, gear, junk, mull, pelf, pelt, raff, ross 5 crawm, dross, offal,

trash, waste, wrack 6 colder, debris, garble, litter, refuse, rubble, trashy 7 baggage, beggary, mullock, rummage 8 nonsense, trumpery 9 worthless 10 clamjamfry 11 foolishness

rube: 4 hick, jake 6 rustic 7 bumpkin, hayseed 10 countryman

rubedity: 7 redness 9 ruddiness

rubellite: 10 tourmaline

rubeola: 7 measles, rubella

rubescent: red 4 pink 8 blushing, flushing 9 reddening 10 erubescent

rubicund: red 4 rosy, ruby 5 ruddy 6 florid 7 flushed, reddish, redness 11 fullblooded

rubor: 9 hyperemia

rubric red 5 title 6 redden

book: 4 ordo 7 ordines(pl.)

ruby: gem, red 5 balas, jewel, stone 6 spinel 7 rubasse

ruck: rut, sit 4 fold, heap, mass, pile, rake, rick 5 cower, crowd, squat, stack 6 crease, crouch, furrow, pucker 7 crumple, wrinkle 9 multitude

ruckus: ado, row 6 rumpus, uproar 7 ruction 9 confusion 11 disturbance

ruction: 4 fray 5 fight, melee 6 uproar 7 quarrel 8 fraction, outbreak 11 disturbance

rudder: *control:* 4 helm 6 tiller

edge: 8 bearding

part: 4 yoke

ruddle: 5 rouge 6 redden

ruddy: red 4 rosy 5 fresh 6 florid, tanned 7 reddish 8 blushing

rude: 4 bold, curt, lewd 5 bluff, crude, harsh, rough, rowdy 6 bloody, borrel, brutal, clumsy, coarse, fierce, rugged, rustic, savage, severe, vulgar 7 artless, boorish, brutish, country, jarring, loutish, uncivil, uncouth, violent 8 churlish, clownish, homespun, ignorant, impolite, impudent, insolent, ungentle, untaught 9 barbarian, barbarous, ferocious, impetuous, inclement, inelegant, insulting, makeshift, truculent, turbulent, unskilled, untrained 10 boisterous, discordant, tumultuous, uncultured, ungracious, unmannerly, unpolished 11 acrimonious, impertinent, uncivilized 12 contumelious, discourteous

rudeness: 6 ferity

rudiment: 4 germ

rudimentary: 7 initial 9 elemental, vestigial 10 elementary 11 abecedarian, fundamental

rue: rew 4 pity, rake 5 dolor, grief, mourn 6 bewail, grieve, lament, regret, repent, sorrow, street, suffer 7 afflict, deplore, remorse 8 penitent 10 bitterness, compassion, repentance 14 disappointment

rueful: 5 sorry 8 penitent

ruff: ree 4 bird, fish 5 perch, plait, reeve, stamp, trump 6 collar, fraise, hackle, pigeon, rabato, rebato, ruffle, tippet 7 applaud, sunfish 8 disorder, drumbeat 9 sandpiper

female: ree 5 reeve

ruffian: 4 pimp, rage, thug 5 bully, cruel, rowdy 6 brutal, cutter, cuttle, pander, roarer, stormy 7 lawless, lustful, violent 8 assassin, gangster, hooligan, paramour 9 cutthroat, desperado, murderous 10 boisterous, licentious

ruffle: vex 4 beat, fret, roil, rool 5 annoy, brawl, crimp, frill, jabot, shake 6 nettle, riffle, ripple, tousel, tousle, tumult 7 agitate, derange, disturb, flounce, flutter, panuelo, roughen, swagger, wrinkle 8 brandish, dishevel, disorder, drumbeat, furbelow, irritate 9 balayeuse, carfuffle, commotion, confusion 10 disarrange, discompose 12 irregularity

neck: 5 jabot, ruche

ruffler: 5 bully, tramp 6 beggar 7 boaster, ruffian 8 braggart 10 attachment

rufous: 5 rusty, tawny 7 reddish

rug: dog, mat, tug 4 Agra, cozy, haul, pull, snug, tear, wrap 5 Herat 6 afghan, carpet, frieze, kaross, liquor, runner, wrench 7 bargain, blanket, drugget, laprobe 8 Akhissar, Amritsar, covering, portiere 9 Samarkind 11 comfortable

Persian: see **Oriental rug**

ruga: 4 fold 6 crease 7 wrinkle 8 membrane

rugby: *formation:* 5 scrum

score: try

rugged: 4 hard, rude, sour 5 asper, hardy, harsh, rough, stern surly 6 craggy, fierce, horrid, robust, seamed, severe, shaggy, stormy, strong, sturdy, uneven 7 austere, crabbed, gnarled, uncivil, unkempt 8 obdurate, vigorous, wrinkled 9 irregular, turbulent 10 ungracious, unpolished 11 tempestuous

rugose: 6 ridged 8 wrinkled 10 corrugated

Ruhr river: 4 Eder

ruin: gin 4 bane, bust, dash, doom, fall, fate, fell, harm, loss, undo 5 blast, break, decay, exile, fordo, havoc, spoil, wrack, wreck 6 beggar, blight, damage, deface, defeat, diddle, dismay, foredo, impair, injure, perish, ravage 7 decayed, despoil, destroy, pervert, ruinate, subvert 8 bankrupt, calamity, demolish, desolate, disaster, downfall 9 overthrow, perdition, ruination 10 bankruptcy, desolation, subversion 11 destruction, devastation, dissolution, ecroulement 12 delapidation

ruined: 4 dead 5 kaput 6 shabby forlorn 10 tumbledown 11 dilapidated
ruinous: 10 pernicious
ruins: 5 ashes 6 debris 7 remains
rule: law 4 lord, norm, sway 5 by-law, canon, guide, maxim, order, regle, reign 6 course, decide, decree, direct, domine, empire, govern, manage, method, regime, screed 7 alidade, brocard, command, conduct, control, counsel, formula, precept, prevail, regency, regimen, theorem 8 behavior, decision, doctrine, domineer, dominion, persuade, practice, regulate, standard 9 authority, criterion, direction, enactment, influence, principle 10 convention, government, regulation 11 aristocracy, predominate 12 prescription 14 administration
pert. to: 5 rutic
rule out: bar 5 debar 6 forbid, refuse 7 prevent, scratch 8 preclude, prohibit
rule over: 6 manage 7 oversee 8 dominate 11 superintend
ruler: dey, min 4 amir, czar, emir, king, lord, tsar, tzar 5 aldor, ameer, emeer, prior 6 archon, author, despot, dynast, ferule, gerent, prince, regent, satrap, sultan, tyrant 7 emperor, monarch, regulus, viceroy 8 autocrat, dictator, governor, hierarch, interrex 9 dominator, governail, imperator, matriarch, potentate, sovereign, yardstick 10 interreges(pl.) 12 straightedge
family: 7 dynasty
former: Nhu 4 czar, Diem, tsar, tzar 5 Lenin 6 Fuhrer, Hitler, Stalin 7 Batista, Fuehrer, Leopold 8 Napoleon, Nicholas 9 Alexander, Mussolini
one of three: 7 triarch 8 triumvir
one of two: 6 duarch
wife: 4 rani 5 queen, ranee 7 czarina, empress, tzarina
rules: 4 code
infraction: 4 foul 8 cheating
ruling: law 7 average, current, inkling, regnant, statute 8 decision, dominant 9 ascendant, ascendent, hegemonic, prevalent 10 prevailing 11 predominant 13 predominating
rum: bad, odd 4 good, grog, poor 5 queer, tafia 6 liquor 7 Bacardi, cachaca, strange 8 beverage, peculiar 9 excellent
rumal: 8 kerchief
Rumania: *capital:* 8 Bucurest 9 Bucharest, Bukharest
coin: ban, leu, ley, lei 4 bani(pl.)
conservative: 5 boyar
king: 5 Carol 7 Michael
mountain: 5 Negoi
queen: 5 Marie
river: Alt, Jiu 5 Aluta, Arges, Schyl, Siret 6 Sereth
river port: 6 Galati, Galatz
town: 4 Arad, Iasi 5 Bacau, Jassy, Neamt, Turnu 6 Braila, Brasov, Galati, Galatz 7 Craiova, Focsani, Ploesti, Severin 8 Cernauti, Irongate, Kishenef, Kolsovar, Temesvar 9 Constanta, Cronstadt, Kronstadt, Nagyvarad, Timisoara 10 Czernovitz, Czernowitz 11 Klausenburg 12 Groswardein
rumble: 4 seat 5 growl, rumor 6 murmur, polish, ramble, report, ripple, uproar 7 grumble 9 complaint 11 disturbance
rumbo: 4 grog
rumen: cud 6 paunch 7 stomach
ruminant: ox; yak 4 deer, goat 5 bison, camel, llama, moose, okapi, sheep, steer 6 alpaca, cattle, vicuna 7 buffalo, chewing, giraffe 8 antelope 10 meditative
female: cow, doe, ewe 5 nanny
genus: bos 5 capra
male: ram 4 buck, bull
stomach: 4 read, reed 5 rumen 6 omasum 8 abomasum, abomasus, roddikin 9 reticulum
ruminate: 4 chaw, chew, mull, muse 5 think, weigh 6 ponder 7 reflect 8 cogitate, consider, meditate
rummage: 4 rout, stow 6 gather, litter, search 7 collect, confuse, derange, examine, fossick, ransack, rubbish, stowage, turmoil 8 upheaval 9 confusion, searching 10 disarrange 11 derangement
rummer: cup 5 glass 6 better
rummy: rum 4 chap, game 5 drunk 8 drunkard
rumor: 4 buzz, sugh, talk, tell, word 5 bruit, noise, sough, story, voice 6 clamor, furphy, gossip, murmur, norate, report, spread, uproar 7 hearsay, message, tidings, whisper 9 grapevine, statement 10 reputation 11 scuttlebutt
personification: 4 Fama
repeat: 5 noise
rump: 4 dock 6 behind, insult 7 hurdies, plunder, remnant 8 bankrupt, buttocks 11 legislature
rump bone: 6 sacrum 8 edgebone 9 aitchbone
rumple: 4 fold, muss, rool, rump, tail 5 plait, touse 6 crease, frowse, tousle 7 crinkle, crumple, wrinkle
rumpus: row 5 brawl 6 barney, fracas, hubbub, uproar 9 confusion 11 disturbance
rumshop: bar 6 saloon, tavern 7 barroom, taproom
run: go; fly, gad, ply, rin(Sc.), sew 4 butt, cast, dart, dash, emit, flow, fuse, galt, grow, hare, hunt, melt, mold, move, pass,

pour, race, roam, rove, sail, scud, tear, tend, trip, trot, turn, work **5** blend, brook, carry, climb, cover, creep, drive, enter, going, hurry, range, ravel, reach, recur, river, route, scoot, score, scour, speed, stand, trace, treat **6** ascend, bicker, career, charge, course, elapse, extend, gallop, govern, hasten, manage, output, pursue, refine, rotate, scurry, spread, spring, sprint, stream, thrust **7** conduct, contend, descend, develop, diffuse, journey, liquefy, migrate, operate, proceed, process, roulade, scamper, scutter, scutttle, smuggle, stretch, trickle **8** continue, dissolve, function, sequence, stampede, traverse **9** discharge, suppurate, transport **11** watercourse

run across: **4** meet **9** encounter **10** transverse

run aground: **7** founder

run away: **4** bolt, flee **5** elope **6** decamp, desert, escape

run down: hit **4** kill, sink, stop **5** crush, decry **6** pursue **7** capture, decline, traduce **8** overbear **9** disparage, exhausted, overthrow **11** dilapidated

run for office: **5** stand

run-in: **4** tiff **5** fight **7** quarrel **11** altercation

run-of-the-mill: **6** common **7** average **8** ordinary

run off: **5** print, waste **7** impress

run out: **4** flow **5** expel, lapse, peter, spill, spilt, waste **6** elapse, expire, spread **8** squander

run over: **6** exceed, strike **8** overflow, rehearse

run through: **4** stab **6** pierce **7** examine, inspect, pervade **8** transfix

run up: **4** grow, rise **5** erect **7** enlarge **8** increase **9** construct **10** accumulate

runagate: **7** runaway **8** deserter, fugitive, renegade, vagabond, wanderer

runaway: **7** escapee **8** fugitive, runagate

rundle (see also **runnel**): **4** ball, drum, rung, step **5** round **6** circle, sphere

rundlet: tun **4** cask **6** barrel

rune: wen **5** magic **6** secret **7** mystery

rung: rod **4** spar, step **5** round, spoke, staff, stair, stake, stave, tread **6** cudgel, degree, rundle **7** girdled

runlet: **4** rush **5** brook **6** barrel, runnel **7** rivulet **9** streamlet

runnel: **4** rill **5** brook, creek, rhine **6** runlet, stream **7** channel, rivulet **9** streamlet **11** watercourse

runner: rug, ski **4** skee **5** agent, miler, racer, ravel, scarf **6** cursor, stolon **8** operator, smuggler, sprinter **9** collector, detective, messenger, solicitor

running: **4** care, trip **6** attack **7** contest, current, cursive, journey **8** skirmish **10** management, successive

running birch: **9** snowberry

running board: **9** footboard

running knot: **5** noose

running toad: **10** natterjack

runt: **4** chit, wrig **5** dwarf, pigmy, pygmy **6** durgan, durgen, titman

runty: **4** puny **5** small **7** stunted **8** dwarfish **10** diminutive, undersized **12** contemptible

runway: **4** file, path, ramp, road **5** chute, strip, track, trail **6** bridge, groove, trough **7** channel **8** platform **10** passageway

rupee, rupia: re., rs.(pl.)

rupia **8** eruption

rupture: **4** part, rend, rent **5** break, burst, split **6** breach, hernia, rhexis **7** ruction, ruption **8** fraction, fracture **10** disruption, separating

rural: **6** rustic **7** bucolic, country **8** agrestic, Arcadian, geoponic, pastoral **11** countrified

life: **7** bucolic, georgic **8** pastoral

rurales: **9** policemen **12** constabulary

ruse: **4** fall, hoax, slip, wile **5** dodge, feint, fraud, shift, trick **6** deceit **8** artifice **9** stratagem **10** subterfuge

rush: sag **4** birr, dart, dash, junk, race, rout, scud, tear **5** break, brook, chute, feeze, haste, hurry, onset, press, sally, scoot, spate, sprat, sprot, straw, surge **6** attack, bustle, charge, combat, defeat, fescue, hasten, hurtle, hustle, runlet, sortie, trifle **7** assault, bulrush, cattail, destroy, rampage, repulse, tantivy **8** eruption, stampede **9** overthrow **11** undergrowth **13** precipitation

family: **9** juncaceae

load: **5** barth, gavel

rush hour: **4** peak

rush nut: **5** chufa

rush toad: **10** natterjack

rusk: **4** cake **5** bread, crisp, toast **7** biscuit

Russ: **7** Russian

Russia (see also **Soviet Union**): **4** USSR **7** Muscovy

alcoholic beverage: **5** kvass, quass, vodka **9** slivovitz

antelope: **5** saiga

apple: **9** astrachan

aristocrat: **5** Boyar **6** Boyard

automobile: Zis

bondman: **4** serf

braid: **8** soutache

cabinet member: **9** commissar

cactus: **7** thistle

calendar: **6** Julian

cap: 4 aska
carriage: 6 drosky, troika 8 tarantas
cathedral: 5 sobor
caviar: 4 ikra 5 ikary
citadel: 7 Kremlin
city: 4 Kiev, Omsk, Orel, Perm 5 Gomel, Kasan, Kazan, Minsk, Pensa, Pskov 6 Kertch, Moscow(c.), Moskva, Nizhni, Odessa, Rostov, Samara, Sartov 7 Bataisk, Ivanovo, Kalinin, Rybinsk 8 Kostroma, Orenburg, Smolensk, Taganrog, Tashkent, Vladimir, Voronezh, Yaroslaf 9 Archangel, Astrakhan, Kuibishev, Petrograd 10 Michurinsk, Sebastopol, Sevastopol, Voznesensk 11 Cheliabinsk, Vladivostok 12 Ekaterinburg 13 Yekaterinburg 14 Nizhni Novgorod 15 Saint Petersburg
coal area: 6 Donets
coin: 5 altin, copec, kopek, ruble 6 copeck, grivna, kopeck 9 altininck, poltinnik 10 chervonets
collective farm: 6 kolhoz 7 kolkhos
commune: 6 kolhoz 7 kolkhos, kolkhoz
composer: Cui 9 Prokofiev 10 Stravinsky 12 Tschaikovsky 13 Shostakovitch 14 Rimsky-Korsakov
cossack: 6 Tartar
council: 4 Duma
country house: 5 dacha
dance: 7 ziganka
decree: 5 ukase
delicacy: 6 caviar 7 caviare
despot: 4 czar, tsar, tzar
devil: 5 chort
diplomat: 5 Malik, Zorin 6 Stalin 7 Gromyko, Molotov, Sobolev 8 Malenkov 9 Kuznetzov, Tsarapkin, Vishinsky 11 Shcherbakov
district: 7 Karelia
dog: 4 alan 6 borzoi 7 owtchah 9 wolfhound
dress: 7 sarafan
emperor: 4 czar, Ivan, tsar, tzar 5 Peter
empress: 7 czarina, tsarina, tzarina 8 tsaritza, tzaritza
exclamation: 7 nichevo 8 nitchevo
farmer: 5 kulak
fish: 6 beluga
flax: 6 bobbin
folk song: 6 bylina
forest: 6 tundra
fox: 6 corsac 7 karagan
gambling game: 6 coocoo
general: 10 Timoshenko 14 Tukhashchevski
government group: 4 duma, rada, tsik 6 soviet 7 zemstvo 9 Politburo, Presidium 10 Praesidium 11 Politbureau
grandmother: 8 babushka
gulf: 4 Azov
hood: 7 bashlik, bashlyk
horse: 6 tarpan
house: 4 isba 5 dacha
image: 4 icon, ikon 5 ikono
imperial order: 5 ukase
kerchief: 6 analav
labor association: 5 artel
lagoon: 5 liman
lake: 4 Aral, Neva, Sego 5 Elton, Ilmen, Onega
language: 4 Russ
leader: 5 Lenin 6 Stalin 7 Molotov 8 Brezhnev 10 Khrushchev
measure: fut, lof 4 duim, fass, loof, stof 5 duime, foute, korec, ligne, osmin, pajak, stoff, vedro, verst 6 arshin, charka, liniya, osmina, paletz, sagene, tchast, versta, verste 7 arsheen, botchka, chkalik, garnetz, verchoc, verchok 8 boutylka, chetvert, krouchka, kroushka 9 chetverik 10 dessiatine 11 polugarnetz
mile: 5 verst
money: 5 ruble
monk: 7 starets 8 Rasputin
mountain range: 4 Alai, Ural
musical instrument: 5 gudok, gusla, gusle 9 balalaika
name: 4 Igor, Ivan, Olga 5 Peter, Sonya
naval academy: 6 Frunze
news agency: 4 Tass
newspaper: 6 Pravda 8 Izvestia
novelist: 5 Gorki 7 Chekhov, Tolstoi, Tolstoy 10 Dostoevsky
peasant: 5 kulak 6 muzhik, muzjik
peninsula: 4 Kola 6 Crimea 7 Karelia
people: Red 4 Lett, Russ, Slav 5 Ersar 7 Cossack, Russine 9 Muscovite 12 Byelorussian
plain: 6 steppe
poet: 6 Jehuda 7 Pushkin 9 Aleksandr, Pasternak, Sholokhov 11 Sergyeevich, Voznesensky, Yevtushenko
port: 4 Eisk 5 Anapa 6 Odessa 9 Archangel 10 Sevastapol 11 Vladivostok
prince: 4 knez 5 knais, knyaz
revolutionist: 5 Lenin, Rykov 6 Stalin, Tomsky 7 Trotsky
river: Ik, Ob; Don, Ili, Ner, Oka, Ros, Ufa 4 Amur, Duna, Kara, Lena, Neva, Orel, Sura, Svir, Ural 5 Dnepr, Dvina, Onega, Terek, Tobol, Volga 6 Donets, Irtish, Irtysh 7 Dnieper
saint: 4 Olga
satellite: 7 sputnik
sea: 4 Aral, Azof, Azov 6 Baikal
soup: 5 shchi 6 borsch 7 borscht
spa: Ems
stockade: 5 etape

tavern: **6** caback
urn: **7** samovar
villa: **5** dacha
village: mir
violinist: **5** Elman
weight: **4** dola, pood
whip: **5** knout
worker: **7** dvornik **12** Stakhanovite
youth organization: **8** Comsomol, Komsomol

russud: **5** grain **6** forage

rust: eat **5** erode **6** aecium, aerugo, blight, canker, patina **7** corrode, erosion, oxidize **9** corrosion, oxidation, verdigris

rustic: hob **4** boor, carl, dull, hick, hind, jake, rube, rude **5** bacon, carle, chuff, churl, clown, doric, hodge, plain, rough, rural, swain, yokel **6** coarse, gaffer, honest, simple, sturdy, sylvan **7** artless, awkward, boorish, bucolic, bumpkin, bushman, Corydon, country, hayseed, peasant, plowboy, plowman, uncouth **8** agrestic, churlish, clownish, pastoral **9** agrestian, campesino, chawbacon, unadorned **10** clodhopper, countryman, unaffected, unpolished

rustle: **5** steal **6** fissle, fistle, scroop **7** crinkle

Rustum: *father:* Zal
son: **6** Sohrab

rut: rat, rit **4** brim **5** ditch, track **6** furrow, groove, strake **7** routine, wrinkle

rutabaga: **6** turnip

ruth: woe **4** pity **5** grief, mercy **6** regret, sorrow **7** remorse, sadness **10** compassion, repentance, tenderness **17** compassionateness

Ruth: *husband:* **4** Boaz
mother-in-law: **5** Naomi
son: **4** Obed

ruthless: **4** grim **5** cruel **6** savage **9** ferocious

rutter: **4** plow **5** guide **7** trooper **8** horseman

ruttle: **6** gurgle, rattle

rye: ree, rie **5** grain, grass **6** whisky **9** gentleman
disease: **5** ergot

ryke: **5** reach(Sc.)

ryot, raiyat: **6** farmer, tenant **7** peasant **10** cultivator

rytina: **12** hydrodamalis

Ryukyu island: **7** Okinawa

S

S-shaped: 4 ogee 7 sigmate, sigmoid
sabana: See **savanna**
sabbat: 8 assembly
saber, sabre: 8 scimitar, scimiter, yataghan
Sabine: *goddess:* 6 Vacuna
people: 7 Vestini
sable: sad 4 dark, ebon 5 black, brush, saber 6 dismal, gloomy, marten, pellet 8 antelope, darkened 10 mysterious 11 threatening
genus of: 7 mustela
pert. to: 8 zibeline 9 zibelline
sablefish: cod 6 beshow 10 candlefish
sabot: 4 shoe
sabotage: 7 destroy 9 undermine 11 destruction
sabre: See **saber**
Sabrina River: 6 Severn
sabulous: 5 dusty, sandy 6 floury, gritty 10 arenaceous
sabutan: 5 fiber, straw
sac: bag, pod 4 cyst, sack 5 ascus, bursa, pouch, theca 6 cavity, saccus 7 cistern, utricle, vesicle 8 sacculus
Sacar's son: 5 Ahiam
sacaton: 5 grass
saccadic: 5 jerky 9 twitching
saccharin: 7 gluside
saccharine: 5 sweet 10 sweetening
saccos: See **sakkos**
sacculate: 7 pouched
sacerdotal: 8 clerical, priestly
sachem: 4 boss 5 chief 8 sagamore
sachet: bat, pad 4 oris 5 pouch, scent 8 reticule
sack (see also **sac**): bag, bed 4 base, fire, loot, poke, ruin 5 bursa, gunny, harry, pouch, purse, waste 6 budget, burlap, jacket, ravage, wallet 7 boucher, dismiss, musette, pillage, plunder 8 desolate 9 container, discharge, dismissal
fiber: 4 jute 5 gunny 6 burlap
sackbut: 8 trombone
sackless: 4 weak 7 bashful 8 harmless, innocent 9 guiltless, peaceable 10 dispirited, unmolested
sacque: 4 sack 6 jacket
sacrament: 4 sign 5 token 6 pledge, symbol 7 baptism, penance, promise, unction 8 ceremony, covenant 9 communion, Eucharist, matrimony 12 confirmation
sacrarium: 5 ambry 6 chapel, shrine 7 oratory 9 sanctuary 10 tabernacle
sacred: 4 holy 5 huaca, santo 6 divine 7 blessed 8 hallowed, reverend 9 geistlich, inviolate, venerated 10 inviolable, sacrosanct 11 consecrated 13 sanctimonious
combining form: 5 hagio, hiero
make: 8 enshrine
most: 10 sacrosanct
sacred bean: 5 lotus
sacred beetle: 10 scarabaeus
sacred bo tree: 5 pipal
sacred fig: 5 pipal
sacred weed: 7 vervain
sacrifice: 4 host, loss 6 corban, homage, korban, victim 8 hecatomb, immolate, oblation, offering 9 holocaust, martyrdom, privation, surrender 10 immolation 11 destruction
sacrilege: 9 blasphemy 11 desecration, profanation
sacristy: 6 vestry
pert. to: 7 vestral
sacrosanct: 6 sacred
sad: bad 4 blue, dark, dram, dull 5 dusky, grave, sober, sorry, trist 6 dismal, dreary, gloomy, solemn, somber, sombre, triste(F.), wicked, woeful 7 doleful, dolente(It.), pensive, serious, unhappy 8 dejected, desolate, dolorous, downcast, grievous, mournful, pathetic, pitiable 9 afflicted, cheerless, depressed, plaintive, sorrowful 10 calamitous, deplorable, despondent, lugubrious 11 distressing, melancholic 12 disconsolate, heavyhearted
combining form: 5 tragi 7 tragico
sadden: 7 attrist

saddle: 4 load 5 ridge 6 howdah 7 aparejo, pillion 8 encumber
blanket: 6 corona, tilpah
bow: 6 pommel
maker: 7 knacker, saddler
pad: 5 panel 7 housing
part: 4 horn, tore 5 arson, cinch, croup, girth, panel, pilch, skirt 6 cantle, corona, crutch, latigo, pommel 7 stirrup 8 sudadero 9 saddlebow
rear part: 6 cantle
saddle horse: 4 pony 5 mount
saddle rock: 6 oyster
saddleback: 4 hill 5 ridge
saddlebag: sag(Sc.) 4 jagg(Sc.) 7 alforja, pannier
saddlecloth: 5 panel 7 housing 8 shabrack 9 shabraque
saddler: 4 seal 5 horse 7 cobbler, knacker, lorimer, loriner 9 shoemaker 11 saddlemaker
sadness: 5 blues, dumps
saeter: 6 meadow 7 pasture
safari: 4 hunt, trek 7 caravan, journey 9 excursion 10 expedition
safe: box 4 sure 5 chest, siker, sound, vault 6 armory, closet, coffer, holder, secure, sicker, unhurt 8 cupboard, unharmed 9 strongbox, untouched 10 depository 11 gardeviance, trustworthy
safe-conduct: 4 pass 5 cowle, guard 6 convoy 10 permission, protection
safecracker: 4 yegg 7 peteman
safeguard: 4 pass 5 guard 6 convoy, escort, safety 7 defense, protect 10 protection
safekeeping: 4 care 7 custody, storage 10 protection
safety: 6 surete(F.) 9 assurance
place of: ark 4 port 5 haven 6 asylum, refuge 7 retreat, sanctum
zone: 6 island
safety lamp: 4 Davy
safety pin: 5 clasp 6 fibula
safety rail: 9 guardrail
saffron: 6 crocus, yellow 9 safflower
sag: 4 bend, flag, reed, rush, sink, wilt 5 drift, droop, sedge, slump 6 settle, weaken
saga: 4 edda, epic, myth, tale 5 story 6 legend 7 history, recital 9 narrative
narrator: 7 sagaman
sagaciate: 4 fare 6 thrive
sagacious: 4 sage, wise 5 acute, quick 6 argute, astute, shrewd 7 knowing, politic, prudent, sapient 9 judicious 10 discerning, farsighted, hardheaded 11 clairvoyant, penetrating 13 perspicacious
sagacity: 6 acumen 8 sapience
sagamore: 5 chief 6 sachem
sage: 4 herb, mint, seer, wise 5 clary, grave, rishi(Ind.), solon, spice 6 pundit, salvia, shrewd, solemn 7 learned, prudent, sapient 8 sagebush 9 counselor, judicious, venerable 10 counsellor, discerning, perceptive 11 philosopher
Sage: *of Chelsea:* 13 Thomas Carlyle
of Concord: 17 Ralph Waldo Emerson
of Emporia: 5 White
of Ferney: 8 Voltaire
of Monticello: 15 Thomas Jefferson
of Pylos: 6 Nestor
sage cheese: 7 cheddar
sage cock: 6 grouse
sage hen: 6 grouse 7 Nevadan
Sagebrush State: 6 Nevada
saginate: 6 fatten
Sagittarius: 6 archer, bowman
sago: 6 starch
sago palm: 7 coontie
sagoin: 8 marmoset
saguaro: 6 cactus
sagum: 5 cloak
Sahara: *people:* 4 Arab 5 nomad 6 Tuareg
plateau: 6 hamada 7 hammada
wind: 5 leste
saic: 4 boat 5 ketch
said (see also **say**): dit(F.) 5 quoth 6 spoken, stated 7 reputed, uttered 8 supposed
Saida: 5 Sidon
saiga: 4 coin 8 antelope
sail: awe, awn, fly, rig, van 4 dart, duck, haul, keel, luff, move, scud, skim, soar, swim, trip 5 fleet, float, glide, sheet 6 canvas, depart, embark, voyage 7 journey 8 navigate 9 excursion
kind of: jib 5 royal 6 lateen, mizzen, square 7 balloon, lugsail, skysail, spanker, topsail, trysail 8 foresail, mainsail, staysail, studding 9 crossjack, foreroyal, spinnaker 10 topgallant 12 forestaysail
nearer wind: 4 luff
part: 4 bunt, clew, yard 5 leach, leech, sheet 6 earing 7 earring, yardarm
pert. to: 5 velic
prepare to: 4 trim
triangular: jib
sail yard: rae(Sc.) 4 spar
sailboat: 4 bark, yawl 5 skiff, sloop, yacht 7 caravel 9 caravelle
sailcloth: 4 duck 6 canvas
sailfish: 8 billfish
sailing: 4 asea
sailing ship: cog 4 bark, brig, saic, yawl 5 sloop 6 barque, cutter, galley, sampan, vessel 7 frigate, galleon 8 schooner 10 barkentine, brigantine 11 barquentine
scoop: 5 skeet

sailor: gob, hat, tar, tot **4** salt **5** Jacky **6** hearty, lascar, ratiny **7** mariner, seafman **8** coxswain, seafarer, waterman **10** bluejacket, lobscouser
assent: aye
associate: **8** messmate
call: **4** ahoy
carving: **9** scrimshaw
chapel: **6** bethel
group: **4** crew **5** hands
jacket: **6** reefer
mess tub: kid
old: **4** salt
patron saint: **4** Elmo
patroness: **11** Mother Carey
potion: **4** grog
song: **6** chanty **7** chantey **9** barcarole
saint (see also **patron saint**): St.; Sao(Port.), Ste. **4** holy **5** santa(Sp.), santo **6** hallow **7** beatify **8** canonize, enshrine
biography: **11** hagiography
image: **5** santo
invocation of: **10** hagiolatry
worship: **10** hagiolatry, hierolatry
Saint Andrew's cross: **7** saltier, saltire
Saint Anthony's cross: tau **4** ankh
Saint Barnabas' prayer: **8** Ave Maria
Saint Catherine's home: **5** Siena
Saint Elmo's fire: **5** flame **6** furole **9** corposant
Saint Francis' birthplace: **6** Assisi
Saint John's-bread: **5** carob
Saint Martin's: *bird:* **7** harrier
feast: **9** Martinmas
Saint Paul: *birthplace:* **6** Tarsus
companion: **4** Luke
Saint Peter: **5** Simon
Saint-Saens opera: **6** Samson
Saint Veronica's handkerchief: **8** sudarium
Saint Vitus' dance: **6** chorea
saintly: **4** holy **5** pious **6** devout **7** angelic **9** angelical **13** sanctimonious
sake: end **5** cause, drink **6** behalf, motive, regard **7** account, benefit, concern, purpose **8** beverage **13** consideration
saker: **6** falcon
saki: **5** drink, yarke **6** monkey, yarkee **8** beverage
sakkos, saccos: **8** vestment
sal: **4** salt
sala: **4** hall
salaam, salam: bow **4** bend **6** salute **8** greeting **9** obeisance **10** compliment, salutation
salacious: **4** lewd **7** lustful, obscene **8** scabrous **9** lecherous **12** pornographic
salad ingredient: **5** cress **6** celery, endive, greens, tomato, **7** cabbage, lettuce, parsley, romaine **8** scallion **9** dandelion **10** watercress
salad tree: **6** redbud
Saladin's foes: **9** Crusaders
salamander: eft, olm **4** evet, newt **6** triton **7** axoloti, axolotl, caudata, urodela, urodele **10** hellbender
order: **7** caudata, urodela
salami: **7** sausage
store: **4** deli
Salammbo author: **8** Flaubert
salary: fee, pay **4** hire **5** wages **6** reward **7** stipend **8** pittance **9** allowance, emolument **10** exhibition, honorarium, recompense **12** compensation, remuneration **13** consideration
sale: net **4** deal, hall, vend **5** bower **6** market, palace, vendue, willow **7** auction, bargain, chamber, rummage **8** contract, transfer **9** utterance, vendition **10** conveyance **11** transaction
sales talk: **4** line **5** pitch, spiel **6** patter
salesman: **5** agent, clerk **6** hawker, pedlar, seller, sutler, vendor **7** drummer, hustler, peddler **8** pitchman, vendeuse(fem.) **9** solicitor **14** representative
salience: **5** point **7** agility **8** emphasis **9** highlight **10** prominence
salient: **4** line **5** cabre, redan **6** trench **7** jumping, leaping **8** bounding, extended, striking **10** noticeable **11** conspicuous
salient angle: **5** arris
salient point: **5** heart **6** detail, source **7** feature
salientia: **5** anura, frogs, toads **7** aglossa, costata **8** Amphibia, linguata
salina: **4** lake, pond **5** marsh **6** salada **9** saltworks
saline: **4** tear **5** brine, briny, salty **8** brackish **10** saliferous
Salisbury steak: **9** hamburger
saliva: **4** spit **7** spittle
salix: **5** genus **6** osiers **7** sallows, willows
salle: **4** room
sallet, salade: **6** helmet
sallow: wan **4** pale, twig **5** muddy, osier, shoot **6** pallid, willow **9** yellowish
sally: **4** leap, quip, rush, trip **5** dance, issue, jaunt, start **6** attack, escape, retort, sortie, spring **7** darting, rushing **8** escapade, outbreak, outburst **9** excursion, witticism **10** liveliness
salmagundi: **4** hash, olio **5** salad **6** medley **7** mixture **9** potpourri
salmi: **6** ragout
salmon: gib, lax **4** chum, coho, kelt, keta, mort, pike, pink, raun, slat **5** color, haddo, holia, nerka, smolt, tecon **6** baggit, **kipper,**

laurel, sauqui, taimen 7 gilling, saumont, shedder 8 schoodic, springer, weakfish 9 ceratodus 10 barramunda
enclosure: 4 weir, yair, yare
female: 4 raun 6 baggit
male: 6 kipper
pool: 5 stell
silver: 4 coho
smoked: lox
trap: 4 slap
young: 4 parr
salmon trout: 5 sewen
salmonoid: 4 ahyu 5 nelma, powan
Salome: *father:* 8 Herodias
grandfather: 5 Herod
salon: 4 hall, room 7 gallery 9 apartment, reception 10 assemblage, exhibition
saloon: bar 4 hall, room 5 cabin, coach, cuddy, divan, sedan 6 tavern 7 barroom, cantina(Sp.) 8 alehouse, groggery 9 apartment, brasserie(F.)
saloop: 5 drink, salep 9 sassafras
salpa, salp: 8 tunicate
salse: 7 volcano
salt: sal, tar, wit 4 alum, corn, cure 5 brine, briny, ester, salic, sharp, witty 6 alkali, flavor, halite, harden, lively, sailor, saline, seaman, season 7 bromate, piquant, pungent, seadust 8 brackish, halinous 9 seasoning
combining form: 4 sali
deposit: 6 saline
oleic acid: 6 oleate
resembling: 5 halid 6 halide, haloid
rock: pig
working: 7 halurgy
salt-like: 6 haloid
salt marsh: 6 salina
salt pit: vat
salt tree: 4 atle 8 tamarisk
salt water: 5 brine
saltate: 4 jump, leap 5 bound, dance
saltcellar: 5 saler
salted: 4 alat 5 cured 6 corned
saltpeter, saltpetre: 5 niter, nitre
saltworks: 7 saltern, saltery
salty: See **salt**
salubrious: 8 salutary 9 benignant, healthful, wholesome 10 beneficial
salutary: 4 good 6 benign 7 healthy, helpful 8 curative 9 desirable, healthful, medicinal, wholesome 10 beneficial 11 restorative
salutation: hi; ave, bow 4 beck, hail 5 aloha, hello, howdy, salam, skoal 6 curtsy, kowtow, Mizpah, Mizpeh, prosit, salaam, salute 7 address, welcome, slainte 8 accolade, chin-chin, farewell, greeting
salute: nod 4 hail 5 greet, halse, salvo 6 accost 7 address 10 salutation
salvage: 4 save 6 rescue 7 reclaim 12 compensation
salvager: 6 salvor
salvation: 6 rescue 10 redemption 12 preservation
pert. to: 8 soterial 9 soterical
salve: 4 balm 6 anoint, cerate, soothe 7 assuage, unguent 8 flattery, ointment, palliate
salver: 4 tray 6 waiter
salvo: 6 excuse, salute 7 pretext, proviso, quibble 9 exception 11 reservation
samadh: 4 tomb 6 shrine
samaj: 6 church 7 society 12 congregation
Samaritan: *alphabet:* i; ba, in, it; jud, mim, nun, phi, sen, tav, tit 4 alaf, bith, goph, kaph, rish, sadi, shan 5 dalat, gaman, labad 6 simcat
god: 6 Tartak
people: 8 Assyrian 9 Israelite
sambar, sambur: elk 4 deer, maha, rusa
same: id; ilk, one 4 ibid, idem, like, meme(F.), self 5 alike, ditto, equal 7 identic 9 identical, unchanged 10 invariable
comb. form: iso 4 homo
sameness: 8 monotony 10 similarity 11 resemblance 14 correspondence
Samhain Eve: 9 Halloween
Samian philosopher: 10 Pythagoras
samisen: 5 banjo
samlet: 4 parr 6 salmon 10 fingerling
sammy: 5 ninny 6 clammy, sodden, watery 9 simpleton
Samoa (see also **Polynesia**): *capital:* 4 Apia
fish: 6 ataata, sesele
hostess: 5 taupo 6 taupou
island: 5 Upolu 6 Savaii
mollusk: asi
mudworm: ipo
owl: 4 lulu
red: 4 mumu
warrior: toa
samovar: urn 6 teapot
samp: 4 meal, mush, soup 6 cereal, hominy 8 porridge
sampaloc: 8 tamarind
sampan: 4 boat 5 skiff
sample: 4 test 5 taste 6 swatch 7 example, pattern 8 specimen 12 illustration
sampleman: 6 taster 12 demonstrator
sampler: 5 model 6 taster 7 example, hanging, pattern 8 original, specimen 9 archetype
Samson: *betrayer:* 7 Delilah
deathplace: 4 Gaza
vulnerable place: 4 hair
Samuel: *home:* 5 Ramah

mentor: Eli
parent: 6 Hannah 7 Elkanah
son: 5 Abiah
victim: 4 Agag, Agog
Samurai: 7 warrior
ostracized: 5 Ronin
San Francisco hill: Nob
San Simeon name: 6 Hearst
sanative: 6 curing 7 healing 8 curative, sanatory 9 healthful
sanatorium: spa 8 hospital
sanatory: 8 sanative
Sancho Panza: *island:* 9 Barataria
master: 10 Don Quixote
mule: 6 Dapple
sanctify: 8 dedicate 10 consecrate
sanctimonious: 4 holy 5 pious 6 devout, sacred 7 saintly 10 sanctified
sanctimoniousness: 4 cant
sanction: 4 amen, fiat 5 allow 6 assent, avouch, permit, placet, ratify 7 approve, confirm, endorse, indorse, support 8 accredit, approval 9 allowance, approbate, authority, authorize, encourage, subscribe 10 imprimatur 11 approbation, countenance, countersign, endorsement 12 ratification 13 authorization, encouragement
sanctity: 5 rites 6 purity 7 halidom 8 halidome, holiness, recesses 9 godliness, solemnity 10 sacredness 11 obligations, saintliness 13 inviolability
place of: 4 fane 5 altar, hiera 6 chapel, church, hieron, shrine, temple 7 chaitya 9 synagogue
sanctuary: ark 4 bema, fane, holy, naos 5 abbey, adyta(pl.), bamah, grith, haven 6 adytum, asylum, bemata, chapel, church, haikal, priory, refuge, shrine, temple 7 alsatia, chancel, convent, halidom, retreat, sanctum, shelter 8 cloister, halidome, holiness 9 monastery 10 penetralia, protection, tabernacle 11 reservation
sanctum: den 5 study 6 adytum, office 9 sanctuary
sand: 4 grit 5 nerve 6 abrade, desert, gravel, smooth 7 courage 8 alluvium, asbestic
and clay: 4 loam
particle: 5 grain
particles: 4 silt
resembling: 7 arenoid
sand cock: 8 redshank
sand dune: 5 towan
sand eel: 4 grig 5 lance 6 launce
sand flea: 6 chigoe 7 chigger
sand flounder: 5 fluke 10 windowpane
sand hill: 4 dene, dune
sand lob: 7 lugworm
sand widgeon: 7 gadwall
sandal (see also **moccasin**): 4 clog, shoe 6 buskin, caliga, charuk 7 rullion, slipper, talaria 9 alpargata 10 espadrille
winged: 7 talaria(pl.)
wooden: 6 patten
sandalwood: 5 algum, almug, maire
Sandalwood Island: 5 Sumba 6 Soemba
sandarac: 7 realgar
tree: 4 arar
wood: 6 alerce, alerse
sandbank: 4 dune, meal
sandbar: 4 dene, dune, reef, spit 5 beach, shelf, shoal
sandia: 10 watermelon
sandpiper: ree 4 bird, knot, ruff 5 reeve, terek 6 dunlin, teeter, tiltup 7 brownie, chorook, fiddler, haybird 8 triddler, redshank 10 canderling
sandstone: 4 grit 5 hazel 6 arkose 8 ganister 9 gritstone
block: 6 sarsen
pert. to: 10 arenilitic
sandy: 6 gritty, plucky 7 arenose, arenous 8 shifting, unstable 9 arenulous 10 arenaceous 13 uninteresting
pert. to: 6 eremic
Sandy: 8 Scotsman
sane: 4 wise 5 lucid, sober, sound 6 normal 7 healthy, sapient 8 rational, sensible 10 reasonable
sang (see also **sing**): 5 blood
sangfroid: 8 calmness, coolness 9 composure 16 imperturbability
sanglier: 4 boar
Sangraal: See **Holy Grail**
sanguinaria: 6 yarrow 9 bloodroot
sanguine: red 4 fond, gory, warm 5 cruel, ruddy 6 ardent, bloody, crayon, savage, yarrow 7 buoyant, hopeful 8 cheerful, hematite 9 confident, ferocious, murderous 10 bloodstone, ensanguine, optimistic, sanguinary 12 bloodthirsty
sanitary: 8 hygienic
sanity: 6 reason 7 balance 8 lucidity, saneness 9 soundness 13 wholesomeness
sans: 7 without
Sanskrit: *dialect:* 4 Pali
dictionary: 10 amara-kosha
division of literature: 5 Sruti 6 Shruti
epic: 8 Ramayana
epic character: 4 Sita
school: tol
soul: 5 atman
verse: 5 sloka
Santa Barbara island: 8 Catalina
Santa Claus's reindeer: 5 Comet, Cupid, Vixen 6 Dancer, Dasher, Donder, Donner 7 Blitzen, Prancer
santo: 5 image, saint

santon: 4 monk 5 image, saint 6 hermit 7 dervish
sap: lac 4 dupe, fool, milk, mine, seve(F.), upas 5 drain, juice, latex, lymph, vigor 6 energy, trench, weaken 7 exhaust, saphead 8 enervate, vitality, weakling 9 exudation, schlemiel, schlemihl, screwball, undermine 10 debilitate, devitalize
dried: gum
lose: 5 bleed
spout: 5 spile
sapajou: 6 monkey
sapanwood, sappanwood: 4 tree 10 brazilwood
saphead: See **sap**
saphie, saffi: 5 charm 6 amulet 8 talisman
sapid: 5 tasty 6 savory 7 savoury 8 engaging 9 palatable 10 flavorable
sapient: 4 sage, sane, wise 6 shrewd 7 knowing 9 sagacious 10 discerning
sapiutan: 4 anoa
sapless: dry 7 insipid 8 withered 9 exsuccous 11 devitalized
sapling: 5 plant, youth
sapo: 4 soap 8 toadfish
sapodilla, sapotilha, sapotilla: 5 chico 6 sapota, sapote, zapote 7 nispero 9 naseberry
saponaceous: 5 soapy 7 elusive 8 slippery
sapor: 5 gusto, savor, taste 6 flavor, relish 7 flavour
sapper: 5 miner 6 digger
Sappho: *consort:* 5 Phaon
home: 6 Lesbos
sappy: 5 juicy, moist, pithy, plump, silly 6 sodden 7 fatuous, foolish 8 vigorous 9 energetic, succulent 11 sentimental
sapsago: 6 cheese
sapsucker: 10 woodpecker
sapwood: 8 alburnum
Saracen: 4 Arab 5 nomad 6 Moslem
knight: 6 Rogero 8 Ruggiero
leader: 7 Saladin
Sarah: *husband:* 7 Abraham
slave: 5 Hagar
son: 5 Isaac
sarcasm: 4 gibe, jeer 5 fling, irony, taunt 6 attack, rebuke, satire 7 mockery 8 acridity, reproach, ridicule 9 criticism
pert. to: 8 ironical
sarcastic: dry 6 biting 7 cutting, mordant 8 incisive, sardonic
sarcenet, sarsenet: 4 silk, soft 6 smooth 8 tempered
sarcina: 8 bacteria 9 bacterium
sarcophagus: 4 tomb 6 coffin, cooler
sard: 7 sardine, sardius 9 carnelian 10 chalcedony
sardine: 4 bang 8 pilchard
Sardinia: *city:* 8 Cagliari
duchy: 5 Savoy 6 Savoie
language: 7 Catalan
seaport: 8 Cagliari
sardonic: 8 derisive 9 sarcastic
Sargon capital: 5 Accad
sarkinite: 8 arsenate
sarment: 4 cion 6 runner 7 cutting
sarong: 6 comboy
sarpler: 4 bale 6 weight 7 wrapper 8 covering
sarrazin: 9 buckwheat
sarsen: 5 block 8 monument 9 sandstone
sartor: 6 tailor
sash: obi 4 band, belt, benn(Sc.) 5 scarf 6 fascia, girdle 8 casement 9 waistband 10 cummerbund
sasin: 4 buck 8 antelope
Saskatchewan capital: 6 Regina
sassaby: 8 antelope
sassafras tea: 6 saloop
Satan: 4 Nick 5 demon, devil, eblis, fiend 6 Belial 7 Lucifer, tempter 8 diabolus 9 archenemy, archfiend 14 Mephistopheles
associate: 9 Beelzebub
son: Imp
satanic: 4 evil 6 wicked 8 devilish, diabolic, infernal 10 diabolical
satchel: bag 4 case, grip 5 cabas 6 valise
sate: 4 cloy, cram, glut 5 gorge, stuff 7 gratify, satiate, surfeit
satellite: Io 4 luna, moon, Rhea, vein 5 Ariel, Dione, Mimas, Titan 6 Europa, planet, Tethys 7 Japetus 8 Callisto, follower, Ganymede, Hyperion 9 attendant, dependent, Enceladus
man-made: Oso 4 Anna, Echo, Mars 5 Ariel, Faith, Lunik, Midas, Relay, Samos, Tiros 6 Cosmos, Flight, Ranger, Syncom, Vostok 7 Courier, Mariner, Pioneer, Sputnik, Telstar, Transit 8 Alouette, Explorer, Telestar, Vanguard 9 Vela-Hotel 10 Discoverer 12 Mercury-Atlas, Project-Score
weather: 5 Tiros
satiat: 7 replete
satiate: 4 cloy, fill, glut, pall, sate 5 gorge, slake 6 pamper 7 content, gratify, overeat, satisfy
satiating: 4 rich 6 stodgy 7 fulsome
satiety: 7 surfeit
satin imitation: 6 sateen 7 satinet 9 satinette
satin pod: 7 honesty
satiny: 6 glossy 8 lustrous
satire: 5 grind, irony 6 banter, parody, satura 7 lampoon, mockery, sarcasm 8 ridicule, travesty

satiric: dry 6 bitter, ironic 7 abusive, atellan, caustic, cutting 8 ironical, poignant 10 censorious 11 reproachful

satirist: 4 Pope, Shaw 5 Swift 8 Voltaire

satirize: 4 lash 5 grind 6 attack, expose 8 denounce 9 criticize

satisfaction: 4 ease, gree 6 amends 7 content, payment 8 pleasure 9 atonement, enjoyment 10 bloodmoney, recompense, reparation, settlement 11 complacence, contentment 12 compensation, propitiation, remuneration 13 gratification 15 indemnification

combat for: 4 duel

payment for killing: cro

satisfactory: pat 4 good 6 enough 8 adequate 9 allowable, expiatory 10 acceptable, satisfying

satisfied: fed 4 paid, smug 5 proud 9 contented, gratified 10 complacent

satisfy: do; pay 4 cloy, feed, fill, free, meet, sate, suit 5 appay, atone, repay, serve, slake 6 defray, please, supply 7 appease, assuage, content, expiate, fulfill, gratify, requite, satiate, suffice, surfeit 8 convince, reparate 9 discharge 10 compensate, remunerate

satrap: 5 ruler 6 prince, tyrant 8 governor, official, overlord

sattva: 5 truth 6 purity, wisdom 8 goodness 12 tranquillity

saturate: ret, sog, sop, wet 4 fill, glut, soak 5 imbue, souse, steep 6 dampen, drench, imbibe, imbrue, seethe 7 ingrain, satiate, satisfy 8 permeate 9 penetrate 10 impregnate

saturated: 6 sodden

Saturday: 7 Sabbath

pert. to: 9 sabbatine

Saturn: 6 Cronus, planet

in alchemy: 4 lead

ring part: 4 ansa 5 ansae(pl.)

satellite: 4 Rhea 5 Dione, Mimas, Titan 6 Tethys 7 Japetus 8 Hyperion 9 Enceladus

temple treasury: 8 aerarium

wife: Ops

saturnalia: 4 orgy 5 feast 7 revelry 8 carnival, festival

saturnine: 4 dull 5 grave, heavy 6 gloomy, morose, sullen 8 sluggish, taciturn

satyr: 4 faun, idol 5 deity 7 demigod 9 butterfly

sauce: dip 5 gravy 6 flavor, relish 8 dressing, matelote 9 condiment

kind: soy 4 alec, lear 5 garum 6 catsup 7 catchup, gascony, ketchup, mustard 8 chawdron, remolade 9 genevoise, remoulade 10 Bordelaise, mayonnaise 11 Hollandaise

sauciness: 10 effrontery

saucy: 4 bold, coxy, pert, rude 5 brash, fresh 6 bantam, cocket 7 forward 8 impudent, malapert 9 audacious, sprightly 11 impertinent

Saudi Arabia (see also **Arabia**): *capital:* 5 Mecca 6 Riyadh

desert: 5 Nefud

port: 5 Jidda

religious center: 5 Mecca 6 Medina

state: 4 Asir, Nejd

sauger: 4 fish 5 perch

Saul: *concubine:* 6 Rizpah

daughter: 6 Michal

father: 4 Kish

grandfather: Ner

herdsman: 4 Doeg

successor: 5 David

uncle: Ner

wife: 7 Ahinoam

Saul of Tarsus: 4 Paul

Sault Sainte Marie: Soo

saumont: 6 salmon

sauna: 4 bath 9 bathhouse

saunter: lag 4 idle, roam, rove, walk 5 range, shool, stray 6 dander, dawdle, loiter, lounge, potter, ramble, stroll, wander 8 ruminate

saunterer: 8 passerby

saurel: 4 fish, scad 5 xurel

saurian: 6 lizard 8 dinosaur

saury: 4 fish

sausage: 5 gigot 6 salame, salami, wiener 7 balloon, balogna, baloney, saveloy 8 cervelat, drisheen, rollejee, rolliche 9 andouille, bratwurst, rollichie 11 wiernerwurst 12 andouillette

casing: 4 bung

poisoning: 11 allantiasis

sausage-shaped: 9 allantoid 11 allantoidal

savage: 4 fell, grim, rude, wild 5 brute, crude, cruel, feral 6 brutal, ferine, fierce 7 brutish, furious, howling, inhuman, untamed 8 pitiless, ruthless 9 aborigine, atrocious, barbarian, barbarous, ferocious, merciless, primitive, truculent 10 unpolished 11 uncivilized 12 uncultivated, unrestrained

Savage Island people: 5 Niuan

savanna, savannah: 5 plain 9 grassland

savant: 4 sage 5 Solon 6 pedant 7 scholar 9 scientist

savarin: 7 brioche 10 coffeecake

save: bar, but 4 hain, keep 5 amass, catch, guard, hoard, salve, spare, store 6 defend, except, redeem, rescue, retain, scrimp, unless 7 deliver, husband, protect, reclaim, reserve, salvage 8 conserve, preserve 9 economize, excepting 10 accumulate

savin, savine: 7 juniper
saving: 6 frugal, thrift 7 thrifty 9 frugality
savings: 7 account, addlins 8 addlings
savoir faire: 4 tact 10 adroitness 11 worldliness 14 sophistication
savor, savour: 4 odor, zest 5 sapor, scent, smack, smell, taste, tinge 6 degust, flavor, relish, season 9 degustate
savory: 5 gusty, salty, sapid, tasty 7 piquant 8 pleasing 9 agreeable, palatable 10 appetizing, delightful
saw (see also **see**): cut 4 talk, word 5 adage, axiom, maxim, motto, rumor 6 cliche, saying 7 proverb 8 aphorism, apothegm 9 platitude 10 apophthegm
combining form: 5 serri
kind: 5 briar, edger, serra 6 stadda, trapan, trepan 8 trephine
part: 4 tine 5 redan, tooth
surgical: 6 trapan, trepan 8 trephine
saw-like: 8 serrated
sawbelly: 7 alewife
sawbones: 7 surgeon
sawder: 7 flatter
sawfish: ray
sawhorse: 4 buck 7 sawbuck
sawyer: 6 beetle, logman 9 lumberman 10 woodcutter
saxhorn: 4 alto, tuba
saxifrage: 6 seseli
Saxon: 9 Sassenach
chief: 5 Horsa
city: Ave
king: Ine 6 Harold
lady: 6 Godiva, Rowena
serf: 4 esne
swineherd: 5 Gurth
warrior: 5 Thane
Saxony city: 7 Dresden
say: 4 aver, deem, silk, tell, wool 5 speak, state, utter 6 advise, allege, answer, assert, bucket, direct, fabric, recite, relate, remark, repeat, report 7 declare, dictate, express, iterate, testify 8 announce, indicate 9 pronounce 10 asseverate
again: 6 repeat 9 reiterate
further: add
saying: mot, saw 4 quip, word 5 adage, axiom, logia, maxim, motto 6 byword, phrase 7 epigram, proverb 8 aphorism, apothegm 9 statement 11 declaration
apt: 6 bon mot
collection: ana 9 gnomology
distinguishing: 10 shibboleth
scab: 5 crust, mange 6 eschar, ratter 8 blackleg 9 scoundrel 13 strike-breaker
scabbard: 4 case 6 sheath, tsubas 7 holster
put in: 7 sheathe
tip: 7 crampit
scabby: low 4 base, mean 5 mangy 6 scurvy, shabby, stingy 12 contemptible
scabies: 4 itch 5 mange
scaddle: 4 wild 6 fierce 7 nervous 8 skittish 11 mischievous
scads: 4 lots 6 oodles
scaffie: 9 scavenger
scaffold: 4 cage, loft 5 easel, stage 7 gallery 8 platform
scalage: 8 estimate 9 allowance 10 percentage
scalar: 10 ladderlike
scalawag, scallawag: 4 pony, runt 5 scamp 6 rascal 10 scapegrace
scald: vex 4 burn 5 worry 6 blanch, excite, scorch 7 inflame, torment
scale: cup, hut 4 bowl, film, husk, peel, rate, rule, scut, shed, size 5 climb, flake, gamut, lepis, palea, scute, shive, weigh 6 ascend, lamina, rament, spread, vessel, weight 7 balance, clamber, coating, compare, lamella, measure, scatter, vernier 8 covering, disperse, separate 9 gradation, steelyard 12 incrustation
bony: 6 scutum
comb. form: 5 lepid 6 lepido
having: 7 leprose, scutate
note: do, fa, la, mi, re, ti; sol 8 dominant 10 supertonic
scale-like: 6 scurfy 7 leprose
scaling device: 6 ladder
scallion: 4 leek 5 onion 7 shallot
scallop: 4 quin 5 crena, notch 7 crenate, mollusk
scalp: rob 4 skin 5 cheat 6 defeat, denude, profit, trophy
disease: 5 favus, scurf 8 dandruff
scalpel: 5 knife 6 lancet 8 bistoury
scalper: 6 punter, trader 10 speculator
scaly: low 4 mean 6 stingy 8 squamous 10 despicable
scamble: 6 sprawl 7 collect, shamble, trample 8 scramble
scamp: imp 5 cheat, knave, rogue 6 rascal 8 scalawag, spalpeen, widdifow 9 scallawag, scoundrel 10 highwayman
scamper: run 4 race 5 speed 6 frolic, hasten, scurry 7 brattle, skitter 9 skedaddle
scan: eye 5 study, watch 6 behold, peruse, survey 7 examine, observe 10 scrutinize 11 contemplate
scandal: 5 eclat, odium, shame 6 gossip 7 calumny, outrage, slander 8 disgrace, ignominy 9 discredit 10 backbiting, defamation, detraction, opprobrium
scandalize: 5 shock 6 malign, offend, vilify
scandalous: 6 unholy 8 libelous, shocking 9 offensive 10 flagitious 11 furciferous
scandent: 8 climbing

Scandinavia (see also **Norse; Teuton**): 4 Dane, Lapp 5 Norse, Swede 8 Norseman, Suiogoth 9 Icelandic, Norwegian
alphabetical character: 4 rune
bard: 5 scald 7 sagaman
division: amt
explorer: 4 Eric
hero's place: 8 Valhalla
king: 4 Atli
land: 4 odal
legend: 4 edda, saga
legendary creature: nis 5 nisse, troll 6 Kraken
measure: ass, lod, ort, vog 4 last, mark, pund, sten, untz 5 carat 6 nylast 7 centner, lispund 8 lispound, skalpund, skeppund, skippund 9 shippound, skaalpund, skibslast 10 bismerpund
minstrel: see *bard* above
money: 5 krone
navigator: 4 Eric
nobleman: 4 jarl
pert. to: 5 Norse
plateau: 5 fjeld
rulers: Ros 10 Varangians
ship: 4 aesc
small bay: 5 fjord
trumpet: 4 lure
scant: few 4 lean 5 chary, stint 6 geason, meager, meagre, narrow, scrimp, slight, sparse 7 limited, sparing, wanting 12 parsimonious
scantling: 4 beam, stud 6 timber
scanty: 4 bare 5 close, small, spare 6 meager, meagre, scarce, sparse 7 limited, niggard, scrimpy, sparing 8 exiguous 9 niggardly 12 insufficient, parsimonious
scape: 4 slip, stem 5 fault, shaft 8 escapade, peduncle
scapegoat: 4 dupe 6 victim 10 substitute
scapegrace: 5 rogue, scamp 6 madcap, rascal 8 scalawag 9 reprobate, scallawag 10 profligate
scar: arr, mar, shy 4 mark, rock, seam, slit, wild 5 chink, cliff, crack, wound 6 cinder, deface, scared 7 blemish, catface, clinker 8 cicatrix, mountain, pockmark 9 disfigure 13 disfigurement
pert. to: 5 uloid
tissue: 6 keloid
scarab: 5 charm 6 beetle
scaramouch, scaramouche: 4 fool 5 scamp 6 rascal 7 buffoon
scarce: 4 dear, rare 5 scant, short 6 geason, meager, meagre, scanty, sparse 8 uncommon 9 deficient 10 infrequent 12 insufficient
scarcely: 6 barely, hardly, merely
scarcity: 4 lack, need, want 6 dearth, famine, penury, rarity 7 paucity, poverty 8 rareness 9 parsimony 10 deficiency, scarcensss 11 infrequency, sparingness 12 uncommonness 13 insufficiency, niggardliness
scare: awe, shy 4 fleg 5 alarm, dread, gliff, gloff, panic 6 fright 7 scarify, startle, terrify 8 affright, frighten
scarecrow: 5 bogle
scared: 6 afraid
scarf: boa, tie 4 band, sash, wrap 5 adorn, ascot, barbe, cloud, cover, orale, shawl, stole, unite 6 cravat, groove, rebozo, runner, tapalo, tippet 7 dopatta(Ind.), muffler, necktie 8 liripipe, liripoop 9 comforter, cormorant 10 fascinator 11 comfortable, neckerchief
feathered: boa
head: 8 babushka
scarfskin: 7 cuticle 9 epidermis
scarify: See **scare**
scarlet: red 4 lewd 5 bawdy 8 flagrant
Scarlett O'Hara: *home:* 4 Tara
husband: 5 Rhett
scarp: cut 5 cliff, slope 6 escarp 7 descent 8 fragment 9 declivity
scart: 4 mark 6 scrape 7 scratch 9 cormorant
scarves: See **scarf**
scary: 4 eery 5 eerie, timid, weird 6 spooky 7 ghostly, uncanny 8 alarming
scat: bop, tax 4 beat, riff, shoo 5 smash 6 begone, rebuff, shower 7 getaway, scatter, tribute, vamoose
scathe: 4 harm, hurt, sear 5 blast 6 assail, damage, injure, injury, scorch, wither 8 denounce 10 misfortune
scathing: 6 biting, severe 7 mordant 8 blasting, injuring, wounding 9 scorching, truculent, withering
scatter: sow, ted 4 deal, rout 5 fling, spray, strew, waste 6 dispel, shower, splash, spread 7 bestrew, confuse, diffuse, disband, fritter, radiate 8 dishevel, disperse, distract, separate, sprinkle, squander 9 bespatter, circulate, discomfit, dissipate 10 disconnect, distribute 11 disseminate
scatter-gun: 7 shotgun
scatterbrained: 5 giddy 7 flighty 9 frivolous
scattered: 6 sparse 7 erratic, strawed 8 rambling, sporadic 9 irregular 10 straggling
scatterer: 6 tedder
scatterling: 7 vagrant, wastrel
scatula: box
scaup: 4 duck 8 grayback 10 canvasback
scavage: tax 4 duty, toll
scavenger: rat 7 vulture
scaw: 8 headland 10 promontory
scena: 10 recitative
scenario: 4 plot 6 script 10 continuity
scend: 4 lift 5 heave

scene: act 4 site, view 5 sight, vista 6 blow-up, locale 7 diorama, display, episode, picture, quarrel, tableau 8 prospect 9 landscape, spectacle
last: 6 finale
scenery: 4 view 7 picture 9 landscape 14 representation
sceneshifter: 4 grip
scenic: 8 dramatic 9 panoramic 10 theatrical 11 picturesque
scenite: 5 nomad
scent: 4 nose, odor 5 aroma, odour, savor, smell, sniff, spoor, track 6 breath, flavor 7 bouquet, essence, flavour, inkling, perfume 8 effluvia 9 emanation, fragrance
scented: 5 olent
scepter, sceptre: rod 4 mace 5 baton, staff 6 emblem 7 trident 8 caduceus 9 authority 11 sovereignty
scerne: 7 discern
schedule: 4 card, list, plan, time 5 slate, table 6 tariff 7 catalog, routine, writing 8 calendar, document, register, tabulate 9 catalogue, inventory, timetable
schefferite: 8 pyroxene
schelm: 5 rogue 6 rascal
schema: 4 plan 6 figure, scheme 7 diagram, outline
scheme: aim, gin, web 4 dart, list, plan, plot 5 angle, cabal, cadre, draft, drift, table 6 design, device, devise, figure, racket 7 complot, concoct, diagram, epitome, outline, program, project, purpose 8 conspire, contrive, forecast, gimcrack, intrigue 9 statement 10 concoction, conspiracy 11 contrivance, machination, proposition
schemer: 6 artist
scheming: 6 artful, crafty, tricky 8 fetching 9 designing 10 intriguing
schism: 4 rent 5 split 6 breach 8 division 10 separation
schist: 5 slate
schizocarp: 5 fruit, regma
schlemiel: dub, oaf 4 clod, goof 5 chump 7 saphead
schmaltz: 4 corn 14 sentimentality
scholar: 5 clerk, pupil 6 pedant, savant 7 bookman, learner, student 8 disciple 11 academician, philologist
day: 6 extern
servant: 7 famulus
scholarly: 7 erudite, learned 8 studious 10 scholastic
scholarship: 7 bursary 8 learning 9 allowance, education, erudition, knowledge 10 fellowship 11 instruction
scholiast: 9 annotator 10 glossarist 11 commentator 13 glossographer
school: gam, pod 4 cult, sect 5 drill, ecole(F.), flock, group, lycee(F.), shoal, teach, train 6 manege 7 academy, college, company, convent, educate, seminar 8 atheneum, document, exercise, instruct, seminary 9 athenaeum, cultivate 10 realschule(G.), university 11 institution, schoolhouse
grounds: 6 campus
group: PTA
kind: 4 high, prep 5 grade 7 primary 8 military 9 finishing, secondary 10 elementary, vocational 11 preparatory
of fish: 5 shoal
of thought: ism
of whales: gam
official: 9 principal, scholarch 10 headmaster 14 superintendent
pert. to: 8 academic
religious: 5 heder 6 cheder 8 seminary
riding: 6 manege
task: 6 lesson 7 problem 10 assignment 11 composition
term: 7 quarter 8 semester 9 trimester
schoolbook: 4 text 5 atlas 6 primer, reader 7 speller 9 geography
schoolfellow: 11 condisciple
schoolmaster: 4 caji, head 7 dominie, manager, pedagog 9 pedagogue
schooner: 4 boat, brig, tern 5 glass 6 vessel 7 measure
builder: 14 Andrew Robinson
schottische: 5 dance, polka
schout: 7 bailiff, sheriff
schrik: 5 panic 6 fright
science: art, sci 5 ology 9 knowledge 10 technology
of crop production: 8 agronomy
of healing: 9 iatrology
of human behavior: 6 ethics 10 psychology
of mountains: 7 orology
of plants: 6 botany
of words: 9 semantics
principle: 5 logic
scient: 4 able 7 knowing 8 skillful 9 knowledge
sciential: 4 able 7 capable 9 competent
scientific: 8 skillful 9 technical
scilicet: 6 namely 9 videlicet
scimitar, scimiter: 4 snee 5 saber, sword
scintilla: 4 atom, iota 5 spark, trace 8 particle
scintillate: 5 flash, gleam, spark 7 glitter, sparkle, twinkle 9 coruscate
scion, cion: bud, son 4 heir, twig 5 shoot, sprig 6 sprout 8 offshoot 9 offspring 10 descendant
scissor: cut 4 clip, trim 5 shear
scissors: 6 shears
scleroid: 4 hard 8 hardened 9 indurated

scoff: 4 food, gibe, gird, jeer, leer, meal, mock, rail 5 fleer, flout, gleek, scout, sneer, steal, taunt 6 deride 7 mockery, plunder 8 ridicule

scoffer: 5 clown 6 jester 10 unbeliever

scoke: 8 pokeweed

scold: nag, yap 4 haze, jump, rail, rant, rate 5 abuse, barge, boast, brawl, chide, score, shrew, slate 6 berate, bounce, rebuff, rebuke, revile 7 reprove, upbraid 8 chastise 9 objurgate 10 vituperate

scolding: 6 dirdum, rating, rebuke 7 combing, hearing, reproof 8 dressing

scombroid fish: 4 tuna 6 bonito 8 mackerel

sconce: 4 fine, fort, head 5 cover, skull 7 bracket, bulwark, lantern, shelter 8 entrench 10 protection 11 candlestick

scone: 4 farl 5 farle 7 biscuit

scoop: dig 4 bail, beat, lade 5 didle, empty, gouge, ladle, skeet, spoon 6 bucket, chisel, dipper, dredge, gather, hollow, shovel, vessel 7 curette 8 excavate

scoot: 4 dart, dray, scud 5 shoot, slide 6 begone, decamp, scurry 9 skedaddle

scooter: toy 4 boat, plow 6 glider

scop: 4 bard, poet

scope: 4 area, goal, room 5 range, reach, theme, tract 6 domain, extent, import, intent, length, object, sphere, target 7 liberty 8 distance, latitude 9 dimension, extension, intention

having: 13 comprehensive

large: 7 general

scopic: 6 visual

scoptical: 7 jeering, jesting 8 scoffing

scorch: cut 4 burn, char, flay, sear, skin 5 adust, parch, score, singe, slash, sting, toast 6 birsle, scathe, wither 7 blister, scratch, shrivel

scorched: 4 sere 5 adust

score: cut, run, tab, taw 4 goal, line, mark, rate 5 chalk, chase, corge, count, judge, notch, scold, slash, tally 6 abrade, barter, berate, furrow, grudge, number, reason, record, scotch, twenty, weight 7 account, arrange, scratch, upbraid 8 incision 9 criticize, grievance, reckoning 10 obligation 11 enumeration, orchestrate 12 indebtedness

scoria: aa 4 lava, slag 5 dross 6 refuse

scorify: 5 smelt

scoring point: ace, hit, run 4 down, goal 5 tally 6 basket

scorn: 4 geck, jeer, mock 5 scoff 6 deride, reject, slight 7 condemn, despise, disdain 8 contempt, derision 9 contumely

scornful: 5 aloof 7 haughty, stuckup 8 arrogant, insolent 10 disdainful, fastidious

scorpion: 4 nepa 6 onager, weapon 7 scourge 8 arachnid, catapult 10 vinegaroon

stinger: 6 telson

Scorpion's Heart: 7 Antares

scorse: 5 trade 6 barter 8 exchange

scot: tax 4 levy 6 assess 7 payment 9 reckoning 10 assessment

Scot: 4 Gael, Pict 10 Caledonian, Highlander

scotch (see also **Scotland**): cut 4 stop 5 check, chock, notch, score, wedge 6 hinder, stingy, whisky 7 scratch, scruple 8 hesitate 9 frustrate

Scotchman: Mac 4 Gael, Scot 7 bluecap, Scottie 10 Highlander

scoter: 4 coot, duck, fowl

genus: 7 oidemia 9 melanitta

Scotland: *accent:* 4 birr, burr

askew or awry: 4 agee 5 agley

at all: ava

author: 5 Scott 6 Barrie

beg: 4 sorn

bird: gae 4 hern 6 grouse, snabby 7 snabbie 8 throstle 9 swinepipe

blessing: 6 rebuke 8 scolding

blood money: cro

bluebell: 8 harebell

boat: 4 zulu 6 scaffy, sexern 7 coracle, skaffie

bonfire: 6 tandle

brain: 4 harn

bread: 5 briar 6 tammie 7 bannock

bread dish: 4 saps

briar: 4 rose

brook: 4 sike

broth: 4 soup

bucket: 5 stoop, stoup

bull: 4 stot

bushel: fou

buxom: 6 sonsie

cake: 5 scone

camp follower: 6 gudget

cap: tam 6 bonnet, tassel, toorie 8 Balmoral 9 Glengarry 11 Tam O'Shanter

cap tassel: 6 toorie

cascade: lin 4 linn 5 force

cat: 6 malkin

cattle: 8 Ayrshire

celebration: 4 kirn

chafing dish: 7 choffer

chair: 5 regal

chief: 5 thegn

child: 4 dalt 5 bairn 6 scuddy 8 smatchet

church: 4 kirk

city: Ayr 5 Alloa, Leith, Perth, Troon 6 Dundee 7 Glasgow, Grunock, Paisley 8 Aberdeen, Stirling 9 Edinburgh, Inverness, St. Andrews 10 Kilmarnock

cloth: 4 kelt 6 tartan
coin: 4 demy 5 bodle, groat 6 baubee, hawbee
colt: 4 stag
congress: Mod
corner: 4 neuk
county: Ayr 4 Bute, Fife, Ross 5 Angus, Banff, Moray, Nairn, Perth 6 Argyll, Lanark, Orkney 7 Berwick, Kinross, Peebles, Renfrew, Selkirk, Wigtown 8 Aberdeen, Ayrshire, Dumfries, Roxburgh, Shetland, Stirling 9 Caithness, Dumbarton, Inverness 10 Kincardine, Midlothian, Sutherland 11 Clackmannan, West Lothian 13 Kirkcudbright
court officer: 5 macer
cross: 8 crantara 9 crostarie
cuddy: 6 draper 7 peddler
cup: 4 tass
curlies: 4 kale
dagger: 5 skean
dance: bob 4 reel 7 walloch 9 ecossaise 10 strathspey 13 Highland-fling
destiny: 5 weird
devil: 4 deil
district: Ayr 5 Rinns 6 Atholl 7 Lothian 8 Galloway 9 Tweeddale 11 Breadalbane
donkey: 5 cuddy
drapery: 4 pand
drinking bout: 6 screed
drinking vessel: 4 tass 6 quaich, quaigh
duck: 10 bufflehead
elm: 4 wych
endure: 4 dree
excuse: 6 sunyie
explorer: Rae
eye: ee
fairy: 4 fane
farmer: 6 cottar, cotter 7 crofter
fashion: 7 Scotice
festival: Mod 7 Uphelya
fiddle: 4 itch
fingering: 4 wool, yarn
fireplace: 5 ingle
firth: Tay 4 Loch, Lorn 5 Clyde, Forth, Moray 6 Linnhe 8 Cromarty
fish: 4 sile 7 sillock 8 spalding
fish trap: 4 yare 5 yaire
fishing expedition: 5 drave
fog: 4 haar
fort: 4 dune 10 roundabout
game: 6 shinty
garment: tam 4 kilt, maud 5 toosh 6 fecket, tartan 7 arisard 8 Balmoral 11 Tam o' Shanter
garter: 8 wooer-bab
ghost: 6 taisch
girl: 4 lass 5 quean 6 lassie, towdie 7 winklot
give: gie
grandchild: oe, oy, oye
grandfather: 8 gudesire
granite: 5 gowan
guess: 4 rede
gutter: 5 siver
hands: 8 paddling
have: hae
hazelnut: nit
heater: 7 choffer
heath: 7 heather
heavy: 5 tharf
hill: 6 strone
hillside: 4 brae
historian: 4 Hume 5 Skene
hoppers: 9 Hopscotch
icicle: 7 shoggle
inlet: gio
island: 4 Iona 5 Arran 6 Orkney 8 Hebrides, Shetland
kale: 8 borecole
king: 6 Robert
kiss: 8 smoorich
lake: dee 4 loch
lament: 6 ochone
land: 6 carses
land tax: 4 cess
landholder: 5 laird, thane
language: 4 Erse 6 Lallan 7 Lalland
liquor: 5 scour 6 athole 8 whittier
lord: 5 laird
loyal: 4 leal
maurauder: 7 cateran
measure: cop 4 cran, fall, mile, peck, pint, rood, rope 5 crane, crans, lippy 6 firlot, lippie 7 auchlet, chalder, choppin 8 mutchkin, stimpart, stimpert 9 particate, shaftment, shaftmont
mist: ure
money: 6 siller
monk: 6 culdee
mountain: 8 Ben Nevis 9 Grampians
muddled: ree
music festival: Mod
musical instrument: 5 pipes 7 bagpipe
musician: 5 piper
must: 4 maun
negative: nae
odd: 4 orra
pastry: 5 scone 7 carcake
patron saint: 6 Andrew
peasant: 6 cottar, cotter
peninsula: 5 Rinns
people: 8 Damnonii 9 Dammonian
person: 4 Gael, Pict, Scot 7 Scottie 9 Lowlander, Scotchman 10 Highlander
physicist: 4 Watt
plaid: 4 maud
poet: 4 Hogg, Moir 5 Burns

pole: 5 caber
pool: lin 4 linn
porridge: 5 brose
proprietor: 5 laird
pouch: 6 sporan 7 sporran
pudding: 6 haggis
queen: 4 Mary
ridge: run
river: Ayr, Dee, Don, Esk, Tay 4 Doon, Find, Norn, Nith, Spey 5 Afton, Annan, Clyde, North, Tweed 6 Teviot 7 Deveron
sausage: 9 whitehass 10 whitehawse
schoolmaster: dux
scurvy grass: 8 seabells
seaport: 4 Leth 5 Alloa 6 Dundee
sect: 9 Buchanite
self: sel
servant: 5 gilly 6 gillie
sheepfold: ree
small: sma
snow: sna 4 snaw
soldier: 7 cateran
song: 6 strowd
student: 5 bejan 6 nejant
tenure: 6 sorren 7 sorehon
tinker: 5 caird
tithe: 5 teind
title: 5 laird
to: tae
toad: ted 4 taed
tobacco: 5 elder
toe: tae
toil: 4 darg
topaz: 6 tassel 9 cairngorm
tourist resort: 4 Oban
tower: 7 toorock
town hall: 8 tolbooth 9 tollbooth
tree: arm
trousers: 5 trews
uncle: eme
unit: ane
vigor: vir
warrior: 4 kemp
water spirit: 5 kelpy 6 kelpie
waterfall: lin 4 linn 5 force
weakling: 4 ribe 5 shilp 7 shilpit
weapon: 5 skean 8 claymore, skeandhu
weight: 4 boll, drop 5 trone 6 bushel
whine: 4 yirn
whirlpool: 7 swilkie 8 swelchie
whisky: 6 athole 9 Glenlivat, Glenlivit 10 Usquebaugh
whitefish: 7 vendace
window: 7 winnock
woodcock: 4 eggs
world: 4 warl
yell: 4 gowl
youth: 5 chiel 7 callant

Scott: *character:* 5 Norna 7 Ivanhoe 9 Lochinvar
novel: 6 Rob Roy 7 Ivanhoe 8 Talisman
poem: 7 Marmion

Scottish: See **Scotland**

scoundrel: cad 4 scab 5 cheat, filth, knave, scamp 6 rascal, varlet 7 glutton, villain, warlock 8 bezonian 9 miscreant, reprobate 10 blackguard

scoup: run 4 leap, skip 7 scamper

scour: rub, run 4 beat, rake, rush, wash 5 clean, purge, scrub 6 decamp, polish, punish, remove 7 cleanse, roister 8 brighten, traverse

scourge: 4 bane, flay, flog, lash, whip 5 harry, shoot, slash 6 plague, punish, swinge, switch 7 afflict, torment 8 chastise 9 devastate 10 affliction, discipline, flagellate, infliction, punishment

Scourge of God: 6 Attila

scout: guy, spy 4 chap, jeer, look 5 scoff, watch 6 fellow, search 7 despise, explore, lookout, observe 8 emissary, informer, ridicule, watchman 11 reconnoiter, reconnoitre
unit: den 4 pack 5 troop

scouth: 4 room 5 range, scope 6 plenty

scovy: 7 blotchy, smeared, streaky

scow: 4 acon(F.), boat 5 barge, float 6 garvey 7 gabbard, gabbart, lighter

scowl: 5 frown, glare, glout, lower 6 glower

scrab: 7 scratch

scraffle: 7 wrangle 8 scramble, struggle

scraggly: 5 rough 6 jagged, ragged 7 unkempt 9 irregular 10 splintered

scraggy: 4 bony, lean, thin 5 rough, weedy 6 meager, rugged, skinny 7 knotted, scrawny

scram: 4 shoo 6 benumb 7 vamoose 8 paralyze, withered

scramble: mix 4 push 5 climb, crowd, crush 6 jostle, sprawl, spread, strive 7 clamber, pushing, scatter 8 struggle

scrambled: 4 pied

scran: 4 grub 6 morsel, refuse 9 leftovers 10 provisions

scrannel: dry 4 lean, poor, thin, weak 5 harsh 6 slight 7 scrawny 11 unmelodious

scrap: bit, end, jag, ort, rag 4 chip, item, junk 5 fight, grain, piece, shred, waste 6 cullet, morsel, refuse 7 cutting, discard, extract, oddment, quarrel, remnant 8 fraction, fragment

scrape: bow, hoe, row, rub, saw 4 claw, grit, harl, rake, rasp, scud, trap 5 claut, erase, grate, graze, gride, hoard, order, shave 6 abrade, dredge, fiddle, gather, harass, re-

fine, remove, sclaff 7 collect, corrode, scratch 9 situation 10 difficulty 11 predicament
scraped linen: 4 lint
scraper: 6 barber, rasper, xyster 7 fiddler, strigil 8 grattoir
scraping: 6 rasion, rasure
scrapper: 5 boxer 7 fighter 8 pugilist
scraps: 5 scran
literary: ana
scratch: dig, mar, rat, rit, rub, wig 4 claw, draw, feed, heap, line, mark, race, rake, rist, tear 5 break, claut, clawk, erase, expel, fluke, frush, score, wound 6 cancel, furrow, gather, injury, rasure, scotch, scrape, scrawl 7 expunge, roughen, scarify, scorify 8 incision, scribble, scrobble, withdraw 12 scratchbrush
scratcher: 6 forger 13 counterfeiter
scratching: 8 rasorial
scratchy: 6 uneven 10 straggling
scrawk: 6 squeak, squawk 7 scratch, screech
scrawl: 4 teem 5 crawl 7 scratch, writing 8 scribble
scrawm: 5 climb 7 clamber 8 scramble
scrawny: 4 lean, poor, thin 7 scraggy, scranny, scrubby 8 rawboned
scrawny animal: 5 scrag
screak: 4 rasp 5 creak, grate 7 screech
scream: cry 4 wail, yarm, yaup, yawl, yell, yowt 6 shriek, squall, yammer 7 screech
screamer: 5 chaja
scree: 5 stone, talus 6 pebble
screech: cry 4 yell 5 quawk 6 outcry, scream, shriek 7 ululate
screed: say 4 land, rend, rent, tear 5 board, shred, strip 6 scrape, smooth, tirade 7 leveler 8 diatribe, fragment, harangue 9 discourse
screen: 4 cage, hide, mask, mesh, reja, sept, sift, veil 5 arras, blind, chick(Ind.), cloak, cover, grill, purda, scarf, shade, sieve, speer, spier 6 defend, filter, grille, purdah, settle, shield 7 conceal, curtain, protect, reredos, shelter 8 bescreen, covering, separate 9 breakwind, partition 10 protection
architectural: 5 spier
chancel: 4 jube 7 reredos
chimney: 6 bonnet
mesh: 4 laun 5 sieve
wind: 8 paravent
screw: key, pay 4 turn, wind, worm 5 cheat, guard, horse, miser, twist 6 gimlet, keeper, salary, spiral 7 contort, distort, robbery, squeeze, tighten, turnkey 9 bargainer, propeller, skinflint 10 contortion, crustacean, instructor
screw-like: 6 spiral, spirod 7 helical
screw pine: 5 vacoa 6 vacona, vacoua 8 pandanus
screw-pine family: 11 pandanaceae
screwball: nut, sap 5 crank, crazy, dippy, goose 7 fanatic, galloot, saphead 8 crackpot, dumbbell 9 blockhead, eccentric 10 crackbrain, muttonhead
screwed: 5 drunk 11 intoxicated
screwy: 5 crazy, wacky 6 absurd, whacky 7 winding 8 freakish, peculiar 9 eccentric, fantastic 10 irrational, misleading, unbalanced 11 impractical 12 crackbrained, preposterous
scribal: 7 clerkly
scribble: 5 write 6 scrawl 7 scratch 8 scrabble
scribe: 5 clerk, write 6 author, copier, doctor, notary, penman, scrive, writer 7 copyist, graffer, teacher 8 inscribe 9 draftsman, scenarist, scrivener, secretary 10 amanuensis, journalist 11 transcriber 13 bibliographer
scriggle: 5 twist 6 squirm, wiggle 7 wriggle 8 curlicue
scrimmage: 4 play 6 battle, splore, tussle 8 football, practice
scrimp: 4 save 5 stint 6 meager, scanty 9 economize
scrimping: 7 miserly, sparing 9 niggardly
scringe: net 4 flog 5 glean, seine 6 cringe, flinch, search
scrip: bag 4 list 6 wallet 7 satchel, writing 8 schedule 11 certificate
script: 5 ronde 8 scenario 10 penmanship 11 chirography, handwriting
Arabic: 5 neski
round: 5 ronde
Syriac: 5 serta
scriptor: See **scribe**
scriptural: 8 Biblical
scripture: 4 text, word, writ 5 Bible, motto 7 passage, writing 10 manuscript, penmanship 11 composition, handwriting, inscription
interpreter: 7 exegete
Moslem: 7 Alcoran
occult interpretation: 6 cabala
part: 6 lesson
version: Vul 4 Vulg 5 Douay, Itala 7 Vulgate
scrive: cut 5 score, write 6 scribe 7 carving, scratch, writing 8 inscribe 11 handwriting
scrivello: 4 tusk
scrivener: See **scribe**
scrofula: 4 evil 6 struma 9 king's evil
scrofulous: 7 corrupt 10 degenerate 12 contaminated

scroll: 4 list, roll 5 draft 6 escrol, record, scrawl, spiral, volute 7 escroll, outline, writing 8 enscribe, inscribe, schedule, streamer
Hebrew: 6 mezuza 7 mezuzah
writing: 8 makimono
scrooch: 6 crouch, huddle
scroop: 5 creak, grate 6 scrape, squeak
scrouge: 5 crowd, press 7 squeeze
scrounge: 5 cadge, steal 6 pilfer, search, sponge
scroyle: 6 fellow, wretch 9 scoundrel
scrub: mop, rub 4 mean, poor, runt, wash 5 clean, dwarf, scour, small 6 drudge, paltry, shabby 7 cleanse 8 inferior 10 undersized 14 undernourished
scrub turkey: 6 leipoa 8 megapode
scrubby: 5 runty, small 7 stunted 8 inferior
scruff: 4 film, nape, scum 5 crust, dross 6 refuse 7 coating 8 covering, dandruff
scrump: 6 shrink 7 shrivel, squeeze
scrumptious: 4 fine, nice 5 dandy 7 capital, elegant 8 splendid 9 delicious
scrunch: 5 crush 6 crunch, huddle 7 squeeze
scruple: 4 part 5 demur, doubt, qualm 6 amount, boggle, weight 7 anxiety, portion 8 question 9 disbelief, misgiving 10 uneasiness
one-half: 5 obole
scrupulous: 4 nice 5 chary, exact 6 honest, proper, strict 7 careful, correct, precise, upright 8 accurate, cautious 9 reluctant 11 punctilious 13 conscientious
to excess: 7 finical, finicky, prudish 9 finicking 10 fastidious
scrutinize: eye, pry 4 scan, sift 5 probe 7 examine, inspect, observe
scrutiny: 4 gaze, look
scrutoire: 10 escritoire
scruze: 5 crush 7 squeeze
scry: cry 4 gaze, look 5 shout 6 descry, outcry
scryer: 4 seer
scud: ale, fly, run 4 beer, blow, foam, gust, mist, move, scum, skim, slap 5 hurry, spank, spray 6 scrape, shower 7 rushing 10 crustacean
scuff: 4 blow, cuff, drag, gust, toss, wipe 5 brush, evade, graze, rowdy, slare, touch, tread 6 buffet, rabble, scruff, shower, slight 7 scatter, shuffle, slipper 9 roughened, scratched
scuffle: 4 cuff 5 amble, fight, melee, scuff, shool 6 affray, bustle, clinch, combat, sclaff, strive, tussle 7 contend, shamble, shuffle 8 struggle
scug: 5 shade 6 shadow 7 protect, shelter 8 pretense, squirrel 9 schoolboy
sculch: 6 cultch, refuse
scull: oar 4 boat 6 basket, propel, wherry 7 rowboat 8 scullion
scullery: 5 ewery
scullion: 4 base 5 gippo, onion 6 menial, wretch 7 servant 8 scallion 10 blackguard
sculp: 4 pelt, skin 5 break, carve, scalp 6 sculpt 7 engrave 9 engraving, sculpture
sculptor: 6 artist, graver, imager
famous: 5 Rodin 7 Phidias 12 Michelangelo
tool: 6 graver
sculpture: 4 bust, head 5 carve, grave, torso 6 emboss, relief, statue 7 engrave, relievo
framework: 8 armature
pert. to: 7 glyphic, glyptic 9 glyptical
slab: 6 metope
scum: 4 brat, foam, scud, silt, skim 5 dross, froth, range, scour, spume, sweep 6 bubble, rabble, refuse, scoria 10 impurities 12 offscourings
scumfish: 5 choke 9 discomfit, overpower, suffocate
scup: 4 fish 5 bream, porgy
scuppernong: 4 wine 5 grape 9 muscadine
scurrilous: low 4 foul, vile 5 gross 6 ribald, vulgar 7 abusive 8 indecent, scurrile 9 insulting, offensive 11 foulmouthed, opprobrious
scurry: hie, run 4 race 5 harry, scoot, scour, skirr 6 flurry, hasten 7 scamper, scuttle, skelter 9 skedaddle
scurvy: low 4 mean 6 shabby 7 disease 8 scorbute 12 contemptible, discourteous
preventative: 6 citrus 13 antiscorbutic
scutage: fee, tax 4 levy 6 impost
scutate: 5 scaly 7 peltate
scuttle: hod, run 4 dish, sink, veto 5 scoot 6 basket, bucket, scotch, scurry, shovel 7 octopus, platter 8 hatchway 10 cuttlefish
scuttlebutt: 5 rumor 6 gossip
scutum: 5 plate, scute 6 shield
Scylla: *father:* 5 Nisus
lover: 5 Minos
scythe: sy(Sc.); lea 6 sickle
handle: 5 snath, thole 6 snathe
sweep: 5 swath
sea: mer(F.) 4 meer(G.)
anemone: 5 polyp 7 actinia
approach: 7 seagate
arm: bay 4 gulf 5 bayou, firth, fjord, frith, inlet, lough 7 estuary
at: 4 asea
bottom: bed
combining form: mer
current: 4 tide 8 undertow
deity: Ler, Ran 5 Aegir, Doris 6 Nereus, Triton 7 Neptune, Phorcus, Phorcyn, Phorcys, Phorkys, Proteus 8 Palaemon, Poseidon
delicacy: roe 4 nori

description: **11** haliography
god: **7** Neptune **8** Poseidon
goddess: Ran **4** Nina **8** Eurynome **9** Leucothea **10** Amphitrite
king: Ler **5** chief **6** pirate, viking
land in: **6** island
life of: **8** halibios
little: **6** sealet
mammal: **4** seal **5** whale
open: **6** midsea
periodic motion: **4** tide
pert. to: **4** vast **5** naval **6** marine **7** oceanic, pelagic **8** maritime, nautical **9** aequoreal, thalassic
plant: **6** enalid
prophetic god: **7** Proteus
roughness: **5** swell, waves **6** lipper
route: **4** lane
spray: **9** spindrift **10** spoondrift
swell: **4** surf
term: **4** ahoy **5** avast, belay, trice
sea biscuit: **7** galette(F.) **8** hardtack
sea cow: **6** dugong, rytina, walrus **7** manatee **8** sirenian **12** hippopotamus
sea cucumber: **6** pedata **7** trepang **11** holothurian
sea dog: tar **4** seal **6** pirate, sailor **7** breaker, dogfish **9** privateer
sea duck: **5** eider **6** scoter **7** scooter
sea eagle: ern **4** erne, tern **6** osprey
sea-ear: **7** abalone
sea eel: **6** conger **7** lamprey
sea-foam: **5** froth **9** sepiolite **10** meerschaum
sea gate: **5** beach **7** channel
sea goose: **7** dolphin **9** phalarope
sea gull: cob, mew **4** cobb, gore
sea hog: **8** porpoise
sea horse: **6** walrus **8** whitecap **11** hippocampus
sea kale: **4** cole
sea lettuce: **5** laver **7** seaweed
sea nettle: **6** medusa **9** jellyfish
sea nymph: **5** siren **6** Nereid **7** Galatea, Oceanid
sea raven: **7** sculpin **9** cormorant **10** squaretail
sea robber: **6** jaeger, pirate **7** corsair **9** buccaneer, privateer
sea slug: **6** trepan **8** cucumber **10** nudibranch
sea soldier: **6** marine
sea squirt: **5** salpa **8** ascidian, tunicate
sea swallow: **4** tern **6** petrel
sea unicorn: **7** narwhal
sea urchin: **6** repkie **7** echinid, echinus **8** echinoid **10** echinoderm
rock hole: **5** geode
sea wolf: **4** seal **6** pirate **7** wolfish **9** privateer, submarine
sea worm: sao **7** annelid
seabird: auk, ern **4** duck, erne, gull, smew, tern **5** solan, yager **6** gannet, petrel **7** pelican **9** albatross **10** shearwater
seaboard: **5** coast **9** coastland, tidewater
seadog: **6** fogbow, fogdog **8** fogeater
seafarer: gob, tar **4** salt **6** sailor, seaman **7** mariner **9** navigator
seagoing: **5** naval **7** capable **9** seafaring **13** weatherbeaten
seal: cap, fix, hem, set, wax **4** bind, bull, cere, lute, rope, seel, shut, sign **5** bulla, chain, close, sigil, stamp, swile, token, wafer **6** attest, cachet, clinch, fasten, pledge, ranger, ratify, scarab, secure, signet **7** closure, confine, confirm, leather **8** breloque, document, guaranty, imprison, sealskin, validate **9** assurance, carnivore, guarantee, sigillate **10** obligation **12** authenticate **14** authentication
bearded: **5** ursuk **6** makluk
decorated with: **9** sigillate
eared: **5** otary
eared genus: **8** zalophus
letter: **6** cachet
limb: **7** flipper
official: **6** signet
pelt: **5** sculp
pert. to: **7** phocine
place: LS **7** rookery
polar: **5** otary, phoca, Ross's, ursal, ursuk **6** makluk **8** bedlamer, Ross seal, seecatch **9** sterrinck
school: pod
young: pup **6** beater, hopper **7** quitter, saddler **11** flipperling, holluschick
seal skin: **5** sculp
sealing wax: lac
seam: sew **4** fash, fold, join, line, load, mark, scar **5** cleft, joint, layer, raphe, ridge, strip, unite **6** groove, streak, suture **7** crevice, fissure, stratum, wrinkle **8** cicatrix **10** packsaddle
pert. to: **7** sutural, suturic
seaman: See **sailor, seafarer**
seamark: **6** beacon **8** landmark **10** lighthouse
seamer: **5** sewer **6** seamer **8** stitcher **10** dressmaker, seamstress
seamless: **5** whole **7** unsewed **12** araphorostic
seamy: **5** rough **8** degraded, wrinkled **12** disreputable
seance: **7** meeting, session, sitting
holder: **6** medium
seaport: **4** port **6** harbor
sear (see also **sere**): **4** burn, mark, scar **5** brand, brown, catch, parch, singe **6** braise, deaden, scorch, wither **9** cauterize

search: 4 comb, grub, hunt, look, nose, rout, seek 5 delve, frisk, probe, quest 6 brevit, ferret, forage, pierce, sphere, survey 7 canvass, examine, explore, inquire, inquiry, inspect, ransack, rummage 8 research, scrounge, scrutiny 9 penetrate 10 scrutinize 11 exploration, investigate

searching: 4 keen 5 acute, sharp 10 discerning

searing: 7 cautery

seascape: 6 marine

seashell: 4 clam 5 conch, snail 7 scallop

seashore: 5 beach, coast, shore 7 seaside 8 seabeach, seacoast
pert. to: 8 littoral

season: age, dry, tid, ver 4 beek, fall, salt, sele, tide, time 5 devil, imbue, inure, ripen, savor, spice, taste, tinge 6 autumn, embalm, flavor, mature, period, soften, spring, steven, summer, temper, winter 7 condite, flavour, Maytide, weather 8 accustom, marinate, occasion 9 habituate 10 impregnate 11 acclimatize, opportunity
religious: 4 Lent 6 careme

seasonable: pat 4 ripe 6 timely 7 apropos 8 suitable 9 opportune 11 appropriate

seasonably: 7 betimes

seasonal: 8 periodic

seasoned: 7 veteran 8 finished

seasoning: 4 herb, mace, sage, salt 5 cumin, onion, spice, thyme 6 celery, cloves, cummin, garlic, nutmeg, pepper, relish 7 caraway, cuminos, mustard, oregano, paprika, vinegar 8 allspice, cardamom, marjoram, rosemary, turmeric 9 condiment, coriander

seasons: 5 Horae
goddess: 4 Dike 5 Horae 6 Eirene, Eunomi

seat: fix, pew, see 4 apse, bank, form, hold, home, loge, room, site 5 asana, bench, chair, floor, place, sella(L.), siege, stool, usher 6 exedra, grange, howdah, locate, sedile, settee, settle, throne 7 capital, install, ottoman, situate, station, taboret, tendoor, tendour 8 bleacher, locality, location, tabouret 9 banquette, establish, residence, situation
chancel: 6 sedile
high: 5 roost
of judgment: 8 tribunal
of justice: 4 banc
on elephant: 6 houdah, howdah
tier of: 6 gradin

seat bone: 7 ischium

seat worm: 7 pinworm

seawan: See **sewan**

seaweed: ore 4 agar, alga, kelp, nori 5 algae, dulse, laver, varec, vraic, wrack 6 delisk, desmid, fucoid, varech 7 oreweek 8 agar-agar, hempweed, sargasso 9 desmidian
culture medium: 4 agar
edible: 5 dulse
extract: 4 agar
genus of: 6 alaria
pert. to: 6 algous
purple: 4 nori 5 laver
red: 5 dulse 6 delisk
study: 6 algology

seaweedy: 6 algous

Seb: See **Geb**

sebaceous: 5 fatty

sec: dry

secant: 7 cutting 12 intersecting

secede: 8 withdraw

seceder: 8 apostate

secern: 7 secrete 8 separate 11 distinguish 12 discriminate

seckel: 4 pear

seclude: bar 4 deny, hide 5 debar, expel 6 recess, remove, retire, screen 7 exclude, isolate, protect, retreat 8 prohibit, separate, withdraw 9 segregate, sequester

secluded: 5 aloof, apart 6 remote, secret 7 private 8 excepted, solitary

second: aid 4 abet, back, echo, time 5 other 6 assist, attend, backer, handle, moment 7 another, confirm, endorse, forward, further, instant, succeed, support, sustain 8 inferior 9 assistant, encourage, imperfect, prototype, reinforce, secondary, viscosity 10 additional 11 corroborate, subordinate 13 supplementary
comb. form: 6 deuter 7 deutero

second childhood: 6 dotage 8 senility

second-rate: 6 shabby 8 inferior, mediocre

second sight: ESP 9 intuition 12 clairvoyance

second-sighted: fey 7 psychic 9 intuitive, visionary 11 clairvoyant 12 precognitive

second-story man: 5 thief 7 burglar

second team: 6 scrubs 9 yannigans 11 substitutes

secondary: bye 5 minor 6 deputy 8 delegate, inferior 9 auxiliary, satellite 10 accidental 11 subordinate
color: 5 green 6 orange, purple
proposition: 5 lemma

secondary school: 4 high, prep 5 lycee(F.) 7 academy 10 realschule(G.), vocational

secondhand: 4 used, worn 6 resold 7 derived 8 borrowed 10 unoriginal
dealer: 6 ragman 7 junkman

secret: 4 dark, dern, hide, rune 5 blind, cabal, close, inner, privy 6 arcane, arcana, closet, covert, hidden, occult, remote, stolen 7 arcanum, cryptic, furtive, mystery, privacy, private, privity, retired, unknown 8 discrete, esoteric, intimate, mys-

tical, reticent, secluded, stealthy 9 clancular, concealed, recondite, seclusion, secretive, underhand 10 confidence 11 clandestine, concealment 12 confidential, hugger-mugger 13 surreptitious
secret agent: spy 8 emissary, saboteur 10 counterspy
secret place: 6 adytum 7 sanctum
secretaire: 9 secretary 10 escritoire
secretary: 4 desk 5 clerk 9 confidant 10 amanuensis
secrete: 4 bury, hide, ooze, stow 5 exude 7 conceal
secretion: gum, sap 4 bile, laap, lerp, milk 5 juice, latex, mucus, resin, sudor, sweat 6 saliva 9 exudation
secretly: 4 inly 5 aside 13 clandestinely
sect: 4 clan, cult, part 5 class, group, order, party 6 school 7 faction, section 9 following 10 philosophy 12 denomination
distinguishing word: 10 shibboleth
sectarian: 7 bigoted, heretic, sectary 8 apostate 9 dissenter 12 narrow-minded 17 denominationalist
sectary: 4 sect 6 votary 8 adherent, disciple, follower, partisan 9 dissenter, sectarian 11 independent 13 non-conformist
section: 4 pane, part 5 piece, slice 6 canton 7 portion, segment 8 division 9 signature 11 subdivision
concluding: 8 epilogue
section hand: 6 worker 7 crewman, laborer
sector: 4 area 8 division
secular: lay 4 laic 5 civil 6 carnal, laique(F.), vulgar 7 earthly, profane, worldly 8 temporal 9 temporary 17 nonecclesiastical
secure: buy, get, pot, tie 4 bail, bind, bolt, easy, fast, firm, gird, moor, nail, safe, sure, tape 5 chain, guard, siker, spike, trice, truss 6 anchor, assure, clinch, defend, ensure, fasten, obtain, sicker, stable, strong 7 acquire, assured, certain, forfend, procure, protect 8 conserve, forefend 9 confident, constrain, guarantee 10 dependable 11 trustworthy, undisturbed 13 overconfident
security: 4 bail, bond, ease, gage 5 frith, grith, guard 6 pledge, safety, surety 7 defense, hostage, shelter 8 guaranty, warranty 9 assurance, certainty, guarantee, insurance 10 confidence, protection
sedan: car 4 auto 5 chair 10 automobile
sedate: 4 calm, cool, dope, drug 5 douce, grave, quiet, sober, staid 6 demure, proper, serene 7 earnest, serious, settled 8 composed, decorous 9 dignified, unruffled 12 tranquillize 13 contemplative, dispassionate
sedative: 6 remedy 7 aconite, bromide, chloral, nervine 8 barbital, lenitive, soothing 9 paregoric 10 palliative 13 tranquillizer
sedent: 6 seated 7 sitting
sedentary: 7 settled, sitting 8 inactive, slothful, tranquil 10 deliberate, motionless, stationary
sederunt: 7 session, sitting 8 assembly
sedge: sag 5 brood, flock 7 bulrush, hassock
genus of: 5 carex 7 scirpus
sediment: lee 4 crap, silt 5 dregs, magma, waste 6 bottom, refuse 7 deposit, grounds 8 settling
sedition: 6 revolt, strife, tumult 7 treason 9 commotion, rebellion 10 dissention, turbulence 12 insurrection
seditionary: 7 inciter 8 promoter 9 seditious 10 factitious, treasonist 12 contumacious
seduce: 4 lure 5 charm, decoy, tempt 6 allure, betray, entice 7 corrupt, debauch, mislead 8 inveigle
seducer: 8 Lothario
sedulous: 4 busy 8 diligent, untiring 9 assiduous, laborious, unwearied 10 persistent 11 industrious, persevering, unremitting
see: spy 4 espy, hear, ibid, look, meet, rank, scry, seat, view 5 besee, chair, power 6 attend, behold, descry, detect, escort, notice, office, throne 7 diocese, discern, examine, inspect, observe, undergo, witness 8 cathedra, consider, discover, perceive 9 accompany, apprehend, authority, bishopric, encounter, interview, visualize 10 comprehend, experience, scrutinize, understand
above: vs(L.) 5 supra
below: vi(L.) 5 infra
seeing: 6 ocular 13 introspective
seed: ben, egg, pea, pip, pit, sow 4 germ, milt, tare 5 acorn, drupe, grain, ovule, plant, spore, stock 6 acinus, bubble, kernel, origin, samara, source 7 capsule, progeny, seedlet 8 ancestry 9 beginning, inoculate, offspring, posterity 10 descendant
apple: pip
aromatic: 5 anise 6 nutmeg 7 aniseed 9 anise-seed
case: pod 4 burr
cell: 4 cyst
coat: 4 aril, bran 5 testa
comb. form: 5 sperm 7 spermat 8 spermato
container: bur, pod 6 carpel, legume, loment
edible: pea 4 bean 6 lentil
expansion: ala
flavoring: 5 anise, cumin 6 cummin, sesame 7 caraway
immature: 5 ovule
organ: 6 pistil

part: pod 4 aril 5 testa 6 tegman, tunica 9 endosperm
part with: 4 core
poisonous: 7 calabar 9 jequirity
remove: gin, pit 5 picul
scar: 4 hila(pl.) 5 hilum
vessel: pod 6 carpel, legume
seed leaf: 9 cotyledon
seedless: 7 agamous
seedy: 4 worn 5 tacky 6 shabby 7 scruffy 11 debilitated
seek: beg, sue, try, woo 4 busk, fand, hunt, sick 5 court, crave, essay, probe, quest, scout, trace 6 aspire, follow, fraist, pursue, search 7 attempt, beseech, entreat, examine, explore, inquire, request, solicit 8 endeavor 9 importune 11 investigate
seeker: 6 prober, tracer 7 pursuer, zetetic 9 applicant 10 petitioner
seel: 5 blind 8 hoodwink
seem: 4 look 5 feign 6 appear, beseem 7 pretend 8 manifest
seeming: 6 proper 9 befitting
seemingly: 5 quasi
seemliness: 5 grace 7 decorum
seemly: fit 6 comely, decent, proper, rather, suited 7 fitting 8 decently, decorous, graceful, handsome, passably, suitable, suitably 10 becomingly 13 appropriately
seen (see also **see**): 7 visible
seep: run 4 leak, ooze 5 exude 8 transude 9 percolate 10 infiltrate
seer: 4 sage 5 augur, sybil 6 mystic, oracle, scryer 7 augurer, diviner, prophet 9 predictor 10 forecaster, foreteller, soothsayer 11 clairvoyant, Nostradamus 14 prognosticator
seesaw: 6 teeter, tilter, totter 9 alternate, crossruff, vacillate 10 reciprocal
seethe: hum 4 boil, soak, stew, teem 5 steep 6 bubble, buller, decoct 7 blubber 8 saturate
segment: arc 4 part 5 piece, tmema 6 cantle, divide, somite 7 isomere, portion, section 8 division, fragment, metamere, separate
body: 8 somatome
of crustacean: 6 telson
segment-shaped: 5 toric
segregate: 4 part 5 sever 6 divide, select 7 isolate, seclude 8 classify, separate
seine: net 5 trawl
Seine tributary: 4 Aube, Eure, Oise 5 Marne
seise: See **seize**
seism: 10 earthquake
seity: 8 selfhood 13 individuality
seize: bag, cap, cly, cop, hap, nab, net 4 bind, bite, claw, fang, grab, grip, hent, hook, prey, take, trap 5 annex, catch, clink, grasp, reave, ravin, usurp, wrest 6 affect, arrest, attach, attack, betake, clinch, clutch, collar, fasten, ravene, snatch, strike 7 afflict, capture, grabble, grapnel, possess, prehend 8 arrogate 9 apprehend, deprehend, raptorize 10 comprehend, confiscate, understand
for debt: 6 attach 8 distrain 9 garnishee
seizure: fit 6 stroke 10 androlepsy 11 androlepsia, manucapture
Sekhet's husband: 4 Ptah
selachian: ray 5 shark 7 dogfish
seladang: 4 gaur 6 animal 7 buffalo
selcouth: 7 strange, unusual 9 marvelous, wonderful
seldom: 4 rare 6 rarely 10 infrequent 12 infrequently
sele: 4 time 6 season 7 welfare 8 occasion 9 happiness 11 opportunity
select: opt 4 cull, draw, name, pick, wale 5 allot, elect, elite 6 assign, choice, choose, chosen, exempt, picked, prefer 8 eximious 9 excellent, exclusive, segregate 10 fastidious 11 outstanding
selection: 5 piece 7 analect, passsage 10 collection
selective: 6 choosy 7 choosey 8 electric 9 demanding
Selene: 4 Luna, moon
selenium: *compound:* 7 selenid 8 selenide
soft acid: 8 selenate
self: ego, own, sel(Sc.), soi(F.) 4 same, very 5 being 6 myself 7 himself 8 personal 9 identical 10 particular 11 personality
combining form: 4 auto
killing of: 7 suicide 8 felo-de-se
pert. to: 8 personal
self-acting: 9 automatic
self-assertion: 6 egoism, vanity
self-centered: 6 stable 7 selfish 10 egocentric, stationary 11 independent
self-confidence: 5 poise 6 aplomb 8 presence 9 composure
self-contained: 4 calm, cool 8 composed, reserved 9 collected 15 uncommunicative
self-control: 4 will 8 calmness 11 forbearance
self-defense: 6 boxing 7 fencing, j(i)ujitsu, j(i)ujutsu 8 fighting
self-denial: 10 abstinence, asceticism, puritanism 11 forbearance
self-esteem: 5 pride 6 egoism, vanity, 7 egotism 9 assurance
self-evident: 5 clear 7 obvious 8 truistic 9 axiomatic 11 postulation
self-examination: 13 introspection
self-generated: 11 spontaneous
self-government: 8 autonomy 12 independence
self-important: 7 pompous

self-love: 6 egoism 7 egotism
self-possessed: 4 calm, cool 6 cooler 8 composed 11 undisturbed
self-reproach: rue 6 regret 7 remorse 9 penitence 10 contrition
self-respect: 5 pride
self-righteous: 11 pharisaical
self-satisfied: 4 smug 6 jaunty 10 complacent
self-subsistence: 12 independence
self-worship: 9 autolatry
selfish: 6 stingy 7 hoggish 9 dissocial, egotistic 10 egocentric 11 egotistical 12 self-centered
selfishness: 12 ego-centricity
selfsameness: 8 identity
sell: 4 bilk, cant, deal, dump, dupe, give, gull, hand, hawk, hoax, vend 5 cheat, trade, trick, yield 6 barter, betray, impose, market, peddle, retail 7 auction, bargain, deceive, deliver, dispose 8 convince, persuade, transfer 9 negotiate, wholesale
over official rate: 5 scalp
seller: 6 dealer, seller, sutler, trader, vender, vendor 7 peddler 8 salesman 9 tradesman 10 saleswoman, saltcellar
selling place: See **market**
selvage: 4 edge, list 5 gouge 6 border, margin 8 sticking
semblable: 7 seeming 8 suitable 10 ostensible
semblance: air 4 copy, face, form, look 5 guise, image 6 aspect, figure 7 pretext 8 likeness, pretense 10 apparition, appearance, conformity, likelihood, similarity, similitude, simulacrum 11 countenance, presumption, resemblance 14 representation
Semele: *father:* 6 Cadmus
husband: 4 Zeus
sister: Ino
son: 7 Bacchus 8 Dionysos 9 Dionysius
semester: 4 half, term 6 course, period
semi: 4 half
semiape: 5 lemur
semidiameter: 6 radius
seminar: 6 course, school 7 meeting
seminary: 6 school 7 academy, college 11 institution
Seminole Indian chief: 7 Osceola
semiopaque: 5 horny 11 translucent
Semiramis' husband: 5 Ninus
Semite: Jew 4 Arab 6 Hebrew 7 Moabite 8 Aramaean, Assyrian 9 Caucasian 10 Babylonian, Phoenician
god: 4 Baal 5 Anath, Hadad 6 Moloch 7 Shamash
language: 4 Geez 6 Arabic, Hebrew, Syrian 7 Hebraic, Maltese
people: 6 Shagia 7 Shaigia 9 Shaikiyeh
semolina: 4 meal, suji 5 flour, sujee 6 groats
semper: 6 always
sempiternal: 4 ever 7 endless, eternal 11 everlasting
senate: 5 boule, divan 7 council 8 assembly 11 legislature
senator: 5 solon 8 lawmaker 10 legislator
senatorship: 4 toga
send: 4 haul, mail, ship 5 drive, grant, impel, issue, relay, speed 6 bestow, commit, convey, depute, ordain, propel 7 address, consign, deliver, dismiss, forward, inflict, project 8 delegate, dispatch, transmit 9 discharge, vouchsafe 10 commission
back: 5 remit 6 remand, return
down: 5 demit
for: 5 order 6 summon
forth: 4 emit 6 effuse
out: 4 emit 5 exile 6 deport, export
to obscurity: 8 relegate
packing: 7 dismiss 9 discharge
up: 4 jail 8 imprison
Senegal: *capital:* 5 Dakar
gazelle: 5 korin
timber: 9 cailcedra
senescent: 5 aging
senile: old 4 aged, weak 5 aging 6 daffle, dotard, infirm 7 ancient, elderly, rickety 8 decrepit 9 doddering 13 deteriorating
senility: 6 dotage 8 caducity
senior: 4 aine, dean 5 elder, older 7 ancient, student 8 alderman, superior 13 undergraduate
seniority: age 5 state 6 status 7 quality 8 priority 10 precedence
by birth: 13 primogeniture
Sennacherib: *father:* 6 Sargon
son: 8 Sharezer
sensation: 5 sense 7 emotion, feeling 8 interest 10 appearance, experience, perception 11 sensibility
lacking: 4 numb
sensational: 5 lurid 6 yellow 8 exciting 9 emotional, startling, thrilling 12 melodramatic
sense: 4 feel, mind 5 touch 6 import, intuit, reason, sanity, wisdom 7 feeling, meaning 8 judgment, perceive, prudence 9 apprehend, awareness, sensation, sentience, soundness 10 appreciate, cognizance, comprehend, perception 11 sensibility 12 intelligence 13 consciousness, sensitiveness, understanding 14 susceptibility
Sense and Sensibility author: 6 Austen
sense organ: ear, eye 4 nose, skin 5 nerve 6 tongue 8 receptor
senseless: mad 4 dumb 5 blind, inane 6 stupid, unwise 7 foolish, idiotic 9 insensate, unfeeling 10 half-witted, insensible, irra-

tional 11 meaningless, nonsensical, purposeless, unconscious 12 unreasonable 13 unintelligent

senselessness: 5 folly

sensible: 5 privy 7 prudent 8 rational 10 responsive

sensitive: raw 4 nice, sore 5 acute, alive 6 tender, touchy 8 delicate 9 receptive 10 compatible, responsive 11 susceptible 14 impressionable

plant: 6 mimosa

sensual: 4 lewd 5 alive, gross 6 carnal, coarse, fleshy 7 bestial, brutish, fleshly, lustful, worldly 9 seductive 10 licentious, voluptuous

sent: See **send**

sentence: rap 4 doom 5 award, axiom, maxim, motto 6 decide, decree, saying 7 adjudge, condemn, opinion, passage, proverb 8 aphorism, decision, judgment 9 destinate, statement 12 adjudication 13 determination

consisting of one word: 7 monepic

construction: 6 syntax

describe: 5 parse

part: 6 clause, phrase, object 7 subject 9 predicate

same backwards and forwards: 10 palindrome

type: 6 simple 7 complex 8 compound

sententious: 5 pithy, short, terse 7 compact, concise, laconic 10 moralistic, proverbial

sentient: 5 alive 6 animal, living 7 feeling 8 sensible 9 conscious

sentiment: 5 maxim, toast 6 lyrics, saying 7 emotion, feeling, meaning, opinion 9 sensation, substance 10 perception 11 sensibility 14 sentimentality, susceptibility

sentimental: 5 gushy 7 maudlin, mawkish, schmalz 8 romantic, schmaltz 9 fantastic 10 idealistic 11 susceptible 13 lackadaisical

sentinel: 5 guard, vedet(Sp.), videt(Sp.), watch 6 bantay(P.I.), sentry, warder 7 soldier 8 watchman 10 factionary, watchtower

sepal: 4 leaf

separate: 4 bolt, cull, deal, free, part, rend, rift, shed, sift, slay, sley, sort 5 alone, aloof, apart, aside, break, hedge, ravel, sever, space, strip 6 assort, breach, cleave, decide, deduct, depart, detach, divide, refine, remove, secede, secern, sejoin, single, sleave, sleeve, sunder, winnow 7 analyse, analyze, disjoin, dispart, diverse, divorce, expanse, isolate, segment, sejunct 8 abstract, alienate, detached, discrete, disperse, dissolve, distinct, disunite, prescind, secluded, solitary, withdraw 9 demarcate, different, disengage, dismember, disparate, eliminate, segregate, withdrawn 10 disconnect, dispossess, dissociate, distribute, individual, sejunctive 11 disembodied, distinctive, distinguish, fractionate, independent, precipitate, unconnected 12 disassociate, disconnected, disintegrate

separated: 4 free, lone 5 alone

separation: 4 gulf 6 schism, tmesis 7 diacope 8 distance 9 cessation, partition 14 discontinuance

prefix; di; dis

separatists: 8 Pilgrims, Zoarites 9 Bimmelers

Sephardim: 4 Jews

country of origin: 5 Spain 8 Portugal

dialect: 6 Ladino

sepia: dun 7 pigment 10 cuttlebone, cuttlefish

sepiment: 5 hedge 7 defense 9 enclosure

sepiolite: 10 meerschaum

sepoy: 9 policeman

seps: 5 snake 6 lizard 7 serpent

sept: 4 clan 5 seven, tribe

septic: 6 putrid, rotten 9 infective

septum: 4 wall 9 partition

sepulcher: 4 bury, tomb 5 grave, inter, vault 6 entomb 8 monument 10 repository

subterranean vault: 8 catacomb

sepulchral: 6 gloomy, hollow 7 charnel 8 funereal

sequacious: 6 pliant 7 ductile, servile 9 attendant, compliant, dependent, following, malleable

sequel (see also **sequence**): 4 next 5 issue 6 effect, result, upshot 7 outcome 8 follower, sequitur 9 aftermath, following, inference 10 conclusion 11 consequence, continuance 12 continuation

sequence (see also **sequel**): run, set 5 gamut, order, suite 6 course, series, tenace 8 straight 10 succession 11 progression

sequent: 8 follower 9 attendant, following 10 succeeding

sequential: 9 following 10 continuous, processive, succeeding 11 consecutive

sequester: 5 seize 6 enisle 7 isolate, seclude 10 confiscate

sequestered: 5 alone 6 lonely, seized 7 private, recluse, removed, retired 8 isolated, secluded, solitary, withdrew 9 renounced, separated, withdrawn 10 cloistered, disclaimed, segregated 11 confiscated 12 appropriated

sequin: 4 disk 7 spangle

sequoia: 7 redwood

serac: 5 block 8 pinnacle

seraglio: 5 harem, serai 6 zenana 8 lodgings 9 enclosure, warehouse

serai: 5 harem 8 lodgings, seraglio 11 caravansary 12 caravanserai
serape: 5 cloak, shawl 7 blanket
seraph: 5 angel 6 cherub
seraphic: 4 pure 7 angelic, refined, sublime 8 cherubic 9 unworldly
seraphim: 5 angel 6 cherub
seraphine: 8 melodeon 10 instrument
Serapis' temple: 7 serapea(pl.) 8 serapeum
Serb: 4 Slav
Serbia: *coin:* 5 dinar
combining form: 5 Serbo
measure: 4 ralo
prince: 4 Cral
sere, sear: dry, wax 4 worn 5 dried, talon 6 yellow 7 parched, several, various 8 scorched, separate, withered 10 desiccated, threadbare
serein: dew 4 mist, rain
serenade: 6 aubade 8 nocturne, serenata
burlesque: 8 shivaree 9 charivari 10 callithump
serenata: 6 serena 7 cantata 8 serenade
serene: 4 calm, cool, damp 5 clear, light, quiet 6 bright, pacify, placid, sedate, serein, steady 7 pacific 8 composed, decorous, peaceful, tranquil 9 collected, impassive, unruffled 10 unobscured 11 tranquilize, undisturbed 13 dispassionate, imperturbable
serenity: 6 repose 7 balance 10 equanimity
serf: 4 esne, peon 5 churl, helot, slave 6 servus, thrall, vassal 7 bondman, peasant, villein 8 bondsman, hireling
female: 5 neife 6 colona
serge: 7 worsted
sergeant: 6 chiaus, tenant 7 esquire, servant, surgeon 9 attendant
sergeant fish: 5 cobia
seriation (see also **series**): 8 position 9 formation 11 arrangement
series: set 4 list 5 chain, gamut, suite, train 6 catena, course 8 beadroll, category, sequence, seriatim 9 gradation 10 succession
arranged in: 6 serial 7 seriate 11 installment
serious: 4 deep, grim, keen 5 grave, heavy, sober, staid 6 demure, sedate, severe, solemn 7 austere, capital, earnest, weighty 9 important, momentous 10 thoughtful 11 considerate
serment: 4 oath 9 sacrament
sermon: 4 talk 5 psalm, speak 6 homily 7 address, lecture 8 harangue 9 collation, discourse, preaching 10 admonition
study of: 10 homiletics
subject: 4 text
sermonic: 5 grave
sermonize: 6 advise, preach 8 admonish
seroon: 4 bale 7 package
serotine: bat
serous: 4 thin 6 watery
serow: 5 goral, jagla
serpent (see also **snake**): 7 entwine, reptile
comb. form: 4 ophi 5 ophio
elapine: 4 naia, naja
mythological: Ahi 5 Apepi, Dahak, Hydra 6 ellops, dragon 8 basilisk 11 Amphisbaena
nine-headed: 5 Hydra
pert. to: 5 anguine
thousand-headed: 5 Sesha 6 Ananta
victim: 7 Laocoon
worship of: 6 ophism
serpentine: 4 file, wily, worm 5 snaky 7 sinuous, turning, winding 8 tempting 10 circuitous, meandering
variety: 10 antigorite
serpigo: 5 tinea 6 herpes, tetter 8 ringworm
serrate: 5 notch, tooth 11 denticulate
serried: 5 dense 6 massed, packed 7 compact, crowded
serum: 4 whey 5 fluid 9 antitoxin
serum-like: 6 serous
servable: 6 usable 10 functional
servant: dey, gyp 4 amah, bata, cook, dasi, esne, girl, help, hewe, hind, maid, maty, mozo, syce 5 alila, biddy, boots, chela, gilly, groom, hamal, nurse, scout, slave, usher, valet 6 abigal, batman, bearer, bildar, butler, chakar, ewerer, flunky, garcon, gillie, hamaul, hammal, harlot, helper, khamal, menial, tenant, varlet, vassal 7 bondman, famulus, flunkey, footman, hummaul 8 chasseur, domestic, sergeant, servitor 9 atriensis 11 chamberlain
female: 4 maid 5 wench 6 slavey
garment: 5 apron 6 livery 7 uniform
head: 6 butler
male: 5 valet 6 butler, lackey
of God: 4 monk, pope 5 friar, rabbi 6 bishop, priest 8 chaplain, minister, preacher 10 Holy Father, missionary
of nobleman: 7 equerry
pert. to: 8 famulary
retired: 8 emeritus
serve: do; act, aid 4 abet, give, help, mess, pass, suit, tend, wait 5 avail, cater, frame, ladle 6 answer, assist, attend, succor 7 advance, benefit, bestead, deliver, forward, further 8 function, minister 9 officiate 10 distribute
server: urn 4 tray 6 salver, waiter 7 caterer 9 assistant, lazy-Susan
Servia: See **Serbia**
service: use 4 mass, rite 5 avera, favor, wages 6 employ, fealty, homage, repair, supply 7 chakari, retinue, **slavery, utility**

8 kindness, ministry 9 servitude 10 recompense 11 maintenance 12 installation, ministration
military: 4 duty 5 hitch 7 stretch 10 enlistment 12 conscription
public: 7 utility
service charge: fee, tip
service tree: 4 sorb
serviceable: 4 kind 6 useful 7 durable, helpful, lasting 8 obliging 9 available 10 beneficial, commodious
serviette: 6 napkin
servile: 4 base, bond, mean 6 abject, menial, sordid 7 fawning, slavish 8 cringing, enslaved 9 dependent, parasitic, truckling 10 obsequious, sequacious, submissive 11 subservient, sycophantic
Servite: 5 friar 9 mendicant
servitor: 6 beadle, menial, squire 7 servant, soldier 8 adherent, follower 9 assistant, attendant 10 apprentice 12 exhibitioner
servitude: 4 yoke 7 bondage, peonage, serfdom, service, slavery 8 sentence 9 captivity, vassalage
sesame: til 4 herb, teel 5 benne 7 passkey 8 ajonjoli, password
seed: 7 gingili, tilseed
session: 4 term 7 meeting, sitting 8 sederunt 10 assemblage
set: fix, gel, lay, put, sit 4 bent, clan, club, cock, crew, gang, laid, park, port, pose, prim, ring, seat, stud, suit 5 align, aline, brood, elect, elite, embed, fixed, group, imbed, place, plant, posit, range, ready, rigid, staid, stake, stand, suite 6 adjust, assign, cement, circle, clique, define, formal, harden, impose, impost, ordain, series, settle 7 appoint, arrange, company, confirm, congeal, coterie, decline, deposit, dispose, instate, platoon, station, stiffen 8 attitude, decorate, exchange, immobile, moveless, regulate, solidify 9 coagulate, collocate, designate, determine, establish, immovable, obstinate, prescribe, stabilize 10 assortment, collection, constitute, stationary
about: 5 begin, start
afloat: 6 launch
apart: 5 elect 6 exempt 7 isolate, reserve, seclude 8 allocate, dedicate, separate 9 segregate, sequester
aside: 4 void 5 annul, table 6 except, reject 7 discard, dismiss, earmark, exclude, reserve 8 overrule, separate
at naught: 4 defy 7 despise 9 disregard
back: 4 loss 5 check 6 hinder 7 backset, relapse, reverse, setback
down: fix 4 seat 5 abase, enter, place, write 6 depose, encamp, ordain, reckon, record, regard, relate 7 appoint, descend, resolve, slacken 8 consider, estimate, register 9 attribute, determine, establish, humiliate, prescribe
forth: 5 adorn, offer, state 6 expone, expose 7 arrange, commend, display, enounce, exhibit, explain, expound, present, promote, propone, publish 8 announce, decorate, manifest 9 interpret, translate 10 promulgate
free: See **liberate**
fresh: 5 relay
in motion: 6 excite 8 activate
in operation: 4 jump, move, skip 5 slide, start 6 launch, plunge, spring
in order: 4 file, tidy 5 align, aline 6 adjust 7 arrange
of players: 4 team 5 squad
of rules: 4 code
on end: 5 upend 10 topsyturvy
on fire: 4 tind 5 light 6 kindle
out: 4 plan 5 adorn, allot, equip, extol, issue, limit, start 6 embark, escort, outfit, recite 7 publish, started 8 describe, proclaim 9 embellish 10 promulgate
right: 4 file 5 align, aline, amend, order 6 adjust, repair 7 arrange, correct, ordered 11 systematize
thickly: 4 stud
to: go 4 bout 5 fight 6 fracas 7 contest 8 struggle
up: 4 post 5 build, erect, exalt, found, hoist, raise, treat 7 appoint, arrange, elevate 8 organize 9 establish
upon: 7 browden
Set, Seth (see also **Seth** below): god 5 deity
brother: 6 Osiris
father: Geb
mother: Nut
victim: 6 Osiris
wife: 8 Nephthys
seta: 6 chaeta 7 bristle
setacceous: 7 bristly
setal: 7 bristly
seth: 6 banker 8 merchant
Seth (see also **Set, Seth** above):
brother: 4 Abel, Cain
descendant: 4 Enos 7 Sethite
father: 4 Adam
son: 4 Enos
seton: 6 suture
setose: 7 bristly 9 setaceous
setout: 4 fuss 6 outfit 7 costume, display, exhibit 10 excitement 13 entertainment
settee: 4 seat, sofa 5 bench, divan
setter: dog 5 Irish 6 Gordon 7 English 10 compositor

setting: 4 eggs, trap, pave 5 decor, scene, snare, scena(It.) 6 locale 7 scenery 8 mounting 10 background 11 environment 12 surroundings

settle: fix, pay, sag, set 4 calm, dais, firm, lend, nest, root, seat, sink, toit 5 affix, agree, audit, bench, clear, couch, lodge, order, perch, plant, quiet, serve, solve 6 accord, adjust, alight, assign, decide, locate, purify, reduce, render, secure, soothe 7 appoint, arrange, clarify, compone, compose, confirm, conform, deposit, depress, dispose, provide, resolve, silence, subside 8 colonize, compound, conclude, ensconce, regulate 9 conjobble, designate, determine, establish, habituate, liquidate, shrinkage 10 accomodate, adjudicate, administer, strengthen 11 tranquilize
strike: 7 mediate

settled: 4 alit, fast 5 fixed, staid 6 formed, sedate 7 certain, decided, peopled, statary, testate 8 decorous 9 inerratic, sedentary, steadfast 10 consistent, determined, unchanging 11 established
in advance: 13 predetermined

settlement: dos 4 camp, lees 5 abode, dregs 6 colony, hamlet 7 payment, village 8 decision, disposal, fixation, sediment 9 aldeament, community, residence 10 adjustment, conclusion, occupation, regulation 11 arrangement 12 colonization, satisfaction 13 clarification, determination, establishment
arrange: 9 negotiate

settler: 6 sooner, vessel 7 planter, pioneer 8 colonist, emigrant 9 colonizer, immigrant 10 forehearth, receptacle
American: 7 Pilgrim, Puritan

seugh, seuch: rut 5 ditch, drain 6 furrow

seven: 4 zeta
combining form: 5 hepta
days and nights: 8 sennight
deadly sins: 4 envy, lust 5 anger, pride, sloth 8 gluttony 12 covetousness
group of: 6 heptad, septet 8 hebdomad

Seven Against Thebes: 6 Tydeus 8 Adrastus, Capaneus 9 Polynices 10 Hippomedon 13 Parthenopaeus

Seven Churches: 6 Sardis, Smyrna 7 Ephesos 8 Laodicea, Pergamos, Thyatira 12 Philadelphia

Seven Dwarfs: Doc 5 Dopey, Happy 6 Grumpy, Sleepy, Sneezy 7 Bashful

seven-faced: 11 heptahedral

seven-fold: 8 septuple

seven hills: See **Rome:** *hill*

seven-sided: 10 heptagonal

sever: cut 4 deal, part, rend, slit 5 break 6 breach, cleave, depart, detach, divide, except, exempt, sunder 7 disjoin, dispart, divorce, scatter 8 disunite, separate 9 dismember, segregate 10 disconnect, dissociate 12 disassociate
from neck: 6 behead 9 decollate 10 decapitate

several: few 4 some 6 divers, single, sundry 7 diverse, various 8 distinct, peculiar 9 different 10 individual, respective
minimum: 5 three

severe: bad 4 dear, dere, dour, dure, hard, keen, sore, tart 5 acute, breme, cruel, grave, gruff, harsh, rethe, rigid, rough, sharp, sober, stark, stern, stiff 6 biting, bitter, chaste, coarse, hetter, sedate, simple, solemn, strict, trying, unkind 7 ascetic, austere, caustic, chronic, condign, crucial, cutting, drastic, extreme, intense, serious, spartan, violent 8 captious, exacting, grievous, rigorous, scathing 9 difficult, draconian, inclement, strenuous, stringent, unsparing 10 afflictive, astringent, censorious, forbidding, methodical, oppressive, restrained 12 unornamented

severed: 5 apart

severity: 8 acerbity, acrimony, asperity

Seville cathedral tower: 7 Giralda

sew: hog, sow 4 bind, darn, join, mend, seam 5 baste, broth, drain, sewer, shirr, smock, unite 6 fasten, needle, stitch, suture 7 pottage
up: end 6 settle 8 conclude 10 monopolize
with gathers: 4 full 5 shirr

sewan: 5 beads, money 6 wampum

Seward's Folly: 6 Alaska

sewer: 5 drain 7 conduit, servant 10 seamstress
opening: 7 manhole

sewing machine: *inventor:* 9 Elias Howe
part: 8 plicator 10 zipperfoot

sex: 6 gender
combining form: 4 geno
hormone: 7 steroid

sexless: 6 neuter 7 epicene

sexton: 6 verger 7 sacrist 9 sacristan 12 underofficer

sextuplet: 7 sestole 8 sestolet

sexual: 5 gamic 6 carnal
continence: 8 chastity
inclination: 4 urge 6 libido

sexy: 5 spicy 6 carnal, erotic 7 amatory, earthly

Seychelles: 4 Mahe 7 La Digue, Praslin
capital: 8 Victoria

sha: 5 sheep, urial 6 nahoor, oorial

shab: 4 itch, scab 7 scratch

shabby: old 4 base, mean, worn 5 dowdy, faded, seedy 6 paltry, ragged, scurvy 7 outworn, unkempt 8 shameful, tattered, unworthy **9** beggardly **10** despicable, threadbare **11** disgraceful **12** contemptible, deteriorated

shack (see also **shuck**): coe, hut **4** feed, plug **5** cabin, catch, chase, hovel, tramp **6** lean-to, refuse, shanty, wander **7** stubble **8** brakeman, retrieve, vagabond

shackle: tie **4** band, bind, bolt, bond, curb, gird, gyve, idle, iron, loaf, ring **5** chain, gyves **6** fetter, hamper, hinder, hobble, pinion, secure **7** confine, manacle, trammel **8** coupling, restrain **10** fetterlock

shad: **5** alose **6** allice **7** crappie, mojarra

shaddock: **5** fruit **6** pomelo **10** grapefruit

shade: bar, dim, hue **4** dark, dull, tint, tone, veil **5** color, cover, ghost, hatch, tinge, trace, umbra, vault **6** awning, canopy, darken, degree, nuance, screen, shadow, spirit, sprite, shield **7** curtain, eclipse, foliage, obscure, parasol, phantom, protect, shelter, spector, shutter, umbrage, vestige **8** clearing, darkness, ornament **9** adumbrate, variation **10** apparition, difference, overshadow, protection, silhouette
light: **6** pastel
lines: **5** hatch
of cap: **5** visor
of meaning: **6** nuance

shaded: **10** umbrageous

shaded walk: **4** mall **6** arcade **8** cloister

shadetail: **8** squirrel

shadow (see also **shade**): dog **4** blot, omen, tail **5** cleek, cloud **6** attend, follow, shroud, symbol **7** remnant **8** penumbra **10** indication, overspread **13** prefiguration
dark cone of: **5** umbra
dispelling: **9** scialytic
figure: **10** silhouette
of death: **5** gloom, Sheol
outline: **10** silhouette
person without: **6** ascian

shadowbox: **4** spar

shadowy: dim **5** faint, vague **6** opaque, shaded, umbral, unreal **7** obscure, retired **8** adumbral **10** impalpable, indistinct, overspread, transitory **12** inaccessible **13** unsubstantial

Shadrach: *companion:* **7** Meshach **8** Abednego
persecutor: **14** Nebuchadnezzar

shady: **7** shadowy, umbrous **11** underhanded **12** disreputable, questionable

shaffle: **4** limp **5** shirk **6** hobble, loiter **7** shuffle

shaft: bar, pit, ray, rod **4** axle, beam, bolt, cone, fust, hole, pole, stem, tige, tole **5** arbor, arrow, helve, heuch, heugh, irony, lance, scape, shank, spear, spire, stalk, stele, thill, trunk **6** arbour, column, groove, handle, pillar, tongue, upcast **7** chamber, chimney, Maypole, missile, obelisk, spindle **8** gatepost **9** flagstaff
column: **4** fust **5** scape, verge
feather: **5** scape
part: **4** orlo
plant: **4** axis
vehicle: **5** thill

shag: mat, nap **4** hair, mane, mass, pile, toss, wool **5** chase, fiber, shake **6** follow, rascal, refuse **7** garment, tobacco **9** cormorant **10** blackguard

shaggy: **5** bushy, furry, nappy, rough **7** hirsute, scrubby, unkempt, villous **8** straggly **10** unpolished

shagreen: **4** skin **7** leather, rawhide **8** galuchat

shaitan, sheitan: **5** devil, fiend

shake: go; bob, jar, jog, wag **4** free, jolt, move, pass, rese, rock, shog, stir, sway, toss, wave **5** churn, drink, eject, quake, shock, steal, swing, trill **6** depart, dither, dodder, goggle, hustle, joggle, quaver, quiver, rattle, shiver, totter, tremor, weaken **7** agitate, chatter, concuss, disturb, fluster, tremble, unnerve, vibrate **8** brandish, convulse, dislodge, enfeeble, flourish **9** agitation, dismissal **10** earthquake
down: bed, con **5** dance **6** extort, settle **9** blackmail
off: **4** shed **6** excuss **8** disagree

Shaker: **4** sect
founder: Lee

Shakespeare: *actor:* **4** Ward **5** Booth **6** Burton **7** Garrick, Geilgud, Olivier, Sothern **8** Modjeska **9** Barrymore
alternate author: **5** Bacon
character: **4** Bone, Iago, Iras, Lear, Snug **5** Biron, Cleon, Henry, Regan, Romeo, Speed, Timon **6** Banquo, Juliet, Oberon, Portia, Simple **7** Antonio, Cassius, Othello, Salerio, Shylock, Silence, Slender, Titania **8** Falstaff
elf: **4** Puck
forest: **5** Arden
home: **4** Avon
play: **4** Lear **6** Caesar, Hamlet **7** Macbeth, Othello **9** Cymbeline
theater: **5** Globe
wife: Ann

shaking: **4** ague **9** tremulant, tremulous **10** concussion

shako: cap **9** headdress
decoration: **6** pompon

shakti: **5** force, power

shaky: **4** weak **5** dicky **6** dickey, groggy, infirm, wabbly, wobbly **7** casalty, caselty,

unsound 8 insecure 9 tottering, trembling, tremulous, uncertain 10 unreliable 12 questionable
shale: cod 4 husk, rock 5 metal, scale, shell, slate 7 shuffle 8 impurity
shall: may 4 must, will 5 would 7 obliged
shallop: 4 boat 6 dinghy, vessel
shallot: 4 tube 5 onion 8 eschalot
shallow: hat 4 cart, tray, weak 5 shoal 6 basket, flimsy, slight 7 cursory, trivial 9 depthless, frivolous 11 superficial
shalom: 5 peace
sham: 4 fake, hoax, mock 5 bogus, cheat, dummy, false, feign, fraud, trick 6 assume, bunyip, chouse, deceit, delude, device, duffer, humbug, shoddy 7 deceive, feigned, forgery, grimace, pretend 8 pretense, trickery 9 brummagem, deception, imitation, imposture, pretended, trickster 10 artificial, factitious, simulacrum, substitute 11 counterfeit, make-believe
shamal: 4 wind
shaman: 4 monk 6 beggar, priest 8 conjurer
Shamash: *consort:* Ai; Aya
messenger: 6 Bunene
worship center: 5 Larsa 6 Sippar
shamble: 5 bandy, bench, stall, stool, table 7 bauchle, butcher, counter, shuffle 9 footstool, malformed, slaughter
shambles: 8 abattoir
shame: 5 abase, abash 6 ashame, assume, bemean, bismer 7 degrade, mortify 8 contempt, disgrace, dishonor 9 embarrass, humiliate 10 repentance 11 degradation, shortcoming 12 illegitimacy 13 embarrassment, mortification
shamefaced: 6 humble, modest 7 bashful 9 diffident
shameful: 4 base, mean 5 gross 7 ignoble 8 flagrant, improper, indecent, infamous 9 degrading, dishonest 10 outrageous, scandalous, slanderous 11 disgraceful, ignominious, opprobrious 12 contumelious, dishonorable, disreputable, vituperative 13 dishonourable
shameless: 6 arrant, brazen 8 immodest, impudent 9 abandoned, audacious, barefaced 10 unblushing 11 brazenfaced
shammer: 4 aper 5 fraud 8 imposter
shammock: 4 loaf 6 dawdle, slouch
shampoo: 4 lave, wash 5 clean
shamrock land: 4 Eire, Erin 5 Irena 7 Ireland
shandrydan: gig 6 chaise 7 vehicle
shandy: 4 wild 5 drink 9 visionary 11 unrealistic
Shang dynasty: Yin
shanghai: 4 drug, ship 6 kidnap
Shangri-la: 6 utopia 8 paradise
shank: leg 4 gamb, shin, stem, tang 5 gambe, knife, ladle, ridge, shaft 8 leggings, stocking
pert. to: 6 crural
shanny: shy 4 fish 5 giddy, silly 6 blenny
shantung: 4 silk 6 pongee, tussah
Shantung's capital: 6 Tsinan
shanty: hut 5 cabin, hovel, hutch, shack 6 leanto 8 chantier, dwelling
shape: fit, hew 4 bend, cast, form, knap, make, mold, plan, tool, trim 5 block, boast, build, carve, feign, frame, guise, model, mould, state, torus 6 create, decree, design, devise, figure, format, happen, ordain 7 appoint, arrange, conform, contour, fashion, incline, phantom, posture, whittle 8 attitude, contrive 9 condition, determine, structure 10 apparition, appearance, figuration 11 arrangement 13 configuration
different: 8 variform
garden: 7 topiary
in: 4 trim
shapeless: 6 deform 8 deformed, formless 9 amorphous, contorted, distorted, misshapen, unshapely
shapely: fit 4 neat, trim 6 decent, gainly 8 suitable 11 symmetrical
shaping machine: 5 edger, lathe 6 shaper
shard: 5 scale, shell 8 fragment
share: cut, lot 4 cant, deal, dole, hand, part, rent 5 divvy, enter, quota, ratio, shear 6 cleave, divide, impart, moiety, ration 7 partake, portion 8 dividend, division 9 allotment, allowance, apportion, communion, plowshare 10 distribute 11 participate
widow's: 5 dower, dowry, terce, third 6 dowery
sharecropper: 7 metayer
Shari River: See **Cameroon**
shark: 4 gata, haye, mako, tope 5 adept 6 expert, lawyer, usurer 7 dogfish, sharper, sponger 8 drunkard, maneater, parasite, swindler, thrasher, thresher 9 porbeagle, selachian, trickster 10 hammerhead
blue pointer: 4 mako
genus of: 11 carcharodon
nurse: 4 gata
pilot: 6 remora
small: 4 tope 5 lamia
young: 8 sharklet
sharp: 4 acid, cold, cute, edgy, fell, gash, gleg, gnib, high, keen, nice, sour, tart 5 acrid, acute, adept, alert, breme, brisk, crisp, eager, edged, fiery, harsh, salty, steep, tangy, witty 6 abrupt, active, acuate, astute, barbed, biting, bitter, clever, crafty, crispy, expert, peaked, severe, shrewd, shrill, snelly(Sc.) 7 angular, aus-

tere, caustic, cunning, cutting, gingery, grating, intense, lyncean, nipping, painful, piquant, pointed, pungent, rasping, sharper, violent, waspish **8** aculeate, distinct, handsome, incisive, piercing, poignant, vigilant, vigorous **9** attentive, beautiful, designing, impetuous, merciless, penetrant, sagacious, sarcastic, trenchant **10** discerning **11** acrimonious, intelligent, penetrating, underhanded
comb. form: oxy
to taste: **4** acid **5** acrid
sharp-sighted: 6 astute
sharpen: nib, ted **4** edge, hone, whet **5** grind, point, reset, strop **6** acuate **7** enhance, quicken **9** intensify **10** cacuminate
sharper: gyp **4** bite **5** cheat, rogue **6** cogger, keener **7** cheater, gambler **8** deceiver, swindler **9** trickster
sharpness: 6 acumen
sharpshooter: 6 sniper **8** marksman
shastra class: 5 sruti **6** purana, smriti, tantra
shatter: 4 blow, dash **5** blast, break, burst, crash, smash, split, wreck **6** batter, damage, impair **7** clatter, derange, destroy, disable, scatter **8** disorder, disperse, splinter **9** dissipate
shattered: 6 broken **8** broozled, doddered
shave: ace, cut **4** pare, poll, trim **5** graze, skive **6** rasure, scrape **7** tonsure, whittle
shaveling: 4 monk **5** youth **6** priest **9** hypocrite, stripling
shaven: 4 bald **6** pilled **8** tonsured
shaver: boy, lad **4** chap **5** cheat **6** barber, fellow, tonsor **8** swindler **9** bargainer, youngster **11** extortioner
shavetail: 4 mule **10** lieutenant
shavie: 4 joke **5** prank, trick
shaving: 5 spale **8** ramentum
shaw: 4 wood **5** copse, grove **7** thicket
shawl (see also **vestment**): **4** maud, wrap **5** manta, orale **6** serape(Mex.) **7** amlikar, paisley **8** epiblema
Shawnee Indian chief: 8 Tecumseh, Tecumtha
shay: 6 chaise **8** carriage
Shea player: Met
sheaf: 4 kern, kirn **5** bunch **6** bundle **7** cluster
group: **6** thrave
shear: cut **4** clip, gnaw, reap, rend, snip, trim **5** carve, force, mince, prune, sever, shave, strip **6** cleave, divest, fleece, nibble, pierce, remove **7** deprive, scissor, whittle **10** circumcise
shearing machine: 7 cropper
shears: 6 forfex **8** scissors, secateur
sheartail: 4 tern **11** hummingbird
shearwater: 4 crew **6** hagdon, haglet
sheatfish: 4 wels **7** catfish
sheath: cot **4** boot, case **5** dress, forel, ocrea, theca, stall **6** forrel, spathe **8** covering, envelope, scabbard
sheathe: 4 bury, case, ceil, dull **5** blunt, cover, glove **6** plunge **7** enclose, envelop
sheave: 5 wheel **6** pulley
sheaves: See **sheaf**
Sheba: 4 Saba
shebang: 4 deal **6** affair, outfit **7** concern **8** business **11** contrivance **13** establishment
Shechem god: 10 Baalberith
shed: cut, hut **4** abri(F.), byre, cast, cote, drop, emit, hull, lair, molt, nest, part, pour **5** booth, cabin, hovel, repel, scale, spill, tease **6** belfry, dingle, divide, effuse, hangar, hemmel, impart, lean-to, slough **7** cottage, diffuse, emanate, radiate, scatter, shelter, testudo **8** disperse, outhouse, separate, sprinkle, woodshed, workshop **9** irradiate, penthouse **11** intersperse, out-building
skin: **7** ecdysis
shedder: 4 crab **6** peeler, salmon **7** lobster
sheen: 4 fair **5** gleam, gloss, shine, shoes **6** bright, glossy, luster **7** exalted, glisten, glitter, radiant, shimmer, shining **8** brightly, lustrous, splendid, splendor **9** beautiful, shininess **10** brightness, glittering **11** beautifully, illustrious, resplendent
sheep: mug, sha **5** argal, dumba, ovine, urial **6** aoudad, argali, wether **7** bighorn, bleater, karakul, mouflon **8** karakule, moufflon, ruminant **9** blackface
breed: **4** Horn **6** Dorset, Exmoor, Merino, Romney **7** Cheviot, Delaine, Lincoln, Suffolk **8** Cotswold, Dartmoor **9** Leicester, Southdown, Teeswater **10** Corriedale, Oxford Down, Shropshire
caretaker: **8** shepherd
coat: **6** fleece
cry: maa **5** bleat
dead: **5** braxy, traik
disease: coe, gid, rot
feed: **5** graze **7** pasture
female: ewe **6** gimmer, sheder
head: **5** jemmy
head broth: **9** powsowdy
kidney extract: **5** venes
male: ram, tup **5** heder **6** wether **10** bellwether
mark: **4** smit **5** brand
pathway: **6** roddin **7** rodding
pen: **5** bught(Sc.) **6** bought(Sc.)
pert. to: **5** ovine
second year: tag, teg

wild: sha 4 arui, udad 5 argal, audad, urial 6 aoudad, argali, bharal, nahoor, nayaur 7 mouflon 8 moufflon
young: hog, teg 4 lamb, tegg 5 heder 6 bident, gimmer, hogget, sheder 7 twinter 8 hoggerel, shearhog 9 four-tooth, shearling
sheep dog: 6 collie 8 shepherd
sheep-like: 4 meek 5 ovine 6 docile
sheepfaced: See **sheepish**
sheepfold: cot, pen, ree(Sc.) 4 cote, fold 7 sheppey 8 sheepcot 9 sheepcote, sheepfold 10 sheephouse
sheepheaded: 5 silly 6 stupid 12 simple-minded
sheepish: shy 4 meek 5 blate, silly, timid 7 abashed, awkward, bashful, daffish 11 embarrassed
sheepskin: 4 bond, cape 5 basil 7 diploma 9 parchment
leather: 4 roan
sheepwalk: run 5 range, slait 7 pasture
sheer: 4 fine, mere, pure, thin, turn 5 brant, clear, steep, utter 6 abrupt, bright, swerve 7 deviate, shining, unmixed, utterly 8 absolute, outright 9 deviation, downright, undiluted 10 diaphanous 11 transparent, unqualified 13 perpendicular
sheet: air 4 fine, page, rope, sail 5 chain, daily, linen, paper, plate 6 expand, lamina, shroud 7 tabloid 8 pamphlet 9 newspaper
twelvemo: 9 duodecimo
sheeting: 5 linen 7 percale
sheldrake, shelldrake: 4 duck
shelf: 4 bank, berm, bink, reef, sill 5 altar, berme, ledge, shoal 6 gradin, mantel 7 bedrock, bracket, gradine, retable, sandbar, stratum 8 credence, credenza, sandbank 9 banquette 10 pigeonhole
shell: hud, pod 4 boat, bomb, coin, hull, husk, lyre, swad, test 5 balat, cameo, conch, cowry, crust, money, murex, scale, shuck, spoon, testa, troca 6 coffin, concha, cowrie, crusta, dolite, dugout, lamina, lorica, strafe 7 abalone, admiral, bombard, capsule, caracol, dariole, grenade 8 caracole, carapace, covering, exterior, frustule 9 cartridge 10 projectile, schoolroom
beads: 4 peag 6 wampum
casing: 5 gaine
defective: dud
explosive: 4 bomb 7 grenade
hole: 6 crater
large: 5 conch
measuring device: 11 conchometer
money: 4 peag 5 cowry, peage, sewan, uhllo 6 cowrie, seawan, wampum
protected with: 8 loricate
ridge: 4 lira 5 varix 7 varices(pl.)
unexploded: dud
shellac: lac 5 resin
shellacking: 6 defeat 7 beating 8 flogging, whipping
shellapple: 9 chaffinch, crossbill
Shelley: *drama:* 5 Cenci
poem: 7 Adonais
shellfire: 6 strafe 7 barrage
shellfish: 5 nacre 6 limpet 7 mollusk 10 crustacean
shelter: cot, hut, lee 4 abri, barn, camp, cote, fold, gite(F.), herd, howf, port, roof, shed, skug, tent 5 benab, bield, boist, bower, cloak, cover, embay, haven, house, hovel, howff, hutch, shack 6 asylum, burrow, covert, defend, garage, hangar, harbor, hostel, refuge, sconce, sconse, screen, shield, trench 7 carport, cottage, defense, embosom, foxhole, harbour, hospice, imbosom, nacelle, pillbox, protect, retreat, trailer, umbrage 8 bescreen, ensconce, mantelet, quarters, security 9 coverture, harbinger, harborage, sanctuary 10 harbourage, protection
sheltered side: 7 leeward
on: 4 alee
shelve: tip 4 tilt 5 defer, ledge, shelf, table 6 mantel, retire 7 dismiss, project 8 overhang, platform 10 pigeonhole
Shem: *father:* 4 Noah
son: Lud 4 Aram, Elam 6 Asshur
shenanigan: 5 trick 7 evasion, foolery 8 mischief, nonsense, trickery
shend: mar 4 harm, lose, ruin 5 blame, shame, spoil, worst 6 damage, defeat, defend, injure, punish, revile, shield 7 degrade, destroy, protect 8 confound, disgrace, dishonor, reproach 10 discomfort
Sheol: 4 hell 5 grave, Hades 10 underworld
shepherd: 4 herd, lead, tend 5 drive, guard, watch 6 attend, escort, feeder, gather, herder, leader, pastor, shadow 8 guardian, minister
band of: 10 pastoureau
clock: 7 salsify 9 pimpernel
dog: 6 Collie 8 Cebalrai
god: Pan 5 Pales
pert. to: 8 pastoral
pipe: 4 reed 7 musette 11 flageolette
purse: 4 herb 9 blindweed
staff: 4 kent 5 crook
shepherdess: 7 bergere 9 Amarillis, Amaryllis
sherbet: ice
sherd: See **shard**
Sheridan play: 6 Rivals
sheriff: 6 grieve 7 bailiff, officer
aides: 5 posse
deputy: 6 elisor 7 bailiff

jurisdiction: 9 bailiwick
Sherlock Holmes: *companion:* 6 Watson
creator: 5 Doyle
sherry: 4 wine 5 tokay 6 Solera 7 oloroso 11 amontillado
Shetland Island: *inlet:* voe
land: 4 odal, udal 6 udaler 7 udalman
measure: ure
musical instrument: gue
ounce: ure
tax: 4 scat
sheugh, sheuch: 5 ditch, gully 6 furrow, ravine, trench
sheyle: 6 squint 7 grimace
shibboleth: 4 test 8 password 9 criterion, watchword
shield: ecu(F.), rim 4 egis, hide, umbo 5 aegis, armor, avert, badge, board, cloak, cover, guard, shade, targe 6 blazon, brooch, canopy, defend, forbid, screen, target 7 buckler, conceal, defense, lirelle, prevent, protect, rotella, shelter, testudo 8 conserve, rondache 9 protector 10 escutcheon, protection
band across: 4 fess
boss: 4 umbo
knob: 4 umbo
large: 5 pavis
Minerva's: 4 egis 5 aegis
on insect's head: 7 clypeus
part of: 4 boss, ente, orle, umbo 6 pointe 7 bordure, impresa
rim: 4 orle
small: ecu
strap: 6 enarme
shield-bearer: 8 escudero
shield-shaped: 7 peltate, scutate 9 clypeolar
shieling: hut 7 cottage, pasture
shift: rid 4 deal, eddy, fend, jibe, move, quit, ruse, stir, tour, turn, veer 5 avoid, dodge, evade, feint, hours, order, shunt, slide 6 assign, bestir, change, device, divide, period 7 arrange, dispose, evasion, replace, shuffle 8 artifice, exchange, mutation, transfer 9 apportion, expedient 10 equivocate, subterfuge, transplant 11 contrivance 12 redistribute 13 transposition
shifting: 6 shifty 8 ambulant, drifting, floating
shiftless: 4 lazy 8 feckless 10 thriftless 11 inefficient
shifty: 4 haft 6 fickle, tricky 7 devious, hangdog 8 shifting 9 changeful, faithless 10 changeable
shikar: 4 hunt 5 sport 7 hunting
shikari, shikaree: 5 guide 6 hunter 9 sportsman
shillelagh: 4 club 6 cudgel
shillibeer: 6 hearse 7 omnibus
shilling: bob
shilly-shally: 5 hedge, waver 6 trifle 8 hesitate 9 vacillate
shilpit: 4 flat, puny, thin, weak 6 feeble, sickly 7 insipid
shim: hoe 5 image, level, wedge 6 shadow, streak, washer 7 glimpse, shingle
Shimei's father: 4 Gera
Shimel's father: Ela
shimmer: 5 flash, light 7 glimmer, glisten
shimmy: 5 dance, shake 6 quiver 7 chemise, tremble, vibrate 10 shimmering
shin: run 4 kick, walk 5 climb, ridge, shank, tibia 6 cnemis, strike
pert. to: 7 cnemial
shindy: row 4 jump, lark, orgy, romp 5 brawl, dance, party, revel, spree 6 fracas, frolic, rumpus, uproar 7 shindig, wassail 8 carousal 9 commotion 11 disturbance, merrymaking
shine: ray 4 beam, beek(Sc.), glow, star 5 black, blaze, blink, excel, glaik, gleam, glent, glint, gloss, gloze, prank, sheen 6 liking, polish 7 glimpse, glisten, glister, glitter, radiate 8 eradiate, fondness, illumine 9 coruscate, irradiate, transluce
shiner: hat 4 chub 6 bruise 8 blackeye 9 bootblack
shingle: 4 sign, whip 7 haircut 9 signboard
splitting tool: 6 prower
shingles: 4 zona 6 herpes
shining: 4 glad, gold 5 aglow, glary, lucid, nitid, sleek 6 ardent, argent, bright, fulgid, glossy, lucent 7 beaming, eminent, fulgent, glowing, radiant 8 flashing, gleaming, luminous, lustrous, radiance, splendid 9 brilliant, effulgent, refulgent, sparkling, unclouded 10 glistening, glittering, remarkable 11 illustrious, irradiating, resplendent
shinplaster: 5 scrip
Shinto: *deity:* 8 Hachiman
gateway: 5 torii
temple: sha 5 Jinja 6 Jinsha 7 Yashiro
shiny: See **shining**
ship: 4 boat, pink 5 setee 7 hagboat 8 balinger
abandoned: 8 derelict
ancient: 7 galleon
Arabian: 6 boutre
arctic: 6 sealer
Argonaut's: 4 Argo
armored: 7 carrack, cruiser 9 destroyer, ironsides, submarine
ascent: 5 scend
attendant: 7 steward
auxiliary: 6 tender
beak: bow, ram 4 prow

berth: 4 dock, slip
biscuit: 8 hardtack
boarding device: 6 ladder 9 gangplank
boat: 4 dory, life 5 barge, dingy 6 dingey, dinghy, tender 7 pinnace
body: 4 hull
breadth of: 4 beam
brutally disciplined: 8 hell ship
burden: 5 cargo
cabin: 6 saloon 9 stateroom
canvas: 4 sail
capacity: 7 tonnage
capacity unit: ton
cargo: 7 gaiassa
cargo invoice: 8 manifest
carpenter: 5 Chips
channel: gat 5 canal 6 narrow, strait
clean: 6 careen
clerk: 6 purser
clock: nef
coast guard: 6 cutter
coastal: hoy 4 dhow, grab 6 droger, trader 7 drogher
codfishing: 6 banker 8 walloper
commercial: 6 trader
company of: 4 crew 5 fleet, hands 6 armada
compass housing: 8 binnacle
cook: 6 slushy
course: 7 sealane
crane: 5 davit
crew leader: 5 bosun
curved planking: sny
desert: 5 camel
deserter: rat
direction: 4 atry 5 abeam
drain: 7 scupper
enemy-watching: 7 vedette
employee: 5 oiler 6 purser, sailor 7 steward 8 deckhand, engineer, helmsman, steerman 9 navigator
fishing: 5 smack 6 hooker, lugger 7 trawler
flat-bottom: 4 keel 5 barge
fleet of: 6 armada
floor: 4 deck
fuel: 5 barge, oiler 6 coaler, tanker 7 collier
fur-hunting: 6 sealer
group: 4 navy 5 fleet 6 armada
hoist: 4 boom 5 dairt 7 capstan
jail: 4 brig
kitchen: 6 galley
lateral movement: 6 leeway
left side: 4 port
lifting device: 5 crane, davit 7 capstan
line: 7 marline, ratline
merchant: 6 argosy, galiot, holcad 7 galliot
middle: 9 amidships
mortgage: 8 bottomry
movement: 6 leeway
oar: 6 bireme, galley, sampan 7 pinnace, rowboat, trireme
officer: 4 mate 5 bosun 6 purser 7 steward 9 boatswain
part: bow 4 beam, brig, deck, helm, hold, hull, keel, mast, prow 5 bilge, stern, waist, wheel 6 bridge, galley, rudder, steven 7 lazaret, scupper 8 binnacle 9 lazarette, lazaretto, sternpost
partition: 8 bulkhead
personnel: 4 crew 5 hands
pirate: 8 gallivat
planking: sny 6 strake
prison: 4 brig
privateer: 10 brigantine
prow: 5 prore
quarters: 6 fo'c'sle 8 steerage 10 forecastle
record: log
repair: 6 careen
repairing device: 7 drydock
rescue: ark
room: 4 brig 5 cabin, salon 6 galley 7 caboose 10 forecastle
rope: 4 line 6 hawser 7 halyard, lanyard, painter, ratline
sailing: 4 buss, dhow, proa, yawl 5 ketch, setee, sloop, smack, xebec 6 caique, chebec, hooker, lugger, mistic, saltie 7 galleon, Geordie, polacre
shovel: 5 skeet
side: 5 abeam
station: 5 berth
structure frame: 7 carcass
table frame: 6 fiddle
tender: 7 collier, pinnace
third-class: AE
tiller: 4 helm
timber: rib 4 bitt, keel, mast, spar 5 stick 7 bollard
twin-hulled: 9 catamaran
unseaworthy: 4 hulk 5 wreck 8 ballahoo, ballahou, derelict
upward movement: 5 scend
Venetian: 9 frigatoon
voyage record: log
war (see also **warship**): sub 7 cruiser, flattop 8 corvette 9 destroyer, submarine 11 dreadnaught
wheel: 4 helm
windless: 7 capstan 8 becalmed
window: 4 port 8 porthole
wood for: 4 teak
worm: 5 borer 6 teredo

Ship of Fools author: 6 Porter
ship out: 6 enlist, export
shipboard: 5 board
shipment: 5 cargo 7 carload 8 delivery
shipping center: 7 seaport
shipshape: 4 neat, taut, tidy, trim 7 orderly

shipwright (launching slide marker): 6 wayman

shire: 5 derby, horse 6 county, region 8 district, province 11 subdivision

shirk: 4 duck, funk 5 avoid, dodge, evade, slack 6 desert 7 neglect 9 fainaigue

shirker: 6 loafer, truant 8 embusque

shirl: 4 slip 5 glide, slide

shirr: 6 gather

shirt: tee 4 jupe, polo, sark 5 dress, haire, kamis, parka, sport 6 camisa, camise, cilice, parkee

button: 4 stud

shirtfront: 5 dicky 6 dickey

shirtwaist: 6 blouse 9 garibaldi

shiver: 4 grue 5 chill, quake, shake 6 dither, quiver, tremor, twitch 7 flicker, frisson, shatter, shudder, tremble, vibrate 8 fragment, splinter

fit: 4 ague 6 chills 10 goosebumps

shivoo: 7 banquet, shindig 9 gathering 13 entertainment

shoal: bar 4 bank, mass, reef 5 barra, crowd, flock 6 school, throng 7 shallow 9 multitude

shoat: hog, pig 5 shote

shock: jar, lot 4 blow, heap, jolt, pile, stun 5 appal, brunt, bushy, gliff, gloff, scare, shake 6 fright, impact, offend, parcel, shaggy, stroke, trauma 7 astound, collect, disgust, horrify, startle, terrify 8 paralyze 9 agitation, collision 10 assemblage, concussion

mental: 6 trauma

to reality: 5 sober

shock absorber: 7 snubber

shocking: 5 awful, lurid 6 horrid, unholy 7 fearful, ghastly, hideous 8 dreadful, horrible 9 egregious, revolting 10 disgusting

shod: 5 soled 6 booted 7 ensoled

shoddy: 4 poor 5 cheap 6 shabby 8 inferior

shoe (see also **overshoe**): cue 4 boot, clog, flat, pump 5 gilly, sabot 6 brogan, brogue, buskin, caliga, crakow, gaiter, galosh, gillic, oxford, patten, sandal 7 blucher, flattie, slipper, sneaker 8 colonial, Congress, mocassin, moccasin, solleret 9 brodequin, pampootee 10 clodhopper, veldschoen

aid: 4 horn

baby: 6 bootee

fix: 5 retap 6 polish, resole

form: 4 last, tree

grip: 5 cleat

gym: 7 sneaker

house: 4 mule 7 slipper

mule's: 6 planch

part: box, cap, toe, top 4 heel, lift, pull, rand, vamp, welt 5 shank, strap 6 insole, tongue 7 counter, outsole 8 backstay, slipsole

paste: 7 clobber

piked: 6 cleats, crakow

repair: tap 5 retap 6 reheel, resole, stitch

rolling: 5 skate

rubber: 6 arctic, galosh 7 galoshe 8 overshoe

wooden: 5 sabot 6 patten

worker: 6 laster 7 cobbler

worn: 7 bauchle

shoebill: 5 stork

shoelace: tie 5 lacet 7 latchet

tip: 5 aglet 6 aiglet

shoemaker: 4 snob 5 soler, sutor(L.) 7 cobbler, crispin, farrier 10 cordonnier(F.)

apprentice: 4 snob

patron saint: 7 Crispin

tool: 4 butt 5 elsin 6 elshin

shoes (see also **shoe**): 5 sheen, shoon

winged: 7 talaria

shoeshine: 9 bootblack

shog: jog 4 jerk, jolt, rock 5 shake 6 jostle

shoggie: 4 sway 5 swing

shoggle: 6 dangle, joggle

Shogun title: 6 tycoon

shole: 5 plank, plate

shoneen: 4 snob 5 toady

shoo: 4 away, scat

shooi: 4 bird, skua 6 jaeger

shook: See **shake**

shool: 4 idle 6 loiter, scrape, shovel 7 saunter, scuffle, shamble, shuffle

shoot: bud, pot 4 bine, cast, chit, cion, dart, emit, film, fire, grow, move, plug, push, twig 5 bough, chute, drive, eject, plant, scion, snipe, spear, spout, spray, sprig, spurt, throw, tuber, utter, wound 6 branch, inject, propel, sprout, stolon, strike, thrust 7 burgeon, project 9 discharge 10 photograph 11 precipitate

objective: 6 target

shooting match: tir(F.) 5 skeet

shooting star: 5 comet 6 meteor 8 fireball

shop: 5 store 6 market, prison, tienda 7 bottega, factory 8 boutique, workshop

coffee: 4 cafe 6 bistro 9 estaminet

dairy: 8 cremerie

kind: 5 stith 6 smithy, stithy 7 mercery 8 saddlery, smithery 12 haberdashery

meat: 7 shamble 10 rotisserie 11 charcuterie

wine: 4 cafe 6 bistro

shophar: 4 horn

shopkeeper: cit 8 merchant, retailer 9 tradesman 11 businessman, storekeeper

shoplifter: 7 booster

shopper: 5 buyer 8 customer
shore: 4 bank, edge, land, prop 5 beach, brink, coast, drain, offer, scold, sewer 6 rivage, strand 7 seaside, support 8 threaten 9 foreshore
pert to: 8 littoral
poetic: 6 strand
recess: bay 4 cove 5 bayou, inlet
shore up: 4 prop
shorebird: ree 4 ruff 5 snipe 6 curlew, plover 9 sandpiper
shorn: See **shear**
short: 4 bain, curt, rude 5 bluff, brief, brusk, crisp, fubsy, harsh, scant, terse 6 abrupt, scanty, scarce 7 briefly, brusque, concise, crisply, curtail, friable, summary 8 abruptly, succinct 9 concisely, crumbling, deficient, shortstop 11 compendious 12 insufficient
and stout: 5 bunty, dumpy 6 stocky, stodgy, stubby 8 rolypoly, thickset
comb. form: 5 brevi 6 brachy
short-breathed: 5 pursy 6 winded 7 puffing
short-lived: 9 ephemeral
short-sighted: 6 myopic
short-spoken: 4 curt 5 gruff 7 laconic
shortage: 7 deficit 10 deficiency 13 insufficiency
shortcoming: 4 flaw 5 fault 6 defect 7 failure 10 deficiency, inadequacy 12 imperfection
shortcut: 5 alley 6 byroad 8 diagonal, gain cope
shorten: bob, cut, lop 4 clip, furl, reef 5 check 6 lessen, reduce 7 abridge, curtail, curtate, deprive 8 condense, contract, decrease, diminish 9 apocopate, decurtate 10 abbreviate 11 incapsulate
shorthand: 11 stenography 12 brachygraphy, speedwriting
system: 5 Gregg 6 Pitman
shortly (see also **short**): 4 soon 7 quickly 9 presently
shortness: 7 brevity
shortsighted: 4 dull 6 myopic, obtuse 11 nearsighted 13 opportunistic
Shoshone Indian: Ute 4 Hopi, Otoe, Utah 5 Piute 6 Paiute 8 Comanche
shot (see also shoot): pop, try 5 blank, carom, drink, guess, masse, photo, range, reach, sally, tired, weary 6 bullet, pellet, stroke 7 attempt, missile 8 marksman, snapshot 9 exhausted, reckoning 10 conjecture, projectile 11 intoxicated
size: B; BB, FF, FT, TT; BBB 4 dust 8 air-rifle, buckshot
shou: 4 deer
should: 5 ought
shoulder: 4 berm, edge 5 bough, raise 6 axilla
angle: 6 epaule
belt: 4 sash 7 baldric
bone: 7 scapula
combining form: omo
muscle: 7 deltoid
ornament: tab 7 epaulet 9 epaulette
pain: 7 omalgia
pert to: 4 alar 7 humeral 8 scapular
protection for: 8 pauldron
to shoulder: 7 serried
shoulder blade: 7 scapula
shout: boo, cry, hoy, hue 4 bark, bawl, call, crow, hoot, roar, root, roup, scry, yell, yelp 5 cheer, huzza, noise, whoop, yodel, yodle 6 clamor, gollar, goller, halloo, hurrah, outcry, yammer 7 acclaim 10 vociferate 11 acclamation
hunting: 5 hallo, holla 6 yoicks 7 tallyho 9 view-haloo
shove: 4 cast, push 5 drive, eject, elbow, hunch, shunt 6 hustle, jostle, propel, thrust
shovel: van 4 pale, peel 5 scoop, shool, skeet, spade 6 thrust 7 shuffle 8 strockle
shoveler: 9 broadbill
shovelfish: 9 spadefish 10 paddlefish
shovelhead: 5 shark 7 catfish 8 flathead, sturgeon
show: 4 bosh, dash, fair, lead, pomp 5 coach, farce, gloss, guide, movie, plead, prove, raree, revue, teach, train 6 accuse, afford, allege, assign, bestow, blazon, cinema, circus, confer, denote, detect, escort, evince, expose, flaunt, gaiety, gayety, inform, locate, parade, reveal, tinsel, unveil, veneer 7 bespeak, betoken, bravura, declare, display, divulge, exhibit, explain, perform, present, produce 8 ceremony, disclose, evidence, flourish, indicate, instruct, manifest 9 barnstorm, burlesque, designate, rareeshow, represent, semblance 10 appearance, exhibition, exposition, expression 11 countenance, demonstrate, performance 13 demonstration
false: 6 tinsel
forth: 7 publish 8 manifest, proclaim 9 publicize
stylized: 4 mime 6 parade 7 pageant 9 cavalcade, pantomime
way: 5 guide, usher, 6 direct, escort 7 conduct
show up: 5 strip 6 appear, arrive, expose 7 display
showcase: 7 vitrine

shower: wet 4 bath, rain, sump, wash 5 bathe, party, spray, water 6 bestow, deluge 7 drizzle, scatter 8 revealer, sprinkle 9 exhibitor
meteor: 6 Leonid
showery: wet 4 damp 5 moist 7 tearful
showing: 4 sign 6 aspect 7 account 10 apocalypse, appearance
first: 8 premiere
showy: gay 4 arty, loud 5 dashy, gaudy, grand 6 flashy, garish, ornate, swanky 7 dashing, gallant, gaudful, pompous 8 gorgeous, splendid, striking 9 brillante, sumptuous 10 pretensive 11 pretentious 12 ostentatious
shrab: 5 drink 6 spirit 8 beverage
shrapnel: 10 projectile
shred: bit, cut, hew, jag, rag 4 fell, jagg, snip, tear, twig, wisp 5 blype, grate, piece, prune, scrap, sever, shard, strip 6 divide, screed, sliver, tailor, tatter 7 fritter, parings, vestige 8 fragment, particle
shrew: 5 curse, scold, vixen 6 mammal, tartar, virago 7 muskrat, villain 9 scoundrel, termagant
long-tailed: 5 sorex
shrewd: bad, sly 4 cagy, cute, evil, foxy, hard, keen, sage, wily 5 acute, canny, harsh, sharp, smart, stern 6 argute, artful, astute, biting, clever, crafty, subtle, wicked 7 abusive, cunning, gnostic, hurtful, knowing, parlous, politic, sapient 8 depraved, grievous, piercing, shrewish 9 gnostical, ingenious, injurious, sagacious 10 discerning, farsighted, hardheaded 11 distressing, mischievous, penetrating, sharpwitted 13 perspicacious
shrewish: 7 nagging 8 vixenish 9 termagant
shriek: cry, yip 4 yell 6 holler, outcry, scream 7 screech
shrift (see also **shrive**): 10 absolution, confession, disclosure 12 confessional 14 acknowledgment
shrill: 4 high, keen 5 acute, sharp 6 argute, biting, piping, shriek, squeak 7 screech 8 piercing, poignant, strident 11 high-pitched, penetrating
shrimp: kid 5 dwarf 6 shaver 9 stripling 10 crustacean
large: 5 prawn
shrine box 4 case, naos, tomb 5 altar, caaba, chest, kaaba, huaca 6 abaton, adytum, chapel, chasse, dagaba(Ind.), dagoba(Ind.), entomb, hallow, temple 7 chaitya, enclose, memoria 8 canonize, enshrine 9 container, reliquary 10 receptacle
goddesses: 9 anaktoran
visitor: 7 pilgrim
shrink: shy 4 fawn, funk, shun, wane 5 cling, cower, quail, rivel, shrug, wizen 6 blench, boggle, cotter, cringe, flinch, gizzen, huddle, humble, lessen, recoil, retire, wither 7 atrophy, dwindle, retract, shrivel 8 condense, contract, decrease, withdraw 9 constrict 10 depreciate
shrinking: shy 5 timid 6 afraid 9 diffident
shrive: rob 4 free 5 purge 6 pardon 7 absolve, confess 8 disclose 9 reconcile
shrivel: 5 blast, crine, parch, rivel, wizen 6 cotter, scrump, shrink, weazen, wither
shriveled: 4 wede
shroff: 6 banker, expert 7 changer, inspect 8 separate 12 moneychanger
shrogs: 9 brushwood
shroud: lop 4 hide, trim, veil 5 array, cloak, cover, crypt, dress, shade, sheet, vault 6 branch, clothe, screen, shadow 7 conceal, curtain, envelop, foliage, garment, plumage, protect, shelter 8 cerement, clothing, covering, envelope 9 cerecloth 10 protection
Shrove Tuesday: 10 Pancake Day
shrub: lop, tea, tod 4 bago, bush, cade, coca, gumi, majo, nabo, olea, sida, sola 5 elder, lilac, prune, punch, salal 6 cudgel, frutex 7 arboret, buckeye, chamise, chamiso, heather, scratch, tarbush 8 abelmosk, barberry, beverage, huisache 9 chaparral, manzanita
aromatic: tea 4 mint, sage 5 batis, thyme 8 rosemary
bean family: 4 ulex
collection: 10 fruticetum
desert: 5 retem 6 alhagi, raetam
evergreen: box 4 ilex, moss, titi 5 furze, heath, salal, savin 6 laurel, myrtle 7 jasmine, juniper 8 oleander 9 mistletoe
fence: box 5 hedge
flowering: 5 lilac, tiara 6 azalea, laurel, myrtle, spirea 7 lantana, rhodora, spiraea, syringa 8 japonica, oleander, oleaster 9 mistletoe 10 mignonette
fruit: 5 salal
genus of: 4 inga 5 erica, ledum 6 aralia
hardy: 7 althaea, heather
indigo: 4 anil
myrtle-like: 7 cajeput, cajuput
ornamental: 6 privet
parasitic: 9 mistletoe
pert. to: 9 fruticose, fruticous
poisonous: 5 sumac 6 sumach
prickly: 4 whin 5 briar, brier, gorse 7 bramble 8 allthorn, hawthorn
rubber: 7 guayule
stunted: 5 scrag, scrub
tea-like: kat 4 coca
tropical: 5 henna 6 olacad 7 lantana 10 frangipane, frangipani
yercum-yielding: 5 madar

shrubbery: 7 boscage, boskage
shruff: 5 dross 7 rubbish
shrug: don, tug 5 hitch 6 fidget, shiver, shrink 7 gesture, shudder 8 contract, hitching 9 handshake 10 convulsion
shrunken (see also **shrink**): 4 lank
Shu: *parent:* Ra 6 Hathor
sister: 6 Tefnut
wife: 6 Tefnut
shuck: pod 4 husk 5 shell, strip 6 recoil, remove 7 discard
shudder: 4 grue 5 quake, shake 6 agrise, shiver 7 frisson, tremble
shuffle: mix 4 gait, plod 5 dance, scuff 6 huddle, juggle, jumble, mingle, remove, sclaff 7 evasion, quibble, scuffle, shamble 8 artifice 10 equivocate 11 prevaricate 12 equivocation
shuffling: 6 shifty 7 evasive 9 deceitful 13 opportunistic
shun: 4 balk, flee, hide 5 avert, avoid, evade, evite 6 eschew 7 forbear, forsake, refrain 8 forebear
shunt: 5 shift, shove 6 divert, remove, switch 9 conductor, rechannel, sidetrack
shut: bar, rid 4 free 5 close 6 climax, fasten, forbid 7 confine, exclude 8 prohibit 10 portcullis
in: hem, pen 4 cage, pent, wall 5 embar, embay, fence 6 bottle, hemmed 7 bottled, confine, enclose, impound 8 imprison 10 quarantine, surrounded
shut-in: 7 invalid, recluse 12 convalescent
shut out: bar 7 exclude 8 preclude
shut up: end, gag 7 seclude 8 conclude 9 terminate
shutter: 5 blind, cover 6 screen 7 buckler 8 jalousie
shuttle: 6 looper
shuttlecock: 4 bird 6 birdie
shy: coy, mim 4 jump, shun, wary 5 aloof, avoid, chary, scant, start, throw, timid 6 anerly, boggle, demure, modest, recoil, shrink 7 bashful, lacking 8 farouche, hesitant, reserved, retiring, secluded, sheepish, skittish 9 diffident, reluctant, shrinking 10 shamefaced, suspicious, unassuming 11 distrustful, unobtrusive 14 unostentatious
Shylock: *coin:* 5 ducat
daughter: 7 Jessica
friend: 5 Tubal
shyster: 11 pettifogger
si: yes
Siam: See **Thailand**
Siamese twin: Eng 5 Chang
sib: kin 4 akin 6 allied, sister 7 brother, kindred, kinship, kinsman, related, sibling 8 friendly, relation, relative 9 congenial, kinswoman, relatives 12 well-disposed
Siberia: *antelope:* 5 saiga
carnivore: 5 sable
city: 4 Enna, Omsk 5 Chita, Tomsk 7 Barnaul, Irkutsk 11 Krasnoyarsk, Vladivostok 15 Blagovestchensk
dog: 7 Samoyed 8 Samoyede
Eskimo: 4 Yuit
fish: 5 nelma
forest: 5 Urman
fur: 7 calabar
gulf: Ob
hunters and fishers: 6 Giliak, Gilyak 7 Samoyed 8 Samoyede
hut: 8 barabara, barabora
leopard: 5 ounce
mountains: 5 Altai
peninsula: 6 Taimir 9 Kamchatka
people: 5 Sagai, Tatar, Yakut 6 Kirgiz, Tartar 7 Kirghis, Kirghiz, Yukagir 8 Yukaghir 9 Mongolian
plain: 6 steppe, tundra
region: 5 taiga
river: Ob, Om; Ili, Tom 4 Amur, Lena, Maya, Onon 5 Sobol, Tobol 6 Olenek 7 Yenisei
squirrel: 7 miniver
squirrel-skin: 7 calabar
storm: 5 buran
tanning plant: 5 badan
tent: 4 yurt 5 yurta
wild cat: 5 manul
wild sheep: 6 argali
sibilant: s, z; ch, sh, zh; ess 7 hissing
sibling (see also **sib**): 6 sister 7 brother
sibness: 7 kinship 10 connection 12 relationship
sibyl: 5 witch 6 Libyan, Samian, Trojan 7 Cumaean, seeress 8 Delphian, Phrygian 9 Cimmerian, Erythrean, sorceress, Tiburtine 10 prophetess 13 fortuneteller, Hellespontine
sibylline: 6 occult 7 cryptic 8 oracular 9 ambiguous, equivocal, prophetic 10 exorbitant, mysterious 11 prophetical
sic: so; set 4 seek, such, thus, urge 5 chase 6 attack, incite
sice: six 8 sixpence
Sicilian: 10 Trinacrian
Sicily: *cape:* 4 Boeo, Faro 7 Passaro
city: 4 Gela 5 Aetna, Bidis 6 Alcamo, Modica, Ragusa 7 Catania, Marsala, Messina, Palermo, Trapani 8 Girgenti 13 Caltanissetta
composer: 7 Bellini
crime society: 5 Mafia

god: 7 Adranus
harbor: 7 Palermo
island: 11 Pantelleria
king: 4 Eryx
measure: 5 salma 7 caffiso
mountain: 4 Etna
people: 5 Elymi, Sicel
river: 5 Salso 6 Belice, Simeto 7 Platani
seaport: Aci 7 Messina
secret society: 5 Mafia
volcano: 4 Etna
whirlpool: 9 Charybdis
youth: 4 Acis

sick: bad, ill, set, wan 4 abed, pale, seek, urge, weak 5 badly, chase, crank, cronk, fed-up, unfit, weary 6 ailing, attack, incite, unwell 7 unsound 8 impaired 9 crapulous, depressed, disgusted, instigate, nauseated, surfeited, unhealthy 10 indisposed 11 exasperated
deathly: 5 amort 7 alamort
person: 7 invalid, patient

sickbay: 6 clinic 8 hospital 9 infirmary 10 dispensary

sicken: 6 affect 8 languish

sickening: 7 fulsome 9 revolting 10 disgusting, nauseating

sicker (see also **sick**): 4 fast, firm, safe, sure 5 fixed 6 assure, pledge, safely, secure, stable 7 assured, certain 8 securely 9 assuredly, certainly, confident 10 dependable 11 established, trustworthy

sickish: 6 sickly 9 sickening

sickle: 6 scythe

sickly: ill, wan 4 flue, pale, puny, weak 5 cothy, faint, frail 6 ailing, cranky, feeble, infirm, weakly 7 cothish, insipid, invalid, languid, mawkish, queechy 8 diseased 9 sickening, unhealthy

sickness: 6 malady, nausea 7 ailment, disease, disgust, illness 9 distemper, infirmity, weariness 12 qualmishness 13 indisposition
feign: 8 malinger
mental: See **mental disorder**

side: far 4 edge, face, line, part, team, wall, wide 5 agree, ample, costa, facet, flank, latus, party, phase, place, proud, shore, slope, space, width 6 aspect, behalf, border, margin, region, severe 7 conceit, distant, faction, lateral, support, surface 8 district, position, spacious 9 declivity, direction, outskirts 10 collateral 15 pretentiousness
on the: 5 apart
pain in: 6 stitch
pert. to: 7 lateral
piece: rib 5 stave
sheltered: lee 4 alee

side arm: 5 sword 6 pistol, weapon 7 bayonet 8 revolver

side by side: 8 parallel, together

side view: 7 profile

sideboard: 6 buffet 8 credence, credenza, cupboard, dressoir

sidekick: pal 4 chum 6 friend 7 partner 8 follower 9 assistant, companion, satellite 11 confederate

sideline: 5 bench 9 avocation

sideling, sidling: 5 askew, slope, steep 7 lateral, sloping 8 inclined, sidelong, sideways 9 inclining, laterally, obliquely

sidelong: 6 subtle 7 lateral, oblique, sloping 8 indirect, sideways, slanting 9 laterally, obliquely

sidepiece: rib 6 border

sidereal: 6 astral, starry 7 stellar 8 starlike

siderite: ore

sideroad: 5 byway

siderolite: 9 meteorite

sideshow: 10 attraction
attraction: 5 freak

sideslip: 4 skid 5 slide 10 digression

sidestep: 4 duck 5 avoid, evade

sidetrack: 4 spur 5 shunt 6 divert, switch

sidewalk: 6 causey 9 banquette, boardwalk
part: 4 curb, kerb 5 crack 6 paving

sideway: 5 byway 6 bypath 7 postern 8 sidewalk, sideways

sideways: 5 aside 6 askant 7 askance, athwart, lateral 8 indirect, sidewise 9 laterally, obliquely

Sidi's wife: 5 Amine

sidle: 4 edge 6 loiter 7 saunter

Sidon's modern name: 5 Saida

sie: 4 drip, drop, sift 6 strain

siege: see 4 rank, seat 5 bench, beset, flock, place, privy 6 attack, throne 7 besiege, sitting, station 8 blockade 9 beleaguer 13 beleaguerment

Siegfried: *mother:* 8 Sieglind
slayer: 5 Hagen
sword: 7 Balmung
vulnerable spot: 4 back 8 shoulder
wife: 9 Kriemhild

sierra: 5 range, ridge

Sierra Nevada: *fog:* 7 pogonip
peak: 4 Dana 7 Whitney

siesta: nap 4 rest 5 sleep

sieve: 4 lawn, sift 5 tamis, temse 6 basket, bolter, filter, ranger, riddle, screen, sifter, strain 7 chaffer, cribble, measure 8 colander, separate, strainer
for clay: 4 laun

sievelike: 8 cribrate

sift: ree, sie, sye 4 bolt, cull, scry, seek 5 sieve, temse 6 dredge, filter, riddle, screen,

search, strain, winnow 7 canvass, examine, inspect, scatter 8 separate 10 scrutinize
sifter: 5 sieve 6 bolter 8 strainer
sigh: sob 4 moan, sugh, wail 5 mourn, sithe, sough, yearn 6 grieve, lament 7 suspire 11 respiration
sight: aim, ken, sum 4 bone, espy, gaze, look, show, vane, view 5 scene 6 aspect, behold, descry, glance, vision 7 discern, display, glimpse, insight, suspire 8 eyesight, quantity 9 spectacle 10 appearance, exhibition, inspection, perception 11 examination, observation, suspiration
defect: 7 anopsia
gun: 4 bead
loss: 9 amaurosis
obscurity: 6 caligo
offending: 7 eyesore
out of: 11 disappeared
pert. to: 6 ocular, visual
second: fey, ESP 7 psychic
sightless: 5 blind 6 unseen 9 invisible
sigil: 4 seal, sign, word 6 device, signet 9 signature
sigmoid: ess
Sigmund: *father:* 7 Volsung
son: 6 Sigurd
sword: 4 Gram
wife: 7 Hiordis
sign (see also **signal**): ad; cue, nod 4 hire, mark, note, omen 5 badge, image, segno(It.), sigil, spoor, token, trace 6 banner, beacon, beckon, caract, effigy, emblem, engage, ensign, figure, motion, notice, poster, signet, symbol, wigwag 7 auspice, endorse, gesture, initial, insigne, message, picture, portent, prodigy, vestige, warning 8 password, pretense, standard 9 character, semaphore, semblance, subscribe, watchword 10 denotation, expression, forerunner, indication, prognostic, underwrite 11 countersign 13 advertisement, constellation, demonstration, foreshadowing
astrological: 5 Aries 6 Gemini, Pisces, Taurus 8 Aquarius 9 Capricorn
diacritical: 5 hamza, tilde 6 hamzah, tittle, umlaut 7 cedilla
direction: 5 arrow
illuminated: ad 4 neon 6 lights
liturgical: 5 selah 6 shelah
magic: 5 sigil
music: 5 presa, segno
pert. to: 5 semic 8 semantic
Zodiac: See **Zodiac** *sign*
sign language: 11 dactylology
sign off: out 6 thirty
sign on: 4 hire, ship 6 engage, enlist, enroll 8 register
signal (see also **sign**): 4 flag 6 buzzer, ensign, notify, sennet 7 betoken, eminent, lantern, notable, presage, signify 9 memorable, prominent, semaphore, symbolize 10 remarkable 11 communicate, conspicuous 13 extraordinary
distress: SOS 6 mayday
electric: 8 teleseme
system: 4 code
warning: 5 alarm, alert, flare, siren 6 alarum, beacon, tocsin 7 blinker
signature: 4 hand, mark, name, sign, visa, vise 5 sigil, stamp 9 allograph, autograph, birthmark, designate 10 directions, impression 11 countersign
signet: 4 mark, seal, sign 5 sigil, stamp 10 impression 12 authenticate
significance: 7 bearing, purport 13 signification
significant: 4 sign 5 grave, token 6 symbol 7 ominous, weighty 8 eloquent, sinister 9 important, momentous 10 expressive, indicative, meaningful, portentous, suggestive 13 consequential
signification: 4 sign 5 sense, token 7 meaning 10 importance, indication 11 consequence 12 apprehension, notification
signify: nod 4 mean, show, sign 5 augur, imply, spell, utter 6 amount, denote, import, inform, matter, signal 7 betoken, compare, declare 8 announce, foreshow, indicate, intimate, manifest 11 communicate
signor: man 4 lord 5 title 9 gentleman
signpost: 5 guide 6 beacon 9 guidepost
signum: 4 bell, mark, sign 9 signature
Sigurd: *father:* 7 Sigmund
foster father: 5 Regin 6 Reginn
horse: 5 Grani
slayer: 5 Hogni
wife: 6 Gudrun
Sigyn's husband: 4 Loki
sike: 4 rill 5 brook, ditch, drain, gully 6 ravine, stream, trench
siker: 4 safe 6 secure 7 assured 9 confident 10 dependable 11 trustworthy
Sikkim (see also **India**): *capital:* 7 Gangtok
people: 4 Rong
silage: 4 feed 6 ensile, fodder 8 ensilage
Silas Marner author: 5 Eliot
sile: fry 4 beam, drop, fall, flow, pour, soil 5 glide, sieve, spawn 6 filter, rafter, strain 8 strainer
silence: gag 4 hush, mute, rest, stun 5 choke, floor, quiet, still, tacet 6 muffle 7

campion, confute, repress, secrecy 8 muteness, suppress 9 obscurity, reticence, stillness 10 silentness
goddess: 8 Angerona
music: 5 tacet
silencer: 4 mute 5 gavel 7 muffler
silene: 7 campion 8 catchfly
silent: mum 4 dumb, flat, mute 5 quiet, still, tacit 8 inactive, overcome, reserved, reticent, taciturn, unspoken 9 noiseless, secretive, unuttered 10 flavorless, speechless, unrecorded 11 unexpressed, unmentioned 15 uncommunicative
Silesian town: 4 Oels 5 Opava, Opole
silex: 5 flint 6 quartz, silica
silica: 4 opal 5 silex 7 dioxide
silicate: 4 mica 6 cerite, iolite 7 epidote 8 calamine, severite, wellsite
silicon derivative: 5 monox
silk: 5 pekin, surah, tulle 7 foulard 8 florence, sarcenet, sarsenet
corded: 6 faille
embroidery thread: 5 floss 8 arrasene
fabric: 4 gros 5 caffa, China, crepe, moire, ninon, pekin, satin, surah, tabby, tulle 6 cendal, faille, mantua, pongee, samite, sendal, tussah, tusser, tussur 7 alamode, marabou, sarsnet, taffeta, tsatlee, tussore 8 sarcenet, sarsenet
fishline: 4 gimp
hank: 4 hasp
hat: 4 tile 6 topper
Indian moth: 4 muga
raw: 5 grege
refuse: 6 strass
source: 6 cocoon
substitute: 5 nylon, rayon
thread: 4 filo
unspun: 6 sleave
waste: 4 noil 5 floss 6 frison
watered: 5 moire
worker: 7 thrower 9 throwster
yarn: 4 tram 7 schappe
yarn size: 6 denier
silk-stocking: 4 ride 5 elite 7 elegant, wealthy 9 exclusive, luxurious 10 Federalist 12 aristocratic
silken: 4 fine, soft 5 quiet, silky, sleek, suave, sweet 6 gentle, glossy, smooth, tender 7 elegant 8 delicate, lustrous, silklike 9 luxurious, sericeous 10 effeminate 12 ingratiating
silkworm: eri 4 eria 6 tussah, tusser, tussur 7 tussore 8 bombycid
silkworm rot: 7 calcino
sill: 4 beam, seat, sile 5 bench, frame, ledge, shelf, stone 6 timber 9 threshold
silliness: 5 folly 6 betise(F.)
silly: mad 4 bete, daft, fond, fool, idle, simp, weak 5 anile, apish, barmy, dazed, dense, frail, goofy, goose, inane, plain 6 absurd, cranky, cuckoo, dotard, dottle(Sc.), feeble, footle, humble, infirm, paltry, rustic, sickly, simple, stupid, unwise 7 asinine, fatuous, foolish, foppish, shallow, witless 8 childish, fopperly, ignorant, imbecile, innocent 9 brainless, childlike, ludicrous, pointless, senseless, simpleton 10 half-witted, indiscreet 12 simple-minded 15 unsophisticated
silt: 4 scum 5 dregs 7 deposit, moraine, residue 8 sediment 9 percolate
silver: 4 pale 5 money, plate, sweet 6 argent, gentle 7 bullion, silvery 8 argentum, eloquent, lustrous, peaceful, precious, sterling 9 tableware 10 silverware 11 resplendent 13 argentiferous
comb. form: 6 argyro 7 argento
containing: 5 lunar
lace: 8 filigree
pert. to: 9 argentine, argentous
reducing kettle: 4 cazo(Sp.)
symbol: Ag
silver and gold: *ornament:* 5 orris
silver-fox fur: 7 platina
silver oak: 11 flannelbush
silver plover: 4 knot(Sc.)
silver thaw: ice 4 rime 5 glaze
silver thistle: 8 acanthus
silver-tongued: 8 eloquent
silverfish: 6 insect, tarpon
silversmith: 9 artificer
silverware: 5 vases 6 dishes 8 platters 9 ornaments, tableware
ornament: 7 gadroon
silverweed: rue 5 tansy 9 jewelweed
silvery: 7 frosted 9 argentine 10 argenteous
silviculture: 8 forestry
simar: 4 robe 6 jacket 7 garment 12 undergarment
Simeon: *father:* 5 Jacob
mother: 4 Leah
simian: ape 6 monkey 7 apelike
similar: sib 4 akin, like, such 5 alike 6 evenly 7 uniform 8 analogic, parallel 9 semblance 9 analogous, resembling 11 counterpart, homogeneous, resemblance 13 correspondent
comb. form: 4 homo 5 homeo 6 homoeo
simile: 10 comparison
similitude: 4 form 5 image 6 simile, symbol 7 analogy, parable 8 allegory, likeness 9 facsimile, semblance 10 similarity 11 counterpart, resemblance 14 representation
similize: 5 liken 7 compare
simmer: 4 boil, stew 6 braise
simmon: 9 persimmon

simnel: 5 bread 7 biscuit 8 cracknel 9 fruitcake
Simon: 5 Peter
Simon Legree: 6 driver 10 taskmaster
simon-pure: 4 real, true 7 genuine 9 authentic 11 unqualified
simony: 8 barratry
simoom, simoon: 4 wind 5 storm 6 tebbad
simper: 5 mince, smile, smirk 7 whimper
simple: 4 bald, bare, dull, easy, fond, mere, poor, pure, real, true, weak 5 folly, lowly, naive, naked, plain, Roman, silly 6 common, Dorian, homely, humble, oafish, rustic, severe, single, stupid 7 artless, austere, babyish, foolish, idyllic, natural, onefold, sincere, Spartan, unmixed 8 absolute, arcadian, childish, complete, gullible, homemade, ignorant, innocent, modestly, ordinary, tailored, trifling 9 childlike, elemental, ingenuous, primitive, unadorned 10 elementary, unaffected, uninvolved 11 homogeneous, undesigning, unimportant 12 inartificial, uncompounded, unpretending 13 insignificant, uncomplicated, unconstrained, unembellished 15 straightforward, undistinguished, unsophisticated
simple-minded: 6 simple, stupid 12 feeble-minded, unsuspecting 13 simple-hearted 15 unsophisticated
simpleton: ass, daw 4 boob, dolt, fool, gaby, gawk, gawp, gowk, lout, simp, tony, zany 5 dunce, goose, idiot, ninny, noddy, sammy 6 dawkin, gander, gawney, gulpin, nincom, nincum, nitwit, noodle 7 gomeral, gomerel, gomeril, muggins, widgeon 8 Abderite, fondling, numskull, omadhaun 10 changeling, nincompoop 11 ninnyhammer
simplify: 7 clarify, expound 9 elucidate, interpret
simulacrum: 4 sham 5 image 7 phantom 8 likeness, pretense, travesty 9 imposture, semblance 11 assemblance, counterfeit
simulate: act, ape 4 fake, mock, sham 5 feign, feiut 6 affect, assume 7 feigned, imitate, pretend 9 dissemble, personate, pretended 10 fictitious 11 counterfeit
simulation: 9 hypocrisy
simurgh, simurg: roc
sin: err 4 debt, envy, evil, lust, vice 5 anger, blame, crime, error, fault, folly, guilt, pride, sloth, wrong 6 acedia, felony 7 offense, violate 8 gluttony, iniquity, peccancy 9 deviation 10 immorality, peccadillo, transgress, wickedness, wrongdoing 11 misdemeanor, ungodliness, viciousness 12 covetousness 13 transgression
canonical: 6 heresy, murder 8 adultery, idolatry
Sinai mountain: 5 Horeb
sinapis: 7 mustard
Sinbad's bird: roc
since: as; ago, for, fro, now 4 ergo, gone, past, sith, syne(Sc.) 5 after, hence, later 7 already, because, whereas 8 inasmuch 9 afterward, therefore, thereupon 11 considering 12 continuously, subsequently
sincere: 4 open, pure, real, true 5 frank, whole 6 candid, devout, hearty, honest 7 cordial, correct, earnest, genuine, unmixed, upright 8 faithful, truthful, virtuous 9 authentic, blameless, heartfelt, unfeigned, veracious 10 unaffected 11 unvarnished 12 wholehearted 13 unadulterated 15 straightforward
sinciput: 8 forehead
Sinclair Lewis character: 7 Babbitt
sind: 5 rinse 6 drench, quench
sinecure: 4 pipe, snap 5 cinch, gravy
sinew: 5 snare 6 tendon
sinewy: 4 firm, wiry 5 thewy, tough 6 brawny, robust, strong 7 fibrose, nervous, stringy 8 forceful, muscular, powerful, vigorous 9 tendinous
sinful (see also **sin**): bad 4 evil 6 wicked 7 immoral, ungodly, vicious 10 iniquitous 11 unrighteous
sing: hum 4 cant, lilt, pipe, ring 5 carol, chant, chirl, croon, ditty, yodel, yodle 6 betray, intone, warble 7 chortle, confess, descant, rejoice, roulade, tweedle
as a round: 5 troll
softly: hum 5 croon
with trills: 6 warble 7 roulade
singable: 7 lyrical, melodic, tuneful 9 cantabile
singe: 4 burn, char, sear 6 scorch
fiber: 6 genapp
singer: 4 alto, bard, bass, diva 5 basso, buffa, buffo, tenor 6 artist, cantor 7 artiste, chanter, crooner, soloist, songman, soprano 8 minstrel, vocalist 9 chanteuse, chorister, contralto, descanter 10 cantatrice 11 entertainer
comic opera: 5 buffa
female: 9 chanteuse
opera: 4 diva
singerie: 6 design 7 picture 10 decoration
singing: 4 cant 5 charm 9 cantation
group: 4 duet, trio 5 choir, octet 6 chorus, sextet 7 octette, quartet 8 chanters, sextette 9 quartette
pert. to: 6 choral 9 cantative
trio: 9 tricinium
single: one 4 lone, only, part, sole, unit 5 alone, unwed 6 unique 7 onefold, unusual 8 celibate, separate, singular, solitary,

withdraw **9** sequester, unmarried **10** individual, particular **11** unsupported
combining form: uni
single out: 6 choose
singlet: 5 shirt **6** jersey **9** waistcoat **10** undershirt
singly: 4 once **5** alone **6** merely, solely **7** unaided **8** honestly **9** severally, sincerely **12** individually, particularly, single-handed
singsong: 5 chime
singular: odd **4** each, rare, sole **5** queer **6** single, unique **7** eminent, private, strange, unusual **8** isolated, peculiar, separate, superior, uncommon **9** eccentric, fantastic, whimsical **10** individual, remarkable, unexampled **11** exceptional **12** unparalleled **13** extraordinary, unprecedented
singult: sob **4** sigh
singultus: hic
sinister: car(Sc.) **4** dark, evil, grim, left **5** wrong **7** adverse, baleful, corrupt, ominous **9** dishonest, injurious, malicious, underhand **10** disastrous, portentous **11** prejudicial, unfortunate **12** inauspicious
sink: bog, dip, ebb, sag **4** cave, drop, fail, fall, ruin, wane **5** avale, drain, droop, embog, heald, hield, lower, plump, sewer, slope **6** debase, dolina, doline, drench, extend, gutter, plunge, settle **7** decline, degrade, depress, descend, destroy, immerse, relapse, subside **8** decrease, diminish, submerge, suppress **9** penetrate
below horizon: set
ship: **7** scuttle
sinker: 6 weight **8** doughnut
Sinkiang: *capital:* **7** Urumchi
river: **5** Tarim
sinking: 10 depression
sinless: 7 perfect **8** innocent **9** righteous
sinner: 5 scamp **8** evildoer, offender, penitent **9** reprobate, wrongdoer **10** backslider, trespasser **12** transgressor
sinning: 7 peccant
sinuous: 4 wavy **5** snaky **7** bending, crooked, curving, devious, sinuate, winding **9** deviating, intricate **10** circuitous, serpentine **11** anfractuous
sinus: bay **4** bend, fold **5** bosom, curve **6** cavity, hollow, recess **7** channel **10** depression
pert. to: **5** sinal **7** sinusal
Sioux: Kaw, Oto **4** Crow, Iowa, Otoe **5** Brule, Omaha, Osage, Sioux **6** Dakota, Santee, Tutelo **8** Catawaba **9** Winnebago
division: **5** Teton
sip: bib, lap, sup **5** draft, drink, quaff, taste **8** toothful
sipe: 4 seep, soak **9** percolate
sipper: 4 tube **5** straw
sir: 4 lord **5** title **6** knight, master **9** gentleman
sirdar: 5 chief, noble **6** bearer **7** officer, servant
sire: 4 lord **5** title **6** father, master, parent **8** ancestor, begetter **10** forefather, procreator, progenitor
siren: 5 lurer **7** charmer, foghorn, Lorelei, mermaid **9** Cleopatra **10** bewitching **11** fascinating
of Nile: **4** Cleo **9** Cleopatra
sirenian: 6 dugong **7** manatee
sirenic: 8 alluring **9** deceptive, melodious **11** fascinating
siriasis: 9 sunstroke
Sirius' master: 5 Orion
sirocco: 4 wind
sisal: 4 hemp **5** sizal
Sisera: *enemy:* **5** Barak
murderer: **4** Jael
siskin: 5 finch, tarin
sissy: 7 girlish **11** mollycoddle
sister: nun, sis **4** girl **5** soror(L.) **7** sibling
murder: **10** sororicide
pert. to: **5** soral **8** sororate, sororial
younger: **7** cadette(F.)
Sister Superior: 6 abbess
sisterhood: 8 sorority
sistrum: 6 rattle
sistrusus: 11 rattlesnake
sit: lie, set **4** meet, pose, rest, seat **5** brood, dwell, model, perch, press, roost, squat **6** occupy, remain, repose **7** convene **8** incubate
carelessly: **4** loll **6** sprawl
sit in: 6 attend **7** protest **11** participate
sit on: 6 confer, rebuke **7** repress, squelch **8** suppress **9** reprimand **11** investigate
site: 4 ruin, seat, spot **5** locus(L.), place, scene, venue **6** locale, locate **8** location, position **9** situation
sitfast: 5 fixed, stone **9** immovable **10** stationary
sithe: 4 sigh
Sitsang: 5 Tibet
sitter: 5 model, rider
sitting: 4 seat **5** abode, place **6** clutch, posing, seance, sedent, sejaul **7** sejeant, session **8** sederunt
court: **6** assize **7** session
Sitting Bull: *enemy:* **6** Custer
tribe: **5** Sioux
sitting duck: 5 decoy **6** target
situated: 4 seat **5** basal **6** nether, placed, plight **7** located, station **8** marginal **13** circumstanced
between folds: **11** interplical
in the middle: **6** medial, median

on membrane enveloping the brain: 8 epidural
on right: 6 dexter
toward rear: 6 astern 7 postern 9 posterior
situation: job 4 case, need, post, seat, site 5 berth, place, siege, situs(L.), state 6 estate, locale, morass, plight, scrape, strait 7 bargain, dilemma, station, vantage 8 locality, location, position, quandary 9 condition, emergency, imbroglio 11 predicament, whereabouts 12 circumstance
situla: 4 pail, vase 6 bucket 10 receptacle
situs: 5 place 8 location, position 9 situation
Siva: *consort:* Uma 4 Devi
son: 6 Skanda
trident: 6 trisul 7 trisula
wife: 4 Sati
six: 6 senary, sestet 7 digamma, sestole 8 senarius
group: 5 hexad 6 hexade, senary, sextet 8 sextette
pert. to: 6 senary
prefix: 4 hexa, hexo
series of: 5 hexad 6 hexade
six-eyed: 9 senocular
six-footed: 7 hexaped 9 hexapodal, hexapodan
six-line stanza: 6 sestet
six on dice: 4 sice
six sheets: 7 sextern
sixfold: 8 sextuple
sixpence: 6 bender 7 cripple, fiddler
size: 4 area, bore, bulk, mass 5 cover, glaze, grade 6 adjust, amount, candle, extent, format, volume 7 arrange, stiffen 8 classify, standard 9 dimension, magnitude 11 measurement
book page: 9 duodecimo
hosiery: 4 pope
indefinite: nth
paper: cap 4 copy, demi, demy, pott 5 atlas, crown, felic, folio, legal 6 bagcap 7 bastard, emperor 8 foolscap, imperial 9 colombier
separation device: 6 grader
type: 4 pica, ruby 5 agate, canon, elite, pearl 6 minion, primer 7 brevier, diamond, English, paragon 9 bourgeois, columbian, nonpareil
yarn: lea 5 forty 6 denier
sizing: 4 glue 6 starch
sizy: 7 viscous 9 glutinous
sizz: 4 hiss
sizzle: fry 4 burn, sear, siss 7 shrivel
sizzling: hot 6 torrid
sjambok: 4 flog, whip
skag: 4 boat, skeg, tear 5 split, wound
skate: jag, ray 4 fish, plug, shoe, skid 5 flair, glide, horse
order: 4 raja 5 raiae 7 rajidae
skate blade: 6 runner
skating arena: 4 rink
skean: 4 dirk 5 sword 6 dagger
skedaddle: 4 bunk, flee 5 scoot 6 scurry 7 scamper
skeeg: 4 flog, lash, slap
skeel: tub 4 pail 6 bucket
skeesicks: 6 rascal 9 skinflint
skeet: 12 trapshooting
skegger: 4 parr
skeigh, skeich: shy 5 proud 10 mettlesome
skein: rap 4 hank, wind 5 flock 6 flight, hurdle, sleeve 7 spireme, thimble
skelder: 5 cheat 7 vagrant 9 panhandle
skelet: 5 mummy 8 skeleton
skeletal: 4 bony
skeleton: 4 past 5 atomy, bones, coral, ilium, mummy 6 sketch 7 outline, remains 9 framework
disease: 7 rickets
hiding place: 6 closet
organization: 5 cadre
sea animal: 5 coral, shell 6 sponge
skeleton key: 4 gilt 5 screw 7 twirler
skell: 5 twist, upset 6 squint
skellum: 5 rogue, scamp 6 rascal
skelly: 4 chub 6 squint 9 chaffinch
skelp: say 4 beat, blow, kick, pare, push, rain, slap, walk 5 write 6 basket, colony, squall, stride, strike 7 beehive, measure, perform, quickly, scratch, scuttle 8 splinter, suddenly
skeppist: 8 apiarist 9 beekeeper
skeptic, sceptic: 7 doubter, infidel 10 pyrrhonist, unbeliever 11 disbeliever, freethinker, nullifidian
skeptical, sceptical: 8 doubting 9 faithless 11 questioning
skerrick: bit 5 scrap, trace 6 morsel
skerry: 4 isle, punt, reef, rock 6 potato
sketch: dot, jot, map 4 draw, limn, plan, play, skit 5 draft, paint, skate, story, trace 6 apercu, design, pastel 7 cartoon, croquis, drawing, outline, schizzo(It.) 8 describe 9 delineate, summarize 11 composition, delineation, description
sketchy: 5 rough, vague 10 inadequate, unfinished
skew: cup, cut, set 4 awry, fail, make, shun, slip, turn 5 askew, avoid, flunk, slant, stone, throw, twist 6 coping, escape, eschew, gauche, glance, offset, squint, swerve 7 blunder, distort, drizzle, oblique, pervert 8 slanting 9 deviating, distorted 12 misrepresent
skewer: pin, rod 5 prick, truss 6 fasten, pierce 7 hairpin 9 brochette
ski: *fall marker:* 8 sitzmark

race: **6** slalom
run: **6** schuss
skid: bar **4** clog, curb, drag, hook, rail, scud, shoe, slip, trig **5** brake, check, slide **6** fender, runner, timber, twitch **7** protect, skidpan, support **8** platform, sideslip
skiff: **4** boat, skif, skim **5** canoe, glide, graze, skift, touch **6** caique, flurry **7** currane, rowboat
skiing salutation: **4** heil
skill: art, can **5** craft, haunt, knack, virtu **7** ability, address, aptness, cunning, finesse, justice, mastery, science **8** artifice, capacity, deftness, facility, industry, judgment, rhetoric, training **9** adeptness, dexterity, knowledge, readiness **10** adroitness, artfulness, astuteness, capability, cleverness, competence, efficiency, experience, expertness **11** discernment, information, proficiency **12** skillfulness **13** judiciousness, understanding
skilled: **5** adept **6** astute, expert, versed **7** capable **10** conversant, proficient
government: **9** statesman
skillful: apt **4** able, deft, fine, good, hend, just **5** adept, handy **6** adroit, artful, aufait, clever, crafty, daedal, expert, habile, proper **7** capable, cleanly, cunning **8** dextrous, tactical **9** daedalian, dexterous, ingenious, righteous **10** proficient, reasonable **11** intelligent **12** accomplished
skillfulness: **5** craft
skilligalee: **5** broth **8** porridge
skim: cut **4** film, flit, sail, scud, scum, skip **5** clear, cover, fleet, glide, graze, ready, study, throw **6** glance, refuse **7** examine
skim over: **5** skirr **6** passim
skimmings: **9** fleetings
skimp: **6** meager, scanty, scrimp **9** economize
skimpy: **5** chary, skimp, spare **6** scanty, stingy **9** niggardly **12** parsimonious
skin: **4** bark, derm, dole, fell, film, flay, hide, pare, peel, pell, pelt, rack, rind, scum **5** balat, cheat, cutis, derma, fraud, layer, plica, purse, scalp, shell, strip, sweep **6** callus, escape, fleece, scrape, spoils **7** callous, cuticle, defraud, plating, profits, sharper, surface, swindle **8** covering, membrane, pellicle, planking **9** epidermis, skinflint **10** integument, pocketbook **11** decorticate, outdistance
animal: fur **4** coat, hide, pelt, plew, rack, robe, vair **5** coney, sculp **6** hackle, peltry
beaver: **4** plew
burning sensation: **5** uredo
comb. form: **4** derm **5** derma **6** dermis
decoration: **6** tattoo
deeper layer: **5** cutis
depression: **6** dimple
disease: **4** acne **5** hives, mange, psora, rupia, tinea **6** eczema, tetter
dressed: fur
dryness: **7** xerosis
excessive pigment: **8** melanism
exudation: **5** sudor, sweat **12** perspiration
fold: **5** plica **7** dewlaps
fruit: **7** epicarp
layer: **4** derm **5** cutis, derma
oil: **5** sebum
opening: **4** pore
pert. to: **5** deric **6** dermal **9** cuticular, epidermal
piece: **5** blype
prepare: taw
presser: **7** sammier
protuberance: **4** mole, wart
remover: **5** parer
resembling: **7** dermoid
sensitive layer: **5** cutis **7** enderon
tan: taw
unsheared pelt: **8** woolfell
without: **8** apellous
worn by Dionysus: **6** nebris
skin game: **5** bunco, bunko, fraud **7** swindle
skinflint: **5** flint, miser **6** huddle **7** niggard
skink: **4** adda, draw, hock, shin **5** drink, serve **6** liquor, lizard
skinker: **7** tapster
skinking: **4** thin **6** watery
skinkle: **5** strew **7** glitter, scatter, sparkle **8** sprinkle
skinned: *dark:* **7** melanic, swarthy
thick: **9** pachyderm **11** pachydermic
skinner: bet, gyp **5** cheat **6** driver **8** swindler
skinny: **4** bony, lean, thin **5** scant **6** meanly, stingy **9** emaciated, niggardly **10** membranous
skip: dap, hip, hop **4** balk, gait, jump, leap, miss, omit, skep, trip **5** bound, caper, elide, frisk, leave, salto, scout, vault **6** basket, bucket, escape, gambol, lackey, spring **7** abscond, captain, footman, servant **8** ricochet
along a surface: **7** skitter
school: tib
skip over: **5** elide
lightly: **4** skim
water: dap
skipjack: fop **4** fish **6** bonito, elater, jockey **7** upstart **8** sailboat **9** stripling **10** butterfish
skipper: ihi **5** saury **6** master **7** captain **9** butterfly
East Indian: **6** serang
skippet: box **4** boat **5** ladle, scoop, skiff **6** basket **8** envelope
skipping: **4** balk

skirl: fly 4 pipe, rain, snow 5 sweep, whirl 6 scream, shriek
skirling: 5 trout 6 salmon
skirmish: 5 brush, fence, fight, melee 6 action, battle, bicker, combat, effort 7 contest 8 conflict, flourish 9 encounter 10 velitation
skirp: 6 splash 7 spatter
skirr: fly, run 4 move, skim, tern 5 scour, whirr 6 scurry
skirt: lie, rim 4 edge, flap, girl 5 trend, woman 6 border, fringe 8 envelope, environs 9 outskirts, periphery, petticoat 10 underskirt
ballet: 4 tutu
coat: 6 lappet
divided: 7 culotte
hoop: 6 peplum 9 crinoline, krinoline 11 farthingale
medieval armor: 4 tace 5 tasse 6 tasset
section: 4 gore 5 panel
short: 4 kilt 6 kirtle
steel: 7 lamboys
velvet: 4 base
skit: act 4 gibe, girl, gust, hoax, jeer, jest, slap 5 caper, pound, revue, story, taunt, trick 6 parody, shower, sketch, splash 7 asperse, flounce 8 ridicule 9 enclosure 10 caricature, reflection
skite: 4 blow, dart, dash, fall, slip 5 boast, smite, trick 6 shower, squirt, strike 7 boaster 9 buffeting, squirting 12 yellowhammer
skitter: 4 pass, skim, skip 5 glide 7 scamper, scatter 8 sprinkle
skittish: coy, shy 5 jumpy 6 fickle, lively 7 nervous, playful, restive 8 spirited 9 excitable, frivolous 10 capricious 12 undependable
skittle: 4 play 5 trash 7 ninepin 8 nonsense, squander 9 enjoyment
skive: 4 dart, pare, skim 5 shave, wheel
skiver: 6 impale, skewer 7 leather, scatter
skivvy: 9 underwear 10 undershirt
sklent: fib 5 slant 7 untruth 8 slanting
skoal: 5 toast 10 salutation 11 exclamation
skua: 4 gull 5 jager 6 jaeger
skulduggery: 8 trickery 10 craftiness, wickedness
skulk: 4 hide, lurk 5 dodge, evade, hedge, miche, shirk, slink, sneak 8 malinger
skull: 4 bean, head, mind 5 brain 6 cobbra, crania(pl.) 7 cranium, harnpan
back part: 7 occiput
bone: 5 vomer 6 zygoma 7 frontal, maxilla 8 mandible, sphenoid
cavity: 5 fossa 7 foramen
pert. to: 5 inial 7 cranial
protuberance: 5 inion
soft spot: 8 fontanel
skull cap: 5 calot 6 beanie 7 calotte 8 capeline, yarmulke, yarmelke(Yid.) 9 zucchetto
Arabian: 7 chechia
cardinal's: 10 berrettino
defensive: 4 coif 9 coiffette
ecclesiastical: 6 callot 7 calotte 9 zucchetto
felt: 6 pileus
skunk: 5 snipe 6 putois(F.) 7 polecat 8 betrayer
skunk-like animal: 5 civet 7 zorille
sky: 4 blue 5 azure, ether 6 welkin 7 heavens 9 firmament
comb. form: 4 uran 5 urano
god: Anu 4 Anat 5 Dyaus
goddess: 5 Frigg 6 Frigga
highest point: 6 zenith
pert. to: 6 coelar 9 celestial
sky-blue: 5 azure 7 celeste 8 cerulean
sky pilot: 8 chaplain, preacher 9 clergyman 10 missionary
skylark: run 4 bird, jump, lark, play, skip, yerk 5 pipit 6 frolic
genus: 6 alauda
skylight: 6 dormer, window 8 abat-jour(F.)
skyline: 7 horizon
slab: 4 tile 5 dalle, plate, slice, stela, stele 6 tablet
slab-like: 6 stelar 7 stelene
slack: lax 4 dull, idle, lull, slow, soft 5 chaff, evade, loose, relax, shirk, slake, tardy 6 abated, loosen, remiss 7 slacken 8 careless, dilatory, inactive, listless, sluggish, unsteady 9 dissolute, impudence, looseness, negligent 10 diminished, inadequate, neglectful 11 inattentive, indifferent
slacken: 4 ease, slow 5 abate, delay, relax 6 loosen, reduce, relent, retard 8 decrease, moderate
slackening: 7 detente(F.)
slacker: 4 spiv 7 coucher, shirker 8 embusque
slacks: 8 trousers
slade: den 4 cave, glen 5 glade, glide, slide 6 ravine, valley 7 peat bog 8 hillside
slag: 4 lava 5 dross, waste 6 cinder, debris, refuse, scoria 7 scoriae(pl.) 9 recrement 11 agglomerate
slain: 4 dead 6 fallen, killed 8 murdered 11 slaughtered 12 assassinated
slainte: 6 health 8 greeting 10 salutation
slaister: 4 idle, mess 5 smear 6 bedaub
slaistery: 4 dirt, miry 6 refuse, sloppy
slake: mud, wet 4 cool, daub, flag, free, lick, mire, sate 5 abate, algae, allay, gully, loose, slack, slime, smear, yield 6 aslake, deaden, lessen, quench, ravine, reduce 7 appease, assuage, crumble, refresh, relaxed, release, relieve, satisfy, slacken 8

decrease, mitigate, moderate 10 extinguish 12 disintegrate
slam: hit 4 bang, beat, blow, cuff, dash, push, shut, vole 5 abuse, clash, close, noise, throw 6 impact 7 flounce 9 criticize
in cards: 4 vole
slammock, slummock: 6 sloven 8 slattern, slipshod, ungainly
slander: 4 tale 5 belie, libel, shame 6 defame, malign, report, vilify 7 asperse, blacken, distort, scandal, traduce 8 derogate, disgrace, dishonor, reproach 10 defamation, depreciate, detraction, scandalize 12 misrepresent
slanderous: 8 libelous, shameful 11 disgraceful
slang: 4 cant 5 abuse, argot 6 jargon, rakish, vulgar 7 license, swindle
slant: tip 4 bend, bias, cant, skew, slab, tilt, turn, view 5 bevel, point, slope 6 biased, breeze, glance, sklent 7 incline, opinion 8 attitude, occasion 10 hypotenuse 11 inclination, opportunity
slanted angle: 5 bevel
slanting: 4 bias, skew 5 askew, aside, atilt 6 askile, aslant, aslope 7 athwart, crooked
slap: box, hit, lap 4 beat, blow, clap, cuff, nick, pass, scud, snub, spat 5 click, clink, cluff, notch, plump, skelp, smack 6 break, buffet, insult, rebuff, slight, strike 7 attempt 8 suddenly
slapdash: 5 abuse, hasty 8 careless 9 impetuous, roughcast 10 abruptness 11 haphazardly 12 carelessness 13 precipitately
slape: 6 crafty, smooth 8 slippery 9 deceitful
slapjack: 7 pancake 11 griddlecake
slapstick: 4 joke 6 comedy
slare: 4 slur 5 scuff, smear, sneer
slash: cut 4 dash, gash, lash, slit 5 crack, slosh, wound 6 attack, defeat, lessen, reduce, splash, strike, stripe 7 censure, scourge, slitter 9 criticize
slasher 5 knife, sword 6 dagger 8 billhook 9 swordsman 12 swashbuckler
slashing: 4 huge 6 severe 7 dashing, driving, immense, violent 8 spirited 9 merciless 10 tremendous 11 criticizing
slat: bar, dab, rib 4 beat, blow, flap, hide, hurl, lath, slab, slap, toss 5 crack, split, throw 6 pummel, strike 8 fragment, splinter
slate: rag 4 list, rock, tile 5 board, color, flesh, hound, plank, scold 6 berate, pummel, punish, pursue, record, roster, tablet, thrash 7 censure, roofing 8 nominate, register, schedule 9 criticize, reprimand, thrashing
break into slabs: 5 sculp
clean: 10 tabula rasa
tool: sax, zax
slater: 5 louse 6 critic 7 hellier
slath: 6 basket
slattern: daw 4 drab, frow, slut 5 dolly, idler, moggy, waste 6 blowze, faggot, sloppy 7 trifler, trollop 8 careless, slovenly
slatternly: 5 dirty, dowdy 6 blowzy, sordid, untidy 8 slovenly
slaty: 6 clayey 7 grayish 9 argillous 12 argillaceous
slaughter: 4 gash, kill, slay 6 battue, murder, pogrom, reduce 7 butcher, carnage, killing 8 butchery, hecatomb, massacre 9 bloodshed, reduction 10 butchering 11 destruction
slaughterhouse: 8 abattoir, butchery, matadero(Sp.)
waste: 7 tankage
Slav: 4 Pole, Serb, Sorb, Wend 5 Croat, Czech, Sider 6 Sclave, Slovak 7 Russian, Serbian, Servian 8 Bohemian, Croatian, Moravian, Silesian 9 Bulgarian 12 Czechoslovak
slave: 4 bond, esne, neif, peon, serf 5 chela, dasir, helot, thane 6 addict, cumhal, drudge, penest(Gr.), thrall, toiler, vassal, wretch 7 bondman, captive, chattel, enslave, odalisk, servant 9 gallerian, hierodule, odalisque
block: 7 catasta
comedy: 5 Davus(L.)
dealer: 5 bichy
free: 7 manumit 10 emancipate
fugitive: 6 maroon
pen: 5 crawl
ship: 6 slaver
The Tempest: 7 Caliban
traveling group: 6 coffle
slave driver: 6 despot, tyrant 8 martinet 11 Simon Legree
Slave States: 5 Texas 7 Alabama, Florida, Georgia 8 Arkansas, Delaware, Kentucky, Maryland, Missouri, Virginia 9 Carolinas, Louisiana, Tennessee 11 Mississippi 13 North Carolina, South Carolina
slaver: 5 drool, smear 6 drivel, saliva 7 slabber, slobber
slavery: 7 bondage, service 8 drudgery 9 captivity, servitude, thralldom, vassalage 11 enslavement 12 enthrallment
release from: 8 liberate 10 emancipate 11 affranchise, enfranchise
Slavic: See **Slav**
slavish: low 4 base, bond, vile 6 abject, menial 7 servile 8 despotic, enslaved 9 barbarous, dependent, imitative 10 oppressive, tyrannical
slaw: 8 coleslaw

slay: 4 kill 5 smite 6 murder, strike 7 butcher, destroy, execute 9 slaughter 10 annihilate 11 assassinate, exterminate
by suffocation: 5 burke
slayer: 4 bane 6 killer 8 criminal, genocide, murderer, regicide, vaticide 9 matricide, patricide, regicidal 10 fratricide, sororicide
sleave: 4 sley 6 cleave, divide, reduce, tangle 8 separate, untangle 11 disentangle
sleazy: 4 thin 6 flimsy
sled: 4 pung 6 jumper, sleigh 7 clipper, coaster, sledger, travois, vehicle 8 toboggan 10 conveyance
log: 4 tode 7 travois
sledge: 4 dray, sled 5 break 6 hammer, hurdle, sleigh, strike
sleech: 4 ooze, silt 5 slime
sleek: nap 4 oily 5 gloss, preen, shiny, slick, smart, suave 6 finish, glossy, polish, smooth, soigne 7 flatter, mollify, soignee 8 polished, unctuous 10 flattering 11 insinuating
sleekit: 5 sleek 6 crafty, smooth 9 deceitful
sleep: nap 4 doss, doze 5 death, sopor 6 drowse, repose, snooze, stupor 7 slumber 8 lethargy 10 somnipathy 11 hibernation 15 unconsciousness
comb. form: 4 hypn 5 hypno
deep: 4 coma 5 sopor 6 stupor
god: 4 Soma 8 Morpheus
inability to: 8 insomnia
inducer of: 6 opiate 7 sandman, sopient 8 sedative
midday: 6 siesta
pert. to: 7 somnial
sleeper: bet, tie 4 beam 5 horse, shark 6 rafter, rester, timber 7 dormant, earmark, Pullman, reposer 8 dormouse 9 dowitcher, slumberer 11 stringpiece
sleepiness: 10 drowsiness, somnolence
sleeping: 4 abed 6 latent 7 dormant 8 dormient, inactive 9 quiescent
place: bed 4 bunk, doss 5 berth, couch 6 pallet 7 cubicle 9 cubiculum, dormitory
sickness: 12 encephalitis
sleepless: 5 alert 7 unquiet, wakeful 8 restless, watchful 9 ceaseless
sleepwalker: 12 noctambulist, somnambulist
sleepy: 4 dull 5 tired 6 drowsy 8 sluggish, soporose, soporous 9 lethargic, somnolent 10 phlegmatic, slumberous
Sleepy Hollow author: 6 Irving
sleet: 5 glaze
sleeve: 5 gigot 6 armlet
bar on: 7 chevron
hole for: 4 scye
sleigh: 4 pung, sled 6 cutter 7 cariole 8 carriole, toboggan
runner: 4 shoe
sleight: sly 5 craft, knack, skill, trick 6 crafty, wisdom 7 agility, conjure, cunning 8 artifice, deftness, prudence, trickery 9 dexterity, dexterous, quickness, stratagem 10 nimbleness
sleight-of-hand: 11 legerdemain
performer: 4 mage 8 conjurer, magician 15 prestidigitator
slender: 4 lean, slim, thin, weak 5 exile, gaunt, lanky, lithe, petit, reedy, small, sylph, wispy 6 feeble, lissom, meager, slight, svelte 7 gracile, tenuous, willowy 8 ethereal 9 attenuate, elongated 10 abstemious
slenderize: 4 slim
slenderness: 7 exility, tenuity
slent: 4 tear 5 slope, split 6 glance 9 declivity
sleuth: tec 6 tracer 7 tracker, trailer 9 detective, operative 12 investigator
slew: lot 4 slue, turn 5 twist 6 slough
sley: 4 part, reed 8 guideway
slice: cut, saw 4 jerk, part 5 carve, piece, share, shave, whang 6 cantle, divide, rasher, shiver, sliver 7 portion 8 separate, splinter
of bacon: 6 rasher
of meat: 6 collop
slick: 4 fine, neat, oily, tidy 5 alert, preen, sleek 6 adroit, chisel, clever, crafty, glossy, paddle, polish, smooth 7 smarten, thicket 8 slippery 9 enjoyable, excellent, ingenious 10 attractive, glistening 12 accomplished
slicker: 4 dude 5 cheat 7 gambler 8 raincoat 9 trickster
slide: 4 fall, skid, sled, slew, slip, slue 5 chute, coast, glide, hurry, scoot 6 sledge 7 incline, slither, sluther 8 glissade, ornament 9 avalanche, backslide, landslide
fastener: 6 zipper
slideway: 8 guideway
slight: cut 4 fine, slap, snub, thin 5 frail, leger(L.), light, minor, scant, scorn, sleek, small 6 flimsy, ignore, meager, scanty, simple, slight, smooth 7 distain, fragile, gracile, neglect, nominal, shallow, slender, trivial 8 careless, delicate 9 disesteem, disparage, disregard, indignity 10 immaterial 11 discourtesy, superficial, unimportant 12 contemptuous 13 disparagement, imperceptible, insignificant, unsubstantial
convexity: 6 camber
sound: 4 peep
variation: 6 nuance 7 shading
slightest: 5 least

slighting remark: 4 slur
slim: sly 4 lean, slur, thin 5 gaunt, small, spare 6 adroit, crafty, meager, meagre, scanty, slight, svelte 7 cunning, slender, tenuous 9 worthless 10 slenderize
slime: mud 4 gore, ooze 5 cover, gleet, smear 6 mucous
slimer: 8 toadfish
slimsy: 5 frail 6 flimsy
slimy: 4 vile 6 filthy, vulgar 7 viscous 9 glutinous, offensive, repulsive 10 disgusting
sling: 4 cast, hurl 5 drink, fling, throw 7 bandage 9 slingshot
slink: 4 lurk 5 crawl, sneak, steal
slip: err, imp 4 balk, clay, fall, omit, pier, shed, skid, slue 5 chute, elude, error, fault, frock, glide, lapse, leash, scion, shoot, slide 6 elapse, miscue 7 blunder, cutting, delapse, descend, faux pas, illapse, misstep, mistake, neglect, slither, sluther 8 pinafore 9 gaucherie 12 undergarment 13 transgression
slip away: die 4 pass 5 steal 6 elapse
slip back: 7 relapse
slip by: 4 pass 6 elapse
slip-up: 5 error 6 miscue 9 oversight
slipe: 4 pare, peel, slip 5 glide, slice, sneak, split, strip 6 sledge, sleigh
slipknot: 5 noose
slipper: 4 mule, shoe 5 moyle, scuff 6 juliet, pliant, sandal 7 bauchle, scuffer, shuffle, willowy 8 babouche, slippery
slippery: 4 eely, glib 5 slick 6 crafty, shifty, tricky, wanton 7 elusive, evasive, glidder 8 glibbery, unstable 9 deceitful, uncertain 10 unreliable 13 untrustworthy
slipshod: 8 careless, slommack, slovenly, slummock 10 disorderly
slipslop, slip-slop: 5 inane, slops 6 gabble 7 blunder, twaddle 10 wishy-washy 11 malapropism
slit: cut, rit 4 fent, gash, kerf, nick, race, rent, tear 5 sever, slash, split, unrip 6 cleave 7 fissure, opening 8 aperture, incision
slither: 4 slip 6 rubble 7 rubbish 8 slippery
slive: cut 4 slip 5 slice, slide, sneak, split 6 cleave, stroke
sliver: cut 5 shred, slice, slops, split 6 strand 7 slobber 8 fragment, splinter
slob: ice, mud 4 mire, ooze, snow 6 sloven, sludge
slobber: mud 4 gush, kiss, slob, slop 5 drool, slime, smarm 6 drivel, slaver, sloven 7 blubber, slabber
slobby: 5 boggy, muddy 8 slobbery
slock: bog 4 lure 5 drink 6 drench, entice, pilfer, quench 7 swallow
slocken: 5 slake 6 quench 8 saturate
sloe: haw 4 plum 10 blackthorn
slog: hit 4 blow, plod, plug, slam, slug, toil, work 5 drive 6 strike
slogan: cry 4 word 5 motto 6 phrase 9 catchword
sloop: 9 raceabout
slop: mud 4 gush, mash 5 slush, smock, spill, swill, waste 6 puddle, refuse, splash 7 cassock, clothes, garment, slobber 8 breeches, clothing, trousers
slope: dip, lie 4 bank, brae(Sc.), brow, cant, hang, ramp, rise, tilt 5 bevel, cliff, hield, scarp, slant, talus 6 ascent, aslant, aslope, bajada, depart, escarp, glacis 7 descent, incline, terrace, versant 8 gradient, hillside 9 acclivity, declivity, obliquely 10 declension 11 inclination
angle-measuring device: 10 clinometer
protective: 6 glacis
sloping: 6 aslant, aslope 7 oblique 8 inclined, slanting 9 declivous, inclining
sloppy: 5 messy 6 slushy 7 splashy 8 careless, slovenly 12 disagreeable
slosh: mud 5 slash, slush, spill, throw 6 wallow 8 flounder
slot: bar, cut 4 bolt, slat, stab 5 track, trail 6 groove, hollow, keyway, spline 7 keyhole, opening 8 aperture, guideway 10 depression
sloth: ai 4 idle, lazy, pack, slow, unau 5 delay 6 acedia, animal 7 accidie, inertia, neglect 8 edentate, idleness, laziness, slowness 9 indolence, tardiness 11 sleuthhound 12 sluggishness, wastefulness
three-toed: ai
two-toed: 4 unau
slothful: 4 argh, idle, lazy 5 inert 8 inactive, indolent, sluggish 9 sedentary
slouch: hat 4 gait, lout, pipe 5 droop 6 bonnet, loafer, lubber 7 posture 8 drooping, laziness 9 pendulous 13 shiftlessness
slough, slew, slue: bog, mud 4 fall, husk, mire, molt, ooze, plod, road, shed, skin, slew, slue 5 bayou, inlet, swamp 6 eschar, sheath, strike 7 channel, discard, mudhole 8 imprison
sloughing: 7 ecdysis
slounge: 4 idle, loaf 6 lounge
sloven: 4 slob 5 besom, clart 6 loafer 7 hallion 8 slovenly 9 scoundrel 11 undeveloped 12 uncultivated
slovenly: 4 lazy 5 dowdy, messy 6 blowzy, frouzy, frowsy, frowzy, grubby, sloppy, untidy 7 unkempt 8 careless, slattern, slipshod, sluttish 9 negligent 10 disorderly, slatternly
slow: lax 4 dull, late, poky 5 brosy, delay, grave, hooly, inert, pokey, slack, tardy 6 boring, hamper, hinder, retard, stolid, strike, stupid 7 dronish, gradual, laggard,

slacken 8 boresome, dilatory, diminish, inactive, sluggard, sluggish 9 leisurely, lingering, slowgoing, unhurried 10 decelerate, deliberate, phlegmatic, retrograde 13 unprogressive
comb. form. 5 brady
music: 5 largo, lento, tardo 6 adagio
slow down: lap 4 idle 6 retard 7 decline 10 decelerate, deliberate
slow loris: 5 kokam
slow-witted: 4 dull 6 stupid
slowness: 6 lentor
slowpoke: 5 snail 7 dawdler
slubber: 4 daub, mire, slur 5 billy, botch, slime, smear, stain 6 darken 7 obscure, slabber
slud: mud 4 mire 5 slush 7 sludder
sludge: ice, mud 4 mire, ooze, slob 5 waste 7 deposit, mixture 8 sediment 9 settlings
slue, slew, slough: 4 turn, veer 5 pivot, swing, twist
sluff: 7 discard
slug: bat, hit 4 blow, dram, slow, snag, stud 5 delay, drink, limax, snail 6 bullet, hinder, loiter, nugget, strike 7 draught, mollusk, trepang 8 sluggard, sluggish 9 gastropod 11 caterpillar, obstruction
genus of: 4 doto 5 limax 6 elysia
pert. to: 8 limacine
sea: 7 trepang 10 nudibranch
sluggard: daw 4 idle, lazy, slug 5 drone 8 faineant, sluggish
slugger: bat 4 goon 5 boxer 6 hitter, mauler 7 batsman 8 operator
sluggish: 4 dull, lazy, logy, slow 5 brosy, faint, heavy, inert 6 bovine, drowsy, leaden, supine, torpid 7 dronish, languor, lumpish 8 dilatory, inactive, indolent, slothful, sluggard, stagnant 10 tardigrade 15 procrastinating
sluice: 4 gash, gote, gout, pipe, race 5 flume, sasse, valve 6 breach, stream, trough 7 channel, launder, opening, passage 8 irrigate 9 floodgate
sluit: 5 ditch, gulch, gully
slum: 4 junk, room 5 alley 6 barrio, ghetto
slumber: 4 coma, doze 5 sleep 6 drowse, repose
slumberous: 4 calm 5 quiet 6 drowsy, sleepy 8 peaceful, tranquil 9 somnolent, soporific 10 slumbering
slump: sag 4 drop, fall, sink, slip 6 settle 7 decline 8 collapse 10 depreciate, depression
slur: 4 blot, blur, slip, soil 5 cheat, decry, elide, glide, slare, slide, smear, stain, sully, trick 6 insult, macule, slight, smirch, stigma 7 blemish, calumny, dimness, traduce 8 besmirch, disgrace, innuendo, reproach 9 aspersion, criticize, discredit, disparage, indignity 10 calumniate 11 contaminate 12 imperfection
slush: mud, wet 4 gush, mire, pulp, slud, wash 5 grout 6 drench, drivel, sloven, sluice, splash 7 mixture, sludder
slut: 4 jade 5 bitch, filth, quean 6 befoul, harlot 8 slattern 9 dratchell
sluther: 4 slip 5 slide 7 shuffle
sluttish: 4 lewd 5 gross 6 filthy, sordid 8 slovenly 10 disorderly
sly: 4 arch, cagy, foxy, ruse, slee, wily 5 coony, snaky 6 artful, clever, crafty, feline, secret, shrewd, slinky, sneaky, subtle, tricky 7 cunning, evasive, furtive, roguish 8 skillful, sneaking 9 cautelous, deceitful, secretive 10 fallacious 11 clandestine, dissembling, mischievous, underhanded 12 hugger-mugger
look: 4 leer, ogle
slyly spiteful: 5 catty
smack: bit, hit 4 blow, boat, buss, kiss, slap, tang 5 crack, savor, sloop, taste, touch, trace 6 cutter, flavor, strike, vessel 7 vestige 8 mouthful, sailboat 10 suggestion
smacking: 5 brisk, sharp 6 lively 8 spanking, vigorous
smaik: 6 rascal 9 scoundrel
small: dab, sma(Sc.), tot, wad, wee(Sc.) 4 cute, lite, mean, puny, thin, tiny, whit, wisp 5 dawny, minim, petty, scant 6 atomic, dapper, grubby, humble, little, mignon, minute, modest, petite(F.), slight 7 minimal, slender, trivial 8 atomical, picayune, trifling 9 miniature, minuscule, thumbnail 10 diminutive 13 insignificant
amount: mot 4 atom, chip, drop, iota, mote, tate 5 speck 6 detail, morsel 7 driblet, handful, modicum, morceau(F.), snippet 8 modecule
bunch: 4 wisp
coin: 4 mite
combining form: 5 lepto, micro
prefix: 5 micro
small-fry: 4 kids, tots 8 children 10 youngsters
small-minded: 4 mean 5 petty 6 narrow 7 selfish 10 prejudiced, ungenerous, vindictive
small talk: 6 babble 7 prattle 8 chitchat
smallage: 6 celery 7 parsley
smaller: 4 less 5 minor 6 lesser
combining form: mi; mio 4 meio
smallest: 5 least
smallness: 7 exility, paucity
smallpox: 7 variola
smalt: 4 flux
smaragd: 7 emerald
smarm: 4 gush 7 slobber
smart: 4 bite, braw, chic, neat, posh, smug, trig, wily, wise 5 acute, alert, brisk, clean,

fresh, natty, nifty, quick, sharp, sting, witty 6 active, astute, bright, cheesy, clever, dressy, jaunty, lively, shrewd, spruce, suffer, swanky 7 capable, knowing, pungent, stylish 8 spirited, talented, vigorous 9 competent, dexterous 10 precocious 11 fashionable, intelligent

smarten: 6 spruce 7 improve 8 brighten, titivate

smash: hit 4 bash, blow, bung, dash, ruin 5 break, crash, crush, stave, wreck 7 destroy, shatter, smash-up, success 8 collapse, stramash(Sc.) 9 collision 10 bankruptcy

smashup: 4 ruin 5 wreck 6 defeat 7 failure 8 collapse 9 collision 10 bankruptcy

smatter: 4 smut, spot 5 break 6 babble, dabble, defile 7 chatter, clatter, crackle, shatter, spatter 9 fragments

smatterer: 7 dabbler 8 sciolist

smear: dab, rub 4 blot, blur, daub, gaum, soil, spot, stop 5 clart, cleam, slake, slare, stain, sully 6 anoint, bedaub, blotch, defame, defeat, defile, grease, malign, smirch, smudge, spread, thwart 7 besmear, plaster, pollute, slander, splatch 8 besmirch, ointment, slaister 9 overwhelm 10 overspread

smearcase: 6 cheese

smeared: 4 foul 6 greasy

smeary: 6 greasy, soiled, sticky 7 smeared

smectic: 9 detergent, purifying

smeddum: 4 dust 5 flour, vigor 6 powder, spirit

smeech: 4 dust 5 smell, smoke, stink, vapor

smeek: 4 reek 5 smoke

smell: 4 funk, fust, odor, olid, reek 5 aroma, fetor, flair, scent, sniff, trace 6 breath 7 hircine, noisome, perfume 9 fragrance 10 suggestion 11 graveolence

comb. form: 4 osmo

having a disagreeable: bad 4 foul, olid, 5 fetid 10 malodorous

loss of sense: 7 anosmia

offensive: 4 reek 5 fetor, nidor, stink 6 stench

pert. to: 9 olfactory

pleasant: 5 aroma 7 perfume

stale: 5 fusty, musty

smell-feast: 7 sponger 8 parasite

smeller: 4 nose 6 feeler 7 antenna, bristle

smelling salts: 9 hartshorn

smelt: 4 fish, flux, fuse, melt, prim 6 iuanga(N.Z.), reduce, refine 7 scorify

smelting: *by-product:* 4 slag

cone: 4 pina

smew: 4 duck 9 merganser

smicker: 5 smile, smirk

smidge, smidgen: bit 4 mite

smile: 4 beam, grin 5 smirk, sneer 6 arride, simper

smirch: 4 blot 5 asoil, smear, stain, sully, taint 6 blotch, smudge, smutch 7 begrime, blacken, blemish, tarnish 8 besmirch, discolor, dishonor

smirched: 5 dingy

smirk: 4 leer, trim, yirn 5 quick, smart, smile 6 simper, spruce 7 grimace, smiling

smit: cut, hit 4 blow, smut, spot 5 brand, stain 6 infect, smirch, stroke, struck 7 tarnish 8 disgrace, punished

smite: hit 4 blow, clap, cuff, gird, hurl, kill, pass, slap, slay, swat 5 blast, knock, skite 6 attack, buffet, defeat, hammer, pierce, punish, strike 7 afflict, chasten, collide, destroy, disease, impress, inspire 8 distress

smith: 6 forger 7 farrier 10 blacksmith 11 metalworker

smithcraft: 6 smithy 8 smithery

smithereens: 4 bits 5 atoms 6 pieces 8 flinders 9 fragments

smithy: 6 forger 7 farrier 10 blacksmith

smitten: 8 affected, enamored, stricken 9 afflicted, enamoured

smock: 5 kamis, shift, tunic 6 camise 7 chemise 11 overgarment

smog: fog 4 mist

smoke: 4 floc, fume, funk, haze, mist, pipe, smog 5 cigar, cubeb, segar, smook(Sc.), vapor 6 smudge 7 cheroot, cigaret 9 cigarette

fragrant: 7 incense

outlet: 7 chimney 8 fumoduct, fumiduct

wisp: 4 floc

smoke out: 5 flush 6 reveal 8 discover

smokejack: 6 funnel

smokeless powder: 6 poudre

smoker: car 4 stag 5 party

smokestack: 4 pipe 6 funnel 7 chimney

smoking equipment: 7 nargile, tabagie

smoky: 4 hazy 5 dingy, fumid 6 fumish 9 fumacious

smolder, smoulder: 5 choke, smoke 6 smudge 7 smother 9 suffocate

smolt: 4 calm 5 clear 6 bright, salmon, smooth

smoodge, smooge: pat 6 pamper 7 wheedle

smooth: 4 clam, ease, easy, even, gleg, glib, iron, lene, mild, pave, sand 5 bland, brent, furry, glace, glary, gloze, level, plane, preen, press, quiet, silky, sleek, slick, soapy, suave 6 creamy, evenly, fluent, glassy, glossy, mangle, serene, sleeky 7 amiable, equable, erugate, flatten, plaster, sadiron 8 explicit, friendly, glabrous, levigate, palliate, pleasant, polished,

soothing **9** courteous, unruffled **10** flattering **11** alabastrine **12** frictionless, ingratiating **13** mellifluently, uninterrupted
combining form: lio
phonetically: **4** lene
smoother: 7 abraser
smorgasbord item: 4 eels
smot: 4 mark **5** brand, stain
smote: hit **7** chasten
smother: 5 choke, smoor, smore **6** stifle, welter **7** overlie, smolder, turmoil **8** suppress **9** suffocate
smudge: 4 blot, blur, smug, smut, soil, soot **5** laugh, prink, smear, smile, stain **6** smutch **7** begrime, chuckle, smolder
smug: dig **4** neat, prig, tidy, trim **5** clean, grind, smart, steal, suave **6** pilfer, spruce **7** correct **9** confident **10** blacksmith, complacent **13** selfsatisfied
smuggler: 6 runner
smurr, smur: 4 mist **5** cloud **7** drizzle
smut: 4 bunt, coom, mark, soil, spot **5** coomb, grime, stain, sully, taint **6** blight, defile, smudge **8** colbrand **9** obscenity
smutch: 4 blot, dirt, smut, soot, spot **5** grime, stain, sully, taint, tinge, touch, trace **6** defile, smudge **7** blacken
smutty: 5 dirty, dusky, sooty **6** soiled, sordid **7** obscene, tainted **8** indecent
Smyrna: 5 Izmir
fig: **5** eleme, elemi
smytrie: 6 litter **10** collection
snack: bit, sip **4** ball, bite, jibe, part, snap **5** acute, alert, chack, lunch, quick, seize, share, smack, taste **6** adroit, morsel, repast, snatch **7** portion, quickly, sharply, teatime **8** grasping, snappish
snaffle: bit **4** loot **5** check, steal **6** pilfer **7** saunter, snuffle **8** restrain **9** restraint
snafu: 4 awry **6** muddle **8** disorder, entangle **9** confusion
snag: cut, hew, nag, nub **4** base, carp, knot, part, slug, tear, tine, tree, trim, unit **5** break, catch, point, snail, stump, tooth **6** branch, damage, hazard, tongue **8** obstacle **9** hindrance **10** difficulty, impediment **11** obstruction **12** protuberance
snagger: 8 billhook
snail: 4 slug, snag, wilk **5** drone, mitra **6** dodman, tritou, winkle **7** driller, mollusk, testudo **8** escargot, neritine, sluggard **9** gastropod **10** hoddy-doddy
clam-killing: **6** winkle
genus of: **5** fusus **6** nerita **9** clausilla
pond: **5** coret
shell: **7** cochlea
snailflower: 7 caracol
snake: asp, boa, bom, esp, nag **4** bind, boma, curl, drag, draw, naga, skid, tail, turn, wind, worm **5** aboma, adder, arrow, braid, cobra, coral, crawl, cribo, filch, kriat, mamba, racer, sneak, steal, viper **6** katuka, python **7** bokadam, camoodi, elapine, hagworm, ingrate, meander, rattler, reptile, serpent **8** anaconda, bungarum, camoodie, moccasin, ophidian, ringhals **9** whipsnake **10** blacksnake, bushmaster, copperhead, massasauga, sidewinder **11** cottonmouth, rattlesnake **12** schaapsteker
big: boa **6** python **8** anaconda **11** constrictor
comb. form: **4** ophi **5** ophio
expert: **13** herpetologist
genus of: boa **7** ophidia
horned: **8** cerastes
killer: **7** mongoos **8** mongoose
marine: **6** chital
movement: **7** slither
mythological: See **serpent**
poison: **5** venom
resembling: **8** viperine
sea: **6** kerril
sound: **4** hiss **6** rattle
suborder: **6** asinea
snake charmer's flute: 5 pungi
snake dancers: 4 Hopi, Taos **5** Moqui
snake doctor: 9 dragonfly **12** hellgrammite
snake-haired woman: 6 Gorgon, Medusa, Stheno **7** Euryale
snake killer: 7 mongoos **8** mongoose
snake-shaped: 9 anguiform
snakeberry: 6 byrony **9** baneberry **11** bittersweet **14** partridge-berry
snakebird: 7 anhinga, wryneck
snakebite antidote: 5 guaco
snakeflower: 7 campion **8** blueweed **10** starflower, stitchwort
snakehead: 7 figwort **10** turtlehead
snakelike: 5 snaky **8** ophidian **9** colubrine **10** anguineous
fish: eel
snakemouth: 6 orchid
snakeroot: 6 seneca, senega **7** sangrel **9** birthwort **10** bitter-bush
snakeskin: 6 exuvia
snakestone: 8 ammonite
snaky: sly **4** evil, wavy **5** angry **6** touchy **7** anguine, sinuous, winding, wriggly **8** spiteful, twisting, venomous **9** snakelike **10** perfidious, serpentine **11** exasperated, treacherous
snap: bit, rod **4** bark, bite, knap, lirp, pass, shut **5** break, catch, chack, cheat, cinch, close, crack, filip, flask, flick, ganch, grasp, hanch, quick, scrap, seize, sever, smart, snack, spell, stamp, steal, vigor, wafer **6** biting, cloyer, cookie, energy, fillip, morsel, report, retort, snatch **7** capture, cozener, crackle, project, sharper, sparkle **8** interval, puncheon, sinecure, snapshot **9** crackling, crispness, fastening,

handcuffs, interrupt, smartness, snatching 10 gingersnap 11 scintillate
with finger: 6 fillip

snape: nip 4 snub 5 bevel, check, stint, taper 6 rebuke 7 snaping 8 beveling 10 disappoint

snapper: 4 bean, sesi 5 error 6 beetle, bonbon, turtle 7 cosoque, stumble, whopper 8 cachucho, fastener 9 castanets 10 stitchwort, woodpecker 11 firecracker, glassworker, phainopepla
black-fin: 4 sesi

snappish: 4 edgy, tart 5 crisp, cross, short, testy 7 brittle, cutting, peevish, uncivil 8 petulant 9 fractious, irascible, irritable 12 sharp-tongued

snappy: 4 frim 5 brisk, quick, sharp, smart 6 strong, sudden 7 stylish 8 pungency 9 briskness, copacetic, smartness

snapshot: 4 shot 5 photo 10 photograph

snare: bag, gin, net, pit, web 4 fang, grin, lure, mesh, toil, trap 5 benet, brake, catch, grasp, noose, steal 6 ambush, cobweb, entice, entoil, entrap, gilder, tangle, trapan, trepan 7 ensnare, involve, overnet, pitfall 8 entangle, inveigle 9 deception 12 entanglement

snarer: 6 spider 7 trapper

snark: 6 boojum

snarl: arr, gin 4 carl, girn, gnar, harl, hurr, knot, yarr, yirr 5 anvil, catch, ganch, gnarl, gnarr, growl, noose, scold, snare 6 tangle 7 confuse, ensnare, grizzle, grumble, involve, quarrel 8 complain, entangle 9 confusion 10 complicate 12 complication

snarly: 5 cross, surly 7 peevish, snarled, tangled 8 confused, snarling 10 illnatured 11 bad-tempered

snash: 5 abuse 6 gibing 9 insolence

snatch: bit, get, hap, nab 4 grab, snap, take, trap, yerk 5 braid, catch, clawk, cleek, erept, grasp, gripe, pluck, seize, snare, spell, stint, swipe, wrest 6 clutch, kidnap, remove, twitch 7 excerpt, grabble 8 fragment

snatchy: 9 irregular, spasmodic 11 interrupted 12 disconnected

snath, snathe: lop 5 prune, shaft, snead 6 handle

sneak: 4 lurk 5 filch, miche, peach, skulk, slink, snoop, steal 6 coward, cringe, pilfer, snudge, tattle 9 fefnicute

sneaking: sly 4 mean, poor 6 craven, hidden, paltry, secret 7 furtive, hangdog 8 cowardly, stealthy 9 dastardly, niggardly, underhand 12 contemptible 13 surreptitious

sneap: spy 5 check, chide, snape, sneak

sneb: bar 4 bolt, snub 6 fasten, rebuke 9 reprimand

sneck: 5 catch, click, close, latch 6 fasten

sned: lop 5 prune

snee: cut 4 dirk 5 knife 6 dagger

sneer: 4 gibe, gird, grin, jeer, mock 5 fleer, fling, flird, flout, flurn, scoff, slare, snirl, snort 7 grimace, snicker 8 belittle, ridicule

sneesh: 5 snuff

sneeze: 5 neese(Sc.) 7 kerchoo 12 sternutation
pert. to: 7 errhine 12 sternutatory

sneezewort: 8 ptarmica, ptarmite 10 gesundheit

snell: 4 hard, keen 5 acute, eager, harsh, quick, sharp, smart, snood, swift 6 active, biting, clever, leader, severe 7 caustic, extreme, pungent, quickly, swiftly 8 piercing 10 vigorously

snib: bar 4 bolt, snub 5 catch, check, snuff 6 entrap, fasten, rebuff, rebuke 7 capture 8 restrain 9 fastening, reprimand

snick: cut, hit 4 blow, draw, kink, knot, move, nick, snip 5 click, notch, share, shoot, snack 6 pierce, strike 8 snicking

snicker: 5 knife, laugh, neigh, sneer, snirl 6 giggle, nicker, titter, whinny

snide: low, sly 4 base, mean 6 tricky 8 inferior, spurious 9 malicious

sniff: 4 nose 5 scent, smell, snuff 6 detect, inhale 7 sniffle 8 perceive 9 recognize

sniffy: 8 scornful 10 disdainful 12 contemptuous, supercilious

snifter: 4 blow, dram, good 5 drink, sniff, snort, storm 6 moment, snivel 7 dilemma, reverse 9 excellent

snig: eel, lop 4 chop, drag, jerk 5 snake, sneak 6 pilfer

snigger: 6 giggle 7 snicker

sniggle: 7 broggle

snip: bit, cut 4 clip, curb, snap 5 check, filch, notch, piece, shred, snack 6 snatch, stripe, stroke, tailor 8 fragment, incision, particle 9 disfigure

snipe: 4 bird, butt, fool 5 skunk 10 sharpshoot
cry: 5 scape
flock: 5 whisp

snipe hawk: 7 harrier

sniper: 8 ambusher

snippy: 4 curt, mean, tart 5 brief, sharp 6 sniffy, stingy 8 snappish, snippety 11 closefisted, fragmentary 12 supercilious

snirl: 5 gnarl, snare, sneer, snort 6 tangle 7 snicker, wrinkle

snirt: 5 sneer, snort 7 snicker

snitch: 4 nose, tell 5 catch, peach, pinch, steal, thief 6 betray, inform, pilfer, smitch, snatch 8 informer, particle

snivel: cry 4 cant, fret 5 sniff, whine 6 pathos 7 emotion, snuffle 8 complain
snivy, snivey: 4 mean, ugly 8 contrary
snob: sob 4 aper, scab 5 toady 6 flunky 7 cobbler, cricket, flunkey, parvenu, plebian, shoneen, upstart 8 blackleg, bluenose, commoner, parvenue, townsman 9 pretender, shoemaker 10 fivestones
snobbish: 7 high-hat 11 overbearing
snod: 4 neat, snug, trim 6 smooth 7 cunning, trimmed 9 plausible
snood: bad, hat, tie 4 bind 5 braid 6 fasten, fillet, ribbon 7 hairnet
snook: pry 5 smell, sneak, sniff 6 follow, robalo, search 7 snuffle 9 barracuda
snool: cow 4 snub 6 craven, cringe
snoop: pry 4 look, nose, peek, peep 5 sneak 6 search 8 busybody
snooper: 7 marplot, meddler 8 busybody
snoot: 4 face, nose 7 grimace
snooty: 7 haughty 8 snobbish 10 hoity-toity 12 contemptuous, supercilious
snooze: nap 4 doze 5 sleep 6 drowse, siesta 7 snoozle
snoozle: 4 doze 5 sleep 6 cuddle, nuzzle, snooze 7 snuggle
snore: 4 rout 5 snork, snort
snoring: 5 stiff 7 roaring, stertor 10 stertorous
snork: pig 5 grunt, snore, snort
snort: 4 rout 5 drink, grunt, laugh, snirl, snore, snork
snotty: 5 dirty, nasty, slimy 6 offish, snooty 7 haughty, viscous 8 impudent, snotlike 9 offensive 12 contemptible, supercilious
snouch: 4 jibe, snub 5 taunt
snout: neb 4 mull, nose 5 groin, spout, trunk 6 nozzle 7 rostrum, tobacco
snout-nose: 7 gruntle 9 proboscis
snow: sna 4 grue, snaw(Sc.) 5 blizz, cover, opium 6 heroin 7 cocaine 8 obstruct 9 whiteness
glacial: 4 firn, neve
granular: 4 corn
half-melted: 5 slush
house: 4 iglu 5 igloo
living in: 5 neval
mushy: 4 slob
resembling: 7 niveous
slide: 8 glissade 9 avalanche
vehicle: 4 pung, sled 6 sleigh
wedding: 4 rice
snow and rain: 5 sleet
snow flurry: 5 skirl
snow goose: 4 chen 5 brant, wavey
snow grouse: 9 ptarmigan
snow mass: 9 avalanche
snow ridges: 8 sastrugi, zastrugi
snow runner: ski 4 skee
snowflake: 4 bird 5 finch 7 crystal
snowshoe: pac, ski 4 skee
snowstorm: 8 blizzard
snowy: 4 pure 5 nival, white 8 spotless, unsoiled
snub: cut, nip 4 chip, curb, slap, stop 5 check, frump, quell, scold, snool 6 ignore, rebuff, rebuke, remark, retort, slight, tauten 7 affront, neglect, repress, upbraid 8 restrain 9 interrupt, reprimand
snudge: 4 sulk 5 miser, sneak
snuff: 4 odor 5 pinch, pique, scent, smell, sniff, snort 6 detect, inhale 7 offense, umbrage 10 extinguish
kind of: 5 musty 6 rappee 8 bergamot, Maccaboy 10 blackguard, Copenhagen
snuff box: 4 mill, mull 9 tabatiere
snuffy: 5 sulky, vexed 6 horrid 7 annoyed 10 displeased 12 disagreeable, unattractive
snug: 4 bein, bien, cosh, cozy, neat, safe, tidy, trim, warm 5 close, quiet, tight 6 modest, secure, silent 7 compact, snuggle 8 reticent, secreted 9 concealed, seaworthy, secretive 10 prosperous 11 comfortable
snuggery: den
snuggle: 4 nest 6 cuddle, nestle
snugly: 6 cosily
sny: 4 bend 5 swarm 6 abound
so: sae, sic, sua 4 ergo, thus, very 5 hence 7 because 9 therefore 11 accordingly 12 consequently
so be it: 4 amen
so far: yet 4 thus
soak: dip, hit, ret, sog, sop, sot, wet 4 bate, blow, bowk, buck, hurl, ooze, pawn, sock 5 drink, drouk, imbue, punch, souse, spree, steep 6 drench, imbibe, imbrue, seethe 8 drunkard, macerate, permeate, saturate 9 distemper, percolate 10 impregnate, instructor, overcharge
flax: ret
in brine: 4 corn, salt 8 marinate
soaked: wet 6 sodden
soaking: 4 slow 6 gentle 7 soakage
soap: 4 sape, sapo 5 money, savon 6 lather 7 cleanse, flatter 8 flattery 9 detergent
convert into: 8 saponify
frame bar: 4 sess
mottled: 7 castile 8 eschwege
pharmaceutical: 4 sapo
plate: 4 sess
substitute: 5 amole, borax
soap plant: 5 amole 8 soapwort
soapmaking substance: lye
soapstone: 4 talc 8 steatite
full of: 7 talcose
soapweed: 5 yucca

soapy: 4 oily, soft 5 suave 6 smooth 7 saponic 8 lathered, unctuous 9 soapsuddy 10 latherable 11 saponaceous 12 ingratiating
soar: fly 4 lift, rise, sail 5 float, glide, hover, mount, plane 6 ascend, aspire 9 transcend
sob: cry, yex 4 sigh, soak, wail, weep 6 boohoo 7 whimper 8 frighten
sober: 4 calm, cool, poor, sane 5 douce, grave, quiet, staid 6 ailing, feeble, gentle, humble, sedate, severe, simple, solemn, somber, steady, subdue, temper 7 chasten, earnest, regular, serious, subdued 8 composed, decorous, moderate, peaceful, rational 9 abstinent, collected, temperate 10 abstemious 11 indifferent 13 unimpassioned, unpretentious
soberly: sad 5 grave 8 demurely
sobol: 5 sable 6 marten
soboles: 5 shoot 6 stolon, sucker
sobriety: 7 gravity 9 restraint, soberness, solemnity, soundness 10 abstinence, moderation, sedateness, temperance 11 seriousness 14 reasonableness
sobriquet, soubriquet: 4 name 5 alias, chuck, title 6 byname 7 affront, epithet 8 nickname 11 appellation
soc: 12 jurisdiction
soccer player: 6 booter
sociability: 10 affability
sociable: 4 cozy, sofa 6 chummy, social 7 affable 8 carriage, familiar, friendly, informal, tricycle 9 aeroplane, agreeable, reception 10 accessible, gregarious 13 communicative, companionable
social: tea 4 stag 5 party 6 smoker 9 agreeable, convivial, gathering 10 gregarious 13 companionable
affair: tea 4 ball 6 soiree 9 reception
career beginning: 5 debut
climber: 4 snob 7 parvenu, upstart
gathering: bee, tea 4 club, stag 5 party 6 smoker 7 reunion 9 reception
group: 4 clan, club 5 caste, class, lodge, tribe 6 estate, family 7 coterie
insect: bee
outcast: 5 leper 6 pariah
person: 4 host 5 mixer 7 hostess
system: 6 feudal, modern, regime, tribal 11 traditional
worker: 7 analyst 8 do-gooder 9 clinician
socialism: 9 Communism 10 utopianism 13 Manchesterism
socialist: Red 9 Anarchist, communist 10 Bolshevist 11 nationalist 12 collectivist
socialize: 6 mingle
society (see also **organization**): 4 bund, clan, gild 5 guild, order, union 6 menage 7 academy, company, hetaera, hetaira 8 academie, alliance 9 accademie, community 10 connection 11 association, cooperation, intercourse, partnership 12 denomination, relationship 13 companionship, confederation, confraternity, participation
girl: deb
low (member): 4 raff 8 riff-raff
kind of: 4 SPCA, frat, Tong 5 elite, order, choir 7 societe 8 sorority 10 fraternity
secret: Hui 4 tong, egbo 5 mafia, lodge 6 maffia, ogboni 7 Camorra 9 Carbonari
symbol: 7 regalia
Society Island: 6 Tahiti
tree: 5 aitoa
Society of Friends: 7 Quakers
founder: Fox
sociology: 8 demotics
sock: hit, sew, udo 4 beat, blow, hurl, shoe, sigh, vamp 5 drive 6 anklet, buskin, comedy, sandal, strike 7 slipper, socking 8 drainage, stocking 9 plowshare
symbol of tragedy: 6 buskin
sockdolager: 4 oner 8 finisher
socket: 5 lance, spear 6 budget, cavity, collet, hollow 7 opening 9 plowshare
kind of: pan 4 birn 5 orbit 8 alveolus
Socrates: *biographer:* 5 Plato
dialogue: 4 Meno 6 Phaedo 8 Apologia
escape plotter: 5 Crito
love: 10 philosophy, Alcibiades
wife: 8 Xantippe 9 Xanthippe
sod: 4 delf, dove, flag, peat, soak, turf 5 delft, divot, glebe, soggy, sward 6 saddle, sodden 7 stratum 9 fermented
pert. to: 8 alkaline
soda: sal 8 beverage 9 saleratus
sodalite: 5 lenad
sodality: 5 union, unity 6 chapel 10 fellowship, fraternity 11 association, brotherhood 13 companionship
sodden: 5 drunk, heavy, moist, sammy, soggy 6 boiled, dulled, soaked, stewed, stupid 7 bloated, drunken, steeped 8 spirited 9 saturated 11 intoxicated
sodium: 7 natrium
carbonate: 4 soda 5 borax, trona 6 natron 7 salsoda
chlorate: 5 NaClo
chloride: sal, tar 4 salt 7 saltcat
compound: 4 soda
nitrate: 5 niter
tetraborate: 5 borax
Sodom: *king:* 4 Bera
neighbor: 8 Gomorrah
sodomite: 6 bugger
sofa: 5 boist, couch, divan 6 lounge, settee 7 bergere, dosados 8 causeuse 9 davenport 12 chesterfield
soft: coy, low 4 feil, fine, limp, mild, saft(Sc.), waxy, weak 5 bland, cushy, downy, dolce, dulce, faint, givey, hooly, mushy, piano,

sooth 6 clammy, dreamy, fluffy, gentle, gently, placid, silken, smooth, tender 7 clement, ductile, lenient, lightly, quietly, squashy, subuded 8 delicate, feminine, flexible, tranquil 9 temperate, tractable, untrained 10 effeminate, peacefully 11 sympathetic 12 nonalcoholic 13 compassionate
and smooth: 5 furry, silky, soapy 6 mellow, supple 7 cottony
and sweet: 5 dolce 6 dulcet
and wet: 5 mushy 7 squashy
food: pap
mass: 4 pulp
music: 5 dulce, piano
palate: 4 cion 5 uvula, velum
soap: 4 gush 7 blarney, flatter, wheedle 8 flattery 9 wheedling
soft drink: ade, pop 4 soda 5 tonic
softa: 7 student 8 beginner
soften: 4 ease, melt 5 allay, malax, relax, yield 6 affect, anneal, gentle, pacify, relent, soothe, subdue, temper, weaken 7 amolish, appease, assuage, mollify 8 attemper, enervate, enfeeble, lenitive, macerate, mitigate, modulate 9 alleviate, emolliate, meliorate 10 emasculate, intenerate 11 tranquilize
softening: 7 lenient 8 emulsive 9 demulcent 11 melioration
of brain: 8 dementia
of decayed fruit: 4 blet
soft-spoken: 4 mild 5 bland, suave 6 gentle, smooth 12 ingratiating
softhearted: 6 tender 13 tenderhearted
softheartedness: 4 pity
softly: low 4 soft 5 piano, sotto 6 fairly, gentle, gently 7 foolish, quietly 10 spiritless 13 unobtrusively
softness: 10 tenderness
sog: 4 soak 6 drowse 8 saturate
soggy: wet 4 damp 5 heavy 6 soaked, sodden, watery 9 saturated
soigne, soignee: 4 neat, tidy 5 sleek 11 well-groomed
soil: 4 blot, blur, daub, dirt, foil, grit, land, moil, mool, slur, spot 5 dirty, earth, filth, glebe, grime, smear, solum, stain, sully 6 assoil, bedaub, befile, befoul, bemire, defile, grease, ground, refuse, sewage, smirch, smudge 7 begrime, benasty, besmear, corrupt, pollute, tarnish 8 alluvium, besmirch, disgrace 9 bedraggle, bespatter, droppings, excrement 11 contaminate
claylike: 4 marl
comb. form: geo 4 agro
goddess of: 7 Demeter
kind of: 4 clay, loam, marl, lair, malm, moss 5 adobe, loess, groot, humus
organic: 5 humus
soiled: 4 foul 5 dingy, grimy 6 smeary
soilure: 5 stain 6 smirch
soiree: 5 party 6 affair
sojourn: 4 bide, howf, rest, stay 5 abide, abode, delay, dwell, howff, lodge, tarry, visit 6 reside, travel 7 allodge, mansion 8 abidance 9 residence 11 peregrinate
sojourner: 7 boarder 8 comeling
sol: sun 4 gold 6 sun-god 7 Phoebus
solace: 5 allay, amuse, cheer 6 lessen, relief, soothe 7 assuage, comfort, console 9 alleviate, diversion, entertain 10 recreation, relaxation 11 alleviation, consolation
solacing: 6 dulcet
solan: 4 fowl 5 goose 6 gannet
solar, soler, sollar: 4 room 5 floor, story 6 garret, heliac, tropic 7 chamber 8 heliacal 9 apartment
deity: Su; Shu
disk: 4 aten, aton
excess over lunar year: 5 epact
solar system: *member:* 6 planet
model: 6 orrery
sold (see also **sell**): 8 marketed
solder: 4 fuse, join, mend 5 braze, patch, unite 6 cement
soldering: *flux:* 5 resin, rosin
piece: lug
soldier: man, vet 4 fogy, swad 5 fogey, guffy, poilu, sammy, shirk 6 galoot, marine, Zouave 7 brigand, feedman, fighter, hobbler, hotspur, palikar, private, regular, trooper, veteran, warrior 8 buffcoat, cavalier, gendarme, malinger, servitor, tolpatch, shackman 9 grenadier, musketeer
detachment: 4 file
drinking flask: 7 canteen
female: 6 W.A.C.
foreign: 4 peon, kern 5 nezam, poilu, sepoy, kerne, spahi 6 sapper, lascar, askari 7 cateran, hoplite, Billjim 8 grognard, miquelet 10 base wallah, carmagnole, carabineer
group of: 4 band, file 5 corps, force, squad, troop 7 brigade, caterva, company, platoon 8 division 9 battalion
mercenary: 7 Hessian, Swisser, Switzer
newly-trained: 5 cadet, plebe, rooky 6 rookie 7 chicken, recruit, trainee 8 bezonian 11 replacement
of fortune: 10 adventurer
old: vet 7 veteran
overcoat: 6 capote
quarters: 7 billets 8 barracks
special functions: 6 lancer, sapper 7 velites, dragoon, trooper 8 fencible, fugleman 9 fantassin, targeteer, flugelman 10 cuiras-

sier, velitation, carabineer, carabinier 12 antesignanus

trenching tools: 8 burgoyne

vacation: 4 pass 5 leave 8 furlough

soldierly: 5 brave 6 heroic 7 martial

sole: 4 dish, fish, foot, lone, mere, only, yoke 5 afald, alone, floor, plate, slade 6 bottom, entire, furrow, halter, hearth, lonely, single, unique, valley 7 outsole, subsoil 8 desolate, flatfish, isolated, solitary, unshared 9 exclusive, threshold, unmarried, unmatched 10 foundation, underframe, unsharable, windowsill

foot: 4 vola 5 pelma

part: 5 shank

pert. to: 7 plantar

solecism: 9 barbarism, deviation 11 impropriety

solely: all 4 only 5 alone 6 merely, singly 8 entirely 9 allenarly 11 exclusively

solement: 4 only 6 solely

solemn: sad 5 budge, grave, sober, usual 6 august, devout, formal, gloomy, ritual, sacred, severe, somber 7 earnest, serious, stately 8 funereal, splendid 9 customary, dignified, sumptuous 10 ceremonial, devotional, noteworthy 11 reverential 13 distinguished

solemnity: 7 gravity 8 ceremony

solemnization: 9 celebrity

solemnize: 5 exalt, marry 7 dignify, glorify, observe 9 celebrate 11 commemorate

solenodon: 6 agouta 7 almique

soler: 7 cobbler 9 shoemaker

solert: 6 crafty 8 skillful

solicit: ask, beg, woo 4 bark, plea, seek, tout 5 court, crave, mooch, tempt 6 accost, entice, incite, invite, manage 7 beseech, canvass, entreat, forward, implore, request 8 campaign, disquiet, petition 9 importune, panhandle, prosecute 10 supplicate

solicitor: 4 tout 6 barker 8 attorney

chambers: 4 inns

solicitous: 5 eager 7 careful 8 desirous, troubled 9 attentive, concerned 10 thoughtful 12 apprehensive

solicitude: 4 care, coda, ease, fear, heed, yeme 7 anxiety, concern 8 business 11 carefulness 12 apprehension

solid: 4 cone, cube, firm, full, hard 5 cubic, dense, level, sound, stiff 6 bodily, sphere, stable, strong 7 bedrock, compact, uniform, weighty 8 constant, reliable, sterling, unbroken 9 estimable 10 consistent, dependable, inflexible 11 homogeneous, responsible, substantial, trustworthy

comb. form: 6 stereo

geometrical: 4 cone, cube 5 prism 7 pyramid 8 cylinder 11 heptahedron, pentahedron 12 dodecahedron

solidified: 8 hardened

solidify: gel, set 4 cake 6 cement, harden 7 compact 8 concrete, condense 9 coagulate 11 consolidate, crystallize

solidity: 8 firmness, hardness 9 solidness, soundness, stability 11 compactness, consistency 13 dependability

solidly: 10 completely

solidum: sum 4 dado

soliloquy: 4 poem 9 discourse, monologue, utterance

solitaire: 4 game 6 hermit, lonely 7 diamond, recluse 8 Canfield, patience, solitary 9 neckcloth

solitary: 4 hole, lone, monk, sole 5 alone 6 hermit, lonely, remote, simple, single 7 dungeon, eremite, recluse 8 desolate, lonesome, solitary 10 individual 12 unfrequented

combining form: 5 eremo

solitude: 6 dearth, desert 7 expanse, privacy, retreat 8 soleness 9 isolation, seclusion 10 loneliness, remoteness, retirement, uniqueness, wilderness 12 solitariness

solo: air 4 aria 5 alone, scena, radel 6 strain

accompaniment: 8 obligato 9 obbligato

soloist: 6 cantor, singer 7 aviator

Solomon: *ally:* 5 Hiram

father: 5 David

gold obtained from: 5 Ophir

mother: 9 Bathsheba

son: 8 Rehoboam

temple: 6 shamir

Solomon Islands: 4 Buka, Gizo, Savo

gulf: 4 Huon, Kula

volcano: 5 Balbi

Solon: 4 sage 7 senator 8 lawmaker 9 publicist 10 legislator

soluble: 4 frim 6 solute

solus: 5 alone

solute: 4 free 5 loose, solve 7 arrange, soluble 8 dissolve, separate 9 dissolved 13 disintegrated

solution: key 6 answer 8 analysis 9 discharge, releasing 10 denouement, resolution 11 deliverance, explanation 14 disintegration 15 disentanglement.

kinds of: lye 5 brine, eusol, iodin, titer, sirup, syrup 6 iodine, phenol

strength of: 5 titer

solve: 4 free, undo 5 break 6 assoil, fathom, unfold 7 explain, resolve, unravel 8 dissolve 9 interpret 11 disentangle

solvent: 8 solution 9 detergent

Somaliland: *city:* 7 Berbera 8 Mogdisho

coin: 4 besa
measure: top 4 caba 5 chela, darat, tabla 6 cubito
weight: 8 parsalah
Somalis division: 6 Hawiya
Somalis Proper: 4 Asha
somatic: 5 somal 6 bodily 8 parietal, physical 9 corporeal 13 somatopleuric
somber, sombre: sad 4 dark, dern, dull 5 dusky, gloom, grave, sober 6 dismal, gloomy, lenten, severe, solemn 7 austere 9 depressed 10 depressing, melancholy
sombrero: hat 8 headgear, sunshade
some: any, few, one 4 part 5 about 7 portion, several 13 approximately
somersault: 4 flip
something: 5 drink 6 liquor 7 aliquid 8 beverage, somewhat
sometime: 4 late, once 6 former 7 quondam 8 formerly 12 occasionally
somewhat: 6 rather 7 aliquid 9 something
Somme city: 6 Amiens
sommelier: 6 butler 9 cellarman
somnambulism: 12 noctambulism
somnolent: 6 drowsy, sleepy
somnus: 5 sleep
son: ben 4 fils 5 child, scion 6 filius, Jesuit, native 8 disciple, follower 9 offspring 10 descendant
as in Welsh names: ap
foster: 7 alumnus
pert. to: 6 filial
Scot.: Mac
youngest: 5 cadet
son-in-law: 5 gener 8 beau-fils
Son of God: 6 Savior 7 Saviour
sonance: 4 tune 5 sound
sonant: 4 oral 5 tonic, vocal 6 voiced 8 sounding 9 intonated
sonata: *closing:* 4 coda
part: 5 rondo 7 scherzo
song: dit, lay, uta 4 aria, cant, dite, duan, fuss, glee, hymn, lied, lilt, noel, poem, tune 5 blues, canto, carol, chant, charm, ditty, lyric, melos, music, psalm, verse 6 ballad, cantic, cantus, canzon, carmen, chanty, clamor, himene, himine, melody, poetry, shanty, sonnet, strain, trifle 7 cancion, cantion, canzone, chantey, descant, shantey 8 canticle, pittance 9 cabaletta 11 composition
baby's: 7 lullaby
choral muse: 11 Terpischore
Christmas: 4 noel 5 carol
college: 4 glee
collection: 9 anthology 10 cancionero
evening: 6 vesper 8 evensong, serenade
folk: 5 blues 6 ballad
funeral: 5 dirge, elegy, elogy 6 elegie, lament, threne 7 elogium, epicede 8 epicedia, threnody 9 epicedium
gay: 4 lilt
German: 4 lied 6 lieder(pl.)
gypsy: 10 zingaresca
love: 6 amoret, ballad, serena 8 serenade
mountaineer's: 5 yodel
mourning: see *funeral* above
obscure: 4 rune
operatic: 4 aria
part: 5 canon, round 8 madrigal
pert. to.: 5 melic
sacred: 4 hymn 5 chant, motet, psalm 6 anthem 7 polymny
sailor's: 6 chanty, shanty 7 chantey, shantey 8 rumbelow 9 barcarole 10 barcarolle
simple: 5 ditty
solo: 4 glee
triumphal: 5 paean
wedding: 5 hymen
song-like: 6 ariose, arioso 7 lyrical
Song of Bernadette author: 6 Werfel
songbird: 4 lark, wren 5 mavie, mavis, robin, veery, vireo 6 canary, linnet, mocker, oriole, oscine, thrush 7 mocking, warbler 8 redstart
songman: 6 singer 7 gleeman 8 minstrel
songster: 4 poet 6 singer 7 chanter, warbler 8 songbird
songstress: 9 chantress
sonnet: 4 poem, song 5 octet, verse 6 sestet
conclusion: 6 sestet
sonority: 9 resonance
sonorous: 7 ringing 8 imposing, resonant 10 impressive
sons, sonse: 6 health 7 fortune 8 felicity 10 prosperity
sonsie, sonsy: 5 buxom, happy, lucky 6 comely 8 handsome, pleasing 9 plentiful 10 prosperous 11 comfortable
soodle: 6 stroll 7 saunter
soodly: 4 slow 9 leisurely
soogan: 4 rope 7 blanket
sook: 4 call 5 booth 6 market
soon: ere 4 anon, yern 5 early, later, quick, yerne 6 belive, rather, speedy 7 betimes, erelong, quickly, readily, shortly 8 directly, promptly, speedily 9 presently, willingly 10 beforetime 11 immediately
sooner: 4 erer, erst 6 before 9 Oklahoman
Sooner State: 8 Oklahoma
soot: 4 coom, smut, stup 5 colly, coomb, grime, sweet, smoke 6 carbon, gentle, smudge 7 blacken 9 melodious
particle: 4 isel, izle
pert. to: 10 fuliginous
sooth: 4 fact, real, soft, true 5 being, sweet, truly, truth 6 augury, smooth 7 comfort, genuine, present, proverb, reality 8 cajol-

ery, pleasing, pleasure, soothing, truthful 10 delightful 11 soothsaying, trustworthy 12 blandishment

soothe: coy, pat, pet 4 balm, calm, dill, ease, lull 5 accoy, allay, charm, dulce, quiet 6 pacify, soften, solace, stroke 7 appease, assuage, comfort, compose, console, demulce, flatter, mollify, placate, relieve 8 mitigate, palliate 9 alleviate, attempter 10 demulceate 11 tranquilize

soother: 4 balm 5 salve 9 emollient

soothing: 4 mild 5 balmy, downy, dulce 6 dreamy, dulcet, gentle 7 anodyne, calming 8 lenitive, sedative 9 appeasing, assuasive, demulcent 13 tranquilizing

soothsay: 4 omen 7 portent, predict, proverb 8 foretell

soothsayer: 4 seer 5 augur, weird, vates 6 ariole, mantis 7 augurer, diviner, prophet, seeress 8 haruspex, chaldean 10 hariolizer 14 prognosticator

sooty: 4 dark 5 black, colly, dusky 6 brokie 9 blackened 10 fuliginous

sop: 4 dunk, gift, heap, lump, mass, mess, soak, tuft 5 bribe, cloud, clump, steep 7 advance, milksop 8 saturate

sophism: 7 fallacy 8 argument

sophist: 7 casuist, teacher, thinker 10 paralogist 11 philosopher

sophistical: 6 captious 9 deceptive 11 adulterated

sophisticate: 5 alter, spoil 6 debase, garble 7 corrupt, falsify, mislead 10 adulterate

sophisticated: 4 wise 7 amended, refined, worldly 11 adulterated

sophistry: 6 deceit 7 fallacy, quibble, sophism 8 argument, trickery 9 deception

Sophocles play: 7 Oedipus

sophy: 4 sage 5 ruler, skill 6 wisdom 7 science 8 religion 9 personage 10 philosophy

sopie: 4 dram 5 drink

sopite: 5 draft, quash, quiet, sleep 6 drowsy 8 drooping

sopor: 5 sleep 6 stupor

soporific: 5 dwale 6 drowsy, opiate 8 hypnotic, narcotic 11 somniferous 12 somnifacient, somnivolency

soppy: wet 5 rainy 6 soaked 7 mawkish 8 drenched 11 sentimental

soprano: 6 singer, treble

operatic: 4 Lind 5 Freni, Patti 6 Callas 7 Nilsson

sora: 4 rail

sorcerer: 4 mage, magi 5 boyla, brujo, Goeta 6 boolya, wizard 7 warlock 8 conjurer, magician 11 necromancer, thaumaturge 13 thaumaturgist

sorceress: 5 Circe, Lamia, sibyl, witch 6 Gorgon 11 enchantress

sorcery: art, obe, obi 5 magic, obeah, spell 6 fetich, fetish, voodoo 8 pishogue, prestige 9 diablerie, diabolism 10 necromancy, witchcraft 11 enchantment

sordellina: 7 bagpipe

sordid: low 4 base, mean, vile 5 dirty, gross 6 chetif, filthy, menial 7 ignoble, selfish, servile, squalid 8 churlish, covetous, grasping, grewsome, gruesome, sluttish, wretched 9 mercenary, niggardly 10 avaricious, despicable, slatternly 12 contemptible

sordo: low 4 deaf, dull 5 muted

sordor: 5 dregs 6 refuse 10 sordidness

sore: 4 boil, buck, evil, harm, kibe, pain, sair 5 angry, blain, botch, grief, ulcer, vexed, wound, wrong 6 bitter, bruise, fester, severe, sorrel, sorrow, tender, touchy 7 angered, annoyed, disease, extreme, grieved, painful, penance, trouble, violent 8 abrasion, grievous, inflamed, offended, sickness 9 detriment, irritated, sensitive, suffering, ulcerated, vexatious 10 affliction, afflictive, contrition, difficulty, distressed, unpleasant 11 disgruntled, distressing 13 temperamental, oversensitive

sorehead: 5 loser 6 griper 10 malcontent

sorely: 7 greatly 8 severely, urgently 9 extremely, painfully, violently 10 grievously

soreness: 4 ache 8 severity, vexation, violence 11 painfulness 12 irritability

sorghum: 4 cush, dura, milo 5 batad, darso, durra, sorgo 7 shallu 8 feterita

sorite: 4 heap 10 collection

sorority: 4 club 7 society 10 fraternity, sisterhood

sorrel: oca 5 brown, horse, plant 6 oxalis 7 roselle

sorrow: rue, woe 4 bale, care, dole, harm, loss, sigh, teen, weal 5 devil, dolor, grief, mourn, rogue, scamp 6 grieve, lament, misery, plague, regret 7 sadness, trouble, waeness 8 calamity, distress, egrimony, mourning 9 adversity, penitence, suffering 10 affliction, compassion, contrition, discomfort, melancholy 11 lamentation, tribulation, unhappiness 12 wretchedness

over: 6 bemoan, bewail, lament 7 deplore

sorrowful: sad 4 teen 5 drear, sadly 6 dismal, dolent, dreary, rueful 7 doleful, grieved, unhappy 8 contrite, dolesome, dolorous, grievous, mournful 9 afflicted, plaintive 10 lamentable, melancholy 11 distressing 12 disconsolate

sorrowing: 11 penitential 13 commiserating

sorry: bad 4 hurt, mean, poor 5 vexed 6 dismal, gloomy, regret, repent 7 chagrin, painful, pitiful 8 contrite, grievous, mournful, penitent, wretched 9 afflicted, chagrined, miserable, mortified, regretful, worthless 10 apologetic, melancholy 12 contemptible, disappointed

sort: ilk, ill, lot, set, way 4 cull, gere, kind, part, race, rank, sift, suit, type 5 adapt, allot, batch, befit, breed, class, crowd, flock, genus, grade, group, order, swarm, vexed 6 adjust, assign, choose, garble, gender, manner, nature, punish, select 7 arrange, company, conform, fashion, quality, species, stripes, variety 8 classify, separate 9 character, disturbed 10 collection, distribute 11 accommodate, description

sorted: 6 chosen 8 assorted, selected 9 separated 10 classified

sortie: 4 knot 5 foray, sally 6 attack

sortilege: 7 sorcery 8 witchery 11 enchantment

sosh: jag 4 dash 5 drunk 11 intoxicated

soso: bad 4 poor 6 unwell 8 mediocre, middling, passable 9 tolerable 11 indifferent

soss: lap 4 mess, slop 5 plump, swill 6 muddle 7 heavily

sossle: 4 mess, slop 10 intoxicate

sot: 4 fool 5 child, fixed, toper, waste 6 befool, guzzle, tipple 7 dastard, foolish, sottish, stupefy, tippler, tosspot 8 drunkard, innocent, squander, stubborn 9 immovable, inebriate, obstinate, simpleton, swillbowl 10 winebibber

sotted: 5 bousy 8 besotted

sottish: 4 dull 6 stupid 7 doltish, drunken, foolish 9 senseless

sotto: 5 below, under

soubise: 5 sauce

soubrette: 4 maid 7 actress 11 entertainer, maidservant

soucar: 6 banker 8 merchant, straight 9 honorable

souchong: tea

soud: pay 4 join 5 unite 6 amount, enlist, fasten, solder 8 quantity 10 strengthen

soudagur: 8 merchant 10 shopkeeper

sough: die, sob 4 moan, sigh, whiz 5 chant, ditch, drain, rumor, whizz 6 murmur, report 7 breathe, moaning, whistle 8 singsong 9 murmuring

soul: ba; ame, God, ker 4 alma 5 atman, force, heart, saint 6 dibbuk, esprit, fervor, leader, pneuma, spirit 7 courage, essence 8 inspirer 10 embodiment, heartiness 11 anilopyrine 15 personification

loss: 9 perdition

personification: 6 Psyche

souled: 5 vital

soulless: 5 brute

sound: cry, din 4 birr, blow, bray, firm, good, hail, hale, rime, safe, sane, test, tone, true 5 alarm, blare, bruit(F.), chang, clang, fresh, grope, hoddy, inlet, legal, loyal, noise, plumb, probe, rhyme, solid, valid, whole 6 bedlam, bratte, clamor, entire, fathom, hearty, honest, hubbub, intact, measure, outcry, racket, report, robust, secure, stable, steven, strong, sturdy, tumult, uproar 7 bluster, clamour, clangor, clatter, clitter, clutter, examine, explore, healthy, hearing, measure, perfect, sonance, sputter 8 complete, flawless, orthodox, profound, reliable, shouting, splutter, thorough 9 honorable, undamaged 10 dependable, hullabaloo, scrutinize 11 trustworthy, undisturbed

amorous: coo

atonic: 4 surd

beating drum: 8 rataplan

bell-like: 4 ding 5 clang, knell 6 tinkle

breathing: 5 snore

bullet: zip 4 ping

buzzing: 4 whiz 5 whirr, whizz

cat's: mew 4 meow, mewl, purr

comb. form: 4 audi, phon 5 audio, phono

contemptuous: 5 snort

contented: 4 purr

derisive: boo 7 catcall

detection instrument: 10 hydrophone

discordant: 6 jangle 9 cacophony

distinctive: 6 timbre

donkey's: 4 bray 6 heehaw

dove's murmuring: 4 curr

drum: 4 roll

dry leaves: 6 rustle

elephant's: 4 roar 7 trumpet

engine: 4 chug, ping

explosive: pop 4 bang, boom, clap, roar 5 blast 6 report

guttural: 4 burr 5 grunt

harsh: 4 bray 5 creak, twang 9 cacophony

high-pitched: 4 ping, ting

hissing: zip 4 siss

hoarse: caw 4 bray

in doctrine: 8 orthodox

in mind: 4 sane

insect's: 5 chirr

jingling: 16 tintinnabulation

light: 5 swish 7 pitapat

loud: 4 boom, peal 5 blare, clang

magnifying device: 9 megaphone 11 loudspeaker

measurement of: bel

menacing: 5 growl, snarl

mentally: 4 sane 5 lucid 6 normal

metallic: 4 ping, ting 5 clang, clank 6 tinkle

monotonous: hum 4 moan 5 drone

mournful: sob

murmuring: 4 purr 5 groan

musical: 4 note

nasal: 5 snore, whine 7 stridor

of bell: 4 ding

of disapproval: boo, bah **4** hiss
of drinking: **4** glub
of hoofbeat: **4** clop
of pain: **4** moan, ouch, yell **5** groan
of rising birds: **5** whirr
of surf: **4** rote
pert. to: **5** tonal **6** sonant **10** acoustical
pleasing in: **8** euphonic
respiratory: **4** rale
ringing: **5** clang **7** tinitus
shallow: **6** lagoon, laguna, lagune
shrill: **5** reedy, skirl
sibilant: **4** hiss, siss
small: **4** peep
solemn: **4** peal
speech: **5** vowel **8** phonetic
splashing: **5** swash
syllabic: **6** sonant
throat: **8** guttural
transposition: **10** spoonerism
trumpet: **5** blare **7** clarion
unvaried: **8** monotone
vibrant: **4** birr
vocal: **4** tone **6** hiccup **8** hiccough
warning: **5** alarm **6** alarum, tocsin
water: **4** klop, rote **5** plash, swish **6** splash
whispering: **8** susurrus
whizzing: **4** ping **5** swish
yelping: yip

sound out: **5** study **7** explore **11** investigate

sounded: **4** blew, rang, rung **5** oaten **6** tooted **7** clanged **8** syllabic

sounding: **6** sonant **8** plangent, resonant, sonorous, strident **9** bombastic **11** mellisonant **12** grandisonant, grandisonous

soundless: **5** quiet **9** noiseless **12** unfathomable

soundly: **6** deeply **7** healthy **8** securely **9** violently **10** completely, forcefully, profoundly, thoroughly

soundness: **5** truth **6** sanity **8** solidity, strength **9** integrity, rectitude **10** heartiness **11** healthiness

sounds: *having melody and rhythm:* **5** music
succession of: **4** peal
vocal symbols: **6** sonant

soup: **5** broth, puree, shchi, slash, stchi **6** borsch, borsht, oxtail **7** garbure, shtchee **8** consomme, gazpacho **12** mulligatawny
dish: **6** tureen
ingredient: **4** lalo, okra **7** noodles
spoon: **5** ladle
thick: **4** bisk **5** hoosh, puree **6** bisque, burgoo **7** burgout, pottage **8** minestra **10** minestrone
thickener: **7** tapioca
thin: **5** broth **8** consomme

soupcon: **5** taste, trace **7** modicum, portion **9** suspicion **10** suggestion

sour: wry **4** acid, dour, grim, hard, tart **5** acerb, acrid, cross, eager, gruff **6** acetic, bitter, cruety, morose, sullen **7** acetose, acetous, acidify, austere, crabbed, painful, peevish **8** acerbate, acescent, embitter **9** acidulate, acidulent, acidulous **10** afflictive, astringent, unpleasant **11** distasteful **12** disagreeable

source: **4** fons, font, germ, head, rise, root, seed **5** fount **6** ascent, origin, parent, spring **7** edition **8** fountain **9** beginning **10** wellspring **12** fountainhead
of caoutchouc: ule
of contrary action: **7** reagent
of gum arabic: **6** acacia
of income: **7** revenue
of indigo: **4** anil
of inspiration: **4** Muse
of iodine: **4** kelp
of knowledge: **7** organon
of metal: ore
of phosphorus: **7** apatite
of vitamin C: **6** orange
of vitamin E: **5** grain

sourdine: **4** mute

sourdook: **10** buttermilk

sourdough: **7** settler **10** prospector

sourness: **7** acidity **8** acerbity, acrimony, asperity **10** moroseness **16** disagreeableness

soursop: **9** guanabana

souse, souce, sowce, sowse: ear, jag **4** blow, cuff, duck, fall, prop, soak, wash **5** bathe, brine, douse, drink, swoop, thump **6** drench, pickle, plunge, pounce, strike, thwack **7** heavily, immerse, tippler **8** clumsily, drunkard, saturate, steeping, submerge **9** drenching

soused: **5** drunk **11** intoxicated

soutache: **5** braid **8** trimming

soutane: **5** cloak **7** cassock, zimarra

soutor: **7** cobbler **9** shoemaker

South: (see also **Confederacy**): **5** Dixie
crop: **6** cotton **7** tobacco
dish: **4** okra **5** gumbo **7** hoecake
inlet: **5** bayou
novelist: **5** Welty **8** Faulkner

South Africa: *animal:* das **5** nenta **8** suricate
antelope: gnu **5** eland, leche, oribi, peele **6** lechee, lechwe, rhebok **7** blaubok, blesbok, boshbok, grysbok, rheeboc, rheebok, sassaby **8** blesbuck, bontebok, boschbok
armadillo: **4** para
ass: **6** quagga
assembly: **4** raad
aunt: **5** tanta
blaubok: **5** etaac

breastwork: 6 scherm
bushman: 4 Qung
camp: 5 lager 6 laager
caterpillar: 6 risper
cattle enclosure: 5 kraal
city: 6 Durban 8 Cape Town, Pretoria 9 Germiston 12 Johannesburg
cliff: 4 klip
club: 10 knobkerrie
coin: 4 cent, pond, rand 6 florin
colonist: 4 Boer
conference: 6 indaba
cony: das
corn: 5 mealy 6 mealie
council: 4 raad
criminal: 8 amalaita
dialect: 4 Taal
diamond: 4 jager 9 schlenter
Dutch: 4 Boer, Taal
Dutch speech: 9 Afrikaans
ferry: 4 pont
foreigner: 9 uitlander
fox: 4 asse 5 caama
garment: 6 caross, kaross
goldfield: 4 rand
government: 8 republic
grass country: 4 veld 5 veldt
greenhorn: 5 ikona
gully: 5 donga
gun: 4 roer
hill: kop 8 spitzkop
hillock: 5 kopje
hippopotamus: 6 zeekoe
hog: 9 boschvark
hut: 8 rondavel, rondawel
javelin: 7 assagai
laborer: 4 togt
legislative assembly: 4 raad
lowland: 4 vlei, vley
monkey: 4 vervet 8 talapoin
mountain: kop
pass: nek
pasture: 5 veldt
people: 4 Xosa 5 Bantu, Namas, Pondo 6 Damara 7 Swahili 8 Bechuana 9 Hottentot
plain: 5 veldt
plant: 4 aloe
plot: erf
polecat: 6 musang
policeman: 4 zarp
province: 9 Transvaal
race: see *people* above
racial policy: 9 apartheid
region: 5 congo
river: 4 Vaal 6 Orange 7 Limpopo
rodent: 5 ratel
settler: 4 Boer
shrub: 6 protea
simpleton: 5 ikona
snake: 5 elaps 8 eggeater
spirit: 8 tikolosh
starling: 5 sprew 7 spreeuw
stream: aar
sumac: 6 karree
thong: 4 riem 7 riempie
tick: 6 tampan
tract: 9 zuurveldt
trader: 7 Swahili
tree: 5 tenio 7 assagai 8 gamdeboo
tribe: see *people* above
village: 5 kraal
warrior: 4 impi
weaverbird: 4 taha
whip: 7 sjambok

South African: 4 Boer 10 Afrikander

South America: *aborigine:* 6 Arawak
animal: ai 4 paca 5 coati, coypu, llama, sloth, tapir 6 alpaca, jaguar, nutria, vicuna 8 anteater 9 armadillo
ant: 5 sauba, sauva
anteater: 7 tamandu
arbor: 6 ramada
armadillo: 4 apar 7 tatouay 10 pichiciago
arrow poison: 6 curara, curare
balsam: 4 tolu
beast of burden: 5 llama
beef: 6 tasajo
beverage: 4 mate
bird: 4 aura, guan, mitu, myna, rara, taha, yeni 5 agami, arara, chaja, mynah 6 barber, barbet 7 aracari, jacamar, oilbird, seriema, tinamou 8 bellbird, boatbill, curassow, guacharo, puffbird, screamer, terutero
blanket: 6 serape
boat: 6 cayuco
cactus: 7 airampo
catfish: 5 dorad
cattle ranch: 8 estancia 9 estantion
country: 4 Peru 5 Chile 6 Brazil 7 Bolivia, Ecuador 8 Colombia 9 Argentina, Patagonia, Venezuela
cowboy: 6 gaucho 7 llanero, planero
cowboy's weapon: 5 bolas
dance: 5 mambo, samba 6 cha-cha
deer: 6 guemal, guemul
dove: 9 talpacoti
estuary: 4 Para 5 Plata
fish: 4 paru 6 aimara, caribe 7 scalare 8 arapaima
fox: 4 asse
game: 6 pelota
garment: 6 serape
gold: oro
griddle cake: 5 arepa
hare: 6 tapeti
hawk: 8 caracara

herb: 9 romerillo
herdsman: 7 llanero
Indian: Ges, Ona 5 Auca, Inca, Tama 5 Carib, Tapas 6 Arawak, Jivaro 7 Cayapos, Goyanas, Guatoan, Pampero, Tapuyan 8 Camacans, Coroados, Timbiras 9 Caingangs, Chavantes 10 Patagonian
Indian hut: 5 toldo
Indian medicine man: 4 peai 6 shaman
Indian poison: 6 curara, curare, curari
island: 5 Aruba
knife: 7 machete 8 machette
language: Ona
lapwing: 8 terutero
liberator: 7 Bolivar
limestone: 5 tosca
liquor: 6 chicha
lizard: 4 teju 5 coati
mammal: ai 4 paca 5 coati, llama, tapir 6 alpaca, guanco 8 kinkajou, pacarana 10 coati-mondi, coati-mundi
marmoset: 7 tamarin
measure: 4 vara 7 manzana
mineral: 4 urso
monkey: sai 4 saki, titi 5 acari, araba 6 grison, teetee 7 ouakari, sapajou 8 marmoset, orabassu 9 barrigudo, beelzebub
mountains: 5 Andes
native: 5 Carib
opossum: 5 quica 7 sarigue
ostrich: 4 rhea
palm: 5 assai, bussu, datil, troly 6 tooroo, ubussu 7 troolie
parrot: 5 macaw
plain: 5 llano, pampa
plains dweller: 7 llanero
plant: 6 ipecac 8 crassula 10 tillandsia
porridge: 5 atole
rabbit: 6 tapeti
raccoon: 5 coati 10 coatimundi
rancher: 10 estanciero
republic: 5 Chile 8 Colombia 9 Argentina, Venezuela
river: 4 Para 5 Plata 6 Amazon 7 Orinoco
rodent: 4 degu, mara, paca 5 coypu 6 agouti, agouty 8 viscacha, vizcacha 10 chinchilla
root: oca
rubber tree: 4 para
ruminant: 5 llama 6 alpaca
scarf: 5 manta
serpent: 5 aboma
shrub: 4 coca
slaughterhouse: 11 frigorifico
snake: bom 4 lora 5 aboma 8 anaconda 10 bushmaster
sorrel: oca
stock: Ona
strait: 8 Magellan
tapir: 5 danta
tiger cat: 5 chati
toucan: 4 toco 7 aracari
tree: 4 fotu, lana, mora, para, vera 5 balsa, cacao, cebil, couma, pekea 6 chicha, simaba, yachan 7 bebeeru, quayabi 9 balaustre, couvatari 11 chichicaste
tribe: Ona
trumpeter: 5 agami
tuber: oca
turtle: 8 matamata
ungulate: 5 tapir
vulture: 6 condor
walnut: 9 conacaste
weapon: 4 bola 5 bolas
wild cat: 4 eyra
wind: 7 pampero

South American: 5 Latin
South Australia: See **Australia**
South Carolina: *county:* Lee 4 York 5 Aiken, Horry, Union 6 Dillon, Saluda, Sumter
dam: 6 Saluda
fort: 6 Sumter
native: 6 weasel
river: 6 Peedee, Saluda, Santee
state tree: 8 palmetto
South Dakota: *capital:* 6 Pierre
county: Day 4 Clay, Hand, Hyde, Lake, Todd 5 Brule, Deuel, Tripp
dam: 4 Oahe
Indian: 5 Brule
state animal: 6 coyote
state flower: 6 pasque
South India: See **India**
South Pacific: *island:* 4 Fiji 5 Samoa, Tonga 7 Society 8 Pitcairn, Woodlark
sea: 5 Coral, Timor 6 Tasman
star: 5 Pinza 6 Martin
South Pole: See **Antarctica**
South Sea: *canoe:* 4 proa
island: 4 Bali, Siam, Sulu
island drink: ava
island food: 5 taros
island money: 6 wakiki
islander: 5 Maori 6 Kanaka, Samoan
plant: 4 taro
product: 5 copra
staple: 4 taro
South Vietnam: *capital:* 6 Saigon
city: Hue 5 Dalat 6 Da Nang
guerillas: 8 Vietcong
holiday: Tet
monetary unit: 7 piastre
river: 6 Mekong
south wind: 5 notus 6 auster
South Wind author: 7 Douglas
Southeast Asia (see also **Asia**): 4 Laos, Siam 5 Burma 6 Ceylon 7 Vietnam 8

Cambodia, Malaysia, Pakistan, Thailand 9 Indonesia 10 Bangladesh 11 Philippines
southeast wind: 5 eurus
southerly: 8 austrine
southern: 7 austral
Southern California: See **California**
Southern dish: See **South:** *dish*
Southern France: 4 Midi
Southern tonic: 4 dope
southernwood: 9 abrotanum
Southwark inn: 6 Tabard
Southwest: *cowboy:* 7 llanero
Indian: 4 Cree
Southwest Pacific island: 5 Samoa
southwest wind: 4 afer
southwester: hat 5 squam, storm
souvenir: 5 curio, relic 6 memory 7 memento 8 keepsake, reminder 12 recollection, remembrancer
sovereign: 4 king 5 chief, liege, royal, ruler 6 couter, Mikado, prince 7 emperor, highest, monarch, supreme 8 autocrat, greatest, princely, reigning, superior, suzerain 9 effectual, excellent, paramount, potentate 11 controlling, efficacious, independent
female: 7 empress 11 autocratrix
petty: 8 tetrarch
sovereign authority: 8 dominion
sovereign power: 6 throne
sovereign prerogative claim: 11 seigniorage
sovereignty: 4 rule, sway 5 realm 6 diadem, empery, empire, status 7 dynasty, majesty, scepter, sceptre 8 dominion 9 supremacy 10 ascendancy, ascendency, domination
absolute: 8 autarchy
joint: 11 condominium
Soviet: 7 council, Russian
Soviet Union (see also **Russia**): 4 USSR
administrative committee: 9 presidium
founder: 5 Lenin
government farm: 7 sovkhos, sovkhoz 8 sovkhose
hero: 5 Lenin 6 Stalin
money: 5 ruble
news agency: 4 Tass
newspaper: 5 Pravda 8 Izvestia
republic: 5 Uzbek 6 Latvia 7 Armenia, Georgia, Kirghiz, Turkmen, Ukraine
secret police: 4 NKVD, OGPU
sow: hog, pig 4 heap, seed, shed 5 ditch, drain, drill, plant, stack, swine 6 runner, sluice, spread 7 channel, furnish, grumphy, implant, scatter 8 disperse, grumphie 9 broadcast, inoculate 10 salamander 11 disseminate
wild: 8 javelina
young: elt 4 gilt
sower: 7 seedman
of dragon's teeth: 6 Cadmus
soy: 4 silk
soy bean: 4 soja
soya: 4 dill 6 fennel 7 soybean
spa: 5 oasis, oases 6 resort, spring 8 Saratoga 10 sanatorium
place: Ems 4 Bath 5 Baden
space: gap 4 area, path, rank, roam, room, rove, void, walk 5 ambit, plena(pl.), range, track 6 course, divide, extent, plenum, region 7 areolae, arrange, expanse 8 capacity, distance, duration, interval, quantity 11 reservation 14 accommodations
agency: 4 NASA
architectural: 8 pediment
between eyes: 4 lore
between two intersecting lines: 5 angle
between two points: 8 distance
blank: 6 lacuna 7 lacunae(pl.)
breathing: 6 recess
cleared: 5 glade
coin: 7 exergue
docking: 6 linkup
empty: 4 void 5 blank, inane 6 vacuum
forest: 5 glade
hallowed: 7 mortice, mortise
included: 8 contents
limitless: 8 infinite
occupied: 6 volume
on surface: 4 area
partitioned: 4 room
pert. to: 5 areal
portion of: 5 place
safekeeping: 7 storage
small: 6 areola, areole 7 aerolae
storage: 4 shed 5 attic 6 cellar 9 storeroom, warehouse
void: 5 chasm 7 inanity
wall: 5 niche
white: 6 margin
space for goods: 7 storage
space full of matter: 6 plenum
space of time: 8 interval
space theory: 7 plenism
spacecraft: 6 rocket 9 satellite
first: 7 Sputnik
part: 6 module 7 capsule
to moon: 6 Apollo
spaceman: 9 astronaut, cosmonaut
spacer: bar
spacious: 4 vast 5 ample, broad, great, large, rangy, roomy 9 capacious, expansive, extensive 13 comprehensive
spack: 7 forward, knowing 11 intelligent
spad: 4 nail
Spad: 7 biplane
spadassin: 5 bravo 7 duelist 9 swordsman

spade: dig 5 graft 6 shovel
Irish: 5 slane
kind of: 6 scavel
narrow: loy
plasterer's: 6 server
sharp: 4 spud
triangular: 5 didle
turf: 5 slane
spadger: boy 7 sparrow
spae: 6 divine 8 foretell, prophecy
spaghetti: 5 pasta
sauce spice: 7 oregano
spahi, spahee: 7 cavalry
Spain: 6 Iberia
adventurer: 9 almogaver
article: el, la, un; las, los, una
aunt: tia
author: 9 Cervantes
bayonet: 5 yucca
beach: 5 plays
belle: 4 maja
blanket: 6 serape
boat: 5 aviso
brandy: 11 aguardiente
bull: 4 toro
cape: 9 Trafalgar
cart: 7 carreta 8 carretta
cathedral city: 7 Seville
cedar: 6 acajou
celery: 4 apio
cellist: 6 Casals
champion: Cid
channel: 4 Cano
chaperone: 6 duenna
cheer: ole
city: See *town* below
clerk: 11 escribiente
cloak: 4 capa 5 manta 6 mantle
coat: 7 zamarra, zamarro
coin: 5 dobla 6 cuarto, doblon, peseta 7 Alfonso, centimo, piaster 8 cuartino 9 cuartillo
conqueror: Cid 7 Pizarro 12 conquistador
contract: 7 asiento 8 assiento
council: 5 junta
count: 5 conde
dance: 4 jota 5 danza, tango 6 bolero, gitano 8 fandango, saraband 9 zapateado 10 seguidilla
dish: 6 posole
district: 5 Xeres
dollar: 4 duro, peso, pezo 7 piaster, piastre
dumpling: 6 tamale
earth: 6 tierra
exclamation: 6 carajo 7 caramba
execution: 7 garotte, garrote 8 garrotte
explorer: 7 Mendoza 8 Coronado
fabric: 5 tiraz
fleet: 6 armada
friend: 5 amigo
frigate: 5 zabra
game: 5 omber 6 pelota 7 jai-alai
gentleman: don 5 senor 8 cavalier 9 caballero
god: 4 dios
goddess: 5 Diosa
gold: oro
governor: 10 idelantado
grass: 5 spart 7 esparto
greeting: 4 hola
griddlecake: 5 arepa
gunboat: 5 barca
gypsy: 7 zincalo
hall: 4 sala
head covering: 8 mantilla
herdsman: 8 ranchero
hero: Cid
hill: 5 cerro, morro
holiday: 6 fiesta
horse: 7 caballo
hotel: 5 venta 6 posada
house: 4 casa
instrument: 8 castanet, zambomba
judge: 7 alcalde
kettle: 4 cazo
king: rey
kingdom: 4 Leon 6 Aragon 7 Castile
lady: 4 dona 6 senora
lagoon: 6 laguna
lake: 4 lago
lariat: 5 reata, riata
leather: 8 cordovan
legislature: 6 cortes
letter: 5 carta
letter carrier: 6 correo
linen cloth: 4 crea
lute: 7 vihuela
magic: 8 brujeria
man: don 6 hombre
mausoleum: 8 Escorial
mayor: 6 alcade 7 alcalde
measure: pie 4 codo, copa, dedo, moyo, paso, vara 5 aroba, braza, cafiz, cahiz, legua, linea, medio, milla, palmo, sesma 6 cordel, cuarta, estado, fanega, league, racion, yugada 7 azumbre, cantara, celemin, estadel, pulgada 8 aranzada, fanegada 9 cuarteron, cuartilla, cuartillo 10 caballeria
miss: 8 senorita
money: 4 duro 6 dinero
monk: 5 padre
mountain: 8 Asturian, Pyrenees 9 Mulahacem 10 Cantabrian, Guardarrama, Pic de Netou 11 La Maladetta 12 Sierra Morena 14 Sierra de Toledo
mouth: 4 boca
muleteer: 7 arriero
native: 7 Catalan, Iberian

nobleman: don 7 grandee, hidalgo
now: 5 ahora
nun: 6 Teresa
officer: 8 alguacil, alguazil
operetta: 8 zarzuela
other: 4 otro
oyster: 5 pinna
painter: 4 Cano, Dali, Goya, Miro, Sert 6 Ribera 7 Murillo, Picasso, Zuloaga 9 Velasquez
palace: 8 Escorial
pancake: 5 arepa
parliament: 6 cortes
pear: 7 avocado
peasant: 7 paisano
peninsula: 6 Iberia
pepper: 5 chili 7 pimento
pickpocket: 6 ratero
plant: aji
poet: 6 Encina
porridge: 5 atole
port: 5 Palos
post office: 6 correo
pot: 4 olla
priest: 4 cura 5 padre
promenade: 5 paseo
pronunciation mark: 5 tilde
raisin: 4 pasa
province: 4 Jaen, Leon, Lugo, Vigo 5 Alava, Avila, Cadiz, Soria 6 Burgos, Coruna, Cuenca, Gerona, Huelva, Huesca, Lerida, Madrid, Malaga, Murcia, Orense, Oviedo, Teruel, Toledo, Zamora 7 Almeria, Badajoz, Caceres, Cordova, Granada, Logrono, Navarra, Segovia, Seville, Vizcaya 8 Albacete, Alicante, Palencia, Valencia 9 Barcelona, Guipuscoa, Salamanca, Santander, Saragossa, Tarragona 10 Ciudad Real, Pontevedra, Valladolid 11 Guadalajara 15 Balearic Islands 18 Castellon de la Plana
rice: 5 arroz
rider: 8 herisson
river: ria, rio 4 Ebro 5 Douro, Tagus 8 Guadiana 12 Guadalquivir
road: 6 camino
room: 4 sala
seaport: 4 Adra 5 Palos
sentinel: 5 vedet, videt 7 vedette, vidette
shawl: 5 manta 6 serape
sherry: 5 Xeres 11 Amontillado
silk: 5 tiraz
sorcerer: 5 brujo
south: sur
stanza: 10 seguidilla
street: 5 calle
sword: 5 bilbo
tax: 8 alcabala
title: don 5 senor 6 senora 7 hidalgo 8 senorita
tomorrow: 6 manana
town: 4 Irun, Jaen, Leon, Olot 5 Cadiz, Gijon, Lorca, Ronda, Siero, Xeres 6 Bilbao, Madrid(c.), Malaga, Murcia, Toledo 7 Cordoba, Cordova, Granada, Seville 8 Valencia, Zaragoza 9 Barcelona, Cartegena, Salamanca, Santander, Saragossa 10 Carthagena, Valladolid 18 Jerez de la Frontiera
trail: 6 camino
trefoil: 7 alfalfa, lucerne
uncle: tio
vase: 4 urna
vehicle: 7 tartana
very: muy
watchword: 6 alerta
water: 4 agua
watercourse: 6 arroyo
weight: 4 onza 5 frail, grano, libra, marco, tomin 6 adarme, arroba, dinero, dracma, ochava 7 arienzo, quilate, quintal 8 caracter, tonelada 9 escrupulo 10 castellano
white: 6 blanco
wind: 6 solano
window: 7 ventana
witchcraft: 8 brujeria
woman: 6 senora

spalpeen: boy, fop, lad 5 scamp 6 rascal 7 laborer, workman 8 braggart 9 youngster
spald: 4 limb, open 5 joint, splay, split 8 shoulder, splinter
spale: bar 4 chip, fine, lath, rail 5 brace, spall 6 timber 7 shaving 8 splinter
spall: 4 chip, fall 5 break 6 reduce 7 breakup, crumble 8 fragment, shoulder
spalt: 4 chip, tear 5 crisp, split 7 brittle
span: 4 cock, pair, rope, swim, team, time 5 cover, grasp, reach, seize 6 attach, bridge, extend, fasten, fetter, hobble, inspan, spread 7 confine, matched, measure, stretch 8 distance, duration, encircle 9 encompass, perfectly 10 completely
spancel: tie 4 clog 6 fetter, hobble
spang: 4 bang, hurl, jump, kick, leap, yoke 5 clasp, crack 6 stride 7 spangle 8 abruptly, directly, ornament, straight
spangle: set 4 boss 5 adorn, aglet, gleam, plate 6 aiglet, sequin, zequin 7 glisten, glitter, sparkle 8 sprinkle, zecchino
spangly: 9 sparkling 10 glittering
Spaniard: 5 Latin 7 Espanol 9 Castilian
imaginary: 9 Espriella
spaniel: 5 trasy 6 cocker 8 springer 9 sycophant
spank: 4 prat, whip 6 strike 8 chastise
spanker: 4 sail
spanking: 4 fine 5 brisk, fresh, large, stout 6 lively, strong 7 dashing 8 vigorous
spanner: 6 wrench

spar: bar, box, rod 4 beam, bolt, boom, gaff, mast, pole, raft, rung, shut, yard 5 close, fight, lunge, sprit, steve 6 barite, bicker, charge, fasten, rafter, strike, thrust, timber 7 contest, dispute, enclose, wrangle, yardarm 8 dolomite, lazulite
end: 7 yardarm
spare: 4 bear, free, gain, hain, lean, part, save, slim, slit, slow, stop, thin 5 avoid, chary, extra, favor, gaunt, grant, lanky, stint 6 desist, endure, favour, frugal, meager, scanty 7 deprive, forbear, forgive, haggard, leisure, opening, placket, refrain, relieve, reserve, sparing 8 dilatory, forebear, preserve, tolerate 9 duplicate, parsimony 11 replacement, superfluous 12 parsimonious
spare time: 7 leisure
sparge: 6 splash 8 sprinkle 9 bespatter
sparing: 5 chary, gnede, scant 6 frugal, meager, saving, scanty 7 careful, limited, thrifty 8 merciful, reticent, stinting 9 scrimping 12 parsimonious
spark: arc, woo 4 beau, funk, soil 5 aizle, belle, blade, court, flash, grain, lover 7 diamond, gallant, sparkle, spatter 8 sparklet 9 scintilla 10 sweetheart 11 scintillate
igniting property: 11 incendivity
sparked: 5 arced 7 courted, spotted 8 streaked 10 variegated
sparker: 5 lover 7 gallant 8 firework
sparkle: 5 blink, flash, gleam, glent, glint, shine, spark, strew, trace 7 diffuse, glisten, glitter, radiate, reflect, scatter, showing, spangle 8 disperse, sprinkle, vivacity 9 coruscate 10 effervesce, illuminate, liveliness 11 coruscation, scintillate 13 scintillation
sparkling: 4 dewy 5 crisp 6 bright, lively, starry 7 shining 8 animated, flashing, gleaming 9 brillante, brilliant, twinkling 10 glittering, reflecting 12 effervescent, effervescing
sparoid fish: 4 scup 5 porgy 10 sheepshead
sparple: 4 rout 7 scatter 8 disperse, sprinkle 11 disseminate
sparrer: 5 boxer 7 sparrow
sparrow: 7 chanter
sparse: 4 thin 5 scant 6 meager, meagre, scanty, thinly 7 scatter 8 disperse 9 scattered 10 distribute, infrequent
Sparta (see also **Attica, Greece**): *army:* 4 mora
bondman: 5 helot
commander: 7 lochage
dog: 10 bloodhound
festival: 6 Carnea 7 Carneia
governor: 7 harmost
king: 8 Leonidas, Menelaus
king's wife: 4 Leda
lawgiver: 8 Lycurgus
magistrate: 5 ephor
method of cipher writing: 7 scytale
native: 8 Laconian
queen: 5 Helen
serf: 5 helot
tyrant: 5 Nabis
spartan: 5 brave, hardy 6 frugal, heroic, severe 7 laconic 9 undaunted 10 courageous
sparver: 4 tent 6 canopy, tester
spasm: fit, tic 4 grip 5 crick 8 paroxysm 10 convulsion 11 contraction
muscle: 5 cramp
of distress: 4 pang
of pain: 5 throe
spasmodic: 6 fitful, sudden 7 snatchy, violent 9 excitable 12 intermittent
disease: 7 tetanus
spat: row 4 blow, clap, fuss, slap, tiff 5 eject 6 gaiter, oyster, splash, strike 7 dispute, legging, quarrel
spate: 4 gush, rain 5 flood 7 freshet, outflow, torrent 9 overwhelm, rainstorm 10 waterspout
spatial: 5 areal 6 steric 8 sterical
spatter: jet 4 dash, drop, soil, spot 5 slart, spurt 6 dabble, defame, injure, splash, spread 7 scatter, spatule, sputter 8 splutter, sprinkle
spatterdash: 7 legging
spatula: 4 tool 5 spade 6 thible
spatulate: 6 lyrate
spawn: roe 4 eggs, germ, seed, spot 5 fungi 6 bulbis, source 7 cormels, deposit, produce 8 generate, mycelium
ascending river to: 10 anadromous
spay: 4 geld 8 castrate 9 sterilize
speak: say 4 carp, chat, hail, talk, tell 5 extol, honor, orate, utter 6 reveal 7 address, bespeak, declaim, declare, deliver, express, publish 8 converse, harangue, manifest, proclaim 9 celebrate, discourse, pronounce 10 articulate
affectedly: 4 mimp 5 mince
against: 6 oppose
at length: 9 expatiate
comb. form: 4 lalo
curtly: 4 snap, birk
evasively: 5 hedge, stall
foolishly: 6 drivel
from memory: 6 recite
imperfectly: 4 lisp 7 stutter
in undertone: 6 mumble, murmur
inability to: 6 alalia, mutism 7 aphasia 8 aglossia
incoherently: 6 gabble, gibber
noisily: 4 fume, rant, rave

of: 4 call 7 mention
offhand: 11 extemporize
oracularly: 11 pontificate
pert. to: 10 oratorical
profusely: 6 dilate 7 palaver
rapidly: 5 troll 6 patter 8 splutter
rhetorically: 5 orate 7 declaim
slightingly: 8 backbite 9 disparage
slowly: 5 drawl
softly: 7 whisper
thoughtlessly: 4 blat 8 splutter
through nose: 9 nasillate
to: 5 greet 6 accost 7 address
under breath: 6 mumble, mutter
with interruption: haw, hem

speaker: 5 drone, sayer 6 lisper, orator, proser, ranter, talker 7 demagog, utterer 8 lecturer 9 demagogue 10 mouthpiece, prolocutor 11 entertainer, spellbinder
inspired: 7 prophet
of many languages: 8 linguist, polyglot

speaker's hammer: 5 gavel

speaking: *style:* 8 staccato, fluently
without preparation: 13 extemporizing

spean: 4 test, wean 5 prong 6 nipple

spear: gad, rod 4 dart, fram, reed, shut, spar 5 apine, blade, lance, shoot, stalk 6 aprout, glaive, impale, pierce, strike 7 feather, harpoon, javelin, missile, trident 9 penetrate
grass: 5 blade
kind of: 4 gaff 5 gidia, gidya 6 bident, fizgig, gidgea, gidgee, gidjee, gidyea 7 assagai, assegai, bourdon, harpoon, leister, trident
three-pronged: 7 trident

spear-shaped: 7 hastate

spearfish: 8 billfish

spearhead: 4 gaff

spearwort: 8 crowfoot

special: 4 dear, rare 5 chief, extra, local 6 unique 7 limited, unusual 8 concrete, detailed, favorite, intimate, paramour, peculiar, personal, specific, uncommon 9 specially 10 especially, individual, noteworthy, particular, restricted 11 distinctive, exceptional 12 particularly 13 distinguished, extraordinary
ability: 6 talent
edition: 5 extra

specialist: *atomic:* 9 physicist
city planning: 8 urbanist
ear: 6 aurist
eye: 7 oculist
medical(see also **doctor**): 7 oculist, surgeon 9 otologist 11 orthopedist 12 obstetrician, orthopaedist, pediatrician 13 paediatrician
mineral: 12 mineralogist
money management: 9 economist
surgical: see **doctor**

specialty: 5 forte, skill 8 aptitude 13 particularity

specie: 4 cash, coin 5 money

species: 4 kind, race, sort, type 5 breed, brood, class, genre, image 7 mankind, variety 8 category, humanity 9 spectacle 10 exhibition, reflection
modified by environment: 4 ecad
spider: 5 acera
various: 5 genus 6 genera

specific: 5 exact 7 precise, special 8 concrete, definite, explicit, peculiar 10 particular, restricted, specifying 11 determinate

specifically: 6 namely 9 specially

specify: 4 name, tell 5 allot, state 6 assign, define, detail 7 mention 8 describe, nominate 9 designate, stipulate 10 articulate
in detail: 4 item 7 itemize
singly: 9 enumerate

specimen: 4 mark 5 model, relic, token 6 cotype, sample, swatch 7 example, pattern 11 examination

specious: gay 4 fair 5 showy 6 glossy, hollow 7 colored 8 coloured 9 colorable, plausible 10 ostensible 12 hyprocritical

speck: bit, dot, nit 4 blot, iota, mark, mite, mote, spot, whit 5 glebe, stain 7 blemish, blubber 8 particle

speckle: dot 5 fleck 7 stipple

speckled: 6 menald 7 bracket

specs: 10 eyeglasses, spectacles

spectacle: 4 show 5 bysen, model, scene, sight 6 mirror 7 display, diorama, example, pageant, pattern 8 panorama, spyglass 9 cyclorama 10 exhibition 14 representation
structure for: 5 arena 7 stadium, theater, theatre 8 coliseum

spectacles: 7 glasses
part of: 6 bridge, temple

spectator: 4 eyer 6 espier 7 witness 8 beholder, kibitzer, looker-on, observer, onlooker

specter, spectre: 4 bogy 5 bogey, bogie, bogle, ghost, shade, spook 6 boggle, spirit, wraith 7 boggard, boggart, bugaboo, bugbear, phantom 8 boggle-bo, guytrash, phantasm, revenant 10 apparition

spectral: 6 ghosty, spooky 7 ghostly, phantom 12 apparitional 13 insubstantial

spectrum: 8 infrared

speculate: 5 guess, think 6 gamble, mirror, ponder, wonder 8 consider, meditate, ruminate, theorize 10 conjecture, deliberate, philosophy 11 contemplate

speculation: 6 bubble, vision 7 surmise 8 decision 9 guesswork, intuition 10 conclusion, conjecture

speculator: spy 4 lamb 7 lookout, scalper 8 explorer, observer, theorist 12 contemplator, investigator

speculum: 6 mirror 7 diopter

sped: 4 hied 5 raced 6 darted, dashed 8 galloped, hastened 11 accelerated

speech: 4 talk 5 idiom, voice, slang 6 dilogy, epilog, orison, steven, tongue 7 address, dialect, oration, oratory, vinegar 8 colloquy, epilogue, harangue, language 9 utterance

abusive: 6 tirade

art: 8 rhetoric

blunder: 8 solecism

conclusion: 9 episcopal 10 peroration

defect: 4 lisp 6 alogia 7 stammer, stutter

denunciation: 5 frump 6 tirade 8 filippic 9 philippic

difficulty: 9 baryphony 10 baryphonia

element: 4 surd

expert: 9 phonetist

figure of: 5 irony, trope 6 aporia, simile 7 imagery 8 metaphor

goddess: Vac

hesitation: haw 7 stutter

impassioned: 6 tirade 9 dithyramb

insane: 9 bedlamism

local: 6 patois 7 dialect

long: 5 spiel

loss: 6 alalia 7 aphasia 8 muteness

part: 4 noun, verb 6 adverb 9 adjective 11 conjunction, preposition 12 interjection

peculiar: 5 idiom

provincial: 6 patois 7 dialect

readiness: 9 facundity

religious: 6 sermon 9 preaching

representing: 8 phonetic

reserved: 8 reticent

summary: 5 notes

violent: 6 tirade

voiceless element: 4 surd 7 spirate

world language: 7 volapuk 9 esperanto

speechify: 5 orate 8 harangue

speechless: mum 4 dumb, mute 6 silent 9 voiceless

speed: go; hie, rip 4 fare, flee, help, race, rate 5 haste, hurry 6 assist, career, hasten, profit, succor 7 execute, prosper 8 celerity, dispatch, expedite, rapidity, velocity 9 advantage, discharge, quickness, swiftness 10 accelerate, expedition, facilitate 12 precipitance

full: 5 amain

great: 4 zoom 5 haste, spurt, amain 6 career 9 posthaste

measuring device: 11 speedometer, velocimeter

note: 4 time 5 clock

rate of: RPM 4 pace 5 tempo

ratio: 4 Mach

speeder: 5 racer 11 accelerator

speedful: 5 rapid 6 expert, speedy 9 efficient, favorable 10 successful

speedily: 4 fast, soon 5 apace 6 presto 7 betimes, hastily, quickly, rapidly 8 promptly 13 expeditiously

speediness: 5 haste 8 dispatch, rapidity 9 quickness 10 promptness

speedometer: 5 clock 8 odometer 10 tachometer

speedy: 4 fast 5 fleet, hasty, quick, rapid, swift 6 active, prompt 7 helpful 12 advantageous

speel: 5 climb, mount 8 splinter

speer: ask 4 seek 5 query 6 screen 7 inquire 9 partition

spell: bar, peg 4 chip, form, lath, mean, rung, save, tale, talk, tell, trap, turn, snap 5 brief, charm, curse, magic, relay, shift, spare, speak, spell, story, utter, weird 6 glamor, gospel, import, period, relate, relief, splint, trance 7 bewitch, cantrip, compose, glamour, relieve, shaving, signify, sorcery, drought, syncope 8 pishogue, splinter 9 discourse 10 constitute, demonifuge 11 conjuration, enchantment, fascination, abracadabra 12 entrancement 13 orthographize, prognosticate

in another alphabet: 13 transliterate

spellbind: 5 orate 7 enchant 9 fascinate

speller (according to pronunciation)**:** 9 phonetist 11 phoneticist

poor: 11 cacographer

spelt: 5 grain, wheat 6 cereal

spelter: 4 zinc

spelunk: den 4 cave, lair 6 cavern

spence, spense: 6 larder, pantry 7 buttery 9 apartment

spencer: wig 4 coat 6 butler, jacket, pantry 7 buttery, steward, trysail

spend: run, use 4 blow, dash, flow, give, jump, pass, span 5 beset, exert, grasp, waste 6 attach, bestow, beware, devote, elapse, expend, fasten, lavish, manage, spread, spring, weaken 7 consume, dispend, exhaust, fatigue, perform 8 confound, disburse, squander 9 dissipate, sacrifice 10 distribute

spend the summer: 8 estivate 9 aestivate

spendful: 8 wasteful 11 extravagant

spendthrift: 6 waster 7 wastrel 8 prodigal, wasteful 10 dingthrift, profligate

Spenserian character: Una

spent: 4 beat, paid, used 5 weary 6 effete, wasted 8 lavished 9 exhausted 10 squandered

speos: 4 cave, tomb 6 grotto, temple

sperm: 4 seed 5 semen 12 spermatozoon

sperm whale: 8 cachalot
spet: 9 barracuda
spetch: 4 mend 5 patch 6 refuse 7 parings
spew, spue: bog 4 ooze, slip 5 eject, exude, strew, vomit 7 extrude, scatter 8 disgorge 10 afterswarm
sphacelate: 7 decayed, mortify 8 withered 9 mortified
sphenic: 11 wedge-shaped
spheral: 7 perfect 10 harmonious 11 symmetrical
sphere: orb, sky 4 ball, rank, star 5 ambit, arena, class, field, globe, orbit, order, range, scope 6 domain, orblet, planet 7 circuit, compass, heavens, stratum, station, theatre, terella 8 idiosome, position, province 9 idioblast 10 atmosphere, department 12 jurisdiction
of action: 5 arena
perforated: 4 bead
spheric: 8 globular 11 globe-shaped
spherical: 5 orbic, round 6 rotund 7 globate, globose 8 globated, globular, obrotund 9 globulous, orbicular
sphericity: 9 rotundity, roundness
spheroid: 4 ball 5 earth
spherule: 7 globule
sphinx: 4 moth 6 enigma 7 monster, prophet
land of: 5 Egypt
mother: 7 Echidna
query of: 6 riddle
site of: 4 Giza 5 Luxor
sphinxian: 10 mysterious 11 enigmatical, inscrutable
sphygmus: 5 pulse
spial: spy 5 scout, watch 6 espial
spica: 7 bandage
spice: 4 dash, kind, mace, mull, nard, odor, sort, vein 5 aroma, taste, touch 6 embalm, flavor, relish, season 7 modicum, perfume, portion, species, variety 8 quantity, specimen 9 admixture, condiment, seasoning 10 appearance
kind of: 4 mace, mull, sage 5 anise, cumin, curry, thyme 6 cloves, ginger, nutmeg, pepper, stacte, tamara 7 cayenne, mustard, oregano, paprika, pimento 8 allspice, cinnamon, marjoram, pimiento, turmeric
mill: 5 quern
package for: 6 robbin
Spice Islands: 6 Indies 7 Molucca
spices: 9 aromatics
spicier: 4 racy 7 nuttier
spick: fat 5 split 6 grease 7 blubber 8 lavender, titmouse
spick-and-span: 4 neat, trim 5 clean, fresh 6 spruce 8 brand-new
spicknel: 9 baldmoney
spicule: rod 4 dart, nail, toxa 5 aster, spine 6 actine 7 prickle, rhabdus 8 sclerite, spikelet
sponge: 5 cymba
spicy: hot 4 keen, racy 5 balmy, natty, showy, smart 6 active, risque 7 gingery, peppery, piquant, pungent 8 aromatic, fragrant, spirited
spider: cob, cop, hub, pan 5 arain 6 eresid, epeira, snarer, tripod, trivet 7 pokomoo, skillet, retiary 8 arachnid, attercop, telarian 9 tarantula 12 candleholder
comb. form: 6 arachn 7 arachno
family of: 7 attidae 9 drassidae 10 citigradae
genus of: 6 aranea, epeira
three-legged: 6 trivet
venomous: 9 tarantula 10 black widow
web-spinning organ: 9 spinneret
spider bug: 5 emesa
spider crab: 4 maia
spider monkey: 9 belzebuth
spider nest: web 5 nidus
spider species: 5 acera
spider web: 8 attercop
resembling: 9 arachnoid
spinner: 9 spinneret
spieler: 5 crier 6 barker, talker 7 sharper, speaker 8 lecturer 9 announcer 11 spellbinder
spiff: PM 5 bonus 7 premium 8 gratuity
spiffy: 4 neat 5 smart 6 spruce
spiflicate, spifflicate: 4 beat, kill 6 stifle 8 astonish, bewilder, confound
spigot: peg, pin, tap 4 cock, plug 5 spile, spout 6 dossil, faucet, pierce
spike: cut, cob, ear, gad 4 brob, chat, nail, tine, umbo 5 ament, block, prong 6 antler, cereal, earlet, fasten, finish, impale, pierce, secure, thwart 7 bayonet, disable, fortify, trenail 8 mackerel 9 frustrate, merganser 10 spadix-tine 13 inflorescence
spike hole: 5 spile
spike let: 4 chat, nail 7 spinule
spikenard: 4 nard 8 ointment
spile: pin, rod, tap 4 bung, heap, pile, plug, rule, tube 5 spill, spout, stake 6 spigot 8 forepole, splinter
spiler: 6 burler
spilikin: peg 7 pushpin 10 jackstraws
spill: die, mar, peg, pin, rod 4 disk, fail, fall, flow, kill, roll, ruin, shed, slip, slop 5 flosh, spile, spoil, spool, waste 6 injure, perish, punish, reveal, sheath, tumble, wasted 7 correct, destroy, divulge, scatter 8 chastise, downpour, gratuity, overflow, spillway, splinter, squander 11 deteriorate
Spillane's hero: 6 Hammer
spiloma: 5 nevus 9 birthmark

spin: 4 birl, burl, gyre, pirl, reel, turn 5 spurt, swirl, twirl, twist, whirl 6 gyrate, rotate 7 prolong, revolve 8 protract
spin a yarn: 7 narrate
spina: 4 wall 5 spine 8 backbone
spinach: 7 epinard, potherb
mountain: 5 orach, savoy 6 orache
spinal: 5 balas
area: 6 dorsal, lumbar, sacral 8 cervical
column: 5 spine 8 backbone 9 vertebrae
cord: 4 alba 6 myelon
disease: 5 polio 8 myelitis
layer: 4 dura
muscle: 5 psoas
spindle: pin, rod 4 axis, axle, hasp, stem 5 arbor, fusee, shaft, stalk, xeres 6 arbour, broach, fuseau, rachis 7 mandrel
spindling: 5 leggy 7 slender
spine (see also **spinal**): awn 4 back, seta, turf 5 chine, ridge, sward, thorn 6 chaeta, needle, spirit 7 acantha, acicula, courage, prickle, spicule 8 backbone, spiculum 9 vertebrae
spine bone: 6 sacrum
spine-tingling: 4 eery 5 eerie 7 ghostly
spinel: gem 5 balas
spinet: 5 piano 7 giraffe 11 harpsichord
spinnaker: 4 sail
spinner: cap, top 5 spoon 6 spider, weaver 8 narrator 10 goatsucker
spinney: 5 copse, grove 7 thicket
spinning: 5 areel 6 rotary 8 whirling 9 revolving
device: 7 distaff
machine: 4 mule 5 jenny 8 throstle
rod: 7 distaff
spinning wheel: 6 charka 7 charkha
spinous: 5 spiny 7 spinose 9 acanthoid, spinelike
Spinoza work: 6 Ethics
spinule: 8 backbone, spikelet
spiny: 6 picked, thorny 7 prickly 9 acanthoid, difficult
spiny-footed: 10 acanthopod 13 acanthopodous
spiny shrub: 4 ulex
spiracles: 4 hole 5 pores, vents 6 breath, spirit 8 blowhole, orifices 9 apertures
spiral: 4 coil, curl 5 curve, helix 7 coiling, curving, helical, winding 8 circling, helicoid 9 corkscrew 11 anfractuous
combining form: 5 helic, helix
spirate: 9 voiceless
spire: 4 coil, curl 5 blade, stalk, tower, twist, whorl 6 fleche, spiral, sprout 7 sapling, steeple
finial: epi 4 epis
ornament: 6 finial
spirit: hag, vim 4 aitu, alma, dash, dook, elan, fire, gimp, life, mood, soul, wind 5 angel, ardor, bugan, dhoul, ethos, fairy, fling, ghost, haunt, metal, pluck, shade, spook, verve, vigor 6 ardour, asuang, breeze, elixir, energy, esprit, ginger, mettle, morale, pneuma, temper, yaksha (mas.), yakshi(fem.) 7 animate, bravery, courage, entrain, hearten, loyalty 8 folletto, phantasm, vivacity 9 animation, encourage 10 apparition, enterprise, enthusiasm 11 disposition, inspiration 12 cheerfulness, entrainement
air: 5 Ariel
animating: 6 animus
animation: pep 4 dash
avenging: Ate 6 alecto, erinys 7 megaera, nemesis 9 tisiphine
evil: Ate, imp, Ker 4 baka, beng, boko, drow, gyre 5 bugan, demon, devil 6 animus, asuang, daemon, daitya, dibbuk, Erynes, Lilith 9 cacodemon 10 cacodaemon
female: 6 undine 7 banshee, banshie
fire: 4 Agni
good: 5 genie, genus 7 eudemon 8 eudaemon
heralding death: 7 banshee, banshie
kinds of: Po; akh, imp, lar, nat 4 arac, gimp, Kuei, Kwei, soul 5 angel, Ariel, duffy, duppy, dusio, ethos, genie, jinni, manes, rakee, shade 6 animus, fulgja, jinnee, mammon, tangie, Undine 7 banshee
lose: 7 despond
mischievous: imp 4 Puck 6 goblin 7 gremlin 11 poltergeist
of censure: 5 Momus
of people: 5 ethos
spirit lamp: 4 etna
spirit-land: 9 fairyland
spirit-leaf: 8 manyroot
spirited: 4 fell, gamy 5 brisk, eager, fiery 6 active, audace, birkie, ginger, lively, spunky 7 animato, dashing 8 animated, desirous, frampoid, generous, vigorous 9 audacious, energetic, spiritoso, sprightly 10 mettlesome
horse: 5 steed 7 charger
spiritedness: 9 animation, animosity
spiritless: 4 cold, dead, meek 5 amort, blate, vapid 6 flashy 7 daviely, hilding 8 dejected, feckless, flagging, lifeless, listless, thewless 9 depressed, exanimate, heartless 10 dispirited
spiritlike: 8 ethereal
spiritous: 6 active, ardent 8 animated 9 vivacious
spirits: *dash of:* 5 lacer
dead: 5 manes
dwelling place of: Po 5 Hades 7 Elysium

kinds of: 6 furies, uplift 7 elation, Sammael 9 firewater 13 aquacaelestis
lift: 5 elate 7 gladden
low: 5 blues, dumps, gloom 6 gloomy 8 doldrums

spirits and water: 4 grog

spirits of hartshorn: 7 ammonia

spiritual: 4 holy, pure, song 5 witty 6 clever, devout, divine, sacred 7 ghostly 8 churchly, internal, platonic, spirited 9 alcoholic, animastic, geistlich, unwordly 10 devotional, immaterial, spirituous 11 animastical, disembodied, incorporeal 14 ecclesiastical
apathy: 6 acedia
being: ens 5 angel, entia(pl.) 6 seraph
darkness: 4 Hell 5 tamas

spiritualistic meeting: 6 seance

spiritualize: 5 endow 6 purify, refine 7 animate 8 idealize 11 etherealize

spirituous: gay 4 airy, hard 5 vivid 6 active, ardent, lively 8 ethereal 9 alcoholic 10 immaterial 11 incorporeal

spiry: 4 tall 6 coiled, curled, spiral 7 slender 8 tapering, wreathed 10 serpentine

spit: dig, fix, rod 4 emit, hang, rain, reef, snow 5 eject, image, light, plant, reach, retch, shoal, spade, stick, sword, utter 6 broach, dagger, impale, saliva, skewer, sputum, thrust 7 spindle, spittle 8 broacher, likeness, sandbank, spadeful, sprinkle 9 brochette, secretion 11 counterpart, expectorate

spital: den 6 refuge, resort 7 shelter 8 hospital 9 lazaretto

spite: vex 4 hate, hurt, mood 5 annoy, depit, pique, shame, venom 6 enmity, grudge, hatred, injury, malice, mauger, maugre, rancor, thwart 7 chagrin, despite, dislike, ill-will, mortify 8 disgrace, dishonor 9 animosity, frustrate, humiliate 10 resentment 11 disposition, malevolence 12 spitefulness 13 mortification

spiteful: 4 mean 5 catty, snaky 6 sullen 7 waspish 8 annoying, venomous 9 malicious, malignant 10 dispiteous, irritating, vindictive 11 troublesome

spitfire: 9 brimstone

spitter: 4 deer 5 spade 7 brocket 8 spitball 12 expectorater

spitting: 6 saliva 10 exspuition

spittle: 4 spit 6 saliva

spittle insect: 10 froghopper

spittoon: 8 crachoir, cuspidor

spiv: 7 slacker

splash: lap 4 dash, daub, gout, lave, plop, pond, pool, spot 5 bathe, blash, plash, slart, slash, spray 6 blotch, dabble, flouse, floush, strike 7 display, scatter, spatter 8 splatter 9 dashingly 10 appearance, excitement 14 ostentatiously

splashboard: 4 gate, trap 5 board, plank 6 fender, screen 8 mudguard

splashy: wet 5 muddy, showy 6 blashy, slushy 8 striking 11 sensational, spectacular 12 ostentatious

splat: 4 open, plot, spot 5 patch 6 blotch 7 flatten

splatter: dab 4 dash, rush 6 hubbub, splash 7 cluster, spatter 9 splashing

splay: hem 4 awry, turn 5 adorn, bevel, carve, slant, slope 6 clumsy, expand, spread 7 awkward, display, sloping 8 ungainly 9 dislocate, expansion, obliquely, slopingly, spreading 10 slantingly 11 enlargement

spleen: fit 4 fire, milt, mood, whim 5 anger, ardor, freak, humor, mirth, organ, spite 6 malice, temper 7 caprice, dislike, impulse 8 laughter 9 lienculus, merriment 10 melancholy 11 impetuosity
pert. to: 6 lienal

spleeny: 5 angry 7 fretful, peevish 9 irritable 10 melancholy

splendent: 6 glossy 7 beaming, shining 8 lustrous, splendid 9 brilliant 11 conspicuous, illustrious, magnificent, resplendent

splendid: gay 4 braw, fine, good, rial 5 grand, regal, showy, tinny 6 bright, candid, costly, superb 7 gallant, ripping, shining, sublime 8 glorious, gorgeous 9 brilliant, excellent, sumptuous 11 illustrious, magnificent, resplendent

splendor, splendour: 4 gite, pomp 5 blaze, eclat, gleam, glory, sheen 6 bright, fulgor, luster, parade 7 display, fulgour 8 elegance, grandeur, radiance, richness 9 pagaentry, showiness 10 brightness, brilliance, brilliancy, effulgence 12 gorgeousness, magnificence, resplendence 14 impressiveness

splenetic: 6 sullen 7 fretful, peevish, splenic 8 spiteful 9 depressed, irritable, malicious, spleenful 10 melancholy

spleuchan: 5 pouch

splice: 4 join 5 marry, unite 6 fasten 7 wedding 8 marriage 10 interweave

spliced: wed 6 joined, united 7 married

splint: 4 coal, lath, tace, scob 5 brace, plate, split, strip, tasse 6 fasten, shiver, tasset 7 confine 8 splinter

splinter: 4 chip, rend 5 break, broom, slice, smash, spale, split 6 fasten, shiver, sliver 7 confine, flinder, shatter 8 fragment

split: cut, rit 4 chap, rend, rent, rive, ruin, tear 5 break, burst, clave, cleft, crack, peach, reave, riven, share, wedge 6 betray, bisect, bottle, breach, broken, cleave, clo-

ven, dilute, divide, rifted, schism, sliver, sunder 7 destroy, dispart, divided, fissure, portion, rupture, shatter 8 fragment, informer, separate, splinter 9 fractured, separated 10 separation
in two parts: 5 bifid 6 cloven, halved 8 bisected 9 bipartite
split pea: dal
splitfruit: 10 schizocarp
splitting: 5 funny 6 severe 7 comical, fission, rending 8 piercing
of mind: 13 schizophrenia
sploit: 5 spout 6 squirt
splore: 4 bout, brag, riot 5 boast, broil, revel 6 frolic 7 debauch, display 8 carousal, escapade 9 commotion, festivity, scrimmage 11 merrymaking
splotch: dab 4 blob, blot, dash, daub, spot 5 smear, stain 6 blotch, splash
splother: 6 splash 8 splutter
splurge: 6 effort 7 display 11 ostentation 13 demonstration
splutter: 4 fuff 5 hurry, noise, stuff 6 bustle, splash 7 dispute, glutter, quarrel, scatter, spatter, sputter, stammer 8 nonsense 9 confusion
Spode: 5 china 6 potter 9 porcelain
Spohr opera: 8 Jessonda
spoil: mar, rob, rot 4 blad, boot, loot, pelf, prey, ruin, swag 5 bitch, blend, booty, carve, cheat, decay, harry, prize, seize, strip, taint, waste 6 coddle, damage, deface, divest, forage, impair, infuse, injure, pamper, perish, ravage 7 connach, corrump, corrupt, estrepe, deprive, despoil, destroy, indulge, pillage, plunder, violate, vitiate 8 confound, unclothe 10 chevisance, corruption, impairment
eggs: 5 addle
spoiled: bad 5 dazed, musty 6 addled, marred, molded, pettod, preyed, rotted 7 botched, decayed, tainted 8 pampered, pillaged 9 plundered
spoiler: 6 robber 7 marplot 8 pillager 9 despoiler, plunderer 10 depredator
spoilsport: 10 wet-blanket
spoke: bar 4 clog, grip, rung, tale, talk 5 block, check, drone, round, spake, stake, stick 6 radius, speech 7 mention, uttered 8 handhold 10 impediment 11 enchantment
spoken: 4 oral, said 5 parol 7 uttered 9 declaimed
spoliate: rob 7 despoil, pillage, plunder
spoliation: 6 rapine 7 pillage, plunder, robbery 8 pillaged 12 despoliation
spondulix: 5 funds, money
spondyl: 8 vertebra
sponge: bum, wet 4 form, swab, wipe 5 ascon, cadge, dough, erase, mooch 6 absorb, ascula, efface, rhagon 7 badiaga, cleanse, destroy, drinker, scrunge, zimocca 8 drunkard, parasite, scrounge
calcareous: 6 leucon
orifice: 6 oscula(pl.) 7 osculum
pen: 5 kraal
pert. to: 9 poriferal
spicule: 4 toxa
vegetable: 5 loofa 6 loofah
sponge tree: 8 huisache
sponger: 6 cadger 8 parasite
spongewood: 4 sola
spongy: 4 fozy 5 rainy 6 porous, quaggy 9 absorbent
sponsor: 4 back 5 angel 6 backer, gossip, patron, surety 9 godfather, godmother, introduce
sponsorship: 4 egis 5 aegis 8 auspices
spontaneous: 4 free, wild 6 native 8 careless, untaught 9 automatic, impulsive 10 indigenous, self-acting 11 instinctive, involuntary
spontoon: 4 club, pike 7 halberd, pantoon 8 spantoon 9 espantoon, truncheon
spoof: guy 4 fool, hoax, joke 5 trick 7 deceive, swindle 8 nonsense 9 deception
spook: 5 ghost, haunt 6 spirit, wraith 7 specter 9 hobgoblin 10 apparition
spooky: 4 eery 5 eerie, weird 7 ghostly, haunted, uncanny 8 spectral
spool: 4 reel, wind 6 bobbin, broach 7 spindle 8 cylinder
spoon: 4 chip, neck 5 ladle, labis, lover, ninny 6 nestle, shovel, spoony 7 student 8 cochlear, splinter 9 simpleton
spoon-fed: 7 coddled 8 pampered
Spoon River poet: 7 Masters
spoon-shaped: 8 cochlear
spoonbill: 5 ajaja 10 paddlefish
spoondrift: 5 spray 9 spindrift
spoony: 5 silly 7 foolish 11 sentimental
spoor: 5 piste, scent, trace, track, trail
spore: 4 germ, seed
spore sac: 5 ascus
sport (see also **game** *official*): bet, fun, gig, toy 4 game, gaud, glee, jest, joke, mock, play, polo, romp 5 dally, freak, mirth, wager 6 frolic, gamble, racing, shikar 7 contest, gambler, jesting, mockery, pastime 8 derision, raillery 9 amusement, diversion, plaything 10 pleasantry, recreation 13 entertainment
attendance: 4 gate
event: 4 game, meet, race
shirt: tee 4 polo
shoe: 6 loafer 7 sneaker
site: gym 4 grid, oval, pool, ring, rink 5 arena, court, field, links, track 6 course 7 diamond, stadium 8 coliseum 10 hippodrome

summer: 6 diving, hiking, quoits, rowing, skiing 7 fishing, sailing 8 swimming
winter: 6 hockey, skiing 7 skating 8 sledding 11 tobogganing
sportive: gay 5 merry 6 frisky, lusory, wanton 7 amorous, festive, jocular, playful 8 frolicky, gamesome, playsome, pleasant 9 lecherous 10 frolicsome
sportiveness: 7 knavery
sports-minded: 8 athletic
sports official: 5 coach, judge 6 umpire 7 referee 8 linesman 10 timekeeper
sportsman: 6 hunter 7 shikari 8 shikaree
sportula: 4 gift 7 largess, present
sporty: 4 loud 5 showy 6 flashy
spot: bit, dab, dot 4 blot, blur, fish, flaw, mark, site 5 blaze, fault, fleck, nevus, patch, place, point, ready, speck, stain, sully, tache, taint 6 blotch, defect, detect, locate, macula, macule, naevus, remove 7 asperse, blemish, freckle, splotch 8 discolor, disgrace, handicap, locality, location, maculate, position, quantity, reproach 9 bespatter, recognize
kinds of: ace, dot, pip, tee 4 blet, fret, gall, rone, spil, wems 5 macle, oasis 6 alcove, bethel, mascle, mottle, mouche 7 freckle 8 bethesda, fenestra, fontanel
on animal's face: 4 star 5 blaze
on playing card: pip
spotless: 5 clean, snowy 9 blameless, unspotted, unsullied 10 immaculate 11 unblemished, untarnished 14 irreproachable
spotlight: arc 4 beam
spotted: 6 bauson, calico, espied, marked, notate, sanded, ticked 7 bracket, dappled, guttate, mottled, noticed, stained, sullied 9 blemished, suspected, tarnished
animal: 4 paco, pard 6 chital, ocelot 7 cheetah, leopard
fever: 6 typhus
spotter: 7 watcher 9 detective
spotty: 5 dotty 6 uneven 9 irregular
spousal: 7 wedlock 8 ceremony, marriage, nuptials
spouse: wed 4 give, join, mate, wife 5 annar, bride, marry, unite 6 fiance 7 consort, espouse, fiancee, husband, partner, promise, wedlock 8 affiance, espousal, marriage 9 companion 10 bridegroom
spout: jet, jut, lip 4 dale, flow, geat, gush, lift, pawn, pipe, rant 5 eject, issue, orate, shoot, speak, spile, spurt, utter 6 pledge, recite, spigot, spring, squirt, stream, trough 7 conduit, declaim 8 downpour, gargoyle, pawnship 9 discharge, waterfall 10 waterspout
sprack: 4 deft 5 alert 6 active, lively, nimble, shrewd
sprag: 4 prop 6 billet
sprain: 5 chink 6 weaken 10 overstrain
sprang: 5 arose, spray 6 branch
sprangle: 5 spray 6 sprawl, spread 8 straggle, struggle
sprat: 5 bleak 6 garvie 7 herring 8 sixpence
sprattle: 6 sprawl 8 scramble, struggle
sprauchie: 6 sprawl 7 clamber 8 scramble
sprawl: 4 loll 7 grabble 8 struggle 9 sprauchie
spray: jet 4 chap, twig 5 bough, shoot, spree, sprig, water 6 boquet, branch, sparge, spread 7 atomize, bouquet, scatter 8 sprinkle 9 aspersion, discharge, spindrift
spread: fan, jam, ted 4 emit, meal, span, taft 5 cover, flare, jelly, reach, smear, splay, strew, widen 6 anoint, dilate, expand, extend, extent, ramify, unfold, unfurl 7 broaden, compass, diffuse, distend, diverge, divulge, enlarge, exhibit, expanse, overlay, overrun, prolong, protect, publish, radiate, scatter, slather, stretch 8 diffused, dispense, disperse, expanded, extended, increase, multiply, permeate, straddle 9 broadcast, circulate, dispersed, displayed, expansion, expatiate, propagate 10 distribute, generalize 11 disseminate
abroad: 5 bruit, noise, libel, rumor 6 delate, rumour, spring 7 delated, radiate 9 broadcast, publicize 11 disseminate
as plaster: 4 teer
for drying: ted
loosely: 5 strew 7 scatter
out: fan, lap, ted 4 bray, open, span 5 flare, widen 6 deploy, flange, sprawl, unfold
spreader: 6 tedder
spreading of light: 8 halation
spreading out: 6 radial
spree: bat, jag 4 bout, bust, gell, lark, orgy, romp, toot, jagg 5 beano, binge, booze, revel 6 bender, buster, bust-up, frolic, high-go, shindy 7 carouse, debauch, wassail 8 carousal 10 indulgence
sprig: 4 brad, nail, trim, twig 5 bough, scion, shoot, smart, spray, youth 6 active, branch, spruce 7 tendril 9 stripling
sprightliness: 6 gaiety, gayety 8 airiness, alacrity, buoyancy 9 animation
sprightly: gay, tid 4 airy, pert 5 agile, alive, brisk, canty, crank, desto, elfin, peart 6 active, blithe, lively 7 briskly, buoyant, chipper, ghostly, quickly 8 animated, vigorous 10 enlivening, spiritedly, spiritlike 11 incorporeal
spring: ain, fly, hop, spa 4 bend, dart, font, head, jump, leap, lilt, rise, warp, well 5 arise, atart, bound, flirt, glent, issue, lymph, shoot, spurt, therm, tower, vault 6 accrue, bounce, emerge, therme, venero 7

diffuse, estuary, thermae 8 fountain 10 intoxicate
abruptly: 4 bolt
back: 6 recoil, resile 7 rebound
deposit: 4 urao 5 trona
hot: 7 balneum, thermae, gipsies
kind of: ain, cee, spa, ver, hop, ojo 4 font 5 lymph 6 geyser, charco, source, saline 7 gambado 9 Castalian
pert. to: 6 vernal
up: 5 arise
spring-like: 6 vernal
springboard: 5 wagon 6 batule
springbok: 7 gazelle
springe: gin, set 4 trap 5 agile, catch, noose, snare 6 supple 7 ensnare
springer: 7 grampus, spaniel 9 springbok
springing back: 7 elastic 9 renascent
springtime: May 8 germinal
springy: wet 6 spongy 7 elastic 8 flexible 9 resilient
sprinkle: deg, dot, wet 4 dart, rain, spot 5 color, flour, spray, strew, twist, water 6 affuse, bedrop, dabble, dredge, sparge 7 asperge, asperse, drizzle, scatter, spairge, sparkle, spatter 8 disperse 9 bespangle, bespatter 10 besprinkle, intoxicate
with flour: 6 dredge
with grains of mustard: 8 sinapize
with grit: 4 sand
with moisture: 5 bedew
with mud: 9 bespatter
with powder: 4 dust
with water: deg
sprinkler: 7 dredger 11 aspergillum
sprinkling: 4 seme 9 aspersion
sprint: run 4 dash, race 5 snare 6 bicker 7 springe
sprinter: 5 racer 6 runner 7 athlete
sprit: bud 4 dart, pole, rush, spar 5 shoot, speck, sprat 6 sprint, sprout 8 bowsprit 9 germinate
sprite: elf, fay, hob, imp 4 elve, life, mind, mood, peri, soul 5 Ariel, bucca, fairy, genie, ghost, gnome, nisse, pixie, shade, vital 6 goblin, person, spirit 7 essence 9 germinate, hobgoblin 10 apparition, woodpecker 11 disposition, inspiration
kind of: nix 5 ariel, demon, Holda, naiad, nixie 6 Kelpie 8 coltpixy 9 coltpixie 10 leprechaun, shoopiltie
sprocket: cam 5 tooth
sproil: 6 active, energy 7 agility 8 activity 9 energetic
sprout: bud, eye, son 4 cion, brod, chit, chun, germ, malt 5 achar, brode, chine, shoot, spire, spout, sprig, spurt 6 braird, expand, germen, growth, ratoon 7 burgeon 8 offshoot 9 germinate
comb. form: 5 blast 6 blasto 7 blastic
spruce: gim 4 deft, neat, posh, smug, trig, trim 5 compt, fussy, natty, Picea, smart, sprig 6 dapper, picked 7 dandify, finical, smarten 8 overnice, titivate
tree: 5 larch 8 epinette
sprue: 4 hole 5 dross 7 opening 8 psilosis 9 asparagus
sprunt: 4 hill, leap 5 brisk, steep 6 active, spring, spruce 8 struggle
spry: 5 agile, brisk, quick, smart 6 active, clever, nimble, spruce 7 knowing 8 vigorous 9 sprightly
spud: dig, man 4 hand 5 child, dough, drill, knife, money, spade 6 dagger, paddle, potato, reamer, remove, shovel 10 projection
spume: 4 foam, scum 5 froth
spumescent: 7 foaming 8 frothing
spumy: 5 foamy 6 frothy 7 spumous
spun: See **spin**
spunk, sponk: 4 punk 5 anger, flame, gleam, match, nerve, pluck, spark 6 kindle, mettle, spirit, sponge, tinder 7 courage, passion 9 touchwood
spunky: 4 game 5 quick 6 plucky, touchy 8 spirited 9 irritable 10 courageous, mettlesome
spur: egg 4 calk, gaff, goad, move, prod, prop, urge 5 arete, brace, drive, hurry, impel, press, prick, range, ridge, rowel, spine, spoor, strut, tower 6 arouse, broach, calcar, digger, excite, foment, griffe, hasten, incite, motive 7 gablock, provoke, publish 8 buttress, stimulus 9 incentive, instigate, stimulate 10 blockhouse 11 publication
having: 7 spicate
of mountain: 5 arete
on gamecock: 4 gaff
railroad: 6 siding
wheel: 5 rowel
spur wheel: 5 rowel
spurge: 4 weed 5 purge 6 purify 8 milkweed 9 euphorbia
spurious: 4 fake 5 bogus, false, phony, snide 6 forced 7 bastard 10 adulterate, apocryphal, artificial, fictitious, fraudulent 11 counterfeit, superficial 12 illegitimate 14 supposititious
spurl: 6 sprawl 8 scramble
spurn: hit 4 blow, dash, kick, rush, spur 5 haste, scorn 6 affray, incite, pillar, rebuff, refuse, reject, scrape, strike 7 contemn, decline, despise, disdain, scratch, stumble 10 engagement
spurt: bud, jet, jut 4 dart, gush 5 expel, shoot, spell, spout 6 sprout, squirt 8 increase, outbreak
Sputnik: 9 satellite

dog: 5 Laika
sputter: ado 4 fuss, spit
sputum: 4 spit 6 saliva 7 spittle
spy: see 4 case, espy, keek, note, tout 5 scout, sneak, snoop, watch 6 behold, descry, detect, espial, gaycat, mouton, search 7 discern, examine, hi-carra, inspect, observe, snooper 8 discover, emissary, hi-carrah, informer, perceive 10 discoverer, scrutinize 13 intelligencer
famous: 4 Hari 5 Andre, Caleb, Fuchs 6 Arnold, Cavell 8 Mata Hari
spying: 9 espionage 16 counter-espionage
Spyri's heroine: 5 Heidi
squab: coy, fat, shy 4 drop, fall, flop, slop, sofa 5 couch, crush, piper, plump, short, thick 6 callow, pigeon, squash 7 cushion, ottoman 8 nestling 9 fledgling, unfledged, upholster
squabble: 5 brawl 6 bicker, jangle 7 bobbery, contend, dispute, quarrel, wrangle 13 collie-shangie
squabbling: 8 bangling
squad: 4 team 5 group, troop
leader of: 8 sergeant
squadron: 6 armada 10 escadrille
squalid: 4 foul, mean, poor 5 dirty, nasty 6 filthy, sordid 7 unclean 8 wretched 9 miserable, repellant, repellent, repulsive
squall: cry, pet 4 dear, drow, gush, gust, wawl 5 storm 6 flurry, scream, shower, squawk, wretch 7 borasca, borasco, dispute, trouble 8 borasque 9 windstorm 11 disturbance
squalor: mud 4 dirt, mire 5 filth 9 roughness 10 filthiness 11 squalidness 12 wretchedness
squander: 4 burn, lash 5 spend, waste 6 befool, lavish, wander 7 consume, debauch, dispend, scatter 8 disperse, embezzle, misspend 9 dissipate
squanderer: 5 loser 7 wastrel
square: 4 even, parc, park, rule, true 5 agora, carre, clear, exact, hunky, plaza 6 dinkum, direct, honest, settle 7 commons, pattern, quarrel, upright 8 justness. quadrate, standard 9 carre-four, criterion, principle 11 unequivocal 13 parallelogram 15 straightforward
public: 5 plaza 6 common
square dance: 4 reel 7 hoedown, lancers
squared circle: 4 ring 5 arena
squarehead: 4 dolt 5 Swede 6 German 8 numskull 9 screwball 12 Scandinavian
squares: 5 panes
squaring tool: 5 edger
squarish: 4 boxy
squark: 5 croak 6 squawk
squarrose: 5 scaly
squash: 4 beat, fall, ooze, pepo, stop 5 crush, press, quash 7 cymling, flatten, pumpkin, squeeze, squelch 8 suppress 9 discomfit 10 disconcert
kind of: 6 banana, cushaw, simnel, summer, turban 7 cymling, Hubbard, Italian 8 cymbling, patty pan, zucchini 9 crookneck
squashy: wet 4 soft 5 boggy, muddy, mushy 8 overripe
squat: sit 4 fall, quat, sink, stub 5 cower, crush, dumpy, pinch, pudgy, quash, quiet, stoop 6 bruise, crouch, fodgel, hurkle, settle, splash, stubby 7 descend, silence, squatty, squeeze 8 thickset
squatter: 4 flap 5 squat 6 crouch, nester, plunge 7 confuse, flutter, nestler, scatter, settler 8 bewilder, squander 9 sandpiper
Squatter State: 6 Kansas
squatting: 8 couchant
squatty: 5 dumpy, squat 8 thickset
squaw: 6 mahala, coween 10 klootchman
husband: 4 buck 6 sannup
squawbush: 5 sumac
squawfish: 4 chub 8 chappaul
squeak: cry, wee 4 peep 5 cheep, creak, noise, speak 6 betray, escape, shrill 7 confess, disturb
squeal: yip 4 blab, sing 5 broil, frail, weary 6 betray, inform 7 dispute, protest, quarrel 8 complain
squealer: 4 duck, fink 5 quail, swift 6 grouse, pigeon, plover 7 traitor 8 informer 9 partridge
squeamish: shy 4 helo, nice, stir 5 dizzy, heloe 6 bustle, dainty, dauncy, modest, queasy 7 finical, prudish 8 overnice, qualmish 9 dizziness, giddiness, reluctant, sensitive 10 fastidious, scrupulous 13 oversensitive
squeeze: eke, hug, jam 4 gain, mull, neck, silk 5 chirt, creem, crowd, crush, force, pinch, press, wring 6 corner, escape, extort, scrump, scruze, thrust, twitch 7 extract, oppress, procure, scrunch, scrunge 8 compress, condense, pressing, pressure, scrounge 9 constrict, influence 10 commission, constraint 11 compression
squeezer: 5 drier, noose 6 juicer, reamer 7 wringer 8 squeegee 9 extractor
squeezy: 7 cramped 8 confined
squelch: 4 blow, fall 5 crush, quash, quell, stamp 6 rebuke, subdue 7 silence, washrag 8 suppress 9 discomfit 10 disconcert
squelcher: 8 blizzard
squib: jet 4 ball, bomb, mote, pipe, skit, tube 5 candy, match, throw, write 6 speech, squirt, writer 7 dispute, explode, lampoon, pasquil, publish, torpedo, writing 9 bespatter 10 pasquinade 11 firecracker

squid: 6 loligo 7 mollusk, octopus 8 calamary 10 cuttlefish
arm: 8 tentacle
pen: 5 quill
secretion: ink
shell: pen
squiffer: 10 concertina
squiggle: 4 curl, line 5 shake, twist 6 squirm 7 wriggle 8 curlicue
squiggly: 4 wavy 8 twisting 9 wriggling
squilla: 5 prawn 6 shrimp
squinch: 4 arch 5 twist 6 lintel, quince, squint, wrench 7 squeeze, squench 9 corbeling
squint: 4 bent, cast, glee, gleg, gley, skew 5 glent, trend 6 gledge, goggle 7 deviate 10 hagioscope, strabismus
squint-eyed: 5 gleed, gleyd
squire: 5 lover, title 6 donzel, escort 7 gallant 8 henchman, servitor 9 accompany, attendant, gentleman, landowner
squirrel: bun 5 sisel, xerus 6 chippy, gyrate 7 assapan 8 archilla, jelerang 9 assapanic, chickaree, shadetail
burrowing: 6 gopher
flying: 7 assapan
genus of: 7 sciurus
nest: 4 dray, drey
shrew: 4 tana
skin: 4 vair
squirrellike: 8 sciuroid
animal: 8 dormouse
squirt: 5 chirt, skite, slirt, spout, spurt 14 whippersnapper
sri: 4 holy 7 Lakshmi 8 glorious, reverend 9 fortunate
stab: dag, jab, jag, try 4 gore, jagg, pink, yerk 5 chive, drive, knife, knive, lunge, prick, sound, stake, stick, stool, stump, wound 6 broach, dagger, pierce, strike, stroke, thrust 7 attempt, poniard, roughen 8 puncture 9 penetrate
in fencing: 4 pink 8 stoccado
stability: 5 poise 7 balance 8 firmance, firmness 9 constancy, fixedness 10 permanence, stableness, steadiness 12 immovability, immutability 13 steadfastness 15 indissolubility
stabilize: fix, set 5 poise 6 steady 8 regulate
stabilizer: 7 ballast
stable: 4 barn, fast, firm, shed, sure 5 fixed, set-up, solid, sound, stall 6 hangar, secure, steady, strong, sturdy 7 durable, equerry, lasting 8 constant, enduring, immobile 9 confirmed, establish, permanent, resistant, steadfast, unabashed, unvarying 10 stationary, unwavering 11 established, trustworthy 12 unchangeable
compartment: 5 stall
range: 4 mews
royal: 4 mews
stableman: 5 groom 6 ostler 7 hostler
stack: set 4 bike, heap, pile, rick, pike, stow, tier 5 group, hovel, mound, scroo, shock 7 chimney, conduit 9 fireplace
stack up: 4 tier 5 total
stackyard: 7 haggard 10 stackgarth
stad: 4 town 7 village
staddle: row 4 cane, tree 5 staff, stain, swath 6 crutch 7 sapling, support
stade: 7 furlong, stadium
stadium: 4 oval 5 arena, stade, stage 7 furlong 8 coliseum
staff: bar, gad, rod 4 cane, club, line, mace, maul, pole, prod, rung, wand 5 aides, baton, crook, lance, pedum, perch, spear, stave, stick, suite 6 baston, cudgel, stanza 7 attache, bailiff, caducei(pl.), scepter, sceptre, support 8 caduceus 9 constable, entourage, personnel 10 assistants, associates 12 quarter-staff
bearer: 5 macer
kinds of: 4 kent, wand 5 filch 6 croche, muleta 7 baculus, bourdon, cambuca, crosier, crozier, distaff, rhabdos 10 alpenstock
officers: 5 aides, cadre
staff of life: 5 bread
stag: 4 colt, hart 7 pollard, shorten 8 informer
horn: 4 rial 9 berantler
stage: era 4 dais, gest, step, tier 5 board, coach, floor, grade, level, phase, shelf, stair, story 6 degree, stadia 7 display, exhibit, produce, rostrum, stadium, theater 8 platform, scaffold 9 condition, gradation 10 proscenium, stagecoach 11 subdivision
extra: 4 supe 5 super
hanging: 7 scenery
on: 7 en scene
part: 4 role
pert. to: 6 scenic
raised: 4 dais 7 estrade
stage direction: all 4 exit, sola 5 aside, enter, manet, omnes, solus 6 exeunt, sennet 8 loquitur
stage whisper: 5 aside
stagecoach: 9 diligence
stager: 5 actor 6 player
stagger: 4 reel, rock, stun, sway 5 lurch, shake, waver 6 hobble, totter, wintle(Sc.) 7 tremble, vibrate 8 hesitate, titubate, unsettle
stagnant: 4 dull, foul 5 inert, stale, still 8 sluggish, standing 10 motionless 13 unprogressive
stagnate: 4 dull 5 inert 10 motionless
stagnation: 6 stasis, stases, torpor
stagy: 8 affected 10 theatrical

staid: set 5 fixed, grave, sober 6 demure, sedate, steady 7 earnest, serious, settled 8 decorous 9 dignified, steadfast 10 coolheaded
stain: dye 4 blot, blur, soil, spot, tint 5 cloud, paint, smear, sully, tache, taint, tinge, trace 6 blotch, infamy macula, smirch, smudge, stigma, vilify 7 blemish, corrupt, tarnish 8 discolor, disgrace, dishonor, maculate, tincture 9 bespatter, pollution 10 attainture 11 contaminate
stainless: 4 pure
stair: 4 step 5 stage, stile 6 degree
face: 5 riser
post: 5 newel
series of: 6 flight
staircase: 5 grece, grice 6 griece
moving: 9 escalator
on ship: 12 companionway
outdoor: 6 perron
part of: 4 rung 5 newel, riser, tread
portable: 6 ladder
spiral: 8 caracole
stake: bet, peg, pin, pot, set 4 ante, back, gage, pale, pile, pole, pool, post, risk, spit, stob 5 anvil, prize, spile, stick, teest, wager 6 chance, gamble, hazard, picket 7 venture 9 grubstake
driver: 4 maul
pert. to: 5 palar
stale: old 4 flat, hoar, lure, rung, worn 5 banal, blown, corny, decoy, frowy, moldy, musty, shaft, trite, vapid, waugh(Sc.) 7 insipid 9 hackneyed, tasteless 10 flavorless, prostitute 11 commonplace 13 uninteresting
stalemate: 4 draw 7 impasse 8 deadlock 10 standstill
stalk: bun 4 axis, halm, hunt, mote, risp, seta, stem 5 haulm, spear, stipe, straw 6 pursue, ratoon, stride 7 pedicel, petiole 8 peduncle
having: 9 petiolate
remove: 5 strig
stalker: 6 hunter
stalking-horse: 5 blind, decoy 7 pretext
stalkless: 7 sessile
stall: bin, cot, pew 4 crib, loge, mire, seat, stop 5 boose, boosy, booth, check, crame, decoy, delay, stand 6 manger, stable 7 pretext, station 8 hesitate 9 enclosure 10 dilly-dally 11 compartment, confederate
stallion: 6 cooser(Sc.)
stalwart: 4 firm 5 brave, stout 6 brawny, robust, strong, sturdy 7 valiant 8 partisan, resolute 10 unyielding
stamina: gut 4 grit 5 vigor 7 essence 8 backbone, capacity, strength 9 endurance, fortitude
stammer: 4 hack, stut 6 falter, hacker 7 fribble, stumble, stutter 8 hesitate
stamp: die 4 beat, coin, form, kind, mark, seal, tool, type 5 brand, class, crush, drive, pound, press, print, stomp 6 signet, strike, thresh 7 impress, imprint, postage, sticker 8 inscribe 9 character 10 impression 11 distinguish
collecting: 9 philately
fencing: 5 appel
madness for: 11 timbromania
paper: 6 pelure
space: 8 spandrel
stampede: 4 bolt, rout, rush 5 panic 6 flight 7 debacle
stamping plate: die
stance: 4 pose 7 posture, station 8 position
stanch, staunch: 4 firm, stem, stop, true 5 allay, check, close, loyal, quell, sound 6 hearty, quench, steady, strong, trusty 7 zealous 8 constant, faithful, resolute 9 steadfast 10 extinguish, unswerving, unwavering, watertight 11 substantial, trustworthy
stanchion: bar 4 beam, post, prop 5 brace, piton 7 confine, support, upright
stand: set 4 bear, dais, ease, halt, hold, last, rack, stop 5 abide, arise, booth, cease, erect, pause, table 6 afford, endure, podium, remain, resist, tripod, trivet 7 etagere, station, sustain, support, taboret, undergo 8 attitude, continue, hesitate, maintain, position, tabouret, tolerate 9 withstand
candles: 7 epergne 10 candelabra
cuplike: 4 zarf
for: 4 mean 8 tolerate 9 represent
for election: run
in awe of: 4 fear 5 dread 7 respect
on end: 5 upend
on hind legs: 4 ramp, rear
opposite: 4 face
ornamental: 7 atagere, etagere
out: jut 6 beetle 7 project 8 overhang, protrude
painter's: 5 easel
small: 7 taboret 8 tabouret
still: ho 4 stop, whoa
three-legged: 6 tripod, trivet
stand-in: 10 substitute
standard: cup, par, set 4 fiar(Sc.), flag, mark, norm, suit, type, unit 5 canon, chest, grade, gauge, ideal, level, model 6 assize, banner, beacon, coffer, ensign, goblet, normal, sample, signal 7 classic, example, labarum(L.), pattern, support, upright 8 accepted, brattach(Sc.), gonfalon, orthodox, vexillum 9 criterion, oriflamme, yardstick 10 touchstone 11 candlestick

bearer: 11 gonfalonier
golf: 5 bogey, bogie
of measurement: 6 metric
Turkish: 4 alem, toug
standardize: 9 calibrate
standing: 4 rank 5 being, erect, fixed 6 estate, stable, stance, status 7 lasting, settled, statant, station, upright 8 constant, duration, location, position, stagnant 9 permanent, situation 10 reputation, stationary
upright: 11 orthostatic
standing room only: S.R.O.
standstill: 4 halt, rest, stop 5 stand, state 8 deadlock 9 cessation, stalemate
stang: bar 4 ache, pang, pole 5 sting, throb
stanhope: 5 buggy
stank: 4 pond, pool 5 ditch
stanza: 5 envoi, stave, verse 7 strophe 8 division 9 apartment
eight line: 6 huitan, octave 7 triolet
five line: 8 cinquain
four line: 8 quatrain
irregular: 13 alloeostropha
six line: 6 sestet
ten line: 6 dizain 7 dizaine
three line: 8 tristich
staple: 4 city, town 5 chief, fiber, shaft 7 chaplet, support 8 fastener 9 principal 10 foundation
star (see also **constellation**): ace, orb, sun 4 hero, lead 5 actor, badge, shine 6 etoile 7 actress, estoile, heroine, ingenue, stellar 8 asterisk, luminary, pentacle, twinkler 9 bespangle, headliner, principal 10 preeminent, topnotcher
apple: 7 caimito
brightest in constellation: 5 alpha
combining form: 5 astro 6 sidero
difference in direction: 8 parallax
divination: 9 astrology
evening: 5 Venus 6 Hesper, Vesper 7 Evestar 8 Hesperus
evil: 8 sidereal
exploding: 4 nova
five-pointed: 8 pentacle
group: 6 galaxy 13 constellation
in Aquila: 6 Altair
in Bootes: 8 Arcturus
in Canis Major: 6 Sirius
in Carina: 7 Canopus
in Centaurus: 5 Agena
in Cetus: 4 Mira
in Cygnus: 5 Deneb 7 Albireo
in Draco: 6 Alsafi 7 Al Rakis, Eltanin
in Gemini: 5 Wasat 6 Alhena, Castor, Pollux
in Leo: 7 Regulus
in Lyra: 4 Vega
in Orion: 5 Rigel, Saiph
in Perseus: 5 Algol
in Scorpius: 7 Antares
in Taurus: 8 Pleiades
in Ursa Major: 5 Alcor, Mizar 6 Alkaid
in Ursa Minor: 7 Polaris
in Virgo: 5 Spica
morning: 4 Mars 5 Venus 6 Saturn 7 Daystar, Jupiter, Mercury
north: 7 polaris 8 loadstar, lodestar, polestar
pert to: 6 astral 7 astrean, stellar 8 sidereal, stellate
representation: 6 etoile
resembling: 8 stellate 9 stellated
shooting: 5 comet 6 Leonid, meteor
six-pointed: 8 hexagram
suddenly flaring: 4 nova
two: 9 bistellar
variable: 4 Mira
worshiper: 7 sabaist
star cluster: 6 nebula
star facet: 4 pane
star-like: 8 stellate
starch: vim 4 arum, sago 5 tikor, vigor 6 amylum, energy, farina, strong 7 cassava, precise, stiffen 8 activity, glycogen, strength 9 arrowroot, formality, stiffness 12 carbohydrate
combining form: 4 amyl
starchy: 5 rigid, stiff 6 formal 7 precise 9 unbending
stare: 4 gape, gaup, gawk, gawp, gaze, gouk, gowk, gype, look, ogle, peer 5 glare, glaze, glore 6 glower, goggle 7 bristle 8 starling
starfish: 7 sun star 8 asteroid
limb: ray
stargazer: 4 fish 10 astrologer, astronomer
staring: 6 astare, gazing 7 glaring 8 wide-eyed
stark: 4 bare, firm, hard, pure 5 bleak, harsh, quite, rigid, rough, sheer, stern, stiff, tense, utter 6 barren, severe, strong, wholly 7 violent 8 absolute, complete, desolate, entirely, obdurate, powerful, stalwart, stripped, vigorous 9 downright, unadorned 10 absolutely, unyielding 11 intractable
starling: 6 pastor
starnose: 4 mole
starry: 6 astral, bright 7 shining, stellar 8 sidereal, starlike, stellate 9 sparkling
Star-Spangled Banner author: 15 Francis Scott Key
start: fit, run, shy 4 dart, head, jerk, jump, lead, rush 5 alarm, begin, dodge, enter, flush, glent, lever, onset, rouse, sally, shock, wince 6 boggle, broach, flinch, fright, loosen, outset, spring, twitch 7 disturb, get away, impulse, provoke, retreat,

startle 8 commence, displace, handicap, outburst 9 advantage, dislocate, introduce, originate
starter: 5 drill, punch 7 entrant 8 official 10 controller
startle: 5 alarm, rouse, scare, shock, start 6 excite 8 affright, frighten, surprise 9 electrify
startling: 7 rousing 8 alarming, restless, skittish 10 surprising
starvation: 6 famine
starve: 4 fast 6 famish, hunger
starveling: 4 lean 6 hungry, pining, wasted
starwort: 5 aster 9 chickweed, colicroot
stash: end 4 stop 5 store
stashie: 6 clamor
state: say 4 acme, aver, etat(F.), mode, pomp, rank, seat, tell, term, weal 5 chair, posit, style, utter 6 affirm, allege, assert, avouch, degree, empire, estate, height, nation, polity, recite, relate, report, status, throne 7 account, country, declare, dignity, enounce, express, narrate 8 ceremony, eminence, grandeur, position, property, propound, standing 9 community, condition, enunciate, pronounce, situation, territory 10 asseverate, possession 11 stateliness 12 circumstance, commonwealth
based on honor: 9 timocracy
bound by treaty: 4 ally
explicitly: 6 define 7 itemize, specify 13 particularize
ideal: 6 Utopia
member: 7 citizen
of balance: 9 equipoise
of excitement: 7 ferment
of mind: 4 mood 5 humor 6 morale
office of: 11 secretariat
pert. to: 7 federal
relating to: 6 statal
under foreign control: 12 protectorate
State Fair author: 5 Stong
state police: 7 trooper
stated: 5 fixed 6 avowed 7 regular 8 declared 10 formulated 11 established
statehouse: 7 capitol
stately: 5 grand, lofty 6 august, formal, superb 7 courtly, gallant, haughty 8 imperial, imposing, majestic 9 dignified 10 deliberate 11 ceremonious, magisterial, magnificent
music: 5 largo
woman: 4 Juno
statement: 4 bill, word 5 audit, dicta 6 dictum, precis, remark, report, resume 7 account, address, article, bromide, epitome, invoice, recital, summary 8 abstract, averment(law), relation, sentence, schedule 9 affadavit, agreement, manifesto, narrative 10 allegation, deposition, expression 11 abridgement, affirmation, assertation, certificate, declaration 12 presentation 13 prevarication 14 circumspection
assumed true: 7 premise
authoritative: 6 dictum
defamatory: 5 libel
formal: 9 affidavit 10 deposition
introductory: 5 proem 6 prolog 7 preface, prelude 8 foreword, prologue
mathematical: 7 theorem
of belief: 5 credo, creed
of facts. 4 case
self-contradictory: 7 paradox
self-evident: 6 truism
stateroom: 5 cabin
statesman: 7 statist 10 politician
static: 7 resting 8 inactive 9 quiescent 10 stationary
station: fix, run, set 4 camp, halt, post, rank, seat, spot, stop 5 berth, depot, field, place, serai, siege 6 assign, church, degree, region, stance 7 appoint, calling, cuartel(Sp.), dignity, habitat, posture 8 attitude, location, position 9 condition, homestead, situation 10 constitute 11 equilibrium, institution
stationary: set 4 fast 5 fixed 6 stable, static 8 immobile, moveless 9 immovable, sedentary 10 unchanging
stationer: 9 publisher 10 bookseller
stationery: ink, pen 4 book 5 blank, paper 6 pencil 10 papeteries
statist: 9 statesman 10 politician
statistics collector: 7 statist 12 statistician
statue: 4 bust, icon, ikon, nude 5 image, orant 6 bronze 7 Madonna 8 Colossus, figurine, likeness, monument
at Thebes: 6 Memnon
base: 6 plinth
gigantic: 8 colossus
in London Guildhall: Gog 5 Magog
praying: 5 orant
primitive: 6 xoanon
that came to life: 7 Galatea
upper part of: 4 bust 5 torso
weeping: 5 Niobe
Statue of Liberty: *poet:* 7 Lazarus
sculptor: 9 Bartholdi
statuesque: 7 stately 8 graceful
statuette: 8 figurine
stature: 6 height
status: 4 rank 5 state 6 aspect, classe(F.) 8 position, relation, standing 9 condition
statute: act, law 4 rule 5 edict 6 assize, decree 9 enactment, ordinance 10 regulation
heading of: 5 title
volume of: 4 code 5 codex 7 codices
staunch: See **stanch**

stave: bar 4 beat, rung, slat, stap(Sc.) 5 break, knock, lathi, staff, stick 6 baculi(pl.), cudgel 7 baculus 8 puncture
bundle of: 5 shook

staver: 6 totter 7 saunter

stavesacre: 8 larkspur

stay: dam, guy, lie, rib 4 bide, calm, halt, hold, live, prop, rely, rest, rope, stem, stop, tack, wait 5 abide, allay, avast, await, brace, cable, cease, check, delay, demur, dwell, pause, quell, stand, stare, tarry 6 arrest, depend, detain, endure, fasten, linger, pacify, remain, reside, resist, secure, shroud, status 7 appease, control, incline, refrain, satisfy, sojourn, support, sustain, triatic 8 continue, restrain 9 anchorage, cessation, hindrance, residence 10 impediment, permanence 12 postponement

staying power: 7 stamina 9 endurance

stead: 4 farm, help, lieu, site, spot 5 avail, beset, place, trace, track 6 assist, behalf 7 benefit, bestead, impress, involve, replace, service, support 8 bedstead, locality, position 9 advantage, farmstead, situation, successor 10 substitute

steadfast, stedfast: 4 fast, firm, true 5 fixed, staid 6 stable, stanch, steady 7 certain, settled, staunch 8 constant, faithful, resolute 9 immovable 10 unchanging, unswerving 11 established, unalterable

steadiness: 5 nerve 7 balance 8 firmness 9 constancy

steading: 9 farmhouse, homestead

steady: 4 calm, even, firm 5 fixed, grave, sober, staid 6 direct, stable, sturdy 7 assured, equable, regular, uniform 8 constant, diligent, faithful, reliable, resolute 9 incessant, steadfast 10 continuous, controlled, invariable, sweetheart, unswerving 11 unfaltering, unmitigated 13 unfluctuating, uninterrupted

steak: 4 club 5 chuck, flank, round, shell, t-bone 7 griskin, New York, sirloin 9 entrecote 11 porterhouse

steal: bag, cly, cop, gyp, nim, rap 4 crib, gain, glom, hook, lift, stem, take 5 bribe, creep, fetch, filch, harry, pinch, poach, shaft, stalk, swipe 6 abduct, burgle, convey, divert, extend, handle, kidnap, pilfer, pirate, rustle, snitch 7 purloin 8 embezzle, peculate 9 condiddle 10 plagiarize 11 appropriate 14 misappropriate

stealage: 5 theft 7 larceny 8 burglary

stealer: 5 thief 6 robber 7 burglar 10 plagiarist 11 biblioklept
cattle: 7 abactor, rustler

stealthy: sly 6 artful, secret 7 catlike, cunning, furtive 11 clandestine 13 surreptitious
walk: 5 stalk

steam: 4 boil, fume, reek 5 force, power, smoke, vapor 6 energy 8 vaporize, vexation 10 exhalation, irritation
jet: 8 soffione, soffioni
pipe: 5 riser

steamer: 4 boat, ship 5 liner 6 vessel 9 steamship
cabin: 5 texas

steaming: 5 aboil

steamship: 5 liner 7 steamer
route: 4 lane
smokestack: 6 funnel

stearic acid: 8 stearate

steatite: 4 talc 9 soapstone

stech: 4 cram 5 gorge 10 gormandize

steed: 4 Arab 5 horse 7 charger, courser

steek: 4 shut 5 close 6 fasten, stitch

steel: 4 rail 5 acier(F.), inure, press 6 damask, harden, smooth, toledo 8 Bessemer, Damascus 10 strengthen
process: 8 Bessemer 11 cementation

steelhead: 5 trout

steely: 10 unyielding

steelyard: 7 balance

steep: ret 4 bate, bath, bold, bowk, brew, buck, high, soak, stew, tall 5 bathe, brant, brent, heavy, hilly, imbue, lofty, proud, sharp, sheer 6 abrupt, bright, clifty, decoct, drench, imbibe, imbrue, infuse, soothe 7 arduous, extract, extreme, immerse 8 elevated, headlong, macerate, saturate, solution 9 difficult, distemper, excessive, precipice 10 exorbitant, impregnate 11 precipitous 13 perpendicular

steeper: vat 6 teapot, vessel 7 cistern

steeple: 5 spire, tower 6 cupola 8 pinnacle 9 campanile

steeply: 5 brant

steepness: 6 height

steer: ox; con, tip 4 conn, helm, lead, stot 5 guide, pilot 6 bovine, direct, govern, manage 7 bullock, control, oversee
close to wind: 4 luff

steerage: 8 guidance 9 direction 10 management, regulation

steering: aim 9 direction, mangement 10 government
apparatus: 4 helm 5 wheel 6 rudder, tiller
part: 10 rudderhead
superintend: con 4 conn

steery: 4 stir 6 tumult

steeve: 4 pack, stow 5 store, stuff

stein: mug 4 toby

steinbock: 8 antelope

steinkirk, steenkirk: 6 cravat 9 neckcloth

stela, stele: 4 slab 6 pillar 8 monument 10 gravestone

stelar: 10 columnlike

stellar: 5 chief 6 astral, starry 7 leading 8 starlike, stellate 9 principal
stellate: 8 starlike 10 star-shaped
Steller's sea cow: 6 rytina
stem: bow, bun, dam, ram 4 axis, base, body, bole, cane, culm, halt, hold, load, prow, race, reed, rise, risp, root, stop, tamp 5 check, haulm, shaft, stalk, steer, stipe, stock, trunk 6 branch, derive, oppose, stanch 7 lineage, pedicel, petiole, spindle 8 ancestry, contract, peduncle, restrain 9 originate, petiolule
bulblike: 4 corm 5 tuber 7 rhizome
climbing: 4 bine 7 tendril
comb. form: 4 caul 5 caulo
fungus: 5 stipe
joint: 4 node
part: 4 pith 5 stele
pert. to: 7 cauline 8 stipular
sheath: 5 ocrea
stemless: 11 acaulescent
stemma: 7 descent, lineage 8 ancestry, pedigree
stemmer: bar
stem-winder: 5 watch
stench: 4 fogo, odor, reek 5 fetor, smell, stink 6 foetor
Stendhal hero: 5 Sorel
stenographer: 5 steno
stenography: 9 shorthand 12 brachygraphy
stent: 5 tight 6 extend, extent 7 stretch 12 outstretched
stentor: 6 roarer
stentorian: 4 loud
step: sty, way 4 gait, pace, rank, rest, rung, walk 5 break, crush, dance, grade, ledge, level, plane, round, shelf, space, stage, stair, stalk, strut, stufe(G.), trace, tread 6 action, degree, manner, squash, stride 7 advance, deprive, imprint, measure 8 distance, footfall, foothold, footrest, footstep, movement 9 footprint, gradation, procedure, promotion 10 proceeding, stepladder 11 translation
dance: pas 5 coule 6 chasse 8 glissade
introductory: 8 rudiment 10 initiative
ladder's: 4 rime, rung
measuring device: 10 passimeter
over fence: 5 stile
part: 5 riser, tread 6 nosing
recording device: 8 odograph
rope ladder: 7 ratline
series of raised: 6 gradin 7 gradine
step up: rev
step-by-step: 8 gradatim(L.)
step-in: 4 shoe 7 slipper
step-ins: 10 underpants
stepbrother: 9 beau-frere(F.) 11 beaux-freres
stepdame: 10 stepmother
steppe: 5 plain 7 prairie 9 wasteland
storm: 5 buran
stepper: 6 dancer
steps: See **step, staircase**
stepson: 8 beau-fils(F.) 9 beaux-fils
stere: 9 kiloliter
sterotype: 6 repeat 7 hackney
sterotyped: 5 trite
sterile: dry 4 arid, dead, geld 6 barren, meager, meagre, otiose 7 aseptic, useless 8 impotent 9 fruitless, infertile 10 unfruitful 11 ineffective 12 unproductive
sterility: 7 asepsis
sterilize: 9 disinfect
sterling: 5 penny 7 genuine 9 excellent
stern: 4 back, dour, firm, grim, hard, helm 5 harsh, rough, steer, stout 6 fierce, gloomy, mighty, rudder, savage, severe, strict, strong, sturdy, sullen, tiller, unkind 7 austere, massive 8 exacting, resolute, rigorous 9 unbending, unfeeling 10 astringent, forbidding, inexorable, inflexible, relentless, uninviting, unyielding 11 hardhearted 14 uncompromising
toward: aft 5 abaft 6 astern
Sterne character: 4 Slop, Toby, Trim 6 Shandy 8 Tristram
sternforemost: 7 awkward 8 backward
sternness: 5 rigor 7 cruelty 8 hardness, severity 9 austerity, harshness, rigidness, stiffness 10 strictness 12 exactingness 13 inflexibility
sternutation: 6 sneeze 8 sneezing
sternward: aft 5 abaft 6 astern
sterol: 7 alcohol
stertor: 5 snore
stevdore: 6 loader, stower 8 cargador 12 longshoreman
steven: din 4 roar 5 noise, voice 6 outcry
Stevenson: *character: Jim* 4 Hyde
home: 5 Samoa
stew: 4 boil, cook, dive, fret, mess, olio 5 bathe, cloud, imbue, steep, study, sweat, worry 6 burgoo, ragout, seethe, simmer 7 brothel, haricot, swelter 8 hothouse 9 Brunswick, confusion 10 capilotade, excitement, hodgepodge, hotchpotch 11 predicament
steward: 4 hind 5 dewan, diwan, graff, grave 6 factor, grieve, waiter 7 bailiff, curator, foreman, granger, manager, officer, proctor 8 bhandari, employee 9 custodian, dispenser, seneschal 10 magistrate 11 chamberlain
monastery: 8 cellarer
ship: 6 flunky 7 flunkey

stewed: 5 drunk 10 inebriated 11 intoxicated
stey: 5 steep
sthenic: 6 active, strong
stib: 6 dunlin 9 sandpiper
stich: 4 line 5 verse
stick: bat, bow, cue, gad, gum, put, rod, set 4 bind, cane, clag, clam, club, fife, glue, kill, mast, poke, pole, push, shut, spit, stab, stem, stop, twig, wand 5 affix, baton, cheat, cleam, cling, close, delay, demur, flute, mount, paste, place, prick, shoot, shove, staff, stalk, stall, stave, trunk 6 adhere, attach, baffle, ballow, billet, branch, cement, cleave, cohere, cudgel, endure, fasten, ferule, fescue, impale, mallet, pierce, puzzle, rammer, strike, thrust 7 confine, defraud, drummer 8 bludgeon, clarinet, hesitate, puncture, revolver, tolerate 9 crabstick, drumstick
bamboo: 5 lathi 6 lathee
bundle of: 5 fagot 6 fasces 7 fascine
conductor's: 5 baton
crooked: 5 caman 7 cammock, gambrel
jumping: 4 pogo
measuring: 5 ruler 7 ellwand 8 yardwand 9 yardstick
mountain climbing: 10 alpenstock
stick out: 7 extrude
stick up: 6 hold up
sticker: bur 4 burr 5 knife, label, poser, thorn 6 paster, puzzle, weapon 7 bramble
sticking: 6 viscid 8 adhering, cohesive 12 stonewalling
stickit: 6 failed 7 botched 9 imperfect 12 unsuccessful
stickle: 5 demur, rapid, rough, steep 6 higgle, pacify 7 contend, current, scruple 8 separate 9 agitation, altercate, intervene 10 perplexity 11 participate 12 perturbation
stickleback: 6 bandie(Sc.)
stickler: 6 purist, second, umpire 7 arbiter, meddler 8 mediator
sticky: 4 clit 5 gluey, gooey, humid, messy 6 claggy, clammy, clarty, slushy, viscid, wooden 7 viscous 8 adhesive 9 difficult, glutinous 10 saccharine 13 uncomfortable
stife: 4 fume 5 smell
stiff: bum 4 deep, firm, hard, high, hobo, taut 5 brave, budge, clung, dense, fixed, grave, harsh, horse, money, rigid, steep, tense, thick, tramp, woody 6 clumsy, corpse, formal, loafer, proper, robust, severe, stanch, strong, sturdy 7 awkward, buckram, cadaver, precise, starchy 8 absorbed, exacting, resolute, rigorous, stalwart, starched, stubborn 9 difficult, laborious, obstinate, unbending 10 ceremonial, consistent, inflexible, unyielding 12 pertinacious 14 uncompromising
stiff-necked: 8 stubborn 9 obstinate 12 contumacious
stiffen: set 5 brace 6 benumb, harden, starch 10 inspissate
stiffness: 5 rigor 8 rigidity 10 constraint 11 starchiness
stifle: gag 4 stop 5 check, choke 6 muffle, quench 7 repress, smother 8 strangle, suppress, throttle 9 suffocate 10 extinguish
stigma: 4 blot, mark, scar, spot 5 brand, cloud, odium, stain, taint 6 defect 7 blemish 10 projection
stigmatize: 5 brand 8 denounce
stile: 4 step 5 style 6 gnomon 9 turnstile
stiletto: 4 kill, stab 6 bodkin, dagger, stylet 9 eyeleteer
still: but, een, low, mum, tho, yet 4 also, calm, cosh, drip, even, ever, hush, lull, stop 5 allay, check, inert, quiet 6 always, distil, gentle, hushed, pacify, serene, soothe 7 appease, however, silence, subdued 8 habitual, inactive, restrain, suppress, tranquil 9 noiseless, uniformly 10 constantly, distillery, motionless, stationary, uneventful 11 continually 12 nevertheless
stillicide: 4 drip, drop
stillness: 5 peace, quiet 7 silence 8 calmness 9 quietness 11 taciturnity
stilly: 4 calm 5 quiet 7 quietly 8 silently
stilt: 4 limp, pile, pole, post 5 shaft 6 crutch
stilted: 6 formal 7 awkward, pompous 8 affected 9 bombastic, dignified 11 sententious
Stilton: 6 cheese
feature: 4 mold
Stilwell's nickname: 10 Vinegar Joe
stimulant: kat 5 drink, tonic 6 bracer 8 beverage 9 sassafras
heart: 8 cardiant, thialdin 9 digitalis, thialdine 10 adrenaline, epinephrin 11 epinephrine
in coffee: 7 caffein
in tea: 5 thein
stimulate: fan, jog, pep 4 goad, move, spur, stir, urge, whet 5 brace, elate, filip, impel, rouse, sting 6 affect, arouse, excite, fillip, incite 7 animate, enliven, inspire, provoke, quicken 8 irritate, motivate 9 encourage, galvanize, instigate 10 exhilarate, invigorate
stimulating: 5 brisk 9 innerving 12 invigorating
stimulus: 4 goad, spur 5 filip, sting 6 fillip, motive 7 impetus 9 incentive
threshold: 5 limen

sting: 4 bite, dupe, goad, mast, pain, pike, pole, post, tang, urge 5 cheat, prick, shaft, smart, wound 6 impale, incite, nettle, pierce, tingle 7 stimuli 8 irritate, stimulus 9 stimulate 10 incitement
stinger: 4 blow 5 drink
stinginess: 9 closeness, frugality, parsimony 13 niggardliness
stinging: 6 biting, bitter 7 caustic, piquant, pungent 8 piercing 10 irritating 11 acrimonious
stingo: ale, vim, zip 4 beer, zest 6 energy
stingray: 6 obispo
stingy: 4 dree(Sc.), hard, mean 5 cheap, light, sharp, stint, tight 6 biting, greedy, meager, scanty 7 miserly, niggard, nipping, selfish 8 covetous 9 illiberal, penurious 10 avaricious 11 closefisted 12 parsimonious
stinking: 4 foul, rank 5 drunk, fetid 6 putrid, rancid 7 noisome 9 offensive 10 malodorous
stint, stent: 4 duty, stay, stop, task 5 bound, cease, check, chore, delay, limit, scant, serve, spare, stunt 6 assign, desist, divide, scrimp 7 confine 8 quantity, restrain, restrict, stoppage 9 cessation, economize, restraint 10 assignment, limitation, proportion 11 restriction
stinting: 7 sparing 8 scanting
stipe: 4 stem 5 stalk 6 caudex 7 petiole
stipend: ann, fee, pay 4 hire, wage 5 annal 6 income, salary 7 payment, prebend 9 allowance 12 compensation, remuneration
stipendiary: 4 beak 7 soldier, teacher 9 clergyman, mercenary 10 magistrate
stipple: dot 6 render 7 engrave, speckle
stipulate: 5 agree 7 bargain, specify 8 contract, covenant
stipulation: 4 bond, item 6 clause, detail 7 article, bargain, proviso 8 contract, covenant 9 agreement, condition, situation 11 arrangement, undertaking
stipule of leaflet: 6 stipel
stir: ado, fan, gog, jog, mix, sir 4 busk, fuss, jail, move, plow, poke, roil, to-do 5 amove, budge, churn, doing, hurry, rally, rouse, shake, shift, shove, stoke, waken 6 arouse, awaken, bestir, bustle, excite, flurry, foment, hubbub, incite, motion, muddle, pother, prison, quetch, tumult 7 agitate, animate, blunder, disturb, flutter, inflame, provoke, trouble 8 activity, brandish, displace, movement 9 commotion, exagitate, stimulate 10 manipulate 12 penitentiary
together: 6 stodge
stirabout: 8 porridge
stirk: cow 4 bull 6 heifer 7 bullock
stirless: 10 motionless
stirps: 4 race 5 stock 6 branch
stirra: boy 6 sirrah 9 stripling
stirring: 5 astir 6 moving, tumult, uproar 7 rousing 8 activity, exciting, movement 9 agitation, animating, inspiring, thrilling 10 incitement 11 stimulating
stirrup: bar 4 ring, rope 5 clamp, strap 6 stapes 7 support 8 footrest
hood: 8 tapadera(Sp.)
straps: 8 chapelet
stirrup bone: 6 stapes
stitch: bit, hem, sew 4 loop, pain, purl 5 baste, picot, ridge, unite 6 pierce, suture, tailor 8 distance 9 embroider
knitting: 4 purl 6 feston
stitchbird: ihi
sticher: 5 sewer 6 seamer 10 dressmaker
stitchwort: 9 chickweed
stithy: 5 anvil, forge 6 smithy 8 smithery
stive: 6 stifle 9 suffocate
stiver: 4 coin 5 money 7 bristle, stagger 8 struggle
stivy: 5 close 8 stifling
stoa: 7 portico 9 colonnade
stoat: 6 ermine, weasel 8 clubster 9 clubstart
stob: 4 post, stab 5 stake 6 pierce
stock: bar, cop, log 4 band, bond, butt, fund, hive, line, post, race, rail, stem 5 banal, block, blood, brace, breed, broth, estoc, flesh, frame, hoard, stake, stick, store, stump, swell, trite, trunk 6 assets, budget, common, cravat, handle, holder, pillar, strain, supply 7 cabbage, capital, catasta, descent, extract, lineage, provide, rhizome, support 8 ancestry, bitstock, colewort, material, ordinary, stoccado 9 extirpate, hackneyed, livestock, provision, replenish, stockfish 10 foundation 11 commonplace, certificate 12 accumulation
framed on: 5 ramed
of food: 5 foray
of goods: 4 line
pair of: 5 cippi 6 cippus
preliminary: 5 scrip
racial: 8 pedigree
stockade: pen 5 etape, pound 6 corral, kennel 7 barrier, fortify, protect 8 poundage 9 enclosure
Africa: 4 boma 5 kraal 6 keddah, zareba 7 zareeba
stock exchange: 6 bourse(F.)
business: 9 arbitrage
patron: 5 buyer 6 seller, trader
stockfish: cod 4 hake, ling 5 torsk 7 haddock
stock-in-trade: 4 tool, ware 5 goods 7 capital 8 material 11 merchandise
stocked: 7 replete

stockholder: 8 investor, stockman
stocking: bas(F.) 4 hose 7 hosiery
bishop's: 6 buskin, caliga
cotton: 5 lisle
footless: 7 hushion
ornament: 5 clock
run: 6 ladder
soleless: 7 traheen
worsted: 7 scogger
stockjobbing: 8 agiotage
stockman: 6 herder 7 rancher 8 beastman
stocky: fat 4 cold, stub 5 cobby, stiff 6 chumpy, formal, stubby, sturdy 7 bunting, defiant 8 thickset 10 boisterous, headstrong
stodge: 6 trudge 7 satiate, satisfy
stodgy: 4 dull 5 bulky, heavy, thick 6 packed 7 crammed, lumpish, stuffed, tedious 8 thickset 9 satiating 10 uninspired 13 uninteresting
stogy: 4 boot, shoe 5 cigar 6 brogan, clumsy, coarse
stoic: 5 porch 7 ascetic, passive 9 impassive
Stoic School: 4 Stoa
founder: 4 Zeno
stoicism: 8 patience 11 impassivity 13 impassiveness
stoit: 5 lurch 7 stagger, stumble
stoke: 4 coal, fire, fuel, poke, stab, tend 5 stick 6 supply, thrust
stoker: 5 firer 7 fireman, greaser
glassworks: 6 teaser
stole: fur 5 scarf 7 garment, orarion 8 vestment 13 epitrachelion
stolen: 5 shoot 6 branch, runner 9 rootstock
stolen property: 4 loot, pelf
buyer of: 5 fence
stolid: 4 dull, firm, slow 5 beefy 6 stupid 7 brutish, clumpse, clumpst, passive 9 impassive, inanimate, unfeeling 10 impassable 12 unexciteable
stolon: 6 runner 7 rhizome
stoma: 4 pore 5 mouth 7 opening, orifice
stomach: gut, maw 4 bear, craw, crop, kyte, vell 5 anger, belly, bingy, brook, pride, rumen 6 bingey, desire, endure, gebbie(Sc.), resent, spirit, temper 7 abdomen, gizzard, gizzern 8 appetite, tolerate 9 arrogance 10 resentment 11 inclination
acidity: 4 acor
bird's: maw 4 craw, crop
comb. form: 6 gastro
lower opening of: 7 pylorus
pert. to: 7 gastric
ruminant's first: 5 rumen
ruminant's fourth: 4 read, reed 8 abomasum, roddikin(Sc.)
ruminant's second: 6 bonnet 9 reticulum
ruminant's third: 6 omasum 9 manyplies 10 psalterium
used as food: 5 tripe
stomach ache: 5 colic 7 gullion
stomacher: 4 gimp 7 echelle 8 forepart
stomachy: 5 proud 8 paunched, spirited 9 irritable, obstinate, resentful 10 potbellied
stomp: See **stamp**
stone (see also **rock**): gem, pit, rub 4 bone, pelt, rock 5 block, brick, lapis(L.), scour, scrub 6 chaton, cobble, domino, harden, marble, mirror 7 diamond, dornick, scruple, sharpen 8 gunflint, lapidate, memorial, monolith, testicle 9 hailstone, hemachate, milestone, millstone, whetstone 10 gravestone, grindstone
abrasive: 5 emery
and clay: 4 sere
architectural 6 abacus
artificial: 8 albolite, albolith 9 granolith
base: 6 plinth
Biblical: 4 ezel
broken: 6 rubble
carved: 5 cameo
chip of: 5 spall 6 gallet
combining form: 5 litho
convert into: 7 petrify
druid: 6 sarsen
drupe: 6 nutlet
eagle: 5 etite
engraving: 8 intaglio
famous: 4 Hope, Pitt 5 Green, Mogul, Sancy, Scone 6 Jonker, Nassak, Orloff, Regent, Vargas 7 Blarney, Dresden, Jubilee, Kohinur, Stewart, Tiffany 8 Braganza, Cullinan, Kohinoor 9 Excelsior, Polar Star 10 Florentine, Great Mogul 12 Plymouth Rock, Star of Africa 14 Star of the South
fruit: pit 4 paip 5 drupe 6 pyrene 7 putamen
gem cutting: 6 adamas
granitic: 6 gneiss
grave: 5 stela, stele 6 marker, stelae, steles 8 memorial, monument
grinding: 6 metate
hammering: 8 lapstone
hand grinding: 4 mano
hard: 5 flint 6 quartz 7 adamant 9 chatoyant
heap: 4 karn 5 cairn
hoist: 5 lewis
hollow: 5 druse, geode
hurling device: 9 trebucket
implement: 4 celt 5 arrow 7 neolith
kidney: 8 calculus
loose: 6 gibber
maize grinding: 4 mano
meteoric: 8 aerolite, aerolith

monumental: 4 lech 6 menhir
of arch: 8 keystone
paving: 4 flag, slab, slat
pert. to: 7 lithoid
philosopher's: 6 carmot, elixir
precious: gem 4 keas, onyx, opal, ruby 5 beryl, pearl, topaz 6 garnet, jasper, lazuli, ligure 7 diamond, peridot 8 astroite, sapphire, tigereye 9 aromatite
pyramid-shape: 6 benben
shaped into pillars: 7 obelisk 9 monoliths
sharpening: oil 4 hone, whet
seam: dry
semiprecious: 4 jade, onyx, sard 5 agate, lapis 6 garnet, lazule, lazuli 7 olivine 8 murrhine 11 lapis lazuli
small: 6 pebble
squared: 6 ashlar
suffix: ith
to death: 8 lapidate
uncut: 4 naif
upright: 5 bauta 6 menhir
used for cameos: 4 onyx
woman turned into: 5 Niobe
worker: 5 mason 6 slater
writing: 5 slate

Stone Age tool: 4 celt 6 eolith 7 neolith 10 palaeolith
stonecrop: 5 orpin 6 orpine
stonecutter: 6 jadder
chisel: 5 drove
disease: 9 silicosis
wooden receptacle of: 7 sebilla
stonelike: 7 lithoid
stoneman: 5 cairn 9 stonehand
stones: *fine* 4 sand
heap of: 5 scree
loose: 6 eratum 8 erratice
mass of loose: 7 clitter
mound of: 4 carn, karn 5 cairn
pile of: 7 warlock
stonewall: 8 stubborn 9 obstinate 10 determined, filibuster
stonewalling: 8 sticking
stoneware: 4 gres 7 ceramic, pottery 11 earthenware
stonework: 7 masonry
stoneworker: 5 mason
stony: 4 cold, hard 5 fixed, rigid, still 7 adamant 8 obdurate, pitiless 9 petrified, unfeeling 10 inexorable, inflexible, petrifying, relentless, stupefying, unyielding 14 expressionless 15 uncompassionate
stood: 5 arose 7 endured
stooge: 4 foil
stook: 5 shock 6 pillar 12 handkerchief
stookie: 4 fool
stool: 4 base, mora, pole, seat, thew 5 bench, chair, decoy, morae, stand, stump 6 buffet, growth, throne, tiller, tripod 7 commode, creepie, taboret, trestle 8 kingship, platform, standard, tabouret 9 footstool 10 foundation 11 chieftaincy
stoolpigeon: spy 5 decoy, narks 7 peacher 8 betrayer, informer, observer
stoop: bow, lay 4 bend, bode, lean, post, sink, tilt 5 deign, lower, porch, slant, souse, stake, stump, swoop, yield 6 alight, boggle, coorie, crouch, debase, gamble, huckle, humble, patron, pillar, pounce, submit 7 decline, degrade, descend, descent, subject, succumb, veranda 8 adherent, overcome, platform, stairway 9 prostrate, supporter 10 condescend 11 humiliation 13 condescension
stop: ho; bar, dam, end, inn, pug, wad 4 bait, bode, bung, call, calk, clog, drop, fill, halt, mend, pawl, plug, quit, stay, stem, stum, wear, weir, whoa 5 avast, basta, block, break, caulk, catch, cease, check, choke, close, delay, embar, estop, holla, hollo, parry, pause, point, repel, stall, stuff, tarry 6 alight, anchor, arrest, behold, boggle, defeat, desist, detain, finish, gravel, hinder, period, reside, scotch, stanch, stench 7 caesura, confine, counter, prevent, sojourn, station, staunch, stopper, suspend 8 caesurae(pl.), obstacle, obstruct, obturate, pinblock, preclude, prohibit, restrain, stoppage, suppress, withhold 9 barricade, cessation, hindrance, intercept, interrupt, punctuate 10 constipate 11 countermand, discontinue, obstruction 12 intermission, interruption, lodginghouse
legally: 5 estop
organ: 5 orage, viola 7 posaune 8 dulciana, gemshorn 9 rohrflote
short: 5 delay, pause 7 respite 8 interval 9 cessation 12 intermission
temporary: 5 pause
stop watch: 5 timer
stopcock: 5 valve 6 faucet
stope: 8 excavate 10 excavation
stopgap: 5 shift 6 resort 9 expedient, makeshift 10 substitute
stoppage: 4 halt 5 block, choke, hitch 6 arrest, devall, strike 7 embargo, seizure 9 cessation, detention 10 arrestment, congestion 11 obstruction
body fluid: 6 stasis
debate: 7 cloture
temporary: 5 delay, pause 6 arrest, recess 10 arrestment 12 interception, intermission, interruption
stopper: wad 4 bung, cork, plug 6 fipple 7 bouchon
stopping: 4 halt 5 block, check 7 seizure 9 detention 11 obstruction
device: 5 brake

stopple: 4 bung, cork, plug 7 stopper
storage: 4 dump 11 safekeeping
battery plate: 4 grid
bin: mow 4 loft 7 granary 8 elevator
charge: 9 demurrage
place: bin 4 shed, silo 5 attic, depot 6 cellar, closet 7 arsenal, granary 8 cupboard, elevator 9 blood bank, reservoir, warehouse
prepare for: can
room: 6 closet, larder 7 lastage, lazaret 9 lazarette, lazaretto
storax: 5 resin 6 balsam
store: bin 4 cave, deck, deep, dose, fond, fund, hold, mass, save, shop, stow 5 amass, breed, cache, hoard, stock 6 amount, budget, garner, repair, shoppe, supply 7 bhandar, collect, deposit, furnish, husband, provide, restore 8 emporium, reserves, supplies, treasure 9 abundance, chandlery, livestock, replenish, reservoir, resources, sweetshop, warehouse 10 accumulate, collection, provisions, storehouse 12 accumulation
cargo: 5 steve
fodder: 6 ensile 8 ensilate
food: 6 market 9 sweetshop 12 delicatessen
fruit: 12 greengrocery
hidden: 5 cache
Hindu: 7 bhandar
in ground: 5 cache
in silo: 6 ensile
large: 4 raff, raft
lumber camp: van
military: PX 7 canteen 10 commissary
milk: 5 dairy
slang: 5 stash
up: 4 hive 6 garner
storehouse: mow 4 barn, bike, crib, shed, silo 5 cache, depot, etape 7 arsenal, bhandar, camalig, camarin, granary 8 building, magazine, treasury 9 repertory, warehouse 10 commissary 11 chalkothoke
military: 5 depot 7 arsenal 10 commissary
public: 5 depot, etape
rural: mow 4 barn, crib, shed, silo 7 granary
wool: 6 lanary
storekeeper: 6 grocer 8 bhandari, merchant, storeman 10 shopkeeper 11 almacenista, stockkeeper
storeroom: 4 cave, gola, loft 6 bodega, cellar 7 buttery, genizah, granary 8 basement 10 repository
stork: 4 ibis 6 simbil 7 marabou 12 xenorhynchus
kin of: 4 ibis 5 heron 10 hammerhead
storken: 7 congeal, stiffen
storklike: 8 pelargic
storm: wap 4 birr, blow, bura, fume, gale, gust, hail, rage, rain, rand, rant, rave, snow, wind 5 blizz, brash, orage 6 attack, burran, expugn, shamal, shower, simoom, simoon, tumult, Wester 7 assault, bluster, borasca, borasco, bravado, cyclone, rampage, tempest, tornado, trouble 8 calamity, eruption, outburst, upheaval, violence 9 agitation, bourasque, commotion, hurricane 10 hurly-burly 11 disturbance
god: Zu 5 Rudra
revolving: 7 cyclone
sand: 6 tebbad
snow: 5 buran
stormcock: 6 petrel, thrush 9 fieldfare 10 woodpecker
stormy: 4 foul 5 dirty, gusty 6 raging 7 furious, riotous, violent 8 agitated, cluttery 9 inclement, turbulent 10 blustering, passionate, tumultuous 11 tempestuous
story: fib, lie 4 myth, plot, saga, tale, tier, yarn 5 etage, fable, floor, rumor, solar, soler 6 fabula, legend, record, report, sollar 7 account, article, episode, history, narrate, parable, recital 8 anecdote, intrigue 9 falsehood, happening, narration, narrative, statement, tradition 11 description
complication in: 4 node 5 nodus
continued: 6 serial, sequel
correspondent's: 8 dispatch
exclusive: 4 beat 5 scoop
heroic: 4 gest, saga 5 geste
kind of: 4 epic, saga, tale, yarn 5 conte, fable 6 canard, legend, script 7 mystery, novella, parable, romance 8 allegory, scenario
short: 5 conte
traditional: 4 myth 6 legend
upper: 5 attic 6 garret
storyteller: 4 liar 5 Aesop 6 disour, fibber 8 narrator 9 raconteur
stot: ox 4 bull 5 bound, horse, steer 6 bounce 7 rebound, stagger, stammer, stumble, stutter
stound: 4 ache, beat, blow, pain, pang, stun, time 5 grief, shock, sight, smart, swoon, throb 6 attack, benumb, bruise, moment, period, season, sorrow, thrill, twinge 7 assault, instant, stupefy 8 astonish, occasion 10 apparition 12 astonishment, stupefaction
stoup, stoop: cup 4 cask, pail 5 basin 6 bucket, flagon, vessel 7 measure, tankard 10 aspersoria 11 aspersorium
holy-water: 8 benitier 11 cantharus-ri(pl.) 12 kantharos-roi(pl.)
stour: fit, fog 4 dust, gale, gush, hard, huge, loud, move, pour, rise, rude, stir, vast 5 agony, chaff, drive, great, hardy, hurry, onset, rough, shock, spray, stern, stiff, storm, throe 6 breeze, coarse, combat, fierce, hoarse, robust, severe, strife,

strong, tumult 7 assault, austere, conflict, meeting, quarrel, turmoil, violent 8 hardship, numerous, paroxysm 9 agitation, commotion, encounter 10 affliction, difficulty, excitement, inflexible, opposition

stourness: 7 bigness 9 greatness 10 sturdiness

stoush: 4 beat, blow 6 attack, strike, tirade 7 assault

stout: ale, fat 4 beer, bold, firm, gnat, hard 5 brave, bulky, burly, cobby, frack, freck, hardy, obese, plump, proud, shock, solid, tough 6 active, flagon, fleshy, liquor, porter, portly, robust, rotund, stable, stanch, stocky, stouty, strong, sturdy 7 defiant, haughty, violent 8 arrogant, bouncing, enduring, forceful, forcible, horsefly, insolent, powerful, resolute, stalwart, stubborn, thickset, vigorous 9 corpulent, energetic, obstinate, undaunted 10 courageous, determined, persistent 11 substantial 14 uncompromising

and rough: 5 burly

and short: 6 stocky 8 thickset

stout-hearted: 4 bold, good 5 brave 10 courageous

stoutly: 7 hardily

stoutness: 8 strength 9 hardihood

stove: 4 dent, etna, kiln 5 grate, plate, range, stave 6 cockle, heater 7 furnace 10 calefactor, glasshouse 12 conservatory

alcohol: 4 etna

charcoal: hod

grated: 8 chauffer

part: 4 oven 7 firebox, griddle

stovepipe: hat 4 flue 7 silk hat

stow: box, cut 4 cram, crop, hide, hold, mass, pack, stop, trim 5 cease, crowd, douse, dowse, grant, lodge, place, shoot, slice, stack, store, stump 6 bestow, commit 7 arrange, contain, entrust, secrete 8 restrain

cargo: 5 steve(var.) 6 steeve

stowage: 6 charge 7 packing

Stowe character: Eva, Tom 5 Topsy 6 Legree

stower: 9 stevedore

strabismus: 6 squint 8 cross-eye

Strad, Stradivarius: 6 violin

straddle: 5 hedge 6 option, sprawl 7 astride, bracket 8 bestride 11 noncommital

straddler: 5 rider

strafe: 4 waif 5 shell, stray 6 punish 7 bombard 9 castigate

straggle: 4 rove 5 stray 6 ramble, wander 7 meander

straggler: 5 tramp 8 vagabond, wanderer

straight: 4 neat 5 brant, erect, euthy, frank, ortho, plain, recti, rigid, stern 6 aright, candid, direct, graith, honest, severe 7 rightly, sincere, stretch, through, unmixed, upright 8 accurate, directly, honestly, reliable, rigorous, sequence, unbroken, virtuous 9 correctly, honorably, undiluted 10 continuous, methodical, unmodified 11 immediately, straightway, undeviating, unqualified 12 continuously, unswervingly 13 unaccompanied, uninterrupted 15 straightforward

combining form: 5 euthy

straight course: 7 beeline

straight edge: 5 ruler

straight-faced: 7 deadpan 9 impassive

straight-haired: 12 leiotrichous 13 lissotrichous

straight man: 4 foil 6 stooge

partner: 8 comedian

straight-out: 6 direct 8 outright 11 unqualified 12 unrestrained 13 thorough-going

straight up and down: 15 perpendicularly

straighten: 5 align, aline, level, order, plumb 7 compose, rectify, unravel 11 disentangle

straightforward: 4 even, open 5 apert, frank 6 aright, candid, dexter, direct, honest 7 sincere 8 directly, outright, straight 9 foreright, outspoken 10 forthright 11 undeviating

straightforwardly: 8 directly

straightness: 9 rectitude

straightway: 4 anon 6 aright, bedene 8 directly 9 downright, forthwith 10 forthright 11 immediately

strain: air, hug, sie, sye, tax, try 4 balk, barb, bend, bind, curb, dash, gain, heft, kind, line, mood, note, ooze, race, sift, solo, sort, tone, tune, turn, urge, vein 5 begte, breed, clasp, class, exert, force, music, press, raise, shade, sieve, stock, style, tenor, touch, trace, track, trail, wield 6 burden, colate, effort, extend, extort, family, fasten, filter, injure, manner, melody, obtain, sprain, strand, stread, stress, strive, temper, thread, weaken, wrench 7 confine, descent, element, embrace, lineage, overtax, progeny, quality, squeeze, stretch, tension, trickle, variety 8 ancestry, brandish, compress, eliquate, exertion, restrain, tendency 9 begetting, character, constrain, constrict, percolate 10 distortion, generation 11 deformation, disposition

blood: 4 race 5 breed, stock 6 family 7 lineage

chief: 5 brunt

combining form: 4 tono

great: tax, tug 5 tense 6 stress 7 tension 8 exertion, overbear 11 tenterhooks

measuring device: 9 telemeter

strained: 4 taut 5 tense 6 forced 7 intense 8 weakened, wrenched 9 distorted 10 farfetched

strainer: 4 cage, sile 5 sieve, strum, tamis 6 filter, milsey, milsie, sifter 8 colander, colature, huckmuck 10 colatorium

strait: 4 area, neck, pass 5 phare 6 narrow 7 channel, isthmus

between Labrador and Newfoundland: 9 Belle Isle

Strait of Gibraltar: 17 Pillars of Hercules

Strait of Messina rock: 6 Scylla

straits: 5 pinch, rigor 7 narrows, poverty 10 difficulty

Straits Settlements: 6 colony

city: 7 Malacca 9 Singapore 10 Georgetown

coin: 4 cent 6 dollar 13 Straits dollar

measure: pau, tun 4 para, pipe 5 parah 6 chupak, parrah 7 gantang

native state: 5 Perak 6 Johore, Pahang 8 Selangor 11 Sungei Ujong 13 Negri Sembilan

weight: 4 chee, hoon, saga 5 bedur, bhara, catty, koyan, picul, tahil

straiten: 5 limit 6 hamper 7 confine 8 contract, distress, restrict 9 embarrass

strait-jacket: 8 camisole

strait-laced: 5 stiff 6 severe, strict 8 stubborn 9 obstinate, puritanic 10 restricted 11 constrained 14 overscrupulous

strake: rut 4 band 5 crack 6 loiter, streak, stripe, stroll, trough, wander 7 stretch

stramineous: 6 chaffy, strawy 9 straw-like, valueless

strand: sea 4 bank, quay, wire 5 beach, fiber, shore, wharf 6 gutter, maroon, region, stream, thread 7 channel, current 8 filament

stranded: 6 ashore 7 aground, beached 8 castaway, marooned

strange: odd 4 fell, rare, unco 5 alien, droll, eerie, fremd, novel, queer 6 exotic, quaint 7 curious, distant, erratic, foreign, uncanny, unknown, unusual 8 abnormal, estrange, fanciful, peculiar, reserved, singular, uncommon 9 couthless, different, eccentric, unnatural 10 outlandish, unfamiliar, unfriendly 12 unaccustomed, unacquainted 13 extraordinary, inexperienced, preternatural

combining form: xen 4 xeno

language: 4 cant 5 lingo 6 jargon 7 dialect

strangely: 5 oddly 6 featly

stranger: goy 5 alien, guest, odder 6 ganger, novice 7 comical, visitor 8 emigrant, estrange, intruder, newcomer, outsider 9 estranger, foreigner, outlander 10 tramontane 12 intermeddler

comb. form: 4 xeno

strangle: 4 kill, slay 5 choke, grane 6 stifle 7 garrote, repress 8 garrotte, suppress, throttle 9 suffocate

strangulate: 5 choke 8 compress, obstruct, strangle 9 constrict

strap: bar, fit, tie 4 band, beat, belt, bind, hang, rein, riem, whip 5 girth, groom, strip, strop, thong 6 billet, chaser, credit, enarme, fillet, halter, latigo, ligule, punish, secure 7 furnish, laniard, lanyard, sharpen 8 chastise

kind of: 4 jess, taws 5 guige, leash, strop, tawse, thong 6 chaser, enarme 8 bretelle 10 boondoggle

strap-shaped: 6 lorate 7 ligular 8 ligulate 9 ligulated

strapping: 6 robust, strong 7 beating 9 thrashing

strass: 5 glass, paste

strata (see also **stratum**): *geological:* 4 lias

later: 7 neozoic

social: 7 classes

stratagem: 4 coup, ruse, wile 5 cheat, fetch, fraud, trick 6 blench, device, humbug, scheme 7 finesse 8 artifice, maneuver 9 chicanery, deception, execution, slaughter 10 artfulness

smart: 8 liripipe, liripoop

strategic: 9 favorable 12 advantageous

strategy: 8 artifice, intrigue, maneuver

stratification: 7 bedding

stratum: bed 5 layer, level 6 couche 7 section 8 division

thin: 4 seam

Strauss work: 5 waltz 6 Salome 7 Electra

stravagant: 7 vagrant 11 extravagant, irrelevance

stravage, stravaig: 6 stroll, wander 7 saunter

Stravinsky work: 8 Firebird 10 Petrouchka

straw: hat, wap 4 gloy, mote, pipe, rush 5 chaff, strae, stree 6 fescue, litter, trifle 9 worthless, yellowish 11 meaningless 12 churchwarden

bed: 6 pallet

bundle of: 6 batten

coat: 4 mino

color: 6 flaxen

colored: 11 stramineous

for hats: 6 sennit

half rotten: 5 mulch

load of: 5 barth

plaited: 6 sennit

threshing floor: 6 bhossa

to protect plants: 5 mulch

used for hats: 7 sabutan

waxed: 6 strass

weaving: 5 rafia

straw in the wind: 4 omen, sign 7 portent
straw vote: 4 poll
strawberry: 6 fraise, runner 8 fragaria
strawlike: 11 stramineous
stray: err, gad 4 cavy, roam, rove, waif 5 range 6 casual, course, errant, estray, random, stroll, swerve, wander 7 decline, deviate, digress, forlorn, habitat, saunter 8 detached, distract, isolated, straggle 9 straggler, unrelated 10 incidental, occasional 12 unenumerated
calf: 4 dogy 5 dogie
straying: 6 astray 7 erratic 8 aberrant 9 deviation, erroneous
streak: rub 4 line, rung, vein, wale 5 fleck, freak, garle, hurry, layer, lined, round, smear, spell, trace, trait 6 period, polish, smooth, strain, strake, stripe, stroke 7 stratum, striped 8 discolor
mottled: roe
narrow: 5 stria 6 striae
regular: 6 stripe
streaked: 4 liny 6 marked 7 alarmed, brindle, striped, worried 8 brindled 10 variegated
streaky: 4 liny 5 liney, mixed 6 uneven 8 variable
stream: ea; run 4 burn, flow, flux, ford, gote, gush, rill, rush 5 bache, bayou, bourn, brook, creek, fleam, floss, flume, fluor, force, issue, river, speed, trend 6 amount, bourne, course, fluent, runnel 7 channel, current, rivulet 8 affluent 9 anabranch 11 watercourse
diminutive: run 4 race 5 brook 6 rillet 7 rivulet 9 streamlet
dry bed: 6 arroyo
lava: 6 coulee
living in: 9 amphibian, rheophile
ravine: 4 ghyl, gill
rushing: jet 7 torrent
small: run 4 rill, sike 5 brook, siket 6 rillet, runlet
sound: 4 purl 6 murmur
underground: aar
upper part of: 6 source 9 headwater
streamer: jet 4 flag 5 strip 6 guidon, ribbon 7 feather, pendant, pennant 8 banderol, headline 9 banderole
streamlet: 4 rill 5 brook 6 rillet, runlet, runnel 7 freshet, rivulet
streamline curve: 10 lissoneoid
streck: 6 direct 8 straight
streel: 7 saunter 8 slattern, straggle
street: rew(Sc.), way 4 char, lane, road 5 calle, chare 6 avenue, causey, spread 7 estreat, highway, roadway, strasse(G.) 8 chaussee, contrada, contrade(pl.), notebook 9 boulevard 12 thoroughfare
Chinese: 6 hutung
degraded: 4 slum
ditch: 6 gutter
India: 5 chawk, chowk
narrow: 5 alley, place
street roister: mun
street urchin: 4 arab 5 gamin
streetcar: 4 tram 7 trolley
driver: 8 motorman
streetwalker: 6 hooker 10 prostitute
strength: arm 4 beef, iron, thew 5 brawn, force, might, power, vigor 6 energy, foison 7 ability, potency, stamina, sthenia 8 capacity, firmness, solidity 9 coherence, endurance, fortitude, intensity, lustiness, puissance, stoutness, toughness, vehemence 10 heartiness, robustness, stronghold 14 impregnability
deprive of: 7 unnerve
diminish: 6 dilute
electric current: 8 amperage
liquor: 5 proof
loss: 8 asthenia
military: 8 armament
of character: 4 guts, sand 9 fortitude
poetic: 9 puissance
regain: 5 rally
solution: 5 titer, titre
source of: 5 asset
strengthen: 4 back, bind, frap, help, prop 5 brace, nerve, steel 6 clench, deepen, endure 7 afforce, comfort, confirm, depthen, educate, fortify, toughen 8 roborate 9 encourage, reinforce 10 invigorate 11 consolidate
with alcohol: 5 spike 7 fortify
strengthener: 6 gusset
strengthening: 7 bracing 8 roborant 10 nourishing, supporting, sustaining 11 corroborant
strenuous: 4 hard 5 eager 6 active, ardent, severe 7 arduous, zealous 8 vigorous 9 energetic
strepent: 4 loud 5 noisy
streperous: 4 loud 5 harsh, noisy 7 noisily 9 turbulent 10 boisterous
strepitant: 5 noisy 9 clamorous 10 strepitous
stress: 5 brunt, force, labor 6 accent, strain 7 afflict, amplify, overtax, tension, urgency 8 ampliate, distrain, distress, emphasis, exertion, pressure 9 emphasize, intensity 10 constraint, importance, overstrain, resistence 12 significance 13 inconvenience
mechanical: 8 erossure
metrical: 5 ictus
music: 6 accent
voice: 5 arsis 6 accent

stretch: eke 4 hang, span, walk 5 reach, retch, space, toise, tract 6 course, dilate, effort, expand, extend, period, spread, strain 7 distend, enlarge, execute, expanse, tension 8 elongate, sentence 9 direction, extension 10 exaggerate
injuriously: 6 sprain
out: eke, lie, out
the neck: 5 crane
stretched: *out:* 6 craned 7 porrect 8 extended, prolated 9 elongated
tight: 4 taut 5 tense
while drying: 8 tentered
stretcher: 6 litter, racker 8 ringhead
neck: 6 craner
stretchy: 7 elastic, rubbery 9 resilient
strew: 6 litter, spread 7 diffuse, scatter 8 disperse, sprinkle 9 bespatter, broadcast 10 besprinkle 11 disseminate
strewing: 4 seme
stria: 4 band, line 5 ridge 6 fillet, furrow, groove, hollow, streak, stripe 7 channel 9 striation
striate: 5 lined 7 grooved 8 furrowed
stricken (see also **strike**): 7 smitten, wounded 13 incapacitated
strickle: 5 rifle 7 pattern 8 template
strict: 4 blue, hard 5 close, exact, harsh, rigid, stern, tense, tight 6 entire, narrow, severe 7 ascetic, austere, binding, correct, perfect, precise 8 absolute, accurate, intimate, limiting, rigorous, straight 9 confining, puritanic, stringent 10 compressed, forbidding, inexorable, inflexible, relentless, scrupulous 11 constricted, punctilious, puritanical, restricting, straitlaced, undeviating 14 uncompromising
disciplinarian: 8 martinet
discipline: 13 regimentation
striction: 12 constriction
strictly: 6 narrow 7 closely 9 precisely 10 positively, rigorously 11 stringently
strictness: 5 rigor 9 closeness
in law: 8 legalism
stricture: 4 sign 5 spark, touch, trace 7 binding, censure, closing 9 criticism 11 contraction 13 animadversion
strid: 5 gorge 6 ravine
stride: 4 step, walk 5 stalk 7 advance 8 bestride, progress, straddle 11 advancement
strident: 5 harsh 6 shrill 7 grating, raucous, yelling 11 cacophonous
stridor: 5 noise
stridulate: 5 cheep, chirk, chirp, creak, crick 7 clitter
strife: war 4 bait, bate, feud 5 fight, flite, flyte, noise, strow 6 combat, debate, estrif 7 contest, discord, hurling, quarrel 8 conflict, endeavor, exertion, struggle 9 emulation 10 contention 11 altercation, competition, controversy
about mere words: 9 logomachy
civil: 6 stasis
striffen: 4 skin 8 membrane
strigil: 7 fluting
strigose, strigous: 5 sharp 6 hispid
strike: bat, bob, box, cob, cop, dab, dad, hew, hit, lam, pat, ram, rap, wap 4 baff, bang, bash, bean, beat, biff, bill, bump, bunt, chap, cope, coup, cuff, dash, daub, daud, dint, dunt, fist, flap, flog, frap, gird, gowf, hurl, hurt, knap, lash, pelt, rout, slap, slay, swat 5 clash, clink, clout, douse, dowse, dunch, fight, filch, gowff, impel, knock, punch, skelp, skite, slash, smear, smite, spank, swipe, touch, trend, whang 6 assail, attack, attain, bounce, buffet, fettle, hammer, hartal, punish, strike, stroke 7 afflict, cacanny, collide, impinge, impress 8 discover, struggle
a balance: 5 agree 6 settle 10 compromise
a mean: 7 average
against: 4 bump 5 crash 7 collide
and rebound: 5 carom 6 carrom 9 carambole
demonstrator: 6 picket
down: 4 fell, kill 5 floor 7 disable
dumb: 4 stun
feature: 7 lockout
gently: dab, pat 4 bump, putt
heavily: lam, ram 4 bash, slog, slug
obliquely: 5 carom
on head: 4 bean
out: fan 4 dele 5 elide, erase 6 cancel, delete 9 eliminate
prepare to: 4 coil
producing musical sound: 5 chime
series of blows: 4 pelt
settler: 8 mediator
together: 5 clash, crash 7 collide
up: 5 begin, start 8 commence
violently: ram 4 slam
with fist: 4 plug 5 punch, pound
with head: 4 butt
with wonder: awe 7 astound
strikebreaker: rat 4 fink, goon, scab
striker: 4 scab, tern 6 batman, batter, helper, hitter, smiter 7 batsman, clapper, mobster 8 blackleg 9 assistant, harpooner
striking: 4 dint 7 salient 8 stunning 9 arresting, effective 10 noticeable, remarkable, surprising 11 conspicuous
effect: 5 eclat
strind: 4 cast, race 6 strain 7 kindred, progeny 9 offspring 10 generation 11 disposition
string: 4 band, cord, hoax, josh, line 5 bound, braid, chain, jolly, strip, twine 6

series, thread 10 conditions, succession 14 qualifications
course: 6 guidon
kinds of: 4 wire 5 lacet, snare 6 amenta, hypate, lachet 7 amentum, langate
of beads: 6 rosary 8 necklace
up: 4 hang, lace 5 lynch
string instrument: uke 4 harp, lute, lyre 5 banjo, cello, piano, viola 6 fiddle, guitar, spinet, violin, zither 7 ukalele, ukelele 8 mandolin 11 harpsichord
old: 4 lute, lyre 6 spinet 8 psaltery 11 harpsichord
stringency: 5 force, rigor 7 cogency 8 scarcity, severity 9 tightness 10 strictness
stringent: 4 hard, ropy 5 rigid, tense, tight 6 cogent, severe, strict 7 binding, extreme 10 convincing 11 restrictive
stringer: tie 4 rope, vein, wire 5 irons 6 string, timber 8 filament 9 handcuffs, libertine 11 stringpiece
stringy: 4 ropy 5 gluey 6 sinewy, viscid 7 fibrous, viscous 11 filamentous
strip: bar, rob, tab, tag, top 4 band, bare, bark, belt, doff, flay, hull, husk, peel, pull, skin, tear 5 clear, flake, fleck, pluck, shred, spoil, swath, unrig 6 border, denude, devest, divest, expose, flense, reduce, remove, runway, swathe 7 bandage, bandeau, bereave, degrade, deprive, despoil, disrobe, pillage, plunder, uncloak, uncover, undress, unleave 8 bandeaux(pl.), denudate, disarray, headland, outstrip, separate 9 dismantle, excoriate 10 disfurnish, dispossess 11 debenzolize, decorticate
blubber: 6 flense
kinds of: 4 came, cove, lead, rand, riem, tirr 5 cleat, ridge, stave 6 inwale, reglet 7 gunwale
leather: 4 welt 5 thong 6 latigo 7 belting
narrow: 4 slat, tape 5 reeve, strap 7 bandeau 8 bandeaux(pl.)
wooden: rib 4 lath, slat 5 stave 6 reglet
strip tease dancer: 9 ecdysiast
stripe: bar, roe 4 band, beat, belt, blow, kind, lash, line, mark, sort, type, wale, weal, welt, zone 5 chest, stria, strip 6 border, frenum, streak, strike, stroke, thrust 7 chevron, fraenum, lineate, pattern, rivulet 8 division 9 character
striped: 5 bandy 6 banded, barred 7 lineate, vittate 8 bayadere, streaked
animal: 5 bongo, zebra
cloth: 6 madras
stripling: boy, lad 5 chiel, youth 6 chield
stripped: 4 bare, nude 6 picked
by trickery: 7 buncoed, bunkoed, fleeced
strive: aim, hie, tew, try, tug, vie 4 seek, toil 5 bandy, ensue, fight, labor, rival 6 battle, buffet, resist, strain 7 compete, contend, contest, emulate 8 contrast, endeavor, struggle
striving: 5 nisus
strobile: 4 chat, cone
strobilophyta: 4 cone
strockle: 6 shovel
stroil: 5 grass, power, weeds 9 dexterity 10 capability
stroke: bat, coy, fit, hew, hit, pat, pet, rub 4 baff, beat, blow, chap, coup, dash, ding, dint, flip, gowf, hurt, lash, mark, milk, oner, shot, walk, whet 5 chare, douse, dowse, flack, fluke, gowff, ictus, knock, power, pulse, rower, strut, throb, trait 6 attack, caress, effort, fondle, ictuse, impact, injury, soothe, stride 7 seizure, sharpen, whample 8 apoplexy, disaster 9 influence
brilliant: ace 4 coup
cutting: 4 chop 5 slice
golf: 4 baff
kinds of: 5 eagle, cerif, serif, wedge 6 birdie 7 virgule
of luck: 8 windfall
short: 4 flip, putt 5 whisk
stroll: 4 mosy, roam, rove, walk 5 mosey, range, stray, tramp 6 dacker, daiker, dander, ramble, soodle, wander 7 saunter 8 flanerie
stroller: 4 cart, pram 5 actor, tramp 6 beggar, gocart, player, shuler 7 peddlar, peddler, shuiler, vagrant 8 bohemian, carriage, wanderer 9 saunterer
strolling: 7 roaming 8 flanerie, fugitive
Stromboli: 6 island 7 volcano
stromming: 7 herring
strone: 4 hill 5 spout 6 stream
strong: fit, hot 4 able, bold, dure, elon, fere, firm, fort, hale, hard, rank, warm, wiry 5 bonny, clear, eager, frack, freck, fresh, great, gross, hardy, heavy, large, lusty, solid, sound, stout, tough, yauld 6 active, ardent, bonnie, brawny, buckra, cogent, feckle, mighty, potent, robust, rugged, sinewy, stable, stouty, strict, sturdy 7 buirdly, durable, fertile, greatly, huffcap, humming, intense, sthenic, violent, zealous 8 athletic, distinct, flagrant, forceful, forcible, muscular, powerful, puissant, resonant, rigorous, severely, stalwart, strongly, vehement, vigorous 9 Atlantean, difficult, effective, impetuous, important, strapping, violently 10 boisterous, forthright, nourishing, outrageous, passionate, persuasive, productive, pronounced, remarkable 11 excessively 12 concentrated
upward movement: 5 surge

strong-arm: rob 4 beat, thug 5 force, power 7 assault, violent 8 violence
man: 4 goon 7 bouncer
strong cloth: 5 scrim
strong man: *Biblical:* 6 Samson 7 Sampson
legendary: 5 Atlas
strong point: 5 forte
strong-smelling: 4 foul, rank 5 fetid 6 foetid 8 mephitic, stinking
strongbox: 4 case, safe 5 chest, vault
stronghold: 4 fort, hold, keep 5 tower 6 castle 7 citadel, fortify 8 fasthold, fastness, fortress 13 fortification
strongly: 5 bigly 6 stably 8 heartily
strop: 4 hone, whet 7 sharpen
strophe: 6 stanza 10 heptastich
stroud: 5 harsh 6 morose 7 blanket
strow: 5 strew 6 strife 7 turmoil 9 confusion 11 disturbance
stroygood: 7 wastrel 11 spendthrift
strub: rob 5 strip 7 despoil
strubbly: 6 untidy 7 unkempt
struck: 4 smit 5 smote 7 smitten 8 punished
with amazement: 6 aghast
with small missiles: 6 pelted
with sudden fear: 7 alarmed
with terror: 6 aghast
with wonder: 6 aghast
struck out: 5 deled 6 elided, erased, fanned 7 deleted
struck smartly: 9 percussed
structural quality: 7 texture
structure: dam 4 form 5 frame 6 bridge, format, make-up 7 edifice, texture 8 building, bulkhead 9 formation 11 arrangement, composition, fabricature 12 constitution, construction
abnormal: 12 malformation
calcareous: 5 coral
conical: 7 pyramid
crown-like: 6 corona
curved: 4 arch
filamentous: 4 hair
floating: 4 raft
funeral: 10 catafalque
hallowed: 6 bethel, chapel, church, temple 8 basilica 9 cathedral, synagogue 10 tabernacle
high: 5 tower
human: 8 physique
keel-like: 6 carina
latticework: 7 trellis
looplike: 4 ansa
monumental: 5 pylon
on roof: 6 cupola, dormer 9 penthouse
Oriental: 6 pagoda
original: 6 isogen
osseous: 4 bone
over obstacles: 6 bridge
pergola-like: 6 ramada
pert. to: 8 tectonic
projecting into water: 4 jiti 5 jetty 6 jettee
raised: 4 dais 5 altar, stage 8 platform
sacrificial: 5 altar
sheltering: cot 4 cote
supporting: 4 pier
tall: 5 tower 7 steeple 9 campanile
tent-like: 10 tabernacle
white: 6 albedo
strudel: 6 pastry
struggle: tug, vie 4 agon, cope, frab, wade 5 fight, heave, labor 6 battle, buckle, bustle, combat, effort, Peniel, strife, strike, strive, throes, tussle, widdle 7 bargain, barrace, contend, contest, flounce, scuffle, warfare, wauchle, wrestle 8 conflict, endeavor, exertion, flounder, scraffle, scramble 10 contention, difficulty
a deux: 4 duel
helplessly: 8 flounder
struggling: 12 colluctation
struma: 6 goiter, goitre
strummed: 8 thrummed
strumpet: 4 brim 5 belie, wench 6 blowen, harlot 7 cocotte, debauch, slander 8 harridan 10 prostitute
strung: 6 beaded
highly: 5 tense 7 nervous
strunt: 4 dock 5 pique, strut, stump 6 liquor 7 stubble
strut: 4 brag, cock, gait, step, walk 5 brace, bulge, swell 6 parade, stride, strife, strunt, thrust 7 distend, peacock, provide, stiffen, stretch, support, swagger, wrangle 8 protrude 10 contention 11 protuberant
struthious: 4 emus 5 rheas 6 ratite 9 ostriches
stub: pen 4 beat, dolt 5 crush, drive, squat, stump 6 coupon, stocky 7 feather, remnant 8 thickset 9 blockhead, extirpate 11 counterfoil
stubble: bun 6 strunt 7 gratten, gratton 8 eelgrass
field: 5 rowen
stubborn: set 4 rude 5 fixed, hardy, harsh, rough, tough 6 coarse, dogged, mulish, sturdy 7 restive 8 obdurate, perverse, resolute, starkish, vigorous 9 camsteary, camsteery, difficult, obstinate, pigheaded 10 bullheaded, calcitrant, determined, hardheaded, headstrong, inflexible, refractory, unyielding 11 intractable 12 pertinacious
stubborness: 8 tenacity 9 contumacy, obstinacy 12 perverseness
stubby: 5 squat 6 stocky, stumpy 8 thickset
stuck: See stick
stuck in the mud: 7 bemired

stuck-up: 4 vain 7 haughty 8 arrogant, snobbish 9 conceited 12 supercilious 13 self-important
stud: dot, pin, rod 4 boss, knob, post, stem, stub 5 adorn, aglet, beset, brace, haras, study, stump 6 aiglet, button, pillar 7 chaplet, support 9 studhorse 10 besprinkle
farm: 5 haras
for shoe: 7 hobnail
with jewels: 5 engem
with radiating bodies: 6 enstar
student: 5 eleve(F.), pupil 6 bursar 7 educand, learner 8 disciple, observer
according to grade: 6 termer
agricultural college: 5 Aggie
college: 4 soph 6 junior, senior 8 freshman 9 sophomore
divinity: 9 theologue 10 theologian
fellow: 9 classmate
first-year: 5 Fuchs(G.)
former: 7 dropout 8 graduate
fourth-year: 6 senior
girl: 4 coed
group: 5 class
hall: 5 burse 9 dormitory
in charge: 7 monitor
law: 8 stagiary
medical: 6 intern 7 interne
military: 5 cadet, plebe
naval academy: 5 cadet 10 midshipman
of birds: 13 ornithologist
of crime: 10 penologist 13 criminologist
of heavens: 13 uranographist
of proverbs: 14 paroemiologist
of punishment: 10 penologist
of relics: 13 archaeologist
of reptiles: 13 herpetologist
of spiders: 13 arachnologist
Oxford: 8 commoner
residence: 5 house 6 hostel 9 dormitory
room: 7 seminar
second-year: 9 sophomore
stipend paid: 6 bursar
third-year: 6 junior
West Point: 5 cadet, plebe
studied: 5 pored 6 intent 7 learned, planned 8 designed, inclined, reasoned 10 ceremonial, deliberate 12 premeditated
studies: *academic:* 4 arts 7 science 10 humanities
advanced: 7 seminar 8 graduate
chosen by students: 9 electives
series of: 6 course
studio: 7 atelier, bottega 8 botteghe, workshop 11 ergasterion
studious: 5 booky 7 bookish, devoted, studied 8 diligent, sedulous 9 assiduous, scholarly 10 deliberate 13 contemplative
study: con, den, mug 4 bone, muse, muzz, pore, read, scan 5 grind 6 lesson, peruse, ponder 7 analyse, analyze, canvass, croquis, examine 8 consider, meditate 11 contemplate 13 consideration, contemplation
animals: 9 zoography
bees: 8 apiology
Bible: 9 isagogics
by lamplight: 9 lucubrate
closely: con 4 pore 7 examine
course: 7 seminar
fingerprints: 13 dactylography
fixed course: 4 rote
flowers: 12 anthoecology
handwriting: 10 graphology
hard: 4 bone
horses: 9 hippology
human generations: 15 anthropogenesis
insect's habits: 10 entomology
laborious: 11 lucubration
mountains: 7 orology
musical: 5 etude
optional: 8 elective
population: 10 larithmics
punishment: 8 penology
sacred edifices: 7 naology
sacred images: 9 iconology
sermons: 10 homiletics
wines: 7 enology
words: 9 etymology
stufe: 4 step 6 degree
stuff: pad, ram, wad 4 copy, cram, fill, gaum, junk, pang 5 crowd, farce, force, grain, pulse, steve 6 amount, fabric, graith, matter, refuse, stifle, supply 7 bombast, element, essence, filling, mixture, portion 8 material, medicine, nonsense, overload, stuffing 9 character, principle, substance, suffocate
full: 4 glut 5 gorge 6 stodge 7 satiate
harvested grain: 7 stubble
sticky: goo
worthless: 4 gear 7 hogwash
stuffed: 6 bourre, stodgy 7 bombast, replete 8 farctate
stuffing: 7 padding 8 dressing 9 forcemeat
prepare with: 8 marinate
stuffy: fat 4 dull, prim 5 angry, close, fubsy, fuggy, stout, sulky 6 froust, frowst, stodgy 8 resolute 9 obstinate 10 mettlesome, old-fogyish 11 strait-laced 12 conservative, old-fashioned
stuggy: 5 short 6 stodgy, sturdy 8 thickset
Stuka: 6 bomber
stulm: 4 adit 8 entrance
stultiloquy: 4 talk 6 babble
stum: 4 must 5 grape, juice
stumble: err 4 fall, slip, trip 5 lurch 6 boggle, chance, faffle, falter, happen, offend 7 blunder, failure, founder, perplex, scrupple, stagger 8 confound, flounder

stumbling: 7 hurting
stumbling block: 8 obstacle 9 hindrance 10 impediment 11 obstruction
stump: cob, lop 4 butt, dare, foil, grub, snag, stab, stub 5 block, clump 6 baffle, corner, hobble, pillar, puzzle, strunt, thwart, travel 7 canvass, nonplus, perplex, rostrum, stumble 8 platform 9 challenge 11 electioneer
stumps: 4 legs
stumpy: 5 bunty 6 stubby 8 thickset
stun: 4 bowl, daze, tear 5 amaze, aston, daunt, daver, deave, dizzy, dover, shock 6 appall, astone, astony, benumb, bruise, crease, deaden, deafen 7 astound, dammish, scratch, stupefy 8 astonish, bewilder 9 dumbfound, overpower, overwhelm
stung (see also **sting**): 7 smarted
stunned: 10 astonished
stunning: 7 stylish 8 dazzling 9 beautiful 10 foudroyant
stunt: act 4 feat 5 angry, blast, blunt, check, cramp, crowl, dwarf, stamp, whale 6 abrupt, hinder 7 curtail, exploit 8 stubborn 10 undersized 11 performance
gymnastic: kip 4 kipp 10 handspring
stunted: 4 runt
stunty: 5 short 6 flashy, stocky 7 dwarfed
stupa: 5 mound, tower 6 shrine
lamaism: 7 chorten
stupe: 6 foment
stupefacient: 4 drug 8 narcotic 10 stupefying
stupefied: 8 benumbed 9 inebriate
stupefy: fox, sot 4 baze, daze, dope, doze, drug, dull, dunt, numb, stun 5 amaze, aston, besot, blunt, daunt, daver, deave, shock 6 astone, bedaze, bemuse, benumb, muddle 7 astound, confuse 8 astonish, bewilder, confound 10 incrassate
with drink: 6 fuddle
stupefying: 8 bemusing
stupend: 4 stun 7 astound, stupefy 10 stupendous
stupendous: 5 great 7 amazing, immense 8 enormous 9 monstrous, wonderful 10 astounding 11 astonishing 12 overpowering, overwhelming
stupent: 9 stupefied 11 dumbfounded
stupid: 4 bete, clod, dull, dumb, dunt, guam, lewd, slow 5 besot, blunt, booby, crass, dazed, dense, dizzy, goosy, heavy, inane, sumph 6 assish, barren, beetle, boring, bovine, dawkin, doiled, doited, drowsey, goosey, hebete, lurdan, oafish, obtuse, simple, stolid, torpid 7 asinine, brutish, buzzard, calvish, daffish, doldrum, doltish, duffing, dullard, fatuous, foolish, foppish, glaiket, glaikit, gomerel, goosish, gullish, lurdane, prosaic, stunned, vacuous, witless 8 anserine, anserous, backward, bayardly, blockish, boeotian, cloddish, deadened, footless, headless, retarded, sluggish 9 blocklike, bourgeois, brainless, codheaded, inanimate, insensate, insipient, plumbeous, pointless, senseless, stupefied 10 hardwitted, hulver-head, irrational, slow-witted 11 claybrained, heavy-headed 12 buffleheaded 13 unintelligent, uninteresting
person: ass, sap 4 clod, clot, coot, dolt, dope, fool, jerk, loon 5 dunce, goose, idiot, moron, ninny 7 dullard, fathead 8 numskull 9 blockhead
render: 8 hebetate
stupidity: 6 betise, stupor 7 density, fatuity 8 dullness, hebetude, idiotism, numbness 9 crassness 12 astonishment, indifference, stupefaction 13 insensibility
stupidly: 10 bullheaded
stupor: fog 4 coma, damp, dote 5 sopor 6 trance 8 lethargy
comb. form: 5 narco
pert. to: 7 carotic, narcose
stuprate: 6 ravish 7 debauch
sturdy: gid, set 4 buff, firm 5 felon, hardy, harsh, lusty, sound, stern, stiff, stout 6 brawny, robust, rugged, rustic, stable, steady, strong 7 violent 8 obdurate, resolute, stalwart, stubborn, vigorous 9 rigidness, obstinate 10 courageous, determined, unyielding 12 stupefaction
sturdy and stout: 5 burly
sturgeon: 6 beluga
small: 7 sterlet
white: 6 beluga
roe: 6 caviar
sturt: vex 4 stir 5 annoy 6 strife 7 startle, trouble 11 disturbance
sturtin, sturtan: 9 staggered 10 frightened
stutter: 7 stammer
stuttering: 8 psellism 9 psellisum
sty, stye: pen 4 boil, soar 5 climb, lodge, mount, stair, steps, stile 6 ascend, aspire, ladder 8 swelling 9 enclosure
stygian: 6 gloomy 7 hellish 8 infernal
style: air, dub, pen, pin, ton 4 call, garb, gere, kind, mode, name, sort, term, type 5 vogue 6 format, gnomon, graver, manner, method, needle, phrase, stylus 7 alamode, diction, entitle, fashion, variety 8 demeanor 9 designate, execution 10 denominate 12 characterize, construction
architecture: 5 Doric, Greek, Ionic, Roman, Saxon 6 Gothic, Norman 7 Italian 8 Colonial, Georgian, Monterey 9 Byzantine 10 Corinthian, Romanesque 11 Elizabethan, Renaissance 13 Mediterranean
art: 5 genre

artistic: **5** gusto
dress: **5** get-up
fantastic: **6** rococo **7** baroque
furniture: **6** Empire
lofty: **4** epic
oratorical: **10** rhetorical
out of: **5** dated, passe
painting: **5** genre
penmanship: **4** hand
performance: **9** execution
styled: **5** named **6** called, formed, yclept
stylet: pro **5** organ, probe **6** dagger **7** poniard **8** stiletto **9** appendage
surgical: **6** trocar
stylish: **4** chic, tony **5** dashy, nifty, smart, swell **6** classy, dressy, jaunty, modish, spiffy, swanky **7** alamode, dashing, doggish, genteel, knowing, swagger **11** fashionable
stylist: **7** modiste
stylites: **7** hermits **8** ascetics
styloid: **8** belonoid
stymie, stymy: **5** block **6** hinder, impede **8** obstruct
Stymphalus: *daughter:* **10** Parthenope
enemy: **6** Pelops
father: **6** Elatus
mother: **7** Laodice
son: **6** Gortys **8** Agamedes
styptic: **4** alum **10** astringent
Styx: **5** nymph, river
father: **7** Oceanus
ferryman: **6** Charon
locale: **5** Hades
mother: **6** Tethys
pert. to: **7** stygian
suant: **4** even **5** grave, quiet **6** demure, placid, smooth, steady **7** equable, regular **9** agreeable, following
suasion: **10** persuasion
suasive: **10** convincing, persuasive
suave: **4** easy, oily, smug **5** bland, civil, soapy, sweet **6** polite, smooth, urbane **7** fulsome **8** gracious, mannered, pleasant, polished, unctuous **9** agreeable **12** ingratiating
suavity: **6** comity **7** amenity **8** urbanity **10** politeness **12** complaisance
sub: **9** auxiliary, submarine
sub rosa: **8** covertly, secretly
subarctic forest: **5** taiga
subbase: **6** plinth
subdivide: **5** carve, mince **8** separate
subdivision: **6** sector, suburb **10** department
defensive position: **6** sector
lateral: **5** aisle
rocks: **5** range
subdue: cow **4** bend, quay, tame **5** accoy, allay, amate, atill, break, charm, crush, daunt, dompt, lower, quell, sober **6** adaunt, bridle, disarm, dismay, evince, master, mellow, reduce, soften, steady, subact **7** affaite, chasten, conquer, control, repress, squelch **8** convince, diminish, overcome, suppress, surmount, vanquish **9** captivate, castigate, overpower, subjugate
suber: **4** cork
subjacent: **10** underlying
subject: try **4** text **5** basis, cause, prone, theme, topic **6** liable, matter, motive, phrase, rēason, submit, vassal **7** article, citizen, conquer, exposed, reality **8** disposed, incident, inferior, obedient **9** dependent, subjugate, substance **10** contingent, predispose, submissive, substratum **11** conditional, subordinate
of discourse: **5** theme, topic
of disease: **4** case **7** patient
of lawsuit: res
of verb: **4** noun
to abuse: **6** revile
to argument: **4** moot
to authority: **6** master
to be taught: **10** didascalic
to change: **7** mutable
to choice: **8** elective
to control: **7** rulable
to death: **6** mortal
to depression: **5** moody
to discussion: **4** moot **9** debatable
to dislike: **8** aversion
to ill treatment: **6** misuse
to mistakes: **7** erratic
to taxation: **8** reteable
to whirling action: **11** centifugate
subjection: **8** thirling **9** captivity
subjoin: add **5** affix, annex **6** append, attach
subjugate: **6** compel, master, reduce, subdue **7** conquer, depress, overawe **8** overcome
sublate: **4** deny **6** cancel, negate, remove **9** eliminate
sublime: **5** exalt, grand, great, lofty, noble, proud **6** purify, refine **7** emotion, exalted, haughty, supreme **8** elevated, empyreal, heavenly, heighten, majestic, splendid, upraised **9** expletive
sublimity: **7** majesty **8** grandeur **12** magnificence
submarine: sub **4** boat **5** diver **9** periscope **11** submersible
detector: **5** sonar
projectile: **7** missile, Polaris, torpedo
submerge: dip **4** bury, dive, hide, sink **5** souse **6** deluge, drench, engulf, plunge **8** inundate, suppress
submerged: **4** sunk **5** awash **6** sunken

continent: 8 Atlantis
submiss: low 6 humble 7 subdued 10 obsequious, submissive
submission: 8 meekness 9 deference, obedience, surrender 10 compliance, confession 11 resignation 13 nonresistance
act of: 5 kneel 6 curtsy 7 curtsey
to destiny: 8 fatalism
submissive: 4 meek 5 buxom 6 docile, humble 7 dutiful, passive, servile 8 obedient, resigned, yielding 9 childlike, compliant
to wife: 8 uxorious
submit: bow 4 bend, obey 5 abide, agree, avale, defer, heald, hield, lower, stoop, yield 6 assent, comply, delate, resign, soften, subdue, suffer, temper 7 exhibit, knuckle, propose, succumb, suggest 8 moderate 9 acquiesce, surrender 10 condescend
for consideration: 5 remit
proposal to: 4 move
to: 4 obey
subordinate: 5 minor, under 6 puisne, subdue 7 control 8 inferior, obedient, servient 9 ancillary, assistant, auxiliary, dependent, secondary, underling 10 accidental, collateral, incidental, submissive 11 subservient
activity: 8 parergon
adjunct: 9 appendage
officer: 4 exon
suborn: 5 adorn, bribe, equip, foist 6 father, incite, induce 7 furnish, procure, provide 9 instigate
subpoena: 4 writ 6 summon
subreption: 6 secret, snatch, unfair 8 unlawful 9 deduction 11 underhanded
subrogate: 10 substitute
subscribe: 5 favor 6 assent, attest 7 ascribe, consent, support 8 sanction 10 acceptance, underwrite
subscriber of newspaper: 6 abonne
subscription to newspaper: 10 abonnement
subsequent: 5 after, later 6 puisne 7 ensuing 8 retainer 9 attendant, companion, following
to birth: 9 postnatal
subsequently: 5 later, since 10 afterwards, thereafter
subservient: 6 vassal 7 duteous, servile 9 accessory, ancillary, auxiliary, truckling 10 obsequious, submissive 11 subordinate
subside: ebb 4 bate, fall, lull, sink, wane 5 abate, cease, lower 6 settle 7 descend, flatten, relapse 8 decrease, withdraw
subsidence: 5 dregs
subsidiary: 7 reserve 9 accessory, assistant, auxiliary, tributary 10 collateral 13 supplementary
subsidy: aid 4 gift, help 5 bonus, grant 6 bounty 7 pension, reserve, support, tribute 10 assistance, subvention
subsist: be 4 feed, hold, live, stay 5 abide, exist, stand 6 obtain, remain 7 support, continue, maintain
subsistence: 6 living 9 allowance, inherency, substance 10 livelihood, provisions 11 persistence
subsoil: bed, pan 4 sole 7 stratum
animal: 4 mole
substance: sum 4 body, core, gist, mass, meat 5 basis, metal, stuff 6 estate, ground, import, matter, realty, spirit, supply, wealth 7 aliment, essence, meaning, purport 8 hardness, majority, material, property, solidity 9 actuality, affluence, resources, solidness 11 consistency
amorphous: 5 resin, rosin 7 ferrite
animal: 7 gelatin
bitter: 4 acid 5 aloes, aloin, linin 6 ilicin 7 amarine, emetine 8 elaterin
dissolving: 9 resolvent
drying: 8 desicant
expansive: gas
reaction-inducing: 7 reagent
rubber-like: 5 gutta
simple: 7 element
sour: 4 acid 7 vinegar
starch-like: 6 inulin, olivil 8 alantine
sticky: goo, gum, tar 4 glue 5 paste
transparent: 9 celluloid
unctuous: oil 6 grease
vegetable: 4 peat 5 resin, rosin
white: 4 alba 6 inulin 7 alanine 8 elaterin
substantial: 4 firm, real, true 5 ample, large, meaty, solid, sound, stout 6 actual, bodily, hearty, stable, strong, sturdy 7 genuine, wealthy 8 tangible 9 corporeal, important 12 considerable
substantiality: See **substance**
substantiate: 5 prove 6 assure, embody, verify 7 confirm 9 establish 11 corroborate
substantive: 4 noun 6 actual, entity 7 pronoun 9 essential 13 self-contained
substitute: 5 extra, fudge, proxy, vicar 6 deputy, ersatz(G.), ringer 7 commute, replace 8 exchange, nominate 9 alternate, makeshift, surrogate 10 viceregent 11 succedaneum 13 succenturiate
for a name: 6 dingus, dodad, widget 9 doohickey 11 thingamabob
temporary: 7 stopgap 9 expedient
substructure: 4 base 6 podium 10 foundation

subsume: 6 assume, deduce 7 contain 8 classify 9 summarize
subterfuge: 4 plan, ruse 5 blind, trick 6 device, escape, refuge 7 evasion 8 artifice, pretense 9 deception 13 prevarication 14 tergiversation
use: 7 chicane 12 tergiversate
subterranean: 4 cave 6 cavern, hidden, secret
subtile: See **subtle**
subtilize: 5 exalt 9 sublimate
subtle: sly 4 deft, keen, nice, wily 5 acute 6 artful, clever, crafty, expert, shrewd 7 cunning, elusive, refined, tenuous 8 abstruse, analytic, delicate, rarefied, skillful 9 beguiling, designing, ingenious, intricate 10 mysterious, perceptive 11 penetrating 14 discriminating
emanation: 4 aura
variation: 6 nuance
subtlety: 7 exility, finesse
subtract: 5 minus 6 deduct, remove 7 detract 8 withdraw, withhold
suburb: 8 environs 9 dissolute, outskirts, periphery
subvention: aid 4 help 5 grant 7 subsidy, support 9 endowment 10 assistance 13 appropriation
subvert: sap 4 ruin 5 evert, upset 6 uproot 7 corrupt, destroy, pervert 8 alienate, overturn 9 overthrow, undermine
subway: 4 tube 5 metro 6 tunnel 11 underground
entrance: 5 kiosk
succade: 8 preserve 10 confection
succedaneum: 6 remedy 8 medicine 10 substitute
succeed: win 4 fare 5 fadge, occur 6 attain, follow, happen, thrive 7 achieve, descend, inherit, prevail, prosper, replace 8 approach, flourish 10 accomplish
succeeding: 7 ensuing, sequent
success: go; hit, wow 4 luck 7 fortune 8 accolade 9 happiness 11 consequence
succession: row, run 6 course, series 7 dynasty 8 sequence 9 gradation
next in line: 4 heir
successive: 9 inherited 10 hereditary 11 consecutive
successor: 4 heir 5 heres 6 haeres, tanist 9 designado(Sp.)
succin: 5 amber
succinct: 4 curt 5 brief, short, terse 6 girded 7 compact, concise, laconic, summary 10 compressed
succor: aid 4 abet, cure, help 5 serve 6 assist, refuge, relief, rescue 7 comfort, deliver, provide, sustain 8 befriend, mitigate 9 alleviate 10 strengthen
succory: 7 chicory
succulent: 4 aloe, lush 5 fresh, juicy, pappy, tasty, vital 6 cactus, tender
fruit: uva
succumb: die 5 yield 6 perish, submit
succursal: 6 branch 9 auxiliary 10 subsidiary
such: as, so; sic(L.) 4 kind, like, some 7 certain, similar
suck: rob, sip 4 draw, lick, swig 5 bleed, draft, drain, drink, nurse 6 absorb, adsorb, imbibe, inhale, suckle 7 consume, extract, suction 14 disappointment
sucker: 4 dupe 5 leech 6 victim 8 lollipop 9 simpleton
sucking fish: 6 remora 7 lamprey
suckle: 4 feed, rear, suck 5 nurse 6 foster 7 nourish 11 honeysuckle
sucrose: 5 sugar 10 saccharose
suction: 6 intake 7 drawing, lifting
sud: 4 foam 6 bubble
Sudan: *animal:* 4 dama 6 oterop
beer: 4 dolo
capital: 7 Khartum
lake: No
language: Ga, Mo; Ewe, Ibo, Kru 4 Efik, Mole, Tshi 6 Yoruba 8 Mandingo
mountain: 4 Nuba
people: 4 Daza, Golo, Sere 5 Fulah, Hausa, Mossi
stockade: 6 zareba, zereba, zeriba 7 zareeba
stretcher: 7 angareb, angarep 8 angareeb
weapon: 8 trombash, trumbash
sudarium: 6 napkin 8 veronica 12 handkerchief
sudden: 4 rash, soon 5 brief, early, ferly, hasty, short, swift 6 abrupt, speedy 7 prerupt, violent 8 headlong, meteoric 9 alertness, impetuous, impromptu 10 unexpected, unforeseen, unprepared 11 precipitate, precipitous
suddenly: 6 presto
suddle: 4 soil 5 stain
Sudra caste member: 5 palli
suds: bog 4 beer, foam 5 dregs, filth, froth 6 lather, refuse 7 bubbles
sue: beg, woo 4 seek, urge 5 chase, court, ensue, plead 6 appeal, follow, guided, pursue 7 beseech, contest, entreat, proceed, request, solicit 8 continue, governed, petition, practice 9 prosecute
suer: 9 plaintiff
suet: fat 6 tallow
Suez Canal: *builder:* 9 de Lesseps
port: 4 Said
suffer: get, let 4 bear, bide, dree(Sc.) 5 admit, allow, groan, thole 6 endure, grieve, permit, submit 7 agonize, undergo 8 tolerate 10 experience

sufferance: 4 pain 6 misery 7 consent, respite 8 patience, sanction 9 passivity, suffering 11 forbearance 12 postponement
sufferer: 3 martyr, victim
suffering: ill 4 bale, dree(Sc.), loss, pain 5 agony 6 ailing, injury 8 distress, sickness 9 adversity 10 affliction 11 tribulation
comb. form: 4 path 5 patho
reliever of: 9 Samaritan
suffice: do 5 serve 6 answer 7 appease, content, satisfy
sufficiency: 4 fill 7 ability, conceit 8 adequacy, capacity 9 abundance 10 capability, competency
sufficient: due, fit 4 able, enow, good 5 ample, valid 6 enough, plenty 7 suffice 8 abundant, adequate 9 competent, effectual, efficient, qualified 11 responsible, substantial 12 satisfactory 13 well-qualified
suffix (see also **combining form, prefix**): For all definitions beginning with this word, look under main word or phrase. EXAMPLES: "suffix for inhabitant": see **inhabitant:** *suffix;* "suffix for sugar": see **sugar:** *suffix.*
sufflate: 7 inflate, inspire
suffocate: 4 kill 5 burke, choke 6 stifle 7 destroy, smother 8 compress, strangle, suppress, throttle 10 asphyxiate, extinguish
suffocation: 8 asphyxia
suffragan: 4 help 5 agent 6 bishop, deputy 9 assistant, auxiliary 11 subordinate
suffrage: aid 4 help, vote 5 right, voice 6 assent, ballot, prayer 7 witness 8 petition 9 franchise, testimony 10 assistance 12 intercession, supplication
suffuse: 4 fill, pour 5 embay 7 diffuse 10 overspread
sugar: gur, ose 4 cane 5 biose, candy, maple, money, oside 6 acrose, aldose, fucose, gulose, hexose, ketose, talose, triose 7 caramel, chitose, glucide, maltose, sucrose, sweeten, tetrose, threose 8 rhodeose 9 muscovado, raffinose, sweetness 10 digitoxose, piloncillo, saccharose 12 carbohydrate 13 dissaccharide 14 monosaccharide
artificial: 6 allose 7 glucose 9 saccharin
boiling kettle: 8 flambeau
burnt: 7 caramel
crystals: 5 candy
fruit: 8 fructose, levulose
liquid: 5 sirup, syrup
lump: 4 cube, loaf
measure: 13 saccharimeter
milk: 7 lactose
mixture: 5 syrup
preparation device: 10 granulator
raw: 9 cassonade
source: sap 4 beet, cane 5 maple
substitute: 5 honey 9 saccharin
syrup: 7 treacle 8 molasses
sugar apple: 6 biriba 8 sweetsop
sugar sand: 5 niter
sugarcane: *disease:* 5 sereh
pulp: 4 marc 6 megass 7 bagasse, megasse
refuse: 4 marc 6 begass 7 bagasse, begasse
stalk: 6 ratoon
sugarloaf: 4 hill 8 conoidal, mountain
sugarplum: 6 bonbon 9 sweetmeat
sugary: 5 sweet 7 honeyed 8 pleasant 10 flattering, saccharine 11 mellifluous
suggest: 4 hint, move 5 imply 6 allude, broach, prompt 7 connote, inspire, mention, propose 8 indicate, intimate 9 insinuate
suggestion: 4 idea 5 tinge, touch, trace 6 advice 7 inkling, remnant, soupcon 8 proposal 9 complaint 10 accusation, incitement, intimation, temptation 11 information
sui juris: 5 adult 11 responsible
suicidal: 4 rash 5 fatal 6 deadly, lethal
suidae: hog 5 swine
suing: 11 prosecution
suint: 5 sweat 6 grease 12 perspiration
suit: do 4 case(law), kind, plea, sort 5 adapt, agree, apply, cards, class, dress, fadge, group, habit, match, order, serve, tally 6 accord, adjust, answer, appeal, assort, attire, behove, outfit, please, prayer, series, trover, wooing 7 arrange, behoove, clothes, comport, conform, costume, request, satisfy, uniform 8 classify, courting, entreaty, petition, sequence 9 harmonize 10 correspond, litigation, succession 11 accommodate 12 solicitation
maker: 6 sartor, tailor
suitable: apt, due, fit, pat 4 able, fair, good, meet 5 right 6 comely, gainly, proper 7 a propos, seeming 8 adequate, apposite, becoming, coherent, eligible, feasible, idoneous, matching 9 competent, congruent, congruous, consonant, expedient 10 commodious, compatible, consistent, convenient, equivalent 11 appropriate 12 commensurate
render: 5 adapt 7 prepare
suitcase: bag 4 grip 6 valise 9 gladstone
suite: set 4 band 5 abode, group, staff, train 6 series 7 retinue 8 equipage 9 apartment, entourage 10 collection
member of: 7 attache
musical: See **musical composition**
suited: See **suitable**
suiting: 4 wool 5 serge

suitor: 4 beau 5 wooer 7 gallant 8 follower 10 petitioner
sukey: 9 teakettle
sulcate: 6 fluted 7 grooved
sulfate: 5 treat 7 convert, sulphur 9 brimstone 10 impregnate
kind: 4 alum 5 hepar, matte 6 barite, blende 7 ilesite, loweite
sulfur: 9 brimstone
substance containing: 5 hepar
sulfuric acid: 7 vitriol
sulk: 4 dort(Sc.), mope, pout 5 grump 6 grouch
sulky: 4 cart, dull, weak 5 chuff, dorty, inert 6 gloomy, gocart, grouty, sullen 7 doggish, peevish 8 carriage, inactive 10 unyielding
sullage: mud 4 silt 5 filth 6 refuse, scoria, sewage 8 drainage 9 pollution 10 filthiness
sullen: sad 4 dour, dull, glum, grim, sour 5 alone, black, cross, felon, gruff, heavy, moody, pouty, stern, sulky, surly 6 crusty, dismal, dogged, gloomy, grouty, morose, silent, somber 7 baleful, boorish, crabbed, peevish, serious 8 churlish, lowering, petulant, solitary 9 obstinate, saturnine 10 depressing, ill-humored, ill-natured, refractory, unsociable 11 intractable, threatening 12 unpropitious
Sullivan's collaborator: 7 Gilbert
sully: 4 blot, blur, foul, soil 5 cloud, dirty, grime, smear, stain, taint 6 darken, defile, smirch 7 attaint, blacken, blemish, corrupt, pollute, tarnish 8 besmirch 9 bespatter 11 contaminate
sulphate: See **sulfate**
sultan: 5 ruler 8 padishah 9 sovereign
decree: 5 irade
sultanate: 4 Oman
sultry: hot 5 close, fiery, humid, lurid 6 coarse, smutty, torrid 7 sensual 8 inflamed 10 oppressive, sweltering 13 uncomfortable
Sulu island: 6 Siassi
sum: add, end, tot 4 gist, host 5 count, gross, issue, total, whole 6 amount, degree, height, number, result, summit 7 integer, numeral, problem, summary 8 addition, assembly, entirety, perorate, quantity 9 aggregate, calculate, gathering, magnitude, substance, summarize, summation 11 epilogation 12 recapitulate
forfeited: 5 dedit
large: gob, pot
small: 4 drab 7 driblet 8 dribblet 11 chickenfeed
subtracted: 9 deduction
unexpended: 7 savings
up: add 9 summarize 12 recapitulate
sumac, sumach: 4 anam 7 dogwood 8 shoemake 11 balinghasay
genus of: 4 rhus
Sumatra: *animal:* 4 balu, tanu 5 orang
ape: 5 orang 6 ourang 9 orangutan
city: 5 Achin, Jambi, Medan 6 Padang 8 Bonkulin 9 Bencoolen, Indrapoor, Palembang
deer: 4 napu
fiber: 6 caloee
lake: 4 Toba
language: 4 Nias
measure: 4 paal
raft: 5 rakit
river: 4 Musi 5 Jambi, Rokan 9 Indragiri
wildcat: 4 balu
Sumer deity: Abu
summarize: sum 5 recap 6 digest 8 abstract 9 epitomize
summary: sum 4 gist 5 brief, recap, short 6 digest, precis, resume, summit 7 concise, epitome, extract, general, medulla 8 abstract, argument, breviate, succinct, synopsis 9 condensed 10 compendium 11 abridgement 13 comprehension 14 recapitulation
summation: See **sum**
summer: ete(F.) 8 estivate 9 aestivate
ailment: 8 heat rash
beverage: ade
pass: 8 estivate
pert. to: 7 estival 8 aestival
summer teal: 8 garganey
summerhouse: 5 kiosk 6 casino, gazebo 7 cottage 8 pavilion 9 belvedere
summery: 5 light 7 estival 8 delicate
summing up: See **sum**
summit (see also **mountain, peak**): bow, cap, tip, top, van 4 acme, apex, knap, roof 5 crest, crown, ridge 6 climax, comble, height, vertex, zenith 8 pinnacle 9 fastigium(L.) 11 culmination
pert. to: 6 apical
summon: ban, bid 4 call, page 5 charm, evoke, rally, rouse 6 accite, appeal, arouse, compel, demand, gather, muster 7 collect, command, convoke, provoke
to court: 4 cite, sist
summoner: 6 beadle 9 apparitor
summons: 4 writ 6 venire 7 command, warning 8 citation 9 challenge 12 notification
sump: mud, pit 4 dirt, pool, pump, tank, well 5 drain 6 puddle, shower 7 cistern, depress 8 cesspool 9 reservoir 10 depression, excavation, receptacle
sumpter: 4 pack 6 burden

sumptuous: 5 grand 6 costly, lavish, superb 8 splendid 9 expensive, luxurious 11 magnificent

sun: orb, sol 4 bask, star 5 Titan 6 bleach 7 daystar, Phoebus 8 luminary 9 Harmachis

combining form: 5 helio

crossing equator: 7 equinox

god: Ra; Tem, Utu 4 Baal, Lleu, Llew, Utug 6 Apollo, Helios 7 Chepera, Khepara, Shamash, Sokaris 8 Hyperion

luminous envelope of: 6 corona

measuring device: 13 pyrheliometer

mock: 9 parhelion

near: 6 heliac

outer layer: 6 corona

part: 6 corona

path: 8 ecliptic

pert. to: 5 solar 6 heliac

protective devices: 7 parasol 8 blindage, havelock

satellite: 6 planet

worshiper: 5 Parsi 6 Parsee 10 heliolater

sun-clock: 7 sundial

sun disk: 4 Aten

sun dog: 4 halo 7 rainbow 9 parhelion

sun room: 7 solaria(pl.) 8 solarium

sun watch: 7 sundial 9 timepiece

sunburn: tan 8 heliosis

sunburst: 6 brooch, ensign

Sunda Island: 4 Bali, Java, Nias 6 Borneo, Lombok 7 Celebes, Sumatra

Sunday: *following Easter:* Low 9 Quasimodo

mid-Lent: 7 Laetare

pert. to: 9 dominical

special: 4 Palm 6 Easter

sunder: rip 4 part, rend, rive 5 break, split 6 divide, severe 7 disjoin, disrupt, divorce 8 dissever, disunite, separate

sundial part: 6 gnomon

sundown: See **sunset**

sundowner: 5 drink, tramp 7 captain 8 nightcap

sundry: 5 apart 6 divers 7 asunder, diverse, several, various 8 distinct, frequent, manifold, numerous, separate, sundered 9 different, disunited 10 respective, separately 12 multifarious 13 miscellaneous

companion of: all

sunfall: See **sunset**

sunfish: 5 bream 8 pondfish

genus of: 4 mola

sunflower: 4 marigold, rockrose 10 balsamroot, heliotrope

maid turned into: 6 Clytie

Sunflower State: 6 Kansas

Sungkiang capital: 6 Harbin

sunk (see also **sink**): pad 4 bank, seat, turf, 5 couch 6 abject, hollow 8 absorbed, overcome 9 depressed

sunken: 6 hollow 9 depressed

fence: 4 ha-ha

sunket: 4 food 6 dainty 8 delicacy

sunless: 4 dark

sunny: gay 4 warm 5 clear, happy, merry 6 bright, golden, sunlit 8 cheerful 9 sparkling, vivacious

sunrise: 4 dawn

song: 6 aubade

sunset: e'en, eve 4 dusk 7 evening, sundown, sunfall 8 twilight

pert. to: 9 acronical

reflection: 9 alpenglow

Sunset State: 6 Oregon 7 Arizona

sunshade: 5 visor 6 awning 7 parasol

sunshine: 5 cheer, light 6 warmth 8 sunburst 9 happiness, sunniness 11 fairweather 12 cheerfulness

Sunshine State: 9 New Mexico 11 South Dakota

sunspot: 6 facula 7 freckle

sunstroke: 8 siriasis 9 calenture

sunwise: 6 deasil, dessil 7 deiseal 9 clockwise

Suomi: 7 Finland

sup: eat, sip 4 dine 5 drink, feast 6 absorb, amount, liquor 7 consume, swallow 8 mouthful, quantity, spoonful

supawn: 4 mush 12 hasty pudding

super: 5 actor, watch 6 square 7 janitor 9 excellent, first-rate

superable: 12 surmountable

superabundance: 5 flood 6 excess 8 plethora 10 exuberance 11 superfluity

superabundant: 4 rank 6 lavish 9 redundant 11 overflowing

superannuate: 6 retire 7 outlast 8 obsolete 9 out-of-date 10 disqualify

superannuated: 5 passe 8 obsolete, outdated 10 antiquated 12 old-fashioned

superb: 4 fine, rich 5 grand, noble, proud 6 lordly 7 elegant, haughty, stately 8 enormous, majestic, splendid 9 excellent, luxurious, sumptuous 13 extraordinary

superbity: 9 arrogance 11 haughtiness

supercilious: 5 lofty, proud 6 uppish 7 haughty 8 arrogant, cavalier, snobbish 9 arbitrary 11 overbearing 12 contemptuous 13 hypercritical

superficial: 4 glib 5 hasty 6 casual, flimsy, slight 7 cursory, outward, shallow, surface 8 external

superfine: 4 luxe, nice, rich 5 extra, plush, prime 6 choice, subtle 8 delicate, overnice 9 excellent

superfluity: 6 excess, luxury 9 abundance 11 prodigality

superfluous: 4 over 5 spare 6 de trop(F.) 7 surplus, useless 8 abnormal, needless, wasteful 9 excessive, redundant, worthless 10 gratuitous, inordinate 11 extravagant, unnecessary 12 nonessential 13 superabundant

superhuman: 6 divine 8 superman 9 herculean 12 supernatural 13 extraordinary

superhumeral: 5 amice

superimpose: 7 overlay

superintend: 4 boss 5 guide 6 direct, manage 7 conduct, control, inspect, oversee 8 engineer 9 supervise 10 administer

superintendence: 4 care 9 authority 14 responsibility

superintendent: 4 boss 6 bishop 7 captain, curator, manager 8 director, minister, overseer 9 inspector 10 supervisor 11 chamberlain

superior: 4 fine, head, lord, over, peer 5 above, eigne, extra, liege, upper 6 better, higher, senior 7 exalted, greater, haughty, palmary, prelate, ranking 8 alderman, arrogant, assuming, dominant, elevated, masterly 9 ascendant, ascendent, excellent, paramount, spiritual 10 preeminant, surpassing 11 predominant 12 supercilious, supernatural 13 comprehensive

superiority: 4 gree(Sc.) 8 priority 9 advantage, meliority, seniority 13 preponderance

position of: 10 domination

superlative: 4 acme, best, peak 6 utmost 7 supreme 8 peerless 9 excessive 11 exaggerated

absolute: 7 elative

suffix: est

Superman's friend: 4 Lois

supernal: 6 divine 8 ethereal, heavenly 9 celestial

supernatural: 5 magic 6 divine 9 marvelous 10 miraculous, superhuman 13 preternatural

supernatural being: elf, god 4 atua 5 angel, deity, demon, fairy, gnome, nymph, troll 6 cherub, seraph, spirit 7 banshee, goddess 10 leprechaun

supernatural happening: 6 vision 7 miracle

supernumerary: 4 supe 5 actor, extra, super

superpower: USA 4 USSR

superscribe: 5 write 6 direct 7 address, engrave

superscription: 5 title 9 direction 11 description, inscription

supersede, supercede: 7 replace, succeed 8 displace, override, supplant

supersensory: 12 extrasensory 13 supersensible

supersonic noise: 4 boom

superstition: 5 freet, freit, magic 6 fetish, voodoo 8 idolatry

supervene: 5 ensue 6 follow, happen 9 supersede

supervise: 4 boss, edit, read, scan 5 check 6 direct, govern, manage, peruse, revise 7 conduct, correct, inspect, oversee 11 superintend

supervisor: 7 foreman 8 alytarch(G.) 9 spectator 10 roadmaster

supine: 5 inert, prone 6 abject, drowsy 7 leaning, passive, sloping, unalert 8 inactive, inclined, indolent, listless, sluggish 9 negligent 11 inattentive, indifferent

supper: tea 4 meal

supplant: 5 upset, usurp 6 follow, remove, uproot 7 replace, succeed 8 displace 9 extirpate, overthrow, supersede, undermine

supple: sly 4 bain, oily 5 agile, lithe 6 limber, lissom, nimble, pliant, swanky 7 cunning, elastic, fawning, lissome, pliable, servile 8 flexible, yielding 9 adaptable, compliant, resilient 10 obsequious, responsive 11 complaisant

supplement: add 8 addendum, addition, appendix 9 accessory 10 complement 13 reinforcement

supplemental: 12 adscititious 13 succenturiate

suppliant: 6 beggar 10 beseeching, entreating, petitioner

supplicate: beg, sue 4 knee, pray 5 crave, plead 6 appeal, invoke, obtest 7 beseech, conjure, entreat, implore, request, solicit 8 petition 9 importune, obsecrate

supplication: 6 litany 8 rogative

supply: aid, fit 4 feed, fill, fund, give, help, load 5 cache, cater, equip, hoard, relay, stock, store, yield 6 afford, employ, foison, purvey, relief, succor 7 fraught, furnish, granary, nourish, plenish, provide, replace, reserve, satisfy 8 minister, ordnance 9 profusion, reinforce, replenish, reservoir 10 administer, assistance, compensate, contribute

support: aid, arm, guy, leg, peg, rib 4 back, base, beam, bear, bibb, fend, help, keep, limb, pier, prop, stay 5 boost, brace, carry, cheer, cleat, easel, favor, found, hinge, shore, sling, staff, strut, truss 6 anchor, behalf, better, defend, endure, lintel, pillar, second, shield, splint, spring, suffer, tripod, trivet, uphold, verify 7 bolster, cherish, comfort, confirm, console, endorse, espouse, fulcrum, nourish, nurture,

protect, provide, reserve, sustain, trestle 8 approval, baluster, befriend, evidence, maintain, pedestal, sanction, tolerate, underlie 9 adminicle, encourage, reinforce, stanchion, vindicate 10 assistance, foundation, strengthen 11 corroborate, countenance 12 alimentation, substantiate
for statue: 5 socle 8 pedestal
one-legged: 6 unipod
slab: 4 tray 6 planch

supporter: 4 ally, knee 6 bearer, patron, rooter 7 abetter, abettor, booster, founder, support 8 adherent, advocate, assertor, follower, henchman, partisan 9 auxiliary

suppose: 4 deem, trow, ween 5 allow, imply, judge, opine, think 6 assume, expect, repute 7 believe, imagine, incline, opinion, presume, suspect 8 conceive, conclude, consider, obligate, supposal 9 apprehend, intention 10 conjecture, presuppose, substitute 11 expectation, supposition

supposed: See **supposititious**

supposition: if 6 notion, theory 7 forgery, surmise 9 postulate 10 alteration, assumption, conjecture, estimation, hypothesis 11 expectation, proposition, uncertainty

supposititious: 7 feigned 8 fabulous, putative, spurious, supposed 9 imaginary, pretended 10 artificial 11 counterfeit 12 hypothetical, illegitimate

suppress: 4 hide, keep, kill, stop 5 check, choke, crush, elide, quash, quell 6 arrest, bridle, censor, harass, ravish, retard, stifle, subdue 7 abolish, conceal, destroy, exclude, oppress, prevent, refrain, repress, silence, smother, squelch 8 compress, prohibit, restrain, withhold 9 interdict, overpower, overthrow 10 dissolving, extinguish

suprarenal: 7 adrenal

supremacy: 4 sway 5 power 7 control, mastery 8 dominion 9 authority, autocracy, dominance, influence 10 ascendancy, ascendency, domination 11 sovereignty 12 predominance 13 preponderance

supreme: 4 last 5 chief, final 6 utmost 7 crucial, highest 8 foremost, greatest, loftiest, peerless, ultimate 9 paramount 10 preeminent

supreme being: 5 Allah, monad 7 creator

surcease: end 4 rest, stay, stop 5 defer, delay 6 desist, relief 7 refrain, respite, suspend 8 postpone 9 cessation

surcharge: tax 4 cost, fill, load 6 burden, impost 7 surfeit 8 overload, surprint 9 overcrowd, overprint, overstock 10 impregnate, overburden, overcharge

surcingle: 4 band, belt 6 girdle 8 cincture

surcoat: 5 jupon 6 cyclas 7 garment

surd: 7 radical 9 insensate, voiceless 10 irrational

sure: 4 fast, firm, safe, true 5 siker(Sc.) 6 indeed, secure, sicker(Sc.), stable, steady strong 7 assured, certain 8 enduring, positive, reliable, unerring 9 authentic, betrothed, confident, convinced, steadfast, undoubted, unfailing 10 dependable, infallible 11 indubitable, trustworthy, unfaltering 12 indisputable 13 incontestable 14 unquestionable

surely: 6 atweel(Sc.), really

sureness: 9 certitude

surety: 4 bail 6 backer, pledge 7 engager, sponsor 8 bailsman, bondsman, security 9 assurance, certainty, guarantee, guarantor 10 confidence
post: 4 bond

surf: 4 foam, wave 5 spray, swell 7 breaker
sound of: 4 rote

surface: 4 area, face, pave, side, skin 5 facet, plane 6 facing, finish, patina 7 outside 8 boundary, exterior 11 superficial
flat: 4 area 5 plane, sheet 7 lateral
geometrical: 5 nappe 6 toroid
inclined: 4 cant, ramp
mellowed: 6 patina
pert. to: 6 facial
rounded: 9 concavity, convexity
toward: 5 ectad

surfacing: 6 gravel 7 asphalt, macadam

surfeit: 4 cloy, feed, glut, sate 6 excess, nausea, supply 7 disgust, replete, satiate, satiety, satisfy 8 disorder 9 satiation 10 discomfort 11 extravagant, overindulge, superfluity 13 overabundance 14 overindulgence

surfeited: 4 sick 5 blase, fed up 8 complete

surge: 4 rise, rush, tide, wave 5 gurge, swell 6 billow 7 estuate, rolling 8 sweeping, swelling

surgeon: 10 chirurgeon

surgeonfish: 4 tang

surgery: 9 operation, resection
appliance: 5 brace 6 crutch, splint
compress: 5 stupe
father of: 4 Pare
instrument: 5 fleam, lance, probe, scala 6 bilabe, gorget, lancet, splint, stylet, trapan, trepan, trocar, vectis 7 forceps, levator, ligator, rongeur, scalpel, trilabe, trochar 8 bistoury, ecraseur, trephine, tweezers 9 goosebill, tenaculum, vulsellum 10 abaptiston, abaptistum, terebellum, tourniquet
perform: 7 operate
plug: 6 tampon
puncture: 8 centesis
roller: 6 fascia 7 fasciae

stitch: 5 seton 6 suture
thread: 6 catgut
Surinam: *capital:* 10 Paramaribo
hut: 5 benab
measure: 7 ketting
toad: 4 pipa 5 pipal
tribe: 4 Boni 5 Djuka
surly: 4 glum, grum, rude 5 bluff, chuff, cross, gruff, gurly 6 abrupt, grumpy, morose, sullen 7 boorish, crabbed, haughty, uncivil 8 arrogant, churlish, growling 10 ill-natured 11 intractable
surmise: 4 deem 5 guess, infer, trace 6 charge 7 imagine, presume, suppose 9 suspicion 10 allegation, assumption, conclusion, conjecture 11 supposition
surmount: top 4 pass, rise, tide 5 climb, crown, excel, mount, total 6 ascend, exceed, hurdle, subdue 7 conquer, surpass 8 overcome 9 negotiate, transcend
surmountable: 9 superable
surmounting: 4 atop
surname: 6 byname 7 agnomen 8 cognomen 11 appellation
surpass: cap, cob, top 4 beat, flog 5 amend, excel, outdo 6 better, exceed, outvie 7 eclipse, outrank, outsoar 8 outclass, outreach, outstrip, surmount 9 transcend
surpassing: 4 fine 6 banner 9 excellent 10 inimitable, preeminent
surplice: 5 cotta, ephod
surplus: 4 over, rest 5 extra 6 excess 7 backlog, reserve 8 overplus 10 redundancy
surprise: awe, cap 5 alarm, amaze, catch, seize, shock 6 dazzle, detect, strike, wonder 7 astound, capture, gloppen, perplex, startle, uncover 8 astonish, bewilder, confound, dumfound, overcome 9 amazement, overwhelm 11 flabbergast
surprised: 5 agape
surprising: 10 unexpected 13 extraordinary
surrealist: 4 Dali
surrender: 4 cede, fall, give 5 remit, yield 6 remise, resign, tender, waiver 7 abandon, cession, concede, deliver, forsake 8 dedition, remittal 9 rendition 10 abdication, capitulate, compromise, relinquish 11 divestiture 12 cancellation
surreptitious: sly 6 secret 7 bootleg 8 sneaking, stealthy 9 underhand 11 clandestine
surrey: 8 carriage
Surrey parish: Kew
surrogate: 6 deputy 8 delegate 9 subrogate 10 substitute
surround: bar, hem 4 belt, fold, gird, ring 5 beset, embay, flood, hedge 6 circle, corral, encase, enring, invest 7 besiege, embosom, enclose, environ, imbosom 8 encircle, envelope, inundate, overflow 9 beleaguer, encompass 12 circumscribe 14 circumnavigate
with water: 4 isle 6 enisle
surrounded: in; mid 4 amid 5 among 6 amidst 7 bounded
surrounding: 5 about, midst 7 context, setting 8 ambiance 9 entourage 11 environment 12 circumjacent, circumstance
surtax: 4 agio, levy 5 extra
surtout: 4 coat, hood 7 garment 8 overcoat
survey: 4 pool, scan, view 5 study 6 regard, review, search 7 examine, history, inspect, oversee 8 consider, traverse 9 delineate, determine, treatment 10 exposition, scrutinize 11 description, reconnoiter, superintend 13 triangulation 14 reconnaissance
surveyor: 6 gauger 9 arpenteur, inspector 14 superintendent
helper: 6 rodman 7 lineman, poleman 8 chainman
instrument: 11 stratameter
nail: 4 spad
tool: 6 alidad 7 alidade, transit 10 theodolite 12 perambulator
survival: 5 relic
survive: 7 outlast, outlive
Susa inhabitant: 7 Elamite
Susanna: *accusers:* 6 elders
husband: 7 Joachim
susceptible: 4 easy, open 6 liable 7 exposed, subject 8 allergic, sensible 9 receptive, sensitive 10 responsive, vulnerable 11 softhearted, unresistant 13 tenderhearted 14 impressionable
to error: 8 fallible
susceptibility: 5 sense 7 emotion, feeling 11 sensibility 13 affectibility
suscitate: 5 rouse 6 excite 7 animate 9 stimulate
suslik: 5 sisel 8 squirrel 11 spermophile
suspect: 4 fear 5 doubt, guess 7 dubious, imagine, inkling, presume, suppose, surmise 8 conceive, distrust, mistrust 9 discredit 10 disbelieve, intimation, suspicious 12 apprehension
suspend: bar 4 hang, hold, oust, stop 5 cease, debar, defer, demur, expel 6 dangle, recess 7 adjourn, exclude 8 intermit, postpone, withhold 9 pretermit
suspended: 4 hung 6 latent 7 abeyant, pendent, pensile 8 inactive 11 inoperaive
suspender: 5 brace 6 garter 7 galluse 9 supporter
suspense: 7 anxiety 8 cautious, hesitant, withheld 11 tenterhooks, uncertainty 12 apprehension 14 indecisiveness
in: 7 pending

suspension: 4 stop 5 delay 7 failure 8 abeyance, buoyancy, stoppage 9 remission 11 withholding 12 intermission, interruption
in air: 5 vapor
of court sentence: 9 probation
of hostilities: 5 truce 9 armistice, cease-fire
suspicion: 4 hint 5 doubt, touch, trace 7 askance, inkling 8 distrust, jealousy, mistrust 9 misgiving 10 diffidence, intimation, suggestion, uneasiness 11 expectation, 12 apprehension
suspicious: 5 fishy, leery 8 doubtful 9 equivocal 11 mistrustful 12 questionable
suspire: 4 sigh 7 respire
Sussex borough: 4 Hove
sustain: 4 abet, back, bear, buoy, dure, feed, help, prop 5 abide, carry 6 assist, endure, foster, second, succor, suffer, supply, uphold 7 comfort, confirm, console, contain, nourish, prolong, provide, support, undergo 8 befriend, continue, maintain 9 encourage, withstand 10 strengthen 11 corroborate
sustenance: 4 food, meat 5 bread, viand 6 living, upkeep 7 aliment, support 9 nutrition, provision 10 exhibition 11 maintenance, nourishment, subsistence 12 alimentation
sustentation: 6 upkeep 7 support 10 sustenance 11 maintenance 12 preservation
susurrus: 6 murmur, rustle 7 whisper
sutler: 9 vivandier 10 vivandiere
suttee: 7 suicide 10 immolation
suture: 4 line, seam 6 stitch 9 arthrosis 12 articulation
suzerain: 8 overlord 9 paramount, sovereign
svelte: 4 slim 5 lithe 6 lissom 7 lissome, slender 8 graceful
swab: mop 4 lout 5 brush, clean 7 epaulet, plunger 8 medicate
swack: 4 blow 5 whack 6 nimble, pliant, supple
swad: pod 4 mass 5 clown, crowd, shell 7 bumpkin, soldier
swaddle: 4 beat, bind, wrap 6 cudgel, swathe 7 bandage 8 restrict, surround
swag: pit, sag, tip 4 list, loot, sway 5 booty, lurch, spoil, swing, tramp 6 bundle, hollow 7 plunder, swagger 10 decoration
swage: 4 tool 5 shape 6 border, groove 7 assuage
swagger: 4 brag 5 bluff, boast, bully, lurch, strut, swell 6 cuttle, hector, prance 7 bluster, gauster, panache, quarrel, roister, ruffler, stagger, stylish 11 braggadocio, fanfaronade 16 ultrafashionable
swaggering: 6 gascon 7 huffcap
swagman: 9 sundowner
bundle: 5 bluey
swain: boy 5 lover, youth 6 rustic, suitor 7 admirer, gallant, peasant, servant 8 shepherd 9 attendant 10 countryman
swale: fen 4 moor, sway 5 marsh, shade, slash, sweal, swing, swirl 6 hollow, meadow, valley 8 coolness 10 depression
swallow: eat, sip, sup 4 bear, bolt, gaup, gawp, glut, gulp, tern 5 drink, merge, quilt, swift 6 absorb, accept, englut, engulf, go-down, gullet, imbibe, ingest, martin, recant, resorb, throat, vanish 7 believe, consume, engorge, retract 8 aperture, suppress, tolerate, withdraw 9 esophagus
swamp: bog, fen 4 mire, moor, muck, ruin, sink, slew, sloo, slue, thin, wham 5 clear, empty, flood, marsh 6 deluge, engulf, hollow, morass, slough 7 cienaga, pocosin, pocoson, slender 8 overcome, quagmire, submerge 9 overwhelm 10 Everglades
gas: 6 miasma 7 methane
grass: 5 sedge
pert. to: 7 miasmal, paludal
swan: cob, elk, pen 5 swear 6 cygnet 7 declare 8 surprise 9 trumpeter
female: pen
genus: 6 cygnus
male: cob
young: 6 cygnet
Swan river: 4 Avon
swank: 6 active, lively 7 stylish, swagger
swanky: ale 4 beer 5 cider 6 active
Swann's Way author: 6 Proust
swap: 4 bang, blow, move, slap 5 fling, smack, swoop, throw, trade 6 barter, dicker, pounce, strike, stroke 8 exchange
swape: bar, oar 4 pole
sward: sod 4 lawn, skin, turf 8 covering 10 greensward
swarm: fry, sny 4 bike(Sc.), byke(Sc.), host, move, shin, swim, teem 5 climb, cloud, crowd, flock, group, horde, mount 6 abound, throng 7 migrate 8 assemble 9 multitude 10 congregate
swarming: 6 aswarm 10 emigration
swart: 4 dark 6 dismal, gloomy 7 baneful, swarthy 8 blackish 9 malignant
swarthy: dun 4 dark 5 dusky 8 blackish
swash: bar 4 blow, move 5 noise, sound 6 strike 7 bluster, channel, dashing, swagger 9 splashing 12 swashbuckler
swashbuckler: 5 bravo 6 gascon 7 ruffian, slasher, soldier 9 daredevil, swaggerer
swashy: 4 weak 6 watery 7 insipid
swastika, svastika, swastica: 5 cross 6 fylfot 9 Gammadion
swat: bat, hit 4 blow 5 clout 6 strike
swatch: 5 swash 6 sample

swath, swathe: row 4 band, crop 5 strip, sweep, 6 stroke 7 windrow
swathe: 4 band, bind, wrap 6 enfold 7 envelop, swaddle 8 surround
sway: 4 bend, bias, lean, move, reel, rock, rule, veer 5 force, grace, guide, lurch, power, shake, swing, waver, wield 6 direct, divert, govern, swerve, totter, waddle 7 command, control, deflect, shoggie 8 dominion, rotation 9 dominance, influence, oscillate, vacillate 10 ascendancy, ascendency 11 fluctuation, inclination, sovereignty 13 lithesomeness
swaying: 5 asway
sweal: 4 burn, melt 5 singe, waste 6 scorch
swear: vow 4 bind 5 curse, utter 6 adjure, affirm, assert, pledge, threat 7 declare, promise 8 execrate 9 blaspheme 10 administer, asseverate
falsely: 7 perjure, slander
to secrecy: 4 tile
sweat: dry 4 emit, ooze, work 5 bleed, exude, hoist, labor, sudor(L.) 6 drudge, fleece 7 excrete, extract, ferment, putrefy, soldier 8 condense, overwork, perspire, transude
sweater: 5 shell 8 cardigan, pullover
Sweden: *artist:* 4 Zorn
botanist: 5 Fries 9 Bromelius
bread: 10 knackebrod
city: 5 Boras, Edane, Falun, Gavle, Malmo, Ystad 6 Orebro, Upsala 7 Uppsala 8 Goteborg, Nykoping 9 Falkoping, Jonkoping, Stockholm 10 Eskilstuna, Gottenburg, Norrkoping 11 Halsingborg
clover: 6 alsike
coin: ore 5 krona
county: lan
dance: 6 polska
division: amt 4 Laen 5 Skane 8 Gotaland, Gothland, Norrland, Swealand
dynasty: 4 Vasa
explorer: 5 Hedin
farm: 4 torp
gulf: 7 Bothnia
island: 5 Oland 6 Oeland 8 Gotaland, Gothland
king: 4 Eric, Wasa 5 Oscar 10 Bernadotte
lake: 5 Asnen, Malar, Wener 6 Siljan, Varern, Vatter, Wennen, Wetter 7 Hielmar, Malaren, Vattern
manual training: 5 sloyd
match: 12 taendstikker
measure: am; aln, fot, mil, ref, tum 4 famn, last, stop 5 carat, foder, kanna, kappe, linje, nymil, spann, stang, tunna 6 fathom, jumfru 7 kollast, oxhuvud, tunland 8 fjarding, kappland, koltunna, tunnland
money: 8 skilling
motion-picture director: 7 Bergman
mountain: 6 Sarjek
noble title: 4 graf
parliament: 7 Riksdag
philologist: 5 Ihre
physicist: 5 Dalen
province: 6 Kalmar, Orebro, Upsala 7 Gotland, Halland 8 Blekinge, Elfsborg, Jemtland, Malmohus, Wermland 9 Gefleborg, Jonkoping, Kronoberg, Skaraborg, Stockholm 10 Kopparberg, Norrbotten 11 Westmanland 12 Oster Gotland, Sodermanland, Westerbotten 13 Christianstad 14 Westernorrland 18 Gottenborgoch Bohus
river: 4 Gota, Klar, Umea 5 Kalix, Lulea, Pitea, Ranea 6 Lainio, Ljusne, Tornea, Windel 7 Ljungan
soprano: 7 Nilsson 10 Jennie Lind
sour milk: 8 tatmjolk
state religion: 8 Lutheran
tribe: 6 Geatas
weight: ass, lod, ort 4 last, mark, pund, sten, untz 5 carat 6 nylast 7 centner, lispund 8 lispound, skalpund, skeppund 9 ship pound
writer: 6 Carlen 7 Bellman 8 Lagerlof 10 Strindberg
Swedish Nightingale: 4 Lind 5 Jenny
sweep: oar 4 line 5 besom, broom, brush, clean, clear, drive, range, scope, scour, strip, surge, swath 6 extend, remove 7 contour, stretch 8 traverse
sweeping: 8 complete 9 extensive 13 comprehensive, thoroughgoing
sweepings: 6 fulyie(Sc.), fulzie(Sc.)
sweer: 4 slow 5 loath 8 indolent 9 reluctant
sweet: 4 dear, fair 5 bonny, candy, dolce, douce(F.), fresh, soave 6 dulcet, gentle, lovely, pretty, sugary, syrupy 7 beloved, caramel, darling, honeyed, musical, winning 8 aromatic, fetching, fragrant, pleasant, pleasing, preserve 9 agreeable, ambrosial, melodious 10 attractive, confection, harmonious 11 mellisonant
sweet flag: 7 calamus
sweet potato: yam 6 batata 7 ocarina
sweetbread: 9 ris de veau
sweetbrier: 9 eglantine
sweeten: 4 mull 5 sugar 6 purify, refine, soften, solace 7 appease, cleanse, freshen, mollify, perfume, relieve 9 disinfect 10 edulcorate
sweetfish: ayu
sweetheart: jo(Sc.); gra 4 agra, beau, dear, doll, doxy, gill, girl, jill, lass, love 5 bully, court, flame, leman 6 adorer, fellow, orpine 8 truelove
sweetly: 8 smoothly 10 pleasantly 11 comfortably 13 mellifluently

sweetmeat: 4 cake 5 candy, goody 6 comfit, dragee, pastry 7 caramel, dessert 8 confetti, conserve, hardbake, marzipan, preserve 9 marchpane, sugarplum 10 confection
sweetsop: 4 ates
swell: nob, sea 4 bell, bulb, bulk, grow, huff, rise, surf, toff, wave 5 bloat, bulge, grand, surge 6 billow, dilate, expand, extend, roller, tiptop, tumefy 7 augment, distend, enlarge, inflate, sea-gate, stylish 8 increase 9 elevation, excellent, first-rate, intumesce 10 prominence, thickening 11 fashionable 12 protuberance 16 ultrafashionable
swelled head: 6 egoist 7 conceit
swellfish: 6 puffer 8 puff-fish
swelling: sty 4 bleb, bubo, node 5 blain, botch, bouge, bunch, edema, tumor 6 aswell, gather, growth 7 gibbous, turgent 8 windgall 9 gibbosity
on plants: 4 gall
pert. to: 5 nodal 9 edematose, edematous
swelt: die 5 broil, faint, swoon 6 perish, scorch 9 suffocate
swelter: 4 fret, heat, rush 5 exude, faint, roast, sweat 6 wallow, welter 8 perspire
swerve: bow 4 skew, turn, veer 5 stray, yield 6 totter 7 deflect, deviate, digress
sweven: 5 dream, sleep 6 vision
swift: 4 cran(Sc.), fast, reel 5 alert, fleet, hasty, quick, rapid, ready 6 lizard, prompt, speedy, winged
Swift: 4 Dean 8 satirist
brute: 5 Yahoo
flying island: 6 Laputa
hero: 8 Gulliver
lady friend: 6 Stella
pen name: 7 Draper 11 Bickerstaff
swiftly: 4 fast 5 apace
swiftness: 5 haste 8 celerity
swig: 4 gulp, rock, sway 5 draft, drink, hoist, swash 6 tackle
swile: 4 seal
swill: 4 fill, wash 5 flood, rinse, swash, waste 6 basket, drench, guzzle, refuse 7 garbage, hogwash
swillbowl: sot 8 drunkard
swim: 4 reel 5 float, swoon 9 dizziness 13 forgetfulness 15 unconsciousness
pert. to: 8 natatory
swimmer: 7 natator
of the English Channel: 6 Ederle
of the Hellespont: 7 Leander
of Tiber river: 7 Cloelia
swimming: 5 aswim 6 filled, naiant, natant 7 flooded, vertigo 9 dizziness
swimming pool: 4 tank 10 natatorium
swimming stroke: 4 back, side 5 crawl 6 breast 9 butterfly
swindle: con, gyp 4 bilk, dupe, fake, mace, rook 5 bunco, bunko, cheat, foist, fraud, spoof, trick 6 diddle, trepan 7 defraud 8 flimflam
swindler: fob 5 biter, cheat, crook, knave, rogue, shark 6 chiaus, chouse, shaver 7 sharper 8 blackleg
swine: hog, pig, sow 4 boar 7 peccary
breed of: 8 Cheshire, Tamworth 9 Berkshire, Hampshire, Yorkshire 11 Duroc-Jersey, Poland China 12 Chester White
feeding of: 7 pannage 8 slopping
female: sow 4 gilt
fever: 6 rouget 7 cholera
flesh: 4 pork
litter of: 6 farrow
male: 4 boar
pert. to: 7 porcine
young: pig 5 shoat 6 piglet
swinelike: 7 porcine
swing: 4 beat, bent, blow, hang, hurl, lilt, slew, slue, sway, whip 5 fling, power, shake, throw, trend, waver 6 dangle, manage, rhythm, stroke, totter 7 flutter, shoggie(Sc.), suspend, trapeze, vibrate 8 brandish; undulate 9 fluctuate, oscillate
swing around: 4 slue
swinge: 4 beat, lash, whip 5 whirl 6 thrash 7 impetus, revolve, scourge
swinish: 5 gross 6 coarse 7 beastly, boarish, piggish, sensual
swink: 4 toil 5 labor, slave 8 drudgery
swipe: cut, hit 4 blow, glom 5 draft, drink, lever, steal, swape, sweep 6 pilfer, snatch, strike
swirl: ess 4 curl, eddy 5 curve, gurge, twist, whirl, whorl
swirly: 7 knotted, tangled, twisted
swish: 4 cane, flog, hiss, lash, whip 5 birch, smart, sound 6 rustle, strike
Swiss: See **Switzerland**
switch: gad, rod 4 beat, flog, lash, turn, twig, wand, whip 5 shift, shunt, swing 6 change, divert, strike 7 scourge 8 transfer 10 disconnect
switchboard: 5 panel
switchman: 7 shunter
Switzerland: 6 Suisse(F.) 7 Schweiz(G.) 8 Helvetia
ax: 6 piolet
bay: Uri
canton: Uri, Zug 4 Bern, Genf, Vaud 5 Basel, Basle, Waadt 6 Aargau, Geneva, Geneve, Glaris, Glarus, Luzern, St. Gall, Schwyz, Tessin, Ticino, Valais, Wallis, Zurich 7 Grisons, Lucerne, Schwytz, Soleure, Thurgau 8 Freiberg 9 Appenzell, Neuchatel, Neuenberg, Solothurn 10 Graubunden

11 Sankt Gallen, Schaffhouse, Unterwalden 12 Schaffhausen
card game: 4 jass
cheese: 7 Gruyere, sapsago 9 schweizer 10 Emmentaler 13 schweizer-kase
city: 4 Bale, Bern, Chur, Genf, Sion 5 Basel, Basle, Berne 6 Geneva, Schwyz, Zurich 7 Fyzabad, Locarno, Lucerne 8 Faizabad, Lausanne, Montreux, St. Gallen 9 Constance, Neuchatel 10 Farukhabad, Winterthur
coin: 5 franc, rappe 6 rappen 7 angster, centime, duplone 8 blaffert
commune: Zug 4 Biel, Wald 5 Aarau, Morat
composer: 4 Raff
district: 6 canton
food: 12 bernerplatte
herdsman: 4 senn
hero: 11 Wilhelm Tell
lake: Uri, Zug 4 Joux, Thon 5 Leman 6 Bienne, Brienz, Geneva, Lugano, Sarnen, Zurich 7 Lucerne, Lungern 8 Viervald 9 Constance, Neuchatel, Sarnersee, Thunersee 10 Stattersee 11 Brienzersee
language: 5 Ladin 6 French, German 7 Italian, Romansh 8 Romansch, Roumansh 14 Switzerdeutsch
legislature: 8 grossrat 9 grosserat, grossrath
measure: imi, pot 4 aune, elle, fuss, immi, muid, pied, saum, zoll 5 lieue, ligne, linie, maass, moule, pouce, schuh, staab, toise 6 perche, setier, strich 7 juchart, klafter, viertel 9 quarteron 11 holzklafter
money: 4 batz
mountain: 4 Alps, Jura, Rigi, Rosa 5 Blanc, Cenis, Genis 7 Pilatus 8 Jungfrau 9 St. Gothard 10 Matterhorn 11 Burgenstock
mountain pass: 5 Furka 7 Gothard, Grimsel, Simplon 8 Lotschen 13 Saint Gotthard
officer: 5 amman
painter: 4 Klee
people: 4 muff 5 French, German 7 Italian, Romansh 8 Rhaetian, Romansch, Roumansh 9 Helvetian
pert. to: 5 Alpen
pine: 6 arolla
psychologist: 4 Jung
resort: 5 Davos
river: Aar, Inn 4 Aare 5 Doubs, Reuss, Rhone
sled: 4 luge 5 luger
song: 5 yodel
tunnel: 5 Cenis 7 Gothard, Simplon 11 Loetschberg
weight: 5 pfund 7 centner, quintal 11 zugtierlast 12 zugthierlast
wind: 4 bise
wine: 7 Dezaley
valley: Aar
swivel: 4 turn
swollen: 4 blub 5 blown, pursy, tumid 6 turgid 7 blubber, bulbous, bulging, pompous 8 enlarged, inflated, varicose 9 distended, increased, tumescent
swoon: fit 4 dwam 5 dwalm(Sc.), faint, sleep, spell 6 attack 7 ecstasy, syncope 8 languish
swoop: cut 5 seize, sweep 6 pounce 7 descend
sword: sax 4 dirk, epee, foil, pata 5 bilbo, brand, estoc, glawe, gully, kukri, saber, sabre 6 barong, creese, cutlas, Damask, dusack, espada, floret, parang, rapier, spatha, Toledo 7 ascalon, askelon, baslard, curtana, curtein, cutlass, espadon, estoque, shabble, simitar 8 acinaces, camplian, claymore, Damascus, falchion, flamberg, scimitar, schlager, whinyard 9 achiavone, flamberge
blade of: 5 forte
cross guard: 7 quillon
curved: 5 saber, sabre 8 scimitar
fencing: 4 epee, foil
handle: 4 haft, hilt
of the Cid: 6 Colada
short: 4 dirk
two-edged: 4 pata
sword lily: 9 gladiolus
swordfish: 6 espada 7 espadon 9 broadbill
swordlike: 5 xypho 6 ensate 8 ensiform, gladiate
swordsman: 6 fencer 7 epeeist
swore: 5 curst 6 cursed
sworn: 7 devoted 8 affirmed, attested 9 confirmed 10 determined, inveterate
swot (see also **swat**): 5 grind, labor, sweat
syagush: 7 caracal
sybarite: 7 epicure 10 voluptuary
Sybil: See **Sibyl**
syce: 5 groom
sycophant: 5 toady 7 fawning, spaniel 8 informer, parasite 9 charlatan, flatterer 10 footlicker, talebearer
sycophantic: 7 servile, slavish
sye: sy; sie 4 fall, sink 7 descend
Syleus' slayer: 8 Heracles, Hercules
syllable: *added:* 6 prefix
deletion: 7 apocope
final: 6 ultima
lacking at end: 10 catalectic
musical: do, fa, la, mi, re, so, ti
next to last: 6 penult
second before last: 10 antepenult
short: 4 mora 5 breve
shortening: 7 apocope, elision, systole
stressed: 5 arsis
unaccented: 6 atonic

syllabus: 7 outline, summary 8 headnote, synopsis 9 statement 10 compendium
sylloge: 10 collection, compendium
syllogism: 7 Sorites 8 argument 9 reasoning 10 epichirema 11 epicheirema
sylph: elf, fay 5 fairy 6 undine
sylphlike: 7 lissome, slender 8 graceful
sylvan: 5 woody 6 rustic, wooded 8 woodsman 10 forestlike
sylvan deity: Pan 4 faun 6 Faunus
sylvatic: 4 rude 11 uncivilized
symbol (see also **element**): 4 icon, ikon, sign, type, word 5 badge, creed, crest, cross, image, token, totem 6 caract, emblem, ensign, figure, letter 7 diagram 9 character, hierogram, trademark 10 expression, similitude 12 abbreviation, contribution
achievement: 5 medal 6 ribbon
comedy: 4 sock
early Christian church: 5 orant
immortality: 6 phenix 7 phoenix
mourning: 5 crepe 7 cypress
peace: 4 dove
put into: 6 notate
saintliness: 4 halo
servitude: 4 yoke
victory: 4 palm 6 laurel
wisdom: owl
symbolical: 7 typical 8 mystical 11 allegorical, sacramental 14 representative
symbolize: 5 agree 6 concur, typify 7 betoken, combine, express, signify 9 harmonize, represent
symmetrical: 7 regular, spheral 13 commensurable
symmetry: 7 balance, harmony 9 congruity 10 conformity, consistency, proportion
sympathetic: 4 soft 6 humane, tender 7 pietoso, piteous 8 affected 9 condolent, congenial, expansive, sensitive 10 responsive 13 compassionate
sympathize: 6 bemoan 7 condole 11 commiserate
sympathy: 4 pity 6 accord, liking 7 harmony 8 interest 9 agreement 10 compassion, condolence, tenderness 13 commiseration, understanding
expression of: 8 clemency 10 condolence
lack of: 8 dyspathy
symphonious: 9 accordant 10 harmonious
symphony: 5 music 7 concord, harmony
division: 8 movement
for Napoleon: 6 Eroica
form: 6 sonata
symposium: 4 talk 7 banquet 8 dialogue 9 symposiac 10 conference, discussion 11 compotation
symptom: 4 mark, note, sign 5 token 10 indication
synagogue: 4 shul 5 group 8 assembly, building, religion 9 communion, community 12 congregation
officer: 6 parnas
platform: 7 almemar
pointer: yad
Sephardic: 5 anoga
singer: 6 cantor, chazan 7 chazzan
synaxis: 7 meeting, service 12 congregation
synchronize: 7 arrange 8 regulate 12 contemporize
synchronous: 8 existing 10 concurrent 11 concomitant 12 contemporary, simultaneous 15 contemporaneous
syncope: 4 loss 5 faint, swoon 7 elision 9 cessation, haplology 10 suspension 11 contraction, hyphaeresis 15 unconsciousness
syndetic: 10 connective
syndic: 5 agent, judge, mayor 7 manager, officer, trustee 8 advocate, official 10 magistrate
syndicate: 4 sell 5 chain, group, trust, unite 6 cartel 7 censure, council 8 monopoly 9 committee 11 association 12 organization
synod: 4 body 5 court 7 council, meeting 8 assembly 10 convention 11 convocation
syne: ago 5 since
synonymous: 4 like 5 alike 10 equivalent
synopsis: 4 plan 7 summary 8 abstract 9 statement 10 compendium, conspectus 11 abridgement
syntax: 5 order 6 system 9 structure 11 arrangement
analyze: 5 parse
mistake: 8 solecism
synthesis: 5 summa 7 complex 11 combination, composition 13 incorporation
syphilis: pox 4 lues
lesion: 7 chancre
old remedy: 9 Salvarsan
Syracuse: *conqueror:* 4 Rome
founder: 7 Archias
tyrant: 5 Gelon
Syria: *ancient name:* 4 Aram
animal: 5 addax, daman
bear: 4 dubb
bishop: 4 abba
buried city: 4 Dura
church plan: 8 triconch
city: 4 Homs 5 Calno, Derra 6 Aleppo, Balbec, Calneh 7 Antioch 8 Damascus, Seleucia 12 Alexandretta
deity: El 4 Baal 5 Allat 6 Mammon 7 Resheph
district: 6 Aleppo, Hauran
goat: 6 angora
grass: 7 Johnson

gypsy: 5 Aptal
lake: 5 Merom 8 Tiberias
mallow: 4 okra
measure: 5 makuk 6 garava
money: 5 pound 6 talent 7 piaster
mountain: 6 Carmel 7 Libanus
peasant: 6 fellah
people: 5 Druse 7 Ansarie, Saracen
plant: 5 cumin
religious sect: 5 Druse
river: 6 Jordan 7 Orontes
script: 5 serta
silk: 4 acca
tetrarchy: 7 abilene
weight: 4 cola, rotl 5 artal, artel, ratel 6 talent
wind: 6 simoon

syringa: 5 lilac, shrub
syrinx: 7 panpipe 8 panpipes
syrt: bog 9 quicksand
syrup: 4 karo, sapa 6 orgeat 7 dhebbus, glucose, sarghum
system: ism 4 code 5 group 6 circle, method, regime, theory 7 regimen 8 religion, treatise, universe 9 procedure 10 assemblage, hypothesis, philosophy, regularity 11 aggregation, arrangement, orderliness
of rules: 4 code
of weights: 4 troy
of worship: 4 cult
systematic: 4 neat 7 orderly, regular 9 organized 10 methodical
systematics: 8 taxonomy
systematize: 6 adjust 7 arrange, catalog 8 organize, regiment 9 catalogue
syzygy: 6 dipody
Szechwan capital: 7 Chengtu

T

t-shaped: tau

taa: 6 pagoda

Taal: 9 Afrikaans

tab: pan, tag 4 bill, drop, flap, loop 5 aglet, check, index, label, score, strap, strip 6 aiglet, eartab, record 7 account, latchet, officer 9 appendage, reckoning 10 accounting

tabac: 5 snuff 7 tobacco

tabanid: 8 horsefly

tabard: inn 4 cape, coat 5 cloak 6 chimer, jacket, mantle 7 pendant

tabasco: 5 sauce

tabatiere: 8 snuffbox

tabby: cat, pad 4 gown, silk 5 dress 6 fabric, gossip, moreen 7 padding, taffeta 8 brindled

tabella: 6 tablet 7 lozenge

taberna: 4 shop, tent 5 booth 7 shelter

tabernacle: 4 tent 5 abode, dwell, hovel, niche 6 church, recess, reside, temple 7 deposit, shelter, support 8 enshrine 9 sanctuary, structure 10 habitation, receptacle

tabes: 7 atrophy 10 emaciation 11 consumption 12 tuberculosis

tabetless: 4 numb 7 foolish 9 senseless

table: hem 4 fare, feed, food, slab, wash 5 bench, board, canon, index, panel, plate, treat 6 indius, lamina, record, repast, tablet 7 console, surface 8 credence, feasting, postpone, schedule, synopsis, tabulate 10 collection 11 concentrate 12 stringcourse
centerpiece: 7 epergne
communion: 5 altar 8 credence, credenza
cover: 5 baize, cloth, tapis
decorative cloth: 6 runner
dish: 6 tureen
game: 4 pool 8 Ping-Pong 9 billiards
linen: 6 napery 7 napkins 11 tablecloths
philosophers: 14 deipnosophists
small: 5 stand, wagon 6 teapoy 7 taboret, tendoor, tendour
working: 5 bench
writing: 4 desk 10 escritoire

table tennis: 8 Ping-Pong

tableland: 4 mesa 5 karoo 6 karroo 7 plateau 8 balaghat, plateaux, plateaus 9 balaghaut 12 altiplanicie

tableau: 7 picture 8 register, schedule 14 representation

tablet: pad 4 bred, slab 5 facia, panel 6 troche 7 lozenge 10 receptacle
medicine: 6 troche
sculptured: 5 stela, stele 6 stelae, steles
stone: 4 slab 5 stele
three-leaved: 8 triptych
two-leaved: 7 diptych
writing: pad 5 slate

tableware item: cup 4 bowl, dish, fork 5 knife, plate, spoon 6 saucer

tablinum: 4 room 6 alcove, recess

tabloid: 5 short 9 condensed 12 concentrated

taboo, tabu: ban 5 debar 6 forbid 8 prohibit 9 forbidden 12 interdiction
opposed to: noa

tabor, tabour: 4 drum 6 atabal 7 attabal, eardrum, timbrel

taboret, tabouret: 4 drum, seat 5 stand, stool, tabor 6 tabour

tabu: See **taboo**

tabulate: 4 list 7 arrange 8 schedule

tabulation: *grammatical:* 8 paradigm
of the year: 8 calendar

taccaceous herb: pia

taccada: 9 fanflower

tache: pan, tie 4 spot 5 clasp, fault, habit, stain 6 attach, buckle 7 blemish, tarnish 11 disposition 14 characteristic

tacit: 6 silent 7 implied 8 implicit, unspoken, wordless 9 noiseless 10 understood

taciturn: 6 silent 8 reserved, reticent 9 saturnine 15 uncommunicative

tack: 4 beat, busk, clap, gear, haul, join, link, nail, rope, slap, trim 5 baste, catch, fetch, rider, spell, strip, tying, unite 6 attach, course, fasten, handle, method, secure, tackle 7 clothes, connect, payment 8

contract 9 agreement, endurance, fastening 10 stickiness, supplement 12 adhesiveness
glazier: 4 brad
nautical: 5 board
to: 4 jibe
to windward: 4 trip
two-pointed: 6 staple
tackle: rig 4 arms, food, gear, tack 5 angle, drink, seize, stuff 6 attach, collar, secure 7 grapple, harness, rigging, weapons 8 mistress, windlass 9 apparatus, encounter, equipment, undertake
football: 4 stop 5 throw
fishing: tew
single and double block: 6 burton
strong: cat
tacky: 5 crude, dowdy, seedy 6 shabby, sticky, untidy 8 adhesive, slovenly
tact: 5 poise, touch 6 stroke 7 address, feeling 8 delicacy, graceful 9 appendage, diplomacy 10 adroitness, cleverness, discretion, perception 11 discernment 14 discrimination
tactfully: 7 happily
tactics: 6 method, system 9 procedure
tactless: 5 brash
tactlessness: 9 gaucherie
tad: 5 child 6 urchin
tadpole: 8 polliwog
taenia: 4 band 6 fillet 8 headband
taffy: 5 gundy 7 glaggum 8 flattery
Taffy: 8 Welshman
tag: dog, end, tab 4 flap, game, join, lock 5 aglet, label, shred, strip, touch 6 aiglet, append, attach, eartab, fasten, follow, rabble 7 refrain, taglock 9 appendage, catchword 11 aiguillette
metal: 5 aglet 6 aiglet
Tagalog (see also **Philippine Islands**): 8 Filipino
child: 4 bata 5 Anacs
deity: 6 Batala 7 Bathala
gambling game: 10 panguingui
learn: 4 aral
mother: Ina
peasant: Tao
race: Ita
wine: 4 alac
tagrag: rag, tag 6 rabble, tatter 8 vagabond
tagtail: 9 sycophant
taha: 4 baya 10 weaverbird
Tahiti: *canoe:* 4 pahi
capital: 7 Papeete
centipede: 4 veri
coronation robe: 4 maro
food plant: 4 taro
god: Oro 6 Taaroa
loincloth: 4 malo, maro
mulberry: 4 aute
old name: 8 Otaheite
people: 10 Polynesian
resident painter: 7 Gauguin
seaport: 7 Papeete
woman: 6 vahine, wahine
Tai, Thai: 7 Siamese
race: Lao
taigle: 4 drag 5 catch, delay, trail 6 entrap, hinder loiter 7 fatigue
tail: bun, cue, end 4 arse, back, bunt, last, rear 5 cauda 6 follow, shadow, switch 7 limited, pendant, reduced 8 abridged, buttocks, encumber, entailed 9 appendage, curtailed, extremity, fundament
having a: 7 caudate
kinds of: bob, bun, fud 4 bunt, scut 5 cauda, plume, stern, twist 6 strunt, wreath 8 streamer 9 empennage
pert. to: 6 caudal
plane: 10 stabilizer
short: bun 4 scut
tailed: 7 caudate
tailing: 5 chaff, waste 6 refuse
taille: fit, tax 4 form 5 build, shape, style, waist 6 figure 10 imposition
tailless: 7 acaudal, anurous 8 acaudate, ecaudate 9 excaudate
tailor: 4 snip 6 darzee, draper, sartor 7 cabbage 9 bushelman 11 bushelwoman
goose: 8 flatiron
iron: 5 goose
lap board: 5 panel
pert. to: 9 sartorial
tailzie: cut 5 agree, shape, slice, tally 6 entail 7 account, appoint, arrange 9 reckoning
taint: dip, dye, hit, hue 4 blow, evil, hogo, spot, tint 5 cloud, color, imbue, prove, spoil, stain, sully, tinge, touch, trace, wound 6 accuse, defile, infect, poison, stigma 7 attaint, blemish, convict, corrupt, debauch, deprave, pollute, vitiate 8 disgrace, empoison, hautgout, tincture 10 conviction, corruption, impregnate 11 contaminate
tainted: bad 5 blown
taipo: 5 demon, devil 10 theodolite
taisch: 5 ghost, voice
taissle: 6 puzzle, tangle 8 disorder
tait: 5 sport 6 lively 8 sportive 9 marsupial 12 cheerfulness
taivers, tavers: 6 babble, shreds 7 tatters
Taiwan: See **Formosa**
taj: cap 8 Taj Mahal
Taj Mahal site: 4 Agra
tajo: 6 trench
take: get, hit, win 4 doff, fang, glom, grip, haul, lead, trap 5 adopt, atone, avail, carry, catch, charm, cheat, check, fetch,

glaum, grasp, infer, seize, snare, spell, steal, swear, touch, trick **6** absorb, accept, affirm, amount, arrest, assume, attach, attack, borrow, choose, convey, deduce, deduct, derive, employ, endure, engage, number, obtain, profit, remove, secure, select, strike, submit, tenure **7** capture, conduct, detract, extract, promise, receive, undergo **8** abstract, contract, proceeds, quantity, receipts, subtract **9** apprehend, interrupt **11** appropriate

aback: **5** check **7** startle **8** astonish, confound, surprise
account of: **6** notice, regard
advantage of: **5** abuse **6** misuse **7** exploit
advice: **4** hear, heed, mind **6** listen
aim: **5** level
another's place: sub **9** alternate **10** substitute
apart: **4** ruin **7** destroy **9** dismantle
as actual: **5** posit
as one's own: **5** adopt **6** borrow
away: **5** adeem, reave **6** adempt, deduct, devest, recant, remove **7** deprive, detract, retract **8** subtract
back: **6** recant **7** retract **8** withdraw
beforehand: **7** pre-empt
bold attitude: **5** brisk
by craft: **6** entoil
by force: **5** erept **8** ereption
by storm: **5** seize **6** attack
by stratagem: **4** trap
care: **4** mind, reck **5** nurse, watch **6** beware, cuiado
care of: **4** tend **5** nurse
chair: sit
cognizance of: **4** note **6** notice
comb from beehive: **4** geld
delight: **5** revel
direction: **5** steer
down: **5** abase, lower **6** escort, humble, record, reduce **7** swallow **8** emaciate, withdraw **10** distribute
evening meal: sup **4** dine
exception: **5** demur **6** object
fire: **5** spunk
first: **7** preempt
five: **4** rest
for granted: **6** assume **7** presume
forcibly: **5** seize
from: **5** wrest **6** deduct, divest **7** deprive, derived, detract **8** derogate, subtract
heed: **4** mind, reck, ware
hold: **5** grasp **6** obtain
in: **4** furl, open **5** admit, annex, brail, cheat, fence, trick, visit **6** attend, escort **7** deceive, embrace, enclose, explore, include, observe, receive **8** commence, comprise, contract **9** encompass **10** comprehend, understand
in hand: **5** seize **7** attempt **9** undertake
in sail: **4** reef
into custody: **6** arrest **9** apprehend
it ill: **6** resent
it easy: **4** rest **5** relax
leave: **6** decamp, depart
legal possession of: **5** seise, seize
liberties: **7** presume
meals for pay: **5** board
no notice of: **9** disregard
notice: NB; see
off: **4** copy, doff, soar **5** abate, begin, deter, mimic, start **6** deduct, depart, lessen, remove **7** detract **8** discount, distract, subtract, withdraw **9** burlesque, calculate, determine, reproduce
off suspended list: **9** reinstate
offense of: **6** resent
on: **4** hire **6** assume, employ, engage, oppose, tackle **7** consort, receive **8** arrogate **9** associate, undertake
on cargo: **4** lade
one's way: **4** wend
orders: **4** obey **5** yield
out: **4** copy, dele, omit **5** elide **6** deduct, delete, efface, escort, except, remove **7** extract, scratch, unhitch **8** overall, separate **9** eliminate
out by roots: **9** extirpate
out curves and bends: **10** straighten
out of pawn: **6** redeem
over: **5** seize **6** assume, convey
part: **4** join **5** share
part in contest: **7** compete
part of: **4** side **5** enact
place: **5** occur
place again: **5** recur
place of: **4** else **8** supplant **9** supersede
pleasure in: **5** enjoy, fancy
positive opinion: **4** side
possession of: **5** enter, seise
rise: **7** emanate
root: **4** grow **6** settle
service as seaman: **4** ship
shape: **4** form **11** crystallize
shelter: **6** nestle
some of: **7** partake
stock: **5** count **6** survey **8** appraise, estimate **9** inventory
the stick: **5** steer
to court: sue
turns: **9** alternate
umbrage at: **6** resent
unawares: **5** seize **7** astound, capture, startle **8** astonish, confound, overcome, surprise **9** overwhelm

unlawfully: rob 5 steal, usurp 6 pilfer
up: buy 4 fill, lift 5 adopt, allow, check, enter, exact, mount, raise, seize 6 absorb, accept, arrest, assume, borrow, employ, gather, occupy, remove, resume 7 collect, dissent, elevate, engross, receive 9 extirpate, reprimand 10 comprehend, understand
up again: 5 renew 6 resume
up weapons: arm 4 rise
with: 4 like 5 brook 6 accept 7 confess 11 acknowledge
without authority: 5 usurp
taken: 8 occupied
in all: 7 overall 9 inclusive
by twos: 5 duple
taker: 5 thief 6 captor 7 catcher 8 pilferer, purveyor 10 plagiarist
of court action: 4 suer
of income or profits: 6 pernor
takin: 7 gazelle 8 antelope
taking: 4 take 5 catch, palsy 6 arrest, attack, blight, plight 7 capture, malefic, seizing, seizure 8 alluring, capitious, catching, engaging, grasping, receipts 9 accepting, rapacious, receiving, reception 10 attachment, attractive, contagious, infectious 11 captivating 12 apprehension
different form: 7 protean 11 metamorphic
precedence: 7 ranking
unauthorized leave: 4 A.W.O.L.
takt: 4 beat 5 beats, pulse, tempo 7 measure
tala: 4 raid, ruin 11 destruction
talapoin: 4 monk 6 monkey 7 poongee 8 poonghee, poonghie
talc: 6 talcum 7 agalite 8 steatite 9 soapstone
tale: lie 4 gest, myth, saga, talk, tell, yarn 5 count, fable, geste, speak, story, tally, total 6 esteem, gossip, legend, reckon, report, speech 7 account, fiction, history, parable, recital 8 anecdote, category, consider, counting, relation 9 discourse, falsehood, narration, narrative, numbering, reckoning 11 declaration, enumeration, information 12 conversation
adventure: 4 gest 5 geste
kind of: lai 4 gest, saga, yarn 5 bourd, geste, roman 6 legend 7 romance 8 allegory, jeremiad 9 storiette
medieval: lai, lay
Tale of Two Cities: *author:* 7 Dickens
hero: 6 Carton
heroine: 5 Lucie
talebearer: 6 buzzer, gossip 7 tattler 8 talepyet, telltale 10 newsmonger 13 scandalmonger
talent: 4 gift 5 anger, dowry, flair, gifts, knack, money, skill, talon 6 custom, desire, flavor, genius, powers, riches, wealth 7 ability, betters, faculty, feature, longing, passion 8 appetite, aptitude, capacity, gamblers, property 9 abilities, abundance, attribute 10 endowments 11 disposition, inclination 14 accomplishment
sale: 8 venality
special: 5 forte
talented: 4 able 5 smart 6 clever, gifted 8 addicted, disposed, inclined
talenter: 4 hawk
talents: 9 endowment
talesman: 5 juror 8 narrator
taletelling: 4 blab
taliation: 5 tally 10 adjustment
taliera: 4 tara
talion: 11 retaliation
talipot: 4 palm
talisman: 4 tara 5 charm, saffi, safie 6 amulet, fetich, fetish, grigri, saphie, scarab, telesm 8 greegree
talitol: 7 alcohol
talk: yap 4 buck, bukh, carp, chat, gaff, knap, talk, word 5 bazoo lingo, parle, prate, rumor, speak, theme, utter 6 confer, debate, gabble, gossip, reason, report, speech, steven, tongue 7 address, chatter, consult, council, dialect, express, meeting, mention, palabra 8 causerie, chitchat, collogue, colloquy, converse, parlance, verbiage 9 dalliance, discourse 10 conference, discussion 11 communicate 12 conversation
about: 6 gossip 7 discuss
abusive: 5 hoker
back: 4 sass 6 retort, ripost 7 riposte 8 repartee
big: 4 brag 5 boast
boastful: 4 gaff, rant
ceremonious: 8 chin-chin
chatty: gab 6 gossip
common: 7 hearsay
complaining: 4 carp
confused: 10 galimatias
desultorily: 6 ramble
deliriously: 4 rave
down: 7 outtalk, silence
down to: 9 patronize 10 condescend
effusively: 4 gush, rave
familiar: 6 confab
fast and idly: 7 gnatter
flattering: 7 palaver
flippant: 10 persiflage
fluent: 7 verbose, voluble
foolish: gab, gas 4 bosh, buff, bunk, gash 5 spiel 6 babble, bunkum, claver, fraise, patter 7 blabber, twaddle 8 buncombe, wishwash 9 poppycock, rigmarole 11 goosecackle, stultiloquy
formal: 7 address, lecture

from pulpit: **6** homily, sermon
glib: **6** patter **7** palaver
idly: gab, gas **5** prate **6** tattle **7** chatter, twaddle
imperfectly: **4** lisp **7** stutter
in sleep: **15** somniloquacious
indiscreetly: **4** blab
indistinctly: **7** sputter
irrationally: **4** rant, rave
light: **5** chaff **6** banter **8** raillery
persuasively: **6** reason
pert: lip **4** sass
profuse: **4** chat **6** patter **7** palaver **10** persiflage
slowly: **5** drawl
small: gab **4** chat, chin **7** prattle **8** chitchat
table: ana **9** symposiac
tediously: **5** prose
to no purpose: **4** blat
together: **4** chat **8** converse
turgid: **4** cant, rant
unintelligible: **6** drivel, jargon, patter **9** gibberish
wildly: **4** rave
with passion: **4** rave
talkative: **4** cozy, gash, glib **5** gabby **6** chatty, clashy, fluent **7** verbose, voluble **8** flippant **9** garrulous **10** babblative, loquacious
talkativeness: **9** garrulity, garrulous, loquacity
talker: **6** proser, ranter, rhetor **7** babbler, spieler **17** conversationalist
incessant: **6** gasbag, magpie **10** chatterbox **12** blabbermouth
talkfest: **9** gathering **10** discussion
talking iron: gun **5** rifle
tall: **4** bold, deft, fine, high, lank, long **5** brave, grand, great, lanky, large, lofty, quick, rangy, ready, steep, tally **6** comely, docile, seemly **7** doughty, skyhigh, unusual **8** obedient, towering, yielding **9** excellent **10** courageous, incredible **11** exaggerated **13** grandiloquent
tallage: aid, due, fee, tax **4** toll **6** custom, impost, tarage
tallet: **5** attic **7** hayloft
talliar: **8** watchman
tallness: **9** procerity
tallote: **5** gourd **7** chayote **8** calabash
tallow: fat **4** suet **5** sevum, smear **6** fatten, grease
pert. to: **7** stearic
pot: **7** fireman
refuse: **9** crackling
sediment: **7** greaves
tallow-berry: **11** locustberry
tally: run, tab, tag **4** deal, goal, mark, mate, suit **5** agree, check, count, grade, label, match, notch, score **6** accord, reckon, record **7** account, compare, loftily **8** estimate **9** agreement, elegantly, reckoning **10** becomingly, correspond, resolutely **11** counterpart **14** correspondence
tallyho: cry **5** coach
crier of: **6** hunter
talma: **4** cape, coat
Talmud commentary: **6** Gemara
Talmudic academy: **7** Yeshiva **8** Yeshibah, Yeshivah **9** Yeshiboth
student: **5** bahur
talon: **4** claw, heel, sere **6** clutch, hallux **7** molding **11** certificate
Talos' slayer: **8** Daedalus
talter: **4** hang
taluk: **5** tract **6** estate **10** dependency **11** subdivision **12** collectorate
talukdar: **9** collector, tahsildar **10** landholder, proprietor
talus: **5** ankle, scree, slope **6** debris **8** clubfoot **9** anklebone **11** knucklebone
tam: cap, hat **5** beret **8** headgear **11** tam-o-shanter
tamarack: **10** hackmatack
tamarind: **8** sampaloc
tamarisk: sal **4** atle, jhow **5** atlee
tamas: **7** inertia **8** dullness **9** ignorance
tamasha: **4** fuss, show **7** pageant **9** commotion, spectacle **10** excitement **13** entertainment
tambo: inn **6** corral, stable, tavern **7** station
tambour: cup **4** desk, drum **5** frame **7** drummer **8** buttress, ornament **9** embroider **10** embroidery, projection
tambourin: **4** drum **5** dance, tabor
tambourine: **4** dove, drum, taar **5** daira **7** timbrel, travale
tambreet: **8** duckbill
tame: cut **4** bust, dead, dull, mild **5** accoy, begin, break, daunt, prune **6** broach, docile, gentle, humble, soften, subdue **7** affaite, crushed, insipid, servile **8** cicurate, civilize, familiar, harmless **9** deficient, tractable **10** accustomed, cultivated, submissive **11** domesticate, ineffectual **12** domesticated **13** pusillanimous
animal: pet **4** cade **6** cosset
poison: **11** swallowwort
tamed: **6** broken, gentle
tameness: **10** mansuetude
Tamil: **9** Dravidian
caste member: **7** Vellala
Taming of the Shrew character: Sly **4** Kate **6** Bianca, Tranio **8** Baptista
tamis: **5** sieve, tammy **8** strainer
Tammany Society: *officer:* **8** Wiskinky **9** Wiskinkie
leader: **6** sachem
Tammuz: *love:* **6** Ishtar

sister: 6 Belili
tamp: ram 5 drive
tamper: fix 4 fool, plot, tool 6 dabble, meddle, potter, scheme 7 machine 9 influence, interfere
Tampico fiber: 5 istle
tampion, tempeon, tampoon: 4 bung, plug 5 cover 7 stopper, turnpin
tampon: 4 plug 6 tympan 9 drumstick
nasal: 9 rhinobyon
tan: dun, taw 4 beat, camp, ecru, flog, tent, whip 5 brown, color, toast 6 almond, bronze, switch, tannin, thrash 7 embrown, imbrown, sunburn, tanbark
derived from: 5 tanic
tana: 8 banxring
tanager: 4 yeni
genus of: 7 piranga
tanbark: 4 bark
tancel: 4 beat 5 abuse 6 thrash
tang: nip 4 butt, capt, fang, foil, odor, pang, pike, ring, root, spur, tine, zest 5 knife, prick, prong, shank, smack, sting, taste, tinge, trace, twang 6 branch, flavor, pierce, tangle, tongue 7 flavour, seatang, seaweed 8 rockweed 10 suggestion 11 surgeonfish
Tanganyika: See **Tanzania**
tangent: 8 touching
tangible: 4 real 6 actual 7 tactile 8 definite, palpable 9 objective, touchable 11 perceptible, substantial
Tangiers measure: 4 kula, mudd
tangle: bar, cot, mat 4 fank, harl, kink, knot, mesh, trap 5 frame, gnarl, ravel, snare, snarl 6 balter, entrap, icicle, medley, muddle, sleave 7 ensnare, involve, quandry 8 obstruct, scrobble 9 embarrass 10 intertwine, perplexity
of thread: 5 snarl
tangle-foot: 5 aster, drink 6 whisky 8 deerweed
tangled: 11 complicated
tango: 5 bingo, dance
tania: 5 aroid
Tanis: 4 Zoan
tank: hit, vat 4 bang, lake, pond, pool 5 basin, knock, trunk 7 cistern, cuvette, drinker, pachuca, piscina, stomach 9 container, reservoir
part: 5 tread 6 turret
tankard: 5 facer, hanap 6 pottle 7 goddard
tanker: 5 oiler
tanned: 5 brown, tawny 8 sixpence, sunburnt
tanner: 6 barker 8 sixpence
Tannhauser composer: 6 Wagner
tannic acid salt: 7 tannate
tannin: 10 astringent
tanning: *extract:* 5 cutch 7 amaltas
material: 5 sumac 6 sumach
method: 4 napa
pert. to: 11 scytodepsic
plant: 5 aldor, sumac 6 sumach
tansy: 9 tanacetum
tanta: 4 aunt
tantadlin: 4 tart 6 dainty 8 dumpling
tantalize: 4 grig 5 taunt, tease 6 harass 7 torment
tantalus: toy 4 case 8 cellaret
Tantalus: *children:* 5 Niobe 6 Pelops
father: 4 Zeus
tantamount: 5 equal 9 identical 10 equivalent
tantara, tantarara: 5 blare 7 fanfare
tantieme: 5 bonus, share 10 percentage
tantivy: cry 4 call, ride, rush, Tory 5 rapid, swift 6 gallop, speedy 7 swiftly 8 headlong, Royalist
tantrum: pet 4 rage
tantum: 5 stint 9 allowance
Tanzania: *island:* 5 Pemba
mountain: 4 Meru
part: 8 Zanzibar 10 Tanganyika
peak: 4 Kibo
people: 4 Goma 6 Wagogo, Wagoma 7 Swahili, Wabunga
title: 5 sayid
weight: 8 farsalah
Taoism: Tao 12 cosmic reason
right conduct: te
tap: bob, cut, hob, pat, rap, tit, vat 4 beat, blow, cock, flip, heat, hole, open, pipe, plug 5 break, fever, flirt, knock, leach, spile, touch, valve 6 broach, faucet, repair, signal, spigot, strike, tapnet 7 censure, connect, penance, reprove
down: 4 tamp
tape: gin, tie 4 band, bind, mole 5 scale, strip 6 fillet, liquor, ribbon, secure 7 bandage, binding
kind of: 4 lear, wick 5 inkle 6 ferret
needle: 6 bodkin
taper: 4 ream, wick 5 light, point, snape 6 candle, cierge, lessen, narrow, trowel 7 conical, dwindle, trindle 8 decrease, diminish 9 acuminate 11 pyramidical
tapered: 7 conical
tapering: 5 conic 6 terete 7 conical 9 acuminate
blades: 6 spires
four-sided pillar: 7 obelisk
piece: 4 gore, shim 5 miter 6 gusset
solid: 4 cone
with circular cross section: 6 terete
tapestry: 5 arras, tapis 6 bayeux, dorser, dosser 7 dossier, gobelin 8 dossiere
comb: 4 reed

kind: 7 Gobelin
warp thread: 5 lisse
tapeworm: 6 taenia 7 taeniae
embryonic form: 10 oncosphere
segments: 8 strobila 9 strobilae
hanging: 5 tapis
provide: 6 arrase
taphouse: bar, inn 6 saloon, tavern 7 taproom
tapioca-like food: 5 salep
source: 7 cassava
tapir: 4 anta 5 danta 8 anteater, ungulate
tapirus Americanus: 4 anta
tapis: 4 band, hide, sash 6 carpet 7 hanging 8 tapestry 10 tablecloth
taplet: 5 block
tapnet: 5 frail 6 basket
tapper: 6 dancer 7 workman 9 decoherer, innkeeper 10 woodpecker
tappet: cam 5 lever 10 projection
taproom: bar, pub 6 saloon, tavern
tapster: 7 barmaid, skinker 9 barkeeper, bartender
Tapuyan: Ge; Ges 5 Gesan 6 Cayapo, Goyana, Timbra 7 Camacan, Coroado 8 Botocudo, Caingang, Chavante
tar: gob 4 brea, salt 5 black, pitch, tease 6 cresol, incite, sailor, seaman 7 blacken, mariner, provoke 8 alkitran, irritate, seafarer, telegram 9 alchitran 10 bluejacket
tar and feathers: 12 plumeopicean
taradiddle: fib, lie 8 nonsense
Taranaki volcano: 6 Egmont
tarantula: 6 spider
tarbet: 7 isthmus, portage
tarboosh: cap, fez
tarde: 4 late, slow 7 evening 9 afternoon
tardigrade: 8 sluggish
tardy: lag, lax 4 late, slow 5 delay, slack 6 remiss, retard 7 belated, lagging, overdue 8 dilatory 10 behindhand, unprepared 11 cunctatious
tare: 4 weed 5 vetch, weigh 6 darnel 7 leakage 9 allowance 13 counterweight
targe: 4 beat 5 paper, scold 6 harass, shield, targer, target 7 buckler, censure 8 document 9 reprimand 10 protection
targer: 5 scold, shrew
target: cut, tee 4 butt, coin, mark, vane 5 shred, sight, slice 6 cymbal, object, shield, tassel, tatter 7 buckler, pendant 8 bullseye, ornament, ridicule 9 indicator, objective, criticism
center: eye 5 clout
shooting gallery: 4 duck
target finder: 5 radar, sonar
Tarheel State: 13 North Carolina
tariff: tax 4 duty, list, rate 5 scale 6 charge, scheme, system 7 average, tribute 8 schedule
favorer: 13 protectionist
Tarkington title: 6 Penrod 9 Seventeen
tarn: 4 lake, pool
tarnish: dim 4 blot, dull, soil, spot 5 cloud, dirty, spoil, stain, sully, taint 6 canker, darken, defile, smirch 7 asperse, blemish, destroy, distain, obscure 8 besmirch, diminish, discolor
taro: 4 coco, eddo, gabi 5 aroid, cocgo, eddoe, tania 7 dasheen 8 caladium
paste: poi
root: edo 4 eddo 6 eddoes
tarpaulin: hat, tar 4 coat, tarp 5 cover 6 sailor 7 sea-bred 10 sailorlike
tarpon: 9 savanilla 10 silverfish
Tarquin's avenger: 7 Porsena
tarriance: 5 delay 7 sojourn 8 awaiting, tarrying 9 hindrance
tarrock: 4 gull, tern
tarrow: 5 delay, tarry 6 linger 7 grumble
tarry: lag, vex 4 bide, loll, rest, stay, stop, wait 5 abide, await, black, dally, defer, delay, demur, dwell, lodge, pause, weary 6 arrest, bundle, hinder, linger, loiter, remain, retard, soiled, tarred, tarrow 7 fatigue, outstay, sojourn, unclean 8 irritate
tarrying: 6 arrest
tarsus: 5 ankle
fore: 4 pala
tart: pie 4 acid, flan, girl, keen, sour 5 acrid, acute, bowla, sharp 6 pastry, pielet, severe, tender, tourte 7 caustic, cutting, painful, piquant, pungent 8 piercing, poignant, turnover 9 acidulous, endearing, sensitive 10 astringent, prostitute
tartan: 4 sett, ship 5 plaid
tartar: 5 argol, shrew, valet 12 incrustation
Tartar: See Tatar
tartarean: 8 infernal
Tartarus: 4 hell 5 Hades
Tartary prince: 4 Agib
tartness: 7 acidity 8 acerbity, acrimony, asperity, piquancy, sourness
Tartuffe: *author:* 7 Moliere
maid: 6 Dorine
tarve: 4 bend, turn
tarweed: 5 Madia
Tarzan's mate: 4 Jane
tash: 4 soil 5 stain 7 fatigue 8 disgrace
task: job, tax 4 busk, char, darg, duty, test, toil, work 5 chare, chore, labor, stent, stint, study 6 amount, burden, dargue, devoir, impost, lesson, strain 7 aufgabe, censure, oppress, overtax 8 quantity 10 accounting, assignment, employment 11 undertaking

easy: 4 pipe, snap 5 cinch 8 sinecure
taskmaster: 6 driver 8 overseer
Tasmania: *animal:* 6 wombat
cape: 4 Grim
capital: 6 Hobart
devil: 7 dasyure
discoverer: 6 Tasman
lake: 12 Westmoreland
mountain: 4 Grey 5 Brown, Drome, Nevis 6 Barrow 8 Humboldt 9 Ben Lomond 10 Wellington
phalanger: 5 tapoa
river: 4 Huon 5 Tamar 6 Arthur, Jordan 7 Derwent
thylacine: 5 tiger
town: 6 Hobart 10 Launceston
wolf: 9 thylacine
tass: cup, mow 4 bowl, heap 5 draft 6 goblet
tassel: 4 tuft 5 adorn, label 6 fringe, toorie, zizith 7 pendant 8 ornament
taste: bit, eat, gab, goo, sip, try 4 bent, dash, gout, gust, heed, hint, rasa, tang, test 5 drink, flair, gusto, prove, sapor, savor, scent, shade, smack, smell, spice, touch, trace 6 degust, flavor, liking, little, palate, relish, relush, ribbon, sample, savour 7 flavour, soupcon, thought 8 appetite, delicacy, elegance, fondness 9 attention, degustate, judgement 10 experience, suggestion 11 discernment, inclination 14 discrimination
absence of: 7 ageusia 8 aguestia
fundamental: 4 acid, salt 5 sweet 6 bitter
kind of: nip, sip 4 tang 5 prose, sapor, savor, smack 8 penchant
lacking in: 4 rude 8 ungentle 9 inelegant 10 unpolished 11 inaesthetic
pert. to: 7 palatal 9 gustative, gustatory
perversion: 7 malacia
refined: 7 elegant
strong: 4 tang
tasted: 4 sipt
tasteful: 4 neat 5 tasty 6 savory 7 elegant
tasteless: 4 dull, flat 5 vapid 7 insipid 8 lifeless 9 savorless 10 inartistic
tasty: 5 sapid 6 savory 7 palatal 8 tasteful 9 flavorful, palatable, toothsome 10 delectable
tat: die, rag, tap 4 pony 5 touch 6 tangle 7 crochet 8 absolute 9 embroider
Tatar, Tartar: Hun 6 ataman, hetman 7 Cossack
dynasty: Kin, Wei
horseman: 7 Cossack
king: 4 khan
militiaman: 4 Ulan 5 Uhlan
mounted band: 4 ulan 5 horde, uhlan 7 chambul
nobleman: 5 murza
principality: 7 Khanate
republic capital: 5 Kazan
tribe: Hun 5 Alani, Alans 7 Shortzy
tatou, tatu: 9 armadillo
tatter: jag, rag 4 jagg, stir, tear 5 hurry, scold, scrap, shred, testy 6 bustle, gabble, ribbon, tattle 7 chatter, flitter, peevish 8 guenille 14 tatterdemalion
tatterdemalion: 6 ragged 8 tattered 10 ragamuffin
tattered: 4 torn 6 broken, jagged, ragged, shaggy 7 slashed 9 disrupted 10 disheveled 11 dilapidated
tattle: 4 blab, chat, gash, talk, tell 5 cheep, clash, clype, prate 6 gossip 7 chatter, clatter, prattle, stammer
tattler: 6 gossip 8 telltale 9 sandpiper 10 talebearer
tattletale: 6 gossip 7 tattler 8 telltale 10 talebearer
tau cross: 4 ankh, crux
Taube: 9 monoplane
taught: See teach
taunt: bob 4 dare, gibe, jeer, jibe, mock, quip, tall, twit 5 check, fleer, glaik, reply, slare, slart, sneer, tease, tempt 6 banter, deride, flaunt, rejoin 7 provoke, upbraid 8 reproach, ridicule 9 aggravate
taurine: 4 bull 6 bovine
taurocol: 4 glue
Taurus: 4 bull
taut: 4 firm, neat, snug, tidy, trim 5 rigid, stiff, tense, tight, tough 6 severe, strict 9 distended, shipshape
tauten: 5 tense 7 tighten
tautog: 9 blackfish
tautological: 9 redundant
tave: 4 rage, toss 5 hurry, labor 6 sprawl 8 struggle
tavern: bar, hut, inn, pub 4 bush, howf 5 booth, hotel, house, howff 6 saloon 7 cabaret, gasthof 8 alehouse, gasthaus, hostelry
tavert: 5 tired 6 stupid 8 confused
taw: tan, tew 4 beat, whip 5 agate 6 harass, marble 7 scourge, shooter, torment, toughen
tawdry: 5 cheap, gaudy, showy 6 sleazy, tinsel
tawny, tawney: tan 5 brown, dusky, olive, swart, tenne 6 Indian, tanned 7 fulvous, tigrine 8 brindled 9 bullfinch
tawse, taws: 4 whip 5 strap
tax: 4 cess, duty, feel, fine, levy, rate, scat, scot, task, toll 5 abuse, agist, exact, order, scatt, stent, stint, tithe, touch, value 6 accuse, assess, avania, burden, charge, demand, excise, extent, handle, hidage, impose, impost, settle, strain 7 censure, dispute, finance, gabelle, license, tailage, tallage, tollage, tribute 8 estimate, exaction,

overtire, reproach 9 prescribe 10 assessment, imposition 12 contribution
assessment: 7 doomage
church: 5 tithe
feudal: 7 tailage, tallage
gatherer: 9 catchpole, catchpoll
hide: 6 hidage
kind of: cro, soc 4 cess, geld, scat 5 finta, tithe 6 abkari, excise, pavage, surtax, taille, vinage 7 boscage, chevage, patente, prisage, scewing, tailage 8 auxilium, carucage 9 surcharge 10 chaukidari
rate: 5 ratal 10 assessment
salt: 7 gabelle
taxable: 10 assessable, censurable
taxation: tax 6 charge 7 finance, reproof, revenue 9 valuation 10 accusation, assessment
degree of: 5 ratal
taxi: cab 4 hack 5 jixie 6 litter 7 vehicle
parking place: 5 stand
taximeter: 5 clock
taxing: 10 accusation
taxman: 8 publican
taxpayer: 9 ratepayer
tazza: cup 4 bowl, vase
tchai: 5 brook, river 6 stream
tea: 5 party 6 repast, supper 8 beverage, function 9 collation, decoction, reception
cake: 5 scone
constituent: 8 caffeine
container: 8 canister
drug: see *stimulant* below
expert: 6 taster
family: 8 Theaceae
genus: 4 thea
kind of: cha 4 chaa, chia, tsia 5 assam, black, bohea, congo, chias, Emesa, green, hyson, Ledum, oopak, pekoe, salop 6 congue, oolong, saloop 7 cambric 8 bouillon, go-widdie 9 gunpowder
plant: 4 thea
receptacle: 8 canister
room: 5 kiosk
serve: 4 pour
stimulant: 5 thein 6 theine
table: 5 tepoy 6 teapoy
urn: 7 samovar
weak: 5 blash
Tea House location: 4 Naha 7 Okinawa
teach: 4 show 5 coach, edify, endue, guide, point, train, tutor 6 commit, direct, lesson, preach, school 7 apprise, apprize, beteach, conduct, educate 8 accustom, amaister, document, instruct 9 enlighten 10 discipline 11 demonstrate
teachable: apt 6 pliant 7 fitting 8 amenable
teacher: 5 coach, guide, Plato, tutor 6 docent, doctor, mentor, pedant, pundit, reader, regent 7 adjunct, edifier, maestro, sophist, trainer 8 civilian, director, educator, gamaliel, moralist, preacher 9 pedagogue, preceptor 10 instructor
Alexandria: 6 Origen
association: NEA
fee: 8 minerval
Indian religion: 4 guru
Jewish: 5 rabbi
Mohammedan: pir 4 alim, imam 5 imaum, molla, mulla 6 mollah, mullah
of eloquence: 6 rhetor 7 sophist
of the deaf: 7 oralist
Russia: 7 starets
teaching: 5 moral 6 docent 7 precept 10 discipline 11 instruction
of a fable: 5 moral
of the Twelve: 7 Didache
pert. to: 9 pedagogic
teakettle: 4 suke, suky 5 sukey, sukie
teal: 5 crick 8 garganey
team: 4 crew, gang, join, pair, race, span, yoke 5 brood, chain, flock, group, wagon 6 convey, couple, number 7 lineage, progeny, vehicle 8 carriage 9 associate, stationed
baseball: 4 nine
kinds of: duo 4 crew 6 scrubs 7 varsity
supporter: fan 6 rooter
two animals: 4 pair, yoke
teamed with: 5 yoked 6 paired 7 matched
teamster: 6 carter, driver 7 carrier
tear: ram, rip, rit, run 4 claw, drag, fine, pull, rage, rend, rent, rive, rush, skag, snag, weep 5 break, claut, larme, reave, split, spree, touse, unrip, waste 6 cleave, dainty, damage, divide, flurry, lament, pierce, remove, screed, tatter, wrench 7 agitate, chatter, consume, destroy, disrupt, fritter, passion, shatter, torment 8 carousal, delicate, lacerate, lachryma, separate
apart: 4 rend 9 dismember
down: 4 rase, raze 11 disassemble
heraldry: 5 larme
into: rip 6 attack
limb from limb: 9 dismember
off: rip, run 4 rush 5 start
to pieces: 6 tatter 10 dilacerate
up by the roots: 6 arache 9 eradicate, extirpate
tearcat: 7 ranting 9 blusterer 10 swaggering
teardrop design: 5 larme
tearful: sad 6 watery 7 flebile, snively, weeping 8 lacrimal
mother: 5 Niobe
tearing: 4 rage 5 hasty, hurry 7 furious, violent 8 splendid 9 furiously, harrowing, impetuous 10 impressive
tearpit: 7 larmier

tears: 5 grief
inducing: 9 rheumatic
pert. to: 8 lacrimal
poetic: 5 rheum
tease: beg, guy, irk, nag, rag, tew, vex 4 card, coax, comb, drag, fret, hare, razz, stir, tear, twit 5 annoy, chevy, chivy, devil, taunt, wrack 6 badger, bother, caddle, chivvy, harass, heckle, molest, pester, plague, teasel 7 disturb, hatchel, provoke, scratch, torment 8 irritate, separate 9 aggravate, importune, tantalize 11 disentangle
wool: tum 4 comb, toom
teasel: 4 comb
teaser: 4 gull 6 carder, curler, sniper, stoker, willow 7 curtain, fireman, problem 8 operator, pesterer, willower
teasing: 11 importunate
teaty: 5 cross 7 fretful, peevish
tebbad: 6 simoom 9 sandstorm
tebeldi: 6 baobab
technology of agriculture: 10 agrotechny
techy: 4 spot 5 habit 6 touchy, vexing 7 blemish, fretful, peevish, quality 9 irascible, irritable
teck: 6 cravat
tectonic: 7 builder, plastic 9 carpenter 10 structural 13 architectural
ted: 4 toad, turn 5 waste 6 spread 7 scatter
tedge: 6 ingate, runner
tedious: dry 4 dead, dree, dull, long, slow 5 bored, prosy 6 boring, borish, elenge, prolix 7 irksome, noxious, peevish, prosaic 8 dilatory, slowness, tiresome 9 exhausted, irritable, laborious, prolixity, wearisome 10 monotonous 11 displeasing, everlasting 13 uninteresting
tedium: 5 ennui 7 boredom, doldrum 11 irksomeness, tediousness 13 wearisomeness
tee: 5 mound
teem: go 4 bear, fill, gush, lead, pour, rain, swim 5 bring, drain, empty, fetch, swarm 6 abound, resort, seethe, summon 7 produce 8 abundant, conceive, generate, prolific
teeming: 4 full 5 agush 7 pouring, replete 8 crowding, prolific 9 abounding 11 overflowing 13 overabounding
teen: vex 4 harm, hate, keen, lose, pain, shut, tell, tind, tune 5 abuse, anger, grief, vexed 6 damage, injure, injury, sorrow 7 provoke, trouble 8 announce, distress, irritate, reproach, vexation 9 vexatious 10 affliction, calumniate
teeny: wee 4 tiny 5 small 7 fretful, peevish 9 malicious
teeny-weeny: 4 tiny 5 small 6 minute
teer: 4 daub 7 plaster
teeter: 4 rock 5 waver 6 jiggle, quiver, seesaw 7 rocking, rolling, tremble 9 sandpiper, vacillate
teeter board: 6 seesaw
teeth: 5 tines 7 canines
decay of: 6 caries
false: 5 plate 8 dentures
grinding of: 7 bruxism
hard tissue: 7 dentine
having all alike: 7 isodont
incrustation on: 6 tartar
large: 4 buck 5 snags
long: 5 fangs 6 tushes
outer covering of: 6 enamel
pert. to: 5 molar 6 dental
serpent: 5 fangs
socket: 7 alveoli(pl.) 8 alveolus
sower of dragon's: 6 Cadmus
without: 10 edentulate, edentulous
teethy: 5 cross 6 biting 7 crabbed 9 irritable
teeting: 7 titlark
teetotal: 6 entire 7 abstain 8 complete
teetotaller: dry 7 nonuser 9 abstainer, rechabite, refrainer
teetotum: top, toy
teewhapp: 7 lapwing
teg: doe 5 sheep, woman 6 fleece
tegmen: 5 cover, plate 6 elytra 8 covering, fore-wing, tegument
tegua: 6 sandal
teguexin: 4 teju 6 lizard
tegula: 4 tile
tegument: 4 coat 5 cover, testa 6 testae 10 integument
tegurium: hut 5 cabin 6 shrine
tehee: 6 giggle, titter 7 snicker
Tehuantepec Gulf Indian: 5 Huave
teicher: 4 ooze 5 bleed
teiidae: 4 teju 7 lizards
teind: 5 tithe
teju: 6 lizard 8 teguexin
tekke: rug 6 carpet 7 convent 9 monastery
tela: web 6 tissue 7 bristle 8 membrane
telamon: 8 atlantes, caryatid
Telamon: *brother:* 6 Peleus
father: 6 Aeacus
friend: 8 Heracles, Hercules
son: 4 Ajax 6 Teucer
teledu: 6 badger
telega: 4 cart 5 wagon
telegraph: 4 wire 5 cable
code: 5 Morse
inventor: 5 Morse
key: 6 tapper
signal: dot 4 dash 9 semaphore
telegraphic communication: 10 lettergram
Telemachus: *father:* 7 Ulysses 8 Odysseus
mother: 8 Penelope

teleost fish: eel 5 apoda
telephone: 4 buzz, call, dial 5 phone
book: 9 directory
inventor: 4 Bell
receiver: 8 cymaphen
Telephus' mother: 4 Auge
telescope: jam 5 glass 7 shorten 8 collapse, condense, simplify
object seen with: 11 debilissima
site: 7 Palomar
telescopic: 9 farseeing
television: TV 4 tube 5 telly, video
award: 4 Emmy
broadcast: 8 telecast
cable: 7 coaxial
camera platform: 5 dolly
comedienne: 4 Lucy
commercial cat: 6 Morris
dragon: 5 Ollie
interference: 4 snow
lens: 4 zoom
network: ABC, CBS, NBC, NET
picture tube: 9 kinescope
type of show: 4 live, news, quiz 5 movie, rerun 6 sitcom, sudser
telic: 9 purposive 10 purposeful 12 teleological
tell: bid, say 4 chat, deem, hill, know, tale, talk, tole, toll 5 aread, areed, breve, count, mound, order, speak, state, utter, value 6 decide, direct, impart, inform, number, recite, reckon, regard, relate, repeat, report, reveal, tattle 7 account, command, dictate, discern, divulge, express, mention, narrate, publish, recount, request 8 acquaint, announce, disclose, rehearse 9 calculate, discourse, enumerate, recognize 11 communicate 12 discriminate
in advance: 4 warn
on: 4 sing 5 peach 6 snitch, squeal
revelatory facts: 6 debunk
romances: 4 gest 5 geste
secrets: 5 clype
stories: 4 yarn 6 tattle
thoughtlessly: 4 blab, blat
without authority: 5 rumor
Tell's home: Uri
teller: 4 blow 5 shoot 6 remark, sprout 8 informer, narrator 9 describer 11 annunciator
telling: 5 valid 6 cogent 8 forceful, relation, striking 9 effective, pertinent 10 convincing
telltale: 4 blab, hint 7 tattler 8 betrayer, informer 9 betraying, indicator 10 indication, talebearer
telltruth: 7 honesty 9 frankness
telluride: 7 altaite
telson: 6 somite 7 segment
of king crab: 5 pleon
temblor: 10 earthquake
temerarious: 4 rash 6 chance 8 heedless, reckless 9 venturous 10 fortuitous, headstrong 11 venturesome
temerity: 4 gall 5 check, nerve 8 audacity, boldness, rashness 9 hardihood 10 effrontery 12 recklessness 13 foolhardiness 15 venturesomeness
temper: fit, ire, mix 4 bait, bate, coll, curb, cure, heal, mean, mood, neal, rage, tone 5 adapt, anger, birse, blend, delay, humor 6 adjust, animus, anneal, attune, church, dander, direct, govern, harden, manage, medium, mingle, modify, puddle, reduce, season, soften, soothe, steady 7 assuage, chasten, control, moisten, mollify, qualify, restore, toughen 8 attemper, chastise, compound, mitigate, moderate, modulate, regulate, restrain 9 composure 10 equanimity, irritation 11 accommodate, disposition
display: 5 scene 7 tantrum
even: 4 calm 5 staid 6 sedate
kind of: ire 4 huff, mood 6 choler, spleen
temperament: 4 mood 5 gemut, humor 6 crasis, crases(pl.), humour, nature, temper 7 caprice, climate, emotion 10 adjustment 11 disposition, temperature 12 constitution
temperance: 8 sobriety 10 abstinence, moderation
temperate: 4 calm, cool, mild 5 sober 6 soften, temper 8 moderate 9 continent 10 abstemious, restrained 13 dispassionate
temperature: 4 heat 5 fever, state 6 temper 7 mixture 8 compound, mildness 10 moderation, proportion 11 disposition, temperament 12 constitution
tempest: 4 gale, wind 5 orage, storm 6 tumult 7 agitate, borasca, borasco, turmoil 9 agitation, bourasque, commotion, hurricane 12 thunderstorm
Tempest characters: 5 Ariel 7 Caliban, Miranda 8 Prospero
tempestuous: 5 galey, gusty 6 stormy 7 violent 9 turbulent
template, templet: 4 beam, mold 5 basil, bezel, bezil, gauge 7 pattern
temple: 4 fane, naos, rath 5 candi, cella, edile, huaca, kovil, ratha, speos 6 aedile, chandi, church, haffet, haffit, hieron
basin: 5 laver
for all gods: 8 pantheon
kind of: sha, taj, wat 4 deul, Rath 5 jinja, Ratha 6 church, jinsha, pagoda 7 capitol 8 pantheon 9 Parthenon
part: 5 cella
sanctuary: 10 penetralia

tempo: 4 pace, rate, time 6 rhythm, timing
pert. to: 6 agogic
rapid: 6 presto
slow: 5 lento
very slow: 5 grave
temporal: 4 laic 5 civil, scale 6 carnal, muscle 7 earthly, secular, worldly 9 ephemeral, political, temporary 10 transitory 11 impermanent 13 chronological
temporarily: 5 nonce
temporary: 6 acting, timely 7 interim, secular, topical 8 temporal 9 adinterim, ephemeral 10 transitory 11 provisional
contrivance: 9 makeshift
temporize: 5 delay, humor, yield 6 demand, parley, soothe 9 negotiate 13 procrastinate
tempt: try 4 defy, fand, lead, lure, test 5 decoy, probe, prove, taunt 6 allure, assail, entice, incite, induce, seduce 7 assault, attempt, attract, provoke 8 endeavor, persuade 9 endeavour, seduction 10 inducement
temptation: 4 bait 5 trial 7 testing 9 seduction 10 allurement, enticement, inducement
tempter: 5 devil, Satan 6 baiter
tempting: 8 alluring 9 seductive 10 attractive
temptress: 4 vamp 5 Circe, siren 7 Delilah, Lorelei, mermaid 10 Parthenope 11 enchantress
temse, tems: 4 sift 5 sieve
temulence: 12 intoxication
ten: 4 iota(Gk.) 5 decad 6 decade, denary
ares: 6 decare
decibels: bel
dollars: 7 sawbuck
group of: 6 decade
prefix: dec 4 deca
Ten Commandments: 7 Decalog 9 Decalogue
ten-footed: 7 decapod
ten-gallon hat: 8 sombrero
ten-sided figure: 7 decagon
ten-stringed: 9 decachord
ten-year periods: 7 decades 9 decenniad, decennium
tenable: 10 defensible 12 maintainable
tenacious: 5 tough 6 cledgy, dogged, grippy, sticky 7 gripple, miserly, viscous 8 adhesive, cohesive, holdfast, sticking, stubborn 9 glutinous, niggardly, retentive 10 persistent 11 closefisted 12 pertinacious
tenaciously: 8 doggedly 10 persistent
tenacity: 8 firmness 9 toughness 11 miserliness, persistence, persistency 12 adhesiveness, cohesiveness, perseverance 13 glutinousness, retentiveness
tenancy: 6 estate, tenure 7 holding 9 occupancy 10 possession
tenant: 4 leud 5 ceile, dreng 6 bordar, drengh, geneat, holder, leaser, lessee, occupy, renter, vassal 7 chakdar, cottier, dweller 8 occupant 9 bordarius, collibert 10 inhabitant
feudal: 4 leud 6 vassal 7 socager
tend: 4 burn, care, lead, move, wait, work 5 apply, await, guard, nurse, offer, reach, serve, swing, treat, watch 6 attend, direct, expect, extend, foster, intend, kindle, listen, manage, supply 7 conduce, hearken, incline, oversee, provide, purpose, stretch, tending 8 minister, tendency 9 accompany, attentive, co-operate, cultivate, gravitate
a fire: 5 stoke
to rise: 8 levitate
toward one point: 8 converge
tendency: set 4 bent, bias, tide 5 drift, drive, tenor, trend 6 course, effect, object, result 7 aptness, bearing, leaning 8 appetite, movement, relation 9 affection, direction, proneness, readiness 10 proclivity, propension, propensity 11 disposition, inclination
monistic: 11 unitariness
structural: 7 peloria
tender: bid, tid 4 boat, dear, fond, gift, keen, kind, mild, nice, soft, sore, thin, warm, weak 5 chary, frail, light, offer, young 6 delate, feeble, gentle, humane, loving, touchy, vessel, waiter 7 amabile, amatory, amorous, careful, fragile, pitiful, present, proffer, slender, sparing, steamer, subdued, tenuous, vehicle 8 delicate, feminine, immature, merciful, precious, proposal, ticklish 9 brotherly, sensitive, succulent 10 charitable, effeminate, scrupulous 11 considerate, softhearted, susceptible, sympathetic, warmhearted 12 affectionate 13 compassionate 14 impressionable
animals: 6 herder 10 husbandman
cattle: 6 cowboy, herder 7 byreman 8 neatherd 9 byrewoman
for cloth: 9 stenterer
horse: 5 groom 6 ostler 7 hostler, stabler
music: 7 amoroso
ship: gig 5 barge, dingy 6 dingey, dinghy 7 collier, pinnace
tenderfoot: 6 novice 7 greenie 8 beginner, neophyte, newcomer 9 cheechaco, cheechako, greenhorn
tenderhearted: 6 humane
tenderloin: 5 steak

tenderness: 4 love, pity 6 cherte 8 kindness, softness, sympathy, weakness 9 affection 10 compassion, gentleness 13 sensitiveness
tendon: 4 band, cord 5 chord, nerve, sinew 11 aponeurosis
comb. form: 4 teno
tendour, tendoor: 4 seat 5 table
tendril: 4 curl 5 clasp, sprig 6 branch, cirrus 7 ringlet, stipule
tendron: bud 5 shoot 6 sprout
tenebrous: 4 dark 5 dusky 6 gloomy 7 obscure 8 darkness
tenement: 5 abode 8 building, dwelling 9 apartment 10 habitation
tenet: ism 4 view 5 adoxy, canon, creed, dogma, maxim 6 belief, decree 7 opinion, paradox 8 doctrine 9 principle
tenfold: 6 denary 7 decuple
tengere: sky 7 heavens
teniente: 6 deputy 7 headman 10 lieutenant
tenmantale: tax 7 tithing 8 carucage
tenne: 5 brown, color
Tennessee: *capital:* 9 Nashville
city: 7 Memphis 11 Chattanooga
county: 4 Clay, Dyer, Knox, Lake, Polk, Rhea
dam: 6 Norris
federal agency: TVA
first governor: 6 Sevier
national park: 6 Shiloh
state flower: 4 iris
tennis: *between four persons:* 7 doubles
between two persons: 7 singles
champion: 4 Ashe, King 5 Budge, Perry, Riggs 6 Gibson, Tilden 8 Gonzalez
cup 5 Davis
game series: set
no score: 4 love
old form: 5 bandy
points: 4 aces
prize cup: 5 Davis
racket: bat
related game: 6 squash 8 handball
score: ace 4 love 5 deuce
shoe: 7 sneaker
stroke: cut, let, lob 4 chop 8 backhand
term: ace, cut, let, lob, set 4 love 5 deuce, fault, serve 6 volley 7 receive, service 9 advantage
trophy donor: 5 Davis
Tennyson: *character:* 4 Enid 5 Arden 6 Elaine
heroine: 4 Enid
"In Memoriam" subject: 6 Hallam
tenon: cog 4 coak 8 dovetail
tenor: 4 copy, feck, gist 5 drift, stamp, trend 6 course, intent, nature, singer 7 holding, purport, writing 8 tendency 9 character, condition, direction, discourse, procedure 10 transcript
falsetto: 8 tenorino
tens of thousands: 7 myriads
tense: 4 rapt, taut, time 5 rigid, stiff, tight 6 intent, tauten 7 intense 8 strained 9 stretched 10 breathless
past: 9 preterite
verb: 4 past 6 aorist, future 7 perfect, present 9 preterite 10 pluperfect 11 conditional
tenseness: 5 rigor
tensile: 6 pliant 7 ductile 8 tensible
tension: 4 bent 6 strain, stress 7 closure 8 pressure
tent: hut 4 camp, care, heed, show, stop, tend, test, wine 5 crame, frame, lodge, probe, teach, tempt 6 attend, beware, encamp, hinder, intent, pulpit, tender 7 observe, prevent, proffer, shelter 9 attention, attentive 10 habitation
dweller: 4 Arab 5 nomad 6 camper, Indian 7 scenite, tourist
flap: fly
kind: 4 pawl, yurt 5 darry, shool, tepee, toldo, yurta 6 abbacy, tienda, wigwam 7 balagan, kibitka, marquee, sparver 8 pavilion 9 pretorium 10 praetorium
large: 8 pavilion
tentacle: 6 feeler 7 tendril 10 tentaculum
animal with: 5 squid 7 octopus 10 cuttlefish
without: 7 acerous
tentage: 5 camps
tentamen: 5 trial 7 attempt
tentative: 9 temporary 11 impermanent, provisional 12 experimental
tenter: 5 frame
tenterhooks: 6 strain 8 suspense
tenth: 5 tithe 6 decima 7 decimae 8 decimate
comb. form: 4 deci
part: 5 tithe
Tentmaker: 4 Omar
tents: 4 camp 7 baggage 10 encampment
tenty: 7 careful 8 watchful 9 attentive, carefully 10 watchfully
tenuity: 6 rarity 7 exility, poverty 8 delicacy, fineness, rareness, thinness 9 faintness, indigence 10 meagerness, slightness 11 slenderness
tenuous: 4 fine, rare, slim, thin 6 flimsy, slight 7 gaseous, slender, subtile 8 delicate, ethereal 13 insignificant, unsubstantial
tenure: 4 term 5 lease 6 manner 8 courtesy 9 condition
tepee, teepee: 6 wigwam
tepid: 4 warm 8 lukewarm
tepidness: 5 tepor

tepor: 9 tepidness
tequila: 5 drink 6 liquor, mescal
tera: 6 church 9 monastery
Terah: *father:* 5 Nahor
son: 7 Abraham
teraph: 4 idol 5 image
teras: 7 monster
teratosis: 11 monstrosity
terceron: 7 mulatto
tercet: 7 triplet
tere, teer: 4 daub 7 plaster
terebene: 10 antiseptic 12 disinfectant
terebra: 5 auger, drill
terebrate: 4 bore 9 perforate
teredo: 7 mollusk 8 shipworm
teres: 6 muscle
terete: 7 centric 8 columnar 11 cylindrical
Tereus: *son:* 4 Itys 6 Itylus
wife: 6 Procne
tergal: 6 dorsal
tergiversate: lie 5 shift 7 shuffle 10 apostatize, equivocate
tergiversation: 6 deceit 7 evasion 8 apostasy 10 subterfuge
tergum: 4 back
term: end 4 call, date, half, name, time, word 5 bound, limit, state 6 period, tenure 7 article, entitle, epithet, session 8 boundary, duration, semester 9 condition, extremity 10 definition, expression 11 appellation, termination
cricket: off, ons 6 yorker
fencing: hai, hay 4 bind 5 coupe 6 touche 8 tacautac
golf: lie, par, tee 4 baff, fore, hook 5 bogey, bogie, divot, eagle, green, slice, stimy 6 birdie, stroke, stymie 7 gallery
grammar: 6 phase, simile, syntax
heraldry: 4 ente, urde
Hindu, of respect: sri
Jewish, of reproach: 4 raca
mathematics: 4 nome, root, sine 6 cosine
of address: sir 4 sire 6 milady, milord, sirrah
of endearment: 5 astor 8 ashstore
of life: age 5 sands
of office: 6 regime
printer: 4 dele, stet
rugby: try 5 scrum
school: 7 seminar 8 semester 9 trimester
science: ame, azo 4 beta 5 stoss
sea: 4 ahoy 5 avast, belay
termagant: 5 shrew 6 Amazon, tartar, virago 7 furious 8 scolding 9 turbulent 10 boisterous, tumultuous 11 quarrelsome
termed: 5 named 6 called, styled, yclept 7 ycleped
terminable: 6 finish, finite 9 limitable 12 determinable 13 discontinuing
terminal: end 5 anode, depot, final, limit 6 finish 7 cathode, closing, limital, station 8 desinent, terminus, ultimate 9 electrode, extremity 10 concluding 11 desinential, termination
negative: 7 cathode, kathode
positive: 5 anode
terminate: end 4 call, halt, stop 5 bound, cease, close, limit 6 define, direct, expire, finish, result 7 achieve, confine, destine, perfect 8 complete, conclude, restrict
terminating: 5 final 6 ending
distinct point: 9 apiculate
trefoil: 6 botone
termination: end 4 amen 5 bound, close, event, limit 6 ending, expiry, finale, finish, period, result, upshot 7 outcome, purpose 8 boundary, decision, finality, terminus 9 extremity 10 completion, concluding, conclusion, expiration 13 determination
malady: 5 lysis
terminative: 8 absolute, bounding, definite 10 concluding 11 determining, terminating
terminus: end 4 goal, post 5 depot, stone 6 marker 8 boundary, terminal 9 extremity 11 termination
termite: ant 4 anai, anay
termless: 8 infinite, nameless, unending 9 boundless, limitless 13 indescribable, inexpressible, unconditional, unconditioned
terms: 9 agreement 10 conditions, provisions 11 limitations 12 propositions 13 circumstances
come to: 5 agree
make: 5 treat 9 negotiate
tern: 4 darr, gull 9 wide-awake
genus: 5 anous 6 sterna
ternary: 6 treble, triple 7 ternion, trinity 9 threefold
ternate: 12 trifoliolate
terne: 8 tinplate
terpsichore: 6 dancer 7 dancing
terra: 5 earth
terra alba: 4 clay 6 gypsum, kaolin
terra cotta: 4 clay 6 statue 7 pottery 11 earthenware
terra firma: 5 earth 6 estate 8 mainland
terrace: 4 bank, dais, mesa, step 5 bench 7 balcony, gallery, portico 8 chabutra, platform 9 colonnade
in series: 8 parterre
wall: 6 podium
terrage: tax 4 toll 7 payment
terrain: 4 terr 5 tract 6 milieu, region 7 estrial, terrane, terrent 11 environment

terrapin: 4 emyd, emys 6 coodle, emydea, heifer, potter, slider, turtle 8 emydidae, emydinae

terrar: 6 bursar

terrene: 4 land 5 earth, realm 6 earthy 7 earthly, mundane, terrain, worldly 11 terrestrial

terrestrial: 6 earthy, layman, mortal 7 earthly, mundane, terrene, worldly 9 planetary

terret: 4 ring 7 cringle

terrible: 4 dire, gast 5 awful, lurid 6 severe, tragic 7 direful, extreme, fearful, ghastly, hideous, intense, painful 8 almighty, dreadful, horrible, terrific 9 appalling, atrocious, excessive, frightful 10 formidable, terrifying, tremendous, unpleasant 12 disagreeable

Terrible one: 4 Ivan

terribly: 4 very 5 felly 6 grisly 9 extremely 11 exceedingly

terrier: fox 4 Bull, Skye 5 Irish, Welsh 6 Boston 8 Scottish, Sealyham 10 Bedlington, Clydesdale

terrific: 7 extreme 8 dreadful, exciting, terrible 9 appalling, excessive, frightful 10 terrifying, tremendous

terrified: 4 awed 6 afraid, aghast 7 ghastly

terrifier: 5 haunt 7 haunter

terrify: awe, cow, hag 4 bree, fray 5 alarm, annoy, appal, daunt, deter, drive, haunt, impel, scare, shock, tease 6 affirm, afread, agrise, appall, bother, dismay, injure 7 torment 8 affright, frighten 9 importune

terrifying: 6 horrid 7 hideous 8 terrible

terrigenous: 9 earthborn 13 autochthonous

terrine: jar 4 stew 6 ragout

territorial division: amt 6 canton 7 commune 10 department 14 arrondissement

territory: 4 area, land 5 field, scope, state, tract 6 extent, ground, region, sphere 7 country, portion 8 district, environs, province 12 neighborhood

kind of: 5 banat 6 canton 7 banlieu, enclave 8 banlieue, Pashalic 10 palatinate

shut in: 7 enclave

terror: awe 4 fear, fray, pest 5 alarm, dread, panic 6 affray, dismay, fright, horror 8 dreddour 12 terribleness 13 consternation

terrorism: 11 subjugation 12 intimidation

terrorist: 5 rebel 8 alarmist 11 scaremonger

terrorize: awe 5 abash, appal, scare 6 appall, coerce 8 frighten 9 embarrass 10 intimidate

terry: 4 loop

terse: 4 curt, neat 5 brief, pithy 6 abrupt, claret, rubbed, smooth 7 compact, concise, laconic, pointed, refined 8 polished, succinct, unprolix 11 sententious, tightlipped 12 accomplished

tertiary period: 7 neocene

tertulia: 4 club 5 party

tervee: 6 writhe 8 struggle

terzina: 6 tercet 7 triplet

terzo: 6 legion 7 brigade

tessel: 11 checkerwork

tessellated: 6 mosiac

tessera: 4 cube, tile 5 glass, label, token 6 billet, marble, pledge, tablet, ticket 7 voucher 8 password 9 rectangle 11 certificate

test: pot, try 4 exam, fand, feel, will 5 assay, check, cupel, grope, proof, prove, shell, taste, testa, trial, weave 6 ordeal, refine, sample 7 approof, approve, examine, witness 8 cupeling, evidence, potsherd, standard 9 construct, criterion, determine, testament, testimony 10 experience, experiment, touchstone 11 examination, performance 12 authenticate

in fineness and weight: pyx

kind: 4 acid

operation: 9 shakedown

ore: 5 assay

series: 7 gantlet

value: 5 assay

testa: 7 coating 8 covering, episperm, tegument 10 integument

testament: Job 4 will 8 covenant, landbook

testator: 7 legator, witness 9 testatrix

beneficiary of: 4 heir 7 heiress, heritor 9 inheritor

tester: 5 crown 6 canopy, conner, helmet, prover, teston 7 assayer, candler, sparver 9 chauffeur, headpiece

testicle: cob 6 testis, testes(pl.)

deer: 6 doucet, dowcet, dowset

testificate: 11 certificate, testimonial

testified under oath: 7 deponed

testifier: 7 witness 8 deponent

testify: 6 affirm, attest, depone, depose 7 declare, express, profess, protest 8 indicate, manifest, proclaim

testimonial: 4 sign 5 token 7 warrant, writing 8 evidence 9 testimony 10 credential 11 certificate

testimony: say 6 attest, avowal 7 witness 8 evidence 10 deposition, profession 11 affirmation, attestation, certificate, declaration 14 recommendation

testing: 5 assay 11 examination

testudo: 4 lyre, shed 5 cover, talpa, tumor, vault 6 screen 7 ceiling

testy: 6 touchy 7 crabbed, fretful, peevish, waspish 8 petulant, snappish 9 impatient, irascible, irritable, obstinate 10 headstrong
tetanus: 7 lockjaw
tetchy: 6 touchy 7 peevish 9 irritable, sensitive
tête-a-tête: 4 chat, seat, sofa 8 causeuse 12 conversation
tetel: 5 torah
tether: tie 4 band, rope 5 cable, chain, leash, limit, noose 6 fasten, picket 7 confine 8 restrain
Tethys: 5 Titan 8 Titaness
brother: 6 Cronus
father: 6 Uranus
husband: 7 Oceanus
tetragon: 6 square 7 rhombus 10 quadrangle
tetric: 5 harsh 6 gloomy 7 austere
tetter: 4 fret 6 eczema, herpes, lichen
Teuton: 4 Goth 6 German
Teutonic: 5 Dutch 6 German, Gothic 7 English 12 Scandinavian
alphabet character: 4 rune
barbarian: 4 Goth
deity: As, Er; Eir, Hel, Tiu, Tyr, Ull 4 Erda, Frea, Frig, Norn, Odin, Thor 5 Aesir, Baldr, Brage, Bragl, Donar, Othin, Tiwaz, Wodin, Wotan 6 Balder, Frigga, Saeter 7 Forseti 8 Heimdall
homicide: 5 morth
land: 4 odal
law: 5 Salic
legendary hero: 4 Offa
race: 4 Ubii 5 Danes, Goths, Jutes 6 Angles, Franks, Saxons 7 Germans, Vandals 8 Lombards 10 Norwegians 11 Burgundians, 13 Scandinavians
water nymph: nis
tew: taw, tow, vex 4 beat, fuss, pull, work 5 knead, tease, tools 6 incite, strive, tackle, tuyere 7 fatigue 8 struggle
tewel: 4 bore, hole, pipe, tool, vent 6 funnel, tuyere 7 chimney, trumpet
tewer: 4 lane 5 alley
tewit: 7 lapwing
tewly: 6 sickly 8 delicate, qualmish
tewsome: 8 restless 11 troublesome
Texas: *battle:* 5 Alamo
bronco, broncho: 7 mustang
capital: 6 Austin
citadel: 5 Alamo
city: 4 Waco 5 Cuero, Mexia, Paris 6 Austin, Dallas, El Paso, Laredo, Odessa 7 Abilene, Denison, Houston, Lubbock 8 Amarillo
cottonwood: 5 alamo
county: Bee 4 Leon, Polk, Rusk 5 Nolan, Starr, Tyler 6 Harris, Sutton, Walker 7 Houston, Madison, Navarro, Trinity 8 Anderson, Angelina, Cherokee 9 Freestone, Limestone 11 Nacogdoches
cowboy jacket: 8 chaqueta
fever carrier: 4 tick
fortress: 5 Alamo
founder: 6 Austin
hat: 7 Stetson 9 ten-gallon
itch: 5 mange 7 scabies
massacre site: 5 Alamo
mission: 5 Alamo
poplar: 5 Alamo
river: Red 5 Pecos 6 Neches, Nueces 9 Rio Grande
shrine: 5 Alamo
shrub: 6 anagua, anaqua
state police: 6 ranger
university: SMU, TCU 4 Rice 6 Baylor
text: 4 copy 5 theme, topic 7 passage, subject 11 handwriting
operatic: 8 libretto
pen: 5 ronde
pert. to: 7 textual
revision: 9 recension
set to music: 8 oratorio
variation: 7 lection
textbook: 6 manual
textile: *dealer:* 6 mercer
goods: 7 mercery
ornament: 8 fagoting
plant refuse: 5 hurds
ring device: 6 poteye
worker: 4 dyer 6 reeder
texture: web 4 wale 5 grain 6 dobweb, fabric, tissue 7 textile 9 structure 11 composition, fabrication
cloth: 4 wale, warp, woof
tez: 7 pungent, violent
tezkirah: 7 license 8 passport 11 certificate
thack: 4 roof, that 5 thump 6 thatch, thwack 8 thatched
Thackeray: *tale country:* 10 Paflagonia
tale hero: 9 Pendennis
Thailand: 4 Siam
cab: 5 samlo 6 samlaw, samlor
canal: 5 klong
city: 6 Bankok 7 Ayuthia, Ayuthya, Bangkok 9 Sukhothai
coin: at; att 4 baht 5 fuang, tical 6 pynung, salung, satang
demon: nat
dialect: Lao
dress: 6 panung
fabric: 8 siamoise
fruit: 5 mango 6 papaya, pumelo
island: 6 Phuket
isthmus: Kra
king: 4 Rama
measure: wa; ken, niu, nmu, rai, sat, sen, sok, wah, yot 4 keup, ngan, tang, yote 5 kwien, laang, sesti, tanan 6 kabiet, kam

meu, kanahn 7 chai meu, roeneng 8 chang awn 9 anukabiet
native: Lao
people: Tai 4 Thai 7 Siamese
provincial capital: 5 Muang
river: 6 Mekong, Meping 7 Meklong 10 Chaophraya
spirit: nat
state: 6 Patani
temple: wat
town: 5 Puket 7 Ayuthia, Bangkok, Lopburi, Singora, Songkla 8 Kiangmai 9 Chiengmai
weight: hap, pai, sen, sok 4 baht, haph, klam, klom 5 catty, chang, coyan, picul, tical 6 fluang, salung, sompay 7 tamlung
Thais composer: 8 Massenet
thalassic: 6 marine 7 oceanic, pelagic
Thalia: *sisters:* 6 Aglaia, Graces 7 Gratiae 8 Charites(Gk.) 10 Euphrosyne
slayer: 5 Erato
Thames: 4 Isis
town: 4 Eton
tributary: 6 Tyburn
Thanatopsis author: 6 Bryant
Thanatos: 5 death
mother: Nyx
thane: 5 churl 7 servant, warrior 8 follower 9 attendant
estate: 5 manor
thank: 7 aggrate 11 acknowledge
thankful: 8 grateful 11 meritorious, thankworthy 12 appreciative
thankfulness: 9 gratitude
thankless: 10 ungrateful 13 unappreciated
person: 7 ingrate
thanks: 7 cumshaw 8 gramercy 9 gratitude 11 gratulation 12 appreciation 15 acknowledgement
thapes: 12 gooseberries
thar: 4 need 7 behoove
tharf: 5 heavy, stiff 9 unbending
tharm: gut 5 belly 6 catgut 9 intestine
that: yon 6 yonder 7 because
that is: e.g., i.e.
to say: 6 namely
that not: 4 lest
thatch: 4 nipa
peg: 4 scob
support: 6 wattle
thatched: 6 reeded, roofed
thatcher: 6 reeder 7 crowder, hellier
thaumaturgists: 6 Goetae 7 wizards 9 magicians, sorcerers
thaumaturgy: 5 magic 11 legerdemain
thaw: 4 melt 6 unbend 8 dissolve
the: se
French: la, le; les
German: der, die, das
Italian: i; il, la, le 4 egli, ella
Spanish: el, la; las, los
the same: 4 idem 5 ditto
theater, theatre: 5 arena, house, odeon, odeum, stage 8 coliseum 9 playhouse
audience: 5 house
award: 4 Tony
box-office sign: SRO
curtain: 4 drop 6 teaser
district: 6 Rialto
Elizabethan: 5 Globe
entrance hall: 5 foyer, lobby
full: SRO
Greek: 5 odeon, odeum
group: 4 ANTA
low-class: 4 gaff
motion-picture: 5 movie 6 cinema 8 bioscope 13 cinematograph, kinematograph
outdoor: 5 arena 7 drive-in, open-air
part: box, pit 4 loge 5 foyer, stage 7 balcony, gallery, parquet 8 parterre 9 orchestra 10 proscenium
pit: 6 circle 7 parquet 8 parterre
sports: 5 arena
theater box: 4 loge
theater-in-the-round: 5 arena
theater stall: 4 loge
theatrical: 5 showy, stagy 6 scenic 7 pompous 8 affected, dramatic 10 artificial, histronic 11 declamation 12 melodramatic
company: 6 troupe
extra: 4 supe 5 super
profession: 5 stage
sign: S.R.O.
spectacle: 7 pageant
star: 4 hero, lead 7 heroine
valet 7 dresser
Thebes: *acropolis:* 6 Cadmea
blind soothsayer: 8 Tiresias
deity: 4 Amon 5 Ament
district: 7 Thebiad
founder: 6 Cadmus
king: 5 Laius 7 Amphion, Oedipus 8 Eteocles, Pentheus
poet: 6 Pindar
prince: 7 Oedipus
queen: 5 Aedon, Niobe 7 Jocasta
statute: 6 Memnon
wicked queen: 5 Dirce
theca: sac, sad 4 case 7 capsule
thee: tha 4 grow 6 thrive 7 prosper 8 increase
theft: 6 furtum, piracy 7 bribery, larceny, robbery 8 burglary 10 conveyance, plagiarism 12 embezzlement
theft-like: 7 piratic
theine: 8 caffeine
source: tea
thelium: 6 nipple 7 papilla

them: 5 hemen
thema: 5 theme, topic 6 thesis 7 subject 12 dissertation
theme: 4 base, text 5 ditty, essay, motif, topic 6 matter, theses, thesis 7 subject 9 discourse 11 composition, proposition 12 dissertation
literary: 5 motif
musical: 4 tema
title: 5 lemma
Themis: *concern of:* law 7 harmony
father: 6 Uranus
mother: 4 Gaea
then: 4 next 5 alors(F.) 7 besides 8 formerly, moreover 9 therefore 11 accordingly
music: poi
then too: 5 again
thence: 4 away 9 elsewhere, therefore 10 henceforth 11 thenceforth
theodolite: 7 alidade
theologian: 6 divine
authority: 4 imam 5 ulema
famous: 5 Arius 6 Calvin, Luther 13 Thomas Aquinas
study of unity: 7 irenics
theorbo: 4 lute
theoreum: 4 rule
theoretical: 5 ideal 8 platonic 11 speculation, speculative, unpractical 12 hypothetical
theorist: 10 ideologist
theorize: 9 postulate, speculate
theory: ism 4 plan 5 guess 6 scheme 7 formula 8 analysis, doctrine 9 principle 10 conjecture, hypothesis 11 explanation, speculation 13 contemplation
kind of: 7 plenism 9 Platonism 13 phenomenalism
theow: 4 bond 5 slave 7 servile
there: ibi(L.), yon 4 able 5 ready 6 yonder 7 thither 8 equipped, reliable 10 dependable
thereafter: 9 afterward 11 accordingly 12 subsequently
thereat: 7 thither
therefore: as, so 4 ergo, then, thus 5 hence, since 6 frothy, thence 9 wherefore 11 accordingly 12 consequently
thereto: 4 also 7 besides 8 moreover
therewith: mit 6 withal 7 besides, thereat 8 moreover 9 forthwith, thereupon
therm, therme: 4 bath, pool
thermal: hot 4 warm
thermal unit: btu 7 calorie
thermometer: 7 Reaumur 8 pyrostat 9 pyrometer 10 Centigrade, Fahrenheit
thesaurus: 7 lexicon 8 treasury 10 dictionary, repository, storehouse 12 encyclopedia
Thesaurus compiler: 5 Roget
Theseus: *father:* 6 Aegeus
lover: 7 Ariadne
wife: 7 Antiope, Phaedra 9 Hippolyte
thesis: 5 essay, point, theme 7 premise 9 postulate, statement 10 assumption, conception 11 affirmation, proposition 12 dissertation
opposed to: 5 arsis
thespian: 5 actor 6 player 7 actress 9 tragedian
Thessaly: *king:* 7 Admetus
mountain: Ida, Osa 4 Ossa 6 Pelion 9 Psiloriti
valley: 5 Tempe
witch: 7 Aganice
thetic: 8 positive 9 arbitrary 10 prescribed
Thetis: *husband:* 6 Peleus
son: 8 Achilles
theurgy: 5 magic 7 miracle, sorcery 9 occultism
thew: 4 form, mode 5 habit, power, press, sinew, stool, trait 6 custom, manner, muscle, virtue 7 oppress, pillory, quality 8 strength 10 discipline, resolution
thewless: 4 lazy 6 feeble 10 spiritless
thewy: 6 sinewy 8 muscular
thick: fat 4 dull, hazy 5 broad, brosy, burly, close, crass, dense, gross, heavy, husky, plump, solid 6 coarse, filled, greasy, hoarse, obtuse, shaggy, stodgy, stupid 7 blubber, compact, crowded, grumous, muffled, thicket, viscous 8 abundant, familiar, friendly, guttural, intimate, profound, thickset 9 excessive, luxuriant 10 indistinct 11 inspissated, marticulate, thickheaded 12 impenetrable
and short: 5 squat
soup: 5 puree 7 pottage
thick-skinned: 4 cold 7 callous 9 pachyderm 11 pachydermic
thicken: gel 4 clot, crud, curd 5 cloud, crowd, flock 6 curdle, deepen, harden 7 confirm, congeal, stiffen 8 condense 9 intensify 10 incrassate, inspissate, strengthen
thicket: 4 bosk, bush, rone, shaw 5 brake, clump, copse, grove, hedge, shola 6 bosket, covert, greave 7 boscage, boskage, bosquet, coppice, spinney 9 brushwood 10 underbrush
kind: 5 brake, hedge, shola 7 chamise, chamiso, coppice, spinney 8 chamisal 9 chaparral
thickheaded: 4 dull 5 dense 6 stupid 7 doltish 11 blockheaded
thickness: ply 5 layer, sheet 8 diameter 9 curdiness, denseness, dimension, heaviness 11 consistency

thickset: 4 stub 5 squat, stout 6 chumpy, chunky, stocky, stodgy, stubby
thickskulled: 4 dull, slow 5 heavy 6 stupid 11 thickheaded
thicky: fat
thief (see also **stealer**): 4 chor, gilt 5 budge, scamp 6 ackman, arrant, bandit, cannon, cloyer, hooker, looter, nimmer, rascal, robber, sucker, waster 7 bramble, brigand, burglar, grifter, sneaker, stealer 8 cutpurse, gangster, larcener 9 larcenist, scoundrel 10 depredator, freebooter, highwayman, plagiarist
crucified beside Christ: 6 Desmas, Dismas, Dysmas
kind of: gun 5 ganef, ganof, gonof, snoop 6 ackman, angler, gonoph, pirate, swiper 7 gorilla, mercury, rustler 9 drawlatch 10 pickpocket
thieveless: 4 cold 5 bleak 6 frigid 7 aimless 8 bootless, listless 10 forbidding
thieves' Latin: 5 slang
thievish: sly 7 furtive, kleptic 8 stealthy 9 Hungarian
thig: ask, beg 6 borrow 7 beggary
thigh: ham 4 hock 5 carve, femur, flank, meros, merus 6 femora(pl.), gammon
armor: 5 cuish
bone: 5 femur, iluim
comb. form: mer 4 mero
muscle: 9 sartorius
pains: 8 sciatica
pert. to: 6 crural
thill: 5 plank, shaft 6 thwart 8 planking, wainscot
thimble: *conjurer:* 6 goblet
machine: 6 sleeve
thimblerigger: 5 cheat 8 swindler
thin: dim 4 bony, flue, lank, lean, pale, poor, rare, slim, weak 5 exile, faint, gaunt, lanky, lathy, scant, sheer, spare, washy, wizen 6 dilute, flimsy, hollow, meager, meagre, papery, rarefy, reduce, scanty, scarce, skinny, slight, slinky, sparse, watery, weaken, weazen 7 gracile, haggard, scrawny, slender, tenuous 8 araneous, gossamer, rarefied, scantily 9 attenuate, emaciated, extenuate, infertile, subtilize 10 inadequate 11 transparent 12 unbelievable, unconvincing 13 unsubstantial
and delicate: 8 araneous
and haggard: 5 gaunt
and slender: 4 lean 5 lanky
and vibrant: 5 reedy
and weak: 6 watery
and withered: 5 wizen 6 weezen
coating or layer: 4 film 6 veneer
disk: 5 wafer
out: 5 peter
plate: 4 leaf, shim 5 wedge 6 lamina, tegmen
scale: 5 flake 6 lamina 7 lamella
Thin Man: dog: 4 Asta
wife: 4 Nora
thin-skinned: 6 touchy 9 sensitive
thine: 4 tuum
thing: act 4 deed, idea, item 5 cause, chose, court, event, point 6 affair, detail, matter, notion, object, reason, wealth 7 article, council 8 assembly, incident, property 9 happening 11 transaction 12 circumstance
accomplished: 4 acta, deed 5 actum, actus
added: ell 6 insert 7 addenda(pl.) 8 addendum, addition, appendix 9 insertion 10 additament, complement, supplement
admitted: 4 fact 5 datum 7 element 9 principle
aforesaid: 5 ditto
assumed: 7 premise, premiss 9 postulate 11 implication, stipulation 14 presupposition
brought into existence: 8 creation
capable of spontaneous motion: 8 automata 9 automaton
complete in itself: 5 unity
consecrated to a deity: 6 hieron, sacrum 8 anathema
cursed: 8 anathema
extra: 5 bonus 6 bounty, lanyap 7 premium 8 lagnappe 9 lagniappe
following: 6 sequel
forfeited to crown: 7 deodand
found: 5 trove
given as security: 4 gage 6 pledge
indefinite, unnamed: 7 so and so 11 nondescript
invariable: 8 constant
known by reasoning: 7 noumena 8 noumenon
known by senses: 9 phenomena 10 phenomenon
of no value: 4 bean 5 nihil 6 fillip, nought, stiver, trifle 7 bauchle, nothing, pinhead, trinket 8 picayune 9 nonentity, resnihili 10 resnullius
of remembrance: 5 token
personal property law: 5 chose
precious: 4 oner 5 curio, relic 6 pippin, rarity 8 treasure
small: dot, jot 4 atom, iota, whit 6 tittle 8 particle, scuddick
to be done: 5 chore 6 agenda 7 agendum
unusual: 5 freak 6 oddity 11 monstrosity 12 malformation
thingamajig: 6 device, gadget, widget 9 doohickey, doohickus, doohinkey, doohinkus, thingummy 10 thingumbob

things: res 4 gear 5 goods 7 clothes, effects 10 belongings 13 appurtenances
between extremes: 13 intermediates
done: 9 res gestae
for sale: 5 goods, wares 8 services 11 merchandise
gained by purchase: 10 acquirenda
hidden: 10 penetralia
holy: 5 hagia
jumble of: 4 mess, muss 14 conglomeration
linked in nature: 8 cognates
movable: 8 chattels 10 resmobiles
obtained from other things: 11 derivatives
prohibited: 7 vetanda
suitable for eating: 9 esculents
to see: 6 sights
worth remembering: 11 memorabilia
thingumbob: See **thingamajig**
think: wis 4 deem, feel, muse, seem, trow, ween 5 judge, opine 6 appear, esteem, expect, intend, reason, repute, scheme 7 believe, bethink, concoct, imagine, purpose, reflect, resolve, suppose, surmise 8 cogitate, conceive, consider, meditate, ruminate 9 calculate, determine, speculate 10 conjecture, deliberate, reconsider 11 contemplate
alike: 5 agree
for: 7 suppose, suspect
logically: 6 reason
out: 4 plán 5 solve 6 devise 7 develop, perfect 8 cogitate, contrive, discover 10 excogitate
over: 5 brood
thinker: 4 mind 5 brain 7 student 9 meditator 11 philosopher
Thinker sculptor: 5 Rodin
thinking: 7 opinion 9 judgement 10 cogitation, reflection 13 ratiocination 17 intellectualizing
marked by exact: 13 ratiocinative
thinly: 6 airily 8 sparsely 14 insufficiently
metallic: 5 tinny
scattered: 6 sparse
thinner: 5 rarer 7 sheerer 10 turpentine
thinness: 6 rarity 7 exility, tenuity 11 attenuation
third: *combining form:* 4 trit
figure mood: 7 ferison
in number: 8 tertiary
music: 6 tierce
power of number: 4 cube
Third Man author: 6 Greene
thirl: 4 hole, hurl, thin 5 drill, gaunt, whirl, wound 6 hungry, hurtle, pierce, sucken, thrill, tingle, window 7 enslave, nostril, opening, vibrate 8 enthrall, restrict, thirlage, traverse 9 penetrate, perforate, shriveled 11 perforation
thirlage: fee, pay 4 dues 5 right 7 multure, service 8 mortgage 9 servitude, thralldom
thirling: 7 bondage 10 subjection
thirst: 4 long 5 crave, dryth 6 desire 7 aridity, craving, longing
absence of: 7 adipsia
excessive: 9 anadipsia
thirsty: dry 4 adry, arid avid 6 desire, drouth 7 athirst, craving, drought, longing, parched 8 droughty
thirty: 6 lambda(Gr.), trente(F.)
thirty nine and thirty seven hundredths inches: 5 meter
this: yis 4 esta(Sp.), haec(L.)
this way: 4 here
Thisbe's love: 7 Pyramus
thistle: 4 weed 7 bedegar, caltrop 8 bedeguar 10 acanaceous
genus of: 5 layia
thistle-like plants: 7 carlina
thistledown: 6 pappus
thither: end, yon 5 hence, there 6 result, yonder 7 farther, thereat
thivel: 5 stick 7 spatula
thixle: ax; adz 7 hatchet
Thjazi: *daughter:* 6 Skathi
home: 9 Thrymheim
tho: 5 still
thole: peg, pin 4 bear 5 allow 6 endure, remain, suffer 7 undergo 8 tolerate
Thomas' opera: 6 Mignon
thong: 4 lace, lash, rein, riem 5 lasso, leash, romal, strap, strip, whang 6 twitch 7 amentum, laniard, lanyard, latchet 8 whiplash
thong-shaped: 6 lorate
Thor: *father:* 4 Odin
hammer: 8 Mjollnir
noise: 7 thunder
stepson: Ull
wife: Sif
thorax: 5 chest
thorn: 4 brod, goad 5 briar, brier, spine, worry 7 acantha 8 vexation 9 annoyance 10 irritation
apple: 5 metel 6 datura
combining form: 5 spini
Egyptian: 5 babul 6 gonake 7 gonakie
full of: 6 briery
small: 7 spinule
thorny: 5 sharp, spiny 6 spinal 7 brambly, bristly, prickly 8 spinated 9 acanthoid, difficult, vexatious 11 contentious
thorough: 4 deep, full 6 arrant 7 through 8 absolute, accurate, complete, finished 9 downright, intensive 10 exhaustive, throughout 11 painstaking 13 thorough-going
thorough-going: 6 arrant 7 radical

thoroughbred: 5 horse 7 trained 8 cultured, educated, well-bred 11 full-blooded
thoroughfare: 4 road 5 alley 6 avenue, street 7 highway, passage, transit 8 waterway 9 boulevard
thoroughly: all 4 inly 6 deeply 9 downright, intensive 10 absolutely, altogether
thoroughwort: 7 boneset
thorp, thorpe: 4 dorp 6 hamlet 7 village 9 community
Thoth: god 6 Tehuti
head: 4 ibis
thou: tha
though: 7 however 12 nevertheless
thought: 4 care, hope, idea, mind, view 5 trace 6 deemed, opined 7 anxiety, concept, judging, opinion 9 cogitated, reasoning 10 cogitation, conception, meditation, melancholy, reflection 11 cerebration, expectation, imagination 12 deliberation, recollection 13 concentration, consideration, ratiocination 16 intellectualized
continuous: 10 meditation
deep in: 10 cogitabund
form: 6 ideate
inability to express: 6 asemia
reader: 8 telepath
transference: 9 telepathy
thoughtful: 4 kind 5 moody 7 careful, earnest, heedful, mindful, pensive, prudent, serious 9 attentive, designing, regardful 10 cogitabund, meditative, melancholy, reflective, ruminative, solicitous 11 circumspect, considerate
thoughtfulness: 14 circumspection
thoughtless: 4 dull, rash 6 remiss, stupid 7 glaiket, glaikit 8 careless, heedless, reckless 9 brainless 10 unthinking 11 harum-scarum, inattentive, lightheaded 13 inconsiderate
thoughtlessness: 12 inadvertence
thousand: *combining form:* 4 kilo 5 mille
one: mil 5 grand 7 chiliad
thousand-headed snake: 5 Sesha 6 Shesha
thousandth: 10 millesimal
of an inch: mil
Thrace: *goddess:* 6 Bendis
king: 6 Tereus
mountaineers: 5 Bessi
musician: 7 Orpheus
people: 6 Satrae 8 Bisaltae
river: 6 Hebrus
town: 6 Sestos
thrall: 4 esne, serf 5 slave, theow 7 bondage, bondman, captive, enslave, slavery, subject 8 enslaved, enthrall 9 suffering 10 oppression, subjugated
thralldom: 7 bondage, slavery 9 captivity, servitude
thrangity: 6 bustle 8 business
thrash: lam, tan 4 bang, beat, bray, ding, drub, flax, flog, lash, rush, sail, whip, yerk 5 array, baste, bless, flail, pound, swing, threp, whang 6 anoint, defeat, fettle, raddle, strike, threap, threep, threip, threpe, thresh, thwack 7 trounce 8 belabour, blathery, vanquish 9 triturate 10 flagellate
thrashing: 4 bean 7 beating, milling 8 drubbing, flogging, whipping
thrast: 5 press 9 constrain
thrave: 4 bind 5 crowd 6 bundle, number, throng 8 quantity
thrawart: 7 adverse, crooked, peevish, twisted 8 backward, perverse, stubborn 9 reluctant 12 unpropitious
thrawn: 7 crooked 8 perverse 9 misshapen 10 unpleasant
thread: ray 4 filo, line, vein, yarn 5 fiber, reeve, weave 6 strata, stream, string 7 quality, stratum 8 filament, fineness, raveling 9 ravelling 11 composition
a needle: 5 reeve
ball of: 4 clew, clue
bits of: 4 lint 9 ravelings
cell: 5 cnida
combining form: nem
cone: cop
division of: 4 beer
in weaving shuttle: 4 weft
inserted beneath skin: 5 seton
kind of: 4 bast, bave, film, silk, yarn 5 floss, linen, lisle, rayon, seton, trame 6 cotton, lingel, lingle 8 arrasene
knot in: 4 burl
on spindle: cop
pert. to: 5 filar
raveled: 6 sleave
shoemaker's: 6 lingel
silk: bur 4 bave, burr 5 floss, trame 9 filoselle
skein of: 4 hasp
surgical: 6 catgut
tape: 5 inkle
tester: 9 serimeter
used as core for tinsel: 4 poil
winding tube: cop
thread-like: 5 filar 6 filose
threadbare: 4 bare, sere, worn 5 stale, trite 6 frayed, pilled, shabby 9 hackneyed
threads: 4 beer, weft, woof 6 filler 8 clothing
combining form: 4 byss
threadworm: 7 filaria 8 nematode
thready: 4 ropy, thin, weak 7 fibrous, stringy

threap, threep, threip, threp, threpe: 4 beat, urge 5 chide, press, scold 6 affirm, assert, haggle, insist, thrash 7 dispute, quarrel, wrangle 8 complain, maintain
threat: vex 4 fail, lack, urge, want, warn 5 chide, crowd, peril, press, troop 6 compel, menace, misery, throng 7 oppress, portend, reprove, trouble, warning 8 maltreat, threaten 10 compulsion 12 denunciation
threaten: 4 brag 5 boast, lower, utter 6 charge, menace 7 portend, promise 8 denounce
threatening: big 6 greasy, lowery 8 lowering, menacing 9 impending 10 formidable
three: 4 drei(G.) 5 crowd, gamma(Gr.), trias 7 Trinity
combination of: 7 triplet, ternary
combining form: ter, tri
consisting of: 7 ternate
group of: tre 4 trio 5 triad, trine 8 triumvir
months: 7 quarter 9 trimester
prefix: tri
ruling group: 11 triumvirate
set of: 4 trio 5 triad 7 ternion
Three B's (in music): 4 Bach 6 Brahms 9 Beethoven
three-card monte: 9 montebank
three-cleft: 6 trifid
three-dimensional: 5 cubic 6 stereo 7 cubical
three-flowered: 9 trifloral
Three Graces: job 5 bloom 6 Aglaia, Thalia 10 brilliance, Euphrosyne
three-headed goddess: 6 Hecate
three-hundredth anniversary: 13 tercentennial, tricentennial
three in one: 6 triune 7 trinity
Three Kingdoms: Wu; Shu, Wei
three L's: 4 lead 7 lookout 8 latitude
three-layered: 10 trilaminar
three-legged stand: 6 tripod, trivet
three-lined: 9 trilinear
three-masted vessel: 5 xebec 8 schooner
Three Musketeers: 5 Athos 6 Aramis 7 Porthos
author: 5 Dumas
friend: 9 D'Artagnan
three-piled: 4 best 6 costly 11 extravagant
three-pointed: 11 tricuspidal
three-score: 5 sixty
three-seeded: 11 trispermous
three-sided figure: 6 trigon 8 triangle
three-spot: 4 trey
three-square: 5 cross 9 irritable, three-fold
three-styled: 10 trystylous
three-toed sloth: ai
Three Wise Men: 6 Gaspar 8 Melchior 9 Balthasar
threefold: 4 tern 5 trine 6 ternal, thrice, treble, trinal, triple, triply
combining form: ter
threescore: 5 sixty
threesome: 4 trio
threne: 5 dirge 8 threnody 11 lamentation
threnody: 4 song 5 dirge 6 hearse
thresh (see also **thrash**): cob 4 beat, flog, lump, rush 5 berry, flail 6 thrash
thresh out: 5 argue 6 debate 7 discuss
threshed grain husks: 5 straw
threshel: 5 flail
thresher: 5 flail, shark 6 beater 7 combine
thresher shark: 6 sea fox 7 foxfish
genus: 7 alopias
threshing: *refuse:* 6 colder
tool: 5 flail
threshold: eve 4 gate, sill 5 limen 6 outset 8 doorsill, entrance 9 beginning
thribble: 6 triple 9 threefold
thrice: 4 very 9 threefold
thrift: 4 work 5 labor 7 economy 9 frugality, husbandry 10 employment, occupation, prosperity, providence 14 forehandedness
thriftily: 4 near
thriftless: 6 lavish 8 prodigal, wasteful 11 extravagant, improvident
thrifty: 4 near 5 fendy, small 6 frugal, narrow, proper, saving, useful, worthy 7 careful, sparing 8 thriving 9 befitting, estimable, provident 10 economical, forehanded, prospering 11 flourishing, serviceable
thrill: 4 bore, cast, dirl, girl, hurl 5 drill, elate, flush, thirl, throw 6 dindle, pierce, quiver, tremor 7 frisson, tremble, vibrate 8 fremitus, transfix 9 penetrate, perforate, throbbing, vibration
thrilling: 9 throbbing, vibrating
thrilly: 8 stirring 11 sensational
thrimble: 6 fumble 7 squeeze, wrestle 8 hesitate
thrimp: 5 press 7 squeeze
thring: 4 cast 5 crowd, crush, press 6 batter, pierce, throng, thrust 7 squeeze
thrive: dow 4 gain, grow 5 addle, moise 6 batten, fatten 7 improve, prosper, succeed 8 flourish, increase
thriven: 4 wise 5 adult, grown 7 prudent 8 thriving 10 prosperous 11 experienced
thriving: 4 bein, bien 10 prosperous, successful 11 flourishing
in shade: 11 sciophilous
thrivingly: 5 gaily, gayly
throat: maw 4 crag, crop, gowl, hals, lane, tube 5 halse 6 groove, gullet, guzzle, weason 7 channel, orifice, weasand 8 guttural
armor: 6 gorget
combining form: 4 lemo
covering: 4 barb

infection: 5 croup 6 angina, quinsy 8 cynanche 9 squinancy 11 strep throat
irritation: 4 frog
lozenge: 6 pastil, troche 7 pastile 8 pastille
part: 7 glottis
pert. to: 5 gular 7 jugular 8 guttural
protector: 5 scarf 7 muffler
sore: 6 housty
swelling: 6 goiter
to clear: hem 4 hawk
upper: 4 gula
throat skin: 6 dewlap
throaty: 6 hoarse 8 guttural 9 voracious
throb: 4 ache, beat, drum, pant 5 flack, pulse 7 flacker, pulsate, vibrate 9 palpitate, pulsation
throbbing: 4 beat
throdden: 4 grow 6 thrive
throddy: 5 plump 6 active 9 well-grown
throe: 4 pang 5 agony 6 effort 7 anguish 8 struggle
thrombus: 4 clot 6 fibrin
throne: see 4 apse, seat 5 asana, chair, exalt, gaddi, gadhi, power, siege 7 anguish, dignity 8 cathedra, enthrone 11 sovereignty
remove from: 6 depose
throng: 4 busy, crew, heap, host, push, rout 5 close, crowd, horde, peril, press, swarm 6 busily, bustle, strain, stress 7 company, hurried 8 distress, familiar, hardship, intimate 9 confusion, frequency, multitude 10 affliction, constantly
thronged: 5 alive 7 peopled 10 celebrious
throttle: gun 5 check, choke 6 throat 7 garrote 8 compress, garrotte, strangle, suppress, windpipe 9 suffocate 11 accelerator
open: gun
through, thru: by; per 4 over 5 athro, ended 6 across, coffin 7 perpend 8 athrough, finished 9 completed, tombstone 11 sarcophagus 12 thoroughfare, unobstructed
comb. form: di; dia
the agency of: per
the mouth: 7 peroral
throughgang: 5 labor 6 energy 11 overhauling 12 thoroughfare
throughgoing: 9 reprimand 11 examination, overhauling 12 thoroughfare
throughout: 5 about 6 bedene, during, sempre 7 perfect 8 thorough 10 completely, everywhere
comb. form: per
throw: boa, cob, don, hit, lob, pat, peg, put, shy, wap 4 bail, bear, blow, cast, dash, fall, form, hike, hove, hurl, pelt, rack, risk, shed, time, toss, turn, yerk 5 check, chuck, chunk, crank, drive, flick, fling, flirt, force, frame, heave, impel, pitch, place, scarf, sling, start, strip, trice, twist, whang, while, whirl 6 change, defeat, divest, elance, hinder, inject, retard, sprain, spread, spring, strike, stroke, thrust, thwart, wrench, writhe 7 advance, discard, fashion, present, produce, project, revolve, venture 8 catapult, coverlet, distance, obstruct 9 prostrate 10 flagellate
a fit: 5 angry 7 excited 9 disturbed, irritated
a scare into: 5 scare 7 terrify
about: 4 tack 5 slosh 6 thrash
at quoits: 6 leaner, ringer
away: 5 waste 6 refuse, reject 7 discard, leaflet 8 handbill, squander
back: 5 check, delay, repel 6 refuse, reject, retort, revert 8 reversal 9 reversion
dice: 4 cast, main, roll
double one at dice: 7 ambsace
down: 4 cast 5 fling 6 defeat, reject 7 refusal, subvert 9 overthrow, rejection 11 precipitate
down the gauntlet: 4 defy 9 challenge
dust in one's eyes: 7 deceive, mislead
from saddle: 7 unhorse
in: add 4 join 6 inject 10 contribute
in the towel: 4 cede, quit 5 yield 9 surrender
into confusion: 4 riot 5 snafu 7 disturb 8 stampede 10 demoralize
into disorder: pif 4 pied 7 derange
into ecstasy: 6 enrapt
into shade: 7 eclipse
lazily: lob
light upon: 6 illume
lightly: 4 toss
obliquely: 4 deal, skew, toss
off: 4 cast, emit, free, molt, shed 5 abate, expel, moult 6 reject 7 abandon, deflect, discard 8 discount 10 disconnect
off the track: 6 derail
one's weight around: 4 push, urge 8 domineer
out: 4 emit, lade 5 egest, eject, evict, expel, utter 6 extend, reject 7 confuse, discard, excrete, project 8 distance 9 eliminate
out of order: 7 derange
over: 4 jilt 7 abandon
overboard: 8 jettison
six at dice: 4 sise 5 sises
stones at: 8 lapidate
together: 7 collect 8 assemble
underhand: lob
up: 4 rise 5 demit, vomit 10 relinquish
water upon: 5 douse
with force: 4 bung
throwing rope: 5 lasso, reata, riata 6 lariat
throwing-stick: 6 atlatl 9 boomerang
thrown: 4 cast 6 hurled 7 twisted 8 unseated
thrum: bit 4 drum, lout, purr, tuft 5 strum, waste 6 fringe, recite, repeat, tangle, thatch 8 particle 10 threepence
thrush: dig 4 bear, birr, bore, butt, dash, ding 5 barge, mavie, mavis, ouzel, robin,

veery 6 missel, oriole, shrike 7 bearing 8 bluebird, throstle 9 blackbird
disease: 4 soor 5 aptha 6 aphtha
European: 4 osel 5 mavis, ossel, ousel, ouzel 6 missel, shrite
ground: 5 pitta
migratory: 5 robin
thrust: dig, jab 4 bear, birr, bore, butt, dush, gird, jerk, pelt, poke, prop, push, stab 5 barge, clash, crowd, drive, force, hunch, impel, longe, lunge, onset, press, shove 6 attack, detude, extend, hustle, pierce, plunge, repost, ripost, spread, stress, throng 7 allonge, assault, collide, extrude, intrude, riposte 8 estocade, pressure, protrude 9 interject, interpose
against wall: 5 crush, mured
aside: 5 shove, shunt
back: 4 rout 6 defeat 7 repulse
thrutch: 4 push 5 crowd, press 6 throng, thrust
thrutchings: 4 whey
thud: 4 baff, blow, gust, move, push 5 press 6 strike 7 tempest 9 windstorm
thug: 5 rough 6 attack, cuttle, gunman 7 ruffian 8 assassin, gangster 9 cutthroat
thuggery: 6 murder 7 thuggee 10 ruffianism
thumb: 6 pollex, thenar 9 peachwort
part: 6 thenar
Thummim's partner: 4 Urim
thump: cob, dad, dub, hit 4 bang, beat, blow, bump, daud, ding, dird, drub, dunt, polt, whip, yerk 5 blaff, bunch, clour, crump, knock, pound, throb 6 bounce, cudgel, hammer, strike, thrash, thunge
thumping: 5 large 6 tattoo 7 bumping 8 whopping
thunder: 4 peal, rage, roar 6 bronte 7 fouldre 9 Fulminate
comb. form: 5 bront 6 bronto
god: 4 Thor, Zeus
witch: 4 baba
thunder and lightning: 8 ceraunic 9 fulminous
thunder-smitten goddess: 6 Semele
thunderbolt: 4 bolt 6 fulmen 7 fouldre 9 fulminant
thunderhead: 4 omen 5 cloud 7 warning
thundering: 5 large 8 thumping, whopping 10 foudroyant
thunderpeal: 4 clap 11 thunderclap
thunderstorm: *Cuba:* 6 bayamo
West Indies: 7 houvari
thunge: 4 bang 5 sound, thump
thurible: 6 censer
Thuringia: *castle:* 8 Wartburg
city: 4 Gera, Jena 5 Gotha 6 Weimar
Thursday: *god of:* 4 Thor
Holy: 5 Skire
thus: so; sae, sic 4 fiat 5 hence 9 therefore 12 consequently
thwack: rap 4 bang, blow, pack 5 crump, crush, drive, force, knock, whack 6 defeat, strike, thrash 7 belabor 8 belabour
thwart: 4 balk, foil, pert, seat 5 bench, block, brace, clash, cross, parry, saucy, spite, zygon 6 across, baffle, defeat, hinder, oppose, outwit, resist 7 athwart, oblique, prevent, quarrel 8 contrair, obstruct, perverse, stubborn, thwartly 9 frustrate, interpose 10 contravene, disappoint, opposition, transverse 11 intractable, obstruction
thy: tha
Thyestes: *brother:* 6 Atreus
father: 6 Pelops
son: 9 Aegisthus
thylacine: 4 wolf 5 tiger, yabbi
thyme: 8 hillwort
thymus: 5 gland
thyroid enlargement: 6 goiter
thyrsus: 5 staff, stick
tiara: 5 crown 6 diadem, fillet 7 cidares, cidaris, coronet 8 frontlet 9 headdress
Tiber county: 7 Etruria
tibert: cat
Tibet: 7 Sitsang
animal: 5 panda
antelope: goa, sus
ass: 5 kiang
banner: 5 tanka
beast of burden: yak
beer: 5 chang
capital: 5 Lassa, Lhasa
city: Noh 5 Lassa, Lhasa
coin: 5 tanga
deer: 4 shou
dialect: 9 Bhutanese
ecclesiastic: 4 lama 5 dalai
food: 6 tsamba
gazelle: goa
goat fleece: 5 pashm
kingdom: 5 Nepal
lama: 5 Dalai
language: 7 Bodskad
leopard: 5 ounce
monastery: 8 lamasery
monk: 4 lama
ox: yak
oxlike animal: 4 zebu
people: 6 Bhotia 7 Bhotiya
pony: 6 tangum, tangun 7 tanghan
priest: 4 lama
religion: Bon
river: 5 Indus
ruminant: 5 takin
sheep: sha 6 bharal, nahoor, nayaur
wild ass: 5 kiang

wildcat: 5 manul
Tibetan: 6 Tangut
tibia: 5 flute 6 cnemis 8 shinbone
pert. to: 7 cnemial
tiburon: 5 shark
Tiburon Island Indian: 4 Seri
tic: 4 jerk 5 spasm 9 twitching 11 vellication
tice: 6 entice, yorker 10 enticement
tichel: lot 5 troop 6 number
tick: dot, fag, ked, pat, tag, tap 4 beat, case, dash, kade, mark, mite, note, pest 5 acari, chalk, click, count, cover, flirt, speck, touch, trust 6 acarid, acarus, credit, fondle, insect, moment, record, second, tampon, talaje 7 acarina, instant, ticking 8 acaridan, arachnid, garapata, indicate, mattress, tickbean 10 pajahuello, pajaroello
fowl: 5 argas
genus of: 5 argas
sheep: ked
ticker: 5 clock, heart, watch
ticket: bid, tag 4 book, card, list, note, slip, tick 5 check, ducat, fiche, label, score, sight, slate, token 6 ballot, billet, notice, permit, record 7 license, placard, voucher, warrant 8 document 9 cardboard, discharge, etiquette 10 memorandum 11 certificate
complimentary: 4 comp, pass 11 Annie Oakley
of leave: 6 parole
receiver of free: 8 deadhead
season: 6 abonne 10 abonnement
sell above cost: 5 scalp
speculator: 7 scalper
tickey, tickie: 10 threepence
tickle: do 4 beat, nice, play, stir, take, whip 5 amuse, annoy, frail, tease, touch 6 arouse, cuitle, divert, excite, please, thrill, tingle, touchy, wanton 7 capture, cuittle, delight, gratify, operate, passage, portray, provoke, tickler 8 chastise, delicate, insecure, tickling, ticklish, unstable, unsteady 9 difficult, squeamish, titillate, vellicate 10 insecurely
tickled: 6 amused 7 pleased 9 gratified
tickler: pad, sip 4 book, cane, file 5 flask, knife, prong, strap 6 pistol, puzzle, record, weapon 7 problem
tickling: 7 craving 13 gratification
ticklish: 4 nice 5 risky 6 fickle, queasy, touchy 7 comical 8 critical, delicate, unstable, unsteady 9 uncertain 10 changeable, precarious, unreliable 13 oversensitive
tid: 4 fond, mood 5 humor, silly 6 lively, tender 8 childish, ill-humor 9 sprightly
tidal: *bore:* 5 eagre
creek: 6 estero
current: 8 tiderace
flow: 4 bore 5 eagre
wave: 5 aigre, eagre
tidbit, titbit: 5 goody 7 saynete 8 beatille
tiddle: 4 rear 6 fidget, fondle, pamper, potter, tickle
tiddley: 5 small 7 trivial
tiddy: 4 girl, tiny 5 child 7 babyish, trivial 8 childish
tide: sea 4 fair, flow, hour, pass, time 5 carry, drift, drive, flood, point, space, surge, tidal 6 befall, betide, endure, happen, moment, period, season, stream 7 current, freshet, proceed 8 continue, festival, occasion, surmount, tendency 11 anniversary, opportunity
low: 4 neap
lowest of high: 4 neap
pert. to: 4 neap
tidewater: 8 seaboard
tidily: 5 fitly 7 smartly 8 cleverly, suitable 9 shipshape
tiding, tidings: ebb 4 flow, news 5 event 6 advice, gospel 7 account, message 9 happening 11 information 12 intelligence
tidy: 4 cosh, fair, good, meet(obs.), neat, redd, smug, tosh, trig, trim 5 clean, douce, great, groom, large, natty, plump 6 comely, fettle, sleeky, tidily, timely, worthy 7 healthy, orderly, upright 8 diligent, pinafore, skillful 9 shipshape 10 receptacle, seasonable 12 antimacassar, considerable, satisfactory
tie: ty; rod, sag 4 band, beam, beat, bind, bond, cord, draw, duty, even, join, knot, lace, link, post, rope, teck 5 angle, ascot, brace, cadge, chain, equal, hitch, marry, nexus, sheaf, trice, union, unite 6 attach, cement, connex, couple, cravat, enlace, fasten, pledge, string, tether, tiewig 7 confine, connect, necktie, oxfords, sleeper 8 alligate, restrain, restrict, shoelace 9 constrain, constrict, influence, stalemate 10 allegiance, obligation
down: 7 confine 8 restrain, restrict
fast: 5 belay
off: 4 snub 5 belay
ornament: pin 4 clip
securely: 4 lash 5 truss 7 shackle, trammel
tightly: 4 bind, lash
up: 4 bind, moor, stop 5 truss 6 hinder, tether 8 obstruct
tie-up: 5 delay 6 strike 7 mooring 10 connection
tied 4 even
tienda: 4 shop, tent 5 booth 6 awning
tier: row 4 bank, rank 5 layer, place, stack, story 6 degree 7 antenna, arrange 8 pinafore

tierce: 4 cask 5 lunge, parry, third 7 measure 8 sequence
Tierra del Fuego Indian: Ona 4 Agni
tiff: fit, pet, sip 4 huff, mood, spat 5 draft, dress, drink, humor, lunch, order, scent, smell, sniff, spell, state, taste 6 liquor 7 quarrel 8 outburst 9 condition 11 altercation
tiffin: 5 lunch 6 eating 8 drinking
tiffle: 4 fray, idle 6 potter, trifle, tumble 7 unravel 8 entangle 10 disarrange
tift: 4 gust, pant, puff 5 hurry, sniff, whiff 6 flight 14 breathlessness
tig: pat, tag, tap 5 touch
tiger: cat, cub 4 howl, rake, yell 5 bully, groom 6 feline, jaguar 7 leopard 9 carnivore, swaggerer, thylacine 12 organization
family: 7 felidae
tiger finch: 8 amadavat
tiger-hunting dog: 5 dhole
tigerish: 5 cruel 6 fierce, flashy 9 ferocious 10 swaggering 12 bloodthirsty
tigers-mouth: 8 foxglove, toadflax 10 snapdragon
tight: 4 fast, firm, hard, held, neat, snug, taut, tidy, trim 5 alert, bound, cheap, close, dense, drawn, drunk, fixed, ready, smart, solid, tense, tipsy 6 climax, comely, firmly, packed, severe, steady, stingy, strait, strict 7 capable, compact, concise, quickly, shapely, soundly, ummoved 8 constant, exacting, faithful 9 competent, condensed, energetic, mercernary, niggardly 10 impervious, vigorously 11 closefisted, intoxicated, restraining 12 parsimonious
making: 7 tensing
tight-fisted: 6 stingy 11 closefisted 12 parsimonious
tight-lipped: 5 terse 9 secretive
tighten: 5 tense 6 tauten 9 constrict
strings of drum: 4 frap
tightness: 9 closeness
tightwad: 4 fist 5 miser, piker 7 niggard 9 skinflint
tigrine: 5 tawny
Tigris River city: 7 Nineveh
til: 6 sesame
tile: hat 5 brick, drain, plate, slate 6 tegula 7 carreau, quarrel
composed of: 7 tegular 9 tessellar
curved: 7 pantile
malting floor: 6 pament 7 pamment
mosaic: 7 tessera 8 abaculus
pert. to: 7 tegular
used in game: 6 domino
tile-like: 5 slaty
tiler: cat 4 kiln 5 field, thief 7 hellier 10 doorkeeper
tilery: 4 kiln
tiles: 8 ceramics
till: at, by, of; box, far, for, get, hoe, sow 4 draw, earn, farm, gain, plow, tray 5 charm, dress, labor, train, while 6 casket, drawer, entice, strive, whilst 7 develop, prepare 9 cultivate 10 concerning
tillable: 6 arable 7 earable
tillage: 7 aration, culture 11 cultivation
fit for: 6 arable
tilled land: 5 arada
tiller: bar, bow 4 helm, hoer 5 lever, stalk, stick 6 farmer, handle, sprout 7 husband, rancher 10 cultivator, husbandman
tilt: tip 4 cant, duel, heel, lean, list, rush, tent 5 argue, fight, forge, heald, hield, joust, pitch, poise, slant, slope, speed, upend, upset 6 awning, canopy, careen, combat, hammer, oppose, seesaw, stroke, thrust, topple 7 contest, dispute, incline 8 covering, tiltyard 10 tournament 11 altercation
hammer: 6 oliver
skyward: 5 upend
tilter: 5 sword 6 avocet, seesaw 7 jouster 9 sandpiper
tilting: 5 alist 7 swaying 8 slanting
tilting match: 5 joust
timarau, timerau: 7 buffalo
timbal: 10 kettledrum
timber: log, rib 4 beam, fuel, gate, land, raff, stay, wood 5 build, cahuy, cover, fence, frame, gripe, spile, stile, trees 6 forest, lumber 7 support 8 building, contrive 9 construct, structure, underpier
bend: sny 6 camber, rafter
central portion: 7 duramen 9 heartwood
cut: 4 bunk 6 lumber 7 fallage 8 teakwood
decay: 4 conk, dote, doze
defect: lag 4 conk, doze
end: 5 tenon
estimator: 6 scaler 7 cruiser
joining peg: 7 trenail, trunnel 8 treenail
partially decayed: 4 doty
parts of building: rib 4 sill 5 joist, spale 6 purlin, rafter 7 purline 8 stringer
peg: 4 coak
ship: bao, rib 4 bibb, bitt, keel, mast, spar, wale 5 snape, spale 7 stemson 8 sternson
sloping: 6 rafter
standing: 4 stud 5 spile 6 forest 8 puncheon, studding, stumpage
tree: ash, fir 4 pine 5 birch, cedar, maple 6 walnut 7 redwood 8 mahogany
wolf: 4 lobo
timber-jack: 10 lumberjack

timberman: 6 sawyer 7 cruiser 8 woodsman 9 carpenter, lumberman
timbre: 4 tone 5 crest, miter 7 coronet, quality, timbrel 9 character
timbrel: 4 drum 5 tabor 10 tambourine
time: age, day, eld, era, tid 4 date, fuss, hint, hour, sele, term, week, year 5 clock, epoch, month, tempo, tense, watch 6 during, indeed, minute, moment, period, season, second, steven 8 duration, occasion, regulate, schedule, yuletide 9 foresooth 13 demonstration
ahead of: 5 early 9 premature
allowed for payment: 6 usance
another: 5 again
at no: 5 never 9 nevermore
before: eve
blossom: 9 blutezeit
break in: 6 hiatus
brief: 4 span 6 moment
Christmas: 8 yuletide
devoted to religion: 8 holytide
error in order of: 11 anachronism
fast: 4 Lent
gone by: 4 yore 10 yesteryear
granted: 4 stay 5 delay, frist 8 reprieve
happy: 4 bust, lark 5 revel, spree 6 soiree 8 jamboree
intervening: 7 interim 8 meantime 9 meanwhile
length: age, eon, era 6 moment, period
long ago: 4 yore
music: 6 presto
musical marker: 9 metronome
of great depression: 5 nadir
of highest strength: 6 heyday
olden: eld 4 syne(Sc.), yore
period of: age, day, eon, era 4 aeon, date, hour, span, term, week, year 5 epoch, month, spell, trice 6 decade, ghurry, minute, moment, recess, season, second 7 century, instant 8 azoic age 9 fortnight
pert. to: 4 eral 8 temporal
present: 5 nonce
right: tid(Sc.)
single: 4 once
to come: 5 tabor
waste: 4 idle, loaf 5 dally 6 dwadle, diddle, loiter 8 flanerie
wrong: 13 anachronistic
time being: 5 nonce
time clock: 8 recorder
Time Machine author: 5 Wells
time out: 4 five 5 break 6 recess
timeless: 4 true 5 valid 6 eterne 7 ageless, eternal, undated 8 dateless, unending, untimely 9 co-eternal, premature 11 everlasting 12 interminable
timeliness: 9 relevance
timely: apt, pat 4 soon 5 early 6 prompt 8 temporal 9 opportune, pertinent 10 forehanded, seasonably 11 opportunity
timepiece: 4 dial 5 clock, watch 8 sunwatch 9 horologue 11 chronometer 17 chronothermometer
water: 9 clepsydra
times: *many:* oft 5 often 10 frequently
olden: eld 9 yesterday 10 yesteryear
prosperous: ups 5 booms
timetable: 8 schedule
timid: shy 4 argh, eery 5 arghe, bauch, blate, eerie, faint, mousy, pavid, scary 6 afraid 7 bashful, fearful, gastful, nervous 8 cowardly, fearsome, ghastful, hesitant, retiring, timorous 9 diffident, shrinking 12 fainthearted 13 pusillanimous 14 chicken-hearted
timidity: 4 fear 7 shyness 9 funkiness 10 diffidence 11 fearfulness
timish: 6 modish 11 fashionable
timon: 4 helm 5 cynic 6 rudder 11 misanthropy
Timon of Athens character: 5 Titus 6 Caphis, Lucius 7 Flavius
timor: 5 dread
Timor: *capital:* 4 Dili
coin: avo 6 pataca
island: 4 Leti
timorous: 5 faint, timid 6 afraid, cowish, sheepy 7 fearful 8 fearsome, hesitant, terrible 9 shrinking 12 fainthearted
timpani: 11 kettledrums
tin: box, can, pan 5 money, terne 6 latten 7 stannic, stannum 8 preserve, prillion 9 container
pert. to: 7 stannic, stranic
rubbish: 5 stent
sheet: 6 latten
symbol: Sn
tin and copper alloy: 6 pewter
Tin Can Island: 7 Niuafoo
tin dioxide: 8 tinstone
tin foil: 4 tain
Tin Pan Alley group: 5 ASCAP
tin-pot: 4 poor 6 paltry 8 inferior, wretched
tinamou: 4 bird, yutu 6 ynambu
tincal: 5 borax
tinct: dye 4 tint 5 color, imbue, tinge 6 tinged, tinted 7 colored 8 coloured, tincture 10 impregnate
tincture: or 4 cast 5 color, gules, imbue, myrrh, smack, stain, taint, tenne, tinge, trace 6 elixir, imbrue 7 vestige 8 coloring 9 admixture, suspicion 10 extraction 12 modification
for sprains: 6 arnica
of opium: 9 paregoric
tinder: *punk:* 6 amadou

vegetable: 6 amadou
tine: tub, vat 4 fine, fork, lose, pain, shut, teen 5 grief, prong, spike, tooth 6 harrow, perish, repair 7 destroy, enclose, forfeit, trouble
tine branch: 4 snag
tinea: 8 ringworm
tinean: 4 moth
tineoidea: 5 moths
tinge: dye, hue 4 cast, odor, tint 5 color, imbue, savor, shade, smack, stain, touch, trace 6 affect, flavor 7 glimpse, quality 8 coloring, discolor, tincture 9 influence 10 suggestion
tinged with purple: 10 violaceous
tinglass: tin 7 bismuth
tingle: 4 dirl, girl, nail, ring, tack 5 alive, patch, sting 6 dindle, tinkle 7 support, tremble, vibrant 9 fastening, sensation, stimulate
tinker: auk 4 fuss, mend, work 5 caird, gypsy, murre, patch, rogue, skate, tramp 6 mender, mugger, potter, putter, rascal, repair, wander 7 botcher, bungler, vagrant 8 mackerel 11 silversides
tinkle: 5 clink 6 dindle, dingle, tingle
tinner: 6 canner 8 tinsmith
tinny: 4 hard, rich, thin 5 cheap 6 bright 7 brittle, wealthy 8 metallic, tinsmith
tinplate: 5 terne
tinsel: 4 sham 5 gaudy, showy 6 tawdry 8 specious, splendor 9 clinquant 10 forfeiture, glittering
tinseled: 9 clinquant 10 glittering
tint: dye, hue 5 blush, color, stain, taste, tinge, trace 6 nuance 9 foretaste
cheeks: 5 rouge
Tintagel Head's prince: 6 Arthur
tinter: 4 dyer
tintinnabulum: 4 bell 5 rhyme 7 rhythem 8 rhymster
tintype: 9 ferrotype
tiny: wee 5 child, small, teeny 6 atomic, infant, minute 9 miniature 10 diminutive 13 infinitesimal
tip: cap, cue, end, fee, neb, tap, toe, top 4 apex, barb, blow, cant, cave, clue, dump, fall, heel, hint, keel, lean, list, pile, tilt, vail 5 aglet, alist, chape, crown, drink, empty, point, slant, snick, spire, steer, touch, upset 6 aiglet, apices, arista, careen, corona, nozzle, summit, topple, unload 7 crampit, crumshaw, ferrule, incline 8 bakshish, bonamano, gratuity, overturn 9 baksheesh, buona-mano, buona-mani, extremity, overthrow, pourboire, protector 10 intoxicate
near to: 6 apical
off: 4 tell, warn 5 alarm 8 forewarn
over: 5 upset 8 overturn
tip-off: tip 4 hint 7 warning
tiple: 6 fuddle, guitar
tippet: boa, fur 4 barb, cape, hood, rope, ruff 5 amice, scarf, snell 6 almuce, sindon 7 hanging, muffler, patagia(pl.) 8 liripipe, liripoop, palatine, patagium 9 comforter, victorine
tipping: 5 alist 7 ripping, topping
up: 5 atilt
tipple: bib, nip, sip, tip 4 drip, gill, lose, suck, whet 5 drink, spend, upset 6 fuddle, liquor, sipple, tumble 8 overturn
tippled: 5 drank 6 beered
tippler: sot 5 souse, toper, winer 6 tipper, tipple, tumble 7 drinker, whetter 9 draftsman 11 draughtsman
tippy: 5 smart 6 tiptop 7 stylish 8 unsteady
tipstaff: 7 bailiff 9 attendant, constable
tipster: 4 tout 8 dopester 10 forecaster
tipsy: ree 4 awry 5 bosky, drunk, shaky, tippy 6 bungfu, groggy 7 crooked, ebriose, ebrious, foolish, fuddled, muddled, puddled, tipsify 8 unsteady 10 staggering 11 intoxicated
tiptoe: 5 alert, eager 6 roused, warily 7 eagerly, exalted, quietly 8 cautious, stealthy 10 cautiously 11 expectantly
tiptop: 4 best 9 first-rate 11 galumptious
tirade: 6 screed, speech 7 censure 8 harangue, jeremiad 9 philippic
tirailleur: 10 skirmisher 12 sharpshooter
tire: fag, lag, rim 4 band, bore, gnaw, hoop, jade, pall, prey, pull, shoe, tear, tier 5 dress, recap, seize, spare, weary 6 attire, casing, harass, satiate, tucker 7 apparel, exhaust, fatigue, frazzle, vesture 8 decorate, enginery, overwork, pinafore 9 adornment, discharge, equipment, furniture, headdress, tiredness, weariness 12 accouterment
burst: 4 flat 7 blowout
casing: 4 shoe
saver: 5 recap 7 retread
tired: 5 blown, spent, weary 6 aweary, fagged, sleepy 7 wearied 8 fatigued 9 exhausted
out: 5 jaded, spent
tireless: 4 busy 8 untiring 10 unwearying 13 indefatigable
Tiresias: 4 seer 10 soothsayer
blinded by: 6 Athena, Athene
home: 6 Thebes
tiresome: dry 4 dull, tame 6 boring, borish, dreary, prolix 7 irksome, prosaic, tedious 8 annoying, ennuyant 9 fatiguing, wearisome 10 irritating, monotonous 13 uninteresting

tirl: rap, tap 4 bout, turn 5 strip, twirl, twist, whirl 6 divest, rattle, thrill, unroof 7 uncover 9 vibration
tiro: See tyro
tirr: 5 strip 6 unroof 7 uncover, undress
tirrivee: 7 tantrum 9 commotion
tirve: 5 strip 6 unroof 7 uncover
tissue: gum, web 4 tela 5 gauze, sheer, telae, weave 6 girdle, ribbon 7 network 8 meshwork 9 embroider, gauzelike 10 interweave
animal: fat, gum 4 bone, seur, suet 6 paxwax 7 keratin 8 gelatine
connective: 6 stroma, tendon
horny: 7 keratin
human: fat, gum 4 suet, tela 5 fiber 6 albedo, diploe, keloid, stroma, tendon 7 tonsils 8 ligament, stromata 10 aerenchyma
layer of: 6 strata 7 stratum
nerve: 8 ganglion
oily: fat
pert. to: 5 telar
resembling: 7 histoid
vegetable: 4 bast 5 xylem 6 lignin 7 endarch 8 meristem
wasting away of: 8 phthisis
tissue-like: 5 telar
tit: nag, pap, pin, tap, tee, tug 4 bird, blow, draw, girl, jade, jerk, plug, pull, teat, tite, twit 5 horse, woman 6 nipple, twitch 7 titlark 8 titmouse
Titan: Ge 4 Bana, Leto, Rhea 5 Coeus, Creus, Dione, giant, Theia 6 Cronus, Kronos, Pallas, Phoebe, Tethys, Themis 7 Iapetus, Oceanus 8 gigantic, Hyperion 9 extensive, Mnemosyne
father: 6 Uranus
mother: Ge 4 Gaia
Titania's husband: 6 Oberon
titanic: 4 huge 5 great 7 immense 8 colossal, gigantic
titanite: 6 sphene 7 ijolite
tite: 4 soon 7 quickly 8 promptly 11 immediately
tithe: tax 5 teind, tiend, tenth 6 decima 7 decimae, decimal
pert. to: 7 decimal
tithing: 6 borrow, decime, denary 8 decenary 9 decennary
titi: 6 monkey
titillate: 6 excite, tickle 9 stimulate, vellicate
titlark: 4 bird 5 pipit
title: Bey, sir 4 Czar, dame, deed, Duke, Earl, Emir, Khan, King, name, Raja, Shah 5 Baron, claim, Count, friar, Major, Mayor, Noble, right 6 assign, Ensign, Kaiser, Knight, legend, madame, Mikado, notice, Prince, record, squire, Sultan 7 Admiral, ascribe, Baronet, Captain, caption, Emperor, epithet, Esquire, General, heading, Justice, Khedive, Marquis, placard, Viceroy 8 Archduke, document, Governor, Viscount 9 Commander, Commodore, designate, President 10 appelation, capitulate, Lieutenant 11 designation 12 championship, denomination 13 Generalissimo
ecclesiastic: dom, fra 4 abba 8 reverend 10 excellency 11 monseigneur
feminine: 4 dame, lady 5 hanum, madam 6 hanoum, milady, missis, missus 8 mistress
foreign: aga, aya, Dan, don, mir, sha, sri 4 baba, Herr, lars, sidi, shri 5 basha, mirza, mpret, pasha, sayid, senor, shree, sieur 6 bashaw, shogun, squire 7 dominus, effendi 8 monsieur
of Athena: 4 Alea
pert. to: 7 titular
royal: hon., sir 4 sire 5 Grace 8 banneret 9 honorable
titled person: 4 peer 5 noble
titmouse: mag, nun, tit 6 fuffit, puffer, titmal, tomtit, verdin 7 jacksaw, titmall, tomnoup 8 heckimal 9 chickadee, mumruffin
pert. to: 6 parine
titter: 5 laugh 6 giggle, rather, seesaw, sooner, totter, wobble 7 tremble
tittered: 7 giggled, teeheed 9 snickered
tittle: dot, jot 4 iota, sign, whit 5 point, tilde 6 accent, gossip, tattle 7 cedilla, whisper 8 particle
tittup: 5 caper, frisk
titubate: 4 reel 6 totter 7 stagger 8 unsteady 11 vacillating
titular: 7 nominal
Titus Andronicus: *daughter:* 7 Lavinia
queen: 6 Tamora
Tivoli's ancient name: 5 Tibur
tizzy: 4 snit 6 dither 7 anxiety
tmema: 7 section, segment
TNT: 6 trotyl 8 dynamite 14 trinitrotoluol 15 trinitrotoluene
to (see also next entries): tae, 4 till, unto 5 until 6 toward 7 forward
a conclusion: out
a place on: 4 onto
a point on: 4 onto
an end: out
be: 4 esse(L.), etre(F.), sein(G.) 5 einai(Gk.) 6 essere(It.)
be sure: 6 indeed
no extent: not
one side: 5 abeam
position into: 4 into
sheltered side: 4 alec
that time: 5 until
the left: haw 5 aport
the opposite side: 6 across

the point that: 5 until
the rear: 5 arear 6 astern
the victor: 4 aboo
this: 6 hereto
this place: 4 here 6 hither
which: 7 whereto
wit: viz. 6 namely 8 scilicet 9 videlicet
your health: 5 skoal 6 prosit
to-deal, to-dele: 6 divide 8 separate 10 distribute 11 distinguish
to-do: ado 4 fuss, stir 6 bustle 9 commotion
to-draw: 4 pull, tear 7 detract 8 postpone, protract
toa: 7 warrior
toad: ted 4 agua, bufo, hyla, pipa, tade 6 anuran, peeper 7 crapaud, paddock, quilkin 9 amphibian, spadefoot
genus of: 4 bufo, hyla 6 alytes
larva: 7 tadpole 8 polliwog
order: 5 anura
tongueless suborder: 7 aglossa
toadeater: 5 toady 8 hanger-on, parasite 9 dependent, sycophant
toadfish: 4 sapo 6 angler, grubby, puffer, slimer 8 frogfish 10 midshipman
toadflax: 7 ransted 8 gallwort, ramstead, ranstead
toady: 4 fawn, snob, ugly, zany 6 flunky 7 flunkey, hideous, shoneen, truckle 8 bootlick, parasite, truckler 9 flatterer, repulsive, sycophant, toadeater
toast: dry, tan 4 soak, warm 5 brede, brown, drink, melba, parch, roast, skoal, worst 6 birsle, pledge, prosit 7 bristle, carouse, drinker, propose, swindle, tippler 8 cinnamon
kind of: 4 rusk 5 melba 8 zwieback
toasted bread: 6 sippet
toastmaster: M.C. 5 emcee
tobacco: *chewing:* 4 quid
coarse: 7 caporal
disease: 6 calico 7 walloon
flavor mixture: 6 petune
holder: 4 pipe 7 humidor
hookah smoking: 7 goracco
ingredient: 8 nicotine
in pipe-bowl: 6 dottel, dottle
juice: 6 ambeer, ambier
kind of: 4 capa, shag 5 bogie, fogus, tabac 6 Burley, cowpen 7 caporal, henbane, Latakia, perique, Turkish 8 domestic, Virginia 9 salvadora
leaf moistener: 5 caser
low grade: 4 shag
paste: 7 goracco
pile: 4 bulk
receptacle: 4 pipe 7 humidor
roll: 5 cigar, segar 7 carotte
small portion: cud, fid, fig 4 quid 6 dottel, dottle 7 carotte
Tobacco Road: *author:* 8 Caldwell
character: 5 Pearl 6 Jeeter
tobacco smoke hater: 11 misocapnist
Tobias: *father:* 5 Tobit
wife: 4 Sara
Tobit: *place of captivity:* 7 Nineveh
son: 6 Tobias
wife: 4 Anna
toboggan: 4 sled 7 coaster, decline
toby: jug, mug, way 5 cigar, stein 6 street 7 highway, pitcher, robbery
toby-man: 10 highwayman
tocher: dot 5 dower 7 portion
toco: 6 toucan 8 flogging 9 thrashing
tocology, tokology: 9 midwifery 10 obstetrics
tocsin: 4 bell, sign 5 alarm 6 alarum, signal
tod: fox, mat 4 bush, load, pack 5 clump, shrub 6 bundle, weight
today: now 4 here, oggi(It.) 7 present
pert. to: 7 diurnal 9 hodiernal
toddle: go 4 walk 5 dance 6 daddle, diddle, stroll 7 saunter
toddler: tot 4 trot 5 child
tode: 4 boat, haul, sled
toe: paw, tae, tai, tip 5 digit, pivot, reach, touch 7 journal 10 projection
comb. form: 6 dactyl
great: 6 hallux
little: 7 minimus
pert. to: 7 digital
thickening of skin: 4 corn 6 callus
without: 10 adactylous
toehold: 7 footing
toff: 5 bloke, dandy, swell
toffish: 5 smart 7 stylish
tog: 4 coat 5 dress 7 clothes, garment
toga: 4 gown, robe 5 tunic 7 garment
togated: 7 stately 9 dignified
together: mix 5 along, chain, union 6 bedene, fasten, unison 7 alongst, concert, contact, harmony 8 ensemble 9 cojointly, collision, courtship 11 association 12 cohabitation, coincidently 13 companionship, consecutively 14 simultaneously
prefix: co; com, con, syn
toggery: set 4 kind 5 dress 7 clothes, harness 9 trappings 12 haberdashery
toggle, toggel: pin, rod 4 bolt 6 cotter 10 crosspiece
Togo: *capital:* 4 Lome
language: Ewe 4 Mina 6 French
tribe: Ewe 4 Mina 6 Cabrai
togs: 7 clothes 8 clothing
togt: 5 draft, labor 7 drawing 10 enterprise 11 undertaking
togue: 9 namaycush

toil: fag, net, tug 4 drag, mesh, moil, plod, pull, rend, roll, task, trap, work 5 broil, cloth, graft, labor, slave, snare, weary 6 battle, canvas, drudge, effort, entrap, harass, strife, writhe 7 contend, ensnare, network, travail, turmoil 8 distress, drudgery, overwork, struggle, writhing 9 enclosure, wallowing 10 accomplish, contention, employment, occupation
toiler: 7 laborer, plodder, workman
toilet: 5 cloth, dress 6 attire 7 costume 8 bathroom, grooming, toilette 9 cleansing
case: 4 etui 5 etwee
toilsome: 4 hard 7 arduous 9 laborious, wearisome
toise: eye 4 look 6 extend 7 stretch
toit: 4 seat 6 dawdle, settle, totter 7 hassock, saunter
tokalon: 6 beauty 9 beautiful
Tokay: 4 wine 5 grape
token: 4 gift, mark, omen, sign 5 badge, check, medal, merit, proof 6 amulet, emblem, hansel, ostent, pledge, signal, symbol 7 betoken, betroth, feature, handsel, memento, portent, presage, signify 8 accolade, evidence, forbysen, keepsake, souvenir, tessella 9 character, symbolize 10 denotation, expression, indication, prognostic 14 characteristic
affection: 6 amoret, mascot 7 handsel 8 accolade
office: 5 badge
servitude: 4 yoke
victory: 4 palm
toko: 4 shop 5 store 8 flogging
Tokyo: Edo 4 Yedo
tolbooth, tollbooth: 4 city, hall, jail, town 5 burgh 6 prison 9 tollhouse 11 customhouse
toldo: hut 4 tent
tole: 5 decoy 6 allure, entice
tolerable: gey 4 fair, so-so 8 bearable, passable 9 allowance, endurable 10 sufferable 11 comportable, supportable, translation 13 entertainment
tolerably: 5 geyah 6 fairly, pretty 7 gaylies, geylies 10 moderately
tolerance: 9 allowance, endurance, variation 10 indulgence 11 forbearance 13 understanding
tolerant: 5 broad 7 lenient, patient 8 enduring 9 indulgent 10 ecumenical 11 forebearing
tolerate: 4 bear, bide 5 abide, allow, broad, brook, stand 6 endure, permit, resist, suffer
toll: due, tax 4 chum, drag, draw, duty, lure, peal, pull, rent, ring 5 annul, decoy, knell, sound 6 allure, charge, custom, entice, excise, impost, invite, vacate 7 scatter, trewage 8 announce, exaction 10 assessment 12 compensation
gatherer: 8 customer, publican 9 collector 11 taxgatherer
kind of: 6 caphar 7 tronage 9 chiminage 10 ballastage
weight: 7 tronage
tolls: 4 dues
tolly: 4 cane 5 spire 6 candle
Toltec: 7 Nahuatl 9 Nahuatlan
site of ruins: 4 Tula
tolu: 6 balsam
toluic acid: 7 toluate
tolypeutine: 4 apar 9 armadillo
Tom of Lincoln: 4 bell
Tom Sawyer: *aunt:* 5 Polly
author: 5 Twain
brother: Sid
girl friend: 5 Becky
pal: 15 Huckleberry Finn
Tom Thumb: 5 dwarf 6 midget
Tom Tulliver's river: 5 Floss
tomahawk: ax; axe, cut 4 kill 6 assail, attack, strike 7 hatchet 9 criticize
toman: 4 coin 5 mound 6 weight 7 hillock 8 division
tomato: 9 loveapple
relish: 6 catsup 7 ketchup
sauce: 6 catsup 7 ketchup
soup: 6 bisque 8 gazpacho
tomb: 4 bury 5 grave, house, huaca, speos, vault 6 burial, casket, cavity, entomb, hearse 7 chamber 8 catacomb, cenotaph, monument 9 sepulcher, tombstone
empty: 8 cenotaph
for bones: 7 ossuary
kind of: 4 cist 7 tritaph 8 cistvaen, kistvaen 9 mauseleum 11 sarcophagus
saint's: 6 shrine
tombe: 4 drum
tomboy: meg 5 rowdy 6 harlot, hoiden, hoyden 8 strumpet
tombstone: 5 stele 8 monument 9 headstone 10 gravestone
Tombstone marshal: 4 Earp 5 Wyatt
tomcat: gib
tome: 4 book 5 atlas 6 ledger, letter, volume 12 encyclopedia
tomfool: 4 fool 5 clown 6 stupid 7 buffoon, doltish, foolish, half-wit 8 rainbird 9 blockhead 10 flycatcher
tomfoolery: 8 nonsense 9 silliness
tommyrot: 8 nonsense 9 silliness
tomorrow: 6 domani(It.), manana(Sp.)
ton: 4 lots, mode 5 heaps, style, tunny, vogue 7 fashion
tonant: 7 blatant
tonca, tonka: 4 bean
wood: 6 camara

tone: 4 mood, note, tint 5 pitch, shade, sound, trend 6 accent, effect, intone, modify, temper, timbre 7 quality 8 coloring, mitigate, modulate 9 character, harmonize 10 atmosphere, inflection, intonation, modulation 12 modification
down: 4 mute 6 soften
lacking: 5 atony 6 atonal, atonic
musical: 5 siren, syren 6 sirene
of cord: 8 concento
quality: 6 timbre
rapid: 7 tremolo
sharp: 4 tang
single: 8 monotone
singsong: 4 sugh 5 sough
succession: 5 melos
system of: 6 tonart
thin: 7 sfogato
third of diatonic scale: 7 mediant
vibrant: 5 twang
tone arm: 6 pickup
tone color: 6 timbre
toneless: 5 atony
tones: *combination of:* 5 chord
series of: 5 scale
Tonga island: Ono
tongs: 5 clamp 6 tenail 7 forceps, pincers, tueiron 8 tenaille
tongue: gab 4 bark, chib, fame, flap, howl, pole, sole, vote 5 chide, clack, lingo, prate, scold, speak, utter 6 report 7 beeweed, dialect, feather, lingula 8 language, lingulae, reproach, suffrage 9 pronounce
bone: 5 hyoid
classical: 5 Greek, Latin 6 Hebrew
comb. form: 6 glosso
disease: 5 agrom
Jesus': 7 Aramaic
mother: 10 vernacular
oxcart: 4 cope
pert. to: 7 glossal, lingual
pivoted: 4 pawl
projection: 7 papilla 8 papillae(pl.)
sacred: 4 Pali
seam: 5 raphe
serpent: 4 fang
tip of: 6 corona
wagon: 4 neap, pole
tongue-lash: 5 baste, scold
tongue-like: 7 lingual
tongued: 6 prated
tongueless: 4 dumb, mute 10 speechless
tonic: 5 aloes 6 bracer 7 bracing 8 medicine, roborant 9 sassafras, stimulant 10 refreshing 11 corroborant 12 invigorating
kind of: 4 dope 6 catnip 7 boneset, nervine
tonic leaf: 4 coca
toning down: 10 modulation
Tonkin See North Vietnam
tonlet: 4 band
tonsil: 5 gland 8 amygdala
inflammation: 6 quinsy
operation: 12 tonsilectomy 13 tonsillectomy
tonsorialist: 6 barber
tonsure: 5 shave 6 barber 7 haircut
tonsured: 4 bald 5 shorn 6 pilled, shaven 7 clipped
tony: 5 smart 7 stylish
too: and, tae 4 also, over, very 6 overly 7 besides 8 likewise 9 extremely 11 exceedingly, excessively 13 superfluously
bad: 4 alas
late: 5 tardy 7 belated
much: 7 nimiety
small to matter: 13 inappreciable
soon: 9 premature
tool (see also **instrument**)**:** ax; adz, axe, saw 4 adze, draw, dupe, file, form, ride 5 drive, plane, shape, sword 6 convey, device, finish, hammer, manage, puppet, weapon 7 cat's-paw, hatchet, utensil 8 ornament 9 appliance, implement 10 manipulate
abrading: 4 file
biting edge: bit
bookbinding: 5 gouge
boring: awl, bit 5 auger, drill 6 gimlet, reamer 7 bradawl
box: see *chest* below
bricklayer: 4 hock 5 float, level 6 hammer, trowel
butcher: saw 5 knife, steel 6 skewer, skiver 7 cleaver
carpenter: ax; bit, saw 4 rasp 5 auger, level, plane, punch 6 chisel, gimlet, hammer, pliers, square 7 handsaw, hatchet, scriber
chest: kit
chopping: 7 dolabra
cobbler's: awl 6 hammer
cultivating: 4 plow 6 harrow, plough 7 leveler
cutting: ax, adz, axe, bit, hob, saw 4 adze 5 bezel, bezil, gouge, knife, plane, razor 6 chisel, graver, reamer, shears
edged: ax; axe 4 adze 5 knife, razor 6 chisel, reamer
engraver's: 5 burin
excavating: 4 pick 6 pickax, shovel
flat: 7 spatula
garden: hoe 4 rake 5 edger, mower 6 sickle, trowel, weeder
gripping: 4 vise 5 clamp, tongs 7 pincers
hole-making: 6 dibble
kind of: awl, fid, fro, loy, tap, zax 4 celt, file, lute, sley 5 burin, edger, flail, lathe, loper, peavy, peevy, punch 6 chisel, cranny, eo-

lith, flange, lifter, peavey, peevey, pommel, taster, trepan, trowel 7 setiron 8 burgoyne 12 straightedge
marble worker's: 6 fraise
mason's: 6 chisel
mining: gad 4 pick
molding: die
pointed: awl, fid, gad 4 barb, brod, brog, pick 6 gimlet, stylet
pounding: 6 pestle
prehistoric: 4 celt 6 eolith 9 paleolith 10 palaoelith
set: kit
shaping: 5 lathe, swage
slate-measuring: 7 scantle
smoothing: 4 file 5 plane 7 sleeker
splitting: 4 froe, frow
temperer: 8 hardener
trimming: ax; axe, saw 6 shears 8 clippers, scissors
woodworking: adz 4 adze 7 edgeman, grainer, scauper, scriber 10 spokeshave
tool handle: *end* 4 butt
fitted part: 4 tang
tools: tew 4 gear 7 gibbles(Sc.)
toom: 4 lank, lean, pour 5 empty 7 leisure
toomly: 4 idly 6 vainly 7 emptily 9 leisurely
toorie: 4 heap, knob 5 tower 6 tassel
toorock: 4 heap 5 tower
toosh: 4 gown, robe 9 nightgown
toot: pry, spy 4 blow, fool, gaze, peep 5 blast, draft, drink, shout, sound, spree 6 spread, sprout 7 carouse, trumpet, whistle 8 carousal, eminence, proclaim 9 elevation
tooter: spy 7 lookout 8 watchman 9 trumpeter
tooth (see also **teeth**): cog, jag 4 bite, dent, fang, jagg, snag, tine, tusk 5 molar, point, prong 6 cuspid, indent 7 consume, grinder, incisor, snaggle 10 projection
canine: 4 tush 6 cuspid, holder 7 laniary
combining form: 6 odonto
diminutive: 13 denticulation
double: 5 molar
drawer: 7 dentist
edge: 7 dentate
facing: 6 enamel
fore: 5 biter 6 cutter
gear wheel: cog 4 dent, tine
grinding surface: 5 mensa
having but one: 8 monodont
tooth covering: 6 enamel
tooth decay: 6 caries 8 cavities 11 saprodontia
tooth for tooth: 6 talion
toothache: 4 worm(Sc.) 8 dentagra 10 odontalgia
toothed: *irregularly:* 5 erose
on edge: 8 serrated
toothful: sip 4 bite 5 drink 6 tipple 9 toothsome
toothless: 4 weak 6 futile 7 edental 8 decrepit, edentate 9 infantile 10 agomphious, edentulate
toothsome: 5 tasty 8 pleasing 9 agreeable, delicious, palatable
toozoo: 8 ringdove
top: ace, cap, fid, lid, tip, toy 4 acme, apex, crop, head, knap, lead, peak, pick, tent, tilt, tuft 5 caput, cream, crest, crown, drain, drink, equal, excel, outdo, prune, ridge, upset 6 apices(pl.), better, capote, culmen, exceed, finial, summit, swells, topple, tumble, upside, vertex, zenith 7 gyrator, highest, surpass, topmost 8 covering, dominate, forelock, foremost, pinnacle, surmount, vertexes(pl.), vertices(pl.) 9 uppermost 10 pre-eminent 11 aristocrats
altar: 5 mensa
head: 4 pate 5 scalp
of card suit: ace
of wave: 5 crest
toy: 8 teetotum
wooden stand: 5 criss
top-hole: 6 tiptop 9 excellent 10 first-class
top kick: 8 sergeant
top-notch: 4 best 6 tiptop 7 highest 9 first-rate 11 unsurpassed
topaz: gem 5 stone
symbol of: 8 fidelity
topaz humming bird: ani, ava 4 avas(pl.), aves(pl.)
topcoat: 6 reefer 8 overcoat
tope: 4 butt, wren 5 clump, drink, grove, shark, stupa 6 guzzle 7 dogfish, orchard
topechee: 12 artilleryman
topee, topi: cat, hat 6 helmet
toper: sot 5 shark 6 boozer, bouser 7 tippler, tosspot 8 drunkard
tophaceous: 5 rough, sandy, stony 6 gritty
tophet, topheth: 4 hell 5 chaos 8 darkness 9 confusion
topi: cap, hat 5 topee 6 helmet 8 antelope
topic: 4 item, text 5 issue, thema, theme 6 reason, remedy 7 heading, subject, themata 8 argument 11 application 13 consideration
topic of discourse: 5 theme
topical: 5 local 9 temporary
topknot: 4 hair, head, tuft 5 crest, onkos 7 commode 8 flounder 9 headdress
toplofty: 5 lofty 7 haughty 10 disdainful 12 contemptuous, supercilious
topmost: 6 apical 7 highest 9 uppermost
topnotcher: ace 4 hero, star
topper: hat 5 cover, float 6 stower 7 cheater, snuffer, topcoat 10 high-rigger 11 highclimber

toppiece: 4 head 6 toupee 11 masterpiece
topping: 4 bran, fine, good 5 icing, proud 6 refuse, tiptop 7 forlock, gallant, highest, topknot, topmost 8 arrogant, pleasant, superior 9 excellent, first-rate, skimmings 11 pretentious
topple: tip 4 fall, tilt 5 pitch, upset 6 totter, tumble 7 overset 8 overhang, overturn 9 overthrow 10 somersault 11 overbalance
toppy: 5 showy 7 stylish
tops: 4 A-one, aces, best 7 supreme
topsman: 5 chief 6 drover 7 hangman, headman
topsy-turvy: 8 confused 10 disordered 11 widdershins, withershins
toque: hat 6 bonnet 9 headdress
tor: taw 4 crag, hill, peak 5 mound 8 pinnacle
tora, torah: law 5 tetel 7 precept 10 hartebeest, Pentateuch, revelation 11 instruction
torch: 4 lamp 5 blaze, brand, flare, fusee 7 lucigen 8 flambeau 8 flambeaux(pl.) 10 flashlight
frame: 7 cresset
tore: 4 knob, plod 5 grass 6 pommel 9 persevere
toreador: 11 bullfighter
torero: 11 bullfighter
torii: 7 gateway
torment: rib, vex 4 bait, pain, rack 5 agony, annoy, chevy, chivy, devil, force, grill, harry, tease, wrack 6 badger, chivvy, harass, harrow, hector, misery, pester, plague, strain 7 afflict, agitate, anguish, bedevil, crucify, distort, hagride, hatchel, tempest, torture, travail 8 distress, vexation 9 martyrdom, suffering, tantalize 10 cruciation 11 persecution
tormenting: 6 plaguy, vexing 9 harassing 11 troublesome
tormina: 5 colic, pains 6 cramps
torn: 4 rent 5 riven 6 broken, ripped 9 lacerated
tornado: 4 wind 6 squall 7 cyclone, thunder, twister 9 hurricane, whirlwind, windstorm 12 thunderstorm
Tornado Junction: 8 Trinidad
toro: 4 bull, tree 7 cavalla, cowfish
torous, torose: 6 brawny 7 bulging, knobbed, swollen 8 muscular 11 protuberant
torpedinous: 9 benumbing 10 stupefying
torpedo: 4 mine, ruin 5 wreck 6 attack, benumb, damage, gunman 7 destroy, explode, shatter 8 firework, gangster, numbfish, paralyze 9 crampfish, detonator
front end: 4 nose
torpedo fish: ray
torpid: 4 boat, dull, numb 5 inert 6 stupid 7 dormant, torpent 8 benumbed, inactive, lifeless, sluggish 9 apathetic, lethargic
torpor: 4 coma 5 sleep 6 acedia, apathy, stupor 7 accidie 8 dormancy, dullness, lethargy 10 inactivity, stagnation 12 sluggishness 13 insensibility
torque: bee 5 chain, sarpe, twist 6 collar
torrefy, torrify: dry 5 parch, roast 6 scorch
torrent: 4 flow, rush 5 flood, parch, roast, spate 6 stream 7 burning, channel, consume, current, roaring, rushing 8 downpour 9 impetuous
torrential: 10 outpouring 12 overwhelming
torrid: hot 4 arid 5 dried 6 ardent 7 burning, parched, zealous 8 inflamed, parching, scorched 9 scorching 10 oppressive, passionate
Torrid Zone boundary: 6 Tropic
tortoise: 6 turtle 8 terrapin 9 chelonian
genus: 4 emys
kind: 4 emyd 5 giant 9 Galapagos
marsh: 6 gopher 7 elodian
order of: 8 chelonia
pert. to: 9 chelonian
shell: 8 carapace
tortuosity: 4 bend, turn 5 twist 7 flexure, winding 9 sinuosity 10 distortion 11 crookedness, deviousness
tortuous: 6 cranky, spiral 7 crooked, devious, immoral, sinuate, sinuous, winding, wriggly 8 wrongful 9 deceitful, injurious 10 circuitous, roundabout 11 anfractuous 12 labyrinthine
torture: 4 pain, rack 5 agony, twist, wheel 6 punish, wrench 7 agonize, anguish, crucify, distort, torment 8 distress, twisting 9 martyrdom 10 affliction, cruciation, distortion, excruciate, perversion, punishment
device: 4 rack
torus: 6 baston 7 molding 9 elevation 12 protuberance
torvity: 8 grimness, severity 9 sternness
torvous: 4 grim 5 stern 6 severe
tory: 6 bandit, outlaw, Papist 8 loyalist, marauder, Royalist 11 reactionary 12 conservative
Tosca's love: 5 Mario
tosh: 4 bath, bosh, neat, tidy 5 souse, trash 6 drench, neatly 7 bathtub 8 familiar, intimate, nonsense 10 intimately
toss: cob, cup, lob 4 cast, cave, flip, hike, hurl, rear, roll 5 chuck, flick, fling, flirt, heave, pitch, raise, serve, throw, wager 6 buffet, chance, fillip, harass, tossup, totter, uplift 7 agitate, disturb 8 disquiet 9 agitation, commotion 10 excitement
a coin: 4 flap, flip

about: **5** bandy **6** thrash, thresh
carelessly: **4** flip
head in derision: **4** geck
side to side: **6** careen
together confusedly: **8** scramble

tosspot: sot **5** toper **7** drinker **8** drunkard
bottle: **6** flagon

tosticate: **6** harass **8** distract **10** intoxicate

tosto: **4** fast **5** quick

tosy: **4** snug **10** comforting **11** intoxicated

tot: add, cup **4** item, note **5** child, count, drink, total, totum **6** amount, toddle, totter, tottum **7** jotting, toddler **8** exercise

tota: **6** grivet, monkey

total: add, all, sum, tot **4** full **5** gross, utter, whole **6** abrupt, amount, entire **7** concise, perfect, summary **8** absolute, complete, entirety **9** aggregate, undivided **10** accumulate

totality: all, sum **6** amount **7** allness **8** entirety **9** aggregate, wholeness **10** altogether

totally: **5** quite **6** wholly **8** entirely **10** altogether, completely

tote: all, lug, tot **4** bear, haul, lead, load **5** carry, count, total **6** handle, reckon **7** conduct **9** abstainer, transport

totem: **6** emblem, fetich, fetish, figure

totem post: xat

toto: **4** baby

totter: **4** fall, hang, reel, rock, sway, toss **5** pitch, shake, swing, waver **6** dodder, falter, quiver, seesaw, staver(Sc.), toddle **7** fribble, stagger, tremble **8** titubate, unstable, unsteady **9** vacillate

tottering: **4** fall **5** shaky **6** groggy **7** adverse, rickety, shaking **8** collapse, unsteady, wavering **9** faltering **10** changeable **11** threatening, vacillating

tottery: **4** weak **5** shaky **8** unsteady **9** tottering

tottle: **4** boil, purl **5** count, total **6** reckon, simmer, toddle, topple, totter **9** reckoning

tottlish: **7** tottery **8** unsteady

tottum, totum: all, tot **5** child, whole

totty: **4** weak **5** child, dotty, shaky **7** tottery **8** unsteady **9** befuddled

toty: **7** laborer **9** messenger

toucan: **4** toco **7** aracari **8** hornbill **13** constellation

touch: dab, hit, rap, rob, tag, tap, tig, toe, use **4** abut, blow, feel, meet, rape **5** equal, reach, rival, steal, taste, trait **6** accuse, adjoin, affect, attain, border, borrow, extend, handle, molest, rebuke, strike, stroke **7** attinge, censure, contact, impinge, palpate, partake **8** perceive **9** mishandle
boundary line: **4** abut
closely: **8** osculate
clumsily: paw
combining form: tac
for medical diagnosis: **7** palpate
lightly: **5** brush **7** attinge, twiddle
measuring device: **10** haptometer
off: **4** fire **5** start
organ of: **4** palp **6** feeler **7** antenna
perceptible by: **7** tactile **8** palpable
pert. to: **6** haptic **7** tactile, tactual

touching: **4** upon **6** moving **7** contact, meeting, tangent **8** adjacent, pathetic **9** affecting, attingent, conjoined **10** contacting, contiguous, contingent
a single point: **7** tangent

touchstone: **4** test **8** basanite, standard **9** criterion

touchwood: **4** funk, punk **5** sponk, spunk **6** amadou, tinder **8** punkwood

touchy: **4** sore **5** cross, risky, snaky, techy, testy **7** peevish **8** ticklish **9** irascible, irritable, sensitive **10** precarious **11** inflammable **13** over-sensitive

tough: **4** thug, wiry **5** hardy, rigid, rough, rowdy, stiff **6** brutal, robust, sinewy, sticky, strong **7** hickory, ruffian, violent, viscous **8** cohesive, enduring, hardened, leathery, rowdyish, stubborn, sturdily, toilsome, vigorous **9** difficult, glutinous, obstinate, ruffianly **10** aggressive, unyielding
and lean: **5** scrag **6** sinewy

tough-minded: **6** shrewd **7** willful **8** stubborn **9** practical, realistic **10** hardheaded **13** unsentimental

toughen: **5** inure **6** anneal, endure, temper

toughened: **5** clung **8** hardened, tempered

toupee: wig **6** peruke **7** periwig

tour: go **4** trip, turn **5** cover, drive, range, round, shift, spell, trick, watch **6** course, travel **7** circuit, compass, journey, proceed **9** barnstorm, excursion **10** appearance, revolution

tourbillion: **5** whirl **6** vortex **8** firework **9** whirlwind

tourelle: **5** tower **6** turret

tourist: **8** traveler

tourmaline: **6** schorl **9** rubellite

tournament: **4** tilt **5** joust, sport, trial **6** battle **7** contest, tourney **9** encounter

tourney: **10** tournament

tournure: pad **6** bustle

touse: **4** fuss, pull, rack, tear **5** worry **6** handle, rumple, tousel, tousle, tussle **7** turmoil **8** dishevel **11** disturbance

tousle, tousel: **4** drag, muss, pull, tear **5** touse **6** ruffle, rumple, tussle **7** rummage **8** dishevel, disorder

tousy: **5** rough **6** shaggy **7** tangled, tousled

tout: spy, vex 4 peep, peer, puff, toot 5 tease, thief, watch 6 praise 7 canvass, lookout, solicit, tipster, touting 8 informer, proclaim, smuggler 9 importune, recommend
tove: 4 emit 5 smoke
tow: tew, tug 4 drag, draw, flax, haul, lead, pull, rope 5 barge, chain 6 hawser 7 towboat, towrope, tugboat 8 cordelle
tow-row: 6 rumpus, uproar 9 racketing
toward: by; tae(Sc.) 4 near 5 anent 6 anenst, coming, future, onward 7 forward, willing 8 imminent, obliging 9 compliant, promising, tractable 11 approaching
center: 5 entad
exterior: 5 ectad
mouth: 4 orad
prefix: ob, oc
stern: aft 5 abaft 6 astern
towardly: 6 docile, gentle, kindly 7 affable 9 compliant, favorable, tractable 10 propitious
towel: dry, rub 5 cloth 6 napkin 8 vesperal 9 handcloth
fabric: 4 huck 5 linen, terry
tower: 4 rise, silo, soar 5 broch, exalt, mount, pylon, raise, reach, sikar, spire, stupa 6 ascend, belfry, castle, donjon, pagoda, prison, turret 7 bastile, bulwark, citadel, clocher, defense, elevate, mansion, minaret, mirador, overtop, shikara, steeple, surpass, zikurat 8 bastille, domineer, fortress, zuggurat, zikkurat 9 campanile 10 protection, stronghold
bell: 6 belfry 9 campanile
castle: 6 donjon
church: 5 spire 7 steeple
famous: 4 Pisa 5 Babel, Minar 6 Eiffel, London
glacier ice: 5 serac
kind of: 5 ivory
mosque: 7 minaret
signal: 6 beacon
small: 6 turret
towering: 4 high, tall 5 great, lofty, steep 7 eminent, intense, violent 11 overweening
towhee: 7 bunting, chewink
town: 4 burg, city, dorp, farm, stad, vill, yard 5 bourg, burgh, court, derby, house, manor, ville(F.), voter 6 ciudad(Sp.), garden, hamlet, parish, podunk, staple 7 borough, burgess, citizen, cluster, village 8 bourgade, township 9 enclosure, farmstead 10 electorate, metropolis 11 aggregation
Attic: 4 deme
official: 6 grieve
pert. to: 5 civic, urban 7 oppidon
plan: 4 plat
small: 11 whistle-stop
witch: 5 Salem
townsman: cit 7 citizen, oppidan 9 selectman 10 inhabitant
township: 4 area 8 district
toxic: 9 poisonous
toxophilite: 6 archer
toy: pet, top 4 ball, daff, doll, fool, play, whim 5 antic, dally, fancy, flirt, panda, sport 6 bauble, finger, gewgaw, hoople, rattle, trifle 7 caprice, conceit, pastime, trinket 8 aversion, flirting, gimcrack, interest, mistress, ornament, teetotum, weakling 9 bandalore, dalliance, headdress, plaything, rattlebox, teddybear 10 knickknack
toyish: 6 wanton 7 playful, trivial, useless 8 sportive, trifling 9 fantastic, frivolous, whimsical 13 unsubstantial
toze: 4 comb, pull 5 tease 11 disentangle
trabant: 9 attendant, bodyguard
trabea: 4 toga
trabeation: 6 beamed 11 entablature
trabuco: 5 cigar 11 blunderbuss
trace: 4 clew, clue, copy, draw, fall, file, hint, line, mark, nose, path, road, seek, sign, step, tang, walk 5 grain, march, probe, route, shade, tinge, track, trail, tread 6 amount, deduce, derive, detect, follow, locate, ramble, sketch, trudge 7 conduct, glimpse, impress, imprint, inquire, outline, remnant, soupcon, uncover, vestige 8 discover, evidence, quantity, traverse 9 ascertain, attribute, delineate, establish, footprint, scintilla 10 indication, procession 11 investigate
tracer: 5 horse 6 bullet, gilder, stylus 7 stainer 9 draftsman
trachea: 4 duct 8 windpipe
trachyte: 6 domite
tracing: 4 copy 6 record 8 ergogram 10 cardiogram
track: rut, way 4 drag, draw, hunt, line, mark, oval, path, rail, road, wake 5 march, route, scent, sight, spoor, trace, trail, tread 6 course, follow, infuse, pursue, teapot, travel 7 circuit, conduct, vestige 8 guideway, sequence, speedway, trackage, traverse 9 ascertain, footprint, spectacle 10 cinder path, succession
animal: run 4 slot 5 spoor
down: 4 hunt 6 pursue, search
official: 5 judge, timer 7 referee, starter
race: 4 mile 5 relay 6 sprint
ship: 4 wake
train: 4 rail 6 siding
tracker: 5 guide, tower
tract (see also **land**): 4 area, mark, path, zone 5 campo, clime, essay, lapse, range, trace, track 6 course, estate, extent, region 7 country, expanse, leaflet, pteryla, quar-

ter, stretch 8 brochure, district, duration, pamphlet, sequence, treatise 9 lineament, narrative, territory 10 exposition 11 subdivision 12 dissertation

tractable: 4 easy 6 docile, gentle, pliant 7 ductile, flexile 8 amenable, flexible, obedient, workable 9 adaptable, compliant, malleable 10 governable

tractate: 5 essay, tract 8 handling, treatise 9 treatment 10 discussion 12 dissertation

tractile: 6 pliant 7 ductile, tensile

traction: 5 power 7 drawing, utility 8 friction 9 influence 10 attraction

tractor: 9 agrimotor

trade: buy, way 4 chap, chop, deal, fuss, path, sell, swap, work 5 cheap, craft, habit, track, trail, tread 6 action, barter, bother, course, employ, manner, method, metier, scorse 7 bargain, calling, dealing, pursuit, traffic 8 activity, business, commerce, exchange, practice, purchase 10 handicraft, occupation, profession 11 intercourse, nundination

association: NAM 5 hansa, hanse

combination: 4 gild 5 guild, hanse 6 cartel, merger

pert. to: 10 emporeutic

unlawful: 10 contraband

votes: 7 logroll

trademark: 5 brand

trader: 6 dealer, monger, seller, slaver, sutler 7 chapman 8 barterer, merchant 9 tradesman 10 shopkeeper

tradesman: 5 buyer 7 artisan, workman 8 merchant 9 craftsman 10 shopkeeper 11 storekeeper

supply: 4 line 5 stock 9 inventory

trading post: P.X. 7 station

trading stamp: 7 premium

tradition: 4 code, lore 6 belief, custom, legend 8 practice 9 surrender 10 convention

traduce: 4 slur 5 abuse, belie 6 debase, defame, malign, vilify 7 asperse, blacken, detract, pervert, slander 8 disgrace 10 calumniate

traffic: buy 4 coup, sell 5 trade 6 barter, market 7 chaffer, dealing 8 business, commerce, exchange 11 intercourse

in holy offices: 6 simony

violator: 9 jaywalker

trafficker: 6 dealer, trader 8 merchant

in narcotics: 6 pusher

tragacanth: gum 4 tree 5 shrub

tragedy: 6 buskin, misery 8 calamity, disaster 10 misfortune

Muse: 9 Melpomene

tragic: sad 4 dire 5 fatal 7 doleful 8 mournful, pathetic, terrible

tragopan: 8 pheasant

tragule: 4 deer 10 chevrotain

trail: lag 4 drag, draw, hang, hunt, mark, path, slot, tail, wake 5 blaze, drail, piste, route, scent, spoor, trace, track, train, tramp, troll 6 camino(Sp.), course, follow, trapse 7 draggle, dwindle, traipse 8 footpath, straggle

blazer: 7 pioneer

marker: 5 cairn

trailer: 4 vine

truck: 4 semi

train: row 4 bait, drag, draw, file, form, gait, lead, line, lure, rack, rank, rear, tail, trap 5 breed, coach, decoy, drawl, drill, flier, guide, local, seine, snare, suite, teach, trace, trail 6 allure, coffle, convoy, cradle, direct, entice, ground, scheme, school, series, shaped 7 caravan, conduct, cortege, educate, prepare, retinue 8 accustom, artifice, equipage, instruct, protract, rehearse, sequence, trickery 9 condition, entourage, following, strategem, treachery 10 attendants, conveyance, discipline, procession 11 streamliner 13 accommodation

end car of: 7 caboose

fast: 7 express, limited

horses: 6 manege

men: 4 crew

of attendants: 5 suite 7 retinue 9 entourage

overhead: el 8 elevated, monorail

slow: 5 local

underground: 4 tube 5 metro(F.) 6 subway

trained: 4 bred 5 aimed 8 educated

trainee: 5 pupil 6 novice 10 apprentice

trainer: 5 tamer 7 lanista 11 gymnasiarch

training: 4 diet 5 drill 8 breeding, exercise 9 education 10 background, discipline 11 supervision

lack of: 11 inappetence

manual: 5 sloid, sloyd

traipse, trapes: gad 4 walk 5 trail, tramp, tread 6 trudge, wander 8 gadabout, slattern

trait: 4 line, mark, note, thew 5 touch 6 streak, stroke 7 feature, quality 9 lineament, mannerism 11 peculiarity 14 characteristic

traitor: 5 Judas 8 betrayer, Iscariot, renegade

Norweigian: 8 Quisling

traitorous: 5 false 9 faithless, felonious 11 disaffected, treacherous, treasonable

traject: way 4 cast 5 ferry, route, throw 6 course 7 passage 8 transmit

trajet: way 5 route 6 course 7 passage, traject

tralatitious: 12 metaphorical

tram, trame: car, leg 4 beam, haul, limb 5 bench, shaft, wagon 6 thread 7 tramcar, trammel, tramway, trolley 9 streetcar 10 conveyance
tier: 4 deck
trammel: net, tie 4 clog, lock 5 check, gauge 6 braids, fasten, fetter, hamper, impede 7 compass, confine, pothook, prevent, shackle, tresses 8 restrain 9 intercept, plaitings 10 instrument
tramontane: 4 boor 5 alien 7 foreign 8 stranger 9 barbarous 10 outlandish 11 transalpine
tramp: bo; boe, bum, vag 4 hike, hobo, hoof, prog, step, tart, vamp, walk 5 caird, jaunt, tread 6 gaycat, trapes, travel, trudge, waffie, wander 7 steamer, traipse, vagrant 8 vagabond 9 excursion 10 prostitute 11 bindle stiff
baggage: 6 bindle
offering to: 7 handout
trample: 4 foil, hurt 5 crush, tread 6 injure 7 destroy, violate
trance: 4 coma, daze 5 spell, swoon 6 prance, raptus, stupor 7 ecstasy, enchant, passage 8 entrance 9 catalepsy, enrapture 10 passageway
traneen: bit 6 trifle
tranquil: 4 calm, cool, easy, even, mild 5 equal, quiet, still 6 gentle, placid, serene, steady 7 equable, pacific, restful 8 composed, peaceful 9 sedentary 10 motionless 11 undisturbed 13 imperturbable
tranquility, tranquillity: kef, kif 5 peace, quiet 8 serenity 10 equanimity 12 peacefulness
tranquilize: 4 lull 5 allay 6 settle, soften, soothe 7 appease, assuage 9 alleviate
transact: do 5 treat 7 conduct, perform 8 complete, transfer 9 negotiate
transaction: 4 deal, sale 6 action, affair 7 bargain 8 business 10 proceeding 11 proposition
unlawful: 10 chevisance
Transcaspian capital: 9 Ashkhabad
Transcaucasia: See **Armenia, Azerbaijan, Georgia**
transcend: 5 climb, excel, mount, raise 6 ascend, exceed 7 elevate, surpass 8 outstrip, overstep, surmount
transcendent: 8 superior 13 extraordinary
transcendental: 5 ideal 8 ethereal 10 superhuman 12 metaphysical, supersensual, supranatural
transcribe: 4 copy 5 write 6 impute, record 7 ascribe, imitate 9 reproduce, translate 10 paraphrase
transcript: 6 record 8 apograph 9 duplicate 12 reproduction
transfer: 4 cede, deed, move, pass, sale, send 5 carry, grant, shift 6 assign, attorn, change, convey, decant, demise, depute, remove 7 dispose 8 alienate, delegate 9 translate, transport 10 abalienate 12 transmission 13 transposition
bus or train: 6 ticket
design: 5 decal
of court suit: 7 remover
property: 4 deed 5 grant 6 convey
transference: 7 passage 10 conveyance
transfigure: 5 exalt 7 glorify 8 idealize 9 transform 12 metamorphose
transfix: fix, pin 5 spear, stick 6 fasten, impale, pierce 11 transpierce
transform: 4 turn 5 alter 6 change 7 convert 9 transmute 11 transfigure 12 metamorphose, transmogrify
transformation: 10 conversion 13 metamorphosis
into human form: 17 anthropomorphosis
transfuse: 5 imbue 6 infuse 7 instill 8 transfer, transmit
transgress: err, sin 5 break, cross 6 offend 7 disobey, violate 8 overstep
transgression: 5 crime, fault 7 misdeed 8 trespass 10 infraction 12 infringement 13 contravention
transient: 8 fleeting, fugitive 9 ephemeral, itinerant, migratory, momentary, temporary, transeunt 10 evanescent, shortlived, transitory 11 impermanent
transit: 6 change 7 passage 10 conveyance, transition 12 thoroughfare
coach: bus
transition: 5 phase, shift 9 metabasis 10 conversion
transitive: 7 flowing 12 transitional
transitory: 5 brief, fleet 8 caducous, temporal 9 ephemeral, temporary 10 evanescent
translate: 4 read, rede 6 change, decode, remove, render 7 convert 8 construe, decipher, entrance, transfer 9 enrapture, interpret 10 paraphrase
translation: 4 pony, trot 7 version 9 rendition 10 paraphrase 14 interpretation 15 transliteration
translucent: 6 limpid 9 alabaster 11 perspicuous, transparent
transmigration: 7 samsara
transmit: 4 emit, hand, send 5 carry, relay 6 convey, render 7 conduct, devolve, forward 8 bequeath 11 communicate
transmutation: 9 evolution
transmute: 6 change 7 convert 8 transfer 9 transform
transom: 5 trave 6 louver, window
transparent: 4 open 5 clear, frank, gauzy, lucid, sheer 6 candid, limpid, lucent 7 obvi-

ous, pelucid 8 luminous, lustrous 9 colorless 10 diaphanous 11 crystalline, perspicuous, translucent

transpierce: 6 pierce 8 transfix 9 penetrate

transpire: 6 happen

transport: dak 4 bear, boat, buss, haul, move, send, ship, tote 5 bring, carry, ferry, flute, truck 6 banish, convey, deport, ravish 7 convict, ecstasy, emotion, fraught, freight, passion, portage, rapture, smuggle 8 entrance, horsecar, overcome, palander, transfer 9 captivate, enrapture, happiness

transportation: *business:* 4 mail 7 air line, express 8 shipping 9 steamship 11 railroading

means: 7 rockets

system: 4 line

transpose: 5 shift 6 change, remove 7 convert, disturb, reverse 8 exchange, transfer 9 rearrange, transform, translate, transmute 11 interchange

transposition: 7 anagram 10 spoonerism 11 permutation

Transvaal: *capital:* 8 Pretoria

district: 4 Rand

policeman: 4 zarp

transverse: bar, way 4 bank, over, pass, rung, turn 5 argue, cross, pivot, route, shift, trace 6 across, denial, stripe, survey, swivel, thwart, travel 7 barrier, discuss, examine, impeach, oblique, pervade, quarrel 9 alternate, crossbeam 10 crosspiece 11 controversy

Transylvania: *city:* 4 Cluj

fabled resident: 7 Dracula, vampire

trap: bag, get, gin, net, pit 4 cage, lure, nail 5 brake, buggy, catch, goods, mouth, rocks, snare, steps, trick 6 ambush, corner, detect, enmesh 7 capture, cunning, ensnare, luggage, pitfall, springe 8 carriage, confound, covering, deadfall, separate, trapball 9 caparison, detective, policeman, stratagem 10 belongings, stepladder

animal: pot, web 4 weir 5 creel 6 bownet, eelpot

police: 7 dragnet 9 roadblock

trapdoor: 4 drop

trapes: See **traipse**

trapeze: bar

trapping: 4 gear 5 cloth 7 harness 8 catching, covering, ornament 9 adornment, caparison, coverture 10 decoration 12 accouterment, accoutrement 13 embellishment, paraphernelia

theatrical: 4 prop 7 scenery 8 property

Trappist: 4 monk

cheese: oka

writer: 6 Merton

traps: 5 bells, drums 7 cymbals

trapshooting: 5 skeet

target: 10 clay pigeon

trash: jog, lop 4 bosh, clog, crop, dirt, jade, pelf, plod, raff, tosh 5 leash, money, tramp, waste, wrack 6 bushwa, debris, halter, hinder, rabble, refuse, retard, rubble, trudge 7 baggage, beggary, blather, rubbish 8 encumber, flummery, nonsense, restrain, riffraff, trumpery 10 balderdash 11 sleuthhound

trashy: 9 worthless

trauma: 5 shock, wound 6 injury

travail: 4 pain, pang, task, toil 5 agony, drive, labor 6 effort, travel 7 journey, torment, trouble 8 exertion 9 suffering 11 parturition

trave: 9 crossbeam

travel: go; run 4 fare, move, mush, post, ride, tour, trek, trip, walk, wend 5 coast 6 motion 7 commute, journey, migrate, passage, proceed, sojourn, torment, travail 8 traverse 9 gallivant, itinerate 10 locomotion 11 peregrinate

company: 7 caravan

pert. to: 6 viatic

yen for: 10 wanderlust

traveler: 5 farer, tramp 6 viator 7 drummer, pilgrim, swagman, tourist, voyager 8 salesman, wanderer, wayfarer 9 itinerant 12 globe-trotter

aid of: 5 guide 7 courier 8 cicerone

commercial: 5 agent 7 drummer 8 salesman

refuge: inn 5 oasis, motel 7 hospice

travels: 7 odyssey

traverse: 4 deny, ford, pass 5 cross, range, rebut 6 patrol, refute, thwart

travesty: 6 parody, satire 8 disguise 9 burlesque, imitation 10 caricature

writer: 8 parodist

trawl: net 4 fish, line 7 boulter, dragnet

tray: hod 4 font 6 hurdle, salver, server 7 coaster

treacherous: 5 false, punic, snaky 6 fickle, hollow 8 disloyal, insecure, plotting, unstable 9 faithless, insidious 10 fraudulent, perfidious, traitorous, unreliable 11 disaffected 12 Machiavelian 13 Machiavellian, untrustworthy

treachery: 5 guile 6 deceit 7 perfidy, treason, untruth 8 betrayal

treacle: 4 cure 6 remedy 7 claggum 8 molasses

treaclewort: 4 herb 10 pennycress

tread: rut 4 gait, mark, pace, rung, step, volt, walk 5 clump, crush, labor, press, stair, stamp, trace, track, trail, tramp 6 balter, course, quench, subdue, trapes 7 conquer, repress, traipse, trample 8 copu-

late, footfall 9 footprint 10 employment, occupation
treadle: 5 pedal 7 chalaza
treason: 7 perfidy 8 betrayal 9 treachery
treasure: 4 roon 5 cache, hoard, pearl, prize, store, trove, value 6 gersum, riches, supply, wealth 7 cherish, finance 8 treasury 9 thesaurus(L.) 10 appreciate, collection 12 accumulation
Treasure State: 7 Montana
treasured: 5 chary
treasurer: 7 cashier, curator 8 bhandari, cofferer, deftodar, guardian, receiver 11 chamberlain
college: 6 bursar
treasury: 4 fisc, fund 5 chest, hoard 6 coffer 7 bursary, revenue 9 exchequer 10 repository, storehouse
Roman: 6 fiscus
treat: use 4 deal, dose, lead, urge 5 argue, besee, Dutch, feast, guide, touch 6 attend, confer, demean, doctor, govern, handle, parley, regale, regard, repast 7 address, bargain, control, discuss, entreat, expound 8 consider, transact, treatise 9 discourse, entertain, negotiate 10 manipulate
improperly: 4 snub 5 flout, scout, spite 6 ill-use, misuse 8 dishonor
tenderly: 5 spare 6 coddle, pamper
treatise: 5 essay, tract 6 thesis, treaty 7 account, grammar 8 brochure 9 discourse, narration, treatment 10 commentary 11 description 12 dissertation
elementary: 6 primer 7 grammar
opening part: 8 exordium
preface: 7 isagoge
treatment: 4 care 5 usage 7 therapy 8 demeanor, entreaty, handling 10 management 13 entertainment
before doctor's arrival: 8 first aid
compassionate: 5 mercy
harsh: 5 abuse 8 misusage, severity
treaty: 4 pact 7 article, concord, entente 8 contract, treatise 9 agreement, discourse 10 convention, discussion 11 arrangement, negotiation 13 understanding
treaty-bound: 6 allied
treble: 6 shrill, triple 7 soprano 9 threefold 11 high-pitched
treble clef: gee
tree (see also next entry): ach, ber, dal, dao, ebo, elm, fir, hur, iba, kou, lin, mee, oak 4 acle, alan, alof, anam, asak, asok, ates, ausu, bael, biti, bogo, bola, dali, dhak, dita, ipil, mabi, mora, odal, palm, pole, post, ship, toon, trap, wood, yaya 5 areca, asoka, betis, bongo, bulak, bumbo, cacao, carob, catch, cebil, couma, dadap, dalli, fulwa, genip, ligas, mahua, neeba, nepal, niepa, nitta, oodal, rohan, roman, salai, sassy, shaft, shift, siman, sissu, spade, staff, stake, stick, tikur, yacca 6 bahera, banyan, barbas, bariba, brauna, bucare, cativo, cedron, chalta, chogak, chupon, cocuyo, colima, corner, cudgel, design, gibbet, gomart, illupi, jarrah, locust, marane, marara, ramoon, sabino, simaba, sissoo, stemma, tikoor, timber 7 anubing, araraba, arboret, assagai, assegai, azarole, capture, champac, champak, cocullo, dhamnoo, diagram, gallows, guaraba, gumihan, hautboy, hollong, madrona, madrono, malpaho, mambong 8 ahueuete, cockspur, gamdeboo, ironbark, magnolia, mangrove, mokihana, phulwara, seedling, tamarack 9 bandoline, betel-palm, bitanhole, canadulce, couratari, currajong, genealogy, sassywood 10 bunyabunya, chaulmugra 11 balinghasay, chaulmaugra, chaulmoogra, guachipilin, hursinghair
alder: arn 5 alnus, birch 12 ament-bearing
algarroba: 5 carob 6 calden
allspice: 7 pimento
apple: 4 sorb
aromatic: 9 sassafras
balsam: fir 9 torchwood
bark: 4 ross, tapa
basswood: 6 linden
bead: nim
bean: 5 sapan
bearing samara: ash
beefwood: 5 belah, belar
betel: 5 areca
bignoniacious: 7 catalpa
blinding sap: 7 alipata
boxwood: 5 seron
breadnut: 6 capomo
buckthorn: 7 cascara
buckwheat: 4 titi 6 teetee
Buddha's: 6 botree
bully: see *gum* below
burned, broken: 7 rampick, rampike
buttonball: 5 plane 8 sycamore
cabbage: 7 angelin
camphor: 5 kapur
candlenut: ama
caoutchouc: ule 6 rubber
caucho-yielding (see also *rubber* below): ule
cemetery: yew
chestnut: 10 chinqua pin
chocolate: 5 cacao
cinchona: 7 quinine 9 quinidine
cinnamon family: 6 cassia
clump: 4 tump 5 motte
coconut: 4 coco
coffee: 6 chicot

conebearing: fir, yew 4 pine 5 alder, cedar, larch 7 conifer 8 gnetales
coral: 6 gabgab
cottonwood: 5 alamo
covering: 4 bark
cranberry: 7 pembina
derivative: 5 pinic
devil: 4 dita
drumstick: 11 canafistolo, canafistula, canafistulo
drupe bearing: 4 bito
dwarf: 5 scrub 7 abuscle 10 chinquapin
dwelling: 4 nest
dye yielding: tua, tui 4 mora 7 annatto 10 hursinghar
ebony: 9 diospyros
elder: 7 trammon
eucalyptus: 4 yati 6 mallee
evergreen: fir, yeu 4 pine, tawa 5 carob, cedar, holly, larch, ocote, olive 6 balsam, carobe, cazaba, coigue, tarata 7 bebeery, juniper, madrona, madrono, taratah
exudation: gum, lac, sap, tar 5 resin, rosin, xylan
fabacious: 5 agati
fiber: 5 bulak, simal, terap 7 bentang
fig family: 4 upas 5 pipal 7 gondang
flowering: 5 agati, elder, titis 6 mimosa, redbud 8 cleaster, oleaster
fodder: 5 mahoe 9 tagasaste
food: 4 akee
fruit: bel, fig, gab 4 gaub, lime 5 araca, lemon, mahis, olive, papaw, topes 6 annona, banana, bearer, biriba, litchi, medlar, pawpaw, sapota 7 avocado, capulin, genipap, tangelo 8 bakupari, tamarind 9 tangerine 12 custard apple
gaucho: ule
group: 4 bosk 5 copse, grove, woods 6 forest 7 coppice, orchard
grower: 8 arborist
gum: 5 babul, balta 6 balata, sapota, sapote, tupelo, zapote 8 banildad 9 sapodilla, sapotilha, sapotilla 10 bansalague, eucalyptus
gum genus: 6 owenia
hardwood: 4 poon 5 aalii, gidia, gidya, mabee, maple, narra, ngaio 6 gidgea, gidgee, gidjee, gidyea, walnut 7 hickory, tindalo 8 macaasin, mahogany 9 quebracho
heartwood: 7 duramen
health: 5 briar, brier
hickory: 5 pecan
holly: 4 ilex
honeberry: 5 genip
horseradish: 4 behn 5 behen
jobber: 10 woodpecker
juniper: 4 cade 5 cedar
kino: 4 bija
koranic: 6 zaggum
laurel: bay 7 tarairi
limb: 5 bough 6 branch
lime: lin 4 linn, teil 6 linden 9 tilicetum
linden: lin 4 lime, teil 8 basswood
locust: 6 acacia 9 courbaril
lotus: sad 4 lote
mafurra: 6 elcaja
magnolia: 5 yulan
mahogany: 4 toon
maple: 4 acer
margosa: 4 neem
marmalade: 5 mamey, mamie 6 mammee, sapote
medicinal: 5 sumac 6 sumach, wahahe
mimosaceous: 5 siris
monkeybread: 6 baobab
mountain ash: 4 sorb 5 rowan 7 service
mulberry: 4 more
nut: 4 cola 6 akhrot, chicha 9 almendron
nymph turned into: 6 Daphne
oil: 5 mahua, mahwa 9 candlenut
old-yielding: bel, ben 4 eboe, shea
olive: 4 olea
olive family: ash
orange-like: 5 osage
palm: ti; tal 4 coco 6 arengs
paradise: 8 aceituna
part: 4 bark, bole, knot, leaf, root, twig 5 shade, trunk 6 branch
pert. to: 8 arboreal
pine: see *evergreen* above
pipal: 6 botree
plane: 8 sycamore 10 buttonwood
plantain: 4 pala
pod-bearing: 7 catalpa
poisonous: 4 upas
poon: 4 dilo 5 keena
poplar: 5 abele, alamo, aspen, tulip 10 cottonwood
pottery: 7 caraipe, caraipi
rain: 5 saman, zaman 6 zamang 8 genisaro 9 algarroba
rare: 6 Joshua
resin: 4 arar
ribbon: 6 akaroa 7 houhere
rowan: see *mountain ash* below
rubber: ule 4 para 6 caucho 7 seringa 10 caoutchouc
rutaceous: 4 lime
salt: 4 atle 5 atlee
sandarac: 4 arar
sandbox: 6 assacu
science: 7 silvics
shade: ash, elm, lin, oak 5 maple 6 linden, poplar 7 catalpa 8 sycamore
smoke: 6 fustet 9 zante-wood
soft-wood: lin 5 ambay, balsa, linde
sour gum: 5 nyssa 6 tupelo
sprout: 5 sprig 7 sapling

streaked wood: 5 baria
stunted: 5 scrub
tallow: 4 cera
tamarisk: see *salt* above
tea: 6 manuka
teak: 4 teca
thorny: bel 4 bael, bito, brea 7 colorin 9 barriguda 11 chichicaste
timber: ash, dar, eng, koa, saj, sal, yew 4 coco, cuya, ipil, pelu, pine, poon, rata, tala, teak, toon, ulmo 5 acana, almon, amate, balao, balau, bayok, beech, birch, cedar, culla, dalli, ebano, fotui, guijo, icica, kauri, kaury, maple, narra, pekea, penda, rauli, tenio, timbo, uadal, yacal, zorro 6 alerce, alerse, alfaje, ausubo, bacury, banaba, banago, banaki, bancal, banuyo, bataan, batino, dagame, dungon, lanete, molave, satine, totara, walnut 7 batulin, becuiba, billian, camagon, capulin, cypress, gateado, gomavel, guacimo, hapiton, redwood 8 flindosa, flindosy, mahogany, zapetero 9 balaustre, guaraguao 10 batikuling
treatise: 5 silva
tropical genus: 8 bauhinia
trunk: 4 bole 5 shaft
tulip: 6 poplar
Turkey oak: 6 cerris
turpentine: 6 tarata 7 taratah 9 terebinth
walnut see *nut* above: 6 akhrot
wattle: 5 boree
wide-spreading: 5 cedar 7 juniper
willow: 5 osier
worship: 11 dendrolatry
yellow alder: 8 sagerose

tree: For trees of specific countries or regions, see under that country or region. EXAMPLES: "African tree", see under Africa: *tree;* "American tree," see under America: *tree*
tree bear: 7 raccoon
tree runner: 8 nuthatch
tree toad: 4 hyla 6 peeper
treelike: 11 arborescent
treeless: 6 barren
plain: 5 llano, pampa 6 steppe 7 prairie, savanna 8 savannah
treen: 6 wooden
treenail: nog, peg, pin 5 spike 7 trunnel
trefoil: 6 claver, clover
tregetour: 7 juggler 8 magician
treillage: 5 grill 7 trellis 8 espalier 11 latticework
trek: 4 draw, pull 5 march 6 travel 7 journey, migrate 10 expedition
trellis: 5 bower, cross 7 lattice, pergola 8 espalier 10 interweave 11 latticework
trematode worms: 8 cercaria 9 flatworms
tremble: 5 bever, quake, shake 6 didder, dither, dodder, falter, quaver, quiver, shiver, totter, tremor 7 flacker, flicker, shudder, vibrate 9 trepidate
trembling: 7 fearful, twitter 9 tremulous
tremendous: big 5 awful, giant, great, large 7 amazing 8 dreadful, enormous, horrible, powerful, terrific 9 frightful, momentous, monstrous 10 terrifying 13 extraordinary
tremolo: 6 quaver
tremor: 5 quake, shake 6 quiver, shiver, thrill 7 tremble 9 vibration
tremplin: 11 springboard
tremulous: 5 aspen, timid 7 fearful, nervous, palsied 8 timorous, unsteady, wavering 9 quavering, sensitive 11 palpitating
trench: cut, gaw 4 bury, gash, moat, sike 5 carve, ditch, drain, fosse, fossa(L.), graff, graft, slash, slice 6 furrow, groove, gutter 7 acequia 8 encroach, entrench, infringe 10 excavation
digger: 6 sapper
digging from within: sap
trenchant: 4 keen 5 acute, sharp 6 biting 7 cutting 8 clear-cut, distinct, forceful, incisive, vigorous 9 energetic 11 penetrating
trencher: 5 board, plate 7 platter 9 parasitic 11 sycophantic
trencherman: 7 sponger 8 hanger-on, parasite 11 gormandizer
trend: run 4 bend, bent, tone, turn, vein 5 drift, swing, tenor 6 extend, strike 7 incline 8 movement, tendency 9 direction 11 inclination
trendle: tub 6 trough
trepan: 4 lure, tool, trap 5 snare, trick 6 entrap 7 deceive, ensnare, swindle 9 perforate, stratagem
trepang: 10 beche-de-mer 22 holothurian-sea-cucumber
trepid: 7 quaking 8 timorous 9 trembling
trepidation: 4 fear 5 alarm, dread 6 dismay, tremor 7 quaking 9 agitation, confusion 11 disturbance 12 perturbation 13 consternation
trespass: sin 5 poach 6 breach, invade, offend 7 intrude 8 encroach, entrench, infringe 9 interlope 10 infraction, transgress 11 misfeasance
tress: 4 curl, hair, lock 5 braid, plait 7 ringlet
tressure: 4 band, caul 6 border, fillet, ribbon 9 headdress
trestle: leg 5 bench, horse, stand, stool 6 tripod, trivet 7 support, viaduct 9 framework
tret: 9 allowance
trew: 5 trust 7 believe
trews: 8 breeches, trousers 9 stockings

triad: 5 three, trine 6 triune 7 trinity 9 trivalent
trial: go; try 4 bout, case, pain, test 5 assay, cross, essay, grief, proof 6 assize, effort, ordeal, sample 7 approof, attempt, contest, hearing, inquiry 8 endeavor, evidence, hardship 10 experience, experiment, tournament 11 examination, tribulation 13 investigation
inconclusive: 8 mistrial
pert. to: 7 empiric
scene of: 5 court
severe: 6 ordeal
trial balloon: 4 kite, test 6 feeler
triangle: 5 delta 6 trigon 7 scalene, trigone 9 isosceles 11 equilateral
draw circle touching: 7 escribe
in heraldry: 5 giron
side: leg 11 hypothenuse
unequal sided: 7 scalene
triangular: 7 deltoid 13 three-cornered
piece: 4 gore 5 miter, mitre, wedge 6 gusset
sail: jib 6 lateen 9 spinnaker
triangular muscle: 7 deltoid
triarchy: 11 triumvirate
tribe: rod 4 band, clan, kind, race, sept 5 class, firca(Ind.), group 6 family 9 community
emblem: 5 totem
Germanic: 8 Alamanni, Alemanni
head: 5 chief 9 patriarch
New Zealand: ati
Roman: 5 Latin 6 Sabine 8 Etruscan
tribulation: 5 agony, trial 6 misery, sorrow 8 distress 9 suffering 10 affliction
tribunal: bar 4 banc, seat 5 bench, court, forum 7 tribune 8 assembly 10 consistory
tribune: 4 dais 6 throne 8 platform 10 magistrate
tributary: 5 ruler, state 6 feeder 7 subject 9 auxiliary, subsidary 11 subordinate 12 contributory
tribute: fee, tax 4 cain, dues, duty, gift, levy, rent, scat 5 grant 6 assign, eulogy, impost, praise, tariff 7 chevage, ovation, payment, respect 8 encomium 9 attribute, gratitude, laudation, panegyric 10 obligation 11 testimonial
tricar: 8 tricycle
trice: 4 bind, gird, haul, lash, pull 5 jiffy 6 moment, secure 7 instant 9 twinkling
trichome: 4 hair 7 bristle, prickle
trichord: 4 lyre
trick: bob, boy, cog, dor, fob, fox, fub, gag, gum, toy 4 bilk, dupe, feat, flam, fool, gaff, gaud, girl, gull, hoax, jest, joke, prat, ruse, trap, turn, wile 5 catch, child, cully, dodge, feint, fraud, gleek, guile, knack, prank, shift, skite, spell, stunt 6 begunk, chouse, delude, humbug, palter, trepan, trifle 7 beguile, cantrip, deceive, defraud, finesse, gimmick, pretext, sleight, swindle 8 artifice, flimflam, illusion, maneuver 9 bamboozle, capriccio, chicanery, diablerie, imposture, mannerism, stratagem 10 subterfuge 11 hornswoggle, legerdemain
trickery: art 5 fraud, hocus 6 cautel, deceit, japery 7 knavery, roguery, slyness 8 cheating, trumpery 9 deception, duplicity 10 hanky-panky
trickle: 4 drip, flow, sipe(Sc.) 5 exude 6 distil 7 distill, dripple
trickster: 5 cheat 6 rascal 7 slicker
tricksy: 5 smart 6 spruce 7 evasive, playful, roguish 8 prankish, sportive 9 deceiving, deceptive, uncertain 11 embellished, mischievous
tricky: sly 5 dodgy 6 artful, catchy 7 devious 8 ticklish 9 deceitful, intricate
tricycle: 6 tricar
trident: 5 spear
bearer: 7 Neptune
tried: 6 ettled(Sc.), proved, select, tested 8 faithful, reliable 11 trustworthy
trier: 5 judge 7 refiner 8 examiner, renderer 12 experimenter, investigator
Trieste measure: 4 orna, orne(pl.)
trifle: bit, fig, rap, toy 4 bean, doit, fike, jest, mock, mote, play 5 dally, flirt, straw, trick 6 bauble, coquet, dabble, dawdle, delude, dibble, doodle, fiddle, fidget, footer, footle, frivol, gewgaw, potter 7 deceive, dessert, fribble, nothing, traneen 8 flimflam, gimcrack, raillery 9 bagatelle 10 equivocate, knickknack, triviality
trifler: 7 flaneur
trifling: 4 airy, idle, mere 5 inane, petty 6 futile, little 7 shallow, wasting 8 badinage, frippery 9 dalliance 10 immaterial 13 insignificant
trifoliolate: 7 ternate 11 three-leaved
plant: 6 clover 8 shamrock
trifolium: 6 clover 8 shamrock
trig: run 4 chic, cram, deck, fill, firm, full, line, neat, prim, prop, stop, tidy, trim, trot 5 brisk, dandy, natty, smart, sound, stiff, stone, stuff, wedge 6 active, lively, spruce, steady, strong, trench 7 distend, foppish, precise, support 10 methodical
trigo: 5 wheat
trigon: 4 harp, lyre 5 trine 8 triangle
trigonometry function: 4 sine 6 cosine, secant 7 tangent
Trilby: *author:* 9 du Maurier
character: 8 Svengali
trill: 4 flow, move, turn 5 shake, twirl 6 gruppo, quaver, quiver, warble 7 mordent, trickle, vibrate, vibrato 8 grupetto 10 coloratura

trim: bob, cut, gay, lop 4 beat, chic, clip, crop, deft, dink, edge, fine, firm, neat, nice, snod(Sc.), snug, tidy, trig 5 adorn, braid, cheat, chide, dress, equip, fitty, natty, nifty, preen, prune, ready, shave, shear 6 adjust, dapper, defeat, modify, petite, punish, spruce, thrash 7 balance, compact, defraud, furnish, orderly 8 chastise, decorate, ornament, pleasant, tailored 9 condition, embellish, excellent, shipshape 10 compromise 11 disposition
coin: nig
dress: 4 gimp 5 ruche 6 sequin
lace: 5 jabot 6 ruffle
trimmer: 5 finer
trimming: 4 gimp, lace 5 braid, ruche 6 frieze, fringe, piping 7 falbala, ruching 8 furbelow, ornament, rick-rack 9 garniture 10 decoration 13 passementerie
trinal: 5 trial 9 threefold
trindle: 4 roll 5 wheel 7 trundle
trine: go 4 hang 5 march, triad 6 trigon, triple, triune 7 Trinity 9 favorable, threefold 10 auspicious
Trinidad: *gulf:* 5 Paria
music: 7 calypso
tree: 4 mora
trinitrotoluene: TNT 6 trotyl 14 trinitrotoluol
trinity: 5 three, triad 6 triune 9 threeness 10 spiderwort
trinket: toy 4 bead, gaud, ring 5 bijou, jewel 6 bangle, bauble, gewgaw, trifle 7 bibelot 8 gimcrack, intrigue, ornament 10 knickknack
trinkle: 4 drip, flow 7 trickle
trio: 9 threesome
trip: run 4 gait, halt, hike, pawl, skip, slip, spin, tour 5 brood, caper, catch, danse, error, flock, jaunt, lapse, tread, wedge 6 cruise, falter, voyage 7 blunder, failure, journey, misstep, mistake, release, stumble 8 obstruct 9 excursion 10 expedition
trip-hammer: *operator:* 6 tilter
tripe: 5 trash 7 rubbish
triple: 5 trine 6 treble 9 threefold
triplet: 4 trin, trio
tripletail: 9 berrugate, spadefish
triplicate: 6 treble, triple 9 threefold
tripod: cat 5 easel, stand 6 trivet
Tripoli ruler: dey
trippet: cam
tripping: 5 quick 6 nimble 7 walking 8 trippant
triptych: *wing:* 5 volet
trisaccharide: 6 triose
trismus: 7 lockjaw, tetanus
Tristam, Tristan: *beloved:* 5 Isolt 6 Iseult, Isolde
uncle: 4 Mark
villain: 5 Melot
wife: 6 Isolde
Tristram Shandy author: 6 Sterne
triste: sad 4 dull 6 dismal 9 sorrowful 10 depressing, melancholy
trite: 4 worn 5 banal, corny, stale, vapid 6 common, jejune 7 bromide, trivial 9 hackneyed 10 threadbare, unoriginal 11 commonplace, stereotyped 12 conventional 13 platitudinous
trite expression: 6 cliche 7 bromide
triton: eft 4 newt 7 demigod 10 salamander
triturate: rub 5 crush, grind 6 bruise 9 comminute, pulverize
triumph: win 4 gain 5 exult, glory 6 defeat, hurrah 7 conquer, prevail, rejoice, success, victory 8 flourish 11 achievement, celebration
triumvirate: *first:* 6 Caesar, Pompey 7 Crassus
second: 6 Antony 7 Lepidus 8 Octavius
trivet: 5 stand 6 tripod 7 support
trivial: 5 banal, fluff, inane, petty, small, trite 6 common, paltry, slight 7 nominal, piperly 8 doggerel, ordinary, trifling 9 frivolous 11 unimportant 13 insignificant 14 inconsiderable
trocar: 6 stylet 7 trochar
troche: 6 pastil, rotula, tablet 7 lozenge, pastile 8 pastille
trochilus: 7 warbler 9 goldcrest 11 hummingbird
trod: 4 path, walk 5 trace, track, tread 8 footpath, footstep
trogon: 4 bird 7 quetzal
Troilus: *beloved:* 8 Cressida
father: 5 Priam
Trojan: 9 Dardanian
epic: 5 Iliad
king: 5 Priam
prince: 5 Eneas, Paris 6 Aeneas, Hector
prisoner: 5 Sinon
serpent victim: 7 Laocoon
soothsayer: 7 Helenus 9 Cassandra
Trojan horse: 8 saboteur 10 subversive
builder: 5 Epeus
Trojan War: *cause:* 5 Helen
hero: 4 Ajax 5 Eneas 6 Aeneas, Agenor, Hector 9 Palamedes
troll: run, wag 4 bowl, fish, lure, reel, roll, sing, song, turn 5 angle, catch, chant, dwarf, giant, gnome, round, spoon 6 trolly 7 revolve, trolley, trollop 9 circulate
trolley: car 4 cart, tram 5 block 6 barrow, sledge 8 handcart 9 streetcar
trollop: 4 hang 5 slump 6 dangle, slouch 8 slattern 10 bedraggled, prostitute
trombone: 7 sackbut

trommel: 5 sieve 6 screen
tronk: 4 jail 6 lockup, prison
troop: lot 4 army, band, ging, line, rout, wave 5 crowd, group 6 number, troupe 7 battery, cavalry, company, echelon, militia, phalanx 8 quantity, soldiers 9 associate, gathering 10 congregate
Anglo-Indian: 6 risala 7 ressala, risalah
arrangement: 7 echelon
assembling: 6 muster
concealed: 6 ambush
German: 6 Panzer
raise: 4 levy 5 draft 9 conscript
sellers to: 6 sutler 10 vivandiere
trooper: 6 hussar 7 soldier 9 policeman, troopship 10 cavalryman
trop: too 4 many
trope: 8 metaphor
trophy: cup 4 palm 5 prize 6 laurel, reward 7 memento 8 memorial, ornament
tropic: 5 limit 8 boundary
animal: 4 alco, eyra 5 agama, coati, potto 6 agouti, iguana 7 peccary
bird: ani 4 tody 5 jalap 7 jacamar
fish: 4 toro 6 salema 7 squetee
fruit: 4 date 5 guava, mango, papaw 6 banana, papaya 8 tamarind
genus of herb: 4 evea, sida 5 tacca, urena 8 laportea
helmet: 4 topi
plant: dal 4 aloe, arum, sida, taro 5 agave 6 alocad 7 cowhage, lantana 8 gardenia
plant genus: 5 rhoeo 6 cannas 7 bomarea, geonoma, hamelia
tree: ebo 4 ceba, coco, dali, eboe, etua, guao, mabi, palm 5 acapu, amate, artar, assai, balsa, banak, bongo, cacao, dalli, guama, guava, icica, nepal, nitta, njave, papaw, seron, zorro 6 baboen, bacury, banana, barbas, cazaba, chupon, dagame, espave, mammee, pawpaw, sapota 7 anubing, gateado, guacimo 8 amarillo, mangrove, sweetsop, tamarind 9 huamuchli, quebracho, sapodilla, sapotilha, sapotilla 10 frangipane, frangipani, manchineel 11 guachipilin
trot: jog, run, tot 4 gait 5 child, hurry 6 hasten 7 toddler 11 translation
troth: 5 certy, faith 6 certie, pledge 8 fidelity 9 betrothal
trottoir: 8 footpath, pavement, sidewalk
trotty: 5 brisk 6 lively
trotyl: TNT 14 trinitrotoluol 15 trinitrotoluene
troubadour, troubador: 4 poet 6 singer 8 minstrel, musician
trouble: ado, ail, irk, vex, woe 4 busy, care, cark, fike, fuss, harm, pain, sore, stir 5 anger, annoy, grief, labor, tease, worry 6 bother, burble, caddle, cumber, dither, effort, harass, impair, matter, mishap, molest, pester, plague, pother, sorrow, unrest 7 afflict, agitate, anxiety, chagrin, concern, disease, disturb, embroil, illness, perturb, travail 8 aggrieve, calamity, disorder, disquiet, distress, exertion 9 adversity, incommode, interfere 10 difficulty, disarrange, discomfort, discommode, misfortune, perplexity, uneasiness 11 displeasure, encumbrance 13 inconvenience
troubled: 6 queasy 12 heart-scalded
troublemaker: 6 gossip 8 agitator
troublesome: 5 pesky 8 fashious 9 pestilent, turbulent, wearisome 10 burdensome, oppressive
troublous: 6 stormy, turbid 7 unquiet 8 restless 9 unsettled
trough: bin 4 boat, bosh, bowl, dale, tank, tomb 5 bakie, basin, canoe, chute 6 buddle, coffin, dugout, gutter, sluice 7 channel, conduit
between waves: 6 valley
inclined: 5 chute
trounce: sue 4 beat, flog 5 scold, tramp 6 cudgel, defeat, indict, punish, ramble, thrash 7 censure, journey
troupe: 4 band 5 group 7 company 9 cuadrilla(Sp.)
trouper: 5 actor
troupial: 6 oriole 7 cacique, cowbird 9 blackbird 10 meadowlark
trousers: 5 pants 6 skilts, slacks 8 breeches, culottes 9 pantalets, shintiyan 10 pantaloons
foreign: 7 shalwar 9 shaksheer, shulwaurs 10 calzoneras(Sp.)
trout: 4 char, peal 5 brook, sewen 6 finnac, grilse 7 gilaroo, rainbow 8 finnacle 9 steelhead 10 squeteague
lake: 9 namaycush
troutlet: 10 fingerling
trovatore: 10 troubadour
trove: 9 discovery
trow: 4 boat, hope 5 faith, fancy, smack, think, troll, trust 6 belief, expect 7 believe, imagine, suppose 9 catamaran
trowing: 5 creed 6 belief 7 opinion
Troy (see also **Trojan, Trojan horse, Trojan War**): 5 Iliac, Ilian, Ilion, Ilium, Troas, Troad 8 Teucrian
defender: 6 Aeneas
founder: 4 Ilus, Tros
king: 5 Priam
mountain: Ida
pert. to: 5 Iliac 6 Trojan
region: 5 Troad
troy weight: 5 grain, ounce, pound 11 pennyweight

truant: 4 idle 5 stray 6 beggar, errant 7 shirker, vagrant 8 vagabond, wanderer 9 shiftless
play: 5 miche
truce: 5 pause, treve(F.) 7 respite 9 armistice, cessation 12 intermission
truck: van 4 deal, dray 5 lorry, trade, trash 6 barrow, barter, camion, peddle, potter 7 bargain, rubbish, traffic, trundle 8 business, exchange, handcart 9 negotiate, transport, vegetable 10 handbarrow 11 association, intercourse
with trailer: 4 semi
truckle: 4 fawn 5 toady, wheel 6 caster, cheese, cringe, submit 7 trundle
truckling: 7 servile
truculent: 4 mean, rude 5 cruel, harsh 6 fierce, savage 8 ruthless, scathing 9 barbarous, ferocious 11 destructive
trudge: pad 4 plod, walk 5 stoge, tramp 6 trapes 7 traipse
true: 4 just, leal(Sc.), pure, real, vera(L.), vrai(F.) 5 align, aline, exact, level, loyal, plumb, right, valid 6 actual, adjust, honest, lawful, proper, steady 7 certain, correct, devoted, factual, genuine, germane, precise, sincere, staunch, upright 8 accurate, bonafide, constant, faithful, reliable, unerring, virtuous 9 authentic, steadfast, truepenny, unfeigned, veracious, veritable 10 legitimate 11 unfaltering
true blue: 5 loyal 7 staunch
truelove: 10 sweetheart
trueness: 7 reality 8 veracity 9 exactness 11 genuineness 12 faithfulness
truffle: 5 tuber 8 earthnut
trug: 4 caul, cawl, pail, tray 5 wench 6 basket, trough 7 measure 10 prostitute
truism: 5 axiom
Truk island: Tol 4 Moen, Udot, Uman 6 Dublon
trull: 4 dell, girl, lass 5 demon, fiend, giant, wench 6 blowze, callet 7 trollop 8 strumpet 10 prostitute
truly: 4 iwis 6 atweel, dinkum, indeed, verily 13 realistically
trump: cap, pam 4 beat, ruff 5 outdo, pedro 7 nonplus, surpass, trumpet 8 jew's-harp
trumpery: 5 fraud, showy, trash, weeds 6 deceit, paltry 7 rubbish 8 gimcrack, nonsense, trickery 9 worthless
trumpet: 4 horn 5 blare 6 bucina(Lat.), funnel, kerana, summon 7 begonia, clarion, publish 8 denounce, proclaim
belt: 7 baldric
blare: 6 sennet 7 fanfare, tantara
caller: 7 Gabriel
muffler: 4 mute
stage direction: 6 sennet
trumpet creeper: 5 plant 6 tecoma
trumpet shell: 6 triton
trumpeter: 4 bird, swan 6 herald, pigeon, tooter 7 yakamik
truncate: cut, lop 6 lessen 7 shorten
truncheon: 4 club, stem 5 baton, staff 6 cudgel 8 fragment, splinter
trundle: bed 4 bowl, cart, hoop, roll 5 truck, twirl, wheel, whirl 6 barrow, caster, pinion, rotate 7 revolve, trindle 11 wheelbarrow
trundler: 6 bowler
trunk: box 4 body, bole, pipe, stem, tank, tube 5 chest, snout, stock, torso 6 caudex, coffer, corpse, thorax 7 baggage 9 proboscis
animal: 4 soma 5 torso, snout
trunkless: 8 bodiless
truss: tie, wap 4 bind, furl, gird, hang, lade, pack 6 bundle, fasten 7 arrange, bracket, enclose, package, support, tighten 10 strengthen
trust: 4 affy, care, duty, hope, task 5 faith 6 belief, cartel, charge, credit, depend, merger 7 believe, confide, consign, custody, keeping, loyalty 8 affiance, commenda, credence, reliance, security 9 assurance, coalition, fiduciary, syndicate 10 commission, confidence 11 combination
trustee: 6 bailee 7 sindico 8 director, guardian 9 garnishee 13 administrator
trustful: 5 liege 7 devoted 9 confiding 13 unquestioning
trustless: 10 unreliable 11 distrustful, treacherous
trustworthy: 4 safe 5 siker, solid, tried 6 honest, sicker 7 certain 8 credible, fiducial, reliable 9 authentic, confiding 10 dependable 12 confidential
trusty: 8 faithful, trustful 9 confiding
truth: 4 fact 5 sooth, troth 6 certes, verity 7 honesty, loyalty 8 accuracy, fidelity, veracity 9 agreement, constancy, integrity, principle, sincerity 11 correctness, genuineness, uprightness 12 faithfulness 14 verisimilitude
goddess: 4 Maat
personification of: Una
seeming: 14 verisimilitude
self-evident: 5 axiom 6 truism
truthful: 6 honest 7 correct 9 veracious, veridical
try: do 4 cull, sift, test 5 annoy, assay, essay, ettle(Sc.), found, prove, trial 6 choose, effort, hansel, harass, purify, refine, render, sample, screen, select, strain, strive 7 adjudge, afflict, approve, attempt, contest, extract, handsel, subject, torment, venture 8 audition, endeavor, irritate, separate, struggle 9 ascertain, undertake 10

experience, experiment 11 demonstrate, investigate
trying: 6 severe 7 irksome, painful 8 annoying 12 exasperating
tryst: 4 fair 5 visit 6 market 7 bespeak, meeting 9 agreement, gathering 10 engagement, rendezvous 11 appointment, assignation
tsamba: 5 flour 6 barley
tsar: 4 czar, Ivan, tzar 5 Peter 6 despot 8 autocrat
tsetse fly: 4 kivu 6 muscid
tsine: 6 wild ox 7 banteng
tuatara, tuatera: 6 lizard 16 rhynchocephalian
tub (see also **barrel, cistern, vat, vessel**): box, kid, soe, vat 4 bath, boat, cask, cool, ship, tram 5 barge, bathe, bowie(Sc.), eshin, keeve, skeel 6 bucket, pulpit, vessel 7 bathtub, cistern, tubfish 9 container
wooden: soe
tuba: 7 helicon
mouthpiece: 5 bocal
tubal: 8 pipelike
Tubal's father: 7 Japheth
Tubalcain's father: 6 Lamech
tubbal: 7 mattock
tubber: 6 cooper, pickax
tubby: 5 squat 6 chubby, portly
tube: 4 duct, hose, lull, pipe 5 chute, diode 6 cannon, siphon, tremie, triode, tunnel 7 cannula, conduit, fistula, pipette, tetrode 8 adjutage, bombilla(Sp.), cylinder 9 telescope
anatomical: 7 salpinx
flexible: 4 hose
for winding silk: cop
glass: 6 sipper 7 pipette
remove by: 6 siphon, syphon
system of: 6 pipage
underground: 6 subway, tunnel
tuber: oca, yam 4 beet, bulb, clog, eddo, root, taro, yamp 5 jalap, salep 6 potato 8 swelling 9 tubercule 10 tuberosity 12 protuberance
orchid: 5 salep
tubercle: 6 nodule 10 prominence
tubiform: 6 tubate
Tubuai island: 4 Rapa
tubular: 4 pipy 5 round 11 cylindrical
tuck: eat, jam, nip 4 cram, draw, fold, hang, poke 5 cramp, feast, pinch, press, scold, stuff, sword 6 energy, gather, hamper, rapier, upraid 7 consume, shorten, tighten 9 sweetmeat
tucked up: 7 cramped 8 hampered 9 exhausted
tucker: bib 4 food, meal, tire 5 board, weary 6 ration 7 fatigue 10 chemisette
Tudesque: 6 German
Tuesday: 5 mardi(F.)
god of: Tiu, Tyr
Shrove: 9 Mardi Gras
tufa: 5 trass
tufan: 5 storm
tuft: 4 beat, coma, disk 5 beard, bunch, clump, crest 6 button, comose, dollop, goatee, pompon, tassel 7 cluster, fetlock, scopula 8 imperial
pert. to: 5 comal
tuft-hunter: 4 snob
tug: lug, tit, tow 4 drag, draw, haul, maul, pull, rope, toil, yank 5 chain, exert, hitch, labor, strap, trace 6 drudge, effort, strain, strife, strive, tussle 7 contend, contest, tugboat, wrestle 8 struggle 11 counterpull
tuition: 4 care 5 watch 6 charge 7 custody 8 teaching 10 protection 11 instruction 12 guardianship
tule: 7 bulrush
tumble: 4 fall, leap, roll, trip, veer 5 pitch, slope, spill, whirl 6 rumple, spring, tousle 7 stumble 8 collapse, dishevel, disorder 9 confusion, overthrow 10 disarrange, handspring, somersault 11 precipitate
down: 10 dilapidate
tumbler: dog 4 cart, pupa 5 glass 6 dunker, pigeon, roller, vessel 7 acrobat, gymnast, tippler, tumbrel
tumbrel, tumbril: 4 cart 5 wagon 8 dumpcart
tumefy: 4 puff 5 swell 7 inflate
tumid: 6 turgid 7 bloated, bulging, fustian, pompous, swollen, teeming 8 bursting, enlarged, inflated 9 bombastic, distended, plethoric 11 protuberant
tumor: wen 4 beal, wart 5 edema, gumma 6 ambury, anbury, glioma, lipoma 7 bombast 8 blastoma, ganglion, hepatoma, neoplasm, papiloma, sarocele, swelling 10 distending 12 adamantinoma, protuberance
brain: 6 glioma
operation: 8 ancotomy
small: wen 7 papilla
suffix: oma
tumorous: 5 tumid 7 swollen 8 inflated 9 bombastic
tump: 4 heap 5 clump 7 hillock, tumulus
tumult: din, mob 4 fray, fuss, riot 5 babel, brawl, broil, noise 6 affray, babble, bedlam, bustle, dirdum(Sc.), emeute, hubbub, uproar 7 bluster, bobbery, ferment, tempest, turmoil 8 disorder, outbreak, outburst, uprising 9 agitation, commotion, confusion, distemper, hurlement 10 convulsion, excitement, turbulence 11 disturbance

tumultuous: 4 high, wild 5 rough 6 stormy 7 furious, violent 10 boisterous, hurly-burly
tumulus: 4 tump 5 mound 6 barrow 7 hillock
tun: cup, jar, tub, vat 4 cask 5 drink 6 guzzle, vessel 7 chimney
tune: air, key, pat 4 lilt, port, song, tone 5 dirge, drant, sound 6 choral, draunt, melody, string 7 chorale, concord, harmony, sonance 8 anglaise 9 agreement 10 adjustment
out: 6 detune
tuneful: 7 musical, tunable 9 melodious 10 concordant, euphonious, harmonious
tungsten ore: cal
tunic: 4 coat, jama, jupe, robe, toga 5 acton, frock, gippo, jamah 6 kirtle 8 colobium 10 cote-hardie, sticharion 11 houppelande
tunicate: 4 salp 5 salpa 12 marine animal
Tunisia: *cape:* bon
capital: 5 Tunis
cities: 4 Sfax, Susa 5 Gabes, Gafsa, Tunis 6 Mateur, Nabeul 7 Bizerte 8 Tebourba, Zaghouan 9 Grombalia 10 Ferryville
gulf: 5 Gabes, Tunis 8 Hammamet
island: 6 Djerba
measure: saa, sah 4 saah 5 cafiz, whiba 6 mettar 9 millerole
river: 8 Medjerda
ruler: bey, dey
weight: saa 4 rotl 5 artal, artel, ratel, uckia 6 kantar
tunk: rap 5 thump
tunnel: net 4 adit, bore, flue, tube 6 burrow, funnel 10 smokestack
long: 5 Otira 6 Hoosac, Severn, Spiral 7 Arlberg, Detroit, Gothard, Holland, Lincoln, Mont D'Or, St. Clair, Simplon 8 Gunnison 9 Baltimore, Cascade Mt., Connaught, Gallitzin, Montcenis, Mt. Roberts 10 Bitterroot, Cumberland, Lotschberg, St. Gotthard, Wasserfluh 11 Busk-Ivanhoe, Loetschberg, Trans-Andine
tunny: 4 tuna 8 albacore
tup: ram 5 cover, sheep 6 mallet 7 cuckold
tupelo: gum 4 tree 5 nyssa
tur: pea 4 goat
turb: 5 clump, crowd
turban: cap, fez, hat 4 pata 5 scarf 6 fillet, mandil 9 headdress
turbid: 4 dark, dull 5 dense, gumly(Sc.), muddy, roily, thick 6 cloudy, grumly(Sc.), impure 7 muddled 8 confused, polluted 9 perplexed
render: 4 roil
turbine: *part:* 6 stator
wheel: 5 rotor
turbot: 5 brill 8 flatfish
turbulence: 4 fury 6 tumult, uproar 7 bluster, ferment, rioting 8 disorder 9 agitation, commotion 11 disturbance
turbulent: 4 wild 5 rough 6 stormy, unruly 7 furious, violent 9 clamorous 10 boisterous, tumultuous 11 tempestuous
turdine bird: 6 thrush
turf: sod 4 flag, peat, vell 5 divot, grass, sward
Turgenev character: 5 Elena
turgid: 5 tumid 7 bloated, pompous, swollen, turgent 8 inflated, swelling 9 bombastic, distended, flatulent, grandiose 12 magniloquent 13 grandiloquent
Turk: aga 5 Tatar 7 Osmanli, Ottoman 9 Kizilbash
turkey: tom 5 poult 7 bustard, failure, gobbler
buzzard: 7 vulture
male: tom
young: 5 poult
Turkey: *agent:* 6 Kehaya
army corps: 4 ordu 8 seraglio
army regiment: 4 alai
bath: 6 hamman
boat: 4 sail 6 mahone
cabinet: 5 divan
camp: 7 palanka
capital: 6 Ankara
carpet: 6 Smyrna
cavalryman: 5 spahi 6 spahee
chief (see also *ruler* below)*:* aga 6 kehaya 7 chambul
city: bir 4 Homs, Sert 5 Adana, Brusa, Izmir, Konya, Siirt, Sivas 6 Aintab, Ankara, Edessa, Edirne, Elaziz, Marash, Samsun, Smyrna 7 Broussa, Erzurum, Kayseri, Scutari, Skutari, Uskudar 8 Istanbul, Stamboul 9 Eskisehir 10 Adrianpole, Diyarbekir 14 Afyonkarahisar, Constantinople
commander: 4 amir, emir 5 ameer, emeer, pacha, pasha 6 sirdar 9 seraskier
council: 5 divan, diwan
court: 5 porte
decree: 5 irade 11 hatti-sherif 12 hatti-humaiun, hatti-humayum
deputy: 6 kahaya
dignitary: 5 pasha
district: 4 Pera 7 Beyoglu, Cilicia
division: 4 caza 5 adana 6 eyalet 7 vilayet 8 villayet
drink: 5 airan
dynasty: 6 seljuk
empire: 7 Ottoman
fig: 5 eleme, elemi
flag: 4 alem, toug 9 horsetail
general: 5 kamal
gold coin: 4 lira 6 mahbub

gulf: Cos
hat: fez 6 calpac
infidel: 6 giaour
inn: 6 imaret 7 cafenet
javelin: 5 jerid 6 jeered
judge: 4 cadi
liquor: 4 raki 5 rakee 6 mastic
man-of-war: 6 carvel 7 caravel 9 caravelle
measures: dra, oka, oke, pic, pik 4 alma, draa, hatt, khat, kile, zira 5 almud, berri, donum, kileh, zirai 6 almude, arshin, chinik, djerib, fortin, halebi, parmak 7 arsheen, arshine, nocktat, parmack 9 pik halebi
military camp: 4 ordu
military rank: 6 chiaus 7 chaoush 8 bimbashi, binbashi
minister: 5 vizir 6 vizier
money: 4 lira, lire, para 5 akcha, asper, attun, pound, rebia 6 akcheh, sequin, zequin 7 altilik, beshlik, chequin, chiquin, pataque, piaster 8 medjidie, zecchino 9 medjidieh
mosque: 4 jami
mountain: 6 Ararat
musical instrument: 5 canum, kanum 7 kussier
musket: 8 tophaike
oak: 6 cerris
official: 4 amir, emir 5 ameer, emeer 6 vizier 7 osmanli, subashi 8 subbassa
palace: 5 serai
policeman: 7 zaptiah, zaptieh
prayer rug: 5 kulah, melas, meles
province: 4 Sert 5 Siirt 6 Angora, Eyalet
religious war: 11 crescentade
reservist: 5 redif
river: 5 Mesta, Sarus 6 Seihun, Seyhan
rug: 5 konia
ruler: bey, dey 4 khan 5 mudir 6 sultan 7 chambul 9 president
saber: 6 odolus
sailor: 8 galionji 9 galiongee
seaport: 4 Enos
slave: 8 mameluke
soldier: 6 nizami 8 janizary 9 janissary 11 bashi-bazouk
statue: 8 tanzimat
storage place: 5 ambar
sultan: Ali 5 Ahmed, calif, Selim 6 caliph 7 Ilderim, Saladin
sword: 7 yatagan 8 yataghan
tambourine: 5 daira
tax: 5 vergi 6 caphar, avania
title: ali 4 amir, baba 5 ameer, basha, pasha 6 bashaw 7 effendi
tobacco: 7 chibouk, Latakia 9 chibouque
treasurer: 8 deftedar
tribe: 4 Kurd
veil: 7 yashmac, yashmak 8 maharmah
vilayet: 4 Urfa
weight: oka, oke 4 dram, kile, ocha, rotl 5 artal, artel, cequi, cheke, kerat, kileh, maund, obolu, ratel 6 batman, dirhem, kantar, miskal 7 drachma, quintal, yusdrum
wheat: 6 bulgar
woman's clothing: 6 jelick 8 charshaf

turkey buzzard: 4 aura 9 gallinazo

Turkish: 7 Osmanli

Turkistan: *cities:* 6 Kokand 7 Andijan 9 Samarkand
highland: 6 Pamirs
land: 5 takyr
moslem: 5 salar
mountain: 4 Alai
peoples: 4 Sart 5 Tatar, Uigur, Usbeg, Usbek, Uzbeg, Yakut 6 Tartan
regiment: 4 alai
river: Ili
salt lake: 4 Shov
sea: 4 Aral

Turkmen: *capital:* 9 Ashkhabad
carpet: 5 Tekke, Yomud 6 Afghan 7 Bokhara
tribe: 5 Ersar 7 Viddhal

turmeric: rea

turmoil: ado, din 4 hurl, toil, toss 5 hurly, labor, touse, upset, worry 6 harass, tumult, unrest, uproar, welter 7 ferment, quarrel, tempest, trouble 8 disquiet, drudgery 9 agitation, commotion, confusion 10 turbulence 11 disturbance 12 perturbation

turn: bow, lap, rev 4 airt, bend, bent, bout, cant, char, head, plow, roll, slew, slue, spin, veer, vert 5 alter, avert, cramp, crook, curve, hinge, pivot, quirk, screw, tarve, wheel, whirl, whorl 6 bought, change, direct, divert, gyrate, invert, ponder, rotate, swerve, swivel, wimple(Sc.), zigzag 7 convert, derange, ferment, meander, rebound, reverse, revolve 8 exchange, nauseate, persuade 9 cinclamen, influence, pirouette, transform, translate 11 disposition 12 metamorphose
about: 9 alternate
another way: 6 obvert
inside out: 5 evert 6 invert
inward: 9 introvert
left: haw 4 port, wynd, wyne
outward: 5 evert, splay 8 extrorse 9 extrovert
rapidly: 4 spin 5 twirl, whirl
right: gee 9 starboard
sour: 5 blink 8 acescent
to one side: 4 awry, skew

turn around: 4 gyre, slue, spin

turn aside: 4 veer 5 shunt 6 detour, divert, swerve
turn away: shy 5 avert, avoid, deter, evade, repel, shunt 6 depart, divert 7 decline, deflect, deviate, dismiss, diverge, swerve
turn back: 4 fold 5 repel 6 return, revert 7 evolute, retrace 9 inversion 10 retroverse
turn down: 4 fold, veto 6 invert, refuse, reject 7 decline
turn off: 4 hang 5 marry, shunt 6 detour, divert 7 consign, deflect, dismiss, putrefy 9 discharge
turn out: 4 oust, trig 5 array, evert, expel, prove 6 outfit, output, siding 7 abandon, dismiss, produce, reverse, striker 8 equipage 9 discharge, equipment, eventuate
turn over: 4 keel 5 spill, upset 6 invert, ponder, reform 7 evolute 8 delegate, overturn, transfer 10 relinquish
turn up: 6 appear, arrive
turnabout: 8 reversal 9 about-face, volte-face
turncoat: 8 apostate, renegade 10 changeling
turned up: 9 retrousse
turner: 7 gymnast, tumbler
turning (see also **turn** above): [illegible] 7 flexion, winding 8 flection, rotative, twisting 10 revolution 11 sinistrorse, vertiginous
turning point: 6 crisis 8 decision, landmark
turnip: 4 neep(Sc.) 5 watch 8 rutabaga 9 blockhead
turnip-shaped: 8 napiform
turnkey: 5 screw 6 jailer, warder
turnover: 4 tart
turnpike: 7 highway 8 tollgate
gatekeeper: 7 pikeman
turnstile: 5 stile
turnstone: 4 bird 6 plover, redleg
turpentine: 4 thus 5 resin, rosin 9 oleoresin
residue: 5 resin, rosin
tree: 4 pine 6 tarata 9 terebinth
turpitude: 6 fedity 8 baseness, vileness 9 depravity
turquoise: 10 chalchuite
turret: 5 tower 8 gunhouse
turse: 4 load, pack 6 bundle
turtle: 5 arrau, caret, torup 6 cooter, emydea, jurara 7 snapper 8 chelonia, emydidae, matamata, shagtail, terrapin, tortoise 10 loggerhead, thalassian 11 leatherback
genus of: 4 emys 7 caretta, testudo 9 chelodina
giant: 5 arrau
part: 7 calipee
shell: 8 carapace
Tuscany: *city:* 4 Pisa
commune: 5 Greve
island: 4 Elba
river: 4 Arno
wine: 7 chianti
tusk: 4 fang 5 tooth 9 scrivello
tusker: 8 elephant
tussis: 5 cough
tussle: 5 fight 6 tousel, tousle 7 contend, contest, scuffle, wrestle 8 struggle 9 scrimmage
tussock: 4 tuft 5 bunch, clump 7 hassock
tut: 4 hush 6 rebuke
tutelage: 7 nurture 8 teaching 9 tutorship 11 instruction 12 guardianship
tutelar: 8 guardian
tutelary: 10 protecting
gods: 5 Lares
tutor: 5 coach, drill, guide, train, watch 6 ground, mentor, school 7 grinder, pedagog, teacher 8 guardian, instruct 9 pedagogue, preceptor 10 discipline
tutta: all 5 whole
tuyere: tew 4 pipe 5 tewel 6 nozzle
TV: See **television**
twaddle: rot 4 bunk 5 haver, prate 6 babble, drivel, footle, gabble 8 nonsense
twangy: 5 nasal
tweak: 4 pull 5 pinch, twist 6 twitch
tweet: 4 peep 5 chirp 7 chirrup
tweezers: 7 pincers 9 merganser
twenty: 5 corge, kappa, score
twenty-faced: 11 icosahedral
twibil: 6 chisel 7 mattock
twice: bis(L.) 6 doubly
prefix: di; dis
twig: 4 beat, mode, pull 5 birch, bough, scion, shoot, spray, sprig, style, tweak, withe 6 branch, fescue, notice, sallow, switch, twitch, wattle 7 fashion, observe 8 perceive 10 comprehend, understand
bundle: 5 fagot 6 barsom
twiggy: 4 thin 6 slight 7 slendor 8 delicate
twilight: 4 dusk 5 gloam 6 dimmet 8 gloaming, glooming 9 cocklight 10 crepuscule
of the Gods: 8 Ragnarok 17 Goetterdaemmerung
pert. to: 11 crepuscular
twill: rib 5 quill, weave
twin: two 4 dual, pair, part 5 gemel, sever, twain 6 couple, double, sunder 7 twofold 8 didymous 11 counterpart
crystal: 5 macle
one: 5 gemel
Siamese: Eng 5 Chang
stars: 6 Castor, gemini, Pollux
twinge: 4 ache, pain, pang 5 pinch, qualm, tweak 6 twitch
twine: ran 4 coil, turn, vine, warp, wind, wrap 5 braid, snarl, twist 6 encurl, enfold, enlace, infold, string, tangle, thread 7 ana-

mite, embrace, entwine, wreathe 8 encircle 9 interlace 10 intertwine, interweave 11 convolution, intermingle
twink: 4 wink 6 punish, thrash 7 twinkle 9 chaffinch
twinkle: 4 wink 5 blink, flash, gleam, shine 7 flicker, flutter, glimmer, glitter, sparkle 11 scintillate
twinkler: 4 star 8 sparkler
twinkling: 4 wink 5 flash, gleam, trice 6 moment 7 instant 13 scintillation
twire: 4 gaze, look, peer 5 gleam 6 glance 7 twinkle
twirl: 4 coil, curl, move, spin, turn 5 querl, twist, whirl 6 gyrate 7 revolve, twizzle 8 flourish, rotation 11 convolution
twist: 4 bend, coil, cord, curl, hang, hurl, silk, skew, slew, slue, spin, tirl(Sc.), turn, wind, yarn 5 crink, crook, curve, gnarl, hinge, quirk, reeve, screw, snarl, swirl, tweak, twine, twirl, unite, wrest, wring 6 branch, enlace, hankle, rotate, spiral, squirm, thread, torque, wrench, writhe 7 confuse, contort, distort, entwine, flexure, meander, perplex, pervert, revolve, scatter, tendril, torment, torsion, torture, twizzle, wreathe 8 appetite, encircle, entangle, separate 9 constrain, deviation, insinuate 10 intertwine, interweave 11 convolution, peculiarity
twisted: cam, wry 6 warped 7 complex, tortile
twister: 4 roll, turn 7 cruller, cyclone, mallard, tornado 8 doughnut 10 somersault, waterspout
twistical: sly 7 evasive 11 underhanded
twistle: 5 twist 6 wrench
twisty (see also **twist** above): 6 tricky 7 bending, evasive, winding 9 dishonest
twit: guy 4 gibe 5 blame, chirp, taunt, tease 7 upbraid 8 reproach, ridicule
twitch: nip, tic, tie, tug 4 draw, jerk, pick, pull, skid, yank 5 pluck, start, thong, tweak 6 fasten, snatch 9 vellicate 11 contraction
twitter: 5 chirp, shake 6 giggle, titter 7 chatter, chitter, flutter, tremble 9 agitation
twizzle: 5 twirl
two: twa(Sc.) 4 beta(Gr.), both, duet, dyad, pair 5 twain, twins 6 couple 7 twosome
chambered: 9 biacameral
edged: 9 ancipital
headed: 11 dicephalous
metrical feet: 6 dipody
months: 8 bi-mester
parts: 6 bident 9 bifurcate 11 dichotomous
pert. to: 4 dual 6 dyadic
prefix: bi, di 5 dioxy
winged: 7 bialate 8 dipteral 9 dipterous
two-bit: 5 cheap
two-faced: 5 false 9 deceitful 11 treacherous 12 hypocritical
god: 5 Janus
two-fisted: 6 virile 8 vigorous
two-foot: 5 biped 7 bipedal
two-pronged: 6 bident
two-sided: 9 bilateral 12 hypocritical
two-spot: 5 deuce
two-time: 5 cheat 7 deceive
two-tone: 7 bicolor
twofold: 4 dual 5 duple 6 bifold, binary, double, duplex 9 bifarious, duplicate
twopenny: ale 4 mean 5 cheap
twosome: 4 duet, pair 6 couple
tycoon: 7 magnate 9 financier 13 industrialist
tyddyn: 4 farm 9 homestead
tydie: 4 bird, wren 8 titmouse
tye: 4 case, rope, wash 5 chain, close 6 common 7 pasture 9 enclosure
tyee: 5 chief
tyke, tike: cur, dog 5 child 6 shaver 7 bumpkin
tylopod: 5 camel
tympan: 4 drum 8 membrane
tympanum: 6 tympan 7 eardrum
tympany: 7 bombast, conceit 9 inflation 10 distention, turgidness
Tyndareus' wife: 4 Leda
typal: 8 symbolic
type: pi; gem 4 font, form, kern, kind, mark, norm, pica, sign, slug, sort 5 agate, class, doric, elite, genre, group, ideal, ionic, metal, model, order, pearl, roman, stamp, token 6 emblem, italic, minion, nature, symbol 7 brevier, English, example, impress, paragon, pattern, species 8 antetype, boldface, classify 9 archetype, bourgeois, character, condensed, nonpareil 11 Baskerville
block: 4 quad 7 quadrat
frame: 5 chase
line: 4 slug
measure: em, en
mixed: pi
mold: 6 matrix
size: 4 pica, ruby 5 pearl 6 minion 7 brevier, diamond 9 nonpareil
slanting: 6 italic
stroke: 5 serif
tray: 6 galley
typeset: 7 compose
typesetter: 8 linotype, monotype 10 compositor
typewriter part: key 6 platen, spacer 9 tabulator
typhoon: 4 wind 5 storm 7 cyclone

typical: 5 typal 6 normal 7 regular 9 schematic 10 emblematic, figurative 13 prefigurative 14 characteristic, representative
typify: 6 embody 9 prefigure, represent, symbolize
typographer: 7 printer
tyrannical: 5 cruel, harsh 6 lordly, unjust 7 slavish 8 despotic 9 arbitrary, imperious 10 oppressive 11 domineering
tyrannosaurus: 8 dinosaur
tyrannous: 5 cruel, harsh 6 severe, unjust 8 despotic 10 tyrannical
tyranny: 5 rigor 8 severity 9 despotism, harshness
tyrant: 4 czar, Ivan, Nero, tsar, tzar 6 despot 7 monarch, usurper 8 martinet 9 oppressor
murder: 11 tyrannicide

Tyre: *king:* 5 Belus, Hiram
noble: 7 Acerbas
prince: 8 Pericles
princess: 4 Dido

tyro: 4 tiro 5 pupil 6 novice 7 amateur 8 beginner, neophyte 9 commencer 10 apprentice 11 abecedarian

tzar, czar, tsar: 4 king 5 ruler 6 tyrant
tzigane: 5 gypsy

U

U-boat: sub 9 submarine
uang: 6 beetle
ubermensch: 8 superman
uberous: 7 copious 8 abundant, fruitful
ubiety: 8 location, position, relation 9 whereness
ubiquitous: 10 everywhere 11 omnipresent
ubiquity: 12 omnipresence
uca: 4 crab
Uffizi site: 8 Florence
Uganda: *capital:* 7 Entebbe
cattle: 6 ankoli
people: 7 Bunyoro
ughten: 4 dawn, dusk 7 evening, morning 8 twilight
ugly: bad 4 vile 5 awful, cross, snivy, toady 6 cranky, homely, snivey 7 crabbed, hideous, ominous 8 grewsome, gruesome, horrible, terrible, unlovely 9 dangerous, fractious, frightful, graceless, loathsome, offensive, repulsive, unsightly 10 ill-favored, ill-natured, unpleasant 11 ill-tempered, quarrelsome, threatening 12 cross-grained, disagreeable 13 objectionable
ugliness symbol: 4 toad
Ugrian: 4 Avar
ugsome: 6 horrid 9 abhorrent, frightful, loathsome
uhlan: 6 lancer 7 soldier 10 cavalryman
uitlander: 9 foreigner, outlander
ukase: 5 edict, order 6 decree 7 command 12 proclamation
ukelele, ukulele: uke
Ukraine: *assembly:* 4 rada
coin: 6 grivna 7 schagiv
dance: 5 gopak
holy city: 4 Kiev
Mother of Cities: 4 Kiev
seaport: 6 Odessa
Ulalume author: Poe
ulcer: 4 noma, sore 7 egilops 8 aegilops, fossette 9 cacoethes
kind of: 6 peptic
ulceration: 8 helcosis
ule: 6 caucho
uliginous: wet 4 oozy 5 moist, muddy 6 swampy
ullage: 7 wantage 8 shortage 10 deficiency
ulna: 4 bone 7 cubitus
end of: 5 ancon
ulster: 4 coat 8 overcoat
ulterior: 5 later 6 future 7 further, remoter 10 subsequent, succeeding 11 undisclosed
ultimate: end 4 dire, last 5 final, telos(Gr.) 6 remote 7 extreme, maximum, primary 8 eventful, eventual, farthest 9 elemental 10 conclusive 11 fundamental
ultimatum: 5 order 6 demand
ultra: 6 beyond 7 extreme, forward, radical 9 excessive, extremist, fanatical 11 extravagant 14 uncompromising
ulu: 5 knife
ululate: bay 4 hoot, howl, wail, yelp 6 lament 7 screech
Ulysses: *antagonist:* 4 Irus
author: 5 Joyce
character: 5 Bloom, Molly
dog: 5 Argos
enchantress of: 5 Circe
enemy: 8 Poseidon
father: 7 Laertes
friend: 6 Mentor
kingdom: 6 Ithaca
mother: 8 Anticlea
plant: 4 moly
son: 9 Telegonus 10 Telemachus
swineherd: 7 Eumaeus
temptress: 5 Circe
voyage: 7 odyssey
wife: 8 Penelope
umber: 5 brown, shade, visor 6 darken, shadow 7 protect, umbrere 8 grayling, umbrette
umbles: 7 numbles 8 entrails
umbra: 4 fish 5 ghost, shade 6 shadow 7 phantom, vestige
umbrage: 5 cloak, doubt, pique, shade, trace 6 offend, shadow 7 foliage, offense, pretext, shelter 8 disfavor, disgrace, disguise 9 disesteem, semblance, suspicion 10 over-

shadow, protection, resentment 11 displeasure
umbrageous: 5 shady 6 shaded
umbrella: 4 gamp 5 blind, guard, shade 6 brolly, chatta, payong, pileus, screen 7 parasol, protect, shelter 8 disguise 11 bumber-shoot
umbrella tree: 8 magnolia
umbrette: 9 hammerkop
Umbrian river: 6 Tevere
umbrous: 5 shady
umiak: 4 boat
umpire: ump 5 judge 6 decide, oddman 7 arbiter, daysman, oddsman, referee 9 supervise 10 arbitrator
Una boat: 7 catboat
unable: 6 cannot 7 disable 8 helpless, impotent 9 incapable 11 incompetent, inefficient, unqualified 13 incapacitated
unaccented: 4 lene 6 atonic
unaccompanied: 4 bare, solo 5 alone
unaccountable: 7 strange 9 countless 10 mysterious 12 inexplicable, unfathomable 13 irresponsible
unaccustomed: new 7 strange 8 uncommon, unwonted 10 unfamiliar
unacquainted: 7 strange, unusual 10 unfamiliar 13 inexperienced
unadorned: 4 bald, bare 5 naked, plain, stark 6 rustic 7 austere
unadulterated: 4 pure 5 clean 6 honest 7 genuine, sincere, unmixed 9 immutable
unaffected: 4 easy, naif, real 5 naive, plain 6 rustic, simple 7 artless, genuine, natural, sincere, unmoved 8 unbiased 9 ingenuous, unaltered, untouched 12 uninfluenced
unaging: 7 eternal
Unalaska native: 5 Aleut
unalike: 9 different
unalleviated: 4 hard
unalloyed: 4 pure 7 genuine, unmixed 11 unqualified
unambiguous: 8 explicit
unanchored: 6 adrift
unanimous: 5 solid 6 united 8 agreeing 11 consentient
unanimously: 7 una voce
unanswerable: 5 final 10 conclusive
unappeasable: 10 implacable
unarmed: 4 bare 5 inerm 11 defenseless
unaspirated: 4 lene
unassailable: 12 invulnerable
unassuming: shy 6 modest 7 natural 8 retiring 9 diffident 14 unostentatious
unattached: 4 free 5 loose 6 single 9 unmarried 11 independent 13 noncollegiate
unattractive: 4 rude, ugly 10 ungracious
unau: 5 sloth
unavailing: 6 futile 8 bootless, gainless
unavowed: 8 ulterior
unaware: 6 unwary 8 heedless, ignorant 11 thoughtless
unbalanced: 6 uneven 8 deranged, lopsided, one-sided
unbecoming: 4 rude 5 inept 8 improper, unseemly, unworthy 10 indecorous, unsuitable 11 disgraceful 12 unattractive
unbefitting: 5 below 10 unsuitable
unbelief: 9 disbelief 10 skepticism 11 agnosticism, incredulity
unbelievable: 9 fantastic 10 incredible 13 inconceivable
unbeliever: 5 pagan 7 atheist, doubter, heretic, infidel, scoffer, skeptic 8 agnostic 11 freethinker
unbend: 4 rest, thaw 5 relax, untie, yield 6 loosen, uncock 7 slacken 8 unfasten
unbending: 5 rigid, stern, stiff 8 obdurate, resolute 10 inexorable, inflexible
unbiased: 4 fair, just 8 detached 9 impartial 12 unprejudiced
unbind: 4 free, undo 5 untie 6 detach, loosen 7 absolve, deliver, release 8 dissolve, unfasten
unbleached: 4 blae, ecru 5 beige 7 natural
unblemished: 4 pure 8 spotless
unblushing: 9 shameless
unbolt: 4 open 5 unbar, unpin 6 unlock 8 unfasten
unbosom: 4 tell 6 reveal
unbound: 4 free 5 loose 10 unconfined
unbounded: 4 open 9 limitless, unchecked, unlimited 11 measureless 12 uncontrolled, unrestrained
unbrace: 4 free, undo 5 carve, relax 6 loosen, reveal, weaken 8 disjoint, enfeeble
unbranched antler: dag
unbridled: 4 free 5 loose 7 violent 9 dissolute, unchecked 10 licentious, ungoverned 12 uncontrolled, unrestrained
unbroken: one 4 flat 5 undug, whole 6 entire, intact 7 untamed 8 unplowed 9 continual, undivided, unsubdued 10 continuous 13 uninterrupted
unburden: 4 ease 5 empty, untax 6 unload 7 disload, relieve
unbury: 6 exhume
uncanny: 4 eery 5 eerie, scary, weird 6 spooky 7 awkward, ghostly, strange 8 careless 9 dangerous, unnatural 10 mysterious
uncanonical: 10 apocryphal
unceasing: 6 eterne 7 endless, eternal 9 continual, incessant, perennial 11 everlasting 14 unintermittent
unceasingly: 7 forever 11 continually, incessantly

unceremonious: 4 curt 5 bluff, blunt 6 abrupt 8 familiar, informal 14 unconventional
uncertain: 4 asea, dark, hazy 5 fluky, vague 6 chancy, fitful, queasy 7 dubious 8 aleatory, doubtful, unsteady, variable 9 ambiguous, equivocal, hazardous, undecided 10 changeable, indefinite, precarious 12 questionable 13 indeterminate, problematical, untrustworthy
uncertainty: 4 were 6 gamble, wonder 7 dubiety 8 suspense 9 dubiosity 10 skepticism
unchanging: 7 eternal, forever, settled, uniform 9 immutable, steadfast, unvarying 10 invariable, stationary
unchaste: 4 lewd 5 bawdy 6 coarse, impure 7 haggard, obscene 8 immodest
unchecked: 4 free 5 loose 7 rampant 9 unbounded, unbridled
unchurch: 13 excommunicate
uncia: 4 coin, inch 5 ounce 7 twelfth
uncivil: 4 rude 5 bluff 7 ill-bred 8 clownish, impolite 9 barbarous 10 indecorous, ungracious, unsuitable 11 uncivilized 12 discourteous 13 disrespectful
uncivilized: 4 rude, wild 5 feral 6 brutal, ferine, savage 8 barbaric 9 barbarian, barbarous, primitive 10 unmannerly 13 unenlightened
uncle: eme, oom, unk 5 nunks 6 nuncle 10 pawnbroker
pert. to: 9 avuncular
Uncle Remus: *author:* 6 Harris
rabbit: 4 Brer
Uncle Tom's Cabin author: 5 Stowe
character: Eva 5 Eliza, Topsy 6 Legree
unclean: 4 foul, tref, vile 5 black, dirty 6 common, filthy, impure 7 defiled, obscene 8 polluted, unchaste 11 unwholesome
unclose: ope 4 open 6 reveal 8 disclose 10 unreserved
unclothe: 5 spoil, strip 6 divest, expose 7 despoil, uncover, undress
unclothed: 4 bare, nude 5 naked
unclouded: 4 open 5 clear, sunny
unco: 5 great, weird 7 foreign, strange, uncanny, unknown 13 extraordinary
uncoil: 6 unwind
uncombined: 4 free 5 loose 10 elementary
uncomfortable: 6 uneasy
uncommon: odd 4 rare 5 novel 6 choice, scarce, unique 7 special, strange, unusual 8 especial, unwonted 10 infrequent, remarkable 11 exceptional 12 unaccustomed 13 extraordinary, preternatural
uncommunicative: 6 silent 8 reserved, reticent
uncompassionate: 5 stony
uncomplaining: 5 stoic 7 stoical
uncomplicated: 5 plain 6 simple
uncompromising: 4 firm 5 rigid, stern 6 strict 9 unbending 10 determined, inflexible, unyielding 12 intransigent
unconcealed: 4 bare, open 5 overt
unconcerned: 4 cool, easy 8 careless, detached 9 apathetic 10 insouciant 11 indifferent 12 uninterested
unconditional: 4 free 8 absolute, explicit
unconfined: lax 4 free 5 loose 9 boundless, limitless, unlimited
unconfused: 4 calm 5 clear 6 steady
unconnected: 5 gappy 6 abrupt 8 detached, rambling, separate 10 incoherent 12 disconnected
unconscious: out 6 asleep, torpid 7 stunned, unaware 8 comatose, ignorant, mindless 9 inanimate, lethargic 10 insensible
render: 4 stun
state: 5 swoon 8 apsychia
unconsciousness: 4 coma 5 faint 6 torpor
unconstrained: 4 easy, free 7 natural 8 familiar 11 spontaneous 12 unrestrained
uncontrollable: 4 wild 11 intractable
uncontrolled: 4 free, wild 5 loose 9 irregular, unbounded, unmanaged 10 hysterical, licentious, ungoverned 11 unregulated 12 unrestrained
unconventional: 5 loose, outre 6 casual 7 devious 8 Bohemian, informal 13 unceremonious
uncooked: raw 6 rawish
uncorrupted: 4 pure 8 pristine
uncouple: 5 loose 8 unfasten 10 disconnect
uncouth: odd 4 rare, rude 5 crude 6 clumsy, dismal, rugged 7 awkward, boorish, loutish, strange, uncanny, unknown 8 desolate, dreadful, ignorant, uncommon, ungainly 9 couthless, unknowing, unrefined, untrained 10 mysterious, outlandish, uncultured, unfamiliar, unpolished 11 comfortless 12 unacquainted, uncultivated
uncouth person: oaf 4 boor, lout 5 yokel 6 bumkin, rustic 7 bumpkin
uncover: 4 bare, open, tirl(Sc.), tirr(Sc.) 6 denude, detect, divest, expose, remove, reveal, unveil 7 display, divulge, undrape, unearth 8 disclose, discover
uncovered: 4 bald, nude, open 5 naked 6 cuerpo 9 developed 10 bareheaded
uncrystallized: 9 amorphous
unction: oil 7 suavity, unguent 8 ointment
give extreme: 5 anele
unctuous: fat 4 oily 5 bland, fatty, soapy, suave 6 fervid, greasy 7 gushing, pinguid, plastic 10 oleaginous
uncultivated: 4 arid, wild 5 feral 6 desert, fallow 7 deserty 9 barbarous

uncultured: 4 rude 7 artless, boorish 9 unrefined
uncurbed: 12 uncontrolled
undamaged: 5 whole 6 intact
undaunted: 4 bold 5 bravo 7 spartan 8 fearless, intrepid, undashed 9 confident, dauntless, turbulent, unbridled, unchecked 10 courageous, undismayed 11 unconquered
undecayed: 5 fresh, green
undeceive: 8 disabuse 11 disillusion
undecided: 4 moot, pend 7 pending 8 doubtful, wavering 9 unsettled 10 inconstant, irresolute, unresolved 13 problematical
undefiled: 4 pure 6 chaste 8 innocent, virtuous 9 unlimited 10 immaculate
undemonstrative: 4 calm, cold, cool 8 reserved 10 restrained
undeniable: 4 true 7 certain 12 indisputable 13 incontestable
undependable: 7 erratic 13 irresponsible
under: 4 alow 5 below, neath, sotto(It.) 6 nether 7 beneath 10 underneath 11 subordinate
obligation: 5 owing 8 beholden, indebted
prefix: hyp, sub
the weather: 4 sick 5 drunk 6 ailing
under-set: 4 prop 6 sublet 7 provide, support 8 maintain, underlet 10 strengthen
underbrush: 6 covert 7 abature
undercover: 6 secret 13 surreptitious
man: spy 5 agent 9 detective 10 counterspy
underdone: 4 rare
underestimate: 8 minimize 9 underrate 10 undervalue
undergarment: bra 4 slip 5 teddy 6 cilice, corset, flimsy, shorts, stepin 7 chemise 9 brassiere, chemilonn, nairshirt, petticoat, teddybear, underwear 10 foundation 11 camiknicker, combination
undergo: 4 bear, pass 5 carry 6 endure, suffer 7 sustain 10 experience
undergraduate: 4 coed 6 junior, senior 7 student 8 freshman 9 sophomore
underground: 5 train 6 hidden, secret, subway 7 beneath 10 undercover 15 surreptitiously
burial place: 5 crypt 8 catacomb
dweller: 5 dwarf, gnome, troll
fighter: 6 maquis 8 partisan
fungus: 7 truffle 8 earthnut
worker: 5 miner 6 mucker, pitman, sapper
undergrowth: 4 rush 5 brush 10 hypotrophy, underbrush
underhanded: sly 4 dern, mean 5 shady 6 byhand, secret, sneaky, unfair 8 sneaking, unfairly 9 deceitful 10 circuitous, fraudulent 11 clandestine, shorthanded, unobtrusive 13 unobtrusively 15 surreptitiously
underlie: 4 bear 7 support
underline: 4 mark 6 stress 9 emphasize
underling: 6 menial, minion 8 inferior 11 subordinate
underlying: 5 basic 7 obscure 8 cardinal 11 fundamental
undermine: sap 4 cave 5 drain, erode 6 impair, weaken 7 founder, subvert 8 discover, enfeeble, excavate 10 demoralize
underneath: 5 below, under 6 secret 7 beneath 13 surreptitious
underpin: 7 justify, support 8 maintain 9 vindicate 12 substantiate
underprop: 4 prop 6 uphold 7 support 8 underpin
underrate: 5 decry 9 extenuate 10 undervalue 13 underestimate
underscore: 9 emphasize, italicize
undersea boat: sub 5 U-boat, wreck 9 submarine 11 submersible
eye: 9 periscope
undershirt: 4 vest 7 chemise
undershrub: 4 bush 7 heather
undersized: 4 puny 5 runty, small 7 scrubby
underskirt: 4 slip 9 petticoat
understand: con, dig, get, ken, see 4 know, sabe, twig 5 grasp, infer, sabby, savey, savvy, sense 6 follow, reason, savvey 7 discern, realize 8 conceive, perceive 9 apprehend, interpret, penetrate 10 comprehend
understandable: 5 clear, lucid
understanding: ken 4 feet, idea, news 5 amity, brain 6 humane, kindly, treaty 7 compact, concept, empathy, entente, knowing 8 attitude, contract, footwear, judgment, skillful, sympathy 9 agreement, diagnosis, knowledge, tolerance 10 acceptance 11 intelligent, sympathetic 12 intelligence
understatement: 7 litotes
understeward: 7 bailiff
understood: 5 clear, lucid, tacit 8 implicit
undertake: try 4 dare, fand, fang 5 chide, grant, seize 6 accept, assume, engage, incept 7 attempt, emprise, emprize, execute, perform, promise, receive, reprove 8 contract, covenant, endeavor, overtake 9 guarantee, underfong
undertaker: 4 bant 5 cerer 6 surety 7 rebuker, sponsor 8 embalmer 9 mortician 12 entrepreneur
undertaking: 4 task 6 charge, pledge 7 calling, project, promise, venture 8 covenant 9 adventure, guarantee 10 enterprise 11 proposition
written: 6 cautio 9 cautiones
undertone: 5 aside

undertow: 4 eddy 6 vortex 7 current, riptide
undervalue: 5 decry 8 disprize, disvalue 10 depreciate
underwater: *apparatus:* 6 tremie 7 caisson
captain: 4 Nemo
chamber: 4 cave 7 caisson
craft: sub 5 U-boat 7 pigboat 9 submarine
missile: 7 torpedo
sound detector: 5 sofar, sonar
underwear: 6 skivvy 7 dessous(F.), stepins 8 lingerie, skivvies 12 underclothes
underwood: 5 frith 7 boscage, coppice 10 underbrush 11 undergrowth
underworld: 4 hell 5 Hades, Orcus, Sheol 6 Amenti, Erebus 7 xibalba 8 gangland 9 antipodes
boatman: 6 Charon
deity: Dis 4 Bran 5 Hades, Pluto 6 Osiris 8 Dispater 9 Enmeshara 11 Ningishzida
goddess: 6 Allatu, Belili, Hecate, Trivia
organization: 5 Mafia
pert. to: 8 chthonic 9 chthonian
river: 4 Styx 5 Lethe 7 Acheron
watchdog: 8 Cerberus
underwrite: 6 insure 7 assure, finance, sponsor 9 subscribe
undesigned: 6 chance 10 accidental
undesigning: 6 simple 7 artless, sincere
undetermined: 5 vague 7 dubious 8 aoristic, doubtful 9 equivocal
undeveloped: 5 crude 6 latent 8 immature
undeviating: 4 even 8 straight
undigested: 5 crude
undiluted: 4 mear, meer, mere, neat, pure 8 straight
undiminished: 6 entire
undine: 5 nymph
undirected: 6 misled 7 aimless 11 misdirected
undisciplined: 4 wild 6 unruly, wanton 9 untrained
undisclosed: 6 secret 8 ulterior
undisguised: 4 bald 5 frank, overt 9 barefaced
undisturbed: 4 calm 5 quiet 6 placid, secure, serene 9 unruffled
undivided: one 5 total, whole 6 entire, intact 8 complete, unbroken 10 continuous
undo: 4 open, ruin 5 annul, fordo, loose, solve 6 betray, cancel, defeat, diddle, foredo, unlash, unwrap 7 defease, destroy, disjoin, explain, nullify, release, uncover, unravel 8 unfasten 10 disappoint, disconnect, invalidate
undoing: 4 ruin 8 downfall 9 overthrow
undomesticated: 4 wild 5 feral 6 ferine
undone: raw 9 neglected 10 defeasible
undoubted: 4 sure 7 certain 8 accepted, admitted 11 indubitable
undraped: 4 bare, nude
undress: 4 doff 5 strip 6 devest, divest 7 disrobe 8 unclothe 10 dishabille
undressed skin: kip 4 pelt
undue: 7 extreme 8 improper 9 excessive 10 exorbitant, immoderate, inordinate, unsuitable 11 unwarranted 12 unreasonable 13 inappropriate
undulant: 7 aripple, sinuous 10 undulating, undulatory
undulate: 4 roll, wave 5 swing 6 billow 9 fluctuate
undulation: 5 crimp, swell 8 waviness
undutiful: 7 impious
undying: 6 eterne 7 ageless, endless, eternal 8 immortal, unending 9 continual, deathless 12 imperishable
unearth: dig 5 learn 6 exhume, expose 7 uncover 8 disclose, discover
unearthly: 4 eery 5 eerie, weird 7 awesome, uncanny, ungodly 8 terrific 9 appalling, fantastic 10 mysterious, outlandish 12 preposterous, supernatural 13 preternatural
uneasiness: 5 worry 6 unrest 7 anxiety, disease, trouble 8 disquiet 10 constraint, discomfort, discontent 11 displeasure, disturbance 12 apprehension 13 inconvenience 15 dissatisfaction
uneasy: 5 stiff 7 anxious, awkward, fidgety, unquiet, restive 8 restless 9 difficult, perturbed, unsettled 13 uncomfortable
uneaten: 5 waste, whole 6 scraps
uneducated: 8 ignorant 10 illiterate, unlettered, unschooled
unemotional: 4 cold 5 stony, stoic 7 stoical 10 phlegmatic
unemployed: 4 idle 6 otiant, otiose 8 inactive, leisured
unenclosed: 4 open 9 fenceless
unencumbered: 4 free
unending: 7 endless, eternal, undying 8 timeless 9 ceaseless 12 interminable
unendurable: 10 impassible, unbearable 11 intolerable
unenthusiastic: 4 cool 9 apathetic 12 uninterested
unequal: 5 impar 6 uneven, unfair, unjust 8 variable 9 disparate, irregular 11 fluctuating 16 disproportionate
comb. form: 5 aniso
condition: 4 odds
unequaled: 7 supreme 9 matchless, unmatched, unrivaled 10 surpassing 12 unparalleled
unequivocal: 5 clear, plain 7 sincere 8 definite, explicit 9 certainly 11 categorical 15 straightforward

unerring: 4 sure, true 5 exact 7 certain 8 inerrant 9 inerrancy, unfailing 10 infallible
unethical: 5 wrong 6 amoral
uneven: odd 5 eroso, gobby, haggy, rough 6 hobbly, rugged, unfair, unjust, unlike 7 unequal, varying 9 irregular 10 ill-matched 11 fluctuating, ill-assorted
unevenness: 8 asperity
unexamined: 7 apriori
unexcelled: 8 champion, superior
unexceptional: 5 usual 7 regular 8 ordinary
unexcitable: 6 stolid
unexcited: 4 calm 7 stoical
unexciting: 4 dead, tame 6 boring 7 prosaic 13 uninteresting
unexpected: 6 abrupt, sudden 9 inopinate, unguarded 10 accidental, unforeseen
unexpended: 6 saving 7 reserve, surplus
unexpired: 5 alive, valid 9 operative
unexpressed: 5 tacit
unextinguished: 5 alive
unface: 6 unmask
unfadable: 4 fast 9 memorable
unfaded: 5 fresh 6 bright
unfading flower: 8 amaranth
unfailing: 4 sure 7 certain 8 reliable, unerring 10 infallible, unflagging, unyielding 13 inexhaustible
unfair: 4 foul, hard 5 wrong 6 biased, uneven, unjust 8 unseemly, wrongful 9 dishonest, unethical 11 inequitable, underhanded, unfavorable 12 dishonorable
unfaithful: 7 infidel, traitor 8 derelict, disloyal, recreant, turncoat 9 dishonest, faithless 10 adulterous, inaccurate, traitorous 13 untrustworthy
unfaltering: 4 true 5 brave 6 steady
unfamed: 5 lowly 6 humble 7 obscure
unfamiliar: new 7 strange, unknown 12 unaccustomed
unfashionable: 5 dated 9 distorted, unshapely
unfast: 6 unfirm, untrue 8 insecure
unfasten: 4 free, open, undo 5 loose, unbar, unfix, unpin, untie 6 detach, loosen, unlace, unlock 8 untether
unfathomable: 10 bottomless 12 impenetrable
unfavorable: bad, ill 4 foul 6 averse 7 adverse 8 contrary 15 disadvantageous
unfeeling: 4 dull, hard 5 cruel, harsh, stern, stony 6 brutal, marble, stolid 7 callous 8 numbness, obdurate 9 apathetic, bloodless, heartless, insensate, senseless 10 impassible, insensible 11 hardhearted, insensitive 13 unsusceptible 16 unimpressionable
unfeigned: 4 real, true 6 hearty 7 genuine, natural, sincere
unfermented grape juice: 4 stum
unfertile: 4 arid 6 barren
unfetter: 6 loosen
unfettered: 4 free 5 broad, loose
unfilled: 5 blank, empty
unfilled cavity: 4 vugg
unfinished: raw 5 crude, rough 7 sketchy 8 immature 9 imperfect 10 incomplete
unfit: bad 4 sick 5 inept, pasul(Heb.) 6 faulty 8 disabled, improper 10 unsuitable 11 handicapped, incompetent, unqualified 12 disqualified 13 incapacitated
unfix: 6 detach, loosen 8 dissolve, unfasten, unsettle
unfixed: 6 adrift, afloat 8 drifting, shifting
unflagging: 8 tireless
unflattering: 4 open 5 blunt, frank 6 candid 10 derogatory, unbecoming
unfledged: 5 green 6 callow 8 immature 11 undeveloped, unfeathered
bird: 4 eyas 8 nestling
unflinching: 4 firm 6 stanch 8 resolute 9 steadfast 10 unwavering, unyielding
unfold: ope 4 open 6 deploy, evolve, expand, explat, flower, reveal, spread, unfurl, unwrap 7 develop, display, divulge, evolute, explain, explate, release 8 develope, disclose 9 explicate
unforced: 4 easy 7 natural, willing 9 voluntary
unforeseen: 6 casual 10 accidental
unformed: 6 callow 9 shapeless, uncreated 11 undeveloped
unfortunate: bad, ill 4 poor 5 worst 6 dismal, wretch 7 hapless, unhappy, unlucky 8 luckless, wretched 9 graceless 10 calamitous, prostitute, ungracious 12 inauspicious, infelicitous, unsuccessful
unfounded: 4 idle, vain 8 baseless 10 chimerical, groundless
unfragrant: 4 olid 5 fetid
unfrequented: 6 lonely 8 isolated, solitary
unfriendly: 4 cool 6 remote 7 asocial, hostile 8 inimical, unsocial 9 dissocial
terms: 4 outs
unfruitful: 5 blunt 6 barren, wasted 7 sterile, useless 9 fruitless, infertile 12 unproductive, unprofitable
unfurl: 4 open 5 enrol 6 enroll, expand, spread, unfold, unroll 7 develop 8 develope
unfurnished: 4 bare 6 vacant
ungainly: 5 lanky 6 clumsy 7 awkward, boorish, uncouth 8 clownish, slammock, slummock 11 elephantine
ungenerous: 4 mean 5 harsh, nasty 6 stingy
ungentlemanly: 7 ill-bred 9 illiberal
ungirt: 5 loose, slack 7 unbound

ungodly: 6 sinful, wicked 7 impious 8 dreadful 9 atheistic, atrocious, unearthly 11 unbelieving 12 hypocritical
ungovernable: 4 wild 6 unruly 7 froward 9 unbridled 10 disorderly, headstrong, licentious, rebellious 11 intractable 13 irrepressible 14 uncontrollable
ungraceful: 6 clumsy 7 angular, awkward 9 inelegant
ungracious: 4 hard, rude 6 wicked 8 churlish, disliked, impolite 9 graceless, offensive 10 unmannerly, unpleasant 11 unfortunate 12 discourteous, unattractive
ungrateful: 9 thankless
ungrounded: 8 baseless 9 unfounded 10 uninformed 12 uninstructed
ungrudging: 8 cheerful
ungual: 4 claw, hoof, nail 6 ungula
unguarded: 6 unwary 8 careless 9 imprudent 10 incautious 11 defenseless, thoughtless, unprotected
unguent: 4 balm 5 salve 6 cerate, ceroma, chrism 8 ointment 9 lubricant
unguinous: 4 oily 8 unctuous
ungula: 4 claw, hoof, nail 6 ungual
ungulate: hog, pig 4 deer 5 horse, tapir 6 hoofed 8 elephant 10 rhinoceros
unhallowed: 6 impure, unholy, wicked 7 impious, profane 10 desecrated
unhamper: 5 loose
unhandsome: 4 mean, rude 5 plain 6 homely, stingy 10 unbecoming
unhandy: 6 clumsy 7 awkward 12 inconvenient
unhap: 6 mishap 7 ill-luck
unhappiness: woe 5 blues, dolor, grief, worry 6 misery, unrest
unhappy: sad 4 evil 6 dismal 7 unlucky 8 dejected, illfated, wretched 9 miserable, sorrowful, woebegone 10 calamitous 11 melancholic, mischievous, unfavorable, unfortunate 12 inauspicious, unsuccessful 13 inappropriate
unharmed: 4 safe 6 unhurt 8 harmless 10 scatheless
unharmonious: 9 dissonant
unharness: 6 disarm, divest, ungear 7 unhitch, unhorse
unhasp: 8 unfasten
unhealthy: ill 4 sick 6 sickly 11 unwholesome
unheard of: 7 strange, unknown 13 unprecedented
unheated: 4 cold
unheeding: 4 deaf 8 careless 12 disregarding
unhesitating: 5 ready
unhidden: 5 overt
unholy: 6 impure, wicked 7 impious, profane 8 dreadful, shocking 9 frightful 10 scandalous, unhallowed
unhonored: 12 dishonorable 13 dishonourable
unhorse: 5 throw 8 dislodge, dismount 9 overthrow, unharness
unhurried: 4 easy, slow 10 deliberate
unhurt: 4 safe 8 unharmed 9 uninjured
unicellular animal: 5 ameba 6 amoeba 9 protozoan 10 paramecium
unicellular plant: 5 spore
unicorn: 4 reem
unicorn fish: 4 unie 7 narwhal 8 filefish
unidentified flying object: UFO
uniform: 4 even, flat, suit 5 equal, level 6 livery, outfit, steady 7 regular, similar 8 constant, equiform 9 continual, equitable, unvarying 10 consistent, equiformal, invariable, monotonous, unchanging 11 homogeneous
cord: 11 aiguillette
in color: 4 flat, flot
servant's: 6 livery
shoulder ornament: 7 epaulet 9 epaulette
uniformly: 6 always
unify: 5 merge, unite 8 coalesce 9 correlate, integrate 11 consolidate
unimaginative: 4 dull 7 literal, prosaic
unimpaired: 4 free 5 fresh 6 entire, intact
unimpassioned: 6 steady
unimpeachable: 9 blameless, faultless 14 irreproachable, unquestionable 15 unexceptionable
unimpeded: 4 free
unimportant: 5 minor, petty, small 6 little, paltry 7 trivial 10 negligible
unimpressed: 6 unawed
uninflected: 7 aptotic
uninformed: 8 ignorant
uninhabited: 5 empty 6 vacant 8 deserted, desolate
uninspired: 4 dull 6 stodgy
unintelligent: 4 dumb 5 brute 6 obtuse, stupid, unwise 7 foolish 8 ignorant 9 senseless 10 irrational
unintentional: 10 accidental 11 inadvertent
uninteresting: dry 4 arid, drab, dull, flat 5 stale 6 boring, jejune, prolix, stupid 7 humdrum, insipid, prosaic, tedious 8 tiresome 9 colorless 10 unexciting
uninterrupted: 7 endless, eternal 9 continual 10 continuous 11 everlasting
unio: 6 mussel
union: AFL, CIO, one, UAW 4 bloc 5 artel, ILGWU, unity 6 accord, copula, fusion, gremio(Sp.), league, merger, unicum 7 amalgam, concord, contact, entente, meeting, oneness, society 8 alliance, junction,

knitting, marriage 9 coalition, coherence, composure 10 connection, copulation, federation, fellowship 11 association, coalescence, combination, concurrence, confederacy, conjunction, consistency
political: 4 bloc 9 coalition
trade: 5 guild, hanse
union jack: 4 flag
Union of South Africa: See **South Africa**
Union of Soviet Socialist Republics (see also **Russia, Soviet Union**): 4 USSR 6 Russia, Soviet
unique: odd, one 4 rare, sole 5 alone, queer 6 single 7 notable, special, unequal, unusual 8 peculiar, singular 9 matchless 13 extraordinary
unison: 5 union 6 accord 7 concord, harmony 9 agreement, consonant, identical, unanimity, unisonant, unisonous 10 concordant, consonance, equivalent
unit: ace, one 4 item 5 digit, group, monad, whole 6 entity 10 individual
conductivity: mho
discord: 4 word
fluidity: rhe
flux density: 5 gauss
force: 4 dyne, volt 5 kinit, tonal
hypothetical: 6 pangen 7 pangene
illumination: 4 phot
inductance: 5 henry
light: lux, pyr 5 lumen
magnetic: 5 weber
measure: are, mil, rod 4 pint 5 meter, stere
measuring sound: 7 decibel
metrical: 4 dyne, mora 5 liter, morae
military: 4 army 5 corps, squad 7 brigade, company, platoon 8 division, regiment 9 battalion
physical: erg 7 atomerg
power: HP; bel 4 watt 5 dynam, horse
pressure: 5 barad, barye
reluctance: rel
resistance: ohm
social: 4 clan, sect 6 family
speed: 4 velo
stellar: 6 parsec
tale: 4 rees
telegraphic: 4 baud
thermal: 6 calory 7 calorie
time: day 4 bell, hour, week, year 5 month 6 minute, season, second
ultimate: 5 monad
velocity: kin 4 kine, velo
volume: oz, pd; cwt, ton 5 ounce, pound 13 hundredweight
weight: ton 4 dram, gram 5 carat, ounce, pound
work: erg 5 ergon, joule 6 kilerg
unite: add, fay, pan, sew, tie, wed 4 ally, band, bind, club, fuse, hasp, join, knit, link, meld, pair, [illegible]am, weld 5 affix, annex, blend, graft, hitch, marry, merge, piece, rally 6 adhere, adjoin, attach, cement, cohere, concur, couple, embody, mingle, pleach, solder, splice 7 combine, conjoin, connect, consort, convene 8 assemble, coalesce, compound, concrete, condense, conspire, continue, federate, regelate 9 affiliate, aggregate, associate, colleague 10 amalgamate, articulate, consociate, federalize 11 concentrate, compaginate, consolidate, incorporate 12 conglutinate
united: one 9 concerted, conjugate, corporate 10 corporated
United Nations Organization: UNO
United Provinces: 7 Holland, Utrecht, Zeeland 9 Friesland, Groningen 10 Gelderland, Overijssel
United States (see also **America**): *admiral:* 4 King, Sims 5 Dewey 6 Halsey, Nimitz 8 Farragut
artist: 4 Pyle, Wood 5 Flagg, Homer, Marin, Moses, Peale, Ryder, Sloan, Wyeth 6 Benton, Eakins, Hopper, Stuart
author: Ade, Poe, Roe 4 Ames, Baum, Buck, Dana, Grey, Pyle, Uris, Ward, Wolf 5 Alger, Barth, Beach, Davis, Field, Harte, Hurst, Lewis, James, Quinn, Stowe, Tripp 6 Alcott, Bellow, Bryant, Cabell, Cooper, Ferber, Hersey, Holmes, Irving, London, Lowell, Jewett, Kantor, O. Henry, O'Neill, Porter, Snyder 7 Barrett, Clemens, Dreiser, Emerson, Hayward, Malamud, Parkman, Saroyan, Stewart, Thoreau, Vaughan, Wallace, Whitman 8 Faulkner, Salinger, Sinclair, Whittier 9 Cenedella, Hawthorne, Hemingway 10 Longfellow, Tarkington
bandleader: 5 Sousa
canal: 4 Erie 6 Panama
capital city: 5 Boise, Dover, Salem 6 Albany, Austin, Boston, Denver, Helena, Juneau, Pierre, St. Paul, Topeka 7 Atlanta, Augusta, Concord, Jackson, Lansing, Lincoln, Madison, Olympia, Phoenix, Raleigh, Santa Fe, Trenton 8 Bismarck, Cheyenne, Columbia, Columbus, Hartford, Honolulu, Richmond 9 Annapolis, Des Moines, Frankfort, Nashville 10 Baton Rouge, Carson City, Charleston, Harrisburg, Little Rock, Montgomery, Montpelier, Providence, Sacramento 11 Springfield, Tallahassee 12 Indianapolis, Oklahoma City, Salt Lake City 13 Jefferson City
cartoonist: 4 Arno, Capp, Nast 5 Petty 6 Addams, Disney 7 Mauldin 8 Herblock
chemist: 4 Urey 5 Moore 7 Pauling

coin: bit 4 cent, dime 5 eagle, penny 6 dollar, nickel 7 quarter
colonists: 5 Dutch 8 Pilgrims, Puritans
composer: 4 Foss, Kern 5 Foote, Grofe, Nevin 6 Berlin, Foster, Porter 7 Copland, Rodgers 8 Gershwin 9 Bernstein
deer: elk 6 wapiti
dramatist: 4 Inge, Rice 5 Barry, Odets 6 Crouse, Miller, O'Neill 8 Crothers, Williams
editor: Bok 4 Dana, Ochs 5 White 7 Greeley
emblem: 5 eagle
essayist: Poe 5 Mabie 6 Lowell, Morley 7 Emerson, Thoreau
explorer: 4 Byrd, Long, Pike 5 Boone, Clark, Lewis, Logan, Perry
falls: 7 Niagara 8 Yosemite 9 Multnomah
flagmaker: 9 Betsy Ross
frontiersman: 4 Cody 5 Boone, Clark, Lewis 8 Crockett
general: Lee, Ord 4 Otis, Pope 5 Bragg, Grant, Meade 7 Bradley, Jackson 8 Burnside, Pershing, Stilwell 10 Eisenhower
historian: 4 Dodd
horse: 5 pinto 6 bronco, morgan 7 mustang
humorist: Ade, Day, Nye 4 Cobb, Nash, Neal 5 Twain 6 Rogers 7 Lardner, Thurber
illustrator: 5 Flagg
Indian: See under **Indian**
inventor: Hoe 4 Bell, Howe 5 Fiske, Fitch, Morse 6 Edison, Fulton 7 Whitney
journalist: 4 Dana, Ochs, Pyle, Reid, Riis 5 Alsop, Block, Broun, White 6 Reston 7 Lorimer 8 Brisbane
jurist: Jay 4 Hand, Reed, Taft 5 Chase, Stone, Story, Taney 6 Holmes 8 Marshall 11 Frankfurter
legendary hero: 6 Bunyan
lexicographer: 4 Funk 7 Webster
measure: lea, mil, rod, ton, tub, vat 4 acre, bolt, cord, drum, foot, gill, hand, hank, heer, inch, iron, last, line, link, mile, nail, pace, palm, peck, pint, pipe, pole, pool, roll, sack, span, typp, vara, yard 5 block, carat, chain, labor, minim, perch, point, prime, quart, skein, stran 6 barrel, basket, bushel, fathom, gallon, league, pottle, square, strand, thread 7 quarter, section, spindle 8 hogshead, quadrant, standard, township 9 board foot, decillion, fluid dram 10 fluid ounce 11 teaspoonful 13 tablespoonful 16 Winchester bushel
measure of weight: bag, keg, kip, ton 5 carat, flask, grain, ounce, pound 6 denier 7 long ton, quarter, quintal 9 troy ounce, troy pound 11 metric carat 13 hundredweight
mountain: 4 Hood 6 Cumbre, Elbert, Helena, Shasta 7 Massive, Rainier, Whitney 8 Katahdin, McKinley
mountain lion: 4 puma 6 cougar
naturalist: 4 Muir 5 Baird, Beebe, Seton 7 Thoreau
novelist: see *author* above
opera singer: 4 Alda 5 Price, Sills 6 Callas, Farrar, Tucker 7 Stevens
orator: 4 Otis 5 Bryan, Henry
ornithologist: 7 Audubon
painter: see *artist* above
personification: 8 Uncle Sam
philanthropist: 4 Ford, Riis 5 Lenox 8 Carnegie 11 Rockefeller
philosopher: 5 James 6 Edmans 7 Thoreau
physician: 4 Mayo, Reed, Rush, Salk 5 Minot
physicist: 5 Tesla 6 Teller 7 Nichols
pianist: 5 Watts 6 Duchin, Levant 7 Cliburn
pioneer: see *frontiersman* above
pirate: 4 Kidd
plains: 7 prairie 8 savannah
poet: Poe 4 Nash 5 Benet, Field, Moore, Reese, Riley, Stein, Towne, Wylie 6 Bryant, Holmes, Kilmer, Lanier, Lowell, Millay 7 Whitman 8 Whittier 10 Longfellow
polar explorer: 4 Byrd 5 Perry
President: See **President (U.S.)**
publisher: 4 Luce, Ochs 6 Cowles, Fields, Hearst, Howard 9 McCormick, Patterson
racetrack: 5 Bowie 6 Goshen, Laurel 7 Hialeah, Jamaica, Pimlico 8 Aqueduct
river: 4 Ohio 6 Hudson, Wabash 8 Missouri 9 Merrimack 11 Mississippi
rodent: 6 beaver, gopher 8 squirrel
sculptor: 6 Calder 7 Borglum
socialist: 4 Debs 6 Thomas
statesman: Jay 5 Baker, Lodge, Logan 6 Baruch, Blaine 7 Acheson, Stimson 9 Stevenson
suffragist: 4 Catt 7 Anthony
Vice President: See **Vice President (U.S.)**
violinist: 5 Stern

units: *aggregate distance:* 7 mileage
biological: 6 idants

unity: one 5 union 6 accord 7 concord, harmony, oneness 8 alliance, identity 9 agreement, communion 10 singleness, solidarity, uniformity 11 conjunction, unification

universal: all 5 local, total, whole 6 common, cosmic, entire, public 7 general 8 catholic, constant 9 continual, unlimited 12 allpervading
language: Ro; ido 9 Esperanto
military training: 5 draft

universe: 5 earth, monad, world 6 cosmos, nature, system 8 creation

comb. form: 5 cosmo
controlling principle: 4 tien 5 logos
pert. to: 6 cosmic
science: 9 cosmology
university (see also **college**): 6 patent 7 academy, college 8 academie 9 accademie
division: 6 school 7 college
grounds: 6 campus
Ivy League: 4 Yale 5 Brown 7 Cornell, Harvard 8 Columbia 9 Dartmouth, Princeton 12 Pennsylvania
official: 4 dean 6 regent
rank: 6 docent 9 professor 10 instructor
team: 7 varsity
univocal: 7 uniform 9 unanimous, unisonous 11 indubitable 12 unmistakable
unjust: 5 cruel 6 unfair 8 improper, wrongful 9 dishonest, faithless 10 inaccurate, iniquitous, unfaithful
unked, unkid: odd 5 weird 6 lonely 7 awkward, ghastly, strange, uncanny, uncouth, unknown 8 desolate 12 inconvenient 13 uncomfortable
unkeeled: 6 ratite
unkempt: 5 crude, messy, rough 6 frouzy, frowsy, frowzy, shaggy, untidy 7 ruffled, squalid, tousled 9 unrefined 10 disarrayed, disheveled, unpolished
unkind: bad, ill 4 vile 5 cruel, harsh, rough, stern 6 severe, wicked 7 foreign, strange 8 ungenial 9 inclement, undutiful, unnatural 10 degenerate, ungenerous, ungracious, ungrateful, unsuitable 11 unfavorable
unknit: 4 undo 5 ravel, relax, untie 6 unknot 7 unravel 8 disperse, dissolve, disunite
unknowable: 8 mystical, noumenon 9 enigmatic
unknown: 4 unco 7 inconnu(F.), strange 9 anonymous, incognito 10 unfamiliar 12 incalculable 13 inexpressible
unlace: 4 undo 5 loose 6 carver 7 undress, unravel 8 unfasten, untangle
unlawful: 7 bastard, illegal, illicit 8 wrongful 9 irregular 10 contraband 12 illegitimate
hunting: 8 poaching
intrusion: 8 trespass
unlearned: 4 lewd 5 gross 6 borrel 7 natural 8 ignorant, untaught 9 untutored 10 illiterate, uneducated 11 instinctive, instinctual
unleashed: 4 free 5 loose 8 released
unleavened: 7 azymous
bread: 4 azym 5 azyme, matzo 7 matzoth(pl.)
unless: 4 lest, nisi(L.), save 6 except 9 excepting, provision 11 reservation
unlettered: 4 lewd 8 ignorant 9 barbarian 10 illiterate, uneducated
unlike: 6 uneven 7 difform, diverse 8 unlikely 9 different, irregular 10 dissimilar, improbable 13 heterogeneous
unlikely: 5 unfit 10 improbable, unsuitable 11 unpromising 12 disagreeable, unattractive 13 objectionable
unlikeness: 8 contrast 12 disagreement 13 dissimilarity
unlimited: 4 vast 9 boundless, limitless, unbounded, undefined, universal 10 indefinite, unconfined 11 illimitable, untrammeled 12 immeasurable, unrestricted 13 indeterminate
unlit: 4 dark
unload: 4 dump 5 empty, trash 6 decant, remove 7 deplete, discard, lighten, relieve 9 disburden, discharge, liquidate, sacrifice
unlock: ope 4 open 5 solve 6 reveal
unlooked for: 6 chance 10 unexpected
unlucky: bad, fey, ill 7 hapless 8 illfated 9 illomened 11 unfortunate
unman: 5 crush 7 monster, unnerve 8 castrate
unmanageable: 5 randy 8 churlish 10 disorderly
unmanly: 8 childish
unmannerly: 4 rude 7 boorish, uncivil 8 impolite 10 ungracious 12 discourteous
unmarried: one 4 lone 6 chaste, single
in law: 4 sole
unmask: 6 expose, reveal, unface 7 uncloak 8 disclose 9 dismantle
unmatched: odd 5 alone 9 matchless
unmeasured: 4 huge, vast 7 immense 9 boundless 12 unrestrained
unmelodious: 9 dissonant 11 cacophonous
unmerciful: 5 cruel 8 pitiless, ruthless 9 inclement 10 relentless
unmethodical: 7 cursory, erratic 9 desultory
unmindful: 8 careless, heedless 9 forgetful, negligent 10 neglectful
unmistakable: 4 open 5 clear, plain 6 patent 7 evident, obvious 8 apparent, definite
unmitigated: 4 mere 5 sheer 6 arrant 8 absolute, clearcut 10 unmodified
unmixed: 4 deep, mear, mere, pure 5 blank, sheer, utter 7 sincere
unmoved: 4 calm, cool, firm 5 stony 6 serene 7 adamant 8 obdurate, stubborn, unshaken 9 apathetic
unmoving: 5 inert
unnatural: 4 eery 5 eerie 7 strange, uncanny 8 abnormal, affected, farcical 9 irregular 10 artificial, factitious 11 counterfeit

unnecessary: 7 useless 8 needless 11 superfluous
unnerve: 5 unman 6 weaken 8 enervate 10 dishearten
unnoble: 7 ignoble
unobservant: 8 heedless
unobstructed: 4 free, open 9 panoramic
unobtrusive: 6 modest 8 retiring
unobtrusively: 9 underhand
unoccupied: 4 idle, void 5 empty 6 vacant 7 leisure 10 unemployed
unofficial: 7 private 8 informal
unorganized: 5 messy 7 chaotic 10 disorderly
unoriginal: 4 copy 5 trite 10 secondhand
unorthodox: 9 heretical
unostentatious: 5 quiet 6 lenten, modest 10 restrained
unpaid: due 6 arrear 10 unrevenged
unpaired: odd
unpalatable: 10 unpleasant 11 distasteful
unparalleled: 5 alone 6 unique 7 unequal 8 peerless 9 matchless, unmatched 10 inimitable
unplaned: 5 rough
unpleasant: bad 7 irksome 9 offensive 10 abominable, forbidding, illfavored, ungracious 11 displeasing, distasteful 12 disagreeable
most: 5 worst
unplowed: lea 6 fallow 8 untilled
unpolished: 5 brull, crude, rough 6 coarse, rugged 8 agrestic, impolite 9 barbarous 10 agrestical
unpopularity: 5 odium
unprecedented: new 5 novel 10 unexampled
unprejudiced: 4 fair 9 impartial 13 dispassionate
unpremeditated: 6 casual 9 extempore 10 accidental
unprepared: raw 5 unfit
unprepossessing: 4 ugly 5 plain 6 homely 11 unappealing 12 unattractive
unpretentious: 5 plain 6 homely, humble, modest, simple 10 unaffected
unprincipled: 4 lewd 9 abandoned 10 perfidious 12 unscrupulous
unprocessed: raw 5 crude
unproductive: 4 arid, dead, lean 6 barren, geason 7 sterile 10 unfruitful
unprofessional: lay 6 laical 7 amateur 9 unskilled 15 nonprofessional
unprofitable: dry 4 dead 6 barren 7 inutile, useless 8 bootless, gainless 9 fruitless, frustrate 10 unfruitful 12 frustraneous 15 disadvantageous
unpropitious: 4 evil 7 adverse, ominous, opposed 12 inauspicious
unprotected: 7 exposed 8 helpless 9 unguarded
unqualified: 4 bare, mear, meer, mere 5 sheer, unfit 6 entire, unable 7 plenary 8 absolute, complete, definite 9 categoric, downright, incapable 11 categorical, incompetent
unquestionable: 7 certain, decided, evident 8 implicit, positive 12 indisputable
unravel: 4 undo 5 feaze, ravel, solve 6 unfold, unlace 8 disorder, disunite, separate, untangle 9 disengage 11 disentangle
unready: 4 slow 5 unfit 6 clumsy 7 awkward 8 hesitant 9 undressed
unreal: 5 false, ideal 6 aerial 7 fancied, fatuous, nominal 8 aeriform, fanciful, illusive, illusory, spurious 9 deceptive, fantastic, imaginary, pretended, visionary 10 apocryphal, artificial, barmecidal, fictitious, mandacious 11 counterfeit, imaginative 13 insubstantial, unsubstantial
unreality: 7 fantasy 9 fantastry
unreasonable: mad 6 absurd 9 excessive, senseless 10 exorbitant, immoderate, irrational 11 extravagant, impractical
unreasonableness: 5 alogy
unrecognized: 6 unsung 7 unknown 13 unappreciated
unrefined: raw 4 dark, loud, rude 5 broad, crass, crude, gross 6 coarse, common, earthy, vulgar 7 uncouth 12 uncultivated
unregenerate: 6 carnal, sinful 9 shameless 10 impenitent 11 unrepentent
unrelated: 5 fremd
unrelaxed: 4 taut 5 tense
unrelenting: 4 grim, hard, iron 5 cruel, stern 6 severe 8 rigorous 9 merciless 10 inexorable, inflexible, relentless, unyielding
unreliable: 5 fishy 6 fickle 7 casalty 10 capricious 12 undependable 13 irresponsible, untrustworthy
unremitting: 4 busy, hard 9 assiduous, continual, incessant 10 persistent 11 persevering
unrepentent: 10 impenitent 12 unregenerate
unreserved: 4 free 5 frank 6 candid 9 outspoken, unlimited
unresponsive: 4 cold, cool
unrest: 5 alarm 6 bustle, motion 8 disquiet 9 commotion 10 uneasiness 12 restlessness
unrestrained: lax 4 free, wild 5 broad, loose 6 wanton 7 riotous 9 abandoned, dissolute, expansive, unbounded, unbridled, unlimited 10 licentious, unmeasured 11 extravagant 12 uncontrolled
unrestraint: 7 license 8 immunity

unrevealed: 6 hidden, latent, masked 7 covered 9 concealed
unripe: 5 crude, green 6 callow 7 uncured, unready 8 immature 9 premature 10 precocious, unseasoned 12 unseasonable 13 inexperienced
unrobe: 7 disrobe, undress
unroll: 6 evolve, unfold 7 display 8 disclose
unruffled: 4 calm, cool 5 quiet 6 placid, poised, sedate, serene, smooth 8 decorous 11 undisturbed 13 dispassionate, philosophical
unruly: 6 haunty, ramage 7 lawless, restive 9 fractious, obstinate, turbulent 10 disorderly, headstrong, licentious, refractory 11 disobedient, intractable 12 recalcitrant, ungovernable, unmanageable
unsafe: 7 exposed 8 insecure, perilous 9 dangerous, hazardous 10 unreliable
unsatisfactory: 9 defective, imperfect 10 inadequate 11 inefficient
unsatisfied: 9 insatiate 15 dissatisfaction
unsatisfying: 6 hollow
unsavory: 7 insipid 9 offensive, tasteless 10 unpleasant 11 distasteful 12 disagreeable
unscrupulous: 8 rascally 9 dishonest, miscreant 12 unprincipled 13 untrustworthy
unseal: ope 4 open 8 disclose
unseasonable: 6 unripe 8 untimely 9 premature 11 inopportune
unseasoned: raw 5 bland, green 8 untimely
unseat: 6 remove 7 unhorse 9 overthrow
unseemly: 8 improper, indecent, unworthy 10 indecorous, unbecoming 13 inappropriate
unseen: 9 invisible, unnoticed 10 unobserved 11 unperceived 12 undiscovered
unselfish: 6 heroic 8 generous 10 altruistic, benevolent
unserviceable: 7 useless
unsettle: 5 upset 7 commove, derange, disturb 8 disorder, displace, disquiet 10 disarrange, discompose
unsettled: 4 moot 6 fickle, queasy 7 dubious 8 restless, unstable 9 ambiguous, desultory, itinerant, uncertain, unquieted 10 changeable, precarious, unoccupied 11 unpopulated 12 undetermined 13 problematical
unshaken: 4 firm 6 steady
unshapely: 8 deformed
unsheathe: 4 draw 6 remove
unsightly: 4 ugly 5 messy 6 homely
unskilled: 4 rude 5 green 6 puisne 7 artless 8 ignorant, malapert
unskillful: 5 inept 6 bungly, clumsy 7 awkward 10 inexpertly 13 inexperienced
unskillfully: 5 badly
unsociable: shy 8 reserved 9 withdrawn
unsocial: 7 asocial 9 dissocial, nonsocial 10 antisocial
unsoiled: 5 clean 10 immaculate
unsophisticated: 4 naif, pure 5 frank, green, naive 6 callow, simple 7 artless, genuine 8 innocent 9 ingenuous, untutored
unsorted flour: 4 atta
unsound: bad 4 evil, sick, weak 5 crazy, dotty, false, frail, risky, shaky 6 addled, fickle, flawed, hollow, rotten, weakly 7 decayed, wracked 8 diseased, impaired, insecure, weakened 9 defective, imperfect, tottering 10 illfounded
unspeakable: bad 4 vile 6 wicked 7 heinous 9 ineffable 11 unutterable
unspoiled: 4 racy 5 fresh
unspoken: 4 oral 5 tacit 6 silent 9 ineffable, unuttered
unspotted: 8 spotless 10 immaculate
unstable: 5 loose, sandy 6 fickle, fitful, flitty, labile 7 astatic, dwaible, dwaibly, erratic, flighty, plastic 8 insecure, ticklish, unhinged, unsteady, variable 9 eccentric, faithless, irregular, unsettled 10 changeable, inconstant, precarious, unreliable 11 fluctuating, vacillating
unstained: 8 spotless 10 immaculate
unsteady: 5 dizzy, fluky, shaky, tippy 6 fickle, flicky, fluffy, groggy, wabbly, wobbly 7 erratic, quavery, rickety, unsound, wayward 8 titubate, unstable, variable, wavering 9 desultory, irregular, uncertain 10 capricious, changeable, flickering, inconstant 11 fluctuating, lightheaded, vacillating
unstinted: 5 ample 8 generous
unstudied: 7 natural 8 careless, unforced, unversed 9 unlearned 10 colloquial, unaffected 11 spontaneous
unsubstantial: 4 airy, slim 5 filmy, light, paper 6 aerial, flimsy, papery, slight, unreal 7 folious, gaseous, nominal, shadowy 8 filigree, footless 9 visionary 10 immaterial
unsuccessful: 6 losing 7 failing, unlucky 8 abortive 9 fruitless 10 disastrous 11 ineffectual, unfortunate
unsuitable: bad 5 inapt, inept, undue, unfit 10 unbecoming 13 inappropriate
unsullied: 4 pure 8 spotless 10 immaculate
unsure: 4 weak 5 timid 6 infirm 8 doubtful 9 dangerous, hazardous 10 precarious 11 vacillating 13 untrustworthy
unsusceptible: 6 immune 8 obdurate
unsweetened: dry, sec 4 sour
unswerving: 4 firm, true 5 loyal 8 straight 9 steadfast

unsymmetrical: 8 lopsided 9 irregular 15 disproportional
unsympathetic: 4 hard 5 stony 6 frozen 7 hostile 9 heartless 11 hardhearted 12 unresponsive
untainted: 4 pure 9 unsullied
untalented: 8 mediocre 11 incompetent
untamed: 4 wild 5 feral 6 ferine, ramage, ramish, savage 9 unsubdued
untangle: 4 free 6 sleave 9 extricate 11 disentangle
untanned skin: kip 4 hide, pelt 8 shagreen
untarnished: 5 clean 8 spotless
untaught: 5 naive 7 natural 8 ignorant 9 unlearned 10 illiterate, uneducated 11 spontaneous 12 uninstructed
untenanted: 5 empty 6 vacant
untended: 9 neglected
untested: new 5 green 7 untried
unthinking: 4 rash 5 brute 6 casual 8 careless, heedless 9 impetuous 11 thoughtless 13 inconsiderate
unthrifty: 6 wanton 7 foolish, profuse 8 prodigal 10 profitless, profligate 11 extravagant
unthrone: 6 unseat 7 decrown 9 overthrow
untidiness: 4 mess, muss 6 litter
untidy: 5 dowdy, messy 7 bunting 8 careless, littered, slovenly 10 disheveled, disordered, slatternly 11 disarranged
untidy person: pig 4 slob 6 sloven 8 slattern
untie: 4 free, undo 5 loose 6 loosen, unbind, unlash 8 disunite, unfasten 9 disengage
until: to; til 4 till, unto
untimely: 8 immature 9 premature 11 inopportune 12 unseasonable
untiring: 4 busy 8 sedulous, tireless 13 indefatigable
unto: to 4 till 5 until
untold: 4 vast 9 boundless, unrelated 10 uninformed, unrevealed 12 immeasurable, incalculable
untouchable: 8 chandala 10 intangible
untouched: 6 intact 9 insensate
untoward: 6 unruly 7 awkward, froward, unlucky 8 improper, perverse, stubborn, unseemly 9 vexatious 10 indecorous, ungraceful 11 troublesome, unfavorable, unfortunate 12 inconvenient, unpropitious
untrained: raw 4 wild 5 green 7 awkward, untamed 8 undocile 9 unskilled 10 amateurish, unprepared
untrammeled: 4 free 5 loose 9 unlimited 10 unhampered
untransferable: 11 inalienable
untraversed: 6 untrod
untried: new 5 fresh, green 8 immature 13 inexperienced
untrue: 4 flam 5 false, wrong 8 disloyal 9 erroneous, faithless, incorrect 10 fallacious, unfaithful 11 disaffected
untrustworthy: 6 tricky 8 slippery 9 dishonest, uncertain 10 perfidious 12 undependable
untruth: lie 5 fable 7 falsity 9 falsehood, mendacity, treachery 11 fabrication, taradiddle
untutored: 5 naive 6 simple 7 artless 8 clownish, ignorant, untaught 9 barbarian, unlearned 10 illiterate 15 unsophisticated
untwine: 5 frese, untie 6 unwind 11 disentangle
untwist: 4 free, open 5 ravel 7 unravel, untwine 8 separate 11 disentangle
Unungun: 5 Aleut
unutterable, inutterable: 7 extreme 9 ineffable 11 unspeakable 13 inexpressible 15 unpronounceable
unused: new 4 idle 5 fresh 8 unwonted 12 unaccustomed
unusual: odd 4 rare 5 novel, queer, weird 6 quaint, unique 7 strange 8 abnormal, uncommon, unwonted 9 anomalous, different, eccentric 10 remarkable 11 exceptional 12 illegitimate 13 extraordinary
unusual person or thing: 4 oner
unvaried: 10 monotonous
unvarnished: 4 bald 5 plain 6 simple 8 unglazed 9 unadorned, unglossed 13 unembellished
unvarying: 7 uniform 8 constant
unveil: 6 reveal 7 uncover 8 disclose
unvitiated: 4 pure 8 pristine
unvoiced: 4 surd 5 tacit 6 secret 9 unuttered
unwarranted: 5 undue 11 unjustified
unwary: 4 rash 7 unaware 8 careless, heedless 9 unguarded 10 groundless 11 precipitate
unwavering: 4 firm 5 solid 6 stable 8 constant 9 steadfast
unwearied: 4 busy 8 tireless 9 assiduous 13 indefatigable
unweave: 4 undo 5 ravel 6 unfold
unwed: 6 single
unwelcome: 8 non grata, unwanted 9 intruding, intrusive
unwell: ill 4 evil, sick 5 badly 6 ailing, wicked
unwholesome: 4 evil 6 impure 7 corrupt, harmful, immoral, noisome, noxious, unclean 11 unhealthful
unwieldy: 5 bulky 6 clumsy 7 awkward, hulking 8 cumbrous, ungainly 9 ponderous 10 cumbersome 12 hippopotamic, unmanageable

unwilling: 4 loth 5 loath 6 averse, mauger, maugre 7 loathly 8 backward 9 eschewing, reluctant 11 disinclined
unwind: 5 ravel 6 uncoil 8 untangle 11 disentangle
unwise: 5 inane 6 simple 7 foolish, witless 9 brainless, impolitic, imprudent, senseless 10 irrational 11 injudicious 12 undiplomatic 13 unintelligent
unwonted: 4 rare 6 unused 7 unusual 8 uncommon 10 infrequent 12 unaccustomed
unworldly: 4 eery 5 eerie, naive, weird 9 spiritual, unearthly
unworthy: 4 base 7 beneath 8 shameful, unseemly 10 despicable, unbecoming 12 contemptible, dishonorable
unwrinkled: 5 brent(Sc.) 6 smooth
unwritten: 4 oral 5 blank, vocal 6 verbal
unwrought: 8 unworked
unyielding: set 4 fast, firm, grim, hard, iron 5 rigid, stern, stiff, stith, stony 6 frozen, steely 7 adamant 8 obdurate, stubborn 9 inelastic, obstinate, unbending 10 determined, immaleable, inexorable, relentless 12 contumacious, unsubmissive 14 uncompromising
unyoke: 4 free, part 5 loose 6 remove 7 disjoin, release 8 separate 10 disconnect
up: 4 busy, rise 5 aloft, astir, raise 6 active 7 success 9 according
up and down: 5 erect 6 direct, uneven 7 upright 8 vertical 9 downright, irregular 10 undulating 13 perpendicular
up to: 5 until
date: new 6 modern 7 stylish 11 fashionable
this time: 6 hereto 8 hitherto
Upanishad: 4 Isha
upas tree gum: 6 antiar
upbraid: 4 draw, twit 5 abuse, blame, braid, chide, scold, score, taunt, twist 6 accuse, charge 7 censure, reprove 8 denounce, reproach 9 exprobate 10 denunciate
upbuilding: 8 increase 11 edification
Updike novel: 7 Centaur, Couples
upeygan: 6 borele 10 rhinoceros
upgrade: 5 raise, slope 6 ascent 7 incline
upheavel: 5 storm 6 revolt 7 rummage 9 agitation, cataclysm, commotion
upheave: 4 lift, rear, rise
uphill: 6 rising, tiring 9 ascending, difficult, laborious
uphold: aid 4 abet, back, bear, stay 5 favor, raise 6 assert, defend, favour, second 7 confirm, support, sustain 8 conserve, maintain 9 encourage 11 countenance
upholder: 6 dealer 8 adherent 9 tradesman 10 undertaker 11 upholsterer
upholstered: 9 cushioned
upholstering material: 6 damask, lampas, mohair 7 valance 8 tapestry
upkeep: 4 cost 6 repair 7 support 8 maintain 11 maintenance
upland: 4 wold 6 coteau 7 plateau
uplift: 4 head, lift, rock 5 erect, raise, tower 7 collect, improve 8 elevated, ennobled, upheaval 9 elevation
Upolu: *city:* 4 Apia
island group: 5 Samoa
upon: on; oer, sur(law) 4 atop 5 about, above 8 touching 10 concerning
prefix: ep; epi
that: 7 thereat 9 thereupon
which: 7 whereat 9 whereupon
upper: 4 bunk, over, vamp 5 above, berth 8 superior
upper case: 7 capital
upper crust: 5 elite 7 segment
upper lips part: 5 flews
upperclassman: 6 junior, senior
uppermost: 5 first 6 upmost, uptown 7 topmost 8 farthest, foremost 9 outermost 11 predominant
uppish: 5 proud 6 elated 7 haughty, peevish 8 arrogant, assuming, snobbish
upraised: 5 atilt 6 lifted, raised 7 erected 8 elevated, extolled, improved 10 encouraged
uprear: 5 erect, exalt, raise
upright: 4 good, just, true 5 erect, moral, piano, right, stela, stele, stile 6 honest, square 7 endwise, sincere 8 straight, vertical, virtuous 9 elevation, equitable, honorable, righteous 10 pianoforte, scrupulous 11 unambiguous 13 perpendicular
comb. form: 5 ortho
support: 4 jamb, stud
uprightness: 9 rectitude
uprising: 4 riot 6 ascent, mutiny, putsch, revolt 7 ensuing 8 reaction 9 ascending, commotion, rebellion 10 increasing, insurgency, revolution 12 insurrection 17 counterrevolution
uproar: din 4 riot, rout 5 brawl, hurly, noise 6 bedlam, bustle, clamor, dirdum, fracas, habble, hubble, hubbub, rattle, tumult 7 clamour, ferment, turmoil 8 outbreak 9 commotion, confusion 10 convulsion, donnybrook, hurlyburly, rumbullion, tintamarre 11 disturbance, pandemonium
uproot: 8 supplant 9 eradicate, extirpate 11 exterminate
upscuddle: 7 quarrel
upset: irk 4 cave, coup, keel, rile 6 defeat, refund, topple 7 capsize, confuse, derange, disturb, outcome, pervert, quarrel, reverse, subvert 8 capsized, overturn 9 dis-

comfit, embarrass, overthrow, perturbed 10 discompose, disconcert, disordered, distressed, overturned 11 disorganize

upshot: end 5 issue, limit 6 result, sequel 7 outcome 10 conclusion 11 termination 12 consummation

upside: top

upstage: shy 5 aloof 6 offish 8 backward, outshine, snobbish 9 conceited 12 supercilious

upstart: 4 snob 6 origin 7 dalteen, parvenu, saffron 8 parvenue 9 cockhorse

upstir: 6 incite 7 agitate 9 stimulate

upsurge: 4 boom 9 inflation

uptake: 4 flue, tube 5 shaft 6 upcast 10 collection, comprehend 13 comprehension, understanding

upupoid bird: 6 hoopoe

upward: 4 more, over 5 above, lofty 7 airward, skyward 8 airwards 9 ascending
comb. form: ano

uraeus: asp 10 decoration

uralite: 9 amphibole

Urania's son: 5 Hymen

uranian: 6 uranic 8 heavenly 9 celestial 12 astronomical

uranium dioxide: 10 ianthinite

Uranus: *children:* 4 Rhea 5 Titan 7 Cyclops
moon: 5 Ariel 6 Oberon 7 Titania, Umbriel
mother: Ge 4 Gaea, Gaia
satellite: 5 Ariel
wife: Ge 4 Gaea, Gaia

urare: rat 6 curare

urban: 5 civic 7 oppidan

urban division: 4 ward

urbane: 5 bland, civil, suave 6 polite, smooth 7 affable, elegant, refined 8 polished 9 courteous 13 sophisticated

urbanity: 6 comity 12 complaisance

urchin: boy, elf, imp, tad 4 arab, brat 5 child, elfin, gamin 8 cylinder, hedgehog, hurcheon 9 dandiprat, hunchback, youngster

ure: use 4 haze, mist 6 custom 8 exercise, practice

urease: 6 enzyme

uredo: 5 hives 9 urticaria

Urfa: 6 Edessa

urge: dun, egg, ert(Sc.), hie, ply, sue 4 brod, coax, goad, prod, push, spur 5 broad, drive, filip, force, hurry, impel, plead, press 6 allege, compel, demand, desire, excite, exhort, fillip, incite, induce, insist 7 animate, augment, commove, entreat, impulse, provoke, solicit 8 advocate, persuade 9 flagitate, importune, influence, prosecute, stimulate 10 exasperate

urgency: 4 need 5 haste, hurry 6 crisis, stress 8 exigency, pressure 10 insistence 11 importunity

urgent: hot 5 grave 7 clamant, exigent 8 critical, pressing 9 important 10 solicitous 11 importunate

Uriah's wife: 9 Bathsheba

urial, oorial: sha 5 sheep

Uriel: 5 angel 9 archangel

Urim's partner: 7 Thummim

Uris novel: 5 QBVII 6 Exodus

urisk: 7 brownie

urn: jar, run 4 bury, ewer, urna, vase 5 grave, inurn, steen, theca 6 spring 7 capsule, cistern, pitcher, samovar, vaselet 8 fountain 9 container 10 jardiniere 11 watercourse
for bones: 7 ossuary
tea: 7 samovar

urn-shaped: 9 urceolate

Urne-Buriall author: 6 Browne

urodela: 5 newts, order 7 Caudata 8 amphibia 10 salamander

Ursa: 4 Bear

ursine: 6 ursoid 8 bearlike

ursine baboon: 6 chacma

ursoid: 6 ursine 8 bearlike

Urth: 4 Norn

urticaria: 5 hives, uredo

urubu: 7 vulture

Uruguay: *city:* 4 Melo 5 Minas 6 Rivera 7 Durazno, Florida 8 Paysandu 9 Maldonado 10 Montevideo
coin: 4 peso 9 centesimo
estuary: 5 Plata
lake: 5 Merin, Mirim
measure: 4 vara 6 cuadra, suerte
river: 4 Malo 5 Negro 6 Ulimar 7 Uruguay 9 Cebollary 10 Tacaurembo
weight: 7 quintal

urus: ox; tur 7 aurochs

us: uns(Gr.) 4 nous(Fr.)

usable: fit 8 servable 9 available, practical 10 convenient, functional 11 serviceable, utilitarian

usage: use 4 wont 5 habit, haunt, idiom 6 custom, method 7 conduct, manners, utility 8 behavior, interest, practice 9 treatment 10 convention, employment, experience

usance: use 5 usage, usury 6 custom, income

use: try 4 boot, hire, vail, wont 5 apply, avail, guide, habit, right, spend, stead, treat, trope, usage, value, wield 6 behoof, custom, employ, expend, handle, hansel, occupy 7 benefit, consume, exhaust, exploit, utility, utilize 8 accustom, exercise, frequent, function, handling, practice 9

habituate, privilege, treatment 10 employment, manipulate 11 application, consumption, utilization
as example: 4 cite
refrain from: 7 boycott
to be of: 5 avail
up: eat 4 tire 5 spend 7 consume, deplete, exhaust, outwear
wastefully: 7 fritter 8 squander 9 dissipate
used: 10 secondhand 11 experienced
useful: 4 good 5 utile 7 helpful 9 practical 10 beneficial, commodious, profitable 11 serviceable 12 advantageous
usefulness: 5 avail, value 6 profit 7 utility
useless: 4 idle, null, vain 6 futile, otiose 7 inutile 8 bootless, hopeless 9 fruitless, worthless 11 ineffectual, inefficient, superfluous 12 unprofitable 13 unserviceable 14 good-for-nothing
user: 4 usee 8 consumer
usher: 4 lead, page 5 guide 6 beadle, escort, herald 7 chobdar, conduct, officer, precede, preface, servant, teacher 9 announcer, assistant, attendant, harbinger, introduce, precursor 10 doorkeeper, forerunner, inaugurate
usings: 8 property 10 belongings
usquebaugh: 6 whisky 7 cordial, whiskey
U.S.S.R.: See **Union of Soviet Socialist Republics**
ustion: 7 burning 13 cauterization
usual: 6 common, normal, wonted 7 average, general, regular, typical 8 familiar, frequent, habitual, ordinary, orthodox 9 customary 10 accustomed, prevailing 11 stereotyped 12 conventional
usurer: 5 shark 6 loaner 11 moneylender
usurp: 4 take 5 seize 6 assume 8 accroach, arrogate
usury: 7 gombeen
Utah: *lake:* 4 Salt, Swan, Utah 6 Sevier
mountain range: 5 Uinta 7 Wasatch
resident: 6 Mormon
river: 5 Grand, Green, Weber 6 Jordan, Sevier 8 Colorado
state tree: 6 spruce
state flower: 4 sego
town: 4 Lehi 5 Delta, Heber, Kanab, Logan, Ogden, Provo 6 Beaver, Eureka, Payson, Tooele 7 Milford 9 Richfield
utensil: pan, pot 4 tool 5 sieve 6 grater, vessel 7 skillet 8 strainer 9 collander, implement 10 instrument
cleaning: mop 5 broom, brush 6 Hoover, ramrod, vacuum 7 Bissell, sweeper
utensils: 7 baggage
Uther's son: 6 Arthur
utile: 6 useful 9 practical 10 profitable 12 advantageous
utilitarian: 5 plain 6 useful 8 economic 9 practical 10 functional 12 matter-of-fact
utility: use 5 avail 6 profit 7 benefit, service
utilize: use 6 employ 9 economize
utmost: end 4 best, last 5 final 7 extreme 8 farthest, greatest 9 uttermost
Uto-Aztecan Indian: 4 Pima 7 Nahuatl 8 Shoshone
Utopia: 4 Eden 9 Shangri La
author: 4 More
Harrington's: 6 Oceana
Utopian: 5 ideal 8 idealist, Quixotic 9 visionary 10 chimerical
utricle: sac 7 vesicle
Uttar Pradesh capital: 7 Lucknow
utter: add, say 4 blat, bray, emit, gasp, pipe, pray, rail, roar, tell, vent 5 blurt, clack, croak, drawl, final, issue, mince, sheer, speak, spill, spout, trill, stark, state, total, voice 6 assert, direct, entire, mumble, reveal, warble 7 bluster, deliver, divulge, enounce, express, extreme, iterate, publish 8 abnormal, absolute, complete, disclose 9 enunciate, pronounce 10 articulate, peremptory 11 unqualified 13 unconditional
utterance: gab 4 osse 5 aside, dicta, ditty 6 dictum, oracle, speech 7 calling 8 effusion, monotone, phonesis, rhapsody 9 phonation 10 expression, forthgoing 12 articulation
soft: 6 breath, murmur 7 whisper
voiced: 6 sonant
voiceless: 4 surd 7 spirate
uttered: 4 oral 5 spake
utterly: 5 fully, stark 6 merely 7 totally 8 entirely 10 absolutely, allutterly, completely 11 diametrally 13 diametrically 17 straightforwardly
uttermost: 5 final 6 utmost 7 extreme, outmost
utu: 6 reward 12 compensation, satisfaction
uva: 5 fruit, grape
ux: 4 uxor(L.), wife
uxorial: 6 wifely
Uzbek capital: 8 Tashkent

V

V: vee 4 five
symbol of: 7 victory
V-shaped piece: 5 wedge
vacancy: gap 5 break, chasm, space 6 cavity, hollow 7 interim, vacuity 10 hollowness, interstice 11 vacuousness
vacant: 4 free, idle, open, void 5 blank, empty, fishy, inane, silly 6 barren, devoid, hollow, lonely 7 foolish, lacking, leisure, vacuous, wanting 8 unfilled 9 destitute 10 disengaged, unemployed, unoccupied, untenanted 12 unencumbered, unreflecting 14 expressionless
vacate: 4 quit, void 5 annul, avoid, empty, leave 7 abandon, abolish 8 abdicate, abrogate, evacuate
vacation: 4 rest 5 leave, spell 6 outing, recess 7 holiday, leisure, nonterm, respite 8 furlough 9 justitium 12 intermission
place: spa 4 city, lake, park 5 beach 6 forest, resort 7 seaside 9 mountains
vacationist: 6 camper 7 tourist
vaccinate: 9 inoculate
vaccination: *inventor:* 6 Jenner
vaccine: 4 sera 5 serum
discoverer of: 4 Salk 6 Jenner
vacillate: 4 sway 5 waver 6 dacker, daiker, seesaw, teeter, totter 7 flutter, stagger 8 hesitate, titubate 9 fluctuate, oscillate
vacillation: 5 doubt 7 halting, swaying 8 wavering 9 faltering, hesitancy, infirmity 10 fickleness, indecision, unsureness 11 uncertainty 12 irresolution 14 changeableness
vacuity: 7 inanity, vacancy
vacuous: 4 dull, idle 5 blank, empty 6 stupid 8 unfilled 9 evacuated, senseless 11 purposeless 13 unintelligent
vacuum: 4 void
opposite of: 6 plenum
vacuum tube: 5 diode 7 tetrode 9 electrode
vacuum pump: 10 pulsometer
vade mecum: 6 manual 8 handbook
vadimonium: 4 bond 6 pledge 8 contract, security
vadium: 4 bail, pawn 6 pledge
vagabond: vag 4 rove 5 scamp 6 beggar, canter, jockey, rascal 7 erratic, gadling, nomadic, vagrant, wayward 8 bohemian, brodyaga, drifting, fugitive, wanderer 9 shiftless, straggler, wandering, worthless 10 blackguard, ne'er-do-well 12 hallanshaker 14 good-for-nothing
vagarious: 7 erratic 13 unpredictable
vagary: 4 roam, whim 5 caper, fancy, freak, jaunt, prank, stray, trick, waver 6 action, breach, notion, oddity, ramble, totter, whimsy 7 caprice, conceit 8 flagarie, rambling 9 departure, excursion, procedure, wandering 10 digression, divergence 13 manifestation
vagrant: bum, vag 4 hobo, prog 5 caird, rogue, tramp 6 arrant, roving, shuler, truant, vagrom 7 devious, drifter, nomadic, prowler, roaming, shuiler 8 brodyaga, vagabond 9 itinerant 10 capricious, circuitous, prostitute 11 extravagant
vague: dim 4 dark, hazy 5 loose, misty, stray 6 dreamy, vagary 7 obscure, shadowy, sketchy, unfixed, vagrant 8 confused, nebulous, vagabond, wanderer 9 ambiguous, uncertain, unsettled, wandering 10 ill-defined, indefinite, indistinct, intangible 13 indeterminate
vail: tip, use 4 doff, dole, veil 5 avail, bribe, lower, yield 6 humble, profit, return, submit 7 benefit, decline, descend, descent, subside 8 downflow, gratuity, proceeds 9 advantage 10 beneficial, profitable 12 advantageous
vain: 4 idle 5 empty, flory, petty, proud, silly 6 flimsy, futile, hollow, otiose, snooty 7 foolish, stuckup, trivial, useless 8 gorgeous, hopeless, ignorant, nugatory 9 conceited, emptiness, fruitless, frustrate, unfounded, worthless 10 chimerical, evanescent, unavailing, unrewarded 11 empty-headed, ineffectual, overweening, unimportant 12 unprofitable, vainglorious

vain boasting: 11 fanfaronade
vain person: fop 5 dandy 7 coxcomb
vainglorious: 4 vain 8 boastful 9 selfproud
vair: fur
Vaishnavas: *deity:* 6 Vishnu
priest: 6 gosain, gusain
Vaisya caste: 6 Aroras
vakass: 5 amice
valance: 5 drape 6 pelmet 7 curtain, drapery, hanging
vale: 4 dale, dean, dell, dene, glen 5 bache, glade 6 dingle, valley 8 farewell
valediction: 5 adieu 7 address 8 farewell
Valence's river: 5 Rhone
valency: 5 power, value 10 importance
valentine: 4 card, gift, love 8 greeting
valerian: 4 drug 5 plant 7 allheal, panacea, setwall
valet: man 4 goad 5 stick 6 andrew, tartar 7 dresser 9 attendant, cameriere, chamberer 10 manservant
Vali's mother: 4 Rind 5 Rindr
valiant: 4 bold, prow 5 aught, brave, proud 6 heroic, robust, strong, sturdy 7 doughty 8 galliard, intrepid, powerful, stalwart, vigorous, virtuous 9 bounteous, excellent, steadfast 10 chivalrous, courageous 11 meritorious 12 stouthearted
valid: 4 good, just, true 5 legal, sound 6 cogent, lawful, robust, strong 7 binding, healthy, telling, weighty 8 forcible, powerful 9 authentic, effective, efficient 10 conclusive, convincing, sufficient 11 efficacious 12 well-grounded
opposite of: 4 null, void
validate: 7 confirm 9 establish
valise: bag 4 case, grip 7 baggage 8 suitcase
Valjean: *discoverer:* 6 Javert
friend: 6 Marius
protege: 7 Cosette
Valkyrie: 8 Brynhild 10 Brunnhilde
vallecula: 6 furrow, groove 7 channel 10 depression
Valletta people: 7 Maltese
valley: dip 4 brae, comb, coom, cove, dale, dean, dell, dene, ghyl, gill, glen, rill, vale, wadi, wady 5 atrio, basin, combe, coomb, dhoon, glack, gorge, goyal, goyle, gully, kloof, swale, waddy 6 bolson, canada, canyon, clough, coombe, coulee, dingle, gutter, hollow, ravine, rincon, strath, trough 7 blowout 10 depression
between volcanic cones: 5 atrio
deep: 5 canon 6 canyon
vallum: 4 wall 7 rampart
valor, valour: 5 arete, merit, value, worth 6 bounty, virtue 7 bravery, courage, heroism, prowess 8 position 9 valuation 10 importance 11 distinction 12 fearlessness 13 signification
valuable: 4 dear 5 asset 6 costly, prized, useful, worthy 8 precious 9 estimable, excellent, treasured 10 worthwhile 11 serviceable
valuable discovery: 4 find
value: use 4 cost, feck(Sc.), rate 5 avail, cheap, price, prize, worth 6 assess, assize, esteem, extend, moment 7 account, apprise, apprize, average, cherish, compute, opinion, respect, utility 8 appraise, estimate, evaluate, treasure 9 inventory, valuation 10 appreciate, estimation, importance
anything of little: 5 plack(Sc.) 6 trifle
equal: 6 parity
mathematical limit of: 8 derivate
mean: 7 average
net: 7 reserve
nominal: par
reduction: 12 depreciation
valued: 4 dear
valve: tap 4 cock, gate 6 faucet, outlet, piston, spigot 7 petcock
heart: 6 mitral
sliding: 6 piston
vamoose: lam 4 scat 5 leave, scram 6 decamp, depart
vamp: 4 hose, plod, sock 5 patch, tramp 6 invent, repair, seduce 7 beguile, concoct, fireman 9 fabricate, improvise
vampire: bat 5 lamia 6 alukah, corpse, usurer 7 seducer 11 blackmailer, bloodsucker, extortioner 12 extortionist
famous: 7 Dracula
van: fan 4 fore, lead, wing 5 front, truck, wagon 6 shovel, summit, winnow 7 fourgon, vehicle 9 forefront
Van Gogh town: 5 Arles
vandal: hun 9 plunderer
vandalize: mar 6 deface
Vandyke: 5 beard 6 artist 7 picture
vane: arm 5 blade 7 feather 11 weathercock
feather: web 8 vexillum
vanguard: 10 avantgarde
vanilla substance: 8 coumarin
vanish: 4 fade, melt 8 disperse, evanesce 9 disappear
vanity (see also **vain**): 4 airs 5 pride 6 egoism 7 compact, conceit, egotism, falsity 8 futility, idleness 9 dizziness, emptiness 10 hollowness 11 fatuousness, foolishness, self-conceit
symbol of: 7 peacock
vanity case: 4 etui 7 compact
Vanity Fair character: 5 Becky 6 Amelia
vanquish: get, win 4 beat, best, rout 5 expel, floor 6 defeat, expugn, master, subdue 7

confute, conquer 8 confound, overcome, suppress, surmount 9 overthrow
vanquisher: 6 victor
vantage: fee 4 gain 6 chance, profit 9 advantage 10 perquisite 11 opportunity, superiority
place of: 5 coign 6 coigne
vapid: dry 4 dull, flat, pall 5 inane, stale, trite 7 insipid, mawkish 8 lifeless 9 pointless, tasteless 10 flavorless, spiritless, unanimated, unexciting 13 uninteresting
vapor: fog, gas 4 fume, haze, idea, mist 5 boast, brume, cloud, ewder, fancy, humor, smoke, steam 6 breath, bubble, humour, nimbus, notion 7 halitus 8 contrail, humidity, phantasm 9 evaporate 10 blustering 11 braggadocio
comb. form: atm 4 atmo
frozen: 4 hail, rime, snow 5 frost, sleet
pressure indicator: 9 tonometer
vaporizable: 8 volatile
vaporize: 5 steam 9 evaporate
vaporous: 8 fleeting 13 unsubstantial
vaquero: 6 cowboy 8 herdsman, horseman 10 equestrian
varec, varech: 4 kelp 7 seaweed
variable (see also **vary**): 6 fickle, fitful 7 protean, unequal, variant, varying 8 floating, unstable, unsteady 9 irregular, uncertain 10 capricious, inconstant
variance (see also **vary**): 7 discord, dispute 10 contention 11 discrepancy
variate: 4 vary 6 varied 8 variable
variation (see also **vary**): 7 variety 8 heterism, mutation 9 tolerance 10 aberration, deflection 11 distinction
varicolored: 6 varied 7 mottled 11 diversified
varicose: 7 dilated, swollen 8 enlarged
varied: 6 daedal 7 several, various 10 variegated
variegate: 9 diversify
variegated: 4 pied, shot 5 lyard(Sc.), lyart(Sc.) 6 daedal, menald, motley, varied 7 dappled, flecked, mottled, painted, piebald, tissued 8 speckled 9 different, enamelled 11 diversified
variety: 4 kind, sort 5 breed, class 7 species 9 diversity, variation 10 difference 16 multifariousness
variola: 6 cowpox 8 horsepox, smallpox
various: 4 many 6 divers, sundry 7 diverse, several 8 manifold, variable 9 different, uncertain, versatile 10 changeable, inconstant
varlet: boy 4 page 5 gippo, knave, noble, youth 6 menial, rabble, rascal, vassal 7 bailiff, footman, servant 8 coistrel, coistril 9 attendant, scoundrel
varmint, varment: 5 sharp 6 clever 7 amateur, cunning, dashing 8 sporting
varnish: 4 spar 5 japan 7 lacquer 8 brighten 9 embellish
ingredient: lac 5 copal, elemi, resin, rosin 6 dammar
vary: 5 alter, range, shift 6 change, depart, differ, modify, swerve 7 deviate, dispute, dissent, diverge, quarrel, variate 8 disagree 9 alternate, diversify, fluctuate, oscillate
vas: 4 duct 6 pledge, surety, vessel
vase: jar, urn 4 asci, vaso 5 ascus, askos, echea, tazza 6 crater, deinoi, deinos, krater 7 amphora 8 amphorae 10 cassolette, jardiniere
handle: 4 ansa
vassal: man 4 bond, esne, rule, serf 5 ceile, helot, liege, slave 6 varlet 7 bondman, feedman, feodary, geneate, homager, servant, servile, subject 8 dominate 9 dependent, feudatory 11 beneficiary, subordinate, subservient
pert. to: 6 feudal
vassalage: 5 valor 6 fealty, homage 7 courage, loyalty, prowess 8 dominion, services 9 authority, servitude
vast: 4 huge 5 broad, great, largo, vasty 6 cosmic, lonely, mighty, untold 7 immense 8 colossal, enormous, gigantic, spacious 9 boundless, cyclopean, extensive 11 farreaching, illimitable
vastness: 7 expanse 8 grandeur 9 magnitude
vat (see also **barrel, tub, vessel**): bac, fat, pit, tub, tun, wit 4 back, beck, cask, coom, gyle, keel, kier, tank 5 coomb, keeve, kieve, press 6 barrel, kettle, vessel 7 caldron, chessel, cistern 8 cauldron, chessart
bleaching: 4 keir, kier
vatic: 8 inspired, oracular 9 prophetic 11 prophetical
Vatican: *chapel:* 7 Sistine
guards' nationality: 5 Swiss
official: 6 datary
statuary group: 7 Laocoon
vaticanism: 9 curialism
vaticinate: 8 foretell
vaticinator: 4 seer 7 prophet
vaudeville: 5 revue
act: 4 skit, song, turn 5 dance
vaudevillist: 5 actor 6 dancer, hoofer, singer 7 acrobat, juggler 9 performer
vaudy: gay 5 gaudy, showy 6 elated, sturdy 8 cheerful
vault: box, pit 4 arch, bend, cave, cope, dome, jump, leap, over, roof, room, safe, tomb 5 bound, croft, crypt, curve, floor, groin, shade 6 cavern, cellar, crater, cupola, curvet, flaunt, grotto, hurdle, spring,

welkin 7 ceiling, chamber, dungeon, glorify, testudo 8 flourish 9 concavity, staircase 10 depository, repository, testudines(pl.)
vaunt: van 4 brag, font 5 boast, roosa, roose 6 avaunt 11 ostentation
vaunty: 4 vain 5 brave, proud
veal: 4 calf, meat, veau(F.)
cutlet: 9 schnitzel
larded: 8 fricando 10 fricandeau
vector: 4 host 7 carrier
opposite of: 6 scalar
vedette: 5 vigil, watch 8 sentinel
Vedic: *artisans of gods:* 6 Ribhus
cosmic order: 4 Rita
fire god: 4 Agni
god: 6 Aditya
hymn: 6 mantra
language: 4 Pali 8 Sanskrit
sky serpent: ahi
sun god: 7 Savitar
text: 5 Sakha, Shaka
veer: yaw 4 slue, sway, turn 5 alter, shift 6 broach, careen, change, swerve 7 deviate, digress 9 fluctuate
veery: 6 thrush
vega: 5 tract 6 meadow
Vega's constellation: 4 Lyra
vegetable: pea, yam 4 bean, beet, corn, kale, leak, ocra, okra, soya 5 onion, pease, plant 6 carrot, celery, lentil, pepper, potato, radish, squash, tomato, turnip 7 brocoli, cabbage, lettuce, parsley, parsnip, peascod, rhubarb, spinach 8 broccoli, cucumber, eggplant, peasecod, rutabaga 9 artichoke 11 cauliflower 15 Brussels sprouts
carbonized: 7 lignite
dealer: 8 huckster 11 greengrocer 12 costermonger
decayed: 4 duff 5 humus
dish: 6 zimmis 10 chiffonade
esculent: 6 legume
exudation: lac, sap 5 resin
ferment: 5 yeast
green: 5 sabzi
grown for sale: 5 truck
oil: 8 macassar
onionlike: 4 leek 7 shallot
pepsin: 6 caroid
pod: 4 hull 8 peasecod
poison: 5 abrin
purple: 8 eggplant
rubbish: 5 wrack
salad: 4 leak 5 chard 6 endive 7 lettuce, romaine, shallot 8 scallion
sponge: 5 loofa 6 loofah
stunted: 5 scrub
sugar-yielding: 4 beet
tinder: 6 amadou
vegetable caterpillar: 5 aweto
vegetable pear: 7 chayote
vegetant: 7 vegetal 9 animating 12 invigorating
vegetation: 6 growth 7 verdure
floating: 4 sadd, sudd
god: 4 Atys, Esus 5 Attis
vegete: 6 lively 7 healthy 11 flourishing
vehement: hot 5 angry, eager, fiery, hefty, irked, yeder 6 ardent, fervid, flashy, heated, raging, urgent 7 animose, animous, fervent, furioso, furious, intense, violent 8 forceful, vigorous 9 impetuous 10 boisterous, passionate
vehemently: 5 amain
vehicle (see also **aircraft, ship**): ark, bus, car, van 4 auto, shay, wain 5 araba, brake, break, buggy, dilly, sedan, sulky, wagon 6 barrow, charet, device, hansom, landau, troika 7 chariot, kibitka(Russ.), tallyho 8 carriage, charette 9 buckboard, velociman 10 automobile, conveyance
army: 4 jeep, tank 9 ambulance
child's: 4 pram 5 buggy 6 walker 7 scooter 8 carriage, stroller, tricycle 10 velocipede
display: 5 float
hauling: van 4 dray, lory, sled 5 truck 7 tractor, trailer
parade: 5 float
passenger: bus, cab 4 hack, taxi, tram 5 train 6 hansom 7 minibus, omnibus, tramcar, trolley 9 charabanc
public: bus, cab, car 4 taxi, tram 5 train 7 omnibus, ricksha 8 rickshaw 10 jinricksha, jinrikisha
snow: 4 pung, sled 6 sleigh
two-wheeled: 4 cart 5 sulky, tonga 6 cisium 7 bicycle, caleche 9 carromata(Fil.) 11 vinaigrette
wheelless: 4 ship, sled 6 cutter, sledge, sleigh
veil: dim 4 caul, film, hide, mask 5 cloak, cover, orale, velum, volet 6 bumble, fannel, masque, screen, shroud, soften 7 conceal, curtain, watcher 8 calyptra, disguise, headrail 11 amphithyron
head: 4 caul
in botany: 5 velum
veiling: 4 veil 5 tulle, voile 7 curtain 10 obvelation
vein: bed, rib 4 dash, hilo, lode, mood, seam, tang, vena, wave 5 costa, crack, scrin, shade, smack, spice, tinge, touch, trend, venae 6 cavity, costae, strain, streak 7 bonanza, channel, crevice, fissure, stratum 8 tendency 11 inclination, variegation
arrangement of: 9 neuration
enlarged: 5 varix
fluid: 4 icor 5 ichor

inflammation: **9** phlebitis
leaf: rib
mining: **4** lode
pert. to: **6** veinal, venous
small: **6** venule **7** veinlet, veinule **8** veinulet
throat: **7** jugular
veinless: 7 avenous
veinstone: 6 gangue, matrix **9** lodestuff
velamen: 5 velum **8** membrane
velar: 7 palatal **8** guttural
velarium: 4 veil **6** awning **8** covering
veldt, veld: 6 meadow, plains **9** grassland
velitation: 7 contest, dispute **8** skirmish
velleity: 4 hope, wish **6** desire **8** volition **11** inclination
vellicate: nip **4** pull **5** pinch, pluck **6** tickle, twitch **9** titillate
veloce: 7 dashing, rapidly **9** direction
velocious: 4 fast **6** speedy
velocipede: 4 ride **7** bicycle, dicycle **8** tricycle **11** quadricycle
velocity: 4 pace **5** speed **8** celerity, rapidity **9** quickness, swiftness
instrument: **11** cinemograph
velum: 4 veil **6** awning, palate **8** membrane
velutinous: 7 velvety
velvet: 4 gain **5** drink **6** birodo(Jap.), profit **7** surplus **8** winnings
fabric like: **5** panne **6** velure
knife: **6** trevet
velvet dock: 6 mullen **7** mullein **10** elecampane
velvetbreast: 9 merganser
venal: 6 venous **7** corrupt, salable **8** saleable, vendible **9** mercenary
vend: 4 hawk, sell **5** utter **6** market, peddle **7** publish **8** transfer
vendetta: 4 feud
vendeuse: 9 salesgirl **10** saleswoman
vendible: 5 venal **7** salable **8** saleable **9** mercenary **10** marketable
vendition: 4 sale
vendor, vender: 6 seller **7** alienor, butcher **8** merchant, salesman
vendue: 4 sale **7** auction
veneer: lac **4** coat, face, show **5** glaze, gloss, layer, plate **6** enamel, facing **7** overlay
venenate: 6 poison **8** poisoned **9** poisonous
venerable: old **4** aged, hoar, sage **5** hoary **6** august **7** ancient, antique, classic
veneration: awe **4** fear **6** esteem **7** respect, worship **8** devotion, idolatry **9** adoration, reverence
of saints and angels: **5** dulia
venerer: 6 hunter **8** huntsman
venery: 5 chase **7** hunting
Venetian: See **Italy, Venice**
Venezuela: *city:* **4** Aroa, Coro **6** Atures, Cumana **7** Barinas, Caracas(c.), Guanare, Maracay, Maturin, Ocumare, San Juan **8** Tacupita, Trujillo, Valencia **9** Barcelona, Los Teques, San Carlos, San Filepe **10** La Asuncion **11** San Fernando **12** Barquisimeto, San Cristobal
coin: **4** real **5** medio **6** fuerte **7** bolivar, centimo **8** morocota **10** venezolano
dam: **4** Guri
fiber: **5** erizo
Indian: **6** Timote
lake: **9** Maracaibo, Tacarigua
language: **4** Pume **7** Spanish
measure: **5** galon, milla **6** fanega **7** estadel
measure of weight: bag **5** libra
mountain: **5** Andes, Icutu **6** Concha, Cuneva, Parima **7** Imutaca, Roraima **9** Pacaraima **20** Sierra-Nevada-de-Merida
patriot: **7** Bolivar
people: **5** Carib **6** Timote **7** Timotex **8** Guarauno
plain: **5** llano
port: **8** La Guayra **9** Maracaibo **13** Ciudad Bolivar, Puerto-Cabello
revolutionist: **7** Miranda
river: **5** Apure, Caura **6** Arausa, Caroni **7** Orinoco, Ventuar
snake: **4** lora
state: **4** Lara **5** Apure, Sucre, Zulia **6** Aragua, Falcon, Merida, Zamora **7** Bolivar, Cojedes, Guarico, Monagas, Tachira, Yaracuy **8** Carabobo, Trujillo **10** Anzoategui, Portuguesa **12** Nueva Esparta
tree: **6** balata
vengeance: 5 wrack **6** wanion **7** revenge **8** reprisal, requital **10** punishment **11** retaliation, retribution
god of: **6** Erinys **7** Alastor
goddess of: Ara, Ate **7** Nemesis
venial: 7 trivial **9** allowable, excusable, tolerable **10** pardonable **13** insignificant **15** unobjectionable
Venice: *beach:* **4** Lido
boat: **7** gondola **9** bucentaur
bridge: **6** Rialto
coin: **5** betso, bezzo, ducat **6** sequin **8** bagatino, gazzetta
court: **8** quaranty
district: **6** Rialto
island: **6** Rialto
magistrate: **4** doge
medal: **5** osela, osele **6** osella, oselle **7** oscella
old silver coin: **5** betso
painter: **6** Titian **7** Bellini **8** Veronese **9** Giorgione **10** Tintoretto
resort: **4** Lido
river: **6** Brenta
traveler and writer: **5** Conti **9** Marco Polo
wine measure: **6** anfora
Venice of the North: 9 Stockholm

venin: 6 poison
venireman: 5 juror
venison: 7 pemican 8 pemmican
vennel: 4 lane 5 alley, sewer 6 gutter
venomous: 5 snaky, toxic 6 attern, deadly 7 baneful, noxious 8 poisoned, spiteful, virulent 9 envenomed, malicious, malignant, poisonous, rancorous 11 mischievous
vent: 4 draw, emit, exit, hole, slit 5 brand, eject 6 cancel, outlet, report 7 fissure, opening, release 8 aperture, avacuate, disgorge, emission 9 discharge, embrasure 10 escapement
ventilate: air, fan 6 aerate, aerify, winnow 9 oxygenate
ventilation: 6 aerage 9 breathing
ventilator: 6 blinds, louver
ventral: 7 sternal
ventriloquist: 12 engastrimyth 13 gastriloquist
venture: hap, try 4 dare, luck, risk, wage 5 brave, essay, stake 6 chance, danger, feeler, hazard 7 attempt, courage, flutter, fortune, risking 8 trespass 9 adventure, speculate 10 enterprise 11 contingency, presumption, speculation, undertaking
ventured: 5 durst
venturesome: 4 bold, rash 5 hardy 6 heroic 8 fearless, heedless, reckless 9 audacious, dangerous, foolhardy, hazardous, venturous 11 adventurous, furthersome, temerarious
venturesomeness: 8 temerity
venturous: 11 venturesome
venue: hit 4 bout, site 5 lunge, match, onset 6 coming, ground, thrust 7 arrival, assault 9 encounter
Venus: 6 Hesper, Vesper 8 Hesperus
as morning star: 7 Lucifer
girdle: 6 cestus
island: 5 Melos
mother: 5 Dione
son: 5 Cupid
sweetheart: 6 Adonis
tree sacred to: 6 myrtle
Venus flytrap: 5 plant 7 dionaea
venust: 6 comely 7 elegant 8 graceful 9 beautiful
veracious: 9 measuring, veridical 10 estimating
veracity: 5 truth 7 honesty 8 accuracy, trueness 9 judgement, precision, sincerity 11 correctness 12 faithfulness, truthfulness
veranda: 5 lanai, porch, stoep 6 loggia, piazza 7 gallery, portico 8 verandah
verb: *auxiliary:* had, has, may, was 4 hast, will 5 might, shall, shalt, would
form: 5 tense
suffix: le; ire, ise 4 esce
table: 8 paradigm
tense: 6 aorist
verbal: 4 oral 5 wordy 7 verbose 9 talkative 10 articulate
verbatim: 6 orally 7 literal 8 verbally
verbena: 7 aloysia
verberate: 4 beat 5 shake 6 quiver, strike 7 tremble
verbiage: 4 talk 7 chatter, diction, fustian, wording 9 verbosity, wordiness 10 redundancy
verbose: 5 windy, wordy 6 prolix 7 diffuse 9 redundant
verboten: 4 tabu 5 taboo 9 forbidden 10 prohibited
verdant: raw 5 fresh, green 8 immature, innocent 13 inexperienced 15 unsophisticated
Verdi: *character:* 7 Amneris, Radames
opera: 4 Aida 6 Ernani, Otello 7 Othello 8 Traviata 9 Rigoletto
verdict: 4 word 7 finding, opinion 8 decision, judgment
verdigris: 6 aerugo
Verdun river: 5 Meuse
verdure: 4 odor 5 scent, smell 6 flavor 7 acidity 8 greenery, strength, tapestry, tartness 9 freshness, greenness
verecund: shy 6 modest 7 bashful
Verein: 7 society 11 association 12 organization
verge: lip, rim, rod 4 edge, tend, twig, wand 5 bound, brink, limit, marge, range, scope, shaft, staff, stick, watch 6 border, margin 7 incline, virgate 8 approach, boundary, yardland 9 extremity, timepiece 13 circumference
verger: 4 dean 6 garden 7 justice, orchard 8 official 9 attendant
Vergil: See Virgil
veridical: 7 genuine 8 accurate, truthful 9 veracious 12 truthtelling
verification: 8 averment 12 confirmation 14 authentication
verify: 4 aver, back, test 5 audit, check, prove 6 affirm, ratify, second 7 certify, collate, confirm, support 8 maintain 9 establish 11 certificate 12 authenticate, substantiate
verily: yea 4 amen 5 parde, pardi, pardy, truly 6 certes, indeed, pardie, really 9 certainly 11 confidently
verisimilitude: 5 truth 10 likelihood 11 probability
veritable: 4 real, true 6 actual, gospel, honest 7 genuine 9 authentic, veracious
verity: 12 faithfulness
verjuice: 5 juice 7 acidity 8 sourness, tartness

vermiform: 4 long, thin 7 sinuous, slender 8 wormlike 10 vermicular
vermifuge: 12 anthelmintic
vermilion: red 8 cinnabar
vermin: 4 lice, mice, rats 5 filth, fleas, flies 7 bedbugs, rodents, weasels
verminous: 5 dirty 6 filthy 7 noxious 9 offensive
Vermont: *city:* 5 Barre 10 Montpelier(c.)
county: 5 Essex 6 Orange 7 Addison, Rutland 8 Lamoille 10 Bennington, Chittenden
mountain range: 7 Taconic
vernacular: 5 lingo 6 jargon, patois 7 dialect
vernal: 4 mild, warm 5 fresh, young 8 youthful 10 springlike
Verne: *character:* 4 Nemo
submarine: 8 Nautilus
verneuk: 5 cheat 6 humbug 7 swindle
verrel: 7 ferrule
versate: 4 turn 7 revolve
versatile: 5 handy 6 fickle 7 flexile 8 unsteady, variable 10 changeable, inconstant, reversible
verse (see also **poem**): 4 turn 5 meter, stave, stich 6 stanza 7 revolve, stichos 8 consider 11 familiarize
Biblo: 4 text
foot: 4 iamb
pert. to: 6 poetic
stress: 5 ictus
verse-maker: 9 metorist
versed: 5 adept 6 beseen 7 erudite, learned, skilled 8 familiar 9 practiced 10 acquainted, conversant, proficient
verset: 7 prelude 8 versicle 9 interlude
versification: 5 rhyme 6 poetry
versifier: 4 poet 5 rimer 6 verser 7 poetess 9 poetaster
versify: 6 berime 7 berhyme
version: 7 edition, turning 9 rendition 10 conversion, paraphrase 11 translation 14 transformation
verso: vo
versus: vs.; con 4 agin 7 against
vertebra: 4 axis 6 spondy 7 spondyl
vertebrae: 5 spine
vertebrate: ray 9 backboned
class: 4 aves
division: 6 somite
feathered: 4 bird
group: 9 amnionata
vertex: top 4 apex 6 summit 11 culmination
vertical: 4 acme 5 apeak, erect, plumb, sheer 6 abrupt, height, summit, vertex 7 upright 13 perpendicular
verticil: 5 whorl
vertiginate: 5 twirl, whirl
vertiginous: 5 dizzy, giddy 6 rotary 8 rotating, unstable, whirling 9 dizziness, giddiness, revolving 10 inconstant 11 vacillating
vertigo: 6 megrim 9 dizziness, giddiness
verve: pep 4 dash, elan 5 ardor, vigor 6 bounce, spirit, talent 7 ability 8 aptitude, vivacity 9 animation 10 enthusiasm
vervet: 6 monkey
very: so; too 4 fell, real, same, tres(F.), true, unco(Sc.) 5 assai(It.), molto(It.), truly, utter 6 actual, lawful, mighty, really 7 dimolto(It.), exactly, genuine 8 absolute, complete, especial, peculiar, rightful, truthful 9 extremely, identical, precisely, veracious, veritable 10 legitimate, mortacious 11 exceedingly
combining form: eri
vesica: 6 vessel 7 bladder
vesicate: 7 blister
vesicle: sac 4 bleb, cell, cyst 5 bulla 6 cavity, vessel 7 bladder, blister, utricle
air: 8 aerocyst
vesper: 7 evening 8 eventide
Vesper: 4 star 5 Venus 8 Hesperus
vespers: 6 prayer 7 service 8 ceremony, evensong
vessel: (see also **aircraft, boat, container, pail, ship**): can, cog, cup, jar, pan, tub, urn, vas 4 bell, cadi, drum, duct, ewer, olla, olpe, tank, tube, vase 5 bocal, cadus, canoe, cogue, craft, cruse, laver, liner, paten 6 aftaba, aludel, barrel, cootie, crater, firkin, funnel, goblet, goulah, holmos, krater, patera, situla, yetlin 7 aleyard, blickey, blickie, cistern, cresset, gabbard, gabbart, paterae, pinnace, pitcher, situlae, steamer, utensil, yetling 8 aiguiere, ciborium 9 alcarraza 10 receptacle
anatomical: vas 4 vasa(pl.), vein 6 artery
assaying: 5 cupel
comb. form: vas 4 vaso
drinking: cup, mug 4 toby 5 flask, glass, gourd, jorum, stein, stoup 6 dipper, flagon, seidel 7 tankard, tumbler 8 schooner
earthen: 5 crock
oil: 5 cruse, cruet
pert. to: 5 vasal
sacred: ama, pix, pyx
small: nog 4 pony, shot 6 noggin
wooden: soe 5 cogue, skeel 6 piggin
vest: 4 robe 5 dress, endow, gilet 6 accrue, clothe, invest, jacket, jerkin, linder, weskit 7 furnish, garment 9 waistcoat 10 undershirt
vesta: 5 match
Vesta: 6 Hestia
vestal: nun 4 pure 6 chaste, virgin

vestibule: 4 hall 5 entry, lobby, porch 7 chamber, narthex, passage 8 anteroom, entrance, vestible 10 antechapel
vestige: bit 4 mark, sign 5 relic, shred, smack, trace, track, umbra 8 footstep, tincture 9 vestigium
vestiture: 4 garb 5 dress 8 clothing
vestment (see also **dress**): 4 garb, gear, gown, hood, robe 5 cotta, dress, orale 6 chimer, chimre, gloves, rochet, tippet 7 cassock, garment, sandals 8 cincture, clothing, covering 10 habiliment
ecclesiastical: alb, cap 4 alba, cope 5 albae, amice, ephod, fanon, miter, orale, stole 6 lappet, palium, saccos 7 cassock, maniple, tunicle 8 chasuble, dalmatic, surplice
pert. to: 8 vestiary
vestry: 4 room 7 meeting 8 sacristy
vesture: 4 corn 5 cover, crops, grass 6 clothe, seizin 7 apparel, envelop, raiment, stubble, wrapper 8 garments, vestment 9 underwood 11 investiture
vesuvian: 5 fusee, match 8 volcanic
vet: 7 veteran 10 veterinary 12 veterinarian
vetch: ers 4 akra, tare, weed 5 fetch 7 arvejon
bitter: ers
veteran: old 7 oldster 8 seasoned 9 practiced 11 experienced
veterinarian: 7 farrier
vetiver: 5 grass 6 cuscus 8 khuskhus
veto: 6 forbid 7 message 8 document, negative, overrule, prohibit 11 disapproval, forbiddance, prohibition 12 interdiction
vettura: 5 coach 8 carriage
veuve: 4 bird 6 whydah
vex: ire, irk, tew 4 cark, chaw, fret, fuss, gall, miff, rile, roil, toss 5 anger, annoy, chafe, harry, shake, spite, tease, worry, wrack 6 bother, cumber, harass, madden, molest, nettle, offend, plague, pother, ruffle 7 afflict, agitate, discuss, dispute, disturb, perplex, provoke, torment, trouble 8 disquiet, irritate, vexation 9 annoyance, displease, infuriate 11 disturbance
vexation: 5 pique, thorn 7 fatigue 9 weariness 13 mortification
vexatious: 4 chaw, sore, vexy 5 pesky 8 annoying, cumbrous, frampoid, untoward 9 disturbed, pestilent 10 afflictive 11 contrarious, troublesome
vexed: 5 sorry 7 grieved
vexillum: web 4 flag, vane 6 banner 8 standard
via: way 4 road 5 right 7 passage, through
viaduct: 6 bridge 7 trestle
vial: 5 ampul, cruet, phial 6 bottle, caster, vessel 7 ampoule
viand: 4 fare, food 6 edible 7 aliment 8 victuals 10 provisions
choice: 4 cate
viaticum: 5 money 8 supplies 9 allowance 10 provisions
viator: 8 traveler, wayfarer
Viaud's pen name: 4 Loti
vibrant: 5 alive, ringy 8 sonorous, vigorous 9 vibrating
vibrate: jar, wag 4 beat, cast, dirl, rock, whir 5 pulse, quake, shake, swing, throb, throw, trill, waver, whirr 6 dindle, launch, quaver, quiver, shimmy, shiver, thrill 7 agitate, resound, tremble 8 brandish, flichter, resonate 9 fluctuate, oscillate, vacillate
vibration: 4 dirl(Sc.), tirl(Sc.) 5 thirl(Sc.) 6 dingle, quaver, quiver, thrill, tremor 7 flutter 8 stirring 11 oscillation, vacillation 14 changeableness
musical: 5 trill 7 sonance, tremolo, vibrato 8 overtone
point without: 4 node
vicar: 5 proxy 6 deputy, priest 8 minister 9 clergyman 10 substitute, vicegerent
assistant: 6 curate
Vicar of Wakefield author: 9 Goldsmith
vicarage: 4 dues 5 house 6 salary, tithes 8 benefice 9 household, pastorate, rectorate, residence
vice: sin 4 evil, grip, hold, turn 5 crime, fault, force, grasp, place, proxy, stead, taint 6 defect 7 blemish, failing, squeeze, stopper 8 iniquity, stairway 9 deformity, depravity 10 corruption, substitute, wickedness 11 harmfulness, viciousness 12 imperfection
Vice President (U.S.): 4 Burr, Ford, King 5 Adams, Agnew, Dawes, Gerry, Nixon, Tyler 6 Arthur, Colfax, Curtis, Dallas, Garner, Hamlin, Hobart, Morton, Truman, Wilson 7 Barkley, Calhoun, Clinton, Johnson, Sherman, Wallace, Wheeler 8 Coolidge, Fillmore, Marshall, Tompkins, Van Buren 9 Fairbanks, Hendricks, Jefferson, Roosevelt, Stevenson 11 Rockefeller 12 Breckinridge
Adams, J.: 9 Jefferson
Adams, J.Q.: 7 Calhoun
Arthur: none
Buchanan: 12 Breckinridge
Cleveland: 9 Hendricks(1), Stevenson(2)
Coolidge: 5 Dawes
Eisenhower: 5 Nixon
Fillmore: none
Ford: 11 Rockefeller
Garfield: 6 Arthur
Grant: 6 Colfax(1), Wilson(2)
Harding: 8 Coolidge

Harrison, B.: 6 Morton
Harrison, W.H.: 5 Tyler
Hayes: 7 Wheeler
Hoover: 6 Curtis
Jackson: 7 Calhoun(1) 8 Van Buren(2)
Jefferson: 4 Burr(1) 7 Clinton(2)
Johnson, A.: none
Johnson, L.B.: 8 Humphrey
Kennedy: 7 Johnson
Lincoln: 6 Hamlin(1) 7 Johnson(2)
Madison: 5 Gerry(2) 7 Clinton(1)
McKinley: 6 Hobart(1) 9 Roosevelt(2)
Monroe: 8 Tompkins
Nixon: 4 Ford(2) 5 Agnew(1)
Pierce: 4 King
Polk: 6 Dallas
Roosevelt, F.D.: 6 Garner(1), Truman(3) 7 Wallace(2)
Roosevelt, T.: 9 Fairbanks
Taft: 7 Sherman
Taylor: 8 Fillmore
Truman: 7 Barkley
Tyler: none
Van Buren: 7 Johnson
Washington: 5 Adams
Wilson: 8 Marshall

viceroy: 5 nabob, nazim 6 exarch, satrap 8 governor 9 butterfly
vicinity: 6 region 8 nearness, vicinage 9 proximity 11 propinquity, resemblance 12 neighborhood 13 neighbourhood
vicious: bad, ill 4 evil, foul, lewd, mean, vile 6 faulty, wicked 7 corrupt, immoral, noxious 8 debasing, depraved, infamous, spiteful 9 dangerous, defective, dissolute, malicious, malignant, nefarious, perverted 10 corrupting, iniquitous, villainous
vicissitude: 6 change 8 mutation 10 difficulty, revolution, succession 11 alternation, interchange
victim: 4 dupe, goat, gull, prey 6 sucker
list: 4 toll
victor: 6 captor, winner 7 conquer 8 bangster, unbeaten 9 conqueror 10 vanquisher, victorious
victory: win 7 mastery, success, triumph 8 conquest 9 landslide, supremacy 11 superiority
celebrating: 9 epinician
crown: bay 6 laurel
goddess: 4 Nike
memorial: 4 arch 6 spoils, trophy
ruinous: 7 Pyrrhic
sign: vee
song: 9 epinicion
symbol: 4 palm
Victory heroine: 4 Lena
victrola: 9 turntable 10 phonograph 12 record player
victualler: 6 sutler 9 innkeeper
victuals: bit 4 bite, food, grub, meat 6 viands 7 vittles 11 nourishment
videlicet: viz 6 namely 8 scilicet
vie: bet, run 4 cope 5 bandy, rival, stake, wager 6 endure, hazard, oppose, strive 7 compete, contend, contest, emulate 8 panorama, prospect, struggle 9 challenge
Vienna: 4 Wien
palace: 10 Schonbrunn
park: 6 Prater
Vietnam: See **North Vietnam, South Vietnam**
view: aim, eye, ken, see, vue(F.) 4 goal, look, scan 5 aview, scape, scene, sight, slant, tenet, vista, watch 6 admire, apercu(F.), aspect, behold, belief, object, regard, sketch, survey, vision 7 examine, inspect, opinion, picture, profile, summary, thought, witness 8 attitude, consider, panorama, prospect, synopsis 9 apprehend 10 appearance, inspection, perception, photograph, scrutinize, standpoint 11 contemplate, examination, expectation 13 contemplation
extended: 8 panorama
mentally: 8 envision
obstruct: 4 hide 7 conceal
open to: 4 bare 5 overt 6 expose
viewer: 9 spectator 11 stereoscope 14 superintendent
viewing instrument: 5 scope 9 telescope 10 binoculars
viewy: 5 showy 8 fanciful 9 visionary 11 spectacular, unpractical 12 ostentatious
vigil: eve 4 wake 5 guard 7 prayers, service 8 devotion, watchman
vigilant: 4 agog, wary 5 alert, awake, aware 7 careful, wakeful 8 cautious, watchful 9 attentive, observant, sleepless 11 circumspect
vigilant person: 5 Argus
vigilantes: 5 posse
vigneron: 10 winegrower 13 viticulturist
vignettist: 6 artist, author, writer 7 painter 8 engraver 12 photographer
vigor, vigour: pep, vim, vir(Sc.), vis 4 birr, zeal 5 flush, force, nerve, power 6 energy, foison, growth, health 7 impetus, potency, stamina 8 activity, boldness, strength, virility, vitality 9 animation, fraicheur, hardihood, intensity, vehemence 10 invigorate
deprive of: sap 6 deaden 8 enervate
lose: fag, sag 4 fail, flag, pine 6 weaken 7 decline
period of: 6 heyday
vigoroso: 8 vigorous 9 direction, energetic

vigorous: yep 4 able, cant, fell, hale, spry, yepe 5 eager, frank, hardy, hefty, lusty 6 florid, hearty, lively, robust, rugged, sturdy 7 cordial 8 athletic, muscular 9 effective, energetic, strenuous 11 efficacious, energetical

vigorously: 5 amain

Viking: 4 Eric 5 rover 6 pirate 8 Norseman, Northman 12 Scandinavian

vilayet: 6 region 8 division

vile: bad, low 4 base, evil, foul, mean 5 cheap, lowly 6 abject, coarse, drasty, filthy, impure, odious, sinful, sordid, wicked 7 bestial, carrion, corrupt, debased, ignoble, unclean, vicious 8 baseborn, befouled, depraved 9 abandoned, degrading, loathsome, nefarious, obnoxious, offensive, repulsive, worthless 10 abominable, despicable, disgusting 12 contaminated

vileness: 6 fedity 9 turpitude

vilify: 5 abuse, avile, libel 6 bemean, debase, defame, malign, revile, slight 7 asperse, blacken, cheapen, debauch, degrade, despise, detract, slander, traduce 8 belittle, disgrace, dishonor, reproach, vilipend 9 blaspheme, disparage 10 calumniate, depreciate

vility: 8 vileness

vill: 4 town 7 village 8 division, township

villa: 5 aldea, dacha(Russ.), house 8 villakin 9 residence, villaette 10 villanette

village: gav, mir(Russ.), rew(Sc.) 4 dorp, home, stad(African), town, vici 5 aldea, bourg, kraal, thorp, vicus 6 bustee, castle, hamlet, pueblo, thorpe 7 borough, caserio(Sp.), endship 8 bourgade, villaget, villakin 9 aldeament 10 settlement 11 aggregation

villain: 4 boor, Iago, lout, serf 5 churl, demon, devil, heavy, knave, rogue 6 rascal 8 scelerat 9 miscreant, scoundrel 10 villainous

mythological: 4 ogre 5 giant 6 dragon

nemesis of: 4 hero

villainous: bad, low 4 base, evil, mean, vile 6 common, slight, vulgar, wicked 7 boorish 8 clownish, criminal, depraved, flagrant, wretched 9 dastardly, felonious 10 detestable, flagitious, iniquitous 12 disagreeable 13 objectionable

villainy: 5 crime 7 knavery 9 depravity

villatic: 5 rural 6 rustic

villein: 4 carl, serf 5 ceorl, churl 7 bondman, cottier

vim: zip 4 gimp 5 force, vigor 6 energy, ginger, spirit 8 strength

vina: 10 instrument

vinaigrette: box 6 bottle 7 vehicle 8 carriage

vincible: 11 conquerable 12 surmountable

vinculum: 4 band, bond 5 brace, union 6 frenum

vindicate: 4 free 5 clear 6 acquit, assert, avenge, defend, excuse, uphold 7 absolve, deliver, justify, propugn, revenge, support, sustain 8 advocate, maintain 9 exculpate, exonerate

vindication: 7 apology

vindicative: See **vindictive**

vindictive: 7 hostile 8 punitive, spiteful, vengeful 10 revengeful 11 retaliatory, retributive, vindicative, vindicatory

vine: hop, ivy 4 akas, bine, gogo, odal, soma 5 betel, buaze, bwazi, guaco, liana, liane 6 maypop 7 creeper, cupseed, trailer 8 clematis 9 grapevine 10 chilicothe

comb. form: 4 viti

covered with: 5 ivied 7 lianaed

fruit-bearing: 5 grape 7 cupseed

parasite: 5 aphid, aphis

twining: 4 bine

vinegar: 4 acid 5 eisel 6 acetum, alegar, eisell 8 vinaigre(F.)

bottle: 5 cruet

dregs: 6 mother

ester: 7 acetate

pert. to: 6 acetic

preserve in: 6 pickle

salt: 7 acetate

spice: 8 tarragon

vinegary: 4 sour 7 acetose, crabbed 9 unamiable 11 ill-tempered

vineyard: cru

protector: 7 Priapus

vinous: 4 winy 9 vinaceous

vintage: 4 crop, wine 5 cuvee, yield

vintner: 8 merchant

viol: 5 gigue, rebec 6 rebeck, vielle 7 quinton 9 violaalta

progenitor: 5 rebec

viola: 4 alto 5 gamba 7 pomposa 12 viola pomposa

Viola's brother: 9 Sebastian

violate: 4 flaw, rape 5 abuse, break, force, harry, spoil, wrong 6 betray, broach, defile, defoil, defoul, injure, insult, invade, offend, ravage, ravish 7 corrupt, debauch, disturb, falsify, outrage, pollute, profane 8 deflower, dishonor, infringe, mistreat 9 constrain, desecrate, disregard 10 contravene, transgress

violation: 5 crime, error 6 breach 10 infraction 11 delinquency 13 nonobservance

sentence structure: 11 anacoluthon

violence: 4 fury 5 ardor 6 bensel, bensil, fervor, hubris, hybris 7 assault, bensail, bensall, bensell, outrage 8 ferocity 9 bloodshed 11 desecration, profanation 12 infringement

violent: 4 high, loud 5 acute, fiery, great, heady, heavy, hefty, rabid, rough, sharp, vivid 6 fierce, mighty, raging, savage, severe, stormy, strong 7 extreme, furious, hotspur, intense, rammish 8 flagrant, forceful, forcible, frenetic, vehement 9 atrocious, impetuous, phrenetic, turbulent 10 headstrong, hotspurred, immoderate, passionate, tumultuous 11 tempestuous

violently: 5 amain 8 slambang

violet: 5 mauve 6 blaver, flower, purple
perfume: 5 irone

violet root: 9 orrisroot

violet tip: 9 butterfly

violin: kit 4 alto, bass 5 Amati, cello, Rocta, Strad 6 fiddle 7 Cremona 8 Guarneri 10 Guadagnini, Guarnerius, Stradivari 11 violincello 12 Stradivarius
city: 7 Cremona
direction: 4 arco 9 pizzicato
forerunner: 5 rabab
part: peg 4 hole, neck 6 string 7 eclisse
rare: 5 Amati, Strad 10 Guarnerius

violin-shaped: 7 waisted

violinist (first): 13 concertmaster 14 concertmeister
comic: 5 Benny
fabled: 4 Nero
famous: 4 Auer 5 Elman, Stern, Ysaye 7 Heifetz, Menuhin 8 Kreisler

V.I.P.: 7 notable

viper: asp 5 adder, snake 8 cerastes 10 bushmaster, copperhead, fer-de-lance 11 rattlesnake
genus of: 5 echis

viperish: 8 spiteful, venomous 9 malicious

vir: 5 green

virago: 5 randy, scold, vixen, woman 6 Amazon, beldam, callet 7 beldame 9 brimstone, termagant

vireo: 7 grasset 8 greenlet, songbird

Virgil: *birthplace:* 6 Mantua
character: 5 Amata, Damon 7 Corydon
family name: 4 Maro
friend: 8 Maecenas
hero: 5 Aneas, Eneas 6 Aeneis
language: 5 Latin
poem: 4 epic 5 Eneid 6 Aeneid
queen: 4 Dido

virgin: new 4 maid, pure 5 first, fresh 6 chaste, maiden, modest, vestal 7 initial 8 maidenly, spinster, virginal 9 unalloyed, undefiled, unsubdued, unsullied, untouched 10 uncaptured 11 undisturbed 12 uncultivated, unfertilized 13 unadulterated

Virgin Island coin: bit 5 daler, franc

Virgin Mary: *flower:* 8 marigold
image: 5 Pieta
mother: 4 Anna, Anne

virginal: 6 spinet, virgin 11 harpsichord

Virginia: *aristocrats:* FFV
dam: 4 Kerr
motto: 17 Sic semper tyrannis
mountain: 5 Cedar
pine: 8 loblolly
quail: 8 bobwhite
river: Dan 5 James 7 Potomac, Rapidan
signature: 4 R. Lee
swamp: 6 Dismal
town: 5 Luray 8 Danville 11 Falls Church

Virginia creeper: ivy 5 plant 8 woodbine 10 ampelopsis

Virginia goat's rue: 6 catgut

Virginia snakeroot: 7 sangrel 9 birthwort 11 sangree-root

Virginia willow: iva 4 itea

Virginian author: 6 Wister

virgularian: 6 searod

viridity: 5 youth 7 verdure 8 verdance 9 freshness, greenness 10 liveliness

virile: 4 male 5 manly 7 lustful 8 forceful, powerful, vigorous 9 masculine, masterful

virl: 7 ferrule

virose: 5 fetid 8 virulent 9 poisonous 10 malodorous

virtu: 5 curio 7 antique

virtually: 6 nearly 7 morally, totally 11 practically

virtue: 4 thew 5 arete, grace 6 bounty, purity 7 probity, quality 8 chastity, efficacy, goodness, morality 9 rectitude, excellence 11 uprightness 13 righteousness
cardinal: 4 hope 5 faith 7 charity, justice 8 prudence 9 fortitude 10 temperance
paragon of: 5 saint

virtuoso: 6 expert, savant 7 scholar 8 aesthete, esthetic 10 empiricist 11 connoisseur, philosopher

virtuous: 4 good, pure 5 brave, moral 6 chaste, honest, potent 7 goddard, thrifty, upright, valiant 8 valorous 9 righteous 11 efficacious, industrious

virulent: 5 acrid, rabid 6 bitter, deadly, potent 7 hostile, noxious 8 spiteful, venomous 9 festering, injurious, malignant, poisonous 10 infectious 12 antagonistic

virus: 5 venom 6 poison 8 acrimony

vis: 5 force, power, vigor, visit 6 visual 7 potency 8 strength

vis-a-vis: 4 seat, sofa 8 carriage, opposite

visage: 4 face, look, show 5 image 6 aspect 8 portrait 9 semblance 10 appearance 11 countenance

viscera: 4 guts 6 vitals 8 entrails 10 intestines
viscid: 7 viscous
viscount: 4 peer 6 deputy 7 sheriff 8 nobleman
viscous: 4 limy, ropy, sizy 5 gobby, gummy, tarry, thick 6 mucous, sirupy, sticky, viscid 7 stringy 8 adhering, sticking 9 glutinous, semisolid
vise: 5 clamp
part: jaw
Vishnu: *bearer:* 6 Garuda
consort: Sri 7 Lakshmi
epithet: 8 Bhagavat
incarnation: 4 Rama 6 avatar 7 Krishna 8 Balarama 11 Ramachandra
serpent: 4 Naga
visible: 4 seen 6 extant 7 evident, glaring, obvious 8 apparent, manifest 9 available 11 conspicuous, discernible, perceivable, perceptible
Visigoth king: 6 Alaric
vision: eye 5 dream, fancy, image, sight 6 beauty, seeing 7 fantasy, imagine
combining form: 4 opto
defect: 6 anopia, myopia 14 metamorphopsae, metamorphopsia
double: 8 diplopia
illusory: 6 mirage
instrument of: 6 retina
lacking in: 8 purblind
measuring device: 9 optometer
pertaining to: 5 optic 6 ocular, visual
visionary: fey 4 aery, airy, wild 5 ideal 6 unreal 7 dreamer, fantast, laputan, utopian 8 delusive, idealist, quixotic, romantic 9 fantastic, imaginary 10 chimerical, ideologist 11 imaginative, impractical, speculative
visit: gam, see, vis 4 call, chat, hawk, slum, stay 5 apply, haunt 6 assail, attend, avenge 7 afflict, ceilidh(Sc.), inflict, sojourn 8 converse 10 inspection, visitation 12 conversation
visitant: 7 visitor
visitation: 8 disaster, visiting 9 migration 10 affliction
visitor: 5 guest 6 caller 7 company 8 visitant
visne: 4 jury, hood 5 venue 8 neighbor, vicinage
vison: 4 mink
vista: 4 view 5 scene 7 outlook 8 panorama, prospect
Vistula tributary: Bug, San
visual: 5 optic 6 ocular, scopic 7 optical, visible 11 perceptible
visualize: 6 ideate 7 imagine, picture 8 envisage 13 conceptualize
vita: 4 life
Vita Nuova author: 5 Dante
vital: 4 live 5 basic, chief, fatal 6 deadly, lively, living, souled, viable 7 animate, capital, exigent, supreme 8 vigorous 9 elemental, energetic, essential, important, necessary, requisite 10 imperative 11 fundamental 13 indispensable
vital fluid: sap 5 blood, lymph
vitality: sap, vim 6 biosis, foison
vitalize: 7 animate
vitals: 7 viscera
vitamin, vitamine: 6 biotin, citrin 7 choline 8 ascorbic, carotene, inositol, thiamine 10 calciferol, pyridoxine, riboflavin, tocopherol
vitellus: 4 yolk
vitiate: 5 pical, spoil, taint 6 debase, faulty, impair, impure, poison, weaken 7 corrupt, deprave, envenom, pervert, pollute 9 defective 10 adulterate, invalidate, neutralize 11 contaminate, ineffective
viticulturist: 8 vigneron 10 winegrower
vitiosity: 4 vice 5 fault 6 defect 9 depravity 11 viciousness 13 defectiveness
vitrella: 11 retinophore
vitrify: 5 glaze
vitrine: 8 showcase
vitriol: 4 acid, sory 7 caustic
vitriolic: 5 sharp 6 biting, bitter 7 caustic 8 scathing, virulent 9 sarcastic
vituperate: 4 rail 5 abuse, curse, scold 6 berate, revile 7 censure
vituperative: 10 scurrilous 10 opprobrious
vivace: 9 direction, vivacious
vivacious: gay 4 airy 5 brisk, merry 6 active, breezy, lively, vivace(It.) 7 buoyant, zestful 8 animated, cheerful, spirited, sportive 9 long-lived, sprightly 12 lighthearted
vivacity: 4 fire, zeal 5 ardor, force, verve, vigor 6 gaiety, gayety 7 gayness 9 longevity 10 liveliness
vivandier: 6 sutler
vivarium: box, zoo 4 cage 6 vivary, warren 9 enclosure
vive: 5 brisk, vivid 6 lively, living 8 forcible, lifelike 9 perceived
vivers: 4 food 8 victuals
vivid: 4 keen, live, rich 5 clear, fresh, sharp 6 active, bright, lively, living, strong 7 eidetic, flaming, glaring, glowing, graphic, intense 8 animated, colorful, distinct, dramatic, spirited, striking, vigorous 9 brilliant
vivificate: 6 vivify
vivify: 5 endue 6 revive 7 animate, enliven, quicken 10 invigorate, vivificate
vivres: 9 foodstuff 10 provisions

vixen: fox, nag 4 fury 5 scold, shrew, woman 9 termagant
viz: 5 to-wit 6 namely 9 videlicet
vizard: 4 mask 5 guise, visor 8 disguise
vizcacha, viscacha: 6 rodent
vocabulary: 5 words 7 diction, lexicon 8 glossary, wordbook 10 dictionary
vocabulist: 13 lexicographer
vocal: 4 oral 5 vowel 9 unwritten
vocalist: 4 alto 5 basso, tenor 6 artist, singer 7 soprano 8 songster 9 performer 10 coloratura
vocalization: 11 melismatics
vocation: 4 call 5 trade 6 career 7 calling, summons 8 business 9 following 10 employment, occupation, profession
vociferate: cry 4 bawl, roar 5 shout, utter 6 assert, bellow, clamor 7 clamour
vociferation: 6 outcry
vociferous: 4 loud 5 noisy 7 blatant 8 brawling, strident 9 turbulent 10 boisterous 11 loud-mouthed, openmouthed 12 obstreperous
voe: bay 5 creek, inlet
vogie: 4 vain 5 merry, proud 6 elated
vogue: cut, ton(F.) 4 mode 5 style 6 custom 7 fashion 8 practice 10 popularity
in: 10 prevailing
voice: say, vox(L.) 4 emit, voce(It.), vote, wish 5 rumor, utter 6 choice, report, speech, steven, tongue 7 divulge, express, opinion 8 announce, falsetto, proclaim 9 utterance 10 expression 12 articulation
handicap: 4 lisp 7 stutter
loss of: 7 anaudia, aphonia
loud: 12 megalophonic 13 megalophonous
male: 4 bass 5 basso, tenor 8 baritone, barytone 12 countertenor
natural singing: 7 dipetto
part: 7 glottis
pert. to: 8 phonetic
principal: 6 cantus
quality: 6 timbre
quiet: 5 sotto
sound: 5 vowel 6 symbol
stop: 9 affricate
stress: 5 arsis
voice box: 6 larynx
voiced: 6 sonant
voiceless: mum 4 dumb, mute, surd 6 atonic, flated, silent 7 aphonic, spirate 8 aphonous 10 speechless
void: gap 4 free, idle, lack, null, vain, want 5 abyss, annul, blank, egest, eject, empty, leave, space 6 devoid, hollow, remove, vacant, vacate, vacuum 7 invalid, lacking, leisure, nullify, opening, useless, vacuity, wanting 8 evacuate 9 destitute, discharge, emptiness, frustrate 10 unemployed, unoccupied 11 ineffective, ineffectual
voile: 5 ninon
voiture: 5 wagon 8 carriage
volage: 5 giddy 6 fickle 7 flighty 8 fleeting
volant: 5 agile, light, quick 6 flying, nimble 7 flounce 8 volitant
volary: 4 cage 6 aviary
volatile: 4 airy, bird 5 ether 6 fickle, figent, flying, lively, volage, volant 7 alcohol, ammonia, buoyant, essence, gaseous, volatic 8 fleeting, fugitive, vaporous 9 fugacious, transient 10 capricious, changeable, transitory 11 hairbrained 12 lighthearted
volatilize: 9 evaporate
volcano: Apo 4 Etna 5 Askja, Pelee 6 Ranier, Shasta 8 Cotopaxi, Krakatao, Krakatau, Mauna Loa, Vesuvius 9 Stromboli 12 Popocatepetl
crater: 4 maar
matter: aa, oo 4 lava, tufa 5 trass 6 pumice
mud from: 5 salse
opening: 5 mouth 6 crater 8 fumarole
rock: 5 trass 6 dacite 8 tephrite
scoria: 4 slag
steam from: 5 stufa
vole: 6 craber, rodent
Volga: Rha
volition: 4 will 6 choice 13 determination
volley: 5 crowd, volee 6 flight 7 barrage, company, platoon
volplane: 5 coast, glide
Volpone character: 5 Mosca
Volsunga Saga: *dragon:* 6 Fafnir
hero: 6 Sigurd
king: 4 Atli
Voltaire: *character:* 8 Pangloss
estate: 6 Ferney
novel: 5 Zadig 7 Candide
real name: 6 Arouet
voluble: 4 glib 5 wordy 6 fickle, fluent 8 rotating, unstable 9 garrulous, revolving, talkative 10 changeable, loquacious
volume: 4 book, bulk, coil, mass, roll, tome, turn 6 amount, cubage, scroll 8 capacity, document, fullness, loudness, quantity, strength 9 aggregate 10 crassitude 11 convolution
large: 4 tome
measure: 11 stereometer
voluminous: 4 full 5 bulky, large
Volund's brother: 4 Egil 5 Egill
voluntary: 4 free 6 freely 7 willful, willing 8 elective 9 volunteer, willingly 10 deliberate, unimpelled 11 intentional, spontaneous 13 unconstrained
volunteer: 5 offer 6 enlist, worker 7 proffer
Volunteer State: 9 Tennessee

voluptuous: 7 sensual 8 sensuous 9 luxurious 11 pleasurable
volute: 4 turn 5 whorl 6 cilery, scroll 7 cillery
volution: 4 coil, turn 5 twist, whorl 7 rolling 9 revolving 11 convolution
vomit: 4 boke, bolk, puke, spew 5 braid, brake, reach, retch 6 emetic 8 disgorge 10 egurgitate 11 regurgitate
vomiting: 6 emesis 12 anacatharsis
voodoo: obe, obi 5 magic, obeah 6 fetish 8 sorcerer
charm: 4 mojo
voracious: 5 eager 6 greedy, hungry 8 esurient, ravening, revenous 9 cormorant, rapacious 10 gargantuan, gluttonous, immoderate, insatiable
voracity: 7 edacity 10 greediness 12 ravenousness
vorago: 4 gulf 5 abyss
vortex: 4 apex, eddy, gyre 5 whirl 7 tornado 9 waterpool, whirlpool, whirlwind 10 waterspout
votary: 6 zealot 7 devoted, devotee 8 adherent, follower, promised 10 enthusiast
vote: aye, con, nay, pro, vow, yes 4 anti, poll, wish 5 elect, grant 6 assign, ballot, choice, confer, prayer 7 declare, opinion 8 dedicate, suffrage 10 plebiscite, referendum
group: 4 bloc
method: 4 hand 5 proxy, straw, voice 6 ballot, secret 7 write-in
of assent: aye, nod, yea 6 placet
of dissent: nay
receptacle: 6 situla 7 situlae
right to: 8 suffrage 9 franchise
solicitation of, for bill: 5 lobby
voter: 6 poller 7 elector 8 balloter, chooser 11 constituent
illegal: 8 repeater, underage 11 nonresident
voters (body of): 10 electorate
votive: 11 consecrated
vouch: vow 4 aver, back, bail, call, pray 6 affirm, allege, assure, attest, second, summon 7 certify, confirm, declare, resolve, support, warrant 8 accredit, maintain, sanction 9 assertion, establish, guarantee 11 attestation 12 authenticate
voucher: 4 chit 7 receipt 9 debenture, statement 10 credential
vouchsafe: 4 give 5 deign, yield 6 assure, bestow, beteem 7 concede 9 guarantee 10 condescend
voussoir: 5 wedge 8 keystone
projection: ear
voust: 5 boast, vaunt
vow: vum 4 bind, hote, oath, wish 5 swear 6 behest, devote, pledge 7 behight, declare, promise 8 dedicate 9 assertion 10 consecrate, obligation 12 asseveration, supplication
dedicated by: 6 votive
vowel: 5 vocal
contraction: 6 crasis, crases 9 diphthong
gradation: 6 ablaut
group of two: 6 digram 7 digraph
mark: 5 breve, tilde 6 umlaut 8 dieresis 10 circumflex
omission: 7 aphesis
sound: 6 dental, labial 7 palatal
unaspirated: 4 lene
vox: 5 voice
voyage: 4 trip 6 cruise, travel 7 journey, passage, passing, project 8 proceeds 9 excursion 10 enterprise, expedition, pilgrimage 11 undertaking
voyageur: 7 boatman, trapper 8 traveler, woodsman
voyaging: 4 asea
vraic: 7 seaweed
vrouw: 4 frow 5 woman 8 mistress 9 housewife
vug, vugg, vugh: 6 cavity, hollow
Vulcan: 5 smith 10 blacksmith, Hephaestus
consort: 4 Maia 5 Venus
epithet: 8 Mulciber
son: 5 Cacus 8 Caeculus
workshop: 4 Etna
vulcanite: 7 ebonite
vulcanize: 4 cure
vulgar: 4 lewd, rude 5 crude, gross 6 coarse, common, public, slangy 7 boorish, general, obscene, popular, profane 8 churlish, ordinary 9 customary, earthbred, inelegant, unrefined
vulgarian: 4 snob
vulgarism: 4 cant 9 vulgarity
Vulgate translator: 6 Jerome
vulnerable: 6 liable 7 exposed 9 pregnable, untenable 10 assailable 11 defenseless, susceptible
point: 12 Achilles heel
vulnerate: 4 hurt 5 wound
vulpine: fox 4 foxy 6 artful, clever, crafty, tricky 7 cunning 9 alopecoid
vult: 4 mien 6 aspect 10 expression 11 countenance
vulture: 4 papa 5 arend, grape, gripe, griph, urubu 6 condor, griphe 8 aasvogel, zopilote 9 gallinazo 11 lammergeier
genus of: 4 gyps
vum: vow

W

waag: 6 grivet, monkey
wabble: See **wobble**
wabby: 4 loon
wabeno: 6 shaman
wachna: cod
wacky, whacky: 5 crazy 6 screwy 7 eratic 9 eccentric 10 irrational
wad: bat, gag, pad, ram 4 cram, heap, lead, line, lump, mass, plug, roll, tuft 5 crowd, money, stuff, trace, track, would 6 bundle, insert, pledge, wealth 7 stopper 8 bankroll, compress, graphite
of paper money: 4 roll
Wadai Muslim: 4 Maba
wadding: 4 hemp 5 kapok 6 cotton
waddle: 5 tread 6 hoddle, toddle, widdle 7 trample
waddy: 4 beat, cane, club 5 stick 6 attack, cowboy
wade: go 4 ford, pass 6 paddle 7 proceed 8 struggle
wader: 4 boot, coot, hern ibis, rail 5 crane, heron, snipe, stork 6 jacana 9 sandpiper
wadi, wady: 5 oasis, river 6 ravine, stream, valley 7 channel 11 watercourse
wading bird: See **bird:** *wading*
wadset: 4 pawn 6 pledge 8 mortgage
wady: See **wadi**
wafer: 4 cake, disk, ring, seal, snap 5 close 6 fasten 7 biscuit, cracker
container for: pix, pyx
waff: wag 4 flap, gust, odor, puff, wave 5 ghost, whiff 6 paltry, wraith 7 flutter, lowborn 8 inferior 9 worthless 12 disreputable
waffie: 5 tramp 7 vagrant 8 vagabond
waffle: 4 cake
waft: 4 blow, buoy, flag, gust, odor, puff, turn, wave, weft 5 carry, drift, float, gleam, sound, taste, whiff 6 beckon, breath, direct, propel, signal, wraith 7 glimpse, pennant 9 transport
wag: wit 4 card, move, stir, sway 5 joker, leave, nudge, rogue, shake, swing 6 beckon, depart, signal 7 farceur, vibrate 8 brandish, flourish, humorist, jokester 9 oscillate
wagang: 5 death 9 departure 11 leavetaking
wage (see also **wager**): fee, pay, utu 4 hire, levy, pawn 5 bribe, fight, incur 6 employ, engage, reward, salary 7 attempt, conduct, contend, stipend 9 emolument 10 recompense 12 compensation
deduct: 4 dock
insurance: 7 chomage
wage earner: 6 worker 7 laborer 8 employee, mechanic 11 proletarian
wager: bet, bid, lay, vie 4 gage, risk 5 prize, sport, stake 6 gamble, hazard, parlay, pledge 7 venture
made in bad faith: 6 levant
waggery: 4 jest, joke 7 foolery 10 pleasantry 11 waggishness
waggish: 4 arch 5 droll, merry 7 jesting, jocular, parlous, playful, roguish 8 humorous, sportive 10 frolicsome 11 mischievous
waggle: wag 6 waddle, wobble
waggly: 8 unsteady
Wagner: *character:* Eva 4 Elsa, Erda 5 Hagen, Senta, Wotan 8 Parsifal
opera: 6 Rienzi 9 Lohengrin 15 Gotterdammerung
wife: 6 Cosima
wagon: bin, van 4 cart, dray, tram, wain 5 araba, aroba, dilly, gilly, lorry, lurry, tonga 6 camion, telega 7 caisson, chariot, fourgon, vehicle 8 carryall, schooner 12 perambulator
maker: 10 wainwright
part: 4 neap, pole, rave 5 thill 6 tongue
shaft: 5 thill
wagon-lit: 7 sleeper
wagonload: 6 fother 8 wagonful
wagonmaker: 10 wagonsmith, wainwright 11 wagonwright
wah: 5 panda
wahine: 4 wife 5 woman 8 mistress 10 sweetheart

wahoo: elm 4 fish, peto 8 nonsense, tommyrot 9 buckthorn, guarapucu
waif: 4 flag 5 stray 7 pennant, vagrant 8 castaway, homeless, wanderer 9 foundling
wail: cry, wow 4 howl, moan, waul, weep, yarm 5 croon, mourn 6 bemoan, bewail, grieve, lament, plaint 7 deplore, ululate 9 complaint 11 lamentation
wain: 4 cart 5 fetch, wagon 6 convey 7 chariot, vehicle
wainscot: 4 line 6 lining 7 ceiling 8 paneling 9 partition
waist: 4 belt, wasp 5 shirt 6 basque, blouse, bodice, camisa, girdle 7 corsage 8 camisole 10 undershirt 12 undergarment
circumference: 5 girth
waistband: 4 sash
waistcoat: 4 vest 5 benjy, gilet 6 fecket, jacket, jerkin
unlined: 7 singlet
wait: 4 bide, rest, stay, stop, tend 5 await, cater, court, dally, defer, delay, guard, serve, tarry, watch 6 ambush, attend, escort, expect, follow, harken, linger, remain 7 hautboy, hearken, observe 8 hesitate, inactive, postpone 9 accompany 10 stationary 11 expectation 12 watchfulness
waiter: spy 4 tray 6 garcon, salver, server, vessel 7 messboy, messman, servant, steward, watcher 8 servitor, watchman, waylayer 9 attendant
waive: put 4 cast, turn 5 cease, defer, forgo, leave, swing, yield 6 desert, forego, refuse, reject, vacate 7 abandon, forbear, forsake, neglect 8 postpone 9 disregard 10 relinquish
waka: 5 canoe
Wakashan: 6 Nootka
wake: 4 call, stir, wauk(Sc.) 5 guard, revel, rouse, track, trail, vigil, waken, watch 6 arouse, awaken, excite, revive 7 passage
wakeful: 5 alert 8 restless, vigilant 9 sleepless
Walden author: 7 Thoreau
Waldensian: 7 Leonist
wale: rib 4 best, flog, mark, pick, weal, welt 5 ridge, wheal 6 choice, choose, select, streak, stripe 7 timber 8 choicest
Wales (see also **Welsh**): 5 Cymru 7 Cambria
bard: 5 ovate
boat: 7 coracle
city: 6 Amlweh, Bangor 7 Cardiff, Rhondda, Swansea 8 Hereford, Holyhead, Pembroke 9 Carnarvon, Worcester 13 Kidderminster
cheese: 10 Caer-philly
deity: 4 Bran 5 Dylan
dog: 5 corgi
emblem: 4 leek
fine: 6 saraad
lake: 4 Bala
language: 6 Cymric, Kymric 7 Cymraeg
law: 7 galanas
legendary prince: 5 Madoc
marriage fee: 6 amober
measure: 5 cover 7 cantred, cantref, lestrad, listred 8 crannock
musical instrument: 7 pibcorn
patron saint: 5 David
people: 5 Cymry, Kymry
person: 5 Taffy 8 Welshman
poet: 6 Thomas
port: 7 Cardiff
river: Dee, Wye 4 Teme 5 Teifi 6 Severn
walk: mog, pad, wag 4 foot, gait, hike, hoof, limp, mall, pace, path, plod, ramp, reel, roam, roll, step, turn, wade 5 allee, amble, haunt, mince, scuff, stalk, stram, stray, strut, stump, trail, tramp, tread 6 arcade, hobble, loiter, lumber, pasear, prance, ramble, resort, stride, stroll, toddle, totter, trapes, trudge, wander 7 alameda, saunter, shuffle, traipse 8 ambulate, frescade, traverse 9 esplanade, promenade, tilicetum 11 perambulate, somnabulate 14 constitutional
a beat: 6 patrol
affectedly: 5 mince
inability to: 6 abasia
lamely: 4 limp
public: 4 mall 6 arcade 7 alameda 9 esplanade, promenade
reeling: 5 lurch
walk off: 5 leave 6 depart
walk off with: win 5 steal
walk-out: 6 strike
walk out on: 5 leave 6 desert 7 abandon
walker: 6 ganger 7 footman 8 stroller 10 pedestrian
walking: 7 passant(her.) 8 ambulant 10 ambulation 11 peripatetic
like a bear: 11 plantigrade
walking meter: 9 pedometer
walking stick: 4 cane 5 kebby, staff, stilt, waddy 6 kebbie
wall: 4 dike, ha-ha 5 fence, levee, redan, scarp 6 bailey, cashel, escarp, haw-haw, paries, podium, septum 7 barrier, bastion, curtain, defense, enclose, parapet, rampart 9 barricade, enclosure, encompass, partition, revetment 13 fortification
bracket: 6 corbel
covering: 4 tile 5 cloth, paint, paper 8 paneling 9 calcimine, draperies, kalsomine, wallpaper
dividing: 5 septa(pl.) 6 septum 9 partition
enclose within: 4 mure 6 immure
hanging: 5 arras
lining: 8 wainscot

masonry: 9 revetment
on: 5 mural
opening: 4 bole, door 6 window 7 scupper
ornament: 4 dado 6 mirror, plaque 7 hanging, molding, picture, placque 8 moulding, tapestry
part: 4 dado, pier 5 bahut, gable 6 coping, plinth 7 cornice
pert. to: 5 mural 8 parietal
plug: 6 outlet
up: 6 immure
wallaba tree: apa
wallaby: 8 kangaroo
wallah, walla: 5 agent, owner 6 fellow, master, person, worker 7 servant
wallet: bag, jag 4 jagg, pack, poke, sack 5 purse, scrip 6 budget 8 billfold, knapsack 10 pocketbook
wallop: 4 beat, blow, flog, lick, whip, whop 6 defeat, strike, thrash
walloping: 5 large 6 strong 8 enormous
wallow: pit 4 fade, mire 5 surge 6 billow, grovel, hollow, trough, welter, wither 7 founder 8 flounder, kommetje 10 depression
wallowish: 4 flat 7 insipid
wallpaper measure: 4 bolt
wally: 4 fine 6 robust, strong, sturdy 8 pleasant, pleasing, splendid 9 agreeable, excellent, first-rate
walnut: 6 bannut
skin: 4 zest
walrus: 5 morse 6 seacat 9 rosmarine
flock: pod
limb: 7 flipper
order: 5 bruta
tooth: 4 tusk
walt: 8 unsteady
waltz: 5 dance, valse
kind of: 6 Boston, Vienna
wambly: 5 faint, shaky 8 unsteady 9 nauseated, squeamish
wame: 5 belly
wampish: 5 swing 9 fluctuate
wampum: 4 peag 5 beads, money 7 roanoke
wamus: 6 jacket 7 doublet 8 cardigan
wan: dim, one, sad 4 dark, fade, pale, sick 5 dusky, faint, livid 6 dismal, feeble, gloomy, pallid, pallor, peaked, sickly 7 ghastly, languid, wanness 8 paleness 9 colorless, sorrowful 10 lusterless
wand: rod 4 pole, twig 5 baton, shoot, staff, stick 6 switch 7 pointer, rhabdos, scepter, sceptre 8 caduceus 9 horsewhip
royal: 4 mace 7 scepter
wand-shaped: 7 virgate
wander: err, gad 4 haik, hake, prog, rave, roam, roil, rove, wind 5 drift, prowl, range, shift, stray 6 cruise, dander, depart, ramble, stroll, trapes, travel 7 deviate, digress, meander, saunter, traipse 8 divagate, straggle, traverse 11 peregrinate
aimlessly: gad 5 stray 7 traipse
wanderer: vag 4 Arab, waif 5 gypsy, nomad 6 truant 7 migrant, pilgrim, vagrant 9 itinerant 11 extravagant
religious: 6 palmer
wandering: 5 vagus(anat.) 6 astray, errant 7 devious, erratic, journey, odyssey 8 aberrant 9 aberrance, planetary 10 circuitous, incoherent 11 noctivigant, perambulant
wandering Jew: ivy 5 plant 7 zebrina
Wandering Jew author: Sue
wanderlust: 8 nomadism 12 restlessness
wanderoo: 6 langur, monkey 7 macaque
wandle: 5 agile, lithe 6 supple
wane: go; ebb 4 fail, làck, sink, want 5 abate, decay, peter 6 absent, defect, repine 7 decline, dwindle, subside 8 decrease, diminish 10 defervesce
opposite of: wax
wang: 4 king 5 ruler 6 prince
wanga: 5 charm, spell 6 voodoo 7 philter, sorcery
wangle: 4 fake 5 shake 6 adjust, change, juggle, totter, wiggle 7 falsify, wriggle 8 contrive 9 extricate 10 manipulate
wanhap: 6 mishap 10 misfortune
wanion: 5 curse 6 plague 9 vengeance
wankle: 6 feeble, fickle, sickly 8 unstable, unsteady 10 irresolute
want: gap 4 hole, lack, lose, miss, mole, need, void, wish 5 crave, fault 6 besoin, dearth, desire, forget, hunger, penury 7 absence, beggary, blemish, craving, lacking, missing, poverty, require, straits, vacancy 8 exigency, scarcity, shortage 9 deficient, indigence, necessary, necessity, privation 10 deficiency, inadequacy 11 deprivation, destitution 12 difficulties
wanted man: 6 outlaw 7 escapee
wanting: 4 less 5 minus 6 devoid 7 without, witless 12 feeble-minded
wanton: gay 4 lewd 5 cadgy, dally, frisk, merry, revel 6 frisky, frolic, giglet, harlot, lavish, trifle, unruly 7 fulsome, haggard, ill-bred, immoral, lustful, playful, sensual, wayward 8 arrogant, flagrant, inhumane, insolent, prodigal, spiteful, sportive, unchaste 9 dissolute, lecherous, luxuriant, luxurious, malicious, merciless 10 capricious, effeminate, frolicsome, gratuitous, lascivious, licentious, refractory, voluptuous 11 extravagant, mollycoddle 12 disregardful, unmanageable, unrestrained 13 undisciplined, unjustifiable
wantwit: 4 fool
wanty: tie 4 rope 5 girth 9 bellyband, surcingle

wap: 4 beat, bind, blow, whop, wrap 5 blast, fight, knock, storm, truss 6 bundle, strike 8 wrapping
wapiti: elk 4 deer, stag
war: *alarm:* 4 flap
club: 4 mace 5 nulla 6 nullah
correspondent: 4 Pyle
fleet: 6 armada
god of: Ira, Tyr 4 Ares, Coel, Mars, Thor 6 Nergal
goddess: 4 Alea 5 Anath, Bella 6 Anunit, Ishtar 7 Bellona
instrument: 7 caltrap, caltrop 9 relocator
machine: ram 4 bomb, tank 6 rocket 7 missile 8 catapult
religious: 7 crusade
restriction: 8 blockade
trophy: 4 star 5 medal, scalp 6 ribbon
vehicle: 4 jeep, tank
vessel: sub 6 corvet 7 cruiser 8 corvette 9 destroyer, submarine 11 dreadnaught
War and Peace author: 7 Tolstoy
war hawk: 5 jingo
war-horse: 5 steed 6 leader 7 charger, standby 8 partisan 10 campaigner, politician
warbird: 7 aviator, tanager 8 airplane
warble: 4 sing 5 carol, chant, chirl, shake, trill, yodel 7 descant, twitter, vibrate
warbler: 4 wren 5 pipit, robin 6 singer, thrush 8 blackcap, grosbeak, redstart, songbird, songster 9 beccafico 10 bluethroat 11 whitethroat
ward: 4 care, jail, rule, warn 5 watch 6 charge, defend, govern, prison, warden, warder 7 counsel, custody, defense, enclose, fortify, keeping, protect 8 district, garrison, guardian, watchman 9 safeguard, storeroom 10 protection 11 confinement 12 guardianship 14 arrondissement(F.)
pert. to: 9 pupillary
ward off: end 4 fend 5 avert, guard, parry, repel 7 forfend, prevent
warden: 4 caid 5 guard, nazir 6 disdar, dizdar, jailer, jailor, keeper, ranger, regent, sexton 7 alcaide, alcayde, turnkey, viceroy 8 director, governor, guardian, overseer, watchman 9 castellan, concierge, constable, custodian 10 doorkeeper, gatekeeper, supervisor
warder (see also **warden**): 5 staff 7 bulwark 8 sentinel 9 caretaker, truncheon 10 stronghold
wardrobe: 4 room 5 privy 6 closet 7 apparel, armoire, bedroom, cabinet, chamber, clothes 8 costumes 9 garderobe 12 clothespress
ware: 4 host, sage, shun, wary, wise 5 avoid, aware, china, goods, ready, spend, stuff, waste 6 people, shrewd 7 careful, chaffer, heedful, pottery, prudent, seaweed 8 cautious, products, squander, vigilant 9 cognizant, conscious, porcelain 11 commodities, earthenware, inhabitants, merchandise
warehouse: 4 silo 5 depot, etape, store 6 fonduk, godown 7 almacen, fondouk, funduck, storage 8 elevator, entrepot, magazine 10 storehouse
fee: 7 storage
warfare: See **war**
warily (see also **wary**): 8 gingerly
warkloom: 4 tool 7 utensil 9 implement
warlike: 7 hostile, martial 8 militant, military 9 bellicose, Bellonian, soldierly 10 battailous, pugnacious 11 belligerent
warlock: 6 wizard 8 conjuror, magician, sorcerer 9 enchanter
warm (see also **hot**): 4 avid, beek, heat, keen, kind, mild 5 angry, brisk, calid, chafe, eager, fiery, fresh, tepid, toast 6 ardent, devout, genial, hearty, heated, kindly, lively, loving, strong, tender, toasty 7 amorous, clement, cordial, earnest, enliven, excited, fervent, glowing, irksome, sincere, thermal, zealous 8 animated, friendly, generous, grateful, vehement, vigorous 9 irascible, irritated, sprightly, strenuous 10 harrassing, overheated, passionate, responsive 11 sympathetic 12 affectionate, disagreeable, enthusiastic 13 uncomfortable
warman: See **warrior**
warming: 7 heating 11 calefacient
warmth: 4 elan, zest 6 spirit
pert. to: 7 thermal
warn: 4 rede 5 alarm, alert 6 advise, exhort, inform, notify 7 apprise, apprize, caution, counsel 8 admonish, threaten 9 reprehend
warning: 4 omen 5 knell 6 alarum, beware, caveat, lesson, signal 7 sematic 13 animadversion
sound of: 4 bell 5 alarm, siren 6 alarum, tocsin
warp: abb, end, hit, mud, wry 4 beat, bend, bias, cast, emit, hurl, line, rope, silt, sway, turn, warf 5 eject, expel, fling, quirk, throw, twist 6 buckle, deform, devise, fasten, swerve 7 contort, deflect, distort, falsify, pervert 8 sediment 9 fabricate 10 aberration, intertwine 12 misinterpret
thread for loom: 6 stamen
warragal, warrigal: 5 dingo, horse
warrant: act 4 earn, save, writ 5 berat, guard, order, right 6 assert, defend, ensure, ground, permit, reason, refuge, safety 7 behight, command, defense, justify, precept, protect, voucher, writing 8 document, guaranty, mittimus, sanction 9 authority, authorize, guarantee, protec-

tor, safeguard 10 commission, foundation, instrument, obligation, protection 11 certificate 13 authorization, justification

warranty: 8 guaranty, sanction 9 assurance, guarantee 13 authorization, justification

warren: 5 hutch 8 rabbitry, tenement

warrener: 10 gamekeeper

warrior: toa 4 hero, impi 5 brave 6 Amazon 7 fighter, martial, soldier
group: 4 army
mythical: 6 Amazon 7 Aslauga
professional: 7 Hessian 9 gladiator, mercenary
Trojan: 6 Agenor, Hector

Warsaw suburb: 5 Praga

warship: sub 5 razee 6 bireme 7 cruiser, dromond, frigate, onebank, trireme 8 corvette 9 destroyer, submarine 10 battleship 11 dreadnaught
deck: 5 orlop
fleet: 6 armada
pert. to: 5 naval
quarters: 7 gunroom
squadron: 10 escadrille
three-bank: 7 trireme
two-bank: 6 bireme

warsle, warstle: 6 tussle 7 wrestle 8 flounder, struggle

wart: 5 tumor 7 verruca 9 subaltern 10 midshipman

wary: shy 5 alert, cagey, canny, chary, leery 7 careful, guarded, knowing, prudent 8 cautious, discreet, stealthy, watchful 9 cautelous, provident 10 economical 11 circumspect

was: See **is**

wase: pad 4 wisp 6 bundle

wash: lap, mud, pan 4 lave, silt, soap 5 bathe, clean, creek, drift, float, leach, rinse, scour, scrub 6 buddle, debris, purify, sperge 7 cleanse, launder, shampoo 8 ablution, alluvium 9 lixiviate
away: 5 erode, purge
out: 4 fail 5 elute, erase, flush 7 discard, launder
up: 6 finish 7 discard, dismiss

washbowl: 4 sink 5 basin 6 lavabo 8 lavatory 9 aljofaina

washed-out: wan 4 pale 5 faded, tired 8 depleted 9 exhausted 10 dispirited, spiritless

washer: 4 rove 5 clove

washing: 8 ablution
chemical: 6 eluate

Washington, D.C.: 7 capital
art gallery: 5 Freer 8 National
hostess: 5 Howar, Mesta
original planner: 7 L'Enfant
river: 7 Potomac
section: NE, NW, SE, SW 10 Georgetown
seeress: 5 Dixon

Washington, George: *portraitist:* 6 Stuart
wife: 6 Martha

Washington, State of: *city:* Roy 4 Yelm 5 Twist 6 Tacoma, Yakima 7 Everett, Hoquiam, Olympia, Rainier, Seattle, Spokane 8 Aberdeen, Chelalis 9 Wenatchee 10 Bellingham, Walla Walla
county: 4 King 5 Adams, Ferry, Lewis 6 Pierce, Yakima
falls: 10 Snoqualmie
fort: 5 Lewis
river: 6 Yakima 8 Quinault 9 Snohomish 10 Snoqualmie
sound: 5 Puget 7 Rosario
volcano: 7 Rainier
wind: 7 chinook

Washington palm: 7 fanleaf

washout: 5 gulch, gully 6 fiasco 7 erosion, failure

washy: 4 oozy, thin, weak 5 loose 6 feeble, watery 7 diluted, insipid 8 slippery 9 frivolous, worthless

wasp: 5 whamp 6 dauber, hornet, insect, vespid 12 hymenopteron, yellow jacket
genus of: 5 sphex
pert. to: 6 vespal 7 vespine

waspish: 5 testy 7 peevish, slender 8 choleric, petulant, snappish, spiteful 9 fractious, irascible, irritable

wassail: 4 lark, orgy, romp 5 drink, revel 6 frolic, shindy 7 carouse 8 carousal 9 festivity, merriment 10 salutation 11 celebration

waste (see also **refuse, wasteland**): 4 fail, idle, loss, pine, ruin, sack 5 decay, dwine, havoc 6 barren, bezzle, devour, molder, ravage 7 atrophy, consume, corrode, destroy, dwindle, exhaust, fritter 8 confound, decrease, demolish, desolate, enfeeble, misspend, squander 9 condiddle, devastate, dissipate, emanciate 11 consumption, destruction, devastation, dissipation, prodigality, superfluous, uninhabited 12 extravagance, improvidence, uncultivated
allowance: 4 tret
lay: 4 sack 5 havoc, spoil 6 ravage

waste matter: 5 ashes, dregs, dross 6 debris 7 garbage

wasted: 7 haggard 8 impaired, phthisic

wasteful: 6 lavish 8 prodigal 10 thriftless 11 extravagant, improvident

wasteland: fen 4 burn, moor 5 heath, marsh, swamp, wilds 6 desert, morass 8 badlands

wasting: 5 tabes 6 awaste 8 cachexia, marasmus 12 malnutrition

wastrel: 4 waif 5 idler 6 waster 8 vagabond 10 profligate 11 spendthrift
wat: 6 temple
watch: eye, spy 4 espy, glom, heed, mark, mind, tend, view, wait 5 await, guard, timer, vigil 6 ambush, behold, defend, patrol, police, regard, sentry 7 bivouac, lookout, observe 8 horologe, meditate, sentinel 9 ambuscade, timepiece 11 observation 13 sleeplessness
crystal rim: 5 basil, bezel, bezil
maker: 10 horologist
part: fob 7 crystal
watchdog: 8 guardian
Hel's: 4 Garm 5 Garmr
underworld: 8 Cerberus
watcher: spy 5 scout 8 observer, watchman
watchful: 4 wary 5 alert, aware 7 careful, wakeful 8 cautious, open-eyed 9 attentive 10 unsleeping 11 circumspect
watchman: 5 guard, scout 6 sentry, warder 8 sentinel 10 gatekeeper
watchtower: 6 beacon, garret 7 lookout, mirador 8 bantayan 10 lighthouse
watchword: 5 motto 6 ensign, signal, parole 8 consigne 10 shibboleth 11 countersign
watchworks: 8 movement
arrangement: 7 caliper
mechanism: 10 escapement
water: eau(F.), wet 4 agua(Sp.), aqua(L.), brim, broo, burn, hose, pani 5 brine, fluid, flume, laver, lough, lymph, spray 6 dilute, liquid 7 moisten 8 calender, beverage, irrigate, sprinkle 10 citronelle
body: (see also **watercourse**): bay, sea 4 deep, gulf, lake, mear, mere, pind, pool, tank, well 5 oasis, ocean 6 lagoon, strait 7 springs 9 reservoir
carrier: 4 duct, pipe 5 barge, canal, flume, zanja 7 aguador 8 aqueduct
comb. form: 5 hydro
congealed: ice 5 glace 6 icicle
covered by: 5 awash 7 flooded
draw: 4 lade
element: 6 oxygen 8 hydrogen
goddess: 4 Nina 7 Anahita
hog: 8 capybara
hole: 5 oasis 7 alberca
living in: 9 amphibian
mineral: 5 Vichy 6 selter, Shasta 7 seltzer
neck: 6 strait
obstruction: bar, dam 4 reef
pert. to: 6 marine 7 aquatic
play in: 5 plash
pure: 8 aqua pura(L.)
raising apparatus: 4 pump 5 sweep 6 siphon 7 shadoof 10 water wheel
rough: rip, sea 4 eddy 5 waves 6 rapids 8 breakers
search for: 5 dowse
soapy: 4 suds
sound: 4 drip 5 plash 6 murmur, splash
still: 6 lagoon
surface: 4 ryme
vessel: jug 4 cowl, ewer, lota, pail 5 cruse, flask, lotah 6 bottle, bucket, goglet 7 pitcher, stamnos 8 decanter
Water Bearer: 8 Aquarius
water bird: 4 coot, loon 5 diver 9 waterfowl
water bottle: 4 lota, olla 6 tinaja
water buffalo: ox 7 carabao
water carrier: 4 pipe 7 aguador(Sp.), bheesty(Ind.), channel 8 bheestie(Ind.)
water cavy: 8 capybara
water centipede: 12 hellgrammite
water chicken: 9 gallinule
water clock: 9 clepsydra
water cooler: 4 icer, olla, tank 11 refrigerant
water cow: 7 manatee
water crow: 4 coot 9 snakebird
water crowfoot: 4 herb 9 buttercup
water cure: 10 hydropathy 12 hydrotherapy 17 hydrotherapeutics
water deep: 10 chevrotain
water eagle: 6 osprey
water elephant: 12 hippopotamus
water gate: 6 sluice 9 floodgate 11 watercourse
water germander: 4 mint
water glass: 6 goblet 7 tumbler 9 clepsydra
water grampus: 12 hellgrammite
water hog: 7 bushpig 8 capybara
water hole: pit 4 lake, pond, pool 5 oasis 7 alberca
water horse: 6 kelpie 11 hippocampus 12 hippopotamus
water ice: 7 sherbet
water lift: 4 pump 5 noria 6 siphon 7 shadoof
water lily: 5 lotos, lotus 6 bobbin, nuphar 7 nelumbo 8 nenuphar
water meter: 7 venturi
water moccasin: 5 snake, viper
water mole: 6 desman 8 duckbill, platypus
water nymph: nix 4 lily 5 Ariel, naiad, nixie 6 flower, kelpie, nereid, Undine 7 goddess, hydriad, Oceanid 9 dragonfly
water on the brain: 13 hydrocephalus
water ouzel: 4 bird 6 dipper, thrush
water pig: 7 gourami 8 capybara
water pipe: 4 duct, hose, tube 6 hookah 8 nargileh
water plant: 7 aquatic 10 hydrophyte
water plug: tap 6 spigot 7 hydrant 8 fireplug
water pocket: 6 tinaja
water rat: 4 vole 7 muskrat

water sprite: See **water nymph**
water thief: 6 pirate
watercourse (see also **water** *body*): run 4 dike, dyke, race, wadi, wady 5 brook, canal, chute, creek, drain, gully, river 6 arroyo(Sp.), course, gutter, nullah, ravine, sluice, stream 7 channel, trinket 8 barranca(Sp.)
watercraft: See **boat; ship**
watercress: 9 brooklime
watered: 5 moire
waterfall: lin 4 linn 5 force 7 cascade, chignon, Niagara 8 cataract, Victoria, Yosemite
waterfowl: 4 coot, loon 5 diver
waterfront worker: 5 navvy 9 stevedore
Watergate judge: 6 Sirica
waterhead: 6 source 9 headwater 12 fountainhead 13 hydrocephalus
watering device: 4 hose, pump 5 spray 6 nozzle
watering place: spa 4 pool 5 oasis 6 aguada(Sp.), battis, resort, spring
waterless: dry 4 arid
watermelon: 6 citrul, sandia 7 anguria
waters: See **watering place**
primeval: 4 Apsu
watershed: 5 ridge 6 divide
waterspout: 5 canal, spate 8 gargoyle 9 hurricano
waterwheel: 5 noria, sakia 6 sakieh 7 sakiyeh 8 tympanum
watery: wet 4 soft, thin, weak 5 fluid, sammy, soggy 6 blashy, serous, soaked, sweaty 7 aqueous, insipid, tearful, weeping 8 humorous 11 transparent
wattle: rod 4 beat, bind, flog, gill, twig, wand 5 cooba, fence, stick, twist, withe 6 acacia, coobah, dewlap, hurdle, lappet 9 boobyalla, framework, hackthorn 10 intertwine, interweave
waugh: 4 weak 5 faint, stale 7 insipid 8 nauseous
wave: ola(Sp.), sea, set, wag 4 bore, curl, flap, surf, sway, tide, vein 5 bless, crimp, curve, eager, eagre, float, flood, ridge, shake, surge, swell, swing, tilde, water, waver 6 beckon, billow, comber, fickle, flaunt, marcel, ripple, roller, signal 7 breaker, flutter, ripplet, seagate, tsunami, vibrate, wavelet 8 brandish, flourish, undulate, whitecap 9 fluctuate, permanent, vibration 10 undulation, unevenness
comb. form: 4 ondo
top: 5 crest
upward motion: 5 scend
waver: 4 reel, sway, twig 5 quake, swing 6 change, falter, teeter, totter, wiggle 7 flicker, flitter, flutter, sapling, stagger, tremble, vibrate 8 hesitate 9 fluctuate, oscillate, vacillate
wavering: 6 fickle 7 lambent 8 doubtful, flexuous, unsteady 9 desultory 10 irresolute
wavy: 4 ente(her.), onde(her.), unde(her.), undy(her.) 5 crisp, curly, snaky, undee(her.) 6 flying 7 billowy, sinuate, sinuous 8 undulant 9 undulated 10 undulating
wawl, waul: 4 howl, wail 6 squall
wax: 4 cere, grow, pela 5 putty 6 become 7 cerumen, suberin 8 adhesive, increase, paraffin 11 zietriskite
candle: 5 taper 6 cierge
cobbler's: 4 code
comb. form: cer
figure: 9 ceroplast
match: 5 vesta
mixture: 6 cerate
myrtle: 8 bayberry
ointment: 6 cerate
opposite of: 4 wane
pert. to: 5 ceral
preparation: 6 cerate
substance: 5 cerin
used for skis: 7 klister
yellow: 7 ceresin
waxbill: 7 astrild
waxen: 4 soft, waxy 6 pallid, viscid 7 cerated, pliable 8 yielding 11 impressible 14 impressionable
waxwing: 9 cedarbird
waxy: 5 angry, vexed
way: via 4 cost, fore, gait, lane, mode, path, plan, road, room 5 alley, going, habit, milky, route, space, style, track 6 ambage, arcade, avenue, career, causey, chemin, course, detour, device, manner, method, scheme, street 7 advance, fashion, highway, opening, passage 8 causeway, contrada, progress 9 banquette, direction, procedure 12 idiosyncrasy
in: 7 contact 8 entrance
on: 7 en route
open: 7 pioneer
out: 4 exit 6 egress, escape
waybill: 8 manifest
wayfarer: 6 viator 8 traveler
waygate: 4 path 9 departure 10 passageway
waylay: 5 await, belay, beset 6 ambush 7 forelay 8 surprise 9 ambuscade
waymark: ahu 5 arrow 9 milestone
wayward: 6 unruly 7 erratic, froward, naughty, willful 8 contrary, perverse, stubborn, unsteady, untoward 9 irregular 10 capricious, headstrong, refractory, self-willed 11 disobedient, fluctuating, intractable 13 unpredictable

waywiser: 8 odometer 9 pedometer 12 perambulator
we: nos(L.) 8 ourselves
weak: 4 puny, soft, thin, worn 5 anile, bauch, chirp, crank, crimp, dicky, faint, frail, seely, washy, waugh, young 6 caduke, debile, dickey, dotish, faulty, feeble, flabby, flaggy, flimsy, foible, infirm, scream, sickly, squeak, tender, unwise, watery 7 brittle, doatish, dwaible, dwaibly, foolish, fragile, pliable 8 childish, decrepit, feckless, feminine, flagging, helpless, impotent 9 childlike, dissolute, enfeebled, nerveless, powerless 10 effeminate, inadequate 11 ineffective 12 unconvincing
weaken: go; sap 4 thin, tire 5 appal, break, craze, delay 6 appall, deaden, defeat, dilute, impair, lessen, rebate, reduce, soften 7 cripple, decline, depress, disable, exhaust, unnerve 8 enervate 9 attenuate, extenuate, undermine 10 debilitate, demoralize
weakling: 5 puler, sissy 6 softie 7 crybaby
weakness: 4 flaw 6 defect, foible 7 acratia, ailment, failing 8 debility, fondness 9 inability 11 attenuation 12 imperfection
of organ or muscle: 5 atony
weal: 4 line, mark, pomp, wale, welt 5 ridge, state, wheal 6 choice, choose, riches, stripe, wealth 7 welfare 9 happiness, wellbeing 10 commonweal, prosperity
wealth: 4 dhan, gear, gold, good, weal 5 money 6 assets, graith, mammon, riches 7 capital, fortune, welfare 8 opulence, property, treasure 9 abundance, affluence, wellbeing 10 prosperity 11 possessions
comb. form: 5 pluto
gained: 8 chevance 9 chievance
god of: 6 Plutus
income from: 6 usance
person of: 5 Midas, nabob 7 Croesus, magnate 9 moneybags, plutocrat
wealthy: 4 full 5 ample, pursy
wean: 4 baby 5 child 6 detach, infant 8 alienate, estrange 9 reconcile
weanie: 4 baby
weanly: 6 feeble 8 childish
weapon: arm, dag, gun 4 beak, bola, bolo, celt, claw, dart, dirk, epee, foil, pike 5 arrow, bolas, glave, knife, lance, rifle, saber, sabre, shaft, sling, spear, sword, talon, vouge 6 bomber, dagger, eolith, glaive, mortar, pistol, poleax, rapier 7 bazooka, carbine, gisarme, halberd, halbert, machete, missile, poleaxe, trident 8 catapult, crossbow, fauchard, leeangle, revolver, stiletto, tomahawk 9 artillery, derringer 11 blunderbuss
lay down: 6 disarm 9 surrender
storage place: 7 arsenal
without: 7 unarmed
wear: don, rub 4 fray, tire 5 chafe, erode, grind, sport, weary 6 abrade, attire, endure, impair 7 apparel, clothes, consume, corrode, display, exhaust, exhibit, fatigue 8 diminish 11 deteriorate
away: 5 erode 6 abrade
wearable: 6 usable 7 garment 8 clothing
weariful: See **wearisome**
weariness (see also **weary**): 5 ennui 6 tedium 7 fatigue 8 vexation 9 lassitude
wearish: 4 weak 5 faint 6 sickly 7 insipid 8 unsavory 9 squeamish
wearisome: 4 hard 6 boring, dismal, dreary, prolix, tiring 7 irksome, tedious 8 tiresome 9 fatiguing, laborious, vexatious 10 monotonous 11 displeasing, everlasting
weary: bad, fag, irk, sad 4 bore, jade, puny, tire, weak, worn 5 annoy, bored, curse, spent, timid, tired 6 harass, plague, sickly 7 exhaust, fatigue, irksome, tedious 8 fatigued, grievous, tiresome 9 forjaskit, forjesket, surfeited 10 defatigate, disastrous 11 unfortunate
Weary Willie: 5 tramp 7 shirker, vagrant 13 featherbedder
weasand: 6 gullet, throat 7 trachea 8 windpipe 9 esophagus
weasel: 4 cane, stot, vare 5 ratel, stoat 6 ermine, ferret 10 equivocate
family: 6 ermine, ferret, marten
weasel cat: 7 linsang
weasel-like: 9 musteline
weather: dry 4 hail, rain, snow, wind 5 erode, sleet 7 climate 8 discolor, windward 12 disintegrate
weather map line: 6 isobar
weather satellite: 5 Tiros
weathercock: 4 fane, vane
weathered: 5 faded 6 tanned 7 bronzed, stained 8 bleached, hardened 9 roughened, toughened
weatherman: 13 meteorologist
weave: 4 darn, knit, lace, spin 5 braid, drape, plait, unite 6 devise, enlace, wattle 7 canille, entwine, fashion 8 cannelle, contrive 9 fabricate, interlace, interwind 10 intertwine, intertwist
twigs: 6 wattle
weaver's tool: 4 loom, reed, sley
weaverbird: 4 baya, taha 6 whidah
weaving: *cylinder:* 4 beam
goddess: 6 Ergane
machine: 4 loom 6 carder 8 jacquard
product: 5 cloth 7 textile
weazen: See **wizen**
web: mat, net, ply 4 caul, trap, veil, warp 5 snare 6 fabric, tissue 7 ensnare, network, texture, webbing 8 entangle, gossamer,

membrane, vexillum 11 fabrication 12 entanglement
pert. to: 6 telary 7 retiary
web-footed: 7 palmate 11 totipalmate
web-like: 4 lacy 7 spidery
half: 11 semi-palmate
webbing: 7 binding
Weber opera: 6 Oberon
wed: 4 join 5 elope, marry, mated, unite 6 joined, pawned 7 espouse, pledged, spliced 9 mortgaged
pert. to: 7 marital
wedding: 6 splice 8 ceremony, espousal, marriage, nuptials 11 anniversary
anniversary: See **wedding anniversary**
attendant: 5 usher 10 bridesmaid
canopy: 5 chupa 6 huppah 7 chuppah
party: 9 breakfast, reception
proclamation: 5 banns
ring: 4 band
wedding anniversary: *fifteenth:* 7 crystal
fifth: 4 wood
first: 5 paper
kind of: tin 4 ruby 5 candy, china, coral, linen, paper, pearl, straw 6 floral, golden, silver, wooden 7 crystal, diamond, emerald, leather
seventy-fifth: 7 diamond
tenth: tin
thirtieth: 5 pearl
twentieth: 5 china
twenty-fifth: 6 silver
wedge: jam 4 club, heel, lump, shoe 5 cleat, crowd, ingot, piece, split 6 cleave, sector, wedgie 7 niblick 8 separate, triangle, voussoir 9 formation
wedge-shaped: 6 cuneal 7 cuneate 8 cuneated, cuniform 9 cuneiform
wedgie: 4 shoe
wedlock (see also **wedding**): 4 wife 9 matrimony
Wednesday (source of name): 5 Woden
wee: 4 tiny 5 bitty, small, teeny 6 little, minute 10 diminutive
weed: 4 band, garb, loco, milk, sida, tare 5 armor, cheat, dress, horse, vetch 6 darnel, datura, nettle, remove, sarcle, spurge 7 allseed, clothes, costume, garment, illness, mallows, purloin, ragweed, relapse, thistle, tobacco 8 clothing, plantain, purslane, sealwort, toadflax, trumpery 9 alfilaria, dandelion, eradicate 11 undergrowth
weed killer: 9 herbicide
weeds: 8 mourning
weedy: 4 foul, lean 5 lanky 7 scraggy 8 ungainly
week: 8 hebdomad
weekday: 5 feria
weekly: 5 aweek 10 hebdomadal, periodical 11 hebdomadary, publication
weeks (two): 9 fortnight
weel: 4 eddy, pool, trap 6 basket 9 whirlpool
weem: pit 4 cave 6 cavern
ween: 4 hope 5 fancy, think 6 expect 7 believe, imagine, suppose 8 conceive
weep: cry, sob 4 leak, tear, wail 5 exude, greet, mourn 6 bewail, beweep, boohoo, lament 7 blubber
Weeping Philosopher: 10 Heraclitus
weeping statue: 5 Niobe
weepy: 5 moist, seepy 6 oozing 7 tearful, weeping 8 mournful
weeshy, weeshie: wee 4 tiny 5 weeny
weet: wet, wit 4 know
weevil: 4 boll, lota 8 circulio
weeze: 4 ooze
weft: web 4 film, warp, woof, yarn 5 shoot, shute 7 filling 12 crossthreads
weigh: 4 bear, lift, tare, test 5 carry, hoist, poise 6 esteem, ponder, regard 7 balance, examine, measure, portion, support 8 consider, dispense, meditate 9 apportion 14 counterbalance
weigh down: sit 4 lade, load 7 depress, oppress
weigher: 5 trone 6 potdar, scaler 7 balance, trutine 8 computer 9 steelyard
weighing machine: 5 scale, trone 7 balance 9 steelyard
weight: bob, CWT, keg, lot, mol, tod, tom, ton, tup 4 beef, dram, gram, heft, lade, last, load, mina, onus, pari, rati, shot, tola 5 carat, clove, flask, grain, ounce, ptund, poise, pound, power, ratti, rider, scale, stein 6 barrel, burden, cental, charge, denier, fother, fotmal, gramme, grivna, import, moment 7 centner, drachma, gravity, oppress, plummet, quarter, quintal, scruple, tonnage 8 decagram, encumber, kilogram, micogram, pressure, vierling, vamfront, vammazsa 9 authority, centigram, hectogram, heaviness, influence, liespfund, milligram, myriagram, quentchen, zollpfund 12 significance 13 hundredweight, ponderability
allowance: 4 tare 7 scalage
comb. form: 4 baro
inspector: 6 sealer
kind of: net 4 troy 5 gross 6 metric 8 jeweler's 10 apothecary 11 avoirdupois
of container: 4 tare
of 100 pounds: 6 cental
of 2000 pounds: ton
official: 6 metage
pert. to: 5 baric 8 ponderal
sash cord: 5 mouse

system of: 4 troy 5 avoir 11 avoirdupois 12 apothecaries
weighted: 5 laden 6 loaded 8 burdened 9 evaluated, oppressed
weightiness: 4 pomp 7 dignity, gravity 9 solemnity
weighty: fat 5 bulky, heavy, hefty, large, massy, obese, solid 6 severe, solemn 7 capital, massive, onerous, serious, telling 8 forcible, grievous, powerful 9 corpulent, momentous, ponderous 10 burdensome, chargeable, cumbersome, impressive, oppressive
weir: dam 4 bank 5 fence, garth, levee 7 barrier, milldam 11 obstruction
weird: lot, odd 4 eery, fate, unco, wild 5 charm, eerie, queer, scary, spell 7 awesome, curious, destine, destiny, fortune, ghostly, macabre, predict, strange, uncanny, unusual 8 foretell, prophecy 9 unearthly 10 mysterious, prediction, soothsayer
weka: 4 bird, rail
welcome: 4 hail 5 adopt, greet 7 acclaim, embrace 8 greeting 9 agreeable, bienvenue, desirable 10 acceptable, salutation
weld: 5 unite 11 consolidate
welding gas: 9 acetylene
welfare: 4 sele, weal 10 prosperity
goddess: 5 Salus
welkin: air, sky 10 atmosphere
well: fit, pit 4 bene(It., L.), bien(F.), fair, flow, gush, hole, sump 5 aweel(Sc.), fount 6 gusher, hearty, spring 7 cistern, gaylies, geylies, gradely, healthy 8 artesian, expertly, fountain 10 gratifying 11 excellently 12 satisfactory
comb. form: 4 bene
drill device: jar
lining: 5 steen
pit: 4 sump
pole: 5 sweep
prefix: eu
well-behaved: 4 good
well-being: 4 good, weal 6 health 7 comfort 8 eucrasia, felicity 9 eudaemony, happiness 10 prosperity
well-bred: 5 civil 6 polite 7 genteel, refined 8 cultured, wellborn 9 pedigreed 10 cultivated 11 gentlemanly 12 thoroughbred
well-defined: 8 distinct 11 distinctive
well-founded: 4 firm
well-groomed: 4 neat 5 clean, sleek 6 soigne 7 soignee
well-grounded: 4 firm 5 valid
well-heeled: 4 rich 7 moneyed 10 prosperous
well-known: 6 famous 7 eminent 8 familiar 9 notorious
well-liked: 7 popular
well-made: 9 affabrous
well-nigh: 6 almost, nearly
well-off: 5 lucky 8 thriving 10 prosperous
well timed: 6 timely 9 opportune
well-versed: 7 erudite
Welland: 4 city 5 canal, river
wellaway: woe 4 alas 5 alack 6 regret 9 alackaday
wellborn: 4 rich 5 noble 7 eugenic
wellhead: 6 source, spring 8 fountain 12 fountainhead
welsh, welch: 5 cheat, evade, renig 6 renege 7 swindle
Welsh, Welch (see also **Wales**): 6 Cymric 8 Cambrian
welsh drake: 7 gadwale, gadwall, gadwell
Welsh onion: 5 cibol
Welsh Rabbit: 7 rarebit
welt: 4 mark, turn, wale 5 ridge, upset 6 stripe, thrash 8 overturn
welter: 4 reel, roll, toss, wilt 5 upset 6 grovel, tumble, wallow, wither 7 stagger, turmoil 8 overturn 9 confusion
wem: 4 flaw, scar, spot 5 stain
wen: 4 cyst, rune 5 tumor 7 blemish 11 excrescence 12 imperfection, protuberance
wench: 4 dell, doxy, drab, gill, girl 5 child, gouge, trull, woman 6 blowen, blowze, damsel, maiden 7 consort, servant 8 strumpet 11 maidservant
wend: go; bow 4 fare, pass 5 alter, shift 6 depart, travel 7 circuit, journey, proceed 9 disappear
Wend: 4 Slav, Sorb 7 Sorbian
Wendy: *brother:* 5 Peter
dog: 4 Nana
went (see also **go**): 4 lane, road 5 alley 7 passage 9 crossroad
wenzel: 4 jack 5 knave
were (see also **are**): 5 check, doubt, dread, guard 10 perplexity 11 uncertainty 12 apprehension
wergild: cro 4 eric
Wessex king: Ine, Ini
West: 8 frontier, Occident
West Africa: See **Africa**
West Germany capital: 4 Bonn
West Indies: 7 Bahamas 8 Antilles
bird: 4 arar, tody 6 mucaro
boat: 6 droger 7 drogher 9 catamaran
coin: 5 daler
fiber: 5 cajun
fish: 4 paru, pega, sesi 5 pelon 6 testar 7 pegador 8 scirenga 9 picudilla
fleas: 7 chigoes
fruit: 4 tuna 5 papaw 6 papaya, pawpaw 7 genipap
handkerchief: 7 malabar

herb: 4 ocra 6 vanglo 7 vangloe
island: 4 Cuba 5 Aruba, Haiti, Nevis 6 Bahama 7 Jamaica 8 Antilles, Barbados, Trinidad
king: 7 Cacique
liquor: 5 mobby, tafia 6 mobbie, taffia
lizard: 6 arbalo
mistletoe: 7 gadbush
palm: 5 yagua, yaray 6 grigri, grugru
people: Ebo 4 Eboe 5 Cuban 6 Creole
pert. to: 9 Antillean
plum: 4 jobo
region: 7 Malabar
republic: 5 Haiti
rodent: 5 hutia, jutia 6 agouti
shrub: 4 anil 7 joewood
snuff: 8 maccaboy, maccoboy
sorcery: ob; obe, obi 6 voodoo
sugar work: 5 usine
taro: 5 tania
tortoise: 7 hicatee 8 hiccatee
tree: 4 ausu, cera 5 acana, acapu, ebony, genip, papaw, yacca 6 aralie, ausubo, balata, cocuyo, gomart, pawpaw, ramoon 7 cocullo 8 aceituna, cockspur, drumwood 9 cocuswood, sapodilla
treewood: 5 galba
volcano: 5 Pelee

West Point: *island:* 4 lona
mascot: 4 mule
student: 4 pleb 5 cadet, plebe 8 yearling

West Virginia city: 5 Logan 10 Charleston(c.)

Western treaty alliance: 4 NATO

Westminster clock: Ben

Westphalian city: 7 Munster

wet: lax, off 4 damp, dank, dewy, lash, mire, rain, soak 5 bedew, bewet, dabby, foggy, humid, leach, misty, moist, mushy, rainy, soggy, soppy, sweat, wrong 6 clashy, dampen, drench, humect, imbrue, jarble, liquor, shower, soaked, sodden, watery 7 flotter, moisten, splashy, squashy 8 dampened, irrigate, moisture, sprinkle 9 misguided 11 intoxicated 18 anti-prohibitionist

wet blanket: 6 dampen 7 depress, killjoy 8 deadhead, dispirit 10 discourage, spoilsport

wet flax: ret

wet one's whistle: 5 drink

weta: 6 insect

wetbird: 9 chaffinch

wether: ram 4 wool 5 sheep 6 eunuch 7 dinmont

whack: hit, try 4 bang, beat, belt, blow 5 share, thump, trial, whang 6 chance, strike, stroke, thwack 7 attempt, portion 8 division 9 allowance, condition

whacking: 5 large 8 whopping 10 tremendous

whale: hit, orc 4 beat, cete, drub, lash, orca, wale, whip, whop 5 poggy, sperm, whack 6 baleen, beluga, blower, strike, thrash 7 Cetacea, grampus, ripsack 8 cachalot, hardhead 9 blackfish, mysticete, mysticeti, zeuglodon 10 bottlehead, zeuglodont 13 sulphur-bottom
blue: 9 sibbaldus
carcass: 5 kreng
constellation: 5 Cetus
cry: 4 fall
fat: 7 blubber
female: cow
food: 4 brit
iron: 7 harpoon
order: 4 cete 7 Cetacea
pert. to: 5 cetic
school: gam, pod
secretion: 9 ambergris
skin: 6 muktuk
strip blubber from: 6 flense
tail part: 5 fluke
young: 4 calf 5 stunt 9 shorthead

whale oil: 10 spermaceti
cask: 4 rier

whaleback: 9 steamship 10 turtleback 12 grain-carrier

whalebird: 4 gull 6 petrel 9 phalarope, turnstone

whalebone: 5 stiff 6 baleen, severe 10 inflexible

whalehead: 8 shoebill

whaler: 4 ship 7 bushman, swagman, whopper 8 whaleman 9 sundowner, whaleboat
visit: gam

whaling: 4 huge 8 whopping
cask: 4 rier 6 cardel
profit: lay
spear: 7 harpoon

whaling ship: 6 Pequod, whaler

whample: 4 blow 6 stroke

whang: 4 bang, beat, blow, chop 5 chunk, slice, thong, throw, whack 6 assail, strike, thrash

whangee, wanghee: 4 cane 5 stick 6 bamboo

wharf: 4 dock, pier, quai(F.), quay 7 landing
space: 7 quayage
worker: 9 stevedore

wharf fish: 6 cunner

wharfmaster: 10 wharfinger

whatnot: 7 etagere

whaup: 4 fuss 6 curlew, outcry

wheal: 4 mark, mine, wale, weal 5 whelk 6 stripe 7 postule 9 suppurate

wheat: 5 durum, spelt, trigo 6 imphee 7 einkorn, semoule

chaff: 4 bran
disease: 4 bunt, rust, smut 5 ergot 6 aecium, fungus
gritty part: 8 semolina
head: ear
outer coat: 4 bran
processed: 4 suji 5 grits 6 bulgur 9 middlings
repository: bin 8 elevator
state: 4 Ohio 5 Idaho 6 Dakota, Kansas 7 Indiana, Montana 8 Illinois, Missouri, Nebraska, Oklahoma 9 Minnesota 10 Washington 12 Pennsylvania
stubble: 6 arrish

wheat duck: 7 widgeon 8 baldpate
wheat louse: 5 aphid
wheat smut: 4 bunt 8 colbrand
wheatbird: 4 lark
wheatear: 4 bird 5 chack 8 chickell 10 gorsehatch
wheedle: cog 4 cant, coax 5 carny, tease, whine 6 banter, butter, cajole, carney, fleech, whilly 7 blarney, cuittle, flatter 8 persuade 9 influence
wheel (see also **gear**): cam, cog 4 bike, disk, helm, roll, turn 5 pivot, rotor, rowel, skeif, skive 6 caster, circle, roller, rotate, sheave 7 bicycle, chukkar, chukker, pedrail, revolve 10 revolution, waterwheel
comb. form: 5 troch 6 trocho
furniture: 6 caster
part: cam, cog, rim 4 tire 5 felly, spoke, sprag 6 felloe 8 sprocket
pert. to: 5 rotal
potters: see **potter's wheel**
rim: 5 felly 6 felloe
shaft: 4 axle
spinning: see **spinning wheel**
spurred: 5 rowel
stopper: 5 brake
toothed: cog
water-raising: see **waterwheel**

wheel-shaped: 6 rotate 8 circular, rotiform
wheelbarrow: hod 10 hurlbarrow
wheeler (see also **wheelman**): 7 cyclist, vulture 11 wheelwright
wheelman: 5 pilot 7 cyclist, steerer, wheeler 8 helmsman, pedalist 9 bicyclist
wheeze: gag 4 hint, joke 5 adage, dodge, hoose, hooze, trick 6 cliche, coghle(Sc.), device, saying 9 witticism
wheezy: 9 asthmatic
whelk: 4 acne 5 snail 6 papule, pimple, winkle 7 pustule
whelm (see also **overwhelm**): 5 cover, crush 9 drainpipe
whelp: cub, dog, pup 4 bear, fawn, lion, wale, welt, wolf 5 child, puppy, tiger, youth 7 leopard
whemmel, whemmle: 5 upset 6 tumble 8 overturn 9 confusion
when: as 5 until 7 whereas 8 although, whenever
where: 7 whither
whereas: as 5 since
wherefore: 5 cause 6 reason 9 therefore 11 accordingly
whereness: 6 ubiety
wherewithal: 5 means 9 resources
wherret: box, hit 4 slap
wherry: 4 boat 5 barge, carry, scull 7 lighter, rowboat, vehicle 9 transport
whet: 4 hone 5 grind, rouse, strop 6 excite 7 quicken, sharpen 9 stimulate
whether: if
whetstone: bur 4 buhr, burr, hone 5 stone 9 sharpener
whewl: cry 4 howl 5 whine
whey: 5 serum
which: who 4 that, whom
which was to be shown: QED
whicker: 5 neigh 6 whinny
whid: fib, lie 4 word 5 frisk
whiff: fan 4 flag, fuff, guff, gust, odor, puff, waft, wave 5 expel, fluff, jiffy, smell 6 breath, exhale, inhale, stench 7 instant 10 inhalation
whiffle: 4 blow, emit, idle, turn, veer, wave 5 expel, shake, shift 6 change, trifle 7 flicker, flutter, scatter 8 disperse 9 vacillate
whig: jog 4 whey 8 beverage 10 buttermilk
Whig poet: Og 8 Shadwell
while: as; yet 5 until 6 whenas 7 whereas
whilly: 4 gull 6 cajole 7 wheedle
whilom: 4 erst, once, past 6 former 8 erewhile, formerly 9 erstwhile
whim: fad, fit, gig 4 idea, mood 5 fancy, humor, winch 6 megrim, notion, trifle, vagary, whimsy 7 boutade, caprice, capstan, whimsey 8 crotchet
whimper: cry, sob 4 mewl, moan, pule, weep 5 whine 6 murmur, yammer 7 grizzle, sniffle
whimsical: odd 5 droll, queer 6 cockle 7 bizzaro, comical 8 fanciful, freakish, notional 9 conceited, eccentric, fantastic, grotesque 10 capricious 11 fantastical
whimsy: See **whim**
whin: 4 rock, whim 5 furze, gorse 9 whinstone
whinchat: 9 gorsechat, grasschat
whine: wow 4 cant, girn, moan, pule 5 croon, whewl 6 snivel, yammer 7 whimper 8 complain
whinnock: 7 whimper
whinny: 4 bray 5 hinny, neigh
whinyard: 5 sword

whip: cat, gad, tan 4 beat, cane, crop, flay, flog, jerk, lace, lash, urge, wind, wrap 5 birch, flick knout, outdo, quirt, spank, strap, swish 6 defeat, punish, stitch, strike, swinge, switch, thrash 7 belabor, chicote, conquer, overlay, scourge, sjambok 8 chawbuck, coachman, hunstman 9 bullwhack, flagellum 10 discipline, flagellate
mark: 4 wale, weal, welt
part: 4 crop 5 snead 6 handle, socket
whir: bur, fly 4 birl, burr, move, whiz 5 hurry, skirr, swirl, whizz 6 bustle, hurtle 7 revolve, vibrate 9 commotion
whirl: 4 eddy, reel, spin, stir, tirl, turn 5 drill, twirl 6 bustle, circle, gyrate, rotate, swinge, tumult, uproar, vortex 7 revolve 9 commotion, pirouette
whirlbone: 7 kneepan, patella 10 hucklebone
whirlpool: 4 eddy 5 gorce, swirl 6 gurges, vortex 9 Charybdis, maelstrom
whirlwind: oe 7 cyclone, tornado 9 maelstrom
whirr: See **whir**
whisht: 4 hush 7 silence
whisk: 4 tuft, whip, wisp 5 flisk
whiskers (see also **beard**): 6 growth 7 stubble 9 sideburns, vibrissae 11 muttonchops
fish: 7 barbels
whiskey, whisky: rye 4 corn 6 poteen, redeye, rotgut, Scotch 8 blockade, busthead 9 moonshine 10 usquebaugh
maker: 9 distiller
punch: 5 facer
whiskin: 4 bowl
whisper: 4 buzz 5 rumor 6 breeze, murmur
whisperer: 7 tattler 9 backbiter, slanderer 10 talebearer
whist: 4 game, hush, mute 5 cards, quiet, still 6 silent 7 silence 8 silently
declaration: 6 misere
dummy: 4 mort
hand: 6 tenace 10 Yarborough
whistle: 4 hiss, pipe, sugh, toot 5 siren, sough
whistle duck: 9 goldeneye
whistle-pig: 9 woodchuck
whistlewing: 9 goldeneye
whit: bit, jot 4 atom, doit, haet, hate, iota 5 speck 8 particle
white: wan 4 ashy, bawn, hoar, pale, pure 5 ashen, happy, hoary, ivory 6 albino, argent, blanch, chalky, grayed, honest, pallid, pearly 7 ivorine, silvery 8 harmless, innocent, spotless 9 colorless, fortunate, honorable 10 auspicious
becoming: 9 canescent
egg's: 5 glair 7 albumen
with age: 4 hoar 5 hoary
white ant: 4 anai, anay 7 termite
white antimony: 11 valentinite
white cell: 9 leukocyte
white cliffs' site: 5 Dover
white-collar: 5 clerk 6 typist 8 salesman 9 secretary 10 bookkeeper
white crow: 7 vulture
white elephant (land of): 4 Siam 5 Burma, India 6 Ceylon 8 Thailand
white feather: 4 fear 9 cowardice
white flag: 5 truce 9 surrender
white gentian: 9 feverroot
white grouse: 9 ptarmigan
white heat: 13 incandescence
white horse nettle: 9 trompillo
White House: *designer:* 5 Hoban
dog: 4 Fala
feature: 7 portico
first resident: 5 Adams
initials: FDR, HST
nickname: Abe, Ike
white Indian hemp: 8 milkweed
white iron pyrites: 9 marcasite
white jade: 9 alabaster
white lead: 6 ceruse
white lead ore: 9 cerussite
white-livered: 8 cowardly 13 pusillanimous
white magic: 7 theurgy
white merganser: 4 smew
white mica: 9 muscovite
White Monk: 10 Cistercian
White Mountain: 5 Adams
white mule: gin 6 liquor, whisky 7 whiskey 9 moonshine
white mundic: 12 arsenopyrite
white nun: 4 smew
white partridge: 9 ptarmigan
white plague: 8 phthisis 11 consumption 12 tuberculosis
white plantain: 9 pussytoes
white poplar: 5 abele, aspen
white pudding: 7 sausage 9 whitehass
white pyrite: 9 marcasite
white sanicle: 9 snakeroot
white snipe: 6 avocet 10 sanderling
White Sunday: 10 Whitsunday
white walnut: 8 shagbark, sycamore 9 butternut
white whale: 6 beluga
white widgeon: 4 smew
whitebelly: 6 grouse, pigeon
whiteboy: pet 8 favorite
whitecap: 4 wave 5 crest
whited sepulcher: 9 hypocrite
whitefish: 5 cisco 6 beluga 8 menhaden
whiten: 4 pale 5 chalk 6 blanch, bleach 8 etiolate
whiteside: 9 goldeneye

whitewash: 6 blanch, defeat, parget 7 conceal
whiteweed: 5 daisy
whitewing: 4 sail 6 scoter 7 sweeper 9 chaffinch
whither: 4 blow, hurl, rush, whiz 5 hurry, shake, throw, where 6 flurry, totter 7 bluster, tremble 8 wherever
whiting: 4 fish 5 chalk
whitlow: 4 sore 5 felon 6 fetlow 12 inflammation
whitster: 8 bleacher
Whitsunday: 9 Pentecost
whittaw: 7 saddler
whitten: 5 rowan
whitterick: 6 curlew
whittle: cut 4 pare, whet 5 knife, shape, shave, shawl 6 mantle, reduce, remove 7 blanket 9 petticoat, whetstone
whiz: go; hum 4 buzz, hiss, pirr, whir 5 hurry 6 corker, rotate 7 bargain
who: quo(L.), Wer(G.), wha(Sc.) 13 interrogative
whoa: 4 halt, stop
whole: all, sum 4 full, hail, hale, sole, unit 5 gross, total 6 entire, healed, intact, wholly 7 perfect 8 absolute, complete, ensemble, entirely, entirety, thorough, unbroken 9 unanimous, undamaged, undivided 10 unimpaired
comb. form: 4 toti, toto
whole note: 9 semibreve
whole number: 7 integer
whole-souled: 7 devoted, sincere, zealous 8 generous 12 whole-hearted
wholehearted: 6 hearty 7 devoted, earnest, sincere 8 complete 10 unreserved 11 unmitigated
wholesale: 4 bulk, lots 7 massive 8 abundant, sweeping 9 extensive
wholesome: 5 sound 6 benign, hearty, robust 7 healthy 8 benedict, halesome, salutary, vigorous 9 favorable, healthful 10 beneficial, healthsome, propitious, salubrious
wholly: 5 quite 7 algates 10 altogether 11 exclusively
comb. form: 4 toto
whoop: 4 hoot, urge, yell 5 cheer, shout 6 halloo
whooping cough: 9 pertussis
whop: 4 beat, blow, bump, flop 5 knock, throw 6 strike, stroke
whopper: lie 5 story 6 bender, bumper 7 bouncer
whopping: 5 great, large 7 banging
whore: 4 drab 5 wench 6 harlot 8 strumpet 9 courtesan 10 prostitute
whorl: 5 spire
why: 9 wherefore
whyo: 6 robber 7 footpad 8 gangster
wick: bay 4 bend, town 5 angle, creek, inlet 6 corner, hamlet, inwick 7 borough, village 9 farmstead
wicked: bad, ill 4 evil, vile 6 fierce, guilty, horrid, sinful, unjust 7 beastly, harmful, heinous, hellish, painful, profane, vicious 8 criminal, depraved, devilish, diabolic, felonous, fiendish, flagrant, indecent 9 atrocious, difficult, malicious, nefandous, nefarious, perverted 10 diabolical, flagitious, impassable, iniquitous, villainous 11 mischievous 12 inaccessible
wicker: 4 twig 5 osier, withe
wicker basket: 4 kish
wicker cradle: 8 bassinet
wicker hut: 5 jacal
wicket: 4 arch, door, gate, hoop 5 hatch 6 window 7 guichet, opening
wickiup: hut 7 shelter
widdershins, withershins: 10 contrarily, topsy-turvy 12 contrariwise
widdle: 7 wriggle 8 struggle
widdrim: 4 fury 7 madness 9 confusion 10 excitement
widdy: 4 rope 5 noose, widow, withy 6 halter 7 gallows
wide: 5 ample, broad, loose, roomy 6 opened 8 expanded, spacious 9 capacious, distended, expansive, extensive 12 farspreading 13 comprehensive
wide-awake: hat 4 keen, tern 5 alert 7 knowing 8 watchful 10 interested
widely: far 4 afar 6 abroad
widen: 4 ream 6 dilate, expand, extend, spread 7 amplify, broaden, enlarge 10 generalize
widespread: 4 rife 7 allover, diffuse, general 8 diffused, sweeping 9 extensive, pervasive, prevalent, universal 13 comprehensive
widgeon: 4 duck 5 goose 8 baldpate 9 simpleton
genus: 6 mareca
widow: 5 widdy 6 relict 7 dowager 8 bereaved
in cards: 4 skat
right: 5 dower 10 quarantine
suicide: 6 suttee
widow monkey: 4 titi
widow's mite: 5 lepta(pl.) 6 lepton
widowhood: 7 viduage
widowman: 7 widower
width: 5 girth 7 breadth 8 diameter, latitude, wideness

wield: ply 4 bear, cope, deal, rule 5 power, swing 6 direct, employ, handle, manage, ordain 7 control 8 brandish 9 determine 10 manipulate
wife: ux(L.); hen 4 frau, frow, mate, uxor(L.) 5 donna, mujer 6 gammer, spouse 7 consort 8 gudewife(Sc.), guidwife(Sc.), helpmate, helpmeet
bequest to: dot 5 dowry
clergyman's: 8 curatess
killer: 9 uxoricide
lord's: 4 lady
pert. to: 7 uxorial
rajah's: 4 rani 5 ranee
slave's: 9 broadwife
wig: 4 gizz 5 busby, caxon, jasey, judge, scold 6 baguio, peruke, rebuke, toupee 7 censure, periwig, spencer 8 Chedreux 9 dignitary, Gregorian, reprimand
repair: 6 careen
wiggle: 5 shake 6 waggle, wobble 7 stagger, wriggle
wight: man 4 loud 5 brave, swift, witch 6 active, nimble, strong 7 swiftly, valiant 8 creature, powerful, strongly
wigwag: 6 signal
wigwam: 4 home, tipi 5 tepee 6 teepee
wild: mad, ree 4 daft, wowf(Sc.) 5 feral, rough, waste, weird 6 desert, ferine, ramage, savage, stormy, unruly 7 bestial, haggard, riotous, skeered(Sc.), untamed, wilsome 8 aberrant, agrestal, desolate, dramatic, farouche, frenetic, hellicat, reckless, untilled 9 agrestial, barbarian, barbarous, dissolute, disturbed, ferocious, hellicate, imprudent, primitive, turbulent, unbridled, visionary 10 chimerical, dissipated, irrational, licentious, tumultuous, wilderness 11 extravagant, harumscarum, uncivilized, uninhabited 12 obstreperous, uncontrolled, uncultivated 14 uncontrollable
wild alder: 8 goutweed
wild allspice: 9 spicebush
wild arum: 10 cuckoopint
wild ass: 6 onager
wild banana: 5 papaw 6 pawpaw
wild carrot: 8 hilltrot
wild coffee: 9 feverroot
wild crocus: 12 pasqueflower
wild dog: 5 dingo
Wild Duck author: 5 Ibsen
wild flower: See **flower**
wild goat: 4 ibex
wild goose: 7 greylag 8 Jacobite
wild hog: 4 boar
wild horse: 7 mustang
wild hyacinth: 6 camass
wild Irishman: 10 tumatakura
wild jalap: 8 mayapple
wild kale: 6 radish 8 charlock
wild masterwort: 8 goutweed
wild musk: 9 alfilaria
wild mustard: 8 charlock
wild passionflower: 6 maypop
wild pineapple: 7 pinguin
wild plum: 4 sloe
wild pumpkin: 11 calabazilla
wild sage: 5 clary
wild sago: 7 coontie
wild sheep: See **sheep**
wild succory: 7 chicory
wild sweet potato: 7 manroot
wild turnip: 6 radish 8 rutabaga 9 breadroot
wildcat: cat 4 balu, eyra 6 ocelot, serval 7 panther 9 promotion
wildebeast: gnu
wilder (see also **wild**): 5 stray 6 wander 7 perplex 8 bewilder
wilderness: 5 waste 6 desert, forest
wildfowl: 4 duck 5 goose, quail 8 pheasant 9 partridge
flight: 5 skein
wildness: 6 ramage 8 ferocity 12 extravagance
wile: art 4 lure, ruse 5 fraud, guile, trick 6 allure, deceit, entice 7 beguile, cunning 8 artifice, trickery 9 stratagem
Wilkes Island: 4 Ashi
will: 4 lust, wish 6 animus, choose, decree, desire, devise, prefer 7 command, longing 8 appetite, pleasure, volition 9 intention, testament 11 disposition, inclination, self-control 13 determination
appendix: 7 codicil
having no: 9 intestate
maker of: 8 testator
proof of: 7 probate
valid: 7 testacy
willful: mad 4 rash 5 heady 7 wayward 8 stubborn 9 camsteary, camsteery, impetuous, obstinate, voluntary 10 hardheaded 11 intentional
willies: 6 creeps 7 jitters
William II's residence: 5 Doorn
William Tell: *canton:* Uri
composer: 7 Rossini
hero: 4 Egil
William The Conqueror's burial place: 4 Caen
willing: apt 4 bain 5 prone, ready 6 minded 7 tending 8 desirous, disposed, unforced 9 agreeable 10 volitional
willingly: 4 fain, lief 5 lieve 6 freely, gladly
willingness: 7 consent 8 alacrity
willow: iva 4 itea 5 osier, salix 6 teaser
willow basket: 7 prickle

willow wren: 10 chiffchaff
willowy: 5 lithe 6 pliant 7 slender 8 flexible, graceful
willpower: 7 purpose 10 resolution 12 resoluteness 13 determination
loss of: 6 abulia 7 aboulia
willy: 4 trap 6 basket, willow
Wilson's thrush: 5 veery
wilt: sag 4 fade, flag 5 droop, quail 6 wither 8 languish
wily: sly 4 foxy 5 canny, smart 6 artful, astute, crafty, shrewd, subtle 7 cunning, subtile 9 cautelous
wimble: awl 4 bore 5 auger, brace, scoop, twist 6 active, gimlet, pierce 9 penetrate, sprightly, whimsical
Wimbledon event: 6 tennis
wimick: cry 7 whimper
wimple: 4 bend, fold, turn, veil, wind 5 curve 6 ripple 7 meander, wriggle 9 headdress
win: get, pot 4 earn, gain, take 5 charm 6 allure, attain, defeat, entice, obtain, secure 7 achieve, acquire, capture, conquer, prevail, succeed, triumph 8 vanquish 9 captivate, influence 10 accomplish, conciliate
all tricks: 4 slam
back: 7 recover 8 retrieve
over: 6 defeat 8 persuade 10 conciliate
wince: 4 crab, reel 5 start 6 cringe, flinch, recoil, shrink 8 windlass
wind: oe; air 4 birr, bise, bora, coil, flaw, gale, gust, kona, reel, wend, wrap 5 belay(naut.), blast, buran, crank, curve, foehn, noser, reeve, samum, siroc, storm, trade, twine, twist, wield 6 boreas, bought, breath, breeze, buster, gibleh, simoom, simoon, solano, squall, writhe, zephyr 7 chamsin, chinook, cyclone, entwine, entwist, etesian, gregale, khamsin, meander, monsoon, pampero, revolve, sirocco, tempest, tornado, typhoon, wreathe, wriggle, wulliwa 8 blizzard, khamseen, libeccio, williwaw, willywaw 9 harmattan, hurricane, libecchio, noreaster 10 euroclydon, tramontana, tramontane
combining form: 5 anemo
desert: 6 simoon 7 sirocco
god of: 4 Adda, Adad, Vayu 5 Eolus 6 Aeolus, Eecatl
periodic: oe 7 etesian, monsoon
personification: 6 Caurus 7 Caecias 8 Favonius
pertaining to: 6 eolian 7 aeolian
summer: 6 breeze, zephyr
wind gauge: 4 vane 10 anemometer 11 weathercock
wind instrument: sax 4 fife, horn, oboe, tuba 5 flute, organ 6 cornet 7 hautboy 8 clarinet
wind up: end 4 coil 5 close 6 finish 8 conclude
windfall: 4 boon, vail 7 bonanza, fortune 8 buckshee
windflower: 7 anemone
windhover: 7 kestrel
windiness: 7 conceit 9 puffiness 11 verboseness 12 boastfulness
winding: 4 wily 6 screwy, spiral, tricky 7 coiling, crinkle, devious, pliable, sinuous, twining, wriggly 8 flexible, rambling, tortuous, twisting 9 deceitful, intricate, meandrous, sinuosity 10 anfracture, circuitous, meandering, serpentine 11 amortisseur, anfractuous
winding device: 4 reel 7 capstan 8 windlass
winding sheet: 6 shroud
windjammer: 4 ship 6 bugler, sailor, talker 8 musician 9 trumpeter
windlass: 4 crab, reel 5 hoist, winch 7 capstan
windle: 7 measure, redwing
windmill: *blade:* 4 vane
fighter of: 7 Quixote
pump: gin
sail: awn, ban
window: bay 5 gable, glaze, oriel 6 dormer 7 balcone, fenetre, lucarne, mirador, opening, winnock(Sc.) 8 aperture, casement
arrangement: 12 fenestration
bay: 5 oriel
frame: 4 sash
leading: 4 came
ledge: 4 sill
part: 4 came, sill
pert. to: 9 fenestral
recess: 6 exedra
roof: 6 dormer 8 skylight
sash weight: 5 mouse
ship's: 4 port
ticket: 6 wicket 7 guichet
worker: 7 glazier
window glass (to supply): 7 impanel
windpipe: 6 artery, gullet, throat, weason 7 trachea, weasand, weazand 9 esophagus
pert. to: 8 trachean
windrow: 5 swath 6 furrow, swathe
windshake: 8 anemosis
windstorm (see also **storm; wind**): 4 gale 7 cyclone, typhoon 9 hurricane
windward: 5 aloof 8 aweather
Windward Island: 7 Grenada
windy: 4 airy 5 empty, gusty, huffy, swift 6 breezy, stormy 7 gustful, pompous, verbose 8 boastful, skittish 9 aeolistic, bom-

bastic 10 boisterous, changeable, intangible 11 harebrained, tempestuous 13 unsubstantial

Windy City: 7 Chicago

wine: vin(F.) 4 alac, Asti, Bual, cote, deal, port, tent 5 Baden, Casel, drink, liane, Medoc, merum(L.), Rhine, Tinta, tokay, Yquem 6 Barolo, Barsac, Beaune, canary, claret, Malaga, Massic, Muscat, Saumur, sherry 7 Alicant, Banyals, Bastard, Chablis, chacoli, Chateau, Chianti, Conthey, Dezaley, Falerno, hollock, Madeira, Margaux, Marsala, Medeira, Moselle, Orvieto 8 Alicante, Ambonnay, beverage, Bordeaux, Bucellas, Burgundy, Florence, Marsalla, muscadel, Muscatel, Rulander, Riesling, Ruchelle, Rulander, sauterne 9 Gladstone, hermitage, teneriffe, Zeltinger, zinfandel 10 Beaujolais, Calon-Segur, Hockheimer, Roussillon 11 Niersteiner, scuppernong 12 Geisenheimer 15 scharlachberger

apple: 5 cider

bag: 8 wineskin

bibber: sot 5 toper 7 tippler 8 drunkard

bottle: 6 fiasco, magnum 8 decanter, jeroboam

cask: tun 4 pipe

cask deposit: 6 tartar

cellar: 6 bodega

comb. form: oen 4 oeno

cruet: 7 burette

cup: ama 5 amula 6 goblet 7 chalice

deposit: 6 tartar

discoverer: 4 Noah

disorder: 5 casse

drink: 5 clary, mulse, negus, punch

dry: 4 brut

film: 8 beeswing

god: 4 Soma 7 Bacchus 8 Dionysus

list: 4 card

lover: 11 oenophilist

maker: 6 abkari, abkary

measure: aam, aum 4 orna, orne

medicinal preparation: 5 mosto

merchant: 6 bistro(F.) 7 vintner 8 gourmand

new: 4 must

pert. to: 5 vinic 6 vinous

pitcher: 4 olpe 5 olpae 8 oenochoe

residue: 4 marc

rice: 4 sake

scene of miracle: 4 Cana

shop: 6 bodega

spiced: 9 hippocras

stock: 6 cellar

study of: 7 enology

strength: 4 seve

sweet: 4 port 5 lunel, tokay 7 malmsey, Moselle 8 Alicante, muscatel

unfermented: 4 must

vessel: ama 5 amula 7 chalice

year: 7 vintage

wine and dine: 4 fete 6 regale

wineberry: 5 grape 7 currant 8 bilberry, makomako 9 raspberry 10 gooseberry

winegrower: 8 vigneron 13 viticulturist

Winesburg Ohio author: 8 Anderson

wineshop: bar 6 bistro, bodega

wineskin: 5 askos

wing: ala, arm, ell, fin, fly, van 4 limb 5 aisle, alula, pinna, shard, speed, volet, wound 6 hasten, pennon, pinion 7 flutter

arrangement: 7 alation

building: ell

pert to: 4 alar 6 pteric

under: 8 subalary

vestigial: 5 alula

wing cover: 7 elytron

wing-footed: 5 swift 6 aliped 9 mercurial

wing-like: 4 alar 5 alary, alate 6 pteric 7 aliform, pteroid

part: ala 4 alae 7 aileron

winged: 4 aile, alar 5 alary, alate, lofty, rapid, swift 6 alated 7 bialate, sublime, wounded 9 aliferous, aligerous, feathered

in heraldry: 4 aile

Winged Horse: 7 Pegasus

wingless: 7 apteral 8 apterous

wingless locust: 4 weta

wings: *being with:* 5 angel 6 cherub, seraph 7 Mercury

conjoined: vol(her.)

wink: bat, nap, nod 4 hint 5 blink, flash, gleam, prink, sleep 6 signal 7 flicker, instant, nictate, slumber, sparkle, twinkle 9 nictation, nictitate, twinkling 10 periwinkle

winking: 13 blepharospasm

winks (forty): nap 6 catnap

winner: 6 earner, reaper, victor 7 faceman, sleeper 8 bangster 9 conqueror 11 breadwinner

Winnie-the-Pooh: *author:* 5 Milne

character: Owl, Roo 5 Kanga 6 Piglet, Rabbit, Tigger

winning (see also **win; winsome**): 5 shaft 6 profit 7 victory

winning three numbers: 4 tern

winninish, winnonish: 6 salmon 10 ouananiche

winnock: 6 window

winnow: fan, van 4 beat, flap, sift 5 dight 6 assort, select 7 analyze, examine, scatter 8 brandish, disperse, separate 9 eliminate

winsome: gay 5 bonny, merry 6 blithe, bonnie 7 likable, winning 8 charming, cheerful, engaging, pleasant 9 agreeable 10 attractive 11 captivating 12 lighthearted
winter: 9 hibernate
pear: 6 seckel, warden
pert. to: 6 brumal, hiemal
winter quarters: 10 hibernacle 12 hibernaculum
winter teal: 9 greenwing
Winter's Tale character: 4 Dion 5 Mopsa 6 Dorcas 7 Camillo, Leontes, Perdita
winterbloom: 6 azalea
wintergreen: 10 pipsissewa
wintle: 4 reel, roll 7 stagger, wriggle
wintry: icy 4 aged, cold 5 snowy, white 6 frigid, hiemal, stormy 8 chilling, hibernal, wintered 9 cheerless
winy: 6 vinous 7 drunken
wipe: dry, hit, mop, rub 4 beat, blow, draw, gibe, jeer, pass 5 brand, cheat, clean, dight, erase, stain, swipe, towel, trick 6 cancel, defeat, remove, sponge, strike, stroke 7 abolish, defraud, exhaust, sarcasm 8 disgrace 10 annihilate, obliterate 11 exterminate 12 handkerchief
wire: 4 coil 5 cable 6 fasten 8 telegram 9 cablegram, telegraph
bundle of: 5 cable
cutters: 6 pliers
measure: mil 5 stone
system: 7 network, reticle
wire cutter: 5 wirer 8 secateur
wiredraw: 5 wrest 7 distort, prolong 8 protract 9 attenuate 10 overrefine
wireless: 5 radio
wirework: 8 filigree
wireworm: 8 myriapod 9 millepede
wiry: 4 lean 5 hardy, stiff, tough 6 sinewy, strong
wis: 4 deem, know 5 think 7 believe, imagine, suppose
Wisconsin: *city:* 6 Beloit, Racine, Sparta 7 Kenosha, Madison(c.), Necedah, Oshkosh 10 Oconomowoc
county: 4 Dane, Polk, Rusk, Sauk 5 Dodge, Pepin, Vilas 6 Barron 7 Kenosha, Ozaukee 8 Bayfield, Walworth, Waushara
native: 6 Badger
wisdom (see also **wise**): 4 lore 8 judgment
god of: 4 Nabu, Nebo 6 Ganesa 7 Ganesha
goddess of: 6 Athena, Pallas 7 Minerva
man of: 6 Nestor
wisdom tooth: 5 molar
wise: 4 mode, sage, sane, show, wary 5 aware, smart, sound, witty 6 advise, crafty, direct, inform, manner, shrewd, subtle, versed, witful 7 beguile, cunning, erudite, explain, fashion, heedful, knowing, learned, politic, prudent, sapient, skilled 8 discreet, informed, instruct, persuade, profound, sensible, skillful 9 cognizant, dexterous, expedient, judicious, provident, sagacious 10 discerning, omniscient 11 calculating, circumspect, enlightened, intelligent, well-advised 13 sophisticated
infinitely: 10 omniscient
wise man: 4 sage 5 magus, solon 6 Casper, Gasper, Nestor, wizard 8 magician, Melchior 9 Balthasar, Balthazar, councilor
Wise Men: 4 Magi
wise saying: saw 5 adage, maxim
wiseacre: 5 dunce 7 prophet 9 simpleton 10 mastermind 11 wisenheimer
wiselike: 6 decent 7 fitting 8 becoming, sensible 9 judicious 11 appropriate
wish: 4 hope, long, want 5 crave, yearn 6 behest, desire, invoke 7 longing, propose, request 8 petition, yearning 10 aspiration, invocation 11 imprecation
grammatical mood expressing: 8 optative
wishbone: 8 furculum 10 fourchette
wishful: 8 desirous 9 desirable 10 attractive
wisht: 5 eerie 6 dismal, dreary 7 uncanny 8 wretched 10 melancholy
wishy-washy: 4 pale, sick, thin, weak 5 tepid 6 feeble, trashy, watery 7 insipid 13 unsubstantial
wisket: 6 basket
wisp: 4 band, ring, wase 5 broom, brush, bunch, clean, flock, shred, torch, whisk 6 bundle, parcel, rumple, wreath 7 crumple, handful 8 fragment
wispy: 5 filmy 6 slight 7 slender 8 gossamer
wissel: 5 money 6 change 8 exchange 11 retribution
wist: 4 know
wistaria 4 bush, fuji 6 purple, violet
wistful: 6 intent 7 longing, pensive 8 yearning 9 attentive, nostalgic
wistfulness: rue 6 regret
wit: wag 4 know 5 humor, irony, learn 6 acumen, esprit(F.), namely, reason, satire, wisdom 7 cunning, faculty, punster 8 comedian, drollery, funnyman, repartee 9 intellect 12 intelligence, perspicacity 13 understanding
low form of: pun
witch: hag, hex 4 baba 5 charm, crone, lamia, woman 6 cummer, kimmer, wizard 7 bewitch 9 fascinate, sorceress
cat: 9 grimalkin
city: 5 Salem
famous: 5 Circe 6 Lilith
male: 7 warlock
means of transportation: 5 broom
witch hazel: 4 tree 5 shrub 8 hornbeam 10 astringent

witchcraft: 5 charm, magic 7 cunning, hexerei, sorcery 8 brujeria(Sp.), pishogue, witchery, wizardry 9 sortilege 11 enchantment, fascination 12 invultuation
goddess of: 5 Obeah 6 Hecate
practice: hex 7 bewitch
witchman: 6 shaman, wizard 8 sorcerer
wite: 4 fine 5 blame, fault 6 accuse 7 censure 8 reproach 9 exemption 14 responsibility
with: wi(Sc.); con(It.), cum(L.), mit(G.) 4 avec(F.), near 5 along 9 alongside 12 accompanying
prefix: col, com, cyn, pro, syn
withdraw: go 4 void 5 avoid 6 absent, depart, detach, divert, recall, recant, recede, remove, retire, secede 7 abscond, decline, detract, extract, forbear, forsake, refrain, retract, retreat, subduce, subside 8 abstract, alienate, derogate, distract, evacuate, renounce, restrain, withhold 9 disengage, sequester 10 relinqish, retrograde
withdrawal (see also **withdraw**): 7 regress
withe: 4 band, bind, herb, rope, twig 5 osier, snare, withy 6 branch, fasten, halter, wattle, willow
wither: age, die, dry 4 fade, pine, sear, sere, wilt 5 blast, cling, daver, decay, wizen 6 blight, cotter, shrink, weaken 7 shrivel, wrinkle 8 languish
withered: 4 arid, sere 7 sapless 10 marcescent 11 sphacelated
withhold: 4 curb, deny, hide, keep 5 check 6 desist, detain, refuse, retain 7 abstain, forbear, prevent, refrain, repress, reserve 8 maintain, postpone, restrain
within: in, on; ben 4 inly, into 5 among 6 during, herein, inside 7 indoors 8 inwardly 10 underneath
comb. form: ent, eso 4 endo, ento
prefix: 5 intra
without: 4 bout, sans, sine(L.) 6 beyond 7 lacking, outside 9 outwardly 10 externally
prefix: se; ect, exo 4 ecto
without this: 7 sine hoc
withstand: 4 bear, bide, defy 5 abide 6 combat, endure, oppose, resist 7 gainsay 8 confront 9 gainstand 10 contradict, controvert
withy: 4 turn, twig, wind, wiry 5 agile, braid 6 branch, willow 8 flexible
witless: mad 5 crazy, gross 6 insane, stupid 7 foolish, unaware 8 heedless 9 brainless, pointless, unknowing 10 dullwitted, indiscreet
witness: eye, see, wit 4 know 5 teste 6 attest, beheld, behold, martyr 7 observe, sponsor, testify 8 beholder, evidence, observer, onlooker 9 spectator, subscribe, testifier, testimony 11 attestation 13 understanding
Witt's planetoid: 4 Eros
witter: tee 4 barb
witticism: mot, pun 4 gibe, jeer, jest, joke, quip 5 sally 11 gauloiserie
witting: 7 tidings 8 judgment 9 knowledge 10 deliberate 11 information, intentional 12 intelligence
wittol: 4 fool 7 cuckold 8 wheatear
witty: 4 gash, wise 5 comic 6 bright, clever, facete, jocose, jocund, versed 7 amusing, comical, jocular, knowing 8 humorous, informed 9 facetious 11 intelligent
witty remark: mot, pun 4 quip
witty reply: 7 riposte 8 repartee
wive: 5 marry
wivern: 6 dragon
wizard: 4 mage, sage 5 fiend 6 genius, Merlin 7 magical, prodigy, warlock 8 charming, conjurer, magician, sorcerer 10 enchanting 11 necromancer, thaumaturge 12 thaumaturgus 13 thaumaturgist
wizardry: art 5 magic 7 sorcery 10 witchcraft
wizen, weazen: dry 6 wither 7 shrivel, wizened
woad: 8 dyestuff
wobble, wabble: 4 boil 5 shake, waver 6 quaver 7 tremble 9 vacillate
wobbly: 5 loose, shaky
woe: 4 bale, bane 5 grief 6 misery, sorrow 7 trouble 8 calamity, disaster 9 dejection 10 affliction, desolation, melancholy, misfortune
tale of: 8 jeremiad 11 lamentation
woeful: sad 4 dire 6 paltry 7 direful, pitiful, unhappy 8 mournful, wretched 9 miserable, sorrowful, woebegone 10 deplorable, dispirited 12 disconsolate
wolaba: 8 kangaroo
wold: lea 5 plain 6 meadow
wolf: 4 lobo 6 canine, chanco, coyote 9 thylacine 10 ladykiller 11 philanderer
cry: 4 howl
gait: 4 lope
genus: 5 canis
pert. to: 6 lupine
young: pup 5 whelp
wolf-like: 6 lupine 9 rapacious
wolfhound: 4 alan 6 borzoi
wolfsbane: 7 aconite 9 monkshood
Wolsey's birthplace: 7 Ipswich
wolverine: 8 carcajou
genus of: 4 gulo
Wolverine State: 8 Michigan
woman (see also **girl; mother**): gin, hen 4 bint, dame, dona, lady, maid, rani 5 begum, broad, chick, donna, femme, madam, mujer, ranee, skirt, squaw 6 calico, cummer, domina, female, heifer, kimmer, maness, senora 7 alewife, servant, signora 8

mistress, senorita 10 klootchman, sweetheart 11 gentlewoman
affected: 5 prude 7 cockney
attractive: 4 doll, peri 5 filly, pin-up, siren, sylph, Venus 6 beauty, looker 7 charmer, Zenobia 8 Musidora
beloved: 9 inamorata
brave: 7 hellcat, heroine
celibate: 7 agapeta
comb. form: gyn 4 gyno
domain: 7 distaff
kept: 8 mistress 9 concubine 12 demimondaine
lawyer: 6 Portia
learned: 4 blue 7 basbleu(F.), seeress 12 bluestocking
little: 4 wife 7 ladykin
loose: tib 4 drab, flap, jilt, slut 5 hussy, quean, queen 6 chippy, giglet, giglot, harlot, wanton 7 cocotte, Jezebel, trollop 9 courtesan, courtezen, dratchell
married: 4 frau, frow, wife 5 vrouw 6 matron
mythical: 6 Gorgon
objectionable: hag 5 fagot, shrew, witch 6 faggot, gorgon, virago 8 harridan 9 grimalkin, termagant
old: gib, hag 4 baba, dame, trot 5 crone, frump 6 carlin, gammer, granny 7 carline, dowager, grandam 8 grandame, spinster 9 cailleach, cailliach
organization: DAR, WAC, WSP 4 AMVS, WAAC, WAVE, Wren 5 Ebell 6 circle 7 sorosis 8 sorority 10 sisterhood
pert. to: 7 gynecic 8 gynaecic 9 muliebral
patient: 8 Griselda
physicist: 5 Curie 7 Meitner
ruler: 5 queen 9 matriarch
sailor: 4 Spar, Wave
serving: See **servant**
single (see also **maiden**): 6 virgin 8 mistress, spinster
soldier: Wac 4 Waac
staid: 4 lady 6 beldam, matron 7 beldame
state of: 10 muliebrity
strong: 6 Amazon, virago 8 titaness
suffragist: 4 Mott 5 Stone 7 Anthony, Stanton
talkative: cat, gad, hen 5 dolly, flirt, scold, shrew, vixen 6 fizgig, virago 7 hellcat 9 termagant
theater: 6 dancer 7 actress, chorine 9 soubrette
unattractive: bag, dog 4 drab 5 crone, dowdy, witch 8 slattern
young (see also **girl**): tib 4 burd, dell, drab, lass 5 filly, trull, wench 6 lassie 7 damozel 10 demoiselle

woman chaser: 4 wolf 8 lothario 10 sheepbiter 11 philanderer
woman hater: 10 misogynist
womanish: 5 anile 6 effete, female 8 feminine 10 effeminate
womb: bag 5 belly 6 uterus
wombat: 6 badger 9 marsupial
won (see also **win**): 4 live 5 abide, dwell 7 inhabit
wonder: awe 4 evil, harm, sign 5 grief, wrong 6 esteem, marvel 7 curious, miracle, prodigy 8 surprise 9 amazement, speculate, uncertain 10 admiration, wonderment 11 destruction 12 astonishment
of the world: 6 Pharos 8 pyramids, Colossus
performance: See **magic**
worker of: See **wizard**
Wonder State: 8 Arkansas
wonderful: 4 fine, good 5 super 6 lovely 7 amazing, amusing, corking, mirific, strange 8 wondrous 9 admirable, excellent, marvelous 10 miraculous, surprising 11 astonishing, interesting 13 extraordinary
wong: 5 field 6 meadow
wonky: off 4 awry 5 shaky 6 feeble 7 tottery 8 unsteady 9 tottering
wont: use 5 dwell, habit, usage, usual 6 custom, reside 8 inclined, practice 10 accustomed
woo: beg, sue 4 coax, seek 5 court, spark 6 assail, invite, splunt(Sc.) 7 address, beseech, entreat, solicit 9 importune
wood: hag, keg, mad 4 bois(F.), bosk, bowl, cask, holt, wold 5 angry, cahuy, grove, hurst, trees, xylem 6 forest, insane, lumber, timber 7 enraged, furious, violent 8 woodland
ash: 6 potash
black: 5 ebony
bundle of: 5 fagot
burned: ash 4 brae 8 charcoal
comb. form: 4 hylo, xylo 5 ligni
core: ame
dealer: 10 xylopolist
derivative: tar 5 turps 6 balsam 10 turpentine
distillation from: tar 5 turps 10 turpentine
edge: 8 woodrime, woodside
fine-grained: yew 6 brauna
firing easily: 4 punk 5 sponk, spunk 6 tinder 8 kindling, punkwood 9 touchwood
flexible: 5 edder, osier 6 willow
fragrant: 5 aloes, cedar
god: See **woodland:** *deity*
growth: 7 coppice
gum: 5 resin, xylan

hard: ash, elm, eng, oak 4 lana, poon, rata, teak 5 ebony, maple, zante 6 walnut 7 hickory 8 mahogany
juice: sap
kind: See **tree**
knot: nur 4 burl, knag, knar 5 gnarl
light: 4 cork 5 balsa
overlaying: 6 veneer
part: fid, nog, peg, rib 4 lath, shim, slat 5 dowel, spile, sprag, stave, tenon 6 batten, billet, reglet, splint 7 dingbat
pert. to: 5 treen
prefix: 4 xylo
steward: 9 woodreeve
strip: 4 lath, slat 6 batten, spline
striped: roe
supporting: 5 cleat
valuable: sal 4 teak
worker: 6 joiner, sawyer 7 paneler 9 carpenter
wood alcohol: 6 methyl 8 methanol
wood-ash salt: 6 potash
wood nymph: 4 moth 5 dryad 8 grayling 11 hummingbird
wood pigeon: 4 dove 6 cushat 8 ringdove
wood pussy: 5 skunk
wood sorrel: oca 6 oxalis 7 begonia 8 haremeat
wood stork: 4 ibis
woodbine: 11 honeysuckle
woodchuck: 6 marmot 9 groundhog
woodcock: 4 dupe, fool 5 pewee 7 becasse(F.) 9 simpleton 10 woodpecker
woodcutter: 6 axeman, logger, sawyer 7 chopper 8 woodsman 9 lumberman
wooded: 6 sylvan
wooden: dry 4 dull, wood 5 oaken, stiff, treen 6 clumsy, stolid 7 awkward 8 lifeless 10 spiritless 11 insensitive 14 expressionless
wooden shoe: 4 clog, geta 5 sabot 6 patten
wooden-headed: 4 dull 6 stupid 8 blockish
Wooden Horse: See **Trojan horse**
woodkern: 6 outlaw, robber
woodland: 6 forest 7 woodlot 10 timberland
burnt over: 6 brulee
deity: Pan 4 faun 5 Diana, satyr, Silen 7 Silenus 8 Seilenos
landscape: 7 boscage
woodness: 4 fury, rage 7 madness 8 insanity
woodpecker: 4 chab 5 picus 6 picule, yaffle, yockel, yuckle, yukkel 7 flicker, piculet, whetile, wryneck, yaffler 8 hickwall, woodcock, woodhack 9 sapsucker, woodchuck, woodspite 10 carpintero, woodhacker, woodjobber 11 hickoryhead, woodknacker
genus: 5 picus
type: 5 downy, hairy 8 imperial, pileated 9 redheaded
pert. to: 6 picine
woods: 6 forest
love of: 9 nemophily
pert. to: 6 sylvan 7 nemoral
woodsman: 5 scout 6 hunter 7 bushman, trapper 8 forester 10 woodcutter 11 woodchopper
woodwind: 4 oboe 5 flute 7 bassoon, piccolo 8 clarinet 9 saxophone
woodworker: 6 joiner, turner 9 carpenter 12 cabinetmaker
machine: saw 5 edger, lathe 6 planer, router, shaper 7 sticker
tool: adz, saw 4 adze 5 plane 6 hammer
woody: 5 bosky 6 sylvan, xyloid 8 ligneous
woody fiber: 4 bast, hemp 5 xylem
wooer: 4 beau 6 suitor 8 courtier
woof: abb 5 cloth, weave 6 fabric 7 filling, texture 9 essential
wool: fur 4 hair, lamb 5 llama, sheep 6 fleece, mohair 8 barragan, barragon 9 cordillas
blemish: 4 mote
clean: 7 garnett
cloth: 5 baize, duroy, tweed 6 alpaca, angora, baline, duffel, frieze, hodden, kersey, melton, merino, mohair, vicuna 7 flannel, ratteen, stammel 8 cashmere, casimire 9 cassimere, hauberget 10 broadcloth, fearnaught, fearnought 11 dreadnaught, dreadnought
comb. form: 4 lani
fat: 5 suint 7 lanolin 8 lanoline
fibers: nep
grower: 5 sheep 7 rancher
implement: 6 carder, shears, teaser 7 distaff, spindle
inferior: 7 cleamer
kind: 4 noil, shag 8 mortling 9 downright, shearling
lock: 5 flock
mixed hues: tum
nap-raising plant: 5 tease
package: 5 fadge
piece: 4 frib, tate(Sc.) 7 cleamer
pulled: 5 slipe
rag: 5 mungo 6 shoddy
reclaimed: 5 mungo 6 shoddy
refuse: 7 backing
spun: 4 yarn
tease: tum 4 card
texture: nap
twisted roll: 4 slub
unravel: 5 tease
waste: fud
weight: tod 5 clove
worker: 8 shedhand

yarn: abb, eis 7 eiswool
wool-colored: 5 beige, camel
wool-dryer: 5 fugal
woolfell: 4 pelt
woolly: 6 fleecy, lanate, lanose 7 lanated 8 peronate
woozy: 5 drunk, shaky 7 muddled, strange, trembly 9 befuddled
word: 4 fame, news, talk, term 5 adage, honor, maxim, motto, order, parol, voice 6 assent, avowal, phrase, pledge, remark, report, repute, saying, signal, speech 7 account, adjunct, command, comment, dispute, message, promise, proverb, tidings 8 acrostic, language, password 9 direction, discourse, statement, watchword 10 expression 11 affirmation, declaration, information 12 intelligence 13 communication
battle 9 logomachy
colorful: 5 slang
complex of ideas: 10 holophrase 11 holophrasis
containing all vowels: 6 oiseau(F.) 7 eulogia, miaoued, sequoia 12 ambidextrous 14 undiscoverably 15 uncopyrightable
containing all vowels in reverse sequence: 10 duoliteral
containing all vowels in sequence: 8 caesious
containing four letters: 9 tetragram
containing no vowels: cwm, nth 5 crwth
containing uu: 6 mutuum, vacuum 7 duumvir, triduum 8 residuum 9 continuum, menstruum, perpetuum, zuurveldt 10 duumvirate
contraction: 9 haplology
corresponding: 8 analogue
derived from another: 7 paronym
figurative use: 5 trope 7 metonym
group: 6 clause, phrase 8 sentence
hard to pronounce: 10 jawbreaker
imitative: 9 onomatope
improper use: 8 solecism
inventor: 6 coiner 9 neologist
last sound omitted: 7 apocope
longest: 45 pneumonoultramicroscopicsilicovolcanokoniosis
magical: 6 presto, sesame 11 abracadabra
meaning: 9 semantics
misuse of: 11 catachresis, malapropism
mystical: 7 anagoge
new: 9 neologism, neoterism
of action: 4 verb
of naming: 4 noun
of opposite meaning: 7 antonym
of same meaning: 7 synonym
pretentious: 10 lexiphanic
root: 6 etymon
sacred: om, um 5 selah 6 sesame, shelah
same backward and forward: 10 palindrome
same sound: 7 homonym 9 homophone
same spelling: 7 homonym 9 homograph
scrambled: 7 anagram
separation: 6 tmesis 7 diacope
square: 10 palindrome
substituted: 5 trope 7 metonym
transposition: 7 anagram
use of imitative: 12 onomatopoeia
use of new: 7 neology
use of unnecessary: 8 pleonasm
very long: 13 sesquipedalia(pl.)
word blindness: 6 alexia
word for word: 7 exactly 8 verbatim 9 literally
Word of God: 5 Logos
word of honor: 6 parole 7 promise
word puzzle: 5 rebus 7 anagram, charade 8 acrostic 9 crossword
word-sign: 8 ideogram, logogram 10 hieroglyph, pictograph
wordbook: 7 lexicon, speller 8 libretto 9 thesaurus 10 cyclopedia, dictionary, vocabulary
wordiness: 8 verbiage
wording: 8 phrasing 9 wrangling 10 expression
wordless: 5 tacit 6 silent
words: 4 text 6 lyrics 7 quarrel 8 libretto
depiction in: 8 vignette
excessive interest in: 10 verbomania
meaningless: 6 drivel 9 gibberish
misuse: 11 catachresis, heterophemy
put into: 5 state 6 phrase 7 express
written: 4 copy, text
wordy: 6 prolix 7 diffuse, verbose 9 garrulous, redundant
wore: See **wear**
work: go; act, job, tew 4 beat, duty, feat, move, opus, plan, task, worm 5 chore, craft, draft, ergon, exert, graft, grind, knead, solve, stint, trade 6 arbeit(G.), design, effort, puddle, strive 7 belabor, ferment, operate, pattern, perform, travail 8 activity, belabour, business, drudgery, exertion, function, industry, struggle 10 accomplish, employment, manipulate, occupation, profession 11 achievement, performance, undertaking
agreement: 4 code, pact 8 contract
aimlessly: 6 potter, putter
aversion to: 10 ergophobia
by day: 4 char 5 chare
defensive: See **fortification**
divine: 7 theurgy
excess: 6 overdo 8 overwork
evade: 4 snib 9 goldbrick

hard: peg, ply 4 char, moil, plod, plug, toil 5 chare, delve, drill, labor, sweat 6 drudge 7 travail 8 scrabble 9 lucubrate
incomplete: 7 ebauche
labored: 11 lucubration
lover of: 9 ergophile
musical: See **musical composition**
period: day 4 hour, turn, week 5 month, shift, spell, trick, watch 8 schedule
slowly: 6 potter, putter 7 cacanny
steadily: ply
together: 4 team 5 co-act 9 co-operate 11 collaborate
unit: erg 5 ergon, joule 7 calorie
women's: 7 distaff
work-a-day: 8 everyday, ordinary 11 commonplace
work-brittle: 11 industrious
work for: 4 earn 5 serve
work of art: 4 song 6 statue 7 classic, etching, picture 8 painting
work on: 6 affect 9 influence
work out: 5 erase, solve 6 efface 7 arrange, develop, exhaust 9 calculate, elaborate 10 accomplish
work over: 6 recast, rehash, revamp 8 persuade 9 brainwash, elaborate, influence
work up: irk 5 raise, rouse 6 arouse, excite, expend 7 advance, develop 9 elaborate 10 manipulate
workable: 4 ripe 6 mellow, pliant 8 feasible 9 practical 11 practicable
workbag: 8 reticule
worked: 7 wrought
worker: 4 arry, doer, hand, hind 5 navvy 6 earner, toiler 7 artisan, laborer 8 operator, opificer 9 artificer, craftsman, operative, performer 11 breadwinner
fellow: 5 buddy, butty 7 comrade 8 confrere
group: 4 crew, gang, team 5 corps, shift, staff 9 personnel
hard: 6 beaver, drudge, fagger
head: 4 boss 5 super 6 ganger 7 foreman 8 employer, overseer 14 superintendent
kind: 5 diver, mason, miner, smith, tuner 6 barman, cocker, hopper, joiner, laster, sapper, sawyer, slater, smithy, tanner, warper, wright 7 analyst, cobbler, collier, geordie, glazier, paneler, plumber, reedman, riveter, sandhog, spinner 8 chaffman, chuckler, enameler, mechanic, shedhand, strapper 9 carpenter, groundhog, machinist, stevedore
migrant: 4 hobo, Okie 5 Arkie 6 boomer 7 floater, wetback
objectionable: 4 scab 7 botcher, bungler 11 scissorbill 13 featherbedder
unskilled: 4 peon 6 coolie 7 laborer
workful: 8 diligent
workhorse: 4 peon, serf 5 slave 6 drudge, toiler 7 trestle 8 sawhorse
workhouse: 6 prison 8 workshop 9 almshouse, poorhouse
working (see also **work**): 4 busy 5 alert 6 active, decree, effort 7 halurgy 8 employed, endeavor 9 ordinance, practical 10 contortion
not: off 4 idle 6 broken 10 unemployed
working-class: 7 laborer 11 proletariat
workman: See **worker**
workman-like: 4 deft 5 adept 8 skillful 10 proficient
workroom: den, lab 4 mill, shop 5 plant, study 6 studio 7 atelier, bottega, factory, library 10 laboratory 11 ergasterion
works: 5 plant
worktable: 5 bench, siege
world: 5 globe, realm 6 cosmos, domain, people, public 7 kingdom, mankind 8 creation, humanity, universe
antedating creation of: 10 premundane
bearer of: 5 Atlas
external: 6 nonego
lower: See **underworld**
miniature: 9 microcosm
pert. to: 7 mundane, secular 11 terrestrial
World War I: *battle:* 5 Marne, Somme, Ypres 6 Verdun 7 Jutland
general: 8 Pershing
hero: 5 York
marshal: 4 Foch
World War II: *battle:* 4 Orel 5 Anzio, Bulge 6 Bataan, Sicily, Tarawa, Warsaw 7 Cassino, Okinawa 8 Normandy
correspondent: 4 Pyle
craft: LST
famous nickname: Ike 5 Monty
worldly: 6 carnal, laical 7 earthen, earthly, mundane, secular, sensual, terrene 11 terrestrial 13 sophisticated
worldwide: 6 global 8 ecumenic, pandemic 9 planetary, universal 10 ecumenical 13 international
worm: bob, eel, eri, ess, ipo, loa, lug, pin 4 grub, nais, nema 5 borer, larva, tinea 6 looper, maggot, palolo, teredo 7 annelid, ascarid, ipomoea, reptile, sagitta, serpent, tagtail 8 cercaria, helminth 9 angleworm, earthworm, nemertina, nemertine, nemertini, trematode 10 nemertinea, serpentine 13 platyhelminth
aquatic: sao 4 naid, nais, nema 5 cadew, leech 6 nereis 7 achaeta, annelid 8 annelida
bait: mad 4 lurg
eye-infecting: loa
genus of: 6 nereis 8 geoplana

parasitic: 5 fluke 7 ascarid, cestode, pinworm 8 tapeworm, trichina 9 roundworm
segment: 6 somite 8 metamere
threadlike: 7 filaria

worm-eaten: old 6 ragged, shabby 7 worn-out 8 decrepit 9 out-of-date, worthless

worm-eating mammal: 4 mole

wormlike: 7 vermian 11 helminthoid

wormweed: 8 pinkroot

wormwood: 4 moxa

wormy: 6 rotten 8 diseased, crawling

worn: See **wear**

worn down: 5 erose 6 eroded 7 abraded, attrite 8 attrited

worn-out: 4 sere, used 5 jaded, passe, seedy, spent, stale, trite 6 frayed, shabby 7 haggard 8 consumed, decrepit, impaired, weakened 9 enfeebled, exhausted, hackneyed 10 bedraggled, threadbare 11 commonplace

worricow: 5 devil 7 bugaboo 9 hobgoblin

worry: hox, nag, vex 4 bait, care, cark, faze, fear, fike, fret, fuss, hare, stew 5 annoy, brood, choke, gally, harry, hurry, touse 6 badger, bother, caddle, fidget, harass, hatter, hector, pester, plague, pother 7 anxiety, bedevil, chagrin, concern, disturb, perturb, torment, trouble 8 distress, strangle 9 worriment 10 disconcert, uneasiness

worse: 8 pejority

worsen: 8 pejorate 10 retrogress 11 deteriorate

worship: 4 cult, fame, love 5 adore, dulia, honor, worth 6 credit, homage, latria, renown, repute, revere 7 dignity, idolism, idolize, liturgy, respect 8 blessing, devotion, hierurgy, idolatry, venerate 9 adoration, deference, monolatry, reverence, theolatry 10 admiration, allotheism, hagiolatry, hierolatry, hyperdulia, reputation, veneration, worthiness
form of: 4 rite 6 ritual
house of: dom 6 chapel, church, mosque, shrine, temple 9 cathedral, synagogue 10 tabernacle
nature: 11 physiolatry
of angels and saints: 5 dulia
object of: 4 icon, idol 5 totem 6 fetich, fetish
pert. to: 8 liturgic 10 liturgical
place of: 5 altar
system of: 4 cult 6 cultus

worshiper: 6 adorer, bhakta, votary 7 devotee 8 disciple, idolater

worshipful: 7 notable 8 esteemed 9 honorable, respected 10 venerating 11 worshipping 13 distinguished

worst: bad 4 beat, best 6 defeat 9 discomfit, overthrow

worsted: 4 garn, yarn 5 serge 6 tamine 8 whipcord 9 gabardine
yarn: 6 caddis, crewel 7 caddice, genappe 9 fingering

wort: 4 herb 8 fleabane

worth: 5 merit, price, value 6 bounty, desert, esteem, riches, virtue, wealth 7 account, fitting 8 eminence 9 deserving, desirable 10 excellence, importance, possession, usefulness
sense of: 5 pride 7 dignity, respect
thing of little: rap 6 stiver, trifle

worthless: bad, rap 4 base, evil, idle, vain, vile 5 inane 6 cheesy, drossy, futile, hollow, paltry, putrid, rotten, trashy 7 fustian, inutile, useless 8 feckless, unworthy 9 frivolous, valueless 11 undeserving 12 contemptible 14 good-for-nothing

worthy: 4 dear, good 7 condign 8 deserved, eligible, meriting, valuable 9 competent, deserving, estimable, excellent, qualified 11 appropriate, meritorious

wound: cut 4 gore, harm, hurt, pain, stab, wing 5 break, ganch, sting 6 breach, damage, grieve, harrow, injury, trauma 7 afflict, attaint 8 distress, puncture
discharge from: pus 5 ichor, serum
dressing: 7 bandage, pledget
in heraldry: 4 vuln
lint to dilate: 4 tent
mark: 4 scab, scar, welt 7 blister
sign: 4 scar 5 blood

woundwort: 7 allheal

wove: See **weave**

woven (see also **weave**): 4 lacy 7 damasse
raised figures: 6 broche 7 brocade

wow: hit, mew 4 howl, rave, wail 5 whine 7 success

wowf: 4 wild 6 crazed

wrack: 4 kelp, rack, ruin 5 goods, trash, weeds, wreck 6 avenge, defeat, injury 7 destroy, seaweed, torment, unsound 8 calamity, mischief, wreckage 9 overthrow, shipwreck, vengeance 10 punishment 11 destruction, persecution

wraith: 5 ghost, spook 7 specter, spectre 10 apparition

wrangle (see also **quarrel**): 4 spar 5 argue, brawl, chide 6 bicker, debate, haggle 7 contend, dispute 11 altercation, controversy 12 disagreement

wrangler: 6 cowboy, hafter 7 student 8 herdsman, opponent 9 disputant 10 antagonist

wrangling: 11 belligerent, contentious

wrap: hap, rug, wap 4 cere, coil, fold, furl, hide, roll, wind 5 cloak, cover, nubia, twine 6 afghan, encowl, enfold, infold, in-

vest, swathe 7 blanket, conceal, enclose, envelop, package 8 enshroud, enswathe, surround 9 encompass
wrapper: 4 gown 6 fardel 8 galabeah 9 undervest 10 undershirt
wrapping: wap 8 cerement
wrasse: 6 ballan
wrath: ire 4 fury, rage 5 anger 6 choler, felony 7 passion 8 violence 10 turbulence 11 indignation 12 exasperation
wrathful: 5 wroth 8 incensed 9 malignant
wreak: 5 exact 6 avenge, punish 7 gratify, indulge, inflict, revenge 9 vengeance
wreath, wreathe: lei 4 bank, coil, orle, roll, turn 5 crown, drift, torse(her.), twine, twist, whorl 6 anadem, corona, crants, crease, laurel, spirea, wrench 7 chaplet, contort, coronet, crownal, entwine, festoon, garland, spiraea, wrinkle 8 encircle, surround
in heraldry: 5 torse
wreck: 4 hulk, ruin 5 crash, ruins, smash, wrack 6 damage, defeat, thwart 7 destroy, disable, founder, shatter 8 demolish, derelict, sabotage 9 overthrow, shipwreck 11 destruction
wreckage: 7 flotsam 8 driftage
wrench (see also **wrest**): 4 jerk, pipe, pull, rack, tear, tool, turn 5 twist, wring 6 injury, monkey, sprain, strain, twinge 7 distort, spanner 8 Stillson 9 alligator, epiltonion 10 distortion
wrest: 4 rend, ruse 5 exact, force, fraud, seize, trick, usurp, wring 6 elicit, extort, snatch 7 pervert, wrestle
wrestle: tug 6 squirm, strive, tussle, wraxle 7 contend, grapple, wriggle 8 struggle
wrestler: 6 mauler
wrestling: *ceremonial:* 4 sumo
hold: 4 lock 6 nelson 8 scissors
pad: mat
place: 4 ring 5 arena 8 palestra 9 palaestra
score: 4 fall
throw: 4 hipe
wretch: bum, dog 5 exile, loser 6 beggar, pauper 7 hilding, scroyle 8 derelict, recreant 9 miscreant 11 rapscallion
wretched: 4 base, foul, lewd, mean, poor 5 dawny 6 dismal, paltry, pilled, woeful 7 baleful, caitiff, forlorn, unhappy 8 dejected, grievous, inferior 9 afflicted, execrable, miserable, niggardly 10 calamitous, deplorable, depressing, despicable, distressed 11 unfortunate 12 contemptible, parsimonious 14 unsatisfactory
wriggle: 4 frig, turn, wind 5 dodge, evade, snake, twist 6 fitter, squirm, widdle, wiggle, wintle, writhe 7 meander 10 equivocate
wriggly: 8 tortuous
wring: 4 fret, rack 5 press, twist 6 elicit, extort, squirm, wrench 7 extract, squeeze, wrestle 8 compress, struggle
wrinkle: fad, rut 4 fold, idea, knit, lirk, ruck, ruga, seam 5 crimp, fancy, knack, reeve, ridge, rivel 6 cockle, crease, device, furrow, notion, pucker, rimple 7 crimple, crinkle, crumple, frumple, novelty, winding 8 contract 9 corrugate 10 prominence
facial: 4 line
wrinkled: 6 crepey, rugate, rugose, rugous 7 savoyed 8 rugulose
free from being: 6 smooth 7 erugate
wrist: 5 joint 6 carpus
bone: 4 ulna 5 carpi(pl.) 6 carpal, carpus 7 carpale 8 carpalia(pl.) 9 capitatum
mark: 7 rasceta
ornament: 4 band 8 bracelet
pert. to: 6 carpal
wristband: 4 cuff 6 bracer
wristlet: 4 band 5 strap 8 bracelet, handcuff 9 wristband 11 comfortable
writ: 5 breve, brief, tales 6 capias, elegit, extent, venire 7 exigent, process, writing 8 detainer, document, mittimus, replevin, subpoena 10 certiorari, distringas, injunction, instrument 11 fierifacias
of execution: 5 outre
write: pen 5 clerk, enrol 6 direct, enface, enroll, indite, record, scrawl, scribe 7 compose, engross, scratch 8 inscribe, scribble 9 character
letters: 10 correspond
write down: 4 list, note 6 record
write off: 4 drop 6 cancel, deduct, remove
writer: 4 hack, poet 5 clerk, odist 6 author, critic, glozer, lawyer, penman, scribe 7 copyist, glosser, hymnist, penster, realist, tropist 8 annalist, composer, gazeteer, literate, lyricist, novelist, parodist, prefacer, scriptor 9 annotater, columnist, craftsman, dramatist, glossator, scrivener, solicitor 10 amanuensis, chronicler, glossarist, journalist 12 calligrapher, epistolarian 13 glossographer
inferior: 4 hack 8 rhymster 9 poetaster, scribbler
prose: 8 prosaist
unscrupulous: 10 plagiarist
verse: 4 bard, poet 5 odist 7 elegist 9 sonneteer
writhe: 4 bend, bind, curl, turn 5 twist, wrest, wring 6 squirm 7 agonize, contort, distort, shrivel 8 encircle, enswathe 9 convolute, insinuate 10 contortion, intertwine
writhing: 4 eely 9 wriggling
writing: ms; ola 4 book, deed, olla, poem, writ 5 diary, essay, prose, verse 6 script 7

epistle, pothook 8 contract, covenant, document, makimono, pleading, spolling 9 allograph, cerograph, enrolment, esoterics 10 enrollment, instrument, literature, penmanship 11 chirography, composition, handwriting, inscription, orthography, pornography, publication
alternate: 13 boustrophedon
ancient manuscript: 6 uncial
character: (see also **word-sign**)*:* 4 sign 6 letter, symbol 9 cuneiform
comb. form: 5 graph 6 grapho
desk: 9 secretary 10 escritoire
excessive interest in: 11 graphomania
master: 7 stylist
material: pad 5 board, paper, slate 6 tablet 7 papyrus 9 parchment 10 stationery
on the wall: 4 mene 5 tekel 8 upharsin
pert. to: 7 scribal
sacred: 5 Bible, Koran 6 psalms, Talmud 9 hagiology, testament 10 scriptures
secret: 4 code 6 cipher 10 cryptogram 12 cryptography
tool: pen 5 chalk, stick 6 pencil, stylus 9 ballpoint

wrizzled: 8 wrinkled 9 shriveled

wrong: bad, car, ill, off, out, sin 4 awry, evil, harm, tort 5 abuse, agley, amiss, crime, error, false, grief, malum, unfit 6 astray, faulty, injure, injury, malign, seduce, sinful, unfair, unjust, wicked 7 crooked, defraud, immoral, misdeed, twisted, violate 8 dishonor, improper, iniquity, mistaken, tortuous, wrongful, wrongous 9 erroneous, incorrect, injurious, injustice, violation 10 dispossess, inaccurate, iniquitous, unsuitable 11 malfeasance, misfeasance 12 illegitimate 14 unsatisfactory
civil: 4 tort
prefix: mis

wrongdoer: 6 sinner 8 criminal, violator 10 malefactor, tort-feasor, trespasser 12 transgressor

wroth: 5 angry, irate 7 violent 8 incensed, wrathful, wrothful 9 turbulent

wrought (see also **work**)**:** 4 agog, made 5 eager 6 formed, shaped, worked 7 excited, operose 9 decorated, disturbed, fashioned, processed 10 elaborated, ornamented, stimulated 11 embroidered 12 manufactured

wrung: See **wring**

wry: 4 awry, bend, bias, sour, tend, turn 5 avert, pinch, twist, wring 6 swerve, warped 7 contort, crooked, deflect, deviate, distort, incline 8 contrary, perverse

wryneck: 5 loxia 9 snakebird 10 woodpecker 11 torticollis
genus: 4 jynx

Wurttemberg: *city:* Ulm 9 Esslingen, Heilbronn, Stuttgart
river: 6 Danube, Neckar
measure: imi

Wuthering Heights author: 6 Bronte

wych: elm

Wycliffe disciple: Hus 4 Huss 7 Lollard

wyliecoat: 9 petticoat, undervest 10 nightdress

wynd, wyne: haw 4 lane 5 alley, close, court

Wyoming: *capital:* 8 Cheyenne
cavern: 8 Shoshone
county: 5 Uinta 6 Goshen, Platte, Weston 7 Natrona 8 Sublette, Washakie
mountain: 5 Moran, Teton
national park: 11 Yellowstone
river: 5 Teton
town: 4 Cody 7 Laramie, Jackson, Rawlins 8 Cheyenne

X

X: chi, ten 4 mark 5 cross 9 signature
X-shaped: 8 cruciate
Xanadu's river: 4 Alph
xanthic: 6 yellow 9 yellowish
Xanthippe: 5 scold, shrew 6 nagger, virago 9 termagent
husband: 8 Socrates
xanthous: 6 yellow 9 Mongolian
xebec: 4 boat, ship 6 vessel
user: 6 pirate 7 corsair
xema: 4 gull
xenagogue: 5 guide
xenagogy: 9 guidebook
xenium: 4 gift 7 present
xenodochy: 11 hospitality
xenogamy: 13 fertilization
xenon: Xe
Xenophanean: 7 eleatic
Xenophon: *teacher:* 8 Socrates
work: 8 Anabasis
Xeres: 4 wine 5 Jerez 6 sherry
xerophyte: 6 cactus
xerosis: 7 dryness
xerotic: dry, sec
Xerox: 4 copy 6 copier 9 duplicate
xerus: 8 squirrel
Xerxes: *composer:* 6 Handel
parent: 6 Atossa, Darius
wife: 6 Esther
Xhosa, Xosa: 5 Bantu, tribe 8 language
xiphoid: 8 ensiform
Xmas: 9 Christmas
X-ray: *inventor:* 8 Roentgen
measuring device: 11 quantimeter
science: 12 rontgenology 13 roentgenology
source: 6 target
type: 8 grenzray
Xtian: 8 Christian
xurel: 4 scad 6 saurel
xylograph: 5 print 9 engraving 10 impression
xyloid: 5 woody 8 ligneous
Xylonite: 9 celluloid
xylophone: 5 saron 6 gender 7 gambang, gamelan, marimba 8 gamelang, gigelira, sticcado
xyrid: 4 iris
xyst, xystos, xystus: 4 stoa, walk 5 porch 7 portico
xyster: 7 scraper 10 instrument

Y

yabber: 4 talk 6 jabber 8 language 12 conversation
yabby, yabbie: 8 crayfish
yacht: 4 boat, race, sail, ship 5 craft 6 cruise, sonder
yacht basin: 6 marina
yacht flag: 6 burgee
yaff: yap 4 bark, yelp
yaffle: 4 yaff 6 armful 7 handful 10 woodpecker
yahoo: 4 lout 5 brute 6 savage 7 bumpkin
creator: 5 Swift
Yahweh: God 4 YHVH, YHWH 5 Yahwe 7 Jehovah
yak: ox 4 zobo 6 sarlak, sarlyk 7 buffalo
cross-bred: 6 yakalo 9 yakattalo
yakamik: 9 trumpeter
yakka: 4 work 5 labor
yaksha: god 4 jinn, ogre 5 angel, demon, dryad, fairy, gnome 6 spirit
Yakut river: 4 Lena
Yale: Eli 4 lock 10 University
Yalta: *conference member:* 6 Stalin 9 Churchill, Roosevelt
location: 6 Crimea
yam: ube, ubi 5 tugui 6 buckra, igname, potato, uviyam 7 boniata 8 cush-cush 9 posthouse 11 sweetpotato
yamen: 6 office 7 mansion 9 residence 12 headquarters
yammadji: 6 native 11 blackfellow
yammer: cry 4 yell 5 crave, shout, whine, yearn 6 clamor, desire, lament, scream 7 chatter, grumble, stammer, whimper 8 complain
yamp: 5 tuber
yang: cry 4 honk
yang-kin: 8 dulcimer
Yangtze River tributary: Han, Kan, Min
yank: 4 blow, jerk, pull 5 hoick 6 twitch
Yank, Yankee: 8 American 10 Northerner
yannigan: 5 scrub
yap: apt, cur, dog, gab 4 bark, keen, talk, yelp 5 cheep, eager, mouth, quick, ready, rowdy, scold 6 active, hungry, jabber 7 bumpkin, chatter, hoodlum 9 greenhorn
Yap Island money: fei 5 stone
yapock, yapok: 6 monkey 7 opossum
yapp: 7 binding
Yaqui: 5 river 6 Indian
yard: rod 4 lawn, spar, wand 5 garth, staff, stick 7 confine 9 courtyard, curtilage, enclosure 10 correction, playground
enclosed: 5 garth, patio
part of: 4 foot, inch
sixteenth of: 4 nail
yards: *five and one-half:* rod
119.6 square: ar
600: 4 heer
two hundred twenty: 7 furlong
yardage: 6 length 8 distance
yardland: 7 virgate
yare: 4 well 5 brisk, eager, quick, ready 6 active, lively, prompt 8 entirely, prepared 10 manageable
yarm: 4 wail, yell 5 whine 6 scream
yarn: abb, eis, tow 4 garn, sley, tale 5 fiber, story 6 caddis, crewel 7 caddice, eiswool, genappe, schappe 9 fingering
ball: 4 clew
croft: 8 ropeyard
holder: cop
quantity: cop, lea 4 clew, clue, hank, hasp 5 skein 7 spangle
reel: 4 pirn
size: 6 denier
spindle: 4 hasp
waste: 5 thrum
yarr: 7 spurrey
yarrow: 7 allheal, milfoil
yashmak, yasmak: 4 veil
yataghan: 5 knife, saber
yatter: 7 chatter
yaud: 4 jade, mare
yauld: 4 mare 5 alert, sharp 6 active, nimble, strong 7 healthy 8 vigorous 10 able-bodied
yaupon: 5 holly 7 cassena, cassina 9 evergreen

yaw: 4 turn, veer 5 steer 6 swerve 7 deviate
yawl: 4 boat, howl 6 scream, vessel
yawn: 4 galp, gant(Sc.), gape, yaup, yawp 5 chasm 7 opening 8 oscitate
yawp: bay, cry, yap 4 bawl, call, gape, yelp 6 bellow, scream 8 complain
yaws: 9 frambesia
yawweed: 7 rhubarb
yclept: 5 named 6 called
ye: you 4 thee, thou
yea: ay; aye, yes 5 truly 6 assent, indeed, verily 11 affirmative
yean: ean 4 bear, lamb 7 produce
yeanling: kid 4 lamb 7 newborn
year: 5 annus(L.)
designation: 4 leap 5 lunar, solar 6 fiscal 7 natural 8 calendar, sidereal, tropical 12 astronomical
difference between lunar and solar: 5 epact
division: 5 raith(Sc.) 6 season
of plenary indulgence: 7 jubilee
one-fourth of calendar: 9 trimester
one-half of academic: 8 semester
one-third of academic: 9 trimester
record: 5 annal 8 calendar
yearbook: 7 almanac
yearling: 4 colt 9 hornotine
Yearling: *author:* 8 Rawlings
boy: 4 Jody
yearly: 6 annual 7 etesian 8 annually
yearn: beg, vex, yen 4 ache, long, pine, sigh 5 crave 6 desire, grieve, hanker, yammer, 7 request
yearning: 4 wish 5 eager 7 anxious
years: age, eon, era 4 time
eight: 9 octennial
fifteen: 9 indiction
five: 6 pentad 7 lustrum
hundred: 9 centenary
ninety: 10 nonagenary
seventy: 12 septuagenary
ten: 6 decade 8 decenary 9 decennary, decenniad, decennium
thousand: 7 chiliad 10 millennium
two: 8 biennium
yeast: bee 4 barm, foam, rise 5 froth 6 leaven 7 ferment 9 agitation 14 tumultuousness
brewer's: 4 barm
yeasty: 5 light 8 restless 9 frivolous, unsettled 11 superficial
yegg: 5 thief 6 robber 7 burglar 8 criminal 11 safebreaker, safecracker
yell: cry 4 gowl, howl, roar, yarm, yowl 5 cheer, shout, whoop 6 outcry, scream, shriek, yammer 7 yelloch
yelling: 8 strident 9 clamorous
yelloch: 4 yell
yellow: or(her.) 4 gull, mean, sere, turn, yolk 5 amber, blake, color, favel, lemon, ochre, tinge 6 butter, canary, fallow, flavic, flavid, flaxen, golden, sallow 7 xanthic 8 cowardly, recreant 9 flavicant, jaundiced, lutescent 10 flavescent, melancholy 11 sensational, treacherous 12 contemptible, dishonorable 13 dishonourable, untrustworthy
brown: dun 4 bran 5 aloma, amber, pablo, straw 6 manila
comb. form: 5 luteo, xanth 6 xantho
dyestuff: 5 morin 6 orlean 7 annatto, annotto, arnatto
egg's: 4 yolk
gray: 4 drab
green: 5 olive 6 privet 8 glaucous, tarragon 10 chartreuse, serpentine
orange: 8 grenadine
red: 4 lava, roan 5 sandy 6 orange 7 nacarat
yellow alloy: 5 brass
yellow bird: 6 canary 7 warbler 9 goldfinch
yellow copper ore: 12 chalcopyrite
yellow copperas: 9 copiapite
yellow jacket: 4 wasp 8 eucalypt
yellow mustard: 8 charlock
yellow ocher: sil
yellow pigment: 7 etiolin 8 orpiment
yellow race: 6 Mongol 9 Mongolian
Yellow River: 7 Hwang Ho
yellow star: 10 sneezeweed
yellow starwort: 10 elecampane
yellowhammer: 4 bird, yite 5 ammer, finch, skite 6 gladdy 7 yeldrin 8 yeldrine, yeldring, yeldrock, yeorling, yoldring 10 woodpecker
Yellowhammer State: 7 Alabama
yellowlegs: 4 bird 9 sandpiper
Yellowstone Park attraction: 4 deer 5 bears 6 geyser 11 Old Faithful
yelp: cry, yip 4 bark, brag 5 boast, cheep, shout 6 greedy, outcry, shriek, squeal 7 ululate 8 complain 9 criticize
yeme: 4 care, heed 5 guard 6 govern, regard 7 observe 10 solicitude
Yemen: *people:* 4 Arab 7 Arabian
seaport: 5 Mocha, Mukha
town: 4 Sana 5 Damar
yen: 4 coin, urge 5 yearn 6 desire 7 longing 10 propensity
one-hundredth: sen
yeoman: 5 clerk 6 butler 8 retainer 9 assistant, attendant 10 freeholder, journeyman, manservant 11 subordinate
of guard officer: 4 exon
yeomanly: 6 sturdy 8 faithful
yerk: 4 carp, cast, gird, goad, jerk, kick, lash, pull, stab 5 crack, throw, thump 6 snatch, thrash, wrench 7 lashing
yes: da(Russ.), ja(G.), si(It., Sp.); aye, iss, oui(F.), yeh, yep 4 yeah 5 agree 6 assent 9 assuredly 11 affirmation, affirmative

yesterday: 6 yester
yet: but 4 also 5 still 7 algates, besides, further, however 10 eventually 11 nonetheless 12 nevertheless 15 notwithstanding
yeti: 7 monster, snowman
yew: ew 4 tree 7 conifer 9 evergreen
genus: 5 taxus
Yiddish: 6 Jewish
pray: 5 daven
synagogue: 4 shul
yield: bow, net, pay, sag 4 bear, bend, cede, cess, elde, fold, give, obey, vail 5 addle, admit, agree, allow, avale, defer, grant, heald, hield, repay, stoop, waive 6 accede, afford, comply, impart, profit, relent, render, return, reward, soften, submit, supply 7 abandon, concede, consent, deliver, produce, revenue, succumb 9 acquiesce, surrender 10 capitulate, recompense, relinquish 11 acknowledge
yielding: 4 meek, soft, waxy 5 buxom 6 feeble, flabby, pliant, supple 7 flaccid 8 flexible, recreant 9 tractable 10 manageable
yill: ale
yin: one 8 feminine, negative
yip: 4 yelp
yird: 5 earth
yirr: 5 growl, snarl
Ymir, Ymer: 5 giant
slayer: Ve 4 Odin, Vili
yodel: 4 call, sing 5 carol, shout 6 warble 7 refrain
yogi: 4 yoga 5 fakir, yogin 6 fakeer 7 ascetic
yoke: tie 4 bail, bond, join, link, pair, span, team 5 bangy, fight(Sc.), marry, seize(Sc.) 6 attack(Sc.), banghy, couple, inspan, tackle(Sc.) 7 bondage, carrier, enslave, harness, oppress, service, slavery 8 restrain 9 associate, servitude
comb. form: 4 zygo
yoked: 9 conjugate
yokefellow: 4 mate, wife 6 spouse 7 husband, partner 9 associate, companion
yokel: oaf 4 boor, clod, lout, rube 6 obtuse, rustic 7 bumpkin, hayseed, plowboy 8 Abderite, gullible 10 countryman, slow-witted
yoking: 4 bout 7 contest, mugging
yolk: 6 yellow 7 essence 8 vitellus
yon: 6 yonder
yond: 4 past 6 raging, yonder
yonder: yon 4 away 5 there 6 beyond 7 distant, farther, further, thither
yore: 4 past
Yorkshire: *district:* 5 Otley, Selby
river: Ure
town: 5 Leeds
you: te, tu(F.), yi; sie(G.), yez
young: fry, raw 4 tyro, weak 5 brood, fetus, fresh, green 6 active, foetus, litter, strong, tender 7 pliable 8 childish, ignorant, immature, juvenile, newcomer, vigorous, workable, youthful 9 offspring, succulent 13 inexperienced
bring forth: ean 4 yean 5 calve, whelp
with: 6 gravid 8 pregnant
young animal: cub, kid, pup 4 calf, colt, fawn, joey 5 chick, puppy 6 kitten 7 tadpole
young hare: 7 leveret
young herring: 4 brit
younger: 6 junior
younger son: 5 cadet
youngling: 5 youth 6 novice 7 student 8 beginner, neophyte
youngster (see also **child**): boy, cub, lad, tad, tot 4 baby, calf, colt, girl, lass, tike 5 filly, youth 6 moppet, shaver, urchin 9 stripling 10 midshipman
younker: 6 knight 7 gallant 8 nobleman 9 gentleman, youngster
your: thy
youth: bud 4 chap 5 chiel(Sc.), chabo 6 hoiden, hoyden 7 callant(Sc.), ephebos, ephebus, gossoon 9 youngster 10 adolescent 11 adolescence, hobbledehoy
goddess of: 4 Hebe
mythological: 5 Etana 6 Adonis, Apollo, Icarus
time of: 9 salad days
youth shelter: 6 hostel
youthful: new 5 early, fresh, young 6 active 7 puerile 8 immature, juvenile, vigorous
yowl: cry 4 howl, wail, yell
yowt: 4 howl, yell, yelp 6 scream
yttrium: Yt
Yucatan: *people:* 4 Maya 5 Mayan
tree: 6 yaxche
yucca: 5 palma
Yugoslavia: *brandy:* 5 rakia 9 slivovitz
city: Nis 5 Agram 6 Morava, Mostar, Prilep, Skopje, Vardar, Zagrab, Zagreb 7 Cattaro 8 Belgrade, Monastir, Sarajevo, Subotica 9 Ljubljana, Subotitsa
coin: 4 para 5 dinar
commune: Pec 4 Stip 5 Veles
island: Rab, Vis 4 Cres, Hvar 5 Solta, Susak
measure: rif 4 akov, ralo 5 donum, khvat, lanaz, stopa 6 motyka, palaze, ralico 9 dan oranja
monarch: 5 Peter
people: 4 Serb 5 Croat 7 Slovene
region: 5 Banat 6 Banate, Bosnia
river: 4 Sava 5 Drava, Drina 6 Danube, Morava, Vardar
weight: oka, oke 5 dramm, tovar, wagon 7 satlijk
yule: 9 Christmas 13 Christmastide

Z

Z: zed 6 izzard
zac: 4 goat, ibex
zacate: hay 5 grass 6 forage
Zacchaeus, Zaccheus: 4 pure 8 innocent
Zadok: 4 just 9 righteous
son: 7 Ahimaaz
Zagreb: See **Yugoslavia**
zaguan: 4 gate 8 entrance 11 entranceway
Zaire: *animal:* 5 okapi
capital: 8 Kinshasa
cool season: 7 cacimba
lake: 5 Tumba
official language: 6 French
people: 5 Bantu, Pygmy 7 Hamitic, Nilotic 8 Sudanese
river: 4 Uele 5 Congo, Zaire 7 Aruwimi
snake: 8 amphiuma
wet season: 6 kundey
Zambales (see also **Philippine Islands**):
capital: Iba
language: 4 Tino
zamia: 4 tree 5 cycad, shrub
Zamindar: *chief:* 6 mirdha 7 mirdaha
overseer: 6 mirdha 7 mirdaha
zampogna: 7 bagpipe, panpipe
zanja: 5 canal, ditch, gully 6 arroyo
zanni: 5 clown
zany: 4 dolt, fool 5 clown, crazy, dotty, nutty, toady 7 acrobat, buffoon, idiotic 8 clownish, follower, imitator 9 assistant, attendant, simpleton 10 lieutenant 11 merry-andrew
Zanzibar: See **Tanzania**
zarf: cup 5 stand 6 holder
zati: 6 monkey
zeal: 4 fire 5 ardor 6 desire, fervor 7 passion 8 devotion, interest 9 eagerness 10 enthusiasm, fanaticism
Zealand: *city:* 10 Copenhagen
zealot: 5 bigot 6 votary 7 devotee, fanatic 8 partisan, votaress 10 enthusiast
zealous: 4 warm 5 rabid 6 ardent, fervid, hearty 7 devoted, earnest, fervent 8 frenetic, vigorous 9 phrenetic, strenuous 12 enthusiastic
Zebedee's son: 4 John 5 James
zebra: 4 dauw
extinct: 6 quagga
zebrawood: 7 arariba 9 nakedwood 10 marblewood
zebu: 8 Brahmany
Zebulon, Zebulun: *brother:* 4 Levi 5 Judah 6 Simeon
father: 5 Jacob
mother: 4 Leah
zecchino: 6 sequin, zequin
Zelus: *brother:* Bia 6 Cratus
father: 6 Pallas
mother: 4 Styx
sister: 4 Nike
zenana: 5 harem 8 seraglio
zenith: 4 acme, peak 6 summit 11 culmination
opposite of: 5 nadir
Zeno: *city:* 4 Elea
follower: 5 Stoic
Zenobia: *country:* 7 Palmyra
husband: 9 Odenathus
zephyr: 4 aura, wind 6 breeze
zeppelin: 5 blimp 9 dirigible
zequin: 6 sequin 8 zecchino
zero: nil 6 cipher, naught, nought 7 nothing
Zeruiah's son: 7 Abishai
zest: 4 tang 5 gusto, savor 6 flavor, relish 8 piquancy 9 enjoyment 10 enthusiasm
zestful: 4 racy 6 hearty 7 pungent
Zeus: 7 Alastor, Jupiter
attendant: 4 Nike
beloved of: Io 6 Europa
brother: 5 Hades 8 Poseidon
cupbearer: 4 Hebe 8 Ganymede
daughter: Ate 4 Hebe, Kore 5 Irene 6 Athena, Athene 7 Artemis, Astraea 8 Despoina 9 Aphrodite 10 Persephone, Proserpina, Proserpine 11 Persephassa
epithet: 5 soter 7 Alastor
form assumed by: 4 bull, swan
messenger: 4 Iris 6 Hermes
mother: 4 Rhea
nurse: 4 goat 8 Amalthea, Cynosura

oracle: 6 Dodona
parent: 4 Rhea 6 Cronus, Kronos
shield: 5 aegis
sister: 4 Hera
son: Gad 4 Ares 5 Arcas, Argus 6 Aeacus, Apollo, Hermes, Tityus 7 Perseus 8 Dardanus, Dionysos, Dionysus, Heracles, Herakles, Hercules, Tantalus 10 Hephaestus
victim: 4 Idas
wife: 4 Hera 5 Danae, Metis 6 Semele
ziarat, ziara: 4 tomb 6 shrine
ziggurat: 5 tower 7 pyramid
zigzag: 4 tack, turn 5 angle, crank, weave 8 flexuous
Zillah: *husband:* 6 Lamech
son: 9 Tubal-cain
Zilpah's son: Gad 5 Asher
zimarra: 5 cloak 7 cassock, soutane
zimb: bug, fly 6 insect
zinc: Zn 7 adamine, adamite, spelter, tutenag 9 galvanize, tutenague
ore: 6 blende
sulphate: 7 ilesite
zing: pep, vim, zip 4 dash, snap 5 force, vigor 6 energy, spirit, stingo 10 enthusiasm
zingaro: 5 gypsy
zingel: 4 fish 5 perch
zinnia: 5 aster 6 flower
Zion: 4 hill 6 heaven
Zionism founder: 5 Herzl
zip: 4 zing
zipper: 8 fastener
Zipporah's father: 6 Jethro
zippy: 5 brisk 6 snappy
zizany: 4 weed 5 tares 6 darnel
zizith: 7 fringes, tassles
Zoan: 5 Tanis
Zobeide's sister: 5 Amina
zodiac sign: Leo, Ram 4 Bull, Crab, Fish, Goat, Lion 5 Aries, decan, Libra, Scale, Twins, Virgo 6 Archer, Cancer, Fishes, Gemini, Pisces, Taurus, Virgin 7 Balance, Scorpio 8 Aquarius, Scorpion 9 Capricorn 11 Capricornus, Sagittarius, Waterbearer
Zola: *defender of:* 7 Dreyfus
character: 4 Nana
work: 4 Nana 6 Verite 7 J'accuse 8 Germinal
zone: 4 area, band, belt, path, zona(L.) 5 layer, tract 6 course, girdle, region, stripe 7 circuit 8 cincture, encircle, engirdle
geological succession: 6 assise
marked by: 6 zonate
zoom: 9 chandelle
zoo: 8 vivarium 9 menagerie
floating: ark
zoophyte: 5 coral
zoril: 7 polecat
Zoroaster's works: 6 Avesta
Zoroastrian: 5 Parsi 6 gheber, ghebre, Parsee
demon: 4 deva
god: 5 Ahura, Mazda 10 Ahura-Mazda
zoster: 4 belt 6 girdle
Zouave: 4 Zuzu
zounds: 4 egad
zoysia: 5 grass
zucchetto: 7 calotte 8 skullcap
zucchini: 5 gourd 6 squash
zufolo: 5 flute 9 flageolet
zuisin: 4 duck 7 widgeon 8 baldpate
Zulu: *boy:* 6 umfaan
headman: 6 induna
language family: 5 Bantu
regiment: 4 impi
spear: 7 assegai
Zuni: 6 Indian, Pueblo
zwieback: 4 rusk 5 toast 7 biscuit
zygomatic bone: 9 cheekbone
zygote: 7 oosperm
zymase: 6 enzyme
source: 5 yeast
zymogen activating substance: 6 kinase
zymosis: 12 fermentation
zythum: 4 beer